NEW • REVISED • EXPANDED
### POCKET-SIZE EDITION

# WEBSTER'S NEW WORLD DICTIONARY
## OF THE AMERICAN LANGUAGE

DAVID B. GURALNIK, Editor in Chief

**WARNER BOOKS**

A Warner Communications Company

# FOREWORD

This latest Paperback Edition of *Webster's New World Dictionary* is an expansion and updating of an earlier revision of the paperback dictionary that has been a best seller since it was first published in 1958. It is based upon and extracted from the materials prepared for *Webster's New World Dictionary*, Second College Edition. The more than 59,000 vocabulary entries in this revised edition include thousands of newer terms and newer senses of established terms not to be found in the first edition.

The selection of vocabulary items has been made largely on the basis of frequency of occurrence within our vast citation file and from various word-count lists. Included in the single alphabetical listing of the dictionary are selected biographical and geographical entries, names from literature and mythology, and common abbreviations. The geographical entries include countries of the world, with area and population, major cities of the world, all cities of the United States with over 100,000 population, and major bodies of water, mountains, and the like.

It has been the intent of the editors of this work to incorporate as much useful information as possible within the available space. As a consequence, in addition to the clear but brief definitions, properly separated and discriminated and, where necessary, identified as to level of usage, there will be found herein illustrative examples of usage to help clarify meanings, a large number of idiomatic expressions, affixes and combining forms, and other features not generally included in a paperback dictionary of this size. Among the unusual features are the etymologies enclosed in boldface brackets following the entry word. These little histories of the origin and development of words often help one to a clearer understanding of the current meanings.

The pronunciations are recorded in a simplified but precise phonemic key, and variant pronunciations, if sufficiently widespread, are given, often in an abbreviated form. The key to pronunciation is printed at the bottom of every right-hand page for the convenience of the user.

Another unusual feature of this paperback dictionary is the inclusion of pictorial illustrations, especially selected and designed to help amplify those definitions that benefit from such illustrations and to brighten the page. The type used is of a modern face in the largest practicable size to facilitate ease of reading.

The members of the dictionary staff involved in preparing this dictionary are: *Managing Editor*, Samuel Solomon; *Supervising Associate Editor*, Clark C. Livensparger; *Associate Editors*, Christopher T. Hoolihan, Ruth K. Kent, Thomas Layman, Paul Murry, Andrew Sparks, Eleanor Rickey Stevens; *Assistant Editors*, Roslyn Block, Jonathan L. Goldman, Judith Clark, *Assistants*, Virginia C. Becker, Dorothy H. Benedict, Cynthia Sadonick, Angie West; *Illustrator*, Anita Rogoff; *Proofreader*, Shirley M. Miller.

David B. Guralnik
Editor in Chief

iii

# GUIDE TO THE USE OF THE DICTIONARY

## I. THE MAIN ENTRY WORD

### A. *Arrangement of Entries*—
All main entries, including single words, hyphenated and unhyphenated compounds, proper names, prefixes, suffixes, and abbreviations, are listed in strict alphabetical order and are set in large, boldface type.

**a** (ə; *stressed,* ā) *adj.* . . .
**a-** *a prefix meaning:* . . .
**a. 1.** about **2.** acre(s) . . .
**aard·vark** (ärd′värk′) *n.* . . . .
**Aar·on** (er′ən) *Bible* . . .
**ab-** [L.] *a prefix meaning* . . .
**A.B.** Bachelor of Arts
**a·back** (ə bak′) *adv.* [Archaic] backward **—taken aback** startled . . .

Note that in biographical entries only the last, or family, name has been considered in alphabetization, but when two or more persons have the same family name, they have been arranged within the entry block in alphabetical order by first names.

**John·son** (jän′s'n) **1.** Andrew . . . **2.** Lyn·don Baines . . . **3.** Samuel . . .

Idiomatic phrases listed after a main entry have also been entered alphabetically within each group.

**fly¹** (flī) *vi.* . . . **—fly into** . . . **—let fly (at)** . . . **—on the fly** . . .

### B. *Variant Spellings & Forms*
—When variant spellings of a word are some distance apart alphabetically, the definition appears with the spelling most frequently used, and the other spellings are cross-referred to this entry. If two commonly used variant spellings are alphabetically close to each other, they are entered as a joint boldface entry, but the order of entry does not necessarily indicate that the form entered first is "more correct" or is to be given preference.

**the·a·ter, the·a·tre** (thē′ə tər) *n.* . . .

If a variant spelling or spellings are alphabetically close to the prevailing spelling, they are given at the end of the entry block in small boldface.

**co·or·di·na·tion** *n.* . . . Also **co·or′-di·na′tion, co·ör′di·na′tion**
**par·af·fin** . . . *n.* . . . : also **par′af·fine** . . .

### C. *Cross-references*— When an entry is cross-referred to another term that has the same meaning but is more frequently used, the entry cross-referred to is usually in small capitals.

**an·aes·the·si·a, an·aes·thet·ic,** etc. *same as* ANESTHESIA, ANESTHETIC, etc.

### D. *Homographs*—Main entries that are spelled alike but are different in meaning and origin, as **bat** (a club), **bat** (the animal), and **bat** (to wink), are given separate entry and are marked by superscript numbers following the boldface spellings.

**bat¹** . . . *n.* . . .
**bat²** . . . *n.* . . .
**bat³** . . . *vt.* . . .

### E. *Foreign Terms*—Foreign words and phrases encountered with some frequency in English but not completely naturalized are marked with a double dagger (‡). The user of the dictionary is thus signaled that such terms are usually printed in italics or underlined in writing.

**‡bon jour** (bôn zhoor′) [Fr.] . . .

### F. *Prefixes, Suffixes, & Combining Forms*—Prefixes and initial combining forms are indicated by a hyphen following the entry form.

**hemi-** . . . *a prefix meaning* half . . .

Suffixes and terminal combining forms are indicated by a hyphen preceding the entry form.

**-a·ble** . . . *a suffix meaning:* **1.** able to . . .

The abundance of these forms, whose syllabification and pronunciation can be determined from the words containing them, makes it possible for the reader to understand and pronounce countless complex terms not entered in the dictionary but formed with affixes and words that are entered.

### G. *Syllabification*—The syllabifications used in this dictionary, indicated by centered dots in the entry words or sometimes by stress marks, are those in general use.

**fun·da·men·tal** (fun′də men′t'l) *adj.* . . . .
**coun′ter·rev′o·lu′tion** *n.* . . . .

## II. PRONUNCIATION

### A. *Introduction*—The pronunciations recorded in this dictionary are those used by cultivated speakers in normal, relaxed conversation. They are symbolized in as broad a manner as is consistent with accuracy so that speakers of every variety of American English can easily read their own pronunciations into the symbols used here. For some words, variant pronunciations that are dialectal, British, slang, etc. are given along with the standard American pronunciations. Contextual differences in pronunciation also have been indicated wherever practicable, as by showing variants in unstressed or shifted stress form.

iv

# Guide to the Dictionary

## B. *Key to Pronunciation*

—An abbreviated form of this key appears at the bottom of every alternate page of the vocabulary.

| Symbol | Key Words | Symbol | Key Words |
|---|---|---|---|
| a | fat | b | bed, dub |
| ā | ape | d | dip, had |
| ä | car | f | fall, off |
| | | g | get, dog |
| e | ten | h | he, ahead |
| ē | even | j | joy, agile |
| | | k | kill, bake |
| i | is | l | let, ball |
| ī | bite | m | met, trim |
| | | n | not, ton |
| ō | go | p | put, tap |
| ô | horn | r | red, dear |
| ᴏᴏ | tool | s | sell, pass |
| ᴏᴏ | look | t | top, hat |
| yᴏᴏ | use | v | vat, have |
| yᴏᴏ | united | w | will, always |
| oi | oil | y | yet, yard |
| ou | out | z | zebra, haze |
| u | up | ch | chin, arch |
| ur | urn | sh | she, dash |
| | | th | thin, truth |
| ə | a in ago | *th* | then, father |
| | e in agent | zh | azure, leisure |
| | i in sanity | ŋ | ring, drink |
| | o in comply | ' | [see explanatory |
| | u in focus | | note in next |
| | | | column] |
| ər | perhaps | | |

A few explanatory notes on some of the more complex of these symbols follow.

**ä** This symbol represents essentially the sound of *a* in *car* but may also represent the low central vowel sometimes heard in New England for *bath*.

**e** This symbol represents the sound of *e* in *ten* and is also used, followed and hence colored by *r*, to represent the vowel sound of *care* (ker).

**ē** This symbol represents the vowel sound in *meet* and is also used for the vowel in the unstressed final syllable of such words as *lucky* (luk′ē), *pretty* (prit′ē), etc.

**i** This symbol represents the vowel sound in *hit* and is also used for the vowel in the unstressed syllables of such words as *garbage* (gär′bij), *deny* (di nī′), etc. In such contexts reductions to *ə* (gär′bəj), (də nī′), etc. are commonly heard and may be assumed as variants. This symbol is also used, followed and hence colored by *r*, to represent the vowel sound of *dear* (dir).

**ô** This symbol represents essentially the sound of *a* in *all*. When followed by *r*, as in *more* (môr), vowels ranging to ō (mōr *or* mō′ər) are often heard and may be assumed as variants.

**ə** This symbol, called the schwa, represents the mid central relaxed vowel of neutral coloration heard in the unstressed syllables of *ago*, *agent*, etc.

**ur** and **ər** These two clusters of symbols represent respectively the stressed and unstressed r-colored vowels heard successively in the two syllables of *murder* (mur′dər). Where these symbols are shown, some speakers, as in the South and along the Eastern seaboard, will, as a matter of course, pronounce them by "dropping their *r*'s."

**ŋ** This symbol represents the voiced velar nasal sound of the -*ng* of *sing* and of the *n* before *k* and *g*, as in *drink* (driŋk) and *finger* (fiŋ′gər).

**'** The apostrophe before an *l*, *m*, or *n* indicates that the following consonant forms the nucleus of a syllable with no appreciable vowel sound, as in *apple* (ap′'l) or *happen* (hap′'n). In some persons' speech, certain syllabic consonants are replaced with syllables containing reduced vowels, as (hap′ən).

## C. *Foreign Sounds*

—In recording the approximate pronunciation of foreign words, it has been necessary to use the following five symbols in addition to those preceding.

**ë** This symbol represents the sound made by rounding the lips as for (ô) and pronouncing (e).

**ö** This symbol represents the sound made by rounding the lips as for (ō) and pronouncing (ā).

**ü** This symbol represents the sound made by rounding the lips as for (ᴏᴏ) and pronouncing (ē).

**kh** This symbol represents the sound made by arranging the speech organs as for (k) but allowing the breath to escape in a continuous stream, as in pronouncing (h).

**n** This symbol indicates that the vowel immediately preceding it is given a nasal sound, as in Fr. *mon* (mōn).

## D. *Styling of Pronunciation*

—Pronunciations are given inside parentheses, immediately following the boldface entry. A primary, or strong, stress is indicated by a heavy stroke (′) immediately following the syllable so stressed. A secondary, or weak, stress is indicated by a lighter stroke (′) following the syllable so stressed. Some compound entries formed of words that are separately entered in the dictionary are syllabified and stressed and repronounced only in part or not repronounced at all.

**hard·ly** (härd′lē) . . .
**hard′-nosed′** (-nōzd′) . . .
**hard sell** . . .
**hard·ship** . . .

## E. *Variants*

—Where two or more pronunciations for a single word are given, the order in which they are entered does not necessarily mean that

# Guide to the Dictionary

the first is preferred to or more correct than another. In most cases the form given first is the most frequent in general cultivated use.

**F.** *Truncation*—Variant pronunciations for a main entry or a run-in entry are truncated, or shortened, whenever possible. A hyphen after the shortened variant marks it as an initial syllable or syllables; one before the variant, as terminal; and hyphens before and after the variant, as internal.

**ab·jure** (əb joor', ab-) . . .
**dom·i·cile** (däm'ə sil', -sil; dō'mə-)
**fu·tu·ri·ty** (fyoo toor'ə tē, -tyoor'-)
. . .

Variant pronunciations involving different parts of speech in the same entry block usually appear as follows:
**a·buse** (ə byōoz'; *for n.* ə byōos') *vt.* . . .

## III. PART-OF-SPEECH LABELS

Part-of-speech labels are given for main entries that are solid or hyphenated forms, except prefixes, suffixes, and abbreviations, and the names of persons, places, etc. When an entry word is used as more than one part of speech in an entry block, long dashes introduce each different part-of-speech label, which appears in boldface italic type.

**round** . . . *adj.* . . . —*n.* . . . —*vt.* . . . —*vi.* . . . —*adv.* . . . —*prep.* . . .

Two or more part-of-speech labels are given jointly for an entry when the definition or definitions, or the cross-reference, will suffice for both or all.

**des·patch** . . . *vt., n. same as* DISPATCH

## IV. INFLECTED FORMS

Inflected forms regarded as irregular or offering difficulty in spelling are entered in small boldface immediately following the part-of-speech labels. They are truncated where possible, and syllabified and pronounced where necessary.

**hap·py** . . . *adj.* -pi·er, -pi·est . . .
**cit·y** . . . *n., pl.* -ies . . .
**a·moe·ba** . . . *n., pl.* -bas, -bae (-bē) . . .

Forms regarded as regular inflections, and hence not normally indicated, include:

*a)* plurals formed by adding -*s* to the singular (or -*es* after *s, x, z, ch,* and *sh*), as *bats, boxes*
*b)* present tenses formed by adding -*s* to the infinitive (or -*es* after *s, x, z, ch,* and *sh*), as *waits, searches*
*c)* past tenses and past participles formed by simply adding -*ed* to the infinitive, as *waited, searched*
*d)* present participles formed by

simply adding -*ing* to the infinitive, as *waiting, searching*
*e)* comparatives and superlatives formed by simply adding -*er* and -*est* to the base of an adjective or adverb, as *taller, tallest* or *sooner, soonest*

Where two inflected forms are given for a verb, the first is the form for the past tense and the past participle, and the second is the form for the present participle.

**make** . . . *vt.* made, mak'ing . . .

Where three forms are given, the first represents the past tense, the second the past participle, and the third the present participle.

**give** . . . *vt.* gave, giv'en, giv'ing . . .

Where there are alternative forms for any of the principal parts, these are given and properly indicated.

**bid** . . . *vt.* bade or bid, bid'den or bid, bid'ding; for vt. 2, 4 & for vi., pt. & pp. bid . . .

## V. ETYMOLOGY

The etymology, or word derivation, appears inside heavy boldface brackets immediately before the definitions proper. The symbols, as < for "derived from," and the abbreviations of language labels, etc. used in the etymologies are dealt with in full in the list immediately preceding page 1 of the vocabulary.

**di·shev·el** . . . [ < OFr. *des-*, dis- + *chevel*, hair] . . .

No etymology is shown where one would be superfluous, as where the elements making up the word are immediately apparent.

## VI. THE DEFINITIONS

**A.** *Order of Senses*—The standard, general senses of a word are given first, and colloquial, slang, etc. senses come next. Technical senses requiring special field labels, as *Astron., Chem.,* etc., follow in order.

**B.** *Numbering & Grouping of Senses*—Senses are numbered consecutively within any given part of speech in boldface numerals. Where a primary sense of a word can easily be subdivided into several closely related meanings, such meanings are indicated by italicized letters.

**time** . . . *n.* . . . 1. every . . . 2. a system . . . 3. the period . . . 11. *Music a)* rhythm . . . *b)* tempo —*vt.* . . . 1. to arrange . . . 2. to adjust . . . —*adj.* 1. having to . . . 2. set to . . . 3. having . . . —in time 1. eventually 2. before . . . 3. keeping . . .

**C.** *Capitalization*—If a main entry word is capitalized in all its

# Guide to the Dictionary

senses, the entry word itself is printed with a capital letter. If a capitalized main entry word has a sense or senses that are uncapitalized, these are marked with the corresponding small-boldface, lower-case letter followed by a short dash and enclosed in brackets.

**Pur·i·tan** . . . *n.* . . . 1. . . . 2. [p-] . . .

Conversely, capitalized letters are shown, where pertinent, with lower-case main entries. In some instances these designations are qualified by the self-explanatory "*often*," "*occas.*," etc.

**left**[1] . . . —*n.* 1. . . . 2. [*often* L-] . . .

D. *Plural Forms*—In a singular noun entry, the designation "[*pl.*]" (or "[*often pl.*]," "[*usually pl.*]," etc.) before a definition indicates that it is (or *often*, *usually*, etc. is) the plural form of the entry word that has the meaning given in the definition.

**look** . . . *vi.* . . . —*n.* 1. . . . 2. . . . 3. [Colloq.] *a*) [*usually pl.*] appearance *b*) [*pl.*] personal appearance . . .

If a plural noun entry or sense is construed as singular, the designation [*with sing. v.*] is added.

**phys·ics** . . . *n.pl.* [*with sing. v.*] . . .

E. *Verbs Followed by Prepositions or Objects*—Where certain verbs are, in usage, invariably or usually followed by a specific preposition or prepositions, this has been indicated in either of the following ways: the preposition has been worked into the definition, italicized and enclosed in parentheses, or a note has been added in parentheses indicating that the preposition is so used.

In definitions of transitive verbs, the specific or generalized objects of the verb, where given, are enclosed in parentheses, since such objects are not part of the definition.

## VII. USAGE LABELS

The editors of this dictionary decided that the familiarity of the conventional usage designations makes their use advisable if the meaning of these labels is kept clearly in mind. The labels, and what they are intended to indicate, are given below.

*Colloquial:* The term or sense is generally characteristic of conversation and informal writing. It is not to be regarded as substandard or illiterate.
*Slang:* The term or sense is not generally regarded as conventional or standard usage, but is used, even by the best speakers, in highly informal contexts. Slang terms either pass into

disuse in time or come to have a more formal status.
*Obsolete:* The term or sense is no longer used but occurs in earlier writings.
*Archaic:* The term or sense is rarely used today except in certain restricted contexts, as in church ritual, but occurs in earlier writings.
*Poetic:* The term or sense is used chiefly in poetry, especially in earlier poetry, or in prose where a poetic quality is desired.
*Dialect:* The term or sense is used regularly only in some geographical areas or in a certain designated area (*South*, *West*, etc.) of the United States.
*British* (or *Canadian*, *Scottish*, etc.): The term or sense is characteristic of British (or Canadian, etc.) English rather than American English. When preceded by *chiefly*, the label indicates an additional, though less frequent, American usage. *British Dialect* indicates that the term or sense is used regularly only in certain geographical areas of Great Britain, usually in northern England.

In addition to the above usage labels, supplementary information is often given after the definition, indicating whether the term or sense is generally regarded as vulgar, substandard, or derogatory, used with ironic, familiar, or hyperbolic connotations, etc.

**pate** . . . *n.* . . . a humorous term

## VIII. RUN-IN DERIVED ENTRIES

It is possible in English to form an almost infinite number of derived forms simply by adding certain prefixes or suffixes to the base word. The editors have included as run-in entries in small-boldface type as many of these common derived words as space permitted, but only when the meaning of such words can be immediately understood from the meanings of the base word and the affix. Thus, **greatness** and **liveliness** are run in at the end of the entries for **great** and **lively**, the suffix **-ness** being found as a separate entry meaning "state, quality, or instance of being." Many words formed with common suffixes, as **-able**, **-er**, **-less**, **-like**, **-ly**, **-tion**, etc. are similarly treated as run-ins with the base word from which they are derived. All such entries are syllabified and either accented to show stress in pronunciation or, where necessary, pronounced in full or in part.

When a derived word has a meaning or meanings different from those that can be deduced from the sum of its parts, it has been given separate entry, pronounced, and fully defined (e.g., **folder**).

# ABBREVIATIONS USED IN THIS DICTIONARY

**abbrev.** abbreviated; abbreviation
**adj.** adjective
**adv.** adverb
**Aeron.** Aeronautics
**Afr.** African
**Afrik.** Afrikaans
**Alb.** Albanian
**alt.** altered; alternative
**Am.** American
**AmInd.** American Indian
**AmSp.** American Spanish
**Anat.** Anatomy
**Ar.** Arabic
**Aram.** Aramaic
**Archit.** Architecture
**art.** article
**Assyr.** Assyrian
**Astron.** Astronomy
**Biochem.** Biochemistry
**Biol.** Biology
**Bot.** Botany
**Braz.** Brazilian
**Brit.** British
**Bulg.** Bulgarian
**C** Celsius; Central
**c.** century; circa
**Canad, Canad.** Canadian
**cap.** capital
**Celt.** Celtic
**Chem.** Chemistry
**Chin.** Chinese
**cf.** compare
**Colloq.** colloquial
**comp.** compound
**compar.** comparative
**conj.** conjunction
**contr.** contracted; contraction
**Dan.** Danish
**deriv.** derivative
**Dial., dial.** dialect; dialectal
**dim.** diminutive
**Du.** Dutch
**E** East; eastern
**E.** East; English (in etym.)
**Eccles.** Ecclesiastical
**Ecol.** Ecology
**Econ.** Economics
**Educ.** Education
**Egypt.** Egyptian
**Elec.** Electricity
**Eng.** English
**equiv.** equivalent
**Esk.** Eskimo
**esp.** especially
**est.** estimated
**etym.** etymology
**Ex.** example
**exc.** except
**F** Fahrenheit
**fem.** feminine
**ff.** following
**fig.** figurative(ly)
**Finn.** Finnish
**Fl.** Flemish
**fl.** flourished
**Fr.** French
**Frank.** Frankish
**fut.** future
**G.** German (in etym.)
**Gael.** Gaelic

**Geog.** Geography
**Geol.** Geology
**Geom.** Geometry
**Ger.** German
**Gmc.** Germanic
**Goth.** Gothic
**Gr.** Greek
**Gram.** Grammar
**Haw.** Hawaiian
**Heb.** Hebrew
**Hung.** Hungarian
**hyp.** hypothetical
**Ind.** Indian
**indic.** indicative
**inf.** infinitive
**infl.** influenced
**interj.** interjection
**Ir.** Irish
**Iran.** Iranian
**It.** Italian
**Jap.** Japanese
**L** Late
**L.** Latin
**Linguis.** Linguistics
**lit.** literally
**LL.** Late Latin
**LowG.** Low German
**M** middle; medieval
**masc.** masculine
**Math.** Mathematics
**MDu.** Middle Dutch
**ME.** Middle English
**Mech.** Mechanics
**Med.** Medicine
**Meteorol.** Meteorology
**Mex.** Mexican
**MexInd.** Mexican Indian
**MHG.** Middle High German
**mi.** mile(s)
**Mil.** Military
**Mod, Mod.** Modern
**Mongol.** Mongolic
**Myth.** Mythology
**N** North; northern
**N.** North
**n.** noun
**NAmInd.** North American Indian
**Naut.** nautical usage
**NE** northeastern
**neut.** neuter
**nom.** nominative
**Norm, Norm.** Norman
**Norw.** Norwegian
**NW** northwestern
**O** Old
**Obs., obs.** obsolete
**occas.** occasionally
**OE.** Old English
**OFr.** Old French
**OHG.** Old High German
**ON.** Old Norse
**orig.** origin; originally
**OS.** Old Saxon
**P** Primitive
**p.** page
**pass.** passive
**Per.** Persian
**Peruv.** Peruvian
**perf.** perfect
**pers.** person

**Philos.** Philosophy
**Phoen.** Phoenician
**Phonet.** Phonetics
**Photog.** Photography
**phr.** phrase
**Physiol.** Physiology
**PidE.** Pidgin English
**pl.** plural
**Poet., poet.** poetic
**Pol.** Polish
**pop.** population
**Port.** Portuguese
**poss.** possessive
**pp.** past participle
**Pr.** Provençal
**prec.** preceding
**prep.** preposition
**pres.** present
**prob.** probably
**pron.** pronoun
**pronun.** pronunciation
**prp.** present participle
**pseud.** pseudonym
**Psychol.** Psychology
**pt.** past tense
**R.C.Ch.** Roman Catholic Church
**Rom.** Roman
**Russ.** Russian
**S** South; southern
**S.** South
**SAmInd.** South American Indian
**Sans.** Sanskrit
**Scand.** Scandinavian
**Scot.** Scottish
**SE** southeastern
**Sem.** Semitic
**sing.** singular
**Slav.** Slavic
**Sp.** Spanish
**sp.** spelling
**specif.** specifically
**sq.** square
**subj.** subjunctive
**superl.** superlative
**SW** southwestern
**Sw., Swed.** Swedish
**t.** tense
**Tag.** Tagalog
**Theol.** Theology
**transl.** translation
**Turk.** Turkish
**TV** television
**ult.** ultimately
**v.** verb
**var.** variant
**v.aux.** auxiliary verb
**vi.** intransitive verb
**VL.** Vulgar Latin
**vt.** transitive verb
**W** West; western
**W.** Welsh; West
**WInd.** West Indian
**Yid.** Yiddish
**Zool.** Zoology

**‡** foreign word or phrase
**<** derived from; from
**?** perhaps; uncertain
**+** plus
**&** and

viii

# A

**A, a** (ā) *n., pl.* **A's, a's** the first letter of the English alphabet

**A** (ā) *n.* **1.** a grade indicating excellence **2.** *Music* the sixth tone in the scale of C major

**a** (ə; *stressed,* ā) *adj., indefinite article* [< *an*] **1.** one; one sort of **2.** each; any one **3.** per *[once a day]* *A* is used before words beginning with a consonant sound *[a child, a union, a history]* See AN

**a-** *a prefix meaning:* **1.** [< OE.] *a)* in, into, on, at, to *[aboard]* *b)* in the act or state of *[asleep]* **2.** [< OE.] *a)* up, out *[arise]* *b)* off, of *[akin]* **3.** [< Gr.] not *[agnostic]*

**a.** **1.** about **2.** acre(s) **3.** adjective **4.** alto **5.** answer

**AA, A.A. 1.** Alcoholics Anonymous **2.** antiaircraft

**A.A.** Associate in (or of) Arts

**aard·vark** (ärd′värk′) *n.* [Du., earth pig] an ant-eating African mammal

**Aar·on** (er′ən) *Bible* the first high priest of the Hebrews

**ab-** [L.] *a prefix meaning* away, from, from off, down *[abdicate]*

**A.B.** Bachelor of Arts

**a.b.** *Baseball* (times) at bat

**a·back** (ə bak′) *adv.* [Archaic] backward —**taken aback** startled and confused; surprised

**ab·a·cus** (ab′ə kəs) *n., pl.* **-cus·es, -ci′** (-sī′) [< Gr. *abax*] a frame with sliding beads for doing arithmetic

**a·baft** (ə baft′) *adv.* [< OE. *on* + *be*, by + *æftan*, aft] aft —*prep. Naut.* behind

ABACUS

**ab·a·lo·ne** (ab′ə lō′nē) *n.* [AmSp.] a sea mollusk with an oval, somewhat spiral shell

**a·ban·don** (ə ban′dən) *vt.* [< OFr. *mettre a bandon*, to put under (another's) ban] **1.** to give up completely **2.** to desert —*n.* unrestrained activity; exuberance —**a·ban′don·ment** *n.*

**a·ban′doned** *adj.* **1.** deserted **2.** shamefully wicked **3.** unrestrained

**a·base** (ə bās′) *vt.* **a·based′, a·bas′-ing** [< ML. *abassare*, to lower] to humble —**a·base′ment** *n.*

**a·bash** (ə bash′) *vt.* [< L. *ex* + *ba*, interj.] to make ashamed and uneasy; disconcert —**a·bash′ed·ly** *adv.*

**a·bate** (ə bāt′) *vt., vi.* **a·bat′ed, a·bat′ing** [< OFr. *abattre*, to beat down] **1.** to make or become less **2.** *Law* to end —**a·bate′ment** *n.*

**ab·at·toir** (ab′ə twär′, ab′ə twär′) *n.* [Fr.: see prec.] a slaughterhouse

**ab·bé** (ä′bā′) *n.* [Fr.: see ABBOT] a French priest's title

**ab·bess** (ab′əs) *n.* [see ABBOT] a woman who heads a convent of nuns

**ab·bey** (ab′ē) *n., pl.* **-beys 1.** a monastery or convent **2.** a church belonging to an abbey

**ab·bot** (ab′ət) *n.* [< Aram. *abbā*, father] a man who heads a monastery

**abbrev., abbr. 1.** abbreviated **2.** abbreviation

**ab·bre·vi·ate** (ə brē′vē āt′) *vt.* **-at′-ed, -at′ing** [< L. *ad-*, to + *brevis*, short] to make shorter; esp., to shorten (a word) by omitting letters

**ab·bre′vi·a′tion** (-ā′shən) *n.* **1.** a shortening **2.** a shortened form of a word or phrase, as *Dr.* for *Doctor*

**A B C** (ā′ bē′ sē′) *n., pl.* **A B C's 1.** [*usually pl.*] the alphabet **2.** the basic elements (of a subject); rudiments

**ab·di·cate** (ab′də kāt′) *vt., vi.* **-cat′-ed, -cat′ing** [< L. *ab-*, off + *dicare*, to proclaim] **1.** to give up formally (a throne, etc.) **2.** to surrender (a right, responsibility, etc.) —**ab′di·ca′tion** *n.*

**ab·do·men** (ab′də mən, ab dō′-) *n.* [L.] the part of the body between the diaphragm and the pelvis; belly —**ab·dom′i·nal** (-dä′mə n'l) *adj.*

**ab·duct** (ab dukt′) *vt.* [< L. *ab-*, away + *ducere*, to lead] to kidnap —**ab·duc′tion** *n.* —**ab·duc′tor** *n.*

**a·beam** (ə bēm′) *adv.* at right angles to a ship's length or keel

**a·bed** (ə bed′) *adv. & adj.* in bed

**A·bel** (ā′b'l) *Bible* the second son of Adam and Eve: See CAIN

**ab·er·ra·tion** (ab′ər ā′shən) *n.* [< L. *ab-*, from + *errare*, wander] **1.** deviation from what is right, true, normal, etc. **2.** mental derangement —**ab·er·rant** (ab er′ənt) *adj.* —**ab′er·ra′tion·al** *adj.*

**a·bet** (ə bet′) *vt.* **a·bet′ted, a·bet′-ting** [< OFr. *a-*, to + *beter*, to bait] to urge on or help, esp. in crime —**a·bet′tor, a·bet′ter** *n.*

---

fat, āpe, cär; ten, ēven; is, bīte; gō, hôrn, tōōl, look; oil, out; up, fur; chin; she; thin, then; zh, leisure; ŋ, ring; ə for *a* in *ago*; ′, (ā′b'l); ë, Fr. coeur; ö, Fr. feu; Fr. mon; ü, Fr. duc; kh, G. ich, doch; ‡ foreign; < derived from

**a·bey·ance** (ə bā′əns) *n.* [< OFr. *a-*, to, at + *bayer*, to gape] temporary suspension, as of an activity or ruling

**ab·hor** (əb hôr′) *vt.* **-horred′**, **-hor′ring** [< L. *ab-*, from + *horrere*, to shudder] to shrink from in disgust, hatred, etc. **—ab·hor′rence** *n.* **—ab·hor′rer** *n.*

**ab·hor·rent** (-ənt) *adj.* causing disgust, etc.; detestable **—ab·hor′rent·ly** *adv.*

**a·bide** (ə bīd′) *vi.* **a·bode′** or **a·bid′ed**, **a·bid′ing** [OE. *abidan*] **1.** to remain **2.** [Archaic] to reside **—vt.** to put up with **—abide by 1.** to live up to (a promise, etc.) **2.** to submit to and carry out **—a·bid′ance** *n.*

**a·bid·ing** *adj.* enduring; lasting **—a·bid′ing·ly** *adv.*

**a·bil·i·ty** (ə bil′ə tē) *n.*, *pl.* **-ties** [< L. *habilitas*] **1.** a being able; power to do **2.** talent; skill

**-a·bil·i·ty** (ə bil′ə tē), *pl.* **-ties** [L. *-abilitas*] a suffix used to form nouns from adjectives ending in **-ABLE** [*washability*]

**ab·ject** (ab′jekt, ab jekt′) *adj.* [< L. *ab-*, from + *jacere*, to throw] **1.** miserable; wretched **2.** degraded **—ab·ject′ly** *adv.* **—ab·jec′tion** *n.*

**ab·jure** (ab joor′, ab-) *vt.* **-jured′**, **-jur′ing** [< L. *ab-*, away + *jurare*, swear] to give up (rights, allegiance, etc.) on oath; renounce **—ab·ju·ra·tion** (ə rā′shən) *n.* **—ab·jur′a·tor′y** (-ə tôr′ē) *adj.* **—ab·jur′er** *n.*

**ab·late** (ab lāt′) *vt.* **-lat′ed**, **-lat′ing** [< L. *ablatus*, carried away] **1.** to remove, as by surgery **2.** to wear away, burn away, or vaporize **—vi.** to be ablated, as a rocket shield in reentry **—ab·la′tion** *n.*

**ab·la·tive** (ab′lə tiv) *n.* [< L. *ablatus*, carried away] in Latin, etc., the case expressing removal, direction from, cause, agency, etc.

**a·blaze** (ə blāz′) *adv.* on fire **—adj. 1.** flaming **2.** greatly excited

**a·ble** (ā′b'l) *adj.* **a′bler**, **a′blest** [< L. *habere*, have] **1.** having power, skill, etc. (*to do something*) **2.** talented; skilled **3.** *Law* competent **—a′bly** *adv.*

**-a·ble** (ə b'l) [< L.] *a suffix meaning:* **1.** able to [*durable*] **2.** capable of being [*drinkable*] **3.** worthy of [*lovable*] **4.** having qualities of [*comfortable*] **5.** tending to [*perishable*]

**a′ble-bod′ied** *adj.* strong; healthy

**able-bodied seaman** a trained or skilled seaman: also **able seaman**

**a·bloom** (ə bloom′) *adj.* in bloom

**ab·lu·tion** (ab loo′shən) *n.* [< L. *ab-*, off + *luere*, wash] a washing of the body, esp. as a religious ceremony

**-a·bly** (ə blē) *a suffix of adverbs corresponding to adjectives in* **-ABLE**

**ABM** anti-ballistic missile

**ab·ne·gate** (ab′nə gāt′) *vt.* **-gat′ed**, **-gat′ing** [< L. *ab-*, from + *negare*, deny] to deny and refuse; renounce (a claim, etc.) **—ab′ne·ga′tion** *n.*

**ab·nor·mal** (ab nôr′m'l) *adj.* not normal, average, or typical; irregular **—ab·nor′mal·ly** *adv.*

**ab·nor·mal·i·ty** (-mal′ə tē) *n.* **1.** an abnormal condition **2.** *pl.* **-ties** an abnormal thing; malformation

**a·board** (ə bôrd′) *adv.*, *prep.* **1.** on or in (a train, ship, etc.) **2.** alongside

**a·bode** (ə bōd′) *alt. pt. & pp. of* ABIDE **—n.** a home; residence

**a·bol·ish** (ə bäl′ish) *vt.* [< L. *abolere*, destroy] to do away with; void

**a·bo·li·tion** (ab′ə lish′ən) *n.* **1.** complete destruction; annulment **2.** [*occas.* A-] the abolishing of slavery in the U.S. **—ab′o·li′tion·ist** *n.*

**A-bomb** (ā′bäm′) *n.* same as ATOMIC BOMB

**a·bom·i·na·ble** (ə bäm′ə nə b'l) *adj.* [see ff.] **1.** disgusting; vile **2.** very bad **—a·bom′i·na·bly** *adv.*

**a·bom′i·nate′** (-nāt′) *vt.* **-nat′ed**, **-nat′ing** [< L. *abominari*, regard as an ill omen] **1.** to hate; loathe **2.** to dislike **—a·bom′i·na′tion** *n.*

**ab·o·rig·i·nal** (ab′ə rij′ə n'l) *adj.* **1.** existing (in a region) from the beginning; first **2.** of aborigines **—n.** an aborigine

**ab′o·rig′i·ne′** (-ə nē′) *n.*, *pl.* **-nes′** [L. < *ab-*, from + *origine*, the beginning] any of the first known inhabitants of a region

**a·born·ing** (ə bôr′niŋ) *adv.* while being born or created [*the plan died aborning*]

**a·bort** (ə bôrt′) *vi.* [< L. *aboriri*, miscarry] to have a miscarriage **—vt. 1.** to check before fully developed **2.** to cut short (a flight, etc.), as because of an equipment failure

**a·bor′tion** *n.* premature expulsion of a fetus so that it does not live, esp. if induced on purpose **—a·bor′tion·ist** *n.*

**a·bor′tive** *adj.* **1.** unsuccessful; fruitless **2.** arrested in development

**a·bound** (ə bound′) *vi.* [< L. *ab-* + *undare*, to rise in waves] to be plentiful (often with *in* or *with*); teem

**a·bout** (ə bout′) *adv.* [< OE. *onbutan*, around] **1.** all around **2.** near **3.** in an opposite direction **4.** nearly [*about ready*] **—adj.** astir [*he is up and about*] **—prep. 1.** on all sides of **2.** near to **3.** with **4.** on the point of **5.** concerning

**a·bout′-face′** (-fās′, -fās′) *n.* a reversal of position or opinion **—vi. -faced′**, **-fac′ing** to turn or face in the opposite direction

**a·bove** (ə buv′) *adv.* [OE. *abufan*] **1.** in a higher place; up **2.** earlier (in a book, etc.) **3.** higher in rank, etc. **—prep. 1.** over; on top of **2.** better or more than [*above average*] **—adj.** mentioned earlier **—above all** most of all; mainly

**a·bove′board′** *adv.*, *adj.* without dishonesty or concealment

**ab·rade** (ə brād′) *vt.*, *vi.* **-rad′ed**, **-rad′ing** [< L. *ab-*, away + *radere*, scrape] to rub off; scrape away

**A·bra·ham** (ā′brə ham′) *Bible* the first patriarch of the Hebrews

**ab·ra·sion** (ə brā′zhən) *n.* **1.** an abrading **2.** an abraded spot

**ab·ra·sive** (-siv) *adj.* causing abrasion **—n.** a substance, as sandpaper, used for grinding, polishing, etc.

**a·breast** (ə brest′) *adv., adj.* **1.** side by side **2.** informed (*of*); aware

**a·bridge** (ə brij′) *vt.* **a·bridged′, a·bridg′ing** [see ABBREVIATE] **1.** to shorten, lessen, or curtail **2.** to shorten by using fewer words but keeping the substance —**a·bridg′ment, a·bridge′ment** *n.*

**a·broad** (ə brôd′) *adv.* **1.** far and wide **2.** in circulation; current **3.** outdoors **4.** to or in foreign lands —**from abroad** from a foreign land

**ab·ro·gate** (ab′rə gāt′) *vt.* **-gat′ed, -gat′ing** [< L. *ab-*, away + *rogare*, propose] to abolish; repeal; annul —**ab′ro·ga′tion** *n.* —**ab′ro·ga′tor** *n.*

**a·brupt** (ə brupt′) *adj.* [< L. *ab-*, off + *rumpere*, break] **1.** sudden; unexpected **2.** brusque **3.** very steep **4.** disconnected, as some writing — **a·brupt′ly** *adv.* —**a·brupt′ness** *n.*

**Ab·sa·lom** (ab′sə ləm) *Bible* David's son who rebelled against him

**ab·scess** (ab′ses) *n.* [< L. *ab(s)-*, from + *cedere*, go] an inflamed area in body tissues, containing pus— *vi.* to form an abscess —**ab′scessed,** *adj.*

**ab·scis·sa** (ab sis′ə) *n., pl.* **-sas, -sae** (-ē) [L. < *ab-*, from + *scindere,* to cut] *Math.* the horizontal distance of a point from a vertical axis

**ab·scond** (ab skänd′) *vi.* [< L. *ab(s)-*, from + *condere,* hide] to leave hastily and secretly, esp. to escape the law

**ab·sence** (ab′s'ns) *n.* **1.** a being absent **2.** the time of this **3.** a lack

**ab·sent** (ab′s'nt; *for v.* ab sent′) *adj.* [< L. *ab-*, away + *esse,* be] **1.** not present **2.** not existing; lacking **3.** not attentive —*vt.* to keep (oneself) away —**ab′sent·ly** *adv.*

**ab·sen·tee** (ab′s'n tē′) *n.* one who is absent, as from work —*adj.* of, by, or from one who is absent [*absentee* landlord] —**ab′sen·tee′ism** *n.*

**absentee ballot** a ballot marked and sent to a board of elections by a voter (**absentee voter**) who cannot be present to vote in an election

**ab′sent-mind′ed** *adj.* **1.** not attentive; preoccupied **2.** habitually forgetful —**ab′sent-mind′ed·ly** *adv.* —**ab′sent-mind′ed·ness** *n.*

**absent without leave** *Mil.* absent from duty without official permission

**ab·sinthe** (ab′sinth) *n.* [Fr., ult. < OPer.] a green, bitter liqueur: also sp. **ab′sinth**

**ab·so·lute** (ab′sə lōōt′) *adj.* [see ABSOLVE] **1.** perfect; complete **2.** not mixed; pure **3.** not limited [*absolute* power] **4.** positive **5.** not doubted; real [*absolute* truth] **6.** not relative —**ab′so·lute′ly** *adv.*

**ab·so·lu′tion** (-lōō′shən) *n.* **1.** a freeing (*from* guilt); forgiveness **2.** remission (*of* sin or its penalty)

**ab·so·lut·ism** (ab′sə lōō′tiz'm) *n.* government by absolute rule; despotism —**ab′so·lut′ist** *n., adj.*

**ab·solve** (ab zälv′, -sälv′) *vt.* **-solved′, -solv′ing** [< L. *ab-*, from + *solvere,*

to loosen] **1.** to free from guilt, a duty, etc. **2.** to give religious absolution to

**ab·sorb** (əb zôrb′, -sôrb′) *vt.* [< L. *ab-*, from + *sorbere,* drink in] **1.** to suck up **2.** to assimilate **3.** to interest greatly; engross **4.** to pay for (costs, etc.) **5.** to take in (a shock) without recoil **6.** to take in and not reflect (light or sound) —**ab·sorb′ing** *adj.*

**ab·sorb′ent** *adj.* capable of absorbing moisture, etc. —*n.* a thing that absorbs —**ab·sorb′en·cy** *n.*

**ab·sorp·tion** (əb zôrp′shən, -sôrp′-) *n.* **1.** an absorbing or being absorbed **2.** great interest —**ab·sorp′tive** *adj.*

**ab·stain** (əb stān′) *vi.* [< L. *ab(s)-*, from + *tenere,* hold] to voluntarily do without; refrain (*from*) —**ab·stain′er** *n.* —**ab·sten′tion** (-sten′shən) *n.*

**ab·ste·mi·ous** (əb stē′mē əs) *adj.* [< L. *ab(s)-*, from + *temetum,* strong drink] moderate in eating and drinking; temperate

**ab·sti·nence** (ab′stə nəns) *n.* an abstaining from some or all food, liquor, etc. —**ab′sti·nent** *adj.*

**ab·stract** (ab strakt′, ab′strakt) *adj.* [< L. *ab(s)-*, from + *trahere,* to draw] **1.** thought of apart from material objects **2.** expressing a quality so thought of **3.** theoretical **4.** *Art* not representing things realistically —*n.* (ab′strakt) a summary —*vt.* **1.** (ab strakt′) to take away **2.** (ab′strakt) to summarize —**ab·stract′ly** *adv.*

**ab·stract′ed** *adj.* absent-minded

**ab·strac′tion** *n.* **1.** an abstracting; removal **2.** an abstract idea, thing, etc. **3.** mental withdrawal **4.** an abstract painting, etc.

**ab·struse** (ab strōōs′) *adj.* [< L. *ab(s)-*, away + *trudere,* to thrust] hard to understand —**ab·struse′ly** *adv.* —**ab·struse′ness** *n.*

**ab·surd** (əb surd′, -zurd′) *adj.* [< L. *absurdus,* not to be heard of] so unreasonable as to be ridiculous —**ab·surd′i·ty** (-sur′də tē) *n., pl.* **-ties** —**ab·surd′ly** *adv.*

**a·bun·dance** (ə bun′dəns) *n.* [see ABOUND] great plenty; more than enough —**a·bun′dant** *adj.* —**a·bun′dant·ly** *adv.*

**a·buse** (ə byōōz′; *for n.* ə byōōs′) *vt.* **a·bused′, a·bus′ing** [< L. *abusus,* misused] **1.** to use wrongly **2.** to mistreat **3.** to insult; revile —*n.* **1.** wrong use **2.** mistreatment **3.** a corrupt practice **4.** insulting language —**a·bu·sive** (ə byōōs′iv) *adj.* —**a·bu′sive·ly** *adv.*

**a·but** (ə but′) *vi.* **a·but′ted, a·but′ting** [< OFr. *a-*, to + *bout,* end] to border (*on* or *upon*)

**a·but′ment** *n.* **1.** an abutting **2.** a part supporting an arch, bridge, etc.

**a·bys·mal** (ə biz′m'l) *adj.* **1.** of or like an abyss; not measurable **2.** very bad —**a·bys′mal·ly** *adv.*

**a·byss** (ə bis′) *n.* [< Gr. *a-*, without + *byssos,* bottom] **1.** a bottomless

---

fat, āpe, cär; ten, ēven; is, bīte; gō, hôrn, tōōl, look; oil, out; up, fur; chin; she; thin, *th*en; zh, leisure; ŋ, ring; ə for *a* in *ago;* ′, (ā′b'l); ë, Fr. coeur; ö, Fr. feu; Fr. mon; ü, Fr. duc; kh, G. ich, doch; ‡ foreign; < derived from gulf **2.** anything too deep for measurement *[an abyss of shame]*

**Ab·ys·sin·i·a** (ə bĭs′ĭn′ē ə) Ethiopia —**Ab′ys·sin′i·an** *adj., n.*

**-ac** (ak, ək) [< Gr.] *a suffix meaning:* **1.** relating to *[cardiac]* **2.** affected by *[maniac]*

**Ac** *Chem.* actinium

**AC, A.C., a.c.** alternating current

**a·ca·cia** (ə kā′shə) *n.* [< Gr. *akakia*; thorny tree] **1.** a tree or shrub with yellow or white flower clusters **2.** the locust tree

**ac·a·dem·ic** (ak′ə dem′ik) *adj.* **1.** of academies or colleges **2.** having to do with liberal arts rather than technical education **3.** formal; pedantic **4.** merely theoretical —**ac′a·dem′i·cal·ly** *adv.*

**a·cad·e·mi·cian** (ə kad′ə mish′ən) *n.* a member of an academy (sense 3)

**a·cad·e·my** (ə kad′ə mē) *n., pl.* **-mies** [< Gr. *akadēmeia*, place where Plato taught] **1.** a private secondary school **2.** a school for special instruction **3.** an association of scholars, writers, etc. for advancing an art or science

**a·can·thus** (ə kan′thəs) *n., pl.* **-thus·es, -thi** (-thī) [< Gr. *acantha*, thorn] **1.** a plant with lobed, often spiny leaves **2.** *Archit.* a representation of these leaves

**a cap·pel·la** (ä′ kə pel′ə) [It., in chapel style] without instrumental accompaniment: said of choral singing

**ac·cede** (ak sēd′) *vi.* **-ced′ed, -ced′ing** [< L. *ad-*, to + *cedere*, go, yield] **1.** to enter upon the duties (of an office) **2.** to assent; agree (*to*)

**ac·cel·er·ate** (ək sel′ə rāt′, ak-) *vt.* **-at′ed, -at′ing** [< L. *ad-*, to + *celerare*, hasten] **1.** to increase the speed of **2.** to cause to happen sooner —*vi.* to go faster —**ac·cel′er·a′tion** *n.* —**ac·cel′er·a′tor** *n.*

**ac·cent** (ak′sent; *for v. also* ak sent′) *n.* [< L. *ad-*, to + *canere*, sing] **1.** emphasis given a spoken syllable or word **2.** a mark showing such emphasis or indicating pronunciation **3.** a distinguishing manner of pronouncing *[an Irish accent]* **4.** special emphasis or attention **5.** *Music & Verse* rhythmic stress —*vt.* **1.** to emphasize; stress **2.** to mark with an accent

**ac·cen·tu·ate** (ak sen′choo wāt′, ək-) *vt.* **-at′ed, -at′ing** to accent; emphasize —**ac·cen′tu·a′tion** *n.*

**ac·cept** (ak sept′, ak-) *vt.* [< L. *ad-*, to + *capere*, take] **1.** to receive, esp. willingly **2.** to approve **3.** to agree to **4.** to believe in **5.** to agree to pay

**ac·cept′a·ble** *adj.* worth accepting; satisfactory —**ac·cept′a·bil′i·ty, ac·cept′a·ble·ness** *n.*

**ac·cept′ance** *n.* **1.** an accepting **2.** approval **3.** belief in; assent **4.** a promise to pay

**ac·cept′ed** *adj.* generally regarded as true, proper, etc.; approved; conventional

**ac·cess** (ak′ses) *n.* [see ACCEDE] **1.** approach or means of approach **2.** the right to enter, use, etc. **3.** an outburst; fit *[in an access of rage]*

**ac·ces′si·ble** *adj.* **1.** that can be approached or entered, esp. easily **2.** obtainable —**ac·ces′si·bil′i·ty, ac·ces′si·ble·ness** *n.* —**ac·ces′si·bly** *adv.*

**ac·ces·sion** (ak sesh′ən) *n.* **1.** the act of attaining (a throne, power, etc.) **2.** assent **3.** *a*) increase by addition *b*) an addition, as to a collection

**ac·ces·so·ry** (ak ses′ər ē, ak-) *adj.* [see ACCEDE] **1.** additional; extra **2.** helping in an unlawful act —*n., pl.* **-ries 1.** something extra or complementary **2.** one who, though absent, helps another to break the law

**ac·ci·dent** (ak′sə dənt) *n.* [< L. *ad-*, to + *cadere*, to fall] **1.** an unintended happening **2.** a mishap **3.** chance

**ac′ci·den′tal** (-den′t'l) *adj.* happening by chance —**ac′ci·den′tal·ly** *adv.*

**ac′ci·dent-prone′** (-prōn′) *adj.* seemingly inclined to become involved in accidents

**ac·claim** (ə klām′) *vt.* [< L. *ad-*, to + *clamare*, to cry out] to greet or announce with loud approval or applause; hail —*n.* loud approval

**ac·cla·ma·tion** (ak′lə mā′shən) *n.* **1.** loud applause or approval **2.** an approving vote by voice

**ac·cli·mate** (ak′lə māt′, ə klī′mət) *vt., vi.* **-mat′ed, -mat′ing** [see AD- & CLIMATE] to accustom or become accustomed to a new climate or environment: also **ac·cli′ma·tize′** (-tīz′) **-tized′, -tiz′ing** —**ac′cli·ma′tion** *n.*

**ac·cliv·i·ty** (ə kliv′ə tē) *n., pl.* **-ties** [< L. *ad-*, to + *clivus*, hill] an upward slope

**ac·co·lade** (ak′ə lād′) *n.* [Fr. < It. *accollare*, to embrace] an approving mention; award

**ac·com·mo·date** (ə käm′ə dāt′) *vt.* **-dat′ed, -dat′ing** [< L. *ad-*, to + *commodare*, to fit] **1.** to adapt **2.** to do a favor for **3.** to have space for; lodge

**ac·com′mo·dat′ing** *adj.* obliging

**ac·com′mo·da′tion** *n.* **1.** adjustment **2.** willingness to do favors **3.** a help; convenience **4.** *[pl.]* *a*) lodgings *b*) traveling space, as in a train

**ac·com·pa·ni·ment** (ə kump′ni mənt) *n.* anything that accompanies something else, as an instrumental part supporting a solo voice, etc.

**ac·com·pa·ny** (ə kum′pə nē, ə kump′nē) *vt.* **-nied, -ny·ing** [see AD- & COMPANION] **1.** to go with **2.** to add to **3.** to play or sing an accompaniment for or to —**ac·com′pa·nist** *n.*

**ac·com·plice** (ə käm′plis) *n.* [< *a* (the article) + L. *complex:* see COMPLEX] a partner in crime

**ac·com·plish** (ə käm′plish) *vt.* [< L. *ad*, intens. + *complere:* see COMPLETE] to succeed in doing; complete

**ac·com′plished** *adj.* **1.** done; completed **2.** skilled; expert

**ac·com′plish·ment** *n.* **1.** completion **2.** work completed; an achievement **3.** a social art or skill

**ac·cord** (ə kôrd′) *vt.* [< L. *ad-*, to + *cor*, heart] **1.** to make agree **2.** to grant —*vi.* to agree; harmonize (*with*) —*n.* mutual agreement; harmony —

of one's own accord willingly —with one accord all agreeing

**ac·cord/ance** *n.* agreement; conformity —**ac·cord/ant** *adj.*

**ac·cord/ing** *adj.* in harmony —*adv.* accordingly —**according to** 1. in agreement with 2. as stated by

**ac·cord/ing·ly** *adv.* 1. in a fitting and proper way 2. therefore

**ac·cor·di·on** (ə kôr/dē ən) *n.* [prob. < It. *accordare*, to be in tune] a keyed musical instrument with a bellows, which is pressed to force air through reeds

ACCORDION

**ac·cost** (ə kôst/) *vt.* [< L. *ad-*, to + *costa*, side] to approach and speak to

**ac·count** (ə kount/) *vt.* [< L. *computare*: see COMPUTE] to judge to be —*vi.* 1. to give a financial reckoning (*to*) 2. to give reasons (*for*) —*n.* 1. a counting 2. [*often pl.*] a record of business transactions 3. *same as a*) BANK ACCOUNT *b*) CHARGE ACCOUNT 4. a credit customer 5. worth; importance 6. an explanation 7. a report —**on account** as partial payment —**on account of** because of —**on no account** under no circumstances —**take into account** to consider —**turn to account** to get use or profit from

**ac·count/a·ble** *adj.* 1. responsible; liable 2. explainable

**ac·count/ant** (ə kount/'nt) *n.* one whose work is accounting

**ac·count/ing** *n.* the figuring and recording of financial accounts

**ac·cou·ter** (ə kōōt/ər) *vt.* [? < L. *consuere*, to sew] to outfit; equip

**ac·cou/ter·ments** (-mənts) *n.pl.* 1. clothes 2. a soldier's equipment

**ac·cred·it** (ə kred/it) *vt.* [see CREDIT] 1. to authorize; certify 2. to believe in 3. to attribute —**ac·cred/it·a/tion** (-ə tā/shən) *n.*

**ac·cre·tion** (ə krē/shən) *n.* [< L. *ad-*, to + *crescere*, grow] 1. growth in size, esp. by addition 2. accumulated matter 3. a growing together of parts

**ac·crue** (ə krōō/) *vi.* -crued/, -cru/ing [see prec.] to come as a natural growth or periodic increase, as interest on money —**ac·cru/al** *n.*

**acct.** account

**ac·cul·tu·rate** (ə kul/chə rāt/) *vi., vt.* -rat/ed, -rat/ing to undergo, or change by, acculturation

**ac·cul·tu·ra·tion** (ə kul/chə rā/shən) *n.* 1. adaptation to a culture, esp. a new or different one 2. mutual influence of different cultures

**ac·cu·mu·late** (ə kyōōm/yə lāt/) *vt., vi.* -lat/ed, -lat/ing [< L. *ad-* + *cumulare*, to heap] to pile up or collect —**ac·cu/mu·la/tion** *n.* —**ac·cu/mu·la/tive** *adj.*

**ac·cu·ra·cy** (ak/yər ə sē) *n.* the state of being accurate; precision

**ac/cu·rate** (-it) *adj.* [< L. *ad-*, to + *cura*, care] 1. careful and exact 2. free from errors —**ac/cu·rate·ly** *adv.* —**ac/cu·rate·ness** *n.*

**ac·curs·ed** (ə kur/sid, -kurst/) *adj.* 1. under a curse 2. damnable Also **ac·curst/** —**ac·curs/ed·ness** *n.*

**ac·cu·sa·tion** (ak/yə zā/shən) *n.* 1. an accusing 2. what one is accused of —**ac·cu·sa·to·ry** (ə kyōō/zə tôr/ē) *adj.*

**ac·cu·sa·tive** (ə kyōō/zə tiv) *adj.* [see ff.] *Gram.* designating or in the case of an object of a verb or preposition; objective —*n.* the accusative case

**ac·cuse** (ə kyōōz/) *vt.* -cused/, -cus/ing [< L. *ad-*, to + *causa*, a cause] 1. to blame 2. to bring charges against (*of* doing wrong) —**ac·cus/er** *n.*

**ac·cus·tom** (ə kus/təm) *vt.* to make familiar by. custom, habit, or use

**ac·cus/tomed** *adj.* 1. customary; usual 2. wont or used (*to*)

**ace** (ās) *n.* [< L. as, unit] 1. a playing card, etc. with one spot 2. a point, as in tennis, won by a single stroke 3. an expert, esp. in combat flying 4. *Golf* a hole in one —*adj.* [Colloq.] first-rate

**ace in the hole** [Slang] any advantage held in reserve

**ac·er·bate** (as/ər bāt/) *vt.* -bat/ed, -bat/ing [< L. *acerbare*] 1. to make sour or bitter 2. to irritate; vex

**a·cer·bi·ty** (ə sur/bə tē) *n., pl.* -ties [< L. *acerbus*, bitter] 1. sourness 2. sharpness of temper, words, etc. —**a·cerb/** *adj.*

**ac·et·an·i·lide** (as/ə tan/ə līd/) *n.* [< ACETIC & ANILINE] a drug used to lessen pain and fever

**ac·e·tate** (as/ə tāt/) *n.* 1. a salt or ester of acetic acid 2. something, esp. a fabric, made of an acetate of cellulose

**a·ce·tic** (ə sēt/ik) *adj.* [< L. *acetum*, vinegar] of the sharp, sour liquid (**acetic acid**) found in vinegar

**a·cet·i·fy** (ə set/ə fī/, -sēt/-) *vt., vi.* -fied/, -fy/ing to change into vinegar or acetic acid

**ac·e·tone** (as/ə tōn/) *n.* [< prec.] a flammable, colorless liquid used as a solvent for certain oils, etc. —**ac/e·ton/ic** (-tän/ik) *adj.*

**a·cet·y·lene** (ə set/'l ēn/) *n.* [< ACETIC + -YL + -ENE] a gas used for lighting, and, with oxygen in a blowtorch, for welding, etc.

**a·ce·tyl·sal·i·cyl·ic acid** (ə sēt/'l-sal/ə sil/ik) aspirin

**ache** (āk) *vi.* ached, ach/ing [< OE. *acan*] 1. to have or give dull, steady pain 2. [Colloq.] to yearn —*n.* a dull, continuous pain —**ach/y** *adj.*

**a·chene** (ā kēn/, ə-) *n.* [< Gr. *a-*, not + *chainein*, to gape] any small, dry fruit with one seed

**a·chieve** (ə chēv/) *vt.* **a·chieved/**, **a·chiev/ing** [< L. *ad-*, to + *caput*, head] 1. to do successfully 2. to get by effort —**a·chiev/a·ble** *adj.*

---

**a·chieve′ment** n. 1. an achieving 2. a thing achieved; feat; exploit

**A·chil·les** (ə kil′ēz) a Greek hero killed in the Trojan War

**Achilles′ heel** (one's) vulnerable spot

**ach·ro·mat·ic** (ak′rə mat′ik) adj. [< Gr. a-, without + chrōma, color] refracting white light without breaking it up into its component colors

**ac·id** (as′id) adj. [< L. acidus, sour] 1. sour; sharp; tart 2. of an acid —n. 1. a sour substance 2. [Slang] same as LSD 3. Chem. any compound that reacts with a base to form a salt —a·cid′i·ty (ə sid′ə tē) n., pl. -ties —ac′id·ly adv.

**a·cid·i·fy** (ə sid′ə fī′) vt., vi. -fied′, -fy′ing 1. to make or become sour 2. to change into an acid

**ac·i·do·sis** (as′ə dō′sis) n. a condition in which the alkali reserve of the body is lower than normal

**acid test** a crucial, final test

**a·cid·u·late** (ə sij′oo lāt′) vt. -lat′ed, -lat′ing to make somewhat acid or sour

**a·cid·u·lous** (ə sij′oo ləs) adj. 1. somewhat acid or sour 2. sarcastic

**-a·cious** (ā′shəs) [< L.] a suffix meaning inclined to, full of [tenacious]

**-ac·i·ty** (as′ə tē) a suffix used to form nouns corresponding to adjectives ending in -ACIOUS [tenacity]

**ack-ack** (ak′ak′) n. [echoic] [Slang] an antiaircraft gun or its fire

**ac·knowl·edge** (ək näl′ij) vt. -edged, -edg·ing [cf. KNOWLEDGE] 1. to admit as true 2. to recognize the authority or claims of 3. to respond to 4. to express thanks for 5. to state that one has received (a letter, etc.) —ac·knowl′edg·ment, ac·knowl′edge·ment n.

**ac·me** (ak′mē) n. [Gr. akmē, a point, top] the highest point; peak

**ac·ne** (ak′nē) n. [? < Gr.: see prec.] a skin disorder usually causing pimples on the face, etc.

**ac·o·lyte** (ak′ə līt′) n. [< Gr. akolouthos, follower] 1. an altar boy 2. an attendant; helper

**ac·o·nite** (ak′ə nīt′) n. [< Gr.] 1. a poisonous plant with hoodlike flowers 2. a sedative drug made from its roots

**a·corn** (ā′kôrn′) n. [< OE. æcern, nut] the nut of the oak tree

**acorn squash** a kind of winter squash, acorn-shaped with dark-green skin and yellow flesh

**a·cous·tic** (ə kōōs′tik) adj. [< Gr. akouein, to hear] having to do with hearing or acoustics: also **a·cous′ti·cal** —a·cous′ti·cal·ly adv.

**a·cous·tics** (-tiks) n.pl. 1. the qualities of a room, etc. that determine how clearly sounds can be heard in it 2. [with sing. v.] the branch of physics dealing with sound, esp. with its transmission

**ac·quaint** (ə kwānt′) vt. [< L. ad-, to + cognoscere, know] 1. to inform 2. to make familiar (with)

**ac·quaint′ance** n. 1. knowledge got from personal experience 2. a person whom one knows slightly

**ac·qui·esce** (ak′wē es′) vi. -esced′, -esc′ing [< L. ad-, to + quiescere, to be at rest] to consent without protest (often with in) —ac′qui·es′cence n. —ac′qui·es′cent adj.

**ac·quire** (ə kwīr′) vt. -quired′, -quir′ing [< L. ad-, to + quærere, to seek] 1. to gain by one's own efforts 2. to get as one's own —ac·quir′a·ble adj. —ac·quire′ment n.

**ac·qui·si·tion** (ak′wə zish′ən) n. 1. an acquiring 2. something acquired

**ac·quis·i·tive** (ə kwiz′ə tiv) adj. eager to acquire (money, etc.); grasping —ac·quis′i·tive·ness n.

**ac·quit** (ə kwit′) vt. -quit′ted, -quit′ting [< L. ad, to + quietare, to quiet] 1. to release from an obligation, etc. 2. to clear (a person) of a charge 3. to conduct (oneself); behave —ac·quit′tal n.

**a·cre** (āk′ər) n. [OE. æcer, field] a measure of land, 43,560 sq. ft.

**a′cre·age** (-ij) n. acres collectively

**ac·rid** (ak′rid) adj. [< L. acris, sharp] 1. sharp or bitter to the taste or smell 2. sharp in speech, etc. —a·crid·i·ty (a krid′ə tē) n. —ac′rid·ly adv.

**ac·ri·mo·ny** (ak′rə mō′nē) n., pl. -nies [< L. acer, sharp] bitterness or harshness of manner or speech —ac′ri·mo′ni·ous adj.

**ac·ro·bat** (ak′rə bat′) n. [< Gr. akrobatos, walking on tiptoe] a performer on the trapeze, tightrope, etc.; gymnast —ac′ro·bat′ic adj.

**ac·ro·bat·ics** (-iks) n.pl. [also with sing. v.] 1. an acrobat's tricks 2. any tricks requiring great skill

**ac·ro·nym** (ak′rə nim) n. [< Gr. akros, at the end + onyma, name] a word formed from the first (or first few) letters of several words, as radar

**ac·ro·pho·bi·a** (ak′rə fō′bē ə) n. [< Gr. akros, at the top + -PHOBIA] an abnormal fear of being in high places

**A·crop·o·lis** (ə kräp′ə ləs) [< Gr. akros, at the top + polis, city] the fortified hill in Athens on which the Parthenon was built

**a·cross** (ə krôs′) adv. 1. crosswise 2. from one side to the other —prep. 1. from one side to the other of 2. on the other side of 3. into contact with by chance [to come across a find]

**a·cross′-the-board′** adj. 1. combining win, place, and show, as a bet 2. affecting all classes or groups

**a·cros·tic** (ə kräs′tik) n. [< Gr. akros, at the end + stichos, line of verse] a poem, etc. in which certain letters in each line, as the first or last, spell out a word, motto, etc.

**a·cryl·ic** (ə kril′ik) adj. 1. designating any of a group of synthetic fibers used to make fabrics 2. designating any of a group of clear, synthetic resins

**act** (akt) n. [< L. agere, to do] 1. a thing done 2. a doing 3. a law 4. a main division of a drama or opera 5. a short performance, as on a variety show 6. something done merely for show —vt. to perform in (a play or part) —vi. 1. to perform on the stage, etc. 2. to behave 3. to function 4. to have an effect (on) 5. to appear to be —act up [Colloq.] to misbehave

**ACTH** [< *a(dreno)c(ortico)t(ropic) h(ormone)*] a pituitary hormone that acts on the adrenal cortex

**act·ing** (ak'tiŋ) *adj.* temporarily doing the duties of another —*n.* the art of an actor

**ac·tin·ic** (ak tin'ik) *adj.* [< Gr. *aktis*, ray] designating one or of light rays (violet or ultraviolet) that produce chemical changes

**ac·ti·nide series** (ak'tə nīd') a group of radioactive chemical elements from element 89 (actinium) through element 103 (lawrencium)

**ac·tin·i·um** (ak tin'ē əm) *n.* [< Gr. *aktis*, ray] a radioactive chemical element

**ac·tion** (ak'shən) *n.* 1. the doing of something 2. a thing done 3. [*pl.*] behavior 4. the way of working, as of a machine 5. the moving parts, as of a gun 6. the sequence of events, as in a story 7. a lawsuit 8. military combat 9. [Slang] activity —**bring** (or **take**) **action** to start a lawsuit

**ac·ti·vate** (ak'tə vāt') *vt.* -**vat·ed**, -**vat'ing** 1. to make active 2. to put (a military unit) on active status 3. to make radioactive 4. to purify sewage by aeration —**ac'ti·va'tion** *n.* —**ac'·ti·va'tor** *n.*

**activated carbon** a form of highly porous carbon that can adsorb gases, vapors, and colloidal particles: also **activated charcoal**

**ac·tive** (ak'tiv) *adj.* 1. acting; working 2. causing motion or change 3. lively; agile 4. indicating the voice of a verb whose subject performs the action —**ac'tive·ly** *adv.*

**ac·tiv·ism** (-tə vis'm) *n.* the doctrine or policy of taking direct action to achieve a political or social end —**ac'tiv·ist** *adj., n.*

**ac·tiv·i·ty** (ak tiv'ə tē) *n., pl.* -**ties** 1. a being active 2. liveliness 3. a specific action [student *activities*]

**ac·tor** (ak'tər) *n.* 1. one who does a thing 2. one who acts in plays, movies, etc. —**ac'tress** *n.fem.*

**ac·tu·al** (ak'choo wəl) *adj.* [< L. *agere*, to do] 1. existing in reality 2. existing at the time —**ac'tu·al·ly** *adv.*

**ac'tu·al'i·ty** (-wal'ə tē) *n.* 1. reality 2. *pl.* -**ties** an actual thing

**ac·tu·al·ize** (ak'choo wə līz') *vt.* -**ized'**, -**iz'ing** 1. to make actual or real 2. to make realistic

**ac·tu·ar·y** (ak'choo wer'ē) *n., pl.* -**ies** [L. *actuarius*, clerk] one who figures insurance risks, premiums, etc. — **ac'tu·ar'i·al** *adj.*

**ac·tu·ate** (ak'choo wāt') *vt.* -**at'ed**, -**at'ing** 1. to put into action 2. to impel to action —**ac'tu·a'tor** *n.*

**a·cu·i·ty** (ə kyōō'ə tē) *n.* [< L. *acus*, needle] keenness of thought or vision

**a·cu·men** (ə kyōō'mən) *n.* [L. < *acuere*, sharpen] keenness of mind or insight

**ac·u·punc·ture** (ak'yoo puŋk'chər) *n.* [< L. *acus*, needle + PUNCTURE]

the ancient practice, esp. among the Chinese, of piercing parts of the body with needles to treat disease or relieve pain

**a·cute** (ə kyōōt') *adj.* [< L. *acuere*, sharpen] 1. sharp-pointed 2. keen of mind 3. sensitive [*acute* hearing] 4. severe, as pain 5. severe but not chronic [an *acute* disease] 6. very serious 7. less than 90° [*acute* angles] —**a·cute'ly** *adv.* —**a·cute'ness** *n.*

**acute accent** a mark (´) showing the quality of a vowel, stress, etc.

**-a·cy** (ə sē) [ult. < Gr.] a suffix meaning quality, condition, etc. [*celibacy*]

**ad** (ad) *n.* [Colloq.] an advertisement

**ad-** [L.] a prefix meaning motion toward, addition to, nearness to: also **a-**, **ac-**, **af-**, **ag-**, **al-**, **an-**, etc. before certain consonants

**A.D.** [L. *Anno Domini*, in the year of the Lord] of the Christian era: used with dates

**ad·age** (ad'ij) *n.* [< L. *ad-*, to + *aio*, I say] an old saying; proverb

**a·da·gio** (ə dä'jō, -zhō) *adv.* [It. *ad agio*, at ease] *Music* slowly —*adj.* slow —*n., pl.* -**gios** 1. a slow movement in music 2. a slow ballet dance

**Ad·am** (ad'əm) [Heb. < *ādām*, human being] *Bible* the first man

**ad·a·mant** (ad'ə mənt) *n.* [< Gr. *a-*, not + *daman*, subdue] a very hard substance —*adj.* inflexible; unyielding

**Ad·ams** (ad'əmz) 1. **John**, 1735–1826; 2d president of U.S. (1797–1801) 2. **John Quin·cy** (kwin'sē), 1767–1848; 6th president of U.S. (1825–29): son of *prec.*

**Adam's apple** the projection of cartilage in the front of the throat, esp. of a man

**a·dapt** (ə dapt') *vt.* [< L. *ad-*, to + *aptare*, to fit] 1. to make suitable, esp. by changing 2. to adjust (oneself) to new circumstances —**ad·ap·ta·tion** (ad'əp tā'shən) *n.*

**a·dapt'a·ble** *adj.* able to adjust or be adjusted —**a·dapt'a·bil'i·ty** *n.*

**add** (ad) *vt.* [< L. *ad-*, to + *dare*, give] 1. to join (to) so as to increase 2. to state further 3. to combine (numbers) into a sum —*vi.* 1. to cause an increase (*to*) 2. to find a sum —**add up** to seem reasonable —**add up to** to mean; signify —**add'·a·ble, add'i·ble** *adj.*

**ad·den·dum** (ə den'dəm) *n., pl.* -**da** (-də) [L.] a thing added, as an appendix

**ad·der** (ad'ər) *n.* [< OE. *nædre*] 1. a poisonous snake of Europe 2. any of several harmless snakes of N. America

**ad·dict** (ə dikt'; *for n.* ad'ikt) *vt.* [< L. *addicere*, give assent] 1. to give (oneself) up (*to* a strong habit) 2. to make become addicted —*n.* one addicted to a habit, as to using drugs —**ad·dic'tion** *n.* —**ad·dic'tive** *adj.*

**Ad·dis A·ba·ba** (ä'dis ä'bə bə) capital of Ethiopia: pop. 443,000

**ad·di·tion** (ə dish'ən) *n.* 1. an adding of numbers to get a sum 2. a joining of one thing to another 3. a part added —**in addition (to)** besides

**ad·di'tion·al** (-əl) *adj.* added; more; extra —**ad·di'tion·al·ly** *adv.*

**ad·di·tive** (ad'ə tiv) *n.* something added —*adj.* of addition

**ad·dle** (ad''l) *vt., vi.* -**dled,** -**dling** [< OE. *adela,* mud] 1. to make or become rotten 2. to make or become confused

**ad·dress** (ə dres'; *for n., esp.* 2 & 3, *also* ad'res) *vt.* [< VL. *directiare,* to direct] 1. to direct (words) *to* 2. to speak or write to 3. to write the destination on (a letter, etc.) 4. to apply (oneself) *to* —*n.* 1. a speech 2. the place where one lives or receives mail 3. the destination indicated on an envelope 4. skill; tact

**ad·dress·ee** (ad'res ē') *n.* the person to whom mail, etc. is addressed

**ad·duce** (ə dōōs') *vt.* -**duced',** -**duc'ing** [< L. *ad-,* to + *ducere,* to lead] to give as a reason or proof

**-ade** (ād) [ult. < L.] *a suffix meaning:* 1. the act of [*blockade*] 2. participant(s) in an action [*brigade*] 3. drink made from [*limeade*]

**A·den** (äd''n, ād''n), Gulf of gulf of the Arabian Sea, south of Arabia

**ad·e·noids** (ad'n oidz') *n.pl.* [< Gr. *adēn,* gland + -OID] lymphoid growths in the throat behind the nose: they can obstruct nasal breathing

**ad·ept** (ə dept'; *for n.* ad'ept) *adj.* [< L. *ad-,* to + *apisci,* attain] highly skilled —*n.* an expert —**ad·ept'ly** *adv.* —**ad·ept'ness** *n.*

**ad·e·quate** (ad'ə kwət) *adj.* [< L. *ad-,* to + *aequare,* make equal] enough for what is required; sufficient; suitable —**ad'e·qua·cy** (-kwə sē) *n.* —**ad'e·quate·ly** *adv.*

**ad·here** (əd hir') *vi.* -**hered',** -**her'ing** [< L. *ad-,* to + *haerere,* to stick] 1. to stick fast; stay attached 2. to give allegiance or support (*to*) — **ad·her'ence** *n.*

**ad·her'ent** *n.* a supporter or follower (*of* a cause, etc.)

**ad·he·sion** (əd hē'zhən) *n.* 1. an adhering or a being stuck together 2. body tissues abnormally joined

**ad·he'sive** (-hēs'iv) *adj.* 1. sticking 2. sticky —*n.* an adhesive substance

**ad hoc** (ad' häk') [L., to this] for a specific purpose [an *ad hoc* committee]

**a·dieu** (ə dyōō', -dōō'; *Fr.* ä dyö') *interj., n., pl.* **a·dieus';** *Fr.* **a·dieux'** (-dyö') [Fr.] goodbye

**ad in·fi·ni·tum** (ad in'fə nīt'əm) [L.] endlessly; without limit

**a·di·os** (a'dē ōs'; *Sp.* ä dyōs') *interj.* [< Sp.] goodbye

**ad·i·pose** (ad'ə pōs') *adj.* [< L. *adeps,* fat] of animal fat; fatty

**Ad·i·ron·dack Mountains** (ad'ə rän'dak) mountain range in NE New York: also **Adirondacks**

**adj.** 1. adjective 2. adjutant

**ad·ja·cent** (ə jās'ənt) *adj.* [< L. *ad-,* to + *jacere,* to lie] near or close (*to*); adjoining —**ad·ja'cen·cy** *n.* —**ad·ja'cent·ly** *adv.*

**ad·jec·tive** (aj'ik tiv) *n.* [< L. *adjicere,* add to] a word used to limit or qualify a noun or other substantive —**ad'jec·ti'val** (-tī'v'l) *adj.* —**ad'jec·ti'val·ly** *adv.*

**ad·join** (ə join') *vt.* [< L. *ad-,* to + *jungere,* join] to be next to —*vi.* to be in contact —**ad·join'ing** *adj.*

**ad·journ** (ə jurn') *vt.* [< OFr. *a,* at + *jorn,* day] to suspend (a meeting, session, etc.) for a time —*vi.* 1. to suspend a meeting, etc. for a time 2. [Colloq.] to retire (*to* another room, etc.) —**ad·journ'ment** *n.*

**ad·judge** (ə juj') *vt.* -**judged',** -**judg'ing** [< L. *ad-,* to + *judicare,* to judge] 1. to decide by law 2. to declare, order, or award by law

**ad·ju·di·cate** (ə jōō'də kāt') *vt.* -**cat'ed,** -**cat'ing** *Law* to hear and decide (a case) —*vi.* to serve as judge (*in* or *on*) —**ad·ju'di·ca'tion** *n.* —**ad·ju'di·ca'tor** *n.* —**ad·ju'di·ca·to'ry** (-kə tôr'ē) *adj.*

**ad·junct** (aj'uŋkt) *n.* [see ADJOIN] a secondary or nonessential addition

**ad·jure** (ə joor') *vt.* -**jured',** -**jur'ing** [< L. *ad-,* to + *jurare,* swear] 1. to charge solemnly under oath 2. to ask earnestly —**ad'ju·ra'tion** *n.*

**ad·just** (ə just') *vt.* [< OFr. *ajoster,* to join] 1. to change so as to fit 2. to regulate (a watch, etc.) 3. to settle rightly 4. to decide the amount to be paid in settling (an insurance claim) —*vi.* to adapt oneself —**ad·just'a·ble** *adj.* —**ad·just'er, ad·jus'tor** *n.* —**ad·just'ment** *n.*

**ad·ju·tant** (aj'ə tənt) *n.* [< L. *ad-,* to + *juvare,* to help] 1. an assistant 2. a military staff officer who assists the commanding officer 3. a large stork of India and Africa

**ad·lib** (ad'lib') *vt., vi.* -**libbed',** -**lib'bing** [< L. *ad libitum,* at pleasure] [Colloq.] to improvise (words, etc. not in the script) —*n.* [Colloq.] an ad-libbed remark —*adv.* [Colloq.] as one pleases: also **ad lib**

**ad·man** (ad'man') *n., pl.* -**men'** a man whose work is advertising

**ad·min·is·ter** (əd min'ə stər) *vt.* [< L. *ad-,* to + *ministrare,* serve] 1. to manage; direct 2. to give out, as punishment 3. to apply (medicine, etc.) 4. to tender (an oath, etc.)

**ad·min'is·trate'** (-strāt') *vt.* -**trat'ed,** -**trat'ing** to administer; manage

**ad·min'is·tra'tion** (-strā'shən) *n.* 1. management 2. [*often* A-] the executive officials of a government, etc. and their policy 3. their term of office 4. the administering (of punishment, medicine, etc.) —**ad·min'is·tra'tive** *adj.*

**ad·min'is·tra'tor** *n.* 1. one who administers 2. *Law* one appointed to settle an estate

**ad·mi·ra·ble** (ad'mər ə b'l) *adj.* deserving admiration; excellent —**ad'mi·ra·bly** *adv.*

**ad·mi·ral** (ad'mər əl) *n.* [< Ar. *amīr a'ālī,* high leader] 1. the commanding officer of a fleet 2. a naval officer of the highest rank

**ad'mi·ral·ty** (-tē) *n., pl.* -**ties** [*often* A-] the governmental department in charge of naval affairs, as in England

**ad·mi·ra·tion** (ad′mə rā′shən) *n.*
1. an admiring 2. pleased approval

**ad·mire** (əd mīr′) *vt.* -mired′, -mir′-
ing [< L. *ad-*, at + *mirari*, wonder]
1. to regard with wonder and delight
2. to esteem highly —**ad·mir′er** *n.*

**ad·mis·si·ble** (əd mis′ə b'l) *adj.* that
can be accepted or admitted —**ad-
mis′si·bil′i·ty** *n.*

**ad·mis·sion** (əd mish′ən) *n.* 1. an
admitting or being admitted 2. an
entrance fee 3. a conceding, confessing, etc. 4. a thing conceded, confessed, etc.

**ad·mit** (əd mit′) *vt.* -mit′ted, -mit′-
ting [< L. *ad-*, to + *mittere*, send]
1. to permit or entitle to enter or use
2. to allow; leave room for 3. to concede or confess —*vi.* to allow (with
*of*) —**ad·mit′tance** *n.*

**ad·mit′ted·ly** *adv.* by admission or
general agreement

**ad·mix·ture** (ad miks′chər) *n.* [<
L. *ad-*, to + *miscere*, to mix] 1. a
mixture 2. a thing added in mixing
—**ad·mix′** *vt., vi.*

**ad·mon·ish** (əd män′ish) *vt.* [< L.
*ad-*, to + *monere*, warn] 1. to warn
2. to reprove mildly 3. to exhort —
**ad·mo·ni·tion** (ad′mə nish′ən) *n.* —
**ad·mon′i·to′ry** (-ə tôr′ē) *adj.*

**ad nau·se·am** (ad′ nô′zē əm, -shē-)
[L.] to the point of disgust

**a·do** (ə dōō′) *n.* fuss; trouble

**a·do·be** (ə dō′bē) *n.* [Sp.] 1. unburnt,
sun-dried brick 2. clay for making
this brick 3. a building of adobe

**ad·o·les·cence** (ad′'l es′'ns) *n.* the
time of life between puberty and
maturity; youth

**ad′o·les′cent** *adj.* [< L. *ad-*, to +
*alescere*, grow up] of or in adolescence
—*n.* a person during adolescence

**A·don·is** (ə dän′is, -dō′nis) *Gr. Myth.*
a young man loved by Aphrodite —*n.*
a handsome young man

**a·dopt** (ə däpt′) *vt.* [< L. *ad-*, to +
*optare*, choose] 1. to take legally into
one's family and raise as one's own
child 2. to take as one's own 3. to
choose or accept —**a·dop′tion** *n.*

**a·dop·tive** (ə däp′tiv) *adj.* that has
become so by adoption

**a·dor·a·ble** (ə dôr′ə b'l) *adj.* 1.
[Rare] worthy of adoration 2. [Colloq.]
delightful; charming —**a·dor′a·bly**
*adv.*

**ad·o·ra·tion** (ad′ə rā′shən) *n.* 1. a
worshiping 2. great love or devotion

**a·dore** (ə dôr′) *vt.* -dored′, -dor′ing
[< L. *ad-*, to + *orare*, speak] 1. to
worship as divine 2. to love greatly
3. [Colloq.] to like very much

**a·dorn** (ə dôrn′) *vt.* [< L. *ad-*, to +
*ornare*, deck out] 1. to be an ornament to 2. to put decorations on
—**a·dorn′ment** *n.*

**ad·re·nal** (ə drē′n'l) *adj.* [AD-
RENAL] 1. near the kidneys 2. of two
ductless glands (**adrenal glands**),
just above the kidneys in mammals

**Ad·ren·al·in** (ə dren′'l in) *a* trade-

*mark for* a hormone secreted by the
adrenal glands or synthesized for use
as a drug —*n.* [a-] this hormone

**A·dri·at·ic** (Sea) (ā′drē at′ik) sea
between Italy and Yugoslavia

**a·drift** (ə drift′) *adv., adj.* floating
without mooring or direction

**a·droit** (ə droit′) *adj.* [Fr. *à*, to +
*droit*, right] skillful and clever —
**a·droit′ly** *adv.* —**a·droit′ness** *n.*

**ad·sorb** (ad sôrb′) *vt.* [< AD- + L.
*sorbere*, drink in] to collect (a gas,
etc.) in condensed form on a surface
—**ad·sorp′tion** (-sôrp′shən) *n.*

**ad·u·late** (aj′ə lāt′) *vt.* -lat′ed,
-lat′ing [< L. *adulari*, fawn upon] to
flatter servilely —**ad′u·la′tion** *n.*

**a·dult** (ə dult′, ad′ult) *adj.* [see
ADOLESCENT] grown up; mature —*n.*
a mature person, animal, or plant
—**a·dult′hood** *n.* —**a·dult′ness** *n.*

**a·dul·ter·ant** (ə dul′tər ənt) *n.* a
substance that adulterates —*adj.*
adulterating

**a·dul·ter·ate** (ə dul′tə rāt′) *vt.* -at′-
ed, -at′ing [< L. *ad-*, to + *alter*,
other] to make inferior, impure, etc.
by adding an improper substance —
**a·dul′ter·a′tion** *n.*

**a·dul·ter·y** (ə dul′tər ē) *n., pl.* -ies
[see prec.] sexual intercourse between
a married person and another not the
spouse—**a·dul′ter·er** *n.* —**a·dul′ter-
ess** *n.fem.* —**a·dul′ter·ous** *adj.*

**ad·um·brate** (ad′um′brāt) *vt.* -brat-
ed, -brat·ing [< L. *ad-*, to + *umbra*,
shade] 1. to outline vaguely 2. to
foreshadow —**ad′um·bra′tion** *n.*

**adv.** 1. adverb 2. advertisement

**ad·vance** (əd vans′) *vt.* -vanced′,
-vanc′ing [< L. *ab-*, from + *ante*,
before] 1. to bring forward 2. to
suggest 3. to promote 4. to raise the
rate of 5. to lend —*vi.* 1. to go
forward 2. to improve; progress 3.
to rise in rank, price, etc. —*n.* 1. a
moving forward 2. an improvement
3. a rise in value 4. [*pl.*] approaches
to get favor 5. a payment before due
—*adj.* 1. in front [*advance* guard] 2.
beforehand —**in advance** 1. in front
2. ahead of time —**ad·vance′ment** *n.*

**ad·vanced′** *adj.* 1. in front 2. old 3.
ahead or higher in progress, price, etc.

**advance man** a person hired to travel in advance of a theatrical company,
political candidate, etc. to arrange
for publicity, appearances, etc.

**ad·van·tage** (əd van′tij) *n.* [< L. *ab*
*ante*, from before] 1. superiority 2. a
favorable circumstance, event, etc. 3.
gain; benefit —*vt.* -taged, -tag·ing to
be a benefit to —**take advantage of**
1. to use for one's own benefit 2. to
impose upon —**ad·van·ta·geous** (ad′
vən tā′jəs) *adj.*

**Ad·vent** (ad′vent) *n.* [< L. *ad-*, to +
*venire*, come] 1. the period including
the four Sundays just before Christmas 2. [a-] a coming

**ad·ven·ti·tious** (ad′vən tish′əs) *adj.*
[see prec.] not inherent; accidental

---

fat, āpe, cär; ten, ēven; is, bīte; gō, hôrn, tōōl, look; oil, out; up, fur;
chin; she; thin, *then*; zh, leisure; ŋ, ring; ə for *a* in *ago*; ′, (ā′b'l); ë, Fr. coeur;
ö, Fr. feu; Fr. mon; ü, Fr. duc; kh, G. ich, doch; ‡foreign; < derived from

**ad·ven·ture** (əd ven′chər) *n.* [see ADVENT] 1. an exciting and dangerous undertaking 2. an unusual, stirring, often romantic experience —*vt., vi.* -tured, -tur·ing to risk; venture —ad·ven′tur·ous, ad·ven′ture·some *adj.* —ad·ven′tur·ous·ly *adv.*

**ad·ven·tur·er** *n.* 1. one who has or looks for adventures 2. one who seeks to become rich, etc. by dubious schemes —ad·ven′tur·ess *n.fem.*

**ad·verb** (ad′vurb) *n.* [< L. *ad-*, to + *verbum*, word] a word used to modify a verb, adjective, or another adverb, by expressing time, place, manner, degree, etc. —ad·ver′bi·al *adj.* —ad·ver′bi·al·ly *adv.*

**ad·ver·sar·y** (ad′vər ser′ē) *n., pl.* -ies [see ADVERT] an opponent; foe

**ad·verse** (ad vurs′, ad′vərs) *adj.* [see ADVERT] 1. hostile; opposed 2. unfavorable —ad·verse′ly *adv.*

**ad·ver·si·ty** (ad vur′sə tē) *n.* 1. misfortune; wretched or troubled state 2. *pl.* -ties a calamity; disaster

**ad·vert** (ad vurt′) *vi.* [< L. *ad-*, to + *vertere*, to turn] to call attention (*to*); refer

**ad·vert·ent** (-′nt) *adj.* attentive; heedful —ad·vert′ence *n.*

**ad·ver·tise** (ad′vər tīz′) *vt.* -tised′, -tis′ing [see ADVERT] to describe or praise publicly, usually to promote for sale —*vi.* 1. to call public attention to things for sale 2. to ask (*for*) by public notice Also **advertize** —ad′ver·tis′er *n.* —ad′ver·tis′ing *n.*

**ad·ver·tise·ment** (ad′vər tīz′mənt, əd vur′tiz-) *n.* a public notice, usually paid for: also **advertizement**

**ad·vice** (əd vīs′) *n.* [< L. *ad-*, at + *videre*, to look] opinion given as to what to do; counsel

**ad·vis·a·ble** (əd vī′zə b'l) *adj.* proper to be advised; wise; sensible —ad·vis′a·bil′i·ty *n.*

**ad·vise** (əd vīz′) *vt.* -vised′, -vis′ing 1. to give advice to; counsel 2. to offer advice 3. to inform —ad·vis′er, ad·vi′sor *n.*

**ad·vis′ed·ly** (-id lē) *adv.* deliberately

**ad·vise·ment** *n.* careful consideration —take under advisement to consider carefully

**ad·vi·so·ry** (əd vī′zər ē) *adj.* advising or empowered to advise —*n., pl.* -ries a report, esp. about weather conditions

**ad·vo·cate** (ad′və kit, -kāt′; *for v.* -kāt′) *n.* [< L. *ad-*, to + *vocare*, to call] one who pleads another's cause or in support of something —*vt.* -cat′ed, -cat′ing to speak or write in support of —ad′vo·ca·cy (-kə sē) *n.*

**advt.** *pl.* **advts.** advertisement

**adz, adze** (adz) *n.* [OE. *adesa*] an axlike tool for dressing wood, etc.

**AEC, A.E.C.** Atomic Energy Commission

**Ae·ge·an (Sea)** (ē jē′ən) sea between Greece and Turkey

**ae·gis** (ē′jis) *n.* [< Gr. *aigis*, shield of Zeus] 1. protection 2. sponsorship

**Ae·ne·as** (i nē′əs) *Gr. & Rom. Myth.* a Trojan whose adventures are told in a poem (the **Aeneid**) by Virgil

**ae·on** (ē′ən, ē′än) *n. same as* EON

**aer·ate** (er′āt′, ā′ər-) *vt.* -at′ed, -at′ing [AER(O)- + -ATE[1]] 1. to expose to air 2. to charge (liquid) with gas, as to make soda water —aer·a′tion *n.* —aer·a′tor *n.*

**aer·i·al** (er′ē əl, ā ir′ē-) *adj.* [< Gr. *aēr*, air + -AL] 1. of, in, or by air 2. unreal; imaginary 3. of aircraft or flying —*n.* a radio or TV antenna —aer′i·al·ly *adv.*

**aer·i·al·ist** (er′ē əl ist) *n.* an acrobat who performs on a trapeze, high wire, etc.

**aer·ie** (er′ē, ir′ē) *n.* [prob. < L. *ager*, field] the high nest of an eagle or other bird of prey: also **aery**

**aero-** [< Gr. *aēr*, air] *a combining form meaning:* 1. air; of the air 2. of aircraft 3. of gases

**aer·o·bat·ics** (er′ə bat′iks) *n.pl.* [prec. + (ACRO)BATICS] stunts done while flying an aircraft

**aer·o·bic** (er ō′bik) *adj.* [< Gr. *aēr*, air + *bios*, life] able to live or grow only where free oxygen is present

**aer·o·dy·nam·ics** (er′ō dī nam′iks) *n.pl.* [*with sing. v.*] the branch of mechanics dealing with forces exerted by air or other gases in motion —aer′o·dy·nam′ic *adj.*

**aer·o·nau·tics** (-ə nôt′iks) *n.pl.* [*with sing. v.*] the science of making and flying aircraft —aer′o·nau′ti·cal *adj.*

**aer·o·plane** (-plān′) *n.* Brit. var. of AIRPLANE

**aer·o·sol** (-sôl′, -säl′) *n.* [AERO- + SOL(UTION)] a suspension of insoluble particles in a gas —*adj.* 1. of a container in which gas under pressure is used to dispense liquid in a spray or foam 2. so dispensed

**aer·o·space** (-ō spās′) *n.* the earth's atmosphere and the space outside it —*adj.* of missiles, etc. for flight in aerospace

**Aes·chy·lus** (es′kə ləs) 525?-456 B.C.; Gr. writer of tragedies

**Ae·sop** (ē′səp, ē′səp) Gr. fable writer: supposedly lived 6th cent. B.C.

**aes·thete** (es′thēt′) *n.* [Gr. *aisthētēs*, one who perceives] a person who is or pretends to be highly sensitive to art and beauty

**aes·thet·ic** (es thet′ik) *adj.* 1. of aesthetics 2. of beauty 3. sensitive to art and beauty

**aes·thet′ics** *n.pl.* [*with sing. v.*] the philosophy of art and beauty

**a·far** (ə fär′) *adv.* [Poet. or Archaic] at or to a distance

**af·fa·ble** (af′ə b'l) *adj.* [< L. *ad-*, to + *fari*, speak] pleasant; friendly —af′fa·bil′i·ty *n.* —af′fa·bly *adv.*

**af·fair** (ə fer′) *n.* [< L. *ad-*, to + *facere*, do] 1. a thing to do 2. [*pl.*] matters of business 3. any matter, event, etc. 4. an amorous episode

**af·fect** (ə fekt′) *vt.* [< L. *ad-*, to + *facere*, do] 1. to have an effect on; influence 2. to stir the emotions of 3. to like to use, wear, etc. 4. to make a pretense of being, feeling, etc.

**af·fec·ta·tion** (af′ek tā′shən) *n.* 1. a pretending to like, have, etc. 2. artificial behavior

**af·fect′ed** *adj.* **1.** afflicted **2.** influenced **3.** emotionally moved **4.** assumed for effect; artificial **5.** behaving in an artificial way

**af·fect′ing** *adj.* emotionally moving

**af·fec·tion** (ə fek′shən) *n.* **1.** fond or tender feeling **2.** a disease

**af·fec′tion·ate** (-it) *adj.* tender and loving —**af·fec′tion·ate·ly** *adv.*

**af·fer·ent** (af′ər ənt) *adj.* [ < L. *ad-,* to + *ferre,* to bear] bringing inward to a central part, as nerves

**af·fi·ance** (ə fī′əns) *vt.* -**anced,** -**anc·ing** [ < ML. *ad-,* to + *fidare,* to trust] to betroth

**af·fi·da·vit** (af′ə dā′vit) *n.* [ML., he has made oath] a written statement made on oath

**af·fil·i·ate** (ə fil′ē āt′; *for n.* -it) *vt.* -**at′ed, -at′ing** [ < ML. *affiliare,* adopt as a son] **1.** to take in as a member **2.** to associate (oneself *with*) —*vi.* to join —*n.* an affiliated person, club, etc. —**af·fil′i·a′tion** *n.*

**af·fin·i·ty** (ə fin′ə tē) *n., pl.* -**ties** [ < L. *affinis,* adjacent] **1.** relationship by marriage **2.** close relationship **3.** a likeness implying common origin **4.** a spontaneous attraction to, or liking for, a person or thing

**af·firm** (ə furm′) *vt.* [ < L. *ad-,* to + *firmare,* make firm] **1.** to declare positively; assert **2.** to confirm; ratify —*vi.* *Law* to make a formal statement, but not under oath —**af·fir·ma·tion** (af′ər mā′shən) *n.*

**af·firm·a·tive** (ə fur′mə tiv) *adj.* affirming; answering "yes" —*n.* **1.** an expression of assent **2.** the side upholding the proposition in a debate

**af·fix** (ə fiks′; *for n.* af′iks) *vt.* [ < L. *ad-,* to + *figere,* fasten] **1.** to fasten; attach **2.** to add at the end —*n.* **1.** a thing affixed **2.** a prefix or suffix

**af·fla·tus** (ə flāt′əs) *n.* [ < L. *ad-,* to + *flare,* to blow] inspiration

**af·flict** (ə flikt′) *vt.* [ < L. *ad-,* to + *fligere,* to strike] to cause pain or suffering to; distress greatly

**af·flic·tion** (ə flik′shən) *n.* **1.** pain; suffering **2.** any cause of suffering

**af·flu·ence** (af′loo wəns) *n.* [ < L. *ad-,* to + *fluere,* to flow] **1.** great plenty; abundance **2.** riches; wealth

**af·flu·ent** *adj.* **1.** plentiful **2.** rich; wealthy —**af′flu·ent·ly** *adv.*

**af·ford** (ə fôrd′) *vt.* [ < OE. *geforthian,* to advance] **1.** to spare (money, time, etc.) without much inconvenience **2.** to give; yield [*affords* pleasure]

**af·for·est** (ə fôr′əst) *vt.* [see AD- & FOREST] to turn (land) into forest —**af·for′est·a′tion** (-əs tā′shən) *n.*

**af·fray** (ə frā′) *n.* [ < OFr. *esfraer,* frighten] a noisy brawl

**af·front** (ə frunt′) *vt.* [ < ML. *ad-,* to + *frons,* forehead] to insult openly —*n.* an open insult

**Af·ghan** (af′gan, -gən) *n.* **1.** a native of Afghanistan **2.** [a-] a crocheted or knitted wool blanket or shawl

**Af·ghan·i·stan** (af gan′ə stan′)

country in SW Asia, east of Iran: c. 250,000 sq. mi.; pop. 15,352,000

**a·fi·cio·na·do** (ə fish′ə nä′dō) *n.* [Sp.] a devotee of some sport, art, etc.

**a·field** (ə fēld′) *adv.* **1.** in or to the field **2.** away (from home); astray

**a·fire** (ə fīr′) *adv., adj.* on fire

**a·flame** (ə flām′) *adv., adj.* **1.** in flames **2.** glowing

**AFL-CIO** American Federation of Labor and Congress of Industrial Organizations: merged in 1955

**a·float** (ə flōt′) *adv.* **1.** floating **2.** at sea **3.** flooded, as a ship's deck

**a·flut·ter** (ə flut′ər) *adv., adj.* in a flutter

**a·foot** (ə foot′) *adv.* **1.** on foot **2.** in motion; in progress

**a·fore·men·tioned** (ə fôr′men′shənd) *adj.* mentioned before

**a·fore·said′** (-sed′) *adj.* spoken of before

**a·fore·thought′** *adj.* thought out beforehand; premeditated

**a·foul** (ə foul′) *adv., adj.* in a collision or tangle —**run** (or **fall**) **afoul of** to get into trouble with

**Afr.** **1.** Africa **2.** African

**a·fraid** (ə frād′) *adj.* [see AFFRAY] frightened (*of, that,* or *to*): often merely indicating regret [I'm *afraid* I must]

**Af·ri·ca** (af′ri kə) second largest continent, south of Europe: c. 11,500,000 sq. mi.; pop. c. 310,000,000 —**Af′ri·can** *adj., n.*

**African violet** a tropical African plant with violet, white, or pinkish flowers and hairy, fleshy leaves, often grown as a house plant

**Af·ri·kaans** (af′ri känz′) *n.* [Afrik. < *Afrika,* Africa] an official language of South Africa, based on Dutch

**Af·ro** (af′rō) *adj.* [ < ff.] designating or of a full, bouffant hair style, as worn by some blacks —*n.* an Afro hair style

**Afro-** [ < L. *Afer,* an African] *a combining form meaning:* **1.** Africa **2.** African

**Af·ro-A·mer·i·can** (af′rō ə mer′ə kən) *adj.* of Negro Americans, their culture, etc. —*n.* a Negro American

**aft** (aft) *adv.* [OE. *æftan*] at, near, or toward the stern of a ship or rear of an aircraft

**af·ter** (af′tər) *adv.* [OE. *æfter*] **1.** behind **2.** later —*prep.* **1.** behind **2.** later than **3.** in search of **4.** as a result of **5.** in spite of [*after* all I've said, he's still going] **6.** lower in rank or order than **7.** in imitation of **8.** for [named *after* Lincoln] —*conj.* following the time when —*adj.* **1.** next; later **2.** nearer the rear

**af·ter·birth′** *n.* the placenta and membranes expelled after childbirth

**af·ter·burn′er** (-bur′nər) *n.* a device attached to some engines for burning or utilizing exhaust gases

**af·ter·ef·fect′** *n.* an effect coming later, or as a secondary result

**af·ter·life′** *n.* a life after death

**af·ter·math′** (-math′) *n.* [ < AFTER

---

fat, āpe, cär; ten, ĕven; is, bīte; gō, hôrn, tōōl, look; oil, out; up, fur; chin; she; thin, *th*en; zh, leisure; ŋ, ring; ə for *a* in ago; ′, (ā′b'l); ӗ, Fr. coeur; ö, Fr. feu; Fr. mon; ü, Fr. duc; kh, G. ich, doch; ‡ foreign; < derived from

**+ OE.** *mæth,* cutting of grass] a result, esp. an unpleasant one

**af'ter·noon'** *n.* the time from noon to evening —*adj.* in the afternoon

**af'ter·thought'** *n.* **1.** an idea, explanation, part, etc. coming or added later **2.** a thought coming too late to be apt

**af'ter·ward** (-wərd) *adv.* later; subsequently: also **af'ter·wards**

**Ag** [L. *argentum*] *Chem.* silver

**a·gain** (ə gen') *adv.* [< OE. *on-*, up to + *gegn,* direct] **1.** back into a former condition **2.** once more **3.** besides **4.** on the other hand —**again and again** often; repeatedly —**as much again** twice as much

**a·gainst** (ə genst') *prep.* [see prec.] **1.** in opposition to **2.** toward so as to strike /thrown *against* the wall/ **3.** next to; adjoining **4.** in preparation for /to provide *against* famine/ **5.** as a charge on —**over against 1.** opposite to **2.** as compared with

**Ag·a·mem·non** (ag'ə mem'nän) *Gr. Myth.* commander of the Greek army in the Trojan War

**a·gape** (ə gāp') *adv., adj.* [A- + GAPE] with the mouth wide open

**a·gar-a·gar** (ä'gär ä'gär) *n.* [Malay] a gelatinous product made from seaweed, used in bacterial cultures

**ag·ate** (ag'ət) *n.* [< Gr. *achatēs*] **1.** a hard, semiprecious stone with striped or clouded coloring **2.** a playing marble made of or like this

**a·ga·ve** (ə gä'vē) *n.* [< proper name in Gr. myth] a desert plant with thick, fleshy leaves

**agcy.** agency

**age** (āj) *n.* [< L. *aetas*] **1.** the length of time that a person or thing has existed **2.** a stage of life **3.** old age **4.** a historical or geological period **5.** [*often pl.*] [Colloq.] a long time —*vi., vt.* **aged, ag'ing** or **age'ing** to grow or make old, ripe, mature, etc. —**of age** having reached the age when one is qualified for full legal rights

**-age** (ij) [< LL. *-aticum*] *a suffix meaning:* **1.** act, state, or result of [*usage*] **2.** amount or number of [*acreage*] **3.** place of [*steerage*] **4.** cost of [*postage*]

**a·ged** (ā'jid; *for 2* ājd) *adj.* **1.** old **2.** of the age of —**the aged** old people

**age·ism** (āj'iz'm) *n.* [AGE + (RAC)ISM] discrimination against older people: also sp. **ag'ism**

**age'less** *adj.* **1.** seemingly not growing older **2.** eternal

**a·gen·cy** (ā'jən sē) *n., pl.* **-cies** [< L. *agere,* to act] **1.** action; power **2.** means **3.** a firm, etc. empowered to act for another **4.** an administrative government division

**a·gen·da** (ə jen'də) *n., pl.* **-das** [< L. *agere,* to do] a list of things to be dealt with at a meeting, etc.

**a·gent** (ā'jənt) *n.* [< L. *agere,* to act] **1.** an active force or substance producing an effect **2.** a person, firm, etc. empowered to act for another **3.** a representative of a government agency

**age·old** (āj'ōld') *adj.* ancient

**ag·er·a·tum** (aj'ə rāt'əm) *n.* [< Gr. *ageratos,* not growing old] a plant

of the composite family having small, thick heads of bluish flowers

**ag·glom·er·ate** (ə gläm'ə rāt'; *for adj. & n.* -ər it) *vt., vi.* **-at'ed, -at'ing** [< L. *ad-,* to + *glomerare,* form into a ball] to gather into a mass or ball —*adj.* gathered into a mass or ball —*n.* a jumbled heap, mass, etc.

**ag·glu·ti·nate** (ə gloot'n it; *for v. -āt') adj.* [< L. *ad-,* to + *gluten,* glue] stuck together —*vt., vi.* **nat'ed, -nat'ing** to stick together, as with glue —**ag·glu'ti·na'tion** *n.*

**ag·gran·dize** (ə gran'dīz', ag'rən-) *vt.* **-dized', -diz'ing** [< Fr. *a-,* to + *grandir,* to increase] to make greater, more powerful, richer, etc. —**ag·gran'dize·ment** (-diz mənt) *n.*

**ag·gra·vate** (ag'rə vāt') *vt.* **-vat'ed, -vat'ing** [< L. *ad-,* to + *gravis,* heavy] **1.** to make worse **2.** [Colloq.] to annoy; vex —**ag'gra·va'tion** *n.*

**ag·gre·gate** (ag'rə gət; *for v.* -gāt') *adj.* [< L. *ad-,* to + *grex,* a herd] total —*n.* a mass of distinct things gathered into a total or whole —*vt.* **-gat'ed, -gat'ing** **1.** to gather into a mass **2.** to total —**ag'gre·ga'tion** *n.*

**ag·gres·sion** (ə gresh'ən) *n.* [< L. *aggredi,* to attack] **1.** an unprovoked attack or warlike act **2.** a being aggressive —**ag·gres'sor** *n.*

**ag·gres·sive** (ə gres'iv) *adj.* **1.** boldly hostile; quarrelsome **2.** bold and active; enterprising —**ag·gres'sive·ly** *adv.* —**ag·gres'sive·ness** *n.*

**ag·grieve** (ə grēv') *vt.* **-grieved', -griev'ing** [see AGGRAVATE] to cause grief or injury to; offend; slight

**a·ghast** (ə gast') *adj.* [< OE. *gast,* ghost] feeling great horror or dismay

**ag·ile** (aj'l) *adj.* [< L. *agere,* to act] quick and easy of movement; nimble —**ag'ile·ly** *adv.* —**a·gil·i·ty** (ə jil'ə tē) *n.*

**ag·i·tate** (aj'ə tāt') *vt.* **-tat'ed, -tat'ing** [< L. *agere,* to act] **1.** to stir up or shake up **2.** to excite the feelings of —*vi.* to stir up people so as to produce changes —**ag'i·ta'tion** *n.* —**ag'i·ta'tor** *n.*

**a·gleam** (ə glēm') *adv., adj.* gleaming

**a·glit·ter** (ə glit'ər) *adv., adj.* glittering

**a·glow** (ə glō') *adv., adj.* in a glow (of color or emotion)

**ag·nos·tic** (ag näs'tik) *n.* [< Gr. *a-,* not + base of *gignōskein,* know] one who believes that it is impossible to know whether God exists —*adj.* of an agnostic —**ag·nos'ti·cism** (-tə siz'm) *n.*

**a·go** (ə gō') *adj.* [< OE. *agan,* pass away] gone by; past /years *ago*/ —*adv.* in the past /long *ago*/

**a·gog** (ə gäg') *adv., adj.* [< OFr. *a-* + *gogue,* joke] with eager anticipation or excitement

**ag·o·nize** (ag'ə nīz') *vi.* **-nized', -niz'ing** **1.** to struggle **2.** to be in agony —*vt.* to torture

**ag·o·ny** (ag'ə nē) *n., pl.* **-nies** [< Gr. *agōn,* a contest] **1.** great mental or physical pain **2.** death pangs **3.** a strong outburst (of emotion)

**a·grar·i·an** (ə grer'ē ən) *adj.* [< L.

*ager*, field] 1. of land or the ownership of land 2. of agriculture

**a·gree** (ə grē′) *vi.* **-greed′, -gree′ing** [< L. *ad*, to + *gratus*, pleasing] 1. to consent (*to*) 2. to be in accord 3. to be of the same opinion (*with*) 4. to arrive at an understanding (*about* prices, etc.) 5. to be suitable, healthful, etc. (*with*) —*vt.* to grant [I agree that it's true]

**a·gree′a·ble** *adj.* 1. pleasing or pleasant 2. willing to consent 3. conformable —**a·gree′a·bly** *adv.*

**a·gree′ment** *n.* 1. an agreeing 2. an understanding between people, countries, etc. 3. a contract

**ag·ri·busi·ness** (ag′rə biz′nis) *n.* [see ff. & BUSINESS] farming and associated businesses and industries

**ag·ri·cul·ture** (ag′ri kul′chər) *n.* [< L. *ager*, field + *cultura*, cultivation] the work of producing crops and raising livestock; farming —**ag′ri·cul′tur·al** *adj.* —**ag′ri·cul′tur·al·ly** *adv.* —**ag′ri·cul′tur·ist** *n.*

**a·gron·o·my** (ə grän′ə mē) *n.* [< Gr. *agros*, field + *nemein*, manage] the science and economics of crop production —**a·gron′o·mist** *n.*

**a·ground** (ə ground′) *adv., adj.* on or onto the shore, a reef, etc.

**agt.** agent

**a·gue** (ā′gyo͞o) *n.* [< ML. (*febris*) *acuta*, violent (fever)] a fever, usually malarial, marked by chills

**ah** (ä, ô) *interj.* an exclamation of pain, delight, surprise, etc.

**a·ha** (ä hä′) *interj.* an exclamation of satisfaction, triumph, etc.

**a·head** (ə hed′) *adv., adj.* 1. in or to the front 2. forward; onward 3. in advance 4. winning or profiting —**get ahead** to advance financially, etc. —**get ahead of** to outdo

**a·hem** (ə hem′) *interj.* a cough, etc. made to gain attention, etc.

**a·hoy** (ə hoi′) *interj. Naut.* a call used in hailing

**aid** (ād) *vt., vi.* [< L. *ad*-, to + *juvare*, to help] to help; assist —*n.* 1. help; assistance 2. a helper

**aide** (ād) *n.* [Fr.] 1. an assistant 2. an aide-de-camp

**aide-de-camp, aid-de-camp** (ād′ də kamp′) *n., pl.* **aides-, aids-** [Fr.] a military officer serving as an assistant to a superior

**aid·man** (ād′man′) *n., pl.* **-men′** *Mil.* an enlisted man in a medical corps attached to a combat unit

**ai·grette, ai·gret** (ā′gret, ā gret′) *n.* [see EGRET] the long, white, showy plumes of the egret, once worn for ornament by women

**ail** (āl) *vt.* [OE. *eglian*, to trouble] to cause pain and trouble to —*vi.* to be in poor health

**ai·le·ron** (ā′lə rän′) *n.* [Fr. < L. *ala*, wing] a hinged section at the trailing edge of an airplane wing, used to control its rolling

**ail·ing** (āl′iŋ) *adj.* in poor health

**ail·ment** (āl′mənt) *n.* a mild illness

**aim** (ām) *vi., vt.* [< L. *ad*-, to + *aestimare*, to estimate] 1. to direct (a weapon, blow, etc.) so as to hit 2. to direct (one's efforts) 3. to intend —*n.* 1. an aiming 2. the direction of a missile, blow, etc. 3. intention —**take aim** to aim a weapon, etc.

**aim′less** *adj.* having no purpose —**aim′less·ly** *adv.* —**aim′less·ness** *n.*

**ain't** (ānt) [< *amn't*, contr. of *am not*] [Colloq.] am not: also a dialectal or substandard contraction for *is not*, *are not*, *has not*, and *have not*

**air** (er) *n.* [< Gr. *aēr*] 1. the invisible mixture of gases surrounding the earth 2. a breeze; wind 3. an outward appearance [*air* of dignity] 4. [*pl.*] affected superior manners 5. public expression 6. a tune —*adj.* of aviation —*vt.* 1. to let air into 2. to publicize —**in the air** prevalent —**on** (or **off**) **the air** that is (or is not) broadcasting —**up in the air** 1. not settled 2. [Colloq.] angry, excited, etc.

**air bag** a bag that inflates automatically inside an automobile in a collision, to protect riders from being thrown forward

**air base** a base for military aircraft

**air′borne** *adj.* 1. carried by or through the air 2. aloft or flying

**air brake** a brake operated by the action of compressed air on a piston

**air′brush′** *n.* an atomizer worked by compressed air and used for spraying on paint, etc.: also **air brush**

**air′bus′** *n.* an extremely large passenger airplane, esp. for short trips

**air conditioning** regulation of air humidity and temperature in buildings, etc. —**air′-con·di′tion** *vt.* —**air′-con·di′tion·er** *n.*

**air′-cooled′** *adj.* cooled by having air passed over, into, or through it

**air′craft′** *n., pl.* **-craft′** any machine for traveling through the air

**aircraft carrier** a warship with a large flat deck, for carrying aircraft

**air curtain** (or **door**) a downward forced air current at an open entrance

**air′drome′** (-drōm′) *n.* [< AIR + Gr. *dromos*, course] the physical facilities of an air base

**air′drop′** *n.* the parachuting of supplies or troops from an aircraft in flight —**air′drop′** *vt.*

**Aire·dale** (er′dāl′) *n.* [< *Airedale*, valley in England] a large terrier with a wiry coat

AIREDALE

**air′field′** *n.* a field where aircraft can take off and land

**air′foil′** *n.* a wing, rudder, etc. of an aircraft

**air force** the aviation branch of a country's armed forces

**air gun** a gun or gunlike device operated by compressed air

**air lane** a route for travel by air; airway

**air′lift′** n. a system of transporting troops, supplies, etc. by aircraft —vt. to transport by airlift

**air′line′** n. a system or company for transportation by aircraft —adj. of or on an airline

**air′lin′er** n. a large passenger aircraft operated by an airline

**air lock** an airtight compartment, with adjustable air pressure, between places of unequal air pressure

**air′mail′** n. mail transported by aircraft —vt. to send by airmail

**air′man** (-mən) n., pl. -men 1. an aviator 2. an enlisted person in the U.S. Air Force

**air′plane′** n. a motor-driven or jet-propelled aircraft kept aloft by the forces of air upon its wings

**air′port′** n. a place where aircraft can land and take off, usually with facilities for repair, etc.

**air power** total capacity of a nation for air war

**air pressure** the pressure of the atmosphere or of compressed air

**air raid** an attack by aircraft, esp. bombers

**air rifle** a rifle operated by compressed air

**air′ship′** n. a self-propelled, steerable aircraft that is lighter than air

**air′sick′** adj. nauseated because of air travel —air′sick′ness n.

**air′space′** n. the space above a nation over which it maintains jurisdiction

**air′strip′** n. a temporary airfield

**air taxi** a small commercial airplane that carries passengers, and often mail, to places not regularly served by scheduled airlines

**air′tight′** adj. 1. too tight for air or gas to enter or escape 2. invulnerable [an airtight alibi]

**air′waves′** n.pl. the medium through which radio signals are transmitted

**air′way′** n. 1. same as AIR LANE 2. [pl.] airways

**air′y** adj. -i·er, -i·est 1. of air 2. open to the air; breezy 3. unsubstantial as air 4. light as air; graceful 5. lighthearted; gay 6. flippant 7. [Colloq.] putting on airs —air′i·ly adv. —air′i·ness n.

**aisle** (Il) n. [< L. ala, wing] a passageway, as between rows of seats

**a·jar** (ə jär′) adv., adj. [OE. cier, a turn] slightly open, as a door

**AK** Alaska

**a·kim·bo** (ə kim′bō) adv., adj. [< ON. keng, bent + bogi, a bow) with hands on hips and elbows bent outward [with arms akimbo]

**a·kin** (ə kin′) adj. 1. of one kin; related 2. similar

**Ak·ron** (ak′rən) city in N Ohio: pop. 275,000

**-al** (əl, 'l) [< L.] a suffix meaning: 1. of, like, or suitable

ARMS AKIMBO

for [comical] 2. the act or process of [avowal]

**Al** Chem. aluminum

**à la, a la** (ä′lə, lä) [Fr.] 1. in the style of 2. according to

**Al·a·bam·a** (al′ə bam′ə) Southern State of SE U.S.: 51,609 sq. mi.; pop. 3,444,000; cap. Montgomery: abbrev. Ala., AL —Al′a·bam′i·an (-ē ən) adj., n.

**al·a·bas·ter** (al′ə bas′tər) n. [< Gr. alabastros, perfume vase] a translucent, whitish variety of gypsum: used for statues, etc.

**à la carte** (ä′ lə kärt′) [Fr.] with a separate price for each item on the menu

**a·lac·ri·ty** (ə lak′rə tē) n. [< L. alacer, lively] eager willingness, often with quick, lively action

**A·lad·din** (ə lad′'n) a boy in The Arabian Nights who found a magic lamp

**à la king** (ä′ lə kiŋ′) in a sauce containing mushrooms, pimentos, etc.

**Al·a·mo** (al′ə mō′) Franciscan mission at San Antonio, Tex.: scene of a massacre of Texans by Mexican troops (1836)

**à la mode** (al′ə mōd′) [< Fr.] 1. in fashion 2. served in a certain style, as pie with ice cream Also à la mode

**a·lar** (ā′lər) adj. [< L. ala, wing] 1. of a wing 2. having wings

**a·larm** (ə lärm′) n. [< It. all′arme, to arms] 1. [Archaic] a sudden call to arms 2. a warning of danger 3. a mechanism that warns of danger, arouses from sleep, etc. 4. fear caused by danger —vt. 1. to warn of danger 2. to frighten

**a·larm′ing** adj. frightening

**a·larm′ist** n. 1. one who spreads alarming rumors 2. one who anticipates the worst —adj. of an alarmist

**a·las** (ə las′) interj. an exclamation of sorrow, pity, etc.

**A·las·ka** (ə las′kə) State of the U.S. in NW N.America: 586,400 sq. mi.; pop. 302,000; cap. Juneau: abbrev. Alas., Ak. —A·las′kan adj., n.

**alb** (alb) n. [< L. albus, white] a white robe worn by a priest at Mass

**al·ba·core** (al′bə kôr′) n. [< Ar. al, the + bukr, young camel] any of various saltwater fishes of the mackerel family, as the tuna

**Al·ba·ni·a** (al bā′nē ə) country in the W Balkans: 11,099 sq. mi.; pop. 1,865,000 —Al·ba′ni·an adj., n.

**Al·ba·ny** (ôl′bə nē) capital of N.Y., on the Hudson: pop. 115,000

**al·ba·tross** (al′bə trôs′) n. [< Sp. < Ar. al qādūs, water container] a large, web-footed sea bird related to the petrel

**al·be·it** (ôl bē′it) conj. [ME. al be it, al(though) it be] although

**Al·ber·ta** (al bur′tə) province of SW Canada: 255,285 sq. mi.; pop. 1,463,000; cap. Edmonton

ALBATROSS

**al·bi·no** (al bī′nō) *n.*, *pl.* **-nos** [< L. *albus*, white] a person, animal, or plant lacking normal coloration: human albinos have white skin, whitish hair, and pink eyes

**al·bum** (al′bəm) *n.* [< L. *albus*, white] 1. a book with blank pages for mounting pictures, stamps, etc. 2. a booklike holder containing phonograph records 3. a single long-playing record or tape recording

**al·bu·men** (al byōō′mən) *n.* [L. < *albus*, white] 1. the white of an egg 2. protein in germinating cells 3. *same as* ALBUMIN

**al·bu′min** (-mən) *n.* [see prec.] a water-soluble protein found in egg, milk, blood, vegetable tissues, etc. —**al·bu′mi·nous** *adj.*

**Al·bu·quer·que** (al′bə kur′kē) city in C N.Mex.: pop. 244,000

**al·che·my** (al′kə mē) *n.* [< ? Gr. *cheein*, to pour] the chemistry of the Middle Ages, the chief aim of which was to change the baser elements into gold —**al′che·mist** *n.*

**al·co·hol** (al′kə hôl′) *n.* [< Ar. *al kuhl*, powder of antimony] 1. a colorless, volatile, pungent liquid, used in various forms as a fuel, an intoxicating ingredient in fermented liquors, etc, 2. any such intoxicating liquor

**al′co·hol′ic** *adj.* 1. of alcohol 2. suffering from alcoholism —*n.* one who has chronic alcoholism

**al′co·hol·ism** *n.* the habitual excessive drinking of alcoholic liquor, or a resulting diseased condition

**al·cove** (al′kōv) *n.* [< Ar. *al*, the + *qubba*, an arch] a recessed section of a room, as a breakfast nook

**al·de·hyde** (al′də hīd′) *n.* [< ALCOHOL + L. *de*, without + HYDROGEN] a colorless fluid oxidized from alcohol

**al·der** (ôl′dər) *n.* [OE. *alor*] a small tree or shrub of the birch family

**al·der·man** (ôl′dər·mən) *n.*, *pl.* **-men** [< OE. *eald*, old + *man*] in some cities, a municipal officer representing a certain district or ward

**ale** (āl) *n.* [OE. *ealu*] a fermented drink made from malt and hops, similar to beer

**a·le·a·to·ry** (ā′lē ə tôr′ē) *adj.* [< L. *aleatorius*, of gambling < *alea*, chance] depending on chance or luck: also **a′le·a·tor′ic** *adj.*

**a·lem·bic** (ə lem′bik) *n.* [< Ar. *al anbīq*, the still < Gr. *ambix*, a cup] 1. an apparatus formerly used for distilling 2. anything that purifies

**a·lert** (ə lurt′) *adj.* [< L. *erigere*, to erect] 1. watchful; vigilantly ready 2. active; nimble —*n.* a warning signal; alarm —*vt.* to warn, as to be ready —**on the alert** vigilant —**a·lert′ly** *adv.* —**a·lert′ness** *n.*

**A·leu·tian Islands** (ə lōō′shən) chain of U.S. islands off the SW tip of Alaska —**A·leu′tian** *adj.*, *n.*

**ale·wife** (āl′wīf′) *n.*, *pl.* **-wives′** [< ?] a N.American fish resembling the

herring, used for food and in fertilizers

**Al·ex·an·der the Great** (al′ig zan′dər) 356-323 B.C.; military conqueror; king of Macedonia (336-323)

**Al′ex·an′dri·a** (-drē ə) seaport in N Egypt: pop. 1,513,000

**al·fal·fa** (al fal′fə) *n.* [Sp. < Ar. *al-fasfasah*, the best fodder] a plant of the pea family, used for fodder, pasture, and as a cover crop

**Al·fred the Great** (al′frid) 849-900? A.D.; king of England (871-900?)

**al·fres·co** (al fres′kō) *adv.* [It. < *al*, in the + *fresco*, cool] outdoors —*adj.* outdoor Also **al fresco**

**al·gae** (al′jē) *n.pl.*, *sing.* **al′ga** (-gə) [pl. of L. *alga*, seaweed] a group of primitive plants, one-celled or many-celled, containing chlorophyll and found in water or damp places

**al·ge·bra** (al′jə brə) *n.* [< Ar. *al*, the + *jabara*, to reunite] a mathematical system used to generalize certain arithmetical operations by using letters or other symbols to stand for numbers —**al′ge·bra′ic** (-brā′ik) *adj.* —**al′ge·bra′ic·al·ly** *adv.*

**Al·ge·ri·a** (al jir′ē ə) country in N Africa: c.919,000 sq. mi.; pop. 11,290,000 —**Al·ge′ri·an** *adj.*, *n.*

**-al·gia** (al′jə) [< Gr. *algos*] a suffix meaning pain [*neuralgia*]

**Al·giers** (al jirz′) seaport and capital of Algeria: pop. 884,000

**Al·gon·qui·an** (al gän′kē ən, -kwē-) *adj.* designating or of a widespread family of N.American Indian languages —*n.* this family of languages

**al·go·rithm** (al′gə rith′m) *n.* [ult. < Ar.] any special way of solving a certain kind of mathematical problem

**a·li·as** (ā′lē əs) *n.*, *pl.* **-as·es** [L. < *alius*, other] an assumed name —*adv.* otherwise named [*Bell alias Jones*]

**A·li Ba·ba** (ä′lē bä′bə, al′ē bab′ə) in *The Arabian Nights*, a poor man who finds the treasure of forty thieves

**al·i·bi** (al′ə bī′) *n.*, *pl.* **-bis′** [L. < *alius ibi*, elsewhere] 1. *Law* the plea that the accused person was elsewhere than at the scene of the crime 2. [Colloq.] any excuse —*vi.* **-bied′**, **-bi′ing** [Colloq.] to offer an excuse

**al·ien** (āl′yən, -ē ən) *adj.* [< L. *alius*, other] 1. foreign; strange 2. of aliens —*n.* 1. a foreigner 2. a foreign-born resident who is not naturalized

**al′ien·a·ble** (-ə b'l) *adj.* capable of being transferred to a new owner

**al′ien·ate′** (-āt′) *vt.* **-at′ed**, **-at′ing** 1. to transfer the ownership of (property) to another 2. to make unfriendly or withdrawn 3. to cause a transference of (affection) —**al′ien·a′tion** *n.*

**al′ien·ist** (-ist) *n.* *Law* a psychiatrist

**a·light¹** (ə līt′) *vi.* **a·light′ed** or **a·lit′**, **a·light′ing** [ME. *alihtan*] 1. to get down or off; dismount 2. to come down after flight

**a·light²** (ə līt′) *adj.* lighted up; burning

**a·lign** (ə līn′) *vt.* [< Fr. *a*, to + *ligne*, LINE¹] 1. to bring into a straight line

**2.** to bring (components or working parts) into adjustment **3.** to bring into agreement, etc. —*vi.* to line up —**a·lign′ment** *n.*

**a·like** (ə līk′) *adj.* [OE. *gelic*] like one another; similar —*adv.* **1.** similarly **2.** equally

**al·i·ment** (al′ə mənt) *n.* [< L. *alere*, nourish] nourishment; food

**al′i·men′ta·ry** (-men′tər ē) *adj.* **1.** of food or nutrition **2.** nourishing

**alimentary canal** (or **tract**) the passage in the body (from the mouth to the anus) that food goes through

**al·i·mo·ny** (al′ə mō′nē) *n.* [< L. *alere*, nourish] money a judge orders paid to a woman by her legally separated or divorced husband

**a·line** (ə līn′) *vt.*, *vi.* **a·lined′**, **a·lin′ing** *same as* ALIGN —**a·line′ment** *n.*

**a·lit** (ə līt′) *alt. pt. & pp.* of ALIGHT[1]

**a·live** (ə līv′) *adj.* [< OE. *on*, in + *life*, life] **1.** having life; living **2.** in existence, operation, etc. **3.** lively; alert —**alive to** aware of —**alive with** teeming with

**al·ka·li** (al′kə lī′) *n.*, *pl.* **-lies′**, **-lis′** [< Ar. *al-qili*, the ashes of a certain plant] **1.** any base, as soda, that is soluble in water and gives off ions in solution **2.** any mineral salt that can neutralize acids

**al′ka·line** (-lin, -līn′) *adj.* of, like, or containing an alkali —**al′ka·lin′i·ty** (-lin′ə tē) *n.*

**al′ka·lize′** (-līz′) *vt.*, *vi.* **-lized′**, **-liz′ing** to make alkaline Also **al′ka·lin·ize′** (-lə nīz′), **-ized′**, **-iz′ing** —**al′ka·li·za′tion** *n.*

**al′ka·loid′** (-loid′) *n.* a bitter, alkaline organic substance, such as caffeine, morphine, quinine, etc., containing nitrogen

**al·kyd** (al′kid) *n.* [< ALKALI & ACID] a synthetic resin used in paints, varnishes, etc.: also **alkyd resin**

**all** (ôl) *adj.* [OE. *eall*] **1.** the whole quantity of [*all* the gold] **2.** every one of [*all* men] **3.** the greatest possible [in *all* sincerity] **4.** any [beyond *all* doubt] **5.** alone; only [*all* work and no play] —*pron.* **1.** [*with pl. v.*] everyone [*all* are going] **2.** everything **3.** every part or bit —*n.* **1.** everything one has [give your *all*] **2.** a totality; whole —*adv.* **1.** wholly; entirely [*all* worn out] **2.** apiece [a score of two *all*] —**after all** nevertheless —**all in** [Colloq.] very tired —**all in all 1.** considering everything **2.** as a whole —**all the** (**better, worse,** etc.) so much the (better, worse, etc.) —**all the same 1.** nevertheless **2.** unimportant —**at all 1.** in the least **2.** in any way **3.** under any considerations —**in all** altogether

**all-** *a prefix meaning:* **1.** entirely [*all*-American] **2.** for every [*all*-purpose] **3.** of everything [*all*-inclusive]

**Al·lah** (al′ə, ä′lə) [< Ar. *al*, the + *ilāh*, god] *the Moslem name for* God

**all′-A·mer′i·can** *adj.* chosen as the best in the U.S. —*n.* **1.** an imaginary football team, etc. made up of U.S. college players voted best of the year **2.** a player on such a team

**all′-a·round′** *adj.* having many abilities, talents, or uses; versatile

**al·lay** (ə lā′) *vt.* **-layed′**, **-lay′ing** [< OE. *a-*, down + *lecgan*, lay] **1.** to calm; quiet **2.** to relieve (pain, etc.)

**all′-clear′** *n.* a siren or other signal that an air raid or alert is over

**al·le·ga·tion** (al′ə gā′shən) *n.* an assertion, esp. one without proof or to be proved

**al·lege** (ə lej′) *vt.* **-leged′**, **-leg′ing** [< L. *ex-*, out of + *litigare*, to dispute] **1.** to declare or assert, esp. without proof **2.** to offer as an excuse

**al·leged′** (ə lejd′, ə lej′id) *adj.* **1.** declared, but without proof **2.** not actual; so-called —**al·leg′ed·ly** *adv.*

**Al·le·ghe·ny Mountains** (al′ə gā′nē) mountain range in C Pa., Md., W.Va., and Va.: also **Alleghenies**

**al·le·giance** (ə lē′jəns) *n.* [< OFr. *liege*, liege] **1.** the duty of being loyal to one's ruler, country, etc. **2.** loyalty; devotion, as to a cause

**al·le·go·ry** (al′ə gôr′ē) *n.*, *pl.* **-ries** [< Gr. *allos*, other + *agoreuein*, speak in assembly] a story in which people, things, and events have a symbolic meaning, often instructive, as in a fable —**al′le·gor′i·cal** *adj.* —**al′le·gor′i·cal·ly** *adv.* —**al′le·go′rist** *n.*

**al·le·gret·to** (al′ə gret′ō) *adj.*, *adv.* [It., dim. of *allegro*] *Music* moderately fast

**al·le·gro** (ə leg′rō, -lā′grō) *adj.*, *adv.* [It.] *Music* fast

**al·le·lu·ia** (al′ə loo͞′yə) *interj.*, *n.* [L.] *same as* HALLELUJAH

**Al·len·town** (al′ən toun′) city in E Pa.: pop. 110,000

**al·ler·gen** (al′ər jən) *n.* [G.] a substance inducing an allergic reaction —**al′ler·gen′ic** (-jen′ik) *adj.*

**al·ler·gic** (ə lur′jik) *adj.* **1.** of, caused by, or having an allergy **2.** averse (*to*)

**al·ler·gist** (al′ər jist) *n.* a doctor who specializes in treating allergies

**al·ler·gy** (al′ər jē) *n.*, *pl.* **-gies** [G. < Gr. *allos*, other + *ergon*, work] **1.** a hypersensitivity to a specific substance (as a food, pollen, dust, etc.) or condition (as heat or cold) **2.** an aversion

**al·le·vi·ate** (ə lē′vē āt′) *vt.* **-at′ed**, **-at′ing** [< L. *ad-*, to + *levis*, light] **1.** to lessen or relieve (pain, etc.) **2.** to decrease (poverty, etc.) —**al·le′vi·a′tion** *n.*

**al·ley** (al′ē) *n.*, *pl.* **-leys** [< OFr. *aler*, go] **1.** a narrow street between or behind buildings **2.** a bowling lane

**alley cat** a homeless, mongrel cat

**al′ley·way′** *n.* an alley between buildings

**all-fired** (ôl′fīrd′) *adv.* [< *hell-fired*] [Slang] completely; extremely

**al·li·ance** (ə līˈəns) *n.* [see ALLY] **1.** an allying or close association, as of nations for a common objective, families by marriage, etc. **2.** an agreement for this **3.** the countries, groups, etc. in such association

**al·lied** (ə līd′, al′īd) *adj.* **1.** united by kinship, treaty, etc. **2.** closely related

**al·li·ga·tor** (al′ə gāt′ər) *n.* [< Sp.

< L. *lacertus*] a large reptile of the U.S., similar to the crocodile but having a short, blunt snout

**al·li·ga·tor pear** same as AVOCADO

**all′-im·por′tant** *adj.* highly important; necessary; essential

**all′-in·clu′sive** *adj.* including everything; comprehensive

**al·lit·er·a·tion** (ə lit′ə rā′shən) *n.* [< L. *ad-*, to + *littera*, letter] repetition of an initial sound in two or more words of a phrase —**al·lit′er·a′tive** *adj.*

**al·lo·cate** (al′ə kāt′) *vt.* -cat′ed, -cat′ing [< L. *ad-*, to + *locus*, a place] 1. to set apart for a specific purpose 2. to distribute or allot — **al′lo·ca′tion** *n.*

**al·lot** (ə lät′) *vt.* -lot′ted, -lot′ting [< OFr. *a-*, to + *lot*, lot] 1. to distribute in arbitrary shares; apportion 2. to assign as one's share —**al·lot′ment** *n.*

**all′-out′** *adj.* complete or wholehearted [an *all-out* effort]

**all′o′ver** *adj.* over the whole surface

**al·low** (ə lou′) *vt.* [< L. *ad-*, to + *locus*, place] 1. to permit; let [I'm not *allowed* to go] 2. to let have [she *allowed* herself no sweets] 3. to acknowledge as valid 4. to provide (a certain amount), as for shrinkage, waste, etc. —**allow for** to leave room, time, etc. for —**al·low′a·ble** *adj.*

**al·low′ance** (-əns) *n.* 1. an allowing 2. something allowed 3. an amount of money, food, etc. given regularly to a child, soldier, etc. 4. a reduction in price, as for a trade-in —**make allowance(s) for** to excuse because of mitigating factors

**al·loy** (al′oi; *also, and for v. usually,* ə loi′) *n.* [< L. *ad-*, to + *ligare*, to bind] 1. a substance that is the mixture of two or more metals 2. something that debases another thing when mixed with it —*vt.* to make into an alloy

**all′-pur′pose** *adj.* useful in many ways

**all right** 1. satisfactory 2. unhurt 3. correct 4. yes; very well

**all′-round′** *adj.* same as ALL-AROUND

**all·spice** (ôl′spīs′) *n.* a spice, combining the tastes of several spices, made from the berry of a West Indian tree of the myrtle family

**all′-star′** *adj.* made up entirely of outstanding or star performers

**all′-time′** *adj.* unsurpassed until now

**al·lude** (ə lōōd′) *vi.* -lud′ed, -lud′ing [< L. *ad-*, to + *ludere*, to play] to refer indirectly (*to*)

**al·lure** (ə loor′) *vt., vi.* -lured′, -lur′ing [< OFr. *a-*, to + *lurer*, to lure] to tempt with something desirable; attract —*n.* fascination; charm — **al·lure′ment** *n.* —**al·lur′ing** *adj.*

**al·lu·sion** (ə lōō′zhən) *n.* 1. an alluding 2. indirect or casual reference

**al·lu·sive** (ə lōō′siv) *adj.* 1. containing an allusion 2. full of allusions —**al·lu′sive·ly** *adv.* —**al·lu′sive·ness** *n.*

**al·lu·vi·um** (ə lōō′vē əm) *n., pl.* -vi·ums, -vi·a (-vē ə) [< L. *ad-*, to + *luere*, wash] sand, clay, etc. deposited by moving water —**al·lu′vi·al** *adj.*

**al·ly** (ə lī′; *also, and for n. usually,* al′ī) *vt., vi.* -lied′, -ly′ing [< L. *ad-*, to + *ligare*, to bind] 1. to unite or join for a specific purpose 2. to relate by similarity of structure, etc. —*n., pl.* -lies a country or person joined with another for a common purpose

**al·ma ma·ter** (al′mə mät′ər, mät′-) [L., fostering mother] 1. the college or school that one attended 2. its anthem

**al·ma·nac** (ôl′mə nak′, al-) *n.* [< LGr. *almenichiaka*, calendar] a calendar with astronomical data, weather forecasts, etc.

**al·might·y** (ôl mīt′ē) *adj.* all-powerful —**the Almighty** God

**al·mond** (ä′mənd, am′ənd) *n.* [< Gr. *amygdalē*] 1. the edible, nutlike kernel of a peachlike fruit 2. the tree that it grows on —*adj.* shaped like an almond; oval and pointed at one or both ends

**al·most** (ôl′mōst, ôl′mōst′) *adv.* very nearly; all but

**alms** (ämz) *n., pl.* **alms** [< Gr. *eleos*, pity] money, food, etc. given to poor people —**alms′giv′er** *n.*

**alms′house′** *n.* 1. formerly, a poorhouse 2. [Brit.] a privately endowed home for the poor

**al·oe** (al′ō) *n., pl.* -oes [< Gr. *aloē*] 1. a South African plant of the lily family 2. [*pl., with sing. v.*] a laxative drug made from the juice of certain aloe leaves

**a·loft** (ə lôft′) *adv.* [ME. < *o*, on + *loft*, loft] 1. high up 2. in the air; flying 3. high above the deck of a ship

**a·lo·ha** (ə lō′a, ä lō′hä) *n., interj.* [Haw., love] a word used as a greeting or farewell

**a·lone** (ə lōn′) *adj., adv.* [ME. < *al*, all + *one*, one] 1. apart from anything or anyone else 2. without any other person 3. only 4. without equal —**let alone** 1. to refrain from interfering with 2. not to speak of [we hadn't a dime, *let alone* a dollar]

**a·long** (ə lôŋ′) *prep.* [< OE. *and-*, over against + *lang*, long] 1. on or beside the length of 2. in conformity with —*adv.* 1. lengthwise 2. progressively onward or advanced 3. together (*with*) 4. with one [take me *along*] —**all along** from the beginning —**be along** [Colloq.] to come or arrive —**get along** 1. to advance 2. to contrive 3. to succeed 4. to agree

**a·long′shore′** *adv.* near or beside the shore

**a·long′side′** *adv.* at or by the side; side by side —*prep.* beside —**alongside of** at the side of

**a·loof** (ə lōōf′) *adv.* [< *a-*, on & Du. *loef*, to windward] at a distance but in view —*adj.* cool and reserved [an *aloof* manner] —**a·loof′ness** *n.*

**a·loud** (ə loud′) *adv.* 1. loudly 2. with the normal voice

---

**alp** (alp) *n.* [ < *Alps* ] a high mountain

**al·pac·a** (al pak'ə) *n.* [Sp. < S.AmInd. *allpaca*] 1. a S.American mammal, related to the llama. 2. its fleecy wool, or cloth woven from it

ALPACA

**al·pha** (al'fə) *n.* the first letter of the Greek alphabet (A, α)

**al'pha·bet'** (-bet') *n.* [ < Gr. *alpha* + *beta*] the letters used in writing a language, esp. as arranged in their usual order —**al'pha·bet'i·cal** *adj.* —**al'pha·bet'i·cal·ly** *adv.*

**al·pha·bet·ize** (al'fə bə tīz') *vt.* -**ized'**, -**iz'ing** to arrange in the usual order of the alphabet —**al'pha·bet/i·za'tion** (-bet'i zā'shən) *n.*

**al'pha·nu·mer'ic** (-nōō mer'ik) *adj.* having both alphabetical and numerical symbols

**alpha particle** a positively charged particle given off by certain radioactive substances

**alpha rays** rays of alpha particles

**Al·pine** (al'pīn) *adj.* 1. of the Alps 2. [a-] of or like high mountains

**Alps** (alps) mountain system in SC Europe

**al·read·y** (ôl red'ē) *adv.* 1. by or before the given or implied time 2. even now or even then

**al·right** (ôl rīt') *adv.* all right: a disputed spelling

**Al·sace** (al säs', al'sas) region and former province of NE France —**Al·sa'tian** (-sā'shən) *adj., n.*

**al·so** (ôl'sō) *adv.* [ < OE. *eal*, all + *swa*, so] likewise; too; in addition

**al'so·ran'** *n.* [Colloq.] a defeated contestant in a race, election, etc.

**alt.** 1. alternate 2. altitude 3. alto

**al·tar** (ôl'tər) *n.* [ < L. *altus*, high] 1. a platform where sacrifices are made to a god, etc. 2. a table, etc. for sacred purposes in a place of worship —**lead to the altar** to marry

**altar boy** a boy or man who helps a priest, etc. at religious services, esp. at Mass

**al·ter** (ôl'tər) *vt., vi.* [ < L. *alter*, other] to change; make or become different —**al'ter·a'tion** *n.*

**al·ter·ca·tion** (ôl'tər kā'shən) *n.* [ < L. *altercari*, to dispute] an angry or heated argument; quarrel

**al·ter e·go** (ôl'tər ē'gō) [L., other I] 1. one's other self 2. a constant companion

**al·ter·nate** (ôl'tər nit; *for v.* -nāt') *adj.* [ < L. *alternus*, one after the other] 1. succeeding each other 2. every other —*n.* a substitute —*vt.* -**nat'ed**, -**nat'ing** to do or use by turns —*vi.* 1. to act, happen, etc. by turns 2. to take turns regularly —**al'ter·nate·ly** *adv.* —**al'ter·na'tion** *n.*

**alternating current** an electric current that reverses its direction periodically

**al·ter·na·tive** (ôl tur'nə tiv) *adj.* providing a choice between things —*n.* 1. a choice between things 2. one of

the things to be chosen 3. something left to choose

**al·ter·na·tor** (ôl'tər nāt'ər) *n.* an electric generator that produces alternating current

**al·though** (ôl thō') *conj.* in spite of the fact that; though: also **altho**

**al·tim·e·ter** (al tim'ə tər) *n.* [ < L. *altus*, high + -METER] an instrument for measuring altitude

**al·ti·tude** (al'tə tōōd') *n.* [ < L. *altus*, high] 1. the height of a thing, esp. above sea level 2. a high place

**al·to** (al'tō) *n., pl.* -**tos** [It. < L. *altus*, high] 1. the range of the lowest female voice 2. a singer with this range —*adj.* of, for, or in the alto

**al·to·geth·er** (ôl'tə geth'ər) *adv.* 1. completely 2. in all 3. on the whole

**al·tru·ism** (al'trōō iz'm) *n.* [ < L. *alter*, other] unselfish concern for the welfare of others —**al'tru·ist** *n.* —**al'tru·is'tic** (-is'tik) *adj.* —**al'tru·is'ti·cal·ly** *adv.*

**al·um** (al'əm) *n.* [ < L. *alumen*] any of a group of double salts of aluminum, etc., used esp. in manufacturing and in medicine

**al·u·min·i·um** (al'yoo min'yəm) *n.* *Brit. var.* of ALUMINUM

**a·lu·mi·num** (ə lōō'mə nəm) *n.* [ < L. *alumen*, alum] a silvery, lightweight metallic chemical element

**a·lum·nus** (ə lum'nəs) *n., pl.* -**ni** (-nī) [L., foster son] a boy or man who has attended or been graduated from a school, college, etc. —**a·lum'na** (-nə) *n.fem., pl.* -**nae** (-nē)

**al·ways** (ôl'wiz, -wāz) *adv.* [OE. *ealne weg*] 1. at all times 2. continually 3. at any time 4. in every instance

**am** (am, əm) [OE. *eom*] *1st pers. sing., pres. indic.,* of BE

**AM** amplitude modulation

**Am.** 1. America 2. American

**A.M., AM** master of arts

**A.M., a.m., AM** [L. *ante meridiem*] before noon: used to designate the time from midnight to noon

**AMA, A.M.A.** American Medical Association

**a·main** (ə mān') *adv.* [A-, on + MAIN] [Archaic] at or with great speed

**a·mal·gam** (ə mal'gəm) *n.* [ < Gr. *malagma*, an emollient] 1. any alloy of mercury with another metal *[a* dental filling of silver *amalgam]* 2. a mixture; blend

**a·mal·ga·mate'** (-gə māt') *vt., vi.* -**mat'ed**, -**mat'ing** to unite; mix; combine —**a·mal'ga·ma'tion** *n.*

**a·man·u·en·sis** (ə man'yoo wen'sis) *n., pl.* -**ses** (-sēz) [L. < *a-*, from + *manus*, hand + -*ensis*, relating to] a secretary: now a jocular usage

**am·a·ranth** (am'ə ranth') *n.* [ < Gr. *amarantos*, unfading] 1. any of a family of plants, some bearing showy flowers 2. [Poet.] an imaginary flower that never dies

**Am·a·ril·lo** (am'ə ril'ō) city in NW Tex.: pop. 127,000

**am·a·ryl·lis** (am'ə ril'əs) *n.* [ < Gr. name for a shepherdess] a bulb plant with white to red lilylike flowers

**a·mass** (ə mas') *vt.* [ < Fr. < L.

*massa*, a lump] to pile up; accumulate

**am·a·teur** (am'ə chər, -tər, -toor) *n.* [Fr. < L. *amare*, to love] 1. one who does something for pleasure, not for pay; nonprofessional 2. one who is somewhat unskillful —*adj.* of or done by amateurs —**am'a·teur'ish** (-choor'-) *adj.* —**am'a·teur'ish·ly** *adv.* —**am'·a·teur·ism** *n.*

**am'a·to'ry** (-tôr'ē) *adj.* [ < L. *amare*, to love] of or showing sexual love

**a·maze** (ə māz') *vt.* **a·mazed', a·maz'ing** [see MAZE] to fill with great surprise or wonder; astonish —**a·maze'ment** *n.* —**a·maz'ing** *adj.* —**a·maz'ing·ly** *adv.*

**Am·a·zon** (am'ə zän') river in N S.America: c.3,300 mi. —*n. Gr. Myth.* any of a race of female warriors

**am·bas·sa·dor** (am bas'ə dər) *n.* [ < Pr. *ambaissador*] the highest-ranking diplomatic representative of one country to another —**am·bas'sa·do'ri·al** (-dôr'ē əl) *adj.* —**am·bas'sa·dor·ship'** *n.*

**am·ber** (am'bər) *n.* [ < Ar. *'anbar*, ambergris] 1. a brownish-yellow fossil resin used in jewelry, etc. 2. its color —*adj.* amberlike or amber-colored

**am'ber·gris'** (-grēs', -gris') *n.* [ < OFr. *ambre gris*, gray amber] a waxy substance secreted by certain whales, used in making perfumes

**am·bi-** (am'bə) [L.] *a combining form meaning both* [*ambidextrous*]

**am·bi·ance** (am'bē əns) *n.* [see AMBIENT] an environment or its distinct atmosphere: also **ambience**

**am·bi·dex·trous** (am'bə dek'strəs) *adj.* [see AMBI- & DEXTEROUS] using both hands with equal ease —**am'bi·dex·ter'i·ty** (-dek ster'ə tē) *n.*

**am'bi·ent** (-ənt) *adj.* [L. < *ambi-*, around + *ire*, to go] surrounding

**am·bi·gu·i·ty** (am'bə gyoo'ə tē) *n.* 1. a being ambiguous 2. *pl.* **-ties** an ambiguous expression

**am·big·u·ous** (am big'yoo wəs) *n.* [ < L. *ambi-*, around + *agere*, to do] 1. having two or more meanings 2. not clear; vague —**am·big'u·ous·ly** *adv.*

**am·bi·tion** (am bi'shən) *n.* [ < L. *ambitio*, a going around (to solicit votes)] 1. strong desire for fame, power, etc. 2. the thing so desired

**am·bi'tious** (-shəs) *adj.* 1. full of or showing ambition 2. showing great effort —**am·bi'tious·ly** *adv.*

**am·biv·a·lence** (am biv'ə ləns) *n.* [AMBI- + VALENCE] simultaneous conflicting feelings —**am·biv'a·lent** *adj.* —**am·biv'a·lent·ly** *adv.*

**am·ble** (am'b'l) *vi.* **-bled, -bling** [ < L. *ambulare*, to walk] 1. to move in an easy gait, as a horse 2. to walk in a leisurely way —*n.* 1. a horse's ambling gait 2. a leisurely walking pace

**am·bro·sia** (am brō'zhə) *n.* [ < Gr. *a-*, not + *brotos*, mortal] 1. *Gr. & Rom. Myth.* the food of the gods 2. anything that tastes or smells delicious —**am·bro'sial** *adj.*

**am·bu·lance** (am'byə ləns) *n.* [ < L. *ambulare*, to walk] a vehicle equipped for carrying the sick or wounded

**am'bu·late'** (-lāt') *vi.* **-lat'ed, -lat'ing** to move about; walk —**am'bu·lant** (-lənt) *adj.* —**am'bu·la'tion** *n.*

**am'bu·la·to'ry** (-lə tôr'ē) *adj.* 1. of or for walking 2. able to walk

**am·bus·cade** (am'bəs kād') *n., vt., vi.* **-cad'ed, -cad'ing** ambush

**am·bush** (am'boosh) *n.* [ < ML. *in-*, in + *boscus*, woods] 1. an arrangement of persons in hiding to make a surprise attack 2. their hiding place —*vt., vi.* to attack from ambush

**a·me·ba** (ə mē'bə) *n., pl.* **-bas, -bae** (-bē) *same as* AMOEBA —**a·me'bic** *adj.*

**a·mel·io·rate** (ə mēl'yə rāt') *vt., vi.* **-rat'ed, -rat'ing** [ < Fr. < OFr. < L. *melior*, better] to make or become better; improve —**a·mel'io·ra'tion** *n.*

**a·men** (ā'men', ä'-) *interj.* [ < Heb. *āmēn*, truly] may it be so!: used after a prayer or to express approval

**a·me·na·ble** (ə mē'nə b'l, -men'ə-) *adj.* [ < OFr. < L. *minare*, to drive (animals)] 1. responsible; answerable 2. able to be controlled; submissive —**a·me'na·bil'i·ty** *n.* —**a·me'na·bly** *adv.*

**a·mend** (ə mend') *vt.* [ < L. *emendare*] 1. to correct; emend 2. to improve 3. to change or revise (a law, etc.) —*vi.* to improve one's conduct —**a·mend'a·ble** *adj.*

**a·mend'ment** *n.* 1. a correction of errors, faults, etc. 2. improvement 3. a revision or change proposed or made in a bill, law, etc.

**a·mends** (ə mendz') *n.pl.* [*sometimes with sing. v.*] [see AMEND] payment made or satisfaction given for injury, loss, etc.

**a·men·i·ty** (ə men'ə tē, -mē'nə-) *n., pl.* **-ties** [ < L. *amoenus*, pleasant] 1. pleasantness 2. an attractive feature or convenience 3. [*pl.*] courteous acts

**am·ent** (am'ənt, ā'mənt) *n.* [ < L. *amentum*, thong] a tassellike spike of small flowers, as on a willow or birch

**a·merce** (ə murs') *vt.* **a·merced', a·merc'ing** [ < OFr. *a merci*, at the mercy of] to punish, esp. by imposing a fine —**a·merce'ment** *n.*

**A·mer·i·ca** (ə mer'ə kə) [associated with *Amerigo* VESPUCCI] *same as* **1.** WESTERN HEMISPHERE: also the Americas 2. NORTH AMERICA 3. SOUTH AMERICA 4. the UNITED STATES

**A·mer'i·can** (-kən) *adj.* 1. of or in America 2. of the U.S., its people, etc. —*n.* 1. a native or inhabitant of America 2. a citizen of the U.S.

**A·mer'i·ca'na** (-kan'ə) *n.pl.* books, papers, objects, etc. having to do with America, its people, and its history

**A·mer'i·can·ism** *n.* 1. a custom or belief of the U.S. 2. a word or idiom originating in American English 3. devotion to the U.S., its customs, etc.

**A·mer'i·can·ize'** (-īz') *vt., vi.* **-ized', -iz'ing** to make or become American in character, manners, etc. —**A·mer′-i·can·i·za′tion** n.

**American plan** a system of hotel operation in which the price charged covers room, service, and meals

**American Revolution** the war (1775–1783) fought by the American colonies to gain independence from England

**Am·er·ind** (am′ə rind′) n. an American Indian or Eskimo —**Am′er·in′di·an** adj., n.

**am·e·thyst** (am′ə thist) n. [< Gr. amethystos, not drunken: the Greeks thought it prevented intoxication] 1. a purple or violet quartz or corundum, used in jewelry 2. purple or violet

**a·mi·a·ble** (ā′mē ə b′l) adj. [< L. amicus, friend] good-natured; friendly —**a′mi·a·bil′i·ty** n. —**a′mi·a·bly** adv.

**am·i·ca·ble** (am′i kə b′l) adj. [see prec.] friendly; peaceable —**am′i·ca·bil′i·ty** n. —**am′i·ca·bly** adv.

**a·mid** (ə mid′) prep. in the middle of; among: also **a·midst** (ə midst′)

**am·ide** (am′īd) n. any of several organic compounds derived from ammonia

**a·mid′ships′** adv. in or toward the middle of a ship: also **a·mid′ship′**

**a·mi·go** (ə mē′gō) n., pl. **-gos** (-gōz) [Sp.] a friend

**amino acids** (ə mē′nō, am′ə nō′) [< AMMONIA] a group of nitrogenous organic compounds found in the proteins and essential to metabolism

**Am·ish** (ä′mish, am′ish) n.pl. [< Jacob Ammann (or Amen), the founder] Mennonites of a sect founded in the 17th cent. —adj. of this sect

**a·miss** (ə mis′) adv. [see A- & MISS¹] in a wrong way; astray —adj. wrong; improper; faulty [what is amiss?]

**am·i·ty** (am′ə tē) n., pl. **-ties** [< L. amicus, friend] peaceful relations

**am·me·ter** (am′mēt′ər) n. [AM(PERE) + -METER] an instrument for measuring an electric current in amperes

**am·mo** (am′ō) n. [Slang] ammunition

**am·mo·nia** (ə mōn′yə) n. [from a salt found near Libyan shrine of Jupiter Ammon] 1. a colorless, pungent gas, a compound of nitrogen and hydrogen 2. a water solution of this gas: in full, **ammonia water**

**am·mu·ni·tion** (am′yə nish′ən) n. [< L. munire, fortify] 1. bullets, gunpowder, bombs, grenades, rockets, etc. 2. any means of attack or defense

**am·ne·sia** (am ne′zhə, -zhē ə) n. [< Gr. a-, not + mnasthai, to remember] partial or total loss of memory

**am·nes·ty** (am′nəs tē) n., pl. **-ties** [< Gr. amnēstia, a forgetting] a general pardon, esp. for political offenses —vt. **-tied, -ty·ing** to pardon

**a·moe·ba** (ə mē′bə) n., pl. **-bas, -bae** (-bē) [< Gr. ameibein, to change] a microscopic, one-celled animal multiplying by fission —**a·moe′bic** adj.

**a·mok** (ə muk′) adj., adv. [Malay amoq] in a frenzy to kill

**a·mong** (ə muŋ′) prep. [< OE. on, in + gemang, a crowd] 1. surrounded by [among friends] 2. in the group of [best among books] 3. to or for each or several of [divide it among the crowd] 4. by the joint action of Also **a·mongst** (ə muŋst′)

**A·mon-Re** (ä′mən rā′) the ancient Egyptian sun god

**a·mon·til·la·do** (ə män′tə lä′dō) n. [Sp. < Montilla, a town in Spain] a pale, relatively dry sherry

**a·mor·al** (ā môr′əl) adj. 1. neither moral nor immoral 2. without moral sense —**a′mor·al′i·ty** n. —**a·mor′al·ly** adv.

**am·o·rous** (am′ər əs) adj. [< L. amor, love] 1. fond of making love 2. full of love 3. of sexual love —**am′o·rous·ly** adv.

**a·mor·phous** (ə môr′fəs) adj. [< Gr. a-, without + morphē, form] 1. without definite form 2. vague or indefinite 3. Chem. not crystalline

**am·or·tize** (am′ər tīz′, ə môr′-) vt. **-tized′, -tiz′ing** [< ME. < L. ad- to + mors, death] to put money aside at intervals for gradual payment of (a debt, etc.) —**am′or·ti·za′tion** n.

**a·mount** (ə mount′) vi. [< OFr. amont, upward < L. ad, to + mons, mountain] 1. to add up (to) 2. to be equal (to) in value, etc. —n. 1. a sum total 2. the whole value or effect 3. a quantity

**a·mour** (ə moor′) n. [< L. amor, love] a love affair, esp. an illicit one

**†a·mour-pro·pre** (a moor prô′pr′) n. [Fr.] self-esteem

**amp.** 1. amperage 2. ampere; amperes

**am·per·age** (am′pər ij, am pir′-) n. the strength of an electric current in amperes

**am·pere** (am′pir) n. [< A. M. Ampère, 19th-c. Fr. physicist] the standard unit for measuring an electric current, equal to one coulomb per second

**am·per·sand** (am′pər sand′) n. [< and per se and, (the sign) & by itself (is) and] a sign (&) meaning and

**am·phet·a·mine** (am fet′ə mēn′, -min) n. a drug used esp. as a stimulant and to lessen appetite

**am·phib·i·an** (am fib′ē ən) n. [see ff.] 1. any animal or plant living both on land and in water 2. an aircraft that can take off from or land on water or land —adj. same as AMPHIBIOUS

**am·phib′i·ous** adj. [< Gr. amphi-, on both sides + bios, life] that can live or operate on land and in water

**am·phi·the·a·ter, am·phi·the·a·tre** (am′fə thē′ə tər) n. [< Gr. amphi-, around + theatron, theater] a round or oval building with rising rows of seats around an open space

**am·ple** (am′p′l) adj. [< L. amplus] 1. large in size, scope, etc. 2. more than enough 3. adequate —**am′ply** adv.

**am·pli·fi·er** (am′plə fī′ər) n. one that amplifies; esp., a device for strengthening electrical signals

**am′pli·fy′** (-fī′) vt. **-fied′, -fy′ing** [< L. amplus, large + facere, to make] 1. to make stronger; esp., to strengthen (electrical signals) 2. to develop more fully —**am′pli·fi·ca′tion** n.

**am·pli·tude** (am′plə tōod′) n. [see AMPLE] 1. scope, extent, breadth, etc. 2. abundance 3. range from mean to extreme, as of an alternating current

**am·pli·tude mod·u·la·tion** the changing of the amplitude of the transmitting radio wave in accordance with the signal being broadcast

**am·pul** (am'pool) n. [< L. *ampulla*, bottle] a small glass container for one dose of a hypodermic medicine: also **am'pule** (-pyool), **am'poule** (-pool)

**am·pu·tate** (am'pyə tāt') vt. **-tat'ed, -tat'ing** [< L. *amb-*, about + *putare*, to prune] to cut off, esp. by surgery —**am'pu·ta'tion** n.

**am'pu·tee'** (-tē') n. one who has had a limb or limbs amputated

**Am·ster·dam** (am'stər dam') constitutional capital of the Netherlands: pop. 866,000

**amt.** amount

**Am·trak** (am'trak') n. [*Am*(erican) *tr*(avel) *tr*(a)(c)k] a nationwide system of passenger railroad service

**a·muck** (ə muk') adj., adv. same as AMOK

**am·u·let** (am'yə lit) n. [< L.] something worn to protect against evil

**a·muse** (ə myōoz') vt. **a·mused', a·mus'ing** [< Fr. < *à*, at + OFr. *muser*, to gaze] 1. to keep pleasantly occupied; entertain 2. to make laugh, etc.

**a·muse'ment** n. 1. a being amused 2. something that amuses

**amusement park** an outdoor place with devices for entertainment, as a merry-go-round, roller coaster, etc.

**am·yl·ase** (am'ə lās') n. [< Gr. *amylon*, starch] an enzyme that helps change starch into sugar, found in saliva, etc.

**an** (ən, 'n; *stressed*, an) adj., *indefinite article* [< OE. *an*, one] 1. one; one sort of 2. each; any one 3. per [two *an* hour] *An* is used before words beginning with a vowel sound [an eye, an honor] See also A. adj.

**-an** (ən, in, 'n) [< L. *-anus*] a suffix meaning: 1. of, belonging to [*diocesan*] 2. born in, living in [*Ohioan*] 3. believing in [*Mohammedan*]

**a·nach·ro·nism** (ə nak'rə niz'm) n. [< Gr. *ana-*, against + *chronos*, time] 1. anything out of its proper historical time 2. the representation of this —**a·nach'ro·nis'tic** adj.

**an·a·con·da** (an'ə kän'də) n. [< ? Sinhalese] a S.American snake that crushes its prey in its coils

**a·nae·mi·a, a·nae·mic,** etc. same as ANEMIA, ANEMIC, etc.

**an·aer·o·bic** (an'er ō'bik) adj. [< Gr. *an-*, without + *āĕr*, air + *bios*, life] able to live and grow without air or free oxygen, as some bacteria

**an·aes·the·si·a, an·aes·thet·ic,** etc. same as ANESTHESIA, ANESTHETIC, etc.

**an·a·gram** (an'ə gram') n. [< Gr. *anagrammatizein*, transpose letters] 1. a word, etc. made by rearranging letters (Ex.: *now*—*won*) 2. [pl., with *sing. v.*] a word game based on this

**An·a·heim** (an'ə hīm') city in SW Calif.: pop. 167,000

**a·nal** (ā'n'l) adj. of or near the anus

**an·al·ge·si·a** (an''l jē'zē ə, -sē ə) n. [< Gr. *an-*, without + *algēsia*, pain] a state of not feeling pain

**an'al·ge'sic** (-zik, -sik) adj. of or causing analgesia —n. a drug that produces analgesia

**an·a·log computer** (an'ə lôg') a computer working on the basis of a physical, esp. electrical, analogy of the mathematical problem to be solved

**a·nal·o·gize** (ə nal'ə jīz') vi., vt. **-gized', -giz'ing** to use, or explain by, analogy

**a·nal·o·gous** (ə nal'ə gəs) adj. [see ANALOGY] similar in some way —**a·nal'o·gous·ly** adv.

**an·a·logue, an·a·log** (an'ə lôg') n. something analogous —adj. of an analog computer: usually **analog**

**a·nal·o·gy** (ə nal'ə jē) n., pl. **-gies** [< Gr. *ana-*, according to + *logos*, ratio] 1. similarity in some way 2. the inference that certain resemblances imply further similarity

**a·nal·y·sand** (ə sand') n. [see ff.] a person undergoing psychoanalysis

**a·nal·y·sis** (-sis) n., pl. **-ses'** (-sēz') [< Gr. < *ana-*, up + *lysis*, a loosing] 1. a breaking up of a whole into its parts to find out their nature, etc. 2. a statement of these findings 3. psychoanalysis 4. *Chem.* separation of compounds and mixtures into their constituents to determine their nature or proportion —**an·a·lyt·i·cal** (an'ə lit'i k'l), **an'a·lyt'ic** adj. —**an'a·lyt'·i·cal·ly** adv.

**an·a·lyst** (an'ə list) n. 1. one who analyzes 2. a psychoanalyst

**an'a·lyze'** (-līz') vt. **-lyzed', -lyz'ing** 1. to make an analysis of; examine in detail 2. to psychoanalyze —**an'a·lyz'a·ble** adj. —**an'a·lyz'er** n.

**an·a·pest** (an'ə pest') n. [< Gr. *ana-*, back + *paiein*, strike] a metrical foot of two unaccented syllables followed by an accented one

**an·ar·chism** (an'ər kiz'm) n. [see ANARCHY] 1. the theory that all organized government is repressive and undesirable 2. resistance to all government

**an'ar·chist** (-kist) n. 1. one who believes in anarchism 2. a promoter of anarchy —**an'ar·chis'tic** adj.

**an'ar·chy** (-kē) n., pl. **-chies** [< Gr. *an-*, without + *archos*, leader] 1. the absence of government 2. political disorder and violence 3. disorder; confusion —**an·ar'chic** (-är'kik), **an·ar'chi·cal** adj. —**an·ar'chi·cal·ly** adv.

**a·nath·e·ma** (ə nath'ə mə) n., pl. **-mas** [Gr., thing devoted to evil] 1. a person or thing accursed or damned 2. anything greatly detested 3. a formal curse, as in excommunicating a person 4. any strong curse

**a·nath'e·ma·tize'** (-tīz') vt., vi. **-tized', -tiz'ing** to utter an anathema (against); curse

**a·nat·o·mize** (ə nat'ə mīz') vt., vi.

**-mized′, -miz′ing** [see ff.] 1. to dissect (animals, etc.) so as to study the structure 2. to analyze —**a·nat′o·mist** n.

**a·nat·o·my** (-mē) n., pl. **-mies** [< Gr. ana-, up + temnein, to cut] 1. dissection of an organism to study its structure 2. the science of the structure of plants or animals 3. the structure of an organism 4. any analysis — **an·a·tom·i·cal** (an′ə täm′i k'l), **an′a·tom′ic** adj. —**an′a·tom′i·cal·ly** adv.

**-ance** (əns) [< L.] a suffix meaning: 1. the act of [utterance] 2. the quality or state of being [vigilance] 3. a thing that [conveyance] 4. a thing that is [inheritance]

**an·ces·tor** (an′ses′tər) n. [< L. ante-, before + cedere, go] 1. a person from whom one is descended; forebear 2. an early kind or type; forerunner — **an·ces′tral** (-trəl) adj. —**an′ces′-tress** (-trəs) n.fem.

**an′ces·try** (-trē) n., pl. **-tries** 1. family descent 2. all one's ancestors

**an·chor** (aŋ′kər) n. [< Gr. ankyra, a hook] 1. a heavy object, as a hooked iron weight, lowered from a ship, as by cable, to prevent drifting 2. anything giving stability —vt. to hold secure as with an anchor —vi. 1. to lower an anchor 2. to be or become fixed —**at anchor** anchored

**an′chor·age** (-ij) n. 1. an anchoring or being anchored 2. a place to anchor

**an·cho·rite** (aŋ′kə rīt′) n. [< Gr. ana-, back + chōrein, retire] a religious recluse; hermit

**anchor man** a newscaster who coordinates reports from various sources

**an·cho·vy** (an′chō′vē, -chə-) n., pl. **-vies** [< Port. anchova] a tiny, herringlike fish, eaten as a relish

**an·cient** (ān′shənt) adj. [< L. ante, before] 1. of times long past 2. very old —n. an aged person —**the ancients** the people of ancient times

**an′cient·ly** adv. in ancient times

**an·cil·lar·y** (an′sə ler′ē) adj. [< L. ancilla, maidservant] 1. subordinate (to) 2. auxiliary

**-an·cy** (ən sē) same as -ance

**and** (ənd, ən; stressed, and) conj. [OE.] 1. also; in addition 2. plus 3. as a result 4. in contrast to; but 5. [Colloq.] to [try and get it]

**an·dan·te** (än dän′tā) adj., adv. [It. < andare, to walk] Music fairly slow

**An·der·sen** (an′dər s'n), **Hans Christian** 1805–75; Dan. writer of fairy stories

**An·des** (**Mountains**) (an′dēz) mountain system of W S.America

**and·i·ron** (and′dī′ərn) n. [< OFr. andier] either of a pair of metal supports for logs in a fireplace

**and/or** either and or or [personal and/or real property]

**An·dor·ra** (an dôr′ə) republic in the E.Pyrenees: 180 sq. mi.; pop. 11,000

ANDIRONS

**an·dro·gen** (an′drə

jən) n. [< Gr. andros, of man + -GEN] a male sex hormone that can give rise to masculine characteristics —**an′dro·gen′ic** (-jen′ik) adj.

**an·droid** (an′droid) n. [< Gr. andros, of man + -OID] in science fiction, an automaton made to look like a human being

**an·ec·dote** (an′ik dōt′) n. [< Gr. anekdotos, unpublished] a short, entertaining account of some event —**an′ec·dot′al** adj.

**a·ne·mi·a** (ə nē′mē ə) n. [< Gr. a-, without + haima, blood] a condition in which the blood is low in red cells or in hemoglobin, resulting in paleness, weakness, etc. —**a·ne′mic** adj.

**an·e·mom·e·ter** (an′ə mäm′ə tər) n. [< Gr. anemos, the wind + -METER] a gauge for determining the force or speed of the wind; wind gauge

**a·nem·o·ne** (ə nem′ə nē′) n. [< Gr. anemos, the wind] 1. a plant with cup-shaped flowers of white, pink, red, or purple 2. a sea anemone

**a·nent** (ə nent′) prep. [< OE. on efen, on even (with)] [Now Rare] concerning; about

**an·er·oid barometer** (an′ər oid) [< Gr. a-, without + nēros, liquid + -OID] a barometer working by the bending of a thin metal plate instead of by the rise or fall of mercury

**an·es·the·sia** (an′əs thē′zhə) n. [< Gr. an-, without + aisthēsis, feeling] a partial or total loss of the sense of pain, touch, etc.

**an′es·the·si·ol′o·gist** (-thē′zē äl′ə jist) n. a doctor who specializes in giving anesthetics —**an′es·the′si·ol′o·gy** n.

**an′es·thet′ic** (-thet′ik) adj. of or producing anesthesia —n. a drug, gas, etc. used to produce anesthesia, as before surgery

**an·es·the·tist** (ə nes′thə tist) n. a person trained to give anesthetics

**an·es′the·tize′** (-tīz′) vt. -tized′, -tiz′ing to cause anesthesia in —**an·es′the·ti·za′tion** n.

**an·eu·rysm, an·eu·rism** (an′yər iz′m) n. [< Gr. ana-, up + eurys, broad] a sac formed by a swelling in a weakened wall of an artery

**a·new** (ə nōō′) adv. 1. once more; again 2. in a new way or form

**an·gel** (ān′j'l) n. [< Gr. angelos, messenger] 1. Theol. a) a messenger of God b) an immortal spirit 2. an image of a human figure with wings and a halo 3. a person regarded as beautiful, good, etc. 4. [Colloq.] a financial backer, as for a play — **an·gel·ic** (an jel′ik), **an·gel′i·cal** adj. —**an·gel′i·cal·ly** adv.

**An·gel·e·no** (an′jə lē′nō) n., pl. **-nos** an inhabitant of Los Angeles

**an·gel·fish** (ān′j'l fish′) n., pl.: see FISH a bright-colored tropical fish with spiny fins

**angel (food) cake** a light, spongy, white cake made with egg whites

**an·ger** (aŋ′gər) n. [< ON. angr, distress] hostile feelings because of opposition, a hurt, etc. —vt., vi. to make or become angry

**an·gi·na** (pec·to·ris) (an ji′nə pek′tər is) [L., distress of the breast] a condition marked by chest pain, caused by a decrease of blood to the heart

**an·gle¹** (aŋ′g′l) *n.* [< Gr. *ankylos*, bent] 1. the shape or space made by two straight lines or plane surfaces that meet 2. the degrees of difference in direction between them 3. a sharp corner 4. a point of view; aspect 5. [Colloq.] a tricky scheme or approach, as for personal gain —*vt.*, *vi.* -gled, -gling 1. to move or bend at an angle 2. [Colloq.] to give a specific aspect to (a story, etc.)

**an·gle²** (aŋ′g′l) *vi.* -gled, -gling [< OE. *angul*, fishhook] 1. to fish with a hook and line 2. to use tricks to get something [to *angle* for a promotion] —**an′gler** *n.*

**angle iron** a piece of iron or steel bent at a right angle, used for joining or reinforcing two beams, etc.

**An·gles** (aŋ′g′lz) *n.pl.* a Germanic people that settled in England in the 5th cent. A.D.

**an′gle·worm**′ *n.* an earthworm

**An·gli·can** (aŋ′gli kən) *adj.* [< ML. *Anglicus*, of the Angles] of or connected with the Church of England —*n.* an Anglican church member

**An·gli·cism** (aŋ′glə siz′m) *n.* a word or trait peculiar to the English

**An′gli·cize**′ (-sīz′) *vt.*, *vi.* -cized′, -ciz′ing to change to English idiom, pronunciation, customs, etc. —**An′gli·ci·za′tion** (-si zā′shən) *n.*

**Anglo-** *a combining form meaning* English or English and

**An′glo-A·mer′i·can** (aŋ′glō-) *adj.* English and American —*n.* an American of English birth or ancestry

**An·glo-Sax·on** (aŋ′glō sak′s′n) *n.* 1. a member of the Germanic peoples in England before the 12th cent. 2. their language, OLD ENGLISH 3. an Englishman —*adj.* of the Anglo-Saxons

**An·go·la** (aŋ gō′lə, an-) country on the SW coast of Africa: 481,351 sq. mi.; pop. 6,761,000

**An·go·ra** (aŋ gôr′ə) *n.* [former name of ANKARA] 1. a breed of animal; specif., a cat, rabbit, or goat, with long, silky fur or hair 2. *a)* yarn of Angora rabbit hair *b)* mohair

**an·gry** (aŋ′grē) *adj.* -gri·er, -gri·est 1. feeling or showing anger 2. wild and stormy —**an′gri·ly** (-grə lē) *adv.*

**ang·strom** (aŋ′strəm) *n.* [< A. J. *Angström*, 19th-c. Swed. physicist] one hundred-millionth of a centimeter, a unit used in measuring the length of light waves: also **angstrom unit**

**an·guish** (aŋ′gwish) *n.* [< L. *angustia*, tightness] great mental or physical pain; agony —*vt.*, *vi.* to feel or make feel anguish —**an′guished** *adj.*

**an·gu·lar** (aŋ′gyə lər) *adj.* 1. having or forming an angle or angles; sharp-cornered 2. lean; gaunt 3. without ease or grace; stiff —**an′gu·lar′i·ty** (-ler′ə tē) *n.*, *pl.* -ties

**an·i·line** (an′′l in) *n.* [< Ar. *al*, the + *nīl*, blue + -INE³] a colorless, poisonous, oily derivative of benzene, used in making dyes, varnishes, etc.

**an·i·mad·vert** (an′ə mad vurt′) *vi.* [< L. *animus*, mind + *advertere*, to turn] to comment adversely (on or upon) —**an′i·mad·ver′sion** (-vur′zhən) *n.*

**an·i·mal** (an′ə m′l) *n.* [< L. *anima*, breath, soul] 1. any living organism except a plant or bacterium, typically able to move about 2. any such organism other than man; esp., any four-footed creature 3. a brutish or bestial person —*adj.* 1. of or like an animal 2. gross, bestial, etc. —**an′i·mal′i·ty** (-mal′ə tē) *n.*

**an·i·mal·cule** (an′ə mal′kyool) *n.* a very small or microscopic animal

**an·i·mate** (an′ə māt′; *for adj.* -mit) *vt.* -mat′ed, -mat′ing [see ANIMAL] 1. to give life or motion to 2. to make gay or spirited 3. to inspire —*adj.* living —**an′i·mat′ed** *adj.* —**an′i·ma′tion** *n.* —**an′i·ma′tor** *n.*

**animated cartoon** a motion picture made by filming a series of cartoons

**an·i·mism** (an′ə miz′m) *n.* [< L. *anima*, soul] the belief that all life is produced by a spiritual force, or that all things in nature have souls —**an′i·mis′tic** *adj.*

**an·i·mos·i·ty** (an′ə mäs′ə tē) *n.*, *pl.* -ties [see ff.] a feeling of strong dislike or hatred; hostility

**an·i·mus** (an′ə məs) *n.* [L., passion] animosity; hostility

**an·i·on** (an′i′ən) *n.* [< Gr. *ana-*, up + *ienai*, to go] a negatively charged ion: in electrolysis, anions move toward the anode

**an·ise** (an′is) *n.* [< Gr. *anēson*] 1. a plant of the parsley family 2. its fragrant seed, used for flavoring: also **an·i·seed** (an′ə sēd′)

**an·i·sette** (an′ə set′, -zet′) *n.* [Fr.] a sweet, anise-flavored liqueur

**An·ka·ra** (aŋ′kər ə, äŋ′-) capital of Turkey: pop. 650,000

**ankh** (aŋk) *n.* [Egypt., life] a cross with a loop at the top, an ancient Egyptian symbol of life

**an·kle** (aŋ′k′l) *n.* [OE. *ancleow*] 1. the joint that connects the foot and leg 2. the part of the leg between the foot and calf

**an′klet** (-klit) *n.* 1. an ornament worn around the ankle 2. a short sock

**an·nals** (an′′lz) *n.pl.* [< L. *annus*, year] 1. a written account of events year by year 2. historical records; history —**an′nal·ist** *n.*

**An·nap·o·lis** (ə nap′ə lis) capital of Md.: pop. 30,000

**Ann Ar·bor** (an är′bər) city in SE Mich.: pop. 100,000

**an·neal** (ə nēl′) *vt.* [< OE. *an-*, on + *æl*, fire] to heat (glass, metals, etc.) and cool slowly to prevent brittleness

**an·ne·lid** (an′′l id) *n.* [< L. dim. of *anulus*, a ring] any of various worms with a body made of joined segments or rings, as the earthworm

**an·nex** (ə neks′; *for n.* an′eks) *vt.* [< L. *ad-*, to + *nectere*, to tie] 1. to attach, esp. to something larger 2. to incorporate into a state the territory of (another state) —*n.* something annexed; esp., an addition to a building —**an′nex·a′tion** *n.*

**an·ni·hi·late** (ə nī′ə lāt′) *vt.* -lat′ed, -lat′ing [< L. *ad*, to + *nihil*, nothing] to destroy entirely; kill off; crush —**an·ni′hi·la′tion** *n.*—**an·ni′hi·la′tor** *n.*

**an·ni·ver·sa·ry** (an′ə vur′sər ē) *n., pl.* -ries [< L. *annus*, year + *vertere*, to turn] the yearly return of the date of some event —*adj.* of an anniversary

**an·no·tate** (an′ə tāt′) *vt., vi.* -tat′ed, -tat′ing [< L. *ad-*, to + *nota*, a sign] to provide explanatory notes for — **an′no·ta′tion** *n.* —**an′no·ta′tor** *n.*

**an·nounce** (ə nouns′) *vt.* -nounced′, -nounc′ing [< L. *ad-*, to + *nuntius*, messenger] 1. to declare publicly or openly 2. to make known the arrival of 3. to be an announcer for —*vi.* to serve as an announcer —**an·nounce′ment** *n.*

**an·nounc′er** *n.* one who announces; specif., one who introduces radio or television programs, identifies the station, etc.

**an·noy** (ə noi′) *vt.* [< VL. *in odio*, in hate] to irritate, bother, etc., as by a repeated action —**an·noy′ance** *n.*— **an·noy′ing** *adj.* —**an·noy′ing·ly** *adv.*

**an·nu·al** (an′yoo wəl) *adj.* [< L. *annus*, year] 1. of or measured by a year 2. yearly 3. living only one year or season —*n.* 1. a periodical published once a year 2. a plant living only one year or season —**an′nu·al·ly** *adv.*

**an·nu·i·ty** (ə nōō′ə tē) *n., pl.* -ties [see prec.] 1. an investment yielding fixed payments, esp. yearly 2. such a payment —**an·nu′i·tant** *n.*

**an·nul** (ə nul′) *vt.* -nulled′, -nul′-ling [< L. *ad-*, to + *nullum*, nothing] 1. to do away with 2. to deprive of legal force; nullify —**an·nul′ment** *n.*

**an·nu·lar** (an′yoo lər) *adj.* [< L. *annulus*, a ring] like or forming a ring

**an·nun·ci·a·tion** (ə nun′sē ā′shən) *n.* 1. an announcing 2. [A-] *a)* the angel Gabriel's announcement to Mary that she would bear Jesus *b)* the church festival commemorating this

**an·ode** (an′ōd) *n.* [< Gr. *ana-*, up + *hodos*, way] 1. the positive electrode in an electrolytic cell 2. the principal electrode for collecting electrons in an electron tube 3. the negative electrode in a battery

**an·o·dize** (an′ə dīz′) *vt.* -dized′, -diz′ing to put a protective oxide film on (a metal) by an electrolytic process in which the metal serves as the anode

**an·o·dyne** (an′ə dīn′) *n.* [< Gr. *an-*, without + *odynē*, pain] anything that relieves pain or soothes

**a·noint** (ə noint′) *vt.* [< L. *in-*, on + *ungere*, to smear] to put oil on, as in consecrating —**a·noint′ment** *n.*

**a·nom·a·lous** (ə näm′ə ləs) *adj.* [< Gr. *an-*, not + *homos*, the same] 1.

deviating from the general rule; abnormal 2. inconsistent or odd

**a·nom′a·ly** (-lē) *n., pl.* -lies 1. departure from the usual; abnormality 2. anything anomalous

**an·o·mie, an·o·my** (an′ə mē) *n.* [Fr. < Gr. *anomia*, lawlessness] lack of purpose, identity, etc.; rootlessness

**a·non** (ə nän′) *adv.* [< OE. *on an*, in one] 1. soon 2. at another time

**anon.** anonymous

**a·non·y·mous** (ə nän′ə məs) *adj.* [< Gr. *an-*, without + *onoma*, name] 1. with no name known 2. given, written, etc. by one whose name is withheld or unknown 3. lacking individuality —**an·o·nym·i·ty** (an′ə nim′ə tē) *n.* —**a·non′y·mous·ly** *adv.*

**a·noph·e·les** (ə näf′ə lēz′) *n.* [< Gr. *anōphelēs*, harmful] the mosquito that can transmit malaria

**an·oth·er** (ə nuth′ər) *adj.* 1. one more; an additional 2. a different —*pron.* 1. one additional 2. a different one 3. one of the same kind

**an·swer** (an′sər) *n.* [< OE. *and-*, against + *swerian*, swear] 1. a reply to a question, letter, etc. 2. any retaliation 3. a solution to a problem —*vi.* 1. to reply 2. to be sufficient 3. to be responsible (*to* a person *for*) 4. to conform (*to*) [he *answers* to the description] —*vt.* 1. to reply or respond to 2. to serve [to *answer* the purpose] 3. to defend oneself against (an accusation, etc.); refute 4. to conform [he *answers* the description] —**answer back** [Colloq.] to reply forcefully or insolently —**an′-swer·a·ble** *adj.*

**ant** (ant) *n.* [< OE. *æmete*] any of a family of insects, generally wingless, that live in colonies

**ant-** *same as* ANTI-

**-ant** (ənt, ′nt) [ult. < L.] *a suffix meaning:* 1. that has, shows, or does [*defiant*] 2. one that [*occupant*]

**ant·ac·id** (ant′as′id) *adj.* counteracting acidity —*n.* an antacid substance

**an·tag·o·nism** (an tag′ə niz′m) *n.* [see ANTAGONIZE] 1. opposition or hostility 2. an opposing force, principle, etc. —**an·tag′o·nis′tic** *adj.* — **an·tag′o·nis′ti·cal·ly** *adv.*

**an·tag′o·nist** *n.* adversary; opponent

**an·tag′o·nize′** (-nīz′) *vt.* -nized′, -niz′ing [< Gr. *anti-*, against + *agōn*, contest] to incur the dislike of

**ant·arc·tic** (ant ärk′tik, -är′-) *adj.* [see ANTI- & ARCTIC] of or near the South Pole or the region around it —**the Antarctic** *same as* ANTARCTICA

**Ant·arc′ti·ca** (-ti kə) land area about the South Pole, completely covered by ice: c.5,000,000 sq. mi.

**Antarctic Circle** [*also* a- c-] an imaginary circle parallel to the equator, 66°33′ south of it

**Antarctic Ocean** popularly, the oceans surrounding Antarctica

**ant bear** a large anteater of tropical S. America

**an·te** (an′tē) *n.* [L., before] *Poker* the stake that each player must put into the pot before receiving cards —*vt.,* *vi.* -ted or -teed, -te·ing *Poker* to put in (one's stake): also **ante up**

**ante-** [see prec.] *a prefix meaning* before [*antecedent*]

**ant′eat′er** *n.* a mammal with a long snout, that feeds mainly on ants

**an·te·bel·lum** (an′ti bel′əm) *adj.* [L.] before the war; specif., before the American Civil War

**an·te·ced·ent** (an′tə sēd′'nt) *adj.* [< L. *ante-*, before + *cedere*, go] prior; previous —*n.* 1. any thing prior to another 2. [*pl.*] one's ancestry, past life, etc. 3. *Gram.* the word or phrase to which a pronoun refers

**an·te·cham·ber** (an′ti chām′bər) *n.* a smaller room leading into a larger or main room

**an′te·date′** (-dāt′) *vt.* -dat′ed, -dat′ing 1. to put a date on that is earlier than the actual date 2. to come before in time

**an·te·di·lu·vi·an** (an′ti də lōō′vē ən) *adj.* [< ANTE- + L. *diluvium*, a flood + -AN] 1. of the time before the Biblical Flood 2. very old or old-fashioned

**an·te·lope** (an′tə lōp′) *n.* [< Gr. *antholops*, deer] a swift, cud-chewing, horned animal resembling the deer

ANTELOPE

**an·te me·ri·di·em** (an′tē mə rid′ē əm) [L.] before noon: abbrev. A.M.

**an·ten·na** (an ten′ə) *n.* [L., sail yard] 1. *pl.* -nae (-ē), -nas either of a pair of feelers on the head of an insect, crab, etc. 2. *pl.* -nas *Radio & TV* an arrangement of wires, rods, etc. used in sending and receiving the electromagnetic waves

**an·te·ri·or** (an tir′ē ər) *adj.* [< L. *ante*, before] 1. at or toward the front 2. earlier; previous

**an·te·room** (an′ti rōōm′) *n.* a room leading to a larger or main room

**an·them** (an′thəm) *n.* [< Gr. *anti-*, over against + *phōnē*, voice] 1. a religious choral song 2. a song of praise or devotion, as to a nation

**an·ther** (an′thər) *n.* [< Gr. *anthos*, a flower] the part of a stamen that contains the pollen

**ant·hill** (ant′hil′) *n.* the soil heaped up by ants around their nest opening

**an·thol·o·gize** (an thäl′ə jīz′) *vi.* -gized′, -giz′ing to make anthologies —*vt.* to include in an anthology

**an·thol·o·gy** (an thäl′ə jē) *n., pl.* -gies [< Gr. *anthos*, flower + *legein*, gather] a collection of poems, stories, etc. —**an·thol′o·gist** *n.*

**An·tho·ny** (an′thə nē, -tə-), Mark see ANTONY

**an·thra·cite** (an′thrə sīt′) *n.* [< Gr. *anthrax*, coal] hard coal, which gives much heat and little smoke

**an·thrax** (an′thraks) *n.* [< Gr., coal, carbuncle] an infectious disease of cattle, sheep, etc. which can be transmitted to man

**anthropo-** [< Gr. *anthrōpos*, man] *a combining form meaning* man, human

**an·thro·po·cen·tric** (an′thrə pə sen′trik) *adj.* [see prec.] centering one's view of everything around man

**an·thro·poid** (an′thrə poid′) *adj.* [< ANTHROPO- + -OID] 1. manlike; esp., designating or of any of the most highly developed apes, as the chimpanzee 2. apelike —*n.* any anthropoid ape

**an·thro·pol·o·gy** (an′thrə päl′ə jē) *n.* [ANTHROPO- + -LOGY] the study of the characteristics, customs, etc. of mankind —**an′thro·po·log′i·cal** (-pə läj′i k'l) *adj.* —**an′thro·pol′o·gist** *n.*

**an·thro·po·mor′phism** (-pə môr′fiz′m) *n.* [< Gr. *anthrōpos*, man + *morphē*, form] the attributing of human characteristics to gods, objects, etc. —**an′thro·po·mor′phic** *adj.* —**an′thro·po·mor′phi·cal·ly** *adv.*

**an·ti** (an′tī, -tē) *n., pl.* -tis [see ff.] [Colloq.] a person opposed to something —*adj.* [Colloq.] opposed

**anti-** [< Gr. *anti*, against] *a prefix meaning:* 1. against, hostile to 2. that operates against 3. that prevents, cures, or neutralizes 4. opposite, reverse 5. rivaling

**an·ti·air·craft** (an′tē er′kraft) *adj.* used against hostile aircraft

**an·ti·bac·te·ri·al** (an′ti bak tir′ē əl) *adj.* that checks the growth or effect of bacteria

**an′ti·bal·lis′tic missile** (-bə lis′tik) a ballistic missile for intercepting an enemy ballistic missile

**an′ti·bi·ot′ic** (-bī ät′ik, -bē-) *n.* [< ANTI- + Gr. *bios*, life] any of certain substances, as penicillin or streptomycin, produced by some microorganisms and capable of destroying or weakening bacteria, etc. —*adj.* of antibiotics

**an·ti·bod·y** (an′ti bäd′ē) *n., pl.* -ies a protein produced in the body to neutralize an antigen

**an·tic** (an′tik) *adj.* [< L.: see ANTIQUE] odd and funny —*n.* a playful or ludicrous act, trick, etc. —*vi.* -ticked, -tick·ing to do antics

**An·ti·christ** (an′ti krist′) *Bible* the great opponent of Christ: I John 2:18

**an·tic·i·pate** (an tis′ə pāt′) *vt.* -pat′ed, -pat′ing [< L. *ante-*, before + *capere*, take] 1. to look forward to 2. to forestall 3. to take care of, use, etc. in advance 4. to be ahead of in doing —**an·tic′i·pa′tion** *n.* —**an·tic′i·pa·to′ry** (-pə tôr′ē) *adj.*

**an·ti·cli·max** (an′ti klī′maks) *n.* 1. a sudden drop from the important to the trivial 2. a descent which is in disappointing contrast to a preceding rise —**an′ti·cli·mac′tic** (-klī mak′tik) *adj.* —**an′ti·cli·mac′ti·cal·ly** *adv.*

**an'ti·co·ag'u·lant** (-kō ag'yə lənt) *n.* a drug or substance that delays or prevents the clotting of blood

**an'ti·de·pres'sant** (-də pres'ənt) *adj.* lessening emotional depression —*n.* an antidepressant drug

**an'ti·dote** (an'tə dōt') *n.* [< Gr. *anti-*, against + *dotos*, given] 1. a remedy to counteract a poison 2. anything that works against an evil

**an'ti·freeze** (an'ti frēz') *n.* a substance used, as in an automobile radiator, to prevent freezing

**an'ti·gen** (an'tə jən) *n.* [ANTI- + -GEN] a substance to which the body reacts by producing antibodies

**an'ti·he·ro** (an'ti hir'ō) *n.* the protagonist of a novel, etc. who lacks the stature of a traditional hero

**an'ti·his·ta·mine** (an'ti his'tə mēn', -mən) *n.* any of several drugs used in treating such allergic conditions as hay fever, asthma, and hives —an'ti·his'ta·min'ic (-min'ik) *adj.*

**an'ti·knock'** (-näk') *n.* a substance added to the fuel of internal-combustion engines to do away with noise resulting from too rapid combustion

**An·til·les** (an til'ēz) group of islands of the West Indies, including Cuba, Jamaica, etc. (**Greater Antilles**) & the Leeward Islands and Windward Islands (**Lesser Antilles**)

**an'ti·log·a·rithm** (an'ti lôg'ə rith'm, -läg'-) *n.* the number corresponding to a logarithm [the *antilogarithm* of 1 is 10]

**an'ti·ma·cas·sar** (an'ti mə kas'ər) *n.* [ANTI- + *macassar*, a hair oil] a small cover on the back or arms of a chair, sofa, etc. to prevent soiling

**an'ti·mag·net'ic** (-mag net'ik) *adj.* made of metals that resist magnetism

**an'ti·mat'ter** (-mat'ər) *n.* a form of matter in which the electrical charge or other property of each particle is the reverse of that in the usual matter of our universe

**an'ti·mis'sile** (-mis''l) *adj.* designed as a defense against ballistic missiles

**an·ti·mo·ny** (an'tə mō'nē) *n.* [< ML.] a silvery-white, metallic chemical element used in alloys to harden them

**an'ti·neu·tron** (an'ti nōō'trän) *n.* the antiparticle of the neutron

**an·ti·par·ti·cle** (an'ti pär'tə k'l) *n.* any particle of antimatter

**an·ti·pas·to** (an'ti pas'tō, -päs'-) *n.* [It. < *anti-*, before + *pasto*, food] an appetizer of salted fish, meat, etc.

**an·tip·a·thy** (an tip'ə thē) *n., pl.* -thies [< Gr. *anti-*, against + *pathein*, feel] 1. strong dislike; aversion 2. an object of this

**an·ti·per·son·nel** (an'ti pur'sə nel') *adj.* intended to destroy people rather than objects [*antipersonnel* mines]

**an'ti·per'spir·ant** (-pur'spər ənt) *n.* a skin lotion, cream, etc. to reduce perspiration

**an·ti·phon** (an'tə fän') *n.* [see ANTHEM] a hymn, psalm, etc. sung in responsive, alternating parts —**an·tiph·o·nal** (an tif'ə n'l) *adj.*

**an·tip·o·des** (an tip'ə dēz') *n.pl.* [<

Gr. *anti-*, opposite + *pous*, foot] two places directly opposite each other on the earth —**an·tip'o·dal** *adj.*

**an·ti·pro·ton** (an'ti prō'tän) *n.* the antiparticle of the proton

**an·ti·quar·i·an** (an'tə kwer'ē ən) *adj.* 1. of antiques or antiquities 2. of antiquaries —*n.* an antiquary

**an'ti·quar'y** (-ē) *n., pl.* -ies a collector or student of antiquities

**an'ti·quate'** (-kwāt') *vt.* -quat'ed, -quat'ing [see ff.] to make old, obsolete, or out-of-date —**an'ti·quat'ed** *adj.* —**an'ti·qua'tion** *n.*

**an·tique** (an tēk') *adj.* [< L. *antiquus*, ancient] 1. of ancient times 2. out-of-date 3. of or in the style of a former period 4. dealing in antiques —*n.* 1. an ancient relic 2. a piece of furniture, etc. of a former period —*vt.* -tiqued', -tiqu'ing to make look antique —**an·tique'ness** *n.*

**an·tiq·ui·ty** (an tik'wə tē) *n., pl.* -ties [see prec.] 1. the ancient period of history 2. ancientness 3. [*pl.*] relics, etc. of the distant past

**an·ti·scor·bu·tic acid** (an'ti skôr·byōō'tik) *same as* VITAMIN C

**an·ti·Se·mit·ic** (an'ti sə mit'ik) *adj.* 1. having prejudice against Jews 2. discriminating against or persecuting Jews —**an'ti·Sem'ite** (-sem'īt) *n.* —**an'ti·Sem'i·tism** (-ə tiz'm) *n.*

**an'ti·sep'sis** (-sep'sis) *n.* 1. a being antiseptic 2. the use of antiseptics

**an'ti·sep'tic** (-sep'tik) *adj.* [ANTI- + SEPTIC] 1. preventing infection, decay, etc.; effective against bacteria, etc. 2. using antiseptics 3. sterile —*n.* any antiseptic substance, as alcohol —an'ti·sep'ti·cal·ly *adv.*

**an'ti·slav'er·y** (-sla'vər ē) *adj.* against slavery

**an'ti·so'cial** *adj.* 1. not sociable 2. harmful to the welfare of people

**an'ti·tank'** *adj.* for use against tanks in war

**an·tith·e·sis** (an tith'ə sis) *n., pl.* -ses' (-sēz') [< Gr. *anti-*, against + *tithenai*, to place] 1. a contrast or opposition, as of ideas 2. the exact opposite —**an'ti·thet'i·cal** (-tə thet'i k'l) *adj.* —**an'ti·thet'i·cal·ly** *adv.*

**an·ti·tox·in** (an'ti täk'sin) *n.* 1. a substance formed in the blood to act against a specific toxin 2. a serum containing an antitoxin, injected into a person to prevent a disease

**an'ti·trust'** *adj.* opposed to or regulating trusts or business monopolies

**an'ti·viv'i·sec'tion·ist** (-viv'ə sek' shən ist) *n.* one opposing vivisection

**ant·ler** (ant'lər) *n.* [< ML. *ante-*, before + *ocularis*, of the eyes] the branched horn of any animal of the deer family —**ant'lered** *adj.*

**An·to·ny** (an'tə nē), Mark or Marc 83?–30 B.C.; Rom. general

**an·to·nym** (an'tə nim') *n.* [< Gr. *anti-*, opposite + *ōnyma*, name] a word meaning the opposite of another

**an·trum** (an'trəm) *n., pl.* -tra (-trə), -trums [< Gr. *antron*, cave] *Anat.* a cavity; esp., a sinus in the upper jaw

**Ant·werp** (ant'wərp) seaport in N Belgium: pop. 247,000

**a·nus** (ā'nəs) *n., pl.* -nus·es, -ni

(-nĭ) [L.] the opening at the lower end of the alimentary canal

**an·vil** (an'vəl) *n.* [OE. *anfilt*] an iron or steel block on which metal objects are hammered into shape

**anx·i·e·ty** (aŋ zī'ə tē) *n., pl.* **-ties** 1. worry or uneasiness about what may happen 2. an eager desire [*anxiety* to do well]

**anx·ious** (aŋk'shəs) *adj.* [< L. *angere*, choke] 1. worried 2. causing anxiety 3. eagerly wishing —**anx'·ious·ly** *adv.*

**an·y** (en'ē) *adj.* [OE. *ænig*] 1. one (no matter which) of more than two [*any* boy may go] 2. some [has he *any* pain?] 3. even one or the least amount of [he hasn't *any* dogs] 4. every [*any* child can tell] 5. without limit [*any* number can play] —*pron. sing. & pl.* any one or ones —*adv.* to any degree or extent; at all [is he *any* better?]

**an'y·bod'y** (-bud'ē, -bäd'ē) *pron.* 1. any person 2. an important person

**an'y·how'** *adv. same as* ANYWAY

**an'y·more'** *adv.* now; nowadays

**an'y·one'** *pron.* any person; anybody

**any one** any single (person or thing)

**an'y·place'** *adv. same as* ANYWHERE

**an'y·thing'** *pron.* any object, event, fact, etc. —*n.* a thing, no matter of what kind —*adv.* in any way —**any·thing** but not at all

**an'y·way'** *adv.* 1. in any manner 2. at any rate 3. haphazardly

**an'y·where'** *adv.* 1. in, at, or to any place 2. [Colloq.] at all —**get any·where** [Colloq.] to achieve anything

**A/o, a/o** account of

**A-OK** (ā'ō kā') *adj.* [A(LL) OK] [Colloq.] excellent, fine, in working order, etc.: also A'-O·kay'

**A one** (ā' wun') [Colloq.] superior; first-class: also A1, A number 1

**a·or·ta** (ā ôr'tə) *n., pl.* **-tas, -tae** (-tē) [< Gr. *aeirein*, to raise] the main artery of the body, carrying blood from the heart

**a·pace** (ə pās') *adv.* at a fast pace

**A·pach·e** (ə pach'ē) *n., pl.* **-es, -e** [prob. < Zuni *ápachu*, enemy] a member of a tribe of SW U.S. Indians

**a·part** (ə pärt') *adv.* [< L. *ad*, to + *pars*, part] 1. aside 2. away in place or time 3. in or to pieces —*adj.* separated —**apart from** other than —**tell apart** to distinguish between

**a·part'heid** (-hāt, -hīt) *n.* [Afrik., apartness] strict racial segregation as practiced in South Africa

**a·part'ment** *n.* [< It. *appartare*, to separate] a room or suite of rooms to live in, esp. one of a number in an **apartment house** (or **building**)

**ap·a·thy** (ap'ə thē) *n., pl.* **-thies** [< Gr. *a-*, without + *pathos*, emotion] 1. lack of emotion 2. indifference; listlessness —**ap'a·thet'ic** (-thet'ik) *adj.* —**ap'a·thet'i·cal·ly** *adv.*

**APC** aspirin, phenacetin, and caffeine, usually in a tablet (**APC tablet**) used for relieving headaches, etc.

**ape** (āp) *n.* [< OE. *apa*] 1. a chimpanzee, gorilla, orangutan, or gibbon 2. any monkey 3. a mimic 4. a gross, clumsy man —*vt.* **aped, ap'ing** to imitate —**ape'like'** *adj.*

**Ap·en·nines** (ap'ə ninz') mountain range of C Italy

**a·pe·ri·ent** (ə pir'ē ənt) *adj., n.* [< L. *aperire*, to open] laxative

**a·pe·ri·tif** (ä'pā rə tēf') *n.* [Fr.] an alcoholic drink taken before meals

**ap·er·ture** (ap'ər chər) *n.* [< L. *aperire*, open] an opening; hole

**a·pex** (ā'peks) *n., pl.* **a'pex·es, ap·i·ces** (ap'ə sēz') [L.] 1. the highest point 2. pointed end; tip 3. a climax

**a·pha·sia** (ə fā'zhə) *n.* [Gr. < *a-*, not + *phanai*, speak] loss of the power to use or understand words —**a·pha'·sic** (-zik) *adj., n.*

**a·phe·li·on** (ə fēl'ē ən) *n., pl.* **-li·ons, -li·a** (-ə) [< Gr. *apo-*, from + *hēlios*, sun] the point farthest from the sun in the orbit of a planet or comet or of a man-made satellite

**a·phid** (ā'fid, af'id) *n.* [< Gr. *apheidēs*, unsparing] an insect that lives on plants by sucking their juices

**aph·o·rism** (af'ə riz'm) *n.* [< Gr. *apo-*, from + *horizein*, to bound] a concise statement of a truth; adage; maxim —**aph'o·ris'tic** *adj.* —**aph'o·ris'ti·cal·ly** *adv.*

**aph·ro·dis·i·ac** (af'rə diz'ē ak') *adj.* [< Gr. *Aphrodítē*] arousing sexual desire —*n.* an aphrodisiac drug, etc.

**Aph·ro·di·te** (af'rə dīt'ē) the Greek goddess of love and beauty

**a·pi·ar·y** (ā'pē er'ē) *n., pl.* **-ies** [< L. *apis*, bee] a place where bees are kept —**a'pi·a·rist** (-ə rist) *n.*

**a·piece** (ə pēs') *adv.* [ME. *a pece*] for each one; each

**a·plen·ty** (ə plen'tē) *adj., adv.* [Colloq.] in abundance

**a·plomb** (ə pläm', -plum') *n.* [Fr.: see PLUMB] self-possession; poise

**APO** Army Post Office

**a·poc·a·lypse** (ə päk'ə lips') *n.* [< Gr. *apokalyptein*, disclose] 1. [A-] *Bible* the book of REVELATION 2. any revelation of a violent struggle in which evil will be destroyed —**a·poc'·a·lyp'tic** (-lip'tik) *adj.*

**A·poc·ry·pha** (ə päk'rə fə) *n.pl.* [< Gr. *apo-*, away + *kryptein*, to hide] fourteen books of the Septuagint rejected in Protestantism and Judaism; eleven are in the Roman Catholic Bible

**a·poc'ry·phal** *adj.* 1. of doubtful authenticity 2. not genuine; spurious; counterfeit

**ap·o·gee** (ap'ə jē') *n.* [< Gr. *apo-*, from + *gē*, earth] the point farthest from a heavenly body, as the earth, in the orbit of a satellite around it

**a·po·lit·i·cal** (ā'pə lit'ə k'l) *adj.* not concerned with political matters — **a'po·lit'i·cal·ly** *adv.*

**A·pol·lo** (ə päl'ō) the Greek and Roman god of music, poetry, proph-

---

ecy, and medicine —*n.* any handsome young man

**a·pol·o·get·ic** (ə päl'ə jet'ik) *adj.* showing apology; expressing regret —**a·pol'o·get'i·cal·ly** *adv.*

**a·pol·o·gist** (ə päl'ə jist) *n.* one who defends or attempts to justify a doctrine, faith, action, etc.

**a·pol'o·gize'** (-jīz') *vi.* **-gized', -giz'-ing** to make an apology

**a·pol'o·gy** (-jē) *n., pl.* **-gies** [< Gr. *apo-*, from + *logos*, speech] **1.** a formal defense of some idea, doctrine, etc.; also **ap·o·lo·gi·a** (ap'ə lō'jē ə) **2.** an expressing of regret for a fault, insult, etc. **3.** a poor substitute

**ap·o·plex·y** (ap'ə plek'sē) *n.* [< Gr. *apo-*, from + *plēssein*, to strike] sudden paralysis caused by the breaking or obstruction of a blood vessel in the brain —**ap'o·plec'tic** *adj.*

**a·pos·ta·sy** (ə päs'tə sē) *n., pl.* **-sies** [< Gr. *apo-*, away + *stasis*, a standing] an abandoning of what one believed in, as a faith, etc.

**a·pos'tate'** (-tāt') *n.* a person guilty of apostasy

**a·pos'ta·tize'** (-tə tīz') *vi.* **-tized', -tiz'ing** to become an apostate

**a pos·te·ri·o·ri** (ā' päs tir'ē ôr'ī) [ML.] **1.** from effect to cause **2.** based on observation or experience

**a·pos·tle** (ə päs''l) *n.* [< Gr. *apo-*, from + *stellein*, send] **1.** [*usually* A-] any of the disciples of Jesus, esp. the original twelve **2.** the leader of a new movement

**ap·os·tol·ic** (ap'əs täl'ik) *adj.* **1.** of the Apostles, their teachings, works, etc. **2.** [*often* A-] of the Pope; papal

**a·pos·tro·phe** (ə päs'trə fē) *n.* [< Gr. *apo-*, from + *strephein*, to turn] the mark (') indicating: **1.** omission of a letter or letters from a word (Ex.: *it's* for *it is*) **2.** the possessive case (Ex.: *Mary's* dress) **3.** certain plural forms (Ex.: five *6's*, dot the *i's*) **4.** an exclamatory address to a person or thing

**a·poth·e·car·y** (ə päth'ə ker'ē) *n., pl.* **-ies** [< Gr. *apothēkē*, storehouse] a druggist; pharmacist

**ap·o·thegm** (ap'ə them') *n.* [< Gr. *apo-*, from + *phthengesthai*, to utter] a short, pithy saying

**a·poth·e·o·sis** (ə päth'ē ō'sis, ap'ə thē'ə sis) *n., pl.* **-ses'** (-sēz') [< Gr. *apo-*, from + *theos*, a god] **1.** the deifying of a person **2.** the glorification of a person or thing **3.** a glorified ideal

**Ap·pa·la·chi·a** (ap'ə lā'chə, -chē ə) the highland region of the E U.S. extending from N Pa. through N Ala., characterized generally by poverty

**Ap·pa·la·chi·an Mountains** (ap'ə lā'chən, -chē ən, -lach'ən) mountain system extending from S Quebec to N Ala.; also **Ap'pa·la'chi·ans**

**ap·pall, ap·pal** (ə pôl') *vt.* **-palled', -pal'ling** [ult. < L. *ad*, to + *pallidus*, pale] to horrify, dismay, or shock

**ap·pa·loo·sa** (ap'ə loō'sə) *n.* [< *Palouse* Indians of NW U.S.] a breed of Western saddle horse with black and white spots on the rump and loins

**ap·pa·rat** (äp'ə rät', ap'ə rat') *n.* [Russ., apparatus] an organization; esp., a political organization

**ap·pa·ra·tus** (ap'ə rat'əs, -rät'-) *n., pl.* **-tus, -tus·es** [< L. *ad-*, to + *parare*, prepare] **1.** the materials, tools, etc. for a specific use **2.** any complex machine, device, or system

**ap·par·el** (ə per'əl) *n.* [ult. < L. *ad-*, to + *parare*, prepare] clothing; attire —*vt.* **-eled** or **-elled, -el·ing** or **-el·ling** to clothe; dress

**ap·par·ent** (ə per'ənt) *adj.* [see APPEAR] **1.** readily seen; visible **2.** evident; obvious **3.** appearing real or true; seeming —**ap·par'ent·ly** *adv.*

**ap·pa·ri·tion** (ap'ə rish'ən) *n.* [see APPEAR] **1.** anything that appears unexpectedly or strangely **2.** a ghost; phantom **3.** a becoming visible

**ap·peal** (ə pēl') *vt.* [< L. *ad-*, to + *pellere*, drive] to make an appeal of (a law case) —*vi.* **1.** to make an appeal in a law case **2.** to make an urgent request (*for* help, etc.) **3.** to be attractive or interesting —*n.* **1.** a request for help, etc. **2.** a request for the transference of a law case to a higher court for rehearing **3.** attraction; interest —**ap·peal'ing** *adj.*

**ap·pear** (ə pir') *vi.* [< L. *ad-*, to + *parere*, become visible] **1.** to come into sight **2.** to become understood or obvious **3.** to seem; look **4.** to present oneself formally in court **5.** to come before the public

**ap·pear'ance** *n.* **1.** an appearing **2.** the outward aspect of anything; look **3.** a pretense or show —**keep up appearances** to maintain an outward show of being proper, etc. —**put in an appearance** to be present for a short time, as at a party

**ap·pease** (ə pēz') *vt.* **-peased', -peas'ing** [ult. < L. *ad*, to + *pax*, peace] to pacify, quiet, or satisfy, esp. by giving in to the demands of —**ap·pease'ment** *n.* —**ap·peas'er** *n.*

**ap·pel·lant** (ə pel'ənt) *n.* a person who appeals, esp. to a higher court

**ap·pel'late court** (-it) a court that can review appeals and reverse the decisions of lower courts

**ap·pel·la·tion** (ap'ə lā'shən) *n.* [see APPEAL] a naming or name; title

**ap·pend** (ə pend') *vt.* [< L. *ad-*, to + *pendere*, suspend] to attach or affix; add as a supplement or appendix

**ap·pend'age** *n.* anything appended; an external organ or part, as a limb

**ap·pen·dec·to·my** (ap'ən dek'tə mē) *n., pl.* **-mies** [see -ECTOMY] the surgical removal of the appendix

**ap·pen·di·ci·tis** (ə pen'də sīt'əs) *n.* [see -ITIS] inflammation of the appendix

**ap·pen·dix** (ə pen'diks) *n., pl.* **-dix·es, -di·ces'** (-də sēz') [see APPEND] **1.** additional material at the end of a book **2.** a small saclike appendage of the large intestine

**ap·per·tain** (ap'ər tān') *vi.* [< L. *ad-*, to + *pertinere*, to reach] to belong as a function, part, etc.; pertain

**ap·pe·ten·cy** (ap'ə tən sē) *n., pl.* **-cies** [see ff.] **1.** a craving; appetite **2.**

a propensity **3.** a natural attraction

**ap·pe·tite** (ap′ə tīt′) *n.* [< L. *ad-*, to + *petere*, seek] **1.** a desire for food **2.** any strong desire; craving

**ap′pe·tiz′er** (-tī′zər) *n.* a tasty food that stimulates the appetite

**ap′pe·tiz′ing** *adj.* **1.** stimulating the appetite **2.** savory; delicious

**ap·plaud** (ə plôd′) *vt., vi.* [< L. *ad-*, to + *plaudere*, clap hands] **1.** to show approval (of) by clapping the hands, etc. **2.** to praise —**ap·plaud′er** *n.*

**ap·plause** (ə plôz′) *n.* approval, esp. as shown by clapping hands

**ap·ple** (ap′'l) *n.* [< OE. *æppel*, fruit, apple] **1.** a round, firm, fleshy, edible fruit **2.** the tree it grows on

**apple butter** jam made of stewed apples

**ap′ple·jack′** (-jak′) *n.* a brandy distilled from apple cider

**ap′ple·sauce′** (-sôs′) *n.* **1.** apples cooked to a pulp in water and sweetened **2.** [Slang] nonsense

**ap·pli·ance** (ə plī′əns) *n.* a device or machine, esp. one for household use

**ap·pli·ca·ble** (ap′li kə b'l) *adj.* that can be applied; appropriate —**ap′pli·ca·bil′i·ty** *n.*

**ap′pli·cant** (-kənt) *n.* one who applies, as for employment, help, etc.

**ap·pli·ca·tion** (ap′lə kā′shən) *n.* **1.** an applying **2.** anything applied, as a remedy **3.** a method of being used **4.** a request, or a form filled out in making one [an employment *application*] **5.** continued effort; diligence **6.** relevance or practicality

**ap′pli·ca′tor** *n.* any device for applying medicine or paint, polish, etc.

**ap·plied** (ə plīd′) *adj.* used in actual practice [*applied* science]

**ap·pli·qué** (ap′lə kā′) *n.* [Fr.] decoration made of one material attached to another —*vt.* -quéd′, -qué′ing to decorate with appliqué

**ap·ply** (ə plī′) *vt.* -plied′, -ply′ing [< L. *ad-*, to + *plicare*, to fold] **1.** to put or spread on [*apply* glue] **2.** to put to practical or specific use [*apply* your knowledge] **3.** to devote (oneself or one's faculties) diligently —*vi.* **1.** to make a request **2.** to be suitable or relevant —**ap·pli′er** *n.*

**ap·point** (ə point′) *vt.* [< L. *ad-*, to + *punctum*, point] **1.** to set (a date, place, etc.) **2.** to name for an office, position, etc. **3.** to furnish [*well-appointed*] —**ap·point′ee′** *n.*

**ap·poin·tive** (ə poin′tiv) *adj.* of or filled by appointment [an *appointive* office]

**ap·point·ment** (ə point′mənt) *n.* **1.** an appointing or being appointed **2.** a position filled by appointing **3.** an engagement to meet someone or be somewhere **4.** [*pl.*] furniture

**Ap·po·mat·tox (Court House)** (ap′ə mat′əks) former village in C Va., where Lee surrendered to Grant

**ap·por·tion** (ə pôr′shən) *vt.* [see AD- & PORTION] to portion out; dis-

tribute in shares —**ap·por′tion·ment** *n.*

**ap·pose** (ə pōz′) *vt.* -posed′, -pos′ing [< L. *ad-*, to + *ponere*, put] to put side by side or opposite —**ap·pos′a·ble** *adj.*

**ap·po·site** (ap′ə zit) *adj.* [see prec.] appropriate; fitting; apt —**ap′po·site·ly** *adv.* —**ap′po·site·ness** *n.*

**ap·po·si·tion** (ap′ə zish′ən) *n.* **1.** an apposing, or the position resulting from this **2.** the placing of a word or phrase beside another in explanation, as in *Jim, my son,* is here —**ap·pos·i·tive** (ə päz′ə tiv) *adj., n.*

**ap·prais·al** (ə prā′z'l) *n.* **1.** an appraising **2.** an appraised value

**ap·praise** (ə prāz′) *vt.* -praised′, -prais′ing [< L. *ad-*, to + *pretium*, value] **1.** to set a price for; estimate the value of **2.** to judge the quality or worth of —**ap·prais′er** *n.* —**ap·prais′ing·ly** *adv.*

**ap·pre·ci·a·ble** (ə prē′shə b'l, -shə b'l) *adj.* [see prec.] enough to be perceived or estimated; noticeable —**ap·pre′ci·a·bly** *adv.*

**ap·pre·ci·ate** (ə prē′shē āt′) *vt.* -at′ed, -at′ing [see APPRAISE] **1.** to think well of; esteem **2.** to recognize gratefully **3.** to estimate the quality of **4.** to be fully or sensitively aware of —*vi.* to rise in value —**ap·pre′ci·a′tor** *n.* —**ap·pre′ci·a·to′ry** (-shə tôr′ē) *adj.*

**ap·pre′ci·a′tion** *n.* **1.** grateful recognition, as of benefits **2.** sensitive awareness, as of art

**ap·pre·ci·a·tive** (ə prē′shə tiv, -shē·ə-) *adj.* feeling or showing appreciation —**ap·pre′ci·a·tive·ly** *adv.*

**ap·pre·hend** (ap′rə hend′) *vt.* [< L. *ad-*, to + *prehendere*, seize] **1.** to capture or arrest **2.** to perceive; understand **3.** to fear; dread

**ap′pre·hen·sion** (-hen′shən) *n.* **1.** capture or arrest **2.** perception or understanding **3.** fear; anxiety

**ap′pre·hen·sive** (-siv) *adj.* anxious; uneasy —**ap′pre·hen·sive·ly** *adv.* —**ap′pre·hen·sive·ness** *n.*

**ap·pren·tice** (ə pren′tis) *n.* [see APPREHEND] **1.** a person being taught a craft or trade, now usually as a member of a labor union **2.** any beginner —*vt.* -ticed, -tic·ing to place or accept as an apprentice —**ap·pren′tice·ship′** *n.*

**ap·prise, ap·prize** (ə prīz′) *vt.* -prised′ or -prized′, -pris′ing or -priz′ing [see APPREHEND] to notify

**ap·prize, ap·prise** (ə prīz′) *vt.* -prized′ or -prised′, -priz′ing or -pris′ing *same as* APPRAISE

**ap·proach** (ə prōch′) *vi.* [< L. *ad,* to + *propius,* nearer] to come closer —*vt.* **1.** to come nearer to **2.** to approximate **3.** to make a proposal or request to **4.** to set about dealing with —*n.* **1.** a coming closer. **2.** an approximation **3.** [*pl.*] overtures (*to* someone) **4.** means of reaching;

access **5.** a preliminary step or movement —**ap·proach′a·ble** *adj.*

**ap·pro·ba·tion** (ap′rə bā′shən) *n.* [see APPROVE] approval or consent

**ap·pro·pri·ate** (ə prō′prē āt′; *for adj.* -it) *vt.* **-at′ed, -at′ing** [< L. *ad-,* to + *proprius,* one's own] **1.** to take for one's own use, often improperly **2.** to set aside (money, etc.) for a specific use —*adj.* suitable; fit; proper —**ap·pro′pri·ate·ly** *adv.* —**ap·pro′pri·ate·ness** *n.* —**ap·pro′pri·a′tor** *n.*

**ap·pro′pri·a′tion** *n.* **1.** an appropriating or being appropriated **2.** money, etc. set aside for a specific use

**ap·prov·al** (ə prōō′v'l) *n.* **1.** the act of approving **2.** favorable attitude or opinion **3.** formal consent —**on approval** for the customer to examine and decide whether to buy or return

**ap·prove** (ə prōōv′) *vt.* **-proved′, -prov′ing** [< L. *ad-,* to + *probus,* good] **1.** to give one's consent to **2.** to consider to be good, satisfactory, etc. —*vi.* to have a favorable opinion (*of*) —**ap·prov′ing·ly** *adv.*

**ap·prox·i·mate** (ə präk′sə mit; *for v.* -māt′) *adj.* [< L. *ad,* to + *proximus,* nearest] **1.** much like **2.** more or less correct or exact —*vt.* **-mat′ed, -mat′ing** to come near to; be almost the same as —**ap·prox′i·mate·ly** *adv.*

**ap·prox·i·ma′tion** (-mā′shən) *n.* **1.** a close estimate **2.** a near likeness

**ap·pur·te·nance** (ə pʉr′t'n əns) *n.* [see APPERTAIN] **1.** something added to a more important thing **2.** [*pl.*] apparatus or equipment **3.** *Law* an additional, subordinate right

**a·pri·cot** (ap′rə kät′, ā′prə-) *n.* [< L. *praecoquus,* early matured (fruit)] **1.** a small, yellowish-orange, peachlike fruit **2.** the tree it grows on

**A·pril** (ā′prəl) *n.* [< L.] the fourth month of the year, having 30 days

**a pri·o·ri** (ā′ prē ôr′ē, ā′ prī ôr′ī) [L.] **1.** from cause to effect **2.** based on theory instead of experience

**a·pron** (ā′prən) *n.* [< L. *mappa,* napkin] **1.** a garment worn over the front part of the body to protect one's clothes **2.** any extending or protecting part **3.** the front part of a stage **4.** a paved area, as where a driveway broadens to meet the road —**a′pron-like′** *adj.*

**apse** (aps) *n.* [< L. *apsis,* an arch] a semicircular or polygonal projection of a church, usually domed or vaulted

**apt** (apt) *adj.* [< L. *aptus*] **1.** appropriate; fitting **2.** tending or inclined; likely **3.** quick to learn —**apt′ly** *adv.* —**apt′ness** *n.*

**apt.** *pl.* **apts.** apartment

**ap·ti·tude** (ap′tə tōōd′, -tyōōd′) *n.* [see APT] **1.** suitability; fitness **2.** a natural tendency, ability, or talent **3.** quickness to learn

**aq·ua** (ak′wə, äk′-) *n., pl.* **-uas, -uae** (-wē) [L.] water —*adj.* [< AQUAMARINE] bluish-green

**aq·ua·cul·ture** (ak′wə kul′chər, äk′-) *n.* [AQUA + CULTURE] the cultivation of water plants and animals for human use

**Aq·ua-lung** (ak′wə luŋ′, äk′-) *a trademark for* an apparatus for breathing under water —*n.* such an apparatus: usually **aq′ua·lung′**

**aq·ua·ma·rine** (ak′wə mə rēn′, äk′-) *n.* [L. *aqua marina,* sea water] **1.** a transparent, pale bluish-green beryl **2.** its color —*adj.* bluish-green

**aq·ua·naut** (ak′wə nôt′) *n.* [AQUA + (ASTRO)NAUT] one trained to use a watertight underwater chamber as a base for undersea experiments

**aq·ua·plane** (ak′wə plān′, äk′-) *n.* [AQUA + PLANE¹] a board on which one rides standing up as it is pulled by a motorboat —*vi.* **-planed′, -plan′ing** to ride on such a board as a sport

**a·quar·ist** (ə kwer′ist) *n.* **1.** a hobbyist with an aquarium **2.** a person in charge of an aquarium (sense 2)

**a·quar·i·um** (-ē əm) *n., pl.* **-i·ums, -i·a** (-ə) [< L. *aquarius,* of water] **1.** a tank, etc. for keeping live water animals and plants **2.** a place where such collections are exhibited

**A·quar·i·us** (-əs) [L., water carrier] the eleventh sign of the zodiac

**a·quat·ic** (ə kwät′ik, -kwat′-) *adj.* **1.** growing or living in water **2.** done in or on the water [*aquatic sports*]

**aq·ua·vit** (ak′wə vēt′, äk′-) *n.* [< L. *aqua vitae,* water of life] a Scandinavian alcoholic liquor distilled from grain or potatoes and flavored with caraway

**aq·ue·duct** (ak′wə dukt′) *n.* [< L. *aqua,* water + *ducere,* to lead] **1.** a large pipe or conduit for bringing water from a distant source **2.** an elevated structure supporting this

**a·que·ous** (ā′kwē əs, ak′wē-) *adj.* of, like, or formed by water

**aqueous humor** a watery fluid between the cornea and the lens of the eye

**aq·ui·line** (ak′wə lin′, -lən) *adj.* [< L. *aquila,* eagle] **1.** of or like an eagle **2.** like an eagle's beak, as a curved nose

**A·qui·nas** (ə kwī′nəs), Saint **Thomas** 1225?–74; It. theologian & philosopher

**Ar** *Chem.* argon

**AR** Arkansas

**Ar·ab** (ar′əb, er′-) *n.* **1.** a native of Arabia **2.** any of a Semitic people in, or orig. from, Arabia; commonly, a Bedouin —*adj.* of the Arabs

**ar·a·besque** (ar′ə besk′) *n.* [< It. *Arabo,* Arab] an elaborate design of flowers, foliage, etc.

**A·ra·bi·a** (ə rā′bē ə) peninsula in SW Asia —**A·ra′bi·an** *adj., n.*

**Arabian Nights, The** a collection of ancient tales from Arabia, India, Persia, etc.

ARABESQUE

**Arabian Peninsula** *same as* ARABIA

**Ar·a·bic** (ar′ə bik) *adj.* **1.** of Arabia **2.** of the Arabs —*n.* the Semitic language of the Arabs, spoken in Arabia, Iraq, Syria, N Africa, etc.

**Arabic numerals** the figures 1, 2, 3, 4, 5, 6, 7, 8, 9, and the 0 (zero)

**ar·a·ble** (ar′ə b′l) *adj.* [ < L. *arare*, to plow] suitable for plowing

**a·rach·nid** (ə rak′nid) *n.* [ < Gr. *arachnē*, spider] any of a group of small animals with eight legs, including spiders and scorpions

**Ar·a·ma·ic** (ar′ə mā′ik) *n.* a group of Semitic languages of Biblical times

**ar·bi·ter** (är′bə tər) *n.* [L., a witness] arbitrator; judge; umpire

**ar·bi·tra·ment** (är bit′rə mənt) *n.* arbitration or an arbitrator's verdict or award

**ar·bi·trar·y** (är′bə trer′ē) *adj.* [see ARBITER] 1. left to one's judgment 2. based on one's preference or whim; capricious 3. absolute; despotic — **ar′bi·trar′i·ly** *adv.* —**ar′bi·trar′i·ness** *n.*

**ar·bi·trate** (är′bə trāt′) *vt., vi.* -**trat·ed**, -**trat′ing** [see ARBITER] 1. to submit (a dispute) to arbitration 2. to decide (a dispute) as an arbitrator —**ar′bi·tra′tion** *n.*

**ar′bi·tra′tor** (-ər) *n.* a person selected to judge a dispute

**ar·bor** (är′bər) *n.* [ < L. *herba*, herb] a place shaded by trees, shrubs, or vines on a latticework; bower

**ar·bo·re·al** (är bôr′ē əl) *adj.* [ < L. *arbor*, tree] 1. of or like a tree 2. living in trees

**ar·bo·re·tum** (är′bə rēt′əm) *n., pl.* -**tums**, -**ta** (-tə) [L.] a place where many kinds of trees and shrubs are grown for study or display

**ar·bor·vi·tae** (är′bər vīt′ē) *n.* [L., tree of life] any of various cypress trees having sprays of scalelike leaves

**ar·bu·tus** (är byōōt′əs) *n.* [L.] 1. a tree or shrub with dark-green leaves and scarlet berries 2. a trailing plant with white or pink flower clusters

**arc** (ärk) *n.* [ < L. *arcus*, a bow, arch] 1. a bowlike curved line or object 2. the band of incandescent light formed when a current leaps a short gap between electrodes 3. any part of a curve, esp. of a circle —*vi.* **arced** or **arcked**, **arc′ing** or **arck′ing** to move in a curved course or form an arc

**ar·cade** (är kād′) *n.* [see prec.] 1. a covered passageway, esp. one lined with shops 2. a line of arches and their supporting columns

**ar·cane** (är kān′) *adj.* [ < L. *arcanus*, hidden] secret or esoteric

**arch**[1] (ärch) *n.* [see ARC] 1. a curved structure used as a support over an open space, as in a doorway 2. the form of an arch 3. anything shaped like an arch —*vt., vi.* 1. to span with or as an arch 2. to form (into) an arch —**arched** (ärcht) *adj.*

**arch**[2] (ärch) *adj.* [ < ff.] 1. chief; principal 2. gaily mischievous; pert

**arch-** [ < Gr. *archos*, ruler] *a prefix meaning* chief, principal [*archbishop*]

**-arch** (ärk) [see prec.] *a suffix meaning* ruler [*matriarch*]

**arch.** 1. archaic 2. architecture

**ar·chae·ol·o·gy** (är′kē äl′ə jē) *n.* [ < Gr. *archaios*, ancient + -LOGY] the study of the life of ancient peoples, as by excavation of ancient cities, etc.: also sp. **archeology** —**ar′chae·o·log′i·cal** (-ə läj′ə k′l) *adj.* —**ar′chae·o·log′i·cal·ly** *adv.* —**ar′chae·ol′o·gist** *n.*

**ar·cha·ic** (är kā′ik) *adj.* [ < Gr. *archaios*, ancient] 1. ancient 2. old-fashioned 3. no longer used except in poetry, church ritual, etc., as the word *begat* —**ar·cha′i·cal·ly** *adv.*

**ar′cha·ism** (-kē iz′m) *n.* an archaic word, usage, style, etc. —**ar′cha·ist** *n.*

**arch·an·gel** (ärk′ān′j′l) *n.* an angel of high rank

**arch·bish·op** (ärch′bish′əp) *n.* a bishop of the highest rank —**arch′-bish′op·ric** (-ə prik) *n.*

**arch′dea′con** (-dēk′'n) *n.* a church official ranking just below a bishop

**arch′di′o·cese** *n.* the diocese of an archbishop —**arch′di·oc′e·san** (-dī-äs′ə sən) *adj.*

**arch′duke′** (-dook′) *n.* a prince of the former Austrian royal family — **arch′duch′ess** *n.fem.*

**arch′en′e·my** *n., pl.* -**mies** a chief enemy —**the archenemy** Satan

**arch·er** (är′chər) *n.* [ < L. *arcus*, a bow] one who shoots with bow and arrow

**arch′er·y** *n.* the practice or art of shooting with bow and arrow

**ar·che·type** (är′kə tīp′) *n.* [ < Gr. *archos*, first + *typos*, a mark] an original pattern or model; prototype —**ar′che·typ′al**, **ar′che·typ′i·cal** (-tīp′i k′l) *adj.*

**ar·chi·e·pis·co·pal** (är′kē ə pis′kə-p′l) *adj.* of an archbishop or arch-bishopric

**Ar·chi·me·des** (är′kə mē′dēz) 287?-212 B.C.; Gr. physicist & inventor

**ar·chi·pel·a·go** (är′kə pel′ə gō′) *n., pl.* -**goes′**, -**gos′** [ < Gr. *archi-*, chief + *pelagos*, sea] 1. a sea with many islands 2. a group of many islands

**ar·chi·tect** (är′kə tekt′) *n.* [ < Gr. *archos*, chief + *tektōn*, carpenter] 1. a person who designs buildings and supervises their construction 2. any builder or planner

**ar·chi·tec·ton·ics** (är′kə tek tän′iks) *n.pl.* [*with sing. v.*] 1. the science of architecture 2. structural design, as of a symphony —**ar′chi·tec·ton′ic** *adj.*

**ar′chi·tec′ture** (-tek′chər) *n.* 1. the science or profession of designing and constructing buildings 2. a style of construction 3. design and construction′ —**ar′chi·tec′tur·al** *adj.* —**ar′-chi·tec′tur·al·ly** *adv.*

**ar·chi·trave** (är′kə trāv′) *n.* [ < L. *archi-*, ARCH- + *trabs*, a beam] in a classical building, the beam resting directly on the tops of the columns

**ar·chives** (är′kīvz) *n.pl.* [ < Gr. *archeion*, town hall] 1. a place where public records are kept **2.** the public records kept in such a place —**ar·chi·vist** (är′kə vist, -kī′-) n.

**arch·way** (ärch′wā′) n. a passage under an arch, or the arch itself

**-ar·chy** (är′kē) [< Gr. archein, to rule] a suffix meaning ruling [monarchy]

**arc lamp** (or **light**) a lamp in which the light is produced by an arc between electrodes

**arc·tic** (ärk′tik, är′-) adj. [< Gr. arktikos, northern] **1.** of or near the North Pole **2.** very cold —**the Arctic** the region around the North Pole

**Arctic Circle** [also **a- c-**] an imaginary circle parallel to the equator, 66°33′ north of it

**Arctic Ocean** ocean surrounding the North Pole

**-ard** (ərd) [< MHG. hart, bold] a suffix meaning one who does something to excess [drunkard]

**ar·dent** (är′d'nt) adj. [< L. ardere, to burn] **1.** passionate **2.** zealous **3.** glowing or burning —**ar′dent·ly** adv.

**ar·dor** (är′dər) n. [< L. ardor, a flame] **1.** emotional warmth; passion **2.** zeal **3.** intense heat Also, Brit. sp., **ardour**

**ar·du·ous** (är′joo wəs) adj. [L. arduus, steep] **1.** difficult to do; laborious **2.** using much energy; strenuous —**ar′du·ous·ly** adv.

**are** (är) [OE. aron] pl. & 2d pers. sing., pres. indic., of BE

**ar·e·a** (er′ē ə) n. [L., vacant place] **1.** an expanse of land; region **2.** a total outside surface, measured in square units **3.** a part of a house, district, etc. [play area, slum area] **4.** scope or extent

**area code** any of the numbers assigned as a telephone code to the areas into which the U.S. and Canada are divided

**a·re·na** (ə rē′nə) n. [L., sandy place] **1.** the center of an ancient Roman amphitheater, where contests were held **2.** any place or sphere of struggle

**arena theater** a theater having a central stage surrounded by seats

**aren't** (ärnt) are not

**Ar·es** (er′ēz) Gr. Myth. the god of war

**ar·gent** (är′jənt) adj. [< L. argentum, silver] [Poet.] silvery

**Ar·gen·ti·na** (är′jən tē′nə) country in S S.America: 1,084,120 sq. mi.; pop. 22,691,000—**Ar′gen·tine** (-tēn′, -tīn′) adj., n.

**ar·gon** (är′gän) n. [Gr., inert] a chemical element, an inert gas found in the air and used in light bulbs, radio tubes, etc.

**Ar·go·naut** (är′gə nôt′) n. Gr. Myth. any of those who sailed with Jason to find the Golden Fleece

**ar·go·sy** (är′gə sē) n., pl. **-sies** [< It. Ragusea, ship of Ragusa, a Sicilian city] [Poet.] a large merchant ship or fleet of such ships

**ar·got** (är′gō, -gət) n. [Fr.] the specialized vocabulary of a particular group, as of criminals, tramps, etc.

**ar·gue** (är′gyōō) vi. **-gued, -gu·ing** [< L. arguere, prove] **1.** to give reasons (for or against) **2.** to dispute; quarrel —vt. **1.** to dispute about; debate **2.** to maintain; contend **3.** to

persuade by giving reasons —**ar′gu·a·ble** adj.

**ar′gu·ment** (-gyə mənt) n. **1.** a reason or reasons offered in arguing **2.** an arguing; debate **3.** a summary

**ar′gu·men·ta′tion** (-men tā′shən) n. the process of arguing; debate

**ar′gu·men′ta·tive** (-men′tə tiv) adj. **1.** controversial **2.** apt to argue; contentious

**ar·gyle** (är′gīl) adj. [< Argyll, Scotland] knitted or woven in a diamond-shaped pattern, as socks

**a·ri·a** (ä′rē ə) n. [It. < L. aer, air] a melody in an opera, etc., esp. for solo voice

**-ar·i·an** (er′ē ən, ar′-) [< L.] a suffix variously denoting age, sect, social belief, or occupation [octogenarian]

**ar·id** (ar′id, er′-) adj. [< L. arere, be dry] **1.** dry and barren **2.** uninteresting; dull —(ə rid′ə tē) —(ə rid′ə tē) n.

**Ar·i·es** (er′ēz, -i ēz′) [L., the Ram] the first sign of the zodiac

**a·right** (ə rīt′) adv. correctly

**a·rise** (ə rīz′) vi. **a·rose** (-rōz′), **a·ris′en** (-riz′n), **a·ris′ing** [< OE. a-, out + risan, rise] **1.** to get up, as from bed **2.** to rise; ascend **3.** to come into being **4.** to result (from)

**ar·is·toc·ra·cy** (ar′ə stä′krə sē, er′-) n., pl. **-cies** [< Gr. aristos, best + kratein, to rule] **1.** government by a privileged minority, usually of inherited wealth **2.** a country with such government **3.** a privileged ruling class; upper class

**a·ris·to·crat** (ə ris′tə krat′, ar′is-) n. **1.** a member of the aristocracy **2.** one with the tastes, manners, etc. of the upper class —**a·ris′to·crat′ic** adj. —**a·ris′to·crat′i·cal·ly** adv.

**Ar·is·toph·a·nes** (ar′ə stäf′ə nēz′) 448?–380? B.C.; Gr. writer of comedies

**Ar·is·tot·le** (ar′is tät′'l) 384–322 B.C.; Gr. philosopher —**Ar·is·to·te·li·an** (ar′is tə tēl′yən) adj., n.

**a·rith·me·tic** (ə rith′mə tik) n. [< Gr. arithmos, number] the science of computing by positive, real numbers —**ar·ith·met·i·cal** (ar′ith met′i k'l, er′-), **ar′ith·met′ic** adj. —**a·rith′me·ti′cian** (-mə tish′ən) n.

**arithmetic mean** the average obtained by dividing a sum by the number of quantities added to make the sum

**Ar·i·zo·na** (ar′ə zō′nə, er′-) State of the SW U.S.: 113,909 sq. mi.; pop. 1,772,000; cap. Phoenix: abbrev. **Ariz.** —**Ar′i·zo′nan** adj., n.

**ark** (ärk) n. [< L. arcere, enclose] **1.** Bible the boat in which Noah, his family, and two of every kind of creature survived the Flood **2.** same as ARK OF THE COVENANT **3.** an enclosure in a synagogue for the scrolls of the Torah

**Ar·kan·sas** (är′k'n sô′) State of the SC U.S.: 53,104 sq. mi.; pop. 1,923,000; cap. Little Rock: abbrev. **Ark.** — **Ar·kan′san** (-kan′z'n) adj., n.

**ark of the covenant** Bible the chest containing the two stone tablets inscribed with the Ten Commandments

**arm¹** (ärm) n. [OE. earm] **1.** an upper limb of the human body **2.** anything like this in shape, function, position, etc. —**with open arms** cordially

**arm²** (ärm) *n.* [< L. *arma*, weapons] **1.** a weapon: *usually used in pl.* **2.** any branch of the military forces —*vt.* to provide with weapons, etc. —*vi.* to prepare for war or any struggle — **under arms** ready for war —**up in arms 1.** prepared to fight **2.** indignant —**armed** *adj.*

**ar·ma·da** (är mä′də) *n.* [Sp. < L. *arma*, weapons] **1.** a fleet of warships **2.** a fleet of warplanes

**ar·ma·dil·lo** (är′mə dil′ō) *n., pl.* -**los** [Sp.: see prec.] a small burrowing mammal of tropical America, covered with bony plates

**Ar·ma·ged·don** (är′mə ged′'n) *n.* **1.** *Bible* the site of the last decisive battle between the forces of good and evil **2.** any great, decisive battle

**ar·ma·ment** (är′mə mənt) *n.* **1.** [*often pl.*] all the military forces and equipment of a nation **2.** all the military equipment of a warship, etc. **3.** an arming or being armed for war

**ar·ma·ture** (är′mə chər) *n.* [< L. *armare*, to arm] **1.** any protective covering **2.** the iron core wound with wire, in which electromotive force is produced in a generator or motor

**arm′chair′** *n.* a chair with supports at the sides for one's arms

**armed forces** all the military, naval, and air forces of a country

**Ar·me·ni·a** (är mēn′ē ə) former kingdom of SW Asia, now mostly a republic of the U.S.S.R. —**Ar·me′ni·an** *adj., n.*

**arm′ful′** (-fool′) *n., pl.* -**fuls′** as much as the arms or an arm can hold

**arm′hole′** *n.* an opening for the arm in a garment

**ar·mi·stice** (är′mə stis) *n.* [< L. *arma*, arms + *stare*, stand still] a truce preliminary to a peace treaty

**Armistice Day** *see* VETERANS DAY

**arm′let** (-lit) *n.* an ornamental band worn around the upper arm

**ar·mor** (är′mər) *n.* [< L. *armare*, to arm] any defensive or protective covering —*vt.,* *vi.* to put armor on — **ar′mored** (-mərd) *adj.*

**armored car** a vehicle covered with armor plate, as a truck for carrying money to or from a bank

**ar·mo·ri·al** (är môr′ē əl) *adj.* of coats of arms; heraldic

**ar·mo·ry** (är′mər ē) *n., pl.* -**ies** [see ARMOR] **1.** an arsenal **2.** an armaments factory **3.** a military drill hall

**arm′pit′** *n.* the hollow under the arm at the shoulder

**arm′rest′** *n.* a support for the arm as on the inside of a car door

**ar·my** (är′mē) *n., pl.* -**mies** [ult. < L. *arma*, weapons] **1.** a large, organized body of soldiers for waging war, esp. on land **2.** any large number of persons, animals, etc.

**Ar·nold** (är′nəld), **Benedict** 1741–1801; Am. Revolutionary general who became a traitor

**a·ro·ma** (ə rō′mə) *n.* [< Gr. *arōma*, spice] a pleasant odor; fragrance

**ar·o·mat·ic** (ar′ə mat′ik) *adj.* of or having an aroma; fragrant or pungent —*n.* an aromatic plant, chemical, etc. —**ar′o·mat′i·cal·ly** *adv.*

**a·rose** (ə rōz′) *pt. of* ARISE

**a·round** (ə round′) *adv.* [ME.] **1.** in a circle **2.** in every direction **3.** in circumference **4.** to the opposite direction **5.** [Colloq.] nearby [stay *around*] —*prep.* **1.** so as to encircle or envelop **2.** on the border of **3.** in various places in or on **4.** [Colloq.] about [*around* 1890]

**a·rouse** (ə rouz′) *vt.* **a·roused′,** **a·rous′ing** **1.** to wake from sleep **2.** to stir, as to action **3.** to evoke [to *arouse* pity] —**a·rous′al** *n.*

**ar·peg·gio** (är pej′ō) *n., pl.* -**gios** [It. < *arpa*, a harp] a chord whose notes are played in quick succession

**ar·raign** (ə rān′) *vt.* [< L. *ad*, to + *ratio*, reason] **1.** to bring before a law court to answer charges **2.** to call to account; accuse —**ar·raign′ment** *n.*

**ar·range** (ə rānj′) *vt.* -**ranged′,** -**rang′ing** [< OFr. *renc*, rank] **1.** to put in the correct order **2.** to classify **3.** to prepare or plan **4.** to arrive at an agreement about **5.** *Music* to adapt (a work) to particular instruments or voices —*vi.* *Music* to write arrangements, esp. as a profession —**ar·rang′er** *n.*

**ar·range·ment** *n.* **1.** an arranging **2.** a result or manner of arranging **3.** [*usually pl.*] a plan **4.** a settlement **5.** *Music a)* an arranging of a composition *b)* the composition as thus arranged

**ar·rant** (ar′ənt) *adj.* [var. of ERRANT] out-and-out; notorious

**ar·ras** (ar′əs) *n.* [< *Arras,* Fr. city] **1.** an elaborate kind of tapestry **2.** a wall hanging, esp. of tapestry

**ar·ray** (ə rā′) *vt.* [< ML. *arredare,* put in order] **1.** to place in order **2.** to dress in finery —*n.* **1.** an orderly grouping, esp. of troops **2.** an impressive display **3.** fine clothes

**ar·rears** (ə rirz′) *n.pl.* [< L. *ad,* to + *retro,* behind] overdue debts —**in arrears** behind in paying a debt, doing one's work, etc.

**ar·rest** (ə rest′) *vt.* [< L. *ad-,* to + *restare,* to stop] **1.** to stop or check **2.** to seize by authority of the law **3.** to catch and keep (the attention, etc.) —*n.* an arresting or being arrested —**under arrest** in legal custody

**ar·rest′ing** *adj.* attracting attention; interesting

**ar·riv·al** (ə rī′v'l) *n.* **1.** an arriving **2.** a person or thing that arrives

**ar·rive** (ə rīv′) *vi.* -**rived′,** -**riv′ing** [< L. *ad-,* to + *ripa,* shore] **1.** to reach one's destination **2.** to come [the time has *arrived*] **3.** to attain fame, etc. —**arrive at** to reach by thinking, etc.

**ar·ri·ve·der·ci** (ä rē′ve der′chē) *interj.* [It.] goodbye

**ar·ro·gant** (ar′ə gənt) *adj.* [see ARRO-

GATE] full of or due to pride; haughty —**ar′ro·gance** *n.* —**ar′ro·gant·ly** *adv.*

**ar′ro·gate′** (-gāt′) *vt.* -**gat′ed**, -**gat′-ing** [< L. *ad*-, for + *rogare*, ask] to claim or seize without right — **ar′ro·ga′tion** *n.*

**ar·row** (ar′ō) *n.* [OE. *arwe*] **1.** a slender, usually pointed shaft, shot from a bow **2.** a sign (⟵) used to indicate direction

**ar′row·head′** (-hed′) *n.* the separable, pointed tip of an arrow

**ar′row·root′** *n.* [< use as antidote for poisoned arrows] **1.** a tropical American plant with starchy roots **2.** a starch made from its roots

**ar·roy·o** (ə roi′ō) *n.*, *pl.* -**os** [Sp. < L. *arrugia*, mine pit] [Southwest] **1.** a dry gully **2.** a rivulet or stream

**ar·se·nal** (är′s'n əl) *n.* [< Ar. *dār* (ēṣ) ṣinā′a, workshop] **1.** a place for making or storing weapons, etc. **2.** a store or collection

**ar·se·nic** (är′s'n ik) *n.* [< L. < Gr.: ult. < Per. *zar*, gold] a silvery-white, very poisonous chemical element, compounds of which are used in insecticides, medicines, etc. —**ar·sen′i·cal** (-sen′ə k'l), **ar·se′ni·ous** (-sē′nē əs) *adj.*

**ar·son** (är′s'n) *n.* [< L. *ardere*, to burn] the crime of purposely setting fire to a building —**ar′son·ist** *n.*

**art**¹ (ärt) *n.* [< L. *ars*] **1.** human creativity **2.** skill **3.** any specific skill or its application **4.** any craft or its principles **5.** a making of things that have form or beauty **6.** any branch of this, as painting, sculpture, etc. **7.** drawings, paintings, statues, etc. **8.** a branch of learning; specif., [*pl.*] *same as* LIBERAL ARTS **9.** cunning **10.** sly trick; wile: *usually used in pl.*

**art**² (ärt) *archaic 2d pers. sing.*, *pres. indic.*, of BE: *used with thou*

**art. 1.** article **2.** artificial

**art dec·o** (dek′ō, dā′kō) a decorative style of the late 1920's and the 1930's, derived from cubism

**ar·te·ri·o·scle·ro·sis** (är tir′ē ō sklə rō′sis) *n.* [see ff. & SCLEROSIS] a thickening and hardening of the walls of the arteries, as in old age

**ar·ter·y** (är′tər ē) *n.*, *pl.* -**ies** [< Gr. *aeirein*, to raise] **1.** any of the large tubes carrying blood from the heart **2.** a main road or channel —**ar·te′ri·al** (-tir′ē əl) *adj.*

**ar·te·sian well** (är tē′zhən) [< Fr. *Artois*, former Fr. province] a deep well in which water is forced up by pressure of underground water draining from higher ground

**art·ful** (ärt′f'l) *adj.* **1.** skillful or clever **2.** cunning; crafty —**art′ful·ly** *adv.* —**art′ful·ness** *n.*

**ar·thri·tis** (är thrīt′is) *n.* [Gr. < *arthron*, a joint + -ITIS] inflammation of a joint or joints —**ar·thrit′ic** (-thrit′ik) *adj.*

**ar·thro·pod** (är′thrə päd′) *n.* [< Gr. *arthron*, a joint + -POD] any of a phylum of invertebrate animals with jointed legs and a segmented body

**Ar·thur** (är′thər) **1.** legendary 6th-cent. king of Britain **2.** Chester A.,

1830–86; 21st president of the U.S. (1881–85) —**Ar·thu′ri·an** (-thoor′ē ən) *adj.*

**ar·ti·choke** (är′tə chōk′) *n.* [ult. < Ar. *al-ḥarṣūf*] **1.** a thistlelike plant **2.** its flower head, cooked as a vegetable

**ar·ti·cle** (är′ti k'l) *n.* [< L. *artus*, a joint] **1.** one of the sections of a document **2.** a complete piece of writing, as in a newspaper, magazine, etc. **3.** a separate item [an *article* of luggage] **4.** *Gram.* any one of the words *a*, *an*, or *the*, used as adjectives

**ar·tic·u·late** (är tik′yə lit; *for v.* -lāt′) *adj.* [< L. *artus*, joint] **1.** jointed: usually **ar·tic′u·lat′ed 2.** spoken distinctly **3.** able to speak **4.** expressing oneself clearly —*vt.* -**lat′ed**, -**lat′ing 1.** to connect by joints **2.** to put together in a connected way **3.** to utter distinctly **4.** to express clearly —*vi.* **1.** to speak distinctly **2.** to be jointed —**ar·tic′u·late·ly** *adv.* —**ar·tic′u·la′tion** *n.*

**ar·ti·fact** (är′tə fakt′) *n.* [see ff.] any object made by human work; esp., a primitive tool, etc.

**ar·ti·fice** (är′tə fis) *n.* [< L. *ars*, art + *facere*, make] **1.** skill or ingenuity **2.** trickery **3.** an artful trick

**ar·tif·i·cer** (är tif′ə sər) *n.* **1.** a skilled craftsman **2.** an inventor

**ar·ti·fi·cial** (är′tə fish′əl) *adj.* [see ARTIFICE] **1.** made by human work or art; not natural **2.** simulated [*artificial* teeth] **3.** affected [an *artificial* smile] —**ar′ti·fi′ci·al′i·ty** (-ē al′ə tē) *n.* —**ar′ti·fi′cial·ly** *adv.*

**artificial respiration** the maintenance of breathing by artificial means, as by forcing breath into the mouth

**ar·til·ler·y** (är til′ər ē) *n.* [ult. < L. *ars*, handicraft] **1.** mounted guns, as cannon **2.** the science of guns; gunnery —**the artillery** the branch of an army using heavy mounted guns —**ar·til′ler·y·man** (-mən) *n.*, *pl.* -**men**

**ar·ti·san** (är′tə z'n) *n.* [ult. < L. *ars*, art] a skilled craftsman

**art·ist** (är′tist) *n.* **1.** one who is skilled in any of the fine arts, esp. in painting, sculpture, etc. **2.** one who does anything very well

**ar·tis·tic** (är tis′tik) *adj.* **1.** of art or artists **2.** done skillfully **3.** sensitive to beauty —**ar·tis′ti·cal·ly** *adv.*

**art·ist·ry** (är′tis trē) *n.* artistic quality, ability, work, etc.

**art·less** (ärt′lis) *adj.* **1.** lacking skill or art **2.** simple; natural **3.** without guile; ingenuous —**art′less·ly** *adv.* —**art′less·ness** *n.*

**art·y** (ärt′ē) *adj.* -**i·er**, -**i·est** [Colloq.] affectedly artistic —**art′i·ness** *n.*

**ar·um** (er′əm) *n.* [L.] any of a family of plants with flowers enveloped within a hoodlike leaf

**Ar·y·an** (ar′ē ən, er′-) *n.* [< Sans. *ārya*, noble] **1.** formerly, the hypothetical parent language of the Indo-European family **2.** a person supposed to be a descendant of the prehistoric peoples who spoke this language *Aryan* has no validity as an ethnological term, as in Nazi use

**as** (az, əz) *adv.* [< ALSO] 1. equally [*as* happy as a lark] 2. for instance [*certain* colors, *as* green and blue] 3. when related in a specified way [this view *as* contrasted with that] —*conj.* 1. to the same amount or degree that [straight *as* an arrow] 2. in the same manner that [do *as* you are told] 3. while [she wept *as* she spoke] 4. because [*as* you object, we won't go] 5. that the consequence is [so clear *as* to be obvious] 6. though [tall *as* he is, he can't reach it] —*pron.* 1. a fact that [he is tired, *as* you can see] 2. that (preceded by *such* or *the same*) [the same color *as* yours] —*prep.* in the role or function of [he poses *as* a friend] —**as for** (or **to**) concerning —**as if** (or **though**) as it (or one) would if —**as is** [Colloq.] just as it is —**as it were** as if it were so

**As** *Chem.* arsenic

**as·a·fet·i·da, as·a·foet·i·da** (as'ə fet'ə də) *n.* [< Per. *āzā*, gum + L. *fetida*, fetid] a bad-smelling resin formerly used in medicine

**as·bes·tos, as·bes·tus** (as bes'təs, az-) *n.* [< Gr. *a-*, not + *sbennynai*, extinguish] a fire-resistant, fibrous mineral used in fireproofing, electrical insulation, etc.

**as·cend** (ə send') *vi., vt.* [< L. *ad-*, to + *scandere*, to climb] 1. to go up; mount 2. to succeed to (a throne)

**as·cend·an·cy, as·cend·en·cy** (-ən sē) *n.* controlling position; domination

**as·cend·ant, as·cend·ent** (-ənt) *adj.* 1. rising 2. in control; dominant —**in the ascendant** at or nearing the height of power, fame, etc.

**as·cen·sion** (ə sen'shən) *n.* 1. an ascending 2. [A-] the fortieth day after Easter, celebrating the Ascension —**the Ascension** *Bible* the bodily ascent of Jesus into heaven

**as·cent** (ə sent') *n.* 1. an ascending 2. an upward slope

**as·cer·tain** (as'ər tān') *vt.* [see AD- & CERTAIN] to find out with certainty

**as·cet·ic** (ə set'ik) *adj.* [< Gr. *askein*, to train the body] self-denying; austere —*n.* one who leads a life of strict self-denial, esp. for religious purposes —**as·cet'i·cism** (-ə siz'm) *n.*

**a·scor·bic acid** (ə skôr'bik) [A- + SCORB(UTIC) + -IC] vitamin C

**as·cot** (as'kət, -kät') *n.* a necktie with very broad ends hanging from the knot

**as·cribe** (ə skrīb') *vt.* -**cribed', -crib'ing** [< L. *ad-*, to + *scribere*, write] 1. to assign (*to* a supposed cause) 2. to regard as belonging (*to*) or coming from someone —**as·crib'a·ble** *adj.* —**as·crip·tion** (ə skrip'shən) *n.*

ASCOT

**a·sep·tic** (ā sep'tik, ə-) *adj.* free from disease-producing germs

**a·sex·u·al** (ā sek'shoo wəl) *adj.* 1. having no sex or sexual organs 2. designating or reproduction without the union of male and female germ cells —**a·sex'u·al·ly** *adv.*

**ash¹** (ash) *n.* [OE. *æsce*] 1. the grayish powder left after something has burned 2. fine, volcanic lava 3. the gray color of wood ash See also ASHES

**ash²** (ash) *n.* [< OE. *æsc*] 1. a shade tree of the olive family 2. its wood

**a·shamed** (ə shāmd') *adj.* 1. feeling shame 2. reluctant because fearing shame beforehand —**a·sham·ed·ly** (ə shā'mid lē) *adv.*

**ash·en** (ash'ən) *adj.* 1. of ashes 2. like ashes, esp. in color; pale

**ash·es** (ash'iz) *n.pl.* 1. the substance remaining after a thing has been burned 2. human remains, esp. the part left after cremation

**a·shore** (ə shôr') *adv., adj.* 1. to or on the shore 2. to or on land

**Ash·to·reth** (ash'tə reth') *same as* ASTARTE

**ash'tray'** *n.* a container for smokers' tobacco ashes: also **ash tray**

**Ash Wednesday** the first day of Lent: from the putting of ashes on the forehead in penitence

**ash'y** *adj.* -**i·er, -i·est** 1. of or covered with ashes 2. ashen; pale

**A·sia** (ā'zhə) largest continent, in the Eastern Hemisphere: c.16,900,000 sq. mi.; pop. c.1,876,351,000 —**A'sian, A·si·at·ic** (ā'zhē at'ik) *adj., n.*

**Asia Minor** large peninsula in W Asia, between the Black Sea and the Mediterranean

**a·side** (ə sīd') *adv.* 1. on or to one side 2. away; in reserve [put one ticket *aside*] 3. apart; notwithstanding [joking *aside*] —*n.* words spoken by an actor but supposedly heard only by the audience —**aside from** 1. with the exception of 2. apart from

**as·i·nine** (as'ə nīn') *adj.* [< L. *asinus*, ass] like an ass; stupid; silly —**as'i·nine'ly** *adv.* —**as'i·nin'i·ty** (-nin'ə tē) *n.*

**ask** (ask) *vt.* [OE. *ascian*] 1. to use words in seeking the answer to (a question) 2. to inquire of (a person) 3. to request or demand 4. to invite —*vi.* 1. to make a request (*for*) 2. to inquire (*about* or *after*) —**ask'er** *n.*

**a·skance** (ə skans') *adv.* 1. with a sidewise glance 2. with suspicion, disapproval, etc.

**a·skew** (ə skyoo') *adv.* to one side; awry —*adj.* on one side; awry

**asking price** the price asked by a seller, esp. as a basis for bargaining

**a·slant** (ə slant') *adv.* on a slant —*prep.* slantingly across —*adj.* slanting

**a·sleep** (ə slēp') *adj.* 1. sleeping 2. inactive; dull 3. numb 4. dead —*adv.* into a sleeping condition

**a·so·cial** (ā sō'shəl) *adj.* 1. avoiding contact with others 2. selfish

---

fat, āpe, cär; ten, ēven; is, bīte; gō, hôrn, tool, look; oil, out; up, fur; chin; she; thin, *then*; zh, leisure; ŋ, ring; ə for *a* in *ago*; ', (ā'b'l); ë, Fr. coeur; ö, Fr. feu; Fr. mon; ü, Fr. duc; kh, G. ich, doch; ‡ foreign; < derived from

**asp** (asp) *n.* [< Gr. *aspis*] a small, poisonous snake of Africa and Europe

**as·par·a·gus** (ə spar'ə gəs, -sper'-) *n.* [< Gr. *asparagos*] 1. any of a genus of plants with small leaves and edible shoots 2. these shoots

**as·pect** (as'pekt) *n.* [< L. *ad-*, to + *specere*, to look] 1. the way one appears 2. the appearance of a thing or idea from a specific viewpoint 3. the side facing a given direction

**as·pen** (as'pən) *n.* [OE. *æspe*] a poplar tree whose leaves flutter in the least breeze: also **quaking aspen**

**as·per·i·ty** (as per'ə tē) *n., pl.* **-ties** [< L. *asper*, rough] 1. roughness or harshness 2. sharpness of temper

**as·perse** (ə spurs') *vt.* **-persed', -pers'ing** [< L. *ad-*, to + *spargere*, to sprinkle] to slander

**as·per·sion** (ə spur'zhən) *n.* a damaging or disparaging remark; slander

**as·phalt** (as'fôlt) *n.* [< Gr. *asphaltos*] a brown or black tarlike substance mixed with sand or gravel and used for paving, roofing, etc. —*vt.* to pave, roof, etc. with asphalt

**as·pho·del** (as'fə del') *n.* [< Gr. *asphodelos*] a plant of the lily family having white or yellow flowers

**as·phyx·i·ate** (as fik'sē āt') *vt., vi.* **-at'ed, -at'ing** [< Gr. *a-*, not + *sphyzein*, to throb] 1. to make or become unconscious from lack of oxygen in the blood 2. to suffocate —**as·phyx'i·a'tion** *n.*

**as·pic** (as'pik) *n.* [< OFr. *aspe*] a jelly of meat juice, tomato juice, etc. used as a relish, salad mold, etc.

**as·pir·ant** (as'pər ənt, ə spir'ənt) *adj.* aspiring —*n.* one who aspires

**as·pi·rate** (as'pə rāt'; *for n.* -pər it) *vt.* **-rat'ed, -rat'ing** [see ASPIRE] 1. to begin (a syllable, etc.) with the sound of English *h* 2. to follow (a consonant) with an audible puff of breath 3. to suck in or suck up —*n.* an aspirated sound

**as·pi·ra·tion** (as'pə rā'shən) *n.* 1. *a)* strong desire or ambition, as for advancement *b)* the thing desired 2. a drawing in by breathing or suction

**as'pi·ra'tor** *n.* an apparatus using suction to remove air, fluids, etc.

**as·pire** (ə spīr') *vi.* **-pired', -pir'ing** [< L. *ad-*, to + *spirare*, breathe] to be ambitious (*to* get or do something); seek (*after*) —**as·pir'ing·ly** *adv.*

**as·pi·rin** (as'pər in) *n.* [G.] a white, crystalline powder used for reducing fever, relieving pain, etc.

**a·squint** (ə skwint') *adv., adj.* with a squint; out of the corner of the eye

**ass** (as) *n.* [< L. *asinus*] 1. a small animal like the horse but with longer ears 2. a stupid or silly person

**as·sail** (ə sāl') *vt.* [< L. *ad-*, to + *salire*, leap] 1. to attack physically and violently 2. to attack with arguments, etc. —**as·sail'a·ble** *adj.*

**as·sail·ant** (-ənt) *n.* an attacker

**as·sas·sin** (ə sas''n) *n.* [< Ar. *hashshāshīn*, hashish users] a murderer who strikes suddenly, esp. a killer of a politically important person

**as·sas'si·nate** (-āt') *vt.* **-nat'ed,** -nat'ing to murder as assassins do —**as·sas'si·na'tion** *n.*

**as·sault** (ə sôlt') *n.* [< L. *ad-*, to + *saltare*, leap] 1. a violent attack 2. rape: a euphemism 3. *Law* an unlawful threat or attempt to harm another physically —*vt., vi.* to make an assault (upon)

**assault and battery** *Law* the carrying out of threatened physical harm

**as·say** (as'ā, a sā'; *for v.* a sā') *n.* [< L. *ex-*, out + *agere*, to deal] 1. a testing 2. the analysis of an ore, etc. to determine the nature, proportion, etc. of the ingredients —*vt.* to make an assay of; test —*vi.* to be shown by assay to have a specified proportion of something —**as·say'er** *n.*

**as·sem·blage** (ə sem'blij) *n.* 1. an assembling 2. a group of persons or things gathered together 3. *Art* things assembled in a sculptural collage

**as·sem'ble** (-b'l) *vt., vi.* **-bled, -bling** [< L. *ad-*, to + *simul*, together] 1. to gather into a group; collect 2. to fit or put together the parts of —**as·sem'bler** *n.*

**as·sem'bly** (-blē) *n., pl.* **-blies** 1. an assembling 2. a group of persons gathered together 3. a legislative body, esp. [A-] the lower house of some State legislatures 4. a fitting together of parts to make a whole

**assembly line** in many factories, an arrangement by which each worker does a single operation in assembling the work as it is passed along

**as·sem'bly·man** *n., pl.* **-men** a member of a legislative assembly

**as·sent** (ə sent') *vi.* [< L. *ad-*, to + *sentire*, feel] to express acceptance of; agree (*to*); concur —*n.* consent or agreement

**as·sert** (ə surt') *vt.* [< L. *ad-*, to + *serere*, join] 1. to declare; affirm 2. to maintain or defend (rights, etc.) —**assert oneself** to insist on one's rights, or on being recognized —**as·sert'er, as·ser'tor** *n.*

**as·ser'tion** (ə sur'shən) *n.* 1. an asserting 2. a positive statement

**as·ser'tive** (-tiv) *adj.* persistently positive or confident —**as·ser'tive·ly** *adv.* —**as·ser'tive·ness** *n.*

**as·sess** (ə ses') *vt.* [< *ad-*, to + *sedere*, sit] 1. to set an estimated value on (property, etc.) for taxation 2. to set the amount of (a tax, a fine, etc.) 3. to impose a fine, tax, etc. on 4. to judge the worth, importance, etc. of —**as·sess'ment** *n.* —**as·ses'sor** *n.*

**as·set** (as'et) *n.* [< L. *ad-*, to + *satis*, enough] 1. anything owned that has value 2. a desirable thing [charm is an *asset*] 3. [*pl.*] all the property, accounts receivable, cash, etc. of a person or business 4. [*pl.*] *Law* property usable to pay debts

**as·sev·er·ate** (ə sev'ə rāt') *vt.* **-at'ed, -at'ing** [< L. *ad-*, to + *severus*, severe] to state positively; assert —**as·sev'er·a'tion** *n.*

**as·sid·u·ous** (ə sij'oo wəs) *adj.* [< L. *assidere*, to assist] diligent; persevering; careful —**as·si·du·i·ty** (as'ə dyo͞o′∂ tē) *n., pl.* **-ties** **—as·sid′u·ous·ly** *adv.* **—as·sid′u·ous·ness** *n.*

**as·sign** (∂ sīn′) *vt.* [< L. *ad-*, to + *signare*, to sign] 1. to set or mark for a specific purpose; designate 2. to appoint, as to a duty 3. to give out as a task; allot 4. to ascribe; attribute 5. *Law* to transfer (a right, property, etc.)—**as·sign′a·ble** *adj.* —**as·sign′er**, *as* **sign′or** *n.*

**as·sig·na·tion** (as′ig nā′shən) *n.* an appointment to meet, esp. one made secretly by lovers

**as·sign·ment** (∂ sīn′mənt) *n.* 1. an assigning or being assigned 2. anything assigned

**as·sim·i·late** (∂ sim′∂ lāt′) *vt.* **-lat′ed, -lat′ing** [< L. *ad-*, to + *similare*, make similar to] 1. to absorb and incorporate; digest 2. to make like or alike —*vi.* 1. to become like 2. to be absorbed and incorporated —**as·sim′i·la′tion** *n.*

**as·sist** (∂ sist′) *vt., vi.* [< L. *ad-*, to + *sistere*, make stand] to help; aid —*n.* an instance or act of helping —**assist at** to be present at; attend

**as·sis′tance** (-∂ns) *n.* help; aid

**as·sis′tant** (-∂nt) *adj.* assisting; helping —*n.* one who assists; helper; aid

**as·siz·es** (∂ sīz′iz) *n.pl.* [see ASSESS] 1. court sessions held periodically in each county of England 2. the time or place of these

**assn.** association

**assoc.** 1. associated 2. association

**as·so·ci·ate** (∂ sō′shē āt′, -sē-; *for n. & adj., usually* -it) *vt.* **-at′ed, -at′ing** [< L. *ad-*, to + *socius*, companion] 1. to connect; combine; join 2. to bring into relationship as partner, etc. 3. to connect in the mind —*vi.* to unite or join (*with*) as a partner, friend, etc. —*n.* 1. a partner, colleague, friend, etc. 2. anything joined with another 3. a degree granted by a junior college at the end of a two-year course —*adj.* 1. united by the same interests, purposes, etc. 2. having secondary status or privileges

**as·so·ci·a′tion** (-ā′shən) *n.* 1. an associating or being associated 2. fellowship; partnership 3. an organization, society, etc. 4. a connection between ideas, etc. —**as·so·ci·a′tive** (-āt′iv) *adj.*

**association football** soccer

**as·so·nance** (as′∂ nəns) *n.* [< L. *ad-*, to + *sonare*, to sound] 1. likeness of sound 2. a partial rhyme made by like vowel sounds, as in *late* and *make* —**as′so·nant** *adj., n.*

**as·sort** (∂ sôrt′) *vt.* [< L. *ad-*, to + *sors*, lot] to separate into classes according to kind; classify

**as·sort′ed** *adj.* 1. various; miscellaneous 2. classified

**as·sort′ment** *n.* 1. classification 2. a miscellaneous collection; variety

**asst.** assistant

**as·suage** (∂ swāj′) *vt.* **-suaged′, -suag′ing** [< L. *ad*, to + *suavis*, sweet] 1. to lessen (pain, etc.) 2. to calm (anger, etc.) 3. to satisfy or slake (thirst, etc.)

**as·sume** (∂ so͞om′) *vt.* **-sumed′, -sum′ing** [< L. *ad-*, to + *sumere*, to take] 1. to take on (the appearance, role, etc. of) 2. to seize; usurp 3. to undertake 4. to take for granted; suppose 5. to pretend to have; feign —**as·sum′ed·ly** *adv.*

**as·sum′ing** *adj.* taking too much for granted; presumptuous

**as·sump·tion** (∂ sump′shən) *n.* 1. [A-] *R.C.Ch.* *a*) the ascent of the Virgin Mary into heaven *b*) the festival celebrating this (Aug. 15) 2. an assuming 3. a supposition —**as·sump′tive** *adj.*

**as·sur·ance** (∂ shoor′∂ns) *n.* 1. an assuring or being assured 2. sureness; confidence 3. a promise, guarantee, etc. 4. self-confidence 5. [Chiefly Brit.] insurance

**as·sure** (∂ shoor′) *vt.* **-sured′, -sur′ing** [< L. *ad*, to + *securus*, secure] 1. to make (a person) sure of something 2. to give confidence to; reassure 3. to tell or promise positively 4. to guarantee 5. [Brit.] to insure against loss

**as·sured′** *adj.* 1. made sure; certain 2. self-confident —**as·sur·ed·ly** (∂ shoor′id lē) *adv.*

**As·syr·i·a** (∂ sir′ē ∂) ancient empire in SW Asia —**As·syr′i·an** *adj., n.*

**As·tar·te** (as tär′tē) ancient Semitic goddess of fertility and sexual love

**as·ter** (as′tər) *n.* [< Gr. *astēr*, star] any of several plants of the composite family with variously colored daisylike flowers

**as·ter·isk** (as′tər isk) *n.* [< Gr. dim. of *astēr*, a star] a starlike sign (*) used in printing to mark footnotes, etc.

**a·stern** (∂ stʉrn′) *adv.* 1. behind a ship or aircraft 2. at or toward the rear of a ship, etc. 3. backward

**as·ter·oid** (as′tə roid′) *n.* [see ASTER & -OID] any of the small planets between Mars and Jupiter

**asth·ma** (az′mə) *n.* [Gr.] a chronic disorder characterized by coughing, difficult breathing, etc. —**asth·mat′ic** (-mat′ik) *adj., n.*

**a·stig·ma·tism** (∂ stig′mə tiz′m) *n.* [< Gr. *a-*, without + *stigma*, a mark + -ISM] a defect of a lens or the eyes that prevents light rays from meeting in a single focal point —**as·tig·mat·ic** (as′tig mat′ik) *adj.*

**a·stir** (∂ stʉr′) *adv., adj.* 1. in motion 2. out of bed

**as·ton·ish** (∂ stän′ish) *vt.* [< L. *ex-*, intens. + *tonare*, to thunder] to fill with sudden surprise; amaze —**as·ton′ish·ing** *adj.* —**as·ton′ish·ing·ly** *adv.* —**as·ton′ish·ment** *n.*

**as·tound** (∂ stound′) *vt.* [see prec.] to astonish greatly —**as·tound′ing** *adj.* —**as·tound′ing·ly** *adv.*

**a·strad·dle** (∂ strad′'l) *adv.* in a straddling position

---

**as·tra·khan** (as′trə kən) *n.* [< *Astrakhan*, U.S.S.R. city] loosely curled fur from young lamb pelts, or a wool fabric resembling this

**as·tral** (as′trəl) *adj.* [< Gr. *astron*, star] of, from, or like the stars

**a·stray** (ə strā′) *adv.* [< OFr. *estraier*, STRAY] 1. off the right path 2. into error

**a·stride** (ə strīd′) *adv.* with a leg on either side —*prep.* 1. with a leg on either side of 2. extending over or across

**as·trin·gent** (ə strin′jənt) *adj.* [< L. *ad-*, to + *stringere*, draw] 1. that contracts body tissues 2. harsh; biting —*n.* an astringent substance —**as·trin′gen·cy** *n.*

**as·tro-** (as′trō) [< Gr. *astron*, a star] *a combining form meaning* of a star or stars [*astrophysics*]

**as·tro·bi·ol·o·gy** (as′trō bī äl′ə jē) *n.* the branch of biology that investigates the existence of living organisms on planets other than earth

**as′tro·dy·nam′ics** (-dī nam′iks) *n.pl.* [*with sing. v.*] the branch of dynamics dealing with the motion and gravitation of objects in space

**as·trol·o·gy** (ə sträl′ə jē) *n.* [< Gr. *astron*, star + *-logia*, -LOGY] a pseudo-science claiming to foretell the future by the supposed influence of the stars, planets, etc. on human affairs —**as·trol′o·ger** *n.* —**as·tro·log·i·cal** (as′trə läj′i k'l) *adj.*

**as·tro·naut** (as′trə nôt′) *n.* [Fr. < Gr. *astron*, star + *nautēs*, sailor] one trained to make flights in outer space —**as′tro·nau′tics** *n.*

**as·tro·nom·i·cal** (as′trə näm′i k'l) *adj.* 1. of astronomy 2. huge, as numbers Also **as′tro·nom′ic** —**as′tro·nom′i·cal·ly** *adv.*

**astronomical unit** a unit of length equal to the mean radius of the earth's orbit, or about 93 million miles

**as·tron·o·my** (ə strän′ə mē) *n.* [< Gr. *astron*, star + *nomos*, law] the science of the stars and other heavenly bodies, their motion, position, size, etc. —**as·tron′o·mer** *n.*

**as·tro·phys·ics** (as′trō fiz′iks) *n.pl.* [*with sing. v.*] the science of the physical properties and phenomena of heavenly bodies —**as′tro·phys′i·cist** (-ə sist) *n.*

**as·tute** (ə stōōt′) *adj.* [< L. *astus*, craft] shrewd; keen; crafty —**as·tute′ly** *adv.* —**as·tute′ness** *n.*

**a·sun·der** (ə sun′dər) *adv.* [< OE. *on sundran*] 1. into pieces 2. apart in direction or position

**a·sy·lum** (ə sī′ləm) *n.* [< Gr. *a-*, without + *sylē*, right of seizure] 1. place of safety; refuge 2. an earlier name for an institution for the mentally ill, orphans, the aged, etc.

**a·sym·me·try** (ā sim′ə trē) *n.* lack of symmetry —**a′sym·met′ri·cal** (-met′ri k'l) *adj.*

**at** (at, ət) *prep.* [< OE. *æt*] 1. on; in; near; by [*at* the office] 2. to or toward [*look at* her] 3. from [visible at one mile] 4. attending [*at* a party] 5. busy with [*at* work] 6. in the state or

manner of [*at* war, *at* a trot] 7. because of [*sad at* his death] 8. with reference to [*good at* tennis] 9. in the amount, etc. of [*at* five cents each] 10. on or near the age or time of [*at* noon]

**At·a·brine** (at′ə brin) *a trademark for* a synthetic drug used in treating malaria, etc. —[a-] this drug

**at·a·vism** (at′ə viz′m) *n.* [< L. *atavus*, ancestor] resemblance or reversion to remotely ancestral characteristics —**at′a·vis′tic** *adj.*

**ate** (āt; *Brit. or U.S. dial.* et) *pt. of* EAT

**-ate¹** (āt, it) [< L. *-atus*, pp. ending] *a suffix meaning:* 1. to become, cause to become, form, provide with [*maturate, ulcerate*] 2. of or characteristic of, characterized by, having [*passionate*]

**-ate²** [L. *-atus*, noun ending] *a suffix denoting* a function, official, or agent [*potentate*]

**at·el·ier** (at′'l yā′) *n.* [Fr.] a studio or workshop, as of an artist or couturier

**Ath·a·pas·can, Ath·a·pas·kan** (ath′ə pas′kən) *adj.* designating or of a widespread family of N. American Indian languages —*n.* this family of languages

**a·the·ism** (ā′thē iz′m) *n.* [< Gr. *a-*, without + *theos*, god] the belief that there is no God —**a′the·ist** *n.* —**a′the·is′tic** *adj.*

**A·the·na** (ə thē′nə) the Greek goddess of wisdom, skills, and warfare

**Ath·ens** (ath′nz) capital of Greece, in the SE part: pop. 1,853,000 —**A·the·ni·an** (ə thē′nē ən) *adj., n.*

**ath·er·o·scle·ro·sis** (ath′ər ō sklə rō′sis) *n.* [< Gr. *athērōma*, grainy tumor + SCLEROSIS] formation of fatty nodules on hardening artery walls

**a·thirst** (ə thurst′) *adj.* 1. [Archaic] thirsty 2. eager; longing (for)

**ath·lete** (ath′lēt′) *n.* [< Gr. *athlon*, a prize] a person trained in exercises or games requiring strength, skill, stamina etc.

**athlete's foot** ringworm of the feet

**ath·let·ic** (-let′ik) *adj.* 1. of or like athletes or athletics 2. physically strong and active —**ath·let′i·cal·ly** *adv.*

**ath·let·ics** *n.pl.* [*sometimes with sing. v.*] athletic sports, games, etc. —

**a·thwart** (ə thwôrt′) *prep.* 1. across 2. against —*adv.* crosswise

**a·tilt** (ə tilt′) *adj., adv.* tilted

**-a·tion** (ā′shən) [< Fr. or L.] *a suffix meaning* act, condition, or result of [*alteration*]

**-a·tive** (ə tiv, āt′iv) [< Fr. or L.] *a suffix meaning* of or relating to, serving to [*demonstrative*]

**At·lan·ta** (ət lan′tə, at-) capital of Ga.: pop. 497,000

**At·lan·tic** (ət lan′tik, at-) ocean touching the Americas to the west and Europe and Africa to the east —*adj.* of, in, or near this ocean

**Atlantic City** ocean resort in SE N.J.: pop. 48,000

**At·lan·tis** (ət lan′tis) [< Gr.] legendary sunken continent in the Atlantic

**At·las** (at'ləs) *Gr. Myth.* a giant whose shoulders supported the heavens —*n.* [a-] a book of maps

**at·mos·phere** (at'məs fir') *n.* [< Gr. *atmos*, vapor + *sphaira*, sphere] 1. all the air surrounding the earth 2. pervading mood or spirit 3. the general tone or effect 4. a unit of pressure equal to 14.69 lb. per sq. in. —**at'mos·pher'ic** (-fer'ik) *adj.* —**at'mos·pher'i·cal·ly** *adv.*

**at·oll** (a'tôl, ā'-) *n.* [< ? Malayalam *adal*, uniting] a ring-shaped coral island surrounding a lagoon

**at·om** (at'əm) *n.* [< Gr. *atomos*, uncut] 1. a tiny particle; jot 2. *Chem., Physics* any of the smallest particles of an element that form compounds with similar particles of other elements —**the atom** atomic energy

**a·tom·ic** (ə täm'ik) *adj.* 1. of an atom or atoms 2. of or using atomic energy or atomic bombs 3. tiny —**a·tom'i·cal·ly** *adv.*

**atomic bomb, atom bomb** a very destructive bomb, whose immense power derives from a chain reaction of nuclear fission

**atomic energy** the energy released from an atom in nuclear reactions, esp. in nuclear fission or nuclear fusion

**at·om·iz·er** (at'ə mī'zər) *n.* a device used to shoot out a fine spray, as of medicine or perfume

**a·to·nal·i·ty** (ā'tō nal'ə tē) *n. Music* lack of tonality through intentional disregard of key —**a·ton·al** (ā tōn'l) *adj.*

**a·tone** (ə tōn') *vi.* **a·toned', a·ton'ing** [< ME. *at one*, in accord] to make amends (*for* wrongdoing, etc.)

ATOMIZER

**a·tone'ment** *n.* 1. an atoning 2. amends; expiation 3. [A-] *Theol.* the redeeming of mankind through Jesus' death

**a·top** (ə täp') *adv.* on or at the top —*prep.* on the top of

**-a·to·ry** (ə tôr'ē) [< L.] *a suffix meaning* of, characterized by [*exclamatory]*

**a·tri·um** (ā'trē əm) *n., pl.* **a'tri·a** (-ə), **a'tri·ums** [L.] 1. the main room of an ancient Roman house 2. an entrance hall 3. an auricle of the heart

**a·tro·cious** (ə trō'shəs) *adj.* [< L. *atrox*, fierce + -OUS] 1. very cruel, evil, etc. 2. [Colloq.] very bad; offensive —**a·tro'cious·ly** *adv.* —**a·tro'cious·ness** *n.*

**a·troc·i·ty** (ə träs'ə tē) *n., pl.* -ties 1. atrocious behavior or act 2. [Colloq.] a very displeasing thing

**at·ro·phy** (a'trə fē) *n.* [< Gr. *a-*, not + *trephein*, nourish] a wasting away or failure to grow, esp. of body tissue, an organ, etc. —*vi.* **-phied, -phy·ing**

to undergo atrophy —*vt.* to cause atrophy in

**at·ro·pine** (at'rə pēn', -pin) *n.* [< Gr. *Atropos*, one of the Fates + -INE[2]] an alkaloid obtained from belladonna, used to relieve spasms

**at·tach** (ə tach') *vt.* [< OFr. *a-*, to + *tach*, a nail] 1. to fasten by tying, etc. 2. to join (often used reflexively) 3. to connect by ties of affection, etc. 4. to affix (a signature, etc.) 5. to ascribe 6. *Law* to take (property, etc.) by writ —**at·tach'a·ble** *adj.*

**at·ta·ché** (at'ə shā'; *chiefly Brit.* ə tash'ā) *n.* [Fr.: see prec.] a member of the diplomatic staff of an ambassador

**attaché case** a flat, rectangular case for carrying papers, etc.

**at·tach'ment** *n.* 1. an attaching or being attached 2. anything that attaches; fastening 3. devotion 4. anything attached 5. an accessory for an electrical appliance, etc. 6. *Law* a taking of property, etc. into custody

**at·tack** (ə tak') *vt.* [< OFr. *atachier*, ATTACH] 1. to use force against in order to harm 2. to speak or write against 3. to undertake vigorously 4. to begin acting upon harmfully —*vi.* to make an assault —*n.* 1. an attacking 2. an onset of a disease 3. a beginning of a task, undertaking, etc. —**at·tack'er** *n.*

**at·tain** (ə tān') *vt.* [< L. *ad-*, to + *tangere*, to touch] 1. to gain; accomplish; achieve 2. to reach; arrive at —**at·tain'a·bil'i·ty** *n.* —**at·tain'a·ble** *adj.* —**at·tain'ment** *n.*

**at·tain·der** (-dər) *n.* [see prec.] loss of civil rights and property of one sentenced to death or outlawed

**at·taint** (ə tānt') *vt.* to punish by attainder

**at·tar** (at'ər) *n.* [< Ar. *'itr*, perfume] a perfume made from flower petals, esp. of roses (attar of roses)

**at·tempt** (ə tempt') *vt.* [< L. *ad-*, to + *temptare*, to try] to try to do, get, etc. —*n.* 1. a try; endeavor 2. an attack, as on a person's life

**at·tend** (ə tend') *vt.* [< L. *ad-*, to + *tendere*, to stretch] 1. to take care of 2. to go with 3. to accompany as a result 4. to be present at —*vi.* 1. to pay attention 2. to wait (on or upon) 3. to apply oneself (to) 4. to give the required care (to)

**at·tend'ance** *n.* 1. an attending 2. the number of persons attending

**at·tend'ant** *adj.* 1. attending or serving 2. being present 3. accompanying —*n.* one who attends or serves

**at·ten·tion** (ə ten'shən) *n.* [see ATTEND] 1. mental concentration or readiness for this 2. notice or observation 3. care or consideration 4. an act of courtesy: *usually used in pl.* 5. the erect posture of soldiers ready for a command

**at·ten·tive** (-tiv) *adj.* 1. paying

attention 2. courteous, devoted, etc. —at·ten'tive·ly adv.

**at·ten·u·ate** (ə ten'yoo wāt'; for adj. -wit) vt. -at'ed, -at'ing [< L. ad-, to + tenuis, thin] 1. to make thin 2. to dilute 3. to lessen or weaken —vi. to become thin, weak, etc. —adj. attenuated —at·ten'u·a'tion n.

**at·test** (ə test') vt. [< L. ad-, to + testari, bear witness] 1. to declare to be true or genuine 2. to certify, as by oath 3. to serve as proof of —vi. to bear witness (to) —at'tes·ta'tion n.

**at·tic** (at'ik) n. [< Gr. Attikos, of Attica (ancient Gr. region): with reference to architectural style] the room or space just below the roof; garret

**At·ti·la** (at''l ə, ə til'ə) 406?-453 A.D.; King of the Huns

**at·tire** (ə tīr') vt. -tired', -tir'ing [< OFr. a-, to + tire, order] to clothe; dress up —n. clothes

**at·ti·tude** (at'ə tōōd') n. [ult. < L. aptus, APT] 1. a bodily posture showing mood, action, etc. 2. a manner showing one's feelings or thoughts 3. one's disposition, opinion, etc.

**at·ti·tu·di·nize** (at'ə tōōd''n īz') vi. -nized', -niz'ing to pose for effect

**at·tor·ney** (ə tur'nē) n., pl. -neys [< OFr. a-, to + torner, to turn] a person legally empowered to act for another; esp., a lawyer

**attorney at law** a lawyer

**attorney general**, pl. **attorneys general, attorney generals** the chief law officer of a government

**at·tract** (ə trakt') vt. [< L. ad-, to + trahere, to draw] 1. to draw to itself or oneself 2. to get the admiration, attention, etc. of; allure —vi. to be attractive —at·tract'a·ble adj.

**at·trac·tion** (ə trak'shən) n. 1. an attracting 2. power of attracting; esp., charm 3. anything that attracts 4. Physics the mutual action by which bodies tend to draw together

**at·trac·tive** (-tiv) adj. that attracts; esp., pleasing, charming, pretty, etc. —at·trac'tive·ly adv. —at·trac'tive·ness n.

**at·trib·ute** (ə trib'yoot; for n. a'trə byōōt') vt. -but·ed, -but·ing [< L. ad-, to + tribuere, assign] to think of as belonging to; ascribe (to) —n. a characteristic or quality of a person or thing —at·trib'ut·a·ble adj. —at'tri·bu'tion n.

**at·trib·u·tive** (ə trib'yoo tiv) adj. 1. attributing 2. preceding the noun it modifies: said of an adjective —at·trib'u·tive·ly adv.

**at·tri·tion** (ə trish'ən) n. [< L. ad-, to + terere, to rub] a wearing away by or as by friction

**at·tune** (ə tōōn') vt. -tuned', -tun'-ing 1. to tune 2. to bring into harmony

**atty.** attorney

**ATV** (ā'tē'vē') n., pl. **ATVs** [A(ll-)T(errain) V(ehicle)] a small motor vehicle for traveling over rough ground, snow, and ice, and in water

**a·twit·ter** (ə twit'ər) adv., adj. twittering

**a·typ·i·cal** (ā tip'i k'l) adj. not typical; abnormal —a·typ'i·cal·ly adv.

**Au** [L. aurum] Chem. gold

**au·burn** (ô'bərn) adj., n. [< L. albus, white: infl. by ME. brun, brown] reddish brown

**auc·tion** (ôk'shən) n. [< L. augere, to increase] a public sale of items to the highest bidders —vt. to sell at auction —**auction off** to sell at auction —auc'tion·eer' n.

**au·da·cious** (ô dā'shəs) adj. [< L. audax, bold] 1. bold; daring 2. too bold; insolent; brazen —au·da'cious·ly adv. —au·da'cious·ness n.

**au·dac·i·ty** (ô das'ə tē) n. 1. bold courage 2. insolence; impudence 3. pl. -ties an audacious act or remark

**au·di·ble** (ô'də b'l) adj. [< L. audire, hear] loud enough to be heard —au'di·bil'i·ty n. —au'di·bly adv.

**au·di·ence** (ô'dē əns) n. [< L. audire, hear] 1. those gathered to hear and see something 2. all those reached by a radio or TV program, book, etc. 3. a hearing, esp. a formal interview

**au·di·o** (ô'dē ō) adj. [< L. audire, hear] 1. of frequencies corresponding to audible sound waves 2. of the sound phase of television

**au·di·ol·o·gy** (-äl'ə jē) n. the science of aiding persons with hearing defects —au'di·ol'o·gist n.

**au·di·om·e·ter** (-äm'ə tər) n. an instrument for measuring the sharpness and range of hearing —au'di·o·met'ric (-ō met'rik) adj.

**au·di·o·phile** (-ə fīl') n. a devotee of high-fidelity sound reproduction, as on record players

**au·di·o·vis·u·al** (ô'dē ō vizh'oo wəl) adj. involving both hearing and sight

**au·dit** (ô'dit) n. [< L. audire, hear] a formal checking of financial records —vt., vi. 1. to check (accounts, etc.) 2. to attend (a college class) to listen without credits

**au·di·tion** (ô dish'ən) n. [< L. audire, hear] a hearing to try out an actor, singer, etc. —vt., vi. to try out in an audition

**au·di·tor** (ô'də tər) n. 1. a listener 2. one who audits accounts 3. one who audits classes

**au·di·to·ri·um** (ô'də tôr'ē əm) n. 1. a room where an audience sits 2. a building or hall for speeches, concerts, etc.

**au·di·to·ry** (ô'də tôr'ē) adj. of hearing or the organs of hearing

**auf Wie·der·se·hen** (ouf vē'dər zā'ən) [G.] goodbye

**au·ger** (ô'gər) n. [< OE. nafogar < nafu, hub (of a wheel) + gar, spear] a tool for boring holes in wood

**aught** (ôt) n. [< OE. a, one + wiht, creature] 1. anything whatever 2. [<

TYPES OF AUGER
(A, screw auger; B, ship auger; C, lip-ring auger)

(N)AUGHT] a zero —*adv.* in any way

**aug·ment** (ôg ment′) *vt., vi.* [< L. *augere*, to increase] to make or become greater —*aug′men·ta′tion* n. —**aug·ment′er** n.

**au gra·tin** (ō grät′'n) [Fr.] with a crust of crumbs and grated cheese

**au·gur** (ô′gər) n. [L., priest at fertility rites] a prophet; soothsayer —*vt., vi.* 1. to prophesy 2. to be an omen —(augur ill (or well) to be a bad (or good) omen

**au·gu·ry** (ô′gyər ē) n., *pl.* -ries 1. the practice of divination 2. an omen

**Au·gust** (ô′gəst) n. [< L. AUGUSTUS] the 8th month of the year, having 31 days: abbrev. Aug.

**au·gust** (ô gust′) *adj.* [L. *augustus*] inspiring awe; imposing —**au·gust′ly** *adv.* —**au·gust′ness** n.

**Au·gus·ta** (ô gus′tə) capital of Me.: pop. 22,000

**Au·gus·tine** (ô′gəs tēn′), Saint 354–430 A.D.; Latin church father

**Au·gus·tus** (ô gus′təs) 63 B.C.,–14 A.D.; first emperor of Rome

**au jus** (ō zhoo′, joos′) [Fr.] served in its natural juices: said of meat

**auk** (ôk) n. [< ON. *alka*] a diving bird of northern seas, with webbed feet and short wings used as paddles

**auld lang syne** (ôld′ laŋ′ zīn′) [Scot., lit., old long since] the good old days

**aunt** (ant, änt) n. [< L. *amita*] 1. a sister of one's mother or father 2. the wife of one's uncle

GREAT AUK

**au·ra** (ôr′ə) n., *pl.* -ras, -rae (-ē) [< Gr., akin to *aēr*, air] 1. an invisible emanation 2. a particular quality surrounding a person or thing

**au·ral** (ôr′əl) *adj.* [< L. *auris*, ear] of the ear or the sense of hearing

**au·re·ole** (ôr′ē ōl′) n. [< L. *aurlum*, gold] 1. a halo 2. a sun's corona

**Au·re·o·my·cin** (ôr′ē ō mīs′'n) [< L. *aureus*, golden + Gr. *mykēs*, fungus] *a trademark for* an antibiotic

**au re·voir** (ō′ rə vwär′) [Fr.] goodbye

**au·ri·cle** (ôr′ə k'l) n. [< L. dim. of *auris*, ear] 1. the outer part of the ear 2. either of the two upper chambers of the heart 3. an earlike part

**au·ric·u·lar** (ô rik′yoo lər) *adj.* 1. of the ear or the sense of hearing 2. said privately 3. of or like an auricle

**Au·ro·ra** (ô rôr′ə) the Rom. goddess of dawn — n. 1. [a-] *pl.* -ras, -rae (-ē) the dawn 2. either of the luminous bands sometimes seen in the night sky: in the S Hemisphere, called the **aurora aus·tra·lis** (ô strā′ləs), in the N Hemisphere, the **aurora bo·re·a·lis** (bôr′ē al′is)

**aus·cul·ta·tion** (ôs′kəl tā′shən) n. [< L. *auscultare*, to listen] a listening, often with a stethoscope, to sounds in

the chest, abdomen, etc. that indicate heart and lung condition, etc. —**aus′cul·tate′** *vt., vi.*

**aus·pice** (ôs′pis) n., *pl.* -pi·ces′ (-pə sēz′) [< L. *auspicium*, omen] 1. an omen 2. a favorable omen or sign 3. [*pl.*] sponsorship; patronage

**aus·pi·cious** (ôs pish′əs) *adj.* 1. favorable; propitious 2. successful —**aus·pi′cious·ly** *adv.*

**Aus·sie** (ôs′ē) *adj., n.* [Slang] Australian

**Aus·ten** (ôs′tən), **Jane** 1775–1817; Eng. novelist

**aus·tere** (ô stir′) *adj.* [< Gr. *austēros*, dry] 1. stern; harsh 2. morally strict 3. unadorned; plain —**aus·tere′ly** *adv.*

**aus·ter·i·ty** (ô ster′ə tē) n., *pl.* -ties 1. sternness 2. [*pl.*] an austere practice 3. tightened economy

**Aus·tin** (ôs′tin) capital of Tex., in the C part: pop. 252,000

**aus·tral** (ôs′trəl) *adj.* [< L. *auster*, the south] southern

**Aus·tral·ia** (ô strāl′yə) 1. island continent between the S Pacific & Indian oceans 2. country comprising this continent & Tasmania: 2,971,081 sq. mi.; pop. 11,633,000 —**Aus·tral′ian** *adj., n.*

**Aus·tri·a** (ôs′trē ə) country in C Europe: 32,375 sq. mi.; pop. 7,273,000 —**Aus′tri·an** *adj., n.*

**au·then·tic** (ô then′tik) *adj.* [< Gr. *authentikos*, genuine] 1. reliable, credible, etc., as a report 2. genuine; real —**au·then′ti·cal·ly** *adv.* —**au·then·tic·i·ty** (ô′thən tis′ə tē) n.

**au·then′ti·cate′** (-tə kāt′) *vt.* -cat′ed, -cat′ing 1. to make valid 2. to verify 3. to prove to be genuine —**au·then′ti·ca′tion** n.

**au·thor** (ô′thər) n. [< L. *augere*, to increase] 1. one who makes or creates something 2. a writer of books, etc. —*vt.* to be the author of —**au′thor·ship′** n.

**au·thor·i·tar·i·an** (ə thôr′ə ter′ēən) *adj.* believing in or characterized by absolute obedience to authority —*n.* an advocate or enforcer of such obedience —**au·thor′i·tar′i·an·ism** n.

**au·thor′i·ta′tive** (-tāt′iv) *adj.* 1. having authority; official 2. based on competent authority; reliable —**au·thor′i·ta′tive·ly** *adv.*

**au·thor′i·ty** (-tē) n., *pl.* -ties [see AUTHOR] 1. the power or right to command, act, etc. 2. [*pl.*] officials with this power 3. influence resulting from knowledge, prestige, etc. 4. a person, writing, etc. cited to support an opinion 5. an expert

**au·thor·ize** (ô′thə rīz′) *vt.* -ized′, -iz′ing 1. to give official approval to 2. to give power or authority to 3. to justify —**au′thor·i·za′tion** n.

**Authorized Version** the revised English translation of the Bible, published in 1611, authorized by King James I

**au·tism** (ô′tiz'm) n. [AUT(O)- + -ISM]

*Psychol.* a mental state marked by disregard of external reality —**au·tis′tic** *adj.*

**au·to** (ôt′ō) *n., pl.* **-tos** an automobile

**auto-** [< Gr. *autos*, self] *a prefix meaning:* **1.** self **2.** by oneself or itself

**au·to·bi·og·ra·phy** (ôt′ə bī ä′grə fē) *n., pl.* **-phies** the story of one's own life written by oneself —**au′to·bi′o·graph′i·cal** (-ə graf′i k'l) *adj.*

**au·toc·ra·cy** (ô tä′krə sē) *n., pl.* **-cies** [see ff.] government in which one person has absolute power

**au·to·crat** (ôt′ə krat′) *n.* [< Gr. *autos*, self + *kratos*, power] **1.** a ruler with absolute power **2.** any domineering person —**au′to·crat′ic** *adj.* —**au′to·crat′i·cal·ly** *adv.*

**au·to·di·dact** (ôt′ō dī′dakt) *n.* [see AUTO- & DIDACTIC] a person who is self-taught

**au·to·graph** (ôt′ə graf′) *n.* [< Gr. *autos*, self + *graphein*, write] a person's own signature or handwriting —*vt.* to write one's signature on or in

**au·to·hyp·no·sis** (ôt′ō hip nō′sis) *n.* a hypnotizing of oneself or the state of being so hypnotized

**au·to·in·tox·i·ca·tion** (ôt′ō in täk′sə kā′shən) *n.* poisoning by toxic substances formed within the body

**au·to·mat** (ôt′ə mat′) *n.* [G.: see AUTOMATIC] a restaurant in which patrons get food from small, coin-operated compartments

**au′to·mate′** (-māt′) *vt.* **-mat′ed, -mat′ing** [< AUTOMATION] to convert to or use automation

**au′to·mat′ic** (-mat′ik) *adj.* [Gr. *automatos*, self-moving] **1.** done unthinkingly, as from habit or by reflex **2.** working by itself **3.** using automatic equipment —*n.* an automatic pistol or rifle —**au′to·mat′i·cal·ly** *adv.*

**automatic pilot** a gyroscopic instrument that automatically keeps an aircraft, missile, etc. to a predetermined course and attitude

**au′to·ma′tion** (-mā′shən) *n.* a manufacturing system in which many or all of the processes are automatically performed or controlled, as by electronic devices

**au·tom·a·tism** (ô täm′ə tiz'm) *n.* automatic quality, condition, or action —**au·tom′a·tize′** (-tīz′) *vt.*

**au·tom′a·ton′** (-tän′, -tən) *n., pl.* **-tons′, -ta** (-tə) [see AUTOMATIC] **1.** any automatic device, esp. a robot **2.** a person acting like a robot

**au·to·mo·bile** (ôt′ə mə bēl′) *n.* [Fr.: see AUTO- & MOBILE] a four-wheeled passenger car with a built-in engine

**au′to·mo′tive** (-mōt′iv) *adj.* [AUTO- + -MOTIVE] **1.** self-moving **2.** having to do with automobiles, trucks, etc.

**au′to·nom′ic** (-näm′ik) *adj.* of or controlled by that part of the nervous system that regulates the motor functions of the heart, lungs, etc.

**au·ton·o·mous** (ô tän′ə məs) *adj.* [< Gr. *autos*, self + *nomos*, law] **1.** having self-government **2.** existing or functioning independently —**au·ton′o·mous·ly** *adv.* —**au·ton′o·my** (-mē) *n.*

**au·to·pi·lot** (ôt′ə pī′lət) *n. same as* AUTOMATIC PILOT

**au·top·sy** (ô′täp′sē) *n., pl.* **-sies** [< Gr. *autos*, self + *opsis*, sight] examination of a corpse to find out the cause of death

**au·tumn** (ôt′əm) *n.* [< L. *autumnus*] the season between summer and winter; fall —**au·tum·nal** (ô tum′n'l) *adj.*

**aux·il·ia·ry** (ôg zil′yər ē) *adj.* [< L. *augere*, to increase] **1.** helping **2.** subsidiary **3.** supplementary —*n., pl.* **-ries** an auxiliary person or thing

**auxiliary verb** a verb that helps form tenses, moods, voices, etc. of other verbs, as *have* or *be*

**aux·in** (ôk′sin) *n.* [< Gr. *auxein*, to increase] a plant hormone that promotes and controls growth

**a·vail** (ə vāl′) *vi., vt.* [< L. *ad*, to + *valere*, be strong] to be of use, help, or worth (to) —*n.* use or help; benefit [to no *avail*] —**avail oneself of** to take advantage of; utilize

**a·vail·a·ble** (ə vāl′ə b'l) *adj.* **1.** that can be used **2.** that can be got or had; handy —**a·vail′a·bil′i·ty** *n.*

**av·a·lanche** (av′ə lanch′) *n.* [Fr. < L. *labi*, to slip] **1.** a large mass of loosened snow, earth, etc. sliding down a mountain **2.** an overwhelming amount

**a·vant-garde** (ä vänt′gärd′) *n.* [Fr.] the leaders in new movements, esp. in the arts —*adj.* of such movements

**av·a·rice** (av′ər is) *n.* [< L. *avere*, desire] greed for money —**av·a·ri·cious** (av′ə rish′əs) *adj.* —**av′a·ri′cious·ly** *adv.*

**a·vast** (ə vast′) *interj.* [< Du. *houd vast*, hold fast] *Naut.* stop! cease!

**av·a·tar** (av′ə tär′) *n.* [Sans. *avatāra*, descent] *Hinduism* a god's coming to earth in bodily form

**a·vaunt** (ə vônt′) *interj.* [< L. *ab*, from + *ante*, before] [Archaic] go away!

**avdp.** avoirdupois

**A·ve Ma·ri·a** (ä′vä mə rē′ə) [L.] *R.C.Ch.* **1.** "Hail, Mary," the first words of a prayer **2.** this prayer

**a·venge** (ə venj′) *vt., vi.* **a·venged′, a·veng′ing** [< L. *ad*, to + *vindicare*, to claim] **1.** to get revenge for (an injury, etc.) **2.** to take vengeance on behalf of —**a·veng′er** *n.*

**a·ve·nue** (av′ə nōō′, -nyōō′) *n.* [< L. *ad*-, to + *venire*, come] **1.** a street, drive, etc., esp. when broad: abbr. **Ave., ave. 2.** a way of approach

**a·ver** (ə vur′) *vt.* **a·verred′, a·ver′ring** [< L. *ad*, to + *verus*, true] to declare to be true; assert

**av·er·age** (av′rij) *n.* [< Fr. *avarie*, damage to ship or cargo; hence, idea of shared losses] **1.** the result of dividing the sum of two or more quantities by the number of quantities **2.** the usual kind, amount, etc. —*adj.* **1.** constituting an average **2.** usual; normal —*vt.* **-aged, -ag·ing 1.** to figure out the average of **2.** to do, take, etc. on an average [to *average* six sales a day] —**average out** to arrive at an average eventually —**on the**

**average** as an average amount, rate, etc.

**a·verse** (ə vʉrs′) *adj.* [see AVERT] unwilling; opposed (*to*)

**a·ver·sion** (ə vʉr′zhən) *n.* 1. intense dislike 2. the object arousing this

**a·vert** (ə vʉrt′) *vt.* [< L. *a-*, from + *vertere*, to turn] 1. to turn (the eyes, etc.) away 2. to ward off; prevent

**avg.** average

**a·vi·ar·y** (ā′vē er′ē) *n.*, *pl.* **-ar′ies** [< L. *avis*, bird] a building or large cage for keeping many birds

**a·vi·a·tion** (ā′vē ā′shən) *n.* [see prec.] 1. the science of flying airplanes 2. the field of airplane design, construction, etc.

**a′vi·a′tor** *n.* an airplane pilot — **a′vi·a′trix** (-triks) *n.fem.*

**av·id** (av′id) *adj.* [< L. *avere*, to desire] very eager or greedy —**a·vid·i·ty** (ə vid′ə tē) *n.* —**av′id·ly** *adv.*

**a·vi·on·ics** (ā′vē än′iks) *n.pl.* [AVI-(ATION) + (ELECTR)ONICS] [*with sing. v.*] electronics as applied in aviation and astronautics

**av·o·ca·do** (av′ə kä′dō, ä′və-) *n.*, *pl.* **-dos** [< MexInd. *ahuacatl*] 1. a thick-skinned, pear-shaped tropical fruit with yellow, buttery flesh 2. the tree it grows on

**av·o·ca·tion** (av′ə kā′shən) *n.* [< L. *a-*, away + *vocare*, to call] occupation in addition to regular work; hobby — **av′o·ca′tion·al** *adj.*

**a·void** (ə void′) *vt.* [< ME. < OFr. *esvuidier*, to empty] to keep away from; shun; shirk —**a·void′a·ble** *adj.* —**a·void′a·bly** *adv.* —**a·void′ance** *n.*

**av·oir·du·pois** (av′ər də poiz′) *n.* [< OFr. *aveir de peis*, goods of weight] 1. a system of weights in which 16 oz. = 1 lb.: also **avoirdupois weight** 2. [Colloq.] weight, esp. of a person

**a·vouch** (ə vouch′) *vt.* [see ADVOCATE] 1. to vouch for 2. to affirm

**a·vow** (ə vou′) *vt.* [see ADVOCATE] to declare; acknowledge —**a·vow′al** *n.* —**a·vowed′** *adj.* —**a·vow′ed·ly** *adv.*

**a·vun·cu·lar** (ə vuŋ′kyə lər) *adj.* [< L. *avunculus*] of an uncle

**aw** (ô) *interj.* a sound of protest, etc.

**a·wait** (ə wāt′) *vt.*, *vi.* 1. to wait for 2. to be in store for

**a·wake** (ə wāk′) *vt.*, *vi.* **a·woke′** or **a·waked′**, **a·waked′**, **a·wak′ing** [< OE.] 1. to rouse from sleep 2. to rouse from inactivity Also **a·wak′en** —*adj.* 1. not asleep 2. active; alert

**a·wak′en·ing** *n.*, *adj.* 1. (a) waking up 2. (an) arousing or reviving

**a·ward** (ə wôrd′) *vt.* [< ME. < ONormFr. *eswarder*] 1. to give, as by legal decision 2. to give (a prize, etc.); grant —*n.* 1. a decision, as by a judge 2. a prize

**a·ware** (ə wer′) *adj.* [< OE. *wær*, cautious] knowing; realizing; conscious —**a·ware′ness** *n.*

**a·wash** (ə wôsh′) *adv.*, *adj.* 1. at a level where the water washes over the surface 2. flooded 3. afloat

**a·way** (ə wā′) *adv.* [< OE. *on weg*] 1. from a place [run *away*] 2. in another place or direction [*away* from here] 3. off; aside [turn *away*] 4. far [*away* behind] 5. from one's possession [give it *away*] 6. at once [fire *away*] 7. continuously [kept working *away*] —*adj.* 1. absent 2. at a distance [a mile *away*] —*interj.* begone! —**away with** go, come, or take away —**do away with** get rid of or kill

**awe** (ô) *n.* [< ON. *agi*] a mixed feeling of reverence, fear, and wonder —*vt.* **awed**, **aw′ing** to fill with awe —**stand (or be) in awe of** to respect and fear

**a·weigh** (ə wā′) *adj.* being weighed (hoisted): said of an anchor

**awe·some** (ô′səm) *adj.* inspiring or showing awe —**awe′some·ly** *adv.* —**awe′some·ness** *n.*

**awe·struck** (ô′struk′) *adj.* filled with awe: also **awe′-strick′en** (-strik′ən)

**aw·ful** (ô′f'l) *adj.* 1. inspiring awe 2. terrifying 3. [Colloq.] very bad —*adv.* [Colloq.] very —**aw′ful·ness** *n.*

**aw·ful·ly** (ô′fə lē, -flē) *adv.* 1. in an awful way 2. [Colloq.] very

**a·while** (ə wīl′, -hwīl′) *adv.* for a short time

**awk·ward** (ôk′wərd) *adj.* [< ON. *öfugr*, turned backward] 1. clumsy; bungling 2. hard to handle; unwieldy 3. uncomfortable [an *awkward* pose] 4. embarrassed or embarrassing —**awk′ward·ly** *adv.* —**awk′ward·ness** *n.*

**awl** (ôl) *n.* [< OE. *æl*] a small, pointed tool for making holes in wood, leather, etc.

**awn** (ôn) *n.* [< ON. *ögn*] the bristly fibers on a head of barley, oats, etc.

**awn·ing** (ô′niŋ) *n.* [? < MFr. *auvent*, window shade] a structure, as of canvas, extended before a window, door, etc. as a protection from sun or rain

**a·woke** (ə wōk′) *alt. pp. of* AWAKE

**A·WOL**, **a·wol** (ā′wôl′) *adj.* absent without leave

**a·wry** (ə rī′) *adv.*, *adj.* [see A- (on) & WRY] 1. with a twist to a side; askew 2. wrong; amiss [our plans went *awry*]

**ax**, **axe** (aks) *n.*, *pl.* **ax′es** [< OE. *æx*] a tool with a long handle and bladed head, for chopping wood, etc. —*vt.* **axed**, **ax′ing** to trim, split, etc. with an ax —**get the ax** [Colloq.] to be discharged from one's job —**have an ax to grind** [Colloq.] to have an object of one's own to gain or promote

**ax·i·al** (ak′sē əl) *adj.* 1. of, like, or forming an axis 2. around, on, or along an axis —**ax′i·al·ly** *adv.*

**ax·i·om** (ak′sē əm) *n.* [< Gr. *axios*, worthy] 1. *a*) a statement universally accepted as true; maxim *b*) a self-evident truth 2. an established principle, scientific law, etc. —**ax′i·o·mat·ic** (-ə mat′ik) *adj.* —**ax′i·o·mat′i·cal·ly** *adv.*

**ax·is** (ak′sis) *n.*, *pl.* **ax′es** (-sēz) [L.]

**1.** a real or imaginary straight line on which an object rotates **2.** a central line around which the parts of a thing, system, etc. are evenly arranged —**the Axis** Germany, Italy, and Japan, in World War II

**ax·le** (ak/s'l) *n.* [< ON. *öxull*] **1.** a rod on or with which a wheel turns **2.** *a*) a bar connecting two opposite wheels, as of an automobile *b*) the spindle at either end of such a bar

**ax/le·tree/** (-trē/) *n.* [< prec. + ON. *tre*, beam] an axle of a wagon, carriage, etc.

**Ax·min·ster** (aks/min/stər) *n.* [< English town where first made] a varicolored, patterned carpet with a cut pile

**ax·o·lotl** (ak/sə lät/'l) *n.* [< MexInd., lit., water toy] a dark salamander of Mexico and the western U.S.

**aye¹** (ā) *adv.* [< ON. *ei*] [Poet.] always; ever: also **ay**

**aye²** (ī) *adv.* [? < prec.] yes —*n.* an affirmative vote or voter   Also **ay**

**AZ** Arizona

**a·zal·ea** (ə zāl/yə) *n.* [< Gr. *azaleos*, dry: it thrives in dry soil] **1.** a shrub of the heath family with flowers of various colors **2.** the flower

**az·i·muth** (az/ə məth) *n.* [< Ar. *al*, the + *samt*, way] *Astron., Surveying* distance clockwise in degrees from the north point or, in the Southern Hemisphere, south point

**A·zores** (ā/zôrz, ə zôrz/) group of Portuguese islands in the N Atlantic, west of Portugal

**Az·tec** (az/tek) *n.* **1.** a member of a people who had an advanced civilization in Mexico before the Spanish conquest in 1519 **2.** their language —*adj.* of the Aztecs, their culture, etc.: also **Az/tec·an**

**az·ure** (azh/ər) *adj.* [< Per. *lāzhuward*, lapis lazuli] sky-blue —*n.* **1.** sky blue or any similar blue color **2.** [Poet.] the blue sky

# B

**B, b** (bē) *n., pl.* **B's, b's** the second letter of the English alphabet

**B** (bē) *n.* **1.** a grade indicating above-average but not outstanding work **2.** *Chem.* boron **3.** *Music* the 7th tone in the scale of C major —*adj.* inferior to the best [a class *B* motion picture]

**B., b. 1.** bachelor **2.** *Baseball a*) base *b*) baseman **3.** *Music* bass **4.** born

**Ba** *Chem.* barium

**B.A.** Bachelor of Arts

**baa** (bä) *n., vi.* [echoic] bleat

**Ba·al** (bā/əl) *n.* [< Heb.] **1.** an ancient Semitic fertility god **2.** an idol

**bab·ble** (bab/'l) *vi.* **-bled, -bling** [echoic] **1.** to talk like a small child; prattle **2.** to talk foolishly or too much **3.** to murmur, as a brook —*vt.* to say incoherently or foolishly —*n.* **1.** incoherent vocal sounds **2.** foolish talk **3.** a murmuring sound —**bab/bler** *n.*

**babe** (bāb) *n.* **1.** a baby **2.** a naive or helpless person: also **babe in the woods 3.** [Slang] a girl or young woman

**Ba·bel** (bā/b'l, bab/'l) *Bible* a city thwarted in building a tower to heaven when God created a confusion of tongues —*n.* [also **b-**] a confusion of voices, sounds, etc., or the scene of this

**ba·boon** (ba bōōn/) *n.* [< OFr. *babuin*, ape, fool] a large, fierce, short-tailed monkey of Africa and Arabia, with a doglike snout

**ba·bush·ka** (bə bōōsh/kə) *n.* [Russ., grandmother] a woman's scarf worn on the head and tied under the chin

BABOON

**ba·by** (bā/bē) *n., pl.* **-bies** [ME. *babi*] **1.** a very young child; infant **2.** one who acts like an infant **3.** a very young animal **4.** the youngest or smallest in a group **5.** [Slang] *a*) a girl or young woman *b*) any person or thing —*adj.* **1.** of or for an infant **2.** very young **3.** small of its kind **4.** childish —*vt.* **-bied, -by·ing** to pamper; coddle —**ba/by·hood/** *n.* —**ba/by·ish** *adj.*

**baby beef** meat from a prime heifer or steer that is one to two years old

**baby carriage** a light carriage for wheeling a baby about: also **baby buggy**

**baby grand** a small grand piano

**Bab·y·lon** (bab/ə lən, -län/) capital of Babylonia, famous for luxury

**Bab·y·lo·ni·a** (bab/ə lō/nē ə) ancient empire in SW Asia —**Bab/y·lo/ni·an** *adj., n.*

**ba·by's breath** (bā/bēz) a plant with small, delicate, white or pink flowers

**baby sitter** a person hired to take care of a child or children, as when the parents are away for the evening —**ba/by-sit/** *vi.* **-sat/, -sit/ting**

**bac·ca·lau·re·ate** (bak/ə lôr/ē it) *n.* [< ML. *baccalaris*, young noble seeking knighthood] **1.** the degree of BACHELOR OF ARTS (or SCIENCE, etc.) **2.** an address delivered at a commencement

**bac·ca·rat, bac·ca·ra** (bak/ə rä/, bak/ə rä/) *n.* [Fr.] a gambling game played with cards

**bac·cha·nal** (bak/ə nəl, -nal/) *n.* **1.** a worshiper of Bacchus **2.** a drunken carouser **3.** a drunken orgy —**bac/cha·na/li·an** (-nā/lē ən) *adj., n.*

**Bac·chus** (bak/əs) the Greek and Roman god of wine and revelry

**Bach** (bäkh; *E. also* bäk), **Jo·hann Se·bas·tian** (yō/hän si bäs/tyən),

1685–1750; Ger. organist & composer

**bach·e·lor** (bach′l ər, bach′lər) *n.* [< ML. *baccalaris:* see BACCALAUREATE] **1.** an unmarried man **2.** one who is a BACHELOR OF ARTS (or SCIENCE, etc.) —**bach′e·lor·hood′** *n.*

**Bachelor of Arts** (or **Science,** etc.) **1.** a degree given by a college or university to one who has completed a four-year course in the humanities (or in science, etc.) **2.** one who has this degree

**bachelor's button** a plant with showy white, pink, or blue flowers, as the cornflower

**ba·cil·lus** (bə sil′əs) *n., pl.* -**cil′li** (-ī) [< L. *bacillum,* little stick] **1.** any of a genus of rod-shaped bacteria **2.** loosely, any bacterium —**bac·il·lar·y** (bas′ə ler′ē, bə sil′ər ē) *adj.*

**back** (bak) *n.* [< OE. *bæk*] **1.** the rear part of the body from the nape of the neck to the end of the spine **2.** the backbone **3.** a part that supports or fits the back **4.** the rear part or reverse of anything **5.** *Sports* a player or position behind the front line —*adj.* **1.** at the rear **2.** remote **3.** of or for the past [*back* pay] **4.** backward —*adv.* **1.** at, to, or toward the rear **2.** to or toward a former condition, time, etc. **3.** in reserve or concealment **4.** in return or requital [pay him *back*] —*vt.* **1.** to move backward **2.** to support **3.** to bet on **4.** to provide or be a back for —*vi.* to go backward —**back and forth** backward and forward —**back down** to withdraw from a position or claim —**back off** (or **away,** etc.) to move back (or away, etc.) —**back out** (**of**) **1.** to withdraw from an enterprise **2.** to evade keeping a promise, etc. —**back up 1.** to support **2.** to move backward **3.** to accumulate because of restricted movement [traffic backed up] —**go back on** [Colloq.] **1.** to be disloyal to; betray **2.** to fail to keep (one's word, etc.) —**turn one's back on 1.** to turn away from, as in contempt **2.** to abandon

**back′ache′** *n.* an ache or pain in the back

**back′bite′** (-bīt′) *vt., vi.* -**bit′**, -**bit′ten** or -**bit′**, -**bit′ing** to slander (someone absent) —**back′bit′er** *n.*

**back′board′** *n.* a board at or forming the back of something; esp., *Basketball* the board behind the basket

**back′bone′** *n.* **1.** the spine **2.** a main support **3.** willpower, courage, etc.

**back′break′ing** *adj.* very tiring

**back′drop′** *n.* **1.** a curtain, often scenic, at the back of a stage **2.** background or setting

**back′er** *n.* **1.** a patron; supporter **2.** one who bets on a contestant

**back′field′** *n. Football* the players behind the line; esp., the offensive unit

**back′fire′** *n.* **1.** the burning out of a small area, as in a forest, to check the spread of a big fire **2.** premature ex-

plosion in an internal-combustion engine **3.** reverse explosion in a gun —*vi.* -**fired′**, -**fir′ing 1.** to explode as a backfire **2.** to go wrong or boomerang, as a plan

**back′gam′mon** (-gam′ən) *n.* [BACK + ME. *gammen,* game] a game for two, with dice governing moves of pieces on a special board

**back′ground′** *n.* **1.** the distant part of a scene **2.** surroundings, sounds, data, etc. behind or subordinate to something **3.** one's training and experience **4.** events leading up to something

**back′hand′** *n.* **1.** handwriting that slants up to the left **2.** a backhand catch, stroke, etc. —*adj.* **1.** done with the back of the hand turned inward, as for a baseball catch, or forward, as for a tennis stroke, and with the arm across the body **2.** written in backhand —*adv.* in a backhand way —*vt.* to hit, catch, swing, etc. backhand

**back′hand′ed** *adj.* **1.** *same as* BACKHAND **2.** not direct and open; devious —*adv.* in a backhanded way

**back′ing** *n.* **1.** something forming a back for support **2.** support given to a person or cause **3.** supporters; backers

**back′lash′** *n.* sharp reaction; recoil

**back′log′** (-lôg′) *n.* an accumulation or reserve —*vi., vt.* -**logged′**, -**log′-ging** to accumulate as a backlog

**back order** an order not yet filled

**back′pack′** *n.* a knapsack, often on a light frame, worn by campers or hikers —*vi., vt.* to wear, or carry in, a backpack —**back′pack′er** *n.*

**back′ped′al** *vi.* -**aled** or -**alled**, -**al·ing** or -**al·ling 1.** to pedal backward, as in braking a bicycle **2.** to move backward; retreat; withdraw

**back′rest′** *n.* a support for the back

**back′side′** *n.* **1.** back part **2.** rump

**back′slap′per** (-slap′ər) *n.* [Colloq.] an effusively friendly person

**back′slide′** *vi.* -**slid′**, -**slid′** or -**slid′den**, -**slid′ing** to slide backward in morals, etc. —**back′slid′er** *n.*

**back′space′** *vi.* -**spaced′**, -**spac′ing** to move a typewriter carriage one or more spaces back along the line

**back′spin′** *n.* backward spin in a ball, etc., making it bound backward upon hitting the ground

**back′stage′** *adv., adj.* behind and off the stage, as in the wings or dressing rooms

**back′stairs′** *adj.* involving intrigue or scandal; secret: also **back′stair′**

**back′stop′** *n.* a screen, fence, etc. to keep balls from going too far, as behind the catcher in baseball

**back′stretch′** *n.* the part of a race track opposite the homestretch

**back′stroke′** *n.* a swimming stroke made while lying face upward

**back talk** [Colloq.] saucy or insolent retorts

**back′-to-back′** *adj.* [Colloq.] one right after another

---

fat, āpe, cär; ten, ēven; is, bīte; gō, hôrn, tōol, look; oil, out; up, fur; chin; she; thin, then; zh, leisure; ŋ, ring; ə for a in ago; ′, (ā′b'l); ë, Fr. coeur; ö, Fr. feu; Fr. mon; ü, Fr. duc; kh, G. ich, doch; ‡ foreign; < derived from

**back'track'** *vi.* **1.** to return by the same path **2.** to retreat or recant

**back'up'**, **back'-up'** *adj.* **1.** standing by as an alternate or auxiliary **2.** supporting —*n.* a backing up; specif., *a*) an accumulation *b*) a support; help

**back'ward** *adv.* **1.** toward the back **2.** with the back foremost **3.** in reverse order **4.** in a way opposite to usual **5.** into the past  Also **back'wards** —*adj.* **1.** turned toward the rear or in the opposite way **2.** hesitant or shy **3.** slow or retarded —**back'wardness** *n.*

**back'wash'** *n.* **1.** water or air moved backward by a ship, propeller, etc. **2.** a reaction caused by some event

**back'wa'ter** *n.* **1.** water moved or held back by a dam, tide, etc. **2.** stagnant water in an inlet, etc. **3.** a backward place or condition

**back'woods'** *n.pl.* [*occas. with sing. v.*] **1.** heavily wooded, remote areas **2.** any remote, thinly populated area —*adj.* of or like the backwoods —**back'woods'man** *n., pl.* -**men**

**ba·con** (bāk'n) *n.* [< OS. *baco,* side of bacon] salted and smoked meat from the back or sides of a hog —**bring home the bacon** [Colloq.] **1.** to earn a living **2.** to succeed

**Ba·con** (bāk'n), **Francis**, 1561–1626; Eng. philosopher and writer

**bac·te·ri·a** (bak tir'ē ə) *n.pl., sing.* -**ri·um** (-əm) [< Gr. *baktērion,* small staff] microorganisms which have no chlorophyll and multiply by simple division: some bacteria cause diseases, but others are necessary for fermentation, etc. —**bac·te'ri·al** *adj.*

**bac·te'ri·cide'** (-tir'ə sīd') *n.* an agent that destroys bacteria —**bacte'ri·cid'al** *adj.*

**bac·te'ri·ol'o·gy** (-tir'ē äl'ə jē) *n.* the science that deals with bacteria —**bac·te'ri·o·log'i·cal** (-ē ə läj'i k'l) *adj.* —**bac·te'ri·ol'o·gist** *n.*

**bad**[1] (bad) *adj.* **worse**, **worst** [ME.] **1.** not good; not as it should be **2.** inadequate or unfit **3.** unfavorable [*bad* news] **4.** rotten or spoiled **5.** incorrect or faulty **6.** *a*) wicked; immoral *b*) mischievous **7.** harmful **8.** severe **9.** ill **10.** sorry; distressed [he feels *bad* about it] **11.** offensive —*adv.* [Colloq.] badly —*n.* anything bad —**in bad** [Colloq.] in trouble or disfavor —**bad'ness** *n.*

**bad**[2] (bad) *archaic pt. of* BID

**bad blood** (mutual) enmity

**bad egg** [Slang] a mean or dishonest person: also **bad actor**, **bad apple**, **bad hat**, **bad lot**, etc.

**badge** (baj) *n.* [ME. *bage*] **1.** an emblem worn to show rank, membership, etc. **2.** any distinctive sign, etc.

**badg·er** (baj'ər) *n.* [< ?] **1.** a burrowing animal with a broad back and thick, short legs —*vt.* to nag at; torment

**bad·i·nage** (bad'ə näzh', bad'n ij) *n.* [Fr. < ML. *badare,* to trifle] playful talk —*vt.* -**naged'**, -**nag'ing** to tease

**bad'lands'** *n.pl.* **1.** an area of barren land with dry soil and soft rocks eroded into odd shapes **2.** [B-] any such W U.S. area: also **Bad Lands**

**bad'ly** *adv.* **1.** in a bad manner **2.** [Colloq.] very much; greatly

**bad'man'** *n., pl.* -**men'** a cattle thief or desperado of the old West

**bad·min·ton** (bad'min t'n) *n.* [< *Badminton,* Eng. estate] a game in which a feathered cork is batted back and forth with rackets across a net

**bad'-mouth'** *vt., vi.* [Slang] to find fault (with)

**bad'tem'pered** *adj.* irritable

**Bae·de·ker** (bā'də kər) *n.* **1.** any of a series of guidebooks to foreign countries first published in Germany **2.** loosely, any guidebook

**baf·fle** (baf'l) *vt.* -**fled**, -**fling** [< ?] **1.** to perplex completely; bewilder **2.** to impede; check —*n.* a screen to deflect air, sound, etc. —**baf'fle·ment** *n.* —**baf'fler** *n.* —**baf'fling** *adj.*

**bag** (bag) *n.* [< ON. *baggi*] **1.** a nonrigid container of paper, plastic, etc., with a top opening that can be closed **2.** a satchel, suitcase, etc. **3.** a purse **4.** game taken in hunting **5.** a baglike shape or part **6.** [Slang] an unattractive woman **7.** [Slang] one's special interest **8.** *Baseball* a base —*vt.* **bagged**, **bag'ging** **1.** to make bulge **2.** to capture **3.** to kill in hunting **4.** [Slang] to get —*vi.* **1.** to swell **2.** to hang loosely —**in the bag** [Slang] certain; assured

**bag·a·telle** (bag'ə tel') *n.* [Fr. < L. *baca,* berry] a trifle

**ba·gel** (bā'g'l) *n.* [Yid.] a hard bread roll shaped like a small doughnut

**bag'ful'** *n., pl.* -**fuls'** as much as a bag will hold

**bag·gage** (bag'ij) *n.* [< ML. *baga,* chest, bag] **1.** the bags, etc. of a traveler; luggage **2.** a lively girl

**bag·gy** (bag'ē) *adj.* -**gi·er**, -**gi·est** puffy or hanging loosely, like a bag —**bag'gi·ly** *adv.* —**bag'gi·ness** *n.*

**Bagh·dad** (bag'dad) capital of Iraq: pop. c.1,000,000: also **Bagdad**

**bag'pipe'** *n.* [*often pl.*] a shrill-toned musical instrument, now chiefly Scottish, played by forcing air from a bag into reed pipes and fingering the stops

**bah** (bä, ba) *interj.* an exclamation of contempt, scorn, or disgust

BAGPIPE

**Ba·ha·mas** (bə hä'məz) country on a group of islands (**Bahama Islands**) in the West Indies: 4,404 sq. mi., pop. 185,000

**bail**[1] (bāl) *n.* [< L. *bajulare,* bear a burden] **1.** money deposited with the court to get an arrested person temporarily released **2.** such a release **3.** the person giving bail —*vt.* **1.** to have (an arrested person) set free by giving bail **2.** to help out of financial or other difficulty  Often with *out*—**bail'a·ble** *adj.*

**bail**[2] (bāl) *n.* [ME. *baille,* bucket] a bucket for dipping up water from a boat —*vi.*, *vt.* to, dip out (water) from (a boat): usually with *out* —**bail out** to parachute from an aircraft

**bail²** (bāl) *n.* [ME. *beil*] a hoop-shaped handle for a bucket, etc.

**bail bond** a bond deposited as bail for an arrested person as surety that he will appear at his trial

**bai·liff** (bā'lif) *n.* [ME. *bailif*] 1. a deputy sheriff 2. a court officer who guards the jurors, keeps order in the court, etc. 3. in England, *a*) a district official *b*) a steward of an estate

**bai·li·wick** (bā'lə wik) *n.* [ME. *bailif*, bailiff + *wik*, village] 1. a bailiff's district 2. one's particular area of activity, authority, interest, etc.

**bails·man** (bālz'mən) *n.*, *pl.* -men a person who gives bail for another

**bairn** (bern) *n.* [Scot.] a child

**bait** (bāt) *vt.* [< ON. *beita*, make bite] 1. to set dogs on for sport [to bait bears] 2. to torment or harass, esp. by verbal attacks 3. to put food on (a hook or trap) as a lure for game 4. to lure; tempt; entice —*n.* 1. food, etc. put on a hook or trap as a lure 2. anything used as a lure; enticement

**bait'-and-switch'** *adj.* of or using an unethical sales technique in which a seller lures customers by advertising an often nonexistent bargain item and then tries to switch their attention to more expensive items

**baize** (bāz) *n.* [< L. *badius*, brown] a coarse, feltlike woolen cloth

**bake** (bāk) *vt.* baked, bak'ing [OE. *bacan*] 1. to cook (food) by dry heat, esp. in an oven 2. to dry and harden (pottery) by heat; fire —*vi.* 1. to bake bread, etc. 2. to become baked —*n.* 1. a baking 2. a social affair at which a baked food is served

**bak·er** (bāk'ər) *n.* one whose work or business is baking bread, etc.

**baker's dozen** thirteen

**bak·er·y** (bāk'ər ē) *n.*, *pl.* -ies 1. a place where bread, etc. is baked or sold 2. baked goods

**baking powder** a leavening agent containing baking soda and an acid-forming substance

**baking soda** sodium bicarbonate, used as a leavening agent and as an antacid

**bal·a·lai·ka** (bal'ə lī'kə) *n.* [Russ.] a Russian stringed instrument somewhat like a guitar

**bal·ance** (bal'əns) *n.* [< LL. *bilanx*, having two scales] 1. an instrument for weighing, esp. one with two matched hanging scales 2. a state of equilibrium in weight, value, etc. 3. bodily or mental stability 4. harmonious proportion of elements in a design, etc. 5. a weight, value, etc. that counteracts another 6. equality of debits and credits, or the difference between them 7. a remainder 8. *same as* BALANCE WHEEL —*vt.* -anced, -anc·ing 1. to weigh in or as in a balance 2. to compare as to relative

value, etc. 3. to counteract; offset 4. to bring into proportion, harmony, etc. 5. to make or be equal to in weight, value, etc. 6. to find the difference between, or to equalize, the debits and credits of (an account) —*vi.* 1. to be in equilibrium 2. to be equal in weight, value, etc. 3. to have the credits and debits equal —**in the balance** not yet settled

**balance sheet** a statement showing the financial status of a business

**bal·co·ny** (bal'kə nē) *n.*, *pl.* -nies [ < It. *balcone*] 1. a platform projecting from an upper story and enclosed by a railing 2. an upper floor of seats in a theater, etc., often projecting over the main floor

**bald** (bôld) *adj.* [< ME.] 1. having a head with white fur, etc. growing on it 2. lacking hair on the head 3. not covered by natural growth 4. plain or blunt [bald truth] —**bald'ly** *adv.* —**bald'ness** *n.*

**bald eagle** a large eagle of N. America, with a white-feathered head

**bal·der·dash** (bôl'dər dash') *n.* [orig. (17th c.), an odd mixture] nonsense

**bald'-faced'** (bôld'fāst') *adj.* brazen; shameless [a baldfaced lie]

**bald'ing** *adj.* becoming bald

**bal·dric** (bôl'drik) *n.* [ult. < L. *balteus*, belt] a belt worn over one shoulder to support a sword, etc.

**bale** (bāl) *n.* [< OHG. *balla*, ball] a large bundle, esp. a standardized quantity of goods, as raw cotton compressed and bound —*vt.* baled, bal'ing to make into bales —**bal'er** *n.*

**ba·leen** (bə lēn') *n.* [ult. < Gr. *phallaina*, whale] *same as* WHALEBONE

**bale·ful** (bāl'fəl) *adj.* [< OE. *bealu*, evil] deadly; harmful; ominous

**Ba·li** (bä'lē) island of Indonesia — **Ba'li·nese'** (-lə nēz') *adj.*, *n.*

**balk** (bôk) *n.* [OE. *balca*, ridge] 1. an obstruction, hindrance, etc. 2. a blunder; error 3. *Baseball* an illegal motion by the pitcher entitling base runners to advance one base —*vt.* to obstruct or foil —*vi.* 1. to stop and refuse to move or act 2. to hesitate or recoil (at)

**Bal·kan** (bôl'kən) *adj.* of the Balkans, their people, etc. —**the Balkans** countries of Albania, Bulgaria, Greece, Romania, Yugoslavia, & European Turkey, in SE Europe

**Balkan Peninsula** peninsula in SE Europe, east of Italy

**balk·y** (bôk'ē) *adj.* -i·er, -i·est stubbornly resisting; balking

**ball¹** (bôl) *n.* [ME. *bal*] 1. any round object; sphere; globe 2. *a*) a round or egg-shaped object used in various games *b*) any of several such games, esp. baseball 3. a throw or pitch of a ball [a fast *ball*] 4. a missile for a cannon, rifle, etc. 5. a rounded part of the body 6. *Baseball* a pitched ball that is not hit and is not a strike —*vi.*, *vt.* to form into a ball —**ball up**

[Slang] to muddle; confuse —**on the ball** [Slang] alert; efficient

**ball²** (bôl) *n.* [< Fr. < Gr. *ballizein*, to dance] **1.** a formal social dance **2.** [Slang] a good time

**bal·lad** (bal'əd) *n.* [OFr. *ballade*, dancing song] **1.** a sentimental song with the same melody for each stanza **2.** a narrative song or poem, usually anonymous, with simple words, short stanzas, and a refrain **3.** a slow, sentimental popular song —**bal'lad·eer'** *n.* —**bal'lad·ry** *n.*

**ball-and-sock·et joint** (bôl'ən säk'it) a joint, as of the hip, formed by a ball in a socket

**bal·last** (bal'əst) *n.* [< ODan. *bar*, bare + *last*, a load] **1.** anything heavy carried in a ship or vehicle to give stability **2.** crushed rock or gravel, used in railroad beds, etc. —*vt.* to furnish with ballast

**ball bearing 1.** a bearing in which the parts turn on freely rolling metal balls **2.** one of those balls

**bal·le·ri·na** (bal'ə rē'nə) *n.* [It.] a woman ballet dancer

**bal·let** (bal'ā, ba lā') *n.* [Fr.] **1.** an intricate group dance using pantomime and conventionalized movements to tell a story **2.** ballet dancers

**bal·let·o·mane** (bə let'ə mān') *n.* [Fr.] a person devoted to the ballet

**ballistic missile** a long-range guided missile designed to fall free as it approaches its target

**bal·lis·tics** (bə lis'tiks) *n.pl.* [with *sing. v.*] the science dealing with the motion and impact of projectiles —**bal·lis'tic** *adj.*

**bal·loon** (bə lōōn') *n.* [< Fr. < It. *palla*, ball] **1.** a large, airtight bag that rises when filled with a gas lighter than air **2.** an airship with such a bag **3.** an inflatable rubber bag, used as a toy —*vt.* to inflate —*vi.* to swell; expand —*adj.* like a balloon —**bal·loon'ist** *n.*

**bal·lot** (bal'ət) *n.* [< It. *palla*, ball] **1.** a ticket, paper, etc. by which a vote is registered **2.** act, method, or right of voting, as by ballots **3.** the total number of votes cast —*vi.* to vote

**ball'park'** *n.* a baseball stadium

**ball'play'er** *n.* a baseball player

**ball point pen** a fountain pen with a small ball bearing instead of a point: also **ball'-point', ball'point'** *n.*

**ball'room'** *n.* a large hall for dancing

**bal·lute** (ba lōōt') *n.* [BALL(OON) + (PARACH)UTE] a heat-resistant, balloonlike device inflated by stored gas and used to slow down a spacecraft reentering the atmosphere

**bal·ly·hoo** (bal'ē hōō') *n.* [< ?] noisy talk, sensational advertising, etc. —*vt., vi.* -hooed', -hoo'ing [Colloq.] to promote with ballyhoo

**balm** (bäm) *n.* [< Gr. *balsamon*] **1.** a fragrant, healing ointment or oil **2.** anything healing or soothing

**balm'y** *adj.* -i·er, -i·est **1.** soothing, mild, etc. **2.** [Brit. Slang] crazy

**ba·lo·ney** (bə lō'nē) *n.* [< ? *bologna*] **1.** bologna **2.** [Slang] nonsense

**bal·sa** (bôl'sə) *n.* [Sp.] **1.** the wood, very light in weight, of a tropical American tree **2.** the tree

**bal·sam** (bôl'səm) *n.* [see BALM] **1.** an aromatic resin obtained from certain trees **2.** any of various aromatic resinous oils or fluids **3.** balm **4.** any of various trees yielding balsam

**Bal·tic Sea** (bôl'tik) sea in N Europe, west of the U.S.S.R.

**Bal·ti·more** (bôl'tə môr') seaport in N Md.: pop. 906,000

**bal·us·ter** (bal'əs tər) *n.* [< Gr. *balaustion*, wild pomegranate flower: from the shape] any of the small posts of a railing, as on a staircase

**bal·us·trade** (bal'ə strād') *n.* a railing held up by balusters

**Bal·zac** (bäl zäk'; E. bôl'zak), **Ho·no·ré de** (ô nô rā' də) 1799–1850; Fr. novelist

**bam·boo** (bam bōō') *n.* [Malay *bambu*] a treelike tropical grass with woody, jointed, often hollow stems used for furniture, canes, etc.

**bamboo curtain** [often B- C-] the political and ideological differences that separate China from the West

**bam·boo·zle** (bam bōō'z'l) *vt.* -zled, -zling [< ?] **1.** to trick; cheat; dupe **2.** to confuse; puzzle

**ban** (ban) *vt.* **banned, ban'ning** [OE. *bannan*, summon] to prohibit or forbid, esp. officially —*n.* **1.** a condemnation by church authorities **2.** a curse **3.** an official prohibition **4.** strong public condemnation

**ba·nal** (bā'n'l, bə nal') *adj.* [Fr.: see prec.] trite; hackneyed —**ba·nal'i·ty** *n., pl.* -ties —**ba'nal·ly** *adv.*

**ba·nan·a** (bə nan'ə) *n.* [Sp. & Port.] **1.** a treelike tropical plant with large clusters of edible fruit **2.** the narrow, somewhat curved fruit, having a creamy flesh and a yellow or red skin

**band¹** (band) *n.* [ON.] **1.** something that binds, ties, or encircles, as a strip or ring of wood, rubber, metal, etc. **2.** a strip of color or of material **3.** a division of a long-playing phonograph record **4.** a range of wavelengths or frequencies —*vt.* to put a band on or around

**band²** (band) *n.* [< Fr.; ult. < Goth. *bandwa*, a sign] **1.** a group of people united for some purpose **2.** a group of musicians playing together, esp. upon wind and percussion instruments —*vi., vt.* to unite for some purpose

**band·age** (ban'dij) *n.* [Fr. < *bande*, a strip] a strip of cloth, etc. used to bind or cover an injury —*vt.* -aged, -ag·ing to put a bandage on

**Band-Aid** (band'dād') [BAND(AGE) + AID] *a trademark for* a small prepared bandage of gauze and adhesive tape —*n.* [b-] a bandage of this type: also **band'aid'**

**ban·dan·na, ban·dan·a** (ban dan'ə) *n.* [Hind. *bāndhnū*, method of dyeing] a large, colored handkerchief

**band·box** (band'bäks') *n.* a light box, as of pasteboard, for hats, etc.

**ban·deau** (ban dō') *n., pl.* **-deaux'** (-dōz') [Fr.] **1.** a narrow ribbon **2.** a narrow brassiere

**ban·dit** (ban'dit) *n.* [ < It.] a robber; highwayman —**ban'dit·ry** *n.*

**ban·do·leer, ban·do·lier** (ban'də lir') *n.* [ < Fr.] a broad belt with pockets for bullets, etc., worn over one shoulder and across the chest

**band saw** an endless toothed steel belt on pulleys, powered for sawing

**bands·man** (bandz'mən, banz'-) *n.*, *pl.* **-men** a member of a band of musicians

**band'stand'** *n.* a platform for a band, esp. one for outdoor concerts

**band'wag'on** *n.* a wagon for a band to ride on, as in a parade —**on the bandwagon** [Colloq.] on the popular or apparently winning side

**ban·dy**[1] (ban'dē) *vt.* **-died, -dy·ing** [Fr. *bander*, bandy at tennis] 1. to toss or hit back and forth 2. to pass (rumors, etc.) freely 3. to exchange (words), esp. angrily

**ban·dy**[2] (ban'dē) *adj.* [Fr. *bandé*, bent] curved outward; bowed

**ban'dy-leg'ged** (-leg'id, -legd') *adj.* having bandy legs; bowlegged

**bane** (bān) *n.* [OE. *bana*] 1. ruin, death, harm, or the cause of this 2. poison —**bane'ful** *adj.*

**bang**[1] (baŋ) *vt.* [ON. *banga*, to pound] to hit, shut, etc. hard and noisily —*vi.* 1. to make a loud noise 2. to hit noisily or sharply —*n.* 1. a hard, noisy blow or impact 2. a loud, sudden noise 3. [Colloq.] a burst of vigor 4. [Slang] a thrill —*adv.* 1. hard and noisily 2. abruptly —**bang up to** damage

**bang**[2] (baŋ) *vt.* [ < ?] to cut (hair) short and straight —*n.* [*usually pl.*] banged hair over the forehead

**Bang·kok** (baŋ'käk) seaport and capital of Thailand: pop. 1,669,000

**Ban·gla·desh** (baŋ'glə desh') country in S Asia, on the Bay of Bengal: 55,134 sq. mi.; pop. 50,840,000

**ban·gle** (baŋ'g'l) *n.* [Hind. *bangrī*] a decorative bracelet or anklet

**bang-up** (baŋ'up') *adj.* [Colloq.] very good; excellent

**ban·ish** (ban'ish) *vt.* [ < OFr. *banir*] 1. to exile 2. to drive away; get rid of —**ban'ish·ment** *n.*

**ban·is·ter** (ban'əs tər) *n.* [ < BAL-USTER] [*often pl.*] a handrail, specif. one with balusters

**ban·jo** (ban'jō) *n.*, *pl.* **-jos, -joes** [of Afr. origin] a musical instrument with a long neck, circular body, and strings that are plucked —**ban'jo·ist** *n.*

**bank**[1] (baŋk) *n.* [ult. < OHG. *bank*, bench] 1. an establishment for receiving or lending money 2. a reserve supply; pool —*vt., vi.* to put into a bank —**bank on** [Colloq.] to rely on

**bank**[2] (baŋk) *n.* [ < ON. *bakki*] 1. a long mound or heap 2. a steep slope 3. a rise of land along a river, etc. 4. a shallow place, as in a sea 5. the lateral, slanting turn of an aircraft —*vt.* 1. to cover (a fire) with ashes and fuel so that it will burn slowly 2. to pile up so as to form a bank 3. to slope (a curve in a road, etc.) 4. to make (an aircraft) slant laterally on a turn 5. to make (a billiard ball) recoil from a cushion

**bank**[3] (baŋk) *n.* [ < OFr. *banc*, bench] 1. a row of oars 2. a row or tier, as of keys in a keyboard —*vt.* to arrange in a row or tier

**bank account** money deposited in a bank and credited to the depositor

**bank'book'** *n.* a book recording a bank depositor's deposits; passbook

**bank'er** *n.* a person who owns or manages a bank

**bank'ing** *n.* the business of a bank

**bank note** a promissory note issued by a bank; a form of paper money

**bank'roll'** *n.* a supply of money —*vt.* [Colloq.] to supply with money; finance

**bank·rupt** (baŋk'rupt') *n.* [ < Fr. < It. *banca*, bench + *rotta*, broken] a person legally declared unable to pay his debts —*adj.* 1. that is a bankrupt; insolvent 2. lacking in some quality [morally *bankrupt*] —*vt.* to make bankrupt —**bank'rupt·cy** *n.*

**ban·ner** (ban'ər) *n.* [ME. *banere* < OFr. *baniere*] 1. a flag 2. a headline running across a newspaper page —*adj.* foremost

**banns** (banz) *n.pl.* [see BAN] the proclamation made in church of an intended marriage

**ban·quet** (baŋ'kwit) *n.* [Fr. < It. *banca*, table] 1. a feast 2. a formal dinner —*vt.* to honor with a banquet

**ban·quette** (baŋ ket') *n.* [Fr.] 1. a gunner's platform inside a trench, etc. 2. an upholstered bench

**ban·shee, ban·shie** (ban'shē) *n.* [ < Ir. *bean*, woman + *sith*, fairy] *Ir. & Scot. Folklore* a female spirit whose wailing warns of impending death

**ban·tam** (ban'təm) *n.* [ < *Bantam*, former province in Java] 1. [*often* B-] any of several breeds of small fowl 2. a small, aggressive person —*adj.* like a bantam

**ban'tam·weight'** *n.* a boxer or wrestler weighing 113 to 118 lbs.

**ban·ter** (ban'tər) *vt.* [17th-c. slang] to tease playfully —*vi.* to exchange banter (*with* someone) —*n.* playful teasing —**ban'ter·ing·ly** *adv.*

**Ban·tu** (ban'tōō) *n.*, *pl.* **-tus, -tu** [Bantu *ba-ntu*, mankind] 1. any member of a group of Negroid tribes of equatorial and southern Africa 2. any of the related languages of these peoples

**Ban'tu·stan'** (-stan') *n.* [prec. + Per. *stān*, a place] any of several territories in South Africa, set aside for native black peoples

**ban·yan** (ban'yən) *n.* [ult. < Sans.] an East Indian fig tree whose branches take root and become trunks

**ba·o·bab** (bā'ō bab', bā'-) *n.* [ < native name] a tall tree of Africa and India, with edible gourdlike fruit

---

fat, āpe, cär; ten, ēven; is, bīte; gō, hôrn, tōōl, look; oil, out; up, fur; chin; she; thin, then; zh, leisure; ŋ, ring; ə for *a* in ago; ', (ā'b'l); ë, Fr. coeur; ö, Fr. feu; Fr. mon; ü, Fr. duc; kh, G. ich, doch; ‡ foreign; < derived from

**bap·tism** (bap'tiz'm) n. [see BAPTIZE]
1. the rite of admitting a person into
a Christian church by dipping him in
water or sprinkling water on him 2. an
initiating experience —**bap·tis'mal**
(-tiz'm'l) adj.

**Bap'tist** (-tist) n. a member of a
Protestant denomination practicing
baptism of believers by immersion

**bap'tis·ter·y** (-tis trē) n., pl. -ies a
place, esp. in a church, used for baptiz-
ing: also **bap'tis·try**, pl. -tries

**bap·tize** (bap'tīz, bap tīz') vt. -tized,
-tiz·ing [ < Gr. baptizein, to immerse]
1. to administer baptism to 2. to
initiate 3. to christen

**bar** (bär) n. [ < ML. barra] 1. any
long, narrow piece of wood, metal, etc.,
often used as a barrier, lever, etc. 2. an
oblong piece, as of soap 3. anything
that obstructs or hinders 4. a band or
strip 5. a law court, esp. that part,
enclosed by a railing, where the lawyers sit 6. lawyers collectively 7. the
legal profession 8. a counter, as for
serving alcoholic drinks 9. a place
with such a counter 10. Music a) a
vertical line dividing a staff into measures b) a measure —vt. barred,
**bar'ring** 1. to fasten with a bar 2. to
obstruct; close 3. to oppose 4. to exclude —prep. excluding [the best, bar
none] —**cross the bar** to die

**barb** (bärb) n. [ < L. barba, beard] 1.
a beardlike growth 2. a sharp point
projecting backward from the main
point of a fishhook, etc. 3. a cutting
remark —vt. to provide with a barb
—**barbed** adj.

**Bar·ba·dos** (bär bā'dōz, -dōs) country on an island in the West Indies:
166 sq. mi.; pop. 245,000

**bar·bar·i·an** (bär ber'ē ən) n. [see
BARBAROUS] 1. a member of a people
considered primitive, savage, etc. 2.
a cruel person —adj. uncivilized, cruel,
etc. —**bar·bar'i·an·ism** n.

**bar·bar'ic** (-ber'ik) adj. 1. primitive;
uncivilized 2. wild, crude, etc.

**bar·ba·rism** (bär'bər iz'm) n. 1. a
word or expression that is not standard
2. the state of being primitive or uncivilized 3. a barbarous act or custom

**bar·bar·i·ty** (bär ber'ə tē) n., pl.
-ties 1. cruelty; brutality 2. a bar-
baric taste, manner, etc.

**bar·ba·rize** (bär'bə rīz') vt., vi.
-rized', -riz'ing to make or become
barbarous —**bar'ba·ri·za'tion** n.

**bar·ba·rous** (bär'bər əs) adj. [ < Gr.
barbaros, foreign] 1. uncivilized; primitive 2. crude, coarse, etc. 3. cruel;
brutal —**bar'ba·rous·ly** adv.

**bar·be·cue** (bär'bə kyōō') n. [Sp.
barbacoa] 1. a) a hog, steer, etc.
roasted whole over an open fire b) any
meat broiled on a spit 2. a party,
picnic, or restaurant featuring this
—vt. -cued', -cu'ing to roast or broil
over an open fire, often with a highly
seasoned sauce (**barbecue sauce**)

**barbed wire** wire with barbs at close
intervals: also **barb'wire'** n.

**bar·bel** (bär'b'l) n. [ < L. barba,
beard] a threadlike growth from the
lips or jaws of certain fishes

**bar·bell** (bär'bel') n. [BAR + (DUMB)-
BELL] a metal bar
with weights at-
tached at each end,
used for weight-
lifting exercises:
also **bar bell**

**BARBELL**

**bar·ber** (bär'bər)
n. [see BARB] one
whose work is cut-
ting hair, shaving
beards, etc. —vt.,
vi. to cut the hair
(of), shave, etc.

**bar·ber·ry** (bär'ber'ē) n., pl. -ries
[ < ML. barberis] 1. a spiny shrub
with sour, red berries 2. the berry

**bar·bi·tu·rate** (bär bich'ər it, bär'
bə tyoor'it) n. [ < C.G.] a salt or ester of
a crystalline acid (**barbituric acid**),
used as a sedative

**bar·ca·role, bar·ca·rolle** (bär'kə
rōl') n. [ < Fr. < It.] a Venetian
gondolier song, or music like this

**Bar·ce·lo·na** (bär'sə lō'nə) seaport
in NE Spain: pop. 1,696,000

**bard** (bärd) n. [Gael. & Ir.] 1. an
ancient Celtic poet 2. a poet

**bare** (ber) adj. [OE. bær] 1. not
covered or clothed; naked 2. without
furnishings; empty 3. simple; plain 4.
mere [bare needs] —vt. bared, bar'-
ing to make bare; uncover —**lay bare**
to uncover; expose —**bare'ness** n.

**bare'back'** adv., adj. on a horse with
no saddle

**bare'faced'** adj. 1. with the face
uncovered 2. open; shameless

**bare'foot'** adj., adv. without shoes
and stockings —**bare'foot'ed** adj.

**bare'hand'ed** adj., adv. 1. with
hands uncovered 2. without weapons,
etc.

**bare'head'ed** adj., adv. with the
head uncovered

**bare'leg'ged** (-leg'id, -legd') adj.,
adv. with the legs bare

**bare'ly** adv. 1. plainly 2. only just;
scarcely 3. scantily

**bar·gain** (bär'g'n) n. [ < OFr. bar-
gaignier, haggle] 1. a mutual agreement or contract 2. an agreement with
regard to its worth [a bad bargain] 3.
something sold at a price favorable to
the buyer —vi. 1. to haggle 2. to
make a bargain —**bargain for** (or on)
to expect; count on —**into the bargain** besides —**bar'gain·er** n.

**bargain counter** a store counter for
displaying goods on sale at reduced
prices

**barge** (bärj) n. [ < ML. barga] 1. a
large, flat-bottomed boat for freight
on rivers, etc. 2. a large pleasure boat
—vi. barged, barg'ing 1. to move
slowly and clumsily 2. to enter rudely
or abruptly (in or into)

**bar·i·tone** (bar'ə tōn', ber'-) n. [ <
Gr. barys, deep + tonos, tone] 1. the
range of a male voice between tenor
and bass 2. a singer or instrument
with this range

**bar·i·um** (ber'ē əm) n. [ < Gr. barys,
heavy] a silver-white metallic chemical element

**bark¹** (bärk) n. [ < ON. börkr] the outside covering of trees and woody plants —vt. **1.** to remove bark from (a tree, etc.) **2.** [Colloq.] to scrape; skin (the knees, etc.)

**bark²** (bärk) vi. [OE. *beorcan*] **1.** to make the sharp, abrupt cry of a dog or a similar sound **2.** to speak sharply; snap —n. the characteristic cry of a dog, or any noise like this —**bark up the wrong tree** to misdirect one's attack, energies, etc.

**bark³** (bärk) n. [< L. *barca*] [Poet.] a boat **2.** a sailing vessel with two forward square-rigged masts and a rear mast rigged fore-and-aft: also **barque**

**bar'keep'er** n. **1.** an owner of a barroom **2.** a bartender Also **bar'keep'**

**bark'er** n. one who talks loud to attract customers to a sideshow, etc.

**bar·ley** (bär'lē) n. [OE. *bærlic*] **1.** a cereal grass **2.** its grain, used in making malts, soups, etc.

**bar'maid'** n. a waitress who serves alcoholic drinks in a bar

**bar mitz·vah** (bär mits'və) [< Heb., son of the commandment] [also **B- M-**] **1.** a Jewish boy who has arrived at the age of religious responsibility, 13 years **2.** a ceremony celebrating this —**bat** (or **bas**) **mitzvah** (bät, bäs) fem.

**barn** (bärn) n. [OE. *bern*] a farm building for sheltering harvested crops, livestock, etc.

**bar·na·cle** (bär'nə k'l) n. [Fr. *bernicle*] a saltwater shellfish that attaches itself to rocks, ship bottoms, etc.

**barn·storm** (bärn'stôrm') vi., vt. to tour (the country, esp. rural areas), giving speeches, plays, etc.

**Bar·num** (bär'nəm), **P(hineas) T(aylor)** 1810–91; U.S. showman

**barn'yard'** n. the yard near a barn —adj. of, like, or fit for a barnyard

**ba·rom·e·ter** (bə räm'ə tər) n. [< Gr. *baros*, weight + -METER] **1.** an instrument for measuring atmospheric pressure and thus forecasting weather **2.** anything that marks change —**bar·o·met·ric** (bar'ə met'rik) adj.

**bar·on** (bar'ən, ber'-) n. [ME.] **1.** a member of the lowest rank of British nobility **2.** a magnate —**bar'on·age** n. —**bar'on·ess** n.fem. —**ba·ro·ni·al** (bə rō'nē əl) adj.

**bar'on·et** (-ə nit, -net') n. a man holding the lowest hereditary British title, below a baron —**bar'on·et·cy** n., pl. **-cies**

**ba·roque** (bə rōk') adj. [Fr. < Port. *barroco*, imperfect pearl] **1.** a) very ornate and full of curved lines, as much art and architecture of about 1550–1750 b) full of highly embellished melodies, fugues, etc., as much music of that time **2.** fantastically ornate

**bar·racks** (bar'iks, ber'-) n.pl. [often with sing. v.] [< Sp. *barro*, clay] a building or buildings for housing soldiers

**bar·ra·cu·da** (bar'ə kōō'də, ber'-) n., pl. **-da, -das** [Sp.] a fierce, pikelike fish of tropical seas

**bar·rage** (bə räzh') n. [Fr. < *barrer*, to stop] **1.** a curtain of artillery fire **2.** any prolonged attack —vi., vt. **-raged', -rag'ing** to subject to a barrage

**barred** (bärd) adj. **1.** having bars or stripes **2.** closed off with bars **3.** not allowed

**bar·rel** (bar'əl, ber'-) n. [< ML. *barillus*] **1.** a) a large, cylindrical container with slightly bulging sides and flat ends b) its standard capacity (31 1/2 gal.) **2.** any similar container or cylinder **3.** the straight tube of a gun —vt. **-reled** or **-relled, -rel·ing** or **-rel·ling** to put in barrels —vi. [Slang] to go at high speed

**barrel organ** a mechanical musical instrument played by turning a crank

**bar·ren** (bar'ən, ber'-) adj. [< OFr.] **1.** that cannot bear offspring; sterile **2.** without vegetation **3.** unproductive **4.** boring; dull **5.** devoid (of) —**bar'ren·ness** n.

**bar·rette** (bə ret') n. [Fr.] a bar or clasp for holding a girl's hair in place

**bar·ri·cade** (bar'ə kād', ber'-; also, esp. for v. bar'ə kād') n. [Fr. < It. *barricare*, to fortify] a barrier, esp. one put up hastily for defense —vt. **-cad'ed, -cad'ing** to block with a barricade

**bar·ri·er** (bar'ē ər, ber'-) n. [see BAR] **1.** an obstruction, as a fence **2.** anything that hinders or blocks

**bar·ring** (bär'iŋ) prep. excepting

**bar·ris·ter** (bar'is tər, ber'-) n. [< *bar* (law court)] in England, a lawyer who pleads cases in court

**bar'room'** n. a room with a bar where alcoholic drinks are sold

**bar·row¹** (bar'ō, ber'-) n. [< OE. *beran*, to bear] a handbarrow or wheelbarrow

**bar·row²** (bar'ō, ber'ō) n. [< OE. *beorg*, hill] a heap of earth or rocks over a grave

**Bart.** Baronet

**bar'tend'er** n. a man who serves alcoholic drinks at a bar

**bar·ter** (bär'tər) vi., vt. [< OFr. *barater*] to trade by exchanging (goods) without money —n. a bartering —**bar'ter·er** n.

**Bar·tók** (bär'tôk), **Bé·la** (bā'lä) 1881–1945; Hung. composer

**bar·y·on** (bar'ē än') n. [< Gr. *barys*, heavy + (ELECTR)ON] any of certain heavy atomic particles

**bas·al** (bā's'l) adj. **1.** of or at the base **2.** basic; fundamental

**basal metabolism** the quantity of energy used by any organism at rest

**ba·salt** (bə sôlt', bäs'ôlt) n. [L. *basaltes*] a hard, dark volcanic rock

**base¹** (bās) n. [see BASIS] **1.** the part of a thing that the thing rests on **2.** the most important element or principal ingredient **3.** the part of a word to which affixes are attached **4.** a basis **5.** any of the four goals a baseball player must reach to score a run **6.** a headquarters or a source of supply **7.** *Chem.* a substance that forms a salt when it reacts with an acid —*adj.* forming a base —*vt.* **based, bas′ing 1.** to make a base for **2.** to establish

**base²** (bās) *adj.* [< VL. *bassus*, low] **1.** ignoble; mean **2.** menial **3.** poor in quality **4.** nonprecious *[base metal]* —**base′ly** *adv.* —**base′ness** *n.*

**base′ball′** *n.* **1.** a game played with ball and bat by two opposing teams on a field with four bases forming a diamond **2.** the ball used in this game

**base′board′** *n.* a board or molding at the base of a wall

**base hit** *Baseball* same as HIT (sense 4)

**base′less** *adj.* having no basis in fact; unfounded —**base′less·ness** *n.*

**base line 1.** a line serving as a base **2.** *Baseball* the lane between any two consecutive bases **3.** the back line at each end of a tennis court

**base′man** (-mən) *n., pl.* **-men** *Baseball* an infielder stationed at first, second, or third base

**base′ment** *n.* the story below a main floor and usually below ground

**base on balls** *Baseball* same as WALK

**base pay** the basic rate of pay, not counting overtime pay, etc.

**base runner** *Baseball* a batter who has reached, or is trying to reach, a base

**bash** (bash) *vt.* [echoic] [Colloq.] to hit hard —*n.* [Slang] a party

**bash·ful** (bash′fəl) *adj.* [(A)BASH + -FUL] easily embarrassed; shy —**bash′ful·ly** *adv.* —**bash′ful·ness** *n.*

**bas·ic** (bās′ik) *adj.* **1.** fundamental **2.** *Chem.* alkaline —*n.* a basic principle, factor, etc. —**bas′i·cal·ly** *adv.*

**bas·il** (baz′′l) *n.* [< Gr. *basilikon*] a fragrant herb of the mint family

**ba·sil·i·ca** (bə·sil′i·kə) *n.* [< Gr. *basilikē* (stoa), royal (portico)] **1.** a church with a broad nave, side aisles, and an apse **2.** *R.C.Ch.* a church with special ceremonial rights

**bas·i·lisk** (bas′ə lisk′) *n.* [< Gr. *basileus*, king] a mythical, lizardlike monster whose glance was fatal

**ba·sin** (bās′′n) *n.* [< VL. *bacca*, water vessel] **1.** a wide, shallow container for liquid **2.** its contents **3.** a sink **4.** any large hollow, often with water in it **5.** same as RIVER BASIN

**ba·sis** (bā′sis) *n., pl.* **-ses** (-sēz) [< Gr., a base] **1.** a base or foundation **2.** a principal constituent **3.** a fundamental principle or theory

**bask** (bask) *vi.* [ME. *basken*, wallow] to expose oneself pleasantly to warmth, another's favor, etc.

**bas·ket** (bas′kit) *n.* [ME.] **1.** a container made of interwoven cane, wood strips, etc. **2.** its contents **3.** *Basketball* a) the goal, a round, open, hanging net b) a scoring toss of the ball through it

**bas′ket·ball′** *n.* **1.** a team game played on a floor with a raised basket at either end through which an inflated ball must be tossed **2.** this ball

**basket weave** a weave of fabrics resembling the weave used in basket making

**bas′ket·work′** *n.* work that is woven like a basket

**Basque** (bask) *n.* **1.** a member of a people living in the W Pyrenees **2.** their language —*adj.* of the Basques

**bas-re·lief** (bä′rə lēf′) *n.* [Fr. < It.: see ff. & RELIEF] sculpture with figures projecting only a little from a flat background

**bass¹** (bās) *n.* [< VL. *bassus*, low] **1.** the range of the lowest male voice **2.** a singer or instrument with this range; specif., a double bass **3.** a low, deep sound —*adj.* of, for, or in the range of a bass

**bass²** (bas) *n., pl.* **bass, bass′es** [OE. *bærs*] a spiny-finned food and game fish of fresh or salt water

**bas·set** (bas′it) *n.* [< OFi. bas, low] a hunting hound with a long body, short forelegs, and long, drooping ears

**bas·si·net** (bas′ə net′) *n.* [see BASIN] a basketlike bed for an infant, often hooded and on wheels

**bas·so** (bas′ō, bäs′ō) *n., pl.* **-sos** [It.] a bass voice or singer

**bas·soon** (bə sōon′, ba-) *n.* [< Fr.] a double-reed bass woodwind instrument

**bast** (bast) *n.* [OE. *bæst*] plant fiber used in ropes, mats, etc.

**bas·tard** (bas′tərd) *n.* [< OFr.] an illegitimate child —*adj.* **1.** of illegitimate birth **2.** inferior, sham, etc. —**bas′tard·y** *n., pl.* **-ies**

BASSOON

**bas′tard·ize′** *vt.* **-ized′, -iz′ing 1.** to make, declare, or show to be a bastard **2.** to make corrupt; debase —**bas′tard·i·za′tion** *n.*

**baste¹** (bāst) *vt.* **bast′ed, bast′ing** [< OHG. *bastian*, sew with bast] to sew temporarily with long, loose stitches until properly sewed

**baste²** (bāst) *vt.* **bast′ed, bast′ing** [< OFr. *bassiner*, moisten] to moisten (roasting meat) with drippings, melted butter, etc.

**baste³** (bāst) *vt.* **bast′ed, bast′ing** [ON. *beysta*] **1.** to beat soundly **2.** to attack with words

**bas·tille, bas·tile** (bas tēl′) *n.* [Fr.: see ff.] a prison —the **Bastille** a prison in Paris destroyed (1789) in the French Revolution

**bas·tion** (bas′chən) *n.* [Fr. < It. *bastire*, build] **1.** a projection from a fortification **2.** any strong defense

**bat¹** (bat) *n.* [OE. *batt*] **1.** a stout club **2.** a club to hit the ball in baseball, etc. **3.** a turn at batting *[at bat]* **4.** [Colloq.] a blow —*vt.* **bat′ted, bat′ting** to hit, as with a bat —*vi.* to take a turn at batting

**bat²** (bat) *n.* [< Scand.] a nocturnal, mouselike, flying mammal with a furry body and membranous wings

**bat³** (bat) *vt.* **bat′ted, bat′ting** [see BATTER¹] [Colloq.] to wink —**not bat an eye** not show surprise

**batch** (bach) *n.* [OE. *bacan*, bake]

1. the amount (of bread, etc.) in one baking 2. one set, lot, group, etc.

**bate** (bāt) *vt.* **bat′ed, bat′ing** [ME.] to abate; lessen —**with bated breath** holding the breath, as in fear

**bath** (bath) *n., pl.* **baths** (bathz, baths) [OE. *bæth*] 1. a washing, esp. of the body, in water 2. water, etc. for bathing or for soaking or treating something 3. a bathtub 4. a bathroom 5. a bathhouse (sense 1)

**bathe** (bāth) *vt.* **bathed, bath′ing** [see prec.] 1. to put into a liquid 2. to give a bath to 3. to cover as with liquid —*vi.* 1. to take a bath 2. to soak oneself in something —**bath′er** *n.*

**bath′house′** *n.* 1. a public building for taking baths 2. a building used by bathers for changing clothes

**bathing suit** a garment worn for swimming

**bath′mat′** *n.* a mat used in or next to a bathtub

**ba·thos** (bā′thäs) *n.* [Gr., depth] 1. anticlimax (sense 1) 2. excessive sentimentality 3. triteness —**ba·thet·ic** (bə thet′ik) *adj.*

**bath′robe′** *n.* a loose-fitting robe worn to and from the bath, etc.

**bath′room′** *n.* a room with a bathtub, toilet, etc.

**bath′tub′** *n.* a tub to bathe in

**bath·y·scaph** (bath′ə skaf′) *n.* [< Gr. *bathys*, deep + *skaphē*, boat] a deep-sea diving apparatus for reaching great depths without a cable: also **bath′y·scaphe′** (-skaf′, -skāf′)

**ba·tik** (bə tēk′) *n.* [Malay] cloth with a design made by dyeing only the parts not coated with wax

**ba·tiste** (ba tēst′, bə-) *n.* [Fr.: < supposed original maker, *Baptiste*] a fine, thin cloth of cotton, rayon, etc.

**ba·ton** (bə tän′) *n.* [Fr.] 1. a staff serving as a symbol of office 2. a slender stick used in directing music 3. a metal rod twirled by a drum major

**Bat·on Rouge** (bat′ ′n rōōzh′) capital of La.: pop. 166,000

**ba·tra·chi·an** (bə trā′kē ən) *n.* [< Gr. *batrachos*, frog] an amphibian without a tail; frog or toad

**bat·tal·ion** (bə tal′yən) *n.* [see BATTLE] a tactical military unit forming part of a division

**bat·ten¹** (bat′′n) *n.* [var. of BATON] 1. a sawed strip of wood 2. a strip of wood put over a seam between boards as a fastening or covering —*vt.* to fasten or supply with battens

**bat·ten²** (bat′′n) *vi., vt.* [ON. *batna,* improve] to fatten; thrive

**bat·ten³** (bat′′n) *n.* [< Fr.: see ff.] in a loom, the frame that is moved to press the woof threads into place

**bat·ter¹** (bat′ər) *vt.* [< L. *battuere,* to beat] 1. to strike with blow after blow 2. to injure by pounding, hard wear, or use —*vi.* to pound noisily

**bat·ter²** (bat′ər) *n.* the baseball or cricket player whose turn it is to bat: also, in cricket, **bats′man** (-mən) *n.*

**bat·ter³** (bat′ər) *n.* [see BATTER¹] a flowing mixture of flour, milk, etc., for making cakes, etc.

**battering ram** a heavy beam, etc. to batter down walls, etc.

**bat·ter·y** (bat′ər ē) *n., pl.* **-ies** [see BATTER¹] 1. a battering 2. a set of things used together 3. *Baseball* the pitcher and the catcher 4. *Elec.* a cell or group of cells storing an electrical charge and able to furnish a current 5. *Law* an illegal beating of another person: see ASSAULT AND BATTERY 6. *Mil.* a set of heavy guns

**bat·ting** (bat′iŋ, -′n) *n.* [see BAT¹] cotton or wool fiber wadded in sheets

**bat·tle** (bat′′l) *n.* [< L. *battuere,* to beat] 1. a large-scale fight between armed forces 2. armed fighting 3. any fight or conflict —*vt., vi.* **-tled, -tling** to fight —**give** (or **do**) **battle** to fight

**bat·tle-ax′, bat·tle-axe′** *n.* 1. a heavy ax formerly used as a weapon 2. [Slang] a harsh, domineering woman

**bat·tle·dore** (bat′′l dôr′) *n.* [< ? Pr. *batedor,* beater] a racket used to hit a shuttlecock in a game like badminton

**bat·tle·field′** *n.* the site of a battle

**bat·tle·ment** (-mənt) *n.* [< OFr. *bataillier,* fortify] a low wall atop a tower, etc., with open spaces for shooting

**battle royal** *pl.* **battles royal** 1. a free-for-all 2. a heated dispute

**bat·tle·ship′** *n.* a large armored warship with big guns

**bat·ty** (bat′ē) *adj.* **-ti·er, -ti·est** [< BAT²] [Slang] 1. insane 2. eccentric

**bau·ble** (bô′b′l) *n.* [< L. *bellus,* pretty] a showy trifle; trinket

**baux·ite** (bôk′sīt, bō′zīt) *n.* [Fr. < (*Les*) *Baux,* town in S France] a clay-like ore, the source of aluminum

**Ba·var·i·a** (bə ver′ē ə) state of S West Germany —**Ba·var′i·an** *adj., n.*

**bawd** (bôd) *n.* [ME. *baude*] 1. a woman who keeps a brothel 2. a prostitute

**bawd·ry** (bô′drē) *n.* obscene language

**bawd·y** (bô′dē) *adj.* **-i·er, -i·est** indecent; obscene —**bawd′i·ness** *n.*

**bawl** (bôl) *vi., vt.* [< ML. *baulare,* to bark] 1. to shout 2. to weep loudly —*n.* 1. a shout 2. a noisy weeping —**bawl out** [Slang] to reprimand

**bay¹** (bā) *n.* [< ML. *baia*] a wide inlet of a sea or lake, along the shore

**bay²** (bā) *n.* [< VL. *batare,* gape] 1. an alcove or recess 2. a bay window

**bay³** (bā) *vi.* [< OFr. *baier,* gape] to bark or howl in long, deep tones —*n.* 1. the sound of baying 2. the situation of a hunted animal forced to turn and fight —**at bay** 1. cornered 2. held off —**bring to bay** to corner

**bay⁴** (bā) *n.* [< L. *baca,* berry] 1. the laurel tree 2. [*pl.*] a laurel wreath

**bay⁵** (bā) *adj.* [< L. *badius*] reddish-brown —*n.* 1. reddish brown 2. a horse, etc. of this color

**bay·ber·ry** (bā′ber′ē) *n., pl.* **-ries** 1. a shrub with small, wax-coated berries 2. any of the berries

---

**bay leaf** the aromatic leaf of the laurel, dried and used as a spice in cooking

**bay·o·net** (bā'ə nit, -net') n. [< Fr. < *Bayonne*, city in France] a detachable blade put on a rifle muzzle, for stabbing —vt., vi. -net'ed or -net'ted, -net'ing or -net'ting to stab with a bayonet

**bay·ou** (bī'ōō) n. [< AmInd.] in the southern U.S., a marshy inlet or outlet of a lake, river, etc.

**bay window 1.** a window or set of windows jutting out from a wall **2.** [Slang] a large, protruding belly

**ba·zaar** (bə zär') n. [Per. *bāzār*] **1.** in Oriental countries, a marketplace **2.** a benefit sale of various articles for a club, church, etc.

**ba·zoo·ka** (bə zōōk'ə) n. [< name of a comic horn] a portable weapon for launching armor-piercing rockets

**bbl.** *pl.* **bbls.** barrel

**BB (shot)** [designation of size] a size of shot (diameter, .18 in.) for an air rifle (**BB gun**) or shotgun

**B.C. 1.** Bachelor of Commerce **2.** before Christ **3.** British Columbia

**be** (bē, bi) vi. was or were, been, being [< OE. *beon*] **1.** to exist; live **2.** to happen; occur **3.** to remain or continue *Note:* be is used to link its subject to a predicate complement [he *is* handsome] or as an auxiliary: (1) with a past participle: *a)* to form the passive voice [he will *be* whipped] *b)* to form the perfect tense [Christ *is* risen] (2) with a present participle to express continuation [the player *is* running] (3) with a present participle or infinitive to express futurity, possibility, obligation, intention, etc. [he *is* going next week, she *is* to scrub the floor] *Be* is conjugated, in the present indicative: (I) *am,* (he, she, it) *is,* (we, you, they) *are;* in the past indicative: (I, he, she, it) *was,* (we, you, they) *were* —be off go away

**be-** [< OE. *be,* by] *a prefix meaning:* **1.** around [*beset*] **2.** completely [*bedeck*] **3.** away [*betake*] **4.** about [*bemoan*] **5.** to make [*besot*] **6.** to furnish with, affect by [*becloud*]

**Be** *Chem.* beryllium

**beach** (bēch) n. [E. dial., pebbles] a sandy shore —vt., vi. to ground (a boat) on a beach

**beach'comb'er** (-kō'mər) n. **1.** a long wave rolling ashore **2.** one who lives on what he finds on beaches, etc.

**beach'head'** n. a position gained, specif. by invading an enemy shore

**bea·con** (bēk'n) n. [< OE. *beacen,* a sign] **1.** a light for warning or guiding **2.** a radio transmitter sending guiding signals for aircraft

**bead** (bēd) n. [< OE. *bed,* prayer bead] **1.** a small ball of glass, etc., pierced for stringing **2.** [*pl.*] a string of beads **3.** [*pl.*] a rosary **4.** any small, round object, as the front sight of a rifle **5.** a drop or bubble **6.** the rim edge of a rubber tire —vt. to decorate with beads —**draw a bead on** to take careful aim at —**say** (or **tell** or **count**) one's **beads** to say prayers with a rosary —**bead'y** adj. **-i·er, -i·est**

**bea·dle** (bē'd'l) n. [ME. *bidel*] a minor officer who keeps order in church

**bea·gle** (bē'g'l) n. [< ? Fr. *bégueule,* wide-throat] a small hound with short legs and drooping ears

**beak** (bēk) n. [< L. *beccus*] **1.** a bird's bill **2.** the beaklike mouth part of various insects, fishes, etc. —**beak'-less** adj. —**beak'like'** adj.

**beak·er** (bēk'ər) n. [< L. *bacar,* wine glass] **1.** a goblet **2.** a glass or metal container used by chemists

**beam** (bēm) n. [ME.] **1.** a long, thick piece of wood, metal, etc. **2.** the crossbar of a balance **3.** a ship's breadth at its widest point **4.** a slender shaft of light, etc. **5.** a radiant look, smile, etc. **6.** a steady radio or radar signal for guiding aircraft or ships —vt. **1.** to give out (shafts of light) **2.** to direct (a radio signal, etc.) —vi. **1.** to shine brightly **2.** to smile warmly

**bean** (bēn) n. [ME. *ben*] **1.** a plant of the legume family, bearing kidney-shaped seeds **2.** a seed or pod of such a plant **3.** any beanlike seed [coffee *beans*] **4.** [Slang] the head or brain —vt. [Slang] to hit on the head —**spill the beans** [Colloq.] to tell, a secret —**bean'like'** adj.

**bear¹** (ber) vt. bore, borne or born, bear'ing [< OE. *beran*] **1.** to carry **2.** to have or show **3.** to give birth to **4.** to produce or yield **5.** to support or sustain **6.** to withstand or endure **7.** to need [this bears watching] **8.** to carry or conduct (oneself) **9.** to give [to bear witness] —vi. **1.** to be productive **2.** to lie, point, or move in a given direction **3.** to be relevant to (with on) **4.** to put up patiently (with) —**bear down (on) 1.** to exert pressure or effort (on) **2.** to approach —**bear out** to confirm —**bear up** to endure —**bear'a·ble** adj. —**bear'er** n.

**bear²** (ber) n. [< OE. *bera*] **1.** a large, heavy mammal with shaggy fur and a short tail **2.** [B-] either of two constellations in the Northern Hemisphere (**Great Bear** and **Little Bear**) **3.** one who is clumsy, rude, etc. **4.** one who sells stocks, etc. hoping to buy them back later at a lower price —adj. falling in price —**bear'like'** adj.

**beard** (bird) n. [OE.] **1.** the hair on the chin and cheeks of a man **2.** any beardlike part **3.** an awn —vt. **1.** to face boldly **2.** to provide with a beard —**beard'ed** adj. —**beard'less** adj.

**bear·ing** (ber'iŋ) n. **1.** way of carrying and conducting oneself **2.** a supporting part **3.** a producing or ability to produce **4.** endurance **5.** [*often pl.*] relative direction or position **6.** [*pl.*] awareness of one's situation **7.** relation; relevance **8.** a part of a machine on which another part revolves, slides, etc.

**bear·ish** adj. **1.** bearlike; rude, rough, etc. **2.** dropping, or causing a drop, in price on the stock exchange —**bear'-ish·ly** adv.

**bear'skin'** n. **1.** the fur or hide of a bear **2.** a rug, coat, etc. made from this

**beast** (bēst) *n.* [< L. *bestia*] 1. any large, four-footed animal 2. one who is brutal, gross, etc.

**beast'ly** *adj.* -li·er, -li·est 1. of or like a beast; brutal, etc. 2. [Colloq.] disagreeable; unpleasant —**beast'li-ness** *n.*

**beast of burden** any animal used for carrying things

**beast of prey** any animal that hunts and kills other animals for food

**beat** (bēt) *vt.* **beat, beat'en, beat'ing** [< OE. *beatan*] 1. to hit repeatedly; pound 2. to punish by so hitting; whip, spank, etc. 3. to dash repeatedly against 4. *a)* to form (a path, way, etc.) by repeated treading or riding *b)* to keep walking on [to *beat* the pavements] 5. to mix (eggs, etc.) by hard stirring 6. to move (esp. wings) up and down 7. to search through (a forest, etc.) 8. to defeat or outdo 9. to mark (time or rhythm) by tapping, etc. 10. [Colloq.] to puzzle 11. [Colloq.] to cheat 12. [Slang] to escape the penalties of —*vi.* 1. to hit, dash, etc. repeatedly 2. to throb —*n.* 1. a beating, as of the heart 2. any of a series of strokes 3. a throb 4. a habitual route 5. the unit of musical rhythm 6. *same as* BEATNIK —*adj.* 1. [Slang] tired out 2. of a group of young persons, esp. of the 1950's, expressing social disillusionment by unconventional dress, actions, etc. —**beat down** to put or force down —**beat it!** [Slang] go away! —**beat off** to drive back —**beat up (on)** [Slang] to give a beating to —**beat'er** *n.* —**beat'nik** *n.*

**be·a·tif·ic** (bē'ə tif'ik) *adj.* 1. making blessed 2. full of bliss

**be·at·i·fy** (bē at'ə fī') *vt.* -fied', -fy'ing [< L. *beatus*, happy + *facere*, make] 1. to make blissfully happy 2. *R.C.Ch.* to declare one who has died to be among the blessed in heaven —**be·at'i·fi·ca'tion** *n.*

**beat'ing** *n.* 1. the act of one that beats 2. a whipping 3. a throbbing 4. a defeat

**be·at·i·tude** (bē at'ə tōōd') *n.* [< L. *beatus*, happy] perfect blessedness or happiness —**the Beatitudes** the pronouncements in the Sermon on the Mount

**beat'-up'** *adj.* [Slang] worn-out, battered, dilapidated, etc.

**beau** (bō) *n.*, *pl.* **beaus, beaux** (bōz) [Fr. < L. *bellus*, pretty] a woman's sweetheart

**Beau·mont** (bō'mänt) city in SE Tex.: pop. 119,000

**beau·te·ous** (byōōt'ē əs) *adj.* beautiful —**beau'te·ous·ly** *adv.*

**beau·ti·cian** (byōō tish'ən) *n.* one who works in a beauty shop

**beau·ti·ful** (byōōt'ə fəl) *adj.* having beauty —**beau'ti·ful·ly** *adv.*

**beau·ti·fy** (-fī') *vt.*, *vi.* -fied', -fy'ing to make or become beautiful —**beau'ti·fi·ca'tion** (-fi kā'shən) *n.* —**beau'ti·fi'er** *n.*

**beau·ty** (byōōt'ē) *n.*, *pl.* -ties [< L. *bellus*, pretty] 1. the quality of being very pleasing, as in form, color, etc. 2. a thing with this quality 3. good looks 4. a very good-looking woman

**beauty shop** (or **salon** or **parlor**) a place where women go for hair styling, manicuring, etc.

**bea·ver** (bē'vər) *n.* [OE. *beofor*] 1. *a)* a large, amphibious rodent with soft, brown fur, webbed hind feet, and a broad tail *b)* its fur 2. a man's high silk hat

BEAVER

**be·calm** (bi käm') *vt.* 1. to make calm 2. to make (a ship) motionless from lack of wind

**be·cause** (bi kôz') *conj.* [ME. *bi*, by + *cause*] for the reason or cause that —**because of** on account of

**beck** (bek) *n.* a beckoning gesture —**at the beck and call of** obedient to the wishes of

**beck·on** (bek''n) *vi.*, *vt.* [< OE. *beacen*, a sign] 1. to summon by a gesture 2. to lure; entice

**be·cloud** (bi kloud') *vt.* 1. to cloud over 2. to muddle

**be·come** (bi kum') *vi.* -came' (-kām'), -come', -com'ing [OE. *becuman*] to come or grow to be —*vt.* to suit; befit —**become of** to happen to

**be·com'ing** *adj.* 1. appropriate; seemly 2. suitable to the wearer

**bed** (bed) *n.* [OE.] 1. a piece of furniture for sleeping on 2. a plot of soil where plants are raised 3. the bottom of a river, lake, etc. 4. any flat surface used as a foundation 5. a stratum —*vt.* **bed'ded, bed'ding** 1. to put to bed 2. to embed 3. to plant in a bed of earth 4. to arrange in layers —*vi.* 1. to go to bed; rest; sleep 2. to stratify

**be·daz·zle** (bi daz''l) *vt.* -zled, -zling to dazzle thoroughly; bewilder

**bed'bug'** *n.* a small, wingless, biting insect that infests beds, etc.

**bed'clothes'** (-klōz', -klōthz') *n.pl.* sheets, blankets, etc., for a bed

**bed'cov'er** *n.* a coverlet; bedspread

**bed'ding** (-iŋ) *n.* 1. mattresses and bedclothes 2. a bottom layer; base

**be·deck** (bi dek') *vt.* to adorn

**be·dev·il** (bi dev''l) *vt.* -iled or -illed, -il·ing or -il·ling to plague or bewilder —**be·dev'il·ment** *n.*

**bed'fast'** *adj.* *same as* BEDRIDDEN

**bed'fel'low** *n.* 1. a person who shares one's bed 2. any associate

**be·dim** (bi dim') *vt.* -dimmed', -dim'ming to make (the eyes or vision) dim

**bed jacket** a woman's short jacket sometimes worn in bed over a nightgown

**bed·lam** (bed'ləm) *n.* [< (the old London mental hospital of St. Mary of) *Bethlehem*] any place or situation of noise and confusion

**bed of roses** [Colloq.] a situation or position of ease and luxury

**Bed·ou·in** (bed′oo win) *n., pl.* **-ins,** **-in** [< Ar. *badāwīn,* desert dwellers] [*also* b-] **1.** an Arab of the desert tribes of Arabia, Syria, or North Africa **2.** any wanderer

**bed′pan′** *n.* a shallow pan used as a toilet by one who is bedridden

**be·drag·gle** (bi drag′'l) *vt.* **-gled,** **-gling** to make wet, limp, and dirty, as by dragging through mire

**bed′rid·den** (-rid′'n) *adj.* confined to bed by illness, infirmity, etc.

**bed′rock′** *n.* **1.** solid rock underlying soil, etc. **2.** the base or bottom

**bed′roll′** *n.* a portable roll of bedding, used esp. by campers

**bed′room′** *n.* a room for sleeping

**bed′side′** *n.* the space beside a bed —*adj.* near a bed

**bed′sore′** *n.* a body sore on a bed-ridden person, caused by chafing

**bed′spread′** *n.* an ornamental cover spread over the blanket on a bed

**bed′stead′** (-sted′) *n.* a framework for the spring and mattress of a bed

**bed′time′** *n.* the time when one usually goes to bed

**bee¹** (bē) *n.* [OE. *beo*] a broad-bodied, four-winged, hairy insect that gathers pollen and nectar and that can sting

**bee²** (bē) *n.* [< OE. *ben,* service] a meeting of people to work together or to compete

**beech** (bēch) *n.* [< OE. *bece*] **1.** a tree with smooth, gray bark, hard wood, and edible nuts **2.** its wood

**beech′nut′** *n.* the small, three-cornered nut of the beech tree

**beef** (bēf) *n., pl.* **beeves** (bēvz); also, and for 3 always, **beefs** [< L. *bos,* ox] **1.** *a)* a full-grown ox, cow, bull, or steer, esp. one bred for meat *b)* these animals, collectively *c)* their meat **2.** [Colloq.] brawn **3.** [Slang] a complaint —*vi.* [Slang] to complain —**beef up** to reinforce

**beef′cake′** *n.* [BEEF (*n.* 2) + (CHEESE)-CAKE] [Slang] photographic display of the figure of a nude, or partly nude, muscular man

**beef′eat′er** *n.* **1.** a person who eats beef **2.** a guard at the Tower of London **3.** [Slang] an Englishman

**beef′steak′** (-stāk′) *n.* a thick cut of beef for broiling or frying

**beef′y** *adj.* **-i·er, -i·est** brawny — **beef′i·ness** *n.*

**bee′hive′** *n.* **1.** a hive for bees **2.** a place of great activity

**bee′keep′er** *n.* one who keeps bees for producing honey —**bee′keep′ing** *n.*

**bee′line′** *n.* a straight line or route from one place to another

**Be·el·ze·bub** (bē el′zə bub′) *Bible* the chief devil; Satan

**been** (bin, ben; *Brit.* bēn) *pp.* of BE

**beep** (bēp) *n.* [echoic] the brief, high-pitched sound of a horn or electronic signal —*vi., vt.* to make or cause to make this sound

**beer** (bir) *n.* [OE. *beor*] **1.** an alcoholic, fermented drink made from malt and

hops **2.** a soft drink made from extracts of roots, etc. [*ginger beer*]

**bees′wax′** *n.* wax secreted by honey-bees, used to make their honeycombs

**beet** (bēt) *n.* [< L. *beta*] **1.** a plant with a thick, fleshy, red or white root **2.** the edible root, also a source of sugar

**Bee·tho·ven** (bā′tō vən), **Lud·wig van** (loot′vikh vän) 1770–1827; Ger. composer

**bee·tle¹** (bēt′'l) *n.* [< OE. *bitan,* to bite] an insect with hard front wings that cover the membranous hind wings when these are folded

**bee·tle²** *n.* [OE. *betel*] a heavy mallet or pestle, usually wooden

**bee·tle³** (bēt′'l) *vi.* **-tled, -tling** [prob. < ff.¹ to overhang —*adj.* over-hanging: also **bee′tling**

**bee′tle-browed′** (-broud′) *adj.* [< ME. < ? *bitel,* sharp + *brouwe,* brow] **1.** having bushy eyebrows **2.** frowning

**be·fall** (bi fôl′) *vi., vt.* **-fell′, -fall′en, -fall′ing** [< OE. *be-* + *feallan,* fall] to happen or occur (to)

**be·fit** (bi fit′) *vt.* **-fit′ted, -fit′ting** to be suitable or proper for; be suited to —**be·fit′ting** *adj.*

**be·fog** (bi fôg′, -fäg′) *vt.* **-fogged′, -fog′ging 1.** to envelop in fog; make foggy **2.** to obscure; confuse

**be·fore** (bi fôr′) *adv.* [< OE. *be-,* by + *foran,* before] **1.** in front **2.** previously **3.** earlier; sooner —*prep.* **1.** ahead of **2.** in front of **3.** in or to the sight, presence, notice, etc. of **4.** earlier than **5.** in preference to —*conj.* **1.** earlier than the time that [*call before you go*] **2.** rather than [*I'd die before I'd tell*]

**be·fore′hand′** (-hand′) *adv., adj.* ahead of time; in anticipation

**be·foul** (bi foul′) *vt.* **1.** to make filthy; soil **2.** to cast aspersions on

**be·friend** (bi frend′) *vt.* to act as a friend to help

**be·fud·dle** (bi fud′'l) *vt.* **-dled, -dling** to confuse or stupefy

**beg** (beg) *vt., vi.* **begged, beg′ging** [ME. *beggen*] **1.** to ask for (alms) **2.** to ask earnestly; entreat —**beg off** to ask to be released from —**go begging** to be available but unwanted

**be·gan** (bi gan′) *pt.* of BEGIN

**be·get** (bi get′) *vt.* **-got′** or archaic **-gat′** (-gat′), **-got′ten** or **-got′, -get′ting** [< OE. *begitan,* acquire] **1.** to become the father of **2.** to cause

**beg·gar** (beg′ər) *n.* **1.** one who begs **2.** a pauper —*vt.* **1.** to impoverish **2.** to make (description, etc.) seem inadequate —**beg′gar·y** *n.*

**beg′gar·ly** *adj.* very poor, worthless, inadequate, etc. —**beg′gar·li·ness** *n.*

**be·gin** (bi gin′) *vi., vt.* **-gan′, -gun′, -gin′ning** [< OE. *beginnan*] **1.** to start doing, acting, etc. **2.** to originate

**be·gin′ner** *n.* one who is just beginning to do or learn something; novice

**be·gin′ning** *n.* **1.** a starting **2.** the time or place of starting; origin **3.** the first part or [*pl.*] early stages

**be·gone** (bi gôn′) *interj., vi.* (to) be gone; go away; get out

**be·gon·ia** (bi gōn′yə) *n.* [after M. *Bégon* (1638–1710), Fr. patron of science] a tropical plant with showy flowers and ornamental leaves

**be·got** (bi gät′) *pt. & alt. pp.* of BEGET

**be·got·ten** (-′n) *alt. pp.* of BEGET

**be·grime** (bi grīm′) *vt.* -grimed′, -grim′ing to cover with grime; soil

**be·grudge** (bi gruj′) *vt.* -grudged′, -grudg′ing 1. to resent another's possession (of something) 2. to give with reluctance —**be·grudg′ing·ly** *adv.*

**be·guile** (bi gīl′) *vt.* -guiled′, -guil′ing 1. to mislead or deprive (of) by guile; deceive 2. to pass (time) pleasantly 3. to charm or delight — **be·guile′ment** *n.* —**be·guil′er** *n.*

**be·gun** (bi gun′) *pp.* of BEGIN

**be·half** (bi haf′) *n.* [ < OE. *be*, by + *healf*, side] support —**in** (or **on**) **behalf of** in the interest of; for

**be·have** (bi hāv′) *vt., vi.* -haved′, -hav′ing [see BE- & HAVE] 1. to conduct (oneself) in a specified way 2. to conduct (oneself) properly

**be·hav·ior** (-yər) *n.* way of behaving; conduct or action —**be·hav′ior·al** *adj.*

**behavioral science** any of the sciences, as sociology or psychology, that study human behavior

**be·head** (bi hed′) *vt.* to cut off the head of

**be·held** (-held′) *pt. & pp.* of BEHOLD

**be·he·moth** (bi hē′məth, bē′ə-) *n.* [ < Heb.] 1. *Bible* some huge animal 2. any huge or powerful animal or thing

**be·hest** (bi hest′) *n.* [ < OE. *behæs*, a vow] a command or earnest request

**be·hind** (bi hīnd′) *adv.* [ < OE. *behindan*] 1. in or to the rear 2. in a former time, place, etc. 3. in or into arrears 4. slow; late —*prep.* 1. in or to the rear of 2. inferior to 3. later than [*behind* schedule] 4. beyond [*behind* the hill] 5. advocating [he is *behind* the plan] 6. hidden by [what's *behind* his smile?] —*n.* [Colloq.] the buttocks

**be·hind′hand′** (-hand′) *adv., adj.* late in payment, time, or progress

**be·hold** (bi hōld′) *vt.* -held′, -held′ or archaic -hold′en, -hold′ing [ < OE. *bihealdan*] to look at; see —*interj.* look! see! —**be·hold′er** *n.*

**be·hold·en** (-ən) *adj.* indebted

**be·hoove** (bi hoov′) *vt.* -hooved′, -hoov′ing [ < OE. *behofian*, to need] to be incumbent upon or proper for [it *behooves* you to go]

**beige** (bāzh) *n.* [Fr.] grayish tan —*adj.* grayish-tan

**be·ing** (bē′iŋ) *n.* [see BE] 1. existence; life 2. fundamental nature 3. one that lives or exists —**being as** (or **that**) [Dial. or Colloq.] since; because —**for the time being** for now

**Bei·rut** (bā root′) seaport and capital of Lebanon: pop. c.500,000

**be·jew·el** (bi joo′əl) *vt.* -eled or -elled, -el·ing or -el·ling to decorate with or as with jewels

**be·la·bor** (bi lā′bər) *vt.* 1. to beat

severely 2. to attack verbally 3. to labor (a point, etc.): popular usage

**be·lat·ed** (bi lāt′id) *adj.* tardy — **be·lat′ed·ly** *adv.*

**be·lay** (bi lā′) *vt., vi.* -layed′ -lay′-ing [ < OE. *belecgan*, make fast] 1. to make (a rope) secure by winding around a cleat, etc. 2. to secure by a rope 3. [Naut. Colloq.] to hold; stop

**bel can·to** (bel′ kän′tō) [It.] a style of singing with brilliant vocal display and purity of tone

**belch** (belch) *vi., vt.* [OE. *bealcian*] 1. to expel (gas) through the mouth from the stomach 2. to throw forth violently [the volcano *belched* flame] —*n.* a belching

**be·lea·guer** (bi lē′gər) *vt.* [ < Du. < *be-*, by + *leger*, a camp] 1. to besiege by encircling 2. to beset or harass

**Bel·fast** (bel′fast) seaport & capital of Northern Ireland: pop. 410,000

**bel·fry** (bel′frē) *n., pl.* -fries [ult. < OHG.] 1. a bell tower 2. the part of a tower that holds the bell(s)

**Belg.** 1. Belgian 2. Belgium

**Bel·gium** (bel′jəm) kingdom in W Europe: 11,779 sq. mi.; pop. 9,499,000 —**Bel′gian** (-jən) *adj., n.*

**Bel·grade** (bel′grād, -grād′) capital of Yugoslavia: pop. 598,000

**be·lie** (bi lī′) *vt.* -lied′, -ly′ing 1. to disguise or misrepresent 2. to leave unfulfilled 3. to prove false

**be·lief** (bə lēf′) *n.* [ < OE. *geleafa*] 1. conviction that certain things are true 2. religious faith 3. trust or confidence 4. creed or doctrine 5. an opinion; expectation; judgment

**be·lieve** (bə lēv′) *vt.* -lieved′, -liev′-ing [ < OE. *geliefan*] 1. to take as true, real, etc. 2. to trust a statement or promise of (a person) 3. to suppose or think —*vi.* to have faith (*in*) —**be·liev′a·ble** *adj.* —**be·liev′er** *n.*

**be·lit·tle** (bi lit′′l) *vt.* -tled, -tling to make seem little, less important, etc. —**be·lit′tle·ment** *n.*

**bell** (bel) *n.* [OE. *belle*] 1. a hollow, cuplike object, as of metal, which rings when struck 2. the sound of a bell 3. anything shaped like a bell 4. *Naut.* a bell rung to mark the periods of the watch —*vt.* to attach a bell to —*vi.* to become bell-shaped

**Bell** (bel), **Alexander Gra·ham** (grā′əm) 1847–1922; U.S. inventor of the telephone, born in Scotland

**bel·la·don·na** (bel′ə dän′ə) *n.* [ < It., beautiful lady: from cosmetic use] 1. a poisonous plant of the nightshade family: source of atropine 2. atropine

**bell′-bot′tom** *adj.* flared at the ankles, as trousers or slacks

**bell′boy′** *n.* a boy or man employed by a hotel, etc. to carry luggage and do errands: also **bell′hop′**

**belle** (bel) *n.* [Fr., fem. of BEAU] a pretty woman or girl

**belles-let·tres** (bel let′rə) *n.pl.* [Fr.] nontechnical literature, as fiction, poetry, drama, etc.

**bel·li·cose** (bel'ə kōs') *adj.* [< L. *bellicus*, of war] quarrelsome; warlike —**bel·li·cos'i·ty** (-käs'ə tē) *n.*

**bel·lig·er·ent** (bə lij'ər ənt) *adj.* [< L. *bellum*, war + *gerere*, carry on] 1. at war 2. of war 3. warlike 4. ready to fight or quarrel —*n.* a belligerent person, group, or nation —**bel·lig'er·ence**, **bel·lig'er·en·cy** *n.* —**bel·lig'er·ent·ly** *adv.*

**bell jar** (or **glass**) a bell-shaped container made of glass, used to keep air, moisture, etc. in or out

**bel·low** (bel'ō) *vi* [< OE. *bylgan*] 1. to roar with a reverberating sound, as a bull 2. to cry out loudly, as in anger —*vt.* to utter loudly or powerfully —*n.* a bellowing sound

**Bel·low** (bel'ō), **Saul** 1915– ; U.S. novelist

**bel·lows** (bel'ōz) *n. sing. & pl.* [see BELLY] 1. a device that puffs out air by compression of its collapsible sides: used for blowing fires, in pipe organs, etc. 2. anything collapsible like a bellows

**bells** (belz) *n.pl.* [Colloq.] bell-bottom trousers

**bell·weth·er** (bel'we*th*'ər) *n.* 1. a male sheep, usually wearing a bell, that leads the flock 2. a leader

BELLOWS

**bel·ly** (bel'ē) *n., pl.* **-lies** [< OE. *belg*, leather bag] 1. the part of the body between the chest and thighs; abdomen 2. the stomach 3. the underside of an animal's body 4. the deep interior, as of a ship —*vt., vi.* **-lied**, **-ly·ing** to swell out

**bel'ly·ache'** (-āk') *n.* pain in the abdomen —*vi.* **-ached'**, **-ach'ing** [Slang] to complain

**bel'ly·but·ton** (-but''n) *n.* [Colloq.] the navel: also **belly button**

**bel'ly·ful'** *n.* 1. more than enough to eat 2. [Slang] all that one can bear

**belly laugh** [Colloq.] a hearty laugh

**be·long** (bi lôŋ') *vi.* [< ME.] 1. to have a proper place [*it belongs here*] 2. to be related (*to*) 3. to be a member (with *to*) 4. to be owned (with *to*)

**be·long'ings** *n.pl.* possessions

**be·lov·ed** (bi luv'id, -luvd') *adj.* dearly loved —*n.* a dearly loved person

**be·low** (bi lō') *adv., adj.* [see BE- & LOW] 1. in or to a lower place; beneath 2. later (in a book, etc.) 3. in or to hell 4. on earth 5. under in rank, amount, etc. —*prep.* 1. lower than 2. unworthy of

**Bel·shaz·zar** (bel shaz'ər) *Bible* the last king of Babylon

**belt** (belt) *n.* [< L. *balteus*] 1. a band of leather, etc. worn around the waist 2. any encircling thing like this 3. an endless band, as for transferring motion or conveying 4. a distinctive area [the corn *belt*] 5. [Slang] a hard blow; punch 6. [Slang] *a*) a gulp of liquor *b*) a thrill —*vt.* 1. to encircle or fasten with a belt 2. *a*) to hit with a belt *b*) [Slang] to hit hard 3. [Colloq.] to *sing* loudly (usually with *out*) 4. [Slang] to gulp (liquor)

**belt'way'** *n.* an expressway passing around an urban area

**be·mire** (bi mīr') *vt.* **-mired'**, **-mir'ing** 1. to make dirty as with mire or mud 2. to cause to bog down in mud

**be·moan** (bi mōn') *vt., vi.* to lament

**be·muse** (bi myōoz') *vt.* **-mused'**, **-mus'ing** [BE- + MUSE] 1. to muddle 2. to preoccupy

**bench** (bench) *n.* [OE. *benc*] 1. a long, hard seat 2. *same as* WORKBENCH 3. the place where judges sit in a court 4. [*sometimes* B-] *a*) the status of a judge *b*) judges collectively *c*) a law court —*vt. Sports* to take (a player) out of a game —**on the bench** 1. serving as a judge 2. *Sports* not taking part in the game

**bench warrant** an order issued by a judge or law court for the arrest of a person

**bend**[1] (bend) *vt.* **bent**, **bend'ing** [< OE. *bendan*, to bind] 1. to make curved or crooked 2. to turn, esp. from a straight line 3. to make submit —*vi.* 1. to turn, esp. from a straight line 2. to yield by curving, as from pressure 3. to curve the body; stoop (*over* or *down*) 4. to give in; yield [he *bent* to her wishes] —*n.* 1. a bending or being bent 2. a bent part —**bend'a·ble** *adj.*

**bend**[2] (bend) *n.* [ME. < prec.] any of various knots for tying rope

**be·neath** (bi nēth') *adv., adj.* [OE. *beneothan*] in a lower place; below; underneath —*prep.* 1. below 2. underneath 3. unworthy of [*beneath* scorn]

**ben·e·dic·tion** (ben'ə dik'shən) *n.* [< L. *bene*, well + *dicere*, speak] 1. a blessing 2. invocation of a blessing, esp. at the end of a church service

**ben·e·fac·tion** (ben'ə fak'shən) *n.* [< L. *bene*, well + *facere*, do] 1. the act of helping, esp. by charitable gifts 2. the money or help given

**ben·e·fac·tor** (ben'ə fak'tər) *n.* one who has given help, esp. financially; patron —**ben'e·fac'tress** *n.fem.*

**ben·e·fice** (ben'ə fis) *n.* [see BENEFACTION] an endowed church office providing a living for a vicar, etc.

**be·nef·i·cence** (bə nef'ə s'ns) *n.* [see BENEFACTION] 1. a being kind 2. a charitable act or gift

**be·nef'i·cent** (-s'nt) *adj.* showing beneficence; doing or resulting in good —**be·nef'i·cent·ly** *adv.*

**ben·e·fi·cial** (ben'ə fish'əl) *adj.* producing benefits; advantageous; favorable —**ben'e·fi'cial·ly** *adv.*

**ben'e·fi·ci·ar'y** (-fish'ē er'ē, -fish'ər ē) *n., pl.* **-ar'ies** 1. anyone receiving benefit 2. a person named to receive an inheritance, income from an insurance policy, etc.

**ben·e·fit** (ben'ə fit) *n.* [see BENEFACTION] 1. anything contributing to improvement; advantage 2. [*often pl.*] payments made by an insurance company, public agency, etc., as during sickness or retirement or for death 3. a public performance, bazaar, etc. the proceeds of which are to help some person or cause —*vt.* **-fit·ed**, **-fit'ing**

to help; aid —vi. to receive advantage; profit

**be·nev·o·lence** (bə nevʹə ləns) n. [< L. bene, well + volere, to wish] 1. an inclination to do good; kindness 2. a kindly, charitable act —**be·nevʹo·lent** adj. —**be·nevʹo·lent·ly** adv.

**Ben·gal** (ben gôlʹ), Bay of part of the Indian Ocean, east of India

**be·night·ed** (bi nītʹid) adj. 1. surrounded by darkness 2. ignorant

**be·nign** (bi nīnʹ) adj. [< L. bene, well + genus, birth] 1. good-natured; kindly 2. favorable; beneficial 3. Med. not malignant —**be·nignʹly** adv.

**be·nig·nant** (bi nigʹnənt) adj. [< prec.] 1. kindly or gracious 2. favorable; beneficial

**be·nig·ni·ty** (-nə tē) n., pl. -ties 1. kindliness 2. a kind act

**ben·i·son** (benʹə zʹn, -sʹn) n. [< L.: see BENEDICTION] a blessing

**ben·ny** (benʹē) n., pl. -nies [Slang] an amphetamine pill, esp. Benzedrine

**bent** (bent) pt. and pp. of BEND¹ —adj. 1. curved or crooked 2. strongly determined (with on) —n. 1. a tendency 2. a mental leaning; propensity

**bent·grass** (bentʹgrasʹ) n. [OE. beonot] a low-growing grass that spreads by putting out runners, used for lawns

**bentʹwoodʹ** adj. made of pieces of wood permanently bent [bentwood furniture]

**be·numb** (bi numʹ) vt. 1. to make numb 2. to deaden the mind, will, etc. of

**Ben·ze·drine** (benʹzə drēnʹ) a trademark for AMPHETAMINE —n. [b-] this drug

**ben·zene** (benʹzēn) n. [< BENZOIN] a flammable liquid obtained from coal tar and used as a solvent, in dyes, etc.

**ben·zine** (benʹzēn) n. [< BENZOIN] a flammable liquid obtained from petroleum and used as a motor fuel, in dry cleaning, etc.

**ben·zo·ate** (benʹzō ātʹ) n. a salt or ester of benzoic acid

**ben·zo·caine** (-kānʹ) n. [< BENZO(IN) + (CO)CAINE] a white powder used in ointments and to protect against sunburn

**ben·zo·ic acid** (ben zōʹik) [< ff.] a crystalline acid used as an antiseptic and preservative

**ben·zo·in** (benʹzō in) n. [< Ar. lubān jāwi, incense of Java] a resin from certain tropical Asiatic trees, used in medicine, perfumes, etc.

**ben·zol** (benʹzōl, -zōl) n. same as BENZENE

**be·queath** (bi kwēthʹ, -kwēthʹ) vt. [< OE. be- + cwethan, say] 1. to leave (property, etc.) to another by one's will 2. to hand down; pass on

**be·quest** (-kwestʹ) n. 1. a bequeathing 2. anything bequeathed

**be·rate** (bi rātʹ) vt. -ratʹed, -ratʹing [BE- + RATE²] to scold severely

**Ber·ber** (burʹbər) n. 1. any of a Moslem people living in N Africa 2.

their language —adj. of the Berbers

**be·reave** (bi rēvʹ) vt. -reavedʹ or -reftʹ (-reftʹ), -reavʹing [< OE. be- + reafian, rob] 1. to deprive: now usually in the pp. (bereft [bereft of hope] 2. to leave in a sad or lonely state, as by death —**be·reaveʹment** n.

**be·ret** (bə rāʹ) n. [< Fr. < L. birrus, a hood] a flat, round, soft cap

**berg** (burg) n. same as ICEBERG

**ber·i·ber·i** (berʹē berʹē) n. [Sinhalese beri, weakness] a disease caused by lack of vitamin B₁ and characterized by nerve disorders, edema, etc.

**Ber·ing Sea** (berʹiŋ) part of the Pacific, between Siberia & Alaska

**Bering Strait** strait joining the Bering Sea with the Arctic Ocean

**Berke·ley** (burkʹlē) city in Calif., near San Francisco: pop. 117,000

**Ber·lin** (bər linʹ) city in E Germany: see EAST BERLIN & WEST BERLIN

**berm, berme** (burm) n. [< MDu. baerm] a ledge or shoulder, as along the edge of a paved road

**Ber·mu·da** (bər myoōʹdə) group of Brit. islands in the W Atlantic

**Bermuda onion** a large onion with a mild flavor, grown in Tex., Calif., etc.

**Bermuda shorts** knee-length trousers

**Bern, Berne** (burn) capital of Switzerland: pop. 167,000

**ber·ry** (berʹē) n., pl. -ries [OE. berie] 1. any small, juicy, fleshy fruit, as a strawberry 2. the dry seed of various plants, as a coffee bean —vi. -ried, -ry·ing 1. to bear berries 2. to pick berries —**berʹry·likeʹ** adj.

**ber·serk** (bər surkʹ, -zurkʹ) adj., adv. [ON. berserkr, warrior] in or into a violent rage or frenzy

**berth** (burth) n. [< base of BEAR¹] 1. a place where a ship anchors or moors 2. a position, job, etc. 3. a built-in bed, as on a ship or train —vt. to put into or furnish with a berth —vi. to occupy a berth —**give a wide berth** to to keep well clear of

**ber·yl** (berʹəl) n. [< Gr. bēryllos] a very hard mineral, of which emerald and aquamarine are two varieties

**be·ryl·li·um** (bə rilʹē əm) n. [ModL. < prec.] a hard, rare, metallic chemical element used in forming alloys

**be·seech** (bi sēchʹ) vt. -soughtʹ or -seechedʹ, -seechʹing [< OE. be- + secan, seek] to ask (for) earnestly; entreat —**be·seechʹing·ly** adv.

**be·seem** (bi sēmʹ) vi. to be suitable or appropriate (to)

**be·set** (bi setʹ) vt. -setʹ, -setʹting [< OE. be- + settan, set] 1. to attack from all sides; harass 2. to surround or hem in

**be·setʹting** adj. constantly harassing

**be·side** (bi sīdʹ) prep. [OE. bi sidan] 1. at the side of; near 2. in comparison with [beside his share hers seems small] 3. in addition to 4. aside from —**beside oneself** wild or upset, as with fear, rage, etc.

**be·sides** (-sīdz′) *adv.* **1.** in addition **2.** except for that mentioned **3.** moreover —*prep.* **1.** in addition to **2.** other than

**be·siege** (bi sēj′) *vt.* **-sieged′, -sieg′-ing 1.** to hem in with armed forces **2.** to close in on **3.** to overwhelm, harass, etc. *[besieged* with queries]

**be·smear** (bi smir′) *vt.* to smear over

**be·smirch** (bi smʉrch′) *vt.* to soil

**be·som** (bē′zəm) *n.* [OE. *besma*] a broom, esp. one made of twigs tied to a handle

**be·sot** (bi sät′) *vt.* **-sot′ted, -sot′ting** to make a sot of; stupefy, as with liquor —**be·sot′ted** *adj.*

**be·sought** (bi sôt′) *alt. pt. and pp. of* BESEECH

**be·span·gle** (bi spaŋ′g'l) *vt.* **-gled, -gling** to cover with or as with spangles

**be·spat·ter** (bi spat′ər) *vt.* to spatter, as with mud or slander

**be·speak** (bi spēk′) *vt.* **-spoke′, -spok′en** or **-spoke′, -speak′ing 1.** to speak for in advance; reserve **2.** to be indicative of; show

**Bes·se·mer process** (bes′ə mər) [< H. *Bessemer*, 19th-c. Eng. inventor] a method of making steel by blasting air through molten iron in a large container (**Bessemer converter**)

**best** (best) *adj. superl. of* GOOD [OE. *betst*] **1.** most excellent **2.** most suitable, desirable, etc. **3.** largest *[the best* part of a day] —*adv. superl. of* WELL² **1.** in the most excellent manner **2.** in the highest degree —*n.* **1.** the most excellent person, thing, etc. **2.** the utmost —*vt.* to defeat or outdo —**all for the best** ultimately good —**at best**, under the most favorable conditions —**get** (or **have**) **the best of 1.** to defeat **2.** to outwit —**make the best of** to do as well as one can with

**bes·tial** (bes′chəl) *adj.* [< L. *bestia*, beast] like a beast; savage, brutal, vile, etc. —**bes′ti·al′i·ty** (-chē al′ə tē) *n., pl.* **-ties**

**bes·tial·ize** (bes′chə līz′, -tyə-) *vt.* **-ized′, -iz′ing** to make bestial

**bes·ti·ar·y** (bes′chē er′ē, -tē-) *n., pl.* **-ies** [see BESTIAL] a medieval book with fables about real or mythical animals

**be·stir** (bi stʉr′) *vt.* **-stirred′, -stir′-ring** to stir to action; busy (oneself)

**best man** the principal attendant of the bridegroom at a wedding

**be·stow** (bi stō′) *vt.* [see BE- & STOW] to present as a gift (often with *on* or *upon*) —**be·stow′al** *n.*

**be·strew** (bi strōō′) *vt.* **-strewed′, -strewed′** or **-strewn′, -strew′ing** to strew or scatter about

**be·stride** (bi strīd′) *vt.* **-strode′, -strid′den, -strid′ing** to sit, mount, or stand astride

**bet** (bet) *n.* [prob. < ABET] **1.** *a)* an agreement that the party proved wrong about something will do or pay what is stipulated *b)* the thing or sum thus staked **2.** a person or thing likely to bring about a desired result —*vt., vi.* **bet** or **bet′ted, bet′ting 1.** to declare as in a bet **2.** to stake (money, etc.) in a bet with (someone)

**be·ta** (bāt′ə) *n.* the second letter of the Greek alphabet (Β, β)

**be·take** (bi tāk′) *vt.* **-took′, -tak′en, -tak′ing** [see BE- & TAKE] to go (used reflexively)

**beta particle** an electron or positron ejected from the nucleus of an atom during radioactive disintegration

**beta ray** a stream of beta particles

**be·tel** (bēt′'l) *n.* [Port. < Malay *veṭṭilai*] a climbing pepper plant of Asia: its leaf, along with lime and the fruit (**betel nut**) of a palm (**betel palm**), is chewed by some Asians

**Beth·le·hem** (beth′lə hem′) ancient town in Palestine: Jesus' birthplace

**be·tide** (bi tīd′) *vi., vt.* **-tid′ed, -tid′ing** [< ME.: see BE- & TIDE] to happen (to); befall

**be·times** (bi tīmz′) *adv.* **1.** early or early enough **2.** [Archaic] promptly

**be·to·ken** (bi tō′k'n) *vt.* **1.** to be a token or sign of; show **2.** to presage

**be·tray** (bi trā′) *vt.* [ult. < L. *tradere*, deliver] **1.** to help the enemy of (one's country, etc.) **2.** to expose treacherously **3.** to fail to uphold *[to betray* a trust] **4.** to deceive; specif., to seduce and fail to marry **5.** to reveal unknowingly —**be·tray′al** *n.* —**be·tray′er** *n.*

**be·troth** (bi trōth′, -trôth′) *vt.* [< ME.: see BE- & TRUTH] to promise in marriage —**be·troth′al** *n.*

**be·trothed′** (-trōthd′, -trôtht′) *adj.* engaged to be married —*n.* a person engaged to be married

**bet·ter** (bet′ər) *adj. compar. of* GOOD [OE. *betera*] **1.** more excellent **2.** more suitable, desirable, etc. **3.** larger *[the better* part of a day] **4.** improved in health —*adv. compar. of* WELL² **1.** in a more excellent manner **2.** in a higher degree **3.** more —*n.* **1.** a person superior in position, etc. **2.** a more excellent thing, condition, etc. —*vt.* **1.** to outdo; surpass **2.** to improve —**better off** in better circumstances —**get** (or **have**) **the better of 1.** to defeat **2.** to outwit

**bet′ter·ment** (-mənt) *n.* a bettering; improvement

**bet′tor, bet′ter** *n.* one who bets

**be·tween** (bi twēn′) *prep.* [< OE. *be*, by + *tweonum*, by twos] **1.** in the space, time, etc. separating (two things) **2.** involving *[a struggle between* powers] **3.** connecting *[a bond between* friends] **4.** in the combined possession of **5.** by the joint action of **6.** from one or the other of *[choose between* us] —*adv.* in an intermediate space, time, etc. —**between ourselves** (or **us** or **you and me**) as a secret

**be·twixt** (bi twikst′) *prep., adv.* [OE. *betwix*] between: archaic except in **betwixt and between**, not altogether one nor altogether the other

**bev·el** (bev′'l) *n.* [< ?] **1.** a tool for measuring or marking angles, etc. **2.** an angle other than a right angle **3.** angled part or surface —*adj.* beveled —*vt.* **-eled** or **-elled, -el·ing** or **-el-**

ling to cut to an angle other than a right angle —*vt.* to slope at an angle

**bevel gear** a gearwheel meshing with another at an angle

**bev·er·age** (bev′rij, -ər ij) *n.* [< L. *bibere*, to drink] any liquid for drinking, esp. one other than water

**bev·y** (bev′ē) *n., pl.* -ies [ME. *bevey*] 1. a group, esp. of girls or women 2. a flock, esp. of quail

BEVEL GEAR

**be·wail** (bi wāl′) *vt.* to wail over; lament; mourn

**be·ware** (bi wer′) *vi., vt.* -wared′, -war′ing [prob. < OE. *bewarian*, to keep watch] to be wary or careful (of)

**be·wigged** (bi wigd′) *adj.* wearing a wig

**be·wil·der** (bi wil′dər) *vt.* [ult. < OE. *wilde*, wild] to confuse hopelessly; befuddle —**be·wil′der·ment** *n.*

**be·witch** (bi wich′) *vt.* [< OE. *wicca*: see WITCH] 1. to cast a spell over 2. to charm and delight greatly

**bey** (bā) *n.* [Turk.] formerly, 1. the governor of a Turkish district 2. the native ruler of Tunis

**be·yond** (bi yänd′) *prep.* [< OE. *be- + geond*, yonder] 1. farther on than; past 2. later than 3. outside the reach of [*beyond* help] 4. more than —*adv.* farther away —**the (great) beyond** whatever follows death

**bez·el** (bez′'l) *n.* [< OFr. *biais*, bias] 1. a sloping cutting edge, as of a chisel 2. the slanting faces of a cut jewel 3. the groove and flange holding a gem or a watch crystal in place

**bhang** (baŋ) *n.* [< Sans. *bhangā*] 1. the hemp plant 2. its dried leaves and flowers, which have intoxicating properties

**Bhu·tan** (bōō tän′) monarchy in the Himalayas: c.18,000 sq. mi.; pop. 750,000

**bi-** [L.] *a prefix meaning:* 1. having two 2. doubly 3. happening every two 4. happening twice during every 5. using two or both 6. joining or involving two

**Bi** *Chem.* bismuth

**bi·an·nu·al** (bī an′yōō wəl, -yool) *adj.* coming twice a year; semiannual

**bi·as** (bī′əs) *n., pl.* -as·es [Fr. *biais*, a slant] 1. a slanting or diagonal line, cut or sewn in cloth 2. partiality; prejudice —*adj.* slanting; diagonal —*adv.* diagonally —*vt.* -ased or -assed, -as·ing or -as·sing to prejudice —**on the bias** diagonally

**bi·ath·lon** (bī ath′län) *n.* [BI- + Gr. *athlon*, contest] an athletic event combining a ski run and marksmanship

**bib** (bib) *n.* [< L. *bibere*, to drink] 1. a cloth or plastic cover tied under a child's neck at meals 2. the upper part of an apron

**Bib.** 1. Bible 2. Biblical

**bibb lettuce** (bib) [after J. *Bibb* (1789–1884), who developed it] a kind of lettuce with loose heads of crisp, dark-green leaves

**Bi·ble** (bī′b'l) *n.* [< Gr. *biblos*, papyrus < *Byblos*, Phoenician city that exported papyrus] 1. the sacred book of Christianity; Old Testament and New Testament 2. the Holy Scriptures of Judaism; Old Testament 3. [b-] any book regarded as authoritative or official —**Bib·li·cal, bib·li·cal** (bib′li k'l) *adj.*

**biblio-** [< Gr. *biblion*, book] *a combining form meaning* book, of books

**bib·li·og·ra·phy** (bib′lē äg′rə fē) *n., pl.* -phies a list of writings on a given subject or by a given author —**bib′li·og′ra·pher** *n.* —**bib′li·o·graph′i·cal** (-ə graf′i k'l) *adj.*

**bib′li·o·phile′** (-ə fīl′) *n.* one who loves or collects books

**bib·u·lous** (bib′yoo ləs) *adj.* [< L. *bibere*, to drink] addicted to or fond of alcoholic liquor

**bi·cam·er·al** (bī kam′ər əl) *adj.* [< BI- + L. *camera*, chamber] having two legislative chambers

**bi·car·bon·ate of soda** (bī kär′bə nit) *same as* SODIUM BICARBONATE

**bi·cen·ten·ni·al** (bī′sen ten′ē əl) *adj.* happening once every 200 years —*n.* a 200th anniversary

**bi·ceps** (bī′seps) *n., pl.* -ceps or -ceps·es [L. < *bis*, two + *caput*, head] a muscle with two points of origin; esp., the large muscle in the front of the upper arm

**bick·er** (bik′ər) *vi., n.* [ME. *bikeren*] squabble; quarrel —**bick′er·er** *n.*

**bi′con·cave′** (-kän′kāv′) *adj.* concave on both surfaces

**bi′con·vex′** (-veks′) *adj.* convex on both surfaces

**bi·cus·pid** (bī kus′pid) *adj.* [< BI- + L. *cuspis*, pointed end] having two points —*n.* any of the eight adult teeth with two-pointed crowns

**bi·cy·cle** (bī′si k'l) *n.* [Fr.: see BI- & CYCLE] a vehicle consisting of a metal frame on two wheels, and having handlebars and a seat —*vi., vt.* -cled, -cling to ride or travel on a bicycle —**bi′cy·clist, bi′cy·cler** *n.*

**bid** (bid) *vt.* **bade** or **bid, bid′den** or **bid, bid′ding;** for vt. 2, 4 & for vi., pt. & pp. **bid** [< OE. *biddan*, to urge & *beodan*, to command] 1. to command or ask 2. to offer (an amount) as the price one will pay or accept 3. to express [to *bid* farewell] 4. *Card Games* to state (a number of tricks) and declare (trump) —*vi.* to make a bid —*n.* 1. a bidding 2. an amount, etc. bid 3. a chance to bid 4. an attempt or try (*for*) 5. [Colloq.] an invitation —**bid fair** to seem likely —**bid′der** *n.*

**bid·dy** (bid′ē) *n., pl.* -dies [< ?] 1. a hen 2. [Slang] an elderly woman who is gossipy, eccentric, etc.

**bide** (bīd) *vi.* **bode** or **bid′ed, bid′ing** [OE. *bīdan*] [Archaic or Dial.] 1. to stay; continue 2. to dwell 3. to wait —*vt.* [Archaic or Dial.] to endure

—**bide one's time** *pt.* **bid'ed** tō wait patiently for an opportunity

**bi·det** (bi dā′) *n.* [Fr.] a low, bowl-shaped bathroom fixture, with running water, for bathing the crotch

**bi·en·ni·al** (bī en′ē əl) *adj.* [< L. *bis*, twice + *annus*, year] 1. happening every two years 2. lasting for two years —*n.* 1. a biennial event 2. *Bot.* a plant that lives two years —**bi·en′ni·al·ly** *adv.*

**bier** (bir) *n.* [OE. *bær*] a portable framework on which a coffin is put

**biff** (bif) *n., v.* [Slang] strike; hit

**bi·fo·cals** (bī′fō′k'lz) *n.pl.* a pair of glasses with lenses having one part ground for close focus and the other for distant focus

**bi·fur·cate** (bī′fər kāt′) *vt., vi.* -**cat·ed**, -**cat'ing** [< L. *bi-* + *furca*, a fork] to divide into two parts or branches —**bi′fur·ca′tion** *n.*

**big** (big) *adj.* **big′ger**, **big′gest** [akin to L. *bucca*, puffed cheek] 1. of great size; large 2. full-grown 3. elder [his *big* sister] 4. noticeably pregnant (*with*) 5. loud 6. important 7. extravagant 8. noble [a *big* heart] —*adv.* [Colloq.] 1. boastfully 2. impressively —**big′ness** *n.*

**big·a·my** (big′ə mē) *n.* [< L. *bis*, twice + *gamos*, marriage] the crime of marrying a second time when one is already legally married —**big′a·mist** *n.* —**big′a·mous** *adj.*

**big game** 1. large wild animals hunted for sport, as lions, tigers, etc. 2. the object of any important or dangerous undertaking

**big′heart′ed** (-härt′id) *adj.* quick to give or forgive; generous

**big′horn′** *n.* a Rocky Mountain wild sheep with long, curved horns

**bight** (bīt) *n.* [ME. *byht*] 1. a bending; corner 2. a slack part in a rope 3. a curve in a coastline 4. a bay

**big mouth** [Slang] a person who talks too much, esp. in an opinionated way

**big·ot** (big′ət) *n.* [Fr. < ?] one who holds blindly and intolerantly to a particular creed, opinion, etc. —**big′-ot·ed** *adj.* —**big′ot·ry** (-ə trē) *n.*

**big shot** [Slang] an important or influential person

**bike** (bīk) *n.* [Colloq.] 1. a bicycle 2. a motorcycle

**bi·ki·ni** (bi kē′nē) *n.* [< *Bikini*, Pacific atoll] an extremely brief two-piece bathing suit for women

**bi·lat·er·al** (bī lat′ər əl) *adj.* 1. of, having, or involving two sides 2. affecting both sides equally; reciprocal —**bi·lat′er·al·ly** *adv.*

**bile** (bīl) *n.* [< L. *bilis*] 1. the bitter, greenish fluid secreted by the liver: it aids digestion 2. bad temper

**bilge** (bilj) *n.* [var. of BULGE] 1. the rounded, lower part of a ship's hold 2. stagnant water that gathers there: also **bilge water** 3. [Slang] nonsense

**bi·lin·gual** (bī lin′gwəl) *adj.* [< L. *bis*, two + *lingua*, tongue] of, in, or speaking two languages

**bil·ious** (bil′yəs) *adj.* 1. of the bile 2. having or resulting from some ailment of the liver 3. bad-tempered

**bilk** (bilk) *vt.* [? < *balk*] to cheat or swindle; defraud —**bilk′er** *n.*

**bill¹** (bil) *n.* [< ML. *bulla*, sealed document] 1. a statement of charges for goods or services 2. a list, as a menu or theater program 3. a poster or handbill 4. a draft of a proposed law 5. *same as* BILL OF EXCHANGE 6. a piece of paper money 7. *Law* a written declaration of charges and complaints filed —*vt.* 1. to make out a bill of (items) 2. to present a statement of charges to 3. *a*) to advertise by bills *b*) to book (a performer) —**fill the bill** [Colloq.] to meet the requirements

**bill²** (bil) *n.* [OE. *bile*] 1. a bird's beak 2. a beaklike mouth part, as of a turtle —*vi.* to touch bills together —**bill and coo** to kiss, talk softly, etc. in a loving way

**bill′board′** *n.* a signboard for advertising posters

**bil·let** (bil′it) *n.* [see BILL¹] 1. *a*) a written order to provide lodging for military personnel *b*) the lodging 2. a position or job —*vt.* to assign to lodging by billet

**bil·let-doux** (bil′ē dōō′) *n., pl.* **bil·lets-doux** (bil′ē dōōz′) [Fr.] a love letter

**bill′fold′** (-fōld′) *n.* a wallet

**bil·liard** (bil′yərd) *adj.* of or for billiards

**bil·liards** (bil′yərdz) *n.* [< Fr. *billard*, orig. a cue] a game played with hard balls driven by a cue on a table with raised, cushioned edges

**bill·ing** (bil′iŋ) *n.* 1. the order in which actors' names are listed, as on a playbill 2. such a listing

**bil·lings·gate** (bil′iŋz gāt′) *n.* [< a London fish market] foul, vulgar, abusive talk

**bil·lion** (bil′yən) *n.* [Fr. < L. *bis*, twice + *million*] 1. a thousand millions (1,000,000,000) 2. formerly, in Great Britain, a million millions (1,000,000,-000,000) —**bil′lionth** *adj., n.*

**bil′lion·aire′** (-yə ner′) *n.* a person whose wealth comes to at least a billion dollars, pounds, francs, etc.

**bill of exchange** a written order to pay a certain sum of money to the person named

**bill of fare** a menu

**bill of lading** a receipt issued to a shipper by a carrier, listing the goods received for shipment

**Bill of Rights** the first ten amendments to the U.S. Constitution, which guarantee civil liberties

**bill of sale** a written statement transferring ownership by sale

**bil·low** (bil′ō) *n.* [ON. *bylgja*] 1. a large wave 2. any large, swelling mass or surge, as of smoke —*vi.* to surge or swell in a billow —**bil′low·y** *adj.*

**bil·ly** (bil′ē) *n., pl.* -**lies** [ult. < OFr. *bille*, tree trunk] a club, esp. a policeman's heavy stick

**billy goat** [Colloq.] a male goat

**bi·met·al·lism** (bī met′'l iz'm) *n.* the use of two metals, esp. gold and silver, as the monetary standard, with fixed values in relation to each other

**bi·month·ly** (bī munth'lē) *adj., adv.* 1. once every two months 2. loosely, twice a month

**bin** (bin) *n.* [OE., crib] a box, crib, etc. for storing grain, coal, etc.

**bi·na·ry** (bī'nər ē) *adj.* [< L. *bis*, double] 1. made up of two parts; double 2. designating or of a number system in which the base used is two, each number being expressed by using only two digits, specif. 0 and 1 —*n., pl.* -ries a set of two

**bind** (bīnd) *vt.* **bound, bind'ing** [< OE. *bindan*] 1. to tie together, as with rope 2. to hold or restrain 3. to encircle with a belt, etc. 4. to bandage (often with *up*) 5. to constipate 6. to reinforce or ornament the edges of by a band, as of tape 7. to fasten together the pages of (a book) and protect with a cover 8. to obligate by duty, love, etc. 9. to compel, as by oath or legal restraint —*vt.* 1. to become tight or stiff 2. to stick together 3. to be obligatory —*n.* 1. anything that binds 2. [Colloq.] a difficult situation

**bind'er** *n.* 1. one who binds 2. a binding substance, as tar 3. a cover for holding sheets of paper together

**bind'er·y** *n., pl.* -ies a place where books are bound

**bind'ing** *n.* a thing that binds, as a band, tape, the covers and backing of a book, a cohesive substance, etc. —*adj.* that binds, obligates, etc.

**binge** (binj) *n.* [Colloq.] a spree

**bin·go** (biŋ'gō) *n.* a gambling game resembling lotto

**bin·na·cle** (bin'ə k'l) *n.* [ult. < L. *habitaculum*, dwelling place] the case enclosing a ship's compass

**bin·oc·u·lar** (bī näk'yə lər, bi-) *adj.* [< L. *bini*, double + *oculus*, eye] using, or for, both eyes —*n.* [*pl.*] a binocular instrument, as field glasses

**bi·no·mi·al** (bī nō'mē əl) *n.* [< L. *bi-*, two + Gr. *nomos*, law] 1. *Math.* an expression consisting of two terms connected by a plus or minus sign 2. a two-word scientific name of a plant or animal

**bio-** [Gr. < *bios*, life] *a combining form meaning* life, of living things

**bi·o·as·tro·nau·tics** (bī'ō as'trə nô'tiks) *n.pl.* [*with sing. v.*] the science dealing with the physical responses of living things to space travel

**bi·o·chem·is·try** (bī'ō kem'is trē) *n.* the branch of chemistry that deals with the life processes of plants and animals —**bi'o·chem'ist** *n.*

**bi·o·cide** (bī'ō sīd') *n.* a poisonous chemical that can kill living organisms

**bi'o·clean'** *adj.* as free as possible from microorganisms; esp., aseptic

**bi·o·de·grad·a·ble** (-di grā'də b'l) *adj.* [BIO- + DEGRAD(E) + -ABLE] readily decomposed by bacterial action, as some detergents in sewage disposal

**bi'o·feed'back** *n.* a technique of seeking to control one's emotions by

using electronic devices to train oneself to modify involuntary body functions, such as heartbeat

**biog.** 1. biographical 2. biography

**bi·og·ra·phy** (bī ag'rə fē) *n., pl.* **-phies** [< Gr.: see BIO- & -GRAPHY] an account of a person's life written by another —**bi·og'ra·pher** *n.* —**bi·o·graph·i·cal** (bī'ə graf'i k'l) *adj.*

**biol.** 1. biological 2. biology

**biological warfare** the use of disease-spreading microorganisms, etc. in war

**bi·ol·o·gy** (bī äl'ə jē) *n.* [BIO- + -LOGY] the science that deals with the origin, history, characteristics, habits, etc. of plants and animals —**bi·o·log·i·cal** (bī'ə läj'i k'l) *adj.* —**bi'o·log'i·cal·ly** *adv.* —**bi·ol'o·gist** *n.*

**bi·o·med·i·cine** (bī'ō med'ə s'n) *n.* a branch of medicine combined with research in biology —**bi'o·med'i·cal** *adj.*

**bi·on·ic** (bī än'ik) *adj.* 1. of bionics 2. having an artificial bodily part or parts, as in science fiction, so as to enhance strength, abilities, etc. 3. very strong, skillful, etc.

**bi·on·ics** (bī än'iks) *n.pl.* [*with sing. v.*] [< Gr. *bion*, living + -ICS] the science of designing instruments or systems modeled after living organisms

**bi·o·phys·ics** (bī'ō fiz'iks) *n.pl.* [*with sing. v.*] the study of biological phenomena in relation to physics —**bi'o·phys'i·cal** *adj.* —**bi'o·phys'i·cist** *n.*

**bi·op·sy** (bī'äp'sē) *n., pl.* -sies [< BIO- + Gr. *opsis*, a sight] *Med.* the removal of bits of living tissue for diagnosis

**bi·o·rhythm** (bī'ō rith''m) *n.* any of three hypothetical biological cycles that determine the regular rise and fall of a person's energy levels

**bi·o·tin** (bī'ə tin) *n.* [< Gr. *bios*, life] a factor of the vitamin B group

**bi·par·ti·san** (bī pär'tə z'n) *adj.* of, representing, or supported by two parties —**bi·par'ti·san·ship'** *n.*

**bi·par·tite** (bī pär'tīt) *adj.* [< L. *bi-*, two + *partire*, divide] 1. having two parts 2. involving two

**bi·ped** (bī'ped) *n.* [< L. *bi-*, two + *pes*, foot] any two-footed animal

**bi·plane** (bī'plān') *n.* an airplane with two sets of wings, one above the other

**bi·ra·cial** (bī rā'shəl) *adj.* consisting of or involving two races

**birch** (burch) *n.* [< OE. *beorc*] 1. a tree having smooth bark in thin layers, and hard, closegrained wood 2. its wood 3. a bunch of birch twigs used for whipping —*vt.* to flog

**bird** (burd) *n.* [< OE. *bridd*, young bird] any of a class of warm-blooded vertebrates with feathers and wings —**birds of a feather** people with the same traits or tastes —**for the birds** [Slang] ridiculous, worthless, etc.

**bird·ie** (bur'dē) *n. Golf* a score of one stroke under par for a hole

**bird's-eye** (burdz'ī') *adj.* 1. seen from high above; overall [a *bird's-eye* view*]* 2. having marks resembling birds' eyes *[bird's-eye maple]*

**bi·ret·ta** (bə ret′ə) *n.* [< LL. *birrettum*, small cloak] a square cap with three projections, worn by Roman Catholic clergy

**Bir·ming·ham** (bur′miŋ əm *for 1*; -ham′ *for 2*) 1. city in C England: pop. 1,116,000 2. city in NC Ala.: pop. 301,000

**birth** (burth) *n.* [< OE. *beran*, to bear] 1. the act of bringing forth offspring 2. a being born 3. origin or descent 4. the beginning of anything 5. natural inclination *[an actor by birth]* —**give birth to** 1. to bring forth (offspring) 2. to create

**birth′day′** *n.* the anniversary of the day of a person's birth

**birth′mark′** *n.* a skin blemish present at birth

**birth′place′** *n.* the place of one's birth or of a thing's origin

**birth′rate′** *n.* the number of births per year per thousand people in a given area, group, etc.

**birth′right′** *n.* any right that a person has by birth

**birth′stone′** *n.* a gem symbolizing the month of one's birth

**bis·cuit** (bis′kit) *n., pl.* **-cuits, -cuit** [< L. *bis*, twice + *coquere*, to cook] 1. [Chiefly Brit.] a cracker or cookie 2. a quick bread baked in small pieces

**bi·sect** (bī′sekt′) *vt.* [< L. *bi-* + *secare*, to cut] 1. to cut in two 2. *Geom.* to divide into two equal parts —*vi.* to divide; fork —**bi′sec′tor** *n.*

**bi·sex·u·al** (bī sek′shoo wəl) *adj.* of, or sexually attracted by, both sexes —*n.* one who is bisexual

**bish·op** (bish′əp) *n.* [< Gr. *episkopos*, overseer] 1. a high-ranking Christian clergyman governing a diocese or church district 2. a chessman that can move in a diagonal direction

**bish′op·ric** (-ə prik) *n.* the district, position, rank, etc. of a bishop

**Bis·marck** (biz′märk) capital of N.Dak.: pop. 35,000

**Bis·marck** (biz′märk), Prince Otto von 1815–98; Prussian chancellor (1871–90) who unified Germany

**bis·muth** (biz′məth) *n.* [< G.] a brittle, grayish-white metallic element used in alloys of low melting point

**bi·son** (bīs′′n) *n., pl.* **bi′son** [Fr. < L., wild ox] a four-legged bovine mammal with a shaggy mane and a humped back, as the American buffalo

**bisque** (bisk) *n.* [Fr.] a thick creamy soup made from shellfish, etc. or strained vegetables

**bis·tro** (bis′trō) *n.* [Fr.] a small café

**bit¹** (bit) *n.* [< OE. *bite*, a bite] 1. a metal mouthpiece on a bridle, used as a control 2. anything that curbs or controls 3. a drilling or boring tool for use in a brace, drill press, etc.

**bit²** (bit) *n.* [< OE. *bita*, piece] 1. *a*) a small piece or quantity *b*) small extent *[a bit bored]* *c*) a short time 2. [Colloq.] 12 1/2 cents: now chiefly in *two bits* 3. *adj.* very small *[a bit role]* —**bit by bit** gradually —**do one's bit** to do one's share

**bitch** (bich) *n.* [< OE. *bicce*] the female of the dog, fox, etc. —*vi.* [Slang] to complain —**bitch′y** *adj.*

**bite** (bīt) *vt.* **bit** (bit), **bit′ten** (bit′′n) or **bit, bit′ing** [< OE. *bītan*] 1. to seize or pierce with or as with the teeth 2. to cut into, as with a sharp weapon 3. to sting, as an insect 4. to cause to smart 5. to eat into; corrode —*vi.* 1. to press or snap the teeth (*into, at,* etc.) 2. to cause a biting sensation 3. to grip 4. to seize a bait 5. to be caught, as by a trick —*n.* 1. a biting 2. biting quality; sting 3. a wound or sting from biting 4. a mouthful 5. a snack 6. [Colloq.] a sum deducted, as by a tax —**bite the bullet** to confront a painful situation bravely: from the patient's biting a bullet during battle-field surgery without anesthetic

**bit·ing** (bīt′iŋ) *adj.* 1. cutting; sharp 2. sarcastic —**bit′ing·ly** *adv.*

**bit·ter** (bit′ər) *adj.* [OE. < base of *bītan*, to bite] 1. having a sharp, often unpleasant taste 2. causing or showing sorrow, pain, etc. 3. sharp and disagreeable; harsh *[a bitter wind]* 4. resentful; cynical —**bit′ter·ly** *adv.* —**bit′ter·ness** *n.*

**bit·tern** (bit′ərn) *n.* [< OFr. *butor*] a heronlike bird with a thumping cry

**bit′ters** *n.pl.* a liquor containing bitter herbs, etc., used in some cocktails

**bit′ter·sweet′** *n.* 1. a woody vine bearing small orange fruits which open to expose bright-red seeds 2. a poisonous vine with purple flowers and red berries 3. pleasure mixed with sadness —*adj.* both bitter and sweet; pleasant and sad

BITTERN

**bi·tu·men** (bi tōō′mən, bī-) *n.* [L. < Celt.] any of several substances obtained as residue in the distillation of coal tar, petroleum, etc., or occurring as natural asphalt —**bi·tu′mi·nous** (-mə nəs) *adj.*

**bituminous coal** coal that yields pitch or tar when it burns; soft coal

**bi·valve** (bī′valv′) *n.* any mollusk having two valves or shells hinged together, as a clam

**biv·ou·ac** (biv′wak, -oo wak′) *n.* [Fr. < OHG. *bi-*, by + *wacht*, a guard] a temporary encampment (esp. of soldiers) in the open —*vi.* **-acked, -ack·ing** to encamp in the open

**bi·week·ly** (bī wēk′lē) *adj., adv.* 1. once every two weeks 2. semiweekly

**bi·zarre** (bi zär′) *adj.* [Fr. < Basque *bizar*, beard] 1. odd; grotesque; eccentric 2. unexpected; fantastic

**bk.** *pl.* **bks.** 1. bank 2. book

**bl.** 1. bale(s) 2. barrel(s)

**B/L** *pl.* **BS/L** bill of lading

**blab** (blab) *vt., vi.* **blabbed, blab′bing** [< dial. *blabber*, babble] 1. to reveal (a secret) 2. to gossip —*n.* gossip

**black** (blak) *adj.* [OE. *blæc*] 1. opposite to white; of the color of coal 2. having dark-colored skin and hair; esp., Negro 3. without light; dark 4. dirty 5. evil; wicked 6. sad; dismal

**7.** sullen —*n.* **1.** black color or pigment **2.** black clothes, esp. when worn in mourning **3.** a Negro: *black* is now generally preferred **4.** darkness —*vt.*, *vi.* to blacken —**black out** to lose consciousness —**in the black** operating at a profit —**black′ish** *adj.*— **black′ly** *adv.* —**black′ness** *n.*

**black′-and-blue′** *adj.* discolored, as by a bruise

**black′ball′** *n.* a vote against —*vt.* **1.** to vote against **2.** to ostracize

**black belt** a black belt awarded to an expert of the highest skill in judo or karate

**black′ber′ry** *n., pl.* **-ries 1.** the fleshy, edible, purple or black fruit of various brambles of the rose family **2.** the plant it grows on

**black′bird′** *n.* any of various birds the male of which is almost all black

**black′board′** *n.* a smooth surface on which to write with chalk

**black′en** (-′n) *vi.* to become black or dark —*vt.* **1.** to make black; darken **2.** to slander; defame

**black eye** a discoloration of the skin around an eye, resulting from a blow or contusion

**black′-eyed′ Su′san** (-Id′ sōō′z′n) a yellow, daisylike wildflower with a dark center

**black·guard** (blag′ərd) *n.* a scoundrel; villain

**black′head′** *n.* a dark plug of dried fatty matter in a pore of the skin

**black′jack′** (-jak′) *n.* **1.** a small, leather-covered bludgeon with a flexible handle **2.** the card game TWENTY-ONE —*vt.* to hit with a blackjack

**black light** ultraviolet or infrared radiation used for fluorescent effects

**black′list′** (-list′) *n.* a list of those censured, refused employment, etc. —*vt.* to put on a blacklist

**black lung (disease)** a disease of the lungs caused by the continual inhalation of coal dust

**black magic** sorcery

**black′mail′** (-māl′) *n.* [lit., black rent < ME. *male,* rent] payment extorted to prevent disclosure of information that would bring disgrace —*vt.* to get or try to get blackmail from —**black′mail′er** *n.*

**black mark** a mark indicating something unfavorable in one's record

**black market** a system for selling goods illegally —**black mar′ket·eer′**

**Black Muslim** a member of a militant Islamic sect of American blacks

**black′out′** (-out′) *n.* **1.** an extinguishing of stage lights to end a scene **2.** a concealing of lights that might be visible to enemy aircraft **3.** lack of lights due to a power failure **4.** momentary unconsciousness

**black power** political and economic power sought by American blacks in the struggle for civil rights

**Black Sea** sea surrounded by the U.S.S.R., Asia Minor, & the Balkans

**black sheep** a person regarded as not respectable by his family or group

**black′smith′** *n.* a smith who works in iron and makes and fits horseshoes

**black′thorn′** *n.* a thorny shrub with purple or black, plumlike fruit; sloe

**black′top′** *n.* a bituminous mixture, usually asphalt, used as a surface for roads, etc. —*vt.* **-topped′, -top′ping** to cover with blacktop

**black widow** a black spider with red underneath; the female has a poisonous bite and eats its mate

**blad·der** (blad′ər) *n.* [OE. *blæddre*] **1.** a sac that fills with fluid, esp. one that holds urine flowing from the kidneys **2.** a thing resembling this *[a football bladder]*

**blade** (blād) *n.* [OE. *blæd*] **1.** *a)* the leaf of a plant, esp. grass *b)* the flat part of a leaf **2.** a broad, flat surface, as of an oar **3.** the cutting part of a tool, knife, etc. **4.** a sword or swordsman **5.** a gay, dashing young man

**blam·a·ble, blame·a·ble** (blām′ə-b'l) *adj.* that deserves blame — **blam′a·bly** *adv.*

**blame** (blām) *vt.* **blamed, blam′ing** [SEE BLASPHEME] **1.** to accuse of being at fault; condemn *(for)* **2.** to put the responsibility of (an error, etc.) *on* —*n.* **1.** a blaming **2.** responsibility for a fault —**be to blame** to deserve blame —**blame′less** *adj.* —**blame′less·ly** *adv.* —**blame′less·ness** *n.*

**blame′wor′thy** (-wur′*th*ē) *adj.* deserving to be blamed

**blanch** (blanch) *vt.* [see BLANK] **1.** to whiten or bleach **2.** to make pale **3.** to scald (vegetables, almonds, etc.) —*vi.* to turn pale

**bland** (bland) *adj.* [L. *blandus*] **1.** gently agreeable **2.** *a)* mild and soothing *b)* insipid —**bland′ly** *adv.* —**bland′ness** *n.*

**blan·dish** (blan′dish) *vt., vi.* [see prec.] to flatter; coax; cajole —**blan′dish·ment** *n.*

**blank** (blank) *adj.* [ < OFr. *blanc,* white] **1.** not written on **2.** empty; vacant **3.** empty of thought *[a blank mind]* **4.** utter; complete *[a blank denial]* —*n.* **1.** an empty space, esp. one to be filled out in a printed form **2.** such a printed form **3.** an empty place or time **4.** a powder-filled cartridge without a bullet —*vt.* to hold (an opponent) scoreless —**blank out** to conceal by covering over —**draw a blank** [Colloq.] **1.** to be unsuccessful **2.** to be unable to remember a particular thing —**blank′ly** *adv.* —**blank′ness** *n.*

**blan·ket** (blan′kit) *n.* [see prec.] **1.** a large, soft piece of cloth used for warmth, esp. as a bed cover **2.** anything like this *[a blanket of leaves]* —*adj.* including many or all items *[blanket insurance]* —*vt.* **1.** to cover; overlie **2.** to obscure

**blank verse** unrhymed verse with five iambic feet per line

**blare** (bler) *vt., vi.* **blared, blar'ing**
[ME. *bleren,* wail] to sound or exclaim
loudly —*n.* a loud, harsh sound

**blar·ney** (blär'nē) *n.* [< *Blarney*
stone in Ireland, traditionally kissed
to gain skill in flattery] flattery —*vt.,
vi.* **-neyed, -ney·ing** to flatter or
coax

**bla·sé** (blä zā') *adj.* [Fr.] satiated
and bored

**blas·pheme** (blas fēm') *vt.* **-phemed',
-phem'ing** [< Gr. *blasphēmein,*
speak evil of] **1.** to speak profanely
of or to (God or sacred things) **2.** to
curse —*vi.* to utter blasphemy —
**blas·phem'er** *n.*

**blas·phe·my** (-fə mē) *n., pl.* **-mies**
profane abuse of God or sacred things
—**blas'phe·mous** *adj.*

**blast** (blast) *n.* [< OE. *blæst*] **1.** a
strong rush of air **2.** the sound of a
sudden rush of air, as through a horn
**3.** a blight **4.** an explosion, as of
dynamite **5.** an outburst of criticism
—*vi.* **1.** to make a loud, harsh sound
**2.** to set off explosives, etc. —*vt.* **1.**
to wither; ruin **2.** to blow up; explode
**3.** to criticize sharply —**blast off** to
take off: said of a rocket or missile
—(**at**) **full blast** at full speed

**blast furnace** a smelting furnace in
which a blast of air produces the
intense heat

**blast'off', blast'-off'** *n.* the launching of a rocket, space vehicle, etc.

**bla·tant** (blāt'nt) *adj.* [prob. < L.
*blaterare,* to babble] **1.** disagreeably
loud; noisy **2.** boldly conspicuous or
obtrusive —**bla'tan·cy** *n., pl.* **-cies**

**blaze¹** (blāz) *n.* [OE. *blæse*] **1.** a
bright burst of flame; fire **2.** a bright
light **3.** a spectacular outburst or
display —*vi.* **blazed, blaz'ing 1.** to
burn rapidly or shine brightly **2.** to
be excited, as with anger

**blaze²** (blāz) *n.* [< ON. *blesi*] **1.** a
white spot on an animal's face **2.** a
mark made on a tree by cutting off
bark —*vt.* **blazed, blaz'ing** to mark
(a tree or trail) with blazes

**blaze³** (blāz) *vt.* **blazed, blaz'ing** [<
OE. or ON.] to proclaim

**blaz·er** (blā'zər) *n.* a light sports
jacket in a solid, often bright color

**bla·zon** (blā'z'n) *n.* [OFr. *blason,* a
shield] **1.** a coat of arms **2.** showy
display —*vt.* **1.** to proclaim **2.** to
adorn

**bldg.** building

**bleach** (blēch) *vt., vi.* [< OE. *blac,*
pale] to make or become white or
colorless —*n.* a substance for bleaching

**bleach'ers** *n.pl.* seats, usually roofless,
for spectators at sporting events

**bleak** (blēk) *adj.* [see BLEACH] **1.**
exposed to wind and cold; bare **2.**
cold; harsh **3.** gloomy **4.** not hopeful
—**bleak'ly** *adv.* —**bleak'ness** *n.*

**blear·y** (blir'ē) *adj.* **-i·er, -i·est** [<
ME. *blere*] dim or blurred, as the eyes
by tears, fatigue, etc.: also **blear**

**bleat** (blēt) *vi.* [OE. *blætan*] to make
the cry of a sheep, goat, or calf —*n.*
a bleating cry or sound

**bleed** (blēd) *vi.* **bled** (bled), **bleed'ing**
[< OE. *blod,* blood] **1.** to emit or lose

blood **2.** to feel pain, grief, or sympathy **3.** to ooze sap, juice, etc. —*vt.*
**1.** to draw blood from **2.** to ooze
(sap, juice, etc.) **3.** [Colloq.] to extort
money from —**bleed'er** *n.*

**bleep** (blēp) *n., vi. same as* BEEP

**blem·ish** (blem'ish) *vt.* [< OFr.
*blesmir,* injure] to mar; spoil —*n.* a
flaw, defect, etc., as a spot

**blench¹** (blench) *vt., vi. same as*
BLANCH

**blench²** (blench) *vi.* [< OE. *blencan,*
deceive] to shrink back; flinch

**blend** (blend) *vt.* **blend'ed** or **blent,
blend'ing** [OE. *blendan*] **1.** to mix
or mingle (varieties of tea, etc.) **2.** to
mix thoroughly —*vi.* **1.** to mix;
merge **2.** to shade gradually into each
other, as colors **3.** to harmonize —*n.*
**1.** a blending **2.** a mixture of varieties

**blend'er** *n.* **1.** a person or thing that
blends **2.** an electrical appliance that
can chop, whip, mix, or liquefy foods

**bless** (bles) *vt.* **blessed** or **blest,
bless'ing** [< OE. *bletsian,* consecrate
with blood] **1.** to make holy **2.** to
ask divine favor for **3.** to endow
(*with*) **4.** to make happy **5.** to praise
**6.** to make the sign of the cross over

**bless·ed** (bles'id, blest) *adj.* **1.** holy;
sacred **2.** fortunate; blissful **3.**
beatified —**bless'ed·ly** *adv.* —**bless'-
ed·ness** *n.*

**bless'ing** *n.* **1.** invocation or bene-
diction **2.** a grace said before or after
eating **3.** good wishes or approval
**4.** anything that gives happiness

**blew** (blōō) *pt. of* BLOW¹

**blight** (blīt) *n.* [? < ME. *bliknen,* to
lose color] **1.** any insect, disease, etc.
that destroys plants **2.** anything
that destroys, frustrates, etc. —*vt.*
**1.** to wither **2.** to destroy

**blimp** (blimp) *n.* [Colloq.] a small
nonrigid or semirigid airship

**blind** (blīnd) *adj.* [OE.] **1.** without
the power of sight **2.** of or for sightless
persons **3.** lacking insight **4.** hard to
see; hidden **5.** closed at one end [a
*blind* alley] **6.** not controlled by
reason [*blind* fate] **7.** *Aeron.* by the
use of instruments only [*blind* flying]
—*vt.* **1.** to make sightless **2.** to dazzle
**3.** to deprive of insight —*n.* **1.** anything that obscures sight or keeps out
light, as a window shade **2.** a place
of concealment **3.** a decoy —**blind'ly**
*adv.* —**blind'ness** *n.*

**blind date** [Colloq.] **1.** a date with
a stranger, arranged by a third person
**2.** either person involved

**blind'fold'** (-fōld') *vt.* [< ME.
*blindfeld,* struck blind] to cover the
eyes, as with a cloth —*n.* a cloth
used to cover the eyes —*adj.* **1.** with
the eyes covered **2.** reckless

**blink** (blink) *vi.* [< ME. *blenchen*]
**1.** to wink one or more times **2.** to
flash on and off **3.** to ignore (with *at*)
—*vt.* **1.** to cause (eyes, light, etc.) to
blink **2.** to evade or avoid —*n.* **1.** a
blinking **2.** a glimmer —**on the blink**
[Slang] out of order

**blink'er** *n.* a flashing warning light

**blintz** (blints) *n.* [Yid. *blintze* <
Russ. *blin,* pancake] a thin pancake

rolled with a filling of cottage cheese, fruit, etc.

**blip** (blip) *n.* [echoic] a luminous image on an oscilloscope

**bliss** (blis) *n.* [< OE. *blithe*, blithe] 1. great happiness 2. spiritual joy — **bliss'ful** *adj.* —**bliss'ful·ly** *adv.* — **bliss'ful·ness** *n.*

**blis·ter** (blis'tər) *n.* [< ON. *blastr*] 1. a raised patch of skin, filled with watery matter and caused as by burning 2. anything like a blister —*vt.* 1. tc raise blisters on 2. to lash with words —*vi.* to form blisters

**blithe** (blīth, blith) *adj.* [OE.] gay; joyful: also **blithe'some** (-səm) — **blithe'ly** *adv.* —**blithe'ness** *n.*

**blitz** (blits) *n.* [< G. *blitz*, lightning] a sudden, destructive or overwhelming attack —*vt.* to subject to a blitz

**bliz·zard** (bliz'ərd) *n.* [< dial. *bliz*, violent blow + -ARD] a violent snow-storm with very cold winds

**bloat** (blōt) *vt., vi.* [< ON. *blautr*, soft] 1. to swell, as with water or air 2. to puff up, as with pride

**blob** (bläb) *n.* [echoic] a small drop or spot —*vt.* **blobbed, blob'bing** to splash, as with blobs

**bloc** (bläk) *n.* [Fr. < LowG. *block*, log] a group of persons, nations, etc. combined for a common purpose

**block** (bläk) *n.* [see prec.] 1. a solid piece of wood, stone, metal, etc. 2. a heavy stand on which chopping, etc. is done 3. an auctioneer's platform 4. an obstruction or hindrance 5. a pulley in a frame 6. a city square 7. a group or row of buildings 8. a number of things regarded as a unit 9. *Printing* a piece of engraved wood, etc. with a design —*vt.* 1. to obstruct; hinder 2. to mount or mold on a block 3. to sketch roughly (often with *out*) —**block'er** *n.*

**block·ade** (blä kād') *n.* [prec. + -ADE] 1. a shutting off of a place by troops or ships to prevent passage 2. any strategic barrier —*vt.* -**ad'ed**, -**ad'ing** to subject to a blockade

**block and tackle** pulley blocks and ropes, used for lifting heavy objects

**block'bust'ing** *n.* [Colloq.] the inducing of owners to sell their homes out of fear that a minority group may move into their neighborhood

**block'head'** *n.* a stupid person

**block'house'** *n.* 1. formerly, a wooden fort 2. a reinforced structure for observers, as of missile launchings

**blond** (bländ) *adj.* [Fr. < ? Gmc.] 1. having light-colored hair and skin 2. light-colored Also **blonde** —*n.* a blond person —**blonde** *n.fem.* — **blond'ness** *n.*

**blood** (blud) *n.* [OE. *blod*] 1. the red fluid circulating in the arteries and veins of animals 2. bloodshed 3. the essence of life; life 4. the sap of a plant 5. passion, temperament, etc. 6. parental heritage; lineage 7. kinship 8. people, esp. youthful people

—**bad blood** anger; hatred —**in cold blood** 1. with cruelty 2. deliberately; dispassionately

**blood bank** a supply of blood stored for future use in transfusion

**blood count** the number of red and white corpuscles in a given volume of blood

**blood'cur'dling** (-kurd'liŋ) *adj.* very frightening; causing terror

**blood'ed** (-id) *adj.* 1. having (a specific kind of) blood [hot-blooded] 2. of fine breed

**blood'hound'** *n.* any of a breed of large, keen-scented tracking dogs

**blood'less** (-ləs) *adj.* 1. without bloodshed 2. anemic or pale 3. having little energy —**blood'less·ly** *adv.* — **blood'less·ness** *n.*

**blood'mo·bile'** (-mō bēl') *n.* a mobile unit for collecting blood from donors for blood banks

**blood poisoning** any of various diseases in which the blood contains microorganisms and their poisonous products

**blood pressure** the pressure of the blood against the blood-vessel walls

**blood relation** (or **relative**) a person related by birth

**blood'shed'** *n.* killing; slaughter

**blood'shot'** *adj.* tinged with red because small blood vessels are broken: said of the eyes

**blood'suck'er** *n.* an animal that sucks blood, esp. a leech

**blood'thirst'y** *adj.* murderous; cruel —**blood'thirst'i·ness** *n.*

**blood vessel** an artery, vein, or capillary

**blood'y** *adj.* -**i·er**, -**i·est** 1. of, containing, or covered with blood 2. involving bloodshed 3. bloodthirsty 4. [Brit. Slang] cursed; damned —*adv.* [Brit. Slang] very —*vt.* -**ied**, -**y·ing** to stain with blood —**blood'i·ly** *adv.* —**blood'i·ness** *n.*

**bloom** (blōōm) *n.* [< ON. *blomi*, flowers] 1. a flower; blossom 2. the state or time of flowering 3. a period of most health, vigor, etc. 4. a youthful, healthy glow 5. the powdery coating on some fruits and leaves —*vi.* 1. to blossom 2. to be at one's prime 3. to glow with health, etc.

**bloom·ers** (blōō'mərz) *n.pl.* [< Amelia *Bloomer*, U.S. feminist] a woman's underpants gathered above the knee

**bloom'ing** *adj.* 1. blossoming 2. flourishing 3. [Colloq.] complete

**bloop·er** (blōōp'ər) *n.* [< imitation of a vulgar noise] [Slang] 1. a stupid mistake 2. *Baseball* a fly that falls just beyond the infield for a hit

**blos·som** (bläs'əm) *n.* [OE. *blostma*] 1. a flower, esp. of a fruit-bearing plant 2. a state or time of flowering —*vi.* 1. to have or open into blossoms 2. to begin to flourish

**blot** (blät) *n.* [ME. < ?] 1. a spot or stain, esp. of ink 2. anything that spoils or mars 3. a moral stain —*vt.*

**blot'ted, blot'ting** 1. to spot; stain 2. to disgrace 3. to erase, obscure, or get rid of ( with *out*) 4. to dry, as with blotting paper —*vi.* 1. to make blots 2. to become blotted 3. to be absorbent

**blotch** (bläch) *n.* [? < prec.] 1. a discoloration on the skin 2. any large blot or stain —*vt.* to mark with blotches —**blotch'y** *adj.* **-i-er, -i-est**

**blot'ter** *n.* 1. a piece of blotting paper 2. a book for recording events as they occur [a police *blotter*]

**blotting paper** a soft, absorbent paper used to dry a surface freshly written on in ink

**blouse** (blous) *n.* [Fr., workman's smock] 1. a shirtlike garment worn by women and children 2. a uniform coat worn by soldiers, etc. —*vi., vt.* **bloused, blous'ing** to gather in and drape at the waistline

**blow¹** (blō) *vi.* **blew, blown** (blōn), **blow'ing** [OE. *blawan*] 1. to move with some force, as the wind 2. to send forth air, as with the mouth 3. to pant 4. to give sound by blowing 5. to spout water and air, as whales do 6. to be carried by the wind 7. to be stormy 8. to burst suddenly (often with *out*) 9. [Colloq.] to brag 10. [Slang] to leave —*vt.* 1. to force air from, into, onto, or through 2. to drive by blowing 3. to sound by blowing 4. to burst by an explosion (often with *up*) 5. to melt (a fuse, etc.) 6. [Colloq.] to spend (money) freely 7. [Slang] to leave 8. [Slang] to bungle —*n.* 1. a blowing 2. a blast or gale —**blow off** [Colloq.] to release emotions, as by shouting —**blow over** to pass over or by —**blow up** [Colloq.] to lose one's temper —**blow'er** *n.*

**blow²** (blō) *n.* [ME. *blowe*] 1. a hard hit, as with the fist 2. a sudden attack 3. a sudden calamity; shock —**come to blows** to begin fighting

**blow³** (blō) *vi.* **blew, blown** (blōn), **blow'ing** [OE. *blowan*] to bloom

**blow'-by-blow'** *adj.* detailed; full

**blow'-dry'** *vt.* **-dried', -dry'ing** to dry (wet hair) with hot air blown from an electric device (**blow'-dry'er**)

**blow'fly'** *n., pl.* **-flies'** a fly that lays its eggs on meat, etc.

**blow'gun'** *n.* a long tube through which darts, etc. are blown

**blow'out'** *n.* 1. the bursting of a tire 2. [Slang] a party, banquet, etc.

**blow'torch'** *n.* a small gasoline torch that shoots out a hot flame

**blow'up'** *n.* 1. an explosion 2. an enlarged photograph 3. [Colloq.] an angry outburst

**blow'y** *adj.* **-i-er, -i-est** windy

**blowz-y** (blou'zē) *adj.* **-i-er, -i-est** [ < obs. *blouze* wench] slovenly: also **blows'y**

**blub-ber** (blub'ər) *n.* [ME. *blober*, a bubble] the fat of the whale —*vi.* to weep loudly —**blub'ber-y** *adj.*

BLOWTORCH

**blu-cher** (blōō'chər, -kər) *n.* [ < *von Blücher*, Prussian general (1742–1819)] a kind of shoe in which the vamp is of one piece with the tongue

**bludg-eon** (bluj'n) *n.* [? < MFr. *bouge*, club] a short club with a heavy end —*vt., vi.* 1. to strike with a bludgeon 2. to bully or coerce

**blue** (blōō) *adj.* [ < Frank. *blao*] 1. of the color of the clear sky 2. livid: said of the skin 3. gloomy 4. puritanical [*blue* laws] 5. [Colloq.] indecent —*n.* 1. the color of the clear sky 2. any blue pigment 3. [*pl.*] [Colloq.] a depressed feeling (with *the*) 4. [*pl.*] Negro folk music having, usually, slow tempo, melancholy words, etc. (often with *the*) —**out of the blue** unexpectedly —**the blue** 1. the sky 2. the sea

**blue baby** a baby born with bluish skin, esp. because of a heart defect

**blue'bell'** *n.* any of various plants with blue, bell-shaped flowers

**blue'ber'ry** *n., pl.* **-ries** 1. a shrub bearing small, edible, blue-black berries 2. any of the berries

**blue'bird'** *n.* a small N.American songbird with a bluish back

**blue blood** an aristocrat: also **blue'-blood'** *n.* —**blue'-blood'ed** *adj.*

**blue cheese** a cheese like Roquefort

**blue'-col'lar** *adj.* designating or of industrial workers

**blue'fish'** *n., pl.:* see FISH a bluish food fish of the Atlantic coast

**blue flu** [from blue police uniforms] a sickout, esp. by police officers

**blue'gill'** (-gil') *n.* a freshwater sunfish of a bluish color

**blue'grass'** *n.* a type of grass with bluish-green stems

**blue'jack'et** *n.* an enlisted man in the U.S. or British navy

**blue jay** a noisy, crested bird with a bluish upper part: also **blue'jay'** *n.*

**blue law** a puritanical law, esp. one prohibiting certain activities on Sunday

**blue'nose'** *n.* [Colloq.] a puritanical person

**blue'-pen'cil** *vt.* **-ciled** or **-cilled, -cil·ing** or **-cil·ling** to edit or correct with or as with a blue pencil

**blue'-plate' special** an inexpensive restaurant meal served at a fixed price

**blue'point'** *n.* [ < *Blue Point*, Long Island] a small oyster, usually eaten raw

**blue'print'** *n.* 1. a photographic reproduction in white on a blue background, as of architectural plans 2. any detailed plan or outline —*vt.* to make a blueprint of

**blue'stock'ing** *n.* a bookish woman

**blu·et** (blōō'it) *n.* [ < Fr. dim. of *bleu*, blue] a small plant with little, pale-blue flowers

**bluff¹** (bluf) *vt., vi.* [prob. < Du. *bluffen*, to baffle] to mislead or frighten by a false, bold front —*n.* 1. a bluffing 2. one who bluffs: also **bluff'er** *n.*

**bluff²** (bluf) *adj.* [ < Du. *blaf*, flat] 1. ascending steeply with a flat front 2. having a rough, frank manner —*n.* a high, steep bank or cliff

**blu·ing** (blōō′iŋ) *n.* a blue rinse used on white fabrics to prevent yellowing: also **blue′ing**

**blu′ish** (-ish) *adj.* somewhat blue: also **blue′ish**

**blun·der** (blun′dər) *vi.* [< ON. *blunda*, shut the eyes] 1. to move clumsily 2. to make a foolish mistake —*vt.* to do poorly —*n.* a foolish mistake —**blun′der·er** *n.*

**blun′der·buss′** (-bus′) *n.* [Du. *donderbus*, thunder box] an obsolete short gun with a broad muzzle

**blunt** (blunt) *adj.* [< ?] 1. having a dull edge, etc. 2. plain-spoken —*vt., vi.* to make or become dull —**blunt′ly** *adv.* —**blunt′ness** *n.*

**blur** (blur) *vt., vi.* **blurred, blur′ring** [? akin to BLEAR(Y)] 1. to smear; blot 2. to make or become indistinct in shape, etc. 3. to dim —*n.* 1. an obscuring stain 2. anything indistinct —**blur′ry** *adj.* —**blur′ri·ness** *n.*

**blurb** (blurb) *n.* [a coinage] [Colloq.] an exaggerated advertisement

**blurt** (blurt) *vt.* [prob. echoic] to say impulsively (with *out*)

**blush** (blush) *vi.* [< OE. *blyscan*, to shine] 1. to become red in the face, as from embarrassment 2. to be ashamed (*at* or *for*) 3. to become rosy —*n.* 1. a reddening of the face, as from shame 2. a rosy color —*adj.* rosy —**at first blush** at first sight

**blush′er** *n.* 1. a person who blushes readily 2. a cosmetic cream, powder, etc. that gives color to the face

**blus·ter** (blus′tər) *vi.* [< LowG. *blüstern*] 1. to blow stormily: said of wind 2. to speak in a noisy or swaggering manner —*n.* 1. noisy commotion 2. noisy or swaggering talk —**blus′ter·er** *n.* —**blus′ter·y** *adj.*

**blvd.** boulevard

**BM** [Colloq.] bowel movement

**BO, B.O.** body odor

**bo·a** (bō′ə) *n.* [L.] 1. a tropical snake that crushes its prey in its coils, as the python 2. a woman's long scarf of fur or feathers

**boar** (bôr) *n.* [OE. *bar*] 1. an uncastrated male pig 2. a wild hog

**board** (bôrd) *n.* [OE. *bord*, plank] 1. a long, flat piece of sawed wood 2. a flat piece of wood, etc. for some special use [a bulletin *board*] 3. pasteboard 4. *a*) a table for meals *b*) meals, esp. as provided regularly for pay 5. a group of administrators; council 6. the side of a ship [*overboard*] —*vt.* 1. to provide with meals, or room and meals, regularly for pay 2. to come onto the deck of (a ship) 3. to get on (a train, bus, etc.) —*vi.* to receive meals, or room and meals, regularly for pay —**board up** to cover with boards —**on board** on a ship, aircraft, etc. —**the boards** the stage (of a theater) —**board′er** *n.*

**board′ing·house′** *n.* a house where meals, or room and meals, can be had for pay: also **boarding house**

**board′walk′** *n.* a walk made of thick boards, esp. one along a beach

**boast** (bōst) *vi.* [< Anglo-Fr.] to talk, esp. about oneself, with too much pride; brag —*vt.* to brag about or glory in —*n.* 1. a boasting 2. anything boasted of —**boast′er** *n.* —**boast′ful** *adj.* —**boast′ful·ly** *adv.*

**boat** (bōt) *n.* [OE. *bat*] 1. a small, open watercraft 2. loosely, a ship 3. a boat-shaped dish —**in the same boat** in the same unfavorable situation —**rock the boat** [Colloq.] to disturb the status quo —**boat′man** (-mən) *n., pl.* **-men**

**boat′er** *n.* a stiff straw hat with a flat crown and brim

**boat′ing** *n.* rowing, sailing, etc.

**boat·swain** (bō′s'n) *n.* a ship's petty officer in charge of the deck crew, the rigging, anchors, etc.

**bob** (bäb) *n.* [ME. *bobbe*, hanging cluster; 3 & 4 < the *v.*] 1. any knoblike hanging weight 2. a woman's or girl's short haircut 3. a quick, jerky motion 4. a float on a fishing line —*vt.* **bobbed, bob′bing** [ME. *bobben*, knock against] 1. to make move with a jerky motion 2. to cut (hair, etc.) short —*vi.* to move with a jerky motion —**bob up** to appear suddenly

**bob·bin** (bäb′in) *n.* [< Fr. *bobiner*, to wind] a spool for thread, etc. used in spinning, machine sewing, etc.

**bob·ble** (bäb′'l) *n.* [Colloq.] *Sports* an awkward juggling of the ball —*vt.* **-bled, -bling** [Colloq.] to make a bobble with

**bob·by** (bäb′ē) *n., pl.* **-bies** [after Sir Robert (*Bobby*) Peel (1788–1850), who reorganized the London police force] [Brit. Colloq.] a policeman

**bobby pin** [from use with *bobbed* hair] a small metal hairpin with the sides pressing close together

**bobby socks** (or **sox**) [< BOB (*vt.* 2)] [Colloq.] girls' ankle-length socks

**bob′by-sox′er, bob′by-sox′er** (-säk′sər) *n.* [Colloq.] a girl in her teens

**bob′cat′** *n.* a wildcat of the E U.S.

**bob-o-link** (bäb′ə liŋk′) *n.* [echoic] a migratory songbird of N.America

**bob′sled′** *n.* a long racing sled —*vi.* **-sled·ded, -sled′ding** to ride or race on a bobsled

**bob-white** (bäb′hwīt′) *n.* [echoic] a small N.American quail

**Boc·cac·cio** (bō kä′chē ō′), **Gio·van·ni** (jō vän′nē) 1313–75; It. writer

**boc·cie, boc·ce, boc·ci** (bäch′ē) *n.* [It. *bocce*, (wooden) balls] an Italian game like bowls

**bock (beer)** (bäk) [< *Einbeck*, Ger. city where first brewed] a dark beer

**bode¹** (bōd) *vt.* **bod′ed, bod′ing** [< OE. *boda*, messenger] to be an omen of —**bode ill** (or **well**) to be a bad (or good) omen

**bode²** (bōd) *alt. pt.* of BIDE

**bod·ice** (bäd′is) *n.* [alt. < *bodies*, pl. of BODY] the upper part of a dress

**bod·i·ly** (bäd′'l ē) *adj.* 1. physical

**2.** of, in, or to the body —*adv.* **1.** in person **2.** as a single group

**bod·kin** (bäd′k′in) *n.* [ME. *bodekin* < ?] **1.** a pointed instrument for making holes in cloth **2.** a thick, blunt needle **3.** [Obs.] a dagger

**bod·y** (bäd′ē) *n., pl.* **-ies** [OE. *bodig*, cask] **1.** the whole physical substance of a man, animal, or plant **2.** the trunk of a man or animal **3.** a corpse **4.** [Colloq.] a person **5.** a distinct mass [a *body* of water] **6.** a distinct group of people or things **7.** the main part **8.** substance or consistency, as of liquid **9.** richness of flavor

**bod′y·guard′** *n.* a person or persons assigned to guard someone

**body language** gestures, unconscious bodily movements, etc. which function as a means of communication

**body stocking** a tightfitting garment, usually of one piece, that covers the torso and, sometimes, the legs

**bod′y·suit′** *n.* a one-piece, tightfitting garment that covers the torso, usually worn with slacks, a skirt, etc.: also **body shirt**

**Boer** (bôr, boor) *n.* [Du. *boer*, peasant] a South African whose ancestors were Dutch colonists

**bog** (bäg, bôg) *n.* [ < Gael. & Ir. *bog*, soft, moist] wet, spongy ground; a small marsh —*vt., vi.* **bogged**, **bog′ging** to sink in or as in a bog (often with *down*) —**bog′gy** *adj.*

**bo·gey** (bō′gē) *n., pl.* **-geys** **1.** same as BOGY **2.** [after an imaginary Colonel *Bogey*] *Golf* one stroke more than par on a hole: also **bo′gie**

**bog·gle** (bäg′'l) *vi.* **-gled**, **-gling** [ < Scot. *bogle*, specter] **1.** to be startled (*at*) **2.** to hesitate (*at*) —*vt.* to confuse (the mind, imagination, etc.)

**Bo·go·tá** (bō′gə tä′) capital of Colombia: pop. 1,697,000

**bo·gus** (bō′gəs) *adj.* [ < ?] not genuine; spurious; counterfeit

**bo·gy** (bō′gē, boog′ē) *n., pl.* **-gies** [ < Scot. *bogle*, specter] an imaginary evil spirit; goblin: also **bo′gie**

**bo·gy·man, bo·gey·man** (bō′gē man′, boog′ē-) *n., pl.* **-men′** an imaginary frightful being

**Bo·he·mi·a** (bō hē′mē ə) region of W Czechoslovakia: a former kingdom

**Bo·he′mi·an** *n.* **1.** a native of Bohemia **2.** same as CZECH (*n.* 2) **3.** [often b-] one who lives unconventionally —*adj.* **1.** of Bohemia, its people, etc. **2.** [often b-] like a Bohemian (*n.* 3) —**Bo·he′mi·an·ism** *n.*

**boil**[1] (boil) *vi.* [ < L. *bulla*, a bubble] **1.** to bubble up and vaporize by being heated **2.** to seethe like boiling liquids **3.** to be agitated, as with rage **4.** to cook in boiling liquid —*vt.* **1.** to heat to the boiling point **2.** to cook in boiling liquid —*n.* the act or state of boiling —**boil down 1.** to lessen in quantity by boiling **2.** to condense

**boil**[2] (boil) *n.* [OE. *byle*] an inflamed, painful, pus-filled swelling on the skin

**boil′er** *n.* **1.** a container in which to boil things **2.** a tank in which water is turned to steam **3.** a tank for heating water and storing it

**Boi·se** (boi′sē, -zē) capital of Idaho: pop. 75,000

**bois·ter·ous** (bois′tər əs) *adj.* [ME. *boistreous*, crude] **1.** rough and stormy; turbulent **2.** loud and exuberant; rowdy —**bois′ter·ous·ly** *adv.*

**bold** (bōld) *adj.* [OE. *beald*] **1.** daring; fearless **2.** too free in manner; impudent **3.** steep **4.** prominent and clear —**bold′ly** *adv.* —**bold′ness** *n.*

**bold′faced′** (-fāst′) *adj.* impudent

**bole** (bōl) *n.* [ON. *bolr*] a tree trunk

**bo·le·ro** (bə ler′ō) *n., pl.* **-ros** [Sp.: see BOIL[1]] **1.** a lively Spanish dance, or music for it **2.** a short, open vest

**Bol·í·var** (bäl′ə vər), **Si·món** (sē′mən) 1783–1830; S.American revolutionary

**Bo·liv·i·a** (bə liv′ē ə) country in WC S.America: 424,000 sq. mi.; pop. 3,748,000 —**Bo·liv′i·an** *adj., n.*

**boll** (bōl) *n.* [ME. *bolle*, bowl] the pod of a plant, esp. of cotton or flax

**boll weevil** a small weevil whose larvae destroy cotton bolls

**bo·lo·gna** (bə lō′nē) *n.* [ < *Bologna*, It. city] a large, smoked sausage of beef, pork, or veal

**Bol·she·vik** (bōl′shə vik′, bäl′-) *n., pl.* **-viks′, -vi′ki** (-vē′kē) [Russ. < *bolshe*, the majority] [also **b-**] **1.** a member of a majority faction that came into power in Russia in 1917 **2.** a Communist, esp. of the Soviet Union —**Bol′she·vism** *n.* —**Bol′she·vist** *n., adj.*

**bol·ster** (bōl′stər) *n.* [OE.] a long, narrow pillow **2.** any bolsterlike object or support —*vt.* to prop up as with a bolster (often with *up*)

**bolt**[1] (bōlt) *n.* [OE.] **1.** a short, blunt arrow used with a crossbow **2.** a flash of lightning **3.** a sudden dash **4.** a sliding bar for locking a door, etc. **5.** a threaded metal rod used with a nut to hold parts together **6.** a roll (*of* cloth, paper, etc.) —*vt.* **1.** to say suddenly; blurt (*out*) **2.** to swallow (food) hurriedly **3.** to fasten as with a bolt **4.** to abandon (a party, group, etc.) —*vi.* **1.** to start suddenly; spring away **2.** to withdraw support from one's party, etc. —*adv.* erectly [to sit *bolt* upright]

**bolt**[2] (bōlt) *vt.* [ < OFr. *buleter*] to sift (flour, grain, etc.)

**bo·lus** (bō′ləs) *n.* [ < Gr. *bōlos*] **1.** a small, round lump **2.** a large pill

**bomb** (bäm) *n.* [ < Gr. *bombos*, hollow sound] **1.** an explosive, incendiary, or chemical-filled container for dropping, hurling, etc. **2.** a small container with compressed gas in it **3.** [Slang] a complete failure —*vt.* to attack with bombs —*vi.* [Slang] to have a failure

**bom·bard** (bäm bärd′) *vt.* [ < Fr. *bombarde*, mortar] **1.** to attack with artillery or bombs **2.** to attack with questions, etc. **3.** to direct particles against the atomic nuclei of (an element) —**bom·bard′ment** *n.*

**bom·bar·dier** (bäm′bə dir′) *n.* one who releases the bombs in a bomber

**bom·bast** (bäm′bast) *n.* [ < Per. *pambak*, cotton] high-sounding, pompous language —**bom·bas′tic** *adj.* — **bom·bas′ti·cal·ly** *adv.*

**Bom·bay** (bäm′bā′) seaport in W India: pop. 2,772,000

**bomb·er** (bäm′ər) *n.* **1.** an airplane for dropping bombs **2.** one who bombs

**bomb′shell′** *n.* **1.** a bomb **2.** any sudden, shocking surprise

**bo·na fi·de** (bō′nə fīd′ *or* fī′dē) [L.] in good faith; without fraud

**bo·nan·za** (bə nan′zə) *n.* [Sp., prosperity] **1.** a rich vein of ore **2.** any source of wealth

**Bo·na·parte** (bō′nə pärt′) *see* NAPOLEON I

**bon·bon** (bän′bän′) *n.* [< Fr. *bon*, good] a small piece of candy

**bond** (bänd) *n.* [ult. < Gothic *bindan*, bind] **1.** anything that binds, fastens, or unites **2.** [*pl.*] shackles **3.** a binding agreement **4.** an obligation imposed by a contract, promise, etc. **5.** the status of goods kept in a warehouse until taxes are paid **6.** an interest-bearing certificate issued by a government or business, redeemable on a specified date **7.** *a)* surety against theft, absconding, etc. *b)* an amount paid as surety or bail —*vt.* **1.** to join; bind **2.** to furnish a bond (*n.* 7 *a*) for **3.** to place or hold (goods) in bond

**bond·age** (bän′dij) *n.* [ult. < ON. *bua*, inhabit] serfdom or slavery

**bond′man** (-mən) *n., pl.* **-men** **1.** a serf **2.** a slave —**bond′wom′an** *n.fem., pl.* **-wom′en**

**bonds·man** (bändz′mən) *n., pl.* **-men** **1.** *same as* BONDMAN **2.** one who furnishes bond (*n.* 7)

**bone** (bōn) *n.* [OE. *ban*] **1.** any of the parts of hard tissue forming the skeleton of most vertebrates **2.** this hard tissue **3.** a bonelike substance or thing —*vt.* **boned, bon′ing** to remove the bones from —*vi.* [Slang] to study hard (usually with *up*) —**have a bone to pick** to have cause to quarrel —**make no bones about** [Colloq.] to admit freely —**bone′less** *adj.*

**bone china** translucent china made of white clay to which the ash of burned bones has been added

**bone′-dry′** *adj.* very dry

**bone meal** crushed or ground bones, used as feed or fertilizer

**bon·er** (bōn′ər) *n.* [Slang] a blunder

**bon·fire** (bän′fīr′) *n.* [ME. *banefyre*, bone fire, pyre] an outdoor fire

**bong** (bôŋ, bäŋ) *n.* [echoic] a deep ringing sound, as of a large bell —*vi.* to make this sound

**bon·go** (bäŋ′gō) *n., pl.* **-gos** [AmSp. < ?] either of a pair of small drums of different pitch struck with the fingers: in full **bongo drum**

**bo·ni·to** (bə nēt′ō) *n., pl.* **-tos, -toes** [Sp.] any of several saltwater food fishes related to the tuna

BONGO DRUM

**bon jour** (bôn zhōōr′) [Fr.] good day; hello

**bon mot** (bôn′ mō′) *pl.* **bons mots** (bôn′ mōz′) [Fr., lit., good word] a clever or witty remark

**Bonn** (bän) capital of West Germany, on the Rhine: pop. 142,000

**bon·net** (bän′it) *n.* [< OFr. *bonet*] a hat with a chin ribbon, worn by children and women

**bon·ny, bon·nie** (bän′ē) *adj.* **-ni·er, -ni·est** [< L. *bonus*, good] [Chiefly Scot.] **1.** handsome or pretty, with a healthy glow **2.** pleasant

**bon·sai** (bän sī′) *n., pl.* **-sai** [Jap.] a tree or shrub grown in a pot and dwarfed by pruning, etc.

**bo·nus** (bō′nəs) *n., pl.* **-nus·es** [L., good] anything given in addition to the customary or required amount

**bon voy·age** (bän′ voi äzh′) [Fr.] pleasant journey

**bon·y** (bō′nē) *adj.* **-i·er, -i·est** **1.** of, like, or having bones **2.** thin; emaciated —**bon′i·ness** *n.*

**boo** (bōō) *interj., n., pl.* **boos** a sound made to express disapproval, etc., or to startle —*vi., vt.* **booed, boo′ing** to shout "boo" (at)

**boo-boo, boo·boo** (bōō′bōō′) *n., pl.* **-boos′** [Slang] a stupid mistake

**boo·by** (bōō′bē) *n., pl.* **-bies** [prob. < Sp. *bobo*] a fool; nitwit: also **boob** (bōōb)

**booby trap** any scheme or device for tricking a person unawares

**boo·dle** (bōō′d'l) *n.* [? < Du. *boedel*, property] [Slang] **1.** something given as a bribe; graft **2.** loot

**book** (book) *n.* [OE. *boc*] **1.** a printed work on sheets of paper bound together, usually between hard covers **2.** a main division of a literary work **3.** a record or account **4.** a libretto **5.** a booklike package, as of matches —*vt.* **1.** to record in a book; list **2.** to engage (rooms, etc.) ahead of time —**by the book** according to the rules —**the (Good) Book** the Bible

**book′bind′ing** *n.* the art or work of binding books —**book′bind′er** *n.* — **book′bind′er·y** *n., pl.* **-ies**

**book′case′** (-kās′) *n.* a set of shelves for holding books

**book′end′** *n.* a weight or bracket that keeps a row of books upright

**book·ie** (-ē) *n.* [Slang] a bookmaker

**book′ing** *n.* an engagement, as for a lecture, performance, etc.

**book·ish** (-ish) *adj.* **1.** inclined to read and study **2.** pedantic

**book′keep′ing** *n.* the work of keeping a systematic record of business transactions —**book′keep′er** *n.*

**book′let** (-lit) *n.* a small book

**book′mak′er** *n.* a person in the business of taking bets, as on horses

**book′mark′** *n.* a thing put between the pages of a book to mark the place

**book matches** safety matches of paper fastened into a small cardboard holder

**book'mo·bile'** (-mō bēl') *n.* a lending library traveling in a truck, etc. to areas lacking libraries

**book'shelf'** *n., pl. -shelves'* a shelf on which books are kept

**book'store'** *n.* a store where books are sold: also **book'shop'**

**book'worm'** *n.* 1. an insect larva that feeds on the binding, paste, etc. of books 2. one who reads much

**boom¹** (bōōm) *vi., vt.* [echoic] to make, or say with, a deep hollow sound —*n.* this sound

**boom²** (bōōm) *n.* [Du., a beam] 1. a spar extending from a mast to hold the bottom of a sail outstretched 2. a long beam extending as from an upright for supporting and guiding anything lifted 3. a barrier, as of logs, to prevent floating logs from dispersing —*vi.* to sail at top speed

**boom³** (bōōm) *vi.* [< *?* prec. *vi.*] to increase or grow rapidly —*vt.* to cause to flourish; support —*n.* 1. swift growth 2. a period of prosperity

**boom·er·ang** (bōōm'ə raŋ') *n.* [< Australian native name] 1. a flat, curved stick that can be thrown so that it returns to the thrower 2. a scheme, etc. that goes awry, to the schemer's harm —*vi.* to act as a boomerang

**boon¹** (bōōn) *n.* [ON. *bon*, petition] a welcome benefit; blessing

**boon²** (bōōn) *adj.* [< L. *bonus*, good] merry; convivial: in **boon companion**

**boon·docks, the** (bōōn'däks) *n.pl.* [< native Philippine name] [Colloq.] 1. a jungle or wilderness 2. any remote rural region

**boon·dog·gle** (bōōn'dôg''l, -däg'-) *vi.* -**gled, -gling** [Colloq.] to do trifling, pointless work —*n.* trifling, pointless work —**boon'dog'gler** *n.*

**boor** (boor) *n.* [Du. *boer*, a peasant] a rude, awkward, ill-mannered person —**boor'ish** *adj.* —**boor'ish·ly** *adv.*

**boost** (bōōst) *vt.* [< *?*] 1. to raise as by a push from below 2. to urge others to support 3. to increase —*n.* 1. a push upward or forward 2. an increase —**boost'er** *n.*

**booster shot** a later injection of a vaccine, for maintaining immunity

**boot¹** (bōōt) *n.* [OFr. *bote*] 1. a covering of leather, rubber, etc. for the foot and part of the leg 2. a patch for the inside of a tire casing 3. a kick —*vt.* 1. to put boots on 2. to kick 3. [Slang] to dismiss —**the boot** [Slang] dismissal

**boot²** (bōōt) *n., vt., vi.* [OE. *bot*, advantage] [Poet.] profit —**to boot** besides; in addition

**boot'black'** *n.* one whose work is shining shoes or boots

**boot·ie, boot·ie** (bōō tē') *n.* [*for 2* bōō'tē) *n.* 1. a short boot for women or children 2. a baby's knitted shoe

**booth** (bōōth) *n., pl.* **booths** (bōōthz) [< ON. *bua*, dwell] 1. a stall for selling goods 2. a small enclosure for voting at elections 3. a small structure to house a public telephone, eating

**boot'leg'** *vt., vi.* -**legged', -leg'ging** [< hiding liquor in a boot] to make or sell (esp. liquor) illegally —*adj.* bootlegged; illegal —*n.* bootlegged liquor —**boot'leg'ger** *n.*

**boot'less** *adj.* [< BOOT²] useless

**boo·ty** (bōōt'ē) *n., pl.* -**ties** [MLowG. *bute*] 1. spoils of war 2. plunder

**booze** (bōōz) *vi.* **boozed, booz'ing** [Du. *buizen*] [Colloq.] to drink too much liquor —*n.* [Colloq.] liquor

**bop** (bäp) *vt.* **bopped, bop'ping** [Slang] to hit; punch

**bo·rax** (bôr'aks) *n.* [< Per. *būrah*] a white, crystalline salt used in glass, soaps, etc.

**Bor·deaux** (bôr dō') seaport in SW France; pop. 250,000

**bor·der** (bôr'dər) *n.* [< OHG. *bord*, margin] 1. an edge or part near an edge; margin 2. a dividing line between two countries, etc. 3. a narrow strip along an edge —*vt.* 1. to provide with a border 2. to extend along the edge of —*adj.* of or near a border —**border on** (or **upon**) to be next to

**bor'der·land'** *n.* 1. land near a border 2. a vague condition

**bor'der·line'** *n.* a boundary —*adj.* 1. on a boundary 2. indefinite

**bore¹** (bôr) *vt.* **bored, bor'ing** [< OE. *bor*, auger] 1. to make a hole in with a drill, etc. 2. to make (a well, etc.) as by drilling 3. to weary by being dull —*vi.* to bore a hole or passage —*n.* 1. a hole made as by boring 2. *a)* the hollow part of a tube or gun barrel *b)* its inside diameter 3. a tiresome, dull person or thing —**bor'er** *n.*

**bore²** (bôr) *pt. of* BEAR¹

**bore·dom** (bôr'dəm) *n.* the condition of being bored or uninterested

**bo·ric acid** (bôr'ik) a white crystalline, weakly acid compound, used as a mild antiseptic

**born** (bôrn) *alt. pp. of* BEAR¹ —*adj.* 1. brought into life 2. natural, as if from birth [a *born* athlete]

**borne** (bôrn) *alt. pp. of* BEAR¹

**Bor·ne·o** (bôr'nē ō) large island in the Malay Archipelago, mostly belonging to Indonesia

**bo·ron** (bôr'än) *n.* [< BORAX] a nonmetallic chemical element

**bor·ough** (bur'ō, bur'-) *n.* [OE. *burg*, town] 1. a self-governing, incorporated town 2. any of the five administrative units of New York City

**bor·row** (bär'ō, bôr'-) *vt., vi.* [OE. *borgian*] 1. to take or receive (something) intending to return it 2. to adopt (an idea, etc.) as one's own —**bor'row·er** *n.*

**borsch** (bôrsh) *n.* [Russ. *borshch*] beet soup, served usually with sour cream: also **borsht** (bôrsht)

**bor·zoi** (bôr'zoi) *n.* [Russ., swift] a large dog with a narrow head, long legs, and silky coat

**bosh** (bäsh) *n., interj.* [Turk., empty] [Colloq.] nonsense

**bos·om** (booz'əm, bōō'zəm) *n.* [OE. *bosm*] 1. the human breast 2. the breast regarded as the source of feelings 3. the interior; midst [the *bosom* of one's family] 4. the part of a garment that covers the breast —*adj.* close; intimate [a *bosom* friend]

**bos·om·y** (-ē) *adj.* having large breasts

**boss**[1] (bôs) *n.* [Du. *baas*, a master] **1.** an employer or manager **2.** one who controls a political organization —*vt.* **1.** to act as boss of **2.** [Colloq.] to order (a person) about —*adj.* [Slang] excellent

**boss**[2] (bôs, bäs) *n.* [OFr. *boce*, a swelling] a protruding ornament or projecting knob —*vt.* to stud

**boss·ism** *n.* control by bosses, esp. of a political machine or party

**boss·y** *adj.* -i·er, -i·est [Colloq.] domineering —**boss·i·ly** *adv.*

**Bos·ton** (bôs't'n, bäs'-) seaport and capital of Mass.; pop. 641,000 — **Bos·to·ni·an** (-tō'nē ən) *adj., n.*

**bo·sun** (bōs'n) *n.* same as BOATSWAIN

**bot·a·ny** (bät'n ē) *n.* [< Gr. *botanē*, a plant] the science that deals with plants and plant life —**bo·tan·i·cal** (bə tan'i k'l), **bo·tan·ic** *adj.* —**bot'a·nist** *n.*

**botch** (bäch) *vt.* [< ? Du. *botsen*, to patch] **1.** to patch clumsily **2.** to bungle —*n.* a bungled or unskilled piece of work

**both** (bōth) *adj., pron.* [OE. *ba tha*, both these] the two [*both* birds sang loudly] —*conj., adv.* together; equally [*both* tired and hungry]

**both·er** (bäth'ər) *vt., vi.* [prob. < *pother*] **1.** to worry; harass **2.** to concern (oneself) —*n.* **1.** worry; trouble **2.** one who gives trouble —**both'er·some** (-səm) *adj.*

**Bot·swa·na** (bät swä'nə) country in S Africa: 222,000 sq. mi.; pop. 576,000

**Bot·ti·cel·li** (bät'ə chel'ē), **San·dro** (sän'drō) 1445?-1510; It. painter

**bot·tle** (bät''l) *n.* [< LL. *buttis*, a cask] **1.** a narrow-necked container for liquids, usually of glass **2.** its contents —*vt.* -tled, -tling to put into a bottle —**bottle up** to restrain —**hit the bottle** [Slang] to drink much alcoholic liquor —**bot'tler** *n.*

**bot·tle·neck** *n.* **1.** a narrow passage or road **2.** any hindrance to movement or progress

**bot·tom** (bät'əm) *n.* [OE. *botm*, ground] **1.** the lowest part or place **2.** the part on which something rests **3.** the side underneath **4.** the seat of a chair **5.** the ground beneath a body of water **6.** basis; cause; source **7.** [Colloq.] the buttocks —*adj.* lowest; last; basic —**at bottom** fundamentally —**bot'tom·less** *adj.*

**bot·u·lism** (bäch'ə liz'm) *n.* [< L. *botulus*, sausage] poisoning from the toxin produced by a bacillus sometimes found in improperly preserved foods

**bou·doir** (bōōd'wär) *n.* [< Fr., pouting room] a woman's private room

**bouf·fant** (bōō fänt') *adj.* [< Fr. *bouffer*, puff out] puffed out; full

**bou·gain·vil·le·a, bou·gain·vil·lae·a** (bōō'gən vil'ē ə) *n.* [ModL.] a woody tropical vine having large purple or red bracts

**bough** (bou) *n.* [OE. *bog*, shoulder] a main branch of a tree

**bought** (bôt) *pt. & pp. of* BUY

**bouil·lon** (bōōl'yän, -yən) *n.* [< Fr. *bouillir*, to boil] a clear broth

**boul·der** (bōl'dər) *n.* [< ME. *bulderstan*, noisy stone] a large rock worn by weather and water

**boul·e·vard** (bōōl'ə värd') *n.* [Fr. < MDu. *bolwerc*, bulwark] a broad street, often lined with trees

**bounce** (bouns) *vi.* **bounced, bounc'ing** [ME. *bounsen*, to thump] **1.** to spring back, as upon impact; rebound **2.** to spring; leap **3.** [Slang] to be returned: said of a worthless check —*vt.* **1.** to cause (a ball, etc.) to bounce **2.** [Slang] to put (a person) out by force **3.** [Slang] to fire from a job —*n.* **1.** a bouncing; rebound **2.** a leap or jump **3.** capacity for bouncing **4.** [Colloq.] energy, dash, etc. —**the bounce** [Slang] dismissal —**bounc'y** *adj.*

**bounc·er** (boun'sər) *n.* [Slang] a man hired to remove disorderly people from nightclubs, etc.

**bounc·ing** *adj.* big, healthy, etc.

**bound**[1] (bound) *vi.* [Fr. *bondir*, to leap] **1.** to move with a leap or leaps **2.** to bounce; rebound —*vt.* to cause to bound or bounce —*n.* **1.** a jump; leap **2.** a bounce; rebound

**bound**[2] (bound) *pt. & pp. of* BIND — *adj.* **1.** tied **2.** closely connected **3.** certain [*bound* to win] **4.** obliged **5.** having a binding, as a book **6.** [Colloq.] determined; resolved

**bound**[3] (bound) *adj.* [< ON. *bua*, prepare] going; headed [*bound* east]

**bound**[4] (bound) *n.* [< ML. *butina*] **1.** a boundary **2.** [*pl.*] an area near a boundary —*vt.* **1.** to limit **2.** to be a limit or boundary to **3.** to name the boundaries of —**out of bounds 1.** beyond the boundaries **2.** forbidden —**bound'less** *adj.* —**bound'less·ly** *adv.*

**bound·a·ry** (boun'drē, -dər ē) *n., pl.* -ries anything marking a limit; bound

**bound·en** (-dən) *adj.* [old pp. of BIND] **1.** obligated **2.** obligatory [one's *bounden* duty]

**bound·er** (-dər) *n.* [< BOUND[1]] [Chiefly Brit. Colloq.] a cad

**boun·te·ous** (boun'tē əs) *adj.* [see ff.] **1.** generous **2.** abundant Also **boun'ti·ful** (-tə f'l)

**boun·ty** (-tē) *n., pl.* -ties [< L. *bonus*, good] **1.** generosity **2.** a generous gift **3.** a reward or premium

**bou·quet** (bō kā', bōō-) *n.* [Fr.] **1.** a bunch of flowers **2.** aroma, as of wine

**bour·bon** (bur'bən, bōōr'-) *n.* [< *Bourbon* County, Ky.] [*sometimes* B-] a whiskey distilled from corn mash

**bour·geois** (boor zhwä') *n., pl.* -geois' [Fr. < LL. *burgus*, castle] a member of the bourgeoisie —*adj.* of the bourgeoisie: used variously to mean commonplace, respectable, smug, etc.

**bour·geoi·sie** (boor'zhwä'zē') *n.* [*with sing. or pl. v.*] the social class between the very wealthy and the working class; middle class

**bourn, bourne** (bôrn, boorn) *n.* [OFr. *bunne*] [Archaic] 1. a limit; boundary 2. a goal

**bout** (bout) *n.* [ME. *bught*] 1. a struggle or contest 2. a period spent in some activity; spell

**bou·tique** (boo tēk′) *n.* [Fr. < Gr. *apothēkē,* storehouse] a small shop which sells fashionable articles

**bou·ton·niere, bou·ton·nière** (boot′'n ir′, -er′) *n.* [Fr., buttonhole] a flower worn in a buttonhole

**bo·vine** (bō′vīn, -vin) *adj.* [ < L. *bos, ox*] 1. of an ox or cow 2. slow, stupid, etc. —*n.* an ox, cow, etc.

**bow**[1] (bou) *vi.* [ < OE. *bugan,* to bend] 1. to bend the head or body in respect, agreement, etc. 2. to submit; yield —*vt.* 1. to bend (the head or body) in agreement, etc. 2. to weigh (*down*) —*n.* a bending of the head or body, as in greeting —**take a bow** to acknowledge applause, etc.

**bow**[2] (bō) *n.* [OE. *boga*] 1. anything curved [a rainbow] 2. a curve; bend 3. a flexible, curved strip of wood with a cord connecting the ends, for shooting arrows 4. a slender stick strung with horsehairs, for playing a violin, etc. 5. *same as* BOWKNOT —*adj.* curved —*vt., vi.* 1. to bend; curve 2. to play (a violin, etc.) with a bow

**bow**[3] (bou) *n.* [ < LowG. *bûg*] the front part of a ship, etc. —*adj.* of or near the bow

**bowd·ler·ize** (boud′lə rīz′) *vt.* -ized′, -iz′ing [ < T. *Bowdler* (1754–1825), Eng. editor] to expurgate —**bowd′ler·ism** *n.* —**bowd′ler·i·za′tion** *n.*

**bow·el** (bou′əl) *n.* [ < L. *botulus,* sausage] 1. an intestine, esp. of a human being 2. [*pl.*] the inner part —**move one's bowels** to defecate

**bow·er** (bou′ər) *n.* [ < OE. *bur,* dwelling] a place enclosed by boughs or vines; arbor

**bow·ie knife** (bōō′ē, bō′-) [ < Col. J. *Bowie* (1799?–1836)] a long single-edged hunting knife

**bow·knot** (bō′nät′) *n.* a knot usually with two loops and two ends

**bowl**[1] (bōl) *n.* [OE. *bolla*] 1. a deep, rounded dish 2. a large drinking cup 3. a bowl-like thing or part 4. an amphitheater 5. the contents of a bowl

**bowl**[2] (bōl) *n.* [ < L. *bulla,* a bubble] 1. a heavy ball used in the game of bowls 2. a roll of the ball in bowling —*vi., vt.* 1. to roll (a ball) or participate in bowling 2. to move swiftly and smoothly —**bowl over** 1. to knock over 2. [Colloq.] to astonish —**bowl′er** *n.*

**bowl·der** (bōl′dər) *n. same as* BOULDER

**bow·leg** (bō′leg′) *n.* a leg with outward curvature —**bow′leg′ged** (-leg′id, -legd′) *adj.*

**bowl′ing** *n.* a game in which a heavy ball is bowled along a wooden lane (**bowling alley**) at ten wooden pins

**bowls** (bōlz) *n.* a bowling game played on a smooth lawn (**bowling green**)

**bow·man** (bō′mən) *n., pl.* -men an archer

**bow·sprit** (bou′sprit, bō′-) *n.* [prob. < Du.] a tapered spar extending forward from the bow of a sailing ship

**bow tie** (bō) a necktie tied in a bow

**box**[1] (bäks) *n.* [ < Gr. *pyxos,* BOX[3]] 1. a container, usually rectangular and lidded; case 2. the contents of a box 3. a boxlike thing or space [a jury *box*] 4. a small, enclosed group of seats, as in a theater 5. a booth 6. *Baseball* an area designated for the batter, pitcher, etc. —*vt.* to put into a box —**box in** (or up) to shut in or keep in; surround or confine —**in a box** [Colloq.] in difficulty —**box′like′** *adj.*

**box**[2] (bäks) *n.* [ < ?] a blow struck with the hand —*vt.* 1. to strike such a blow 2. to fight by boxing with —*vi.* to fight with the fists

**box**[3] (bäks) *n.* [ < Gr. *pyxos*] an evergreen shrub with small leathery leaves: also **box′wood′**

**box′car′** *n.* a fully enclosed railroad freight car

**box′er** *n.* 1. a man who boxes; prizefighter 2. a medium-sized dog with a sturdy body and a smooth coat

**box′ing** *n.* the skill or sport of fighting with the fists, esp. in padded leather mittens (**boxing gloves**)

**box office** 1. a place where admission tickets are sold, as in a theater 2. [Colloq.] the power, as of a performer, to attract a paying audience

**boy** (boi) *n.* [ME. *boie*] 1. a male child 2. any man: familiar term 3. a male servant: patronizing term —*interj.* [Slang] an exclamation of pleasure, surprise, awe, etc.: often oh, boy! —**boy′hood′** *n.* —**boy′ish** *adj.*

**boy·cott** (boi′kät) *vt.* [ < Capt. *Boycott,* Irish land agent so treated] to join together in refusing to deal with, buy, etc. so as to punish or coerce —*n.* a boycotting

**boy′friend′** *n.* [Colloq.] 1. a sweetheart or escort of a girl or woman 2. a boy who is one's friend

**boy scout** a member of the **Boy Scouts,** a boys' club that stresses outdoor life and service to others

**boy·sen·ber·ry** (boi′z'n ber′ē) *n., pl.* -ries [ < R. *Boysen,* U.S. horticulturist] a berry that is a cross of the raspberry, loganberry, and blackberry

**Br** *Chem.* bromine

**Br.** 1. Britain 2. British

**bra** (brä) *n.* [ < BRASSIERE] a brassiere

**brace** (brās) *vt.* braced, brac′ing [ < Gr. *brachiōn,* arm] 1. to bind 2. to strengthen by supporting the weight of, etc. 3. to make ready for an impact, shock, etc. 4. to stimulate —*n.* 1. a couple; pair 2. a thing that clamps or connects 3. [*pl.*] [Brit.] suspenders 4. a device for setting up or maintaining tension 5. either of the signs { }, used to connect words, lines, etc. 6. any propping device 7. *a)* a device for supporting a weak part of the body *b)* [often *pl.*] a device worn for straightening the teeth 8. a tool for holding a

BOWIE
KNIFE

drilling bit —**brace up** [Colloq.] to call forth one's courage, etc.

**brace and bit** a boring tool consisting of a removable drill (*bit*) in a rotating handle (*brace*)

**brace·let** (brās′lit) *n.* [< Gr. *brachiōn*, arm] an ornamental band or chain worn about the wrist or arm

**brack·en** (brak′n) *n.* [ME. *braken*] a large, coarse, weedy fern found in meadows, woods, and wastelands

**brack·et** (brak′it) *n.* [< Fr. *brague*, knee pants] 1. a support projecting from a wall, etc. 2. any angle-shaped support 3. either of the signs [ ], used to enclose a word, etc. 4. a classification *[high income bracket]* —*vt.* 1. to support with brackets 2. to enclose within brackets 3. to classify together

**brack·ish** (brak′ish) *adj.* [< MDu. *brak*] 1. salty 2. nauseating

**bract** (brakt) *n.* [L. *bractea*, thin metal plate] a modified leaf growing at the base of a flower or on its stalk

**brad** (brad) *n.* [ON. *broddr*, a spike] a thin wire nail with a small head

**brae** (brā) *n.* [ON. *bra*, brow] [Scot.] a sloping bank; hillside

**brag** (brag) *vt.*, *vi.* **bragged, brag′ging** [prob. < OFr. *braguer*] to boast —*n.* boastful talk —**brag′ger** *n.*

**brag′gart** (-ərt) *n.* an offensively boastful person —*adj.* boastful

**Brah·ma** (brä′mə) the chief member of the Hindu trinity (Brahma, Vishnu, and Siva), regarded as the creator of the universe

**Brah·man** (brä′mən) *n.*, *pl.* **-mans** [Hind. < Sans., worship] 1. a member of the priestly Hindu caste 2. a breed of domestic cattle related to the zebu of India

**Brahms** (brämz), **Jo·han·nes** (yō hän′əs) 1833–97; Ger. composer

**braid** (brād) *vt.* [< OE. *bregdan*, move quickly] 1. to interweave three or more strands of (hair, straw, etc.) 2. to make by such interweaving —*n.* 1. a strip, as of hair, formed by braiding 2. a woven band of cloth, etc., used to bind or decorate clothing

**Braille** (brāl) *n.* [< Louis *Braille*, its 19th-c. Fr. inventor] [*also* b-] a system of printing for the blind, using raised dots felt with the fingers

**brain** (brān) *n.* [OE. *brægen*] 1. the mass of nerve tissue in the cranium of vertebrates 2. [*often pl.*] intelligence —*vt.* to dash out the brains of

**brain′child′** *n.* [Colloq.] an idea, plan, etc. produced by one's mental labor

**brain drain** [Colloq.] an exhausting of the intellectual or professional resources of a country or region, esp. through emigration

**brain′less** *adj.* foolish or stupid

**brain′storm′** *n.* [Colloq.] a sudden inspiration or idea

**brain′storm′ing** *n.* the unrestrained offering of ideas by all members of a group to seek solutions to problems

**brain′wash′** *vt.* [Colloq.] to indoctri-

nate so thoroughly as to effect a radical change of beliefs

**brain wave** 1. rhythmic electric impulses from the nerve centers in the brain 2. [Colloq.] a brainstorm

**brain′y** *adj.* **-i·er, -i·est** [Colloq.] having a good mind; intelligent

**braise** (brāz) *vt.* **braised, brais′ing** [< Fr. *braise*, live coals] to brown (meat) and then simmer slowly

**brake** (brāk) *n.* [< MLowG. *breken*, to break] any device for slowing or stopping a vehicle or machine, as by pressing a block or band against a moving part —*vt.*, *vi.* **braked, brak′ing** to slow down or stop as with a brake —**brake′less** *adj.*

**brake′man** (-mən) *n.*, *pl.* **-men** formerly, an operator of brakes on a railroad train, now, assistant to the conductor

**bram·ble** (bram′b'l) *n.* [< OE. *brom*, broom] a prickly shrub of the rose family, as the raspberry, blackberry, etc. —**bram′bly** *adj.*

**bran** (bran) *n.* [OFr. *bren*] the husk of grains of wheat, rye, etc. separated from the flour, as by sifting

**branch** (branch) *n.* [< LL. *branca*, a claw] 1. any woody extension from a tree or shrub; limb 2. a tributary stream 3. any part or extension of a main body or system, as a division of a family or a separately located unit of a business —*vi.* 1. to put forth branches 2. to come out (*from* the main part) as a branch —**branch off** 1. to separate into branches 2. to diverge —**branch out** to extend one's interests, activities, etc. —**branched** *adj.* —**branch′like′** *adj.*

**brand** (brand) *n.* [OE. < *biernan*, to burn] 1. a burning or partially burned stick 2. a mark burned on the skin, formerly used to punish criminals, now used on cattle to show ownership 3. the iron used in branding 4. a stigma 5. *a)* an identifying mark or label *b)* the make of a commodity *[a brand of tea] c)* a special kind —*vt.* 1. to mark with a brand 2. to put a stigma on —**brand′er** *n.*

**bran·dish** (bran′dish) *vt.* [< Gmc. *brand*, sword] to wave menacingly or as a challenge; to flourish

**brand name** the name by which a certain brand or make of commodity is known —**brand′-name′** *adj.*

**brand′-new′** *adj.* [orig., fresh from the fire: see BRAND] entirely new

**bran·dy** (bran′dē) *n.*, *pl.* **-dies** [< Du. *brandewijn*, distilled wine] an alcoholic liquor distilled from wine or from fermented fruit juice —*vt.* **-died, -dy·ing** to flavor or preserve with brandy

**brash** (brash) *adj.* [orig. Scot. < ?] 1. hasty and reckless 2. insolent; impudent —**brash′ness** *n.*

**brass** (bras) *n.* [OE. *bræs*] 1. a yellowish metal, an alloy of copper and zinc 2. [*often pl.*] brass-wind musical instruments 3. [Colloq.] bold impudence 4. [Slang] officers or officials of high rank —*adj.* of brass —**brass'y** *adj.* **-i·er, -i·est**

**bras·siere, bras·sière** (brə zir') *n.* [Fr. < *bras*, an arm] an undergarment worn by women to support the breasts

**brass tacks** [Colloq.] basic facts

**brass winds** musical instruments made of coiled metal tubes and having a cup-shaped mouthpiece, as the trumpet and tuba —**brass'-wind'** *adj.*

**brat** (brat) *n.* [ < Gael. *bratt*, cloth, rag] a child, esp. an impudent, unruly child: scornful or playful term

**brat·wurst** (brat'wərst) *n.* [G. < OHG. *brato*, lean meat + *wurst*, sausage] highly spiced, fresh sausage of veal and pork

**braun·schwei·ger** (broun'shwī'gər) *n.* [ < *Braunschweig*, Germany, where orig. made] smoked liver sausage

**bra·va·do** (brə vä'dō) *n.* [ < Sp. < *bravo*, BRAVE] pretended courage or feigned confidence

**brave** (brāv) *adj.* [Fr. < It. *bravo*] 1. not afraid; having courage 2. having a fine appearance —*n.* 1. any brave man 2. a N. American Indian warrior —*vt.* **braved, brav'ing** 1. to face with courage 2. to defy; dare —**brave'ly** *adv.* —**brave'ness** *n.*

**brav·er·y** (brā'vər ē) *n.* courage; valor

**bra·vo** (brä'vō) *interj.* [It.] well done! excellent! —*n.* a shout of "bravo"

**bra·vu·ra** (brə vyoor'ə) *n.* [It. < *bravo*, brave] 1. bold daring; dash 2. a brilliant musical passage or technique

**brawl** (brôl) *vi.* [ < Du. *brallen*, to boast] to quarrel or fight noisily —*n.* a noisy quarrel or fight

**brawn** (brôn) *n.* [ < OFr. *braon*, muscle] 1. strong, well-developed muscles 2. muscular strength — **brawn'i·ness** *n.* —**brawn'y** *adj.* **-i·er, -i·est**

**bray** (brā) *vi.* [ < VL. *bragire*, cry out] to make the loud, harsh cry of a donkey —*n.* the harsh cry of a donkey, or a sound like this

**braze** (brāz) *vt.* **brazed, braz'ing** [Fr. *braser*] to solder with a metal having a high melting point

**bra·zen** (brā'z'n) *adj.* [ < OE. *bræs*, brass] 1. of brass 2. like brass in color, etc. 3. shameless; bold 4. harsh and piercing —**brazen it out** to act in a bold, unashamed way —**bra'zen·ly** *adv.* —**bra'zen·ness** *n.*

**bra·zier¹** (brā'zhər) *n.* [see BRAISE] a metal container to hold burning coals

**bra·zier²** (brā'zhər) *n.* [see BRASS] a person who works in brass

**Bra·zil** (brə zil') country in C & NE S.America: c.3,287,000 sq. mi.; pop. 84,829,000 —**Bra·zil'ian** *adj., n.*

**Brazil nut** the edible, three-sided seed of a tree of S. America

**breach** (brēch) *n.* [ < OE. *brecan*, to break] 1. a failure to observe a law, promise, etc. 2. an opening made by a breakthrough 3. a break in friendship —*vt.* to make a breach in — **breach of promise** a breaking of a promise to marry

**bread** (bred) *n.* [OE., crumb] 1. a

baked food made of flour or meal mixed with water, etc. 2. livelihood [to earn one's *bread*] —*vt.* to coat with bread crumbs before cooking —**break bread** to eat

**breadth** (bredth) *n.* [ < OE. *brad*, broad] 1. width 2. scope; extent

**bread'win'ner** *n.* one who supports dependents by his earnings

**break** (brāk) *vt.* **broke, bro'ken, break'ing** [OE. *brecan*] 1. to split or crack into pieces; smash 2. to cut open the surface of (soil, the skin, etc.) 3. to make unusable by cracking, disrupting, etc. 4. to tame as with force 5. to get rid of (a habit) 6. to demote 7. to make poor, ill, bankrupt, etc. 8. to surpass (a record) 9. to violate (a promise, etc.) 10. to disrupt the order of [to *break* ranks] 11. to interrupt (a journey, electric circuit, etc.) 12. to reduce the force of by interrupting (a fall, etc.) 13. to bring to an end suddenly or by force 14. to penetrate (silence, darkness, etc.) 15. to disclose 16. to decipher or solve [*break* a code] —*vi.* 1. to split into pieces; come apart 2. to force one's way (*through* obstacles, etc.) 3. to stop associating (*with*) 4. to become unusable 5. to change suddenly [his voice *broke*] 6. to begin suddenly [to *break* into song] 7. to come into being, notice, etc. [the story *broke*] 8. to stop activity temporarily 9. to suffer a collapse, as of spirit —*n.* 1. a breaking 2. a broken place 3. a beginning or appearance [the *break* of day] 4. an interruption of regularity 5. an interval, gap, or rest 6. a sudden change 7. an escape 8. [Slang] a chance piece of luck —**break down** 1. to go out of working order 2. to have a physical or emotional collapse 3. to analyze —**break in** 1. to enter forcibly 2. to interrupt 3. to train (a beginner) 4. to work the stiffness out of —**break off** to stop abruptly — **break out** 1. to become covered with pimples, etc. 2. to escape suddenly —**break up** 1. to separate; disperse 2. to stop 3. [Colloq.] to make laugh —**break'a·ble** *adj.*

**break'age** (-ij) *n.* 1. a breaking 2. things broken 3. loss due to breaking 4. the sum allowed for such loss

**break'down'** *n.* 1. a breaking down 2. a failure of health 3. an analysis

**break'er** *n.* 1. a thing that breaks 2. a wave that breaks into foam

**break·fast** (brek'fast) *n.* the first meal of the day —*vi.* to eat breakfast

**break·front** (brāk'frunt') *adj.* having a projecting center section in front —*n.* a breakfront cabinet

**break'-in'** *n.* the act of forcibly entering a building, esp. in order to rob

**break·neck** (brāk'nek') *adj.* highly dangerous [*breakneck* speed]

**break'through'** *n.* 1. the act of forcing a way through against resistance, as in warfare 2. a very important advance or discovery

**break'up'** *n.* 1. a dispersion 2. a disintegration 3. a collapse

**break'wa'ter** *n.* a barrier to break

the impact of waves, as before a harbor

**breast** (brest) *n.* [OE. *breost*] **1.** either of two milk-secreting glands on a woman's body **2.** the upper, front part of the body **3.** the part of a garment, etc. over the breast **4.** the breast regarded as the center of emotions —*vt.* to face firmly; oppose

**breast′bone′** *n. same as* STERNUM

**breast′-feed′** *vt.* -fed′, -feed′ing to feed (a baby) milk from the breast

**breast′plate′** *n.* a piece of armor for the breast

**breast stroke** a swimming stroke in which both arms are brought out sideways from the chest

**breast′work′** *n.* a low wall put up quickly as a defense in battle

**breath** (breth) *n.* [OE. *bræth*, odor] **1.** air taken into the lungs and then let out **2.** respiration **3.** the power to breathe easily **4.** life; spirit **5.** a fragrant odor **6.** a slight breeze **7.** a whisper; murmur —**below** (or **under**) **one's breath** in a whisper —**catch one's breath 1.** to gasp or pant **2.** to pause or rest —**out of breath** breathless, as from exertion —**take one's breath away** to thrill

**breathe** (brēth) *vi., vt.* **breathed, breath′ing 1.** to take (air) into the lungs and let it out again; inhale and exhale **2.** to live **3.** to speak or sing softly; whisper **4.** to rest —**breathe again** (or **freely**) to have a feeling of relief —**breath′a·ble** *adj.*

**breath·er** (brē′thər) *n.* **1.** one who breathes **2.** [Colloq.] a pause for rest

**breath·less** (breth′lis) *adj.* **1.** without breath **2.** panting; gasping **3.** unable to breathe easily because of emotion —**breath′less·ly** *adv.*

**breath′tak′ing** *adj.* very exciting

**breath·y** (breth′ē) *adj.* marked by an audible emission of breath

**bred** (bred) *pt. & pp. of* BREED

**breech** (brēch) *n.* [OE. *brec*] **1.** the buttocks **2.** the part of a gun behind the barrel

**breech′cloth′** *n. same as* LOINCLOTH

**breech·es** (brich′iz) *n.pl.* **1.** trousers reaching to the knees **2.** [Colloq.] any trousers

**breed** (brēd) *vt.* **bred, breed′ing** [< OE. *brod*, fetus] **1.** to bring forth (offspring) **2.** to be the source of; produce **3.** to raise (animals) **4.** to rear; train —*vi.* **1.** to be produced; originate **2.** to reproduce —*n.* **1.** a stock; strain **2.** a sort; type —**breed′er** *n.*

**breed·ing** *n.* **1.** the producing of young **2.** good upbringing **3.** the producing of plants and animals, esp. for improving the stock

**breeze** (brēz) *n.* [< Fr. *brise*] **1.** a gentle wind **2.** [Colloq.] a thing easy to do —*vi.* **breezed, breez′ing** [Slang] to move or go briskly

**breeze′way′** *n.* a covered passageway, as between a house and garage

**breez·y** (brēz′ē) *adj.* **-i·er, -i·est 1.** having a breeze **2.** light and gay —**breez′i·ly** *adv.* —**breez′i·ness** *n.*

**Bre·men** (brem′ən; *G.* brā′mən) seaport in N West Germany: pop. 588,000

**breth·ren** (breth′rən) *n.pl.* [ME. *bretheren*] brothers: chiefly religious

**bre·vet** (brə vet′) *n.* [< L. *brevis*, brief] *Mil.* a commission giving higher honorary rank without extra pay —*vt.* **-vet′ted** or **-vet′ed, -vet′ting** or **-vet′ing** to give a brevet to

**bre·vi·ar·y** (brē′vē er′ē) *n., pl.* **-ies** [< L. *brevis*, brief] a book of prayers, hymns, etc. to be recited daily by priests, nuns, etc.

**brev·i·ty** (brev′ə tē) *n.* [< L. *brevis*, brief] briefness

**brew** (brōō) *vt.* [OE. *breowan*] **1.** to make (beer, ale, etc.) from malt and hops by boiling and fermenting **2.** to steep (tea, etc.) **3.** to plot; scheme —*vi.* to begin to form —*n.* a beverage brewed —**brew′er** *n.*

**brew·er·y** (brōō′ər ē) *n., pl.* **-ies** a place where beer, etc. is brewed

**Brezh·nev** (brezh′nef), **Le·o·nid** (lā′ô nēt′) 1906-  ; general secretary of the Communist Party of the U.S.S.R. (1964- )

**bri·ar** (brī′ər) *n. same as* BRIER

**bribe** (brīb) *n.* [< OFr. *briber*, beg] anything given or promised as an inducement, esp. to do something illegal or wrong —*vt.* **bribed, brib′ing** to offer or give a bribe to —**brib′er·y** *n.*

**bric-a-brac** (brik′ə brak′) *n.* [< Fr. *à bric et à brac*, by hook or crook] **1.** small artistic objects used to ornament a room **2.** knickknacks

**brick** (brik) *n.* [< MDu. *breken*, piece of baked clay] **1.** an oblong block of baked clay, used in building, etc. **2.** anything shaped like a brick —*adj.* built or paved with brick —*vt.* to build or cover with brick

**brick′bat′** *n.* **1.** a piece of brick used as a missile **2.** an unfavorable remark

**brick′lay′ing** *n.* the work of building with bricks —**brick′lay′er** *n.*

**brid·al** (brīd′'l) *n.* [< OE. *bryd ealo*, bride feast] a wedding —*adj.* **1.** of a bride **2.** of a wedding

**bride** (brīd) *n.* [OE. *bryd*] a woman just married or about to be married

**bride′groom′** *n.* [< OE. *bryd*, bride + *guma*, man] a man just married or about to be married

**brides·maid** (brīdz′mād′) *n.* a young woman attending the bride during a wedding

**bridge¹** (brij) *n.* [OE. *brycge*] **1.** a structure built over a river, etc. to provide a way across **2.** a thing that provides connection, contact, etc. **3.** the bony part of the nose **4.** a raised platform on a ship **5.** a mounting for false teeth —*vt.* **bridged, bridg′ing** to build or be a bridge over —**burn one's bridges (behind one)** to follow a course from which there is no retreat —**bridge′a·ble** *adj.*

**bridge²** (brij) *n.* [< ? Russ.] a card game for two pairs of players in which they bid for the right to name the trump suit or declare no-trump

**bridge'head'** *n.* a fortified position established by an attacking force in enemy territory

**Bridge·port** (brij'pôrt') seaport in SW Conn.: pop. 157,000

**bridge'work'** *n.* a dental bridge or bridges

**bri·dle** (brīd''l) *n.* [< OE. *bregdan*, to pull] 1. a head harness for guiding a horse 2. anything that controls or restrains —*vt.* **-dled, -dling** 1. to put a bridle on 2. to curb or control —*vi.* to draw one's head back as an expression of anger, scorn, etc.

**bridle path** a path for horseback riding

BRIDLE

**brief** (brēf) *adj.* [< L. *brevis*] 1. short 2. concise —*n.* 1. a summary, specif. of the main points of a law case 2. [*pl.*] legless undershorts —*vt.* 1. to summarize 2. to supply with all pertinent information —**brief'ing** *n.* —**brief'ly** *adv.* —**brief'ness** *n.*

**brief'case'** *n.* a flat, flexible case for carrying papers, books, etc.

**bri·er¹** (brī'ər) *n.* [OE. *brer*] any thorny bush, as a bramble

**bri·er²** (brī'ər) *n.* [Fr. *bruyère*] a variety of heath, whose root is used for making tobacco pipes

**brig** (brig) *n.* 1. [< *brigantine*] a two-masted ship with square sails 2. [< ?] a prison on a warship

**bri·gade** (bri gād') *n.* [< It. *briga*, strife] 1. a militar unit composed of two or more battalions with service and administrative units 2. a group of people organized to function as a unit in some work [a fire *brigade*]

**brig·a·dier general** (brig'ə dir') a military officer ranking just above a colonel

**brig·and** (brig'ənd) *n.* [see BRIGADE] a bandit, esp. one of a roving band

**brig'and·age** (-ən dij) *n.* 1. plundering by brigands 2. brigands collectively

**brig·an·tine** (brig'ən tēn') *n.* [< It. *brigantino*, pirate vessel] a ship with the foremast square-rigged and a fore-and-aft mainsail

**bright** (brīt) *adj.* [OE. *bryht*] 1. shining with light 2. brilliant in color or sound; vivid 3. lively; cheerful 4. mentally quick; clever 5. favorable or hopeful 6. illustrious —**bright'ly** *adv.* —**bright'ness** *n.*

**bright'en** (-'n) *vt., vi.* to make or become bright or brighter

**Brigh·ton** (brīt''n) resort city in S England: pop. 163,000

**bril·liant** (bril'yənt) *adj.* [< Fr. < It. *brillare*, to sparkle] 1. shining brightly 2. vivid 3. very splendid 4. very intelligent, talented, etc. —**bril'liance, bril'lian·cy** *n.* —**bril'liant·ly** *adv.*

**bril·lian·tine** (bril'yən tēn') *n.* [< Fr.] an oily dressing for the hair

**brim** (brim) *n.* [OE., sea] 1. the topmost edge of a cup, glass, etc. 2. a projecting rim, as of a hat —*vt., vi.* **brimmed, brim'ming** to fill or be full to the brim —**brim'less** *adj.*

**brim'ful** *adj.* full to the brim

**brim'stone'** *n.* [< OE. *biernan*, burn + *stan*, stone] sulfur

**brin·dle** (brin'd'l) *adj. same as* BRINDLED —*n.* a brindled color

**brin'dled** (-d'ld) *adj.* [prob. < ME. *brennen*, to burn] having a gray or tawny coat marked with darker streaks

**brine** (brīn) *n.* [OE.] 1. water full of salt 2. the ocean —**brin'y** *adj.*

**bring** (brin) *vt.* **brought, bring'ing** [OE. *bringan*] 1. to carry or lead "here" or to the place where the speaker will be 2. to cause to happen 3. to lead to an action or belief 4. to sell for —**bring about** to cause —**bring forth** to give birth to; produce —**bring off** to accomplish —**bring out** 1. to reveal 2. to offer (a play, book, etc.) to the public —**bring to** to revive (an unconscious person) —**bring up** 1. to rear (children) 2. to introduce, as into discussion 3. to cough or vomit up

**brink** (brink) *n.* [< MLowG. or Dan., shore] the edge, esp. at the top of a steep place; verge

**brink'man·ship'** (-mən ship') *n.* the policy of pursuing a risky course of action to the brink of disaster: also **brinks'man·ship'**

**bri·oche** (brē ōsh') *n.* [Fr.] a light, rich roll made with flour, eggs, etc.

**bri·quette, bri·quet** (bri ket') *n.* [Fr. < *brique*, brick] a brick of compressed coal dust, etc.

**Bris·bane** (briz'bān) seaport in E Australia: pop. 664,000

**brisk** (brisk) *adj.* [< ? Fr. *brusque*, brusque] 1. quick in manner; energetic 2. keen, bracing, etc. —**brisk'ly** *adv.* —**brisk'ness** *n.*

**bris·ket** (bris'kit) *n.* [ME. *brusket*] meat from the breast of an animal

**bris·ling** (bris'lin, brīz'-) *n.* [Norw.] a small sprat canned as a sardine

**bris·tle** (bris''l) *n.* [OE. *byrst*] any short, stiff hair —*vi.* **-tled, -tling** 1. to be stiff and erect 2. to have the bristles become erect 3. to become tense with fear, anger, etc. 4. to be thickly covered (*with*) —**bris'tly** (-lē) *adj.* **-tli·er, -tli·est**

**Bris·tol** (bris't'l) seaport in SW England: pop. 434,000

**Brit.** 1. Britain 2. British

**Brit·ain** (brit'n) *same as* GREAT BRITAIN

**britch·es** (brich'iz) *n.pl.* [Colloq.] *same as* BREECHES (sense 2)

**Brit·i·cism** (brit'ə siz'm) *n.* a word or idiom peculiar to the British

**Brit·ish** (brit'ish) *adj.* 1. of Great Britain or its people 2. of the British Commonwealth —*n.* English as spoken and written in England —**the British** the people of Great Britain

**British Columbia** province of SW Canada: 366,255 sq. mi.; pop. 1,629,000; cap. Victoria

**British Commonwealth (of Nations)** confederation of nations, including the United Kingdom, united under the British crown

**British Isles** group of islands including Great Britain, Ireland, etc.

**British thermal unit** a unit of heat equal to about 252 calories

**Brit·on** (brit'n) n. 1. a member of an early Celtic people of S Britain 2. a native or inhabitant of Great Britain; esp., an Englishman

**brit·tle** (brit''l) adj. [< OE. breotan, to break] easily broken or shattered —n. a brittle, crunchy candy with nuts in it —brit'tle·ness n.

**bro.** pl. **bros.** brother

**broach** (brōch) n. [< ML. brocca, spike] a tapered bit for boring holes —vt. 1. to make a hole in so as to let out liquid 2. to ream with a broach 3. to start a discussion of

**broad** (brôd) adj. [OE. brad] 1. of large extent from side to side; wide 2. extending about; full [broad daylight] 3. obvious [a broad hint] 4. tolerant; liberal [a broad view] 5. wide in range [a broad variety] 6. not detailed; general [in a broad sense] —broad'ly adv. —broad'ness n.

**broad·cast** (-kast') vt., vi. -cast' or, in radio, occas. -cast'ed, -cast'ing 1. to scatter or spread widely 2. to transmit by radio or television —adj. 1. widely scattered 2. of or for radio or television broadcasting —n. 1. a sowing by broadcasting 2. a radio or television program —adv. far and wide —broad'cast'er n.

**broad·cloth** n. a fine, smooth woolen, cotton, or silk cloth

**broad·en** (-'n) vt., vi. to widen

**broad jump** same as LONG JUMP

**broad·loom** adj. woven on a wide loom [broadloom carpeting]

**broad·mind·ed** adj. tolerant of unconventional behavior, etc.; liberal —broad'-mind'ed·ly adv. —broad'-mind'ed·ness n.

**broad·side** n. 1. the side of a ship above the waterline 2. the firing of all guns on one side of a ship 3. a vigorous critical attack —adv. with the side facing

**broad·sword** n. a broad-bladed sword for slashing

**Broad·way** (-wā') street in New York City with many theaters, etc.

**bro·cade** (brō kād') n. [< Sp. < It. broccare, embroider] a rich cloth with a raised design woven into it —vt. -cad'ed, -cad'ing to weave a raised design into (cloth)

**broc·co·li** (bräk'ə lē) n. [It. < ML. brocca, a spike] a kind of cauliflower with loose heads of tiny green buds

**bro·chette** (brō shet') n. [Fr.] a skewer for broiling chunks of meat

**bro·chure** (brō shoor') n. [Fr. < brocher, to stitch] a pamphlet

**bro·gan** (brō'g'n) n. [Ir.] a heavy work shoe, fitting high on the ankle

**brogue¹** (brōg) n. [prob. < Ir. barróg, a grip] a dialectal pronunciation, esp. that of English by the Irish

**brogue²** (brōg) n. [< Ir. brōg, a shoe] a man's heavy oxford shoe

**broil** (broil) vt., vi. [< OFr. bruillir] to cook by exposure to direct heat —n. a broiling

**broil·er** n. 1. a pan, part of a stove, etc. for broiling 2. a chicken suitable for broiling

**broke** (brōk) pt. of BREAK —adj. [Colloq.] having little or no money; bankrupt

**bro·ken** (brō'k'n) pp. of BREAK —adj. 1. splintered, fractured, etc. 2. not in working order 3. violated [a broken vow] 4. ruined 5. interrupted; discontinuous 6. imperfectly spoken 7. tamed —bro'ken·ly adv. —bro'ken·ness n.

**bro·ken-down'** adj. 1. sick or worn out 2. out of order; useless

**bro·ken-heart·ed** adj. crushed by sorrow, grief, etc.

**bro·ker** (brō'kər) n. [< OFr. brokier, to tap; orig. sense "wine dealer"] a person hired as an agent in making contracts, selling stocks, etc.

**bro·ker·age** (-ij) n. 1. the business of a broker 2. a broker's fee

**bro·mide** (brō'mīd) n. 1. a compound of bromine with another element or a radical 2. potassium bromide, used as a sedative 3. a trite saying

**bro·mid·ic** (-mid'ik) adj. trite; dull

**bro·mine** (brō'mēn) n. [< Gr. brōmos, stench] a chemical element, a reddish-brown, corrosive liquid

**bron·chi** (brän'kī) n.pl., sing. -chus (-kəs) [< Gr. bronchos, windpipe] the two main branches of the windpipe —bron'chi·al (-kē əl) adj.

**bron·chi·tis** (-kīt'is) n. inflammation of the bronchial tubes

**bron·co** (brän'kō) n., pl. -cos [Sp., rough] a wild or only partly tamed horse or pony of the western U.S.: also **bron'cho**, pl. -chos

**bron·co·bust·er** n. [Colloq.] a tamer of broncos —bron'co·bust'ing n.

**Bron·të** (brän'të) 1. **Charlotte**, 1816–55; Eng. novelist 2. **Emily**, 1818–48; Eng. novelist: sister of prec.

**bron·to·sau·rus** (brän'tə sôr'əs) n., pl. -sau'rus·es, -sau'ri (-ī) [< Gr. brontē, thunder + sauros, lizard] an extinct American dinosaur

**Bronx** (bränks) borough of New York City: pop. 1,472,000

**bronze** (bränz) n. [Fr., prob. ult. < Per. biring, copper] 1. an alloy of copper and tin 2. a reddish-brown color —adj. of or like bronze —vt. bronzed, bronz'ing to make bronze in color

**brooch** (brōch) n. [see BROACH] a large ornamental pin with a clasp

**brood** (brood) n. [OE. brod] 1. a group of birds hatched at one time 2. the children in a family —vi. 1. to sit on and hatch eggs 2. to worry (often with on, over, or about)

**brood′er** *n.* **1.** one that broods **2.** a heated shelter for raising fowl

**brook**[1] (brook) *n.* [OE. *broc*] a small stream

**brook**[2] (brook) *vt.* [OE. *brucan*, to use] to put up with; endure

**Brook·lyn** (brook′lən) borough of New York City: pop. 2,602,000

**brook trout** a mottled stream trout of NE N. America

**broom** (broom, broom) *n.* [OE. *brom*, brushwood] **1.** a flowering shrub of the legume family **2.** a bundle of fibers or straws attached to a long handle (**broom′stick′**), used for sweeping

**bros.** brothers

**broth** (brôth) *n.* [OE.] a thin soup made by boiling meat, etc. in water

**broth·el** (brôth′əl) *n.* [ < OE. *broethan*, go to ruin] a house of prostitution

**broth·er** (bruth′ər) *n., pl.* -ers; chiefly religious **breth′ren** [OE. *brothor*] **1.** a male related to one by having the same parents **2.** a friend who is like a brother **3.** a fellow member of the same race, creed, profession, etc. **4.** a lay member of a men's religious order

**broth′er·hood′** *n.* **1.** the bond between brothers **2.** an association of men united in some interest, work, etc.

**broth′er-in-law′** *n., pl.* **broth′ers-in-law′** **1.** the brother of one's spouse **2.** the husband of one's sister **3.** the husband of the sister of one's spouse

**broth′er·ly** *adj.* **1.** of or like a brother **2.** friendly, kind, loyal, etc.

**brougham** (broom, broo′əm) *n.* [ < Lord *Brougham* (1778–1868)] a closed carriage (or automobile) with the driver's seat outside

**brought** (brôt) *pt. & pp. of* BRING

**brou·ha·ha** (broo′hä hä′) *n.* [Fr.] an uproar or commotion

**brow** (brou) *n.* [OE. *bru*] **1.** the eyebrow **2.** the forehead **3.** the edge of a cliff

**brow′beat′** (-bēt′) *vt.* -beat′, -beat′en, -beat′ing to intimidate with harsh looks and talk; bully

**brown** (broun) *adj.* [OE. *brun*] **1.** having the color of chocolate, a mixture of red, black, and yellow **2.** tanned; dark-skinned —*n.* brown color —*vt., vi.* to make or become brown —**brown′ish** *adj.*

**Brown** (broun), **John** 1800–59; U.S. abolitionist: hanged for treason

**brown′-bag′** *vt.* -bagged′, -bag′-ging to carry one's lunch to work or school, as in a brown paper bag

**brown·ie** (broun′ē) *n.* **1.** a small, helpful elf in stories **2.** a small bar cut from a flat chocolate cake

**Brown·ing** (broun′iŋ), **Robert** 1812–89; Eng. poet

**brown′out′** *n.* a turning off of some lights in a city, as during an electric power shortage

**brown rice** unpolished rice

**brown′stone′** *n.* a reddish-brown sandstone, used for building

**brown study** deep thought; reverie

**brown sugar** sugar whose crystals retain a brown coating of syrup

**browse** (brouz) *n.* [ < OS. *brustian*, to sprout] leaves, shoots, etc. which animals feed on —*vt., vi.* **browsed, brows′ing 1.** to nibble at (leaves, shoots, etc.) **2.** to examine (a book, articles for sale, etc.) in a casual way —**brows′er** *n.*

**bru·in** (broo′ən) *n.* [Du., brown] a bear

**bruise** (brooz) *vt.* **bruised, bruis′ing** [ < OE. *brysan*, crush] **1.** to injure and discolor (body tissue) without breaking the skin **2.** to injure the surface of, causing spoilage, denting, etc. **3.** to hurt (the feelings, spirit, etc.) —*vi.* **1.** to bruise tissue, etc. **2.** to be or become bruised —*n.* a bruised area, as of tissue

**bruis′er** *n.* a strong, pugnacious man

**bruit** (broot) *vt.* [ < OFr., noise, rumor] to spread (*about*) by rumor

**brunch** (brunch) *n.* [Colloq.] a combined breakfast and lunch

**bru·net** (broo net′) *adj.* [ < OFr., dim. of *brun*, brown] having black or dark-brown hair, often with dark eyes and complexion —*n.* a brunet person

**bru·nette** (-net′) *adj.* same as BRUNET —*n.* a brunette woman or girl

**Bruns·wick** (brunz′wik) city in NC West Germany: pop. 239,000

**brunt** (brunt) *n.* [ME. *bront*] **1.** the shock (of an attack) or impact (of a blow) **2.** the hardest part

**brush**[1] (brush) *n.* [ < OFr. *broce*, bush] **1.** brushwood **2.** sparsely settled country **3.** a device for cleaning, painting, etc., having bristles, wires, etc. fastened into a back **4.** a brushing **5.** a light, grazing stroke **6.** a bushy tail, as of a fox —*vt.* **1.** to clean, paint, etc. with a brush **2.** to apply, remove, etc. as with a brush **3.** to touch or graze in passing —*vi.* to graze past something —**brush up** to refresh one's memory

**brush**[2] (brush) *vi.* [ME. *bruschen*] to rush; hurry —*n.* a short, quick fight

**brush′off′** *n.* [Slang] curt dismissal: esp. in the phrase **give** (or **get**) **the brushoff**

**brush′wood′** *n.* **1.** chopped-off tree branches **2.** underbrush

**brusque** (brusk) *adj.* [ < Fr. < ML. *bruscus*, brushwood] rough and abrupt in manner or speech; curt: also **brusk** —**brusque′ly** *adv.* —**brusque′ness** *n.*

**Brus·sels** (brus′lz) capital of Belgium: pop. (with suburbs) 1,058,000

**Brussels sprouts 1.** a plant that bears small cabbagelike heads on an erect stem **2.** its edible heads

BRUSSELS SPROUTS

**bru·tal** (broot′l) *adj.* **1.** like a brute; very savage, cruel, etc. **2.** very harsh —**bru′tal·ly** *adv.*

**bru·tal·i·ty** (broo tal′ə tē) *n.* **1.** a being brutal **2.** *pl.* -ties a brutal act

**bru·tal·ize** (broot′l īz′) *vt.* -ized′, -iz′ing **1.** to make brutal 2. to treat brutally —**bru′-tal·i·za′tion** n.

**brute** (brōōt) adj. [< L. brutus, irrational] 1. lacking the ability to reason [a brute beast] 2. of or like an animal; specif., savage, stupid, etc. —n. 1. an animal 2. a brutal person —**brut′ish·ly** adv.

**B.S., B.Sc.** Bachelor of Science

**b.s.** bill of sale

**B.t.u.** British thermal unit(s)

**bu.** bushel(s)

**bub·ble** (bub′'l) n. [echoic] 1. a film of liquid forming a ball around air or gas 2. a tiny ball of air or gas in a liquid or solid 3. a transparent dome 4. a plausible scheme that proves worthless —vi. **-bled, -bling** 1. to rise in bubbles; boil 2. to make a gurgling sound —**bub′bly** adj.

**bubble gum** a kind of chewing gum that can be blown into large bubbles

**bub′bler** (-lər) n. a drinking fountain in which water spurts up from a nozzle

**bub′ble-top′** n. a bulletproof, transparent dome, as over an automobile

**bu·bo** (byōō′bō) n., pl. **-boes** [< Gr. boubōn, groin] an inflamed swelling of a lymph gland, esp. in the groin

**bu·bon′ic plague** (-bän′ik) a contagious disease characterized by buboes, fever, and delirium

**buc·ca·neer** (buk′ə nir′) n. [< Fr. boucanier] a pirate

**Bu·chan·an** (byōō kan′ən), **James** 1791–1868; 15th president of the U.S. (1857–61)

**Bu·cha·rest** (bōō′kə rest′) capital of Romania: pop. 1,511,000

**buck¹** (buk) n. [OE. bucca, male goat] 1. a male deer, goat, etc. 2. the act of bucking 3. [Colloq.] a bold, vigorous young man —vi. 1. to rear upward quickly, as to throw off a rider: said of a horse 2. [Colloq.] to resist something as if plunging against it —vt. 1. to charge against, as in football 2. to throw by bucking 3. [Colloq.] to resist stubbornly —**buck** for [Slang] to work eagerly for (a promotion, raise, etc.) —**buck up** [Colloq.] to cheer up

**buck²** (buk) n. [Du. zaagbok] 1. a sawbuck; sawhorse 2. a gymnastic apparatus for vaulting over

**buck³** (buk) n. [< ?] [Slang] a dollar —**pass the buck** [Colloq.] to throw the responsibility on another

**buck′board′** n. [< ?] an open carriage whose floorboards rest directly on the axles

**buck·et** (buk′it) n. [< OE. buc, pitcher] 1. a cylindrical container with a curved handle, for carrying water, etc.; pail 2. the amount held by a bucket: also **buck′et·ful′**, pl. **-fuls′** 3. a thing like a bucket, as a scoop on a steam shovel —**kick the bucket** [Slang] to die

**bucket seat** a single contoured seat with a movable back, as in sports cars

**buck·eye** (buk′ī′) n. [BUCK¹ + EYE:

the appearance of the seed] 1. a horse chestnut with large burs enclosing shiny brown seeds 2. the seed

**buck·le¹** (buk′'l) n. [< L. buccula, cheek strap of a helmet] a clasp for fastening a strap, belt, etc. —vt., vi. **-led, -ling** to fasten with a buckle —**buckle down** to apply oneself

**buck·le²** (buk′'l) vt., vi. **-led, -ling** [prob. < Du. bukken, to bend] to bend or crumple —n. a bend, bulge, etc.

**buck·ler** (buk′lər) n. [OFr. bocler] a small, round shield

**buck′-pass′er** n. [Colloq.] one who regularly shifts blame or responsibility to someone else —**buck′-pass′ing** n.

**buck·ram** (buk′rəm) n. [< ? Bokhara, in Asia Minor] a coarse, stiffened cloth used in bookbinding, etc.

**buck·saw** (buk′sô′) n. a wood-cutting saw set in a frame

**buck′shot′** n. a large lead shot for shooting deer and other large game

**buck′skin′** n. 1. a soft leather made from the skins of deer or sheep 2. [pl.] clothes made of buckskin

**buck′tooth′** n., pl. **-teeth′** a projecting front tooth —**buck′toothed′** adj.

**buck′wheat′** n. [< OE. boc-, BEECH + WHEAT] 1. a plant with beechnut-shaped seeds 2. a dark flour made from the seeds

**bu·col·ic** (byōō käl′ik) adj. [< Gr. boukolos, herdsman] 1. of shepherds; pastoral 2. rural; rustic —n. a pastoral poem —**bu·col′i·cal·ly** adv.

**bud** (bud) n. [ME. budde] 1. a small swelling on a plant, from which a shoot, leaf, or flower develops 2. an early stage of development —vi. **bud′ded, bud′ding** 1. to put forth buds 2. to begin to develop —**in (the) bud** 1. in a budding condition 2. in an early stage —**bud′like′** adj.

**Bu·da·pest** (bōō′də pest′) capital of Hungary: pop. 1,900,000

**Bud·dha** (bood′ə) a religious leader who lived in India 563?–483? B.C.: founder of Buddhism

**Bud·dhism** (bood′iz'm) n. a religion of Asia teaching that by right living and right thinking one achieves Nirvana —**Bud′dhist** n., adj.

**bud·dy** (bud′ē) n., pl. **-dies** [< ? Brit. dial.] [Colloq.] a comrade

**budge** (buj) vt., vi. **budged, budg′-ing** [Fr. bouger, to move] to move even a little

**budg·er·i·gar** (buj′ə ri gär′) n. [native name] a greenish-yellow Australian parakeet: also [Colloq.] **budg′ie**

**budg·et** (buj′it) n. [< L. bulga, bag] 1. a stock of items 2. a plan adjusting expenses to income 3. estimated cost of living, operating, etc. —vt. 1. to put on a budget 2. to schedule; plan [budget your time] —**budg′et·ar′y** adj. —**budg′et·er** n.

**Bue·nos Ai·res** (bwā′nəs er′ēz) capital of Argentina: pop. 3,876,000

**buff** (buf) *n.* [< It. *bufalo*, buffalo]
1. a heavy, soft, brownish-yellow
leather 2. a military coat made of this
3. a dull brownish yellow 4. [Colloq.]
a devotee; fan —*adj.* 1. made of buff
2. of the color buff —*vt.* to clean or
shine with leather or a leather-covered
wheel —**in the buff** naked —**buff′er** *n.*

**Buf·fa·lo** (buf′ə lō′) city in W N.Y.,
on Lake Erie: pop. 463,000

**buf·fa·lo** (buf′ə lō′) *n., pl.* **-loes′,**
**-loe′** [< It. < Gr. *bous*, ox] 1. any of
various wild oxen, as the water buffalo
of India 2. popularly, the American
bison —*vt.* **-loed′, -lo′ing** [Slang] to
baffle, bluff, etc.

**buff·er** (buf′ər) *n.* [< OFr. *buffe*, a
blow] anything that lessens shock, as
of collision

**buf·fet¹** (buf′it) *n.* [OFr. < *buffe*, a
blow] a blow or shock —*vt.* 1. to
punch; fight 2. to thrust about

**buf·fet²** (bə fā′, boo′ā) *n.* [Fr.] 1. a
sideboard 2. a sideboard or table at
which guests serve themselves food
3. a meal served thus

**buf·foon** (bə foon′) *n.* [< Fr. < It.
*buffare*, to jest] one who is always
trying to be funny; clown —**buf-
foon′er·y** *n.* —**buf·foon′ish** *adj.*

**bug** (bug) *n.* [? < ME. *bugge*] 1. an
insect with sucking mouth parts 2.
any insect 3. [Colloq.] a germ or virus
4. [Slang] a defect, as in a machine
5. [Slang] a hidden microphone —*vt.*
**bugged, bug′ging** [Slang] 1. to
annoy, anger, etc. 2. to hide a microphone in (a room, etc.)

**bug′bear′** *n.* [< W. *bwg* + BEAR²] 1.
a bogy 2. a cause of needless fear Also
**bug′a·boo′** (-ə boo′) *n., pl.* **-boos′**

**bug′-eyed′** *adj.* [Slang] with bulging
eyes

**bug·gy** (bug′ē) *n., pl.* **-gies** [< ?] 1.
a light, one-horse carriage with one
seat 2. a small carriage for a baby

**bu·gle** (byoo′g'l) *n.* [< L. *buculus*,
young ox] a brass-wind instrument like
a small trumpet, usually without
valves —*vi., vt.* **-gled, -gling** to
signal by blowing a bugle —**bu′gler** *n.*

**build** (bild) *vt.* **built** (bilt), **build′ing**
[< OE. *bold*, house] 1. to make by
putting together materials, parts, etc.;
construct 2. to establish; base [*build* a
theory on facts] 3. to create or
develop (often with *up*) —*vi.* 1. to
put up buildings 2. to grow or intensify (often with *up*) —*n.* the way
a thing is built or shaped [a stocky
*build*] —**build up** to make more attractive, healthy, etc. —**build′er** *n.*

**build′ing** *n.* 1. anything that is built;
structure 2. the work or business of
making houses, etc.

**build′up′, build′-up′** *n.* [Colloq.]
1. favorable publicity or praise 2. a
gradual increase or expansion

**built′-in′** *adj.* 1. made as part of
the structure 2. inherent

**built′-up′** *adj.* 1. made higher,
stronger, etc. with added parts [*built-up*
heels] 2. having many buildings on it

**bulb** (bulb) *n.* [< Gr. *bolbos*] 1. an
underground bud with roots and a
short, scaly stem, as in a lily or onion

2. a tuber or tuberous root resembling
a bulb, as in a crocus 3. anything
shaped like a bulb [an electric light
*bulb*] —**bul′bous** *adj.*

**Bul·gar·i·a** (bul ger′ē ə) country in
SE Europe: 42,796 sq. mi.; pop.
8,230,000 —**Bul·gar′i·an** *adj., n.*

**bulge** (bulj) *n.* [< L. *bulga*, leather
bag] an outward swelling; protuberance —*vi., vt.* **bulged, bulg′ing** to
swell or bend outward; protrude —
**bulg′y** *adj.*

**bulk** (bulk) *n.* [ON. *bulki*, a heap] 1.
size, mass, or volume, esp. if great
2. the main mass; largest part —*vi.* to
have, or to increase in, size or importance —*adj.* 1. total; aggregate 2. not
packaged —**bulk′y** *adj.* **-i·er, -i·est**

**bulk·head** (bulk′hed′) *n.* [< ON.
*balkr*, partition + HEAD] 1. an upright
partition, as in a ship, that is watertight, fireproof. etc. 2. a retaining wall
3. a boxlike structure over an opening

**bull¹** (bool) *n.* [< OE. *bula*, a steer]
1. the adult male of any bovine animal,
as the ox, or of certain other large
animals, as the elephant, whale, etc.
2. a speculator who buys stocks expecting their prices to rise, or seeks
to bring about such a rise 3. [Slang]
insincere talk; nonsense —*adj.* 1. male
2. rising in price —**bull′ish** *adj.*

**bull²** (bool) *n.* [< LL. *bulla*, a seal]
an official document from the Pope

**bull′dog′** *n.* a short-haired, square-
jawed, heavily built dog —*adj.* like a
bulldog; stubborn —*vt.* **-dogged′,**
**-dog′ging** to throw (a steer) by holding its horns and twisting its neck

**bull′doze′** (-dōz′) *vt.* **-dozed′, -doz′-
ing** [< *bull*, a flogging + DOSE] 1.
[Colloq.] to force or frighten by threatening; bully 2. to move, make level,
etc. with a bulldozer

**bull′doz′er** *n.* a tractor with a large
shovellike blade in front for pushing
earth, debris, etc.

**bul·let** (bool′it) *n.* [< L. *bulla*, a
knob] a small, shaped piece of lead,
steel, etc. to be shot from a firearm

**bul·le·tin** (bool′ət 'n) *n.* [< L. *bulla*,
a seal] 1. a brief statement of late
news 2. a regular publication, as of
an organization, etc.

**bulletin board** a board or wall on
which bulletins, notices, etc. are put up

**bul′let-proof′** *adj.* that bullets cannot pierce —*vt.* to make bulletproof

**bull′fight′** (-fīt′) *n.* a spectacle in
which a bull is provoked in various
ways and then killed with a sword by
the matador —**bull′fight′er** *n.* —
**bull′fight′ing** *n.*

**bull′finch′** (-finch′) *n.* a small European songbird

**bull′frog′** *n.* a large N.American frog
with a deep, loud croak

**bull′head′ed** (-hed′id) *adj.* stubborn; headstrong

**bull′horn′** *n.* a portable electronic
voice amplifier

**bul·lion** (bool′yən) *n.* [< OFr. *billon*,
small coin] ingots of gold or silver

**bull′ish** *adj.* 1.- of or like a bull
2. rising, or causing a rise, in price on
the stock exchange 3. optimistic

**bull′ock** (-ək) n. [ < OE. dim. of *bula*, steer ] a castrated bull; steer

**bull′pen′** (-pen′) n. 1. [Colloq.] a temporary detention room in a jail 2. *Baseball* a practice area for relief pitchers

**bull′s-eye** (boolz′ī′) n. 1. the central mark of a target 2. a direct hit

**bul·ly** (bool′ē) n., *pl.* **-lies** [ < MHG. *buole*, lover; infl. by BULL[1] ] one who hurts or browbeats those who are weaker —*vt., vi.* **-lied, -ly·ing** to act the bully (toward) —*adj., interj.* [Colloq.] fine; good

**bul·rush** (bool′rush′) n. [ < OE. *bol*, tree trunk + *risc*, a rush ] a tall plant of the sedge family, found in wet places

**bul·wark** (bool′wərk) n. [MDu. *bol-werc*] 1. a defensive wall; rampart 2. a defense; protection

**bum** (bum) n. [prob. < G. *bummeln*, go slowly] [Colloq.] 1. a vagrant; loafer 2. a devotee, as of golf or skiing —*vi.* **bummed, bum′ming** [Colloq.] to live as a bum or by begging —*vt.* [Slang] to get by begging [to *bum* a cigar] —*adj.* **bum′mer, bum′mest** [Slang] 1. poor in quality 2. false 3. lame —**on the bum** [Colloq.] 1. living as a vagrant 2. out of repair

**bum·ble·bee** (bum′b'l bē′) n. [ < ME. *bomblen*, buzz] a large, hairy, yellow-and-black bee

**bum′bling** adj. [ < obs. *bumble*, buzz] self-important in a blundering way

**bum·mer** (bum′ər) n. [Slang] an unpleasant experience, esp. with drugs

**bump** (bump) vt., vi. [echoic] 1. to collide (with); hit against 2. to move with jolts —n. 1. a knock; light jolt 2. a swelling, esp. one caused by a blow —**bump into** [Colloq.] to meet unexpectedly —**bump off** [Slang] to murder —**bump′y** adj.

**bump′er**[1] n. a device to absorb the shock of a collision; esp., a bar at the front or back of an automobile

**bump′er**[2] n. [prob. < *bombard*, liquor jug] a cup or glass filled to the brim —*adj.* unusually abundant [a *bumper* crop]

**bumper sticker** a slogan, witticism, etc. printed on gummed paper for sticking on an automobile bumper

**bump·kin** (bump′k'n) n. [prob. < MDu. *bommekijn*, small cask] an awkward or simple person from the country

**bump′tious** (-shəs) adj. [prob. < BUMP] disagreeably conceited or forward —**bump′tious·ly** adv.

**bun** (bun) n. [prob. < OFr. *buigne*, a swelling] 1. a small roll, usually somewhat sweetened 2. hair worn in a roll or knot

**bunch** (bunch) n. [ < Fl. *boudje*, little bundle] 1. a cluster of similar things growing or grouped together 2. [Colloq.] a group of people —*vt., vi.* to collect into a bunch —**bunch′y** adj.

**bun·combe** (buŋ′kəm) n. [ < *Buncombe* County, N.C., loquaciously represented in 16th Congress] [Colloq.] empty insincere talk: also **bunkum**

**bun·dle** (bun′d'l) n. [MDu. *bondel*] 1. a number of things bound together 2. a package 3. a bunch; collection —*vt.* **-dled, -dling** 1. to make into a bundle 2. to hustle (*away, off, out, into*) —**bundle up** to dress warmly

**bung** (buŋ) n. [ < MDu. *bonge*] a stopper for a bunghole

**bun·ga·low** (buŋ′gə lō′) n. [ < Hind. *bānglā*, thatched house] a small, one-storied house or cottage

**bung′hole′** (buŋ′hōl′) n. a hole in a barrel or keg for pouring in or drawing out liquid

**bun·gle** (buŋ′g'l) vt., vi. **-gled, -gling** [ < ? ] to do clumsily; spoil; botch —n. 1. a bungling 2. a bungled piece of work —**bun′gler** n.

**bun·ion** (bun′yən) n. [prob. < OFr.: see BUN] an inflamed swelling at the base of the big toe

**bunk**[1] (buŋk) n. [prob. < Scand. cognate of BENCH] 1. a shelflike bed built against a wall, as in a ship 2. [Colloq.] any sleeping place —*vi.* to sleep in a bunk —*vt.* to provide sleeping place for

**bunk**[2] (buŋk) n. [Slang] buncombe

**bunk′er** n. [Scot. < ? ] 1. a large bin, as for a ship's fuel 2. an underground fortification 3. a mound serving as an obstacle on a golf course

**bunk′house′** n. a barracks for ranch hands, etc.

**bun·ny** (bun′ē) n., *pl.* **-nies** [dim. of dial. *bun*] a rabbit: a child's term

**Bun·sen burner** (bun′s'n) [ < R. W. *Bunsen*, 19th-c. G. chemist] a small tubular gas burner that produces a hot, blue flame

**bunt** (bunt) vt., vi. [ < ? Bret. *bounta*, to butt] *Baseball* to bat (a pitch) lightly so that it does not go beyond the infield —n. a bunted ball

**bun·ting**[1] (bun′tiŋ) n. [ < ? ME. *bonten*, sift] 1. a thin cloth for making flags, etc. 2. decorative flags

**bun·ting**[2] (bun′tiŋ) n. [ME.] a small, brightly colored, short-billed bird

**buoy** (boo′ē, boi) n. [ < L. *boia*, fetter] 1. a floating object anchored in water to warn of rocks, etc. or to mark a channel 2. same as LIFE PRESERVER —*vt.* [ < Sp. *boyar*, to float] 1. to mark with a buoy 2. to keep afloat 3. to lift up in spirits

**buoy·ant** (boi′ənt, boo′yənt) adj. [ < ? Sp. *boyar*, to float] 1. having the ability or tendency to float 2. cheerful —**buoy′an·cy** n.

**bur** (bur) n. [ < Scand.] 1. a rough prickly seed capsule of certain plants 2. a plant with burs 3. same as BURR

**bur·den**[1] (burd′n) n. [ < OE. *beran*, to bear] 1. anything that is carried; load 2. heavy load, as of work, care, etc. 3. the carrying capacity of a ship —*vt.* to put a burden on; oppress —**bur′den·some** adj.

**bur·den**[2] n. [ < OFr. *bourdon*, a humming] 1. a chorus or refrain of a song 2. a repeated, central idea; theme

**bur·dock** (bur′däk′) n. [BUR +

**bock³]** a plant with large leaves and purple-flowered heads with prickles

**bu·reau** (byoor'ō) *n.*, *pl.* **-reaus**, **-reaux** (-rōz) [Fr., desk] **1.** a chest of drawers for clothing, etc. **2.** an agency [a credit *bureau*] **3.** a government department

**bu·reau·cra·cy** (byoo rä'krə sē) *n.*, *pl.* **-cies 1.** government by departmental officials following an inflexible routine **2.** the officials collectively **3.** governmental officialism **4.** the concentration of authority in administrative bureaus —**bu·reau·crat** (byoor'ə krat') *n.* —**bu'reau·crat'ic** *adj.* —**bu'reau·crat'i·cal·ly** *adv.*

**bu·reau·cra·tize'** (-tīz') *vt.*, *vi.* **-tized'**, **-tiz'ing** to develop into a bureaucracy —**bu·reau·cra·ti·za'tion** *n.*

**burg** (burg) *n.* [var. of BOROUGH] [Colloq.] a quiet or dull town

**bur·geon** (bur'jən) *vi.* [< OFr. *burjon*, a bud] **1.** to put forth buds, etc. **2.** to grow or develop rapidly

**-burg·er** (bur'gər) [< (HAM)BURGER] *a combining form meaning:* **1.** sandwich of ground meat, etc. [*turkeyburger*] **2.** hamburger and [*cheeseburger*]

**burgh** (burg; *Scot.* bu'rə) *n.* [Scot. var. of BOROUGH] **1.** [Brit.] a borough **2.** in Scotland, a chartered town

**burgh'er** *n.* a citizen of a town

**bur·glar** (bur'glər) *n.* [< OFr. *burgeor*] one who commits burglary

**bur'glar·ize'** *vt.* **-ized'**, **-iz'ing** [Colloq.] to commit burglary in

**bur'gla·ry** *n.*, *pl.* **-ries** the act of breaking into a building to commit a felony, as theft, or a misdemeanor

**bur·gle** (bur'g'l) *vt.*, *vi.* **-gled**, **-gling** [Colloq.] to burglarize or commit burglary

**bur·go·mas·ter** (bur'gə mas'tər) *n.* [< MDu. *burg*, town + *meester*, MASTER] the mayor of a town in the Netherlands, Flanders, Austria, or Germany

**Bur·gun·dy** (bur'gən dē) *n.* [*occas.* b-] *pl.* **-dies** a red or white wine, orig. made in Burgundy, a region in SE France —**Bur·gun'di·an** *adj.*, *n.*

**bur·i·al** (ber'ē əl) *n.* the burying of a dead body in a grave, tomb, etc.

**burl** (burl) *n.* [< VL. *burrula*, wool tuft] **1.** a knot in thread or yarn that makes cloth look nubby **2.** a knot on some tree trunks **3.** veneer from wood with burls —**burled** *adj.*

**bur·lap** (bur'lap) *n.* [< ? ME. *borel*] a coarse cloth of jute or hemp, used for making bags, etc.

**bur·lesque** (bər lesk') *n.* [Fr. < It. *burla*, a jest] **1.** any broadly comic or satirical imitation; parody **2.** a sort of vaudeville characterized by low comedy, striptease acts, etc. —*vt.*, *vi.* **-lesqued'**, **-lesqu'ing** to imitate comically

**bur·ly** (bur'lē) *adj.* **-li·er**, **-li·est** [ME. *borlich*, excellent] **1.** big and strong **2.** hearty in manner; bluff —**bur'li·ness** *n.*

**Bur·ma** (bur'mə) country in SE Asia: 261,789 sq. mi.; pop. 24,732,000 — **Bur·mese'** (-mēz') *adj.*, *n.*

**burn** (burn) *vt.* **burned** or **burnt**, **burn'ing** [OE. *biernan*] **1.** to set on fire, as in order to produce heat, light, or power **2.** to destroy by fire **3.** to injure or damage by fire, acid, etc. **4.** to consume as fuel **5.** to sunburn **6.** to cause (a hole, etc.) as by fire **7.** to cause a sensation of heat in —*vi.* **1.** to be on fire **2.** to give out light or heat **3.** to be destroyed or injured by fire or heat **4.** to feel hot **5.** to be excited —*n.* **1.** an injury or damage caused by fire, heat, etc. **2.** the process or result of burning —**burn down** to burn to the ground —**burn up** [Slang] to make or become angry —**burn'a·ble** *adj.*, *n.*

**burn'er** *n.* the part of a stove, lamp, etc. from which the flame comes

**bur·nish** (bur'nish) *vt.*, *vi.* [< OFr. *brunir*, make brown] to make or become shiny by rubbing —*n.* gloss; polish —**bur'nish·er** *n.*

**bur·noose** (bər nōōs') *n.* [< Ar. *burnus*] a hooded cloak worn by Arabs

**burn·out** (burn'out') *n.* the point at which missile fuel is burned up and the missile enters free flight

**Burns** (burnz), **Robert** 1759–96; Scot. poet

**burnt** (burnt) *alt. pt. & pp.* of BURN

**burp** (burp) *n.*, *vi.* [echoic] [Slang] belch —*vt.* to cause (a baby) to belch

**burp gun** [Mil. Slang] a type of automatic pistol or small submachine gun

**burr¹** (bur) *n.* **1.** a bur **2.** a rough edge left on metal, etc. by cutting or drilling —*vt.* to form a rough edge on

**burr²** (bur) *n.* [prob. echoic] **1.** the trilling of *r*, as in Scottish speech **2.** a whir

**bur·ro** (bur'ō) *n.*, *pl.* **-ros** [Sp. < LL. *burricus*, small horse] a donkey

**bur·row** (bur'ō) *n.* [see BOROUGH] **1.** a hole dug in the ground by an animal **2.** any similar hole —*vi.* **1.** to make a burrow **2.** to live or hide in a burrow **3.** to search, as if by digging —*vt.* **1.** to make burrows in **2.** to make by burrowing

**bur·sa** (bur'sə) *n.*, *pl.* **-sae** (-sē), **-sas** [< Gr. *byrsa*, a hide] *Anat.* a sac or cavity with a lubricating fluid, as between a tendon and bone

**bur·sar** (bur'sər) *n.* [< ML. *bursa*, a purse] a college treasurer

**bur·si·tis** (bər sīt'is) *n.* [< BURSA + -ITIS] inflammation of a bursa

**burst** (burst) *vi.* **burst**, **burst'ing** [OE. *berstan*] **1.** to come apart suddenly and violently; explode **2.** to give sudden vent; break (*into* tears, etc.) **3.** to appear, start, etc. suddenly **4.** to be as full or crowded as possible —*vt.* to cause to burst —*n.* **1.** a bursting **2.** a break or rupture **3.** a sudden action or effort; spurt **4.** a volley of shots

**Bu·run·di** (boo roon'dē) country in EC Africa: 10,745 sq. mi.; pop. 2,800,000

**bur·y** (ber'ē) *vt.* **-ied**, **-y'ing** [OE. *byrgan*] **1.** to put (a dead body) into the earth, a tomb, etc. **2.** to hide or cover **3.** to put away **4.** to immerse

**bus** (bus) *n.*, *pl.* **bus'es**, **bus'ses** [< (OMNI)BUS] a large motor coach for many passengers, usually following a

regular route —*vt.* **bused** or **bussed,**
**bus'ing** or **bus'sing** to transport by
bus —*vi.* 1. to go by bus 2. to do the
work of a busboy

**bus'boy'** *n.* a waiter's assistant who
clears tables, brings water, etc.

**bus·by** (buz'bē) *n., pl.* **-bies** [prob. <
name *Busby*] a tall fur hat worn with
a full-dress uniform, as by guardsmen

**bush** (boosh) *n.* [OE. *busc*] 1. a low
woody plant with spreading branches;
shrub 2. anything like a bush 3. un-
cleared land —*vi.* to grow thickly —
**beat around the bush** to talk around
a subject without getting to the point
—**bush'y** *adj.* **-i·er, -i·est**

**bushed** (boosht) *adj.* [Colloq.] very
tired; exhausted

**bush·el** (boosh''l) *n.* [< OFr. *boisse,*
grain measure] a dry measure equal to
4 pecks, or 32 quarts

**bush·ing** (boosh'iŋ) *n.* [< MDu.
*busse,* box] a removable metal lining,
for reducing friction on moving parts

**bush league** [Slang] *Baseball* a
small or second-rate minor league —
**bush'-league'** *adj.* —**bush leaguer**

**bush'man** (-mən) *n., pl.* **-men** one
who lives in the Australian bush

**bush'mas'ter** (-mas'tər) *n.* a large
poisonous snake of C and S.America

**bush'whack'er** (-hwak'ər) *n.* a
guerrilla fighter

**bus·i·ly** (biz'ə lē) *adv.* in a busy
manner

**busi·ness** (biz'nis) *n.* [OE. *bisignes:*
see BUSY] 1. one's work; occupation
2. a special task, duty, etc. 3. rightful
concern 4. a matter or affair 5. commerce; trade 6. a commercial or industrial establishment —*adj.* of or for
business —**mean business** [Colloq.]
to be in earnest

**business college** (or **school**) a
school of typing, bookkeeping, etc.

**busi'ness·like'** *adj.* efficient, methodical, systematic, etc.

**busi'ness·man'** *n., pl.* **-men'** a man
in business, esp. as an owner —**busi'-
ness·wom'an** *n.fem., pl.* **-wom'en**

**bus·ing, bus·sing** (bus'iŋ) *n.* the
transporting of children by bus to a
school outside of their neighborhood,
esp. so as to desegregate the school

**bus·kin** (bus'kin) *n.* [? < MDu.
*brosekin,* small boot] 1. a high, laced
boot worn in ancient tragedy 2. a
tragedy

**buss** (bus) *n., vt., vi.* [< ?] [Archaic
or Dial.] kiss

**bust**[1] (bust) *n.* [< It. *busto*] 1. a
sculpture of a person's head and
shoulders 2. a woman's bosom

**bust**[2] (bust) *vt., vi.* [< BURST] [Slang]
1. to burst or break 2. to make or
become bankrupt or demoted 3. to hit
4. to arrest —*n.* [Slang] 1. a failure 2.
financial collapse 3. a punch 4. a
spree 5. an arrest

**bus·tle**[1] (bus''l) *vi., vt.* **-tled, -tling**
[< ME. *busken,* prepare] to hurry
busily —*n.* busy and noisy activity

**bus·tle**[2] (bus''l) *n.* [< ? G. *buschel,*
pad] a padding worn to fill
out the upper back of a
woman's skirt

**bus·y** (biz'ē) *adj.* **-i·er,
-i·est** [OE. *bisig*] 1. active; at work 2. full of activity 3. in use, as a telephone
4. too detailed —*vt.* **-ied,
-y·ing** to make or keep
busy —**bus'y·ness** *n.*

**bus'y·bod'y** (-bäd'ē) *n.,
pl.* **-ies** a meddler in the
affairs of others

**but** (but) *prep.* [OE. *butan,* BUSTLE
without] except; save [no-
body went *but* me] —*conj.* 1. yet; still
[it's good, *but* not great] 2. on the
contrary [I am old, *but* he is young]
3. unless [it never rains *but* it pours]
4. that [I don't doubt *but* he's right]
5. that . . . not [I never gamble *but* I
lose] —*adv.* 1. only [if I had *but*
known] 2. merely [he is *but* a child]
3. just [I heard it *but* now] —*pron.*
who . . . not; which . . . not [not a man
*but* felt it] —**but for** if it were not for

**bu·tane** (byoo'tān) *n.* [ult. < *buty-
rum,* butter] a hydrocarbon used as a
fuel, in organic synthesis, etc.

**butch** (booch) *adj.* [< ? BUTCHER]
[Slang] 1. designating a man's closely
cropped haircut 2. masculine: said
of a lesbian

**butch·er** (booch'ər) *n.* [< OFr. *bouc,*
he-goat] 1. one whose work is killing
and dressing animals for meat 2. one
who cuts meat for sale 3. a brutal
killer —*vt.* 1. to kill or dress (animals)
for meat 2. to kill brutally or sense-
lessly 3. to botch —**butch'er·y** *n.,
pl.* **-ies**

**but·ler** (but'lər) *n.* [< OFr. *bouteille,*
bottle] a manservant, usually the head
servant of a household

**butt**[1] (but) *n.* [< ?] 1. the thick end
of anything 2. a stub or stump, as of a
cigar 3. a target 4. an object of ridicule 5. [Slang] a cigarette —*vt., vi.*
to join end to end

**butt**[2] (but) *vt., vi.* [< OFr. *buter,* to
thrust against] 1. to ram with the
head 2. to project —*n.* a butting
—**butt in(to)** [Slang] to mix into
(another's business, etc.)

**butt**[3] (but) *n.* [< LL. *bottis,* cask] a
large cask for wine or beer

**butte** (byoot) *n.* [Fr., mound] a steep
hill standing alone in a plain

**but·ter** (but'ər) *n.* [< Gr. *bous,* cow
+ *tyros,* cheese] 1. the thick, yellowish product that results from churning
cream 2. any substance somewhat like
butter —*vt.* 1. to spread with butter
2. [Colloq.] to flatter (with *up*) —
**but'ter·y** *adj.*

**butter bean** *same as:* 1. LIMA BEAN
2. WAX BEAN

**but'ter·cup'** *n.* a plant with yellow,
cup-shaped flowers

**but'ter·fat'** *n.* the fatty part of milk,
from which butter is made

---

fat, āpe, cär; ten, ēven; is, bīte; gō, hôrn, tōōl, look; oil, out; up, fur;
chin; she; thin, then; zh, leisure; ŋ, ring; ə for a in ago; ', (ā'b'l); ë, Fr. coeur;
ö, Fr. feu; Fr. mon; ü, Fr. duc; kh, G. ich, doch; ‡ foreign; < derived from

**but·ter·fin·gers** *n.* one who often fumbles and drops things

**but·ter·fly** *n.*, *pl.* **-flies** [OE. *buttorfleoge*] an insect with a slender body and four broad, usually brightly colored wings

**but·ter·milk** *n.* the sour liquid left after churning butter from milk

**but·ter·nut** *n.* **1.** a walnut tree of E N.America **2.** its edible, oily nut

**but·ter·scotch** (-skäch´) *n.* **1.** a hard, sticky candy made with brown sugar, butter, etc. **2.** a syrup with the flavor of this

**but·tocks** (but´əks) *n.pl.* [< OE. *buttuc*, end] the fleshy, rounded parts of the hips; rump

**but·ton** (but´'n) *n.* [< OFr. *boton*] **1.** any small disk or knob used as a fastening, ornament, etc., as on a garment **2.** anything small and shaped like a button —*vt.*, *vi.* to fasten with a button or buttons

**but·ton-down** *adj.* **1.** designating a collar, as on a shirt, fastened down by small buttons **2.** conservative, unimaginative, etc. [a *button-down* mind]

**but·ton·hole** *n.* a slit or loop through which a button is inserted —*vt.* **-holed´**, **-hol´ing 1.** to make buttonholes in **2.** to detain and talk to

**but·tress** (but´ris) *n.* [see BUTT²] **1.** a structure built against a wall to support or reinforce it **2.** a support or prop —*vt.* to prop up; bolster

**bux·om** (buk´səm) *adj.* [ME., humble] healthy, comely, plump, etc.: specif. said of a full-bosomed woman —**bux´om·ness** *n.*

**buy** (bī) *vt.* **bought**, **buy´ing** [OE. *bycgan*] **1.** to get by paying money; purchase **2.** to get by an exchange [to *buy* time by negotiating] **3.** to bribe **4.** [Slang] to accept as true [I can't *buy* his excuse] —*n.* **1.** anything bought **2.** [Colloq.] something worth its price —**buy off** to bribe —**buy out** to buy all the stock, rights, etc. of —**buy up** to buy all that is available

**buy´er** *n.* **1.** one who buys; consumer **2.** one whose work is to buy merchandise for a retail store

**buzz** (buz) *vi.* [echoic] **1.** to hum like a bee **2.** to gossip **3.** to be filled with noisy activity or talk —*vt.* to fly an airplane low over —*n.* a sound like a bee's hum

**buz·zard** (buz´ərd) *n.* [< L. *buteo*, kind of hawk] **1.** a kind of hawk that is slow and heavy in flight **2.** *same as* TURKEY BUZZARD

**buzz´er** *n.* an electrical device that makes a buzzing sound as a signal

**buzz saw** a circular saw rotated by machinery

**bx.** box

**by** (bī) *prep.* [OE. *be*, *bi*] **1.** near; at [sit *by* the fire] **2.** *a*) in or during [travel *by* day] *b*) for a fixed time [to work *by* the hour] *c*) not later than [be back *by* noon] **3.** *a*) through; via [to Boston *by* Route 6] *b*) past; beyond [he walked right *by* me] **4.** in behalf of [he did well *by* me] **5.** through the agency of [gained *by* fraud] **6.** *a*) according to [to go *by* the book] *b*) in [to die *by* degrees] *c*) following in series [marching two *by* two] **7.** *a*) in or to the amount of [apples *by* the peck] *b*) and in another dimension [two *by* four] *c*) using (the given number as multiplier or divisor —*adv.* **1.** close at hand [stand *by*] **2.** aside [to put money *by*] **3.** past [he sped *by*] **4.** at the place specified [stop *by* on your way] —**by and by** soon or eventually —**by and large** considering everything —**by the by** incidentally

**by-** *a prefix meaning:* **1.** near **2.** secondary [*by*product]

**by-and-by** (bī´'n bī) *n.* a future time

**bye** (bī) *n.* [see BY] the advantage obtained by an unpaired contestant in a tournament, who advances to the next round without playing

**bye-bye** (bī´bī´) *n.*, *interj.* goodbye

**Bye·lo·rus·sian Soviet Socialist Republic** (bye´lō rush´ən) republic of the U.S.S.R., in W European Russia: 80,154 sq. mi.; pop. 8,633,000: also **Bye´lo·rus´sia**

**by·gone** (bī´gôn´, -gän´) *adj.* past; former —*n.* anything gone or past

**by·law** (bī´lô´) *n.* [< ME. *bi*, village + *laue*, law] a law or rule adopted by an organization or assembly for its own meetings or affairs

**by´line´** *n.* a line above a newspaper or magazine article, telling who wrote it

**by´pass´** *n.* a way, pipe, channel, etc. between two points that avoids or is auxiliary to the main way —*vt.* **1.** to detour **2.** to furnish with a bypass **3.** to ignore

**by´path´, by´·path´** *n.* a secluded, little-used path; byway

**by´play´** *n.* action, gestures, etc. going on aside from the main action or conversation

**by´prod´uct, by´-prod´uct** *n.* anything produced, as from residues, in the course of making another thing

**by´road´** *n.* a road that is not a main road

**By·ron** (bī´rən), **George Gordon** 1788–1824; Eng. poet

**by´stand´er** *n.* a person who stands near but does not participate

**by´way´** *n.* a side road or path

**by´word´** *n.* **1.** a proverb **2.** an object of scorn, ridicule, etc. to many

**By·zan·tine Empire** (biz´'n tēn´) empire (395–1453 A.D.) in SE Europe & SW Asia

# C

**C, c** (sē) *n.*, *pl.* **C's, c's** the third letter of the English alphabet

**C** (sē) *n.* **1.** a Roman numeral for 100 **2.** a grade for average work **3.** *Chem.* carbon **4.** *Music* the first tone in the scale of C major

**C, C.** Celsius or centigrade

**C., c. 1.** carat **2.** catcher **3.** Catholic **4.** cent **5.** center **6.** centimeter **7.** century **8.** circa **9.** college **10.** copyright **11.** cycle

**Ca** *Chem.* calcium

**CA** California

**cab** (kab) *n.* [< CABRIOLET] **1.** a carriage, esp. one for public hire **2.** a taxicab **3.** the place in a locomotive, motor truck, crane, etc. where the operator sits

**ca·bal** (kə bal') *n.* [Fr., intrigue] **1.** a small group joined in a secret intrigue **2.** the intrigue itself

**cab·a·la** (kab'ə lə, kə bäl'ə) *n.* [< Heb. *qabbālāh*, tradition] **1.** a medieval occult Jewish philosophy **2.** occultism

**ca·bal·le·ro** (kab'ə ler'ō, -əl yer'ō) *n.*, *pl.* **-ros** [Sp.] **1.** a Spanish gentleman **2.** [Southwest] *a)* a horseman *b)* a lady's escort

**ca·ba·na** (kə bän'ə, -ban'ə) *n.* [Sp. < LL. *capanna*] **1.** a cabin or hut **2.** a small shelter used as a bathhouse

**cab·a·ret** (kab'ə rā') *n.* [Fr.] a café providing musical entertainment

**cab·bage** (kab'ij) *n.* [< L. *caput*, the head] a vegetable with thick leaves formed into a round compact head

**cab·by, cab·bie** (kab'ē) *n.*, *pl.* **-ies** [Colloq.] one who drives a cab

**cab·in** (kab'n) *n.* [< LL. *capanna*, hut] **1.** a small, crudely or simply built house; hut **2.** a room on a ship or boat **3.** the space for passengers, crew, or cargo in an aircraft

**cab·i·net** (kab'ə nit) *n.* [Fr. < ?] **1.** a case with drawers or shelves **2.** a boxlike structure for the components of a record player, radio, etc. **3.** [*often* C-] a body of official advisers to a chief executive —**cab'i·net·mak'er** *n.* a workman who makes fine furniture —**cab'i·net·work'k** *n.*

**ca·ble** (kā'b'l) *n.* [< L. *capere*, to take hold] **1.** a thick, heavy rope, often of wire strands **2.** a bundle of insulated wires to carry an electric current **3.** a cablegram —*vt.* **-bled, -bling 1.** to fasten with a cable **2.** to transmit by undersea cable **3.** to send a cablegram to —*vi.* to send a cablegram

**cable car** a car drawn by a moving cable, as up a steep incline

**ca'ble·gram'** (-gram') *n.* a message sent by undersea cable

**ca·bo·chon** (kab'ə shän') *n.* [Fr. < *caboche*, the head] any precious stone cut in convex shape

**ca·boo·dle** (kə bōōd''l) *n.* [< BOODLE] [Colloq.] lot; group [the whole *caboodle*]

**ca·boose** (kə bōōs') *n.* [MDu. *kambuis*, cabin house] the trainmen's car at the rear of a freight train

**cab·ri·o·let** (kab'rē ə lā') *n.* [< Fr. *cabriole*, a leap] **1.** a light, two-wheeled, one-horse carriage **2.** a former style of convertible coupe

**ca·ca·o** (kə kā'ō, -kä'ō) *n.*, *pl.* **-os** [Sp. < MexInd. *cacauatl*] **1.** the seed of a tropical American tree from which cocoa and chocolate are made: also **cacao bean 2.** this tree

**cache** (kash) *n.* [Fr. < VL. *coacticare*, store up] **1.** a place in which stores of food, supplies, etc. are hidden **2.** anything so hidden —*vt.*, *vi.* **cached, cach'ing** to place in a cache

**cache·pot** (kash'pät. -pō) *n.* [Fr. < *cacher*, to hide] a decorative jar for holding potted plants: also **cache pot**

**ca·chet** (ka shā') *n.* [Fr.] **1.** a stamp or official seal, as on a document **2.** any sign of official approval, or of quality, prestige, etc. **3.** a design, slogan, advertisement, etc. stamped or printed on mail

**cack·le** (kak''l) *vi.* **-led, -ling** [echoic] **1.** to make the shrill, broken sounds of a hen **2.** to laugh or chatter with similar sounds —*n.* a cackling

**ca·coph·o·ny** (kə käf'ə nē) *n.*, *pl.* **-nies** [< Gr. *kakos*, bad + *phōnē*, voice] harsh, jarring sound; discord —**ca·coph'o·nous** *adj.*

**cac·tus** (kak'təs) *n.*, *pl.* **-tus·es, -ti** (-tī) [< Gr. *kaktos*, a kind of thistle] any of a family of desert plants with fleshy stems and spinelike leaves

**cad** (kad) *n.* [< CADET] a man whose behavior is not gentlemanly —**cad'dish** *adj.* —**cad'dish·ly** *adv.* —**cad'dish·ness** *n.*

**ca·dav·er** (kə dav'ər) *n.* [L., prob. < *cadere*, to fall] a corpse, as for dissection

**ca·dav·er·ous** (-əs) *adj.* [< L.] of or like a cadaver; pale; ghastly

**cad·die, cad·dy¹** (kad'ē) *n.* [Scot. form of Fr. *cadet*: see CADET] one who attends a golf player, carrying his clubs, etc. —*vi.* **-died, -dy·ing** to act as a caddie

**cad·dy²** (kad'ē) *n.*, *pl.* **-dies** [< Malay *kati*, unit of weight] a small container, specif. one used for tea

**-cade** (kād) [< (CAVAL)CADE] *a suffix meaning* procession, parade [*motorcade*]

**ca·dence** (kād'ns) *n.* [< L. *cadere*, to fall] 1. fall of the voice in speaking 2. flow of rhythm 3. measured movements, as in marching

**ca·den·za** (kə den'zə) *n.* [It.: see prec.] an elaborate passage for the solo instrument in a concerto

**ca·det** (kə det') *n.* [Fr. < L. dim. of *caput*, head] 1. a student in training at an armed forces academy 2. any trainee, as a practice teacher

**cadge** (kaj) *vt.,* **cadged, cadg'ing** [ME. *caggen*, to tie] to beg or get by begging —**cadg'er** *n.*

**cad·mi·um** (kad'mē əm) *n.* [< L. *cadmia*, zinc ore (with which it occurs)] a metallic chemical element used in alloys, pigment, etc.

**ca·dre** (kad'rē) *n.* [< Fr. < L. *quadrum*, a square] a nucleus around which an expanded organization, as a military unit, can be built

**ca·du·ce·us** (kə dōō'sē əs) *n., pl.* **-ce·i** (-sē i') [L.] the winged staff of Mercury: now a symbol of the medical profession

**cae·cum** (sē'kəm) *n., pl.* **-ca** (-kə) *same as* CECUM

**Cae·sar** (sē'zər), **Julius** 100?–44 B.C.; Rom. general & dictator

**Cae·sar·e·an section** (si zer'ē ən) the delivery of a baby by cutting through the mother's abdominal and uterine walls: Caesar was supposedly born thus

**cae·su·ra** (si zhoor'ə, -zyoor'ə) *n., pl.* **-ras, -rae** (-ē) [L. < *caedere*, to cut] a break or pause in a line of verse, usually in the middle

**ca·fé, ca·fe** (ka fā', kə-) *n.* [Fr., coffeehouse] a small restaurant or a barroom, nightclub, etc.

**caf·e·te·ri·a** (kaf'ə tir'ē ə) *n.* [AmSp., coffee store] a self-service restaurant

**caf·feine, caf·fein** (kaf'ēn) *n.* [G. *kaffein*] the alkaloid present in coffee, tea, and kola: it is a stimulant

**caf·tan** (kaf'tən) *n.* [Turk. *qaftān*] a long-sleeved robe, worn in eastern Mediterranean countries

**cage** (kāj) *n.* [< L. *cavea*, hollow place] 1. a structure of wires, bars, etc. for confining animals 2. any openwork frame or structure —*vt.* **caged, cag'ing** to put or confine, as in a cage

**cag·er** (kā'jər) *n.* [Slang] a basketball player

**ca·gey, ca·gy** (kā'jē) *adj.* **-gi·er, -gi·est** [< ?] [Colloq.] 1. sly; tricky; cunning 2. cautious —**ca'gi·ly** *adv.* —**ca'gi·ness** *n.*

**ca·hoots** (kə hōōts') *n.pl.* [< ?] [Slang] partnership: implying scheming in phr. **in cahoots**

**Cain** (kān) *Bible* oldest son of Adam and Eve: he killed his brother Abel —**raise Cain** [Slang] to create a great commotion

**cairn** (kern) *n.* [Scot.] a conical heap of stones built as a monument

**Cai·ro** (ki'rō) capital of Egypt: pop. 3,346,000

**cais·son** (kā'sän) *n.* [Fr. < L. *capsa*, box] 1. a two-wheeled wagon with a chest for ammunition 2. a watertight box for underwater construction work

**cai·tiff** (kāt'if) *n.* [< L. *captivus*, CAPTIVE] a mean, evil, or cowardly person —*adj.* evil, mean, or cowardly

**ca·jole** (kə jōl') *vt., vi.* **-joled', -jol'ing** [< Fr.] to coax with flattery and insincere talk —**ca·jol'er** *n.* —**ca·jol'er·y** *n.*

**Ca·jun, Ca·jan** (kā'jən) *n.* 1. a native of Louisiana of Canadian French ancestry 2. the dialect of Cajuns

**cake** (kāk) *n.* [< ON.] 1. a small, flat mass of baked or fried dough, batter, hashed food, etc. 2. a mixture of flour, eggs, sugar, etc. baked as in a loaf and often covered with icing 3. a shaped, solid mass, as of soap —*vt., vi.* **caked, cak'ing** to form into a hard mass or crust —**take the cake** [Slang] to win the prize —**cak'y** *adj.*

**cal.** 1. caliber 2. calorie

**cal·a·bash** (kal'ə bash') *n.* [< Sp. *calabaza* < ?] 1. the gourdlike fruit of a tropical American tree 2. a gourd; specif., the bottle gourd or a smoking pipe made from it

**cal·a·boose** (kal'ə bōōs') *n.* [Sp. *calabozo*] [Slang] a jail

**cal·a·mine** (kal'ə min') *n.* [Fr. < L. *cadmia*, zinc ore] a zinc oxide powder used in skin lotions, etc.

**cal·am·i·ty** (kə lam'ə tē) *n., pl.* **-ties** [< L. *calamitas*] a great misfortune; disaster —**ca·lam'i·tous** *adj.* —**ca·lam'i·tous·ly** *adv.* —**ca·lam'i·tous·ness** *n.*

**cal·car·e·ous** (kal ker'ē əs) *adj.* [< L. *calx,* lime] of or like limestone, calcium, or lime

**cal·ci·fy** (kal'sə fi') *vt., vi.* **-fied', -fy'ing** [< L. *calx,* lime + -FY] to change into a hard, stony substance by the deposit of lime or calcium salts —**cal'ci·fi·ca'tion** *n.*

**cal·ci·mine'** (-min') *n.* [< L. *calx,* lime] a white or colored liquid used as a wash for plastered surfaces —*vt.* **-mined', -min'ing** to cover with calcimine

**cal·cine** (kal'sin) *vt., vi.* **-cined, -cin·ing** [< ML. *calcinare*] to change to an ashy powder by heat

**cal·cite** (kal'sit) *n.* calcium carbonate, a mineral found as limestone, chalk, and marble

**cal·ci·um** (kal'sē əm) *n.* [< L. *calx,* lime] a soft, silver-white metallic chemical element found combined in limestone, chalk, etc.

**calcium carbonate** a white powder or crystalline compound found in limestone, chalk, bones, shells, etc.

**cal·cu·late** (kal'kyə lāt') *vt.* **-lat'ed, -lat'ing** [< L. *calculare,* reckon] 1. to determine by using mathematics; compute 2. to determine by reasoning; estimate 3. to plan or intend for a purpose —*vi.* 1. to reckon 2. to rely (*on*) —**cal'cu·la·ble** (-lə b'l) *adj.*

**cal'cu·lat'ed** *adj.* deliberately planned or carefully considered

**cal'cu·lat'ing** *adj.* shrewd or cunning; scheming

**cal'cu·la'tion** *n.* 1. a calculating 2. something deduced by calculating 3. careful planning or forethought —**cal'cu·la'tive** *adj.*

**cal·cu·la'tor** *n.* **1.** one who calculates **2.** a machine for doing arithmetic rapidly: also **calculating machine**

**cal·cu·lus** (kal'kyə ləs) *n., pl.* **-li'** (-lī'), **-lus·es** [L., pebble used in counting] **1.** an abnormal stony mass in the body **2.** a method of calculation or analysis in higher mathematics

**Cal·cut·ta** (kal kut'ə) seaport in NE India: pop. 2,927,000

**cal·dron** (kôl'drən) *n.* [< L. *calidus*, warm] **1.** a large kettle or boiler **2.** a state of violent agitation

**cal·en·dar** (kal'ən dər) *n.* [< L. *kalendarium*, account book] **1.** a system of determining the length and divisions of a year **2.** a table that shows the days, weeks, and months of a given year **3.** a schedule, as of pending court cases

**cal·en·der** (kal'ən dər) *n.* [< Gr. *kylindros*, cylinder] a machine with rollers for giving paper, cloth, etc. a smooth or glossy finish —*vt.* to process (paper, etc.) in a calender

**calf¹** (kaf) *n., pl.* **calves**; esp. for 3, **calfs** [OE. *cealf*] **1.** a young cow or bull **2.** the young of some other large animals, as the elephant, seal, etc. **3.** leather from a calf's hide

**calf²** (kaf) *n., pl.* **calves** [ON. *kalfr*] the fleshy back part of the leg below the knee

**calf'skin'** *n.* **1.** the skin of a calf **2.** a soft leather made from this

**Cal·ga·ry** (kal'gər ē) city in S Alberta, Canada: pop. 331,000

**cal·i·ber, cal·i·bre** (kal'ə bər) *n.* [Fr. & Sp. < Ar. *qālib*, a mold] **1.** the diameter of a cylindrical body, esp. the diameter of a bullet or shell **2.** the diameter of the bore of a gun **3.** quality; ability

**cal·i·brate** (kal'ə brāt') *vt.* **-brat'ed, -brat'ing 1.** to determine the caliber of **2.** to fix or correct the graduations of (a measuring instrument) —**cal'i·bra'tion** *n.* —**cal'i·bra'tor** *n.*

**cal·i·co** (kal'ə kō') *n., pl.* **-coes', -cos'** [< *Calicut*, city in India] a kind of coarse, printed, cotton fabric —*adj.* spotted like a calico [*a calico cat*]

**Cal·i·for·ni·a** (kal'ə fôr'nyə, -nē ə) State of the SW U.S., on the Pacific: 158,693 sq. mi.; pop. 19,953,000; cap. Sacramento: abbrev. **Calif.** —**Cal'i·for'ni·an** *adj., n.*

**cal·i·per** (kal'ə pər) *n.* [var. of CALIBER] [*usually pl.*] an instrument consisting of a pair of hinged legs, for measuring thickness or diameter —*vt., vi.* to measure with calipers

CALIPERS

**ca·liph, ca·lif** (kā'lif, kal'if) *n.* [Ar. *khalifa*] supreme ruler: the title taken by Mohammed's successors as heads of Islam —**cal'iph·ate** *n.*

**cal·is·then·ics** (kal'əs then'iks) *n.pl.* [< Gr. *kallos*, beauty + *sthenos*, strength] athletic exercises

**calk** (kôk) *vt. same as* CAULK

**call** (kôl) *vt.* [< ON. *kalla*] **1.** to say in a loud tone; shout **2.** to summon **3.** to give or apply a name to **4.** to describe as specified **5.** to awaken **6.** to telephone **7.** to give orders for **8.** to stop (a game, etc.) **9.** to demand payment of (a loan, etc.) **10.** *Poker* to require (a player) to show his hand by equaling his bet —*vi.* **1.** to shout **2.** to visit for a while (often with *on*) **3.** to telephone —*n.* **1.** a calling **2.** a loud utterance **3.** the distinctive cry of an animal or bird **4.** a summons; invitation **5.** an economic demand, as for a product **6.** need [*no call for tears*] **7.** a demand for payment **8.** a brief visit —**call down** [Colloq.] to scold —**call for 1.** to demand **2.** to come and get —**call off** to cancel (a scheduled event) —**call up 1.** to recall **2.** to summon for duty **3.** to telephone —**on call** available when summoned —**call'er** *n.*

**cal·la** (kal'ə) *n.* [< L., a plant (of unc. kind)] a plant with a large, white leaf surrounding a yellow flower spike: also **calla lily**

**call girl** a prostitute who is called by telephone to assignations

**cal·lig·ra·phy** (kə lig'rə fē) *n.* [< Gr. *kallos*, beauty + *graphein*, write] handwriting, esp. when attractive —**cal·lig'ra·pher** *n.* —**cal·li·graph·ic** (kal'ə graf'ik) *adj.*

**call'ing** *n.* **1.** act of one that calls **2.** one's work or profession **3.** an inner urging toward some vocation

**cal·li·o·pe** (kə lī'ə pē', kal'ē ōp') *n.* [< Gr. *kallos*, beauty + *ops*, voice] a keyboard instrument like an organ, having a series of steam whistles

**call letters** the letters, and sometimes numbers, that identify a radio station

**cal·los·i·ty** (ka läs'ə tē) *n.* **1.** the state of being callous **2.** a callus

**cal·lous** (kal'əs) *adj.* [< L. *callum*, hard skin] **1.** hardened **2.** unfeeling —**cal'lous·ly** *adv.* —**cal'lous·ness** *n.*

**cal·low** (kal'ō) *adj.* [OE. *calu*, bare, bald] immature; inexperienced —**cal'low·ness** *n.*

**cal·lus** (kal'əs) *n., pl.* **-lus·es** [L., var. of *callum*, hard skin] a hardened, thickened place on the skin

**calm** (käm) *n.* [< Gr. *kauma*, heat] stillness; tranquility —*adj.* still; quiet; tranquil —*vt., vi.* to make or become calm (often with *down*) —**calm'ly** *adv.* —**calm'ness** *n.*

**cal·o·mel** (kal'ə mel', -məl) *n.* [Fr. < Gr. *kalos*, beautiful + *melas*, black] a white, tasteless powder, formerly used as a cathartic, etc.

**ca·lor·ic** (kə lôr'ik, -lär'-) *adj.* **1.** of heat **2.** of calories

**cal·o·rie** (kal'ə rē) *n.* [Fr. < L. *calor*, heat] a unit for measuring heat, esp. for measuring the energy produced by food when oxidized in the body

**cal·o·rif·ic** (kal'ə rif'ik) *adj.* [< L. *calor*, heat + *facere*, make] producing heat

**cal·u·met** (kal′yə met′) *n.* [Fr. < L. *calamus*, reed] a long-stemmed ceremonial pipe smoked by N.American Indians as a token of peace

**ca·lum·ni·ate** (kə lum′nē āt′) *vt.*, *vi.* -at′ed, -at′ing [see ff.] to slander —**ca·lum′ni·a′tion** *n.* —**ca·lum′ni·a′tor** *n.*

**cal·um·ny** (kal′əm nē) *n.*, *pl.* -nies [< L. *calumnia*, slander] a false and malicious statement; slander

**Cal·va·ry** (kal′vər ē) *Bible* the place where Jesus was crucified

**calve** (kav) *vi.*, *vt.* **calved, calv′ing** to give birth to (a calf)

**calves** (kavz) *n. pl. of* CALF

**Cal·vin** (kal′vin), **John** 1509–64; Fr. Protestant reformer

**Cal·vin·ism** (-iz′m) *n.* the theological system of John Calvin and his followers, stressing predestination —**Cal′vin·ist** *n.*, *adj.* —**Cal′vin·is′tic** *adj.*

**cal·vi·ti·es** (kal vish′i ēz′) *n.* [L.] baldness

**ca·lyp·so** (kə lip′sō) *n.* [< ?] a lively, topical folk song, orig. of Trinidad

**ca·lyx** (kā′liks, kal′iks) *n.*, *pl.* **-lyx·es, -ly·ces** (-lə sēz′) [L., pod] the outer whorl of protective leaves, or sepals, of a flower

**cam** (kam) *n.* [Du. *cam*, orig., a comb] a wheel, projection on a wheel, etc. which gives an irregular motion as to a wheel or shaft, or receives such motion from it

**ca·ma·ra·de·rie** (käm′ə räd′ər ē) *n.* [Fr.] good fellowship; comradeship

**cam·ber** (kam′bər) *n.* [OFr. < L. *camur*, arched] a slight convex curve of a surface, as of a road —*vt.*, *vi.* to arch slightly

**cam·bi·um** (kam′bē əm) *n.* [LL., change] a layer of cells between the wood and bark in woody plants, from which new wood and bark grow

**Cam·bo·di·a** (kam bō′dē ə) country in S Indochina: 69,884 sq. mi.; pop. 6,250,000: official name **Kam·pu·che·a** (kam′poo chē′ə) —**Cam·bo′di·an** *adj.*, *n.*

**cam·bric** (kām′brik) *n.* [< *Cambrai*, Fr. city] a fine linen or cotton cloth

**Cam·bridge** (kām′brij) **1.** city in EC England: pop. 100,000 **2.** city in E Mass.: pop. 100,000

**Cam·den** (kam′dən) city in SW N.J.: pop. 103,000

**came** (kām) *pt. of* COME

**cam·el** (kam′'l) *n.* [ult. < Heb. *gāmāl*] a large, domesticated mammal with a humped back and long neck: because it can store water in its body, it is used in Asian and African deserts

**ca·mel·lia** (kə mēl′yə) *n.* [after G. J. *Kamel*, 17th-c. missionary to the Far East] **1.** an Asiatic evergreen tree or shrub with dark-green leaves and roselike flowers **2.** the flower

**ca·mel·o·pard** (kə mel′ə pärd′) *n.* [< Gr. *kamēlos*, camel + *pardalis*, leopard: from its neck and spots] *early name for the* GIRAFFE

**Cam·em·bert (cheese)** (kam′əm ber′) [< *Camembert*, Fr. village] a soft, creamy, rich cheese

**cam·e·o** (kam′ē ō′, kam′yō) *n.*, *pl.* -os [< It. < ML. *camaeus*] **1.** a gem carved with a figure raised in relief **2.** *a)* an outstanding bit role *b)* a bit of fine writing

**cam·er·a** (kam′er ə) *n.* [L., a vault] **1.** the private office of a judge **2.** a device for taking photographs, a closed box containing a sensitized plate or film on which an image is formed when light enters through a lens **3.** *TV* the device that receives the image and transforms it into a flow of electrical impulses for transmission —**in camera** in privacy or secrecy

**cam′er·a·man′** *n.*, *pl.* -men′ an operator of a motion-picture or television camera

**Cam·e·roon** (kam′ə rōōn′) country in WC Africa: c.183,000 sq. mi.; pop. 5,229,000 —**Cam′e·roon′i·an** *adj.*, *n.*

**cam·i·sole** (kam′ə sōl′) *n.* [Fr. < VL. *camisia*, shirt] a woman's lace-trimmed underwaist

**cam·o·mile** (kam′ə mīl′, -mēl′) *n.* *same as* CHAMOMILE

**cam·ou·flage** (kam′ə fläzh′, -fläj′) *n.* [Fr. < *camoufler*, to disguise] **1.** a disguising, as of ships or guns, to conceal them from the enemy **2.** a disguise; deception —*vt.*, *vi.* **-flaged′, -flag′ing** to disguise in order to conceal —**cam′ou·flag′er** *n.*

**camp** (kamp) *n.* [< L. *campus*, field] **1.** *a)* a place where temporary tents, huts, etc. are put up, as for soldiers *b)* a group of such tents, etc. **2.** the supporters of a particular cause **3.** a recreational place in the country for vacationers, esp. children **4.** the people living in a camp **5.** [Slang] banality, artifice, etc. so extreme as to amuse or have a perversely sophisticated appeal —*vi.* **1.** to set up a camp **2.** to live or stay in a camp (often with *out*) —**break camp** to dismantle a camp and depart

**cam·paign** (kam pān′) *n.* [Fr. < L. *campus*, field] **1.** a series of military operations with a particular objective **2.** a series of planned actions, as for electing a candidate —*vi.* to participate in a campaign —**cam·paign′er** *n.*

**cam·pa·ni·le** (kam′pə nē′lē) *n.*, *pl.* **-les, -li** (-lē) [It. < LL. *campana*, a bell] a bell tower

**camp·er** (kamp′ər) *n.* **1.** a vacationer at a camp **2.** a motor vehicle or trailer equipped for camping out

**camp′fire′** *n.* **1.** an outdoor fire at a camp **2.** a social gathering around such a fire

**cam·phor** (kam′fər) *n.* [< Sans. *karpurah*, camphor tree] a crystalline substance with a strong odor, derived chiefly from an Oriental evergreen tree (**camphor tree**): used to repel moths, in medicine as a stimulant, etc. — **cam′phor·at′ed** *adj.*

**camp meeting** a religious meeting held outdoors or in a tent, etc.

**camp′site′** *n.* **1.** any site for a camp **2.** an area in a park set aside for camping

**cam·pus** (kam′pəs) *n.*, *pl.* **-pus·es** [L., a field] the grounds, and sometimes buildings, of a school or college

—*adj.* of a school or college [*campus* politics]

**camp·y** *adj.* -i·er, -i·est [Slang] characterized by camp (*n.* 5)

**can¹** (kan, kən) *vi. pt.* **could** [< OE. *cunnan,* know] 1. to know how to 2. to be able to 3. to be likely to [*can* that be true?] 4. to have the right to 5. [Colloq.] to be permitted to; may —**can** but can only

**can²** (kan) *n.* [OE. *canne,* cup] 1. a container, usually metal, with a separate cover [a garbage *can*] 2. a tinned metal container in which foods, etc. are sealed for preservation 3. the contents of a can —*vt.* **canned, can′-ning** 1. to put up in cans or jars for preservation 2. [Slang] to dismiss

**Ca·naan** (kā′nən) Promised Land of the Israelites, a region between the Jordan and the Mediterranean

**Can·a·da** (kan′ə də) country in N. N.America: 3,852,000 sq. mi.; pop. 20,015,000; cap. Ottawa: abbrev. **Can.** —**Ca·na·di·an** (kə nā′dē ən) *adj., n.*

**Ca·na′di·an·ism** *n.* 1. a custom or belief of Canada 2. a word or idiom originating in Canadian English

**ca·nal** (kə nal′) *n.* [< L. *canalis,* channel] 1. an artificial waterway for transportation or irrigation 2. *Anat.* a tubular passage or duct

**Canal Zone** strip of land in Panama, extending 5 miles on either side of the Panama Canal: leased by the U.S.

**ca·na·pé** (kan′ə pē, -pā′) *n.* [Fr.] a cracker, etc. spread with spiced meat, cheese, etc., served as an appetizer

**ca·nard** (kə närd′) *n.* [Fr., a duck] a false, esp. malicious report

**ca·nar·y** (kə ner′ē) *n., pl.* -ies [< *Canary* Islands] 1. a yellow songbird of the finch family 2. a light yellow

**Canary Islands** group of Sp. islands off NW Africa

**ca·nas·ta** (kə nas′tə) *n.* [Sp., basket] a double-deck card game

**Can·ber·ra** (kan′bər ə) capital of Australia: pop. 67,000

**can·can** (kan′kan′) *n.* [Fr.] a gay dance with much high kicking

**can·cel** (kan′s'l) *vt.* -celed or -celled, -cel·ing or -cel·ling [< L. *cancellus,* lattice] 1. to mark over with lines, etc., as in deleting written matter or marking a postage stamp, check, etc. as used 2. to make invalid 3. to do away with; abolish 4. to neutralize or balance (often with *out*) 5. *Math.* to remove (a common factor, equivalents, etc.) —**can′cel·la′tion** *n.*

**can·cer** (kan′sər) [< L., a crab] [C-] the fourth sign of the zodiac —*n.* 1. a malignant tumor that can spread. 2. any spreading evil —**can′cer·ous** *adj.*

**can·de·la·brum** (kan′də lä′brəm, -lab′rəm) *n., pl.* -bra (-brə), -brums [L.: see CHANDELIER] a large branched candlestick: also **can′de·la′bra,** *pl.* -**bras**

**can·did** (kan′did) *adj.* [< L. *candidus,* white, sincere] 1. honest; frank 2. un-posed and informal [a *candid* photo] —**can′did·ly** *adv.* —**can′did·ness** *n.*

**can·di·date** (kan′də dāt′, -dit) *n.* [L. *candidatus,* white-robed, as office seekers] one seeking an office, award, etc. —**can′di·da·cy** (-də də sē) *n.*

**can·died** (kan′dēd) *adj.* 1. cooked in sugar 2. sugary

**can·dle** (kan′d'l) *n.* [< L. *candela*] a cylinder of tallow or wax with a wick through it, which gives light when burned —*vt.* -**dled, -dling** to examine (eggs) for freshness by holding in front of a light —**can′dler** *n.*

**candle power** luminous intensity measured in units called candles

**can′dle·stick′** *n.* a cupped or spiked holder for a candle or candles

**can·dor** (kan′dər) *n.* [L., sincerity] honesty or frankness in expressing oneself: Brit. sp., **candour**

**can·dy** (kan′dē) *n., pl.* -dies [< Per. *qand,* cane sugar] a solid confection of sugar or syrup with flavoring, fruit, nuts, etc. —*vt.* -died, -dy·ing 1. to cook in sugar, esp. to preserve 2. to crystallize into sugar

**cane** (kān) *n.* [< Gr. *kanna*] 1. the slender, jointed stem of certain plants, as bamboo 2. a plant with such a stem, as sugar cane 3. a walking stick 4. split rattan —*vt.* **caned, can′ing** 1. to flog with a cane 2. to make (chair seats, etc.) with cane —**can′er** *n.*

**cane·brake** (kān′brāk′) *n.* a dense growth of cane plants

**ca·nine** (kā′nīn) *adj.* [< L. *canis,* dog] 1. of or like a dog 2. of the family of animals that includes dogs, wolves, and foxes —*n.* 1. a dog or other canine animal 2. any of the four sharp-pointed teeth next to the incisors: in full **canine tooth**

**can·is·ter** (kan′is tər) *n.* [< Gr. *kanistron,* wicker basket] a small box or can for coffee, tea, etc.

**can·ker** (kaŋ′kər) *n.* [< L.: see CANCER] a spreading sore, esp. in the mouth —**can′ker·ous** *adj.*

**can·na·bis** (kan′ə bis) *n.* [L., hemp] 1. *same as* HEMP 2. the female flowering tops of the hemp

**canned** (kand) *adj.* 1. preserved, as in cans 2. [Slang] recorded for reproduction as on radio or TV

**can·nel (coal)** (kan′'l) [< ? *candle coal*] a tough bituminous coal that burns with a bright flame

**can·ner·y** (kan′ər ē) *n., pl.* -ies a factory where foods are canned

**can·ni·bal** (kan′ə b'l) *n.* [Sp. *canibal*] 1. a person who eats human flesh 2. an animal that eats its own kind —*adj.* of or like cannibals —**can′ni·bal·ism** *n.* —**can′ni·bal·is′tic** *adj.*

**can′ni·bal·ize′** (-īz′) *vt., vi.* -ized′, -iz′ing to strip (old equipment) of parts for use in other units

**can·non** (kan′ən) *n., pl.* -nons, -non [< L. *canna,* cane] 1. a large, mounted piece of artillery 2. an automatic gun on an aircraft

**can·non·ade′** (-ād′) *n.* a continuous firing of artillery —*vt.*, *vi.* -ad′ed, -ad′ing to fire artillery (at)

**can·not** (kan′ät, kə nät′) can not —cannot but have no choice but to

**can·ny** (kan′ē) *adj.* -ni·er, -ni·est [< CAN¹] 1. cautious and shrewd 2. wise and well-informed —can′ni·ly *adv.* —can′ni·ness *n.*

**ca·noe** (kə nōō′) *n.* [Sp. *canoa* < AmInd.] a narrow, light boat moved by paddles —*vi.* -noed′, -noe′ing to paddle, or go in, a canoe —ca·noe′ist *n.*

**can·on** (kan′ən) *n.* [OE., a rule < L.] 1. a law or body of laws of a church 2. *a)* a basic law or principle *b)* a criterion 3. an official list, as of books of the Bible 4. a clergyman serving in a cathedral 5. *Music* a round

**ca·ñon** (kan′yən) *n. same as* CANYON

**ca·non·i·cal** (kə nän′i k'l) *adj.* 1. of or according to church law 2. of or belonging to a canon

**can·on·ize** (kan′ə nīz′) *vt.* -ized′, -iz′ing 1. to declare (a dead person) a saint 2. to glorify —can′on·i·za′tion *n.*

**can·o·py** (kan′ə pē) *n.*, *pl.* -pies [< Gr. *kōnōpeion*, couch with mosquito nets] 1. a drapery, etc. fastened above a bed, throne, etc., or held over a person 2. a rooflike projection —*vt.* -pied, -py·ing to place or form a canopy over

**cant¹** (kant) *n.* [< L. *canere*, sing] 1. the secret slang of beggars, thieves, etc.; argot 2. the special vocabulary of those in a certain occupation; jargon 3. insincere talk, esp. when pious —*vi.* to use cant

**cant²** (kant) *n.* [< L. *cant(h)us*, tire of a wheel] 1. an outside angle 2. a beveled edge 3. a tilt, slant, turn, etc. —*vt.*, *vi.* to slant; tilt

**can't** (kant, känt) cannot

**can·ta·loupe, can·ta·loup** (kan′tə lōp′) *n.* [Fr. < It. *Cantalupo*, estate near Rome, where first grown in Europe] a muskmelon, esp. one with a rough rind and juicy orange flesh

**can·tan·ker·ous** (kan taŋ′kər əs) *adj.* [prob. < ME. *contakour*, troublemaker] bad-tempered; quarrelsome —can·tan′ker·ous·ly *adv.* —can·tan′ker·ous·ness *n.*

**can·ta·ta** (kən tät′ə) *n.* [It. < *cantare*, sing] a choral composition for a story to be sung but not acted

**can·teen** (kan tēn′) *n.* [< Fr. < It. *cantina*, wine cellar] 1. a recreation center for servicemen, teen-agers, etc. 2. a small flask for carrying water

**can·ter** (kan′tər) *n.* [< *Canterbury gallop*, a riding pace] a moderate gallop —*vt.*, *vi.* to ride at this pace

**can·ti·cle** (kan′ti k'l) *n.* [< L. *canere*, sing] a song or chant, esp. a hymn with words from the Bible

**can·ti·le·ver** (kan′t'l ē′vər, -ev′ər) *n.* [< ?] a bracket or block projecting as a support; esp., a projecting structure anchored at one end to a pier or wall —*vt.* to support by means of cantilevers —can′ti·le′vered *adj.*

**can·to** (kan′tō) *n.*, *pl.* -tos [It. < L.

*canere*, sing] any of the main divisions of certain long poems

**Can·ton** (kan tän′; *for 2* kan′tən) 1. *former name of* KWANGCHOW 2. city in EC Ohio: pop. 110,000

**can·ton** (kan′tən, kan tän′) *n.* [Fr. < LL. *cantus*, corner] any of the states in the Swiss Republic

**Can·ton·ese** (kan′tə nēz′) *adj.* of Canton, China, its people, or language

**can·ton·ment** (kan tän′mənt, -tōn′-) *n.* [< Fr.: see CANTON] temporary quarters for troops

**can·tor** (kan′tər) *n.* [L., singer] a singer of liturgical solos in a synagogue

**can·vas** (kan′vəs) *n.* [< L. *cannabis*, hemp] 1. a coarse cloth of hemp, cotton, etc., used for tents, sails, etc. 2. a sail, tent, etc. 3. an oil painting on canvas

**can′vas·back′** *n.* a N. American wild duck with a grayish back

**can·vass** (kan′vəs) *vt.*, *vi.* [< *canvas* (? used for sifting)] to go through (places) or among (people) asking for votes, opinions, orders, etc. —*n.* a canvassing —can′vass·er *n.*

**can·yon** (kan′yən) *n.* [Sp. *cañón*, tube < L. *canna*, reed] a long, narrow valley between high cliffs

**cap** (kap) *n.* [< LL. *cappa*, hooded cloak] 1. any closefitting head covering, visored or brimless 2. a caplike thing; cover or top —*vt.* capped, cap′ping 1. to put a cap on 2. to cover (the end of) 3. to equal or excel

**cap.** 1. capacity 2. *pl.* caps. capital

**ca·pa·ble** (kā′pə b'l) *adj.* [< L. *capere*, take] having ability; skilled; competent —capable of 1. having the qualities necessary for 2. able or ready to —ca′pa·bil′i·ty (-bil′ə tē) *n.*, *pl.* -ties —ca′pa·bly *adv.*

**ca·pa·cious** (kə pā′shəs) *adj.* [< L. *capere*, take] roomy; spacious —ca·pa′cious·ly *adv.* —ca·pa′cious·ness *n.*

**ca·pac·i·tor** (kə pas′ə tər) *n.* a device for storing an electrical charge

**ca·pac·i·ty** (-tē) *n.*, *pl.* -ties [< L. *capere*, take] 1. the ability to contain, absorb, or receive 2. all that can be contained; volume 3. ability 4. maximum output 5. position; function

**ca·par·i·son** (kə par′ə s'n) *n.* [< LL. *cappa*, cloak] trappings for a horse —*vt.* to cover (a horse) with trappings

**cape¹** (kāp) *n.* [see prec.] a sleeveless garment fastened at the neck and hanging over the back and shoulders

**cape²** (kāp) *n.* [< L. *caput*, head] a piece of land projecting into water

**ca·per¹** (kā′pər) *vi.* [? < Fr. *capriole*, a leap] to skip about in a playful manner —*n.* 1. a gay, playful leap 2. a prank —cut a caper (or capers) 1. to caper 2. to play silly tricks

**ca·per²** (kā′pər) *n.* [< Gr. *kapparis*] the green flower bud of a Mediterranean bush, pickled and used as a seasoning

**cape′skin′** *n.* fine leather made from goatskin or sheepskin, orig. from the Cape of Good Hope

**Cape Town** seaport in South Africa; seat of the legislature: pop. 807,000

**cap·il·lar·y** (kap′ə ler′ē) *adj.* [< L.

*capillus,* hair] very slender —*n., pl.* **-ies** 1. a tube with a very small bore: also **capillary tube** 2. any of the tiny blood vessels connecting arteries with veins

**capillary attraction** (or **action**) the action by which liquids in contact with solids, as in a capillary tube, rise or fall: also **cap'il·lar'i·ty** (-ə tē) *n.*

**cap·i·tal** (kap'ə t'l) *adj.* [< L. *caput,* head] 1. punishable by death 2. principal; chief 3. of, or being, the seat of government 4. of capital, or wealth 5. excellent —*n.* 1. a capital letter 2. a city that is the seat of government of a state or nation 3. money or property owned or used in business 4. [*often* C-] capitalists collectively 5. the top part of a column

CAPITAL

**capital gain** profit made from the sale of capital investments, as stocks

**cap'i·tal·ism** (-iz'm) *n.* the economic system in which the means of production and distribution are privately owned and operated for profit

**cap'i·tal·ist** *n.* 1. an owner of wealth used in business 2. an upholder of capitalism 3. a wealthy person —**cap'i·tal·is'tic** *adj.*

**cap'i·tal·ize'** (-iz') *vt.* **-ized', -iz'ing** 1. to use as or convert into capital 2. to use to one's advantage (with *on*) 3. to supply capital to or for 4. to begin (a word) with a capital letter —**cap'i·tal·i·za'tion** *n.*

**capital letter** the form of an alphabetical letter used to begin a sentence or proper name, as A, B, C, etc.

**cap'i·tal·ly** *adv.* very well

**capital punishment** penalty of death for a crime

**capital stock** the capital of a corporation, divided into shares

**Cap·i·tol** (kap'ə t'l) [< L. *Capitolium,* temple of Jupiter] the building in which the U.S. Congress meets, at Washington, D.C. —*n.* [*usually* c-] the building in which a state legislature meets

**ca·pit·u·late** (kə pich'ə lāt') *vi.* **-lat'ed, -lat'ing** [< L. *capitulare,* arrange conditions] 1. to give up (*to* an enemy) on prearranged conditions 2. to stop resisting —**ca·pit'u·la'tion** *n.*

**ca·pon** (kā'pän) *n.* [< L. *capo*] a castrated rooster fattened for eating

**ca·price** (kə prēs') *n.* [Fr. < It.] 1. a sudden, impulsive change in thinking or acting 2. a capricious quality

**ca·pri·cious** (kə prish'əs) *adj.* subject to caprices; erratic —**ca·pri'cious·ly** *adv.* —**ca·pri'cious·ness** *n.*

**Cap·ri·corn** (kap'rə kôrn') [< L. *caper,* goat + *cornu,* horn] the tenth sign of the zodiac

**cap·size** (kap'sīz) *vt., vi.* **-sized, -siz·ing** [< ?] to overturn or upset: said esp. of a boat

**cap·stan** (kap'stən) *n.* [< L. *capere,* take] an upright drum, as on ships,

around which cables are wound so as to haul them in

**cap·sule** (kap's'l, -syool) *n.* [Fr. < L. *capsa,* chest] 1. a soluble gelatin container enclosing a dose of medicine 2. a detachable compartment to hold men, instruments, etc. in a rocket 3. *Bot.* a seedcase —*adj.* in a concise form —**cap'su·lar** *adj.*

**cap'sul·ize'** (-īz') *vt.* **-ized', -iz'ing** 1. to enclose in a capsule 2. to condense

**cap·tain** (kap'tən) *n.* [< L. *caput,* head] 1. a chief; leader 2. *U.S. Mil.* an officer ranking just above lieutenant 3. a navy officer ranking just above commander 4. the master of a ship 5. the leader of a team, as in sports Abbrev. **Capt.** —*vt.* to be captain of —**cap'tain·cy** *n., pl.* **-cies**

**cap·tion** (kap'shən) *n.* [< L. *capere,* take] 1. a heading or title, as of a newspaper article or an illustration 2. *Motion Pictures* a subtitle —*vt.* to supply a caption for

**cap·tious** (-shəs) *adj.* [see prec.] 1. made for the sake of argument, as a remark 2. quick to find fault —**cap'tious·ly** *adv.* —**cap'tious·ness** *n.*

**cap·ti·vate** (kap'tə vāt') *vt.* **-vat'ed, -vat'ing** to capture the attention or affection of —**cap'ti·va'tion** *n.*

**cap·tive** (kap'tiv) *n.* [< L. *capere,* take] a prisoner —*adj.* 1. taken or held prisoner 2. obliged to listen —**cap·tiv'i·ty** *n.*

**cap'tor** (-tər) *n.* one who captures

**cap'ture** (-chər) *vt.* **-tured, -tur·ing** [< L. *capere,* take] 1. to take or seize by force, surprise, etc. 2. to represent in a more permanent form [a picture *capturing* her charm] —*n.* a capturing or being captured

**car** (kär) *n.* [< L. *carrus,* chariot] 1. any vehicle on wheels 2. a vehicle that moves on rails 3. an automobile 4. an elevator cage

**Ca·ra·cas** (kə räk'əs, -rak'-) capital of Venezuela: pop. 787,000

**car·a·cul** (kar'ə kəl) *n.* same as KARAKUL

**ca·rafe** (kə raf') *n.* [Fr.] a glass or metal bottle for water, coffee, etc.

**car·a·mel** (kar'ə m'l, kär'm'l) *n.* [Fr.] 1. burnt sugar used to color or flavor food 2. chewy candy made from sugar, milk, etc.

**car'a·mel·ize'** (-mə līz') *vt., vi.* **-ized', -iz'ing** to turn into caramel

**car·a·pace** (kar'ə pās') *n.* [Fr. < Sp.] an upper shell, as of the turtle

**car·at** (kar'ət) *n.* [Fr. < Gr. *keration*] 1. a unit of weight for precious stones, equal to 200 milligrams 2. same as KARAT

**car·a·van** (kar'ə van') *n.* [< Per. *kārwān*] 1. a company of people traveling together for safety, as through a desert 2. same as VAN²

**car·a·van·sa·ry** (kar'ə van'sə rē) *n., pl.* **-ries** [< Per. *kārwān,* caravan + *sarāi,* palace] in the Orient, an inn for caravans

**car·a·way** (kar′ə wā′) *n.* [< Ar. *karawiyā′*] the spicy seeds of a plant, used to flavor bread, etc.

**car·bide** (kär′bīd) *n.* a compound of a metal with carbon

**car·bine** (kär′bīn, -bēn) *n.* [< Fr. *scarabée*, beetle] 1. a short-barreled rifle 2. *U.S. Armed Forces* a light, semiautomatic or automatic .30-caliber rifle

**carbo-** *a combining form meaning* carbon: also **carb-**

**car·bo·hy·drate** (kär′bə hī′drāt) *n.* [CARBO- + HYDRATE] an organic compound composed of carbon, hydrogen, and oxygen, as a sugar or starch

**car·bol·ic acid** (kär bäl′ik) *same as* PHENOL

**car·bon** (kär′bən) *n.* [< L. *carbo*, coal] 1. a nonmetallic chemical element found esp. in all organic compounds: diamond and graphite are pure carbon: a radioactive isotope of carbon (**carbon 14**) is used in dating fossils, etc. 2. carbon paper 3. a copy made with carbon paper: in full **carbon copy** —*adj.* of or like carbon

**car·bon·ate** (-bə nit, -nāt′) *n.* a salt or ester of carbonic acid —*vt.* (-nāt′) -at′ed, -at′ing to charge with carbon dioxide —**car′bon·a′tion** *n.*

**carbon black** finely divided carbon produced by the incomplete burning of oil or gas

**car′bon-date′** *vt.* -dat′ed, -dat′ing to establish the approximate age of (fossils, etc.) by measuring the carbon 14 content

**carbon dioxide** a heavy, colorless, odorless gas: it passes out of the lungs in respiration

**car·bon·ic acid** (kär bän′ik) a weak acid formed by carbon dioxide in water

**car·bon·if·er·ous** (kär′bə nif′ər əs) *adj.* containing carbon or coal

**carbon monoxide** a colorless, odorless, highly poisonous gas

**carbon paper** thin paper coated on one side, as with a carbon preparation, used to make copies of letters, etc.

**carbon tet·ra·chlo·ride** (tet′rə klôr′īd) a nonflammable liquid used in cleaning mixtures, etc.

**Car·bo·run·dum** (kär′bə run′dəm) [CARB(ON) + (c)*orundum*] *a trademark for* a hard abrasive, esp. of carbon and silicon —*n.* [c-] such a substance

**car·boy** (kär′boi) *n.* [< Per.] a large bottle to hold corrosive liquids, enclosed in a protective container

**car·bun·cle** (kär′buŋ k'l) *n.* [< L. dim. of *carbo*, coal] a painful, pus-bearing inflammation of the tissue beneath the skin —**car·bun′cu·lar** (-kyoo lər) *adj.*

**car·bu·ret·or** (kär′bə rāt′er) *n.* a device for mixing air with gasoline spray to make an explosive mixture in an internal-combustion engine

**car·cass** (kär′kəs) *n.* [< Fr. *carcasse*] 1. the dead body of an animal 2. a framework or shell

**car·cin·o·gen** (kär sin′ə jən) *n.* [< ff. + -GEN] any substance that produces cancer —**car·ci·no·gen·ic** (kär′sə nō jen′ik) *adj.*

**car·ci·no·ma** (kär′sə nō′mə) *n., pl.* **-mas, -ma·ta** (-mə tə) [L. < Gr. *karkinos*, a crab] any of several kinds of epithelial cancer

**car coat** a short overcoat

**card**[1] (kärd) *n.* [< Gr. *chartēs*, leaf of paper] 1. a flat, stiff piece of paper or pasteboard; specif., *a*) any of a pack of playing cards *b*) a card identifying a person, esp. as a member, agent, etc. *c*) a post card *d*) a card bearing a greeting *e*) any of a series of cards on which information is recorded 2. an attraction [drawing *card*] 3. [Colloq.] a witty or clowning person —**put (or lay) one's cards on the table** to reveal something frankly

**card**[2] (kärd) *n.* [< L. *carere*, to card] a metal comb or a machine with wire teeth for combing fibers of wool, cotton, etc. —*vt.* to use a card on

**card′board′** *n.* stiff, thick paper or pasteboard, for cards, boxes, etc.

**car·di·ac** (kär′dē ak′) *adj.* [< Gr. *kardia*, heart] of or near the heart

**car·di·gan** (kär′də gən) *n.* [< 7th Earl of *Cardigan*] a sweater or jacket that opens down the front

**car·di·nal** (kärd′n əl) *adj.* [< L. *cardo*, pivot] 1. principal; chief 2. bright-red —*n.* 1. an official appointed by the Pope to his council 2. bright red 3. a bright-red American songbird 4. a cardinal number

**cardinal number** any number used in counting or showing how many (e.g., two, forty, 627, etc.)

**cardio-** [< Gr. *kardia*, heart] *a combining form meaning of* the heart

**car·di·o·gram** (kär′dē ə gram′) *n.* *same as* ELECTROCARDIOGRAM —**car′-di·o·graph′** *n.*

**car·di·ol·o·gy** (-äl′ə jē) *n.* the branch of medicine dealing with the heart

**car·di·o·vas·cu·lar** (-ō vas′kyoo lər) *adj.* of the heart and the blood vessels as a unified system

**cards** (kärdz) *n.pl.* any game played with a deck of playing cards, as poker

**card′sharp′** *n.* [Colloq.] a professional cheater at cards: also **card shark**

**care** (ker) *n.* [< OE. *caru*, sorrow] 1. *a*) a troubled state of mind; worry *b*) a cause of such a mental state 2. close attention; heed 3. a liking or regard (*for*) 4. charge; protection 5. a responsibility —*vi.* **cared, car′ing** 1. to feel concern 2. to feel love or liking (*for*) 3. to look after; provide (*for*) 4. to wish (*for*); want —*vt.* 1. to feel concern about or interest in 2. to wish —**care of** at the address of —**take care of** 1. to attend to 2. to provide for

**ca·reen** (kə rēn′) *vt., vi.* [< L. *carina*, keel] to lean or cause to lean sideways; tip; tilt; lurch

**ca·reer** (kə rir′) *n.* [< Fr. < It. *carro*, car] 1. a swift course 2. one's progress through life 3. a profession or occupation —*vi.* to rush wildly

**care′free′** *adj.* without care

**care′ful** *adj.* 1. cautious; wary 2. accurately or thoroughly done —**care′ful·ly** *adv.* —**care′ful·ness** *n.*

**care′less** *adj.* 1. carefree; untroubled 2. not paying enough heed; neglectful

**3.** done or made without enough attention, precision, etc. —**care′less·ly** adv. —**care′less·ness** n.

**ca·ress** (kə res′) vt. [ult. < L. carus, dear] to touch lovingly or gently —n. an affectionate touch, kiss, etc.

**car·et** (kar′it, ker′-) n. [L., there is lacking] a mark (∧) used to show where something is to be added in a written or printed line

**care′tak′er** n. **1.** a person hired to take care of something or someone **2.** one acting as temporary replacement

**care′worn′** adj. haggard or worn out by troubles and worry

**car·fare** (kär′fer′) n. the price of a ride on a streetcar, bus, etc.

**car·go** (kär′gō) n., pl. **-goes, -gos** [< Sp. cargar, to load] the load carried by a ship, truck, etc.; freight

**car′hop′** n. [CAR + (BELL)HOP] one who serves food at a drive-in restaurant

**Car·ib·be·an (Sea)** (ker′ə bē′ən, kə rib′ē an) sea bounded by the West Indies, Central America, & S.America

**car·i·bou** (kar′ə bōō′) n. [CanadFr.] a large N. American deer

**car·i·ca·ture** (kar′ə kə chər) n. [Fr. < It. caricare, exaggerate] **1.** the exaggerated imitation of a person, literary style, etc. for satirical effect **2.** a picture, etc. in which this is done —vt. **-tured, -tur·ing** to depict as in a caricature —**car′i·ca·tur·ist** n.

**car·ies** (ker′ēz) n. [L., decay] decay of bones or, esp., of teeth

**car·il·lon** (kar′ə län′) n. [Fr., chime of four bells < L. quattuor, four] a set of bells tuned to the chromatic scale

**car′il·lon·neur′** (-lə nur′) n. [Fr.] a carillon player

**car′load′** n. a load that fills a car

**car·min·a·tive** (kär min′ə tiv) adj. [< L. carminare, cleanse] expelling gas from the stomach and intestines —n. a carminative medicine

**car·mine** (kär′min, -mīn) n. [ult. < Ar. qirmis, crimson] a red or purplish-red color —adj. red or purplish-red

**car·nage** (kär′nij) n. [Fr. < L. caro, flesh] extensive slaughter; massacre

**car′nal** (-n′l) adj. [< L. caro, flesh] **1.** of the flesh; material; worldly **2.** sensual —**car·nal′i·ty** (-nal′ə tē) n. —**car′nal·ly** adv.

**car·na·tion** (kär nā′shən) n. [< L. caro, flesh] **1.** a variety of the pink **2.** its pink, white, or red flower

**Car·ne·gie** (kär′nə gē′, kär nā′gē), Andrew 1835–1919; U.S. industrialist

**car·nel·ian** (kär nēl′yən) n. [< L. carnis, of flesh (color)] a red kind of chalcedony, used as a gem

**car·ni·val** (kär′nə vəl) n. [< Fr. or It.] **1.** the period of feasting and revelry just before Lent **2.** a reveling; festivity **3.** an entertainment with sideshows, rides, etc.

**car·ni·vore** (kär′nə vôr′) n. a carnivorous animal or plant

**car·niv·o·rous** (kär niv′ə rəs) adj.

[< L. caro, flesh + vorare, devour, eat] **1.** flesh-eating **2.** insect-eating, as certain plants **3.** of the carnivores —**car·niv′o·rous·ness** n.

**car·ol** (kar′əl) n. [< OFr. carole, kind of dance] a song of joy or praise; esp., a Christmas song —vi., vt. **-oled** or **-olled, -ol·ing** or **-ol·ling** to sing; warble —**car′ol·er, car′ol·ler** n.

**car·om** (kar′əm) n. [< Sp. carambola] **1.** Billiards a shot in which the cue ball successively hits two balls **2.** a hitting and rebounding —vi. **1.** to make a carom **2.** to hit and rebound —n. a carotid artery

**ca·rot·id** (kə rät′id) adj. [Gr. karōtis] designating or of either of the two main arteries, one on each side of the neck, which convey blood to the head —n. a carotid artery

**ca·rous·al** (kə rou′zəl) n. a carouse

**ca·rouse** (kə rouz′) vi. **-roused′, -rous′ing** [< G. gar austrinken, to drink] to engage in a noisy drinking party —n. a noisy drinking party

**carp¹** (kärp) n., pl. **carp, carps** [< Gmc. carpa] an edible freshwater fish living in tranquil waters

**carp²** (kärp) vi. [< ON. karpa, to brag] to find fault pettily or unfairly

**car·pel** (kär′pəl) n. [< Gr. karpos, fruit] a simple pistil, regarded as a modified leaflike structure

**car·pen·ter** (kär′pən tər) n. [< L. carpentum, a cart] one who builds and repairs wooden things, esp. buildings, ships, etc. —vi. to do a carpenter's work —**car′pen·try** (-trē) n.

**carpenter ant** any of the large, black ants that build nests by gnawing the wood in buildings, tree trunks, etc.

**car·pet** (kär′pit) n. [< L. carpere, to card] **1.** a heavy fabric for covering a floor **2.** anything that covers like a carpet —vt. to cover as with a carpet —**on the carpet** being reprimanded

**car′pet·bag′** n. an old-fashioned traveling bag, made of carpeting —vi. **-bagged′, -bag′ging** to act as a carpetbagger

**car′pet·bag′ger** n. a Northerner who went South to profit from unsettled conditions after the Civil War

**car′pet·ing** n. carpets; carpet fabric

**car pool** a plan by a group to use their cars in rotation, to and from work

**car·port** (kär′pôrt′) n. an automobile shelter built as a roof at the side of a building

**car·rel, car·rell** (kar′əl) n. [< ML. carula] a small enclosure in a library, for privacy in studying

**car·riage** (kar′ij) n. [ult. < L. carrus, car] **1.** a carrying; transportation **2.** manner of carrying oneself; bearing **3.** a) a four-wheeled, horse-drawn passenger vehicle b) a baby buggy **4.** a moving part, as on a typewriter, that supports and shifts something

**car·ri·er** (kar′ē ər) n. **1.** one that carries **2.** one in the business of transporting **3.** one that transmits disease germs **4.** an aircraft carrier

**carrier pigeon** *same as* HOMING PIGEON

**car·ri·on** (kar′ē ən) *n.* [ < L. *caro*, flesh] decaying flesh of a dead body

**Car·roll** (kar′əl), **Lewis** (pseud. of *C. L. Dodgson*) 1832–98; Eng. writer

**car·rot** (kar′ət) *n.* [ < Gr. *karōton*] 1. a plant with an edible, fleshy, orange-red root 2. the root —**car′rot·y** *adj.*

**car·rou·sel** (kar′ə sel′, -zel′) *n.* [Fr.; < It. dial. *carusiello*, kind of tournament] a merry-go-round: also **carousel**

**car·ry** (kar′ē) *vt.* **-ried, -ry·ing** [ < L. *carrus*, car] 1. to hold or support 2. to take from one place to another 3. to lead or impel 4. to transmit [air *carries* sounds] 5. to transfer or extend 6. to involve; imply 7. to bear (oneself) in a specified way 8. *a)* to gain support for *b)* to win (an election, debate, etc.) 9. *a)* to keep in stock *b)* to keep on one's account books, etc. —*vi.* 1. to act as a bearer, conductor, etc. 2. to cover a range, as a voice —*n., pl.* **car′ries** 1. the distance covered by a gun, ball, etc. 2. a portage —be (or get) **carried away** to become very emotional or enthusiastic —**carry on** 1. to engage in 2. to continue 3. [Colloq.] to behave wildly or childishly —**carry out** (or **through**) 1. to put (plans, etc.) into practice 2. to accomplish —**carry over** to postpone; continue

**carrying charge** interest paid on the balance owed in installment buying

**car′ry·out′** *adj.* designating or of prepared food or beverages sold as by a restaurant to be consumed elsewhere

**car′ry·o′ver** *n.* something carried over, as a remainder of crops or goods

**car′sick′** *adj.* nauseated from riding in an automobile, bus, etc.

**Car·son City** (kär′s'n) capital of Nev., in the W part: pop. 15,000

**cart** (kärt) *n.* [ < ON. *kartr*] a small wagon —*vt., vi.* to carry in a cart, truck, etc.; transport —**cart′er** *n.*

**cart·age** (kär′tij) *n.* 1. the work of carting 2. the charge for this

**carte blanche** (kärt′ blänsh′) [Fr., blank card] full authority

**car·tel** (kär tel′) *n.* [Fr.: see CARD[1]] an association of business firms, etc. for establishing a national or international monopoly; trust

**Car·ter** (kär′tər), **James E.** 1924– ; 39th president of the U.S. (1977– )

**car·ti·lage** (kärt′'l ij) *n.* [ < L. *cartilago*] a tough, elastic tissue forming parts of the skeleton; gristle —**car′ti·lag′i·nous** (-aj′ə nəs) *adj.*

**car·tog·ra·phy** (kär täg′rə fē) *n.* [see CARD[1] & -GRAPHY] the art of making maps or charts —**car·tog′ra·pher** *n.*

**car·ton** (kärt′'n) *n.* [Fr. < It. *carta*, card] a cardboard box or container

**car·toon** (kär tōōn′) *n.* [ < Fr.: see prec.] 1. a drawing that caricatures some person or event 2. *same as* COMIC STRIP 3. a motion picture in which drawn figures seem to move —*vi., vt.* to draw cartoons (of) —**cartoon′ist** *n.*

**car·tridge** (kär′trij) *n.* [ < Fr. < It. *carta*, card] 1. a cylindrical case of cardboard, metal, etc. containing the charge and primer, and usually the projectile, for a firearm 2. a small container, as for camera film, a phonograph needle, etc.

**cart′wheel′** *n.* 1. a handspring performed sidewise 2. [Slang] a large coin

**carve** (kärv) *vt.* [OE. *ceorfan*] 1. to make or shape by or as by cutting 2. to decorate the surface of with cut designs 3. to divide by cutting; slice —*vi.* 1. to carve statues or designs 2. to carve meat —**carv′er** *n.* —**carv′ing** *n.*

CARTWHEEL

**car′wash′** *n.* an establishment at which automobiles are washed

**car·y·at·id** (kar′ē at′id) *n., pl.* **-ids, -id·es′** (-ə dēz′) [ < Gr. *karyatides*, priestesses at Karyai, in ancient Greece] a supporting column having the form of a draped female figure

**ca·sa·ba** (kə sä′bə) *n.* [ < *Kassaba*, town in Asia Minor] a kind of muskmelon with a yellow rind

**Ca·sa·blan·ca** (kas′ə blaŋ′kə, kä′sə bläŋ′-) seaport in NW Morocco: pop. 1,177,000

**Ca·sa·no·va** (kas′ə nō′və, kaz′-), **Gio·van·ni** (jō vän′nē) 1725–98; It. adventurer and writer

**cas·cade** (kas kād′) *n.* [Fr. < L. *cadere*, to fall] 1. a small, steep waterfall 2. a shower, as of sparks, etc. —*vt., vi.* **-cad′ed, -cad′ing** to fall or drop in a cascade

**cas·car·a** (kas ker′ə) *n.* [ < Sp., bark] 1. a thorny tree growing on the Pacific coast of the U.S. 2. a laxative made from its bark

**case**[1] (kās) *n.* [ < L. *casus*, event < *cadere*, to fall] 1. an example or instance [a *case* of flu] 2. a person being helped by a doctor, etc. 3. any matter requiring study 4. a statement of the facts, as in a law court 5. convincing arguments [he has no *case*] 6. a lawsuit 7. a form taken by a noun, pronoun, or adjective to show its relation to neighboring words —*vt.* **cased, cas′ing** [Slang] to look over carefully —**in any case** anyhow —**in case** in the event that; if —**in case of** in the event of —**in no case** by no means

**case**[2] (kās) *n.* [ < L. *capsa*, box] 1. a container, as a box 2. a protective cover [a watch *case*] 3. a frame, as for a window —*vt.* **cased, cas′ing** 1. to put in a container 2. to enclose

**ca·se·in** (kā′sē in, -sēn) *n.* [ < L. *caseus*, cheese] a protein that is one of the chief constituents of milk

**case′load′** *n.* the number of cases being handled by a court, social agency, caseworker, etc.

**case·ment** (kās′mənt) *n.* [ < OFr. *encassement*, a frame] a window frame that opens on hinges along the side

**case′work′** *n.* social work in which guidance is given in cases of personal and family maladjustment —**case′work′er** *n.*

**cash** (kash) *n.* [Fr. *caisse*, money box] 1. money that one actually has; esp., ready money 2. money, a check, etc. paid at the time of purchase —*vt.* to give or get cash for —*adj.* of or for cash —**cash in** to turn into cash

**cash·ew** (kash′ōō, ka shōō′) *n.* [< SAmInd. *acajú*] 1. a tropical tree bearing kidney-shaped nuts 2. the nut

**cash·ier¹** (ka shir′) *n.* [Fr. *caissier*] a person in charge of the cash transactions of a bank or store

**cash·ier²** (ka shir′) *vt.* [< LL. *cassare*, destroy] to dismiss in dishonor

**cash·mere** (kazh′mir) *n.* [< *Kashmir*, region in India] 1. a fine carded wool from goats of N India and Tibet 2. a soft, twilled cloth as of this wool

**cash register** a device, usually with a money drawer, used for registering visibly the amount of a sale

**cas·ing** (kās′iŋ) *n.* 1. the skin of a sausage 2. the outer covering of a pneumatic tire 3. a frame, as for a door

**ca·si·no** (kə sē′nō) *n.*, *pl.* -**nos** [It. < L. *casa*, cottage] 1. a room or building for dancing, gambling, etc. 2. *same as* CASSINO

**cask** (kask) *n.* [< Sp. < L. *quassare*, shatter] 1. a barrel of any size, esp. one for liquids 2. its contents

**cas·ket** (kas′kit) *n.* [prob. < OFr. *casse*, box] 1. a small box or chest, as for valuables 2. a coffin

**Cas·pi·an Sea** (kas′pē ən) inland sea between Caucasia and Asiatic U.S.S.R.

**Cas·san·dra** (kə san′drə) *Gr. Myth.* a Trojan prophetess of doom whose prophecies were never believed

**cas·sa·va** (kə sä′və) *n.* [< Fr. < WInd. *casávi*] 1. a tropical plant with starchy roots 2. a starch made from these roots, used in tapioca

**cas·se·role** (kas′ə rōl′) *n.* [Fr. < Gr. *kyathos*, a bowl] 1. a dish in which food can be baked and served 2. food baked in such a dish

**cas·sette** (ka set′, kə-) *n.* [Fr. < L. *capere*, contain] a case with magnetic tape or film in it, for loading a tape recorder or movie projector quickly

**cas·sia** (kash′ə) *n.* [ult. < Heb. *qeṣī′āh*] 1. *a*) the bark of a tree of SE Asia: used as a source of cinnamon *b*) the tree 2. any of various tropical plants whose leaves yield senna

**cas·si·no** (kə sē′nō) *n.* [see CASINO] a card game for two to four players

**cas·sock** (kas′ək) *n.* [< Fr. < Per. *kazh*, raw silk] a long, closefitting vestment worn by clergymen

**cast** (kast) *vt.* **cast**, **cast′ing** [< ON. *kasta*] 1. to throw with force; fling; hurl 2. to deposit (a ballot or vote) 3. to direct [to *cast* one's eyes] 4. to project [to *cast* light] 5. to throw off or shed (a skin) 6. to shape (molten metal, etc.) by pouring into a mold 7. to select (an actor) for (a role or play) —*vi.* to throw; hurl —*n.* 1. a casting; throw 2. something formed in a mold 3. a plaster form for immobilizing a

limb 4. the set of actors in a play or movie 5. an appearance, as of features 6. kind; quality 7. a tinge; shade —**cast about** to search; look (*for*) —**cast aside** (or **away**) to discard; abandon —**cast off** 1. to discard 2. to free a ship from a dock, etc. —**cast up** 1. to turn upward 2. to add up

**cas·ta·nets** (kas′tə nets′) *n.pl.* [< Sp. < L. *castanea*, chestnut: from the shape] a pair of small, hollowed pieces of hard wood or ivory, clicked together in the hand in time to music

**cast′a·way′** *n.* 1. a person or thing cast off 2. a shipwrecked person —*adj.* 1. discarded 2. shipwrecked

**caste** (kast) *n.* [Fr. < L. *castus*, pure] 1. any of the hereditary Hindu social classes of a formerly segregated system of India 2. any exclusive group 3. class distinction based on birth, wealth, etc. —**lose caste** to lose social status

**cast′er** *n.* 1. a container for vinegar, oil, etc. at the table 2. any of a set of small wheels for supporting and moving furniture: also **cas′tor**

**cas·ti·gate** (kas′tə gāt′) *vt.* -**gat′ed**, -**gat′ing** [< L. *castigare*] to rebuke severely, esp. by public criticism —**cas′ti·ga′tion** *n.* —**cas′ti·ga′tor** *n.*

**cast′ing** *n.* a thing, esp. of metal, cast in a mold

**cast iron** a hard, brittle alloy of iron made by casting —**cast′-i′ron** *adj.*

**cas·tle** (kas′'l) *n.* [< L. *castrum*, fort] 1. a large fortified building or group of buildings 2. any massive dwelling like this 3. *same as* ROOK²

**cast′off′** *adj.* discarded; abandoned —*n.* a person or thing cast off

**cas·tor-oil plant** (kas′tər oil′) [< Gr. *kastōr*, beaver] a tropical plant with large seeds which yield an oil (**castor oil**) used as a cathartic

**cas·trate** (kas′trāt) *vt.* -**trat·ed**, -**trat·ing** [< L. *castrare*] to remove the testicles of; emasculate —**cas·tra′tion** *n.*

**cas·u·al** (kazh′oo wəl) *adj.* [< L. *casus*, chance] 1. happening by chance; not planned; incidental 2. occasional 3. careless or cursory 4. nonchalant 5. for informal use —**cas′u·al·ly** *adv.* —**cas′u·al·ness** *n.*

**cas·u·al·ty** (-əl tē, -oo wəl-) *n.*, *pl.* -**ties** 1. an accident, esp. a fatal one 2. a member of the armed forces killed, wounded, captured, etc. 3. anyone hurt or killed in an accident

**cas·u·ist·ry** (kazh′oo wis trē) *n.*, *pl.* -**ries** [< L. *casus*, CASE¹] subtle but false reasoning, esp. about moral issues; sophistry —**cas′u·ist** *n.*

**cat** (kat) *n.* [OE.] 1. a small, softfurred animal, often kept as a pet or for killing mice 2. any flesh-eating mammal related to this, as the lion, tiger, leopard, etc. 3. a spiteful woman —**let the cat out of the bag** to let a secret be found out

**cat·a·clysm** (kat′ə kliz′m) *n.* [< Gr. *kata-*, down + *klyzein*, wash] any sudden, violent change, as in war — **cat′a·clys′mic** (-klĭz′mĭk) *adj.*

**cat·a·comb** (kat′ə kōm′) *n.* [ < ? L. *cata*, by + *tumba*, tomb] a gallery in an underground burial place

**cat′a·falque** (-falk′, -fôlk′) *n.* [Fr. < It. *catafalco*, funeral canopy] a wooden framework on which a body in a coffin lies in state

**cat·a·lep·sy** (kat′′l ep′sē) *n.* [ < Gr. *katalēpsis*, a seizing] a condition of muscle rigidity and sudden, temporary loss of consciousness, as in epilepsy —**cat′a·lep′tic** *adj., n.*

**cat·a·log, cat·a·logue** (kat′′l ôg′) *n.* [ < Gr. *kata-*, down + *legein*, to count] a complete list, as an alphabetical card file of the books in a library, a list of articles for sale, etc. —*vt., vi.* -loged′ or -logued′, -log′ing or -logu′ing to arrange in a catalog —**cat′a·log′er** or **cat′a·logu′er** *n.*

**ca·tal·pa** (kə tal′pə) *n.* [ < AmInd.] a tree with large, heart-shaped leaves and slender, beanlike pods

**ca·tal·y·sis** (kə tal′ə sis) *n., pl.* -ses′ (-sēz′) [ < Gr. *katalysis*, dissolution] the speeding up or, sometimes, slowing down of a chemical reaction by adding a substance which itself is not changed thereby —**cat·a·lyt·ic** (kat′′l it′ik) *adj.*

**cat·a·lyst** (kat′′l ist) *n.* a substance serving as the agent in catalysis

**cat·a·ma·ran** (kat′ə mə ran′) *n.* [Tamil *kattumaram*] 1. a narrow log raft propelled by sails or paddles 2. a boat like this with two parallel hulls

**cat·a·mount** (kat′ə mount′) *n.* [CAT + a, of + MOUNT] 1. a puma 2. a lynx

**cat·a·pult** (kat′ə pult′) *n.* [ < Gr. *kata-*, down + *pallein*, hurl] 1. an ancient military device for throwing stones, etc. 2. a device for launching an airplane, rocket missile, etc. as from a deck or ramp —*vt.* to shoot as from a catapult —*vi.* to leap

**cat·a·ract** (kat′ə rakt′) *n.* [ < Gr. *kata-*, down + *rhēgnusthai*, to break] 1. a large waterfall 2. a) an eye disease in which the lens becomes opaque, causing partial or total blindness b) the opaque area

**ca·tarrh** (kə tär′) *n.* [ < Gr. *kata-*, down + *rhein*, to flow] inflammation of the mucous membrane of the nose or throat: old-fashioned term

**ca·tas·tro·phe** (kə tas′trə fē) *n.* [ < Gr. *kata-*, down + *strephein*, to turn] any sudden, great disaster —**cat·a·stroph·ic** (kat′ə sträf′ik) *adj.*

**cat·a·ton·ic** (kat′ə tän′ik) *adj.* [ < Gr. *kata*, down + *tonos*, tension] designating or of a state of stupor or catalepsy, as in schizophrenia

**cat′bird′** *n.* a slate-gray N.American songbird with a call like a cat's

**cat′boat′** *n.* a sailboat with a single sail and mast set well forward

**cat′call′** *n.* a shrill noise or whistle expressing derision, etc. —*vt., vi.* to make catcalls (at)

**catch** (kach) *vt.* **caught, catch′ing** [ < L. *capere*, take] 1. to seize and hold; capture 2. to take by a trap 3. to deceive 4. to surprise 5. to get to in time [to *catch* a bus] 6. to lay hold of; grab [*catch* a ball] 7. to become infected with [he *caught* a cold] 8. to understand 9. to get entangled 10. [Colloq.] to see, hear, etc. —*vi.* 1. to become held, fastened, etc. 2. to take hold, as fire 3. to keep hold, as a lock —*n.* 1. a catching 2. a thing that catches 3. something caught 4. one worth catching as a spouse 5. a snatch or fragment 6. a break in the voice 7. [Colloq.] a tricky qualification —**catch at** to seize desperately —**catch on** 1. to understand 2. to become popular —**catch up** 1. to snatch 2. to overtake

**catch′all′** (-ôl′) *n.* a container for holding all sorts of things

**catch′er** *n. Baseball* the player behind home plate, who catches pitched balls

**catch′ing** *adj.* 1. contagious 2. attractive

**catch·up** (kech′əp, kach′-) *n.* same as KETCHUP

**catch′y** *adj.* -i·er, -i·est 1. easily caught up and remembered 2. tricky

**cat·e·chism** (kat′ə kiz′m) *n.* [ < Gr. *kata-*, thoroughly + *ēchein*, to sound] 1. a handbook of questions and answers for teaching the tenets of a religion 2. a close questioning

**cat′e·chize′** (-kīz′) *vt.* -chized′, -chiz′ing [see prec.] to question searchingly: also **catechise**

**cat·e·gor·i·cal** (kat′ə gôr′ə k'l) *adj.* 1. positive; explicit: said of a statement, etc. 2. of, as, or in a category —**cat′e·gor′i·cal·ly** *adv.*

**cat·e·go·rize** (kat′ə gə rīz′) *vt.* -rized′, -riz′ing to place in a category; classify

**cat′e·go′ry** (-gôr′ē) *n., pl.* -ries [ < Gr. *katēgorein*, assert] a class or division in a scheme of classification

**ca·ter** (kā′tər) *vi.* [ < L. *ad-*, to + *capere*, take] 1. to provide food and service, as for parties 2. to seek to gratify another's desires (with *to*) —**ca′ter·er** *n.*

**cat·er-cor·nered** (kat′ē kôr′nərd) *adj.* [ < OFr. *catre*, four + CORNERED] diagonal —*adv.* diagonally Also **cat′er-cor′ner**

**cat·er·pil·lar** (kat′ər pil′ər) *n.* [ < L. *catta pilosus*, hairy cat] the wormlike larva of a butterfly, moth, etc.

**cat·er·waul** (kat′ər wôl′) *vi.* [prob. echoic] to make a shrill sound like that of a cat; wail —*n.* such a sound

**cat′fish′** *n., pl.:* see FISH a scaleless fish with long, whiskerlike feelers about the mouth

**cat′gut′** *n.* a tough thread made from dried intestines, as of sheep, and used for surgical sutures, etc.

**ca·thar·sis** (kə thär′sis) *n.* [ < Gr. *katharos*, pure] 1. a purging, esp. of the bowels 2. a relieving of the emotions, as through the arts or psychotherapy

**ca·thar·tic** *adj.* purging —*n.* a medicine for purging the bowels; laxative

**ca·the·dral** (kə thē′drəl) *n.* [ < Gr. *kata-*, down + *hedra*, a seat] 1. the main church of a bishop's see  **2.** any large, imposing church

**cath·e·ter** (kath′ə tər) *n.* [< Gr. *kata-*, down + *hienai*, to send] a slender tube inserted into a body passage, as into the bladder for drawing off urine —**cath′e·ter·ize′** (-īz′) *vt.* **-ized′, -iz′ing**

**cath·ode** (kath′ōd) *n.* [< Gr. *kata-*, down + *hodos*, way] **1.** the negative electrode in an electrolytic cell **2.** the electron emitter in a vacuum tube **3.** the positive terminal in a battery

**cathode rays** streams of electrons projected from a cathode: they produce X-rays when they strike solids

**cath·o·lic** (kath′ə lik, kath′lik) *adj.* [< Gr. *kata-*, completely + *holos*, whole] **1.** universal; all-inclusive **2.** broad in sympathies, tastes, etc. **3.** [C-] *same as* ROMAN CATHOLIC —*n.* [C-] *same as* ROMAN CATHOLIC — **Ca·thol·i·cism** (kə thäl′ə siz'm) *n.* —**cath·o·lic·i·ty** (kath′ə lis′ə tē) *n.*

**cat·i·on** (kat′ī′ən) *n.* [< Gr. *kata*, downward + *ienai*, to go] a positively charged ion: in electrolysis, cations move toward the cathode

**cat·kin** (kat′kin) *n.* [< Du. *katte*, cat] a drooping, scaly spike of small flowers without petals, as on a willow

**cat′nap′** *n.* a short nap —*vi.* **-napped′, -nap′ping** to doze briefly

**cat′nip** *n.* [< CAT + dial. *nep*, catnip] a plant of the mint family: cats like its odor: also, Brit. var., **cat′mint′**

CATKIN

**cat-o′-nine-tails** (kat′ə nīn′tālz′) *n., pl.* **-tails′** a whip made of nine knotted cords attached to a handle

**cat's cradle** a game in which a piece of string is looped back and forth over the fingers to make various designs

**Cats·kill Mountains** (kat′skil′) mountain range in SE N.Y.: also **Cats′kills′**

**cat's-paw** (kats′pô′) *n.* a person used by another to do distasteful or unlawful work; dupe

**cat·sup** (kech′əp, kat′səp) *n.* *same as* KETCHUP

**cat·tail** (kat′tāl′) *n.* a tall marsh plant with long, brown, fuzzy spikes

**cat·tle** (kat′'l) *n.* [ult. < L. *caput*, the head] **1.** [Archaic] livestock **2.** cows, bulls, steers, or oxen —**cat′tle·man** (-mən) *n., pl.* **-men**

**cat·ty** (kat′ē) *adj.* **-ti·er, -ti·est 1.** of or like a cat **2.** spiteful, mean, malicious, etc. —**cat′ti·ness** *n.*

**cat′ty-cor′nered** *adj., adv. same as* CATER-CORNERED: also **cat′ty-cor′ner**

**CATV** community antenna television

**cat′walk′** *n.* a narrow, elevated walk, as over an engine room

**Cau·ca·sia** (kô kā′zhə) *same as* CAUCASUS (sense 1)

**Cau·ca·sian** (kô kā′zhən) *adj.* **1.** of the Caucasus, its people, etc. **2.** *same as* CAUCASOID —*n.* **1.** a native of the Caucasus **2.** *same as* CAUCASOID

**Cau·ca·soid** (kô′kə soid′) *adj.* designating or of one of the major groups of mankind, loosely called the *white race* —*n.* a member of the Caucasoid group

**Cau·ca·sus** (kô′kə səs) **1.** region in SE European U.S.S.R., between the Black Sea and the Caspian **2.** mountain range in this region

**cau·cus** (kô′kəs) *n.* [< ?] a meeting of a party or faction to decide policy, pick candidates, etc. —*vi.* **-cused** or **-cussed, -cus·ing** or **-cus·sing** to hold a caucus

**cau·dal** (kôd′'l) *adj.* [< L. *cauda*, tail + -AL] of, like, at, or near the tail

**caught** (kôt) *pt. & pp.* of CATCH

**caul** (kôl) *n.* [< OE. *cawl*, basket] the membrane enclosing a fetus, esp. the part sometimes covering the head at birth

**caul·dron** (kôl′drən) *n. same as* CALDRON

**cau·li·flow·er** (kôl′ə flou′ər) *n.* [< It. *cavolo*, cabbage + *fiore*, flower] **1.** a variety of cabbage with a dense white head of fleshy flower stalks **2.** this head, eaten as a vegetable

**caulk** (kôk) *vt.* [< L. *calx*, a heel] **1.** to make (a boat, etc.) watertight by filling the seams with oakum, tar, etc. **2.** to stop up (cracks) with a filler —**caulk′er** *n.*

**caus·al** (kôz′'l) *adj.* **1.** of, being, or expressing a cause **2.** relating to cause and effect —**cau·sal·i·ty** (kô zal′ə tē) *n.* —**caus′al·ly** *adv.*

**cau·sa·tion** (kô zā′shən) *n.* **1.** a causing **2.** a causal agency; anything producing an effect

**cause** (kôz) *n.* [< L. *causa*] **1.** anything producing an effect or result **2.** a reason or motive for producing an effect **3.** any objective or movement that people are interested in and support **4.** a case to be decided by a court —*vt.* **caused, caus′ing** to be the cause of; bring about —**caus′a·tive** *adj.* —**cause′less** *adj.* —**caus′er** *n.*

**cau·se·rie** (kō′zə rē′) *n.* [Fr.] **1.** a chat **2.** a short, chatty composition

**cause·way** (kôz′wā′) *n.* [ult. < L. *calx*, lime + WAY] a raised path or road, as across wet ground

**caus·tic** (kôs′tik) *adj.* [< Gr. *kaiein*, to burn] **1.** that can burn tissue by chemical action; corrosive **2.** sarcastic; biting —*n.* a caustic substance —**caus′ti·cal·ly** *adv.* —**caus·tic′i·ty** (-tis′ə tē) *n.*

**cau·ter·ize** (kôt′ər īz′) *vt.* **-ized′, -iz′ing** [see prec.] to burn with a hot iron, or with a caustic substance, so as to destroy dead tissue, etc. —**cau′ter·i·za′tion** *n.*

**cau·tion** (kô′shən) *n.* [< L. *cautio*] **1.** a warning **2.** wariness; prudence —*vt.* to warn —**cau′tion·ar′y** *adj.*

**cau·tious** (kô'shəs) *adj.* full of caution; careful to avoid danger —**cau'-tious·ly** *adv.* —**cau'tious·ness** *n.*

**cav·al·cade** (kav''l kād') *n.* [Fr. < L. *caballus,* horse] a procession, as of horsemen, carriages, etc.

**cav·a·lier** (kav'ə lir') *n.* [Fr.: see prec.] **1.** an armed horseman; knight **2.** a gallant gentleman, esp. a lady's escort —*adj.* **1.** casual **2.** arrogant —**cav'a·lier'ly** *adv.*

**cav·al·ry** (kav''l rē) *n., pl.* **-ries** [< Fr.: see CAVALCADE] combat troops mounted originally on horses but now often on motorized armored vehicles —**cav'al·ry·man** (-mən) *n., pl.* **-men**

**cave** (kāv) *n.* [< L. *cavus,* hollow] a hollow place inside the earth; cavern —*vt., vi.* **caved, cav'ing** to collapse or make collapse (with *in*)

**ca·ve·at emp·tor** (kā'vē at' emp'tôr) [L.] let the buyer beware

**cave'-in'** *n.* **1.** a caving in **2.** a place where the ground, etc. has caved in

**cave man** a prehistoric human being of the Stone Age who lived in caves

**cav·ern** (kav'ərn) *n.* a cave, esp. a large cave —**cav'ern·ous** *adj.*

**cav·i·ar, cav·i·are** (kav'ē är') *n.* [Fr. < Per. *khāya,* egg + *-dār,* bearing] the salted eggs of sturgeon, etc. eaten as an appetizer

**cav·il** (kav''l) *vi.* **-iled** or **-illed, -il·ing** or **-il·ling** [< L. *cavilla,* quibbling] to object unnecessarily; carp —*n.* a trivial objection; quibble —**cav'il·er, cav'il·ler** *n.*

**cav·i·ty** (kav'ə tē) *n., pl.* **-ties** [see CAVE] a hollow place, as in a tooth

**ca·vort** (kə vôrt') *vi.* [< ?] **1.** to prance or caper **2.** to romp; frolic

**caw** (kô) *n.* [echoic] the harsh cry of a crow —*vi.* to make this sound

**cay·enne** (**pepper**) (kī en', kā-) [< native Braz. *kynnha*] very hot red pepper made from the dried fruit of a pepper plant

**cay·use** (kī'ōōs, kī ōōs') *n., pl.* **-us·es** [< AmInd. tribal name] a small Western horse used by cowboys

**CB** (sē'bē') *adj.* [citizens' band] designating or of shortwave radio frequencies set aside by the FCC for local use by private persons

**cc., c.c.** cubic centimeter(s)

**Cd** *Chem.* cadmium

**cease** (sēs) *vt., vi.* **ceased, ceas'ing** [see CEDE] to end; stop

**cease'-fire'** *n.* a temporary cessation of warfare; truce

**cease'less** (-lis) *adj.* unceasing; continual —**cease'less·ly** *adv.*

**ce·cro·pi·a moth** (si krō'pē ə) [after *Cecrops,* legendary Gr. king] the largest moth of the U.S., with a white spot on each wing

**ce·cum** (sē'kəm) *n., pl.* **-ca** (-kə) [< L. *caecus,* blind] the pouch at the beginning of the large intestine

**ce·dar** (sē'dər) *n.* [< Gr. *kedros*] **1.** a pine tree having fragrant, durable wood **2.** its wood —*adj.* of cedar

**cede** (sēd) *vt.* **ced'ed, ced'ing** [< L. *cedere,* to yield] **1.** to surrender formally **2.** to transfer the title of

**ce·dil·la** (si dil'ə) *n.* [Sp. dim. of *zeda,*

---

*zeta*] a mark put under *c* in some French words (Ex.: *façade*) to show that it has an *s* sound

**ceil·ing** (sēl'iŋ) *n.* [< L. *caelum,* heaven] **1.** the inside top part of a room, opposite the floor **2.** an upper limit [a price *ceiling*] **3.** the upper limit of visibility —**hit the ceiling** [Slang] to lose one's temper

**cel·an·dine** (sel'ən dīn', -dēn') *n.* [< Gr. *chelidōn,* a swallow] **1.** a variety of poppy with yellow flowers **2.** a variety of buttercup

**cel·e·brate** (sel'ə brāt') *vt.* **-brat'ed, -brat'ing** [< L. *celebrare,* to honor] **1.** to perform (a ritual, etc.) **2.** to commemorate (an anniversary, holiday, etc.) with festivity **3.** to honor publicly —*vi.* [Colloq.] to have a good time —**cel'e·brant** (-brənt) *n.* —**cel'e·bra'tion** *n.* —**cel'e·bra'tor** *n.*

**cel'e·brat'ed** *adj.* famous; renowned

**ce·leb·ri·ty** (sə leb'rə tē) *n.* **1.** fame **2.** *pl.* **-ties** a famous person

**ce·ler·i·ty** (sə ler'ə tē) *n.* [< L. *celer,* swift] swiftness; speed

**cel·er·y** (sel'ə rē) *n.* [< Gr. *selinon,* parsley] a plant whose crisp leaf stalks are eaten as a vegetable

**ce·les·tial** (sə les'chəl) *adj.* [< L. *caelum,* heaven] **1.** of the heavens or sky **2.** heavenly; divine **3.** perfect

**cel·i·ba·cy** (sel'ə bə sē) *n.* **1.** the state of being unmarried **2.** complete sexual abstinence

**cel·i·bate** (sel'ə bət, -bāt') *n.* [< L. *caelebs*] an unmarried person —*adj.* of or in a state of celibacy

**cell** (sel) *n.* [< L. *cella*] **1.** a small room, as in a prison **2.** a small hollow, as in a honeycomb **3.** a small unit of protoplasm: all plants and animals are made up of one or more cells **4.** a receptacle for generating electricity by chemical reactions **5.** a small unit of an organization —**celled** (seld) *adj.*

**cel·lar** (sel'ər) *n.* [see prec.] a room or rooms below ground and usually under a building

**cel·lo, 'cel·lo** (chel'ō) *n., pl.* **-los, -li** (-ē) [< VIOLONCELLO] an instrument of the violin family, between the viola and double bassin pitch —**cel'list, 'cel'list** *n.*

CELLO

**cel·lo·phane** (sel'ə fān') *n.* a thin, transparent material made from cellulose, used as a wrapping

**cel·lu·lar** (sel'yoo lər) *adj.* of, like, or containing a cell or cells

**Cel·lu·loid** (sel'yoo loid') [CELLUL(OSE) + -OID] *a trademark* for a flammable plastic substance made from nitrocellulose and camphor —*n.* [c-] this substance

**cel·lu·lose** (sel'yoo lōs') *n.* [Fr. < L. *cella,* cell + -OSE[1]] the chief substance in the cell walls of plants, used in making paper, textiles, etc.

**cellulose acetate** a cellulose resin used in making acetate fiber, plastics, lacquers, etc.

**cellulose nitrate** *same as* NITROCEL-LULOSE

**Cel·si·us** (sel′sē əs) *adj.* [< A. *Celsius* (1701-44), Swed. inventor] designating, of, or according to a thermometer on which 0° is the freezing point and 100° is the boiling point of water

**Celt** (selt, kelt) *n.* [< L.] a Celtic-speaking person

**Cel·tic** (sel′tik, kel′-) *adj.* of the Celts, their languages, etc. —*n.* a subfamily of languages including Gaelic and Welsh

**ce·ment** (si ment′) *n.* [< L. *caementum*, rough stone] **1.** a powdered substance of lime and clay, mixed with water, etc. to make mortar or concrete: it hardens upon drying **2.** any adhesive substance —*vt.* **1.** to unite as with cement **2.** to cover with cement —*vi.* to be cemented —**ce·ment′er** *n.*

**cem·e·ter·y** (sem′ə ter′ē) *n.*, *pl.* **-ies** [< Gr. *koiman*, put to sleep] a place for the burial of the dead

**cen·o·bite** (sen′ə bīt′) *n.* [< LGr. *koinos*, common + *bios*, life] a member of a religious order in a monastery or convent

**cen·o·taph** (sen′ə taf′) *n.* [Fr. < Gr. *kenos*, empty + *taphos*, tomb] a monument honoring a dead person buried elsewhere

**Ce·no·zo·ic** (sē′nə zō′ik, sen′ə-) *adj.* [< Gr. *kainos*, recent + *zo(o)-* + *-IC*] designating the geologic era that includes the present, during which the various mammals have developed

**cen·ser** (sen′sər) *n.* a container in which incense is burned

**cen·sor** (sen′sər) *n.* [L. < *censere*, to judge] an official with the power to examine literature, mail, etc. and remove or prohibit anything considered obscene, objectionable, etc. —*vt.* to act as a censor of (a book, etc.) —**cen′sor·ship′** *n.*

**cen·so·ri·ous** (sen sôr′ē əs) *adj.* inclined to find fault; harshly critical

**cen·sure** (sen′shər) *n.* [see CENSOR] strong disapproval; condemnation —*vt.* -sured, -sur·ing to condemn as wrong —**cen′sur·a·ble** *adj.*

**cen·sus** (sen′səs) *n.* [L. < *censere*, enroll] an official count of population and recording of age, sex, etc.

**cent** (sent) *n.* [< L. *centum*, hundred] a 100th part of a dollar, or a coin of this value; penny

**cent. 1.** centigrade **2.** century

**cen·taur** (sen′tôr) *n.* [< Gr. *Kentauros*] *Gr. Myth.* a monster with a man's head and trunk and a horse's body

**cen·ta·vo** (sen tä′vō) *n.*, *pl.* **-vos** [Sp.: see CENT] a small coin of the Philippines, Mexico, and some S.American countries; one 100th of a peso

**cen·te·nar·i·an** (sen′tə ner′ē ən) *n.* [< ff.] a person at least 100 years old

**cen·te·nar·y** (sen ten′ər ē; sen′tə ner′ē) *adj.* [< L. *centum*, hundred] **1.** of a century **2.** of a centennial —*n.*, *pl.* **-ies 1.** a century **2.** a centennial

**cen·ten·ni·al** (sen ten′ē əl) *adj.* [< L. *centum*, hundred + *annus*, year] of or lasting 100 years —*n.* a 100th anniversary or its celebration

**cen·ter** (sen′tər) *n.* [< Gr. *kentron*, a point] **1.** a point equally distant from all points on the circumference of a circle or surface of a sphere **2.** a pivot **3.** the approximate middle point or part of anything **4.** a focal point of activity **5.** [*often* C-] a political party between left (liberals) and right (conservatives) **6.** *Sports* a player at the center of a line, floor, etc. —*vt.* **1.** to place in or near the center **2.** to gather to one place —*vi.* to be centered

**cen′ter·board′** *n.* a movable keellike board in a shallow sailboat

**cen′ter·fold′** *n.* the center facing pages of a magazine, often with an extra fold or folds, showing a photograph, as of a nude woman or man

**center of gravity** that point in a body around which its weight is evenly balanced

**cen·ter·piece** (sen′tər pēs′) *n.* an ornament for the center of a table

**centi-** [L.] a combining form meaning: **1.** hundred **2.** a 100th part of

**cen·ti·grade** (sen′tə grād′) *adj.* [Fr.: see CENTI- & GRADE] *same as* CELSIUS

**cen′ti·gram′,    cen′ti·gramme′** (-gram′) *n.* [Fr.: see CENTI- & GRAM] a unit of weight, 1/100 gram

**cen·time** (sän′tēm) *n.* [Fr.] the 100th part of a franc

**cen·ti·me·ter, cen·ti·me·tre** (sen′tə mēt′ər) *n.* [Fr.: see CENTI- & -METER] a unit of measure, 1/100 meter

**cen·ti·pede** (sen′tə pēd′) *n.* [Fr. < L. *centum*, hundred + *pes*, foot] a wormlike animal with a pair of legs for each body segment

**cen·tral** (sen′trəl) *adj.* **1.** in, near, or of the center **2.** equally accessible from various points **3.** basic; chief **4.** of a controlling source in a system —**cen′tral·ly** *adv.*

**Central African Republic** country in C Africa: 238,224 sq. mi.; pop. 1,352,000

**Central America** part of N.America between Mexico and S.America —**Central American**

**central city** the crowded, industrial central area of a large city

**cen′tral·ize′** (-īz′) *vt.* -ized′, -iz′ing **1.** to make central; bring to a center **2.** to organize under one control —*vi.* to become centralized —**cen′tral·i·za′tion** *n.* —**cen′tral·iz′er** *n.*

**cen·tre** (sen′tər) *n.*, *vt.*, *vi.* -tred, -tring *Brit. sp. of* CENTER

**centri-** *same as* CENTRO-

**cen·trif·u·gal** (sen trif′yə gəl, -ə gəl) *adj.* [< CENTRI- + L. *fugere*, flee] using or acted upon by a force (**centrifugal force**) that tends to make rotating bodies move away from the center of rotation

**cen·tri·fuge** (sen′trə fyōōj′) *n.* a machine using centrifugal force to separate particles of varying density

**cen·trip·e·tal** (sen trip′ət ′l) *adj.* [< CENTRI- + L. *petere*, seek] using or acted upon by a force (**centripetal force**) that tends to make rotating bodies move toward the center of rotation

**cen·trist** (sen′trist) *n.* a member of a political party of the center

**centro-** [< L. *centrum*, CENTER] *a combining form meaning* center

**cen·tu·ri·on** (sen tyoor′ē ən) *n.* [see ff.] the commanding officer of an ancient Roman military unit, originally of 100 men

**cen·tu·ry** (sen′chər ē) *n.*, *pl.* **-ries** [< L. *centum*, hundred] a period of 100 years, esp. as reckoned from 1 A.D.

**ce·phal·ic** (sə fal′ik) *adj.* [< Gr. *kephalē*, head] 1. of the head or skull 2. in, on, or near the head

**ce·ram·ic** (sə ram′ik) *adj.* [< Gr. *keramos*, clay] 1. of pottery, porcelain, etc. 2. of ceramics —*n.* 1. [*pl., with sing. v.*] the art or work of making pottery, porcelain, etc. 2. an object made of such materials

**ce·ram·ist** (sə ram′ist) *n.* an expert in ceramics; ceramic artist: also **ce·ram·i·cist** (-ə sist)

**ce·re·al** (sir′ē əl) *adj.* [< L. *Cerealis*, of Ceres, Rom. goddess of agriculture] of grain —*n.* 1. any grain used for food, as wheat, oats, etc. 2. any grass producing such grain 3. food made from grain, as oatmeal

**cer·e·bel·lum** (ser′ə bel′əm) *n.*, *pl.* **-lums**, **-la** [L., dim. of *cerebrum*] the section of the brain behind and below the cerebrum

**cer·e·bral** (ser′ə brəl, sə rē′-) *adj.* of the brain or the cerebrum

**cerebral palsy** spastic paralysis due to brain damage

**cer·e·brate** (ser′ə brāt′) *vi.* **-brat′ed**, **-brat′ing** [< L. *cerebrum*, the brain] to think —**cer′e·bra′tion** *n.*

**cer·e·brum** (ser′ə brəm, sə rē′-) *n.*, *pl.* **-brums**, **-bra** [L.] the upper, main part of the brain

**cere·ment** (ser′ə mənt, sir′mənt) *n.* [< Gr. *kēros*, wax] 1. a shroud for a dead person 2. [*usually pl.*] any burial clothes

**cer·e·mo·ni·al** (ser′ə mō′nē əl) *adj.* of or consisting of ceremony; formal —*n.* 1. a set system of forms or rites 2. a rite —**cer′e·mo′ni·al·ly** *adv.*

**cer′e·mo′ni·ous** (-nē əs) *adj.* 1. full of ceremony 2. very polite or formal —**cer′e·mo′ni·ous·ly** *adv.*

**cer·e·mo·ny** (ser′ə mō′nē) *n.*, *pl.* **-nies** [L. *caerimonia*] 1. a set of formal acts proper to a special occasion, as a religious rite 2. behavior that follows rigid etiquette 3. *a)* formality *b)* empty formality —**stand on ceremony** to insist on formality

**ce·rise** (sə rēs′, -rēz′) *n.*, *adj.* [Fr., a cherry] bright red

**cer·tain** (surt′'n) *adj.* [< L. *cernere*, decide] 1. fixed; settled 2. inevitable 3. reliable; dependable 4. sure; positive 5. definite, but unnamed [a *certain* person] 6. some [to a *certain* extent] —**for certain** without doubt

**cer′tain·ly** *adv.* undoubtedly; surely

**cer′tain·ty** (-tē) *n.* 1. the state or fact of being certain 2. *pl.* **-ties** anything certain

**cer·tif·i·cate** (sur tif′ə kit) *n.* [see ff.] a document attesting to a fact, qualification, etc. —*vt.* (-kāt′) **-cat′ed**, **-cat′ing** to issue a certificate to

**certificate of deposit** a bank certificate issued for a specified large deposit of money drawing a higher rate of interest if not withdrawn during a specified period

**certified public accountant** a public accountant certified as passing a State examination

**cer·ti·fy** (sur′tə fī′) *vt.* **-fied′**, **-fy′ing** [< L. *certus*, certain + *facere*, to make] 1. to declare (a thing) true, accurate, etc. by formal statement 2. to guarantee (a check, document, etc.) 3. to grant a certificate to —**cer′ti·fi′a·ble** *adj.* —**cer′ti·fi·ca′tion** *n.*

**cer·ti·tude** (surt′ə tood′, -tyood′) *n.* sureness; inevitability

**ce·ru·le·an** (sə roo′lē ən) *adj.* [< L. *caelum*, heaven] sky-blue; azure

**Cer·van·tes** (sər van′tēz), **Mi·guel** (mē gel′) **de** 1547–1616; Sp. writer

**cer·vix** (sur′viks) *n.*, *pl.* **-vi·ces** (-və sēz′), **-vix·es** [L., neck] a necklike part, as of the uterus —**cer′vi·cal** (-vi kəl) *adj.*

**ces·sa·tion** (se sā′shən) *n.* [< L. *cessare*, to cease] a ceasing or stopping

**ces·sion** (sesh′ən) *n.* [< L. *cedere*, to yield] a ceding or giving up (of rights, etc.) to another

**cess·pool** (ses′pool′) *n.* [< It. *cesso*, privy] a deep hole in the ground to receive drainage or sewage from sinks, toilets, etc.

**ce·ta·cean** (si tā′shən) *adj.* [< L. *cetus*, whale] of water mammals such as whales and dolphins —*n.* any of these

**Cey·lon** (sə län′) country on an island off the SE tip of India: 25,332 sq. mi.; pop. 11,500,000: official name *Sri Lanka* —**Cey·lo·nese** (sel′ə nēz′) *adj.*, *n.*

**cf.** [L. *confer*] compare

**cg, cg.**, **cgm, cgm.** centigram(s)

**Ch., ch.** 1. chapter 2. church

**Cha·blis** (shab′lē) *n.* a dry, white Burgundy wine, orig. from Chablis, France

**Chad** (chad) country in NC Africa: c.495,000 sq. mi.; pop. 3,361,000

**chafe** (chāf) *vt.* **chafed**, **chaf′ing** [< L. *calefacere*, make warm] 1. to rub so as to make warm 2. to wear away or make sore by rubbing 3. to annoy; irritate —*vi.* 1. to rub (*on* or *against*) 2. to be vexed

**chaff** (chaf) *n.* [OE. *ceaf*] 1. threshed or winnowed husks of grain 2. anything worthless 3. teasing; banter —*vt.*, *vi.* to tease

**chaf·ing dish** (chāf′iŋ) a pan with a heating device beneath it, to cook food at the table or to keep food hot

**cha·grin** (shə grin′) *n.* [Fr.] embarrassment due to disappointment, failure, etc. —*vt.* **-grined′**, **-grin′ing** to make feel chagrin

**chain** (chān) *n.* [< L. *catena*] 1. a flexible series of joined links 2. [*pl.*] *a*) bonds; fetters *b*) captivity 3. a chainlike measuring instrument, as for surveying 4. a series of related things or events 5. a group of stores, etc. owned by one company —*vt.* 1. to fasten with chains 2. to restrain, confine, etc.

**chain gang** a gang of prisoners chained together, as when working

**chain'-re·act'** *vi.* to be involved in or subjected to a chain reaction

**chain reaction** 1. a self-sustaining series of chemical or nuclear reactions in which reaction products keep the process going 2. a series of events each of which results in the following

**chain saw** a portable power saw with an endless chain carrying cutting teeth

**chair** (cher) *n.* [< L. *cathedra*: see CATHEDRAL] 1. a piece of furniture with a back, for one person to sit on 2. an important or official position 3. a chairman —*vt.* 1. to seat 2. to preside over as chairman

**chair'lift'** *n.* a line of seats suspended from a power-driven endless cable, used to carry skiers up a slope

**chair'man** (-mən) *n., pl.* -men a person in charge of a meeting, committee, etc.: also **chair'per'son** — **chair'man·ship'** *n.*

**chaise** (shāz) *n.* [Fr.] a lightweight carriage, having two or four wheels

**chaise longue** (lôn') *pl.* **chaise longues** (lônz') [Fr., long chair] a couchlike chair with a long seat: also **chaise lounge** (lounj)

**chal·ced·o·ny** (kal sed'n ē, kal'sə dō'nē) *n., pl.* -nies [< Gr.] a kind of colored quartz with the luster of wax

**cha·let** (sha lā', shal'ē) *n.* [Swiss-Fr.] 1. a Swiss house with overhanging eaves 2. any similar building

**chal·ice** (chal'is) *n.* [< L. *calix*] 1. a cup 2. the cup for the wine of Holy Communion

**chalk** (chôk) *n.* [< L. *calx*, limestone] 1. a soft, whitish limestone 2. a piece of chalk or chalklike substance used for writing on a blackboard —*adj.* made with chalk —*vt.* to mark or rub with chalk —**chalk up** 1. to score, get, or achieve 2. to charge or credit — **chalk'i·ness** *n.* —**chalk'y** *adj.*

**chalk'board'** *n.* *same as* BLACKBOARD

**chal·lenge** (chal'ənj) *n.* [< L. *calumnia*, false accusation] 1. a demand for identification 2. a calling into question 3. a call to a duel, contest, etc. 4. anything that calls for special effort —*vt.* -lenged, -leng·ing to subject to a challenge —*vi.* to make a challenge —**chal'leng·er** *n.*

**chal·lis, chal·lie** (shal'ē) *n.* [< ?] a lightweight fabric of wool, etc.

**cham·ber** (chām'bər) *n.* [< L. *camera*, a vault] 1. a room; esp., a bedroom 2. [*pl.*] a judge's office near the courtroom 3. an assembly hall 4. a legislative or judicial body 5. a council

[*chamber* of commerce] 6. an enclosed space 7. the part of a gun holding the charge or of a revolver holding the cartridge —**cham'bered** *adj.*

**cham·ber·lain** (chām'bər lin) *n.* [< OHG. *chamarlinc*] 1. an officer in charge of the household of a ruler or lord 2. a high official in certain royal courts 3. [Brit.] a treasurer

**cham'ber·maid'** *n.* a woman whose work is taking care of bedrooms

**chamber music** music for performance by a small group, as a string quartet

**chamber of commerce** an association established to further the business interests of its community

**cham·bray** (sham'brā) *n.* [< *Cambrai*, Fr. city] a smooth cotton fabric of white threads woven across a colored warp

**cha·me·le·on** (kə mēl'yən, -mē'lē ən) *n.* [< Gr. *chamai*, on the ground + *leōn*, lion] any of various lizards that can change the color of their skin

**cham·ois** (sham'ē) *n., pl.* **cham'ois** [Fr.] 1. a small, goatlike antelope of the mountains of Europe and the Caucasus 2. a soft leather made from the skin of chamois, sheep, etc.: also **cham'my** (sham'ē)

**cham·o·mile** (kam'ə mīl', -mēl') *n.* [< Gr. *chamai*, on the ground + *melon*, apple] a plant with dried flower heads used in a medicinal tea

**champ¹** (champ) *vt., vi.* [prob. echoic] to chew or bite hard and noisily

**champ²** (champ) *n.* [Slang] a champion

**cham·pagne** (sham pān') *n.* an effervescent white wine, orig. from Champagne, region in NE France

**cham·paign** (sham pān') *n.* [< L. *campus*, field] flat, open country

**cham·pi·on** (cham'pē ən) *n.* [< LL. *campio*, gladiator] 1. one who fights for another or for a cause; defender 2. a winner of first place in a competition —*adj.* excelling all others —*vt.* to fight for; defend; support —**cham'pi·on·ship'** *n.*

**chance** (chans) *n.* [< L. *cadere*, to fall] 1. the way things happen without apparent cause; luck 2. an unpredictable event 3. a risk or gamble 4. a ticket in a lottery 5. an opportunity 6. a possibility or probability —*adj.* accidental —*vi.* chanced, chanc'ing to have the luck or occasion (*to*) —*vt.* to risk —**by chance** accidentally — **chance on** (or **upon**) to find or meet by chance —**on the** (off) **chance** relying on the (remote) possibility

**chan·cel** (chan's'l) *n.* [< L. *cancelli*, lattices] the part of a church around the altar, for the clergy and the choir

**chan'cel·ler·y** (-sə lə rē) *n., pl.* -ies the position or office of a chancellor

**chan'cel·lor** (-lər) *n.* [< LL. *cancellarius*, secretary] 1. a high government official, as, in certain countries, a prime minister 2. in some universities, the president or other executive officer

**3.** a chief judge of a court of chancery or equity in some States **4.** any of several church officials —**chan'cel·lor·ship'** *n.*

**chance'-med'ley** *n.* **1.** accidental homicide **2.** haphazard action

**chan·cer·y** (chan'sər ē) *n.*, *pl.* **-ies** [< ML. *cancellaria*] **1.** a court of equity **2.** an office of public archives **3.** a chancellery

**chan·cre** (shan'kər) *n.* [Fr.: see CANCER] a sore or ulcer of syphilis

**chanc·y** (chan'sē) *adj.* **-i·er, -i·est** risky; uncertain

**chan·de·lier** (shan'də lir') *n.* [Fr. < L. *candela*, candle] a lighting fixture hung from a ceiling, with branches for candles, electric bulbs, etc.

**chan·dler** (chan'dlər) *n.* [< L. *candela*, candle] **1.** a maker of candles **2.** a retailer of supplies, as for ships —**chan'dler·y** *n.*

**change** (chānj) *vt.* **changed, chang'ing** [< L. *cambire*, to barter] **1.** to put or take (a thing) in place of something else [*change jobs*] **2.** to exchange [*change seats*] **3.** to make different; alter —*vi.* **1.** to alter; vary **2.** to leave one train, bus, etc. and board another **3.** to put on other clothes **4.** to make an exchange —*n.* **1.** a substitution, alteration, or variation **2.** variety **3.** another set of clothes **4.** *a)* money returned as the difference between the price and the greater sum presented *b)* coins or bills that together equal the larger value of a single coin or bill *c)* loose coins —**change off** to take turns —**ring the changes 1.** to ring a set of bells with all possible variations **2.** to do or say a thing in many ways —**change'a·ble** *adj.* —**change'less** *adj.*

**change'ling** *n.* a child secretly put in the place of another

**change of life** menopause

**change'o'ver** *n.* a complete change, as in goods produced

**chan·nel** (chan'l) *n.* [see CANAL] **1.** the bed or deeper part of a river, harbor, etc. **2.** a body of water joining two larger ones **3.** any means of passage **4.** [*pl.*] the official course of transmission of communications **5.** a groove or furrow **6.** a frequency band assigned to a radio or television station —*vt.* **-neled** or **-nelled, -nel·ing** or **-nel·ling 1.** to make a channel in **2.** to send through a channel

**Channel Islands** group of Brit. islands in the English Channel

**chan·nel·ize'** (-īz') *vt.* **-ized', -iz'ing** to provide a channel for

‡**chan·son** (shän sōn') *n.*, *pl.* **-sons'** (-sōn') [Fr.] a song

**chant** (chant) *n.* [< L. *cantare*, sing] **1.** a song; esp., a liturgical song with a series of words sung to each tone **2.** a singsong way of speaking —*vi.*, *vt.* **1.** to sing or say in a chant **2.** to celebrate in song —**chant'er** *n.*

**chan·teuse** (shän tooz') *n.* [Fr.] a woman singer, esp. of popular ballads

**chan·tey** (shan'tē, chan'-) *n.*, *pl.* **-teys** a song that sailors sing in rhythm with their motions while working: also **chan'ty**, *pl.* **-ties**

**chan·ti·cleer** (chan'tə klir') *n.* [see CHANT & CLEAR] a rooster

**Cha·nu·kah** (khä'noo kä') *same as* HANUKA

**cha·os** (kā'äs) *n.* [< Gr., space] extreme confusion or disorder —**cha·ot'ic** (-ät'ik) *adj.*

**chap¹** (chäp, chap) *n.* [< ?] *same as* CHOP²

**chap²** (chap) *n.* [< Brit. *chapman*, peddler] [Colloq.] a man; fellow

**chap³** (chap) *vt.*, *vi.* **chapped** or **chapt, chap'ping** [ME. *chappen*, cut] to crack open; split; roughen, as skin —*n.* a chapped place in the skin

**chap.** **1.** chaplain **2.** chapter

**chap·ar·ral** (chap'ə ral', shap'-) *n.* [Sp. < *chaparro*, evergreen oak] [Southwest] a dense thicket of shrubs, etc.

**cha·peau** (sha pō') *n.*, *pl.* **-peaus', -peaux'** (-pōz') [Fr.] a hat

**chap·el** (chap'l) *n.* [< VL. *cappa*, cape] **1.** a small church **2.** a private place of worship, as in a school

**chap·er·on, chap·er·one** (shap'ə rōn') *n.* [Fr., hood] a person, esp. an older woman, who accompanies young unmarried people for propriety —*vt.*, *vi.* **-oned', -on'ing** to act as chaperon (to) —**chap'er·on·age** *n.*

**chap·lain** (chap'lən) *n.* [see CHAPEL] **1.** a clergyman attached to a chapel **2.** a clergyman serving in a religious capacity with the armed forces, or in a prison, hospital, etc.

**chap·let** (chap'lit) *n.* [< LL. *cappa*, hood] **1.** a garland for the head **2.** a string of beads, esp. prayer beads

**chaps** (chaps, shaps) *n.pl.* [< MexSp. *chaparreras*] leather trousers without a seat, worn over ordinary trousers by cowboys to protect their legs

CHAPS

**chap·ter** (chap'tər) *n.* [< L. *caput*, head] **1.** a main division, as of a book **2.** a local branch of an organization

**char¹** (chär) *vt.*, *vi.* **charred, char'ring** [< CHARCOAL] **1.** to reduce to charcoal **2.** to burn partly; scorch

**char²** (chär) *n.* [< Gael. *ceara*, red] a kind of red-bellied trout

**char·ac·ter** (kar'ik tər) *n.* [< Gr. *charattein*, engrave] **1.** any letter, figure, or symbol used in writing and printing **2.** a distinctive trait **3.** kind or sort **4.** behavior typical of a person or group **5.** moral strength **6.** reputation **7.** status; position **8.** a person in a play, novel, etc. **9.** [Colloq.] an eccentric person

**char'ac·ter·is'tic** (-tə ris'tic) *adj.* typical; distinctive —*n.* a distinguishing trait or quality —**char'ac·ter·is'ti·cal·ly** *adv.*

**char'ac·ter·ize'** (-tə rīz') *vt.* **-ized', -iz'ing 1.** to describe the particular traits of **2.** to be a characteristic of —**char'ac·ter·i·za'tion** *n.*

**cha·rade** (shə rād') *n.* [Fr. < Pr. *charrar*, to gossip] [*often pl.*] a game in which words to be guessed are pantomimed, often syllable by syllable

**char·coal** (chär'kōl') *n.* [ME. *char cole*] a black form of carbon made by partially burning wood, etc. in an airless kiln or retort

**chard** (chärd) *n.* [< L. *carduus,* thistle] a kind of beet with large, edible leaves and stalks

**charge** (chärj) *vt.* **charged, charg'-ing** [ult. < L. *carrus,* car] **1.** to load or fill (*with* something) **2.** to add an electrical charge to (a battery, etc.) **3.** to give as a duty, command, etc. to **4.** to accuse **5.** to make liable for (an error, etc.) **6.** to ask as a price **7.** to record as a debt **8.** to attack vigorously —*vi.* **1.** to ask payment (*for*) **2.** to attack vigorously —*n.* **1.** a load or burden **2.** the necessary quantity, as of fuel, for a container or device **3.** the amount of chemical energy stored in a battery **4.** responsibility or care (*of*) **5.** a person or thing entrusted to one's care **6.** instruction; command **7.** accusation; indictment **8.** cost **9.** a debt, debit, or expense **10.** an onslaught **11.** [Slang] a thrill —**in charge** (*of*) in control (of) —**charge'a·ble** *adj.*

**charge account** an arrangement by which a customer may pay for purchases within a specified future period

**charge plate** a metal or plastic plate embossed with the owner's name, used as a stamp on bills in making purchases on credit: also **charge'-a-plate'** *n.*

**charg'er** *n.* **1.** a person or thing that charges **2.** a horse ridden in battle

**char·i·ot** (char'ē ət) *n.* [see CAR] a horse-drawn, two-wheeled cart used in ancient times for war, racing, etc. —**char'i·o·teer'** (-ə tir') *n.*

**cha·ris·ma** (kə riz'mə) *n., pl.* -**ma·ta** (-mə tə) [< Gr., favor, grace] a special, inspiring quality of leadership

**char·is·mat·ic** (kar'iz mat'ik) *adj.* **1.** of or having charisma **2.** designating or of a religious group seemingly inspired by God, as in healing powers —*n.* a member of a charismatic group

**char·i·ta·ble** (char'i tə b'l) *adj.* **1.** generous to the needy **2.** of or for charity **3.** kind and forgiving —**char'i·ta·ble·ness** *n.* —**char'i·ta·bly** *adv.*

**char·i·ty** (-ə tē) *n., pl.* -**ties** [< L. *caritas,* affection] **1.** *Christian Theol.* love for one's fellow men **2.** leniency in judging others **3.** *a*) generosity toward the needy *b*) the help given **4.** a welfare institution, fund, etc.

**char·la·tan** (shär'lə t'n) *n.* [ult. < LL. *cerretanus,* seller of papal indulgences] a fraud; quack; impostor —**char'la·tan·ism** *n.*

**Char·le·magne** (shär'lə mān') 742–814 A.D.; emperor of the Western Roman Empire (800–814)

**Charles·ton** (chärl'stən) capital of W.Va., in the W part: pop. 72,000 —*n.* a lively dance of the 1920's, in 4/4 time

**char·ley horse** (chär'lē) [Colloq.] a cramp in the leg or arm muscles

**Char·lotte** (shär'lət) city in S N.C.: pop. 241,000

**charm** (chärm) *n.* [< L. *carmen*] **1.** an action, object, or words assumed to have magic power **2.** a trinket worn on a bracelet, etc. **3.** a quality that attracts or delights —*vt., vi.* **1.** to act on as if by magic **2.** to fascinate; delight —**charm'er** *n.* —**charm'-ing** *adj.* —**charm'ing·ly** *adv.*

**char·nel** (**house**) (chär'n'l) [< LL. *carnale,* graveyard] a building, etc. used for dead bodies and bones

**Cha·ron** (ker'ən) *Gr. Myth.* the ferryman on the river Styx

**chart** (chärt) *n.* [< Gr. *chartēs,* leaf of paper] **1.** a map, esp. for use in navigation **2.** an information sheet with tables, graphs, etc. **3.** a table, graph, etc. —*vt.* **1.** to make a chart of **2.** to plan (a course of action)

**char·ter** (chär'tər) *n.* [see prec.] **1.** a franchise given by a government **2.** a written statement of basic laws or principles; constitution **3.** written permission to form a local chapter of a society —*vt.* **1.** to grant a charter to **2.** to hire (a bus, plane, etc.) for private use —**char'ter·er** *n.*

**charter member** a founding member

**char·treuse** (shär trōoz') *n.* [Fr.] pale, yellowish green

**char·wom·an** (chär'-) *n., pl.* -**wom'-en** [see CHORE] a cleaning woman

**char·y** (cher'ē) *adj.* -**i·er, -i·est** [< OE. *cearu,* care] **1.** not taking chances; cautious **2.** sparing —**char'i·ly** *adv.* —**char'i·ness** *n.*

**chase¹** (chās) *vt.* **chased, chas'ing** [ult. < L. *capere,* take] **1.** to follow so as to catch **2.** to run after **3.** to drive away **4.** to hunt —*vi.* **1.** to go in pursuit **2.** [Colloq.] to rush —*n.* **1.** a chasing; pursuit **2.** the hunting of game for sport **3.** anything hunted; quarry —**give chase** to pursue

**chase²** (chās) *vt.* **chased, chas'ing** [< Fr. *enchâsser,* enshrine] to ornament (metal) as by engraving

**chas'er** *n.* [Colloq.] a mild drink, as water, taken after whiskey, etc.

**chasm** (kaz''m) *n.* [< Gr. *chasma*] **1.** a deep crack in the earth's surface; abyss **2.** any break or gap; rift

**chas·sis** (chas'ē, shas'ē) *n., pl.* -**sis** (-ēz) [Fr. < L. *capsa,* a box] **1.** the frame, wheels, etc. of a motor vehicle, but not the body or engine **2.** *a*) a frame, as for the parts of a TV set *b*) the assembled frame and parts

**chaste** (chāst) *adj.* [< L. *castus,* pure] **1.** not indulging in unlawful sexual activity **2.** decent; modest **3.** simple in style —**chaste'ly** *adv.* —**chaste'ness** *n.*

**chas·ten** (chās''n) *vt.* [< L. *casti-gare,* punish] **1.** to punish so as to correct **2.** to restrain or subdue

**chas·tise** (chas tīz') *vt.* -**tised',** -**tis'ing** [see prec.] **1.** to punish, esp.

by beating **2.** to scold sharply —
**chas·tise·ment** n. —**chas·tis·er** n.

**chas·ti·ty** (chas′tə tē) n. **1.** abstention from unlawful sexual activity **2.** celibacy or virginity **3.** decency; modesty **4.** simplicity of style

**chas·u·ble** (chaz′yoo b′l, chas′-) n. [< ML. *casula*] a sleeveless outer vestment worn by priests at Mass

**chat** (chat) vi. **chat′ted, chat′ting** [< CHATTER] to talk in a light, informal manner —n. light, informal talk

**châ·teau** (sha tō′) n., pl. **-teaux′** (-tōz′, -tō′), **-teaus′** [Fr. < L. *castellum*, castle] **1.** a French feudal castle **2.** a large country house and estate, esp. in France Also **cha·teau′**

**chat·e·laine** (shat′'l ān′) n. [Fr.] **1.** the mistress of a château or large household **2.** a clasp or chain ornament

**Chat·ta·noo·ga** (chat′ə nōō′gə) city in SE Tenn.: pop. 119,000

**chat·tel** (chat′'l) n. [see CATTLE] a movable item of personal property

**chat·ter** (chat′ər) vi. [echoic] **1.** to make short, rapid, indistinct sounds, as apes do **2.** to talk much and foolishly **3.** to click together rapidly as teeth do from cold —n. **1.** a chattering **2.** foolish talk —**chat′ter·er** n.

**chat′ter·box′** n. an incessant talker

**chat·ty** (chat′ē) adj. **-ti·er, -ti·est** fond or full of chatting —**chat′ti·ness** n.

**Chau·cer** (chô′sər), **Geoffrey** 1340?–1400; Eng. poet

**chauf·feur** (shō′fər, shō fur′) n. [Fr., lit., stoker] one hired to drive a private automobile for someone else —vt. to act as chauffeur for

**chau·vin·ism** (shō′və niz′m) n. [< N. *Chauvin*, fanatical Fr. patriot] **1.** militant and fanatical patriotism **2.** unreasoning devotion to one's race, sex, etc. —**chau′vin·ist** n., adj. —**chau′vin·is′tic** adj. —**chau′vin·is′ti·cal·ly** adv.

**cheap** (chēp) adj. [ult. < L. *caupo*, tradesman] **1.** low in price **2.** worth more than the price **3.** easily got **4.** of little value **5.** contemptible **6.** [Colloq.] stingy —adv. at a low cost —**cheap′ly** adv. —**cheap′ness** n.

**cheap·en** (chēp′'n) vt., vi. to make or become cheap or cheaper —**cheap′en·er** n.

**cheap′skate′** n. [Slang] a stingy person

**cheat** (chēt) n. [< L. *ex-*, out + *cadere*, fall] **1.** a fraud; swindle **2.** a swindler —vt. **1.** to defraud; swindle **2.** to foil or elude [to *cheat* death] —vi. **1.** to be dishonest or deceitful **2.** [Slang] to be sexually unfaithful (often with *on*) —**cheat′er** n.

**check** (chek) n. [< OFr. *eschec*, a check at chess] **1.** a sudden stop **2.** any restraint **3.** one that restrains **4.** a supervision or test of accuracy, etc. **5.** a mark (√) to show verification **6.** an identification ticket, token, etc. [a hat *check*] **7.** one's bill at a restaurant or bar **8.** a written order to a bank to pay a sum of money **9.** a pattern of squares, or one of the squares **10.** *Chess* the state of a

king that is in danger —interj. [Colloq.] agreed! right! —vt. **1.** to stop suddenly **2.** to restrain; curb; block **3.** to test, verify, etc. by examination or comparison (often with *out*) **4.** to mark with a check (√) (often with *off*) **5.** to mark with a pattern of squares **6.** to deposit temporarily **7.** to clear (esp. luggage) for shipment **8.** *Chess* to place (the opponent's king) in check —vi. **1.** to agree with one another, item for item (often with *out*) **2.** to investigate or verify (often with *on, up on*) —**check in 1.** to register at a hotel, etc. **2.** [Colloq.] to present oneself, as at work —**check out 1.** to pay and leave a hotel, etc. **2.** to add up the prices of (items selected) for payment **3.** to prove to be accurate, etc. —**in check** under control —**check′er** n.

**check′book′** n. a book of forms for writing checks (sense **8**)

**checked** (chekt) adj. having a pattern of squares

**check′er·board′** n. a board with 64 squares of two alternating colors, used in checkers and chess

**check′ered** (-ərd) adj. **1.** having a pattern of squares **2.** varied

**check′ers** (-ərz) n.pl. **1.** [with sing. v.] a game for two played with flat disks on a checkerboard **2.** the disks

**checking account** a bank account against which the depositor can draw checks

**check′list′** n. a list of things, names, etc. to be referred to: also **check list**

**check′mate′** (-māt′) n. [ult. < Per. *shāh māt*, the king is dead] **1.** *Chess a)* the winning move that puts the opponent's king in a position where it cannot be saved *b)* this position **2.** total defeat, frustration, etc. —vt. **-mat′ed, -mat′ing 1.** to place in checkmate **2.** to defeat completely

**check′off′** n. the withholding of dues for the union by the employer

**check′out′** n. **1.** the act or place of checking out purchases **2.** the time by which one must check out of a hotel, etc.

**check′point′** n. a place on a road, etc. where traffic is inspected

**check′room′** n. a room for checking hats, coats, etc.

**check′up′** n. a medical examination

**Ched·dar** (**cheese**) (ched′ər) [< *Cheddar*, England] a hard, smooth cheese

**cheek** (chēk) n. [OE. *ceoke*, jaw] **1.** either side of the face below the eye **2.** [Colloq.] sauciness; impudence —**tongue in cheek** jestingly

**cheek′bone′** n. the bone of the upper cheek, just below the eye

**cheek′y** adj. **-i·er, -i·est** saucy; impudent —**cheek′i·ness** n.

**cheep** (chēp) n. [echoic] the short, shrill sound made by a young bird —vt., vi. to make, or utter with, this sound —**cheep′er** n.

**cheer** (chir) n. [ult. < Gr. *kara*, the head] **1.** a state of mind or of feeling; spirit [be of good *cheer*] **2.** gladness; joy **3.** festive food or entertainment

**4.** encouragement **5.** *a*) a glad, excited shout to urge on, greet, etc. *b*) a rallying cry —*vt.* **1.** to comfort or gladden (often with *up*) **2.** to urge on, greet, etc. with cheers —*vi.* **1.** to become cheerful (usually with *up*) **2.** to shout cheers

**cheer′ful** *adj.* **1.** full of cheer; gay **2.** bright and attractive **3.** willing [a *cheerful* helper] —**cheer′ful·ly** *adv.* —**cheer′ful·ness** *n.*

**cheer′i·o′** (-ē ō′) *interj., n., pl.* -os′ [Brit. Colloq.] **1.** goodbye **2.** good health: used as a toast

**cheer′lead′er** (-lē′dər) *n.* a leader of cheers, as at a football game

**cheer′less** *adj.* not cheerful; dismal; dreary —**cheer′less·ly** *adv.* —**cheer′-less·ness** *n.*

**cheers** (chirz) *interj.* [Chiefly Brit.] good health: used as a toast

**cheer′y** *adj.* -i·er, -i·est cheerful; gay; bright —**cheer′i·ly** *adv.* —**cheer′i·ness** *n.*

**cheese** (chēz) *n.* [OE. *cyse*] a solid food made from milk curds

**cheese′burg′er** (-bur′gər) *n.* a hamburger topped with melted cheese

**cheese′cake′** *n.* **1.** a cake made with cottage cheese or cream cheese **2.** [Slang] photographic display of the figure, esp. the legs, of a pretty girl

**cheese′cloth′** *n.* [from its use for wrapping cheese] a thin, cotton cloth with a very loose weave

**chees·y** (chēz′ē) *adj.* -i·er, -i·est **1.** like cheese **2.** [Slang] inferior; poor

**chee·tah** (chēt′ə) *n.* [< Hind. < Sans. *citra*, spotted] a swift, leopard-like animal of Africa and S Asia

**chef** (shef) *n.* [Fr., head, chief] **1.** a head cook **2.** any cook

**Che·khov** (chek′ôf), **An·ton** (än tôn′) 1860–1904; Russ. writer

**che·la** (kē′lə) *n.* [< Gr. *chēlē*, claw] a pincerlike claw, as of a crab

**chem. 1.** chemical **2.** chemistry

**chem·i·cal** (kem′i k'l) *adj.* **1.** of, made by, or used in chemistry **2.** made with ·or operated by chemicals —*n.* any substance used in or obtained by a chemical process —**chem′i·cal·ly** *adv.*

**chemical engineering** the science or profession of applying chemistry to industrial uses

**chemical warfare** warfare using poisonous gases, napalm, etc.

**che·mise** (shə mēz′) *n.* [< VL. *camisia*, tunic] **1.** a woman's loose, short slip **2.** a straight, loose dress

**chem·ist** (kem′ist) *n.* [< ALCHEMIST] **1.** a specialist in chemistry **2.** [Brit.] a pharmacist, or druggist

**chem·is·try** (kem′is trē) *n.* [< CHEMIST] the science dealing with the composition and properties of substances, and with the reactions by which substances are produced from or converted into other substances

**chem·o·sur·ger·y** (kem′ō sur′jər ē, kē′mō-) *n.* the removal of diseased tissue, etc. with chemicals

**chem′o·ther′a·py** (-ther′ə pē) *n.* the use of chemical drugs in medicine

**chem·ur·gy** (kem′ər jē) *n.* chemistry dealing with the use of organic, esp. farm, products in industrial manufacture

**che·nille** (shi nēl′) *n.* [Fr., caterpillar] **1.** a tufted, velvety yarn **2.** a fabric woven with this

**cheque** (chek) *n. Brit. sp. of* CHECK (*n.* 8)

**cher·ish** (cher′ish) *vt.* [< L. *carus*, dear] **1.** to hold dear **2.** to cling to; hold to; nurture

**Cher·o·kee** (cher′ə kē′) *n., pl.* -kees′, -kee′ a member of a tribe of N.American Indians now chiefly of SW U.S.

**che·root** (shə rōōt′) *n.* [< Tamil] a cigar with both ends cut square

**cher·ry** (cher′ē) *n., pl.* -ries [< Gr. *kerasion*] **1.** a small, fleshy fruit with a smooth, hard pit **2.** the tree that it grows on **3.** the wood of this tree **4.** a bright red

**cher′ry·stone′** (**clam**) a small quahog, a variety of clam

**cher·ub** (cher′əb) *n., pl.* -ubs; for 1 usually -u·bim (-ə bim, -yoo bim) [< Heb. *kerūbh*] **1.** any of a kind of angel, often represented as a chubby, rosy-faced child with wings **2.** an innocent or lovely child —**che·ru·bic** (chə rōō′bik) *adj.* —**che·ru′bi·cal·ly** *adv.*

**cher·vil** (chur′vəl) *n.* [< Gr. *chaire-phyllon*] a plant like parsley, with leaves used to flavor salads, soups, etc.

**Ches·a·peake Bay** (ches′ə pēk′) arm of the Atlantic, extending into Va. & Md.

**chess** (ches) *n.* [< OFr. *eschec*, a check at chess] a game played on a checkerboard by two players, using a variety of pieces (**chessmen**)

**chess′board′** *n.* a checkerboard used for playing chess

**chest** (chest) *n.* [< Gr. *kistē*, a box] **1.** a box with a lid **2.** a cabinet with drawers, as for clothes **3.** a cabinet with shelves, as for medicines **4.** the part of the body enclosed by the ribs and breastbone

**ches·ter·field** (ches′tər fēld′) *n.* [< a 19th-c. Earl of *Chesterfield*] a single-breasted topcoat, usually with a velvet collar

**chest·nut** (ches′nut′) *n.* [< Gr. *kastaneia*] **1.** the edible nut of a tree of the beech family **2.** this tree, or its wood **3.** reddish brown **4.** [Colloq.] an old, stale joke, story, etc.

**che·val glass** (shə val′) [Fr. *cheval*, horse] a full-length mirror mounted on swivels in a frame

**chev·i·ot** (shev′ē ət) *n.* [< *Cheviot* Hills, on the Scottish-English border] a rough, twilled wool fabric

**chev·ron** (shev′rən) *n.* [OFr., rafter] a V-shaped bar on the sleeves of a uniform, showing rank

**chew** (chōō) *vt., vi.* [OE. *ceowan*] to bite and crush with the teeth —*n.* **1.**

a chewing **2.** something chewed or for chewing —**chew′a·ble** *adj.* —**chew′er** *n.* —**chew′y** *adj.* **-i·er, -i·est**

**chewing gum** a sweet, flavored substance, as chicle, used for chewing

**Chey·enne** (shī an′, -en′) capital of Wyo., in the SE part: pop. 41,000

**chg.** *pl.* **chgs.** charge

**chi** (kī) *n.* the 22d letter of the Greek alphabet (Χ, χ)

**Chi·an·ti** (kē än′tē, -an′/-) *n.* [It.] a dry, red wine

**chi·a·ro·scu·ro** (kē är′ə skyoor′ō) *n., pl.* **-ros** [It. < L. *clarus*, clear + *obscurus*, dark] **1.** treatment of light and shade in a painting, etc., esp. when emphasized **2.** a painting, drawing, etc. notable for this

**chic** (shēk) *n.* [Fr. < MLowG. *schick*, skill] smart elegance —*adj.* **chic′quer, chic′quest** smartly stylish

**Chi·ca·go** (shə kä′gō, -kô′-) city and port in NE Ill.: pop. 3,367,000

**chi·can·er·y** (shi kān′ər ē) *n., pl.* **-ies** [< Fr.] **1.** trickery **2.** a trick

**Chi·ca·no** (chē kä′nō) *n., pl.* **-nos** [< AmSp.] [*also* **c-**] a U.S. citizen or inhabitant of Mexican descent

**chi·chi, chi-chi** (shē′shē, chē′chē) *adj.* [Fr.] extremely chic, in an affected or showy way

**chick** (chik) *n.* [ME. *chike*] **1.** a young chicken or bird **2.** a child **3.** [Slang] a young woman

**chick·a·dee** (chik′ə dē′) *n.* [echoic] a small bird related to the titmouse

**chick·en** (chik′ən) *n.* [< OE. *cycen*, little cock] **1.** a common farm bird raised for its edible eggs and flesh; hen or rooster, esp. a young one **2.** its flesh —*adj.* [Slang] cowardly —**chicken (out)** [Slang] to quit from fear

**chicken feed** [Slang] a paltry sum

**chick′en-heart′ed** *adj.* cowardly; timid: also **chick′en-liv′ered**

**chicken pox** an acute, contagious virus disease, esp. of children, characterized by skin eruptions

**chicken wire** light, pliable, wire fencing

**chick′pea′** *n.* [< L. *cicer*, pea] **1.** a bushy annual plant with short, hairy pods **2.** the edible seeds

**chick′weed′** *n.* a low-growing plant often found as a lawn weed

**chic·le** (chik′′l) *n.* [< MexInd.] gumlike substance from a tropical American tree, used in chewing gum

**chic·o·ry** (chik′ə rē) *n., pl.* **-ries** [< Gr. *kichora*] **1.** a plant with blue flowers and with leaves used for salad **2.** its root, ground for mixing with coffee or as a coffee substitute

**chide** (chīd) *vt., vi.* **chid′ed** or **chid** (chid), **chid′ed** or **chid** or **chid·den** (chid′n), **chid′ing** [OE. *cidan*] to scold; rebuke mildly —**chid′ing·ly** *adv.*

**chief** (chēf) *n.* [< L. *caput*, head] a leader; head —*adj.* foremost; main; principal

**chief′ly** *adv.* **1.** most of all **2.** mainly —*adj.* of or like a chief

**chief′tain** (-tən) *n.* [< L. *caput*, head] a chief, esp. of a clan or tribe

**chif·fon** (shi fän′) *n.* [Fr.] a sheer, silky cloth —*adj.* **1.** of chiffon **2.** made fluffy as with beaten egg whites

**chif·fo·nier, chif·fon·nier** (shif′ə nir′) *n.* [Fr.] a high bureau or chest of drawers, often with a mirror

**chig·ger** (chig′ər) *n.* [of Afr. origin] the tiny, red larva of certain mites, whose bite causes itching

**chi·gnon** (shēn′yän) *n.* [Fr. < L. *catena*, chain] a coil of hair worn at the back of the neck by women

**Chi·hua·hua** (chi wä′wä) *n.* [< *Chihuahua*, a Mex. state] a breed of tiny dog with large, pointed ears

CHIHUAHUA

**chil·blain** (chil′blān′) *n.* [CHIL(L) + *blain* < OE. *blegen*, a sore] a painful swelling or sore on the foot or hand, caused by exposure to cold

**child** (chīld) *n., pl.* **chil′dren** [OE. *cild*] **1.** an infant **2.** a boy or girl before puberty **3.** a son or daughter —**with child** pregnant —**child′hood′** *n.* —**child′less** *adj.*

**child′birth′** *n.* the act of giving birth to a child

**child′ish** *adj.* of or like a child; specif., immature, foolish, etc. —**child′ish·ly** *adv.* —**child′ish·ness** *n.*

**child′like′** *adj.* of or like a child; specif., innocent, trusting, etc.

**chil·dren** (chil′drən) *n. pl. of* CHILD

**child′s play** any very simple task

**Chil·e** (chil′ē) country on the SW coast of S.America: 286,397 sq. mi.; pop. 8,690,000 —**Chil′e·an** *adj., n.*

**chil·i** (chil′ē) *n., pl.* **-ies** [MexSp.] **1.** the very hot dried pod of red pepper, often ground (**chili powder**) **2.** a highly seasoned dish of beef, chilies or chili powder, beans, and often tomatoes: in full **chili con car·ne** (kən kär′nē) Also **chile**

**chili sauce** a spiced sauce of chopped tomatoes, sweet peppers, onions, etc.

**chill** (chil) *n.* [OE. *ciele*] **1.** coldness or coolness causing shivers **2.** a moderate coldness **3.** a sudden fear, etc. **4.** unfriendliness —*adj.* same as CHILLY —*vi., vt.* **1.** to make or become cold **2.** to cause a chill (in)

**chill factor** the combined effect of low temperatures and high winds on exposed skin

**chill′y** *adj.* **-i·er, -i·est 1.** moderately cold **2.** chilling **3.** unfriendly —**chill′i·ness** *n.*

**chime** (chīm) *n.* [< Gr. *kymbalon*, cymbal] **1.** [*usually pl.*] *a)* a set of tuned bells or metal tubes *b)* the musical sounds made by these **2.** a single bell, as in a clock —*vi.* **chimed, chim′ing 1.** to sound as a chime or chimes **2.** to agree —*vt.* to give (the time) by chiming —**chime in 1.** to join in **2.** to agree —**chim′er** *n.*

**Chi·me·ra, Chi·mae·ra** (ki mir′ə, kī-) [< Gr. *chimaira*, orig., goat] *Gr. Myth.* a monster with a lion's head, goat's body, and serpent's tail —*n.* [**c-**] an impossible fancy

**chi·mer′i·cal** (-mir′i k′l, -mer′-) *adj.*
1. imaginary; unreal 2. visionary

**chim·ney** (chim′nē) *n., pl.* **-neys**
[ult. < Gr. *kaminos*, oven] 1. the
passage or structure through which
smoke escapes from a fire, often extending above the roof 2. a glass tube
around the flame of a lamp

**chim·pan·zee** (chim′pan zē′, chim
pan′zē) *n.* [< Afr. native name] a
medium-sized anthropoid ape of
Africa: also [Colloq.] **chimp** (chimp)

**chin** (chin) *n.* [OE. *cin*] the part of
the face below the lower lip —*vt.*
**chinned, chin′ning** to pull (oneself)
up, while hanging by the hands from
a bar, until the chin is just above
the bar

**Chin.** 1. China 2. Chinese

**Chi·na** (chī′nə) country in E Asia:
3,691,000 sq. mi.; pop. 646,530,000

**chi′na** *n.* 1. *a)* porcelain, orig. made
in China *b)* vitrified ceramic ware
*c)* any earthenware 2. dishes, etc.
made of china Also **chi′na·ware′**

**chinch** (bug) (chinch) [< Sp. < L.
*cimex*, bug] a small, white-winged,
black bug that damages grain plants

**chin·chil·la** (chin chil′ə) *n.* [prob.
dim. of Sp. *chinche*, chinch] 1. *a)* a
small rodent of S.America *b)* its
expensive, gray fur 2. a heavy wool
cloth used for making overcoats

**chine** (chīn) *n.* [OFr. *eschine*] 1. the
backbone 2. a cut of meat from the
backbone 3. a ridge

**Chi·nese** (chī nēz′, -nēs′) *n.* 1. *pl.*
**-nese′** a native of China 2. the language of the Chinese —*adj.* of China,
its people, language, etc.

**Chinese checkers** a game-like
checkers, using marbles on a board
with holes in a star-shaped pattern

**Chinese lantern** a paper lantern
that can be folded up

**chink¹** (chiŋk) *n.* [OE. *cine*] a crack
—*vt.* to close up the chinks in

**chink²** (chiŋk) *n.* [echoic] a sharp,
clinking sound —*vi., vt.* to make or
cause to make this sound

**chi·no** (chē′nō, shē′-) *n.* [< ?] 1. a
strong, twilled cotton cloth 2. [*pl.*]
men's pants of chino for casual wear

**Chi·nook** (chi nōōk′) *n., pl.* **-nooks′,
-nook′** [< AmInd. name] a member
of a tribe of American Indians of
Wash. and Oreg.

**chintz** (chints) *n.* [< Hind. *chhīnt*] a
cotton cloth printed in colored designs
and usually glazed

**chintz′y** *adj.* **-i·er, -i·est** 1. like
chintz 2. [Colloq.] cheap, stingy, etc.

**chip** (chip) *vt.* **chipped, chip′ping**
[< OE.] to break or cut off small
pieces from —*vi.* to break off in small
pieces —*n.* 1. a small piece of wood,
etc. cut or broken off 2. a place where
a small piece has been chipped off
3. a small disk used in gambling
games as a counter 4. a thin slice of
food [a potato *chip*] —**chip in**
[Colloq.] to contribute (money, etc.)

—**chip on one's shoulder** [Colloq.]
an inclination to fight —**in the chips**
[Slang] wealthy

**chip′munk′** (-muŋk′) *n.* [<
AmInd.] a small, striped N. American
squirrel

**chipped beef** dried or smoked beef
sliced into shavings

**chip·per** (chip′ər) *adj.* [< Brit. dial.]
[Colloq.] in good spirits; lively; spry

**chiro-** [< Gr. *cheir*, hand] *a combining form meaning* hand

**chi·rog·ra·phy** (kī räg′rə fē) *n.* [CHI-
RO- + -GRAPHY] handwriting

**chi·rop·o·dy** (kə räp′ə dē, kī-) *n.*
[CHIRO- + -POD + -Y³] *same as*
PODIATRY —**chi·rop′o·dist** *n.*

**chi·ro·prac·tic** (kī′rə prak′tik) *n.*
[< CHIRO- + Gr. *praktikos*, practical]
a method of treating disease by
manipulation of the body joints, esp.
of the spine —**chi′ro·prac′tor** *n.*

**chirp** (churp) *vi., vt.* [echoic] to
make, or utter in, short, shrill tones, as
some birds do —*n.* this sound

**chir·rup** (chur′əp) *vi.* [< prec.] to
chirp repeatedly —*n.* this sound

**chis·el** (chiz′'l) *n.* [< L. *caedere*, to
cut] a sharp-edged tool for cutting
or shaping wood, stone, etc. —*vi., vt.*
**-eled** or **-elled, -el·ing** or **-el·ling**
1. to cut or shape with a chisel 2.
[Colloq.] to swindle or get by swindling
—**chis′el·er, chis′el·ler** *n.*

**chit** (chit) *n.* [< Hind.] a voucher of
a sum owed for drink, food, etc.

**chit·chat** (chit′chat′) *n.* [< CHAT]
1. light, informal talk 2. gossip

**chi·tin** (kīt′n) *n.* [< Gr. *chitōn*,
tunic] the tough, horny outer covering of insects, crustaceans, etc.

**chit·ter·lings, chit·lins, chit·
lings** (chit′lənz) *n.pl.* [< Gmc. base]
small intestines of pigs, used for food

**chiv·al·rous** (shiv′'l rəs) *adj.* 1.
gallant, courteous, etc. like an ideal
knight 2. of chivalry Also **chiv·al·ric**
(shi val′rik, shiv′'l-) —**chiv′al·rous·
ly** *adv.* —**chiv′al·rous·ness** *n.*

**chiv′al·ry** *n.* [< OFr. *chevaler*, knight]
1. medieval knighthood 2. the qualities of an ideal knight, as courage,
courtesy, etc.

**chives** (chīvz) *n.pl.* [< L. *cepa*,
onion] [*often with sing. v.*] a plant with
slender, hollow leaves and a mild
onion odor, used for flavoring

**chlo·ral** (klôr′əl) *n.* 1. a thin, oily,
pungent liquid made from chlorine
and alcohol 2. chloral hydrate

**chloral hydrate** a colorless, crystalline compound used as a sedative

**chlor′dane** (-dān) *n.* a chlorinated,
poisonous, volatile oil used as an
insecticide: also **chlor′dan** (-dan)

**chlo·ride** (-īd) *n.* a compound of
chlorine and another element or radical

**chlo·ri·nate** (klôr′ə nāt′) *vt.* **-nat′
ed, -nat′ing** to combine (a substance)
with chlorine; esp., to treat (water or
sewage) with chlorine for purification
—**chlo′ri·na′tion** *n.*

---

fat, āpe, cär; ten, ēven; is, bīte; gō, hôrn, tōōl, look; oil, out; up, fur;
chin; she; thin, then; zh, leisure; ŋ, ring; ə for *a* in *ago*; ', (ā′b'l); ë, Fr. coeur;
ö, Fr. feu; Fr. mon; ü, Fr. duc; kh, G. ich, doch; ‡ foreign; < derived from

**chlo·rine** (klôr′ēn, -in) n. [< Gr. *chlōros*, pale green] a greenish-yellow, poisonous, gaseous chemical element with a disagreeable odor, used in bleaching, water purification, etc.

**chlo·ro·form** (klôr′ə fôrm′) n. [< Fr.: see prec. & FORMIC] a colorless, volatile liquid used as an anesthetic and solvent —vt. to anesthetize or kill with chloroform

**chlo·ro·phyll, chlo·ro·phyl** (-fil′) n. [< Gr. *chlōros*, green + *phyllon*, leaf] the green pigment in plant cells, a factor in photosynthesis

**chock** (chäk) n. [ONormFr. *choque*, a block] a block or wedge placed under a wheel, etc. to prevent motion —vt. to wedge fast as with chocks —adv. as close or tight as can be

**chock′-full′** adj. as full as possible

**choc·o·late** (chôk′lət, chäk′-; -ə lət) n. [< MexInd. *chocolatl*] 1. a substance made from roasted and ground cacao seeds 2. a drink or candy made with chocolate 3. reddish brown —adj. 1. made of or flavored with chocolate 2. reddish-brown

**choice** (chois) n. [< OFr. < Gothic *kausjan*, to test] 1. a choosing; selection 2. the right or power to choose 3. a person or thing chosen 4. the best part 5. a variety from which to choose 6. an alternative —adj. choic′er, choic′est 1. of special excellence 2. carefully chosen

**choir** (kwīr) n. [< L. < Gr. *choros*] 1. a group of singers, esp. in a church 2. the part of a church they occupy

**choke** (chōk) vt. choked, chok′ing [< OE. *aceocian*] 1. to prevent from breathing by blocking the windpipe; strangle; suffocate 2. to obstruct by clogging 3. to hinder the growth or action of 4. to cut off some air from the carburetor of (a gasoline engine) so as to make a richer gasoline mixture —vi. 1. to be suffocated 2. to be obstructed —n. 1. a choking 2. a sound of choking 3. the valve that chokes a carburetor —choke back to hold back (feelings, sobs, etc.) —choke down to swallow with difficulty —choke off to bring to an end —choke up to obstruct

**choke collar** a training collar for a dog, that tightens when the dog strains at the leash

**chok′er** n. a close-fitting necklace

**chol·er** (käl′ər) n. [< Gr. *cholē*, bile] [Now Rare] anger or ill humor

**chol·er·a** (käl′ər ə) n. [see prec.] any of several severe, infectious intestinal diseases

**chol·er·ic** adj. easily angered

**cho·les·ter·ol** (kə les′tə rōl′, -rôl′) n. [< Gr. *cholē*, bile + *stereos*, solid] a crystalline alcohol found esp. in animal fats, blood, and bile

**chomp** (chämp) vt., vi. same as CHAMP[1]

**choose** (chooz) vt., vi. chose, cho′sen, choos′ing [OE. *ceosan*] 1. to take as a choice; select 2. to decide or prefer [I choose to go] —cannot choose but cannot do otherwise —choos′er n.

**choos·y, choos′ey** adj. -i·er, -i·est [Colloq.] fussy in choosing

**chop[1]** (chäp) vt. chopped, chop′ping [ME. *choppen*] 1. to cut by blows with a sharp tool 2. to cut into small bits —vi. to make quick, cutting strokes —n. 1. a short, sharp stroke 2. a cut of meat and bone from the rib, loin, or shoulder 3. a short, broken movement of waves

**chop[2]** (chäp) n. [< ?] 1. a jaw 2. [pl.] the mouth and lower cheeks

**chop′house′** n. a restaurant that specializes in chops and steaks

**Cho·pin** (shō′pan; Fr. shô pan′), **Fré·dé·ric** (frā dā rēk′) 1810–49; Pol. composer in France after 1831

**chop′per** n. 1. one that chops 2. [pl.] [Slang] teeth 3. [Colloq.] a helicopter

**chop·py** (chäp′ē) adj. -pi·er, -pi·est 1. rough with short, broken waves, as the sea 2. making abrupt starts and stops —chop′pi·ness n.

**chop′sticks′** n.pl. [PidE.] two small sticks held together in one hand and used in some Asian countries in eating

**chop su·ey** (chäp′ soo′ē) [< Chin. *tsa-sui*, various pieces] a Chinese-American dish of meat, bean sprouts, etc., served with rice

**cho·ral** (kôr′əl) adj. of, for, or sung by a choir or chorus —cho′ral·ly adv.

CHOPSTICKS

**cho·rale, cho·ral** (kə ral′) n. 1. a hymn tune 2. a choir or chorus

**chord[1]** (kôrd) n. [alt. (after L. *chorda*) < CORD] 1. [Poet.] the string of a musical instrument 2. a straight line joining any two points on an arc

**chord[2]** (kôrd) n. [< ACCORD] *Music* a combination of three or more tones sounded together in harmony

**chore** (chôr) n. [< OE. *cierr*, job] 1. a routine task 2. a hard task

**chor·e·o·graph** (kôr′ē ə graf′) vt., vi. [see ff.] to design or plan the movements of (a dance) —chor′e·o·graph′ic adj.

**chor·e·og·ra·phy** (kôr′ē äg′rə fē) n. [< Gr. *choreia*, dance + -GRAPHY] 1. dancing, esp. ballet dancing 2. the art of devising dances or ballets —chor′e·og′ra·pher n.

**chor·is·ter** (kôr′is tər) n. [see CHORUS] a member of a choir

**chor·tle** (chôr′t'l) vi., vt. -tled, -tling [prob. < CHUCKLE + SNORT] to make, or utter with, a gleeful chuckling or snorting sound —n. such a sound

**cho·rus** (kôr′əs) n. [< Gr. *choros*] 1. a group of dancers and singers performing together 2. the part of a drama, song, etc. performed by a chorus 3. a group singing or speaking something together 4. music written for group singing 5. the refrain of a song, following each verse —vt., vi. to sing, speak, or say in unison —in chorus in unison

**chose** (chōz) pt. of CHOOSE

**cho·sen** (chō′z'n) pp. of CHOOSE —adj. selected; choice

**Chou En-lai** (jō′ en lī′) 1898–1976; Chin. prime minister (1949–76)

**chow** (chou) *n.* [< Chin.] 1. any of a breed of medium-sized dog, originally from China 2. [Slang] food

**chow·der** (chou′dər) *n.* [< Fr. *chaudière,* pot ] a thick soup usually of onions and potatoes and, often, clams and milk

**chow mein** (chou mān′) [Chin. *ch'ao,* fry + *mien,* flour] a Chinese-American dish of meat, bean sprouts, etc., served with fried noodles

**chrism** (kriz′m) *n.* [< Gr. *chrisma,* oil] holy oil used in baptism

**Christ** (krīst) [< Gr. *christos,* the anointed] Jesus of Nazareth, regarded by Christians as the Messiah

**chris·ten** (kris′n) *vt.* 1. to take into a Christian church by baptism; baptize 2. to give a name to, esp. at baptism —**chris′ten·ing** *n.*

**Chris′ten·dom** (-dəm) *n.* 1. Christians collectively 2. those parts of the world where most of the inhabitants profess Christianity

**Chris·tian** (kris′chən) *n.* a believer in Jesus as the Christ, or in the religion based on the teachings of Jesus —*adj.* 1. of Jesus Christ 2. of or professing the religion based on his teachings 3. having the qualities taught by Jesus, as love, kindness, etc. 4. of Christians or Christianity

**Chris·ti·an·i·ty** (kris′chē an′ə tē) *n.* 1. Christians collectively 2. the Christian religion 3. the state of being a Christian

**Chris·tian·ize** (kris′chə nīz′) *vt.* -ized′, -iz′ing 1. to convert to Christianity 2. to cause to conform with Christian character or precepts

**Christian name** the baptismal name or given name, as distinguished from the surname or family name

**Christian Science** a religion and system of healing: official name **Church of Christ, Scientist**

**chris·tie, chris·ty** (kris′tē) *n., pl.* -ties [< *Christiania,* former name of Oslo] a high-speed turn in skiing with the skis parallel

**Christ·mas** (kris′məs) *n.* [see CHRIST & MASS] a holiday on Dec. 25 celebrating the birth of Jesus Christ

**chro·mat·ic** (krō mat′ik) *adj.* [< Gr. *chrōma,* color] 1. of or having color or colors 2. *Music* progressing by half tones —**chro·mat′i·cal·ly** *adv.*

**chrome** (krōm) *n.* [Fr. < Gr. *chrōma,* color] chromium or chromium alloy —*adj.* designating any of various pigments (**chrome red, chrome yellow,** etc.) made from chromium compounds —*vt.* chromed, **chrom′ing** to plate with chromium

**-chrome** (krōm) [< Gr. *chrōma,* color] a suffix meaning: 1. color or coloring agent 2. chromium

**chro·mi·um** (krō′mē əm) *n.* [see CHROME] a hard metallic chemical element resistant to corrosion

**chromo-** [< Gr. *chrōma*] a combining form meaning color or pigment [*chromosome*]: also **chrom-**

**chro·mo·some** (krō′mə sōm′) *n.* [prec. + -SOME²] any of the microscopic rod-shaped bodies bearing genes

**chron·ic** (krän′ik) *adj.* [< Gr. *chronos,* time] 1. lasting a long time or recurring: said of a disease 2. having had an ailment for a long time 3. habitual —**chron′i·cal·ly** *adv.*

**chron·i·cle** (krän′i k'l) *n.* [< Gr. *chronika,* annals] a historical record of events in the order in which they happened —*vt.* -cled, -cling to tell the history of; recount; record —**chron′i·cler** *n.*

**chrono-** [< Gr. *chronos*] a combining form meaning time: also **chron-**

**chro·nol·o·gy** (krə näl′ə jē) *n., pl.* -gies [CHRONO- + -LOGY] 1. the science of measuring time and of dating events 2. the arrangement of events in the order of occurrence —**chron·o·log·i·cal** (krän′ə läj′i k'l) *adj.* —**chron′o·log′i·cal·ly** *adv.*

**chro·nom·e·ter** (krə näm′ə tər) *n.* [CHRONO- + -METER] a highly accurate kind of clock or watch

**chrys·a·lis** (kris′'l əs) *n.* [< Gr. *chrysallis*] 1. the pupa of a butterfly, encased in a cocoon 2. the cocoon

**chrys·an·the·mum** (kri san′thə məm) *n.* [< Gr. *chrysos,* gold + *anthemon,* flower] 1. a late-blooming plant of the composite family, with showy flowers 2. the flower

**chub** (chub) *n.* [ME. *chubbe*] a freshwater fish related to the carp

**chub·by** (chub′ē) *adj.* -bi·er, -bi·est [< prec.] round and plump —**chub′bi·ness** *n.*

**chuck¹** (chuk) *vt.* [< ? Fr. *choquer,* strike against] 1. to tap playfully, esp. under the chin 2. to throw; toss 3. [Slang] to get rid of —*n.* a chucking

**chuck²** (chuk) *n.* [? var. of CHOCK] 1. a cut of beef from around the neck and shoulder blade 2. a clamplike holding device, as on a lathe

**chuck′-full′** *adj.* same as CHOCK-FULL

**chuck′hole′** *n.* [see CHOCK & HOLE] a rough hole in pavement

**chuck·le** (chuk′'l) *vi.* -led, -ling [? var. of CLUCK] to laugh softly in a low tone —*n.* a soft, low-toned laugh

**chuck wagon** a wagon equipped as a kitchen for feeding cowboys, etc.

**chug** (chug) *n.* [echoic] a puffing or explosive sound, as of a locomotive —*vi.* chugged, **chug′ging** to make, or move with, such sounds

**chuk·ka boot** (chuk′ə) [ult. < Sans. *cakra,* wheel] a man's ankle-high shoe

**chum** (chum) *n.* [prob. < *chamber* (mate)] [Colloq.] a close friend —*vi.* chummed, **chum′ming** [Colloq.] to be close friends —**chum′mi·ness** *n.* —**chum′my** *adj.* -mi·er, -mi·est

**chump** (chump) *n.* [< ?] [Colloq.] a stupid person; fool

**Chung·king** (choon′kiŋ′, chuŋ′-) city in SC China: pop. 4,070,000

**chunk** (chuŋk) *n.* [< ? CHUCK²] a short, thick piece

**chunk·y** *adj.* **-i·er, -i·est** 1. short and thick 2. stocky —**chunk′i·ness** *n.*

**church** (church) *n.* [< Gr. *kyriakē* (*oikia*), Lord's (house)] 1. a building for public worship, esp. Christian worship 2. religious service 3. [*usually* C-] *a*) all Christians *b*) a particular Christian denomination 4. ecclesiastical, as opposed to secular, government

**church′go′er** (-gō′ər) *n.* a person who attends church regularly —**church′go′ing** *n., adj.*

**Church·ill** (chur′chil), **Win·ston** (win′stən) 1874–1965; Brit. prime minister (1940–45; 1951–55)

**church′man** (-mən) *n., pl.* **-men** 1. a clergyman 2. a church member

**Church of England** the episcopal church of England: it is an established church headed by the sovereign

**church′ward′en** (-wôr′d'n) *n.* a lay officer handling certain secular affairs of a church

**church′yard′** *n.* the yard adjoining a church, often used as a cemetery

**churl** (churl) *n.* [OE. *ceorl*, peasant] 1. a peasant 2. a surly, ill-bred person; boor —**churl′ish** *adj.* —**churl′ish·ness** *n.*

**churn** (churn) *n.* [OE. *cyrne*] a container in which milk or cream is stirred and shaken to form butter —*vt., vi.* 1. to stir and shake (milk or cream) in a churn 2. to make (butter) thus 3. to stir up or move vigorously

**chute¹** (shōōt) *n.* [Fr., a fall] an inclined or vertical trough or passage down which things slide or drop

**chute²** (shōōt) *n.* [Colloq.] a parachute

**chut·ney** (chut′nē) *n., pl.* **-neys** [Hind. *chatni*] a relish of fruits, spices, and herbs: also **chutnee**

**chutz·pah, chutz·pa** (khoots′pə) *n.* [Heb. via Yid.] [Colloq.] impudence; brass

**CIA, C.I.A.** Central Intelligence Agency

**ci·ca·da** (si kā′də) *n., pl.* **-das, -dae** (-dē) [L.] a large, flylike insect with transparent wings: the male makes a loud, shrill sound

**cic·a·trix** (sik′ə triks) *n., pl.* **cic·a·tri·ces** (si kat′rə sēz′) [L.] fibrous tissue that forms at a healing wound; scar

**Cic·er·o** (sis′ə rō′) 106–43 B.C.; Rom. statesman and orator

**-cide** (sīd) [< L. *caedere*, kill] *a suffix meaning:* 1. killer 2. killing

**ci·der** (sī′dər) *n.* [< Gr. *sikera*, intoxicant] juice pressed from apples, used as a drink or for making vinegar

**ci·gar** (si gär′) *n.* [< Sp.] a compact roll of tobacco leaves for smoking

**cig·a·rette** (sig′ə ret′) *n.* [Fr.] a small roll of finely cut tobacco wrapped in thin paper for smoking

**ci·ga·ril·lo** (-ril′ō) *n., pl.* **-los** [Sp.] a small, thin cigar

**cil·i·a** (sil′ē ə) *n.pl., sing.* **-i·um** (-ē əm) [L.] 1. the eyelashes 2. *Biol.* small hairlike processes

**cinch** (sinch) *n.* [< Sp. < L. *cingulum*, girdle] 1. a saddle or pack girth 2. [Slang] a thing easy to do or sure to happen —*vt.* 1. to tighten a girth on 2. [Slang] to make sure of

**cin·cho·na** (sin kō′nə) *n.* [< 17th-c. Peruv. Countess del *Chinchón*] 1. a tropical tree with a bitter bark 2. the bark, from which quinine is made

**Cin·cin·nat·i** (sin′sə nat′ē, -ə) city in SW Ohio: pop. 453,000

**cinc·ture** (sink′chər) *n.* [L. *cinctura*] a belt or girdle —*vt.* **-tured, -tur·ing** to encircle with a cincture

**cin·der** (sin′dər) *n.* [OE. *sinder*] 1. a tiny piece of partly burned wood, etc. 2. [*pl.*] ashes from coal or wood

**Cin·der·el·la** (sin′də rel′ə) in a fairy tale, a household drudge who eventually marries a prince

**cin·e·ma** (sin′ə mə) *n.* [< Gr. *kinēma*, motion] [Chiefly Brit.] 1. a motion picture 2. a motion-picture theater —**the cinema** motion pictures collectively —**cin′e·mat′ic** *adj.*

**cin·e·ma·tog·ra·phy** (sin′ə mə täg′rə fē) *n.* the art of photography in making motion pictures —**cin′e·ma·tog′ra·pher** *n.* —**cin′e·mat′o·graph′ic** (-mat′ə graf′ik) *adj.*

**cin·na·bar** (sin′ə bär′) *n.* [ult. < Per.] mercuric sulfide, a heavy bright-red mineral

**cin·na·mon** (sin′ə mən) *n.* [< Heb. *qinnāmōn*] 1. the light-brown spice made from the inner bark of a laurel tree of the East Indies 2. this bark

**ci·pher** (sī′fər) *n.* [< Ar. *şifr*] 1. the symbol 0; zero 2. a nonentity 3. secret writing based on a key; code 4. the key to such a code —*vi.* [Now Rare] to solve arithmetical problems

**cir·ca** (sur′kə) *prep.* [L.] about: used to indicate an approximate date

**cir·ca·di·an** (sur kā′dē ən) *adj.* [< L. *circa*, about + *dies*, day] of the physiological rhythms associated with the 24-hour cycle of the earth's rotation

**Cir·ce** (sur′sē) in the *Odyssey*, an enchantress who turned men to swine

**cir·cle** (sur′k'l) *n.* [< Gr. *kirkos*] 1. a plane figure bounded by a single curved line every point of which is equally distant from the center 2. this curved line 3. anything like a circle, as a ring 4. a complete or recurring series; cycle 5. a group of people with common interests 6. extent; scope, as of influence —*vt.* **-cled, -cling** 1. to form a circle around 2. to move around, as in a circle —*vi.* to go around in a circle —**cir′cler** *n.*

**cir′clet** (-klit) *n.* 1. a small circle 2. a circular band for the finger, etc.

**cir·cuit** (sur′kit) *n.* [< L. *circum-*, around + *ire*, go] 1. a boundary line or its length 2. a going around something 3. the regular journey through a district of a person in his work 4. a chain or association, as of theaters or resorts 5. the path or line of an electric current —*vi.* to go in a circuit —*vt.* to make a circuit about —**cir′cuit·al** *adj.*

**circuit breaker** a device that automatically interrupts the flow of an electric current

**cir·cu·i·tous** (sər kyōō′ə təs) *adj.* roundabout; indirect —**cir·cu′i·tous·ly** *adv.* —**cir·cu′i·ty** *n.*

**cir·cuit·ry** (sur′kə trē) *n.* the system or the elements of an electric circuit

**cir·cu·lar** (sur′kyə lər) *adj.* **1.** in the shape of a circle; round **2.** moving in a circle **3.** circuitous —*n.* an advertisement, etc. intended for many —cir′cu·lar′i·ty (-ler′ə tē) *n.*

**cir·cu·lar·ize** (-lə rīz′) *vt.* -ized′, -iz′ing **1.** to make circular **2.** to send circulars to **3.** to canvass —cir′cu·lar·i·za′tion *n.* —cir′cu·lar·iz′er *n.*

**cir·cu·late** (sur′kyə lāt′) *vi.* -lat′ed, -lat′ing [< L. *circulari*, form a circle] **1.** to move in a circle or circuit and return, as the blood **2.** to go from person to person or from place to place —*vt.* to make circulate —cir′cu·la′tor *n.* —cir′cu·la·to′ry (-lə tôr′ē) *adj.*

**cir·cu·la′tion** *n.* **1.** a circulating **2.** the movement of the blood through veins and arteries **3.** distribution of newspapers, magazines, etc.

**circum-** [< L. *circum*] *a prefix meaning* around, about, surrounding

**cir·cum·cise** (sur′kəm sīz′) *vt.* -cised′, -cis′ing [< L. *circum*-, around + *caedere*, to cut] to cut off all or part of the foreskin of —cir′cum·ci′sion (-sizh′ən) *n.*

**cir·cum·fer·ence** (sər kum′fər əns) *n.* [< L. *circum*-, around + *ferre*, carry] **1.** the line bounding a circle, ball, etc. **2.** length of this line

**cir·cum·flex** (sur′kəm fleks′) *n.* [< L. *circum*-, around + *flectere*, to bend] a mark (^, `, ~) used over a vowel to indicate pronunciation

**cir·cum·lo·cu′tion** (-lō kyōō′shən) *n.* [< L.: see CIRCUM- & LOCUTION] a roundabout way of saying something

**cir·cum·nav′i·gate′** (-nav′ə gāt′) *vt.* -gat′ed, -gat′ing [< L.: see CIRCUM- & NAVIGATE] to sail or fly around (the earth, etc.) —cir′cum·nav′i·ga′tion *n.*

**cir·cum·scribe′** (-skrīb′) *vt.* -scribed′, -scrib′ing [< L.: see CIRCUM- & SCRIBE] **1.** to trace a line around; encircle **2.** to limit; confine —cir′cum·scrip′tion (-skrip′shən) *n.*

**cir·cum·spect′** (-spekt′) *adj.* [< L. *circum*-, around + *specere*, look] cautious —cir′cum·spec′tion *n.*

**cir·cum·stance′** (-stans′) *n.* [< L. *circum*-, around + *stare*, stand] **1.** a fact or event accompanying another **2.** [*pl.*] conditions affecting one, esp. financial conditions **3.** mere chance **4.** much ceremony —under no circumstances never —cir′cum·stanced′ *adj.*

**cir′cum·stan′tial** (-stan′shəl) *adj.* **1.** having to do with or depending on circumstances **2.** incidental **3.** complete in detail

**circumstantial evidence** *Law* indirect evidence of a fact at issue, based on attendant circumstances

**cir′cum·stan′ti·ate′** (-stan′shē āt′) *vt.* -at′ed, -at′ing to give detailed proof or support of —cir′cum·stan′ti·a′tion *n.*

**cir′cum·vent′** (-vent′) *vt.* [< L. *circum*-, around + *venire*, come] to get the better of or prevent by craft or ingenuity —cir′cum·ven′tion *n.*

**cir·cus** (sur′kəs) *n.* [L., a circle] **1.** in ancient Rome, an amphitheater **2.** a traveling show of clowns, acrobats, trained animals, etc. **3.** [Colloq.] a source of much fun

**ci·ré** (sə rā′) *adj.* [< Fr. *cire*, wax] having a smooth, glossy finish

**cirque** (surk) *n.* [see CIRCUS] a natural amphitheater in a mountainside

**cir·rho·sis** (sə rō′sis) *n.* [< Gr. *kirrhos*, tawny + -OSIS] a degenerative disease, esp. of the liver, marked by excess formation of connective tissue

**cir·rus** (sir′əs) *n.* [L., a curl] a formation of clouds in wispy filaments or feathery tufts

**cis·tern** (sis′tərn) *n.* [< L. *cista* chest] a large tank for storing water

**cit·a·del** (sit′ə d'l, -del′) *n.* [< L. *civitas*, city] a fortress

**cite** (sīt) *vt.* cit′ed, cit′ing [< L. *citare*, summon] **1.** to summon before a court of law **2.** to quote **3.** to mention by way of example, proof, etc. **4.** to mention in an official report as meritorious —ci·ta′tion *n.*

**cit·i·fied** (sit′i fīd′) *adj.* having the ways, dress, etc. of city people

**cit·i·zen** (sit′ə zən) *n.* [< L. *civis*] a member of a state or nation who owes allegiance to it by birth or naturalization and is entitled to full civil rights —cit′i·zen·ship′ *n.*

**cit′i·zen·ry** (-rē) *n.* all citizens as a group

**cit·ric** (si′trik) *adj.* designating or of an acid obtained from citrus fruits

**cit′ron** (-trən) *n.* [Fr. < L.: see CITRUS] **1.** a yellow, thick-skinned, lemonlike fruit **2.** its rind candied

**cit·ron·el·la** (si′trə nel′ə) *n.* [ModL.] a sharp-smelling oil used in perfume, soap, insect repellents, etc.

**cit·rus** (si′trəs) *n.* [L.] **1.** any of the trees bearing oranges, lemons, limes, etc. **2.** any such fruit —*adj.* of these trees: also citrous

**cit·y** (sit′ē) *n., pl.* -ies [< L. *civis*, citizen] **1.** a population center larger or more important than a town **2.** in the U.S., an incorporated municipality with boundaries, powers, etc. defined by state charter **3.** the people of a city —*adj.* of a city

**city hall** a building housing a municipal government

**civ·et** (siv′it) *n.* [< Ar. *zabād*] **1.** the musky secretion of a catlike, flesh-eating animal (civet cat) of Africa and S Asia: used in some perfumes **2.** the animal, or its fur

**civ·ic** (siv′ik) *adj.* [< L. *civis*, citizen] of a city, citizens, or citizenship

**civ′ics** (-iks) *n.pl.* [*with sing. v.*] the study of civic affairs and the duties and rights of citizenship

**civ·il** (siv′'l) *adj.* [see CIVIC] **1.** of a

citizen or citizens **2.** civilized **3.** polite **4.** of citizens in matters not military or religious —**civ′il·ly** adv.

**civil disobedience** nonviolent opposition to a law by refusing to comply with it, on the grounds of conscience

**civil engineering** engineering dealing with the construction of bridges, roads, etc. —**civil engineer**

**ci·vil·ian** (sə vil′yən) n. [see CIVIC] a person not in military or naval service —adj. of civilians; nonmilitary

**ci·vil·i·ty** (-ə tē) n., pl. -ties **1.** politeness **2.** a civil, or polite, act

**civ·i·li·za·tion** (siv′ə lə zā′shən) n. **1.** a civilizing or being civilized **2.** the total culture of a people, period, etc. **3.** the peoples considered to have reached a high social development

**civ·i·lize** (siv′ə līz′) vt., vi. -lized′, -liz′ing [see CIVIC] **1.** to bring out of a condition of savagery or barbarism to a higher level of social organization, esp. in the arts and sciences **2.** to refine —**civ′i·lized′** adj.

**civil law** the body of law having to do with private rights

**civil liberties** liberties guaranteed to the individual by law; rights of thinking, speaking, and acting as one likes without hindrance except in the interests of public welfare

**civil rights** those rights guaranteed to the individual, esp. by the 13th, 14th, 15th, and 19th Amendments to the U.S. Constitution

**civil servant** a civil service employee

**civil service** those employed in government service, esp. through public competitive examination

**civil war** war between different factions of the same nation —**the Civil War** the war between the North and the South in the U.S. (1861–1865)

**civ·vies** (siv′ēz) n.pl. [Colloq.] civilian clothes; also sp. **civ′ies**

**ck.** pl. **cks. 1.** cask **2.** check

**Cl** Chem. chlorine

**clack** (klak) vi., vt. [prob. echoic < ON.] to make or cause to make a sudden, sharp sound —n. this sound

**clad** (klad) alt. pt. & pp. of CLOTHE —adj. clothed; dressed

**claim** (klām) vt. [< L. clamare, cry out] **1.** to demand as rightfully belonging to one **2.** to require; deserve [to claim attention] **3.** to assert —n. **1.** a claiming **2.** a right to something **3.** something claimed —**claim′a·ble** adj. —**claim′ant, claim′er** n.

**clair·voy·ance** (kler voi′əns) n. [Fr. < clair, clear + voyant, seeing] the supposed ability to perceive things not in sight —**clair·voy′ant** n., adj.

**clam** (klam) n. [< earlier clam, a clamp] a hard-shelled bivalve mollusk —vi. clammed, clam′ming to dig for clams —**clam up** [Colloq.] to keep silent

**clam·bake′** n. **1.** a picnic at which steamed or baked clams are served **2.** [Colloq.] any large, noisy party

**clam·ber** (klam′bər) vi., vt. [ME. clambren] to climb clumsily, esp. by using both hands and feet

**clam·my** (klam′ē) adj. -mi·er, -mi-

est [ME. < clam, mud] moist, cold, and sticky —**clam′mi·ness** n.

**clam·or** (klam′ər) n. [< L. clamare, cry out] **1.** a loud outcry; uproar **2.** a loud demand or complaint —vi. to make a clamor —**clam′or·ous** adj.

**clamp** (klamp) n. [< MDu. klampe] a device for clasping or fastening things together —vt. to fasten or brace, as with a clamp —**clamp down (on)** to become more strict (with)

**clan** (klan) n. [< Gael. < L. planta, offshoot] **1.** a group of families claiming descent from a common ancestor **2.** a group of people with interests in common —**clan′nish** adj. —**clans·man** (klanz′mən) n., pl. -men

**clan·des·tine** (klan des′t'n) adj. [< L. clam, secret] secret or hidden; furtive —**clan·des′tine·ly** adv.

**clang** (klaŋ) vi., vt. [echoic] to make or cause to make a loud, ringing sound, as by striking metal —n. this sound

**clan′gor** (-ər) n. [L. < clangere, to sound] a continuous clanging sound

**clank** (klaŋk) n. [echoic] a sharp metallic sound —vi., vt. to make or cause to make this sound

**clap** (klap) vi. clapped, clap′ping [OE. clæppan, to beat] **1.** to make the explosive sound of two flat surfaces struck together **2.** to strike the hands together, as in applause —vt. **1.** to strike together briskly **2.** to strike with an open hand **3.** to put, move, etc. abruptly [clapped into jail] —n. **1.** the sound or act of clapping **2.** a sharp slap

**clap·board** (klab′ərd, klap′bôrd′) n. [transl. of MDu. klapholt < klappen, to fit + holt, wood] a thin board with one thicker edge, used as siding —vt. to cover with clapboards

**clap′per** n. a thing that makes a clapping sound, as the tongue of a bell

**clap′trap′** n. [CLAP + TRAP[1]] insincere, empty talk intended to get applause —adj. showy and cheap

**claque** (klak) n. [Fr. < claquer, to clap] a group of people paid to applaud at a play, opera, etc.

**clar·et** (klar′it) n. [< L. clarus, clear] a dry red wine

**clar·i·fy** (klar′ə fī′) vt., vi. -fied′, -fy′ing [< L. clarus, clear + facere, make] to make or become clear —**clar′i·fi·ca′tion** n.

**clar·i·net** (klar′ə net′) n. [< Fr. < L. clarus, clear] a single-reed, woodwind instrument played by means of holes and keys —**clar′i·net′ist, clar′i·net′tist** n.

**clar·i·on** (klar′ē ən) adj. [< L. clarus, clear] clear, sharp, and ringing [a clarion call]

**clar·i·ty** (klar′ə tē) n. [< L. clarus, clear] clear quality; clearness

CLARINET

**clash** (klash) vi. [echoic] **1.** to collide with a loud, harsh, metallic noise **2.** to conflict; disagree —vt. to strike with a clashing noise —n. **1.** the sound of clashing **2.** conflict

**clasp** (klasp) *n.* [ME. *claspe*] 1. a fastening, as a hook, to hold things together 2. a grasping; embrace 3. a grip of the hand —*vt.* 1. to fasten with a clasp 2. to hold or embrace tightly 3. to grip with the hand

**class** (klas) *n.* [< L. *classis*] 1. a number of people or things grouped together because of likenesses; kind; sort 2. social or economic rank [*the working class*] 3. *a)* a group of students taught together *b)* a group graduating together 4. grade or quality 5. [Slang] excellence, as of style —*vt.* to classify —*vi.* to be classified —**class′less** *adj.*

**class action** (**suit**) a legal action brought by one or more persons on behalf of themselves and a much larger group

**clas·sic** (klas′ik) *adj.* [< L. *classis*, class] 1. being an excellent model of its kind 2. of the art, literature, etc. of the ancient Greeks and Romans 3. balanced, formal, simple, etc. 4. famous as traditional or typical —*n.* 1. a literary or artistic work of the highest excellence 2. a creator of such a work 3. a famous traditional or typical event —**the classics** ancient Greek and Roman literature

**clas′si·cal** (-i k′l) *adj.* 1. *same as* CLASSIC (senses 1, 2, 3) 2. versed in Greek and Roman literature, etc. 3. designating or of music conforming to certain standards of form, complexity, etc. 4. standard and traditional [*classical economics*] —**clas′si·cal·ly** *adv.*

**clas′si·cism** (-ə siz′m) *n.* 1. the aesthetic principles of ancient Greece and Rome 2. adherence to these principles 3. knowledge of classical art and literature —**clas′si·cist** *n.*

**classified advertising** advertising under such listings as *help wanted*

**clas·si·fy** (klas′ə fi′) *vt.* -**fied′**, -**fy′ing** 1. to arrange in classes according to a system 2. to designate (government documents) to be secret or restricted —**clas′si·fi·ca′tion** *n.* —**clas′si·fi′er** *n.*

**class′mate′** *n.* a member of the same class at a school or college

**class′room′** *n.* a room where a class is taught at a school or college

**class′y** *adj.* -**i·er**, -**i·est** [Slang] first-class, esp. in style; elegant

**clat·ter** (klat′ər) *vi., vt.* [ME. *clateren*] to make or cause to make a clatter —*n.* 1. a rapid succession of loud, sharp noises 2. a tumult; hubbub

**clause** (klôz) *n.* [< L. *claudere*, to close] 1. a group of words containing a subject and verb: an independent (principal) clause can stand alone as a sentence; a dependent (subordinate) clause functions as a noun, adjective, or adverb 2. a particular article or provision in a document

**claus·tro·pho·bi·a** (klôs′trə fō′bē ə) *n.* [< L. *claustrum*, enclosure + -PHOBIA] a fear of enclosed places —**claus′tro·pho′bic** *adj.*

**clav·i·chord** (klav′ə kôrd′) *n.* [< L. *clavis*, key + *chorda*, a string] a stringed musical instrument with a keyboard: predecessor of the piano

**clav·i·cle** (klav′ə k′l) *n.* [< L. *clavis*, key] a bone connecting the breastbone with the shoulder blade

**cla·vi·er** (klə vir′; *for 1, also* klav′ē ər) *n.* [Fr. < L. *clavis*, key] 1. the keyboard of an organ, piano, etc. 2. any stringed keyboard instrument

**claw** (klô) *n.* [OE. *clawu*] 1. a sharp, hooked nail on an animal's or bird's foot 2. the pincers of a lobster, etc. —*vt., vi.* to scratch, clutch, etc. as with claws

**clay** (klā) *n.* [OE. *clæg*] 1. a firm, plastic earth, used in making bricks, etc. 2. *a)* earth *b)* the human body —**clay′ey** *adj.* **clay′i·er**, **clay′i·est**

**clean** (klēn) *adj.* [OE. *clæne*] 1. free from dirt and impurities; unsoiled 2. morally pure 3. fair; sportsmanlike 4. neat and tidy 5. free from flaws; 6. thorough —*adv.* completely —*vt., vi.* to make or be made clean —**clean up** 1. to make neat 2. [Colloq.] to finish 3. [Slang] to make much profit —**come clean** [Slang] to confess —**clean′ly** *adv.* —**clean′ness** *n.*

**clean′-cut′** *adj.* 1. clearly outlined 2. well-formed 3. trim, neat, etc.

**clean′er** *n.* a person or thing that cleans; esp., one who dry-cleans

**clean·ly** (klen′lē) *adj.* -**li·er**, -**li·est** 1. having clean habits 2. always kept clean —**clean′li·ness** *n.*

**clean room** a room, as in a computer center, designed to be nearly 100% free of dust, pollen, etc.

**cleanse** (klenz) *vt.* **cleansed, cleans′ing** [OE. *clænsian*] to make clean, pure, etc. —**cleans′er** *n.*

**clean′up′** *n.* 1. a cleaning up 2. elimination of crime 3. [Slang] profit; gain

**clear** (klir) *adj.* [< L. *clarus*] 1. bright; free from clouds 2. transparent 3. easily seen or heard; distinct 4. keen or logical [*a clear mind*] 5. not obscure; obvious 6. certain; positive 7. free from guilt 8. free from deductions; net 9. free from debt 10. free from obstruction; open —*adv.* 1. in a clear manner 2. all the way; completely —*vt.* 1. to make clear 2. to free from impurities, blemishes, etc. 3. to make lucid 4. to open [*clear a path*] 5. to get rid of 6. to prove the innocence of 7. to pass or leap over, by, etc., esp. without touching 8. to be passed or approved by 9. to make as profit —*vi.* to become clear —**clear away** (or **off**) 1. to remove so as to leave a cleared space 2. to go away —**clear out** [Colloq.] to depart —**clear up** to make or become clear —**in the clear** 1. free from obstructions 2. [Colloq.] guiltless —**clear′ly** *adv.* —**clear′ness** *n.*

**clear′ance** (-əns) *n.* 1. the clear space between an object and that which it is passing 2. the adjustment of accounts in a clearinghouse

---

fat, āpe, cär; ten, ēven; is, bīte; gō, hôrn, tōōl, look; oil, out; up, fur; chin; she; thin, then; zh, leisure; ŋ, ring; ə for a in ago; ', (ā′b'l); ë, Fr. coeur; ö, Fr. feu; Fr. mon; ü, Fr. duc; kh, G. ich, doch; ‡ foreign; < derived from

**clear'-cut'** *adj.* 1. clearly outlined 2. distinct; definite

**clear'ing** *n.* an area of land cleared of trees

**clear'ing·house'** *n.* an office maintained by several banks for exchanging checks, balancing accounts, etc.

**cleat** (klēt) *n.* [< ME.] a piece of wood or metal fastened to something to strengthen it or give secure footing

**cleav·age** (klē'vij) *n.* 1. a cleaving; dividing 2. a cleft; fissure; division

**cleave¹** (klēv) *vt., vi.* **cleaved** or **cleft** or **clove**, **cleaved** or **cleft** or **clo'ven**, **cleav'ing** [OE. *cleofan*] to divide by a blow; split; sever —**cleav'a·ble** *adj.*

**cleave²** (klēv) *vi.* **cleaved**, **cleav'ing** [OE. *cleofian*] 1. to adhere; cling (*to*) 2. to be faithful (*to*)

**cleav'er** *n.* a heavy cutting tool with a broad blade, used by butchers

**clef** (klef) *n.* [Fr. < L. *clavis*, key] a symbol used in music to indicate the pitch of the notes on the staff

**cleft** (kleft) *alt. pt. & pp. of* CLEAVE¹ —*adj.* split; divided —*n.* an opening made by cleaving; crack; crevice

**clem·a·tis** (klem'ə tis) *n.* [< Gr. *klēma*, vine] a vine of the buttercup family, with bright-colored flowers

**Clem·ens** (klem'ənz), **Samuel L.** (pseud. *Mark Twain*) 1835–1910; U.S. writer

**clem·ent** (klem'ənt) *adj.* [L. *clemens*] 1. lenient; merciful 2. mild, as weather —**clem'en·cy** (-ən sē) *n.*

**clench** (klench) *vt.* [< OE. (*be-)clencan*, make cling] 1. to close (the teeth or fist) firmly 2. to grip tightly —*n.* a firm grip

**Cle·o·pa·tra** (klē'ə pat'rə, -pā'trə) 69?–30 B.C.; queen of Egypt (51–30)

**clere·sto·ry** (klir'stôr'ē) *n., pl.* **-ries** [< ME. *cler*, CLEAR + *storie*, STORY²] an outside wall with windows that rises above a roofed section of a building

**cler·gy** (klur'jē) *n., pl.* **-gies** [see CLERK] ministers, priests, rabbis, etc., collectively

**cler'gy·man** (-mən) *n., pl.* **-men** a minister, priest, rabbi, etc.

**cler·ic** (kler'ik) *n.* a clergyman

**cler'i·cal** (-i k'l) *adj.* 1. of a clergyman or the clergy 2. of an office clerk or clerks; of office work

**cler'i·cal·ism** (-iz'm) *n.* political power of the clergy —**cler'i·cal·ist** *n.*

**clerk** (klurk) *n.* [< Gr. *klēros*, clergy] 1. a layman with minor duties in a church 2. an office worker who types, files, etc. 3. a public official who keeps the records of a court, town, etc. 4. a salesclerk —*vi.* to work as a salesclerk

**Cleve·land** (klēv'lənd) city and port in NE Ohio: pop. 751,000

**Cleveland, (Stephen) Gro·ver** (grō'vər) 1837–1908; 22d and 24th president of the U.S. (1885–89; 1893–97)

**clev·er** (klev'ər) *adj.* [? < Norw. *klöver*] 1. skillful; adroit 2. intelligent; ingenious; smart —**clev'er·ly** *adv.* —**clev'er·ness** *n.*

**clev·is** (klev'is) *n.* [see CLEAVE²] a U-shaped piece of iron with holes for a pin for attaching one thing to another

**clew** (klōō) *n.* [OE. *cliwen*] 1. a ball of thread or yarn 2. *same as* CLUE 3. a metal loop in the corner of a sail

**cli·ché** (klē shā') *n.* [Fr. < *clicher*, to stereotype] a trite expression

**click** (klik) *n.* [echoic] a slight, sharp sound like that of a door latch snapping into place —*vi., vt.* to make or cause to make a click

**cli·ent** (klī'ənt) *n.* [< L. *cliens*, follower] 1. a person or company for whom a lawyer, accountant, etc. is acting 2. a customer

**cli·en·tele** (klī'ən tel') *n.* [< Fr. < L. *clientela*, patronage] all one's clients or customers, collectively

**cliff** (klif) *n.* [OE. *clif*] a high, steep face of rock, esp. on a coast

**cliff'hang'er** (-haŋ'ər) *n.* a suspenseful movie, story, situation, etc.

**cli·mac·ter·ic** (klī mak'tər ik, klī' mak ter'ik) *n.* [< Gr. *klimax*, ladder] a crucial period in life, esp. the menopause —*adj.* crucial

**cli·mate** (klī'mət) *n.* [< Gr. *klima*, region] 1. the prevailing weather conditions of a place 2. a region with reference to its prevailing weather —**cli·mat'ic** (-mat'ik) *adj.*

**cli·max** (klī'maks) *n.* [L. < Gr. *klimax*, ladder] 1. the final, culminating element in a series; highest point of interest, excitement, etc. 2. the turning point of action in a drama, story, etc. —*vi., vt.* to reach, or bring to, a climax —**cli·mac'tic** (-mak'tik) *adj.*

**climb** (klīm) *vi., vt.* **climbed**, **climb'ing** [OE. *climban*] 1. to move up by using the feet and often the hands 2. to move (*down, over, along*, etc.) using the hands and feet 3. to ascend gradually 4. to grow upward —*n.* 1. a climbing 2. a place to be climbed —**climb'er** *n.*

**clime** (klīm) *n.* [see CLIMATE] [Poet.] a region, esp. with regard to climate

**clinch** (klinch) *vt.* [var. of CLENCH] 1. to fasten (a driven nail, etc.) by bending the projecting end 2. to settle (an argument, bargain, etc.) definitely —*vi.* 1. *Boxing* to grip the opponent with the arms so as to hinder his punching 2. [Slang] to embrace —*n.* a clinching

**clinch'er** *n.* 1. one that clinches 2. a decisive point, argument, etc.

**cling** (kliŋ) *vi.* **clung**, **cling'ing** [OE. *clingan*] 1. to adhere; hold fast, as by embracing 2. to be or stay near 3. to be emotionally attached

**clin·ic** (klin'ik) *n.* [< Gr. *klinē*, bed] 1. the teaching of medicine by treating patients in the presence of students 2. a place where medical specialists practice as a group 3. an outpatient department, as of a hospital

**clin'i·cal** (-i k'l) *adj.* 1. of or connected with a clinic or sickbed 2. having to do with the treatment and observation of patients, as distinguished from theoretical study 3. purely scientific; impersonal —**clin'i·cal·ly** *adv.*

**cli·ni·cian** (kli nish'ən) *n.* one who practices clinical medicine, psychology, etc.

**clink** (kliŋk) vi., vt. [echoic] to make or cause to make a slight, sharp sound, as of glass struck —n. 1. such a sound 2. [Colloq.] a jail

**clink′er** n. [Du. klinker] 1. [Archaic] a hard brick 2. a hard mass of fused matter, formed as from burned coal 3. [Slang] a mistake

**clip¹** (klip) vt. clipped, clip′ping [< ON. klippa] 1. to cut as with shears 2. to cut short 3. to cut the hair of 4. [Colloq.] to hit sharply 5. [Slang] to swindle —vi. to move rapidly —n. 1. a clipping 2. a thing clipped 3. a rapid pace 4. [Colloq.] a quick, sharp punch 5. same as CLIPPED FORM

**clip²** (klip) vt., vi. clipped, clip′ping [OE. clyppan, to embrace] to grip tightly; fasten —n. anything that clips or fastens [a paper clip]

**clip′board′** n. a writing board with a clip at the top to hold papers

**clip joint** [Slang] a nightclub, store, etc. that charges excessive prices

**clipped form** (or **word**) a shortened form of a word, as pike (for turnpike)

**clip·per** (klip′ər) n. 1. [usually pl.] a tool for cutting or trimming 2. a sailing ship built for great speed

CLIPPER SHIP

**clip′ping** n. a piece cut out or off, as an item clipped from a newspaper

**clique** (klēk) n. [Fr. < cliquer, make a noise] a small, exclusive circel of people; coterie —cliqu′ish adj. —cliqu′ish·ly adv. —cliqu′ish·ness n.

**cli·to·ris** (klit′ər əs) n. [< Gr.] a small, sensitive organ of the vulva

**cloak** (klōk) n. [< ML. clocca, bell: from its shape] 1. a loose, usually sleeveless outer garment 2. something that covers or conceals; disguise —vt. 1. to cover with a cloak 2. to conceal

**clob·ber** (kläb′ər) vt. [< ?] [Slang] 1. to beat or hit repeatedly 2. to defeat decisively

**cloche** (klōsh) n. [Fr. < ML. clocca, a bell] a closefitting, bell-shaped hat for women

**clock¹** (kläk) n. [ME. clokke, orig., clock with bells < ML. clocca, bell] a device for measuring and indicating time, usually by means of pointers moving over a dial —vt. to record the time of (a race, etc.) with a stopwatch

**clock²** (kläk) n. [< ? prec., because of orig. bell shape] a woven or embroidered ornament on a sock, going up from the ankle

**clock′wise′** (-wīz′) adv., adj. in the direction in which the hands of a clock rotate

**clock′work′** (-wurk′) n. 1. the mechanism of a clock 2. any similar mechanism, with springs and gears —like clockwork very regularly

**clod** (kläd) n. [OE.] 1. a lump, esp. of earth or clay 2. a dull, stupid fellow —clod′dish adj. —clod′dy adj.

**clod′hop′per** (-häp′ər) n. [prec. + HOPPER] 1. a plowman 2. a clumsy, stupid fellow 3. a coarse, heavy shoe

**clog** (kläg) n. [ME. clogge, lump of wood] 1. anything that hinders or obstructs 2. a shoe with a thick, usually wooden, sole —vt. clogged, clog′ging 1. to hinder 2. to obstruct (a passage); stop up; jam —vi. to become stopped up —clog′gy adj.

**cloi·son·né** (kloi′zə nā′) adj. [Fr., lit., partitioned] denoting enamel work in which the surface decoration is set in hollows formed by thin strips of wire

**clois·ter** (klois′tər) n. [< L. claudere, to close] 1. a monastery or convent 2. monastic life 3. a covered walk along a courtyard wall with an open colonnade —vt. to confine as in a cloister

**clomp** (klämp) vi. to walk heavily or noisily

**clone** (klōn) n. [< Gr. klōn, a twig] an identical duplicate of an organism produced by replacing the nucleus of an unfertilized ovum with the nucleus of a body cell from the organism —vt. cloned, clon′ing to produce as a clone

**clop** (kläp) n. a clapping sound as of a hoofbeat —vi. clopped, clop′ping to make, or move with, such sounds

**close¹** (klōs) adj. clos′er, clos′est [see ff.] 1. confined or confining [close quarters] 2. hidden; secluded 3. secretive; reserved 4. miserly; stingy 5. warm and stuffy, as stale air 6. with little space between; near together 7. compact; dense [a close weave] 8. near to the surface [a close shave] 9. intimate; familiar [a close friend] 10. strict; careful [close attention] 11. nearly alike [a close resemblance] 12. nearly equal or even [a close contest] 13. hard to get [credit is close] —adv. in a close manner —close′ly adv. —close′ness n.

**close²** (klōz) vt. closed, clos′ing [< L. claudere, to close] 1. to shut 2. to stop up (an opening) 3. to finish; conclude —vi. 1. to undergo shutting 2. to come to an end 3. to come close or together —n. an end or conclusion —**close down** (or **up**) to shut or stop entirely —**close in** to draw near from all directions; surround —**close out** to dispose of (a stock of goods) by sale

**close call** (klōs) [Colloq.] a narrow escape from danger: also **close shave**

**closed circuit** a system for telecasting by cable only to receivers connected in the circuit —**closed′-cir′cuit** adj.

**close-fist·ed** (klōs′fis′tid) adj. stingy

**close′-fit′ting** adj. fitting tightly

**close′-knit′** adj. closely united

**close′mouthed′** (-mouthd′, -moutht′) adj. not talking much; taciturn

**clos·et** (kläz′it) n. [< L. claudere, to close] 1. a small room or cupboard for clothes, supplies, etc. 2. a small room for privacy —*vt.* to shut up in a private room for confidential talk

**close-up** (klōs'up') *n.* a photograph, etc. taken at very close range

**clo·sure** (klō'zhər) *n.* [< L. *claudere,* to close] 1. a closing or being closed 2. a finish; end 3. anything that closes 4. *same as* CLOTURE

**clot** (klät) *n.* [OE.] a soft lump or thickened mass *[a blood clot]* —*vt., vi.* **clot'ted, clot'ting** to form into a clot or clots; coagulate

**cloth** (klôth) *n., pl.* **cloths** (klôthz, klôths) [OE. *clath*] 1. a woven, knitted, or pressed fabric of fibrous material, as cotton, wool, silk, synthetic fibers, etc. 2. a tablecloth, washcloth, dustcloth, etc. —*adj.* made of cloth —**the cloth** the clergy

**clothe** (klōth) *vt.* **clothed** or **clad, cloth'ing** [see prec.] 1. to provide with or dress in clothes 2. to cover

**clothes** (klōz, klōthz) *n.pl.* [OE. *clathas*] clothing; wearing apparel

**clothes'pin'** *n.* a small clip for fastening clothes on a line

**cloth·ier** (klōth'yər) *n.* a dealer in clothes or cloth

**cloth·ing** (klō'thin) *n.* 1. wearing apparel; clothes 2. a covering

**clo·ture** (klō'chər) *n.* [see CLOSURE] the ending of legislative debate by having the bill put to immediate vote

**cloud** (kloud) *n.* [OE. *clud,* mass of rock] 1. a visible mass of vapor in the sky 2. a mass of smoke, dust, steam, etc. 3. a crowd; swarm *[a cloud of locusts]* 4. anything that darkens, obscures, etc. —*vt.* 1. to darken or obscure as with clouds 2. to make gloomy 3. to sully —*vi.* to become cloudy, gloomy, etc. —**in the clouds** 1. impractical 2. in a daydream —**under a cloud** under suspicion — **cloud'less** *adj.* —**cloud'y** *adj.* **-i·er, -i·est**

**cloud'burst'** *n.* a sudden, heavy rain

**clout** (klout) *n.* [< OE. *clut,* a patch] a blow, as with the hand —*vt.* 1. [Colloq.] to strike, as with the hand 2. [Slang] to hit (a ball) a far distance

**clove¹** (klōv) *n.* [< L. *clavus,* nail: from its shape] 1. the dried flower bud of a tropical evergreen tree, used as a spice 2. the tree

**clove²** (klōv) *n.* [OE. *clufu*] a segment of a bulb, as of garlic

**clove³** (klōv) *alt. pt.* of CLEAVE¹

**clo·ven** (klō'v'n) *alt. pp.* of CLEAVE¹ —*adj.* divided; split

**clo·ver** (klō'vər) *n.* [OE. *clafre*] any of various herbs with leaves of three leaflets and small flowers in dense heads: some are used for forage

**clo·ver·leaf'** (-lēf') *n., pl.* **-leafs'** a highway interchange with overpass and curving ramps, letting traffic move unhindered in any of four directions

**clown** (kloun) *n.* [< ? Fr. *colon,* farmer] 1. a clumsy or boorish person 2. one who entertains, as in a circus, by antics, jokes, etc. —*vi.* to act the clown —**clown'ish** *adj.*

**cloy** (kloi) *vt., vi.* [< OFr. *encloyer,* nail up < L. *clavus,* nail] to surfeit by too much that is sweet, rich, etc.

**club** (klub) *n.* [< ON. *klumba,* mass] 1. a heavy stick used as a weapon 2. any stick used in a game, as golf 3. *a)* a group of people associated for a common purpose *b)* its meeting place 4. *a)* any of a suit of playing cards marked with a black trefoil (♣) *b)* *[pl.]* this suit —*vt.* **clubbed, club'bing** to strike as with a club —*vi.* to unite for a common purpose

**club'foot'** *n., pl.* **-feet'** a congenitally misshapen, often clublike, foot

**club'house'** (-hous') *n.* 1. the building used by a club 2. a locker room used by an athletic team

**club soda** *same as* SODA WATER

**cluck** (kluk) *vi.* [echoic] to make a low, clicking sound, as of a hen calling her chicks —*n.* a clucking sound

**clue** (klōō) *n.* a fact, object, etc. that helps to solve a mystery or problem —*vt.* **clued, clu'ing** to provide with clues or needed facts

**clump** (klump) *n.* [< LowG. *klump*] 1. a lump; mass 2. a cluster, as of trees 3. the sound of heavy footsteps —*vi.* 1. to tramp heavily 2. to form clumps —**clump'y** *adj.* **-i·er, -i·est**

**clum·sy** (klum'zē) *adj.* **-si·er, -si·est** [ME. *clumsid,* numb with cold] 1. lacking grace or skill; awkward 2. awkwardly shaped or made —**clum'si·ly** *adv.* —**clum'si·ness** *n.*

**clung** (klun) *pt. & pp.* of CLING

**clunk·er** (klunk'ər) *n.* [echoic of its noisiness] [Slang] an old machine or automobile in poor repair

**clus·ter** (klus'tər) *n.* [OE. *clyster*] a number of persons or things grouped together —*vi., vt.* to gather or grow in a cluster

**clutch¹** (kluch) *vt.* [OE. *clyccan,* clench] to grasp or hold eagerly or tightly —*vi.* to snatch or seize (*at*) —*n.* 1. *[usually pl.]* power; control 2. a grasp; grip 3. a device for engaging and disengaging a motor or engine

**clutch²** (kluch) *n.* [< ON. *klekja,* hatch] 1. a nest of eggs 2. a brood of chicks 3. a cluster

**clut·ter** (klut'ər) *n.* [< CLOT] a number of things scattered in disorder; jumble —*vt.* to put into disorder; jumble (often with *up*)

**cm.** centimeter(s)

**co-** (kō) *a prefix shortened from* COM-, *meaning:* 1. together with *[cooperation]* 2. joint *[co-owner]* 3. equally *[coextensive]*

**Co** *Chem.* cobalt

**CO** Colorado

**Co., co.** *pl.* **Cos., cos.** 1. company 2. county

**C/O, c.o.** care of

**C.O., CO** Commanding Officer

**coach** (kōch) *n.* [< *Kócs,* village in Hungary] 1. a large, covered, four-wheeled carriage 2. a railroad passenger car 3. a bus 4. the lowest-priced class of airline accommodations 5. an instructor or trainer, as of athletes, actors, singers, etc. —*vt., vi.* to instruct and train (students, etc.)

**coach'man** (-mən) *n., pl.* **-men** the driver of a coach, or carriage

**co·ad·ju·tor** (kō aj'ə tər, kō'ə jōō'-)

*n.* [ < L. *co-*, together + *adjuvare*, help] an assistant, esp. to a bishop

**co·ag·u·late** (kō ag'yoo lāt') *vt.* **-lat'ed, -lat'ing** [ < L. *co-*, together + *agere*, drive] to cause (a liquid) to become semisolid; clot —*vi.* to become coagulated —**co·ag'u·lant** (-lənt) *n.* —**co·ag'u·la'tion** *n.* —**co·ag'u·la'tive** *adj.* —**co·ag'u·la'tor** *n.*

**coal** (kōl) *n.* [OE. *col*] 1. a black, combustible mineral used as fuel 2. a piece of coal 3. an ember —*vt., vi.* to supply or be supplied with coal —**haul (or rake, drag, call) over the coals** to criticize sharply

**co·a·lesce** (kō'ə les') *vi.* **-lesced', -lesc'ing** [ < L. *co-*, together + *alescere*, grow up] to unite into a single body or group —**co'a·les'cence** *n.*

**co'a·li'tion** (-lish'ən) *n.* [see prec.] a combination or union, esp. a temporary one

**coal oil** kerosene

**coal tar** a black, thick liquid obtained by the distillation of coal: used in dyes, medicines, etc.

**coarse** (kôrs) *adj.* [ < COURSE in sense of "usual"] 1. of poor quality; common 2. consisting of rather large particles [*coarse* sand] 3. rough; harsh 4. unrefined; vulgar; crude —**coarse'ly** *adv.* —**coarse'ness** *n.*

**coars'en** *vt., vi.* to make or become coarse

**coast** (kōst) *n.* [ < L. *costa*, rib, side] 1. land alongside the sea; seashore 2. a slide down an incline, as on a sled —*vi.* 1. to sail near or along a coast 2. to go down an incline, as on a sled 3. to continue in motion on momentum —**coast'al** *adj.*

**coast'er** *n.* 1. a person or thing that coasts 2. a small mat, etc. placed under a glass to protect a table

**coaster brake** a brake on a bicycle operated by reverse pressure on the pedals

**coast guard** a governmental force employed to defend a nation's coast, aid vessels in distress, etc.; specif. [C- G-], such a branch in the U.S. armed forces

**coast'line'** *n.* the outline of a coast

**coat** (kōt) *n.* [ < ML. *cota*, tunic] 1. a sleeved outer garment opening down the front 2. the natural covering of a plant or animal 3. a layer of a substance, as paint, over a surface —*vt.* to cover with a coat or layer

**coat'ing** *n.* a surface coat or layer

**coat of arms** heraldic insignia, as on a family escutcheon

**coat'tail'** (-tāl') *n.* either half of the divided lower back part of a coat

**co·au·thor** (kō ô'thər) *n.* a joint author; collaborator

**coax** (kōks) *vt., vi.* [ < obs. slang *cokes*, a fool] to urge or get with soft words, flattery, etc. —**coax'er** *n.* —**coax'ing·ly** *adv.*

**co·ax·i·al** (kō ak'sē əl) *adj.* 1. having a common axis 2. designating

a double-conductor high-frequency transmission line, as for television

**cob** (käb) *n.* [prob. < LowG.] 1. a corncob 2. a male swan 3. a short, thickset horse

**co·balt** (kō'bôlt) *n.* [ < G. *kobold*, demon of the mines] a hard, steel-gray metallic chemical element

**cob·ble** (käb'l) *vt.* **-bled, -bling** [ < ?] 1. to mend (shoes, etc.) 2. to mend or put together clumsily

**cob·bler** (käb'lər) *n.* 1. one who mends shoes 2. a deep-dish fruit pie

**cob'ble·stone'** *n.* a rounded stone formerly much used for paving streets

**co·bra** (kō'brə) *n.* [Port.] a very poisonous snake of Asia and Africa

**cob·web** (käb'web') *n.* [ < ME. *coppe*, spider + WEB] 1. a web spun by a spider 2. anything flimsy, gauzy, or ensnaring like this

**co·caine, co·cain** (kō kān') *n.* [ < *coca*, tropical shrub from whose leaves it is extracted] an alkaloid drug used as a narcotic and local anesthetic

**coc·cus** (käk'əs) *n., pl.* **coc'ci** (-sī) [ < Gr. *kokkos*, kernel] a spherically shaped bacterium

**coc·cyx** (käk'siks) *n., pl.* **coc·cy·ges** (käk sī'jēz) [ < Gr. *kokkyx*, cuckoo: it is shaped like a cuckoo's beak] a small, triangular bone at the base of the spine

**coch·i·neal** (käch'ə nēl') *n.* [ult. < L. *coccum*, a (red) berry] a red dye made from a dried Mexican insect

**coch·le·a** (käk'lē ə) *n., pl.* **-ae'** (-ē'), **-as** [ < Gr. *kochlias*, snail] the spiral-shaped part of the internal ear

**cock¹** (käk) *n.* [OE. *coc*] 1. a rooster or other male bird 2. a faucet or valve 3. *a)* the hammer of a gun *b)* its firing position 4. a jaunty tilt, as of a hat —*vt.* 1. to tilt jauntily 2. to raise or turn alertly 3. to set (a gun hammer) in firing position

**cock²** (käk) *n.* [ME. *cokke*] a small, cone-shaped pile, as of hay

**cock·ade** (kä kād') *n.* [ < Fr. *coq*, a cock] a rosette, knot of ribbon, etc., worn on the hat as a badge

**cock·a·ma·mie** (käk'ə mā'mē) *adj.* [ < DECALCOMANIA] [Slang] poor; inferior

**cock-and-bull story** (käk' 'n bool') an absurd, improbable story

**cock·a·too** (käk'ə too') *n., pl.* **-toos'** [ < Malay *kakatua*] a large, crested parrot of Australia & the East Indies

**cock·a·trice** (käk'ə tris') *n.* [ < L. *calcare*, to tread] a fabulous serpent supposedly able to kill by a look

**cock·crow** (käk'krō') *n.* dawn

**cocked hat** a three-cornered hat

**cock·er·el** (käk'ər əl) *n.* a young rooster, less than a year old

**cock·er (spaniel)** (käk'ər) [ < use in hunting woodcock] a small spaniel with long, silky hair and drooping ears

**cock·eyed'** (-īd') *adj.* [ < COCK¹, *v.* + EYE] 1. cross-eyed 2. [Slang] *a)* crooked; awry *b)* silly; foolish *c)* drunk

**cock′fight′** *n.* a fight between game-cocks, usually wearing metal spurs

**cock·le¹** (käk′′l) *n.* [< Gr. *konchē*, mussel] an edible shellfish with two heart-shaped shells —**cockles of one's heart** one's deepest emotions

**cock·le²** (käk′′l) *n.* [OE. *coccel*] any of various weeds in grainfields

**cock·ney** (käk′nē) *n., pl.* **-neys** [ME. *cokenei*, spoiled child, milksop] [*often* **C-**] **1.** a native of the East End of London, England, speaking a characteristic dialect **2.** this dialect

**cock′pit′** *n.* **1.** a pit for cockfighting **2.** the space in a small airplane for the pilot and passengers or in a large airplane for the pilot and crew

**cock′roach′** (-rōch′) *n.* [Sp. *cucaracha*] an insect with long feelers and a flat body: a common household pest

**cocks·comb** (käks′kōm′) *n.* **1.** the red, fleshy growth on a rooster's head **2.** a plant with flowers like this

**cock·sure** (käk′shoor′) *adj.* [< COCK¹ + SURE] absolutely sure or self-confident, esp. in an arrogant way

**cock′tail′** (-tāl′) *n.* [< ?] **1.** a mixed alcoholic drink, usually iced **2.** an appetizer, as of shrimp or juice

**cock·y** (käk′ē) *adj.* **-i·er, -i·est** [< COCK¹ + -Y²] [Colloq.] jauntily conceited —**cock′i·ly** *adv.* —**cock′i·ness** *n.*

**co·co** (kō′kō) *n., pl.* **-cos** [< Gr. *kokkos*, berry] **1.** the coconut palm **2.** its fruit; coconut

**co·coa** (kō′kō) *n.* [see CACAO] **1.** powder made from roasted cacao seeds **2.** a drink made of this and hot milk, etc. **3.** a reddish-yellow brown

**cocoa butter** a yellowish-white fat made from cacao seeds

**co·co·nut, co·coa·nut** (kō′kə nut′) *n.* the fruit of a tropical tree (**coconut palm**), a thick, brown, oval husk with edible white meat and a sweet, milky fluid (**coconut milk**) inside

**co·coon** (kə kōōn′) *n.* [< ML. *coco*, shell] the silky case which the larvae of some insects spin about themselves as a shelter during the pupa stage

**cod** (käd) *n., pl.* **cod, cods** [ME.] a food fish of northern seas

**C.O.D., c.o.d.** collect on delivery

**Cod** (käd), **Cape** hook-shaped peninsula in E Mass.: 65 mi. long

**co·da** (kō′də) *n.* [It. < L. *cauda*, tail] *Music* a final passage

**cod·dle** (käd′′l) *vt.* **-dled, -dling** [< ?] **1.** to cook (esp. eggs) in water not quite boiling **2.** to pamper

**code** (kōd) *n.* [< L. *codex*, wooden tablet] **1.** a systematized body of laws **2.** a set of principles, as of ethics **3.** a set of signals for sending messages **4.** a system of symbols for secret writing, etc. —*vt.* **cod′ed, cod′ing** to put into code

**co·de·ine** (kō′dēn) *n.* [< Gr. *kōdeia*, poppy head] an alkaloid derived from opium: used for pain relief and in cough medicines: also **co′dein**

**co·dex** (kō′deks) *n., pl.* **-di·ces′** (-də sēz′) [see CODE] a manuscript volume, esp. of the Scriptures or a classic text

**cod′fish′** *n., pl.:* see FISH same as COD

**codg·er** (käj′ər) *n.* [< ?] [Colloq.] an eccentric fellow, esp. an older one

**cod·i·cil** (käd′i s′l) *n.* [< L. dim.: see CODE] an addition to a will

**cod·i·fy** (käd′ə fī′, kō′də-) *vt.* **-fied′, -fy′ing** to arrange (laws, etc.) systematically —**cod′i·fi·ca′tion** *n.* —**cod′i·fi′er** *n.*

**co-ed, co·ed** (kō′ed′) *n.* [Colloq.] a girl attending a coeducational college —*adj.* [Colloq.] **1.** coeducational **2.** of a coed

**co·ed·u·ca·tion** (kō′ej ə kā′shən) *n.* the educational system in which students of both sexes attend classes together —**co′ed·u·ca′tion·al** *adj.*

**co·ef·fi·cient** (kō′ə fish′ənt) *n.* [co- + EFFICIENT] **1.** a factor contributing to a result or measuring some physical property **2.** a multiplier of a variable or unknown quantity (as *6* in *6x*)

**co·e·qual** (kō ē′kwəl) *adj., n.* equal —**co′e·qual′i·ty** (-i kwäl′ə tē) *n.* —**co·e′qual·ly** *adv.*

**co·erce** (kō ʉrs′) *vt.* **-erced′, -erc′ing** [< L. *co-*, together + *arcere*, confine] **1.** to restrain by force **2.** to compel **3.** to enforce —**co·er′cion** (-ʉr′shən) *n.* —**co·er′cive** (-siv) *adj.*

**co·e·val** (kō ē′v′l) *adj., n.* [< L. *co-*, together + *aevum*, age] contemporary

**co′ex·ist′** (-ig zist′) *vi.* **1.** to exist together at the same time or in the same place **2.** to live together peacefully, despite differences —**co′ex·ist′ence** *n.* —**co′ex·ist′ent** *adj.*

**co′ex·ten′sive** (-ik sten′siv) *adj.* extending equally in time or space

**cof·fee** (kôf′ē) *n.* [< Ar. *qahwa*] **1.** a drink made from the roasted, ground, beanlike seeds of a tropical shrub of the madder family **2.** the seeds, whole or ground, or the shrub **3.** milky brown

**coffee break** a brief respite from work when coffee, etc. is taken

**cof′fee·cake′** *n.* a kind of cake or roll to be eaten with coffee, etc.

**cof′fee·house′** *n.* a place where coffee is served and people gather for talk, entertainment, etc.

**cof′fee·pot′** *n.* a pot with a spout, for brewing or serving coffee

**coffee shop** a small restaurant serving coffee and light refreshments or meals

**coffee table** a small, low table for serving refreshments

**cof·fer** (kôf′ər) *n.* [see ff.] **1.** a chest for holding money or valuables **2.** [*pl.*] a treasury; funds

**cof·fin** (kôf′in) *n.* [< Gr. *kophinos*, basket] the case or box in which a corpse is buried

**cog** (käg) *n.* [< Scand.] **1.** one of the teeth on the rim of a cogwheel **2.** a cogwheel

**co·gent** (kō′jənt) *adj.* [< L. *co-*, together + *agere*, drive] convincingly to the point —**co′gen·cy** *n.*

**cog·i·tate** (käj′ə tāt′) *vi., vt.* **-tat′ed, -tat′ing** [< L.] to think deeply (about); ponder —**cog′i·ta′tion** *n.* —**cog′i·ta′tive** *adj.* —**cog′i·ta′tor** *n.*

**co·gnac** (kōn′yak) *n.* [Fr.] brandy; specif., a brandy from Cognac, France

**cog·nate** (käg′nāt) *adj.* [< L. *co-*,

together + (g)*nasci*, be born] 1. related by family 2. from a common original form, as two words 3. related; similar —n. a cognate person or thing

**cog·ni·tion** (käg nish'ən) *n.* [< L. *co-*, together + *gnoscere*, know] 1. the process of knowing, perceiving, etc. 2. an idea, perception, etc.

**cog·ni·za·ble** (käg'ni zə b'l) *adj.* 1. that can be known or perceived 2. *Law* within the jurisdiction of a court

**cog·ni·zance** (käg'nə zəns) *n.* 1. perception or knowledge 2. notice; heed —**cog'ni·zant** *adj.*

**cog·no·men** (käg nō'mən) *n.* [< L. *co-*, with + *nomen*, name] 1. surname 2. any name; esp., a nickname

**cog'wheel'** *n.* a wheel rimmed with teeth that mesh with those of another wheel, etc., to transmit or receive motion

COGWHEELS

**co·hab·it** (kō hab'it) *vi.* [< L. *co-*, together + *habitare*, dwell] to live together as husband and wife, esp. when not legally married —**co·hab'i·ta'tion** *n.*

**co·heir** (kō'er') *n.* one who inherits jointly with another or others

**co·here** (kō hir') *vi.* -**hered'**, -**her'ing** [< L. *co-*, together + *haerere*, to stick] 1. to stick together 2. to be connected naturally or logically

**co·her'ent** (-ənt) *adj.* 1. sticking together; cohering 2. logically connected and intelligible —**co·her'ence** *n.* —**co·her'ent·ly** *adv.*

**co·he·sion** (kō hē'zhən) *n.* a cohering; tendency to stick together —**co·he'sive** (-hēs'iv) *adj.*

**co·ho** (kō'hō) *n., pl.* -**ho**, -**hos** [< ?] a small salmon of the North Pacific, introduced into fresh waters of N U.S.

**co·hort** (kō'hôrt) *n.* [< L. *cohors, enclosure*] 1. a band of soldiers 2. a group 3. an associate

**coif** (koif; *for 2, usually* kwäf) *n.* [< LL. *cofea*, cap] a closefitting cap 2. [< ff.] a hair style

**coif·fure** (kwä fyoor') *n.* [Fr.] 1. a headdress 2. a hair style

**coil** (koil) *vt., vi.* [< L. *com-*, together + *legere*, gather] to wind into circular or spiral form —*n.* 1. a series of rings or a spiral, or anything in this form 2. a single turn of a coil 3. *Elec.* a spiral of wire

**coin** (koin) *n.* [< L. *cuneus*, a wedge] 1. a piece of stamped metal, issued by a government as money 2. such pieces collectively —*vt.* 1. to stamp (metal) into (coins) 2. to invent (a new word, phrase, etc.) —**coin'age** *n.*

**co·in·cide** (kō'in sīd') *vi.* -**cid'ed**, -**cid'ing** [< L. *co-*, together + *incidere*, fall upon] 1. to take up the same place in space 2. to occur at the same time 3. to agree exactly

**co·in·ci·dence** (kō in'sə dəns) *n.* 1. a coinciding 2. an accidental occurrence of related or identical events, ideas, etc. at the same time —**co·in'-**

ci·dent, co·in'ci·den'tal *adj.* —co·in'ci·den'tal·ly *adv.*

**co·i·tus** (kō'it əs) *n.* [< L. < *co-*, together + *ire*, go] sexual intercourse: also **co·i·tion** (kō ish'ən)

**coke** (kōk) *n.* [ME. *colke*, a core] coal from which most of the gases have been removed by heating: used as an industrial fuel

**col-** (käl) *same as* COM-: used before *l*

**Col.** Colonel

**col.** 1. color(ed) 2. column

**co·la** (kō'lə) *n.* [< WAfr. name] 1. an African tree with nuts that yield an extract used in soft drinks and medicine 2. a carbonated soft drink flavored with this extract

**col·an·der** (kul'ən dər, käl'-) *n.* [prob. < L. *colum*, strainer] a perforated pan for draining off liquids

**cold** (kōld) *adj.* [OE. *cald*] 1. of a temperature much lower than that of the human body 2. too cool; chilly 3. unfriendly, indifferent, or depressing 4. devoid of feeling; emotionless 5. *a)* not fresh: said of a hunting scent *b)* off the track 6. [Colloq.] unprepared [to enter a game *cold*] 7. [Slang] perfectly memorized 8. [Slang] unconscious [knocked *cold*] —*n.* 1. lack of heat or warmth 2. cold weather 3. a virus infection of the respiratory tract, causing sneezing, coughing, etc. —**catch** (or **take**) **cold** to become ill with a cold —**have** (or **get**) **cold feet** [Colloq.] to be (or become) timid —**in the cold** neglected —**cold'ly** *adv.* —**cold'ness** *n.*

**cold'blood'ed** *adj.* 1. having a body temperature that varies with the surrounding air, water, etc., as fish and reptiles 2. cruel or callous

**cold cream** a creamy preparation for softening and cleansing the skin

**cold cuts** a variety of sliced cold meats and, usually, cheeses

**cold duck** a drink that is a mixture of burgundy and champagne

**cold front** the forward edge of a cold air mass advancing into a warmer mass

**cold shoulder** [Colloq.] a slight; snub; rebuff —**cold'-shoul'der** *vt.*

**cold sore** little blisters about the mouth during a cold or fever

**cold turkey** [Slang] 1. the abrupt and total withdrawal of drugs from an addict 2. without preparation

**cold war** hostility and conflict without actual warfare

**cole** (kōl) *n.* [< L. *caulis*, cabbage] any of various plants of the mustard family; esp., rape

**cole'slaw'** (-slô') *n.* [< Du.: see prec. & SLAW] a salad of shredded raw cabbage: also **cole slaw**

**col·ic** (käl'ik) *n.* [< Gr. *kōlon*, colon] acute abdominal pain —**col'ick·y** *adj.*

**col·i·se·um** (käl'ə sē'əm) *n.* [< L. *colosseum*] a large stadium

**co·li·tis** (kō līt'is) *n.* [< COLON² + -ITIS] inflammation of the colon

**coll.** 1. collect 2. college

**col·lab·o·rate** (kə lab'ə rāt') vi. -rat'ed, -rat'ing [< L. com-, with + laborare, to work] 1. to work together, esp. in literary or scientific work 2. to cooperate with the enemy —col·lab'o·ra'tion n. —col·lab'o·ra'tor n.

**col·lage** (kə läzh') n. [Fr., a pasting] an art form in which bits of materials are pasted on a surface

**col·lapse** (kə laps') vi. -lapsed', -laps'ing [< L. com-, together + labi, to fall] 1. to fall down or cave in 2. to break down suddenly 3. to fail suddenly in health 4. to fold together compactly —vt. to make collapse —n. a collapsing —col·laps'i·ble adj.

**col·lar** (käl'ər) n. [< L. collum, neck] 1. the part of a garment encircling the neck 2. a band of leather, etc., for an animal's neck 3. anything like a collar —vt. 1. to put a collar on 2. to seize, as by the collar

**col'lar·bone'** n. the clavicle

**col·lard** (käl'ərd) n. [< ME.] a kind of kale, with coarse leaves

**col·late** (kə lāt') vt. -lat'ed, -lat'ing [< L. com-, together + latus, brought] 1. to compare (texts) carefully 2. to put (pages) in proper order —col·la'tor n.

**col·lat·er·al** (kə lat'ər əl) adj. [< L. com-, together + latus, a side] 1. parallel or corresponding 2. accompanying or supporting [collateral evidence] 3. having the same ancestors but in a different line 4. designating or of security given as a pledge for the repayment of a loan, etc. —n. 1. a collateral relative 2. collateral security

**col·la·tion** (kä lā'shən) n. 1. act or result of collating 2. a light meal

**col·league** (käl'ēg) n. [< Fr. < L. com-, with + legare, appoint as deputy] a fellow worker; associate in office

**col·lect** (kə lekt') vt. [< L. com-, together + legere, gather] 1. to gather together 2. to gather (stamps, etc.) as a hobby 3. to call for and receive (money) for (bills, etc.) 4. to regain control of (oneself) —vi. to assemble or accumulate —adj., adv. with payment to be made by the receiver [to telephone collect] —n. (käl'ekt) [also C-] a short prayer used in certain services —col·lect'a·ble, col·lect'i·ble adj. —col·lec'tor n.

**col·lect'ed** adj. 1. gathered together 2. in control of oneself; calm

**col·lec'tion** n. 1. a collecting 2. things collected 3. a mass or pile; accumulation 4. money collected

**col·lec'tive** adj. 1. formed by collecting 2. of or as a group [collective effort] 3. designating a singular noun, as tribe, denoting a collection of individuals —n. 1. a) any collective enterprise; specif., a collective farm b) the people who work together in it 2. a collective noun —col·lec'tive·ly adv.

**collective bargaining** negotiation between organized workers and their employer concerning wages, hours, etc.

**col·lec'tiv·ism** n. collective ownership and control, esp. under socialism —col·lec'tiv·ist n., adj. —col·lec'·tiv·ize' vt. -ized', -iz'ing

**col·leen** (käl'ēn, kə lēn') n. [< Ir. caile, girl] [Ir.] a girl

**col·lege** (käl'ij) n. [see COLLEAGUE] 1. a group of individuals with certain powers and duties [the electoral college] 2. an institution of higher education that grants degrees 3. any of the schools of a university 4. a school offering specialized instruction [a business college]

**col·le·gian** (kə lē'jən) n. a college student

**col·le'giate** (-jət, -jē ət) adj. of or like a college or college students

**col·lide** (kə līd') vi. -lid'ed, -lid'ing [< L. com-, together + laedere, to strike] 1. to come into violent contact; crash 2. to conflict; clash

**col·lie** (käl'ē) n. [< ?] a large, long-haired dog, orig. bred in Scotland

**col·lier** (käl'yər) n. [ME. < col, charcoal] [Chiefly Brit.] 1. a coal miner 2. a coal freighter

**col'lier·y** n., pl. -ies [Chiefly Brit.] a coal mine and its buildings, etc.

**col·li·sion** (kə lizh'ən) n. 1. a colliding 2. a clash or conflict

**col·lo·cate** (käl'ə kāt') vt. -cat'ed, -cat'ing [< L. com-, together + locare, to place] to arrange together, esp. side by side —col·lo·ca'tion n.

**col·lo·di·on** (kə lō'dē ən) n. [< Gr. kolla, glue + eidos, form] a nitrocellulose solution that dries into a tough, elastic film: used to protect wounds, in photographic films, etc.

**col·loid** (käl'oid) n. [< Gr. kolla, glue + -oid] a substance made up of tiny, insoluble, nondiffusible particles that remain suspended in a medium of different matter —col·loid'al adj.

**colloq.** colloquial

**col·lo·qui·al** (kə lō'kwē əl) adj. [see ff.] designating or of the words, phrases, etc. characteristic of informal speech and writing; conversational —col·lo'qui·al·ism n. —col·lo'qui·al·ly adv.

**col·lo'qui·um** n., pl. -qui·a, -qui·ums [L.: see ff.] an organized conference or seminar on some subject

**col·lo·quy** (käl'ə kwē) n., pl. -quies [< L. com-, together + loqui, speak] a conversation or conference

**col·lu·sion** (kə lōō'zhən) n. [< L. com-, with + ludere, to play] a secret agreement for fraudulent or illegal purpose; conspiracy —col·lu'sive (-siv) adj.

**Colo.** Colorado

**Co·logne** (kə lōn') city in W West Germany, on the Rhine; pop. 857,000

**co·logne** (kə lōn') n. [< Fr. eau de Cologne, lit., water of Cologne] a perfumed toilet water made of alcohol and aromatic oils

**Co·lom·bi·a** (kə lum'bē ə) country in NW S.America: 455,335 sq. mi.; pop. 18,068,000 —Co·lom'bi·an adj., n.

**co·lon¹** (kō'lən) n. [< Gr. kōlon, verse part] a mark of punctuation (:) used before a long quotation, explanation, example, series, etc. and after the salutation of a formal letter

**co·lon²** (kō'lən) n., pl. -lons, -la (-lə) [< Gr. kolon] that part of the large intestine extending from the cecum to the rectum

**colo·nel** (kur'n'l) *n.* [< It. *colonna*, (military) column] a military officer ranking just above a lieutenant colonel —**colo'nel·cy** *n., pl.* **-cies**

**co·lo·ni·al** (kə lō'nē əl) *adj.* 1. of, in, or having a colony 2. [*often* C-] of or in the thirteen British colonies that became the U.S. —*n.* an inhabitant of a colony —**co·lo'ni·al·ly** *adv.*

**co·lo'ni·al·ism** (-iz'm) *n.* the system by which a country maintains foreign colonies, esp. for economic exploitation —**co·lo'ni·al·ist** *n., adj.*

**col·o·nist** (käl'ə nist) *n.* a settler or inhabitant of a colony

**col'o·nize'** (-nīz') *vt., vi.* **-nized', -niz'ing** 1. to found a colony (in) 2. to settle in a colony —**col'o·ni·za'tion** *n.* —**col'o·niz'er** *n.*

**col·on·nade** (käl'ə nād') *n.* [< L. *columna*, column] *Archit.* a row of columns, as along a side of a building

**col·o·ny** (käl'ə nē) *n., pl.* **-nies** [< L. *colere*, to cultivate] 1. *a)* a group of settlers in a distant land, under the jurisdiction of their native land *b)* the region settled 2. any territory ruled over by a distant state 3. a community of the same nationality or pursuits, as within a city 4. *Biol.* a group living or growing together

**col·o·phon** (käl'ə fän') *n.* [LL. < Gr. *kolophon*, top] a publisher's emblem

**col·or** (kul'ər) *n.* [L.] 1. the property of reflecting light of a particular visible wavelength: the *colors* of the spectrum are red, orange, yellow, green, blue, indigo, and violet 2. any coloring matter; pigment; dye; paint 3. color of the face or skin 4. [*pl.*] a colored badge, etc. to identify the wearer 5. [*pl.*] a flag 6. outward appearance 7. vivid quality —*vt.* 1. to give color to; paint, dye, etc. 2. to change the color of 3. to alter, as by distorting *[to color a story]* —*vi.* 1. to become colored 2. to change color 3. to blush or flush —**show one's colors** to show one's true self

**Col·o·rad·o** (käl'ə rad'ō) Western State of the U.S., in the Rockies: 104,247 sq. mi.; pop. 2,207,000; cap. Denver —**Col'o·rad'an** *adj., n.*

**col·or·ant** (kul'ər ənt) *n.* a dye or other coloring agent

**col'or·a'tion** (-ə rā'shən) *n.* coloring

**col·o·ra·tu·ra** (soprano) (kul'ər ə toor'ə, -tyoor'-) [It.] a soprano skilled at singing brilliant trills, etc.

**color bar** *same as* COLOR LINE

**col'or·blind'** *adj.* 1. unable to distinguish certain colors or any colors 2. not influenced by considerations of race —**col'or·blind'ness** *n.*

**col'or·cast'** *n.* a color television broadcast —*vt., vi.* **-cast'** or **-cast'ed, -cast'ing** to televise in color

**col'ored** (-ərd) *adj.* 1. having color 2. non-Caucasoid; specif., Negro

**col'or·fast'** (-fast') *adj.* with color not subject to fading or running

**col'or·ful** (-fəl) *adj.* 1. full of color 2. picturesque, vivid, etc. —**col'or·ful·ly** *adv.* —**col'or·ful·ness** *n.*

**col'or·ing** *n.* 1. anything applied to impart color; pigment, etc. 2. the way a thing is colored 3. false appearance

**col'or·less** *adj.* 1. without color 2. lacking variety or interest; dull —**col'or·less·ly** *adv.* —**col'or·less·ness** *n.*

**color line** any barrier of social, political, or economic restrictions imposed on Negroes or other nonwhites

**co·los·sal** (kə läs''l) *adj.* 1. like a colossus in size; huge 2. [Colloq.] extraordinary —**co·los'sal·ly** *adv.*

**co·los·sus** (kə läs'əs) *n., pl.* **-si** (-ī), **-sus·es** [< Gr.] 1. a gigantic statue 2. anything huge or important

**col·our** (kul'ər) *n., vt., vi.* Brit. *sp.* of COLOR

**colt** (kōlt) *n.* [OE.] a young horse, zebra, etc.; esp., a young male horse

**colt'ish** *adj.* of or like a colt; esp., frisky, frolicsome, etc.

**Co·lum·bi·a** (kə lum'bē ə) 1. capital of S.C.: pop. 114,000 2. river flowing from Canada, through Wash., & along the Wash.-Oreg. border into the Pacific

**col·um·bine** (käl'əm bīn') *n.* [< L. *columbinus*, dovelike] a plant of the buttercup family, with showy, spurred flowers

**Co·lum·bus** (kə lum'bəs) 1. capital of Ohio, in the C part: pop. 540,000 2. city in W Ga.: pop. 154,000

**Columbus, Christopher** 1451?-1506; It. discoverer of America (1492)

**col·umn** (käl'əm) *n.* [< L. *columna*] 1. a slender upright structure, usually a supporting member in a building 2. anything like a column *[the spinal column]* 3. a file formation of troops, etc. 4. any of the vertical sections of printed matter on a page 5. a feature article appearing regularly in a newspaper, etc. —**co·lum·nar** (kə lum'nər) *adj.*

COLUMN

**col·um·nist** (käl'əm nist) *n.* a writer of a column (sense 5)

**com-** [L. < *cum*, with] a prefix meaning with or together: also an intensive

**Com.** 1. Commission(er) 2. Committee

**com.** 1. commerce 2. common

**co·ma** (kō'mə) *n.* [< Gr. *kōma*, deep sleep] deep, prolonged unconsciousness caused by injury or disease

**co·ma·tose** (kō'mə tōs', käm'ə-) *adj.* 1. of, like, or in a coma 2. lethargic

**comb** (kōm) *n.* [< OE. *camb*] 1. a thin strip of hard rubber, plastic, etc., with teeth, used to arrange or clean the hair 2. any similar tool, as for cleaning and straightening wool, flax, etc. 3. a red, fleshy outgrowth on the head, as of a rooster 4. a honeycomb —*vt.* 1. to arrange, etc. with a comb 2. to search thoroughly

---

fat, āpe, cär; ten, ēven; is, bīte; gō, hôrn, tōōl, look; oil, out; up, fur; chin; she; thin, *then*; zh, leisure; ŋ, ring; ə for *a* in *ago*; ', (ā'b'l); ë, Fr. coeur; ö, Fr. feu; Fr. mon; ü, Fr. duc; kh, G. ich, doch; ‡ foreign; < derived from

**com·bat** (for v. kəm bat′, käm′bat; for n. käm′bat) vt., vi. **-bat′ed** or **-bat′ted, -bat′ing** or **-bat′ting** [< Fr. < L. com-, with + battuere, to fight] to fight or actively oppose —n. 1. armed fighting; battle 2. any struggle or conflict —**com·bat·ant** (käm′bə tənt, kəm bat′′nt) adj., n.

**combat fatigue** a psychoneurosis with anxiety, depression, etc., as after prolonged combat in warfare

**com·bat·ive** (kəm bat′iv; käm′bə tiv) adj. ready or eager to fight

**comb·er** (kō′mər) n. 1. one that combs 2. a wave, curling at the top

**com·bi·na·tion** (käm bə nā′shən) n. 1. a combining or being combined 2. a thing formed by combining 3. an association formed for a common purpose 4. the series of numbers to which a dial is turned on a lock (**combination lock**) to open it

**com·bine** (kəm bīn′; for n. käm′bīn) vt., vi. **-bined′, -bin′ing** [< L. com-, together + bini, two by two] to join into one, as by blending; unite —n. 1. a machine for harvesting and threshing grain 2. an association formed for commercial or political, often unethical, purposes —**com·bin′er** n.

**comb·ings** (kō′miŋz) n.pl. loose hair, wool, etc. removed in combing

**combining form** a word form occurring only in compounds and derivatives (Ex.: cardio- in cardiograph)

**com·bo** (käm′bō) n., pl. **-bos** [Colloq.] a combination; specif., a small jazz ensemble

**com·bus·ti·ble** (kəm bus′tə b'l) adj. that can burn; flammable —**com·bus′ti·bil′i·ty** n. —**com·bus′ti·bly** adv.

**com·bus′tion** (-chən) n. [< L. com-, intens. + urere, to burn] the act or process of burning

**Comdr.** Commander

**come** (kum) vi. **came, come, com′ing** [< OE. cuman] 1. to move from "there" to "here" 2. to arrive or appear 3. to extend; reach 4. to happen 5. to occur in a certain order [after 8 comes 9] 6. to be derived or descended 7. to be caused; result 8. to become [to come loose] 9. to be available [it comes in four sizes] 10. to amount (to) —interj. see here!: used to express impatience, etc. —**come about** 1. to happen 2. to turn about —**come across** (or upon) to find or meet by chance —**come along** 1. to appear or arrive 2. to proceed or succeed —**come around** (or round) 1. to recover 2. to yield —**come by** to get; gain —**come into** 1. to enter into 2. to inherit —**come off** 1. to become detached 2. to end up 3. [Colloq.] to prove effective, etc. —**come out** 1. to be disclosed 2. to make a debut 3. to end up —**come out for** to announce endorsement of —**come through** 1. to complete something successfully 2. [Slang] to do or give what is wanted —**come to** to recover consciousness —**come up** to arise, as a point in a discussion —**how come?** [Colloq.] why?

**come′back′** n. [Colloq.] 1. a return to a previous position, as of power 2. a witty answer; retort

**co·me·di·an** (kə mē′dē ən) n. an actor who plays comic parts —**co·me′di·enne′** (-en′) n.fem.

**co·me·dic** (kə mē′dik, -med′ik) adj. of or having to do with comedy

**come′down′** n. a loss of status

**com·e·dy** (käm′ə dē) n., pl. **-dies** [< Gr. kōmos, festival + aeidein, sing] 1. a humorous play, etc. with a nontragic ending 2. an amusing event

**come·ly** (kum′lē) adj. **-li·er, -li·est** [< OE. cymlic] attractive; fair —**come′li·ness** n.

**come′-on′** n. [Slang] an inducement

**co·mes·ti·ble** (kə mes′tə b'l) n. [< L. com-, intens. + edere, to eat] [usually pl.] food

**com·et** (käm′ət) n. [< Gr. komē, hair] a heavenly body with a starlike nucleus and, usually, a long, luminous tail: comets move in orbits around the sun

**come·up·pance** (kum′up′ns) n. [Colloq.] deserved punishment

**com·fit** (kum′fit) n. [< L. com-, with + facere, do] a candy; sweetmeat

**com·fort** (kum′fərt) vt. [< L. com-, intens. + fortis, strong] to soothe in distress or sorrow; console —n. 1. relief from distress, etc. 2. one that comforts 3. a state of, or thing that provides, ease and quiet enjoyment —**com′fort·ing** adj. —**com′fort·less** adj.

**com·fort·a·ble** (kumf′tər b'l, kum′fər tə b'l) adj. 1. providing comfort 2. at ease in body or mind 3. [Colloq.] sufficient to satisfy [a comfortable salary] —**com′fort·a·bly** adv.

**com′fort·er** n. 1. one that comforts 2. a quilted bed covering

**comfort station** a public toilet or restroom

**com·fy** (kum′fē) adj. **-fi·er, -fi·est** [Colloq.] comfortable

**com·ic** (käm′ik) adj. 1. of comedy 2. amusing; funny —n. 1. a comedian 2. the humorous part of art or life 3. a) same as COMIC STRIP b) [pl.] a section of comic strips

**com′i·cal** (-i k'l) adj. causing amusement; humorous; funny —**com′i·cal′i·ty** (-kal′ə tē) n. —**com′i·cal·ly** adv.

**comic strip** a series of cartoons telling a humorous or adventurous story, as in a newspaper or in a booklet (**comic book**)

**com·ing** (kum′iŋ) adj. 1. approaching; next 2. showing promise of being successful, etc. —n. arrival; approach

**com·i·ty** (käm′ə tē) n., pl. **-ties** [< L. comis, polite] courtesy

**comm.** 1. commission 2. committee

**com·ma** (käm′ə) n. [< Gr. komma, clause] a mark of punctuation (,) used to indicate a slight separation of sentence elements

**com·mand** (kə mand′) vt. [< L. com-, intens. + mandare, entrust] 1. to give an order to; direct 2. to have authority over; control 3. to have for use [to command a fortune] 4. to deserve and get [to command respect]

**5.** to control (a position); overlook —*vi.* to have authority —*n.* **1.** order; direction **2.** controlling power or position **3.** mastery **4.** a military or naval force, or district, under a specified authority

**com·man·dant** (käm'ən dant') *n.* a commanding officer, as of a fort

**com·man·deer** (käm'ən dir') *vt.* [see COMMAND] to seize (property) for military or governmental use

**com·mand'er** *n.* **1.** one who commands **2.** *U.S. Navy* an officer ranking just above a lieutenant commander

**commander in chief** *pl.* **commanders in chief** the supreme commander of the armed forces of a nation

**com·mand'ment** *n.* **1.** a command **2.** any of the Ten Commandments

**com·man·do** (kə man'dō) *n., pl.* **-dos, -does** [Afrik. < Port.] a member of a small force trained to raid enemy territory

**command post** the field headquarters of a military unit, from which operations are directed

**com·mem·o·rate** (kə mem'ə rāt') *vt.* **-rat'ed, -rat'ing** [< L. *com-*, intens. + *memorare*, remind] **1.** to honor the memory of, as by a ceremony **2.** to serve as a memorial to —**com·mem'o·ra'tion** *n.* —**com·mem'o·ra'tive** *adj.* —**com·mem'o·ra'tor** *n.*

**com·mence** (kə mens') *vi., vt.* **-menced', -menc'ing** [< L. *com-*, together + *initiare*, begin] to begin

**com·mence'ment** *n.* **1.** a beginning **2.** the ceremony of conferring degrees or diplomas at a school

**com·mend** (kə mend') *vt.* [see COMMAND] **1.** to put in the care of another; entrust **2.** to recommend **3.** to praise —**com·mend'a·ble** *adj.* —**com·mend'a·bly** *adv.* —**com·men·da·tion** (käm'ən dā'shən) *n.*

**com·mend·a·to·ry** (kə men'də tôr'ē) *adj.* praising or recommending

**com·men·su·ra·ble** (kə men'shər ə b'l) *adj.* [< L. *com-*, together + *mensura*, measurement] measurable by the same standard or measure

**com·men'su·rate** (-shər it) *adj.* [see prec.] **1.** equal in measure or size **2.** proportionate **3.** commensurable

**com·ment** (käm'ent) *n.* [< L. *com-*, intens. + *meminisse*, remember] **1.** an explanatory or critical note **2.** a remark or observation **3.** talk; gossip —*vi.* to make a comment or comments

**com·men·tar·y** (käm'ən ter'ē) *n., pl.* **-ies** a series of explanatory notes or remarks

**com'men·tate'** (-tāt') *vi.* **-tat'ed, -tat'ing** to perform as a commentator

**com'men·ta'tor** (-tāt'ər) *n.* one who reports and analyzes events, trends, etc., as on television

**com·merce** (käm'ərs) *n.* [< L. *com-*, together + *merx*, merchandise] trade on a large scale, as between countries

**com·mer·cial** (kə mur'shəl) *adj.* **1.** of commerce or business **2.** made or done for profit —*n. Radio & TV* a paid advertisement —**com·mer'cial·ism** *n.* —**com·mer'cial·ly** *adv.*

**com·mer'cial·ize'** (-iz') *vt.* **-ized', -iz'ing** to put on a business basis, esp. so as to make profit —**com·mer'cial·i·za'tion** *n.*

**com·min·gle** (kə miŋ'g'l) *vt., vi.* **-gled, -gling** to mingle together

**com·mis·er·ate** (kə miz'ə rāt') *vt.* **-at·ed, -at'ing** [< L. *com-*, intens. + *miserari*, to pity] to feel or show pity for —*vi.* to condole (*with*) —**com·mis'er·a'tion** *n.* —**com·mis'er·a'tive** *adj.*

**com·mis·sar** (käm'ə sär') *n.* [Russ. *komissar*] the head of any former U.S.S.R. commissariat (sense 2): now called *minister*

**com·mis·sar·i·at** (-ser'ē ət) *n.* [Fr. < L.: see COMMIT] **1.** an army branch providing food and supplies **2.** formerly, a government department in the U.S.S.R.: now called *ministry*

**com·mis·sar·y** (käm'ə ser'ē) *n., pl.* **-ies** [see COMMIT] **1.** formerly, an army officer in charge of supplies **2.** a store, as in an army camp, where food and supplies are sold **3.** a restaurant in a movie or TV studio

**com·mis·sion** (kə mish'ən) *n.* [see COMMIT] **1.** a document authorizing certain duties and powers **2.** authority to act for another, or that which one is authorized to do **3.** a group of people chosen to do something **4.** a committing; doing **5.** a percentage of money from sales, allotted to the agent **6.** *Mil.* a) an official certificate conferring rank b) the rank conferred —*vt.* **1.** to give a commission to **2.** to authorize **3.** *Naut.* to put (a vessel) into service —**in** (or **out of**) **commission** in (or not in) working order

**commissioned officer** an officer in the armed forces holding a commission

**com·mis'sion·er** *n.* **1.** a member of a commission **2.** an official in charge of a governmental department **3.** a man selected to regulate and control a professional sport

**com·mit** (kə mit') *vt.* **-mit'ted, -mit'ting** [< L. *com-*, together + *mittere*, to send] **1.** to give in charge; consign **2.** to put in custody or confinement [*committed* to prison] **3.** to do or perpetrate (a crime) **4.** to bind, as by a promise; pledge —**com·mit'ment** *n.* —**com·mit'ta·ble** *adj.* —**com·mit'tal** *n.*

**com·mit·tee** (kə mit'ē) *n.* [see prec.] a group of people chosen to report or act upon a certain matter —**com·mit'tee·man** (-mən) *n., pl.* **-men** —**com·mit'tee·wom'an** *n.fem., pl.* **-wom'en**

**com·mode** (kə mōd') *n.* [Fr. < L.: see COM- & MODE] **1.** a chest of drawers **2.** a movable washstand **3.** a toilet

**com·mo·di·ous** (kə mō'dē əs) *adj.* [see prec.] spacious; roomy

---

fat, āpe, cär; ten, ēven; is, bīte; gō, hôrn, tōōl, look; oil, out; up, fur; chin; she; thin, *then*; zh, leisure; ŋ, ring; ə for *a* in ago; ', (ā'b'l); ë, Fr. coeur; ö, Fr. feu; Fr. mon; ü, Fr. duc; kh, G. ich, doch; ‡ foreign; < derived from

**com·mod·i·ty** (kə mäd'ə tē) *n., pl.*
**-ties** [see COMMODE] 1. any useful
thing 2. anything bought and sold

**com·mo·dore** (käm'ə dôr') *n.* [<
Fr.: see COMMAND] *U.S. Navy* formerly, an officer ranking just above
a captain

**com·mon** (käm'ən) *adj.* [< L. *communis*] 1. belonging to or shared by
each or all 2. of an entire community;
public 3. general; widespread 4.
familiar; usual 5. below ordinary 6.
vulgar; coarse 7. designating a noun
(as book) that refers to any of a group
—*n.* [*sometimes pl.*] land owned or used
by all the inhabitants of a place —**in
common** shared by each or all —
**com'mon·ly** *adv.*

**com'mon·al·ty** (-əl tē) *n., pl.* **-ties**
the common people; public

**common carrier** a person or company in the business of transporting
people or goods for a fee

**common denominator** 1. a common multiple of the denominators of
two or more fractions 2. a characteristic in common

**common divisor** (or **factor**) a factor common to two or more numbers

**com'mon·er** *n.* a person not of the
nobility; one of the common people

**common law** law based on custom,
usage, and judicial decisions

**common market** an association of
countries for closer economic union

**common multiple** *Math.* a multiple
of each of two or more quantities

**com'mon·place'** *n.* 1. a trite remark; platitude 2. anything common
or ordinary —*adj.* trite or ordinary

**common pleas** *Law* in some States,
a court having jurisdiction over civil
and criminal trials

**com·mons** (käm'ənz) *n.pl.* 1. the
common people 2. [C-] *same as* HOUSE
OF COMMONS 3. a dining room, as at
college

**common sense** good sense or practical judgment —**com'mon-sense'**
*adj.*

**com'mon·weal'** (-wēl') *n.* the public
good; general welfare

**com'mon·wealth'** (-welth') *n.* 1.
the people of a nation or state 2. a
democracy or republic 3. a federation
of states

**com·mo·tion** (kə mō'shən) *n.* [< L.
*com-,* together + *movere,* move] 1.
violent motion 2. confusion; bustle

**com·mu·nal** (käm'yoon 'l, kə
myōon 'l) *adj.* 1. of a commune 2. of
the community; public 3. marked by
common ownership of property —
**com'mu·nal·ize'** *vt.* **-ized', -iz'ing**
—**com·mu'nal·ly** *adv.*

**com·mune¹** (kə myōon') *vi.* **-muned',
-mun'ing** [< OFr. *comuner,* share]
to talk together intimately

**com·mune²** (käm'yōon) *n.* [< L.
*communis,* common] 1. the smallest
administrative district of local government in some European countries,
esp. France 2. a small group of people
living communally

**com·mu·ni·ca·ble** (kə myōo'ni kə
b'l) *adj.* that can be communicated, as

an idea, or transmitted, as a disease
—**com·mu'ni·ca·bil'i·ty** *n.*

**com·mu'ni·cant** (-kənt) *n.* one who
receives Holy Communion

**com·mu·ni·cate** (kə myōo'nə kāt')
*vt.* **-cat'ed, -cat'ing** [< L. *communi-
care*] 1. to impart; transmit 2. to give
(information, etc.) —*vi.* 1. to receive
Holy Communion 2. to give or exchange information 3. to have a
meaningful relationship 4. to be connected, as rooms —**com·mu'ni·ca'
tor** *n.*

**com·mu·ni·ca'tion** *n.* 1. a transmitting 2. *a)* a giving or exchanging of
information, messages, etc. *b)* a message, letter, etc. 3. [*often pl.*] a means
of communicating —**com·mu'ni-
ca'tive** *adj.*

**com·mun·ion** (kə myōon'yən) *n.*
[see COMMON] 1. possession in common 2. a communing 3. a Christian
denomination 4. [C-] *same as* HOLY
COMMUNION

**com·mu·ni·qué** (kə myōo'nə kā')
*n.* [Fr.] an official communication

**com·mu·nism** (käm'yə niz'm) *n.*
[see COMMON] 1. any theory or system
of common ownership of property 2.
[*often* C-] *a)* socialism as formulated
by Marx, Lenin, etc. *b)* any government or political movement supporting
this

**com'mu·nist** (-nist) *n.* 1. an advocate or supporter of communism 2.
[C-] a member of a Communist Party
—*adj.* of, like, or supporting communism or communists —**com'munis'tic** *adj.*

**com·mu·ni·ty** (kə myōo'nə tē) *n.,
pl.* **-ties** [see COMMON] 1. *a)* any group
living in the same area or having interests, work, etc. in common *b)* such an
area 2. the general public 3. a sharing
in common

**community antenna television**
a system by which telecasts from
distant stations are received by a
single, high antenna and sent to subscribers by direct cable

**community college** a junior college
serving a certain community

**com·mute** (kə myōot') *vt.* **-mut'ed,
-mut'ing** [< L. *com-,* intens. +
*mutare,* to change] 1. to exchange;
substitute 2. to change (an obligation,
punishment, etc.) to a less severe one
—*vi.* to travel regularly, esp. by train,
etc., between two points at some distance —**com·mu·ta·tion** (käm'yə
tā'shən) *n.* —**com·mut'er** *n.*

**comp.** 1. comparative 2. compound

**com·pact** (kəm pakt', käm'pakt; *for
n.* käm'pakt) *adj.* [< L. *com-,* with +
*pangere,* fix] 1. closely and firmly
packed 2. taking little space 3. terse
—*vt.* 1. to pack or join firmly together
2. to make by putting together —*n.*
1. a small cosmetic case, usually containing face powder and a mirror 2. a
smaller model of car 3. an agreement;
covenant —**com·pact'ly** *adv.* —
**com·pact'ness** *n.*

**com·pac'tor** (-pak'tər) *n.* a device
that compresses trash into small
bundles

**com·pan·ion** (kəm pan'yən) n. [ < L. com-, with + panis, bread] 1. an associate; comrade 2. a person paid to live or travel with another 3. one of a pair or set —**com·pan'ion·a·ble** adj. —**com·pan'ion·ship'** n.

**com·pan·ion·way'** n. a stairway from a ship's deck to the space below

**com·pa·ny** (kum'pə nē) n., pl. -nies 1. companionship; society 2. a group of people gathered or associated for some purpose 3. a guest or guests 4. companions 5. a body of troops 6. a ship's crew —**keep company** 1. to associate (with) 2. to go together, as a couple intending to marry —**part company** to stop associating (with)

**com·pa·ra·ble** (käm'pər ə b'l) adj. 1. that can be compared 2. worthy of comparison —**com'pa·ra·bly** adv.

**com·par·a·tive** (kəm par'ə tiv) adj. 1. involving comparison 2. not absolute; relative 3. Gram. designating the second degree of comparison of adjectives and adverbs —n. Gram. the comparative degree [finer is the comparative of fine] —**com·par'a·tive·ly** adv.

**com·pare** (kəm per') vt. -pared', -par'ing [ < L. com-, with + par, equal] 1. to liken (to) 2. to examine for similarities or differences 3. Gram. to form the degrees of comparison of —vi. 1. to be worth comparing (with) 2. to make comparisons —**beyond** (or **past** or **without**) **compare** without equal

**com·par·i·son** (kəm par'ə s'n) n. 1. a comparing or being compared 2. likeness; similarity 3. Gram. change in an adjective or adverb to show the positive, comparative, and superlative degrees —**in comparison with** compared with

**com·part·ment** (kəm pärt'mənt) n. [ < L. com-, intens. + partire, divide] 1. any of the divisions into which a space is partitioned off 2. a separate section or category —**com·part'men·tal·ize'** (-men'tə līz') vt. -ized', -iz'ing

**com·pass** (kum'pəs) vt. [ < L. com-, together + passus, a step] 1. to go round 2. to surround 3. to understand 4. to achieve or contrive —n. 1. [often pl.] an instrument with two pivoted legs, for drawing circles, measuring, etc. 2. a boundary 3. an enclosed area 4. range; scope 5. an instrument for showing direction, esp. one with a swinging magnetic needle pointing north **DRAWING COMPASS**

**com·pas·sion** (kəm pash'ən) n. [ < L. com-, together + pati, suffer] deep sympathy; pity —**com·pas'sion·ate** adj. —**com·pas'sion·ate·ly** adv.

**com·pat·i·ble** (kəm pat'ə b'l) adj. [see prec.] getting along or going well together —**com·pat'i·bil'i·ty** n.

**com·pa·tri·ot** (kəm pā'trē ət) n. [see COM- & PATRIOT] a countryman —adj. of the same country

**com·peer** (käm'pir) n. [see COMPARE] 1. an equal; peer 2. a comrade

**com·pel** (kəm pel') vt. -pelled', -pel'ling [ < L. com-, together + pellere, drive] to force or get by force —**com·pel'ling·ly** adv.

**com·pen·di·um** (kəm pen'dē əm) n., pl. -ums, -a (-ə) [ < L. com-, together + pendere, weigh] a concise but comprehensive summary

**com·pen·sate** (käm'pən sāt') vt. -sat'ed, -sat'ing [ < L. com-, with + pendere, weigh] 1. to make up for; counterbalance 2. to pay —vi. to make amends (for) —**com'pen·sa'tion** n. —**com·pen·sa·to·ry** (kəm pen'sə tôr'ē) adj.

**com·pete** (kəm pēt') vi. -pet'ed, -pet'ing [ < L. com-, together + petere, seek] to be in rivalry; contend; vie (in a contest, etc.)

**com·pe·tence** (käm'pə təns) n. 1. sufficient means for one's needs 2. ability; fitness 3. legal jurisdiction, power, etc. Also **com'pe·ten·cy**

**com'pe·tent** (-tənt) adj. [see COMPETE] 1. capable; fit 2. sufficient; adequate 3. having legal competence —**com'pe·tent·ly** adv.

**com·pe·ti·tion** (käm'pə tish'ən) n. 1. a competing; rivalry, esp. in business 2. a contest; match —**com·pet·i·tive** (kəm pet'ə tiv) adj.

**com·pet·i·tor** (kəm pet'ə tər) n. one who competes, as a business rival

**com·pile** (kəm pīl') vt. -piled', -pil'ing [ < L. com-, together + pilare, to compress] 1. to collect and assemble (data, writings, etc.) 2. to compose (a book, etc.) of materials from various sources —**com·pi·la·tion** (käm'pə lā'shən) n. —**com·pil'er** n.

**com·pla·cen·cy** (kəm pläs'ʼn sē) n., pl. -cies [ < L. com-, intens. + placere, please] contentment; often, specif., self-satisfaction, or smugness: also **com·pla'cence** —**com·pla'cent** adj.

**com·plain** (kəm plān') vi. [ < L. com-, intens. + plangere, strike (the breast)] 1. to express pain, displeasure, etc. 2. to find fault 3. to make an accusation —**com·plain'er** n.

**com·plain·ant** (-ənt) n. a plaintiff

**com·plaint'** (-plānt') n. 1. a complaining 2. a cause for complaining 3. an ailment 4. Law a formal charge

**com·plai·sant** (kəm plā'z'nt, -s'nt) adj. [see COMPLACENCY] willing to please; obliging —**com·plai'sance** n.

**com·plect·ed** (kəm plek'tid) adj. [Colloq.] same as COMPLEXIONED

**com·ple·ment** (käm'plə mənt; for v. -ment') n. [see ff.] 1. that which completes or perfects 2. the amount needed to fill or complete 3. an entirety —vt. to make complete —**com'ple·men'ta·ry** (-men'tər ē) adj.

**com·plete** (kəm plēt') adj. [ < L. com-, intens. + plere, fill] 1. whole;

entire 2. finished 3. thorough —*vt.* -**plet′ed, -plet′ing** 1. to finish 2. to make whole or perfect —**com·plete′- ly** *adv.* —**com·plete′ness** *n.* —**com· ple′tion** (-plē′shən) *n.*

**com·plex** (kəm pleks′; *also, and for n.* *always,* käm′pleks) *adj.* [ < L. *com-,* with + *plectere,* to weave] 1. consist- ing of two or more related parts 2. complicated —*n.* 1. a complex whole 2. a unified grouping, as of buildings 3. *Psychoanalysis a)* a group of mostly unconscious impulses, etc. strongly influencing behavior *b)* loosely, an obsession —**com·plex′i·ty** *n.*

**com·plex·ion** (kəm plek′shən) *n.* [see prec.] 1. the color, texture, etc. of the skin, esp. of the face 2. nature; character; aspect

**com·plex′ioned** *adj.* having a (spec- ified) complexion [light-*complexioned*]

**complex sentence** a sentence con- sisting of a main clause and one or more subordinate clauses

**com·pli·ance** (kəm plī′əns) *n.* 1. a complying; acquiescence 2. a tendency to give in to others Also **com·pli′an- cy** —**com·pli′ant** *adj.*

**com·pli·cate** (käm′plə kāt′) *vt., vi.* -**cat′ed, -cat′ing** [ < L. *com-,* to- gether + *plicāre,* to fold] to make or become intricate, difficult, or involved —**com′pli·ca′tion** *n.*

**com′pli·cat′ed** *adj.* intricately in- volved; hard to solve, analyze, etc.

**com·plic·i·ty** (kəm plis′ə tē) *n., pl.* -**ties** [see COMPLEX] partnership in wrongdoing

**com·pli·ment** (käm′plə mənt; *for v.* -ment′) *n.* [Fr. < L.: see COMPLETE] 1. a formal act of courtesy; esp., some- thing said in praise 2. [*pl.*] respects —*vt.* to pay a compliment to

**com′pli·men′ta·ry** (-men′tər ē) *adj.* 1. paying or containing a compliment 2. given free as a courtesy

**com·ply** (kəm plī′) *vi.* -**plied′, -ply′- ing** [see COMPLETE] to act in accord- ance (*with* a request, order, etc.)

**com·po·nent** (kəm pō′nənt) *adj.* [ < L. *com-,* together + *ponere,* put] serv- ing as one of the parts of a whole —*n.* a part, element, or ingredient

**com·port** (kəm pôrt′) *vt.* [ < L. *com-,* together + *portāre,* bring] to behave (oneself) in a specified way —*vi.* to accord (*with*) —**com·port′ment** *n.*

**com·pose** (kəm pōz′) *vt.* -**posed′, -pos′ing** [ < OFr. *com-,* with + *poser,* to place] 1. to make up; constitute 2. to put in proper form 3. to create (a musical or literary work) 4. to make calm 5. to set (type) —*vi.* to create musical works, etc. —**com·pos′er** *n.*

**com·posed′** *adj.* calm; self-possessed

**com·pos·ite** (kəm päz′it) *adj.* [ < L. *com-,* together + *ponere,* put] 1. com- pound 2. *Bot.* of a family of plants, as the daisy, with flower heads composed of clusters of small flowers —*n.* a composite thing —**com·pos′ite·ly** *adv.*

**com·po·si·tion** (käm′pə zish′ən) *n.* 1. a composing, esp. of literary or musical works 2. the makeup of a thing or person 3. something composed

**com·pos·i·tor** (kəm päz′ə tər) *n.* a person who sets type; typesetter

**com·post** (käm′pōst) *n.* [see COM- POSITE] a mixture of decomposing vegetation for fertilizing soil

**com·po·sure** (kəm pō′zhər) *n.* [see COMPOSE] calmness; self-possession

**com·pote** (käm′pōt) *n.* [Fr.: see COMPOSITE] 1. a dish of stewed fruits 2. a long-stemmed dish, as for candy

**com·pound¹** (käm pound′, kam-; *for adj. usually, and for n. always,* käm′pound) *vt.* [see COMPOSITE] 1. to mix or combine 2. to make by com- bining parts 3. to compute (compound interest) 4. to intensify by adding new elements —*adj.* made up of two or more parts —*n.* 1. a thing formed by combining parts 2. a substance con- taining two or more elements chemi- cally combined —**compound a felony** (or crime) to agree, for payment, not to prosecute a felony (or crime)

**com·pound²** (käm′pound) *n.* [Malay *kampong*] an area enclosing a building or buildings, esp. in the Orient

**compound fracture** a fracture in which the broken bone pierces the skin

**compound interest** interest paid on both the principal and the accumu- lated unpaid interest

**compound sentence** a sentence consisting of two or more independent, coordinate clauses

**com·pre·hend** (käm′prə hend′) *vt.* [ < L. *com-,* with + *prehendere,* seize] 1. to grasp mentally; understand 2. to include; take in; comprise — **com·pre·hen·si·ble** (käm′prə hen′- sə b'l) *adj.* —**com′pre·hen′sion** *n.*

**com′pre·hen′sive** *adj.* wide in scope; inclusive —**com′pre·hen′- sive·ly** *adv.* —**com′pre·hen′sive- ness** *n.*

**com·press** (kəm pres′; *for n.* käm′ pres) *vt.* [ < L. *com-,* together + *premere,* press] 1. to press together and make more compact 2. to put (air) under pressure —*n.* a pad of folded cloth, often wet or medicated, applied to the skin —**com·pressed′** *adj.* —**com·pres′sion** *n.*

**com·pres′sor** (-ər) *n.* a machine for compressing air, gas, etc.

**com·prise′** (-prīz′) *vt.* -**prised′, -pris′ing** [see COMPREHEND] 1. to include; contain 2. to consist of 3. to make up; form: a loose usage

**com·pro·mise** (käm′prə mīz′) *n.* [ < L. *com-,* together + *promittere,* to promise] 1. a settlement in which each side makes concessions 2. something midway —*vt., vi.* -**mised′, -mis′ing** 1. to adjust by compromise 2. to lay open to suspicion, disrepute, etc.

**comp·trol·ler** (kən trō′lər) *n.* [al- tered (after Fr. *compte,* account) < CONTROLLER] *same as* CONTROLLER (sense 1)

**com·pul·sion** (kəm pul′shən) *n.* a compelling or being compelled; force —**com·pul′sive** (-siv) *adj.* —**com· pul′sive·ly** *adv.* —**com·pul′sive- ness** *n.*

**com·pul·so·ry** (-sər ē) *adj.* 1. oblig- atory; required 2. compelling

**com·punc·tion** (kəm puŋk′shən) *n.* [< L. *com*-, intens. + *pungere*, to prick] an uneasy feeling prompted by guilt

**com·pute** (kəm pyōōt′) *vt.*, *vi.* **-put′ed**, **-put′ing** [< L. *com*-, with + *putare*, reckon] to determine (an amount, etc.) by reckoning —**com·pu·ta·tion** (käm′pyoo tā′shən) *n.*

**com·put′er** *n.* an electronic machine that performs rapid, complex calculations or compiles and correlates data —**com·put′er·ize′** *vt.* **-ized′** **-iz′ing**

**com·rade** (käm′rad) *n.* [< Sp. *camarada*, chamber mate < L. *camera*, room] **1.** a friend; close companion **2.** an associate —**com′rade·ship′** *n.*

**com·sat** (käm′sat) *n.* a communications satellite for relaying microwave transmissions, as of television

**con¹** (kän) *adv.* [< L. *contra*] against —*n.* an opposing reason, vote, etc.

**con²** (kän) *vt.* **conned, con′ning** [< OE. *cunnan*, know] to study carefully

**con³** (kän) *adj.* [Slang] confidence [*con* game] —*vt.* **conned, con′ning** [Slang] to swindle or trick

**con⁴** (kän) *n.* [Slang] a convict

**con-** (kän) same as COM-: used before *c, d, g, j, n, q, s, t,* and *v*

**con·cat·e·na·tion** (kän kat″n ā′shən) *n.* [< L. *com*-, together + *catena*, chain] a connected series, as of events

**con·cave** (kän kāv′, kän′kāv) *adj.* [< L. *com*-, intens. + *cavus*, hollow] hollow and curved like the inside half of a hollow ball —**con·cav′i·ty** (-kav′ə tē) *n.*, *pl.* **-ties**

**con·ceal** (kən sēl′) *vt.* [< L. *com*-, together + *celare*, hide] **1.** to hide **2.** to keep secret —**con·ceal′ment** *n.*

**con·cede** (kən sēd′) *vt.* **-ced′ed, -ced′ing** [< L. *com*-, with + *cedere*, cede] **1.** to admit as true, valid, certain, etc. **2.** to grant as a right

**con·ceit** (kən sēt′) *n.* [see CONCEIVE] **1.** an exaggerated opinion of oneself, one's merits, etc.; vanity **2.** a fanciful expression or notion

**con·ceit′ed** *adj.* vain

**con·ceiv·a·ble** (kən sēv′ə b'l) *adj.* that can be understood or believed —**con·ceiv′a·bil′i·ty** *n.* —**con·ceiv′a·bly** *adv.*

**con·ceive** (kən sēv′) *vt.*, *vi.* **-ceived′, -ceiv′ing** [< L. *com*-, together + *capere*, take] **1.** to become pregnant with **2.** to form in the mind; imagine **3.** to understand —*vi.* **1.** to become pregnant **2.** to form an idea (*of*)

**con·cel·e·brate** (kän sel′ə brāt′) *vt.* **-brat′ed, -brat′ing** [< L. *com*-, together + *celebrare*, to honor] to celebrate (the Eucharistic liturgy) jointly, two or more priests officiating —**con′cel·e·bra′tion** *n.*

**con·cen·trate** (kän′sən trāt′) *vt.* **-trat′ed, -trat′ing** [< L. *com*-, together + *centrum*, a center + -ATE¹] **1.** to focus (one's thoughts, efforts, etc.) **2.** to increase the strength, den-

sity, etc. of —*vi.* to fix one's attention (*on* or *upon*) —*n.* a concentrated substance —**con′cen·tra′tion** *n.*

**concentration camp** a place of confinement for political foes, members of minority ethnic groups, etc.

**con·cen·tric** (kən sen′trik) *adj.* [< L. *com*-, together + *centrum*, center] having a common center, as circles —**con·cen′tri·cal·ly** *adv.*

**con·cept** (kän′sept) *n.* [see CONCEIVE] an idea; general notion

**con·cep·tion** (kən sep′shən) *n.* **1.** a conceiving or being conceived in the womb **2.** the beginning, as of a process **3.** the formulation of ideas **4.** a concept **5.** an original idea or design

**con·cep·tu·al** (-choo wəl) *adj.* of conception or concepts —**con·cep′-tu·al·ly** *adv.*

**con·cep′tu·al·ize′** (-choo wəl īz′) *vt.* **-ized′, -iz′ing** to form a concept of —**con·cep′tu·al·i·za′tion** *n.*

**con·cern** (kən surn′) *vt.* [< L. *com*-, with + *cernere*, sift] **1.** to have a relation to **2.** to engage or involve —*n.* **1.** a matter; affair **2.** interest in or regard for a person or thing **3.** reference **4.** worry **5.** a business firm —**as concerns** in regard to —**concern oneself 1.** to busy oneself **2.** to be worried

**con·cerned′** *adj.* **1.** involved or interested (*in*) **2.** uneasy or anxious

**con·cern′ing** *prep.* relating to

**con·cert** (kän′sərt) *n.* [< L. *com*-, with + *certare*, strive] **1.** mutual agreement; concord **2.** a performance of music —**in concert** in unison

**con·cert·ed** (kən sur′tid) *adj.* mutually arranged or agreed upon; combined —**con·cert′ed·ly** *adv.*

**con·cer·ti·na** (kän′sər tē′nə) *n.* [< CONCERT] a small accordion

**con·cert·ize** (kän′sər tīz′) *vi.* **-ized′, -iz′ing** to perform as a soloist in concerts, esp. on a tour

**con·cert·mas·ter** *n.* the leader of the first violin section of a symphony orchestra, and often the assistant to the conductor

**con·cer·to** (kən cher′tō) *n.*, *pl.* **-tos, -ti** (-tē) [It.] a musical composition for one or more solo instruments and an orchestra

**con·ces·sion** (kən sesh′ən) *n.* **1.** a conceding **2.** a thing conceded; acknowledgment **3.** a privilege granted by a government, company, etc., as the right to sell food at a park

**con·ces′sion·aire′** (-ə ner′) *n.* [< Fr.] the holder of a concession (sense 3)

**conch** (käŋk, känch) *n.*, *pl.* **conchs** (käŋks), **conch·es** (kän′chəz) [< Gr. *konchē*] **1.** the spiral, one-piece shell of various sea mollusks **2.** the mollusk

**con·cierge** (kän′sē urzh′; Fr. kôn syerzh′) *n.* [Fr. < L. *conservus*, fellow slave] an attendant, custodian, etc. guarding an apartment house, etc.

**con·cil·i·ar** (kən sil′ē ər) *adj.* of, from, or by means of a council

**con·cil·i·ate** (-āt′) *vt.* **-at′ed,**

**-at'ing** [see COUNCIL] to win over; make friendly; placate —**con·cil'i·a'tion** *n.* —**con·cil'i·a'tor** *n.* —**con·cil'i·a·to'ry** (-ə tôr'ē) *adj.*

**con·cise** (kən sīs') *adj.* [< L. *com-*, intens. + *caedere*, to cut] brief and to the point; terse —**con·cise'ly** *adv.* —**con·cise'ness, con·ci'sion** (-sizh' ən) *n.*

**con·clave** (kän'klāv, käŋ'-) *n.* [< L. *com-*, with + *clavis*, key] a private meeting; specif., one held by cardinals to elect a pope

**con·clude** (kən klōōd') *vt.*, *vi.* **-clud'ed, -clud'ing** [< L. *com-*, together + *claudere*, to shut] 1. to end; finish 2. to deduce 3. to decide; determine 4. to arrange (a treaty, etc.)

**con·clu'sion** (-klōō'zhən) *n.* 1. the end 2. a judgment or opinion formed after thought 3. an outcome 4. a concluding (*of* a treaty, etc.) —**in conclusion** lastly; in closing

**con·clu'sive** (-siv) *adj.* decisive; final —**con·clu'sive·ly** *adv.* —**con·clu'sive·ness** *n.*

**con·coct** (kən käkt', kän-) *vt.* [< L. *com-*, together + *coquere*, to cook] 1. to make by combining ingredients 2. to devise; plan —**con·coc'tion** *n.*

**con·com'i·tant** (-käm'ə tənt) *adj.* [< L. *com-*, together + *comes*, companion] accompanying; attendant —*n.* a concomitant thing —**con·com'i·tant·ly** *adv.*

**Con·cord** (käŋ'kərd) capital of N.H.; pop. 30,000 —*n.* a large, dark-blue grape: also **Concord grape**

**con·cord** (kän'kôrd, käŋ'-) *n.* [< L. *com-*, together + *cor*, heart] 1. agreement; harmony 2. peaceful relations, as between nations

**con·cord·ance** (kən kôr'd'ns, kän-) *n.* 1. agreement 2. an alphabetical list of the words in a book, with references to the passages where they occur

**con·cord'ant** *adj.* agreeing

**con·cor·dat** (kən kôr'dat, kän-) *n.* [see CONCORD] a formal agreement

**con·course** (kän'kôrs, käŋ'-) *n.* [see CONCUR] 1. a crowd; throng 2. an open space for crowds, as in a park 3. a broad boulevard

**con·crete** (kän krēt'; *also, and for n. & vt. 2 usually,* kän'krēt) *adj.* [< L. *com-*, together + *crescere*, grow] 1. having a material existence; real; actual 2. specific, not general 3. made of concrete —*n.* 1. anything concrete 2. a hard building material made of sand and gravel, bonded together with cement —*vt.*, *vi.* **-cret'ed, -cret'ing** 1. to solidify 2. to cover with concrete —**con·crete'ly** *adv.* —**con·crete'ness** *n.*

**con·cre'tion** (-krē'shən) *n.* 1. a solidifying 2. a solidified mass

**con·cu·bine** (käŋ'kyə bīn', kän'-) *n.* [< L. *com-*, with + *cubare*, to lie down] in some societies, a secondary wife having inferior status

**con·cu·pis·cence** (kän kyōō'pə s'ns) *n.* [< L. *com-*, intens. + *cupiscere*, to desire] strong desire, esp. sexual desire; lust —**con·cu'pis·cent** *adj.*

**con·cur** (kən kur') *vi.* **-curred', -cur'ring** [< L. *com-*, together + *currere*, to run] 1. to occur at the same time 2. to act together 3. to agree —**con·cur'rence** *n.*

**con·cur'rent** *adj.* 1. occurring at the same time 2. acting together 3. *Law* having equal authority —**con·cur'rent·ly** *adv.*

**con·cus·sion** (kən kush'ən) *n.* [< L. *com-*, together + *quatere*, to shake] 1. a violent shaking; shock, as from impact 2. impaired functioning, esp. of the brain, caused by a violent blow

**con·demn** (kən dem') *vt.* [< L. *com-*, intens. + *damnare*, to harm] 1. to disapprove of strongly 2. to declare guilty 3. to inflict a penalty upon 4. to doom 5. to appropriate (property) for public use 6. to declare unfit for use —**con·dem·na·tion** (kän'dem nā'shən) *n.* —**con·dem'na·to'ry** (-nə-tôr'ē) *adj.* —**con·demn'er** *n.*

**con·dense** (kən dens') *vt.* **-densed', -dens'ing** [< L. *com-*, intens. + *densus*, dense] 1. to make more dense or compact 2. to express in fewer words 3. to change to a denser form, as from gas to liquid —*vi.* to become condensed —**con·den·sa·tion** (kän'dən sā'shən) *n.*

**condensed milk** a thick milk made by evaporating part of the water from cow's milk and adding sugar

**con·dens'er** *n.* one that condenses; specif., *a*) an apparatus for liquefying gases *b*) a lens for concentrating light rays *c*) *Elec.* *same as* CAPACITOR

**con·de·scend** (kän'də send') *vi.* [< L. *com-*, together + *descendere*, descend] 1. to be gracious about doing a thing considered beneath one's dignity 2. to deal with others patronizingly —**con'de·scend'ing·ly** *adv.* —**con'de·scen'sion** *n.*

**con·dign** (kən dīn') *adj.* [< L. *com-*, intens. + *dignus*, worthy] deserved; suitable: said esp. of punishment

**con·di·ment** (kän'də mənt) *n.* [< L. *condire*, to pickle] a seasoning or relish, as pepper, mustard, sauces, etc.

**con·di·tion** (kən dish'ən) *n.* [< L. *com-*, together + *dicere*, speak] 1. anything required for the performance, completion, or existence of something else; provision or prerequisite 2. *a*) state of being *b*) [Colloq.] an illness *c*) a healthy state 3. social position; rank —*vt.* 1. to stipulate 2. to impose a condition on 3. to bring into fit condition 4. to make accustomed (*to*) —**on condition that** provided that —**con·di'tion·er** *n.*

**con·di'tion·al** *adj.* containing, expressing, or dependent on a condition; qualified —**con·di'tion·al·ly** *adv.*

**con·di'tioned** (-ənd) *adj.* 1. subject to conditions 2. in a desired condition 3. affected by conditioning 4. accustomed (*to*)

**con·do** (kän'dō) *n.*, *pl.* **-dos, -does** *short for* CONDOMINIUM (sense 2)

**con·dole** (kən dōl') *vi.* **-doled', -dol'ing** [< L. *com-*, with + *dolere*, grieve] to express sympathy; commiserate —**con·do'lence** *n.*

**con·dom** (kun'dəm, kän'-) n. [? after a 17th-c. Brit. colonel] a thin, rubber sheath for the penis, used as a prophylactic or contraceptive

**con·do·min·i·um** (kän'də min'ē əm) n. [ModL. < com-, with + dominium, ownership] 1. joint rule by two or more states 2. the territory ruled 3. one of the units in a multiunit dwelling, each separately owned

**con·done** (kən dōn') vt. -doned', -don'ing [< L. com-, intens. + donare, give] to forgive or overlook (an offense) —con·don'a·ble adj.

**con·dor** (kän'dər) n. [< Sp. < Peruv-Ind.] 1. a large vulture of the S. American Andes, with a bare head 2. a similar vulture of S Calif.

**con·duce** (kən dōōs') vi. -duced', -duc'ing [< L. com-, together + ducere, to lead] to tend or lead (to an effect) —con·du'cive adj.

**con·duct** (kän'dukt'; for v. kən dukt') n. [see prec.] 1. management 2. behavior —vt., vi. 1. to lead 2. to manage 3. to direct (an orchestra, etc.) 4. to behave (oneself) 5. to transmit or convey —con·duc'tion n. —con·duc'tive adj. —con·duc·tiv'i·ty (-tiv'ə tē) n.

**con·duct·ance** (kən duk'təns) n. the ability to conduct electricity

**con·duc·tor** n. 1. the leader of an orchestra, etc. 2. one in charge of passengers on a train, etc. 3. a thing that conducts electricity, heat, etc.

**con·duit** (kän'dit, -doo wit) n. [see CONDUCE] 1. a channel for conveying fluids 2. a tube for electric wires

**con·dyle** (kän'dīl) n. [< Gr. kondylos, hard knob] a rounded process at the end of a bone

**cone** (kōn) n. [< Gr. kōnos] 1. a solid with a circle for its base and a curved surface tapering evenly to a point 2. any cone-shaped object 3. the scaly fruit of evergreen trees

**co·ney** (kō'nē) n., pl. -neys [< L. cuniculus] a rabbit or its fur

**Co·ney Island** (kō'nē) beach and amusement park in Brooklyn, N.Y.

**con·fab** (kän'fab') n. [ult. < L. com-, together + fabulari, to converse] [Colloq.] an informal talk; chat

**con·fec·tion** (kən fek'shən) n. [< L. com-, with + facere, make] a candy, ice cream, preserves, etc.

**con·fec'tion·er** n. one who makes or sells candy and other confections

**con·fec'tion·er·y** (-er'ē) n., pl. -ies a confectioner's shop; candy store

**con·fed·er·a·cy** (kən fed'ər ə sē) n., pl. -cies a league or alliance —the Confederacy the eleven Southern States that seceded from the U.S. in 1860 & 1861

**con·fed·er·ate** (kən fed'ər it; for v. -ə rāt') adj. [< L. com-, together +

foedus, a league] 1. united in an alliance 2. [C-] of the Confederacy —n. 1. an ally; associate 2. an accomplice 3. [C-] a Southern supporter of the Confederacy —vt., vi. -at'ed, -at'ing to unite in a confederacy; ally

**con·fed·er·a'tion** n. an alliance; federation —the Confederation the United States from 1781 to 1789

**con·fer** (kən fur') vt. -ferred', -fer'ring [< L. com-, together + ferre, bring] to give; bestow —vi. to have a conference —con·fer·ee (kän'fə rē') n. —con·fer'ment n. —con·fer'rer n.

**con·fer·ence** (kän'fər əns) n. 1. a formal meeting for discussion 2. an association of schools, churches, etc.

**con·fess** (kən fes') vt., vi. [< L. com-, together + fateri, acknowledge] 1. to admit or acknowledge (a fault, crime, belief, etc.) 2. a) to tell (one's sins) to a priest b) to hear the confession of (a person) —confess to to acknowledge

**con·fess'ed·ly** (-id lē) adv. admittedly

**con·fes·sion** (kən fesh'ən) n. 1. a confessing 2. something confessed 3. a creed 4. a sect; denomination

**con·fes'sion·al** n. an enclosure in a church where a priest hears confessions

**con·fes'sor** n. 1. one who confesses 2. a priest who hears confessions

**con·fet·ti** (kən fet'ē) n.pl. [with sing. v.] [< It.] bits of colored paper scattered about at celebrations, etc.

**con·fi·dant** (kän'fə dant') n. a close, trusted friend —con'fi·dante' n.fem.

**con·fide** (kən fīd') vi. -fid'ed, -fid'ing [< L. com-, intens. + fidere, to trust] to trust (in someone), esp. by sharing secrets —vt. 1. to tell about as a secret 2. to entrust (to)

**con·fi·dence** (kän'fə dəns) n. 1. trust; reliance 2. assurance 3. belief in one's own abilities 4. the belief that another will keep a secret 5. something told as a secret —adj. swindling or used to swindle

**confidence game** a swindle effected by one (confidence man) who first gains the confidence of his victim

**con·fi·dent** (-dənt) adj. full of confidence; specif., a) certain b) sure of oneself —con'fi·dent·ly adv.

**con·fi·den·tial** (-den'shəl) adj. 1. secret 2. of or showing confidence 3. entrusted with private matters —con'fi·den·ti·al'i·ty (-shē al'ə tē) n. —con'fi·den'tial·ly adv.

**con·fig·u·ra·tion** (kən fig'yə rā'shən) n. [< L. com-, together + figurare, to form] contour; outline

**con·fine** (kən fīn'; for n. kän'fīn') n. [< L. com-, with + finis, an end] [usually pl.] a boundary or bounded region —vt. -fined', -fin'ing 1. to keep within limits; restrict 2. to keep shut up, as in prison, a sickbed, etc. —con·fine'ment n.

**con·firm** (kən furm') vt. [< L. com-, intens. + firmare, strengthen] 1. to make firm 2. to give formal approval to 3. to prove the truth of 4. to admit to full church membership

**con·fir·ma·tion** (kän′fər mā′shən) *n.* 1. a confirming 2. something that confirms 3. a ceremony admitting a person to full membership in a church

**con·firmed′** *adj.* 1. firmly established; habitual 2. corroborated

**con·fis·cate** (kän′fə skāt′) *vt.* **-cat′ed, -cat′ing** [< L. *com-*, together + *fiscus*, treasury] 1. to seize (private property) for the public treasury 2. to seize as by authority; appropriate — **con′fis·ca′tion** *n.*

**con·fis·ca·to·ry** (kən fis′kə tôr′ē) *adj.* of or effecting confiscation

**con·fla·gra·tion** (kän′flə grā′shən) *n.* [< L. *com-*, intens. + *flagrare*, to burn] a big, destructive fire

**con·flict** (kən flikt′; *for n.* kän′flikt) *vi.* [< L. *com-*, together + *fligere*, to strike] to be antagonistic, incompatible, etc. —*n.* 1. a fight or war 2. sharp disagreement, as of interests or ideas 3. emotional disturbance

**conflict of interest** a conflict between the obligation to the public and the self-interest of a public officeholder, etc.

**con·flu·ence** (kän′floo əns) *n.* [< L. *com-*, together + *fluere*, flow] 1. a flowing together, esp. of streams 2. the place of this 3. a coming together; crowd —**con′flu·ent** *adj.*

**con·form** (kən fôrm′) *vt.* [< L. *com-*, together + *formare*, to form] 1. to make similar 2. to bring into agreement —*vi.* 1. to be or become similar 2. to be in agreement 3. to act in accordance with rules, customs, etc. —**con·form′ism** *n.*—**con·form′ist** *n.*

**con·for·ma·tion** (kän′fôr mā′shən) *n.* 1. a symmetrical arrangement of the parts of a thing 2. the shape or outline, as of an animal

**con·form·i·ty** (kən fôr′mə tē) *n., pl.* **-ties** 1. agreement; correspondence; similarity 2. conventional behavior

**con·found** (kən found′, kän-) *vt.* [< L. *com-*, together + *fundere*, pour] 1. to confuse; bewilder 2. to damn: a mild oath —**con·found′ed** *adj.*

**con·fra·ter·ni·ty** (kän′frə tur′nə tē) *n., pl.* **-ties** [see COM- & FRATERNAL] 1. brotherhood 2. a religious society, usually of laymen

**con·frere** (kän′frer, kôn′-) *n.* [OFr.] a colleague; associate

**con·front** (kən frunt′) *vt.* [< L. *com-*, together + *frons*, front] 1. to face, esp. boldly or defiantly 2. to bring face to face (*with*) —**con·fron·ta·tion** (kän′frən tā′shən) *n.*

**Con·fu·cius** (kən fyōō′shəs) 551?–479? B.C.; Chin. philosopher & teacher —**Con·fu′cian** *adj., n.*

**con·fuse** (kən fyōōz′) *vt.* **-fused′, -fus′ing** [see CONFOUND] 1. to mix up; put into disorder 2. to bewilder or embarrass 3. to mistake the identity of —**con·fus′ed·ly** *adv.*

**con·fu·sion** (-fyōō′zhən) *n.* a confusing or being confused; specif., disorder, bewilderment, etc.

**con·fute** (kən fyōōt′) *vt.* **-fut′ed,**

**-fut′ing** [< L. *confutare*] to prove to be in error or false —**con·fu·ta·tion** (kän′fyoo tā′shən) *n.*

**Cong.** 1. Congregational 2. Congress

**con·geal** (kən jēl′) *vt., vi.* [< L. *com-*, together + *gelare*, freeze] 1. to freeze 2. to thicken; coagulate; jell —**con·geal′a·ble** *adj.* —**con·geal′ment** *n.*

**con·gen·ial** (kən jēn′yəl) *adj.* [see COM- & GENIAL] 1. kindred; compatible 2. of the same temperament; friendly 3. suited to one's needs; agreeable —**con·ge′ni·al′i·ty** (-jēn′ē al′ə tē) *n.* —**con·gen′ial·ly** *adv.*

**con·gen·i·tal** (kən jen′ə t'l) *adj.* [< L. *congenitus*, born with] existing as such at birth —**con·gen′i·tal·ly** *adv.*

**con·ger** (eel) (käŋ′gər) [< Gr. *gongros*] a large, edible, saltwater eel

**con·ge·ries** (kän′jə rēz′) *n., pl.* **-ries** [L.: see ff.] a heap or pile of things

**con·gest** (kən jest′) *vt.* [< L. *com-*, together + *gerere*, carry] 1. to cause too much blood to accumulate in (a part of the body) 2. to fill to excess; overcrowd —**con·ges′tion** *n.*

**con·glom·er·ate** (kən gläm′ə rāt′; *for adj. & n.* -ər it) *vt., vi.* **-at′ed, -at′ing** [< L. *com-*, together + *glomus*, ball] to form into a rounded mass —*adj.* 1. formed into a rounded mass 2. formed of substances collected into a single mass, esp. of rock fragments or pebbles cemented together by clay, silica, etc. —*n.* 1. a conglomerate mass 2. a large corporation formed by merging many diverse companies 3. a conglomerate rock —**con·glom′er·a′tion** *n.*

**Con·go** (käŋ′gō) 1. river in C Africa, flowing into the Atlantic 2. country mostly west of Zaire: 132,046 sq. mi.; pop. 826,000 3. *former name of* ZAIRE —**Con′go·lese′** (-gə lēz′) *adj., n.*

**con·grat·u·late** (kən grach′ə lāt′) *vt.* **-lat′ed, -lat′ing** [< L. *com-*, together + *gratulari*, wish joy] to express to (a person) one's pleasure at his good fortune, etc.; felicitate —**con·grat′u·la·to·ry** (-lə tôr′ē) *adj.*

**con·grat·u·la·tion** *n.* 1. a congratulating 2. [*pl.*] expressions of pleasure over another's good fortune

**con·gre·gate** (käŋ′grə gāt′) *vt., vi.* **-gat′ed, -gat′ing** [< L. *com-*, together + *grex*, a flock] to gather into a crowd; assemble

**con′gre·ga′tion** *n.* 1. a gathering; assemblage 2. an assembly of people for religious worship —**con′gre·gant** *n.*

**con′gre·ga′tion·al** *adj.* 1. of or like a congregation 2. [C-] of a Protestant denomination in which each member church is self-governing

**con·gress** (käŋ′grəs) *n.* [< L. *com-*, together + *gradi*, to walk] 1. an association or society 2. an assembly or conference 3. a legislature, esp. of a republic 4. [C-] the legislature of the U.S.; the Senate and the House of Representatives —**con·gres·sion·al** (kən gresh′ən 'l) *adj.* —**con·gres′sion·al·ly** *adv.*

**con·gress·man** (-mən) *n., pl.* **-men** a member of Congress, esp. of the House of Representatives

**con·gru·ent** (kän′groo wənt) *adj.* [ < L. *congruere*, agree] corresponding; harmonious —**con′gru·ence** *n.*

**con·gru·ous** (kän′groo wəs) *adj.* 1. congruent 2. fitting; suitable; appropriate —**con·gru·i·ty** (kən groō′ə tē) *n.*, *pl.* **-ties** —**con′gru·ous·ly** *adv.*

**con·i·cal** (kän′i k'l) *adj.* 1. of a cone 2. resembling or shaped like a cone Also **con′ic** —**con′i·cal·ly** *adv.*

**con·i·fer** (kän′ə fər, kō′nə-) *n.* [L. < *conus*, cone + *ferre*, to bear] any of an order of cone-bearing trees and shrubs, mostly evergreens —**co·nif·er·ous** (kə nif′ər əs) *adj.*

**conj.** 1. conjugation 2. conjunction

**con·jec·ture** (kən jek′chər) *n.* [ < L. *com-*, together + *jacere*, throw] 1. an inferring, theorizing, or predicting from incomplete evidence; guesswork 2. a guess —*vt.*, *vi.* **-tured, -tur·ing** to guess —**con·jec′tur·al** *adj.*

**con·join** (kən join′) *vt.*, *vi.* [ < L. *com-*, together + *jungere*, join] to join together; unite —**con·joint′** *adj.*

**con·ju·gal** (kän′jə gəl) *adj.* [ < L. *conjunx*, spouse] of marriage or the relation between husband and wife

**con·ju·gate** (kän′jə gət, -gāt′) *adj.* [ < L. *com-*, together + *jugare*, join] joined together, esp. in a pair —*vt.* (-gāt′) **-gat·ed, -gat·ing** 1. [Archaic] to join together; couple 2. *Gram.* to give in order the inflectional forms of (a verb) —**con′ju·ga′tion** *n.*

**con·junc·tion** (kən junk′shən) *n.* [see CONJOIN] 1. a joining together; union; combination 2. coincidence 3. a word used to connect words, phrases, or clauses (Ex.: *and, but, if*, etc.) —**con·junc′tive** *adj.*

**con·junc·ti·va** (kän′jəŋk tī′və) *n.*, *pl.* **-vas, -vae** (-vē) [see CONJOIN] the mucous membrane covering the inner eyelid and the front of the eyeball

**con·junc·ti·vi·tis** (kən juŋk′tə vīt′is) *n.* inflammation of the conjunctiva

**con·junc·ture** (kən juŋk′chər) *n.* [see CONJOIN] a combination of events creating a crisis

**con·jure** (kän′jər, kun′-; *for vt. 1* kən joor′) *vi.* **-jured, -jur·ing** [ < L. *com-*, together + *jurare*, swear] 1. to summon a demon, spirit, etc. by magic 2. to practice magic —*vt.* 1. to adjure 2. to cause to appear, come (*up*), etc. by or as by magic —**con′ju·ra′tion** *n.* —**con′jur·er, con′jur·or** *n.*

**conk** (käŋk) *n.*, *vt.* [ < CONCH] [Slang] hit on the head —**conk out** [Slang] 1. to fail suddenly, as a motor 2. to fall asleep from fatigue; pass out

**con man** [Slang] *same as* CONFIDENCE MAN

**con·nect** (kə nekt′) *vt.* [ < L. *com-*, together + *nectere*, fasten] 1. to join (two things together, or one thing *with* or *to* another) 2. to show or think of as related —*vi.* to join —**con·nec′tor, con·nect′er** *n.*

**Con·nect·i·cut** (kə net′ə kət) New England State of the U.S.: 5,009 sq.

mi.; pop. 3,032,000; cap. Hartford: abbrev. **Conn.**

**con·nec·tion** (kə nek′shən) *n.* 1. a connecting or being connected 2. a thing that connects 3. a relation; association 4. *a)* a relative, esp. by marriage *b)* an associate, etc.: *usually used in pl.* 5. [*usually pl.*] a transferring from one bus, plane, etc. to another Brit. sp., **con·nex′ion**

**con·nec′tive** (-tiv) *adj.* connecting —*n.* that which connects, esp. a connecting word, as a conjunction

**con·nip·tion** (fit) (kə nip′shən) [pseudo-L.] [Colloq.] a fit of anger, hysteria, etc.: also **con·nip′tions**

**con·nive** (kə niv′) *vi.* **-nived′, -niv′ing** [ < L. *conivere*, to wink, connive] 1. to pretend not to look (*at* crime, etc.), thus giving tacit consent 2. to cooperate secretly (*with* someone), esp. in wrongdoing; scheme —**con·niv′ance** *n.* —**con·niv′er** *n.*

**con·nois·seur** (kän′ə sur′) *n.* [ < Fr. < L. *cognoscere*, know] one who has expert knowledge and keen discrimination, esp. in the fine arts

**con·note** (kə nōt′) *vt.* **-not′ed, -not′ing** [ < L. *com-*, together + *notare*, to mark] to suggest or convey (associations, etc.) in addition to the explicit, or denoted, meaning —**con·no·ta·tion** (kän′ə tā′shən) *n.* —**con′no·ta′tive** *adj.*

**con·nu·bi·al** (kə nōō′bē əl) *adj.* [ < L. *com-*, together + *nubere*, marry] of marriage; conjugal

**con·quer** (käŋ′kər) *vt.* [ < L. *com-*, intens. + *quaerere*, seek] 1. to get control of as by winning a war 2. to overcome; defeat —**con′quer·or** *n.*

**con·quest** (käŋ′kwest, kän′-) *n.* 1. a conquering 2. something conquered 3. a winning of someone's affection or favor

**con·quis·ta·dor** (kän kwis′tə dôr′, -kēs′-) *n.*, *pl.* **-dors, -dores** [Sp., conqueror] any of the 16th-c. Spanish conquerors of Mexico, Peru, etc.

**con·san·guin·e·ous** (kän′saŋ gwin′ē əs) *adj.* [see COM- & SANGUINE] related by blood —**con′san·guin′i·ty** *n.*

**con·science** (kän′shəns) *n.* [ < L. *com-*, with + *scire*, know] an awareness of right and wrong, with a compulsion to do right —**con′science·less** *adj.*

**con·sci·en·tious** (kän′shē en′shəs) *adj.* 1. governed by one's conscience; scrupulous 2. painstaking —**con′sci·en′tious·ly** *adv.* —**con′sci·en′tious·ness** *n.*

**conscientious objector** one who refuses to take part in warfare because his conscience prohibits killing

**con·scious** (kän′shəs) *adj.* [ < L.: see CONSCIENCE] 1. having an awareness (*of* or *that*) 2. able to feel and think; awake 3. aware of oneself as a thinking being 4. intentional [*conscious* humor] —**con′scious·ly** *adv.*

**con′scious·ness** *n.* 1. the state of

being conscious; awareness 2. the totality of one's thoughts and feelings

**con·script** (kən skript'; *for n.* kän' skript) *vt.* [ < L. *com-,* with + *scribere,* write] to enroll for compulsory service in the armed forces; draft —*n.* a draftee —**con·scrip'tion** *n.*

**con·se·crate** (kän'sə krāt') *vt.* -crat'ed, -crat'ing [ < L. *com-,* together + *sacrare,* make holy] to set apart as holy; devote to sacred or serious use —**con'se·cra'tion** *n.*

**con·sec·u·tive** (kən sek'yə tiv) *adj.* [see CONSEQUENCE] following in order, without interruption; successive — **con·sec'u·tive·ly** *adv.*

**con·sen·sus** (kən sen'səs) *n.* [see ff.] 1. an opinion held by all or most 2. general agreement, esp. in opinion

**con·sent** (kən sent') *vi.* [ < L. *com-,* with + *sentire,* feel] to agree, permit, or assent —*n.* 1. permission; approval 2. agreement [by common *consent*]

**con·se·quence** (kän'sə kwens') *n.* [ < L. *com-,* with + *sequi,* follow] 1. a result; effect 2. importance —**take the consequences** to accept the results of one's actions

**con'se·quent'** (-kwent', -kwənt) *adj.* following as a result; resulting —**con'-se·quent'ly** *adv.*

**con'se·quen'tial** (-kwen'shəl) *adj.* 1. consequent 2. important

**con·ser·va·tion** (kän'sər vā'shən) *n.* 1. a conserving 2. the official care and protection of natural resources —**con'ser·va'tion·ist** *n.*

**con·ser·va·tive** (kən sur'və tiv) *adj.* 1. tending to conserve 2. tending to preserve established institutions, etc.; opposed to change 3. moderate; cautious —*n.* a conservative person —**con·ser'va·tism** *n.* —**con·ser'-va·tive·ly** *adv.*

**con·ser·va·to·ry** (kən sur'və tôr'ē) *n., pl.* -ries 1. a greenhouse 2. a school, or academy, of music, art, etc.

**con·serve** (kən surv') *vt.* -served', -serv'ing [ < L. *com-,* with + *servare,* keep] to keep from being damaged, lost, or wasted; save —*n. (usually* kän'sərv) *[often pl.]* a jam of two or more fruits

**con·sid·er** (kən sid'ər) *vt.* [ < L. *considerare,* observe] 1. to think about in order to understand or decide 2. to keep in mind 3. to be thoughtful of (others) 4. to regard as; believe

**con·sid'er·a·ble** *adj.* 1. worth considering; important 2. much or large —**con·sid'er·a·bly** *adv.*

**con·sid'er·ate** (-it) *adj.* having regard for others and their feelings — **con·sid'er·ate·ly** *adv.*

**con·sid'er·a'tion** (-ə rā'shən) *n.* 1. the act of considering; deliberation 2. thoughtful regard for others 3. something considered in making a decision 4. a recompense; fee —**take into consideration** to keep in mind — **under consideration** being thought over

**con·sid'ered** (-ərd) *adj.* arrived at after careful thought

**con·sid'er·ing** *prep.* in view of; taking into account

**con·sign** (kən sīn') *vt.* [ < L. *con-signare,* to seal] 1. to hand over; deliver 2. to entrust 3. to assign 4. to send or deliver (goods)

**con·sign'ment** (-mənt) *n.* 1. a consigning or being consigned 2. a shipment of goods sent to an agent for sale, etc. —**on consignment** with payment due after sale of the consignment

**con·sist** (kən sist') *vi.* [ < L. *com-,* together + *sistere,* stand] 1. to be formed or composed *(of)* 2. to be contained or inherent *(in)*

**con·sis·ten·cy** (-ən sē) *n., pl.* -cies 1. firmness or thickness, as of a liquid 2. agreement; harmony 3. conformity with previous practice

**con·sis·tent** (-ənt) *adj.* 1. in harmony or agreement; compatible 2. holding to the same principles or practice —**con·sis'tent·ly** *adv.*

**con·sis·to·ry** (kən sis'tər ē) *n., pl.* -ries [see CONSIST] 1. a church council or court, as the papal senate 2. a session of such a body

**con·so·la·tion** (kän'sə lā'shən) *n.* 1. comfort; solace 2. one that consoles

**con·sole¹** (kən sōl') *vt.* -soled', -sol'-ing [ < L. *com-,* with + *solari,* to solace] to make feel less sad or disappointed; comfort —**con·sol'a·to·ry** *adj.* —**con·sol'ing·ly** *adv.*

**con·sole²** (kän'sōl) *n.* [Fr.] 1. the desklike frame containing the keys, stops, etc. of an organ 2. a radio, television, or phonograph cabinet designed to stand on the floor 3. a control panel for operating aircraft, computers, electronic systems, etc.

**con·sol·i·date** (kən sä'lə dāt') *vt., vi.* -dat'ed, -dat'ing [ < L. *com-,* together + *solidus,* solid] 1. to combine into one; unite 2. to make or become strong or stable —**con·sol'i-da'tion** *n.* —**con·sol'i·da'tor** *n.*

**con·som·mé** (kän'sə mā') *n.* [Fr.] a clear, strained meat soup

**con·so·nance** (kän'sə nəns) *n.* [ < L. *com-,* with + *sonus,* sound] harmony, esp. of musical tones; agreement: also **con·so·nan·cy**

**con'so·nant** (-nənt) *adj.* in harmony or accord —*n.* a letter representing a speech sound made by obstructing the air stream, as *p, t, l, f,* etc. —**con'so·nan'tal** (-nant'l) *adj.*

**con·sort** (kän'sôrt; *for v.* kən sôrt') *n.* [ < L. *com-,* with + *sors,* a share] a wife or husband, esp. of a reigning king or queen —*vi.* to associate

**con·sor·ti·um** (kən sôr'shē əm) *n., pl.* -ti·a [see prec.] an international alliance, as of business firms or banks

**con·spec·tus** (kən spek'təs) *n.* [L.: see ff.] 1. a general view 2. a summary; digest

**con·spic·u·ous** (kən spik'yoo wəs) *adj.* [ < L. *com-,* intens. + *specere,* see] 1. easy to see 2. outstanding; striking —**con·spic'u·ous·ly** *adv.*

**con·spir·a·cy** (kən spir'ə sē) *n., pl.* -cies 1. a conspiring 2. an unlawful plot 3. a conspiring group

**con·spire** (-spīr') *vi.* -spired', -spir'ing [ < L. *com-,* together + *spirare,* to breathe] 1. to plan together secretly, as to commit a crime 2. to work together toward a single end —**con·spir'a·tor** (-spir'ə tər) *n.* —**con·spir'a·to'ri·al** (-spir'ə tôr'ē əl) *adj.*

**con·sta·ble** (kän'stə b'l, kun'-) *n.* [< LL. *comes stabuli,* lit., count of the stable] [Chiefly Brit.] a policeman

**con·stab·u·lar·y** (kən stab'yə ler'ē) *n., pl.* **-ies** 1. constables, collectively 2. a militarized police force

**con·stant** (kän'stənt) *adj.* [< L. *com-,* together + *stare,* to stand] 1. not changing; regular; faithful 2. continual; persistent —*n.* anything that does not change or vary —**con'stan·cy** *n.* —**con'stant·ly** *adv.*

**Con·stan·tine** (kän'stən tēn', -tīn') 280?–337 A.D.; first Christian emperor of Rome (306–337 A.D.)

**Con·stan·ti·no·ple** (kän'stan tə nō'p'l) *former name of* ISTANBUL

**con·stel·la·tion** (kän'stə lā'shən) *n.* [< L. *com-,* with + *stella,* star] a group of fixed stars

**con·ster·na·tion** (kän'stər nā'shən) *n.* [< L. *consternare,* terrify] great fear or shock

**con·sti·pate** (kän'stə pāt') *vt.* **-pat'ed, -pat'ing** [< L. *com-,* together + *stipare,* cram] to cause constipation in —**con'sti·pa'tion** *n.* infrequent and difficult movement of the bowels

**con·stit·u·en·cy** (kən stich'oo wən sē) *n., pl.* **-cies** the voters in a district

**con·stit·u·ent** (-wənt) *adj.* [see ff.] 1. necessary to the whole; component 2. that elects 3. authorized to make or revise a constitution —*n.* 1. a voter in a district 2. a component

**con·sti·tute** (kän'stə tōōt', -tyōōt') *vt.* **-tut'ed, -tut'ing** [< L. *com-,* together + *statuere,* to set] 1. to establish (a law, government, etc.) 2. to set up (an assembly, etc.) in a legal form 3. to appoint 4. to form; compose —**con'sti·tu'tive** *adj.*

**con·sti·tu·tion** (-tōō'shən, -tyōō'-) *n.* 1. a constituting 2. structure; organization 3. *a)* the system of basic laws and principles of a government, society, etc. *b)* a document stating these; specif., [C-] the Constitution of the U.S.

**con·sti·tu·tion·al** *adj.* 1. of or in one's constitution or structure; basic 2. of or in accordance with the constitution of a government, society, etc.—*n.* a walk taken for one's health —**con'sti·tu'tion·al'i·ty** (-al'ə tē) *n.* —**con'sti·tu'tion·al·ly** *adv.*

**con·strain** (kən strān') *vt.* [< L. *com-,* together + *stringere,* draw tight] 1. to confine 2. to restrain 3. to compel

**con·straint'** *n.* 1. confinement; restriction 2. force; compulsion 3. forced, unnatural manner

**con·strict** (kən strikt') *vt.* [see CON-STRAIN] to make smaller or narrower by squeezing, etc. —**con·stric'tion** *n.*

**con·struct** (kən strukt') *vt.* [< L. *com-,* together + *struere,* pile up] to build, devise, etc. —**con·struc'tor** *n.*

**con·struc·tion** (-struk'shən) *n.* 1. a constructing or manner of being constructed 2. a structure 3. an interpretation, as of a statement 4. the arrangement of words in a sentence

**con·struc·tion·ist** *n.* a person who interprets a law, document, etc. in a specified way

**con·struc·tive** *adj.* helping to construct; leading to improvement

**con·strue** (kən strōō') *vt., vi.* **-strued', -stru'ing** [see CONSTRUCT] 1. to analyze the grammatical construction of (a sentence) 2. to translate 3. to explain; interpret

**con·sul** (kän's'l) *n.* [< L. *consulere,* to deliberate] 1. a chief magistrate of ancient Rome 2. a government official appointed to live in a foreign city and look after his country's citizens and business there —**con'su·lar** *adj.*

**con'sul·ate** (-it) *n.* 1. the position, powers, etc. of a consul 2. the office or residence of a consul

**con·sult** (kən sult') *vi.* [< L. *consulere,* consider] to talk things over; confer —*vt.* 1. to seek information or instruction from 2. to consider —**con·sul·ta·tion** (kän's'l tā'shən) *n.*

**con·sult'ant** *n.* 1. a person who consults another 2. one who gives professional or technical advice

**con·sume** (kən sōōm') *vt.* **-sumed', -sum'ing** [< L. *com-,* together + *sumere,* to take] 1. to destroy, as by fire 2. to use up or waste (time, money, etc.) 3. to eat or drink up

**con·sum'er** *n.* a person or thing that consumes; specif., one who uses goods or services for his own needs rather than to produce other goods

**con·sum'er·ism** (-iz'm) *n.* a movement for protecting the consumer against defective products, misleading business practices, etc.

**con·sum·mate** (kən sum'it; *for v.* kän'sə māt') *adj.* [< L. *com-,* together + *summa,* a sum] complete; perfect —*vt.* **-mat'ed, -mat'ing** 1. to complete 2. to complete (marriage) by sexual intercourse —**con·sum'mate·ly** *adv.* —**con'sum·ma'tion** *n.*

**con·sump·tion** (kən sump'shən) *n.* 1. a consuming or being consumed 2. the using up of goods or services 3. the amount consumed 4. a wasting disease, esp. tuberculosis of the lungs

**con·sump'tive** (-tiv) *adj.* 1. consuming or tending to consume 2. of or having tuberculosis of the lungs —*n.* one who has tuberculosis of the lungs

**cont., contd.** continued

**con·tact** (kän'takt) *n.* [< L. *com-,* together + *tangere,* to touch] 1. a touching or meeting 2. the state of being in association (*with*) 3. a connection —*vt.* 1. to place in contact 2. to get in touch with —*vi.* to come into contact

**contact flying** piloting an airplane by observing objects on the ground

**contact lens** a tiny, thin correctional

lens placed in the fluid over the cornea of the eye

**con·ta·gion** (kən tā′jən) *n.* [see prec.] **1.** the spreading of disease by contact **2.** a contagious disease **3.** the spreading of an emotion, idea, etc.

**con·ta′gious** (-jəs) *adj.* **1.** spread by contact: said of diseases **2.** carrying the causative agent of a contagious disease **3.** spreading from person to person —**con·ta′gious·ness** *n.*

**con·tain** (kən tān′) *vt.* [< L. *com-*, together + *tenere*, to hold] **1.** to have in it; hold **2.** to have the capacity for holding **3.** to hold back or restrain within fixed limits —**con·tain′ment** *n.*

**con·tain′er** *n.* a thing for containing something; box, can, etc.

**con·tain′er·ize** *vt.* -ized′, -iz′ing to pack (cargo) into huge, standardized containers for shipment

**con·tam·i·nant** (kən tam′ə nənt) *n.* a contaminating substance

**con·tam′i·nate′** (-nāt′) *vt.* -nat′ed, -nat′ing [< L. *com-*, together + *tangere*, to touch] to make impure, corrupt, etc. by contact; pollute; taint —**con·tam′i·na′tion** *n.*

**con·temn** (kən tem′) *vt.* [< L. *com-*, intens. + *temnere*, to scorn] to treat with contempt; scorn

**con·tem·plate** (kän′təm plāt′) *vt.* -plat′ed, -plat′ing [< L. *contemplari*, observe] **1.** to gaze at or think about intently **2.** to expect or intend —*vi.* to muse —**con′tem·pla′tion** *n.* —**con·tem·pla·tive** (kən tem′plə tiv, kän′təm plāt′iv) *adj.*, *n.*

**con·tem·po·rar·y** (kən tem′pə rer′ē) *adj.* [< L. *com-*, with + *tempus*, time] **1.** living or occurring in the same period **2.** of about the same age **3.** modern Also **con·tem′po·ra·ne·ous** (-rā′nē əs) —*n.*, *pl.* -ies one existing in the same period as another or others

**con·tempt** (kən tempt′) *n.* [see CONTEMN] **1.** the feeling one has toward someone or something he considers low, worthless, etc. **2.** the condition of being despised **3.** *Law* a showing disrespect for the dignity of a court (or legislature)

**con·tempt′i·ble** *adj.* deserving contempt or scorn; despicable —**con·tempt′i·bly** *adv.*

**con·temp·tu·ous** (kən temp′choo wəs) *adj.* full of contempt; scornful —**con·temp′tu·ous·ly** *adv.*

**con·tend** (kən tend′) *vi.* [< L. *com-*, together + *tendere*, extend] **1.** to fight or argue **2.** to compete —*vt.* to assert —**con·tend′er** *n.*

**con·tent¹** (kən tent′) *adj.* [see CONTAIN] **1.** satisfied **2.** willing; assenting —*vt.* to satisfy —*n.* contentment

**con·tent²** (kän′tent) *n.* [see CONTAIN] **1.** [*usually pl.*] *a)* what is in a container *b)* what is in a book, etc. **2.** what is dealt with in a talk, etc. **3.** substance or meaning **4.** amount contained

**con·tent′ed** *adj.* satisfied —**con·tent′ed·ly** *adv.* —**con·tent′ed·ness** *n.*

**con·ten·tion** (kən ten′shən) *n.* [see CONTEND] **1.** dispute; strife **2.** a point argued for —**con·ten′tious** *adj.* —**con·ten′tious·ly** *adv.* —**con·ten′tious·ness** *n.*

**con·tent′ment** *n.* the state or fact of being contented

**con·ter·mi·nous** (kən tur′mə nəs) *adj.* [< *com-*, together + *terminus*, end] **1.** having a common boundary **2.** contained within the same boundaries —**con·ter′mi·nous·ly** *adv.*

**con·test** (kən test′; *for n.* kän′test) *vt.* [< L. *com-*, together + *testis*, witness] **1.** to dispute (a point, etc.) **2.** to fight for (a position, etc.) —*vi.* to struggle (*with* or *against*) —*n.* **1.** a fight; struggle **2.** a competitive game, race, etc. —**con·test′a·ble** *adj.*

**con·test′ant** *n.* [Fr.] **1.** a competitor in a game, etc. **2.** one who contests

**con·text** (kän′tekst) *n.* [< L. *com-*, together + *texere*, weave] the parts just before and after a word or passage, that determine its meaning —**con·tex·tu·al** (kən teks′choo wəl) *adj.*

**con·tig·u·ous** (kən tig′yoo wəs) *adj.* [see CONTACT] **1.** in contact; touching **2.** near; next —**con·ti·gu·i·ty** (kän′tə gyōō′ə tē) *n.*, *pl.* -ties

**con·ti·nence** (känt′′n əns) *n.* [see CONTAIN] **1.** self-restraint **2.** self-restraint in sexual activity, esp. total abstinence —**con′ti·nent** *adj.*

**con′ti·nent** (-ənt) *n.* [see CONTAIN] any of the main large land areas of the earth —**the Continent** the mainland of Europe

**con′ti·nen′tal** (-en′t′l) *adj.* **1.** of a continent **2.** [*sometimes* C-] European **3.** [C-] of the American colonies at the time of the American Revolution

**con·tin·gen·cy** (kən tin′jən sē) *n.*, *pl.* -cies **1.** dependence on chance **2.** a possible or chance event

**con·tin′gent** *adj.* [see CONTACT] **1.** possible **2.** accidental **3.** dependent (*on* or *upon* an uncertainty) —*n.* **1.** a chance happening **2.** a quota, as of troops **3.** a part of a large group

**con·tin·u·al** (kən tin′yoo wəl) *adj.* **1.** repeated often **2.** continuous —**con·tin′u·al·ly** *adv.*

**con·tin′u·ance** *n.* **1.** a continuing **2.** duration **3.** an unbroken succession **4.** *Law* postponement or adjournment

**con·tin′u·a′tion** (-wā′shən) *n.* **1.** a continuing **2.** a beginning again; resumption **3.** a part added; sequel

**con·tin·ue** (kən tin′yōō) *vi.* -ued, -u·ing [< L. *continuare*, join] **1.** to last; endure **2.** to go on in a specified action or condition **3.** to stay **4.** to extend **5.** to go on again after an interruption —*vt.* **1.** to go on with **2.** to extend **3.** to cause to remain, as in office **4.** *Law* to postpone

**con·ti·nu·i·ty** (känt′ə nōō′ə tē, -nyōō′-) *n.*, *pl.* -ties **1.** a continuous state or quality **2.** an unbroken, coherent whole **3.** the script for a motion picture, radio program, etc.

**con·tin·u·ous** (kən tin′yoo wəs) *adj.* going on without interruption; unbroken —**con·tin′u·ous·ly** *adv.*

**con·tin′u·um** (-yoo wəm) *n.*, *pl.* -u·a, -u·ums [L.] a continuous whole, quantity, or series

**con·tort** (kən tôrt′) *vt.*, *vi.* [< L.

com-, together + *torquere*, to twist] to twist or wrench out of shape; distort —con·tor′tion n.

con·tor′tion·ist n. one who can twist his body into unnatural positions

con·tour (kän′toor) n. [Fr. < L. com-, intens. + *tornare*, to turn] the outline of a figure, land, etc. —vt. to shape to the contour of —adj. conforming to or following the shape or contour of something

contr. contraction

contra- [< L. *contra*] a prefix meaning against, opposite, opposed to

con·tra·band (kän′trə band′) n. [< Sp. < It.] smuggled goods —adj. illegal to import or export

con·tra·cep·tion (kän′trə sep′shən) n. [CONTRA- + (CON)CEPTION] prevention of the fertilization of the human ovum —con′tra·cep′tive adj., n.

con·tract (kän′trakt′ for n. & usually for vt. 1 & vi. 1; kən trakt′ for v. generally) n. [< L. com-, together + *trahere*, draw] an agreement, esp. a written one enforceable by law, between two or more people —vt. 1. to undertake by contract 2. to get or incur (a debt, disease, etc.) 3. to reduce in size; shrink 4. to shorten (a word or phrase) —vi. 1. to make a contract 2. to become smaller

con·trac·tile (kən trak′t'l) adj. having the power of contracting

con·trac·tion (kən trak′shən) n. 1. a contracting or being contracted 2. the shortened form of a word or phrase [Ex.: don't for do not]

con·trac·tor (kän′trak tər, kən trak′-) n. a builder, etc. who contracts to supply materials or do work

con·trac·tu·al (kən trak′choo wəl) adj. of or constituting a contract

con·tra·dict (kän′trə dikt′) vt. [< L. *contra*-, against + *dicere*, speak] 1. to assert the opposite of or deny (a statement) 2. to deny the statement of (a person) 3. to be contrary to —con′tra·dic′tion n. —con′tra·dic′to·ry adj.

con·tra·dis·tinc·tion (-dis tiŋk′shən) n. distinction by contrast —con′tra·dis·tinc′tive adj.

con·trail (kän′trāl′) n. a white trail of condensed water vapor in the wake of an aircraft

con·tra·in·di·cate vt. -cat′ed, -cat′ing Med. to make (the indicated drug or treatment) inadvisable

con·tral·to (kən tral′tō) n., pl. -tos, -ti (-tē) [It.: see CONTRA- & ALTO] 1. a female voice of the lowest range 2. a woman with such a voice

con·trap·tion (kən trap′shən) n. [< ?] [Colloq.] a contrivance; gadget

con·tra·pun·tal (kän′trə pun′t'l) adj. [< It. *contrapunto*, counterpoint] of or characterized by counterpoint

con·tra·ri·wise (kän′trer ē wiz′) adv. 1. on the contrary 2. in the opposite way, order, etc.

con·tra·ry (kän′trer ē; for adj. 4, often kən trer′ē) adj. [< L. *contra*, against] 1. opposed 2. opposite in nature, order, etc.; quite different 3. unfavorable 4. always resisting; perverse —n., pl. -ries the opposite —on the contrary as opposed to what has been said —to the contrary to the opposite effect —con′tra·ri·e·ty (-trə rī′ə tē) n. —con′trar·i·ly adv. —con′trar·i·ness n.

con·trast (kən trast′; for n. kän′trast) vt. [< L. *contra*, against + *stare*, to stand] to compare so as to point out the differences —vi. to show differences when compared —n. 1. a contrasting or being contrasted 2. a striking difference between things being compared 3. a person or thing showing differences when compared with another —con′trast′a·ble adj.

con·tra·vene (kän′trə vēn′) vt. -vened′, -ven′ing [< L. *contra*, against + *venire*, come] 1. to go against; violate 2. to contradict

con·tre·temps (kōn′trə tän′) n., pl. -temps′ (-tän′) [Fr.] a confusing, embarrassing, or awkward occurrence

con·trib·ute (kən trib′yoot) vt., vi. -ut·ed, -ut·ing [< L.: see COM- & TRIBUTE] 1. to give together with others 2. to write (an article, etc.) as for a magazine 3. to furnish (ideas, etc.) —contribute to to share in bringing about —con·trib′u·tor n. —con·trib′u·to′ry adj.

con·tri·bu·tion (kän′trə byoo′shən) n. 1. a contributing 2. something contributed, as money

con·trite (kən trīt′) adj. [< L. com-, together + *terere*, to rub] deeply sorry for having done wrong; penitent —con·trite′ly adv. —con·trite′ness n. —con·tri′tion (-trish′ən) n.

con·triv·ance (kən trī′vəns) n. 1. the act, way, or power of contriving 2. something contrived; device, etc.

con·trive (kən trīv′) vt. -trived′, -triv′ing [ult. < VL. *contropare*, compare] 1. to think up, devise, design, etc. 2. to make inventively 3. to bring about; manage —con·triv′er n.

con·trol (kən trōl′) vt. -trolled′, -trol′ling [< ML. *contrarotulus*, a register] 1. to regulate or direct 2. to verify (an experiment) by comparison 3. to exercise authority over; direct 4. to restrain —n. 1. power to direct or regulate 2. a means of controlling; check 3. an apparatus to regulate a mechanism: usually used in pl. —con·trol′la·ble adj.

con·trol′ler n. 1. a person in charge of finances, as in a business 2. a person or device that controls

con·tro·ver·sial (kän′trə vur′shəl) adj. subject to controversy; debatable

con′tro·ver′sy (-sē) n., pl. -sies [< L. *contra*, against + *vertere*, to turn] a conflict of opinion; dispute

con′tro·vert′ (-vurt′) vt. 1. to argue against; dispute 2. to argue about; debate —con′tro·vert′i·ble adj.

fat, āpe, cär; ten, ēven; is, bīte; gō, hôrn, tōōl, look; oil, out; up, fur; chin; she; thin, then; zh, leisure; ŋ, ring; ə for a in ago; ', (ā′b'l); ë, Fr. coeur; ö, Fr. feu; Fr. mon; ü, Fr. duc; kh, G. ich, doch; ‡ foreign; < derived from

**con·tu·ma·cy** (kän′too mə sē) *n.*, *pl.* **-cies** [< L. *contumax*, stubborn] stubborn resistance to authority — **con′tu·ma′cious** (-mā′shəs) *adj.*

**con·tu·me·ly** (kän′too mə lē) *n.*, *pl.* **-lies** [< L. *contumelia*, abuse] humiliating treatment or scornful insult — **con′tu·me′li·ous** (-mē′lē əs) *adj.*

**con·tuse** (kən tōōz′) *vt.* **-tused′**, **-tus′ing** [see ff.] to bruise

**con·tu·sion** (kən tōō′zhən) *n.* [< L. *com-*, intens. + *tundere*, to beat] a bruise

**co·nun·drum** (kə nun′drəm) *n.* [pseudo-L.] 1. a riddle whose answer is a pun 2. any puzzling problem

**con·ur·ba·tion** (kän′ər bā′shən) *n.* a vast urban area around and including a large city

**con·va·lesce** (kän′və les′) *vi.* **-lesced′**, **-lesc′ing** [< L. *com-*, intens. + *valere*, be strong] to regain health and strength; get better — **con′va·les′cence** *n.* — **con′va·les′cent** *adj.*, *n.*

**con·vec·tion** (kən vek′shən) *n.* [< L. *com-*, together + *vehere*, carry] 1. a transmitting 2. *a)* movement of parts of a fluid within the fluid because of differences in heat, etc. *b).* heat transference by such movement — **con·vec′tion·al** *adj.* — **con·vec′tive** *adj.*

**con·vene** (kən vēn′) *vi.*, *vt* **-vened′**, **-ven′ing** [< L. *com-*, together + *venire*, come] to assemble for a meeting — **con·ven′er** *n.*

**con·ven·ience** (kən vēn′yəns) *n.* [see prec.] 1. the quality of being convenient 2. comfort 3. anything that adds to one's comfort or saves work —**at one's convenience** at a time or place suitable to one

**con·ven·ient** (-yənt) *adj.* easy to do, use, or get to; handy —**con·ven′ient·ly** *adv.*

**con·vent** (kän′vənt, -vent) *n.* [see CONVENE] 1. a community of nuns 2. the place where they live

**con·ven·ti·cle** (kən ven′ti k′l) *n.* [see CONVENE] an assembly, esp. a religious assembly, held secretly

**con·ven·tion** (kən ven′shən) *n.* 1. an assembly, often periodical, or its members. 2. an agreement, as between nations 3. custom; usage

**con·ven·tion·al** (-′l) *adj.* 1. having to do with a convention 2. sanctioned by or following custom or usage; customary 3. formal —**con·ven′tion·al′i·ty** (-al′ə tē) *n.*, *pl.* **-ties** —**con·ven′tion·al·ly** *adv.*

**con·ven·tion·al·ize′** (-īz′) *vt.* **-ized′**, **-iz′ing** to make conventional

**con·verge** (kən vurj′) *vi.*, *vt.* **-verged′**, **-verg′ing** [< L. *com-*, together + *vergere*, to turn] to come or bring together at a point —**con·ver′gence** *n.* —**con·ver′gent** *adj.*

**con·ver·sant** (kən vur′s′nt, kän′vər-) *adj.* familiar or acquainted (*with*)

**con·ver·sa·tion** (kän′vər sā′shən) *n.* a talking together; informal talk — **con′ver·sa′tion·al** *adj.* —**con′ver·sa′tion·al·ist** *n.* —**con′ver·sa′tion·al·ly** *adv.*

**conversation piece** something, as an unusual article of furniture, that attracts attention or invites comment

**con·verse′** (kən vurs′; *for n.* kän′vərs) *vi.* **-versed′**, **-vers′ing** [< L. *conversari*, to live with] to hold a conversation; talk —*n.* conversation

**con·verse²** (kän′vərs; *also for adj.* kən vurs′) *adj.* [see CONVERT] reversed in position, order, etc.; opposite; contrary —*n.* a converse thing; the opposite —**con·verse′ly** *adv.*

**con·ver·sion** (kən vur′zhən) *n.* a converting or being converted

**con·vert** (kən vurt′; *for n.* kän′vərt) *vt.* [< L. *com-*, together + *vertere*, to turn] 1. to change; transform 2. to change from one religion, doctrine, etc. to another 3. to exchange for something equal in value 4. to misappropriate —*vi.* to be converted —*n.* a person converted, as to a religion —**con·vert′er, con·ver′tor** *n.*

**con·vert·i·ble** (kən vur′tə b′l) *adj.* that can be converted —*n.* an automobile with a folding top

**con·vex** (kän veks′, kän′veks) *adj.* [< L. *com-*, together + *vehere*, bring] curving outward like the surface of a sphere —**con·vex′i·ty** *n.*, *pl.* **-ties**

**con·vey** (kən vā′) *vt.* [< L. *com-*, together + *via*, way] 1. to take from one place to another; transport; carry 2. to transmit —**con·vey′a·ble** *adj.* —**con·vey′or, con·vey′er** *n.*

**con·vey′ance** *n.* 1. a conveying 2. a means of conveying, esp. a vehicle

**con·vict** (kən vikt′; *for n.* kän′vikt) *vt.* [see CONVINCE] to prove or find (a person) guilty —*n.* a convicted person serving a prison sentence

**con·vic·tion** (kən vik′shən) *n.* 1. a convicting or being convicted 2. a being convinced; strong belief

**con·vince** (kən vins′) *vt.* **-vinced′**, **-vinc′ing** [< L. *com-*, intens. + *vincere*, conquer] to persuade by argument or evidence; make feel sure — **con·vinc′er** *n.* —**con·vinc′ing** *adj.* —**con·vinc′ing·ly** *adv.*

**con·viv·i·al** (kən viv′ē əl) *adj.* [< L. *com-*, together + *vivere*, to live] 1. festive 2. fond of eating, drinking, and good company; sociable —**con·viv′i·al′i·ty** (-al′ə tē) *n.*

**con·vo·ca·tion** (kän′və kā′shən) *n.* 1. a convoking 2. an assembly

**con·voke** (kən vōk′) *vt.* **-voked′**, **-vok′ing** [< L. *com-*, together + *vocare*, to call] to call together; convene

**con·vo·lut·ed** (kän′və lōōt′id) *adj.* 1. coiled 2. complicated; involved

**con·vo·lu·tion** (-lōō′shən) *n.* [< L. *com-*, together + *vol-vere*, to roll] 1. a twisting, coiling, or winding together 2. a fold, twist, or coil

**con·voy** (kän′voi; *also for v.* kən voi′) *vt.* [see CONVEY] to escort in order to protect —*n.* 1. a convoying 2. a protecting escort 3. ships, vehicles, etc. being convoyed

CONVOLUTIONS OF BRAIN

**con·vulse** (kən vuls′) *vt.* **-vulsed′**, **-vuls′ing** [< L. *com-*, together +

*vellere,* to pluck] 1. to shake violently; agitate 2. to cause to shake with laughter, rage, etc.

**con·vul·sion** (-vul′shən) *n.* 1. a violent, involuntary spasm of the muscles: *often in pl.* 2. a fit of laughter 3. a violent disturbance —**con·vul′sive** *adj.* —**con·vul′sive·ly** *adv.*

**co·ny** (kō′nē) *n., pl.* -**nies** *same as* CONEY

**coo** (kōō) *vi.* [echoic] to make the soft, murmuring sound of pigeons or doves —*n.* this sound

**cook** (kook) *vt.* [< L. *coquere*] to prepare (food) by boiling, baking, frying, etc. —*vi.* 1. to be a cook 2. to undergo cooking —*n.* one who prepares food —**cook up** [Colloq.] to devise; invent —**cook′er** *n.*

**cook′book′** *n.* a book with recipes and other information for preparing food

**cook′er·y** *n.* [Chiefly Brit.] the art or practice of cooking

**cook′ie** (-ē) *n.* [prob. < Du. *koek,* cake] a small, sweet, flat cake: also **cook′y,** *pl.* -**ies**

**cook′out′** *n.* a meal cooked and eaten outdoors

**cool** (kōōl) *adj.* [OE. *col*] 1. moderately cold 2. tending to reduce the effects of heat [*cool* clothes] 3. not excited; composed 4. showing dislike or indifference 5. calmly bold 6. [Colloq.] without exaggeration [a *cool* $1,000] 7. [Slang] very good —*n.* 1. a cool place, time, etc. [the *cool* of the night] 2. [Slang] cool, dispassionate manner —*vt., vi.* to make or become cool —**cool′ly** *adv.* —**cool′ness** *n.*

**cool′ant** (-ənt) *n.* a fluid or other substance for cooling engines, etc.

**cool′er** *n.* 1. a place for keeping things cool 2. [Slang] jail

**Coo·lidge** (kōō′lij), (**John**) **Calvin** 1872–1933; 30th president of the U.S. (1923–29)

**coo·lie** (kōō′lē) *n.* [Hind. *qūlī,* servant] an unskilled native laborer, esp. formerly, in India, China, etc.

**coon** (kōōn) *n. short for* RACCOON

**coon′skin′** *n.* the skin of a raccoon, used as a fur

**coop** (kōōp) *n.* [< L. *cupa,* cask] 1. a small pen for poultry, etc. 2. [Slang] jail —*vt.* to confine as in a coop

**co-op** (kō′äp) *n.* a cooperative

**coop′er** *n.* [see COOP] one whose work is making or repairing barrels and casks —**coop′er·age** (-ij) *n.*

**co·op·er·ate** (kō äp′ə rāt′) *vi.* -**at′ed,** -**at′ing** [< L. *co-,* with + *opus,* work] to act or work together with another or others Also **co-op′er·ate′, co·öp′er·ate′** —**co·op′er·a′tion** *n.*

**co·op·er·a·tive** (-ər ə tiv, -ə rāt′iv) *adj.* 1. cooperating 2. owned collectively by members who share in its benefits —*n.* a cooperative store, etc. Also **co-op′er·a·tive, co·öp′er·a·tive**

**co-opt** (kō äpt′) *vt.* [< L. *co-,* with + *optare,* choose] 1. to elect or appoint

as an associate 2. to get (an opponent) to join one's side

**co·or·di·nate** (kō ôr′d'n it; *also, and for v. always,* -də nāt′) *adj.* [< L. *co-,* with + *ordo,* order] 1. of equal order, rank, or importance [*coordinate* clauses in a sentence] 2. of coordination or coordinates —*n.* a coordinate person or thing —*vt.* -**nat′ed,** -**nat′ing** 1. to make coordinate 2. to bring into proper order or relation; adjust Also **co-or′di·nate, co·ör′di·nate** — **co·or′di·na′tor** *n.*

**coordinating conjunction** a conjunction connecting coordinate words, clauses, etc. (Ex.: *and, but*)

**co·or·di·na′tion** *n.* 1. a coordinating or being coordinated 2. harmonious action, as of muscles Also **co-or′di·na′tion, co·ör′di·na′tion**

**coot** (kōōt) *n.* [ME. *cote*] 1. a ducklike water bird 2. [Colloq.] a fool

**coot·ie** (kōōt′ē) *n.* [Slang] a louse

**cop** (käp) *vt.* copped, cop′ping [< ? L. *capere,* take] [Slang] to seize; steal —*n.* [Slang] a policeman —**cop out** [Slang] 1. to confess to police 2. to renege 3. to give up; quit

**co·part·ner** (kō pärt′nər) *n.* a partner

**cope¹** (kōp) *vi.* coped, cop′ing [< OFr. *couper,* to strike] to fight or contend (*with*) successfully

**cope²** (kōp) *n.* [< LL. *cappa*] 1. a large capelike vestment worn by priests 2. any cover like this

**Co·pen·hag·en** (kō′pən hā′gən, -hä′-) capital of Denmark: pop. 874,000

**Co·per·ni·cus** (kō pur′ni kəs), **Nic·o·la·us** (nik′ə lā′əs) 1473–1543; Pol. astronomer —**Co·per′ni·can** *adj., n.*

**cop·i·er** (käp′ē ər) *n.* 1. one who copies 2. a duplicating machine

**co·pi·lot** (kō′pī′lət) *n.* the assistant pilot of an airplane

**cop·ing** (kō′piŋ) *n.* [< COPE²] the top layer of a masonry wall

**co·pi·ous** (kō′pē əs) *adj.* [< L. *copia,* abundance] plentiful; abundant — **co′pi·ous·ly** *adv.* —**co′pi·ous·ness** *n.*

**cop′-out′** *n.* [Slang] a copping out, as by confessing, reneging, or quitting

**cop·per** (käp′ər) *n.* [< LL. *cuprum*] 1. a reddish-brown, ductile, metallic element 2. [Chiefly Brit.] a penny 3. a reddish brown —*adj.* 1. of copper 2. reddish-brown —**cop′per·y** *adj.*

**cop·per·as** (käp′ər əs) *n.* [< ML. (*aqua*) *cuprosa,* copper (water)] a green sulfate of iron used in making dyes, inks, etc.

**cop′per·head′** *n.* a poisonous N. American snake

**co·pra** (kō′prə, käp′rə) *n.* [Port. < Hindi *khoprā*] dried coconut meat, the source of coconut oil

**copse** (käps) *n.* [< OFr. *couper,* to cut] a thicket of small trees or shrubs: also **cop′pice** (käp′is)

**cop·ter** (käp′tər) *n. shortened form of* HELICOPTER

**cop·u·la** (käp′yə lə) *n., pl.* -**las** [L.,

a link] a verb form, as of *be*, *seem*, *appear*, etc., that links a subject with a predicate —**cop′u·la′tive** (-lāt′iv) *adj.*

**cop·u·late** (käp′yə lāt′) *vi.* -**lat′ed,** -**lat′ing** [< L. *co-*, together + *apere*, to join] to have sexual intercourse — **cop′u·la′tion** *n.*

**cop·y** (käp′ē) *n., pl.* -**ies** [< L. *copia*, plenty] **1.** a thing made just like another **2.** any of a number of books, magazines, etc. having the same contents **3.** matter to be set in type **4.** the words of an advertisement —*vt., vi.* **cop′ied,** **cop′y·ing** **1.** to make a copy of **2.** to imitate —**cop′y·ist** *n.*

**cop′y·cat′** (-kat′) *n.* an imitator

**cop′y·right′** *n.* the exclusive legal right to the publication, sale, etc. of a literary or artistic work —*vt.* to protect (a book, etc.) by copyright

**cop′y·writ′er** *n.* a writer of copy, esp. for advertisements

**co·quette** (kō ket′) *n.* [Fr.] a girl or woman flirt —*vi.* -**quet′ted,** -**quet′ting** to flirt —**co·quet′tish** *adj.* — **co·quet′tish·ly** *adv.*

**cor-** *same as* COM-: used before *r*

**cor·al** (kôr′əl) *n.* [< Gr. *korallion*] **1.** the hard skeleton secreted by certain marine polyps: reefs and atolls of coral occur in tropical seas **2.** a yellowish red —*adj.* of coral

**cor·bel** (kôr′bəl) *n.* [< L. *corvus*, raven] a piece of stone, wood, etc. projecting from a wall, to support a cornice, arch, etc.

**cord** (kôrd) *n.* [< Gr. *chordē*] **1.** thick string **2.** a measure of wood cut for fuel (128 cu. ft.) **3.** a rib on the surface of a fabric **4.** ribbed fabric **5.** *Anat.* any part like a cord **6.** *Elec.* a slender cable —*vt.* to fasten with a cord

**cord′age** (-ij) *n.* cords and ropes

**cor·dial** (kôr′jəl) *adj.* [< L. *cor*, heart] warm; hearty; sincere —*n.* a liqueur —**cor′di·al′i·ty** (-jē al′ə tē) *n., pl.* -**ties** —**cor′dial·ly** *adv.*

**cor·dil·le·ra** (kôr′dil yer′ə, kôr dil′ər ə) *n.* [Sp. < L. *chorda*, a cord] a system or chain of mountains

**cord·ite** (kôr′dīt) *n.* [< CORD: it is stringy] a smokeless explosive made of nitroglycerin, guncotton, etc.

**cord·less** (kôrd′lis) *adj.* operated by batteries, as an electric shaver

**cor·don** (kôr′d'n) *n.* [see CORD] **1.** a line or circle of police, troops, etc. guarding an area **2.** a cord or braid worn as a decoration —*vt.* to encircle with a cordon

**cor·do·van** (kôr′də vən) *n.* [< *Córdoba*, Spain] a soft, colored leather

**cor·du·roy** (kôr′də roi′) *n.* [prob. < CORD + obs. *duroy*, coarse fabric] a heavy, ribbed cotton fabric

**core** (kôr) *n.* [prob. < L. *cor*, heart] **1.** the central part of an apple, pear, etc. **2.** the central part of anything **3.** the most important part —*vt.* **cored, cor′ing** to remove the core of

**co·re·spond·ent** (kō′ri spän′dənt) *n.* [CO- + RESPONDENT] *Law* a person charged with having committed adultery with the husband or wife from whom a divorce is sought

**co·ri·an·der** (kôr′ē an′dər) *n.* [< Gr. *koriandron*] **1.** an annual herb of the parsley family **2.** its strong-smelling seedlike fruit, used as a flavoring

**cork** (kôrk) *n.* [ult. < L. *quercus*, oak] **1.** the light, thick, elastic outer bark of an oak tree (**cork oak**) **2.** a piece of cork; esp., a stopper for a bottle, etc. **3.** any stopper —*adj.* of cork —*vt.* to stop with a cork

**cork′screw′** *n.* a spiral-shaped device for pulling corks out of bottles —*adj.* spiral —*vi., vt.* to twist

**corm** (kôrm) *n.* [< Gr. *kormos*, log] the fleshy, underground stem of certain plants, as the gladiolus

**cor·mo·rant** (kôr′mə rənt) *n.* [< L. *corvus*, raven + *marinus*, marine] a large, voracious sea bird

**corn¹** (kôrn) *n.* [OE.] **1.** a small, hard seed, esp. of a cereal grass **2.** *a)* an American cereal plant with kernels growing in rows along a woody, husk-enclosed core (**corncob**); maize *b)* the kernels **3.** [Brit.] grain, esp. wheat **4.** in Scotland and Ireland, oats **5.** [Slang] ideas, humor, etc. regarded as old-fashioned, trite, etc. —*vt.* to pickle (meat, etc.) in brine

**corn²** (kôrn) *n.* [< L. *cornu*, horn] a hard, thick, painful growth of skin, esp. on a toe

**corn′ball′** (-bôl′) *adj.* [CORN¹, *n.* 5 + (SCREW)BALL] [Slang] corny

**cor·ne·a** (kôr′nē ə) *n.* [< L. *cornu*, horn] the transparent outer coat of the eyeball —**cor′ne·al** *adj.*

**cor·ner** (kôr′nər) *n.* [< L. *cornu*, horn] **1.** the point or place where lines or surfaces join and form an angle **2.** the angle formed **3.** any of the angles formed at a street intersection **4.** a remote, secluded place **5.** a region; quarter **6.** a position hard to escape from **7.** a monopoly acquired on a stock or commodity so as to raise the price —*vt.* **1.** to force into a corner (sense 6) **2.** to get a monopoly on (a stock, etc.) —*adj.* at, on, or for a corner —**cut corners** to cut down expenses, time, etc. —**cor′nered** *adj.*

**cor′ner·back′** *n.* *Football* either of two defensive backs stationed between the line of scrimmage and the safety men

**cor′ner·stone′** *n.* **1.** a stone at the corner of a building, often laid at a ceremony **2.** the basic or main part; foundation

**cor·net** (kôr net′) *n.* [< L. *cornu*, a horn] a brass-wind musical instrument of the trumpet class

**corn′flow′er** *n.* an annual plant of the composite family with showy flowers

**cor·nice** (kôr′nis) *n.* [< Gr. *korōnis*, wreath] a horizontal molding projecting along the top of a wall, etc.

**corn′meal′** *n.* **1.** meal made from corn (maize) **2.** meal made from other grain

**corn snow** coarse granules of snow formed by partial melting then freezing

**corn′starch′** *n.* a starch made from corn (maize), used in cooking

**corn syrup** a sweet syrup made from cornstarch

**cor·nu·co·pi·a** (kôr'nə kō'pē ə, -nyoo-) *n.* [L. *cornu copiae*, horn of plenty] 1. a horn-shaped container overflowing with fruits, flowers, etc. 2. an abundance

**corn·y** (kôr'nē) *adj.* -i·er, -i·est [Colloq.] hackneyed, trite, etc.

**co·rol·la** (kə räl'ə) *n.* [< L. *corona*, crown] the petals of a flower

CORNUCOPIA

**cor·ol·lar·y** (kôr'ə ler'ē) *n., pl.* -ies [see prec.] 1. a proposition following from one already proved 2. a normal result

**co·ro·na** (kə rō'nə) *n., pl.* -nas, -nae (-nē) [L.] 1. a crown or crownlike part 2. a circle of light around the sun or moon; esp., the halo seen around the sun during a total eclipse

**cor·o·nar·y** (kôr'ə ner'ē) *adj.* 1. of or like a crown 2. of the arteries supplying blood to the heart muscle —*n.* -ies a thrombosis in a coronary artery: in full **coronary thrombosis**

**cor·o·na·tion** (kôr'ə nā'shən) *n.* the crowning of a sovereign

**cor·o·ner** (kôr'ə nər) *n.* [ME., officer of the crown] a public officer who must determine the cause of any death not obviously due to natural causes

**cor·o·net** (kôr'ə net') *n.* [< OFr. *corone*, crown] 1. a small crown worn by nobility 2. a band of jewels, flowers, etc. for the head

**corp., corpn.** corporation

**cor·po·ral¹** (kôr'pər əl) *n.* [< L. *caput*, head] the lowest-ranking noncommissioned officer, just below a sergeant: abbrev. **Corp., Cpl.**

**cor·po·ral²** (kôr'pər əl) *adj.* [< L. *corpus*, body] of the body; bodily

**corporal punishment** bodily punishment, as flogging

**cor·po·rate** (kôr'pər it) *adj.* [< L. *corpus*, body] 1. of, like, or being a corporation 2. shared; joint

**cor·po·ra·tion** (kôr'pə rā'shən) *n.* a group of people organized, as to operate a business, under a charter granting them as a body some of the legal rights, etc. of an individual

**cor·po·re·al** (kôr pôr'ē əl) *adj.* [< L. *corpus*, body] 1. of or for the body 2. of a material nature; physical

**corps** (kôr) *n., pl.* **corps** (kôrz) [< L. *corpus*, body] 1. a body of people associated under common direction 2. *a)* a specialized branch of the armed forces [the Marine *Corps*] *b)* a tactical subdivision of an army

**corpse** (kôrps) *n.* [var. of prec.] a dead body, esp. of a person

**cor·pu·lence** (kôr'pyoo ləns) *n.* [< L. *corpus*, body] fatness; obesity — **cor'pu·lent** *adj.*

**cor·pus** (kôr'pəs) *n., pl.* **cor'po·ra** (-pər ə) [L.] 1. a body, esp. a dead one 2. a body of laws, writings, etc.

**Cor·pus Christ·i** (kôr'pəs kris'tē) city in SE Tex.: pop. 205,000

**cor·pus·cle** (kôr'pəs 'l, -pus''l) *n.* [< L. *corpus*, body] 1. a very small particle 2. any of the cells in the blood, lymph, etc. of vertebrates

**corpus de·lic·ti** (di lik'tī) [ModL., lit., body of the crime] 1. the facts constituting a crime 2. loosely, the body of a murder victim

**cor·ral** (kə ral') *n.* [Sp. < L. *currere*, to run] an enclosure for horses, cattle, etc.; pen —*vt.* -ralled', -ral'ling 1. to drive into or confine in a corral 2. to surround or capture

**cor·rect** (kə rekt') *vt.* [< L. *com-*, together + *regere*, to direct] 1. to make right 2. to mark the errors of 3. to punish or discipline 4. to remove or counteract (a defect) —*adj.* 1. conforming to an established standard 2. true; accurate; right —**cor·rec'tive** *adj., n.* —**cor·rect'ly** *adv.* —**cor·rect'ness** *n.*

**cor·rec·tion** (kə rek'shən) *n.* 1. a correcting or being corrected 2. a change that corrects a mistake 3. punishment to correct faults —**cor·rec'tion·al** *adj.*

**cor·re·late** (kôr'ə lāt') *vi., vt.* -lat'ed, -lat'ing [COR- + RELATE] to be in or bring into mutual relation —**cor'·re·la'tion** *n.*

**cor·rel·a·tive** (kə rel'ə tiv) *adj.* 1. having a mutual relationship 2. *Gram.* expressing mutual relation and used in pairs, as the conjunctions *neither . . . nor* —*n.* a correlative word, etc.

**cor·re·spond** (kôr'ə spänd') *vi.* [< L. *com-*, together + *respondere*, to answer] 1. to be in agreement (*with* something); tally 2. to be similar or equal (*to*) 3. to communicate by letters —**cor're·spond'ing·ly** *adv.*

**cor're·spond'ence** *n.* 1. agreement 2. similarity 3. *a)* communication by letters *b)* the letters

**cor're·spond'ent** *adj.* corresponding —*n.* 1. a thing that corresponds 2. one who exchanges letters with another 3. a journalist supplying news from a place away from the home office

**cor·ri·dor** (kôr'ə dər, -dôr') *n.* [< L. *currere*, to run] a long hall

**cor·rob·o·rate** (kə räb'ə rāt') *vt.* -rat'ed, -rat'ing [< L. *com-*, intens. + *robur*, strength] to confirm; support —**cor·rob'o·ra'tion** *n.* —**cor·rob'o·ra'tive** *adj.*

**cor·rode** (kə rōd') *vt., vi.* -rod'ed, -rod'ing [< L. *com-*, intens. + *rodere*, gnaw] to eat into or wear away gradually, as by chemical action —**cor·ro'sion** (-rō'zhən) *n.* —**cor·ro'sive** (-siv) *adj., n.* —**cor·ro'sive·ly** *adv.*

**cor·ru·gate** (kôr'ə gāt') *vt., vi.* -gat'ed, -gat'ing [< L. *com-*, intens. + *rugare*, to wrinkle] to form into parallel ridges and grooves —**cor'ru·ga'tion** *n.*

**cor·rupt** (kə rupt') *adj.* [< L. *com-*, together + *rumpere*, to break] 1. evil;

depraved; debased **2.** taking bribes; dishonest —*vt.*, *vi.* to make or become corrupt —**cor·rupt′i·ble** *adj.* —**cor·rup′tion** *n.* —**cor·rupt′ly** *adv.*

**cor·sage** (kôr säzh′) *n.* [see CORPS + -AGE] a small bouquet for a woman to wear, as at the waist or shoulder

**cor·sair** (kôr′ser) *n.* [< Fr. < L. *cursus*, course] a pirate or pirate ship

**cor·set** (kôr′sit) *n.* [see CORPS] [*sometimes pl.*] a closefitting undergarment worn, chiefly by women, to give support to or shape the torso

**cor·tege, cor·tège** (kôr tezh′, -tāzh′) *n.* [< Fr. < L. *cohors*, retinue] **1.** a retinue **2.** a ceremonial procession

**cor·tex** (kôr′teks) *n.*, *pl.* **-ti·ces** (-tə sēz′) [L., bark of a tree] **1.** the outer part of an internal organ; esp., the layer of gray matter over most of the brain **2.** an outer layer of plant tissue —**cor′ti·cal** (-ti k'l) *adj.*

**cor·ti·sone** (kôr′tə sōn′, -zōn′) *n.* [< CORTEX (of adrenals)] a hormone used in adrenal insufficiency and for inflammatory diseases, etc.

**co·run·dum** (kə run′dəm) *n.* [< Sans. *kuruvinda*, ruby] a very hard mineral used for grinding and polishing

**cor·us·cate** (kôr′əs kāt′) *vi.* **-cat′ed**, **-cat′ing** [< L. *coruscus*, vibrating] to glitter; sparkle —**cor′us·ca′tion** *n.*

**cor·vette** (kôr vet′) *n.* [Fr.] a small, fast, British warship for convoy duty

**co·ry·za** (kə rī′zə) *n.* [< Gr.] a cold in the head

**co·sign** (kō′sīn′) *vt.*, *vi.* **1.** to sign (a promissory note) along with the maker, thus becoming responsible if the maker defaults **2.** to sign jointly —**co′sign′er** *n.*

**co·sig·na·to·ry** (kō sig′nə tôr′ē) *n.*, *pl.* **-ries** one of two or more joint signers, as of a treaty

**cos·met·ic** (käz met′ik) *adj.* [< Gr. *kosmos*, order] beautifying, or correcting faults in, the face, hair, etc. —*n.* a cosmetic preparation, as lipstick —**cos·met′i·cal·ly** *adv.*

**cos·me·tol·o·gy** (käz′mə täl′ə jē) *n.* the work of a beautician —**cos′me·tol′o·gist** *n.*

**cos·mic** (käz′mik) *adj.* [< Gr. *kosmos*, universe] **1.** of the cosmos **2.** vast

**cosmic rays** streams of highly penetrating charged particles bombarding the earth from outer space

**cos·mog·o·ny** (käz mäg′ə nē) *n.* [< Gr. *kosmos*, universe + *gignesthai*, produce] **1.** the origin of the universe **2.** *pl.* **-nies** a theory of this

**cos·mol·o·gy** (-mäl′ə jē) *n.* [< ML.] the study of the physical nature, form, etc. of the universe as a whole —**cos′·mo·log′i·cal** (-mə läj′ə k'l) *adj.*

**cos·mo·naut** (käz′mə nôt′) *n.* [< Russ.] *same as* ASTRONAUT

**cos·mo·pol·i·tan** (käz′mə päl′ə t'n) *adj.* [< Gr. *kosmos*, world + *polis*, city] **1.** common to or representative of all or many parts of the world **2.** not narrow in outlook, habits, etc.; at home anywhere in the world —*n.* a cosmopolitan person or thing: also **cos·mop′o·lite′** (-mäp′ə līt′)

**cos·mos** (käz′məs, -mōs) *n.* [< Gr. *kosmos*, universe] **1.** the universe considered as an orderly system **2.** any complete and orderly system

**co·spon·sor** (kō′spän′sər) *n.* a joint sponsor, as of a proposed piece of legislation —*vt.* to be a cosponsor of —**co′spon′sor·ship′** *n.*

**Cos·sack** (käs′ak, -ək) *n.* any of a people of S Russia famous as horsemen

**cost** (kôst) *vt.* **cost**, **cost′ing** [< L. *com-*, together + *stare*, to stand] **1.** to be obtained for (a certain price) **2.** to require the expenditure, loss, etc. of —*n.* **1.** the amount of money, effort, etc. asked or paid for a thing; price **2.** loss; sacrifice —**at all costs** by any means required

**co·star** (kō′stär′; *for v.. usually* kō′stär′) *n.* any of the leading actors or actresses given equal prominence in a movie or play —*vt.*, *vi.* **-starred′**, **-star′ring** to make or be a costar

**Cos·ta Ri·ca** (käs′tə rē′kə, kôs′-) country in Central America: 19,575 sq. mi.; pop. 1,502,000 —**Cos′ta Ri′can**

**cos·tive** (käs′tiv, kôs′-) *adj.* [see CONSTIPATE] constipated or constipating

**cost′ly** *adj.* **-li·er**, **-li·est 1.** costing much; dear **2.** magnificent; sumptuous —**cost′li·ness** *n.*

**cost of living** the average cost of the necessities of life, as food, shelter, and clothes

**cos·tume** (käs′tōōm) *n.* [Fr. < L. *consuetudo*, custom] **1.** *a)* style of clothes typical of a certain country, period, etc. *b)* a set of such clothes **2.** a set of outer clothes —*vt.* **-tumed**, **-tum·ing** to provide with a costume

**co·sy** (kō′zē) *adj.* **-si·er**, **-si·est** & *n.*, *pl.* **-sies** *same as* COZY —**co′si·ly** *adv.* —**co′si·ness** *n.*

**cot¹** (kät) *n.* [< Hind. *khāt*] a narrow, collapsible bed, as one made of canvas on a folding frame

**cot²** (kät) *n.* [ME.] **1.** a small shelter **2.** a sheath, as for a hurt finger

**cote** (kōt) *n.* [ME.] a small shelter for fowl, sheep, etc.

**co·te·rie** (kōt′ər ē) *n.* [Fr.] a close circle of friends or colleagues; clique

**co·ter·mi·nous** (kō tur′mə nəs) *adj.* *same as* CONTERMINOUS

**co·til·lion** (kō til′yən) *n.* [< Fr.] **1.** an intricate, formal group dance **2.** a formal ball Also **co·til′lon**

**cot·tage** (kät′ij) *n.* [ME.] **1.** a small house **2.** a house used for vacations —**cot′tag·er** *n.*

**cottage cheese** a soft, white cheese made from the curds of sour milk

**cot·ter, cot·tar** (kät′ər) *n.* [Scot.] a tenant farmer

**cot·ter pin** (kät′ər) [ME.] a split pin fastened in place by spreading apart its ends after insertion

**cot·ton** (kät′'n) *n.* [< Ar. *qutun*] **1.** the soft, white, fibrous substance around the seeds of certain mallow plants **2.** such a plant or plants **3.** thread or cloth made of cotton —**cotton to** [Colloq.] **1.** to take a liking to **2.** to

COTTER PIN

become aware of (a situation) —**cot/ton·y** *adj.*

**cot·ton gin** [see GIN²] a machine for separating cotton from the seeds

**cot/ton·mouth/** *n. same as* WATER MOCCASIN

**cot/ton·seed/** *n.* the seed of the cotton plant, yielding an oil used in margarine, cooking oil, soap, etc.

**cot/ton·tail/** *n.* a common American rabbit with a fluffy tail

**cot/ton·wood/** *n.* a poplar that has seeds thickly covered with cottony or silky hairs

**cot·y·le·don** (kät/'l ēd'n) *n.* [< Gr. *kotylē,* cavity] the first leaf or a leaf of the first pair produced by the embryo of a flowering plant

**couch** (kouch) *n.* [< OFr. *couchier,* lie down] an article of furniture on which one may lie down; sofa —*vt., vi.* **1.** to recline as on a couch **2.** to put in words; express

**cou·gar** (kōō/gər) *n.* [< Fr. < S. Am-Ind.] a large, tawny-brown wild cat

**cough** (kôf) *vi.* [ME. *coughen*] to expel air suddenly and noisily from the lungs —*vt.* to expel by coughing —*n.* **1.** a coughing **2.** a condition of coughing frequently

**could** (kood) **1.** *pt.* of CAN¹ **2.** an auxiliary generally equivalent to *can,* expressing esp. a shade of doubt [it *could* be so]

**couldn't** (-'nt) could not

**cou·lomb** (kōō läm/) *n.* [after C. A. de *Coulomb* (1736–1806), Fr. physicist] a unit of electric charge equal to 6.25 x $10^{18}$ electrons passing a point in one second

**coun·cil** (koun/s'l) *n.* [< L. *com-,* together + *calere,* to call] **1.** a group of people called together for discussion, advice, etc. **2.** an administrative or legislative body [a city *council*] —**coun/cil·man** (-mən) *n., pl.* -men

**coun/ci·lor, coun/cil·lor** (-ər) *n.* a member of a council

**coun·sel** (koun/s'l) *n.* [< L. *consilium*] **1.** mutual exchange of ideas, etc.; discussion **2.** advice **3.** a lawyer or group of lawyers **4.** a consultant —*vt.* **-seled** or **-selled, -sel·ing** or **-sel·ling 1.** to give advice to **2.** to recommend (an action, etc.) —*vi.* to give or take advice

**coun/se·lor, coun/sel·lor** (-ər) *n.* **1.** an adviser **2.** a lawyer

**count¹** (kount) *vt.* [< L. *computare,* compute] **1.** to name or add up, unit by unit, to reach a total **2.** to take account of; include **3.** to believe to be; consider —*vi.* **1.** to name numbers or add up items in order **2.** to be taken into account; have importance **3.** to have a specified value (often with *for*) **4.** to rely or depend (on or *upon*) —*n.* **1.** a counting **2.** the total number **3.** a reckoning **4.** *Law* any of the charges in an indictment

**count²** (kount) *n.* [< L. *comes,* companion] a European nobleman with a

rank equal to that of an English earl

**count/down/** *n.* **1.** the schedule of operations just before firing a rocket, etc. **2.** the counting off, in reverse order, of time units in this schedule

**coun·te·nance** (koun/tə nəns) *n.* [< L. *continentia,* bearing] **1.** facial expression **2.** the face; visage **3.** approval; support —*vt.* **-nanced, -nanc·ing** to approve or tolerate

**count·er¹** (koun/tər) *n.* **1.** a person, device, etc. that counts something **2.** a small disk for keeping count in games **3.** an imitation coin, or token **4.** a long table, board, etc. for serving customers, displaying goods, etc.

**coun·ter²** (koun/tər) *adv.* [< L. *contra,* against] in opposition; contrary —*adj.* opposed; contrary —*n.* the opposite or contrary —*vt., vi.* to act, do, etc. in opposition to; oppose

**counter-** [< L. *contra-,* against] *a combining form meaning:* **1.** contrary to [*counterclockwise*] **2.** in retaliation [*counterattack*] **3.** complementary [*counterpart*]

**coun/ter·act/** *vt.* to act against; neutralize —**coun/ter·ac/tion** *n.*

**coun/ter·at·tack/** *n.* an attack made in opposition to another attack —*vt., vi.* to attack in opposition

**coun/ter·bal/ance** *n.* a weight, force, etc. that balances another —*vt., vi.* **-anced, -anc·ing** to be a counterbalance (to); offset

**coun/ter·claim/** *n.* an opposing claim to offset another —*vt., vi.* (koun/tər·klām/) to make a counterclaim (of)

**coun/ter·clock/wise** (-wīz) *adj., adv.* in a direction opposite to that in which the hands of a clock move

**coun/ter·cul/ture** *n.* the culture of those young people whose life style is opposed to the prevailing culture

**coun/ter·es/pi·on·age/** *n.* actions to prevent or thwart enemy espionage

**coun·ter·feit** (koun/tər fit) *adj.* [< OFr. *contre-,* counter- + *faire,* make] **1.** made in imitation of the genuine so as to defraud; forged **2.** pretended; sham —*n.* an imitation made to deceive —*vt., vi.* **1.** to make an imitation (of money, etc.) so as to defraud **2.** to pretend —**coun/ter·feit/er** *n.*

**count/er·man/** *n., pl.* **-men** a man who serves customers at the counter of a lunchroom or cafeteria

**coun·ter·mand** (koun/tər mand/) *vt.* [< L. *contra,* against + *mandare,* to command] to revoke or call back by a contrary order

**coun/ter·pane/** (-pān/) *n.* [ult. < L. *culcita puncta,* embroidered quilt] a bedspread

**coun/ter·part/** *n.* **1.** a person or thing that closely resembles another **2.** a copy or duplicate

**coun/ter·point/** *n.* [< It.: see COUNTER- & POINT] **1.** the art of adding related, independent melodies to a basic melody **2.** such a composition

**coun/ter·poise/** *n.* [see COUNTER² &

POISE] **1.** a counterbalance **2.** equilibrium —*vt.* **-poised′, -pois′ing** to counterbalance

**coun′ter·pro·duc′tive** *adj.* having results contrary to those intended

**coun′ter·rev′o·lu′tion** *n.* a political movement to restore the system overthrown by a revolution —**coun′ter·rev′o·lu′tion·ar′y** *adj., n.*

**coun′ter·sign′** *n.* **1.** a signature added to a previously signed document to confirm it **2.** a secret signal given to identify oneself as to a sentry —*vt.* to confirm with one's own signature

**coun′ter·sink′** *vt.* **-sunk′, -sink′-ing 1.** to enlarge the top part of (a hole) for receiving the head of a bolt, screw, etc. **2.** to sink (a bolt, etc.) into such a hole

**coun′ter·ten′or** (-ten′ər) *n.* **1.** range of the highest male voice, above tenor **2.** a singer with this range

**coun′ter·weight′** *n.* a counterbalance

**count·ess** (koun′tis) *n.* the wife or widow of a count or earl

**count·less** (kount′lis) *adj.* too many to count; innumerable; myriad

**coun·try** (kun′trē) *n., pl.* **-tries** [< VL. *contrata*, region] **1.** an area; region **2.** the whole territory, or the people, of a nation **3.** the land of one's birth or citizenship **4.** land with farms and small towns

**country club** a social club in or near a city, with a golf course, etc.

**coun′try·man** (-mən) *n., pl.* **-men** a man of one's own country

**country music** rural folk music, esp. of the Southern U.S.

**coun′try·side′** *n.* a rural region

**coun·ty** (koun′tē) *n., pl.* **-ties** [< ML. *comitatus*, jurisdiction of a count] an administrative district of a country or State, or its people

**coup** (kōō) *n., pl.* **coups** (kōōz) [Fr. < L. *colaphus*, a blow] a sudden, brilliantly successful move

‡**coup de grâce** (kōō də gräs′) [Fr., lit., stroke of mercy] the blow, shot, etc. that brings death to a sufferer

‡**coup d'é·tat** (kōō dā tä′) [Fr., lit., stroke of state] the sudden, forcible overthrow of a government

**coupe** (kōōp; *now rarely* kōō pā′) *n.* [< Fr. *couper*, to cut] a closed, two-door automobile: also **coupé**

**cou·ple** (kup′'l) *n.* [< L. *copula*, a link] **1.** anything joining two things together; link **2.** a pair of persons or things; esp., a man and woman who are engaged, married, or partners in a dance, game, etc. **3.** [Colloq.] a few —*vt., vi.* **-pled, -pling** to link or unite

**cou·plet** (kup′lit) *n.* two successive rhyming lines of poetry

**cou·pling** (kup′liŋ) *n.* **1.** a joining together **2.** a mechanical device for joining parts or things together

**cou·pon** (kōō′pän, kyōō′-) *n.* [Fr. < *couper*, to cut] **1.** a detachable certificate on a bond, presented for payment of interest **2.** a certificate entitling one to a discount, gift, etc., or for use in ordering goods

**cour·age** (kur′ij) *n.* [< L. *cor*, heart] the quality of being brave; valor

**cou·ra·geous** (kə rā′jəs) *adj.* brave; valorous —**cou·ra′geous·ly** *adv.*

**cou·ri·er** (koor′ē ər, kur′-) *n.* [< L. *currere*, to run] **1.** a messenger **2.** a person hired to take care of hotel accommodations, etc. for a traveler

**course** (kôrs) *n.* [< L. *currere*, to run] **1.** an onward movement; progress **2.** a way, path, or channel **3.** the direction taken **4.** a regular mode of procedure or conduct [our wisest *course*] **5.** a series of like things in order **6.** a part of a meal served at one time **7.** *Educ. a)* a complete series of studies *b)* any of the studies —*vi.* **coursed**, **cours′ing 1.** to run or race **2.** to hunt with hounds —**in due course** in the usual sequence (of events) —**in the course of** during —**of course 1.** naturally **2.** certainly

**cours·er** (kôr′sər) *n.* [Poet.] a graceful, spirited or swift horse

**court** (kôrt) *n.* [< L. *cohors*, enclosure] **1.** an uncovered space surrounded by buildings or walls **2.** a short street **3.** a playing space, as for tennis **4.** *a)* the palace, or the family, attendants, etc., of a sovereign *b)* a sovereign and his councilors, etc. as a governing body *c)* a formal assembly held by a sovereign **5.** courtship; wooing **6.** *a)* a judge or judges *b)* a place where trials, etc. are held *c)* a judicial assembly —*vt.* **1.** to pay attention to (a person) so as to get something **2.** to seek as a mate; woo **3.** to try to get [to court favor] —*vi.* to carry on a courtship —**pay court to** to court, as for favor or love —**court′er** *n.*

**cour·te·ous** (kur′tē əs) *adj.* [see prec. & -EOUS] polite and gracious —**cour′te·ous·ly** *adv.*

**cour·te·san, cour·te·zan** (kôr′tə z'n) *n.* [see COURT] a prostitute

**cour·te·sy** (kur′tə sē) *n., pl.* **-sies 1.** courteous behavior **2.** a polite or considerate act or remark

**court′house′** *n.* **1.** a building housing law courts **2.** a building housing offices of a county government

**cour·ti·er** (kôr′tē ər, -tyər) *n.* an attendant at a royal court

**court′ly** *adj.* **-li·er, -li·est** suitable for a king's court; dignified; elegant —**court′li·ness** *n.*

**court′-mar′tial** (-mär′shəl) *n., pl.* **courts′-mar′tial 1.** a military or naval court to try offenses against military law **2.** a trial by such a court —*vt.* **-tialed** or **-tialled, -tial·ing** or **-tial·ling** to try by such a court

**court′room′** *n.* a room in which a law court is held

**court′ship′** *n.* the act, process, or period of courting, or wooing

**court′yard′** *n.* a space enclosed by walls, adjoining or in a large building

**cous·in** (kuz′'n) *n.* [ult. < L. *com-*, with + *soror*, sister] the son or daughter of one's uncle or aunt

‡**cou·tu·rier** (kōō tü ryā′; *E.* -toor′ē ā′) *n.* [Fr.] a male designer of women's fashions —**cou·tu·riere** (-ryer′; *E.* -ē er′) *n.fem.*

**cove** (kōv) *n.* [< OE. *cofa*, cave] a small bay or inlet

**cov·en** (kuv'ən) *n.* [see CONVENE] a gathering or meeting of witches

**cov·e·nant** (kuv'ə nənt) *n.* [see CONVENE] an agreement; compact —*vt.* to promise by a covenant —*vi.* to make a covenant

**cov·er** (kuv'ər) *vt.* [< L. *co-*, intens. + *operire*, to hide] 1. to place something on or over 2. to extend over 3. to clothe 4. to conceal; hide 5. to shield 6. to include or deal with [to *cover* a subject] 7. to protect financially [to *cover* a loss] 8. to travel over 9. to point a firearm at 10. *Journalism* to get news, pictures, etc. of —*vi.* 1. to spread over, as a liquid does 2. to provide an excuse (*for*) —*n.* 1. anything that covers, as a lid, top, etc. 2. a shelter for protection 3. a tablecloth and setting 4. something used to hide one's real actions, etc. —**take cover** to seek shelter —**under cover** in secrecy or concealment

**cov·er·age** (-ij) *n.* the amount, extent, etc. covered by something

**cov·er·all** *n.* [*usually pl.*] a one-piece protective outer garment, often worn over regular clothing, as by mechanics

**cover charge** a fixed charge, as at a nightclub, besides food and drink cost

**cover crop** a crop, as clover, grown to keep soil fertile and uneroded

**covered wagon** a large wagon with an arched cover of canvas

**cov·er·ing** *n.* anything that covers

**cov·er·let** (kuv'ər lit) *n.* [< OFr. *covrir*, cover + *lit*, bed] a bedspread

...the article in a magazine ...that deals with the subject shown on the cover

**cov·ert** (kuv'ərt) *adj.* [see COVER] hidden or disguised —*n.* a protective shelter, as for game —**cov'ert·ly** *adv.*

**cov·er-up** *n.* something used for hiding one's real activities, etc.

**cov·et** (kuv'it) *vt., vi.* [< L. *cupiditas*, cupidity] to want ardently (something that another person has)

**cov·et·ous** (-əs) *adj.* tending to covet; greedy —**cov'et·ous·ness** *n.*

**cov·ey** (kuv'ē) *n., pl.* -**eys** [< OFr. *cover*, to hatch] a small flock of birds, esp. partridges or quail

**cow¹** (kou) *n.* [< OE. *cu*] 1. the mature female of domestic cattle, valued for its milk 2. the mature female of certain other animals, as the elephant

**cow²** (kou) *vt.* [< ON. *kuga*, subdue] to make timid; intimidate

**cow·ard** (kou'ərd) *n.* [ult. < L. *cauda*, tail] one who lacks courage or is shamefully afraid —*adj.* cowardly

**cow'ard·ice** (-is) *n.* lack of courage

**cow'ard·ly** *adj.* of or like a coward —*adv.* in the manner of a coward —**cow'ard·li·ness** *n.*

**cow'boy'** *n.* a ranch worker who herds cattle: also **cow'hand'**

**cow·er** (kou'ər) *vi.* [ME.] to crouch or huddle up, as from fear or cold; shrink; cringe

**cow'hide'** *n.* 1. the hide of a cow 2. leather from it 3. a whip of this

**cowl** (koul) *n.* [< L. *cucullus*, hood] 1. *a*) a monk's hood *b*) a monk's cloak with a hood 2. the top part at the front of a car body, to which the windshield and dashboard are attached

**cow'lick** *n.* [< its looking as if licked by a cow] a tuft of hair that cannot easily be combed flat

**cowl·ing** (kou'liŋ) *n.* [see COWL] a metal covering for an airplane engine

**co'-work'er** *n.* a fellow worker

**cow'poke'** *n.* [Colloq.] *same as* COWBOY

**cow pony** a pony used in herding cattle

**cow-pox** (kou'päks') *n.* a disease of cows: vaccination with its virus gives temporary immunity to smallpox

**cox·comb** (käks'kōm') *n.* [for *cock's comb*] a silly, vain, foppish fellow

**cox·swain** (käk's'n, -swān') *n.* [< *cock* (small boat) + SWAIN] one who steers a boat or racing shell

**coy** (koi) *adj.* [ME., quiet] 1. bashful; shy 2. pretending to be shy —**coy'ly** *adv.* —**coy'ness** *n.*

**coy·o·te** (kī ōt'ē, kī'ōt) *n.* [< Mex.-Ind.] a small wolf of W N.America

**coz·en** (kuz'n) *vt., vi.* [ME.] to cheat; deceive —**coz'en·age** *n.*

**co·zy** (kō'zē) *adj.* -**zi·er**, -**zi·est** [Scot. < ?] warm and comfortable; snug —*n., pl.* -**zies** a padded cover for a teapot, to keep the tea hot —**co'zi·ly** *adv.* —**co'zi·ness** *n.*

**CPA** Certified Public Accountant

**Cpl, Cpl.** Corporal

**CPO, C.P.O.** Chief Petty Officer

**cps, c.p.s.** cycles per second

**Cr** *Chem.* chromium

**crab** (krab) *n.* [OE. *crabba*] 1. a crustacean with four pairs of legs and a pair of pincers 2. a peevish person —*vi.* **crabbed, crabbing** [Colloq.] to complain

**crab apple** 1. a small, very sour apple 2. a tree bearing such apples

EDIBLE CRAB

**crab·bed** (krab'id) *adj.* [< CRAB (APPLE)] 1. crabby 2. hard to read, as writing —**crab'bed·ness** *n.*

**crab'by** *adj.* -**bi·er**, -**bi·est** [see prec.] ill-tempered; peevish; cross —**crab'bi·ly** *adv.* —**crab'bi·ness** *n.*

**crab grass** a weedy grass, with freely rooting stems, that spreads rapidly

**crack** (krak) *vi.* [< OE. *cracian*, resound] 1. to make a sudden, sharp noise, as in breaking 2. to break or split, usually without separation of parts 3. to rasp or shift erratically in vocal tone 4. [Colloq.] to collapse from strain —*vt.* 1. to cause to make a sharp, sudden noise 2. to cause to break or split 3. to break down (petroleum hydrocarbons) into the lighter hydrocarbons of gasoline, etc.

4. [Colloq.] to hit hard 5. to solve 6. [Colloq.] to break into or force open 7. [Slang] to make (a joke) —n. 1. a sudden, sharp noise 2. a partial break; fracture 3. a chink; crevice 4. a cracking of the voice 5. [Colloq.] a sudden, sharp blow 6. [Colloq.] an attempt or try 7. [Slang] a joke or gibe —adj. [Colloq.] excelling; first-rate —**crack down** (on) to become strict (with) —**cracked up to be** [Colloq.] believed to be —**crack up** 1. to crash 2. [Colloq.] to break down physically or mentally —**get cracking** to start moving fast

**crack'down'** n. a resorting to strict or stricter discipline or punishment

**cracked** (krakt) adj. 1. having a crack or cracks 2. sounding harsh or strident 3. [Colloq.] insane

**crack'er** n. 1. a firecracker 2. a thin, crisp wafer or biscuit

**crack'er-jack'** adj. [Slang] first-rate; excellent —n. [Slang] a first-rate person or thing

**crack·le** (krak''l) vi. -led, -ling [ME.] to make a series of slight, sharp, popping sounds —n. 1. a series of such sounds 2. a finely cracked surface, as on some pottery

**crack'pot'** n. [Colloq.] an eccentric person —adj. [Colloq.] eccentric

**crack'up'** n. 1. a crash 2. [Colloq.] a mental or physical breakdown

**-cra·cy** (krə sē) [< Gr. kratos, rule] a combining form meaning a (specified) type of government, rule by [autocracy]

**cra·dle** (krā'd'l) n. [OE. cradol] 1. a baby's small bed, usually on rockers 2. infancy 3. the place of a thing's beginning 4. anything like a cradle —vt. -dled, -dling 1. to place or rock in or as in a cradle 2. to take care of in infancy

**cra'dle-song'** n. a lullaby

**craft** (kraft) n. [OE. cræft, power] 1. a special skill or art 2. an occupation requiring special manual skill 3. the members of a skilled trade 4. guile; slyness 5. pl. **craft** a boat, ship, or aircraft

**crafts·man** (krafts'mən) n., pl. -men a skilled worker; artisan —**crafts'man·ship'** n.

**craft'y** adj. -i·er, -i·est subtly deceitful; sly; cunning —**craft'i·ly** adv. —**craft'i·ness** n.

**crag** (krag) n. [< Celt.] a steep, rugged rock rising from a rock mass —**crag'gy** adj. -gi·er, -gi·est

**cram** (kram) vt. **crammed, cram'ming** [OE. crammian] 1. to pack full or too full 2. to stuff; force 3. to feed to excess —vi. 1. to eat too much or too quickly 2. [Colloq.] to prepare for an examination in a hurried, intensive way

**cramp** (kramp) n. [< OFr. crampe, bent] 1. a sudden, painful contraction of muscles from chill, strain, etc. 2. [usually pl.] abdominal spasms and pain —vt. 1. to cause a cramp or cramps in 2. to hamper; restrain

**cramped** (krampt) adj. 1. confined or restricted 2. irregular and crowded, as some handwriting

**cran·ber·ry** (kran'ber'ē, -bər i) n., pl. -ries [< Du. kranebere] 1. a firm, sour, edible, red berry, the fruit of an evergreen shrub 2. the shrub

**crane** (krān) n. [OE. cran] 1. a large wading bird with very long legs and neck 2. a machine for lifting and moving heavy weights, using a movable projecting arm or a horizontal traveling beam —vt., vi. **craned, cran'ing** to stretch (the neck)

**cra·ni·um** (krā'nē əm) n., pl. -ni·ums, -ni·a (-ə) [Gr. kranion] the skull, esp. the part containing the brain —**cra'ni·al** adj.

**crank** (kraŋk) n. [ME.] 1. a handle, etc. bent at right angles and connected to a machine shaft to transmit motion 2. [Colloq.] an eccentric or peevish person —vt. to start or operate by a crank

**crank'case'** n. the metal casing that encloses the crankshaft of an engine

**crank'shaft'** n. a shaft with one or more cranks for transmitting motion

**crank'y** adj. -i·er, -i·est 1. peevish 2. eccentric —**crank'i·ly** adv.

**cran·ny** (kran'ē) n., pl. -nies [< LL. crena, notch] a crevice; crack

**crap** (krap) n. [< OFr. crape, ordure] [Vulgar Slang] 1. nonsense 2. junk; trash —**crap'py** adj. -pi·er, -pi·est

**crape** (krāp) n. crepe; esp., black crepe as a sign of mourning

**crap·pie** (krap'ē) n. a small N.American sunfish

**craps** (kraps) n.pl. [with sing. v.] a gambling game played with ▬▬▬

**crap·shoot·er** (krap'shoot er, ▬▬ gambler at craps

**crash**[1] (krash) vi. [ME.] 1. to fall, collide, break, etc. with a loud noise; smash 2. to collapse; fail —vt. 1. to cause (a car, airplane, etc.) to crash 2. to force with a crashing noise (in, out, through, etc.) 3. [Colloq.] to get into (a party, etc.) without an invitation —n. 1. a loud, sudden noise 2. a crashing 3. a sudden collapse, as of business —adj. [Colloq.] using all possible resources, effort, and speed [a crash program to build roads]

**crash**[2] (krash) n. [? < Russ. krashenina] a coarse linen cloth

**crash'-land'** vt., vi. to bring (an airplane) down in a forced landing, esp. without use of the landing gear —**crash landing**

**crash pad** [Slang] a temporary sleeping place or quarters

**crass** (kras) adj. [L. crassus] grossly stupid or dull —**crass'ly** adv.

**-crat** (krat) [see -CRACY] a combining form meaning member or supporter of (a specified kind of) government

**crate** (krāt) n. [L. cratis] a packing case made of slats of wood —vt. **crat'ed, crat'ing** to pack in a crate

**cra·ter** (krāt'ər) n. [< Gr. kratēr, bowl] 1. a bowl-shaped cavity, as at the mouth of a volcano 2. a pit made by an explosion, as of a bomb

**cra·vat** (krə vat') n. [< Fr. < Cravate, Croatian: from scarves worn by Croatian soldiers] a necktie

**crave** (krāv) vt. **craved, crav'ing**

[OE. *crafian*] 1. to ask for earnestly; beg 2. to long for eagerly

**cra·ven** (krā'vən) *adj.* [< L. *crepare*, to creak] cowardly —*n.* a coward —**cra'ven·ly** *adv.* —**cra'ven·ness** *n.*

**crav·ing** (krā'viŋ) *n.* an intense and prolonged desire, as for food

**craw** (krô) *n.* [ME. *craue*] 1. the crop of a bird 2. the stomach

**craw·fish** (krô'fish') *n., pl.:* see FISH *same as* CRAYFISH

**crawl** (krôl) *vi.* [< ON. *krafla*] 1. to move slowly by dragging the body along the ground 2. to go on hands and knees; creep 3. to move slowly 4. to swarm (*with* crawling things) 5. to feel as if insects were crawling on the skin —*n.* 1. a slow movement 2. an overarm swimming stroke

**crawl space** a narrow space, as under a floor, allowing access to wiring, plumbing, etc.

**crawl'y** *adj.* -i·er, -i·est *same as* CREEPY

**cray·fish** (krā'fish') *n., pl.:* see FISH [< OHG.] 1. a freshwater crustacean somewhat like a little lobster 2. *same as* SPINY LOBSTER

**cray·on** (krā'ən, -än') *n.* [Fr., pencil < L. *creta*, chalk] 1. a small stick of white or colored chalk, waxy material, etc. used for drawing or writing 2. a drawing made with crayons —*vt.* to draw or color with crayons —**cray'on·ist** *n.*

CRAYFISH

**craze** (krāz) *vt., vi.* crazed, **craz'ing** [ME. *crasen*, to crack] to make or become insane —*n.* a fad

**cra·zy** (krā'zē) *adj.* -zi·er, -zi·est [< prec.] 1. unsound of mind; insane 2. [Colloq.] foolish; not sensible 3. [Colloq.] very enthusiastic or eager —*n., pl.* -zies [Slang] a crazy person —**cra'zi·ly** *adv.* —**cra'zi·ness** *n.*

**crazy bone** *same as* FUNNY BONE

**crazy quilt** a patchwork quilt with no regular design

**creak** (krēk) *vi.* [echoic] to make, or move with, a harsh, squeaking sound —*n.* such a sound —**creak'y** *adj.* -i·er, -i·est —**creak'i·ly** *adv.* —**creak'i·ness** *n.*

**cream** (krēm) *n.* [< Gr. *chrisma*, ointment] 1. the oily, yellowish part of milk 2. a creamlike cosmetic ointment 3. the finest part 4. a yellowish white —*adj.* made of or with cream —*vt.* 1. to add cream to 2. to beat into a soft, smooth consistency —**cream of** creamed purée of —**cream'y** *adj.* -i·er, -i·est —**cream'i·ness** *n.*

**cream cheese** a soft, white cheese made of cream or of milk and cream

**cream'er** *n.* a pitcher for cream

**cream'er·y** (-ər ē) *n., pl.* -ies a place where dairy products are processed or sold

**crease** (krēs) *n.* [< ME. *creste*, ridge] 1. a line made by folding and pressing 2. a fold or wrinkle —*vt.* creased, **creas'ing** 1. to make a crease in 2. to wrinkle —*vi.* to become creased

**cre·ate** (krē āt') *vt.* -at'ed, -at'ing [< L. *creare*] 1. to cause to come into existence; make; originate 2. to bring about; give rise to; cause

**cre·a·tion** (krē ā'shən) *n.* 1. a creating or being created 2. the universe 3. anything created —**the Creation** God's creating of the world

**cre·a·tive** (krē āt'iv) *adj.* 1. creating or able to create 2. inventive 3. stimulating the inventive powers —**cre'a·tiv'i·ty** *n.*

**cre·a·tor** (krē āt'ər) *n.* [L.] 1. one who creates 2. [C-] God

**crea·ture** (krē'chər) *n.* [< L. *creatura*] a living being, animal or human

**crèche** (kresh) *n.* [Fr.] a display of the stable scene of Jesus' birth

**cre·dence** (krēd'ns) *n.* [< L. *credere*, believe] belief, esp. in the reports or testimony of another

**cre·den·tial** (kri den'shəl) *n.* [see prec.] [*usually pl.*] a letter or certificate showing one's right to a certain position or authority

**cre·den·za** (kri den'zə) *n.* [It.] a type of buffet, or sideboard

**credibility gap** 1. a disparity between a statement and the true facts 2. inability to have one's truthfulness or honesty accepted

**cred·i·ble** (kred'ə b'l) *adj.* [< L. *credere*, believe] that can be believed; reliable —**cred'i·bil'i·ty** *n.*

**cred·it** (kred'it) *n.* [< L. *credere*, believe] 1. belief; confidence 2. favorable reputation 3. praise or approval 4. a person or thing bringing approval or honor 5. [*pl.*] a list of acknowledgments of work done, as on a motion picture 6. a sum available to one, as in a bank account 7. the entry in an account of payment on a debt 8. trust in one's ability to meet payments 9. the time allowed for payment 10. a completed unit of study in a school —*vt.* 1. to believe; trust 2. to give credit to or commendation for 3. to give credit in a bank account, etc. —**credit one with** to ascribe to one —**do credit to** to bring honor to —**on credit** agreeing to pay later

**cred'it·a·ble** *adj.* deserving some credit or praise —**cred'it·a·bly** *adv.*

**credit card** a card entitling one to charge bills at certain places

**cred·i·tor** (kred'it ər) *n.* one to whom money is owed

**credit union** a cooperative association for pooling savings of members and making low-interest loans to them

**cre·do** (krē'dō, krā'-) *n., pl.* -dos [L., I believe] a creed

**cred·u·lous** (krej'oo ləs) *adj.* [< L. *credere*, believe] tending to believe too readily —**cre·du·li·ty** (krə doo'lə tē) *n.* —**cred'u·lous·ly** *adv.*

**creed** (krēd) *n.* [< L. *credo*, lit., I believe] 1. a brief statement of religious belief, esp. one accepted as authoritative by a church 2. any statement of belief, principles, etc.

**creek** (krēk, krik) *n.* [< ON. *-kriki*, a winding] a small stream, somewhat larger than a brook —**up the creek** [Slang] in trouble

**creel** (krēl) *n.* [< L. *cratis*, wickerwork] a wicker basket for holding fish

**creep** (krēp) *vi.* **crept**, **creep′ing** [OE. *creopan*] 1. to move with the body close to the ground, as on hands and knees 2. to move slowly or stealthily 3. to grow along the ground or a wall, as ivy —*n.* [Slang] an annoying or disgusting person —**make one's flesh creep** to make one feel fear, disgust, etc. —**the creeps** [Colloq.] a feeling of fear, repugnance, etc. —**creep′er** *n.*

**creep′y** *adj.* **-i·er**, **-i·est** having or causing a feeling of fear or disgust —**creep′i·ly** *adv.* —**creep′i·ness** *n.*

**cre·mate** (krē′māt) *vt.* **-mat·ed**, **-mat·ing** [< L. *cremare*] to burn (a dead body) to ashes —**cre·ma′tion** *n.*

**cre·ma·to·ry** (krē′mə tôr′ē) *n., pl.* **-ries** a furnace for cremating: also **cre′ma·to′ri·um** (-ē əm), *pl.* **-ums**, **-a** (-ə) —*adj.* of or for cremation

**crème de menthe** (krem′ də mänt′) [Fr.] a green, mint-flavored liqueur

**cren·el·ate**, **cren·el·late** (kren′l-āt′) *vt.* **-el·at′ed** or **-el·lat′ed**, **-el·at′ing** or **-el·lat′ing** [< VL. *crena*, a notch] to furnish with battlements or with squared notches

**Cre·ole** (krē′ōl) *n.* [Fr. < Port. *crioulo*, native] 1. a person descended from the original French settlers of Louisiana 2. a person of mixed Creole and Negro descent —*adj.* [*usually* c-] prepared with sautéed tomatoes, green peppers, onions, etc. [*creole* sauce]

**cre·o·sote** (krē′ə sōt′) *n.* [< Gr. *kreas*, flesh + *sōtein*, save] an oily liquid with a pungent odor, distilled from wood tar or coal tar: used as an antiseptic and as a wood preservative

**crepe**, **crêpe** (krāp; *for 5, also* krep) *n.* [< Fr. < L. *crispus*, curly] 1. a thin, crinkled cloth of silk, rayon, wool, etc. 2. *same as* CRAPE 3. thin paper crinkled like crepe: also **crepe paper** 4. wrinkled soft rubber: also **crepe rubber** 5. a thin pancake, rolled and filled

**crêpes su·zette** (krāp′ sōō zet′; Fr. krep′) [Fr.] thin pancakes folded in orange sauce and served in flaming brandy

**crept** (krept) *pt. & pp. of* CREEP

**cre·scen·do** (krə shen′dō) *adj., adv.* [It. < L. *crescere*, grow] *Music* gradually increasing in loudness —*n., pl.* **-dos** a gradual increase in loudness

**cres·cent** (kres′nt) *n.* [< L. *crescere*, grow] 1. the shape of the moon in its first or last quarter 2. anything shaped like this —*adj.* shaped like a crescent

**cress** (kres) *n.* [OE. *cressa*] a plant of the mustard family, as water cress, whose leaves are used in salads

**crest** (krest) *n.* [< L. *crista*] 1. a comb, tuft, etc. on the head of an animal or bird 2. a heraldic device, as on note paper, etc. 3. the top line or surface; summit 4. the highest point, level, degree, etc. —*vi.* to form or reach a crest —**crest′ed** *adj.*

**crest′fall′en** (-fôl′ən) *adj.* dejected, disheartened, or humbled

**Crete** (krēt) Gr. island in the E Mediterranean

**cre·tin** (krēt′n) *n.* [< Fr. *chrétien*, Christian, hence human being] a person suffering from cretinism

**cre′tin·ism** *n.* a congenital deficiency of thyroid secretion with resulting deformity and idiocy

**cre·tonne** (krē′tän, kri tän′) *n.* [Fr. < *Creton*, village in Normandy] a heavy, printed cotton or linen cloth, used for curtains, slipcovers, etc.

**cre·vasse** (kri vas′) *n.* [Fr., crevice] a deep crack, esp. in a glacier

**crev·ice** (krev′is) *n.* [< L. *crepare*, to rattle] a narrow opening caused by a crack or split; fissure

**crew**[1] (krōō) *n.* [< L. *crescere*, grow] a group of people working together [a road *crew*, a ship's *crew*] —**crew′man** (-mən) *n., pl.* **-men**

**crew**[2] (krōō) *alt. pt. of* CROW[2]

**crew cut** a man's closely cropped haircut

**crew·el** (krōō′əl) *n.* [< ?] a loosely twisted, worsted yarn used in embroidery —**crew′el·work**′ *n.*

**crib** (krib) *n.* [OE., ox stall] 1. a rack or box for fodder 2. a small bed with high sides, for a baby 3. an enclosure for storing grain 4. an underwater structure serving as a pier, water intake, etc. 5. [Colloq.] a translation or other aid used dishonestly in doing schoolwork —*vt.* **cribbed**, **crib′bing** 1. to confine 2. to furnish with a crib 3. [Colloq.] to plagiarize —*vi.* [Colloq.] to use a crib for schoolwork

**crib·bage** (krib′ij) *n.* [< prec. + -AGE] a card game in which the object is to form combinations for points

**crick** (krik) *n.* [< ? ON.] a painful cramp in the neck or back

**crick·et**[1] (krik′it) *n.* [< OFr. *criquer*, to creak] a leaping insect related to the grasshoppers

**crick·et**[2] (krik′it) *n.* [prob. < MDu. *cricke*, a stick] an outdoor game played by two teams of eleven men each, using a ball, bats, and wickets

**cried** (krīd) *pt. & pp. of* CRY

**cri·er** (krī′ər) *n.* one who shouts out news, announcements, etc.

**crime** (krīm) *n.* [< L. *crimen*, offense] 1. an act committed or omitted in violation of a law 2. a sin

**Cri·me·a** (krī mē′ə) peninsula in SW U.S.S.R., extending into the Black Sea

**crim·i·nal** (krim′ə n'l) *adj.* 1. being a crime 2. relating to or guilty of crime —*n.* a person guilty of a crime —**crim′i·nal′i·ty** (-nal′ə tē) *n.* —**crim′i·nal·ly** *adv.*

**crim·i·nol·o·gy** (krim′ə näl′ə jē) *n.* the scientific study of crime and criminals —**crim′i·nol′o·gist** *n.*

**crimp** (krimp) *vt.* [< MDu. *crimpen*, to wrinkle] 1. to press into narrow folds; pleat 2. to curl (hair) —*n.* 1. a crimping 2. anything crimped —**put a crimp in** [Colloq.] to hinder

**crim·son** (krim′z'n) n. [< Sans. *kṛmi*, insect] deep red —*adj.* deep-red —*vt.*, *vi.* to make or become crimson

**cringe** (krinj) *vi.* **cringed, cring′ing** [< OE. *cringan*, fall (in battle)] 1. to draw back, crouch, etc., as when afraid; cower 2. to fawn

**crin·kle** (kriŋ′k'l) *vt.*, *vi.* **-kled, -kling** [see prec.] 1. to wrinkle; ripple 2. to rustle, as crushed paper —**crin′kly** *adj.* **-kli·er, -kli·est**

**crin·o·line** (krin′'l in) n. [Fr. < It. < *crino*, horsehair + *lino*, linen] 1. a coarse, stiff cloth used as a lining in garments 2. *same as* HOOP SKIRT

**crip·ple** (krip′'l) n. [< OE. *creopan*, to creep] one who is lame or otherwise disabled —*vt.* **-pled, -pling** 1. to lame 2. to disable; impair

**cri·sis** (krī′sis) n., *pl.* **-ses** (-sēz) [L. < Gr. *krinein*, to separate] 1. the turning point in a disease, when it becomes clear whether the patient will recover 2. any crucial situation

**crisp** (krisp) *adj.* [< L. *crispus*, curly] 1. brittle; easily crumbled 2. sharp and clear 3. fresh and firm 4. bracing 5. curly and wiry Also **crisp′y** —**crisp′ly** *adv.* —**crisp′ness** n.

**criss·cross** (kris′krôs′) n. [ME. *Christcros*, Christ's cross] a mark or pattern made of crossed lines —*adj.* marked by crossing lines —*vt.* to mark with crossing lines —*vi.* to move crosswise —*adv.* 1. crosswise 2. awry

**cri·ter·i·on** (krī tir′ē ən) n., *pl.* **-i·a** (-ē ə), **-i·ons** [< Gr. *kritēs*, judge] a standard, rule, or test by which something can be judged

**crit·ic** (krit′ik) n. [< Gr. *krinein*, discern] 1. one who writes judgments of books, plays, music, etc. professionally 2. one who finds fault

**crit′i·cal** (-i k'l) *adj.* 1. tending to find fault 2. of critics or criticism 3. of or forming a crisis; crucial —**crit′i·cal·ly** *adv.*

**crit′i·cism** (-ə siz′m) n. 1. the act of making judgments, esp. of literary or artistic work 2. a review, article, etc. expressing such judgment 3. a finding fault 4. the art, principles, or methods of critics

**crit′i·cize′** (-ə sīz′) *vi.*, *vt.* **-cized′, -ciz′ing** 1. to analyze and judge as a critic 2. to find fault (with) Brit. sp. **criticise** —**crit′i·ciz′a·ble** *adj.* —**crit′i·ciz′er** n.

**cri·tique** (kri tēk′) n. [Fr.] a critical analysis or review

**crit·ter** (krit′ər) n. [Dial.] a creature

**croak** (krōk) *vi.* [echoic] 1. to make a deep, hoarse sound *[frogs croak]* 2. [Slang] to die —*vt.* to utter in deep, hoarse tones —n. a croaking sound

**Cro·a·tia** (krō ā′shə) a republic of Yugoslavia —**Cro·a′tian** *adj.*, n.

**cro·chet** (krō shā′) n. [Fr. a small hook] needlework done with one hooked needle —*vt.*, *vi.* **-cheted**

(-shād′), **-chet′ing** to do, or make by, crochet —**cro·chet′er** n.

**crock** (kräk) n. [OE. *crocca*] an earthenware pot or jar —**crock′er·y** n.

**crocked** (kräkt) *adj.* [< *crock*, to disable] [Slang] drunk

**croc·o·dile** (kräk′ə dīl′) n. [< Gr. *krokodilos*, lizard] a large, lizardlike reptile of tropical streams, having a long, narrow head with massive jaws

**cro·cus** (krō′kəs) n., *pl.* **-cus·es, -ci** (-sī) [< Gr. *krokos*, saffron] a spring-blooming plant of the iris family, with grasslike leaves and a yellow, purple, or white flower

**Croe·sus** (krē′səs) a wealthy king of ancient times —n. a very rich man

**crois·sant** (krə sänt′; Fr. krwä sän′) n. [Fr.] a crescent-shaped roll

**Cro-Ma·gnon** (krō mag′nən) *adj.* [< *Cro-Magnon* cave in France] of a prehistoric type of tall man on the European continent in the Stone Age

**Crom·well** (kräm′wel). **Oliver** 1599-1658; Eng. revolutionary leader and head of England (1653-1658)

**crone** (krōn) n. [< MDu. *kronje*, old ewe] an ugly, withered old woman

**cro·ny** (krō′nē) n., *pl.* **-nies** [< Gr. *chronios*, long-time] a close friend

**crook** (krook) n. [< ON. *krōkr*, hook] 1. a hook; hooked or curved staff, etc. 2. a bend or curve 3. [Colloq.] a swindler —*vt.*, *vi.* **crooked** (krookt), **crook′ing** to bend or curve

**crook·ed** (krookt; *for 2 & 3* krook′id) *adj.* 1. having a crook 2. not straight; bent 3. dishonest —**crook′ed·ly** *adv.* —**crook′ed·ness** n.

**crook′neck′** n. a squash with a long, curved neck

**croon** (krōōn) *vi.*, *vt.* [ME.] to sing or hum in a low, gentle tone —n. a low, gentle singing or humming —**croon′er** n.

**crop** (kräp) n. [OE. *croppa*, cluster] 1. a saclike part of a bird's gullet, in which food is stored before digestion 2. any agricultural product, growing or harvested 3. the yield of any product in one season or place 4. a group 5. the handle of a whip 6. a riding whip 7. hair cut close to the head —*vt.* **cropped, crop′ping** 1. to cut or bite off the tops or ends of 2. to reap 3. to cut short —**crop out** (or **up**) to appear unexpectedly

**crop′-dust′ing** n. the spraying of crops with pesticides from an airplane —**crop′-dust′** *vi.*, *vt.*

**crop′per** n. 1. one that crops 2. a sharecropper —**come a cropper** [Colloq.] to come to ruin; fail

**cro·quet** (krō kā′) n. [Fr.: see CROTCHET] an outdoor game in which the players use mallets to drive a ball through hoops in the ground

**cro·quette** (krō ket′) n. [Fr. < *croquer*, to crunch] a small mass of meat, fish, etc. fried in deep fat

**cro·sier** (krō′zhər) n. [< OFr. *croce*] the staff of a bishop or abbot

**cross** (krôs) *n.* [< L. *crux*] **1.** an upright post with another across it, on which the ancient Romans executed people **2.** [*often* C-] a representation of this as a symbol of the crucifixion of Jesus, and hence of Christianity **3.** any trouble or affliction **4.** any mark or design made by intersecting lines, bars, etc. **5.** a crossing of varieties or breeds —*vt., vi.* **1.** to make the sign of the cross upon **2.** to place or lie across or crosswise **3.** to intersect **4.** to draw a line or lines across **5.** to go or extend across **6.** to meet and pass (each other) **7.** to thwart; oppose **8.** to interbreed (animals or plants) —*adj.* **1.** lying or passing across **2.** contrary; opposed **3.** cranky; irritable **4.** of mixed variety or breed —**cross off** (or **out**) to cancel as by drawing lines across —**cross one's mind** to come to mind briefly —**cross one's path** to meet one —**cross'ly** *adv.*

**cross'bar'** *n.* a bar, line, or stripe placed crosswise

**cross'beam'** *n.* a beam placed across another or from one wall to another

**cross'bones'** *n.* a representation of two bones placed across each other, under a skull, used to symbolize death

**cross'bow'** (-bō') *n.* a medieval weapon consisting of a bow set transversely on a wooden stock —**cross'-bow'man** (-mən) *n., pl.* -men

**cross'breed'** *vt., vi.* -bred', -breed'ing to hybridize —*n.* a hybrid

**cross'-coun'try** *adj.* across open country or fields, as a race

**cross'cut'** *adj.* **1.** used for cutting across [a *crosscut* saw] **2.** cut across —*n.* a cut across —*vt., vi.* -cut', -cut'ting to cut across

**cross'-ex·am'ine** *vt., vi.* *Law* to question (a witness already questioned by the opposing side) to determine the validity of his testimony —**cross'-ex·am'i·na'tion** *n.*

**cross'-eye'** *n.* an abnormal condition in which the eyes are turned toward each other —**cross'-eyed'** *adj.*

**cross'hatch'** (-hach') *vt., vi.* to shade (a drawing) with two sets of parallel lines that cross each other

**cross'ing** *n.* **1.** the act of passing across, thwarting, etc. **2.** an intersection, as of streets **3.** a place where a street, etc. may be crossed

**cross'piece'** *n.* a piece lying across another

**cross'-pol'li·nate'** *vt., vi.* -nat'ed, -nat'ing to transfer pollen from the anther of (one flower) to the stigma of (another) —**cross'-pol'li·na'tion** *n.*

**cross'-pur'pose** *n.* a contrary purpose —**at cross-purposes** having a misunderstanding as to each other's purposes

**cross'-ref'er·ence** *n.* a reference from one part of a book, etc. to another —**cross'-re·fer'** *vt., vi.*

**cross'road'** *n.* **1.** a road that crosses another **2.** [*usually pl.*] the place where roads intersect

**cross section 1.** *a)* a cutting through something *b)* a piece so cut off, or a representation of this **2.** a representative part of a whole

**cross'-town'** *adj.* going across the main avenues of a city

**cross'walk'** *n.* a lane marked off for pedestrians to use crossing a street

**cross'wise** (-wīz') *adv.* so as to cross; across: also **cross'ways'** (-wāz')

**cross'word' puzzle** an arrangement of numbered squares to be filled in with words whose definitions are given

**crotch** (kräch) *n.* [see CRUTCH] **1.** a place where two branches fork from a tree **2.** the place where the legs fork from the human body

**crotch·et** (kräch'it) *n.* [< OFr. *croc*, a hook] a peculiar whim or stubborn notion —**crotch'et·y** (-ē) *adj.*

**crouch** (krouch) *vi.* [< OFr. *croc*, a hook] **1.** to stoop or bend low **2.** to cringe —*n.* a stooping position

**croup** (krōōp) *n.* [< obs. *croup*, speak hoarsely] an inflammation of the respiratory passages, with labored breathing and hoarse coughing

**crou·pi·er** (krōō'pē ā') *n.* [Fr.] a person in charge of a gambling table

**crou·ton** (krōō'tän, krōō tän') *n.* [< Fr.: see CRUST] a small piece of toasted bread served in soup

**crow**[1] (krō) *n.* [OE. *crawa*] a large, glossy-black bird with a harsh call —**as the crow flies** in a straight, direct line —**eat crow** [Colloq.] to admit an error, recant, etc.

**crow**[2] (krō) *vi.* crowed, or for **1** crew, crowed, crow'ing [OE. *crawan*] **1.** to make the shrill cry of a rooster **2.** to boast in triumph **3.** to make a sound of pleasure —*n.* a crowing sound

**crow·bar** (krō'bär') *n.* a long, metal bar used as a lever for prying, etc.

**crowd** (kroud) *vi.* [OE. *crudan*] **1.** to push one's way (*into*) **2.** to throng —*vt.* **1.** to press or push **2.** to fill too full; cram —*n.* **1.** a large number of people or things grouped closely **2.** [Colloq.] a set; clique —**crowd'ed** *adj.*

**crow'foot'** *n., pl.* -foots' a plant of the buttercup family, with leaves resembling a crow's foot

**crown** (kroun) *n.* [< Gr. *korōnē*, wreath] **1.** a wreath worn on the head in victory **2.** a reward; honor **3.** the head covering of a monarch **4.** [*often* C-] *a)* the power of a monarch *b)* the monarch **5.** the top part, as of the head, a hat, etc. **6.** a British coin equal to five shillings **7.** the highest quality, point, state, etc. of anything **8.** the part of a tooth projecting beyond the gum line —*vt.* **1.** to put a crown on **2.** to cause to be a monarch **3.** to honor **4.** to be the highest part of **5.** to put the finishing touch on

**crown prince** the male heir apparent to a throne

**crow's-foot** (krōz'foot') *n., pl.* -feet' any of the wrinkles that often develop at the outer corners of the eyes

**crow's-nest** (-nest') *n.* a lookout platform high on a ship's mast

**cro·zier** (krō'zhər) *n.* *same as* CROSIER

**cru·cial** (krōō'shəl) *adj.* [< L. *crux*, a cross] **1.** decisive; critical **2.** severe; trying —**cru'cial·ly** *adv.*

**cru·ci·ble** (krōō'sə b'l) *n.* [< ML. *crucibulum*, lamp, crucible] **1.** a heat-resistant container for melting ores, metals. etc. **2.** a severe trial

**cru·ci·fix** (krōō'sə fiks') *n.* [< L. *crux*, a cross + *figere*, fasten] a representation of a cross with Jesus crucified on it: a Christian symbol

**cru·ci·fix·ion** (-fik'shən) *n.* **1.** a crucifying **2.** [C-] the crucifying of Jesus, or a representation of this

**cru·ci·form** *adj.* formed in a cross

**cru·ci·fy'** (-fī') *vt.* -fied', -fy'ing [see CRUCIFIX] **1.** to execute by nailing to a cross and leaving to die **2.** to be very cruel to; torment

**crude** (krōōd) *adj.* [< L. *crudus*, raw] **1.** in a raw or natural condition **2.** lacking grace, taste, etc. **3.** roughly made —**crude'ly** *adv.* —**cru·di·ty** (krōō'də tē), **crude'ness** *n.*

**cru·el** (krōō'əl) *adj.* [see prec.] causing pain and suffering; pitiless —**cru'el·ly** *adv.* —**cru'el·ty** *n.*, *pl.* -**ties**

**cru·et** (krōō'it) *n.* [< OFr. *crue*, earthen pot] a small glass bottle to hold vinegar, oil, etc. for the table

**cruise** (krōōz) *vi.* **cruised**, **cruis'ing** [< Du. *kruisen*, to cross] **1.** to sail or drive about from place to place, as for pleasure or in search of something **2.** to move at the most efficient speed for sustained travel —*vt.* to sail or journey over or about —*n.* a cruising voyage

**cruise missile** a long-range, jet-propelled winged bomb, launched from an airplane, submarine, or ship and guided by remote control

**cruis'er** *n.* **1.** anything that cruises, as a police car **2.** a fast warship smaller than a battleship

**crul·ler** (krul'ər) *n.* [Du. < *krullen*, to curl] a kind of twisted doughnut

**crumb** (krum) *n.* [< OE. *cruma*] **1.** a small piece broken off, as of bread **2.** any bit or scrap [*crumbs* of knowledge] —*vt.* *Cooking* to cover with crumbs —**crum·by** (krum'ē) *adj.*

**crum·ble** (krum'b'l) *vt.* -**bled**, -**bling** [freq. of prec.] to break into crumbs —*vi.* to fall to pieces —**crum'bly** *adj.* -**bli·er**, -**bli·est**

**crum·my** (krum'ē) *adj.* -**mi·er**, -**mi·est** [Slang] shabby, mean, etc.

**crum·pet** (krum'pit) *n.* [OE. *crompeht*] a batter cake baked on a griddle

**crum·ple** (krum'p'l) *vt.*, *vi.* -**pled**, -**pling** [ME. *crumplen*] to crush together into wrinkles

**crunch** (krunch) *vi.*, *vt.* [echoic] to chew, press, grind, etc. with a noisy, crackling or crushing sound —*n.* **1.** the act or sound of crunching **2.** [Slang] a showdown or tight situation —**crunch'y** *adj.* -**i·er**, -**i·est**

**crup·per** (krup'ər, kroop'-) *n.* [< OFr. *crope*, rump] a leather strap attached to a saddle or harness and passed under a horse's tail

**cru·sade** (krōō sād') *n.* [ult. < L. *crux*, a cross] **1.** [*often* C-] any of the Christian military expeditions (11th-13th cent.) to recover the Holy Land from the Moslems **2.** vigorous, con-

certed action for some cause, or against some abuse —*vi.* -**sad'ed**, -**sad'ing** to engage in a crusade —**cru·sad'er** *n.*

**cruse** (krōōz, krōōs) *n.* [OE.] a small container for water, oil. etc.

**crush** (krush) *vt.* [< OFr. *croisir*] **1.** to press with force so as to break or put out of shape **2.** to grind or pound into small bits **3.** to subdue; overwhelm **4.** to extract by squeezing —*vi.* to become crushed —*n.* **1.** a crushing **2.** a crowded mass of people **3.** [Colloq.] an infatuation —**crush'er** *n.*

**crust** (krust) *n.* [< L. *crusta*] **1.** the hard, outer part of bread **2.** any dry, hard piece of bread **3.** the pastry shell of a pie **4.** any hard surface layer, as of snow **5.** [Slang] insolence —*vt.*, *vi.* to cover or become covered with a crust —**crust'y** *adj.* -**i·er**, -**i·est**

**crus·ta·cean** (krus tā'shən) *n.* [see prec.] any of a class of arthropods, including shrimps, crabs, lobsters, etc., that have a hard outer shell

**crutch** (kruch) *n.* [OE. *crycce*] **1.** a staff with a top crosspiece that fits under the armpit, used to aid the lame in walking **2.** any prop or support

**crux** (kruks) *n.* [L., a cross] **1.** a difficult problem **2.** the essential or deciding point

**cry** (krī) *vi.* **cried**, **cry'ing** [< L. *quiritare*, to wail] **1.** to utter a loud sound, as in pain, fright, etc. **2.** to sob and shed tears; weep **3.** to plead or clamor (*for*) **4.** to utter its characteristic call: said of an animal —*vt.* **1.** to utter loudly; shout **2.** to call out (wares for sale, etc.) —*n.*, *pl.* **cries 1.** a loud vocal sound; call; shout **2.** a plea; appeal **3.** a fit of weeping **4.** the characteristic call of an animal —**a far cry** a great distance or difference

**cry·ba·by** *n.*, *pl.* -**bies** one who complains constantly, in a childish way

**cry·o·gen·ics** (krī'ə jen'iks) *n.* [< Gr. *kryos*, cold + -GEN + -ICS] the science that deals with the production of very low temperatures and their effect on the properties of matter

**cry·o·sur·ger·y** (krī'ə sur'jə rē) *n.* [< Gr. *kryos*, cold + SURGERY] surgery that destroys tissues by freezing

**crypt** (kript) *n.* [< Gr. *kryptein*, hide] an underground vault, esp. one under a church, used for burial

**cryp·tic** (krip'tik) *adj.* **1.** hidden or mysterious; baffling **2.** obscure and curt —**cryp'ti·cal·ly** *adv.*

**cryp·to·gram** (krip'tə gram') *n.* [see ff.] a message in code or cipher

**cryp·tog·ra·phy** (krip täg'rə fē) *n.* [< Gr. *kryptos*, hidden + -GRAPHY] the art of writing or deciphering messages in code —**cryp·tog'ra·pher** *n.*

**crys·tal** (kris't'l) *n.* [< Gr. *kryos*, frost] **1.** a clear, transparent quartz **2.** *a)* a very clear, brilliant glass *b)* articles of such glass, as goblets **3.** anything clear like crystal, as the covering over a watch face **4.** a solidified form of a substance having plane faces arranged in a symmetrical, three-dimensional pattern —*adj.* 1. of crystal 2. like crystal; clear

**crys'tal·line** (-tə lin) *adj.* 1. made of crystals 2. like crystals in clearness, structure, etc.

**crys'tal·lize'** (-līz') *vi.*, *vt.* **-lized', -liz'ing** 1. to become or cause to become crystalline 2. to take on or cause to take on a definite form — **crys'tal·li·za'tion** *n.*

**cs.** case(s)

**CST, C.S.T.** Central Standard Time

**CT** Connecticut

**ct.** 1. *pl.* **cts.** cent 2. court

**Cu** [L. *cuprum*] *Chem.* copper

**cu,** cubic

**cub** (kub) *n.* [< ? OIr. *cuib*, whelp] 1. a young fox, bear, lion, whale, etc. 2. a youth or novice

**Cu·ba** (kyōō'bə) island country in the West Indies, south of Fla.: 44,218 sq. mi.; pop. 7,833,000 —**Cu'ban** *adj., n.*

**cub·by·hole** (kub'ē hōl') *n.* [< Brit. dial. *cub*, little shed + HOLE] a small, enclosed space: also **cub'by**

**cube** (kyōōb) *n.* [< Gr. *kybos*] 1. a solid with six equal, square sides 2. the product obtained by multiplying a given number by its square [the *cube* of 3 is 27] —*vt.* **cubed, cub'ing** 1. to obtain the cube of (a number) 2. to cut or shape into cubes —**cub'er** *n.*

**cube root** the quantity of which a given quantity is the cube [the *cube root* of 8 is 2]

**cu·bic** (kyōō'bik) *adj.* 1. having the shape of a cube: also **cu'bi·cal** 2. having three dimensions: a cubic foot is the volume of a cube one foot in length, width, and breadth

**cu·bi·cle** (kyōō'bi k'l) *n.* [< L. *cubare*, lie down] a small compartment

**cub·ism** (kyōō'biz'm) *n.* a school of modern art characterized by the use of cubes and other geometric forms —**cub'ist** *adj., n.* —**cu·bis'tic** *adj.*

**cu·bit** (kyōō'bit) *n.* [< L. *cubitum*] an ancient measure of length, about 18 to 22 inches

**cuck·old** (kuk'ld) *n.* [see ff.] a man whose wife has committed adultery —*vt.* to make a cuckold of —**cuck'old·ry** (-rē) *n.*

**cuck·oo** (kōō'kōō', kook'ōō) *n.* [< OFr. *cucu*, echoic] 1. a gray-brown bird with a long, slender body: one species lays eggs in the nests of other birds 2. its call —*adj.* [Slang] crazy

**cu·cum·ber** (kyōō'kum bər) *n.* [< L. *cucumis*] a long, green-skinned fruit with firm, white flesh, used in salads or preserved as pickles

**cud** (kud) *n.* [OE. *cudu*] a mouthful of swallowed food regurgitated from the first stomach of cattle and other ruminants and chewed again

**cud·dle** (kud'l) *vt.* **-dled, -dling** [< ?] to embrace and fondle —*vi.* to lie close and snug

**cud'dly** (-lē) *adj.* **-dli·er, -dli·est** that invites cuddling; lovable: also **cud'dle·some** (-səm)

**cudg·el** (kuj'əl) *n.* [OE. *cycgel*] a short, thick stick or club —*vt.* **-eled**

or **-elled, -el'ing** or **-el'ling** to beat with a cudgel

**cue¹** (kyōō) *n.* [< *q* (? for L. *quando*, when) found in 16th-c. plays] 1. a signal in dialogue, etc. for an actor's entrance or speech 2. any signal to do something 3. a hint —*vt.* **cued, cu'ing** or **cue'ing** to give a cue to

**cue²** (kyōō) *n.* [var. of QUEUE] a long, tapering rod used in billiards and pool to strike the ball (**cue ball**)

**cuff** (kuf) *n.* [ME. *cuffe*, glove] 1. a band at the wrist end of a sleeve 2. a turned-up fold at the bottom of a trouser leg 3. a slap —*vt.* to slap —**off the cuff** [Slang] offhandedly —**on the cuff** [Slang] on credit

**cuff link** a pair of linked buttons, etc. for fastening a shirt cuff

**cui·sine** (kwi zēn') *n.* [Fr. < L. *coquere*, to cook] 1. a style of cooking or preparing food 2. the food prepared, as at a restaurant

**cul-de-sac** (kul'də sak') *n., pl.* **-sacs'** [Fr., lit., bottom of a sack] a blind alley

**cu·li·nar·y** (kyōō'lə ner'ē) *adj.* [< L. *culina*, kitchen] of cooking

**cull** (kul) *vt.* [< L. *colligere*, collect] to pick out; select and gather —*n.* something picked out for rejection as not being up to standard

**cul·len·der** (kul'ən dər) *n.* same as COLANDER

**cul·mi·nate** (kul'mə nāt') *vi.* **-nat'ed, -nat'ing** [< L. *culmen*, peak] to reach its highest point or climax —**cul'mi·na'tion** *n.*

**cu·lotte** (koo lät', kyoo-) *n.* [Fr. < L. *culus*, posterior] [*often pl.*] a women's garment consisting of trousers made to resemble a skirt

**cul·pa·ble** (kul'pə b'l) *adj.* [< L. *culpa*, fault] deserving blame —**cul'pa·bil'i·ty** *n.* —**cul'pa·bly** *adv.*

**cul·prit** (kul'prit) *n.* [< early law Fr. *culpable*, guilty + *prit*, ready (to prove)] a person accused, or found guilty, of a crime

**cult** (kult) *n.* [< L. *cultus*, care] 1. a system of religious worship 2. devoted attachment to a person, principle, etc. 3. a sect —**cult'ism** *n.* —**cult'ist** *n.*

**cul·ti·vate** (kul'tə vāt') *vt.* **-vat'ed, -vat'ing** [see prec.] 1. to prepare (land) for growing crops; till 2. to grow (plants) 3. to loosen the soil and kill weeds around (plants) 4. to develop or improve [*cultivate* your mind] 5. to seek to become familiar with —**cul'ti·va·ble** (-və b'l), **cul'ti·vat'a·ble** *adj.* —**cul'ti·va'tor** *n.*

**cul·ti·va'tion** *n.* 1. the act of cultivating 2. refinement, or culture

**cul·ture** (kul'chər) *n.* [see CULT] 1. cultivation of the soil 2. a growth of bacteria, etc. in a prepared substance 3. improvement of the mind, manners, etc. 4. development by special training or care 5. the skills, arts, etc. of a given people in a given period; civilization —*vt.* **-tured, -tur·ing** to cultivate —**cul'tur·al** *adj.* —**cul'tur·al·ly** *adv.*

**cul·vert** (kul'vərt) *n.* [< ?] a drain or conduit under a road or embankment

**cum·ber** (kum′bər) vt. [< OFr. combrer, barrier] to hinder; hamper

**cum′ber·some** (-səm) adj. burdensome; unwieldy: also **cum′brous** (-brəs)

**cum·in** (kum′in) n. [< Gr. kyminon] 1. a plant of the parsley family 2. its aromatic fruits, used for flavoring

**cum·mer·bund** (kum′ər bund′) n. [< Ar.-Per. kamar, loins + Per. band, band] a wide sash worn as a waistband, esp. with men's formal dress

**cu·mu·la·tive** (kyōom′yə lāt′iv, -lə tiv) adj. [< L. cumulus, a heap] increasing in effect, size, etc. by successive additions

**cu·mu·lus** (kyōom′yə ləs) n., pl. -li′ (-lī′) [L., a heap] a thick cloud type with upper parts resembling domes

**cu·ne·i·form** (kyōo nē′ə fôrm′) adj. [< L. cuneus, a wedge + -FORM] wedge-shaped, as the characters used in ancient Assyrian and Babylonian inscriptions —n. cuneiform characters

**cun·ning** (kun′iŋ) adj. [< ME. cunnen, know] 1. sly; crafty 2. made with skill 3. pretty; cute —n. slyness; craftiness —**cun′ning·ly** adv.

**cup** (kup) n. [< L. cupa, tub] 1. a small, bowl-shaped container for beverages, usually with a handle 2. a cup and its contents 3. a cupful 4. anything shaped like a cup —vt. **cupped, cup′ping** to shape like a cup

**cup·board** (kub′ərd) n. a closet or cabinet with shelves for cups, plates, food, etc.

**cup′cake′** n. a small cake

**cup′ful′** n., pl. -fuls′ as much as a cup will hold; specif., eight ounces

**Cu·pid** (kyōo′pid) Rom. Myth. the god of love —n. [c-] a representation of Cupid as a winged boy with bow and arrow

**cu·pid·i·ty** (kyōo pid′ə tē) n. [< L. cupere, to desire] strong desire for wealth; avarice

**cu·po·la** (kyōo′pə lə) n. [It. < L. cupa, a tub] a small dome, etc. on a roof —**cu′po·laed** (-ləd) adj.

**cu·pro·nick·el** (kyōo′prō nik′'l) n. [< L. cuprum, copper + NICKEL] an alloy of copper and nickel, used in coins

**cur** (kur) n. [prob. < ON. kurra, to growl] 1. a dog of mixed breed; mongrel 2. a contemptible person

**cu·rate** (kyoor′it) n. [< L. cura, care] a clergyman who assists a vicar or rector —**cu′ra·cy** (-ə sē) n., pl. -cies

**cur·a·tive** (kyoor′ə tiv) adj. having the power to cure —n. a remedy

**cu·ra·tor** (kyoo rāt′ər) n. [< L. curare, take care of] a person in charge of a museum, library, etc. —**cu·ra·to·ri·al** (kyoor′ə tôr′ē əl) adj.

**curb** (kurb) n. [< L. curvus, bent] 1. a chain or strap attached to a horse's bit, used to check the horse 2. anything that checks or restrains 3. a stone or concrete edging along a street 4. a market dealing in stocks and bonds not listed on the exchange —vt. to restrain; control

**curb service** service offered to customers who wish to remain in their cars

**curb′stone′** n. the stone or stones making up a curb: also **curb′ing**

**curd** (kurd) n. [< ME. crud, coagulated substance] the coagulated part of soured milk from which cheese is made

**cur·dle** (kur′d'l) vt., vi. -dled, -dling to form into curd; coagulate

**cure** (kyoor) n. [< L. cura, care] 1. a healing or being healed 2. a remedy 3. a method of medical treatment —vt. cured, cur′ing 1. to restore to health 2. to get rid of (an ailment, evil, etc.) 3. a) to preserve (meat), as by salting or smoking b) to process (tobacco, leather, etc.), as by drying or aging —**cur′a·ble** adj. —**cur′er** n.

**cu·ré** (kyoo rā′) n. [Fr. < L. cura, care] in France, a parish priest

**cure′-all′** n. something supposed to cure all ailments or evils

**cu·ret·tage** (kyoor′ə täzh′) n. [Fr.] the process of cleaning or scraping the walls of a body cavity with a spoonlike instrument

**cur·few** (kur′fyōo) n. [< OFr. covrefeu, lit., cover fire: orig. a nightly signal to cover fires and retire] a time in the evening beyond which children, etc. may not appear on the streets

**Cu·ri·a** (kyoor′ē ə) n., pl. -ri·ae (-ē) [L.] the official body governing the Roman Catholic Church under the authority of the Pope

**Cu·rie** (kyoo rē′, kyoor′ē), **Marie** 1867–1934; Pol. chemist in France

**cu·ri·o** (kyoor′ē ō′) n., pl. -os′ [contr. of ff.] an unusual or rare article

**cu·ri·os·i·ty** (kyoor′ē äs′ə tē) n., pl. -ties 1. a desire to learn 2. inquisitiveness 3. anything curious or rare

**cu·ri·ous** (kyoor′ē əs) adj. [< L. curiosus, careful] 1. eager to learn or know 2. prying or inquisitive 3. unusual; strange —**cu′ri·ous·ly** adv.

**curl** (kurl) vt. [< ME. crul, curly] 1. to twist (esp. hair) into ringlets 2. to cause to bend around —vi. to become curled —n. 1. a ringlet of hair 2. anything with a curled shape —**curl′er** n. —**curl′y** adj. -i·er, -i·est

**cur·lew** (kur′lōo) n. [echoic] a large, brownish wading bird with long legs

**curl·i·cue** (kur′li kyōo′) n. [< CURLY + CUE²] a fancy curve, flourish, etc.

**curl·ing** (kur′liŋ) n. a game played on ice by sliding a flat stone at a mark

**cur·rant** (kur′ənt) n. [ult. < Corinth, ancient Gr. city] 1. a small, seedless raisin from the Mediterranean region 2. a) the sour berry of several species of hardy shrubs b) the shrub

CURLEW

**cur·ren·cy** (kur'ən sē) *n., pl.* **-cies** [see ff.] **1.** circulation **2.** the money in circulation in any country **3.** general use or acceptance

**cur·rent** (kur'ənt) *adj.* [< L. *currere*, to run] **1.** now going on; of the present time **2.** circulating **3.** commonly accepted; prevalent —*n.* **1.** a flow of water or air in a definite direction **2.** a general tendency **3.** the flow or rate of flow of electricity in a conductor —**cur'rent·ly** *adv.*

**cur·ric·u·lum** (kə rik'yə ləm) *n., pl.* **-la** (-lə), **-lums** [L., course for racing] a course of study in a school — **cur·ric'u·lar** *adj.*

**cur·ry**[1] (kur'ē) *vt.* **-ried, -ry·ing** [< OFr. *correier*, put in order] **1.** to rub down and clean the coat of (a horse, etc.) with a comb or brush **2.** to prepare (tanned leather) **3.** to try to win (favor) by flattery, etc.

**cur·ry**[2] (kur'ē) *n., pl.* **-ries** [Tamil *kari*] **1.** a powder prepared from various spices, or a sauce made with this **2.** a stew made with curry —*vt.* **-ried, -ry·ing** to prepare with curry

**cur'ry·comb'** *n.* a comb with teeth or ridges, for currying a horse — *vt.* to use a currycomb on

**curse** (kurs) *n.* [OE. *curs*] **1.** a calling on God or the gods to bring evil on some person or thing **2.** a profane or obscene oath **3.** evil coming as if in answer to a curse —*vt.* **cursed** or **curst, curs'ing 1.** to call evil down on **2.** to swear at **3.** to afflict —*vi.* to swear; blaspheme —**be cursed with** to suffer from

**curs·ed** (kur'sid, kurst) *adj.* **1.** under a curse **2.** deserving to be cursed; evil; hateful

**cur·sive** (kur'siv) *adj.* [ult. < L. *currere*, to run] designating writing in which the letters are joined

**cur·so·ry** (kur'sər ē) *adj.* [< L. *cursor*, runner] hastily, often superficially, done —**cur'so·ri·ly** *adv.*

**curt** (kurt) *adj.* [L. *curtus*, short] brief, esp. to the point of rudeness —**curt'ly** *adv.* —**curt'ness** *n.*

**cur·tail** (kər tāl') *vt.* [< L. *curtus*, short] to cut short; reduce —**cur·tail'ment** *n.*

**cur·tain** (kur't'n) *n.* [< L. *cors*, a court] a piece of cloth, etc. hung at a window, in front of a stage, etc. to decorate or conceal —*vt.* to provide or shut off as with a curtain

**curtain call 1.** a call, usually by applause, for performers to return to the stage **2.** such a return

**curt·sy** (kurt'sē) *n., pl.* **-sies** [var. of COURTESY] a woman's bow of greeting, respect, etc. made by bending the knees and dipping the body slightly —*vi.* **-sied, -sy·ing** to make a curtsy Also **curtsey**

**cur·va·ceous** (kər vā'shəs) *adj.* [< CURVE] [Colloq.] having a full, shapely figure: said of a woman

**cur·va·ture** (kur'və chər) *n.* **1.** a curving or being curved **2.** a curve

**curve** (kurv) *n.* [L. *curvus*, bent] **1.** a line having no straight part; bend with no angles **2.** something shaped like, or moving in, a curve —*vt., vi.* **curved, curv'ing 1.** to form a curve by bending **2.** to move in a curve —**curv'y** *adj.* **-i·er, -i·est**

**cush·ion** (koosh'ən) *n.* [< ML. *coxinum*] **1.** a pillow or pad **2.** a thing like this in shape or use **3.** anything that absorbs shock —*vt.* to provide with a cushion

**cush·y** (koosh'ē) *adj.* **-i·er, -i·est** [< Per. *khūsh*, pleasant] [Slang] easy; comfortable

**cusp** (kusp) *n.* [L. *cuspis*] a point, as on the chewing surface of a tooth

**cus·pi·dor** (kus'pə dôr') *n.* [< Port. *cuspir*, to spit] a spittoon

**cuss** (kus) *n., vt., vi.* [Colloq.] same as CURSE

**cus·tard** (kus'tərd) *n.* [< L. *crusta*, crust] **1.** a mixture of eggs, milk, sugar, etc., boiled or baked **2.** a somewhat similar frozen mixture: in full **frozen custard**

**cus·to·di·an** (kəs tō'dē ən) *n.* **1.** one who has the custody or care of something; caretaker **2.** a janitor

**cus·to·dy** (kus'tə dē) *n.* [< L. *custos*, a guard] a guarding or keeping safe; care —**in custody** under arrest — **cus·to·di·al** (kəs tō'dē əl) *adj.*

**cus·tom** (kus'təm) *n.* [< L. *com-*, intens. + *suere*, be accustomed] **1.** a usual practice; habit **2.** social conventions carried on by tradition **3.** [*pl.*] duties or taxes imposed on imported goods **4.** the regular patronage of a business —*adj.* **1.** made to order **2.** making things to order

**cus'tom·ar'y** (-tə mer'ē) *adj.* in keeping with custom; usual; habitual —**cus'tom·ar'i·ly** *adv.*

**cus'tom-built'** *adj.* built to order, to the customer's specifications

**cus'tom·er** *n.* a person who buys, esp. one who buys regularly

**cus'tom·house'** *n.* an office where customs or duties are paid

**cus'tom·ize'** (-īz') *vt., vi.* **-ized', -iz'ing** to make according to individual specifications

**cus'tom-made'** *adj.* made to order, to the customer's specifications

**cut** (kut) *vt.* **cut, cut'ting** [ME. *cutten*] **1.** to make an opening in with a sharp-edged instrument; gash **2.** to pierce sharply so as to hurt **3.** to have (a new tooth) grow through the gum **4.** to divide into parts with a sharp-edged instrument; sever **5.** to hew **6.** to reap **7.** to reduce; curtail **8.** to trim; pare **9.** to divide (a pack of cards) **10.** to make or do as by cutting **11.** to hit (a ball) so that it spins **12.** [Colloq.] to pretend not to recognize (a person) **13.** [Colloq.] to be absent from (a school class, etc.) **14.** [Slang] to stop —*vi.* **1.** to pierce, sever, gash, etc. **2.** to take cutting [*pine cuts* easily] **3.** to go (*across* or *through*) **4.** to swing a bat, etc. (*at* a ball) **5.** to change direction suddenly —*adj.* **1.** that has been cut **2.** made or formed by cutting —*n.* **1.** a cutting or being cut **2.** a stroke or opening made by a sharp-edged instrument **3.** a piece cut off, as of meat **4.** a reduction **5.** a passage or channel cut out **6.** the style in which a thing is cut **7.** an act, remark, etc. that hurts one's feelings **8.** a block or plate engraved for printing, or the impression from this **9.** [Colloq.] an unauthorized absence from school, etc. **10.** [Slang] a share, as of profits —**cut and dried 1.** arranged beforehand **2.** lifeless; dull —**cut down (on)** to reduce; lessen —**cut it out** [Colloq.] to stop what one is doing —**cut off 1.** to sever **2.** to stop abruptly; shut off —**cut out for** suited for —**cut up 1.** to cut into pieces **2.** [Slang] to clown, joke, etc.

**cu·ta·ne·ous** (kyōō tā′nē əs) *adj.* [< L. *cutis*, skin] of or on the skin

**cut′a·way′** *n.* a man's formal coat cut so as to curve back to the tails

**cut′back′** *n.* a reduction or discontinuance, as of production

**cute** (kyōōt) *adj.* cut′er, cut′est [< ACUTE] [Colloq.] **1.** clever; shrewd **2.** pretty or attractive, esp. in a dainty way —**cute′ly** *adv.* —**cute′ness** *n.*

**cut·i·cle** (kyōōt′i k'l) *n.* [L. *cuticula*, skin] **1.** the outer layer of the skin **2.** hardened skin as at the base and sides of a fingernail

**cut·lass** (kut′ləs) *n.* [< L. *culter*, knife] a short, thick, curved sword

**cut·ler·y** (kut′lər ē) *n.* [< L. *culter*, knife] cutting implements, as knives; often, specif., eating implements

**cut·let** (kut′lit) *n.* [< L. *costa*, a rib] **1.** a small slice of meat from the ribs or leg **2.** a small, flat croquette of chopped meat or fish

**cut′off′** *n.* **1.** a road, etc. that is a shortcut **2.** any device for shutting off the flow of a fluid, a connection, etc.

**cut′-rate′** *adj.* selling or on sale at a lower price

**cut·ter** (kut′ər) *n.* **1.** a person or thing that cuts **2.** a small, swift vessel **3.** a small, light sleigh

**cut′throat′** *n.* a murderer —*adj.* **1.** murderous **2.** merciless; ruthless

**cut·ting** (kut′iŋ) *n.* a shoot cut away from a plant for rooting or grafting —*adj.* **1.** that cuts; sharp **2.** chilling or piercing **3.** sarcastic; wounding

**cut·tle·fish** (kut′'l fish′) *n., pl.:* see FISH [OE. *cudele*] a sea mollusk with ten sucker-bearing arms and a hard internal shell (**cuttlebone**)

**cwt.** hundredweight

**-cy** (sē) [< Gr. *-kia*] a suffix meaning: **1.** quality, condition, or fact of being [*hesitancy*] **2.** position, rank, or office of [*captaincy*]

**cy·a·nide** (sī′ə nīd′) *n.* a highly poisonous, white, crystalline compound

**cy·ber·na·tion** (sī′bər nā′shən) *n.* [CYBERN(ETICS) + -ATION] the use of computers coupled to automatic machinery to do routine, repetitive tasks, etc.

**cy·ber·net·ics** (sī′bər net′iks) *n.pl.* [*with sing. v.*] [< Gr. *kybernētēs*, helmsman] the comparative study of electronic computers and the human

nervous system —**cy′ber·net′ic** *adj.*

**cy·cla·mate** (sik′lə māt′, sī′klə-) *n.* a salt of an organic acid, esp. sodium or calcium salt with a sweet taste

**cy·cla·men** (sik′lə mən) *n.* [< Gr. *kyklaminos*] a plant of the primrose family with heart-shaped leaves

**cy·cla·zo·cine** (sī′klə zō′sēn) *n.* a pain-killing drug that blocks the effects of heroin or morphine

**cy·cle** (sī′k'l) *n.* [< Gr. *kyklos*, a circle] **1.** *a)* a period of time within which a round of regularly recurring events is completed *b)* a complete set of such events **2.** a series of poems or songs on one theme **3.** a bicycle, motorcycle, etc. —*vi.* -**cled,** -**cling** to ride a bicycle, etc. —**cy·clic** (sī′klik) *adj.*

**cy·clist** (sī′klist) *n.* a cycle rider

**cyclo-** [< *kyklos*, circle] *a combining form meaning* of a circle or wheel

**cy·clom·e·ter** (sī kläm′ə tər) *n.* [prec. + -METER] an instrument that records the revolutions of a wheel for measuring distance traveled

**cy·clone** (sī′klōn) *n.* [< Gr. *kyklos*, circle] a storm with strong winds rotating about a center of low pressure

**cy·clo·pe·di·a, cy·clo·pae·di·a** (sī′klə pē′dē ə) *n.* same as ENCYCLOPEDIA

**Cy·clops** (sī′kläps) *n., pl.* **Cy·clo·pes** (sī klō′pēz) *Gr. Myth.* any of a race of one-eyed giants

**cy·clo·tron** (sī′klə trän′) *n.* [CYCLO- + (ELEC)TRON] an apparatus for giving high energy to particles, as protons, etc.: used in atomic research

**cyg·net** (sig′nət) *n.* [< Gr. *kyknos*, swan] a young swan

**cyl·in·der** (sil′ən dər) *n.* [< Gr. *kylindein*, to roll] **1.** a solid figure described by the edge of a rectangle rotated around the parallel edge as axis **2.** anything with this shape; specif., *a)* the turning part of a revolver *b)* the piston chamber of an engine —**cy·lin·dri·cal** (sə lin′dri k'l) *adj.*

**cym·bal** (sim′b'l) *n.* [< Gr. *kymbē*, hollow of a vessel] *Music* a circular brass plate that makes a sharp, ringing sound when hit —**cym′bal·ist** *n.*

**cyn·ic** (sin′ik) *n.* a cynical person

**cyn′i·cal** (-i k'l) *adj.* [< Gr. *kyōn*, dog] **1.** denying the sincerity of people's motives and actions **2.** sarcastic, sneering, etc. —**cyn′i·cal·ly** *adv.*

**cyn′i·cism** (-ə siz′m) *n.* the attitude or beliefs of a cynic

**cy·no·sure** (sī′nə shoor′, sin′ə-) *n.* [< Gr. *kynosoura*, dog's tail] a center of attention or interest

**cy·pher** (sī′fər) *n., vi.* Brit. var. of CIPHER

**cy·press** (sī′prəs) *n.* [< Gr. *kyparissos*] **1.** an evergreen tree with cones and dark foliage **2.** its wood

**Cy·prus** (sī′prəs) country on an island at the E end of the Mediterranean: 3,572 sq. mi.; pop. 607,000 —**Cyp·ri·ot** (sip′rē ət) *adj., n.*

**cyst** (sist) *n.* [ < Gr. *kystis*, sac] a sac-like structure in plants or animals, esp. one filled with diseased matter —**cyst·ic** (sis′tik) *adj.*

**cystic fibrosis** a children's disease in which there is fibrosis of the pancreas and respiratory infections

**cy·tol·o·gy** (sī tät′ə jē) *n.* [ < Gr. *kytos*, a hollow + -LOGY] the branch of biology dealing with cells

**C.Z., CZ** Canal Zone

**czar** (zär) *n.* [ < Russ. < L. *Caesar*] 1. the title of any of the former emperors of Russia 2. an autocrat —**cza·ri·na** (zä rē′nə) *n.fem.*

**Czech** (chek) *n.* 1. a member of a Slavic people of central Europe 2. the West Slavic language of the Czechs 3. loosely, a native or inhabitant of Czechoslovakia —*adj.* of Czechoslovakia, its people, or their language: also **Czech′ish**

**Czech·o·slo·va·ki·a** (chek′ə slō vä′kē ə) country in C Europe: 49,367 sq. mi.; pop. 14,274,000 —**Czech′o·slo′-vak, Czech′o·slo·va′ki·an** *adj., n.*

# D

**D, d** (dē) *n., pl.* **D's, d's** the fourth letter of the English alphabet

**D** (dē) *n.* 1. a Roman numeral for 500 2. a grade for below-average work 3. *Music* the second tone in the scale of C major

**d.** 1. day(s) 2. degree 3. diameter 4. died 5. [L. *denarii*] pence

**D.A.** District Attorney

**dab** (dab) *vt., vi.* **dabbed, dab′bing** [ME. *dabben*, to strike] 1. to touch lightly and quickly; pat 2. to put on (paint, etc.) with light, quick strokes —*n.* 1. a tap; pat 2. a soft or moist bit of something

**dab·ble** (dab′'l) *vi.* **-bled, -bling** [ < Du. *dabben*, to strike] 1. to play in water, as with the hands 2. to do something superficially (with *in* or *at*)

**dace** (dās) *n., pl.* **dace, dac′es** [ < VL. *darsus*] a small freshwater fish of the carp family

**dachs·hund** (däks′hoond) *n.* [G. < *dachs*, badger + *hund*, dog] a small dog with a long body, short legs, and drooping ears

**Da·cron** (dā′krän, dak′rän) *a trademark for* a synthetic wrinkle-resistant fabric —*n.* [also **d–**] this fabric

**dac·tyl** (dak′t'l) *n.* [ < Gr. *daktylos*, finger] a metrical foot of three syllables, the first accented and the others unaccented —**dac·tyl′ic** (-til′ik) *adj.*

**dad** (dad) *n.* [ < child's cry *dada*] [Colloq.] father: also **dad′dy,** *pl.* **-dies**

**dad′dy-long′legs′** *n., pl.* **-long′-legs′** a spiderlike animal with long legs

**da·do** (dā′dō) *n., pl.* **-does** [It. < L. *datum*, a die] 1. the part of a pedestal between the cap and the base 2. the lower part of a wall if decorated differently from the upper part

**dae·mon** (dē′mən) *n.* [ < Gr. *daimōn*] 1. *Gr. Myth.* a secondary deity 2. a guardian spirit 3. *same as* DEMON —**dae·mon·ic** (di män′ik) *adj.*

**daf·fo·dil** (daf′ə dil′) *n.* [ < Gr. *asphodelos*] a narcissus with long leaves and yellow flowers

**daf·fy** (daf′ē) *adj.* **-fi·er, -fi·est** [ < ME. *dafte*, daft] [Colloq.] crazy; silly —**daf′fi·ness** *n.*

**daft** (daft) *adj.* [ < OE. (*ge*)*dæfte*, mild] 1. silly 2. insane

**dag·ger** (dag′ər) *n.* [ < ML. *daggarius*] 1. a weapon with a short, pointed blade, used for stabbing 2. *Printing* a reference mark (†)

**da·guerre·o·type** (də ger′ə tīp′) *n.* [ < L.J.M. *Daguerre*, 19th-c. Fr. inventor] an early kind of photograph made on a chemically treated plate—*vt.* **-typed′, -typ′ing** to photograph by this method

**dahl·ia** (dal′yə, däl′-) *n.* [ < A. *Dahl*, 18th-c. Swed. botanist] a perennial plant with large, showy flowers

**dai·ly** (dā′lē) *adj.* done, happening, or published every (week)day —*n., pl.* **-lies** a daily newspaper —*adv.* every day

**daily double** a bet or betting procedure in which a bettor wins by choosing both winners in two specified races on the same program

**dain·ty** (dān′tē) *n., pl.* **-ties** [ < L. *dignitas*, worth] a delicacy —*adj.* **-ti·er, -ti·est** 1. delicious and choice 2. delicately pretty 3. *a)* of refined taste; fastidious *b)* squeamish —**dain′ti·ly** *adv.* —**dain′ti·ness** *n.*

**dai·qui·ri** (dak′ər ē) *n.* [after *Daiquiri*, Cuban village] a cocktail made of rum, sugar, and lime or lemon juice

**dair·y** (der′ē) *n., pl.* **-ies** [ME. *daie, dairymaid*] 1. a place where milk and cream are made into butter, cheese, etc. 2. a farm that produces, or a store that sells, milk and milk products —**dair′y·man** (-mən) *n., pl.* **-men**

**dair′y·ing** *n.* the business of producing or selling dairy products

**da·is** (dā′is) *n., pl.* **da′is·es** [ < ML. *discus*, table] a raised platform

**dai·sy** (dā′zē) *n., pl.* **-sies** [OE. *dæges eage*, day's eye] a plant of the composite family, bearing flowers with white rays around a yellow disk

**dale** (dāl) *n.* [OE. *dæl*] a valley

**Dal·las** (dal′əs) city in NE Tex.: pop. 844,000

**dal·ly** (dal′ē) *vi.* **-lied, -ly·ing** [ < OFr. *dalier*, to trifle] 1. to make love in a playful way 2. to deal carelessly (*with*); trifle 3. to waste time; loiter —**dal′li·ance** (-ē əns) *n.*

**Dal·ma·tian** (dal mā'shən) *n.* a large, short-haired dog with dark spots on a white coat

**dam¹** (dam) *n.* [ME.] a barrier built to hold back flowing water —*vt.* **dammed, dam'ming** 1. to build a dam in 2. to keep back or confine

DALMATIAN

**dam²** (dam) *n.* [see DAME] the female parent of any four-legged animal

**dam·age** (dam'ij) *n.* [ < L. *damnum*] 1. injury or harm resulting in a loss 2. [*pl.*] *Law* money compensating for injury, loss, etc. —*vt.* **-aged, -ag·ing** to do damage to —**dam'age·a·ble** *adj.*

**Da·mas·cus** (da mas'kəs) capital of Syria: pop. 530,000

**dam·ask** (dam'əsk) *n.* [ < It. < prec.] 1. a reversible fabric in figured weave, used for table linen, etc. 2. steel decorated with wavy lines 3. deep pink or rose —*adj.* 1. of or like damask 2. deep-pink or rose

**dame** (dām) *n.* [ < L. *domina*, lady] 1. [D-] in Great Britain, a woman's title of honor 2. [Slang] any woman

**damn** (dam) *vt.* **damned, damn'ing** [ < L. *damnare*, condemn] 1. to condemn to an unhappy fate or, *Theol.*, to hell 2. to condemn as bad, inferior, etc. 3. to swear at by saying "damn" —*n.* the saying of "damn" as a curse —*adj., adv.* [Colloq.] *clipped form of* DAMNED —*interj.* an expression of anger, etc.

**dam·na·ble** (dam'nə b'l) *adj.* 1. deserving damnation 2. deserving to be sworn at —**dam'na·bly** *adv.*

**dam·na·tion** (-nā'shən) *n.* a damning or being damned —*interj.* an expression of anger, etc.

**damned** (damd) *adj.* 1. condemned, as to hell 2. [Colloq.] deserving cursing; outrageous —*adv.* [Colloq.] very

**Dam·o·cles** (dam'ə klēz') *Gr. Legend* a man whose king seated him under a sword hanging by a hair to show him the perils of a ruler's life

**Da·mon and Pyth·i·as** (dā'mən ən pith'ē əs) *Classical Legend* two very devoted friends

**damp** (damp) *n.* [MDu., vapor] 1. a slight wetness 2. a harmful gas sometimes found in mines —*adj.* somewhat moist or wet —*vt.* 1. to bank (a fire) 2. to check or reduce —**damp'ness** *n.*

**damp·dry** (-drī') *vt.* **-dried', -dry'ing** to dry (laundry) so that some moisture is retained —*adj.* designating or of laundry so treated

**damp·en** (dam'pən) *vt.* 1. to make damp; moisten 2. to deaden, depress, or reduce —*vi.* to become damp— **damp'en·er** *n.*

**damp·er** (-pər) *n.* 1. anything that deadens or depresses 2. a valve in a flue to control the draft 3. a device to check vibration in piano strings

**dam·sel** (dam'z'l) *n.* [see DAME] [Archaic] a girl; maiden

**dam·son** (dam'z'n) *n.* [ < DAMASCUS] a variety of small, purple plum

**Dan.** Danish

**dance** (dans) *vi.* **danced, danc'ing** [ < OFr. *danser*] 1. to move the body and the feet in rhythm, ordinarily to music 2. to move lightly, rapidly, gaily, etc. —*vt.* 1. to perform (a dance) 2. to cause to dance —*n.* 1. rhythmic movement, ordinarily to music 2. a particular kind of dance 3. the art of dancing 4. a party for dancing 5. a piece of music for dancing 6. rapid movement —**danc'er** *n.*

**dan·de·li·on** (dan'də lī'ən) *n.* [ < OFr. *dent*, tooth + *de*, of + *lion*, lion] a common weed with yellow flowers

**dan·der** (dan'dər) *n.* [ < ?] [Colloq.] anger or temper

**dan·dle** (dan'd'l) *vt.* **-dled, -dling** [ < ?] to dance (a child) up and down on the knee or in the arms

**dan·druff** (dan'drəf) *n.* [ < earlier *dandro* + dial. *hurf*, scab] little scales of dead skin on the scalp

**dan·dy** (dan'dē) *n., pl.* **-dies** [ < ?] 1. a man overly attentive to his clothes and appearance 2. [Colloq.] something very good —*adj.* **-di·er, -di·est** [Colloq.] very good; fine

**Dane** (dān) *n.* a native or inhabitant of Denmark

**dan·ger** (dān'jər) *n.* [ult. < L. *dominus*, a master] 1. liability to injury, damage, loss, etc.; peril 2. a thing that may cause injury, pain, etc.

**dan'ger·ous** *adj.* full of danger; unsafe —**dan'ger·ous·ly** *adv.*

**dan·gle** (dan'g'l) *vi.* **-gled, -gling** [ < Scand.] to hang swinging loosely —*vt.* to cause to dangle —**dan'gler** *n.*

**Dan·iel** (dan'yəl) *Bible* a Hebrew prophet whose faith saved him in the lions' den

**Dan·ish** (dā'nish) *adj.* of Denmark, the Danes, or their language —*n.* 1. the language of the Danes 2. [*also d-*] rich, flaky pastry filled with fruit, cheese, etc.: in full **Danish pastry**

**dank** (dank) *adj.* [ME.] disagreeably damp —**dank'ly** *adv.* —**dank'ness** *n.*

**dan·seuse** (dän sooz') *n.* [Fr.] a woman dancer, esp. a ballet dancer

**Dan·te (Alighieri)** (dän'tā, dan'tē) 1265–1321; It. poet

**Dan·ube** (dan'yōōb) river flowing from SW Germany into the Black Sea

**dap·per** (dap'ər) *adj.* [ < ? MDu.] 1. small and active 2. trim; neat

**dap·ple** (dap''l) *adj.* [ < ON. *depill*, a spot] marked with spots; mottled: also **dap'pled** —*vt.* **-pled, -pling** to cover with spots

**Dar·da·nelles** (där'də nelz') W strait separating the Balkan Peninsula from Asia Minor

**dare** (der) *vt., vi.* **dared** *or archaic* **durst, dared, dar'ing** [OE. *durran*] 1. to have enough courage for (some act) 2. to face (something) bravely 3.

fat, āpe, cär; ten, ēven; is, bīte; gō, hôrn, tōōl, look; oil, out; up, fur; chin; she; thin, *th*en; zh, leisure; ŋ, ring; ə for *a* in *ago*; ', (ā'b'l); ĕ, Fr. cœur; ö, Fr. feu; Fr. mon; ü, Fr. duc; *kh*, G. ich, doch; ‡ foreign; < derived from to challenge (someone) to do something —*n.* a challenge —**dare say** to think probable —**dar′er** *n.*

**dare′devil** (-dev′'l) *adj.* bold and reckless —*n.* a bold, reckless person

**dar′ing** *adj.* fearless; bold —*n.* bold courage —**dar′ing·ly** *adv.*

**dark** (därk) *adj.* [OE. *deorc*] **1.** entirely or partly without light **2.** *a)* almost black *b)* not light in color **3.** hidden **4.** gloomy **5.** evil **6.** ignorant —*n.* **1.** the state of being dark **2.** night —**dark′ly** *adv.* —**dark′ness** *n.*

**Dark Ages** [ < prec., *adj.* 6] the Middle Ages, esp. the earlier part

**dark′en** *vt., vi.* to make or become dark or darker —**dark′en·er** *n.*

**dark horse** [Colloq.] a little-known contestant thought unlikely to win

**dark′room′** *n.* a darkened room for developing photographs

**dar·ling** (där′liŋ) *n.* [OE. *deorling*] a person much loved by another —*adj.* **1.** very dear; beloved **2.** [Colloq.] cute

**darn**[1] (därn) *vt., vi.* [ < MFr. dial. *darner*] to mend (cloth, etc.) by sewing a network of stitches across the gap —*n.* a darned place in fabric

**darn**[2] (därn) *vt., n., adj., adv., interj.* [Colloq.] damn: a euphemism —**darned** *adj., adv.*

**dar·nel** (där′n'l) *n.* [ < Fr. dial. *darnelle*] a weedy rye grass

**dart** (därt) *n.* [ < OFr.] **1.** a small, pointed missile for throwing or shooting **2.** a sudden movement **3.** a short, tapered seam —*vt., vi.* to send out or move suddenly and fast

**Dar·von** (där′vän) *a trademark* for a pain-killing drug containing an analgesic related to methadone

**Dar·win** (där′win), **Charles Robert** 1809–82; Eng. naturalist and propounder of theory of evolution

**dash** (dash) *vt.* [ < Scand.] **1.** to smash; destroy **2.** to strike violently (*against*) **3.** to throw or spray (*away, down,* etc.) **4.** to splash —*vi.* **1.** to strike violently against **2.** to rush —*n.* **1.** a splash **2.** a bit of something added **3.** a rush **4.** a short, fast race **5.** spirit; vigor **6.** the mark of punctuation (—) used to indicate a break, omission, etc. —**dash off** to do, write, etc. hastily —**dash′er** *n.*

**dash′board′** *n.* a panel with instruments and gauges, as in an automobile

**da·shi·ki** (dä shē′kē) *n.* a loosefitting, brightly colored robe modeled after an African tribal garment

**dash′ing** *adj.* **1.** full of dash or spirit; lively **2.** showy; striking —**dash′ing·ly** *adv.*

**das·tard** (das′tərd) *n.* [ME., a craven] a sneaky, cowardly evildoer

**das′tard·ly** *adj.* mean, cowardly, etc.

**dat.** dative

**da·ta** (dāt′ə, dat′ə) *n.pl.* [*often with sing. v.*] [see DATUM] facts or figures from which conclusions may be drawn

**da·ta·ma·tion** (dā′tə mā′shən) *n.* [DATA + (AUTO)MATION] electronic data processing

**data processing** the handling of information by mechanical means or computer

**date**[1] (dāt) *n.* [ < L. *dare,* give] **1.** the time at which a thing happens, was made, etc. **2.** the day of the month **3.** *a)* an appointment *b)* a social engagement with a person of the opposite sex *c)* this person —*vt.* **dat′ed, dat′ing 1.** to mark (a letter, etc.) with a date **2.** to find out or give the date of **3.** to make seem old-fashioned **4.** to have social engagements with —*vi.* **1.** to belong to a definite period in the past **2.** to date persons of the opposite sex —**out of date** old-fashioned —**up to date** modern —**dat′er** *n.*

**date**[2] (dāt) *n.* [ < Gr. *daktylos,* lit., a finger] the sweet, fleshy fruit of a tall palm tree (**date palm**)

**date′line′** *n.* the date and place of writing or issue, as given in a line in a newspaper story, etc.

**dating bar** a bar frequented by persons seeking casual acquaintances, as for sexual purposes

**da·tive** (dāt′iv) *n.* [see DATE[1]] the case expressing an indirect object

**da·tum** (dāt′əm, dat′əm) *n.* [L., what is given] *sing.* of DATA

**daub** (dôb) *vt., vi.* [ < L. *de-,* intens. + *albus,* white] **1.** to cover or smear with sticky, soft matter **2.** to paint badly —*n.* **1.** anything daubed on **2.** a daubing stroke **3.** a poorly painted picture —**daub′er** *n.*

**daugh·ter** (dôt′ər) *n.* [OE. *dohtor*] **1.** a girl or woman as she is related to either or both parents **2.** a female descendant —**daugh′ter·ly** *adj.*

**daugh′ter-in-law′** *n., pl.* **daugh′ters-in-law′** the wife of one's son

**Dau·mier** (dō myā′), **Ho·no·ré** (ô nô rā′) 1809–79; Fr. painter

**daunt** (dônt) *vt.* [ < L. *domare,* tame] to frighten or dishearten

**daunt′less** *adj.* that cannot be daunted, intimidated, etc.; fearless —**daunt′less·ly** *adv.* —**daunt′less·ness** *n.*

**dau·phin** (dô′fin) *n.* [Fr., dolphin] the eldest son of the king of France: a title used from 1349 to 1830

**dav·en·port** (dav′ən pôrt′) *n.* [ < ?] a large couch or sofa

**Da·vid** (dā′vid) *Bible* the second king of Israel and Judah

**Da·vis** (dā′vis), **Jefferson** 1808–89; president of the Confederacy (1861–65)

**dav·it** (dav′it) *n.* [ < OFr. dim. of *David*] either of a pair of curved uprights on a ship for suspending and for lowering a small boat

**daw·dle** (dôd′'l) *vi., vt.* **-dled, -dling** [ < ?] to waste (time) in trifling; loiter —**daw′dler** *n.*

**dawn** (dôn) *vi.* [OE. *dagian*] **1.** to begin to be day **2.** to begin to appear, develop, etc. **3.** to begin to be understood or felt —*n.* **1.** daybreak **2.** the beginning (*of* something)

**day** (dā) *n.* [OE. *dæg*] **1.** the period of light between sunrise and sunset **2.** the time (24 hours) that it takes the earth to revolve once on its axis **3.** [*also pl.*] a period; era **4.** a time of power, glory, etc. **5.** daily work period [*an 8-hour day*] —**day after day** every day: also **day in, day out**

**day'bed'** *n.* a couch that can also be used as a bed

**day'break'** *n.* the time in the morning when light first appears

**day'dream'** *n.* 1. a pleasant, dreamy series of thoughts 2. a visionary scheme —*vi.* to have daydreams

**day'light'** *n.* 1. the light of day 2. dawn 3. daytime 4. understanding

**day'light'-sav'ing time** time that is one hour later than standard time

**day nursery** a place for daytime care of preschool children, as of working mothers: also **day-care center**

**Day of Atonement** *same as* YOM KIPPUR

**day'time'** *n.* the time between dawn and sunset

**day'-to-day'** *adj.* daily; routine

**Day·ton** (dāt'n) city in SW Ohio: pop. 244,000

**daze** (dāz) *vt.* **dazed, daz'ing** [ < ON. *dasi,* tired] to stun or bewilder —*n.* a dazed condition —**daz'ed·ly** *adv.*

**daz·zle** (daz''l) *vt., vi.* **-zled, -zling** [ < prec.] 1. to overpower or be overpowered by the glare of bright light 2. to surprise or arouse admiration with brilliant qualities, display, etc. —*n.* a dazzling —**daz'zler** *n.*

**db** decibel(s)

**DC, D.C., d.c.** direct current

**D.C., DC** District of Columbia

**D.D.** Doctor of Divinity

**D.D.S.** Doctor of Dental Surgery

**DDT** [ < its chemical name] a powerful insecticide

**de-** [ < Fr. *dé* or L. *de*] *a prefix meaning:* 1. away from, off [*derail*] 2. down [*decline*] 3. entirely [*defunct*] 4. reverse the action of [*decode*]

**DE** Delaware

**de·ac·ces·sion** (dē'ak sesh'ən) *vt.* to remove (a work of art) from a museum collection preparatory to selling it

**dea·con** (dēk'n) *n.* [ < Gr. *diakonos,* servant] 1. a cleric ranking just below a priest 2. a church officer who helps the minister —**dea'con·ess** *n.fem.*

**de·ac·ti·vate** (dē ak'tə vāt') *vt.* **-vat'ed, -vat'ing** 1. to make (an explosive, chemical, etc.) inactive 2. *Mil.* to demobilize

**dead** (ded) *adj.* [OE.] 1. no longer living 2. without life 3. deathlike 4. lacking warmth, interest, brightness, etc. 5. without feeling, motion, or power 6. extinguished; extinct 7. no longer used; obsolete 8. unerring [a *dead* shot] 9. complete [a *dead* stop] 10. [Colloq.] very tired —*n.* the time of most cold, most darkness, etc. [the *dead* of night] —*adv.* 1. completely 2. directly —**the dead** those who have died

**dead·beat** (ded'bēt') *n.* [Slang] one who tries to evade paying for things

**dead·en** (ded''n) *vt.* 1. to lessen the vigor or intensity of; dull 2. to make numb 3. to make soundproof

**dead end** a street, alley, etc. closed at one end —**dead'-end'** *adj.*

**dead heat** a race in which two or more contestants finish even

**dead letter** 1. a rule, law, etc. no longer enforced 2. an unclaimed letter

**dead'line'** (-līn') *n.* the latest time by which something must be done

**dead'lock'** (-läk') *n.* a standstill resulting from the action of equal and opposed forces —*vt., vi.* to bring or come to a deadlock

**dead'ly** *adj.* **-li·er, -li·est** 1. causing or likely to cause death 2. implacable 3. typical of death [*deadly* pallor] 4. extreme 5. very boring 6. very accurate —*adv.* extremely —**dead'li·ness** *n.*

**dead'pan'** (-pan') *adj., adv.* [Slang] without expression; blank(ly)

**Dead Sea** inland body of salt water between Israel and Jordan

**dead'wood'** (-wood') *n.* anything useless or burdensome

**deaf** (def) *adj.* [OE.] 1. unable to hear 2. unwilling to respond, as to a plea —**deaf'ness** *n.*

**deaf'en** (-'n) *vt.* 1. to make deaf 2. to overwhelm with noise

**deaf'-mute'** (-myōōt') *n.* a person who is deaf and has not learned to speak

**deal¹** (dēl) *vt.* **dealt** (delt), **deal'ing** [OE. *dælen*] 1. to portion out or distribute 2. to give; administer (a blow, etc.) —*vi.* 1. to have to do (*with*) [*science deals* with facts] 2. to conduct oneself [*deal* fairly with others] 3. to do business; trade (*with* or in) —*n.* 1. the distributing of playing cards 2. a business transaction 3. an agreement, esp. when secret 4. [Colloq.] treatment [a fair *deal*] —**deal'er** *n.*

**deal²** (dēl) *n.* [OE. *dæl,* a part] an indefinite amount —**a good** (or **great**) **deal** 1. a large amount 2. very much

**deal'er·ship'** (-ship') *n.* a franchise to sell a product in a specified area

**deal'ing** *n.* 1. way of acting 2. [*usually pl.*] transactions or relations

**dean** (dēn) *n.* [ < LL. *decanus,* chief of ten (monks, etc.)] 1. the presiding official of a cathedral 2. a college official in charge of students or faculty 3. the senior member of a group

**dean's list** a list of the students at a college getting high grades

**dear** (dir) *adj.* [OE. *deore*] 1. much loved 2. esteemed: a polite form of address [*Dear* Sir] 3. high-priced; costly 4. earnest [our *dearest* wish] —*n.* a loved one; darling —**dear'ly** *adv.* —**dear'ness** *n.*

**Dear·born** (dir'bərn, -bôrn') city in SE Michigan: pop. 104,000

**Dear John (letter)** [Colloq.] a letter, as to a fiancé, breaking off a close relationship

**dearth** (durth) *n.* [ < ME. *dere,* dear] scarcity or lack

**death** (deth) *n.* 1. the act or fact of dying 2. the state of being dead 3. end or destruction 4. the cause of death —**death'like'** *adj.*

---

**death′bed′** n. 1. the bed on which a person dies 2. a person's last hours

**death′blow′** n. 1. a blow that kills 2. a thing fatal (to something)

**death′less** adj. that cannot die; immortal —**death′less·ly** adv.

**death′ly** adj. 1. causing death; deadly 2. like or characteristic of death —adv. extremely [deathly ill]

**death′trap′** n. any unsafe structure

**Death Valley** dry, hot desert basin in E Calif. & S Nev.

**deb** (deb) n. [Colloq.] a debutante

**de·ba·cle** (di bäk′′l, -bak′-) n. [< Fr. débâcler, break up] 1. a crushing defeat 2. a ruinous collapse

**de·bar** (dē bär′) vt. -barred′, -bar′ring [< Fr.: see DE- & BAR] 1. to keep (from) some right, etc. 2. to prevent or prohibit —**de·bar′ment** n.

**de·bark** (di bärk′) vt., vi. [< Fr.: see DE- & BARK³] to unload from or leave a ship or aircraft —**de·bar·ka·tion** (dē′bär kā′shən) n.

**de·base** (di bās′) vt. -based′, -bas′ing [DE- + BASE²] to make lower in value, dignity, etc. —**de·base′ment** n.

**de·bate** (di bāt′) vi., vt. -bat′ed, -bat′ing [< OFr.: see DE- & BATTER¹] 1. to discuss reasons for and against (something) 2. to take part in a debate with (a person) or about (a question) —n. 1. a discussion of opposing reasons 2. a formal contest of skill in reasoned argument —**de·bat′a·ble** adj. —**de·bat′er** n.

**de·bauch** (di bôch′) vt. [< OFr. desbaucher, seduce] to lead astray morally; corrupt —n. an orgy —**de·bauch′er·y** n., pl. -ies

**deb·au·chee** (di bôch′ē′; deb′ô chē′, -shē′) n. a dissipated person

**de·ben·ture** (di ben′chər) n. [< L.: see DEBT] 1. a voucher acknowledging a debt 2. an interest-bearing bond, often issued without security

**de·bil·i·tate** (di bil′ə tāt′) vt. -tat′ed, -tat′ing [< L. debilis, weak] to make weak; enervate

**de·bil′i·ty** (-tē) n., pl. -ties [see prec.] weakness; feebleness

**deb·it** (deb′it) n. [< L. debere, owe] 1. an entry in an account of money owed 2. the total of such entries —vt. to enter as a debit

**deb·o·nair, deb·o·naire** (deb′ə ner′) adj. [< OFr. de bon aire, lit., of good breed] 1. genial; affable 2. carefree; jaunty —**deb′o·nair′ly** adv.

**de·brief** (dē brēf′) vt. [DE- + BRIEF] to receive information from (a pilot, etc.) about a recent mission

**de·bris, dé·bris** (də brē′) n. [Fr. < OFr. desbrisier, break apart] bits and pieces of stone, rubbish, etc.

**debt** (det) n. [< L. debere, owe] 1. something owed to another 2. the condition of owing (to be in debt)

**debt′or** (-ər) n. one who owes a debt

**de·bug** (dē bug′) vt. -bugged′, -bug′ging [Slang] 1. to correct defects in 2. to find and remove hidden electronic listening devices from

**de·bunk** (dē bunk′) vt. [DE- + BUNK²] [Colloq.] to expose the false or exaggerated claims, etc. of

**De·bus·sy** (də bü sē′; E. deb′yoo sē′), Claude 1862–1918; Fr. composer

**de·but, dé·but** (di byoo′, dā′byoo) n. [Fr. < débuter, to lead off] 1. a first public appearance 2. the formal introduction of a girl into society

**deb·u·tante** (deb′yoo tänt′, deb′yoo tänt′) n. [Fr.] a girl making a debut into society

**Dec.** December

**deca-** [< Gr. deka, ten] a combining form meaning ten: also **dec-**

**dec·ade** (dek′ād) n. [< Gr. deka, ten] a period of ten years

**dec·a·dence** (dek′ə dəns, di kād′′ns) n. [< L. de-, from + cadere, to fall] a process, condition, or period of decline, as in morals, art, etc.; deterioration —**dec′a·dent** adj., n.

**de·cal·co·ma·ni·a** (di kal′kə mā′nē ə) n. [< Fr. < L. calcare, to tread + Gr. mania, madness] a picture or design transferred from prepared paper to glass, wood, etc.: also **de·cal′**

**Dec·a·logue, Dec·a·log** (dek′ə lôg′) n. [see DECA- & -LOGUE] [sometimes d-] same as TEN COMMANDMENTS

**de·camp** (di kamp′) vi. [< Fr.: see DE- & CAMP] 1. to break camp 2. to go away suddenly and secretly

**de·cant** (di kant′) vt. [< Fr. < L. de-, from + canthus, tire of a wheel] to pour off (a liquid) gently without stirring up the sediment

**de·cant′er** n. a decorative glass bottle for serving wine, etc.

**de·cap·i·tate** (di kap′ə tāt′) vt. -tat′ed, -tat′ing [< L. de-, off + caput, head] to behead —**de·cap′i·ta′tion** n.

**de·cath·lon** (di kath′län) n. [DEC- + Gr. athlon, contest] an athletic contest in which each contestant takes part in ten track and field events

DECANTER

**de·cay** (di kā′) vi. [see DECADENCE] 1. to lose strength, prosperity, etc. gradually; deteriorate 2. to rot 3. to undergo radioactive disintegration —vt. to cause to decay —n. 1. deterioration 2. a rotting or rottenness

**de·cease** (di sēs′) n. [< L. de-, from + cedere, go] death —vi. -ceased′, -ceas′ing to die

**de·ceased′** adj. dead —**the deceased** the dead person or persons

**de·ceit** (di sēt′) n. 1. a deceiving or lying 2. a lie; dishonest action 3. deceitful quality

**de·ceit′ful** adj. 1. apt to lie or cheat 2. deceptive —**de·ceit′ful·ly** adv.

**de·ceive** (di sēv′) vt., vi. -ceived′, -ceiv′ing [< L. de-, from + capere, take] to make (a person) believe what is not true; mislead —**de·ceiv′er** n. —**de·ceiv′ing·ly** adv.

**de·cel·er·ate** (dē sel′ə rāt′) vt., vi. -at′ed, -at′ing [DE- + (AC)CELERATE] to reduce the speed (of); slow down —**de·cel′er·a′tion** n.

**De·cem·ber** (di sem′bər) n. [< L. decem, ten: tenth month in Rom. calendar] the twelfth and last month of the year, having 31 days

**de·cen·cy** (dē's'n sē) *n., pl.* **-cies** a being decent; propriety, courtesy, etc.

**de·cen·ni·al** (di sen'ē əl) *adj.* [< L. *decem*, ten + *annus*, year] 1. of or for ten years 2. occurring every ten years

**de·cent** (dē's'nt) *adj.* [< L. *decere*, befit] 1. proper and fitting 2. not obscene 3. respectable 4. adequate [*decent* wages] 5. fair and kind —**de'cent·ly** *adv.*

**de·cen·tral·ize** (dē sen'trə līz') *vt.* **-ized', -iz'ing** to break up a concentration of (governmental authority, industry, etc.) and distribute more widely —**de·cen'tral·i·za'tion** *n.*

**de·cep·tion** (di sep'shən) *n.* 1. a deceiving or being deceived 2. an illusion or fraud —**de·cep'tive** *adj.*

**dec·i·bel** (des'ə bel') *n.* [< L. *decem*, ten + A.G. BELL] a unit for measuring relative loudness of sound

**de·cide** (di sīd') *vt.* **-cid'ed, -cid'ing** [< L. *de-*, off + *caedere*, to cut] 1. to end (a contest, dispute, etc.) by giving one side the victory 2. to reach a decision about; resolve —*vi.* to reach a decision —**de·cid'a·ble** *adj.*

**de·cid·ed** *adj.* 1. definite; clear 2. determined —**de·cid'ed·ly** *adv.*

**de·cid·u·ous** (di sij'ŏŏ wəs) *adj.* [< L. *de-*, off + *cadere*, to fall] 1. falling off at a certain season, as some leaves or antlers 2. shedding leaves annually

**dec·i·mal** (des'ə m'l) *adj.* [< L. *decem*, ten] of or based on the number 10 —*n.* a fraction with a denominator of ten or some power of ten, shown by a point (**decimal point**) before the numerator (Ex.: .5 = 5/10)

**dec·i·mate** (des'ə māt') *vt.* **-mat'ed, -mat'ing** [< L. *decem*, ten] to destroy or kill a large part of (lit., a tenth part of) —**dec'i·ma'tion** *n.*

**de·ci·pher** (di sī'fər) *vt.* [DE- + CIPHER] 1. *same as* DECODE 2. to make out the meaning of (a scrawl, etc.)

**de·ci·sion** (di sizh'ən) *n.* 1. the act of deciding or settling a dispute or question 2. the act of making up one's mind 3. a judgment or conclusion 4. determination; firmness of mind

**de·ci·sive** (di sī'siv) *adj.* 1. that settles a dispute, question, etc. 2. showing decision —**de·ci'sive·ly** *adv.*

**deck**[1] (dek) *n.* [prob. < MLowG. *verdeck*] 1. a floor of a ship 2. a pack of playing cards

**deck**[2] (dek) *vt.* [MDu. *decken*, to cover] to array or adorn

**de·claim** (di klām') *vi., vt.* [< L. *de-*, intens. + *clamare*, to cry] to recite or speak in a studied, dramatic, or impassioned way —**dec·la·ma·tion** (dek'lə mā'shən) *n.* —**de·clam·a·to·ry** (di klam'ə tôr'ē) *adj.*

**dec·la·ra·tion** (dek'lə rā'shən) *n.* 1. a declaring; announcement 2. a formal statement

**de·clar·a·tive** (di klar'ə tiv) *adj.* making a statement or assertion

**de·clare** (di kler') *vt.* **-clared', -clar'ing** [< L. *de-*, intens. + *clarus,*

clear] 1. to announce openly or formally 2. to show or reveal 3. to say emphatically 4. *Card Games* to establish by a successful bid —**de·clar'er** *n.*

**de·clas·si·fy** (dē klas'ə fī') *vt.* **-fied', -fy'ing** to make (secret documents) available to the public

**de·clen·sion** (di klen'shən) *n.* [see ff.] 1. a descent 2. a decline 3. *Gram.* the inflection of nouns, pronouns, or adjectives

**de·cline** (di klīn') *vi.* **-clined', -clin'ing** [< L. *de-*, from + *-clinare*, to bend] 1. to bend or slope downward 2. to deteriorate 3. to refuse something —*vt.* 1. to cause to bend or slope downward 2. to refuse politely 3. *Gram.* to give the inflected forms of (a noun, pronoun, or adjective) —*n.* 1. a declining; a dropping, failing, decay, etc. 2. a period of decline 3. a downward slope —**dec·li·na·tion** (dek'lə nā'shən) *n.* —**de·clin'er** *n.*

**de·cliv·i·ty** (di kliv'ə tē) *n., pl.* **-ties** [< L. *de-*, down + *clivus,* a slope] a downward slope

**de·code** (dē kōd') *vt.* **-cod'ed, -cod'ing** to translate (a coded message) into understandable language

**dé·col·le·té** (dā kä'lə tā') *adj.* [Fr. < L. *de,* from + *collum,* neck] cut low so as to bare the neck and shoulders

**de·col·o·ni·za·tion** (dē käl'ə nə zā'shən) *n.* a freeing or being freed from colonialism or colonial status —**de·col'o·nize'** (-ə nīz') *vt., vi.* **-nized', -niz'ing**

**de·com·pose** (dē'kəm pōz') *vt., vi.* **-posed', -pos'ing** [< Fr.: see DE- & COMPOSE] 1. to break up into basic parts 2. to rot —**de'com·po·si'tion** (-käm pə zish'ən) *n.*

**de·com·press** (dē'kəm pres') *vt.* to free from pressure, esp. from air pressure —**de'com·pres'sion** *n.*

**de'con·gest'ant** *n.* a medication that relieves congestion, as in the nose

**de'con·tam'i·nate'** (-tam'ə nāt') *vt.* **-nat'ed, -nat'ing** to rid of a harmful substance, as radioactive products

**dé·cor, de·cor** (dā kôr') *n.* [Fr.] a decorative scheme, as of a room

**dec·or·ate** (dek'ə rāt') *vt.* **-at'ed, -at'ing** [< L. *decus,* an ornament] 1. to adorn; ornament 2. to paint or wallpaper 3. to give a medal or similar honor to —**dec'o·ra·tive** (-ər ə tiv, -ə rāt'iv) *adj.* —**dec'o·ra'tor** *n.*

**dec'o·ra'tion** *n.* 1. a decorating 2. an ornament 3. a medal, etc.

**Decoration Day** Memorial Day

**dec·o·rous** (dek'ər əs, di kôr'əs) *adj.* having or showing decorum, good taste, etc. —**dec'o·rous·ly** *adv.*

**de·co·rum** (di kôr'əm) *n.* [< L. *decorus,* proper] 1. whatever is suitable or proper 2. propriety in behavior, speech, etc.

**de·cou·page, dé·cou·page** (dā'kōō päzh') *n.* [Fr.] the art of cutting out designs from paper, foil, etc. and mounting them on a surface

**de·coy** (di koi′; *for n. also* dē′koi) *n.* [< Du. *de kooi*, the cage] 1. an artificial or trained bird, etc. used to lure game within gun range 2. a thing or person used to lure into danger —*vt.* to lure into a trap

**de·crease** (di krēs′; *esp. for n.* dē′krēs) *vi., vt.* -creased′, -creas′ing [< L. *de-*, from + *crescere*, grow] to become or make gradually less, smaller, etc.; diminish —*n.* 1. a decreasing 2. amount of decreasing

**de·cree** (di krē′) *n.* [< L. *de-*, from *cernere*, see] an official order or decision —*vt.* -creed′, -cree′ing to order or decide by decree

**de·crep·it** (di krep′it) *adj.* [< L. *de-*, intens. + *crepare*, to creak] broken down or worn out by old age or long use —**de·crep′i·tude** (-ə tōōd′) *n.*

**de·crim·i·nal·ize** (dē krim′ə n'l īz′) *vt.* -ized′, -iz′ing to eliminate or reduce the penalties for (a crime)

**de·cry** (di krī′) *vt.* -cried′, -cry′ing [< Fr.: see DE- & CRY] to speak out against openly; denounce

**ded·i·cate** (ded′ə kāt′) *vt.* -cat′ed, -cat′ing [< L. *de-*, intens. + *dicare*, proclaim] 1. to set apart for, or devote to, a special purpose 2. to address (a book, etc.) to someone as a sign of honor —**ded′i·ca′tion** *n.*

**de·duce** (di dōōs′, -dyōōs′) *vt.* -duced′, -duc′ing [< L. *de-*, down + *ducere*, to lead] to infer or decide by reasoning —**de·duc′i·ble** *adj.*

**de·duct** (di dukt′) *vt.* [see prec.] to take away or subtract (a quantity) —**de·duct′i·ble** *adj.*

**de·duc′tion** (-duk′shən) *n.* 1. a deducting 2. an amount deducted 3. *a*) reasoning from the general to the specific *b*) a conclusion reached by such reasoning —**de·duc′tive** *adj.*

**deed** (dēd) *n.* [< OE. *ded*] 1. a thing done; act 2. a feat of courage, skill, etc. 3. a legal document which transfers a property —*vt.* to transfer (property) by deed —**in deed** in fact

**deem** (dēm) *vt., vi.* [OE. *deman*, to judge] to think, believe, or judge

**de·em·pha·size** (dē em′fə sīz′) *vt.* -sized′, -siz′ing to lessen the importance of —**de·em′pha·sis** (-sis) *n.*

**deep** (dēp) *adj.* [OE. *deop*] 1. extending far downward, inward, or backward 2. hard to understand; abstruse 3. serious; profound 4. dark and rich [a *deep* red] 5. absorbed by (with *in*) [*deep* in thought] 6. great in degree; intense 7. of low pitch [a *deep* voice] —*n.* a deep place —*adv.* far down, far back, etc. —**the deep** [Poet.] the ocean —**deep′ly** *adv.* —**deep′ness** *n.*

**deep·en** (-'n) *vt., vi.* to make or become deep or deeper

**deep′freeze′** *vt.* -froze′ or -freezed′, -fro′zen or -freezed′, -freez′ing *same as* QUICK-FREEZE

**deep′-fry′** *vt.* -fried′, -fry′ing to fry in a deep pan of boiling fat

**deep′-root′ed** *adj.* 1. having deep roots 2. firmly fixed

**deep′-seat′ed** *adj.* 1. buried deep 2. firmly fixed

**deep′-six′** *vt.* [< six fathoms] [Slang] to get rid of, as by throwing into water

**deep space** *same as* OUTER SPACE

**deer** (dir) *n., pl.* **deer, deers** [OE. *deor*, wild animal] a hoofed, cud-chewing animal, the male of which bears antlers that are shed annually

**de·es·ca·late** (dē es′kə lāt′) *vi., vt.* -lat′ed, -lat′ing to reduce in scope, magnitude, etc. —**de·es′ca·la′tion** *n.*

**de·face** (di fās′) *vt.* -faced′, -fac′ing [see DE- & FACE] to spoil the look of; mar —**de·face′ment** *n.*

**de fac·to** (di fak′tō) [L.] actually existing but not officially approved

**de·fal·cate** (di fal′kāt) *vi.* -cat·ed, -cat·ing [< L. *de-*, from + *falx*, a sickle] to steal or misuse funds entrusted to one; embezzle —**de·fal·ca′tion** (dē′fal kā′shən) *n.*

**de·fame** (di fām′) *vt.* -famed′, -fam′ing [< L. *dis-*, from + *fama*, fame] to attack the reputation of; slander or libel —**def·a·ma·tion** (def′ə mā′shən) *n.* —**de·fam·a·to·ry** (di fam′ə tôr′ē) *adj.* —**de·fam′er** *n.*

**de·fault** (di fôlt′) *n.* [< L. *de-*, away + *fallere*, fail] failure to do or appear as required; specif., failure to pay money due —*vi., vt.* 1. to fail to do or pay when required 2. to lose (a contest) by default —**de·fault′er** *n.*

**de·feat** (di fēt′) *vt.* [< L. *dis-*, from + *facere*, do] 1. to win victory over 2. to bring to nothing; frustrate —*n.* a defeating or being defeated

**de·feat′ist** *n.* one who too readily accepts defeat —**de·feat′ism** *n.*

**def·e·cate** (def′ə kāt′) *vi.* -cat′ed, -cat′ing [< L. *de-*, from + *faex*, dregs] to excrete waste matter from the bowels —**def′e·ca′tion** *n.*

**de·fect** (dē′fekt; *also, and for v. always,* di fekt′) *n.* [< L. *de-*, from + *facere*, do] 1. lack of something necessary for completeness 2. an imperfection; fault —*vi.* to forsake a party, cause, etc., esp. so as to join the opposition —**de·fec′tion** *n.* —**de·fec′tor** *n.*

**de·fec·tive** (di fek′tiv) *adj.* having defects; imperfect; faulty

**de·fend** (di fend′) *vt.* [< L. *de-*, away + *fendere*, to strike] 1. to guard from attack; protect 2. to support or justify 3. *Law a*) to oppose (an action, etc.) *b*) to act as lawyer for (an accused) —**de·fend′er** *n.*

**de·fend·ant** (di fen′dənt) *n. Law* the person sued or accused

**de·fense** (di fens′, dē′fens) *n.* 1. a defending against attack 2. something that defends 3. justification by speech or writing 4. *a*) the arguments of a defendant *b*) the defendant and his counsel *Brit. sp.* **defence** —**de·fense′less** *adj.* —**de·fen′si·ble** *adj.*

**defense mechanism** any thought process used unconsciously to protect oneself against painful feelings

**de·fen·sive** *adj.* 1. defending 2. of or for defense —*n.* a position of defense —**de·fen′sive·ly** *adv.*

**de·fer** (di fur′) *vt., vi.* -ferred′, -fer′ring [see DIFFER] 1. to postpone; delay 2. to postpone the induction of (a person) into the armed forces — **de·fer'ment** n.

**de·fer²** (di fur') vi. **-ferred', -fer'ring** [< L. de-, down + ferre, to bear] to yield with courtesy (to)

**def·er·ence** (def'ər əns) n. 1. a yielding in opinion, judgment, etc. 2. courteous respect

**def·er·en'tial** (-ə ren'shəl) adj. showing deference; very respectful

**de·fi·ance** (di fī'əns) n. a defying; open, bold resistance to authority — **de·fi'ant** adj. **—de·fi'ant·ly** adv.

**de·fi·cien·cy** (di fish'ən sē) n. [< L. de-, from + facere, do] 1. a being deficient 2. pl. **-cies** a shortage

**deficiency disease** a disease due to a lack of vitamins, minerals, etc. in the diet

**de·fi'cient** (-ənt) adj. [see prec.] 1. lacking in some essential; incomplete 2. inadequate in amount

**def·i·cit** (def'ə sit) n. [L. < deficere, to lack] the amount by which a sum of money is less than the required amount

**de·file¹** (di fīl') vt. **-filed', -fil'ing** [< OFr. defouler, tread underfoot] 1. to make filthy 2. to profane; sully — **de·file'ment** n. **—de·fil'er** n.

**de·file²** (di fīl', dē'fīl) vi. **-filed', -fil'ing** [< Fr. dé-, from + fil, a thread] to march in single file —n. a narrow passage, valley, etc.

**de·fine** (di fīn') vt. **-fined', -fin'ing** [< L. de-, from + finis, boundary] 1. to determine the limits or nature of; describe exactly 2. to state the meaning of (a word, etc.) **—de·fin'er** n.

**def·i·nite** (def'ə nit) adj. [see prec.] 1. having exact limits 2. precise in meaning; explicit 3. certain; positive 4. Gram. limiting or specifying ["the" is the definite article] **—def'i·nite·ly** adv. **—def'i·nite·ness** n.

**def·i·ni'tion** (-nish'ən) n. 1. a defining or being defined 2. a statement of the meaning of a word 3. clarity of outline, sound, etc.

**de·fin·i·tive** (di fin'ə tiv) adj 1. conclusive; final 2. most nearly complete 3. serving to define

**de·flate** (di flāt') vt., vi. **-flat'ed, -flat'ing** [DE- + (IN)FLATE] 1. to collapse by letting out air or gas 2. to lessen in size, importance, etc. 3. to cause deflation of (currency)

**de·fla'tion** n. 1. a deflating 2. a lessening of the amount of money in circulation, making it rise in value

**de·flect** (di flekt') vt., vi. [< L. de-, from + flectere, to bend] to turn or make go to one side **—de·flec'tion** n. **—de·flec'tive** adj. **—de·flec'tor** n.

**De·foe** (di fō'), **Daniel** 1660?-1731; Eng. writer

**de·fo·li·ant** (dē fō'lē ənt) n. [< L. de-, from + folium, leaf] a chemical spray that strips growing plants of their leaves **—de·fo'li·ate** (-āt') vt. **-at'ed, -at'ing**

**de·form** (di fôrm') vt. [< L. de-,

from + forma, form] 1. to impair the form of 2. to make ugly **—de·for·ma·tion** (dē'fôr mā'shən, def'ər-) n.

**de·formed'** adj. misshapen

**de·form·i·ty** (di fôr'mə tē) n., pl. **-ties** 1. a deformed part, as of the body 2. ugliness or depravity

**de·fraud** (di frôd') vt. to take property, rights, etc. from by fraud; cheat **—de·fraud'er** n.

**de·fray** (di frā') vt. [Fr. défrayer] to pay (the cost or expenses) **—de·fray'a·ble** adj. **—de·fray'al** n.

**de·frost** (di frôst') vt., vi. to rid or get rid of frost or ice **—de·frost'er** n.

**deft** (deft) adj. [see DAFT] skillful; dexterous **—deft'ly** adv.

**de·funct** (di funkt') adj. [< L. defungi, to finish] no longer existing; dead or extinct

**de·fy** (di fī') vt. **-fied', -fy'ing** [< LL. dis-, from + fidus, faithful] 1. to resist boldly or openly 2. to dare to do or prove something

**de·gen·er·ate** (di jen'ər it; for v. -ə rāt') adj. [< L. de-, from + genus, race] 1. having sunk below a former or normal condition, etc.; deteriorated 2. depraved —n. a degenerate person —vi. **-at'ed, -at'ing** to lose former, normal, or higher qualities **—de·gen'er·a·cy** (-ə sē) n. **—de·gen'er·a'tion** n. **—de·gen'er·a·tive** adj.

**de·grade** (di grād') vt. **-grad'ed, -grad'ing** [< L. de-, down + gradus, a step] 1. to demote 2. to lower in quality, moral character, dignity, etc.; debase, dishonor, etc. **—deg·ra·da·tion** (deg'rə dā'shən) n.

**de·gree** (di grē') n. [see prec.] 1. any of the successive steps in a process 2. social or official rank 3. extent, amount, or intensity 4. a rank given by a college or university to one who has completed a course of study, or to a distinguished person as an honor 5. a grade of comparison of adjectives and adverbs [the superlative degree] 6. Law the seriousness of a crime [murder in the first degree] 7. a unit of measure for angles or arcs, 1/360 of the circumference of a circle 8. a unit of measure for temperature **—to a degree** somewhat

**de·hu·man·ize** (dē hyōō'mə nīz') vt. **-ized', -iz'ing** to deprive of human qualities; make machinelike **—de·hu'man·i·za'tion** n.

**de·hu·mid·i·fy** (dē'hyōō mid'ə fī') vt. **-fied', -fy'ing** to remove moisture from (air, etc.) **—de·hu·mid'i·fi'er** n.

**de·hy·drate** (dē hī'drāt) vt. **-drat'ed, -drat'ing** to remove water from; dry —vi. to lose water **—de·hy·dra'tion** n. **—de·hy'dra·tor** n.

**de·ice** (dē īs') vt. **-iced', -ic'ing** to melt ice from **—de·ic'er** n.

**de·i·fy** (dē'ə fī') vt. **-fied', -fy'ing** [< L. deus, god + facere, make] 1. to make a god of 2. to look upon as a god **—de'i·fi·ca'tion** (-fi kā'shən) n.

**deign** (dān) *vi., vt.* [< L. *dignus,* worthy] to condescend (to do or give)

**de·ism** (dē′iz′m) *n.* [< L. *deus,* god] the belief that God exists and created the world but thereafter assumed no control over it —**de′ist** *n.*

**de·i·ty** (dē′ə tē) *n., pl.* **-ties** [< L. *deus,* god] 1. the state of being a god 2. a god or goddess —**the Deity** God

**de·ject** (di jekt′) *vt.* [< L. *de-,* down + *jacere,* throw] to dishearten; depress —**de·ject′ed** *adj.* —**de·jec′-tion** *n.*

**Del·a·ware** (del′ə wer′) Eastern State of the U.S.: 2,057 sq. mi.; pop. 548,000; cap. Dover: abbrev. **Del.** —**Del′a·war′e·an** *adj., n.*

**de·lay** (di lā′) *vt.* [< OFr. *de-,* intens. + *laier,* to leave] 1. to put off; postpone 2. to make late; detain —*vi.* to linger —*n.* a delaying or being delayed

**de·lec·ta·ble** (di lek′tə b'l) *adj.* [see DELIGHT] delightful or delicious

**de·lec·ta·tion** (dē′lek tā′shən) *n.* [see DELIGHT] delight; enjoyment

**del·e·gate** (del′ə gāt′; *also for n.* -git) *n.* [< L. *de-,* from + *legare,* send] a person authorized to act for others; representative —*vt.* **-gat′ed, -gat′-ing** 1. to appoint as a delegate 2. to entrust (authority, etc.) to another

**del·e·ga·tion** *n.* 1. a delegating or being delegated 2. a body of delegates

**de·lete** (di lēt′) *vt.* **-let′ed, -let′ing** [< L. *delere,* destroy] to take out (a word, etc.); cross out —**de·le′tion** *n.*

**del·e·te·ri·ous** (del′ə tir′ē əs) *adj.* [< Gr. *dēleisthai,* injure] harmful to health, well-being, etc.; injurious

**delft′·ware** (delft′wer′) *n.* [< *Delft,* city in Holland] glazed earthenware, usually blue and white: also **delft**

**Del·hi** (del′ē) city in N India: pop. 2,062,000

**del·i** (del′ē) *clipped form of* DELICATESSEN

**de·lib·er·ate** (di lib′ər it; *for v.* -āt′) *adj.* [< L. *de-,* intens. + *librare,* weigh] 1. carefully thought out; premeditated 2. not rash or hasty 3. unhurried —*vi., vt.* **-at′ed, -at′ing** to consider carefully —**de·lib′er·ate·ly** *adv.* —**de·lib′er·a′tive** *adj.*

**de·lib·er·a′tion** *n.* 1. a deliberating 2. [*often pl.*] consideration of alternatives 3. carefulness; slowness

**del·i·ca·cy** (del′i kə sē) *n., pl.* **-cies** 1. the quality or state of being delicate; fineness, weakness, sensitivity, etc. 2. a choice food

**del·i·cate** (-kit) *adj.* [< L. *delicatus,* delightful] 1. pleasing in its lightness, mildness, etc. 2. beautifully fine in texture, workmanship, etc. 3. slight and subtle 4. easily damaged 5. frail in health 6. *a)* needing careful handling *b)* showing tact, consideration, etc. 7. finely sensitive —**del′i·cate·ly** *adv.* —**del′i·cate·ness** *n.*

**del·i·ca·tes·sen** (del′i kə tes′'n) *n.* [< G. *pl.* < Fr. *délicatesse,* delicacy] 1. prepared cooked meats, fish, cheeses, salads, etc. 2. a shop where such foods are sold

**de·li·cious** (di lish′əs) *adj.* [see ff.] 1. delightful 2. very pleasing to taste

or smell —**de·li′cious·ly** *adv.* —**de·li′cious·ness** *n.*

**de·light** (di līt′) *vt.* [< L. *de-,* from + *lacere,* entice] to give great pleasure to —*vi.* 1. to give great pleasure 2. to be highly pleased; rejoice —*n.* 1. great pleasure 2. something giving great pleasure —**de·light′ed** *adj.*

**de·light′ful** *adj.* giving delight; very pleasing —**de·light′ful·ly** *adv.*

**De·li·lah** (di lī′lə) *Bible* the mistress and betrayer of Samson

**de·lim·it** (di lim′it) *vt.* to fix the limits of —**de·lim′i·ta′tion** *n.*

**de·lin·e·ate** (di lin′ē āt′) *vt.* **-at′ed, -at′ing** [< L. *de-,* from + *linea,* a line] 1. to draw; sketch 2. to depict in words —**de·lin·e·a′tion** *n.*

**de·lin·quent** (di lin′kwənt) *adj.* [< L. *de-,* from + *linquere,* leave] 1. failing to do what duty or law requires 2. overdue, as taxes —*n.* a delinquent person; esp., *same as* JUVENILE DELINQUENT —**de·lin′quen·cy** *n., pl.* **-cies** —**de·lin′quent·ly** *adv.*

**de·li·quesce** (del′ə kwes′) *vi.* **-quesced′, -quesc′ing** [< L. *de-,* from + *liquere,* be liquid] to become liquid by absorbing moisture from the air —**del′i·ques′cent** *adj.*

**de·lir·i·ous** (di lir′ē əs) *adj.* 1. in a state of delirium 2. of or caused by delirium 3. wildly excited —**de·lir′i·ous·ly** *adv.* —**de·lir′i·ous·ness** *n.*

**de·lir·i·um** (-əm) *n.* [< L. *de-,* from + *lira,* a line] 1. a temporary mental disturbance, as during a fever, marked by confused speech and hallucinations 2. uncontrollably wild excitement

**de·liv·er** (di liv′ər) *vt.* [< L. *de-,* from + *liber,* free] 1. to set free or rescue 2. to assist at the birth of 3. to make (a speech, etc.) 4. to hand over 5. to distribute (mail, etc.) 6. to strike (a blow) 7. to throw (a ball)

**de·liv·er·ance** *n.* a freeing or being freed; rescue

**de·liv·er·y** *n., pl.* **-ies** 1. a handing over 2. a distributing, as of mail 3. a giving birth 4. any giving forth 5. the act or manner of delivering a speech, ball, etc. 6. something delivered

**dell** (del) *n.* [OE. *del*] a small, secluded valley or glen, usually wooded

**del·phin·i·um** (del fin′ē əm) *n.* [< Gr. *delphin,* dolphin] a tall plant bearing spikes of flowers, usually blue

**del·ta** (del′tə) *n.* 1. the fourth letter of the Greek alphabet (Δ, δ) 2. a deposit of soil, usually triangular, formed at the mouth of some rivers

DELTA

**de·lude** (di lōōd′) *vt.* **-lud′ed, -lud′ing** [< L. *de-,* from + *ludere,* to play] to mislead; deceive

**del·uge** (del′yōōj) *n.* [< L. *dis-,* off + *lavere,* to wash] 1. a great flood 2. a heavy rainfall —*vt.* **-uged, -ug·ing** 1. to flood 2. to overwhelm

**de·lu·sion** (di lōō′zhən) *n.* 1. a deluding or being deluded 2. a false belief, specif. one that persists psychotically —**de·lu′sive** *adj.*

**de·luxe** (di luks′, -looks′) *adj.* [Fr., of luxury] of extra fine quality —*adv.* in a deluxe manner

**delve** (delv) *vi.* **delved, delv′ing** [OE. *delfan*] **1.** [Archaic or Brit. Dial.] to dig **2.** to search (*into*) —**delv′er** *n.*

**Dem.** **1.** Democrat **2.** Democratic

**de·mag·net·ize** (dē mag′nə tīz′) *vt.* **-ized′, -iz′ing** to deprive of magnetic properties —**de·mag′net·i·za′tion** *n.*

**dem·a·gogue, dem·a·gog** (dem′ə gäg′, -gôg′) *n.* [< Gr. *dēmos*, the people + *agōgos*, leader] one who tries to stir up people's emotions so as to further his own interests —**dem′a·gog′y** (-gō′jē, -gäg′ē), **dem′a·gog′·uer·y** (-gäg′ər ē) *n.*

**de·mand** (di mand′) *vt.* [< L. *de-*, from + *mandare*, entrust] **1.** to ask for boldly or urgently **2.** to ask for as a right **3.** to require; need —*vi.* to make a demand —*n.* **1.** a demanding **2.** a thing demanded **3.** a strong request **4.** an urgent requirement **5.** *Econ.* the desire for a commodity together with ability to pay for it; also, the amount people are ready to buy —**in demand** wanted or sought —**on demand** when presented for payment

**de·mand′ing** *adj.* making difficult demands on one's patience, energy, etc. —**de·mand′ing·ly** *adv.*

**de·mar·ca·tion** (dē′mär kā′shən) *n.* [< Sp. *de-*, from + *marcar*, to mark] **1.** the act of setting and marking boundaries **2.** a limit or boundary

**de·mean¹** (di mēn′) *vt.* [DE- + MEAN²] to degrade; humble

**de·mean²** (di mēn′) *vt.* [see ff.] to behave or conduct (oneself)

**de·mean·or** (di mēn′ər) *n.* [< OFr. *demener*, to lead] outward behavior; conduct; deportment: Brit. sp. **de·meanour**

**de·ment·ed** (di ment′id) *adj.* [see ff.] mentally deranged; insane

**de·men·tia** (di men′shə) *n.* [< L. *de-*, out from + *mens*, the mind] loss or impairment of mental powers

**de·mer·it** (di mer′it) *n.* [< L. *de-*, intens. + *merere*, deserve, with *de-* taken as negative] **1.** a fault; defect **2.** a mark recorded against a student, etc. for poor conduct or work

**de·mesne** (di mān′, -mēn′) *n.* [see DOMAIN] a region or domain

**De·me·ter** (di mēt′ər) *Gr. Myth.* the goddess of agriculture

**demi-** [< L. *dimidius*, half] a *prefix* meaning: **1.** half **2.** less than usual in size, power, etc. [*demigod*]

**dem·i·god** (dem′ē gäd′) *n.* **1.** a minor deity **2.** a godlike person

**dem′i·john** (-jän′) *n.* [Fr. *dame-jeanne*] a large bottle of glass or earthenware in a wicker casing

**de·mil·i·ta·rize** (dē mil′ə tə rīz′) *vt.* **-rized′, -riz′ing** to free from organized military control

**dem·i·monde** (dem′ē mänd′) *n.* [Fr. < *demi-* + *monde*, world] the class of women who have lost social standing because of sexual promiscuity

**de·mise** (di mīz′) *n.* [< L. *de-*, down + *mittere*, send] **1.** *Law* transfer of an estate by lease **2.** death —*vt.* **-mised′, -mis′ing** to transfer (an estate) by lease

**dem·i·tasse** (dem′ē tas′, -täs′) *n.* [Fr. < *demi-*, DEMI- + *tasse*, cup] a small cup of or for after-dinner coffee

**dem·o** (dem′ō) *n.* [Colloq.] a phonograph or tape recording made to demonstrate a performer's talent, etc.

**de·mo·bi·lize** (dē mō′bə līz′) *vt.* **-lized′, -liz′ing** to disband (troops) —**de·mo′bi·li·za′tion** *n.*

**de·moc·ra·cy** (di mäk′rə sē) *n., pl.* **-cies** [< Gr. *dēmos*, the people + *kratein*, to rule] **1.** government by the people, directly or through representatives **2.** a country, etc. with such government **3.** equality of rights, opportunity, and treatment

**dem·o·crat** (dem′ə krat′) *n.* **1.** one who supports or practices democracy **2.** [D-] a Democratic Party member

**dem′o·crat′ic** *adj.* **1.** of or for democracy **2.** of or for all the people **3.** not snobbish **4.** [D-] of the Democratic Party —**dem′o·crat′i·cal·ly** *adv.*

**Democratic Party** one of the two major political parties in the U.S.

**de·mod·u·la·tion** (dē mäj′oo lā′shən) *n. Radio* the recovery, at the receiver, of a signal that has been modulated on a carrier wave

**de·mog·ra·phy** (di mäg′rə fē) *n.* [< Gr. *dēmos*, people + -GRAPHY] the statistical study of populations —**de·mog′ra·pher** *n.* —**de′mo·graph′ic** *adj.* —**de′mo·graph′i·cal·ly** *adv.*

**de·mol·ish** (di mäl′ish) *vt.* [< L. *de-*, down + *moliri*, build] to wreck —**dem·o·li·tion** (dem′ə lish′ən) *n.*

**de·mon** (dē′mən) *n.* [< L. *daemon*] **1.** a devil; evil spirit **2.** a person or thing regarded as evil, cruel, etc. —**de·mon·ic** (di män′ik) *adj.*

**de·mon·e·tize** (dē män′ə tīz′) *vt.* **-tized′, -tiz′ing** to deprive (currency) of its standard value

**de·mo·ni·ac** (di mō′nē ak′) *adj.* of or like a demon; fiendish; frenzied: also **de·mo·ni·a·cal** (dē′mə nī′ə k′l)

**de·mon·stra·ble** (di män′strə b′l) *adj.* that can be demonstrated, or proved —**de·mon′stra·bly** *adv.*

**dem·on·strate** (dem′ən strāt′) *vt.* **-strat′ed, -strat′ing** [< L. *de-*, from + *monstrare*, to show] **1.** to show by reasoning; prove **2.** to explain by using examples, etc. **3.** to show how something works —*vi.* to show feelings or views publicly by meetings, etc. —**dem′on·stra′tion** *n.* —**dem′on·stra′tor** *n.*

**de·mon·stra·tive** (di män′strə tiv) *adj.* **1.** illustrative **2.** giving proof (*of*) **3.** showing feelings openly **4.** *Gram.*

pointing out /"this" is a *demonstrative pronoun*/ —*n.* a demonstrative pronoun or adjective

**de·mor·al·ize** (di môr'ə līz') *vt.* -ized', -iz'ing 1. to lower the morale of 2. to throw into confusion —**de·mor'al·i·za'tion** *n.*

**De·mos·the·nes** (di mäs'thə nēz') 384?-322 B.C.; Athenian orator

**de·mote** (di mōt') *vt.* -mot'ed, -mot'ing [DE- + (PRO)MOTE] to reduce to a lower rank —**de·mo'tion** *n.*

**de·mul·cent** (di mul's'nt) *adj.* [< L. *de-*, down + *mulcere*, to stroke] soothing —*n.* a soothing ointment

**de·mur** (di mur') *vi.* -murred', -mur'ring [< L. *de-*, from + *mora*, a delay] to hesitate, as because of doubts; have scruples; object —*n.* a demurring: also **de·mur'ral**

**de·mure** (di myoor') *adj.* [< *de-* (prob. intens.) + OFr. *meur*, mature] 1. decorous; modest 2. affectedly modest; coy —**de·mure'ly** *adv.*

**de·mur·rage** (di mur'ij) *n.* 1. the delaying of a ship, freight car, etc., as by failure to load, unload, etc. 2. the compensation paid for this

**de·mur·rer** (di mur'ər) *n.* [see DE-MUR] 1. a plea that a lawsuit be dismissed because statements supporting a claim are defective 2. an objection

**den** (den) *n.* [OE. *denn*] 1. the lair of a wild animal 2. a haunt, as of thieves 3. a small, cozy room where one can be alone to read, work, etc.

**de·na·ture** (dē nā'chər) *vt.* -tured, -tur·ing 1. to change the nature of 2. to make (alcohol) unfit to drink

**de·ni·al** (di nī'əl) *n.* 1. a denying; saying "no" (to a request, etc.) 2. a contradiction 3. a refusal to believe or accept (a doctrine, etc.) 4. *same as* SELF-DENIAL —**de·ni'er** *n.*

**de·nier** (den'yər) *n.* [< L. *deni*, by tens] a unit of weight for measuring fineness of threads of silk, nylon, etc.

**den·i·grate** (den'ə grāt') *vt.* -grat'ed, -grat'ing [< L. *de-*, entirely + *nigrare*, blacken] to blacken, or belittle, the character of; defame —**den'i·gra'tion** *n.*

**den·im** (den'əm) *n.* [< Fr. (*serge*) *de Nîmes*, serge of Nîmes, town in France] a coarse, twilled cotton cloth

**den·i·zen** (den'i zən) *n.* [< L. *de intus*, from within] an inhabitant or frequenter of a particular place

**Den·mark** (den'märk) country in Europe, on a peninsula & several islands in the North & Baltic seas: 16,615 sq. mi.; pop. 4,797,000

**de·nom·i·nate** (di näm'ə nāt') *vt.* -nat'ed, -nat'ing [< L. *de-*, intens. + *nominare*, to name] to name; call

**de·nom·i·na·tion** (-nā'shən) *n.* 1. the act of naming 2. a name 3. a class or kind, as of coins, having a specific name or value 4. a religious sect

**de·nom'i·na'tion·al** *adj.* of, or under the control of, a religious sect

**de·nom'i·na'tor** (-nāt'ər) *n.* 1. a shared characteristic 2. *Math.* the term below the line in a fraction

**de·note** (di nōt') *vt.* -not'ed, -not'-

ing [< L. *de-*, down + *notare*, to mark] to indicate or signify —**de·no·ta·tion** (dē'nō tā'shən) *n.*

**de·noue·ment, dé·noue·ment** (dā nōō'män) *n.* [Fr.] the outcome or unraveling of a plot in a drama, etc.

**de·nounce** (di nouns') *vt.* -nounced', -nounc'ing [see DENUNCIATION] 1. to accuse publicly; inform against 2. to condemn strongly 3. to give formal notice of the ending of (a treaty, etc.) —**de·nounce'ment** *n.*

**dense** (dens) *adj.* [< L. *densus*, compact] 1. packed tightly together 2. difficult to get through 3. stupid —**dense'ly** *adv.* —**dense'ness** *n.*

**den·si·ty** (den'sə tē) *n., pl.* -ties 1. a dense condition 2. stupidity 3. number per unit, as of area 4. ratio of the mass of an object to its volume

**dent** (dent) *n.* [ME., var. of DINT] 1. a slight hollow made in a surface by a blow 2. a slight impression —*vt., vi.* to make or receive a dent (in)

**den·tal** (den't'l) *adj.* [< L. *dens*, tooth] of or for the teeth or dentistry

**dental floss** thread for removing food particles between the teeth

**den·ti·frice** (den'tə fris') *n.* [< L. *dens*, tooth + *fricare*, rub] any preparation for cleaning teeth

**den·tin** (den'tin) *n.* [see DENTAL] the hard tissue under the enamel of a tooth: also **den'tine** (-tēn, -tin)

**den·tist** (den'tist) *n.* one whose profession is the care and repair of teeth —**den'tist·ry** *n.*

**den·ture** (den'chər) *n.* [see DENTAL] a set of artificial teeth

**de·nu·cle·ar·ize** (dē nōō'klē ə rīz') *vt.* -ized', -iz'ing to prohibit the possession of nuclear weapons in (an area or nation)

**de·nude** (di nōōd', -nyōōd') *vt.* -nud'ed, -nud'ing [< L. *de-*, off + *nudare*, to strip] to make bare or naked; strip

**de·nun·ci·a·tion** (di nun'sē ā'shən) *n.* [< L. *de-*, intens. + *nuntiare*, announce] the act of denouncing

**Den·ver** (den'vər) capital of Colo.: pop. 515,000

**de·ny** (di nī') *vt.* -nied', -ny'ing [< L. *de-*, intens. + *negare*, to deny] 1. to declare (a statement) untrue 2. to refuse to accept as true or right 3. to repudiate 4. to refuse to grant or give 5. to refuse the request of —**deny oneself** to do without desired things

**de·o·dor·ant** (dē ō'dər ənt) *adj.* that can counteract undesired odors —*n.* any deodorant preparation

**de·o'dor·ize'** (-də rīz') *vt.* -ized', -iz'ing to counteract the odor of —**de·o'dor·iz'er** *n.*

**de·part** (di pärt') *vi.* [< L. *dis-*, apart + *partire*, divide] 1. to go away; leave 2. to die 3. to deviate (*from*)

**de·part'ed** *adj.* 1. gone away 2. dead —**the departed** the dead

**de·part·ment** (-mənt) *n.* 1. a separate part or division, as of a business 2. a field of activity, etc. —**de·part'men'tal** (-men't'l) *adj.*

**de·part'men·tal·ize'** (-men'tə līz') *vt.* -ized', -iz'ing to organize into departments —de·part'men'tal·i·za'tion n.

**department store** a large retail store for the sale of many kinds of goods arranged in departments

de·par·ture (di pär'chər) n. 1. a departing 2. a starting out, as on a trip 3. a deviation (from something)

de·pend (di pend') vi. [< L. de-, down + pendere, to hang] 1. to be determined by something else; be contingent (on) 2. to rely (on) 3. to rely (on) for support or aid

de·pend'a·ble adj. trustworthy; reliable —de·pend'a·bil'i·ty n.

de·pend'ence n. 1. a being dependent 2. reliance (on) for support or aid 3. reliance; trust

de·pend'en·cy n., pl. -cies 1. dependence 2. something dependent 3. a territory, as a possession, subordinate to its governing country

de·pend'ent adj. 1. hanging down 2. determined by something else 3. relying (on) for support, etc. 4. subordinate —n. one relying on another for support, etc. Also de·pend'ant —de·pend'ent·ly adv.

de·pict (di pikt') vt. [< L. de-, intens. + pingere, to paint] 1. to represent by drawing, painting, etc. 2. to describe —de·pic'tion n.

de·pil·a·to·ry (di pil'ə tôr'ē) adj. [< L. de-, from + pilus, hair] serving to remove unwanted hair —n., pl. -ries a depilatory substance or device

de·plane (dē plān') vi. -planed', -plan'ing to leave an airplane after it lands

de·plete (di plēt') vt. -plet'ed, -plet'ing [< L. de-, from + plere, fill] 1. to use up (funds, etc.) 2. to use up the resources, etc. of —de·ple'tion n.

de·plor·a·ble (di plôr'ə b'l) adj. regrettable or wretched

de·plore (di plôr') vt. -plored', -plor'ing [< L. de-, intens. + plorare, weep] to regret deeply

de·ploy (dē ploi') vt., vi. [< L. dis-, apart + plicare, to fold] Mil. to spread out so as to form a wider front —de·ploy'ment n.

de·po·lar·ize (dē pō'lə rīz') vt. -ized', -iz'ing to destroy or counteract the polarization of —de·po'lar·i·za'tion n.

de·po·lit·i·cize (dē'pə lit'ə sīz') vt. -cized', -ciz'ing to remove from political influence

de·po·nent (di pō'nənt) adj. [< L. de-, down + ponere, put] Law one who gives written testimony under oath

de·pop·u·late (dē päp'yə lāt') vt. -lat'ed, -lat'ing to reduce the population of —de·pop'u·la'tion n.

de·port (di pôrt') vt. [< L. de-, from + portare, carry] 1. to behave (oneself) 2. to expel (an alien) —de·por·ta·tion (dē'pôr tā'shən) n.

de·port'ment n. conduct; behavior

de·pose (di pōz') vt. -posed', -pos'-

ing [< OFr. de-, from + poser, cease] 1. to remove from office 2. to testify

de·pos·it (di päz'it) vt. [< L. de-, down + ponere, put] 1. to place (money, etc.) for safekeeping, as in a bank 2. to give as a pledge or partial payment 3. to set down 4. to leave (sediment, etc.) lying —n. 1. something placed for safekeeping, as money in a bank 2. a pledge or part payment 3. something deposited or left lying —de·pos'i·tor n.

dep·o·si·tion (dep'ə zish'ən) n. 1. a deposing or being deposed 2. testimony 3. something deposited

de·pos·i·to·ry (di päz'ə tôr'ē) n., pl. -ries a place where things are put for safekeeping

de·pot (dē'pō; military & Brit. dep'ō) n. [< Fr. see DEPOSIT] 1. a warehouse 2. a railroad or bus station 3. a storage place for military supplies

de·prave (di prāv') vt. -praved', -prav'ing [< L. de-, intens. + pravus, crooked] to make morally bad; corrupt —de·praved' adj. —de·prav'i·ty (-prav'ə tē) n., pl. -ties

dep·re·cate (dep'rə kāt') vt. -cat'ed, -cat'ing [< L. de-, off + precari, pray] 1. to express disapproval of 2. to belittle —dep're·ca'tion n. —dep're·ca·to'ry (-kə tôr'ē) adj.

de·pre·ci·ate (di prē'shē āt') vt., vi. -at'ed, -at'ing [< L. de-, from + pretium, price] 1. to lessen in value 2. to belittle —de·pre'ci·a'tion n.

dep·re·da·tion (dep'rə dā'shən) n. [< L. de-, intens. + praedari, to plunder] a robbing or plundering

de·press (di pres') vt. [< L. de-, down + premere, to press] 1. to press down 2. to sadden; deject 3. to make less active 4. to lower in value, price, etc. —de·pressed' adj. —de·press'ant n.

de·pres·sion (di presh'ən) n. 1. a depressing or being depressed 2. a hollow or low place 3. low spirits; dejection 4. a decrease in force, activity, etc. 5. a period of reduced business, much unemployment, etc.

de·prive (di prīv') vt. -prived', -priv'ing [< L. de-, intens. + privare, to separate] 1. to take away from forcibly 2. to keep from having, etc. —dep·ri·va·tion (dep'rə vā'shən) n.

dept. 1. department 2. deputy

depth (depth) n. [< ME. dep, deep + -TH] 1. the distance from the top downward, or from front to back 2. deepness 3. intensity 4. [usually pl.] the deepest or inmost part —in depth comprehensively

dep·u·ta·tion (dep'yoo tā'shən) n. 1. a deputing 2. a delegation

de·pute (di pyoot') vt. -put'ed, -put'ing [< L. de-, from + putare, cleanse] 1. to give (authority, etc.) to a deputy 2. to appoint as one's substitute

dep·u·tize (dep'yə tīz') vt. -tized', -tiz'ing to appoint as deputy

dep·u·ty (dep'yə tē) n., pl. -ties a person appointed to act for another

**de·rail** (di rāl′) *vt.*, *vi.* to run off the rails, as a train —**de·rail′ment** *n.*

**de·rail·leur** (di rā′lər) *n.* [Fr.] a gearshifting mechanism on a bicycle for shifting the sprocket chain from one size of sprocket wheel to another

**de·range** (di rānj′) *vt.* -ranged′, -rang′ing [< OFr. *des-*, apart + *rengier*, to range] 1. to upset the arrangement or working of 2. to make insane —**de·range′ment** *n.*

**Der·by** (dur′bē; *Brit.* där′-) *n.*, *pl.* -bies 1. any of certain famous horse races; orig., one founded (1780) by an Earl of Derby 2. [d-] a stiff felt hat with a round crown

**de·reg·u·late** (dē reg′ yə lāt′) *vt.* -lat′ed, -lat′ing to remove regulations governing —**de·reg′u·la′tion** *n.*

DERBY

**der·e·lict** (der′ə likt′) *adj.* [< L. *de-*, intens. + *relinquere*: see RELINQUISH] 1. deserted by the owner; abandoned 2. negligent —*n.* 1. a ship deserted at sea 2. a destitute and rejected person

**der·e·lic·tion** (-lik′shən) *n.* 1. a forsaking or being forsaken 2. a neglect of, or failure in, duty

**de·ride** (di rīd′) *vt.* -rid′ed, -rid′ing [< L. *de-*, down + *ridere*, to laugh] to laugh at in scorn; ridicule —**de·ri′sion** (-rizh′ən) *n.* —**de·ri′sive** (-rī′siv) *adj.* —**de·ri′sive·ly** *adv.*

**der·i·va·tion** (der′ə vā′shən) *n.* 1. a deriving or being derived 2. the source or origin of something 3. the origin and development of a word

**de·riv·a·tive** (də riv′ə tiv) *adj.* derived —*n.* something derived

**de·rive** (di rīv′) *vt.* -rived′, -riv′ing [< L. *de-*, from + *rivus*, a stream] 1. to get or receive (*from* a source) 2. to deduce or infer 3. to trace from or to a source —*vi.* to be derived

**der·ma·ti·tis** (dur′mə tīt′is) *n.* [< Gr. *derma*, skin + -ITIS] inflammation of the skin

**der·ma·tol·o·gy** (dur′mə täl′ə jē) *n.* [< Gr. *derma*, skin + -LOGY] the branch of medicine dealing with the skin —**der′ma·tol′o·gist** *n.*

**der·o·gate** (der′ə gāt′) *vi.*, *vt.* -gat′ed, -gat′ing [< L. *de-*, from + *rogare*, ask] to detract or disparage —**der′o·ga′tion** *n.*

**de·rog·a·to·ry** (di räg′ə tôr′ē) *adj.* [see prec.] 1. detracting 2. disparaging; belittling

**der·rick** (der′ik) *n.* [after *Derrick*, 17th-c. London hangman: orig. applied to a gallows] 1. a pivoted beam for lifting and moving heavy objects 2. a tall framework, as over an oil well, to support drilling machinery, etc.

**der·ri·ère** (der′ē er′) *n.* [Fr., back part] the buttocks

**der·vish** (dur′vish) *n.* [< Per. *darvēsh*, beggar] a member of any of various Moslem ascetic orders

**de·sal·i·na·tion** (dē sal′ə nā′shən) *n.* [DE- + SALIN(E) + -ATION] the removal of salt, esp. from sea water to make it drinkable —**de·sal′i·nate′** *vt.* -nat′ed, -nat′ing

**des·cant** (des′kant, des kant′) *vi.* [< L. *dis-*, apart + *cantus*, song] 1. to discourse (*on* or *upon*) 2. to sing

**Des·cartes** (dā kärt′), **Re·né** (rə nā′) 1596-1650; Fr. philosopher

**de·scend** (di send′) *vi.* [< L. *de-*, down + *scandere*, climb] 1. to move down to a lower place 2. to pass from an earlier to a later time, from greater to less, etc. 3. to slope downward 4. to come down (*from* a source) 5. to stoop (*to*) 6. to make a sudden attack or visit (*on*) —*vt.* to move down along

**de·scend·ant** *n.* an offspring of a certain ancestor, family, group, etc.

**de·scent** (di sent′) *n.* 1. a coming or going down 2. ancestry 3. a downward slope 4. a way down 5. a sudden attack 6. a decline

**de·scribe** (di skrīb′) *vt.* -scribed′, -scrib′ing [< L. *de-*, from + *scribere*, write] 1. to tell or write about 2. to trace the outline of —**de·scrib′er** *n.*

**de·scrip·tion** (di skrip′shən) *n.* 1. the act or technique of describing 2. a statement or passage that describes 3. sort; kind 4. a tracing or outlining —**de·scrip′tive** (-tiv) *adj.*

**de·scry** (di skrī′) *vt.* -scried′, -scry′ing [< OFr. *descrier*, proclaim] 1. to catch sight of; discern 2. to detect

**des·e·crate** (des′ə krāt′) *vt.* -crat′ed, -crat′ing [< DE- (in CON-) SECRATE] to violate the sacredness of; profane —**des′e·cra′tion** *n.*

**de·seg·re·gate** (dē seg′rə gāt′) *vt.*, *vi.* -gat′ed, -gat′ing to abolish racial segregation in (public schools, etc.) —**de·seg′re·ga′tion** *n.*

**de·sen·si·tize** (dē sen′sə tīz′) *vt.* -tized′, -tiz′ing to make less sensitive, as to an allergen

**de·sert¹** (di zurt′) *vt.*, *vi.* [< L. *de-*, from + *serere*, join] 1. to abandon; forsake 2. to leave (one's military post, etc.) without permission and with no intent to return —**de·sert′er** *n.* —**de·ser′tion** (-zur′shən) *n.*

**des·ert²** (dez′ərt) *n.* [see prec.] 1. an uninhabited region; wilderness 2. a dry, barren, sandy region

**de·sert³** (di zurt′) *n.* [see ff.] [*often pl.*] deserved reward or punishment

**de·serve** (di zurv′) *vt.*, *vi.* -served′, -serv′ing [< L. *de-*, intens. + *servire*, serve] to be worthy (of); merit —**de·serv′ed·ly** *adv.* —**de·serv′ing** *adj.*, *n.*

**des·ic·cate** (des′i kāt′) *vt.*, *vi.* -cat′ed, -cat′ing [< L. *de-*, intens. + *siccus*, dry] to dry out completely —**des′ic·ca′tion** *n.* —**des′ic·ca′tor** *n.*

**de·sid·er·a·tum** (di sid′ə rāt′əm) *n.*, *pl.* -ta (-ə) [see DESIRE] something needed and wanted

**de·sign** (di zīn′) *vt.* [< L. *de-*, out + *signum*, a mark] 1. to sketch an outline for; plan 2. to contrive 3. to plan to do; intend —*vi.* to make original plans, etc. —*n.* 1. a plan; scheme 2. purpose; aim 3. a working plan; pattern 4. arrangement of parts, form, color, etc.; artistic invention —**by design** purposely —**de·sign′er** *n.*

**des·ig·nate** (dez′ig nāt′) *vt.* -nat′-

ed, -nat'ing [see prec.] 1. to point out; specify 2. to name 3. to appoint —des'ig·na'tion n.

de·sign'ing adj. scheming; artful —n. the art of creating designs, etc.

de·sir·a·ble (di zir' b'l) adj. worth having; pleasing —de·sir'a·bil'i·ty n. —de·sir'a·bly adv.

de·sire (di zir') vt. -sired', -sir'ing [< L. desiderare] 1. to long for; crave 2. to ask for —vi. to have a desire —n. 1. a wish; craving 2. sexual appetite 3. a request 4. thing desired

de·sir'ous (-əs) adj. desiring

de·sist (di zist') vi. [< L. de-, from + stare, to stand] to cease; stop

desk (desk) n. [< ML. desca, table] a table for writing, drawing, or reading

Des Moines (də moin') capital of Iowa; pop. 201,000

des·o·late (des'ə lit; for v. -lāt') adj. [< L. de-, intens. + solus, alone] 1. lonely; solitary 2. uninhabited 3. laid waste 4. forlorn —vt. -lat'ed, -lat'ing 1. to rid of inhabitants 2. to lay waste 3. to make forlorn —des'o·late·ly adv. —des'o·late·ness n.

des'o·la'tion n. 1. a making desolate 2. a desolate condition or place 3. misery 4. loneliness

de·spair (di sper') vi. [< L. de-, without + sperare, to hope] to lose hope —n. 1. loss of hope 2. a person or thing causing despair

des·patch (di spach') vt., n. same as DISPATCH —des·patch'er n.

des·per·a·do (des'pə rä'dō, -rä'-) n., pl. -does, -dos [< OSp.: see DESPAIR] a dangerous criminal; bold outlaw

des·per·ate (des'pər it) adj. 1. rash or violent because of despair 2. having a very great need 3. very serious 4. drastic —des'per·ate·ly adv.

des·per·a·tion (des'pə rā'shən) n. 1. the state of being desperate 2. recklessness resulting from despair

des·pi·ca·ble (des'pik ə b'l, di spik'-) adj. deserving scorn; contemptible

de·spise (di spīz') vt. -spised', -spis'ing [< L. de, down + specere, look at] 1. to scorn 2. to loathe

de·spite (di spīt') prep. [see prec.] in spite of; notwithstanding

de·spoil (di spoil') vt. [< L. de-, intens. + spoliare, to strip] to rob; plunder —de·spoil'ment n.

de·spond·en·cy (di spän'dən sē) n. [< L. de-, from + spondere, to promise] loss of hope; dejection: also de·spond'ence —de·spond'ent adj.

des·pot (des'pət) n. [< Gr. despotēs, a master] 1. an absolute ruler 2. a tyrant —des·pot·ic (de spät'ik) adj. —des'pot·ism (-pə tiz'm) n.

des·sert (di zurt') n. [< L. de-, from + servire, serve] the final course of a meal, typically cake, fruit, etc.

des·ti·na·tion (des'tə nā'shən) n. 1. the purpose for which something or someone is destined 2. the place toward which one is going or sent

des·tine (des'tin) vt. -tined, -tin-ing [< L. de-, intens. + stare, to stand] 1. to predetermine, as by fate 2. to intend —destined for 1. bound for 2. intended for

des·tin·y (des'tə nē) n., pl. -ies 1. the seemingly inevitable succession of events 2. (one's) fate

des·ti·tute (des'tə tōōt') adj. [< L. de, down + statuere, to set] 1. lacking (with of) 2. totally impoverished —des'ti·tu'tion n.

de·stroy (di stroi') vt. [< L. de-, down + struere, to build] 1. to tear down; demolish 2. to wreck; ruin 3. to do away with 4. to kill

de·stroy'er n. 1. one that destroys 2. a small, fast warship

de·struct (di strukt', dē'strukt') n. [< DESTRUCTION] deliberate destruction of a rocket, etc. after its launch —vi. to be automatically destroyed

de·struc·tion (di struk'shən) n. 1. a destroying or being destroyed 2. a cause or means of destroying —de·struc'tive adj. —de·struc'tive·ly adv. —de·struc'tive·ness n.

des·ue·tude (des'wi tōōd') n. [< L. de-, from + suescere, be accustomed] disuse

des·ul·to·ry (des''l tôr'ē) adj. [< L. de-, from + salire, to leap] 1. aimless; disconnected 2. random

de·tach (di tach') vt. [< Fr.: see DE- & ATTACH] 1. to unfasten and remove; disconnect; disengage 2. to send (troops, etc.) on a special mission —de·tach'a·ble adj.

de·tached' adj. 1. not connected 2. aloof; disinterested; impartial

de·tach'ment n. 1. a detaching 2. a unit of troops, etc. on a special mission 3. impartiality or aloofness

de·tail (di tāl', dē'tāl) n. [< Fr. < dé-, from + tailler, to cut] 1. a dealing with things item by item 2. a minute account 3. a small part; item 4. a) one or more soldiers, etc. on special duty b) the duty —vt. 1. to tell, item by item 2. to assign to special duty in detail with particulars

de·tain (di tān') vt. [< L. de-, off + tenere, to hold] 1. to keep in custody; confine 2. to keep from going on —de·tain'ment n.

de·tect (di tekt') vt. [< L. de-, from + tegere, to cover] to discover (something hidden, not clear, etc.) —de·tect'a·ble, de·tect'i·ble adj. —de·tec'tion n. —de·tec'tor n.

de·tec'tive n. one whose work is solving crimes, tracking people, etc.

dé·tente (dā tänt') n. [Fr.] a lessening of tension, esp. between nations

de·ten·tion (di ten'shən) n. a detaining or being detained

detention home a place where juvenile offenders are held in custody

de·ter (di tur') vt. -terred', -ter'ring [< L. de-, from + terrere, frighten] to keep or discourage (a person) from doing something through fear, doubt, etc. —de·ter'ment n.

**de·ter·gent** (di tur′jənt) *adj.* [< L. *de-*, off + *tergere*, wipe] cleansing —*n.* a soaplike cleansing substance

**de·te·ri·o·rate** (di tir′ē ə rāt′) *vt., vi.* -rat′ed, -rat′ing [< L. *deterior*, worse] to make or become worse — **de·te′ri·o·ra′tion** *n.*

**de·ter·mi·nant** (di tur′mi nənt) *n.* a thing or factor that determines

**de·ter′mi·nate** (-nit) *adj.* clearly determined; fixed; settled

**de·ter·mi·na·tion** (di tur′mə nā′shən) *n.* 1. a determining or being determined 2. a firm intention 3. firmness of purpose

**de·ter·mine** (di tur′mən) *vt.* -mined, -min·ing [< L. *de-*, from + *terminus*, a limit] 1. to set limits to 2. to settle conclusively 3. to decide or decide upon 4. to be the deciding factor in; direct 5. to find out exactly —*vi.* to decide —**de·ter′mi·na·ble** *adj.*

**de·ter′mined** *adj.* 1. having one's mind made up 2. resolute; firm

**de·ter·rent** (di tur′ənt) *adj.* deterring —*n.* something that deters

**de·test** (di test′) *vt.* [< L. *detestari*, to curse by the gods] to dislike intensely; hate —**de·test′a·ble** *adj.* —**de·tes·ta·tion** (dē′tes tā′shən) *n.*

**de·throne** (dē thrōn′) *vt.* -throned′, -thron′ing to depose (a monarch)

**det·o·nate** (det′'n āt′) *vi., vt.* -nat′ed, -nat′ing [< L. *de-*, intens. + *tonare*, to thunder] to explode violently —**det′o·na′tion** *n.* —**det′o·na′tor** *n.*

**de·tour** (dē′toor, di toor′) *n.* [< Fr.: see DE- & TURN] 1. a roundabout way 2. a road used when the regular route is closed —*vi., vt.* to go or route on a detour

**de·tract** (di trakt′) *vt.* [< L. *de-*, from + *trahere*, to draw] to take away —*vi.* to take something desirable (from) —**de·trac′tion** *n.* —**de·trac′tor** *n.*

**det·ri·ment** (det′rə mənt) *n.* [< L. *de-*, off + *terere*, to rub] 1. damage; injury 2. anything that causes this —**det′ri·men′tal** *adj.*

**de·tri·tus** (di trīt′əs) *n.* [L., a rubbing away: see prec.] rock fragments, etc. from disintegration or erosion —**de·tri′tal** (-′l) *adj.*

**De·troit** (di troit′) city & port in SE Mich.: pop. 1,511,000

**deuce** (dōōs) *n.* [< L. *duo*, two] 1. a playing card or side of a die with two spots 2. *Tennis* a tie score after which one side must score twice in a row to win 3. the devil: a mild oath

**deu·te·ri·um** (dōō tir′ē əm) *n.* [ModL.] a heavy isotope of hydrogen

**Deu·ter·on·o·my** (dōōt′ər än′ə mē) [< Gr. *deuteros*, second + *nomos*, law] the fifth book of the Pentateuch

**de·val·ue** (dē val′yōō) *vt.* -ued, -u·ing 1. to lessen the value of 2. to lower the exchange value of (a currency) —**de·val′u·a′tion** *n.*

**dev·as·tate** (dev′ə stāt′) *vt.* -tat′ed, -tat′ing [< L. *de-*, intens. + *vastus*, empty] 1. to lay waste; ravage; destroy 2. to overwhelm —**dev′as·ta′tion** *n.* —**dev′as·ta′tor** *n.*

**de·vel·op** (di vel′əp) *vt.* [< Fr. *dé-*, apart + OFr. *voloper*, to wrap] 1. to make fuller, bigger, better, etc. 2. to show or work out by degrees; disclose 3. *Photog.* to put (a film, etc.) in chemical solutions to make the picture visible —*vi.* 1. to come into being or activity; occur or happen 2. to become developed —**de·vel′op·er** *n.* —**de·vel′op·ment** *n.*

**de·vi·ant** (dē′vē ənt) *adj.* deviating, esp. from what is considered normal —*n.* one whose behavior is deviant

**de·vi·ate** (dē′vē āt′; for *adj.* & *n.* -it) *vi.* -at′ed, -at′ing [< L. *de-*, from + *via*, road] to turn aside (from a course, standard, etc.); diverge —*adj.* deviant —*n.* a deviant, esp. in sexual behavior —**de′vi·a′tion** *n.* —**de′vi·a′tor** *n.*

**de·vice** (di vīs′) *n.* [see DEVISE] 1. a thing devised; plan, scheme, or trick 2. a mechanical contrivance 3. an ornamental design, esp. on a coat of arms —**leave to one's own devices** to allow to do as one wishes

**dev·il** (dev′'l) *n.* [ult. < Gr. *diabolos*, slanderer] 1. [*often* D-] *Theol. a)* the chief evil spirit; Satan (with *the*) *b)* any demon of hell 2. a very wicked person 3. a person who is mischievous, reckless, unlucky, etc. 4. anything hard to operate, control, etc. 5. a printer's apprentice —*vt.* -iled or -illed, -il·ing or -il·ling 1. to prepare (food) with hot seasoning 2. to annoy; tease —**dev′il·ish** *adj.*

**dev′il-may-care′** *adj.* reckless

**dev′il·ment** *n.* mischievous action

**devil's advocate** a person upholding the wrong side for argument's sake

**dev′il's-food′ cake** a rich chocolate cake

**dev′il·try** (-trē) *n., pl.* -tries reckless mischief, fun, etc.: also **dev′il·ry**

**de·vi·ous** (dē′vē əs) *adj.* [< L. *de-*, off + *via*, road] 1. not direct; roundabout or deviating 2. not straightforward —**de′vi·ous·ness** *n.*

**de·vise** (di vīz′) *vt., vi.* -vised′, -vis′ing [< L. *dividere*, to divide] 1. to work out or create (a plan, device, etc.) 2. to bequeath (real property) by will —*n.* a bequest of property

**de·vi·tal·ize** (dē vīt′'l īz′) *vt.* -ized′, -iz′ing to deprive of vitality

**de·void** (di void′) *adj.* [see DE- & VOID] completely without; empty (of)

**de·voir** (də vwär′) *n.* [< L. *debere*, to owe] 1. duty 2. [*pl.*] courteous acts or greetings

**de·volve** (di välv′) *vt., vi.* -volved′, -volv′ing [< L. *de-*, down + *volvere*, to roll] to pass (on) to another: said of duties, responsibilities, etc.

**de·vote** (di vōt′) *vt.* -vot′ed, -vot′ing [< L. *de-*, from + *vovere*, to vow] to set apart for or give up to some purpose, activity, or person; dedicate

**de·vot′ed** *adj.* very loving, loyal, or faithful —**de·vot′ed·ly** *adv.*

**dev·o·tee** (dev′ə tē′, -tā′) *n.* one strongly devoted to something

**de·vo·tion** *n.* 1. a devoting or being devoted 2. piety 3. religious worship 4. [*pl.*] prayers 5. loyalty or deep affection —**de·vo′tion·al** *adj.*

**de·vour** (di vour′) *vt.* [< L. *de-*, intens. + *vorare*, swallow whole] 1. to eat hungrily 2. to swallow up 3. to take in greedily, as with the eyes

**de·vout** (di vout′) *adj.* [see DEVOTE] 1. very religious; pious 2. earnest; sincere —**de·vout′ly** *adv.*

**dew** (dōō) *n.* [OE. *deaw*] 1. atmospheric moisture that condenses in drops on cool surfaces at night 2. anything refreshing, pure, etc., like dew —**dew′y** *adj.* **-i·er, -i·est**

**dew·ber′ry** *n., pl.* **-ries** 1. a trailing blackberry plant 2. its berry

**dew·claw′** *n.* a functionless digit as on the inner side of a dog's leg

**dew·drop′** *n.* a drop of dew

**dew·lap′** *n.* [see DEW + LAP¹] loose skin under the throat of cattle, etc.

**dex·ter·i·ty** (dek ster′ə tē) *n.* [see ff.] skill in using one's hands, body, or mind; adroitness

**dex·ter·ous** (dek′strəs, -stər əs) *adj.* [< L. *dexter*, right] having or showing dexterity; adroit: also **dex′trous**

**dex·trose** (dek′strōs) *n.* a glucose found in plants and animals

DEWLAP

**dho·ti** (dō′tē) *n.* [Hind. *dhoti*] a loincloth worn by Hindu men

**di-¹** [Gr. *di-* < *dis*, twice] *a prefix meaning* twice, double, twofold

**di-²** *same as* DIS-

**di·a·be·tes** (dī′ə bēt′is, -ēz) *n.* [< Gr. *dia-*, through + *bainein*, to go] a disease characterized by excess sugar in the blood and urine, hunger, thirst, etc.: also **sugar diabetes** —**di′a·bet′ic** (-bet′ik) *adj., n.*

**di·a·bol·ic** (dī′ə bäl′ik) *adj.* [see DEVIL] very wicked or cruel; fiendish: also **di′a·bol′i·cal**

**di·a·crit·ic** (dī′ə krit′ik) *adj.* [< Gr. *dia-*, across + *krinein*, to separate] distinguishing: also **di′a·crit′i·cal** —*n.* a mark, as a macron, added to a letter or symbol to show pronunciation, etc.: in full **diacritical mark**

**di·a·dem** (dī′ə dem′) *n.* [< Gr. *dia-*, through + *dein*, to bind] 1. a crown 2. an ornamental headband

**di·ag·nose** (dī′əg nōs′) *vt., vi.* **-nosed′, -nos′ing** to make a diagnosis (of)

**di·ag·no·sis** (-nō′sis) *n., pl.* **-ses** (-sēz) [< Gr. *dia-*, through + *gignōskein*, know] 1. the act of deciding the nature of a disease, situation, problem, etc. by examination and analysis 2. the resulting decision —**di′ag·nos′tic** (-näs′tik) *adj.* —**di′ag·nos·ti′cian** (-tish′ən) *n.*

**di·ag·o·nal** (dī ag′ə n'l) *adj.* [< Gr. *dia-*, through + *gōnia*, an angle] 1. extending slantingly between opposite corners 2. slanting; oblique —*n.* a diagonal line, plane, course, part, etc. —**di·ag′o·nal·ly** *adv.*

**di·a·gram** (dī′ə gram′) *n.* [< Gr. *dia-*, across + *graphein*, write] a sketch, plan, graph, etc. that explains something, as by outlining its parts —*vt.* **-gramed′** or **-grammed′, -gram′ing** or **-gram′ming** to make a diagram of —**di′a·gram·mat′ic** (-grə mat′ik) *adj.*

**di·al** (dī′əl, dīl) *n.* [< L. *dies*, day] 1. the face of a clock, etc. 2. the face of a meter, etc. for indicating, as by a pointer, an amount, direction, etc. 3. a graduated disk on a radio, etc., esp. for tuning in stations 4. a rotating disk on a telephone, to make automatic connections —*vt., vi.* **-aled** or **-alled, -al·ing** or **-al·ling** 1. to show on or measure with a dial 2. to tune in (a radio station, etc.) 3. to call by using a telephone dial

**di·al.** 1. dialect(al) 2. dialectic(al)

**di·a·lect** (dī′ə lekt′) *n.* [< Gr. *dia-*, between + *legein*, to talk] the form of a spoken language peculiar to a region, social group, etc. —**di′a·lec′tal** *adj.*

**di·a·lec·tic** (-lek′tik) *n.* 1. [*often pl.*] a logical examination of ideas to test their validity 2. logical argumentation —*adj.* dialectical

**di·a·lec·ti·cal** *adj.* 1. of or using dialectics 2. of a dialect

**di·a·logue, di·a·log** (dī′ə lôg′) *n.* [see DIALECT] 1. interchange of ideas by open discussion 2. the passages of talk in a play, story, etc.

**Dialogue Mass** *R.C.Ch.* a Mass at which the congregation responds aloud

**di·am·e·ter** (dī am′ət ər) *n.* [< Gr. *dia-*, through + *metron*, a measure] 1. a straight line passing through the center of a circle, sphere, etc. from one side to the other 2. its measure

**di·a·met·ri·cal** (dī′ə met′ri k'l) *adj.* 1. of or along a diameter 2. designating an opposite altogether such

**di·a·mond** (dī′mənd, -ə mənd) *n.* [< Gr. *adamas*, adamant] 1. a nearly pure, brilliant, crystalline carbon, the hardest mineral known 2. a gem, etc. cut from it 3. *a)* the plane figure ◊ *b)* a playing card so marked 4. *Baseball* the infield or the whole field

**di·a·mond·back′** *n.* a large, poisonous rattlesnake of the S U.S.

**Di·an·a** (dī an′ə) *Rom. Myth.* the goddess of the moon and of hunting

**di·a·pa·son** (dī′ə pāz′'n) *n.* [< Gr. *dia*, through + *pas*, all] an organ stop covering the instrument's entire range

**di·a·per** (dī′pər, dī′ə pər) *n.* [< ML. *diasprum*, flowered cloth] a soft, absorbent cloth folded around a baby's loins —*vt.* to put a diaper on (a baby)

**di·aph·a·nous** (dī af′ə nəs) *adj.* [< Gr. *dia-*, through + *phainein*, to show] letting much light through

**di·a·phragm** (dī′ə fram′) *n.* [< Gr. *dia-*, through + *phragma*, fence] 1. the muscular partition between the chest and abdominal cavities 2. a vibrating disk producing sound waves 3. a vaginal contraceptive device —**di′a·phrag·mat′ic** (-frag mat′ik) *adj.*

**di·ar·rhe·a** (dī′ə rē′ə) *n.* [< Gr. *dia-*,

through + *rhein*, to flow] too frequent
and loose bowel movements

**di·a·ry** (dī'ə rē) *n., pl.* **-ries** [ < L.
*dies*, day] a daily written record of
one's experiences, etc. —**di'a·rist** *n.*

**di·as·to·le** (dī as'tə lē') *n.* [ < Gr.
*dia-*, apart + *stellein*, put] the usual
rhythmic expansion of the heart —
**di·a·stol·ic** (dī'ə stäl'ik) *adj.*

**di·a·ther·my** (dī'ə thur'mē) *n.* [ <
Gr. *dia-*, through + *thermē*, heat] *Med.*
high-frequency electrical induction of
heat into tissues below the skin

**di·a·tom** (dī'ə täm', -ət əm) *n.* [ <
Gr. *diatomos*, cut in two] any of various
microscopic algae that are an important
source of food for marine life

**di·a·ton·ic** (dī'ə tän'ik) *adj.* [ < Gr.
*dia-*, through + *tenein*, to stretch]
designating or of any standard major
or minor scale of eight tones

**di·a·tribe** (dī'ə trīb') *n.* [ < Gr. *dia-*,
through + *tribein*, to rub] a bitter,
abusive denunciation

**dib·ble** (dib''l) *n.* [ME. *dibbel*] a
pointed tool for making holes in the
soil for seeds, bulbs, etc.

**dice** (dīs) *n.pl., sing.* **die** or **dice** [see
DIE²] small cubes marked on each side
with from one to six dots, used in
games of chance —*vi.* **diced, dic'ing**
to play or gamble with dice —*vt.* to
cut (vegetables, etc.) into small cubes
—**no dice** [Colloq.] 1. no: used in
refusing a request 2. no luck

**di·chot·o·my** (dī kät'ə mē) *n., pl.*
**-mies** [ < Gr. *dicha*, in two + *temnein*,
to cut] division into two parts

**dick** (dik) *n.* [Slang] a detective

**Dick·ens** (dik'nz), **Charles** (pseud.
*Boz*) 1812–70; Eng. novelist

**dick·er** (dik'ər) *vi., vt.* [ult. < L.
*decem*, ten] to bargain or haggle

**dick·ey** (dik'ē) *n., pl.* **-eys** [ < nickname *Dick*] 1. a detachable collar or
shirt front 2. a small bird: also **dickey
bird** 3. a back seat in a carriage
Also **dick'y**, *pl.* **-ies**

**di·cot·y·le·don** (dī'kät 'l ēd''n) *n.*
a plant with two seed leaves (cotyle-
dons) —**di'cot·y·le'don·ous** *adj.*

**dict.** 1. dictator 2. dictionary

**Dic·ta·phone** (dik'tə fōn') [DICTA-
(TE) + -PHONE] *a trademark for* a
machine that records and plays back
speech for typed transcripts, etc. —*n.*
this machine

**dic·tate** (dik'tāt; *also for v.* dik tāt')
*vt., vi.* **-tat·ed, -tat·ing** [ < L. *dicere*,
speak] 1. to speak (something) aloud
for someone else to write down 2. to
command expressly 3. to give (orders)
with authority —*n.* an authoritative
order —**dic·ta'tion** *n.*

**dic'ta·tor** *n.* one who dictates; esp.,
a ruler or tyrant with absolute power
—**dic'ta·to'ri·al** (-tə tôr'ē əl) *adj.*
—**dic·ta'tor·ship'** *n.*

**dic·tion** (dik'shən) *n.* [ < L. *dicere*,
say] 1. manner of expression in words;
choice of words 2. enunciation

**dic'tion·ar'y** (-er'ē) *n., pl.* **-ies** [see
prec.] a book of alphabetically listed
words in a language, with definitions,
pronunciations, etc.

**dic·tum** (dik'təm) *n., pl.* **-tums, -ta**

(-tə) [L. < *dicere*, speak] a formal
statement of opinion; pronouncement

**did** (did) *pt. of* DO¹

**di·dac·tic** (dī dak'tik) *adj.* [ < Gr.
*didaskein*, teach] 1. intended for
instruction 2. morally instructive

**did·dle** (did''l) *vt., vi.* **-dled, -dling**
[ < ?] [Colloq.] 1. to cheat 2. to
waste (time) in trifling

**did·n't** (did''nt) did not

**di·do** (dī'dō) *n., pl.* **-does, -dos** [ < ?]
[Colloq.] a mischievous trick; prank

**die¹** (dī) *vi.* **died, dy'ing** [ < ON.
*deyja*] 1. to stop living 2. to stop
functioning; end 3. to lose force or
activity 4. [Colloq.] to wish very much
[I'm *dying* to go] —**die away** (or
**down**) to cease gradually —**die off** to
die one by one until all are gone —**die
out** to stop existing

**die²** (dī) *n., pl.,* for 2, **dies** (dīz) [ < L.
*dare*, give] 1. *sing.* of DICE 2. a tool
for shaping, punching, etc. metal or
other material

**die'hard'** *n.* a person stubbornly resistant to new ideas, reform, etc.

**diel·drin** (dēl'drin) *n.* [*Diel*(*s-Al*)*d*-
(*e*)*r reaction* + -IN¹] a highly toxic
insecticide

**di·e·lec·tric** (dī'ə lek'trik) *n.* [ <
*dia-*, across + ELECTRIC] a material
that does not conduct electricity

**di·er·e·sis** (dī er'ə sis) *n., pl.* **-ses'**
(-sēz') [ < Gr. *dia-*, apart + *hairein*,
to take] a mark (¨) placed over the
second of two consecutive vowels to
show that it is pronounced separately

**die·sel** (dē'z'l, -s'l) *n.* [ < R. *Diesel*,
Ger. inventor] [*often* D-] an internal-
combustion engine that burns oil
ignited by the heat from air compression: also **diesel engine** (or **motor**)

**di·et¹** (dī'ət) *n.* [ < Gr. *diaita*, way of
life] 1. what a person or animal
usually eats or drinks 2. a regimen of
special or limited food and drink, as to
lose weight —*vi., vt.* to adhere to or
place on a diet —**di'e·tar'y** (-ə ter'ē)
*adj.* —**di'et·er.** *n.*

**di·et²** (dī'ət) *n.* [ < ML. *dieta*] a
formal assembly

**di'e·tet'ic** (-ə tet'ik) *adj.* of or for a
particular diet of food and drink

**di'e·tet'ics** (-ə tet'iks) *n.pl.* [*with sing.
v.*] the study of the kinds and quantities of food needed for health

**di'e·ti'tian, di'e·ti'cian** (-tish'ən)
*n.* a specialist in dietetics

**dif–** (dif) *same as* DIS-: used before *f*

**dif·fer** (dif'ər) *vi.* [ < L. *dis-*, apart
+ *ferre*, carry] 1. to be different 2. to
be of a different opinion; disagree

**dif·fer·ence** (dif'ər əns, dif'rəns) *n.*
1. a being different 2. the way in
which people or things are different 3.
a differing in opinion; disagreement 4.
a quarrel 5. the amount by which one
quantity is less than another

**dif'fer·ent** *adj.* 1. not alike 2. not
the same 3. various 4. unusual —
**dif'fer·ent·ly** *adv.*

**dif'fer·en'tial** (-ə ren'shəl) *adj.* of,
showing, or constituting a difference
—*n.* 1. a differentiating amount,
degree, etc. 2. a differential gear
3. *Math.* an infinitesimal difference

between values of a variable quantity

**dif·fer·en·ti·al gear** (or **gearing**) a gear arrangement allowing one axle to turn faster than the other

**dif·fer·en·ti·ate** (-ren'shē āt') *vt.* **-at'ed, -at'ing** 1. to constitute a difference in or between 2. to make unlike 3. to distinguish between —*vi.* 1. to become different or differentiated 2. to note a difference —**dif'fer·en'ti·a'tion** *n.*

**dif·fi·cult** (dif'i kəlt, -kult') *adj.* 1. hard to do, understand, etc. 2. hard to satisfy, deal with, etc.

**dif·fi·cul'ty** *n., pl.* **-ties** [< L. *dis-*, not + *facilis*, easy] 1. a being difficult 2. something difficult; problem, obstacle, or objection 3. trouble

**dif·fi·dent** (dif'ə dənt) *adj.* [< L. *dis-*, not + *fidere*, to trust] lacking self-confidence; shy —**dif'fi·dence** *n.*

**dif·frac·tion** (di frak'shən) *n.* [< L. *dis-*, apart + *frangere*, to break] 1. the breaking up of a ray of light into dark and light bands or into the colors of the spectrum 2. a similar breaking up of other waves, as of sound

**dif·fuse** (di fyoos'; *for v.* -fyooz') *adj.* [< L. *dis-*, apart + *fundere*, pour] 1. spread out; not concentrated 2. using more words than are needed —*vt., vi.* **-fused', -fus'ing** to pour in every direction; spread widely —**dif·fuse'ly** *adv.* —**dif·fuse'ness** *n.* —**dif·fu'sion** *n.* —**dif·fu'sive** *adj.*

**dig** (dig) *vt.* **dug, dig'ging** [< OFr. < Du. *dijk*, dike] 1. to turn up or remove (ground, etc.) as with a spade, the hands, etc. 2. to make (a hole, etc.) by digging 3. to get out by digging 4. to find out, as by careful study 5. to jab 6. [Slang] *a)* to understand *b)* to like —*vi.* to excavate —*n.* 1. *a)* [Colloq.] a poke, nudge, etc. *b)* a taunt 2. an archaeological excavation —**dig'ger** *n.*

**di·gest** (di'jest; *for v.* di jest', di-) *n.* [< L. *di-*, apart + *gerere*, to bear] a collection of condensed, systematic information; summary —*vt.* 1. to summarize 2. to change (food taken into the body) into an absorbable form 3. to absorb mentally —*vi.* to undergo digestion —**di·gest'i·ble** *adj.*

**di·ges'tion** *n.* 1. a digesting or being digested 2. the ability to digest —**di·ges'tive** *adj.*

**dig·it** (dij'it) *n.* [< L. *digitus*] 1. a finger or toe 2. any number from 0 to 9 —**dig'it·al** *adj.*

**digital clock** (or **watch**) a timepiece that shows the time in a row of digits

**digital computer** a computer using numbers to perform calculations

**dig·i·tal·is** (dij'ə tal'is) *n.* [ModL., foxglove: see DIGIT] 1. a plant with long spikes of thimblelike flowers; foxglove 2. a medicine made from the leaves of the purple foxglove, used as a heart stimulant

**dig·ni·fied** (dig'nə fīd') *adj.* having or showing dignity

**dig·ni·fy** (dig'nə fī') *vt.* **-fied', -fy'ing** [< L. *dignus*, worthy + *facere*, to make] to give dignity to; exalt

**dig·ni·tar'y** (-ter'ē) *n., pl.* **-ies** [< L. *dignitas*, dignity + -ARY] a person holding a high position

**dig·ni·ty** (-tē) *n., pl.* **-ties** [< L. *dignus*, worthy] 1. honorable quality; worthiness 2. high repute or honor, or the degree of this 3. a high position, rank, or title 4. stately appearance or manner 5. self-respect

**di·graph** (dī'graf) *n.* a combination of two letters to express a simple sound, as *sh* in *show*

**di·gress** (di gress', dī-) *vi.* [< L. *dis-*, apart + *gradi*, to go] to turn aside, esp. from the main subject, in talking or writing —**di·gres'sion** (-gresh'ən) *n.* —**di·gres'sive** *adj.*

**Di·jon mustard** (dē zhōn') [after *Dijon*, city in France] a mild mustard paste blended with white wine

**dike** (dīk) *n.* [OE. *dic*, ditch] an embankment or dam made to prevent flooding by the sea or by a stream

**di·lap·i·dat·ed** (di lap'ə dāt'id) *adj.* [< L. *dis-*, apart + *lapidare*, throw stones at] falling to pieces; broken down —**di·lap'i·da'tion** *n.*

**di·late** (dī lāt', di-) *vt., vi.* **-lat'ed, -lat'ing** [< L. *dis-*, apart + *latus*, wide] 1. to make or become wider or larger 2. to speak or write at length (*on* or *upon* a subject) —**di·la'tion, dil·a·ta·tion** (dil'ə tā'shən) *n.*

**dil·a·to·ry** (dil'ə tôr'ē) *adj.* [see prec.] 1. causing delay 2. inclined to delay; slow; tardy

**di·lem·ma** (di lem'ə) *n.* [< LGr. *di-*, two + *lēmma*, proposition] any situation requiring a choice between unpleasant alternatives

**dil·et·tante** (dil'ə tänt', -tän'tē, -tan'tē) *n., pl.* **-tantes', -tan'ti** (-tän'tē) [It. < L. *delectare*, to delight] one who dabbles in art, literature, etc. in a superficial way —**dil'et·tant'ish** *adj.* —**dil'et·tant'ism** *n.*

**dil·i·gent** (dil'ə jənt) *adj.* [< L. *di-*, apart + *legere*, choose] 1. persevering and careful in work; hard-working 2. done carefully —**dil'i·gence** *n.* —**dil'i·gent·ly** *adv.*

**dill** (dil) *n.* [OE. *dile*] a plant of the parsley family, with aromatic leaves and seeds, used to flavor pickles, etc.

**dil·ly** (dil'ē) *n.* [? < DEL(IGHTFUL) + -Y] [Slang] a remarkable person or thing

**dil·ly·dal·ly** (dil'ē dal'ē) *vi.* **-lied, -ly·ing** [redupl. form of DALLY] to waste time by hesitating; loiter or dawdle

**di·lute** (di loot', dī-) *vt.* **-lut'ed, -lut'ing** [< L. *dis-*, off + *lavere*, to wash] to thin down or weaken as by mixing with water —*adj.* diluted —**di·lu'tion** *n.*

**dim** (dim) *adj.* **dim'mer, dim'mest** [OE.] 1. not bright, clear, or distinct; dull, obscure, etc. 2. not clearly seeing, hearing, or understanding —*vt., vi.*

**dimmed, dim′ming** to make or grow dim —**dim′ly** adv. —**dim′ness** n.

**dim.** 1. diminuendo 2. diminutive

**dime** (dīm) n. [< L. *decem*, ten] a U.S. and Canadian 10-cent coin

**di·men·sion** (də men′shən) n. [< L. *dis*-, off + *metiri*, to measure] 1. any measurable extent, as length, width, etc. 2. [*pl.*] measurements in length, width, and often depth 3. [*often pl.*] extent; scope —**di·men′sion·al** adj.

**dime store** same as FIVE-AND-TEN-CENT STORE

**di·min·ish** (də min′ish) vt., vi. [< L. *deminuere*, reduce] to make or become smaller in size, degree, importance, etc.; lessen —**dim·i·nu·tion** (dim′ə nyōō′shən, -nōō′-) n.

**di·min·u·en·do** (də min′yōō wen′dō) adj., adv. [It.: see prec.] *Music* with gradually diminishing volume

**di·min·u·tive** (də min′yoo tiv) adj. [see DIMINISH] very small; tiny —n. a word having a suffix that expresses smallness, endearment, etc.

**dim·i·ty** (dim′ə tē) n., pl. -ties [< Gr. *dis*-, two + *mitos*, a thread] a thin, strong, corded cotton cloth

**dim′mer** n. a device for dimming electric lights

**dim·ple** (dim′p'l) n. [ME. *dimpel*] a small, natural hollow, as on the cheek or chin —vi., vt. -pled, -pling to form dimples (in) —**dim′ply** (-plē) adj.

**dim′wit′** n. [Slang] a stupid person; simpleton —**dim′wit′ted** adj.

**din** (din) n. [OE. *dyne*] a loud, continuous noise; confused uproar —vt. **dinned, din′ning** 1. to beset with a din 2. to repeat insistently or noisily

**din-din** (din′din′) n. [Colloq.] dinner

**dine** (dīn) vi. **dined, din′ing** [ult. < L. *dis*-, away + *jejunus*, fasting] to eat dinner —vt. to provide dinner for

**din·er** (dī′nər) n. 1. a person eating dinner 2. a railroad car equipped to serve meals 3. a small restaurant built to look like such a car

**din·ette** (dī net′) n. an alcove or small space used as a dining room

**ding** (diŋ) n. [< Scand.] the sound of a bell: also **ding′-dong′** (-dôŋ′)

**din·ghy** (diŋ′gē, diŋ′ē) n., pl. -ghies [Hind. *ḍiṅgī*] any of various small boats, as a ship's tender

**din·gle** (diŋ′g'l) n. [ME. *dingel*, abyss] a small, deep, wooded valley

**din·go** (diŋ′gō) n., pl. -goes [native name] the Australian wild dog, usually tawny in color

**ding·us** (diŋ′əs) n. [< Du. *ding*, thing] [Colloq.] any device; gadget

**din·gy** (din′jē) adj. -gi·er, -gi·est [orig. dial. var. < DUNG] 1. not clean or bright; grimy 2. dismal; shabby —**din′gi·ness** n.

**din·ky** (diŋ′kē) adj. -ki·er, -ki·est [< Scot. *dink*, trim] [Colloq.] small

**din·ner** (din′ər) n. [see DINE] 1. the chief meal of the day 2. a banquet honoring a person or event

**din′ner·ware′** (-wer′) n. 1. plates, cups, saucers, etc., collectively 2. a set of such dishes

**di·no·saur** (dī′nə sôr′) n. [< Gr. *deinos*, terrible + *sauros*, lizard] a prehistoric, extinct reptile, often huge

DINOSAUR

**dint** (dint) n. [OE. *dynt*] 1. force; exertion 2. a dent

**di·o·cese** (dī′ə sis, -sēs′) n. [< Gr. *dioikein*, keep house] the district under a bishop's jurisdiction —**di·oc′e·san** (-äs′ə s'n) adj.

**di·ode** (dī′ōd) n. [DI-] + -ODE] an electron tube used esp. as a rectifier

**Di·og·e·nes** (dī äj′ə nēz′) 412?–323? B.C.; Gr. philosopher

**Di·o·ny·sus, Di·o·ny·sos** (dī′ə nī′səs) *Gr. Myth.* the god of wine

**di·o·ra·ma** (dī′ə ram′ə) n. [< Gr. *dia*-, through + *horama*, a view] a scenic display, as of three-dimensional figures against a painted background

**di·ox·ide** (dī äk′sīd) n. an oxide with two atoms of oxygen per molecule

**dip** (dip) vt. **dipped, dip′ping** [OE. *dyppan*] 1. to immerse briefly 2. to scoop (liquid) up or out 3. to lower (a flag, etc.) and immediately raise again —vi. 1. to plunge into a liquid and quickly come out 2. to sink suddenly 3. to decline slightly 4. to slope down 5. to lower a container, the hand, etc. as into water 6. to read or inquire superficially (with *into*) —n. 1. a dipping or being dipped 2. a brief plunge into water, etc. 3. a liquid, sauce, etc. into which something is dipped 4. whatever is removed by dipping 5. a downward slope or plunge

**diph·the·ri·a** (dif thir′ē ə, dip-) n. [< Gr. *diphthera*, leather] an acute infectious disease marked by high fever and difficult breathing

**diph·thong** (dif′thôŋ, dip′-) n. [< Gr. *di*-, two + *phthongos*, sound] a sound made by gliding from one vowel to another in one syllable, as in *oil*

**di·plo·ma** (di plō′mə) n. [< Gr. *diplōma*, folded letter] a certificate issued by a school, college, etc. indicating graduation or conferring a degree

**di·plo·ma·cy** (-sē) n., pl. -cies [see ff.] 1. the conducting of relations between nations 2. tact

**dip·lo·mat** (dip′lə mat′) n. 1. a representative of a government who conducts relations with another government 2. a tactful person

**dip′lo·mat′ic** adj. 1. of diplomacy 2. tactful —**dip′lo·mat′i·cal·ly** adv.

**di·pole** (antenna) (dī′pōl′) a straight, level antenna separated at its center by a line to a transmitter or receiver

**dip·per** (dip′ər) n. 1. a long-handled cup, etc. for dipping 2. [D-] either of two groups of stars in the shape of a dipper (**Big Dipper, Little Dipper**)

**dip·so·ma·ni·a** (dip′sə mā′nē ə) n. [< Gr. *dipsa*, thirst + *mania*, madness] an abnormal craving for alcoholic drink —**dip′so·ma′ni·ac′** (-ak′) n.

**dip′stick′** n. a graduated rod for measuring quantity or depth

**dire** (dīr) *adj.* **dir′er, dir′est** [L. *dirus*] **1.** dreadful; terrible: also **dire′-ful 2.** urgent [*dire* need]

**di·rect** (di rekt′, dī-) *adj.* [< L. *di-*, apart + *regere*, to rule] **1.** not round-about or interrupted; straight **2.** honest; frank **3.** with nothing be-tween; immediate **4.** in unbroken line of descent; lineal **5.** exact; complete [the *direct* opposite] **6.** in the exact words [a *direct* quote] —*vt.* **1.** to manage; guide **2.** to order; command **3.** to turn or point; aim; head **4.** to tell (a person) the way to a place **5.** to address (a letter, etc.) **6.** to supervise the action and effects of (a play, etc.) —*adv.* directly —**di·rect′ness** *n.*

**direct current** an electric current flowing in one direction

**di·rec·tion** (də rek′shən, dī-) *n.* **1.** a directing **2.** [*usually pl.*] instructions for doing, using, etc. **3.** a command **4.** the point toward which something faces or the line along which it moves or lies —**di·rec′tion·al** *adj.*

**di·rec·tive** (-tiv) *adj.* directing —*n.* a general order issued authoritatively

**di·rect·ly** *adv.* **1.** in a direct way or line; straight **2.** with nothing coming between **3.** exactly [*directly* opposite] **4.** instantly; right away

**direct object** the word or words that denote the receiver of the action of a verb (Ex.: *me* in he *hit* me)

**di·rec·tor** *n.* one who directs a school, corporation, etc. or a play, choir, etc. —**di·rec′tor·ship′** *n.*

**di·rec′to·ry** (-tə rē) *n., pl.* **-ries** a book listing the names, addresses, etc. of a specific group of persoon

**dirge** (durj) *n.* [< L. *dirige* (direct), first word of a prayer] a song, poem, etc. of grief or mourning

**dir·i·gi·ble** (dir′i jə b'l) *n.* [see DIRECT & -IBLE] *same as* AIRSHIP

**dirk** (durk) *n.* [< ?] a short dagger

**dirn·dl** (durn′d'l) *n.* [< G. *dirne*, girl] a full skirt gathered at the waist

**dirt** (durt) *n.* [< ON. *drit*, excre-ment] **1.** any unclean matter, as mud, trash, etc.; filth **2.** earth; soil **3.** dirtiness, corruption, etc. **4.** obscenity **5.** malicious gossip

**dirt′-cheap′** *adj., adv.* [Colloq.] very inexpensive

**dirt′y** *adj.* **-i·er, -i·est 1.** not clean **2.** obscene **3.** contemptible or nasty **4.** unfair; dishonest **5.** rough, as weather —*vt., vi.* **-ied, -y·ing** to make or become dirty —**dirt′i·ness** *n.*

**dis-** [< L.] *a prefix meaning* separa-tion, negation, reversal [*disjoint, dis-honest, disown*]

**dis·a·bil·i·ty** (dis′ə bil′ə tē) *n., pl.* **-ties 1.** a disabled condition **2.** that which disables or disqualifies

**dis·a′ble** (-ā′b'l) *vt.* **-bled, -bling** to make unable, unfit, or disqualified

**dis·a·buse** (dis′ə byōōz′) *vt.* **-bused′, -bus′ing** to rid of false ideas

**dis·ad·van·tage** (dis′əd van′tij) *n.* **1.** an unfavorable situation or circum-stance **2.** detriment —**dis·ad′van-ta′geous** (-ad′vən tā′jəs) *adj.*

**dis′ad·van′taged** *adj.* underprivi-leged

**dis·af·fect** (dis′ə fekt′) *vt.* to make unfriendly, discontented, or disloyal —**dis·af·fec′tion** *n.*

**dis·af·fil·i·ate** (-ə fil′ē āt′) *vt., vi.* **-at′ed, -at′ing** to end an affiliation (with) —**dis·af·fil′i·a′tion** *n.*

**dis·a·gree** (-ə grē′) *vi.* **-greed′, -gree′ing 1.** to fail to agree; differ **2.** to differ in opinion; quarrel **3.** to give distress (with *with*) —**dis′a-gree′ment** *n.*

**dis·a·gree·a·ble** *adj.* **1.** unpleasant; offensive **2.** quarrelsome —**dis′a-gree′a·bly** *adv.*

**dis·al·low** (dis′ə lou′) *vt.* to refuse to allow (a claim, etc.); reject

**dis·ap·pear** (-ə pir′) *vi.* **1.** to cease to be seen; vanish **2.** to cease existing —**dis′ap·pear′ance** *n.*

**dis·ap·point** (-ə point′) *vt.* to fail to satisfy the hopes or expectations of —**dis′ap·point′ment** *n.*

**dis·ap·pro·ba·tion** (dis ap′rə bā′shən) *n.* a disapproving; disapproval

**dis·ap·prove** (dis′ə prōōv′) *vt., vi.* **-proved′, -prov′ing 1.** to have or express an unfavorable opinion (of) **2.** to refuse to approve —**dis′ap-prov′al** *n.* —**dis′ap·prov′ing·ly** *adv.*

**dis·arm** (dis ärm′) *vt.* **1.** to take away weapons from **2.** to make harm-less **3.** to make friendly —*vi.* to reduce armed forces and armaments —**dis-ar′ma·ment** (-är′mə mənt) *n.*

**dis·ar·range** (dis′ə rānj′) *vt.* **-ranged′, -rang′ing** to undo the order of —**dis′ar·range′ment** *n.*

**dis·ar·ray** (-ə rā′) *vt.* to throw into disorder —*n.* disorder

**dis·as·sem′ble** (-ə sem′b'l) *vt.* **-bled, -bling** to take apart

**dis·as·so′ci·ate** (-ə sō′shē āt′, -sē-) *vt.* **-at′ed, -at′ing** to sever associa-tion with; dissociate

**dis·as·ter** (di zas′tər) *n.* [< L. *dis-* + *astrum*, a star] any happening that causes great harm or damage; calamity —**dis·as′trous** (-trəs) *adj.*

**dis·a·vow** (dis′ə vou′) *vt.* to deny any knowledge of or responsibility for; disclaim —**dis′a·vow′al** *n.*

**dis·band** (dis band′) *vi., vt.* to break up, as an organization

**dis·bar′** (-bär′) *vt.* **-barred′, -bar′-ring** to deprive (a lawyer) of the right to practice law —**dis·bar′ment** *n.*

**dis·be·lieve** (dis′bə lēv′) *vt., vi.* **-lieved′, -liev′ing** to refuse to believe —**dis′be·lief′** (-lēf′) *n.*

**dis·burse** (dis burs′) *vt.* **-bursed′, -burs′ing** [< OFr. *desbourser*] to pay out; expend —**dis·burse′ment** *n.*

**disc** (disk) *n.* **1.** *same as* DISK **2.** a phonograph record

**dis·card** (dis kärd′; *for n.* dis′kärd) *vt.* [< OFr.: see DIS- & CARD[1]] **1.** Card Games to throw away (undesired cards) **2.** to get rid of as no longer useful —*n.* **1.** a discarding or being discarded **2.** something discarded

**disc brake** a brake, as on an automobile, with two friction pads that press on a disc rotating along with the wheel

**dis·cern** (di surn', -zurn') *vt.* [< L. *dis-*, apart + *cernere*, to separate] to perceive or recognize clearly —**dis·cern'i·ble** *adj.* —**dis·cern'ment** *n.*

**dis·cern'ing** *adj.* having good judgment; astute —**dis·cern'ing·ly** *adv.*

**dis·charge** (dis chärj'; *for n., usually* dis'chärj) *vt.* -**charged'**, -**charg'ing** [< L. *dis-*, from + *carrus*, wagon] **1.** to release or dismiss **2.** to unload (a cargo) **3.** to shoot (a gun or projectile) **4.** to emit [to *discharge* pus] **5.** to pay (a debt) or perform (a duty) **6.** *Elec.* to remove stored energy from (a battery, etc.) —*vi.* **1.** to get rid of a load, etc. **2.** to go off, as a gun —*n.* **1.** a discharging or being discharged **2.** that which discharges or is discharged

**dis·ci·ple** (di sī'p'l) *n.* [< L. *dis-*, apart + *capere*, to hold] **1.** a pupil or follower of any teacher or school **2.** an early follower of Jesus; esp., one of the Apostles —**dis·ci'ple·ship'** *n.*

**dis·ci·pli·nar·i·an** (dis'ə pli ner'ē ən) *n.* one who believes in or enforces strict discipline

**dis·ci·pline** (dis'ə plin) *n.* [see DISCIPLE] **1.** training that develops self-control, efficiency, etc. **2.** strict control to enforce obedience **3.** orderly conduct **4.** a system of rules, as for a monastic order **5.** treatment that corrects or punishes —*vt.* -**plined**, -**plin·ing 1.** to train; control **2.** to punish —**dis'ci·pli·nar'y** (-pli ner'ē) *adj.*

**disc jockey** one who conducts a radio program of recorded music

**dis·claim** (dis klām') *vt.* **1.** to give up any claim to **2.** to repudiate

**dis·claim'er** *n.* a denial or renunciation, as of responsibility

**dis·close** (dis klōz') *vt.* -**closed'**, -**clos'ing** to uncover; reveal —**dis·clo'sure** (-klō'zhər) *n.*

**dis·co** (dis'kō) *n., pl.* -**cos** *clipped form of* DISCOTHÈQUE

**dis·col·or** *vt., vi.* to change in color by streaking, staining, etc.: Brit. sp. **discolour** —**dis·col'or·a'tion** *n.*

**dis·com·fit** (dis kum'fit) *vt.* [< L. *dis-*, away + *conficere*, prepare] **1.** to frustrate the plans of **2.** to disconcert —**dis·com'fi·ture** (-fi chər) *n.*

**dis·com·fort** *n.* **1.** lack of comfort; uneasiness **2.** anything causing this —*vt.* to cause discomfort

**dis·com·mode** (dis'kə mōd') *vt.* -**mod'ed**, -**mod'ing** [< DIS- + L. *commodare*, make suitable] to cause bother to; inconvenience

**dis'com·pose'** (-kəm pōz') *vt.* -**posed'**, -**pos'ing** to disturb; fluster —**dis'com·po'sure** (-pō'zhər) *n.*

**dis'con·cert'** (-kən surt') *vt.* to upset; embarrass; confuse

**dis'con·nect'** (-kə nekt') *vt.* to break the connection of; separate —**dis'con·nec'tion** *n.*

**dis'con·nect'ed** *adj.* **1.** separated **2.** incoherent

**dis·con·so·late** (dis kän'sə lit) *adj.* [see DIS- & CONSOLE[1]] inconsolable; dejected —**dis·con'so·late·ly** *adv.*

**dis·con·tent** (dis'kən tent') *adj. same as* DISCONTENTED —*n.* dissatisfaction with one's situation: also **dis'con·tent'ment** —*vt.* to make discontented

**dis'con·tent'ed** *adj.* not contented; wanting something more or different

**dis·con·tin·ue** (dis'kən tin'yōō) *vt., vi.* -**ued**, -**u·ing** to stop; cease; give up —**dis'con·tin'u·ance**, **dis'con·tin'u·a'tion** *n.*

**dis·con·tin·u·ous** *adj.* not continuous; having interruptions or gaps

**dis·cord** (dis'kôrd) *n.* [< L. *dis-*, apart + *cor*, heart] **1.** disagreement **2.** a harsh noise **3.** a lack of musical harmony —**dis·cord'ant** *adj.*

**dis·co·thèque** (dis'kə tek) *n.* [Fr.] a place for dancing to recorded music

**dis·count** (dis'kount; *for v. also* dis kount') *n.* [see DIS- & COMPUTE] **1.** a reduction from the usual or list price **2.** the rate of interest charged on a discounted bill —*vt.* **1.** to pay or receive the value of (a bill, promissory note, etc.) minus a deduction for interest **2.** to deduct an amount from (a bill, price, etc.) **3.** to sell at less than the regular price **4.** *a)* to allow for exaggeration, bias, etc. in (a story, etc.) *b)* to disregard **5.** to lessen the effect of by anticipating

**dis·coun·te·nance** (dis kount'ə nəns) *vt.* -**nanced**, -**nanc·ing 1.** to make ashamed or embarrassed; disconcert **2.** to refuse approval or support to

**discount house** (or **store**) a retail store that sells goods for less than regular prices

**dis·cour·age** (dis kur'ij) *vt.* -**aged**, -**ag·ing 1.** to deprive of courage or confidence **2.** to persuade (a person) to refrain **3.** to try to prevent by disapproving —**dis·cour'age·ment** *n.*

**dis·course** (dis'kôrs; *for v., usually* dis kôrs') *n.* [< L. *dis-*, from + *currere*, to run] **1.** talk; conversation **2.** a formal treatment of a subject, spoken or written —*vi.* -**coursed'**, -**cours'ing** to talk

**dis·cour·te·ous** (dis kur'tē əs) *adj.* impolite; ill-mannered

**dis·cour·te·sy** (-tə sē) *n.* **1.** lack of courtesy; rudeness **2.** *pl.* -**sies** a rude or impolite act or remark

**dis·cov·er** (dis kuv'ər) *vt.* [see DIS- & COVER] **1.** to be the first to find out, see, etc. **2.** to learn the existence of —**dis·cov'er·er** *n.*

**dis·cov'er·y** *n., pl.* -**ies 1.** a discovering **2.** anything discovered

**dis·cred·it** (dis kred'it) *vt.* **1.** to disbelieve **2.** to cast doubt on **3.** to disgrace —*n.* **1.** loss of belief; doubt **2.** disgrace —**dis·cred'it·a·ble** *adj.*

**dis·creet** (dis krēt') *adj.* [see DISCERN] careful about what one says or does; prudent —**dis·creet'ly** *adv.*

**dis·crep·an·cy** (dis krep'ən sē) *n., pl.* -**cies** [< L. *dis-*, from + *crepare*, to rattle] disagreement; inconsistency

**dis·crete** (dis krēt') *adj.* [see DISCERN] separate and distinct; unrelated

**dis·cre·tion** (dis kresh'ən) *n.* **1.** the freedom to make decisions **2.** the quality of being discreet; prudence —**dis·cre'tion·ar'y** (-er'ē) *adj.*

**dis·crim·i·nate** (dis krim' nāt') *vi.* -**nat'ed, -nat'ing** [see DISCERN] **1.** to distinguish **2.** to make distinctions in treatment; show partiality or prejudice —**dis·crim'i·nat'ing** *adj.* —**dis·crim'i·na'tion** *n.*

**dis·crim·i·na·to·ry** (-nə tôr'ē) *adj.* showing discrimination or bias

**dis·cur·sive** (dis kur'siv) *adj.* [see DISCOURSE] wandering from one topic to another; rambling

**dis·cus** (dis'kəs) *n.* [< Gr. *diskos*] a disk, as of metal and wood, thrown in a contest of strength and skill

**dis·cuss** (dis kus') *vt.* [< L. *dis-*, apart + *quatere*, to shake] to talk or write about; consider the pros and cons of —**dis·cus'sion** (-kush'ən) *n.*

**dis·cus·sant** (-ənt) *n.* a participant in an organized discussion

**dis·dain** (dis dān') *vt.* [< L. *dis-*, not + *dignari*, deign] to regard as beneath one's dignity; scorn —*n.* aloof contempt —**dis·dain'ful** *adj.*

**dis·ease** (di zēz') *n.* [< OE. *des*, dis- + *aise*, ease] **1.** illness in general **2.** a particular destructive process in an organism; specif., an illness —**dis·eased'** *adj.*

**dis·em·bark** (dis'im bärk') *vi.*, *vt.* to leave, or unload from, a ship, aircraft, etc. —**dis'em·bar·ka'tion** *n.*

**dis·em·bod·y** (dis'im bäd'ē) *vt.* -**ied, -y·ing** to free from bodily existence —**dis'em·bod'i·ment** *n.*

**dis·em·bow·el** (-im bou'əl) *vt.* -**eled** or -**elled, -el·ing** or -**el·ling** to take out the entrails of

**dis·em·ployed** (dis'im ploid') *adj.* out of work, esp. because of lack of training or education

**dis·en·chant'** (-in chant') *vt.* to free from an enchantment; disillusion —**dis'en·chant'ment** *n.*

**dis·en·cum·ber** (-in kum'bər) *vt.* to relieve of a burden

**dis·en·gage** *vt.*, *vi.* -**gaged', -gag'-ing** to release or get loosed from something that engages, holds, entangles, etc.; unfasten —**dis'en·gage'ment** *n.*

**dis·en·tan·gle** *vt.* -**gled, -gling** to free from something that entangles, confuses, etc.; extricate; untangle

**dis·es·teem'** *n.* lack of esteem

**dis·fa·vor** (dis fā'vər) *n.* **1.** an unfavorable opinion; dislike; disapproval **2.** the state of being disliked, etc.

**dis·fig·ure** (dis fig'yər) *vt.* -**ured, -ur·ing** to hurt the appearance of; mar —**dis·fig'ure·ment** *n.*

**dis·fran·chise** (dis fran'chīz) *vt.* -**chised, -chis·ing** to deprive of a right, privilege, etc., esp. the right to vote; also **dis·en·fran'chise**

**dis·gorge** (-gôrj') *vt.*, *vi.* -**gorged', -gorg'ing** [< OFr.: see DIS- & GORGE] **1.** to vomit **2.** to pour forth (its contents); empty (itself)

**dis·grace'** (-grās') *n.* [< It. *dis-*, not + *grazia*, favor] **1.** loss of favor or respect; shame; disrepute **2.** a person or thing bringing shame —*vt.* -**graced', -grac'ing** to bring shame or dishonor upon —**dis·grace'ful** *adj.*

**dis·grun·tle** (-grun't'l) *vt.* -**tled, -tling** [ult. < DIS- + GRUNT] to make peevishly discontented; make sulky

**dis·guise'** (-gīz') *vt.* -**guised', -guis·ing** [< OFr.: see DIS- & GUISE] **1.** to make appear, sound, etc. so different as to be unrecognizable **2.** to hide the real nature of —*n.* **1.** anything that disguises **2.** a being disguised —**dis·guise'ment** *n.*

**dis·gust'** (-gust') *n.* [< DIS- + L. *gustus*, taste] a sickening dislike —*vt.* to make feel disgust —**dis·gust'ed** *adj.* —**dis·gust'ing** *adj.*

**dish** (dish) *n.* [see DISCUS] **1.** a container, generally shallow and concave, for holding food **2.** as much as a dish holds **3.** a particular kind of food —*vt.* to serve in a dish (with *up* or *out*)

**dis·ha·bille** (dis'ə bēl') *n.* [< Fr. *dés-*, dis- + *habiller*, to dress] the state of being dressed only partially or in night clothes

**dish antenna** a radio antenna with a dish-shaped reflector

**dis·har·mo·ny** (dis här'mə nē) *n.* lack of harmony; discord —**dis'har·mo'ni·ous** (-mō'nē əs) *adj.*

**dish'cloth'** *n.* a cloth for washing dishes; also **dish'rag'**

**dis·heart·en** (dis härt'n) *vt.* to discourage; depress

**di·shev·el** (di shev''l) *vt.* -**eled** or -**elled, -el·ing** or -**el·ling** [< OFr. *des-*, dis- + *chevel*, hair] to cause (hair, clothes, etc.) to become disarranged; rumple —**di·shev'el·ment** *n.*

**dis·hon·est** *adj.* not honest; not to be trusted —**dis·hon'est·ly** *adv.*

**dis·hon·es·ty** *n.* **1.** a being dishonest **2.** *pl.* -**ties** a dishonest act

**dis·hon·or** *n.* **1.** loss of honor or respect; shame; disgrace **2.** a cause of dishonor —*vt.* to insult or disgrace —**dis·hon'or·a·ble** *adj.*

**dish'wash'er** *n.* a person or machine that washes dishes, etc.

**dis·il·lu·sion** *vt.* **1.** to free from illusion **2.** to take away the idealism of and make bitter, etc. —**dis·il·lu'sion·ment** *n.*

**dis·in·cline** (dis'in klīn') *vt.* -**clined', -clin'ing** to make unwilling

**dis·in·fect** (dis'in fekt') *vt.* to destroy the harmful bacteria, viruses, etc. in; sterilize —**dis'in·fect'ant** *n.*

**dis·in·gen·u·ous** (dis'in jen'yoo-wəs) *adj.* not candid or frank

**dis·in·her·it** (dis'in her'it) *vt.* to deprive of an inheritance

**dis·in·te·grate** (dis in'tə grāt') *vt.*, *vi.* -**grat'ed, -grat'ing** to separate into parts or fragments; break up —**dis·in'te·gra'tion** *n.*

**dis·in·ter** (dis'in tur') *vt.* -**terred', -ter'ring** to remove from a grave, etc.

**dis·in·ter·est·ed** (dis in′trist id, -tər ist id) *adj.* 1. impartial; unbiased 2. uninterested; indifferent

**dis·joint′** *vt.* 1. to put out of joint; dislocate 2. to dismember 3. to destroy the unity, connections, etc. of —**dis·joint′ed** *adj.*

**disk** *n.* [see DISCUS] 1. any thin, flat, circular thing 2. *same as* DISC

**dis·like′** *vt.* -liked′, -lik′ing to have a feeling of not liking —*n.* a feeling of not liking; distaste

**dis·lo·cate** (dis′lō kāt′) *vt.* -cat′ed, -cat′ing 1. to displace (a bone) from its proper position 2. to disarrange; disrupt —**dis′lo·ca′tion** *n.*

**dis·lodge′** *vt., vi.* -lodged′, -lodg′ing to force from or leave a place where lodged, hiding, etc.

**dis·loy′al** *adj.* not loyal or faithful —**dis·loy′al·ty** *n., pl.* -ties

**dis·mal** (diz′m'l) *adj.* [< ML. *dies mali,* evil days] 1. causing gloom or misery 2. dark and gloomy; dreary

**dis·man·tle** (dis man′t'l) *vt.* -tled, -tling [see DIS- & MANTLE] 1. to strip (a house, etc.) as of furniture 2. to take apart —**dis·man′tle·ment** *n.*

**dis·may′** (-mā′) *vt.* [< Anglo-Fr.] to make afraid at the prospect of trouble; daunt —*n.* consternation

**dis·mem′ber** (-mem′bər) *vt.* [see DIS- & MEMBER] 1. to cut or tear the limbs from 2. to pull or cut to pieces —**dis·mem′ber·ment** *n.*

**dis·miss′** (-mis′) *vt.* [< L. *dis-,* from + *mittere,* send] 1. to cause or allow to leave 2. to discharge from an office, employment, etc. 3. to put aside mentally —**dis·miss′al** *n.*

**dis·mount′** *vi.* to get off, as from a horse —*vt.* 1. to remove (a thing) from its mounting 2. to take apart

**dis·o·be·di·ence** (dis′ə bē′dē əns) *n.* refusal to obey; insubordination —**dis′o·be′di·ent** *adj.*

**dis′o·bey′** *vt., vi.* to refuse or fail to obey

**dis′o·blige′** *vt.* -bliged′, -blig′ing 1. to refuse to oblige 2. to offend

**dis·or′der** *n.* 1. a lack of order; confusion 2. a breach of public peace; riot 3. an upset of normal function; ailment —*vt.* 1. to throw into disorder 2. to upset the normal functions of

**dis·or′der·ly** *adj.* 1. not orderly; untidy 2. unruly; riotous 3. violating public peace, safety, etc. —**dis·or′der·li·ness** *n.*

**dis·or′gan·ize** (dis ôr′gə nīz′) *vt.* -ized′, -iz′ing to break up the order or system of; throw into confusion —**dis·or′gan·i·za′tion** *n.*

**dis·o′ri·ent′** (-ôr′ē ent′) *vt.* [see DIS- & ORIENT, *v.*] 1. to cause to lose one's bearings 2. to confuse mentally

**dis·own′** *vt.* to refuse to acknowledge as one's own; repudiate

**dis·par·age** (dis par′ij) *vt.* -aged, -ag·ing [< OFr. *des-* (see DIS-) + *parage,* rank] 1. to discredit 2. to belittle —**dis·par′age·ment** *n.*

**dis·pa·rate** (dis′pər it) *adj.* [< L. *dis-,* not + *par,* equal] distinct or different in kind; unequal —**dis·par′i·ty** (-par′ə tē) *n., pl.* -ties

**dis·pas·sion·ate** *adj.* free from passion or bias; calm; impartial —**dis·pas′sion·ate·ly** *adv.*

**dis·patch** (dis pach′) *vt.* [< L. *dis-,* away + *pes,* foot] 1. to send promptly, as on an errand 2. to kill 3. to finish quickly —*n.* 1. a sending off 2. a killing 3. speed; promptness 4. a message 5. a news story sent to a newspaper, radio station, etc. —**dis·patch′er** *n.*

**dis·pel** (dis pel′) *vt.* -pelled′, -pel′ling [< L. *dis-,* apart + *pellere,* to drive] to scatter and drive away

**dis·pen·sa·ble** (dis pen′sə b'l) *adj.* 1. that can be dealt out 2. that can be dispensed with; not important

**dis·pen·sa·ry** (-sə rē) *n., pl.* -ries a room or place where medicines and first-aid treatment are available

**dis·pen·sa·tion** (dis′pən sā′shən) *n.* 1. a dispensing 2. anything distributed 3. an administrative system 4. a release from an obligation 5. *Theol. a)* the ordering of events under divine authority *b)* any religious system

**dis·pense** (dis pens′) *vt.* -pensed′, -pens′ing [< L. *dis-,* out + *pendere,* weigh] 1. to give out; distribute 2. to prepare and give out (medicines) 3. to administer (the law or justice) —**dispense with** 1. to get rid of 2. to do without —**dis·pen′ser** *n.*

**dis·perse′** (-purs′) *vt.* -persed′, -pers′ing [< L. *dis-,* out + *spargere,* strew] 1. to break up and scatter 2. to dispel (mist, etc.) —*vi.* to scatter —**dis·per′sal** *n.* —**dis·per′sion** *n.*

**dis·pir·it** (di spir′it) *vt.* to depress; discourage —**dis·pir′it·ed** *adj.*

**dis·place′** *vt.* -placed′, -plac′ing 1. to move from its usual place 2. to remove from office 3. to replace

**displaced person** one forced from his country, esp. as a result of war, and left homeless elsewhere

**dis·place′ment** *n.* 1. a displacing or being displaced 2. the weight or volume of air, water, or other fluid displaced by a floating object

**dis·play** (dis plā′) *vt.* [< L. *dis-,* apart + *plicare,* to fold] 1. to unfold; spread out 2. to exhibit —*n.* 1. an exhibition 2. anything displayed

**dis·please′** *vt., vi.* -pleased′, -pleas′ing to fail to please; offend

**dis·pleas′ure** (-plezh′ər) *n.* a being displeased; dissatisfaction

**dis·port** (dis pôrt′) *vi.* [< OFr. *des-* (see DIS-) + *porter,* carry] to play; frolic —*vt.* to amuse (oneself)

**dis·pose** (dis pōz′) *vt.* -posed′, -pos′ing [see DIS- & POSITION] 1. to arrange 2. to settle (affairs) 3. to make willing —**dispose of** 1. to settle 2. to give away or sell 3. to get rid of —**dis·pos′a·ble** *adj.* —**dis·pos′al** *n.*

**dis·pos′er** *n.* 1. one that disposes 2. a device in the drain of a kitchen sink for grinding up garbage

**dis·po·si·tion** (dis′pə zish′ən) *n.* 1. arrangement 2. management of affairs 3. a selling or giving away 4. the authority to settle, etc.; control 5. a tendency 6. one's temperament

**dis′pos·sess′** *vt.* to deprive of the

possession of land, a house, etc.; oust

**dis·praise** (dis prāz´) *vt.* -praised´, -prais´ing [< OFr. *despreisier*] to blame; censure —*n.* blame

**dis·pro·por·tion** *n.* a lack of proportion —**dis´pro·por´tion·ate** *adj.*

**dis·prove´** *vt.* -proved´, -prov´ing to prove to be false —**dis·proof´** *n.*

**dis·pu·ta·tion** (dis´pyoo tā´shən) *n.* 1. a disputing 2. debate

**dis´pu·ta´tious** (-pyoo tā´shəs) *adj.* inclined to dispute; contentious —**dis´pu·ta´tious·ly** *adv.*

**dis·pute** (dis pyoot´) *vi.* -put´ed, -put´ing [< L. *dis-*, apart + *putare*, think] 1. to argue; debate 2. to quarrel —*vt.* 1. to argue (a question) 2. to doubt 3. to oppose in any way —*n.* 1. a disputing; debate 2. a quarrel —**in dispute** not settled —**dis·pu´ta·ble** *adj.* —**dis·pu´tant** *adj.*, *n.*

**dis·qual·i·fy´** *vt.* -fied´, -fy´ing to make or declare unqualified, unfit, or ineligible —**dis·qual´i·fi·ca´tion** *n.*

**dis·qui·et** (dis kwī´ət) *vt.* to make uneasy; disturb —*n.* restlessness: also **dis·qui´e·tude´** (-ə tood´)

**dis·qui·si·tion** (dis´kwə zish´ən) *n.* [< L. *dis-*, apart + *quaerere*, seek] a formal discussion; treatise

**dis·re·gard** (dis´ri gärd´) *vt.* 1. to pay little or no attention to 2. to treat without due respect —*n.* 1. lack of attention 2. lack of due regard or respect —**dis´re·gard´ful** *adj.*

**dis·re·pair´** *n.* the condition of needing repairs; state of neglect

**dis·rep´u·ta·ble** *adj.* 1. not reputable 2. not fit to be seen

**dis·re·pute´** *n.* lack or loss of repute; bad reputation; disgrace

**dis·re·spect´** *n.* lack of respect; discourtesy —**dis´re·spect´ful** *adj.*

**dis·robe** (dis rōb´) *vt.*, *vi.* -robed´, -rob´ing to undress

**dis·rupt** (dis rupt´) *vt.*, *vi.* [< L. *dis-*, apart + *rumpere*, to break] 1. to break apart 2. to disturb or interrupt —**dis·rup´tion** *n.* —**dis·rup´tive** *adj.*

**dis·sat·is·fy´** *vt.* -fied´, -fy´ing to fail to satisfy; displease —**dis·sat´is·fac´tion** *n.*

**dis·sect** (di sekt´) *vt.* [< L. *dis-*, apart + *secare*, to cut] 1. to cut apart piece by piece, as a body for purposes of study 2. to analyze closely —**dis·sec´tion** *n.* —**dis·sec´tor** *n.*

**dis·sem·ble** (di sem´b'l) *vt.*, *vi.* -bled, -bling [< OFr. *dessembler*] to conceal the truth; one's feelings, etc.) under a false appearance —**dis·sem´blance** *n.* —**dis·sem´bler** *n.*

**dis·sem·i·nate** (di sem´ə nāt´) *vt.* -nat´ed, -nat´ing [< L. *dis-*, apart + *seminare*, to sow] to scatter about; spread widely —**dis·sem´i·na´tion** *n.*

**dis·sen·sion** (di sen´shən) *n.* a dissenting; disagreement or quarreling

**dis·sent** (di sent´) *vi.* [< L. *dis-*, apart + *sentire*, feel] 1. to disagree 2. to reject the doctrines of an estab-

lished church —*n.* a dissenting —**dis·sent´er** *n.*

**dis·ser·ta·tion** (dis´ər tā´shən) *n.* [< L. *dis-*, apart + *serere*, join] a formal discourse or treatise; thesis

**dis·serv·ice** (dis sur´vis) *n.* harm

**dis·sev·er** (di sev´ər) *vt.* 1. to sever 2. to divide into parts —*vi.* to separate; disunite

**dis·si·dence** (dis´ə dəns) *n.* [< L. *dis-*, apart + *sidere*, sit] disagreement —**dis´si·dent** (-dənt) *adj.*, *n.*

**dis·sim·i·lar** (di sim´ə lər) *adj.* not similar; different —**dis·sim´i·lar´i·ty** (-lar´ə tē) *n.*, *pl.* -ties

**dis·si·mil·i·tude** (dis´si mil´ə tood´) *n.* dissimilarity; difference

**dis·sim·u·late** (di sim´yə lāt´) *vt.*, *vi.* -lat´ed, -lat´ing [see DIS- & SIMULATE] to dissemble —**dis·sim´u·la´tion** *n.* —**dis·sim´u·la´tor** *n.*

**dis·si·pate** (dis´ə pāt´) *vt.* -pat´ed, -pat´ing [< L. *dis-*, apart + *supare*, to throw] 1. to scatter; disperse 2. to make disappear 3. to waste or squander —*vi.* 1. to vanish 2. to indulge in pleasure to the point of harming oneself —**dis´si·pa´tion** *n.*

**dis·so·ci·ate** (di sō´shē āt´) *vt.* -at´ed, -at´ing [< L. *dis-*, apart + *sociare*, join] to break the connection between; disunite —**dis·so´ci·a´tion** *n.*

**dis·so·lute** (dis´ə loot´) *adj.* [see DISSOLVE] dissipated and immoral —**dis´so·lute´ly** *adv.* —**dis´so·lute´ness** *n.*

**dis·so·lu·tion** (dis´ə loo´shən) *n.* a dissolving or being dissolved; specif., *a)* a breaking up or into parts *b)* a termination *c)* death

**dis·solve** (di zälv´, -zôlv´) *vt.*, *vi.* -solved´, -solv´ing [< L. *dis-*, apart + *solvere*, loosen] 1. to make or become liquid; melt 2. to pass or make pass into solution 3. to break up 4. to end as by breaking up 5. to disappear or make disappear

**dis·so·nance** (dis´ə nəns) *n.* [< L. *dis-*, apart + *sonus*, a sound] 1. an inharmonious combination of sounds; discord 2. any lack of harmony or agreement —**dis´so·nant** *adj.*

**dis·suade** (di swād´) *vt.* -suad´ed, -suad´ing [< L. *dis-*, away + *suadere*, persuade] to turn (a person) aside (*from* a course, etc.) by persuasion or advice —**dis·sua´sion** *n.*

**dis·taff** (dis´taf) *n.* [< OE. *dis-*, flax + *stæf*, staff] a staff on which flax, wool, etc. is wound for use in spinning —*adj.* female

**dis·tal** (dis´t'l) *adj.* [DIST(ANT) + -AL] *Anat.* farthest from the point of attachment or origin —**dis´tal·ly** *adv.*

**dis·tance** (dis´təns) *n.* [< L. *dis-*, apart + *stare*, to stand] 1. a being separated in space or time; remoteness 2. an interval between two points in space or time 3. a remoteness in behavior; reserve 4. a faraway place

**dis´tant** (-tənt) *adj.* 1. far away in space or time 2. away ⁄ 100 miles *distant*] 3. far apart in relationship 4. aloof; reserved 5. from or at a distance —**dis'tant·ly** *adv.*

**dis·taste** (dis tāst') *n.* dislike —**dis·taste'ful** *adj.*

**dis·tem·per** (dis tem'pər) *n.* [< ML. *distemperare*, to disorder] an infectious virus disease of young dogs

**dis·tend** (dis tend') *vt., vi.* [< L. *dis-*, apart + *tendere*, to stretch] 1. to stretch out 2. to make or become swollen —**dis·ten'tion** *n.*

**dis·till, dis·til** (dis til') *vi., vt.* -tilled', -till'ing [< L. *de-*, down + *stillare*, to drop] 1. to fall or let fall in drops 2. to undergo, subject to, or produce by distillation —**dis·till'er** *n.*

**dis·til·late** (dis'tə lāt', -t'l it) *n.* a liquid obtained by distilling

**dis·til·la·tion** (dis'tə lā'shən) *n.* 1. the process of heating a mixture and condensing the resulting vapor to produce a more nearly pure substance 2. anything distilled

**dis·till'er·y** *n., pl.* -ies a place where alcoholic liquors are distilled

**dis·tinct** (dis tiŋkt') *adj.* [see DISTINGUISH] 1. not alike 2. separate 3. clearly marked off; plain 4. unmistakable —**dis·tinct'ly** *adv.*

**dis·tinc'tion** (-tiŋk'shən) *n.* 1. the act of making or keeping distinct 2. difference 3. a quality or feature that differentiates 4. fame; eminence 5. the quality that makes one seem superior 6. a mark of honor

**dis·tinc'tive** *adj.* making distinct; characteristic —**dis·tinc'tive·ly** *adv.* —**dis·tinc'tive·ness** *n.*

**dis·tin·guish** (dis tiŋ'gwish) *vt.* [< L. *dis-*, apart + *-stinguere*, to prick] 1. to perceive or show the difference in 2. to characterize 3. to perceive clearly 4. to classify 5. to make famous —*vi.* to make a distinction (*between* or *among*) —**dis·tin'guish·a·ble** *adj.*

**dis·tin'guished** *adj.* celebrated; famous

**dis·tort** (dis tôrt') *vt.* [< L. *dis-*, intens. + *torquere*, to twist] 1. to twist out of shape 2. to misrepresent (facts, etc.) —**dis·tor'tion** *n.*

**dis·tract** (dis trakt') *vt.* [< L. *dis-*, apart + *trahere*, draw] 1. to draw (the mind, etc.) away in another direction; divert 2. to confuse; bewilder —**dis·tract'ed** *adj.* —**dis·tract'ing** *adj.*

**dis·trac'tion** *n.* 1. a distracting or being distracted 2. anything that distracts confusingly or amusingly; diversion 3. great mental distress

**dis·trait** (dis trā') *adj.* [see DISTRACT] absent-minded; inattentive

**dis·traught** (-trôt') *adj.* [var. of prec.] 1. distracted; confused 2. driven mad; crazed

**dis·tress** (dis tres') *vt.* [ult. < L. *dis-*, apart + *stringere*, to stretch] to cause misery or suffering to —*n.* 1. pain, suffering, etc. 2. an affliction 3. a state of danger or trouble

**dis·trib·ute** (dis trib'yoot) *vt.* -ut·ed, -ut·ing [< L. *dis-*, apart + *tribuere*, allot] 1. to give out in shares 2. to spread out 3. to classify 4. to put (things) in various distinct places —**dis'tri·bu'tion** *n.*

**dis·trib'u·tor** *n.* one that distributes; specif., *a*) a dealer who distributes goods to consumers *b*) a device for distributing electric current to the spark plugs of a gasoline engine

**dis·trict** (dis'trikt) *n.* [< L. *dis-*, apart + *stringere*, to stretch] 1. a division of a state, city, etc. made for a specific purpose 2. any region

**district attorney** the prosecuting attorney for the State or the Federal government in a specified district

**District of Columbia** federal district of the U.S., on the Potomac: coextensive with city of Washington

**dis·trust'** *n.* a lack of trust; doubt —*vt.* to have no trust in; doubt —**dis·trust'ful** *adj.*

**dis·turb** (dis turb') *vt.* [< L. *dis-*, intens. + *turbare*, to disorder] 1. to break up the quiet or settled order of 2. to make uneasy; upset 3. to interrupt —**dis·turb'er** *n.*

**dis·turb'ance** *n.* 1. a disturbing or being disturbed 2. anything that disturbs 3. commotion; disorder

**dis·u·nite** (dis'yoo nīt') *vt., vi.* -nit'ed, -nit'ing to divide or separate into parts, factions, etc. —**dis·u'ni·ty** *n.*

**dis·use** (dis yoos') *n.* lack of use

**ditch** (dich) *n.* [OE. *dic*] a long, narrow channel dug into the earth, as for drainage —*vt.* 1. to make a ditch in 2. [Slang] to get rid of

**dith·er** (dith'ər) *n.* [ME. *dideren*] a nervously excited or confused state

**dit·to** (dit'ō) *n., pl.* -tos [It. < L. *dicere*, speak] 1. the same (as above or before) 2. *same as* DITTO MARK

**ditto mark** a mark (") used in lists or tables to show that the item above is to be repeated

**dit·ty** (dit'ē) *n., pl.* -ties [< L. *dicere*, speak] a short, simple song

**di·u·ret·ic** (dī'yoo ret'ik) *adj.* [< Gr. *dia-*, through + *ourein*, urinate] increasing the flow of urine —*n.* a diuretic drug or substance

**di·ur·nal** (dī ur'n'l) *adj.* [< L. *dies*, day] 1. daily 2. of the daytime —**di·ur'nal·ly** *adv.*

**div.** 1. dividend 2. division

**di·va** (dē'və) *n., pl.* -vas; It. -ve (-ve) [It. < L., goddess] *same as* PRIMA DONNA

**di·van** (dī'van, di van') *n.* [< Per. *dīwan*] a large, low couch or sofa

**dive** (dīv) *vi.* dived or dove, dived, div'ing [OE. *dyfan*] 1. to plunge headfirst into water 2. to submerge 3. to plunge suddenly into something 4. to make a steep descent, as an airplane —*n.* 1. a diving 2. any sudden plunge 3. a sharp descent 4. [Colloq.] a cheap, disreputable saloon, etc. —**div'er** *n.*

**di·verge** (də vurj', dī-) *vi.* -verged', -verg'ing [< L. *dis-*, apart + *vergere*, to turn] 1. to go or move in different directions; branch off 2. to differ, as in opinion —**di·ver'gence** *n.* —**di·ver'gent** *adj.*

**di·vers** (dī'vərz) *adj.* [see ff.] various

**di·verse** (dī vurs', də-) *adj.* [< L.

*dis-*, apart + *vertere,* to turn] **1.** different **2.** varied —**di·verse′ly** *adv.*

**di·ver·si·fy** (də vur′sə fī′) *vt.* **-fied′,** **-fy′ing** to make diverse; vary —**di·ver′si·fi·ca′tion** *n.*

**di·ver·sion** (də vur′zhən, dī-) *n.* **1.** a diverting or turning aside **2.** distraction of attention **3.** a pastime —**di·ver′sion·ar′y** *adj.* serving to divert or distract [*diversionary* tactics]

**di·ver·si·ty** (də vur′sə tē, dī-) *n., pl.* **-ties 1.** difference **2.** variety

**di·vert′** (-vurt′) *vt.* [see DIVERSE] **1.** to turn aside (*from* a course) **2.** to amuse

**di·ver·tic·u·li·tis** (dī′vər tik′yoo līt′əs) *n.* [ < L. *de-*, from + *vertere,* to turn + -ITIS] inflammation of a sac (**diverticulum**) opening out from a tubular organ or main cavity

**di·vest′** (-vest′) *vt.* [ < L. *dis-*, from + *vestire,* to dress] **1.** to strip (of clothing, etc.) **2.** to deprive (*of* rank, rights, etc.) **3.** to rid (*of* something unwanted)

**di·vide** (də vīd′) *vt.* **-vid′ed, -vid′ing** [ < L. *dividere*] **1.** to separate into parts; sever **2.** to classify **3.** to make or keep separate **4.** to apportion **5.** to cause to disagree **6.** *Math.* to separate into equal parts by a divisor —*vi.* **1.** to be or become separate **2.** to disagree **3.** to share **4.** *Math.* to do division —*n.* a ridge that divides two drainage areas —**di·vid′er·n.**

**div·i·dend** (div′ə dend) *n.* **1.** the number or quantity to be divided **2.** *a)* a sum to be divided among stockholders, etc. *b)* a single share of this **3.** a bonus

**di·vid′ers** *n.pl.* an instrument for dividing lines, etc.; compasses

**div·i·na·tion** (div′ə nā′shən) *n.* [see ff.] the practice of trying to foretell the future or the unknown

**di·vine** (də vīn′) *adj.* [ < L. *divus,* a god] **1.** of, like, or from God or a god; holy **2.** devoted to God; religious **3.** supremely great, good, etc. —*n.* a clergyman —*vt.* **-vined′, -vin′ing 1.** to prophesy **2.** to guess **3.** to find out by intuition —**di·vine′ly** *adv.*

**divining rod** a forked stick alleged to dip downward when held over an underground supply of water, etc.

**di·vin·i·ty** (də vin′ə tē) *n., pl.* **-ties 1.** a being divine **2.** a god **3.** theology —**the Divinity** God

**di·vis·i·ble** (də viz′ə b'l) *adj.* that can be divided, esp. without leaving a remainder —**di·vis′i·bil′i·ty** *n.*

**di·vi·sion** (də vizh′ən) *n.* **1.** a dividing or being divided **2.** a sharing **3.** a difference of opinion **4.** anything that divides **5.** a segment, section, department, class, etc. **6.** the process of finding how many times a number (the **divisor**) is contained in another (the **dividend**) **7.** a major military unit

**di·vi·sive** (də vī′siv) *adj.* causing disagreement or dissension —**di·vi′sive·ly** *adv.* —**di·vi′sive·ness** *n.*

**di·vi·sor** (də vī′zər) *n.* the number by which the dividend is divided

**di·vorce** (də vôrs′) *n.* [ < L. *dis-*, apart + *vertere,* to turn] **1.** legal dissolution of a marriage **2.** complete separation —*vt.* **-vorced′, -vorc′ing 1.** to dissolve legally a marriage between **2.** to separate from (one's spouse) by divorce **3.** to separate —**di·vorce′ment** *n.*

**di·vor·cée, di·vor·cee** (də vôr′sā′, -sē′) *n.* [Fr.] a divorced woman

**div·ot** (div′ət) *n.* [Scot.] *Golf* a lump of turf dislodged in hitting a ball

**di·vulge** (də vulj′) *vt.* **-vulged′, -vulg′ing** [ < L. *dis-*, apart + *vulgare,* make public] to make known; reveal

**div·vy** (div′ē) *vt., vi.* **-vied, -vy·ing** [Slang] to share; divide (*up*)

**Dix·ie** (dik′sē) [ < *Dixie,* the minstrel song] the Southern States of the U.S.

**Dix′ie·land′** *adj.* in, of, or like a style of jazz with a ragtime tempo

**diz·zy** (diz′ē) *adj.* **-zi·er, -zi·est** [OE. *dysig,* foolish] **1.** feeling giddy or unsteady **2.** causing giddiness **3.** confused **4.** [Colloq.] silly —**diz′zi·ly** *adv.* —**diz′zi·ness** *n.*

**D.J., DJ** disc jockey

**DNA** [ < *d(eoxyribo)n(ucleic)* *a(cid)*] an essential component of all living matter and the basic chromosomal material transmitting the hereditary pattern

**Dne·pr** (nē′pər) river in W U.S.S.R. flowing into the Black Sea

**do¹** (dōō) *vt.* **did, done, do′ing** [OE. *don*] **1.** to perform (an action, etc.) **2.** to finish; complete **3.** to cause [it *does* no harm] **4.** to exert [*do* your best] **5.** to deal with as required [*do* the ironing] **6.** to have as one's occupation; work at **7.** [Colloq.] to cheat **8.** [Colloq.] to serve (a jail term) —*vi.* **1.** to behave [*do* as you please] **2.** to be active [*up* and *doing*] **3.** to get along; fare [how is he *doing?*] **4.** to be adequate [the red hat will *do*] **5.** to take place [anything *doing* tonight?] Auxiliary uses of *do:* **1.** to give emphasis [please *do* stay] **2.** to ask a question [*did* you go?] **3.** to serve as a substitute verb [act as I do (act)] —**do in** [Slang] to kill —**do over** [Colloq.] to redecorate —**do up** [Colloq.] to wrap up —**do with** to make use of —**do without** to get along without —**have to do with** to be related to —**make do** to get along with what is available

**do²** (dō) *n.* [It.] *Music* the first or last tone of the diatonic scale

**do·a·ble** (dōō′ə b'l) *adj.* that can be done

**Do·ber·man pin·scher** (dō′bər mən pin′shər) [ < *Dobermann,* 19th-c. Ger. breeder + G. *pinscher,* terrier] a large dog with short, dark hair

**doc** (däk) *n.* [Slang] doctor

**do·cent** (dō′s'nt) *n.* [ < L. *docere,* to teach] in some American universities, a teacher not on the regular faculty

fat, āpe, cär, ten, ēven; is, bīte; gō, hôrn, tōōl, look; oil, out; up, fur; chin; she; thin, *th*en; zh, leisure; ŋ, ring; ə for *a* in ago; ' (ā'b'l); ë, Fr. coeur; ö, Fr. feu; Fr. mon; ü, Fr. duc; kh, G. ich; doch. ‡foreign; < derived from

**doc·ile** (däs´'l) *adj.* [< L. *docere*, teach] easy to discipline; tractable —**do·cil·i·ty** (dä sil´ə tē, dō-) *n.*

**dock**[1] (däk) *n.* [< It. *doccia*, canal] 1. an excavated basin for receiving ships between voyages 2. a wharf; pier 3. the water between two piers 4. a platform for loading and unloading trucks, etc. —*vt.* to pilot (a ship) to a dock —*vi.* to come into a dock

**dock**[2] (däk) *n.* [< Fl. *dok*, a cage] the place where the accused stands or sits in court

**dock**[3] (däk) *n.* [OE. *docce*] a coarse weed of the buckwheat family

**dock**[4] (däk) *n.* [ME. *dok*] the solid part of an animal's tail —*vt.* 1. to cut off the end of (a tail, etc.); bob 2. to deduct from (wages, etc.)

**dock·et** (däk´it) *n.* [< ?] 1. a list of cases to be tried by a law court 2. an agenda —*vt.* to enter in a docket

**dock´yard´** *n.* a place with docks, etc. for repairing or building ships

**doc·tor** (däk´tər) *n.* [< L., teacher] 1. a person on whom a university has conferred a high degree, as a Ph.D. 2. a physician or surgeon 3. a person licensed to practice any of the healing arts —*vt.* [Colloq.] 1. to try to heal 2. to mend 3. to tamper with —**doc´tor·al** *adj.*

**doc´tor·ate** (-it) *n.* the degree of doctor conferred by a university

**doc·tri·naire** (däk´trə ner´) *adj.* [Fr.] adhering to a doctrine dogmatically —**doc´tri·nair´ism** *n.*

**doc·trine** (däk´trən) *n.* [see DOCTOR] something taught, esp. as the principles of a religion, political party, etc.; tenet or tenets; dogma —**doc´tri·nal** (-trə nəl) *adj.*

**doc·u·ment** (däk´yə mənt; *for v.* -ment´) *n.* [< L. *documentum*, proof] anything printed, written, etc., relied upon to record or prove something —*vt.* to provide with or support by documents —**doc´u·men·ta´tion** *n.*

**doc´u·men·ta·ry** (-men´tə rē) *adj.* 1. of or supported by documents 2. showing or analyzing news events, social conditions, etc. in nonfictional but dramatic form —*n.*, *pl.* -**ries** a documentary film, TV show, etc.

**dod·der** (däd´ər) *vi.* [ME. *daderen*] 1. to shake or tremble, as from old age 2. to totter —**dod´der·ing** *adj.*

**dodge** (däj) *vi.*, *vt.* **dodged, dodg´ing** [< ?] 1. to move quickly aside, or avoid by so moving 2. to use tricks or evasions, or evade by so doing —*n.* 1. a dodging 2. a trick used in evading or cheating —**dodg´er** *n.*

**do·do** (dō´dō) *n.*, *pl.* -**dos, -does** [Port. *doudo*, lit., stupid] a large, flightless bird, now extinct

**doe** (dō) *n.* [OE. *da*] the female of the deer, antelope, rabbit, etc.

**do·er** (dōo´ər) *n.* 1. one who does something 2. one who gets things done

**does** (duz) *3d pers. sing., pres. indic.,* of DO[1]

DODO

**doe´skin´** *n.* 1. leather from the skin of a female deer 2. a soft wool cloth

**does·n´t** (duz´'nt) does not

**doff** (däf, dôf) *vt.* [see DO[1] & OFF] to take off (one's hat, etc.)

**dog** (dôg) *n.* [OE. *docga*] 1. a domesticated animal related to the fox, wolf, and jackal 2. a mean, contemptible fellow 3. a mechanical device for holding or grappling 4. [*pl.*] [Slang] feet 5. [Slang] an unsatisfactory person or thing —*vt.* **dogged, dog´ging** to follow or hunt like a dog —**go to the dogs** [Colloq.] to deteriorate

**doge** (dōj) *n.* [It. < L. *dux*, leader] the chief magistrate in the former republics of Venice and Genoa

**dog´ear´** *n.* a turned-down corner of the leaf of a book —**dog´eared´** *adj.*

**dog´fish´** *n.*, *pl.*: see FISH any of various small sharks

**dog·ged** (dôg´id) *adj.* persistent; stubborn —**dog´ged·ly** *adv.*

**dog·ger·el** (dôg´ər əl) *n.* [prob. < It. *doga*, barrel stave] trivial verse, poorly constructed and usually comic

**dog´gie bag** (-ē) a bag supplied to a restaurant patron, in which he may place leftovers, as for his dog

**dog´gone´** *interj.* damn! darn! —*vt.* -**goned´, -gon´ing** [Colloq.] to damn

**dog´house´** *n.* a dog's shelter —**in the doghouse** [Slang] in disfavor

**do·gie, do·gy** (dō´gē) *n.*, *pl.* -**gies** [< ?] in the western U.S., a stray calf

**dog·ma** (dôg´mə) *n.* [< Gr., opinion] a doctrine; belief; esp., a body of theological doctrines strictly adhered to

**dog·mat·ic** (-mat´ik) *adj.* 1. of or like dogma 2. asserted without proof 3. positive or arrogant in stating opinion —**dog·mat´i·cal·ly** *adv.*

**dog·ma·tism** (-tiz´m) *n.* dogmatic assertion of opinion —**dog´ma·tist** *n.*

**do´-good´er** *n.* [Colloq.] an idealistic, but impractical person who seeks to correct social ills

**dog´-tired´** *adj.* [Colloq.] very tired

**dog´tooth´** *n.*, *pl.* -**teeth** a canine tooth; eyetooth

**dog´trot´** *n.* a slow, easy trot

**dog´wood´** *n.* a small tree bearing pink or white flowers in early spring

**doi·ly** (doi´lē) *n.*, *pl.* -**lies** [after a 17th-c. London draper] a small mat, as of lace, put under a plate, etc. as a decoration or to protect a surface

**do·ings** (dōo´ingz) *n.pl.* things done; actions

**do´-it-your·self´** *n.* the practice of making or repairing things oneself, not hiring it done

**dol·drums** (däl´drəmz, dōl´-) *n.pl.* [< ? DULL] 1. *a)* low spirits *b)* sluggishness 2. equatorial ocean regions noted for dead calms

**dole** (dōl) *n.* [OE. *dal*, a share] 1. money or food given in charity 2. money paid by a government to the unemployed —*vt.* **doled, dol´ing** to give sparingly or as a dole

**dole´ful** (-fəl) *adj.* [< L. *dolere*, suffer] sad; mournful —**dole´ful·ly** *adv.*

**doll** (däl) *n.* [< nickname for *Dorothy*] 1. a child's toy made to resemble a human being 2. [Slang] any attractive or lovable person —*vt., vi.* [Colloq.] to dress stylishly or showily (with *up*)

**dol·lar** (däl′ər) *n.* [< G. *thaler*] 1. the monetary unit of the U.S., equal to 100 cents 2. the monetary unit of certain other countries, as Canada 3. a coin or paper bill of the value of a dollar

**dol·lop** (däl′əp) *n.* [< ?] 1. a soft mass 2. a quantity, often a small one

**dol·ly** (däl′ē) *n., pl.* **-lies** 1. a doll: child's word 2. a low, flat, wheeled frame for moving heavy objects

**dol·men** (däl′mən, dōl′-) *n.* [Fr.] a prehistoric monument consisting of a large, flat stone laid across upright stones

**do·lor·ous** (dō′lər əs, däl′ər-) *adj.* [< L. *dolere*, suffer] 1. sorrowful; sad 2. painful —**do′lor·ous·ly** *adv.*

**dol·phin** (däl′fən, dôl′-) *n.* [< Gr. *delphis*] a water-dwelling mammal, often with a beaklike snout

**dolt** (dōlt) *n.* [prob. < ME. *dolte*] a stupid person —**dolt′ish** *adj.*

**-dom** (dəm) [OE. *dom*, state] *a suffix meaning:* 1. rank or domain of [*kingdom*] 2. fact or state of being [*martyrdom*] 3. a body of [*officialdom*]

**do·main** (dō mān′) *n.* [< L. *dominus*, a lord] 1. territory under one government or ruler 2. field of activity or influence

**dome** (dōm) *n.* [< Gr. *dōma*, housetop] 1. a rounded roof or ceiling 2. any dome-shaped object

**do·mes·tic** (də mes′tik) *adj.* [< L. *domus*, house] 1. of the home or family 2. of or made in one's country 3. tame: said of animals 4. home-loving —*n.* a maid. cook, etc. —**do·mes′ti·cal·ly** *adv.*

**do·mes′ti·cate′** (-tə kāt′) *vt.* **-cat′ed, -cat′ing** 1. to accustom to home life 2. to tame for man's use —**do·mes′ti·ca′tion** *n.*

**do·mes·tic·i·ty** (dō′mes tis′ə tē) *n.* home life, or devotion to it

**dom·i·cile** (däm′ə sīl′, -sil; dō′mə-) *n.* [see DOMESTIC] a home; residence —*vt.* **-ciled′, -cil′ing** to establish in a domicile

**dom·i·nant** (däm′ə nənt) *adj.* dominating; ruling; prevailing —**dom′i·nance** *n.* —**dom′i·nant·ly** *adv.*

**dom′i·nate′** (-nāt′) *vt., vi.* **-nat′ed, -nat′ing** [< L. *dominus*, a master] 1. to rule or control by superior power 2. to rise above (the surroundings) —**dom′i·na′tion** *n.*

**dom·i·neer** (däm′ə nir′) *vi., vt.* [< Du.: see prec.] to rule (*over*) in a harsh or arrogant way; tyrannize

**dom′i·neer′ing** *adj.* overbearing

**Do·min·i·can Republic** (də min′i kən) country in the E part of Hispaniola: 18,816 sq. mi.; pop. 3,889,000

**do·min·ion** (də min′yən) *n.* [see DOMINATE] 1. rule or power to rule 2. a governed territory, or, sometimes, a self-governing nation

**dom·i·no** (däm′ə nō′) *n., pl.* **-noes′, -nos′** [Fr. & It.] 1. a loose cloak with a hood and mask, worn at masquerades 2. a mask for the eyes 3. a small, oblong tile marked with dots 4. [*pl., with sing. v.*] a game played with such tiles

**domino theory** a theory that if one country should become Communistic its neighbors would quickly follow, like a row of dominoes falling down

**Don** (dän) river in C European U.S.S.R., flowing into the Black Sea

**don**[1] (dän) *n.* [Sp. < L. *dominus*, master] 1. [D-] Sir; Mr.: a Spanish title of respect 2. a Spanish gentleman 3. [Colloq.] a tutor at a British college

**don**[2] (dän) *vt.* **donned, don′ning** [contr. of *do on*] to put on (clothes)

‡**Do·ña** (dō′nyä) *n.* [Sp.] Lady; Madam: a Spanish title of respect

**do·nate** (dō′nāt) *vt., vi.* **-nat·ed, -nat·ing** [< L. *donum*, gift] to give or contribute —**do·na′tion** *n.*

**done** (dun) *pp.* of DO[1] —*adj.* 1. completed 2. cooked —**done in** [Colloq.] exhausted —**done (for)** [Colloq.] dead, ruined, finished, etc.

**Don Juan** (dän′ jōō′ən, dän′ wän′) Sp. *Legend* a dissolute nobleman and seducer of women

**don·key** (dän′kē, dôn′-, dun′-) *n., pl.* **-keys** [< ?] 1. the domesticated ass 2. a stupid or foolish person

**don·ny·brook** (dän′ē brook′) *n.* [< a fair formerly held near Dublin, Ireland] a rowdy fight or free-for-all

**do·nor** (dō′nər) *n.* one who donates

**Don Quix·o·te** (dän′ kē hōt′ē, kwik′sət) 1. a satirical romance by Cervantes 2. its chivalrous, unrealistic hero

**don't** (dōnt) do not

**do·nut** (dō′nut′) *n.* same as DOUGHNUT

**doo·dle** (dōōd′'l) *vi.* **-dled, -dling** [G. *dudeln*, to trifle] to scribble aimlessly —*n.* a mark made in doodling —**doo′dler** *n.*

**doom** (dōōm) *n.* [OE. *dom*] 1. a judgment; sentence 2. fate 3. ruin or death —*vt.* 1. to pass judgment on; condemn 2. to destine to a tragic fate

**dooms′day′** *n.* Judgment Day

**door** (dôr) *n.* [OE. *duru*] 1. a movable structure for opening or closing an entrance 2. a doorway 3. a means of access —**out of doors** outdoors

**door′bell′** *n.* a bell rung by one who wishes to enter a building or room

**door′man′** (-man′, -mən) *n., pl.* **-men** (-men′, -mən) a man whose work is opening the door of a building, hailing taxicabs, etc.

**door′mat′** *n.* a mat to wipe the shoes on before entering a house, etc.

**door′step′** *n.* a step leading from an outer door to a path, lawn, etc.

**door′way′** *n.* 1. an opening in a wall that can be closed by a door 2. any means of access

**door′yard′** *n.* a yard onto which a door of a house opens

---

fat, āpe, cär; ten, ēven; is, bīte; gō, hôrn, tōōl, look; oil, out; up, fur; chin; she; thin, *then*; zh, leisure; ŋ, ring; ə for a in *ago*; ‚ (ā′b'l); ë, Fr. coeur; ö, Fr. feu; Fr. mon; ü, Fr. duc; kh, G. ich, doch; ‡ foreign; < derived from

**do·pa** (dō′pə) *n.* [< chemical name] an amino acid converted into an essential amine in the bloodstream: one isomer (**L-dopa**) is used in treating Parkinson's disease

**dope** (dōp) *n.* [Du. *doop*, sauce] 1. any thick liquid used as a lubricant, varnish, filler, etc. 2. [Slang] a drug or narcotic 3. a stupid person 4. [Slang] information —*vt.* doped, dop′ing to drug —**dope out** [Colloq.] to solve

**dop·ey, dop·y** (dō′pē) *adj.* dop′i·er, dop′i·est [Slang] 1. under the influence of a narcotic 2. lethargic or stupid

**Dor·ic** (dôr′ik) *adj.* designating or of a Greek style of architecture marked by fluted columns with plain capitals

**dorm** (dôrm) *n.* [Colloq.] a dormitory

**dor·mant** (dôr′mənt) *adj.* [< L. *dormire*, to sleep] 1. inactive 2. *Biol.* in a resting or torpid state —**dor′·man·cy** *n.*

**dor·mer** (dôr′mər) *n.* [see prec.] a window set upright in a structure projecting from a sloping roof: also **dormer window**

DORMER

**dor·mi·to·ry** (dôr′mə tôr′ē) *n.,* *pl.* -ries [see DORMANT] 1. a room with beds for a number of people 2. a building, as at a college, with many rooms for sleeping and living in

**dor·mouse** (dôr′mous′) *n., pl.* -mice′ (-mīs′) [ME. *dormous*] a small European rodent resembling a squirrel

**dor·sal** (dôr′s'l) *adj.* [< L. *dorsum*, the back] of, on, or near the back

**do·ry** (dôr′ē) *n., pl.* -ries [Central AmInd. *dori*, dugout] a small, flat-bottomed fishing boat with high sides

**dose** (dōs) *n.* [< Gr. *dosis*, a giving] an amount of medicine to be taken at one time —*vt.* dosed, dos′ing to give doses to —**dos′age** *n.*

**do·sim·e·ter** (dō sim′ə tər) *n.* a device for measuring the roentgens absorbed in a single exposure to radiation

**dos·si·er** (däs′ē ā′) *n.* [Fr.] a collection of documents about some person or matter

**dost** (dust) *archaic 2d pers. sing., pres. indic.,* of DO¹: *used with* thou

**Dos·to·ev·ski** (dôs′tô yef′skē), **Feodor** (fyô′dôr) 1821–81; Russ. novelist: also **Dos′to·yev′sky**

**dot** (dät) *n.* [OE. *dott*, head of boil] 1. a tiny speck or mark 2. a small, round spot —*vt.* dot′ted, dot′ting to mark as with a dot or dots —**on the dot** [Colloq.] at the exact time

**DOT** Department of Transportation

**dot·age** (dōt′ij) *n.* [ME. < *doten*, DOTE] childish state due to old age

**dot′ard** (-ərd) *n.* one in his dotage

**dote** (dōt) *vt.* dot′ed, dot′ing [ME. *doten*] 1. to be weak-minded, esp. because of old age 2. to be excessively fond (with *on* or *upon*) —**dot′ing** *adj.*

**doth** (duth) *archaic 3d pers. sing., pres. indic.,* of DO¹ (in auxiliary uses)

**Dou·ay Bible** (dōō ā′) [< *Douai*, France, where one part was first published] an English version of the Bible for the use of Roman Catholics

**dou·ble** (dub′'l) *adj.* [< L. *duplus*] 1. twofold 2. having two layers 3. having two of one kind 4. being of two kinds [a *double* standard] 5. twice as much, as many, etc. 6. made for two —*adv.* 1. twofold or twice 2. in a pair —*n.* 1. anything twice as much, as many, etc. as normal 2. a duplicate; counterpart 3. a fold 4. [*pl.*] a game of tennis, etc. with two players on each side 5. *Baseball* a hit on which the batter reaches second base 6. *Bridge* the doubling of an opponent's bid —*vt.* -bled, -bling 1. to make twice as much or many 2. to fold 3. to repeat or duplicate 4. *Bridge* to increase the point value or penalty of (an opponent's bid) —*vi.* 1. to become double 2. to turn sharply backward [to *double* on one's tracks] 3. to serve as a double 4. to serve an additional purpose 5. *Baseball* to hit a double —**double up** 1. to clench (one's fist) 2. to bend over, as in pain 3. to share a room, etc. with someone

**double agent** a spy who infiltrates an enemy espionage organization

**dou·ble-bar·reled** *adj.* 1. having two barrels, as a kind of shotgun 2. having a double purpose or meaning

**double bass** (bās) the largest, deepest-toned instrument of the violin family

**double boiler** a cooking utensil with an upper pan for food, fitting into a lower one in which water is boiled

**dou′ble-breast′ed** *adj.* overlapping across the breast, as a coat

**dou′ble-cross′** *vt.* [Colloq.] to betray —**dou′ble-cross′er** *n.*

**double date** [Colloq.] a social engagement shared by two couples —**dou′ble-date′** *vi., vt.* -dat′ed, -dat′ing

**dou′ble-deal′ing** *n.* duplicity

**dou′ble-deck′er** *n.* 1. any structure or vehicle with an upper deck 2. [Colloq.] a two-layer sandwich made with three slices of bread

**dou·ble-en·ten·dre** (dōō′blän tän′drə, dub′′l än-) *n.* [Fr. (now obs.), double meaning] a term with two meanings, esp. when one is risqué

**dou′ble-head′er** *n.* two games played in succession on the same day

**dou′ble-joint′ed** *adj.* having joints that permit limbs, fingers, etc. to bend at other than the usual angles

**dou′ble-knit′** *adj.* knit with a double stitch that makes the fabric extra thick

**double play** *Baseball* a play in which two players are put out

**dou′ble-reed′** *adj.* designating or of a woodwind instrument, as the oboe, having two reeds separated by a narrow opening

**double standard** a system, code, etc. applied unequally; specif., a moral code stricter for women than for men

**dou·blet** (dub′lit) *n.* [< OFr. *double*, orig., something folded] 1. a man's closefitting jacket of the 14th-16th cent. 2. a pair, or one of a pair

**double take** a delayed, startled reaction to the unexpected, following initial unthinking acceptance

**double talk** 1. ambiguous and deceptive talk 2. meaningless syllables made to sound like talk

**dou·bloon** (du blōōn′) n. [< Fr. < Sp. < L. duplus, double] an obsolete Spanish gold coin

**dou·bly** (dub′lē) adv. 1. twice 2. two at a time

**doubt** (dout) vi. [< L. dubitare] to be uncertain or undecided —vt. 1. to be uncertain about 2. to tend to disbelieve —n. 1. a) a wavering of opinion or belief b) lack of trust 2. a condition of uncertainty 3. an unsettled point or matter —beyond (or without) doubt certainly —no doubt 1. certainly 2. probably —doubt′er n. —doubt′ing·ly adv.

**doubt′ful** adj. 1. uncertain 2. causing doubt or suspicion 3. feeling doubt —doubt′ful·ly adv.

**doubt′less** adv. 1. certainly 2. probably —doubt′less·ly adv.

**douche** (dōōsh) n. [Fr. < It. doccia] 1. a jet of liquid applied externally or internally to the body 2. a device for douching —vt., vi. douched, douch′ing to apply a douche (to)

**dough** (dō) n. [OE. dag] 1. a mixture of flour, liquid, etc. worked into a soft mass for baking 2. [Slang] money

**dough′nut** n. a small, usually ring-shaped cake, fried in deep fat

**dough·ty** (dout′ē) adj. -ti·er, -ti·est [OE. dohtig] valiant; brave: now humorous and somewhat archaic

**dough′y** adj. -i·er, -i·est of or like dough; soft, pasty, etc.

**dour** (door, dōōr, dour) adj. [< L. durus, hard] 1. [Scot.] stern; severe 2. sullen; gloomy —dour′ness n.

**douse** (dous) vt. doused, dous′ing [< ?] 1. to thrust suddenly into liquid 2. to drench 3. [Colloq.] to extinguish, as a light

**dove¹** (duv) n. [ME. douve] 1. a bird of the pigeon family, with a cooing cry: a symbol of peace 2. an advocate of peaceful international relationships

**dove²** (dōv) alt. pt. of DIVE

**Do·ver** (dō′vər) capital of Del.: pop. 17,000

**dove·tail** (duv′tāl′) n. a projecting part that fits into a corresponding indentation to form a joint —vt., vi. to join or fit together closely or by means of dovetails

**dow·a·ger** (dou′ə jər) n. [< L. dotare, endow] 1. a widow with title or property derived from her dead husband 2. an elderly, dignified woman of wealth

DOVETAIL

**dow·dy** (dou′dē) adj. -di·er, -di·est [< ME. doude, plain woman] not neat or smart in dress —dow′di·ness n.

**dow·el** (dou′əl) n. [ME. doule] a peg

of wood, etc., usually fitted into corresponding holes in two pieces to fasten them together —vt. -eled or -elled, -el·ing or -el·ling to fasten with dowels

**dow·er** (dou′ər) n. [< L. dare, give] 1. that part of a man's property which his widow inherits for life 2. a dowry —vt. to endow (with)

**down¹** (doun) adv. [OE. adune, from the hill] 1. to, in, or on a lower place or level 2. in or to a low or lower condition, amount, etc. 3. from an earlier to a later period 4. out of one's hands [put it down] 5. in a serious manner [get down to work] 6. completely [loaded down] 7. in cash [$5 down and $5 a week] 8. in writing [take down notes] —adj. 1. descending 2. in a lower place 3. gone, brought, etc. down 4. dejected; discouraged 5. ill 6. finished [four down, six to go] 7. in cash [a down payment] —prep. down toward, along, through, into, or upon —vt. to put or throw down —n. 1. a misfortune [ups and downs] 2. Football one of a series of plays in which a team tries to advance the ball —down and out penniless, ill, etc. —down on [Colloq.] angry or annoyed with —down with! away with!

**down²** (doun) n. [< ON. dūnn] 1. soft, fine feathers 2. soft, fine hair

**down³** (doun) n. [OE. dun, hill] open, high, grassy land: usually used in pl.

**down′beat′** n. Music the downward stroke of the conductor's hand indicating the first beat of each measure

**down′cast′** adj. 1. directed downward 2. unhappy; dejected

**Down East** [Colloq.] New England, esp. Maine: also **down east**

**down′er** n. [Slang] any depressant or sedative

**down′fall′** n. 1. a) a sudden fall, as from power b) the cause of this 2. a heavy fall, as of snow

**down′fall′en** adj. fallen; ruined

**down′grade′** n. a downward slope —adv., adj. downward —vt. -grad′ed, -grad′ing 1. to demote 2. to belittle —on the downgrade declining

**down′heart′ed** adj. discouraged

**down′hill′** adv., adj. toward the bottom of a hill; downward

**Down′ing Street** a street in London containing British government offices

**down′pour′** n. a heavy rain

**down′right′** adv. utterly —adj. 1. absolute; utter 2. plain; frank

**Down's syndrome** (dounz) [after J. Down, 19th-c. Eng. physician] same as MONGOLISM

**down′stage′** adj., adv. of or toward the front of the stage

**down′stairs′** adv. 1. down the stairs 2. on or to a lower floor —adj. on a lower floor —n. a lower floor

**down′state′** adj., adv. in, to, or from the southerly part of a State

**down′stream′** adv., adj. in the direction of the current of a stream

**down'swing'** *n.* **1.** a downward swing, as of a golf club **2.** a downward trend: also **down'turn'**

**down'-to-earth'** *adj.* realistic or practical

**down'town'** *adj., adv.* in or toward the main business section of a city —*n.* the downtown section of a city

**down'trod'den** *adj.* oppressed

**down'ward** (-wərd) *adv., adj.* toward a lower place, position, etc.: also **down'wards** *adv.*

**down·y** (dou'nē) *adj.* **-i·er, -i·est 1.** covered with soft, fine feathers or hair **2.** soft and fluffy, like down

**dow·ry** (dou'rē) *n., pl.* **-ries** [see DOWER] the property that a woman brings to her husband at marriage

**dowse** (douz) *vi.* **dowsed, dows'ing** [< ?] to use a divining rod

**dox·ol·o·gy** (däk säl'ə jē) *n., pl.* **-gies** [< Gr. *doxa*, praise + *-logia*, -LOGY] a hymn of praise to God

**doz.** dozen(s)

**doze** (dōz) *vi.* **dozed, doz'ing** [prob. < Scand.] to sleep lightly; nap —*n.* a light sleep —**doz'er** *n.*

**doz·en** (duz''n) *n., pl.* **-ens** or, esp. after a number, **-en** [< L. *duo*, two + *decem*, ten] a set of twelve —**doz'enth** *adj.*

**dpt. 1.** department **2.** deponent

**Dr. 1.** Doctor **2.** Drive

**drab** (drab) *n.* [< VL. *drappus*, cloth] a dull yellowish brown —*adj.* **drab'ber, drab'best 1.** dull yellowish-brown **2.** dull —**drab'ness** *n.*

**drach·ma** (drak'mə) *n.* [see DRAM] a Greek coin and monetary unit

**draft** (draft) *n.* [OE. *dragan*, to draw] **1.** a drawing or pulling, as of a vehicle or load **2.** *a)* a drawing in of a fish net *b)* the amount of fish caught in one draw **3.** *a)* a drinking or the amount taken at one drink *b)* [Colloq.] a portion of beer, etc. drawn from a cask **4.** an inhalation **5.** a preliminary or tentative piece of writing **6.** a plan or drawing of a work to be done **7.** a current of air **8.** a device for regulating the current of air in a heating system **9.** a written order for payment of money; check **10.** *a)* the choosing or taking of persons, esp. for compulsory military service *b)* those so taken **11.** the depth of water that a ship displaces —*vt.* **1.** to take, as for military service, by drawing from a group **2.** to make a sketch of or plans for —*adj.* **1.** used for pulling loads **2.** drawn from a cask [*draft* beer] —**draft'er** *n.*

**draft·ee** (draf tē') *n.* a person drafted, esp. for military service

**drafts·man** (drafts'mən) *n., pl.* **-men** one who draws plans of structures or machinery —**drafts'man·ship'** *n.*

**draft'y** *adj.* **-i·er, -i·est** full of or exposed to drafts of air

**drag** (drag) *vt., vi.* **dragged, drag'ging** [see DRAW] **1.** to pull or be pulled with effort, esp. along the ground **2.** to search (a lake bottom, etc.) with a dragnet or the like **3.** to draw (something) out over a period of time; move or pass too slowly (often

with *on* or *out*) —*n.* **1.** something dragged along the ground, as a harrow **2.** a dragnet, grapnel, etc. **3.** anything that hinders **4.** a dragging **5.** [Slang] influence **6.** [Slang] a puff of a cigarette, etc. **7.** [Slang] street [the main *drag*] **8.** [Slang] *same as* DRAG RACE **9.** [Slang] a dull person, situation, etc.

**drag·gy** (drag'ē) *adj.* **-gi·er, -gi·est** dragging; slow-moving, dull, etc.

**drag'net'** *n.* **1.** a net dragged along a lake bottom, etc., as for catching fish **2.** an organized system or network for catching criminals, etc.

**drag·on** (drag'ən) *n.* [< Gr. *drakōn*] a mythical monster, typically a large, winged reptile breathing out fire

**drag'on·fly'** *n., pl.* **-flies'** a large, long-bodied insect with narrow, transparent wings

**dra·goon** (drə gōōn') *n.* [see DRAGON] a heavily armed cavalryman —*vt.* to force (into) doing something; coerce

**drag race** [Slang] a race between hot-rod cars accelerating from a standstill on a short, straight course (**drag strip**) —**drag'-race'** *vi.* -raced', -rac'ing

**drain** (drān) *vt.* [< OE. *dryge*, dry] **1.** to draw off (liquid) gradually **2.** to draw liquid from gradually **3.** to exhaust (strength, resources, etc.) gradually —*vi.* **1.** to flow off or trickle through gradually **2.** to become dry by draining —*n.* **1.** a channel or pipe for draining **2.** a draining —**drain'er** *n.*

**drain'age** (-ij) *n.* **1.** a draining **2.** a system of drains **3.** that which is drained off **4.** an area drained

**drain'pipe'** *n.* a large pipe used to carry off water, sewage, etc.

**drake** (drāk) *n.* [ME.] a male duck

**dram** (dram) *n.* [< Gr. *drachmē*, handful] **1.** *Apothecaries' Weight* a unit equal to 1/8 oz. **2.** *Avoirdupois Weight* a unit equal to 1/16 oz. **3.** a small drink of alcoholic liquor

**dra·ma** (drä'mə, dram'ə) *n.* [< Gr.] **1.** a literary composition to be performed by actors; play **2.** the art of writing, acting, or producing plays **3.** a series of events suggestive of those of a play **4.** dramatic quality

**Dram·a·mine** (dram'ə mēn') a trademark for a drug to relieve motion sickness —*n.* [d-] a tablet of this drug

**dra·mat·ic** (drə mat'ik) *adj.* **1.** of drama **2.** like a play **3.** vivid, striking, etc. —**dra·mat'i·cal·ly** *adv.*

**dra·mat'ics** *n.pl.* **1.** [*usually with sing. v.*] the performing or producing of plays **2.** exaggerated emotionalism

**dram·a·tist** (dram'ə tist) *n.* a playwright

**dram'a·tize'** (-tīz') *vt.* **-tized', -tiz'ing 1.** to make into a drama **2.** to regard or show in a dramatic manner —**dram'a·ti·za'tion** *n.*

**drank** (drank) *pt.* of DRINK

**drape** (drāp) *vt.* **draped, drap'ing** [< VL. *drappus*, cloth] **1.** to cover or hang as with cloth in loose folds **2.** to arrange (a garment, etc.) in folds or hangings —*n.* cloth hanging in loose folds; drapery: *usually used in pl.*

**drap·er** (drā'pər) *n.* [Brit.] a dealer in cloth and dry goods

**dra/per·y** n., pl. **-ies** 1. [Brit.] *same as* DRY GOODS 2. hangings or clothing arranged in loose folds 3. [pl.] curtains of heavy material

**dras·tic** (dras'tik) adj. [< Gr. *drastikos*, active] having a violent effect; severe; harsh —**dras'ti·cal·ly** adv.

**draught** (draft) n., vt., adj. now *chiefly Brit. sp.* of DRAFT

**draughts** (drafts) n.pl. [Brit.] the game of checkers

**draw** (drô) vt. drew, drawn, draw'-ing [OE. *dragan*] 1. to make move toward one; pull 2. to pull up, down, back, in, or out 3. to need (a specified depth of water) to float in: said of a ship 4. to attract 5. to breathe in 6. to elicit (a reply, etc.) 7. to bring on; provoke 8. to receive [to *draw* a salary] 9. to withdraw (money) held in an account 10. to write (a check or draft) 11. to deduce 12. to take or get (cards, etc.) 13. to stretch 14. to make (lines, pictures, etc.), as with a pencil 15. to make (comparisons, etc.) —vi. 1. to draw something 2. to be drawn 3. to come; move 4. to shrink 5. to allow a draft, as of smoke, to move through 6. to make a demand (on) —n. 1. a drawing or being drawn 2. the result of drawing 3. a thing drawn 4. a tie; stalemate 5. a thing that attracts —**draw out** 1. to extend 2. to take out 3. to get (a person) to talk —**draw up** 1. to arrange in order 2. to draft (a document) 3. to stop

**draw/back/** n. anything that prevents or lessens satisfaction; shortcoming

**draw/bridge/** n. a bridge that can be raised, lowered, or drawn aside

**draw·er** (drô'ər; *for 2* drôr) n. 1. a person or thing that draws 2. a sliding box in a table, chest, etc.

**draw·ers** (drôrz) n.pl. an undergarment for the lower part of the body

**draw/ing** n. 1. the act of one that draws; specif., the art of making pictures, etc. as with a pencil 2. a picture, etc. thus made 3. a lottery

**drawing card** an entertainer, show, etc. that draws a large audience

**drawing room** [< *withdrawing room:* guests withdrew there after dinner] a room where guests are received or entertained

**drawl** (drôl) vt., vi. [prob. < DRAW, v.] to speak slowly, prolonging the vowels —n. a manner of speaking thus

**drawn** (drôn) pp. of DRAW —adj. 1. disemboweled 2. tense; haggard

**drawn butter** melted butter

**draw/string/** n. a string drawn through a hem, etc. to tighten a garment

**dray** (drā) n. [< OE. *dragan*, to draw] a wagon for carrying heavy loads

**dread** (dred) vt. [< OE. *ondraedan*] to anticipate with fear or distaste —n. 1. intense fear 2. fear mixed with awe —adj. inspiring dread

**dread/ful** adj. 1. inspiring dread; awesome; terrible 2. [Colloq.] very bad,

offensive, etc. —**dread/ful·ly** adv.

**dread/nought/**, **dread/naught/** (-nôt') n. a large battleship with big guns

**dream** (drēm) n. [< OE., joy, music] 1. a sequence of images, etc. passing through a sleeping person's mind 2. a daydream; reverie 3. a fond hope 4. anything dreamlike—vi., vt. dreamed or dreamt (dremt), dream'ing to have a dream or remote idea (of) —dream up [Colloq.] to devise (a fanciful plan, etc.) —dream'er n. —dream'less adj. —dream'like' adj.

**dream/land/** n. 1. any lovely but imaginary place 2. sleep

**dream world** 1. *same as* DREAMLAND 2. the realm of fantasy

**dream/y** adj. -i·er, -i·est 1. of or like a dream 2. filled with dreams 3. visionary 4. soothing 5. [Slang] wonderful —dream'i·ly adv.

**drear·y** (drir'ē) adj. -i·er, -i·est [OE. *dreorig*, sad] dismal: also [Poet.] drear —drear'i·ly adv. —drear'i·ness n.

**dredge¹** (drej) n. [? < MDu.] an apparatus for scooping up mud, etc., as in deepening channels —vt., vi. dredged, dredg'ing 1. to search (for) or gather (up) as with a dredge 2. to enlarge or clean out with a dredge

**dredge²** (drej) vt. dredged, dredg'-ing [ME. *dragge*, sweetmeat] to coat (food) with flour or the like

**dregs** (dregz) n.pl. [< ON. *dregg*] 1. particles settling at the bottom in a liquid 2. the most worthless part

**Drei·ser** (drī'sər, -zər), **Theodore** (**Herman Albert**) 1871–1945; U.S. novelist

**drench** (drench) vt. [OE. *drincan*, to make drink] to make wet all over; soak

**Dres·den** (drez'dən) city in SC East Germany; pop. 508,000

**dress** (dres) vt. dressed or drest, dress'ing [< L. *dirigere*, lay straight] 1. to put clothes on; clothe 2. to trim; adorn 3. to arrange (the hair) in a certain way 4. to align (troops, etc.) 5. to apply medicines and bandages to (a wound, etc.) 6. to prepare for use, esp. for cooking [to *dress* a fowl] 7. to smooth or finish (leather, stone, etc.) —vi. 1. to clothe oneself 2. to dress formally 3. to line up in rank —n. 1. clothing 2. the usual outer garment of women, generally of one piece with a skirt —adj. 1. of or for dresses 2. for formal wear —**dress down** to scold —**dress up** to dress formally, elegantly, etc.

**dres·sage** (drə säzh') n. [< Fr. *dresser*, to train] horsemanship using slight movements to control the horse

**dress circle** a semicircle of seats in a theater, etc., usually behind and above the orchestra seats

**dress/er** n. 1. one who dresses (in various senses) 2. a chest of drawers for clothes, usually with a mirror

**dress/ing** n. 1. the act of one that dresses 2. bandages, etc. applied to wounds **3.** a sauce for salads, etc. **4.** a stuffing for roast fowl

**dress'ing-down'** *n.* a sound scolding

**dressing gown** a loose robe for one not fully clothed, as when lounging

**dress'mak'er** *n.* one who makes dresses, etc. —**dress'mak'ing** *n.*

**dress rehearsal** a final rehearsal, as of a play, with costumes, etc.

**dress'y** *adj.* **-i·er, -i·est 1.** showy or elaborate in dress or appearance **2.** elegant; smart —**dress'i·ness** *n.*

**drew** (drōō) *pt. of* DRAW

**drib·ble** (drib''l) *vt., vi.* **-bled, -bling** [< DRIP] **1.** to flow, or let flow, in drops **2.** to drool **3.** *Sports* to move (a ball or puck) along by repeated bouncing, kicking, or tapping —*n.* **1.** a dribbling **2.** a tiny amount: also **drib'let** (-lit) —**drib'bler** *n.*

**dried** (drīd) *pt. & pp. of* DRY

**dri·er** (drī'ər) *n.* **1.** a substance added to paint, etc. to make it dry fast **2.** *same as* DRYER —*adj. compar. of* DRY

**dri'est** (-ist) *adj. superl. of* DRY

**drift** (drift) *n.* [OE. *drifan*, to drive] **1.** *a)* a being carried along, as by a current *b)* the course of this **2.** a tendency; trend **3.** general meaning **4.** a heap of snow, etc. piled up by wind **5.** gravel, etc. deposited by a glacier —*vi.* **1.** to be carried along, as by a current **2.** to go along aimlessly **3.** to pile up in drifts —*vt.* to make drift —**drift'er** *n.*

**drift'wood'** *n.* wood drifting in the water or washed ashore

**drill¹** (dril) *n.* [Du. *drillen*, to bore] **1.** a tool for boring holes **2.** *a)* systematic military or physical training *b)* the method or practice of teaching by repeated exercises —*vt., vi.* **1.** to bore with a drill **2.** to train in, or teach by means of, drill (sense 2) —**drill'er** *n.*

**drill²** (dril) *n.* [< ? prec.] a planting machine for making holes or furrows and dropping seeds into them

**drill³** (dril) *n.* [< L. *trilix*, three-threaded] a coarse, twilled cotton cloth, used for uniforms, etc.

**drill'mas'ter** *n.* **1.** an instructor in military drill **2.** one who teaches by drilling

**drill press** a power-driven machine for drilling holes in metal, etc.

**dri·ly** (drī'lē) *adv. same as* DRYLY

**drink** (driŋk) *vt.* **drank, drunk, drink'ing** [OE. *drincan*] **1.** to swallow (liquid) **2.** to absorb (liquid) **3.** to swallow the contents of —*vi.* **1.** to swallow liquid **2.** to drink alcoholic liquor, esp. to excess —*n.* **1.** any liquid for drinking **2.** alcoholic liquor —**drink in** to take in eagerly with the senses or mind —**drink to** to drink a toast to —**drink'a·ble** *adj.* —**drink'er** *n.*

**drip** (drip) *vi., vt.* **dripped** or **dript, drip'ping** [OE. *dryppan*] to fall, or let fall, in drops —*n.* **1.** a dripping **2.** [Slang] a person regarded as unpleasant —**drip'per** *n.*

**drip'-dry'** *adj.* designating garments that dry quickly when hung wet and need little or no ironing

**drip grind** a fine grind of coffee

**drive** (drīv) *vt.* **drove, driv'en** (driv''n), **driv'ing** [OE. *drifan*] **1.** to force to go **2.** to force into or from a state or act **3.** to force to work, esp. to excess **4.** to hit (a ball, etc.) hard **5.** to make penetrate **6.** *a)* to control the movement of; operate (a car, bus, etc.) *b)* to transport in a car, etc. **7.** to push (a bargain, etc.) through —*vi.* **1.** to advance violently **2.** to try hard, as to reach a goal **3.** to drive a ball, blow, etc. **4.** to be driven: said of a car, bus, etc. **5.** to operate, or go in, a car, etc. —*n.* **1.** a driving **2.** a trip in a car, etc. **3.** *a)* a road for cars, etc. *b)* a driveway **4.** a rounding up of animals **5.** a campaign **6.** energy and initiative **7.** a strong impulse or urge **8.** the propelling mechanism of a machine, etc. —**drive at** to mean; intend —**drive in 1.** to force in, as by a blow **2.** *Baseball* to cause (a runner) to score or (a run) to be scored

**drive'-in'** *n.* a restaurant, movie theater, bank, etc. designed to serve people seated in their cars

**driv·el** (driv''l) *vi., vt.* **-eled** or **-elled, -el·ing** or **-el·ling** [OE. *dreflian*] **1.** to let (saliva) drool **2.** to speak or say in a silly, stupid way —*n.* silly, stupid talk —**driv'el·er, driv'el·ler** *n.*

**driv'er** *n.* a person or thing that drives, as *a)* one who drives a car, etc. *b)* one who herds cattle *c)* the golf club for hitting the ball from the tee

**drive shaft** a shaft that transmits motion, as to the rear axle of a car

**drive'way'** *n.* a path for cars, from a street to a garage, house, etc.

**driz·zle** (driz''l) *vi., vt.* **-zled, -zling** [prob. < ME.] to rain in fine, misty drops —*n.* such rain —**driz'zly** *adj.*

**drogue** (drōg) *n.* [prob. < Scot. *drug*, drag] a funnel-shaped device towed behind an aircraft for drag effect, use as a target, etc.

**droll** (drōl) *adj.* [< Fr. < MDu. *drol*, stout fellow] amusing in an odd way —**droll'er·y** (-ər ē) *n., pl.* **-ies** —**droll'ness** *n.* —**drol'ly** *adv.*

**drom·e·dar·y** (dräm'ə der'ē) *n., pl.* **-ies** [< LL. *dromedarius (camelus)*, running (camel)] the one-humped or Arabian camel

**drone¹** (drōn) *n.* [OE. *dran*] **1.** a male honeybee, which does no work **2.** an idler; loafer

**drone²** (drōn) *vi.* **droned, dron'ing** [< prec.] **1.** to make a continuous humming sound **2.** to talk in a monotonous way —*vt.* to utter in a monotonous tone —*n.* a droning sound

**drool** (drōōl) *vi.* [< DRIVEL] **1.** to let saliva flow from one's mouth **2.** to flow from the mouth, as saliva

**droop** (drōōp) *vi.* [< ON. *drūpa*] **1.** to sink, hang, or bend down **2.** to lose vitality **3.** to become dejected —*vt.* to let sink or hang down —*n.* a drooping —**droop'y** *adj.* **-i·er, -i·est** —**droop'i·ness** *n.*

**drop** (dräp) *n.* [OE. *dropa*] **1.** a bit of liquid rounded in shape by falling, etc. **2.** anything like this in shape, etc. **3.** a very small quantity **4.** a sudden fall, slump, descent, etc. **5.** something that drops, as a curtain or trapdoor **6.** the distance between a higher and lower level —*vi.* **dropped, drop′ping 1.** to fall in drops **2.** *a)* to fall suddenly down *b)* to fall exhausted, wounded, or dead **3.** to pass into a specified state *[to drop* off to sleep*]* **4.** to come to an end *[let the matter drop]* —*vt.* **1.** to let or make fall **2.** to utter (a hint, etc.) casually **3.** to send (a letter) **4.** to stop, end, or dismiss **5.** to lower **6.** [Colloq.] to deposit at a specified place —**drop in** (or **over, by,** etc.) to pay a casual visit —**drop out** to stop participating —**drop′let** *n.*

**drop kick** *Football* a kick of the ball made just as it rebounds from the ground after being dropped —**drop′-kick′** *vt., vi.* —**drop′-kick′er** *n.*

**drop′off′** *n.* **1.** a very steep drop **2.** a decline, as in sales or prices

**drop′out′** *n.* a student who withdraws from school before graduating

**drop′per** *n.* a small tube with a hollow rubber bulb at one end, used to measure out a liquid in drops

**drop·sy** (dräp′sē) *n.* [< Gr. *hydrōps* < *hydōr,* water] *an earlier term for* EDEMA —**drop′si·cal** (-si k′l) *adj.*

DROPPER

**dross** (drôs) *n.* [OE. *dros*] **1.** scum on molten metal **2.** refuse; rubbish

**drought** (drout, drouth) *n.* [< OE. *drugóth,* dryness] prolonged dry weather: also **drouth** (drouth, drout)

**drove¹** (drōv) *n.* [OE. *draf*] **1.** a number of cattle, sheep, etc. driven or moving along as a group; flock; herd **2.** a moving crowd of people

**drove²** (drōv) *pt.* of DRIVE

**dro·ver** (drō′vər) *n.* one who herds animals, esp. to market

**drown** (droun) *vi.* [ME. *drounen*] to die by suffocation in water —*vt.* **1.** to kill by such suffocation **2.** to flood **3.** to be so loud as to overcome (another sound): usually with *out*

**drowse** (drouz) *vi.* drowsed, drows′ing [< OE. *drusian,* become sluggish] to be half asleep; doze —*n.* a doze

**drow′sy** *adj.* **-si·er, -si·est** being or making sleepy or half asleep —**drow′si·ly** *adv.* —**drow′si·ness** *n.*

**drub** (drub) *vt.* drubbed, drub′bing [< Ar. *daraba,* to cudgel] **1.** to beat as with a stick **2.** to defeat soundly —**drub′ber** *n.* —**drub′bing** *n.*

**drudge** (druj) *n.* [ME. *druggen*] a person who does hard, menial, or tedious work —*vi.* drudged, drudg′ing to do such work —**drudg′er·y** *n., pl.* **-ies**

**drug** (drug) *n.* [< OFr. *drogue*] **1.** any substance used as or in a medicine **2.** a narcotic, hallucinogen, etc. —*vt.* drugged, drug′ging **1.** to put a narcotic, etc. in (a drink, etc.) **2.** to stupefy as with a drug —**a drug on the market** a thing in much greater supply than demand

**drug′gist** (-ist) *n.* **1.** a dealer in drugs, medical supplies, etc. **2.** a pharmacist **3.** a drugstore owner or manager

**drug′store′** *n.* a store where drugs, medical supplies, and various items are sold and prescriptions are filled

**dru·id** (drōo′id) *n.* [< Celt.] *[often* D-] a member of a Celtic religious order in ancient Britain, Ireland, and France —**dru′id·ism** *n.*

**drum** (drum) *n.* [< Du. *trom*] **1.** a percussion instrument consisting of a hollow cylinder with a membrane stretched over the end or ends. **2.** the sound produced by beating a drum **3.** any drumlike cylindrical object **4.** the eardrum —*vi.* drummed, drum′ming **1.** to beat a drum **2.** to tap continually —*vt.* **1.** to play (a rhythm, etc.) as on a drum **2.** to instill (ideas, facts, etc. *into*) by continued repetition —**drum out of** to expel from in disgrace —**drum up** to get (business, etc.) by soliciting

**drum·lin** (drum′lin) *n.* [< Ir.] a long ridge formed of glacial drift

**drum major** a person who twirls a baton at the head of a marching band —**drum ma′jor·ette′** (-et′) *fem.*

**drum′mer** *n.* **1.** a drum player **2.** [Colloq.] a traveling salesman

**drum′stick′** *n.* **1.** a stick for beating a drum **2.** the lower half of the leg of a cooked fowl

**drunk** (drunk) *adj.* **1.** overcome by alcoholic liquor; intoxicated **2.** [Colloq.] *same as* DRUNKEN (sense 2) —*n.* [Slang] **1.** a drunken person **2.** a drinking spree

**drunk·ard** (drun′kərd) *n.* a person who often gets drunk

**drunk′en** (-kən) *adj.* [*used before the noun*] **1.** intoxicated **2.** caused by or occurring during intoxication —**drunk′en·ly** *adv.* —**drunk′en·ness** *n.*

**drupe** (drōop) *n.* any fleshy fruit with an inner stone, as a peach

**dry** (drī) *adj.* dri′er, dri′est [OE. *dryge*] **1.** not under water *[dry land]* **2.** not wet or damp **3.** lacking rain or water; arid **4.** thirsty **5.** not yielding milk **6.** solid; not liquid **7.** not sweet *[dry wine]* **8.** prohibiting alcoholic liquors *[a dry town]* **9.** funny in a quiet but sharp way *[dry wit]* **10.** unproductive **11.** boring; dull —*n., pl.* drys [Colloq.] a prohibitionist —*vt., vi.* dried, dry′ing to make or become dry —**dry up 1.** to make or become thoroughly dry **2.** to make or become unproductive **3.** [Slang] to stop talking —**dry′ly** *adv.* —**dry′ness** *n.*

**dry·ad** (drī′ad) *n.* [< Gr. *drys,* tree] *Classical Myth. [also* D-] a tree nymph

**dry cell** a voltaic cell containing an absorbent so that its contents cannot spill

**dry′-clean′** *vt.* to clean (garments, etc.) with a solvent other than water, as naphtha —**dry cleaner**

**Dry·den** (drĭd'n), **John** 1631–1700; Eng. poet, critic, & playwright

**dry dock** a dock from which the water can be emptied, used for building and repairing ships

**dry'er** n. 1. a person or thing that dries: specif., an appliance for drying clothes with heat 2. *same as* DRIER

**dry farming** farming without irrigation, by conserving the soil's moisture

**dry goods** cloth, cloth products, etc.

**dry ice** a refrigerant consisting of solidified carbon dioxide

**dry run** [Slang] a simulated or practice performance; rehearsal

**dry wall** a wall made of wallboard, etc., without using wet plaster

**D.S.C.** Distinguished Service Cross

**D.S.T., DST** Daylight Saving Time

**Du.** 1. Duke 2. Dutch

**du·al** (dŏŏ'əl) adj. [< L. *duo*, two] 1. of two 2. double; twofold —**du'al·ism** n. —**du·al'i·ty** (-ăl'ə tē) n.

**dub¹** (dub) vt. dubbed, dub'bing [< OE. *dubbian*, to strike] 1. a) to confer a title or rank upon b) to name or nickname 2. to smooth by hammering, scraping, etc. 3. [Slang] to bungle (a golf stroke, etc.) —**dub'ber** n.

**dub²** (dub) vt. dubbed, dub'bing [< DOUBLE] to insert (dialogue, etc.) in a sound track of a movie, etc. —**dub'ber** n.

**dub·bin** (dub'n) n. [< DUB¹] a greasy substance used for waterproofing leather

**du·bi·e·ty** (dŏŏ bī'ə tē) n. 1. a being dubious 2. pl. -ties a doubtful thing

**du·bi·ous** (dŏŏ'bē əs) adj. [< L. *dubius*, uncertain] 1. causing doubt 2. feeling doubt; skeptical 3. questionable —**du'bi·ous·ly** adv.

**Dub·lin** (dub'lən) capital of Ireland: pop. 568,000

**Du Bois** (dŏŏ bois'), **W(illiam) E. B.** 1868–1963; U.S. historian & educator

**du·cal** (dŏŏ'k'l) adj. [< LL. *ducalis*, of a leader] of a duke or dukedom

**duc·at** (duk'ət) n. [see DUCHY] any of several former European coins

**duch·ess** (duch'is) n. 1. a duke's wife or widow 2. a woman ruling a duchy

**duch'y** (-ē) n., pl. -ies [< L. *dux*, leader] the territory ruled by a duke or duchess

**duck¹** (duk) n. [< OE. *duce*, lit., diver] 1. a swimming fowl with a flat bill, short neck, and webbed feet 2. the flesh of a duck as food

**duck²** (duk) vt., vi. [ME. *douken*] 1. to plunge or dip under water for a moment 2. to lower or bend (the head, body, etc.) suddenly, as to avoid a blow 3. [Colloq.] to avoid (a task, person, etc.) —n. a ducking

**duck³** (duk) n. [Du. *doek*] a cotton or linen cloth like canvas but finer and lighter in weight

**duck'bill** n. *same as* PLATYPUS

**duck'ling** n. a young duck

**duck'pins** n.pl. [*with sing. v.*] a game like bowling, played with smaller pins and balls

**duck'y** adj. -i·er, -i·est [Slang] pleasing, delightful, etc.

**duct** (dukt) n. [< L. *ducere*, to lead]

a tube, channel, or pipe, as for passage of a liquid —**duct'less** adj.

**duc·tile** (duk't'l) adj. [see prec.] 1. that can be drawn or hammered thin without breaking: said of metals 2. easily led; tractable —**duc·til·i·ty** (duk til'ə tē) n.

**ductless gland** an endocrine gland

**dud** (dud) n. [prob. < Du. *dood*, dead] [Colloq.] 1. a bomb or shell that fails to explode 2. a failure

**dude** (dŏŏd) n. [< ?] 1. a dandy; fop 2. [Western Slang] a city fellow or tourist

**due** (dŏŏ, dyŏŏ) adj. [< L. *debere*, owe] 1. owed or owing as a debt; payable 2. suitable; proper 3. enough [due care] 4. expected or scheduled to arrive —adv. exactly; directly [due west] —n. anything due; specif., [pl.] fees or other charges [membership dues] —**due to** 1. caused by 2. [Colloq.] because of —**pay one's dues** [Slang] to earn certain rights as by having suffered in struggle

**du·el** (dŏŏ'əl) n. [< OL. *dvellum*, war] 1. a prearranged fight between two persons armed with deadly weapons 2. any contest like this —vi., vt. -eled or -elled, -el·ing or -el·ling to fight a duel with —**du'el·ist** or **du'el·list, du'el·er** or **du'el·ler** n.

**‡duen·de** (dwen'de) n. [Sp., lit., goblin] a special, irresistible charm

**due process (of law)** legal proceedings established to protect individual rights and liberties

**du·et** (dŏŏ et') n. [< L. *duo*, two] 1. a composition for two voices or instruments 2. the two performers of this

**duf·fel** (or **duf·fle**) **bag** (duf'l) [< *Duffel*, town in Belgium] a large cloth bag for carrying clothing, etc.

**duf·fer** (duf'ər) n. [< thieves' slang *duff*, to fake] [Slang] an awkward or incompetent person

**dug** (dug) pt. & pp. of DIG

**dug'out'** n. 1. a boat hollowed out of a log 2. a shelter, as in warfare, dug in the ground 3. *Baseball* a covered shelter for the players

**duke** (dŏŏk) n. [< L. *dux*, leader] 1. a prince ruling an independent duchy 2. a nobleman next in rank to a prince —**duke'dom** n.

**dul·cet** (dul'sit) adj. [< L. *dulcis*, sweet] soothing or pleasant to hear

**dul·ci·mer** (dul'sə mər) n. [< L. *dulce*, sweet + *melos*, song] a musical instrument with metal strings, struck with two small hammers or plucked with a plectrum or quill

**dull** (dul) adj. [< OE. *dol*, stupid] 1. mentally slow; stupid 2. physically slow; sluggish 3. boring; tedious 4. not sharp; blunt 5. not feeling or felt keenly 6. not vivid or bright [a dull color] —vt., vi. to make or become dull —**dull'ness** n. —**dul'ly** adv.

**dull'ard** (-ərd) n. a stupid person

**Du·luth** (də lŏŏth') city in NE Minn., on Lake Superior: pop. 101,000

**du·ly** (dŏŏ'lē) adv. in due manner; in the proper way, time, etc.

**Du·mas** (dŏŏ'mä), **Alexandre** 1802–70; Fr. writer

**dumb** (dum) *adj.* [OE.] **1.** lacking the power of speech; mute **2.** silent **3.** [G. *dumm*] [Colloq.] stupid —**dumb′ly** *adv.* —**dumb′ness** *n.*

**dumb·bell** (dum′bel′) *n.* **1.** a device consisting of round weights joined by a short bar, used for muscular exercise **2.** [Slang] a stupid person

**dumb·found, dum·found** (dum′found′) *vt.* [DUMB + (CON)FOUND] to make speechless by shocking; amaze

**dumb′wait′er** *n.* a small elevator for sending food, etc. from one floor to another

**dum·dum (bullet)** (dum′dum′) [< *Dumdum*, arsenal in India] a soft-nosed bullet that expands when it hits

**dum·my** (dum′ē) *n., pl.* **-mies 1.** a figure made in human form, as for displaying clothing **2.** an imitation; sham **3.** [Slang] a stupid person **4.** *Bridge*, etc. the declarer's partner, whose hand is exposed on the board and played by the declarer —*adj.* sham

**dump** (dump) *vt.* [prob. < ON.] **1.** to unload in a heap or mass **2.** to throw away (rubbish, etc.) —*n.* **1.** a place for dumping rubbish, etc. **2.** *Mil.* a temporary storage center in the field **3.** [Slang] an ugly, run-down place —**(down) in the dumps** in low spirits

**dump·ling** (dump′liŋ) *n.* [< ?] **1.** a small piece of steamed or boiled dough served with meat or soup **2.** a crust of baked dough filled with fruit

**dump·y** (dum′pē) *adj.* **-i·er, -i·est 1.** short and thick; squat **2.** [Slang] ugly, run-down, etc.

**dun¹** (dun) *adj., n.* [OE.] dull grayish brown

**dun²** (dun) *vt., vi.* **dunned, dun′ning** [? dial. var. of DIN] to ask (a debtor) repeatedly for payment —*n.* an insistent demand for payment

**dunce** (duns) *n.* [< *Duns* Scotus, follower of *Duns* Scotus, 13th-c. Scot. scholar] a dull, ignorant person

**dune** (dōōn) *n.* [< ODu. *duna*] a rounded hill or ridge of drifted sand

**dune buggy** [orig. used on sand dunes] a small, light automobile generally made from a standard, compact chassis and a prefabricated body

**dung** (duŋ) *n.* [OE.] animal excrement; manure

**dun·ga·ree** (duŋ′gə rē′) *n.* [Hind. *dungrī*] **1.** a coarse cotton cloth **2.** [*pl.*] work trousers or overalls made of this

**dun·geon** (dun′jən) *n.* [< OFr. *donjon*] a dark underground cell or prison

**dung′hill′** *n.* a heap of dung

**dunk** (duŋk) *vt.* [G. *tunken*] **1.** to dip (bread, etc.) into coffee, etc. before eating it **2.** to immerse briefly

**Dun·kirk** (dun′kərk) seaport in N France: scene of evacuation of Allied troops under fire (May, 1940)

**du·o** (dōō′ō) *n., pl.* **-os** [It.] *same as* DUET (sense 2)

**du·o·de·num** (dōō′ə dē′nəm) *n., pl.* **-na** (-nə), **-nums** [< L. *duodeni*, twelve each: it is about 12 fingers'-breadth long] the first section of the small intestine, below the stomach —**du′o·de′nal** *adj.*

**dup.** duplicate

**dupe** (dōōp) *n.* [< L. *upupa*, bird easily tricked] a person easily tricked —*vt.* duped, dup′ing to deceive; fool; trick —**dup′er** *n.*

**du·plex** (dōō′pleks) *adj.* [L.] double —*n.* **1.** an apartment with rooms on two floors **2.** a house consisting of two separate family units

**du·pli·cate** (dōō′plə kit; *for v.* -kāt′) *adj.* [< L. *duplicare*, to double] **1.** double **2.** corresponding exactly —*n.* an exact copy; facsimile —*vt.* -cat′ed, -cat′ing **1.** to make an exact copy of **2.** to cause to happen again —**du′pli·ca′tion** *n.*

**duplicating machine** a machine for making copies of a letter, drawing, etc.: also **du′pli·ca′tor** (-kāt′ər) *n.*

**du·plic·i·ty** (dōō plis′ə tē) *n., pl.* **-ties** [< LL. *duplicitas*] hypocritical cunning or deception

**du·ra·ble** (door′ə b'l) *adj.* [< L. *durare*, to last] **1.** lasting in spite of hard wear or frequent use **2.** stable —**du′ra·bil′i·ty** *n.* —**du′ra·bly** *adv.*

**dur·ance** (door′əns) *n.* [see prec.] imprisonment: esp. in **in durance vile**

**du·ra·tion** (doo rā′shən) *n.* [see DURABLE] the time that a thing continues or lasts

**du·ress** (doo res′) *n.* [< L. *durus*, hard] **1.** imprisonment **2.** compulsion or coercion

**dur·ing** (door′iŋ) *prep.* [see DURABLE] **1.** throughout the entire time of **2.** in the course of

**durst** (durst) *archaic pt. of* DARE

**du·rum** (door′əm) *n.* [< L. *durus*, hard] a hard wheat that yields flour used for macaroni, spaghetti, etc.

**dusk** (dusk) *n.* [< OE. *dox*, dark-colored] **1.** the dim part of twilight **2.** gloom —**dusk′y** *adj.* **-i·er, -i·est**

**dust** (dust) *n.* [OE.] **1.** powdery earth or any finely powdered matter **2.** earth **3.** disintegrated mortal remains **4.** anything worthless —*vt.* **1.** to sprinkle with dust, powder, etc. **2.** to rid of dust, as by wiping —*vi.* to remove dust, as from furniture —**bite the dust** to be killed, esp. in battle —**dust′less** *adj.*

**dust bowl** an arid region with eroded topsoil easily blown off by winds

**dust′er** *n.* **1.** a person or thing that dusts **2.** a lightweight housecoat

**dust′pan′** *n.* a shovellike receptacle into which floor dust is swept

**dust′y** *adj.* **-i·er, -i·est 1.** covered with or full of dust **2.** powdery **3.** dust-colored —**dust′i·ness** *n.*

**Dutch** (duch) *adj.* **1.** of the Netherlands, its people, language, etc. **2.** [Slang] German —*n.* the language of the Netherlands —**go Dutch** [Colloq.] to have each pay his own expenses —**in Dutch** [Colloq.] in trouble or disfavor —**the Dutch** Dutch people

**Dutch door** a door with upper and lower halves opening separately

**Dutch oven** a heavy pot with an arched lid, for pot roasts, etc.

**Dutch treat** [Colloq.] any entertainment, etc. at which each pays his own expenses

**Dutch uncle** [Colloq.] one who bluntly and sternly lectures another

**du·te·ous** (dōōt′ē əs) *adj.* dutiful; obedient —**du′te·ous·ly** *adv.*

**du·ti·a·ble** (dōōt′ē ə b'l) *adj.* necessitating payment of a duty

**du·ti·ful** (dōōt′ə fəl) *adj.* showing, or resulting from, a sense of duty; obedient —**du′ti·ful·ly** *adv.*

**du·ty** (dōōt′ē) *n., pl.* **-ties** [see DUE & -TY] **1.** obedience or respect to be shown to one's parents, elders, etc. **2.** any action required by one's position or by moral or legal considerations, etc. **3.** service, esp. military service [overseas *duty*] **4.** a tax, as on imports —**on** (or **off**) **duty** at (or temporarily relieved from) one's work

**dwarf** (dwôrf) *n., pl.* **dwarfs, dwarves** (dwôrvz) [OE. *dweorg*] any abnormally small person, animal, or plant —*vt.* **1.** to stunt the growth of **2.** to make seem small in comparison —*vi.* to become dwarfed —*adj.* abnormally small —**dwarf′ish** *adj.* —**dwarf′ism** *n.*

**dwell** (dwel) *vi.* **dwelt** or **dwelled, dwell′ing** [OE. *dwellan,* to hinder] to make one's home; live —**dwell on** (or **upon**) to linger over in thought or speech —**dwell′er** *n.*

**dwell′ing (place)** an abode; residence

**DWI, D.W.I.** driving while intoxicated

**dwin·dle** (dwin′d'l) *vi., vt.* **-dled, -dling** [< OE. *dwinan,* waste away] to keep on becoming or making smaller or less; diminish; shrink

**dyb·buk** (dib′ək) *n.* [Heb. *dibbūq*] *Jewish Folklore* a spirit of one deceased that enters the body of a person

**dye** (dī) *n.* [OE. *deag*] a substance or solution for coloring fabric, hair, etc.; also, the color produced —*vt., vi.* **dyed, dye′ing** to color with dye —**dy′er** *n.*

**dyed′-in-the-wool′** *adj.* thoroughgoing; unchanging

**dye′stuff′** *n.* any substance constituting or yielding a dye

**dy·ing** (dī′iŋ) *prp.* of DIE[1] —*adj.* **1.** about to die or end **2.** at death

**dy·nam·ic** (dī nam′ik) *adj.* [< Gr. *dynasthai,* be able] **1.** of energy or physical force in motion **2.** energetic; forceful —**dy·nam′i·cal·ly** *adv.*

**dy·nam′ics** *n.pl.* [with sing. v. for 1] **1.** the science dealing with motions produced by given forces **2.** the forces operative in any field

**dy·na·mism** (dī′nə miz'm) *n.* dynamic quality; forcefulness

**dy·na·mite** (dī′nə mīt′) *n.* [see DYNAMIC] a powerful explosive made with nitroglycerin —*vt.* **-mit′ed, -mit′ing** to blow up with dynamite

**dy·na·mo** (dī′nə mō′) *n., pl.* **-mos′** [see DYNAMIC] **1.** earlier term for GENERATOR **2.** a dynamic person

**dy·nas·ty** (dī′nəs tē) *n., pl.* **-ties** [< Gr. *dynasthai,* be strong] a succession of rulers, members of the same family —**dy·nas′tic** (-nas′tik) *adj.*

**dys-** [Gr.] *a prefix meaning* bad, ill, difficult, etc.

**dys·en·ter·y** (dis′'n ter′ē) *n.* [< Gr. *dys-,* bad + *entera,* bowels] an intestinal inflammation characterized by bloody diarrhea and abdominal pain

**dys·func·tion** (dis fuŋk′shən) *n.* abnormal or impaired functioning

**dys·lex·i·a** (dis lek′sē ə) *n.* [< Gr. *dys-,* bad + *lexis,* speech] impairment of reading ability, as because of brain injury

**dys·pep·si·a** (dis pep′shə, -sē ə) *n.* [< Gr. *dys-,* bad + *peptein,* to digest] indigestion —**dys·pep′tic** *adj., n.*

**dz.** dozen(s)

# E

**E, e** (ē) *n., pl.* **E's, e's** the fifth letter of the English alphabet

**E** (ē) *n.* **1.** *Music* the third tone in the scale of C major **2.** *symbol for* energy

**e-** *a prefix meaning* out, out of, from, without: see EX-

**E, E., e, e. 1.** east **2.** eastern

**E. 1.** Earl **2.** Easter **3.** English

**each** (ēch) *adj., pron.* [OE. *ælc*] every one of two or more considered separately —*adv.* apiece Abbrev. **ea.**

**ea·ger** (ē′gər) *adj.* [< L. *acer,* keen] keenly desiring; impatient or anxious —**ea′ger·ly** *adv.* —**ea′ger·ness** *n.*

**ea·gle** (ē′g'l) *n.* [< L. *aquila*] **1.** a large bird of prey, with sharp vision and powerful wings **2.** a representation of an eagle, as the U.S. emblem **3.** a former U.S. $10 gold coin **4.** *Golf* a score of two under par on a hole

**ea′gle-eyed′** *adj.* having keen vision

**ea·glet** (ē′glit) *n.* a young eagle

**ear**[1] (ir) *n.* [OE. *eare*] **1.** the part of the body that perceives sound **2.** the outer part of the ear **3.** one's sense of hearing or hearing ability **4.** anything like an ear —**be all ears** to listen attentively —**give** (or **lend**) **ear** to give attention; heed —**play by ear** to play (music) without using notation —**play it by ear** [Colloq.] to improvise

**ear**[2] (ir) *n.* [OE. *ær*] the grain-bearing spike of a cereal plant, as of corn —*vi.* to sprout ears

**ear′ache′** *n.* an ache in an ear

**ear′drum′** *n.* the tympanic membrane

**earl** (url) *n.* [OE. *eorl,* warrior] a British nobleman ranking just above a viscount —**earl′dom** *n.*

**ear·ly** (ur′lē) *adv., adj.* **-li·er, -li·est** [< OE. *ær,* before + *-lice, -ly*] **1.**

near the beginning **2.** before the expected or usual time **3.** in the distant past **4.** in the near future —**early on** at an early stage —**ear′li·ness** *n.*

**ear′mark′** *n.* **1.** a brand put on the ear of livestock **2.** an identifying mark or feature —*vt.* **1.** to set such a brand or mark on **2.** to reserve for a special purpose

**ear′muffs′** *n.pl.* coverings for the ears, worn in cold weather

**earn** (ʉrn) *vt.* [OE. *earnian*] **1.** to receive (wages, etc.) for one's work **2.** to get as deserved **3.** to gain (interest, etc.) as profit

**ear·nest** (ʉr′nist) *adj.* [OE. *eornost*] **1.** serious and intense; not joking **2.** important —**in earnest 1.** serious **2.** with determination —**ear′nest·ly** *adv.* —**ear′nest·ness** *n.*

**ear·nest²** (ʉr′nist) *n.* [ult. < Heb. *'ērābōn*] money, etc. given as a pledge in binding a bargain

**earn′ings** *n.pl.* **1.** wages or other recompense **2.** profits, interest, etc.

**ear′phone′** *n.* a receiver for radio, etc., held to, or put into, the ear

**ear′ring′** *n.* a ring or other small ornament for the lobe of the ear

**ear′shot′** (-shät′) *n.* the distance within which a sound can be heard

**ear′split′ting** *adj.* so loud as to hurt the ears; very loud

**earth** (ʉrth) *n.* [OE. *eorthe*] **1.** the planet we live on, the fifth largest of the solar system: see PLANET **2.** this world, as distinguished from heaven and hell **3.** land, as distinguished from sea or sky **4.** soil; ground —**down to earth** practical; realistic

**earth′en** *adj.* made of earth or clay

**earth′en·ware′** *n.* pots, jars, dishes, etc. made of baked clay

**earth′ling** *n.* a person who lives on the earth; human being

**earth′ly** *adj.* **1.** *a)* terrestrial *b)* worldly *c)* temporal **2.** conceivable

**earth mother** a buxom, sensuous woman who is inclined to mother others

**earth′quake′** *n.* a shaking of the earth's crust, caused by underground volcanic forces or shifting of rock

**earth′ward** (-wərd) *adv., adj.* toward the earth: also **earth′wards** *adv.*

**earth′work′** *n.* an embankment or fortification made by piling up earth

**earth′worm′** *n.* a round, segmented worm that burrows in the soil

**earth·y** (ʉr′thē) *adj.* **-i·er, -i·est 1.** of or like earth **2.** coarse; unrefined

**ease** (ēz) *n.* [< L. *adjacens,* lying nearby] **1.** freedom from pain or trouble; comfort **2.** natural manner; poise **3.** freedom from difficulty; facility **4.** affluence —*vt.* **eased, eas′ing 1.** to free from pain or trouble; comfort **2.** to lessen (pain, anxiety, etc.) **3.** to facilitate **4.** to reduce the strain or pressure of **5.** to move by careful shifting, etc. —*vi.* to become less tense, severe, etc. —**ease′ful** *adj.*

**ea·sel** (ē′z'l) *n.* [ult. < L. *asinus,* ass] an upright frame to hold an artist's canvas, etc.

EASEL

**ease·ment** (ēz′mənt) *n.* **1.** an easing or being eased **2.** *Law* a right that one may have in another's land

**eas·i·ly** (ē′z'l ē) *adv.* **1.** with ease **2.** without a doubt **3.** very likely

**east** (ēst) *n.* [OE.] **1.** the direction in which sunrise occurs (90° on the compass, opposite west) **2.** a region in or toward this direction **3.** [E-] Asia and the nearby islands; Orient —*adj.* **1.** in, of, or toward the east **2.** from the east —*adv.* in or toward the east

**East Berlin** E section of Berlin; capital of East Germany: pop. 1,077,000

**East China Sea** part of the Pacific Ocean, between China & Japan

**East·er** (ēs′tər) *n.* [< OE. *Eastre,* dawn goddess] an annual Christian festival in the spring celebrating the resurrection of Jesus

**east′er·ly** *adj., adv.* **1.** toward the east **2.** from the east

**east′ern** *adj.* **1.** in, of, or toward the east **2.** from the east **3.** [E-] of the East

**east′ern·er** *n.* a native or inhabitant of the east

**Eastern Hemisphere** that half of the earth which includes Europe, Africa, Asia, and Australia

**East Germany** E section of Germany; country in NC Europe: c. 41,800 sq. mi.; pop. 17,067,000

**East In·dies** (in′dēz) the Malay Archipelago —**East Indian**

**east′ward** (-wərd) *adv., adj.* toward the east: also **east′wards** *adv.*

**eas·y** (ē′zē) *adj.* **-i·er, -i·est** [see EASE] **1.** not difficult **2.** free from anxiety, pain, etc. **3.** comfortable; restful **4.** free from constraint; not stiff **5.** not strict or severe **6.** *a)* unhurried *b)* gradual —*adv.* [Colloq.] easily —**take it easy** [[Colloq.] **1.** to refrain from anger, haste, etc. **2.** to relax; rest —**eas′i·ness** *n.*

**easy chair** a stuffed or padded arm-chair

**eas′y·go′ing** *adj.* dealing with things in a relaxed or lenient way

**eat** (ēt) *vt.* **ate, eat′en, eat′ing** [OE. *etan*] **1.** to chew and swallow (food) **2.** to consume or ravage (with *away* or *up*) **3.** to destroy, as acid does; corrode **4.** to make by eating [acid *eats* holes in cloth] **5.** [Slang] to worry or bother —*vi.* to eat food; have a meal —**eat′er** *n.*

**eat′a·ble** *adj.* fit to be eaten —*n.* a thing fit to be eaten: *usually in pl.*

**eat·er·y** *n., pl.* **-ies** [Colloq.] a restaurant

**eats** (ēts) *n.pl.* [Colloq.] food

**eaves** (ēvz) *n.pl.* [< OE. *efes*] the projecting lower edge or edges of a roof

**eaves'drop'** (-dräp') *vi.* **-dropped',** **-drop'ping** [prob. < *eavesdropper*, one standing under eaves to overhear] to listen secretly to a private conversation —**eaves'drop'per** *n.*

**ebb** (eb) *n.* [OE. *ebba*] 1. the flow of the tide back toward the sea 2. a lessening; decline —*vi.* 1. to recede, as the tide 2. to lessen; decline

**eb·on·ite** (eb'ən it') *n.* *same as* VULCANITE

**eb·on·y** (eb'ən ē) *n.,* *pl.* **-ies** [< Gr. *ebenos*] the hard, heavy, dark wood of certain tropical trees —*adj.* 1. of ebony 2. like ebony; black

**e·bul·lient** (i bool'yənt, -bul'-) *adj.* [< L. *e-*, out + *bullire*, to boil] 1. boiling or bubbling up 2. enthusiastic; exuberant —**e·bul'lience** *n.*

**e·bul·li·tion** (eb'ə lish'ən) *n.* [see prec.] 1. a boiling or bubbling up 2. a sudden outburst, as of emotion

**ec·cen·tric** (ik sen'trik) *adj.* [< Gr. *ek-*, out of + *kentron*, center] 1. not having the same center, as two circles 2. having the axis off center 3. not exactly circular 4. odd, as in conduct; unconventional —*n.* 1. a disk set off center on a shaft, for converting circular motion into back-and-forth motion 2. an eccentric person —**ec·cen'tri·cal·ly** *adv.* —**ec·cen·tric·i·ty** (ek'sen tris'ə tē, -sən-) *n.,* *pl.* **-ties**

**Ec·cle·si·as·tes** (i klē'zē as'tēz) [< Gr. *ek-*, out + *kalein*, to call] a book of the Old Testament: abbrev. Eccles., Eccl.

**ec·cle·si·as·tic** (-tik) *adj.* [see prec.] ecclesiastical —*n.* a clergyman

**ec·cle·si·as·ti·cal** *adj.* of the church or the clergy

**ECG** electrocardiogram

**ech·e·lon** (esh'ə län') *n.* [< Fr. < L. *scala*, ladder] 1. a steplike formation of ships, troops, or aircraft 2. a subdivision of a military force 3. any of the levels of responsibility in an organization

**ech·o** (ek'ō) *n.,* *pl.* **-oes** [< Gr. *ēchō*] 1. the repetition of a sound by reflection of the sound waves from a surface 2. a sound so produced —*vi.* **-oed,** **-o·ing** 1. to reverberate 2. to make an echo —*vt.* to repeat (another's words, etc.)

**e·cho·ic** (e kō'ik) *adj.* imitative in sound, as the word *tinkle*

**é·clair** (ā kler', ē-) *n.* [Fr., lit., lightning] an oblong frosted pastry shell filled with custard, etc.

**é·clat** (ā klä') *n.* [Fr. < *éclater*, to burst (out)] 1. brilliant success 2. striking effect 3. acclaim; fame

**ec·lec·tic** (i klek'tik, e-) *adj.* [< Gr. *ek-*, out + *legein*, to pick] selecting or selected from various sources —*n.* one who uses eclectic methods —**ec·lec'ti·cal·ly** *adv.* —**ec·lec'ti·cism** *n.*

**e·clipse** (i klips') *n.* [< Gr. *ek-*, out + *leipein*, to leave] 1. the obscuring of the sun when the moon comes between it and the earth (**solar eclipse**), or of the moon when the earth's shadow is cast upon it (**lunar eclipse**) 2. any obscuring of light, or of fame, glory, etc. —*vt.* **e·clipsed',** **e·clips'ing** 1. to cause an eclipse of 2. to surpass

**e·clip·tic** (i klip'tik) *n.* the sun's apparent annual path; great circle of the celestial sphere

**ec·logue** (ek'lôg) *n.* [see ECLECTIC] a short pastoral poem

**e·co·cide** (ē'kō sīd') *n.* [< Gr. *oikos*, house + -CIDE] the destruction of the environment, as by pollutants

**e·col·o·gy** (ē käl'ə jē) *n.* [< Gr. *oikos*, house + *-logia*, -LOGY] the branch of biology that deals with the relations between living organisms and their environment —**e'co·log'i·cal** *adj.* —**e'co·log'i·cal·ly** *adv.* —**e·col'o·gist** *n.*

**econ.** 1. economic(s) 2. economy

**e·co·nom·ic** (ē'kə näm'ik, ek'ə-) *adj.* 1. of the management of income, expenditures, etc. 2. of economics 3. of the satisfaction of the material needs of people

**e'co·nom'i·cal** *adj.* 1. not wasting money, time, etc.; thrifty 2. of economics —**e'co·nom'i·cal·ly** *adv.*

**e'co·nom'ics** *n.pl.* [*with sing. v.*] 1. the science that deals with the production, distribution, and consumption of wealth 2. economic factors

**e·con·o·mist** (i kän'ə mist) *n.* a specialist in economics

**e·con'o·mize'** (-mīz') *vi.* **-mized',** **-miz'ing** to reduce waste or expenses —*vt.* to manage or use with thrift —**e·con'o·miz'er** *n.*

**e·con'o·my** (-mē) *n.,* *pl.* **-mies** [< Gr. *oikos*, house + *nomos*, managing] 1. the management of the income, expenditures, etc. of a household, government, etc. 2. careful management of wealth, etc.; thrift 3. an instance of thrift 4. a system of producing and distributing wealth

**e·co·sys·tem** (ē'kō sis'təm) *n.* [< Gr. *oikos*, house + SYSTEM] a community of animals and plants and the environment with which it is interrelated

**ec·ru** (ek'rōō) *adj.,* *n.* [< Fr. < L. *ex-*, intens. + *crudus*, raw] light tan

**ec·sta·sy** (ek'stə sē) *n.,* *pl.* **-sies** [< Gr. *ek-*, out + *histanai*, to place] a state or feeling of overpowering joy; rapture —**ec·stat·ic** (ik stat'ik) *adj.* —**ec·stat'i·cal·ly** *adv.*

**-ec·to·my** (ek'tə mē) [< Gr. *ek-*, out + *temnein*, to cut] a combining form meaning a surgical excision of [*appendectomy*]

**Ec·ua·dor** (ek'wə dôr') country on the NW coast of S. America: 104,506 sq. mi.; pop. 5,508,000

**ec·u·men·i·cal** (ek'yoo men'i k'l) *adj.* [< Gr. *oikoumenē* (*gē*), the inhabited (world)] 1. general or universal; esp., of the Christian Church as a whole 2. furthering religious unity, esp. among Christian churches —**ec'u·men'i·cal·ism** *n.* —**ec'u·men'i·cal·ly** *adv.*

**ec'u·men·ism** (-mə niz'm, e kyōō'-) *n.* the ecumenical movement, esp. among Christian churches: also **ec·u·men·i·cism** (ek'yoo men'i siz'm)

**ec·ze·ma** (ek'sə mə, eg'zə-; ig zē'mə) *n.* [< Gr. *ek-*, out + *zein*, to boil] a skin disease characterized by inflammation, itching, and scaliness

**-ed** [OE.] a suffix used: a) to form the past tense and past participle of many verbs   b) to form adjectives from nouns or verbs [cultured]

**ed.** 1. edited 2. pl. **eds.** a) edition b) editor

**E·dam (cheese)** (ē′dəm) [< Edam, Netherlands] a mild yellow cheese

**ed·dy** (ed′ē) n., pl. **-dies** [prob. < ON. itha] a little whirlpool or whirlwind —vi. **-died, -dy·ing** to whirl

**e·del·weiss** (ā′d'l vīs′) n. [G. < edel, noble + weiss, white] a small, flowering plant, esp. of the Alps, with white, woolly leaves

**e·de·ma** (i dē′mə) n. [< Gr. oidēma, swelling] an abnormal accumulation of fluid in body tissues or cavities

**E·den** (ēd′n) Bible the garden where Adam and Eve first lived; Paradise —n. any delightful place

**edge** (ej) n. [OE. ecg] 1. the sharp, cutting part of a blade 2. sharpness; keenness 3. the projecting ledge of a cliff, etc.; brink 4. the part farthest from the middle; border or margin 5. [Colloq.] advantage [he has the edge on me] —vt., vi. **edged, edg′ing** 1. to form an edge (on) 2. to make (one's) way sideways 3. to move gradually —**on edge** 1. very tense; irritable 2. impatient —**take the edge off** to dull the intensity, force, or pleasure of —**edg′er** n.

**edge′ways** (-wāz′) adv. with the edge foremost: also **edge′wise** (-wīz′)

**edg′ing** n. trimming along an edge

**edg·y** (ej′ē) adj. **-i·er, -i·est** irritable; on edge —**edg′i·ness** n.

**ed·i·ble** (ed′ə b'l) adj. [< L. edere, eat] fit to be eaten —n. [usually pl.] food —**ed′i·bil′i·ty** n.

**e·dict** (ē′dikt) n. [< L. e-, out + dicere, speak] a public order; decree

**ed·i·fice** (ed′ə fis) n. [see ff.] a building, esp. a large, imposing one

**ed·i·fy** (ed′ə fī′) vt. **-fied′, -fy′ing** [< L. aedificare, build] to instruct; esp., to instruct or improve morally —**ed′i·fi·ca′tion** n. —**ed′i·fi′er** n.

**Ed·in·burgh** (ed′'n bur′ə, -ō) capital of Scotland: pop. 469,000

**Ed·i·son** (ed′ə s'n), **Thomas A.** 1847–1931; U.S. inventor

**ed·it** (ed′it) vt. [< EDITOR] 1. to prepare (a manuscript, etc.) for publication by arranging, revising, etc. 2. to control the policy and contents of (a newspaper, etc.) 3. to prepare (a film, tape, etc.) for presentation by cutting, dubbing, etc.

**edit.** 1. edited 2. edition 3. editor

**e·di·tion** (i dish′ən) n. [see ff.] 1. the size or form in which a book is published 2. the total number of copies of a book, etc. published at one time 3. any particular issue of a newspaper

**ed·i·tor** (ed′i tər) n. [L. < e-, out + dare, give] 1. one that edits 2. a writer of editorials

**ed·i·to·ri·al** (ed′ə tôr′ē əl) adj. of or by an editor —n. an article in a newspaper, etc., explicitly stating opinions of the editor or publisher —**ed′i·to′ri·al·ly** adv.

**ed′i·to′ri·al·ize′** (-īz′) vi. **-ized′, -iz′ing** to express editorial opinions

**editor in chief** pl. **editors in chief** the editor who heads the editorial staff of a publication

**Ed·mon·ton** (ed′mən tən) capital of Alberta, Canada: pop. 377,000

**educ.** 1. education 2. educational

**ed·u·ca·ble** (ej′ə kə b'l) adj. that can be educated or trained —**ed′u·ca·bil′i·ty** n.

**ed·u·cate** (ej′ə kāt′) vt. **-cat′ed, -cat′ing** [< L. e-, out + ducere, to lead] 1. to develop the knowledge, skill, or character of, esp. by formal schooling; teach 2. to pay for the schooling of —**ed′u·ca′tor** n.

**ed·u·ca·tion** n. 1. the process of educating; teaching 2. knowledge, etc. thus developed 3. formal schooling —**ed′u·ca′tion·al** adj.

**e·duce** (i dōōs′, ē-) vt. **-duced′, -duc′ing** [see EDUCATE] 1. to draw out; elicit 2. to deduce

**-ee** (ē) [< Anglo-Fr. pp. ending] a suffix designating: 1. the recipient of an action [appointee] 2. one in a specified condition [absentee]

**EEG** electroencephalogram

**eel** (ēl) n. [OE. æl] a long, slippery, snakelike fish —**eel′y** (-ē) adj.

**e′er** (er, ar) adv. [Poet.] ever

**-eer** (ir) [< L. -arius] a suffix denoting a person involved with or an action involving [auctioneer]

**ee·rie, ee·ry** (ir′ē) adj. **-ri·er, -ri·est** [< OE. earg, timid] mysterious, uncanny, or weird —**ee′ri·ly** adv.

**ef-** same as EX-: used before f

**ef·face** (i fās′, e-) vt. **-faced′, -fac′ing** [< L. ex-, out + facies, face] 1. to rub out; erase 2. to make (oneself) inconspicuous —**ef·face′ment** n.

**ef·fect** (ə fekt′, i-) n. [< L. ex-, out + facere, do] 1. anything brought about by a cause; result 2. the power to cause results 3. influence 4. meaning [spoke to this effect] 5. an impression made on the mind, or its cause 6. a being operative or in force 7. [pl.] belongings; property —vt. to bring about; accomplish —**in effect** 1. actually 2. virtually 3. in operation —**take effect** to become operative

**ef·fec·tive** adj. 1. producing a desired effect; efficient 2. in effect; operative 3. impressive —**ef·fec′tive·ly** adv. —**ef·fec′tive·ness** n.

**ef·fec·tu·al** (ə fek′choo wəl, i-) adj. 1. producing, or able to produce, the desired effect 2. having legal force; valid —**ef·fec′tu·al·ly** adv.

**ef·fec′tu·ate′** (-wāt′) vt. **-at′ed, -at′ing** to bring about; effect

**ef·fem·i·nate** (i fem′ə nit) adj. [< L. ex-, out + femina, woman] showing qualities attributed to women, as

---

fat, āpe, cär; ten, ēven; is, bīte; gō, hôrn, tōōl, look; oil, out; up, fur; chin; she; thin, then; zh, leisure; ŋ, ring; ə for a in ago; ′, (ā′b'l); ë, Fr. coeur; ö, Fr. feu; Fr. mon; ü, Fr. duc; kh, G. ich, doch; ‡ foreign; < derived from weakness, delicacy, etc.; unmanly —**ef·fem′i·na·cy** (-nə sē) n.

**ef·fer·ent** (ef′ər ənt) adj. [< L. ex-, out + ferre, BEAR¹] carrying away from a central part, as nerves

**ef·fer·vesce** (ef′ər ves′) vi. -vesced′, -vesc′ing [< L. ex-, out + fervere, to boil] 1. to give off gas bubbles; bubble 2. to be lively —**ef′fer·ves′cence** n. —**ef′fer·ves′cent** adj.

**ef·fete** (e fēt′, i-) adj. [< L. ex-, out + fetus, productive] 1. no longer able to produce; sterile 2. decadent —**ef·fete′ly** adv. —**ef·fete′ness** n.

**ef·fi·ca·cious** (ef′ə kā′shəs) adj. [see EFFECT] that produces the desired effect —**ef′fi·ca′cious·ly** adv. —**ef′fi·ca·cy** (-kə sē) n.

**ef·fi·cient** (ə fish′ənt, i-) adj. [see EFFECT] producing the desired result with a minimum of effort, expense, or waste —**ef·fi′cien·cy** n. —**ef·fi′cient·ly** adv.

**ef·fi·gy** (ef′ə jē) n., pl. -gies [< L. ex-, out + fingere, to form] a statue or other image; esp., a crude representation (for hanging or burning) of a despised person

**ef·flu·ent** (ef′loo wənt) adj. [< L. effluere, to flow out] flowing out —n. the outflow of a sewer, septic tank, etc. —**ef′flu·ence** n.

**ef·flu·vi·um** (e floo′vē əm) n., pl. -vi·a (-ə), -vi·ums [see prec.] a disagreeable vapor or odor

**ef·fort** (ef′ərt) n. [< L. ex-, intens. + fortis, strong] 1. the use of energy to do something 2. a try; attempt 3. a result of working or trying —**ef′fort·less** adj. —**ef′fort·less·ly** adv.

**ef·fron·ter·y** (e frun′tər ē, i-) n., pl. -ies [< L. ex-, from + frons, forehead] impudence; audacity

**ef·ful·gence** (e ful′jəns, i-) n. [< L. ex-, forth + fulgere, shine] radiance; brilliance —**ef·ful′gent** adj.

**ef·fuse** (e fyooz′, i-) vt., vi. -fused′, -fus′ing [< L. ex-, out + fundere, pour] 1. to pour out or forth 2. to spread; diffuse

**ef·fu·sion** (-fyoo′zhən) n. 1. a pouring forth 2. unrestrained expression in speaking or writing —**ef·fu′sive** adj. —**ef·fu′sive·ly** adv. —**ef·fu′sive·ness** n.

**e.g.** [L. exempli gratia] for example

**e·gad** (i gad′, ē-) interj. [prob. < oh God] a softened oath

**e·gal·i·tar·i·an** (i gal′ə ter′ē ən) adj. [< Fr. égalité, equality] advocating full political and social equality for all people —n. one advocating this

**egg¹** (eg) n. [ON.] 1. the oval body laid by a female bird, fish, etc., containing the germ of a new individual 2. a female reproductive cell; ovum 3. a hen's egg, raw or cooked

**egg²** (eg) vt. [< ON. eggja, give edge to] to urge or incite (with on)

**egg′beat′er** n. a kitchen utensil for beating eggs, cream, etc.

**egg foo yong** (or **young**) (eg′ foo yuŋ′) a Chinese-American dish of eggs beaten and cooked with bean sprouts, onions, minced pork, etc.

**egg′head′** n. [Slang] an intellectual

**egg′nog′** (-näg′, -nôg′) n. [EGG¹ + nog, strong ale] a drink made of eggs, milk, sugar, and, often, whiskey

**egg′plant′** n. a plant with a large purple-skinned fruit, eaten as a vegetable

**e·gis** (ē′jis) n. same as AEGIS

**eg·lan·tine** (eg′lən tīn′, -tēn′) n. [< L. aculeus, a sting] a European pink rose with sweet-scented leaves

EGGPLANT

**e·go** (ē′gō) n., pl. -gos [L., I] 1. the individual as aware of himself; the self 2. conceit 3. Psychoanalysis the part of the psyche which governs action rationally

**e′go·cen′tric** (-sen′trik) adj. viewing everything in relation to oneself —n. an egocentric person

**e′go·ism** n. 1. selfishness; self-interest 2. conceit —**e′go·ist** n. —**e′go·is′tic, e′go·is′ti·cal** adj.

**e·go·tism** (ē′gə tiz′m) n. 1. excessive reference to oneself in speaking or writing 2. conceit —**e′go·tist** n. —**e′go·tis′tic, e′go·tis′ti·cal** adj.

**ego trip** an experience, activity, etc. that is self-fulfilling or increases one's vanity

**e·gre·gious** (i grē′jəs) adj. [< L. e-, out + grex, a herd] outstandingly bad; flagrant —**e·gre′gious·ly** adv.

**e·gress** (ē′gres) n. [< L. e-, out + gradi, go] a way out; exit

**e·gret** (ē′grit, eg′rit) n. [OFr. aigrette] 1. a heronlike bird with long white plumes 2. such a plume

**E·gypt** (ē′jipt) country in NE Africa, on the Mediterranean: 386,000 sq. mi.; pop. 34,383,000; cap. Cairo

**E·gyp·tian** (i jip′shən, ē-) adj. of Egypt, its people, etc. —n. 1. a native or inhabitant of Egypt 2. the language of the ancient Egyptians

**eh** (ā, e) interj. a sound expressing: 1. surprise 2. doubt or inquiry

**EHF** extremely high frequency

**ei·der** (ī′dər) n. [ult. < ON. æthr] 1. a large sea duck of northern regions 2. eiderdown

**ei′der·down′** n. the soft, fine down of the eider duck, used as a stuffing for quilts, pillows, etc.

**eight** (āt) adj., n. [OE. eahta] one more than seven; 8; VIII —**eighth** (ātth, āth) adj., n.

**eight ball** a black ball with the number eight on it, used in playing pool —**behind the eight ball** [Slang] in a very unfavorable position

**eight·een** (ā′tēn′) adj., n. eight more than ten; 18; XVIII —**eight′eenth′** (-tēnth′) adj., n.

**eight·y** (āt′ē) adj., n., pl. -ies eight times ten; 80; LXXX —**the eighties** the numbers or years, as of a century, from 80 through 89 —**eight′i·eth** (-ith) adj., n.

**Ein·stein** (īn′stīn) **Albert** 1879-1955; U.S. physicist born in Germany; formulated theory of relativity

**Eir·e** (er′ə) Gaelic name of IRELAND (sense 2)

**Ei·sen·how·er** (ī′z'n hou′ər), **Dwight**

**David** 1890–1969; U.S. general & 34th president of the U.S. (1953–1961)

**ei·ther** (ē′thər, ī′-) *adj.* [OE. ǣghwæther] **1.** one or the other (of two) **2.** each (of two) —*pron.* one or the other —*conj.* a correlative used with *or* to denote a choice of alternatives [*either* go or stay] —*adv.* any more than the other; also [if you don't go, I won't *either*]

**e·jac·u·late** (i jak′yə lāt′) *vt.*, *vi.* -lat′ed, -lat′ing [see ff.] **1.** to eject (esp. semen) **2.** to utter suddenly; exclaim —**e·jac′u·la′tion** *n.*

**e·ject** (i jekt′) *vt.* [< L. *e-*, out + *jacere*, throw] to throw or force out; expel; discharge —**e·jec′tion** *n.*

**eke** (ēk) *vt.* eked, ek′ing [< OE. *eacan*, to increase] to manage to make (a living) with difficulty: with *out*

**EKG** electrocardiogram

**e·kis·tics** (i kis′tiks) *n.pl.* [*with sing. v.*] [< Gr. *oikos*, house + -ICS] the science of city and area planning to meet both individual and community needs

**e·lab·o·rate** (i lab′ər it; *for v.* -ə rāt′) *adj.* [< L. *e-*, out + *labor*, work] developed in great detail; complicated —*vt.* -rat′ed, -rat′ing to work out in great detail —*vi.* to add more details (usually with *on* or *upon*) —**e·lab′o·rate·ly** *adv.* —**e·lab′o·rate·ness** *n.* —**e·lab′o·ra′tion** *n.*

**é·lan** (ā län′) *n.* [Fr. < *élancer*, to dart] spirited self-assurance; dash

**e·lapse** (i laps′) *vi.* e·lapsed′, e·laps′ing [< L. *e-*, out + *labi*, to glide] to slip by; pass: said of time

**e·las·tic** (i las′tik) *adj.* [< Gr. *elaunein*, set in motion] **1.** able to return immediately to its original size, shape, etc. after being stretched, squeezed, etc.; flexible **2.** able to recover easily, as from dejection; buoyant **3.** adaptable —*n.* an elastic band or fabric —**e·las′tic′i·ty** (-tis′ə tē) *n.*

**e·las′ti·cize′** (-tə sīz′) *vt.* -cized′, -ciz′ing to make (fabric) elastic

**e·late** (i lāt′, ē-) *vt.* -lat′ed, -lat′ing [< L. *ex-*, out + *ferre*, BEAR¹] to raise the spirits of; make very proud, happy, etc. —**e·la′tion** *n.*

**el·bow** (el′bō) *n.* [see ELL² & BOW²] **1.** the joint between the upper and lower arm; esp., the outer angle made by a bent arm **2.** anything bent like an elbow —*vt.*, *vi.* to shove as with the elbows —**out at (the) elbows** shabby

**elbow grease** [Colloq.] hard work

**el′bow·room′** *n.* ample space or room

**eld·er¹** (el′dər) *adj.* [< OE. *ald*, old] **1.** older **2.** of superior rank, position, etc. **3.** earlier; former —*n.* **1.** an older or aged person **2.** an older person with some authority, as in a tribe **3.** any of certain church officers

**el·der²** (el′dər) *n.* [OE. *ellern*] a shrub or tree of the honeysuckle family, with red or purple berries

**el′der·ber′ry** *n.*, *pl.* -ries **1.** same as

ELDER² **2.** its berry, used for making wines, jelly, etc.

**eld′er·ly** *adj.* somewhat old

**eld·est** (el′dist) *adj.* oldest

**El Do·ra·do, El·do·ra·do** (el′də rä′dō) *pl.* -dos [Sp., the gilded] any place supposed to be rich in gold, opportunity, etc.

**e·lect** (i lekt′) *adj.* [< L. *e-*, out + *legere*, choose] **1.** chosen **2.** elected but not yet installed in office [mayor-*elect*] —*vt.*, *vi.* **1.** to select for an office by voting **2.** to choose

**e·lec·tion** (i lek′shən) *n.* **1.** a choosing or choice **2.** a choosing by vote

**e·lec′tion·eer′** (-shə nir′) *vi.* to canvass votes in an election

**e·lec′tive** (-tiv) *adj.* **1.** *a)* filled by election [an *elective* office] *b)* chosen by election **2.** having the power to choose **3.** optional —*n.* an optional course or subject in a school curriculum

**e·lec′tor** (-tər) *n.* **1.** one who elects; specif., a qualified voter **2.** a member of the electoral college —**e·lec′tor·al** *adj.*

**electoral college** an assembly elected by the voters to perform the formal duty of electing the president and vice-president of the U.S.

**e·lec′tor·ate** (-it) *n.* all those qualified to vote in an election

**E·lec·tra** (i lek′trə) *Gr. Myth.* a daughter of Agamemnon: she plotted the death of her mother

**e·lec·tric** (i lek′trik) *adj.* [< Gr. *ēlektron*, amber: from the effect of friction upon amber] **1.** of or charged with electricity **2.** producing, or produced by, electricity **3.** operated by electricity **4.** thrilling; exciting Also **e·lec′tri·cal** —**e·lec′tri·cal·ly** *adv.*

**electric chair** a chair used in electrocuting those sentenced to death

**e·lec·tri·cian** (i lek′trish′ən, ē′lek-) *n.* a person whose work is the construction and repair of electric apparatus

**e·lec·tric′i·ty** (-tris′ə tē) *n.* **1.** a property of certain fundamental particles of all matter, as electrons (negative charges) and protons or positrons (positive charges): electric charge is generated by friction, induction, or chemical change **2.** an electric current **3.** electric current as a public utility for lighting, etc.

**e·lec·tri·fy** (i lek′trə fī′) *vt.* -fied′, -fy′ing **1.** to charge with electricity **2.** to excite; thrill **3.** to equip for the use of electricity —**e·lec′tri·fi·ca′tion** *n.* —**e·lec′tri·fi′er** *n.*

**electro-** *a combining form meaning* electric, electricity

**e·lec·tro·car·di·o·gram** (i lek′trō kär′dē ə gram′) *n.* [prec. + CARDIO- + -GRAM] a tracing showing the changes in electric potential produced by contractions of the heart

**e·lec′tro·car′di·o·graph′** (-graf′) *n.* an instrument for making electrocardiograms

**e·lec·tro·chem·is·try** *n.* the science dealing with chemical changes produced by electrical energy

**e·lec·tro·cute** (i lek'trə kyōōt') *vt.* -cut'ed, -cut'ing [ELECTRO- + (EXE)CUTE] to kill or execute with electricity —e·lec'tro·cu'tion *n.*

**e·lec·trode** (i lek'trōd) *n.* [ELECTR(O)- + -ODE] any terminal by which electricity enters or leaves a battery, etc.

**e·lec·tro·en·ceph·a·lo·gram'** (-trō en sef'ə lə gram') *n.* [see ENCEPHALITIS & -GRAM] a tracing showing the changes in electric potential produced by the brain

**e·lec·tro·en·ceph·a·lo·graph'** (-graf') *n.* an instrument for making electroencephalograms

**e·lec·trol·o·gist** (i lek'träl'ə jist) *n.*, a practitioner of electrolysis (sense 2)

**e·lec·trol·y·sis** (i lek'träl'ə sis) *n.* [ELECTRO- + -LYSIS] 1. the decomposition of an electrolyte by the action of an electric current passing through it 2. the eradication of unwanted hair with an electrified needle

**e·lec·tro·lyte** (i lek'trə līt') *n.* [ELECTRO- + -LYTE] any substance which in solution is capable of conducting an electric current by the movement of its dissociated ions —e·lec'tro·lyt'ic (-lit'ik) *adj.*

**e·lec·tro·mag·net** (i lek'trō mag'nit) *n.* a soft iron core that becomes a magnet when an electric current flows through a coil surrounding it —e·lec'·tro·mag·net'ic (-net'ik) *adj.*

**electromagnetic wave** a wave generated by an oscillating electric charge

**e·lec·tro·mo·tive** (i lek'trə mōt'iv) *adj.* producing an electric current through differences in potential

**e·lec·tron** (i lek'trän) *n.* [see ELECTRIC] any of the negatively charged particles that form a part of all atoms

**e·lec·tron·ic** (i lek'trän'ik, ē'lek-) *adj.* 1. of electrons 2. operating, produced, or done by the action of electrons —e·lec'tron'i·cal·ly *adv.*

**electronic music** music in which the sounds are originated by electronic devices and recorded on tape

**e·lec·tron'ics** *n.pl.* [with sing. v.] the science that deals with electron action and the use of electron tubes, transistors, etc.

**electron microscope** a device that focuses a beam of electrons to form a greatly enlarged image of an object, as on a fluorescent screen

**electron tube** a sealed glass or metal tube with a gas or a vacuum inside, used to control the flow of electrons

**e·lec·tro·plate** (i lek'trə plāt') *vt.* -plat'ed, -plat'ing to deposit a coating of metal on by electrolysis —*n.* anything so plated

**e·lec·tro·shock' therapy** shock therapy using electricity

**e·lec·tro·ther·a·py** (-ther'ə pē) *n.* the treatment of disease by means of electricity, as by diathermy

**e·lec·tro·type** (-tīp') *n. Printing* a facsimile plate made by electroplating a wax or plastic impression of the surface to be reproduced

**el·ee·mos·y·nar·y** (el'i mäs'ə ner'ē, el'ē ə-) *adj.* [< Gr. *eleēmosynē*, pity] of, for, or supported by charity

**el·e·gant** (el'ə gənt) *adj.* [< L. *e-*, out + *legere*, choose] 1. having dignified richness and grace, as of manner, design, dress, etc.; tastefully luxurious 2. [Colloq.] excellent —el'e·gance *n.* —el'e·gant·ly *adv.*

**el·e·gi·ac** (el'ə jī'ək, i lē'jē ak') *adj.* 1. of, like, or fit for an elegy 2. sad; mournful Also el'e·gi'a·cal

**el·e·gy** (el'ə jē) *n., pl.* -gies [< Gr. *elegos*, a lament] a mournful poem, esp. of lament and praise for the dead

**el·e·ment** (el'ə mənt) *n.* [< L. *elementum*] 1. the natural or suitable environment for a person or thing 2. a component part or quality, often one that is basic or essential 3. *Chem.* any substance that cannot be separated into different substances except by radioactive decay or by nuclear reactions: all matter is composed of such substances —**the elements** 1. the first principles; rudiments 2. wind, rain, etc.; forces of the atmosphere

**el·e·men·tal** (el'ə men't'l) *adj.* 1. of or like basic, natural forces; primal 2. *same as* ELEMENTARY (sense 2) 3. being an essential part or parts

**el·e·men·ta·ry** (-tər ē, -trē) *adj.* 1. *same as* ELEMENTAL 2. of first principles or fundamentals; basic; simple

**elementary particle** a subatomic particle, as a neutron, electron, etc.

**elementary school** a school of the first six (or eight) grades, where basic subjects are taught

**el·e·phant** (el'ə fənt) *n.* [< Gr. *elephas*] a huge, thick-skinned mammal with a long flexible snout, or trunk, and, usually, two ivory tusks

**el·e·phan·ti·a·sis** (el'ə fən tī'ə sis) *n.* a chronic disease of the skin causing enlargement of certain bodily parts

**el·e·phan·tine** (el'ə fan'tēn, -tīn) *adj.* like an elephant; huge, clumsy, etc.

**el·e·vate** (el'ə vāt') *vt.* -vat'ed, -vat'ing [< L. *e-*, out + *levare*, to lift] 1. to lift up; raise 2. to raise in rank 3. to raise to a higher moral or intellectual level 4. to elate; exhilarate

**el'e·va'tion** *n.* 1. an elevating or being elevated 2. a high place or position 3. height above the surface of the earth or above sea level

**el'e·va'tor** *n.* 1. one that elevates, or lifts up 2. a suspended cage for hoisting or lowering people or things 3. a warehouse for storing and discharging grain 4. a device like a horizontal rudder, for making an aircraft go up or down

**el·ev·en** (i lev'ən) *adj., n.* [OE. *endleofan*] one more than ten; 11; XI —el·ev'enth (-ənth) *adj., n.*

**elf** (elf) *n., pl.* **elves** (elvz) [OE. *ælf*] *Folklore* a tiny, often mischievous fairy —**elf'in, elf'ish** *adj.*

**El Grec·o** (el grek'ō) 1541?-1614?; painter in Spain, born in Crete

**e·lic·it** (i lis'it) *vt.* [< L. *e-*, out + *lacere*, entice] to draw forth; evoke (a response, etc.) —e·lic'i·ta'tion n.

e·lide (i līd') vt. e·lid'ed, e·lid'ing [< L. e-, out + laedere, to strike] to leave out; esp., to slur over (a letter, etc.) in pronunciation —e·li·sion (i lizh'ən) n.

el·i·gi·ble (el'i jə b'l) adj. [see ELECT] fit to be chosen; qualified —n. an eligible person —el'i·gi·bil'i·ty n.

E·li·jah (i lī'jə) Bible a prophet of Israel in the 9th c. B.C.

e·lim·i·nate (i lim'ə nāt') vt. -nat'ed, -nat'ing [< L. e-, out + limen, threshold] 1. to get rid of; remove 2. to leave out of consideration; omit 3. to excrete —e·lim'i·na'tion n.

El·i·ot (el'ē ət) 1. George (pseud. of Mary Ann Evans) 1819–80; Eng. novelist 2. T(homas) S(tearns), 1888–1965; Brit. poet, born in the U.S.

e·lite, é·lite (i lēt', ā-) n. [Fr. < L.: see ELECT] [also used with pl. v.] the group or part of a group regarded as the best, most powerful, etc.

e·lit'ism n. government or control by an elite —e·lit'ist adj., n.

e·lix·ir (i lik'sər) n. [Ar. al-iksīr] 1. a hypothetical substance sought for by medieval alchemists to prolong life indefinitely: in full elixir of life 2. a medicine in alcoholic solution

E·liz·a·beth (i liz'ə bəth) city in NE N.J.; pop. 113,000

E·liz·a·beth I 1533–1603; queen of England (1558–1603)

E·liz·a·be'than (-bē'thən, -beth'ən) adj. of or characteristic of the time of Elizabeth I —n. an English person, esp. a writer, of that time

elk (elk) n., pl. elk, elks [OE. eolh] 1. a large, mooselike deer of N Europe and Asia 2. the wapiti

ell¹ (el) n. 1. an extension or wing at right angles to the main structure 2. an L-shaped joint, as of pipes

ell² (el) n. [OE. eln] a former measure of length (in England, 45 in.)

ELK

el·lipse (i lips') n., pl. -lip'ses (-lip'-siz) [< Gr. elleipein, to fall short] a closed curve in the form of a symmetrical oval

el·lip·sis (i lip'sis) n., pl. -ses (-sēz) [see prec.] 1. the omission of a word or words understood in the context, as in "if (it is) possible" 2. a mark (. . .) indicating an omission of words

el·lip·ti·cal (i lip'ti k'l) adj. 1. of, or having the form of, an ellipse 2. of or characterized by ellipsis Also el·lip'tic —el·lip'ti·cal·ly adv.

elm (elm) n. [OE.] 1. a tall, hardy shade tree 2. its hard, heavy wood

el·o·cu·tion (el'ə kyōō'shən) n. [see ELOQUENT] the art of public speaking —el'o·cu'tion·ist n.

e·lon·gate (i lôn'gāt) vt., vi. -gat·ed, -gat·ing [< L. e-, out + longus, long] to make or become longer; lengthen —e·lon'ga'tion n.

e·lope (i lōp') vi. e·loped', e·lop'ing [prob. < OE. a-, away + hleapan, to run] to run away secretly, esp. in order to get married —e·lope'ment n.

el·o·quent (el'ə kwənt) adj. [< L. e-, out + loqui, speak] vivid, forceful, fluent, etc. in speech or writing —el'o·quence n. —el'o·quent·ly adv.

El Pas·o (el pas'ō) city in westernmost Tex.: pop. 322,000

El Sal·va·dor (el sal'və dôr') country in Central America, on the Pacific: 8,260 sq. mi.; pop. 3,037,000

else (els) adj. [OE. elles] 1. different; other [somebody else] 2. in addition [is there anything else?] —adv. 1. differently; otherwise [where else can I go?] 2. if not [study, (or) else you will fail]

else'where' (-hwer', -wer') adv. in or to some other place

e·lu·ci·date (i lōō'sə dāt') vt., vi. -dat'ed, -dat'ing [< L. e-, out + lucidus, clear] to make (something) clear; explain —e·lu'ci·da'tion n.

e·lude (i lōōd') vt. e·lud'ed, e·lud'ing [< L. e-, out + ludere, to play] 1. to avoid or escape from by quickness, cunning, etc.; evade 2. to escape the mental grasp of —e·lud'er n.

e·lu·sive (i lōō'siv) adj. tending to elude —e·lu'sive·ness n.

elves (elvz) n., pl. of ELF

E·ly·si·um (i lizh'ē əm, -liz'-) Gr. Myth. the place where virtuous people dwell after death —n. any state of ideal bliss; paradise —E·ly'sian (-lizh'ən, -ē ən) adj.

em (em) n. [< the letter M] Printing a unit of measure, as of column width

'em (əm, 'm) pron. [Colloq.] them

em- same as EN-: used before p, b, or m

e·ma·ci·ate (i mā'shē āt', -sē-) vt. -at'ed, -at'ing [< L. e-, out + macies, leanness] to cause to become abnormally lean —e·ma'ci·a'tion n.

em·a·nate (em'ə nāt') vi. -nat'ed, -nat'ing [< L. e-, out + manare, to flow] to come forth; issue, as from a source —em'a·na'tion n.

e·man·ci·pate (i man'sə pāt') vt. -pat'ed, -pat'ing [< L. e-, out + manus, the hand + capere, to take] 1. to set free (a slave, etc.) 2. to free from restraint —e·man'ci·pa'tion n. —e·man'ci·pa'tor n.

e·mas·cu·late (i mas'kyə lāt') vt. -lat'ed, -lat'ing [< L. e-, out + masculus, male] 1. to castrate 2. to weaken —e·mas'cu·la'tion n.

em·balm (im bäm') vt. [see EN- & BALM] to preserve (a dead body) with various chemicals —em·balm'er n.

em·bank (im baŋk') vt. to protect, support, or enclose with a bank of earth, etc. —em·bank'ment n.

em·bar·go (im bär'gō) n., pl. -goes

[Sp. < L. *in-*, in + ML. *barra*, a bar]
1. a government order prohibiting the entry or departure of commercial ships at its ports 2. any legal restriction of commerce —*vt.* **-goed, -go·ing** to put an embargo upon

**em·bark'** (-bärk') *vt.* [ < L. *in-*, in + *barca*, small boat] to put or take aboard a ship, airplane, etc. —*vi.* 1. to go aboard a ship, airplane, etc. 2. to begin a journey 3. to engage in an enterprise —**em'bar·ka'tion** *n.*

**em·bar·rass** (im ber'əs) *vt.* [< It. *in-*, in + *barra*, a bar] 1. to cause to feel self-conscious 2. to hinder 3. to cause to be in debt —**em·bar'rass·ing** *adj.* —**em·bar'rass·ment** *n.*

**em·bas·sy** (em'bə sē) *n., pl.* **-sies** [see AMBASSADOR] 1. the residence or offices of an ambassador 2. an ambassador and his staff 3. a group sent on an official mission

**em·bat·tled** (im bat''ld) *adj.* [< OFr.] ready for battle

**em·bed** (im bed') *vt.* **-bed'ded, -bed'ding** to set or fix firmly in a surrounding mass —**em·bed'ment** *n.*

**em·bel·lish** (im bel'ish) *vt.* [< OFr. *em-*, in + *bel*, beautiful] 1. to decorate; adorn 2. to improve (a story, etc.) by adding details, often fictitious —**em·bel'lish·ment** *n.*

**em·ber** (em'bər) *n.* [OE. *æmerge*] 1. a glowing piece of coal, wood, etc. 2. [*pl.*] the smoldering remains of a fire

**em·bez·zle** (im bez''l) *vt.* **-zled, -zling** [ < OFr. *en-*, in + *besillier*, destroy] to steal (money, etc. entrusted to one) —**em·bez'zle·ment** *n.* —**em·bez'zler** *n.*

**em·bit·ter** (-bit'ər) *vt.* to make bitter

**em·bla·zon** (im blā'z'n) *vt.* [see BLAZON] 1. to decorate (*with* coats of arms, etc.) 2. to display brilliantly 3. to extol —**em·bla'zon·ment** *n.*

**em·blem** (em'bləm) *n.* [ < Gr. *en-*, in + *ballein*, to throw] a visible symbol of a thing, idea, etc.; sign; badge —**em'blem·at'ic** (-blə mat'ik) *adj.*

**em·bod·y** (im bäd'ē) *vt.* **-ied, -y·ing** 1. to give bodily form to 2. to give definite form to 3. to form into, or make part of, an organized whole; incorporate —**em·bod'i·ment** *n.*

**em·bold·en** (im bōl'd'n) *vt.* to give courage to; cause to be bold

**em·bo·lism** (em'bə liz'm) *n.* [ < Gr. *en-*, in + *ballein*, to throw] the obstruction of a blood vessel as by a blood clot or air bubble

**em·boss** (im bôs') *vt.* [see EN- & BOSS²] 1. to decorate with raised designs, patterns, etc. 2. to raise (a design, etc.) in relief —**em·boss'ment** *n.*

**em·bou·chure** (äm'boo shoor') *n.* [Fr. < L. *in*, in + *bucca*, cheek] the method of applying the lips to the mouthpiece of a wind instrument

**em·brace** (im brās') *vt.* **-braced', -brac'ing** [ < L. *im-*, in + *brachium*, an arm] 1. to clasp in the arms lovingly; hug 2. to accept readily 3. to take up (a profession, etc.) 4. to encircle 5. to include —*vi.* to clasp each other in the arms —*n.* an embracing; hug —**em·brace'a·ble** *adj.*

**em·bra·sure** (im brā'zhər) *n.* [Fr. < *embraser*, widen an opening] 1. an opening (for a door or window) wider on the inside than on the outside 2. an opening in a wall for a gun, with the sides slanting outward

**em·bro·cate** (em'brō kāt', -brə-) *vt.* **-cat'ed, -cat'ing** [ < Gr. *en-*, in + *brechein*, to wet] to moisten and rub (a part of the body) with an oil, liniment, etc. —**em'bro·ca'tion** *n.*

**em·broi·der** (im broi'dər) *vt., vi.* [ < OFr. *en-*, on + *brosder*, embroider] 1. to make (a design, etc.) on (fabric) with needlework 2. to embellish (a story); exaggerate

**em·broi·der·y** *n., pl.* **-ies** 1. the art of embroidering 2. embroidered work or fabric 3. embellishment

**em·broil** (im broil') *vt.* [ < OFr. *en-*, in + *brouillier*, to dirty] 1. to confuse; muddle 2. to involve in conflict or trouble —**em·broil'ment** *n.*

**em·bry·o** (em'brē ō') *n., pl.* **-os'** [ < Gr. *en-*, in + *bryein*, to swell] 1. an animal in the earliest stages of its development in the uterus 2. the rudimentary plant contained in a seed 3. an early stage of something —**em'bry·on'ic** (-än'ik) *adj.*

**em·bry·ol·o·gy** (-äl'ə jē) *n.* [EMBRYO + -LOGY] the branch of biology dealing with the formation and development of embryos —**em'bry·ol'o·gist** *n.*

**em·cee** (em'sē') *vt., vi.* **-ceed', -cee'ing** [ < M.C.] [Colloq.] to act as master of ceremonies (for) —*n.* [Colloq.] a master of ceremonies

**e·mend** (i mend') *vt.* [ < L. *emendare*, to correct] to make scholarly corrections in (a text) —**e·men·da·tion** (ē'man dā'shən, em'ən-) *n.*

**em·er·ald** (em'ər əld) *n.* [ < Gr. *smaragdos*] 1. a bright-green, transparent precious stone 2. bright green

**e·merge** (i murj') *vi.* **e·merged', e·merg'ing** [ < L. *e-*, out + *mergere*, to dip] 1. to rise as from a fluid 2. to become visible or apparent 3. to evolve —**e·mer'gence** *n.* —**e·mer'gent** *adj.*

**e·mer·gen·cy** (i mur'jən sē) *n., pl.* **-cies** [orig. sense, an emerging] a sudden, generally unexpected occurrence demanding immediate action

**e·mer·i·tus** (i mer'ə təs) *adj.* [L. < *e-*, out + *mereri*, to serve] retired from active service, usually for age, but retaining one's title [professor *emeritus*]

**Em·er·son** (em'ər sən), **Ralph Wal·do** (wôl'dō) 1803–82; U.S. writer

**em·er·y** (em'ər ē) *n.* [ < Gr. *smyris*] a dark, hard variety of corundum used for grinding, etc.

**e·met·ic** (i met'ik) *adj.* [ < Gr. *emein*, to vomit] causing vomiting —*n.* an emetic substance

**-e·mi·a** (ēm'ē ə) [ < Gr. *haima*, blood] a suffix meaning a (specified) condition of the blood [leukemia]

**em·i·grate** (em'ə grāt') *vi.* **-grat'ed, -grat'ing** [ < L. *e-*, out + *migrare*, to move] to leave a country or region to settle in another —**em'i·grant** (-grənt) *adj., n.* —**em'i·gra'tion** *n.*

**é·mi·gré, e·mi·gré** (em'ə grā', ā'mə-grā') *n.* [Fr.] a person forced to flee his country for political reasons

**em·i·nence** (em'ə nəns) *n.* [< L. *eminere*, stand out] 1. a high place, thing, etc. 2. superiority in rank, position, etc. 3. [E-] a title of honor of a cardinal, preceded by *His* or *Your*

**em'i·nent** *adj.* [see prec.] 1. high; lofty 2. projecting; prominent 3. renowned; distinguished 4. outstanding —**em'i·nent·ly** *adv.*

**eminent domain** the right of a government to take (usually by purchase) private property for public use

**e·mir** (i·mir') *n.* [< Ar. *amara*, to command] a Moslem ruler

**em·is·sar·y** (em'ə ser'ē) *n., pl.* -**ies** [see EMIT] a person, esp. a secret agent, sent on a specific mission

**e·mis·sion** (i mish'ən) *n.* 1. an emitting 2. something emitted; discharge

**e·mit** (i mit') *vt.* **e·mit'ted, e·mit'ting** [< L. *e-*, out + *mittere*, send] 1. to send out; give forth; discharge 2. to utter (sounds, etc.) —**e·mit'ter** *n.*

**e·mol·li·ent** (i mäl'yənt) *adj.* [< L. *e-*, out + *mollire*, soften] softening; soothing —*n.* a medicine that softens or soothes surface tissues

**e·mol·u·ment** (-yoo mənt) *n.* [< L. *e-*, out + *molere*, grind] gain from employment or position; salary, fees, etc.

**e·mote** (i mōt') *vi.* **e·mot'ed, e·mot'ing** [Colloq.] to display one's emotions dramatically

**e·mo·tion** (i mō'shən) *n.* [< L. *e-*, out + *movere*, to move] 1. strong feeling 2. any specific feeling, as love, hate, fear, anger, etc.

**e·mo'tion·al** *adj.* 1. of or showing emotion 2. easily aroused to emotion 3. appealing to the emotions —**e·mo'tion·al·ism** *n.* —**e·mo'tion·al·ly** *adv.*

**e·mo'tion·al·ize'** *vt.* -**ized'**, -**iz'ing** to deal with in an emotional way

**em·path·ic** (im path'ik) *adj.* of or showing empathy

**em·pa·thize** (em'pə thīz') *vi.* -**thized'**, -**thiz'ing** to feel empathy (with)

**em'pa·thy** (-thē) *n.* [< Gr. *en-*, in + *pathos*, feeling] intellectual or emotional identification with another

**em·pen·nage** (em'pə näzh') *n.* [Fr. < *em*, in + *penne*, a feather] the tail assembly of an airplane, including the fin, rudder, elevators, etc.

**em·per·or** (em'pər ər) *n.* [< L. *imperare*, to command] the supreme ruler of an empire

**em·pha·sis** (em'fə sis) *n., pl.* -**ses'** (-sēz') [< Gr. *en-*, in + *phainein*, to show] 1. force of expression, action, etc. 2. special stress given to a syllable, word, etc. in speaking 3. importance; stress

**em'pha·size'** (-sīz') *vt.* -**sized'**, -**siz'ing** to give emphasis to; stress

**em·phat·ic** (im fat'ik) *adj.* 1. felt or done with emphasis 2. using emphasis in speaking, etc. 3. forcible; striking —**em·phat'i·cal·ly** *adv.*

**em·phy·se·ma** (em'fə sē'mə) *n.* [< Gr. *en-*, in + *physaein*, to blow] a disease of the lungs in which the air sacs become distended and lose elasticity

**em·pire** (em'pīr) *n.* [see EMPEROR] 1. supreme rule 2. government by an emperor or empress 3. a group of states or territories under one ruler

**em·pir·i·cal** (em pir'i k'l) *adj.* [< Gr. *en-*, in + *peira*, trial] relying or based on experiment or experience —**em·pir'i·cism** (-ə siz'm) *n.*

**em·place·ment** (im plās'mənt) *n.* the prepared position from which a heavy gun or guns are fired

**em·ploy** (im ploi') *vt.* [< L. *in-*, in + *plicare*, to fold] 1. to use 2. to keep busy or occupied 3. to engage the services of; hire —*n.* employment

**em·ploy'a·ble** *adj.* physically and mentally fit to be hired for work

**em·ploy·ee, em·ploy·e** (im ploi'ē, em'ploi ē') *n.* a person employed by another for wages or salary

**em·ploy'er** *n.* one who employs others for wages or salary

**em·ploy'ment** *n.* 1. an employing or being employed 2. work; occupation 3. the number or percentage of persons gainfully employed

**em·po·ri·um** (em pôr'ē əm) *n., pl.* -**ri·ums, -ri·a** (-ə) [< Gr. *en-*, in + *poros*, 'way] a large store with a wide variety of things for sale

**em·pow·er** (im pou'ər) *vt.* 1. to give power to; authorize 2. to enable

**em·press** (em'pris) *n.* 1. an emperor's wife 2. a woman ruler of an empire

**emp·ty** (emp'tē) *adj.* -**ti·er, -ti·est** [OE. *æmettig*] 1. having nothing or no one in it; unoccupied 2. worthless [*empty* pleasure] 3. insincere [*empty* promises] —*vt.* -**tied, -ty·ing** 1. to make empty 2. to remove (the contents) of something —*vi.* 1. to become empty 2. to pour out; discharge —*n., pl.* -**ties** an empty truck, bottle, etc. —**emp'ti·ly** *adv.* —**emp'ti·ness** *n.*

**emp'ty-hand'ed** *adj.* bringing or carrying away nothing

**em·py·re·an** (em'pī rē'ən) *n.* [< Gr. *en-*, in + *pyr*, fire] 1. the highest heaven 2. the sky; firmament

**e·mu** (ē'myoō) *n.* [prob. < Port. *ema*, a crane] a large, nonflying Australian bird, like the ostrich but smaller

**em·u·late** (em'yə lāt') *vt.* -**lat'ed, -lat'ing** [< L. *aemulus*, trying to equal or excel] 1. to try to equal or surpass 2. to rival successfully —**em'u·la'tion** *n.* —**em'u·la'tive** *adj.* —**em'u·la'tor** *n.* —**em'u·lous** *adj.*

**e·mul·si·fy** (i mul'sə fī') *vt., vi.* -**fied', -fy'ing** to form into an emulsion —**e·mul'si·fi·ca'tion** *n.*

**e·mul·sion** (i mul'shən) *n.* [< L. *e-*, out + *mulgere*, to milk] a fluid formed by the suspension of one liquid in another; specif., *Pharmacy* a preparation of an oily substance suspended in a watery liquid

**en-** [< L. *in-*, in] *a prefix meaning:* 1. to put or get into or on [*enthrone*] 2. to make, cause to be [*endanger, enfeeble*] 3. in or into [*enclose*]

**-en** (ən, 'n) [OE.] *a suffix used:* 1. to form plurals [*children*] 2. to form diminutives [*chicken*] 3. to mean: *a*) to become or cause to be [*weaken*] *b*) to cause to have [*heighten*] *c*) made of [*woolen*]

**en·a·ble** (in ā'b'l) *vt.* **-bled, -bling** to make able; provide with means, power, etc. (*to do something*)

**en·act** (in akt') *vt.* 1. to pass (a bill, law, etc.); decree 2. to represent as in a play —**en·act'ment** *n.* —**en·ac'tor** *n.*

**en·am·el** (i nam'l) *n.* [< OFr. *esmail*] 1. a glassy, opaque substance fused to metal, pottery, etc. as an ornamental or protective coating 2. the hard, white coating of teeth 3. paint or varnish producing a hard, glossy surface —*vt.* **-eled** or **-elled, -el·ing** or **-el·ling** to coat with enamel —**en·am'el·er, en·am'el·ler** *n.*

**en·am'el·ware'** (-wer') *n.* kitchen utensils, etc. made of enameled metal

**en·am·or** (in am'ər) *vt.* [ult. < L. *in-*, in + *amor*, love] to fill with love; charm: mainly in the passive voice, with *of* [*enamored of her*]

**en bloc** (en bläk) [Fr., lit., in a block] all together; as a whole

†**en bro·chette** (än brô shet') [Fr.] broiled on small skewers

**en·camp** (in kamp') *vi., vt.* to set up, or put in, a camp —**en·camp'ment** *n.*

**en·cap·su·late** (in kap'sə lāt') *vt.* **-lat·ed, -lat·ing** 1. to enclose in a capsule 2. to make concise; condense Also **en·cap'sule** (-s'l, -syool), **-suled, -sul·ing** —**en·cap'su·la'tion** *n.*

**en·case** (in kās') *vt.* **-cased', -cas'ing** to enclose, as in a case

**en cas·se·role** (en kas'ə rōl') [Fr.] (baked and served) in a casserole

**-ence** (əns, 'ns) [< L.] *a suffix meaning* act, state, or result [*conference*]

**en·ceph·a·li·tis** (in sef'ə lit'is) *n.* [< Gr. *en-*, in + *kephalē*, the head + -ITIS] inflammation of the brain

**en·chain** (in chān') *vt.* to bind with or as with chains; fetter

**en·chant** (in chant') *vt.* [< L. *in-*, in + *cantare*, sing] 1. to cast a spell over 2. to charm greatly; delight —**en·chant'er** *n.* —**en·chant'ing** *adj.* —**en·chant'ment** *n.*

**en·chi·la·da** (en'chə lä'də) *n.* [Am-Sp.] a tortilla rolled with meat inside, served with a chili-flavored sauce

**en·cir·cle** (in sur'k'l) *vt.* **-cled, -cling** 1. to surround 2. to move in a circle around —**en·cir'cle·ment** *n.*

**en·clave** (en'klāv) *n.* [< L. *in-*, in + *clavis*, a key] a territory surrounded by another country's territory

**en·close** (in klōz') *vt.* **-closed', -clos'ing** 1. to shut in all around; surround 2. to insert in an envelope, etc., often along with a letter, etc.

**en·clo'sure** (-klō'zhər) *n.* 1. an enclosing or being enclosed 2. something that encloses 3. something enclosed, as in an envelope or by a wall

**en·code** (in kōd') *vt.* **-cod'ed, -cod'ing** to put (a message) into code

**en·co·mi·um** (en kō'mē əm) *n., pl.* **-ums, -a** (-ə) [< Gr. *en-*, in + *kōmos*, a revel] high praise; eulogy

**en·com·pass** (in kum'pəs) *vt.* 1. to surround 2. to contain; include

**en·core** (än'kôr) *interj.* [Fr.] again; once more —*n.* a further performance in response to an audience's applause

**en·coun·ter** (in koun'tər) *vt., vi.* [< L. *in*, in + *contra*, against] 1. to meet unexpectedly 2. to meet in conflict —*n.* 1. a battle; fight 2. an unexpected meeting

**encounter group** a small group that meets for therapy in personal interrelationship, with open exchange of feelings, etc.

**en·cour·age** (in kur'ij) *vt.* **-aged, -ag·ing** 1. to give courage, hope, or confidence to 2. to give support to; help —**en·cour'age·ment** *n.*

**en·croach** (in krōch') *vi.* [< OFr. *en-*, in + *croc*, a hook] to trespass or intrude (*on* or *upon*) —**en·croach'ment** *n.*

**en·crust** (in krust') *vt., vi. same as* INCRUST —**en·crus·ta'tion** *n.*

**en·cum·ber** (in kum'bər) *vt.* [see EN- & CUMBER] 1. to hold back the motion or action of; hinder 2. to burden; load down —**en·cum'brance** *n.*

**-en·cy** (ən sē) [L. *-entia*] *a suffix meaning* act, state, or result [*efficiency*]

**en·cyc·li·cal** (in sik'li k'l) *n.* [< Gr. *en-*, in + *kyklos*, a circle] a letter from the Pope to the bishops

**en·cy·clo·pe·di·a** (in sī'klə pē'dē ə) *n.* [< Gr. *enkyklios*, general + *paideia*, education] a book or set of books with alphabetically arranged articles on all branches, or on one field, of knowledge: also **en·cy'clo·pae'di·a** —**en·cy'clo·pe'dic** *adj.*

**en·cyst** (en sist') *vt., vi.* to enclose or become enclosed in a cyst, capsule, or sac —**en·cyst'ment** *n.*

**end** (end) *n.* [OE. *ende*] 1. a boundary; limit 2. the last part of anything; finish; conclusion 3. a ceasing to exist; death or destruction 4. the part at or near an extremity; tip 5. an aim; purpose 6. an outcome; result 7. *Football* a player at either end of the line —*vt., vi.* to bring or come to an end; finish; stop —*adj.* at the end; final —**make (both) ends meet** to manage to keep one's expenses within one's income —**put an end to** 1. to stop 2. to do away with

**en·dan·ger** (in dān'jər) *vt.* to expose to danger, harm, etc.; imperil

**en·dear** (in dir') *vt.* to make dear or beloved —**en·dear'ing** *adj.*

**en·dear'ment** *n.* 1. an endearing 2. a word or act expressing affection

**en·deav·or** (in dev'ər) *vt.* [< EN- + OFr. *devoir*, duty] to try (*to do something*) —*n.* an earnest attempt or effort Brit. sp. **en·deav'our**

**en·dem·ic** (en dem′ik) *adj.* [< Gr. *en-*, in + *dēmos*, people] prevalent in or restricted to a particular locality, as a disease —**en·dem′i·cal·ly** *adv.*

**end·ing** (en′diŋ) *n.* 1. the last part; finish 2. death

**en·dive** (en′dīv, än′dēv) *n.* [< Gr. *entybon*] a cultivated plant with curled, narrow leaves used in salads

**end′less** *adj.* 1. having no end; eternal; infinite 2. lasting too long [an *endless* speech] 3. with the ends joined to form a closed ring [an *endless* chain] —**end′less·ly** *adv.* —**end′less·ness** *n.*

**end′most′** *adj.* at the end; farthest

**endo-** [< Gr. *endon*] *a combining form meaning* within, inner

**en·do·crine** (en′də krin, -krīn′) *adj.* [ENDO- + Gr. *krinein*, to separate] designating of any gland producing an internal secretion carried by the blood to some body part whose functions it regulates

**end organ** a structure at the end of nerve fibers having either sensory or motor functions

**en·dorse** (in dôrs′) *vt.* -dorsed′, -dors′ing [< L. *in*, on + *dorsum*, back] 1. to write on the back of (a document); specif., to sign (one's name) as payee on the back of (a check, etc.) 2. to sanction, approve, or support 3. to recommend (an advertised product) for a fee —**en·dorse′ment** *n.* —**en·dors′er** *n.*

**en·do·scope** (en′də skōp′) *n.* an instrument for examining visually the inside of a hollow organ, as the rectum

**en·dow** (in dou′) *vt.* [ult. < L. *in*, in + *dotare*, endow] 1. to provide with some talent, quality, etc. [endowed with courage] 2. to give money to (a college, etc.) —**en·dow′ment** *n.*

**end product** the final result of a series of changes, processes, etc.

**end table** a small table placed at the end of a sofa, etc.

**en·due** (in dōo′) *vt.* -dued′, -du′ing [< L. *in-*, in + *ducere*, to lead] to provide (*with* qualities)

**en·dur·ance** (in door′əns) *n.* the ability to last, stand pain, etc.

**en·dure** (in door′) *vt.* -dured′, -dur′ing [< L. *in-*, in + *durus*, hard] 1. to stand (pain, fatigue, etc.) 2. to tolerate —*vi.* 1. to last; continue 2. to bear pain, etc. without flinching —**en·dur′a·ble** *adj.*

**end′ways′** (-wāz′) *adv.* 1. on end; upright 2. with the end foremost 3. lengthwise Also **end′wise′** (-wīz′)

**-ene** (ēn) [after Gr. *-enos*, adj. suffix] a suffix used to form names for certain hydrocarbons [benzene]

**en·e·ma** (en′ə mə) *n.* [< Gr. *en-*, in + *hienai*, send] the injection of a liquid, as a purgative, medicine, etc., into the colon through the anus

**en·e·my** (en′ə mē) *n., pl.* -mies [< L. *in-*, not + *amicus*, friend] 1. a person who hates another and wishes

to injure him 2. *a*) a nation hostile to another *b*) a soldier, citizen, etc. of a hostile nation 3. one hostile to a cause, idea, etc. 4. anything injurious

**en·er·get·ic** (en′ər jet′ik) *adj.* having or showing energy; vigorous —**en′er·get′i·cal·ly** *adv.*

**en·er·gize** (en′ər jīz′) *vt.* -gized′, -giz′ing to give energy to; activate —**en′er·giz′er** *n.*

**en·er·gy** (en′ər jē) *n., pl.* -gies [< Gr. *en-*, in + *ergon*, work] 1. force of expression 2. *a*) inherent power; capacity for action *b*) [often *pl.*] such power, esp. in action 3. *Physics* the capacity for doing work

**en·er·vate** (en′ər vāt′) *vt.* -vat′ed, -vat′ing [< L. *enervis*, weak] to deprive of strength, force, vigor, etc.; devitalize —**en′er·va′tion** *n.*

**en·fee·ble** (in fē′b'l) *vt.* -bled, -bling to make feeble; weaken

**en·fi·lade** (en′fə lād′) *n.* [Fr.] gunfire directed along a line of troops

**en·fold** (in fōld′) *vt.* 1. to wrap in folds; wrap up 2. to embrace

**en·force** (in fôrs′) *vt.* -forced′, -forc′ing 1. to impose by force [to *enforce* one's will] 2. to compel observance of (a law, etc.) —**en·force′a·ble** *adj.* —**en·force′ment** *n.*

**en·fran·chise** (in fran′chīz) *vt.* -chised, -chis·ing 1. to free from slavery 2. to give the right to vote —**en·fran′chise·ment** (-chiz mənt, -chīz-) *n.*

**Eng.** 1. England 2. English

**en·gage** (in gāj′) *vt.* -gaged′, -gag′ing [see EN- & GAGE¹] 1. to pledge (oneself) 2. to bind by a promise of marriage 3. to hire 4. to involve or occupy 5. to attract and hold (the attention, etc.) 6. to enter into conflict with (the enemy) 7. to mesh together (gears, etc.) —*vi.* 1. to pledge oneself 2. to involve or occupy oneself [to *engage* in dramatics] 3. to enter into conflict 4. to mesh

**en·gaged′** *adj.* 1. betrothed 2. occupied; employed 3. involved in combat, as troops 4. meshed

**en·gage′ment** *n.* an engaging or being engaged; specif., *a*) a betrothal *b*) an appointment *c*) employment *d*) a conflict; battle

**en·gag′ing** *adj.* attractive; charming —**en·gag′ing·ly** *adv.*

**en·gen·der** (in jen′dər) *vt.* [< L. *in-*, in + *generare*, to beget] to bring into being; cause; produce

**en·gine** (en′jən) *n.* [< L. *in-*, in + base of *gignere*, to produce] 1. any machine that uses energy to develop mechanical power 2. a railroad locomotive 3. any machine

**en·gi·neer** (en′jə nir′) *n.* 1. one skilled in some branch of engineering 2. one who operates or supervises the operation of engines or technical equipment [a locomotive *engineer*] —*vt.* 1. to plan, construct, etc. as an engineer 2. to manage skillfully

**en·gi·neer·ing** n. 1. the putting of scientific knowledge in various branches to practical uses 2. the planning, designing, construction, etc. of machinery, roads, bridges, etc.

**Eng·land** (iŋ'glənd) division of the United Kingdom, in S Great Britain: 50,331 sq. mi.; pop. 43,461,000

**Eng·lish** (iŋ'glish) adj. 1. of England, its people, etc. 2. of their language —n. 1. the language of the people of England, the official language of the British Commonwealth, the U.S., etc. 2. [sometimes e-] a spinning motion given to a ball —the English the people of England

**English Channel** arm of the Atlantic, between England & France

**English horn** a double-reed instrument of the woodwind family

**Eng·lish·man** (-mən) n., pl. -men a native or inhabitant of England —**Eng·lish·wom·an** n.fem., pl. -wom·en

ENGLISH HORN

**en·graft** (in graft') vt. to graft (a shoot, etc.) from one plant onto another

**en·grave** (in grāv') vt. -graved', -grav·ing [< Fr. en-, in + graver, to incise] 1. to cut or etch (letters, designs, etc.) in or on (a metal plate, wooden block, etc.) 2. to print from such a plate, etc. 3. to impress deeply —en·grav·er n.

**en·grav·ing** n. 1. the act or art of one who engraves 2. an engraved plate, design, etc. 3. a printed impression made from an engraved surface

**en·gross** (in grōs') vt. [< OFr. engroissier, become thick] to take the entire attention of; occupy wholly —en·gross·ing adj. —en·gross·ment n.

**en·gulf** (in gulf') vt. to swallow up

**en·hance** (in hans') vt. -hanced', -hanc·ing [ult. < L. in, in + altus, high] to make better, greater, etc.; heighten —en·hance·ment n.

**e·nig·ma** (ə nig'mə) n., pl. -mas [< Gr. ainigma] 1. a riddle 2. a perplexing or baffling matter, person, etc. —**e·nig·mat·ic** (e'nig mat'ik, ē'nig-), **e·nig·mat'i·cal** adj.

**en·jamb·ment, en·jambe·ment** (in jam'mənt) n. [< Fr. enjamber, to encroach] the running on of a sentence from one line to the next of a poem

**en·join** (in join') vt. [< L. in-, in + jungere, join] 1. to command; order 2. to prohibit, esp. by legal injunction

**en·joy** (in joi') vt. [< OFr. en-, in + joir, rejoice] 1. to get joy or pleasure from; relish 2. to have the use or benefit of —**enjoy oneself** to have a good time —en·joy'a·ble adj. —en·joy'ment n.

**en·large** (in lärj') vt. -larged', -larg·ing to make larger; expand —vi. 1. to become larger; expand 2. to discuss at greater length (with on or upon) —en·large·ment n.

**en·light·en** (in līt''n) vt. to free from ignorance, prejudice, etc. 2. to inform —en·light'en·ment n.

**en·list** (in list') vt., vi. 1. to enroll in some branch of the armed forces 2. to engage in support of a cause or movement —en·list'ment n.

**enlisted man** any man in the armed forces who is not a commissioned officer or warrant officer

**en·liv·en** (in līf'v'n) vt. to make active, cheerful, etc.; liven up

**en masse** (en mas') [Fr., lit., in mass] in a group; as a whole

**en·mesh** (en mesh') vt. to catch as in the meshes of a net; entangle

**en·mi·ty** (en'mə tē) n., pl. -ties [see ENEMY] the attitude or feelings of an enemy or enemies; hostility

**en·no·ble** (i nō'b'l) vt. -bled, -bling to give a noble quality to; dignify —en·no'ble·ment n.

**en·nui** (än'wē) n. [Fr.: see ANNOY] a feeling of boredom and weariness

**e·nor·mi·ty** (i nôr'm tē) n., pl. -ties [< L. enormis, nmense] 1. great wickedness 2. an outrageous act 3. loosely, enormous size or extent

**e·nor·mous** (i nôr'məs) adj. [see prec.] of great size, number, etc.; huge; vast —e·nor'mous·ly adv.

**e·nough** (i nuf') adj. [OE. genoh] as much or as many as necessary; sufficient —n. the amount needed —adv. 1. sufficiently 2. fully; quite [oddly enough] 3. tolerably

**e·now** (i nou') adj., n., adv. [Archaic] enough

**en·plane** (en plān') vi. -planed', -plan·ing to board an airplane

**en·quire** (in kwīr') vt., vi. -quired', -quir·ing same as INQUIRE —en·quir'y (-ē) n., pl. -ies

**en·rage** (in rāj') vt. -raged', -rag·ing to put into a rage; infuriate

**en·rap·ture** (in rap'chər) vt. -tured, -tur·ing to fill with delight

**en·rich** (in rich') vt. to make rich or richer; give greater value, better quality, etc. to —en·rich'ment n.

**en·roll, en·rol** (in rōl') vt., vi. -rolled', -roll·ing 1. to record or be recorded in a roll or list 2. to enlist 3. to make or become a member —en·roll'ment, en·rol'ment n.

**en route** (än rōōt') [Fr.] on the way

**en·sconce** (in skäns') vt. -sconced', -sconc·ing [< Du. schans, small fort] to place or settle snugly or securely

**en·sem·ble** (än säm'b'l) n. [Fr. < L. in-, in + simul, at the same time] 1. total effect 2. a whole costume of matching parts 3. a) a small group of musicians playing or singing together b) the performance of such a group, or of an orchestra, chorus, etc.

**en·shrine** (in shrīn') vt. -shrined', -shrin·ing 1. to enclose in a shrine 2. to hold as sacred; cherish

**en·shroud** (in shroud') vt. to cover as with a shroud; hide; obscure

**en·sign** (en'sīn; also, and for 2 always, -s'n) n. [see INSIGNIA] 1. a flag or banner 2. U.S. Navy a commissioned officer of the lowest rank

**en·si·lage** (en's'l ij) n. [Fr.] green fodder preserved in a silo

**en·sile** (en sīl') vt. -siled', -sil·ing [Fr.] to store (green fodder) in a silo

**en·slave** (in slāv′) *vt.* -slaved′, -slav′ing 1. to make a slave of 2. to subjugate —en·slave′ment *n.*

**en·snare** (in sner′) *vt.* -snared′, -snar′ing to catch as in a snare

**en·sue** (in sōō′) *vi.* -sued′, -su′ing [< L. *in-*, in + *sequi*, follow] 1. to come afterward 2. to result

**en·sure** (in shoor′) *vt.* -sured′, -sur′ing 1. to make sure 2. to protect

**-ent** (ənt) [< Fr. *-ent*, L. *-ens*, prp. ending] *a suffix meaning:* 1. that has, shows, or does [*insistent*] 2. a person or thing that [*superintendent, solvent*]

**en·tail** (in tāl′) *vt.* [< OFr. *taillier*, to cut] 1. *Law* to limit the inheritance of (property) to a specific line of heirs 2. to make necessary; require

**en·tan·gle** (in·gled, -gling 1. to involve in a tangle 2. to involve in difficulty 3. to confuse 4. to complicate —en·tan′gle·ment *n.*

**en·tente** (än tänt′) *n.* [Fr. < OFr. *entendre*, to understand] 1. an understanding or agreement, as between nations 2. the parties to this

**en·ter** (en′tər) *vt.* [< L. *intra*, within] 1. to come or go into 2. to penetrate 3. to insert 4. to write down in a list, etc. 5. to become a member of or participant in 6. to get (someone) admitted 7. to begin 8. to put on record, formally or before a law court —*vi.* 1. to come or go into some place 2. to penetrate —enter into 1. to take part in 2. to form a part of — enter on (or upon) to begin; start

**en·ter·i·tis** (en′tə rīt′is) *n.* [< Gr. *enteron*, intestine + -ITIS] inflammation of the intestine

**en·ter·prise** (en′tər prīz′) *n.* [ult. < L. *inter*, in + *prehendere*, take] 1. an undertaking, esp. a big, bold, or difficult one 2. energy and initiative

**en′ter·pris′ing** *adj.* showing enterprise; full of energy and initiative

**en·ter·tain** (en′tər tān′) *vt.* [ult. < L. *inter*, between + *tenere*, to hold] 1. to amuse; divert 2. to have as a guest 3. to have in mind; consider —*vi.* to give hospitality to guests

**en′ter·tain′er** *n.* one who entertains; esp., a popular singer, comedian, etc.

**en′ter·tain′ing** *adj.* interesting and pleasurable; amusing

**en′ter·tain′ment** *n.* 1. an entertaining or being entertained 2. something that entertains; esp., a show

**en·thrall, en·thral** (in thrôl′) *vt.* -thralled′, -thral′ing [see EN- & THRALL] to fascinate; captivate

**en·throne′** *vt.* -throned′, -thron′ing 1. to place on a throne 2. to exalt

**en·thuse** (in thōōz′) *vi.* -thused′, -thus′ing [Colloq.] to express enthusiasm —*vt.* [Colloq.] to make enthusiastic

**en·thu·si·asm** (in thōō′zē az′m) *n.* [< Gr. *enthous*, inspired] intense or eager interest; zeal —en·thu′si·ast′ (-ast′) *n.* —en·thu′si·as′tic *adj.* — en·thu′si·as′ti·cal·ly *adv.*

**en·tice** (in tīs′) *vt.* -ticed′, -tic′ing [< L. *in*, in + *titio*, a burning brand] to tempt with hope of reward or pleasure —en·tice′ment *n.*

**en·tire** (in tīr′) *adj.* [< L. *integer*, whole] not lacking any parts; complete; whole; intact —en·tire′ly *adv.*

**en·tire·ty** (-tē) *n., pl.* -ties 1. the state or fact of being entire; wholeness 2. an entire thing; whole

**en·ti·tle** (in tīt′'l) *vt.* -tled, -tling 1. to give a title or name to 2. to give a right or claim to

**en·ti·ty** (en′tə tē) *n., pl.* -ties [ult. < L. *esse*, to be] 1. existence 2. a thing that has real existence

**en·tomb** (in tōōm′) *vt.* to place in a tomb; bury —en·tomb′ment *n.*

**en·to·mol·o·gy** (en′tə mäl′ə jē) *n.* [< Gr. *entomon*, insect + -LOGY] the branch of zoology that deals with insects —en′to·mo·log′i·cal (-mə läj′i k'l) *adj.* —en′to·mol′o·gist *n.*

**en·tou·rage** (än′too räzh′) *n.* [Fr. < *entourer*, surround] a group of associates or attendants; retinue

**en·trails** (en′trālz, -trəlz) *n.pl.* [< L. *interaneus*, internal] the inner organs; specif., the intestines; viscera

**en·train** (in trān′) *vt., vi.* to put or go aboard a train

**en·trance¹** (en′trəns) *n.* 1. the act of entering 2. a place for entering; door, etc. 3. permission or right to enter; admission

**en·trance²** (in trans′) *vt.* -tranced′, -tranc′ing [see EN- & TRANCE] to fill with delight; enchant

**en·trant** (en′trənt) *n.* one who enters

**en·trap** (in trap′) *vt.* -trapped′, -trap′ping to catch as in a trap

**en·treat** (in trēt′) *vt., vi.* [< OFr. *en-*, in + *traiter*: see TREAT] to ask earnestly; beseech; implore —entreat′ing·ly *adv.* —en·treat′ment *n.*

**en·treat′y** *n., pl.* -ies an earnest request; prayer

**en·tree, en·trée** (än′trā) *n.* [Fr. < OFr. *entrer*: see ENTER] 1. right to enter 2. the main course of a meal

**en·trench** (in trench′) *vt.* 1. to surround with trenches 2. to establish securely —en·trench′ment *n.*

**en·tre·pre·neur** (än′trə pro nur′) *n.* [Fr.: see ENTERPRISE] one who organizes a business undertaking, assuming the risk for the sake of the profit

**en·tro·py** (en′trə pē) *n.* [< Gr. *entropē*, a turning toward] 1. a measure of the energy unavailable for useful work in a system 2. the tendency of an energy system to run down

**en·trust** (in trust′) *vt.* 1. to charge with a trust or duty 2. to turn over for safekeeping

**en·try** (en′trē) *n., pl.* -tries [< OFr.: see ENTER] 1. an entering; entrance 2. a way by which to enter 3. an item or note entered in a list, journal, etc. 4. one entered in a race, etc.

**en·twine** (in twīn′) *vt., vi.* -twined′, -twin′ing to twine together or around

**e·nu·mer·ate** (i nōō'mə rāt') *vt.* **-at'ed, -at'ing** [< L. *e-*, out + *numerare*, to count] 1. to count 2. to name one by one —**e·nu'mer·a'tion** *n.*

**e·nun·ci·ate** (i nun'sē āt') *vt., vi.* **-at'ed, -at'ing** [< L. *e-*, out + *nuntiare*, announce] 1. to state definitely 2. to announce 3. to pronounce (words) —**e·nun'ci·a'tion** *n.*

**en·u·re·sis** (en'yoo rē'sis) *n.* [< Gr. *enourein*, to urinate in] inability to control urination, esp. during sleep

**en·vel·op** (in vel'əp) *vt.* [< OFr.: see EN- & DEVELOP] 1. to wrap up; cover completely 2. to surround 3. to conceal; hide —**en·vel'op·ment** *n.*

**en·vel·ope** (en'və lōp', än'-) *n.* 1. a thing that envelops; covering 2. a folded paper container for letters, etc., usually with a gummed flap

**en·ven·om** (in ven'əm) *vt.* 1. to put venom into 2. to fill with hate

**en·vi·a·ble** (en'vē ə b'l) *adj.* good enough to be envied or desired —**en'vi·a·bly** *adv.*

**en·vi·ous** (en'vē əs) *adj.* feeling or showing envy —**en'vi·ous·ly** *adv.*

**en·vi·ron·ment** (in vī'rən mənt) *n.* [see ENVIRONS] 1. surroundings 2. all the conditions, etc. surrounding, and affecting the development of, an organism —**en·vi'ron·men'tal** *adj.*

**en·vi'ron·men'tal·ist** *n.* a person working to solve environmental problems, as air and water pollution

**en·vi·rons** (in vī'rəns) *n.pl.* [< OFr. *en-*, in + *viron*, a circuit] 1. the districts surrounding a city; suburbs 2. surrounding area; vicinity

**en·vis·age** (en viz'ij) *vt.* **-aged, -ag·ing** [see EN- & VISAGE] to form an image of in the mind; visualize

**en·vi·sion** (en vizh'ən) *vt.* [EN- + VISION] to imagine (something not yet in existence)

**en·voy** (en'voi, än'-) *n.* [< Fr. < L. *in*, in + *via*, way] 1. a messenger 2. a diplomatic agent ranking just below an ambassador

**en·vy** (en'vē) *n., pl.* **-vies** [< L. *invidia*] 1. discontent and ill will over another's advantages, possessions, etc. 2. desire for something that another has 3. an object of such feeling —*vt.* **-vied, -vy·ing** to feel envy toward or because of —**en'vy·ing·ly** *adv.*

**en·zyme** (en'zīm) *n.* [< Gr. *en-*, in + *zymē*, leaven] a proteinlike substance, formed in plant and animal cells, acting as a catalyst in chemical reactions

**e·on** (ē'ən, ē'än) *n.* [< Gr. *aiōn*, an age] an extremely long, indefinite period of time

**-e·ous** (ē əs) [< L. *-eus*] *a suffix meaning* having the nature of, like [*beauteous*]

**EPA** Environmental Protection Agency

**ep·au·let, ep·au·lette** (ep'ə let') *n.* [< Fr.: see SPATULA] a shoulder ornament, as on military uniforms

**e·pee, é·pée** (e pā') *n.* [Fr.] a fencing sword like a foil, but more rigid

**e·pergne** (i purn') *n.* an ornamental dish or stand with several compartments for candy, flowers, etc.

**e·phed·rine** (i fed'rin) *n.* [< L. *ephedra*, the plant horsetail] an alkaloid used to relieve nasal congestion and asthma

**e·phem·er·al** (i fem'ər əl) *adj.* [< Gr. *epi-*, upon + *hēmera*, day] 1. lasting one day 2. short-lived; transitory

**epi-** [< Gr. *epi*, at, on] *a prefix meaning* on, upon, over, among [*epiglottis*]

**ep·ic** (ep'ik) *n.* [< Gr. *epos*, a word, song, epic] a long narrative poem in a dignified style about the deeds of a hero or heroes —*adj.* of or like an epic; heroic; grand

**ep·i·cen·ter** (ep'ə sen'tər) *n.* 1. the area of the earth's surface directly above the place of origin of an earthquake 2. a focal or central point

**ep·i·cure** (ep'i kyoor') *n.* [< *Epicurus*, ancient Gr. philosopher] one who enjoys and has a discriminating taste for fine foods and drinks

**ep·i·cu·re·an** (ep'i kyoo rē'ən) *adj.* 1. fond of sensuous pleasure 2. having to do with an epicure —*n.* same as EPICURE

**ep·i·dem·ic** (ep'ə dem'ik) *adj.* [< Fr. < Gr. *epi-*, among + *dēmos*, people] spreading rapidly among many people in a community, as a disease —*n.* 1. an epidemic disease 2. the spreading of such a disease —**ep·i·dem'i·cal·ly** *adv.*

**ep·i·der·mis** (-dur'mis) *n.* [< Gr. *epi-*, upon + *derma*, the skin] the outermost layer of the skin —**ep'i·der'mal, ep'i·der'mic** *adj.*

**ep·i·glot·tis** (-glät'is) *n.* [see EPI- & GLOTTIS] the thin cartilage lid that covers the windpipe during swallowing

**ep·i·gram** (ep'ə gram') *n.* [< Gr. *epi-*, upon + *graphein*, write] a terse, witty, pointed statement —**ep·i·gram·mat·ic** (ep'i grə mat'ik) *adj.*

**ep·i·graph·y** (i pig'rə fē) *n.* the study of inscriptions, esp. ancient ones

**ep·i·lep·sy** (ep'ə lep'sē) *n.* [< Gr. *epi-*, upon + *lambanein*, seize] a chronic nervous disease, characterized by convulsions and unconsciousness

**ep'i·lep'tic** (-tik) *adj.* of or having epilepsy —*n.* one who has epilepsy

**ep·i·logue** (ep'ə lôg') *n.* [< Gr. *epi-*, upon + *legein*, speak] a closing section added to a novel, play, etc. providing further comment; specif., a speech to the audience by an actor

**E·piph·a·ny** (i pif'ə nē) *n.* [< Gr. *epiphainein*, show forth] a Christian festival (Jan. 6) commemorating the revealing of Jesus as the Christ to the Gentiles

**e·pis·co·pa·cy** (i pis'kə pə sē) *n., pl.* **-cies** [< Gr. *epi-*, upon + *skopein*, to look] 1. church government by bishops 2. same as EPISCOPATE

**e·pis·co·pal** (-p'l) *adj.* 1. of or governed by bishops 2. [E-] designating or of any of various churches governed by bishops

**E·pis·co·pa'li·an** (-pāl'yən, -pā'lē ən) *adj.* same as EPISCOPAL —*n.* a member of the Protestant Episcopal Church

**e·pis·co·pate** (i pis'kə pit, -pāt') *n.*

1. the position, rank, etc. of a bishop
2. bishops collectively

**ep·i·sode** (ep′ə sōd′) *n.* [ < Gr. *epi-*, upon + *eisodos*, entrance] 1. any part of a novel, poem, etc. that is complete in itself 2. an event or series of events complete in itself —**ep′i·sod′ic** (-säd′ik) *adj.* —**ep·i·sod′i·cal·ly** *adv.*

**e·pis·tle** (i pis′'l) *n.* [ < Gr. *epi-*, to + *stellein*, send] 1. a letter 2. [E-] any of the letters in the New Testament —**e·pis′to·lar′y** (-tə ler′ē) *adj.*

**ep·i·taph** (ep′ə taf′) *n.* [ < Gr. *epi-*, upon + *taphos*, tomb] an inscription, as for a tomb, in memory of a dead person

**ep·i·the·li·um** (ep′ə thē′lē əm) *n.* [ < Gr. *epi-*, upon + *thēlē*, nipple] membranelike tissue that covers body surfaces and lines body cavities —**ep′i·the′li·al** (-əl) *adj.*

**ep·i·thet** (ep′ə thet′) *n.* [ < Gr. *epi-*, on + *tithenai*, put] a word or phrase characterizing some person or thing

**e·pit·o·me** (i pit′ə mē) *n., pl.* **-mes** [ < Gr. *epi-*, upon + *temnein*, to cut] 1. an abstract; summary 2. a person or thing that typifies a whole class

**e·pit′o·mize′** (-mīz′) *vt.* **-mized′, -miz′ing** to make or be an epitome of

**‡e plu·ri·bus u·num** (ē′ ploor′ə bəs yōō′nəm) [L.] out of many, one: a motto of the U.S.

**ep·och** (ep′ək) *n.* [ < Gr. *epi-*, upon + *echein*, hold] 1. the start of a new period of something [radio marked an *epoch* in communication] 2. a period of time in terms of noteworthy events, persons, etc. —**ep′och·al** *adj.*

**ep·ox·y** (e päk′sē) *adj.* [EP(I)- + OXY(GEN)] designating a resin used in strong, resistant glues, enamels, etc. —*n., pl.* **-ies** an epoxy resin

**ep·si·lon** (ep′sə län′) *n.* the fifth letter of the Greek alphabet (E, ε)

**Ep·som salts** (or **salt**) (ep′səm) [ < *Epsom*, town in England] a white, crystalline salt, magnesium sulfate, used as a cathartic

**e·qua·ble** (ek′wə b'l) *adj.* [see ff.] steady; uniform; even; tranquil —**eq′ua·bil′i·ty** *n.* —**eq′ua·bly** *adv.*

**e·qual** (ē′kwəl) *adj.* [ < L. *aequus*, even] 1. of the same quantity, size, value, etc. 2. having the same rights, ability, rank, etc. 3. evenly proportioned 4. having the necessary ability, strength, etc. (with *to*) —*n.* any person or thing that is equal —*vt.* **e·qualed** or **e′qualled, e′qual·ing** or **e′qual·ling** 1. to be equal to 2. to do or make something equal to —**e·qual·i·ty** (i kwäl′ə tē, -kwôl′-) *n., pl.* **-ties** —**e′qual·ly** *adv.*

**e·qual·ize** (ē′kwə līz′) *vt.* **-ized′, -iz′ing** to make equal or uniform —**e′qual·i·za′tion** *n.* —**e′qual·iz′er** *n.*

**equal sign** (or **mark**) the arithmetical sign (=), indicating that the terms on either side of it are equal

**e·qua·nim·i·ty** (ek′wə nim′ə tē, ē′kwə-) *n.* [ < L. *aequus*, even +

*animus*, mind] calmness of mind; composure

**e·quate** (i kwāt′) *vt.* **e·quat′ed, e·quat′ing** 1. to make equal 2. to treat, regard, or express as equal —**e·quat′a·ble** *adj.*

**e·qua·tion** (i kwā′zhən) *n.* 1. an equating or being equated 2. a statement of equality between two quantities, as shown by the equal sign (=)

**e·qua·tor** (i kwāt′ər) *n.* an imaginary circle around the earth, equally distant from both the North Pole and the South Pole —**e·qua·to·ri·al** (ē′kwə tôr′ē əl, ek′wə-) *adj.*

**Equatorial Guinea** country in C Africa: 10,832 sq. mi.; pop. 246,000

**eq·uer·ry** (ek′wər ē, i kwer′ē) *n., pl.* **-ries** [ < Fr.] 1. formerly, an officer in charge of royal horses 2. an officer who attends a person of royalty

**e·ques·tri·an** (i kwes′trē ən) *adj.* [ < L. *equus*, horse] 1. of horses or horsemanship 2. on horseback —*n.* a rider or circus performer on horseback —**e·ques′tri·enne′** (-trē en′) *n.fem.*

**equi-** *a combining form meaning* equal, equally [*equidistant*]

**e·qui·an·gu·lar** (ē′kwə aŋ′gyə lər) *adj.* having all angles equal

**e·qui·dis·tant** (ē′kwə dis′tənt) *adj.* equally distant

**e′qui·lat′er·al** (-lat′ər əl) *adj.* [ < L. *aequus*, equal + *latus*, side] having all sides equal

**e′qui·lib′ri·um** (-lib′rē əm) *n., pl.* **-ri·ums, -ri·a** (-ə) [ < L. *aequus*, equal + *libra*, a balance] a state of balance between opposing forces

**e·quine** (ē′kwīn, ek′wīn) *adj.* [ < L. *equus*, horse] of or like a horse

**e·qui·nox** (ē′kwə näks′) *n.* [ < L. *aequus*, equal + *nox*, night] the time when the sun crosses the equator, making night and day of equal length in all parts of the earth —**e′qui·noc′tial** (-näk′shəl) *adj.*

**e·quip** (i kwip′) *vt.* **e·quipped′, e·quip′ping** [ < OFr. *esquiper*, embark] to provide with what is needed

**eq·ui·page** (ek′wə pij) *n.* a carriage with horses and liveried servants

**e·quip·ment** (i kwip′mənt) *n.* 1. an equipping or being equipped 2. whatever one is equipped with; supplies, furnishings, etc.

**e·qui·poise** (ek′wə poiz′) *n.* [EQUI- + POISE] 1. state of equilibrium 2. counterbalance

**eq′ui·ta·ble** (-wit ə b'l) *adj.* [see EQUITY] fair; just —**eq′ui·ta·bly** *adv.*

**eq·ui·ta·tion** (ek′wə tā′shən) *n.* [ < L. *equitare*, to ride] horsemanship

**eq·ui·ty** (ek′wət ē) *n., pl.* **-ties** [ < L. *aequus*, equal] 1. fairness; impartiality; justice 2. the value of property beyond the amount owed on it 3. *Law* a system of doctrines supplementing common and statute law

**e·quiv·a·lent** (i kwiv′ə lənt) *adj.* [ < L. *aequus*, equal + *valere*, be strong] equal in quantity, value, force, mean-

---

fat, āpe, cär; ten, ēven; is, bīte; gō, hôrn, tōōl, look; oil, out; up, fur; chin; she; thin, then; zh, leisure; ŋ, ring; ə for *a* in *ago*; ′, (ā′b'l); ë, Fr. coeur; ö, Fr. feu; Fr. mon; ü, Fr. duc; kh, G. ich, doch; ‡ foreign; ‹ derived from ing, etc. —*n.* an equivalent thing — **e·quiv′a·lence** *n.*

**e·quiv·o·cal** (i kwiv′ə k'l) *adj.* [< L. *aequus,* equal + *vox,* voice] 1. having two or more meanings; purposely ambiguous 2. uncertain; doubtful 3. suspicious —**e·quiv′o·cal·ly** *adv.* —**e·quiv′o·cal·ness** *n.*

**e·quiv·o·cate′** (-kāt′) *vi.* -**cat′ed,** -**cat′ing** to use equivocal terms in order to deceive or mislead —**e·quiv′o·ca′tion** *n.* —**e·quiv′o·ca′tor** *n.*

**-er** (ər) [< OE.] 1. *a suffix meaning: a)* a person or thing having to do with [*hatter*] *b)* a person living in [*New Yorker*] *c)* a person or thing that [*sprayer*] *d)* repeatedly [*flicker*] 2. a suffix forming the comparative degree [*greater*]

**e·ra** (ir′ə, er′ə) *n.* [LL. *aera*] 1. a period of time measured from some important event 2. a period of history having some special characteristic

**ERA** 1. *Baseball* earned run average 2. Equal Rights Amendment

**e·rad·i·cate** (i rad′ə kāt′) *vt.* -**cat′ed,** -**cat′ing** [< L. *e-,* out + *radix,* root] to uproot; wipe out; destroy —**e·rad′i·ca′tion** *n.* —**e·rad′i·ca′tor** *n.*

**e·rase** (i rās′) *vt.* **e·rased′, e·ras′ing** [< L. *e-,* out + *radere,* scrape] 1. to rub, scrape, or wipe out (esp. writing) 2. to obliterate, as from the mind —**e·ras′a·ble** *adj.*

**e·ras′er** *n.* a thing that erases; specif., a rubber device for erasing ink or pencil marks, or a pad for removing chalk marks from a blackboard

**E·ras·mus, Des·i·der·i·us** (des′ə dir′ē əs) 1466?-1536; Du. humanist and writer

**e·ra·sure** (i rā′shər) *n.* 1. an erasing 2. an erased word, mark, etc.

**ere** (er) *prep.* [OE. *ær*] [Archaic] before (in time) —*conj.* [Archaic] 1. before 2. rather than

**e·rect** (i rekt′) *adj.* [< L. *e-,* up + *regere,* make straight] upright —*vt.* 1. to construct (a building, etc.) 2. to set in an upright position 3. to set up; assemble —**e·rec′tion** *n.* —**e·rect′ly** *adv.* —**e·rect′ness** *n.* —**e·rec′tor** *n.*

**e·rec·tile** (i rek′t'l) *adj.* that can become erect, as tissue that becomes rigid when filled with blood

**erg** (ʉrg) *n.* [< Gr. *ergon,* work] *Physics* a unit of work or energy

**ter·go** (ʉr′gō) *adv.* [L.] therefore

**er·gos·ter·ol** (ər gäs′tə rōl′) *n.* a steroid alcohol prepared from yeast, that produces vitamin D when exposed to ultraviolet rays

**Er·ie** (ir′ē) 1. city in NW Pa.: pop. 129,000 2. **Lake,** one of the Great Lakes, between Lake Huron & Lake Ontario

**Er·in** (er′in) *poet.* name for IRELAND

**er·mine** (ʉr′mən) *n.* [prob. < OHG. *harmo,* weasel] 1. a weasel whose fur is white in winter 2. its white fur

**e·rode** (i rōd′) *vt.* **e·rod′ed, e·rod′ing** [< L. *e-,* out + *rodere,* gnaw] 1. to

ERMINE

wear away 2. to form by wearing away gradually (the stream *eroded* a gully) —*vi.* to become eroded

**e·ro·sion** (i rō′zhən) *n.* an eroding or being eroded —**e·ro′sive** (-siv) *adj.*

**e·rot·ic** (i rät′ik) *adj.* [< Gr. *erōs,* love] of or arousing sexual feelings or desires; amatory —**e·rot′i·cal·ly** *adv.*

**e·rot′i·ca** (-i kə) *n.pl.* [*often with sing. v.*] erotic books, pictures, etc.

**e·ro·to·gen·ic** (i rät′ə jen′ik) *adj.* [see EROTIC & -GENIC] designating or of those areas of the body that are sensitive to sexual stimulation

**err** (ʉr, er) *vi.* [< L. *errare,* wander] 1. to be wrong or mistaken 2. to deviate from the established moral code

**er·rand** (er′ənd) *n.* [< OE. *ærende,* mission] 1. a trip to do a thing, as for someone else 2. the thing to be done

**er·rant** (er′ənt) *adj.* [see ERR] 1. roving or wandering, esp. in search of adventure 2. erring 3. shifting about

**er·rat·ic** (i rat′ik) *adj.* [see ERR] 1. irregular; random 2. eccentric; queer —**er·rat′i·cal·ly** *adv.*

**er·ra·tum** (e ra′təm, -rät′-) *n., pl.* -**ta** [see ERR] an error in printing or writing

**er·ro·ne·ous** (ə rō′nē əs) *adj.* containing error; mistaken; wrong —**er·ro′ne·ous·ly** *adv.*

**er·ror** (er′ər) *n.* [see ERR] 1. the state of believing what is untrue 2. a wrong belief 3. something incorrectly done; mistake 4. a transgression 5. *Baseball* any misplay in fielding

**er·satz** (ʉr′zäts, er′-) *adj.* [G.] substitute or synthetic and inferior

**Erse** (ʉrs) *adj., n.* [< ME. var. of *Irisc,* IRISH] *same as* GAELIC

**erst** (ʉrst) *adv.* [< OE. *ær,* ere] [Archaic] formerly

**erst′while′** (-hwīl′) *adv.* [Archaic] formerly —*adj.* former

**e·ruct** (i rukt′) *vt., vi.* [< L. < *e-,* out + *ructare,* belch] to belch —**e·ruc′ta′tion** *n.*

**er·u·dite** (er′yoo dīt′, -oo-) *adj.* [< L. *e-,* out + *rudis,* rude] learned; scholarly —**er′u·dite′ly** *adv.*

**er′u·di′tion** (-dish′ən) *n.* learning acquired by reading and study

**e·rupt** (i rupt′) *vi.* [< L. *e-,* out + *rumpere,* to break] 1. to burst forth or out [*erupting* lava] 2. to throw forth lava, water, etc. 3. to break out in a rash —*vt.* to cause to burst forth

**e·rup·tion** (i rup′shən) *n.* 1. a bursting forth or out 2. *a)* a breaking out in a rash *b)* a rash

**-er·y** (ə rē) [< LL. -*aria*] *a suffix meaning:* 1. a place to [*tannery*] 2. a place for [*nunnery*] 3. the practice or act of [*robbery*] 4. the product of [*pottery*] 5. a collection of [*crockery*] 6. the condition of [*drudgery*]

**er·y·sip·e·las** (er′ə sip′l əs, ir′-) *n.* [< Gr. *erythros,* red + -*pelas,* skin] an acute, infectious skin disease with local inflammation and fever

**e·ryth·ro·cyte** (i rith′rə sīt′) *n.* [< Gr. *erythros,* red + *kytos,* a hollow] a red corpuscle in the blood: it contains hemoglobin, which carries oxygen to the body tissues

**-es** (iz, əz) [< OE.] a suffix used to form: **1.** certain plurals *(fishes)* **2.** the third person singular, present indicative, of verbs *((he) kisses)*

**E·sau** (ē′sô) *Bible* Isaac's son, who sold his birthright to his brother, Jacob

**es·ca·late** (es′kə lāt′) *vi.* **-lat′ed, -lat′ing** **1.** to rise as on an escalator **2.** to expand step by step **3.** to increase rapidly —**es′ca·la′tion** *n.*

**es·ca·la·tor** (es′kə lāt′ər) *n.* [ult. < L. *scala*, ladder] a moving stairway on an endless belt

**es·cal·lop, es·cal·op** (e skal′əp, -skäl′-) *n., vt.* same as SCALLOP

**es·ca·pade** (es′kə pād′) *n.* [Fr.: see ff.] a reckless adventure or prank

**es·cape** (ə skāp′, e-) *vi.* **-caped′, -cap′ing** [< L. *ex-*, out of + *cappa*, a cloak] **1.** to get free **2.** to avoid harm, injury, etc. **3.** to leak away —*vt.* **1.** to get away from **2.** to avoid *(he escaped death)* **3.** to come from involuntarily **4.** to be forgotten or not noticed by —*n.* **1.** an escaping **2.** a means of escape **3.** a leakage **4.** a temporary mental release from reality —*adj.* providing an escape

**es·cap·ee** (ə skā′pē′, e-) *n.* a person who has escaped, as from prison

**es·cape′ment** *n.* a notched wheel with a detaining catch that controls the action of a clock or watch

**escape velocity** the minimum speed required for a space vehicle, etc. to escape permanently from the gravitational field of a planet, star, etc.

**es·cap·ism** (-iz′m) *n.* a tendency to escape from reality, responsibilities, etc. through the imagination —**es·cap′ist** *adj., n.*

**es·ca·role** (es′kə rōl′) *n.* [Fr. < L. *esca*, food] a kind of endive with wide leaves

**es·carp·ment** (e skärp′mənt) *n.* [< Fr.] a steep slope or cliff

**-es·cence** (es′ns) a noun suffix corresponding to the suffix -ESCENT

**-es·cent** (es′nt) [< L. *-escens*] an adjective suffix meaning: **1.** starting to be, being, or becoming *(putrescent)* **2.** giving off light *(incandescent)*

**es·chew** (es chōō′) *vt.* [< OHG. *sciuhan*, to fear] to shun; avoid

**es·cort** (es′kôrt; *for v.* i skôrt′) *n.* [< L. *ex-*, out + *corrigere*, set right] **1.** one or more persons, cars, etc. accompanying another to protect it or show honor **2.** a man accompanying a woman —*vt.* to go with as an escort

**es·cri·toire** (es′krə twär′) *n.* [< L. *scribere*, to write] a writing desk

**es·crow** (es′krō) *n.* [see SCROLL] the state of a deed, etc. put in the care of a third party until certain conditions are fulfilled

**es·cutch·eon** (i skuch′ən) *n.* [< L. *scutum*, shield] a shield on which a coat of arms is displayed

**-ese** (ēz, ēs) [< L. *-ensis*] a suffix meaning: **1.** (an inhabitant) of *(Japanese)* **2.** (in) the language of *(Cantonese)*

**Es·ki·mo** (es′kə mō′) *n.* [< Fr. < Algonquian] **1.** *pl.* **-mos, -mo** a member of a people living in Greenland, arctic N. America, etc. **2.** either of their two languages —*adj.* of the Eskimos, their language, etc.

**Eskimo dog** a strong breed of dog used by the Eskimos to pull sleds

ESKIMO DOG

**e·soph·a·gus** (i säf′ə gəs) *n., pl.* **-gi′** (-jī′) [< Gr. *oisophagos*] the passage for food from the pharynx to the stomach

**es·o·ter·ic** (es′ə ter′ik) *adj.* [< Gr. *esōteros*, inner] meant for or understood by only a chosen few

**ESP** extrasensory perception

**esp., espec.,** especially

**es·pa·drille** (es′pə dril′) *n.* [Fr. < Sp. *esparto*, coarse grass] a casual shoe with a canvas upper and a rope or rubber sole

**es·pal·ier** (es pal′yər) *n.* [Fr. < It. *spalla*, shoulder] **1.** a lattice on which trees or shrubs are trained to grow flat **2.** such a tree or shrub

**es·pe·cial** (es pesh′əl) *adj.* special; particular —**es·pe′cial·ly** *adv.*

**Es·pe·ran·to** (es′pə rän′tō, -ran′-) *n.* an artificial international language based on European word roots

**es·pi·o·nage** (es′pē ə näzh′, -nij′) *n.* [< Fr. < It. *spia*, spy] the act or practice of spying

**es·pla·nade** (es′plə nād′, -näd′) *n.* [< Fr. < It. < L. *explanare*, to level] a level stretch of ground, esp. a public walk

**es·pous·al** (i spou′z'l) *n.* **1.** *(often pl.)* a wedding **2.** an espousing (of some cause, idea, etc.); advocacy

**es·pouse** (i spouz′) *vt.* **-poused′, -pous′ing** [see SPOUSE] **1.** to marry **2.** to advocate (some cause, idea, etc.)

**es·pres·so** (es pres′ō) *n., pl.* **-sos** [It.] coffee made by forcing steam through finely ground coffee beans

**es·prit de corps** (es prē′ də kôr′) [Fr.] group spirit; pride, etc. shared by those in the same group

**es·py** (ə splī′) *vt.* **-pied′, -py′ing** [see SPY] to catch sight of; make out

**-esque** (esk) [Fr.] a suffix meaning: **1.** in the manner or style of *(Romanesque)* **2.** like *(picturesque)*

**es·quire** (es′kwīr, ə skwīr′) *n.* [< LL. *scularius*, shield-bearer] **1.** formerly, an attendant on a knight **2.** in England, a member of the gentry ranking just below a knight **3.** [E-] a title of courtesy, usually abbrev. **Esq.** or **Esqr.**, placed after a man's surname

**es·say** (e sā′) *vt.* [< L. *exagium*, a weighing] to try; attempt —*n.* **1.** (es′ā, e sā′) an attempt; trial **2.** (es′ā) a short, personal literary composition dealing with a single subject —**es·say′er** *n.* —**es·say·ist** (es′ā ist) *n.*

**es·sence** (es′ns) *n.* [< L. *esse*, to be] **1.** the basic nature (of something) **2.**

*a)* a concentrated substance that keeps the flavor, etc. of that from which it is extracted *b)* perfume

**Es·sene** (es′ēn, ə sēn′) *n.* a member of an ancient Jewish ascetic sect (2d cent. B.C. to 2d cent. A.D.)

**es·sen·tial** (ə sen′shəl) *adj.* 1. of or constituting the essence of something; basic 2. absolutely necessary; indispensable —*n.* something necessary or fundamental —**es·sen′tial·ly** *adv.*

**-est** (ist, əst) a suffix forming the superlative degree *[greatest]*

**EST, E.S.T.** Eastern Standard Time

**est.** 1. established 2. estimate 3. estimated

**es·tab·lish** (ə stab′lish) *vt.* [< L. *stabilis*, stable] 1. to ordain or appoint (a law, official, etc.) permanently 2. to found (a nation, business, etc.) 3. to cause to be; bring about 4. to set up in a business, etc. 5. to cause to be accepted 6. to prove; demonstrate

**es·tab′lish·ment** *n.* 1. an establishing or being established 2. a thing established, as a business —**the Establishment** an inner circle thought of as holding decisive power in a nation, institution, etc.

**es·tate** (ə stāt′) *n.* [ME. *estat*] 1. a condition or stage of life 2. property; possessions 3. a large, individually owned piece of land containing a large residence

**es·teem** (ə stēm′) *vt.* [< L. *aestimare*, to value] 1. to value highly; respect 2. to consider —*n.* favorable opinion

**es·ter** (es′tər) *n.* [G. < *essig*, vinegar + *äther*, ether] an organic compound formed by the reaction of an acid and an alcohol

**Es·ther** (es′tər) *Bible* the Jewish wife of a Persian king: she saved her people from slaughter

**es·thete, es·thet·ics,** etc. same as AESTHETE, AESTHETICS, etc.

**es·ti·ma·ble** (es′tə mə b'l) *adj.* worthy of esteem; fine

**es·ti·mate** (es′tə māt′; *for n.* -mit) *vt.* -mat′ed, -mat′ing [see ESTEEM] 1. to form an opinion about 2. to calculate approximately (size, cost, etc.) —*n.* 1. a general calculation; esp., an approximate computation of probable cost 2. an opinion or judgment —**es′ti·ma′tor** *n.*

**es′ti·ma′tion** *n.* 1. an opinion or judgment 2. esteem; regard

**Es·to·ni·a** (es tō′nē ə) republic of the U.S.S.R., in NE Europe —**Es·to′ni·an** *adj., n.*

**es·trange** (ə strānj′) *vt.* -tranged′, -trang′ing [< L. *extraneus*, strange] to turn (a person) from an affectionate attitude to an indifferent or unfriendly one —**es·trange′ment** *n.*

**es·tro·gen** (es′trə jən) *n.* [< Gr. *oistros*, frenzy] any of several female sex hormones

**es·tu·ar·y** (es′choo wer′ē) *n., pl.* -ies [< L. *aestus*, tide] the wide mouth of a river into which the tide flows

**-et** (it, ət) [< LL. *-itus*] a suffix meaning little *[islet]*

**e·ta** (āt′ə, ēt′ə) *n.* the seventh letter of the Greek alphabet (H, η)

**†é·ta·gère** (ā tä zher′) *n.* [Fr.] a stand with open shelves, for displaying art objects, ornaments, etc.

**et al.** [L. *et alii*] and others

**et cet·er·a** (et set′ər ə, set′rə) [L.] and others; and so forth: abbrev. etc.

**etch** (ech) *vt.* [< MHG. *etzen*, eat] to make (a drawing, design, etc.) on (metal plate, glass, etc.) by the action of an acid —**etch′er** *n.*

**etch′ing** *n.* 1. the art of an etcher 2. a print made from an etched plate

**e·ter·nal** (i tur′n'l) *adj.* [< L. *aeternus*] 1. without beginning or end; everlasting 2. always the same 3. seeming never to stop —**e·ter′nal·ly** *adv.* —**e·ter′nal·ness** *n.*

**e·ter·ni·ty** (i tur′nə tē) *n., pl.* -ties 1. the state or fact of being eternal 2. infinite or endless time 3. a long period of time that seems endless 4. the endless time after death

**eth·ane** (eth′ān) *n.* [see ETHYL] an odorless, colorless, gaseous hydrocarbon, found in natural gas and used as a fuel

**e·ther** (ē′thər) *n.* [< Gr. *aithein*, to burn] 1. the upper regions of space 2. a volatile, colorless, highly flammable liquid, used as an anesthetic and solvent 3. an invisible substance once thought to pervade space

**e·the·re·al** (i thir′ē əl) *adj.* 1. very light; airy; delicate 2. not earthly; heavenly —**e·the′re·al·ly** *adv.*

**eth·ic** (eth′ik) *n.* [see ff.] ethics or a system of ethics

**eth·i·cal** (eth′i k'l) *adj.* [< Gr. *ethos*, character] 1. having to do with ethics; of or conforming to moral standards 2. conforming to professional standards of conduct —**eth′i·cal·ly** *adv.*

**eth·ics** (eth′iks) *n.pl.* [*with sing. v.*] 1. the study of standards of conduct and moral judgment 2. the system of morals of a particular person, religion, group, etc.

**E·thi·o·pi·a** (ē′thē ō′pē ə) country in E Africa, on the Red Sea: 457,000 sq. mi.; pop. 23,000,000 —**E′thi·o′pi·an** *adj., n.*

**eth·nic** (eth′nik) *adj.* [< Gr. *ethnos*, nation] of any of the basic divisions of mankind, as distinguished by customs, language, etc. —*n.* a member of a minority or nationality group that is part of a larger community —**eth′ni·cal·ly** *adv.*

**eth·nic·i·ty** (eth nis′ə tē) *n.* ethnic classification or affiliation

**eth·nol·o·gy** (eth näl′ə jē) *n.* [< Gr. *ethnos*, nation + -LOGY] the branch of anthropology that deals with the distribution, culture, etc. of various peoples —**eth′no·log′i·cal** (-nə läj′i k'l) *adj.* —**eth·nol′o·gist** *n.*

**e·thos** (ē′thäs) *n.* [Gr. *ēthos*, character] the characteristic attitudes, habits, etc. of an individual or group

**eth·yl** (eth′'l) *n.* [< ETHER] the hydrocarbon radical which forms the base of common alcohol, ether, etc.

**ethyl alcohol** same as ALCOHOL (n. 1)

**eth·yl·ene** (eth′ə lēn′) *n.* [ETHYL + -ENE] a colorless, flammable, gaseous hydrocarbon with a disagreeable odor e·ti·ol·o·gy (ēt'ē äl'ə jē) n., pl. -gies [< Gr. aitia, cause + logia, description] 1. the cause assigned, as for a disease 2. the science of causes or origins —e'ti·o·log'ic (-ə läj'ik) adj.

et·i·quette (et'i kət, -ket') n. [Fr. étiquette, a ticket] the forms, manners, etc. conventionally acceptable or required in society, a profession, etc.

Et·na (et'nə) volcanic mountain in E Sicily

E·trus·can (i trus'kən) adj. of an ancient country (Etruria) in WC Italy

et seq. [L. et sequens] and the following

-ette (et) [Fr.] a suffix meaning: 1. little [statuette] 2. female [majorette]

é·tude (ā'tōōd) n. [Fr., study] a musical composition for a solo instrument, designed to give practice in some point of technique

ETV educational television

et·y·mol·o·gy (et'ə mäl'ə jē) n., pl. -gies [< Gr. etymos, true + logos, word] 1. the origin and development of a word 2. the scientific study of word origins Abbrev. etym. —etym. —et'y·mo·log'i·cal (-mə läj'ə k'l) adj. — et'y·mol'o·gist n.

eu- [Fr. < Gr.] a prefix meaning good, well [eulogy, euphony]

eu·ca·lyp·tus (yōō'kə lip'təs) n. [< Gr. eu-, well + kalyptos, covered] a tall, aromatic, chiefly Australian evergreen of the myrtle family

Eu·cha·rist (yōō'kə rist) n. [< Gr. eucharistia, gratitude] 1. same as HOLY COMMUNION 2. the consecrated bread and wine used in this —Eu'cha·ris'tic adj.

eu·chre (yōō'kər) n. [< ?] a card game played with thirty-two cards

Eu·clid (yōō'klid) fl. 300 B.C.; Gr. mathematician: author of a basic work in geometry —Eu·clid'e·an, Eu·clid'i·an (-ē ən) adj.

eu·gen·ics (yoo jen'iks) n.pl. [with sing. v.] [see EU- & GENESIS] the movement devoted to improving the human species by controlling heredity —eu·gen'ic adj. —eu·gen'i·cal·ly adv. —eu·gen'i·cist (-ə sist) n.

eu·lo·gize (yōō'lə jīz') vt. -gized', -giz'ing [see ff.] to praise highly —eu'lo·gist, eu'lo·giz'er n.

eu·lo·gy (-jē) n., pl. -gies [< Gr. eulegein, speak well of] 1. speech or writing praising a person or thing; esp., a funeral oration 2. high praise — eu'lo·gis'tic (-jis'tik) adj.

eu·nuch (yōō'nək) n. [< Gr. eunē, bed + echein, have] a castrated man

eu·phe·mism (yōō'fə miz'm) n. [< Gr. eu-, good + phēmē, voice] 1. the use of a less direct word or phrase for one considered offensive 2. a word or phrase so substituted —eu'phe·mis'tic adj. —eu'phe·mis'ti·cal·ly adv.

eu·pho·ni·ous (yoo fō'nē əs) adj. having a pleasant sound; harmonious

eu·pho·ny (yōō'fə nē) n., pl. -nies [< Gr. eu-, well + phōnē, voice] a

pleasant combination of agreeable sounds, as in speech

eu·pho·ri·a (yoo fôr'ē ə) n. [< Gr. eu-, well + pherein, to bear] a feeling of well-being —eu·phor'ic adj.

Eu·phra·tes (yoo frāt'ēz) river flowing from EC Turkey through Syria & Iraq into the Persian Gulf: cf. TIGRIS

Eur·a·sia (yoo rā'zhə) land mass of Europe & Asia

Eur·a·sian adj. 1. of Eurasia 2. of mixed European and Asian descent —n. a person of Eurasian descent

eu·re·ka (yoo rē'kə) interj. [< Gr. heurēka, I have found (it)] an exclamation of triumphant achievement

Eu·rip·i·des (yoo rip'ə dēz') 479?-406? B.C.; Gr. writer of tragedies

Eu·rope (yoor'əp) continent between Asia & the Atlantic: c.3,750,000 sq. mi.; pop. c.628,000,000 —Eu'ro·pe'an (-ə pē'ən) adj., n.

European plan a system of hotel operation in which guests are charged for rooms, and pay for meals separately

eu·ryth·mics (yoo ri th'miks) n.pl. [with sing. v.] [< Gr. eu-, well + rhythmos, rhythm] the art of performing bodily movements in rhythm, usually to music

Eu·sta·chi·an tube (yoo stā'shən, -kē ən) [after B. Eustachio, 16th-c. It. anatomist] a slender tube between the middle ear and the pharynx

eu·tha·na·si·a (yōō'thə nā'zhə) n. [< Gr. eu-, well + thanatos, death] act of causing death painlessly, so as to end suffering

eu·then·ics (yoo then'iks) n.pl. [with sing. v.] [< Gr. euthēnein, flourish] a movement to improve the human species by controlling the environment

e·vac·u·ate (i vak'yoo wāt') vt. -at'ed, -at'ing [< L. e-, out + vacuus, empty] 1. to make empty 2. to discharge (bodily waste, esp. feces) 3. to withdraw from; remove —vi. to withdraw —e·vac'u·a'tion n. —e·vac'u·ee' (-wē') n.

e·vade (i vād') vi., vt. e·vad'ed, e·vad'ing [< L. e-, out + vadere, go] 1. to avoid or escape (from) by deceit or cleverness 2. to avoid doing or answering directly —e·vad'er n.

e·val·u·ate (i val'yoo wāt') vt. -at'ed, -at'ing [ult. < L. ex-, out + valere, be worth] 1. to find the value or amount of 2. to judge the worth of —e·val'u·a'tion n.

ev·a·nes·cent (ev'ə nes''nt) adj. [< L. e-, out + vanescere, vanish] tending to fade from sight; fleeting; ephemeral —ev'a·nes'cence n.

e·van·gel·i·cal (ē'van jel'i k'l, ev' ən-) adj. [< Gr. euangelos, bringing good news] 1. of or according to the Gospels or the New Testament 2. of those Protestant churches that emphasize salvation by faith in Jesus

e·van·gel·ist (i van'jə list) n. 1. [E-] any of the four writers of the Gospels 2. a preacher of the gospel;

esp., a traveling preacher; revivalist —e·van'gel·ism n. —e·van'gel·is'-tic adj. —e·van'gel·is'ti·cal·ly adv.

e·van'gel·ize' (-līz') vt. -ized', -iz'-ing to convert to Christianity —vi. to preach the gospel

**Ev·ans·ville** (ev'anz vil') city in SW Ind.: pop. 139,000

e·vap·o·rate (i vap'ə rāt') vt. -rat'-ed, -rat'ing [< L. e-, out + vaporare, emit vapor] 1. to change (a liquid or solid) into vapor 2. to remove moisture from (milk, etc.), as by heating, so as to get a concentrated product —vi. 1. to become vapor 2. to give off vapor 3. to vanish —e·vap'o·ra'tion n. —e·vap'o·ra'tor n.

e·va·sion (i vā'zhən) n. 1. an evading; specif., an avoiding of a duty, question, etc. by deceit or cleverness 2. a way of doing this; subterfuge

e·va·sive (-siv) adj. 1. tending or seeking to evade; tricky 2. elusive —e·va'sive·ly adv. —e·va'sive·ness n.

**Eve** (ēv) Bible Adam's wife, the first woman

eve (ēv) n. [< OE. æfen, evening] 1. [Poet.] evening 2. [often E-] the evening or day before a holiday 3. the period just prior to some event

e·ven (ē'vən) adj. [OE. efne] 1. flat; level; smooth 2. not varying; constant [an even tempo] 3. calm; tranquil [an even temper] 4. in the same plane or line [even with the rim] 5. owing and being owed nothing 6. equal in number, quantity, etc. 7. exactly divisible by two 8. exact [an even mile] —adv. 1. however improbable; indeed 2. exactly; just [it happened even as I expected] 3. still; yet [he's even better] —vt., vi. to make or become even —break even [Colloq.] to finish as neither a winner nor a loser —even if though —e'ven·ly adv. —e'ven·ness n.

e'ven·hand'ed adj. impartial; fair

eve·ning (ēv'niŋ) n. [< OE. æfnung] 1. the last part of the day and early part of night 2. [Dial.] afternoon

even money equal stakes in betting, with no odds

e·vent (i vent') n. [< L. e-, out + venire, come] 1. an occurrence, esp. when important 2. an outcome 3. a particular contest in a program of sports —in any event anyhow —in the event of in case of —in the event that if it should happen that

e'ven-tem'pered adj. not quickly angered; calm

e·vent'ful adj. 1. full of outstanding events 2. having an important outcome —e·vent'ful·ly adv. —e·vent'-ful·ness n.

e·ven·tide (ē'vən tīd') n. [Archaic] evening

e·ven·tu·al (i ven'choo wəl) adj. ultimate; final —e·ven'tu·al·ly adv.

e·ven·tu·al·i·ty (-wal'ə tē) n., pl. -ties a possible event or outcome

e·ven·tu·ate' (-wāt') vi. -at'ed, -at'ing to happen in the end; result

ev·er (ev'ər) adv. [< OE. æfre] 1. always [ever the same] 2. at any time [do you ever see her?] 3. at all; by any

chance [how can I ever repay you?] —ever so [Colloq.] very

**Ev·er·est** (ev'ər ist), **Mount** peak of the Himalayas: highest known mountain in the world: 29,028 ft.

ev'er·glade' (-glād') n. swampy land

ev'er·green' adj. having green leaves all year long, as most conifers —n. an evergreen plant or tree

ev'er·last'ing adj. lasting forever; eternal —n. eternity

ev'er·more' adv. forever; constantly

ev·er·y (ev'rē, ev'ər ē) adj. [OE. æfre ælc, lit., ever each] 1. each, individually and separately 2. the greatest possible [to make every effort] 3. each interval of [a dose every two hours] —every other each alternate, as the first, third, fifth, etc. —every so often [Colloq.] occasionally —every which way [Colloq.] in complete disorder

ev'er·y·bod'y (-bäd'ē, -bud'ē) pron. every person; everyone

ev'er·y·day' adj. 1. daily 2. suitable for ordinary days [everyday shoes] 3. usual; common

ev'er·y·one' pron. every person

every one every person or thing of those named [every one of the boys]

ev'er·y·thing' pron. every thing; all

ev'er·y·where' adv. in or to every place

e·vict (i vikt') vt. [< L. e-, intens. + vincere, conquer] to remove (a tenant) by legal procedure —e·vic'tion n.

ev·i·dence (ev'ə dəns) n. 1. the state of being evident 2. something that makes another thing evident; sign 3. a statement of a witness, an object, etc. bearing on or establishing the point in question in a court of law —vt. -denced, -denc·ing to make evident —in evidence plainly seen

ev'i·dent (-dənt) adj. [< L. e-, from + videre, see] easy to see or perceive; clear —ev'i·dent·ly adv.

e·vil (ē'v'l) adj. [OE. yfel] 1. morally bad or wrong; wicked 2. harmful; injurious 3. unlucky; disastrous —n. 1. wickedness; sin 2. anything causing harm, pain, etc. —e'vil·ly adv.

e'vil·do'er (-dōō'ər) n. one who does evil —e'vil·do'ing n.

e·vince (i vins') vt. e·vinced', e·vinc'ing [< L. e-, intens. + vincere, conquer] to show plainly; make clear

e·vis·cer·ate (i vis'ə rāt') vt. -at'ed, -at'ing [< L. e-, out + viscera, VISCERA] 1. to remove the entrails from 2. to deprive of an essential part —e·vis'cer·a'tion n.

e·voke (i vōk') vt. e·voked', e·vok'-ing [< L. e-, out + vox, voice] 1. to call forth 2. to elicit (a reaction, etc.) —ev·o·ca·tion (ev'ə kā'shən) n.

ev·o·lu·tion (ev'ə lōō'shən) n. [see ff.] 1. an unfolding; process of development or change 2. a thing evolved 3. a movement that is part of a series 4. Biol. a) the development of a species, organism, etc. from its original to its present state b) the theory that all species developed from earlier forms —ev'o·lu'tion·ar'y adj. —ev'o·lu'tion·ist n.

**e·volve** (i välv′) *vt., vi.* **e·volved′, e·volv′ing** [< L. *e-,* out + *volvere,* to roll] 1. to develop gradually; unfold 2. to develop by evolution

**ewe** (yōō) *n.* [OE. *eowu*] a female sheep

**ew·er** (yōō′ər) *n.* [< L. *aqua,* water] a large, wide-mouthed water pitcher

**ex-** [< OFr. or L.] *a prefix meaning:* 1. from, out [*expel*] 2. beyond [*excess*] 3. thoroughly [*exterminate*] 4. upward [*exalt*] 5. former [*ex*-president]

EWER

**Ex.** Exodus

**ex.** 1. example 2. except(ed)

**ex·ac·er·bate** (ig zas′ər bāt′) *vt.* **-bat′ed, -bat′ing** [< L. *ex-,* intens. + *acerbus,* sour] 1. to aggravate (pain, annoyance, etc.) 2. to exasperate; irritate —**ex·ac′er·ba′tion** *n.*

**ex·act** (ig zakt′) *adj.* [< L. *ex-* + *agere,* do] 1. characterized by or requiring accuracy; methodical; correct 2. without variation; precise —*vt.* 1. to extort 2. to demand; require —**ex·act′ly** *adv.* —**ex·act′ness** *n.*

**ex·act′ing** *adj.* 1. making severe demands; strict 2. demanding great care, effort, etc.; arduous —**ex·act′ing·ly** *adv.* —**ex·act′ing·ness** *n.*

**ex·ac′tion** *n.* 1. an exacting 2. an extortion 3. something exacted

**ex·ac·ti·tude′** (-tə tōōd′) *n.* the quality of being exact; accuracy

**ex·ag·ger·ate** (ig zaj′ə rāt′) *vt., vi.* **-at′ed, -at′ing** [< L. *ex-,* out + *agger,* a heap] to think or tell of (something) as greater than it is; overstate —**ex·ag′ger·a′tion** *n.* —**ex·ag′ger·a′tive** *adj.* —**ex·ag′ger·a′tor** *n.*

**ex·alt** (ig zôlt′) *vt.* [< L. *ex-,* up + *altus,* high] 1. to raise in status, dignity, etc. 2. to praise; glorify 3. to fill with joy, pride, etc.; elate —**ex·al·ta·tion** (eg′zôl tā′shən) *n.*

**ex·am·i·na·tion** (ig zam′ə nā′shən) *n.* 1. an examining or being examined 2. a set of questions asked in testing: also [Colloq.] **ex·am′**

**ex·am·ine** (ig zam′ən) *vt.* **-ined, -in·ing** [< L. *examinare,* weigh] 1. to look at critically or methodically; investigate; inspect 2. to test by questioning —**ex·am′in·er** *n.*

**ex·am·ple** (ig zam′p'l) *n.* [< L. *eximere,* take out] 1. something selected to show the character of the rest; sample 2. a case that serves as a warning 3. a model; pattern 4. an instance that illustrates a principle

**ex·as·per·ate** (ig zas′pə rāt′) *vt.* **-at′ed, -at′ing** [< L. *ex-,* out + *asper,* rough] to irritate; anger; vex —**ex·as′per·a′tion** *n.*

**ex·ca·vate** (eks′kə vāt′) *vt.* **-vat′ed, -vat′ing** [< L. *ex-,* out + *cavus,* hollow] 1. to make a hole or cavity in 2. to form (a tunnel, etc.) by hollowing out 3. to unearth 4. to dig out (earth, etc.) —**ex′ca·va′tion** *n.* —**ex′ca·va′tor** *n.*

**ex·ceed** (ik sēd′) *vt., vi.* [< L. *ex-,* out + *cedere,* go] 1. to go or be beyond (a limit, etc.) 2. to surpass

**ex·ceed′ing** (-in) *adj.* surpassing; extreme —**ex·ceed′ing·ly** *adv.*

**ex·cel** (ik sel′) *vi., vt.* **-celled′, -cel′ling** [< L. *ex-,* out of + *-cellere,* to rise] to be better or greater than (another or others)

**ex·cel·lence** (ek′s'l əns) *n.* 1. the fact or state of excelling; superiority 2. a particular virtue

**ex·cel·len·cy** (-ən sē) *n., pl.* **-cies** 1. [E-] a title of honor for certain dignitaries 2. *same as* EXCELLENCE

**ex′cel·lent** *adj.* [see EXCEL] outstandingly good of its kind; of exceptional merit —**ex′cel·lent·ly** *adv.*

**ex·cel·si·or** (ek sel′sē ôr′; *for n.* ik sel′sē ər) *adj., interj.* [see EXCEL] always upward —*n.* long, thin wood shavings used for packing

**ex·cept** (ik sept′) *vt.* [< L. *ex-,* out + *capere,* take] to leave out or take out; exclude —*prep.* leaving out; but —*conj.* [Colloq.] were it not that; only —except for if it were not for

**ex·cept′ing** *prep. same as* EXCEPT

**ex·cep′tion** *n.* 1. an excepting 2. a person or thing different from others of the same class; case to which a rule does not apply 3. an objection —take exception to object

**ex·cep′tion·a·ble** *adj.* liable to exception; open to objection

**ex·cep′tion·al** *adj.* 1. unusual; esp., unusually good 2. requiring special education, as because mentally handicapped —**ex·cep′tion·al·ly** *adv.*

**ex·cerpt** (ik surpt′; *for n.* ek′surpt′) *vt.* [< L. *ex-,* out + *carpere,* to pick] to select or quote (passages from a book, etc.); extract —*n.* a passage selected or quoted; extract

**ex·cess** (ik ses′; *also & for adj. usually* ek′ses′) *n.* [see EXCEED] 1. action that goes beyond a reasonable limit 2. an amount greater than is necessary 3. the amount by which one thing exceeds another; surplus —*adj.* extra; surplus —in excess of more than

**ex·ces′sive** *adj.* being too much; immoderate —**ex·ces′sive·ly** *adv.*

**ex·change** (iks chānj′) *vt., vi.* **-changed′, -chang′ing** [see EX- & CHANGE] 1. to give or receive (something) for another thing; barter; trade 2. to interchange (similar things) —*n.* 1. an exchanging; interchange 2. a thing exchanged 3. a place for exchanging [a stock *exchange*] 4. a central office providing telephone service 5. the value of one currency in terms of another —**ex·change′a·ble** *adj.*

**exchange rate** the ratio of the value of one currency in relation to the value of another

**ex·cheq·uer** (iks chek′ər, eks′chek-) *n.* [< ML. *scaccarium,* chessboard: accounts of revenue were kept on a squared board] 1. a national treasury 2. funds; finances

**ex·cise¹** (ek'sīz, -sīs) n. [ult. < L. *assidere*, assist (in office)] a tax on various commodities, as tobacco, within a country: also **excise tax**

**ex·cise²** (ik sīz') vt. -cised', -cis'ing [< L. ex-, out + caedere, to cut] to remove by cutting out —**ex·ci'sa·ble** adj. —**ex·ci'sion** (-sizh'ən) n.

**ex·cit·a·ble** (ik sīt'ə b'l) adj. easily excited —**ex·cit'a·bil'i·ty** n.

**ex·cite** (ik sīt') vt. -cit'ed, -cit'ing [< L. ex-, out + ciere, to call] 1. to make active; stimulate 2. to arouse; provoke 3. to arouse the feelings of — **ex·ci·ta·tion** (ek'sī tā'shən) n. —**ex·cit'ed·ly** adv. —**ex·cit'er** n.

**ex·cite'ment** n. 1. an exciting or being excited 2. that which excites

**ex·cit'ing** adj. causing excitement; stirring, thrilling, etc.

**ex·claim** (iks klām') vi., vt. [< L. ex-, out + clamare, to shout] to cry out; say suddenly and vehemently

**ex·cla·ma·tion** (eks'klə mā'shən) n. 1. an exclaiming 2. something exclaimed; interjection —**ex·clam·a·to·ry** (iks klam'ə tôr'ē) adj.

**exclamation mark** (or **point**) a mark (!) used in punctuating to show surprise, strong emotion, etc.

**ex·clude** (iks klōōd') vt. -clud'ed, -clud'ing [< L. ex-, out + claudere, shut] 1. to refuse to admit, consider, etc.; reject 2. to put or force out; expel —**ex·clu'sion** (-klōō'zhən) n.

**ex·clu·sive** (-klōō'siv) adj. 1. excluding all others 2. not shared or divided; sole [an exclusive right.] 3. excluding certain people, as for social or economic reasons —**exclusive of** not including —**ex·clu'sive·ly** adv. —**ex·clu'sive·ness** n.

**ex·com·mu·ni·cate** (eks'kə myōō'nə kāt') vt. -cat'ed, -cat'ing to exclude from communion with a church —**ex'com·mu'ni·ca'tion** n.

**ex·co·ri·ate** (ik skôr'ē āt') vt. -at'ed, -at'ing [< L. ex-, off + corium, the skin] to denounce harshly —**ex·co'ri·a'tion** n.

**ex·cre·ment** (eks'krə mənt) n. waste matter excreted from the bowels

**ex·cres·cence** (iks kres''ns) n. [< L. ex-, out + crescere, grow] an abnormal outgrowth, as a bunion

**ex·cre·ta** (eks krēt'ə) n.pl. waste matter excreted from the body

**ex·crete** (iks krēt') vt., vi. -cret'ed, -cret'ing [< L. ex-, out of + cernere, sift] to eliminate (waste matter) from the body —**ex·cre'tion** n. —**ex·cre·to·ry** (eks'krə tôr'ē) adj.

**ex·cru·ci·at·ing** (iks krōō'shē āt'in) adj. [< L. ex-, intens. + cruciare, crucify] 1. intensely painful; agonizing 2. intense; extreme [excruciating care]

**ex·cul·pate** (eks'kəl pāt') vt. -pat'ed, -pat'ing [< L. ex, out + culpa, fault] to free from blame; prove guiltless —**ex'cul·pa'tion** n.

**ex·cur·sion** (ik skur'zhən) n. [< L. ex-, out + currere, to run] 1. a short trip, as for pleasure 2. a round trip at reduced rates 3. a digression —adj. for an excursion —**ex·cur'sion·ist** n.

**ex·cur·sive** (-siv) adj. rambling; digressive —**ex·cur'sive·ly** adv. —**ex·cur'sive·ness** n.

**ex·cuse** (ik skyōōz') vt. -cused', -cus'ing [< L. ex-, from + causa, a charge] 1. to apologize or give reasons for 2. to overlook (an offense or fault) 3. to release from an obligation, etc. 4. to permit to leave 5. to justify —n. 1. a defense of some action; apology 2. something that excuses 3. a pretext —**excuse oneself** 1. to apologize 2. to ask for permission to leave —**ex·cus'a·ble** adj.

**ex·e·cra·ble** (ek'si krə b'l) adj. [see ff.] 1. detestable 2. very inferior

**ex'e·crate'** (-krāt') vt. -crat'ed, -crat'ing [< L. execrare, to curse] 1. to denounce scathingly 2. to loathe; abhor —**ex'e·cra'tion** n.

**ex·e·cute** (ek'sə kyōōt') vt. -cut'ed, -cut'ing [see EXECUTOR] 1. to carry out; do 2. to administer (laws, etc.) 3. to put to death by a legal sentence 4. to create in accordance with a plan, etc. 5. to make valid (a deed, will, etc.)

**ex'e·cu'tion** n. 1. an executing; specif., a) a carrying out, performing, etc. b) a putting to death by a legal sentence 2. the manner of performing

**ex'e·cu'tion·er** n. one who carries out a court-imposed death penalty

**ex·ec·u·tive** (ig zek'yə tiv) adj. [see ff.] 1. of or capable of carrying out duties, functions, etc. 2. empowered to administer (laws, government affairs, etc.) —n. 1. the branch of government administering the laws and affairs of a nation 2. one who administers or manages affairs

**ex·ec·u·tor** (ig zek'yə tər) n. [< L. ex-, intens. + sequi, follow] a person appointed to carry out the provisions of another's will

**ex·e·ge·sis** (ek'sə jē'sis) n., pl. -ses (-sēz) [< Gr. ex-, out + hēgeisthai, to guide] interpretation of a word, passage, etc., esp. in the Bible

**ex·em·plar** (ig zem'plär) n. [< L. exemplum, a pattern] 1. a model; pattern 2. a typical specimen

**ex·em·pla·ry** (ig zem'plə rē) adj. [< L. exemplum, a pattern] serving as a model or example [an exemplary life]

**ex·em·pli·fy** (ig zem'plə fī') vt. -fied', -fy'ing [< L. exemplum, example + facere, make] to show by example —**ex·em'pli·fi·ca'tion** n.

**ex·empt** (ig zempt') vt. [< L. ex-, out + emere, take] to free from a rule or obligation which applies to others — adj. freed from a usual rule, duty, etc. —**ex·emp'tion** n.

**ex·er·cise** (ek'sər sīz') n. [< L. exercere, to put to work] 1. active use or operation 2. performance (of duties; etc.) 3. activity for developing the body or mind 4. a task to be practiced for developing some skill 5. [pl.] a program of speeches, etc. —vt. -cised', -cis'ing 1. to put into action; use 2. to put into use so as to develop or train 3. to exert (influence, etc.) 4. to worry; disturb —vi. to do exercises

**ex·ert** (ig zurt') vt. [< L. exserere, stretch out] 1. to put into action 2.

to apply (oneself) with great effort
**ex·er′tion** n. 1. the act, fact, or process of exerting 2. effort
**ex·hale** (eks hāl′) vt., vi. -haled′, -hal′ing [< L. ex-, out + halare, breathe] 1. to breathe forth (air) 2. to give off (vapor, etc.) —ex·ha·la·tion (eks′hə lā′shən) n.
**ex·haust** (ig zôst′) vt. [< L. ex-, out + haurire, to draw] 1. to use up 2. to empty completely; drain 3. to tire out 4. to deal with thoroughly —n. 1. a) the discharge of used steam, gas, etc. from an engine b) the pipe through which it is released 2. fumes, etc. given off —ex·haust′i·ble adj.
**ex·haus·tion** (ig zôs′chən) n. 1. an exhausting 2. great fatigue
**ex·haus′tive** adj. leaving nothing out
**ex·hib·it** (ig zib′it) vt. [< L. ex-, out + habere, to hold] 1. to show; display 2. to present to public view —vi. to put art objects, etc. on public display —n. 1. a display 2. a thing exhibited 3. Law an object produced as evidence in a court —ex·hib′i·tor n.
**ex·hi·bi·tion** (ek′sə bish′ən) n. 1. an exhibiting 2. that which is exhibited 3. a public showing
**ex′hi·bi′tion·ism** n. 1. a tendency to call attention to oneself or show off 2. a tendency to expose oneself sexually —ex′hi·bi′tion·ist n.
**ex·hil·a·rate** (ig zil′ə rāt′) vt. -rat′ed, -rat′ing [< L. ex-, intens. + hilaris, glad] 1. to make lively and gay 2. to stimulate —ex·hil′a·ra′tion n. —ex·hil′a·ra′tive adj.
**ex·hort** (ig zôrt′) vt., vi. [< L. ex-, out + hortari, to urge] to urge earnestly; advise strongly —ex·hor·ta·tion (eg′zôr tā′shən, ek′sər-) n.
**ex·hume** (ig zyo͞om′, iks hyo͞om′) vt. -humed′, -hum′ing [< L. ex, out + humus, the ground] to dig out of the earth; disinter —ex·hu·ma·tion (eks′hyoo mā′shən) n.
**ex·i·gen·cy** (ek′sə jən sē) n., pl. -cies [< L. ex-, out + agere, to do] 1. urgency 2. a situation calling for immediate attention 3. [pl.] pressing needs —ex′i·gent adj.
**ex·ig·u·ous** (eg zig′yoo wəs) adj. [< L.: see prec.] scanty; meager
**ex·ile** (eg′zīl, ek′sīl) n. [< L. exul, an exile] 1. a prolonged living away from one's country, usually enforced 2. a person in exile —vt. -iled, -il·ing to force (one) into exile; banish
**ex·ist** (ig zist′) vi. [< L. ex-, out + sistere, to set, place] 1. to have reality or being; be 2. to occur or be present 3. to continue being; live
**ex·ist′ence** n. 1. the state or fact of being 2. life; living 3. occurrence —ex·ist′ent adj.
**ex·is·ten·tial** (eg′zis ten′shəl) adj. 1. of existence 2. of existentialism
**ex·is·ten·tial·ism** (eg′zis ten′shəl iz′m) n. a philosophical movement stressing individual existence and holding that man is totally free and

responsible for his acts —ex′is·ten′tial·ist adj., n.
**ex·it** (eg′zit, ek′sit) n. [< L. ex-, out + ire, go] 1. an actor's departure from the stage 2. a going out; departure 3. a way out —vi. to leave a place
**exo-** [< Gr. exō] a prefix meaning outside, outer, outer part
**ex′o·bi·ol′o·gy** n. the branch of biology studying the possible existence of living organisms elsewhere in the universe than on earth
**ex·o·dus** (ek′sə dəs) n. [< Gr. ex-, out + hodos, way] a going out or forth —[E-] 1. the departure of the Israelites from Egypt (with -the) 2. the second book of the Bible, describing this
**ex of·fi·ci·o** (eks′ ə fish′ē ō′) [L., lit., from office] because of one's position
**ex·on·er·ate** (ig zän′ə rāt′) vt. -at′ed, -at′ing [< L. ex-, out + onerare, to load] to declare or prove blameless —ex·on′er·a′tion n.
**ex·or·bi·tant** (ig zôr′bə tənt) adj. [< L. ex-, out + orbita, a track] going beyond what is reasonable, just, etc.; excessive —ex·or′bi·tance n.
**ex·or·cise, ex·or·cize** (ek′sôr sīz′) vt. -cised′ or -cized′, -cis′ing or -ciz′ing [< Gr. ex-, out + horkos, oath] 1. to expel (an evil spirit) by incantations, etc. 2. to free from such a spirit —ex′or·cism (-siz′m) n. —ex′or·cist n.
**ex·ot·ic** (ig zät′ik) adj. [< Gr. exō, outside] 1. foreign 2. strangely beautiful, enticing, etc.
**ex·pand** (ik spand′) vt., vi. [< L. ex-, out + pandere, to spread] 1. to spread out; unfold 2. to increase in size, scope, etc.; enlarge; develop
**ex·panse** (ik spans′) n. a large area or unbroken surface; wide extent
**ex·pan·si·ble** adj. that can be expanded: also ex·pand′a·ble
**ex·pan′sion** n. 1. an expanding or being expanded; enlargement 2. an expanded thing or part 3. the degree or extent of expansion
**expansion bolt** a bolt with an attachment that expands in use to act as a wedge
**ex·pan′sive** adj. 1. that can expand 2. broad; extensive 3. effusive; demonstrative —ex·pan′sive·ly adv.
**ex·pa·ti·ate** (ik spā′shē āt′) vi. -at′ed, -at′ing [< L. ex(s)patiari, wander] to speak or write at length (on or upon) —ex·pa′ti·a′tion n.
**ex·pa·tri·ate** (eks pā′trē āt′; for n. -it) vt., vi. -at′ed, -at′ing [< L. ex, out of + patria, fatherland] to exile (a person or oneself) —n. an expatriated person —ex·pa′tri·a′tion n.
**ex·pect** (ik spekt′) vt. [< L. ex-, out + spectare, to look] 1. to look for as likely to occur or appear 2. to look for as proper or necessary 3. [Colloq.] to suppose; guess —be expecting [Colloq.] to be pregnant
**ex·pect′an·cy** n., pl. -cies 1. same as EXPECTATION 2. that which is

expected, esp. on a statistical basis

**ex·pect'ant** *adj.* that expects; expecting —**ex·pect'ant·ly** *adv.*

**ex·pec·ta·tion** (ek'spek tā'shən) *n.* 1. an expecting; anticipation 2. a thing looked forward to 3. [*also pl.*] a reason for expecting something

**ex·pec·to·rant** (ik spek'tər ənt) *n.* [see ff.] a medicine that helps to bring up phlegm

**ex·pec'to·rate'** (-tə rāt') *vt.,* *vi.* -rat'ed, -rat'ing [< L. *ex-,* out + *pectus,* breast] to spit —**ex·pec'to·ra'tion** *n.*

**ex·pe·di·en·cy** (ik spē'dē ən sē) *n.,* *pl.* -cies 1. a being expedient; suitability for a given purpose 2. the doing of what is selfish rather than of what is right or just; self-interest 3. an expedient Also **ex·pe'di·ence**

**ex·pe'di·ent** *adj.* [see ff.] 1. useful for effecting a desired result; convenient 2. based on or guided by self-interest —*n.* an expedient thing; means to an end

**ex·pe·dite** (ek'spə dīt') *vt.* -dit'ed, -dit'ing [< L. *expedire,* lit., to free the foot] 1. to speed up the progress of; facilitate 2. to do quickly

**ex'pe·dit'er** *n.* one employed to expedite urgent or involved projects

**ex'pe·di'tion** (-dish'ən) *n.* [see EXPEDITE] 1. *a)* a voyage, march, etc., as for exploration or battle *b)* those on such a journey 2. efficient speed — **ex'pe·di'tion·ar'y** *adj.*

**ex'pe·di'tious** (-dish'əs) *adj.* efficient and speedy; prompt —**ex·pe·di'tious·ly** *adv.*

**ex·pel** (ik spel') *vt.* -pelled', -pel'ling [< L. *ex-,* out + *pellere,* to thrust] 1. to drive out by force 2. to dismiss by authority [*expelled* from college] —**ex·pel'la·ble** *adj.* —**ex·pel'ler** *n.*

**ex·pend** (ik spend') *vt.* [< L. *ex-,* out + *pendere,* weigh] 1. to spend 2. to use up

**ex·pend'a·ble** *adj.* 1. that can be expended 2. *Mil.* designating equipment (or men) expected to be used up (or sacrificed) in service

**ex·pend'i·ture** (-spen'də chər) *n.* 1. an expending of money, time, etc. 2. the amount of money, etc. expended

**ex·pense** (ik spens') *n.* [see EXPEND] 1. financial cost; charge 2. any cost or sacrifice 3. [*pl.*] charges met with in one's work, etc.

**ex·pen·sive** *adj.* costly; high-priced

**ex·pe·ri·ence** (ik spir'ē əns) *n.* [< L. *experiri,* to try] 1. the act of living through an event 2. anything ever experienced or lived through 3. *a)* training and personal participation *b)* knowledge, skill, etc. resulting from this —*vt.* -enced, -enc·ing to have experience of; undergo

**ex·pe'ri·enced** *adj.* having had or having learned from experience

**ex·per·i·ment** (ik sper'ə mənt) *n.* [see EXPERIENCE] a test or trial undertaken to discover or demonstrate something —*vi.* to make an experiment —**ex·per'i·men·ta'tion** (-mən tā'shən) *n.* —**ex·per'i·ment'er** *n.*

**ex·per'i·men'tal** *adj.* 1. based on or used for experiments 2. testing; trial —**ex·per'i·men'tal·ly** *adv.*

**ex·pert** (ek'spərt) *adj.* [see EXPERIENCE] very skillful —*n.* one who is very skillful or well-informed in some special field —**ex'pert·ly** *adv.* —**ex'pert·ness** *n.*

**ex·per·tise** (ek'spər tēz') *n.* [Fr.] the skill or knowledge of an expert

**ex·pi·ate** (ek'spē āt') *vt.* -at'ed, -at'ing [< L. *ex-,* out + *piare,* appease] to make amends for (wrongdoing or guilt); atone for —**ex'pi·a'tion** *n.* —**ex'pi·a·to'ry** (-ə tôr'ē) *adj.*

**ex·pire** (ik spīr') *vi.* -pired', -pir'ing [< L. *ex-,* out + *spirare,* breathe] 1. to exhale 2. to die 3. to come to an end —**ex·pi·ra·tion** (ek'spə rā'shən) *n.*

**ex·plain** (ik splān') *vt.* [< L. *ex-,* out + *planus,* level] 1. to make plain or understandable 2. to give the meaning of; expound 3. to account for —*vi.* to give an explanation —**ex·plain'a·ble** *adj.*

**ex·pla·na·tion** (eks'plə nā'shən) *n.* 1. an explaining 2. something that explains; interpretation, meaning, etc.

**ex·plan·a·to·ry** (ik splan'ə tôr'ē) *adj.* explaining or intended to explain

**ex·ple·tive** (eks'plə tiv) *n.* [< L. *ex-,* out + *plere,* to fill] an oath or exclamation

**ex·pli·ca·ble** (eks'pli kə b'l) *adj.* [see ff.] that can be explained

**ex'pli·cate'** (-kāt') *vt.* -cat'ed, -cat'ing [< L. *ex-,* out + *plicare,* to fold] to make clear; explain fully

**ex·plic·it** (ik splis'it) *adj.* [see prec.] 1. clearly stated or shown; definite 2. outspoken —**ex·plic'it·ly** *adv.*

**ex·plode** (ik splōd') *vt.* -plod'ed, -plod'ing [orig., to drive off the stage < L. *ex-,* off + *plaudere,* applaud] 1. to expose as false 2. to make burst with a loud noise 3. to cause to change suddenly or violently, as from a solid to an expanding gas —*vi.* to burst forth noisily —**ex·plod'a·ble** *adj.*

**ex·ploit** (eks'ploit; *for v., usually* ik sploit') *n.* [see EXPLICATE] a daring act; bold deed —*vt.* 1. to make use of 2. to make unethical use of for one's own profit —**ex'ploi·ta'tion** *n.* —**ex·ploit'a·tive** *adj.* —**ex·ploit'er** *n.*

**ex·plore** (ik splôr') *vt.,* *vi.* -plored', -plor'ing [< L. *ex-,* out + *plorare,* cry out] 1. to examine (something) carefully; investigate 2. to travel in (a little-known region) for discovery —**ex·plo·ra·tion** (eks'plə rā'shən) *n.* —**ex·plor'a·to'ry** (-ə tôr'ē) *adj.* —**ex·plor'er** *n.*

**ex·plo·sion** (ik splō'zhən) *n.* 1. an exploding 2. the noise made by exploding 3. a noisy outburst 4. a sudden, widespread increase

**ex·plo'sive** (-siv) *adj.* 1. of, causing, or like an explosion 2. tending to explode —*n.* a substance that can explode, as gunpowder —**ex·plo'sive·ly** *adv.* —**ex·plo'sive·ness** *n.*

**ex·po·nent** (ik spō'nənt; *for n.* 3, *usually* ek'spō'nənt) *n.* [see EXPOUND] 1. one who expounds or promotes (principles, etc.) **2.** a person or thing that is an example or symbol (*of something*) **3.** *Math.* a symbol placed at the upper right of another to show how many times the latter is to be used as a factor (Ex.: $b^2 = b \times b$) —**ex·po·nen·tial** (eks'pō nen'shəl) *adj.*

**ex·port** (ik spôrt'; *also, and for n. always,* eks'pôrt) *vt.* [ < L. *ex-,* out + *portare,* carry] to send (goods, etc.) to another country, esp. for sale —*n.* **1.** something exported **2.** an exporting Also **ex'por·ta'tion** —**ex·port'er** *n.*

**ex·pose** (ik spōz') *vt.* -**posed'**, -**pos'-ing** [see EXPOUND] **1.** to lay open (*to danger, attack, etc.*) **2.** to reveal; exhibit; make known **3.** *Photography* to subject (a sensitized film or plate) to actinic rays

**ex·po·sé** (eks'pō zā') *n.* [Fr.] a public disclosure of a scandal, crime, etc.

**ex·po·si·tion** (eks'pə zish'ən) *n.* [see EXPOUND] **1.** a detailed explanation **2.** writing or speaking that explains **3.** a large public exhibition

**ex·pos·i·tor** (ik späz'ə tər) *n.* one who expounds or explains

**ex·pos'i·to'ry** (-ə tôr'ē) *adj.* of or containing exposition; explanatory

**ex post fac·to** (eks pōst fak'tō) [L., from (the thing) done afterward] done afterward, but retroactive

**ex·pos·tu·late** (ik späs'chə lāt') *vi.* -**lat'ed**, -**lat'ing** [ < L. *ex-,* intens. + *postulare,* to demand] to reason with a person earnestly, objecting to his actions —**ex·pos'tu·la'tion** *n.*

**ex·po·sure** (ik spō'zhər) *n.* **1.** an exposing or being exposed **2.** facing position of a house, etc. [a *southern* exposure] **3.** frequent appearance before the public **4.** the time during which photographic film is exposed **5.** a section of film for one picture

**ex·pound** (ik spound') *vt.* [ < L. *ex-,* out + *ponere,* put] **1.** to set forth; state in detail **2.** to explain

**ex·press** (ik spres') *vt.* [ < L. *ex-,* out + *premere,* to press] **1.** to squeeze out (juice, etc.) **2.** to put into words; state **3.** to reveal; show **4.** to signify or symbolize **5.** to send by express —*adj.* **1.** expressed; stated; explicit **2.** exact **3.** specific **4.** fast and direct [an *express* bus, highway, etc.] **5.** related to express —*adv.* by express —*n.* **1.** an express train, bus, etc. **2.** *a)* a service for transporting things rapidly *b)* the things sent by express

**ex·pres'sion** (-spresh'ən) *n.* **1.** a putting into words; stating **2.** a manner of expressing, esp. with eloquence **3.** a particular word or phrase **4.** a showing of feeling, character, etc. **5.** a look, intonation, etc. that conveys meaning **6.** a mathematical symbol or symbols —**ex·pres'sion·less** *adj.*

**ex·pres'sion·ism** *n.* a movement in art, literature, etc. seeking to give symbolic, objective expression to inner experience —**ex·pres'sion·ist** *adj., n.* —**ex·pres'sion·is'tic** *adj.*

**ex·pres'sive** *adj.* **1.** that expresses **2.** full of meaning or feeling —**ex·pres'-sive·ly** *adv.* —**ex·pres'sive·ness** *n.*

**ex·press'ly** *adv.* **1.** plainly; definitely **2.** especially; particularly

**ex·press'way** *n.* a divided highway for high-speed, through traffic, with grade separations at intersections

**ex·pro·pri·ate** (eks prō'prē āt') *vt.* -**at'ed**, -**at'ing** [ < L. *ex,* out + *proprius,* one's own] to take (land, etc.) from its owner, esp. for public use —**ex·pro'pri·a'tion** *n.*

**ex·pul·sion** (ik spul'shən) *n.* an expelling or being expelled

**ex·punge** (ik spunj') *vt.* -**punged'**, -**pung'ing** [ < L. *ex-,* out + *pungere,* to prick] to blot or strike out; erase

**ex·pur·gate** (eks'pər gāt') *vt.* -**gat'-ed**, -**gat'ing** [ < L. *ex-,* out + *purgare,* cleanse] to remove passages considered obscene, etc. from (a book, etc.) —**ex'pur·ga'tion** *n.*

**ex·qui·site** (eks'kwi zit, ik skwiz'it) *adj.* [ < L. *ex-,* out + *quaerere,* ask] **1.** carefully or elaborately done **2.** very beautiful, delicate, etc. **3.** of highest quality **4.** very intense; keen

**ex·tant** (ek'stənt, ik stant') *adj.* [ < L. *ex-,* out + *stare,* stand] still existing

**ex·tem·po·ra·ne·ous** (ik stem'pə rā'nē əs) *adj.* [see ff.] done or spoken with little preparation; offhand —**ex·tem'po·ra'ne·ous·ly** *adv.*

**ex·tem·po·re** (ik stem'pə rē) *adv., adj.* [L. < *ex,* out of + *tempus,* time] with little preparation; offhand

**ex·tem'po·rize'** (-rīz') *vi., vt.* -**rized'**, -**riz'ing** to speak, perform, etc. extempore; improvise

**ex·tend** (ik stend') *vt.* [ < L. *ex-,* out + *tendere,* to stretch] **1.** to make longer; stretch out; prolong **2.** to en-large in area, scope, etc.; expand **3.** to stretch forth **4.** to offer; grant **5.** to make (oneself) work very hard —*vi.* to be extended —**ex·tend'ed** *adj.* —**ex·tend'er** *n.* —**ex·ten'si·ble** (-sten'sə-b'l), **ex·tend'i·ble** *adj.*

**extended care** nursing care in a facil-ity for convalescents, the disabled, etc.

**extended family** a social unit con-sisting of parents and their children along with other relatives, living as one family

**ex·ten·sion** (-sten'shən) *n.* **1.** an extending or being extended **2.** range; extent **3.** a part forming a continua-tion or addition

**ex·ten'sive** (-siv) *adj.* having great extent; vast; comprehensive; far-reaching —**ex·ten'sive·ly** *adv.* —**ex-ten'sive·ness** *n.*

**ex·tent** (ik stent') *n.* **1.** the space, amount, or degree to which a thing extends; size **2.** scope; limits **3.** an extended space; vast area

**ex·ten·u·ate** (ik sten'yoo wāt') *vt.* -**at'ed**, -**at'ing** [ < L. *ex-,* out + *tenuis,* thin] to make (an offense, etc.) seem less serious —**ex·ten'u·a'tion** *n.*

**ex·te·ri·or** (ik stir′ē ər) *adj.* [see EXTERNAL] **1.** on the outside; outer **2.** for use on the outside **3.** coming from without —*n.* an outside or outside surface —**ex′te′ri·or·ly** *adv.*

**ex·ter·mi·nate** (ik stur′mə nāt′) *vt.* **-nat′ed, -nat′ing** [ < L. *ex-*, out + *terminus,* boundary] to destroy entirely; wipe out —**ex·ter′mi·na′tion** *n.* —**ex·ter′mi·na′tor** *n.*

**ex·tern** (ek′sturn) *n.* [see ff.] a doctor, etc. connected with an institution, as a hospital, but not living in it

**ex·ter·nal** (ik stur′n'l) *adj.* [ < L. *externus*] **1.** on the outside; outer **2.** material; existing apart from the mind **3.** coming from without **4.** superficial **5.** foreign —*n.* an outside surface or part —**ex·ter′nal·ly** *adv.*

**ex·tinct** (ik stiŋkt′) *adj.* [see EXTINGUISH] **1.** having died down; extinguished **2.** no longer in existence

**ex·tinc·tion** *n.* **1.** an extinguishing **2.** a destroying or being destroyed **3.** a dying out, as a species

**ex·tin·guish** (ik stiŋ′gwish) *vt.* [ < L. *ex-*, out + *stinguere,* extinguish] **1.** to put out (a fire, etc.) **2.** to destroy —**ex·tin′guish·er** *n.*

**ex·tir·pate** (ek′stər pāt′) *vt.* **-pat′ed, -pat′ing** [ < L. *ex-*, out + *stirps,* root] **1.** to pull up by the roots **2.** to destroy completely —**ex′tir·pa′tion** *n.*

**ex·tol, ex·toll** (ik stōl′) *vt.* **-tolled′, -tol′ling** [ < L. *ex-*, up + *tollere,* raise] to praise highly; laud

**ex·tort** (ik stôrt′) *vt.* [ < L. *ex-*, out + *torquere,* twist] to get (money, etc.) from someone by force or threats

**ex·tor·tion** (-stôr′shən) *n.* **1.** an extorting **2.** something extorted —**ex·tor′tion·ate** *adj.* —**ex·tor′tion·er** *n.* —**ex·tor′tion·ist** *n.*

**ex·tra** (eks′trə) *adj.* [ < L. *extra,* more than] more or better than normal, expected, etc.; additional —*n.* an extra person or thing; specif., *a)* a special edition of a newspaper *b)* an extra benefit *c)* an actor hired by the day for a minor part —*adv.* more than usually; esp., exceptionally

**extra-** [see EXTERNAL] *a prefix meaning* outside, beyond, besides

**ex·tract** (ik strakt′; *for n.* eks′trakt) *vt.* [ < L. *ex-*, out + *trahere,* draw] **1.** to draw out by effort **2.** to obtain by pressing, distilling, etc. **3.** to deduce; derive **4.** to select or quote (a passage, etc.) —*n.* something extracted; specif., *a)* a concentrate [beef extract] *b)* an excerpt

**ex·trac·tion** *n.* **1.** the act or process of extracting **2.** origin; descent

**ex·tra·cur·ric·u·lar** (eks′trə kə rik′yə lər) *adj.* not part of the required curriculum

**ex·tra·dite** (eks′trə dīt′) *vt.* **-dit′ed, -dit′ing** [ < L. *ex,* out + *traditio,* a surrender] to turn over (an alleged criminal, etc.) to the jurisdiction of another country, State, etc. —**ex′tra·di′tion** (-dish′ən) *n.*

**ex′tra·le′gal** *adj.* not regulated by law

**ex·tra·ne·ous** (ik strā′nē əs) *adj.* [L. *extraneus,* foreign] **1.** coming from outside; foreign **2.** not pertinent; irrelevant —**ex·tra′ne·ous·ly** *adv.*

**ex·traor·di·nar·y** (ik strôr′d'n er′ē) *adj.* [ < L. *extra ordinem,* out of order] **1.** not ordinary **2.** going far beyond the ordinary; unusual; remarkable

**ex·trap·o·late** (ik strap′ə lāt′) *vt., vi.* **-lat′ed, -lat′ing** [see EXTRA- & INTERPOLATE] to estimate (something unknown) on the basis of known facts —**ex·trap′o·la′tion** *n.*

**ex·tra·sen·so·ry** (eks′trə sen′sər ē) *adj.* apart from, or in addition to, normal sense perception

**ex·trav·a·gant** (ik strav′ə gənt) *adj.* [ < L. *extra,* beyond + *vagari,* wander] **1.** going beyond reasonable limits; excessive **2.** costing or spending too much; wasteful —**ex·trav′a·gance** *n.*

**ex·trav·a·gan·za** (ik strav′ə gan′zə) *n.* [ < It. *estravaganza,* extravagance] a spectacular theatrical production

**ex·tra·ve·hic·u·lar** (eks′trə vē hik′yoo lər) *adj.* designating activity by an astronaut outside a vehicle in space

**ex·treme** (ik strēm′) *adj.* [ < L. *exterus,* outer] **1.** farthest away; utmost **2.** very great; excessive **3.** unconventional or radical, as in politics **4.** harsh; drastic —*n.* **1.** either of two things that are as different or far as possible from each other **2.** an extreme act, state, etc. —**ex·treme′ly** *adv.* —**ex·treme′ness** *n.*

**ex·trem·ism** (-iz′m) *n.* a going to extremes, esp. in politics —**ex·trem′ist** *adj., n.*

**ex·trem·i·ty** (ik strem′ə tē) *n., pl.* **-ties 1.** the outermost part; end **2.** the greatest degree **3.** great need, danger, etc. **4.** an extreme measure **5.** [*pl.*] the hands and feet

**ex·tri·cate** (eks′trə kāt′) *vt.* **-cat′ed, -cat′ing** [ < L. *ex-*, out + *tricae,* vexations] to set free (*from* a net, difficulty, etc.) —**ex′tri·ca′tion** *n.*

**ex·trin·sic** (ek strin′sik) *adj.* [ < L. *exter,* without + *secus,* otherwise] not essential; not inherent —**ex·trin′si·cal·ly** *adv.*

**ex·tro·vert** (eks′trə vurt′) *n.* [ < L. *extra-*, outside + *vertere,* to turn] one whose interest is more in his environment and in other people than in himself —**ex′tro·ver′sion** (-vur′zhən) *n.* —**ex′tro·vert′ed** *adj.*

**ex·trude** (ik strōōd′) *vt.* **-trud′ed, -trud′ing** [ < L. *ex-*, out + *trudere,* to thrust] to force out, as through a small opening —*vi.* to be extruded; esp., to protrude —**ex·tru′sion** (-strōō′zhən) *n.* —**ex·tru′sive** *adj.*

**ex·u·ber·ant** (ig zōō′bər ənt) *adj.* [ < L. *ex-*, intens. + *uberare,* bear abundantly] **1.** growing profusely; luxuriant **2.** characterized by good health and high spirits; full of life —**ex·u′ber·ance** *n.* —**ex·u′ber·ant·ly** *adv.*

**ex·ude** (ig zōōd′) *vt., vi.* **-ud′ed, -ud′ing** [ < L. *ex-*, out + *sudare,* to sweat] **1.** to pass out in drops, as through pores; ooze **2.** to seem to radiate [to *exude* joy] —**ex·u·da·tion** (eks′yə dā′shən) *n.*

**ex·ult** (ig zult′) *vi.* [ < L. *ex-*, intens.

+ *saltare*, to leap] to rejoice greatly; glory —ex·ult′ant *adj.* —ex·ul·ta·tion (eg′zəl tā′shən, ek′səl-) *n.*

ex·ur·bi·a (eks ur′bē ə) *n.* [EX- + (SUB)URBIA] the semirural communities beyond the suburbs, lived in by upper-income families —ex·ur′ban *adj.* — ex·ur′ban·ite′ *n., adj.*

eye (ī) *n.* [OE. *eage*] 1. the organ of sight in man and animals 2. *a)* the eyeball *b)* the iris [blue *eyes*] 3. the area around the eye [a black *eye*] 4. [*often pl.*] sight; vision 5. a look; glance 6. attention; observation 7. the power of judging, etc. by eyesight [an *eye* for distances] 8. [*often pl.*] judgment; opinion [in the *eyes* of the law] 9. a thing like an eye in appearance or function —*vt.* eyed, eye′ing or ey′ing to look at; observe —**have an eye for** to have a keen appreciation of —**keep an eye on** to look after —**lay** (or **set** or **clap**) **eyes on** to look at —**make eyes at** to look at amorously —**see eye to eye** to agree completely —**with an eye to** paying attention to; considering

eye′ball′ *n.* the ball-shaped part of the eye

eye′brow′ *n.* the bony arch over each eye, or the hair growing on this

eye′-catch′er *n.* something that especially attracts one's attention —eye′-catch′ing *adj.*

eye′ful′ (-fool′) *n.* [Slang] a person or thing that looks striking

eye′glass′ *n.* 1. a lens to help faulty vision 2. [*pl.*] a pair of such lenses in a frame; glasses

eye′lash′ *n.* any of the hairs on the edge of the eyelid

eye′let (-lit) *n.* 1. a small hole for receiving a cord, hook, etc. 2. a metal ring, etc. for lining it 3. a small hole edged by stitching in embroidery

eye′lid′ *n.* either of two folds of flesh that cover and uncover the eyeball

eye′-o′pen·er (-ō′p'n ər) *n.* a surprising piece of news, sudden realization, etc.

eye′piece′ *n.* in a telescope, microscope, etc., the lens or lenses nearest the viewer's eye

eye′sight′ *n.* 1. the power of seeing; sight 2. the range of vision

eye′sore′ *n.* an unpleasant sight

eye′strain′ *n.* a tired or strained condition of the eye muscles

eye′tooth′ *n., pl.* -teeth′ a canine tooth of the upper jaw

eye′wit′ness *n.* one who has himself seen a specific thing happen

ey·rie, ey·ry (er′ē, ir′ē) *n., pl.* -ries *same as* AERIE

# F

F, f (ef) *n., pl.* F's, f's the sixth letter of the English alphabet

F (ef) *n.* 1. *Chem.* fluorine 2. *Educ.* a grade for failing work or, sometimes, fair or average work 3. *Music* the fourth tone in the scale of C major

F, F: 1. Fahrenheit 2. Friday

F., f. 1. feminine 2. folio(s) 3. following 4. *Music* forte 5. franc(s)

fa (fä) *n.* [< ML.] *Music* the fourth tone of the diatonic scale

fa·ble (fā′b'l) *n.* [< L. *fabula*, a story] 1. a fictitious story, usually about animals, meant to teach a moral lesson 2. a myth or legend 3. a falsehood

fa′bled *adj.* 1. legendary; mythical 2. unreal; fictitious

fab·ric (fab′rik) *n.* [< L. *fabrica*, workshop] 1. a framework; structure 2. a material made from fibers, etc. by weaving, felting, etc., as cloth

fab·ri·cate (fab′rə kāt′) *vt.* -cat′ed, -cat′ing [see prec.] 1. to make, construct, etc.; manufacture 2. to make up (a story, lie, etc.); invent —fab′ri·ca′tion *n.* —fab′ri·ca′tor *n.*

fab·u·lous (fab′yoo ləs) *adj.* [see FABLE] 1. of or like a fable; fictitious 2. incredible 3. [Colloq.] wonderful —fab′u·lous·ly *adv.*

fa·cade, fa·cade (fə säd′) *n.* [Fr.: see ff.] 1. the front or main face of a building 2. an imposing appearance concealing something inferior

face (fās) *n.* [< L. *facies*] 1. the front of the head 2. the expression of the countenance 3. the main or front surface 4. the surface that is marked, as of a clock, fabric, etc. 5. appearance; outward aspect 6. dignity; self-respect: usually in to **lose** (or **save**) **face** —*vt.* faced, fac′ing 1. to turn, or have the face turned, toward 2. to confront with boldness, etc. 3. to cover with a new surface —*vi.* to turn, or have the face turned, in a specified direction —**face to face** 1. confronting one another 2. very close (with *with*) —**face up to** to face with courage —**in the face of** 1. in the presence of 2. in spite of —**make a face** to grimace —**on the face of it** apparently

face′less *adj.* lacking a distinct character; anonymous

face lifting 1. plastic surgery to remove wrinkles, etc. from the face 2. an altering, repairing, etc., as of a building's exterior Also face lift —face′-lift′ *vt.*

face′-off′ *n. Hockey* the start or resumption of play when the referee drops the puck between two opposing players

**face′-sav′ing** *adj.* preserving one's dignity or self-respect

**fac·et** (fas′it) *n.* [see FACE] 1. any of the polished plane surfaces of a cut gem 2. any of a number of sides or aspects, as of a personality —*vt.* -et·ed or -et′ted, -et·ing or -et′ting to cut or make facets on

**fa·ce·tious** (fə sē′shəs) *adj.* [< L. *facetus*, witty] joking, esp. at an inappropriate time —**fa·ce′tious·ly** *adv.*

**face value** 1. the value written on a bill, bond, etc. 2. the seeming value

**fa·cial** (fā′shəl) *adj.* of or for the face —*n.* a cosmetic treatment, massage, etc. for the skin of the face

**facial tissue** a sheet of soft tissue paper used as a handkerchief, etc.

**fac·ile** (fas′'l) *adj.* [Fr. < L. *facere*, do] 1. not hard to do 2. working or done easily; fluent 3. superficial

**fa·cil·i·tate** (fə sil′ə tāt′) *vt.* -tat′ed, -tat′ing [see prec.] to make easy or easier —**fa·cil′i·ta′tion** *n.*

**fa·cil′i·ty** (-tē) *n., pl.* -ties 1. absence of difficulty 2. skill; dexterity 3. [*usually pl.*] the means by which something can be done 4. a building, etc. that facilitates some activity

**fac·ing** (fās′iŋ) *n.* 1. a lining on the edge of a garment 2. a covering of contrasting material on a building

**fac·sim·i·le** (fak sim′ə lē) *n.* [< L. *facere*, make + *simile*, like] (an) exact reproduction or copy

**fact** (fakt) *n.* [< L. *facere*, do] 1. a deed, esp. a criminal deed [an accessory before (or after) the *fact*] 2. a thing that has actually happened or is true 3. reality; truth 4. something stated as being true —**as a matter of fact** really: also **in fact**

**fac·tion** (fak′shən) *n.* [see prec.] 1. a group of people in an organization working in a common cause against the main body 2. dissension —**fac′-tion·al** *adj.* —**fac′tion·al·ism** *n.*

**fac′tious** (-shəs) *adj.* of, produced by, or tending to produce faction

**fac·ti·tious** (fak tish′əs) *adj.* [see FACT] forced or artificial

**fac·tor** (fak′tər) *n.* [< L. *facere*, do] 1. one who transacts business for another 2. any of the conditions, etc. that bring about a result 3. *Math.* any of the quantities which form a product when multiplied together —*vt. Math.* to resolve into factors

**fac·to·ry** (fak′tə rē) *n., pl.* -ries [see prec.] a building or buildings in which things are manufactured

**fac·to·tum** (fak tōt′əm) *n.* [< L. *facere*, do + *totum*, all] a handyman

**fac·tu·al** (fak′choo wəl) *adj.* of or containing facts; real; actual

**fac·ul·ty** (fak′'l tē) *n., pl.* -ties [see FACILE] 1. any natural or specialized power of a living organism 2. special aptitude 3. all the teachers of a school or of one of its departments

**fad** (fad) *n.* [< Brit. dial.] a style, etc. that interests many people for a short time; passing fashion —**fad′dish** *adj.*

**fade** (fād) *vi.* **fad′ed, fad′ing** [< OFr. *fade*, pale] 1. to lose color, brilliance, etc. 2. to lose freshness or strength 3. to disappear slowly; die out —*vt.* to cause to fade —**fade in** (or **out**) *Motion Pictures & TV* to appear (or disappear) gradually

**faer·ie, faer·y** (fer′ē) *n.* [Archaic] 1. fairyland 2. *pl.* -ies a fairy

**fag** (fag) *vt., vi.* **fagged, fag′ging** [< ?] to make or become very tired by hard work —*n.* [Slang] a male homosexual

**fag·ot, fag·got** (fag′ət) *n.* [ult. < Gr. *phakelos*, a bundle] a bundle of sticks or twigs, esp. for use as fuel

**fag′ot·ing, fag′got·ing** *n.* 1. a hemstitch with wide spaces 2. openwork with crisscross or barlike stitches across the open seam

**Fahr·en·heit** (fer′ən hīt′) *adj.* [< G. D. *Fahrenheit*, 18th-c. G. physicist] designating or of a thermometer on which 32° is the freezing point and 212° is the boiling point of water —*n.* this thermometer or its scale

**fail** (fāl) *vi.* [< L. *fallere*, deceive] 1. to be insufficient; fall short 2. to weaken; die away 3. to stop operating 4. to be negligent in a duty, expectation, etc. 5. to be unsuccessful 6. to become bankrupt 7. *Educ.* to get a grade of failure —*vt.* 1. to be of no help to; disappoint 2. to leave; abandon 3. to neglect [to *fail* to go] 4. *Educ.* to give a grade of failure or get such a grade in —**without fail** without failing (to do, occur, etc.)

**fail′ing** *n.* 1. a failure 2. a fault —*prep.* without; lacking

**faille** (fīl, fāl) *n.* [Fr.] a ribbed, soft fabric of silk or rayon

**fail′-safe′** *adj.* of an intricate procedure for preventing accidental operation, as of nuclear weapons

**fail·ure** (fāl′yər) *n.* 1. *a)* a falling short *b)* a weakening *c)* a breakdown in operation *d)* neglect *e)* a not succeeding *f)* a becoming bankrupt 2. one that does not succeed 3. *Educ.* a failing to pass, or a grade showing this

**fain** (fān) *adj., adv.* [< OE. *fægen*, glad] [Archaic] glad(ly); willing(ly)

**faint** (fānt) *adj.* [see FEIGN] 1. weak; feeble 2. timid 3. feeling weak and dizzy 4. dim; indistinct —*n.* a state of temporary unconsciousness —*vi.* to fall into a faint —**faint′ly** *adv.* —**faint′ness** *n.*

**fair¹** (fer) *adj.* [OE. *fæger*] 1. attractive; beautiful 2. unblemished; clean 3. blond [*fair* hair] 4. clear and sunny 5. easy to read [a *fair* hand] 6. just and honest 7. according to the rules 8. moderately large 9. average [in *fair* condition] 10. that may be hunted [*fair* game] 11. *Baseball* that is not foul —*adv.* 1. in a fair manner 2. squarely —**fair′ness** *n.*

**fair²** (fer) *n.* [< L. *feriae*, festivals] 1. a regular gathering for barter and sale of goods 2. a carnival or bazaar, often for charity 3. a competitive exhibition of farm, household, and manufactured products, with various amusements and educational displays

**fair′-haired′** *adj.* 1. having blond hair 2. [Colloq.] favorite

**fair'ly** *adv.* 1. justly; honestly 2. somewhat; moderately 3. completely or really

**fair shake** [Colloq.] fair or just treatment

**fair'-trade'** *adj.* designating or of an agreement whereby a seller of a product charges no less than the minimum price set by the producer

**fair'way'** (-wā') *n.* the mowed part of a golf course between a tee and a green

**fair·y** (fer'ē) *n., pl.* **-ies** [ < OFr. *feie*] 1. a tiny, graceful imaginary being in human form, with magic powers 2. [Slang] a male homosexual —*adj.* 1. of fairies 2. fairylike

**fair'y·land'** *n.* 1. the imaginary land where the fairies live 2. a lovely, enchanting place

**fairy tale** 1. a story about fairies 2. an unbelievable or untrue story

**‡fait ac·com·pli** (fe tä kôⁿ plē') [Fr.] a thing done that cannot be changed

**faith** (fāth) *n.* [ < L. *fidere*, to trust] 1. unquestioning belief, specif. in God, religion, etc. 2. a particular religion 3. complete trust or confidence 4. loyalty —**good** (or **bad**) **faith** (in)sincerity; (dis)honesty

**faith'ful** (-fəl) *adj.* 1. loyal 2. conscientious 3. accurate; reliable —**faith'ful·ly** *adv.* —**faith'ful·ness** *n.*

**faith'less** (-lis) *adj.* untrue, dishonest, or disloyal —**faith'less·ly** *adv.* —**faith'less·ness** *n.*

**fake** (fāk) *vt., vi.* **faked, fak'ing** [ < ?] to make (something) seem real, etc. by deception —*n.* a fraud; counterfeit —*adj.* sham; false —**fak'er** *n.*

**fa·kir** (fə kir') *n.* [Ar. *faqīr*, lit., poor] 1. one of a Moslem holy sect of beggars 2. a Hindu ascetic

**fal·con** (fal'kən, fôl'-, fô'-) *n.* [ult. < L. *falx*, sickle] a hawk trained to hunt small game —**fal'con·er** *n.* —**fal'con·ry** *n.*

**fall** (fôl) *vi.* **fell, fall'en, fall'ing** [OE. *feallan*] 1. to come down by gravity; drop; descend 2. to come down suddenly from an upright position; tumble or collapse 3. to be wounded or killed in battle 4. to take a downward direction 5. to become lower, less, weaker, etc. 6. to lose power, status, etc. 7. to do wrong; sin 8. to be captured 9. to take on a sad look [his face *fell*] 10. to pass into a specified condition [to *fall ill*] 11. to take place; occur 12. to be directed by chance 13. to come by inheritance, lot, etc. 14. to be divided (*into*) —*n.* 1. a dropping; descending 2. a coming down suddenly from an upright position 3. a downward direction or slope 4. a becoming lower or less 5. a capture 6. a loss of status, reputation, etc. 7. a yielding to temptation 8. autumn 9. the amount of what has fallen [a six-inch *fall* of snow] 10. the distance something falls 11. [*pl.*, *often with sing. v.*] water falling over a cliff, etc. 12. a long tress

of hair, added to a woman's hairdo —*adj.* of, for, or in the autumn —**fall back** to withdraw; retreat —**fall flat** to fail completely —**fall for** [Colloq.] 1. to fall in love with 2. to be tricked by —**fall in** to line up in formation —**fall off** to become smaller, worse, etc. —**fall on** (or **upon**) to attack —**fall out** 1. to quarrel 2. to leave one's place in a formation —**fall through** to fail —**fall to** 1. to begin 2. to start eating

**fal·la·cious** (fə lā'shəs) *adj.* [see ff.] 1. erroneous 2. misleading or deceptive —**fal·la'cious·ly** *adv.*

**fal·la·cy** (fal'ə sē) *n., pl.* **-cies** [ < L. *fallere*, deceive] 1. a mistaken idea; error 2. a flaw in reasoning

**fall·en** (fôl'ən) *adj.* that fell; dropped; prostrate, ruined, dead, etc.

**fal·li·ble** (fal'ə b'l) *adj.* [ < L. *fallere*, deceive] liable to be mistaken, deceived, or erroneous —**fal'li·bil'i·ty, fal'li·ble·ness** *n.* —**fal'li·bly** *adv.*

**fall'ing-out'** *n.* a quarrel

**falling star** *same as* METEOR (sense 1)

**fall'off'** *n.* a decline

**Fal·lo·pi·an tube** (fə lō'pē ən) [< G. *Fallopius*, 16th-c. It. anatomist] either of two tubes that carry ova to the uterus

**fall'out'** *n.* 1. the descent to earth of radioactive particles, as after a nuclear explosion 2. these particles

**fal·low** (fal'ō) *adj.* [ < OE. *fealh*] 1. left unplanted 2. inactive

**Fall River** seaport in SE Mass.: pop. 97,000

**false** (fôls) *adj.* **fals'er, fals'est** [< L. *fallere*, deceive] 1. not true; incorrect; wrong 2. untruthful; lying 3. unfaithful 4. misleading 5. not real; artificial —*adv.* in a false manner —**false'ly** *adv.* —**false'ness** *n.*

**false'hood'** *n.* 1. falsity 2. a lie

**fal·set·to** (fôl set'ō) *n., pl.* **-tos** [It., dim. of *falso*, false] an artificial way of singing in which the voice is much higher-pitched than normal

**fal·si·fy** (fôl'sə fī') *vt.* **-fied', -fy'ing** 1. to misrepresent 2. to alter (a record, etc.) fraudulently —**fal'si·fi·ca'tion** *n.* —**fal'si·fi'er** *n.*

**fal·si·ty** (-tē) *n., pl.* **-ties** 1. the quality of being false 2. a lie

**Fal·staff**, Sir John (fôl'staf) a character in Shakespeare's plays, a fat, blustering, witty knight

**fal·ter** (fôl'tər) *vi.* [prob. < ON.] 1. to move unsteadily; stumble 2. to stammer 3. to act hesitantly; waver —**fal'ter·ing·ly** *adv.*

**fame** (fām) *n.* [ < L. *fama*] 1. reputation, esp. for good 2. the state of being well known —**famed** *adj.*

**fa·mil·ial** (fə mil'yəl) *adj.* of or common to a family

**fa·mil·iar** (fə mil'yər) *adj.* [see FAMILY] 1. friendly; intimate 2. too friendly; unduly intimate 3. closely acquainted (*with*) 4. common; ordinary —**fa·mil'iar·ly** *adv.*

---

**fa·mil'i·ar'i·ty** (-yar'ə tē) *n., pl.* **-ties** 1. intimacy 2. free and intimate behavior 3. undue intimacy 4. close acquaintance (*with* something)

**fa·mil'iar·ize'** (-yə rīz') *vt.* **-ized', -iz'ing** 1. to make commonly known 2. to make (another or oneself) fully acquainted —**fa·mil'iar·i·za'tion** *n.*

**fam·i·ly** (fam'ə lē, fam'lē) *n., pl.* **-lies** [< L. *famulus*, servant] 1. a household 2. parents and their children 3. relatives 4. all those descended from a common ancestor; lineage 5. a group of similar or related things

**family room** a room in a home set apart for relaxation and recreation

**fam·ine** (fam'ən) *n.* [< L. *fames*, hunger] 1. an acute and general shortage of food 2. any acute shortage

**fam'ish** (-ish) *vt., vi.* [see prec.] to make or be very hungry

**fa·mous** (fā'məs) *adj.* 1. having fame; renowned 2. [Colloq.] excellent; very good —**fa'mous·ly** *adv.*

**fan¹** (fan) *n.* [< L. *vannus*, basket for winnowing grain] any device used to set up a current of air for ventilating or cooling —*vt., vi.* **fanned, fan'ning** 1. to move (air) as with a fan 2. to direct air toward as with a fan 3. to stir up; excite 4. *Baseball* to strike out —**fan out** to spread out

**fan²** (fan) *n.* [< FAN(ATIC)] [Colloq.] a person enthusiastic about a specified sport, performer, etc.

**fa·nat·ic** (fə nat'ik) *adj.* [< L. *fanum*, temple] unreasonably enthusiastic; overly zealous: also **fa·nat'i·cal** —*n.* a fanatic person —**fa·nat'i·cal·ly** *adv.* —**fa·nat'i·cism** *n.*

**fan·ci·er** (fan'sē ər) *n.* a person with a special interest in something, esp. plant or animal breeding

**fan·ci·ful** (fan'si fəl) *adj.* 1. full of fancy; imaginative 2. imaginary; not real —**fan'ci·ful·ly** *adv.*

**fan·cy** (fan'sē) *n., pl.* **-cies** [contr. < ME. *fantasie*, FANTASY] 1. imagination when light, playful, etc. 2. a mental image 3. a notion; caprice; whim 4. an inclination or fondness —*adj.* **-ci·er, -ci·est** 1. capricious; whimsical 2. extravagant [a *fancy* price] 3. ornamental; elaborate [a *fancy* necktie] 4. of superior skill or quality —*vt.* **-cied, -cy·ing** 1. to imagine 2. to be fond of 3. to suppose —**fan'ci·ly** *adv.* —**fan'ci·ness** *n.*

**fan'cy-free'** *adj.* 1. not married, engaged, etc. 2. carefree

**fan'cy·work'** *n.* embroidery, crocheting, and other ornamental needlework

**fan·dom** (fan'dəm) *n.* fans, collectively, as of a sport or entertainer

**fan·fare** (fan'fer') *n.* [Fr., prob. < *fanfaron*, braggart] 1. a loud flourish of trumpets 2. noisy or showy display

**fang** (faŋ) *n.* [OE. < *fon*, seize] 1. one of the long, pointed teeth of meat-eating mammals 2. one of the long, hollow teeth through which poisonous snakes inject venom

FANGS

**fan·ta·size** (fan'tə

**fan·ta·size** (... sīz') *vt., vi.* **-sized', -siz'ing** to indulge in fantasies or have daydreams (about) —**fan'ta·sist** (-sist) *n.*

**fan·tas·tic** (fan tas'tik) *adj.* [see ff.] 1. imaginary; unreal 2. grotesque; odd 3. extravagant —**fan·tas'ti·cal·ly** *adv.* —**fan·tas'ti·cal·ness** *n.*

**fan·ta·sy** (fan'tə sē) *n., pl.* **-sies** [< Gr. *phainein*, to show] 1. imagination or fancy 2. an illusion or reverie 3. an imaginative poem, play, etc.

**FAO** Food and Agriculture Organization (of the UN)

**far** (fär) *adj.* **far'ther, far'thest** [OE. *feorr*] 1. distant in space or time 2. more distant [the *far* side] —*adv.* 1. very distant in space, time, or degree 2. to or from a distance in time or position 3. very much [*far* better] —**as far as** to the distance or degree that —**by far** very much; considerably: also **far and away** —(in) **so far as** to the extent that —**so far** up to this place, time, or degree

**far'a·way'** *adj.* 1. distant in time or place 2. dreamy

**farce** (färs) *n.* [Fr. < L. *farcire*, to stuff] 1. (an) exaggerated comedy based on broadly humorous situations 2. an absurd or ridiculous action, pretense, etc. —**far'ci·cal** (fär'si k'l) *adj.*

**fare** (fer) *vi.* **fared, far'ing** [< OE. *faran*, go] 1. to happen; result 2. to be in a specified condition [to *fare* well] 3. to eat —*n.* 1. money paid for transportation 2. a passenger who pays a fare 3. food

**Far East** E Asia; China, Japan, etc.

**fare·well** (fer'wel'; *for adj.* -wel') *interj.* goodbye —*n.* good wishes at parting —*adj.* parting; final [a *farewell* gesture]

**far-fetched** (fär'fecht') *adj.* forced; strained; unlikely

**far'-flung'** (-fluŋ') *adj.* extending over a wide area

**fa·ri·na** (fə rē'nə) *n.* [< L., meal] flour or meal made from cereal grains, potatoes, etc., eaten as a cooked cereal

**far·i·na·ceous** (far'ə nā'shəs) *adj.* [see prec.] 1. consisting of or made from flour or meal 2. like meal

**farm** (färm) *n.* [< ML. *firma*, fixed payment] a piece of land (with house, barns, etc.) on which crops or animals are raised; orig., such land let out to tenants —*vt.* 1. to cultivate (land) 2. to turn over to another for a fee —*vi.* to work on or operate a farm

**farm'er** *n.* a person who manages or operates a farm

**farm'hand'** *n.* a hired farm worker

**farm'house'** *n.* a house on a farm

**farm'ing** *n.* the business of operating a farm; agriculture

**farm'yard'** *n.* the yard surrounding or enclosed by farm buildings

**far·o** (fer'ō) *n.* [< ? PHARAOH] a gambling game played with cards

**far-off** (fär'ôf') *adj.* distant; remote

**far'-out'** *adj.* [Colloq.] nonconformist; esp., avant-garde

**far·ra·go** (fə rä'gō, -rä'-) *n., pl.* **-goes** [< L. *far*, kind of grain] a jumble

**far'-reach'ing** *adj.* having a wide range, extent, influence, or effect

**far·ri·er** (far'ē ər) *n.* [< L. *ferrum*, iron] [Brit.] a blacksmith

**far·row** (far'ō) *n.* [< OE. *fearh*, young pig] a litter of pigs —*vt., vi.* to give birth to (a litter of pigs)

**far'sight'ed** *adj.* 1. planning ahead; provident: also **far'see'ing** 2. seeing distant objects more clearly than near ones —**far'sight'ed·ness** *n.*

**far·ther** (fär'thər) *compar.* of FAR —*adj.* 1. more distant 2. additional; more —*adv.* 1. at or to a greater distance 2. to a greater degree 3. in addition Cf. FURTHER

**far·thest** (fär'thist) *superl.* of FAR —*adj.* most distant —*adv.* at or to the greatest distance or degree

**far·thing** (fär'thiŋ) *n.* [OE. *feorthing*] a former British coin worth 1/4 penny

**fas·ci·nate** (fas'ə nāt') *vt.* -nat'ed, -nat'ing [< L. *fascinum*, an enchanting] 1. to hold motionless, as by inspiring terror 2. to charm; captivate —**fas'ci·na'tion** *n.*

**fas·cism** (fash'iz'm) *n.* [< It. < L. *fasces*, rods bound about an ax, ancient Roman symbol of authority] [*occas.* F-] a system of government characterized by dictatorship, belligerent nationalism and racism, militarism, etc.: first instituted in Italy (1922–43) —**fas'cist** *n., adj.*

**fash·ion** (fash'ən) *n.* [< L. *factio*, a making] 1. the form or shape of a thing 2. way; manner 3. the current style of dress, conduct, etc. —*vt.* 1. to make; form 2. to fit; accommodate (*to*) —**after** (or **in**) **a fashion** to some extent —**fash'ion·er** *n.*

**fash·ion·a·ble** *adj.* 1. stylish 2. of or used by people who follow fashion —**fash'ion·a·bly** *adv.*

**fast¹** (fast) *adj.* [OE. *fæst*] 1. firm; firmly fastened 2. loyal; devoted 3. nonfading [*fast* colors] 4. swift; quick 5. ahead of time [a *fast* watch] 6. wild, promiscuous, or dissipated 7. [Colloq.] glib —*adv.* 1. firmly; fixedly 2. thoroughly [*fast* asleep] 3. rapidly —**fast'ness** *n.*

**fast²** (fast) *vi.* [OE. *fæstan*] to abstain from all or certain foods —*n.* 1. a fasting 2. a period of fasting

**fast'back'** *n.* an automobile body whose roof forms an unbroken curve from windshield to rear bumper

**fas·ten** (fas''n) *vt.* [see FAST¹] 1. to attach; connect 2. to make secure, as by locking, buttoning, etc. 3. to fix (the attention, etc. *on*) —*vi.* to become fastened —**fas'ten·er** *n.*

**fas'ten·ing** *n.* anything used to fasten; bolt, clasp, hook, etc.

**fast'-food'** *adj.* designating a business, as a hamburger stand, that offers food prepared and served quickly

**fas·tid·i·ous** (fas tid'ē əs) *adj.* [< L. *fastus*, disdain] 1. not easy to please 2. daintily refined; oversensitive —**fas·tid'i·ous·ly** *adv.* —**fas·tid'i·ous·ness** *n.*

**fast'-talk'** *vt.* [Colloq.] to persuade

with smooth, but often deceitful talk

**fast time** *same as* DAYLIGHT-SAVING TIME

**fat** (fat) *adj.* **fat'ter, fat'test** [OE. *fætt*] 1. containing fat; oily 2. *a)* fleshy; plump *b)* too plump 3. thick; broad 4. fertile [*fat* land] 5. profitable [a *fat* job] 6. plentiful —*n.* 1. an oily or greasy material found in animal tissue and plant seeds 2. the richest part of anything 3. superfluous part —**chew the fat** [Slang] to chat —**fat'ly** *adv.* —**fat'ness** *n.*

**fa·tal** (fāt''l) *adj.* 1. fateful; decisive 2. resulting in death 3. destructive; disastrous —**fa'tal·ly** *adv.*

**fa'tal·ism** *n.* the belief that all events are determined by fate and are hence inevitable —**fa'tal·ist** *n.* —**fa'tal·is'tic** *adj.* —**fa'tal·is'ti·cal·ly** *adv.*

**fa·tal·i·ty** (fə tal'ə tē, fā-) *n., pl.* -ties 1. a deadly effect; deadliness 2. a death caused by a disaster or accident

**fat'back'** *n.* fat from a hog's back, usually dried and salted in strips

**fat cat** [Slang] a wealthy, influential donor, esp. to a political campaign

**fate** (fāt) *n.* [< L. *fatum*, oracle] 1. the power supposed to determine the outcome of events; destiny 2. one's lot or fortune 3. final outcome 4. death; destruction —**the Fates** *Gr. & Rom. Myth.* the three goddesses who control human destiny and life

**fat·ed** (fāt'id) *adj.* 1. destined 2. doomed

**fate'ful** (-fəl) *adj.* 1. prophetic 2. significant; decisive 3. controlled as if by fate 4. bringing death or destruction —**fate'ful·ly** *adv.*

**fa·ther** (fä'thər) *n.* [OE. *fæder*] 1. a male parent 2. [F-] God 3. an ancestor 4. an originator, founder, or inventor 5. a Christian priest: used esp. as a title —*vt.* to be the father of —**fa'ther·hood'** *n.* —**fa'ther·less** *adj.*

**fa'ther-in-law'** *n., pl.* **fa'thers-in-law'** the father of one's spouse

**fa'ther·land'** *n.* one's native land

**fa'ther·ly** *adj.* of or like a father; kindly —**fa'ther·li·ness** *n.*

**fath·om** (fath'əm) *n.* [OE. *fæthm*, the two arms outstretched] a nautical unit of depth or length, equal to 6 feet —*vt.* 1. to measure the depth of 2. to understand thoroughly —**fath'om·a·ble** *adj.* —**fath'om·less** *adj.*

**fa·tigue** (fə tēg') *n.* [Fr. < L. *fatigare*, to weary] 1. exhaustion; weariness 2. [*pl.*] soldiers' work clothing —*vt., vi.* -tigued', -tigu'ing to tire out

**fat·ten** (fat''n) *vt., vi.* to make or become fat (in various senses)

**fat'ty** *adj.* -ti·er, -ti·est 1. of or containing fat 2. like fat; greasy

**fat·u·ous** (fach'oo wəs) *adj.* [L. *fatuus*] complacently stupid; foolish —**fa·tu·i·ty** (fə too'ə tē) *n.* —**fat'u·ous·ly** *adv.* —**fat'u·ous·ness** *n.*

**fau·cet** (fô'sit) *n.* [prob. < OFr. *faulser*, to breach] a device with a valve for regulating the flow of a liquid from a pipe, etc.; tap

**Faulk·ner** (fôk'nər), **William** 1897-1962; U.S. novelist

**fault** (fôlt) *n.* [ < L. *fallere*, deceive] 1. something that mars; flaw; defect 2. a misdeed or mistake 3. blame for something wrong 4. a fracture in rock strata —**at fault** deserving blame —**find fault (with)** to criticize

**fault/find'ing** *n.*, *adj.* criticizing

**fault/less** *adj.* perfect

**fault/y** *adj.* -**i·er**, -**i·est** having a fault or faults; defective —**fault/i·ly** *adv.* —**fault/i·ness** *n.*

**faun** (fôn) *n.* [ < L. *faunus*] any of a class of minor Roman deities, half man and half goat

**fau·na** (fô'nə) *n.* [ < LL. *Fauna*, Rom. goddess] the animals of a specified region or time

**Faust** (foust) a man in legend and literature who sells his soul to the devil for knowledge and power

**faux pas** (fō'pä') *pl.* **faux pas** (fō'päz') [Fr., lit., false step] a social blunder

**fa·vor** (fā'vər) *n.* [ < L. *favere*, to favor] 1. friendly regard; approval 2. partiality 3. a kind or obliging act 4. a small gift or token —*vt.* 1. to approve or like 2. to be partial to 3. to support; advocate 4. to help 5. to do a kindness for 6. to resemble [to *favor* one's mother] Brit. sp. **favour** —**in favor of** 1. approving 2. to the advantage of —**fa'vor·er** *n.*

**fa'vor·a·ble** *adj.* 1. approving 2. helpful 3. pleasing —**fa'vor·a·bly** *adv.*

**fa·vor·ite** (fā'vər it) *n.* 1. a person or thing regarded with special liking 2. a contestant regarded as most likely to win —*adj.* highly regarded; preferred

**fa'vor·it·ism** *n.* partiality; bias

**fawn¹** (fôn) *vi.* [ < OE. *fægen*, glad] 1. to show friendliness by licking hands, etc.: said of a dog 2. to cringe and flatter —**fawn'er** *n.*

**fawn²** (fôn) *n.* [ < L. *fetus*, FETUS] 1. a deer less than one year old 2. a pale, yellowish brown —*adj.* of this color

**fay** (fā) *n.* [see FATE] a fairy

**faze** (fāz) *vt.* **fazed, faz'ing** [ < OE. *fesan*, to drive] [Colloq.] to disturb

**FBI, F.B.I.** Federal Bureau of Investigation

**FCC, F.C.C.** Federal Communications Commission

**FDA, F.D.A.** Food and Drug Administration

**FDIC, F.D.I.C.** Federal Deposit Insurance Corporation

**Fe** [L. *ferrum*] *Chem.* iron

**fe·al·ty** (fē'əl tē) *n.*, *pl.* -**ties** [ < L. *fidelitas*, fidelity] loyalty, esp. as owed to a feudal lord

**fear** (fir) *n.* [ < OE. *fær*, danger] 1. anxiety caused by real or possible danger, pain, etc.; fright 2. awe; reverence 3. apprehension; concern 4. a cause for fear —*vt.*, *vi.* 1. to be afraid (of) 2. to be in awe (of) 3. to expect with misgiving —**fear'less** *adj.* —**fear'less·ly** *adv.*

**fear'ful** *adj.* 1. causing, feeling, or showing fear 2. [Colloq.] very bad, great, etc. —**fear'ful·ly** *adv.* —**fear'ful·ness** *n.*

**fear'some** *adj.* 1. causing fear; frightful 2. frightened; timid

**fea·si·ble** (fē'zə b'l) *adj.* [ < OFr. *faire*, to do] 1. capable of being done; possible 2. likely; probable 3. suitable —**fea'si·bil'i·ty** *n.* —**fea'si·bly** *adv.*

**feast** (fēst) *n.* [ < L. *festus*, festal] 1. a religious festival 2. a rich and elaborate meal —*vi.* to have a feast —*vt.* 1. to entertain at a feast 2. to delight [to *feast* one's eyes on a sight]

**feat** (fēt) *n.* [ < L. *factum*, a deed] a deed of unusual daring or skill

**feath·er** (feth'ər) *n.* [OE. *fether*] 1. any of the soft, light growths covering the body of a bird 2. [*pl.*] *a*) plumage *b*) attire 3. class; kind [birds of a *feather*] —*vt.* 1. to provide or adorn with feathers 2. to turn (an oar or propeller blade) so that the edge is foremost —**feather in one's cap** a distinctive achievement —**feath'er·y** *adj.*

**feath'er·bed'ding** (-bed'iŋ) *n.* the employment of extra, standby workers

**feath'er·weight'** *n.* 1. a boxer weighing from 119 to 126 lbs. 2. a wrestler weighing from 124 to 134 lbs.

**fea·ture** (fē'chər) *n.* [ < L. *facere*, make] 1. *a*) [*pl.*] facial form or appearance *b*) any of the parts of the face 2. a distinct or outstanding part or quality of something 3. a special attraction, sale item, newspaper article, etc. 4. a full-length motion picture —*vt.*, *vi.* -**tured, -tur·ing** to make or be a feature of (something)

**fe·brile** (fē'brəl, -bril) *adj.* [ < L. *febris*, fever] feverish

**Feb·ru·ar·y** (feb'rə wer'ē, feb'yoo-) *n.* [ < L. *Februarius (mensis)*, orig. month of expiation] the second month of the year, having 28 days (or 29 days in leap years): abbrev. **Feb., F.**

**fe·ces** (fē'sēz) *n.pl.* [ < L. *faeces*, dregs] excrement —**fe'cal** (-kal) *adj.*

**feck·less** (fek'lis) *adj.* [Scot. < *feck*, effect + -LESS] 1. weak; ineffective 2. irresponsible —**feck'less·ly** *adv.*

**fe·cund** (fē'kənd, fek'ənd) *adj.* [ < L. *fecundus*] fertile; productive —**fe·cun·di·ty** (fi kun'də tē) *n.*

**fe·cun·date** (fē'kən dāt', fek'ən-) *vt.* -**dat'ed, -dat'ing** 1. to make fecund 2. to fertilize

**fed** (fed) *pt.* & *pp.* of FEED —**fed up** [Colloq.] having had enough to become disgusted, bored, etc.

**Fed.** 1. Federal 2. Federation

**fed·a·yeen** (fed'ä yēn') *n.pl.* [Ar., lit., the sacrificers] Arab guerrillas

**fed·er·al** (fed'ər əl) *adj.* [ < L. *foedus*, a league] 1. designating or of a union of states, etc. in which each member subordinates its power to a central authority 2. designating or of a central government of this sort; specif., [*usually* **F-**] the central government of the U.S. 3. [**F-**] of or supporting a former U.S. political party (**Federalist Party**) which favored a strong centralized government 4. [**F-**] of or supporting the Union in the Civil War —n. [F-] a supporter or soldier of the Union in the Civil War —**fed'er·al·ism** n. —**fed'er·al·ist** adj., n. —**fed'er·al·ly** adv.

**fed·er·al·ize** (-ə liz') vt. **-ized', -iz'ing** 1. to unite (states, etc.) in a federal union 2. to put under federal authority —**fed'er·al·i·za'tion** n.

**fed·er·ate** (fed'ə rāt') vt., vi. **-at·ed, -at'ing** to unite in a federation

**fed·er·a·tion** (fed'ə rā'shən) n. [see FEDERAL] 1. a union of states, groups, etc. in which each subordinates its power to that of the central authority 2. a federated organization

**fe·do·ra** (fə dôr'ə) n. [Fr.] a soft felt hat worn by men

**fee** (fē) n. [ult. < Gmc.] 1. a charge for professional services, licenses, etc. 2. *Law* an inheritance in land

**fee·ble** (fē'b'l) adj. **-bler, -blest** [< L. *flere,* weep] 1. weak; infirm [a *feeble* old man] 2. without force or effectiveness [a *feeble* attempt] —**fee'ble·ness** n. —**fee'bly** adv.

**fee·ble-mind·ed** (-mīn'did) adj. mentally retarded

**feed** (fēd) vt. **fed, feed'ing** [< OE. *foda,* food] 1. to give food to 2. to provide something necessary for the growth, operation, etc. of 3. to gratify [to *feed* one's vanity] —vi. to eat: said esp. of animals —n. 1. food for animals 2. a) the material fed into a machine b) the part of a machine supplying this material —**feed'er** n.

**feed'back'** n. the transfer of part of the output back to the input, as of electricity or of information

**feel** (fēl) vt. **felt, feel'ing** [OE. *felan*] 1. to touch; examine by handling 2. to be aware of through physical sensation 3. to experience (an emotion or condition); be affected by 4. to be aware of 5. to think or believe —vi. 1. to have physical sensation 2. to appear to be to the senses [it *feels* warm] 3. to grope 4. to be aware of being [I *feel* sad] 5. to be moved to sympathy, pity, etc. (for) —n. 1. the act of feeling 2. the sense of touch 3. the nature of a thing perceived through touch —**feel (a person) out** to find out the opinions of (a person) cautiously —**feel like** [Colloq.] to have a desire for —**feel one's way** to advance cautiously —**feel up to** [Colloq.] to feel capable of

**feel'er** n. 1. a specialized organ of touch in an animal or insect, as an antenna 2. a remark, offer, etc. made to feel another out

**feel'ing** n. 1. the sense of touch 2. the ability to experience physical sensation 3. an awareness; sensation 4. an emotion 5. [pl.] sensitivities [hurt *feelings*] 6. sympathy; pity 7. an opinion or sentiment

**feet** (fēt) n. pl. of FOOT

**feign** (fān) vt., vi. [< L. *fingere,* to shape] 1. to make up (an excuse, etc.) 2. to pretend; dissemble

**feint** (fānt) n. [see prec.] a pretended attack intended to take the opponent off his guard, as in boxing —vi., vt. to deliver (such an attack)

**feld·spar** (feld'spär') n. [< G. *feld,* field + *spath,* a mineral] any of several hard, crystalline minerals

**fe·lic·i·tate** (fə lis'ə tāt') vt. **-tat'ed, -tat'ing** [< L. *felix,* happy] to wish happiness to; congratulate —**fe·lic'i·ta'tion** n. —**fe·lic'i·ta'tor** n.

**fe·lic'i·tous** (-təs) adj. [< f.] used or expressed in a way suitable to the occasion; appropriate

**fe·lic'i·ty** n., pl. **-ties** [< L. *felix,* happy] 1. happiness; bliss 2. anything producing happiness 3. apt and pleasing expression in writing, etc.

**fe·line** (fē'līn) adj. [< L. *feles,* cat] 1. of a cat or the cat family 2. catlike; sly —n. any animal of the cat family

**fell**[1] (fel) pt. of FALL

**fell**[2] (fel) vt. [OE. *fellan*] 1. to knock down 2. to cut down (a tree)

**fell**[3] (fel) adj. [< ML. *fello*] fierce; cruel

**fell**[4] (fel) n. [OE.] an animal's hide

**fel·low** (fel'ō, -ə) n. [Late OE. *feolaga,* partner] 1. an associate 2. one of the same rank; equal 3. one of a pair; mate 4. one holding a fellowship in a college, etc. 5. a member of a learned society 6. [Colloq.] a man or boy —adj. having the same position, work, etc. [fellow workers]

**fel'low-ship'** n. 1. companionship 2. a mutual sharing 3. a group of people with the same interests 4. an endowment for the support of a student or scholar doing advanced work

**fellow traveler** a nonmember who supports the cause of a party

**fel·on**[1] (fel'ən) n. [< ML. *fello*] a person guilty of a felony; criminal

**fel·on**[2] (fel'ən) n. [ME.] a painful, pus-producing infection at the end of a finger or toe, near the nail

**fel·o·ny** (fel'ə nē) n., pl. **-nies** [< ML.] a major crime, as murder, arson, etc. —**fe·lo·ni·ous** (fə lō'nē əs) adj.

**felt**[1] (felt) n. [OE.] a fabric of wool, often mixed with fur or hair, worked together by pressure, etc. —adj. made of felt —vt. to make into felt

**felt**[2] (felt) pt. & pp. of FEEL

**fe·male** (fē'māl) adj. [< L. *femina,* woman] 1. designating or of the sex that bears offspring 2. of, like, or suitable to women or girls; feminine 3. having a hollow part (as a pipe fitting) for receiving an inserted part —n. a female person, animal, or plant

**fem·i·nine** (fem'ə nin) adj. [< L. *femina,* woman] 1. of women or girls 2. having qualities characteristic of or suitable to women; gentle, delicate, etc. 3. *Gram.* designating or of the gender of words referring to females or things orig. regarded as female —**fem'i·nin'i·ty** n.

**fem′i·nism** n. the movement to win political, economic, and social equality for women —**fem′i·nist** n., adj.

**fe·mur** (fē′mər) n., pl. **fe′murs, fem·o·ra** (fem′ər ə) [< L., thigh] the thighbone —**fem′o·ral** adj.

**fen** (fen) n. [OE.] an area of low, flat, marshy land; swamp; bog

**fence** (fens) n. [< ME. defens, defense] 1. a protective or confining barrier of posts, wire mesh, etc. 2. one who deals in stolen goods —vt. **fenced, fenc′ing** 1. to enclose as with a fence (with in, off, etc.) 2. to keep (out) as by a fence —vi. 1. to practice the art of fencing 2. to avoid giving a direct reply —**fenc′er** n.

**fenc′ing** n. 1. the art of fighting with a foil or other sword 2. material for making fences 3. a system of fences

**fend** (fend) vi. [ME. fenden, defend] to resist —**fend for oneself** to manage by oneself —**fend off** to ward off

**fend′er** n. anything that fends off or protects something else, as the part of an automobile body over the wheel

**fen·nel** (fen′'l) n. [< L. faenum, hay] a tall herb of the parsley family, with aromatic seeds used in cooking

**fe·ral** (fir′əl) adj. [< L. ferus, wild] 1. untamed; wild 2. savage

**fer·ment** (fur′ment; for v. fər ment′) n. [< L. fervere, to boil] 1. a substance causing fermentation, as yeast 2. excitement or agitation —vt. 1. to cause fermentation in 2. to excite; agitate —vi. 1. to be in the process of fermentation 2. to be excited or agitated; seethe

**fer·men·ta·tion** (fur′mən tā′shən, -men-) n. 1. the breakdown of complex molecules in organic compounds, caused by the influence of a ferment [bacteria cause milk to curdle by fermentation] 2. excitement; agitation

**fern** (furn) n. [OE. fearn] any of a large class of nonflowering plants having roots, stems, and fronds, and reproducing by spores

**fe·ro·cious** (fə rō′shəs) adj. [< L. ferus, wild] 1. fierce; savage; violently cruel 2. [Colloq.] very great [a ferocious appetite] —**fe·ro′cious·ly** adv. —**fe·roc′i·ty** (ə räs′ə tē) n.

FERN

**-fer·ous** (fər əs) [< L. ferre, to bear] a suffix meaning bearing, yielding

**fer·ret** (fer′it) n. [< L. fur, thief] a weasellike animal, tamed for hunting rats, etc. —vt. 1. to force out of hiding with a ferret 2. to search (out)

**Fer·ris wheel** (fer′is) [after G. Ferris, 1859–96, U.S. engineer] a large, upright wheel revolving on a fixed axle and having suspended seats: used as an amusement ride

**ferro-** [< L. ferrum, iron] a combining form meaning: 1. iron 2. iron and

**fer·rous** (fer′əs) adj. [< L. ferrum, iron] of, containing, or derived from iron: also **fer′ric** (-ik)

**fer·rule** (fer′əl, -ool) n. [< L. viriae, bracelets] a metal ring or cap put around the end of a cane, tool handle, etc. to give added strength

**fer·ry** (fer′ē) vt., vi. **-ried, -ry·ing** [OE. ferian] 1. to take across or cross (a river, etc.) in a boat 2. to deliver (airplanes) by flying them 3. to transport by airplane —n., pl. **-ries** 1. a system for carrying people, goods, etc. across a river, etc. by boat 2. a boat (also **ferryboat**) used for this —**fer′ry·man** (-mən) n., pl. **-men**

**fer·tile** (furt′'l) adj. [< L. ferre, to bear] 1. producing abundantly; fruitful 2. able to produce young, seeds, fruit, pollen, spores, etc. 3. fertilized —**fer·til′i·ty** (fər til′ə tē) n.

**fer′til·ize′** (-īz′) vt. **-ized′, -iz′ing** 1. to make fertile 2. to spread fertilizer on 3. to make (the female cell or female) fruitful by introducing the male germ cell; impregnate —**fer′til·iz′a·ble** adj. —**fer′til·i·za′tion** n.

**fer′til·iz′er** n. manure, chemicals, etc. used to enrich the soil

**fer·ule** (fer′əl, -ool) n. [< L. ferula, a whip, rod] a flat stick or ruler used for punishing children

**fer·vent** (fur′vənt) adj. [< L. fervere, to glow] showing great warmth of feeling; intensely devoted or earnest —**fer′ven·cy** n. —**fer′vent·ly** adv.

**fer·vid** (fur′vəd) adj. [see prec.] impassioned; fervent —**fer′vid·ly** adv.

**fer·vor** (fur′vər) n. [see FERVENT] great warmth of emotion; ardor; zeal

**-fest** (fest) [< G. fest, a feast] a combining form meaning an occasion of much [gabfest]

**fes·tal** (fes′t'l) adj. [< L. festum, feast] of or like a joyous celebration; gay

**fes·ter** (fes′tər) n. [< L. fistula, ulcer] a small sore filled with pus —vi. 1. to form pus 2. to rankle

**fes·ti·val** (fes′tə v'l) n. [see ff.] 1. a time or day of feasting or celebration 2. a celebration or series of performances 3. merrymaking

**fes·tive** (fes′tiv) adj. [< L. festum, feast] of or for a feast or festival; merry; joyous —**fes′tive·ly** adv. —**fes′tive·ness** n.

**fes·tiv·i·ty** (fes tiv′ə tē) n., pl. **-ties** 1. merrymaking; gaiety 2. a festival 3. [pl.] things done in celebration

**fes·toon** (fes tōōn′) n. [< It. festa, feast] a curved garland of flowers, etc. —vt. to adorn with festoons

**fet·a (cheese)** (fet′ə) [< ModGr. < It. fetta, a slice] a white, soft cheese made in Greece

**fe·tal** (fēt′'l) adj. of a fetus

**fetch** (fech) vt. [OE. feccan] 1. to go after and bring back; get 2. to cause to come 3. to sell for

**fetch′ing** adj. attractive; charming

**fete, fête** (fāt) n. [Fr. fête: see FEAST] a festival; entertainment, esp. outdoors —vt. **fet′ed** or **fêt′ed, fet′ing** or **fêt′ing** to honor with a fete

**fet·id** (fet′id, fēt′-) adj. [< L. foetere, to stink] having a bad smell; stinking; putrid —**fet′id·ness** n.

**fet·ish** (fet′ish, fēt′-) n. [< Port. feitiço] 1. any object believed to have magical power 2. anything to which one is irrationally devoted **3.** any non-sexual object that abnormally excites erotic feelings Also **fetich** —**fet′ish-ism** n. —**fet′ish-ist** n.

**fet·lock** (fet′läk′) n. [< ME. fet, feet + lok, LOCK²] **1.** a tuft of hair on the back of a horse's leg above the hoof **2.** the joint bearing this tuft

**fet·ter** (fet′ər) n. [< OE. fot, foot] **1.** a shackle or chain for the feet **2.** any check or restraint —vt. **1.** to bind with fetters **2.** to restrain

**fet·tle** (fet′'l) n. [ME. fetlen, make ready] condition; state [in fine fettle]

**fe·tus** (fēt′əs) n., pl. **-tus·es** [L., a bringing forth] **1.** the unborn young of an animal, esp. in its later stages **2.** in man, the offspring in the womb from the fourth month until birth

**feud** (fyōōd) n. [< OFr.] a deadly quarrel, esp. between clans or families —vi. to carry on a feud; quarrel

**feu·dal** (fyōōd′'l) adj. [< OHG. feho, property] of or like feudalism

**feu′dal·ism** n. the economic and social system in medieval Europe, in which land, worked by serfs, was held by vassals in exchange for military and other services to overlords

**fe·ver** (fē′vər) n. [< L. febris] **1.** an abnormally increased body temperature **2.** any disease marked by a high fever **3.** a restless excitement —**fe′ver·ish** adj. —**fe′ver·ish·ly** adv.

**fever blister** (or **sore**) same as COLD SORE

**few** (fyōō) adj. [OE. feawe, pl.] not many —pron., n. a small number — **quite a few** [Colloq.] a rather large number —**the few** the minority

**fey** (fā) adj. [OE. fæge] **1.** [Archaic] fated **2.** strange or unusual

**fez** (fez) n., pl. **fez′zes** [< Fez, city in Morocco] a red, tapering felt hat, worn, esp. formerly, by Turkish men

**ff. 1.** folios (pages, etc.) **2.** following (pages, etc.)

**FHA** Federal Housing Administration

**fi·an·cé** (fē′än sā′) n. [Fr. < OFr. fiance, a promise] the man to whom a woman is engaged to be married

**fi·an·cée** (fē′än sā′) n. [Fr.: see prec.] the woman to whom a man is engaged to be married

**fi·as·co** (fē as′kō) n., pl. **-coes**, **-cos** [Fr. < It.] a complete, ridiculous failure

**fi·at** (fī′at, -ət) n. [L., let it be done] **1.** a decree; order **2.** a sanction

**fib** (fib) n. [< ? FABLE] a lie about something unimportant —vi. **fibbed**, **fib′bing** to tell a fib —**fib′ber** n.

**fi·ber, fi·bre** (fī′bər) n. [< L. fibra] **1.** a threadlike structure that combines with others to form animal or vegetable tissue **2.** any substance that can be separated into threadlike parts for weaving, etc. **3.** texture **4.** character or nature —**fi′brous** (-brəs) adj.

**fi′ber·board′** n. a boardlike material made from pressed fibers of wood, etc.

**Fi′ber·glas′** (-glas′) a trademark for finespun filaments of glass made into

textiles or insulating material —n. [f-] this substance: also **fiberglass**

**fi·bril·la·tion** (fib′rə lā′shən) n. [< L. fibra, fiber + -ATION] a rapid series of contractions of the heart, causing weak, irregular heartbeats

**fi·brin** (fī′brən) n. a threadlike, elastic protein formed in blood clots

**fi·brin·o·gen** (fī brin′ə jən) n. [prec. + -GEN] a protein in the blood from which fibrin is formed

**fi·broid** (fī′broid) adj. like or composed of fibrous tissue, as a tumor

**fi·bro·sis** (fī brō′sis) n. an abnormal increase in the amount of fibrous connective tissue in an organ, part, etc.

**fib·u·la** (fib′yoo lə) n., pl. **-lae** (-lē′), **-las** [L., a clasp] the long, thin outer bone of the lower leg —**fib′u·lar** adj.

**-fic** (fik) [< L. facere, make] a suffix meaning making [terrific]

**FICA** Federal Insurance Contributions Act

**-fi·ca·tion** (fi kā′shən) [see -FIC] a suffix meaning a making [glorification]

**fich·u** (fish′ōō) n. [Fr.] a triangular lace or muslin cape for women, worn with the ends fastened in front

**fick·le** (fik′'l) adj. [< OE. ficol, tricky] changeable or unstable; capricious

**fic·tion** (fik′shən) n. [< L. fingere, to form] **1.** an imaginary statement, story, etc. **2.** a) any literary work with imaginary characters and events, as a novel, play, etc. b) such works collectively —**fic′tion·al** adj.

**fic′tion·al·ize′** (-'l īz′) vt. **-ized′**, **-iz′ing** to deal with (historical events) as fiction

**fic·ti·tious** (fik tish′əs) adj. **1.** of or like fiction; imaginary **2.** false **3.** assumed for disguise [a fictitious name]

**fic·tive** (fik′tiv) adj. **1.** of fiction **2.** imaginary —**fic′tive·ly** adv.

**fid·dle** (fid′'l) n. [< L. fithele] [Colloq.] a violin —vi. **-dled**, **-dling 1.** [Colloq.] to play on a violin **2.** to tinker (with) nervously —**fid′dler** n.

**fid′dle·sticks′** interj. nonsense!

**fi·del·i·ty** (fə del′ə tē, fī-) n., pl. **-ties** [< L. fides, faith] **1.** faithful devotion to duty; loyalty **2.** accuracy of description, sound reproduction, etc.

**fidg·et** (fij′it) n. [< ME. < ?] a restless or nervous state, esp. in phr. **the fidgets** —vi. to make restless or nervous movements —**fidg′et·y** adj.

**fi·du·ci·ar·y** (fi dōō′shē er′ē) adj. [< L. fiducia, trust] holding or held in trust —n., pl. **-ies** a trustee

**fie** (fī) interj. for shame!

**fief** (fēf) n. [Fr.: see FEE] in feudalism, heritable land held by a vassal

**field** (fēld) n. [OE. feld] **1.** a stretch of open land **2.** a piece of cleared land for crops or pasture **3.** a piece of land used for a particular purpose [a landing field] **4.** any wide unbroken expanse [a field of ice] **5.** a) a battlefield b) a battle **6.** a realm of knowledge or work **7.** the background, as on a flag **8.** all the entrants in a contest **9.** Physics a space within which magnetic or electrical lines of force are active —vt. **1.** to stop or catch and return (a baseball, etc.) **2.** to put (a player or a team) into active play —**play the field** to expand one's activities to a broad area — **field′er** n.

**field glass(es)** a small, portable, binocular telescope

**field goal 1.** *Basketball* a basket toss made from play, scoring two points **2.** *Football* a goal kicked from the field, scoring three points

**field hand** a hired farm laborer

**field hockey** *same as* HOCKEY (sense 2)

**field marshal** in some armies, an officer of the highest rank

**field′-test′** vt. to test (a device, method, etc.) under operating conditions

**fiend** (fēnd) n. [OE. *feond*] **1.** an evil spirit; devil **2.** an inhumanly wicked person **3.** [Colloq.] an addict [a dope *fiend*, fresh-air *fiend*] —**fiend′ish** adj.

**fierce** (firs) adj. **fierc′er, fierc′est** [< L. *ferus*, wild] **1.** savage **2.** violent **3.** intense [a *fierce* effort] **4.** [Colloq.] very distasteful —**fierce′ly** adv. — **fierce′ness** n.

**fi·er·y** (fī′ər ē) adj. **-i·er, -i·est 1.** like fire; glaring, hot, etc. **2.** ardent; spirited **3.** excitable **4.** inflamed

**fi·es·ta** (fē es′tə) n. [Sp. < L. *festus*, festal] **1.** a religious festival **2.** any gala celebration; holiday

**fife** (fīf) n. [G. *pfeife*] a small, shrill musical instrument like a flute

**fif·teen** (fif′tēn′) adj., n. [OE. *fiftene*] five more than ten; 15; XV —**fif′teenth′** (-tēnth′) adj., n.

**fifth** (fifth) adj. [< OE. *fif*, five] preceded by four others in a series; 5th —n. **1.** the one following the fourth **2.** any of the five equal parts of something; 1/5 **3.** a fifth of a gallon

**Fifth Amendment** an amendment to the U.S. Constitution assuring certain legal safeguards, as that no person shall be compelled in any criminal case to be a witness against himself

**fif·ty** (fif′tē) adj., n., pl. **-ties** [OE. *fiftig*] five times ten; 50; L —**the fifties** the numbers or years, as of a century, from 50 through 59 —**fif′ti·eth** (-ith) adj., n.

**fif′ty-fif′ty** adj. [Colloq.] equal; even —adv. [Colloq.] equally

**fig** (fig) n. [< L. *ficus*] **1.** a) a small, sweet, pear-shaped fruit that grows on a tree related to the mulberry b) the tree **2.** a trifle [not worth a *fig*]

**fig. 1.** figurative(ly) **2.** figure(s)

**fight** (fīt) vi. fought, fight′ing [OE. *feohtan*] to take part in a struggle, contest, etc. esp. against a foe or for a cause —vt. **1.** to oppose physically or in battle **2.** to struggle against **3.** to engage in (a war, etc.) **4.** to gain (one's way) by struggle —n. **1.** any struggle, contest, or quarrel **2.** power or readiness to fight

**fight′er** n. **1.** one that fights; esp., a prizefighter **2.** a fast, highly maneuverable combat airplane

**fig·ment** (fig′mənt) n. [< L. *fingere*,

to make] something merely imagined

**fig·u·ra·tion** (fig′yə rā′shən) n. [see FIGURE] **1.** a forming; shaping **2.** form; appearance

**fig·u·ra·tive** (fig′yər ə tiv) adj. **1.** representing by means of a figure or symbol **2.** not in its usual or exact sense; metaphorical **3.** using figures of speech —**fig′u·ra·tive·ly** adv.

**fig·ure** (fig′yər) n. [< L. *fingere*, to form] **1.** an outline or shape; form **2.** the human form **3.** a person thought of in a specified way [a historical *figure*] **4.** a likeness of a person or thing **5.** an illustration; diagram **6.** a design; pattern **7.** the symbol for a number **8.** [pl.] arithmetic **9.** a sum of money **10.** *Geom.* a surface or space bounded by lines or planes —vt. **-ured, -ur·ing 1.** to represent in definite form **2.** to imagine **3.** to ornament with a design **4.** to compute with figures **5.** [Colloq.] to believe; consider —vi. **1.** to appear prominently **2.** to do arithmetic — **figure in** to include —**figure on** to rely on —**figure out 1.** to solve **2.** to understand —**figure up** to add; total

**fig′ure·head′** n. **1.** a carved figure on the bow of a ship **2.** one put in a position of leadership, but having no real power or authority

**figure of speech** an expression, as a metaphor or simile, using words in a nonliteral or unusual sense

**fig·u·rine** (fig′yə rēn′) n. [Fr.] a small sculptured or molded figure

**Fi·ji** (fē′jē) country on a group of islands (**Fiji Islands**) in the SW Pacific, north of New Zealand: 7,000 sq. mi.; pop. 535,000

**fil·a·ment** (fil′ə mənt) n. [< L. *filum*, thread] a very slender thread or threadlike part; specif., the fine wire in a light bulb or electron tube

**fil·bert** (fil′bərt) n. [ME. *filberde*] *same as* HAZELNUT

**filch** (filch) vt. [ME. *filchen*] to steal (usually something small or petty)

**file¹** (fīl) vt. filed, fil′ing [< L. *filum*, thread] **1.** to put (papers, etc.) in order for future reference **2.** to dispatch or register (a news story, application, etc.) **3.** to put on public record —vi. **1.** to move in a line **2.** to make application (for divorce, etc.) —n. **1.** a container for keeping papers, etc. in order **2.** an orderly arrangement of papers, etc. **3.** a line of persons or things —**file′a·ble** adj. —**fil′er** n.

**file²** (fīl) n. [OE. *feol*] a steel tool with a rough, ridged surface for smoothing or grinding —vt. filed, fil′ing to smooth or grind, as with a file

**fi·let mi·gnon** (fi lā′ min yōn′) [Fr., lit., tiny fillet] a thick, round cut of lean beef tenderloin broiled

**fil·i·al** (fil′ē əl, fil′yəl) adj. [< L. *filius*, son] of, suitable to, or due from a son or daughter

**fil·i·bus·ter** (fil′ə bus′tər) n. [< Sp. < MDu. *vrijbuiter*, freebooter] **1.** a member of a legislature who obstructs a bill by making long speeches **2.** such obstruction of a bill —vt., vi. to obstruct (a bill) by such methods

**fil·i·gree** (fil′ə grē′) n. [< L. *filum*,

thread + *granum*, grain] lacelike ornamental work of intertwined wire of gold, silver, etc. —*vt.* -greed′, -gree′ing to ornament with filigree

**fil·ing** (fīl′iŋ) *n.* a small piece scraped off with a file: *usually in pl.*

**Fil·i·pi·no** (fil′ə pē′nō) *n.*, *pl.* -nos [Sp.] a native of the Philippines — *adj.* Philippine

**fill** (fil) *vt.* [OE. *fyllan*] 1. to put as much as possible into 2. to occupy wholly 3. to put a person into or to occupy (a position, etc.) 4. to supply the things called for in (an order, etc.) 5. to close or plug (holes, etc.) —*vi.* to become full —*n.* 1. enough to make full or to satisfy 2. anything that fills —**fill in** 1. to complete by supplying something 2. to supply for completion 3. to be a substitute —**fill out** 1. to make or become larger, etc. 2. to make (a document, etc.) complete with data —**fill up** to make or become completely full —**fill′er** *n.*

**fil·let** (fil′it; *for n. 2 & v. usually* fil′ā, fi lā′) *n.* [< L. *filum*, thread] 1. a thin strip or band 2. a boneless, lean piece of fish or meat —*vt.* to bone and slice (fish or meat)

**fill′-in′** *n.* 1. one that fills a vacancy or gap 2. [Colloq.] a brief summary of the pertinent facts

**fill′ing** *n.* a substance used to fill something, as gold in a tooth cavity

**filling station** *same as* SERVICE STATION

**fil·lip** (fil′əp) *n.* [< FLIP¹] 1. an outward snap of a finger from the thumb 2. something stimulating —*vt.* to strike or toss with a fillip

**Fill·more** (fil′môr), **Mill·ard** (mil′ərd) 1800–74; 13th president of the U.S. (1850–53)

**fil·ly** (fil′ē) *n.*, *pl.* -lies [< ON. *fylja*] a young female horse

**film** (film) *n.* [OE. *filmen*] 1. a fine, thin skin, coating, etc. 2. a flexible cellulose material covered with a substance sensitive to light and used in photography 3. a haze or blur 4. a motion picture —*vt.*, *vi.* 1. to cover or be covered as with a film 2. to photograph or make a motion picture (of)

**film′strip′** *n.* a strip of film for projection, with stills of pictures, charts, etc. on some subject

**film′y** *adj.* -i·er, -i·est 1. gauzy; sheer; thin 2. blurred; hazy

**fil·ter** (fil′tər) *n.* [< ML. *filtrum*, FELT¹] 1. a device or substance for straining out solid particles, impurities, etc. from a liquid or gas 2. a device or substance for screening out electric oscillations, light waves, etc. of certain frequencies —*vt.*, *vi.* 1. to pass through or as through a filter 2. to remove with a filter —**fil′ter·a·ble**, **fil′tra·ble** (-trə b′l) *adj.*

**filter tip** 1. a cigarette with a tip of cellulose, cotton, etc. for filtering the smoke 2. such a tip

**filth** (filth) *n.* [OE. *fylthe*] 1. foul dirt 2. obscenity —**filth′i·ness** *n.* — **filth′y** *adj.* -i·er, -i·est

**fil·trate** (fil′trāt) *vt.* -trat·ed, -trat·ing to filter —*n.* a filtered liquid — **fil·tra′tion** *n.*

**fin** (fin) *n.* [OE. *finn*] 1. any of several winglike organs on the body of a fish, dolphin, etc., used in swimming 2. anything like this in shape or use

**fi·na·gle** (fə nā′g′l) *vt.*, *vi.* -gled, -gling [< ?] [Colloq.] to use, or get by, craftiness or trickery —**fi·na′gler** *n.*

**fi·nal** (fī′n′l) *adj.* [< L. *finis*, end] 1. of or coming at the end; last 2. deciding; conclusive —*n.* 1. anything final 2. [*pl.*] the last of a series of contests 3. a final examination —**fi·nal′i·ty** (-nal′ə tē) *n.* —**fi′nal·ly** *adv.*

**fi·na·le** (fə nä′lē) *n.* [It.] the concluding part of a musical work, etc.

**fi′nal·ist** *n.* a contestant in the final, deciding contest of a series

**fi′nal·ize** *vt.* -ized′, -iz′ing to make final; complete —**fi′nal·i·za′tion** *n.*

**fi·nance** (fə nans′, fī′nans) *n.* [< L. *finis*, end] 1. [*pl.*] money resources, income, etc. 2. the science of managing money —*vt.* -nanced′, -nanc′ing to supply or get money for —**fi·nan′cial** (-nan′shəl) *adj.* —**fi·nan′cial·ly** *adv.*

**fin·an·cier** (fin′ən sir′, fī′nan-) *n.* [Fr.] one skilled in finance

**finch** (finch) *n.* [OE. *finc*] any of a group of small songbirds, including the canary, cardinal, etc.

**find** (fīnd) *vt.* found, find′ing [OE. *findan*] 1. to discover by chance; come upon 2. to get by searching 3. to perceive; learn 4. to recover (something lost) 5. to reach; attain 6. to decide and declare to be —*vi.* to reach a decision [the jury *found* for the accused] —*n.* 1. a finding 2. something found —**find out** to discover; learn

**find′er** *n.* 1. one that finds 2. a camera device for sighting the field of view

**find′ing** *n.* 1. discovery 2. something found 3. [*often pl.*] the verdict of a judge, scholar, etc.

**fine¹** (fīn) *adj.* fin′er, fin′est [< L. *finis*, end] 1. very good; excellent 2. with no impurities; refined 3. clear and bright [*fine* weather] 4. not heavy or coarse [*fine* sand] 5. very thin or small [*fine* print] 6. sharp [a *fine* edge] 7. subtle; delicate [a *fine* distinction] 8. elegant —*adv.* 1. in a fine manner 2. [Colloq.] very well —**fine′ly** *adv.* —**fine′ness** *n.*

**fine²** (fīn) *n.* [see prec.] a sum of money paid as a penalty —*vt.* fined, fin′ing to order to pay a fine

**fine arts** any of certain art forms, esp. drawing, painting, sculpture, etc.

**fin·er·y** (fīn′ər ē) *n.*, *pl.* -ies elaborate clothes, jewelry, etc.

**fi·nesse** (fi nes′) *n.* [Fr.: see FINE¹] 1. adroitness; skill 2. the ability to handle delicate situations diplomatically 3. cunning; artfulness

**fin·ger** (fiŋ′gər) *n.* [OE.] 1. any of the five jointed parts extending from the palm of the hand, esp. one other than the thumb 2. anything like a finger in shape or use —*vt.* 1. to touch with the fingers; handle 2. *Music* to use the fingers in a certain way in playing —**have** (or **keep**) **one's fingers crossed** to hope for something —**put one's finger on** to ascertain exactly

**fin·ger·board′** *n.* the part of a stringed instrument against which the strings are pressed to produce the desired tones

**fin·ger·ling** (-liŋ) *n.* a small fish

**fin·ger·nail′** *n.* the horny substance at the upper end of a finger

**finger painting** a painting done by using the fingers, hand, or arm to spread paints made of starch, glycerine, and pigments (**finger paints**) on wet paper —**fin′ger-paint′** *vi., vt.*

**fin·ger·print′** *n.* an impression of the lines and whorls on a finger tip, used to identify a person —*vt.* to take the fingerprints of

**finger tip** the tip of a finger —**have at one's finger tips** to have available for instant use

**fin·i·al** (fin′ē əl) *n.* [ult. < L. *finis*, end] a decorative terminal part at the tip of a spire, lamp, etc.

**fin·ick·y** (fin′i kē) *adj.* [< FINE¹] too particular; fussy: also **fin′i·cal** (-k′l), **fin′ick·ing**

**fi·nis** (fin′is, fē nē′) *n., pl.* **-nis·es** [L.] the end; finish

FINIAL

**fin·ish** (fin′ish) *vt.* [< L. *finis*, end] 1. *a)* to bring to an end *b)* to come to the end of 2. to consume all of 3. to give final touches to; perfect 4. to give a desired surface effect to —*vi.* to come to an end —*n.* 1. the last part; end 2. *a)* anything used to finish a surface *b)* the finished effect 3. means or manner of completing or perfecting 4. polished manners, speech, etc. —**finish off** 1. to end 2. to kill or ruin —**finish with** to bring to an end —**fin′ished** *adj.* —**fin′ish·er** *n.*

**fi·nite** (fī′nīt) *adj.* [< L. *finis*, end] having definable limits; not infinite

**fink** (fiŋk) *n.* [< ?] [Slang] an informer or strikebreaker

**Fin·land** (fin′lənd) country in N Europe: 130,119 sq. mi.; pop. 4,664,000

**Finn** (fin) *n.* a native or inhabitant of Finland

**fin·nan had·die** (fin′ən had′ē) [prob. < *Findhorn* (Scotland) *haddock*] smoked haddock

**Finn·ish** (fin′ish) *adj.* of Finland, its people, their language, etc. —*n.* the language of the Finns: abbrev. **Finn.**

**fin·ny** (fin′ē) *adj.* 1. having fins 2. like a fin 3. of, full of, or being fish

**fiord** (fyôrd) *n.* [Norw. < ON. *fjörthr*] a narrow inlet of the sea bordered by steep cliffs

**fir** (fur) *n.* [OE. *fyrh*] 1. a cone-bearing evergreen tree of the pine family 2. its wood

**fire** (fīr) *n.* [OE. *fyr*] 1. the flame, heat, and light of combustion 2. something burning 3. a destructive burning [a forest *fire*] 4. strong feeling 5. a discharge of firearms —*vt., vi.* **fired, fir′ing** 1. to start burning; ignite 2. to supply with fuel 3. to bake (bricks, etc.) in a kiln 4. to excite or become excited 5. to shoot (a gun, bullet, etc.) 6. to hurl or direct with force 7. to dismiss from a position; discharge —**catch (on) fire** to ignite —**on fire** 1. burning 2. greatly excited —**under fire** under attack —**fir′er** *n.*

**fire′arm′** *n.* any hand weapon from which a shot is fired by explosive force, as a rifle or pistol

**fire′base′** *n.* a military base in a combat zone, from which artillery, rockets, etc. are fired

**fire′bomb′** *n.* an incendiary bomb —*vt.* to attack or damage with a firebomb

**fire′brand′** *n.* 1. a piece of burning wood 2. one who stirs up others to revolt or strife

**fire′break′** (-brāk′) *n.* a strip of forest or prairie land cleared or plowed to stop the spread of fire

**fire′brick′** *n.* a highly heat-resistant brick for lining fireplaces or furnaces

**fire′bug′** *n.* [Colloq.] one who compulsively starts destructive fires

**fire′crack′er** *n.* a roll of paper containing an explosive, set off as a noisemaker at celebrations, etc.

**fire′damp′** *n.* same as DAMP (sense 2)

**fire′dog′** (-dôg′) *n.* same as ANDIRON

**fire engine** a motor truck with equipment for fighting fires

**fire escape** an outside stairway, etc. for escape from a burning building

**fire′fight′er** *n.* a person who helps fight fires —**fire′fight′ing** *n.*

**fire′fly′** *n., pl.* **-flies′** a winged beetle whose abdomen glows with a luminescent light

**fire′man** (-mən) *n., pl.* **-men** 1. a man whose work is fighting fires 2. a man who tends a fire in a furnace, etc.

**fire′place′** *n.* a place for a fire, esp. an open place built in a wall

**fire′plug′** *n.* a street hydrant supplying water for fighting fires

**fire′proof′** *adj.* not easily destroyed by fire —*vt.* to make fireproof

**fire′side′** *n.* 1. the space around a fireplace 2. home or home life

**fire′storm′** *n.* an intense fire over a wide area, as one caused by an atomic explosion with its high winds

**fire tower** a tower used as a lookout for forest fires

**fire′trap′** *n.* a building easily set afire or hard to get out of if afire

**fire′wa′ter** *n.* [Colloq.] alcoholic liquor

**fire′wood′** *n.* wood used as fuel

**fire′works′** *n.pl.* firecrackers, rockets, etc., for noisy effects or brilliant displays: *sometimes used in sing.*

**firing line** 1. the line from which gunfire is directed at the enemy 2. any vulnerable front position

**firm¹** (furm) *adj.* [< L. *firmus*] 1. solid; hard 2. not moved easily; fixed 3. unchanging; steady 4. resolute; constant 5. showing determination;

strong **6.** definite *[a firm contract]*
—*vt.*, *vi.* to make or become firm —
**firm′ly** *adv.* —**firm′ness** *n.*

**firm²** (furm) *n.* [< It. < L. *firmus*,
firm] a business company

**fir·ma·ment** (fur′mə mənt) *n.* [< L.
*firmus*, firm] the sky, viewed poetically
as a solid arch or vault

**first** (furst) *adj.* [OE. *fyrst*] **1.** before
all others in a series; 1st **2.** earliest **3.**
foremost, as in rank, quality, etc. —
*adv.* **1.** before anyone or anything else
**2.** for the first time **3.** sooner; preferably —*n.* **1.** any person or thing that
is first **2.** the beginning **3.** the winning
place, as in a race **4.** low gear

**first aid** emergency treatment for
injury, etc. before regular medical aid
is available —**first′-aid′** *adj.*

**first′born′** *adj.* born first in a family;
oldest —*n.* the firstborn child

**first′-class′** *adj.* **1.** of the highest
class, quality, etc. **2.** of the most expensive regular class of sealed mail
—*adv.* **1.** with first-class accommodations **2.** by first-class mail

**first′hand′** *adj.*, *adv.* from the
original producer or source; direct

**first lady** [*often* F- L-] the wife of
the U.S. president

**first lieutenant** a military officer
ranking just above a second lieutenant

**first′ly** *adv.* in the first place; first

**first person** that form of a pronoun
or verb which refers to the speaker

**first′-rate′** *adj.* highest in quality,
rank, etc. —*adv.* [Colloq.] very well

**first′-string′** *adj.* [Colloq.] *Sports*
that is the first choice for regular play
at the specified position

**firth** (furth) *n.* [< ON. *fjörthr*] a
narrow inlet or arm of the sea

**fis·cal** (fis′kəl) *adj.* [< L. *fiscus*,
public chest] **1.** relating to the public
treasury or revenues **2.** financial
—**fis′cal·ly** *adv.*

**fish** (fish) *n.*, *pl.* **fish**; in referring to
different species, **fish′es** [OE. *fisc*] **1.**
any of a large group of coldblooded
animals living in water and having
backbones, gills for breathing, and fins
**2.** the flesh of a fish used as food —*vi.*
**1.** to catch or try to catch fish **2.** to
try to get something indirectly (often
with *for*) —*vt.* to grope for, find, and
bring to view (often with *out*)

**fish′er** (-ər) *n.* **1.** an animal related to
the marten, with dark fur **2.** this fur

**fish′er·man** (-ər mən) *n.*, *pl.* **-men**
**1.** a person who fishes for sport or for
a living **2.** a ship used in fishing

**fish′er·y** *n.*, *pl.* **-ies** **1.** the business
of catching fish **2.** a place where fish
are caught or bred

**fish′eye′ lens** a camera lens designed
for a full 180° field of vision

**fish′hook′** *n.* a hook, usually barbed,
for catching fish

**fish′ing** *n.* the catching of fish for
sport or for a living

**fish′wife′** *n.*, *pl.* **-wives′** a coarse,
scolding woman

**fish′y** *adj.* **-i·er**, **-i·est** **1.** like a fish in
odor, taste, etc. **2.** dull; without
expression *[a fishy stare]* **3.** [Colloq.]
questionable; odd —**fish′i·ness** *n.*

**fis·sion** (fish′ən) *n.* [< L. *findere*, to
split] **1.** a splitting apart; cleavage **2.**
*same as* NUCLEAR FISSION —**fis′sion-
a·ble** *adj.*

**fis·sure** (fish′ər) *n.* [see prec.] a cleft
or crack

**fist** (fist) *n.* [OE. *fyst*] a hand with the
fingers closed tightly into the palm

**fis·ti·cuffs** (fis′ti kufs′) *n.pl.* **1.** a
fight with the fists **2.** *same as* BOXING

**fis·tu·la** (fis′choo lə) *n.*, *pl.* **-las**, **-lae′**
(-lē′) [L.] an abnormal passage, as
from an abscess to the skin

**fit¹** (fit) *vt.* **fit′ted** or **fit**, **fit′ted**, **fit′-
ting** [ME. *fitten*] **1.** to be suitable to
**2.** to be the proper size, shape, etc. for
**3.** to adjust so as to fit **4.** to equip;
outfit —*vi.* **1.** to be suitable or proper
**2.** to have the proper size or shape
—*adj.* **fit′ter**, **fit′test** **1.** suited to
some purpose, function, etc. **2.**
proper; right **3.** healthy **4.** [Colloq.]
inclined; ready —*n.* the manner of
fitting *[a tight fit]* —**fit′ly** *adv.* —
**fit′ness** *n.* —**fit′ter** *n.*

**fit²** (fit) *n.* [OE. *fitt*, conflict] **1.** any
sudden, uncontrollable attack, as of
coughing **2.** an outburst, as of anger
**3.** a seizure involving convulsions or
loss of consciousness —**by fits (and
starts)** in an irregular way —**have
(or throw) a fit** [Colloq.] to become
very angry or upset

**fit′ful** (-fəl) *adj.* characterized by
intermittent activity; spasmodic —
**fit′ful·ly** *adv.* —**fit′ful·ness** *n.*

**fit′ting** *adj.* suitable; proper —*n.* **1.**
an adjustment or trying on of clothes,
etc. **2.** a small part used to join or
adapt other parts **3.** [*pl.*] fixtures

**five** (fiv) *adj.*, *n.* [OE. *fif*] one more
than four; 5; V

**five′-and-ten′-cent′ store** a store
that sells a wide variety of inexpensive
merchandise: also **five′-and-ten′** *n.*

**fix** (fiks) *vt.* **fixed**, **fix′ing** [< L. *figere*,
fasten] **1.** to fasten firmly **2.** to set
firmly in the mind **3.** to direct (one's
eyes) steadily at something **4.** to make
rigid **5.** to make permanent **6.** to
establish (a date, etc.) definitely **7.** to
set in order; adjust **8.** to repair **9.** to
prepare (food or meals) **10.** [Colloq.]
to influence the result or action of (a
race, jury, etc.) as by bribery **11.**
[Colloq.] to punish —*vi.* **1.** to become
fixed **2.** [Dial.] to prepare or intend
—*n.* **1.** the position of a ship, etc.
determined from the bearings of two
known positions **2.** [Colloq.] a predicament **3.** [Slang] a situation that has
been fixed (sense 10) **4.** [Slang] an
injection of a narcotic by an addict
—**fix up** [Colloq.] **1.** to repair **2.** to
arrange; set in order —**fix′a·ble** *adj.*
—**fix′er** *n.*

**fix·a·tion** (fik sā′shən) *n.* **1.** a fixing
or being fixed **2.** an obsession **3.** a

fat, āpe, cär; ten, ēven; is, bīte; gō, hôrn, tōōl, look; oil, out; up, fur;
chin; she; thin, then; zh, leisure; ŋ, ring; ə for a in *ago*; ', (ā′b'l); ë, Fr. coeur;
ö, Fr. feu; Fr. mon; ü, Fr. duc; kh, G. ich, doch; ‡ foreign; < derived from

remaining at an early stage of psycho-
sexual development

**fix·a·tive** (fik′sə tiv) *adj.* that can, or
tends to, make permanent, prevent
fading, etc. —*n.* a fixative substance

**fixed** (fikst) *adj.* 1. firmly in place 2.
clearly established 3. resolute; unchanging 4. persistent [a *fixed* idea]
—**fix·ed·ly** (fik′sid lē) *adv.*

**fix·ings** (fik′sinz) *n.pl.* [Colloq.] ac-
cessories or trimmings

**fix·i·ty** (fik′sə tē) *n.* the quality or
state of being fixed or steady

**fix·ture** (fiks′chər) *n.* [see FIX] 1. anything firmly in place 2. any attached
piece of equipment in a house, etc. 3.
a person long-established in a job, etc.

**fizz** (fiz) *n.* [echoic] 1. a hissing,
bubbling sound 2. an effervescent
drink —*vi.* fizzed, fizz′ing 1. to make
a bubbling sound 2. to effervesce

**fiz·zle** (fiz′′l) *vi.* -zled, -zling [< 
ME.] 1. *same as* FIZZ 2. [Colloq.] to
fail, esp. after a good start —*n.* 1. a
hissing sound 2. [Colloq.] a failure

**fjord** (fyôrd) *n. same as* FIORD

**fl.** 1. floor 2. [L. *floruit*] (he or she)
flourished 3. fluid

**Fla.,** FL Florida

**flab** (flab) *n.* [back-formation <
FLABBY] [Colloq.] sagging flesh

**flab·ber·gast** (flab′ər gast′) *vt.*
[18th-c. slang < ?] to dumbfound

**flab·by** (flab′ē) *adj.* -bi·er, -bi·est
[< FLAP] 1. limp and soft 2. weak —
**flab′bi·ly** *adv.* —**flab′bi·ness** *n.*

**flac·cid** (flak′sid, flas′id) *adj.* [< L.
*flaccus*] soft and limp; flabby

**flack** (flak) *n.* [< ?] [Slang] *same as*
PRESS AGENT

**‡fla·con** (flä kōn′) *n.* [Fr.] a small
flask with a stopper, for perfume, etc.

**flag¹** (flag) *n.* [< ? FLAG⁴, to flutter] a
cloth with colors, patterns, etc. used as
a symbol, as of a nation, or as a signal
—*vt.* flagged, flag′ging to signal as
with a flag; esp., to signal to stop
(often with *down*)

**flag²** (flag) *n.* [< ON. *flaga,* slab of
stone] a flagstone —*vt.* flagged,
flag′ging to pave with flagstones

**flag³** (flag) *n.* [ME. *flagge*] any of
various irises, or a flower or leaf of one

**flag⁴** (flag) *vi.* flagged, flag′ging [< ?
ON. *flakka,* flutter] 1. to become limp
2. to grow weak or tired

**flag·el·late** (flaj′ə lāt′) *vt.* -lat′ed,
-lat′ing [< L. *flagellum,* a whip] to
whip —**flag′el·la′tion** *n.*

**flag·on** (flag′ən) *n.* [< LL. *flasca*] a
container for liquids, with a handle,
narrow neck, spout, and, often, a lid

**flag′pole′** *n.* a pole on which a flag is
raised and flown: also **flag′staff′**

**fla·grant** (flā′grənt) *adj.* [< L.
*flagrare,* to blaze] glaringly bad; outrageous —**fla′gran·cy** (-grən sē),
**fla′grance** *n.* —**fla′grant·ly** *adv.*

**flag′ship′** *n.* the ship that carries the
commander of a fleet or squadron

**flag′stone′** *n.* a flat paving stone

**flail** (flāl) *n.* [< L. *flagellum,* a whip]
a farm tool for threshing grain by
hand —*vt., vi.* 1. to thresh with a
flail 2. to beat 3. to move (one's arms)
like flails

**flair** (fler) *n.* [< L. *fragrare,* to smell]
1. a natural talent; aptitude 2.
[Colloq.] a sense of style; dash

**flak** (flak) *n.* [G. acronym] 1. the fire
of antiaircraft guns 2. strong criticism: also **flack**

**flake** (flāk) *n.* [< Scand.] 1. a small,
thin mass 2. a piece split off; chip
—*vt., vi.* flaked, flak′ing 1. to form
into flakes 2. to peel off in flakes —
**flak′y** *adj.* -i·er, -i·est

**‡flam·bé** (flän bā′) *adj.* [Fr.] served
with a brandy or rum sauce set afire
to flame —*n.* a dessert so served

**flam·boy·ant** (flam boi′ənt) *adj.* [<
Fr. < L. *flamma,* a flame] 1. flamelike
or brilliant 2. ornate; too showy
—**flam·boy′ance** *n.* —**flam·boy′ant-
ly** *adv.*

**flame** (flām) *n.* [< L. *flamma*] 1. the
burning gas of a fire, appearing as a
tongue of light 2. the state of burning
with a blaze 3. a thing like a flame
4. an intense emotion 5. a sweetheart:
now humorous —*vi.* flamed, flam′ing
1. to burst into flame 2. to grow red
or hot 3. to become excited

**fla·men·co** (flə men′kō) *n.* [Sp.]
Spanish gypsy style of music or
dancing

**flame′out′** *n.* a failure of combustion
in a jet engine during flight

**flame thrower** a military weapon
that shoots flaming gasoline, oil, etc.

**fla·min·go** (flə miŋ′gō) *n., pl.* -gos,
-goes [Port.] a tropical wading bird
with long legs and pink or red feathers

**flam·ma·ble** (flam′ə b′l) *adj.* easily
set on fire; that will burn readily
—**flam′ma·bil′i·ty** *n.*

**Flan·ders** (flan′dərz) region in NW
Europe, in France, Belgium, & the
Netherlands

**flange** (flanj) *n.* [< ? ME.] a projecting rim on a wheel,
etc., as to hold it in
place or give it strength

**flank** (flaŋk) *n.* [<
OFr. *flanc*] 1. the
side of an animal
between the ribs and
the hip 2. the side of
anything 3. *Mil.* the
right or left side of a formation —*vt.*
1. to be at the side of 2. to attack, or
pass around, the side of (enemy troops)

**flank·en** (flaŋ′k′n, fläŋ′-) *n.* [Yid. <
G. *flanke,* flank] a thin cut of beef
from the forequarter, usually boiled

**flan·nel** (flan′′l) *n.* [prob. < W.
*gwlan,* wool] 1. a loosely woven cloth
of wool or cotton 2. [*pl.*] trousers, etc.
made of this

**flan·nel·ette, flan·nel·et** (flan′ə
let′) *n.* a soft, fleecy, cotton cloth

**flap** (flap) *n.* [ME. *flappe*] 1. anything
flat and broad hanging loose at one
end 2. the motion or sound of a
swinging flap 3. a slap 4. [Slang] a
commotion; stir —*vt., vi.* flapped,
flap′ping 1. to slap 2. to move back
and forth or up and down, as wings

**flap′jack′** *n.* a pancake

**flap·per** (flap′ər) *n.* 1. one that flaps
2. [Colloq.] in the 1920's, a bold,
unconventional young woman

**flare** (fler) *vi.* **flared, flar′ing** [ME. *fleare* < ?] **1.** *a)* to blaze brightly *b)* to burn unsteadily **2.** to burst out suddenly, as in anger (often with *up* or *out*) **3.** to curve outward, as a bell lip —*n.* **1.** a bright, unsteady blaze **2.** a brightly flaming light for signaling, etc. **3.** an outburst, as of emotion **4.** a curving outward

**flare′-up′** *n.* a sudden outburst of flame or of anger, trouble, etc.

**flash** (flash) *vi.* [ME. *flashen*, to splash] **1.** to send out a sudden, brief light **2.** to sparkle **3.** to come or pass suddenly —*vt.* **1.** to cause to flash **2.** to send (news, etc.) swiftly —*n.* **1.** a sudden, brief light **2.** a brief moment **3.** a sudden, brief display **4.** a brief news item sent by radio, etc. **5.** a gaudy display —*adj.* happening swiftly or suddenly —**flash′er** *n.*

**flash′back′** *n.* an interruption in the continuity of a story, etc. by telling or showing an earlier episode

**flash′bulb′** *n.* a bulb giving a brief, dazzling light, for taking photographs

**flash′cube′** *n.* a rotating cube containing flashbulbs in four sides

**flash′-for′ward** *n.* an interruption in the continuity of a story, etc. by telling or showing a future episode

**flash′ing** *n.* sheets of metal used to weatherproof roof joints or edges

**flash′light′** *n.* **1.** a portable electric light **2.** a brief, dazzling light for taking photographs, esp. indoors

**flash point** the lowest temperature at which vapor, as of an oil, will ignite with a flash

**flash′y** *adj.* **-i·er, -i·est** **1.** dazzling **2.** gaudy; showy —**flash′i·ness** *n.*

**flask** (flask) *n.* [< LL. *flasca*, bottle] **1.** any of various bottles used in laboratories, etc. **2.** a small, flat pocket container for liquor, etc.

**flat¹** (flat) *adj.* **flat′ter, flat′test** [< ON. *flatr*] **1.** having a smooth, level surface **2.** lying spread out **3.** broad, even, and thin **4.** absolute [a *flat* denial] **5.** not fluctuating [a *flat* rate] **6.** tasteless; insipid **7.** not interesting **8.** emptied of air [a *flat* tire] **9.** without gloss [*flat* paint] **10.** *Music* below true pitch —*adv.* **1.** in a flat manner or position **2.** exactly **3.** *Music* below true pitch —*n.* **1.** anything flat, esp. a surface, part, or expanse **2.** a deflated tire **3.** *Music* *a)* a note one half step below another *b)* the symbol (♭) for this —*vt., vi.* **flat′ted, flat′ting** to make or become flat —**flat′ly** *adv.* —**flat′ness** *n.* —**flat′tish** *adj.*

**flat²** (flat) *n.* [< Scot. dial. *flet*, floor] an apartment or suite of rooms

**flat′bed′, flat′-bed′** *n.* a truck, trailer, etc. having a platform without sides or stakes

**flat′boat′** *n.* a flat-bottomed boat for carrying freight on rivers, etc.

**flat′car′** *n.* a railroad freight car without sides or a roof

**flat′fish′** *n., pl.*: see FISH a flat-bodied fish with both eyes on the upper side, as the flounder

**flat′foot′** *n.* **1.** a condition of the foot in which the instep arch is flattened **2.** *pl.* **-foots** [Slang] a policeman —**flat′-foot′ed** *adj.*

**flat′i′ron** *n. same as* IRON (sense 2)

**flat′ten** (-′n) *vt., vi.* to make or become flat or flatter

**flat·ter** (flat′ər) *vt.* [< OFr. *flater*, to smooth] **1.** to praise insincerely **2.** to try to please, as by praise **3.** to make seem more attractive than is so **4.** to gratify the vanity of —**flat′ter·er** *n.* —**flat′ter·ing·ly** *adv.* —**flat′ter·y** *n.*

**flat′top′** *n.* [Slang] an aircraft carrier

**flat·u·lent** (flach′ə lənt) *adj.* [ult. < L. *flare*, to blow] **1.** having or producing gas in the stomach or intestines **2.** pompous —**flat′u·lence** *n.*

**flat′ware′** *n.* flat tableware

**flaunt** (flônt) *vi., vt.* [< ? dial. *flant*, to strut] to show off proudly or defiantly —**flaunt′ing·ly** *adv.*

**flau·tist** (flôt′ist, flout′-) *n.* [< It.] one who plays the flute; flutist

**fla·vor** (flā′vər) *n.* [ult. < L. *flare*, to blow] **1.** that quality of a substance that is a mixing of its characteristic taste and smell **2.** flavoring **3.** characteristic quality —*vt.* to give flavor to Brit. sp. **flavour** —**fla′vor·ful** *adj.* —**fla′vor·less** *adj.*

**fla′vor·ing** *n.* an essence, extract, etc. that adds flavor to food or drink

**flaw** (flô) *n.* [prob. < Scand.] **1.** a crack, as in a gem **2.** a defect; fault —**flaw′less** *adj.* —**flaw′less·ly** *adv.* —**flaw′less·ness** *n.*

**flax** (flaks) *n.* [OE. *fleax*] **1.** a slender, erect plant with delicate, blue flowers: its seed (**flaxseed**) is used to make linseed oil **2.** the threadlike fibers of this plant, spun into linen thread

**flax′en** (-′n) *adj.* **1.** of or made of flax **2.** pale-yellow

**flay** (flā) *vt.* [OE. *flean*] **1.** to strip off the skin of **2.** to criticize harshly

**flea** (flē) *n.* [OE. *fleah*] a small, wingless, jumping insect that is a blood-sucking parasite as an adult

**flea market** an outdoor bazaar dealing mainly in cheap, secondhand goods

**fleck** (flek) *n.* [ON. *flekkr*] a spot, speck, or flake —*vt.* to spot; speckle

**fled** (fled) *pt. & pp. of* FLEE

**fledg·ling** (flej′liŋ) *n.* [< ME. *flegge*, fit to fly] **1.** a young bird just able to fly **2.** a young, inexperienced person Also, chiefly Brit., **fledgeling**

**flee** (flē) *vi., vt.* **fled, flee′ing** [OE. *fleon*] **1.** to go swiftly or escape, as from danger, etc. **2.** to vanish

**fleece** (flēs) *n.* [OE. *fleos*] **1.** the wool covering a sheep or similar animal **2.** a soft, napped fabric —*vt.* **fleeced, fleec′ing** **1.** to shear the fleece from **2.** to swindle —**fleec′er** *n.*

**fleec′y** *adj.* **-i·er, -i·est** of or like fleece; soft and light —**fleec′i·ness** *n.*

**fleet¹** (flēt) *n.* [OE. *fleot*] **1.** a number of warships under one command **2.** any group of ships, trucks, etc. under one control

**fleet²** (flēt) *adj.* [< OE. *fleotan*, to float] swift; rapid —**fleet'ness** *n.*

**fleet'ing** *adj.* passing swiftly —**fleet'-ing-ly** *adv.* —**fleet'ing-ness** *n.*

**Flem·ish** (flem'ish) *adj.* of Flanders, its people, or their language —*n.* the West Germanic language of Flanders

**flesh** (flesh) *n.* [OE. *flæsc*] 1. the soft substance of the body; esp., the muscular tissue 2. the pulpy part of fruits and vegetables 3. meat 4. the body as distinct from the soul 5. all mankind 6. yellowish pink —**in the flesh** 1. alive 2. in person —**one's (own) flesh and blood** one's close relatives —**flesh'y** *adj.* -i·er, -i·est

**flesh'ly** *adj.* -li·er, -li·est 1. of the body; corporeal 2. sensual 3. fleshy

**fleur-de-lis** (flur'də lē') *n., pl.* **fleurs'-de-lis'** (-lēz') [< OFr. *flor de lis*, lit., flower of the lily] a lilylike emblem: the coat of arms of the former French royal family

**flew** (flōō) *pt.* of FLY¹

**flex** (fleks) *vt., vi.* [< L. *flectere*, to bend] 1. to bend (an arm, etc.) 2. to contract (a muscle)

**flex·i·ble** (flek'sə b'l) *adj.* 1. able to bend without breaking; pliant 2. easily influenced 3. adjustable to change —**flex'i·bil'i·ty** *n.*

**flib·ber·ti·gib·bet** (flib'ər tē jib'it) *n.* [< ?] a frivolous, flighty person

**flick¹** (flik) *n.* [echoic] a light, quick stroke —*vt.* to strike, throw, etc. with a light, quick stroke

**flick²** (flik) *n.* [< ff.] [Slang] a movie —**the flicks** a showing of a movie

**flick'er** *vi.* [OE. *flicorian*] 1. to move with a quick, light, wavering motion 2. to burn or shine unsteadily —*n.* 1. a flickering 2. a dart of flame or light

**fli·er** (flī'ər) *n.* 1. a thing that flies 2. an aviator 3. a bus, train, etc. with a fast schedule 4. a widely distributed handbill 5. [Colloq.] a reckless gamble

**flight¹** (flīt) *n.* [OE. *flyht*] 1. the act, manner, or power of flying 2. the distance flown 3. a group of things flying together 4. an airplane scheduled to fly a certain trip 5. a trip by airplane 6. a soaring above the ordinary [a *flight* of fancy] 7. a set of stairs, as between landings

**flight²** (flīt) *n.* [< OE. *fleon*, flee] a fleeing, as from danger

**flight'less** *adj.* not able to fly

**flight line** the part of an airfield where planes are parked and serviced

**flight strip** an emergency runway

**flight'y** *adj.* -i·er, -i·est 1. given to sudden whims; frivolous 2. slightly demented or silly —**flight'i·ness** *n.*

**flim·sy** (flim'zē) *adj.* -si·er, -si·est [< ?] 1. easily broken or damaged; frail 2. ineffectual [a *flimsy* excuse] —**flim'si·ly** *adv.* —**flim'si·ness** *n.*

**flinch** (flinch) *vi.* [< OFr. *flenchir*] to draw back from a blow or anything difficult or painful —*n.* a flinching

**fling** (fliŋ) *vt.* **flung**, **fling'ing** [< ON. *flengja*, to whip] 1. to throw, esp. with force; hurl 2. to put abruptly or violently 3. to move (one's arms,

legs, etc.) suddenly —*n.* 1. a flinging 2. a brief time of wild pleasures 3. a spirited dance 4. [Colloq.] a try

**Flint** (flint) city in SE Mich.: pop. 193,000

**flint** (flint) *n.* [OE.] a very hard, siliceous rock, usually gray, that produces sparks when struck against steel —**flint'y** *adj.* -i·er, -i·est

**flip¹** (flip) *vt.* **flipped**, **flip'ping** [echoic] 1. to toss with a quick jerk; flick 2. to snap (a coin) into the air, with the thumb 3. to turn or turn over —*vi.* 1. to move jerkily 2. [Slang] to lose self-control —*n.* a flipping —**flip one's lid** [Slang] to go berserk

**flip²** (flip) *adj.* **flip'per**, **flip'pest** *colloq. var. of* FLIPPANT

**flip'pant** (-ənt) *adj.* [prob. < FLIP¹] frivolous and disrespectful; saucy —**flip'pan·cy** *n., pl.* **-cies** —**flip'pant·ly** *adv.*

**flip'per** (-ər) *n.* [< FLIP¹] 1. a broad, flat limb adapted for swimming, as in seals 2. a paddlelike rubber device worn on each foot by swimmers

**flip side** [Colloq.] the reverse side (of a phonograph record), esp. the less popular side

**flirt** (flurt) *vt.* [< ?] to move jerkily [the bird *flirted* its tail] —*vi.* 1. to make love without serious intentions 2. to trifle or toy [to *flirt* with an idea] —*n.* 1. a quick, jerky movement 2. one who plays at love

**flir·ta·tion** (flar tā'shən) *n.* a frivolous love affair —**flir·ta'tious** *adj.*

**flit** (flit) *vi.* **flit'ted**, **flit'ting** [< ON. *flytja*] to move lightly and rapidly

**flitch** (flich) *n.* [OE. *flicce*] the cured and salted side of a hog; side of bacon

**float** (flōt) *n.* [< OE. *flota*, a ship] 1. anything that stays on the surface of a liquid, as a raft, a cork on a fishing line, etc. 2. a low, flat vehicle decorated for exhibit in a parade —*vi.* 1. to stay on the surface of a liquid 2. to drift easily on water, in air, etc. 3. to move about aimlessly —*vt.* 1. to cause to float 2. to put into circulation [to *float* a bond issue] 3. to arrange for (a loan) —**float'er** *n.*

**flock** (fläk) *n.* [OE. *flocc*] 1. a group of certain animals, as birds, sheep, etc., living or feeding together 2. a group of people or things —*vi.* to assemble or travel in a flock or crowd

**flock·ing** (fläk'iŋ) *n.* [< L. *floccus*, tuft of wool] 1. tiny fibers of wool, cotton, etc. applied to a fabric, wallpaper, etc. as a velvetlike surface: also **flock** 2. such a fabric, etc.

**floe** (flō) *n.* [< ON. *flo*, layer] *same as* ICE FLOE

**flog** (fläg, flôg) *vt.* **flogged**, **flog'ging** [< ? L. *flagellare*] to beat with a stick, whip, etc. —**flog'ger** *n.*

**flood** (flud) *n.* [OE. *flod*] 1. an overflowing of water on an area normally dry 2. the rising of the tide 3. a great outpouring, as of words —*vt.* 1. to cover or fill, as with a flood 2. to put too much water, fuel, etc. on or in —*vi.* 1. to gush out in a flood 2. to become flooded —**the Flood** *Bible* the great flood in Noah's time

**flood′light′** n. 1. a lamp that casts a broad beam of bright light 2. such a beam of light —vt. -light′ed or -lit′, -light′ing to illuminate by a floodlight

**flood tide** the rising tide

**floor** (flôr) n. [OE. flor] 1. the inside bottom surface of a room 2. the bottom surface of anything [the ocean floor] 3. a story in a building 4. the right to speak in an assembly —vt. 1. to furnish with a floor 2. to knock down 3. [Colloq.] a) to defeat b) to shock, confuse, etc.

**floor′board′** n. 1. a board in a floor 2. the floor of an automobile, etc.

**floor exercise** any gymnastic exercise, as a cart wheel, done without apparatus

**floor′ing** n. 1. a floor or floors 2. material for making a floor

**floor show** a show presenting singers, dancers, etc. in a nightclub, restaurant, etc.

**floor′walk′er** n. formerly, a person employed by a department store to direct customers, supervise sales, etc.: now usually **floor** (or **sales**) **manager**

**flop** (fläp) vt. flopped, flop′ping [var. of FLAP] to flap or throw noisily and clumsily —vi. 1. to move, drop, or flap around loosely or clumsily 2. [Colloq.] to fail —n. 1. the act or sound of flopping 2. [Colloq.] a failure —flop′py adj. -pi·er, -pi·est

**flop′house′** n. [Colloq.] a cheap hotel

**flop′o′ver** n. TV faulty reception when the picture seems to move repeatedly up or down the screen

**flo·ra** (flôr′ə) n. [L. < flos, a flower] the plants of a specified region or time

**flo′ral** (-əl) adj. of or like flowers

**Flor·ence** (flôr′əns) city in C Italy: pop. 454,000 —**Flor′en·tine′** (-ən tēn′) adj., n.

**flo·res·cence** (flô res′ns) n. [< L. flos, a flower] a blooming or flowering —flo·res′cent adj.

**flor·id** (flôr′id) adj. [< L. flos, a flower] 1. ruddy: said of the complexion 2. ornate; showy; gaudy

**Flor·i·da** (flôr′ə də) SE State of the U.S.: 58,560 sq. mi.; pop. 6,789,000; cap. Tallahassee —**Flo·rid·i·an** (flô rid′ē ən) adj., n.

**flor·in** (flôr′in) n. [< L. flos, a flower] any of various European or S. African silver or gold coins

**flo·rist** (flôr′ist) n. [< L. flos, a flower] one who grows or sells flowers

**floss** (flôs, fläs) n. [ult. < L. floccus, tuft of wool] 1. the short, downy waste fibers of silk 2. a soft, loosely twisted thread or yarn, as of silk, used in embroidery 3. a substance like this —floss′y adj. -i·er, -i·est

**flo·ta·tion** (flô tā′shən) n. the act or condition of floating

**flo·til·la** (flō til′ə) n. [Sp., dim. of flota, a fleet] 1. a small fleet 2. a fleet of boats or small ships

**flot·sam** (flät′səm) n. [< MDu. vloten, to float] the wreckage of a ship or its cargo found floating on the sea: chiefly in **flotsam and jetsam**

**flounce¹** (flouns) vi. flounced, flounc′ing [prob. < Scand.] to move with quick, flinging motions of the body, as in anger —n. a flouncing

**flounce²** (flouns) n. [< OFr. froncir, to wrinkle] a wide ruffle sewed to a skirt, sleeve, etc. —flounc′y adj.

**floun·der¹** (floun′dər) vi. [< ? FOUNDER] 1. to struggle awkwardly, as in deep snow 2. to speak or act in an awkward, confused manner

**floun·der²** (floun′dər) n. [< Scand.] any of various flatfishes caught for food, as the halibut

**flour** (flour) n. [orig. flower (i.e., best) of meal] 1. a fine, powdery substance produced by grinding and sifting grain, esp. wheat 2. any finely powdered substance —flour′y adj.

**flour·ish** (flur′ish) vi. [< L. flos, a flower] 1. to grow vigorously; thrive 2. to be at the peak of development, etc. —vt. to brandish (a sword, etc.) —n. 1. anything done in a showy way 2. a brandishing 3. decorative lines in writing 4. a musical fanfare

**flout** (flout) vt., vi. [< ? ME. flouten, play the flute] to mock or scorn —n. a scornful act or remark —flout′er n.

**flow** (flō) vi. [OE. flowan] 1. to move as a liquid does 2. to pour out 3. to move gently and smoothly 4. to proceed; issue 5. to be plentiful 6. to hang loose [flowing hair] —n. 1. a flowing 2. the rate of flow 3. anything that flows 4. the rising of the tide

**flow chart** a diagram showing the progress of work in a series of operations

**flow·er** (flou′ər, flour) n. [< L. flos] 1. the seed-producing structure of a flowering plant; blossom 2. a plant cultivated for its blossoms 3. the best or finest part —vi. 1. to produce blossoms 2. to reach the best stage —in flower flowering

**flow′er·pot′** n. a container to hold earth for a plant to grow in

**flow′er·y** adj. -i·er, -i·est 1. covered or decorated with flowers 2. full of ornate expressions and fine words —flow′er·i·ness n.

**flown** (flōn) pp. of FLY¹

**flu** (flōō) n. 1. short for INFLUENZA 2. popularly, a respiratory or intestinal infection caused by a virus

**flub** (flub) vt., vi. flubbed, flub′bing [< ? FL(OP) + (D)UB¹] [Colloq.] to bungle (a job, stroke, etc.) —n. [Colloq.] a blunder

**fluc·tu·ate** (fluk′choo wāt′) vi. -at′ed, -at′ing [< L. fluctus, a wave] to be continually varying in an irregular way —fluc′tu·a′tion n.

**flue** (flōō) n. [< ? OFr. fluie, a flowing] a shaft for the passage of smoke, hot air, etc., as in a chimney

**flu·ent** (flōō′ənt) adj. [< L. fluere, to flow] 1. flowing smoothly 2. able to write or speak easily, expressively, etc. —flu′en·cy n. —flu′ent·ly adv.

**fluff** (fluf) *n.* [? blend of *flue,* soft mass + PUFF] **1.** soft, light down **2.** a loose, soft mass, as of hair —*vt.* **1.** to shake or pat until loose or fluffy **2.** to bungle (one's lines), as in acting

**fluff′y** (-ē) *adj.* **-i·er, -i·est** like fluff; soft and light; feathery

**flu·id** (flōō′id) *adj.* [< L. *fluere,* to flow] **1.** that can flow as a liquid or gas does **2.** that can change rapidly or easily **3.** available for investment or as cash —*n.* a liquid or gas —**flu·id′i·ty** *n.* —**flu′id·ly** *adv.*

**fluke** (flōōk) *n.* [< ?] **1.** either of the pointed ends of an anchor, which catch in the ground **2.** a barb of a harpoon, etc. **3.** a lobe of a whale's tail **4.** [Colloq.] a stroke of luck

**flume** (flōōm) *n.* [< L. *flumen,* river] an inclined chute for carrying water, as to transport logs, furnish power, etc.

FLUKES OF A WHALE

**flung** (fluŋ) *pt. & pp.* of FLING

**flunk** (fluŋk) *vt., vi.* [< ?] [Colloq.] to fail, as in schoolwork

**flun·ky** (fluŋ′kē) *n., pl.* **-kies** [orig. Scot.] **1.** orig., a liveried manservant **2.** a toady **3.** a person with menial tasks Also **flunkey**

**flu·o·resce** (flōō′ə res′, floo res′) *vi.* **-resced′, -resc′ing** to show or undergo fluorescence

**flu·o·res·cence** (flōō′ə res′ns; floo res′-) *n.* [ult. < L. *fluor,* flux] **1.** the property of producing light when acted upon by radiant energy **2.** light so produced —**flu′o·res′cent** *adj.*

**fluorescent lamp** (or **tube**) a glass tube coated on the inside with a fluorescent substance that gives off light (**fluorescent light**) when mercury vapor in the tube is acted upon by a stream of electrons

**fluor·i·date** (flôr′ə dāt′, floor′-) *vt.* **-dat′ed, -dat′ing** to add fluorides to (a water supply) in order to reduce tooth decay —**fluor′i·da′tion** *n.*

**flu·o·ride** (floor′id, flōō′ə rīd′) *n.* any of various compounds of fluorine

**flu·o·rine** (floor′ēn; flōō′ə rēn′, -rin) *n.* [< L. *fluor,* flux] a greenish-yellow gaseous chemical element

**fluor·o·scope** (floor′ə skōp′) *n.* a machine for examining internal structures by viewing the shadows cast on a fluorescent screen by objects through which X-rays are directed

**flur·ry** (flur′ē) *n., pl.* **-ries** [< ?] **1.** a sudden gust of wind, rain, or snow **2.** a sudden commotion —*vt.* **-ried, -ry·ing** to confuse; agitate

**flush¹** (flush) *vi.* [blend of FLASH & ME. *flusshen,* fly up suddenly] **1.** to flow rapidly **2.** to blush or glow **3.** to be washed out with a sudden flow of water **4.** to start up from cover: said of birds —*vt.* **1.** to wash out with a sudden flow of water **2.** to make blush or glow **3.** to excite **4.** to drive (birds) from cover —*n.* **1.** a rapid flow, as of water **2.** a sudden, vigorous growth **3.** sudden excitement **4.** a blush; glow

**5.** a sudden feeling of heat, as in a fever —*adj.* **1.** well supplied, esp. with money **2.** abundant **3.** level or even (*with*) **4.** direct; full [a blow *flush* in the face] —*adv.* **1.** so as to be level **2.** directly

**flush²** (flush) *n.* [< L. *fluere,* to flow] a hand of cards all in the same suit

**flus·ter** (flus′tər) *vt., vi.* [prob. < Scand.] to make or become confused —*n.* a being flustered

**flute** (flōōt) *n.* [< Pr. *flaut*] **1.** a high-pitched wind instrument consisting of a long, slender tube with finger holes and keys **2.** a groove in the shaft of a column, etc. —**flut′ed** *adj.* —**flut′ing** *n.* —**flut′ist** *n.*

**flut·ter** (flut′ər) *vi.* [< OE. *fleotan,* to float] **1.** to flap the wings rapidly, without flying **2.** to wave, move, or beat rapidly and irregularly —*vt.* to cause to flutter —*n.* **1.** a fluttering movement **2.** an excited or confused state —**flut′ter·y** *adj.*

**flux** (fluks) *n.* [< L. *fluere,* to flow] **1.** a flowing **2.** a continual change **3.** any abnormal discharge from the body **4.** a substance used to help metals fuse together, as in soldering

**fly¹** (flī) *vi.* **flew, flown, fly′ing** [OE. *fleogan*] **1.** to move through the air by using wings, as a bird, or in an aircraft **2.** to wave or float in the air **3.** to move or pass swiftly **4.** to flee **5.** flied, fly′ing *Baseball* to hit a fly —*vt.* **1.** to cause to float in the air **2.** to operate (an aircraft) **3.** to flee from —*n., pl.* **flies 1.** a flap that conceals the zipper, etc. in a garment **2.** a flap serving as the door of a tent **3.** *Baseball* a ball batted high in the air **4.** *Theater* [*pl.*] the space above a stage —**fly into** to have a violent outburst of —**let fly (at) 1.** to hurl (at) **2.** to direct a verbal attack (at) —**on the fly** [Colloq.] while in a hurry

**fly²** (flī) *n., pl.* **flies** [OE. *fleoge*] **1.** any of a large group of insects with two transparent wings; esp., the housefly **2.** an artificial fly used as a fish lure

**fly·a·ble** *adj.* suitable for flying

**fly′by′,** **fly′-by′** *n., pl.* **-bys** a flight past a designated point or place by an aircraft or spacecraft

**fly′-by-night′** *adj.* financially irresponsible —*n.* an absconding debtor

**fly′-by-wire′** *adj.* of a system for controlling an airplane or spacecraft electronically, as from a computer

**fly′-cast′** *vi.* to fish by casting artificial flies

**fly′catch′er** *n.* a small bird, as the phoebe, that catches insects in flight

**fly′er** *n. same as* FLIER

**flying buttress** a buttress connected with a wall by an arch, serving to resist outward pressure

**flying colors** notable success

**flying fish** a fish with winglike fins used in gliding through the air

**flying saucer** *same as* UFO

**fly′leaf′** *n., pl.* **-leaves′** a blank leaf at the beginning or end of a book

**fly′pa′per** *n.* a sticky or poisonous paper set out to catch flies

**fly′speck′** *n.* **1.** a speck of fly excrement 2. any tiny spot or petty flaw

**fly/way/** *n.* a route flown by birds migrating to and from breeding grounds

**fly/weight/** *n.* a boxer who weighs 112 pounds or less

**fly/wheel/** *n.* a heavy wheel on a machine, for regulating its speed

**FM** frequency modulation

**foal** (fōl) *n.* [OE. *fola*] a young horse, mule, etc.; colt or filly —*vt., vi.* to give birth to (a foal)

**foam** (fōm) *n.* [OE. *fam*] 1. the froth formed on liquids by shaking, etc. 2. something like foam, as frothy saliva 3. a rigid or spongy cellular mass, made from liquid rubber, plastic, etc. —*vi.* to froth —**foam/y** *adj.*

**fob** (fäb) *n.* [prob. < dial. G. *fuppe*, a pocket] 1. a short ribbon or chain attached to a watch 2. any ornament worn on such a chain, etc.

**F.O.B., f.o.b.** free on board

**fo·cal** (fō'k'l) *adj.* of or at a focus

**focal length** the distance from the optical center of a lens to the point where the light rays converge

**fo'c's'le** (fōk's'l) *n.* *phonetic spelling of* FORECASTLE

**fo·cus** (fō'kəs) *n., pl.* **-cus·es, -ci** (-sī) [L., hearth] 1. the point where rays of light, heat, etc. come together; specif., the point where rays of reflected or refracted light meet 2. *same as* FOCAL LENGTH 3. an adjustment of this length to make a clear image [*move the lens into focus*] 4. any center of activity, attention, etc. —*vt.* **-cused** or **-cussed, -cus·ing** or **-cus·sing** 1. to bring into focus 2. to adjust the focal length of (the eye, a lens, etc.) so as to produce a clear image 3. to concentrate —**in focus** clear —**out of focus** blurred

**fod·der** (fäd'ər) *n.* [OE. *fodor*] coarse food for cattle, horses, etc., as hay

**foe** (fō) *n.* [OE. *fah*, hostile] an enemy; opponent

**foe·tus** (fēt'əs) *n. same as* FETUS

**fog** (fôg, fäg) *n.* [prob. < Scand.] 1. a large mass of water vapor condensed to fine particles, just above the earth's surface 2. a state of mental confusion —*vt., vi.* **fogged, fog/ging** to make or become foggy

**fog bank** a dense mass of fog

**fog/gy** *adj.* **-gi·er, -gi·est** 1. full of fog 2. dim; blurred 3. confused

**fog/horn/** *n.* a horn blown to give warning to ships in a fog

**fo·gy** (fō'gē) *n., pl.* **-gies** [< ?] one who is old-fashioned in ideas and actions: also **fo/gey,** *pl.* **-geys**

**foi·ble** (foi'b'l) *n.* [< Fr. *faible*, feeble] a small weakness in character

**foil¹** (foil) *vt.* [< OFr. *fuler*, trample] to keep from success; thwart

**foil²** (foil) *n.* [< L. *folium*, leaf] 1. a very thin sheet of metal 2. a person or thing that sets off or enhances another by contrast 3. [etym. unc.] a long, thin, blunted fencing sword

**foist** (foist) *vt.* [prob. < dial. Du.

*vuisten*, to hide in the hand] to get (a thing) accepted, sold, etc. by fraud, deception, etc.; palm off (*on* or *upon*)

**fold¹** (fōld) *vt.* [OE. *faldan*] 1. to double (material) up on itself 2. to draw together and intertwine [*fold your arms*] 3. to embrace 4. to wrap up; envelop —*vi.* 1. to be or become folded 2. [Colloq.] *a*) to fail, as a play, business, etc. *b*) to collapse —*n.* a folded part

**fold²** (fōld) *n.* [OE. *fald*] 1. a pen for sheep 2. a flock of sheep 3. a group of people, esp. in a church

**-fold** (fōld) [< OE. *-feald*] *a suffix meaning:* 1. having (a specified number of) parts 2. (a specified number of) times as many or as much

**fold/a·way/** *adj.* that can be folded together for easy storage

**fold/er** *n.* 1. a sheet of heavy paper folded for holding papers 2. a booklet of folded, unstitched sheets

**fo·li·age** (fō'lē ij) *n.* [< L. *folia* leaves, as of a plant or tree

**fo·li·o** (fō'lē ō') *n., pl.* **-os** [< L. *folium*, leaf] 1. a large sheet of paper folded once 2. the largest regular size of book, made of sheets so folded 3. the number of a page in a book

**folk** (fōk) *n., pl.* **folk, folks** [OE. *folc*] 1. *a*) a people; nation *b*) the common people of a nation 2. [*pl.*] people; persons —*adj.* of or originating among the common people —(**one's**) **folks** [Colloq.] (one's) family

**folk/lore/** *n.* the traditional beliefs, legends, etc. of a people

**folk/-rock/** *n.* rock-and-roll music using lyrics like those of a folk song

**folk song** a song made and handed down among the common people, or one like it of known authorship —**folk singer**

**folk/sy** (-sē) *adj.* **-si·er, -si·est** [Colloq.] friendly or sociable

**fol·li·cle** (fäl'i k'l) *n.* [< L. *follis*, bellows] any small sac, cavity, or gland [*a hair follicle*]

**fol·low** (fäl'ō) *vt.* [< OE. *folgian*] 1. to come or go after 2. to pursue 3. to go along [*follow the road*] 4. to take up (a trade, etc.) 5. to result from 6. to take as a model; imitate 7. to obey 8. to watch or listen to closely 9. to understand —*vi.* 1. to come or go after something else in place, time, etc. 2. to result —**follow out** (or **up**) to carry out fully —**follow through** to continue and finish a stroke or action

**fol·low·er** *n.* one that follows; specif., *a*) one who follows another's teachings; disciple *b*) an attendant

**fol·low·ing** *adj.* that follows; next after —*n.* a group of followers —*prep.* after [*following* dinner he left]

**fol·low-up/** *n.* a letter, visit, etc. that follows as a review or addition

**fol·ly** (fäl'ē) *n., pl.* **-lies** [see FOOL] 1. a lack of sense; foolishness 2. a foolish action or belief

**fo·ment** (fō ment′) *vt.* [< L. *fovere*, keep warm] to stir up (trouble); incite —**fo′men·ta′tion** *n.*

**fond** (fänd) *adj.* [< ME. *fonnen*, be foolish] **1.** tender and affectionate; loving or doting **2.** cherished [a *fond* hope] —**fond of** having a liking for —**fond′ly** *adv.* —**fond′ness** *n.*

**fon·dle** (fän′d'l) *vt.* -**dled**, -**dling** [< FOND] to caress or handle lovingly

**fon·due, fon·du** (fän′dōō′) *n.* [Fr. < *fondre*, melt] melted cheese, etc. used for dipping cubes of bread

**font**[1] (fänt) *n.* [< L. *fons*, spring] **1.** a bowl to hold baptismal water **2.** a basin for holy water **3.** a source

**font**[2] (fänt) *n.* [see FOUND[2]] *Printing* a complete assortment of type in one size and style

**food** (fōōd) *n.* [OE. *foda*] **1.** any substance, esp. a solid, taken in by a plant or animal to enable it to live and grow **2.** anything that nourishes

**food chain** *Ecol.* a sequence (as fox, rabbit, grass) of organisms in a community in which each feeds on the member below it

**food cycle** (or **web**) *Ecol.* all the individual food chains in a community

**food poisoning** the sickness resulting from eating food contaminated by bacteria, chemicals, etc.

**food stamp** any of the Federal stamps sold at less than face value to persons with low income for use in buying food

**food′stuff**′ *n.* any material amde into or used as food

**fool** (fōōl) *n.* [< L. *follis*, windbag] **1.** a silly person; simpleton **2.** a jester **3.** a dupe —*vi.* **1.** to act like a fool **2.** to joke **3.** [Colloq.] to meddle (*with*) —*vt.* to trick; deceive —**fool around** [Colloq.] to trifle —**fool′er·y** *n.*

**fool′har′dy** *adj.* -**di·er**, -**di·est** foolishly daring; reckless —**fool′har′di·ly** *adv.* —**fool′har′di·ness** *n.*

**fool′ish** *adj.* silly; unwise; absurd —**fool′ish·ly** *adv.* —**fool′ish·ness** *n.*

**fool′proof**′ *adj.* so harmless, simple, etc. as not to be mishandled, damaged, etc. even by a fool

**fools·cap** (fōōlz′kap′) *n.* [from a watermark of a jester's cap] a size of writing paper, 13 by 16 in. in the U.S.

**foot** (foot) *n.*, *pl.* **feet** [OE. *fot*] **1.** the end part of the leg, on which one stands **2.** the base or bottom [the *foot* of a page] **3.** a measure of length, equal to 12 inches: symbol ′ **4.** [Brit.] infantry **5.** a group of syllables serving as a unit of meter in verse —*vt.* **1.** to add (a column of figures) (often with *up*) **2.** [Colloq.] to pay (costs, etc.) —**foot it** [Colloq.] to dance or walk —**on foot** walking —**put one's foot down** [Colloq.] to be firm —**under foot** in the way

**foot′age** (-ij) *n.* measurement in feet

**foot′ball**′ *n.* **1.** a field game played with an inflated leather ball by two teams **2.** the ball used

**foot′bridge**′ *n.* a narrow bridge for pedestrians

**foot′ed** *adj.* having feet of a specified number or kind [four-*footed*]

**foot′fall**′ *n.* the sound of a footstep

**foot′hill**′ *n.* a low hill at the foot of a mountain or mountain range

**foot′hold**′ *n.* **1.** a place for the feet, as in climbing **2.** a secure position

**foot′ing** *n.* **1.** a secure placing of the feet **2.** a foothold **3.** a secure position **4.** a basis for relationship

**foot′less** *adj.* **1.** without feet **2.** without basis **3.** [Colloq.] clumsy; inept

**foot′lights**′ *n.pl.* a row of lights along the front of a stage floor —**the footlights** the theater or acting

**foot′lock′er** *n.* a small trunk, usually kept at the foot of a bed

**foot′loose**′ (-lōōs′) *adj.* free to go where or do as one likes

**foot′man** (-mən) *n.*, *pl.* -**men** a male servant who assists the butler

**foot′note**′ *n.* a note of comment or reference at the bottom of a page —*vt.* -**not′ed**, -**not′ing** to add a footnote or footnotes to

**foot′path**′ *n.* a narrow path for use by pedestrians only

**foot′print**′ *n.* a mark left by a foot

**foot′sore**′ *adj.* having sore or tender feet, as from much walking

**foot′step**′ *n.* **1.** the distance covered in a step **2.** the sound of a step **3.** a footprint

**foot′stool**′ *n.* a low stool for supporting the feet of a seated person

**foot′wear**′ *n.* shoes, boots, etc.

**foot′work**′ *n.* the manner of using the feet, as in boxing, dancing, etc.

**fop** (fäp) *n.* [ME. *foppe*, a fool] *same as* DANDY (*n.* 1) —**fop′per·y** *n.*, *pl.* -**ies** —**fop′pish** *adj.*

**for** (fôr, far) *prep.* [OE.] **1.** in place of [use a rope *for* a belt] **2.** in the interest of [acting *for* another] **3.** in favor of [vote *for* the levy] **4.** in honor of [a party *for* him] **5.** in order to have, get, keep, find, reach, etc. [walk *for* exercise, start *for* home] **6.** meant to be received by [flowers *for* a girl] **7.** suitable to [a room *for* sleeping] **8.** with regard to; concerning [an ear *for* music] **9.** as being [to know *for* a fact] **10.** considering the nature of [cool *for* July] **11.** because of [to cry *for* pain] **12.** to the length, amount, or duration of **13.** at the price of [two *for* a dollar] —*conj.* because

**for-** (fôr, far) [OE.] *a prefix meaning* away, apart, off [*forbid*, *forgo*]

**for·age** (fôr′ij, fär′-) *n.* [< Frank. *fodr*, food] **1.** food for domestic animals **2.** a search for food —*vi.* -**aged**, -**ag·ing** to search for food —*vt.* to get or take food from; raid —**for′ag·er** *n.*

**fo·ra·men** (fō rā′mən) *n.*, *pl.* -**ram′i·na** (-ram′ə nə), -**ra′mens** [L., a hole] a small opening, as in a bone

**for·ay** (fôr′ā) *vt.*, *vi.* [< OFr. *forrer*, to forage] to plunder —*n.* a raid in order to seize things

**for·bear**[1] (fôr ber′) *vt.* -**bore**′, -**borne**′, -**bear′ing** [see FOR- & BEAR[1]] to refrain from (doing, saying, etc.) —*vi.* **1.** to refrain **2.** to control oneself

**for·bear**[2] (fôr′ber′) *n. same as* FOREBEAR

**for·bear·ance** (-əns) *n.* **1.** the act of forbearing **2.** self-restraint

**for·bid** (fər bid′, fôr-) *vt.* -**bade**′ (-bad′) or -**bad**′, -**bid′den**, -**bid′ding**

[see FOR- & BID] 1. to order (a person) not to do (something); prohibit 2. to prevent

**for·bid′ding** adj. looking dangerous or disagreeable; repellent —**for·bid′ding·ly** adv.

**force** (fôrs) n. [< L. fortis, strong] 1. strength; power 2. physical coercion against a person or thing 3. the power to control, persuade, etc.; effectiveness 4. military power 5. any group of people organized for some activity [a sales force] 6. energy that causes or alters motion —vt. forced, forc′ing 1. to make do something by force; compel 2. to break open, into, or through by force 3. to take by force; extort 4. to impose as by force (with on or upon) 5. to produce as by force [she forced a smile] 6. to cause (plants, etc.) to develop faster by artificial means —**in force** 1. in full strength 2. in effect; valid —**force′less** adj.

**forced** (fôrst) adj. 1. compulsory [forced labor] 2. not natural; strained [a forced smile]

**force′-feed′** vt. -fed′, -feed′ing to feed as by a tube through the throat to the stomach

**force′ful** (-fəl) adj. full of force; powerful, vigorous, effective, etc. —**force′ful·ly** adv. —**force′ful·ness** n.

**for·ceps** (fôr′səps) n., pl. -ceps [L. < formus, warm + capere, to take] small pincers for grasping, pulling, etc.

**for·ci·ble** (fôr′sə b′l) adj. 1. done by force 2. having force —**for′ci·bly** adv.

**ford** (fôrd) n. [OE.] a shallow place in a stream, etc. that can be crossed by wading —vt. to cross at a ford

**Ford** (fôrd) 1. Gerald R., 1913– ; 38th president of the U.S. (1974–77) 2. Henry, 1863–1947; U.S. automobile manufacturer

**fore** (fôr) adv., adj. [OE.] at, in, or toward the front part, as of a ship —n. the front —interj. Golf a shout warning that one is about to hit the ball

**fore-** (fôr) [OE.] a prefix meaning: 1. before in time, place, etc. [forenoon] 2. the front part of [forearm]

**fore′-and-aft′** adj. from the bow to the stern; set lengthwise, as a rig

**fore·arm′**[1] n. the part of the arm between the elbow and the wrist

**fore·arm′**[2] vt. to arm in advance

**fore′bear′** (-ber′) n. [< FORE + BE + -ER] an ancestor

**fore·bode′** (-bōd′) vt., vi. -bod′ed, -bod′ing [< OE.] 1. to foretell; predict 2. to have a presentiment of (something evil) —**fore·bod′ing** n.

**fore·cast′** vt. -cast′ or -cast′ed, -cast′ing 1. to predict 2. to serve as a prediction of —n. a prediction —**fore′cast′er** n.

**fore·cas·tle** (fōk′s′l) n. 1. the upper deck of a ship in front of the foremast 2. the front part of a merchant ship, where the sailors' quarters are located

**fore·close′** (fôr klōz′) vt., vi. -closed′, -clos′ing [< OFr. fors, outside + clore, CLOSE[2]] to take away the right to redeem (a mortgage, etc.) —**fore·clo′sure** (-klō′zhər) n.

**fore·doom′** vt. to doom in advance

**fore′fa′ther** n. an ancestor

**fore′fin′ger** n. the finger nearest the thumb

**fore′foot′** n., pl. -feet′ either of the front feet of an animal

**fore′front′** n. 1. the extreme front 2. the position of most importance

**fore·go′**[1] vt., vi. -went′, -gone′, -go′ing to precede

**fore·go′**[2] vt. same as FORGO

**fore·go′ing** adj. previously said, written, etc.; preceding

**fore·gone′** adj. 1. previous 2. previously determined; inevitable

**fore′ground′** n. the part of a scene, etc. nearest the viewer

**fore′hand′** n. a stroke, as in tennis, made with the palm of the hand turned forward —adj. done as with a forehand

**fore·head** (fôr′id, -hed′; fär′-) n. the part of the face between the eyebrows and the hairline

**for·eign** (fôr′in, fär′-) adj. [< L. foras, out-of-doors] 1. situated outside one's own country, locality, etc. 2. of, from, or having to do with other countries 3. not characteristic or belonging to another country; not native

**for′eign-born′** adj. born in some other country; not native

**for′eign·er** n. a person from another country; alien

**foreign minister** a member of a governmental cabinet in charge of foreign affairs for his country

**fore·know′** vt. -knew′, -known′, -know′ing to know beforehand —**fore′knowl′edge** (-näl′ij) n.

**fore′leg′** n. either of the front legs of an animal

**fore′lock′** n. a lock of hair growing just above the forehead

**fore′man** (-mən) n., pl. -men 1. the chairman of a jury 2. the head of a group of workers —**fore′la′dy** n.fem.

**fore′mast′** n. the mast nearest the bow of a ship

**fore′most′** (-mōst′) adj. first in place, time, rank, etc. —adv. first

**fore′noon′** n. the time from sunrise to noon; morning

**fo·ren·sic** (fə ren′sik) adj. [< L. forum, marketplace] of or suitable for public debate —**fo·ren′si·cal·ly** adv.

**fore′or·dain′** vt. to ordain beforehand; predestine —**fore′or·di·na′tion** (-d′n ā′shən) n.

**fore′quar′ter** n. the front half of a side of beef or the like

**fore′run′ner** n. 1. a herald 2. a sign that tells or warns of something to follow 3. a predecessor; ancestor

**fore′sail′** (-sāl′, -səl) n. the main sail on the foremast of a schooner

**fore·see′** vt. -saw′, -seen′, -see′ing to see or know beforehand —**fore·see′a·ble** adj. —**fore·se′er** n.

**fore·shad′ow** vt. to indicate or suggest beforehand; presage

**fore·short·en** *vt.* in drawing, etc. to shorten some lines of (an object) to give the illusion of proper relative size

**fore·sight** *n.* 1. *a)* a foreseeing *b)* the power to foresee 2. prudent regard or provision for the future

**fore·skin** *n.* the fold of skin that covers the end of the penis

FORESHORTENED ARM

**for·est** (fôr'ist) *n.* [< L. *foris*, out-of-doors] a thick growth of trees, etc. covering a large tract of land —*vt.* to plant with trees

**fore·stall** (fôr stôl') *vt.* [< OE. *foresteall*, ambush] 1. to prevent by doing something ahead of time 2. to act in advance of; anticipate

**for·est·a·tion** (fôr'is tā'shən) *n.* the planting or care of forests

**for·est·er** *n.* one trained in forestry

**for·est·ry** *n.* the science of planting and taking care of forests

**fore·taste** *n.* a taste or sample of what can be expected

**fore·tell** *vt.* -told', -tell'ing to tell or indicate beforehand; predict

**fore·thought** *n.* 1. a thinking or planning beforehand 2. foresight

**for·ev·er** (fər ev'ər, fôr-) *adv.* 1. for always; endlessly 2. always; at all times Also **for·ev'er·more'**

**fore·warn** *vt.* to warn beforehand

**fore·word** *n.* an introductory remark or preface

**for·feit** (fôr'fit) *n.* [< OFr. *forfaire*, transgress] 1. a fine or penalty for some crime, fault, or neglect 2. the act of forfeiting —*adj.* lost or taken away as a forfeit —*vt.* to lose or be deprived of as a forfeit

**for·fei·ture** (-fə chər) *n.* 1. the act of forfeiting 2. anything forfeited

**for·gath·er** (fôr ga*th*'ər) *vi.* to come together; assemble; meet

**for·gave** (fər gāv') *pt.* of FORGIVE

**forge¹** (fôrj) *n.* [< L. *faber*, workman] 1. a furnace for heating metal to be wrought 2. a place where metal is heated and wrought; smithy —*vt., vi.* forged, forg'ing 1. to shape (metal) by heating and hammering 2. to form; shape 3. to imitate (a signature, etc.) fraudulently; counterfeit (a check, etc.) —forg'er *n.*

**forge²** (fôrj) *vt., vi.* forged, forg'ing [prob. alt. < FORCE] to move forward steadily: often with *ahead*

**for·ger·y** *n., pl.* -ies 1. the act or crime of forging documents, signatures, etc. to deceive 2. anything forged

**for·get** (fər get', fôr-) *vt., vi.* -got', -got'ten or -got', -get'ting [OE. *forgitan*] 1. to be unable to remember 2. to overlook or neglect —forget oneself to act in an improper manner —for·get'ta·ble *adj.*

**for·get'ful** *adj.* 1. apt to forget 2. heedless or negligent —for·get'ful·ly *adv.* —for·get'ful·ness *n.*

**for·get'-me-not'** *n.* a marsh plant

with small blue, white, or pink flowers

**for·give** (fər giv', fôr-) *vt., vi.* -gave', -giv'en, -giv'ing [OE. *forgiefan*] to give up resentment against or the desire to punish; pardon (an offense or offender) —for·giv'a·ble *adj.* —for·give'ness *n.* —for·giv'er *n.*

**for·giv'ing** *adj.* inclined to forgive —for·giv'ing·ly *adv.*

**for·go** (fôr gō') *vt.* -went', -gone', -go'ing [OE. *forgan*] to do without; abstain from; give up —for·go'er *n.*

**for·got** (fər gät', fôr-) *pt. & alt. pp.* of FORGET

**for·got'ten** (-'n) *pp.* of FORGET

**fork** (fôrk) *n.* [< L. *furca*] 1. an instrument of varying size with prongs at one end, as for eating food, pitching hay, etc. 2. something like a fork in shape, etc. 3. the place where a road, etc. divides into branches 4. any of these branches —*vi.* to divide into branches —*vt.* to pick up or pitch with a fork —**fork over** (or **out, up**) [Colloq.] to pay out; hand over —fork'ful *n., pl.* -fuls'

**fork'lift'** *n.* a device for lifting heavy objects by means of projecting prongs slid under the load

**for·lorn** (fər lôrn', fôr-) *adj.* [< OE. *forleosan*, lose utterly] 1. abandoned 2. wretched; miserable 3. without hope —for·lorn'ly *adv.*

**form** (fôrm) *n.* [< L. *forma*] 1. shape; general structure 2. the figure of a person or animal 3. a mold 4. a particular mode, kind, type, etc. [ice is a *form* of water, the *forms* of poetry] 5. arrangement; style 6. a way of doing something requiring skill 7. a customary or conventional procedure; formality; ceremony 8. a printed document with blanks to be filled in 9. condition of mind or body 10. a chart giving information about horses in a race 11. a changed appearance of a word to show inflection, etc. 12. type, etc. locked in a frame for printing —*vt.* 1. to shape; fashion 2. to train; instruct 3. to develop (habits) 4. to make up; constitute —*vi.* to be formed

**-form** (fôrm) [< L.] *a suffix meaning* having the form of [*cuneiform*]

**for·mal** (fôr'məl) *adj.* [< L. *formalis*] 1. according to fixed customs, rules, etc. 2. stiff in manner 3. *a)* designed for wear at ceremonies, etc. *b)* requiring clothes of this kind 4. done or made in explicit, definite form [a *formal* contract] —*n.* 1. a formal dance 2. a woman's evening dress —for'mal·ly *adv.*

**form·al·de·hyde** (fôr mal'də hīd') *n.* [FORM(IC) + ALDEHYDE] a colorless, pungent gas used in solution as a disinfectant and preservative

**for·mal·ism** *n.* strict attention to outward forms and customs

**for·mal·i·ty** (fôr mal'ə tē) *n., pl.* -ties 1. *a)* an observing of customs, rules, etc.; propriety *b)* excessive attention to convention; stiffness 2. a formal act; ceremony

**for·mal·ize** (fôr'mə līz') *vt.* -ized', -iz'ing 1. to shape 2. to make formal —for'mal·i·za'tion *n.*

**for·mat** (fôr′mat) n. [ < L. *formatus*, formed] 1. the shape, size, and arrangement of a book, etc. 2. the arrangement or plan of a presentation

**for·ma·tion** (fôr mā′shən) n. 1. a forming or being formed 2. a thing formed 3. the way in which something is formed; structure 4. an arrangement or positioning, as of troops

**form·a·tive** (fôr′mə tiv) adj. helping or involving formation or development

**for·mer** (fôr′mər) adj. [ME. *formere*] 1. previous; past 2. being the first mentioned of two

**for′mer·ly** adv. in the past

**for·mic** (fôr′mik) adj. [ < L. *formica*, ant] designating a colorless acid found in ants, spiders, etc.

**For·mi·ca** (fôr mīk′ə) a trademark for a laminated, heat-resistant plastic used for table and sink tops, etc.

**for·mi·da·ble** (fôr′mə də b'l) adj. [ < L. *formidare*, to dread] 1. causing dread, fear, or awe 2. hard to handle

**form′less** adj. shapeless; amorphous

**form letter** a standardized letter, usually one of many, with the date, address, etc. added separately

**For·mo·sa** (fôr mō′sə) former (Portuguese) name of TAIWAN

**for·mu·la** (fôr′myə lə) n., pl. **-las, -lae′** (-lē′) [L. < *forma*, form] 1. a fixed form of words, esp. a conventional expression 2. any conventional rule for doing something 3. a prescription or recipe 4. fortified milk for a baby 5. a set of symbols expressing a mathematical equation 6. *Chem.* an expression of the composition, as of a compound, using symbols and figures

**for·mu·late** (-lāt′) vt. **-lat′ed, -lat′ing** 1. to express in a formula 2. to express in a definite way —**for′mu·la′tion** n. —**for′mu·la′tor** n.

**for·ni·cate** (fôr′nə kāt′) vi. **-cat′ed, -cat′ing** [ < L. *fornix*, brothel] to commit fornication —**for′ni·ca′tor** n.

**for·ni·ca·tion** n. sexual intercourse between unmarried persons

**for·sake** (fər sāk′, fôr-) vt. **-sook′** (-sook′), **-sak′en, -sak′ing** [ < OE. *for-* + *sacan*, strive] 1. to give up (a habit, etc.) 2. to leave; abandon

**for·sooth** (fər sooth′, fôr-) adv. [ME. *forsoth*] [Archaic] indeed

**for·swear** (fôr swer′) vt. **-swore′, -sworn′, -swear′ing** to deny or renounce on oath —vi. to commit perjury

**for·syth·i·a** (fər sith′ē ə, fôr-) n. [ < W. *Forsyth*, 18th-c. Eng. botanist] a shrub with yellow, bell-shaped flowers in early spring

**fort** (fôrt) n. [ < L. *fortis*, strong] 1. a fortified place for military defense 2. a permanent army post

**forte¹** (fôrt) n. [ < OFr.: see prec.] that which one does particularly well

**for·te²** (fôr′tā, -tē) adj., adv. [It. < L. *fortis*, strong] *Music* loud

**forth** (fôrth) adv. [OE.] 1. forward; onward 2. out into view

**Forth** (fôrth), **Firth of** estuary of the Forth River in SE Scotland

**forth′com′ing** adj. 1. approaching; about to appear 2. ready when needed

**forth′right′** adj. direct and frank

**forth′with′** adv. without delay

**for·ti·fy** (fôr′tə fī′) vt. **-fied′, -fy′ing** [ < L. *fortis*, strong + *facere*, make] 1. to strengthen physically, emotionally, etc. 2. to strengthen against attack, as with forts 3. to support 4. to add alcohol to (wine, etc.) 5. to add vitamins, etc. to (milk, etc.) —**for′ti·fi·ca′tion** n. —**for′ti·fi′er** n.

**for·tis·si·mo** (fôr tis′ə mō′) adj., adv. [It., superl. of *forte*, strong] *Music* very loud

**for·ti·tude** (fôr′tə tood′) n. [ < L. *fortis*, strong] courage; patient endurance of trouble, pain, etc.

**Fort Knox** (näks) military reservation in N Ky.: U.S. gold depository

**Fort Lau·der·dale** (lô′dər dāl′) city on the SE coast of Fla.: pop. 140,000

**fort·night** (fôrt′nīt′) n. [ME. *fourte(n) niht*] [Chiefly Brit.] two weeks —**fort′night′ly** adv., adj.

**for·tress** (fôr′trəs) n. [ < L. *fortis*, strong] a fortified place; fort

**for·tu·i·tous** (fôr too′ə təs) adj. [ < L. *fors*, luck] 1. happening by chance 2. lucky —**for·tu′i·tous·ly** adv.

**for·tu·nate** (fôr′chə nit) adj. 1. having good luck 2. coming by good luck; favorable —**for′tu·nate·ly** adv.

**for·tune** (fôr′chən) n. [ < L. *fors*, chance] 1. luck; chance; fate 2. one's future lot, good or bad 3. good luck; success 4. wealth; riches

**for′tune·tell′er** n. one who professes to foretell the future of others —**for′tune·tell′ing** n., adj.

**Fort Wayne** (wān) city in NE Ind.: pop. 178,000

**Fort Worth** (wurth) city in N Tex.: pop. 393,000

**for·ty** (fôr′tē) adj., n., pl. **-ties** [OE. *feowertig*] four times ten; 40; XL —**the forties** the numbers or years, as of a century, from 40 through 49 —**for′ti·eth** (-ith) adj., n.

**fo·rum** (fôr′əm) n. [L.] 1. the public square of an ancient Roman city 2. an assembly, program, etc. for the discussion of public matters

**for·ward** (fôr′wərd) adj. [OE. *foreweard*] 1. at, toward, or of the front 2. advanced 3. onward 4. prompt; ready 5. bold; presumptuous 6. of or for the future —adv. toward the front; ahead —n. *Basketball, Hockey, etc.* a player in a front position —vt. 1. to promote 2. to send on

**for′wards** adv. *same as* FORWARD

**fos·sil** (fäs′'l) n. [ < L. *fossilis*, dug up] 1. any hardened remains of a plant or animal of a previous geological age, preserved in the earth's crust 2. a person with outmoded ideas or ways —adj. 1. of or like a fossil 2. dug from the earth [coal is a *fossil* fuel] 3. antiquated

---

fat, āpe, cär; ten, ēven; is, bīte; gō, hôrn, tōōl, look; oil, out; up, fur; chin; she; thin, then; zh, leisure; ŋ, ring; ə for a in ago; ', (ā′b'l); ë, Fr. coeur; ö, Fr. feu; Fr. mon; ü, Fr. duc; kh, G. ich, doch; ‡ foreign; < derived from

**fos·sil·ize'** (-ɪz') *vt., vi.* **-ized', -iz'- ing 1.** to change into a fossil **2.** to make or become outdated, rigid, etc. **—fos'sil·i·za'tion** *n.*

**fos·ter** (fôs'tər) *vt.* [OE. *fostrian*, nourish] **1.** to bring up; rear **2.** to help to develop; promote **—adj.** having a specified standing in a family but not by birth [a *foster* brother]

**fought** (fôt) *pt. & pp. of* FIGHT

**foul** (foul) *adj.* [OE. *ful*] **1.** stinking; loathsome **2.** extremely dirty **3.** indecent; profane **4.** wicked; abominable **5.** stormy [*foul* weather] **6.** tangled [a *foul* rope] **7.** not within the limits or rules set **8.** designating lines setting limits on a playing area **9.** dishonest **10.** [Colloq.] unpleasant, disagreeable, etc. **—adv.** in a foul manner **—n.** *Sports* a hit, blow, move, etc. that is foul (sense 7) **—vt. 1.** to make filthy **2.** to dishonor **3.** to obstruct [grease *fouls* drains] **4.** to entangle (a rope, etc.) **5.** to make a foul against, as in a game **6.** *Baseball* to bat (the ball) foul **—vi.** to be or become fouled **—foul up** [Colloq.] to bungle **—foul'ly** *adv.* **—foul'ness** *n.*

**fou·lard'** (fōō lärd') *n.* [Fr.] a lightweight fabric of silk, rayon, etc., usually printed with small figures

**foul'-up'** *n.* [Colloq.] a mix-up

**found¹** (found) *vt.* [< L. *fundus*, bottom] **1.** to set for support; base **2.** to bring into being; set up; establish **—found'er** *n.*

**found²** (found) *vt.* [< L. *fundere*, pour] **1.** to melt and pour (metal) into a mold **2.** to make by founding metal

**found³** (found) *pt. & pp. of* FIND

**foun·da·tion** (foun dā'shən) *n.* **1.** a founding or being founded; establishment **2.** *a)* an endowment for an institution *b)* such an institution **3.** basis **4.** the base of a wall, house, etc.

**foun·der** (foun'dər) *vi.* [< L. *fundus*, bottom] **1.** to stumble, fall, or go lame **2.** to fill with water and sink: said of a ship **3.** to break down

**found·ling** (found'liŋ) *n.* an infant of unknown parents, found abandoned

**found·ry** (foun'drē) *n., pl.* **-ries** a place where metal is cast

**fount** (fount) *n.* [< L. *fons*] **1.** [Poet.] a fountain; spring **2.** a source

**foun·tain** (foun't'n) *n.* [< L. *fons*] **1.** a natural spring of water **2.** a source **3.** *a)* an artificial jet or flow of water [a drinking *fountain*] *b)* the basin where this flows **4.** a reservoir, as for ink

**foun·tain·head'** *n.* the source, as of a stream

**fountain pen** a pen which is fed ink from its own reservoir

**four** (fôr) *adj., n.* [OE. *feower*] one more than three; 4; IV

**four'flush'er** (-flush'ər) *n.* [< FLUSH²] [Colloq.] one who bluffs

**four'-in-hand'** *n.* a necktie tied in a slipknot with the ends left hanging

**four'score'** *adj., n.* four times twenty; eighty

**four'some** (-səm) *n.* four people

**four'square'** *adj.* **1.** square **2.** unyielding; firm **3.** frank; forthright **—adv.** in a square form or manner

**four'teen'** (-tēn') *adj., n.* [OE. *feowertyne*] four more than ten; 14; XIV **—four'teenth'** *adj., n.*

**fourth** (fôrth) *adj.* [OE. *feortha*] preceded by three others in a series; 4th **—n. 1.** the one following the third **2.** any of the four equal parts of something; 1/4 **3.** the fourth forward gear

**fourth'-class'** *adj., adv.* of or in a class of mail including parcels over 1 lb. in weight and books, films, etc.

**fourth dimension** in the theory of relativity, time added as a dimension to those of length, width, and depth

**fourth estate** [often F- E-] journalism or journalists

**Fourth of July** *see* INDEPENDENCE DAY

**fourth world** [often F- W-] the poorest countries of the third world

**fowl** (foul) *n.* [OE. *fugol*] **1.** any bird **2.** any of the domestic birds used as food, as the chicken, duck, etc. **3.** the flesh of these birds used for food

**fox** (fäks) *n.* [OE.] **1.** a small, wild animal of the dog family, considered sly and crafty **2.** its fur **3.** a sly, crafty person **—vt.** to trick by slyness

**fox'glove'** *n.* common name for DIGITALIS (sense 1)

**fox'hole'** *n.* a hole dug in the ground as a protection against enemy gunfire

**fox'hound'** *n.* a hound with a keen scent, bred and trained to hunt foxes

**fox terrier** a small, active terrier with a smooth or wiry coat, formerly trained to drive foxes out of hiding

**fox trot** a dance for couples in 4/4 time, or music for it **—fox'-trot'** *vi.* **-trot'ted, -trot'ting**

**fox·y** (fäk'sē) *adj.* **-i·er, -i·est 1.** foxlike; crafty; sly **2.** [Slang] attractive or sexy: used esp. of women

**foy·er** (foi'ər, foi yā') *n.* [Fr. < L. *focus*, hearth] an entrance hall or lobby, as in a theater or hotel

**FPO** Fleet Post Office

**Fr. 1.** Father **2.** French **3.** Friday

**frab·jous** (frab'jəs) *adj.* [coined by Lewis Carroll] [Colloq.] splendid; fine

**fra·cas** (frā'kəs) *n.* [Fr. < It. *fracassare*, smash] a noisy fight; brawl

**frac·tion** (frak'shən) *n.* [< L. *frangere*, break] **1.** a small part, amount, etc. **2.** *Math. a)* a quantity less than a whole, expressed as a decimal *b)* a quantity with a numerator and denominator **—frac'tion·al** *adj.*

**frac·tious** (frak'shəs) *adj.* [< ?] **1.** unruly; rebellious **2.** irritable; cross

**frac·ture** (frak'chər) *n.* [< L. *frangere*, to break] a breaking or break, esp. of a bone **—vt., vi. -tured, -tur·ing** to break, crack, or split

**frag** (frag) *vt.* **fragged, frag'ging** [< *frag(mentation grenade)*] [Mil. Slang] to intentionally kill or wound (a superior officer), as with a hand grenade

**frag·ile** (fraj'l) *adj.* [< L. *frangere*, to break] easily broken or damaged; delicate **—fra·gil·i·ty** (frə jil'ə tē) *n.*

**frag·ment** (frag'mənt) *n.* [< L. *frangere*, to break] **1.** a part broken away **2.** an incomplete part, as of a novel **—vt., vi.** to break up **—frag'men·ta'tion** (-mən tā'shən) *n.*

**frag'men·tar'y** (-mən ter'ē) *adj.* consisting of fragments; not complete

**fra·grant** (frā'grənt) *adj.* [ < L. *fragrare*, emit a (sweet) smell] having a pleasant odor —**fra'grance** *n.*

**frail** (frāl) *adj.* [see FRAGILE] 1. easily broken 2. not robust; weak 3. easily tempted; morally weak —**frail'ly** *adv.*

**frail'ty** (-tē) *n.* 1. a being frail; esp., moral weakness 2. *pl.* -**ties** a fault arising from such weakness

**frame** (frām) *vt.* framed, fram'ing [prob. < ON. *frami*, profit] 1. to form according to a pattern; design [to *frame* laws] 2. to construct 3. to put into words [to *frame* an excuse] 4. to enclose (a picture, etc.) in a border 5. [Colloq.] to falsify evidence in order to make appear guilty —*n.* 1. body structure 2. the framework, as of a house 3. the structural case enclosing a window, door, etc. 4. an ornamental border, as around a picture 5. the way that anything is put together; form 6. mood; temper [good *frame* of mind] 7. one exposure in a filmstrip or movie film 8. *Bowling,* etc. a division of a game —*adj.* having a wooden framework [a *frame* house] —**fram'er** *n.*

**frame'-up'** *n.* [Colloq.] a secret, deceitful scheme, as a falsifying of evidence to make a person seem guilty

**frame'work'** *n.* 1. a structure to hold together or to support something 2. a basic structure, system, etc.

**franc** (fraŋk) *n.* [Fr. < L. *Francorum rex*, king of the French, on the coin in 1360] the monetary unit and a coin of France, Belgium, Switzerland, etc.

**France** (frans, fräns) country in W Europe: 212,821 sq. mi.; pop. 49,750,000

**fran·chise** (fran'chīz) *n.* [ < OFr. *franc*, free] 1. any special right or privilege granted by a government 2. the right to vote; suffrage 3. the right to sell a product or service —*vt.* -**chised**, -**chis·ing** to grant a franchise to

**Franco-** *a combining form meaning:* 1. of France or the French 2. France and

**fran·gi·ble** (fran'jə b'l) *adj.* [ < L. *frangere*, to break] breakable; fragile

**Frank** (fraŋk) *n.* a member of the Germanic tribes whose 9th-cent. empire extended over what is now France, Germany, and Italy

**frank** (fraŋk) *adj.* [ < OFr. *franc*, free] free in expressing oneself; candid —*vt.* to send (mail) free of postage —*n.* 1. the right to send mail free 2. a mark indicating this right — **frank'ly** *adv.* —**frank'ness** *n.*

**Frank·en·stein** (fraŋ'kən stīn') the title character in a novel (1818), creator of a monster that destroys him —*n.* popularly, the monster

**Frank·fort** (fraŋk'fərt) capital of Ky.: pop. 21,000

**frank·furt·er** (fraŋk'fər tər) *n.* [G. < *Frankfurt*, city in Germany] a smoked sausage of beef, beef and

pork, etc.; wiener: also [Colloq.] **frank**

**frank·in·cense** (fraŋ'kən sens') *n.* [see FRANK & INCENSE] a gum resin burned as incense

**Frank·ish** (fraŋ'kish) *n.* the West Germanic language of the Franks

**Frank·lin** (fraŋk'lin), **Benjamin** 1706–90; Am. statesman, scientist, inventor, & writer

**fran·tic** (fran'tik) *adj.* [ < Gr. *phrenitis*, madness] wild with anger, pain, worry, etc. —**fran'ti·cal·ly** *adv.*

**frap·pé** (fra pā') *n.* [Fr. < *frapper*, to strike] 1. a dessert made of partly frozen fruit juices, etc. 2. a beverage poured over shaved ice 3. [Eastern] a milk shake Also **frappe** (frap)

**fra·ter·nal** (frə tur'n'l) *adj.* [ < L. *frater*, brother] 1. of brothers; brotherly 2. designating or of a society organized for fellowship

**fra·ter·ni·ty** (frə tur'nə tē) *n.,* *pl.* -**ties** 1. brotherliness 2. a group of men joined together for fellowship, etc., as in college 3. a group of people with the same beliefs, work, etc.

**frat·er·nize** (frat'ər nīz') *vi.* -**nized'**, -**niz'ing** to associate in a friendly way —**frat'er·ni·za'tion** *n.*

‡**Frau** (frou) *n.,* *pl.* **Frau'en** (-ən) [G.] a wife: a title corresponding to *Mrs.*

**fraud** (frôd) *n.* [ < L. *fraus*] 1. deceit; trickery 2. *Law* intentional deception 3. a trick 4. an impostor

**fraud·u·lent** (frô'jə lənt) *adj.* 1. based on or using fraud 2. done or obtained by fraud —**fraud'u·lence** *n.* —**fraud'u·lent·ly** *adv.*

**fraught** (frôt) *adj.* [ < MDu. *vracht,* a load] filled or loaded (*with*) [a situation *fraught* with danger]

‡**Fräu·lein** (froi'līn) *n.,* *pl.* -**lein,** E. -**leins** [G.] an unmarried woman: a title corresponding to *Miss*

**fray¹** (frā) *n.* [ < AFFRAY] a noisy quarrel or fight; brawl

**fray²** (frā) *vt., vi.* [ < L. *fricare,* rub] 1. to make or become worn or ragged 2. to make or become weak

**fraz·zle** (fraz''l) *vt., vi.* -**zled,** -**zling** [ < dial. *fasle*] [Colloq.] 1. to wear to tatters 2. to tire out —*n.* [Colloq.] a being frazzled

**freak** (frēk) *n.* [ < ?] 1. an odd notion; whim 2. an unusual happening 3. any abnormal animal, person, or plant 4. [Slang] *a)* a drug user *b)* a devotee: buff [a chess *freak*] —**freak out** [Slang] 1. to have hallucinations, etc., as from a psychedelic drug 2. to become a hippie —**freak'ish** *adj.*

**freak'out'** *n.* [Slang] the act of freaking out

**freck·le** (frek''l) *n.* [ < Scand.] a small, brownish spot on the skin —*vt., vi.* -**led,** -**ling** to make or become spotted with freckles

**Fred·er·ick the Great** (fred'ər ik) 1712–86; king of Prussia (1740–86)

**free** (frē) *adj.* fre'er, fre'est [OE. *freo*] 1. not under the control or power of another; having liberty; independent **2.** having civil and political liberty **3.** able to move in any direction; loose **4.** not burdened by obligations, debts, discomforts, etc. **5.** not confined to the usual rules [*free* verse] **6.** not exact [a *free* translation] **7.** generous; profuse [a *free* spender] **8.** frank **9.** with no cost or charge **10.** exempt from taxes, duties, etc. **11.** clear of obstructions [a *free* road] **12.** not fastened [a rope's *free* end] —*adv.* **1.** without cost **2.** in a free manner —*vt.* **freed, free'ing** to make free; specif., *a*) to release from bondage or arbitrary power, obligation, etc. *b*) to clear of obstruction, etc. —**free from** (or **of**) without —**make free with** to use freely —*free'ly adv.* —*free'ness n.*

**free·bie, free·by** (frē'bē) *n., pl.* -**bies** [Slang] something given free of charge, as a theater ticket

**free'boot'er** (-bōōt'ər) *n.* [< Du. *frij*, free + *buit*, plunder] a pirate

**freed'man** (frēd'mən) *n., pl.* -**men** a man legally freed from slavery

**free·dom** (frē'dəm) *n.* **1.** a being free; esp., *a*) independence *b*) civil or political liberty *c*) exemption from an obligation, discomfort, etc. *d*) a being able to act, use, etc. freely *e*) ease of movement *f*) frankness **2.** a right or privilege

**free fall** the unchecked fall of a body through the air, as of a parachutist before the parachute opens

**free flight** the flight of a rocket after the fuel supply has been used up or shut off —**free'-flight'** *adj.*

**free'-for-all'** *n.* a disorganized, general fight; brawl —*adj.* open to all

**free'hand'** *adj.* drawn by hand without the use of instruments, etc.

**free'hold'** *n.* an estate held for life or with the right to pass it on through inheritance —**free'hold'er** *n.*

**free lance** a writer, actor, etc. who sells his services to individual buyers —**free'-lance'** (-lans') *adj., vi.*

**free'load'er** (-lō'dər) *n.* [Colloq.] one who habitually imposes on others for free food, etc. —**free'load'** *vi.*

**free'man** (-mən) *n., pl.* -**men 1.** a person not in slavery **2.** a citizen

**Free·ma·son** (frē'mās''n) *n.* a member of an international secret society based on brotherliness and mutual aid —**Free'ma'son·ry** *n.*

**free on board** delivered (by the seller) aboard the train, ship, etc. at no extra charge

**free'stone'** *n.* a peach, etc. in which the pit does not cling to the pulp

**free'think'er** *n.* one who forms his opinions about religion independently

**free trade** trade conducted without protective tariffs, quotas, etc.

**free university** a loosely organized forum for studying subjects not normally offered at universities

**free'way'** *n.* a multiple-lane divided highway with fully controlled access

**free'will'** *adj.* voluntary

**freeze** (frēz) *vi.* **froze, fro'zen, freez'-ing** [OE. *freosan*] **1.** to be formed into, or become covered with, ice **2.** to

become very cold **3.** to be damaged or killed by cold **4.** to become motionless **5.** to be made speechless by strong emotion **6.** to become formal or unfriendly —*vt.* **1.** to form into, or cover with, ice **2.** to make very cold **3.** to preserve (food) by rapid refrigeration **4.** to kill or damage by cold **5.** to make motionless **6.** to make formal or unfriendly **7.** *a*) to fix (prices, etc.) at a given level by authority *b*) to make (funds, etc.) unavailable to the owners —*n.* **1.** a freezing or being frozen **2.** a period of freezing weather —**freeze out 1.** to die out through freezing, as plants **2.** [Colloq.] to keep out by a cold manner, competition, etc. —**freeze over** to become covered with ice —**freez'a·ble** *adj.*

**freeze'-dry'** *vt.* -**dried', -dry'ing** to quick-freeze (food, etc.) and then dry under high vacuum

**freez'er** *n.* **1.** a refrigerator, compartment, etc. for freezing and storing perishable food **2.** a machine for making ice cream

**freight** (frāt) *n.* [< MDu. *vracht*, a load] **1.** the transporting of goods by water, land, or air **2.** the cost for this **3.** the goods transported **4.** a railroad train for transporting goods: in full **freight train** —*vt.* **1.** to load with freight **2.** to send by freight

**freight'er** *n.* a ship for freight

**Fre·mont** (frē'mänt) city in W Calif. on San Francisco Bay: pop., 101,000

**French** (french) *adj.* of France, its people, language, etc. —*n.* the language of France —**the French** the French people —**French'man** (-mən) *n., pl.* -**men**

**French cuff** a shirt-sleeve cuff turned back and fastened with a link

**French doors** a pair of doors hinged at the sides to open in the middle

**French dressing** a salad dressing made of vinegar, oil, and seasonings

**French fried** fried in hot, deep fat

**French fries** [Colloq.] potatoes cut into strips and then French fried

**French Guiana** Fr. overseas department in NE S. America

**French horn** a brass-wind instrument: its coiled tube ends in a flaring bell

**French leave** an unauthorized departure

**French toast** sliced bread dipped in a batter of egg and milk and fried

**fre·net·ic** (frə net'ik) *adj.* [see PHRENETIC] frantic; frenzied —**fre·net'i·cal·ly** *adv.*

**fren·zy** (fren'zē) *n., pl.* -**zies** [< Gr. FRENCH HORN *phrenitis*, madness] wild excitement; delirium

**fre·quen·cy** (frē'kwən sē) *n., pl.* -**cies 1.** frequent occurrence **2.** the number of times any event recurs in a given period **3.** *Physics* the number of oscillations or cycles per unit of time

**frequency modulation** the variation of the frequency of the transmitting radio wave in accordance with the signal transmitted

**fre·quent** (frē'kwənt; *for v. usually* frē kwent') *adj.* [< L. *frequens*, crowded] 1. occurring often 2. constant; habitual —*vt.* to go to or be at or in habitually —**fre·quent·ly** *adv.*

**fres·co** (fres'kō) *n., pl.* -**coes**, -**cos** [It., fresh] a painting with water colors on wet plaster

**fresh¹** (fresh) *adj.* [OE. *fersc*] 1. recently made, grown, etc. [*fresh* coffee] 2. not salted, pickled, etc. 3. not spoiled 4. not tired; lively 5. not worn, soiled, faded, etc. 6. new; recent 7. inexperienced 8. cool and refreshing [a *fresh* spring day] 9. brisk: said of wind 10. not salt: said of water —**fresh'ly** *adv.* —**fresh'ness** *n.*

**fresh²** (fresh) *adj.* [< G. *frech*, bold] [Slang] bold; impertinent; impudent

**fresh'en** (-ən) *vt., vi.* to make or become fresh —**freshen up** to bathe, put on fresh clothes, etc.

**fresh·et** (fresh'it) *n.* a flooding of a stream, as because of melting snow

**fresh'man** (-mən) *n., pl.* -**men** 1. a beginner 2. a person in his first year in college, Congress, etc.

**fresh'wa·ter** *adj.* 1. of or living in water that is not salty 2. sailing only on inland waters

**Fres·no** (frez'nō) city in C Calif.: pop. 166,000

**fret¹** (fret) *vt., vi.* fret'ted, fret'ting [OE. *fretan*, devour] 1. to gnaw, wear away, rub, etc. 2. to ripple or ruffle 3. to irritate or be irritated; worry —*n.* irritation; worry —**fret'ter** *n.*

**fret²** (fret) *n.* [< OFr. *frette*, a band] any of the ridges on the fingerboard of a banjo, guitar, etc.

**fret³** (fret) *n.* [ME. *frette*] a running design of interlacing small bars —*vt.* fret'ted, fret'ting to furnish with frets

FRETS

**fret'ful** *adj.* irritable; peevish —**fret'ful·ly** *adv.* —**fret'ful·ness** *n.*

**fret'work'** *n.* decorative carving or openwork, as of interlacing lines

**Freud** (froid), **Sigmund** 1856–1939; Austrian psychiatrist: founder of psychoanalysis —**Freud'i·an** *adj., n.*

**fri·a·ble** (frī'ə b'l) *adj.* [Fr. < L. *friare*, to rub] easily crumbled

**fri·ar** (frī'ər) *n.* [< L. *frater*, brother] R.C.Ch. a member of certain religious orders

**fric·as·see** (frik'ə sē', frik'ə sē') *n.* [< Fr. *fricasser*, cut up and fry] meat cut into pieces and stewed —*vt.* -**seed'**, -**see'ing** to prepare in this way

**fric·tion** (frik'shən) *n.* [< L. *fricare*, to rub] 1. a rubbing of one object against another 2. conflict, as because of differing opinions 3. the resistance to motion of surfaces that touch —**fric'tion·al** *adj.*

**Fri·day** (frī'dē, -dā) *n.* [< *Frig*, Germanic goddess] 1. the sixth day of the week 2. [< the devoted servant of ROBINSON CRUSOE] a faithful helper: usually **man** (or **girl**) **Friday**

**fried** (frīd) *pt. & pp.* of FRY¹

**fried'cake'** *n.* a small cake fried in deep fat; doughnut or cruller

**friend** (frend) *n.* [ME. *freond*] 1. a person whom one knows well and is fond of 2. an ally, supporter, or sympathizer 3. [F-] a member of the Society of Friends; Quaker —**make** (or **be**) **friends with** to become (or be) a friend of —**friend'less** *adj.*

**friend'ly** *adj.* -**li·er**, -**li·est** 1. of or like a friend; kindly 2. not hostile; amicable 3. supporting; helping —**friend'li·ly** *adv.* —**friend'li·ness** *n.*

**friend'ship** *n.* 1. the state of being friends 2. friendly feeling

**frieze** (frēz) *n.* [< ML. *frisium*] a horizontal band with designs or carvings along a wall or around a room

**frig·ate** (frig'it) *n.* [< It. *fregata*] a fast, medium-sized sailing warship of the 18th and early 19th cent.

**fright** (frīt) *n.* [OE. *fyrhto*] 1. sudden fear; alarm 2. something unsightly

**fright'en** *vt.* 1. to make suddenly afraid; scare 2. to force (*away, off*, etc.) by scaring —**fright'en·ing·ly** *adv.*

**fright'ful** *adj.* 1. causing fright; alarming 2. shocking; terrible 3. [Colloq.] *a*) unpleasant *b*) great —**fright'ful·ly** *adv.*

**frig·id** (frij'id) *adj.* [< L. *frigus*, coldness] 1. extremely cold 2. not warm or friendly 3. sexually unresponsive: said of a woman —**fri·gid'i·ty** *n.* —**frig'id·ly** *adv.*

**Frigid Zone** either of two zones (**North** or **South Frigid Zone**) between the polar circles and the poles

**frill** (fril) *n.* [< ?] 1. any unnecessary ornament 2. a ruffle —**frill'y** *adj.*

**fringe** (frinj) *n.* [< L. *fimbria*] 1. a border of threads, etc. hanging loose, often tied in bunches 2. an outer edge; border 3. a marginal or minor part —*vt.* **fringed**, **fring'ing** to be or make a fringe for —*adj.* 1. at the outer edge 2. additional 3. minor

**fringe benefit** payment other than wages, as in pension, insurance, etc.

**frip·per·y** (frip'ər ē) *n., pl.* -**ies** [< OFr. *frepe*, rag] 1. cheap, gaudy clothes 2. showy display in dress, etc.

**Fris·bee** (friz'bē) [after "Mother Frisbie's" cookie jar lids] *a trademark for* a plastic, saucer-shaped disk tossed back and forth in a game —*n.* [f-] such a disk

**fri·sé** (fri zā') *n.* [Fr. < *friser*, to curl] an upholstery fabric with a thick pile of loops

**Fri·sian** (frizh'ən) *n.* the West Germanic language of an island chain (**Frisian Islands**) along the coast of the Netherlands, West Germany, & Denmark

**frisk** (frisk) *vi.* [< OHG. *frisc*, lively] to frolic —*vt.* [Slang] to search (a person) for weapons, etc. by passing the hands quickly over his clothing

**frisk′y** adj. **-i·er**, **-i·est** lively; frolicsome —**frisk′i·ly** adv. —**frisk′i·ness** n.

**frit·ter¹** (frit′ər) vt. [< L. *frangere*, to break] to waste (money, time, etc.) bit by bit (usually with *away*)

**frit·ter²** (frit′ər) n. [< VL. *frigere*, to fry] a small cake of fried batter, usually containing corn, fruit, etc.

**friv·o·lous** (friv′ə ləs) adj. [< L. *frivolus*] 1. of little value; trivial 2. silly and light-minded; flighty —**fri·vol·i·ty** (fri väl′ə tē) n., pl. **-ties** —**friv′o·lous·ly** adv.

**frizz, friz** (friz) vt., vi. **frizzed, friz′zing** [Fr. *friser*] to form into small, tight curls —n. hair, etc. that is frizzed —**friz′zly, friz′zy** adj.

**friz·zle¹** (friz′'l) vt., vi. **-zled, -zling** [< FRY¹] to sizzle, as in frying

**friz·zle²** (friz′'l) n., vt., vi. **-zled, -zling** same as FRIZZ

**fro** (frō) adv. [< ON. *frā*] backward; back: now only in *to and fro*: see under TO

**frock** (fräk) n. [< OFr. *froc*] 1. a robe worn by friars, monks, etc. 2. a dress

**frog** (frôg, fräg) n. [OE. *frogga*] 1. a tailless, leaping amphibian with long hind legs and webbed feet 2. a fancy braided loop used to fasten clothing —**frog in the throat** hoarseness

**frog′man′** (-man′) n., pl. **-men** (-mən) one trained and equipped for underwater demolition, exploration, etc.

**frol·ic** (fräl′ik) n. [< MDu. *vrō*, merry] 1. a lively party or game 2. merriment; fun —vi. **-icked, -icking** 1. to make merry; have fun 2. to romp about; gambol —**frol′ick·er** n.

**frol′ic·some** (-səm) adj. playful; gay

**from** (frum, främ) prep. [OE.] 1. beginning at; starting with [*from* noon to midnight] 2. out of [*from* her purse] 3. originating with [a letter *from* me] 4. out of the possibility or use of [kept *from* going] 5. as not being like [to know good *from* evil] 6. because of [to tremble *from* fear]

**frond** (fränd) n. [L. *frons*, leafy branch] the leaf of a fern or palm

**front** (frunt) n. [< L. *frons*, forehead] 1. a) outward behavior [a bold *front*] b) [Colloq.] an appearance of social standing, wealth, etc. 2. the part facing forward 3. the first part; beginning 4. a forward or leading position 5. the land bordering a lake, street, etc. 6. the advanced battle area in warfare 7. an area of activity [the home *front*] 8. a person or group used to hide another's activity 9. *Meteorology* the boundary between two differing air masses —adj. at, to, in, on, or of the front —vt., vi. 1. to face 2. to serve as a front (*for*) —**in front of** before —**front′al** adj.

**front′age** (-ij) n. 1. the front part of a building 2. the front boundary line of a lot or the length of this line 3. land bordering a front, etc.

**fron·tier** (frun tir′) n. [see FRONT] 1. the border between two countries

2. the part of a country which borders an unexplored region 3. any new field of learning, etc. —adj. of or on the frontier —**fron·tiers′man** (-tirz′mən) n., pl. **-men**

**fron·tis·piece** (frun′tis pēs′) n. [< L. *frons*, front + *specere*, to look] an illustration facing the title page of a book

**front office** the management or administration, as of a company

**front′-run′ner** n. a leading contestant

**frost** (frôst, fräst) n. [OE. < *freosan*, freeze] 1. a temperature low enough to cause freezing 2. frozen dew or vapor —vt. 1. to cover with frost 2. to cover with frosting 3. to give a frostlike, opaque surface to (glass) —**frost′y** adj. **-i·er, -i·est** —**frost′i·ness** n.

**Frost** (frôst, fräst), Robert (Lee) 1874–1963; U.S. poet

**frost′bite′** vt. **-bit′, -bit′ten, -bit′ing** to injure the tissues of (a body part) by exposure to intense cold —n. injury caused by such exposure

**frost′ing** n. 1. a mixture of sugar, butter, etc. for covering a cake; icing 2. a dull finish on glass, metal, etc.

**froth** (frôth, fräth) n. [< ON. *frotha*] 1. foam 2. foaming saliva 3. light, trifling talk, ideas, etc. —vi. to foam —**froth′y** adj. **-i·er, -i·est**

**frou-frou** (frōō′frōō′) n. [Fr.] [Colloq.] excessive ornateness

**fro·ward** (frō′ərd, -wərd) adj. [see FRO & -WARD] not easily controlled; willful; contrary —**fro′ward·ness** n.

**frown** (froun) vi. [< OFr. *froigne*, sullen face] 1. to contract the brows, as in displeasure 2. to show disapproval (with *on* or *upon*) —n. a frowning

**frow·zy** (frou′zē) adj. **-zi·er, -zi·est** [< ?] dirty and untidy; slovenly —**frow′zi·ly** adv. —**frow′zi·ness** n.

**froze** (frōz) pt. of FREEZE

**fro·zen** (-'n) pp. of FREEZE —adj. 1. turned into or covered with ice 2. damaged or killed by freezing 3. preserved by freezing 4. made motionless 5. kept at a fixed level 6. not readily convertible into cash

**fruc·ti·fy** (fruk′tə fī′) vi., vt. **-fied′, -fy′ing** [< L. *fructificare*] to bear or cause to bear fruit

**fruc·tose** (fruk′tōs, frook′-) n. [< L. *fructus*, fruit + -OSE¹] a sugar found in sweet fruit, honey, etc.

**fru·gal** (frōō′g'l) adj. [< L. *frugi*, fit for food] 1. not wasteful; thrifty 2. inexpensive or meager —**fru·gal′i·ty** (-gal′ə tē) n. —**fru′gal·ly** adv.

**fruit** (frōōt) n. [< L. *fructus*] 1. any plant product, as grain, vegetables, etc.: *usually used in pl.* 2. a) a sweet, edible plant structure, containing the seeds inside a juicy pulp b) *Bot.* the seed-bearing part of any plant 3. the result or product of any action

**fruit′cake′** n. a rich cake containing nuts, preserved fruit, citron, etc.

**fruit′ful** adj. 1. bearing much fruit 2. productive; prolific 3. profitable

**fru·i·tion** (frōō ish′ən) n. 1. the bearing of fruit 2. a coming to fulfillment; realization

**fruit·less** *adj.* **1.** without results; unsuccessful **2.** bearing no fruit; sterile; barren —**fruit′less·ly** *adv.* —**fruit′less·ness** *n.*

**frump** (frump) *n.* [prob. < Du. *rompelen*, rumple] a dowdy woman —**frump′ish, frump′y** *adj.*

**frus·trate** (frus′trāt) *vt.* -**trat·ed**, -**trat·ing** [< L. *frustra*, in vain] **1.** to cause to have no effect **2.** to prevent from achieving a goal or gratifying a desire —**frus·tra′tion** *n.*

**fry**[1] (frī) *vt., vi.* fried, fry′ing [< L. *frigere*] to cook over direct heat, usually in hot fat —*n., pl.* fries **1.** [*pl.*] fried potatoes **2.** a social gathering at which food is fried and eaten

**fry**[2] (frī) *n., pl.* fry [< OFr. *freier*, to spawn] young fish —**small fry 1.** children **2.** insignificant people

**fry′er** (-ər) *n.* **1.** a utensil for deep-frying foods **2.** a chicken young and tender enough to fry

**ft.** foot; feet

**FTC** Federal Trade Commission

**fuch·sia** (fyōō′shə) *n.* [< L. *Fuchs* (1501–66), G. botanist] **1.** a shrubby plant with pink, red, or purple flowers **2.** purplish red

**fud·dle** (fud′'l) *vt.* -**dled**, -**dling** [< ?] to confuse or stupefy as with alcoholic liquor —*n.* a fuddled state

**fud·dy-dud·dy** (fud′ē dud′ē) *n., pl.* -**dies** [Slang] a fussy, critical, or old-fashioned person

**fudge** (fuj) *n.* [< ?] a soft candy made of butter, milk, sugar, flavoring, etc. —*vi.* **1.** to refuse to commit oneself; hedge **2.** to be dishonest; cheat

**fu·el** (fyōō′əl) *n.* [ult. < L. *focus*, fireplace] **1.** coal, oil, gas, wood, etc., burned to supply heat or power **2.** material from which atomic energy can be obtained **3.** anything that intensifies strong feeling —*vt., vi.* -**eled** or -**elled**, -**el·ing** or -**el·ling** to supply with or get fuel

**fuel cell** a device that converts chemical energy directly into electrical energy

**fu·gi·tive** (fyōō′jə tiv) *adj.* [< L. *fugere*, flee] **1.** fleeing, as from danger or justice **2.** fleeting —*n.* one who is fleeing from justice, etc.

**fugue** (fyōōg) *n.* [< L. *fugere*, flee] a musical work in which a theme is taken up successively and developed by the various parts in counterpoint

**-ful** (fəl, f'l; *for 3* fool) [< FULL[1]] *a suffix meaning:* **1.** full of, having [*joyful*] **2.** having the qualities of or tendency to [*helpful*] **3.** *pl.* -**fuls** the quantity that will fill [*handful*]

**ful·crum** (fool′krəm, ful′-) *n.* [L., a support] the support on which a lever turns in raising something

**ful·fill, ful·fil** (fool fil′) *vt.* -**filled′**, -**fill′ing** [OE. *fullfyllan*]

FULCRUM

**1.** to carry out (a promise, etc.) **2.** to do (a duty, etc.) **3.** to satisfy (a condition) **4.** to bring to an end; complete —**ful·fill′ment, ful·fil′ment** *n.*

**full**[1] (fool) *adj.* [OE.] **1.** having in it all there is space for; filled **2.** having eaten all that one wants **3.** having a great deal or number (*of*) **4.** complete [*a full dozen*] **5.** having reached the greatest size, extent, etc. **6.** plump; round **7.** with wide folds; flowing [*a full skirt*] —*n.* the greatest amount, extent, etc. —*adv.* **1.** to the greatest degree; completely **2.** directly; exactly —**full′ness, ful′ness** *n.*

**full**[2] (fool) *vt., vi.* [< L. *fullo*, cloth fuller] to shrink and thicken (wool cloth) —**full′er** *n.*

**full′back′** *n. Football* a member of the offensive backfield, stationed behind the quarterback

**full′-blood′ed** *adj.* **1.** of unmixed breed or race **2.** vigorous

**full′-blown′** *adj.* **1.** in full bloom **2.** fully developed; matured

**full′-fledged′** *adj.* completely developed or trained; of full status

**full moon** the moon when it reflects light as a full disk

**full′-scale′** *adj.* **1.** according to the original or standard scale **2.** to the utmost degree; all-out

**full′-time′** *adj.* of or engaged in work, study, etc. that takes all of one's regular working hours

**ful·ly** *adv.* **1.** completely; thoroughly **2.** at least

**ful·mi·nate** (ful′mə nāt′) *vi., vt.* -**nat′ed**, -**nat′ing** [< L. *fulmen*, lightning] **1.** to explode **2.** to shout forth —**ful′mi·na′tion** *n.*

**ful·some** (fool′səm) *adj.* [see FULL[1] & -SOME[1], but infl. by ME. *ful*, foul] disgusting, esp. because excessive

**fum·ble** (fum′b'l) *vi., vt.* -**bled**, -**bling** [prob. < ON. *famla*] **1.** to grope (*for*) or handle (a thing) clumsily **2.** to lose one's grasp on (a football, etc.) —*n.* a fumbling —**fum′bler** *n.*

**fume** (fyōōm) *n.* [< L. *fumus*] a gas, smoke, or vapor, esp. if offensive or suffocating —*vi.* fumed, fum′ing **1.** to give off fumes **2.** to show anger

**fu·mi·gate** (fyōō′mə gāt′) *vt.* -**gat′ed**, -**gat′ing** [< L. *fumus*, smoke + *agere*, do] to expose to fumes, esp. to disinfect or kill the vermin in —**fu′mi·ga′tion** *n.* —**fu′mi·ga′tor** *n.*

**fum·y** (fyōō′mē) *adj.* -**i·er**, -**i·est** full of or producing fumes; vaporous

**fun** (fun) *n.* [< ME. *fonne*, foolish] **1.** *a*) lively, gay play or playfulness *b*) pleasure **2.** a source of merriment —**make fun of** to ridicule

**func·tion** (funk′shən) *n.* [< L. *fungi*, perform] **1.** the normal or characteristic action of anything **2.** a special duty required in work **3.** a formal ceremony or social occasion **4.** a thing that depends on and varies with something else —*vi.* to act in a required manner; work; be used —**func′tion·less** *adj.*

**func·tion·al** *adj.* **1.** of a function **2.** performing a function **3.** *Med.* affecting a function of some organ without apparent organic changes

**func·tion·ar·y** (-er'ē) *n., pl.* **-ies** an official performing some function

**function word** a word, as an article or conjunction, serving mainly to show grammatical relationship

**fund** (fund) *n.* [L. *fundus*, bottom] **1.** a supply that can be drawn upon; stock **2.** *a)* a sum of money set aside for a purpose *b)* [*pl.*] ready money —*vt.* to put or convert into a long-term debt that bears interest

**fun·da·men·tal** (fun'də men't'l) *adj.* [see prec.] of or forming a foundation or basis; basic; essential —*n.* a principle, theory, law, etc. serving as a basis —**fun'da·men'tal·ly** *adv.*

**fun'da·men'tal·ism** *n.* [*sometimes* F-] religious beliefs based on a literal interpretation of the Bible —**fun'da·men'tal·ist** *n., adj.*

**fu·ner·al** (fyōō'nər əl) *n.* [< L. *funus*] the ceremonies connected with burial or cremation of the dead

**funeral director** the manager of an establishment (**funeral home** or **parlor**) where funeral services can be held

**fu·ne·re·al** (fyoo nir'ē əl) *adj.* suitable for a funeral; sad and solemn; dismal —**fu·ne're·al·ly** *adv.*

**fun·gi·cide** (fun'jə sīd') *n.* [see -CIDE] any substance that kills fungi

**fun·gus** (fuŋ'gəs) *n., pl.* **-gi** (fun'jī), **-gus·es** [< Gr. *spongos*, sponge] any of various plants, as molds, mildews, mushrooms, etc., that lack chlorophyll, stems, and leaves and reproduce by spores —**fun'gous** *adj.*

**fu·nic·u·lar** (fyoo nik'yoo lər) *adj.* [< L. *funiculus*, little rope] worked by a rope or cable —*n.* a mountain railway with counterbalanced cable cars on parallel sets of rails

**funk** (fuŋk) *n.* [< ? Fl. *fonck*, dismay] [Colloq.] **1.** a cowering through fear; panic **2.** a depressed mood

**fun·ky** (fuŋ'kē) *adj.* **-ki·er, -ki·est** [orig., earthy] *Jazz* of an earthy style derived from early blues

**fun·nel** (fun'l) *n.* [ult. < L. *fundere*, pour] **1.** a tapering tube with a cone-shaped mouth, for pouring things into small-mouthed containers **2.** the smokestack of a steamship —*vi., vt.* **-neled** or **-nelled, -nel·ing** or **-nel·ling** to move or pour as through a funnel

**fun·ny** (fun'ē) *adj.* **-ni·er, -ni·est** **1.** causing laughter; humorous **2.** [Colloq.] *a)* strange; queer *b)* tricky —*n., pl.* **-nies** [Colloq.] *same as* COMIC STRIP: *usually in pl.* —**fun'ni·ly** *adv.* —**fun'ni·ness** *n.*

**funny bone** a place on the elbow where a sharp impact on a nerve causes a strange, tingling sensation

**fur** (fur) *n.* [< OFr. *fuerre*, sheath] **1.** the soft, thick hair covering certain animals **2.** a processed skin bearing such hair —*adj.* of fur —**furred** *adj.*

**fur·be·low** (fur'bə lō') *n.* [ult. < Fr. *falbala*] **1.** a flounce or ruffle **2.** [*usually pl.*] showy, useless trimming

**fur·bish** (fur'bish) *vt.* [< OFr. *forbir*] **1.** to polish; burnish **2.** to renovate

**Fu·ries** (fyoor'ēz) *n.pl. Gr. & Rom. Myth.* the three terrible female spirits who punished unavenged crimes

**fu·ri·ous** (fyoor'ē əs) *adj.* **1.** full of fury; very angry **2.** very great, intense, wild, etc. —**fu'ri·ous·ly** *adv.*

**furl** (furl) *vt.* [< L. *firmus*, FIRM[1] + *ligare*, to tie] to roll up (a sail, flag etc.) tightly and make secure

**fur·long** (fur'lôŋ) *n.* [< OE. *furh*, a furrow + *lang*, LONG[1]] a measure of distance equal to 1/8 of a mile

**fur·lough** (fur'lō) *n.* [< Du. *verlof*] a leave of absence, esp. for military personnel —*vt.* to grant a furlough to

**fur·nace** (fur'nəs) *n.* [< L. *fornus*, oven] an enclosed structure in which heat is produced, as by burning fuel

**fur·nish** (fur'nish) *vt.* [< OFr. *furnir*] **1.** to supply with furniture, etc.; equip **2.** to supply; provide

**fur'nish·ings** *n.pl.* **1.** the furniture, carpets, etc. as for a house **2.** things to wear (men's *furnishings*)

**fur·ni·ture** (fur'ni chər) *n.* [Fr. *fourniture*] **1.** the things in a room, etc. which equip it for living, as chairs, beds, etc. **2.** necessary equipment

**fu·ror** (fyoor'ôr) *n.* [< L.] **1.** fury; frenzy **2.** *a)* a widespread enthusiasm; craze *b)* a commotion or uproar Also for 2, [Chiefly Brit.] **fu'rore** (-ôr)

**fur·ri·er** (fur'ē ər) *n.* one who processes furs or deals in fur garments

**fur·ring** (fur'iŋ) *n.* thin strips of wood fixed on a wall, floor, etc. before adding boards or plaster

**fur·row** (fur'ō) *n.* [OE. *furh*] **1.** a narrow groove made in the ground by a plow **2.** anything like this, as a deep wrinkle —*vt.* to make furrows in —*vi.* to become wrinkled

**fur·ry** (fur'ē) *adj.* **-ri·er, -ri·est** **1.** of or like fur **2.** covered with fur —**fur'ri·ness** *n.*

**fur·ther** (fur'thər) *adj.* [OE. *furthra*] **1.** additional **2.** more distant; farther —*adv.* **1.** to a greater degree or extent **2.** in addition **3.** at or to a greater distance; farther In sense 2 of the *adj.* and sense 3 of the *adv.*, FARTHER is more commonly used —*vt.* to give aid to; promote —**fur'ther·ance** *n.*

**fur'ther·more'** *adv.* in addition; besides; moreover

**fur·thest** (fur'thist) *adj.* most distant; farthest: also **fur'ther·most'** —*adv.* at or to the greatest distance or degree

**fur·tive** (fur'tiv) *adj.* [< L. *fur*, thief] done or acting in a stealthy manner; sneaky —**fur'tive·ly** *adv.* —**fur'tive·ness** *n.*

**fu·ry** (fyoor'ē) *n., pl.* **-ries** [< L. *furere*, to rage] **1.** violent anger; wild rage **2.** violence; vehemence

**furze** (furz) *n.* [OE. *fyrs*] a prickly evergreen shrub native to Europe

**fuse[1]** (fyōōz) *vt., vi.* **fused, fus'ing** [< L. *fundere*, to shed] **1.** to melt **2.** to unite as if by melting together

**fuse[2]** (fyōōz) *n.* [< L. *fusus*, spindle] **1.** a tube or wick filled with combustible material, for setting off an explosive charge **2.** *Elec.* a strip of easily melted metal placed in a circuit: it melts and breaks the circuit if the current becomes too strong

**fu·see** (fyōō zē′) *n.* [Fr. *fusée,* a rocket] a colored flare used as a signal, as by truck drivers

**fu·se·lage** (fyōō′sə läzh′) *n.* [Fr.] the body of an airplane, exclusive of the wings, tail assembly, and engines

**fu·si·ble** (fyōō′zə b'l) *adj.* that can be fused or easily melted

**fu·sil·ier, fu·sil·eer** (fyōō′zə lir′) *n.* [Fr.] formerly, a soldier armed with a flintlock musket

**fu·sil·lade** (fyōō′sə lād′) *n.* [Fr. < *fusiller,* to shoot] a simultaneous or rapid discharge of many firearms

**fu·sion** (fyōō′zhən) *n.* **1.** a fusing or melting together **2.** a blending; coalition **3.** *same as* NUCLEAR FUSION

**fuss** (fus) *n.* [prob. echoic] **1.** nervous, excited activity; bustle **2.** a nervous state **3.** [Colloq.] a quarrel **4.** [Colloq.] a showy display of approval, etc. —*vi.* **1.** to bustle about or worry over trifles **2.** to whine, as a baby

**fuss′budg′et** (-buj′it) *n.* [FUSS + BUDGET] [Colloq.] a fussy person: also **fuss′pot′** (-pät′)

**fuss′y** *adj.* **-i·er, -i·est 1.** *a)* worrying over trifles *b)* hard to please *c)* whining, as a baby **2.** full of needless, showy details —**fuss′i·ness** *n.*

**fus·tian** (fus′chən) *n.* [< L. *fustis,* wooden stick] pompous, pretentious talk or writing; bombast

**fus·ty** (fus′tē) *adj.* **-ti·er, -ti·est** [< OFr. *fust,* cask] **1.** musty; moldy

**2.** old-fashioned —**fus′ti·ly** *adv.* —**fus′ti·ness** *n.*

**fut.** future

**fu·tile** (fyōōt′'l) *adj.* [< L. *futilis,* that easily pours out] useless; vain —**fu·til·i·ty** (fyōō til′ə tē) *n.*

**fu·ton** (fōō′tän) *n.* [Jap.] a thin mattress, placed on the floor for use as a bed

**fu·ture** (fyōō′chər) *adj.* [< L. *futurus,* about to be] **1.** that is to be or come **2.** indicating time to come [the *future* tense] —*n.* **1.** the time that is to come **2.** what is going to be **3.** the chance to succeed —**fu′tur·is′tic** *adj.*

**future shock** [after A. Toffler's book *Future Shock* (1970)] an inability to cope with rapid social changes that have not been properly anticipated

**fu·tu·ri·ty** (fyōō toor′ə tē, -tyoor′-) *n., pl.* **-ties 1.** the future **2.** a future condition or event

**fu·tur·ol·o·gy** (fyōō′chər äl′ə jē) *n.* [FUTUR(E) + -OLOGY] a method of stating the probable form of future conditions by making assumptions based on known facts —**fu′tur·ol′o·gist** *n.*

**futz** (futs) *vi.* [? < Yid.] [Slang] to trifle or fool (*around*)

**fuze** (fyōōz) *n., vt., vi.* **fuzed, fuz′ing** *same as* FUSE

**fuzz** (fuz) *n.* [< ?] loose, light particles of down, wool, etc.; fine hairs or fibers —**the fuzz** [Slang] a policeman or the police —**fuzz′y** *adj.* **-i·er, -i·est**

**-fy** (fī) [< L. *facere,* to make] *a suffix meaning:* **1.** to make [*liquefy*] **2.** to cause to have [*glorify*] **3.** to become [*putrefy*]

# G

**G, g** (jē) *n., pl.* **G's, g's 1.** the 7th letter of the English alphabet **2.** *Physics* gravity

**G** (jē) *n. Music* the fifth tone in the scale of C major

**G** a motion-picture rating for a film considered suitable for general audiences, with no age restriction

**G.** German

**G., g. 1.** gauge **2.** gram(s) **3.** gulf

**Ga., GA** Georgia

**gab** (gab) *n., vi.* **gabbed, gab′bing** [ON. *gabba,* mock] [Colloq.] chatter

**gab·ar·dine** (gab′ər dēn′) *n.* [< OFr. *gaverdine,* kind of cloak] a twilled cloth of wool, cotton, etc., with a fine, diagonal weave Also [Brit.] **gab′er·dine**

**gab·ble** (gab′'l) *vi., vt.* **-bled, -bling** [< GAB] to talk or utter rapidly or incoherently —*n.* such talk

**gab·by** (gab′ē) *adj.* **-bi·er, -bi·est** [Colloq.] talkative —**gab′bi·ness** *n.*

**gab′fest′** (-fest′) *n.* [Colloq.] an informal gathering to talk or gab

**ga·ble** (gā′b'l) *n.* [< Gmc.] the triangular wall enclosed by the sloping ends of a ridged roof —**ga′bled** *adj.*

**Ga·bon** (gä bōn′) country on the W coast of Africa: 103,089 sq. mi.; pop. 473,000

**Ga·bri·el** (gā′brē əl) *Bible* an archangel, the herald of good news

**gad** (gad) *vi.* **gad′ded, gad′ding** [LME. *gadden,* to hurry] to wander about idly or restlessly —**gad′der** *n.*

**gad′a·bout′** *n.* [Colloq.] one who gads about, looking for fun, etc.

**gad′fly′** *n., pl.* **-flies′** [see GOAD & FLY²] **1.** a large fly that bites livestock **2.** one who annoys others

**gadg·et** (gaj′it) *n.* [< ?] any small mechanical contrivance or device

**Gael·ic** (gāl′ik) *adj.* of the Celtic people of Ireland, Scotland, or the Isle of Man —*n.* any Celtic language spoken by these people Abbrev. **Gael.**

**gaff** (gaf) *n.* [< Pr. *gaf* or Sp. *gafa*] **1.** a large hook on a pole for landing fish **2.** a spar supporting a fore-and-aft sail —**stand the gaff** [Slang] to bear up well under punishment, ridicule, etc.

**gaffe** (gaf) *n.* [Fr.] a blunder

**gag** (gag) *vt.* **gagged, gag′ging** [echoic] 1. to cause to retch 2. to keep from speaking, as by stopping the mouth of —*vi.* to retch —*n.* 1. something put into or over the mouth to prevent talking, etc. 2. any restraint of free speech 3. a joke

**gage**[1] (gāj) *n.* [< OFr., a pledge] 1. something pledged; security 2. a glove, etc. thrown down as a challenge to fight 3. a challenge

**gage**[2] (gāj) *n., vt.* **gaged, gag′ing** *same as* GAUGE (esp. in technical use)

**gag·gle** (gag′′l) *n.* [echoic] 1. a flock of geese 2. any group

**gai·e·ty** (gā′ə tē) *n., pl.* **-ties** 1. the quality of being gay; cheerfulness 2. merrymaking 3. showy brightness

**gai·ly** (gā′lē) *adv.* in a gay manner; specif., *a)* merrily *b)* brightly

**gain** (gān) *n.* [< OFr. *gaaigne*] 1. an increase; specif., *a)* [*often pl.*] profit *b)* an increase in advantage 2. acquisition —*vt.* 1. to earn 2. to win 3. to attract 4. to get as an addition, profit, or advantage 5. to make an increase in 6. to get to; reach —*vi.* 1. to make progress 2. to increase in weight —**gain on** to draw nearer to (an opponent in a race, etc.)

**gain′er** *n.* 1. a person or thing that gains 2. a fancy dive forward, but with a backward somersault

**gain′ful** *adj.* producing gain; profitable —**gain′ful·ly** *adv.*

**gain·say** (gān′sā′) *vt.* **-said′** (-sed′, -sād′), **-say′ing** [< OE. *gegn*, against + *seggen*, say] 1. to deny 2. to contradict —**gain′say′er** *n.*

**gait** (gāt) *n.* [< ON. *gata*, path] 1. manner of walking or running 2. any of the various foot movements of a horse, as a trot, pace, canter, etc.

**gai·ter** (gāt′ər) *n.* [< Fr. *guêtre*] a cloth or leather covering for the instep, ankle, and lower leg

**gal** (gal) *n.* [Colloq.] a girl

**gal.** gallon(s)

**ga·la** (gā′lə, gal′ə) *n.* [It. < OFr. *gale*, pleasure] a celebration —*adj.* festive

**gal·a·bi·a, gal·a·bi·ya** (gal′ə bē′ə) *n.* [< Ar.] a long, loose cotton gown, worn in Arabic countries

**Gal·a·had** (gal′ə had′) *Arthurian Legend* the knight who, because of his purity, found the Holy Grail

**gal·ax·y** (gal′ək sē) [< Gr. *gala*, milk] [*often* G-] *same as* MILKY WAY —*n., pl.* **-ies** 1. any similar group of stars 2. a group of illustrious people —**ga·lac·tic** (gə lak′tik) *adj.*

**gale** (gāl) *n.* [< ?] 1. a strong wind 2. an outburst [a gale of laughter]

**ga·le·na** (gə lē′nə) *n.* [L., lead ore] native lead sulfide, a lead-gray mineral with metallic luster

**Gal·i·lee** (gal′ə lē′), **Sea of** lake in NE Israel

**Gal·i·le·o** (gal′ə lē′ō, -lā′-) 1564-1642; It. astronomer & physicist

**gall**[1] (gôl) *n.* [OE. *galla*] 1. bile, the bitter, greenish fluid secreted by the liver 2. something bitter or distasteful 3. bitter feeling 4. [Colloq.] impudence

**gall**[2] (gôl) *n.* [see ff.] a sore on the skin caused by chafing —*vt.* 1. to make sore by rubbing 2. to annoy

**gall**[3] (gôl) *n.* [< L. *galla*] a tumor on plant tissue caused by irritation due to fungi, insects, or bacteria

**gal·lant** (gal′ənt; *for adj. 3 & n., usually* gə lant′ *or* -länt′) *adj.* [< OFr. *gale*, pleasure] 1. stately; imposing 2. brave and noble 3. polite and attentive to women —*n.* [Rare] 1. a high-spirited, stylish man 2. a man attentive to women

**gal·lant·ry** (gal′ən trē) *n., pl.* **-ries** 1. heroic courage 2. the behavior of a gallant 3. a courteous act or remark

**gall·blad·der** (gôl′blad′ər) *n.* a membranous sac attached to the liver, in which excess gall or bile is stored

**gal·le·on** (gal′ē ən) *n.* [ult. < MGr. *galaia*, kind of ship] a large Spanish ship of the 15th and 16th cent.

**gal·ler·y** (gal′ə rē) *n., pl.* **-ies** [< ML. *galeria*] 1. a covered walk or porch open at one side 2. a long, narrow, outside balcony 3. *a)* a balcony in a theater, etc.; esp., the highest balcony with the cheapest seats *b)* the people in these seats 4. the spectators at a sports event, etc. 5. an establishment for exhibitions, etc.

**gal·ley** (gal′ē) *n., pl.* **-leys** [< MGr. *galaia*, kind of ship] 1. a long, low ship of ancient times, propelled by oars and sails 2. a ship's kitchen 3. *Printing a)* a shallow tray for holding composed type *b)* proof printed from such type: in full, **galley proof**

GALLEY

**Gal·lic** (gal′ik) *adj.* 1. of ancient Gaul or its people 2. French

**Gal′li·cism** (-ə siz′m) *n.* [< prec.] [*also* g-] a French idiom, custom, etc.

**gal·li·vant** (gal′ə vant′) *vi.* [arbitrary elaboration of GALLANT] to go about in search of amusement

**gal·lon** (gal′ən) *n.* [< ML. *galo*, jug] a liquid measure, equal to 4 quarts

**gal·lop** (gal′əp) *vi., vt.* [< OFr. *galoper*] to go, or cause to go, at a gallop —*n.* the fastest gait of a horse, etc., a succession of leaping strides

**gal·lows** (gal′ōz) *n., pl.* **-lows·es, -lows** [OE. *galga*] an upright frame with a crossbeam and a rope, for hanging condemned persons

**gall·stone** (gôl′stōn′) *n.* a small solid mass sometimes formed in the gallbladder or bile duct

**ga·lore** (gə lôr′) *adv.* [Ir. *go leor*, enough] in abundance; plentifully

**ga·losh, ga·loshe** (gə läsh′) *n.* [OFr. *galoche*] a high, warmly lined overshoe of rubber and fabric

**gal·van·ic** (gal van′ik) *adj.* [< L. *Galvani*, 18th-c. It. physicist] 1. of or producing an electric current, esp. from a battery 2. startling

**gal′va·nism** (-və niz′m) *n.* electricity produced by chemical action

**gal·va·nize** (gal′və nīz′) *vt.* **-nized′, -niz′ing 1.** to apply an electric current to **2.** to startle; excite **3.** to plate (metal) with zinc

**Gam·bi·a** (gam′bē ə) country on the W coast of Africa: c.4,000 sq. mi.; pop. 343,000

**gam·bit** (gam′bit) *n.* [< Sp. *gambito*, a tripping] **1.** *Chess* an opening in which a pawn, etc. is sacrificed to get an advantage in position **2.** an action intended to gain an advantage

**gam·ble** (gam′b'l) *vi.* **-bled, -bling** [OE. *gamenian*, to play] **1.** to play games of chance for money, etc. **2.** to take a risk for some advantage —*vt.* to risk in gambling; bet —*n.* an undertaking involving risk —**gam′bler** *n.*

**gam·bol** (gam′b'l) *n.* [< It. *gamba*, leg] a gamboling; frolic —*vi.* **-boled** or **-bolled, -bol·ing** or **-bol·ling** to jump and skip about in play; frolic

**gam·brel** (roof) (gam′brəl) [< ML. *gamba*, leg] a roof with two slopes on each side

**game**[1] (gām) *n.* [OE. *gamen*] **1.** any form of play; amusement **2.** *a)* amusement or sport involving competition under rules *b)* a single contest in such a competition **3.** the number of points required for winning **4.** a scheme; plan **5.** wild birds or animals hunted for sport or food **6.** [Colloq.] a business or job, esp. one involving risk —*vi.* **gamed, gam′ing** to play cards, etc. for stakes; gamble —*adj.* **1.** designating or of wild birds or animals hunted for sport or food **2.** *a)* plucky; courageous *b)* enthusiastic; ready (for) —**the game is up** failure is certain —**game′ly** *adv.* —**game′ness** *n.*

**game**[2] (gām) *adj.* [< ?] [Colloq.] lame or injured [a *game* leg]

**game′cock′** *n.* a specially bred rooster trained for cockfighting

**game′keep′er** *n.* a person who takes care of game birds and animals, as on an estate

**game plan 1.** the strategy planned before a game **2.** any long-range strategy

**game point 1.** the situation when the next point scored could win a game **2.** the winning point

**games·man·ship** (gāmz′mən ship′) *n.* skill in using ploys to gain an advantage

**game·ster** (gām′stər) *n.* a gambler

**gam·ete** (gam′ēt, gə mēt′) *n.* [< Gr. *gamos*, marriage] a reproductive cell that unites with another to form the cell that develops into a new individual

**game theory** a mathematical method of selecting the best strategy for a game, war, competition, etc. so as to minimize one's maximum losses

**gam·in** (gam′ən) *n.* [Fr.] **1.** a homeless child who roams the streets **2.** a girl with a roguish, saucy charm: also **ga·mine** (ga mēn′)

**gam·ma** (gam′ə) *n.* the third letter of the Greek alphabet (Γ, γ)

**gamma glob·u·lin** (gläb′yə lin) that fraction of blood serum which contains most antibodies

**gamma rays** strong electromagnetic radiation from a radioactive substance

**gam·ut** (gam′ət) *n.* [< Gr. letter *gamma*, for the lowest note of the medieval scale] **1.** any complete musical scale **2.** the entire range or extent

**gam·y** (gā′mē) *adj.* **-i·er, -i·est 1.** having the strong flavor of cooked game **2.** slightly tainted **3.** plucky **4.** risqué —**gam′i·ness** *n.*

**gan·der** (gan′dər) *n.* [OE. *gan(d)ra*] **1.** a male goose **2.** [Slang] a look

**Gan·dhi** (gän′dē), **Mo·han·das K.** (mō hän′dəs) 1869–1948; Hindu nationalist leader: called *Mahatma Gandhi*

**gang** (gaŋ) *n.* [< OE. *gang*, a going] a group of people working or acting together [a school *gang*] —**gang up on** [Colloq.] to attack as a group

**Gan·ges** (gan′jēz) river in N India & Bangladesh

**gan·gling** (gaŋ′gliŋ) *adj.* [< ?] thin, tall, and awkward; lanky: also **gan′gly**

**gan·gli·on** (gaŋ′glē ən) *n., pl.* **-gli·a** (-ə), **-gli·ons** [ult. < Gr., tumor] a mass of nerve cells from which nerve impulses are transmitted

**gang′plank′** *n.* a movable ramp by which to board or leave a ship

**gan·grene** (gaŋ′grēn, gaŋ grēn′) *n.* [< Gr. *gran*, gnaw] decay of body tissue when the blood supply is obstructed —**gan′gre·nous** (-grə nəs) *adj.*

**gang·ster** (gaŋ′stər) *n.* a member of a gang of criminals —**gang′ster·ism** *n.*

**gang′way′** *n.* [OE. *gangweg*] a passageway; specif., *a)* an opening in a ship's side for loading, etc. *b)* a gangplank —*interj.* clear the way!

**gan·net** (gan′it) *n.* [OE. *ganot*] a large, web-footed sea bird

**gant·let** (gônt′lit, gant′-) *n.* [< Sw. *gata*, lane + *lopp*, a run] **1.** a former punishment in which the offender ran between two rows of men who struck him **2.** a series of troubles, etc. Now equally sp. **gaunt′let**

**gan·try** (gan′trē) *n., pl.* **-tries** [< L. *canterius*, beast of burden] **1.** a framework, often on wheels, for a traveling crane **2.** a wheeled framework with a crane, platforms, etc., for readying a rocket to be launched

**gaol** (jāl) *n. Brit. sp. of* JAIL

**gap** (gap) *n.* [< ON. *gapa*, to gape] **1.** an opening made by breaking or parting **2.** a mountain pass or ravine **3.** a blank space **4.** a lag; disparity

**gape** (gāp) *vi.* **gaped, gap′ing** [< ON. *gapa*] **1.** to open the mouth wide, as in yawning **2.** to stare with the mouth open **3.** to open wide —*n.* **1.** a gaping **2.** a wide opening

**gar** (gär) *n., pl.* **gar, gars** [< OE. *gar*, a spear] a long fish with a beaklike snout: also **gar′fish′**

**ga·rage** (gə räzh′, -räj′) *n.* [Fr. < *garer*, protect] **1.** a shelter for automotive vehicles **2.** a business place where such vehicles are repaired, stored, serviced, etc.

**garb** (gärb) *n.* [ < It. *garbo*, elegance] **1.** clothing; style of dress **2.** external appearance —*vt.* to clothe

**gar·bage** (gär′bij) *n.* [ME., entrails of fowls] waste parts of food

**gar·ban·zo** (gär ban′zō, -bän′-) *n.*, *pl.* -zos [Sp.] *same as* CHICKPEA

**gar·ble** (gär′b'l) *vt.* -bled, -bling [ < Ar. *ghirbāl*, a sieve] to distort or confuse (a story, etc.) so as to mislead

**†gar·çon** (gär sōn′) *n.* [Fr.] a waiter

**gar·den** (gär′d'n) *n.* [ < Frank.] **1.** a piece of ground for growing flowers, vegetables, etc. **2.** an area of fertile land **3.** [*often pl.*] a public parklike place, often having displays of animals or plants —*vi.* to make, or work in, a garden —*adj.* of, for, or grown in a garden —**gar′den·er** *n.*

**Garden Grove** city in SW Calif.: pop. 123,000

**gar·de·ni·a** (gär dēn′yə) *n.* [ < A. *Garden* (1730–91), U.S. botanist] a fragrant flower with waxy, white petals

**Gar·field** (gär′fēld), **James Abram** 1831–81; 20th president of the U.S. (1881); assassinated

**Gar·gan·tu·a** (gär gan′choo wə) a giant king in a satire by Rabelais —**Gar·gan′tu·an, gar·gan′tu·an** *adj.*

**gar·gle** (gär′g'l) *vt., vi.* -gled, -gling [ < Fr. *gargouille*, throat] to rinse (the throat) with a liquid kept in motion by the expulsion of air from the lungs —*n.* a liquid for gargling

**gar·goyle** (gär′goil) *n.* [see prec.] a waterspout formed like a fantastic creature, projecting from a building

**Gar·i·bal·di** (gar′ə bôl′dē), **Giu·sep·pe** (jōō zep′pe) 1807–82; It. patriot

**gar·ish** (ger′ish) *adj.* [prob. < ME. *gauren*, to stare] too gaudy; showy —**gar′ish·ly** *adv.* —**gar′ish·ness** *n.*

**gar·land** (gär′lənd) *n.* [ < OFr. *garlande*] a wreath of flowers, leaves, etc. —*vt.* to decorate with garlands

**gar·lic** (gär′lik) *n.* [ < OE. *gar*, a spear + *leac*, a leek] **1.** a plant of the lily family **2.** its strong-smelling bulb, used as seasoning —**gar′lick·y** *adj.*

**gar·ment** (gär′mənt) *n.* [see GARNISH] any article of clothing

**gar·ner** (gär′nər) *vt.* [ < L. *granum*, grain] to gather up and store

**gar·net** (gär′nit) *n.* [ < ML. *granatum*] a hard, glasslike mineral: deep-red varieties are often used as gems

**gar·ni** (gär nē′) *adj.* [Fr.] garnished: said of food

**gar·nish** (gär′nish) *vt.* [ < OFr. *garnir*, furnish] **1.** to decorate; trim **2.** to decorate (food) with something that adds color or flavor **3.** to garnishee —*n.* **1.** a decoration **2.** something used to garnish food, as parsley

**gar·nish·ee** (gär′nə shē′) *vt.* -eed′, -ee′ing [ < prec.] *Law* to attach (a debtor's property, wages, etc.) so that it can be used to pay the debt

**gar·ret** (gar′it) *n.* [ < OFr. *garite*, watchtower] an attic

**gar·ri·son** (gar′ə s'n) *n.* [ < OFr. *garir*, to watch] **1.** troops stationed in a fort **2.** a fortified place with troops, etc. —*vt.* to station (troops) in (a fortified place) for its defense

**gar·rote** (gə rät′, -rōt′) *n.* [Sp.] **1.** a cord, thong, etc. used in strangling a person **2.** strangulation with a cord, thong, etc. —*vt.* -rot′ed or -rot′ted, -rot′ing or -rot′ting to execute or attack by such strangling  Also **ga·rotte′, gar·rotte′** or **gar·rot′er** *n.*

**gar·ru·lous** (gar′ə ləs, -yoo-) *adj.* [ < L. *garrire*, to chatter] talking much, esp. about unimportant things — **gar·ru·li·ty** (gə rōō′lə tē) *n.*

**gar·ter** (gär′tər) *n.* [ < OFr. *garet*, the back of the knee] an elastic band or strap for holding a stocking in place —*vt.* to fasten with a garter

**garter snake** a small, harmless snake, common in N. America

**Gar·y** (ger′ē) city in NW Ind.: pop. 175,000

**gas** (gas) *n.* [coined < Gr. *chaos*, chaos] **1.** the fluid form of a substance in which it can expand indefinitely; vapor **2.** any mixture of flammable gases used for lighting or heating **3.** any gas used as an anesthetic **4.** any poisonous substance dispersed in the air, as in war **5.** [Colloq.] *a)* gasoline *b)* the accelerator in an automobile, etc. —*vt.* gassed, gas′sing to attack or kill by gas —**gas′e·ous** (-ē əs) *adj.*

**gas chamber** a room in which people are put to be killed with poison gas

**gash** (gash) *vt.* [ < OFr. *garser*] to make a long, deep cut in; slash —*n.* a long, deep cut

**gas·ket** (gas′kit) *n.* [prob. < OFr. *garcette*, small cord] a piece or ring of rubber, metal, etc. used to make a piston or joint leakproof

**gas mask** a filtering mask to protect against breathing in poisonous gases

**gas·o·line, gas·o·lene** (gas′ə lēn′, gas′ə lēn′) *n.* [ < *gas* + L. *oleum*, oil] a volatile, flammable liquid distilled from petroleum and used chiefly as a fuel in internal-combustion engines

**gasp** (gasp) *vi.* [ < ON. *geispa*, to yawn] to catch the breath with effort —*vt.* to say with gasps —*n.* a gasping

**gas station** *same as* SERVICE STATION

**gas·sy** (gas′ē) *adj.* -si·er, -si·est **1.** full of gas; esp., flatulent **2.** like gas

**gas·tric** (gas′trik) *adj.* [GASTR(O)- + -IC] of, in, or near the stomach

**gastric juice** the thin, acid digestive fluid produced by glands in the stomach lining

**gas·tri·tis** (gas trīt′is) *n.* [GASTR(O)- + -ITIS] inflammation of the stomach

**gastro-** [ < Gr. *gastēr*] *a combining form meaning* the stomach (and)

**gas·tron·o·my** (gas trän′ə mē) *n.* [ < Gr. *gastēr*, stomach + *nomos*, a rule] the art of good eating —**gas′tro·nom′i·cal** (-trə näm′i k'l) *adj.*

**gas·tro·pod** (gas′trə päd′) *n.* [GASTRO- + -POD] a mollusk of the class including snails, slugs, etc.

**gate** (gāt) *n.* [OE. *geat*] **1.** a movable structure controlling passage through an opening in a fence or wall **2.** a gateway **3.** a movable barrier **4.** a structure controlling the flow of water, as in a canal **5.** the total amount or number of paid admissions to a performance —**give (someone) the gate** [Slang] to get rid of

**gate′-crash′er** *n.* [Colloq.] one who attends an affair without an invitation or a performance without paying

**gate′fold′** *n.* an oversize page in a magazine or book, bound so that it can be folded out

**gate′way′** *n.* **1.** an entrance in a wall, etc. fitted with a gate **2.** a means of entrance or access

**gath·er** (ga*th*′ər) *vt.* [OE. *gad(e)rian*] **1.** to bring together in one place or group **2.** to gather gradually; accumulate **3.** to collect by picking; harvest **4.** to infer; conclude **5.** to draw into folds or pleats —*vi.* **1.** to assemble **2.** to increase —*n.* a pleat

**gath′er·ing** *n.* **1.** a meeting; crowd **2.** a series of folds in a cloth

**gauche** (gōsh) *adj.* [Fr. < MFr. *gauchir*, become warped] lacking social grace; awkward; tactless

**gau·che·rie** (gō′shə rē′) *n.* gauche behavior or a gauche act

**gau·cho** (gou′chō) *n.*, *pl.* **-chos** [Am-Sp.] a S. American cowboy

**gaud·y** (gôd′ē) *adj.* **-i·er**, **-i·est** [ME. *gaude*] bright and showy, but in bad taste —**gaud′i·ly** *adv.* —**gaud′i·ness** *n.*

**gauge** (gāj) *n.* [ONormFr.] **1.** a standard measure or criterion **2.** any device for measuring **3.** the distance between rails of a railway **4.** the size of the bore of a shotgun **5.** the thickness of sheet metal, wire, etc. —*vt.* **gauged**, **gaug′ing 1.** to measure the size, amount, etc. of **2.** to judge

**Gaul** (gôl) ancient division of the Roman Empire, in W Europe —*n.* any of the people of Gaul

**Gaul′ish** *n.* the Celtic language spoken in ancient Gaul

**gaunt** (gônt) *adj.* [ME. *gawnte*] **1.** thin and bony; haggard, as from great hunger or age **2.** looking grim or forbidding —**gaunt′ness** *n.*

**gaunt·let¹** (gônt′lit, gänt′-) *n.* [< OFr. *gant*, glove] **1.** a knight's armored glove **2.** a long glove with a flaring cuff —**throw down the gauntlet** to challenge, as to combat

**gaunt′let²** *n.* same as GANTLET

**gauze** (gôz) *n.* [Fr. *gaze*] any very thin, transparent, loosely woven material, as of cotton or silk —**gauz′y** *adj.*

**ga·vage** (gə väzh′) *n.* [Fr.] forced feeding of liquids through a stomach tube

**gave** (gāv) *pt.* of GIVE

**gav·el** (gav′'l) *n.* [< Scot. *gable*, fork] a small mallet used, as by a presiding officer, to call for attention, etc.

**ga·votte** (gə vät′) *n.* [Fr.] a 17th-c. dance like the minuet, but livelier

**gawk** (gôk) *vi.* [prob. < *gowk*, stupid person] to stare stupidly

**gawk·y** (gô′kē) *adj.* **-i·er**, **-i·est** clumsy; ungainly —**gawk′i·ness** *n.*

**gay** (gā) *adj.* [OFr. *gai*] **1.** joyous and lively; merry **2.** bright; brilliant [*gay* colors] **3.** [Slang] homosexual

**gay·e·ty** (gā′ə tē) *n.* same as GAIETY

**gay·ly** (gā′lē) *adv.* same as GAILY

**gaze** (gāz) *vi.* **gazed**, **gaz′ing** [< Scand.] to look steadily; stare —*n.* a steady look —**gaz′er** *n.*

**ga·ze·bo** (gə zē′bō, -zā′-) *n.*, *pl.* **-bos**, **-boes** [ < ? prec.] a windowed balcony, summerhouse, etc. for gazing at scenery

**ga·zelle** (gə zel′) *n.* [ < Ar. *ghazāl*] a small, swift antelope of Africa and Asia, with large, lustrous eyes

**ga·zette** (gə zet′) *n.* [Fr. < It. dial. *gazeta*, a small coin, price of the paper] **1.** a newspaper: now mainly in newspaper titles **2.** in England, an official publication —*vt.* **-zet′ted**, **-zet′ting** [Chiefly Brit.] to announce or list in a gazette

**gaz·et·teer** (gaz′ə tir′) *n.* a dictionary or index of geographical names

**gaz·pa·cho** (gäz pä′chō) *n.* [Sp.] a cold Spanish soup of tomatoes, chopped cucumbers, peppers, onions, oil, vinegar, etc.

**G.B.** Great Britain

**Ge** *Chem.* germanium

**gear** (gir) *n.* [ < ON. *gervi*, preparation] **1.** clothing **2.** equipment, esp. for some task **3.** *a)* a toothed wheel designed to mesh with another *b)* [*often pl.*] a system of such gears meshed together to pass motion along *c)* a specific adjustment of such a system [*high gear*] *d)* a part of a mechanism with a specific function [*steering gear*] —*vt.* **1.** to connect by or furnish with gears **2.** to adapt (one thing) to conform with another [to *gear* supply to demand] —**in** (or **out**) **of gear 1.** (not) connected to the motor **2.** (not) in proper working order

**gear′shift′** *n.* a device for connecting or disconnecting any of several sets of transmission gears to a motor, etc.

**gear′wheel′** *n.* a toothed wheel in a system of gears; cogwheel

**gee** (jē) *interj.* [ < JE(SUS)] [Slang] an exclamation of surprise, etc.

**geese** (gēs) *n.* *pl.* of GOOSE

**gee·zer** (gē′zər) *n.* [ < GUISE] [Slang] an eccentric old man

**ge·fil·te fish** (gə fil′tə) [Yid.] chopped, seasoned fish, boiled and served in balls or cakes

**Gei·ger counter** (gī′gər) [ < H. *Geiger* (1882-1945), G. physicist] an instrument for detecting and counting ionizing particles, as from radioactive ores

**gei·sha** (gā′shə) *n.*, *pl.* **-sha**, **-shas** [Jap.] a Japanese girl trained as an entertainer to serve as a hired companion to men

**gel** (jel) *n.* [ < ff.] a jellylike substance formed by a colloidal solution —*vi.* **gelled**, **gel′ling** to form a gel

**gel·a·tin**, **gel·a·tine** (jel′ət 'n) *n.* [ < L. *gelare*, freeze] a tasteless, odorless substance extracted by boiling bones, hoofs, etc., or a similar vegetable substance: dissolved and cooled, it forms a jellylike substance used in foods, photographic film, etc. —**ge·lat·i·nous** (jə lat′n əs) *adj.*

**geld** (geld) *vt.* **geld′ed** or **gelt**, **geld′ing** [ < ON. *geldr*, barren] to castrate (esp. a horse)

**geld′ing** *n.* a castrated horse

**gel·id** (jel′id) *adj.* [ < L. *gelu*, frost] extremely cold; frozen

**gem** (jem) *n.* [ < L. *gemma*] 1. a precious stone, cut for use as a jewel 2. something very precious or valuable

**Gem·i·ni** (jem′ə nī′, -nē′) [L., twins] the third sign of the zodiac

**gem′stone′** *n.* any mineral that can be used as a gem when cut and polished

†**ge·müt·lich** (gə müt′likh) *adj.* [G.] agreeable, cheerful, cozy, etc.

**-gen** (jən, jen) [ < Gr. *-genēs*, born] *a suffix meaning:* 1. something that produces *[oxygen]* 2. something produced (in a specified way)

**Gen.** 1. General 2. Genesis

**gen·darme** (zhän′därm) *n.* [Fr. < *gens d'armes*, men-at-arms] an armed policeman in France, etc.

**gen·der** (jen′dər) *n.* [ < L. *genus*, origin] *Gram.* the classification by which words are grouped as masculine, feminine, or neuter

**gene** (jēn) *n.* [see -GEN] any of the units in the chromosomes by which hereditary characters are transmitted

**ge·ne·al·o·gy** (jē′nē äl′ə jē, -al′-) *n.*, *pl.* **-gies** [ < Gr. *genea*, race + *-logia*, -LOGY] 1. a recorded history of one's ancestry 2. the study of family descent 3. descent from an ancestor; lineage —**ge′ne·a·log′i·cal** (-ə läj′i k'l) *adj.* —**ge′ne·al′o·gist** *n.*

**gen·er·a** (jen′ər ə) *n. pl. of* GENUS

**gen·er·al** (jen′ər əl) *adj.* [ < L. *genus*, class] 1. of, for, or from all; not local, special, or specialized 2. of or for a whole genus, kind, etc. 3. widespread *[general unrest]* 4. most common; usual 5. not specific or precise *[in general terms]* 6. highest in rank *[attorney general]* —*n.* 1. a military officer ranking just above a lieutenant general: also **full general** 2. a military officer ranking above a colonel —**in general** 1. usually 2. without specific details —**gen′er·al·ship′** *n.*

**general assembly** 1. the legislative assembly in some States 2. [G- A-] the legislative assembly of the UN

**general delivery** delivery of mail at the post office to addressees who call for it

**gen′er·al·is′si·mo′** (-ə lis′ə mō′) *n.*, *pl.* **-mos′** [It.] in some countries, the commander in chief of the armed forces

**gen·er·al·i·ty** (jen′ə ral′ə tē) *n.*, *pl.* **-ties** 1. the quality of being general 2. a nonspecific or vague statement, idea, etc. 3. the bulk; main body

**gen·er·al·ize** (jen′ər ə līz′) *vt.* **-ized′**, **-iz′ing** 1. to state in terms of a general law 2. to infer or derive (a general law) from (particular instances) —*vi.* 1. to formulate general principles 2. to talk in generalities —**gen′er·al·i·za′tion** *n.*

**gen′er·al·ly** *adv.* 1. widely; popularly 2. usually 3. not specifically

**general practitioner** a practicing physician who does not specialize in a particular field of medicine

**gen·er·ate** (jen′ə rāt′) *vt.* **-at′ed**, **-at′ing** [ < L. *genus*, race] 1. to produce (offspring); beget 2. to bring into being; produce —**gen′er·a·tive** *adj.*

**gen′er·a′tion** *n.* 1. the producing of offspring 2. production 3. a single stage in the succession of descent 3. the average time (c.30 years) between human generations 4. all the people born and living at about the same time —**gen′er·a′tion·al** *adj.*

**gen′er·a′tor** *n.* a machine for changing mechanical energy into electrical energy; dynamo

**ge·ner·ic** (jə ner′ik) *adj.* [ < L. *genus*, race, kind] 1. of a whole class, kind, or group; inclusive 2. that is not a trademark 3. of or characteristic of a genus —**ge·ner′i·cal·iy** *adv.*

**gen·er·ous** (jen′ər əs) *adj.* [ < L. *generosus*, noble] 1. noble-minded; magnanimous 2. willing to give or share; unselfish 3. large; ample —**gen·er·os·i·ty** (jen′ə räs′ə tē) *n.*, *pl.* **-ties** —**gen′er·ous·ly** *adv.*

**gen·e·sis** (jen′ə sis) *n.*, *pl.* **-ses′** (-sēz′) [Gr.] the beginning; origin —[G-] the first book of the Bible

**genetic code** the order in which four chemical constituents are arranged in huge molecules of DNA

**ge·net·ics** (jə net′iks) *n.pl.* [*with sing. v.*] [ < prec.] the branch of biology dealing with heredity and variation in animal and plant species —**ge·net′ic** *adj.* —**ge·net′i·cal·ly** *adv.* —**ge·net′i·cist** (-ə sist) *n.*

**Ge·ne·va** (jə nē′və) city in SW Switzerland: pop. 175,000

**Gen·ghis Khan** (geŋ′gis kän′, jeŋ′-) 1162?-1227; Mongol conqueror

**ge·nial** (jēn′yəl) *adj.* [see GENIUS] 1. good for life and growth *[a genial climate]* 2. cordial and kindly; amiable —**ge·ni·al·i·ty** (jē′nē al′ə tē) *n.* —**ge′nial·ly** *adv.*

**ge·nie** (jē′nē) *n.* [ < Fr. < Ar. *jinnī*] *same as* JINNI

**gen·i·tal** (jen′ə t'l) *adj.* [ < L. *genere*, to beget] of reproduction or the sexual organs

**gen′i·tals** *n.pl.* [see prec.] the reproductive organs; esp., the external sex organs: also **gen′i·ta′li·a** (-tāl′yə)

**gen·i·tive** (jen′ə tiv) *adj.* [ < Gr. *genos*, genus] designating or in the grammatical case expressing possession, source, etc. —*n.* the genitive case

**gen·i·to·u·ri·nar·y** (jen′ə tō yoor′ə-ner′ē) *adj.* of the genital and urinary organs

**gen·ius** (jēn′yəs) *n.* [L., guardian spirit] 1. particular spirit of a nation, place, age, etc. 2. natural ability; strong inclination *(for)* 3. great mental capacity and inventive ability 4. one having such capacity or ability

**Gen·o·a** (jen′ə wə) seaport in NW Italy: pop. 848,000

**gen·o·cide** (jen′ə sīd′) *n.* [ < Gr.

*gĕnos*, race + -CIDE] the systematic killing of a whole people or nation

**gen·re** (zhän′rə) *n.* [Fr. < L. *genus*, a kind] 1. a kind or type 2. painting in which subjects from everyday life are treated realistically

**gent** (jent) *n.* [Colloq.] a gentleman: humorous or vulgar term

**gen·teel** (jen tēl′) *adj.* [< Fr. *gentil*] polite or well-bred; now, esp., affectedly refined, polite, etc.

**gen·tian** (jen′shən) *n.* [< L. *gentiana*] a plant typically with blue, fringed flowers

**gen·tile** (jen′tīl) *n.* [*also* G-] [< L. *gentilis*, of the same clan] any person not a Jew —*adj.* not Jewish

**gen·til·i·ty** (jen til′ə tē) *n., pl.* -ties [see ff.] 1. the gentry (sense 1) or their status 2. the quality of being genteel

**gen·tle** (jent′'l) *adj.* -tler, -tlest [< L. *gentilis*, of the same clan] 1. of the upper classes 2. refined; courteous 3. generous; kind 4. tame [a *gentle* dog] 5. kindly; patient 6. not harsh or rough; mild [a *gentle* tap] 7. gradual [a *gentle* slope] —**gen′tle·ness** *n.* —**gen′tly** *adv.*

**gen′tle·folk′** *n.pl.* people of good social standing: also **gen′tle·folks′**

**gen′tle·man** (-mən) *n., pl.* -men 1. a man of good family and social standing 2. a courteous, gracious, and honorable man 3. any man: polite term, as (chiefly in pl.) of address —**gen′tle·man·ly** *adj.* —**gen′tle·wom·an** *n.fem., pl.* -wom′en

**gen·try** (jen′trē) *n.* [see GENTLE] 1. people of high social standing 2. people of a particular class or group

**gen·u·flect** (jen′yə flekt′) *vi.* [< L. *genu*, knee + *flectere*, bend] to bend the knee, as in worship —**gen′u·flec′tion** *n.*

**gen·u·ine** (jen′yoo wən) *adj.* [L. *genuinus*, inborn] 1. not fake or artificial; real; true 2. sincere —**gen′u·ine·ly** *adv.* —**gen′u·ine·ness** *n.*

**ge·nus** (jē′nəs) *n., pl.* **gen·er·a** (jen′ər ə), **ge′nus·es** [L., race, kind] 1. a class; kind; sort 2. a classification of related plants or animals

**geo-** [< Gr. *gē*] a *prefix* meaning earth, of the earth [*geology*]

**ge·o·bot·a·ny** (jē′ō bät′'n ē) *n.* the science that studies how specific plant species are nourished by their substrata

**ge·o·cen·tric** (jē′ō sen′trik) *adj.* 1. viewed as from the center of the earth 2. having the earth as a center Also **ge′o·cen′tri·cal**

**ge·o·des·ic** (jē′ə des′ik) *adj.* 1. *same as* GEODETIC (sense 1) 2. *a*) designating the shortest line between two points on a curved surface *b*) of the geometry of such lines 3. having a surface formed of straight bars in a grid of polygons [*geodesic* dome]

**ge·o·det·ic** (-det′ik) *adj.* [< Gr. *gē*, earth + *daiein*, divide] 1. of or concerned with the measurement of the

earth and its surface 2. *same as* GEODESIC (sense 2)

**ge·og·ra·phy** (jē äg′rə fē) *n., pl.* -phies [< Gr. *gē*, earth + *graphein*, write] 1. the science dealing with the earth's surface, continents, climates, plants, animals, resources, etc. 2. the physical features of a region —**ge·og′ra·pher** *n.* —**ge′o·graph′i·cal** (-ō graf′i k'l), **ge′o·graph′ic** *adj.*

**ge·ol·o·gy** (jē äl′ə jē) *n.* [see GEO- & -LOGY] the science dealing with the development of the earth's crust, its rocks and fossils, etc. —**ge′o·log′ic** (-ə läj′ik), **ge′o·log′i·cal** *adj.* —**ge·ol′o·gist** *n.*

**ge·o·mag·net·ic** (jē′ō mag net′ik) *adj.* of the magnetic properties of the earth —**ge′o·mag′ne·tism** *n.*

**ge·om·e·try** (jē äm′ə trē) *n., pl.* -tries [< Gr. *gē*, earth + *metrein*, measure] the branch of mathematics dealing with the properties, measurement, and relationships of points, lines, planes, and solids —**ge′o·met′ric** (-ə met′rik), **ge′o·met′ri·cal** *adj.* —**ge′o·met′ri·cal·ly** *adv.*

**ge·o·phys·ics** (jē′ō fiz′iks) *n.pl.* [*with sing. v.*] the science dealing with the effects of weather, winds, tides, etc. on the earth —**ge′o·phys′i·cal** *adj.*

**George III** (jôrj) 1738–1820; king of England (1760–1820)

**Geor·gia** (jôr′jə) 1. SE State of the U.S.: 58,876 sq. mi.; pop. 4,590,000; cap. Atlanta 2. republic of the U.S.S.R., on the Black Sea —**Geor′gian** *adj., n.*

**ge·o·syn·chro·nous** (jē′ō siŋ′krə nəs) *adj.* designating or of a satellite in orbit above the equator at the same speed that the earth rotates, so as to seem to hover over the same point: also **ge′o·sta′tion·ar′y**

**ge·o·ther·mic** (jē′ō thur′mik) *adj.* [< GEO- + Gr. *thermē*, heat] of the heat inside the earth: also **ge′o·ther′mal**

**ge·ra·ni·um** (jə rā′nē əm) *n.* [< Gr. *geranos*, a crane] 1. a common garden plant with showy red, pink, or white flowers 2. a related wildflower

**ger·bil** (jur′b'l) *n.* [ult. < Ar.] a small rodent with long hind legs

**ger·i·at·rics** (jer′ē at′riks) *n.pl.* [*with sing. v.*] [< Gr. *gēras*, old age + -IATRICS] the branch of medicine dealing with the diseases of old age —**ger′i·at′ric** *adj.*

**germ** (jurm) *n.* [< L. *germen*] 1. the rudimentary form from which a new organism is developed; seed, bud, etc. 2. any microscopic, disease-causing organism, esp. one of the bacteria 3. an origin [the *germ* of an idea]

**Ger·man** (jur′mən) *adj.* of Germany, its people, language, etc. —*n.* 1. a native or inhabitant of Germany 2. the language of Germany, Austria, etc.

**ger·mane** (jər mān′) *adj.* [see GERM] 1. truly relevant; pertinent 2. akin

**Ger·man·ic** (jər man′ik) *adj.* 1. German 2. designating or of the original language of the German peoples or the languages descended from it —*n.* the Germanic branch of languages including English, Dutch, Danish; etc.

**ger·ma·ni·um** (jər mā′nē əm) *n.* [< L. *Germania*, Germany] a rare, metallic chemical element used in transistors

**German measles** *same as* RUBELLA

**Ger·ma·ny** (jur′mə nē) former country in NE Europe: divided (1945) into EAST GERMANY & WEST GERMANY

**germ cell** an ovum or sperm cell

**ger·mi·cide** (jur′mə sīd′) *n.* [< GERM + -CIDE] any antiseptic, etc. used to destroy germs —**ger′mi·ci′dal** *adj.*

**ger·mi·nal** (jur′mə n′l) *adj.* 1. of or like germ cells 2. in the first stage of growth or development

**ger·mi·nate** (jur′mə nāt′) *vi., vt.* -**nat′ed**, -**nat′ing** [< L. *germen*, a sprout] to start developing; sprout, as from a seed —**ger′mi·na′tion** *n.*

**ger·on·tol·o·gy** (jer′ən täl′ə jē) *n.* [< Gr. *gerōn*, old man + -LOGY] the study of aging and the problems of the aged —**ger′on·tol′o·gist** *n.*

**ger·ry·man·der** (jer′i man′dər, ger′-) *vt., vi.* [< E. *Gerry*, governor of Mass. (1812) + SALAMANDER, from shape of the county redistricted then] to divide (a voting area) so as to give unfair advantage to one political party

**ger·und** (jer′ənd) *n.* [< L. *gerere*, carry out] a verbal noun ending in -*ing*

**Ge·sta·po** (gə stä′pō) *n.* [< G. *Ge(heime) Sta(ats)po(lizei)*, secret state police] the terrorist secret state police force of Nazi Germany

**ges·ta·tion** (jes tā′shən) *n.* [< L. *gerere*, to bear] the act or period of carrying young in the uterus; pregnancy —**ges′tate** *vt.* -**tat·ed**, -**tat·ing**

**ges·tic·u·late** (jes tik′yə lāt′) *vi.* -**lat′ed**, -**lat′ing** [see ff.] to make gestures —**ges·tic′u·la′tion** *n.*

**ges·ture** (jes′chər) *n.* [< L. *gerere*, to bear] 1. movement of part of the body to express or emphasize ideas, emotions, etc. 2. any act or remark conveying a state of mind, intention, etc., often made merely for effect —*vi.* -**tured**, -**tur·ing** to make gestures

**get** (get) *vt.* **got**, **got** or **got′ten**, **get′ting** [< ON. *geta*] 1. to come into the state of having; receive; obtain; acquire 2. to arrive at [*get* home early] 3. to go and bring [*get* your books] 4. to catch 5. to persuade [*get* him to go] 6. to cause to be [*get* the jar open] 7. to prepare [to *get* lunch] 8. [Colloq.] *a)* to be obliged to (with *have* or *has*) [he's *got* to pass] *b)* to possess (with *have* or *has*) [he's *got* red hair] *c)* to strike, kill, baffle, defeat, etc. *d)* to understand 9. [Slang] to cause an emotional response in [her singing *gets* me] —*vi.* 1. to come, go, or arrive 2. to come to be [to *get* caught] 3. to manage or contrive [to *get* to do something] *Get* is used as an auxiliary for emphasis in passive construction [to *get* praised] —*n.* the young of an animal —**get around** 1. to move from place to place; circulate: also **get about** 2. to circumvent 3. to influence as by flattery —**get away** 1. to go away 2. to escape —**get away with** [Slang] to do something without being discovered or punished —**get by** [Colloq.] to survive; manage —**get it** [Colloq.] 1. to understand 2. to be punished —**get off** 1. to come off, down, or out of 2. to leave or start 3. to escape or help to escape —**get on** 1. to go on or into 2. to put on 3. to proceed 4. to grow older 5. to succeed —**get out** 1. to go out or away 2. take out 3. to be disclosed 4. to publish —**get over** 1. to recover from 2. to forget —**get through** 1. to finish 2. to manage to survive —**get together** 1. to assemble 2. [Colloq.] to reach an agreement —**get up** 1. to rise (from sleep, etc.) 2. to organize

**get′a·way′** *n.* 1. the act of starting, as in a race 2. the act of escaping

**get′-to·geth′er** *n.* an informal social gathering or meeting

**Get·tys·burg** (get′iz burg′) town in S Pa.: site of crucial Civil War battle

**get′-up′** *n.* [Colloq.] costume; dress

**gew·gaw** (gyōo′gô) *n.* [ME.] a trinket

**gey·ser** (gī′zər, -sər) *n.* [< ON. *gjosa*, to gush] a spring from which columns of boiling water and steam gush into the air at intervals

**Gha·na** (gä′nə) country in W Africa: 91,843 sq. mi.; pop. 8,143,000

**ghast·ly** (gast′lē) *adj.* -**li·er**, -**li·est** [< OE. *gast*, spirit] 1. horrible; frightful 2. ghostlike; pale 3. [Colloq.] very bad or unpleasant —**ghast′li·ness** *n.*

**ghat, ghaut** (gôt, gät) *n.* [Hindi *ghāṭ*] in India, a flight of steps at a river landing for ritual bathers

**gher·kin** (gur′kin) *n.* [< Per. *angārah*, watermelon] a small pickled cucumber

**ghet·to** (get′ō) *n., pl.* -**tos**, -**toes** [It.] 1. a section of some European cities to which Jews were restricted 2. any section of a city in which many members of a minority group live

**ghet′to·ize′** (-īz′) *vt.* -**ized′**, -**iz′ing** 1. to keep in a ghetto 2. to make into a ghetto

**ghost** (gōst) *n.* [< OE. *gast*] 1. the supposed disembodied spirit of a dead person, appearing as a pale, shadowy apparition 2. a slight trace; shadow [not a *ghost* of a chance] —**give up the ghost** to die —**ghost′ly** *adj.*

**ghost′writ′er** *n.* one who writes speeches, articles, etc. for another who professes to be the author —**ghost′write′** *vt., vi.*

**ghoul** (gōōl) *n.* [< Ar. *ghāla*, seize] *Oriental Folklore* an evil spirit that robs graves and feeds on the dead —**ghoul′ish** *adj.* —**ghoul′ish·ly** *adv.*

**GHQ, G.H.Q.** General Headquarters

**GI** (jē′ī′) *adj.* 1. government issue: designating clothing, etc. issued to military personnel 2. [Colloq.] of or characteristic of the U.S. armed forces [a *GI* haircut] —*n., pl.* GI's, GIs [Colloq.] a U.S. enlisted soldier

**gi·ant** (jī′ənt) *n.* [< Gr. *gigas*] 1. an imaginary being of superhuman size 2. a person or thing of great size, strength, intellect, etc. —*adj.* like a giant —**gi'ant·ess** *n.fem.*

**gib·ber** (jib'ər, gib'-) *vi., vt.* [echoic] to speak rapidly and incoherently

**gib'ber·ish** *n.* unintelligible chatter

**gib·bet** (jib'it) *n.* [< Frank. *gibb,* forked stick] 1. a gallows 2. a structure from which bodies of executed criminals were hung and exposed to public scorn —*vt.* to hang on a gibbet

**gib·bon** (gib'ən) *n.* [Fr.] a small, slender, long-armed ape of India, S China, and the East Indies

**gibe** (jīb) *vi., vt.* **gibed, gib'ing** [< ? OFr. *giber,* to handle roughly] to jeer or taunt —*n.* a jeer or taunt

**gib·let** (jib'lit) *n.* [< OFr. *gibelet,* stew made of game] any of the edible internal parts of a fowl, as the gizzard

**Gi·bral·tar** (ji brôl'tər) Brit. colony occupying a peninsula consisting mostly of a rocky hill (**Rock of Gibraltar**) at the S tip of Spain

**gid·dy** (gid'ē) *adj.* **-di·er, -di·est** [< OE. *gydig,* insane] 1. having or causing a whirling, dazed sensation; dizzy 2. frivolous —**gid'di·ness** *n.*

**Gid·e·on** (gid'ē ən) *Bible* a judge of Israel and victorious leader in battle

**gift** (gift) *n.* [< OE. *giefan,* give] 1. something given; present 2. the act of giving 3. a natural ability —*vt.* to present with or as a gift

**gift'ed** *adj.* 1. having a natural ability; talented 2. of superior intelligence

**gig** (gig) *n.* [ME. *gigge,* whirligig] 1. a light, two-wheeled, open carriage 2. a long, light ship's boat

**gi·gan·tic** (jī gan'tik) *adj.* [see GIANT] huge; enormous; immense

**gig·gle** (gig'l) *vi.* **-gled, -gling** [< Du. *giggelen*] to laugh with high, quick sounds in a silly or nervous way —*n.* such a laugh —**gig'gly** *adj.*

**gig·o·lo** (jig'ə lō) *n., pl.* **-los** [Fr.] a man paid to be a woman's escort

**Gi·la monster** (hē'lə) [< the *Gila* River, Ariz.] a poisonous, black-and-orange lizard of the SW U.S. deserts

**gild** (gild) *vt.* **gild'ed** or **gilt, gild'ing** [< OE. *gyldan*] 1. to coat with gold leaf or a gold color 2. to make seem more attractive or valuable than is so —**gild'er** *n.* —**gild'ing** *n.*

**gill¹** (gil) *n.* [ME. *gile*] the breathing organ of most water animals, as fish

**gill²** (jil) *n.* [< LL. *gillo,* cooling vessel] a liquid measure, equal to 1/4 pint

**gilt** (gilt) *alt. pt. & pp. of* GILD —*n.* gold leaf or color —*adj.* coated with gilt

**gilt·edged'** *adj.* of the highest quality or value [*gilt-edged* securities]: also **gilt'-edge'**

**gim·bals** (gim'b'lz, jim'-) *n.pl.* [with sing. v.] [< L. *gemellus,* twin] a pair of rings so pivoted that one swings freely within the other: used to keep a ship's compass level

**gim·crack** (jim'krak') *adj.* [< ME. *gibbecrak,* an ornament] showy but

cheap and useless —*n.* a gimcrack thing —**gim'crack'er·y** *n.*

**gim·let** (gim'lit) *n.* [< MDu. *wimpel*] a small boring tool with a spiral cutting edge

**gim·mick** (gim'ik) *n.* [< ?] 1. [Colloq.] a tricky device 2. [Slang] an attention-getting feature or device, as for promoting a product, etc.

**gimp** (gimp) *n.* [< ?] 1. a lame person 2. a limp —**gimp'y** *adj.*

**gin¹** (jin) *n.* [< L. *juniperus,* juniper] a distilled alcoholic liquor flavored typically with juniper berries

GIMLET

**gin²** (jin) *n.* [< OFr. *engin,* ENGINE] 1. a snare, as for game 2. a cotton gin —*vt.* **ginned, gin'ning** to remove seeds from (cotton) with a gin

**gin·ger** (jin'jər) *n.* [< Gr. *zingiberi*] 1. a tropical plant with rhizomes used esp. as a spice 2. this spice 3. [Colloq.] vigor; spirit —**gin'ger·y** *adj.*

**ginger ale** a carbonated soft drink flavored with ginger

**gin'ger·bread'** *n.* 1. a cake flavored with ginger 2. showy ornamentation

**gin'ger·ly** *adv.* very carefully —*adj.* very careful; cautious

**gin'ger·snap'** *n.* a crisp cookie flavored with ginger and molasses

**ging·ham** (giŋ'əm) *n.* [< Malay *ginggang*] a cotton cloth, usually woven in stripes, checks, or plaids

**gin·gi·vi·tis** (jin'jə vīt'əs) *n.* [< L. *gingiva,* the gum + -ITIS] inflammation of the gums

**gink·go** (giŋ'kō) *n., pl.* **gink'goes** [Jap. *ginkyo*] an Asian tree with fan-shaped leaves: also **ging'ko**

**gin rummy** a variety of the card game rummy: also **gin rum'my**

**gip** (jip) *n., vt., vi. same as* GYP

**Gip·sy** (jip'sē) *n., adj., vi. same as* GYPSY

**gi·raffe** (jə raf') *n.* [< Ar. *zarāfa*] a large cud-chewing animal of Africa, with a very long neck and legs

**gird** (gurd) *vt.* **gird'ed** or **girt, gird'ing** [OE. *gyrdan*] 1. to encircle or fasten with a belt 2. to surround 3. to prepare (oneself) for action

**gird·er** (gur'dər) *n.* a large wooden or steel beam for supporting joists, the framework of a building, etc.

**gir·dle** (gur'd'l) *n.* [OE. *gyrdel*] 1. a belt for the waist 2. anything that encircles 3. a woman's elasticized undergarment supporting the waist and hips —*vt.* **-dled, -dling** to encircle or bind, as with a girdle

**girl** (gurl) *n.* [ME. *girle,* youngster] 1. a female child 2. a young, unmarried woman 3. a female servant 4. [Colloq.] a sweetheart —**girl'hood'** *n.* —**girl'ish** *adj.*

**girl scout** a member of the **Girl Scouts,** a girls' club providing healthful, character-building activities

**girt**[1] (gurt) *alt. pt. & pp.* of GIRD

**girt**[2] (gurt) *vt.* 1. *same as* GIRD 2. to fasten with a girth

**girth** (gurth) *n.* [< ON. *gyrtha*, encircle] 1. a band put around the belly of a horse, etc. to hold a saddle or pack 2. the circumference, as of a tree trunk or person's waist

**gist** (jist) *n.* [< OFr. *giste*, point at issue] the essence or main point, as of an article or argument

**give** (giv) *vt.* **gave, giv'en, giv'ing** [OE. *giefan*] 1. to hand over as a present 2. to hand over [to *give* the porter a bag] 3. to hand over in or for payment 4. to pass (regards, etc.) along 5. to cause to have [to *give* pleasure] 6. to act as host or sponsor of 7. to produce; supply [cows *give* milk] 8. to concede; yield 9. to offer [*give* advice] 10. to perform [to *give* a concert] 11. to utter [*give* a reply] 12. to inflict (punishment, etc.) 13. to devote or sacrifice —*vi.* to bend, move, etc. from force or pressure —*n.* a bending, moving, etc. under pressure —**give away** 1. to make a gift of 2. to give (the bride) to the bridegroom 3. [Colloq.] to reveal or betray —**give forth** (or **off**) to emit —**give in** to yield —**give it to** [Colloq.] to beat or scold —**give or take** plus or minus —**give out** 1. to make public 2. to distribute 3. to become worn out, etc. —**give up** 1. to hand over 2. to cease 3. to stop trying 4. to despair of 5. to devote wholly —**giv'er** *n.*

**give'-and-take'** *n.* 1. mutual concession 2. banter or repartee

**give'a·way'** *n.* [Colloq.] 1. an unintentional revelation 2. something given free or sold cheap 3. a radio or television program giving prizes

**giv·en** (giv'n) *pp.* of GIVE —*adj.* 1. accustomed (*to*) by habit, etc. 2. specified 3. assumed; granted

**given name** a person's first name

**giz·mo, gis·mo** (giz'mō) *n.* [< ?] [Slang] a gadget or gimmick

**giz·zard** (giz'ərd) *n.* [< L. *gigeria*, cooked entrails of poultry] the muscular second stomach of a bird

**Gk.** Greek

**gla·cé** (gla sā') *adj.* [Fr.] 1. glossy, as silk 2. candied, as fruits —*vt.* **-céed', -cé'ing** to glaze (fruits, etc.)

**gla·cial** (glā'shəl) *adj.* of or like ice, glaciers, or a glacial epoch —**gla'cial·ly** *adv.*

**glacial epoch** any period when much of the earth was covered with glaciers

**gla·cier** (glā'shər) *n.* [< L. *glacies*, ice] a large mass of ice and snow moving slowly down a mountain or valley

**glad**[1] (glad) *adj.* **glad'der, glad'dest** [OE. *glæd*] 1. happy 2. causing joy 3. very willing 4. bright —**glad'ly** *adv.* —**glad'ness** *n.*

**glad**[2] (glad) *n.* [Colloq.] *same as* GLADIOLUS

**glad·den** (glad'n) *vt., vi.* to make or become glad

**glade** (glād) *n.* [ME.] 1. an open space in a forest 2. an everglade

**glad hand** [Slang] a cordial or effusive welcome —**glad'-hand'** *vt., vi.*

**glad·i·a·tor** (glad'ē āt'ər) *n.* [L. < *gladius*, sword] 1. in ancient Rome, a man, often a slave, who fought in an arena as a public show 2. any person involved in a fight —**glad'i·a·to'ri·al** (-ə tôr'ē əl) *adj.*

**glad·i·o·lus** (glad'ē ō'ləs) *n.*, *pl.* **-lus·es, -li** (-lī) [L., small sword] a plant of the iris family with swordlike leaves and tall spikes of funnel-shaped flowers: also **glad'i·o'la** (-lə)

**glad·some** (glad'səm) *adj.* joyful or cheerful —**glad'some·ly** *adv.*

**Glad·stone (bag)** (glad'stōn) [after W. *Gladstone*, 19th-c. Brit. statesman] a traveling bag hinged to open flat

**glam·or·ize** (glam'ə rīz') *vt.* **-ized', -iz'ing** to make glamorous —**glam'or·i·za'tion** *n.*

**glam·our, glam·or** (glam'ər) *n.* [Scot. var. of *grammar*, magic] seemingly mysterious allure; bewitching charm —**glam'or·ous, glam'our·ous** *adj.*

**glance** (glans) *vi.* **glanced, glanc'ing** [ME. *glansen*] 1. to strike obliquely and go off at an angle 2. to flash 3. to look quickly —*n.* 1. a glancing off 2. a flash 3. a quick look

**gland** (gland) *n.* [< L. *glans*, acorn] any organ that separates certain elements from the blood and secretes them for the body to use or throw off —**glan·du·lar** (glan'jə lər) *adj.*

**glans** (glanz) *n.*, *pl.* **glan·des** (glan'dēz) [L., lit., acorn] 1. the head of the penis 2. the tip of the clitoris

**glare** (gler) *vi.* **glared, glar'ing** [ME. *glaren*] 1. to shine with a steady, dazzling light 2. to stare fiercely —*vt.* to express with a glare —*n.* 1. a steady, dazzling light 2. a fierce stare 3. a bright, glassy surface, as of ice

**glar'ing** *adj.* 1. dazzlingly bright 2. too showy 3. staring fiercely 4. flagrant [a *glaring* mistake] —**glar'ing·ly** *adv.*

**Glas·gow** (glas'kō, glaz'gō) seaport in SC Scotland: pop. 980,000

**glass** (glas) *n.* [OE. *glæs*] 1. a hard, brittle substance, usually transparent, made by fusing silicates with soda, lime, etc. 2. glassware 3. *a*) a glass article, as a drinking container *b*) [*pl.*] eyeglasses or binoculars 4. the amount held by a drinking glass —*vt.* to equip with glass panes —*adj.* of or made of glass —**glass'ful** *n.*, *pl.* **-fuls**

**glass'ware'** *n.* articles made of glass

**glass'y** *adj.* **-i·er, -i·est** 1. like glass, as in smoothness 2. expressionless [a *glassy* stare] —**glass'i·ly** *adv.*

**glau·co·ma** (glô kō'mə) *n.* [< Gr. *glaukos*, gleaming] a disease of the eye, with hardening of the eyeball

**glaze** (glāz) *vt.* **glazed, glaz'ing** [ME. *glasen*] 1. to provide (windows, etc.) with glass 2. to give a hard, glossy finish to (pottery, etc.) 3. to cover (foods) with a coating of sugar syrup, etc. —*vi.* to become glassy or glossy —*n.* a glassy finish or coating

**gla·zier** (glā'zhər) *n.* one whose work is fitting glass in windows

**gleam** (glēm) *n.* [OE. *glæm*] 1. a flash or beam of light 2. a faint light 3. a

faint manifestation, as of hope —*vi.*
1. to shine with a gleam 2. to appear suddenly —**gleam′y** *adj.*

**glean** (glēn) *vt., vi.* [< Celt.] 1. to collect (grain left by reapers) 2. to collect (facts, etc.) gradually

**glee** (glē) *n.* [OE. *gleo*] lively joy; merriment —**glee′ful** *adj.*

**glee club** a group singing part songs

**glen** (glen) *n.* [Late MScot.] a narrow, secluded valley

**Glen·dale** (glen′dāl) city in SW Calif.: pop. 133,000

**glen plaid** [also G-] a plaid pattern with thin crossbarred stripes

**glib** (glib) *adj.* **glib′ber, glib′best** [< or akin to Du. *glibberig*, slippery] speaking or spoken smoothly, often too smoothly to be convincing — **glib′ly** *adv.* —**glib′ness** *n.*

**glide** (glīd) *vi.* **glid′ed, glid′ing** [OE. *glidan*] 1. to move smoothly and easily 2. *Aeron.* to descend with little or no engine power —*vt.* to make glide —*n.* 1. a gliding 2. a disk or ball, as of nylon, under a furniture leg to allow easy sliding

**glid′er** *n.* 1. one that glides 2. an engineless aircraft carried along by air currents 3. a porch swing suspended in a frame

**glim·mer** (glim′ər) *vi.* [< OE. *glæm*, gleam] 1. to give a faint, flickering light 2. to appear faintly —*n.* 1. a faint, flickering light 2. a faint manifestation —**glim′mer·ing** *n.*

**glimpse** (glimps) *vt.* **glimpsed, glimps′ing** [OE. *glæm*, gleam] to catch a brief, quick view of —*vi.* to look quickly —*n.* a brief, quick view

**glint** (glint) *vi.* [ME. *glenten*] to gleam or glitter —*n.* a glinting

**glis·san·do** (gli sän′dō) *n., pl.* **-di** (-dē), **-dos** [as if It. < Fr. *glisser*, to slide] *Music* a sliding effect, with tones sounded in rapid succession —*adj., adv.* (performed) with such an effect

**glis·ten** (glis′n) *vi.* [OE. *glisian*] to shine with reflected light, as a wet surface —*n.* a glistening

**glit·ter** (glit′ər) *vi.* [prob. < ON. *glitra*] 1. to shine brightly; sparkle 2. to be showy and bright —*n.* 1. bright, sparkling light 2. showiness or brightness 3. bits of glittering material —**glit′ter·y** *adj.*

**glitz·y** (glit′sē) *adj.* **-i·er, -i·est** [< G. *glitzern*, to glitter] [Slang] 1. glittery; sparkling 2. showy

**gloam·ing** (glō′miŋ) *n.* [< OE. *glom*] evening dusk; twilight

**gloat** (glōt) *vi.* [prob. < ON. *glotta*, grin scornfully] to gaze or think with malicious pleasure

**glob** (gläb) *n.* [prob. < GLOBULE] a rounded mass or lump, as of mud

**glo·bal** (glō′b'l) *adj.* worldwide — **glob′al·ly** *adv.*

**glob·al·ism** (-iz'm) *n.* a policy, outlook, etc. that is worldwide in scope

**globe** (glōb) *n.* [< L. *globus*] 1. anything spherical or somewhat spherical

2. the earth, or a model of the earth

**globe′-trot′ter** *n.* one who travels widely about the world

**glob·u·lar** (gläb′yə lər) *adj.* 1. spherical 2. made up of globules

**glob′ule** (-yōol) *n.* [< L. *globus*, ball] a tiny ball; very small drop

**glock·en·spiel** (gläk′ən spēl′) *n.* [G. < *glocke*, bell + *spiel*, play] a percussion instrument with tuned metal bars in a frame, played with hammers

**gloom** (glōom) *n.* [< Scand.] 1. darkness; dimness 2. deep sadness; dejection —**gloom′y** *adj.* **-i·er, -i·est**

**glop** (gläp) *n.* [< ? GL(UE) + (SL)OP] [Slang] any soft, gluey substance

**glo·ri·fy** (glôr′ə fī′) *vt.* **-fied′, -fy′ing** [< L. *gloria*, glory + *facere*, make] 1. to give glory to 2. to exalt (God), as in worship 3. to honor; extol 4. to make seem better, greater, etc. than is so —**glo′ri·fi·ca′tion** *n.*

**glo·ri·ous** (-ē əs) *adj.* 1. full of, receiving, or deserving glory 2. splendid —**glo′ri·ous·ly** *adv.*

**glo·ry** (glôr′ē) *n., pl.* **-ries** [< L. *gloria*] 1. great honor or fame, or its source 2. adoration 3. great splendor, prosperity, etc. 4. heavenly bliss 5. *same as* HALO (sense 2) —*vi.* **-ried, -ry·ing** to exult (*in*)

**gloss¹** (glôs) *n.* [< ? Scand.] 1. the shine of a polished surface 2. a deceptive outward show —*vt.* 1. to give a shiny surface to 2. to hide (an error, etc.) or make seem right or trivial —**gloss′y** *adj.* **-i·er, -i·est**

**gloss²** (glôs) *n.* [< Gr. *glōssa*, tongue] a note of comment or explanation, as in a footnote —*vt.* to annotate

**glos·sa·ry** (gläs′ə rē, glôs′-) *n., pl.* **-ries** [see prec.] a list of difficult terms with explanations, as for a book

**glos·so·la·li·a** (gläs′ə lā′lē ə, glôs′-) *n.* [< Gr. *glōssa*, tongue + *lalein*, to speak] an uttering of unintelligible sounds, as in a religious ecstasy

**glot·tis** (glät′is) *n.* [< Gr. *glōssa*, tongue] the opening between the vocal cords in the larynx —**glot′tal** *adj.*

**glove** (gluv) *n.* [OE. *glof*] 1. a covering for the hand, with separate sheaths for the fingers and thumb 2. a baseball player's mitt 3. a boxing glove —*vt.* **gloved, glov′ing** to cover with a glove

**glow** (glō) *vi.* [OE. *glowan*] 1. to give off a bright light due to great heat 2. to give out a steady light 3. to give out heat 4. to be elated 5. to be bright with color —*n.* 1. light given off, due to great heat 2. steady, even light 3. brightness, warmth, etc.

**glow·er** (glou′ər) *vi.* [prob. < ON.] to stare with sullen anger; scowl —*n.* a sullen, angry stare; scowl

**glow′worm′** (glō′-) *n.* a luminescent, wingless insect or insect larva

**glu·cose** (glōō′kōs) *n.* [Fr. < Gr. *gleûkos*, sweetness] 1. a crystalline sugar occurring naturally in fruits, honey, etc. 2. a sweet syrup prepared by the hydrolysis of starch

---

fat, āpe, cär; ten, ēven; is, bīte; gō, hôrn, tōōl, look; oil, out; up, fʉr; chin; she; thin, *then*; zh, leisure; ŋ, ring; ə for *a* in *ago*; ′, (ā′b'l); ë, Fr. coeur; ö, Fr. feu; Fr. mon; ü, Fr. duc; kh, G. ich; doch. ‡foreign; < derived from

**glue** (glōō) n. [< LL. *glus*] **1.** a sticky, viscous liquid made from animal gelatin, used as an adhesive **2.** any similar substance —vt. **glued, glu′ing** to make stick as with glue —**glue′y** adj. **glu′i·er, glu′i·est**

**glum** (glum) adj. **glum′mer, glum′mest** [prob. < ME. *glomen*, look morose] gloomy; sullen —**glum′ly** adv. —**glum′ness** n.

**glut** (glut) vi. **glut′ted, glut′ting** [< L. *gluttire*, to swallow] to eat to excess —vt. **1.** to feed, fill, etc. to excess **2.** to supply (the market) beyond demand —n. **1.** a glutting or being glutted **2.** a supply beyond demand

**glu·ten** (glōōt′'n) n. [L., glue] a gray, sticky, nutritious protein substance found in wheat, etc. —**glu′ten·ous** adj.

**glu·ti·nous** (-əs) adj. [see prec.] gluey; sticky —**glu′ti·nous·ly** adv.

**glut·ton** (glut′'n) n. [see GLUT] **1.** one who eats to excess **2.** one with a great capacity for something —**glut′ton·ous** adj. —**glut′ton·ous·ly** adv.

**glut′ton·y** n., pl. **-ies** the habit or act of eating too much

**glyc·er·in, glyc·er·ine** (glis′ər in) n. [< Gr. *glykeros*, sweet] *popular and commercial name for* GLYCEROL

**glyc·er·ol** (glis′ər ōl′, -ôl′) n. [< prec.] a colorless, syrupy liquid made from fats and oils: used in skin lotions, in making explosives, etc.

**gly·co·gen** (glī′kə jən) n. [see prec.] a substance in animal tissues that is changed into a simple sugar as the body needs it

**gm.** gram(s)·

**Gmc.** Germanic

**gnarl** (närl) n. [< ME. *knorre*] a knot on a tree trunk or branch —vt. to make knotted; twist —**gnarled** adj.

**gnash** (nash) vt., vi. [prob. < ON.] to grind (the teeth) together, as in anger —n. a gnashing

**gnat** (nat) n. [OE. *gnæt*] any of various small, two-winged insects that bite or sting

**gnaw** (nô) vt., vi. [OE. *gnagen*] **1.** to bite away bit by bit; consume **2.** to torment, as by constant pain

**gneiss** (nīs) n. [< OHG. *gneisto*, a spark] a granitelike rock formed of layers of quartz, mica, etc.

**gnome** (nōm) n. [LL. < Gr. *gnōmē*, thought] *Folklore* a dwarf who dwells in the earth and guards its treasures —**gnom′ish** adj.

**GNP** gross national product

**gnu** (nōō) n. [< the native name] a large African antelope with an oxlike head and a horse-like tail

GNU

**go** (gō) vi. **went, gone, go′ing** [OE. *gan*] **1.** to move along; travel; proceed **2.** to work properly; operate [the motor won′t go] **3.** to act, sound, etc. as specified [the balloon went "pop"] **4.** to result; turn out [the game went badly] **5.** to pass: said of time **6.** to become [to go mad] **7.** to be expressed, sung, etc. [as the saying goes] **8.** to harmonize; agree [blue goes with gold] **9.** to be accepted, valid, etc. **10.** to leave; depart **11.** to come to an end; fail [his eyesight is going] **12.** to be allotted or sold **13.** to reach, extend, etc. **14.** to be able to pass (through), fit (into), etc. **15.** to be capable of being divided (into) [5 goes into 10 twice] **16.** to belong [socks go in this drawer] —vt. **1.** to travel along [to go the wrong way] **2.** [Colloq.] a) to put up with b) to furnish (bail) for an arrested person —n., pl. **goes** [Colloq.] **1.** a success [make a go of marriage] **2.** [Colloq.] energy; animation **3.** [Colloq.] a try; attempt —**go back on** [Colloq.] **1.** to betray **2.** to break (a promise, etc.) —**go for** **1.** to try to get **2.** [Colloq.] to attack **3.** [Colloq.] to be attracted by —**go in for** [Colloq.] to engage or indulge in —**go off** **1.** to depart **2.** to explode —**go on** **1.** to proceed; continue **2.** to happen —**go out** **1.** to be extinguished, become outdated, etc. **2.** to attend social affairs, etc. —**go over** **1.** to examine thoroughly **2.** to do again **3.** [Colloq.] to be successful —**go through** **1.** to endure; experience **2.** to look through —**go through with** to pursue to the end —**go together** **1.** to match; harmonize **2.** [Colloq.] to be sweethearts —**go under** to fail, as in business —**let go** **1.** to let escape **2.** to release one's hold —**let oneself go** to be unrestrained —**on the go** [Colloq.] in constant motion or action —**to go** [Colloq.] **1.** to be taken out: said of food in a restaurant **2.** still to be done, etc.

**goad** (gōd) n. [OE. *gad*] **1.** a sharp-pointed stick used in driving oxen **2.** any driving impulse; spur —vt. to drive as with a goad; urge on

**go′-a·head′** n. permission or a signal to proceed: usually with *the*

**goal** (gōl) n. [ME. *gol*, boundary] **1.** the place at which a race, trip, etc. is ended **2.** an end that one strives to attain **3.** in some games, a) the place over or into which the ball or puck must go to score b) the score made

**goal′keep′er** n. in some games, a player stationed at a goal to prevent the ball or puck from crossing it: also **goal′ie** (-ē), **goal′tend′er**

**goat** (gōt) n. [OE. *gat*] **1.** a cud-chewing mammal with hollow horns, related to the sheep **2.** a lecherous man **3.** [Colloq.] a scapegoat —**get one's goat** [Colloq.] to irritate one

**goat·ee** (gō tē′) n. a small, pointed beard on a man's chin

**goat′herd′** n. one who herds goats

**goat′skin′** n. the skin of a goat, or leather made from this skin

**gob**[1] (gäb) n. [< OFr. *gobe*, mouthful] **1.** a soft lump or mass **2.** [pl.] [Colloq.] a large quantity

**gob**[2] (gäb) n. [< ?] [Slang] a sailor in the U.S. Navy

**gob·ble**[1] (gäb′'l) n. [echoic] the

throaty sound made by a male turkey —*vi.* **-bled, -bling** to make this sound

**gob·ble²** (gäb′'l) *vt., vi.* **-bled, -bling** [prob. < OFr. *gobe*, mouthful] **1.** to eat quickly and greedily **2.** to seize eagerly; snatch (*up*)

**gob′ble·dy·gook′** (-dē gook′) *n.* [? echoic] [Slang] pompous, wordy, usually meaningless talk or writing

**gob′bler** (gäb′lər) *n.* a male turkey

**go-be·tween** (gō′bi twēn′) *n.* one who makes arrangements between each of two sides; intermediary

**Go·bi** (gō′bē) large desert plateau in E Asia, chiefly in Mongolia

**gob·let** (gäb′lit) *n.* [< OFr. *gobel*] a drinking glass with a base and stem

**gob·lin** (gäb′lin) *n.* [< ML. *gobelinus*] *Folklore* an evil or mischievous sprite

**go-by** (gō′bī′) *n.* [Colloq.] an intentional disregard or slight

**god** (gäd) *n.* [OE.] **1.** any of various beings conceived of as supernatural and immortal; esp., a male deity **2.** an idol **3.** a person or thing deified —[G-] in monotheistic religions, the creator and ruler of the universe; Supreme Being —**god′like′** *adj.*

**god′child′** *n., pl.* **-chil′dren** the person a godparent sponsors

**god′daugh′ter** *n.* a female godchild

**god·dess** (gäd′is) *n.* **1.** a female god **2.** a woman of great beauty, charm, etc.

**god′fa′ther** *n.* a male godparent

**god′head′** (-hed′) *n.* **1.** *same as* GOD-HOOD **2.** [G-] God (usually with *the*)

**god′hood** (-hood) *n.* the state of being a god

**Go·di·va** (gə dī′və) *Eng. Legend* an 11th-cent. noblewoman who rode naked through the streets on condition that her husband would abolish a heavy tax

**god′less** *adj.* **1.** irreligious **2.** wicked —**god′less·ness** *n.*

**god′ly** *adj.* **-li·er, -li·est** devoted to God; devout —**god′li·ness** *n.*

**god′moth′er** *n.* a female godparent

**god′par′ent** *n.* a person who sponsors a child, as at baptism, taking responsibility for its faith

**god′send′** *n.* anything that comes unexpectedly and when needed or desired, as if sent by God

**god′son′** *n.* a male godchild

**God′win Aus·ten** (ôs′win) mountain in N India: 2d highest in the world: 28,250 ft.

**Goe·the** (gö′tə; *Eng.* gur′tə), **Jo·hann Wolf·gang von** (yō′hän vôlf′gäŋ fôn) 1749–1832; Ger. poet

**go-get·ter** (gō′get′ər) *n.* [Colloq.] an enterprising and aggressive person who usually gets what he wants

**gog·gle** (gäg′'l) *vi.* **-gled, -gling** [ME. *gogelen*] to stare with bulging eyes —*n.* [*pl.*] large spectacles to protect the eyes against dust, wind, sparks, etc. —*adj.* bulging or staring: said of the eyes

**go-go** (gō′gō′) *adj.* [< Fr. *à gogo*, in plenty] of rock-and-roll dancing per-

formed in cafés, often in topless costumes

**go·ing** (gō′iŋ) *n.* **1.** a departure **2.** the condition of the ground or land as it affects traveling, walking, etc. —*adj.* **1.** moving; working **2.** commonly accepted —**be going to** will or shall

**go′ing-o′ver** *n.* [Colloq.] **1.** a thorough inspection **2.** a severe scolding or beating

**go′ings-on′** *n.pl.* [Colloq.] actions or events, esp. when disapproved of

**goi·ter, goi·tre** (goit′ər) *n.* [< L. *guttur*, throat] an enlargement of the thyroid gland, often seen as a swelling in the front of the neck

**gold** (gōld) *n.* [OE.] **1.** a heavy, yellow, metallic, highly malleable chemical element: it is a precious metal **2.** money; wealth **3.** bright yellow —*adj.* of gold —**gold′en** *adj.* **1.** made of or containing gold **2.** bright-yellow **3.** very valuable; excellent **4.** flourishing

**gold′brick′** (-brik′) *n.* **1.** [Colloq.] anything worthless passed off as valuable **2.** [Mil. Slang] one who avoids work: also **gold′brick′er** —*vi.* [Mil. Slang] to avoid work

**gold·en ag·er** (āj′ər) [Colloq.] [*also* G- A-] an elderly person, esp. one 65 or older and retired

**Golden Fleece** *Gr. Myth.* the fleece of gold captured by Jason

**Golden Gate** strait between San Francisco Bay & the Pacific

**gold′en·rod′** *n.* a N.American plant with long, branching stalks bearing clusters of small, yellow flowers

**golden rule** the precept that one should act toward others as he would want them to act toward him

**gold′-filled′** *adj.* made of a base metal overlaid with gold

**gold′finch′** *n.* [OE. *goldfinc*] a small American finch, the male of which has a yellow body

**gold′fish′** *n., pl.:* see FISH a small, golden-yellow or orange fish, often kept in ponds or fishbowls

**gold leaf** gold beaten into very thin sheets, used for gilding

**gold′smith′** *n.* a skilled worker who makes articles of gold

**gold standard** a monetary standard in which the basic currency unit equals a specified quantity of gold

**golf** (gôlf, gälf) *n.* [< ? Du. *kolf*, club] an outdoor game played with a small, hard ball and a set of clubs, the object being to hit the ball into each of a series of 9 or 18 holes with the fewest possible strokes —*vi.* to play golf —**golf′er** *n.*

**golf course** (or **links**) a tract of land for playing golf

**Go·li·ath** (gə lī′əth) *Bible* the Philistine giant killed by David

**gol·ly** (gäl′ē) *interj.* an exclamation of surprise, etc.

**-gon** (gän) [< Gr. *gōnia*, an angle] *a combining form meaning* a figure having (a specified number of) angles

---

**go·nad** (gō′nad) *n.* [ < Gr. *gonē*, seed] an animal organ that produces reproductive cells; ovary or testis

**gon·do·la** (gän′də lə) *n.* [It.] 1. a long, narrow boat used on the canals of Venice 2. a railroad freight car with low sides and no top: also **gondola car** 3. a cabin suspended under a dirigible or balloon

**gon·do·lier′** (-lir′) *n.* a man who rows or poles a gondola

**gone** (gôn, gän) *pp.* of GO —*adj.* 1. departed 2. ruined 3. lost 4. dead 5. consumed 6. ago; past

**gon′er** *n.* [Colloq.] a person or thing certain to die, be ruined, etc.

**gong** (gôŋ, gäŋ) *n.* [Malay *gun*] a slightly convex metallic disk that gives a loud, resonant tone when struck

**gon·or·rhe·a, gon·or·rhoe·a** (gän′ə rē′ə) *n.* [ < Gr. *gonos*, semen + *rheein*, to flow] a venereal disease with inflammation of the genital organs

**goo** (gōō) *n.* [Slang] 1. anything sticky, or sticky and sweet 2. sentimentality —**goo′ey** *adj.* -i·er, -i·est

**goo·ber** (gōō′bər) *n.* [ < Afr. *nguba*] [Chiefly South] a peanut

**good** (good) *adj.* bet′ter, best [OE. *god*] 1. having the proper qualities 2. beneficial 3. valid; real [good money] 4. healthy or sound [good eyesight] 5. honorable [one's good name] 6. enjoyable, pleasant, etc. 7. thorough 8. virtuous, devout, kind, dutiful, etc. 9. skilled 10. considerable [a good many] —*n.* something good; worth, benefit, etc. —*adv.* [Dial. or Colloq.] well; fully —**as good as** virtually; nearly —**for good (and all)** permanently —**good and** [Colloq.] very or altogether —**good for** 1. able to endure or be used for (a period of time) 2. worth 3. able to pay or give —**make good** 1. to repay or replace 2. to fulfill 3. to succeed —**no good** useless; worthless

**good′bye, good′-bye′** (-bī′) *interj., n.* (contr. of *God be with ye*] farewell: also **good′by′, good′-by′**

**Good Friday** the Friday before Easter, commemorating the Crucifixion

**good′-heart′ed** *adj.* kind; generous —**good′-heart′ed·ly** *adv.* —**good′-heart′ed·ness** *n.*

**Good Hope, Cape of** cape at the SW tip of Africa

**good humor** a cheerful, agreeable mood —**good′-hu′mored** *adj.* —**good′-hu′mored·ly** *adv.*

**good′-look′ing** *adj.* handsome

**good′ly** *adj.* -li·er, -li·est 1. of good appearance or quality 2. ample

**good′-na′tured** *adj.* agreeable; affable —**good′-na′tured·ly** *adv.*

**good′ness** *n.* the state or quality of being good; virtue, kindness, etc. —*interj.* an exclamation of surprise

**goods** (goodz) *n.pl.* 1. movable personal property 2. merchandise; wares 3. fabric; cloth —**get (or have) the goods on** [Slang] to discover (or know) something incriminating about

**good Sa·mar·i·tan** (sə mer′ə t'n) anyone who helps others unselfishly: see Luke 10:30–37

**good′-sized′** *adj.* ample; fairly big

**good′-tem′pered** *adj.* amiable

**good turn** a friendly, helpful act

**good will** 1. benevolence 2. willingness 3. the value of a business in patronage, reputation, etc.; beyond its tangible assets Also **good′will′** *n.*

**good′y** *n., pl.* **-ies** [Colloq.] something good to eat, as a candy —*interj.* a child's exclamation of delight

**good′y-good′y** *adj.* [Colloq.] affectedly moral or pious —*n.* [Colloq.] a goody-goody person

**goof** (gōōf) *n.* [Slang] 1. a stupid person 2. a mistake; blunder —*vi.* [Slang] 1. to err or blunder 2. to waste time, shirk duties, etc. (with *off* or *around*) —**goof′y** *adj.*

**goof′-off′** *n.* [Slang] one who wastes time, shirks duties, etc.

**gook** (gook, gōōk) *n.* [GOO + (GUN)K] [Slang] any sticky or slimy substance

**goon** (gōōn) *n.* [Slang] 1. a ruffian or thug, esp. one hired as a strikebreaker 2. a stupid person

**goop** (gōōp) *n.* [Slang] any sticky, semiliquid substance

**goose** (gōōs) *n., pl.* **geese** [OE. *gos*] 1. a long-necked, web-footed bird like a duck but larger 2. its flesh as food 3. a silly person —**cook one's goose** [Colloq.] to spoil one's chances

**goose′ber′ry** *n., pl.* **-ries** 1. a small, sour berry used for preserves, pies, etc. 2. the shrub it grows on

**goose flesh (or bumps or pimples)** a roughened condition of the skin, caused by cold, fear, etc.

**GOP, G.O.P.** Grand Old Party (Republican Party)

**go·pher** (gō′fər) *n.* [ < ? Fr. *gaufre*, honeycomb: from its burrowing] 1. a burrowing rodent with wide cheek pouches 2. a striped ground squirrel of the prairies

**gore¹** (gôr) *n.* [OE. *gor*, filth] blood from a wound, esp. clotted blood

**gore²** (gôr) *vt.* **gored, gor′ing** [OE. *gar*, a spear] 1. to pierce as with a horn or tusk 2. to insert gores in —*n.* a tapering piece of cloth inserted in a skirt, sail, etc. to give it fullness

**gorge** (gôrj) *n.* [ < L. *gurges*, whirlpool] 1. the gullet 2. what has been swallowed 3. resentment, disgust, etc. 4. a deep, narrow pass between steep heights —*vi., vt.* **gorged, gorg′ing** to eat greedily or glut (oneself)

**gor·geous** (gôr′jəs) *adj.* [ < OFr. *gorgias*] 1. brilliantly colored; magnificent 2. [Slang] beautiful, delightful, etc. —**gor′geous·ly** *adv.*

**go·ril·la** (gə ril′ə) *n.* [ < WAfr.] the largest and most powerful of the manlike apes native to Africa

**Gor·ki** (gôr′kē) city in W U.S.S.R., on the Volga: pop. 1,100,000

**gor·mand·ize** (gôr′mən dīz′) *vi., vt.* **-ized, -iz·ing** [ < Fr. *gourmandise*, gluttony] to eat like a glutton

GORILLA

**gorse** (gôrs) *n.* [OE. *gorst*] *same as* FURZE

**gor·y** (gôr′ē) *adj.* **-i·er, -i·est** 1. covered with gore; bloody 2. with much bloodshed —**gor′i·ness** *n.*

**gosh** (gäsh) *interj.* an exclamation of surprise, etc.: a euphemism for *God*

**gos·ling** (gäz′liŋ) *n.* a young goose

**gos·pel** (gäs′p'l) *n.* [OE. *gōdspel*, good news] 1. [*often* G-] the teachings of Jesus and the Apostles 2. [G-] any of the first four books of the New Testament 3. anything proclaimed or accepted as the absolute truth: also **gospel truth**

**gos·sa·mer** (gäs′ə mər) *n.* [ME. *gosesomer*, lit., goose summer] 1. a filmy cobweb 2. a very thin, filmy cloth —*adj.* light, thin, and filmy

**gos·sip** (gäs′əp) *n.* [< Late OE. *godsibbe*, godparent] 1. one who chatters idly about others 2. such talk —*vi.* to be a gossip —**gos′sip·y** *adj.*

**got** (gät) *pt. & alt. pp.* of GET

**Goth** (gäth) *n.* any member of a Germanic people that conquered most of the Roman Empire in the 3d, 4th, and 5th c. A.D.

**Goth·ic** (gäth′ik) *adj.* 1. of the Goths or their language 2. designating or of a style of architecture developed in W Europe between the 12th & 16th c., with pointed arches, steep roofs, etc. 3. [*sometimes* g-] uncivilized —*n.* 1. the East Germanic language of the Goths 2. Gothic architecture

**got·ten** (gät′'n) *alt. pp.* of GET

**Gou·da** (**cheese**) (gou′də, gōō′-) [< *Gouda*, Netherlands] a mild cheese made from curds, usually coated with red wax

**gouge** (gouj) *n.* [< LL. *gulbia*] 1. a chisel for cutting grooves or holes in wood 2. such a groove or hole —*vt.* **gouged, goug′ing** 1. to scoop out as with a gouge 2. [Colloq.] to defraud or overcharge —**goug′er** *n.*

**gou·lash** (gōō′läsh, -lash) *n.* [< Hung. *gulyás*] a beef or veal stew seasoned with paprika

**gou·ra·mi** (goor′ə mē, goo rä′mē) *n.*, *pl.* **-mis, -mi** [Malay *gurami*] 1. a food fish of SE Asia 2. a related fish, brightly colored, often kept in aquariums

**gourd** (gôrd, goord) *n.* [< L. *cucurbita*] 1. any trailing or climbing plant of a family that includes the squash, melon, etc. 2. the fruit of one species or its dried, hollowed-out shell, used as a cup, dipper, etc.

**gour·mand** (goor′mand, goor mänd′) *n.* [OFr.] one who likes good food and drink, often to excess

**gour·met** (goor′mā) *n.* [Fr. < OFr., wine taster] one who likes and is an excellent judge of fine foods and drinks

**gout** (gout) *n.* [< L. *gutta*, a drop] a disease characterized by painful swelling of the joints, esp. in the big toe —**gout′y** *adj.* **-i·er, -i·est**

**gov., Gov.** 1. government 2. governor

**gov·ern** (guv′ərn) *vt., vi.* [< Gr. *kybernan*, to steer] 1. to exercise authority over; rule, control, etc. 2. to influence the action of; guide 3. to determine —**gov′ern·a·ble** *adj.*

**gov′ern·ance** (-ər nəns) *n.* the action, function, or power of government

**gov′ern·ess** (-ər nəs) *n.* a woman employed in a private home to train and teach the children

**gov·ern·ment** (guv′ər mənt, -ərn mənt) *n.* 1. the exercise of authority over a state, organization, etc.; control; rule 2. a system of ruling, political administration, etc. 3. those who direct the affairs of a state, etc.; administration —**gov′ern·men′tal** *adj.*

**gov·er·nor** (guv′ə nər, -ər nər) *n.* 1. one who governs; esp., *a*) one appointed to govern a province, etc. *b*) the elected head of any State of the U.S. 2. a mechanical device for automatically controlling the speed of an engine —**gov′er·nor·ship′** *n.*

**governor general** *pl.* **governors general, governor generals** a governor who has deputy governors under him

**govt., Govt.** government

**gown** (goun) *n.* [< LL. *gunna*] a long, loose outer garment; specif., *a*) a woman's formal dress *b*) a nightgown *c*) a long, flowing robe worn by judges, clergymen, scholars, etc.

**Gr.** Greek

**gr.** 1. grain(s) 2. gram(s) 3. gross

**grab** (grab) *vt.* **grabbed, grab′bing** [prob. < MDu. *grabben*] 1. to snatch suddenly 2. to get by unscrupulous methods 3. [Slang] to affect; impress —*n.* a grabbing —**grab′ber** *n.*

**grab·by** (grab′ē) *adj.* **-bi·er, -bi·est** grasping; avaricious

**grace** (grās) *n.* [< L. *gratus*, pleasing] 1. beauty or charm of form, movement, or expression 2. good will; favor 3. a delay granted for payment of an obligation 4. a short prayer of thanks for a meal 5. [G-] a title of an archbishop, duke, or duchess 6. the love and favor of God toward man —*vt.* **graced, grac′ing** 1. to decorate 2. to dignify —**in the good** (or **bad**) **graces of** in favor (or disfavor) with

**grace′ful** *adj.* having beauty of form, movement, or expression —**grace′ful·ly** *adv.* —**grace′ful·ness** *n.*

**grace′less** *adj.* 1. lacking any sense of what is proper 2. clumsy —**grace′less·ly** *adv.* —**grace′less·ness** *n.*

**gra·cious** (grā′shəs) *adj.* 1. having or showing kindness, charm, courtesy, etc. 2. compassionate 3. polite to supposed inferiors 4. marked by luxury, ease, etc. [*gracious living*] —**gra′cious·ly** *adv.* —**gra′cious·ness** *n.*

**grack·le** (grak′'l) *n.* [< L. *graculus*, jackdaw] any of various blackbirds somewhat smaller than a crow

**grad** (grad) *n.* [Colloq.] a graduate

**gra·da·tion** (grā dā′shən) *n.* 1. an arranging in grades, or stages 2. a gradual change by stages 3. a step or degree in a graded series

**grade** (grād) *n.* [< L. *gradus*] 1. a stage or step in a progression 2. *a)* a degree in a scale of quality, rank, etc. *b)* a group of people of the same rank, merit, etc. 3. *a)* the degree of slope *b)* a sloping part 4. any of the divisions of a school course, by years 5. a mark or rating in an examination, etc. —*vt.* **grad′ed, grad′ing** 1. to classify by grades; sort 2. to give a grade (sense 5) to 3. to make (ground) level or evenly sloped, as for a road —**make the grade** to succeed

**grade crossing** the place where a railroad intersects another railroad or a roadway on the same level

**grade school** *same as* ELEMENTARY SCHOOL

**grade separation** a crossing with an overpass or underpass

**gra·di·ent** (grā′dē ənt) *n.* [< L. *gradi*, to step] 1. a slope, as of a road 2. the degree of slope

**grad·u·al** (graj′ōō wəl) *adj.* [< L. *gradus*, a step] taking place by degrees; little by little —**grad′u·al·ly** *adv.*

**grad′u·al·ism** *n.* the principle of promoting gradual rather than rapid change

**grad·u·ate** (graj′ōō wit; *for v.* -wāt′) *n.* [< L. *gradus*, a step] one who has completed a course of study at a school or college —*vt.* **-at′ed, -at′ing** 1. to give a degree or diploma to upon completion of a course of study 2. to mark with degrees for measuring 3. to classify into grades according to size, quality, etc. —*vi.* to become a graduate of a school, etc. —*adj.* 1. being a graduate of a school, etc. 2. of or for graduates —**grad′u·a′tor** *n.*

**grad′u·a′tion** *n.* 1. a graduating from a school or college 2. the ceremony connected with this

**graf·fi·to** (grə fēt′ō) *n., pl.* **-ti** (-ē) [It. < L.: see ff.] a crude inscription or drawing on a wall or other public surface

**graft** (graft) *n.* [< Gr. *grapheion*, stylus] 1. *a)* a shoot or bud of one plant or tree inserted into another, where it grows permanently *b)* the inserting of such a shoot 2. the transplanting of skin, bone, etc. 3. *a)* the dishonest use of one's position to gain money, etc., as in politics *b)* anything so gained —*vt., vi.* 1. to insert (a graft) 2. to obtain (money, etc.) by graft —**graft′er** *n.*

**gra·ham** (grā′əm) *adj.* [< S. *Graham*, 19th-c. U.S. dietary reformer] designating or made of finely ground, wholewheat flour [*graham* crackers]

**Grail** (grāl) [< ML. *gradalis*, cup] *Medieval Legend* the cup used by Jesus at the Last Supper

**grain** (grān) *n.* [< L. *granum*] 1. the small, hard seed of any cereal plant, as wheat, corn, etc. 2. cereal plants 3. a tiny, solid particle, as of salt or sand 4. a tiny bit 5. the smallest unit of weight 6. *a)* the arrangement of fibers, layers, etc. of wood, leather, etc. *b)* the markings or texture due to this 7. disposition; nature

**grain′y** *adj.* **-i·er, -i·est** 1. having a clearly defined grain, as wood 2. coarsely textured; granular —**grain′i·ness** *n.*

**gram** (gram) *n.* [< Gr. *gramma*, small weight] the basic unit of weight in the metric system, equal to about 1/28 of an ounce: also **gramme**

**-gram** (gram) [< Gr. *gramma*, writing] *a combining form meaning:* 1. something written [*telegram*] 2. a specified number of grams [*kilogram*]

**gram·mar** (gram′ər) *n.* [< Gr. *gramma*, writing] 1. language study dealing with the forms of words and with their arrangement in sentences 2. a system of rules for speaking and writing a given language 3. one's manner of speaking or writing as judged by such rules —**gram·mar·i·an** (grə mer′ē ən) *n.* —**gram·mat·i·cal** (grə mat′i k'l) *adj.*

**grammar school** [Now Rare] *same as* ELEMENTARY SCHOOL

**gran·a·ry** (gran′ər ē, grā′nər ē) *n., pl.* **-ries** [< L. *granum*, grain] a building for storing grain

**grand** (grand) *adj.* [< L. *grandis*, large] 1. higher in rank than others [a *grand* duke] 2. most important; main [the *grand* ballroom] 3. imposing in size, beauty, extent, etc. 4. distinguished; illustrious 5. overall; comprehensive [the *grand* total] 6. [Colloq.] very good; delightful —*n.* [Slang] a thousand dollars —**grand′ly** *adv.*

**grand-** *a combining form meaning of* the generation older (or younger) than [*grandfather, grandson*]

**gran·dam** (gran′dam, -dəm) *n.* [see prec. & DAME] [Archaic or Rare] 1. a grandmother 2. an old woman

**grand′child** *n., pl.* **-chil′dren** a child of one's son or daughter

**grand′daugh′ter** *n.* a daughter of one's son or daughter

**grande dame** (gränd däm) [Fr.] a woman, esp. an older one, of great dignity

**gran·dee** (gran dē′) *n.* [< Sp. & Port.: see GRAND] a man of high rank

**gran·deur** (gran′jər, -joor) *n.* [see GRAND] 1. splendor; magnificence 2. nobility; dignity

**grand′fa′ther** *n.* 1. the father of one's father or mother 2. a forefather

**grandfather** (or **grandfather's**) **clock** a large clock with a pendulum, in a tall, upright case

**gran·dil·o·quent** (gran dil′ə kwənt) *adj.* [< L. *grandis*, grand + *loqui*, speak] using pompous, bombastic words —**gran·dil′o·quence** *n.*

**gran·di·ose** (gran′dē ōs′) *adj.* [< L. *grandis*, great] 1. having grandeur 2. pompous and showy —**gran′di·os′i·ty** (-äs′ə tē) *n.*

**grand jury** a jury that investigates accusations and indicts persons for trial if there is sufficient evidence

**grand·ma** (gran′mä) *n.* [Colloq.] grandmother

**grand′mas′ter** *n.* any highly skilled chess player: also **grand master**

**grand′moth′er** *n.* the mother of one's father or mother

**grand opera** opera in which the whole text is set to music

**grand·pa** (gran'pä) n. [Colloq.] grandfather

**grand'par'ent** n. a grandfather or grandmother

**grand piano** a large piano with a horizontal, harp-shaped case

**Grand Rapids** city in SW Mich.: pop. 198,000

**grand slam 1.** Baseball a home run hit when there is a runner on each base **2.** Bridge the winning of all the tricks in a deal

**grand·son'** n. a son of one's son or daughter

**grand'stand'** n. the main structure for spectators at a sporting event

**grange** (grānj) n. [< L. granum, grain] **1.** a farm **2.** [G-] an association of farmers or a local lodge of this

**gran·ite** (gran'it) n. [< L. granum, grain] a hard, igneous rock consisting chiefly of feldspar and quartz

**gran·ny, gran·nie** (gran'ē) n., pl. **-nies** [Colloq.] **1.** a grandmother **2.** an old woman **3.** any fussy person

**gran·o·la** (gra nō'la) n. [? < L. granum, grain] a breakfast cereal of rolled oats, wheat germ, sesame seeds, brown sugar or honey, nuts or dried fruit, etc.

**grant** (grant) vt. [< L. credere, believe] **1.** to give (what is requested, as permission, etc.) **2.** to give or transfer by legal procedure **3.** to admit as true; concede —n. **1.** a granting **2.** something granted, as property, a right, etc. —**take for granted** to consider as true, already settled, etc.

**Grant** (grant), **Ulysses S.** 1822–85; 18th president of the U.S. (1869–77); Union commander in Civil War

**grant'-in-aid'** n., pl. **grants'-in-aid'** a grant of funds, as by a foundation to a scientist, artist, etc., to support a specific project

**grants·man·ship** (grants'mən-ship') n. the skill of getting grants-in-aid

**gran·u·lar** (gran'yə lər) adj. **1.** containing or consisting of grains **2.** like grains or granules —**gran'u·lar·ly** adv.

**gran·u·late'** (-lāt') vt., vi. **-lat'ed, -lat'ing** to form into grains or granules —**gran'u·la'tion** n.

**gran·ule** (gran'yool) n. [< L. granum, a grain] a small grain or particle

**grape** (grāp) n. [< OFr. graper, gather with a hook] **1.** a small, round, juicy berry, growing in clusters on a vine **2.** a grapevine **3.** a dark purplish red

**grape'fruit'** n. a large, round, sour citrus fruit with a yellow rind

**grape hyacinth** a small plant of the lily family, with spikes of blue or white, small, bell-shaped flowers

**grape'vine'** n. **1.** a woody vine bearing grapes **2.** a secret means of spreading information **3.** a rumor

**graph** (graf) n. [short for graphic formula] a diagram representing the successive changes in the value of a variable quantity or quantities —vt. to represent by a graph

**-graph** (graf) [< Gr. graphein, write] a combining form meaning: **1.** something that writes or records [telegraph] **2.** something written [autograph]

**graph·ic** (graf'ik) adj. [< Gr. graphein, write] **1.** described in realistic detail **2.** of those arts (**graphic arts**) that include any form of visual artistic representation, esp. painting, drawing, etching, etc. Also **graph'i·cal** — **graph'i·cal·ly** adv.

**graph'ics** (-iks) n.pl. [with sing. v.] **1.** the graphic arts **2.** design as used in the graphic arts

**graph·ite** (graf'īt) n. [< Gr. graphein, write] a soft, black form of carbon used in pencils, for lubricants, etc.

**graph·ol·o·gy** (gra fäl'ə jē) n. [< Fr.: see GRAPHIC & -LOGY] the study of handwriting, esp. as a clue to character, attitudes, etc. —**graph-ol'o·gist** n.

**-graph·y** (grə fē) [< Gr. graphein, write] a combining form meaning: **1.** a process or method of writing, or graphically representing [lithography] **2.** a descriptive science [geography]

**grap·nel** (grap'n'l) n. [< Pr. grapa, a hook] **1.** a small anchor with several flukes **2.** an iron bar with claws at one end for grasping things

**grap·ple** (grap''l) n. [OFr. grappil] **1.** same as GRAP-NEL (sense 2) **2.** a hand-to-hand fight —vt. **-pled, -pling** to grip and hold —vi. **1.** to use a grapnel (sense 2) **2.** to wrestle **3.** to try to cope (with)

GRAPNEL

**grappling iron** (or **hook**) same as GRAPNEL (sense 2)

**grasp** (grasp) vt. [ME. graspen] **1.** to grip, as with the hand **2.** to take hold of eagerly; seize **3.** to comprehend —vi. **1.** to try to seize (with at) **2.** to accept eagerly (with at) —n. **1.** a grasping; grip **2.** control; possession **3.** the power to hold or seize **4.** comprehension —**grasp'a·ble** adj.

**grasp'ing** adj. avaricious; greedy

**grass** (gras) n. [OE. græs] **1.** a plant with narrow leaves, jointed stems, and seedlike fruit, as wheat, rye, etc. **2.** any of various green plants with narrow leaves, growing densely in meadows, lawns, etc. **3.** pasture or lawn **4.** [Slang] marijuana —**grass'y** adj.

**grass'hop'per** n. any of a group of plant-eating, winged insects with powerful hind legs for jumping

**grass roots** [Colloq.] **1.** the common people **2.** the basic source or support, as of a movement —**grass'-roots'** adj.

**grass widow** a woman divorced or separated from her husband

**grate¹** (grāt) vt. **grat'ed, grat'ing** [< OFr. grater] **1.** to grind into particles by scraping **2.** to rub against (an object) or grind (the teeth) together with a harsh sound **3.** to irritate —vi. **1.** to rub with or make a rasping sound **2.** to be irritating —**grat′er** n.

**grate²** (grāt) n. [ < L. cratis, a hurdle] **1.** same as GRATING¹ **2.** a frame of metal bars for holding fuel in a fireplace, etc. **3.** a fireplace

**grate·ful** (grāt′fəl) adj. [obs. grate ( < L. gratus), pleasing] **1.** thankful **2.** welcome —**grate′ful·ly** adv. —**grate′ful·ness** n.

**grat·i·fy** (grat′ə fī′) vt. -**fied′**, -**fy′ing** [ < L. gratus, pleasing + facere, make] **1.** to please or satisfy **2.** to indulge; humor —**grat′i·fi·ca′tion** n.

**grat·ing¹** (grāt′iŋ) n. a framework of bars set in a window, door, etc.

**grat′ing²** adj. **1.** rasping **2.** irritating

**gra·tis** (grat′is, grāt′-) adv., adj. [L. < gratia, a favor] free of charge

**grat·i·tude** (grat′ə tōōd′) n. [ < L. gratus, pleasing] thankful appreciation for favors received

**gra·tu·i·tous** (grə tōō′ə təs, -tyōō′-) adj. [ < L. gratus, pleasing] **1.** given free of charge **2.** uncalled-for —**gra·tu′i·tous·ly** adv.

**gra·tu·i·ty** (-tē) n., pl. -**ties** a gift as of money, esp. for a service; tip

**grave¹** (grāv) adj. [ < L. gravis, heavy] **1.** important **2.** serious [a grave illness] **3.** solemn **4.** somber; dull —**grave′ly** adv. —**grave′ness** n.

**grave²** (grāv) n. [ < OE. grafan, dig] **1.** a) a hole in the ground in which to bury a dead body b) any burial place; tomb **2.** death —vt. **graved, grav′en** or **graved, grav′ing 1.** to sculpture **2.** to impress sharply

**grave accent** a mark (`) showing the quality of a vowel, stress, etc.

**grav·el** (grav′l) n. [ < OFr. grave, coarse sand] a loose mixture of pebbles and rock fragments coarser than sand

**grav′el·ly** (-ē) adj. **1.** full of or like gravel **2.** harsh or rasping

**grav·en** (grāv′'n) alt. pp. of GRAVE²

**grave′stone′** n. a tombstone

**grave′yard′** n. a cemetery

**graveyard shift** [Colloq.] a night work shift, esp. one starting at midnight

**grav·id** (grav′id) adj. [ < L. gravis, heavy] pregnant

**gra·vim·e·ter** (grə vim′ə tər) n. [ < L. gravis, heavy + Fr. -mètre, -METER] **1.** a device for determining specific gravity **2.** an instrument for measuring the earth's gravitational pull

**grav·i·tate** (grav′ə tāt′) vi. -**tat′ed, -tat′ing 1.** to move or tend to move in accordance with the force of gravity **2.** to be attracted (toward)

**grav·i·ta′tion** n. **1.** a gravitating **2.** Physics the force by which every mass attracts and is attracted by every other mass —**grav′i·ta′tion·al** adj.

**grav·i·ty** (grav′ə tē) n., pl. -**ties** [ < L. gravis, heavy] **1.** graveness; seriousness **2.** weight [specific gravity] **3.** Physics gravitation; esp., the pull on all bodies in the earth's sphere toward the earth's center

**gra·vy** (grā′vē) n., pl. -**vies** [ < ?] **1.** the juice given off by meat in cooking **2.** a sauce made from this juice **3.** [Slang] money easily obtained

**gray** (grā) n. [ < OE. græg] a color made by mixing black and white —adj. **1.** of this color **2.** having hair this color **3.** a) darkish b) dreary **4.** designating a vague, intermediate area —vt., vi. to make or become gray —**gray′ish** adj. —**gray′ness** n.

**gray′beard′** (-bird′) n. an old man

**gray′ling** (-liŋ) n., pl. -**ling, -lings** a freshwater salmonlike game fish

**gray matter 1.** grayish nerve tissue of the brain and spinal cord **2.** [Colloq.] intelligence

**graze¹** (grāz) vt. **grazed, graz′ing** [ < OE. græs, grass] **1.** to put livestock to graze on (growing grass, etc.) **2.** to tend (grazing livestock) —vi. to feed on growing grass, etc.

**graze²** (grāz) vt., vi. **grazed, graz′ing** [prob. < prec.] to scrape or rub lightly in passing —n. a grazing

**Gr. Brit., Gr. Br.** Great Britain

**grease** (grēs; for v., also grēz) n. [ < L. crassus, fat] **1.** melted animal fat **2.** any thick, oily substance or lubricant —vt. **greased, greas′ing** to smear or lubricate with grease

**grease′paint′** n. greasy coloring matter used in making up for the stage

**greas·y** (grē′sē, -zē) adj. -**i·er, -i·est 1.** soiled with grease **2.** containing or like grease; oily —**greas′i·ness** n.

**great** (grāt) adj. [OE.] **1.** of much more than ordinary size, extent, etc. **2.** much above the average, as, a) intense [great pain] b) eminent [a great writer] **3.** most important; main **4.** designating a relationship one generation removed [great-grandparent] **5.** [Colloq.] skillful (often with at) **6.** [Colloq.] excellent; fine —n. a distinguished person —**great′ly** adv. —**great′ness** n.

**Great Britain** England, Scotland, & Wales

**Great Dane** a large, powerful dog with short, smooth hair

**great′-grand′child′** n. a child of any of one's grandchildren

**great′-grand′par′ent** n. a parent of any of one's grandparents

**great′heart′ed** adj. **1.** brave; fearless **2.** generous; unselfish

**Great Lakes** chain of five freshwater lakes in EC N. America

**Great Salt Lake** shallow saltwater lake in NW Utah

**grebe** (grēb) n. [Fr. grèbe] a diving and swimming bird related to the loons

**Gre·cian** (grē′shən) adj., n. Greek

**Gre·co-** (grē′kō) a combining form meaning Greek or Greek and

**Greece** (grēs) country in the S Balkan peninsula, on the Mediterranean: 50,534 sq. mi.; pop. 8,614,000

**greed** (grēd) n. [ < ff.] excessive desire, esp. for wealth; avarice

**greed′y** adj. -**i·er, -i·est** [OE. grædig] **1.** wanting more than one needs or deserves **2.** having too strong a desire for food and drink; gluttonous —**greed′i·ly** adv. —**greed′i·ness** n.

**Greek** (grēk) n. **1.** a native or inhabitant of Greece **2.** the language, ancient or modern, of Greece —adj. of Greece, its people, language, etc

**green** (grēn) *adj.* [OE. *grene*] 1. of the color of growing grass 2. covered with plants or foliage 3. sickly or bilious 4. unripe 5. inexperienced or naive 6. not dried or seasoned 7. [Colloq.] jealous —*n.* 1. the color of growing grass 2. [*pl.*] green leafy vegetables, as spinach, etc. 3. an area of smooth turf [a putting *green*] —**green'ish** *adj.* —**green'ness** *n.*

**green'back'** *n.* any U.S. paper money printed in green on the back

**green bean** the edible, immature green pod of the kidney bean

**green'belt'** *n.* a beltlike area around a city, reserved for park land or farms

**green'er·y** *n., pl.* -**ies** green vegetation; verdure

**green'-eyed'** *adj.* very jealous

**green'gro'cer** (-grō'sər) *n.* [Brit.] a retail dealer in fruit and vegetables

**green'horn'** *n.* 1. an inexperienced person 2. a person easily duped

**green'house'** *n.* a heated building, mainly of glass, for growing plants

**Green·land** (grēn'lənd) Danish island northeast of N. America

**green manure** a crop, as of clover, plowed under to fertilize the soil

**green onion** an immature onion with green leaves, eaten raw; scallion

**green pepper** the green, immature fruit of the sweet red pepper

**green power** money, as the source of power

**Greens·bor·o** (grēnz'bur'ō) city in NC N.C.; pop. 144,000

**greens fee** a fee paid to play golf

**green'sward'** (-swôrd') *n.* green turf

**green thumb** a knack for growing plants

**Green·wich** (gren'ich, grin'ij) borough of London, on the prime meridian

**Green·wich Village** (gren'ich) section of New York City, a center for artists, writers, etc.

**green'wood'** *n.* a forest in leaf

**greet** (grēt) *vt.* [OE. *gretan*] 1. to address with friendliness 2. to meet or receive (a person, event, etc.) in a specified way 3. to present itself to

**greet'ing** *n.* 1. the act or words of one who greets 2. [*often pl.*] a message of regards

**gre·gar·i·ous** (grə ger'ē əs) *adj.* [< L. *grex*, herd] 1. living in herds 2. fond of the company of others; sociable

**Gre·go·ri·an calendar** (grə gôr'ē ən) the calendar now widely used, introduced by Pope Gregory XIII in 1582

**grem·lin** (grem'lən) *n.* [< ?] an imaginary small creature humorously blamed for disruption of any procedure

**gre·nade** (grə nād') *n.* [Fr. < OFr., pomegranate] a small bomb detonated by a fuse and usually thrown by hand

**gren·a·dier** (gren'ə dir') *n.* 1. orig., a soldier who threw grenades 2. a member of a special regiment

**gren·a·dine** (gren'ə dēn') *n.* [Fr.] a syrup made from pomegranate juice

**grew** (grōō) *pt.* of GROW

**grey** (grā) *adj., n., v. Brit. sp.* of GRAY

**grey'hound'** *n.* a tall, slender, swift hound with a narrow head

**grid** (grid) *n.* [< GRIDIRON] 1. a gridiron or grating 2. a metallic plate in a storage battery 3. an electrode, as of wire mesh, for controlling the flow of electrons in an electron tube

**grid·dle** (grid'l) *n.* [< L. *craticula*, gridiron] a heavy, flat metal pan for cooking pancakes, etc.

**grid'dle-cake'** *n.* a pancake

**grid·i·ron** (grid'ī'ərn) *n.* [see GRIDDLE] 1. a framework of metal bars or wires for broiling 2. anything resembling this, as a football field

**grief** (grēf) *n.* [see GRIEVE] 1. intense emotional suffering caused by loss, disaster, etc. 2. a cause of such suffering —**come to grief** to fail or be ruined

**griev·ance** (grē'vəns) *n.* 1. a circumstance thought to be unjust and ground for complaint 2. complaint against a real or imagined wrong

**grieve** (grēv) *vi., vt.* **grieved, griev'ing** [< L. *gravis*, heavy] to feel or cause to feel grief —**griev'er** *n.*

**griev·ous** (grē'vəs) *adj.* 1. causing grief 2. showing or full of grief 3. severe 4. deplorable; atrocious —**griev'ous·ly** *adv.* —**griev'ous·ness** *n.*

**grif·fin** (grif'ən) *n.* [< Gr.] a mythical animal, part eagle and part lion

**grill** (gril) *n.* [see GRIDDLE] 1. a gridiron 2. grilled food 3. a restaurant that specializes in grilled foods —*vt.* 1. to broil 2. to question relentlessly

**grille** (gril) *n.* [see GRIDDLE] an open grating forming a screen

**grim** (grim) *adj.* **grim'mer, grim'mest** [OE. *grimm*] 1. hard and unyielding; stern 2. appearing forbidding, harsh, etc. 3. repellent; ghastly —**grim'ly** *adv.* —**grim'ness** *n.*

**gri·mace** (gri mās', grim'əs) *n.* [Fr.] a distortion of the face, as in expressing pain, disgust, etc. —*vi.* -**maced'**, -**mac'ing** to make grimaces

**grime** (grīm) *n.* [prob. < Fl. *grijm*] sooty dirt rubbed into a surface, as of the skin —**grim'y** *adj.* -**i·er**, -**i·est**

**Grimm** (grim), **Ja·kob** (yä'kôp) 1785–1863; Ger. philologist and collector (with his brother **Wilhelm**) of fairy tales

**grin** (grin) *vi.* **grinned, grin'ning** [< OE. *grennian*, bare the teeth] 1. to smile broadly as in amusement 2. to show the teeth in pain, scorn, etc. —*n.* the act or look of grinning

**grind** (grīnd) *vt.* **ground, grind'ing** [OE. *grindan*] 1. to crush into fine particles; pulverize 2. to oppress 3. to sharpen or smooth by friction 4. to rub (the teeth, etc.) together gratingly 5. to operate by turning the crank of —*n.* 1. a grinding 2. long, difficult work or study 3. [Colloq.] a student who studies hard

**grind·er** (grīn'dər) *n.* 1. a person or thing that grinds 2. [*pl.*] [Colloq.] the teeth 3. *same as* HERO SANDWICH

---

fat, āpe, cär; ten, ēven; is, bīte; gō, hôrn, tōōl, look; oil, out; up, fur; chin; she; thin, *then*; zh, leisure; ŋ, ring; ə for *a* in *ago*; ', (ā'b'l); ë, Fr. coeur; ö, Fr. feu; Fr. mon; ü, Fr. duc; kh, G. ich, doch; ‡ foreign; < derived from

**grind'stone'** *n.* a revolving stone disk for sharpening tools or polishing things —**keep one's nose to the grindstone** to work steadily

**grip** (grip) *n.* [ < OE. *gripan*, seize] 1. a secure grasp; firm hold 2. the manner of holding a bat, club, etc. 3. the power of grasping firmly 4. mental grasp 5. firm control; mastery 6. a handle 7. a small traveling bag —*vt.* **gripped** or **gript, grip'ping** 1. to take firmly and hold fast 2. to get and hold the attention of —*vi.* to get a grip —**come to grips** to struggle (*with*) —**grip'per** *n.*

**gripe** (grip) *vt.* **griped, grip'ing** [OE. *gripan*, seize] 1. formerly, to distress 2. to cause sharp pain in the bowels of 3. [Slang] to annoy —*vi.* [Slang] to complain —*n.* 1. a sharp pain in the bowels: *usually in pl.* 2. [Slang] a complaint —**grip'er** *n.*

**grippe** (grip) *n.* [Fr.] *earlier term for* INFLUENZA: also **grip**

**gris-gris** (grē'grē) *n., pl.* **gris'-gris** [of Afr. origin] an amulet, charm, or spell associated with voodoo

**gris-ly** (griz'lē) *adj.* **-li-er, -li-est** [OE. *grislic*] terrifying; ghastly

**grist** (grist) *n.* [OE.] grain that is to be or has been ground

**gris-tle** (gris'l) *n.* [OE.] cartilage —**gris'tly** (-lē) *adj.*

**grist-mill** (grist'mil') *n.* a mill for grinding grain

**grit** (grit) *n.* [ < OE. *greot*] 1. rough particles as of sand 2. coarse sandstone 3. stubborn courage; pluck —*vt.* **grit'ted, grit'ting** to grind (the teeth) as in determination —*vi.* to grate —**grit'ty** *adj.* **-ti-er, -ti-est**

**grits** (grits) *n.pl.* [OE. *grytte*] coarsely ground grain

**griz-zled** (griz'ld) *adj.* [ < OFr. *gris*, gray] 1. gray or streaked with gray 2. having gray hair

**griz-zly** (-lē) *adj.* **-zli-er, -zli-est** grayish; grizzled

**grizzly** (**bear**) a large, ferocious brown or grayish bear of W N. America

**groan** (grōn) *vi., vt.* [ < OE. *granian*] to utter (with) a deep sound expressing pain, distress, etc. —*n.* such a sound

**gro-cer** (grō'sər) *n.* [ < OFr. *grossier*] a dealer in food and household supplies

**gro'cer-y** *n., pl.* **-ies** 1. a grocer's store 2. [*pl.*] the goods a grocer sells

**grog** (gräg) *n.* [after Old *Grog*, nickname of an 18th-c. Brit. admiral] 1. orig., rum diluted with water 2. any alcoholic liquor

**grog'gy** *adj.* **-gi-er, -gi-est** [ < prec.] 1. orig., intoxicated 2. dizzy; dazed

**groin** (groin) *n.* [ < ? OE. *grynde*, abyss] 1. the fold where the abdomen joins either thigh 2. *Archit.* the sharp, curved edge at the intersection of two vaults

**grom-met** (gräm'it, grum'-) *n.* [ < obs. Fr. *gromette*, a curb] 1. a ring of rope 2. a metal eyelet in cloth, etc.

GROIN

**groom** (grōōm) *n.* [ME. *grom*, boy] 1. one whose work is tending horses 2. a bridegroom —*vt.* 1. to clean and curry (a horse, etc.) 2. to make neat and tidy 3. to train (a person) for a particular purpose

**groove** (grōōv) *n.* [ < ON. *grof*, a pit] 1. a long, narrow furrow cut with a tool 2. any channel or rut 3. a settled routine —*vt.* **grooved, groov'ing** to make a groove in —*vi.* [Slang] to react with empathy to persons, situations, etc. around one (often with *on*)

**groov'y** *adj.* **-i-er, -i-est** [Slang] very pleasing or attractive

**grope** (grōp) *vi.* **groped, grop'ing** [ < OE. *grapian*, to touch] to feel or search about blindly or uncertainly —*vt.* to seek or find by groping

**gros-beak** (grōs'bēk') *n.* [ < Fr.: see GROSS & BEAK] a finchlike bird with a thick, conical bill

**gros-grain** (grō'grān') *n.* [Fr., lit., coarse grain] a ribbed silk or rayon fabric for ribbons, etc.

**gross** (grōs) *adj.* [ < LL. *grossus*, thick] 1. fat and coarse-looking; burly 2. flagrant; very bad 3. dense; thick 4. lacking in refinement 5. coarse; vulgar 6. total; with no deductions —*n.* 1. overall total 2. *pl.* **gross** twelve dozen —*vt., vi.* [Colloq.] to earn (a specified total amount) before expenses are deducted —**gross'ly** *adv.*

**gross national product** the total value of a nation's annual output of goods and services

**gro-tesque** (grō tesk') *adj.* [ < It. *grotta*, grotto: from designs found in grottoes] 1. distorted or fantastic in appearance, shape, etc. 2. ridiculous; absurd —**gro-tesque'ly** *adv.*

**grot-to** (grät'ō) *n., pl.* **-toes, -tos** [ < It. < L. *crypta*, crypt] 1. a cave 2. a cavelike shrine, summerhouse, etc.

**grouch** (grouch) *vi.* [ < ME. *grucchen*] to grumble or complain sulkily —*n.* 1. one who grouches 2. a sulky mood —**grouch'y** *adj.* **-i-er, -i-est**

**ground¹** (ground) *n.* [OE. *grund*, bottom] 1. the solid surface of the earth 2. soil; earth 3. [*often pl.*] a tract of land [*grounds* of an estate] 4. area, as of discussion 5. [*often pl.*] a) basis; foundation b) valid reason or motive 6. the background, as in a design 7. [*pl.*] sediment [coffee *grounds*] 8. the connection of an electrical conductor with the ground —*adj.* of, on, or near the ground —*vt.* 1. to set on the ground 2. to cause to run aground 3. to base; found; establish 4. to instruct in the first principles of 5. to keep (an aircraft or pilot) from flying 6. *Elec.* to connect (a conductor) with the ground —*vi.* 1. to run ashore 2. *Baseball* to be put out on a grounder (usually with *out*) —**gain** (or **lose**) **ground** to gain (or lose) in achievement, popularity, etc. —**give ground** to retreat; yield —**hold** (or **stand**) **one's ground** to remain firm, not yielding —**run into the ground** [Colloq.] to overdo

**ground²** (ground) *pt. & pp. of* GRIND

**ground cover** low, dense-growing

plants used for covering bare ground

**ground crew** a group of workers who repair and maintain aircraft

**ground′er** *n. Baseball* a batted ball that travels along the ground

**ground floor** the floor of a building more or less level with the ground; first floor —**in on the ground floor** in at the start (of a business, etc.)

**ground glass** non-transparent glass, whose surface has been ground to diffuse light

**ground′hog′** *n. same as* WOODCHUCK

**ground′less** *adj.* without reason

**ground rule 1.** *Baseball* a rule adapted to playing conditions in a specific ballpark **2.** any basic rule

**ground′swell′** *n.* **1.** a large, rolling wave **2.** a wave of popular feeling

**ground′work′** *n.* a foundation; basis

**group** (grōōp) *n.* [< It. *gruppo*] a number of persons or things gathered or classified together —*vt., vi.* to form into a group or groups

**group·er** (grōōp′ər) *n.* [Port. *garoupa*] a large fish found in warm seas

**group·ie** (grōōp′ē) *n.* [Colloq.] a girl fan of rock groups or other popular personalities, who follows them about

**group therapy** (or **psychothera·py**) a form of treatment for a group of patients with similar emotional problems, as by mutual criticism

**grouse**[1] (grous) *n., pl.* **grouse** [< ?] a game bird with a round, plump body, feathered legs, and mottled feathers

**grouse**[2] (grous) *vi.* groused, grous′ing [< ?] [Colloq.] to complain

**grout** (grout) *n.* [ME.] a thin mortar used as between tiles

**grove** (grōv) *n.* [OE. *graf*] a group of trees, often without undergrowth

**grov·el** (gruv′'l, gräv′-) *vi.* -eled or -elled, -el·ing or -el·ling [< ME. *grufelinge*, down on one's face] **1.** to lie or crawl in a prostrate position, esp. abjectly **2.** to behave abjectly

**grow** (grō) *vi.* grew, grown, grow′ing [< OE. *growan*] **1.** to come into being or be produced naturally **2.** to develop or thrive, as a living thing **3.** to increase in size, quantity, etc. **4.** to become [to grow weary] —*vt.* to cause to or let grow; raise; cultivate —**grow on** to have an increasing effect on —**grow up** to mature —**grow′er** *n.*

**growl** (groul) *n.* [ME. *groulen*] a rumbling, menacing sound such as an angry dog makes —*vi., vt.* to make, or express by, such a sound

**grown** (grōn) *pp.* of GROW —*adj.* having completed its growth; mature

**grown′-up′** *adj., n.* adult: also, for *n.,* **grown′up′**

**growth** (grōth) *n.* **1.** a growing or developing **2.** *a)* increase in size, etc. *b)* the full extent of this **3.** something that grows or has grown **4.** an abnormal mass of tissue, as a tumor

**growth stock** a stock that is expected to grow in value and that pays relatively low dividends

**grub** (grub) *vi.* grubbed, grub′bing [ME. *grubben*] **1.** to dig in the ground **2.** to work hard —*vt.* **1.** to clear (ground) of roots **2.** to uproot —*n.* **1.** a wormlike larva, esp. of a beetle **2.** a drudge **3.** [Slang] food

**grub′by** *adj.* -bi·er, -bi·est dirty; untidy —**grub′bi·ness** *n.*

**grub′stake′** (-stāk′) *n.* [GRUB, *n.* 3 + STAKE] [Colloq.] money or supplies advanced as to a prospector

**grudge** (gruj) *vt.* grudged, grudg′ing [< OFr. *grouchier*] **1.** *same as* BEGRUDGE **2.** to give with reluctance —*n.* resentment or ill will over some grievance —**grudg′ing·ly** *adv.*

**gru·el** (grōō′əl) *n.* [< ML. *grutum,* meal] a thin broth of meal cooked in water or milk

**gru·el·ing, gru·el·ling** *adj.* [prp. of obs. v. *gruel,* punish] very trying; exhausting

**grue·some** (grōō′səm) *adj.* [< dial. *grue,* to shudder + -SOME[1]] causing horror or loathing; grisly

**gruff** (gruf) *adj.* [Du. *grof*] **1.** rough or surly **2.** harsh and throaty; hoarse —**gruff′ly** *adv.* —**gruff′ness** *n.*

**grum·ble** (grum′b'l) *vi.* -bled, -bling [prob. < Du. *grommelen*] **1.** to growl **2.** to mutter in discontent **3.** to rumble —*vt.* to express by grumbling —*n.* a grumbling —**grum′bler** *n.*

**grump·y** (grum′pē) *adj.* -i·er, -i·est [prob. echoic] peevish; grouchy

**grun·gy** (grun′jē) *adj.* -gi·er, -gi·est [Slang] dirty, messy, slovenly, etc.

**grunt** (grunt) *vi., vt.* [< OE. *grunian*] to utter (with) the deep, throaty sound of a hog —*n.* this sound

**GSA, G.S.A.** General Services Administration

**G-suit** (jē′sōōt′) *n.* [G for *gravity*] an astronaut's or pilot's garment, pressurized to counteract the effects as of rapid acceleration

**Guam** (gwäm) island in the W Pacific: a possession of the U.S.

**gua·no** (gwä′nō) *n., pl.* **-nos** [Sp. < SAmInd.] manure of sea birds, used as fertilizer

**guar·an·tee** (gar′ən tē′) *n.* **1.** *same as* GUARANTY (sense 1) **2.** *a)* a pledge to replace something if it is not as represented *b)* assurance that something will be done as specified **3.** a guarantor —*vt.* -teed′, -tee′ing **1.** to give a guarantee for **2.** to promise

**guar·an·tor** (gar′ən tôr′, -tər) *n.* one who gives a guaranty or guarantee

**guar′an·ty** (-tē) *n., pl.* **-ties** [< OFr. *garant,* a warrant] **1.** a pledge or security for another's debt or obligation **2.** an agreement that secures the existence or maintenance of something

**guard** (gärd) *vt.* [< OFr. *garder*] **1.** to watch over and protect; defend **2.** to keep from escape or trouble —*vi.* **1.** to keep watch (*against*) **2.** to act as a guard —*n.* **1.** defense; protection **2.** a posture of readiness for defense **3.** any device to protect against injury or loss **4.** a person or group that guards **5.** a defensive basketball player or offensive football lineman —**on** (one's) **guard** vigilant

**guard'ed** adj. **1.** kept safe **2.** cautious [a guarded reply] —**guard'ed·ly** adv.

**guard'house'** n. Mil. **1.** a building used by a guard when not walking a post **2.** a jail for temporary confinement

**guard'i·an** (-ĕ ən) n. **1.** one who guards or protects; custodian **2.** a person legally in charge of a minor or of someone incapable of taking care of his own affairs —adj. protecting — **guard'i·an·ship'** n.

**guard'rail'** n. a protective railing, as along a highway

**Gua·te·ma·la** (gwä'tə mä'lə) country in Central America: 42,042 sq. mi.; pop. 4,717,000

**gua·va** (gwä'və) n. [< native name] a yellow, pear-shaped tropical fruit

**gu·ber·na·to·ri·al** (gōō'bər nə tôr'ē əl) adj. [L. gubernator, governor] of a governor or his office

**Guern·sey** (gurn'zē) n., pl. **-seys** [< Guernsey, one of the Channel Islands] a breed of dairy cattle, usually fawn-colored with white markings

**guer·ril·la, gue·ril·la** (gə ril'ə) n. [Sp., dim. of guerra, war] a member of a small defensive force of irregular soldiers, making surprise raids

**guess** (ges) vt., vi. [ME. gessen] **1.** to form a judgment or estimate of without actual knowledge; surmise **2.** to judge correctly by doing this **3.** to think or suppose —n. **1.** a guessing **2.** something guessed; conjecture

**guess'work'** n. **1.** a guessing **2.** a judgment, result, etc. arrived at by guessing

**guest** (gest) n. [< ON. gestr] **1.** a person entertained at the home, club, etc. of another **2.** any paying customer of a hotel, restaurant, etc. —adj. **1.** for guests **2.** performing by special invitation [a guest artist]

**guff** (guf) n. [echoic] [Slang] **1.** nonsense **2.** brash or insolent talk

**guf·faw** (gə fô') n., vi. [echoic] laugh in a loud, coarse burst

**guid·ance** (gīd'ns) n. **1.** a guiding; leadership **2.** advice or counsel

**guide** (gīd) vt. guid'ed, guid'ing [< OFr. guier] **1.** to point out the way for; lead **2.** to direct the course of; control —n. **1.** one whose work is conducting tours, etc. **2.** a controlling device **3.** a book of basic instruction

**guide'book'** n. a book containing directions and information for tourists

**guided missile** a military missile whose course is controlled by radar, etc.

**guide'line'** n. a principle by which to determine a course of action

**guild** (gild) n. [< OE. gieldan, to pay] an association for mutual aid and the promotion of common interests

**guil·der** (gil'dər) n. [< MDu. gulden, golden] the monetary unit and a coin of the Netherlands

**guile** (gīl) n. [< OFr.] slyness and cunning in dealing with others — **guile'ful** adj. —**guile'less** adj.

**guil·lo·tine** (gil'ə tēn'; for v., usually gil'ə tēn') n. [Fr. < J. Guillotin, who advocated its use in 18th c.] an instrument for beheading, having a heavy blade dropped between two grooved uprights —vt. -tined', -tin'ing to behead with a guillotine

**guilt** (gilt) n. [OE. gylt, a sin] **1.** the fact of having done a wrong or committed an offense **2.** a feeling of self-reproach from believing that one has done a wrong —**guilt'less** adj.

**guilt'y** adj. -i·er, -i·est **1.** having guilt **2.** legally judged an offender **3.** of or showing guilt [a guilty look] —**guilt'i·ly** adv. —**guilt'i·ness** n.

**Guin·ea** (gin'ē) country on the W coast of Africa: 94,925 sq. mi.; pop. 3,702,000

**guin·ea** (gin'ē) n. [first coined of gold from Guinea] a former English gold coin equal to 21 shillings

**guinea fowl** (or **hen**) [orig. imported from Guinea] a domestic fowl with a rounded body and speckled feathers

**guinea pig** [prob. orig. brought to England by ships plying between England, Guinea, and S. America] **1.** a small, fat rodent used in biological experiments **2.** any subject used in an experiment

**guise** (gīz) n. [< OHG. wisa, manner] **1.** manner of dress; garb **2.** semblance **3.** a false appearance; pretense

**gui·tar** (gi tär') n. [< Sp. < Gr. kithara, lyre] a musical instrument with usually six strings plucked with the fingers or a plectrum —**gui·tar'ist** n.

**gulch** (gulch) n. [prob. < dial. gulch, swallow greedily] a deep, narrow ravine

**gulf** (gulf) n. [ult. < Gr. kolpos, bosom] **1.** a large area of ocean reaching into land **2.** a wide, deep chasm **3.** a vast separation

**Gulf Stream** warm ocean current flowing from the Gulf of Mexico northward toward Europe

**gull¹** (gul) n. [< Celt.] a gray and white water bird with webbed feet

**gull²** (gul) n. [< ?] a person easily tricked; dupe —vt. to cheat or trick

**gul·let** (gul'ət) n. [< L. gula, throat] **1.** the esophagus **2.** the throat

**gul·li·ble** (gul'ə b'l) adj. easily gulled; credulous —**gul'li·bil'i·ty** n.

**gul·ly** (gul'ē) n., pl. **-lies** [see GULLET] a small, narrow ravine

**gulp** (gulp) vt., vi. [prob. < Du. gulpen] **1.** to swallow hastily or greedily **2.** to choke back as if swallowing —n. a gulping or swallowing

**gum¹** (gum) n. [< L. gumma] **1.** a sticky substance found in certain trees and plants **2.** an adhesive **3.** same as CHEWING GUM —vt. **gummed, gum'ming** to coat or unite with gum —vi. to become sticky or clogged —**gum up** [Slang] to cause to go awry —**gum'my** adj. -mi·er, -mi·est

**gum²** (gum) n. [OE. goma] [often pl.] the firm flesh surrounding the teeth —vt. **gummed, gum'ming** to chew with toothless gums

**gum arabic** a gum from certain acacia trees, used in medicine, candy, etc.

**gum·bo** (gum'bō) *n.* [ < Bantu name for okra] a soup thickened with unripe okra pods

**gum·drop'** *n.* a small, firm candy made of sweetened gelatin, etc.

**gump·tion** (gump'shən) *n.* [ < Scot.] [Colloq.] initiative; enterprise

**gun** (gun) *n.* [ < ME. *gonnilde*, cannon < ON.] 1. a weapon with a metal tube from which a projectile is discharged by the force of an explosive 2. any similar device not discharged by an explosive *[an air gun]* 3. anything like a gun —*vi.* **gunned, gun'ning** to shoot or hunt with a gun —*vt.* 1. [Colloq.] to shoot (a person) 2. [Slang] to advance the throttle of (an engine) —**gun for** [Slang] to try to get —**jump the gun** [Slang] to begin before the proper time —**stick to one's guns** to stand fast; be firm

**gun'boat'** *n.* a small armed ship

**gun'fight'** *n.* a fight between persons using pistols or revolvers

**gun'fire'** *n.* the firing of guns

**gung-ho** (gun'hō') *adj.* [Chin., lit., work together] enthusiastic

**gunk** (guŋk) *n.* [Slang] a viscous or thick, messy substance

**gun'man** (-mən) *n., pl.* **-men** an armed gangster or hired killer

**gun'met'al** *n.* 1. bronze with a dark tarnish 2. its dark-gray color

**gun'ner** *n.* 1. a soldier, etc. who helps fire artillery 2. a naval warrant officer in charge of a ship's guns

**gun'ner·y** *n.* the science of making and using heavy guns and projectiles

**gun·ny** (gun'ē) *n.* [ < Sans. *gōnī*, sack] a coarse fabric of jute or hemp

**gun'ny·sack'** *n.* a sack made of gunny

**gun'play'** *n.* an exchange of gunshots, as between gunmen and police

**gun'pow'der** *n.* an explosive powder used in guns, for blasting, etc.

**gun'ship'** *n.* a heavily armed helicopter used to assault enemy ground forces

**gun'shot'** *n.* shot fired from a gun

**gun'-shy'** *adj.* easily frightened at the firing of a gun *[a gun-shy dog]*

**gun'smith'** *n.* one who makes or repairs small guns

**gun·wale** (gun''l) *n.* [ < supporting a ship's guns] the upper edge of the side of a ship or boat

**gup·py** (gup'ē) *n., pl.* **-pies** [ < R. *Guppy*, of Trinidad] a tiny freshwater fish of the West Indies, etc.

**gur·gle** (gur'g'l) *vi.* **-gled, -gling** [ < L. *gurgulio*, gullet] to make, or flow with, a bubbling sound —*n.* a gurgling sound

**gu·ru** (goor'oo, goo roo') *n.* [ < Sans. *guru-h*, venerable] in Hinduism, one's personal spiritual adviser or teacher

**gush** (gush) *vi.* [ME. *guschen*] 1. to flow out plentifully 2. to have a sudden flow 3. to talk or write effusively —*vt.* to cause to gush —*n.* a gushing —**gush'y** *adj.* **-i·er, -i·est**

**gush'er** *n.* 1. one who gushes 2. an oil well from which oil spouts forth

**gus·set** (gus'it) *n.* [ < OFr. *gousset*] a triangular piece inserted to strengthen or enlarge a garment

**gus·sie, gus·sy** (gus'ē) *vt., vi.* **-sied, -sy·ing** [Slang] to dress (*up*) in a showy way

**gust** (gust) *n.* [ < ON. *gjosa*, gush] 1. a sudden, strong rush of air 2. a sudden outburst of rain, laughter, etc. —**gust'y** *adj.* **-i·er, -i·est**

**gus·ta·to·ry** (gus'tə tôr'ē) *adj.* [ < L. *gustus*, taste] of the sense of taste

**gus·to** (gus'tō) *n.* [see prec.] 1. zest; relish 2. great vigor or liveliness

**gut** (gut) *n.* [ < OE. *geotan*, pour] 1. [*pl.*] the bowels or the stomach 2. the intestine 3. tough cord made from animal intestines 4. [*pl.*] [Slang] daring; courage —*vt.* **gut'ted, gut'ting** 1. to remove the intestines from 2. to destroy the interior of —*adj.* [Slang] 1. basic 2. not hard; easy

**gut'less** *adj.* [Slang] lacking courage

**guts·y** (gut'sē) *adj.* **-i·er, -i·est** [Slang] courageous, forceful, etc.

**gut·ter** (gut'ər) *n.* [ < L. *gutta*, a drop] a channel to carry off water, as along the eaves of a roof or the side of a street —*vi.* to flow in a stream

**gut·tur·al** (gut'ər əl) *adj.* [L. *guttur*, throat] 1. of the throat 2. produced in the throat; rasping

**guy¹** (gī) *n.* [ < OFr. *guier*, to guide] a wire, rope, etc. used to steady or guide something —*vt.* to guide or steady with a guy

**guy²** (gī) *n.* [ < *Guy* Fawkes, Eng. conspirator] [Slang] a man or boy —*vt.* to tease

**Guy·a·na** (gī an'ə) country in NE S. America: 83,000 sq.mi.; pop. 662,000

**guz·zle** (guz''l) *vi., vt.* **-zled, -zling** [ < ? OFr. *gosier*, throat] to drink greedily or immoderately

**gym** (jim) *n.* [Colloq.] *same as:* 1. GYMNASIUM 2. PHYSICAL EDUCATION

**gym·na·si·um** (jim nā'zē əm) *n., pl.* **-si·ums, -si·a** (-ə) [ < Gr. *gymnos*, naked] a room or building equipped for physical training and sports

**gym·nas·tics** (jim nas'tiks) *n.pl.* exercises to develop and train the muscles —**gym'nast** *n.* —**gym·nas'tic** *adj.* —**gym·nas'ti·cal·ly** *adv.*

**gyn·e·col·o·gy** (gī'nə käl'ə jē, jin'ə-, jī'nə-) *n.* [ < Gr. *gynē*, woman + -LOGY] the branch of medicine dealing with women's diseases, etc. —**gyn'e·col'o·gist** *n.*

**gyp** (jip) *n.* [prob. < GYPSY] [Colloq.] 1. a swindle 2. a swindler: also **gyp'per, gyp'ster** —*vt., vi.* **gypped, gyp'ping** [Colloq.] to swindle; cheat

**gyp·sum** (jip'səm) *n.* [ < Gr. *gypsos*] a sulfate of calcium used for making plaster of Paris, in treating soil, etc.

**Gyp·sy** (jip'sē) *n., pl.* **-sies** [ < *Egipcien*, Egyptian: orig. thought to be from Egypt] 1. [*also* g-] a member of a wandering Caucasoid people, perhaps orig. from India, with dark skin and black hair 2. their language 3.

[g-] one who looks or lives like a Gypsy

**gypsy moth** a European moth now common in the E. U.S.: its larvae feed on leaves, damaging trees

**gy·rate** (jī′rāt) *vi.* -rat·ed, -rat·ing [< Gr. *gyros*, a circle] to move in a circular or spiral path; whirl — **gy·ra′tion** *n.* —**gy′ra′tor** *n.*

**gyro-** [see prec.] *a combining form meaning:* 1. gyrating [*gyroscope*] 2. gyroscope

**gy·ro·pi·lot** (jī′rō pī′lət) *n.* *same as* AUTOMATIC PILOT

**gy·ro·scope** (jī′rə skōp′) *n.* [GYRO- + -SCOPE] a wheel mounted in a ring so that its axis is free to turn in any direction: when the wheel is spun rapidly, it will keep its original plane of rotation

**gyve** (jīv) *n.,* *vt.* **gyved, gyv′ing** [ME. *give*] [Archaic] fetter; shackle

GYROSCOPE

# H

**H, h** (āch) *n.,* *pl.* **H's, h's** the eighth letter of the English alphabet

**H** *Chem.* hydrogen

**H., h.** 1. height 2. high 3. *Baseball* hits 4. hour(s)

**ha** (hä) *interj.* an exclamation of wonder, surprise, anger, triumph, etc.

**tha·be·as cor·pus** (hā′bē əs kôr′pəs) [L., (that) you have the body] *Law* a writ requiring that a prisoner be brought before a court to decide the legality of his detention

**hab·er·dash·er** (hab′ər dash′ər) *n.* [< ME.] a dealer in men's hats, shirts, neckties, etc. —**hab′er·dash′er·y** *n.*

**ha·bil·i·ment** (hə bil′ə mənt) *n.* [< MFr. *habiller*, clothe] 1. [*usually pl.*] clothing; attire 2. [*pl.*] trappings

**hab·it** (hab′it) *n.* [< L. *habere*, have] 1. a distinctive costume, as of a religious order 2. a thing done often and, hence, easily; custom 3. a usual way of doing 4. an addiction, esp. to narcotics

**hab′it·a·ble** *adj.* fit to be lived in

**hab·i·tat** (hab′ə tat′) *n.* [L., it inhabits] 1. the region where a plant or animal naturally lives 2. the place where a person is ordinarily found

**hab·i·ta′tion** (-tā′shən) *n.* 1. an inhabiting 2. a dwelling; home

**hab′it-form′ing** *adj.* leading to the formation of a habit or addiction

**ha·bit·u·al** (hə bich′ōō wəl) *adj.* 1. done or acquired by habit 2. steady; inveterate [a *habitual* smoker] 3. much seen, done, or used; usual —**ha·bit′u·al·ly** *adv.* —**ha·bit′u·al·ness** *n.*

**ha·bit′u·ate′** (-wāt′) *vt.* -at·ed, -at′ing to accustom (*to*)

**ha·bit·u·é** (hə bich′ōō wā′) *n.* [Fr.] one who frequents a certain place

**ha·ci·en·da** (hä′sē en′də) *n.* [Sp. < L. *facere*, do] in Spanish America, a large estate, ranch, or plantation, or the main dwelling on any of these

**hack¹** (hak) *vt.* [OE. *haccian*] to chop or cut roughly —*vi.* 1. to make rough cuts 2. to give harsh, dry coughs —*n.* 1. a tool for hacking 2. a gash or notch 3. a harsh, dry cough —**hack′er** *n.*

**hack²** (hak) *n.* [< HACKNEY] 1. a horse for hire 2. an old, worn-out horse 3. a literary drudge 4. a coach for hire

5. [Colloq.] a taxicab —*adj.* 1. employed as, or done by, a hack 2. trite; hackneyed

**hack·le** (hak′'l) *n.* [ME. *hechele*] 1. the neck feathers of a rooster, pigeon, etc., collectively 2. [*pl.*] the hairs on a dog's neck and back that bristle

**hack·ney** (hak′nē) *n.,* *pl.* -neys [< *Hackney*, England] 1. a horse for driving or riding 2. a carriage for hire

**hack′neyed′** (-nēd′) *adj.* made trite by overuse

**hack′saw′** *n.* a fine-toothed saw for cutting metal: also **hack saw**

**had** (had) *pt.* & *pp.* of HAVE

**had·dock** (had′ək) *n.,* *pl.* -dock, -docks [ME. *hadok*] an Atlantic food fish, related to the cod

HACKSAW

**Ha·des** (hā′dēz) *Gr. Myth.* the home of the dead —*n.* [*often* h-] [Colloq.] hell

**had·n't** (had′'nt) had not

**haft** (haft) *n.* [OE. *hæft*] the handle or hilt of a knife, ax, etc.

**hag** (hag) *n.* [< OE. *hægtes*] 1. a witch 2. an ugly, often vicious old woman —**hag′gish** *adj.*

**hag·gard** (hag′ərd) *adj.* [MFr. *hagard*, untamed (hawk)] having a wild, wasted, worn look; gaunt

**hag·gle** (hag′'l) *vi.* -gled, -gling [< Scot. *hag*, to hack] to argue about terms, price, etc. —*n.* a haggling —**hag′gler** *n.*

**Hague** (hāg), **The** political capital of the Netherlands: pop. 593,000

**hah** (hä) *interj.* same as HA

**hai·ku** (hī′kōō) *n.* [Jap.] 1. a Japanese verse form of three unrhymed lines of 5, 7, and 5 syllables respectively 2. *pl.* -ku a poem in this form

**hail¹** (hāl) *vt.* [< ON. *heill*, whole, sound] 1. to greet with cheers; acclaim 2. to call out to —*n.* a greeting —*interj.* an exclamation of tribute, greeting, etc. —**hail from** to be from

**hail²** (hāl) *n.* [OE. *hægel*] 1. frozen raindrops falling during thunderstorms 2. a shower of or like hail —*vt.,* *vi.* to pour down like hail

**hail′stone′** *n.* a pellet of hail

**hail'storm'** n. a storm with hail
**hair** (her) n. [OE. hær] 1. any of the threadlike outgrowths from the skin 2. a growth of these, as on the human head 3. a very small space, degree, etc. 4. a threadlike growth on a plant —**get in one's hair** [Slang] to annoy one —**split hairs** to quibble —**hair'-less** adj. —**hair'like'** adj.
**hair'ball'** n. a ball of hair often found in the stomach of a cow, cat, or other animal that licks its coat
**hair'breadth'** (-bredth') n. a very small space or amount —adj. very narrow; close Also **hairs'breadth'**
**hair'cut'** n. the act of, or a style of, cutting the hair
**hair'do'** n., pl. -**dos** the style in which (a woman's) hair is arranged
**hair'dress'er** n. one whose work is dressing (women's) hair
**hair'line'** n. 1. a very thin line 2. the outline of the hair on the head
**hair'piece'** n. a toupee or wig
**hair'pin'** n. a small, bent piece of wire, etc. for keeping the hair in place —adj. U-shaped [a hairpin turn]
**hair'-rais'ing** adj. [Colloq.] terrifying or shocking
**hair'split'ting** adj., n. making petty distinctions; quibbling
**hair'spring'** n. a slender, hairlike coil spring, as in a watch
**hair'y** adj. -**i**-er, -**i**-est covered with hair —**hair'i**-ness n.
**Hai·ti** (hāt'ē) country occupying the W portion of Hispaniola: 10,714 sq. mi.; pop. 4,485,000 —**Hai·tian** (hā'shən, hāt'ē ən) adj., n.
**hake** (hāk) n., pl. **hake, hakes** [prob. < ON.] a marine food fish related to the cod
**hal·berd** (hal'bərd) n. [< MHG. helmbarte] a combination spear and battle-ax of the 15th and 16th c.
**hal·cy·on** (hal'sē ən) adj. [< Gr. alkyōn, kingfisher (fabled calmer of the sea)] tranquil, happy, idyllic, etc.
**hale**[1] (hāl) adj. [OE. hal] vigorous and healthy
**hale**[2] (hāl) vt. **haled, hal'ing** [< OFr. haler] to force (a person) to go
**half** (haf) n., pl. **halves** [OE. healf] 1. either of the two equal parts of something 2. either of the two equal periods of some games —adj. 1. being a half 2. incomplete; partial —adv. 1. to the extent of a half 2. [Colloq.] partly [half done] 3. [Colloq.] at all: used with not [not half bad]
**half'-and-half'** n. something half one thing and half another, as a mixture of milk and cream —adj. partly one thing and partly another —adv. in two equal parts
**half'back'** n. Football either of two backs, in addition to the fullback and the quarterback
**half'-breed'** n. one whose parents are of different races: also **half'-caste'**
**half brother** a brother through one parent only

**half dollar** a coin of the U.S. and Canada, worth 50 cents
**half'heart'ed** adj. with little enthusiasm, determination, interest, etc. —**half'heart'ed·ly** adv.
**half'-mast'** n. the position of a flag halfway down its staff, as a sign of mourning or a distress signal
**half note** Music a note (♩) having one half the duration of a whole note
**half·pen·ny** (hā'pə nē, hāp'nē) n., pl. -**pence** (hā'pəns), -**pen·nies** a British coin equal to half a penny
**half sister** a sister through one parent only
**half sole** a sole (of a shoe or boot) from the arch to the toe
**half'track'** n. an army truck, armored vehicle, etc. with a continuous tread instead of rear wheels
**half'way'** adj. 1. midway between two points, etc. 2. partial [halfway measures] —adv. 1. to the midway point 2. partially —**meet halfway** to be willing to compromise with
**halfway house** a place for helping people adjust to society after being imprisoned, hospitalized, etc.
**half'-wit'** n. a stupid, silly, or imbecilic person —**half'-wit'ted** adj.
**hal·i·but** (hal'ə bət) n., pl. -**but**, -**buts** [ME. hali, holy + butt, a flounder: eaten on holidays] a large, edible flatfish found in northern seas
**Hal·i·fax** (hal'ə faks') capital of Nova Scotia: pop. 87,000
**hal·ite** (hal'īt, hā'līt) n. [< Gr. hals, salt + -ITE] same as ROCK SALT
**hal·i·to·sis** (hal'ə tō'sis) n. [< L. halitus, breath] bad-smelling breath
**hall** (hôl) n. [OE. heall] 1. the main dwelling on an estate 2. a public building with offices, etc. 3. a large room for gatherings, exhibits, etc. 4. a college building 5. a vestibule at the entrance of a building 6. a hallway
**hal·le·lu·jah, hal·le·lu·iah** (hal'ə lōō'yə) interj. [< Heb. hallelū, praise + yāh, Jehovah] praise (ye) the Lord! —n. a hymn of praise to God
**hall'mark'** (hôl'märk') n. [< the mark stamped on gold and silver articles at Goldsmith's Hall in London] a mark or symbol of genuineness or high quality
**hal·loo** (hə lōō') interj., n. a shout to attract attention —vi., vt. -**looed'**, -**loo'ing** to shout or call
**hal·low** (hal'ō) vt. [OE. halgian] to make or regard as holy
**hal·lowed** (hal'ōd; in liturgy, often hal'ə wid) adj. holy or sacred
**Hal·low·een, Hal·low·e'en** (hal'ə wēn') n. [contr. < all hallow even] the evening of October 31, followed by All Saints' Day
**hal·lu·ci·nate** (hə lōō'sə nāt') vi., vt. -**nat'ed**, -**nat'ing** [see ff.] to have or cause to have hallucinations
**hal·lu·ci·na·tion** (hə lōō'sə nā'shən) n. [< L. hallucinari, to wander mentally] the apparent perception of

sights, sounds, etc. that are not actually present —**hal·lu·ci·na·to·ry** (-nə tôr/ē) *adj.*

**hal·lu·ci·no·gen** (-nə jen, hal/yoo sin/ə jen) *n.* a drug or other substance that produces hallucinations

**hall/way/** *n.* a passageway; corridor

**ha·lo** (hā/lō) *n., pl.* **-los, -loes** [< Gr. *halos*, circular threshing floor] **1.** a ring of light, as around the sun **2.** a symbolic ring of light around the head of a saint in pictures

**hal·o·gen** (hal/ə jen) *n.* [< Gr. *hals*, salt] any of the very active chemical elements, fluorine, chlorine, bromine, astatine, and iodine

**halt¹** (hôlt) *vi., vt.* [< Fr. *faire halte* and G. *halt machen*] stop

**halt²** (hôlt) *vi.* [< OE. *healt*] **1.** [Archaic] to limp **2.** to hesitate —*adj.* lame —**the halt** those who are lame

**hal·ter** (hôl/tər) *n.* [OE. *hælftre*] **1.** a rope or strap for tying or leading an animal **2.** a hangman's noose **3.** a woman's upper garment, held up by a loop around the neck

**halve** (hav) *vt.* **halved, halv/ing 1.** to divide into two equal parts **2.** to reduce to half

**halves** (havz) *n. pl.* of HALF —**by halves** halfway; imperfectly —**go halves** to share expenses equally

**hal·yard** (hal/yərd) *n.* [< ME. *halier* (see HALE²)] a rope or tackle for raising or lowering a flag, sail, etc.

**ham** (ham) *n.* [OE. *hamm*] **1.** the back of the thigh **2.** the upper part of a hog's hind leg, salted, smoked, etc. **3.** [Colloq.] an amateur radio operator **4.** [Slang] an actor who overacts —**ham/my** *adj.* **-mi·er, -mi·est**

**Ham·burg** (ham/bərg) seaport in N West Germany: pop. 1,854,000

**ham·burg·er** (ham/bür/gər) *n.* [< prec.] **1.** ground beef **2.** a cooked patty of such meat, often in a sandwich Also **Ham/burg**

**Ham·il·ton** (ham/əl t'n) city & port in SE Ontario: pop. 298,000

**Ham·let** (ham/lit) the title hero of a tragedy by Shakespeare

**ham·let** (ham/lit) *n.* [< LowG. *hamm*, enclosed area] a very small village

**ham·mer** (ham/ər) *n.* [OE. *hamor*] **1.** a tool for pounding, having a metal head and a handle **2.** a thing like this in shape or use, as the part of a gun that strikes the firing pin **3.** a bone of the middle ear —*vt., vi.* **1.** to strike repeatedly, as with a hammer **2.** to drive, force, or shape, as with hammer blows —**hammer (away) at** to keep emphasizing —**ham/mer·er** *n.*

**ham/mer·head/** *n.* **1.** the head of a hammer **2.** a shark with a mallet-shaped head having an eye at each end

**ham/mer·toe/** *n.* a toe that is deformed, with its first joint bent downward

**ham·mock** (ham/ək) *n.* [Sp. *hamaca*, of WInd. origin] a bed of canvas, etc. swung from ropes at both ends

**Ham·mond** (ham/ənd) city in NW Ind., near Chicago: pop. 108,000

**ham·per¹** (ham/pər) *vt.* [ME. *hampren*] to hinder; impede; encumber

**ham·per²** (ham/pər) *n.* [< OFr. *hanap*, a cup] a large basket, usually covered

**Hamp·ton** (hamp/tən) seaport in SE Va.: pop. 121,000

**ham·ster** (ham/stər) *n.* [< OHG. *hamustro*] a ratlike animal of Europe and Asia used in scientific experiments

**ham·string** (ham/striŋ/) *n.* a tendon at the back of the knee —*vt.* **-strung/, -string/ing** to disable, as by cutting a hamstring

**hand** (hand) *n.* [OE.] **1.** the part of the arm below the wrist, used for grasping **2.** a side or direction [at my right *hand*] **3.** possession or care [the land is in my *hands*] **4.** control [to strengthen one's *hand*] **5.** an active part [take a *hand* in the work] **6.** a promise to marry **7.** skill **8.** one having a special skill **9.** manner of doing something **10.** handwriting **11.** applause **12.** help [to lend a *hand*] **13.** a hired worker [a farm *hand*] **14.** a source [to get news at first *hand*] **15.** anything like a hand, as a pointer on a clock **16.** the breadth of a hand **17.** *Card Games a)* the cards held by a player at one time *b)* a round of play —*adj.* of, for, or controlled by the hand —*vt.* **1.** to give as with the hand **2.** to help or conduct with the hand —**at hand** near —**hand in hand** together —**hand it to** [Slang] to give credit to —**hand over fist** [Colloq.] easily and in large amounts —**hands down** easily —**on hand 1.** near **2.** available **3.** present —**on the one (or other) hand** from one (or the opposed) point of view

**hand/bag/** *n.* a woman's purse

**hand/ball/** *n.* a game in which players bat a small rubber ball against a wall or walls with the hand

**hand/bar/row** *n.* a frame carried by two people by handles at the ends

**hand/bill/** *n.* a small printed notice to be passed out by hand

**hand/book/** *n.* a compact reference book; manual

**hand/breadth/** *n.* the breadth of the human palm, about 4 inches

**hand/cart/** *n.* a small cart pulled or pushed by hand

**hand/clasp/** *n. same as* HANDSHAKE

**hand/craft/** *n. same as* HANDICRAFT —*vt.* to make skillfully by hand

**hand/cuff/** *n.* either of a pair of connected rings for shackling the wrists of a prisoner: *usually used in pl.* —*vt.* to put handcuffs on; manacle

**hand/ed** *adj.* having or involving (a specified kind or number of) hands [right-*handed*, two-*handed*]

**Han·del** (han/d'l), **George Frederick** 1685–1759; Eng. composer, born in Germany

**hand/ful** *n., pl.* **-fuls/ 1.** as much or as many as the hand will hold **2.** a few; not many **3.** [Colloq.] someone or something hard to manage

**hand/gun/** *n.* any firearm that is held and fired with one hand, as a pistol

**hand·i·cap** (han/dē kap/) *n.* [< *hand in cap*, former kind of lottery] **1.** a competition in which difficulties are imposed on, or advantages given to, the various contestants to equalize their chances **2.** such a difficulty or advantage **3.** any hindrance —*vt.* **-capped′, -cap′ping 1.** to give a handicap to **2.** to hinder —**the handicapped** those who are physically disabled or mentally retarded

**hand′i·cap′per** *n.* a person, as a sports writer, who tries to predict the winners in horse races

**hand·i·craft** (han′dē kraft′) *n.* skill with the hands, or work calling for it

**hand′i·work′** *n.* **1.** *same as* HANDWORK **2.** work done by a person himself

**hand·ker·chief** (haŋ′kər chif) *n.* [HAND + KERCHIEF] a small cloth for wiping the nose, face, etc.

**han·dle** (han′d'l) *n.* [OE. < *hand*] that part of a tool, etc. by which it is held or lifted —*vt.* **-dled, -dling 1.** to touch, lift, operate, etc. with the hand **2.** to manage; control **3.** to deal with; treat **4.** to sell or deal in —*vi.* to respond to control *[the car handles well]* —**han′dler** *n.*

**han·dle·bar′** *n.* [*often pl.*] a curved metal bar with handles on the ends, for steering a bicycle, etc.

**hand·made′** *adj.* made by hand, not by machine

**hand′maid′en** *n.* [Archaic] a woman or girl servant: also **hand′maid′**

**hand′-me-down′** *n.* [Colloq.] a used garment, etc. passed on to one

**hand′out′** *n.* **1.** a gift of food, clothing, etc., as to a beggar **2.** a leaflet handed out **3.** an official news release

**hand′pick′** *vt.* **1.** to pick by hand **2.** to choose with care or for a purpose

**hand′rail′** *n.* a rail serving as a support or guard, as along a stairway

**hand′set′** *n.* a telephone mouthpiece and receiver in a single unit

**hand′shake′** *n.* a gripping of each other's hand in greeting, promise, etc.

**hands′-off′** *adj.* designating or of a policy of not interfering

**hand·some** (han′səm) *adj.* [orig., easily handled] **1.** considerable **2.** generous; gracious **3.** good-looking, esp. in a manly or impressive way

**hand′spring′** *n.* a spring in which one turns over in midair with one or both hands touching the ground

**hand′-to-hand′** *adj.* at close quarters: said of fighting

**hand′-to-mouth′** *adj.* consuming all that is obtained

**hand′work′** *n.* handmade work

**hand′writ′ing** *n.* **1.** writing done by hand, as with a pen **2.** a style of such writing —**hand′writ′ten** *adj.*

**hand′y** *adj.* **-i·er, -i·est 1.** close at hand; easily reached **2.** easily used; convenient **3.** clever with the hands —**hand′i·ly** *adv.* —**hand′i·ness** *n.*

**han·dy·man′** *n., pl.* **-men′** a man who does odd jobs

**hang** (haŋ) *vt.* **hung, hang′ing;** for vt. **3** & vi. **5 hanged** is preferred pt. & pp. [OE. *hangian*] **1.** to attach from above with no support from below;

suspend **2.** to attach (a door, etc.) so as to move freely **3.** to kill by suspending from a rope about the neck **4.** to attach (wallpaper, etc.) to walls **5.** to let (one's head) droop downward **6.** to deadlock (a jury) —*vi.* **1.** to be attached above with no support from below **2.** to hover in the air **3.** to swing freely **4.** to fall or drape, as cloth **5.** to die by hanging **6.** to droop; bend —*n.* the way a thing hangs —**get (or have) the hang of 1.** to learn (or have) the knack of **2.** to understand the meaning or idea of —**hang around (or about)** [Colloq.] to loiter around —**hang back (or off)** to be reluctant, as from shyness —**hang on 1.** to go on; persevere **2.** to depend on **3.** to listen attentively to —**hang out** [Slang] to spend much time —**hang up 1.** to put on a hanger, hook, etc. **2.** to end a telephone call by replacing the receiver **3.** to delay

**hang·ar** (haŋ′ər) *n.* [Fr.] a repair shed or shelter for aircraft

**hang′dog′** *adj.* abject or ashamed

**hang′er** *n.* **1.** one who hangs things **2.** that on which something is hung

**hang gliding** the sport of gliding through the air while hanging by a harness from a large type of kite **(hang glider)**

**hang′ing** *adj.* that hangs —*n.* **1.** a killing by hanging **2.** something hung on a wall, etc., as a drapery

**hang′man** (-mən) *n., pl.* **-men** a man who hangs convicted criminals

**hang′nail′** *n.* [< OE. *angnægl*, a corn (on the toe)] a bit of torn skin hanging next to a fingernail

**hang′o′ver** *n.* **1.** a survival **2.** nausea, headache, etc. from drinking much alcoholic liquor

**hang′-up′** *n.* [Slang] an unresolvable personal or emotional problem

**hank** (haŋk) *n.* [prob. < Scand.] a skein of yarn or thread

**hank·er** (haŋ′kər) *vi.* [prob. < Du. or LowG.] to long or yearn *(for)* —**hank′er·ing** *n.*

**Ha·noi** (hä noi′, ha-) capital of Vietnam: pop. 1,378,000

**han·som (cab)** (han′səm) [< J. A. *Hansom,* 19th-c. Eng. inventor] a two-wheeled covered carriage, pulled by one horse, with the driver's seat behind

HANSOM

**Ha·nu·ka** (khä′ noo kä′, -kə; hä′-) *n.* [< Heb., dedication] an 8-day Jewish festival commemorating the rededication of the Temple: also **Ha′nuk·kah′**

**hap** (hap) *n.* [< ON. *happ*] luck

**hap·haz·ard** (hap′haz′ərd) *adj.* not planned; random —*adv.* by chance

**hap·less** (hap′lis) *adj.* unlucky

**hap′ly** *adv.* [Archaic] by chance

**hap·pen** (hap′n) *vi.* [ME. *happenen*] 1. to take place; occur 2. to be, occur, or come by chance 3. to have the luck or occasion [I *happened* to see it] —**happen on** (or **upon**) to meet or find by chance

**hap′pen·ing** *n.* an occurrence; event

**hap′pen·stance′** (-stans′) *n.* [Colloq.] chance or accidental happening

**hap·pi coat** (hap′ē) [ < Jap.] a short, light Japanese coat worn with a sash

**hap·py** (hap′ē) *adj.* **-pi·er, -pi·est** [ < HAP] 1. lucky; fortunate 2. having, showing, or causing great pleasure or joy 3. suitable and clever; apt —**hap′pi·ly** *adv.* —**hap′pi·ness** *n.*

**hap′py-go-luck′y** *adj.* easygoing

**ha·ra-ki·ri** (här′ə kir′ē) *n.* [Jap. *hara*, belly + *kiri*, a cutting] ritual suicide by ripping out the bowels

**ha·rangue** (hə raŋ′) *n.* [ < OIt. *aringo*, site for public assemblies] a long, blustering speech; tirade —*vi., vt.* **-rangued′, -rangu′ing** to speak or address in a harangue

**har·ass** (hə ras′, har′əs) *vt.* [ < OFr. *harer*, set a dog on] 1. to worry or torment 2. to trouble by constant raids or attacks —**har·ass′ment** *n.*

**Har·bin** (här′bin) city in NE China: pop. 1,800,000

**har·bin·ger** (här′bin jər) *n.* [ < OFr. *herberge*, a shelter] a forerunner; herald

**har·bor** (här′bər) *n.* [ < OE. *here*, army + *beorg*, shelter] 1. a shelter 2. a protected inlet for anchoring ships; port —*vt.* 1. to shelter or house 2. to hold in the mind [to *harbor* envy] —*vi.* to take shelter Brit. sp. **harbour**

**hard** (härd) *adj.* [OE. *heard*] 1. firm and unyielding to the touch; solid and compact 2. powerful [a *hard* blow] 3. difficult to do, understand, or deal with 4. *a)* unfeeling [a *hard* heart] *b)* unfriendly [*hard* feelings] 5. harsh; severe 6. having mineral salts that interfere with lathering 7. energetic [a *hard* worker] 8. containing much alcohol [*hard* liquor] 9. addictive and harmful [heroin is a *hard* drug] —*adv.* 1. energetically [work *hard*] 2. with strength [hit *hard*] 3. with difficulty [*hard*-earned] 4. close; near [we live *hard* by] 5. so as to be solid [frozen *hard*] 6. sharply [turn *hard* right] —**hard and fast** invariable; strict —**hard of hearing** partially deaf —**hard up** [Colloq.] in great need of money —**hard′ness** *n.*

**hard′back′** *n.* a hard-cover book

**hard′ball′** *n. same as* BASEBALL

**hard′-bit′ten** *adj.* tough; dogged

**hard′-boiled′** *adj.* 1. boiled until solid: said of eggs 2. [Colloq.] unfeeling; tough; callous

**hard′-core′** *adj.* absolute; unqualified

**hard′-cov′er** *adj.* designating any book bound in a stiff cover

**hard·en** (här′d′n) *vt., vi.* to make or become hard —**hard′en·er** *n.*

**hard hat** 1. a protective helmet worn by construction workers, miners, etc. 2. [Slang] such a worker

**hard′head′ed** *adj.* 1. shrewd and unsentimental; practical 2. stubborn

**hard′heart′ed** *adj.* unfeeling; cruel

**har·di·hood** (här′dē hood′) *n.* boldness

**Har·ding** (här′diŋ), **Warren G.** 1865–1923; 29th president of the U.S. (1921–23)

**hard′-line′** *adj.* aggressive; unyielding

**hard·ly** (härd′lē) *adv.* 1. only just; scarcely 2. probably not; not likely

**hard′-nosed′** (-nōzd′) *adj.* [Slang] tough and stubborn or shrewd

**hard sell** high-pressure salesmanship

**hard′ship′** *n.* a thing hard to bear, as poverty, pain, etc.

**hard′stand′** *n.* a paved area for parking aircraft or other vehicles

**hard′tack′** (-tak′) *n.* unleavened bread made in hard, large wafers

**hard′top′** *n.* an automobile like a convertible but having a fixed metal top

**hard′ware′** (-wer′) *n.* 1. articles made of metal, as tools, nails, fittings, etc. 2. the mechanical, magnetic, and electronic devices of a computer

**hard′wood′** *n.* 1. any tough, heavy timber with a compact texture 2. the wood of any tree with broad, flat leaves, as the oak, maple, etc.

**har·dy** (här′dē) *adj.* **-di·er, -di·est** [ < OFr. *hardir*, make bold] 1. bold and resolute 2. robust; vigorous— **har′di·ly** *adv.* —**har′di·ness** *n.*

**hare** (her) *n.* [OE. *hara*] a mammal related to and resembling the rabbit

**hare′brained′** *adj.* giddy, rash, etc.

**hare′lip′** *n.* a congenital deformity consisting of a cleft of the upper lip

**ha·rem** (her′əm) *n.* [Ar. *harim*, prohibited (place)] 1. that part of a Moslem's house in which the women live 2. the women in a harem

**hark** (härk) *vi.* [ME. *herkien*] to listen carefully: usually in the imperative —**hark back** to go back in thought or speech

**hark·en** (här′k′n) *vi., vt. same as* HEARKEN

**Har·le·quin** (här′lə kwin, -kin) a comic character in pantomime, who wears a mask and gay, spangled tights —*n.* [h-] a clown; buffoon

**har·lot** (här′lət) *n.* [ < OFr., rogue] a prostitute —**har′lot·ry** (-rē) *n.*

**harm** (härm) *n.* [OE. *hearm*] hurt; injury; damage —*vt.* to do harm to

**harm′ful** *adj.* causing harm; hurtful —**harm′ful·ly** *adv.*

**harm′less** *adj.* causing no harm —**harm′less·ly** *adv.*

**har·mon·ic** (här män′ik) *adj. Music* of or in harmony —*n.* an overtone —**har·mon′i·cal·ly** *adv.*

**har·mon·i·ca** (-i kə) *n.* a small wind instrument with a series of metal reeds that produce tones when air is blown or sucked across them

**har·mon·ics** *n.pl.* [*with sing. v.*] the science of musical sounds

**har·mo·ni·ous** (här mō′nē əs) *adj.* 1. having parts arranged in an orderly or pleasing way 2. having similar ideas, interests, etc. 3. having musical tones combined to give a pleasing effect —**har·mo′ni·ous·ly** *adv.*

**har·mo·ni·um** (här mō′nē əm) *n.* [Fr.] a small kind of reed organ

**har·mo·nize** (här′mə nīz′) *vi.* -nized′, -niz′ing 1. to be in harmony 2. to sing in harmony —*vt.* to make harmonious —**har·mo·ni·za′tion** *n.* —**har′mo·niz′er** *n.*

**har·mo·ny** (här′mə nē) *n., pl.* -nies [< Gr. *harmos,* a fitting] 1. pleasing agreement of parts in color, size, etc. 2. agreement in action, ideas, etc.; friendly relations 3. the pleasing combination of tones in a chord

**har·ness** (här′nis) *n.* [< OFr. *harneis,* armor] the leather straps and metal pieces by which a horse, mule, etc. is fastened to a vehicle, plow, etc. —*vt.* 1. to put a harness on 2. to control so as to use the power of

**harp** (härp) *n.* [OE. *hearpe*] a musical instrument with strings stretched across a triangular frame, played by plucking —*vi.* 1. to play a harp 2. to persist in talking or writing tediously (*on* or *upon* something) —**harp′ist** *n.*

**har·poon** (här poon′) *n.* [< ON. *harpa,* to squeeze] a barbed spear with an attached line, for spearing whales, etc. —*vt.* to strike with a harpoon

**harp·si·chord** (härp′si kôrd′) *n.* [< It. *arpa,* harp + *corda,* CORD] a pianolike keyboard instrument whose strings are plucked rather than struck

**Har·py** (här′pē) *n., pl.* -pies [< Gr. *harpazein,* snatch] 1. *Gr. Myth.* any of several hideous monsters, part woman and part bird 2. [h-] a greedy person

**har·ri·dan** (har′i d′n) *n.* [< Fr. *haridelle,* worn-out horse] a disreputable, shrewish old woman

**har·ri·er** (har′ē ər) *n.* [< HARE + -IER] 1. a small dog used for hunting hares 2. a cross-country runner

**Har·ris·burg** (har′is burg′) capital of Pa.; pop. 68,000

**Har·ri·son** (har′s n) 1. **Benjamin,** 1833–1901; 23d president of the U.S. (1889–93) 2. **William Henry,** 1773–1841; 9th president of the U.S. (1841); grandfather of *prec.*

**har·row** (har′ō) *n.* [prob. < ON.] a heavy frame with spikes or disks, used for breaking up and leveling plowed ground, etc. —*vt.* 1. to draw a harrow over (land) 2. to cause mental distress to —**har′row·ing** *adj.*

**har·ry** (har′ē) *vt.* -ried, -ry·ing [< OE. *here,* army] 1. to raid and ravage or rob 2. to torment or worry

**harsh** (härsh) *adj.* [ME. *harsk*] 1. unpleasantly rough to the eye, ear, taste, or touch 2. offensive to the mind or feelings 3. cruel or severe —**harsh′ly** *adv.* —**harsh′ness** *n.*

**hart** (härt) *n.* [OE. *heorot*] a full-grown, male European red deer

**Hart·ford** (härt′fərd) capital of Conn.; pop. 158,000

**har·um·scar·um** (her′əm sker′əm) *adj.* [< ?] reckless or irresponsible —*adv.* in a harum-scarum way

**har·vest** (här′vist) *n.* [OE. *hærfest*] 1. the time of the year when grain, fruit, etc. are gathered in 2. a season's crop 3. the gathering in of a crop 4. the outcome of any effort —*vt., vi.* to gather in (a crop) —**har′vest·er** *n.*

**has** (haz; *before* "*to*" has) 3d *pers. sing., pres. indic., of* HAVE

**has′-been′** *n.* [Colloq.] a person or thing whose popularity is past

**hash** (hash) *vt.* [< Fr. *hacher,* to chop] to chop up (meat or vegetables) for cooking —*n.* 1. a chopped mixture of cooked meat and vegetables, usually baked 2. a mixture 3. a muddle; mess 4. [Slang] hashish —**hash out** [Colloq.] to settle by long discussion —**hash over** [Colloq.] to discuss at length

**hash·ish** (hash′ēsh, -ish) *n.* [Ar. *hashīsh,* dried hemp] a narcotic and intoxicant made from Indian hemp

**has·n't** (haz′′nt) has not

**hasp** (hasp) *n.* [OE. *hæsp*] a hinged fastening for a door, etc.; esp., a metal piece fitted over a staple and fastened as by a bolt or padlock

**has·sle** (has′′l) *n.* [< ?] [Colloq.] a heated argument; squabble —*vi.* -sled, -sling [Colloq.] to argue heatedly

HASP

**has·sock** (has′ək) *n.* [OE. *hassuc,* (clump of) coarse grass] a firm cushion used as a footstool or seat

**hast** (hast) *archaic* 2d *pers. sing., pres. indic., of* HAVE: *used with* thou

**haste** (hāst) *n.* [OFr.] 1. quickness of motion; rapidity —*vt., vi.* [Rare] *same as* HASTEN —**make haste** to hurry

**has·ten** (hās′′n) *vt.* to make be or come faster; speed up —*vi.* to move or act swiftly; hurry

**hast·y** (hās′tē) *adj.* -i·er, -i·est 1. done with haste; hurried 2. done, made, or acting too quickly or rashly —**hast′i·ly** *adv.* —**hast′i·ness** *n.*

**hat** (hat) *n.* [OE. *hætt*] a head covering, usually with a brim and a crown —**pass the hat** to take up a collection —**talk through one's hat** to talk nonsense —**throw one's hat into the ring** to enter a contest, esp. for political office —**under one's hat** [Colloq.] confidential

**hatch¹** (hach) *vt.* [ME. *hacchen*] 1. to bring forth (young) from (an egg or eggs) 2. to contrive (a plan, plot, etc.) —*vi.* 1. to bring forth young: said of eggs 2. to emerge from the egg

**hatch²** (hach) *n.* [OE. *hæcc,* grating] 1. a hatchway 2. a lid for a hatchway

**hatch′back′** *n.* [HATCH² + BACK] an automobile with a rear that swings up, giving wide entry to a storage area

**hat′check′** *adj.* of or working in a checkroom for hats, coats, etc.

**hatch′er·y** *n., pl.* -ies a place for

hatching eggs, esp. of fish or poultry

**hatch·et** (hach′it) *n.* [ < OFr. *hache,* ax] a small ax with a short handle —**bury the hatchet** to make peace

**hatchet job** [Colloq.] a biased, malicious attack on another's character

**hatch′way′** *n.* an opening in a ship's deck, or in a floor or roof

**hate** (hāt) *vt.* **hat′ed, hat′ing** [OE. *hatian*] **1.** to have strong dislike or ill will for **2.** to wish to avoid [to *hate* fights] —*vi.* to feel hatred —*n.* **1.** a strong feeling of dislike or ill will **2.** a person or thing hated

**hate′ful** *adj.* deserving hate —**hate′ful·ly** *adv.* —**hate′ful·ness** *n.*

**hath** (hath) *archaic 3d pers. sing., pres. indic., of* HAVE

**ha·tred** (hā′trid) *n.* strong dislike or ill will; hate

**hat·ter** (hat′ər) *n.* a person who makes or sells men's hats

**hau·berk** (hô′bərk) *n.* [ < Frank. *hals,* neck + *bergan,* protect] a medieval coat of armor, usually of chain mail

**haugh·ty** (hôt′ē) *adj.* **-ti·er, -ti·est** [ < OFr. *haut,* high] having or showing great pride in oneself and contempt for others; arrogant —**haugh′ti·ly** *adv.* —**haugh′ti·ness** *n.*

**haul** (hôl) *vt., vi.* [ < OFr. *haler*] **1.** to move by pulling; drag **2.** to transport by wagon, truck, etc. —*n.* **1.** the act of hauling; pull **2.** the amount gained, caught, etc. at one time **3.** the distance over which something is transported —**haul off** [Colloq.] to draw the arm back before hitting —**in** (or **over**) **the long haul** over a long period of time

**haunch** (hônch) *n.* [ < OFr. *hanche* < Gmc.] **1.** the hip, buttock, and upper thigh together **2.** an animal's loin and leg together

**haunt** (hônt) *vt.* [ < OFr. *hanter,* to frequent] **1.** to visit often or continually **2.** to recur repeatedly to [*haunted* by memories] —*n.* a place often visited

**haunt′ed** *adj.* supposedly frequented by ghosts [a *haunted* house]

**haunt′ing** *adj.* recurring often to the mind; not easily forgotten

**hau·teur** (hō tur′) *n.* [Fr. < *haut,* high] disdainful pride; haughtiness

**Ha·van·a** (hə van′ə) capital of Cuba: pop. 788,000 —*n.* a cigar made of Cuban tobacco

**have** (hav; *before* "to" haf) *vt.* **had, hav′ing** [OE. *habban*] **1.** to hold; own; possess [to *have* money, a week has 7 days] **2.** to experience [*have* a good time] **3.** to hold mentally [to *have* an idea] **4.** to state [so rumor has it] **5.** to get, take, consume, etc. [*have* a drink] **6.** to bear or beget (offspring) **7.** to engage in [to *have* a fight] **8.** to cause to; cause to be [*have* her leave] **9.** to permit; tolerate [I won't *have* this noise!] **10.** [Colloq.] *a)* to hold at a disadvantage *b)* to deceive; cheat *Have* is used as an auxiliary to express completed action (Ex.: I *had* left), and with infinitives to express obligation or necessity (Ex.:

we *have* to go). *Have got* often replaces *have. Have* is conjugated in the present indicative: (I) *have,* (he, she, it) *has,* (we, you, they) *have* —*n.* a wealthy person or nation —**have it out** to settle an issue by fighting or discussion —**have on** to be wearing

**ha·ven** (hā′vən) *n.* [OE. *hæfen*] **1.** a port **2.** any sheltered place; refuge

**have-not** (hav′nät′) *n.* a person or nation with little or no wealth

**have·n't** (hav′nt) have not

**hav·er·sack** (hav′ər sak′) *n.* [ < G. *habersack,* lit., sack of oats] a canvas bag for rations, worn over one shoulder, as by soldiers or hikers

**hav·oc** (hav′ək) *n.* [ < OFr. *havot*] great destruction and devastation —**play havoc with** to devastate; ruin

**haw**[1] (hô) *n.* [OE. *haga*] **1.** the berry of the hawthorn **2.** the hawthorn

**haw**[2] (hô) *n.* [echoic] to grope for words: in HEM AND HAW (see HEM[2])

**Ha·wai·i** (hə wä′ē, -yē) **1.** State of the U.S., consisting of a group of islands (**Hawaiian Islands**) in the N Pacific: 6,424 sq. mi.; pop. 769,000; cap. Honolulu **2.** largest of these islands —**Ha·wai′ian** (-yən) *adj., n.*

**hawk**[1] (hôk) *n.* [OE. *hafoc*] **1.** a bird of prey with short, rounded wings, a long tail, and a hooked beak and claws **2.** an advocate of war

**hawk**[2] (hôk) *vt., vi.* [ < HAWKER] to advertise or peddle (goods) in the streets by shouting

**hawk**[3] (hôk) *vi., vt.* [echoic] to clear the throat (of) audibly

**hawk·er** (hôk′ər) *n.* [ < MLowG. *hoker*] one who hawks goods; huckster

**hawk′-eyed′** (-īd′) *adj.* keen-sighted

**haw·ser** (hô′zər) *n.* [ < OFr. *haucier* < L. *altus,* high] a rope or cable by which a ship is anchored, towed, etc.

**haw·thorn** (hô′thôrn′) *n.* [ < OE. *haga,* hedge + THORN] a thorny shrub or small tree of the rose family, with flowers and small, red fruits

**Haw·thorne** (hô′thôrn′), **Nathaniel** 1804–64; U.S. writer

**hay** (hā) *n.* [ < OE. *hieg*] grass, clover, etc. cut and dried for fodder —*vi.* to mow and dry grass, etc. for hay —**hit the hay** [Slang] to go to sleep

**hay′cock′** (-käk′) *n.* a small, conical heap of hay drying in a field

**Hay·dn** (hīd′n), **Franz Jo·seph** (fränts yō′zef) 1732–1809; Austrian composer

**Hayes** (hāz), **Ruth·er·ford B.** (ruth′ər fərd) 1822–93; 19th president of the U.S. (1877–81)

**hay fever** an acute inflammation of the eyes and respiratory tract: an allergic reaction to some kinds of pollen

**hay′loft′** *n.* a loft, or upper story, in a barn or stable, for storing hay

**hay′mow′** (-mou′) *n.* **1.** a pile of hay in a barn **2.** *same as* HAYLOFT

**hay′stack′** *n.* a large heap of hay piled up outdoors

**hay′wire′** *adj.* [Slang] **1.** out of order; disorganized **2.** crazy: usually in **go haywire,** to become crazy

**haz·ard** (haz′ərd) *n.* [ < OFr. *hasard,*

game of dice] **1.** risk; danger **2.** an obstacle on a golf course —*vt.* to risk

**haz'ard·ous** *adj.* risky; dangerous

**haze**[1] (hāz) *n.* [prob. < HAZY] **1.** a thin vapor of fog, smoke, etc. in the air **2.** slight vagueness of mind —*vi.*, *vt.* **hazed, haz'ing** to make or become hazy (often with *over*)

**haze**[2] (hāz) *vt.* **hazed, haz'ing** [< ?] to force to do ridiculous or painful things, as in initiation

**ha·zel** (hā'z'l) *n.* [OE. *hæsel*] **1.** a shrub or tree of the birch family, with edible nuts **2.** a reddish brown —*adj.* light reddish-brown

**ha'zel·nut'** *n.* the small, edible, roundish nut of the hazel; filbert

**ha·zy** (hā'zē) *adj.* **-zi·er, -zi·est** [prob. < OE. *hasu,* dusky] **1.** somewhat foggy or smoky **2.** somewhat vague —**ha'zi·ly** *adv.* —**ha'zi·ness** *n.*

**H-bomb** (āch'bäm') *n.* same as HYDROGEN BOMB

**he** (hē) *pron., for pl. see* THEY [OE.] **1.** the man, boy, or male animal previously mentioned **2.** anyone [*he* who laughs last laughs best] —*n.* a male

**He** *Chem.* helium

**head** (hed) *n.* [OE. *heafod*] **1.** the part of the body containing the brain, and the jaws, eyes, ears, nose, and mouth **2.** the mind; intelligence **3.** *pl.* **head** a unit of counting [ten *head* of cattle] **4.** the main side of a coin **5.** the uppermost part or thing; top **6.** the topic or title of a section, chapter, etc. **7.** the foremost or projecting part; front **8.** the part designed for holding, striking, etc. [the *head* of a nail] **9.** the membrane across the end of a drum, etc. **10.** the source of a river, etc. **11.** froth, as on beer **12.** the pressure in an enclosed fluid, as steam **13.** a position of leadership or honor **14.** a leader, ruler, etc. —*adj.* **1.** most important; principal **2.** at the top or front **3.** striking against the front [*head* current] —*vt.* **1.** to be the chief of; command **2.** to lead; precede **3.** to cause to go in a specified direction —*vi.* to set out; travel [to *head* eastward] —**come to a head 1.** to be about to suppurate, as a boil **2.** to culminate, or reach a crisis —**go to one's head 1.** to confuse or intoxicate one **2.** to make one vain —**head off** to get ahead of and intercept —**head over heels** deeply; completely —**heads up!** [Colloq.] look out! —**keep (or lose) one's head** to keep (or lose) one's poise, self-control, etc. —**on (or upon) one's head** as one's responsibility or misfortune —**over one's head 1.** too difficult for one to understand **2.** to a higher authority —**turn one's head** to make one vain —**head'less** *adj.*

**head'ache'** (-āk') *n.* **1.** a continuous pain in the head **2.** [Colloq.] a cause of worry, annoyance, or trouble

**head'board'** (-bôrd') *n.* a board that forms the head of a bed, etc.

**head cold** a common cold with congestion of the nasal passages

**head'dress'** *n.* **1.** a decorative covering for the head **2.** a hairdo; coiffure

**-head·ed** (hed'id) *a combining form meaning* having a head or heads [clearheaded, two-headed]

**head'first'** *adv.* **1.** with the head in front; headlong **2.** recklessly; rashly

**head'gear'** *n.* a hat, cap, etc.

**head'ing** *n.* **1.** something forming the head, top, or front **2.** the title, topic, etc., as of a chapter **3.** the direction in which a ship, plane, etc. is moving

**head'land'** *n.* a point of land reaching out into the water; promontory

**head'light'** *n.* a light with a reflector and lens, at the front of a vehicle

**head'line'** *n.* printed lines at the top of a newspaper article, giving the topic —*vt.* **-lined', -lin'ing** to give featured billing or publicity to

**head'long'** (-lôŋ') *adv., adj.* [ME. *hedelinge(s)*] **1.** with the head first **2.** with uncontrolled speed and force **3.** reckless(ly); rash(ly)

**head'mas'ter** *n.* the principal of a private school —**head'mis'tress** *n.fem.*

**head'-on'** *adj., adv.* with the head or front foremost [hit *head-on*]

**head'phone'** *n.* a telephone or radio receiver held to the head by a band

**head'quar'ters** (-kwôr'tərz) *n.pl.* [often with sing. v.] **1.** the main office, or center of operations, of one in command, as in an army **2.** the main office in any organization

**head'rest'** *n.* a support for the head

**head'room'** *n.* space overhead, as in a doorway or tunnel

**head start** an early start or other competitive advantage

**head'stone'** *n.* a stone marker placed at the head of a grave

**head'strong'** *adj.* determined to do as one pleases

**head'wa'ters** *n.pl.* the small streams that are the sources of a river

**head'way'** *n.* **1.** forward motion **2.** progress or success

**head·y** (hed'ē) *adj.* **-i·er, -i·est 1.** impetuous; rash **2.** intoxicating

**heal** (hēl) *vt., vi.* [OE. *hælan*] **1.** to make or become well or healthy again **2.** to cure (a disease) or mend, as a wound —**heal'er** *n.*

**health** (helth) *n.* [OE. *hælth*] **1.** physical and mental well-being; freedom from disease, etc. **2.** condition of body or mind [poor *health*] **3.** a wish for one's health and happiness, as in a toast **4.** soundness, as of a society

**health food** food thought to be very healthful, as food grown with natural fertilizers and free of additives

**health'ful** *adj.* helping to produce or maintain health; wholesome

**health·y** (hel'thē) *adj.* **-i·er, -i·est 1.** having good health **2.** showing or resulting from good health [a *healthy* appetite] 3. *same as* HEALTHFUL —health'i·ness *n*.

**heap** (hēp) *n*. [< OE. *heap*, a troop] 1. a pile or mass of jumbled things 2. [Colloq.] a large amount —*vt*. 1. to make a heap of 2. to give in large amounts 3. to fill (a plate, etc.) full or to overflowing —*vi*. to rise in a heap

**hear** (hir) *vt*. **heard** (hurd), **hear'ing** [OE. *hieran*] 1. to be aware of (sounds) by the ear 2. to listen to 3. to conduct a hearing of (a law case, etc.) 4. to be informed of; learn —*vi*. 1. to be able to hear sounds 2. to be told (*of* or *about*) —**hear from** to get a letter, etc. from —**not hear of** to refuse to consider —**hear'er** *n*.

**hear'ing** *n*. 1. the act or process of perceiving sounds 2. the ability to hear 3. opportunity to be heard 4. an appearance before a judge, investigative committee, etc. 5. the distance a sound will carry [*within hearing*]

**heark·en** (här'kən) *vi*. [OE. *heorcnean*] to listen carefully; pay heed

**hear·say** (hir'sā') *n*. rumor; gossip

**hearse** (hurs) *n*. [< L. *hirpex*, a harrow] a vehicle used in a funeral for carrying the corpse

**heart** (härt) *n*. [OE. *heorte*] 1. the hollow, muscular organ that circulates the blood by alternate dilation and contraction 2. the central, vital, or main part; core 3. the human heart considered as the center of emotions, personality attributes, etc.; specif., *a*) inmost thought and feeling *b*) love, sympathy, etc. *c*) spirit or courage 4. a conventionalized design of a heart (♥) 5. any of a suit of playing cards marked with such symbols in red —**after one's own heart** that pleases one perfectly —**at heart** in one's innermost nature —**by heart** by or from memorization —**set one's heart on** to have a fixed desire for —**take to heart** 1. to consider seriously 2. to be troubled by

**heart'ache'** (-āk') *n*. sorrow or grief

**heart attack** any sudden instance of heart failure; esp., a CORONARY THROMBOSIS

**heart'beat'** *n*. one full contraction and dilation of the heart

**heart'break'** *n*. overwhelming sorrow or grief —**heart'bro'ken** *adj*.

**heart'burn'** *n*. a burning, acid sensation beneath the breastbone

**heart·en** (här't'n) *vt*. to encourage

**heart failure** the inability of the heart to pump enough blood to supply the body tissues adequately

**heart'felt'** *adj*. sincere; genuine

**hearth** (härth) *n*. [OE. *heorth*] 1. the stone or brick floor of a fireplace 2. *a*) the fireside *b*) family life; home

**heart'less** *adj*. unkind; unfeeling —**heart'less·ly** *adv*. —**heart'less·ness** *n*.

**heart'-rend'ing** *adj*. causing much grief or mental anguish

**heart'sick'** *adj*. sick at heart; extremely unhappy or despondent

**heart'strings'** *n.pl*. deepest feelings or affections

**heart'-to-heart'** *adj*. intimate and candid

**heart'warm'ing** *adj*. such as to cause genial feelings

**heart'y** *adj*. **-i·er, -i·est** 1. warm and friendly; cordial 2. strongly felt; unrestrained [*hearty* laughter] 3. strong and healthy 4. nourishing and plentiful [a *hearty* meal] —*n*., *pl*. **-ies** [Archaic] a fellow sailor —**heart'i·ly** *adv*. —**heart'i·ness** *n*.

**heat** (hēt) *n*. [OE. *hætu*] 1. the quality of being hot; hotness, or the perception of this 2. much hotness 3. hot weather or climate 4. the warming of a house, etc. 5. *a*) strong feeling; ardor, anger, etc. *b*) the period of this 6. a single bout, round, or trial 7. the period of sexual excitement in animals, esp. females 8. [Slang] coercion —*vt*., *vi*. 1. to make or become warm or hot 2. to make or become excited

**heat'ed** *adj*. 1. hot 2. vehement or angry —**heat'ed·ly** *adv*.

**heat'er** *n*. an apparatus for giving heat; stove, furnace, radiator, etc.

**heath** (hēth) *n*. [OE. *hæth*] 1. a tract of open wasteland, esp. in the British Isles 2. any of various shrubs that grow on heaths, as heather

**hea·then** (hē'thən) *n*., *pl*. **-thens, -then** [OE. *hæthen*] 1. anyone not a Jew, Christian, or Moslem 2. a person regarded as irreligious, uncivilized, etc. —*adj*. 1. pagan 2. irreligious, uncivilized, etc. —**hea'then·ish** *adj*.

**heath·er** (heth'ər) *n*. [ME. *haddyr*] a plant of the heath family, esp. common in the British Isles, with small, bell-shaped, purplish flowers

**heating pad** a pad with a fabric cover containing an electric heating element, for applying heat to the body

**heat lightning** lightning without thunder, seen on hot evenings

**heat'stroke'** *n*. a condition of high fever, collapse, etc., resulting from exposure to intense heat

**heave** (hēv) *vt*. **heaved** or (esp. *Naut*.) **hove, heav'ing** [OE. *hebban*] 1. to lift, esp. with effort 2. to lift in this way and throw 3. to utter (a sigh, etc.) with effort 4. *Naut*. to raise, haul, etc. by pulling as with a rope —*vi*. 1. to swell up 2. to rise and fall rhythmically 3. *a*) to vomit *b*) to pant; gasp 4. *Naut*. to haul (*on* or *at* a rope, etc.) —*n*. the act or effort of heaving —**heave to** *Naut*. to stop —**heav'er** *n*.

**heave'-ho'** (-hō') *n*. [Colloq.] dismissal, as from a job: chiefly in **give** (or **get**) **the** (**old**) **heave-ho**

**heav·en** (hev''n) *n*. [OE. *heofon*] 1. [*usually pl*.] the visible sky; firmament 2. *Theol*. [H-] *a*) the dwelling place of God and his angels, where the blessed go after death *b*) God 3. any place or state of great happiness —**heav'en·ly** *adj*.

**heav'en·ward** (-wərd) *adv*., *adj*. toward heaven: also **heav'en·wards** *adv*.

**heav·y** (hev'ē) *adj*. **-i·er, -i·est** [OE. *hefig*] 1. hard to lift because of great weight 2. **●**f more than the usual, expected, or defined weight 3. larger greater, or more intense than usual [a *heavy* blow, a *heavy* vote, *heavy* applause] 4. to an unusual extent [a *heavy* drinker] 5. hard to do [*heavy* work] 6. sorrowful [a *heavy* heart] 7. burdened with sleep [*heavy* eyelids] 8. hard to digest [a *heavy* meal] 9. clinging; penetrating [a *heavy* odor] 10. cloudy; gloomy [a *heavy* sky] 11. using massive machinery to produce basic materials, as steel —*adv.* in a heavy manner —*n., pl.* **-ies** Theater a villain —**heav′i·ly** *adv.* —**heav′i·ness** *n.*

**heav·y-du′ty** *adj.* made to withstand great strain, bad weather, etc.

**heav·y-hand′ed** *adj.* 1. clumsy or tactless 2. oppressive or tyrannical

**heav·y-heart′ed** *adj.* sad; unhappy

**heavy hydrogen** *same as* DEUTERIUM

**heav·y-set′** (-set′) *adj.* having a stout or stocky build

**heav′y·weight′** *n.* a boxer or wrestler who weighs over 175 pounds

**Heb.** 1. Hebrew 2. Hebrews

**He·bra·ic** (hi brā′ik) *adj.* of or characteristic of the Hebrews, their language, culture, etc.; Hebrew

**He·brew** (hē′brōō) *n.* 1. *a)* a member of an ancient Semitic people; Israelite *b)* a Jew 2. *a)* the ancient Semitic language of the Israelites *b)* its modern form, the language of Israel —*adj.* of Hebrew or the Hebrews

**Heb·ri·des** (heb′rə dēz′) group of Scottish islands off NW Scotland

**heck** (hek) *interj., n.* [Colloq.] *a euphemism for* HELL

**heck·le** (hek′'l) *vt.* **-led, -ling** [ME. *hekelin*] to harass (a speaker) with questions or taunts —**heck′ler** *n.*

**hec·tare** (hek′ter) *n.* [Fr.] a metric measure of area, 10,000 square meters

**hec·tic** (hek′tik) *adj.* [ < Gr. *hektikos*, habitual] 1. feverish; flushed 2. confused, rushed, excited, etc.—**hec′ti·cal·ly** *adv.*

**Hec·tor** (hek′tər) in Homer's *Iliad*, a Trojan hero killed by Achilles —*vt.* [h-] to browbeat; bully

**he′d** (hēd) 1. he had 2. he would

**hedge** (hej) *n.* [OE. *hecg*] 1. a dense row of shrubs, etc. forming a boundary 2. any fence or barrier 3. a hedging —*vt.* **hedged, hedg′ing** 1. to put a hedge around 2. to hinder or guard as with a barrier 3. to try to avoid loss in (a bet, etc.) as by making counterbalancing bets —*vi.* to refuse to commit oneself or give direct answers

**hedge′hog′** *n.* 1. a small, insect-eating mammal of the Old World, with sharp spines on the back 2. the American porcupine

**he·don·ism** (hēd′'n iz′m) *n.* [ < Gr. *hēdonē*, pleasure] the doctrine that pleasure

HEDGEHOG

is the principal good —**he′don·ist** *n.* —**he′do·nis′tic** *adj.*

**-he·dron** (hē′drən) [ < Gr.] a combining form meaning a figure or crystal with (a specified number of) surfaces

**heed** (hēd) *vt., vi.* [OE. *hedan*] to pay close attention (to) —*n.* close attention —**heed′ful** *adj.* —**heed′less** *adj.* —**heed′less·ly** *adv.* —**heed′less·ness** *n.*

**hee·haw** (hē′hô′) *n., vi.* [echoic] bray

**heel¹** (hēl) *n.* [OE. *hela*] 1. the back part of the foot, under the ankle 2. that part of a stocking or shoe at the heel 3. anything like a heel in location, shape, crushing power, etc. 4. [Colloq.] a despicable person —*vt.* 1. to furnish with a heel 2. to follow closely 3. [Colloq.] to provide with money, etc. —*vi.* to follow along at the heels of someone —**down at the heel(s)** shabby; seedy —**kick up one's heels** to have fun —**on** (or **upon**) **the heels of** close behind

**heel²** (hēl) *vi.* [OE. *hieldan*] to lean to one side; list: said esp. of a ship —*vt.* to make (a ship) list

**heft** (heft) *n.* [ < base of HEAVE] [Colloq.] 1. weight; heaviness 2. importance; influence —*vt.* [Colloq.] to try to judge the weight of by lifting

**heft·y** (hef′tē) *adj.* **-i·er, -i·est** [Colloq.] 1. heavy 2. large and strong 3. big —**heft′i·ness** *n.*

**he·gem·o·ny** (hi jem′ə nē) *n., pl.* **-nies** [ < Gr. *hēgemōn*, leader] leadership or dominance, esp. that of one nation over others

**he·gi·ra** (hi jī′rə) *n.* [ < Ar. *hijrah*, flight] 1. [often H-] the flight of Mohammed from Mecca in 622 A.D. 2. any journey for safety or escape

**Hei·del·berg** (hīd′'l burg′) city in SW West Germany: pop. 125,000

**heif·er** (hef′ər) *n.* [OE. *heahfore*] a young cow that has not borne a calf

**height** (hīt) *n.* [ < OE. *heah*, high] 1. the topmost point 2. the highest limit; extreme 3. the distance from the bottom to the top 4. elevation above a given level; altitude 5. a relatively great distance above a given level 6. [often pl.] an eminence; hill

**height′en** (- ′n) *vt., vi.* 1. to bring or come to a higher position 2. to make or become larger, greater, etc.

**hei·nous** (hā′nəs) *adj.* [ < OFr. *haine*, hatred] outrageously evil —**hei′nous·ly** *adv.* —**hei′nous·ness** *n.*

**heir** (er) *n.* [ < L. *heres*] one who inherits or is entitled to inherit another's property, title, etc.

**heir apparent** the heir whose right to inherit cannot be denied if he outlives the ancestor

**heir·ess** (-is) *n.* a woman or girl who is an heir, esp. to great wealth

**heir′loom′** (-lōōm′) *n.* [see HEIR & LOOM¹] any possession handed down from generation to generation

**heist** (hīst) *n.* [ < HOIST] [Slang] a robbery —*vt.* [Slang] to rob or steal

**held** (held) *pt. & pp.* of HOLD[1]

**Hel·e·na** (hel'i nə) capital of Mont.: pop. 23,000

**Helen of Troy** *Gr. Legend* the beautiful wife of the king of Sparta: the Trojan War was started by her elopement with Paris to Troy

**hel·i·cal** (hel'i kəl) *adj.* [see HELIX] shaped like a helix; spiral

**hel·i·cop·ter** (hel'ə käp'tər, hē'lə-) *n.* [ < Gr. *helix*, spiral + *pteron*, wing] a kind of aircraft lifted and moved, or kept hovering, by large rotary blades mounted horizontally

**he·li·o·cen·tric** (hē'lē ō sen'trik) *adj.* [ < Gr. *hēlios*, the sun + *kentron*, a point] having or regarding the sun as the center

**he·li·o·trope** (hē'lē ə trōp') *n.* [ < Gr. *hēlios*, the sun + *trepein*, to turn] 1. a plant with fragrant clusters of small, white or reddish-purple flowers 2. reddish purple —*adj.* reddish-purple

**hel·i·port** (hel'ə pôrt') *n.* a flat area where helicopters land and take off

**he·li·um** (hē'lē əm) *n.* [Gr. *hēlios*, sun] a chemical element, a very light, inert gas having the lowest known boiling and melting points: used for inflating balloons, etc.: symbol, He

**he·lix** (hē'liks) *n., pl.* **-lix·es, -li·ces'** (hel'ə sēz') [L. & Gr.] a spiral

**hell** (hel) *n.* [ < OE. *helan*, to hide] 1. *often* H-] *Christianity* the place to which sinners and unbelievers go to eternal punishment after death 2. any place or state of misery, cruelty, etc. —**catch** (or **get**) **hell** [Slang] to be severely scolded, punished, etc.

**he'll** (hēl) 1. he will 2. he shall

**hell'bent'** *adj.* [Slang] 1. recklessly determined 2. moving fast

**hell'cat'** *n.* an evil, spiteful woman

**hel·le·bore** (hel'ə bôr') *n.* [ < Gr. *helleboros*] a plant of the buttercup family whose rhizomes were used in medicine

**Hel·len·ic** (hə len'ik) *adj.* 1. Greek 2. of the history, language, or culture of the ancient Greeks —**Hel·len·ism** (hel'ən iz'm) *n.* —**Hel'len·is'tic** *adj.*

**hell·gram·mite** (hel'grə mīt') *n.* [ < ?] the dark-brown aquatic larva of a fly, used as fish bait

**hel·lion** (hel'yən) *n.* [ < Scot. dial. *hallion*, a low fellow] [Colloq.] a person fond of deviltry; troublemaker

**hell'ish** *adj.* 1. devilish; fiendish 2. [Colloq.] very unpleasant —**hell'ish·ly** *adv.* —**hell'ish·ness** *n.*

**hel·lo** (he lō', hel'ō) *interj.* an exclamation of greeting

**helm** (helm) *n.* [OE. *helma*] 1. the wheel or tiller by which a ship is steered 2. the control or leadership of an organization, government, etc.

**hel·met** (hel'mət) *n.* [ < OFr. *helme*] a protective, rigid head covering for use in combat, certain sports, etc.

**helms·man** (helmz'mən) *n., pl.* **-men** the man who steers a ship

**he·lot** (hel'ət, hēl'ət) *n.* [? < *Helos*, ancient Greek town] a serf or slave

**help** (help) *vt.* [OE. *helpan*] 1. to make things easier or better for; aid; assist 2. to remedy [to *help* a cough] 3. to

keep from; avoid [can't *help* crying] 4. to serve or wait on (a customer, etc.) —*vi.* to give aid; be useful —*n.* 1. a helping; aid; assistance 2. a remedy 3. one that helps; esp., a hired person or persons; servant(s), farm hand(s), etc. —**help oneself to** to take without asking —**help out** to help in getting or doing something —**help'er** *n.*

**help·ful** (help'fəl) *adj.* giving help; useful —**help'ful·ly** *adv.* —**help'ful·ness** *n.*

**help'ing** (-iŋ) *n.* a portion of food served to one person

**help'less** *adj.* 1. not able to help oneself; weak 2. lacking help or protection 3. incompetent —**help'less·ly** *adv.* —**help'less·ness** *n.*

**help'mate'** *n.* [ < ff.] a helpful companion; specif., a wife or husband

**help'meet'** *n.* [misreading of "an *help meet* for him" (Gen. 2:18)] *same as* HELPMATE

**Hel·sin·ki** (hel'siŋ kē) capital of Finland: pop. 519,000

**hel·ter-skel·ter** (hel'tər skel'tər) *adv., adj.* in or showing haste or confusion

**helve** (helv) *n.* [OE. *helfe*] the handle of an ax, hatchet, etc.

**Hel·ve·tian** (hel vē'shən) *adj., n.* Swiss

**hem**[1] (hem) *n.* [OE.] the border on a garment, etc. made by folding and sewing down the edge.—*vt.* **hemmed, hem'ming** to fold back the edge of and sew down —**hem in** (or **around** or **about**) 1. to surround 2. to confine

**hem**[2] (hem) *interj., n.* the sound made in clearing the throat —*vi.* **hemmed, hem'ming** 1. to make this sound, as for attracting attention 2. to grope about in speech for the right words: usually used in the phrase **to hem and haw**

**he'-man'** *n.* [Colloq.] a strong, virile man

**hem·a·tite** (hem'ə tīt', hē'mə-) *n.* [ < Gr. *haimatitēs*, bloodlike] native ferric oxide, an important iron ore

**he·ma·tol·o·gy** (hē'mə täl'ə jē) *n.* [ < Gr. *haima*, blood + -LOGY] the study of blood and its diseases —**he'·ma·tol'o·gist** *n.*

**heme** (hēm) *n.* [ < Gr. *haima*, blood] the iron-containing pigment in hemoglobin

**hemi-** [Gr. *hēmi-*] *a prefix meaning* half [*hemisphere*]

**hem·i·sphere** (hem'ə sfir') *n.* 1. half of a sphere or globe 2. any of the halves (northern, southern, eastern, or western) of the earth —**hem'i·spher'i·cal** (-sfer'i kəl) *adj.*

**hem·line** (hem'līn') *n.* the bottom edge of a dress, skirt, coat, etc.

**hem·lock** (hem'läk) *n.* [OE. *hemlic*] 1. *a)* a poisonous plant of the parsley family *b)* a poison made from this plant 2. *a)* an evergreen tree of the pine family *b)* the wood of this tree

**hemo-** [ < Gr. *haima*] *a combining form meaning* blood

**he·mo·glo·bin** (hē'mə glō'bin) *n.* [ < *prec.* + GLOBULE] the red coloring matter of the red blood corpuscles

**he·mo·phil·i·a** (hē′mə fil′ē ə) *n.* [see HEMO- & -PHILE] a hereditary condition in which the blood fails to clot normally, causing prolonged bleeding from even minor injuries —**he′mo·phil′i·ac** (-ak) *n.*

**hem·or·rhage** (hem′ər ij, hem′rij) *n.* [< Gr. *haima*, blood + *rhēgnynai*, to break] the escape of blood from a blood vessel; heavy bleeding —*vi.* **-rhaged, -rhag·ing** to have a hemorrhage —**hem′or·rhag′ic** (-ə-raj′ik) *adj.*

**hem·or·rhoid** (hem′ə roid′, hem′ roid) *n.* [< Gr. *haima*, blood + *rhein*, to flow] a painful swelling of a vein in the region of the anus, often with bleeding: *usually used in pl.*

**hemp** (hemp) *n.* [OE. *hænep*] 1. a tall Asiatic plant having tough fiber 2. its fiber, used to make rope, sailcloth, etc. 3. a substance, as hashish, made from its leaves and flowers

**hemp·en** (hem′pən) *adj.* of or like hemp

**hem·stitch** (hem′stich′) *n.* an ornamental stitch, used esp. at a hem, made by pulling out several parallel threads and tying the cross threads into small bunches —*vt.* to put hemstitches on

**hen** (hen) *n.* [OE. *henn*] 1. the female of the chicken (the domestic fowl) 2. the female of various other birds

**hence** (hens) *adv.* [< OE. *heonan*, from here] 1. from this place; away [go *hence*] 2. from this time [a year *hence*] 3. as a result; therefore 4. [Archaic] from this origin or source

**hence′forth′** *adv.* from this time on: also **hence′for′ward**

**hench·man** (hench′mən) *n.*, *pl.* **-men** [< OE. *hengest*, stallion + *-man*] a trusted helper or follower

**hen·na** (hen′ə) *n.* [Ar. *hinnā′*] 1. an old-world plant with minute flowers 2. a dye extracted from its leaves, used to tint the hair auburn 3. reddish brown —*adj.* reddish-brown —*vt.* **-naed, -na·ing** to tint with henna

**hen·peck** (hen′pek′) *vt.* to nag and domineer over (one's husband)

**Hen·ry VIII** (hen′rē) 1491-1547; king of England (1509-47)

**hep** (hep) *adj.* [Slang] *same as* HIP²

**hep·a·rin** (hep′ər in) *n.* [Gr. *hēpar*, the liver + -IN¹] a substance in body tissues, esp. in the liver, that prevents the clotting of blood

**he·pat·ic** (hi pat′ik) *adj.* [< Gr. *hēpar*, liver] of or like the liver

**hep·a·ti·tis** (hep′ə tīt′is) *n.* [< Gr. *hēpar*, liver + -ITIS] inflammation of the liver

**her** (hur) *pron.* [OE. *hire*] objective case of SHE —*poss. pronominal adj.* of, belonging to, or done by her

**He·ra** (hir′ə) *Gr. Myth.* the wife of Zeus and queen of the gods

**her·ald** (her′əld) *n.* [< OFr. *heralt*] 1. formerly, an official who made proclamations, carried state messages, etc. 2. one who announces significant news, etc. 3. a forerunner; harbinger —*vt.* to announce, foretell, etc.

**he·ral·dic** (he ral′dik) *adj.* of heraldry or heralds

**her·ald·ry** *n.* 1. the science dealing with coats of arms, genealogies, etc. 2. ceremony or pomp

**herb** (urb, hurb) *n.* [< L. *herba*] 1. any seed plant whose stem withers away annually 2. any plant used as a medicine, seasoning, etc. —**her·ba·ceous** (hər bā′shəs, ər-) *adj.* —**herb′al** *adj.*

**herb·age** (ur′bij, hur′-) *n.* herbs collectively; esp., pasturage; grass

**herb·al·ist** (hur′b'l ist, ur′-) *n.* one who grows or deals in herbs

**her·bi·cide** (hur′bə sīd′, ur′-) *n.* any chemical substance used to destroy plants, esp. weeds —**her′bi·ci′dal** *adj.*

**her·biv·o·rous** (hər biv′ər əs) *adj.* [< L. *herba*, herb + *vorare*, devour] feeding chiefly on grass or plants

**her·cu·le·an** (hur′kyə lē′ən, hər kyoo′lē ən) *adj.* [*sometimes* H-] 1. having the great size or strength of Hercules 2. calling for great strength, size, or courage

**Her·cu·les** (hur′kyə lēz′) *Gr. & Rom. Myth.* a hero famous for feats of strength —*n.* [h-] a very strong man

**herd** (hurd) *n.* [OE. *heord*] 1. a number of cattle or other large animals feeding or living together 2. *a)* a crowd *b)* the common people; masses: contemptuous term —*vt.*, *vi.* to gather or move as a herd

**herds·man** (hurdz′mən) *n.*, *pl.* **-men** one who keeps or tends a herd

**here** (hir) *adv.* [OE. *her*] 1. at or in this place: often used as an intensive [John *here* is an actor] 2. to or into this place [come *here*] 3. at this point; now 4. on earth —*n.* this place —**neither here nor there** irrelevant

**here′a·bout′** *adv.* in this general vicinity: also **here′a·bouts′**

**here·af·ter** *adv.* 1. from now on; in the future 2. following this —*n.* 1. the future 2. the state after death

**here′by′** *adv.* by this means

**he·red·i·tar·y** (hə red′ə ter′ē) *adj.* 1. *a)* of, or passed down by, inheritance from an ancestor *b)* having title, etc. by inheritance 2. of or passed down by heredity

**he·red·i·ty** (hə red′ə tē) *n.*, *pl.* **-ties** [< L. *heres*, heir] the transmission of characteristics from parent to offspring by means of genes

**here·in** (hir in′) *adv.* 1. in here 2. in this writing, container, etc.

**here·of′** *adv.* of or concerning this

**her·e·sy** (her′ə sē) *n.*, *pl.* **-sies** [< Gr. *hairesis*, selection, sect] 1. a religious belief opposed to the orthodox doctrines of a church 2. any opinion opposed to established views

**her′e·tic** (-tik) *n.* one who professes

a heresy; esp., a church member who holds beliefs opposed to church dogma —**he·ret·i·cal** (hə ret′i k'l) adj.

**here′to·fore′** adv. up to now

**here′up·on′** adv. 1. at once; following this 2. concerning this point

**here·with′** adv. 1. along with this 2. by this method or means

**her·it·a·ble** (her′it ə b'l) adj. that can be inherited

**her·it·age** (her′ət ij) n. 1. property that is or can be inherited 2. a tradition, etc. handed down from one's ancestors or the past

**her·maph·ro·dite** (hər maf′rə dīt′) n. [< Gr. Hermaphroditos, son of Hermes and Aphrodite, united in a single body with a nymph] a person, animal, or plant with the sexual organs of both the male and the female — **her·maph′ro·dit′ic** (-dit′ik) adj.

**Her·mes** (hur′mēz) Gr. Myth. a god who was messenger of the other gods

**her·met·ic** (hər met′ik) adj. [< prec. (reputed founder of alchemy)] airtight: also **her·met′i·cal** —**her·met′i·cal·ly** adv.

**her·mit** (hur′mit) n. [< Gr. erēmos, desolate] one who lives by himself in a lonely or secluded spot; recluse

**her′mit·age** (-ij) n. a secluded retreat, as the place where a hermit lives

**her·ni·a** (hur′nē ə) n., pl. -as, -ae′ (-ē′) [L.] the protrusion of an organ, esp. a part of the intestine, through a tear in the wall of the surrounding structure; rupture —**her′ni·al** adj.

**her′ni·ate′** (-āt′) vi. -at′ed, -at′ing to protrude so as to form a hernia —**her′ni·a′tion** n.

**he·ro** (hir′ō, hē′rō) n., pl. -roes [< Gr. hērōs] 1. a man of great courage, nobility, etc. or one admired for his exploits 2. the central male character in a novel, play, etc.

**He·rod·o·tus** (hə räd′ə təs) 485?-425? B.C.; Gr. historian

**he·ro·ic** (hi rō′ik) adj. 1. of or like a hero 2. of or about heroes and their deeds 3. daring and risky —n. [pl.] extravagant talk or action —**he·ro′i·cal·ly** adv.

**her·o·in** (her′ə·win) n. [G., orig. a trademark] a habit-forming narcotic derived from morphine

**her·o·ine** (her′ə win) n. a girl or woman hero in life or literature

**her′o·ism** (-wiz'm) n. the qualities and actions of a hero or heroine

**her·on** (her′ən) n. [< OFr. hairon] a wading bird with a long neck, long legs, and a long bill

**hero sandwich** a large roll sliced lengthwise and filled with cold meats, cheeses, etc.

**her·pes** (hur′pēz) n. [L. < Gr. herpein, to creep] a virus disease causing small blisters on the skin

**herpes zos·ter** (zäs′tər) [< prec. + Gr. zōstēr, a girdle] same as SHINGLES

‡**Herr** (her) n., pl. **Her′ren** (-ən) [G.] 1. a man; gentleman 2. Mr.; Sir

**her·ring** (her′iŋ) n. [OE. hæring] a small food fish of the N Atlantic

**her′ring·bone′** n. 1. the spine of a herring with the ribs extending in rows

of parallel, slanting lines 2. anything having such a pattern

**hers** (hurz) pron. that or those belonging to her [hers are better]

**her·self** (hər self′) pron. 1. the intensive form of SHE [she went herself] 2. the reflexive form of SHE [she hurt herself] 3. her true self [she's not herself today]

**hertz** (hurts) n., pl. **hertz** [after H. R. Hertz, 19th-c. G. physicist] the international unit of frequency, equal to one cycle per second

**Hertz·i·an waves** (hurt′sē ən) [see prec.] [sometimes h-] electromagnetic radiation resulting from the oscillations of electricity in a conductor

**he's** (hēz) 1. he is 2. he has

**hes·i·tant** (hez′ə tənt) adj. hesitating or undecided; doubtful —**hes′i·tan·cy** n. —**hes′i·tant·ly** adv.

**hes′i·tate′** (-tāt′) vi. -tat′ed, -tat′ing [< L. haerere, to stick] 1. to stop in indecision; waver 2. to pause 3. to be reluctant [I hesitate to ask] 4. to pause continually in speaking —**hes′i·tat′ing·ly** adv. —**hes′i·ta′tion** n.

**hetero-** [Gr. hetero-] a combining form meaning other, another, different

**het·er·o·dox** (het′ər ə däks′) adj. [< prec. + Gr. doxa, opinion] opposed to the usual beliefs, esp. in religion; unorthodox —**het′er·o·dox′y** n.

**het·er·o·ge·ne·ous** (het′ər ə jē′nē əs) adj. [< HETERO- + Gr. genos, a kind] 1. differing in structure, quality, etc.; dissimilar 2. composed of unlike parts

**het′er·o·sex′u·al** (-sek′shoo wəl) adj. 1. of or having sexual desire for those of the opposite sex 2. of different sexes —n. a heterosexual individual

**heu·ris·tic** (hyoo ris′tik) adj. [< Gr. heuriskein, invent] helping to learn, as by a method of self-teaching

**hew** (hyoo) vt. hewed, hewed or hewn, hew′ing [OE. heawan] 1. to chop or cut with an ax, knife, etc. 2. to make or shape thus —vi. to conform (to a rule, principle, etc.)

**HEW** (Department of) Health, Education, and Welfare

**hex** (heks) n. [< G. hexe, witch] something supposed to bring bad luck —vt. to cause to have bad luck

**hexa-** [< Gr. hex, six] a combining form meaning six

**hex·a·gon** (hek′sə gän′) n. [< Gr. hex, six + gōnia, an angle] a plane figure with six angles and six sides —**hex·ag′o·nal** (-sag′ə n'l) adj.

**hex·am·e·ter** (hek sam′ə tər) n. [see HEXA- & METER[1]] 1. a line of verse containing six metrical feet 2. verse consisting of hexameters

**hey** (hā) interj. an exclamation used to attract attention, etc.

**hey·day** (hā′dā′) n. the time of greatest vigor, prosperity, etc.; prime

**Hg** [L. hydrargyrum] Chem. mercury

**hi** (hī) interj. an exclamation of greeting

**HI** Hawaii

**hi·a·tus** (hī āt′əs) n., pl. -tus·es, -tus [L. < hiare, to gape] a gap or break, as where a part is missing

**hi·ba·chi** (hi bä´chē) n., pl. **-chis** [Jap. < hi, fire + bachi, bowl] a charcoal-burning brazier and grill

**hi·ber·nate** (hī´bər nāt´) vi. **-nat´ed, -nat´ing** [< L. hibernus, wintry] to spend the winter in a dormant state —**hi´ber·na´tion** n.

**hi·bis·cus** (hī bis´kəs, hi-) n. [< L.] a plant of the mallow family, with large, colorful flowers

**hic·cup** (hik´əp) n. [echoic] an involuntary contraction of the diaphragm that closes the glottis at the moment of breathing in so that a sharp sound is produced —vi. **-cupped, -cup·ing** or **-cup·ping** to make a hiccup Also **hic·cough** (hik´əp)

**hick** (hik) n. [< Richard] [Colloq.] an awkward, unsophisticated person, esp. from a rural area

**hick·ey** (hik´ē) n., pl. **-eys, -ies** [Colloq.] any device or gadget

**hick·o·ry** (hik´ər ē) n., pl. **-ries** [< AmInd. pawcohiccora] 1. a N. American tree of the walnut family 2. its hard, tough wood 3. its smooth-shelled, edible nut: also **hickory nut**

**hide¹** (hīd) vt. hid (hid), **hid´den** (hid´'n) or **hid, hid´ing** [OE. hydan] 1. to put or keep out of sight; conceal 2. to keep secret 3. to keep from sight by obscuring, etc. —vi. 1. to be concealed. 2. to conceal oneself

**hide²** (hīd) n. [OE. hid] an animal skin or pelt, either raw or tanned

**hide´a·way´** (-ə wā´) n. [Colloq.] a place where one can hide, be secluded, etc.

**hide´bound´** adj. obstinately conservative and narrow-minded

**hid·e·ous** (hid´ē əs) adj. [< OFr. hide, fright] horrible; very ugly —**hid´e·ous·ly** adv. —**hid´e·ous·ness** n.

**hide´-out´** n. [Colloq.] a hiding place, as for gangsters

**hie** (hī) vi., vt. hied, hie´ing or hy´ing [< OE. higian] to hasten

**hi·er·ar·chy** (hī´ə rär´kē) n., pl. **-chies** [< Gr. hieros, sacred + archos, ruler] 1. church government by clergy in graded ranks 2. the highest officials in such a system 3. a group of persons or things arranged in order of rank, grade, etc. —**hi´er·ar´chi·cal** adj.

**hi·er·o·glyph·ic** (hī´ər ə glif´ik, hī´rə-) n. [< Gr. hieros, sacred + glyphein, carve] 1. a picture or symbol representing a word, sound, etc., in a system used by ancient Egyptians and others 2. a symbol, etc. hard to understand —adj. of or like hieroglyphics

**hi·er·o·phant** (hī´ər ə fant´) n. [< Gr. hieros, sacred + phainein] a priest in ancient Greece who presided at sacred mysteries

**hi-fi** (hī´fī´) n. a phonograph, etc. having high fidelity —adj. of or having high fidelity of sound reproduction

**high** (hī) adj. [OE. heah] 1. lofty; tall 2. extending upward a (specified) distance 3. reaching to, situated at, or done from a height 4. above others in rank, position, etc.; superior 5. grave [high treason]´ 6. greater in size, amount, cost, etc. than usual [high prices] 7. luxurious [high living] 8. raised or acute in pitch; shrill 9. slightly tainted, as meat 10. elated [high spirits] 11. [Slang] a) drunk b) under the influence of a drug —adv. in or to a high level, degree, rank, etc. —n. 1. a high level, place, etc. 2. that gear of a motor vehicle, etc. producing the greatest speed 3. [Slang] a euphoric condition induced as by drugs —**high and low** everywhere —**on high** in heaven

**high´ball´** n. whiskey or brandy mixed with soda water, ginger ale, etc.

**high´born´** adj. of noble birth

**high´boy´** n. a high chest of drawers mounted on legs

**high´brow´** n. [Colloq.] one having or affecting highly cultivated tastes; intellectual — adj. [Colloq.] of or for highbrows

**high´er-up´** n. [Colloq.] a person of higher rank or position

**high´fa·lu·tin(g)** (-fə lōōt´'n) adj. [Colloq.] pretentious or pompous

HIGHBOY

**high fidelity** in radio, sound recording, etc., nearly exact reproduction of a wide range of sound waves

**high´-flown´** (-flōn´) adj. 1. extravagantly ambitious 2. bombastic

**high frequency** any radio frequency between 3 and 30 megahertz

**High German** the West Germanic dialects spoken in C and S Germany

**high´hand´ed** adj. overbearing — **high´hand´ed·ly** adv. —**high´hand´ed·ness** n.

**high´-hat´** adj. [Slang] snobbish —vt. **-hat´ted, -hat´ting** [Slang] to snub

**high´land** (-lənd) n. a region with many hills or mountains —the **Highlands** mountainous region occupying most of N Scotland —**High´land·er** n.

**high´-lev´el** adj. 1. of or by persons of high office 2. in a high office

**high´light´** n. 1. the part on which light is brightest: also **high light** 2. the most important or interesting part, scene, etc. —vt. 1. to give highlights to 2. to give prominence to

**high´ly** adv. 1. very much 2. favorably 3. at a high level, wage, rank, etc.

**high´-mind´ed** adj. having high ideals, principles, etc.

**high´ness** n. 1. height 2. [H-] a title used in speaking to or of royalty

**high´-pres´sure** adj. 1. having or withstanding high pressure 2. using forcefully persuasive or insistent methods —vt. **-sured, -sur·ing** [Colloq.] to urge with such methods

**high´-rise´** n. an apartment house, office building, etc. of many stories

**high'road'** n. 1. [Chiefly Brit.] a highway 2. an easy or direct way

**high school** a secondary school offering academic or vocational subjects to students in grades 10, 11, and 12, and sometimes grade 9

**high seas** open ocean waters outside the territorial limits of any nation

**high sign** a signal given secretly, as in warning

**high'-spir'it·ed** adj. 1. courageous 2. lively; spirited

**high'-strung'** adj. highly sensitive or nervous and tense; excitable

**high'-ten'sion** adj. having or carrying a high voltage

**high tide** the highest level to which the tide rises

**high time** time beyond the proper time but before it is too late

**high'way'** n. 1. a public road 2. a main road; thoroughfare

**high'way·man** (-mən) n., pl. **-men** one who robs travelers on a highway

**high wire** a wire stretched high above the ground, used by aerialists; tightrope

**hi·jack** (hī'jak') vt. [Colloq.] 1. to steal (goods in transit, etc.) by force 2. to force (an aircraft) to make a nonscheduled flight —**hi'jack'er** n.

**hike** (hīk) vi. **hiked**, **hik'ing** [ < dial. heik'] to take a long walk; tramp —vt. [Colloq.] 1. to pull up; hoist 2. to raise (prices, etc.) —n. 1. a long walk 2. [Colloq.] a rise —**hik'er** n.

**hi·lar·i·ous** (hi ler'ē əs, hī-) adj. [ < Gr. hilaros, cheerful] noisily merry; very gay —**hi·lar'i·ty** (-ə tē) n.

**hill** (hil) n. [OE. hyll] 1. a natural raised part of the earth's surface, smaller than a mountain 2. a small pile, as of soil heaped around plants

**hill'bil'ly** n., pl. **-lies** [ < nickname Billy] [Colloq.] one who lives in or comes from the mountains or backwoods, esp. of the South

**hill'ock** (-ək) n. a small hill

**hill'side'** n. the side of a hill

**hill'top'** n. the top of a hill

**hill'y** adj. **-i·er, -i·est** 1. full of hills 2. like a hill; steep —**hill'i·ness** n.

**hilt** (hilt) n. [OE.] the handle of a sword, dagger, tool, etc.

**him** (him) pron. objective case of HE

**Hi·ma·la·yas** (him'ə lā'əz, hi mäl'-yəz) mountain system of SC Asia, mostly in India —**Hi'ma·la'yan** adj.

**him·self'** pron. 1. the intensive form of HE [he went himself] 2. the reflexive form of HE [he hurt himself] 3. his true self [he is not himself today]

**hin·di¹** (hīnd) adj. **hind'er, hind'-most'** or **hind'er·most'** [prob. < HINDER²] back; rear; posterior

**hind²** (hīnd) n. [OE.] the female of the red deer

**Hind.** 1. Hindi 2. Hindu

**hin·der¹** (hin'dər) vt. [OE. hindrian] 1. to keep back; stop 2. to thwart

**hind·er²** (hīn'dər) adj. [OE.] rear

**Hin·di** (hin'dē) n. the main (and official) language of India

**hind'most'** adj. farthest back; last

**hind'quar'ter** n. the hind half of a side of veal, beef, lamb, etc.

**hin·drance** (hin'drəns) n. 1. the act of hindering 2. a person or thing that hinders; obstacle

**hind'sight'** n. ability to see, after the event, what should have been done

**Hin·du** (hin'dōō) n. 1. any of several peoples of India 2. a follower of Hinduism —adj. 1. of the Hindus, their language, etc. 2. of Hinduism

**Hin'du·ism** n. the religion and social system of the Hindus

**Hin·du·stan** (hin'doo stan') 1. region in N India 2. the Indian peninsula 3. the republic of India

**hinge** (hinj) n. [ < ME. hengen, hang] 1. a joint on which a door, lid, etc. swings 2. a natural joint, as of the shell of a clam —vt. **hinged**, **hing'-ing** to attach by a hinge —vi. to hang as on a hinge; depend

**hint** (hint) n. [prob. < OE. hentan, to grasp] a slight indication; indirect allusion —vt., vi. to give a hint (of)

**hin·ter·land** (hin'tər land') n. [G.] 1. the land behind that bordering a coast or river 2. a remote area

**hip¹** (hip) n. [OE. hype] the part of the body around the joint formed by each thigh bone and the pelvis

**hip²** (hip) adj. **hip'per, hip'pest** [ < ? hep] [Slang] 1. sophisticated; aware; fashionable 2. of hippies —**get** (or **be**) **hip to** [Slang] to become (or be) informed about

**hip'pie** n. [Slang] a young person who, in his alienation from conventional society, has turned to mysticism, psychedelic drugs, communal living, etc.: also **hippy**, pl. **-pies**

**hip·po** (hip'ō) n., pl. **-pos** [Colloq.] same as HIPPOPOTAMUS

**Hip·poc·ra·tes** (hi päk'rə tēz') 460?-370? B.C.; Gr. physician

**Hip·po·crat'ic oath** (hip'ə krat'ik) the oath, attributed to Hippocrates, generally taken by medical graduates: it sets forth their ethical code

**hip·po·drome** (hip'ə drōm') n. [ < Gr. hippos, horse + dromos, course] an arena for a circus, games, etc.

**hip·po·pot·a·mus** (hip'ə pät'ə məs) n., pl. **-mus·es, -a·mi** (-mī') [ < Gr. hippos, horse + potamus, river] a large, plant-eating mammal with a heavy, thick-skinned body: it lives in or near rivers in Africa

**hire** (hīr) vt. **hired**, **hir'ing** [ < OE. hyr, wages] to pay for the services of (a person) or the use of (a thing) —n. 1. a hiring 2. the amount paid in hiring —**hire out** to work for pay

**hire'ling** n. one who will follow anyone's orders for pay; mercenary

**Hi·ro·shi·ma** (hir'ə shē'mə) seaport in SW Honshu, Japan: largely destroyed (Aug. 6, 1945) by a U.S. atomic bomb, the first ever used in warfare: pop. 504,000

**hir·sute** (hur'sōōt, hir'-; hər sōōt') adj. [L. hirsutus] hairy; shaggy

**his** (hiz) pron. [OE.] that or those belonging to him [his are better] — poss. pronominal adj. of, belonging to, or done by him

**His·pan·io·la** (his'pən yō'lə) island in the West Indies

**hiss** (his) *vi.* [echoic] 1. to make a sound like that of a prolonged *s* 2. to show disapproval by hissing —*vt.* to say or indicate by hissing —*n.* the act or sound of hissing

**hist** (st, hist) *interj.* be quiet!

**his·ta·mine** (his′tə mēn′) *n.* [ < Gr. *histos*, tissue + AMMONIA] an ammonia derivative released by the tissues in allergic reactions

**his·tol·o·gy** (his täl′ə jē) *n.* [ < Gr. *histos*, tissue + -LOGY] *Biol.* the microscopic study of tissue structure —**his·tol′o·gist** *n.*

**his·to·ri·an** (his tôr′ē ən) *n.* a writer of, or authority on, history

**his·tor′ic** (-ik) *adj.* 1. same as HISTORICAL 2. famous in history

**his·tor′i·cal** (-i k'l) *adj.* 1. of or concerned with history 2. based on people or events of the past 3. established by history; factual —**his·tor′i·cal·ly** *adv.*

**his·to·ric·i·ty** (his′tə ris′ə tē) *n.* historical authenticity

**his·to·ri·og·ra·phy** (his tôr′ē äg′rə fē) *n.* the study of the techniques of historical research

**his·to·ry** (his′tə rē, -trē) *n.*, *pl.* **-ries** [ < Gr. *histōr*, learned] 1. an account of what has happened, esp. in the life of a people, country, etc. 2. all recorded past events 3. the branch of knowledge that deals with the recording, analysis, etc. of past events 4. a known past [my coat has a *history*]

**his·tri·on·ic** (his′trē än′ik) *adj.* [ < L. *histrio*, actor] 1. of acting or actors 2. overacted or overacting

**his′tri·on′ics** *n.pl.* [sometimes with sing. v.] 1. dramatics 2. an artificial or affected manner or outburst

**hit** (hit) *vt.*, *vi.* **hit**, **hit′ting** [ < ON. *hitta*, meet with] 1. to come against (something) with force; knock; bump 2. to give a blow (to); strike 3. to strike with a missile 4. to affect strongly [a town hard *hit* by floods] 5. to come (upon) by accident or after search 6. to arrive at [stocks *hit* a new high] 7. *Baseball* to get (a hit) —*n.* 1. a blow that strikes its mark 2. a collision 3. a successful and popular song, book, etc. 4. *Baseball* a ball struck fairly by which a batter gets on base —**hit it off** to get along well together —**hit or miss** in a haphazard way —**hit′ter** *n.*

**hit′-and-run′** *adj.* hitting with a vehicle, usually an automobile, and then escaping: also **hit′-skip′**

**hitch** (hich) *vi.* [ME. *hicchen*] 1. to move jerkily 2. to become fastened or caught —*vt.* 1. to move, pull, etc. with jerks 2. to fasten with a hook, knot, etc. 3. [Slang] to get (a ride) in hitchhiking —*n.* 1. a tug; jerk 2. a limp 3. a hindrance; obstacle 4. a catching or fastening 5. a kind of knot 6. [Slang] a period of time served, as of military service

**hitch′hike′** (-hīk′) *vi.* **-hiked′,**

**-hik′ing** to travel by asking for rides from motorists along the way —**hitch′hik′er** *n.*

**hith·er** (hi*th*′ər) *adv.* [ < OE.] to this place —*adj.* nearer

**hith′er·to′** *adv.* until this time

**Hit·ler** (hit′lər), **Adolf** 1889–1945; Nazi dictator of Germany (1933–45)

**hit man** [Slang] a hired murderer

**hit′-or-miss′** *adj.* haphazard; random

**hive** (hīv) *n.* [ < OE.] 1. a shelter for a colony of bees; beehive 2. the bees of a hive 3. a crowd of busy people 4. a place of great activity —*vt.* **hived**, **hiv′ing** to gather (bees) into a hive —*vi.* to enter a hive

**hives** (hīvz) *n.* [orig. Scot. dial.] same as URTICARIA

**H.M.S.** 1. His (or Her) Majesty's Service 2. His (or Her) Majesty's Ship

**hoa·gie, hoa·gie** (hō′gē) *n.*, *pl.* **-gies** [ < ?] same as HERO SANDWICH

**hoard** (hôrd) *n.* [OE. *hord*] a supply stored up and hidden —*vi.*, *vt.* to accumulate and store away (money, goods, etc.) —**hoard′er** *n.*

**hoar·frost** (hôr′frôst′) *n.* white, frozen dew on the ground, leaves, etc.

**hoarse** (hôrs) *adj.* [OE. *has*] 1. harsh and grating in sound 2. having a rough, husky voice —**hoarse′ness** *n.*

**hoar·y** (hôr′ē) *adj.* **-i·er**, **-i·est** [ < OE. *har*] 1. white or gray 2. having white or gray hair from old age 3. very old Also **hoar** —**hoar′i·ness** *n.*

**hoax** (hōks) *n.* [ < ? HOCUS-POCUS] a trick or fraud; esp., a practical joke —*vt.* to deceive with a hoax

**hob** (häb) *n.* [ < *Robin* or *Robert*] [Eng. Dial.] an elf or goblin —**play** (or **raise**) **hob** with to make trouble for

**hob·ble** (häb′'l) *vi.* **-bled**, **-bling** [ME. *hobelen*] to go haltingly; limp —*vt.* 1. to cause to limp 2. to hamper (a horse, etc.) by tying two feet together 3. to hinder —*n.* 1. a limp 2. a rope, etc. used to hobble a horse

**hob·by** (häb′ē) *n.*, *pl.* **-bies** [ME. *hoby*] 1. same as HOBBYHORSE 2. something that a person likes to do in his spare time —**hob′by·ist** *n.*

**hob′by·horse′** *n.* 1. a child's toy consisting of a stick with a horse's head 2. same as ROCKING HORSE

**hob·gob·lin** (häb′gäb′lin) *n.* [HOB + GOBLIN] 1. an elf 2. a bugbear

**hob·nail′** *n.* [*hob*, a peg + NAIL] a broad-headed nail put on the soles of heavy shoes to prevent wear, etc. —*vt.* to put hobnails on

**hob′nob′** (-näb′) *vi.* **-nobbed′**, **-nob′bing** [ < ME. *habben*, have + *nabben*, not have] to be on close terms (with)

**ho·bo** (hō′bō) *n.*, *pl.* **-bos**, **-boes** 1. a migratory worker 2. a tramp

**hock¹** (häk) *n.* [ < OE. *hoh*, heel] the joint bending backward in the hind leg of a horse, ox, etc.

**hock²** (häk) *vt.*, *n.* [ < Du. *hok*, prison, debt] [Slang] same as PAWN¹

**hock·ey** (häk′ē) *n.* [prob. < OFr. *hoquet,* bent stick] **1.** a team game played on ice skates, with curved sticks and a rubber disk (*puck*) **2.** a similar game played on foot on a field, with a small ball

**hock′shop′** *n.* [Slang] a pawnshop

**ho·cus-po·cus** (hō′kəs pō′kəs) *n.* [imitation L.] **1.** meaningless words used as a formula by conjurers **2.** *same as* SLEIGHT OF HAND **3.** trickery

**hod** (häd) *n.* [prob. < MDu. *hodde*] **1.** a long-handled wooden trough used for carrying bricks, mortar, etc. on the shoulder **2.** a coal scuttle

**hodge·podge** (häj′päj′) *n.* [< OFr. *hochepot,* a stew] a jumbled mixture

**hoe** (hō) *n.* [< OHG. *houwan,* hew] a tool with a thin blade set across the end of a long handle, for weeding, loosening soil, etc. —*vt., vi.* **hoed, hoe′ing** to cultivate with a hoe

**hoe′cake′** (-kāk′) *n.* a thin bread made of cornmeal

**hoe′down′** *n.* **1.** a lively, rollicking dance **2.** a party with such dances

**hog** (hôg, häg) *n.* [OE. *hogg*] **1.** a pig; esp., a full-grown pig raised for its meat **2.** [Colloq.] a selfish, greedy, or filthy person —*vt.* **hogged, hog′ging** [Slang] to take all of or an unfair share of —**go (the) whole hog** [Slang] to go all the way —**high on (or off) the hog** [Colloq.] in a luxurious or costly way —**hog′gish** *adj.* —**hog′gish·ly** *adv.*

**ho·gan** (hō′gôn, -gən) *n.* [< AmInd.] a Navaho Indian dwelling, built of earth walls supported by timbers

**hogs·head** (hôgz′hed′, hägz′-) *n.* **1.** a large barrel or cask holding from 63 to 140 gallons **2.** a liquid measure, esp. one equal to 63 gallons

**hog′tie′** *vt.* **-tied′, -ty′ing** or **-tie′ing 1.** to tie the four feet or the hands and feet of **2.** [Colloq.] to make incapable of effective action

**hog′wash′** *n.* **1.** refuse fed to hogs; swill **2.** insincere talk, writing, etc.

**hoi pol·loi** (hoi′ pə loi′) [Gr., the many] the common people; the masses

**hoist** (hoist) *vt.* [< Du. *hijschen*] to raise aloft; lift, esp. with a pulley, crane, etc. —*n.* **1.** a hoisting **2.** an apparatus for lifting; elevator or tackle

**hoke** (hōk) *vt.* **hoked, hok′ing** [< ff.] [Slang] to treat in a too sentimental or crudely comic way: usually with up —**hok′ey** *adj.*

**ho·kum** (hōk′əm) *n.* [< HOCUS-POCUS] [Slang] **1.** mawkish sentiment in a play, story, etc. **2.** nonsense; humbug

**hold¹** (hōld) *vt.* **held, hold′ing** [OE. *haldan*] **1.** to keep in the hands, arms, etc.; grasp **2.** to keep in a certain position or condition **3.** to restrain or control; keep back **4.** to possess; occupy *[hold* an office*]* **5.** to guard; defend *[hold* the fort*]* **6.** to carry on (a meeting, etc.) **7.** to contain *[the* jar *holds* a pint*]* **8.** to regard; consider *[I hold* the story to be true*]* —*vi.* **1.** to go on being firm, loyal, etc. **2.** to remain unbroken or unyielding *[the* rope *held]* **3.** to be true or valid *[this* rule *holds* for most cases*]* **4.** to con- tinue *[the* wind *held* steady*]* —*n.* **1.** a grasping or seizing; grip **2.** a thing to hold on by **3.** a thing for holding something else **4.** a dominating force *[she* has a *hold* over him*]* **5.** a prison —**get (catch, lay,** or **take) hold of** to take, seize, acquire, etc. —**hold forth** to preach; lecture **2.** to offer —**hold out 1.** to last; endure **2.** to stand firm **3.** to offer **4.** [Slang] to refuse to hand over something —**hold over 1.** to postpone **2.** to stay for an additional period —**hold up 1.** to prop up **2.** to show **3.** to last; endure **4.** to stop; delay **5.** to stop forcibly and rob —**hold′er** *n.*

**hold²** (hōld) *n.* [< HOLE or MDu. *hol*] **1.** the interior of a ship below decks, in which the cargo is carried **2.** the compartment for cargo in an aircraft

**hold′ing** *n.* **1.** land, esp. a farm, rented from another **2.** *[usually pl.]* property owned, esp. stocks or bonds

**hold′o′ver** *n.* [Colloq.] one staying on from a previous period

**hold′up′** *n.* **1.** a delay **2.** the act of stopping forcibly and robbing

**hole** (hōl) *n.* [OE. *hol*] **1.** a hollow place; cavity **2.** an animal's burrow **3.** a small, dingy, squalid place **4.** an opening in anything; gap; tear; rent **5.** *Golf a)* a small cavity into which the ball is to be hit *b)* the tee, fairway, etc. leading to this —**hole up** [Colloq.] to hibernate, as in a hole —**in the hole** [Colloq.] financially embarrassed or behind

**hol·i·day** (häl′ə dā′) *n.* **1.** a religious festival; holy day **2.** a day of freedom from labor, often set aside by law to celebrate some event **3.** *[often pl.]* [Chiefly Brit.] a vacation —*adj.* of or for a holiday; joyous; gay

**ho·li·er-than-thou** (hō′lē ər *th*ən *th*ou′) *adj.* annoyingly self-righteous

**hol·i·ness** (hō′lē nis) *n.* **1.** a being holy **2.** [H-] a title of the Pope (with *His* or *Your*)

**Hol·land** (häl′ənd) *same as* NETHERLANDS —**Hol′land·er** *n.*

**hol·lan·daise sauce** (häl′ən dāz′) [Fr., of Holland] a creamy sauce made of butter, egg yolks, lemon juice, etc.

**hol·ler** (häl′ər) *vi., vt., n.* [Colloq.] shout; yell

**hol·low** (häl′ō) *adj.* [OE. *holh*] **1.** having a cavity inside; not solid **2.** shaped like a bowl; concave **3.** sunken *[hollow* cheeks*]* **4.** empty or worthless *[hollow* praise*]* **5.** hungry **6.** deep-toned and dull —*n.* **1.** a hollow place; cavity **2.** a valley —*vt., vi.* to make or become hollow —**hol′low·ness** *n.*

**hol·ly** (häl′ē) *n., pl.* **-lies** [OE. *holegn*] an evergreen shrub with glossy leaves and red berries

**hol·ly·hock** (häl′ē häk′) *n.* [< OE. *halig,* holy + *hoc,* mallow] a tall plant of the mallow family, with large, showy flowers

**Hol·ly·wood** (häl′ē wood′) **1.** section of Los Angeles: once the site of many U.S. motion-picture studios **2.** city on the SE coast of Fla.: pop. 107,000

**Holmes** (hōmz), **Oliver Wendell**

1841–1935; associate justice, U.S. Supreme Court (1902–32)

**hol·o·caust** (häl′ə kôst′, hō′lə-) *n.* [< Gr. *holos*, whole + *kaustos*, burnt] great destruction of life, esp. by fire — **the Holocaust** the destruction of millions of Jews by the Nazis

**hol·o·graph** (häl′ə graf′) *n.* [< Gr. *holos*, whole + *graphein*, to write] a document, letter, etc. in the handwriting of the person under whose name it appears —**hol′o·graph′ic** *adj.*

**Hol·stein** (hōl′stēn, -stīn) *n.* [< Schleswig-*Holstein*, Germany] a breed of large, black-and-white dairy cattle

**hol·ster** (hōl′stər) *n.* [Du.] a pistol case, usually of leather and attached to a belt

**ho·ly** (hō′lē) *adj.* **-li·er, -li·est** [OE. *halig*] **1.** dedicated to religious use; sacred **2.** spiritually pure; sinless **3.** deserving reverence or adoration

**Holy Communion** a Christian rite in which bread and wine are consecrated and received as (symbols of) the body and blood of Jesus

**Holy Land** *same as* PALESTINE

**Holy Roman Empire** empire of WC Europe, from 962 A.D. until 1806

**Holy Spirit** (or **Ghost**) the third person of the Trinity; spirit of God

**hom·age** (häm′ij, äm′-) *n.* [< L. *homo*, man] anything given or done to show reverence, honor, etc.

**hom·burg** (häm′bərg) *n.* [after *Homburg*, Prussia] a man's felt hat with a crown dented front to back and a stiff, curved brim

**home** (hōm) *n.* [OE. *ham*] **1.** the place where one lives **2.** the city, state, etc. where one was born or reared **3.** a place thought of as home or as a place of origin **4.** a household and its affairs **5.** an institution for orphans, the aged, etc. **6.** the natural environment of an animal, plant, etc. **7.** *same as* HOME PLATE —*adj.* **1.** of one's home or country; domestic [*home office*] —*adv.* **1.** at, to, or in the direction of home **2.** to the point aimed at [to drive a nail *home*] —**at home 1.** in one's home **2.** at ease —**bring home** to impress upon— **home′less** *adj.* —**home′like′** *adj.*

**home economics** the science and art of homemaking, including nutrition, clothing, budgeting, etc.

**home′land′** *n.* the country in which one was born or makes one's home

**home′ly** *adj.* **-li·er, -li·est 1.** suitable for home life; everyday **2.** crude **3.** not good-looking —**home′li·ness** *n.*

**home′made′** *adj.* made, or as if made, at home

**home′mak′er** *n.* a housewife or one who manages a home

**home plate** *Baseball* the slab that the batter stands beside: it is the last base touched in scoring a run

**Ho·mer** (hō′mər) semilegendary Gr. epic poet of c. 8th cent. B.C. —**Ho·mer·ic** (hō mer′ik) *adj.*

**home run** *Baseball* a hit that allows the batter to touch all bases and score a run: also [Colloq.] **hom′er** *n.*

**home′sick′** *adj.* longing for home —**home′sick′ness** *n.*

**home′spun′** *n.* **1.** cloth made of yarn spun at home **2.** coarse cloth like this —*adj.* **1.** spun at home **2.** made of homespun **3.** plain; homely

**home′stead′** (-sted′) *n.* **1.** a place for a family's home, including the land and buildings **2.** a 160-acre tract of U.S. public land, granted as a farm —**home′stead′er** *n.*

**home′stretch′** *n.* **1.** the part of a race track between the last turn and the finish line **2.** the final part

**home′ward** (-wərd) *adv., adj.* toward home: also **home′wards** *adv.*

**home′work′** *n.* **1.** work, esp. piecework, done at home **2.** schoolwork to be done outside the classroom **3.** study or research to get ready for some project or activity: usually in **do one's homework**

**home′y** (-ē) *adj.* **hom′i·er, hom′i·est** cozy, familiar, etc. —**home′y·ness** *n.*

**hom·i·cide** (häm′ə sīd′, hō′mə-) *n.* [< L. *homo*, man + *caedere*, kill] **1.** the killing of one person by another **2.** a person who kills another —**hom′i·ci′dal** *adj.*

**hom·i·let·ics** (häm′ə let′iks) *n.pl.* [*with sing. v.*] [see ff.] the art of writing and preaching sermons

**hom·i·ly** (häm′ə lē) *n., pl.* **-lies** [< Gr. *homilos*, assembly] **1.** a sermon **2.** a solemn moral talk or writing

**homing pigeon** a pigeon trained to find its way home from distant places

**hom·i·ny** (häm′ə nē) *n.* [< AmInd.] dry corn hulled and coarsely ground (**hominy grits**): it is boiled for food

**homo-** [< Gr. *homos*] *a combining form meaning* same, equal, like

**ho·mo·ge·ne·ous** (hō′mə jē′nē əs, häm′ə-; -jēn′yəs) *adj.* [see prec. & GENUS] **1.** the same in structure, quality, etc.; similar **2.** composed of similar parts —**ho′mo·ge·ne′i·ty** (-jə nē′ə tē) *n.*

**ho·mog·e·nize** (hə mäj′ə nīz′) *vt.* **-nized′, -niz′ing** to make homogeneous, or more uniform throughout; specif., to process (milk) so that fat particles are so finely emulsified that the cream does not separate

**hom·o·graph** (häm′ə graf′, hō′mə-) *n.* [HOMO- + -GRAPH] a word with the same spelling as another but different in meaning and origin

**ho·mol·o·gous** (hō mäl′ə gəs) *adj.* [Gr. *homologos*, agreeing] matching in structure, position, origin, etc.

**hom·o·nym** (häm′ə nim) *n.* [< Gr. *homos*, same + *onyma*, name] a word with the same pronunciation as another but with a different meaning, origin, and, usually, spelling (Ex.: *bore* and *boar*)

**Ho·mo sa·pi·ens** (hō′mō sā′pē enz′)

**homosexual** [ModL. *homo*, man + *sapiens*, prp. of *sapere*, know] man; human being

**ho·mo·sex·u·al** (-mə sek/shoo wəl) *adj.* of or having sexual desire for those of the same sex —*n.* a homosexual person —**ho/mo·sex/u·al/i·ty** *n.*

**Hon., hon.** honorable

**Hon·du·ras** (hän door/əs, -dyoor/-) country in Central America: 43,227 sq. mi.; pop. 2,445,000

**hone** (hōn) *n.* [OE. *han*, a stone] a hard stone used to sharpen cutting tools, esp. razors —*vt.* **honed, hon/ing** to sharpen, as with a hone

**hon·est** (än/əst) *adj.* [< L. *honor, honor*] **1.** truthful; trustworthy **2.** *a)* sincere or genuine [*honest* effort] *b)* gained by fair means [*honest* living] **3.** frank and open [*honest* face] —**hon/est·ly** *adv.* —**hon/es·ty** *n.*

**hon·ey** (hun/ē) *n.*, *pl.* **-eys** [OE. *hunig*] **1.** a sweet, syrupy substance that bees make as food from the nectar of flowers **2.** sweetness **3.** darling

**hon/ey·comb/** (-kōm/) *n.* **1.** the structure of six-sided wax cells made by bees to hold their honey, eggs, etc. **2.** anything like this —*vt.* to fill with holes like a honeycomb —*adj.* of or like a honeycomb

HONEYCOMB

**hon/ey·dew/ melon** (-doō/) a variety of melon with a smooth, whitish rind and sweet, green flesh

**hon/ey·moon/** *n.* the vacation spent together by a newly married couple —*vi.* to have or spend a honeymoon

**hon/ey·suck/le** (-suk/'l) *n.* any of a genus of plants with small, fragrant flowers of red, yellow, or white

**Hong Kong** (häŋ/ käŋ/, hôŋ/ kôŋ/) Brit. colony in SE China

**honk** (hôŋk, häŋk) *n.* [echoic] **1.** the call of a wild goose **2.** a similar sound, as of an automobile horn —*vi., vt.* to make or cause to make such a sound

**hon·ky-tonk** (hôŋ/kē tôŋk/) *n.* [Slang] a cheap, noisy nightclub —*adj.* designating music played on a piano with a tinkling sound

**Hon·o·lu·lu** (hän/ə loō/loō) capital of Hawaii, on Oahu: pop. 325,000

**hon·or** (än/ər) *n.* [L.] **1.** high regard or respect; esp., *a)* glory; fame *b)* good reputation **2.** adherence to principles considered right; integrity **3.** chastity **4.** high rank; distinction **5.** [H-] a title of certain officials, as judges (with *His, Her,* or *Your*) **6.** something done or given as a token of respect **7.** a source of respect and fame —*vt.* **1.** to respect greatly **2.** to show high regard for **3.** to do or give something in honor of **4.** to accept and pay [to *honor* a check] —**do the honors** to act as host Brit. sp. **honour**

**hon/or·a·ble** *adj.* **1.** worthy of being honored **2.** honest; upright **3.** bringing honor [*honorable* mention] —**hon/or·a·bly** *adv.*

**hon·o·ra·ri·um** (än/ə rer/ē əm) *n.*, *pl.* **-ri·ums, -ri·a** (-ə) [L.] a payment as to a professional person for services on which no fee is set

**hon/or·ar/y** (-rer/ē) *adj.* **1.** given as an honor **2.** designating or in an office held as an honor, without service or pay —**hon/or·ar/i·ly** *adv.*

**hon·or·if·ic** (än/ə rif/ik) *adj.* conferring honor [an *honorific* title]

**Hon·shu** (hän/shoō/) largest of the islands forming Japan

**hood** (hood) *n.* [OE. *hod*] **1.** a covering for the head and neck, often part of a cloak **2.** anything like a hood, as the metal cover over an automobile engine —*vt.* to cover as with a hood —**hood/ed** *adj.*

**-hood** (hood) [OE. *had*] a suffix meaning: **1.** state or quality [*childhood*] **2.** the whole group of [*priesthood*]

**hood·lum** (hoōd/ləm) *n.* [prob. < G. dial. *hudilump*, wretch] a member of a lawless gang

**hoo·doo** (hoō/doō) *n.*, *pl.* **-doos** [var. of VOODOO] **1.** same as VOODOO **2.** [Colloq.] bad luck or a person or thing that causes it

**hood·wink** (hood/wiŋk/) *vt.* [HOOD + WINK] to mislead by trickery; dupe

**hoo·ey** (hoō/ē) *interj., n.* [echoic] [Slang] nonsense; bunk

**hoof** (hoof, hoōf) *n.*, *pl.* **hoofs,** rarely **hooves** [OE. *hof*] the horny covering on the feet of cattle, horses, etc., or the entire foot —*vt., vi.* [Colloq.] to walk —**hoofed** *adj.*

**hook** (hook) *n.* [OE. *hoc*] **1.** a bent piece of metal, etc. used to catch, hold, or pull something **2.** a fishhook **3.** something shaped like a hook **4.** a strike, blow, etc. in which a curving motion is involved —*vt.* **1.** to catch, fasten, throw, hit, etc. with a hook **2.** [Colloq.] to steal —*vi.* **1.** to curve as a hook does **2.** to be fastened or caught by a hook —**by hook or by crook** by any means, honest or dishonest —**hook up** to connect (a radio, etc.) —**off the hook** [Colloq.] out of trouble

**hook·ah, hook·a** (hook/ə) *n.* [Ar. *ḥuqqah*] an Oriental tobacco pipe with a long tube for drawing smoke through water to cool it

**hooked** (hookt) *adj.* **1.** like a hook **2.** made with a hook [*hooked* rug] **3.** [Slang] *a)* obsessed with or addicted to (often with *on*) *b)* married

**hook/er** *n.* [Slang] a prostitute

**hook/up/** *n.* the arrangement and connection of parts, circuits, etc., as in (a) radio

**hook/worm/** *n.* a small, parasitic roundworm with hooks around the mouth, infesting the small intestine

**hoo·li·gan** (hoō/li gən) *n.* [< ? *Hooligan*, a family name] a hoodlum

**hoop** (hoōp) *n.* [OE. *hop*] **1.** a circular band for holding together the staves of a barrel **2.** anything like this, as a ring in a hoop skirt —*vt.* to bind or fasten as with a hoop

**hoop·la** (hoōp/lä) *n.* [< ?] [Colloq.] **1.** great excitement **2.** showy publicity

**hoop skirt** a woman's skirt worn spread over a framework of hoops

**hoo·ray** (hoo rā/, hə-, hoō-) *interj., n., vi.* same as HURRAH

**hoose·gow** (hoos'gou) *n.* [< Sp. *juzgado*, court of justice] [Slang] a jail

**Hoo·sier** (hoo'zhər) *n.* [Colloq.] a native or inhabitant of Indiana

**hoot** (hoot) *n.* [echoic] 1. the sound that an owl makes 2. any sound like this, as a shout of scorn —*vi.* to utter a hoot —*vt.* to express (scorn) of (someone) by hooting —**hoot'er** *n.*

**hoot·en·an·ny** (hoot'n an'ē) *n., pl.* **-nies** a gathering or performance of folk singers

**Hoo·ver** (hoo'vər), Herbert C. 1874–1964; 31st president of the U.S. (1929–33)

**hop¹** (häp) *vi.* **hopped, hop'ping** [OE. *hoppian*] 1. to make a short leap or leaps on one foot 2. to leap with all feet at once, as a frog, etc. 3. [Colloq.] to go briskly —*vt.* 1. to jump over 2. to get aboard —*n.* 1. a hopping 2. [Colloq.] *a)* a dance *b)* a short flight in an airplane

**hop²** (häp) *n.* [< MDu. *hoppe*] 1. a twining vine with small, cone-shaped flowers 2. [*pl.*] the dried ripe cones, used for flavoring beer, ale, etc. —**hop up** [Slang] 1. to stimulate, as by a drug 2. to supercharge (an automobile engine, etc.)

**hope** (hōp) *n.* [OE. *hopa*] 1. a feeling that what is wanted will happen 2. the object of this 3. a person or thing on which one may base some hope —*vt.* **hoped, hop'ing** to want and expect —*vi.* to have hope (*for*) —**hope'ful** *adj.* —**hope'ful·ly** *adv.* —**hope'less** *adj.* —**hope'less·ly** *adv.*

**hop'head'** *n.* [Slang] a drug addict

**hop·per** (häp'ər) *n.* 1. one that hops 2. a hopping insect 3. a container from which the contents can be emptied slowly and evenly

**hop·sack·ing** (häp'sak'iŋ) *n.* a sturdy fabric somewhat like a coarse material for bags, used for suits, coats, etc.: also **hopsack**

**hop'scotch'** *n.* [HOP¹ + *scotch*, line] a game in which children hop about in figures drawn on the ground

**Hor·ace** (hôr'is, här'-) 65–8 B.C.; Rom. poet

**horde** (hôrd) *n.* [ult. < Tatar *urdu*, a camp] a crowd or throng; swarm —*vi.* **hord'ed, hord'ing** to form or gather in a horde

**hore·hound** (hôr'hound') *n.* [OE. *harhune*] 1. a bitter mint plant 2. medicine or candy made from its juice

**ho·ri·zon** (hə rī'z'n) *n.* [< Gr. *horos*, boundary] 1. the line where the sky seems to meet the earth 2. the limit of one's experience, interest, etc.

**hor·i·zon·tal** (hôr'ə zän't'l, här'-) *adj.* 1. parallel to the plane of the horizon; not vertical 2. flat and even; level —**hor'i·zon'tal·ly** *adv.*

**hor·mone** (hôr'mōn) *n.* [< Gr. *hormē*, impulse] a substance formed in some organ of the body and carried to another part, where it takes effect — **hor·mo'nal** *adj.*

**horn** (hôrn) *n.* [OE.] 1. a hard, bone-like projection growing on the head of a cow, goat, etc. 2. the substance horns are made of 3. anything like a horn in position, shape, etc. 4. any brass-wind instrument 5. a device sounded to give a warning —*adj.* made of horn —**horn in (on)** [Colloq.] to intrude or meddle (*in*) —**horned** *adj.* —**horn'less** *adj.* —**horn'like'** *adj.*

**Horn, Cape** southernmost point of S. America, on an island of Chile

**horned toad** a small, scaly, insect-eating lizard with hornlike spines

**hor·net** (hôr'nit) *n.* [OE. *hyrnet*] a large, yellow and black wasp

**horn of plenty** same as CORNUCOPIA

**horn'pipe'** *n.* a lively dance formerly popular with sailors

**horn'y** *adj.* **-i·er, -i·est** 1. made of horn 2. having horns 3. toughened and calloused [*horny* hands] 4. [Slang] sexually aroused

**ho·rol·o·gy** (hô räl'ə jē) *n.* [< Gr. *hōra*, hour + -LOGY] the science of measuring time or making timepieces

**hor·o·scope** (hôr'ə skōp', här'-) *n.* [< Gr. *hōra*, hour + *skopos*, watcher] a chart of the zodiacal signs and positions of planets, etc., by which astrologers profess to tell fortunes

**hor·ren·dous** (hô ren'dəs) *adj.* [see HORROR] horrible; dreadful

**hor·ri·ble** (hôr'ə b'l, här'-) *adj.* [see HORROR] 1. causing horror; terrible; dreadful 2. [Colloq.] very bad, ugly, unpleasant, etc. —**hor'ri·bly** *adv.*

**hor'rid** (-id) *adj.* 1. causing horror; terrible 2. very bad, ugly, unpleasant, etc. —**hor'rid·ly** *adv.*

**hor·ri·fy** (hôr'ə fī', här'-) *vt.* **-fied', -fy'ing** 1. to cause to feel horror 2. [Colloq.] to shock or disgust

**hor·ror** (hôr'ər, här'-) *n.* [< L. *horrere*, to bristle] 1. the strong feeling caused by something frightful or shocking 2. strong dislike 3. something that causes horror, disgust, etc. —**hor'ror·ful** *adj.*

**‡hors de com·bat** (ôr' də kôn bä') [Fr., lit., out of combat] disabled

**hors d'oeuvre** (ôr' dɜrv') *pl.* **d'oeuvres'** (dɜrvz') [Fr., lit., outside of work] an appetizer, as olives, canapés, etc., served before a meal

**horse** (hôrs) *n.* [OE. *hors*] 1. a large, four-legged, solid-hoofed animal with flowing mane and tail, domesticated for drawing loads, carrying riders, etc. 2. a frame with legs to support something —*vt.* **horsed, hors'ing** to supply with a horse or horses; put on horseback —*adj.* of or on horses —**hold one's horses** [Slang] to curb one's impatience —**horse around** [Slang] to engage in horseplay

**horse'back'** *n.* the back of a horse —*adv.* on horseback

**horse chestnut** 1. a flowering tree with large leaves and glossy brown seeds 2. its seed

**horse'feath'ers** *n., interj.* [Slang] nonsense; bunk

---

fat, āpe, cär; ten, ēven; is, bīte; gō, hôrn, tool, look; oil, out; up, fur; chin; she; thin, then; zh, leisure; ŋ, ring; ə for *a* in *ago*; ', (ä'b'l); ē, Fr. coeur; ö, Fr. feu; Fr. mon; ü, Fr. duc; kh, G. ich, doch; ‡ foreign; < derived from

**horse′fly′** *n., pl.* **-flies′** a large fly that sucks the blood of horses, etc.

**horse′hair′** *n.* **1.** hair from the mane or tail of a horse **2.** a stiff fabric made from this hair

**horse′hide′** *n.* **1.** the hide of a horse **2.** leather made from this

**horse′laugh′** *n.* a boisterous, usually derisive laugh; guffaw

**horse′man** (-mən) *n., pl.* **-men** a man skilled in the riding or care of horses **—horse′man·ship′** *n.* **—horse′wom′an** *n., pl.* **-wom′en**

**horse opera** [Slang] a cowboy movie

**horse′play′** *n.* rough, boisterous fun

**horse′pow′er** *n.* a unit for measuring the power of engines, etc., equal to 746 watts or 33,000 foot-pounds per minute

**horse′rad′ish** *n.* **1.** a plant of the mustard family, with a pungent root **2.** a relish made by grating this root

**horse sense** [Colloq.] ordinary common sense

**horse′shoe′** *n.* **1.** a flat, U-shaped, protective metal plate nailed to a horse's hoof **2.** anything shaped like this **3.** [*pl.*] a game in which the players toss horseshoes at a stake

**horse′whip′** *n.* a whip for driving horses **—vt. -whipped′, -whip′ping** to lash with a horsewhip

**hors·y** (hôr′sē) *adj.* **-i·er, -i·est** **1.** of, like, or suggesting a horse **2.** of or like people who are fond of horses, fox hunting, or horse racing Also **horsey**

**hor·ta·to·ry** (hôr′tə tôr′ē) *adj.* [< L. *hortari,* incite] exhorting; advising

**hor·ti·cul·ture** (hôr′tə kul′chər) *n.* [< L. *hortus,* garden + *cultura,* culture] the art or science of growing flowers, fruits, and vegetables **—hor′ti·cul′tur·al** *adj.*

**ho·san·na** (hō zan′ə) *n., interj.* [< Heb. *hōshī′āh nnā,* lit., save, we pray] an exclamation of praise to God

**hose** (hōz) *n., pl.* **hose;** for 2, usually **hos′es** [OE. *hosa*] **1.** [*pl.*] *a)* stockings *b)* socks **2.** a flexible tube, used to convey fluids, esp. water from a hydrant **—vt. hosed, hos′ing** to water with a hose

**ho·sier·y** (hō′zhər ē) *n.* stockings

**hos·pice** (häs′pis) *n.* [< L. *hospes,* host, guest] a shelter for travelers

**hos·pi·ta·ble** (häs′pi tə b′l, häs pit′ə-) *adj.* [see prec.] friendly and solicitous toward guests, new arrivals, etc. **—hos′pi·ta·bly** *adv.*

**hos·pi·tal** (häs′pi t′l) *n.* [< L. *hospes,* host, guest] an institution where the ill or injured may receive medical treatment, nursing, etc.

**hos·pi·tal·i·ty** (häs′pə tal′ə tē) *n., pl.* **-ties** the act, practice, or quality of being hospitable

**hos·pi·tal·ize** (häs′pi t′l īz′) *vt.* **-ized′, -iz′ing** to put in, or admit to, a hospital **—hos′pi·tal·i·za′tion** *n.*

**host¹** (hōst) *n.* [< L. *hospes,* host, guest] **1.** a man who entertains guests, esp. in his own home **2.** a man who keeps an inn or hotel **3.** an organism on or in which another lives **—vt., vi.** to act as host (to)

**host²** (hōst) *n.* [< ML. *hostis,* army] **1.** an army **2.** a great number

**host³** (hōst) *n.* [< ML. *hostia*] a wafer of bread used in the Eucharist

**hos·tage** (häs′tij) *n.* [< OFr.] a person kept or given as a pledge until certain conditions are met

**hos·tel** (häs′t′l) *n.* [see HOSPITAL] a lodging place; inn: also **hos′tel·ry** (-rē), *pl.* **-ries —hos′tel·er** *n.*

**host·ess** (hōs′tis) *n.* **1.** a woman who entertains guests, esp. in her home; often, the host's wife **2.** a woman employed in a restaurant to supervise the waitresses, seating, etc.

**hos·tile** (häs′t′l) *adj.* [< L. *hostis,* enemy] **1.** of or characteristic of an enemy **2.** unfriendly; antagonistic **—hos′tile·ly** *adv.*

**hos·til·i·ty** (häs til′ə tē) *n., pl.* **-ties** **1.** a feeling of enmity, ill will, etc. **2.** *a)* a hostile act *b)* [*pl.*] warfare

**hos·tler** (häs′lər, äs′-) *n.* [contr. of HOSTELER] one who takes care of horses at an inn, stable, etc.

**hot** (hät) *adj.* **hot′ter, hot′test** [OE. *hat*] **1.** *a)* having a temperature higher than that of the human body *b)* having a relatively high temperature **2.** producing a burning sensation [*hot* pepper] **3.** full of intense feeling, as, *a)* impetuous [a *hot* temper] *b)* violent [a *hot* battle] *c)* lustful *d)* very controversial **4.** following closely [in *hot* pursuit] **5.** electrically charged [a *hot* wire] **6.** [Colloq.] recent; fresh [*hot* news] **7.** [Slang] *a)* recently stolen or smuggled *b)* [Slang] excellent; good **—make it hot for** [Colloq.] to make things uncomfortable for **—hot′ly** *adv.* **—hot′ness** *n.*

**hot air** [Slang] empty talk

**hot′bed′** *n.* **1.** a bed of earth covered with glass and heated by manure, for forcing plants **2.** any place that fosters rapid growth or extensive activity

**hot′-blood′ed** *adj.* easily excited; passionate, reckless, etc.

**hot′box′** *n.* an overheated bearing on an axle or shaft

**hot cake** a griddlecake **—sell like hot cakes** [Colloq.] to be sold rapidly and in large quantities

**hot dog** [Colloq.] a wiener, esp. one served in a long, soft roll

**ho·tel** (hō tel′) *n.* [see HOSPITAL] an establishment providing lodging, and often food, for travelers, etc.

**ho·tel·ier** (hō′tel yā′, -tə lir′) *n.* [Fr.] an owner or manager of a hotel

**hot′head′ed** *adj.* **1.** quick-tempered **2.** impetuous **—hot′head′** *n.*

**hot′house′** *n. same as* GREENHOUSE

**hot line** a telephone or telegraph line for immediate communication, as between heads of state in a crisis

**hot plate** a small stove for cooking

**hot potato** [Colloq.] a troubling problem that no one wants to handle

**hot rod** [Slang] an automobile, often an old one, whose engine has been supercharged **—hot rod′der**

**hot seat** [Slang] **1.** *same as* ELECTRIC CHAIR **2.** a difficult situation

**hot′shot′** *n.* [Slang] one who is expert at something in an aggressive way

**hot′-tem′pered** *adj.* having a fiery temper

**Hot·ten·tot** (hät′'n tät′) *n.* 1. a member of a nomadic people of SW Africa 2. their language

**hound** (hound) *n.* [OE. *hund*, dog] 1. any of several breeds of hunting dog 2. any dog —*vt.* 1. to hunt or chase with or as with hounds 2. to urge on

**hounds′·tooth check** (houndz′-tōōth′) a pattern of irregular broken checks, used in woven material

**hour** (our) *n.* [< Gr. *hōra*] 1. one of the twenty-four·parts of a day; sixty minutes 2. the time for a particular activity [lunch *hour*] 3. [*pl.*] a period fixed for work, etc. [office *hours*] 4. the time of day [the *hour* is 2:30] 5. *Educ.* a credit, equal to each hour spent in class per week —**after hours** after the regular hours for business, school, etc. —**hour after hour** every hour

**hour′glass′** *n.* an instrument for measuring time by the trickling of sand, etc. from one part to another

**hou·ri** (hoor′ē, hou′rē) *n., pl.* **-ris** [< Ar. *ḥūriyah*, black-eyed woman] a beautiful nymph of the Moslem paradise

**hour′ly** *adj.* 1. happening every hour 2. done during an hour 3. frequent —*adv.* 1. at every hour 2. often

HOURGLASS

**house** (hous; *for v.* houz) *n., pl.* **hous·es** (hou′ziz) [OE. *hus*] 1. a building to live in; specif., a building occupied by one family or person 2. the people who live in a house; household 3. a family as including kin, ancestors, and descendants 4. shelter, living or storage space, etc. 5. *a*) a theater *b*) the audience in a theater 6. a business firm 7. a legislative assembly —*vt.* **housed, hous′ing** 1. to provide a house or lodgings for 2. to cover, shelter, etc. —**keep house** to take care of a home —**on the house** at the expense of the establishment

**house′boat′** *n.* a large, flat-bottomed boat used as a residence

**house′break′ing** *n.* the breaking into and entering another's house to commit theft or some other felony

**house′bro′ken** *adj.* trained to live in a house (i.e., to void in a special place): said of a dog, cat, etc.

**house′fly′** *n., pl.* **-flies′** a two-winged fly found in and around houses

**house′hold′** *n.* 1. all those living in one house 2. the home and its affairs

**house′hold′er** *n.* 1. one who owns or maintains a house 2. the head of a household or family

**household word** a common saying or thing, familiar to nearly everyone

**house′hus′band** *n.* a married man whose job is keeping house and doing the work usually done by a housewife

**house′keep′er** *n.* a woman who runs a home, esp. one hired to do so

**house′maid′** *n.* a maid for housework

**House of Commons** the lower branch of the legislature of Great Britain or Canada

**House of Lords** the upper branch of the legislature of Great Britain

**House of Representatives** the lower branch of the legislature of the U.S., or of most States of the U.S.

**house′wares′** (-werz′) *n.pl.* articles for household use, esp. in the kitchen

**house′warm′ing** *n.* a party to celebrate moving into a new home

**house′wife′** *n., pl.* **-wives′** a woman in charge of her own household

**house′work′** *n.* the work involved in housekeeping; cleaning, cooking, etc.

**hous·ing** (hou′ziŋ) *n.* 1. the providing of shelter or lodging 2. shelter or lodging 3. houses collectively 4. an enclosing frame, box, etc.

**Hous·ton** (hyōōs′tən) city & port in SE Tex.: pop. 938,000

**hove** (hōv) *alt. pt. & pp. of* HEAVE

**hov·el** (huv′'l, häv′-) *n.* [ME.] any small, miserable dwelling; hut

**hov·er** (huv′ər, häv′-) *vi.* [< ME. *hoven*, to stay (suspended)] 1. to flutter in the air near one place 2. to linger close by 3. to waver (*between*)

**how** (hou) *adv.* [OE. *hu*] 1. in what manner or way 2. in what state or condition 3. for what reason 4. to what extent, degree, etc. *How* is also used as an intensive —**how about** what is your thought concerning?

**how·be·it** (hou bē′it) *adv.* [Archaic] however it may be; nevertheless

**how·dah** (hou′də) *n.* [Hind. *hauda*] a seat for riding on the back of an elephant or camel

**how·ev′er** *adv.* 1. in whatever manner 2. to whatever degree 3. nevertheless Also [Poet.] **how·e′er′** (-er′)

**how·itz·er** (hou′it sər) *n.* [< Czech *haufnice*, orig., a sling] a short cannon, firing shells in a high trajectory

**howl** (houl) *vi.* [ME. *hulen*] 1. to utter the long, wailing cry of wolves, dogs, etc. 2. to utter a similar cry of pain, anger, etc. 3. to shout or laugh in scorn, mirth, etc. —*vt.* 1. to utter with a howl 2. to drive by howling —*n.* 1. the wailing cry of a wolf, dog, etc. 2. any similar sound 3. [Colloq.] a joke

**howl′er** *n.* 1. one who howls 2. [Colloq.] a ludicrous blunder

**how·so·ev′er** (hou′sō ev′ər) *adv.* 1. to whatever degree or extent 2. by whatever means

**hoy·den** (hoid′'n) *n.* [< ? Du.] a bold, boisterous girl; tomboy

**Hoyle** (hoil) *n.* a book of rules for card games, orig. compiled by E. Hoyle (1672–1769) —**according to Hoyle** according to the rules

**HP, H.P., hp, h.p.** horsepower

**HQ, H.Q.** headquarters

**hr.** *pl.* **hrs.** hour(s)

**H.R.** House of Representatives

**H.R.H.** His (or Her) Royal Highness

**H.S., h.s.** high school

**ht.** 1. heat 2. *pl.* **hts.** height

**hua·ra·ches** (hə rä′chēz, wə-) *n.pl.*
[MexSp.] flat sandals with uppers
made of straps or woven leather strips

**hub** (hub) *n.* [< ?] 1. the center part
of a wheel 2. a center of activity

**hub·bub** (hub′ub) *n.* [prob. < Irish
exclamation] an uproar; tumult

**hu·bris** (hyōō′bris) *n.* [Gr. *hybris*]
arrogance caused by too great pride

**huck·le·ber·ry** (huk′′l ber′ē) *n.*, *pl.*
**-ries** [prob. < ME. *hurtilberye*] 1. a
shrub with dark-blue berries 2. this
berry

**huck·ster** (huk′stər) *n.* [< MDu.
*hoeken*, peddle] a peddler, esp. of
fruits, vegetables, etc. —*vt.* to peddle

**HUD** (Department of) Housing and
Urban Development

**hud·dle** (hud′′l) *vi.*, *vt.* **-dled**,
**-dling** [prob. < ME. *hoderen*, cover
up] 1. to crowd close together 2. to
draw (oneself) up —*n.* 1. a confused
crowd or heap 2. [Slang] a private
conference 3. *Football* a grouping of a
team to get signals before a play

**Hud·son** (hud′s′n) river in E N.Y.

**Hudson Bay** inland sea in NE
Canada; arm of the Atlantic

**hue¹** (hyōō) *n.* [OE. *heow*] 1. color 2.
a particular shade or tint of a color

**hue²** (hyōō) *n.* [< OFr. *hu*, outcry] a
shouting: now only in **hue and cry**

**huff** (huf) *vi.* to blow; puff —*n.* state
of smoldering anger or resentment —
**huff′y** *adj.* **-i·er**, **-i·est**

**hug** (hug) *vt.* **hugged**, **hug′ging**
[prob. < ON. *hugga*, to comfort] 1.
to clasp closely and fondly in the arms;
embrace 2. to cling to (a belief, etc.)
3. to keep close to —*vi.* to embrace
one another —*n.* a close embrace

**huge** (hyōōj) *adj.* [< OFr. *ahuge*] very
large; gigantic; immense —**huge′ly**
*adv.* —**huge′ness** *n.*

**Hu·go** (hyōō′gō), **Victor Marie** 1802-
85; Fr. poet, novelist, & playwright

**Hu·gue·not** (hyōō′gə nät′) *n.* a
French Protestant of the 16th or 17th
century

**huh** (hu, hun) *interj.* an exclamation
used to express contempt, surprise,
etc., or to ask a question

**hu·la** (hōō′lə) *n.* [Haw.] a native
Hawaiian dance: also **hu′la-hu′la**

**hulk** (hulk) *n.* [< Gr. *holkas*, towed
ship] 1. the body of a ship, esp. if old
and dismantled 2. a big, clumsy
person or thing

**hulk′ing** *adj.* bulky and clumsy

**hull** (hul) *n.* [OE. *hulu*] 1. the outer
covering of a seed or fruit, as the husk
of grain, shell of nuts, etc. 2. the frame
or main body of a ship, airship, etc.
3. any outer covering —*vt.* to take the
hulls off (nuts, etc.) —**hull′er** *n.*

**hul·la·ba·loo** (hul′ə bə lōō′) *n.*
[echoic] clamor; hubbub

**hum** (hum) *vi.* **hummed**, **hum′-
ming** [echoic] 1. to make a low, continuous, murmuring sound 2. to sing
with closed lips 3. [Colloq.] to be full
of activity —*vt.* to sing (a tune) with
closed lips —*n.* a continuous murmur

**hu·man** (hyōō′mən) *adj.* [< L.
*humanus*] of, characteristic of, or
having the qualities typical of man-

kind —*n.* a person: also **human being**
—**hu′man·ness** *n.*

**hu·mane** (hyōō mān′) *adj.* [var. of
prec.] 1. kind, tender, merciful, etc.
2. civilizing; refining —**hu·mane′ly**
*adv.* —**hu·mane′ness** *n.*

**hu·man·ism** (hyōō′mə niz′m) *n.* 1.
any system of thought based on the
interests and ideals of man 2. [H-] the
intellectual movement that stemmed
from the study of Greek and Latin
classics during the Middle Ages —
**hu′man·ist** *n.*, *adj.* —**hu′man·is′-
tic** *adj.* —**hu′man·is′ti·cal·ly** *adv.*

**hu·man·i·tar·i·an** (hyōō man′ə
ter′ē ən) *n.* a person devoted to
promoting the welfare of humanity;
philanthropist —*adj.* helping humanity —**hu·man′i·tar′i·an·ism** *n.*

**hu·man·i·ty** (hyōō man′ə tē) *n.*, *pl.*
**-ties** 1. the fact or quality of being
human or humane 2. mankind; people
—**the humanities** the branches of
learning concerned with human
thought and relations; esp., literature,
philosophy, the fine arts, etc.

**hu·man·ize** (hyōō′mə nīz′) *vt.*, *vi.*
**-ized′**, **-iz′ing** to make or become
human or humane —**hu′man·i·za′-
tion** *n.* —**hu′man·iz′er** *n.*

**hu′man·kind′** *n.* mankind; people

**hu′man·ly** *adv.* 1. in a human
manner 2. by human means

**hu′man·oid′** (-oid′) *adj.* nearly
human —*n.* a nearly human creature

**hum·ble** (hum′b′l, um′-) *adj.* **-bler**,
**-blest** [< L. *humilis*, low] 1. having
or showing a consciousness of one's
defects; modest 2. lowly; unpretentious —*vt.* **-bled**, **-bling** 1. to lower
in condition or rank 2. to lower in
pride; make modest —**hum′ble·ness**
*n.* —**hum′bly** *adv.*

**hum·bug** (hum′bug′) *n.* [< ?] 1.
fraud; sham; hoax 2. an impostor
—*vt.* **-bugged′**, **-bug′ging** to dupe;
deceive —*interj.* nonsense!

**hum·drum** (hum′drum′) *adj.*
[echoic] dull; monotonous

**hu·mer·us** (hyōō′mər əs) *n.*, *pl.*
**-mer·i′** (-ī′) [L.] the bone of the upper arm or forelimb —**hu′mer·al** *adj.*

**hu·mid** (hyōō′mid) *adj.* [< L.
*umere*, be moist] damp; moist

**hu·mid·i·fy** (hyōō mid′ə fī′) *vt.*
**-fied′**, **-fy′ing** to make humid —
**hu·mid′i·fi′er** *n.*

**hu·mid·i·ty** *n.* 1. moistness; dampness 2. amount of moisture in the air

**hu·mi·dor** (hyōō′mə dôr′) *n.* a case
or jar for keeping tobacco moist

**hu·mil·i·ate** (hyōō mil′ē āt′) *vt.*
**-at′ed**, **-at′ing** [< L. *humilis*,
humble] to hurt the pride or dignity
of; mortify —**hu·mil′i·a′tion** *n.*

**hu·mil′i·ty** (-ə tē) *n.* the state or
quality of being humble

**hum·ming·bird** (hum′iŋ burd′) *n.*
a very small, brightly colored bird with
narrow wings that vibrate rapidly,
making a humming sound

**hum·mock** (hum′ək) *n.* [< ?] a low,
rounded hill; knoll

**hu·mor** (hyōō′mər, yōō′-) *n.* [< L.
*humor*, fluid: after former belief in four
body fluids (humors) held responsible

for one's disposition] 1. mood; state of mind 2. whim; caprice 3. a comical quality 4. *a)* the ability to appreciate or express what is funny, amusing, etc. *b)* the expression of this —*vt.* to comply with the mood or whim of; indulge —**out of humor** not in a good mood; disagreeable Brit. sp. **humour** —**hu′mor·ist** *n.*

**hu′mor·ous** *adj.* funny; amusing; comical —**hu′mor·ous·ly** *adv.*

**hump** (hump) *n.* [< ?] a rounded, protruding lump, as on a camel's back —*vt.* to hunch; arch —**over the hump** [Colloq.] past the difficult part

**hump′back′** *n.* 1. a humped, deformed back 2. a person having this —**hump′backed′** *adj.*

**hu·mus** (hyōō′məs) *n.* [L., earth] the dark part of the soil, resulting from the partial decay of leaves, etc.

**Hun** (hun) *n.* a member of a warlike Asiatic people who invaded Europe in the 4th and 5th centuries A.D.

**hunch** (hunch) *vt.* [< ?] to arch into a hump —*vi.* to move forward jerkily —*n.* 1. a hump 2. [Colloq.] a feeling that something is going to happen

**hunch′back′** *n.* same as HUMPBACK

**hun·dred** (hun′drid) *n., adj.* [OE.] ten times ten; 100; C —**hun′dredth** (-dridth) *adj., n.*

**hun′dred·fold′** *adj., adv.* a hundred times as much or as many

**hun′dred·weight′** *n.* a unit of weight, equal to 100 pounds in the U.S. and 112 pounds in England

**hung** (hung) *pt. & pp.* of HANG —**hung over** [Slang] having a hangover —**hung up (on)** [Slang] emotionally disturbed, frustrated, or obsessed (by)

**Hung.** 1. Hungarian 2. Hungary

**Hun·gar·i·an** (hung ger′ē ən) *adj.* of Hungary, its people, etc. —*n.* 1. a native or inhabitant of Hungary 2. the language of the Hungarians

**Hun·ga·ry** (hung′gə rē) country in SC Europe: 35,919 sq. mi.; pop. 10,231,000

**hun·ger** (hung′gər) *n.* [OE. *hungor*] 1. discomfort caused by a need for food 2. starvation 3. a desire for food 4. any strong desire —*vi.* 1. to be hungry 2. to desire —**hun′gri·ly** *adv.* —**hun′gry** *adj.* **-gri·er, -gri·est**

**hunger strike** a refusal of a prisoner, protester, etc. to eat until certain demands are granted

**hunk** (hungk) *n.* [Fl. *hunke*] [Colloq.] a large piece, lump, etc.

**hun·ker** (hung′kər) *vi.* [< dial.] to squat —*n.* [*pl.*] haunches or buttocks

**hunt** (hunt) *vt., vi.* [OE. *huntian*] 1. to kill or catch (game) for food or sport 2. to try to find; search; seek 3. to chase; harry —*n.* 1. a hunting 2. a group of people who hunt together 3. a search —**hunt′er, hunts′man** *n., pl.* **-men** —**hunt′ress** *n.fem.*

**Hun·ting·ton Beach** (hun′tiŋ tən) city in SW Calif.: pop. 116,000

**Hunts·ville** (hunts′vil′) city in N Ala.: pop. 138,000

**hur·dle** (hur′d'l) *n.* [OE. *hyrdel*] 1. a framelike barrier which horses or runners must leap in a race 2. an obstacle —*vt.* **-dled, -dling** 1. to jump over 2. to overcome (an obstacle) —**hur′dler** *n.*

HURDLES

**hur·dy-gur·dy** (hur′dē gur′dē) *n., pl.* **-dies** [? echoic] same as BARREL ORGAN

**hurl** (hurl) *vt.* [prob. < ON.] 1. to throw with force or violence 2. to cast down 3. to utter vehemently —*vi.* [Colloq.] *Baseball* to pitch —**hurl′er** *n.*

**hurl·y-burl·y** (hur′lē bur′lē) *n., pl.* **-burl′ies** a turmoil; uproar

**Hu·ron** (hyoor′ən), **Lake** one of the Great Lakes, between Mich. & Canada

**hur·rah** (hə rô′, -rä′) *interj., n.* [echoic] a shout of joy, approval, etc. —*vi.* to shout "hurrah"; cheer Also **hur·ray′** (-rā′)

**hur·ri·cane** (hur′ə kān′) *n.* [< WInd. *huracan*] a violent tropical cyclone

**hurricane lamp** 1. an oil lamp or candlestick with a glass chimney to protect the flame 2. an electric lamp like this

**hur·ry** (hur′ē) *vt.* **-ried, -ry·ing** [prob. akin to HURL] 1. to move or send with haste 2. to cause to occur or be done more rapidly or too rapidly 3. to urge to act soon or too soon —*vi.* to move or act with haste —*n.* 1. rush; urgency 2. eagerness to do, go, etc. quickly —**hur′ried·ly** *adv.*

**hurt** (hurt) *vt., vi., hurt, hurt′ing* [< OFr. *hurter*, to hit] 1. to cause pain or injury to 2. to harm 3. to offend —*vi.* 1. to cause pain, injury, etc. 2. to have pain; be sore —*n.* 1. a pain or injury 2. harm; damage

**hurt′ful** *adj.* causing hurt; harmful

**hur·tle** (hurt′'l) *vi., vt.* **-tled, -tling** [ME. *hurtlen*] to move or throw with great speed or much force

**hus·band** (huz′bənd) *n.* [< ON. *hūs*, house + *bondi*, freeholder] a married man —*vt.* to manage economically; conserve

**hus′band·man** (-mən) *n., pl.* **-men** [Archaic] a farmer

**hus′band·ry** *n.* 1. careful, thrifty management 2. farming

**hush** (hush) *vt., vi.* [< ME. *huscht*, quiet] 1. to make or become quiet or silent 2. to soothe; lull —*n.* quiet; silence —*interj.* an exclamation calling for silence

**hush′-hush′** *adj.* [Colloq.] very secret

**hush puppy** [South] a cornmeal fritter

**husk** (husk) *n.* [prob. < MDu. *huus*, house] 1. the dry outer covering of various fruits or seeds, as of corn 2. any dry, rough, or useless covering —*vt.* to remove the husk from

**hus·ky**[1] (hus′kē) *n., pl.* **-kies** [< ? ESKIMO] [*also* H-] *same as* ESKIMO DOG

**husk·y**[2] (hus′kē) *adj.* **-i·er, -i·est** 1. dry in the throat; hoarse 2. [< toughness of a HUSK] big and strong

**hus·sar** (hoo zär′) *n.* [< Serb. *husar*] a European light-armed cavalryman, usually with a brilliant dress uniform

**hus·sy** (huz′ē, hus′ē) *n., pl.* **-sies** [< ME. *huswife*, housewife] 1. a woman of low morals 2. a bold, saucy girl

**hus·tings** (hus′tiŋz) *n.pl.* [*usually with sing. v.*] [OE. *hūsthing*, house council] the process of, or a place for, political campaigning

**hus·tle** (hus′l) *vt.* **-tled, -tling** [Du. *husselen,* shake up] 1. to push about; jostle 2. to force in a rough, hurried manner —*vi.* 1. to move hurriedly 2. [Colloq.] to work energetically 3. [Slang] to obtain money aggressively or immorally —*n.* 1. a hustling 2. [Colloq.] energetic action; drive —**hus′tler** *n.*

**hut** (hut) *n.* [< OHG. *hutta*] a very plain or crude little house or cabin

**hutch** (huch) *n.* [< ML. *hutica,* chest] 1. a chest or cupboard 2. a pen or coop for small animals 3. a hut

**hutz·pah** (hoots′pə) *n. same as* CHUTZPAH

**huz·zah, huz·za** (hə zä′) *interj., n., vi. former var. of* HURRAH

**Hwang Ho** (hwäŋ′ hō′) river in N China, flowing into the Yellow Sea

**hwy.** highway

**hy·a·cinth** (hī′ə sinth′) *n.* [< Gr. *hyakinthos*] a plant of the lily family, with spikes of bell-shaped flowers

**hy·brid** (hī′brid) *n.* [L. *hybrida*] 1. the offspring of two animals or plants of different species, varieties, etc. 2. anything of mixed origin —*adj.* of or like a hybrid —**hy′brid·ism** *n.*

**hy·brid·ize** (hī′brə dīz′) *vt., vi.* **-ized′, -iz′ing** to produce or cause to produce hybrids; crossbreed

**Hy·der·a·bad** (hī′dər ə bad′) city in SC India: pop. 1,119,000

**hy·dra** (hī′drə) *n., pl.* **-dras, -drae** (-drē) [< Gr. water serpent] a small, freshwater polyp with a soft, tubelike body

**hy·dran·ge·a** (hī drān′jə, -dran′-, -jē ə) *n.* [< HYDRO- + Gr. *angeion,* vessel] a shrub with large, showy clusters of white, blue, or pink flowers

**hy·drant** (hī′drənt) *n.* [< Gr. *hydōr,* water] a large pipe with a valve for drawing water from a water main

**hy·drate** (hī′drāt) *n.* [HYDRO(-) + -ATE[2]] a chemical compound of water and some other substance

**hy·drau·lic** (hī drô′lik) *adj.* [ult. < Gr. *hydōr,* water + *aulos,* tube] 1. of hydraulics 2. operated by the movement and force of liquid [*hydraulic brakes*] —**hy·drau′li·cal·ly** *adv.*

**hy·drau′lics** *n.pl.* [*with sing. v.*] the science dealing with the mechanical properties of liquids, as water, and their application in engineering

**hydro-** [< Gr. *hydōr,* water] *a combining form meaning:* 1. water [*hydrometer*] 2. hydrogen [*hydrocarbon*]

**hy·dro·car·bon** (hī′drə kär′bən) *n.*

any compound containing only hydrogen and carbon

**hy·dro·chlo·ric acid** (hī′drə klôr′ik) a strong, highly corrosive acid, that is a solution of the gas hydrogen chloride in water

**hy·dro·e·lec·tric** (hī′drō i lek′trik) *adj.* producing, or relating to the production of, electricity by water power —**hy′dro·e·lec′tric′i·ty** *n.*

**hy·dro·fluor·ic acid** (hī′drə flôr′ik, -floor′-) a colorless, corrosive acid, used in etching glass

**hy·dro·foil** (hī′drə foil′) *n.* [HYDRO- + (AIR)FOIL] 1. a winglike structure that lifts and carries a watercraft just above the water at high speed 2. such a watercraft

**hy·dro·gen** (hī′drə jən) *n.* [see HYDRO- & -GEN] a flammable, colorless, odorless, gaseous chemical element: the lightest known substance

**hy·dro·gen·ate** (hī′drə jə nāt′, hī-dräj′ə-) *vt.* **-at′ed, -at′ing** to combine with or treat with hydrogen [*oil is hydrogenated to make a solid fat*]

**hydrogen bomb** an extremely destructive atom bomb in which atoms of hydrogen are fused by explosion of a nuclear-fission unit in the bomb

**hydrogen peroxide** an unstable liquid used as a bleach or disinfectant

**hy·drol·y·sis** (hī dräl′ə sis) *n., pl.* **-ses′** (-sēz′) [HYDRO- + -LYSIS] a chemical reaction in which a compound reacts with the ions of water to produce a weak acid, a weak base, or both

**hy·drom·e·ter** (hī dräm′ə tər) *n.* [HYDRO- + -METER] an instrument for determining the specific gravity of liquids

**hy·dro·pho·bi·a** (hī′drə fō′bē ə) *n.* [see HYDRO- & -PHOBIA] 1. an abnormal fear of water 2. [from the symptomatic inability to swallow liquids] *same as* RABIES

**hy·dro·plane** (hī′drə plän′) *n.* [HYDRO- + PLANE[1]] 1. a small, high-speed motorboat with hydrofoils or a flat bottom 2. *same as* SEAPLANE

**hy·dro·pon·ics** (hī′drə pän′iks) *n.pl.* [*with sing. v.*] [< HYDRO- & Gr. *ponos,* labor] the science of growing plants in liquid mineral solutions

**hy′dro·ther′a·py** (-ther′ə pē) *n.* the treatment of disease, etc. by the use of water

**hy·drous** (hī′drəs) *adj.* [HYDR(O)- + -OUS] containing water, esp. in chemical combination

**hy·drox·ide** (hī dräk′sīd) *n.* [HYDR(O)- + OXIDE] a compound consisting of an element or radical combined with the radical OH

**hy·e·na** (hī ē′nə) *n.* [< Gr. *hyaina*] a wolflike, flesh-eating animal of Africa and Asia, with a shrill cry

**hy·giene** (hī′jēn) *n.* [Gr. *hygiēs,* healthy] 1. a system of principles for preserving health 2. cleanliness

**hy·gi·en·ic** (hī′jē en′ik, -jē′nik, -jen′ik) *adj.* 1. of hygiene or health 2. sanitary —**hy′gi·en′i·cal·ly** *adv.*

**hy·grom·e·ter** (hī gräm′ə tər) *n.* [< Gr. *hygros,* wet + -METER] an instrument for measuring humidity

**hy·men** (hī′mən) *n.* [Gr. *hymēn*, membrane] the thin mucous membrane that usually closes part of the opening of the vagina in a virgin

**hy·me·ne·al** (hī′mə nē′əl) *adj.* [< *Hymen*, Gr. god of marriage] of a wedding or marriage

**hymn** (him) *n.* [< Gr. *hymnos*] a song of praise, esp. in honor of God

**hym·nal** (him′nəl) *n.* a collection of hymns: also **hymn′book′**

**hype** (hīp) *n.* [Slang] **1.** *same as* HYPODERMIC **2.** a drug addict **3.** deception, esp. exaggerated promotion —*vt.* **hyped, hyp′ing** [Slang] **1.** to stimulate, excite, etc. as by a drug injection: usually with *up* **2.** to promote in a sensational way

**hyper-** [Gr. < *hyper*] a prefix meaning over, above, excessive

**hy·per·bo·le** (hī pur′bə lē) *n.* [L. < Gr. < *hyper-*, above + *ballein*, throw] exaggeration for effect, not meant to be taken literally —**hy·per·bol·ic** (hī′pər bäl′ik) *adj.*

**hy·per·crit·i·cal** (hī′pər krit′i k'l) *adj.* too critical

**hy·per·sen·si·tive** (hī′pər sen′sə tiv) *adj.* excessively sensitive —**hy′per·sen′si·tiv′i·ty** *n.*

**hy·per·ten·sion** (hī′pər ten′shən) *n.* abnormally high blood pressure

**hy′per·thy′roid·ism** (-thī′roid iz′m) *n.* excessive activity of the thyroid gland, causing nervousness, rapid pulse, etc. —**hy′per·thy′roid** *adj., n.*

**hy·per·tro·phy** (hī pur′trə fē) *n.* [< HYPER- + Gr. *trephein*, to nourish] abnormal increase in the size of an organ or tissue —*vi., vt.* **-phied, -phy·ing** to increase abnormally in size

**hy·phen** (hī′f'n) *n.* [< Gr. *hypo-*, under + *hen*, one] a mark (-) used between the parts of a compound word or the syllables of a divided word, as at the end of a line —*vt.* to hyphenate

**hy′phen·ate′** (-āt′) *vt.* **-at′ed, -at′ing** to join or write with a hyphen —**hy′phen·a′tion** *n.*

**hyp·no·sis** (hip nō′sis) *n., pl.* **-ses** (-sēz) [< Gr. *hypnos*, sleep + -OSIS] a sleeplike condition psychically induced, in which the subject responds to the suggestions of the hypnotist

**hyp·not·ic** (hip nät′ik) *adj.* **1.** causing sleep; soporific **2.** of, like, or inducing hypnosis —*n.* any agent causing sleep —**hyp·not′i·cal·ly** *adv.*

**hyp·no·tism** (hip′nə tiz′m) *n.* the act or practice of inducing hypnosis —**hyp′no·tist** *n.*

**hyp′no·tize′** (-tīz′) *vt.* **-tized′, -tiz′ing** to induce hypnosis in

**hy·po** (hī′pō) *n., pl.* **-pos** *short for* HYPODERMIC

**hypo-** [Gr. < *hypo*, less than] a prefix meaning: **1.** under, beneath [*hypodermic*] **2.** less than [*hypothyroid*]

**hy·po·chon·dri·a** (hī′pə kän′drē ə) *n.* [LL., pl., abdomen (supposed seat of this condition)] abnormal anxiety over one's health, often with imaginary illnesses —**hy′po·chon′dri·ac′** (-ak′) *n., adj.*

**hy·poc·ri·sy** (hi päk′rə sē) *n., pl.* **-sies** [< Gr. *hypokrisis*, acting a part] a pretending to be what one is not, or to feel what one does not; esp., a pretense of virtue, piety, etc.

**hyp·o·crite** (hip′ə krit) *n.* [see prec.] one who pretends to be pious, virtuous, etc. without really being so —**hyp′o·crit′i·cal** *adj.*

**hy·po·der·mic** (hī′pə dur′mik) *adj.* [< HYPO- + Gr. *derma*, skin] injected under the skin —*n.* a hypodermic syringe, needle, or injection

**hypodermic syringe** a syringe attached to a hollow needle (**hypodermic needle**) used for the injection of a medicine or drug under the skin

**hy·pot·e·nuse** (hī pät′'n ōōs′) *n.* [< Gr. *hypo-*, under + *teinein*, stretch] the side of a right-angled triangle opposite the right angle

**hy·poth·e·sis** (hī päth′ə sis, hi-) *n., pl.* **-ses** (-sēz′) [< Gr. *hypo-*, under + *tithenai*, to place] an unproved theory, etc. tentatively accepted to explain certain facts —**hy·poth′e·size′** (-sīz′) *vt., vi.* **-sized′, -siz′ing**

**hy·po·thet·i·cal** (hī′pə thet′i k'l) *adj.* based on a hypothesis; assumed; supposed —**hy′po·thet′i·cal·ly** *adv.*

**hy·po·thy·roid·ism** (hī′pō thī′roid iz′m) *n.* deficient activity of the thyroid gland, causing sluggishness, goiter, etc. —**hy′po·thy′roid** *adj., n.*

**hys·sop** (his′əp) *n.* [< Heb. *ēzōbh*] a fragrant, blue-flowered plant of the mint family

**hys·ter·ec·to·my** (his′tə rek′tə mē) *n., pl.* **-mies** [< Gr. *hystera*, uterus + -ECTOMY] surgical removal of the uterus

**hys·te·ri·a** (his tir′ē ə, -ter′-) *n.* [< Gr. *hystera*, uterus: orig. attributed to disturbances of the uterus] **1.** a psychiatric condition characterized by excitability, anxiety, the simulation of organic disorders, etc. **2.** any outbreak of wild, uncontrolled feeling: also **hys·ter′ics** (-ter′iks) —**hys·ter′i·cal** (-ter′-), **hys·ter′ic** *adj.* —**hys·ter′i·cal·ly** *adv.*

**Hz, hz** hertz

# I

**I, i** (ī) *n., pl.* **I's, i's** the ninth letter of the English alphabet

**I**[1] (ī) *n.* **1.** a Roman numeral for 1 **2.** *Chem.* iodine

**I**[2] (ī) *pron., for pl.* see WE [OE. *ic*] the person speaking or writing

**I., i.** **1.** island(s) **2.** isle(s)

**Ia., IA** Iowa

**-i·al** (ē əl, yəl) [L. *-ialis*] *same as* -AL

**i·am·bic** (ī am'bik) *n.* [< Gr. *iambos*] a metrical foot of two syllables, the first unaccented and the other accented —*adj.* in iambics

**-i·at·rics** (ē at'riks) [< Gr. *iatros,* physician] *a combining form meaning* treatment of disease [*pediatrics*]

**-i·a·try** (ī'ə trē) [< Gr. *iatreia,* healing] *a combining form meaning* medical treatment [*psychiatry*]

**I·be·ri·a** (ī bir'ē ə) the Spanish-Portuguese peninsula: also **Iberian Peninsula** —**I·be'ri·an** *adj., n.*

**i·bex** (ī'beks) *n., pl.* **i'bex·es, i·bi·ces** (ib'ə sēz') [L.] a wild goat of Europe, Asia, or Africa, with large, backward-curved horns

**ibid.** [L. *ibidem*] in the same place, i.e., the book, page, etc. just cited

**i·bis** (ī'bis) *n.* [< Egypt. *hib*] a large wading bird related to the herons

**-i·ble** (i b'l, ə b'l) [L. *-ibilis*] *same as* -ABLE —**-i·bil·i·ty** (ə bil'ə tē)

**Ib·sen** (ib's'n), **Hen·rik** (hen'rik) 1828–1906; Norw. playwright

**-ic** (ik) [< Gr. *-ikos*] *a suffix meaning:* **1.** *a)* of, having to do with [*volcanic*] *b)* like [*angelic*] *c)* produced by [*photographic*] *d)* consisting of, containing [*alcoholic*] **2.** a person or thing *a)* having [*paraplegic*] *b)* supporting [*Socratic*] *c)* producing [*hypnotic*] Also **-i·cal** (i k'l, ə k'l)

**ICBM** intercontinental ballistic missile

**ICC, I.C.C.** Interstate Commerce Commission

**ice** (īs) *n.* [OE. *is*] **1.** water frozen solid by cold **2.** a frozen dessert of fruit juice, sugar, etc. **3.** [Slang] diamonds —*vt.* **iced, ic'ing** **1.** to change into ice; freeze **2.** to cool with ice **3.** to cover with icing —*vi.* to freeze (often with *up* or *over*) —**break the ice** to make a start, as in getting acquainted —**cut no ice** [Colloq.] to have no influence —**on thin ice** [Colloq.] in danger

**Ice.** **1.** Iceland **2.** Icelandic

**ice age** *same as* GLACIAL EPOCH

**ice'berg'** (-bʉrg') *n.* [prob. < Du. *ijsberg,* lit., ice mountain] a great mass of ice broken off from a glacier and floating in the sea

**ice'bound'** (-bound') *adj.* held fast or shut in by ice

**ice'box'** (-bäks') *n.* a refrigerator, esp. one in which ice is used

**ice'break'er** *n.* a sturdy boat for breaking a channel through ice

**ice'cap'** *n.* a mass of glacial ice spreading slowly from a center

**ice cream** a sweet, frozen food made from flavored cream or milk —**ice'-cream'** *adj.*

**ice floe** a piece of floating sea ice

**ice hockey** *same as* HOCKEY (sense 1)

**Ice·land** (īs'lənd) island country in the N. Atlantic, southeast of Greenland: 39,768 sq. mi.; pop. 192,000 —**Ice'land·er** *n.*

**Ice·lan·dic** (īs lan'dik) *adj.* of Iceland, its people, etc. —*n.* the Germanic language of the Icelanders

**ice'man'** (-man', -mən) *n., pl.* **-men'** one who sells or delivers ice

**ice milk** a frozen dessert like ice cream, but with less butterfat

**ice skate** *see* SKATE[1] (sense 1) —**ice'-skate'** *vi.*

**ich·thy·ol·o·gy** (ik'thē äl'ə jē) *n.* [< Gr. *ichthys,* a fish + -LOGY] the branch of zoology dealing with fishes —**ich'thy·ol'o·gist** *n.*

**i·ci·cle** (ī'si k'l) *n.* [< OE. *is,* ice + *gicel,* piece of ice] a hanging piece of ice, formed by the freezing of dripping water

**ic·ing** (ī'sin) *n.* a mixture of sugar, flavoring, egg whites, etc. for covering a cake; frosting

**ick·y** (ik'ē) *adj.* **-i·er, -i·est** [< STICKY] [Slang] **1.** unpleasantly sticky or sweet **2.** very distasteful

**i·con** (ī'kän) *n.* [< Gr. *eikōn,* image] **1.** an image; figure **2.** *Orthodox Eastern Ch.* a sacred image or picture of Jesus, Mary, etc.

**i·con·o·clast** (ī kän'ə klast') *n.* [< LGr. *eikōn,* image + *klaein,* to break] one who attacks venerated institutions or ideas —**i·con'o·clas'tic** *adj.*

**-ics** (iks) [see -IC] *a suffix meaning* art, science, study [*physics*]

**i·cy** (ī'sē) *adj.* **i'ci·er, i'ci·est** **1.** full of or covered with ice **2.** of ice **3.** like ice; slippery or very cold **4.** cold in manner; unfriendly —**i'ci·ly** *adv.* —**i'ci·ness** *n.*

**id** (id) *n.* [L., it] *Psychoanalysis* that part of the psyche which is the source of psychic energy

**I'd** (īd) **1.** I had **2.** I would **3.** I should

**ID, I.D.** identification

**I·da·ho** (ī'də hō') Northwestern State of the U.S.: 83,557 sq. mi.; pop. 713,000; cap. Boise: abbrev. **Ida.,** ID

**i·de·a** (ī dē'ə) *n.* [< Gr. *idea,* appearance of a thing] **1.** a thought; mental conception or image **2.** an opinion or belief **3.** a plan; scheme **4.** meaning or significance

**i·de·al** (ī dē'əl) *adj.* [see prec.] **1.** existing as an idea, model, etc. **2.** thought of as perfect **3.** existing only in the mind; imaginary —*n.* **1.** a conception of something in its most

excellent form  2. a perfect model
3. a goal or principle

**i·de·al·ism** n.  1. behavior or thought based on a conception of things as one thinks they should be  2. a striving to achieve one's ideals —**i·de′al·ist** n. —**i′de·al·is′tic** adj.

**i·de·al·ize** (ī dē′ə līz′) vt. **-ized′, -iz′ing** to regard or show as perfect or more nearly perfect than is true —**i·de′al·i·za′tion** n.

**i·de′al·ly** adv.  1. in an ideal manner; perfectly  2. in theory

**i·den·ti·cal** (ī den′ti k'l) adj. [< L. idem, the same]  1. the very same  2. exactly alike —**i·den′ti·cal·ly** adv.

**i·den·ti·fi·ca·tion** (ī den′tə fi kā′shən, i-) n.  1. an identifying or being identified  2. anything by which one can be identified

**i·den·ti·fy** (ī den′tə fī′, i-) vt. **-fied′, -fy′ing**  1. to make identical; treat as the same  2. to fix the identity of  3. to connect or associate closely

**i·den·ti·ty** (ī den′tə tē, i-) n., pl. **-ties**  1. the state or fact of being the same  2. a) the state or fact of being some specific person or thing; individuality  b) the state of being as described

**identity crisis** the state of being uncertain about oneself, one's character, goals, etc., esp. in adolescence

**id·e·o·gram** (id′ē ə gram′, ī′dē-) n. [see IDEA & -GRAM] a symbol representing an object or idea without expressing the word for it: also **id′e·o·graph′**

**i·de·ol·o·gy** (ī′dē äl′ə jē, id′ē-) n., pl. **-gies** [< Gr. idea, idea + logos, word] the doctrines, opinions, etc. of an individual, class, etc. —**i′de·o·log′i·cal** (-ə läj′i k'l) adj.

**ides** (īdz) n.pl. [< L. idus] in the ancient Roman calendar, the 15th day of March, May, July, or October, or the 13th of the other months

**id·i·o·cy** (id′ē ə sē) n., pl. **-cies**  1. great foolishness or stupidity  2. an idiotic act or remark

**id·i·om** (id′ē əm) n. [< Gr. idios, one's own]  1. the dialect of a people, region, etc.  2. the usual way in which words of a language are joined together to express thought  3. an accepted phrase or expression having a meaning different from the literal  4. a characteristic style, as in art or music —**id′i·o·mat′ic** (-ə mat′ik) adj. —**id′i·o·mat′i·cal·ly** adv.

**id·i·o·path·ic** (id′ē ə path′ik) adj. [< Gr. idios, one's own + -PATHIC] of a disease whose cause is unknown

**id·i·o·syn·cra·sy** (id′ē ə siŋ′krə sē) n., pl. **-sies** [< Gr. idio-, one's own + synkrasis, a mixture] any personal peculiarity; mannerism, etc.

**id·i·ot** (id′ē ət) n. [< Gr. idiōtēs, ignorant person]  1. an adult mentally inferior to a child of three: an obsolescent term  2. a very foolish or stupid person —**id′i·ot′ic** (-ät′ik) adj. —**id′i·ot′i·cal·ly** adv.

**i·dle** (ī′d'l) adj. **i′dler, i′dlest** [OE. idel, empty]  1. useless; futile  2. un-

founded [idle rumors]  3. a) unemployed; not busy  b) inactive; not in use  4. lazy —vi. **i′dled, i′dling**  1. to move slowly or aimlessly  2. to be unemployed or inactive  3. to operate without transmitting power [the motor idled] —vt.  1. to waste  2. to cause (a motor, etc.) to idle —**i′dle·ness** n. —**i′dler** n. —**i′dly** adv.

**i·dol** (ī′d'l) n. [< Gr. eidōlon, image]  1. an image of a god, used as an object of worship  2. any object of ardent or excessive devotion

**i·dol·a·try** (ī däl′ə trē) n., pl. **-tries**  1. worship of idols  2. excessive devotion to or reverence for some person or thing —**i·dol′a·ter** n. —**i·dol′a·trous** adj.

**i·dol·ize** (ī′d'l īz′) vt. **-ized′, -iz′ing**  1. to make an idol of  2. to love or admire excessively

**i·dyll, i·dyl** (ī′d'l) n. [< Gr. eidos, a form]  1. a short poem or prose work describing a simple, pleasant scene of rural or pastoral life  2. a scene or incident suitable for such a work —**i·dyl·lic** (ī dil′ik) adj.

**-ie** (ē) [earlier form of -y¹] a suffix meaning:  1. small, little [lassie]  2. one that is as specified [a softie]

**IE.** Indo-European

**i.e.** [L. id est] that is (to say)

**-ier** (ir, ər, ē′ər) [< L. -arius] a suffix meaning a person concerned with (a specified action or thing) [bombardier]

**if** (if) conj. [OE. gif]  1. on condition that; in case that [if I were you, I'd quit]  2. allowing that [if he was there, I didn't see him]  3. whether [ask him if he knows her] —as if as it would be if

**if·fy** (if′ē) adj. [Colloq.] containing doubtful elements; not definite

**ig·loo** (ig′lōō) n., pl. **-loos** [Esk. igdlu] an Eskimo hut, usually dome-shaped and built of blocks of packed snow

IGLOO

**ig·ne·ous** (ig′nē əs) adj. [< L. ignis, a fire]  1. of fire  2. produced by volcanic action or intense heat [igneous rock]

**ig·nite** (ig nīt′) vt. **-nit′ed, -nit′ing** [see prec.] to set fire to —vi. to catch fire; start burning —**ig·nit′a·ble, ig·nit′i·ble** adj.

**ig·ni·tion** (ig nish′ən) n.  1. an igniting or being ignited  2. the system for igniting the explosive mixture in the cylinder of an internal-combustion engine

**ig·no·ble** (ig nō′b'l) adj. [< L. in-, not + (g)nobilis, known] not noble; base; mean —**ig·no′bly** adv.

**ig·no·min·y** (ig′nə min′ē) n., pl. **-ies** [< L. in-, without + nomen, name] loss of reputation; shame; disgrace —**ig′no·min′i·ous** adj. —**ig′no·min′i·ous·ly** adv.

**ig·no·ra·mus** (ig'nə rā'məs) n., pl. **-mus·es** an ignorant person

**ig'no·rant** adj. [see ff.] 1. lacking knowledge or experience 2. caused by or showing lack of knowledge 3. unaware (of) —**ig'no·rance** n. —**ig'no·rant·ly** adv.

**ig·nore** (ig nôr') vt. **-nored'**, **-nor'ing** [< L. in-, not + gnarus, knowing] to disregard; pay no attention to

**i·gua·na** (i gwä'nə) n. [< SAmInd.] a large tropical American lizard

**il-** same as: 1. IN-1 2. IN-2 Used before l-

**Il·i·ad** (il'ē əd) [< Gr. Ilios, Troy] a Greek epic poem, ascribed to Homer, about the Trojan War

**ilk** (ilk) n. [< OE. ilca, same] kind; sort; class: only in of that (or his, her, etc.) ilk

**ill** (il) adj. **worse**, **worst** [< ON. illr] 1. bad [ill repute, ill will, an ill omen] 2. not well; sick —n. an evil or disease —adv. **worse**, **worst** 1. badly 2. scarcely [I can ill afford it] —ill at ease uncomfortable

**I'll** (Il) 1. I shall 2. I will

**Ill., IL** Illinois

**ill'-ad·vised'** adj. showing or resulting from poor advice; unwise

**ill'-bred'** adj. rude; impolite

**il·le·gal** (i lē'gəl) adj. prohibited by law; against the law —**il·le·gal·i·ty** (il'ē gal'i tē) n. —**il·le'gal·ly** adv.

**il·leg·i·ble** (i lej'ə b'l) adj. hard or impossible to read because badly written or printed —**il·leg'i·bly** adv.

**il·le·git·i·mate** (il'ə jit'ə mit) adj. 1. born of parents not married to each other 2. contrary to law, rules, or logic —**il'le·git'i·ma·cy** (-mə sē) n.

**ill'-fat'ed** adj. 1. certain to have an evil fate or unlucky end 2. unlucky

**ill'-fa'vored** adj. ugly or unpleasant

**ill'-got'ten** adj. obtained by evil, unlawful, or dishonest means

**il·lib·er·al** (i lib'ər əl) adj. 1. narrow-minded 2. not generous

**il·lic·it** (i lis'it) adj. [< L. illicitus, not allowed] unlawful; improper —**il·lic'it·ly** adv. —**il·lic'it·ness** n.

**il·lim·it·a·ble** (i lim'i tə b'l) adj. without limit; immeasurable

**Il·li·nois** (il'ə noi') Middle Western State of the U.S.: 56,400 sq. mi.; pop. 11,114,000; cap. Springfield —**Il'li·nois'an** adj., n.

**il·lit·er·ate** (i lit'ər it) adj. uneducated; esp., not knowing how to read or write —n. an illiterate person —**il·lit'er·a·cy** (-ə sē) n.

**ill'-man'nered** adj. having bad manners; rude; impolite

**ill nature** a disagreeable or mean disposition —**ill'-na'tured** adj.

**ill'ness** n. the condition of being in poor health; sickness; disease

**il·log·i·cal** (i läj'i k'l) adj. not logical or reasonable —**il·log'i·cal·ly** adv.

**ill'-starred'** (il'stärd') adj. unlucky

**ill'-suit'ed** adj. not suited or appropriate

**ill'-tem'pered** adj. sullen; irritable

**ill'-timed'** adj. inopportune

**ill'-treat'** vt. to treat unkindly, unfairly, etc. —**ill'-treat'ment** n.

**il·lu·mi·nate** (i lōō'mə nāt') vt. **-nat'ed**, **-nat'ing** [< L. in- + luminare, to light] 1. to give light to; light up 2. a) to make clear; explain b) to inform 3. to decorate as with lights —**il·lu'mi·na·ble** adj.

**il·lu'mi·na'tion** n. 1. an illuminating 2. the intensity of light

**il·lu'mine** (-min) vt. **-mined**, **-min·ing** to light up

**illus.** illustration

**ill-us·age** (il'yōō'sij, -zij) n. unkind or cruel treatment: also **ill usage**

**ill'-use'** (-yōōz'; for n. -yōōs') vt. **-used'**, **-us'ing** to abuse —n. same as **ILL-USAGE**

**il·lu·sion** (i lōō'zhən) n. [< L. illudere, to mock] 1. a false idea or conception 2. an unreal or misleading appearance or image —**il·lu'so·ry** (-sər ē), **il·lu'sive** (-siv) adj.

**il·lus·trate** (il'ə strāt') vt. **-trat'ed**, **-trat'ing** [< L. in- + lustrare, illuminate] 1. to explain; make clear, as by examples 2. to furnish (books, etc.) with explanatory or decorative pictures, etc. —**il'lus·tra'tor** n.

**il'lus·tra'tion** n. 1. an illustrating 2. an example, etc. used to help explain 3. a picture, diagram, etc. used to decorate or explain

**il·lus·tra·tive** (i lus'trə tiv) adj. serving as an illustration or example

**il·lus·tri·ous** (i lus'trē əs) adj. [< L. illustris, clear] distinguished; famous; outstanding —**il·lus'tri·ous·ly** adv. —**il·lus'tri·ous·ness** n.

**ill will** hostility; hate; dislike

**I'm** (Im) I am

**im-** same as: 1. IN-1 2. IN-2 Used before b, m, and p

**im·age** (im'ij) n. [< L. imago] 1. a representation of a person or thing; esp., a statue 2. the visual impression of something in a lens, mirror, etc. 3. a copy; likeness 4. a) a mental picture; idea b) the concept of a person, product, etc. held by the general public 5. a metaphor or simile —vt. **-aged**, **-ag·ing** 1. to make a representation of 2. to reflect 3. to imagine

**im·age·ry** (im'ij rē) n. 1. mental images 2. figurative language

**i·mag·i·na·ble** (i maj'ə nə b'l) adj. that can be imagined

**i·mag'i·nar'y** (-ner'ē) adj. existing only in the imagination; unreal

**i·mag'i·na'tion** (-nā'shən) n. 1. a) the act or power of forming mental images of what is not present b) the act or power of creating new ideas by combining previous experiences 2. the ability to understand the imaginative creations of others 3. resourcefulness

**i·mag'i·na·tive** (-nə tiv) adj. 1. having, using, or showing imagination 2. of or resulting from imagination —**i·mag'i·na·tive·ly** adv.

**i·mag·ine** (i maj'in) vt., vi. **-ined**, **-in·ing** [< L. imago, image] 1. to make a mental image (of); conceive in the mind 2. to suppose; think

**im·bal·ance** (im bal'əns) n. lack of balance, as in proportion or force

**im·be·cile** (im'bə s'l) n. [< L.

*imbecilis,* feeble] **1.** an adult mentally equal to a child between three and eight : an obsolescent term **2.** a foolish or stupid person —*adj.* foolish or stupid: also **im'be·cil'ic** (-sil'ik) —**im'be·cil'i·ty** *n.*

**im·bed** (im bed') *vt. same as* EMBED

**im·bibe** (im bīb') *vt.* **-bibed'**, **-bib'ing** [ < L. *in-,* in + *bibere,* to drink] **1.** to drink (esp. alcoholic liquor) **2.** to absorb into the mind —*vi.* to drink, esp. alcoholic liquor

**im·bro·glio** (im brōl'yō) *n., pl.* **-glios** [It. < *imbrogliare,* embroil] **1.** an involved, confusing situation **2.** a confused misunderstanding

**im·bue** (im byōō') *vt.* **-bued'**, **-bu'ing** [ < L. *imbuere,* to wet] **1.** to dye **2.** to permeate (*with* ideas, feelings, etc.)

**im·i·tate** (im'ə tāt') *vt.* **-tat'ed**, **-tat'ing** [ < L. *imitari*] **1.** to seek to follow the example of **2.** to mimic **3.** to reproduce in form, color, etc. **4.** to resemble —**im'i·ta'tor** *n.*

**im'i·ta'tion** *n.* **1.** an imitating **2.** the result of imitating; copy —*adj.* not real; sham [*imitation* leather] —**im'i·ta'tive** *adj.*

**im·mac·u·late** (i mak'yə lit) *adj.* [ < L. *in-,* not + *macula,* a spot] **1.** perfectly clean **2.** without a flaw or error **3.** pure; innocent; sinless —**im·mac'u·late·ly** *adv.* —**im·mac'u·late·ness** *n.*

**im·ma·nent** (im'ə nənt) *adj.* [ < L. *in-,* in + *manere,* remain] **1.** operating within; inherent **2.** present throughout the universe: said of God —**im'ma·nence** *n.* —**im'ma·nent·ly** *adv.*

**im·ma·te·ri·al** (im'ə tir'ē əl) *adj.* **1.** spiritual **2.** unimportant

**im·ma·ture** (im'ə toor', -tyoor', -choor') *adj.* **1.** not mature; not completely developed **2.** not finished or perfected —**im'ma·tu'ri·ty** *n.*

**im·meas·ur·a·ble** (i mezh'ər ə b'l) *adj.* that cannot be measured; boundless; vast —**im·meas'ur·a·bly** *adv.*

**im·me·di·a·cy** (i mē'dē ə sē) *n.* a being immediate; esp., direct relevance to the present time or purpose

**im·me'di·ate** (-it) *adj.* [see IN-² & MEDIATE] **1.** not separated in space; closest **2.** without delay; instant **3.** next in order or relation **4.** direct; first-hand —**im·me'di·ate·ly** *adv.*

**im·me·mo·ri·al** (im'ə môr'ē əl) *adj.* extending back beyond memory or record; ancient

**im·mense** (i mens') *adj.* [ < L. *in-,* not + *metiri,* to measure] very large; vast; huge —**im·mense'ly** *adv.* —**im·men'si·ty** *n.*

**im·merse** (i murs') *vt.* **-mersed'**, **-mers'ing** [ < L. *immergere*] **1.** to plunge into or as if into a liquid **2.** to baptize by dipping under water **3.** to absorb deeply; engross [*immersed* in study] —**im·mer'sion** *n.*

**immersion heater** an electric coil or rod immersed in water to heat it

**im·mi·grant** (im'ə grənt) *n.* one who immigrates —*adj.* immigrating

**im'mi·grate'** (-grāt') *vi.* **-grat'ed**, **-grat'ing** [see IN-¹ & MIGRATE] to come into a new country, etc., esp. in order to settle there —**im'mi·gra'tion** *n.*

**im·mi·nent** (im'ə nənt) *adj.* [ < L. *in-,* on + *minere,* to project] likely to happen without delay; impending —**im'mi·nence** *n.*

**im·mo·bile** (i mō'b'l) *adj.* **1.** firmly placed; stable **2.** motionless —**im'mo·bil'i·ty** *n.* —**im·mo'bi·lize'** (-līz') *vt.* **-lized'**, **-liz'ing**

**im·mod·er·ate** (i mäd'ər it) *adj.* without restraint; excessive

**im·mod·est** (i mäd'ist) *adj.* **1.** indecent **2.** not shy; forward —**im·mod'est·ly** *adv.* —**im·mod'es·ty** *n.*

**im·mo·late** (im'ə lāt') *vt.* **-lat'ed**, **-lat'ing** [ < L. *immolare,* sprinkle with sacrificial meal] to kill as a sacrifice —**im'mo·la'tion** *n.*

**im·mor·al** (i môr'əl, i mär'-) *adj.* not moral; specif., unchaste; lewd —**im·mor'al·ly** *adv.*

**im·mo·ral·i·ty** (im'ə ral'ə tē, im'ô-) *n.* **1.** a being immoral **2.** *pl.* **-ties** an immoral act or practice; vice

**im·mor·tal** (i môr't'l) *adj.* **1.** not mortal; living forever **2.** enduring **3.** having lasting fame —*n.* an immortal being —**im'mor·tal'i·ty** (-tal'ə tē) *n.* —**im·mor'tal·ize'** (-ə līz') *vt.* **-ized'**, **-iz'ing** to make immortal, as in fame

**im·mov·a·ble** (i mōōv'ə b'l) *adj.* **1.** firmly fixed **2.** unyielding; steadfast

**im·mune** (i myōōn') *adj.* [ < L. *in-,* without + *munia,* duties] **1.** exempt from or protected against something disagreeable or harmful **2.** not susceptible to some specified disease

**im·mu·ni·ty** (i myōōn'ə tē) *n., pl.* **-ties 1.** exemption from something burdensome, as a legal obligation **2.** resistance to a specified disease

**im·mu·nize** (im'yə nīz') *vt.* **-nized'**, **-niz'ing** to make immune, as by inoculation —**im'mu·ni·za'tion** *n.*

**im·mu·nol·o·gy** (im'yoo näl'ə jē) *n.* the branch of medicine dealing with immunity to disease or with allergic reactions —**im'mu·nol'o·gist** *n.*

**im·mure** (i myoor') *vt.* **-mured'**, **-mur'ing** [ < L. *in-,* in + *murus,* wall] to shut up within walls; confine

**im·mu·ta·ble** (i myōōt'ə b'l) *adj.* unchangeable —**im·mu'ta·bly** *adv.*

**imp** (imp) *n.* [ < Gr. *em-,* in + *phyton,* growth] **1.** a young demon **2.** a mischievous child —**imp'ish** *adj.*

**im·pact** (im pakt'; *for n.* im'pakt) *vt.* [ < L. *impingere,* press firmly together] to force tightly together —*n.* **1.** violent contact **2.** a shocking effect

**im·pact·ed** (-pak'tid) *adj.* abnormally lodged in the jaw: said of a tooth

**im·pair** (im per') *vt.* [ < L. *in-,* intens. + *pejor,* worse] to make worse, less, etc.; damage —**im·pair'ment** *n.*

**im·pa·la** (im pä'lə) *n., pl.* **-la, -las**

a reddish antelope of C and S Africa

**im·pale** (im pāl′) vt. -paled′, -pal′ing [< L. in-, on + palus, a pole] to pierce through with, or fix on, something pointed —im·pale′ment n.

**im·pal·pa·ble** (im pal′pə b'l) adj. 1. not perceptible to the touch 2. too subtle to be easily understood

**im·pan·el** (im pan′'l) vt. -eled or -elled, -el·ing or -el·ling 1. to enter the name(s) of on a jury list 2. to choose (a jury) from such a list

**im·part** (im pärt′) vt. [see IN-¹ & PART] 1. to give a share of; give 2. to make known; reveal

**im·par·tial** (im pär′shəl) adj. without bias; fair —im·par′ti·al′i·ty (-shē al′ə tē) n. —im·par′tial·ly adv.

**im·pass·a·ble** (im pas′ə b'l) adj. that cannot be passed or traveled over

**im·passe** (im′pas, im pas′) n. [Fr.] a situation offering no escape; deadlock

**im·pas·sioned** (im pash′ənd) adj. passionate; fiery; ardent

**im·pas·sive** (im pas′iv) adj. not feeling or showing emotion; calm —im·pas·siv·i·ty (im′pə siv′ə tē) n.

**im·pas·to** (im päs′tō) n. [It.] 1. painting in which the paint is laid thickly on the canvas 2. such paint

**im·pa·tient** (im pā′shənt) adj. lacking patience; specif., a) annoyed because of delay, opposition, etc. b) restlessly eager to do something, etc. —im·pa′tience n.

**im·peach** (im pēch′) vt. [< L. in-, in + pedica, a fetter] 1. to discredit (a person's honor, etc.) 2. to try (a public official) on a charge of wrongdoing —im·peach′ment n.

**im·pec·ca·ble** (im pek′ə b'l) adj. [< L. in-, not + peccare, to sin] without defect or error; flawless —im·pec′ca·bil′i·ty n. —im·pec′ca·bly adv.

**im·pe·cu·ni·ous** (im′pi kyoo′nē əs) adj. [< L. in-, not + pecunia, money] having no money; poor

**im·ped·ance** (im pēd′ns) n. [< ff. + -ANCE] the total resistance in an electric circuit to the flow of an alternating current of a single frequency

**im·pede** (im pēd′) vt. -ped′ed, -ped′ing [< L. in-, in + pes, foot] to hinder the progress of; obstruct

**im·ped·i·ment** (im ped′ə mənt) n. anything that impedes; specif., a speech defect

**im·ped·i·men·ta** (-men′tə) n.pl. encumbrances, as baggage or supplies

**im·pel** (im pel′) vt. -pelled′, -pel′ling [< L. in-, in + pellere, to drive] 1. to drive or move forward 2. to force, compel, or urge

**im·pend** (im pend′) vi. [< L. in-, in + pendere, hang] to be about to happen; be imminent [impending disaster]

**im·pen·e·tra·ble** (im pen′i trə b'l) adj. 1. that cannot be penetrated 2. that cannot be solved or understood

**im·pen·i·tent** (im pen′ə tənt) adj. not penitent; without regret or shame

**im·per·a·tive** (im per′ə tiv) adj. [< L. imperare, to command] 1. indicating authority or command 2. necessary; urgent 3. designating or of the mood of a verb that expresses a command, etc. —n. a command

**im·per·cep·ti·ble** (im′pər sep′tə b'l) adj. not easily perceived by the senses or the mind; very slight, subtle, etc. —im′per·cep′ti·bly adv.

**im′per·cep′tive** (-tiv) adj. not perceiving —im′per·cep′tive·ness n.

**im·per·fect** (im pur′fikt) adj. 1. not complete 2. not perfect 3. designating a verb tense that indicates a past action or state as incomplete or continuous —im·per′fect·ly adv.

**im·per·fec·tion** (im′pər fek′shən) n. 1. a being imperfect 2. a defect; fault

**im·pe·ri·al** (im pir′ē əl) adj. [< L. imperium, empire] 1. of an empire, emperor, or empress 2. having supreme authority 3. majestic; august 4. of great size or superior quality —n. a small, pointed chin beard

**imperial gallon** the standard British gallon, equal to c. 1 1/5 U.S. gallons

**im·pe·ri·al·ism** n. 1. imperial state or authority 2. the policy of forming and maintaining an empire, as by subjugating territories, establishing colonies, etc. 3. the policy of seeking to dominate the affairs of weaker countries —im·pe′ri·al·ist n., adj. —im·pe′ri·al·is′tic adj.

**im·per·il** (im per′əl) vt. -iled or -illed, -il·ing or -il·ling to put in peril; endanger

**im·pe·ri·ous** (im pir′ē əs) adj. [< L. imperium, empire] 1. overbearing, arrogant, etc. 2. urgent; imperative —im·pe′ri·ous·ly adv.

**im·per·ish·a·ble** (im per′ish ə b'l) adj. not perishable; indestructible

**im·per·ma·nent** (im pur′mə nənt) adj. not permanent; temporary —im·per′ma·nent·ly adv.

**im·per·son·al** (im pur′s'n əl) adj. 1. without reference to any particular person 2. not existing as a person [an impersonal force] 3. designating or of a verb occurring only in the third person singular, usually with it as subject —im·per′son·al·ly adv.

**im·per·son·ate** (im pur′sə nāt′) vt. -at′ed, -at′ing to assume the role of, for purposes of entertainment or fraud —im·per′son·a′tion n. —im·per′son·a′tor n.

**im·per·ti·nent** (im pur′t'n ənt) adj. 1. not pertinent 2. impudent; insolent —im·per′ti·nence n.

**im·per·turb·a·ble** (im′pər tur′bə b'l) adj. that cannot be perturbed; calm; impassive

**im·per·vi·ous** (im pur′vē əs) adj. 1. incapable of being penetrated, as by moisture 2. not affected by (with to)

**im·pe·ti·go** (im′pə tī′gō) n. [see IMPETUS] a contagious skin disease with eruption of pustules

**im·pet·u·ous** (im pech′oo wəs) adj. [see ff.] acting or done suddenly with little thought; rash —im·pet′u·os′i·ty (-wäs′ə tē) n. —im·pet′u·ous·ly adv.

**im·pe·tus** (im′pə təs) n. [< L. in-, in + petere, rush at] 1. the force with which a body moves against resistance 2. driving force or motive

**im·pi·e·ty** (im pī′ə tē) n. 1. lack of reverence for God 2. disrespect

**im·pinge** (im pinj′) vi. -pinged′, -ping′ing [< L. in-, in + pangere, to strike] 1. to strike, hit, etc. (on or upon) 2. to encroach (on or upon) —im·pinge′ment n.

**im·pi·ous** (im′pē əs) adj. not pious; specif., lacking reverence for God

**im·plac·a·ble** (im plak′ə b'l, -plā′kə-) adj. not to be placated or appeased; relentless —im·pla′ca·bly adv.

**im·plant** (im plant′) vt. 1. to plant firmly 2. to fix firmly in the mind

**im·plau·si·ble** (im plô′zə b'l) adj. not plausible —im·plau′si·bly adv.

**im·ple·ment** (im′plə mənt; for v. -ment′) n. [< L. in-, in + plere, to fill] something used in a given activity; tool, instrument, etc. —vt. to carry into effect; accomplish —im′ple·men·ta′tion n.

**im·pli·cate** (im′plə kāt′) vt. -cat′ed, -cat′ing [< L. in-, in + plicare, to fold] to show to be a party to a crime, etc. —im′pli·ca′tive adj.

**im′pli·ca′tion** n. 1. an implicating or being implicated 2. an implying or being implied 3. something implied

**im·plic·it** (im plis′it) adj. [see IMPLICATE] 1. suggested though not plainly expressed; implied 2. necessarily involved though not apparent; inherent 3. without reservation; absolute —im·plic′it·ly adv.

**im·plode** (im plōd′) vt., vi. -plod′ed, -plod′ing [< IN-¹ + (EX)PLODE] to burst inward —im·plo′sion (-plō′zhən) n. —im·plo′sive adj.

**im·plore** (im plôr′) vt. -plored′, -plor′ing [< L. in-, intens. + plorare, cry out] 1. to ask earnestly for 2. to beg (a person) to do something —im·plor′ing·ly adv.

**im·ply** (im plī′) vt. -plied′, -ply′ing [< L. implicare, involve] 1. to have as a necessary part, condition, etc. 2. to indicate indirectly; hint; suggest

**im·po·lite** (im′pə līt′) adj. not polite; discourteous —im′po·lite′ly adv.

**im·pol·i·tic** (im päl′ə tik) adj. unwise; not politic

**im·pon·der·a·ble** (im pän′dər ə b'l) adj. that cannot be weighed or measured —n. anything imponderable

**im·port** (im pôrt′; also, and for n. always, im′pôrt) vt. [< L. in-, in + portare, carry] 1. to bring (goods) into one country from another in commerce 2. to mean; signify —vi. to be of importance; matter —n. 1. something imported 2. meaning; signification 3. importance —im′por·ta′tion n. —im·port′er n.

**im·por·tant** (im pôr′t'nt) adj. [see prec.] 1. meaning a great deal; having much significance or value 2. having, or acting as if having, power, authority, etc. —im·por′tance n. —im·por′tant·ly adv.

**im·por·tu·nate** (im pôr′chə nit) adj. persistent in asking or demanding

**im·por·tune** (im′pôr tōōn′) vt., vi. -tuned′, -tun′ing [< L. importunus, troublesome] to urge or entreat persistently or repeatedly —im′por·tu′ni·ty n., pl. -ties

**im·pose** (im pōz′) vt. -posed′, -pos′ing [< L. in-, on + ponere, to place] 1. to place (a burden, tax, etc. on or upon) 2. to force (oneself) on others —impose on (or upon) 1. to take advantage of 2. to cheat or defraud —im′po·si′tion (-pə zish′ən) n.

**im·pos′ing** adj. impressive because of great size, strength, dignity, etc. —im·pos′ing·ly adv.

**im·pos·si·ble** (im päs′ə b'l) adj. 1. not capable of being, being done, or happening 2. not capable of being endured, used, etc. because disagreeable or unsuitable —im·pos′si·bil′i·ty n., pl. -ties —im·pos′si·bly adv.

**im·post** (im′pōst) n. [see IMPOSE] a tax; esp., a duty on imported goods

**im·pos·tor** (im päs′tər) n. [see IMPOSE] one who deceives or cheats others by pretending to be what he is not

**im·pos·ture** (-chər) n. the act or practice of an impostor; fraud

**im·po·tent** (im′pə tənt) adj. 1. lacking physical strength 2. ineffective; powerless 3. unable to engage in sexual intercourse: said of males —im′po·tence, im′po·ten·cy n. —im′po·tent·ly adv.

**im·pound** (im pound′) vt. 1. to shut up (an animal) in a pound 2. to take and hold in legal custody 3. to gather and enclose (water), as for irrigation

**im·pov·er·ish** (im päv′ər ish) vt. [< L. in-, in + pauper, poor] 1. to make poor 2. to deprive of strength, resources, etc. —im·pov′er·ish·ment n.

**im·prac·ti·ca·ble** (im prak′ti kə b'l) adj. not capable of being carried out in practice

**im·prac·ti·cal** (im prak′tə k'l) adj. not practical

**im·pre·cate** (im′prə kāt′) vt. -cat′ed, -cat′ing [< L. in-, on + precari, pray] to invoke (evil, a curse, etc.) —im′pre·ca′tion n.

**im·pre·cise** (im′pri sīs′) adj. not precise; vague —im′pre·cise′ly adv. —im′pre·ci′sion (-sizh′ən) n.

**im·preg·na·ble** (im preg′nə b'l) adj. 1. that cannot be overcome or entered by force 2. unyielding —im·preg′na·bil′i·ty n. —im·preg′na·bly adv.

**im·preg·nate** (im preg′nāt) vt. -nat·ed, -nat·ing 1. to make pregnant; fertilize 2. to saturate 3. to imbue (with ideas, etc.) —im·preg′na·ble adj. —im′preg·na′tion n.

**im·pre·sa·ri·o** (im′prə sär′ē ō) n., pl. -os [It.] the manager of an opera, concert series, etc.

**im·press¹** (im pres′) vt. [< IN-¹ + PRESS²] 1. to force into military service 2. to seize for public use

**im·press²** (im pres′; for n. im′pres) vt. [see IN-¹ + PRESS¹] 1. to stamp; imprint 2. to affect strongly the mind or emotions of **3.** to fix in the memory —*n.* **1.** an impressing **2.** an imprint

**im·press'i·ble** (-ə b'l) *adj.* that can be impressed —**im·press'i·bil'i·ty** *n.*

**im·pres·sion** (im presh'ən) *n.* **1.** an impressing **2.** *a)* a mark, imprint, etc. *b)* an effect produced on the mind **3.** a vague notion **4.** an amusing impersonation; mimicking

**im·pres'sion·a·ble** *adj.* easily impressed or influenced; sensitive

**im·pres'sion·ism** *n.* a theory of art, music, etc., whose aim is to reproduce the immediate, overall impression —**im·pres'sion·ist** *adj., n.* —**im·pres'sion·is'tic** *adj.*

**im·pres'sive** (im pres'iv) *adj.* tending to impress the mind or emotions; eliciting wonder or admiration —**im·pres'sive·ly** *adv.*

**im·pri·ma·tur** (im'pri mät'ər, -māt'-) *n.* [ModL., lit., let it be printed] permission or license, esp. to publish

**im·print** (im print'; *for n.* im'print) *vt.* [< L. *in-,* on + *premere,* to press] to mark or fix as by pressing or stamping —*n.* **1.** a mark made by imprinting **2.** a lasting effect **3.** a note in a book giving facts of its publication

**im·pris·on** (im priz'n) *vt.* to put in or as in prison —**im·pris'on·ment** *n.*

**im·prob·a·ble** (im präb'ə b'l) *adj.* not probable; unlikely —**im'prob·a·bil'i·ty** *n.* —**im·prob'a·bly** *adv.*

**im·promp·tu** (im prämp'tōō) *adj., adv.* [< L. *in promptu,* in readiness] without preparation; offhand

**im·prop·er** (im präp'ər) *adj.* **1.** not suitable; unfit **2.** incorrect **3.** not in good taste —**im·prop'er·ly** *adv.*

**im·pro·pri·e·ty** (im'prə prī'ə tē) *n., pl.* **-ties 1.** a being improper **2.** an improper act, usage, etc.

**im·prove** (im prōōv') *vt.* **-proved'**, **-prov'ing** [ult. < L. *in-,* in + *prodesse,* to be of profit] **1.** to use (time) well **2.** to make better **3.** to make (land or structures) more valuable by cultivation, construction, etc. —*vi.* to become better —**improve on** (or **upon**) to do or make better than —**im·prov'a·ble** *adj.*

**im·prove'ment** *n.* **1.** an improving or being improved **2.** a change that improves or adds value to something

**im·prov·i·dent** (im präv'ə dənt) *adj.* lacking foresight or thrift —**im·prov'i·dence** *n.* —**im·prov'i·dent·ly** *adv.*

**im·pro·vise** (im'prə vīz') *vt., vi.* **-vised'**, **-vis'ing** [< L. *in-,* not + *providere,* foresee] **1.** to compose and perform without preparation **2.** to make or do with whatever is at hand —**im·prov'i·sa'tion** (-präv'ə zā'shən) *n.* —**im·prov'i·sa'tion·al** *adj.*

**im·pru·dent** (im prōōd'nt) *adj.* not prudent; rash —**im·pru'dence** *n.*

**im·pu·dent** (im'pyōō dənt) *adj.* [< L. *in-,* not + *pudere,* feel shame] shamelessly bold; insolent —**im'pu·dence** *n.* —**im'pu·dent·ly** *adv.*

**im·pugn** (im pyōōn') *vt.* [< L. *in-,* against + *pugnare,* to fight] to oppose or challenge as false

**im·pulse** (im'puls) *n.* [see IMPEL] **1.** *a)* a driving forward *b)* an impelling

force; impetus *c)* the motion or effect caused by such a force **2.** *a)* incitement to action by a stimulus *b)* a sudden inclination to act

**im·pul·sion** (im pul'shən) *n.* **1.** an impelling or being impelled **2.** an impelling force **3.** impetus **4.** *same as* IMPULSE (sense 2)

**im·pul·sive** (im pul'siv) *adj.* **1.** driving forward **2.** given to acting on impulse —**im·pul'sive·ly** *adv.*

**im·pu·ni·ty** (im pyōō'nə tē) *n.* [< L. *in-,* without + *poena,* punishment] freedom from punishment, harm, etc.

**im·pure** (im pyoor') *adj.* **1.** unclean; dirty **2.** immoral; obscene **3.** mixed with foreign matter; adulterated —**im·pure'ly** *adv.* —**im·pure'ness** *n.*

**im·pu·ri·ty** *n.* **1.** a being impure **2.** *pl.* **-ties** an impure thing or part

**im·pute** (im pyōōt') *vt.* **-put'ed**, **-put'ing** [< L. *in-,* to + *putare,* to think] to attribute (esp. a fault or misconduct) to another —**im'pu·ta'tion** (-pyoo tā'shən) *n.*

**in** (in) *prep.* [OE.] **1.** contained by [in the room] **2.** wearing [in formal dress] **3.** during [done in a day] **4.** at the end of [due in an hour] **5.** not beyond [in sight] **6.** employed at [a man in business] **7.** out of a group of [one in ten] **8.** amidst [in a storm] **9.** affected by [in trouble] **10.** with regard to [to vary in size] **11.** using [speak in English] **12.** because of; for [he cried in pain] **13.** into [come in the house] —*adv.* **1.** to the inside [he went in] **2.** to or at a certain place **3.** so as to be contained by a certain space, condition, etc. —*adj.* **1.** that is in power [the in group] **2.** inner; inside **3.** gathered, counted, etc. **4.** [Colloq.] currently smart, popular, etc. —*n.* **1.** one that is in power: *usually used in pl.* **2.** [Colloq.] special influence or favor —**have it in for** [Colloq.] to hold a grudge against —**ins and outs** all the details and intricacies —**in that** because; since —**in with** associated with

**in-¹** [< the prep. IN or L. *in,* in] *a prefix meaning* in, into, within, on, toward [inbreed, infer]

**in-²** [L.] *a prefix meaning* no, not, without, non- The following list includes some common compounds formed with *in-,* with no special meanings; they will be understood if *not* or *lack of* is used with the meaning of the base word:

inability
inaccessible
inaccuracy
inaccurate
inaction
inactive
inadequacy
inadequate
inadmissible
inadvisable
inanimate
inapplicable
inappropriate
inapt
inartistic
inaudible
inauspicious
incapable

incautious
incivility
incombustible
incommensurate
incommunicable
incomprehensible
inconceivable
inconclusive
inconsistency
inconsistent
incorrect
incurable
indecorous
indefinable
indiscernible
indisputable
indistinct
indistinguishable

indivisible

inedible

ineffective

ineffectual

inefficacy

inelastic

ineligible

inequality

inequitable

inequity

inexact

inexcusable

inexpensive

infertile

inharmonious

inhospitable

inhumane

injudicious

inoperable

inopportune

inseparable

insignificance

insignificant

insolvable

insufficient

insurmountable

insusceptible

invariable

**-in** (in) a combining form used in forming words analogous to SIT-IN to describe similar demonstrations [*teach-in, be-in*]

**IN** Indiana

**in.** inch(es)

**in ab·sen·ti·a** (in əb sen′shə, -shē ə) [L.] although not present [to receive a college degree *in absentia*]

**in·ac·ti·vate** (in ak′tə vāt′) *vt.* -vat′ed, -vat′ing to make no longer active —**in·ac′ti·va′tion** *n.*

**in·ad·vert·ent** (in′əd vur′tənt) *adj.* 1. not attentive or observant 2. due to oversight —**in′ad·vert′ence** *n.* —**in′ad·vert′ent·ly** *adv.*

**in·al·ien·a·ble** (ān′lyən ə b'l) *adj.* [see ALIEN] that cannot be taken away or transferred —**in·al′ien·a·bly** *adv.*

**in·am·o·ra·ta** (in am′ə rät′ə) *n.* [It.] one's sweetheart or mistress

**in·ane** (in ān′) *adj.* [L. *inanis*] 1. empty 2. lacking sense; silly —**in·an·i·ty** (in an′ə tē) *n.*

**in·ar·tic·u·late** (in′är tik′yə lit) *adj.* 1. without the articulation of normal speech [an *inarticulate* cry] 2. mute 3. unable to speak clearly or coherently 4. unexpressed or inexpressible

**in·as·much as** (in′əz much′ əz) 1. since; because 2. to the extent that

**in·at·ten·tion** (in′ə ten′shən) *n.* failure to pay attention; negligence —**in′at·ten′tive** *adj.*

**in·au·gu·ral** (in ô′gyə rəl) *adj.* [Fr.] 1. of an inauguration 2. first in a series —*n.* 1. a speech made at an inauguration 2. an inauguration

**in·au·gu·rate′** (-rāt′) *vt.* -rat′ed, -rat′ing [< L. *inaugurare*, to practice augury] 1. to induct into office with a formal ceremony 2. to make a formal beginning of 3. to dedicate formally —**in·au′gu·ra′tion** *n.*

**in·board** (in′bôrd′) *adv., adj.* 1. inside the hull of a ship or boat 2. close to the fuselage of an aircraft —*n.* a marine motor mounted inboard

**in·born** (in′bôrn′) *adj.* present in the organism at birth; innate; natural

**in′bound′** (-bound′) *adj.* traveling or going inward

**in·bred** (in′bred′) *adj.* 1. inborn; natural 2. resulting from inbreeding

**in·breed** (in′brēd′) *vt., vi.* -bred′, -breed′ing 1. to breed by continual mating of individuals of the same or closely related stocks 2. to make or become too refined, effete, etc.

**inc.** 1. incorporated 2. increase

**In·ca** (iŋ′kə) *n.* a member of the highly civilized Indian people that dominated ancient Peru until the Spanish conquest

**in·cal·cu·la·ble** (in kal′kyə lə b'l) *adj.* 1. that cannot be calculated; too great or too many to be counted 2. unpredictable —**in·cal′cu·la·bly** *adv.*

**in·can·des·cent** (in′kən des′'nt) *adj.* [< L. *in-*, in + *candere*, to shine] 1. glowing with intense heat 2. very bright —**in′can·des′cence** *n.*

**incandescent lamp** a lamp with a filament in a vacuum heated to incandescence by an electric current

**in·can·ta·tion** (in′kan tā′shən) *n.* [< L. *in-*, in + *cantare*, to chant] words chanted in magic spells or rites

**in·ca·pac·i·tate** (in′kə pas′ə tāt′) *vt.* -tat′ed, -tat′ing 1. to make unable or unfit 2. *Law* to disqualify

**in′ca·pac′i·ty** *n., pl.* -ties 1. lack of capacity, power, or fitness 2. legal ineligibility

**in·car·cer·ate** (in kär′sə rāt′) *vt.* -at′ed, -at′ing [< L. *in*, in + *carcer*, prison] to imprison —**in·car′cer·a′tion** *n.*

**in·car·na·dine** (in kär′nə dīn′) *vt.* -dined′, -din′ing to make red

**in·car·nate** (in kär′nit; *for v.* -nāt) *adj.* [< L. *in-*, in + *caro*, flesh] endowed with a human body; personified —*vt.* -nat·ed, -nat·ing 1. to give bodily form to 2. to be the type or embodiment of —**in′car·na′tion** *n.*

**in·cen·di·ar·y** (in sen′dē er′ē) *adj.* [< L. *incendium*, a fire] 1. having to do with the willful destruction of property by fire 2. designed to cause fires, as certain bombs 3. willfully stirring up strife, riot, etc. —*n., pl.* -ies one who willfully stirs up strife, riot, etc.

**in·cense¹** (in′sens) *n.* [< L. *in-*, in + *candere*, to burn] 1. any substance burned to produce a pleasant odor 2. the fragrance from this 3. any pleasant odor

**in·cense²** (in sens′) *vt.* -censed′, -cens′ing [see prec.] to make very angry; enrage —**in·cense′ment** *n.*

**in·cen·tive** (in sen′tiv) *n.* [< L. *in-*, on + *canere*, sing] a stimulus; motive

**in·cep·tion** (in sep′shən) *n.* [see INCIPIENT] the act of beginning; start

**in·cer·ti·tude** (in sur′tə tood′, -tyood′) *n.* 1. doubt 2. insecurity

**in·ces·sant** (in ses′'nt) *adj.* [< L. *in-*, not + *cessare*, cease] never ceasing; continuing without stopping; constant —**in·ces′sant·ly** *adv.*

**in·cest** (in′sest) *n.* [< L. *in-*, not + *castus*, chaste] sexual intercourse between persons too closely related to marry legally —**in·ces·tu·ous** (in ses′choo wəs) *adj.* —**in·ces′tu·ous·ly** *adv.* —**in·ces′tu·ous·ness** *n.*

**inch** (inch) *n.* [< L. *uncia*, twelfth part] a measure of length equal to 1/12 foot; symbol, ″ —*vt., vi.* to move very slowly, or by degrees —**every**

**inch** in all respects —**inch by inch** gradually; also **by inches** —**within an inch of** very close to

**in·cho·ate** (in kō′it) *adj.* [< L. *inchoare*, begin] 1. just begun; rudimentary 2. not yet clearly formed

**in·ci·dence** (in′si dəns) *n.* the degree or range of occurrence or effect

**in′ci·dent** (-dənt) *adj.* [< L. *in-*, on + *cadere*, to fall] 1. likely to happen as a result 2. falling upon or affecting —*n.* 1. something that happens; an event, esp. a minor one 2. a minor conflict

**in′ci·den′tal** (-den′t′l) *adj.* 1. happening in connection with something more important; casual 2. secondary or minor —*n.* 1. something incidental 2. [*pl.*] miscellaneous items

**in′ci·den′tal·ly** *adv.* 1. in an incidental manner 2. by the way

**in·cin·er·ate** (in sin′ə rāt′) *vt.*, *vi.* -at′ed, -at′ing [< L. *in*, in + *cinis*, ashes] to burn to ashes; burn up —**in·cin′er·a′tion** *n.*

**in·cin′er·a′tor** *n.* a furnace for burning trash

**in·cip·i·ent** (in sip′ē ənt) *adj.* [< L. *in-*, on + *capere*, take] just beginning to exist or appear —**in·cip′i·ence** *n.*

**in·cise** (in sīz′) *vt.* -cised′, -cis′ing [< L. *in-*, into + *caedere*, to cut] to cut into with a sharp tool; specif., to engrave, or carve

**in·ci·sion** (in sizh′ən) *n.* 1. an incising 2. cut; gash 3. incisive quality

**in·ci·sive** (in sī′siv) *adj.* 1. cutting into 2. sharp; penetrating; acute —**in·ci′sive·ly** *adv.* —**in·ci′sive·ness** *n.*

**in·ci·sor** (in sī′zər) *n.* any of the front cutting teeth between the canines

**in·cite** (in sīt′) *vt.* -cit′ed, -cit′ing [< L. *in-*, on + *citare*, urge] to urge to action; rouse —**in·cite′ment** *n.*

**incl.** 1. including 2. inclusive

**in·clem·ent** (in klem′ənt) *adj.* [< L. *in-*, not + *clemens*, lenient] 1. rough; stormy 2. lacking mercy; harsh —**in·clem′en·cy** *n.*

**in·cli·na·tion** (in′klə nā′shən) *n.* 1. a bending, leaning, or sloping 2. an inclined surface; slope 3. *a*) a bias; tendency *b*) a preference

**in·cline** (in klīn′; *for n. usually* in′klīn) *vi.* -clined′, -clin′ing [< L. *in-*, on + *clinare*, lean] 1. to lean; slope 2. to have a tendency 3. to have a preference or liking —*vt.* 1. to cause to lean, slant, etc. 2. to make willing; influence —*n.* a slope; grade

**in·close** (in klōz′) *vt.* -closed′, -clos′ing *same as* ENCLOSE —**in·clo′sure** (-klō′zhər) *n.*

**in·clude** (in klōōd′) *vt.* -clud′ed, -clud′ing [< L. *in-*, in + *claudere*, to close] 1. to enclose 2. to have as part of a whole; contain; comprise 3. to take into account —**in·clu′sion** (-klōō′zhən) *n.*

**in·clu·sive** (-klōō′siv) *adj.* 1. taking everything into account 2. including the terms or limits mentioned (*the first to the tenth inclusive*) —**inclusive of** including —**in·clu′sive·ly** *adv.*

**in·cog·ni·to** (in′käg nēt′ō, in käg′

**ni tō′**) *adv.*, *adj.* [It. < L. *in-*, not + *cognitus*, known] disguised under an assumed name, rank, etc.

**in·co·her·ent** (in′kō hir′ənt) *adj.* 1. not logically connected; disjointed 2. characterized by incoherent speech, etc. —**in′co·her′ence** *n.* —**in′co·her′ent·ly** *adv.*

**in·come** (in′kum′) *n.* the money, etc. received for labor or services, or from property, investments, etc.

**in·com·mu·ni·ca·do** (in′kə myōō′ nə kä′dō) *adj.* [Sp.] not allowed to communicate with others

**in·com·pa·ra·ble** (in käm′pər ə b′l) *adj.* 1. having no basis of comparison 2. beyond comparison; matchless

**in·com·pat·i·ble** (in′kəm pat′ə b′l) *adj.* not compatible; specif., unable to live together harmoniously —**in′com·pat′i·bil′i·ty** *n.*

**in·com·pe·tent** (in käm′pə tənt) *adj.* without adequate ability, knowledge, fitness, etc. —*n.* an incompetent person —**in·com′pe·tence** *n.* —**in·com′pe·tent·ly** *adv.*

**in·com·plete** (in′kəm plēt′) *adj.* 1. lacking a part or parts 2. unfinished; not concluded 3. not perfect

**in·con·gru·ous** (in käŋ′grŏō wəs) *adj.* 1. lacking harmony or agreement of parts, etc. 2. unsuitable; inappropriate —**in′con·gru′i·ty** (-kən grŏō′ ə tē) *n.*

**in·con·se·quen·tial** (in kän′sə kwen′shəl) *adj.* of no consequence

**in·con·sid·er·a·ble** (in′kən sid′ər ə b′l) *adj.* trivial; small

**in′con·sid′er·ate** (-it) *adj.* without thought or consideration for others; thoughtless —**in′con·sid′er·ate·ly** *adv.* —**in′con·sid′er·ate·ness** *n.* —**in′con·sid′er·a′tion** (-ə rā′shən) *n.*

**in·con·sol·a·ble** (in′kən sōl′ə b′l) *adj.* that cannot be consoled

**in·con·spic·u·ous** (in′kən spik′yoo wəs) *adj.* attracting little attention

**in·con·stant** (in kän′stənt) *adj.* not constant; changeable, fickle, irregular, etc. —**in·con′stan·cy** *n.*

**in·con·test·a·ble** (in′kən tes′tə b′l) *adj.* unquestionable; indisputable —**in′con·test′a·bil′i·ty** *n.* —**in′con·test′a·bly** *adv.*

**in·con·ti·nent** (in känt′′n ənt) *adj.* 1. without self-restraint, esp. in sexual activity 2. unable to restrain a natural discharge, as of urine —**in·con′ti·nence** *n.*

**in·con·ven·ience** (in′kən vēn′yəns) *n.* 1. lack of comfort, ease, etc. 2. anything inconvenient —*vt.* -ienced, -ienc·ing to cause inconvenience to

**in′con·ven′ient** *adj.* not favorable to one's comfort; causing bother, etc.

**in·cor·po·rate** (in kôr′pə rāt′) *vt.* -rat′ed, -rat′ing [see IN-¹ & CORPORATE] 1. to combine; include; embody 2. to bring together into a single whole; merge 3. to form into a corporation —*vi.* to unite into one group or substance; form a corporation —**in·cor′po·ra′tion** *n.*

**in·cor·ri·gi·ble** (in kôr′i jə b′l, -kär′-) *adj.* [see IN-² & CORRECT] that cannot be corrected or reformed, esp.

because set in bad habits —**in·cor·ri·gi·bil′i·ty** n. —**in·cor′ri·gi·bly** adv.,

**in·cor·rupt·i·ble** (in′kə rup′tə b'l) adj. that cannot be corrupted, esp. morally

**in·crease** (in krēs′; for n. in′krēs) vt. -**creased′**, -**creas′ing** [< L. in-, in + crescere, grow] to become greater in size, amount, number, etc. —vi. to make greater in size, etc. —n. 1. an increasing or becoming increased 2. the result or amount of an increasing —**on the increase** increasing

**in·creas′ing·ly** adv. more and more

**in·cred·i·ble** (in kred′ə b'l) adj. not credible; seeming too unusual to be possible —**in·cred′i·bly** adv.

**in·cred·u·lous** (in krej′oo ləs) adj. 1. unwilling to believe 2. showing doubt or disbelief —**in·cre·du·li·ty** (in′krə dōō′lə tē) n.

**in·cre·ment** (in′krə mənt, iŋ′-) n. [< L. incrementum] 1. an increase 2. amount of increase

**in·crim·i·nate** (in krim′ə nāt′) vt. -**nat′ed**, -**nat′ing** [< L. in-, in + crimen, offense] 1. to accuse of a crime 2. to involve in, or make appear guilty of, a crime or fault —**in·crim′i·na′tion** n.

**in·crust** (in krust′) vt. to cover as with a crust —vi. to form a crust —**in′crus·ta′tion** n.

**in·cu·bate** (in′kyə bāt′) vt., vi. -**bat′ed**, -**bat′ing** [< L. in-, on + cubare, to lie] 1. to sit on and hatch (eggs) 2. to keep (eggs, embryos, etc.) in a favorable environment for hatching or developing 3. to develop, as by planning —**in′cu·ba′tion** n.

**in′cu·ba′tor** n. 1. a heated container for hatching eggs 2. a similar apparatus in which premature babies are kept for a period

**in·cu·bus** (iŋ′kyə bəs) n. [LL.] 1. a nightmare 2. an oppressive burden

**in·cul·cate** (in kul′kāt, in′kul kāt′) vt. -**cat·ed**, -**cat·ing** [< L. in-, in + calcare, trample underfoot] to impress upon the mind, as by insistent urging —**in′cul·ca′tion** n.

**in·cul·pate** (in kul′pāt, in′kul pāt′) vt. -**pat·ed**, -**pat·ing** [< L. in, on + culpa, blame] same as INCRIMINATE

**in·cum·ben·cy** (in kum′bən sē) n., pl. -**cies** 1. a duty or obligation 2. a term of office

**in·cum′bent** (-bənt) adj. [< L. in-, on + cubare, lie down] 1. resting (on or upon one) as a duty or obligation 2. currently in office —n. the holder of an office, etc.

**in·cum·ber** (in kum′bər) vt. same as ENCUMBER —**in·cum′brance** n.

**in·cu·nab·u·la** (in′kyoo nab′yə lə) n.pl. sing. -**u·lum** (-ləm) [L., pl., swaddling clothes] 1. infancy; beginnings 2. books printed before 1500

**in·cur** (in kur′) vt. -**curred′**, -**cur′ring** [< L. in-, in + currere, to run] to meet with or bring upon oneself (something undesirable)

**in·cu·ri·ous** (in kyoor′ē əs) adj. not curious; uninterested

**in·cur·sion** (in kur′zhən) n. [see prec.] an invasion or raid

**in·cus** (iŋ′kəs) n., pl. **in·cu·des** (in-kyōō′dēz) [< L., anvil] the central one of the three small bones in the middle ear

**Ind.** 1. India 2. Indian 3. Indiana

**ind.** 1. independent 2. index

**in·debt·ed** (in det′id) adj. 1. in debt 2. obliged; owing gratitude

**in·debt′ed·ness** n. 1. a being indebted 2. the amount owed

**in·de·cent** (in dē′s'nt) adj. not decent; specif., a) improper b) morally offensive; obscene —**in·de′cen·cy** n. —**in·de′cent·ly** adv.

**in·de·ci·pher·a·ble** (in′di sī′fər ə b'l) adj. that cannot be deciphered

**in·de·ci·sion** (in′di sizh′ən) n. inability to decide; vacillation

**in′de·ci′sive** (-sī′siv) adj. 1. not decisive 2. showing indecision —**in·de·ci′sive·ly** adv. —**in′de·ci′sive·ness** n.

**in·deed** (in dēd′) adv. certainly; truly —interj. an exclamation of surprise, doubt, sarcasm, etc.

**in·de·fat·i·ga·ble** (in′di fat′i gə b'l) adj. [< L. in-, not + defatigare, tire out] not tiring; tireless

**in·de·fen·si·ble** (in′di fen′sə b'l) adj. 1. that cannot be defended 2. that cannot be justified

**in·def·i·nite** (in def′ə nit) adj. 1. having no exact limits 2. not precise in meaning; vague 3. not certain; unsure 4. Gram. not limiting or specifying [a and an are indefinite articles] —**in·def′i·nite·ly** adv.

**in·del·i·ble** (in del′ə b'l) adj. [< L. in-, not + delere, destroy] 1. that cannot be erased, blotted out, etc. 2. leaving an indelible mark

**in·del·i·cate** (in del′i kit) adj. lacking propriety or modesty; coarse —**in·del′i·ca·cy** n., pl. -**cies**

**in·dem·ni·fy** (in dem′nə fī′) vt. -**fied′**, -**fy′ing** [< L. indemnis, unhurt + -FY] 1. to insure against loss, damage, etc. 2. to repay for (loss or damage) —**in·dem′ni·fi·ca′tion** n.

**in·dem′ni·ty** n., pl. -**ties** 1. insurance against loss, damage, etc. 2. repayment for loss, damage, etc.

**in·dent¹** (in dent′) vt., vi. [< L. in, in + dens, tooth] 1. to notch 2. to space (the beginning of a paragraph, etc.) in from the regular margin

**in·dent²** (in dent′) vt. [IN-¹ + DENT] to make a dent in

**in′den·ta′tion** (-den tā′shən) n. 1. a being indented 2. a notch, cut, inlet, etc. 3. a dent 4. a spacing in from the margin, or a blank space so made: in this sense, usually, in·den′tion

**in·den·ture** (in den′chər) n. 1. a written contract 2. [often pl.] a contract binding one person to work for another —vt. -**tured**, -**tur·ing** to bind by indenture

---

fat, āpe, cär; ten, ēven; is, bīte; gō, hôrn, tōōl. look; oil, out; up, fur; chin; she; thin, then; zh, leisure; ŋ, ring; ə for a in ago; ′, (ā′b'l); ë, Fr. coeur; ö, Fr. feu; Fr. mon; ü, Fr. duc; kh, G. ich, doch; ‡ foreign; < derived from

**In·de·pend·ence** (in'di pen'dəns) city in W Mo.: pop. 112,000

**in·de·pend·ence** (in'di pen'dəns) *n.* a being independent; freedom from the control of another

**Independence Day** the anniversary of the adoption of the American Declaration of Independence on July 4, 1776

**in'de·pend'ent** (-dənt) *adj.* 1. free from the influence or control of others; specif., *a)* self-governing *b)* self-determined, self-reliant, etc. *c)* not adhering to any political party *d)* not connected with others [an *independent* grocer] 2. not depending on another for financial support —*n.* one who is independent in thinking, action, etc. —**in'de·pend'ent·ly** *adv.*

**independent clause** *same as* MAIN CLAUSE

**in'-depth'** *adj.* profound; thorough

**in·de·scrib·a·ble** (in'di skrī'bə b'l) *adj.* beyond the power of description —**in'de·scrib'a·bly** *adv.*

**in·de·struct·i·ble** (in'di struk'tə b'l) *adj.* that cannot be destroyed

**in·de·ter·mi·nate** (in'di tur'mi nit) *adj.* 1. indefinite; vague 2. unsettled; inconclusive

**in·dex** (in'deks) *n., pl.* **-dex·es, -di·ces'** (-də sēz') [L.: see INDICATE] 1. the forefinger: also **index finger** 2. a pointer, as the needle on a dial 3. an indication [an *index* of ability] 4. an alphabetical list of names, subjects, etc. indicating pages where found, as in a book 5. a figure showing ratio or relative change 6. [I-] *R.C.Ch.* formerly, a list of books forbidden to be read —*vt.* to make an index of or for

**In·di·a** (in'dē ə) 1. region in S Asia, south of the Himalayas 2. republic in the Brit. Commonwealth, in C & S India: 1,177,000 sq. mi.; pop. 507,386,000

**India ink** a black liquid ink

**In'di·an** *n.* 1. a native of India or the East Indies 2. a member of any of the aboriginal peoples of the Americas: also **American Indian** 3. any of the languages spoken by the American Indians —*adj.* 1. of India or the East Indies, their people, etc. 2. of the American Indians or their culture

**In·di·an·a** (in'dē an'ə) Middle Western State of the U.S.: 36,291 sq. mi.; pop. 5,194,000; cap. Indianapolis —**In'di·an'i·an** *adj., n.*

**In·di·an·ap·o·lis** (in'dē ə nap'ə lis) capital of Indiana: pop. 745,000

**Indian corn** *same as* CORN[1] (sense 2)

**Indian file** *same as* SINGLE FILE

**Indian Ocean** ocean south of Asia, between Africa & Australia

**Indian summer** mild, warm weather after the first frosts of late autumn

**India paper** 1. a thin, absorbent paper used in taking proofs from engraved plates 2. a thin, strong, opaque printing paper, as for Bibles

**indic.** indicative

**in·di·cate** (in'də kāt') *vt.* **-cat'ed, -cat'ing** [< L. *in-*, in + *dicare*, declare] 1. to direct attention to;

point out 2. to be a sign of; signify 3. to show the need for 4. to express briefly or generally —**in'di·ca'tion** *n.*

**in·dic·a·tive** (in dik'ə tiv) *adj.* 1. giving an indication 2. designating that mood of a verb used to express an act, state, etc. as actual, or to ask a question —*n.* the indicative mood

**in'di·ca'tor** *n.* a person or thing that indicates; specif., a gauge, dial, etc. that measures something

**in·dict** (in dīt') *vt.* [ult. < L. *in*, against + *dicere*, speak] to charge with a crime —**in·dict'ment** *n.*

**in·dif·fer·ent** (in dif'ər ənt) *adj.* 1. showing no bias; neutral 2. unconcerned; apathetic 3. of no importance 4. fair; average —**in·dif'fer·ence** *n.* —**in·dif'fer·ent·ly** *adv.*

**in·dig·e·nous** (in dij'ə nəs) *adj.* [< OL. *indu*, in + L. *gignere*, be born] existing or growing naturally in a region or country; native

**in·di·gent** (in'di jənt) *adj.* [< OL. *indu*, in + *egere*, to need] poor; needy —*n.* an indigent person —**in'di·gence** *n.* —**in'di·gent·ly** *adv.*

**in·di·gest·i·ble** (in'di jes'tə b'l) *adj.* not easily digested

**in'di·ges'tion** (-jes'chən) *n.* difficulty in digesting food

**in·dig·nant** (in dig'nənt) *adj.* [< L. *in-*, not + *dignus*, worthy] feeling or expressing anger, esp. at unjust or mean action —**in·dig'nant·ly** *adv.*

**in·dig·na·tion** (in'dig nā'shən) *n.* righteous anger

**in·dig·ni·ty** (in dig'nə tē) *n., pl.* **-ties** an insult or affront to one's dignity or self-respect

**in·di·go** (in'di gō') *n., pl.* **-gos', -goes'** [Sp. < Gr. *Indikos*, Indian] 1. a blue dye obtained from certain plants or made synthetically 2. a deep violet blue —*adj.* of this color

**in·di·rect** (in'di rekt', -dī-) *adj.* 1. not straight 2. not straight to the point 3. dishonest [indirect dealing] 4. not immediate; secondary [an *indirect* result] —**in'di·rect'ly** *adv.* —**in'di·rect'ness** *n.*

**indirect object** the word or words denoting the person or thing indirectly affected by the action of the verb (Ex.: *us* in *give us* time)

**in·dis·creet** (in'dis krēt') *adj.* lacking prudence; unwise

**in·dis·cre·tion** (in'dis kresh'ən) *n.* 1. lack of discretion 2. an indiscreet act or remark

**in·dis·crim·i·nate** (in'dis krim'ə nit) *adj.* 1. confused; random 2. making no distinctions —**in'dis·crim'i·nate·ly** *adv.*

**in·dis·pen·sa·ble** (in'dis pen'sə b'l) *adj.* absolutely necessary

**in·dis·posed** (in'dis pōzd') *adj.* 1. slightly ill 2. unwilling; disinclined —**in·dis·po·si·tion** (-pə zish'ən) *n.*

**in·dis·sol·u·ble** (in'di säl'yoo b'l) *adj.* that cannot be dissolved or destroyed; lasting

**in·dite** (in dīt') *vt.* **-dit'ed, -dit'ing** [see INDICT] to compose and write

**in·di·vid·u·al** (in'di vij'oo wəl) *adj.* [< L. < *in-*, not + *dividere*, to divide]

1. existing as a separate thing or being; single 2. of, for, by, or relating to a single person or thing —*n.* 1. a single thing or being 2. a person

**in·di·vid·u·al·ism** *n.* 1. individuality 2. the doctrine that the state exists for the individual 3. the leading of one's life in one's own way —**in'di·vid'u·al·ist** *n.* —**in'di·vid'u·al·is'tic** *adj.*

**in·di·vid·u·al·i·ty** (-wal'ə tē) *n., pl.* **-ties** 1. the sum of the characteristics that set one person or thing apart 2. existence as an individual

**in·di·vid·u·al·ize** (-wə līz') *vt.* **-ized', -iz'ing** 1. to make individual 2. to treat as an individual —**in'di·vid'u·al·i·za'tion** *n.*

**in·di·vid·u·al·ly** *adv.* 1. as individuals; separately 2. distinctively

**In·do·chi·na** (in'dō chī'nə) 1. large peninsula south of China 2. E part of this peninsula, consisting of Laos, Cambodia, & Vietnam

**in·doc·tri·nate** (in dăk'trə nāt') *vt.* **-nat'ed, -nat'ing** to instruct in doctrines, theories, beliefs, etc. —**in·doc'tri·na'tion** *n.*

**In·do·Eu·ro·pe·an** (in'dō yoor'ə pē'ən) *adj.* designating a family of languages including most of those of Europe and some of those of Asia

**in·do·lent** (in'də lənt) *adj.* [< L. *in-*, not + *dolere*, feel pain] idle; lazy —**in'do·lence** *n.* —**in'do·lent·ly** *adv.*

**in·dom·i·ta·ble** (in dăm'ĭt ə b'l) *adj.* [< L. *in-*, not + *domare*, to tame] not easily discouraged or defeated

**In·do·ne·si·a** (in'də nē'zhə, -shə) republic in the Malay Archipelago, including Java, Sumatra, & most of Borneo: 736,510 sq. mi.; pop. 100,795,000 —**In'do·ne'sian** *adj., n.*

**in·door** (in'dôr') *adj.* living, belonging, etc. in a building

**in·doors** (in'dôrz') *adv.* in or into a building

**in·dorse** (in dôrs') *vt.* **-dorsed', -dors'ing** *same as* ENDORSE

**in·du·bi·ta·ble** (in dōō'bi tə b'l) *adj.* that cannot be doubted —**in·du'bi·ta·bly** *adv.*

**in·duce** (in dōōs') *vt.* **-duced', -duc'ing** [< L. *in-*, in + *ducere*, to lead] 1. to persuade 2. to bring on [*sleep induced* by drugs] 3. to draw (a conclusion) from particular facts 4. to bring about (an electric or magnetic effect) in a body by placing it within a field of force —**in·duc'er** *n.*

**in·duce'ment** *n.* 1. an inducing or being induced 2. a motive; incentive

**in·duct** (in dukt') *vt.* [see INDUCE] 1. to place formally in an office, a society, etc. 2. to enroll (esp. a draftee) in the armed forces

**in·duct·ance** (in duk'təns) *n.* the property of an electric circuit by which a varying current in it produces a magnetic field that induces voltages in the same or a nearby circuit

**in·duct·ee** (in duk'tē') *n.* a person

inducted, esp. into the armed forces

**in·duc·tion** (in duk'shən) *n.* 1. an inducting or being inducted 2. reasoning from particular facts to a general conclusion 3. the inducing of an electric or magnetic effect by a field of force —**in·duc'tive** *adj.*

**in·due** (in dōō') *vt.* **-dued', -du'ing** *same as* ENDUE

**in·dulge** (in dulj') *vt.* **-dulged', -dulg'ing** [L. *indulgere*, be kind to] 1. to satisfy (a desire) 2. to gratify the wishes of; humor —*vi.* to give way to one's desires —**in·dulg'er** *n.*

**in·dul·gence** (in dul'jəns) *n.* 1. an indulging or being indulgent 2. a thing indulged in 3. a favor or privilege 4. *R.C.Ch.* a remission of punishment still due for a sin after the guilt has been forgiven

**in·dul·gent** *adj.* indulging or inclined to indulge; kind or lenient, often to excess —**in·dul'gent·ly** *adv.*

**in·dus·tri·al** (in dus'trē əl) *adj.* having to do with industries or with the people working in industries —**in·dus'tri·al·ly** *adv.*

**industrial arts** the mechanical and technical skills used in industry

**in·dus·tri·al·ism** *n.* social and economic organization characterized by large industries, machine production, urban workers, etc.

**in·dus·tri·al·ist** *n.* one who owns or manages an industrial enterprise

**in·dus·tri·al·ize** (-ə līz') *vt.* **-ized', -iz'ing** 1. to establish or develop industrialism in 2. to organize as an industry —**in·dus'tri·al·i·za'tion** *n.*

**industrial park** an area zoned for industrial and business use, usually on the outskirts of a city

**in·dus·tri·ous** (in dus'trē əs) *adj.* hard-working; diligent —**in·dus'tri·ous·ly** *adv.* —**in·dus'tri·ous·ness** *n.*

**in·dus·try** (in'dəs trē) *n., pl.* **-tries** [< L. *industrius*, active] 1. earnest, steady effort 2. any branch of productive, manufacturing enterprise, or all of these collectively 3. any large-scale business activity 4. the owners and managers of industry

**-ine¹** (*variously* In, in, ēn, ən) [< L. *-inus*] *a suffix meaning of*, having the nature of, like [*divine, crystalline*]

**-ine²** (in, ən) [< L. *-ina*] a suffix used to form certain abstract nouns [*medicine, doctrine*]

**-ine³** (*variously* ēn, in, ĭn, ən) [< L. *-inus*] a suffix used to form the chemical names of: 1. halogens [*iodine*] 2. alkaloids or nitrogen bases [*morphine*] Often used to form commercial names [*Vaseline*]

**in·e·bri·ate** (in ē'brē āt'; *for n.*, *usually* -it) *vt.* **-at'ed, -at'ing** [ult. < L. *in-*, intens. + *ebrius*, drunk] to make drunk; intoxicate —*n.* a drunkard —**in·e'bri·a'tion** *n.*

**in·ed·u·ca·ble** (in ej²ə kə b'l) *adj.* thought to be incapable of being educated

**in·ef·fa·ble** (in ef'ə b'l) *adj.* [< L. *in-*, not + *effabilis*, utterable] 1. inexpressible 2. too sacred to be spoken

**in·ef·fi·cient** (in'ə fish'ənt) *adj.* 1. not producing the desired effect with a minimum of energy, time, etc. 2. incapable —**in'ef·fi'cien·cy** *n.* —**in'·ef·fi'cient·ly** *adv.*

**in·el·e·gant** (in el'ə gənt) *adj.* not elegant; crude —**in·el'e·gant·ly** *adv.*

**in·e·luc·ta·ble** (in'i luk'tə b'l) *adj.* [< L. *in-*, not + *eluctari*, to struggle] not to be avoided or escaped —**in'e·luc'ta·bly** *adv.*

**in·ept** (in ept') *adj.* [< L. *in-*, not + *aptus*, apt] 1. unsuitable; unfit 2. foolish 3. awkward; clumsy —**in·ept'·i·tude** (-ep'tə tood'), **in·ept'ness** *n.*

**in·ert** (in urt') *adj.* [< L. *in-*, not + *ars*, skill] 1. without power to move or to resist 2. inactive; dull; slow 3. with few or no active properties

**in·er·tia** (in ur'shə) *n.* [see prec.] 1. *Physics* the tendency of matter to remain at rest (or continue in a fixed direction) unless affected by an outside force 2. disinclination to act —**in·er'tial** *adj.*

**in·es·cap·a·ble** (in'ə skap'ə b'l) *adj.* that cannot be escaped or avoided

**in·es·ti·ma·ble** (in es'tə mə b'l) *adj.* too great to be properly estimated

**in·ev·i·ta·ble** (in ev'ə tə b'l) *adj.* [< L. *in-*, not + *evitabilis*, avoidable] that must happen; unavoidable —**in·ev'i·ta·bil'i·ty** *n.* —**in·ev'i·ta·bly** *adv.*

**in·ex·haust·i·ble** (in'ig zôs'tə b'l) *adj.* 1. that cannot be used up or emptied 2. tireless

**in·ex·o·ra·ble** (in ek'sər ə b'l) *adj.* [< L. *in-*, not + *exorare*, move by entreaty] 1. that cannot be influenced by persuasion or entreaty; unrelenting 2. that cannot be altered, checked, etc. —**in·ex'o·ra·bly** *adv.*

**in·ex·pe·ri·ence** (in'ik spir'ē əns) *n.* lack of experience or of the knowledge or skill resulting from experience —**in'ex·pe'ri·enced** *adj.*

**in·ex·pert** (in ek'spərt, in'ik spurt') *adj.* not expert; unskillful

**in·ex·pi·a·ble** (in ek'spē ə b'l) *adj.* that cannot be expiated or atoned for

**in·ex·pli·ca·ble** (in eks'pli kə b'l) *adj.* that cannot be explained

**in·ex·press·i·ble** (in'ik spres'ə b'l) *adj.* that cannot be expressed

**in·ex·tin·guish·a·ble** (in'ik stiŋ'gwish ə b'l) *adj.* that cannot be put out or stopped

†**in ex·tre·mis** (in' ik strē'mis) [L., in extremity] at the point of death

**in·ex·tri·ca·ble** (in eks'tri kə b'l) *adj.* 1. that one cannot extricate himself from 2. that cannot be disentangled or untied 3. insolvable

**inf.** 1. infantry 2. infinitive

**in·fal·li·ble** (in fal'ə b'l) *adj.* [see IN-² & FALLIBLE] 1. incapable of error 2. dependable; reliable —**in·fal'li·bil'i·ty** *n.* —**in·fal'li·bly** *adv.*

**in·fa·mous** (in'fə məs) *adj.* 1. having a bad reputation; notorious 2. causing a bad reputation; scandalous

**in'fa·my** (-mē) *n., pl.* -**mies** 1. very bad reputation; disgrace 2. great wickedness 3. an infamous act

**in·fan·cy** (in'fən sē) *n., pl.* -**cies** 1. the state or period of being an infant 2. the earliest stage of anything

**in·fant** (in'fənt) *n.* [< L. *in-*, not + *fari*, speak] a very young child; baby —*adj.* 1. of or for infants 2. in a very early stage

**in·fan·ti·cide** (in fan'tə sīd') *n.* 1. the murder of a baby 2. a person guilty of this

**in·fan·tile** (in'fən tīl', -til) *adj.* 1. of infants 2. like an infant; babyish

**infantile paralysis** poliomyelitis

**in·fan·try** (in'fən trē) *n., pl.* -**tries** [< It. *infante*, a youth] that branch of an army consisting of soldiers trained to fight on foot —**in'fan·try·man** (-mən) *n., pl.* -**men**

**in·farct** (in färkt') *n.* [< L. *in-*, in + *farcire*, to stuff] an area of dying or dead tissue caused by obstruction of blood vessels: also **in·farc'tion** (-färk'shən)

**in·fat·u·ate** (in fach'oo wāt') *vt.* -**at'ed**, -**at'ing** [< L. *in-*, intens. + *fatuus*, foolish] to inspire with foolish love or affection —**in·fat'u·a'tion** *n.*

**in·fect** (in fekt') *vt.* [< L. *inficere*, to stain] 1. to contaminate, or cause to become diseased, with a germ or virus 2. to imbue with one's feelings or beliefs, esp. so as to harm

**in·fec·tion** (in fek'shən) *n.* 1. an infecting or being infected 2. an infectious disease

**in·fec·tious** (-shəs) *adj.* 1. likely to cause infection 2. designating a disease caused by the presence in the body of certain microorganisms 3. tending to spread to others —**in·fec'·tious·ly** *adv.* —**in·fec'tious·ness** *n.*

**in·fe·lic·i·tous** (in'fə lis'ə təs) *adj.* not felicitous; unsuitable; not apt —**in'fe·lic'i·ty** *n., pl.* -**ties**

**in·fer** (in fur') *vt.* -**ferred'**, -**fer'ring** [< L. *in-*, in + *ferre*, bring] 1. to conclude by reasoning from something known or assumed 2. to imply: still sometimes regarded as a loose usage —**in'fer·ence** *n.*

**in·fer·en·tial** (in'fə ren'shəl) *adj.* based on or relating to inference

**in·fe·ri·or** (in fir'ē ər) *adj.* [< L. *inferus*, low] 1. lower in space 2. lower in order, status, quality, etc. (with *to*) 3. poor in quality; below average —*n.* an inferior person or thing —**in·fe'ri·or'i·ty** (-ôr'ə tē) *n.*

**in·fer·nal** (in fur'n'l) *adj.* [< L. *inferus*, below] 1. of hell or Hades 2. hellish; fiendish

**in·fer·no** (in fur'nō) *n., pl.* -**nos** [It. < L.: see prec.] *same as* HELL

**in·fest** (in fest') *vt.* [< L. *infestus*, hostile] 1. to overrun in large numbers, usually so as to be harmful 2. to be parasitic in or on —**in'fes·ta'·tion** *n.* —**in·fest'er** *n.*

**in·fi·del** (in'fə d'l) *n.* [< L. *in-*, not + *fidelis*, faithful] 1. one who does not believe in a certain religion 2. one who has no religion

**in·fi·del·i·ty** (in'fə del'ə tē) *n.* unfaithfulness, esp. in marriage

**in·field** (in′fēld′) *n.* **1.** the area enclosed by the four base lines on a baseball field **2.** the players (**infielders**) whose field positions are there

**in′fight′ing** *n.* **1.** fighting, esp. boxing at close range **2.** personal conflict within a group —**in′fight′er** *n.*

**in·fil·trate** (in fil′trāt, in′fil trāt′) *vi., vt.* **-trat·ed, -trat·ing 1.** to filter or pass gradually through or into **2.** to penetrate (enemy lines, a region, etc.) gradually or stealthily, so as to attack or seize control from within —**in′fil·tra′tion** *n.* —**in′fil·tra′tor** *n.*

**in·fi·nite** (in′fə nit) *adj.* [see IN-² & FINITE] **1.** lacking limits; endless **2.** very great; vast —*n.* something infinite —**in′fi·nite·ly** *adv.*

**in·fin·i·tes·i·mal** (in′fin ə tes′ə məl) *adj.* [< L. *infinitus*, infinite] too small to be measured; very minute —**in′fin·i·tes′i·mal·ly** *adv.*

**in·fin·i·tive** (in fin′ə tiv) *n.* [see INFINITE] the form of a verb without reference to person, number, or tense: usually with *to*, as in "I want to go"

**in·fin′i·tude** (-tōōd′) *n.* **1.** a being infinite **2.** an infinite quantity or extent

**in·fin′i·ty** (-tē) *n., pl.* **-ties** [< L. *infinitas*] **1.** the quality of being infinite **2.** unlimited space, time, etc. **3.** an indefinitely large quantity

**in·firm** (in furm′) *adj.* **1.** weak; feeble **2.** not firm; unstable; frail; shaky — **in·firm′ly** *adv.* —**in·firm′ness** *n.*

**in·fir·ma·ry** (in fur′mə rē) *n., pl.* **-ries** a place for the care of the sick, injured, or infirm; hospital

**in·fir′mi·ty** (-mə tē) *n., pl.* **-ties** physical weakness or defect

**in·flame** (in flām′) *vt., vi.* **-flamed′, -flam′ing** [see IN-¹ & FLAME] **1.** to arouse, excite, etc. or become aroused, excited, etc. **2.** to undergo or cause to undergo inflammation

**in·flam·ma·ble** (in flam′ə b'l) *adj.* **1.** *same as* FLAMMABLE **2.** easily excited —**in·flam′ma·bil′i·ty** *n.*

**in·flam·ma·tion** (in′flə mā′shən) *n.* **1.** an inflaming or being inflamed **2.** redness, pain, heat, and swelling in some part of the body, caused by injury or disease

**in·flam·ma·to·ry** (in flam′ə tôr′ē) *adj.* **1.** rousing excitement, anger, etc. **2.** of or caused by inflammation

**in·flate** (in flāt′) *vt.* **-flat′ed, -flat′ing** [< L. *in-*, in + *flare*, blow] **1.** to blow full with air or gas **2.** to puff up with pride **3.** to increase beyond what is normal; specif., to cause inflation of (money, credit, etc.) —*vi.* to become inflated —**in·flat′a·ble** *adj.*

**in·fla′tion** *n.* **1.** an inflating or being inflated **2.** an increase in the currency in circulation or a marked expansion of credit, resulting in a fall in currency value and a sharp rise in prices —**in·fla′tion·ar′y** *adj.*

**in·flect** (in flekt′) *vt.* [< L. *in-*, in + *flectere*, to bend] **1.** to vary the tone of (the voice) **2.** to change the form of (a word) by inflection

**in·flec·tion** (in flek′shən) *n.* **1.** a change in the tone of the voice **2.** the change of form in a word to indicate number, case, tense, etc. Brit. sp. **inflexion** —**in·flec′tion·al** *adj.*

**in·flex·i·ble** (in flek′sə b'l) *adj.* not flexible; stiff, rigid, fixed, unyielding, etc. —**in·flex′i·bil′i·ty** *n.*

**in·flict** (in flikt′) *vt.* [< L. *in-*, on + *fligere*, to strike] **1.** to cause (wounds, pain, etc.) as by striking **2.** to impose (a punishment, etc. on or upon) —**in·flic′tion** *n.* —**in·flic′tive** *adj.*

**in·flight** (in′flīt′) *adj.* done, shown, etc. while an aircraft is in flight

**in·flo·res·cence** (in′flô res′'ns) *n.* **1.** the producing of blossoms **2.** the arrangement of flowers on a stem **3.** a flower cluster **4.** flowers collectively

**in·flu·ence** (in′floo wəns) *n.* [< L. *in-*, in + *fluere*, to flow] **1.** power to affect others **2.** power to produce effects because of wealth, position, ability, etc. **3.** one that has influence —*vt.* **-enced, -enc·ing** to have influence or effect on

**in′flu·en′tial** (-wen′shəl) *adj.* exerting influence, esp. great influence

**in·flu·en·za** (in′floo wen′zə) *n.* [It., an influence] an acute, contagious virus infection, characterized by inflammation of the respiratory tract, fever, muscular pain, etc.

**in·flux** (in′fluks′) *n.* [see INFLUENCE] a flowing in or streaming in

**in·fold** (in fōld′) *vt. same as* ENFOLD

**in·form** (in fôrm′) *vt.* [see IN-¹ & FORM] **1.** to give knowledge of something to —*vi.* to give information, esp. in accusing another —**in·form′er** *n.*

**in·for·mal** (in fôr′məl) *adj.* not formal; specif., *a)* not according to fixed customs, rules, etc. *b)* casual, relaxed, etc. *c)* not requiring formal dress *d)* colloquial —**in′for·mal′i·ty** (-mal′ə tē) *n., pl.* **-ties** —**in·for′mal·ly** *adv.*

**in·form·ant** (in fôr′mənt), *n.* a person who gives information

**in·for·ma·tion** (in′fər mā′shən) *n.* **1.** an informing or being informed **2.** something told or facts learned; news or knowledge **3.** data stored in or retrieved from a computer

**in·for·ma·tive** (in fôr′mə tiv) *adj.* giving information; instructive

**infra-** [< L.] *a prefix meaning* below

**in·frac·tion** (in frak′shən) *n.* [see INFRINGE] a violation of a law, pact, etc.

**in·fran·gi·ble** (in fran′jə b'l) *adj.* [see IN-² & FRANGIBLE] unbreakable or inviolable —**in·fran′gi·bly** *adv.*

**in·fra·red** (in′frə red′) *adj.* designating or of those invisible rays just beyond the red of the visible spectrum: they have a penetrating heating effect

**in′fra·struc′ture** (-struk′chər) *n.* basic installations and facilities, as roads, power plants, transportation and communication systems, etc.

**in·fre·quent** (in frē′kwənt) *adj.* not frequent; happening seldom; rare — **in·fre′quen·cy, in·fre′quence** *n.* —**in·fre′quent·ly** *adv.*

**in·fringe** (in frinj′) *vt.* **-fringed′, -fring′ing** [< L. *in-*, in + *frangere*, to break] to break (a law or pact) —**infringe on** (or **upon**) to encroach on (the rights, etc. of others) —**in·fringe′ment** *n.*

**in·fu·ri·ate** (in fyoor′ē āt′) *vt.* **-at′ed, -at′ing** [< L. *in-*, in + *furia*, rage] to make very angry; enrage

**in·fuse** (in fyōōz′) *vt.* **-fused′, -fus′ing** [< L. *in-*, in + *fundere*, pour] **1.** to instill or impart (qualities, etc.) **2.** to fill; inspire **3.** to steep (tea leaves, etc.) to extract the essence —**in·fus′er** *n.* —**in·fu′sion** *n.*

**-ing** (iŋ) [< OE.] a suffix used to form the present participle or verbal nouns [*talking, painting*]

**in·gen·ious** (in jēn′yəs) *adj.* [< L. *in-*, in + *gignere*, to produce] **1.** clever, resourceful, etc. **2.** made or done in a clever or original way —**in·gen′ious·ly** *adv.*

**in·gé·nue** (an′zhə nōō′, -jə-) *n.* [Fr., ingenuous] *Theater* the role of an inexperienced young woman, or an actress in this role

**in·ge·nu·i·ty** (in′jə nōō′ə tē) *n.* ingenious quality; cleverness

**in·gen·u·ous** (in jen′yoo wəs) *adj.* [< L. *in-*, in + *gignere*, to produce] **1.** frank; open **2.** simple; naive — **in·gen′u·ous·ly** *adv.* —**in·gen′u·ous·ness** *n.*

**in·gest** (in jest′) *vt.* [< L. *in-*, into + *gerere*, carry] to take (food, etc.) into the body —**in·ges′tion** *n.*

**in·glo·ri·ous** (in glôr′ē əs) *adj.* shameful; disgraceful

**in·got** (iŋ′gət) *n.* [prob. < OFr. *lingo*, tongue] a mass of metal cast into a bar or other convenient shape

**in·grained** (in grānd′) *adj.* **1.** firmly established, as habits **2.** inveterate [*an ingrained bias*]

**in·grate** (in′grāt) *n.* [< L. *in-*, not + *gratus*, grateful] an ungrateful person

**in·gra·ti·ate** (in grā′shē āt′) *vt.*-at′ed, -at′ing [< L. *in*, in + *gratia*, favor] to bring (oneself) into another's favor —**in·gra′ti·a′tion** *n.*

**in·grat·i·tude** (in grat′ə tōōd″) *n.* lack of gratitude; ungratefulness

**in·gre·di·ent** (in grē′dē ənt) *n.* [see ff.] any of the things that make up a mixture; component

**in·gress** (in′gres) *n.* [< L. *in-*, into + *gradi*, to go] entrance

**in·grown** (in′grōn′) *adj.* grown inward, esp. into the flesh, as a toenail

**in·gui·nal** (iŋ′gwə n′l) *adj.* [< L. *inguen*, groin] of or near the groin

**in·hab·it** (in hab′it) *vt.* [< L. *in-*, *habitare*, dwell] to live in —**in·hab′it·a·ble** *adj.*

**in·hab·it·ant** (-i tənt) *n.* a person or animal inhabiting a specified place

**in·hal·ant** (in hāl′ənt) *n.* a medicine, etc. to be inhaled

**in·ha·la·tor** (in′hə lāt′ər) *n.* **1.** an apparatus used in inhaling medicinal vapors **2.** *same as* RESPIRATOR (sense 2)

**in·hale** (in hāl′) *vt., vi.* **-haled′, -hal′ing** [< L. *in-*, in + *halare*, breathe] to breathe in (air or smoke) —**in·ha·la·tion** (in′hə lā′shən) *n.*

**in·hal·er** (-ər) *n.* **1.** one who inhales **2.** *same as* RESPIRATOR (sense 1) **3.** *same as* INHALATOR (sense 1)

**in·here** (in hir′) *vi.* **-hered′, -her′ing** [< L. *in-*, in + *haerere*, to stick] to be inherent

**in·her·ent** (in hir′ənt, -her′-) *adj.* existing in someone or something as a natural and inseparable quality

**in·her·it** (in her′it) *vt., vi.* [< L. *in*, in + *heres*, heir] **1.** to receive (property, etc.) as an heir **2.** to have (certain characteristics) by heredity

**in·her′it·ance** *n.* **1.** the action of inheriting **2.** something inherited

**in·hib·it** (in hib′it) *vt.* [< L. *in-*, in + *habere*, to hold] to check or repress

**in·hi·bi·tion** (in′hi bish′ən, in′ə-) *n.* **1.** an inhibiting or being inhibited **2.** a mental process that restrains an action, emotion, or thought

**in·hu·man** (in hyōō′mən) *adj.* not having worthy human characteristics; heartless, cruel, brutal, etc. —**in′hu·man′i·ty** (-man′ə tē) *n.*

**in·im·i·cal** (in im′i k′l) *adj.* [< L. *in-*, not + *amicus*, friend] **1.** hostile; unfriendly **2.** in opposition; adverse

**in·im·i·ta·ble** (in im′ə tə b′l) *adj.* that cannot be imitated; matchless

**in·iq·ui·ty** (in ik′wə tē) *n.* [< L. *in-*, not + *aequus*, equal] **1.** wickedness **2.** *pl.* **-ties** a wicked or unjust act —**in·iq′ui·tous** *adj.*

**in·i·tial** (i nish′əl) *adj.* [< L. *in-*, in + *ire*, go] of or at the beginning; first —*n.* the first letter of a name —*vt.* **-tialed** or **-tialled, -tial·ing** or **-tial·ling** to mark with initials —**in·i′tial·ly** *adv.*

**in·i·ti·ate** (i nish′ē āt′) *vt.* **-at′ed, -at′ing** [see prec.] **1.** to bring into practice or use **2.** to teach the fundamentals of a subject to **3.** to admit as a member into a fraternity, club, etc., esp. with a special or secret ceremony —**in·i′ti·a′tion** *n.* —**in·i′ti·a·to′ry** (-ə tôr′ē) *adj.*

**in·i·ti·a·tive** (i nish′ē ə tiv, -nish′ə-) *n.* **1.** the action of taking the first step or move **2.** ability in originating new ideas or methods **3.** the introduction of proposed legislation, as to popular vote, by voters′ petitions

**in·ject** (in jekt′) *vt.* [< L. *in-*, in + *jacere*, to throw] **1.** to force (a fluid) into a vein, tissue, etc. with a syringe or the like **2.** to introduce (a remark, quality, etc.) —**in·jec′tion** *n.* —**in·jec′tor** *n.*

**in·junc·tion** (in juŋk′shən) *n.* [< L. *in-*, in + *jungere*, join] **1.** a command; order **2.** a court order prohibiting or ordering a given action

**in·jure** (in′jər) *vt.* **-jured, -jur·ing** [see INJURY] **1.** to do harm or damage to; hurt **2.** to wrong or offend

**in·ju·ri·ous** (in joor′ē əs) *adj.* injuring or likely to injure; harmful

**in·ju·ry** (in′jər ē) *n., pl.* **-ries** [< L.

*in-*, not + *jus*, right] 1. harm or damage 2. an injurious act

**in·jus·tice** (in jus'tis) *n.* 1. a being unjust 2. an unjust act; wrong

**ink** (iŋk) *n.* [< Gr. *en-*, in + *kaiein*, to burn] a colored liquid used for writing, printing, etc. —*vt.* to cover, mark, or color with ink

**ink'blot'** *n.* any of the patterns made by blots of ink that are used in the RORSCHACH TEST

**ink·ling** (iŋk'liŋ) *n.* [ME. *ingkiling*] 1. a hint 2. a vague notion

**ink'well'** *n.* a container for ink

**ink'y** *adj.* **-i·er, -i·est** 1. like very dark ink in color; black 2. covered with ink —**ink'i·ness** *n.*

**in·laid** (in'lād', in lād') *adj.* set into a surface or formed, decorated, etc. by inlaying

**in·land** (in'lənd; *for n. & adv. usually* -land') *adj.* of or in the interior of a country —*n.* inland region —*adv.* into or toward this region

**in-law** (in'lô') *n.* [< (MOTHER)-IN-LAW, etc.] [Colloq.] a relative by marriage

INLAID WOOD

**in·lay** (in'lā'; *for v., also* in lā') *vt.* **-laid', -lay'ing** 1. to set (pieces of wood, etc.) into a surface, specif. for decoration 2. to decorate thus —*n., pl.* **-lays'** 1. inlaid decoration or material 2. a shaped filling, as of gold, cemented into the cavity of a tooth

**in·let** (in'let) *n.* a narrow strip of water extending into a body of land

**in·mate** (in'māt') *n.* a person confined with others in a prison or institution

**in·most** (in'mōst') *adj.* 1. farthest within 2. most secret

**inn** (in) *n.* [OE.] 1. a small hotel 2. a restaurant or tavern Now usually only in the names of such places

**in·nards** (in'ərdz) *n.pl.* [< INWARDS] [Colloq.] inner organs or parts

**in·nate** (i nāt', in'āt) *adj.* [< L. *in-*, in + *nasci*, be born] inborn; natural

**in·ner** (in'ər) *adj.* 1. farther within 2. more secret

**inner circle** the small, exclusive, most influential part of a group

**inner city** the crowded or blighted central sections of a large city

**in'ner·most'** *adj. same as* INMOST

**in'ner·sole'** *n. same as* INSOLE

**in'ner·spring' mattress** a mattress with built-in coil springs

**in·ner·vate** (i nur'vāt, in'ər vāt') *vt.* **-vat·ed, -vat·ing** 1. to supply (a part) with nerves 2. to stimulate (a muscle, etc.) —**in'ner·va'tion** *n.*

**in·ning** (in'iŋ) *n.* [< OE. *innung*, getting in] *Baseball & (pl.) Cricket* 1. a team's turn at bat 2. a numbered round of play in which both teams have a turn at bat

**inn'keep'er** *n.* the owner of an inn

**in·no·cent** (in'ə sənt) *adj.* [< L. *in-*, not + *nocere*, to harm] 1. free from sin, evil, etc.; specif., not guilty of a specific crime 2. harmless 3. knowing no evil 4. without guile —*n.* an innocent person, as a child —**in'no·cence** *n.* —**in'no·cent·ly** *adv.*

**in·noc·u·ous** (i näk'yoo wəs) *adj.* [see prec.] harmless —**in·noc'u·ous·ly** *adv.* —**in·noc'u·ous·ness** *n.*

**in·no·va·tion** (in'ə vā'shən) *n.* [< L. *in-*, in + *novus*, new] 1. the process of making changes 2. a new method, custom, device, etc. —**in'no·vate' vi.,** *vt.* **-vat·ed, -vat·ing** —**in'no·va'tor** *n.*

**in·nu·en·do** (in'yoo wen'dō) *n., pl.* **-does, -dos** [L. < *in-*, in + *nuere*, to nod] a hint or sly remark, usually derogatory; insinuation

**in·nu·mer·a·ble** (i noo'mər ə b'l) *adj.* too numerous to be counted

**in·oc·u·late** (in äk'yoo lāt') *vt.* **-lat·ed, -lat·ing** [< L. *in-*, in + *oculus*, eye] to inject a serum or vaccine into, esp. in order to create immunity — **in·oc'u·la'tion** *n.*

**in·of·fen·sive** (in'ə fen'siv) *adj.* causing no harm or annoyance; unobjectionable —**in'of·fen'sive·ly** *adv.*

**in·op·er·a·tive** (in äp'ər ə tiv, -ə rāt'iv) *adj.* not working or functioning

**in·or·di·nate** (in ôr'd'n it) *adj.* [< L. *in-*, not + *ordo*, an order] excessive; immoderate —**in·or'di·nate·ly** *adv.*

**in·or·gan·ic** (in'ôr gan'ik) *adj.* not organic; specif., designating or of matter not animal or vegetable; not living

**in·put** (in'poot') *n.* what is put in, as power into a machine, information into a computer, etc.

**in·quest** (in'kwest) *n.* [see ff.] a judicial inquiry, esp. before a jury, as a coroner's investigation of a death

**in·qui·e·tude** (in kwī'ə tōōd', -tyōōd') *n.* restlessness; uneasiness

**in·quire** (in kwīr') *vi.* **-quired', -quir'ing** [< L. *in-*, into + *quaerere*, seek] 1. to ask a question or questions 2. to investigate (usually with *into*) —*vt.* to seek information about

**in·quir·y** (in'kwə rē, in kwīr'ē) *n., pl.* **-ies** 1. an inquiring; investigation 2. a question

**in·qui·si·tion** (in'kwə zish'ən) *n.* 1. an investigation or inquest 2. [I-] *R.C.Ch.* formerly, the tribunal for suppressing heresy and heretics 3. any relentless questioning or harsh suppression —**in·quis'i'tor** *n.*

**in·quis·i·tive** (in kwiz'ə tiv) *adj.* 1. inclined to ask many questions 2. unnecessarily curious; prying —**in·quis'i·tive·ness** *n.*

**in re** (in rē, rā) [L.] in the matter (of); concerning

**in-res'i·dence** *adj.* having specific duties, often as a teacher, but given time to work at one's profession

**in·road** (in'rōd') *n.* 1. a raid 2. [*usually pl.*] any injurious encroachment

**in·sane** (in sān′) *adj.* 1. not sane; mentally ill or deranged 2. of or for insane people 3. very foolish —**in·sane′ly** *adv.* —**in·san′i·ty** (-san′ə tē) *n.*

**in·sa·ti·a·ble** (in sā′shə b′l, -shē ə-) *adj.* [see IN-² & SATIATE] that cannot be satisfied —**in·sa′ti·a·bly** *adv.*

**in·scribe** (in skrīb′) *vt.* -**scribed′**, -**scrib′ing** [< L. *in-*, in + *scribere*, write] 1. to mark or engrave (words, etc.) on (a surface) 2. to add (a person's name) to a list 3. *a)* to dedicate (a book, etc.) to someone *b)* to autograph 4. to fix in the mind —**in·scrip′tion** (-skrip′shən) *n.*

**in·scru·ta·ble** (in skrōōt′ə b′l) *adj.* [< L. *in-*, not + *scrutari*, examine] not easily understood; enigmatic —**in·scru′ta·bly** *adv.*

**in·seam** (in′sēm′) *n.* an inner seam; specif., the seam from the crotch to the bottom of a trouser leg

**in·sect** (in′sekt) *n.* [< L. *insectum*, lit., notched] any of a large class of small, usually winged, invertebrates, as beetles, flies, wasps, etc., having three pairs of legs

**in·sec·ti·cide** (in sek′tə sīd′) *n.* any substance used to kill insects —**in·sec′ti·cid′al** *adj.*

**in·sec·tiv·o·rous** (-tiv′ər əs) *adj.* [< INSECT + L. *vorare*, devour] feeding chiefly on insects

**in·se·cure** (in′si kyoor′) *adj.* 1. not safe 2. feeling anxiety 3. not firm or dependable —**in′se·cure′ly** *adv.* —**in′se·cu′ri·ty** *n.*

**in·sem·i·nate** (in sem′ə nāt′) *vt.* -**nat′ed**, -**nat′ing** [< L. *in-*, in + *semen*, seed] 1. to fertilize; impregnate 2. to imbue (with ideas, etc.) —**in·sem′i·na′tion** *n.*

**in·sen·sate** (in sen′sāt, -sit) *adj.* 1. not feeling sensation 2. stupid 3. without regard or feeling; cold

**in·sen·si·ble** (in sen′sə b′l) *adj.* 1. unable to perceive with the senses 2. unconscious 3. unaware; indifferent 4. so slight as to be virtually imperceptible —**in·sen′si·bil′i·ty** *n.*

**in·sen·si·tive** (-sə tiv) *adj.* not sensitive; not responsive —**in·sen′si·tive·ly** *adv.* —**in·sen′si·tiv′i·ty** *n.*

**in·sen·ti·ent** (in sen′shē ənt, -shənt) *adj.* not sentient; without life or consciousness —**in·sen′ti·ence** *n.*

**in·sert** (in surt′; *for n.* in′sərt) *vt.* [< L. *in-*, in + *serere*, join] to put or fit (something) into something else —*n.* anything inserted or to be inserted —**in·ser′tion** *n.*

**in·set** (in set′; *for n.* in′set) *vt.* -**set′**, -**set′ting** to set in; insert —*n.* something inserted

**in·shore** (in′shôr′, in shôr′) *adv.*, *adj.* near or in toward the shore

**in·side** (in′sīd′, in′sīd′; *for prep. & adv. usually* in sīd′) *n.* 1. the inner side, surface, or part 2. [*pl.*] [Colloq.] the viscera —*adj.* 1. internal 2. known only to insiders; secret —*adv.* 1. on or in the inside; within 2. indoors —*prep.* in or within —**inside of** within the space or time of —**inside out** 1. reversed 2. [Colloq.] thoroughly

**in·sid·er** *n.* 1. a person inside a given place or group 2. one having secret or confidential information

**in·sid·i·ous** (in sid′ē əs) *adj.* [< L. *insidiae*, an ambush] 1. characterized by treachery or slyness 2. more dangerous than seems evident

**in·sight** (in′sīt′) *n.* 1. the ability to see and understand clearly the inner nature of things, esp. by intuition 2. an instance of such understanding

**in·sig·ni·a** (in sig′nē ə) *n.pl., sing.* -**sig′ni·a, -sig′ne** (-nē) [ult. < L. *in-*, in + *signum*, a mark] distinguishing marks, as emblems of rank, membership, etc.

**in·sin·cere** (in′sin sir′) *adj.* not sincere; deceptive or hypocritical —**in′sin·cer′i·ty** (-ser′ə tē) *n.*

**in·sin·u·ate** (in sin′yoo wāt′) *vt.* -**at′ed, -at′ing** [< L. *in-*, in + *sinus*, a curve] 1. to work in or introduce slowly, indirectly, etc. 2. to hint or suggest indirectly; imply —**in·sin′u·a′tion** *n.* —**in·sin′u·a′tor** *n.*

**in·sip·id** (in sip′id) *adj.* [< L. *in-*, not + *sapidus*, savory] 1. without flavor; tasteless 2. not exciting; dull

**in·sist** (in sist′) *vi.* [< L. *in-*, on + *sistere*, to stand] to take and maintain a stand (often with *on* or *upon*) —*vt.* 1. to demand strongly 2. to declare firmly —**in·sist′ing·ly** *adv.*

**in·sist·ent** *adj.* insisting or demanding —**in·sist′ence** *n.*

**in si·tu** (in sī′tōō) [L.] in position; in its original place

**in·so·far** (in′sə fär′) *adv.* to such a degree or extent (usually with *as*)

**in·sole** (in′sōl′) *n.* 1. the inside sole of a shoe 2. a removable sole put inside a shoe for comfort

INSOLE

**in·so·lent** (in′sə lənt) *adj.* [< L. *in-*, not + *solere*, be accustomed] boldly disrespectful; impudent —**in′so·lence** *n.*

**in·sol·u·ble** (in säl′yoo b′l) *adj.* 1. that cannot be solved 2. that cannot be dissolved —**in·sol′u·bil′i·ty** *n.*

**in·sol·vent** (in säl′vənt) *adj.* not solvent; unable to pay debts; bankrupt —**in·sol′ven·cy** *n.*

**in·som·ni·a** (in säm′nē ə) *n.* [< L. *in-*, without + *somnus*, sleep] abnormal inability to sleep —**in·som′ni·ac′** (-ak′) *n.*

**in·so·much** (in′sō much′) *adv.* 1. to such an extent (*that*) 2. inasmuch (*as*)

**in·sou·ci·ant** (in sōō′sē ənt) *adj.* [Fr. < *in-*, not + *soucier*, to care] calm and unbothered; carefree

**in·spect** (in spekt′) *vt.* [< L. *in-*, at + *specere*, look at] 1. to look at carefully 2. to examine or review officially —**in·spec′tion** *n.*

**in·spec·tor** *n.* 1. one who inspects 2. an officer on a police force, ranking next below a superintendent

**in·spi·ra·tion** (in′spə rā′shən) *n.* 1. an inhaling 2. an inspiring or being inspired mentally or emotionally 3. *a)* any stimulus to creative thought or action *b)* an inspired idea, action, etc. —**in·spi·ra′tion·al** *adj.*

**in·spire** (in spīr′) *vt.* **-spired′, -spir′-ing** [< L. *in-*, in + *spirare*, breathe] 1. to inhale 2. to stimulate or impel, as to some creative effort 3. to motivate by divine influence 4. to arouse (a thought or feeling) in (someone) 5. to occasion or cause —*vi.* 1. to inhale 2. to give inspiration

**in·spir·it** (in spir′it) *vt.* to put spirit into; cheer; hearten

**Inst.** 1. Institute 2. Institution

**in·sta·bil·i·ty** (in′stə bil′ə tē) *n.* lack of firmness, determination, etc.

**in·stall, in·stal** (in stôl′) *vt.* **-stalled′, -stall′ing** [< ML. *in-*, in + *stallum*, a place] 1. to place in an office, rank, etc. with formality 2. to establish in a place 3. to fix in position for use [*to install* new fixtures] —**in·stal·la·tion** (in′stə lā′shən) *n.* —**in·stall′er** *n.*

**in·stall·ment, in·stal·ment** *n.* 1. an installing or being installed 2. any of the parts of a sum of money to be paid at regular specified times 3. any of several parts, as of a serial

**installment plan** a system by which debts, as for purchased articles, are paid in installments

**in·stance** (in′stəns) *n.* [see ff.] 1. an example; case 2. a step in proceeding; occasion [*in the first instance*] —*vt.* **-stanced, -stanc·ing** to give as an example; cite —**at the instance of** at the suggestion or instigation of

**in·stant** (in′stənt) *adj.* [< L. *in-*, upon + *stare*, to stand] 1. urgent; pressing 2. of the current month: an old usage [*your letter of the 8th instant*] 3. imminent 4. immediate 5. concentrated or precooked for quick preparation, as a food or beverage —*n.* 1. a moment 2. a particular moment —**the instant** as soon as

**in·stan·ta·ne·ous** (in′stən tā′nē əs) *adj.* done or happening in an instant —**in′stan·ta′ne·ous·ly** *adv.*

**in·stan·ter** (in stan′tər) *adv.* [L.] immediately

**in′stant·ly** *adv.* immediately

**in·state** (in stāt′) *vt.* **-stat′ed, -stat′-ing** [IN-¹ + STATE] to put in a particular rank, etc. [install]

**in·stead** (in sted′) *adv.* [IN + STEAD] in place of the one mentioned —**instead of** in place of

**in·step** (in′step′) *n.* the upper part of the arch of the foot, between the ankle and the toes

**in·sti·gate** (in′stə gāt′) *vt.* **-gat′ed, -gat′ing** [< L. *in-*, on + *stigare*, to prick] 1. to urge on to some action 2. to foment (rebellion, etc.) —**in′sti·ga′tion** *n.* —**in′sti·ga′tor** *n.*

**in·still, in·stil** (in stil′) *vt.* **-stilled′, -still′ing** [< L. *in-*, in + *stilla*, a drop] 1. to put in drop by drop 2. to

put (an idea, etc.) in or into gradually

**in·stinct** (in′stiŋkt) *n.* [< L. *instinguere*, impel] 1. (an) inborn tendency to behave in a way characteristic of a species 2. a natural or acquired tendency; knack —**in·stinc′tive** *adj.* —**in·stinc′tu·al** *adj.*

**in·sti·tute** (in′stə tōōt′) *vt.* **-tut′ed, -tut′ing** [< L. *in-*, in + *statuere*, set up] 1. to set up; establish 2. to start; initiate —*n.* something instituted; specif., *a)* an organization for the promotion of art, science, etc. *b)* a school or college specializing in some field —**in′sti·tut′er, in′sti·tu′tor** *n.*

**in·sti·tu′tion** (-tōō′shən) *n.* 1. an instituting or being instituted 2. an established law, custom, etc. 3. *a)* an organization having a social, educational, or religious purpose *b)* the building housing it 4. [Colloq.] a person or thing long established in a place —**in′sti·tu′tion·al** *adj.*

**in′sti·tu′tion·al·ize′** (-īz′) *vt.* **-ized′, -iz′ing** 1. to make into an institution 2. to make institutional 3. to place in an institution, as for treatment —**in′-sti·tu′tion·al·i·za′tion** *n.*

**in·struct** (in strukt′) *vt.* [< L. *in-*, in + *struere*, pile up] 1. to teach; educate 2. to inform 3. to order or direct

**in·struc′tion** (-struk′shən) *n.* 1. an instructing; education 2. something taught 3. [*pl.*] orders or directions

**in·struc′tive** *adj.* giving knowledge

**in·struc′tor** *n.* 1. a teacher 2. a college teacher of the lowest rank

**in·stru·ment** (in′strə mənt) *n.* [see INSTRUCT] 1. a thing by means of which something is done; means 2. a tool or implement 3. any of various devices for indicating, measuring, controlling, etc. 4. any of various devices producing musical sound 5. *Law* a formal document

**in′stru·men′tal** (-men′t'l) *adj.* 1. serving as a means; helpful 2. of, performed on, or written for a musical instrument or instruments

**in′stru·men′tal·ist** *n.* a person who performs on musical instruments

**in′stru·men·tal′i·ty** (-tal′ə tē) *n.*, *pl.* **-ties** a means; agency

**in′stru·men·ta′tion** (-tā′shən) *n.* 1. the writing or scoring of music for instruments 2. use of or equipment with instruments

**instrument flying** the flying of an aircraft by instruments only

**in·sub·or·di·nate** (in′sə bôr′d'n it) *adj.* not submitting to authority; disobedient —**in′sub·or′di·na′tion** *n.*

**in·sub·stan·tial** (in′səb stan′shəl) *adj.* not substantial; specif., *a)* unreal; imaginary *b)* weak or flimsy

**in·suf·fer·a·ble** (in suf′ər ə b'l) *adj.* not sufferable; intolerable; unbearable

**in·su·lar** (in′sə lər) *adj.* [< L. *insula*, island] 1. of or like an island or islanders 2. narrow-minded; illiberal

**in′su·late′** (-lāt′) *vt.* **-lat′ed, -lat′ing**

[ < L. *insula*, island] **1.** to set apart; isolate **2.** to cover with a nonconducting material in order to prevent the escape of electricity, heat, sound, etc. —**in′su·la′tor** *n.*

**in·su·la′tion** *n.* **1.** an insulating or being insulated **2.** material for this

**in·su·lin** (in′sə lin) *n.* [ < L. *insula*, island] **1.** a hormone vital to carbohydrate metabolism, secreted by islets of tissue in the pancreas **2.** an extract from the pancreas of sheep, oxen, etc., used in the treatment of diabetes

**in·sult** (in sult′; *for n.* in′sult) *vt.* [ < L. *in-*, on + *salire*, to leap] to subject to an act, remark, etc. meant to hurt the feelings or pride —*n.* an insulting act, remark, etc.

**in·su·per·a·ble** (in soo′pər ə b′l) *adj.* [ < L. *in-*, not + *superare*, overcome] that cannot be overcome

**in·sup·port·a·ble** (in′sə pôrt′ə b′l) *adj.* not supportable; incapable of being borne, upheld, proved, etc.

**in·sur·ance** (in shoor′əns) *n.* **1.** an insuring or being insured **2.** a contract (**insurance policy**) purchased to guarantee compensation for a specified loss by fire, death, etc. **3.** the amount for which something is insured **4.** the business of insuring against loss

**in·sure** (in shoor′) *vt.* -**sured′**, -**sur′ing** [see IN-¹ & SURE] **1.** to take out or issue insurance on **2.** *same as* ENSURE —**in·sur′a·ble** *adj.*

**in·sured′** *n.* a person whose life, property, etc. is insured against loss

**in·sur′er** *n.* a person or company that insures others against loss

**in·sur·gent** (in sur′jənt) *adj.* [ < L. *in-*, upon + *surgere*, rise] rising up against established authority —*n.* an insurgent person —**in·sur′gence** *n.*

**in·sur·rec·tion** (in′sə rek′shən) *n.* [see prec.] a rising up against established authority; rebellion —**in·sur·rec′tion·ist** *n.*

**int. 1.** interest **2.** international

**in·tact** (in takt′) *adj.* [ < L. *in-*, not + *tactus*, touched] unimpaired or uninjured; kept or left whole

**in·tagl·io** (in tal′yō) *n., pl.* -**ios** [It. < *in-*, in + *tagliare*, to cut] a design carved or engraved below the surface

**in·take** (in′tāk′) *n.* **1.** a taking in **2.** amount taken in **3.** the place in a pipe, etc. where a fluid is taken in

**in·tan·gi·ble** (in tan′jə b′l) *adj.* **1.** that cannot be touched; incorporeal **2.** representing value, but either without material being or without intrinsic value, as good will or stocks **3.** that cannot be easily defined; vague —*n.* something intangible

**in·te·ger** (in′tə jər) *n.* [L., whole] a whole number (e.g., 5, -10) or zero

**in′te·gral** (-grəl) *adj.* [see prec.] **1.** necessary for completeness; essential **2.** whole or complete **3.** made up of parts forming a whole

**in′te·grate′** (-grāt′) *vt., vi.* -**grat′ed**, -**grat′ing** [ < L. *integer*, whole] **1.** to make or become whole or complete **2.** to bring (parts) together into a whole **3.** *a)* to remove barriers imposing segregation upon (racial groups)

*b)* to abolish segregation in —**in′te·gra′tion** *n.* —**in′te·gra′tive** *adj.*

**integrated circuit** an electronic circuit with many interconnected circuit elements formed on a single body of semiconductor material

**in·teg·ri·ty** (in teg′rə tē) *n.* [see INTEGER] **1.** completeness; wholeness **2.** unimpaired condition; soundness **3.** honesty, sincerity, etc.

**in·teg·u·ment** (in teg′yoo mənt) *n.* [ < L. *in-*, upon + *tegere*, to cover] an outer covering; skin, shell, etc.

**in·tel·lect** (in′t′l ekt′) *n.* [ < L. *inter-*, between + *legere*, choose] **1.** the ability to reason or understand **2.** high intelligence **3.** a very intelligent person

**in·tel·lec·tu·al** (in′t′l ek′choo wəl) *adj.* **1.** of, involving, or appealing to the intellect **2.** requiring intelligence **3.** showing high intelligence —*n.* one with intellectual interests or tastes —**in′tel·lec′tu·al·ly** *adv.*

**in′tel·lec′tu·al·ize′** (-īz′) *vt.* -**ized′**, -**iz′ing** to examine rationally, often without proper regard for emotional considerations

**in·tel·li·gence** (in tel′ə jəns) *n.* [see INTELLECT] **1.** *a)* the ability to learn or understand *b)* the ability to cope with a new situation **2.** news or information **3.** those engaged in gathering secret, esp. military, information

**intelligence quotient** *see* IQ

**in·tel′li·gent** (-jənt) *adj.* having or showing intelligence; clever, wise, etc. —**in·tel′li·gent·ly** *adv.*

**in·tel′li·gent′si·a** (-jent′sē ə) *n.* [ < Russ.] intellectuals collectively

**in·tel·li·gi·ble** (in tel′i jə b′l) *adj.* that can be understood; clear —**in·tel′li·gi·bly** *adv.*

**in·tem·per·ate** (in tem′pər it) *adj.* **1.** not temperate or moderate; excessive **2.** drinking too much alcoholic liquor —**in·tem′per·ance** *n.*

**in·tend** (in tend′) *vt.* [ < L. *in-*, at + *tendere*, to stretch] **1.** to plan; purpose **2.** to mean (something) to be or be used (*for*) **3.** to mean; signify

**in·tend′ed** *n.* [Colloq.] one's prospective wife or husband; fiancé(e)

**in·tense** (in tens′) *adj.* [see INTENSE] **1.** very strong [an *intense* light] **2.** strained to the utmost; strenuous [*intense* thought] **3.** characterized by much action, strong emotion, etc. —**in·tense′ly** *adv.*

**in·ten·si·fy** (in ten′sə fī′) *vt., vi.* -**fied′**, -**fy′ing** to make or become more intense —**in·ten′si·fi·ca′tion** *n.*

**in·ten′si·ty** *n., pl.* -**ties 1.** a being intense **2.** great energy or vehemence, as of emotion **3.** the amount of force or energy of heat, light, sound, etc.

**in·ten·sive** *adj.* **1.** of or characterized by intensity; thorough **2.** designating very attentive care given to patients right after surgery, etc. **3.** *Gram.* giving force or emphasis ["very" is an *intensive* adverb] —*n. Gram.* an intensive word, prefix, etc. —**in·ten′sive·ly** *adv.* —**in·ten′sive·ness** *n.*

**in·tent** (in tent′) *adj.* [see INTEND] **1.** firmly directed; earnest **2.** having one's attention or purpose firmly fixed [*intent* on going] —*n.* 1. an intending 2. something intended; purpose or meaning —**to all intents and purposes** in almost every respect —**intent′ly** *adv.* —**in·tent′ness** *n.*

**in·ten·tion** (in ten′shən) *n.* 1. a determination to act in a specified way 2. anything intended; purpose

**in·ten′tion·al** *adj.* done purposely

**in·ter** (in tur′) *vt.* -**terred′**, -**ter′ring** [< L. *in-*, in + *terra,* earth] to put (a dead body) into a grave or tomb

**inter-** [L.] *a combining form meaning:* 1. between, among, or involving individual elements named in the base adjective or singular noun

| | |
|---|---|
| **intercultural** | **interfaith** |
| **interdepartmental** | **intergroup** |

2. with or on each other (or one another)

| | |
|---|---|
| **interact** | **interaction** |

**in·ter·breed** (in′tər brēd′) *vt., vi.* -**bred′**, -**breed′ing** *same as* HYBRIDIZE

**in′ter·cede′** (-sēd′) *vi.* -**ced′ed**, -**ced′ing** [< L. *inter-,* between + *cedere,* go] 1. to plead in behalf of (another 2. to mediate

**in′ter·cept′** (-sept′) *vt.* [< L. *inter-,* between + *capere,* take] 1. to stop or seize in its course [to *intercept* a message] 2. *Math.* to cut off or mark off between two points, lines, etc. —**in′ter·cep′tion** *n.*

**in′ter·ces′sion** (-sesh′ən) *n.* an interceding; mediation or prayer in behalf of another —**in′ter·ces′sor** (-ses′ər) *n.* —**in′ter·ces′so·ry** *adj.*

**in·ter·change** (in′tər chānj′; *for n.* in′tər chānj′) *vt.* -**changed′**, -**chang′ing** 1. to give and take mutually; exchange 2. to put (each of two things) in the other's place 3. to alternate —*n.* 1. an interchanging 2. a place on a freeway where traffic can enter or depart —**in′ter·change′·a·ble** *adj.*

**in′ter·col·le′gi·ate** *adj.* between or among colleges and universities

**in·ter·com** (in′tər käm′) *n.* a radio or telephone intercommunication system, as between rooms

**in′ter·com·mu′ni·cate′** *vt., vi.* -**cat′ed**, -**cat′ing** to communicate with or to each other or one another —**in′ter·com·mu′ni·ca′tion** *n.*

**in′ter·con·nect′** (-kə nekt′) *vt., vi.* to connect with one another —**in′ter·con·nec′tion** *n.*

**in′ter·con′ti·nen′tal** *adj.* 1. between or among continents 2. able to travel from one continent to another, as a missile, etc.

**in·ter·course** (in′tər kôrs′) *n.* [see INTER- & COURSE] 1. communication or dealings between people, countries, etc. 2. the sexual joining of two individuals: in full, **sexual intercourse**

**in′ter·de·nom′i·na′tion·al** *adj.* between or among religious denominations

**in′ter·de·pend′ence** *n.* mutual de-

pendence —**in′ter·de·pend′ent** *adj.*

**in·ter·dict** (in′tər dikt′; *for n.* in′tər dikt′) *vt.* [ < L. *inter-,* between + *dicere,* say] 1. to prohibit (an action) 2. to restrain from doing or using something —*n.* an official prohibition —**in′ter·dic′tion** *n.*

**in′ter·dis′ci·pli·nar′y** *adj.* involving two or more disciplines, or branches of learning

**in·ter·est** (in′trist, in′tər ist) *n.* [< L. *inter-,* between + *esse,* be] 1. a right to, or share in, something 2. anything in which one has a share 3. [*often pl.*] advantage; benefit 4. [*usually pl.*] those having a common concern or power in some industry, cause, etc. [the steel *interests*] 5. *a*) a feeling of concern, curiosity, etc. about something *b*) the power of causing this feeling *c*) something causing this feeling 6. *a*) money paid for the use of money *b*) the rate of such payment —*vt.* 1. to involve or excite the interest or attention of 2. to cause to have an interest, or share, in —**in the interest(s) of** for the sake of —**in′ter·est·ed** *adj.* 1. having an interest or share 2. influenced by personal interest; biased 3. feeling or showing interest

**in′ter·est·ing** *adj.* exciting curiosity or attention; of interest

**in·ter·face** (in′tər fās′) *n.* a surface that forms the common boundary between two parts of matter or space

**in·ter·fere** (in′tər fir′) *vi.* -**fered′**, -**fer′ing** [ult. < L. *inter-,* between + *ferire,* to strike] 1. to clash; collide 2. *a*) to come between; intervene *b*) to meddle 3. *Sports* to hinder an opposing player in any of various illegal ways —**interfere with** to hinder —**in′ter·fer′ence** *n.*

**in·ter·im** (in′tər im) *n.* [L. < *inter,* between] the period of time between; meantime —*adj.* temporary

**in·te·ri·or** (in tir′ē ər) *adj.* [ < L. *inter,* between] 1. situated within; inner 2. inland 3. private —*n.* 1. the interior part, as of a room, country, etc. 2. the internal, or domestic, affairs of a country

**interior decoration** the art or business of decorating and furnishing interiors of homes, offices, etc. —**interior decorator**

**in·te′ri·or·ize′** (-īz′) *vt.* -**ized′**, -**iz′ing** to make (a concept, value, etc.) part of one's inner nature

**interj.** interjection

**in·ter·ject** (in′tər jekt′) *vt.* [< L. *inter-,* between + *jacere,* to throw] to throw in between; interrupt with

**in′ter·jec′tion** (-jek′shən) *n.* 1. an interjecting 2. something interjected 3. *Gram.* an exclamation

**in′ter·lace′** *vt., vi.* -**laced′**, -**lac′ing** to lace or weave together

**in′ter·lard′** (-lärd′) *vt.* [see INTER- & LARD] to intersperse; diversify [to *interlard* a talk with quotations]

---

fat, āpe, cär; ten, ēven; is, bīte; gō, hôrn, tōōl, look; oil, out; up, fur; chin; she; thin, *then*; zh. leisure; ŋ, ring; ə for *a* in ago; ′, (ā′b'l); ë, Fr. coeur; ö, Fr. feu; Fr. mon; ü, Fr. duc; kh, G. ich, doch; ‡ foreign; < derived from

**in·ter·line**/1 vt. -lined/, -lin/ing to write (something) between the lines of (a text, etc.)

**in·ter·line**/2 vt. -lined/, -lin/ing to put an inner lining under the ordinary lining of (a garment)

**in·ter·lock** vt., vi. to lock together; join with one another

**in·ter·loc·u·to·ry** (in′tər läk′yə tôr′ē) adj. [< L. inter-, between + loqui, speak] Law not final, as a decree

**in·ter·lop·er** (in′tər lō′pər) n. [prob. < INTER- + LOPE] one who meddles

**in·ter·lude** (in′tər lood′) n. [< L. inter, between + ludus, play] anything that fills time between two events, as music between acts of a play

**in·ter·mar·ry** vi. -ried, -ry·ing 1. to become connected by marriage: said of different clans, races, etc. 2. to marry: said of closely related persons —in′ter·mar′riage n.

**in·ter·me·di·ar·y** (-mē′dē er′ē) adj. 1. acting as a go-between or mediator 2. intermediate —n., pl. -ies a go-between; mediator

**in·ter·me·di·ate** (-mē′dē it) adj. [< L. inter-, between + medius, middle] in the middle; in between

**in·ter·ment** (in tur′mənt) n. the act of interring; burial

**in·ter·mez·zo** (in′tər met′sō) n., pl. -zos, -zi (-sē) [It. < L.: see INTERMEDIATE] a short piece of music, as between parts of a composition

**in·ter·mi·na·ble** (in tur′mi nə b′l) adj. lasting, or seeming to last, forever; endless —in·ter′mi·na·bly adv.

**in·ter·min·gle** vt., vi. -gled, -gling to mix together; mingle

**in·ter·mis·sion** (in′tər mish′ən) n. [< L. inter-, between + mittere, send] an interval of time between periods of activity, as between acts of a play

**in′ter·mit′tent** (-mit′′nt) adj. [see prec.] stopping and starting again at intervals; periodic

**in·tern** (in′tərn; for vt. usually in turn′) n. [< L. internus, inward] 1. a doctor serving as assistant resident in a hospital, usually just after graduation from medical school 2. an apprentice teacher, journalist, etc. Also **interne** —vi. to serve as an intern —vt. to detain and confine within an area [to intern aliens in wartime] —in·tern′ment n.

**in·ter·nal** (in tur′n′l) adj. [< L. internus] 1. of or on the inside; inner 2. to be taken inside the body [internal remedies] 3. intrinsic [internal evidence] 4. domestic [internal revenue] —in·ter′nal·ly adv.

**in·ter′nal-com·bus′tion engine** an engine, as in an automobile, powered by the explosion of a fuel-and-air mixture within the cylinders

**in·ter′nal·ize** (-īz′) vt. -ized′, -iz′-ing to make (others' ideas, etc.) a part of one's own way of thinking

**internal medicine** the branch of medicine dealing with the diagnosis and nonsurgical treatment of diseases

**internal revenue** governmental income from taxes on income, profits, etc.

**in·ter·na·tion·al** (in′tər nash′ə n′l) adj. 1. between or among nations 2. concerned with the relations between nations 3. for the use of all nations 4. of or for people in various nations —in′ter·na′tion·al·ize′ vt. -ized′, -iz′ing —in′ter·na′tion·al·ly adv.

**in·ter·ne·cine** (in′tər nē′sin) adj. [< L. inter-, between + necare, kill] extremely destructive to both sides

**in·ter·nist** (in′tər nist, in tur′nist) n. a doctor who specializes in the nonsurgical treatment of diseases

**in·ter·of·fice** (in′tər ôf′is) adj. between the offices of an organization

**in′ter·per′son·al** (-pur′sə n′l) adj. between persons

**in′ter·plan′e·tar′y** (-plan′ə ter′ē) adj. between planets

**in′ter·play′** n. action, effect, or influence on each other

**in·ter·po·late** (in tur′pə lāt′) vt. -lat′ed, -lat′ing [< L. inter-, between + polire, to polish] 1. to change (a text, etc.) by inserting new material 2. to insert between or among others —in·ter′po·la′tion n.

**in·ter·pose** (in′tər pōz′) vt., vi. -posed′, -pos′ing 1. to place or come between 2. to intervene (with) 3. to interrupt (with) —in′ter·po·si′tion (-pə zish′ən) n.

**in·ter·pret** (in tur′prit) vt. [< L. interpres, negotiator] 1. to explain or translate 2. to construe [to interpret a silence as contempt] 3. to give one's own conception of, as a role in a play —vi. to translate —in·ter′pre·ta′tion n. —in·ter′pret·er n.

**in·ter·pre·tive** (in tur′prə tiv) adj. that interprets: also **in·ter′pre·ta′tive** (-tāt′iv)

**in·ter·ra·cial** (in′tər rā′shəl) adj. between, among, or for persons of different races: also **in′ter·race′**

**in′ter·re·late′** (-ri lāt′) vt., vi. -lat′-ed, -lat′ing to make or be mutually related —in′ter·re·lat′ed adj.

**in·ter·ro·gate** (in ter′ə gāt′) vt., vi. -gat′ed, -gat′ing [< L. inter-, between + rogare, ask] to question, esp. formally —in·ter′ro·ga′tion n. —in·ter′ro·ga′tor n.

**in·ter·rog·a·tive** (in′tə räg′ə tiv) adj. asking a question: also **in′ter·rog′a·to′ry** (-ə tôr′ē)

**in·ter·rupt** (in′tə rupt′) vt. [< L. inter-, between + rumpere, to break] 1. to break into (a discussion, etc.) or break in upon (a speaker, worker, etc.) 2. to make a break in the continuity of —vi. to interrupt an action, talk, etc. —in′ter·rup′tion n.

**in·ter·scho·las·tic** (in′tər skə las′tik) adj. between or among schools

**in·ter·sect** (in′tər sekt′) vt. [< L. inter-, between + secare, to cut] to divide into two parts by passing through —vi. to cross each other

**in′ter·sec′tion** (-sek′shən) n. 1. an intersecting 2. the place where two lines, roads, etc. meet or cross

**in′ter·serv′ice** adj. between or among branches of the armed forces

**in′ter·ses′sion** n. a short session between regular college sessions, for concentration on specialized projects

**in·ter·sperse** (in'tər spurs') *vt.* -spersed', -spers'ing [< L. *inter-*, among + *spargere*, scatter] 1. to put here and there; scatter 2. to vary with things scattered here and there

**in'ter·state'** *adj.* between or among states of a federal government

**in'ter·stel'lar** (-stel'ər) *adj.* between or among the stars

**in·ter·stice** (in tur'stis) *n., pl.* -stic·es [< L. *inter-*, between + *sistere*, to set] a crack; crevice

**in'ter·twine'** *vt., vi.* -twined', -twin'ing to twine together

**in'ter·ur'ban** (-ur'bən) *adj.* between cities or towns

**in·ter·val** (in'tər v'l) *n.* [< L. *inter-*, between + *vallum*, wall] 1. a space between things 2. the time between events 3. the difference in pitch between two tones —**at intervals** 1. now and then 2. here and there

**in·ter·vene** (in'tər vēn') *vi.* -vened', -ven'ing [< L. *inter-*, between + *venire*, come] 1. to come or be between 2. to occur between two events, etc. 3. to come in to modify, settle, or hinder some action, etc.

**in·ter·ven·tion** (-ven'shən) *n.* 1. an intervening 2. interference, esp. of one state in the affairs of another

**in'ter·view'** (-vyoo') *n.* 1. a meeting of people face to face to confer 2. *a)* a meeting in which a person is asked about his views, etc., as by a reporter *b)* a published account of this —*vt.* to have an interview with —**in'ter·view·ee'** *n.* —**in'ter·view'er** *n.*

**in'ter·weave'** *vt., vi.* -wove', -wov'en, -weav'ing 1. to weave together 2. to connect closely

**in·tes·tate** (in tes'tāt, -tit) *adj.* [< L. *in-*, not + *testari*, make a will] having made no will

**in·tes·tine** (in tes'tin) *n.* [< L. *intus*, within] [*usually pl.*] the lower part of the alimentary canal, extending from the stomach to the anus and consisting of a long, winding upper part (**small intestine**) and a shorter, thicker lower part (**large intestine**); bowel(s) —**in·tes'tin·al** *adj.*

**in·ti·mate** (in'tə mit; *for v.* -māt') *adj.* [< L. *intus*, within] 1. most private or personal 2. very close or familiar 3. deep and thorough —*n.* an intimate friend —*vt.* -mat'ed, -mat'ing to hint or imply —**in'ti·ma·cy** (-mə sē) *n., pl.* -cies —**in'ti·mate·ly** *adv.* —**in'ti·ma'tion** *n.*

**in·tim·i·date** (in tim'ə dāt') *vt.* -dat'ed, -dat'ing [< L. *in-*, in + *timidus*, afraid] to make afraid, as with threats —**in·tim'i·da'tion** *n.*

INTESTINES

**in·to** (in'too, -too) *prep.* [OE.] 1. toward and within [*into* a room] 2. continuing to the midst of [to talk *into* the night] 3. to the form, substance, or condition of [divided *into* parts] 4. so as to strike [to run *into* a wall] 5. [Colloq.] involved in [she's *into* jazz now]

**in·tol·er·a·ble** (in täl'ər ə b'l) *adj.* unbearable; too severe, painful, etc. to be endured —**in·tol'er·a·bly** *adv.*

**in·tol·er·ant** (-ənt) *adj.* unwilling to tolerate others' beliefs, etc. —**intolerant of** not able or willing to tolerate —**in·tol'er·ance** *n.*

**in·to·na·tion** (in'tə nā'shən) *n.* 1. an intoning 2. the manner of producing tones with regard to accurate pitch 3. variations in pitch within an utterance

**in·tone** (in tōn') *vt., vi.* -toned', -ton'ing to speak or recite in a singing tone; chant —**in·ton'er** *n.*

**in to·to** (in tō'tō) [L.] as a whole

**in·tox·i·cate** (in täk'sə kāt') *vt.* -cat'ed, -cat'ing [< L. *in-*, in + *toxicum*, poison] 1. to make drunk 2. to excite greatly —**in·tox'i·cant** *n.* —**in·tox'i·ca'tion** *n.*

**intra-** [L., within] *a combining form meaning* within, inside of

**in·tra·cit·y** (in'trə sit'ē) *adj.* of or within a large municipality, often specif. the inner city

**in·trac·ta·ble** (in trak'tə b'l) *adj.* hard to manage; unruly or stubborn

**in·tra·mu·ral** (in'trə myoor'əl) *adj.* [INTRA- + MURAL] between or among members of the same school, college, etc.

**in·tran·si·gent** (in tran'sə jənt) *adj.* [< L. *in-*, not + *transigere*, to settle] refusing to compromise —**in·tran'si·gence** *n.*

**in·tran·si·tive** (in tran'sə tiv) *adj.* not transitive; designating a verb that does not take a direct object —**in·tran'si·tive·ly** *adv.*

**in·tra·u·ter·ine device** (in'trə yoot'ər in) a device, as a plastic loop, inserted in the uterus as a contraceptive

**in'tra·ve'nous** (-vē'nəs) *adj.* [INTRA- + VENOUS] directly into a vein —**in'tra·ve'nous·ly** *adv.*

**in·trench** (in trench') *vt., vi. same as* ENTRENCH

**in·trep·id** (in trep'id) *adj.* [< L. *in-*, not + *trepidus*, alarmed] bold; fearless; brave —**in·trep'id·ly** *adv.*

**in·tri·cate** (in'tri kit) *adj.* [< L. *in-*, in + *tricae*, vexations] 1. hard to follow or understand because full of puzzling parts, details, etc. 2. full of elaborate detail —**in'tri·ca·cy** (-kə sē) *n.* —**in'tri·cate·ly** *adv.*

**in·trigue** (in trēg') *vi.* -trigued', -trigu'ing [see prec.] to plot secretly or underhandedly —*vt.* to excite the interest or curiosity of —*n.* 1. secret or underhanded plotting 2. a secret or underhanded plot or scheme 3. a

fat, āpe, cär; ten, ēven; is, bīte; gō, hôrn, tool, look; oil, out; up, fur; chin; she; thin, then; zh, leisure; ŋ, ring; ə for a in ago; ', (ā'b'l); ë, Fr. coeur; ö, Fr. feu; Fr. mon; ü, Fr. duc; kh, G. ich, doch; ‡ foreign; < derived from secret love affair —**in·tri·gu'er** n. —**in·trigu'ing·ly** adv.

**in·trin·sic** (in trin'sik) adj. [< L. intra-, within + secus, close] belonging to the real nature of a thing; inherent —**in·trin'si·cal·ly** adv.

**in·tro·duce** (in'trə dōōs') vt. -duced', -duc'ing [< L. intro-, in + ducere, to lead] 1. to put in; insert 2. to bring in as a new feature 3. to bring into use or fashion 4. a) to make acquainted; present [introduce me to her] b) to give experience of [they introduced him to music] 5. to bring forward 6. to start; begin [to introduce a talk over a joke]

**in'tro·duc'tion** (-duk'shən) n. 1. an introducing or being introduced 2. the preliminary section of a book, speech, etc.; preface

**in'tro·duc'to·ry** (-duk'tər ē) adj. serving to introduce; preliminary

**in·tro·it** (in trō'it, in'troit) n. [< L. intro-, in + ire, to go] 1. a psalm or hymn at the opening of a Christian worship service 2. [I-] R.C.Ch. the first variable part of the Mass

**in·tro·spec·tion** (in'trə spek'shən) n. [< L. intro-, within + specere, to look] a looking into one's own mind, feelings, etc. —**in'tro·spec'tive** adj.

**in·tro·vert** (in'trə vurt') n. [< L. intro-, within + vertere, to turn] one who is more interested in his own thoughts, feelings, etc. than in external objects or events —**in'tro·ver'sion** (-vur'zhən) n. —**in'tro·vert'ed** adj.

**in·trude** (in trōōd') vt., vi. -trud'ed, -trud'ing [< L. in-, in + trudere, to push] to force (oneself) upon others without being asked or welcomed —**in·trud'er** n.

**in·tru·sion** (in trōō'zhən) n. an intruding —**in·tru'sive** (-siv) adj. — **in·tru'sive·ly** adv. —**in·tru'sive·ness** n.

**in·trust** (in trust') vt. same as ENTRUST

**in·tu·i·tion** (in'too wish'ən) n. [< L. in-, in + tueri, look at] the immediate knowing of something without the conscious use of reasoning —**in·tu·i·tive** (in tōō'i tiv) adj.

**in·un·date** (in'ən dāt') vt. -dat'ed, -dat'ing [< L. in-, in + unda, a wave] to cover with or as with a flood; deluge —**in'un·da'tion** n.

**in·ure** (in yoor') vt. -ured', -ur'ing [< ME. in ure, in practice] to accustom to pain, trouble, etc.

**in·vade** (in vād') vt. -vad'ed, -vad'ing [< L. in-, in + vadere, go] 1. to enter forcibly or hostilely 2. to intrude upon; violate —**in·vad'er** n.

**in·va·lid¹** (in'və lid) adj. [< L. in-, not + validus, strong] 1. weak and sickly 2. of or for invalids —n. one who is ill or disabled

**in·val·id²** (in val'id) adj. not valid; having no force; null or void

**in·val'i·date'** (-ə dāt') vt. -dat'ed, -dat'ing to make invalid; deprive of legal force —**in·val'i·da'tion** n.

**in·val·u·a·ble** (in val'yoo wə b'l, -yə b'l) adj. too valuable to be meas-

ured; priceless —**in·val'u·a·bly** adv.

**in·va·sion** (in vā'zhən) n. an invading or being invaded, as by an army

**in·vec·tive** (in vek'tiv) n. [see ff.] a violent verbal attack; vituperation

**in·veigh** (in vā') vi. [< L. in-, in + vehere, carry] to make a violent verbal attack; rail (against)

**in·vei·gle** (in vē'g'l, -vā'-) vt. -gled, -gling [< MFr. aveugler, to blind] to entice or trick into doing something —**in·vei'gler** n.

**in·vent** (in vent') vt. [< L. in-, on + venire, come] 1. to think up [invent excuses] 2. to think out or produce (a new device, process, etc.); originate —**in·ven'tor** n.

**in·ven'tion** (-ven'shən) n. 1. an inventing 2. the power of inventing 3. something invented

**in·ven'tive** (-tiv) adj. 1. of invention 2. skilled in inventing —**in·ven'tive·ly** adv. —**in·ven'tive·ness** n.

**in·ven·to·ry** (in'vən tôr'ē) n., pl. -ries [see INVENT] 1. an itemized list of goods, property, etc., as of a business 2. the store of goods, etc. for such listing; stock —vt. -ried, -ry·ing to make an inventory of

**in·verse** (in vurs'; also in'vurs') adj. inverted; directly opposite —n. any inverse thing —**in·verse'ly** adv.

**in·ver·sion** (in vur'zhən) n. 1. an inverting or being inverted 2. something inverted; reversal

**in·vert** (in vurt') vt. [< L. in-, to + vertere, to turn] 1. to turn upside down 2. to reverse the order, position, direction, etc. of

**in·ver·te·brate** (in vur'tə brit, -brāt') adj. not vertebrate; having no backbone —n. any invertebrate animal

**in·vest** (in vest') vt. [< L. in-, in + vestis, clothing] 1. to clothe 2. to install in office with ceremony 3. to furnish with power, authority, etc. 4. to put (money) into business, bonds, etc., in order to get a profit —vi. to invest money —**in·ves'tor** n.

**in·ves·ti·gate** (in ves'tə gāt') vt., vi. -gat'ed, -gat'ing [< L. in-, in + vestigare, to track] to search (into); inquire —**in·ves'ti·ga'tor** n.

**in·ves'ti·ga'tion** n. an investigating; careful search; systematic inquiry

**in·ves·ti·ture** (in ves'tə chər) n. a formal investing, as with an office

**in·vest·ment** (in vest'mənt) n. 1. an investing or being invested 2. a) money invested b) anything in which money is or may be invested

**in·vet·er·ate** (in vet'ər it) adj. [< L. inveterare, to age] firmly established; habitual —**in·vet'er·a·cy** n.

**in·vid·i·ous** (in vid'ē əs) adj. [< L. invidia, envy] such as to excite ill will; giving offense, as by discriminating unfairly —**in·vid'i·ous·ly** adv. —**in·vid'i·ous·ness** n.

**in·vig·or·ate** (in vig'ə rāt') vt. -at'ed, -at'ing to give vigor to; fill with energy —**in·vig'or·a'tion** n.

**in·vin·ci·ble** (in vin'sə b'l) adj. [< L. in-, not + vincere, overcome] that cannot be overcome; unconquerable —**in·vin'ci·bil'i·ty** n.

**in·vi·o·la·ble** (in vī′ə lə b′l) *adj.* 1. not to be violated; not to be profaned or injured; sacred 2. indestructible —**in·vi′o·la·bil′i·ty** *n.*

**in·vi′o·late** (-lit) *adj.* not violated; kept sacred or unbroken

**in·vis·i·ble** (in viz′ə b′l) *adj.* 1. not visible; that cannot be seen 2. out of sight 3. imperceptible —**in·vis′i·bil′i·ty** *n.* —**in·vis′i·bly** *adv.*

**in·vi·ta·tion** (in′və tā′shən) *n.* 1. an inviting 2. a message used in inviting

**in′vi·ta′tion·al** *adj.* only for those invited to take part, as an art show

**in·vite** (in·vīt′) *vt.* -vit′ed, -vit′ing [< L. *invitare*] 1. to ask to come somewhere or do something 2. to ask for 3. to give occasion for [his conduct *invites* gossip] 4. to tempt; entice —*n.* [Colloq.] an invitation

**in·vit′ing** *adj.* tempting; enticing

**in·vo·ca·tion** (in′və kā′shən) *n.* an invoking of God, the Muses, etc.

**in·voice** (in′vois) *n.* [prob. < ME. *envoie*, message] a list of goods shipped to a buyer, stating prices, etc. —*vt.* -voiced, -voic·ing to present an invoice for or to

**in·voke** (in vōk′) *vt.* -voked′, -vok′ing [< L. *in-*, on + *vocare*, to call] 1. to call on (God, the Muses, etc.) for blessing, help, etc. 2. to resort to (a law, ruling, etc.) as pertinent 3. to conjure 4. to beg for; implore

**in·vol·un·tar·y** (in väl′ən ter′ē) *adj.* 1. not done by choice 2. not consciously controlled —**in·vol′un·tar′i·ly** *adv.* —**in·vol′un·tar′i·ness** *n.*

**in·vo·lu·tion** (in′və lōō′shən) *n.* 1. an involving or being involved; entanglement 2. a complication; intricacy

**in·volve** (in välv′) *vt.* -volved′, -volv′ing [< L. *in-*, in + *volvere*, to roll] 1. to make intricate; complicate 2. to entangle in difficulty, danger, etc.; implicate 3. to affect or include [the riot *involved* thousands] 4. to require [saving *involves* thrift] 5. to make busy; occupy [*involved* in study] —**in·volved′** *adj.* —**in·volve′ment** *n.*

**in·vul·ner·a·ble** (in vul′nər ə b′l) *adj.* 1. that cannot be wounded or injured 2. proof against attack

**in·ward** (in′wərd) *adj.* 1. situated within; internal 2. mental or spiritual 3. directed toward the inside —*adv.* 1. toward the inside 2. into the mind or soul Also **in′wards**, *adv.*

**in′ward·ly** *adv.* 1. in or on the inside 2. in the mind or spirit 3. toward the inside or center

**i·o·dine** (ī′ə dīn′, -din) *n.* [< Gr. *iōdēs*, violetlike] 1. a nonmetallic chemical element used in medicine, etc. 2. tincture of iodine, used as an antiseptic

**i′o·dize′** (-dīz′) *vt.* -dized′, -diz′ing to treat with iodine

**i·on** (ī′ən, -än) *n.* [< Gr. *ienai*, to go] an electrically charged atom or group of atoms

**-ion** [< L. *-io*] *a suffix meaning:* 1. the act or condition of [*translation*] 2. the result of [*correction*]

**I·on·ic** (ī än′ik) *adj.* designating or of a Greek style of architecture characterized by ornamental scrolls on the capitals

IONIC CAPITAL

**i·on·ize** (ī′ə nīz′) *vt., vi.* -ized′, -iz′ing to dissociate into ions, as a salt dissolved in water, or become electrically charged, as a gas under radiation —**i′on·i·za′tion** *n.* —**i′on·iz′er** *n.*

**i·on·o·sphere** (ī än′ə sfir′) *n.* the outer layers of the earth's atmosphere, with some electron and ion content

**i·o·ta** (ī ōt′ə, ē-) *n.* 1. the ninth letter of the Greek alphabet (Ι, ι) 2. a very small quantity; jot

**IOU, I.O.U.** (ī′ō′yōō′) 1. I owe you 2. a signed note bearing these letters, acknowledging a specified debt

**-ious** (ē əs, yəs, əs) [see -OUS] *a suffix meaning* having, characterized by [*furious*]

**I·o·wa** (ī′ə wə) Middle Western State of the U.S.: 56,290 sq. mi.; pop. 2,825,000; cap. Des Moines —**I′o·wan** *adj., n.*

**ip·e·cac** (ip′ə kak′) *n.* [< SAmInd. name] an emetic made from the dried roots of a S. American plant

**ip·so fac·to** (ip′sō fak′tō) [L.] by the fact (or act) itself

**IQ, I.Q.** [intelligence quotient] a number indicating a person's level of intelligence, based on a test

**ir-** *same as:* 1. IN-[1] 2. IN-[2] Used before *r*

**Ir.** 1. Ireland: also Ire. 2. Irish

**I·ran** (i ran′, ī-; ē rän′) country in SW Asia: formerly called *Persia:* 636,000 sq. mi.; pop. 26,015,000 —**I·ra·ni·an** (i rā′nē ən, ī-) *adj., n.*

**I·raq** (i räk′, -rak′; ē-) country in SW Asia, west of Iran: 171,599 sq. mi.; pop. 8,338,000 —**I·ra·qi** (i rä′kē, -rak′ē) *adj., n.*

**i·ras·ci·ble** (i ras′ə b′l) *adj.* [see ff.] easily angered; hot-tempered

**i·rate** (ī rāt′, ī′rāt) *adj.* [< L. *ira*, anger] angry; wrathful; incensed —**i·rate′ly** *adv.* —**i·rate′ness** *n.*

**ire** (īr) *n.* [< L. *ira*] anger; wrath

**Ire·land** (īr′lənd) 1. one of the British Isles, west of Great Britain 2. republic comprising most of this island: 27,136 sq. mi.; pop. 2,884,000

**i·ren·ic** (ī ren′ik) *adj.* [< Gr. *eirēnē*, peace] promoting peace

**ir·i·des·cent** (ir′ə des′ənt) *adj.* [< Gr. *iris*, rainbow] having or showing an interplay of rainbowlike colors —**ir′i·des′cence** *n.*

**i·rid·i·um** (i rid′ē əm) *n.* [see ff.] a white, metallic chemical element: symbol, **Ir**

**i·ris** (ī′ris) *n., pl.* **i′ris·es** [Gr., rainbow] 1. the round, pigmented membrane surrounding the pupil of the eye

**2.** a plant with sword-shaped leaves and a showy flower

**I·rish** (ī'rish) *adj.* of Ireland, its people, language, etc. —*n.* **1.** the Celtic language of Ireland **2.** the English dialect of Ireland —**the Irish** the people of Ireland —**I'rish·man** *n., pl.* -men —**I'rish·wom'an** *n.fem., pl.* -wom'en

**Irish coffee** brewed coffee with Irish whiskey, topped with whipped cream

**Irish Sea** arm of the Atlantic between Ireland & Great Britain

**irk** (urk) *vt.* [ME. *irken*, be weary of] to annoy, irritate, tire out, etc.

**irk'some** (-səm) *adj.* that tends to irk; annoying or tiresome

**i·ron** (ī'ərn) *n.* [OE. *īren*] **1.** a metallic chemical element, the most common of all the metals **2.** any device of iron; esp., such a device with a flat undersurface, heated for pressing cloth **3.** [*pl.*] shackles of iron **4.** firm strength; power **5.** any of certain golf clubs with angled metal heads —*adj.* **1.** of iron **2.** like iron; strong; firm —*vt., vi.* to press with a hot iron —**iron out** to smooth out; eliminate

**i'ron·clad'** (-klad') *adj.* **1.** covered or protected with iron **2.** difficult to change or break [an *ironclad* lease]

**iron curtain** a barrier of secrecy and censorship, esp. around the U.S.S.R.

**i·ron·i·cal** (ī rän'i k'l) *adj.* **1.** meaning the contrary of what is expressed **2.** using irony **3.** opposite to what might be expected Also **i·ron'ic** — **i·ron'i·cal·ly** *adv.*

**iron lung** a large respirator enclosing all of the body but the head

**i'ron·stone'** *n.* **1.** any rock rich in iron **2.** a hard, white ceramic ware

**i'ron·ware'** *n.* things made of iron

**i·ro·ny** (ī'rən ē, ī'ər nē) *n., pl.* -nies [< Gr. *eirōn*, dissembler in speech] **1.** expression in which the intended meaning of the words is the opposite of their usual sense **2.** an event or result that is the opposite of what is expected

**Ir·o·quois** (ir'ə kwoi') *n., pl.* -quois' (-kwoi', -kwoiz') a member of a tribe of N. American Indians that lived in and near W and N New York —*adj.* of the Iroquois —**Ir'o·quoi'an** *adj., n.*

**ir·ra·di·ate** (i rā'dē āt') *vt.* -at'ed, -at'ing **1.** to shine upon; light up **2.** to enlighten **3.** to radiate **4.** to expose to X-rays or other radiant energy —*vi.* to emit rays; shine —**ir·ra'di·a'tion** *n.*

**ir·ra·tion·al** (i rash'ə n'l) *adj.* **1.** lacking the power to reason **2.** senseless; unreasonable; absurd —**ir·ra'·tion·al'i·ty** (-ə nal'ə tē) *n., pl.* -ties —**ir·ra'tion·al·ly** *adv.*

**ir·re·claim·a·ble** (ir'i klā'mə b'l) *adj.* that cannot be reclaimed

**ir·rec·on·cil·a·ble** (i rek'ən sīl'ə b'l) *adj.* that cannot be brought into agreement; incompatible

**ir·re·cov·er·a·ble** (ir'i kuv'ər ə b'l) *adj.* that cannot be recovered, rectified, or remedied

**ir·re·deem·a·ble** (ir'i dēm'ə b'l) *adj.* **1.** that cannot be bought back **2.** that

cannot be converted into coin, as certain paper money **3.** that cannot be changed or reformed

**ir·ref·u·ta·ble** (i ref'yoo tə b'l, ir'i fyoot'ə b'l) *adj.* indisputable

**ir·re·gard·less** (ir'i gärd'lis) *adj., adv. a substandard or humorous redundancy for* REGARDLESS

**ir·reg·u·lar** (i reg'yə lər) *adj.* **1.** not conforming to established rule, standard, etc. **2.** not straight, even, or uniform **3.** Gram. not inflected in the usual way —**ir·reg'u·lar'i·ty** *n.*

**ir·rel·e·vant** (i rel'ə vənt) *adj.* not pertinent; not to the point —**ir·rel'·e·vance** *n.* —**ir·rel'e·vant·ly** *adv.*

**ir·re·li·gious** (ir'i lij'əs) *adj.* **1.** not religious; indifferent or hostile to religion **2.** profane; impious

**ir·re·me·di·a·ble** (ir'i mē'dē ə b'l) *adj.* that cannot be remedied or corrected —**ir're·me'di·a·bly** *adv.*

**ir·rep·a·ra·ble** (i rep'ər ə b'l) *adj.* that cannot be repaired, mended, etc.

**ir·re·place·a·ble** (ir'i plās'ə b'l) *adj.* that cannot be replaced

**ir·re·press·i·ble** (ir'i pres'ə b'l) *adj.* that cannot be repressed

**ir·re·proach·a·ble** (ir'i prō'chə b'l) *adj.* blameless; faultless

**ir·re·sist·i·ble** (ir'i zis'tə b'l) *adj.* that cannot be resisted; too strong, fascinating, etc. to be withstood

**ir·res·o·lute** (i rez'ə lōōt') *adj.* not resolute; wavering; indecisive —**ir·res'o·lu'tion** *n.*

**ir·re·spec·tive** (ir'i spek'tiv) *adj.* regardless (*of*)

**ir·re·spon·si·ble** (ir'i spän'sə b'l) *adj.* **1.** not responsible for actions **2.** lacking a sense of responsibility —**ir'·re·spon'si·bil'i·ty** *n.*

**ir·re·triev·a·ble** (ir'i trēv'ə b'l) *adj.* that cannot be retrieved

**ir·rev·er·ent** (i rev'ər ənt) *adj.* not reverent; showing disrespect —**ir·rev'er·ence** *n.*

**ir·re·vers·i·ble** (ir'i vur'sə b'l) *adj.* that cannot be reversed; esp., that cannot be annulled or turned back

**ir·rev·o·ca·ble** (i rev'ə kə b'l) *adj.* that cannot be revoked or undone —**ir·rev'o·ca·bly** *adv.*

**ir·ri·ga·ble** (ir'i gə b'l) *adj.* that can be irrigated

**ir·ri·gate** (ir'ə gāt') *vt.* -gat'ed, -gat'ing [< L. *in-*, in + *rigare*, to water] **1.** to supply (land) with water as by means of artificial ditches **2.** Med. to wash out (a cavity, wound, etc.) —**ir'ri·ga'tion** *n.*

**ir·ri·ta·ble** (ir'i tə b'l) *adj.* **1.** easily irritated or provoked **2.** Med. excessively sensitive to a stimulus —**ir'ri·ta·bil'i·ty** *n.* —**ir'ri·ta·bly** *adv.*

**ir·ri·tant** (-tənt) *adj.* causing irritation —*n.* a thing that irritates

**ir·ri·tate** (-tāt') *vt.* -tat'ed, -tat'ing [< L. *irritare*, excite] **1.** to provoke to anger; annoy **2.** to make inflamed or sore —**ir'ri·ta'tion** *n.*

**ir·rupt** (i rupt') *vi.* [< L. *in-*, in + *rumpere*, to break] **1.** to burst suddenly or violently (*into*) **2.** Ecology to increase abruptly in size of population —**ir·rup'tion** *n.* —**ir·rup'tive** *adj.*

**IRS, I.R.S.** Internal Revenue Service

**is** (iz) [OE.] *3d pers. sing., pres. indic., of* BE

**is.** 1. island(s) 2. isle(s)

**I·saac** (I'zək) *Bible* one of the patriarchs, son of Abraham, and father of Jacob and Esau

**I·sa·iah** (I zā'ə) *Bible* 1. a Hebrew prophet of the 8th cent. B.C. 2. the book containing his teachings: abbrev. **Isa.**

**-ise** (Iz) *chiefly Brit. var. of* -IZE

**-ish** (ish) [OE. *-isc*] *a suffix meaning:* a) of (a specified people) *[Irish]* b) like *[boyish]* c) somewhat *[tallish]* d) [Colloq.] approximately *[thirtyish]*

**Ish·tar** (ish'tär) the Babylonian and Assyrian goddess of fertility

**i·sin·glass** (I'z'n glas', -ziŋ-) *n.* [< MDu. *huizen*, sturgeon + *blas*, bladder] 1. a gelatin prepared from fish bladders 2. mica, esp. in thin sheets

**I·sis** (I'sis) the Egyptian goddess of fertility

**isl.** *pl.* **isls.** 1. island 2. isle

**Is·lam** (is'läm, iz'-; is läm') *n.* [Ar. *islām*, lit., submission (to God's will)] 1. the Moslem religion, a monotheistic religion founded by Mohammed 2. Moslems collectively or the lands in which they predominate

**is·land** (I'lənd) *n.* [< OE. *igland*, lit., island land: sp. after *isle*] 1. a land mass smaller than a continent and surrounded by water 2. anything like this in position or isolation

**is'land·er** *n.* a native or inhabitant of an island

**isle** (Il) *n.* [< L. *insula*] an island, esp. a small one

**is·let** (I'lit) *n.* a very small island

**ism** (iz'm) *n.* any doctrine, theory, system, etc. whose name ends in *-ism*

**-ism** (iz'm) [< Gr. *-ismos*] *a suffix meaning:* 1. act or result of *[terrorism]* 2. condition, conduct, or qualities of *[patriotism]* 3. theory of *[socialism]* 4. devotion to *[nationalism]* 5. an instance of *[witticism]*

**isn't** (iz'nt) is not

**iso-** [< Gr. *isos*] *a combining form meaning* equal, similar, identical

**i·so·bar** (I'sə bär') *n.* [< prec. + Gr. *baros*, weight] a line on a map connecting points of equal barometric pressure

**i·so·late** (I'sə lāt') *vt.* -lat'ed, -lat'ing [< It. *isola* (< L. *insula*), island] to set apart from others; place alone —*n.* a person or thing that is isolated —i'so·la'tion *n.* —i'so·la'tor *n.*

**i·so·la'tion·ist** *n.* one who believes his country should not take part in international alliances, etc. —*adj.* of isolationists —i'so·la'tion·ism *n.*

**i·so·mer** (I'sə mər) *n.* [< Gr. *isos*, equal + *meros*, a part] any of two or more chemical compounds whose molecules contain the same atoms but in different arrangements —i'so·mer'·ic (-mer'ik) *adj.*

**i·so·met·ric** (-met'rik) *adj.* [< Gr. *isos*, equal + Gr. *metron*, measure] 1. equal in measure 2. of isometrics —*n.* [*pl.*] exercise in which muscles are briefly tensed in opposition to other muscles or to an immovable object —i'so·met'ri·cal·ly *adv.*

**i·sos·ce·les** (I säs'ə lēz') *adj.* [< Gr. *isos*, equal + *skelos*, leg] designating a triangle with two equal sides

**i·so·tope** (I'sə tōp') *n.* [< *iso-* + Gr. *topos*, place] any of two or more forms of an element having the same atomic number but different atomic weights

ISOSCELES
TRIANGLE

**Is·ra·el** (iz'rē əl) 1. *Bible* Jacob 2. ancient land of the Hebrews at the SE end of the Mediterranean 3. kingdom in the N part of this land 4. country between the Mediterranean & the country of Jordan: 7,992 sq. mi.; pop. 2,813,000 5. the Jewish people

**Is·rae·li** (iz rā'lē) *adj.* of modern Israel or its people —*n., pl.* -**lis**, -**li** a native or inhabitant of modern Israel

**Is·ra·el·ite** (iz'rē ə līt', -rā-) *n.* any of the people of ancient Israel

**is·su·ance** (ish'oo wəns) *n.* an issuing; issue

**is·sue** (ish'oo) *n.* [< L. *ex-*, out + *ire*, go] 1. an outgoing; outflow 2. an outlet; exit 3. a result; consequence 4. offspring 5. a point under dispute 6. a sending or giving out 7. all that is put forth at one time *[an issue of* bonds, a periodical, etc.] 8. *Med.* a discharge of blood, etc. —*vi.* -sued, -su·ing 1. to go or flow out; emerge 2. to result *(from)* or end *(in)* 3. to be published —*vt.* 1. to let out; discharge 2. to give or deal out, as supplies 3. to publish —**at issue** in dispute —**take issue** to disagree

**-ist** (ist, əst) [< Gr. *-istēs*] *a suffix meaning:* 1. one who does, makes, or practices *[satirist]* 2. one skilled in or occupied with *[druggist, violinist]* 3. an adherent of *[anarchist]*

**Is·tan·bul** (is'tan bool', -tän-) seaport in NW Turkey: pop. 1,467,000

**isth·mus** (is'məs) *n., pl.* -mus·es, -mi (-mi) [< Gr. *isthmos*, a neck] a narrow strip of land having water at each side and connecting two larger bodies of land

**it** (it) *pron.* [for *pl.* see THEY] [< OE. *hit*] the animal or thing previously mentioned *It* is also used as: a) the subject of an impersonal verb *[it* is snowing] b) a subject or object of indefinite sense in various idiomatic constructions *[it's* all right, he lords *it* over us] —*n.* the player, as in tag, who must try to catch another —**with it** [Slang] alert, informed, or hip

**It., Ital.** 1. Italian 2. Italy

---

fat, āpe, cär; ten, ēven; is, bīte; gō, hôrn, tōōl, look; oil, out; up, fur; chin; she; thin, then; zh, leisure; ŋ, ring; ə for *a* in ago; ', (ā'b'l); ë, Fr. coeur; ö, Fr. feu; Fr. mon; ü, Fr. duc; kh, G. ich, doch; ‡ foreign; < derived from

**I·tal·ian** (i tal′yən) *adj.* of Italy, its people, language, etc. —*n.* **1.** a native or inhabitant of Italy **2.** the Romance language of Italy

**i·tal·ic** (i tal′ik) *adj.* [< its early use in *Italy*] designating a type in which the letters slant upward to the right [*this is italic type*] —*n.* [*usually pl.*, *sometimes with sing. v.*] italic type or print: abbrev. *ital.*

**i·tal·i·cize** (i tal′ə sīz′) *vt.* **-cized′, -ciz′ing** to print in italics

**It·a·ly** (it′'l ē) country in S Europe: 116,304 sq. mi.; pop. 51,945,000

**itch** (ich) *vi.* [OE. *giccan*] **1.** to feel a tingling of the skin, with the desire to scratch **2.** to have a restless desire —*n.* **1.** an itching **2.** a restless desire —**the itch** an itching skin disorder —**itch′y** *adj.* **-i·er, -i·est**

**-ite** (īt) [< Gr. *-itēs*] *a suffix meaning:* **1.** an inhabitant of [*Akronite*] **2.** an adherent of [*laborite*] **3.** a manufactured product [*dynamite*]

**i·tem** (īt′əm) *n.* [< L. *ita*, so, thus] **1.** an article; unit; separate thing **2.** a bit of news or information

**i′tem·ize′** (-īz′) *vt.* **-ized′, -iz′ing** to specify the items of; set down by items —**i′tem·i·za′tion** *n.*

**it·er·ate** (it′ə rāt′) *vt.* **-at′ed, -at′ing** [< L. *iterum*, again] to utter or do again; repeat —**it′er·a′tion** *n.*

**i·tin·er·ant** (ī tin′ər ənt) *adj.* [< L. *iter*, a walk] traveling from place to place —*n.* a traveler

**i·tin·er·ar·y** (-ə rer′ē) *n.*, *pl.* **-ies 1.** a route **2.** a record of a journey **3.** a detailed plan of a journey

**-i·tis** (īt′əs) [< Gr. *-itis*] *a suffix meaning* inflammation of (a specified part or organ) [*neuritis*]

**it′ll** (it′'l) **1.** it will **2.** it shall

**its** (its) *pron.* that or those belonging

to it —*possessive pronominal adj.* of, belonging to, or done by it

**it's** (its) **1.** it is **2.** it has

**it·self** (it self′) *pron.* **1.** *the intensive form of* IT [*the work itself is easy*] **2.** *the reflexive form of* IT [*the dog bit itself*] **3.** its true self [*the cat is not itself today*]

**it·ty-bit·ty** (it′ē bit′ē) *adj.* [baby talk < *little bit*] [Colloq.] very small; tiny Also **it·sy-bit·sy** (it′sē bit′sē)

**-i·ty** (ə tē, i-) [< L. *-itas*] *a suffix meaning* state, quality, or instance [*chastity*]

**IUD** intrauterine device

**i.v.** intravenous(ly)

**I've** (īv) I have

**-ive** (iv) [L. *-ivus*] *a suffix meaning:* **1.** of or having the nature of [*substantive*] **2.** tending to [*creative*]

**i·vied** (ī′vēd) *adj.* covered or overgrown with ivy

**i·vo·ry** (ī′vər ē, īv′rē) *n.*, *pl.* **-ries** [ult. < Egypt. *ābu*] **1.** the hard, white substance forming the tusks of elephants, walruses, etc. **2.** any substance like ivory **3.** creamy white **4.** [*pl.*] [Slang] *a)* piano keys *b)* dice —*adj.* **1.** of or like ivory **2.** creamy-white

**Ivory Coast** country in WC Africa: 124,500 sq. mi.; pop. 3,750,000

**ivory tower** a retreat away from reality or action

**i·vy** (ī′vē) *n.*, *pl.* **i′vies** [OE. *īfig*] **1.** a climbing vine with a woody stem and evergreen leaves **2.** any of various similar climbing plants

**-ize** (īz) [< Gr. *-izein*] *a suffix meaning:* **1.** to cause to be [*sterilize*] **2.** to become (like) [*crystallize*] **3.** to combine with [*oxidize*] **4.** to engage in [*soliloquize*] —**-i·za·tion** (ə zā′shən, ī-)

# J

**J, j** (jā) *n.*, *pl.* **J's, j's** the tenth letter of the English alphabet

**jab** (jab) *vt.*, *vi.* **jabbed, jab′bing** [< ME. *jobben*, to peck] **1.** to poke, as with a sharp instrument **2.** to punch with short, straight blows —*n.* a quick thrust or blow

**jab·ber** (jab′ər) *vi.*, *vt.* [prob. echoic] to talk quickly, incoherently, or foolishly; chatter —*n.* chatter —**jab′ber·er** *n.*

**ja·bot** (zha bō′, ja-) *n.* [Fr., bird's crop] a ruffle or frill down the front of a blouse, etc.

**jack** (jak) *n.* [< the name *Jack*] **1.** [*often* J-] a man or boy **2.** any of various machines used to lift something heavy a short distance [an automobile *jack*] **3.** a playing-card with a page boy's picture on it **4.** a small flag flown on a ship's bow as a signal or to show nationality **5.** any of the small 6-pronged metal pieces tossed and picked up in the game of jacks

**6.** a plug-in receptacle used to make electric contact **7.** [Slang] money —*vt.* to raise by means of a jack —**jack up** [Colloq.] to raise (prices, wages, etc.)

**jack-** [see prec.] *a combining form meaning:* **1.** male [*jackass*] **2.** large or strong [*jackknife*] **3.** boy, fellow [*jack-in-the-box*]

**jack·al** (jak′əl, -ôl) *n.* [< Sans.] a wild dog of Asia and N Africa

**jack·ass** (jak′as′) *n.* [*jack-* + *ass*] **1.** a male donkey. **2.** a fool

JACK (sense 2)

**jack·daw** (jak′dô′) *n.* [< *jack* +

ME. *dawe*, jackdaw] a European black bird like the crow, but smaller

**jack·et** (jak′it) *n.* [ < Ar. *shakk*] **1.** a short coat **2.** an outer covering, as the removable paper cover on a book, the cardboard holder of a phonograph record, the skin of a potato, etc.

**Jack Frost** frost or cold weather personified

**jack′-in-the-box′** *n., pl.* **-box′es** a toy consisting of a box from which a figure on a spring jumps up when the lid is lifted: also **jack′-in-a-box′**

**jack′-in-the-pul′pit** (-pool′pit) *n., pl.* **-pits** a plant with a flower spike partly arched over by a hoodlike covering

**jack′knife′** *n., pl.* **-knives′ 1.** a large pocketknife **2.** a dive in which the diver touches his feet with knees unbent and then straightens out —*vi., vt.* **-knifed′, -knif′ing** to bend or fold at the middle or at a connection

**jack′-of-all′-trades′** *n., pl.* **jacks′-** [see JACK-] [*often* J-] one who can do many kinds of work acceptably

**jack-o′-lan·tern** (jak′ə lan′tərn) *n., pl.* **-terns** a hollow pumpkin cut to look like a face and used as a lantern

**jack′pot′** *n.* [*jack*, playing card + *pot*] cumulative stakes, as in a poker game, slot machine, etc.

**jack rabbit** a large hare of W N. America, with strong hind legs

**Jack·son** (jak′s'n) capital of Miss.: pop. 154,000

**Jack·son** (jak′s'n), **Andrew** 1767–1845; 7th U.S. president (1829–1837)

**Jack·son·ville** (jak′s'n vil′) port in NE Fla.: pop. 529,000

**Ja·cob** (jā′kəb) *Bible* a son of Isaac: Gen. 25–50

**Jac·quard** (jə kärd′) *n.* [ < J. M. *Jacquard* (1752–1834), Fr. inventor] a fabric with a figured weave

**jade¹** (jād) *n.* [ < Sp. *piedra de ijada*, stone of the side: supposed to cure pains in the side] **1.** a hard, ornamental stone, usually green **2.** the green color of this stone

**jade²** (jād) *n.* [ < ON. *jalda*, mare] **1.** a worn-out, worthless horse **2.** a disreputable woman —*vt.* **jad′ed, jad′ing 1.** to tire **2.** to satiate — **jad′ed·ly** *adv.* —**jad′ed·ness** *n.*

**jade·ite** (jā′dīt) *n.* a hard, translucent variety of jade

**jade plant** a plant with thick, green leaves, native to S Africa and Asia

**jag** (jag) *n.* [ME. *jagge*] a sharp, toothlike projection

**jag·ged** (jag′id) *adj.* having sharp projecting points; notched or ragged —**jag′ged·ly** *adv.* —**jag′ged·ness** *n.*

**jag·uar** (jag′wär) *n.* [Port. < SAm.-Ind.] a large leopardlike cat found from SW U.S. to Argentina

**jai a·lai** (hī′ lī′, ə lī′) [ < Basque *jai*, celebration + *alai*, merry] a game like handball, played with a basketlike racket

**jail** (jāl) *n.* [ult. < L. *cavea*, cage] a prison, esp. for minor offenders or persons awaiting trial —*vt.* to put or keep in jail

**jail′break′** (-brāk′) *n.* a breaking out of jail

**jail′er, jail′or** *n.* a person in charge of a jail or of prisoners

**Ja·kar·ta** (jə kär′tə) capital of Indonesia: pop. c.3,500,000

**ja·lop·y** (jə läp′ē) *n., pl.* **-ies** [ < ?] [Slang] an old, ramshackle car

**jal·ou·sie** (jal′ə sē) *n.* [Fr.: see JEALOUS] a window, shade, door, etc. formed of adjustable horizontal slats of wood, metal, or glass

**jam¹** (jam) *vt.* **jammed, jam′ming** [ < ?] **1.** to squeeze into a confined space **2.** to crush **3.** to crowd **4.** to crowd into or block (a passageway, etc.) **5.** to cause to be stuck tight and unworkable **6.** to make (radio broadcasts, etc.) unintelligible, as by sending out other signals on the same wavelength —*vi.* **1.** *a*) to become stuck fast *b*) to become unworkable because of jammed parts **2.** to become squeezed into a confined space **3.** [Slang] *Jazz* to improvise —*n.* **1.** a jamming or being jammed [a traffic *jam*] **2.** [Colloq.] a difficult situation

**jam²** (jam) *n.* [ < ? prec.] fruit boiled with sugar to a thick mixture

**Ja·mai·ca** (jə mā′kə) country on an island in the West Indies, south of Cuba: 4,411 sq. mi.; pop. 1,876,000 —**Ja·mai′can** *adj., n.*

**jamb** (jam) *n.* [ < LL. *gamba*, leg] a side post of a doorway, etc.

**jam·bo·ree** (jam′bə rē′) *n.* [ < ?] **1.** [Colloq.] a noisy revel **2.** a large assembly of boy scouts from many places

**James·town** (jāmz′toun′) former village in Va.: 1st Eng. colonial settlement in America (1607)

**jam·packed** (jam′pakt′) *adj.* tightly packed

**jan·gle** (jaŋ′g'l) *vi.* **-gled, -gling** [ < OFr. *jangler*] to make a harsh, usually metallic sound —*vt.* **1.** to cause to jangle **2.** to irritate [*jangled* nerves] —*n.* a jangling —**jan′gler** *n.*

**jan·i·tor** (jan′i tər) *n.* [L., doorkeeper] one who takes care of a building, doing routine repairs, etc. —**jan′i·to′ri·al** (-ə tôr′ē al) *adj.*

**Jan·u·ar·y** (jan′yoo wer′ē) *n., pl.* **-ies** [ < L. < *Janus*, Roman god who was patron of beginnings and endings] the first month of the year, having 31 days: abbrev. **Jan.**

**Ja·pan** (jə pan′) **1.** island country in the Pacific, off the E coast of Asia: 142,726 sq. mi.; pop. 100,020,000 **2. Sea of**, arm of the Pacific, between Japan & Asia

**ja·pan** (jə pan′) *n.* [ < *Japan*] a hard lacquer giving a glossy finish —*vt.* **-panned′, -pan′ning** to lacquer with japan

**Jap·a·nese** (jap′ə nēz′) *adj.* of Japan, its people, language, etc. —*n.*

1. *pl.* **-nese/** a native of Japan 2. the language of Japan

**Japanese beetle** a shiny, green-and-brown beetle, orig. from Japan, damaging to crops

**jape** (jāp) *vi., vt., n.* **japed, jap/ing** [ME. *japen*] joke; trick

**jar¹** (jär) *vi.* **jarred, jar/ring** [ult. echoic] 1. to make a harsh sound; grate 2. to have an irritating effect (*on one*) 3. to vibrate from an impact 4. to clash; conflict —*vt.* to jolt —*n.* 1. a grating sound 2. a vibration due to impact 3. a jolt

**jar²** (jär) *n.* [< Ar. *jarrah*, earthen container] 1. a container made of glass, earthenware, etc., with a large opening 2. as much as a jar will hold: also **jar/ful/**

**jar·di·niere** (jär/d'n ir/) *n.* [< Fr. < *jardin*, a garden] an ornamental pot or stand for flowers or plants

**jar·gon** (jär/gən) *n.* [< MFr., a chattering] 1. unintelligible talk 2. the specialized vocabulary of those in the same work, way of life, etc.

**jas·mine** (jaz/min; *chiefly Brit.* jas/-) *n.* [< Per. *yāsamin*] any of certain plants of warm regions, with fragrant flowers of yellow, red, or white

**Ja·son** (jās/'n) *Gr.Myth.* the leader of the Argonauts: cf. ARGONAUT

**jas·per** (jas/pər) *n.* [< Gr. *iaspis*] an opaque variety of colored quartz

**ja·to, JA·TO** (jā/tō) *n.* [*j*(*et*)-*a*(*ssisted*) *t*(*ake*)*o*(*ff*)] an airplane takeoff assisted by a jet-producing unit or units

**jaun·dice** (jōn/dis) *n.* [ult. < L. *galbus*, yellow] a diseased condition in which the eyeballs, skin, and urine become abnormally yellow as a result of bile in the blood —*vt.* **-diced, -dic·ing** 1. to cause to have jaundice 2. to make prejudiced through envy, etc.

**jaunt** (jōnt) *vi.* [< ?] to take a short pleasure trip —*n.* such a trip

**jaun·ty** (jōnt/ē) *adj.* **-ti·er, -ti·est** [< Fr. *gentil*, genteel] showing an easy confidence; perky or sprightly —**jaun/ti·ly** *adv.* —**jaun/ti·ness** *n.*

**Ja·va** (jä/və, jav/ə) large island of Indonesia —*n.* 1. a coffee grown there 2. [*often* **j-**] [Slang] any coffee —**Jav/a·nese/** (-nēz/) *adj., n., pl.* **-nese/**

**jav·e·lin** (jav/lin, -ə lin) *n.* [MFr. *javeline*] a light spear, esp. one thrown for distance in a contest

**jaw** (jô) *n.* [< ? OFr. *joue*, cheek] 1. either of the two bony parts that hold the teeth and frame the mouth 2. either of two movable parts that grasp or crush something, as in a vise —*vi.* [Slang] to talk

**jaw/bone/** *n.* a bone of a jaw, esp. of the lower jaw —*vt., vi.* **-boned/, -bon/ing** to try to persuade by using the influence of one's office

**jaw/break/er** (-brā/kər) *n.* 1. a machine for crushing rocks, ore, etc. 2. a hard, usually round candy 3. [Slang] a word hard to pronounce

**jay** (jā) *n.* [< LL. *gaius*, jay] 1. any of several birds of the crow family 2. *same as* BLUE JAY

**jay/walk/** *vi.* [Colloq.] to walk across a street carelessly without obeying traffic rules or signals —**jay/walk/er** *n.*

**jazz** (jaz) *n.* [< ?] 1. a kind of syncopated, highly rhythmic music originated by New Orleans musicians, esp. Negroes 2. [Slang] talk, acts, etc. regarded disparagingly —*vt.* 1. to play as jazz 2. [Slang] to enliven or embellish (with *up*)

**jazz/y** *adj.* **-i·er, -i·est** 1. of or like jazz 2. [Slang] lively, flashy, etc.

**jeal·ous** (jel/əs) *adj.* [see ZEAL] 1. watchful in guarding [*jealous* of his rights] 2. *a*) resentfully suspicious of rivalry [a *jealous* lover] *b*) resentfully envious *c*) resulting from such feelings [a *jealous* rage] —**jeal/ous·ly** *adv.*

**jeal/ous·y** *n., pl.* **-ies** the quality, condition, or feeling of being jealous

**jean** (jēn) *n.* [< L. *Genua*, Genoa] 1. a durable, twilled cotton cloth 2. [*pl.*] trousers of this or of denim

**jeep** (jēp) *n.* [< creature in a comic strip by E. C. Segar] a small, rugged, military automobile of World War II

**jeer** (jir) *vi., vt.* [? < *cheer*] to make fun of in a rude, sarcastic manner; scoff (at) —*n.* a jeering cry or remark

**Jef·fer·son** (jef/ər s'n), **Thomas** 1743–1826; 3d U.S. president (1801–09)

**Jefferson City** capital of Mo.: pop. 132,000

**Je·ho·vah** (ji hō/və) [< Heb.] God

**je·june** (ji jōōn/) *adj.* [L. *jejunus*, empty] 1. not satisfying or interesting 2. not mature; childish

**je·ju·num** (ji jōō/nəm) *n., pl.* **-na** (-nə) [< L. *jejunus*, empty] the middle part of the small intestine

**jell** (jel) *vi., vt.* [< ff.] 1. to become, or make into, jelly 2. to crystallize, as a plan

**jel·ly** (jel/ē) *n., pl.* **-lies** [< L. *gelare*, freeze] 1. a soft, gelatinous food made from cooked fruit syrup or meat juice 2. any substance like this —*vi., vt.* **-lied, -ly·ing** to jell (sense 1)

**jel/ly·bean/** *n.* a small, bean-shaped, gelatinous candy

**jel/ly·fish/** *n., pl.* see FISH 1. a sea animal with an umbrella-shaped, jelly-like body and long tentacles 2. [Colloq.] a weak-willed person

**jel/ly·roll/** *n.* a thin sheet of sponge cake spread with jelly and rolled up

**jeop·ard·ize** (jep/ər dīz/) *vt.* **-ized/, -iz/ing** to put in jeopardy

**jeop/ard·y** (-dē) *n., pl.* **-ies** [< OFr. *jeu parti*, lit., a game with even chances] great danger or risk

**jer·e·mi·ad** (jer/ə mī/əd, -ad) *n.* a tale of woe: in allusion to the *Lamentations of Jeremiah*

**Jer·e·mi·ah** (jer/ə mī/ə) *Bible* a Hebrew prophet of the 7th and 6th cent. B.C.

**Jer·i·cho** (jer/ə kō/) city in W Jordan: site of an ancient city in Canaan

**jerk** (jurk) *n.* [< ?] 1. a sharp, abrupt pull, twist, etc. 2. a sudden muscular contraction or reflex 3. [Slang] a person regarded as stupid, foolish, etc. —*vi., vt.* 1. to move with a jerk; pull sharply 2. to twitch

**jer·kin** (jur′kin) *n.* [< ?] a short, closefitting jacket, often sleeveless

**jerk′wa′ter** *adj.* [Colloq.] small, unimportant, as of a *jerkwater town*]

**jerk·y¹** (jurk′ē) *adj.* **-i·er, -i·est** 1. moving by jerks; spasmodic 2. [Slang] stupid, foolish, etc. —**jerk′i·ly** *adv.*

**jer·ky²** (jur′kē) *n.* [< Sp. *charqui*] meat preserved by being sliced into strips and dried in the sun

**jer·ry-built** (jer′ē bilt) *adj.* built poorly, or of cheap materials

**jer·sey** (jur′zē) *n., pl.* **-seys** [< *Jersey,* Brit. island in the English Channel] 1. [J-] a breed of reddish-brown dairy cattle originally from Jersey 2. a soft knitted cloth 3. a closefitting, knitted upper garment

**Jersey City** city in N.J., across the Hudson from New York: pop. 261,000

**Je·ru·sa·lem** (jə rōō′sə ləm) capital of Israel (sense 4): pop. 250,000

**jest** (jest) *n.* [< L. *gerere,* perform] 1. a mocking remark; taunt 2. a joke 3. fun; joking 4. a thing to be laughed at —*vi.* 1. to jeer 2. to joke

**jest′er** *n.* one who jests; esp., a man kept by a medieval ruler to amuse him by joking and clowning

**Jes·u·it** (jezh′ōō wit, jez′-) *n.* a member of the Society of Jesus, a R.C. religious order, founded 1534

**Je·sus** (jē′zəs) the founder of the Christian religion: also **Jesus Christ**

**jet¹** (jet) *vt., vi.* **jet′ted, jet′ting** [< L. *jacere,* to throw] 1. to gush out in a stream 2. to travel or convey by jet airplane —*n.* 1. a stream of liquid or gas suddenly emitted 2. a spout for emitting a jet 3. a jet-propelled airplane: in full, **jet (air)plane** —*adj.* driven by jet propulsion

**jet²** (jet) *n.* [< Gr. *Gagas,* town in Asia Minor] 1. a hard, black mineral like coal, polished and used in jewelry 2. a lustrous black —*adj.* black

**jet lag** a disruption of the daily body rhythms, associated with high-speed travel by jet airplane

**jet′lin′er** *n.* a commercial jet aircraft for carrying passengers

**jet′port′** *n.* an airport with long runways, for use by jet airplanes

**jet propulsion** propulsion of airplanes, boats, etc. by the discharge of gases under pressure from a rear vent —**jet′-pro·pelled′** (-prə peld′) *adj.*

**jet·sam** (jet′səm) *n.* [var. of JETTISON] cargo thrown overboard to lighten a ship in danger

**jet set** fashionable people who travel widely for pleasure, esp. in jets

**jet·ti·son** (jet′ə s′n) *vt.* [< L. *jactare,* to throw] 1. to throw (goods) overboard so as to lighten a ship in danger 2. to discard

**jet·ty** (jet′ē) *n., pl.* **-ties** [see JET¹] 1. a wall built out into the water to restrain currents, protect a harbor, etc. 2. a landing pier

**Jew** (jōō) *n.* [< Heb. *yehūdī,* citizen of Judah] 1. a person descended, or regarded as descended, from the ancient Hebrews 2. a person whose religion is Judaism

**jew·el** (jōō′əl) *n.* [ult. < L. *jocus,* a joke] 1. a precious stone; gem 2. any person or thing very dear to one 3. a small gem used as a bearing in a watch —*vt.* **-eled** or **-elled, -el·ing** or **-el·ling** to decorate or set with jewels

**jew′el·er, jew′el·ler** (-ər) *n.* one who makes or deals in jewelry

**jew′el·ry** *n.* jewels collectively

**Jew·ish** (jōō′ish) *adj.* of or having to do with Jews or Judaism —*n.* [Colloq.] same as YIDDISH —**Jew′ish·ness** *n.*

**Jew·ry** (jōō′rē) *n.* the Jewish people

**jew's-harp** (jōōz′härp′) *n.* [< Du. *jeugd-tromp,* child's trumpet] a small, metal musical instrument held between the teeth and plucked to produce twanging tones: also **jews'-harp**

**Jez·e·bel** (jez′ə bel′) *Bible* a wicked queen of Israel

**jg, j.g.** junior grade

**jib** (jib) *n.* [Dan. *gib*] a triangular sail projecting ahead of the foremast

**jibe¹** (jīb) *vi.* **jibed, jib′ing** [< Du. *gijpen*] 1. to shift from one side of a ship to the other, as a fore-and-aft sail 2. to change the course of a ship so that the sails jibe 3. [Colloq.] to be in agreement or accord

**jibe²** (jīb) *n., vi., vt.* same as GIBE

**jif·fy** (jif′ē) *n., pl.* **-fies** [< ?] [Colloq.] a very short time: also **jiff**

**jig** (jig) *n.* [prob. < MFr. *giguer,* to dance] 1. a fast, springy dance in triple time, or music for this 2. a device used to guide a tool —*vi., vt.* **jigged, jig′ging** to dance (a jig) —**in jig time** [Colloq.] very quickly —**the jig is up** [Slang] no chance is left

**jig·ger** (jig′ər) *n.* 1. a small glass, usually of 1 1/2 ozs., used to measure liquor 2. the contents of a jigger

**jig·gle** (jig′l) *vi., vt.* **-gled, -gling** [< JIG] to move in quick, slight jerks —*n.* a jiggling

**jig·saw** (jig′sô′) *n.* a saw consisting of a narrow blade set in a frame, used for cutting along irregular lines

**jigsaw puzzle** a puzzle consisting of disarranged, irregularly cut pieces of a picture that are to be fitted together

**jilt** (jilt) *vt.* [< *Jill,* sweetheart] to reject or cast off (a lover or sweetheart) after encouraging him

**Jim Crow** [name of an early Negro minstrel song] [also **j- c-**] [Colloq.] discrimination against or segregation of Negroes —**Jim′Crow′** *vt., adj.*

**jim·my** (jim′ē) *n., pl.* **-mies** [< *James*] a short crowbar, used by burglars to pry open windows, etc. —*vt.* **-mied, -my·ing** to pry open with or as with a jimmy

**jim·son weed** (jim′s′n) [< *Jamestown weed*] a poisonous weed with white or purplish, trumpet-shaped flowers

**jin·gle** (jiŋ′g′l) *vi.* **-gled, -gling** [echoic] to make light, ringing sounds, as small bells —*vt.* to cause to jingle —*n.* **1.** a jingling sound **2.** a catchy verse or song with easy rhythm, simple rhymes, etc.

**jin·go·ism** (jiŋ'gō iz'm) *n.* [< phr. *by jingo* in a patriotic Brit. song] chauvinistic advocacy of an aggressive, warlike foreign policy —**jin'·go·ist** *n.* —**jin'go·is'tic** *adj.*

**jin·ni** (ji nē', jin'ē) *n., pl.* **jinn** [Ar.] Moslem Legend a supernatural being that can influence human affairs

**jin·rik·i·sha** (jin rik'shô) *n.* [Jap. < *jin*, a man + *riki*, power + *sha*, carriage] a small, two-wheeled carriage pulled by a man, esp. formerly in the Orient: also **jin·rick'sha, jin·rik'sha**

**jinx** (jiŋks) *n.* [< Gr. *iynx*, the wryneck (bird used in black magic)] [Colloq.] a person or thing supposed to bring bad luck —*vt.* [Colloq.] to be a jinx to

**jit·ney** (jit'nē) *n., pl.* **-neys** [< ? Fr. *jeton*, a token] **1.** [Old Slang] a five-cent coin **2.** a bus or car carrying passengers for a small fare

**jit'ter·bug'** *n.* a fast, acrobatic dance for couples, esp. in the 1940's —*vi.* **-bugged', -bug'ging** to do this dance

**jit·ters** (jit'ərz) *n.pl.* [Colloq.] an uneasy, nervous feeling; fidgets (with *the*) —**jit'ter·y** *adj.*

**jive** (jīv) *n.* [< JIBE²] **1.** [Slang] foolish, exaggerated, or insincere talk **2.** *former term for* JAZZ *or* SWING

**Joan of Arc** (jōn' əv ärk'), Saint 1412–31; Fr. military heroine: burned at the stake

**Job** (jōb) *Bible* a man who suffered much but kept his faith in God

**job** (jäb) *n.* [< ?] **1.** a piece of work done for pay **2.** task; duty **3.** the thing or material being worked on **4.** employment; work —*adj.* hired or done by the job —*vt., vi.* **jobbed, job'bing 1.** to deal in (goods) as a jobber **2.** to sublet (work, etc.) —**job'hold'er** *n.* —**job'less** *adj.*

**job action** a refusal by a group of employees to perform their duties, in order to win certain demands, esp. by a group forbidden by law to strike

**job·ber** (jäb'ər) *n.* **1.** one who buys goods in quantity and sells them to dealers **2.** one who does piecework

**job lot** an assortment of goods for sale as one quantity

**jock** (jäk) *n.* [Slang] *short for* DISC JOCKEY

**jock·ey** (jäk'ē) *n., pl.* **-eys** [< Scot. dim. of *Jack*] one whose job is riding horses in races —*vt., vi.* **-eyed, -ey·ing 1.** to cheat; swindle **2.** to maneuver for position or advantage

**jock·strap** (jäk'strap') *n.* [*jock*, penis + STRAP] **1.** an elastic belt with a pouch for supporting the genitals, worn by male athletes **2.** [Slang] an athlete Also **jock**

**jo·cose** (jō kōs') *adj.* [< L. *jocus*, a joke] joking or playful —**jo·cose'ly** *adv.* —**jo·cos'i·ty** (-käs'ə tē) *pl.* **-ties,** jo·cose'ness n.

**joc·u·lar** (jäk'yə lər) *adj.* [< L. *jocus*, a joke] joking; full of fun —**joc'u·lar'i·ty** (-lar'ə tē) *n., pl.* **-ties**

**joc·und** (jäk'ənd) *adj.* [< L. *jucundus*, pleasant] cheerful; genial; gay —**joc'und·ly** *adv.*

**jodh·purs** (jäd'pərz) *n.pl.* [< *Jodhpur*, former state in India] riding breeches made loose and full above the knees and closefitting below

**jog¹** (jäg) *vt.* **jogged, jog'ging** [ME. *joggen*, to spur (a horse)] **1.** to give a little shake to; nudge **2.** to rouse (the memory) —*vi.* to move along at a slow, steady, jolting pace —*n.* **1.** a little shake or nudge **2.** a slow, steady, jolting motion —**jog'ger** *n.*

**jog²** (jäg) *n.* [var. of JAG¹] **1.** a projecting or notched part in a surface or line **2.** a sharp, brief change of direction, as in a road

**jog·gle** (jäg'l) *vt., vi.* **-gled, -gling** [< JOG¹] to shake or jolt slightly —*n.* a slight jolt

**Jo·han·nes·burg** (jō han'is burg', yō hän'is-) city in NE South Africa: pop. 1,153,000

**John** (jän) *Bible* **1.** a Christian apostle, the reputed author of the fourth Gospel **2.** this book

**john** (jän) *n.* [Slang] **1.** a toilet **2.** [*also* J-] a prostitute's customer

**John Bull** (bool) England, or an Englishman, personified

**John Doe** (dō) a fictitious name used in legal papers for an unknown person

**John·son** (jän's'n) **1. Andrew,** 1808–75; 17th president of the U.S. (1865–69) **2. Lyn·don Baines** (lin' dən bānz), 1908–73; 36th president of the U.S. (1963–69) **3. Samuel,** 1709–84; Eng. lexicographer & writer

**John the Baptist** *Bible* the forerunner and baptizer of Jesus

**join** (join) *vt., vi.* [< L. *jungere*] **1.** to bring or come together (with); connect; unite **2.** to become a part or member of (a club, etc.) **3.** to participate (*in* a conversation, etc.)

**join·er** *n.* **1.** a carpenter who finishes interior woodwork **2.** [Colloq.] one who joins many organizations

**joint** (joint) *n.* [< L. *jungere*, join] **1.** a place where, or way in which, two things are joined **2.** any of the parts of a jointed whole **3.** a large cut of meat with the bone still in it **4.** [Slang] a cheap bar, restaurant, etc., or any house, building, etc. **5.** [Slang] a marijuana cigarette —*adj.* **1.** common to two or more [*joint* property] **2.** sharing with another [*a joint* owner] —*vt.* **1.** to fasten together by or provide with a joint or joints **2.** to cut (meat) into joints —**out of joint 1.** dislocated **2.** disordered

**joint'ly** *adv.* in common

**joist** (joist) *n.* [< OFr. *giste*, a bed] any of the parallel beams that hold up the planks of a floor or the laths of a ceiling

JOISTS

**joke** (jōk) *n.* [L. *jocus*] **1.** anything said or done to arouse laughter, as a funny anecdote **2.** a thing done or said merely in fun **3.** a person or thing to be laughed at

—*vi.* joked, jok′ing to make jokes —jok′ing·ly *adv.*

**jok′er** *n.* 1. one who jokes 2. a hidden provision, as in a legal document, to make it different from what it seems to be 3. an extra playing card used in some games

**jol·li·ty** (jäl′ə tē) *n.* a being jolly; gaiety

**jol·ly** (jäl′ē) *adj.* -li·er, -li·est [OFr. *joli*] 1. full of high spirits and good humor; merry 2. [Colloq.] enjoyable —*vt., vi.* -lied, -ly·ing [Colloq.] 1. to try to make (a person) feel good, as by coaxing (often with *along*) 2. to make fun of (someone) —jol′li·ly *adv.* —jol′li·ness *n.*

**jolt** (jōlt) *vt.* [< earlier *jot*] 1. to shake up, as with a bumpy ride 2. to shock or surprise —*vi.* to move along in a bumpy manner —*n.* 1. a sudden jerk, bump, etc. 2. a shock or surprise

**Jo·nah** (jō′nə) 1. *Bible* a Hebrew prophet: cast overboard and swallowed by a big fish, he was later cast up unharmed 2. a person whose presence brings bad luck

**Jones** (jōnz), **John Paul** 1747–92; Am. naval officer in the Revolutionary War, born in Scotland

**jon·quil** (jän′kwəl, jän′-) *n.* [< L. *juncus*, a rush] a species of narcissus with small yellow flowers

**Jon·son** (jän′s'n), **Ben** 1572?–1637; Eng. dramatist & poet

**Jor·dan** (jôr′d'n) 1. river in the Near East, flowing into the Dead Sea 2. country east of Israel: 37,300 sq. mi.; pop. 2,101,000

**Jo·seph** (jō′zəf) *Bible* 1. one of Jacob's sons, who became a high official in Egypt 2. the husband of Mary, mother of Jesus

**josh** (jäsh) *vt., vi.* [< ?] [Colloq.] to tease; banter —josh′er *n.*

**Josh·u·a** (jäsh′oo wə) *Bible* Moses' successor, and leader of the Israelites into the Promised Land

**jos·tle** (jäs′'l) *vt., vi.* -tled, -tling [see JOUST] to push, as in a crowd; shove roughly —*n.* a jostling

**jot** (jät) *n.* [< Gr. *iōta*, the smallest letter] a very small amount —*vt.* jot′ted, jot′ting to make a brief note of (usually with *down*) —jot′ter *n.*

**jounce** (jouns) *vt., vi.* jounced, jounc′ing [< ?] to jolt or bounce —*n.* a jolt —jounc′y *adj.*

**jour·nal** (jur′n'l) *n.* [< L. *diurnalis*, daily] 1. a daily record of happenings, as a diary 2. a newspaper or periodical 3. *Bookkeeping* a book of original entry for recording transactions 4. [orig. Scot.] the part of an axle or shaft that turns in a bearing

**jour·nal·ese** (jur′n'l ēz′) *n.* a facile style of writing found in many newspapers, magazines, etc.

**jour·nal·ism** (-iz'm) *n.* the work of gathering news for, or producing, a newspaper, etc. —jour′nal·ist *n.* —jour′nal·is′tic *adj.*

**jour·ney** (jur′nē) *n.*, *pl.* -neys [< OFr. *journee*; ult. < L. *dies*, day] a traveling from one place to another; trip —*vi.* -neyed, -ney·ing to travel —jour′ney·er *n.*

**jour·ney·man** (-mən) *n.*, *pl.* -men [ME. < *journey*, day's work + *man*] 1. a worker who has learned his trade 2. an average or mediocre performer

**joust** (joust, just) *n.* [ult. < L. *juxta*, close to] a combat with lances between two knights on horseback —*vi.* to engage in a joust

**jo·vi·al** (jō′vē əl) *adj.* [< LL. *Jovialis*, of Jupiter: from astrological notion of planet's influence] full of hearty, playful good humor; gay —jo′vi·al′i·ty (-al′ə tē) *n.* —jo′vi·al·ly *adv.*

**jowl**[1] (joul) *n.* [OE. *ceafl*, jaw] 1. the lower jaw 2. the cheek, esp. of a hog

**jowl**[2] (joul) *n.* [OE. *ceole*, throat] [often *pl.*] the fleshy, hanging part under the jaw —jowl′y *adj.*

**joy** (joi) *n.* [ult. < L. *gaudium*, joy] 1. a very glad feeling; happiness; delight 2. anything causing this

**Joyce** (jois), **James** 1882–1941; Ir. novelist & poet

**joy·ful** *adj.* feeling, expressing, or causing joy; glad —joy′ful·ly *adv.*

**joy·ous** (-əs) *adj.* joyful; gay —joy′ous·ly *adv.* —joy′ous·ness *n.*

**joy ride** [Colloq.] an automobile ride, often at reckless speed, just for pleasure —joy rider —joy riding

**J.P.** justice of the peace

**Jpn.** 1. Japan 2. Japanese

**Jr., jr.** junior

**ju·bi·lant** (jōō′b'l ənt) *adj.* [< L. *jubilum*, wild shout] joyful and triumphant; rejoicing; elated

**ju·bi·la·tion** (jōō′bə lā′shən) *n.* a rejoicing 2. a happy celebration

**ju·bi·lee** (jōō′bə lē′) *n.* [< Heb. *yōbēl*, a ram's horn (trumpet)] 1. a 50th or 25th anniversary 2. a time of rejoicing 3. jubilation

**Ju·dah** (jōō′də) 1. *Bible* one of Jacob's sons 2. kingdom in the S part of ancient Palestine

**Ju·da·ism** (jōō′də iz'm) *n.* the Jewish religion —Ju·da′ic (-dā′ik) *adj.*

**Ju·das** (**Is·car·i·ot**) (jōō′dəs is ker′ē ət) the disciple who betrayed Jesus for money —*n.* a traitor; betrayer

**judge** (juj) *n.* [< L. *jus*, law + *dicere*, say] 1. a public official with authority to hear and decide cases in a court of law 2. a person designated to determine the winner, settle a controversy, etc. 3. a person qualified to decide on the relative worth of anything —*vt., vi.* judged, judg′ing 1. to hear and pass judgment (on) in a court of law 2. to determine the winner of (a contest) or settle (a controversy) 3. to form an opinion about 4. to criticize or censure 5. to think; suppose —judge′ship′ *n.*

**judg′ment** *n.* 1. a judging; deciding 2. a legal decision; order given by a judge, etc. **3.** an opinion **4.** the ability to come to an opinion **5.** [J-] *short for* LAST JUDGMENT Also **judgement** —**judg·men'tal** (-men'ť'l) *adj.*

**Judgment Day** *Theol.* the time of God's final judgment of all people

**ju·di·ca·to·ry** (jōō'di kə tôr'ē) *adj.* [see JUDGE] having to do with administering justice —*n., pl.* **-ries** a law court, or law courts collectively

**ju'di·ca·ture** (-chər) *n.* **1.** the administering of justice **2.** jurisdiction **3.** judges or courts collectively

**ju·di·cial** (jōō dish'əl) *adj.* **1.** of judges, courts, or their functions **2.** allowed, enforced, etc. by a court **3.** befitting a judge **4.** fair; impartial

**ju·di·ci·ar·y** (jōō dish'ē er'ē) *adj.* of judges or courts —*n., pl.* **-ies 1.** the part of government that administers justice **2.** judges collectively

**ju·di·cious** (-dish'əs) *adj.* having or showing sound judgment —**ju·di'cious·ly** *adv.*

**ju·do** (jōō'dō) *n.* [Jap. < *jū*, soft + *dō*, art] a form of jujitsu

**jug** (jug) *n.* [a pet form of *Judith* or *Joan*] **1.** a container for liquids, with a small opening and a handle **2.** [Slang] a jail

**jug·ger·naut** (jug'ər nôt') *n.* [< Sans. *Jagannātha*, lord of the world] a terrible, irresistible force

**jug·gle** (jug'ľ) *vt.* **-gled, -gling** [< L. *jocus*, a joke] **1.** to perform skillful tricks of sleight of hand with (balls, etc.) **2.** to manipulate so as to deceive —*vi.* to toss up balls, etc. and keep them in the air —**jug'gler** *n.* —**jug'gler·y** *n.*

**jug·u·lar** (jug'yoo lər) *adj.* [< L. *jugum*, a yoke] of the neck or throat —*n.* either of two large veins in the neck carrying blood from the head: in full, **jugular vein**

**juice** (jōōs) *n.* [< L. *jus*, broth] **1.** the liquid part of a plant, fruit, etc. **2.** a liquid in or from animal tissue **3.** [Colloq.] vitality **4.** [Slang] *a)* electricity *b)* alcoholic liquor —*vt.* **juiced, juic'ing** to extract juice from

**juic·er** (jōō'sər) *n.* a device for extracting juice from fruit

**juic·y** (jōō'sē) *adj.* **-i·er, -i·est 1.** full of juice **2.** [Colloq.] *a)* very interesting *b)* highly profitable —**juic'i·ness** *n.*

**ju·jit·su, ju·jut·su** (jōō jit'sōō) *n.* [< Jap. *jū*, pliant + *jutsu*, art] a Japanese system of wrestling in which the strength and weight of an opponent are used against him

**ju·ju·be** (jōō'jōō bē') *n.* [< Gr.] a gelatinous fruit-flavored candy

**juke·box** (jōōk'bäks') *n.* [< Am. Negro *juke*, wicked] a coin-operated electric phonograph

**ju·lep** (jōō'ləp) *n.* [< Per. *gul*, rose + *āb*, water] *same as* MINT JULEP

**ju·li·enne** (jōō'lē en') *adj.* [Fr.] cut into strips: said of vegetables

**Ju·li·et** (jōō'lyət, jōō'lē et') the heroine of Shakespeare's tragedy *Romeo and Juliet*

**Ju·ly** (joo lī', jə-) *n.* [< L. < *Julius* Caesar], the seventh month of the

year, having 31 days: abbrev. **Jul.**

**jum·ble** (jum'b'l) *vt., vi.* **-bled, -bling** [? blend of JUMP + TUMBLE] to mix or be mixed in a confused heap —*n.* a confused mixture or heap

**jum·bo** (jum'bō) *n., pl.* **-bos** [< Am. Negro *jamba*, elephant] a large person, animal, or thing —*adj.* very large

**jump** (jump) *vi.* [< ?] **1.** to spring or leap from the ground, a height, etc. **2.** to jerk; bob **3.** to move or act eagerly (often with *at*) **4.** to pass suddenly, as to a new topic **5.** to rise suddenly, as prices **6.** [Slang] to be lively —*vt.* **1.** *a)* to leap over *b)* to pass over **2.** to cause to leap **3.** to leap upon **4.** to cause (prices, etc.) to rise **5.** [Colloq.] *a)* to attack suddenly *b)* to react to prematurely **6.** [Slang] to leave suddenly *[to jump town]* —*n.* **1.** a jumping **2.** a distance jumped **3.** a sudden transition **4.** a sudden rise, as in prices **5.** a sudden, nervous start —**get (or have) the jump on** [Slang] to get (or have) an advantage over —**jump bail** to forfeit bail by running away —**jump'er** *n.*

**jump·er** (jum'pər) *n.* [< dial. *jump*, short coat] **1.** a loose jacket **2.** a sleeveless dress for wearing over a blouse, etc. **3.** [*pl.*] *same as* ROMPERS

**jump suit 1.** a coverall worn by paratroops, etc. **2.** any one-piece garment like this

**jump'y** *adj.* **-i·er, -i·est 1.** moving in jumps, etc. **2.** easily startled —**jump'i·ly** *adv.* —**jump'i·ness** *n.*

**jun·co** (juŋ'kō) *n., pl.* **-cos** [< Sp.] a small bird with a gray or black head

**junc·tion** (juŋk'shən) *n.* [< L. *jungere*, join] **1.** a joining or being joined **2.** a place of joining, as of roads —**junc'tion·al** *adj.*

**junc·ture** (juŋk'chər) *n.* **1.** a junction **2.** a point of time **3.** a crisis

**June** (jōōn) *n.* [< L. *Junius*, of Juno] the sixth month of the year, having 30 days

**Ju·neau** (jōō'nō) capital of Alas., on the SE coast: pop. 6,000

**jun·gle** (juŋ'g'l) *n.* [< Sans. *jaṅgala*, wasteland] **1.** land densely covered with trees, vines, etc., as in the tropics **2.** [Slang] a situation in which people struggle fiercely to survive

**jun·ior** (jōōn'yər) *adj.* [L. < *juvenis*, young] **1.** the younger: written *Jr.* after a son's name if it is the same as his father's **2.** of more recent position or lower status *[a junior partner]* **3.** of juniors —*n.* **1.** one who is younger, of lower rank, etc. **2.** a student in the next-to-last year, as of a college

**junior college** a school offering courses two years beyond high school

**junior high school** a school usually including 7th, 8th, and 9th grades

**ju·ni·per** (jōō'nə pər) *n.* [L. *juniperus*] a small evergreen shrub or tree with berrylike cones

**junk¹** (juŋk) *n.* [< ?] **1.** old metal, paper, rags, etc. **2.** [Colloq.] trash **3.** [Slang] heroin —*vt.* [Colloq.] to scrap

**junk²** (juŋk) *n.* [< Javanese *joṅ*] a Chinese flat-bottomed ship

**Jun·ker** (yooŋ'kər) *n.* [G.] a Prussian

of the land-owning, militaristic class

**junk·er** (juŋ'kər) *n.* [Slang] an old, dilapidated car or truck

**jun·ket** (juŋ'kit) *n.* [ME. *joncate*, cream cheese] 1. milk sweetened, flavored, and thickened into curd 2. a picnic 3. an excursion, esp. one by an official at public expense —*vi.* to go on a junket —**jun'ket·eer'** (-kə-tir'), **jun'ket·er** *n.*

**junk food** snack food with chemical additives and little food value

**junk·ie, junk·y** (juŋ'kē) *n., pl.* **-ies** [Slang] a narcotics addict

**Ju·no** (jōō'nō) *Rom. Myth.* the wife of Jupiter and queen of the gods

**jun·ta** (hoon'tə, jun'-) *n.* [Sp. < L. *jungere*, join] a group of political intriguers, esp. military men, in power after a coup d'état: also **jun·to** (jun'tō), *pl.* **-tos**

**Ju·pi·ter** (jōō'pə tər) 1. the chief Rom. god 2. the largest planet of the solar system: see PLANET

**ju·rid·i·cal** (joo rid'i k'l) *adj.* [< L. *jus*, law + *dicere*, declare] of judicial proceedings or law

**ju·ris·dic·tion** (joor'is dik'shən) *n.* [see prec.] 1. the administering of justice 2. authority or its range — **ju'ris·dic'tion·al** *adj.*

**ju·ris·pru·dence** (joor'is prōō'd'ns) *n.* [< L. *jus*, law + *prudentia*, a foreseeing] 1. the science or philosophy of law 2. a division of law

**ju·rist** (joor'ist) *n.* [< L. *jus*, law] an expert in law or writer on law

**ju·ror** (joor'ər) *n.* a member of a jury: also **ju'ry·man** (-mən), *pl.* **-men**

**ju·ry** (joor'ē) *n., pl.* **-ries** [< L. *jurare*, swear] 1. a group of people sworn to hear evidence in a law case and to give a decision 2. a committee that decides winners in a contest

**just** (just) *adj.* [< L. *jus*, law] 1. right or fair *[a just decision]* 2. righteous *[a just man]* 3. deserved *[just praise]* 4. lawful 5. proper 6.

correct or true 7. accurate; exact —*adv.* 1. exactly *[just one o'clock]* 2. nearly 3. only *[just a taste]* 4. barely *[just missed him]* 5. a very short time ago *[she's just left]* 6. immediately *[just east of here]* 7. [Colloq.] really *[just beautiful]* —**just the same** [Colloq.] nevertheless —**just'ly** *adv.* —**just'ness** *n.*

**jus·tice** (jus'tis) *n.* 1. a being righteous 2. fairness 3. rightfulness 4. reward or penalty as deserved 5. the use of authority to uphold what is just 6. the administration of law 7. same as: a) JUDGE (sense 1) b) JUS-TICE OF THE PEACE —**do justice to** to treat fairly

**justice of the peace** a local magistrate who decides minor cases, performs marriages, etc.

**jus·ti·fy** (jus'tə fī') *vt.* **-fied'**, **-fy'ing** [< L. *justus*, just + *facere*, to do] 1. to show to be just, right, etc. 2. *Theol.* to free from blame or guilt 3. to supply grounds for —**jus'ti·fi'a·ble** *adj.* —**jus'ti·fi·ca'tion** *n.*

**Jus·tin·i·an I** (jəs tin'ē ən) 483–565 A.D.; Eastern Roman emperor (527–565): codified Roman law

**jut** (jut) *vi., vt.* **jut'ted**, **jut'ting** [prob. var. of JET[1]] to stick out; project —*n.* a part that juts

**jute** (jōōt) *n.* [< Sans. *jūta*, matted hair] 1. a strong fiber used for making burlap, rope, etc. 2. an Indian plant having this fiber

**ju·ven·ile** (jōō'və n'l, -nīl') *adj.* [< L. *juvenis*, young] 1. young; immature 2. of or for young persons —*n.* 1. a young person 2. an actor who plays youthful roles 3. a book for children

**juvenile delinquency** antisocial or illegal behavior by minors, usually 18 or younger —**juvenile delinquent**

**jux·ta·pose** (juk'stə pōz') *vt.* **-posed'**, **-pos'ing** [< L. *juxta*, beside + POSE] to put side by side —**jux'-ta·po·si'tion** *n.*

# K

**K, k** (kā) *n., pl.* **K's, k's** the eleventh letter of the English alphabet

**K** [ModL. *kalium*] *Chem.* potassium

**K., k.** 1. karat (carat) 2. kilo 3. king

**kad·dish** (käd'ish) *n.* [Aram. *qaddish*, holy] *Judaism* a hymn in praise of God, recited at the daily service or as a mourner's prayer

**kaf·fee·klatsch** (kä'fē kläch', kô'fē klach') *n.* [G. < *kaffee*, coffee + *klatsch*, gossip] *[also* K-*]* an informal gathering to drink coffee and chat

**kai·ser** (kī'zər) *n.* [< L. *Caesar*, emperor: the title [K-] of the former rulers of Austria and Germany

**kale, kail** (kāl) *n.* [var. of COLE] a

hardy cabbage with spreading leaves

**ka·lei·do·scope** (kə lī'də skōp') *n.* [< Gr. *kalos*, beautiful + *eidos*, form + -SCOPE] 1. a small tube containing bits of colored glass reflected by mirrors to form symmetrical patterns as the tube is rotated 2. anything that constantly changes —**ka·lei'do·scop'ic** (-skäp'ik) *adj.*

**Ka·ma·su·tra** (kä'mə sōō'trə) [Sans.] a Hindu love manual of the 8th century

**kan·ga·roo** (kaŋ'gə rōō') *n.* [< ?] a leaping, marsupial mammal of Australia and nearby islands, with short forelegs and strong, large hind legs

---

fat, āpe, cär, ten, ēven; is, bīte; gō, hôrn, tōōl, look; oil, out; up, fur; chin; she; thin, *then*; zh, leisure; ŋ, ring; ə for *a* in *ago*; ʼ (ā'b'l); ë, Fr. coeur; ö, Fr. feu; Fr. mon; ü, Fr. duc; kh, G. ich; doch. ‡foreign; <derived from

**kangaroo court** [Colloq.] a mock court illegally passing and executing judgment, as among frontiersmen

**Kan·sas** (kan'zəs) Middle Western State of the U.S.: 82,264 sq. mi.; pop. 2,249,000; cap. Topeka: abbrev. **Kans.**

**Kansas City 1.** city in W Mo., on the Missouri River: pop. 507,000 **2.** city opposite this, in NE Kansas: pop. 168,000

**Kant** (kant), **Im·man·u·el** (i man' yoo wəl) 1724–1804; Ger. philosopher

**ka·o·lin** (kā'ə lin) n. [Fr. < Chin. name of hill where found] a white clay used in porcelain, etc.

**ka·pok** (kā'päk) n. [Malay *kapoq*] the silky fibers around the seeds of certain tropical trees, used for stuffing mattresses, etc.

**kap·pa** (kap'ə) n. the tenth letter of the Greek alphabet (K, κ)

**ka·put** (kä poot') adj. [G. *kaputt*] [Slang] ruined, destroyed, etc.

**Ka·ra·chi** (kə rä'chē) seaport in SW Pakistan: pop. 1,913,000

**kar·a·kul** (kar'ə kəl) n. [< *Kara Kul*, lake in the U.S.S.R.] **1.** a sheep of C Asia **2.** the curly black fur from the fleece of its lambs: usually sp. *caracul*

**kar·at** (kar'ət) n. [var. of CARAT] one 24th part (of pure gold)

**ka·ra·te** (kə rät'ē) n. [Jap.] a Japanese system of self-defense by blows with the side of the open hand

**kar·ma** (kär'mə) n. [Sans., act] **1.** *Buddhism & Hinduism* the totality of one's acts in each state of one's existence **2.** loosely, fate

**kart** (kärt) n. [< CART] a small, flat motorized vehicle, used in racing

**ka·ty·did** (kāt'ē did') n. [echoic of its shrill sound] a large, green, tree insect resembling the grasshopper

**kay·ak** (kī'ak) n. [Esk.] an Eskimo canoe made of skins on a wooden frame

**kay·o** (kā'ō') vt. -**oed'**, -**o'ing** [< KO] [Slang] *Boxing* to knock out —n. [Slang] *Boxing* a knockout

**ka·zoo** (kə zōō') n. [echoic] a toy musical instrument, a small tube with a paper-covered hole that makes buzzing tones when hummed into

KAYAK

**kc, kc.** kilocycle(s)

**Keats** (kēts), **John** 1795–1821; Eng. poet

**ke·bab** (kə bäb') n. [Ar. *kabāb*] [often *pl.*] a dish of small pieces of marinated meat stuck on a skewer, often with vegetables, and broiled

**keel** (kēl) n. [< ON. *kjölr*] the chief timber or piece extending along the length of the bottom of a boat or ship —**keel over** [Colloq.] **1.** to capsize **2.** to fall over suddenly —**on an even keel** in an upright, level position

**keen** (kēn) adj. [OE. *cene*, wise] **1.** having a sharp edge or point [a *keen* knife] **2.** cutting; piercing [a *keen* wind] **3.** very perceptive [*keen* eyes] **4.** shrewd **5.** eager **6.** strongly felt; in-tense —**keen'ly** adv. —**keen'ness** n.

**keep** (kēp) vt. **kept**, **keep'ing** [OE. *cepan*, behold] **1.** to celebrate; observe [*keep* the Sabbath] **2.** to fulfill (a promise, etc.) **3.** to protect; guard; take care of; tend **4.** to preserve **5.** to provide for; support **6.** to make regular entries in [to *keep* books] **7.** to maintain in a specified state, position, etc. [*keep* prices down] **8.** to hold for the future; retain **9.** to hold and not let go; detain, withhold, restrain, etc. **10.** to stay in or on (a course, place, etc.) —vi. **1.** to stay in a specified state, position, etc. **2.** to continue; go on **3.** to refrain [to *keep* from eating] **4.** to stay fresh; not spoil —n. **1.** care or custody **2.** food and shelter; support **3.** the inner stronghold of a castle —**for keeps** [Colloq.] **1.** with the winner keeping what he wins **2.** permanently —**keep to oneself 1.** to avoid others **2.** to refrain from telling —**keep up 1.** to maintain in good condition **2.** to continue **3.** to maintain the pace **4.** to remain informed (with *on* or *with*)

**keep'er** n. one that keeps; specif., *a*) a guard *b*) a guardian *c*) a custodian

**keep'ing** n. **1.** observance (of a rule, etc.) **2.** care; charge —**in keeping with** in conformity or accord with

**keep'sake'** n. something kept, or to be kept, in memory of the giver

**keg** (keg) n. [< ON. *kaggi*] **1.** a small barrel **2.** a unit of weight for nails, equal to 100 lb.

**kelp** (kelp) n. [ME. *culp*] large, coarse, brown seaweed, rich in iodine

**Kelt** (kelt) n. same as CELT

**ken** (ken) vt. **kenned**, **ken'ning** [OE. *cennan*, cause to know] [Scot.] to know —n. range of knowledge

**Ken·ne·dy** (ken'ə dē), **John F.** 1917–63; 35th president of the U.S. (1961–63)

**ken·nel** (ken'l) n. [< L. *canis*, dog] **1.** a doghouse **2.** [often *pl.*] a place where dogs are bred or kept —vt. -**neled** or -**nelled**, -**nel·ing** or -**nel·ling** to keep in a kennel

**Ken·tuck·y** (kən tuk'ē) EC State of the U.S.: 40,395 sq. mi.; pop. 3,219,000; cap. Frankfort

**Ken·ya** (ken'yə, kēn'-) country in EC Africa: 224,960 sq. mi.; pop. 9,948,000

**kept** (kept) pt. & pp. of KEEP —adj. maintained as a mistress [a *kept* woman]

**ker·a·tin** (ker'ət 'n) n. [< Gr. *keras*, horn + -IN] a tough, fibrous protein, the basic substance of hair, nails, etc.

**kerb** (kurb) n. Brit. sp. of CURB (n. 3)

**ker·chief** (kur'chif) n. [< OFr. *covrir*, to cover + *chef*, head] **1.** a piece of cloth worn over the head or around the neck **2.** a handkerchief

**ker·nel** (kur'n'l) n. [OE. *cyrnel*] **1.** a grain or seed, as of corn **2.** the inner, softer part of a nut, etc. **3.** the central, most important part; essence

**ker·o·sene** (ker'ə sēn')* n. [< Gr. *kēros*, wax] a thin oil distilled from petroleum, used as a fuel, solvent, etc.: also **kerosine**

**kes·trel** (kes'trəl) n. [echoic] a small European falcon

**ketch** (kech) *n.* [ME. *cache*] a fore-and-aft rigged sailing vessel

**ketch-up** (kech'əp) *n.* [Malay *kēchap,* sauce] a sauce for meat, fish, etc.; esp., a thick sauce (**tomato ketchup**) of tomatoes, onions, spices, etc.

**ket-tle** (ket''l) *n.* [ < L. *catinus,* bowl] 1. a metal container for boiling or cooking things 2. a teakettle

**ket'tle-drum'** *n.* a hemispheric percussion instrument of copper with a parchment top that can be tightened or loosened to change the pitch

**key¹** (kē) *n., pl.* **keys** [OE. *cæge*] 1. a device for moving the bolt of a lock and thus locking or unlocking something 2. any somewhat similar device, as a lever pressed in operating a piano, typewriter, etc. 3. a thing that explains or solves, as a code, the legend of a map, etc. 4. a controlling person or thing 5. style or mood of expression 6. [*Music*] a system of related tones based on a keynote and forming a given scale —*adj.* controlling; important —*vt.* keyed, key'ing 1. to furnish with a key 2. to regulate the tone or pitch of 3. to bring into harmony —**key up** to make nervous

**key²** (kē) *n., pl.* **keys** [Sp. *cayo*] a reef or low island

**key'board'** *n.* the row or rows of keys of a piano, typewriter, etc.

**key club** a private nightclub, etc., to which each member has a key

**key'hole'** *n.* an opening (in a lock) into which a key is inserted

**key'note'** *n.* 1. the lowest, basic note or tone of a musical scale 2. the basic idea or ruling principle —*vt.* -not'ed, -not'ing 1. to give the keynote of 2. to give the keynote speech at —**key'not'er** *n.*

**keynote speech** (or **address**) a speech, as at a convention, setting forth the main line of policy

**key punch** a machine with a keyboard for recording data by punching holes in cards for use in data processing

**key'stone'** *n.* 1. the central, topmost stone of an arch 2. essential part

**Key West** westernmost island of the Florida Keys

**kg, kg.** kilogram(s)

**kha-ki** (kak'ē, kä'kē) *adj.* [ < Per. *khāk,* dust] 1. dull yellowish-brown 2. made of khaki (cloth) —*n., pl.* -kis 1. a dull yellowish brown 2. strong, twilled cloth of this color 3. [*often pl.*] a khaki uniform or trousers

**khan** (kän, kan) *n.* [Turki *khān,* lord] 1. a title of Tatar or Mongol rulers in the Middle Ages 2. a title of various dignitaries in India, Iran, etc.

**Khar-kov** (kär'kôf) city in NE Ukrainian S.S.R.: pop. 1,092,000

**Khar-toum** (kär tōōm') capital of Sudan: pop. 135,000

**Khmer Republic** (k'mer) *official name of* CAMBODIA

**kHz** kilohertz

**kib-butz** (ki bōōts', -boots') *n., pl.* -but-zim (kē'bōō tsēm') [ModHeb.] an Israeli collective settlement, esp. a collective farm

**kib-itz-er** (kib'its ər) *n.* [Yid. < G. *kiebitz*] [Colloq.] an onlooker at a card game, etc., esp. one who volunteers advice —**kib'itz** *vi.*

**ki-bosh** (kī'bäsh) *n.* [ < ?] [Slang] end: usually in **put the kibosh on,** to check, squelch, etc.

**kick** (kik) *vi.* [ME. *kiken*] 1. to strike out with the foot 2. to recoil, as a gun 3. [Colloq.] to complain 4. *Football* to kick the ball —*vt.* 1. to strike with the foot 2. to drive, force, etc. as by kicking 3. to score (a goal, etc.) by kicking 4. [Slang] to get rid of (a habit) —*n.* 1. an act or method of kicking 2. a sudden recoil 3. [Colloq.] a complaint 4. [Colloq.] an intoxicating effect 5. [Colloq.] [*often pl.*] pleasure —**kick in** [Slang] to pay (one's share) —**kick over** to start working, as an internal-combustion engine —**kick'er** *n.*

**kick'back'** *n.* [Slang] 1. a giving back of part of money received as payment 2. the money so returned

**kick'off'** *n.* 1. *Football* a kick that puts the ball into play 2. a beginning, as of a campaign

**kick'stand'** *n.* a pivoted metal bar that can be kicked down to support a bicycle, etc. in an upright position

**kick-y** (kik'ē) *adj.* -i-er, -i-est [Slang] 1. fashionable 2. exciting

**kid** (kid) *n.* [ME. *kide*] 1. a young goat 2. leather from the skin of young goats: also **kid'skin'** 3. [Colloq.] a child —*vt., vi.* **kid'ded, kid'ding** [Colloq.] to tease or fool playfully

**kid'dy, kid'die** (-ē) *n., pl.* -dies [dim. of KID, *n.* 3] [Colloq.] a child

**kid'nap'** (-nap') *vt.* -napped' or -naped', -nap'ping or -nap'ing [KID, *n.* 3 + dial. *nap,* to snatch] to seize and hold (a person) by force or fraud, as for ransom —**kid'nap'per, kid'nap'er** *n.*

**kid-ney** (kid'nē) *n., pl.* -neys [ < ?] 1. either of a pair of glandular organs that separate waste products from the blood and excrete them as urine 2. an animal's kidney used as food 3. *a*) disposition *b*) class; kind

**kidney bean** the kidney-shaped seed of the common garden bean

**kidney stone** a hard, mineral depoits sometimes formed in the kidney

**kiel-ba-sa** (kēl bä'sə) *n., pl.* -si (-sē), -sas [Pol.] a smoked Polish sausage spiced with garlic

**Ki-ev** (kē'ef) capital of the Ukrainian S.S.R.: pop. 1,371,000

**kill** (kil) *vt.* [ < ? OE. *cwellan*] 1. to cause the death of; slay 2. to destroy; put an end to 3. to defeat or veto (legislation) 4. to spend (time) on trivial matters 5. to turn off (an engine, etc.) 6. to stop publication of —*n.* 1. the act of killing 2. an animal or animals killed —**kill'er** *n.*

**kill'ing** adj. 1. causing death; deadly 2. exhausting; fatiguing —n. 1. slaughter; murder 2. [Colloq.] a sudden great profit

**kill'-joy'** n. one who destroys or lessens other people's enjoyment

**kiln** (kil, kiln) n. [< L. culina, cook-stove] a furnace or oven for drying, burning, or baking bricks, pottery, etc.

**ki·lo** (kē'lō, kil'ō) n., pl. **-los** [Fr.] short for: 1. KILOGRAM 2. KILOMETER

**kilo-** [< Gr. chilioi] a combining form meaning a thousand

**kil·o·cy·cle** (kil'ə sī'k'l) n. former name for KILOHERTZ

**kil'o·gram'** (-gram') n. a unit of weight and mass, equal to 1,000 grams (2.2046 lb.): also, chiefly Brit., **kil'o·gramme'**

**kil'o·hertz'** (-hurts') n., pl. **-hertz'** one thousand hertz

**ki·lo·me·ter** (ki läm'ə tər, kil'ə mēt'ər) n. a unit of length, equal to 1,000 meters (3,280.8 ft.): also, chiefly Brit., **ki·lo'me·tre**

**kil·o·watt** (kil'ə wät') n. a unit of electrical power, equal to 1,000 watts

**kilt** (kilt) n. [prob. < ON.] a knee-length, pleated tartan skirt worn sometimes by men of the Scottish Highlands

**kil·ter** (kil'tər) n. [< ?] [Colloq.] good condition; proper order: now chiefly in **out of kilter**

**ki·mo·no** (kə mō'nə) n., pl. **-nos** [Jap.] 1. a loose outer garment with a sash, part of the traditional Japanese costume 2. a woman's dressing gown

**kin** (kin) n. [OE. cynn] relatives; family —adj. related, as by blood

**-kin** (kin) [< MDu. -ken] a suffix meaning little [lambkin]

**kind** (kīnd) n. [OE. cynd] 1. a natural group or division 2. essential character 3. sort; variety; class —adj. sympathetic, gentle, benevolent, etc. —**in kind** in the same way —**kind of** [Colloq.] somewhat; rather —**of a kind** alike

**kin·der·gar·ten** (kin'dər gär't'n) n. [G. < kinder, children + garten, garden] a school or class of young children, usually four to six years old, that develops basic skills and social behavior by games, handicraft, etc. —**kin'der·gart'ner, kin'der·gar'ten·er** n.

**kind'heart'ed** adj. kind

**kin·dle** (kin'd'l) vt. **-dled, -dling** [< ON. kynda] 1. to set on fire; ignite 2. to excite (interest, feelings, etc.) —vi. 1. to catch fire 2. to become aroused or excited

**kin·dling** (kin'dliŋ) n. material, as bits of dry wood, for starting a fire

**kind'ly** adj. **-li·er, -li·est** 1. kind; gracious 2. agreeable; pleasant —adv. 1. in a kind, gracious manner 2. agreeably; favorably 3. please [kindly shut the door] —**kind'li·ness** n.

**kind'ness** n. 1. the state, quality, or habit of being kind 2. a kind act

**kin·dred** (kin'drid) n. [< OE. cynn, kin + ræden, condition] relatives or family —adj. similar [kindred spirits]

**kine** (kīn) n.pl. [< OE. cy, cows] [Archaic] cows; cattle

**ki·net·ic** (ki net'ik) adj. [< Gr. kinein, to move] of or resulting from motion

**kin·folk** (kin'fōk') n.pl. family; relatives: also **kin'folks'**

**king** (kiŋ) n. [< OE. cyning] 1. a male ruler of a state 2. a man who is supreme in some field 3. something supreme in its class 4. a playing card with a picture of a king on it 5. Chess the chief piece —adj. chief (in size, importance, etc.) —**king'ly** adj.

**King, Martin Luther, Jr.,** 1929–68; U.S. clergyman; civil rights leader

**king'dom** (-dəm) n. 1. a country headed by a king or queen; monarchy 2. a realm; domain [the kingdom of poetry] 3. any of three divisions into which all natural objects have been classified (the animal, vegetable, and mineral kingdoms)

**king'fish'er** n. a short-tailed diving bird that feeds chiefly on fish

**King James Version** same as AUTHORIZED VERSION

**King Lear** (lir) the title character of a tragedy by Shakespeare

**king'-size'** (-sīz') adj. [Colloq.] larger than the usual size: also **king'-sized'**

**kink** (kiŋk) n. [< Scand.] 1. a short twist or curl in a rope, hair, etc. 2. a painful cramp in the neck, back, etc. 3. a mental twist; queer notion; whim —vt., vi. to form or cause to form a kink or kinks —**kink'y** adj.

**kin·ship** (kin'ship') n. 1. family relationship 2. close connection

**kins·man** (kinz'mən) n., pl. **-men** a relative; esp., a male relative —**kins'wom'an** n.fem., pl. **-wom'en**

**ki·osk** (kē'äsk, kē äsk') n. [< Per. kūshk, palace] a small, open structure, used as a newsstand, etc.

**kip·per** (kip'ər) vt. [< ?] to cure (herring, salmon, etc.) by salting and drying or smoking —n. a kippered herring, etc.

**kirk** (kurk, kirk) n. [Scot. & North Eng.] a church

**kis·met** (kiz'met) n. [< Ar. qasama, to divide] fate; destiny

**kiss** (kis) vt., vi. [< OE. cyssan] 1. to touch or caress with the lips as an act of affection, greeting, etc. 2. to touch lightly or gently —n. 1. an act of kissing 2. a light, gentle touch 3. any of various candies —**kiss'a·ble** adj.

**kit** (kit) n. [ME. kyt, tub] 1. a) personal equipment, esp. as packed for travel b) a set of tools c) equipment for some particular activity, etc. d) a set of parts to be put together 2. a box, bag, etc. for carrying such parts, tools, or equipment —**the whole kit and caboodle** [Colloq.] the whole lot

**kitch·en** (kich'ən) n. [ult. < L. coquere, to cook] a room or place for the preparation and cooking of food

**kitch'en·ette', kitch'en·et'** (-et') n. a small, compact kitchen

**kitch'en·ware'** (-wer') n. kitchen utensils

**kite** (kīt) n. [< OE. cyta] 1. any of several long-winged birds of the hawk family 2. a light, wooden frame covered with paper or cloth, to be flown in the wind at the end of a string

**kith** (kith) *n.* [< OE. *cyth*] friends: now only in **kith and kin,** friends and relatives; also, relatives, or kin

**kitsch** (kich) *n.* [G., gaudy trash] pretentious but worthless art or writing —**kitsch′y** *adj.*

**kit·ten** (kit′'n) *n.* [< OFr. dim. of *chat*, cat] a young cat —**kit′ten·ish** *adj.*

**kit·ty¹** (kit′ē) *n., pl.* **-ties** 1. a kitten 2. *a pet name for* a cat

**kit·ty²** (kit′ē) *n., pl.* **-ties** [prob. < KIT] 1. the stakes in a poker game 2. money pooled for some purpose

**kit′ty-cor′nered** (-kôr′nərd) *adj., adv.* same as CATER-CORNERED: also **kit′ty-cor′ner**

**ki·wi** (kē′wē) *n., pl.* **-wis** [of echoic origin] a flightless bird of New Zealand

**K.K.K., KKK** Ku Klux Klan

**klep·to·ma·ni·a** (klep′tə mā′nē ə) *n.* [< Gr. *kleptēs*, thief + MANIA] an abnormal, persistent impulse to steal —**klep′to·ma′ni·ac′** *n., adj.*

**Klon·dike** (klän′dīk) gold-mining region in W Yukon Territory, Canada

**klutz** (kluts) *n.* [< Yid. *klots*, a block] [Slang] a clumsy or stupid person

**km, km.** kilometer(s)

**knack** (nak) *n.* [ME. *knak*, sharp blow] 1. a clever expedient 2. ability to do something easily

**knack·wurst** (näk′wurst′) *n.* [G. < *knacken*, to split + *wurst*, sausage] a thick, highly seasoned sausage

**knap·sack** (nap′sak′) *n.* [< Du. *knappen*, eat + *zak*, a sack] a leather or canvas bag for carrying equipment or supplies on the back

**knave** (nāv) *n.* [< OE. *cnafa*, boy] 1. a dishonest, deceitful person; rogue 2. a jack (playing card) —**knav′ish** *adj.*

**knav·er·y** (nāv′ər ē) *n., pl.* **-ies** rascality; dishonesty

**knead** (nēd) *vt.* [< OE. *cnedan*] 1. to work (dough, clay, etc.) into a plastic mass by pressing and squeezing 2. to massage —**knead′er** *n.*

**knee** (nē) *n.* [< OE. *cneow*] 1. the joint between the thigh and the lower leg 2. anything shaped like a bent knee —*vt.* **kneed, knee′ing** to hit or touch with the knee

**knee′cap′** *n.* a movable bone at the front of the human knee

**knee′-deep′** *adj.* 1. up to the knees 2. very much involved

**knee′-jerk′** *adj.* [< the reflex when the kneecap is tapped] designating, or reacting with, an automatic response

**kneel** (nēl) *vi.* **knelt** or **kneeled, kneel′ing** [< OE. *cneow*, knee] to bend or rest on one's knee or knees

**knell** (nel) *vi.* [< OE. *cnyllan*] 1. to ring slowly; toll 2. to sound ominously —*vt.* to call or announce as by a knell —*n.* 1. the sound of a bell rung slowly, as at a funeral 2. an omen of death, failure, etc.

**knelt** (nelt) *alt. pt. and pp. of* KNEEL

**knew** (nōō, nyōō) *pt. of* KNOW

**knick·ers** (nik′ərz) *n.pl.* [< D. *Knickerbocker*, fictitious Du. author

of W. Irving's *History of New York*] loose breeches gathered just below the knees: also **knick′er·bock′ers** (-bäk′ərz)

**knick·knack** (nik′nak′) *n.* [< KNACK] a small ornamental article

**knife** (nīf) *n., pl.* **knives** (nīvz) < OE. *cnif*] 1. a cutting instrument with a sharp-edged blade set in a handle 2. a cutting blade, as in a machine —*vt.* **knifed, knif′ing** 1. to cut or stab with a knife 2. [Colloq.] to injure or defeat by treachery —**under the knife** [Colloq.] undergoing surgery

**knight** (nīt) *n.* [< OE. *cniht*, boy] 1. in medieval times, a man formally raised to honorable military rank and pledged to chivalrous conduct 2. in Britain, a man who for some achievement is given honorary rank entitling him to use *Sir* before his given name 3. a chessman shaped like a horse's head —*vt.* to make (a man) a knight

**knight′-er′rant** (-er′ənt) *n., pl.* **knights′-er′rant** 1. a medieval knight wandering in search of adventure 2. a chivalrous or quixotic person

**knight′hood′** (-hood′) *n.* 1. the rank, status, or vocation of a knight 2. chivalry 3. knights collectively

**knight′ly** *adj.* of or like a knight; chivalrous, brave, etc.

**knit** (nit) *vt., vi.* **knit′ted** or **knit, knit′ting** [< OE. *cnotta*, a knot] 1. to make (a fabric) by looping yarn or thread together with special needles 2. to join or grow together closely and firmly, as a broken bone 3. to draw or become drawn together in wrinkles, as the brows —**knit′ter** *n.*

**knit′wear′** (-wer′) *n.* knitted clothing

**knob** (näb) *n.* [prob. < MLowG. *knobbe*, a knot] 1. a rounded lump or protuberance 2. a handle, usually round, of a door, drawer, etc.

**knob′by** *adj.* **-bi·er, -bi·est** 1. covered with knobs 2. like a knob

**knock** (näk) *vi.* [< OE. *cnocian*] 1. to strike a blow 2. to rap on a door 3. to bump; collide 4. to make a thumping noise: said of an engine, etc. —*vt.* 1. to hit; strike 2. to hit so as to cause to fall (with *down* or *off*) 3. to make by hitting [to *knock* a hole in the wall] 4. [Colloq.] to find fault with —*n.* 1. a knocking 2. a hit; rap 3. a thumping noise in an engine, etc. 4. [Colloq.] an adverse criticism —**knock about** (or **around**) [Colloq.] to wander about —**knock down** 1. to take apart 2. to indicate the sale of (an article) at an auction —**knock off** 1. [Colloq.] to stop working 2. [Colloq.] to deduct 3. [Slang] to kill, overcome, etc. —**knock out** to make unconscious or exhausted —**knock together** [Colloq.] to make or compose hastily

**knock′er** *n.* one that knocks; esp., a small ring, knob, etc. on a door for use in knocking

**knock′-kneed′** (-nēd′) *adj.* having legs that bend inward at the knees

---

fat, āpe, cär; ten, ēven; is, bīte; gō, hôrn, tōōl, look; oil, out; up, fur; chin; she; thin, *then*; zh, leisure; ŋ, ring; ə for *a* in ago; ', (ā′b'l); ë, Fr. coeur; ö, Fr. feu; Fr. mon; ü, Fr. duc; kh, G. ich, doch; ‡ foreign; < derived from

**knock·out** *n.* 1. a knocking out or being knocked out 2. [Slang] a very attractive person or thing 3. *Boxing* a victory won when an opponent is unable to continue to fight, as by being knocked unconscious

**knock·wurst** (näk′wurst′) *n.* same as KNACKWURST

**knoll** (nōl) *n.* [< OE. *cnoll*] a little rounded hill; mound

**knot** (nät) *n.* [< OE. *cnotta*] 1. a lump in a thread, etc. formed by a tightened loop or tangle 2. a fastening made by tying together pieces of string, rope, etc. 3. an ornamental bow of ribbon, etc. 4. a small group or cluster 5. something that ties closely; esp., the bond of marriage 6. a problem; difficulty 7. a hard lump on a tree where a branch grows out, or a cross section of such a lump in a board 8. *Naut.* a unit of speed of one nautical mile (6,076.12 feet) an hour —*vt.*, *vi.* **knot′ted, knot′ting** 1. to make or form a knot (in) 2. to entangle or become entangled —**tie the knot** [Colloq.] to get married

**knot′hole′** *n.* a hole in a board, etc. where a knot has fallen out

**knot′ty** *adj.* **-ti·er, -ti·est** 1. full of knots [*knotty* pine] 2. hard to solve; puzzling [a *knotty* problem]

**know** (nō) *vt.* **knew, known, know′ing** [< OE. *cnawan*] 1. to be well-informed about 2. to be aware of [he *knew* why we left] 3. to be acquainted with 4. to recognize or distinguish [to *know* right from wrong] —*vi.* 1. to have knowledge 2. to be sure or aware —**in the know** [Colloq.] having confidential information

**know′-how′** *n.* [Colloq.] technical skill

**know′ing** *adj.* 1. having knowledge 2. shrewd; clever 3. implying shrewd or secret understanding [a *knowing* look] —**know′ing·ly** *adv.*

**know′-it-all′** *n.* [Colloq.] one who acts as if he knows much about nearly everything: also **know′-all′**

**knowl·edge** (näl′ij) *n.* 1. the fact or state of knowing 2. range of information or understanding 3. what is known; learning 4. the body of facts, etc. accumulated by mankind —**to (the best of) one's knowledge** as far as one knows

**knowl·edge·a·ble** (-ə b'l) *adj.* having knowledge or intelligence —**knowl′edge·a·bly** *adv.*

**known** (nōn) *pp.* of KNOW

**Knox·ville** (näks′vil) city in E Tenn.: pop. 175,000

**knuck·le** (nuk′'l) *n.* [< or akin to MDu. & MLowG. *knokel*, dim. of *knoke*, bone] 1. a joint of the finger; esp., the joint connecting a finger to the rest of the hand 2. the knee or hock joint of an animal, used as food —**knuckle down** to work hard —**knuckle under** to yield; give in

**knuck′le·head′** (-hed′) *n.* [Colloq.] a stupid person

**KO** (kā′ō′) *vt.* **KO'd, KO'ing** [Slang] *Boxing* to knock out —*n.*, *pl.* **KO's** [Slang] *Boxing* a knockout Also **K.O., k.o.**

**ko·a·la** (kō ä′lə) *n.* [< native name] an Australian tree-dwelling marsupial with thick, gray fur

KOALA

**kohl·ra·bi** (kōl′rä′bē) *n.*, *pl.* **-bies** [< It. *cavolo rapa*] a kind of cabbage with an edible, turniplike stem

**ko·la** (kō′lə) *n.* same as COLA

**kook** (kook) *n.* [prob. < CUCKOO] [Slang] a person regarded as silly, eccentric, etc. —**kook′y, kook′ie** *adj.*

**kook·a·bur·ra** (kook′ə bur′ə) *n.* [< native name] an Australian kingfisher with a harsh cry like loud laughter

**ko·peck, ko·pek** (kō′pek) *n.* [Russ. < *kopye*, a lance] a coin equal to 1/100 of a Russian ruble

**Ko·ran** (kō ran′, kô rän′) *n.* [< Ar. *qur'ān*, book] the sacred book of the Moslems

**Ko·re·a** (kô rē′ə) peninsula northeast of China, divided into *a)* North Korea, 47,255 sq. mi.; pop. 11,568,000 *b)* South Korea, 38,030 sq. mi.; pop. 30,010,000 —**Ko·re′an** *adj.*, *n.*

**ko·sher** (kō′shər) *adj.* [Heb. *kāshēr*, proper] *Judaism* clean or fit to eat according to the dietary laws

**Kos·suth** (käs′ōōth), **Louis** 1802–94; Hung. patriot & statesman

**kow·tow** (kou′tou′, kō′-) *vi.* [Chin. *k'o-t'ou*, lit., knock head] to show great deference, submissive respect, etc. (*to*)

**KP, K.P.** kitchen police, a detail to assist the cooks in an army kitchen

**kraal** (kräl) *n.* [Afrik.] 1. a village of South African natives 2. an enclosure for cattle or sheep in S Africa

**Krem·lin** (krem′lin) [< Russ. *kreml'*] 1. the citadel of Moscow, formerly housing many Soviet government offices 2. the Soviet government

**Krem′lin·ol·o·gy** (-äl′ə jē) *n.* the study of the government, policies, etc. of the Soviet Union —**Krem′lin·ol′o·gist** *n.*

**Krish·na** (krish′nə) a Hindu god, an incarnation of Vishnu

**kro·na** (krō′nə) *n.*, *pl.* **-nor** (-nôr) [ult. < L. *corona*, crown] 1. the monetary unit and a coin of Sweden 2. *pl.* **-nur** (-nər) the monetary unit and a coin of Iceland

**kro·ne** (krō′nə) *n.*, *pl.* **-ner** (-nər) [see prec.] the monetary unit and a coin of Denmark or Norway

**KS** Kansas

**ku·chen** (kōō′kən) *n.* [G., cake] a kind of cake made of yeast dough, often filled with raisins, nuts, etc.

**ku·dos** (kōō′däs) *n.* [Gr. *kydos*] [Colloq.] credit for an achievement; glory; fame

**Ku Klux Klan** (kōō′ kluks′ klan′, kyōō′) [< Gr. *kyklos*, circle] a U.S. secret society that is anti-Negro, anti-Semitic, anti-Catholic, etc. and uses terrorist methods

**kum·quat** (kum′kwät) *n.* [< Chin.

*chin-chü*, lit., golden orange] a small, orange-colored, oval citrus fruit, with a sour pulp and a sweet rind

**kung fu** (koon′ foo′, goon′) [< Chin.] a Chinese system of self-defense, like karate but with circular movements

**Ku·wait** (koo wāt′, -wĭt′) independent Arab state in E Arabia: 6,000 sq. mi.; pop. 491,000

**kw.** kilowatt(s)

**Kwang-chow** (kwän′chō′) port in SE China: pop. 2,200,000

**Ky., KY** Kentucky

**Kyo·to** (kyō′tō) city in S Honshu, Japan: pop. 1,365,000

# L

**L, l** (el) *pl.* **L's, l's** the twelfth letter of the English alphabet

**L** (el) *n.* **1.** a Roman numeral for 50 **2.** an extension forming an L with the main structure

**L.** Latin

**L., l. 1.** lake **2.** latitude **3.** left **4.** length **5.** *pl.* **LL., ll.** line **6.** liter **7.** [L. *libra*, pl. *librae*] pound(s)

**la** (lä) *n.* [< L.] *Music* the sixth tone of the diatonic scale

**La., LA** Louisiana

**L.A.** [Colloq.] Los Angeles

**lab** (lab) *n.* [Colloq.] a laboratory

**la·bel** (lā′b'l) *n.* [< OFr., a rag] **1.** a card, paper, etc. marked and attached to an object to indicate its contents, destination, owner, producer, etc. **2.** a term of generalized classification —*vt.* **-beled** or **-belled, -bel·ing** or **-bel·ling 1.** to attach a label to **2.** to classify by; call

**la·bi·al** (lā′bē əl) *adj.* [< L. *labium*, lip] **1.** of the lips **2.** *Phonetics* formed mainly with the lips, as *b, m,* and *p*

**la′bi·um** (-əm) *n., pl.* **-bi·a** (-ə) [L., lip] any one of two pairs of liplike folds of the vulva

**la·bor** (lā′bər) *n.* [< L.] **1.** physical or mental exertion; work **2.** a specific task **3.** all wage-earning workers **4.** labor unions collectively **5.** the process of childbirth —*vi.* **1.** to work **2.** to work hard **3.** to move slowly and with difficulty **4.** to suffer (*under* a false idea, etc.) **5.** to be in childbirth —*vt.* to develop in too great detail [to *labor* a point]

**lab·o·ra·to·ry** (lab′rə tôr′ē, lab′ər ə-) *n., pl.* **-ries** [see prec.] a room or building for scientific work or research

**Labor Day** the first Monday in September, a legal holiday honoring labor

**la·bored** (lā′bərd) *adj.* made or done with great effort; strained

**la′bor·er** *n.* one who labors; esp., a wage-earning worker whose work is characterized by physical exertion

**la·bo·ri·ous** (lə bôr′ē əs) *adj.* **1.** involving much hard work; difficult **2.** hard-working —**la·bo′ri·ous·ly** *adv.*

**labor union** an association of workers to promote and protect the welfare, rights, etc. of its members

**la·bour** (lā′bər) *n., vi., vt. Brit. sp.* of LABOR

**Lab·ra·dor** (lab′rə dôr′) **1.** large peninsula in NE Canada, between the Atlantic & Hudson Bay **2.** its E section, the mainland of Newfoundland

**la·bur·num** (lə bur′nəm) *n.* [< L.] a small tree or shrub of the legume family, with drooping yellow flowers

**lab·y·rinth** (lab′ə rinth′) *n.* [< Gr. *labyrinthos*] a structure containing winding passages hard to follow without losing one's way; maze

**lac** (lak) *n.* [< Sans. *lākṣā*] a resinous substance secreted on certain Asiatic trees by a scale insect: source of shellac

**lace** (lās) *n.* [< L. *laqueus*, noose] **1.** a string, etc. used to draw together and fasten the parts of a shoe, corset, etc. **2.** an openwork fabric of linen, silk, etc., woven in ornamental designs —*vt.* **laced, lac′ing 1.** to fasten with a lace **2.** to weave together; intertwine **3.** to thrash; whip

**lac·er·ate** (las′ə rāt′) *vt.* **-at′ed, -at′ing** [< L. *lacer*, mangled] to tear jaggedly; mangle —**lac′er·a′tion** *n.*

**lace·work** (lās′wurk′) *n.* lace, or any openwork decoration like lace

**lach·ry·mal** (lak′rə məl) *adj.* [< L. *lacrima*, TEAR²] **1.** of or producing tears **2.** *same as* LACRIMAL (sense 1)

**lach′ry·mose′** (-mōs′) *adj.* [see prec.] shedding, or causing to shed, tears; tearful or sad

**lack** (lak) *n.* [< or akin to MLowG. *lak*] **1.** the fact or state of not having enough or of not having any **2.** the thing that is needed —*vi., vt.* to be deficient in or entirely without

**lack·a·dai·si·cal** (lak′ə dā′zi k'l) *adj.* [< archaic *lackaday*, an exclamation of regret, etc.] showing lack of interest or spirit; listless

**lack·ey** (lak′ē) *n., pl.* **-eys** [< Sp. *lacayo*] **1.** a male servant of low rank **2.** a servile follower; toady

**lack·lus·ter** (lak′lus′tər) *adj.* lacking brightness; dull: also, chiefly Brit., **lack′lus′tre**

**la·con·ic** (lə kän′ik) *adj.* [< Gr. *Lakōn*, a Spartan] terse in expression; using few words; concise —**la·con′i·cal·ly** *adv.*

**lac·quer** (lak′ər) *n.* [< Fr. < Port. *laca*, lac] **1.** a coating substance made of shellac, gum resins, etc. dissolved in ethyl alcohol or other solvent that evaporates quickly  2. a resinous varnish obtained from certain Oriental trees  3. a wooden article coated with this —*vt.* to coat with lacquer

**lac·ri·mal** (lak'rə məl) *adj.* 1. of or near the glands that secrete tears  2. *same as* LACHRYMAL (sense 1)

**la·crosse** (lə krôs') *n.* [CanadFr. < Fr. *la*, the + *crosse*, crutch] a ball game played by two teams using long-handled, pouched rackets

LACROSSE

**lac·te·al** (lak'tē əl) *adj.* [< L. *lac*, milk] of or like milk; milky

**lac·tic** (lak'tik) *adj.* [< L. *lac*, milk] of or obtained from milk

**lactic acid** a clear, syrupy acid formed when milk sours

**lac·tose** (lak'tōs) *n.* [< L. *lac*, milk] a sugar found in milk: used in foods

**la·cu·na** (lə kyōō'nə) *n., pl.* **-nas, -nae** (-nē) [L., a ditch] a blank space; esp., a missing portion in a text, etc.

**lac·y** (lā'sē) *adj.* **-i·er, -i·est** of or like lace —**lac'i·ness** *n.*

**lad** (lad) *n.* [ME. *ladde*] a boy; youth

**lad·der** (lad'ər) *n.* [OE. *hlæder*] 1. a framework of two sidepieces connected by a series of rungs, for use in climbing up or down  2. any means of climbing

**lad·die** (lad'ē) *n.* [Chiefly Scot.] a lad

**lade** (lād) *vt., vi.* **lad'ed, lad'ed** or **lad'en, lad'ing** [OE. *hladan*] 1. to load  2. to bail; ladle

**lad'en** *alt. pp. of* LADE —*adj.* 1. loaded  2. burdened; afflicted

**la-di-da, la-de-da** (lä'dē dä') *adj.* [imitative] [Colloq.] affectedly refined

**lad'ing** *n.* a load; cargo; freight

**la·dle** (lā'd'l) *n.* [OE. *hlædel*] a long-handled, cuplike spoon —*vt.* **-dled, -dling** to dip out with a ladle

**la·dy** (lā'dē) *n., pl.* **-dies** [< OE. *hlaf*, loaf + base of *dæge*, kneader] 1. *a)* a woman of high social position  *b)* a woman who is polite, refined, etc.  2. any woman: used to address a group  3. [L-] a British title given to women of certain ranks —*adj.* female

**la'dy·bug'** *n.* a small, roundish beetle with a spotted back: also **la'dy·bird'**

**la'dy·fin'ger** *n.* a small spongecake shaped somewhat like a finger

**la'dy-in-wait'ing** *n., pl.* **la'dies-in-wait'ing** a woman waiting upon a queen or princess

**la'dy·like'** *adj.* like or suitable for a lady; refined; well-bred

**la'dy·love'** *n.* a sweetheart

**la'dy·ship'** *n.* 1. the rank or position of a lady  2. a title used in speaking to or of a titled Lady: with *your* or *her*

**la'dy-slip'per** *n.* an orchid with flowers somewhat like slippers: also **la'dy's-slip'per**

**la·e·trile** (lā'ə tril') *n.* any of several compounds got from certain substances, as almond seeds, and claimed to be effective in treating cancer

**La·fa·yette** (lä'fä yet'), marquis de 1757–1834; Fr. general; served in the American Revolutionary army

**lag** (lag) *vi.* **lagged, lag'ging** [< ?] 1. to fall behind or move slowly; loiter  2. to become less intense —*n.* 1. a falling behind  2. the amount of this

**la·ger (beer)** (lä'gər) [G. *lager bier*, storehouse beer] a beer that has been aged for several months

**lag·gard** (lag'ərd) *n.* [< LAG + -ARD] a slow person, esp. one who falls behind —*adj.* slow; falling behind

**la·gniappe, la·gnappe** (lan yap') *n.* [Creole < Fr. & Sp.] 1. [Chiefly South] a present given to a customer with a purchase  2. a gratuity

**la·goon** (lə gōōn') *n.* [< L. *lacuna*, pool] 1. a shallow lake or pond, esp. one connected with a larger body of water  2. the water enclosed by a circular coral reef  3. shallow water separated from the sea by sand dunes

**La·hore** (lə hôr') city in NE Pakistan: pop. 1,296,000

**laid** (lād) *pt. & pp. of* LAY[1]

**laid'back'** *adj.* [Slang] relaxed, easygoing, etc.; not hurried

**lain** (lān) *pp. of* LIE[1]

**lair** (ler) *n.* [OE. *leger*] a resting place of a wild animal; den

**lais·sez faire** (les'ā fer', lez'-) [Fr., allow to do] noninterference; specif., absence of governmental control over industry and business

**la·i·ty** (lā'ət ē) *n., pl.* **-ties** [< LAY[2]] laymen collectively

**lake** (lāk) *n.* [< L. *lacus*] 1. a large inland body of usually fresh water  2. a pool of oil or other liquid

**lal·ly·gag** (lä'lē gag') *vi.* **-gagged', -gag'ging** [Colloq.] *same as* LOLLYGAG

**lam** (lam) *n.* [< ?] [Slang] headlong flight —*vi.* **lammed, lam'ming** [Slang] to flee; escape —**on the lam** [Slang] in flight, as from the police

**la·ma** (lä'mə) *n.* [Tibetan *blama*] a priest or monk in Lamaism

**La·ma·ism** (lä'mə iz'm) *n.* a form of Buddhism in Tibet and Mongolia

**la·ma·ser·y** (lä'mə ser'ē) *n., pl.* **-ies** a monastery of lamas

**La·maze** (lə mäz') *n.* [< F. *Lamaze*, 20th-c. Fr. physician] a training program in natural childbirth, involving the help of the father

**lamb** (lam) *n.* [OE.] 1. a young sheep  2. its flesh used as food  3. a gentle, innocent, or gullible person

**lam·baste** (lam bāst', -bast') *vt.* **-bast'ed, -bast'ing** [< *lam*, to beat + *baste*, to flog] [Colloq.] 1. to beat soundly  2. to scold severely

**lamb·da** (lam'də) *n.* the eleventh letter of the Greek alphabet (Λ, λ)

**lam·bent** (lam'bənt) *adj.* [< L. *lambere*, to lick] 1. playing lightly over a surface: said of a flame  2. giving off a soft glow  3. light and graceful [*lambent wit*] —**lam'ben·cy** *n.*

**lamb'kin** *n.* a little lamb

**lame** (lām) *adj.* [OE. *lama*] 1. crippled; esp., having an injury that makes one limp  2. stiff and painful  3. poor; ineffectual [*a lame excuse*] —*vt.* **lamed, lam'ing** to make lame —**lame'ly** *adv.* —**lame'ness** *n.*

**la·mé** (la mā') *n.* [< Fr. *lame*, metal plate] a cloth interwoven with metal threads, especially of gold or silver

**lame duck** an elected official whose term extends beyond the time of his defeat for reelection

**la·mel·la** (lə mel′ə) n., pl. **-lae** (-ē), **-las** [L.] a thin plate, scale, or layer

**la·ment** (lə ment′) vi., vt. [< L. lamentum, a wailing] to feel or express deep sorrow (for); mourn —n. 1. a lamenting 2. an elegy, dirge, etc. mourning some loss or death —**lam·en·ta·ble** (lam′ən tə b′l, lə men′-) adj. —**lam′en·ta′tion** n.

**lam·i·na** (lam′ə nə) n., pl. **-nae′** (-nē′), **-nas** [L.] a thin scale or layer, as of metal, tissue, etc.

**lam′i·nate′** (-nāt′; for adj. usually -nit) vt. **-nat′ed, -nat′ing** 1. to cover with one or more thin layers 2. to make by building up in layers —adj. built in thin sheets or layers: also **lam′i·nat′ed** —**lam′i·na′tion** n.

**lamp** (lamp) n. [< Gr. lampein, to shine] 1. a container with a wick for burning oil, etc. to produce light or heat 2. any device for producing light or therapeutic rays 3. a holder or base for such a device

**lamp′black′** n. fine soot used as a black pigment

**lam·poon** (lam pōōn′) n. [< Fr. lampons, let us drink: used as a refrain] a satirical writing attacking someone —vt. to attack in a lampoon

**lamp·post** (lamp′pōst′, lamp′-) n. a post supporting a street lamp

**lam·prey** (lam′prē) n., pl. **-preys** [< ML. lampreda] an eellike water animal with a jawless, sucking mouth

**la·nai** (lä ni′, lä-) n. [Haw.] a veranda or open-sided living room

**lance** (lans) n. [< L. lancea] 1. a long wooden spear with a sharp metal head 2. same as: a) LANCER b) LANCET 3. any instrument like a lance —vt. **lanced, lanc′ing** 1. to pierce with a lance 2. to cut open with a lancet

**Lan·ce·lot** (lan′sə lät′) the bravest of the Knights of the Round Table

**lan·cer** (lan′sər) n. a cavalry soldier armed with a lance

**lan·cet** (lan′sit) n. [< OFr. dim. of lance, LANCE] a small, pointed surgical knife, usually two-edged

**land** (land) n. [OE.] 1. the solid part of the earth's surface 2. a country or nation 3. ground or soil 4. real estate —vt. 1. to put on shore from a ship 2. to bring to a particular place [it landed him in jail] 3. to set (an aircraft) down on land or water 4. to catch [to land a fish] 5. [Colloq.] to get or secure [to land a job] 6. [Colloq.] to deliver (a blow) —vi. 1. to leave a ship and go on shore 2. to come to a port, etc.: said of a ship 3. to arrive at a specified place 4. to come to rest

**land contract** a contract in which the seller of real estate transfers his interest to the buyer only after the purchase price is fully paid in regular payments over a specified period

**land·ed** (lan′did) adj. owning land [landed gentry]

**land′fall′** n. 1. a sighting of land from a ship at sea 2. the land sighted

**land′fill′** n. disposal of garbage or rubbish by burying it in the ground

**land grant** a grant of land by the government for a college, railroad, etc.

**land′hold′er** n. an owner of land —**land′hold′ing** adj., n.

**land·ing** (lan′diŋ) n. 1. the act of coming to shore 2. the place where a ship is loaded or unloaded 3. a platform at the end of a flight of stairs 4. the act of alighting

**landing gear** the undercarriage of an aircraft, including wheels, etc.

**land′locked′** adj. 1. surrounded by land, as a bay 2. cut off from the sea and confined to fresh water [landlocked salmon]

**land′lord′** n. 1. a man who leases land, houses, etc. to others 2. a man who keeps a rooming house, inn, etc. —**land′la′dy** n.fem., pl. **-dies**

**land′lub·ber** (-lub′ər) n. one who has had little experience at sea

**land′mark′** n. 1. an object that marks the boundary of a piece of land 2. any prominent feature of the landscape, distinguishing a locality 3. an important event or turning point

**land′mass′** n. a very large area of land; esp., a continent

**land office** a government office that handles the sales of public lands

**land′-of′fice business** [Colloq.] a booming business

**land′scape′** (-skāp′) n. [< Du. land, land + -schap, -ship] 1. a picture of natural, inland scenery 2. an expanse of natural scenery seen in one view —vt. **-scaped′, -scap′ing** to make (a plot of ground) more attractive, as by adding lawns, bushes, etc. —**land′scap′er** n.

**land′slide′** n. 1. the sliding of a mass of earth or rocks down a slope 2. the mass sliding down 3. an overwhelming victory, esp. in an election

**land′ward** (-wərd) adv., adj. toward the land: also **land′wards** adv.

**lane** (lān) n. [OE. lanu] 1. a narrow way, path, road, etc. 2. a path or strip designated, for reasons of safety, for ships, aircraft, automobiles, etc.

**lan·guage** (laŋ′gwij) n. [< L. lingua, tongue] 1. human speech or the written symbols for speech 2. a) any means of communicating b) a special set of symbols used in a computer 3. the speech of a particular nation, etc. [the French language] 4. the particular style of verbal expression characteristic of a person, group, profession, etc.

**lan·guid** (laŋ′gwid) adj. [< L. langue.e, be faint] 1. without vigor or vitality; weak 2. listless; indifferent 3. slow; dull —**lan′guid·ly** adv.

**lan·guish** (-gwish) vi. [see prec.] 1. to become weak; droop 2. to long; pine 3. to put on a wistful air

**lan·guor** (laŋ'gər) *n.* [see LANGUID] lack of vigor or vitality; weakness; listlessness —**lan'guor·ous** *adj.*

**lank** (laŋk) *adj.* [OE. *hlanc*] 1. long and slender; lean 2. straight and limp: said of hair —**lank'ness** *n.*

**lank·y** (laŋ'kē) *adj.* **-i·er, -i·est** awkwardly tall and lean

**lan·o·lin** (lan'ʼl in) *n.* [< L. *lana*, wool + *oleum*, oil] a fatty substance obtained from wool and used in ointments, cosmetics, etc.

**Lan·sing** (lan'siŋ) capital of Mich., in the SC part: pop. 132,000

**lan·tern** (lan'tərn) *n.* [ult. < Gr. *lampein*, to shine] a transparent case for holding and shielding a light

**lan'tern-jawed'** *adj.* having long, thin jaws and sunken cheeks

**lan·yard** (lan'yərd) *n.* [< OFr. *lasne*, noose] a short rope used on board ship for holding or fastening something

**La·os** (lä'ōs) kingdom in NW Indochina: 91,429 sq. mi.; pop. 2,635,000 —**La·o·tian** (lä ō'shən) *adj., n.*

**lap¹** (lap) *n.* [OE. *læppa*] 1. the front part from the waist to the knees of a sitting person 2. the part of the clothing covering this 3. that in which a person or thing is cared for 4. *a)* an overlapping *b)* a part that overlaps 5. one complete circuit of a race track —*vt.* lapped, **lap'ping** 1. to fold (*over* or *on*) 2. to wrap; enfold 3. to overlap 4. to get a lap ahead of (an opponent) in a race —*vi.* 1. to overlap 2. to extend beyond something in space or time (with *over*)

**lap²** (lap) *vi., vt.* lapped, **lap'ping** [OE. *lapian*] 1. to drink (a liquid) by dipping it up with the tongue as a dog does 2. to strike gently with a light splash: said of waves —*n.* 1. a lapping 2. the sound of lapping —**lap up** [Colloq.] to accept eagerly

**La Paz** (lä päs') city & seat of government of Bolivia: pop. 461,000

**lap'board'** *n.* a board placed on the lap for use as a table or desk

**lap dog** any pet dog small enough to be held in the lap

**la·pel** (lə pel') *n.* [dim. of LAP¹] the front part of a coat folded back and forming a continuation of the collar

**lap·i·dar·y** (lap'ə der'ē) *n., pl.* **-ies** [< L. *lapis*, a stone] a workman who cuts and polishes precious stones

**lap·in** (lap'in) *n.* [Fr., rabbit] rabbit fur, often dyed to resemble other fur

**lap·is laz·u·li** (lap'is laz'yoo li', lazh'-; -lē') [< L. *lapis*, a stone + ML. *lazulus*, azure] an azure, opaque, semiprecious stone

**Lap·land** (lap'land') region of N Europe, including the N parts of Norway, Sweden, & Finland

**Lapp** (lap) *n.* a member of a Mongoloid people living in Lapland

**lap·pet** (lap'it) *n.* [dim. of LAP¹] a small, loose flap or fold of a garment or head covering

**lap robe** a heavy blanket, fur covering, etc. laid over the lap for warmth

**lapse** (laps) *n.* [< L. *labi*, to slip] 1. a small error 2. *a)* a moral slip *b)* a falling into a lower condition 3. a passing, as of time 4. the termination as of a privilege through failure to meet requirements —*vi.* lapsed, **laps'ing** 1. to fall into a specified state [he *lapsed* into silence] 2. to backslide 3. to elapse 4. to come to an end; stop 5. to become void because of failure to meet requirements

**lar·board** (lär'bərd) *n., adj.* [< OE. *hladan*, lade + *bord*, side] port; left

**lar·ce·ny** (lär'sə nē) *n., pl.* **-nies** [ult. < L. *latro*, robber] the unlawful taking of another's property; theft —**lar'ce·nist** *n.* —**lar'ce·nous** *adj.*

**larch** (lärch) *n.* [< L. *larix*] 1. a tree of the pine family, that sheds its needles annually 2. its tough wood

**lard** (lärd) *n.* [< L. *lardum*] the fat of hogs, melted and clarified —*vt.* 1. to put strips of bacon or fat pork on (meat, etc.) before cooking 2. to embellish [a talk *larded* with jokes]

**lard'er** *n.* 1. a place where food supplies are kept 2. food supplies

**la·res and pe·na·tes** (ler'ēz ənd pi nāt'ēz) the household gods of the ancient Romans

**large** (lärj) *adj.* larg'er, larg'est [< L. *largus*] 1. of great extent or amount; big, bulky, spacious, etc. 2. bigger than others of its kind 3. operating on a big scale [a *large* producer] —*adv.* in a large way [write *large*] —**at large** 1. free; not confined 2. fully; in detail 3. representing no particular district [a congressman at *large*] —**large'ness** *n.* —**larg'ish** *adj.*

**large'heart'ed** *adj.* generous; kindly

**large'ly** *adv.* 1. much; in great amounts 2. for the most part; mainly

**large'-scale'** *adj.* 1. drawn to a large scale 2. of wide scope; extensive

**lar·gess, lar·gesse** (lär jes', lär'jis) *n.* [see LARGE] 1. generous giving 2. a gift generously given

**lar·go** (lär'gō) *adj., adv.* [It., slow] *Music* slow and stately

**lar·i·at** (lar'ē it) *n.* [Sp. *la reata*, the rope] 1. a rope used for tethering grazing horses, etc. 2. *same as* LASSO

**lark¹** (lärk) *n.* [< OE. *læwerce*] any of a large family of chiefly old-world songbirds; esp., the skylark

**lark²** (lärk) *vi.* [< ? ON. *leika*] to play or frolic —*n.* a frolic or spree

**lark·spur** (lärk'spur') *n.* a common name for DELPHINIUM

**lar·va** (lär'və) *n., pl.* **-vae** (-vē), **-vas** [L., ghost] the early form of any animal that changes structurally when it becomes an adult [the tadpole is the *larva* of the frog] —**lar'val** *adj.*

**lar·yn·gi·tis** (lar'ən jīt'əs) *n.* an inflammation of the larynx, often with a temporary loss of voice

**lar·ynx** (lar'iŋks) *n., pl.* **lar'ynx·es, ła·ryn·ges** (lə rin'jēz) [< Gr.] the structure at the upper end of the trachea, containing the vocal cords

**la·sa·gna** (lə zän'yə) *n.* [It., the noodle] a dish of wide noodles baked in layers with cheese, tomato sauce, and ground meat

**las·civ·i·ous** (lə siv'ē əs) *adj.* [< L. *lascivus*, wanton] 1. characterized by or expressing lust 2. exciting lust

**la·ser** (lā′zər) *n.* [*l*(*ight*) *a*(*mplification by*) *s*(*timulated*) *e*(*mission of*) *r*(*adiation*)] a device that amplifies light waves and concentrates them in an intense, penetrating beam

**lash**¹ (lash) *n.* [< ?] 1. the flexible striking part of a whip 2. a stroke as with a whip 3. an eyelash —*vt.* 1. to strike or drive as with a lash 2. to switch energetically [the cat *lashed* her tail] 3. to censure or rebuke —*vi.* to make strokes as with a whip —**lash out** 1. to strike out violently 2. to speak angrily

**lash**² (lash) *vt.* [see LACE] to fasten or tie with a rope, etc.

**lass** (las) *n.* [prob. < ON. *lọskr*, weak] a young woman

**Las·sa fever** (läs′ə) [< *Lassa*, Nigerian village] an acute virus disease endemic to western Africa, causing high fever and inflammation

**las·sie** (las′ē) *n.* [Scot.] a young girl

**las·si·tude** (las′ə tōōd′) *n.* [< L. *lassus*, faint] weariness; languor

**las·so** (las′ō) *n., pl.* **-sos, -soes** [< Sp. < L. *laqueus*, noose] a long rope with a sliding noose at one end, used in catching cattle, etc. —*vt.* to catch with a lasso —**las′so·er** *n.*

**last**¹ (last) *alt. superl. of* LATE —*adj.* 1. being or coming after all others in place or time; final 2. only remaining 3. most recent [*last* month] 4. least likely [the *last* person to suspect] 5. conclusive [the *last* word] —*adv.* 1. after all others 2. most recently 3. finally —*n.* the one coming last —**at (long) last** finally

**last**² (last) *vi.* [OE. *læstan*] to remain in existence, use, etc.; endure —*vt.* 1. to continue during 2. to be enough for

**last**³ (last) *n.* [< OE. *last*, footstep] a form shaped like a foot, used in making or repairing shoes

**last hurrah** a final attempt or appearance, as in politics

**last′ing** *adj.* that lasts a long time

**Last Judgment** *Theol.* the final judgment at the end of the world

**last′ly** *adv.* in conclusion; finally

**last straw** [< the straw that broke the camel's back in the fable] a final annoyance or trouble that results in a defeat, loss of patience, etc.

**Las Ve·gas** (läs vā′gəs) city in SE Nev.: pop. 126,000

**lat.** latitude

**latch** (lach) *n.* [< OE. *læccan*] a fastening for a door, gate, or window; esp., a bar, etc. that fits into a notch —*vt., vi.* to fasten with a latch —**latch onto** [Colloq.] to get or obtain

**late** (lāt) *adj.* **lat′er** or **lat′ter, lat′est** or **last** [OE. *læt*] 1. happening, coming, etc. after the usual or expected time, or at a time far advanced in a period [*late* to class, *late* Victorian] 2. *a*) recent *b*) having recently died —*adv.* **lat′er, lat′est** or **last** 1. after the expected time 2. at or until an advanced time of the day, year, etc. 3. toward the end of a period 4. recently —**of late** recently —**late′-ness** *n.* —**lat′ish** *adj., adv.*

**late′ly** *adv.* not long ago; recently

**la·tent** (lāt′'nt) *adj.* [< L. *latere*, lurk] lying hidden and undeveloped in a person or thing —**la′ten·cy** *n.*

**lat·er·al** (lat′ər əl) *adj.* [< L. *latus*, a side] of, at, from, or toward the side; sideways —**lat′er·al·ly** *adv.*

**la·tex** (lā′teks) *n.* [L., a fluid] a milky liquid in certain plants and trees: a latex is the basis of rubber

**lath** (lath) *n., pl.* **laths** (la*thz*, laths) [< OE. *lætt*] 1. any of the thin, narrow strips of wood used as a groundwork for plastering, etc. 2. any framework for plaster

**lathe** (lā*th*) *n.* [prob. < MDu. *lade*] a machine for shaping wood, metal, etc. by holding and turning it rapidly against a cutting tool —*vt.* **lathed, lath′ing** to shape on a lathe

**lath·er** (la*th*′ər) *n.* [OE. *leathor*, soap] 1. the foam formed by soap and water 2. foamy sweat 3. [Slang] an excited state —*vt., vi.* to cover with or form lather —**lath′er·y** *adj.*

**Lat·in** (lat′'n) *adj.* [< L. *Latium*, ancient country in C Italy] 1. of ancient Rome, its people, their language, etc. 2. designating or of the languages derived from Latin, the peoples who speak them, their countries, etc. —*n.* 1. a native or inhabitant of ancient Rome 2. the language of ancient Rome 3. a person, as a Spaniard or Italian, whose language is derived from Latin

**Latin America** that part of the Western Hemisphere south of the U.S. in which Spanish, Portuguese, & French are the official languages

**lat·i·tude** (lat′ə tōōd′) *n.* [< L. *latus*, wide] 1. extent; scope 2. freedom from narrow restrictions 3. *a*) distance north or south from the equator, measured in degrees *b*) a region with reference to this distance

**la·trine** (lə trēn′) *n.* [< L. *lavare*, to wash] a toilet for the use of many people, as in an army camp

**lat·ter** (lat′ər) *adj. alt. compar. of* LATE 1. *a*) later; more recent *b*) nearer the end or close 2. being the last mentioned of two—**lat′ter·ly** *adv.*

**lat·tice** (lat′is) *n.* [< MHG. *latte*, lath] an openwork structure of crossed strips of wood, metal, etc. used as a screen, support, etc.

**lat′tice·work′** (-wurk′) *n.* 1. a lattice 2. lattices collectively

**Lat·vi·a** (lat′vē ə) republic of the U.S.S.R., in NE Europe —**Lat′vi·an** *adj., n.*

**laud** (lôd) *n.* [< L. *laus*] praise —*vt.* to praise; extol

**laud′a·ble** *adj.* praiseworthy; commendable

**laud·a·num** (lôd′n əm) *n.* [ < L. *ladanum*, a dark resin] 1. formerly, any of various opium preparations 2. a solution of opium in alcohol

**laud·a·to·ry** (lôd′ə tôr′ē) *adj.* expressing praise; commendatory

**laugh** (laf) *vi.* [ < OE. *hleahhan*] to make the sounds and facial movements that express mirth, ridicule, etc. —*n.* 1. the act or sound of laughing 2. a cause of laughter —**laugh at** 1. to be amused by 2. to make fun of

**laugh′a·ble** *adj.* amusing or ridiculous —**laugh′a·bly** *adv.*

**laughing gas** nitrous oxide used as an anesthetic: inhaling it may cause a reaction of laughter

**laugh′ing·stock′** (-stäk′) *n.* an object of ridicule

**laugh′ter** (-tər) *n.* the action or sound of laughing

**launch¹** (lônch) *vt.* [ < L. *lancea*, lance] 1. to hurl or send forth with some force [to *launch* a rocket] 2. to slide (a vessel) into the water 3. to set in operation or on some course; start [to *launch* an attack] —*vi.* 1. *a)* to put to sea *b)* to start something new With *out* or *forth* 2. to plunge (*into*) —*n.* a launching —*adj.* designating or of facilities, sites, etc. used in launching spacecraft or missiles

**launch²** (lônch) *n.* [Sp. or Port. *lancha*] an open, or partly enclosed, motorboat

**launch pad** the platform from which a rocket, guided missile, etc. is launched: also **launching pad**

**launch window** a favorable time period for launching a spacecraft

**laun·der** (lôn′dər) *vt., vi.* [ < L. *lavare*, to wash] to wash, or wash and iron, (clothes, etc.) —**laun′der·er** *n.* —**laun′dress** (-dris) *n.fem.*

**Laun·dro·mat** (lôn′drə mat′) *a service mark for* a self-service laundry —*n.* [l-] such a laundry

**laun·dry** (lôn′drē) *n., pl.* **-dries** 1. a place for laundering 2. clothes, etc. laundered or to be laundered

**laun′dry·man** (-mən) *n., pl.* **-men** a man who collects and delivers laundry

**lau·re·ate** (lôr′ē it) *adj.* [ < L. *laurus*, laurel] honored: as with a crown of laurel —*n. same as* POET LAUREATE

**lau·rel** (lôr′əl) *n.* [ < L. *laurus*] 1. an evergreen tree or shrub of S Europe, with large, glossy leaves 2. its foliage, esp. as woven into crowns 3. [*pl.*] fame; honor 4. any of various trees and shrubs resembling the true laurel

**la·va** (lä′və, lav′ə) *n.* [It. < L. *labi*, to slide] 1. melted rock issuing from a volcano 2. such rock when solidified by cooling

**la·va·bo** (lə vä′bō, -vā′-) *n., pl.* **-boes** [L., I shall wash] 1. a washbasin and water tank hung on a wall 2. a wall planter resembling this

**lav·a·liere, lav·a·lier** (lav′ə lir′, lä′və-) *n.* [ < Fr.] an ornament on a chain, worn around the neck

**lav·a·to·ry** (lav′ə tôr′ē) *n., pl.* **-ries** [ < L. *lavare*, to wash] 1. a washbowl with faucets and drain 2. a room with a washbowl and a toilet

**lave** (lāv) *vt., vi.* **laved, lav′ing** [ < L. *lavare*] [Poet.] to wash; bathe

**lav·en·der** (lav′ən dər) *n.* [ < ML. *lavandula*] 1. a fragrant European mint, with spikes of pale-purplish flowers 2. its dried flowers and leaves, used to perfume clothes, etc. 3. a pale purple —*adj.* pale-purple

**lav·ish** (lav′ish) *adj.* [ < OFr. *lavasse*, downpour] 1. very generous; prodigal 2. very abundant —*vt.* to give or spend liberally —**lav′ish·ly** *adv.*

**law** (lô) *n.* [OE. *lagu*] 1. *a)* all the rules of conduct established by the authority or custom of a nation, etc. *b)* any one of such rules 2. obedience to such rules 3. the study of such rules; jurisprudence 4. the seeking of justice in courts under such rules 5. the profession of lawyers, judges, etc. 6. *a)* a sequence of natural events occurring with unvarying uniformity under the same conditions *b)* the stating of such a sequence 7. any rule expected to be observed [the *laws* of health] —**the Law** 1. the Mosaic law, or the part of the Bible containing it 2. [l-] [Colloq.] a policeman or the police

**law′-a·bid′ing** *adj.* obeying the law

**law′break′er** *n.* one who violates the law —**law′break′ing** *adj., n.*

**law′ful** *adj.* 1. in conformity with the law 2. recognized by law [*lawful* debts] —**law′ful·ly** *adv.*

**law′giv·er** *n.* a lawmaker; legislator

**law′less** *adj.* 1. not regulated by the authority of law 2. not in conformity with law; illegal 3. not obeying the law; unruly —**law′less·ness** *n.*

**law′mak′er** *n.* one who makes or helps to make laws; esp., a legislator

**lawn¹** (lôn) *n.* [ < OFr. *launde*, heath] land covered with grass kept closely mowed, esp. around a house

**lawn²** (lôn) *n.* [ < *Laon*, city in France] a fine, sheer cloth of linen or cotton

**lawn mower** a hand-propelled or power-driven machine to cut lawn grass

**law·ren·ci·um** (lô ren′sē əm) *n.* [after E. O. *Lawrence* (1901-58), U.S. physicist] a radioactive chemical element produced by nuclear bombardment

**law′suit′** (-sōt′) *n.* a suit between private parties in a law court

**law·yer** (lô′yər) *n.* one whose profession is advising others in matters of law or representing them in lawsuits

**lax** (laks) *adj.* [ < L. *laxus*] 1. loose; slack; not tight 2. not strict or exact

**lax·a·tive** (lak′sə tiv) *adj.* [see prec.] making the bowels loose and relieving constipation —*n.* any laxative medicine

**lax′i·ty** *n.* lax quality or condition

**lay¹** (lā) *vt.* **laid, lay′ing** [ < OE. *lecgan*] 1. to cause to fall with force; knock down 2. to place or put in a resting position (often with *on* or *in*) 3. to put down (bricks, carpeting, etc.) in the correct position or way 4. to place; put; set [to *lay* emphasis on accuracy] 5. to produce (an egg) 6. to allay, suppress, etc. 7. to bet (a specified sum, etc.) 8. to devise [to *lay* plans] 9. to present or assert [to *lay* claim to property] —*n.* the way or position in which something is situated *[the lay of the land]* —**lay aside** to put away for future use; save: also **lay away, lay by** —**lay in** to get and store away —**lay off 1.** to discharge (an employee), esp. temporarily **2.** [Slang] to cease —**lay open 1.** to cut open **2.** to expose —**lay out 1.** to spend **2.** to arrange according to a plan **3.** to spread out (clothes, etc.) ready for wear, etc. —**lay over** to stop a while in a place before going on —**lay up 1.** to store for future use **2.** to confine to a sickbed

**lay²** (lā) *pt. of* LIE¹

**lay³** (lā) *adj.* [ < Gr. *laos*, the people] **1.** of a layman **2.** not belonging to a given profession

**lay⁴** (lā) *n.* [ME. & OFr. *lai*] **1.** a short poem, esp. a narrative poem, for singing **2.** [Archaic] a song

**lay analyst** a psychoanalyst who is not a medical doctor

**lay'a·way' plan** a method of buying by making a deposit on something which is delivered only after full payment

**lay'er** *n.* **1.** a person or thing that lays **2.** a single thickness, fold, etc.

**lay·ette** (lā et') *n.* [ < MDu. *lade*, chest] a complete outfit of clothes, bedding, etc. for a newborn baby

**lay·man** (lā'mən) *n., pl.* **-men** a person not a clergyman or one not belonging to a given profession

**lay·off** (lā'ôf') *n.* a putting out of work temporarily, or the period of this

**lay'out'** *n.* **1.** the manner in which anything is laid out; specif., the makeup of a newspaper, advertisement, etc. **2.** the thing laid out

**lay'o'ver** *n.* a stop in a journey

**Laz·a·rus** (laz'ə rəs) *Bible* a man raised from the dead by Jesus

**laze** (lāz) *vi., vt.* **lazed, laz'ing** to idle or loaf

**la·zy** (lā'zē) *adj.* **-zi·er, -zi·est** [prob. < MLowG. or MDu.] **1.** not eager or willing to work or exert oneself **2.** sluggish —*vi., vt.* **-zied, -zy·ing** to laze —**la'zi·ly** *adv.* —**la'zi·ness** *n.*

**la'zy·bones'** *n.* [Colloq.] a lazy person

**Lazy Su·san** (sōō'z'n) a revolving tray for food

**lb.** [L. *libra*, pl. *librae*] **1.** pound **2.** pounds: also **lbs.**

**l.c.** [L. *loco citato*] in the place cited

**lea** (lē) *n.* [OE. *leah*] [Chiefly Poet.] a meadow or grassy field

**leach** (lēch) *vt.* [prob. < OE. *leccan*, to water] **1.** to wash (wood ashes, etc.) with a filtering liquid **2.** to extract (a soluble substance) from some material —*vi.* to lose soluble matter through a filtering liquid

**lead¹** (lēd) *vt.* **led, lead'ing** [OE. *lædan*] **1.** to direct, as by going before or along with, by physical contact, pulling a rope, etc.; guide **2.** to direct by influence **3.** to be the head of (an expedition, orchestra, etc.) **4.** to be at the head of *[to lead one's class]* **5.** to be ahead of in a contest **6.** to live; spend *[to lead a full life]* —*vi.* **1.**

to show the way, as by going before **2.** to tend in a certain direction (with *to, from,* etc.) **3.** to bring as a result (with *to)* *[hate led to war]* **4.** to be or go first —*n.* **1.** the role or example of a leader **2.** first or front place **3.** the amount or distance ahead *[to hold a safe lead]* **4.** anything that leads, as a clue **5.** the leading role in a play, etc. **6.** the right of playing first in cards or the card played —**lead off** to begin —**lead on** to lure —**lead up to** to prepare the way for

**lead²** (led) *n.* [OE.] **1.** a heavy, soft, bluish-gray metallic chemical element used for piping, etc. **2.** a weight for sounding depths at sea, etc. **3.** bullets **4.** a thin stick of graphite, used in pencils —*adj.* made of or containing lead —*vt.* to cover, line, or weight with lead

**lead·en** (led'n) *adj.* **1.** made of lead **2.** heavy **3.** sluggish **4.** gloomy **5.** of a dull gray

**lead·er** (lē'dər) *n.* one that leads; guiding head —**lead'er·ship'** *n.*

**lead·ing** (lē'diŋ) *adj.* **1.** that leads; guiding *[a leading question]* **2.** principal; chief

**lead poisoning** (led) poisoning caused by absorbing lead or a lead salt into the body

**lead time** (lēd) the period of time needed from the decision to make a product to the start of production

**leaf** (lēf) *n., pl.* **leaves** (lēvz) [OE.] **1.** any of the flat, thin parts, usually green, growing from the stem of a plant **2.** a petal **3.** a sheet of paper **4.** a very thin sheet of metal **5.** a hinged or removable part of a table top —*vi.* **1.** to bear leaves **2.** to turn the pages of (with *through)* —**leaf'less** *adj.*

**leaf'let** (-lit) *n.* **1.** a small or young leaf **2.** a separate sheet of printed matter, often folded

**leaf'y** *adj.* **-i·er, -i·est** having many or broad leaves *[a leafy vegetable]*

**league¹** (lēg) *n.* [ < L. *ligare*, bind] **1.** an association of nations, groups, etc. for promoting common interests **2.** *Sports* a group of teams formed to play one another —*vt., vi.* **leagued, leagu'ing** to form into a league

**league²** (lēg) *n.* [ult. < Celt.] a measure of distance, about 3 miles

**League of Nations** an association of nations (1920–46) succeeded by UN

**leak** (lēk) *vi.* [ < ON. *leka*, to drip] **1.** to let a fluid out or in accidentally **2.** to enter or escape in this way, as a fluid **3.** to become known gradually, accidentally, etc. *[news leaked out]* —*vt.* to allow to leak —*n.* **1.** an accidental crack, etc. that lets something out or in **2.** any accidental means of escape **3.** leakage —**leak'y** *adj.*

**leak'age** (-ij) *n.* **1.** a leaking **2.** that which or the amount that leaks

**lean¹** (lēn) *vi.* **leaned** or **leant** (lent), **lean'ing** [OE. *hlinian]* **1.** to bend or slant from an upright position **2.** to bend the body and rest part of one's weight on something **3.** to rely (on or *upon*) **4.** to tend (*toward* or *to*) —*vt.* to cause to lean —**lean′er** *n.*

**lean²** (lēn) *adj.* [OE. *hlǽne*] **1.** with little flesh or fat; thin; spare **2.** meager —*n.* meat containing little or no fat —**lean′ness** *n.*

**lean′ing** *n.* tendency; inclination

**lean′-to′** *n., pl.* **-tos′** a structure whose sloping roof abuts a wall, etc.

**leap** (lēp) *vi.* **leaped** or **leapt** (lept, lēpt), **leap′ing** [OE. *hleapan*] **1.** to jump; spring; bound **2.** to accept eagerly something offered (with *at*) —*vt.* **1.** to pass over by a jump **2.** to cause to leap —*n.* **1.** a jump; spring **2.** the distance covered in a jump **3.** a sudden transition —**leap′er** *n.*

**leap′frog′** *n.* a game in which each player in turn leaps over the bent backs of the others —*vt., vi.* **-frogged′, -frog′ging** to leap or jump in or as in this way; skip (*over*)

**leap year** every fourth year, containing an extra day in February

**learn** (lurn) *vt., vi.* **learned** (lurnd) or **learnt** (lurnt), **learn′ing** [OE. *leornian*] **1.** to get knowledge of or skill in (an art, trade, etc.) by study, experience, etc. **2.** to come to know; hear (of or *about*) **3.** to memorize —**learn′er** *n.*

**learn·ed** (lur′nid; *for 2* lurnd) *adj.* **1.** having or showing much learning **2.** acquired by study, experience, etc.

**learn′ing** *n.* **1.** the acquiring of knowledge or skill **2.** acquired knowledge or skill

**lease** (lēs) *n.* [< L. *laxus,* loose] a contract by which a landlord rents lands, buildings, etc. to a tenant for a specified time —*vt.* **leased, leas′ing** to give or get by a lease —**leas′er** *n.*

**lease′hold′** (-hōld′) *n.* **1.** the act of holding by lease **2.** land, buildings, etc. held by lease —**lease′hold′er** *n.*

**leash** (lēsh) *n.* [< L. *laxus,* loose] a cord, strap, etc. by which a dog or the like is held in check —*vt.* to check or control as by a leash

**least** (lēst) *alt. superl. of* LITTLE—*adj.* [OE. *lǽst*] smallest in size, degree, etc.; slightest —*adv.* in the smallest degree —*n.* the smallest in amount, importance, etc. —**at (the) least 1.** at the lowest **2.** at any rate —**not in the least** not at all

**least′wise′** *adv.* [Colloq.] at least; anyway: also **least′ways′**

**leath·er** (le*th*′ər) *n.* [< OE. *lether*-] animal skin prepared for use by removing the hair and tanning —*adj.* of leather

**leath′er·neck′** *n.* [< former leather-lined collar] [Slang] a U.S. Marine

**leath′er·y** *adj.* like leather; tough and flexible —**leath′er·i·ness** *n.*

**leave¹** (lēv) *vt.* **left, leav′ing** [OE. *lǽfan,* let remain] **1.** to allow to remain /leave a sip for me, *leave* it open/ **2.** to have remaining behind or after one **3.** to bequeath **4.** to go away from **5.** to abandon **6.** [Dial. or Slang] to let /*leave* us go/ —*vi.* to go away or set out —**leave off** to stop —**leave out** to omit —**leav′er** *n.*

**leave²** (lēv) *n.* [OE. *leaf*] **1.** permission **2.** *a)* permission to be absent from duty *b)* the period for which this is granted —**take leave of** to say goodbye to —**take one's leave** to depart

**leave³** (lēv) *vi.* **leaved, leav′ing** to put forth, or bear, leaves; leaf

**leav·en** (lev′'n) *n.* [< L. *levare,* raise] **1.** a substance, as fermenting dough from a previous baking, yeast, etc., used to make dough rise **2.** a tempering or modifying quality or thing —*vt.* **1.** to make (dough) rise **2.** to spread through, causing gradual change

**leav′en·ing** *n.* **1.** *same as* LEAVEN **2.** a causing to be leavened

**leave of absence** leave from work or duty, esp. for a long time; also, the period of time

**leaves** (lēvz) *n., pl. of* LEAF

**leave′-tak′ing** *n.* a parting; farewell

**leav·ings** (lēv′iŋz) *n.pl.* leftovers, remnants, refuse, etc.

**Leb·a·non** (leb′ə nən) country in SW Asia, on the Mediterranean: 4,000 sq. mi.; pop. 2,367,000 —**Leb′a·nese′** (-nēz′) *adj., n., pl.* **-nese′**

**lech** (lech) *vi., n.* [see ff.] [Slang] lust

**lech·er** (lech′ər) *n.* [OFr. *lechier,* live debauchedly] a lustful, grossly sensual man —**lech′er·ous** *adj.* —**lech′er·y** *n.*

**lec·i·thin** (les′ə thin) *n.* [< Gr. *lekithos,* egg yolk] a nitrogenous, fatty compound found in animal and plant cells: used in medicine, foods, etc.

**lec·tern** (lek′tərn) *n.* [< L. *legere,* read] a reading stand

**lec·ture** (lek′chər) *n.* [< L. *legere,* read] **1.** an informative talk to a class, etc. **2.** a lengthy scolding —*vt., vi.* **-tured, -tur·ing** **1.** to give a lecture (to) **2.** to scold —**lec′tur·er** *n.*

LECTERN

**led** (led) *pt. & pp. of* LEAD¹

**ledge** (lej) *n.* [ME. *legge*] **1.** a shelf **2.** a projecting ridge of rocks

**ledg·er** (lej′ər) *n.* [ME. *legger*] a book of final entry, in which a record of debits, credits, etc. is kept

**lee** (lē) *n.* [OE. *hleo,* shelter] **1.** shelter **2.** *Naut.* the side or part away from the wind —*adj.* of or on the lee

**Lee** (lē), **Robert E.** 1807-70; commander of the Confederate army

**leech** (lēch) *n.* [OE. *lǽce*] **1.** a blood-sucking worm living in water and used, esp. formerly, to bleed patients **2.** one who clings to another to get what he can from him —*vi.* to cling (*onto*) thus

**leek** (lēk) *n.* [OE. *leac*] a vegetable that resembles a thick green onion

**leer** (lir) *n.* [OE. *hleor*] a sly, sidelong look showing lust, malicious triumph, etc. —*vi.* to look with a leer

**leer·y** (lir′ē) *adj.* **-i·er, -i·est** wary; suspicious

**lees** (lēz) *n.pl.* [< ML. *lia*] dregs or sediment, as of wine

**lee·ward** (lē′wərd; *naut.* lōō′ərd) *adj.* away from the wind —*n.* the lee side —*adv.* toward the lee

**Lee·ward Islands** (lē′wərd) group of islands in the E West Indies

**lee·way** (lē′wā′) *n.* **1.** leeward drift

of a ship or aircraft from its course
2. [Colloq.] *a)* margin of time, money,
etc. *b)* room for freedom of action
**left**[1] (left) *adj.* [< OE. *lyft*, weak]
1. of or on the side that is toward the
west when one faces north  2. closer
to the left side of one facing the thing
mentioned —*n.* 1. the left side  2. *[often
L-] Politics* a radical or liberal position,
party, etc. (often with *the*) —*adv.* on
or toward the left hand or side
**left**[2] (left) *pt. & pp.* of LEAVE[1]
**left'-hand'** *adj.* 1. on the left
2. of, for, or with the left hand
**left'-hand'ed** *adj.* 1. using the left
hand more skillfully than the right
2. done with or made for use with the
left hand  3. ambiguous or backhanded
*[a left-handed compliment]* —*adv.* with
the left hand *[to write left-handed]*
**left'ist** *n., adj.* radical or liberal
**left'o'ver** *n.* something left over
**left wing** the more radical or liberal
section of a political party, group, etc.
—**left'-wing'** *adj.* —**left'-wing'er** *n.*
**left'y** *n., pl.* **-ies** [Slang] a left-
handed person or a nickname
**leg** (leg) *n.* [ON. *leggr*]  1. one of the
parts of the body by means of which
men and animals stand and walk  2. the
part of a garment covering the leg
3. anything like a leg in shape or use
4. a stage, as of a trip —*vi.* **legged,
leg'ging** [Colloq.] to walk or run
(usually with *it*)
**leg·a·cy** (leg'ə sē) *n., pl.* **-cies** [ult.
< L. *lex*, law]  1. money or property
left to one by a will  2. anything
handed down as from an ancestor
**le·gal** (lē'gəl) *adj.* [< L. *lex*, law]  1.
of or based on law  2. permitted by
law  3. of or for lawyers —**le'gal·ly** *adv.*
**le·gal·ese** (lē'gə lēz') *n.* the special
vocabulary and formulations of legal
forms, documents, etc.
**legal holiday** a holiday set by law
**le'gal·ism** *n.* strict or too strict adherence to the law —**le'gal·is'tic** *adj.*
**le·gal·i·ty** (li gal'ə tē) *n., pl.* **-ties**
quality, condition, or instance of
being legal or lawful
**le·gal·ize** (lē'gə līz') *vt.* **-ized', -iz'-
ing** to make legal or lawful
**legal tender** money acceptable by
law in payment of an obligation
**leg·ate** (leg'it) *n.* [< L. *lex*, law] an
envoy, esp. of the Pope
**leg·a·tee** (leg'ə tē') *n.* one to whom a
legacy is bequeathed
**le·ga·tion** (li gā'shən) *n.* a diplomatic
minister and his staff and headquarters
**le·ga·to** (li gät'ō) *adj., adv.* [< It.
*legare*, to tie] *Music* in a smooth, even
style, with no breaks between notes
**leg·end** (lej'ənd) *n.* [< L. *legere*, read]
1. a story or body of stories handed
down for generations and popularly
believed to have a historical basis  2. a
notable person or the stories of his
exploits  3. an inscription on a coin,
etc.  4. a title, key, etc. accompanying
an illustration or map

**leg·end·ar·y** (lej'ən der'ē) *adj.* of,
based on, or presented in legends
**leg·er·de·main** (lej'ər di mān') *n.*
[< MFr. *leger de main*, light of hand]
1. sleight of hand  2. trickery
**leg·ged** (leg'id, legd) *adj.* having (a
specified number or kind of) legs
*[long-legged]*
**leg·ging** (leg'iŋ) *n.* a covering for the
leg: *usually used in pl.*
**leg·horn** (leg'hôrn, -ərn) *n.* [< *Leg-
horn*, It. seaport] *[often L-]* any of a
breed of small chicken
**leg·i·ble** (lej'ə b'l) *adj.* [< L. *legere*,
read] that can be read, esp. easily
—**leg'i·bil'i·ty** *n.* —**leg'i·bly** *adv.*
**le·gion** (lē'jən) *n.* [< L. *legere*, to
select]  1. a large group of soldiers;
army  2. a large number; multitude
—**le'gion·ar'y** *adj., n.* —**le'gion-
naire'** (-jə ner') *n.*
**Legionnaires' disease** [after an outbreak at an American Legion convention
in July, 1976] [Colloq.] a severe bacterial disease occurring sporadically
**leg·is·late** (lej'is lāt') *vi.* **-lat'ed,
-lat'ing** [see ff.] to make or pass laws
—*vt.* to cause to be, go, etc. by making
laws —**leg'is·la'tor** *n.*
**leg'is·la'tion** *n.* [< L. *lex*, law +
*latio*, a bringing]  1. the making of
laws  2. the laws made
**leg'is·la'tive** *adj.* 1. of legislation or
a legislature  2. having the power to
make laws —**leg'is·la'tive·ly** *adv.*
**leg'is·la'ture** (-lā'chər) *n.* a body of
persons given the power to make laws
**le·git·i·mate** (lə jit'ə mit; *for v.* -māt')
*adj.* [< L. *lex*, law]  1. born of parents
married to each other  2. lawful  3. *a)*
reasonable *b)* justifiable  4. conforming
to accepted rules, standards, etc.  5. of
stage plays, as distinguished from
burlesque, etc. —**le·git'i·ma·cy** (-mə
sē) *n.* —**le·git'i·mate·ly** *adv.*
**le·git'i·mize'** (-mīz') *vt.* **-mized',
-miz'ing** to make or declare legiti-
mate: also **le·git'i·ma·tize'**
**leg·man** (leg'man') *n., pl.* **-men'**  1. a
reporter who turns in news from on
the scene  2. an assistant who does
routine tasks outside the office
**leg'room'** *n.* adequate space for the
legs while seated, as in a car
**leg·ume** (leg'yōōm, li gyōōm') *n.* [<
L. *legere*, gather]  1. any of a large
family of plants having seeds growing
in pods, including peas, beans, etc.
2. the pod or seed of such a plant
—**le·gu·mi·nous** (li gyōō'min əs) *adj.*
**leg'work'** *n.* [Colloq.] necessary
routine travel as part of a job
**lei** (lā, lā'ē) *n., pl.* **leis** [Haw.] a garland of flowers
**Leip·zig** (līp'sig) city in SC East
Germany: pop. 596,000
**lei·sure** (lē'zhər, lezh'ər) *n.* [< L.
*licere*, be permitted] free time during
which one may indulge in rest, recreation, etc. —*adj.* free and unoccupied
**lei'sure·ly** *adj.* without haste; slow
—*adv.* in an unhurried manner

---

fat, āpe, cär; ten, ēven; is, bīte; gō, hôrn, tōōl, look; oil, out; up, fur;
chin; she; thin, *then*; zh, leisure; ŋ, ring; ə for *a* in *ago*; ', (ā'b'l); ĕ, Fr. coeur;
ö, Fr. feu; Fr. mon; ü, Fr. duc; kh, G. ich; doch. ‡foreign; < derived from

**leit·mo·tif, leit·mo·tiv** (līt′mō-tēf′) n. [G. leitmotiv < leiten, to LEAD[1] + motiv, motive] a dominant theme

**lem·ming** (lem′iŋ) n. [< ON. læmingi] a small arctic rodent with a short tail

**lem·on** (lem′ən) n. [< Per. limūn] 1. a small, sour, pale-yellow citrus fruit 2. the spiny, semitropical tree that it grows on 3. [Slang] something that is defective —adj. pale-yellow

**lem′on·ade′** (-ə nād′) n. a drink made of lemon juice, sugar, and water

**le·mur** (lē′mər) n. [< L. lemures, ghosts] a small primate related to the monkey

**lend** (lend) vt. lent, lend′ing [< OE. lǣn, a loan] 1. to let another use or have (a thing) temporarily 2. to let out (money) at interest 3. to give; impart —vi. to make loans —lend itself (or oneself) to to be useful for or open to —lend′er n.

**lend′-lease′** n. in World War II, material aid granted countries whose defense the U.S. deemed vital

**length** (leŋkth) n. [< OE. lang, long] 1. the distance from end to end of a thing 2. extent in space or time 3. a long stretch or extent 4. a piece of a certain length —at length 1. finally 2. in full

**length′en** vt., vi. to make or become longer

**length′wise′** (-wīz′) adv., adj. in the direction of the length: also **length′ways′** (-wāz′)

**length′y** adj. -i·er, -i·est long; esp., too long —length′i·ly adv.

**le·ni·ent** (lē′nī ənt, lēn′yənt) adj. [< L. lenis, soft] not harsh or severe; merciful —le′ni·en·cy, le′ni·ence n.

**Len·in** (len′in), V. I. 1870-1924; leader of the Soviet revolution

**Len·in·grad** (len′in grad′) seaport in NW R.S.F.S.R.; pop. 3,665,000

**len·i·tive** (len′ə tiv) adj. [< L. lenire, to soften] lessening pain or distress

**lens** (lenz) n. [L., lentil: < its shape] 1. a curved piece of glass, plastic, etc. for bringing together or spreading rays of light passing through it: used in optical instruments to form an image 2. any device used to focus electromagnetic waves, sound waves, etc. 3. a similar transparent part of the eye: it focuses light rays upon the retina

**Lent** (lent) n. [OE. lengten, the spring] Christianity the forty weekdays of fasting and penitence, from Ash Wednesday to Easter —Lent′en, lent′en adj.

**lent** (lent) pt. & pp. of LEND

**len·til** (lent′'l) n. [< L. lens] 1. a kind of legume, with small, edible seeds 2. this seed

**Le·o** (lē′ō) [L., lion] the fifth sign of the zodiac

**le·o·nine** (lē′ə nīn′) adj. [< L. leo, lion] of or like a lion

**leop·ard** (lep′ərd) n. [< Gr. leōn, lion + pardos, panther] 1. a large, wild animal of the cat family, with a black-spotted tawny coat, found in Africa and Asia 2. same as JAGUAR

**le·o·tard** (lē′ə tärd′) n. [< J. Léotard]

19th-c. Fr. aerial performer] a tight-fitting garment for an acrobat or dancer

**lep·er** (lep′ər) n. [< Gr. lepros, scaly] a person having leprosy

**lep·re·chaun** (lep′rə kôn′) n. [< OIr. lu, little + corp, body] Ir. Folklore a fairy who can reveal hidden treasure

**lep·ro·sy** (lep′rə sē) n. [see LEPER] a chronic infectious disease of the skin, flesh, nerves, etc., characterized by ulcers, white scaly scabs, deformities, etc. —lep′rous adj.

**les·bi·an** (lez′bē ən) n. [< Lesbos, Gr. island home of the poetess Sappho] a homosexual woman —les′bi·an·ism n.

**lese maj·es·ty** (lēz′ maj′is tē) [< Fr. < L. laesa majestas, injured majesty] 1. a crime against the sovereign 2. any lack of proper respect as toward one in authority

**le·sion** (lē′zhən) n. [< L. laedere, to harm] an injury of an organ or tissue resulting in impairment of function

**Le·so·tho** (le sut′hō, le sō′thō) country in SE Africa: 11,716 sq. mi.; pop. 975,000

**less** (les) alt. compar. of LITTLE —adj. [OE. lǣs(sa)] not so much, so great, etc.; smaller; fewer —adv. to a smaller extent —n. a smaller amount —prep. minus —less and less decreasingly

**-less** (lis, ləs) [OE. leas, free] a suffix meaning: 1. without [valueless] 2. that does not [tireless] 3. that cannot be [dauntless]

**les·see** (les ē′) n. [see LEASE] one to whom a lease is given; tenant

**less·en** (les′'n) vt., vi. to make or become less; decrease, diminish, etc.

**less·er** (les′ər) alt. compar. of LITTLE —adj. smaller, less, or less important

**les·son** (les′'n) n. [< L. legere, to read] 1. an exercise for a student to learn 2. something learned for one's safety, etc. 3. [pl.] course of instruction 4. a selection read from the Bible

**les·sor** (les′ôr) n. [see LEASE] one who gives a lease; landlord

**lest** (lest) conj. [< OE. thy lǣs the, by the less that] for fear that

**let[1]** (let) vt. let, let′ting [OE. lǣtan, leave behind] 1. to leave; now only in let alone, let be 2. a) to rent b) to assign (a contract) 3. to cause to escape [let blood] 4. to allow; permit Also used as an auxiliary in commands or suggestions [let us go] —vi. to be rented —let down 1. to lower 2. to slow up 3. to disappoint —let off 1. to give forth 2. to deal leniently with —let on [Colloq.] 1. to pretend 2. to indicate one's awareness —let out 1. to release 2. to rent out 3. to make a garment larger —let up 1. to relax 2. to cease

**let[2]** (let) n. [< OE. lettan, make late] an obstacle: in without let or hindrance

**-let** (lit, lət) [MFr. -el + -et, dim. suffixes] a suffix meaning small [ringlet]

**let′down′** n. 1. a slowing up 2. the descent of an airplane about to land 3. a disappointment

**le·thal** (lē′thəl) adj. [< L. letum, death] causing death; fatal

**leth·ar·gy** (leth′ər jē) n., pl. -gies

[ < Gr. *lēthē*, oblivion + *argos*, idle] **1.** an abnormal drowsiness **2.** sluggishness; apathy —**le·thar·gic** (li thär′jik) *adj.* —**le·thar′gi·cal·ly** *adv.*

**let's** (lets) let us

**let·ter** (let′ər) *n.* [ < L. *littera*] **1.** any character of the alphabet **2.** a written or printed message, usually sent by mail **3.** [*pl.*] *a)* literature *b)* learning; knowledge **4.** literal meaning —*vt.* to mark with letters —**let′ter·er** *n.*

**letter box** *same as* MAILBOX

**letter carrier** a postman; mailman

**let′tered** *adj.* **1.** literate **2.** well-educated **3.** marked with letters

**let′ter·head′** *n.* the name, address, etc. of a person or firm as a heading on stationery; also, a sheet of this

**let′ter·ing** *n.* the act of making or inscribing letters, or such letters

**let′ter-per′fect** *adj.* entirely correct

**letters patent** a document granting a patent

**let·tuce** (let′is) *n.* [ < L. *lac*, milk] **1.** a plant with crisp, green leaves **2.** the leaves, much used for salads

**let·up** (let′up′) *n.* [Colloq.] **1.** a slackening **2.** a stop; pause

**leu·ke·mi·a** (lōō kē′mē ə) *n.* [see ff. & -EMIA] a disease characterized by abnormal increase in the number of leukocytes: also **leu·kae′mi·a**

**leu·ko·cyte** (lōō′kə sīt′) *n.* [ < Gr. *leukos*, white + *kytos*, hollow] a white corpuscle in the blood: it destroys disease-causing organisms

**lev·ee** (lev′ē) *n.* [ult. < L. *levare*, raise] an embankment to prevent a river from flooding bordering land

**lev·el** (lev′'l) *n.* [ < L. *libra*, a balance] **1.** an instrument for determining the horizontal **2.** a horizontal plane or line [*sea level*] **3.** a horizontal area **4.** normal position with reference to height [*water seeks its level*] **5.** position in a scale of values [*income level*] —*adj.* **1.** perfectly flat and even **2.** not sloping **3.** even in height (*with*) **4.** equal in importance, advancement, quality, etc. **5.** calm or steady —*vt.*, *vi.* -eled or -elled, -el·ing or -el·ling **1.** to make or become level **2.** to demolish **3.** to raise and aim (a gun, etc.) —**level with** [Slang] to be honest with —**lev′el·er**, **lev′el·ler** *n.*

**lev′el-head′ed** *adj.* having an even temper and sound judgment

**lev·er** (lev′ər, lē′vər) *n.* [ < L. *levare*, raise] **1.** a bar used as a pry **2.** a means to an end **3.** a device consisting of a bar turning about a fixed point, using force at a second point to lift a weight at a third

**lev′er·age** (-ij) *n.* the action or mechanical power of a lever

**LEVERS**

**le·vi·a·than** (lə vī′ə thən) *n.* [ < Heb. *liwyāthān*] **1.** Bible a sea monster **2.** any huge thing

**Le·vi's** (lē′vīz) [ < *Levi* Strauss, U.S. manufacturer] *a trademark for* close-fitting trousers of heavy denim

**lev·i·ta·tion** (lev′ə tā′shən) *n.* [ < L. *levis*, light] the illusion of raising a body in the air with no support —**lev′i·tate′** *vt.*, *vi.* -tat′ed, -tat′ing

**Le·vit·i·cus** (lə vit′i kəs) the third book of the Pentateuch

**lev·i·ty** (lev′ə tē) *n.*, *pl.* -ties [ < L. *levis*, light] frivolity; improper gaiety

**lev·y** (lev′ē) *n.*, *pl.* -ies [ < L. *levare*, to raise] **1.** an imposing and collecting of a tax, fine, etc. **2.** the amount collected **3.** compulsory enlistment for military service **4.** a group so enlisted —*vt.* -ied, -y·ing **1.** to impose (a tax, fine, etc.) **2.** to enlist (troops) **3.** to wage (war)

**lewd** (lood) *adj.* [OE. *læwede*, unlearned] indecent; lustful; obscene —**lewd′ly** *adv.* —**lewd′ness** *n.*

**lex·i·cog·ra·phy** (lek′sə käg′rə fē) *n.* [see ff. & -GRAPHY] the act, art, or work of writing a dictionary —**lex′i·cog′ra·pher** *n.*

**lex·i·con** (lek′si kən) *n.* [ < Gr. *lexis*, word] **1.** a dictionary **2.** a special vocabulary

**Lex·ing·ton** (lek′siŋ tən) city in NC Ky.; pop. 108,000

**Li** *Chem.* lithium

**L.I.** Long Island

**li·a·bil·i·ty** (lī′ə bil′ə tē) *n.*, *pl.* -ties **1.** the state of being liable **2.** anything for which a person is liable **3.** [*pl.*] the debts of a person or business **4.** something that works to one's disadvantage

**li·a·ble** (lī′ə b'l) *adj.* [ < L. *ligare*, bind] **1.** legally bound or responsible **2.** subject to [*liable to suspicion*] **3.** likely (*to*) [*liable to die*]

**li·ai·son** (lē′ə zän′, -zōn′) *n.* [ < L. *ligare*, bind] **1.** intercommunication as between units of a military force **2.** an illicit love affair

**li·ar** (lī′ər) *n.* one who tells lies

**lib** (lib) *n. short for* LIBERATION

**li·ba·tion** (lī bā′shən) *n.* [ < L. *libare*, pour out] **1.** the ritual of pouring out wine or oil in honor of a god **2.** this liquid **3.** an alcoholic drink

**li·bel** (lī′b'l) *n.* [ < L. *liber*, book] **1.** any written or printed matter tending to injure a person's reputation unjustly **2.** the act or crime of publishing such a thing —*vt.* -beled or -belled, -bel·ing or -bel·ling to make a libel against —**li′bel·er**, **li′bel·ier** *n.* —**li′bel·ous**, **li′bel·lous** *adj.*

**lib·er·al** (lib′ər əl) *adj.* [ < L. *liber*, free] **1.** generous **2.** ample; abundant **3.** not literal or strict **4.** tolerant; broad-minded **5.** favoring reform or progress —*n.* one who favors reform or progress —**lib′er·al·ism** *n.* —**lib′er·al·ly** *adv.* —**lib′er·al·ness** *n.*

**liberal arts** literature, languages, history, etc. as courses of study

**lib·er·al′i·ty** (-ə ral′ə tē) *n.*, *pl.* -ties **1.** generosity **2.** broad-mindedness

**lib·er·al·ize′** (-ə līz′) *vt.*, *vi.* -ized′,

**-iz′ing** to make or become liberal —**lib′er·al·i·za′tion** n.

**lib·er·ate** (lib′ə rāt′) vt. **-at′ed, -at′ing** [< L. liber, free] **1.** to release from slavery, enemy occupation, etc. **2.** to secure equal rights for (women, etc.) —**lib′er·a′tion** n. —**lib′er·a′tor** n.

**Li·be·ri·a** (lī bir′ē ə) country on the W coast of Africa, founded by freed U.S. slaves: 43,000 sq. mi.; pop. 1,090,000 —**Li·ber′i·an** adj., n.

**lib·er·tar·i·an** (lib′ər ter′ē ən) n. **1.** a believer in free will **2.** an advocate of full civil liberties

**lib·er·tine** (lib′ər tēn′) n. [< L. liber, free] a man who is sexually promiscuous —adj. licentious

**lib·er·ty** (lib′ər tē) n., pl. **-ties** [< L. liber, free] **1.** freedom from slavery, captivity, etc. **2.** a particular right, freedom, etc. **3.** an impertinent attitude **4.** leave given to a sailor to go ashore  See also CIVIL LIBERTIES —**at liberty 1.** not confined **2.** permitted (to) **3.** not busy or in use —**take liberties 1.** to be impertinent or too familiar **2.** to deal inaccurately (with facts, data, etc.)

**Liberty Bell** the bell of Independence Hall, Philadelphia, rung July 4, 1776, to proclaim U.S. independence

**li·bid·i·nize** (li bid′′n īz′) vt. **-nized′, -niz′ing** to regard as a source of sexual gratification

**li·bid·i·nous** (li bid′′n əs) adj. [see ff.] lustful; lascivious

**li·bi·do** (li bē′dō, -bī′-) n. [< L. desire] **1.** the sexual urge **2.** Psychoanalysis psychic energy generally; specif., that comprising the positive, loving instincts

**Li·bra** (lī′brə, lē′-) [L., a balance] the seventh sign of the zodiac

**li·brar·i·an** (lī brer′ē ən) n. one in charge of a library or trained in library science

**li·brar·y** (lī′brer′ē) n., pl. **-ies** [< L. liber, book] **1.** a collection of books, etc. **2.** a room or building for, or an institution in charge of, such a collection

**li·bret·to** (li bret′ō) n., pl. **-tos, -ti** (-ē) [It. < L. liber, book] the words, or text, of an opera, oratorio, etc. —**li·bret′tist** n.

**Lib·y·a** (lib′ē ə) country in N Africa, on the Mediterranean: 679,359 sq. mi.; pop. 1,738,000 —**Lib′y·an** adj., n.

**lice** (līs) n. pl. of LOUSE

**li·cense** (līs′′ns) n. [< L. licere, be permitted] **1.** formal or legal permission to do something specified **2.** a document indicating such permission **3.** freedom to deviate from rule, practice, etc. [poetic license] **4.** excessive freedom, constituting an abuse of liberty  Brit. sp. **licence** —vt. **-censed, -cens·ing** to permit formally

**li′cen·see′** (-′n sē′) n. a person to whom a license is granted

**li·cen·ti·ate** (lī sen′shē it, -āt′) n. a person having a professional license

**li·cen·tious** (lī sen′shəs) adj. [see LICENSE] morally unrestrained; lascivious —**li·cen′tious·ness** n.

**li·chen** (lī′kən) n. [< Gr. leichein, to lick] a mosslike plant growing in patches on rock, wood, soil, etc.

**lic·it** (lis′it) adj. [< L. licitus, permitted] lawful —**lic′it·ly** adv.

**lick** (lik) vt. [OE. liccian] **1.** to pass the tongue over **2.** to pass lightly over like a tongue **3.** [Colloq.] a) to whip b) to vanquish —n. **1.** a licking with the tongue **2.** a small quantity **3.** short for SALT LICK **4.** [Colloq.] a) a sharp blow b) a short, rapid burst of activity: also **lick and a promise** —**lick up** to consume as by licking

**lic·o·rice** (lik′ər ish, -is) n. [< Gr. glykys, sweet + rhiza, root] **1.** a black flavoring extract made from the root of a European plant **2.** candy flavored with this extract

**lid** (lid) n. [OE. hlid] **1.** a movable cover, as for a box, etc. **2.** an eyelid **3.** [Colloq.] a restraint —**lid′ded** adj.

**li·dar** (lī′där) n. [LI(GHT) + (RA)DAR] an instrument using laser light to detect pollutants in the atmosphere

**lie¹** (lī) vi. lay, lain, ly′ing [OE. licgan] **1.** to be or put oneself in a reclining or horizontal position **2.** to rest on a support in a horizontal position **3.** to be in a specified condition **4.** to be situated [Canada lies to the north] **5.** to exist [love lies in her eyes] —n. the way in which something is situated; lay

**lie²** (lī) vi. lied, ly′ing [OE. leogan] to make a statement that one knows is false —vt. to bring, put, accomplish, etc. by lying —n. a false statement made with intent to deceive

**Liech·ten·stein** (lēkh′tən shtīn′) country between Switzerland & Austria: 61 sq. mi.; pop. 19,000

**lie detector** same as POLYGRAPH

**lief** (lēf) adv. [< OE. leof, dear] [Archaic] willingly; gladly: only in **would** (or **had**) as **lief**, etc.

**liege** (lēj) adj. [< OFr.] loyal; faithful —n. Feudal Law **1.** a lord or sovereign **2.** a subject or vassal

**li·en** (lēn, lē′ən) n. [Fr. < L. ligare, to bind] a legal claim on another's property as security for the payment of a just debt

**lieu** (loo) n. [< L. locus] place: in phrase **in lieu of**, instead of

**lieu·ten·ant** (loo ten′ənt) n. [< MFr. lieu, place + tenant, holding] **1.** one who acts for a superior **2.** U.S. Mil. an officer ranking below a captain: see FIRST LIEUTENANT, SECOND LIEUTENANT **3.** U.S. Navy an officer ranking just above a lieutenant junior grade  Abbrev. **Lieut., Lt.** —**lieu·ten′an·cy** n.

**lieutenant colonel** U.S. Mil. an officer ranking just above a major

**lieutenant commander** U.S. Navy an officer ranking just above a lieutenant

**lieutenant general** U.S. Mil. an officer ranking just above a major general

**lieutenant governor** an elected official of a State who ranks below and substitutes for the governor

**lieutenant junior grade** U.S.

*Navy* an officer ranking just above an ensign

**life** (līf) *n., pl.* **lives** [OE. *lif*] **1.** that property of plants and animals (ending at death) which makes it possible for them to take in food, get energy from it, grow, etc. **2.** the state of having this property **3.** a human being *[100 lives were lost]* **4.** living things collectively *[plant life]* **5.** the time a person or thing is alive or exists **6.** one's manner of living *[a life of ease]* **7.** the people and activities of a given time, place, etc. *[military life]* **8.** *a)* one's animate existence *b)* a biography **9.** the source of liveliness *[the life of the party]* **10.** vigor; liveliness

**life belt** a life preserver in belt form

**life/blood/** *n.* **1.** the blood necessary to life **2.** a vital element

**life/boat/** *n.* one of the small rescue boats carried by a ship

**life/guard/** *n.* a swimmer employed at beaches, etc. to prevent drownings

**life insurance** insurance in which a stipulated sum is paid at the death of the insured

**life jacket** (or **vest**) a life preserver like a sleeveless jacket or vest

**life/less** *adj.* **1.** without life; specif., *a)* inanimate *b)* dead **2.** dull

**life/like/** *adj.* resembling real life or a real person or thing

**life/line/** *n.* **1.** the rope for raising or lowering a diver **2.** a very important commercial route

**life/long/** *adj.* lasting or not changing during one's whole life

**life net** a strong net used by firemen, etc. as to catch people jumping from a burning building

**life preserver** a buoyant device for saving a person from drowning by keeping his body afloat

**lif/er** *n.* [Slang] a person sentenced to prison for life

**life raft** a small, inflatable raft or boat for emergency use at sea

**life/sav/er** *n.* **1.** a lifeguard **2.** [Colloq.] a help in time of need

LIFE
PRESERVER

**life/-size/** *adj.* as big as the person or thing represented: said of a statue, picture, etc.: also **life/-sized/**

**life style** an individual's whole way of living

**life/time/** *n.* the length of time that one lives or that a thing lasts

**life/work/** *n.* the work to which a person devotes his life

**lift** (lift) *vt.* [< ON. *lopt*, air] **1.** to bring up to or to a higher position; raise **2.** to raise in rank, condition, etc.; exalt **3.** to pay off (a mortgage, debt, etc.) **4.** to end (a blockade, etc.) **5.** [Slang] to steal —*vi.* **1.** to exert strength in raising something **2.** to rise; go up —*n.* **1.** a lifting or rising **2.** the amount

lifted **3.** the distance something is lifted **4.** lifting power or influence **5.** elevation of mood, etc. **6.** elevated position or carriage **7.** a ride in the direction one is going **8.** help of any kind **9.** [Brit.] an elevator —**lift up one's voice** to speak out loudly

**lift/off/** *n.* **1.** the vertical thrust of a spacecraft, missile, etc. at launching **2.** the time of this

**lig·a·ment** (lig/ə mənt) *n.* [< L. *ligare*, bind] a band of tissue connecting bones or holding organs in place

**lig·a·ture** (lig/ə chər) *n.* [< L. *ligare*, bind] **1.** a tying or binding together **2.** a tie, bond, etc. **3.** two or more letters united, as æ, th **4.** *Surgery* a thread used to tie up an artery, etc.

**li·ger** (lī/gər) *n.* [LI(ON) + (TI)GER] the offspring of a male lion and a female tiger

**light¹** (līt) *n.* [OE. *leoht*] **1.** *a)* the form of radiant energy acting on the retina of the eye to make sight possible *b)* ultraviolet or infrared radiation **2.** brightness; illumination **3.** a source of light, as the sun, a lamp, etc. **4.** daylight **5.** a thing used to ignite something **6.** a window or windowpane **7.** knowledge; enlightenment **8.** public view *[to bring new facts to light]* **9.** aspect *[viewed in another light]* **10.** an outstanding person —*adj.* **1.** having light; bright **2.** pale in color; fair —*adv.* palely *[a light blue color]* —*vt.* **light/ed** or **lit, light/ing 1.** to ignite *[to light a bonfire]* **2.** to cause to give off light **3.** to furnish with light **4.** to brighten; animate —*vi.* **1.** to catch fire **2.** to be lighted (usually with *up*) —**in the light of** considering —**see the light (of day) 1.** to come into being **2.** to come into public view **3.** to understand

**light²** (līt) *adj.* [OE. *leoht*] **1.** having little weight; not heavy, esp. for its size **2.** less than usual in weight, amount, force, etc. *[a light blow]* **3.** of little importance **4.** easy to bear *[a light tax]* **5.** easy to do *[light work]* **6.** gay; happy **7.** dizzy; giddy **8.** not serious *[light reading]* **9.** moderate *[a light meal]* **10.** moving with ease *[light on her feet]* **11.** producing small products *[light industry]* —*adv. same as* LIGHTLY —*vi.* **light/ed** or **lit, light/ing 1.** to come to rest after traveling through the air **2.** to come or happen (*on* or *upon*) **3.** to strike suddenly, as a blow —**light out** [Colloq.] to depart suddenly —**make light of** to treat as unimportant

**light/en¹** *vt., vi.* **1.** to make or become light or brighter **2.** to shine; flash

**light/en²** *vt., vi.* **1.** to make or become lighter in weight **2.** to make or become more cheerful

**light/er¹** *n.* a person or thing that starts something burning

**light/er²** *n.* [< MDu. *licht*, LIGHT²] a large barge used in loading or unloading larger ships lying offshore

**light′-fin′gered** *adj.* skillful at stealing, esp. by picking pockets

**light′-foot′ed** *adj.* stepping lightly and gracefully

**light′head′ed** *adj.* 1. giddy; dizzy 2. flighty; frivolous

**light′heart′ed** *adj.* gay; cheerful —**light′heart′ed·ly** *adv.* —**light′-heart′ed·ness** *n.*

**light heavyweight** a boxer or wrestler weighing 161 to 175 lb.

**light′house′** *n.* a tower with a bright light to guide ships at night

**light′ing** *n.* the act or manner of giving light, or illuminating

**light′ly** *adv.* 1. with little weight or pressure; gently 2. to a small degree or amount 3. nimbly; deftly 4. cheerfully 5. with indifference

**light′-mind′ed** *adj.* silly; frivolous

**light′ness¹** *n.* 1. the amount of light; brightness 2. paleness in color

**light′ness²** *n.* 1. a being light, not heavy 2. mildness, carefreeness, etc.

**light′ning** (-niŋ) *n.* a flash of light in the sky caused by the discharge of atmospheric electricity

**lightning bug** *same as* FIREFLY

**lightning rod** a metal rod placed high on a building and grounded to divert lightning from the structure

**light opera** *same as* OPERETTA

**light′weight′** *adj.* light in weight —*n.* a boxer or wrestler weighing 127 to 135 lb.

**light′-year′** *n.* the distance that light travels in one year, c. 6 trillion miles

**lig·nite** (lig′nīt) *n.* [< L. *lignum*, wood] a soft, brownish-black coal with the texture of the original wood

**lik·a·ble** (līk′ə b'l) *adj.* attractive, pleasant, genial, etc.: also **likeable** —**lik′a·ble·ness, lik′a·bil′i·ty** *n.*

**like¹** (līk) *adj.* [OE. *gelic*] having the same characteristics; similar; equal —*adv.* [Colloq.] likely [*like* as not, he'll go] —*prep.* 1. similar to 2. similarly to [to sing *like* a bird] 3. characteristic of [not like him to cry] 4. in the mood for [to feel *like* eating] 5. indicative of [it looks *like* rain] 6. as for example [fruit, *like* pears and plums] —*conj.* [Colloq.] 1. as [it's just *like* he said] 2. as if [it looks *like* he's late] —*n.* an equal; counterpart [the *like* of it] —**and the like** and others of the same kind —**like blazes** (or **crazy, the devil, mad,** etc.) [Colloq.] with furious energy, speed, etc. —**the like** (or **likes**) **of** [Colloq.] any person or thing like

**like²** (līk) *vi.* **liked, lik′ing** [OE. *lician*] to be so inclined [do as you *like*] —*vt.* 1. to be pleased with; enjoy 2. to wish [I'd *like* to go] —*n.* [*pl.*] preferences; tastes —**lik′er** *n.*

**-like** (līk) *a suffix meaning* like, characteristic of [*ball-like, homelike*]

**like·li·hood** (līk′lē hood′) *n.* a being likely to happen; probability

**like′ly** *adj.* **-li·er, -li·est** [OE. *geliclic*] 1. credible [a *likely* story] 2. reasonably to be expected [*likely* to rain] 3. suitable [a *likely* place to swim] —*adv.* probably [*likely* he'll win]

**like′-mind′ed** *adj.* having the same

ideas, plans, tastes, etc. —**like′-mind′ed·ness** *n.*

**lik·en** (līk′'n) *vt.* to compare

**like′ness** *n.* 1. a being like 2. (the same) form 3. a copy, portrait, etc.

**like′wise′** *adv.* [< *in like wise*] 1. in the same manner 2. also; too

**lik·ing** (līk′iŋ) *n.* 1. fondness; affection 2. preference; taste; pleasure

**li·lac** (lī′lək, -läk) *n.* [ult. < Per. *lilak*, bluish] 1. a shrub with large clusters of tiny, fragrant flowers 2. a pale purple —*adj.* pale-purple

**Lil·li·pu·tian** (lil′ə pyōō′shən) *adj.* [< *Lilliput*, place in J. Swift's *Gulliver's Travels*] 1. tiny 2. petty

**lilt** (lilt) *n.* [ME. *lilten*, to sound] a light, swingy rhythm or tune

**lil·y** (lil′ē) *n., pl.* **-ies** [< L. *lilium*] 1. a plant grown from a bulb and having typically trumpet-shaped flowers 2. its flower 3. any similar plant, as the water lily —*adj.* like a lily, as in whiteness, purity, etc.

**lil·y-liv′ered** (-liv′ərd) *adj.* cowardly; timid

**lily of the valley** *pl.* **lilies of the valley** a low plant with a spike of fragrant, white, bell-shaped flowers

**Li·ma** (lē′mə) capital of Peru: pop. 1,716,000

**li·ma bean** (lī′mə) [< *Lima*, Peru] [*also* L- b-] 1. a bean with broad pods 2. its broad, flat, edible seed

**limb** (lim) *n.* [OE. *lim*] 1. an arm, leg, or wing 2. a large branch of a tree —**out on a limb** [Colloq.] in a precarious position —**limb′less** *adj.*

**lim·ber** (lim′bər) *adj.* [< ? prec.] 1. easily bent; flexible 2. able to bend the body easily —*vt., vi.* to make or become limber

**lim·bo** (lim′bō) *n.* [< L. (*in*) *limbo*, (on) the border] 1. [*often* L-] in some Christian theologies, the abode after death of unbaptized children, etc. 2. a place of oblivion 3. a vague condition

**Lim·bur·ger (cheese)** (lim′bər gər) [< *Limburg*, Belgian province] a semisoft cheese with a strong odor

**lime¹** (līm) *n.* [OE. *līm*] a white substance, calcium oxide, obtained from limestone, etc. and used in mortar and cement and to neutralize acid soil —*vt.* **limed, lim′ing** to treat with lime

**lime²** (līm) *n.* [< Ar. *līma*] a small, lemon-shaped, greenish-yellow citrus fruit with a juicy, sour pulp

**lime′ade′** (-ād′) *n.* a drink made of lime juice and water, usually sweetened

**lime′light′** *n.* 1. a brilliant light created by the incandescence of lime: formerly used in theaters 2. a prominent position before the public

**lim·er·ick** (lim′ər ik) *n.* [prob. < *Limerick*, Ir. county] a rhymed nonsense poem of five lines

**lime′stone′** *n.* rock consisting mainly of calcium carbonate

**lim·it** (lim′it) *n.* [< L. *limes*] 1. the point, line, etc. where something ends; boundary 2. [*pl.*] bounds 3. the greatest amount allowed —*vt.* to set a limit to; restrict —**lim′i·ta′tion** *n.* —**lim′it·er** *n.* —**lim′it·less** *adj.*

**lim′it·ed** *adj.* 1. confined within

bounds 2. making a restricted number of stops: said of a train, bus, etc.

**limn** (lim) vt. [ < L. *illuminare*, make light] 1. to paint or draw 2. to describe

**lim·ou·sine** (lim′ə zēn′) n. [Fr., lit., a hood] a large, luxury automobile, esp. one driven by a chauffeur

**limp** (limp) vi. [ < OE. *limpan*] to walk with or as with a lame leg —n. a halt or lameness in walking —adj. lacking firmness; wilted, flexible, etc. —limp′ly adv. —limp′ness n.

**limp·et** (lim′pit) n. [ < ML. *lempreda*] a mollusk that clings to rocks, etc.

**lim·pid** (lim′pid) adj. [ < L. *limpidus*] perfectly clear; transparent — lim·pid′i·ty n. —lim′pid·ly adv.

**lim·y** (lī′mē) adj. -i·er, -i·est of, like, or containing lime

**lin·age** (lī′nij) n. the number of written or printed lines, as on a page

**linch·pin** (linch′pin′) n. [OE. *lynis*, linchpin] a pin in an axle to keep the wheel from coming off

**Lin·coln** (liŋ′kən) capital of Nebr.: pop. 150,000

**Lincoln, Abraham** 1809–65; 16th president of the U.S. (1861–65)

**lin·den** (lin′dən) n. [OE.] a tree with dense, heart-shaped leaves

**line**[1] (līn) n. [ < L. *linea*, lit., linen thread] 1. a cord, rope, wire, etc. 2. any wire, pipe, etc., or system of these, conducting fluid, electricity, etc. 3. a thin, threadlike mark 4. a border or boundary 5. a limit 6. outline; contour 7. a row of persons or things, as of printed letters across a page 8. a succession of persons or things 9. lineage 10. a transportation system of buses, ships, etc. 11. the course a moving thing takes 12. a course of conduct, action, explanation, etc. 13. a person's trade or occupation 14. a stock of goods 15. a piece of information 16. a short letter, note, etc. 17. a verse of poetry 18. [pl.] all the speeches of a character in a play 19. the forward combat position in warfare 20. *Football* the players in the forward row 21. *Math.* the path of a moving point —vt. lined, lin′ing 1. to mark with lines 2. to form a line along —bring (or come) into line to bring or come into alignment or conformity —draw the (or a) line to set a limit —hold the line to stand firm —in line for being considered for —line up to form, or bring into, a line

**line**[2] (līn) vt. lined, lin′ing [ < L. *linum*, flax] to put, or serve as, a lining in

**lin·e·age** (lin′ē ij) n. [see LINE[1]] 1. direct descent from an ancestor 2. ancestry; family

**lin·e·al** (lin′ē əl) adj. 1. in the direct line of descent from an ancestor 2. hereditary 3. of lines; linear

**lin·e·a·ment** (lin′ē ə mənt) n. [ < L. *linea*, LINE[1]] a distinctive feature, esp. of the face: usually used in pl.

**lin·e·ar** (lin′ē ər) adj. 1. of, made of, or using a line or lines 2. narrow and long 3. in relation to length only

**line·back·er** (līn′bak′ər) n. *Football* a defensive player directly behind the line

**line drive** a baseball hit in a straight line parallel to the ground

**line′man** (-mən) n., pl. -men 1. a man who sets up and repairs telephone or electric power lines 2. *Football* a player in the line

**lin·en** (lin′ən) n. [ < OE. *lin*, flax: see LINE[2]] 1. thread or cloth made of flax 2. [often pl.] sheets, cloths, etc. of linen, or of cotton, etc.

**lin·er** (lī′nər) n. 1. a steamship, airplane, etc. in regular service for some line 2. a cosmetic applied in a fine line, as along the eyelid

**lines·man** (līnz′mən) n., pl. -men 1. *Football* an official who marks the gains or losses in ground 2. *Tennis* an official who determines if the balls land outside the foul lines

**line′up′** n. an arrangement of persons or things in or as in a line

**lin·ey** (lī′nē) adj. lin′i·er, lin′i·est same as LINY

**-ling** (liŋ) [OE.] a suffix meaning: 1. small [duckling] 2. contemptible; unimportant [princeling]

**lin·ger** (liŋ′gər) vi. [OE. *lengan*, to delay] 1. to continue to stay, as through reluctance to leave 2. to loiter —lin′ger·er n. —lin′ger·ing adj.

**lin·ge·rie** (län′zhə rā′, -rē′; -jə-) n. [Fr.] women's underwear

**lin·go** (liŋ′gō) n., pl. -goes [ < L. *lingua*, tongue] a dialect, jargon, etc. that one is not familiar with

**lin·gua fran·ca** (liŋ′gwə fraŋ′kə) a hybrid language used for communication by speakers of different languages

**lin·gual** (liŋ′gwəl) adj. [see ff.] of, or pronounced with, the tongue

**lin·guist** (-gwist) n. [ < L. *lingua*, tongue] 1. a specialist in linguistics 2. same as POLYGLOT (sense 1)

**lin·guis·tics** (-gwis′tiks) n.pl. [with sing. v.] 1. the science of language 2. the study of a particular language —lin·guis′tic adj.

**lin·i·ment** (lin′ə mənt) n. [ < L. *linere*, to smear] a soothing medicated liquid to be rubbed on the skin

**lin·ing** (lī′niŋ) n. the material covering an inner surface

**link** (liŋk) n. [ < Scand.] 1. any of the loops forming a chain 2. a) a section of something like a chain [a link of sausage] b) an element in a series [a weak link in evidence] 3. anything that connects [a link with the past] —vt., vi. to join; connect

**link·age** (liŋ′kij) n. 1. a linking 2. a series or system of links

**links** (liŋks) n.pl. [OE. *hlinc*, a slope] a golf course

**link′up′** n. a linking together

**Lin·nae·us** (li nē′əs), **Car·o·lus** (kar′ə ləs) 1707–78; Swed. botanist

**lin·net** (lin′it) *n.* [< L. *linum*, flax: it feeds on flaxseed] a small finch of Europe, Asia, and Africa

**li·no·le·um** (li nō′lē əm) *n.* [< L. *linum*, flax + *oleum*, oil] a hard floor covering made of ground cork and linseed oil on a backing, as of canvas

**lin·seed** (lin′sēd′) *n.* [OE. *linsæd*] the seed of flax

**linseed oil** a yellowish oil extracted from flaxseed, used in oil paints, etc.

**lint** (lint) *n.* [< L. *linum*, flax] 1. scraped and softened linen 2. bits of thread, fluff, etc. from cloth or yarn —lint′y *adj.* -i·er, -i·est

**lin·tel** (lin′t′l) *n.* [ult. < L. *limen*, threshold] the horizontal crosspiece over a door, window, etc.

**lin·y** (lī′nē) *adj.* -i·er, -i·est 1. line-like 2. marked with lines

**li·on** (lī′ən) *n.* [< Gr. *leōn*] 1. a large, powerful mammal of the cat family, found in Africa and SW Asia 2. a person of great courage or strength 3. a celebrity —li′on·ess *n.fem.*

**li′on·heart′ed** *adj.* very brave

**li·on·ize** (lī′ə nīz′) *vt.* -ized′, -iz′ing to treat as a celebrity

**lip** (lip) *n.* [OE. *lippa*] 1. either of the two fleshy folds forming the edges of the mouth 2. anything like a lip, as the rim of a pitcher 3. [Slang] insolent talk —adj. spoken, but insincere *[lip* service] —keep a stiff upper lip [Colloq.] to bear pain or distress bravely

**lip′py** *adj.* -pi·er, -pi·est [Slang] impudent; insolent —lip′pi·ness *n.*

**lip reading** recognition of a speaker's words, as by the deaf, by watching the movement of his lips —lip′-read′ *vt., vi.* —lip reader

**lip′stick′** *n.* a small stick of cosmetic paste for coloring the lips

**lip′-sync′, lip′-synch′** (-siŋk′) *vt., vi.* [< *lip synchronization*] to move the lips silently so as to seem to be speaking or singing (something recorded) —*n.* a lip-syncing

**liq·ue·fy** (lik′wə fī′) *vt., vi.* -fied′, -fy′ing [< L. *liquere*, be liquid + *facere*, make] to change to a liquid —liq′ue·fac′tion (-fak′shən) *n.*

**li·queur** (li kur′) *n.* [Fr.] a sweet, syrupy, flavored alcoholic liquor

**liq·uid** (lik′wid) *adj.* [< L. *liquidus*] 1. readily flowing; fluid 2. clear; limpid 3. flowing smoothly and musically, as verse 4. readily convertible into cash —*n.* a substance that, unlike a solid, flows readily but, unlike a gas, does not expand indefinitely —liq·uid′i·ty *n.*

**liq·ui·date** (lik′wə dāt′) *vt.* -dat′ed, -dat′ing [see prec.] 1. to settle the accounts of (a business) by apportioning assets and debts 2. to pay (a debt) 3. to convert into cash 4. to get rid of, as by killing —liq′ui·da′tion *n.* —liq′ui·da′tor *n.*

**liq′uid·ize′** (-dīz′) *vt.* -ized′, -iz′ing to make of liquid quality

**liq·uor** (lik′ər) *n.* [L.] 1. any liquid 2. an alcoholic drink, esp. a distilled drink, as whiskey or rum

**li·ra** (lir′ə) *n., pl.* li′re (-ā), li′ras [< L. *libra*, pound] the monetary unit of Italy

**Lis·bon** (liz′bən) capital of Portugal: pop. 802,000

**lisle** (līl) *n.* [< *Lisle* (now, *Lille*), in France] 1. a fine, hard, extra-strong cotton thread 2. a fabric, or stockings, gloves, etc., woven of this

**lisp** (lisp) *vi.* [< OE. *wlisp*, a lisping] 1. to substitute the sounds (th) and (*th*) for the sounds of *s* and *z* 2. to speak imperfectly —*vt.* to utter with a lisp —*n.* the act or sound of lisping —lisp′er *n.*

**lis·some** (lis′əm) *adj.* [< *lithesome*] lithe, supple, agile, etc.

**list¹** (list) *n.* [< OE. *liste*, border] a series of names, words, etc. set forth in order —*vt.* to set forth or enter in a list, directory, etc.

**list²** *vt., vi.* [prob. ult. < OE. *lust*, desire] to tilt to one side, as a ship —*n.* such a tilting

**lis·ten** (lis′n) *vi.* [OE. *hlysnan*] 1. to make a conscious effort to hear 2. to give heed; take advice —lis′ten·er *n.*

**list·ing** (lis′tiŋ) *n.* 1. the making of a list 2. an entry in a list

**list·less** (list′lis) *adj.* [< OE. *lust*, desire + -LESS] indifferent because of illness, dejection, etc.; languid —list′less·ly *adv.* —list′less·ness *n.*

**list price** retail price as given in a list or catalog

**lists** (lists) *n.pl.* [< ME. *liste*, border] a fenced area in which knights jousted

**Liszt** (list), **Franz** (fränts) 1811–86; Hung. composer & pianist

**lit** (lit) *alt. pt. & pp. of* LIGHT

**lit.** 1. liter(s) 2. literal(ly) 3. literature

**lit·a·ny** (lit′n ē) *n., pl.* -nies [< Gr. *litē*, a request] prayer in which the congregation recites responses

**li·tchi** (lē′chē′) *n.* [< Chin.] the raisinlike fruit of a Chinese evergreen tree, enclosed in a papery shell

**li·ter** (lēt′ər) *n.* [< Gr. *litra*, a pound] the basic unit of capacity in the metric system, equal to 1.0567 liquid quarts or .908 dry quart: Brit. sp. **li′tre**

**lit·er·a·cy** (lit′ər ə sē) *n.* the ability to read and write

**lit·er·al** (lit′ər əl) *adj.* [< L. *littera*, a letter] 1. following the exact words of the original *[a literal* translation] 2. in a basic or strict sense *[the literal* meaning] 3. prosaic; matter-of-fact *[a literal* mind] 4. real *[the literal* truth] —lit′er·al·ly *adv.*

**lit·er·ar·y** (lit′ə rer′ē) *adj.* 1. of or dealing with literature 2. familiar with or versed in literature

**lit·er·ate** (lit′ər it) *adj.* [< L. *littera*, a letter] 1. able to read and write 2. well-educated —*n.* a literate person

**lit·e·ra·ti** (lit′ə rät′ē) *n.pl.* [It. < L. *litterati*: see prec.] scholarly people

**lit·er·a·ture** (lit′ər ə chər) *n.* [< L. *littera*, a letter] 1. *a)* all writings in prose or verse of an imaginative character *b)* all such writings having permanent value, excellence of form, etc. *c)* all the writings of a particular time, country, etc. *d)* all the writings on a particular subject 2. [Colloq.] any printed matter

**lithe** (līth) *adj.* [OE. *lithe*, soft] bending easily; flexible; supple

**lith·i·um** (lith'ē əm) *n.* [< Gr. *lithos*, stone] a soft, silver-white chemical element

**lithium carbonate** a white, powdery salt, used in making glass, dyes, etc. and in treating manic-depressive disorders

**lith·o·graph** (lith'ə graf') *n.* a print made by lithography —*vi., vt.* to make (prints or copies) by this process —**li·thog·ra·pher** (li thäg'rə fər) *n.*

**li·thog·ra·phy** (li thäg'rə fē) *n.* [< Gr. *lithos*, stone + -GRAPHY] printing from a flat stone or metal plate, parts of which have been treated to repel ink —**lith·o·graph·ic** (lith'ə graf'ik) *adj.*

**Lith·u·a·ni·a** (lith'oo wā'nē ə) republic of the U.S.S.R., in NE Europe —**Lith'u·a'ni·an** *adj., n.*

**lit·i·gant** (lit'ə gənt) *n.* [see ff.] a party to a lawsuit

**lit'i·gate'** (-gāt') *vt., vi.* -gat'ed, -gat'ing [< L. *lis*, dispute + *agere*, do] to contest in a lawsuit —**lit'i·ga'tion** *n.* —**lit'i·ga'tor** *n.*

**lit·mus** (lit'məs) *n.* [< ON. *litr*, color + *mosi*, moss] a purple coloring matter obtained from lichens: paper treated with it (**litmus paper**) turns blue in bases and red in acids

**Litt.D.** Doctor of Letters

**lit·ter** (lit'ər) *n.* [< L. *lectus*, a couch] **1.** a framework enclosing a couch on which a person can be carried **2.** a stretcher for carrying the sick or wounded **3.** straw, hay, etc. used as bedding for animals **4.** the young borne at one time by a dog, cat, etc. **5.** things lying about in disorder, esp. bits of rubbish —*vt.* **1.** to make untidy **2.** to scatter about carelessly

**lit'ter·bug'** (-bug') *n.* one who litters public places with rubbish

**lit·tle** (lit'l) *adj.* **lit'tler** or **less** or **less'er, lit'tlest** or **least** [OE. *lytel*] **1.** small in size, amount, degree, etc. **2.** short in duration; brief **3.** small in importance or power [the *little* man] **4.** narrow-minded [a *little* mind] —*adv.* **less, least 1.** slightly; not much **2.** not in the least —*n.* **a.** small amount, degree, etc. —**little by little** gradually —**make** (or **think**) **little of** to consider as not very important —**lit'tle·ness** *n.*

**Little Rock** capital of Ark.: pop. 132,000

**little slam** *Bridge* the winning of all but one trick in a deal

**lit·to·ral** (lit'ər əl) *adj.* [< L. *litus*, seashore] of or along the shore

**lit·ur·gy** (lit'ər jē) *n., pl.* -gies [ult. < Gr. *leōs*, people + *ergon*, work] prescribed ritual for public worship —**li·tur·gi·cal** (li tur'jə k'l) *adj.* —**lit'ur·gist** *n.*

**liv·a·ble** (liv'ə b'l) *adj.* **1.** fit or pleasant to live in [a *livable* house] **2.** endurable Also **liveable**

**live¹** (liv) *vi.* **lived, liv'ing** [OE. *libban*] **1.** to have life **2.** *a*) to remain alive *b*) to endure **3.** to pass life in a specified manner **4.** to enjoy a full life **5.** to feed [to *live* on fruit] **6.** to reside —*vt.* **1.** to carry out in one's life [to *live* one's faith] **2.** to spend; pass [to *live* a useful life] —**live down** to live so as to wipe out the shame of (a misdeed, etc.) —**live up to** to act in accordance with (one's ideals, etc.)

**live²** (līv) *adj.* [< ALIVE] **1.** having life **2.** of the living state or living beings **3.** of present interest [a *live* issue] **4.** still burning [a *live* spark] **5.** unexploded [a *live* shell] **6.** carrying electrical current [a *live* wire] **7.** *a*) in person *b*) broadcast, recorded, etc. during the actual performance **8.** *Sports* in play [a *live* ball]

**-lived** (līvd; *occas.* livd) *a combining form meaning* having a (specified kind of) life [short-lived]

**live·li·hood** (līv'lē hood') *n.* [< OE. *lif*, life + *-lad*, course] means of living or of supporting life

**live·long** (liv'lôŋ') *adj.* [ME. *lefe longe*, lief long: *lief* is merely intens.] long in passing; whole; entire

**live·ly** (līv'lē) *adj.* -li·er, -li·est [OE. *liflic*] **1.** full of life; vigorous **2.** full of spirit; exciting **3.** gay; cheerful **4.** vivid; keen **5.** bounding back with great resilience [a *lively* ball] —**live'li·ness** *n.*

**liv·en** (lī'vən) *vt., vi.* to make or become lively or gay; cheer (*up*)

**liv·er** (liv'ər) *n.* [OE. *lifer*] **1.** the largest glandular organ in vertebrate animals: it secretes bile and is important in metabolism **2.** this organ of an animal used as food

**liv·er·ied** (liv'ər ēd) *adj.* wearing a livery

**Liv·er·pool** (liv'ər pool') seaport in NW England: pop. 740,000

**liv·er·wurst** (liv'ər wurst') *n.* [< G. *leber*, liver + *wurst*, sausage] a sausage containing ground liver

**liv·er·y** (liv'ər ē) *n., pl.* -ies [ME., gift of clothes to a servant] **1.** an identifying uniform as of a servant **2.** *a*) the care and feeding of horses for a fee *b*) the keeping of horses or vehicles for hire

**lives** (līvz) *n. pl. of* LIFE

**live·stock** (līv'stäk') *n.* domestic animals kept for use on a farm or raised for sale

**liv·id** (liv'id) *adj.* [< L. *lividus*] **1.** discolored by a bruise; black-and-blue **2.** grayish-blue or pale [*livid* with rage]

**liv·ing** (liv'iŋ) *adj.* **1.** alive; having life **2.** in active operation or use [a *living* language] **3.** of persons alive [within *living* memory] **4.** true; lifelike **5.** of life [*living* conditions] —*n.* **1.** a being alive **2.** livelihood **3.** manner of existence —**the living** those that are still alive

**living room** a room in a home, with sofas, chairs, etc., for social activities, entertaining guests, etc.

**living wage** a wage sufficient to maintain a reasonable level of comfort

**liz·ard** (liz'ərd) *n.* [ < L. *lacerta*] any of a group of slender, scaly reptiles with four legs and a tail

**LL.** Late Latin

**ll., 11** lines

**lla·ma** (lä'mə) *n.* [Sp. < Peruv. native name] a S.American beast of burden related to the camel but smaller

**lla·no** (lä'nō) *n., pl.* **-nos** [Sp. < L. *planus*, plain] any of the level, grassy plains of Spanish America

**LL.B.** Bachelor of Laws

**LL.D.** Doctor of Laws

**lo** (lō) *interj.* [OE. *la*] look! see!

**load** (lōd) *n.* [ < OE. *lad*, a course] 1. an amount carried at one time 2. something borne with difficulty; burden 3. [*often pl.*] [Colloq.] a great amount —*vt.* 1. to put (a load) into or upon (a carrier) 2. to burden; oppress 3. to supply in large quantities 4. to put a charge of ammunition into (a firearm) —*vi.* to take on a load —**load′er** *n.* —**load′ing** *n.*

**load′star′** *n. same as* LODESTAR

**load′stone′** *n. same as* LODESTONE

**loaf**[1] (lōf) *n., pl.* **loaves** [OE. *hlaf*] 1. a portion of bread baked in one piece 2. any food baked in this shape

**loaf**[2] (lōf) *vi.* [prob. < ff.] to spend time idly; idle, dawdle, drift

**loaf′er** *n.* [prob. < G. *landläufer*, vagabond] one who loafs; idler

**loam** (lōm) *n.* [OE. *lam*] a rich soil, esp. one composed of clay, sand, and some organic matter —**loam′y** *adj.*

**loan** (lōn) *n.* [ < ON. *lān*] 1. the act of lending 2. something lent, esp. money at interest —*vt., vi.* to lend

**loan′word′** (-wurd′) *n.* a word of one language taken and used in another

**loath** (lōth) *adj.* [ < OE. *lath*, hostile] reluctant [to be loath to depart]

**loathe** (lōth) *vt.* **loathed, loath′ing** [ < OE. *lathian*, be hateful] to feel intense dislike or disgust for; abhor

**loath·ing** (lō'thiŋ) *n.* intense dislike, disgust, or hatred

**loath′some** (-səm) *adj.* causing loathing; disgusting

**loaves** (lōvz) *n. pl. of* LOAF[1]

**lob** (läb) *vt., vi.* **lobbed, lob′bing** [ME. *lobbe-*, heavy] to toss or hit (a ball) in a high curve —**lob′ber** *n.*

**lob·by** (läb'ē) *n., pl.* **-bies** [LL. *lobia*] 1. an entrance hall, as of a hotel, theater, etc. 2. a group of lobbyists representing the same interest —*vi.* **-bied, -by·ing** to act as a lobbyist

**lob′by·ist** *n.* one who tries to get legislators to support certain measures

**lobe** (lōb) *n.* [ < Gr. *lobos*] a rounded projection, as the lower end of the ear or any of the divisions of the lung

**lob·ster** (läb'stər) *n.* [ < OE. *loppe*, spider + *-estre*, -ster] an edible sea crustacean with four pairs of legs and a pair of large pincers

**lobster tail** the edible tail of any of various crayfish

**lo·cal** (lō'k'l) *adj.* [ < L. *locus*, a place] 1. of, characteristic

LOBSTER

of, or confined to a particular place 2. of or for a particular part of the body 3. making all stops along its run [a *local* bus] —*n.* 1. a local train, bus, etc. 2. a branch, as of a labor union —**lo′cal·ly** *adv.*

**lo·cale** (lō kal′) *n.* [Fr. *local*] a locality, esp. with reference to events, etc. associated with it

**lo·cal·i·ty** (lō kal′ə tē) *n., pl.* **-ties** 1. position with regard to surrounding objects, etc. 2. a place or district

**lo·cal·ize** (lō′kə līz′) *vt.* **-ized′, -iz′ing** to limit, confine, or trace to a particular place —**lo′cal·i·za′tion** *n.*

**lo·cate** (lō′kāt) *vt.* **-cat·ed, -cat·ing** [ < L. *locus*, a place] 1. to establish in a certain place [offices *located* downtown] 2. to discover the position of 3. to show the position of [*locate* Guam on this map] —*vi.* [Colloq.] to settle [he *located* in Ohio]

**lo·ca′tion** *n.* 1. a locating or being located 2. position; place —**on location** *Movies* away from the studio

**loc. cit.** [L. *loco citato*] in the place cited

**loch** (läk, läkh) *n.* [ < Gael. & OIr.] [Scot.] 1. a lake 2. an arm of the sea

**lock**[1] (läk) *n.* [ < OE. *loc*, a bolt] 1. a mechanical device for fastening a door, strongbox, etc. as with a key or combination 2. an enclosed part of a canal, etc. equipped with gates for raising or lowering the level of the water 3. the mechanism of a firearm that explodes the charge —*vt.* 1. to fasten with a lock 2. to shut (*up, in,* or *out*); confine 3. to fit; link [to *lock* arms] 4. to jam together so as to make immovable —*vi.* 1. to become locked 2. to interlock

**lock**[2] (läk) *n.* [OE. *loc*] 1. a curl of hair 2. a tuft of wool, etc.

**lock′er** *n.* 1. a chest, closet, etc. which can be locked 2. a large compartment for freezing and storing food

**lock·et** (läk′it) *n.* [ < OFr. *loc*, a lock] a small, hinged case for holding a picture, lock of hair, etc.: usually worn on a necklace

**lock′jaw′** *n.* a form of tetanus, in which the jaws become firmly closed

**lock′out′** *n.* the shutdown of a plant to bring the workers to terms

**lock′smith′** *n.* one whose work is making or repairing locks and keys

**lock·up** (läk′up′) *n.* a jail

**lo·co** (lō′kō) *adj.* [Sp., mad] [Slang] crazy; demented

**lo·co·mo·tion** (lō′kə mō′shən) *n.* [ < L. *locus*, a place + MOTION] motion, or the power of moving, from one place to another

**lo′co·mo′tive** (-mōt′iv) *adj.* of locomotion —*n.* an electric, steam, or diesel engine on wheels, designed to push or pull a railroad train

**lo·co·weed** (lō′kō wēd′) *n.* a plant of W N.America that causes a nervous disease in horses, cattle, etc.

**lo·cus** (lō′kəs) *n., pl.* **lo·ci** (-sī) [L.] 1. a place 2. *Math.* a line, plane, etc. every point of which satisfies a given condition

**lo·cust** (lō′kəst) *n.* [ < L. *locusta*] 1.

a large grasshopper often traveling in swarms and destroying crops **2.** *same as* SEVENTEEN-YEAR LOCUST **3.** a tree of the S U.S., with clusters of fragrant white flowers

**lo·cu·tion** (lō kyōō′shən) *n.* [< L. *loqui,* speak] a word, phrase, etc.

**lode** (lōd) *n.* [< OE. *lad,* course] a vein, stratum, etc. of metallic ore

**lode′star′** *n.* a star by which one directs his course; esp., the North Star

**lode′stone′** *n.* a strongly magnetic iron ore

**lodge** (läj) *n.* [< OFr. *loge,* arbor] **1.** *a)* a small house for some special use [a hunting *lodge] b)* a resort hotel or motel **2.** the local chapter or hall of a fraternal society —*vt.* **lodged, lodg′-ing 1.** to house temporarily **2.** to shoot, thrust, etc. firmly (*in*) **3.** to bring (a complaint, etc.) before legal authorities **4.** to confer (powers) upon (with *in*) —*vi.* **1.** to live in a place for a time **2.** to live (*with* or *in*) as a paying guest **3.** to come to rest and stick firmly (*in*)

**lodg′er** *n.* one who lives in a rented room in another's home

**lodg′ing** *n.* **1.** a place to live in, esp. temporarily **2.** [*pl.*] a room or rooms rented in a private home

**loft** (lôft, läft) *n.* [< ON. *lopt,* upper room, air] **1.** the space just below the roof of a house, barn, etc. **2.** an upper story of a warehouse or factory **3.** a gallery [a choir *loft] ***4.** height given to a ball hit or thrown —*vt.* to send (a ball) into a high curve

**loft′y** *adj.* **-i·er, -i·est 1.** very high **2.** elevated; noble **3.** haughty; arrogant —**loft′i·ness** *n.*

**log¹** (lôg, läg) *n.* [ME. *logge*] **1.** a section of the trunk or of a large limb of a felled tree **2.** a device for measuring the speed of a ship **3.** a record of progress, speed, etc., specif. one kept on a ship's voyage or aircraft's flight —*vt.* **logged, log′ging 1.** to saw (trees) into logs **2.** to record in a log **3.** to sail or fly (a specified distance) —*vi.* to cut down trees and remove the logs —**log′ger** *n.*

**log²** (lôg, läg) *n. short for* LOGARITHM

**-log** (lôg, läg) *same as* -LOGUE

**lo·gan·ber·ry** (lō′gən ber′ē) *n., pl.* **-ries** [< J. H. *Logan,* who developed it (1881)] **1.** a hybrid developed from the blackberry and the red raspberry **2.** its purplish-red fruit

**log·a·rithm** (lôg′ə ri*th*′m, läg′-) [< Gr. *logos,* ratio + *arithmos,* number] the exponent expressing the power to which a fixed number must be raised to produce a given number —**log′a·rith′mic** *adj.*

**loge** (lōzh) *n.* [Fr.: see LODGE] a theater box or mezzanine section

**log·ger·head** (lôg′ər hed′, läg′-) *n.* [dial. *logger,* block of wood + HEAD] a blockhead —**at loggerheads** in sharp disagreement

**log·ic** (läj′ik) *n.* [ult. < Gr. *logos,* word] **1.** correct reasoning, or the science of this **2.** way of reasoning [bad *logic] ***3.** what is expected by the working of cause and effect —**lo·gi·cian** (lō jish′ən) *n.*

**log′i·cal** (-i k′l) *adj.* **1.** based on or using logic **2.** expected because of what has gone before —**log′i·cal·ly** *adv.*

**lo·gis·tics** (lō jis′tiks) *n.pl.* [*with sing. v.*] [< Fr. *loger,* to quarter] the military science of procuring, maintaining, and transporting materiel and personnel —**lo·gis′tic, lo·gis′ti·cal** *adj.* —**lo·gis′ti·cal·ly** *adv.*

**log′jam′** *n.* **1.** an obstacle of logs jamming together in a stream **2.** piled-up work, etc. that obstructs progress

**log·o·type** (lôg′ə tīp′, läg′-) *n.* [< Gr. *logos,* a word + -TYPE] a distinctive company signature, trademark, etc.: also **log·o** (lôg′ō, läg′ō, lō′gō)

**log′roll′ing** *n.* **1.** mutual exchange of favors, esp. among legislators **2.** the sport of balancing oneself while revolving a floating log with one's feet

**-logue** (lôg) [see LOGIC] *a combining form meaning* a (specified kind of) speaking or writing [monologue]

**lo·gy** (lō′gē) *adj.* **-gi·er, -gi·est** [< ? Du. *log,* dull] [Colloq.] dull or sluggish

**-lo·gy** (lə jē) [see LOGIC] *a combining form meaning:* **1.** a (specified kind of) speaking [eulogy] **2.** science, doctrine, or theory of [biology]

**loin** (loin) *n.* [< L. *lumbus*] **1.** [*usually pl.*] the lower part of the back between the hipbones and the ribs **2.** the front part of the hindquarters of beef, lamb, etc. **3.** [*pl.*] the hips and the lower abdomen regarded as the region of strength, etc.

**loin′cloth′** *n.* a cloth worn about the loins, as by some tropical tribes

**loi·ter** (loit′ər) *vi.* [< MDu. *loteren*] **1.** to spend time idly; linger **2.** to move slowly and idly —**loi′ter·er** *n.*

**loll** (läl) *vi.* [< MDu. *lollen*] **1.** to lean or lounge about lazily **2.** to hang loosely; droop, as the head on the shoulders —*vt.* to let hang loosely

**lol·li·pop, lol·ly·pop** (läl′ē päp′) *n.* [prob. < dial. *lolly,* tongue + *pop*] a piece of candy on the end of a stick

**lol·ly·gag** (läl′ē gag′) *vi.* **-gagged′, -gag′ging** [var. of *lallygag* < ?] [Colloq.] to waste time in aimless activity

**Lon·don** (lun′dən) **1.** capital of England, the United Kingdom, & the Brit. Commonwealth, in SE England: pop. (incl. suburbs) 8,183,000 **2.** city in SE Ontario, Canada: pop. 194,000

**lone** (lōn) *adj.* [< *alone*] **1.** by oneself; solitary **2.** isolated

**lone′ly** *adj.* **-li·er, -li·est 1.** solitary or isolated **2.** unhappy at being alone —**lone′li·ness** *n.*

**lon·er** (lō′nər) *n.* [Colloq.] one who avoids the company, counsel, etc. of others

**lone′some** *adj.* **1.** having or causing a lonely feeling **2.** unfrequented

**long**[1] (lôŋ) *adj.* [< OE.] **1.** measuring much in space or time **2.** in length *[six feet long]* **3.** of greater than usual length, quantity, etc. *[a long list]* **4.** tedious; slow **5.** far-reaching *[a long view of the matter]* **6.** well-supplied *[long on excuses]* —*adv.* **1.** for a long time **2.** from start to finish *[all day long]* **3.** at a remote time *[long ago]* —**as** (or **so**) **long as 1.** during the time that **2.** since **3.** provided that —**before long** soon

**long**[2] (lôŋ) *vi.* [< OE. *langian*] to feel a strong yearning; wish earnestly

**long.** longitude

**Long Beach** seaport in SW Calif., on the Pacific; pop. 359,000

**long distance** a telephone exchange for calls to and from distant places —**long′-dis′tance** *adj., adv.*

**lon·gev·i·ty** (län jev′ə tē) *n.* [< L. *longus,* long + *aevum,* age] long life

**long′-faced′** *adj.* glum

**long′hair′** *adj.* [Colloq.] of intellectuals or intellectual tastes

**long′hand′** *n.* ordinary handwriting, as distinguished from shorthand

**long′ing** *n.* strong desire; yearning —*adj.* feeling or showing a yearning

**Long Island** island in SE N.Y., in the Atlantic south of Conn.

**lon·gi·tude** (län′jə tood′) *n.* [< L. *longus,* long] distance east or west of the prime meridian, expressed in degrees or time

**lon′gi·tu′di·nal** (-tood′'n əl) *adj.* **1.** of or in length **2.** running or placed lengthwise **3.** of longitude

**long jump** *Sports* a jump for distance, made either from a stationary position or with a running start

**long′-lived′** (-līvd′, -livd′) *adj.* having or tending to have a long life span

**long play** a long-playing record

**long′-play′ing** *adj.* designating or of a phonograph record having microgrooves and playing at 33⅓ revolutions per minute

**long′-range′** *adj.* reaching over a long distance or period of time

**long·shore·man** (lôŋ′shôr′mən) *n., pl.* -**men** [< *alongshore* + MAN] a person who works on a waterfront loading and unloading ships

**long shot** [Colloq.] in betting, a choice that is little favored and, hence, carries great odds

**long′-stand′ing** *adj.* having continued for a long time

**long′-suf′fer·ing** *adj.* bearing trouble, etc. patiently for a long time

**long′-term′** *adj.* for or extending over a long time

**long ton** 2,240 pounds: see TON

**long′-wind′ed** (-win′did) *adj.* **1.** speaking or writing at great length **2.** tiresomely long

**look** (look) *vi.* [< OE. *locian*] **1.** to direct one's eyes in order to see **2.** to search **3.** to appear; seem **4.** to be facing in a specified direction —*vt.* **1.** to direct one's eyes on **2.** to have an appearance befitting *[to look the part]* —*n.* **1.** a looking; glance **2.** appearance; aspect *3.* [Colloq.] *a)* [*usually pl.*] appearance *b)* [*pl.*] personal appearance —*interj.* **1.** see! **2.** pay attention! —**look after** to take care of —**look down on** (or **upon**) to regard with contempt —**look for** to expect —**look forward to** to anticipate —**look in** (on) to pay a brief visit (to) —**look into** to investigate —**look out** to be careful —**look over** to examine —**look to 1.** to take care of **2.** to rely on —**look up 1.** to search for as in a reference book **2.** [Colloq.] to call on —**look up to** to admire —**look′er** *n.*

**look′er-on′** *n., pl.* **look′ers-on′** an observer or spectator; onlooker

**looking glass** a (glass) mirror

**look′out′** *n.* **1.** a careful watching **2.** a place for keeping watch **3.** a person detailed to watch **4.** [Colloq.] concern

**look′-see′** *n.* [Slang] a quick look

**loom**[1] (loom) *n.* [< OE. *(ge)loma,* tool] a machine for weaving thread or yarn into cloth —*vt.* to weave on a loom

**loom**[2] (loom) *vi.* [< ?] to come into sight indistinctly, esp. in a large or threatening form

**loon**[1] (loon) *n.* [< ON. *lomr*] a fish-eating, diving bird, similar to a duck

**loon**[2] (loon) *n.* [< ?] **1.** a clumsy, stupid person **2.** a crazy person

**loon·y** (loo′nē) *adj.* -**i·er**, -**i·est** [< LUNATIC] [Slang] crazy; demented

**loop** (loop) *n.* [ME. *loup*] **1.** the figure made by a line, thread, etc. that curves back to cross itself **2.** anything forming this figure **3.** an intrauterine contraceptive device —*vt.* **1.** to make a loop of **2.** to fasten with a loop —*vi.* to form a loop or loops

**loop′hole′** *n.* [prob. < MDu. *lupen,* to peer + HOLE?] **1.** a hole in a wall for looking or shooting through **2.** a means of evading an obligation, etc.

**loose** (loos) *adj.* [< ON. *lauss*] **1.** not confined or restrained; free **2.** not firmly fastened **3.** not tight or compact **4.** not precise; inexact **5.** sexually immoral **6.** [Colloq.] relaxed —*adv.* loosely —*vt.* **1.** to set free; unbind **2.** to make less tight, compact, etc. **3.** to relax **4.** to release (an arrow, etc.) —*vi.* to become loose —**on the loose** not confined; free —**loose′ly** *adv.* —**loose′ness** *n.*

**loose′-leaf′** *adj.* having leaves, or sheets, that can easily be removed or replaced

**loose ends** unsettled details —**at loose ends** unsettled, idle, etc.

**loos·en** (loos′'n) *vt., vi.* to make or become loose or looser

**loot** (loot) *n.* [Hind. *lūt*] **1.** goods stolen or taken by force; plunder **2.** [Slang] money, presents, etc. —*vt., vi.* to plunder

**lop**[1] (läp) *vt.* lopped, lop′ping [< OE. *loppian*] **1.** to trim (a tree, etc.) by cutting off branches, etc. **2.** to remove as by cutting off —*lop′per n.*

**lop**[2] (läp) *vi.* lopped, lop′ping [prob. akin to LOB] to hang down loosely

**lope** (lōp) *vi.* loped, lop′ing [< ON. *hlaupa,* to leap] to move with a long, swinging stride —*n.* such a stride

**lop·sid·ed** (läp′sīd′id) *adj.* noticeably heavier, bigger, or lower on one side

**lo·qua·cious** (lō kwā′shəs) *adj.* [<

L. *loqui*, speak] very talkative —**lo-quac′i·ty** (-kwas′ə tē) *n.*

**lord** (lôrd) *n.* [< OE. *hlaf*, loaf + *weard*, keeper] **1.** a ruler; master **2.** the head of a feudal estate **3.** [L-] *a)* God *b)* Jesus Christ **4.** in Great Britain, a titled nobleman —**lord it** (**over**) to be overbearing (toward)

**lord′ly** *adj.* **-li·er, -li·est 1.** noble; magnificent **2.** haughty —*adv.* in the manner of a lord

**Lord′s day** Sunday

**lord′ship′** *n.* **1.** the rank or authority of a lord **2.** rule; dominion **3.** a title used in speaking of or to a lord: with *his* or *your*

**Lord′s Prayer** the prayer beginning *Our Father*: Matt. 6:9–13

**lore** (lôr) *n.* [< OE. *lar*] knowledge; learning, esp. of a traditional nature

**lor·gnette** (lôr nyet′) *n.* [Fr. < OFr. *lorgne*, squinting] eyeglasses, or opera glasses, attached to a handle

**lorn** (lôrn) *adj.* [ME. < *losen*, lose] [Archaic] forsaken, forlorn, etc.

**lor·ry** (lôr′ē, lär′-) *n., pl.* **-ries** [prob. < dial. *lurry*, to pull] [Brit.] a motor truck

**Los An·gel·es** (lôs an′jə ləs, läs an′gə ləs) seaport on the SW coast of Calif.: pop. 2,816,000

**lose** (lōōz) *vt.* **lost, los′ing** [< OE. *losian*] **1.** to become unable to find *[to lose* one's keys*]* **2.** to have taken from one by accident, death, removal, etc. **3.** to fail to keep *[to lose* one's temper*]* **4.** to fail to see, hear, or understand **5.** to fail to have, get, etc. *[to lose* one's chance*]* **6.** to fail to win **7.** to cause the loss of **8.** to wander from (one's way, etc.) **9.** to squander —*vi.* **1.** to suffer (a) loss —**lose oneself** to become absorbed —**los′er** *n.*

**loss** (lôs) *n.* [< ? OE. *los*, ruin] **1.** a losing or being lost **2.** the damage, trouble, etc. caused by losing **3.** the person, thing, or amount lost —**at a loss 1.** uncertain (how to)

**lost** (lôst) *pt. & pp.* of LOSE —*adj.* **1.** ruined; destroyed **2.** not to be found; missing **3.** no longer held, seen, heard, etc. **4.** not gained or won **5.** having wandered astray **6.** wasted

**lot** (lät) *n.* [< OE. *hlot*] **1.** the deciding of a matter by chance, as by drawing counters **2.** the decision thus arrived at **3.** one's share by lot **4.** fortune *[his unhappy lot]* **5.** a plot of ground **6.** a group of persons or things **7.** *[often pl.]* [Colloq.] a great amount **8.** [Colloq.] sort *[he's a bad lot]* —*adv.* very much: also **lots** —**draw** (or **cast**) **lot** to decide by lot

**Lo·thar·i·o** (lō ther′ē ō′) *n., pl.* **-i·os′** [< the rake in the play *The Fair Penitent*] a gay seducer of women

**lo·tion** (lō′shən) *n.* [< L. *lavare*, to wash] a liquid preparation used, as on the skin, for washing, healing, etc.

**lot·ter·y** (lät′ər ē) *n., pl.* **-ies** [< MDu. *lot*, lot] a game of chance in which people buy numbered tickets on

prizes, winners being chosen by lot **2.** a drawing, event, etc. based on chance

**lot·to** (lät′ō) *n.* [It. < MDu. *lot*, lot] a game of chance played on cards with numbered squares: counters are placed on numbers chosen by lot

**lo·tus** (lōt′əs) *n.* [< Gr. *lōtos*] **1.** *Gr. Legend* a plant whose fruit induced forgetfulness **2.** any of several tropical waterlilies

**lotus position** an erect sitting posture in yoga, with the legs crossed close to the body

**loud** (loud) *adj.* [< OE. *hlud*] **1.** strongly audible: said of sound **2.** sounding with great intensity **3.** noisy **4.** emphatic *[loud* denials*]* **5.** [Colloq.] *a)* flashy *b)* vulgar —*adv.* in a loud manner —**loud′ly** *adv.* —**loud′ness** *n.*

**loud′mouthed′** (-moutht′, -mouthd′) *adj.* talking in a loud, irritating voice

**loud′speak′er** *n.* a device for converting electrical energy to sound and amplifying it

**Lou·is** (lōō′ē) **1.** XIV 1638–1715; king of France (1643–1715) **2.** XV 1710–74; king of France (1715–74) **3.** XVI 1754–93; king of France (1774–92): guillotined

**Lou·i·si·an·a** (lōō wē′zē an′ə, lōō′ə zē-) Southern State of the U.S.: 48,523 sq. mi.; pop. 3,643,000; cap. Baton Rouge

**Lou·is·ville** (lōō′ē vil) city in N Ky.: pop. 361,000

**lounge** (lounj) *vi.* **lounged, loung′ing** [Scot. dial. < ? *lungis*, a laggard] **1.** to move, sit, lie, etc. in a relaxed way **2.** to spend time in idleness —*n.* **1.** a room with comfortable furniture for lounging **2.** a couch or sofa

**louse** (lous) *n., pl.* **lice** [< OE. *lus*] **1.** a small, wingless insect parasitic on man and other animals **2.** any similar insect parasitic on plants **3.** [Slang] a mean, contemptible person —**louse up** [Slang] to spoil; ruin

**lous·y** (lou′zē) *adj.* **-i·er, -i·est 1.** infested with lice **2.** [Slang] *a)* disgusting *b)* poor; inferior *c)* well supplied (*with*) —**lous′i·ness** *n.*

**lout** (lout) *n.* [prob. < or akin to ME. *lutien*, lurk] a clumsy, stupid fellow —**lout′ish** *adj.*

**lou·ver** (lōō′vər) *n.* [< MDu. *love*, gallery] **1.** an opening, window, etc. fitted with a series of sloping slats arranged so as to admit light and air but shed rain **2.** any of these slats

**Lou·vre** (lōō′vrə, lōōv) national art museum in Paris

**love** (luv) *n.* [< OE. *lufu*] **1.** strong affection or liking for someone or something **2.** a passionate affection for one of the opposite sex **3.** the object of such affection; sweetheart **4.** *Tennis* a score of zero —*vt., vi.* **loved, lov′ing** to feel love (for) —**in love** feeling love —**make love 1.** to woo, embrace, etc. **2.** to have sexual intercourse —**lov′a·ble, love′a·ble** *adj.* —**love′less** *adj.*

---

**love′lorn′** *adj.* pining from love

**love′ly** *adj.* **-li·er, -li·est 1.** beautiful **2.** [Colloq.] highly enjoyable —**love′·li·ness** *n.*

**lov·er** (luv′ər) *n.* one who loves; specif., *a*) sweetheart *b*) a paramour *c*) [*pl.*] a couple in love with each other *d*) a devotee, as of music

**love seat** a small sofa for two people

**lov′ing** *adj.* feeling or expressing love —**lov′ing·ly** *adv.*

**loving cup** a large drinking cup with two handles, often given as a prize

**low¹** (lō) *adj.* [< ON. *lagr*] **1.** not high or tall **2.** below the normal level [*low* ground] **3.** shallow **4.** less in size, degree, etc. than usual [*low* speed] **5.** deep in pitch **6.** depressed in spirits **7.** not of high rank; humble **8.** vulgar; coarse **9.** poor; inferior **10.** not loud —*adv.* in or to a low level, degree, etc. —*n.′* **1.** a low level, degree, etc. **2.** an arrangement of gears giving the lowest speed and greatest power —**lay low** to overcome or kill —**lie low** to keep oneself hidden —**low′ness** *n.*

**low²** (lō) *vi., n.* [< OE. *hlowan*] same as MOO

**low′born′** *adj.* of humble birth

**low′boy′** *n.* a chest of drawers mounted on short legs

**low′brow′** *n.* [Colloq.] one considered to lack cultivated tastes

**Low Countries** the Netherlands, Belgium, & Luxembourg

**low′-down′** (lō′doun′; *for adj.* -doun′) *n.* [Slang] the true, pertinent facts (with *the*) —*adj.* [Colloq.] mean; contemptible

**low·er¹** (lō′ər) *adj. compar. of* LOW¹ **1.** below in place, rank, etc. **2.** less in amount, degree, etc. —*vt.* **1.** to let or put down [to *lower* a window] **2.** to reduce in height, amount, etc. **3.** to bring down in respect, etc. —*vi.* to become lower

**low·er²** (lou′ər) *vi.* [ME. *louren*] **1.** to scowl or frown **2.** to appear black and threatening, as the sky —**low′er·ing** *adj.* —**low′er·ing·ly** *adv.*

**lower case** small-letter type used in printing, as distinguished from capital letters —**low′er-case′** *adj.*

**low frequency** any radio frequency between 30 and 300 kilohertz

**Low German 1.** the vernacular dialects of N Germany **2.** the branch of Germanic languages including English, Dutch, Flemish, etc.

**low′-grade′** *adj.* of low quality, degree, etc.

**low′-key′** *adj.* of low intensity, tone, etc.; subdued: also **low′-keyed′**

**low′land′** *n.* land below the level of the surrounding land —**the Lowlands** lowlands of SC Scotland

**low′ly** *adj.* **-li·er, -li·est 1.** of low position or rank **2.** humble; meek —*adv.* humbly —**low′li·ness** *n.*

**low′-mind′ed** *adj.* having or showing a coarse, vulgar mind

**low profile** a barely noticeable presence or concealed activity

**low′-spir′it·ed** *adj.* sad; melancholy

**low tide** the lowest level reached by the ebbing tide

**lox¹** (läks) *n.* [< Yid. < G. *lachs*, salmon] a kind of smoked salmon

**lox²** (läks) *n.* liquid oxygen, used in a fuel mixture for rockets

**loy·al** (loi′əl) *adj.* [see LEGAL] **1.** faithful to one's country, friends, ideals, etc. **2.** showing such faithfulness —**loy′al·ly** *adv.* —**loy′al·ty** *n., pl.* **-ties**

**loy′al·ist** *n.* one who supports the government during a revolt

**loz·enge** (läz′nj) *n.* [< OFr. *losenge*] a cough drop, candy, etc., orig. diamond-shaped

**LP** [*L(ong) P(laying)*] *a trademark for* a long-playing record —*n.* a long-playing record

**LPN, L.P.N.** Licensed Practical Nurse

**Lr** *Chem.* lawrencium

**LSD** [*l(y)s(ergic acid) d(iethylamide)*] a chemical compound used in the study of mental disorders and as a psychedelic drug

**Lt.** Lieutenant

**Ltd., ltd.** limited

**lu·au** (lōō′ou′) *n.* a Hawaiian feast

**lub·ber** (lub′ər) *n.* [< ME. *lobbe*, heavy] **1.** a big, slow, clumsy person **2.** an inexperienced, clumsy sailor

**Lub·bock** (lub′ək) city in NW Tex.: pop. 149,000

**lube** (lōōb) *n.* **1.** a lubricating oil for machinery: also **lube oil 2.** [Colloq.] a lubrication

**lu·bri·cant** (lōō′brə kənt) *adj.* reducing friction by providing a smooth surface film over parts coming into contact —*n.* a lubricant oil, etc.

**lu′bri·cate′** (-kāt′) *vt.* **-cat′ed, -cat′ing** [< L. *lubricus*, smooth] **1.** to make slippery or smooth **2.** to apply a lubricant to (machinery, etc.) —**lu′bri·ca′tion** *n.* —**lu′bri·ca′tor** *n.*

**lu·cid** (lōō′sid) *adj.* [< L. *lucere*, shine] **1.** shining **2.** transparent **3.** sane **4.** clear; readily understood —**lu·cid′i·ty** *n.* —**lu′cid·ly** *adv.*

**Lu·ci·fer** (lōō′sə fər) Satan; the Devil

**luck** (luk) *n.* [prob. < MDu. *gelucke*] **1.** the seemingly chance happening of events which affect one; fortune; lot **2.** good fortune —**luck out** [Colloq.] to be lucky —**luck′less** *adj.*

**luck′y** *adj.* **-i·er, -i·est 1.** having good luck **2.** resulting fortunately **3.** believed to bring good luck —**luck′i·ly** *adv.* —**luck′i·ness** *n.*

**lu·cra·tive** (lōō′krə tiv) *adj.* [< L. *lucrum*, riches] producing wealth or profit; profitable

**lu·cre** (lōō′kər) *n.* [< L. *lucrum*] riches; money: chiefly derogatory

**lu·cu·brate** (lōō′kyŏŏ brāt′) *vi.* **-brat′ed, -brat′ing** [< L. *lucubrare*, work by candlelight] to work, study, or write laboriously, esp. late at night —**lu′cu·bra′tion** *n.*

**lu·di·crous** (lōō′di krəs) *adj.* [< L. *ludus*, a game] causing laughter because absurd or ridiculous —**lu′di·crous·ly** *adv.* —**lu′di·crous·ness** *n.*

**luff** (luf) *vi.* [< ODu. *loef*, windward side (of a ship)] to turn the bow of a ship toward the wind

**lug** (lug) *vt.* **lugged, lug′ging** [prob. < Scand.] to carry or drag with effort —*n.* **1.** an earlike projection by which a thing is held or supported **2.** a heavy nut for securing a wheel to an axle

**lug·gage** (lug′ij) *n.* [< prec.] suitcases, trunks, etc.; baggage

**lu·gu·bri·ous** (loo goo′brē əs) *adj.* [< L. *lugere*, mourn] very sad or mournful, esp. in an exaggerated way —**lu·gu′bri·ous·ly** *adv.* —**lu·gu′bri·ous·ness** *n.*

**Luke** (look) *Bible* **1.** an early Christian, the reputed author of the third Gospel **2.** this book

**luke·warm** (look′wôrm′) *adj.* [< ME. *luke*, tepid + *warm*, warm] **1.** barely warm; tepid **2.** lacking enthusiasm —**luke′warm′ly** *adv.* —**luke′warm′ness** *n.*

**lull** (lul) *vt.* [ME. *lullen*] **1.** to calm by gentle sound or motion **2.** to bring into a specified condition by soothing and reassuring —*vi.* to become calm —*n.* a short period of calm

**lull′a·by′** (-ə bī′) *n., pl.* **-bies′** a song for lulling a baby to sleep

**lum·ba·go** (lum bā′gō) *n.* [L. < *lumbus*, loin] pain in the lower back

**lum·bar** (lum′bər, -bär) *adj.* [< L. *lumbus*, loin] of or near the loins

**lum·ber¹** (lum′bər) *n.* [< ? pawnbrokers of *Lombardy*, Italy; hence, stored articles] **1.** discarded household articles, furniture, etc. **2.** timber sawed into boards, etc. —*vi.* to cut down timber and saw it into lumber —**lum′ber·ing** *n.*

**lum·ber²** (lum′bər) *vi.* [< ? Scand.] to move heavily and noisily —**lum′ber·ing** *adj.*

**lum·ber·jack** (lum′bər jak′) *n.* a man whose work is cutting down timber and preparing it for the sawmill

**lum′ber·man** (-mən) *n., pl.* **-men** one who deals in lumber

**lu·mi·nar·y** (loo′mə ner′ē) *n., pl.* **-ies** [< L. *lumen*, light] **1.** a body that gives off light, such as the sun **2.** a famous or notable person

**lu·mi·nes·cence** (loo′mə nes′′ns) *n.* [< L. *lumen*, light¹ + -ESCENCE] the giving off of light without heat, as in fluorescence or phosphorescence —**lu′mi·nes′cent** *adj.*

**lu·mi·nous** (loo′mə nəs) *adj.* [< L. *lumen*, light] **1.** giving off light; bright **2.** clear; readily understood —**lu′mi·nos′i·ty** (-näs′ə tē) *n.*

**lum·mox** (lum′əks) *n.* [< ?] [Colloq.] a clumsy, stupid person

**lump¹** (lump) *n.* [ME. *lompe*] **1.** an indefinitely shaped mass of something **2.** a swelling **3.** [*pl.*] [Colloq.] hard blows, criticism, etc. —*adj.* in a lump or lumps —*vt.* **1.** to put together in a lump or lumps **2.** to treat or deal with in a mass —*vi.* to become lumpy —**lump′i·ness** *n.* —**lump′y** *adj.*

**lump²** (lump) *vt.* [Early ModE., look sour] [Colloq.] to have to put up with (something disagreeable)

**lump sum** a gross, or total, sum paid at one time

**lu·na·cy** (loo′nə sē) *n., pl.* **-cies** [< LUNATIC] **1.** insanity **2.** utter folly

**lu·nar** (loo′nər) *adj.* [< L. *luna*, the moon] of or like the moon

**lu·na·tic** (loo′nə tik) *adj.* [< L. *luna*, the moon] **1.** insane or for the insane **2.** utterly foolish —*n.* an insane person

**lunch** (lunch) *n.* [< ? Sp. *lonja*, slice of ham] a light meal; esp., the midday meal between breakfast and dinner —*vi.* to eat lunch

**lunch·eon** (lun′chən) *n.* a lunch; esp., a formal lunch

**lunch′eon·ette′** (-chə net′) *n.* a small restaurant serving light lunches

**luncheon meat** meat processed in loaves, sausages, etc. and ready to eat

**lung** (lun) *n.* [OE. *lungen*] either of the two spongelike breathing organs in the thorax of vertebrates

**lunge** (lunj) *n.* [< Fr. *allonger*, lengthen] **1.** a sudden thrust as with a sword **2.** a sudden plunge forward —*vi., vt.* **lunged, lung′ing** to move, or cause to move, with a lunge

**lung·fish** (lun′fish′) *n., pl.:* see FISH any of various fishes having lungs as well as gills

**lunk·head** (lunk′hed′) *n.* [prob. echoic alt. of LUMP¹ + HEAD] [Colloq.] a stupid person: also **lunk**

**lu·pine** (loo′pin) *adj.* [< L. *lupus*, wolf] of or like a wolf —*n.* a plant with long spikes of white, rose, or blue flowers

**lu·pus** (loo′pəs) *n.* [< L. wolf] any of various diseases with skin lesions

**lurch¹** (lurch) *vi.* [< ?] **1.** to pitch or sway suddenly to one side **2.** to stagger —*n.* a lurching movement

**lurch²** (lurch) *n.* [prob. < OFr. *lourche*, duped] a difficult situation: only in **leave in the lurch**

**lure** (loor) *n.* [< OFr. *loirre*] **1.** anything that tempts or entices **2.** a bait used in fishing —*vt.* **lured, lur′ing** to attract; tempt; entice

**lu·rid** (loor′id) *adj.* [L. *luridus*, ghastly] **1.** glowing through a haze, as flames enveloped by smoke **2.** shocking; sensational —**lu′rid·ness** *n.*

**lurk** (lurk) *vi.* [ME. *lurken*] **1.** to stay hidden, ready to attack, etc. **2.** to move furtively

**lus·cious** (lush′əs) *adj.* [ME. *lucius*] **1.** highly gratifying to taste or smell; delicious **2.** delighting any of the senses —**lus′cious·ness** *n.*

**lush¹** (lush) *adj.* [< OFr. *lasche*, lax] **1.** of or showing luxuriant growth **2.** rich, abundant, extravagant, etc.

**lush²** (lush) *n.* [Slang] an alcoholic

**lust** (lust) *n.* [OE., pleasure] **1.** bodily appetite; esp., excessive sexual desire **2.** overmastering desire [a *lust* for power] —*vi.* to feel an intense desire —**lust′ful** *adj.* —**lust′ful·ly** *adv.*

**lus·ter** (lus′tər) *n.* [< L. *lustrare*, illumine] **1.** gloss; sheen **2.** brightness; radiance **3.** brilliant beauty or

fat, āpe, cär; ten, ēven; is, bīte; gō, hôrn, tool, look; oil, out; up, fur; chin; she; thin, *then*; zh, leisure; ŋ, ring; ə for *a* in *ago*; ', (ā′b'l); ë, Fr. coeur; ö, Fr. feu; Fr. mon; ü, Fr. duc; kh, G. ich, doch; ‡ foreign; < derived from fame; glory Also, chiefly Brit., **lustre**

**lus·trous** *adj.* having luster; shiny

**lust·y** (lus'tē) *adj.* -i·er, -i·est full of vigor; robust —lust'i·ly *adv.* — lust'i·ness *n.*

**lute** (lōōt) *n.* [ult. < Ar. *al'ūd*, the wood] an old stringed instrument like the guitar, with a rounded body

**Lu·ther** (lōō'thər), **Martin** 1483–1546; Ger. Reformation leader

LUTE

**Lu·ther·an** *adj.* of the Protestant denomination founded by Luther —*n.* a member of a Lutheran Church

**lut·ist** (lōōt'ist) *n.* a lute player: also **lu·ta·nist** (lōōt'n ist)

**Lux·em·bourg** (luk'səm burg') grand duchy in W Europe, north of France; 998 sq. mi.; pop. 335,000

**lux·u·ri·ant** (lug zhoor'ē ənt) *adj.* [see LUXURY] 1. growing with vigor and in abundance 2. having rich ornamentation, etc. —lux·u'ri·ance*n.*

**lux·u'ri·ate'** (-āt') *vi.* -at'ed, -at'ing 1. to live in great luxury 2. to revel (*in*) —lux·u'ri·a'tion *n.*

**lux·u'ri·ous** *adj.* 1. fond of or indulging in luxury 2. constituting luxury; rich, comfortable, etc. —lux·ur'·i·ous·ly *adv.*

**lux·u·ry** (luk'shə rē, lug'zhə-) *n., pl.* -ries [< L. *luxus*] 1. the enjoyment of the best and most costly things 2. anything contributing to such enjoyment, usually not necessary

**Lu·zon** (lōō zän') main island of the Philippines

**-ly** (lē) [< OE. *-lic* ] a *suffix meaning:* 1. like or characteristic of [*manly*] 2. in a (specified) manner, to a (specified) extent or direction, in or at a (specified) time or place [*harshly, outwardly, hourly*] 3. in sequence [*thirdly*] 4. happening (once) every (specified period) [*monthly*]

**ly·ce·um** (lī sē'əm, lī'sē-) *n.* [< Gr. *Lykeion*, grove at Athens where Aristotle taught] 1. a lecture hall 2. an organization providing lectures, etc.

**lye** (lī) *n.* [OE. *leag*] any strongly alkaline substance, used in cleaning and in making soap

**ly·ing**[1] (lī'in) *prp.* of LIE[1]

**ly·ing**[2] (lī'in) *prp.* of LIE[2] —*adj.* false; not truthful —*n.* the telling of a lie or lies

**ly'ing-in'** *n.* confinement in childbirth —*adj.* of or for childbirth

**lymph** (limf) *n.* [L. *lympha*, spring water] a clear, yellowish body fluid resembling blood plasma, found in intercellular spaces and in the lymphatic vessels

**lym·phat·ic** (lim fat'ik) *adj.* 1. of or containing lymph 2. sluggish

**lymph node** any of the compact structures lying in groups along the course of the lymphatic vessels

**lymph·oid** (lim'foid) *adj.* of or like lymph or tissue of the lymph nodes

**lynch** (linch) *vt.* [< W. *Lynch*, vigilante in Va. in 1780] to murder (an accused person) by mob action, without lawful trial, as by hanging

**lynx** (links) *n.* [< Gr. *lynx*] a wildcat found throughout the N Hemisphere, having a short tail and tufted ears

**lynx'-eyed'** (-īd') *adj.* keen-sighted

**Lyon** (lyôn) city in EC France: pop. 529,000

**ly·on·naise** (lī'ə nāz') *adj.* [Fr.] prepared with sliced, fried onions

**lyre** (līr) *n.* [< Gr. *lyra*] a small stringed instrument of the harp family, used by the ancient Greeks

**lyr·ic** (lir'ik) *adj.* [< Gr. *lyrikos*] 1. suitable for singing; specif., designating or of poetry expressing the poet's personal emotion 2. of or having a high voice with a light, flexible quality [*a lyric tenor*] —*n.* 1. a lyric poem 2. [*usually pl.*] the words of a song

**lyr'i·cal** *adj.* 1. lyric 2. expressing rapture or enthusiasm

**lyr·i·cist** (lir'i sist) *n.* a writer of lyrics, esp. for popular songs

**ly·ser·gic acid** (lī sur'jik) *see* LSD

**-ly·sis** (lə sis) [< Gr. *lysis*, a loosening] *a combining form meaning* a loosing, dissolution, dissolving, destruction [*electrolysis, paralysis*]

**-lyte** (līt) [see prec.] *a combining form meaning* a substance undergoing decomposition [*electrolyte*]

# M

**M, m** (em) *n., pl.* **M's, m's** the 13th letter of the English alphabet

**M** (em) *n.* 1. a Roman numeral for 1,000 2. *symbol for* mass

**M.** 1. Medieval 2. Monday 3. *pl.* MM. Monsieur

**M., m.** 1. male 2. married 3. masculine 4. mile(s) 5. minute(s) 6. month 7. [L. *meridies*] noon

**m., m** meter(s)

**ma** (mä) *n.* [Colloq.] mother

**MA** Massachusetts

**MA, M.A.** Master of Arts

**ma'am** (mam, mäm, məm) *n.* [Colloq.] madam: used in direct address

**ma·ca·bre** (mə käb'rə, mə käb') *adj.* [< OFr. (*danse*) *Macabré*, (dance) of death] gruesome; grim and horrible

**mac·ad·am** (mə kad'əm) *n.* [< J. L. *McAdam* (1756–1836), Scot. engineer] small broken stones, or a road made by rolling successive layers of these, often with tar or asphalt —mac·ad'am·ize' *vt.* -ized', -iz'ing

**Ma·cao** (mə kou') Port. territory in SE China, near Hong Kong

**mac·a·ro·ni** (mak′ə rō′nē) *n.* [It. *maccaroni*, ult. < Gr. *makar*, blessed] pasta in the form of tubes, etc.

**mac·a·roon** (mak′ə rōōn′) *n.* [see prec.] a small, sweet cookie made with crushed almonds or coconut

**ma·caw** (mə kô′) *n.* [prob. < Braz. native name] a large, bright-colored parrot of Central and South America

**Mac·beth** (mək beth′) the title hero of a tragedy by Shakespeare

**Mac·ca·bees** (mak′ə bēz′) a family of Jewish patriots who headed a successful revolt against Syria (175–164 B.C.)

**Mace** (mās) [< ff.] *a trademark for* a combined tear gas and nerve gas

**mace**[1] (mās) *n.* [OFr. *masse*] 1. a heavy, spiked war club, used in the Middle Ages 2. a staff used as a symbol of authority by certain officials

**mace**[2] (mās) *n.* [< ML. *macis*] a spice made from the husk of the nutmeg

**Mac·e·do·ni·a** (mas′ə dō′nē ə) ancient kingdom in SE Europe —**Mac′·e·do′ni·an** *adj., n.*

**mac·er·ate** (mas′ə rāt′) *vt.* -at′ed, -at′ing [< L. *macerare*, soften] 1. to soften or separate the parts of by soaking in liquid 2. to tear, chop, etc. into bits —**mac′er·a′tion** *n.*

**mach.** 1. machine 2. machinery

**ma·che·te** (mə shet′ē, -chet′ē) *n.* [Sp. < L. *marcus*, hammer] a large knife used for cutting sugar cane, underbrush, etc., esp. in S. America

**Mach·i·a·vel·li·an** (mak′ē ə vel′ē ən) *adj.* [< N. *Machiavelli*, (1469–1527), It. statesman] crafty; deceitful

**mach·i·na·tion** (mak′ə nā′shən) *n.* [< L. *machinari*, to plot] a plot or scheme, esp. an evil one

**ma·chine** (mə shēn′) *n.* [< Gr. *mēchos*, contrivance] 1. a vehicle, as an automobile: an old term 2. a structure consisting of a framework with various moving parts, for doing some kind of work 3. an organization functioning like a machine 4. the controlling group in a political party 5. a device, as the lever, etc., that transmits, or changes the application of, energy —*adj.* 1. of machines 2. done by machinery —*vt.* -chined′, -chin′ing to shape, etc. by machinery

**machine gun** an automatic gun, firing a rapid stream of bullets

**machine language** the system of signs, symbols, etc. used by a computer

**ma·chin·er·y** (mə shēn′ər ē, -shēn′rē) *n., pl.* -ies 1. machines collectively 2. the working parts of a machine 3. the means for keeping something going

**ma·chin′ist** *n.* one who makes, repairs, or operates machinery

**‡ma·chis·mo** (mä chēz′mō) *n.* [Sp. < *macho*, masculine] strong or assertive masculinity; virility

**Mach (number)** (mäk) [< E. *Mach* (1838–1916), Austrian physicist] a number indicating the ratio of an object's speed to the speed of sound

**ma·cho** (mä′chō) *adj.* [Sp., masculine] masculine, virile, courageous, etc.

**mack·er·el** (mak′ər əl) *n., pl.* -el, -els [< OFr. *makerel*] an edible fish of the North Atlantic

**Mack·i·naw coat** (mak′ə nô′) [< *Mackinac* Is. in N Lake Huron] a short, heavy, double-breasted coat, usually plaid: also **mackinaw** *n.*

**mack·in·tosh** (mak′in täsh′) *n.* [< C. *Macintosh*, 19th-c. Scot. inventor] a raincoat of rubberized cloth

**Ma·con** (mā′kən) city in C Ga.: pop. 122,000

**mac·ra·mé** (mak′rə mā′) *n.* [Fr., ult. < Ar. *miqramah*, a veil] coarse string or lace knotted in designs

**macro-** [< Gr. *makros*, long] *a combining form meaning* long, large

**mac·ro·bi·ot·ics** (mak′rō bī ät′iks) *n.pl.* [*with sing. v.*] [< prec. & Gr. *bios*, life] the art of prolonging life, as by diet —**mac′ro·bi·ot′ic** *adj.*

**mac·ro·cosm** (mak′rə käz′m) *n.* [see MACRO- & COSMOS] 1. the universe 2. any large, complex entity

**ma·cron** (mā′krən) *n.* [< Gr. *makros*, long] a mark (‾) placed over a vowel to indicate its pronunciation

**mad** (mad) *adj.* **mad′der, mad′dest** [< OE. (*ge*)*mædan*, make mad] 1. mentally ill; insane 2. frantic [*mad* with fear] 3. foolish and rash 4. infatuated [she's *mad* about him] 5. wildly gay 6. having rabies [a *mad* dog] 7. angry —*n.* an angry mood —**mad′ly** *adv.* —**mad′ness** *n.*

**Mad·a·gas·car** (mad′ə gas′kar) an island country off the SE coast of Africa: 229,000 sq. mi.; pop. 6,750,000

**mad·am** (mad′əm) *n., pl.* -ams; for 1, usually **mes·dames** (mā däm′) [< Fr., orig. *ma dame*, my lady] 1. a woman; lady: a polite term of address 2. a woman in charge of a brothel

**mad·ame** (mad′əm; *Fr.* mä däm′) *n., pl.* **mes·dames** (mā däm′) [Fr.] a married woman: equivalent to *Mrs.*

**mad′cap′** *n.* [MAD + CAP, fig. for head] a reckless, impulsive person —*adj.* reckless and impulsive

**mad·den** (mad′'n) *vt., vi.* to make or become insane, angry, or wildly excited —**mad′den·ing** *adj.*

**mad·der** (mad′ər) *n.* [OE. *mædere*] 1. any of various plants; esp., a vine with yellow flowers and a red root 2. a red dye made from the root

**made** (mād) *pt. & pp. of* MAKE

**ma·de·moi·selle** (mad′ə mə zel′; *Fr.* mäd mwà zel′) *n., pl.* **mes·de·moi·selles** (mād mwà zel′) [Fr. < *ma*, my + *demoiselle*, young lady] an unmarried woman or girl: title equivalent to *Miss*

**made′-to-or′der** *adj.* made to conform to the customer's specifications

**made′-up′** *adj.* 1. put together 2. invented; false [a *made-up* story] 3. with cosmetics applied

**mad′house′** *n.* 1. an insane asylum 2. any place of turmoil, noise, etc.

**Mad·i·son** (mad′i s′n) capital of Wis.: pop. 173,000

**Madison, James** 1751–1836; 4th president of the U.S. (1809–17)

**mad/man′** n., pl. **-men′** an insane person; lunatic —**mad/wom′an** n.fem., pl. **-wom′en**

**Ma·don·na** (mə dän′ə) [It. < ma, my + donna, lady] Mary, mother of Jesus —n. a picture or statue of Mary

**Ma·dras** (mə dras′, -dräs′) seaport on SE coast of India: pop. 1,729,000

**ma·dras** (mad′rəs, mə dras′) n. [< prec.] a fine, firm cotton cloth, usually striped or plaid

**Ma·drid** (mə drid′) capital of Spain, in the C part: pop. 2,559,000

**mad·ri·gal** (mad′ri gəl) n. [< It.] a part song, without accompaniment, popular in the 15th to 17th c.

**mael·strom** (māl′strəm) n. [< Du. malen, grind + stroom, a stream] 1. a large or violent whirlpool 2. an agitated state of mind, affairs, etc.

**ma·es·tro** (mīs′trō, mä es′-) n., pl. **-tros, -tri** (-trē) [It. < L. magister, master] a master in any art; esp., a great composer or conductor of music

**Ma·fi·a, Maf·fi·a** (mä′fē ə) n. [It.] an alleged secret society of criminals

**mag.** 1. magazine 2. magnetism

**mag·a·zine** (mag′ə zēn′) n. [< Ar. makhzan, granary] 1. a warehouse or military supply depot 2. a space in which explosives are stored, as in a fort 3. a supply chamber, as in a rifle, camera, etc. 4. a periodical publication containing stories, articles, etc.

**Ma·gel·lan** (mə jel′ən), **Ferdinand** 1480?–1521; Port. navigator

**ma·gen·ta** (mə jen′tə) n. [< Magenta, town in Italy] 1. a purplish-red dye 2. purplish red —adj. purplish-red

**mag·got** (mag′ət) n. [ME. magotte] a wormlike larva, as of the housefly —**mag′got·y** adj.

**Ma·gi** (mā′jī) n.pl., sing. **-gus** (-gəs) [< OPer. magus, magician] Douay Bible the wise men who came bearing gifts to the infant Jesus

**mag·ic** (maj′ik) n. [< Gr. magikos, of the Magi] 1. the use of charms, spells, etc. in seeking or pretending to control events 2. any mysterious power [the magic of love] 3. the art of producing illusions by sleight of hand, etc. —adj. 1. of, produced by, or using magic 2. producing extraordinary results, as if by magic —**mag′i·cal** adj. —**mag′i·cal·ly** adv.

**ma·gi·cian** (mə jish′ən) n. [< OFr. magicien] an expert in magic

**mag·is·te·ri·al** (maj′is tir′ē əl) adj. 1. of or suitable for a magistrate 2. authoritative

**mag·is·trate** (maj′is trāt) n. [< L. magister, master] 1. a civil officer empowered to administer the law 2. a minor official, as a justice of the peace

**Mag·na Char·ta** (or **Car·ta**) (mag′nə kär′tə) [ML., great charter] the charter, granted in 1215, that guaranteed certain civil and political liberties to the English people

**mag·nan·i·mous** (mag nan′ə məs, adj. [< L. magnus, great + animus)

soul] generous in overlooking injury or insult; rising above pettiness; noble —**mag′na·nim′i·ty** (-nə nim′ə tē) n. —**mag·nan′i·mous·ly** adv.

**mag·nate** (mag′nāt) n. [< L. magnus, great] a very influential person

**mag·ne·sia** (mag nē′zhə, -shə) n. [< LGr. Magnēsia, district in ancient Greece] a white powder, an oxide of magnesium, used as a laxative

**mag·ne′si·um** (-zē əm, -zhē-) n. [< prec.] a light metallic chemical element

**mag·net** (mag′nit) n. [see MAGNESIA] 1. any piece of iron, steel, or lodestone that has the property of attracting iron or steel 2. anything that attracts

**mag·net·ic** (mag net′ik) adj. 1. having the properties of a magnet 2. of, producing, or caused by magnetism 3. of the earth's magnetism 4. that can be magnetized 5. powerfully attractive —**mag·net′i·cal·ly** adv.

**magnetic field** any space in which there is an appreciable magnetic force

**magnetic tape** a thin plastic ribbon with a magnetized coating for recording sound, digital computer data, etc.

**mag·net·ism** (mag′nə tiz′m) n. 1. the property, quality, or condition of being magnetic 2. the force to which this is due 3. personal charm

**mag′net·ite′** (-tīt′) n. [< G.] a black iron oxide, an important iron ore

**mag′net·ize′** (-tīz′) vt. **-ized′, -iz′ing** 1. to give magnetic properties to (steel, iron, etc.) 2. to charm (a person) —**mag′net·i·za′tion** n.

**mag·ne·to** (mag nēt′ō) n., pl. **-tos** a small generator in which one or more permanent magnets produce the magnetic field

**mag·ne·tom·e·ter** (mag′nə täm′ə tər) n. an instrument for measuring magnetic forces: one form is used to check airline passengers for concealed metal weapons

**magnet school** a public school offering new and special courses to attract students from a broad urban area so as to promote desegregation

**mag·nif·i·cent** (mag nif′ə s′nt) adj. [< L. magnus, great + facere, do] 1. splendid, stately, or sumptuous, as in form 2. exalted: said of ideas, etc. 3. [Colloq.] excellent —**mag·nif′i·cence** n. —**mag·nif′i·cent·ly** adv.

**mag·ni·fy** (mag′nə fī′) vt., vi. **-fied′, -fy′ing** [see prec.] 1. to exaggerate 2. to increase the apparent size of (an object), as (with) a lens 3. [Archaic] to praise —**mag′ni·fi·ca′tion** n. —**mag′ni·fi′er** n.

**mag·ni·tude** (mag′nə tōōd′) n. [< L. magnus, great] 1. greatness of size, extent, etc. 2. a) size b) loudness (of sound) c) importance 3. the degree of brightness of a fixed star

**mag·no·li·a** (mag nōl′ē ə, -nōl′yə) n. [< P. Magnol (1638–1715), Fr. botanist] a tree with large, fragrant flowers of white, pink, or purple

**mag·num** (mag′nəm) n. [< L. magnus, great] a wine bottle holding about 2/5 of a gallon

**†mag·num o·pus** (mag′nəm ō′pəs) [L.] a great work; masterpiece

**mag·pie** (mag′pī′) *n.* [< *Mag*, dim. of *Margaret* + *pie*, magpie] **1.** a noisy, black-and-white bird of the crow family **2.** one who chatters

**Mag·yar** (mag′yär) *n.* **1.** a member of the main ethnic group in Hungary **2.** the Hungarian language

**ma·ha·ra·jah, ma·ha·ra·ja** (mä′ hə rä′jə) *n.* [< Sans. *mahā*, great + *rājā*, king] in India, a prince; formerly the ruler of a native state —**ma′ha·ra′ni, ma′ha·ra′nee** (-nē) *n.fem.*

**ma·ha·ri·shi** (mä′hä rish′ē) *n.* [Hindi <*mahā*, great + *ṛshi*, sage] a Hindu teacher of mysticism and meditation

**ma·hat·ma** (mə hat′mə, -hät′-) *n.* [< Sans. *mahā*, great + *ātman*, soul] *Buddhism* any of a class of wise and holy persons held in special regard

**mah-jongg, mah·jong** (mä′jôṅ′) *n.* [< Chin. *ma-ch′iao*, sparrow (a figure on one of the tiles)] a game of Chinese origin, played with small tiles

**ma·hog·a·ny** (mə häg′ə nē, -hôg′-) *n., pl.* **-nies** [< ?] **1.** *a)* the reddish-brown wood of a tropical American tree *b)* this tree **2.** reddish brown

**Ma·hom·et** (mə häm′it) *same as* MOHAMMED

**ma·hout** (mə hout′) *n.* [Hind. < Sans.] in India, an elephant driver or keeper

**maid** (mād) *n.* **1.** *same as* MAIDEN **2.** a girl or woman servant

**maid′en** (-′n) *n.* [OE. *mægden*] a girl or young unmarried woman —*adj.* **1.** of or suitable for a maiden **2.** unmarried or virgin **3.** untried; new **4.** first or earliest [a *maiden* voyage] — **maid′en·hood′** *n.* —**maid′en·ly** *adj., adv.*

**maid′en·hair′** *n.* a fern with delicate fronds and slender stalks

**maid′en·head′** *n.* the hymen

**maiden name** the surname that a woman had when not yet married

**maid of honor** an unmarried woman acting as chief attendant to a bride

**maid′ser′vant** *n.* a girl or woman servant

**mail¹** (māl) *n.* [< OHG. *malaha*, wallet] **1.** letters, packages, etc. transported and delivered by the post office **2.** a postal system —*adj.* of mail —*vt.* to send by mail —**mail′er** *n.*

**mail²** (māl) *n.* [< L. *macula*, mesh of a net] a body armor made of small metal rings, scales, etc. —**mailed** *adj.*

**mail′box′** *n.* a box into which mail is delivered or a box for depositing outgoing mail  Also **mail box**

**mail′man′** *n., pl.* **-men′** a man who carries and delivers mail

**mail order** an order for goods to be sent by mail — **mail′-or′der** *adj.*

**maim** (mām) *vt.* [OFr. *mahaigner*] to cripple; mutilate

**main** (mān) *n.* [OE. *mægen*, strength]

COAT OF
MAIL

**1.** a principal pipe in a distributing system for water, gas, etc. **2.** [Poet.] the ocean —*adj.* chief in size, importance, etc.; principal —**by main force** (or **strength**) by sheer force (or strength) —**in the main** mostly; chiefly —**with might and main** with all one's strength

**main clause** a clause that can function as a complete sentence

**main drag** [Slang] the principal street of a city or town

**Maine** (mān) New England State of the U.S.: 33,215 sq. mi.; pop. 992,000; cap. Augusta

**main·land** (mān′land′, -lənd) *n.* the principal land mass of a continent, as distinguished from nearby islands

**main′line′** *n.* the principal road, course, etc. —*vt.* **-lined′, -lin′ing** [Slang] to inject (a narcotic drug) directly into a large vein

**main′ly** *adv.* chiefly; principally

**main′mast** (-məst, -mast′) *n.* the principal mast of a vessel

**main′sail** (-s′l, -sāl′) *n.* the principal sail of a vessel, set from the mainmast

**main′spring′** *n.* **1.** the principal spring in a clock, watch, etc. **2.** the chief motive, incentive, etc.

**main′stay′** (-stā′) *n.* **1.** the supporting line extending forward from the mainmast **2.** a chief support

**main′stream′** (-strēm′) *n.* a major trend or line of thought, action, etc.

**main·tain** (mān tān′) *vt.* [< L. *manu tenere*, hold in the hand] **1.** to keep or keep up; carry on **2.** to keep in continuance or in a certain state, as of repair **3.** to defend **4.** to affirm or assert **5.** to support by supplying what is needed —**main·tain′a·ble** *adj.*

**main·te·nance** (mān′t′n əns) *n.* a maintaining or being maintained

**maî·tre d'hô·tel** (me′tr′ dô tel′) [Fr., master of house] a headwaiter or steward: also [Colloq.] **maî·tre d'** (māt′ər dē′)

**maize** (māz) *n.* [< WInd. *mahiz*] **1.** *same as* CORN¹ (*n.* 2.) **2.** yellow

**Maj.** Major

**ma·jes·tic** (mə jes′tik) *adj.* grand; stately; dignified —**ma·jes′ti·cal·ly** *adv.*

**maj·es·ty** (maj′is tē) *n., pl.* **-ties** [< L. *magnus*, great] **1.** [M-] a title used in speaking to or of a sovereign: with *His, Her,* or *Your* **2.** grandeur

**ma·jol·i·ca** (mə jäl′i kə) *n.* [It.] Italian glazed pottery

**ma·jor** (mā′jər) *adj.* [L., compar. of *magnus*, great] **1.** greater in size, importance, amount, etc. **2.** *Music* higher than the corresponding minor by a half tone —*vi. Educ.* to specialize (*in* a field of study) —*n.* **1.** *U.S. Mil.* an officer ranking just above a captain **2.** *Educ.* a principal field of study

**ma′jor-do′mo** (-dō′mō) *n., pl.* **-mos** [< L. *major*, greater + *domus*, house] a man in charge of a great household

**major general** *pl.* **major generals**

*U.S. Mil.* an officer ranking just above a brigadier general

**ma·jor·i·ty** (mə jôr′ə tē) *n., pl.* **-ties** [see MAJOR] **1.** the greater number; more than half of a total **2.** the excess of the larger number of votes cast for one candidate, etc. over all the rest of the votes **3.** full legal age **4.** the military rank of a major

**major scale** a musical scale with half steps between the third and fourth and the seventh and eighth tones

**make** (māk) *vt.* **made, mak′ing** [OE. *macian*] **1.** to bring into being; build, create, produce, etc. **2.** to cause to be or become [*made* king, *made* sad] **3.** to prepare for use [*make* the beds] **4.** to amount to [two pints *make* a quart] **5.** to have the qualities of [to make a fine leader] **6.** to acquire; earn **7.** to cause the success of [that venture *made* him] **8.** to understand [what do you *make* of that?] **9.** to execute, do, etc. [to *make* a speech] **10.** to cause or force [*make* him go] **11.** to arrive at; reach [the ship *made* port] **12.** [Colloq.] to get on or in [to *make* the team] —*vi.* **1.** to start (to do something) **2.** to behave as specified [*make* bold] **3.** to cause something to be as specified [*make* ready] —*n.* **1.** the way in which something is made; style **2.** type; brand —**make away with 1.** to steal **2.** to kill —**make believe** to pretend —**make for 1.** to go toward **2.** to help effect —**make it** [Colloq.] to achieve a certain thing —**make off with** to steal —**make out 1.** to see with difficulty **2.** to understand **3.** to fill out (a blank form, etc.) **4.** to (try to) show or prove to be **5.** to succeed; get along **6.** [Slang] to make love: see phr. under LOVE —**make over 1.** to change; renovate **2.** to transfer the ownership of —**make up 1.** to put together **2.** to form; constitute **3.** to invent **4.** to provide (what is lacking) **5.** to compensate (*for*) **6.** to become friends again after a quarrel **7.** to put on cosmetics, etc. **8.** to decide (one's mind) —**make up to** to try to win over, as by flattering —**mak′er** *n.*

**make′-be·lieve′** *n.* pretense; feigning —*adj.* pretended; feigned

**make′shift′** (-shift′) *n.* a temporary substitute or expedient —*adj.* that will do as a temporary substitute

**make′up′, make′-up′** *n.* **1.** the way something is put together; composition **2.** nature; disposition **3.** the cosmetics, etc. used by an actor **4.** cosmetics generally

**make′-work′** *adj.* that serves no other purpose than to give an idle or unemployed person something to do [a *make-work* project]

**mal-** [< L. *malus*, bad] *a prefix meaning* bad or badly, wrong, ill

**mal·ad·just·ed** (mal′ə jus′tid) *adj.* poorly adjusted, esp. to the environment —**mal′ad·just′ment** *n.*

**mal·a·droit** (mal′ə droit′) *adj.* [Fr.: see MAL- & ADROIT] awkward; clumsy; bungling —**mal′a·droit′ly** *adv.*

**mal·a·dy** (mal′ə dē) *n., pl.* **-dies** [< VL. *male habitus*, badly kept] the fact of being sick; disease; illness

**ma·laise** (ma lāz′) *n.* [Fr. < *mal*, bad + *aise*, ease] a vague feeling of physical discomfort or of uneasiness

**mal·a·mute** (mal′ə myoot′) *n.* [< *Malemute*, an Eskimo tribe] a strong dog developed as a sled dog by Eskimos

**mal·a·prop·ism** (mal′ə prap iz′m) *n.* [< Mrs. *Malaprop* in Sheridan's *The Rivals* (1775)] a ludicrous misuse of words that sound alike

**ma·lar·i·a** (mə ler′ē ə) *n.* [It. < *mala aria*, bad air] an infectious disease transmitted by the anopheles mosquito, characterized by intermittent chills and fever —**ma·lar′i·al** *adj.*

**ma·lar·key, ma·lar·ky** (mə lär′kē) *n.* [< ?] [Slang] nonsensical talk

**mal·a·thi·on** (mal′ə thī′ən) *n.* [< chem. names] an organic insecticide

**Ma·la·wi** (mä′lä wē) country in SE Africa, in the Brit. Commonwealth: 46,066 sq. mi.: pop. 4,042,000

**Ma·lay** (mā′lā, mə lā′) *n.* **1.** a member of a group of brown-skinned peoples living chiefly in the Malay Peninsula and the Malay Archipelago **2.** their language —*adj.* of the Malays, their language, etc. Also **Ma·lay′an**

**Mal·a·ya·lam** (mal′ə yä′ləm) *n.* a language of the SW coast of India

**Malay Archipelago** large group of islands between SE Asia & Australia

**Malay Peninsula** peninsula in SE Asia

**Ma·lay·sia** (mə lā′zhə) country in SE Asia, mostly on the Malay Peninsula, in the Brit. Commonwealth: 128,654 sq. mi.; pop. 10,223,000 —**Ma·lay′sian** *adj., n.*

**mal·con·tent** (mal′kən tent′) *adj.* [see MAL- & CONTENT[1]] dissatisfied; rebellious —*n.* a malcontent person

**Mal·dive Islands** (mal′dīv) sultanate on a group of islands in the Indian Ocean: 115 sq. mi.; pop. 93,000

**male** (māl) *adj.* [< L. *mas*, a male] **1.** designating or of the sex that fertilizes the ovum **2.** of, like, or suitable for men or boys; masculine **3.** *Mechanics* having a part shaped to fit into a corresponding hollow part —*n.* a male person, animal, or plant

**mal·e·dic·tion** (mal′ə dik′shən) *n.* [see MAL- & DICTION] a curse

**mal·e·fac·tor** (mal′ə fak′tər) *n.* [< L. *male*, evil + *facere*, do] an evildoer or criminal —**mal′e·fac′tion** *n.*

**ma·lef·i·cent** (mə lef′ə s'nt) *adj.* [< L.: see MALEFACTOR] harmful; evil —**ma·lef′i·cence** *n.*

**ma·lev·o·lent** (mə lev′ə lənt) *adj.* [< L. *male*, evil + *velle*, to wish] wishing evil or harm to others; malicious —**ma·lev′o·lence** *n.*

**mal·fea·sance** (mal fē′z'ns) *n.* [< Fr. *mal*, evil + *faire*, do] wrongdoing, esp. by a public official

**mal·for·ma·tion** (mal′fôr mā′shən) *n.* faulty or abnormal formation of a body or part —**mal·formed′** *adj.*

**mal·func·tion** (mal funk′shən) *vi.* to fail to function as it should —*n.* an instance of malfunctioning

**Ma·li** (mä′lē) country in W Africa: 464,873 sq. mi.; pop. 4,305,000

**mal·ice** (mal′is) *n.* [< L. *malus*, bad] 1. active ill will; desire to harm another 2. *Law* evil intent

**ma·li·cious** (mə lish′əs) *adj.* having, showing, or caused by malice; spiteful —**ma·li′cious·ly** *adv.*

**ma·lign** (mə līn′) *vt.* [< L. *male*, ill + *genus*, born] to speak evil of; slander —*adj.* 1. malicious 2. evil; baleful 3. very harmful

**ma·lig·nant** (mə lig′nənt) *adj.* [see prec.] 1. having an evil influence 2. wishing evil 3. very harmful 4. causing or likely to cause death [a *malignant* tumor] —**ma·lig′nan·cy** *n.* —**ma·lig′ni·ty** (-nə tē) *n.*

**ma·lin·ger** (mə lin′gər) *vi.* [< Fr. *malingre*, sickly] to feign illness so as to escape duty —**ma·lin′ger·er** *n.*

**mall** (môl) *n.* [< *maul*, mallet: from use in a game on outdoor lanes] 1. a shaded walk or public promenade 2. *a*) a shop-lined street for pedestrians only *b*) an enclosed shopping center

**mal·lard** (mal′ərd) *n.* [< OFr. *malart*] the common wild duck

**mal·le·a·ble** (mal′ē ə b′l) *adj.* [< L. *malleus*, a hammer] 1. that can be hammered, pounded, or pressed into various shapes without breaking 2. adaptable —**mal′le·a·bil′i·ty** *n.*

**mal·let** (mal′it) *n.* [see prec.] 1. a short-handled hammer with a wooden head, for driving a chisel, etc. 2. any similar long-handled hammer, as for use in croquet or polo 3. a small hammer for playing a xylophone, etc.

MALLET

**mal·low** (mal′ō) *n.* [< L. *malva*] any of a family of plants, including the hollyhock, cotton, and okra, with large, showy flowers

**mal·nour·ished** (mal nur′isht) *adj.* improperly nourished

**mal·nu·tri·tion** (mal′nōō trish′ən) *n.* faulty or inadequate nutrition; poor nourishment

**mal·oc·clu·sion** (-ə klōō′zhən) *n.* a faulty position of the teeth so that they do not meet properly

**mal·o·dor·ous** (mal ō′dər əs) *adj.* having a bad odor; stinking

**mal·prac·tice** (mal prak′tis) *n.* professional misconduct or improper practice, esp. by a physician

**malt** (môlt) *n.* [OE. *mealt*] 1. barley or other grain soaked and then kiln-dried: used in brewing and distilling 2. beer, ale, etc. —*adj.* made with malt —**malt′y** *adj.* -**i·er**, -**i·est**

**Mal·ta** (môl′tə) country on a group of islands in the Mediterranean, south of Sicily, in the Brit. Commonwealth: 122 sq. mi.; pop. 328,000 —**Mal′tese′** (-tēz′) *adj.*, *n.*

**malted milk** powdered malt and dried milk, used in a drink with milk, etc.

**malt liquor** beer, ale, or the like made from malt by fermentation

**mal·treat** (mal trēt′) *vt.* [see MAL- & TREAT] to treat roughly or brutally; abuse —**mal·treat′ment** *n.*

**mam·ma** (mä′mə; *occas.* mə mä′) *n.* mother: a child's word

**mam·mal** (mam′əl) *n.* [< L. *mamma*, breast] any of a group of vertebrates the females of which have milk-secreting glands (**mam′ma·ry glands**) for feeding their offspring —**mam·ma·li·an** (mə mā′lē ən) *adj.*, *n.*

**mam·mog·ra·phy** (mə mäg′rə fē) *n.* [< L. *mamma*, breast + -GRAPHY] an X-ray technique for detecting breast tumors before they can be seen or felt

**mam·mon** (mam′ən) *n.* [< Aram.] [*often* M-] riches regarded as an object of worship and greedy pursuit

**mam·moth** (mam′əth) *n.* [Russ. *mamont*] an extinct elephant with long tusks —*adj.* very big; huge

**man** (man) *n.*, *pl.* **men** [OE. *mann*] 1. a human being; person 2. the human race; mankind 3. an adult male person 4. an adult male servant, employee, etc. 5. a husband 6. any of the pieces used in chess, checkers, etc. —*vt.* **manned**, **man′ning** 1. to furnish with men for work, defense, etc. 2. to strengthen; brace [to *man* oneself for an ordeal] —**as a** (or **one**) **man** in unison; unanimously —**to a man** with no exception

**-man** (mən, man) *a combining form meaning* man or person of a specified kind, in a specified activity, etc. [*Frenchman*, *sportsman*]

**Man.** Manitoba

**Man, Isle of** one of the Brit. Isles, between Northern Ireland & England

**man·a·cle** (man′ə k′l) *n.* [< L. *manus*, hand] a handcuff: *usually used in pl.* —*vt.* -**cled**, -**cling** 1. to put handcuffs on 2. to restrain

**man·age** (man′ij) *vt.* -**aged**, -**ag·ing** [< L. *manus*, hand] 1. to control the movement or behavior of 2. to have charge of; direct [to *manage* a hotel] 3. to succeed in accomplishing —*vi.* 1. to carry on business 2. to contrive to get along —**man′age·a·ble** *adj.*

**man′age·ment** *n.* 1. a managing or being managed; control, direction, etc. 2. the persons managing a business, institution, etc.

**man′ag·er** *n.* one who manages; esp., one who manages a business, etc.

**man·a·ge·ri·al** (man′ə jir′ē əl) *adj.* of a manager or management

‡**ma·ña·na** (mä nyä′nä) *n.*, *adv.* [Sp.] tomorrow or an indefinite future time

**man·a·tee** (man′ə tē′) *n.* [< WInd. native name] a large, plant-eating aquatic mammal of tropical waters

**Man·ches·ter** (man′ches′tər) seaport in NW England: pop. 661,000

**Man·chu** (man chōō′) *n.* 1. *pl.* -**chus′**, -**chu′** a member of a Mongolian people of Manchuria who ruled China from 1644 to 1912 2. their language

**Man·chu·ri·a** (man choor′ē ə) region in NE China —**Man·chu′ri·an** *adj., n.*

**man·da·rin** (man′də rin) *n.* [< Sans. *mantra*, counsel] **1.** a high official of the former Chinese Empire **2.** [M-] the main dialect of Chinese

**man·date** (man′dāt) *n.* [< L. *mandare*, to command] **1.** an order or command **2.** *a)* formerly, a League of Nations' commission to a country to administer some region *b)* this region **3.** the will of constituents expressed to their representative, legislature, etc.

**man·da·to·ry** (man′də tôr′ē) *adj.* **1.** of or containing a mandate **2.** authoritatively commanded; obligatory

**man·di·ble** (man′də b'l) *n.* [< L. *mandere*, chew] the jaw; specif., *a)* the lower jaw of a vertebrate *b)* either jaw of a beaked animal —**man·dib′u·lar** (-dib′yoo lər) *adj.*

**man·do·lin** (man′d'l in′, man′də lin′) *n.* [< LGr. *pandoura*, kind of lute] a musical instrument with four or five pairs of strings

**man·drake** (man′drāk) *n.* [< Gr. *mandragoras*] a poisonous plant of the nightshade family, with a thick, forked root suggesting the human form

**man·drel, man·dril** (man′drəl) *n.* [prob. < Fr. *mandrin*] a spindle inserted into a lathe center to support work while it is being machined

**man·drill** (man′dril) *n.* [MAN + *drill*, W Afr. monkey] a large, strong baboon of W Africa: the male has blue and scarlet patches on the face and rump

**mane** (mān) *n.* [OE. *manu*] the long hair growing on the neck of the horse, lion, etc. —**maned** *adj.*

**man′-eat′er** *n.* an animal that eats human flesh —**man′-eat′ing** *adj.*

**ma·nège, ma·nege** (ma nezh′) *n.* [Fr. < It. *maneggiare*, MANAGE] the art of riding and training horses

**ma·neu·ver** (mə noo′vər) *n.* [< L. *manu operare*, to work by hand] **1.** a planned and controlled movement of troops, warships, etc. **2.** a skillful or shrewd move; stratagem —*vi., vt.* **1.** to perform or cause to perform maneuvers **2.** to manage or plan skillfully **3.** to move, get, make, etc. by some scheme —**ma·neu′ver·a·ble** *adj.*

**man·ful** (man′fəl) *adj.* manly; brave, resolute, etc. —**man′ful·ly** *adv.*

**man·ga·nese** (man′gə nēs′, -nēz′) *n.* [ult. < ML. *magnesia*] a grayish, metallic chemical element, used in alloys

**mange** (mānj) *n.* [< OFr. *mangeue*, an itch] a skin disease of mammals, causing itching, loss of hair, etc.

**man·ger** (mān′jər) *n.* [< L. *mandere*, to chew] a box or trough to hold hay, etc. for horses or cattle to eat

**man·gle¹** (maŋ′g'l) *vt.* -gled, -gling [< OFr. *mehaigner*, maim] **1.** to mutilate by roughly cutting, tearing, crushing, etc. **2.** to spoil; botch; mar

**man·gle²** (maŋ′g'l) *n.* [< Gr. *manganon*, war machine] a machine for ironing sheets, etc. between rollers

**man·go** (maŋ′gō) *n., pl.* -goes, -gos [< Tamil *mān-kāy*] **1.** the yellow-red, somewhat acid fruit of a tropical tree **2.** the tree

**man·grove** (maŋ′grōv) *n.* [< WInd. name] a tropical tree with branches that spread and send down roots, thus forming more trunks

**man·gy** (mān′jē) *adj.* -gi·er, -gi·est **1.** having the mange **2.** filthy, low, etc. —**man′gi·ly** *adv.* —**man′gi·ness** *n.*

**man′han′dle** *vt.* -dled, -dling to handle roughly

**Man·hat·tan** (man hat′'n) island borough of New York City: pop. 1,525,000 —*n.* [*often* m-] a cocktail made of whiskey and sweet vermouth

**man′hole′** *n.* a hole through which one can enter a sewer, conduit, etc.

**man′hood′** *n.* **1.** the state or time of being a man **2.** virility, courage, etc. **3.** men collectively

**man′-hour′** *n.* a time unit equal to one hour of work done by one person

**man′hunt′** *n.* a hunt for a fugitive

**ma·ni·a** (mā′nē ə) *n.* [Gr.] **1.** wild or violent mental disorder **2.** an excessive enthusiasm; obsession; craze

**-ma·ni·a** (mā′nē ə) [see prec.] *a combining form meaning* a (specified) type of mental disorder [*kleptomania*]

**ma·ni·ac** (mā′nē ak′) *adj.* wildly insane —*n.* a violently insane person —**ma·ni·a·cal** (mə ni′ə k'l) *adj.*

**man·ic** (man′ik) *adj.* having, characterized by, or like mania

**man′ic-de·pres′sive** *adj.* characterized by alternating periods of mania and mental depression

**man·i·cure** (man′ə kyoor′) *n.* [< L. *manus*, a hand + *cura*, care] a trimming, polishing, etc. of fingernails —*vt.* -cured′, -cur′ing to trim, polish, etc. (fingernails) —**man′i·cur′ist** *n.*

**man·i·fest** (man′ə fest′) *adj.* [< L. *manifestus*, lit., struck by the hand] apparent to the senses or the mind; obvious —*vt.* to show plainly; reveal —*n.* an itemized list of a ship's cargo or passengers —**man′i·fest′ly** *adv.*

**man·i·fes·ta·tion** (-fes tā′shən) *n.* **1.** a manifesting or being manifested **2.** something that manifests

**man·i·fes·to** (man′ə fes′tō) *n., pl.* -toes [It. < L.: see MANIFEST] a public declaration of intention by an important person or group

**man·i·fold** (man′ə fōld′) *adj.* [see MANY & -FOLD] **1.** having many forms, parts, etc. **2.** of many sorts **3.** being such in many ways [*a manifold villain*] **4.** operating several parts of one kind —*n.* a pipe with several outlets, as for conducting cylinder exhaust from an engine —*vt.* to make copies of, as with carbon paper

**man·i·kin, man·ni·kin** (man′ə k'n) *n.* [< Du. *manneken*, little man] *same as* MANNEQUIN

**Ma·ni·la** (mə nil′ə) capital of the Philippines, on Luzon: pop. 1,438,000

**Manila hemp** a strong fiber from the leafstalk of a Philippine plant, used for making rope, paper, etc.

**Manila paper** a strong, buff-colored paper, orig. made of Manila hemp

**man in the street** the average person

**man·i·ple** (man′ə p'l) *n.* [ult. < L. *manus*, a hand] a silk band worn over the left forearm by priests at Mass

**ma·nip·u·late** (mə nip′yə lāt′) *vt.* -lat′ed, -lat′ing [ult. < L. *manus*, a hand + *plere*, to fill] **1.** to work or handle skillfully **2.** to manage artfully or shrewdly, often in an unfair way **3.** to alter (figures, etc.) for one's own purposes —**ma·nip′u·la′tion** *n.*

**Man·i·to·ba** (man′ə tō′bə) province of SC Canada: 251,000 sq. mi.; pop. 963,000; cap. Winnipeg

**man·kind** *n.* **1.** (man′kīnd′) the human race **2.** (-kīnd′) all human males

**man′ly** *adj.* -li·er, -li·est having the qualities regarded as suitable for a man; virile, brave, etc. —*adv.* in a manly way —**man′li·ness** *n.*

**man′-made′** *adj.* artificial; synthetic

**Mann** (män), **Thomas** 1875–1955; Ger. novelist in the U.S., etc.

**man·na** (man′ə) *n.* [< Heb. *mān*] **1.** *Bible* food miraculously provided for the Israelites in the wilderness **2.** any help that comes unexpectedly

**man·ne·quin** (man′ə kin) *n.* [see MANIKIN] **1.** a model of the human body, used by tailors, etc. **2.** a woman who models clothes in stores, etc.

**man·ner** (man′ər) *n.* [< L. *manus*, a hand] **1.** a way of doing something; mode of procedure **2.** a way, esp. a usual way, of acting; habit **3.** [*pl.*] *a)* ways of social behavior [*bad manners*] *b)* polite ways of social behavior [to learn *manners*] **4.** kind; sort

**man′nered** (-ərd) *adj.* **1.** having manners of a specified kind [*well-mannered*] **2.** artificial, stylized, etc.

**man′ner·ism** *n.* **1.** excessive use of some distinctive manner in art, literature, etc. **2.** a peculiarity of manner in behavior, speech, etc.

**man′ner·ly** *adj.* polite

**man·nish** (man′ish) *adj.* like a man or man's [*her mannish stride*]

**ma·noeu·vre** (mə nōō′vər) *n.*, *vi.*, *vt.* -vred, -vring *chiefly Brit. sp.* of MANEUVER

**man of letters** a writer, scholar, etc., esp. in the field of literature

**man′-of-war′** *n.*, *pl.* **men′-of-war′** an armed naval vessel; warship

**man·or** (man′ər) *n.* [< L. *manere*, dwell] **1.** in England, a landed estate **2.** the main house on an estate — **ma·no·ri·al** (mə nôr′ē əl) *adj.*

**man′pow′er** *n.* **1.** power furnished by human strength **2.** the collective strength or availability for work of the people in a given area, nation, etc.

‡**man·qué** (män kā′) *adj.* [Fr.] unfulfilled; would-be [*a poet manqué*]

**man·sard (roof)** (man′särd) [< F. *Mansard*, 17th-c. Fr. architect] a roof with two slopes on each of four sides, the lower steeper than the upper

MANSARD ROOF

**manse** (mans) *n.* [see MANSION] the residence of a minister; parsonage

**man′ser′vant** *n.*, *pl.* **men′ser′vants** a male servant: also **man servant**

**-man·ship** (mən ship) *a combining form meaning* talent or skill (esp. in gaining advantage) in [*gamesmanship*]

**man·sion** (man′shən) *n.* [< L. *manere*, dwell] a large, imposing house

**man′-sized′** *adj.* [Colloq.] of a size fit for a man; big: also **man′-size′**

**man′slaugh′ter** (-slôt′ər) *n.* the killing of a human being by another, esp. when unlawful but without malice

**man·tel** (man′t'l) *n.* [see MANTLE] **1.** the facing about a fireplace, including a projecting shelf **2.** this shelf: also **man′tel·piece′**

**man·til·la** (man til′ə, -tē′ə) *n.* [Sp. < L.: see MANTLE] a woman's scarf, as of lace, worn over the hair and shoulders

**man·tis** (man′tis) *n.*, *pl.* -tis·es, -tes (-tēz) [< Gr. *mantis*, prophet] an insect with forelegs held as if praying

**man·tis·sa** (man tis′ə) *n.* [L. (useless) addition] the decimal part of a logarithm

**man·tle** (man′t'l) *n.* [< L. *mantellum*] **1.** a loose, sleeveless cloak **2.** anything that envelops or conceals **3.** a small hood which when placed over a flame becomes white-hot and gives off light —*vt.* -tled, -tling to cover as with a mantle —*vi.* **1.** to be or become covered **2.** to blush or flush

**man·tra** (mun′trə, man′-) *n.* [Sans.] a chant of a Vedic hymn, text, etc.

**man·u·al** (man′yoo wəl) *adj.* [< L. *manus*, a hand] **1.** of the hands **2.** made, done, or worked by hand **3.** involving skill or hard work with the hands —*n.* **1.** a handy book for use as a guide, reference, etc. **2.** prescribed drill in the handling of a weapon — **man′u·al·ly** *adv.*

**manual training** training in practical arts and crafts, as woodworking

**man·u·fac·ture** (man′yə fak′chər) *n.* [< L. *manus*, a hand + *facere*, make] **1.** the making of goods, esp. by machinery and on a large scale **2.** the making of any product, as of bile by the liver —*vt.* -tured, -tur·ing **1.** to make, esp. by machinery **2.** to make up (excuses, etc.); invent —**man′u·fac′tur·er** *n.*

**man·u·mit** (man′yə mit′) *vt.* -mit′-ted, -mit′ting [< L. *manus*, a hand + *mittere*, send] to free from slavery —**man′u·mis′sion** *n.*

**ma·nure** (mə noor′, -nyoor′) *vt.* -nured′, -nur′ing [< OFr. *manouvrer*, work with the hands] to put manure on or into —*n.* animal excrement, etc. used to fertilize soil

**man·u·script** (man′yə skript′) *adj.* [< L. *manus*, hand + *scriptus*, written] **1.** written by hand or typewritten **2.** written with printlike letters —*n.* **1.** a written or typewritten document, book, etc., as submitted to a publisher **2.** writing as opposed to print

**Manx** (maŋks) *adj.* of the Isle of Man, its people, etc. —*n.* the language spoken on the Isle of Man

**man·y** (men′ē) *adj.* **more, most** [OE. *manig*] numerous —*n.* a large number (of persons or things) —*pron.* many persons or things

**Mao·ri** (mou′rē) *n.* **1.** *pl.* **-ris, -ri** any of the Polynesians native to New Zealand **2.** their language —*adj.* of the Maoris, their language, etc.

**Mao Tse-tung** (mou′ dzu′dŏŏŋ′) 1893–1976; Chin. communist leader — **Mao′ism** *n.* —**Mao′ist** *n.*

**map** (map) *n.* [ < L. *mappa*, napkin, cloth] **1.** a representation of all or part of the earth's surface, showing countries, bodies of water, etc. **2.** a representation of the sky, showing the stars, etc. —*vt.* **mapped, map′ping 1.** to make a map of **2.** to plan

**ma·ple** (mā′p'l) *n.* [OE. *mapel*] **1.** any of a large group of trees with two-winged fruits, grown for wood, sap, or shade **2.** the hard, light-colored wood **3.** the flavor of the syrup or sugar made from the sap

**mar** (mär) *vt.* **marred, mar′ring** [OE. *mierran*, hinder] to injure so as to make imperfect, etc.; spoil

**mar·a·bou** (mar′ə bŏŏ′) *n.* [Fr. < Ar. *murābit*, hermit] **1.** a large stork of Africa or India **2.** its plumes

**ma·ra·ca** (mə rä′kə) *n.* [ < the Braz. native name] a percussion instrument made of a dried gourd or gourd-shaped rattle with pebbles in it

**mar·a·schi·no** (mar′ə skē′nō, -shē′) *n.* [It. < *marasca*, cherry] a liqueur made from the black wild cherry

**maraschino cherries** cherries in a syrup flavored with maraschino

**mar·a·thon** (mar′ə thän′) *n.* [ < *Marathon*, in ancient Greece] **1.** a foot race of 26 miles, 385 yards **2.** any endurance contest

**ma·raud** (mə rôd′) *vi., vt.* [ < Fr. *maraud*, vagabond] to raid and plunder —**ma·raud′er** *n.*

**mar·ble** (mär′b'l) *n.* [ < Gr. *marmaros*, white stone] **1.** a hard limestone, white or colored, which takes a high polish **2.** a piece of this stone, used in sculpture, etc. **3.** anything like marble in hardness, coldness, etc. **4.** *a)* a little ball of stone, glass, etc. *b)* [*pl. with sing. v.*] a children's game played with such balls **5.** [*pl.*] [Slang] brains; good sense —*adj.* of or like marble —*vt.* **-bled, -bling 1.** to make (book edges) look mottled like marble **2.** to cause (meat) to be streaked with fat

**mar′ble·ize′** *vt.* **-ized′, -iz′ing** to make look like marble

**March** (märch) *n.* [ < L. *Mars,* Mars] the third month of the year, having 31 days; abbrev. **Mar.**

**march**[1] (märch) *vi.* [Fr. *marcher*] **1.** to walk with regular steps, as in military formation **2.** to advance steadily —*vt.* to cause to march —*n.* **1.** a marching **2.** a steady advance; progress **3.** a regular, steady step **4.** the distance covered in marching **5.** a piece of music for marching —**on the march** marching —**steal a march on**

to get an advantage over secretly —**march′er** *n.*

**march**[2] (märch) *n.* [ < OFr.] a boundary, border, or frontier

**March hare** a hare in breeding time, proverbially an example of madness

**marching orders** orders to march, go, or leave

**mar·chion·ess** (mär′shə nis) *n.* **1.** the wife or widow of a marquess **2.** a lady of the rank of a marquess

**Mar·co·ni** (mär kō′nē), **Gu·gliel·mo** (gŏŏ lyel′mō) 1874–1937; It. physicist: developed wireless telegraphy

**Mar·di gras** (mär′di grä′) [Fr., fat Tuesday] the last day before Lent: a day of carnival in New Orleans, etc.

**mare**[1] (mer) *n.* [ < OE. *mere*] a mature female horse, mule, donkey, etc.

**ma·re**[2] (mer′ē) *n., pl.* **-ri·a** [L., sea] a large, dark area on the moon

**mare's-nest** (merz′nest′) *n.* **1.** a hoax **2.** a jumble; mess

**mar·ga·rine** (mär′jə rin) *n.* [Fr.] a spread or cooking fat of vegetable oils processed, often with skim milk, to the consistency of butter

**mar·gin** (mär′jən) *n.* [ < L. *margo*] **1.** a border; edge **2.** the blank border of a printed or written page **3.** an amount beyond what is needed **4.** provision for increase, error, etc. **5.** the difference between the cost and selling price of goods —**mar′gin·al** *adj.*

**mar·gi·na·li·a** (mär′jə nā′lē ə) *n.pl.* notes in the margins, as of a book

**ma·ri·a·chi** (mär′ē ä′chē) *n., pl.* **-chis** [Mex. Sp. < ?] **1.** one of a strolling band of musicians in Mexico **2.** such a band **3.** its music

**Mar·i·an** (mer′ē ən, mar′-) *adj.* of the Virgin Mary

**Ma·rie An·toi·nette** (mə rē′ an′twə net′) 1755–93; wife of Louis XVI: guillotined

**mar·i·gold** (mar′ə gōld′) *n.* [ < Virgin *Mary* + *gold*] a plant of the composite family, with yellow or orange flowers

**ma·ri·jua·na, ma·ri·hua·na** (mar′ə wä′nə) *n.* [AmSp.] **1.** *same as* HEMP (*n.* 1) **2.** its dried leaves and flowers, smoked, esp. as cigarettes, for the psychological and euphoric effects

**ma·rim·ba** (mə rim′bə) *n.* [ < native Afr. name] a kind of xylophone with a resonant tube beneath each bar

**ma·ri·na** (mə rē′nə) *n.* [ < L. *mare,* sea] a small harbor with docks, services, etc. for pleasure craft

**mar·i·nade** (mar′ə nād′) *n.* [Fr. < Sp. *marinar,* to pickle] **1.** a spiced pickling solution for steeping meat, fish, etc., often before cooking **2.** meat or fish thus steeped —*vt.* **-nad′ed, -nad′ing** *same as* MARINATE

**mar·i·nate** (mar′ə nāt′) *vt.* **-nat′ed, -nat′ing** [ < It. *marinare,* to pickle] to steep (meat or fish) in a marinade

**ma·rine** (mə rēn′) *adj.* [ < L. *mare,* sea] **1.** of or found in the sea **2.** *a)* maritime; nautical *b)* naval —*n.* **1.** [*often* M-] a member of the MARINE CORPS **3.** naval or merchant ships

**Marine Corps** a branch of the U.S.

armed forces trained for land, sea, and aerial combat

**mar·i·ner** (mar′ə nər) *n.* a sailor

**mar·i·o·nette** (mar′ē ə net′) *n.* [Fr. < *Marie*, Mary] a little jointed doll moved by strings or wires

**mar·i·tal** (mar′ə t'l) *adj.* [< L. *maritus*, a husband] of marriage; matrimonial —**mar′i·tal·ly** *adv.*

**mar·i·time** (mar′ə tīm′) *adj.* [< L. *mare*, sea] 1. on, near, or living near the sea 2. of navigation, shipping, etc.

**mar·jo·ram** (mär′jər əm) *n.* [? ult. < Gr. *amarakos*] a fragrant plant of the mint family, used in cooking

**Mark** (märk) *Bible* 1. a Christian apostle, the reputed author of the second Gospel 2. this book

**mark¹** (märk) *n.* [OE. *mearc*, boundary] 1. a spot, scratch, etc. on a surface 2. a printed or written symbol [*punctuation marks*] 3. a brand or label on an article showing the maker, etc. 4. an indication of some quality, character, etc. 5. a grade [a *mark* of B in Latin] 6. a standard of quality 7. impression, influence, etc. 8. an object of known position, serving as a guide 9. a line, dot, etc. indicating position, as on a graduated scale 10. a target; goal —*vt.* 1. to put or make a mark or marks on 2. to identify as by a mark 3. to indicate by a mark 4. to show plainly [her smile *marked* her joy] 5. to set off; characterize 6. to take notice of; heed [*mark* my words] 7. to grade; rate —**make one's mark** to achieve fame —**mark down** (or **up**) to mark for sale at a reduced (or an increased) price —**mark time** 1. to keep time while at a halt by lifting the feet as if marching 2. to suspend progress for a time —**mark′er** *n.*

**mark²** (märk) *n.* [< ON. *mork*] the monetary unit of Germany

**mark′down′** *n.* 1. a selling at a reduced price 2. the amount of reduction

**marked** (märkt) *adj.* 1. having a mark or marks 2. noticeable; obvious —**mark·ed·ly** (mär′kid lē) *adv.*

**mar·ket** (mär′kit) *n.* [ult. < L. *merx*, merchandise] 1. a gathering of people for buying and selling things 2. an open space or building where goods are shown for sale: also **mar′ket·place′** 3. a shop for the sale of provisions [a meat *market*] 4. a region in which goods can be bought and sold [the European *market*] 5. trade; buying and selling 6. demand for (goods, etc.) [a good *market* for tea] —*vt.* 1. to offer for sale 2. to sell —*vi.* to buy provisions —**mar′ket·a·ble** *adj.* —**mar′ket·er, mar′ket·eer′** (-kə tir′) *n.*

**mark′ing** *n.* 1. a mark or marks 2. the characteristic arrangement of marks, as on fur or feathers

**marks·man** (märks′mən) *n.*, *pl.* **-men** one who shoots, esp. one who shoots well —**marks′man·ship′** *n.*

**mark′up′** *n.* 1. a selling at an increased price 2. the amount of increase

**mar·lin** (mär′lin) *n.*, *pl.* **-lin, -lins** [< ff.] a large, slender deep-sea fish

**mar·line·spike** (mär′lin spīk′) *n.* [< Du. *marlijn*, small cord & SPIKE] a pointed iron tool for splicing rope

**mar·ma·lade** (mär′mə lād′) *n.* [ult. < Gr. *meli*, honey + *melon*, apple] a jamlike preserve of oranges, etc.

**mar·mo·set** (mär′mə zet′) *n.* [< OFr. *marmouset*, grotesque figure] a small monkey of S. and C. America

**mar·mot** (mär′mət) *n.* [prob. < L. *mus montanus*, mountain mouse] any of a group of thick-bodied rodents, as the woodchuck or prairie dog

**ma·roon¹** (mə rōōn′) *n.*, *adj.* [Fr. *marron*, chestnut] dark brownish red

**ma·roon²** (mə rōōn′) *vt.* [< AmSp. *cimarrón*, wild] 1. to put (a person) ashore in a lonely place and leave him 2. to leave helpless and alone

**marque** (märk) *n.* [Fr., a sign] a distinctive emblem on an automobile

**mar·quee** (mär kē′) *n.* [< Fr. *marquise*, awning] a rooflike projection over an entrance, as to a theater

**mar·quess** (mär′kwis) *n.* [see MARQUIS] 1. a British nobleman ranking above an earl 2. *same as* MARQUIS

**mar·que·try** (mär′kə trē) *n.* [see MARQUE] decorative inlaid work, as in furniture

**mar·quis** (mär′kwis; Fr. mär kē′) *n.* [< ML. *marchisus*, a prefect] in some European countries, a nobleman ranking above an earl or count

**mar·quise** (-kēz′) *n.* 1. the wife or widow of a marquis 2. a lady of the rank of a marquis

**mar·qui·sette** (mär′ki zet′, -kwi-) *n.* [see MARQUEE] a thin, meshlike fabric used for curtains

**mar·riage** (mar′ij) *n.* 1. the state of being married 2. a wedding 3. a close union —**mar′riage·a·ble** *adj.*

**mar·ried** *adj.* 1. being husband and wife 2. having a husband or wife 3. of marriage —*n.* a married person

**mar·row** (mar′ō) *n.* [OE. *mearg*] the soft, fatty tissue that fills the cavities of most bones

**mar·ry** (mar′ē) *vt.* **-ried, -ry·ing** [< L. *maritus*, husband] 1. to join as husband and wife 2. to take as husband or wife 3. to unite —*vi.* to get married —**marry off** to give in marriage

**Mars** (märz) 1. the Roman god of war 2. a planet of the solar system; see PLANET

**Mar·seille** (mär sā′) seaport in SE France: pop. 778,000 Eng. sp. **Marseilles**

**marsh** (märsh) *n.* [OE. *merisc*] a tract of low, wet, soft land; swamp —**marsh′y** *adj.* **-i·er, -i·est**

**mar·shal** (mär′shəl) *n.* [< OHG. *marah*, horse + *scalh*, servant] 1. in various foreign armies, a general officer of the highest rank **2.** an official in charge of ceremonies, parades, etc. **3.** in the U.S., *a)* a Federal officer appointed to a judicial district with duties like those of a sheriff *b)* the head of some police or fire departments —*vt.* **-shaled** or **-shalled, -shal·ing** or **-shal·ling 1.** to arrange (troops, ideas, etc.) in order **2.** to guide

**Mar·shall** (mär′shəl), **John** 1755–1835; chief justice, U.S. Supreme Court (1801–35)

**marsh·mal·low** (märsh′mel′ō, -mal′ō) *n.* [orig. made of the root of a mallow found in marshes] a soft, spongy confection of sugar, gelatin, etc.

**mar·su·pi·al** (mär sōō′pē əl) *adj.* [< Gr. *marsypos*, pouch] of a group of mammals that carry their incompletely developed young in an external abdominal pouch on the mother —*n.* an animal of this kind, as a kangaroo

**mart** (märt) *n.* [MDu. *markt*] a market

**mar·ten** (mär′t'n) *n.* [< OFr. *martre*] **1.** a small mammal like a weasel, with soft, thick fur **2.** the fur

**mar·tial** (mär′shəl) *adj.* [< L. *martialis*, of Mars] **1.** of or suitable for war **2.** warlike; bold **3.** military —*mar′tial·ly adv.*

**martial law** rule by military authorities over civilians, as during a war

**Mar·tian** (mär′shən) *adj.* of Mars —*n.* an imagined inhabitant of Mars

**mar·tin** (mär′t'n) *n.* [Fr.] any of several birds of the swallow family

**mar·ti·net** (mär′t'n et′) *n.* [< *Martinet*, 17th-c. Fr. general] a very strict disciplinarian

**mar·ti·ni** (mär tē′nē) *n., pl.* **-nis** [< ?] a cocktail made of gin (or vodka) and dry vermouth

**mar·tyr** (mär′tər) *n.* [< Gr. *martyr*, a witness] **1.** one who chooses to suffer or die for his faith or principles **2.** one who suffers misery for a long time —*vt.* to kill or persecute for adherence to a belief —*mar′tyr·dom n.*

**mar·vel** (mär′v'l) *n.* [< L. *mirari*, admire] a wonderful or astonishing thing —*vt., vi.* **-veled** or **-velled, -vel·ing** or **-vel·ling** to become full of wonder (often followed by a clause)

**mar·vel·ous** (mär′v'l əs) *adj.* **1.** causing wonder; extraordinary, etc. **2.** improbable; incredible **3.** [Colloq.] fine; splendid Also, *chiefly Brit.* **mar′vel·lous** —*mar′vel·ous·ly adv.*

**Marx** (märks), **Karl** 1818–83; Ger. founder of modern socialism

**Marx·ism** (märk′siz′m) *n.* the system of thought developed by Karl Marx and Friedrich Engels, serving as a basis for socialism and communism — **Marx′ist, Marx′i·an** *adj., n.*

**Mar·y** (mer′ē) *Bible* mother of Jesus

**Mar·y·land** (mer′ə lənd) E State of the U.S.: 10,577 sq. mi.; pop. 3,922,000; *cap.* Annapolis

**Mary Mag·da·lene** (mag′də lēn) *Bible* a woman out of whom Jesus cast devils

**mar·zi·pan** (mär′zi pan′) *n.* [G. < It. *marzapane*] a pasty confection of

ground almonds, sugar, and egg white

**masc., mas.** masculine

**mas·ca·ra** (mas kar′ə) *n.* [< Ar. *maskhara*, a clown] a cosmetic for coloring the eyelashes and eyebrows — *vt.* **-ca′raed, -ca′ra·ing** to put mascara on

**mas·con** (mäs′kän′) *n.* [*mas(s) con(centration)*] dense material beneath the moon's surface

**mas·cot** (mas′kät) *n.* [< Fr. *masco*, sorcerer] any person, animal, or thing supposed to bring good luck

**mas·cu·line** (mas′kyə lin) *adj.* [< L. *mas*, male] **1.** male; of men or boys **2.** suitable to or characteristic of men; strong, vigorous, manly, etc. **3.** mannish: said of women **4.** *Gram.* designating or of the gender of words referring to males or things originally regarded as male —*mas′cu·lin′i·ty n.*

**ma·ser** (mā′zər) *n.* [*m(icrowave) a(mplification by) s(timulated). e(mission of) r(adiation)*] a device that stimulates atoms, as in a gas, to emit radiation in a narrow beam

**mash** (mash) *n.* [< OE. *mascwyrt*] **1.** crushed malt or meal soaked in hot water for making wort **2.** a mixture of watered bran, meal, etc. for feeding horses, etc. **3.** any soft mass —*vt.* **1.** to change into a soft mass by beating, crushing, etc. **2.** to crush or injure — *mash′er n.*

**mask** (mask) *n.* [ult. < Ar. *maskhara*, a clown] **1.** a covering to conceal or protect the face **2.** anything that conceals or disguises **3.** a masquerade **4.** *a)* a molded likeness of the face *b)* a grotesque representation of the face, worn to amuse or frighten —*vt.* to cover or conceal as with a mask — **masked** *adj.*

**mas·och·ism** (mas′ə kiz′m) *n.* [< L. von Sacher-*Masoch*, 19th-c. Austrian writer] the getting of pleasure, often sexual, from being hurt or humiliated —*mas′och·ist n.* —*mas′och·is′tic adj.* —*mas′och·is′ti·cal·ly adv.*

**ma·son** (mā′s'n) *n.* [< ML. *matio*] **1.** one whose work is building with stone, brick, etc. **2.** [M-] *same as* FREEMASON

**Ma·son-Dix·on line** (mā′s'n dik′s'n) [< C. *Mason* & J. *Dixon*, who, surveyed it, 1763–67] boundary line between Pa. & Md., regarded as separating the North from the South

**Ma·son·ic** (mə sän′ik) *adj.* [also m-] of Freemasons or Freemasonry

**ma·son·ry** (mā′s'n rē) *n., pl.* **-ries 1.** a mason's trade **2.** something built by a mason; brickwork or stonework **3.** [*also* M-] *same as* FREEMASONRY

**masque** (mask) *n.* [see MASK] **1.** *same as* MASQUERADE (sense 1) **2.** a former kind of dramatic entertainment, with a mythical or allegorical theme

**mas·quer·ade** (mas′kə rād′) *n.* [see MASK] **1.** a ball or party at which masks and fancy costumes are worn **2.** *a)* a disguise *b)* an acting under false pretenses —*vi.* **-ad′ed, -ad′ing 1.** to take part in a masquerade **2.** to act under false pretenses

**Mass** (mas) *n.* [< L. *missa* in the

words said by the priest *ite, missa est,
go,* (you) are dismissed [also **m-**]
R.C.Ch. the service of the Eucharist
**mass** (mas) *n.* [< Gr. *maza,* barley
cake] **1.** a quantity of matter of indefinite shape and size; lump **2.** a large
quantity or number [*a mass* of bruises]
**3.** bulk; size **4.** the main part **5.**
*Physics* the quantity of matter in a
body as measured in its relation to
inertia —*adj.* of or for the masses or
for a large number —*vt., vi.* to gather
or form into a mass —**the masses** the
common people; specif., the lower
social classes
**Mas·sa·chu·setts** (mas'ə chōō'sits)
New England State of the U.S.: 8,257
sq. mi.; pop. 5,689,000; cap. Boston:
abbrev. **Mass.**
**mas·sa·cre** (mas'ə kər) *n.* [< OFr.
*maçacre,* shambles] the indiscriminate,
cruel killing of many people or animals
—*vt.* **-cred, -cring** to kill in large
numbers
**mas·sage** (mə säzh') *n.* [Fr. < Ar.
*massa,* to touch] a rubbing, kneading,
etc. of part of the body, as to stimulate
circulation —*vt.* **-saged', -sag'ing**
to give a massage to
**mass·cult** (mas'kult') *n.* [MASS +
CULT(URE)] [Colloq.] a commercialized
culture popularized through the mass
media
**mas·seur** (ma sur', mə-) *n.* [Fr.] a
man whose work is giving massages —
**mas·seuse'** (-sooz', -sōōz') *n.fem.*
**mas·sive** (mas'iv) *adj.* **1.** forming or
consisting of a large mass; big and
solid **2.** large and imposing —**mas'-
sive·ly** *adv.* —**mas'sive·ness** *n.*
**mass media** newspapers, magazines,
radio, and television as the means of
reaching the mass of people
**mass number** the number of neutrons and protons in the nucleus of an
atom
**mass production** quantity production of goods, esp. by machinery and
division of labor
**mast** (mast) *n.* [OE. *mæst*] **1.** a tall
vertical spar used to support the sails,
yards, etc. on a ship **2.** a vertical pole
**mas·tec·to·my** (mas tek'tə mē) *n.,
pl.* **-mies** surgical removal of a breast
**mas·ter** (mas'tər) *n.* [< L. *magister*]
**1.** a man who rules others or has control over something; specif., *a)* one
who is head of a household *b)* an
employer *c)* an owner of an animal or
slave *d)* the captain of a merchant ship
*e)* [Chiefly Brit.] a male teacher **2.** an
expert; specif., *a)* a workman skilled
in his trade *b)* an artist regarded as
great **3.** [M-] a title applied to: *a)* a
boy too young to be addressed as *Mr.
b)* one holding an advanced academic
degree [*Master* of Arts] —*adj.* **1.**
being a master **2.** of a master **3.** chief;
main; controlling —*vt.* **1.** to be or
become master of **2.** to become an
expert in (art, etc.)
**mas·ter·ful** *adj.* **1.** acting the part of

a master; domineering **2.** expert;
skillful —**mas'ter·ful·ly** *adv.*
**master key** a key that will open up
every one of a set of locks
**mas'ter·ly** *adj.* expert; skillful —*adv.*
in a masterly manner
**mas'ter·mind'** *n.* a very clever
person, esp. one who plans or directs a
project —*vt.* to be the mastermind of
**master of ceremonies** a person
who presides over an entertainment
**mas'ter·piece'** *n.* **1.** a thing made or
done with masterly skill **2.** the greatest work of a person or group
**master sergeant** *U.S. Mil.* a noncommissioned officer of high rank
**mas'ter·stroke'** *n.* a masterly action,
move, or achievement
**mas'ter·work'** *n. same as* MASTER-
PIECE
**mas'ter·y** *n., pl.* **-ies 1.** control as by
a master **2.** ascendancy or victory **3.**
expert skill or knowledge
**mast'head'** *n.* **1.** the top part of a
ship's mast **2.** that part of a newspaper or magazine giving its address,
publishers, etc.
**mas·ti·cate** (mas'tə kāt') *vt.* **-cat'-
ed, -cat'ing** [ult. < Gr. *mastax,*
mouth] to chew up —**mas'ti·ca'-
tion** *n.*
**mas·tiff** (mas'tif) *n.* [< L. *mansuetus,*
tame] a large, smooth-coated dog
with powerful jaws
**mas·to·don** (mas'tə dän') *n.* [< Gr.
*mastos,* breast + *odous,* tooth: from
the nipplelike processes on its molars]
a large, extinct animal resembling the
elephant but larger
**mas·toid** (mas'toid) *adj.* [< Gr.
*mastos,* breast + *eidos,* form] designating, of, or near a projection of the
temporal bone behind the ear —*n.* the
mastoid projection
**mas·tur·bate** (mas'tər bāt') *vi.*
**-bat'ed, -bat'ing** [< L. *masturbari*]
to manipulate the genitals for sexual
gratification —**mas'tur·ba'tion** *n.*
**mat¹** (mat) *n.* [< LL. *matta*] **1.** a flat
piece of cloth, woven straw, rubber,
etc., variously used for protection, as
under a vase, etc. or on the floor **2.** a
thickly padded floor covering used for
wrestling, etc. **3.** anything interwoven
or tangled into a thick mass —*vt., vi.*
**mat'ted, mat'ting 1.** to cover as
with a mat **2.** to interweave or tangle
into a thick mass
**mat²** (mat) *n.* [< OFr.] **1.** *same as*
MATTE **2.** a border, as of cardboard,
put around a picture —*vt.* **mat'ted'
mat'ting 1.** to put a dull finish on
**2.** to frame with a mat
**mat³** (mat) *n.* [Colloq.] *Printing* a
matrix
**mat·a·dor** (mat'ə dôr') *n.* [< Sp.
*matar,* to kill] the bullfighter who
kills the bull with a sword
**match¹** (mach) *n.* [< ? L. *myxa,*
candlewick] a slender piece of wood,
cardboard, etc. tipped with a composition that catches fire by friction

---

fat, āpe, cär; ten, ēven; is, bīte; gō, hôrn, tōōl, look; oil, out; up, fur;
chin; she; thin, *then;* zh, leisure; ŋ, ring; ə for *a* in *ago;* ', (ä'b'l); ë, Fr. coeur;
ö, Fr. feu; Fr. mon; ü, Fr. duc; kh, G. ich, doch; ‡ foreign; < derived from

**match²** (mach) *n.* [OE. (*ge*)*mæcca*, mate] 1. any person or thing equal or similar to another 2. two persons or things that go well together 3. a contest or game 4. a marriage or mating —*vt.* 1. to join in marriage; mate 2. to put in opposition (*with*, *against*) 3. to be equal or similar to 4. to make or get a counterpart or equivalent to 5. to suit (one thing) to another —*vi.* to be equal, similar, suitable, etc.

**match/book/** *n.* a folder of paper matches

**match/less** *adj.* having no equal

**match/mak/er** *n.* one who arranges marriages for others

**mate** (māt) *n.* [< MDu.] 1. a companion or fellow worker 2. one of a matched pair 3. *a*) a husband or wife *b*) the male or female of paired animals 4. an officer of a merchant ship, ranking below the captain —*vt.*, *vi.* mat/ed, mat/ing 1. to join as a pair 2. to couple in marriage or sexual union

**ma·te·ri·al** (mə tir/ē əl) *adj.* [< L. *materia*, matter] 1. of matter; physical [a *material* object] 2. of the body or bodily needs, comfort, etc.; not spiritual 3. important, essential, etc. —*n.* 1. what a thing is, or may be made of; elements or parts; cloth; fabric 3. [*pl.*] tools, etc. needed to make or do something

**ma·te/ri·al·ism** (-iz'm) *n.* 1. the doctrine that everything in the world, including thought, can be explained only in terms of matter 2. the tendency to be more concerned with material than with spiritual or intellectual values —**ma·te/ri·al·ist** *adj.*, *n.* —**ma·te/ri·al·is/tic** *adj.*

**ma·te/ri·al·ize/** (-ə liz/) *vt.* -ized/, -iz/ing to give material form to —*vi.* 1. to become fact; be realized 2. to take on bodily form: said of spirits, etc. —**ma·te/ri·al·i·za/tion** *n.*

**ma·te/ri·al·ly** *adv.* 1. physically 2. to a great extent; substantially

**ma·te·ri·el, ma·té·ri·el** (mə tir/ē el/) *n.* [Fr.: see MATERIAL] the necessary materials and tools; specif., military weapons, supplies, etc.

**ma·ter·nal** (mə tur'n'l) *adj.* [< L. *mater*, mother] 1. of, like, or from a mother 2. related through the mother's side of the family —**ma·ter/nal·ly** *adv.*

**ma·ter·ni·ty** (-nə tē) *n.* the state of being a mother; motherhood —*adj.* 1. for pregnant women 2. for the care of mothers and their newborn babies

**math·e·mat·i·cal** (math/ə mat/i k'l) *adj.* 1. of, like, or concerned with mathematics 2. very precise, accurate, etc. —**math/e·mat/i·cal·ly** *adv.*

**math·e·mat·ics** (math/ə mat/iks) *n.pl.* [*with sing. v.*] [< Gr. *manthenein*, learn] the science dealing with quantities, forms, etc. and their relationships by the use of numbers and symbols: also **math** —**math/e·ma·ti/cian** (-mə tish/ən) *n.*

**mat·i·nee, mat·i·née** (mat'n ā/) *n.* [< Fr. *matin*, morning] an afternoon performance of a play, etc.

**mat·ins** (mat/nz) *n.pl.* [< L. *matutinus*, of the morning] [*often* M-] a church service of morning prayer

**Ma·tisse** (mä tēs/), **Hen·ri** (än rē/) 1869–1954; Fr. painter

**matri-** [< L. *mater*] *a combining form meaning* mother

**ma·tri·arch** (mā/trē ärk/) *n.* [prec. + -ARCH] a woman who rules a family, tribe, etc. —**ma/tri·ar/chal** *adj.* —**ma/tri·ar/chy** *n.*, *pl.* -chies

**ma·tric·u·late** (mə trik/yoo lāt/) *vt.*, *vi.* -lat/ed, -lat/ing [see MATRIX] to enroll, esp. as a student in a college —**ma·tric/u·la/tion** *n.*

**mat·ri·mo·ny** (mat/rə mō/nē) *n.*, *pl.* -nies [< L. *mater*, mother] 1. the act or rite of marriage 2. the married state —**mat/ri·mo/ni·al** *adj.*

**ma·trix** (mā/triks) *n.*, *pl.* -tri·ces/ (mā/trə sēz/, mat/rə-), -trix·es [LL., womb < L. *mater*, mother] that within which something originates, takes form, etc.; specif., a mold for the face of a type or for a printing plate

**ma·tron** (mā/trən) *n.* [< L. *mater*, mother] 1. a wife or widow, esp. one who has a mature appearance and manner 2. a woman manager of the domestic arrangements of a hospital, prison, etc. —**ma/tron·ly** *adj.*

**matron of honor** a married woman acting as chief attendant to a bride

**matte** (mat) *n.* [var. of MAT?] a dull surface or finish —*adj.* not glossy

**mat·ted** (mat/id) *adj.* closely tangled in a dense mass

**mat·ter** (mat/ər) *n.* [< L. *materia*] 1. what a thing is made of; material 2. whatever occupies space and is perceptible to the senses 3. any specified substance [coloring *matter*] 4. content of thought or expression 5. an amount or quantity 6. *a*) a thing or affair *b*) cause or occasion [no laughing *matter*] 7. importance; significance [it's of no *matter*] 8. trouble; difficulty [what's the *matter*?] 9. pus 10. mail —*vi.* 1. to be of importance 2. to form pus —**as a matter of fact** in fact; really —**no matter** 1. it is not important 2. in spite of

**mat/ter-of-fact/** *adj.* sticking to facts; literal, practical, etc.

**Mat·thew** (math/yōō) *Bible* 1. a Christian apostle, reputed author of the first Gospel 2. this book: abbrev. Matt.

**mat·ting** (mat/iŋ) *n.* 1. a fabric of straw, hemp, etc. for mats, floor covering, etc. 2. mats collectively

**mat·tock** (mat/ək) *n.* [OE. *mattuc*] a tool like a pickax, for loosening the soil, digging roots, etc.

**mat·tress** (mat/ris) *n.* [< Ar. *matrah*, cushion] a casing of strong cloth filled with cotton, foam rubber, coiled springs, etc., used on a bed

MATTOCK

**ma·ture** (mə toor/, -choor/, -tyoor/) *adj.* [< L. *maturus*, ripe] 1. full-grown; ripe 2. fully developed, perfected, etc. 3. due: said of a note, bond, etc. —*vt.*, *vi.* -tured′, -tur′ing to make or become mature —mat·u·ra·tion (mach′ŏŏ rā′shən) *n.* —ma·tu′ri·ty, *n.*

mat·zo (mät′sə, -sô) *n.*, *pl.* mat′zot, mat′zoth (-sōt), mat′zos [Heb. *matstsāh*, unleavened] flat, thin unleavened bread eaten during the Passover, or a piece of this

maud·lin (môd′lin) *adj.* [< ME. *Maudeleyne*, (Mary) Magdalene (often represented as weeping)] foolishly, often tearfully, sentimental

maul (môl) *n.* [< L. *malleus*, a hammer] a heavy hammer for driving stakes, etc. —*vt.* 1. to bruise or lacerate 2. to handle roughly; manhandle —maul′er *n.*

maun·der (môn′dər) *vi.* [prob. < obs. *maund*, to beg] to talk or move in a confused or aimless way

Mau·pas·sant (mō′pə sänt′), Guy de (gē də) 1850–93; Fr. writer

Mau·ri·ta·ni·a (môr′ə tā′nē ə) country in W Africa: 419,230 sq. mi.; pop. 1,100,000

Mau·ri·ti·us (mô rish′ē əs) island country in the Indian Ocean, in the Brit. Commonwealth: 809 sq. mi.; pop. 780,000

mau·so·le·um (mô′sə lē′əm, -zə-) *n.*, *pl.* -le′ums, -le′a (-ə) [< the tomb of King *Mausolus*, in ancient Asia Minor] a large, imposing tomb

mauve (mōv, môv) *n.* [Fr. < L. *malva*, mallow] any of several shades of pale purple —*adj.* of this color

mav·er·ick (mav′ər ik) *n.* [after S. *Maverick*, 19th-c. Texan whose cattle had no brand] 1. an unbranded animal, esp. a lost calf 2. [Colloq.] a person who acts independently of any organization, political party, etc.

maw (mô) *n.* [OE. *maga*] 1. orig., the stomach 2. the throat, gullet, jaws, or oral cavity of a voracious animal

mawk·ish (mô′kish) *adj.* [< ON. *mathkr*, maggot] sentimental in a weak, insipid way —mawk′ish·ly *adv.*

maxi- [< MAXI(MUM)] *a combining form meaning* maximum, very large, very long

max·il·la (mak sil′ə) *n.*, *pl.* -lae (-ē) [L.] the upper jawbone —max·il·lar·y (mak′sə ler′ē) *adj.*

max·im (mak′sim) *n.* [< LL. *maxima* (*propositio*), the greatest (premise)] a concise rule of conduct; precept

max·i·mize (mak′sə mīz′) *vt.* -mized′, -miz′ing to increase to a maximum

max·i·mum (mak′sə məm) *n.*, *pl.* -mums, -ma (-mə) [< L. superl. of *magnus*, great] 1. the greatest quantity, number, etc., possible 2. the highest degree or point reached —*adj.* greatest possible, permissible, or reached —max′i·mal (-m′l) *adj.*

May (mā) *n.* [< L. *Maius*] the fifth month of the year, having 31 days

may (mā) *v.* *pt.* might [OE. *mæg*] an auxiliary expressing: 1. possibility [it *may* rain] 2. permission [you *may* go]: see also CAN[1] 3. contingency [be quiet so that we *may* hear] 4. wish or hope [*may* he live!]

Ma·ya (mä′yə) *n.* 1. a member of a tribe of Indians of C. America, who had a highly developed civilization 2. their language —Ma′yan *adj.*, *n.*

may·be (mā′bē) *adv.* [ME. (for *it may be*)] perhaps

May Day May 1: celebrated as a traditional spring festival: observed in many countries as a labor holiday

may·flow·er (mā′flou′ər) *n.* an early spring flower; esp., the trailing arbutus —[M-] the ship on which the Pilgrims came to America (1620)

may·hem (mā′hem, -əm) *n.* [see MAIM] 1. *Law* the offense of maiming a person 2. any violent destruction

may·n′t (mā′nt, mānt) may not

may·o (mā′ō) *n.* [Colloq.] *clipped form of* MAYONNAISE

may·on·naise (mā′ə nāz′) *n.* [< *Mahón*, port on a Sp. island] a creamy salad dressing made with egg yolks

may·or (mā′ər, mer) *n.* [< L. *major*, greater] the chief administrative officer of a municipality

may′or·al·ty (-əl tē) *n.*, *pl.* -ties the office or term of office of a mayor

maze (māz) *n.* [< OE. *amasian*, amaze] 1. a confusing, intricate network of pathways 2. a confused state —in a maze bewildered

‡maz·el tov (mä′z′l tōv′) [Heb.] good luck: also maz′el·tov′

ma·zur·ka (mə zur′kə) *n.* [Pol.] a lively Polish dance in 3/4 or 3/8 time

M.C. 1. master of ceremonies 2. Member of Congress

Mc·Kin·ley (mə kin′lē), Mount mountain in Alas.: highest peak in N.America

McKinley, William 1843–1901; 25th president of the U.S. (1897–1901)

Md., MD Maryland

M.D. Doctor of Medicine

me (mē) *pron.* [OE.] *objective case of* I

Me., ME Maine

mead[1] (mēd) *n.* [OE. *meodu*] an alcoholic liquor made from fermented honey

mead[2] (mēd) *n.* *poet. var. of* MEADOW

mead·ow (med′ō) *n.* [< OE. *mæd*] 1. a piece of land where grass is grown for hay 2. low, level, moist grassland

mea·ger (mē′gər) *adj.* [< L. *macer*, lean] 1. thin; lean 2. poor; not full or rich; inadequate Brit. sp. mea′gre —mea′ger·ly *adv.* —mea′ger·ness *n.*

meal[1] (mēl) *n.* [OE. *mæl*] 1. any of the times for eating, as lunch, dinner, etc. 2. the food served at such a time

meal[2] (mēl) *n.* [OE. *melu*] 1. any edible grain, coarsely ground [*cornmeal*] 2. any substance similarly ground —meal′y *adj.* -i·er, -i·est

meal′y-mouthed′ (-ē mou′thd′) *adj.* not outspoken or blunt; euphemistic

mean[1] (mēn) *vt.* meant (ment),

**mean'ing** [OE. *mænan*] 1. to have in mind; intend *[he means to go]* 2. to intend to express *[say what you mean]* 3. to signify; denote *["oui" means "yes"]* —*vi.* to have a (specified) degree of importance, effect, etc. *[honors mean little to him]* —**mean well** to have good intentions

**mean²** (mēn) *adj.* [OE. *(ge)mæne*] 1. low in quality or value; paltry; inferior 2. poor in appearance; shabby 3. ignoble; petty 4. stingy 5. contemptibly selfish, bad-tempered, etc. 6. [Slang] *a)* difficult *b)* expert —**mean'ly** *adv.* —**mean'ness** *n.*

**mean³** (mēn) *adj.* [< L. *medius*, middle] 1. halfway between extremes 2. average —*n.* 1. what is between extremes 2. *Math.* a number between the smallest and largest values of a set of quantities; esp., an average

**me·an·der** (mē an'dər) *vi.* [< Gr. *Maiandros*, a winding river in Asia Minor] 1. to take a winding course: said of a stream 2. to wander idly

**mean'ie, mean'y** *n., pl.* **-ies** [Colloq.] one who is mean, selfish, etc.

**mean'ing** *n.* what is meant; what is intended to be signified, understood, etc.; import *[a look full of meaning]* —**mean'ing·ful** *adj.* —**mean'ing·less** *adj.*

**means** (mēnz) *n.pl.* [< MEAN³, *n.*] 1. *[with sing. or pl. v.]* that by which something is done or obtained; agency *[a means to an end]* 2. resources; wealth —**by all means** 1. without fail 2. certainly —**by means of** by using —**by no means** not at all

**meant** (ment) *pt. & pp. of* MEAN¹

**mean'time'** *adv.* 1. in or during the intervening time 2. at the same time —*n.* the intervening time Also **mean'while'**

**mea·sles** (mē'z'lz) *n.pl.* *[with sing. v.]* [ME. *maseles*] 1. an acute, infectious, communicable virus disease, usually of children, characterized by small red spots on the skin, high fever, etc. 2. a similar but milder disease: in full **German measles**

**mea·sly** (mēz'lē) *adj.* **-sli·er, -sli·est** 1. infected with measles 2. [Colloq.] contemptibly slight or worthless

**meas·ure** (mezh'ər) *n.* [< L. *metiri*, to measure] 1. the extent, dimensions, capacity, etc. of anything 2. a determining of this; measurement 3. *a)* a unit of measurement *b)* any standard of valuation 4. a system of measurement 5. an instrument for measuring 6. a definite quantity measured out 7. a course of action *[reform measures]* 8. a statute; law 9. a rhythmical pattern or unit; specif., the notes and rests between two bars on a musical staff —*vt.* **-ured, -ur·ing** 1. to find out or estimate the extent, dimensions, etc. of, esp. by a standard 2. to mark off by measuring 3. to be a measure of —*vi.* 1. to take measurements 2. to be of specified measurements —**beyond measure** exceedingly —**for good measure** as something extra —**in a measure to** some extent —**measure up** to prove

to be competent —**meas'ur·a·ble** *adj.* —**meas'ur·a·bly** *adv.* —**meas'ure·less** *adj.*

**meas'ured** *adj.* 1. set or marked off by a standard *[a measured mile]* 2. regular or steady *[measured steps]* 3. planned with care *[measured words]*

**meas'ure·ment** *n.* 1. a measuring or being measured 2. extent or quantity determined by measuring 3. a system of measuring or of measures

**meat** (mēt) *n.* [OE. *mete*] 1. food: now archaic except in **meat and drink** 2. the flesh of animals, esp. of mammals, used as food 3. the edible part *[a nut meat]* 4. the substance or essence —**meat'y** *adj.* **-i·er, -i·est**

**meat'pack'ing** *n.* the industry of preparing the meat of animals for market

**Mec·ca** (mek'ə) one of the two capitals of Saudi Arabia: birthplace of Mohammed, hence Moslem pilgrimage center: pop. 200,000 —*n.* *[often* **m-**] any place that one yearns to go to

**me·chan·ic** (mə kan'ik) *n.* [< Gr. *mēchanē*, machine] a worker skilled in using tools or repairing machines

**me·chan'i·cal** *adj.* 1. having to do with machinery or tools 2. produced or operated by machinery 3. of the science of mechanics 4. machinelike; spiritless —**me·chan'i·cal·ly** *adv.*

**me·chan'ics** *n.pl.* *[with sing. v.]* 1. the science of motion and the action of forces on bodies 2. knowledge of machinery 3. the technical aspect *[the mechanics of poetry]*

**mech·a·nism** (mek'ə niz'm) *n.* [see MECHANIC] 1. the working parts of a machine 2. any system of interrelated parts 3. any physical or mental process by which a result is produced —**mech'a·nis'tic** *adj.*

**mech'a·nize'** (-nīz') *vt.* **-nized', -niz'ing** 1. to make mechanical 2. to equip (an industry) with machinery or (an army, etc.) with motor vehicles, tanks, etc. —**mech'a·ni·za'tion** *n.*

**mech'an·o·ther'a·py** *n.* the treatment of disease by mechanical means, as massage —**mech'an·o·ther'a·pist** *n.*

**med·al** (med'l) *n.* [< LL. *medialis*, medial] 1. a small, flat piece of inscribed metal, commemorating some event or awarded for some distinguished action, merit, etc. 2. a disk bearing a religious symbol

**med'al·ist** *n.* one awarded a medal

**me·dal·lion** (mə dal'yən) *n.* [< Fr.] 1. a large medal 2. a design, portrait, etc. shaped like a medal

**med·dle** (med'l) *vi.* **-dled, -dling** [< L. *miscere*, mix] to interfere in another's affairs —**med'dler** *n.* —**med'dle·some** (-səm) *adj.*

**me·di·a** (mē'dē ə) *n. alt. pl. of* MEDIUM: see MEDIUM *(n. 3)*

**me·di·al** (mē'dē əl) *adj.* [< L. *medius*] 1. middle 2. ordinary

**me·di·an** (mē'dē ən) *n.* 1. middle; intermediate 2. designating the middle number in a series —*n.* a median number, point, line, etc.

**me·di·ate** (mē'dē āt') *vi.* **-at'ed,**

**-at′ing 1.** to be in an intermediate position **2.** to be an intermediary — *vt.* to settle (differences) between persons, nations, etc. by intervention —**me′di·a′tion** *n.* —**me′di·a′tor** *n.*

**med·ic** (med′ik) *n.* [Colloq.] **1.** a physician or surgeon **2.** a member of a military medical corps

**Med′i·caid′** (-ād′) *n.* [*also* **m-**] a State and Federal health program for paying certain medical expenses of persons having a low income

**med·i·cal** (med′i k′l) *adj.* of or connected with the practice or study of medicine —**med′i·cal·ly** *adv.*

**Med′i·care′** (-ker′) *n.* [*also* **m-**] a Federal health program for paying certain medical expenses of the aged

**med′i·cate′** (-kāt′) *vt.* **-cat′ed, -cat′ing** [< L. *medicari*, heal] to treat with medicine —**med′i·ca′tion** *n.*

**me·dic·i·nal** (mə dis′′n ′l) *adj.* of, or having the properties of, medicine

**med·i·cine** (med′ə s′n) *n.* [< L. *medicus*, physician] **1.** the science of treating and preventing disease **2.** any substance, as a drug, used in treating disease, relieving pain, etc.

**medicine man** among N.American Indians, etc., a man supposed to have supernatural powers to heal the sick

**me·di·e·val** (mē′dē ē′v′l) *adj.* [< L. *medius*, middle + *aevum*, age] of or characteristic of the Middle Ages

**me·di·o·cre** (mē′dē ō′kər) *adj.* [< L. *medius*, middle + *ocris*, peak] **1.** ordinary; average **2.** inferior —**me′di·oc′ri·ty** (-äk′rə tē) *n., pl.* **-ties**

**med·i·tate** (med′ə tāt′) *vt.* **-tat′ed, -tat′ing** [< L. *meditari*] to plan or intend —*vi.* to think deeply —**med′i·ta′tion** *n.* —**med′i·ta′tive** *adj.*

**Med·i·ter·ra·ne·an** (med′i tə rā′nē ən) *adj.* **1.** of the large sea (**Mediterranean Sea**) surrounded by Europe, Africa, & Asia **2.** designating furniture made to simulate heavy, ornately carved Renaissance furniture

**me·di·um** (mē′dē əm) *n., pl.* **-di·ums, -di·a** (-ə) [L. < *medius*, middle] **1.** *a)* something intermediate  *b)* a middle state or degree; mean **2.** an intervening thing through which a force acts **3.** any means, agency, etc.; specif., a means of communication that reaches the general public: a singular form **media** (*pl.* **medias**) is sometimes heard **4.** any surrounding substance or environment **5.** *pl.* **-di·ums** one through whom messages are supposedly sent from the dead —*adj.* intermediate in size, quality, etc.

**med·ley** (med′lē) *n., pl.* **-leys** [ult. < L. *miscere*, mix] **1.** a mixture of dissimilar things **2.** a musical piece made up of various tunes or passages

**me·dul·la** (mi dul′ə) *n., pl.* **-las, -lae** (-ē) [L., the marrow] *Anat.* **1.** a widening of the spinal cord forming the lowest part of the brain: in full **medulla ob·lon·ga·ta** (äb′lôṅ gät′ə) **2.** the inner substance of an organ

**meek** (mēk) *adj.* [< ON. *miukr*, gentle] **1.** patient and mild **2.** too submissive; spiritless —**meek′ly** *adv.* —**meek′ness** *n.*

**meer·schaum** (mir′shəm) *n.* [G. < *meer*, sea + *schaum*, foam] **1.** a white, claylike mineral used for tobacco pipes **2.** a pipe made of this

**meet¹** (mēt) *vt.* **met, meet′ing** [OE. *metan*] **1.** to come upon; encounter **2.** to be present at the arrival of [to *meet* a bus] **3.** to come into contact with **4.** to be introduced to **5.** to contend with; deal with **6.** to experience [to *meet* disaster] **7.** to be perceived by (the eye, etc.) **8.** *a)* to satisfy (a demand, etc.) *b)* to pay (a bill, etc.) —*vi.* **1.** to come together **2.** to come into contact, etc. **3.** to be introduced **4.** to assemble —*n.* a meeting [a track *meet*] —**meet with 1.** to experience **2.** to receive

**meet²** (mēt) *adj.* [< OE. (ge)*mæte*, fitting] [Now Rare] suitable; proper

**meet′ing** *n.* **1.** a coming together **2.** a gathering of people **3.** a junction

**mega-** [Gr. < *megas*, great] *a combining form meaning:* **1.** large, great, powerful **2.** a million of

**meg·a·hertz** (meg′ə hurts′) *n., pl.* **-hertz**′ [MEGA- + HERTZ] one million hertz: formerly **meg′a·cy′cle** (-sī′k′l)

**meg·a·lo·ma·ni·a** (meg′ə lō mā′nē ə) *n.* [< Gr. *megas*, large + -MANIA] a mental disorder characterized by delusions of grandeur, power, etc.

**meg·a·lop·o·lis** (meg′ə läp′ə ləs) *n.* [Gr., great city] a vast urban area

**meg·a·phone** (meg′ə fōn′) *n.* [MEGA- + -PHONE] a funnel-shaped device for increasing the volume of the voice

**meg′a·ton′** (-tun′) *n.* the explosive force of a million tons of TNT

**Me·kong** (mā′käṅ′, -kôṅ′) river in SE Asia, flowing into the South China Sea

**mel·a·mine** (mel′ə mēn′) *n.* [G. *melamin*] a white crystalline compound used in making synthetic resins

**mel·an·cho·li·a** (mel′ən kō′lē ə) *n.* a mental disorder, often psychotic, characterized by extreme depression

**mel·an·chol·y** (mel′ən käl′ē) *n.* [< Gr. *melas*, black + *cholē*, bile] sadness and depression of spirits —*adj.* **1.** sad and depressed **2.** causing sadness

**Mel·a·ne·sia** (mel′ə nē′zhə) a group of islands in the South Pacific —**Mel′a·ne′sian** *adj., n.*

**mé·lange** (mā länzh′, -länj′) *n.* [Fr. < *mêler*, to mix] a mixture; medley

**mel·a·nin** (mel′ə nin) *n.* [< Gr. *melas*, black] a brownish-black pigment found in skin, hair, etc.

**mel·a·no·ma** (mel′ə nō′mə) *n., pl.* **-mas, -ma·ta** (-mə tə) a tumor containing melanin

**Mel·ba toast** (mel′bə) [< N. *Melba* (1861–1931), Australian soprano] very crisp, thinly sliced toast

**Mel·bourne** (mel′bərn) seaport in SE Australia: pop. 2,108,000

**meld** (meld) *vt., vi.* [G. *melden*, announce] *Card Games* to expose and declare (certain cards) for a score —*n.* the cards melded

**me·lee, mê·lée** (mā'lā, mā lā') *n.* [Fr.] a confused fight or hand-to-hand struggle among a number of people

**mel·io·rate** (mēl'yə rāt') *vt., vi.* **-rat'ed, -rat'ing** [< L. *melior*, better] to make or become better

**mel·lif·lu·ous** (mə lif'loo wəs) *adj.* [< L. *mel*, honey + *fluere*, to flow] sounding sweet and smooth: also **mel·lif'lu·ent** —**mel·lif'lu·ence** *n.*

**mel·low** (mel'ō) *adj.* [prob. < OE. *melu*, MEAL²] 1. soft, sweet, etc. because ripe: said of fruit 2. full-flavored: said of wine, etc. 3. full, rich, soft, etc.: said of sound, light, etc. 4. grown gentle and understanding —*vt., vi.* to make or become mellow

**me·lo·di·ous** (mə lō'dē əs) *adj.* 1. producing melody 2. pleasing to hear; tuneful —**me·lo'di·ous·ly** *adv.*

**mel·o·dra·ma** (mel'ə drä'mə, -dram'ə) *n.* [< Fr. < Gr. *melos*, song + LL. *drama*, drama] a drama with sensational action, extravagant emotions, stereotyped characters, etc. — **mel'o·dra·mat'ic** (-drə mat'ik) *adj.* **mel'o·dra·mat'ics** (-drə mat'iks) *n.pl.* melodramatic behavior

**mel·o·dy** (mel'ə dē) *n., pl.* **-dies** [< Gr. *melos*, song + *aeidein*, sing] 1. pleasing sounds in sequence 2. *Music* a) a tune, song, etc. b) the leading part in a harmonic composition — **me·lod·ic** (mə läd'ik) *adj.* —**mel·od'i·cal·ly** *adv.*

**mel·on** (mel'ən) *n.* [< Gr. *mēlon*, apple] the large, juicy many-seeded fruit of certain trailing plants, as the watermelon, cantaloupe, etc.

**melt** (melt) *vt., vi.* [OE. *m(i)eltan*] 1. to change from a solid to a liquid state, generally by heat 2. to dissolve 3. to disappear or cause to disappear gradually 4. to soften in feeling

**melting pot** a country, etc. in which people of various nationalities and races are assimilated

**Mel·ville** (mel'vil), **Herman** 1819–91; U.S. novelist

**mem·ber** (mem'bər) *n.* [< L. *membrum*] 1. a limb or other part of a person, animal, or plant 2. a distinct part of a whole 3. any of the persons constituting an organization or group

**mem'ber·ship'** *n.* 1. the state of being a member 2. all the members of a group or organization 3. the number of members

**mem·brane** (mem'brān) *n.* [< L. *membrum*, member] a thin, soft layer of animal or plant tissue that covers or lines an organ or part —**mem'bra·nous** (-brə nəs) *adj.*

**me·men·to** (mi men'tō, mə-) *n., pl.* **-tos, -toes** [< L. *meminisse*, remember] a reminder; esp., a souvenir

**mem·o** (mem'ō) *n., pl.* **-os** *clipped form of* MEMORANDUM

**mem·oirs** (mem'wärz) *n.pl.* [< L. *memoria*, memory] 1. an autobiography 2. a record of events based on the writer's personal observation and knowledge

**mem·o·ra·bil·i·a** (mem'ər ə bil'ē ə) *n.pl.* [L.] things worth remembering

**mem·o·ra·ble** (mem'ər ə b'l) *adj.* worth remembering; notable; remarkable —**mem'o·ra·bly** *adv.*

**mem·o·ran·dum** (mem'ə ran'dəm) *n., pl.* **-dums, -da** (-də) [L.] 1. a short note written to remind oneself of something 2. an informal written communication, as within an office

**me·mo·ri·al** (mə môr'ē əl) *adj.* [see MEMORY] serving as a remembrance —*n.* anything meant to help people remember a person, event, etc., as a monument, holiday, etc. —**me·mo'ri·al·ize'** (-iz') *vt.* **-ized', -iz'ing**

**Memorial Day** a legal holiday in the U.S. (the last Monday in May in most States) in memory of dead servicemen of all wars

**mem·o·rize** (mem'ə rīz') *vt.* **-rized', -riz'ing** to commit to memory

**mem·o·ry** (mem'ər ē) *n., pl.* **-ries** [< L. *memor*, mindful] 1. the power or act of remembering 2. all that one remembers 3. something remembered 4. the period of remembering [not within my *memory*] 5. commemoration

**Mem·phis** (mem'fis) city in SW Tenn.: pop. 624,000

**men** (men) *n., pl. of* MAN

**men·ace** (men'is) *n.* [< L. *minari*, threaten] a threat or danger —*vt., vi.* **-aced, -ac·ing** to threaten —**men'ac·ing·ly** *adv.*

**mé·nage, me·nage** (mā näzh', mə-) *n.* [Fr. < L. *mansio*, a dwelling] a household

**me·nag·er·ie** (mə naj'ər ē) *n.* [see prec.] a collection of wild animals kept in cages, etc. for exhibition

**mend** (mend) *vt.* [see AMEND] 1. to repair 2. to make better; reform [mend your manners] —*vi.* 1. to improve, esp. in health 2. to heal, as a fracture —*n.* 1. a mending 2. a mended place —**on the mend** improving, esp. in health —**mend'er** *n.*

**men·da·cious** (men dā'shəs) *adj.* [< L. *mendax*] not truthful; lying —**men·dac'i·ty** (-das'ə tē) *n.*

**Men·del** (men'd'l), **Gre·gor** (grā'gôr) 1822–84; Austrian geneticist

**Men·dels·sohn** (men'd'l sən), **Fe·lix** (fā'liks) 1809–47; Ger. composer

**men·di·cant** (men'di kənt) *adj.* [< L. *mendicus*, needy] begging —*n.* 1. a beggar 2. a mendicant friar

**men'folk'** *n.pl.* [Dial. or Colloq.] men

**me·ni·al** (mē'nē əl) *adj.* [< L. *mansio*, house] 1. of or fit for servants 2. servile; low —*n.* 1. a domestic servant 2. a servile, low person — **me'ni·al·ly** *adv.*

**men·in·gi·tis** (men'in jīt'is) *n.* [< Gr. *mēninx*, membrane] inflammation of the membranes enveloping the brain and spinal cord

**me·nis·cus** (mi nis'kəs) *n., pl.* **-nis'cus·es, -nis'ci** (-nis'ī, -kī) [< Gr. dim. of *mēnē*, the moon] 1. a crescent 2. the convex or concave upper surface of a column of liquid

**Men·non·ite** (men'ə nīt') *n.* [< *Menno* Simons, 16th-c. Du. reformer] a member of an evangelical Christian sect living and dressing plainly and rejecting military service, oaths, etc.

**men·o·pause** (men'ə pôz') *n.* [< Gr. *mēn*, month + *pauein*, to end] the permanent cessation of menstruation

**men·o·rah** (mə nō'rə, -nôr'ə) *n.* [Heb., lamp stand] *Judaism* a candelabrum with seven (or nine) branches

**men·ses** (men'sēz) *n.pl.* [L., pl. of *mensis*, month] the periodic flow, usually monthly, of blood from the uterus

**men·stru·ate** (men'stroo wāt', -strāt) *vi.* -at'ed, -at'ing [< L. *mensis*, month] to have a discharge of the menses —**men'stru·al** *adj.* — **men'stru·a'tion** *n.*

**men·su·ra·tion** (men'shə rā'shən) *n.* [< L. *mensura*, measure] a measuring —**men'sur·a·ble** (-shər ə b'l) *adj.*

**-ment** (mənt, mint) [< L. *-mentum*] *a suffix meaning:* 1. a result [*improvement*] 2. a means [*adornment*] 3. an act [*movement*] 4. a state [*bereavement*]

**men·tal** (men't'l) *adj.* [< L. *mens*, the mind] 1. of, for, by, or in the mind 2. ill in mind [*mental* patients] 3. for the ill in mind —**men'tal·ly** *adv.*

**men'tal·ist** *n.* same as MIND READER

**men·tal·i·ty** (men tal'ə tē) *n., pl.* -ties mental capacity or power

**mental reservation** qualification of (a statement) that one makes to oneself but does not express

**mental retardation** congenital lowness of intelligence

**men·ta·tion** (men tā'shən) *n.* the act or process of using the mind

**men·thol** (men'thōl, -thôl) *n.* [G. < L. *mentha*, MINT²] a white, crystalline alcohol obtained from oil of peppermint and used in medicine, cosmetics, etc. —**men'tho·lat'ed** (-thə lāt'id) *adj.*

**men·tion** (men'shən) *n.* [< L. *mens*, the mind] 1. a brief reference 2. a citing for honor —*vt.* to refer to briefly or incidentally —**make mention** of to mention —**not to mention** without even mentioning

**men·tor** (men'tər, -tôr) *n.* [< *Mentor*, friend of Odysseus] 1. a wise adviser 2. a teacher or coach

**men·u** (men'yōō) *n., pl.* -us [Fr. < L. *minutus*, small] a detailed list of the foods served at a meal

**me·ow, me·ou** (mē ou') *n.* [echoic] the characteristic vocal sound made by a cat —*vi.* to make this sound

**mer·can·tile** (mur'kən til) *adj.* of or characteristic of merchants or trade

**mer·ce·nar·y** (mur'sə ner'ē) *adj.* [< L. *merces*, wages] working or done for payment only —*n., pl.* -ies a soldier hired to serve in a foreign army

**mer·cer** (mur'sər) *n.* [< L. *merx*, wares] [Brit.] a dealer in textiles

**mer·cer·ize** (mur'sə rīz') *vt.* -ized', -iz'ing [< J. *Mercer*, 19th-c. Eng. calico dealer] to treat (cotton thread or fabric) with an alkali solution to strengthen it, give it a gloss, etc.

**mer·chan·dise** (mur'chən dīz'; *for n. also* -dīs') *n.* [see ff.] things bought and sold; wares —*vt., vi.* -dised', -dis'ing 1. to buy and sell 2. to promote the sale of (a product) Also, for v., **mer'chan·dize** —**mer'chan·dis'er, mer'chan·diz'er** *n.*

**mer·chant** (mur'chənt) *n.* [ult. < L. *merx*, wares] 1. one whose business is buying and selling goods 2. a dealer at retail; storekeeper —*adj.* mercantile

**mer'chant·man** (-mən) *n., pl.* -men a ship used in commerce

**merchant marine** all the ships of a nation that are used in commerce

**‡mer·ci** (mer sē') *interj.* [Fr.] thanks

**mer·ci·ful** (mur'si fəl) *adj.* having or showing mercy —**mer'ci·ful·ly** *adv.*

**mer'ci·less** *adj.* without mercy; pitiless —**mer'ci·less·ly** *adv.*

**mer·cu·ri·al** (mər kyoor'ē əl) *adj.* having qualities suggestive of mercury; quick, changeable, fickle, etc.

**Mer·cu·ro·chrome** (mər kyoor'ə krōm') [see ff., *n. & -*CHROME] *a trademark* for a red solution of a compound of mercury, used as an antiseptic

**Mer·cu·ry** (mur'kyoo rē) 1. a Roman god who was the messenger of the other gods 2. the smallest planet in the solar system: see PLANET —*n.* [m-] a heavy, silver-white metallic chemical element, liquid at ordinary temperatures, used in thermometers, etc. —**mer·cu·ric** (mər kyoor'ik) *adj.* — **mer'cu'rous** *adj.*

**mer·cy** (mur'sē) *n., pl.* -cies [< L. *merces*, payment] 1. a refraining from harming offenders, enemies, etc. 2. imprisonment rather than death for a capital crime 3. a disposition to forgive or be kind 4. the power to forgive 5. a lucky thing; blessing —**at the mercy of** in the power of

**mercy killing** same as EUTHANASIA

**mere** (mir) *adj. superl.* **mer'est** [< L. *merus*, pure] nothing more or other than; bare [a *mere* trifle]

**mere'ly** *adv.* only; simply

**mer·e·tri·cious** (mer'ə trish'əs) *adj.* [< L. *meretrix*, a prostitute] 1. alluring but tawdry 2. specious

**mer·gan·ser** (mər gan'sər) *n.* [< L. *mergus*, diver (bird) + *anser*, goose] a large, fish-eating, diving duck

**merge** (murj) *vi., vt.* merged, merg'ing [L. *mergere*, to dip] 1. to lose or cause to lose identity by being absorbed or combined 2. to unite

**merg'er** *n.* a merging; specif., a combining of several companies in one

**me·rid·i·an** (mə rid'ē ən) *n.* [< L. *meridies*, noon] 1. the highest point of power, etc. 2. a) a circle on the earth's surface passing through the geographical poles and any given point b) any of the lines of longitude

**me·ringue** (mə raŋ') *n.* [Fr. < ?] egg whites beaten stiff and mixed with sugar: used as a pie covering, etc.

**me·ri·no** (mə rē'nō) *n., pl.* -nos [Sp.] 1. one of a hardy breed of sheep with long, fine, silky wool 2. the wool 3. yarn or cloth made of it

---

fat, āpe, cär; ten, ēven; is, bīte; gō, hôrn, tool, look; oil, out; up, fur; chin; she; thin, then; zh, leisure; ŋ, ring; ə for a in ago; ', (ā'b'l); ë, Fr. coeur; ö, Fr. feu; Fr. mon; ü, Fr. duc; kh, G. ich, doch; ‡ foreign; < derived from

**mer·it** (mer′it) n. [< L. *merere*, deserve] 1. worth; value; excellence 2. something deserving reward, praise, etc. 3. [pl.] intrinsic rightness or wrongness —vt. to deserve

**mer·i·to·ri·ous** (mer′ə tôr′ē əs) adj. having merit; deserving reward, praise, etc. —mer′i·to·ri·ous·ly adv. —mer′i·to·ri·ous·ness n.

**Mer·lin** (mur′lin) *Arthurian Legend* a magician, helper of King Arthur

**mer·maid** (mur′mād′) n. [< OE. *mere*, sea + MAID] an imaginary sea creature with the head and upper body of a woman and the tail of a fish —mer′man′ n.*masc.*, pl. -men

**mer·ri·ment** (mer′i mənt) n. merrymaking; gaiety and fun; mirth

**mer·ry** (mer′ē) adj. -ri·er, -ri·est [< OE. *myrge*, pleasing] 1. full of fun; gay 2. festive —make merry to be gay or festive —mer′ri·ly adv. —mer′ri·ness n.

MERMAID

**mer·ry-go-round′** n. 1. a circular, revolving platform with wooden animals and seats on it, used as an amusement ride 2. a whirl, as of work

**mer·ry·mak·ing** n. a having fun; festivity —mer′ry·mak′er n.

**me·sa** (mā′sə) n. [Sp. < L. *mensa*, table] a high plateau with steep sides

**mes·ca·line** (mes′kə lēn′, -lin) n. [< MexInd. *mexcalli*, a spineless cactus] a psychedelic drug obtained from a cactus plant (mescal)

**mes·dames** (mā däm′) n. pl. of MADAME, MADAM (sense 1), or MRS.

**mes·de·moi·selles** (mā′də mə zel′) n. pl. of MADEMOISELLE

**mesh** (mesh) n. [prob. < MDu. *maesche*] 1. any of the open spaces of a net, screen, etc. 2. a net or network 3. a netlike material, as for stockings 4. the engagement of the teeth of gears —vt., vi. 1. to entangle or become entangled 2. to engage or become engaged: said of gears 3. to interlock

**mes·mer·ize** (mez′mər īz′, mes′-) vt. -ized′, -iz′ing [< F. A. *Mesmer*, 18th-c. G. physician] to hypnotize —mes′mer·ism n. —mes′mer·ist n.

**Mes·o·po·ta·mi·a** (mes′ə pə tā′mē ə) ancient country in SW Asia, between the Tigris & Euphrates rivers

**Mes·o·zo·ic** (mes′ə zō′ik, mez′-) adj. [< Gr. *mesos*, middle + zo(o)- + -ic] designating the geologic era (c.230–65 million years ago) characterized by dinosaurs, the appearance of birds, etc.

**mes·quite, mes·quit** (mes kēt′) n. [< MexInd. *mizquitl*] a thorny shrub of the SW U.S. and Mexico

**mess** (mes) n. [< L. *missus*, course (at a meal)] 1. a serving, as of porridge 2. a group of people who regularly eat together, as in the army 3. the meal they eat 4. a jumble 5. a state of trouble, disorder, untidiness, etc. —vt. 1. to make dirty or untidy 2. to bungle; botch (up) —vi. 1. to eat as one of a mess 2. to make a mess 3. to putter or meddle (in, with, around, etc.) —mess′y adj. -i·er, -i·est —mess′i·ly adv. —mess′i·ness n.

**mes·sage** (mes′ij) n. [< L. *mittere*, send] 1. a communication sent between persons 2. the chief idea that a writer, artist, etc. seeks to communicate in a work —get the message [Colloq.] to understand a hint

**mes·sen·ger** (mes′n jər) n. one who carries messages, or does errands

**mess hall** a room or building where soldiers, etc., regularly have meals

**Mes·si·ah** (mə sī′ə) [< Heb. *māshīah*, anointed] 1. *Judaism* the expected deliverer of the Jews 2. *Christianity* Jesus —Mes·si·an·ic (mes′ē an′ik) adj.

**mes·sieurs** (mes′ərz; Fr. mā syö′) n. pl. of MONSIEUR

**Messrs.** (mes′ərz) Messieurs: now used chiefly as the pl. of MR.

**mes·ti·zo** (mes tē′zō) n., pl. -zos, -zoes [Sp. < L. *miscere*, mix] a person of mixed parentage, esp. Spanish and American Indian

**met** (met) pt. & pp. of MEET[1]

**met.** metropolitan

**meta-** [< Gr. *meta*, after] a prefix meaning: 1. changed [*metamorphosis*] 2. after, beyond, higher [*metaphysics*]

**me·tab·o·lism** (mə tab′ə liz′m) n. [< Gr. *meta*, beyond + *ballein*, throw] the process in organisms by which protoplasm is formed from food and broken down into waste matter, with release of energy —met·a·bol·ic (met′ə bäl′ik) adj. —me·tab′o·lize′ (-līz′) vt., vi. -lized′, -liz′ing

**met·a·car·pus** (met′ə kär′pəs) n., pl. -pi (-pī) [ModL. < Gr. *meta-*, over + *karpos*, wrist] the part of the hand between the wrist and the fingers —met′a·car′pal adj., n.

**met·al** (met′l) n. [< Gr. *metallon*, a mine] 1. *a)* any of a class of chemical elements, as iron, gold, copper, etc., that have luster, can conduct heat and electricity, etc. *b)* an alloy of such elements, as brass, bronze, etc. 2. anything consisting of metal —me·tal·lic (mə tal′ik) adj. —me·tal′li·cal·ly adv.

**met·al·lur·gy** (met′l ur′jē) n. [< Gr. *metallon*, metal + *ergon*, work] the science of separating metals from their ores and preparing them for use by smelting, refining, etc. —met′al·lur′gi·cal adj. —met′al·lur′gist n.

**met·a·mor·phose** (met′ə môr′fōz, -fōs) vt., vi. -phosed, -phos·ing to change in form; transform

**met·a·mor·pho·sis** (met′ə môr′fə sis, -môr fō′-) n., pl. -ses (-sēz) [< Gr. *meta*, over + *morphē*, form] 1. a change in form, structure, or function; specif., the physical change undergone by some animals, as of the tadpole to the frog 2. any marked change, as in character, appearance, or condition —met′a·mor′phic adj.

**met·a·phor** (met′ə fôr′) n. [< Gr. *meta*, over + *pherein*, to bear] a figure of speech in which one thing is spoken of as if it were another (Ex.: "all the world's a stage") —**met'a·phor'i·cal** *adj.* —**met'a·phor'i·cal·ly** *adv.*

**met·a·phys·i·cal** (met'ə fiz'i k'l) *adj.* **1.** of, or having the nature of, metaphysics **2.** very abstract or subtle **3.** supernatural

**met'a·phys'ics** (-iks) *n.pl.* [*with sing. v.*] [ < Gr. *meta* (*ta*) *physika*, after (the) *Physics* (of Aristotle)] **1.** the branch of philosophy that seeks to explain the nature of being and reality **2.** speculative philosophy in general

**me·tas·ta·sis** (mə tas'tə sis) *n., pl.* **-ses'** (-sēz') [ < Gr. *meta*, after + *histanai*, to place] the transfer, as of malignant cells, from one part of the body to another through the bloodstream —**me·tas'ta·size'** (-sīz') *vi.* **-sized', -siz'ing**

**met·a·tar·sus** (met'ə tär'səs) *n., pl.* **-si** (-sī) [ModL. < Gr. *meta-*, over + *tarsos*, flat of the foot] the part of the foot between the ankle and toes —**met'a·tar'sal** *adj., n.*

**me·tath·e·sis** (mə tath'ə sis) *n., pl.* **-ses'** (-sēz') [LL. < Gr. *meta*, over + *tithenai*, to place] transposition, specif. of letters or sounds in a word

**mete** (mēt) *vt.* **met'ed, met'ing** [OE. *metan*] to allot; portion (*out*)

**met·em·psy·cho·sis** (mi temp'si kō'sis, met'əm sī-) *n., pl.* **-ses** (-sēz) [LL. < Gr. < *meta*, over + *en*, in + *psyche*, soul] transmigration of souls

**me·te·or** (mēt'ē ər) *n.* [ < Gr. *meta*, beyond + *eōra*, a hovering] **1.** the streak of light, etc. occurring when a meteoroid enters the earth's atmosphere **2.** a meteoroid or meteorite

**me·te·or·ic** (mēt'ē ôr'ik) *adj.* **1.** of a meteor **2.** like a meteor; swift, momentarily brilliant, etc.

**me·te·or·ite** (mēt'ē ə rīt') *n.* a stone or metal mass remaining from a meteoroid fallen to earth

**me'te·or·oid'** (-roid') *n.* a small, solid body traveling through outer space, seen as a streak of light when falling to earth

**me·te·or·ol·o·gy** (mēt'ē ə räl'ə jē) *n.* [see METEOR & -LOGY] the science of the atmosphere and its phenomena; study of weather and climate —**me'te·or·o·log'i·cal** (-ər ə läj'i k'l) *adj.* —**me'te·or·ol'o·gist** *n.*

**me·ter¹** (mēt'ər) *n.* [ < Gr. *metron*, measure] **1.** rhythmic pattern in verse; measured arrangement of syllables according to stress **2.** rhythmic pattern in music **3.** the basic unit of length in the metric system, equal to 39.37 in.

**me·ter²** (mēt'ər) *n.* [ < METE] **1.** an apparatus for measuring and recording the quantity of gas, water, etc. passing through it **2.** *same as* PARKING METER **-me·ter** (mēt'ər, mi tər) [see METER¹] *a suffix meaning:* **1.** a device for measuring [*barometer*] **2.** meter(s) in length [*kilometer, centimeter*]

**meter maid** a woman employed by a

police department to issue summonses for illegal parking, jaywalking, etc.

**meth·a·done** (meth'ə dōn') *n.* [ < its chemical name] a synthetic narcotic drug used in medicine, more potent than morphine and not so habitforming

**meth·ane** (meth'ān) *n.* [ < METHYL] a colorless, odorless, flammable gas formed by the decomposition of vegetable matter, as in marshes

**meth·a·nol** (meth'ə nôl') *n.* [ < METHAN(E) + (ALCOH)OL] a poisonous liquid used as a fuel, solvent, antifreeze, etc.: also called **methyl alcohol**

**me·thinks** (mi thinks') *v.impersonal pt.* **-thought'** [ < OE. *me*, to me + *thyncth*, it seems] [Archaic] it seems to me

**meth·od** (meth'əd) *n.* [ < Fr. < Gr. *meta*, after + *hodos*, a way] **1.** a way of doing anything; process **2.** system in doing things or handling ideas

**me·thod·i·cal** (mə thäd'i k'l) *adj.* characterized by method; orderly; systematic —**me·thod'i·cal·ly** *adv.*

**Meth·od·ist** (meth'ə dist) *n.* a member of a Protestant Christian denomination that developed from the teachings of John Wesley —**Meth'od·ism** *n.*

**meth·od·ol·o·gy** (meth'ə däl'ə jē) *n.* a system of methods, as in a science

**Me·thu·se·lah** (mə thōō'zə lə) *Bible* a patriarch who lived 969 years

**meth·yl** (meth'əl) *n.* [ < Gr. *methy*, wine + *hylē*, wood] a hydrocarbon radical found in methanol

**me·tic·u·lous** (mə tik'yoo ləs) *adj.* [ < L. *metus*, fear] very careful or too careful about details; scrupulous or finicky —**me·tic'u·lous·ly** *adv.*

**mé·tier** (mā tyā') *n.* [Fr., trade] work that one is particularly suited for

**me·tre** (mēt'ər) *n. Brit. sp. of* METER

**met·ric** (met'rik) *adj.* **1.** *same as* METRICAL **2.** *a*) of the meter (unit of length) *b*) of the metric system

**met'ri·cal** *adj.* **1.** of or composed in meter or verse **2.** of or used in measurement —**met'ri·cal·ly** *adv.*

**met·ri·ca·tion** (met'rə kā'shən) *n.* [METRIC + -ATION] a changing over to the metric system of weights and measures —**met'ri·cate'** *vt.* **-cat'ed, -cat'ing**

**met'ri·cize'** (-sīz') *vt.* **-cized', -ciz'ing** to change to the metric system

**metric system** a decimal system of weights and measures whose basic units are the gram (.0022046 pound), the meter (39.37 inches), and the liter (61.025 cubic inches)

**met·ro·nome** (met'rə nōm') *n.* [ < Gr. *metron*, measure + *nomos*, law] a device that beats time at a desired rate, as for piano practice

**me·trop·o·lis** (mə träp'l is) *n., pl.* **-lis·es** [ < Gr. *mētēr*, mother + *polis*, city] **1.** the main city, often the capital, of a country, state, etc. **2.** any large or important city —**met·ro·pol·i·tan** (met'rə päl'i t'n) *adj.*

**met·tle** (met′'l) n. [var. of METAL] spirit; courage; ardor —**on one's mettle** prepared to do one's best

**met′tle·some** (-səm) adj. full of mettle; spirited, ardent, brave, etc.

**mew¹** (myōō) vt. [ult. < L. mutare, to change] to confine: see also MEWS

**mew²** (myōō) n. [echoic] the characteristic vocal sound made by a cat —vi. to make this sound

**mewl** (myōōl) vi. [< MEW²] to cry weakly, like a baby; whimper

**mews** (myōōz) n.pl. [usually with sing. v.] [< MEWS] [Chiefly Brit.] stables or carriage houses, now often made into dwellings, in a court or alley

**Mex.** 1. Mexican 2. Mexico

**Mex·i·co** (mek′si kō′) 1. country in N.America, south of the U.S.: 760,373 sq. mi.; pop. 45,671,000 2. Gulf of, arm of the Atlantic, east of Mexico —**Mex′l·can** (-kən) adj., n.

**Mexico City** capital of Mexico: pop. 3,353,000

**mez·za·nine** (mez′ə nēn′) n. [< It. mezzano, middle] 1. a low-ceilinged story between two main stories, often a balcony over the main floor 2. the lowest balcony section of a theater

**mez′zo-so·pra′no** (met′sō-, mez′ō-) n., pl. -nos, -ni (-nē) [It. < mezzo, medium + SOPRANO] a voice or singer between soprano and contralto

**mfg.** manufacturing

**mfr.** pl. mfrs. manufacturer

**Mg** Chem. magnesium

**mg, mg.** milligram(s)

**Mgr.** Manager

**MHz, Mhz** megahertz

**mi** (mē) n. [ML.] Music the third tone of the diatonic scale

**MI** Michigan

**mi.** 1. mile(s) 2. mill(s)

**Mi·am·i** (mī am′ē) city on the SE coast of Fla.: pop. 335,000

**mi·as·ma** (mī az′mə) n. [< Gr., pollution] a vapor as from marshes, formerly supposed to poison the air

**mi·ca** (mī′kə) n. [L., a crumb] a mineral that crystallizes in thin, flexible layers, resistant to heat

**mice** (mīs) n. pl. of MOUSE

**Mi·chel·an·ge·lo** (mī′k'l an′jə lō′) 1475–1564; It. painter & sculptor

**Mich·i·gan** (mish′ə gən) 1. Middle Western State of the U.S.: 58,216 sq. mi.; pop. 8,875,000; cap. Lansing: abbrev. **Mich.** 2. Lake, one of the Great Lakes, between Mich. & Wis.

**micro-** [< Gr. mikros, small] a combining form meaning: 1. little, small [microfilm] 2. enlarging [microscope] 3. microscopic [microbiology] 4. one millionth [microgram]

**mi·crobe** (mī′krōb) n. [< Gr. mikros, small + bios, life] a microorganism, esp. one causing disease

**mi·cro·cosm** (mī′krə käz′m) n. [see MICRO- & COSMOS] an organism or organization regarded as a world in miniature

**mi′cro·fiche′** (-fēsh′) n. [Fr. < micro- + fiche, small card] a film card on which many pages of greatly reduced microfilm copy are recorded

**mi′cro·film′** n. film on which docu-

ments, etc. are photographed in a reduced size for convenience —vt., vi. to photograph on microfilm

**mi′cro·groove′** n. a very narrow needle-groove, as for a long-playing phonograph record

**mi·crom·e·ter** (mī kräm′ə tər) n. [< Fr.: see MICRO- & -METER] an instrument for measuring very small distances, angles, etc.

**mi·cron** (mī′krän) n. [< Gr. mikros, small] one millionth of a meter

**Mi·cro·ne·sia** (mī′krə nē′zhə) the groups of islands in the Pacific east of Philippines —**Mi′cro·ne′sian** adj., n.

**mi·cro·or·gan·ism** (mī′krō ôr′gə niz′m) n. any microscopic animal or vegetable organism; esp., any of the bacteria, protozoans, viruses, etc.

**mi·cro·phone** (mī′krə fōn′) n. [MICRO- + -PHONE] an instrument for transforming sound waves into corresponding electrical signals

**mi′cro·scope** (-skōp′) n. [see MICRO- & -SCOPE] an instrument consisting of a combination of lenses, for making very small objects, as microorganisms, look larger

**mi′cro·scop′ic** (-skäp′ik) adj. 1. so small as to be invisible or obscure except through a microscope; minute 2. of, with, or like a microscope — **mi′cro·scop′i·cal·ly** adv.

**mi′cro·wave′** n. an electromagnetic wave between 300,000 megahertz and 300 megahertz in frequency

**mid¹** (mid) adj. [OE. midd] middle

**mid²** (mid) prep. [Poet.] amid: also **'mid**

**mid-** a combining form meaning middle or middle part of

**mid′air′** n. any point not in contact with the ground or other surface

**Mi·das** (mī′dəs) Gr. Myth. a king granted the power of turning everything that he touched into gold

**mid·day** (mid′dā′) n., adj. noon

**mid·dle** (mid′'l) adj. [OE. middel] 1. halfway between two given points, times, etc. 2. intermediate 3. [M-] designating a stage in language development intermediate between Old and Modern [Middle English] —n. 1. a point or part halfway between extremes; middle point, time, etc. 2. something intermediate 3. the middle part of the body; waist

**middle age** the time of life between youth and old age —**mid′dle-aged′** adj.

**Middle Ages** the period of European history between ancient and modern times, 476 A.D.–c.1450 A.D.

**Middle America** the conventional or conservative American middle class

**mid′dle-brow′** (-brou′) n. [Colloq.] one regarded as having conventional, middle-class tastes or opinions

**middle class** the social class between the aristocracy or very wealthy and the lower working class

**middle ear** the part of the ear including the eardrum and a cavity containing three small bones; tympanum

**Middle East** 1. area from Afghanistan to Egypt, including the Arabian

Peninsula & Asiatic Turkey 2. the Near East, excluding the Balkans

**Middle English** the English language between c.1100 and c.1500

**mid'dle-man'** *n., pl.* **-men'** 1. a trader who buys from a producer and sells at wholesale or retail 2. a go-between

**mid'dle-most'** *adj. same as* MIDMOST

**mid'dle-of-the-road'** *adj.* avoiding extremes, esp. political extremes

**middle school** in some school systems, a school with usually grades 5 to 8

**mid'dle-weight'** *n.* a boxer or wrestler between a welterweight and a light heavyweight (in boxing, 148-160 lb.)

**Middle West** region of the NC U.S., between the Rocky Mountains & the E border of Ohio —**Middle Western**

**mid·dling** (mid'liŋ) *adj.* of middle size, quality, state, etc.; medium —*adv.* [Colloq.] fairly; moderately —**fair to middling** [Colloq.] moderately good or well

**mid·dy** (mid'ē) *n., pl.* **-dies** 1. [Colloq.] a midshipman 2. a loose blouse with a sailor collar, worn by women and children

**midge** (mij) *n.* [OE. *mycg*] a small, gnatlike insect

**midg·et** (mij'it) *n.* 1. a very small person 2. anything very small of its kind —*adj.* miniature

**mid·land** (mid'lənd) *n.* the middle region of a country; interior —*adj.* in or of the midland; inland

**mid'most'** *adj.* exactly in the middle, or nearest the middle

**mid'night'** (-nīt') *n.* twelve o'clock at night —*adj.* 1. of or at midnight 2. like midnight; very dark

**mid'point'** *n.* a point at or close to the middle or center

**mid·riff** (mid'rif) *n.* [< OE. *midd,* MID¹ + *hrif,* belly] 1. *same as* DIAPHRAGM (sense 1) 2. the middle part of the torso, between the abdomen and the chest

**mid'ship'man** (-ship'mən) *n., pl.* **-men** a student in training to be a naval officer

**midst¹** (midst) *n.* the middle; central part —**in the midst of** 1. in the middle of 2. during

**midst²** (midst) *prep.* [Poet.] in the midst of; amidst: also **'midst**

**mid·stream** (mid'strēm') *n.* the middle of a stream

**mid'sum'mer** *n.* 1. the middle of summer 2. the time of the summer solstice, about June 21

**mid'term'** *adj.* in the middle of the term —*n.* [Colloq.] a midterm examination

**mid'way'** (-wā') *n.* that part of a fair where sideshows, etc. are located —*adj., adv.* in the middle of the way or distance; halfway

**Mid'west'** *n. same as* MIDDLE WEST

**mid'wife'** (-wīf') *n., pl.* **-wives'** [< ME. *mid,* with + *wif,* woman] a

woman who helps women in childbirth —**mid'wife'ry** (-wī'fə rē, -wīf'rē) *n.*

**mid'win'ter** *n.* 1. the middle of winter 2. the time of the winter solstice, about Dec. 22

**mid'year'** *adj.* in the middle of the year —*n.* [Colloq.] a midyear examination

**mien** (mēn) *n.* [short for DEMEAN²] one's appearance, bearing, or manner

**miff** (mif) *vt.* [prob. orig. cry of disgust] [Colloq.] to offend

**MIG** (mig) *n.* [< *Mi*koyan & *Gu*revich, its Soviet designers] a small, fast, highly maneuverable jet military aircraft: also **MiG**

**might¹** (mīt) *v.* [OE. *mihte*] 1. *pt. of* MAY 2. *an auxiliary generally equivalent to* MAY *[it might* rain*]*

**might²** (mīt) *n.* [OE. *miht*] strength, power, or vigor

**might'y** (-ē) *adj.* **-i·er, -i·est** 1. powerful; strong 2. remarkably large, etc.; great —*adv.* [Colloq.] very —**might'i·ly** *adv.* —**might'i·ness** *n.*

**mi·gnon·ette** (min'yə net') *n.* [< Fr. *mignon,* small] a plant with spikes of small, fragrant flowers

**mi·graine** (mī'grān) *n.* [< Gr. *hēmi-,* half + *kranion,* skull] an intense, periodic headache, usually limited to one side of the head

**mi·grant** (mī'grənt) *adj.* migrating —*n.* one that migrates; specif., a farm laborer who moves from place to place to harvest seasonal crops

**mi·grate** (mī'grāt) *vi.* **-grat·ed, -grat·ing** [< L. *migrare*] 1. to settle in another country or region 2. to move to another region with the change in season, as many birds —**mi·gra·to·ry** (mī'grə tôr'ē) *adj.*

**mi·gra·tion** (mī grā'shən) *n.* 1. a migrating 2. a group of people, birds, etc. migrating together

**mi·ka·do** (mi kä'dō) *n., pl.* **-dos** [< Jap. *mi,* exalted + *kado,* gate] [Obs.] an emperor of Japan

**mike** (mīk) *n.* [Colloq.] a microphone

**mil** (mil) *n.* [L. *mille,* thousand] a unit of length, .001 of an inch

**mil.** military

**mi·la·dy, mi·la·di** (mi lā'dē) *n.* [Fr. < Eng. *my lady*] 1. a noblewoman 2. a woman of fashion: advertisers' term

**Mi·lan** (mi lan') city in NW Italy: pop. 1,673,000

**milch** (milch) *adj.* [ME. *milche*] kept for milking *[milch* cows*]*

**mild** (mīld) *adj.* [OE. *milde*] 1. gentle or kind; not severe 2. having a soft, pleasant flavor *[a mild* cheese*]* —**mild'ly** *adv.* —**mild'ness** *n.*

**mil·dew** (mil'dōō') *n.* [OE. *meledeaw,* lit., honeydew] a fungus that attacks some plants or appears on damp cloth, etc. as a whitish coating —*vt., vi.* to affect or be affected with mildew

**mile** (mīl) *n.* [< L. *milia (passuum),* thousand (paces)] a unit of linear measure, equal to 5,280 ft.: the **nautical mile** is 6,076.12 feet

**mile·age** (-ij) *n.* **1.** an allowance per mile for traveling expenses **2.** total miles traveled **3.** the average number of miles that can be traveled, as per gallon of fuel

**mile·post′** *n.* a signpost showing the number of miles to or from a place

**mil·er** (-ər) *n.* one who competes in mile races

**mile·stone′** *n.* **1.** a stone set up to show the distance in miles from some place **2.** a significant event

**mi·lieu** (mēl yoo′) *n.* [Fr. < L. *medius*, middle + *locus*, a place] environment; esp., social setting

**mil·i·tant** (mil′i tənt) *adj.* [< L. *miles*, soldier] **1.** fighting **2.** ready to fight, esp. for some cause —*n.* a militant person —**mil′i·tan·cy** *n.* —**mil′i·tant·ly** *adv.*

**mil′i·ta·rism** (-tər iz′m) *n.* **1.** military spirit **2.** a policy of aggressive military preparedness —**mil′i·ta·rist** *n.* —**mil′i·ta·ris′tic** *adj.*

**mil′i·ta·rize′** (-tə riz′) *vt.* -rized′, -riz′ing to equip and prepare for war

**mil′i·tar′y** (-ter′ē) *adj.* [< L. *miles*, soldier] **1.** of, for, or done by soldiers **2.** of, for, or fit for war **3.** of the army —**the military** the army

**military police** soldiers assigned to carry on police duties for the army

**mil·i·tate** (mil′ə tāt′) *vi.* -tat′ed, -tat′ing [< L. *militare*, be a soldier] to operate or work (*against*)

**mi·li·tia** (mə lish′ə) *n.* [< L. *miles*, soldier] an army composed of citizens called out in time of emergency —**mi·li′tia·man** (-mən) *n., pl.* -men

**milk** (milk) *n.* [OE. *meolc*] **1.** a white liquid secreted by special glands of female mammals for suckling their young; esp., cow's milk **2.** any liquid like this *[coconut milk]* —*vt.* **1.** to squeeze milk from (a cow, goat, etc.) **2.** to extract money, ideas, etc. from as if by milking —**milk′er** *n.*

**milk glass** a nearly opaque whitish glass

**milk′maid′** *n.* a girl or woman who milks cows or works in a dairy

**milk′man′** *n., pl.* -men′ a man who sells or delivers milk for a dairy

**milk of magnesia** a milky-white suspension of magnesium hydroxide in water, used as a laxative and antacid

**milk′shake′** *n.* a drink of milk, flavoring, and ice cream, shaken until frothy

**milk′sop′** (-säp′) *n.* a sissy

**milk tooth** any of the temporary, first teeth of a child or animal

**milk′weed′** *n.* any of a group of plants with a milky juice

**milk·y** (-ē) *adj.* -i·er, -i·est **1.** like milk; esp., white as milk **2.** of or containing milk —**milk′i·ness** *n.*

**Milky Way** a broad, faintly luminous band of very distant stars and clouds of gas, seen across the sky at night

**mill¹** (mil) *n.* [< L. *mola*, millstone] **1.** a building with machinery for grinding grain into flour or meal **2.** any of various machines for grinding, crushing, cutting, etc. **3.** a factory *[a textile mill]* —*vt.* to grind, form, etc.

by or in a mill —*vi.* to move (*around* or *about*) confusedly, as a crowd —**in the mill** in preparation —**through the mill** [Colloq.] through a hard, painful, instructive experience

**mill²** (mil) *n.* [< L. *mille*, thousand] 1/10 of a cent: unit used in calculating

**mil·lage** (mil′ij) *n.* taxation in mills per dollar of valuation

**mil·len·ni·um** (mi len′ē əm) *n., pl.* -ni·ums, -ni·a (-ə) [< L. *mille*, thousand + *annus*, year] **1.** a thousand years **2.** *Theol.* the period of a thousand years during which Christ will reign on earth (with *the*) **3.** any period of great happiness, peace, etc.

**mill·er** (mil′ər) *n.* one who owns or operates a mill, esp. a flour mill

**mil·let** (mil′it) *n.* [< L. *milium*] **1.** a cereal grass whose grain is used for food in Europe and Asia **2.** any of several similar grasses used for forage

**milli-** [< L. *mille*, thousand] *a combining form meaning* a 1000th part of *[millimeter]*

**mil·li·gram** (mil′ə gram′) *n.* one thousandth of a gram: chiefly Brit. sp. **mil′li·gramme′**

**mill′li·me·ter** (-mēt′ər) *n.* one thousandth of a meter (.03937 inch): chiefly Brit. sp. **mil′li·me′tre**

**mil·li·ner** (mil′ə nər) *n.* [< *Milaner*, importer of dress wares from Milan] one who makes or sells women's hats

**mil·li·ner·y** (mil′ə ner′ē) *n.* **1.** women's hats, headdresses, etc. **2.** the work or business of a milliner

**mil·lion** (mil′yən) *n.* [< L. *mille*, thousand] a thousand thousands; 1,000,000 —**mil′lionth** *adj., n.*

**mil·lion·aire′** (-yə ner′) *n.* a person whose wealth comes to at least a million dollars, pounds, francs, etc.

**mill′race′** *n.* the channel in which the water driving a mill wheel runs

**mill′stone′** *n.* **1.** either of a pair of flat, round stones used for grinding grain, etc. **2.** a heavy burden

**mill′stream′** *n.* water flowing in a millrace

**mill′wright′** (-rīt′) *n.* a worker who builds, installs, or repairs the machinery in a mill

**milt** (milt) *n.* [prob. < Scand.] the sex glands or sperm of male fishes

**Mil·ton** (mil′t′n), **John** 1608–74; Eng. poet

**Mil·wau·kee** (mil wô′kē) city in SE Wis.: pop. 717,000

**mime** (mīm) *n.* [< Gr. *mimos*] **1.** the representation of an action, mood, etc. by gestures, not words **2.** a mimic or pantomimist —*vt.* to mimic or pantomime

**mim·e·o·graph** (mim′ē ə graf′) *n.* [< Gr. *mimeomai*, I imitate] a machine for making copies of graphic matter by means of an inked stencil —*vt.* to make (such copies) of

**mi·met·ic** (mi met′ik, mī-) *adj.* [< Gr. *mimeisthai*, to imitate] **1.** imitative **2.** characterized by mimicry

**mim·ic** (mim′ik) *adj.* [< Gr. *mimos*, a mime] **1.** imitative **2.** make-believe —*n.* an imitator; esp., an actor skilled in mimicry —*vt.* -icked, -ick·ing **1.**

to imitate, often so as to ridicule 2.
to copy or resemble closely

**mim'ic·ry** (-rē) *n., pl.* **-ries** the
practice, art, or way of mimicking

**mi·mo·sa** (mi mō'sə) *n.* [see MIME] a
tree, shrub, or herb growing in warm
regions and usually having spikes of
white or pink flowers

**min.** 1. minimum 2. minute(s)

**min·a·ret** (min'ə ret') *n.* [< Ar.
*manārah*, lighthouse] a
high, slender tower at-
tached to a Moslem
mosque

**min·a·to·ry** (min'ə
tôr'ē) *adj.* [< L. *min-
ari*, threaten] menac-
ing

**mince** (mins) *vt.*
minced, minc'ing
[< L. *minutus*, small]
1. to cut up (meat,
etc.) into small pieces
2. to express or do
with affected dainti-      MINARET
ness 3. to lessen the force of [to mince
no words] —*vi.* to speak or act with
affected daintiness —minc'ing *adj.*

**mince'meat'** *n.* a mixture of chopped
apples, spices, raisins, etc., and sometimes meat, used as a filling for a pie
(**mince pie**)

**mind** (mīnd) *n.* [OE. (ge)*mynd*] 1.
memory [to bring to *mind* a story] 2.
opinion [to speak one's *mind*] 3. the
seat of consciousness, in which thinking, feeling, etc. take place 4. intellect
5. *same as* PSYCHE (sense 2) 6. reason;
sanity —*vt.* 1. to pay attention to;
heed 2. to obey 3. to take care of
[*mind* the baby] 4. to be careful about
[*mind* the stairs] 5. to care about;
object to [don't *mind* the noise] —*vi.*
1. to pay attention 2. to be obedient
3. to be careful 4. to care; object
—**bear** (or **keep**) **in mind** to remember —**blow one's mind** [Slang] to
undergo hallucinations, etc. as from
psychedelic drugs —**change one's
mind** to change one's opinion, purpose, etc. —**have in mind** to intend
—**make up one's mind** to reach a
decision —**on one's mind** 1. filling
one's thoughts 2. worrying one —**out
of one's mind** frantic (with worry,
etc.)

**mind'ed** *adj.* 1. having a specified
kind of mind [high-*minded*] 2. inclined

**mind'ful** *adj.* having in mind; aware
or careful (*of*) —**mind'ful·ly** *adv.*
—**mind'ful·ness** *n.*

**mind reader** one who professes ability
to perceive another's thoughts

**mind's eye** the imagination

**mine**[1] (mīn) *pron.* [OE. *min*] that or
those belonging to me [this is mine]

**mine**[2] (mīn) *n.* [MFr.] 1. a large
excavation made in the earth, from
which to extract ores, coal, etc. 2. a
deposit of ore, coal, etc. 3. any great
source of supply 4. *Mil. a)* a tunnel

dug under an enemy's fort, etc., in
which an explosive is placed *b)* an
explosive charge hidden underground
or in the sea, for destroying enemy
vehicles, ships, etc. —*vt., vi.* mined,
min'ing 1. to dig (ores, etc.) from
(the earth) 2. to dig or lay military
mines in or under .3. to undermine

**min'er** *n.* one whose work is digging
coal, ore, etc. in a mine

**min·er·al** (min'ər əl) *n.* [< ML.
*minera*, a mine] 1. an inorganic
substance found naturally in the earth,
as metallic ore 2. any substance
neither vegetable nor animal —*adj.*
of or containing minerals

**mineral jelly** *same as* PETROLATUM

**min·er·al·o·gy** (min'ə räl'ə jē, -ral'-)
*n.* the scientific study of minerals
—**min'er·al'o·gist** *n.*

**mineral oil** a colorless, tasteless oil
derived from petroleum and used as
a laxative

**mineral water** water impregnated
with mineral salts or gases

**Mi·ner·va** (mi nur'və) the Roman
goddess of wisdom and invention

**mi·ne·stro·ne** (min'ə strō'nē) *n.* [It.:
ult. < L. *ministrare*, serve] a thick
vegetable soup in a meat broth

**min·gle** (min'g'l) *vt.* -gled, -gling
[< OE. *mengan*, mix] to mix together;
blend —*vi.* 1. to become mixed or
blended 2. to join or unite with others

**mini-** [< MINI(ATURE)] *a combining
form meaning* miniature, very small,
very short [*miniskirt*]

**min·i·a·ture** (min'ē ə chər, min'i
chər) *n.* [< L. *miniare*, paint red] 1.
a small painting, esp. a portrait 2. a
copy or model on a very small scale
—*adj.* done on a very small scale

**min'i·a·tur·ize'** (-īz') *vt.* -ized',
-iz'ing to make in a small and compact form —**min'i·a·tur'i·za'tion** *n.*

**min·i·bus** (min'ē bus') *n.* a very
small bus

**min·im** (min'im) *n.* [< L. *minimus*,
least] 1. the smallest liquid measure,
about a drop 2. *Music* a half note

**min·i·mize** (min'ə mīz') *vt.* -mized',
-miz'ing to reduce to or estimate at a
minimum

**min'i·mum** (-məm) *n., pl.* -mums,
-ma (-mə) [L., least] 1. the smallest
quantity, number, etc. possible 2. the
lowest degree or point reached —*adj.*
smallest possible, permissible, or
reached: also **min'i·mal**

**min·ion** (min'yən) *n.* [Fr. *mignon*,
darling] 1. a favorite, esp. one who is
a servile follower: term of contempt
2. a subordinate official

**min·is·cule** (min'ə skyōōl') *adj.*
*erroneous sp. of* MINUSCULE

**min·i·skirt** (min'ē skurt') *n.* a very
short skirt ending well above the knee

**min·is·ter** (min'is tər) *n.* [L., a
servant] 1. a person appointed to
head a governmental department 2. a
diplomat representing his government
in a foreign nation 3. one authorized

fat, āpe, cär; ten, ēven; is, bīte; gō, hôrn, tōōl, look; oil, out; up, fur;
chin; she; thin, then; zh, leisure; ŋ, ring; ə for *a* in ago; ', (ä′b'l); ĕ, Fr. coeur;
ŏ, Fr. feu; Fr. mon; ü, Fr. duc; kh, G. ich, doch; ‡ foreign; < derived from

to conduct religious services in a church; pastor —*vi.* **1.** to serve as a minister in a church **2.** to give help (*to*) —**min′is·te′ri·al** (-tir′ē əl) *adj.* —**min′is·trant** (-trənt) *adj., n.*

**min·is·tra′tion** (-trā′shən) *n.* the act of giving help or care; service

**min′is·try** (-trē) *n., pl.* **-tries 1.** the act of ministering, or serving **2.** *a)* the office or function of a clergyman *b)* the clergy **3.** *a)* the department under a minister of government *b)* his term of office *c)* the ministers of a particular government as a group

**mink** (miŋk) *n.* [< Scand.] **1.** a weasellike mammal living on land and in water **2.** its valuable fur

**Min·ne·ap·o·lis** (min′ē ap′ ′l is) city in E Minn.: pop. 434,000

**Min·ne·so·ta** (min′ə sōt′ə) Middle Western State of the U.S.: 84,068 sq. mi.; pop. 3,805,000; cap. St. Paul: abbrev. **Minn.** —**Min′ne·so′tan** *adj., n.*

**min·now** (min′ō) *n.* [< OE. *myne*] any of a number of usually small freshwater fishes, commonly used as bait

**Mi·no·an** (mi nō′ən) *adj.* [< *Minos,* mythical king of Crete] of an advanced prehistoric culture in Crete (c.2800–c.1100 B.C.)

**mi·nor** (mī′nər) *adj.* [L.] **1.** lesser in size, amount, importance, etc. **2.** *Music* lower than the corresponding major by a half tone —*vi. Educ.* to have a secondary field of study (*in*) —*n.* **1.** a person under full legal age **2.** *Educ.* a secondary field of study

**mi·nor·i·ty** (mə nôr′ə tē, mī-) *n., pl.* **-ties 1.** the lesser part or smaller number; less than half **2.** a racial, religious, or political group that differs from the larger, controlling group **3.** the state of being under full legal age

**min·strel** (min′strəl) *n.* [see MINISTER] **1.** a traveling singer of the Middle Ages **2.** a member of a comic variety show (**minstrel show**) in which the performers blacken their faces — **min′strel·sy** (-sē) *n., pl.* **-sies**

**mint¹** (mint) *n.* [< L. < *Juno Moneta,* whose temple was the mint] **1.** a place where money is coined by the government **2.** a large amount —*adj.* new, as if freshly minted —*vt.* to coin (money) —**mint′age** *n.*

**mint²** (mint) *n.* [< Gr. *mintha*] **1.** an aromatic plant whose leaves are used for flavoring **2.** a mint-flavored candy

**mint julep** an iced drink of whiskey or brandy, sugar, and mint leaves

**min·u·end** (min′yoo wend′) *n.* [< L. *minuere,* lessen] the number from which another is to be subtracted

**min·u·et** (min′yoo wet′) *n.* [< Fr. < OFr. *menu,* small] **1.** a slow, stately dance **2.** the music for this

**mi·nus** (mī′nəs) *prep.* [< L. *minor,* less] **1.** less [*four minus two*] **2.** [Colloq.] without [*minus a toe*] —*adj.* **1.** involving subtraction [*a minus sign*] **2.** negative **3.** less than [*a grade of A minus*] —*n.* a sign (—), indicating subtraction or negative quantity: in full **minus sign**

**mi·nus·cule** (mi nus′kyool, min′ə skyool′) *adj.* [L. *minusculus*] tiny

**min·ute¹** (min′it) *n.* [see ff.] **1.** the sixtieth part of an hour or of a degree of an arc **2.** a moment **3.** a specific point in time **4.** [*pl.*] an official record of a meeting, etc. —**the minute** (**that**) just as soon as

**mi·nute²** (mī noot′) *adj.* [< L. *minor,* less] **1.** very small **2.** of little importance **3.** of or attentive to tiny details; precise —**mi·nute′ly** *adv.*

**min′ute·man′** *n., pl.* **-men′** [*also* M-] a member of the American citizen army at the time of the Revolution

**minute steak** (min′it) a small, thin steak that can be cooked quickly

**mi·nu·ti·ae** (mi noo′shi ē′) *n.pl., sing.* **-ti·a** (-shē ə) [see MINUTE²] small or unimportant details

**minx** (miŋks) *n.* [< ?] a pert girl

**mir·a·cle** (mir′ə k′l) *n.* [< L. *mirus,* wonderful] **1.** an event or action that apparently contradicts known scientific laws **2.** a remarkable thing

**mi·rac·u·lous** (mi rak′yoo ləs) *adj.* **1.** having the nature of, or like, a miracle **2.** able to work miracles — **mi·rac′u·lous·ly** *adv.*

**mi·rage** (mi räzh′) *n.* [< VL. *mirare,* look at] an optical illusion, caused by the refraction of light, in which a distant object appears to be nearby

**mire** (mīr) *n.* [< ON. *myrr*] **1.** an area of wet, soggy ground **2.** deep mud; slush —*vt.* **mired, mir′ing 1.** to cause to get stuck as in mire **2.** to soil with mud, etc. —*vi.* to sink in mud —**mir′y** *adj.* **-i·er, -i·est**

**mir·ror** (mir′ər) *n.* [< ML. *mirare,* look at] **1.** a smooth, reflecting surface; esp., a glass coated as with silver **2.** anything giving a true representation —*vt.* to reflect, as in a mirror

**mirth** (murth) *n.* [< OE. *myrig,* pleasant] joyfulness or gaiety, esp. with laughter —**mirth′ful** *adj.*

**MIRV** (murv) *n., pl.* **MIRV's** [*m(ultiple) i(ndependently targeted) r(eentry) v(ehicle)*] an intercontinental ballistic missile whose several warheads can be scattered

**mis-** [< OE. *mis-* or OFr. *mes-*] a *prefix meaning:* **1.** wrong(ly), bad(ly) **2.** no, not

**mis·ad·ven·ture** (mis′əd ven′chər) *n.* a mishap; bad luck

**mis·an·thrope** (mis′ən thrōp′) *n.* [< Gr. *misein,* to hate + *anthrōpos,* man] one who hates or distrusts all people: also **mis·an′thro·pist** (-an′thrə pist) —**mis·an·throp′ic** (-thräp′ik) *adj.* —**mis·an′thro·py** *n.*

**mis′ap·ply′** *vt.* **-plied′, -ply′ing** to apply badly or improperly

**mis·ap·pre·hend** (mis′ap rə hend′) *vt.* to misunderstand —**mis′ap·pre·hen′sion** *n.*

**mis′ap·pro′pri·ate′** *vt.* **-at′ed, -at′ing** to appropriate to a wrong or dishonest use —**mis′ap·pro′pri·a′tion** *n.*

**mis′be·got′ten** *adj.* wrongly or unlawfully begotten; illegitimate

**mis′be·have′** *vt., vi.* **-haved′, -hav′ing** to behave (oneself) wrongly — **mis′be·hav′ior** (-yər) *n.*

**misc. 1.** miscellaneous **2.** miscellany

**mis·cal·cu·late′** *vt., vi.* **-lat′ed,**

-lat'ing to calculate incorrectly; mis-judge —mis'cal·cu·la'tion n.

mis·call' vt. to call by a wrong name

mis·car·ry (mis kar'ē) vi. -ried, -ry·ing 1. to fail; go wrong [the plan miscarried] 2. to fail to arrive: said of mail, etc. 3. to give birth to a fetus before it has developed enough to live —mis·car'riage (-ij) n.

mis·cast' vt. -cast', -cast'ing to cast (an actor or a play) unsuitably

mis·ce·ge·na·tion (mis'i jə nā'shən, mi sej'ə-) n. [< L. miscere, mix + genus, race] marriage or sexual relations between a man and woman of different races

mis·cel·la·ne·ous (mis'ə lā'nē əs) adj. [< L. miscere, mix] consisting of various kinds or qualities

mis·cel·la·ny (mis'ə lā'nē) n., pl. -nies a miscellaneous collection, esp. of literary works

mis·chance' n. bad luck

mis·chief (mis'chif) n. [< OFr. mes-, MIS- + chief, end] 1. harm or damage 2. a cause of harm or annoyance 3. a) a prank b) gay teasing

mis·chie·vous (mis'chi vəs) adj. 1. causing mischief; specif., a) harmful b) prankish 2. inclined to annoy with playful tricks —mis'chie·vous·ly adv.

mis·ci·ble (mis'ə b'l) adj. [< L. miscere, to mix] that can be mixed

mis·con·ceive (mis'kən sēv') vt., vi. -ceived', -ceiv'ing to misunderstand —mis'con·cep'tion (-sep'shən) n.

mis·con·duct n. 1. bad or dishonest management 2. improper behavior

mis·con·strue (mis'kən strōō') vt. -strued', -stru'ing to misinterpret —mis'con·struc'tion n.

mis'count' vt., vi. to count incorrectly —n. an incorrect count

mis·cre·ant (mis'krē ənt) adj. [< OFr. mes-, MIS- + croire, believe] villainous; evil —n. a villain

mis·deal' vt., vi. -dealt', -deal'ing to deal (playing cards) wrongly —n. a wrong deal

mis·deed' n. a wrong or wicked act; crime, sin, etc.

mis·de·mean·or (mis'di mēn'ər) n. Law any minor offense bringing a lesser punishment than a felony

mis'di·rect' vt. to direct wrongly or badly —mis'di·rec'tion n.

mis·do'ing n. wrongdoing

mi·ser (mī'zər) n. [L., wretched] a greedy, stingy person who hoards money for its own sake —mi'ser·ly adj. —mi'ser·li·ness n.

mis·er·a·ble (miz'ər ə b'l) adj. 1. in misery 2. causing misery, discomfort, etc. 3. bad; inadequate 4. pitiable —mis'er·a·bly adv.

mis·er·y (miz'ər ē) n., pl. -ies [see MISER] 1. a condition of great suffering; distress 2. a cause of such suffering; pain, poverty, etc.

mis·file' vt. -filed', -fil'ing to file (papers, etc.) in the wrong place

mis·fire' vi. -fired', -fir'ing 1. to fail to go off or ignite properly 2. to fail to achieve a desired effect —n. a misfiring

mis·fit' vt., vi. -fit'ted, -fit'ting to fit badly —n. 1. an improper fit 2. a maladjusted person

mis·for·tune n. 1. ill fortune; trouble 2. a mishap, calamity, etc.

mis·giv·ing (-giv'iŋ) n. [often pl.] a disturbed feeling of fear, doubt, etc.

mis·gov·ern vt. to govern badly —mis·gov'ern·ment n.

mis·guide' (-gīd') vt. -guid'ed, -guid'ing to lead into error or misconduct; mislead —mis·guid'ance n.

mis·han'dle vt. -died, -dling to handle badly or roughly; abuse

mis·hap (mis'hap) n. an unlucky or unfortunate accident

mis·hear' vt., vi. -heard', -hear'ing to hear wrongly

mish·mash (mish'mash') n. a jumble

mis'in·form' vt. to supply with false or misleading information —mis'in·for·ma'tion n.

mis'in·ter'pret vt. to interpret wrongly; understand or explain incorrectly —mis'in·ter'pre·ta'tion n.

mis·judge' vt., vi. -judged', -judg'ing to judge wrongly or unfairly

mis·la'bel vt., vi. -beled or -belled, -bel·ing or -bel·ling to label incorrectly or improperly

mis·lay' (-lā') vt. -laid', -lay'ing 1. to put in a place afterward forgotten 2. to put down or install improperly

mis·lead' (-lēd') vt. -led', -lead'ing 1. to lead in a wrong direction 2. to deceive or delude 3. to lead into wrongdoing

mis·man'age vt., vi. -aged, -ag·ing to manage badly or dishonestly —mis·man'age·ment n.

mis·match' vt. to match badly or unsuitably —n. a bad match

mis·mate' vt., vi. -mat'ed, -mat'ing to mate badly or unsuitably

mis·name' vt. -named', -nam'ing to give an inappropriate name to

mis·no·mer (mis nō'mər) n. [< MIS- + L. nomen, name] a wrong name

mi·sog·y·ny (mi säj'ə nē) n. [< Gr. misein, to hate + gynē, woman] hatred of women —mi·sog'y·nist n.

mis·place' vt. -placed', -plac'ing 1. to put in a wrong place 2. to bestow (one's trust, etc.) unwisely 3. same as MISLAY (sense 1)

mis·play' vt., vi. to play wrongly or badly, as in games or sports —n. a wrong or bad play

mis·print' vt. to print incorrectly —n. a printing error

mis·pri·sion (-prizh'ən) n. [< OFr. mesprendre, take wrongly] misconduct or neglect of duty by a public official

mis'pro·nounce' vt., vi. -nounced', -nounc'ing to pronounce differently from the accepted pronunciations —mis'pro·nun'ci·a'tion n.

mis·quote' vt., vi. -quot'ed, -quot'-

**ing** to quote incorrectly —**mis'quo·ta'tion** (-kwō tā'shən) n.

**mis·read'** (-rēd') vt., vi. -**read'** (-red'), -**read'ing** to read wrongly, esp. so as to misunderstand

**mis'rep·re·sent'** vt. to represent falsely; give an untrue idea of —**mis'rep·re·sen·ta'tion** n.

**mis·rule'** vt. -**ruled'**, -**rul'ing** to rule badly; misgovern —n. misgovernment

**miss**[1] (mis) vt. [OE. missan] 1. to fail to hit, meet, catch, do, attend, see, hear, etc. 2. to let (a chance, etc.) go by 3. to avoid [he missed being hit] 4. to notice or feel the absence or loss of —vi. 1. to fail to hit 2. to fail to be successful 3. to misfire, as an engine —n. a failure to hit, obtain, etc.

**miss**[2] (mis) n., pl. **miss'es** [< MISTRESS] 1. [M-] a title used before the name of an unmarried woman or girl 2. a young unmarried woman or girl

**mis·sal** (mis'l) n. [< LL. missa, Mass] R.C.Ch. the official, liturgical book containing the prayers used in celebrating Mass throughout the year

**mis·shape'** vt. -**shaped'**, -**shap'ing** to shape badly; deform —**mis·shap'en** adj.

**mis·sile** (mis'l) n. [< L. mittere, send] an object, as a bullet, spear, rocket, etc., to be thrown, fired, or launched toward a target

**mis'sile·ry, mis'sil·ry** (-rē) n. 1. the science of building and launching guided missiles 2. such missiles

**miss·ing** (mis'iŋ) adj. absent; lost

**mis·sion** (mish'ən) n. [< L. mittere, send] 1. a sending out or being sent out to perform a special duty 2. a) a group of missionaries b) its headquarters 3. a diplomatic delegation 4. a group of technicians, specialists, etc. sent to a foreign country 5. the special duty for which one is sent 6. a special task to which one devotes his life; calling

**mis·sion·ar·y** (-er'ē) adj. of religious missions —n., pl. -**ies** a person sent out by his church to preach and make converts in a foreign country

**Mis·sis·sip·pi** (mis'ə sip'ē) 1. river in C U.S., flowing from N Minn. to the Gulf of Mexico 2. Southern State of the U.S.: 47,716 sq. mi.; pop. 2,217,000; cap. Jackson: abbrev. **Miss.** —**Mis'sis·sip'pi·an** adj., n.

**mis·sive** (mis'iv) n. [< L. mittere, send] a letter or written message

**Mis·sour·i** (mi zoor'ē) 1. river in WC U.S., flowing from NW Mont. to the Mississippi 2. Middle Western State of the U.S.: 69,686 sq. mi.; pop. 4,677,000; cap. Jefferson City — **Mis·sour'i·an** adj., n.

**mis·spell'** vt., vi. -**spelled'** or -**spelt'**, -**spell'ing** to spell incorrectly

**mis·spend'** vt. -**spent'**, -**spend'ing** to spend improperly or wastefully

**mis·state'** vt. -**stat'ed**, -**stat'ing** to state incorrectly or falsely —**mis·state'ment** n.

**mis·step'** n. 1. a wrong or awkward step 2. a mistake in conduct

**mist** (mist) n. [OE.] 1. a large mass of water vapor, less dense than a fog 2. anything that dims or obscures —vt., vi. to make or become misty

**mis·take** (mi stāk') vt. -**took'**, -**tak'en**, -**tak'ing** [< ON. mistaka, take wrongly] to understand or perceive wrongly —vi. to make a mistake —n. an idea, answer, act, etc. that is wrong; error or blunder —**mis·tak'a·ble** adj.

**mis·tak'en** adj. 1. wrong; having an incorrect understanding 2. incorrect: said of ideas, etc.

**mis·ter** (mis'tər) n. [< MASTER] 1. [M-] a title used before the name of a man or his office and usually written Mr. 2. [Colloq.] sir

**mis·time** (mis tīm') vt. -**timed'**, -**tim'ing** to do or say at the wrong time

**mis·tle·toe** (mis'l tō') n. [< OE. mistel, mistletoe + tan, a twig] a parasitic evergreen plant with yellowish flowers and waxy white, poisonous berries

**mis·took** (mi stook') pt. of MISTAKE

**mis·treat'** vt. to treat wrongly or badly —**mis·treat'ment** n.

**mis·tress** (mis'tris) n. [< OFr., fem. of maistre, master] 1. a woman who is head of a household or institution 2. a woman, nation, etc. that has control or power 3. a woman with whom a man is having a prolonged affair 4. [Chiefly Brit.] a woman schoolteacher 5. [M-] formerly, a title used before the name of a woman: now replaced by Mrs. or Miss

**mis·tri·al** (mis trī'əl) n. Law a trial made void as because of an error in proceedings or the inability of the jury to reach a verdict

**mis·trust'** n. lack of trust or confidence —vt., vi. to have no trust in; doubt —**mis·trust'ful** adj.

**mist·y** (mis'tē) adj. -**i·er**, -**i·est** 1. of, like, or covered with mist 2. blurred, as by mist; vague —**mist'i·ly** adv.

**mis·un·der·stand'** vt. -**stood'**, -**stand'ing** to fail to understand correctly; misinterpret

**mis'un·der·stand'ing** n. 1. a failure to understand; mistake of meaning, etc. 2. a quarrel or disagreement

**mis·use** (mis yōōz'; for n. -yōōs') vt. -**used'**, -**us'ing** 1. to use improperly 2. to treat badly or harshly; abuse —n. incorrect or improper use

**mite** (mīt) n. [OE.] 1. a tiny arachnid, often parasitic upon animals or plants 2. a very small sum of money 3. a very small creature or object

**mi·ter** (mīt'ər) n. [< Gr. mitra, headband] 1. a tall, ornamented cap worn by bishops and abbots 2. Carpentry a joint formed by fitting together two pieces beveled to form a corner: also **miter joint**

MITER JOINT

**mit·i·gate** (mit'ə gāt') vt., vi. -**gat'ed**, -**gat'ing** [< L. mitis, mild] to make or become less severe, less painful, etc. —**mit'i·ga'tion** n.

**mi·to·sis** (mī tō′sis) *n.* [< Gr. *mitos*, thread] the process by which a cell divides into two so that the nucleus of each new cell has the full number of chromosomes —**mi·tot′ic** (-tät′ik) *adj.*

**mitt** (mit) *n.* [< ff.] **1.** a glove covering the hand and forearm, but only part of the fingers **2.** [Slang] a hand **3.** *a*) *Baseball* a padded glove, worn for protection *b*) a boxing glove

**mit·ten** (mit′n) *n.* [< OFr. *mitaine*] a glove with a thumb but no separately divided fingers

**mix** (miks) *vt.* **mixed** or **mixt, mix′-ing** [< L. *miscere*] **1.** to blend together in a single mass **2.** to make by blending ingredients [to *mix* a cake] **3.** to combine [*mix* work and play] —*vi.* **1.** to be mixed or blended **2.** to get along together —*n.* **1.** a mixture **2.** a beverage for mixing with alcoholic liquor —**mix up 1.** to mix thoroughly **2.** to confuse **3.** to involve or implicate (*in*) —**mix′a·ble** *adj.* —**mix′er** *n.*

**mixed** (mikst) *adj.* **1.** blended **2.** made up of different parts, classes, races, sexes, etc. **3.** confused

**mixed number** a number made up of a whole number and a fraction, as 8⅔

**mix·ture** (miks′chər) *n.* **1.** a mixing or being mixed **2.** something mixed

**mix′-up′** *n.* confusion; tangle

**miz·zen·mast** (miz′′n məst, -mast′) *n.* [< L. *medius*, middle] the mast closest to the stern of a ship

**Mlle.** *pl.* **Mlles.** Mademoiselle

**mm, mm.** millimeter; millimeters

**MM.** Messieurs

**Mme.** *pl.* **Mmes.** Madame

**Mn** *Chem.* manganese

**MN** Minnesota

**mne·mon·ic** (nē män′ik) *adj.* [< Gr. *mnēmōn*, mindful] of or helping the memory

**Mo., MO** Missouri

**mo.** *pl.* **mos.** month

**moan** (mōn) *n.* [prob. < OE. *mænan*, complain] a low, mournful sound as of sorrow or pain —*vi., vt.* **1.** to say with or utter a moan **2.** to complain

**moat** (mōt) *n.* [< OFr. *mote*, mound] a deep, broad ditch, often filled with water, around a fortress or castle

**mob** (mäb) *n.* [< L. *mobile* (*vulgus*), movable (crowd)] **1.** a disorderly, lawless crowd **2.** any crowd **3.** the masses: contemptuous term **4.** [Slang] a gang of criminals —*vt.* **mobbed, mob′bing 1.** to crowd around and attack, annoy, etc. **2.** to throng

**Mo·bile** (mō bēl′) seaport in SW Ala.: pop. 190,000

**mo·bile** (mō′b′l, -bēl) *adj.* [< L. *movere,* to move] **1.** moving or movable **2.** movable by means of a motor vehicle [a *mobile* X-ray unit] **3.** that can change rapidly or easily; adaptable **4.** characterized by ease in change of social status —*n.* (-bēl) a piece of abstract sculpture which aims to depict movement, as by an arrangement of thin forms, rings, etc. suspended and set in motion by air currents —**mo·bil′i·ty** (-bil′ə tē) *n.*

**mobile home** a large trailer outfitted as a home

**mo′bi·lize′** (-bə līz′) *vt., vi.* **-lized′, -liz′ing** to make or become organized and ready, as for war —**mo′bi·li·za′-tion** *n.*

**mob·ster** (mäb′stər) *n.* [Slang] a gangster

**moc·ca·sin** (mäk′ə s′n) *n.* [< Am-Ind.] **1.** a heelless slipper of soft, flexible leather **2.** any similar heeled slipper **3.** *same as* WATER MOCCASIN

**mo·cha** (mō′kə) *n.* a choice grade of coffee grown orig. in Arabia —*adj.* flavored with coffee and, often, chocolate

**mock** (mäk) *vt.* [< OFr. *mocquer*] **1.** to ridicule **2.** to mimic, as in fun or derision **3.** to defy and make futile —*vi.* to express scorn, ridicule, etc. —*adj.* sham; imitation

**mock′er·y** *n., pl.* **-ies 1.** a mocking **2.** one receiving or deserving ridicule **3.** a false or derisive imitation

**mock′ing·bird′** *n.* an American bird that imitates the calls of other birds

**mock′-up′** *n.* [< Fr. *maquette*] a model built to scale, often full-sized, for teaching, testing, etc.

**mod** (mäd) *adj.* [< MODERN] ultra-stylish in the mode of the 1960's

**mode** (mōd) *n.* [< L. *modus*] **1.** a manner or way of acting, doing, or being **2.** customary usage, or current fashion **3.** *Gram. same as* MOOD²

**mod·el** (mäd′′l) *n.* [< L. *modus*, a measure] **1.** a small representation of a planned or existing object **2.** a person or thing regarded as a standard of excellence to be imitated **3.** a style or design **4.** *a*) one who poses for an artist or photographer *b*) one employed to display clothes by wearing them —*adj.* **1.** serving as a model **2.** representative of others of the same style, etc. [a *model* home] —*vt.* **-eled** or **-elled, -el·ing** or **-el·ling 1.** *a*) to make a model of *b*) to plan or form after a model **2.** to display (clothes) by wearing —*vi.* to serve as a model (sense 4)

**mod·er·ate** (mäd′ər it; *for v.* -ə rāt′) *adj.* [< L. *moderare,* restrain] **1.** within reasonable limits; avoiding extremes **2.** mild; calm **3.** of medium quality, amount, etc. —*n.* one holding moderate opinions —*vt., vi.* **-at′ed, -at′ing 1.** to make or become moderate **2.** to preside over (a meeting, etc.) —**mod′er·ate·ly** *adv.*

**mod′er·a′tion** *n.* **1.** a moderating **2.** avoidance of extremes **3.** calmness

**mod′er·a′tor** *n.* one who presides at an assembly, debate, etc.

**mod·ern** (mäd′ərn) *adj.* [< L. *modo,* just now] **1.** of the present or recent times; specif., up-to-date **2.** [*often* M-] designating the most recent form of a language —*n.* a person living in modern times, with modern ideas, etc.

**Modern English** the English language since about the mid-15th cent.

**mod′ern·ism** n. (a) modern usage, practice, thought, etc. —**mod′ern·ist** n., adj. —**mod′ern·is′tic** adj.

**mod′ern·ize′** vt., vi. **-ized′, -iz′ing** to make or become modern —**mod′ern·i·za′tion** n.

**mod·est** (mäd′ist) adj. [< L. modus, measure] **1.** not vain or boastful; unassuming **2.** shy or reserved **3.** decorous; decent **4.** not extreme; unpretentious —**mod′est·ly** adv. —**mod′es·ty** n.

**mod·i·cum** (mäd′i kəm) n. [L., moderate] a small amount; bit

**mod·i·fy** (mäd′ə fī′) vt. **-fied′, -fy′ing** [< L. modificare, to limit] **1.** to change partially in character, form, etc. **2.** to limit slightly **3.** Gram. to limit in meaning; qualify —**mod′i·fi·ca′tion** n. —**mod′i·fi′er** n.

**mod·ish** (mōd′ish) adj. fashionable; stylish —**mod′ish·ness** n.

**mod·u·lar** (mäj′ə lər) adj. of modules

**mod·u·late′** (-lāt′) vt. **-lat′ed, -lat′ing** [< L. modus, measure] **1.** to regulate or adjust **2.** to vary the pitch, intensity, etc. of (the voice) **3.** to vary the frequency of (radio waves, etc.) —**mod′u·la′tion** n. —**mod′u·la′tor** n.

**mod·ule** (mäj′ool) n. [Fr. < L. modus, measure] **1.** a standard or unit of measurement, as of building materials **2.** any of a set of units to be variously fitted together **3.** a detachable unit with a specific function, as in a spacecraft

**mo·gul** (mō′gul) n. [Per. Mughul, Mongol] a powerful or important person

**mo·hair** (mō′her) n. [< Ar. mukhayyar] **1.** the hair of the Angora goat **2.** yarn or fabric made of this

**Mo·ham·med** (mō ham′id) 570?-632 A.D.; Arabian prophet; founder of the Moslem religion

**Mo·ham′med·an** adj., n. same as Moslem —**Mo·ham′med·an·ism** n.

**moi·e·ty** (moi′ə tē) n., pl. **-ties** [< L. medius, middle] **1.** a half **2.** an indefinite part

**moire** (mwär, môr) n. [Fr.] a fabric, esp. silk, etc., having a wavy pattern: also **moi·ré** (mwä rā′, mô-)

**moist** (moist) adj. [< L. mucus, mucus] slightly wet; damp —**moist′ly** adv. —**moist′ness** n.

**mois·ten** (mois′'n) vt., vi. to make or become moist

**mois′ture** (-chər) n. water or other liquid causing a slight wetness

**mois′tur·ize′** (-īz′) vt., vi. **-ized′, -iz′ing** to make (the skin, air, etc.) moist —**mois′tur·iz′er** n.

**Mo·ja·ve Desert** (mō hä′vē) desert in SE Calif.: also **Mohave Desert**

**mo·lar** (mō′lər) adj. [< L. mola, millstone] designating a tooth or teeth adapted for grinding —n. a molar tooth

**mo·las·ses** (mə las′iz) n. [< L. mel, honey] a thick, dark syrup produced during the refining of sugar

**mold¹** (mōld) n. [< L. modus, meas-

ure] **1.** a hollow form for giving a certain shape to something plastic or molten **2.** a frame on which something is modeled **3.** a pattern; model **4.** something formed in or on a mold **5.** distinctive character —vt. **1.** to make in or on a mold **2.** to form; shape

**mold²** (mōld) n. [ME. moul] **1.** a fungus producing a furry growth on the surface of organic matter **2.** this growth —vi. to become moldy

**mold³** (mōld) n. [OE. molde] loose, soft soil rich in decayed organic matter

**mold′board** n. a curved plate on a plowshare, for turning over the soil

**mold·er** (mōl′dər) vi. [< OE. molde, dust] to crumble into dust

**mold·ing** (mōl′diŋ) n. **1.** the act of one that molds **2.** something molded **3.** a shaped strip of wood, etc., as around the upper walls of a room

**mold·y** (mōl′dē) adj. **-i·er, -i·est 1.** covered or overgrown with mold **2.** musty or stale —**mold′i·ness** n.

**mole¹** (mōl) n. [OE. mal] a small, congenital spot on the human skin, usually dark-colored and raised

**mole²** (mōl) n. [ME. molle] a small, burrowing mammal with soft fur

**mole³** (mōl) n. [< L. moles, dam] a breakwater

MOLE

**mol·e·cule** (mäl′ə kyool′) n. [< L. dim. of moles, a mass] **1.** the smallest particle of an element or compound that can exist in the free state and still retain the characteristics of the substance **2.** a small particle —**mo·lec·u·lar** (mə lek′yə lər) adj.

**mole′hill′** n. a small ridge of earth formed by a burrowing mole

**mole·skin** (mōl′skin) n. **1.** the fur of the mole **2.** a napped cotton fabric

**mo·lest** (mə lest′) vt. [< L. moles, a burden] **1.** to annoy or to meddle with so as to trouble or harm **2.** to make improper sexual advances to —**mo·les·ta·tion** (mō′les tā′shən) n.

**Mo·lière** (mōl yer′) 1622-73; Fr. dramatist

**moll** (mäl) n. [Slang] a gangster's mistress

**mol·li·fy** (mäl′ə fī′) vt. **-fied′, -fy′ing** [< L. mollis, soft + facere, make] **1.** to soothe; appease **2.** to make less severe or violent

**mol·lusk, mol·lusc** (mäl′əsk) n. [< L. mollis, soft] any of a group of invertebrates, as oysters, snails, squids, etc., characterized by a soft body often enclosed in a shell

**mol·ly·cod·dle** (mäl′ē käd′'l) n. [< Molly, dim. of Mary + coddle] a man or boy used to being coddled —vt. **-dled, -dling** to pamper; coddle

**molt** (mōlt) vi. [< L. mutare, to change] to shed hair, skin, horns, etc. prior to replacement by a new growth, as reptiles, birds, etc.

**mol·ten** (mōl′t'n) adj. [archaic pp. of melt] **1.** melted by heat **2.** made by being melted and cast in a mold

**mo·lyb·de·num** (mə lib/də nəm) *n.*
[ < Gr. *molybdos*, lead] a silvery metallic chemical element, used in alloys

**mom** (mäm) *n.* [Colloq.] mother

**mo·ment** (mō/mənt) *n.* [ < L. *momentum*, movement] 1. an indefinitely
brief period of time; instant 2. a
definite point in time 3. a brief time of
importance 4. importance

**mo·men·tar·i·ly** (mō/mən ter/ə lē)
*adv.* 1. for a short time 2. in an
instant 3. at any moment

**mo·men·tar·y** (mō/mən ter/ē) *adj.*
lasting only for a moment; passing

**mo·men·tous** (mō men/təs) *adj.* of
great moment; very important

**mo·men·tum** (mō men/təm) *n., pl.*
**-tums, -ta** (-tə) [L.: see MOMENT] the
impetus of a moving object, equal to
the product of its mass and its velocity

**mom·my** (mäm/ē) *n., pl.* **-mies**
mother: a child's word

**Mon·a·co** (män/ə kō′) principality on
the Mediterranean; enclave in SE
France: 1/2 sq. mi.; pop. 25,000

**mon·arch** (män/ərk) *n.* [ < Gr.
*monos*, alone + *archein*, to rule] a
hereditary ruler; king, queen, etc. —
**mo·nar·chi·cal** (mə när/ki k′l) *adj.*

**mon·arch·ist** (-ər kist) *n.* one who
favors monarchical government

**mon·arch·y** (-kē) *n., pl.* **-ies** a
government or state headed by a
monarch

**mon·as·ter·y** (män/ə ster/ē) *n., pl.*
**-ies** [ < Gr. *monos*, alone] the residence of a group of monks or nuns

**mo·nas·tic** (mə nas/tik) *adj.* of or
characteristic of monks or nuns,
ascetic: also **mo·nas/ti·cal** —**mo·
nas/ti·cism** (-tə siz′m) *n.*

**mon·au·ral** (män ôr/əl) *adj.* of sound
reproduction using a single channel to
carry and reproduce sound

**Mon·day** (mun/dē, -dā) *n.* [OE.
*monandæg*, moon's day] the second
day of the week: abbrev. **Mon.**

**mon·e·tar·y** (män/ə ter/ē, mun/-)
*adj.* [ < L. *moneta*, a MINT¹] 1. of the
coinage or currency of a country 2. of
money; pecuniary

**mon·ey** (mun/ē) *n., pl.* **-eys, -ies** [ <
L. *moneta*, a MINT¹] 1. stamped pieces
of metal, or any paper notes, authorized by a government as a medium of
exchange 2. property; wealth —**in
the money** [Slang] 1. among the
winners in a race, etc. 2. wealthy —
**make money** to gain profits —**put
money into** to invest money in

**mon·ey·bag** *n.* 1. a bag for money
2. [*pl., with sing. v.*] [Colloq.] a rich
person

**money belt** a belt with a compartment to hold money

**mon·eyed** (mun/ēd) *adj.* rich; wealthy

**mon·ey·mak·er** *n.* 1. one good at
acquiring money 2. something financially profitable —**mon/ey·mak/ing**
*adj., n.*

**money of account** a monetary denomination not issued as currency or

a coin but used in keeping accounts

**money order** an order for payment
of a specified sum of money, issued for
a fee at one post office, bank, etc.
and payable at another

**mon·ger** (muŋ/gər) *n.* [ < OE.
*mangere*] [Chiefly Brit.] a dealer;
trader

**Mon·gol** (mäŋ/gəl, -gōl) *adj., n. same
as* MONGOLIAN

**Mon·go·li·a** (mäŋ gō/lē ə) region in
EC Asia, consisting of a country
(**Mongolian People's Republic**,
592,600 sq. mi.; pop. 1,121,000) and a
region in China (**Inner Mongolia**)

**Mon·go/li·an** *adj.* 1. of Mongolia,
its people, or their culture 2. *same as:*
a) MONGOLOID b) MONGOLIC —*n.* 1.
a native of Mongolia 2. *same as:* a)
MONGOLOID b) MONGOLIC

**Mon·gol·ic** (mäŋ gäl/ik) *adj.* designating or of a subfamily of languages
spoken in Mongolia —*n.* any of these
languages

**Mon·gol·oid** (mäŋ/gə loid′) *adj.* 1.
of the Mongolians 2. designating or of
one of the major groups of mankind,
including most of the peoples of Asia
—*n.* a member of the Mongoloid group

**mon·goose** (mäŋ/gōōs) *n., pl.* **-goos-
es** [ < native Indian name] a ferret-
like, flesh-eating mammal of the Old
World, that kills snakes, etc.

**mon·grel** (muŋ/grəl, mäŋ/-) *n.* [ <
OE. *gemong*, mixture] an animal or
plant, esp. a dog, of mixed breed —*adj.*
of mixed breed, origin, character, etc.

**mon·ied** (mun/ēd) *adj. same as*
MONEYED

**mon·i·ker, mon·ick·er** (män/i kər)
*n.* [ < ?] [Slang] a person's name

**mo·ni·tion** (mō nish/ən) *n.* [ < L.
*monere*, warn] admonition; warning

**mon·i·tor** (män/ə tər) *n.* [ < L.
*monere*, warn] 1. a student chosen to
help the teacher 2. any device for
regulating the performance of a machine, aircraft, etc. 3. *Radio & TV* a
receiver for checking the quality of
transmission —*vt., vi.* to watch or
check on (a person or thing)

**monk** (muŋk) *n.* [ < Gr. *monos*, alone]
a man who joins a religious order living
in retirement —**monk/ish** *adj.*

**mon·key** (muŋ/kē) *n., pl.* **-keys** [ < ?
Fr. or Sp. *mona*, ape + LowG. -*ke*,
-KIN] any of the primates except man
and the lemurs; specif., any of the
smaller, long-tailed primates —*vi.*
[Colloq.] to play, trifle, or meddle

**monkey business** [Colloq.] foolishness, mischief, or deceit

**mon/key·shines** (-shīnz′) *n.pl.*
playful tricks or pranks

**monkey wrench** a wrench with an
adjustable jaw —**throw a monkey
wrench into** [Colloq.] to disrupt the
orderly functioning of

**monk's cloth** a heavy cloth with a
basket weave, used for drapes, etc.

**mon·o** (män/ō) *n. short for* MONO-
NUCLEOSIS

---

fat, āpe, cär; ten, ēven; is, bīte; gō, hôrn, tōōl, look; oil, out; up, fur;
chin; she; thin, then; zh, leisure; ŋ, ring; ə for *a* in ago; ′, (ā′b'l); ë, Fr. coeur;
ö, Fr. feu; Fr. mon; ü, Fr. duc; kh, G. ich, doch; ‡ foreign; < derived from

**mono-** [< Gr. *monos*, single] *a prefix meaning* one, alone, single

**mon·o·cle** (män′ə k'l) *n.* [ult. < Gr. *monos*, single + L. *oculus*, eye] an eyeglass for one eye only

**mo·nog·a·my** (mə näg′ə mē) *n.* [ult. < Gr. *monos*, single + *gamos*, marriage] the practice or state of being married to only one person at a time —**mo·nog′a·mous** *adj.*

**mon·o·gram** (män′ə gram′) *n.* [< Gr. *monos*, single + *gramma*, letter] the initials of a name, combined in a single design —*vt.* -**grammed′**, -**gram′ming** to put a monogram on

**mon·o·graph** (män′ə graf′) *n.* [MONO- + -GRAPH] a book or paper, esp. a scholarly one, on a single subject

**mon·o·lin·gual** (män′ə liŋ′gwəl) *adj.* using or knowing only one language

**mon′o·lith′** (-lith′) *n.* [< Gr. *monos*, single + *lithos*, stone] 1. a single large block of stone, as one made into an obelisk, etc. 2. any massive, unyielding structure —**mon′o·lith′ic** *adj.*

**mon′o·logue′**, **mon′o·log′** (-lôg′) *n.* [< Gr. *monos*, single + *legein*, speak] 1. a long speech 2. a soliloquy 3. a skit, etc. for one actor only

**mon·o·ma·ni·a** (män′ə mā′nē ə) *n.* an excessive interest in or enthusiasm for some one thing; craze —**mon′o·ma′ni·ac′** (-ak′) *n.* —**mon′o·ma·ni′a·cal** (-mə nī′ə k'l) *adj.*

**mon′o·nu·cle·o′sis** (-nōō′klē ō′sis) *n.* [MONO- + NUCLE(US) + -OSIS] an acute disease, esp. of young people, with fever, swollen lymph nodes, etc.

**mon′o·phon′ic** (-fän′ik) *adj.* of sound reproduction using a single channel to carry and reproduce sounds

**mo·nop·o·list** (mə näp′ə list) *n.* one who has a monopoly or favors monopoly —**mo·nop′o·lis′tic** *adj.*

**mo·nop′o·lize′** (-līz′) *vt.* -**lized′**, -**liz′ing** 1. to get, have, or exploit a monopoly of 2. to get full control of

**mo·nop′o·ly** (-lē) *n., pl.* -**lies** [< Gr. *monos*, single + *pōlein*, sell] 1. exclusive control of a commodity or service in a given market 2. such control granted by a government 3. something held as a monopoly 4. a company that has a monopoly

**mon·o·rail** (män′ə rāl′) *n.* a single rail that is a track for cars suspended from it or balanced on it

**mon′o·syl′la·ble** (-sil′ə b'l) *n.* a word of one syllable —**mon′o·syl·lab′ic** (-si lab′ik) *adj.*

**mon′o·the·ism** (-thē iz′m) *n.* [MONO- + THEISM] the doctrine or belief that there is only one God —**mon′o·the·ist** *n.* —**mon′o·the·is′tic** *adj.*

**mon′o·tone′** (-tōn′) *n.* [see MONO- & TONE] 1. utterance of successive words without change of pitch or key 2. tiresome sameness of style, color, etc. 3. a single, unchanging tone

**mo·not·o·nous** (mə nät′'n əs) *adj.* 1. going on in the same tone 2. having no variety 3. tiresome because unvarying —**mo·not′o·ny** *n.*

**mon·ox·ide** (mə näk′sīd) *n.* an oxide with one atom of oxygen per molecule

**Mon·roe** (mən rō′), **James** 1758–1831; 5th president of the U.S. (1817–25)

**mon·sieur** (mə syur′; *Fr.* mə syö′) *n., pl.* **mes·sieurs** (mes′ərz; *Fr.* mâ syö′) [*Fr.*, lit., my lord] a man; gentleman: French title [M-] equivalent to *Mr.* or *Sir*

**Mon·si·gnor** (män sēn′yər) *n.* [It., lit., my lord] a title given to certain Roman Catholic prelates

**mon·soon** (män sōōn′) *n.* [< Ar. *mausim*, a season] 1. a seasonal wind of the Indian Ocean and S Asia 2. the rainy season during which this wind blows from the southwest

**mon·ster** (män′stər) *n.* [< L. *monere*, warn] 1. any greatly malformed plant or animal 2. any grotesque imaginary creature 3. a very wicked person 4. any huge animal or thing —*adj.* huge

**mon·strance** (män′strəns) *n.* [ult. < L. *monstrare*, to show] *R.C.Ch.* a receptacle for displaying the consecrated host

**mon·strous** (män′strəs) *adj.* 1. greatly malformed 2. huge 3. horrible; hideous 4. hideously evil —**mon·stros′i·ty** (-sträs′ə tē) *n.*

**mon·tage** (män tä zh′) *n.* [Fr. < *monter*, to mount] 1. a composite picture 2. a rapid sequence of movie scenes, often superimposed

**Mon·tan·a** (män tan′ə) Northwestern State of the U.S.: 147,138 sq. mi.; pop. 694,000; cap. Helena: abbrev. **Mont.** —**Mon·tan′an** *adj., n.*

**Mon·te Car·lo** (män′ti kär′lō) town in Monaco: gambling resort

**Mon·tes·so·ri method** (män′tə sôr′ē) a method of teaching young children, emphasizing training of the senses

**Mon·te·vid·e·o** (män′tə vi dā′ō) capital of Uruguay: pop. 1,204,000

**Mont·gom·er·y** (mənt gum′ər ē, mänt-) capital of Ala.: pop. 133,000

**month** (munth) *n.* [OE. *monath*] 1. any of the twelve divisions of the calendar year 2. a period of four weeks or 30 days 3. one twelfth of the solar year

**month′ly** *adj.* 1. continuing for a month 2. done, happening, payable, etc. every month —*n., pl.* -**lies** a periodical published once a month —*adv.* once a month; every month

**Mont·pel·ier** (mänt pēl′yər) capital of Vt.: pop. 9,000

**Mont·re·al** (män′trē ôl′) seaport in SW Quebec, on an island in the St. Lawrence River: pop. 1,222,000

**mon·u·ment** (män′yə mənt) *n.* [< L. *monere*, remind] 1. something set up to keep alive the memory of a person or event, as a tablet, statue, etc. 2. a work of enduring significance

**mon′u·men′tal** (-men′t'l) *adj.* 1. of or serving as a monument 2. like a monument: massive, enduring, etc.

**moo** (mōō) *n., pl.* **moos** [echoic] the vocal sound made by a cow —*vi.* **mooed, moo′ing** to make this sound

**mooch** (mōōch) *vt., vi.* [ult. < OFr. *muchier*, to hide] [Slang] to get (food, money, etc.) by begging, imposition, etc. —**mooch′er** n.

**mood**¹ (m○̄ōd) n. [< OE. *mōd*, mind] 1. a particular state of mind or feeling 2. a predominant feeling or spirit

**mood**² (m○̄ōd) n. [< MODE] *Gram.* that aspect of verbs which indicates whether the action or state expressed is a fact, supposition, or command

**mood′y** adj. **-i·er**, **-i·est** characterized by gloomy or changing moods —**mood′i·ly** adv. —**mood′i·ness** n.

**moon** (m○̄ōn) n. [OE. *mona*] 1. the satellite of the earth, that revolves around it once about every 29 1/2 days and shines by reflected sunlight 2. anything shaped like the moon (i.e., an orb or crescent) 3. any satellite of a planet —vi. to behave in an idle or abstracted way

**moon′beam′** n. a ray of moonlight

**moon′light′** n. the light of the moon

**moon′light′ing** n. the holding of a second job along with one's main job

**moon′lit′** adj. lighted by the moon

**moon′quake′** n. a trembling of the moon's surface, as because of internal rock shifting or meteorite impact

**moon′scape′** (-skāp′) n. [MOON + (LAND)SCAPE] the surface of the moon or a representation of it

**moon′shine′** n. 1. same as MOONLIGHT 2. [Colloq.] whiskey unlawfully distilled —**moon′shin′er** n.

**moon′shot′** n. the launching of a spacecraft to the moon

**moon′stone′** n. a feldspar with a pearly luster, used as a gem

**moon′struck′** adj. 1. crazed; lunatic 2. romantically dreamy

**moon′walk′** n. a walking about by an astronaut on the surface of the moon

**Moor** (moor) n. any of a Moslem people of NW Africa —**Moor′ish** adj.

**moor**¹ (moor) n. [OE. *mor*] [Brit.] a tract of open wasteland, usually covered with heather and often marshy

**moor**² (moor) vt. [< ? MDu. *maren*, to tie] 1. to hold (a ship, etc.) in place by cables to the shore, or by anchors 2. to secure —vi. to moor a ship, etc.

**moor′ings** n.pl. 1. the lines, cables, etc. by which a ship is moored 2. a place where a ship is moored

**moose** (m○̄ōs) n., pl. **moose** [< AmInd.] the largest animal of the deer family, native to N U.S. and Canada

**moot** (m○̄ōt) adj. [OE. *mot*, a meeting] 1. debatable 2. hypothetical

**mop** (mäp) n. [earlier *mappe*] 1. a bundle of rags, a sponge, etc. at the end of a stick, as for washing floors 2. anything suggesting this, as a thick head of hair —vt. mopped, mop′ping to wash or wipe with a mop —mop up 1. to clear of remnants of beaten enemy forces 2. [Colloq.] to finish

**mope** (mōp) vi. moped, mop′ing [< ?] to be gloomy and apathetic —mop′ey, mop′y, mop′ish adj.

**mop·pet** (mäp′it) n. [< ME. *moppe*, rag doll] [Colloq.] a little child

**mo·raine** (mə rān′) n. [Fr.] a mass of rocks, sand, etc. left by a glacier

**mor·al** (môr′əl, mär′-) adj. [< L. *mos*, pl. *mores*, morals] 1. dealing with, or capable of distinguishing between, right and wrong 2. of, teaching, or in accordance with the principles of right and wrong 3. good in conduct or character; specif., sexually virtuous 4. involving sympathy without action [moral support] 5. virtually such because of effects on thoughts or attitudes [a moral victory] 6. based on probability [a moral certainty] —n. 1. a moral lesson taught by a fable, event, etc. 2. [pl.] principles or standards with respect to right and wrong in conduct —**mor′al·ly** adv.

**mo·rale** (mə ral′, mô-) n. moral or mental condition with respect to courage, discipline, confidence, etc.

**mo·ral·i·ty** (mə ral′ə tē) n., pl. **-ties** 1. rightness or wrongness, as of an action 2. right or moral conduct 3. moral principles

**mor·al·ize** (môr′ə līz′, mär′-) vi. **-ized′**, **-iz′ing** to consider or discuss moral questions, often in a self-righteous or tedious way —**mor′al·ist** n. —**mor′al·is′tic** adj.

**mo·rass** (mə ras′, mô-) n. [< Frank.] a bog; marsh; swamp

**mor·a·to·ri·um** (môr′ə tôr′ē əm) n., pl. **-ri·ums**, **-ri·a** (-ə) [< L. *mora*, a delay] 1. a legally authorized delay in the payment of money due 2. an authorized delay of any activity

**mo·ray (eel)** (môr′ā) [< Gr. *myraina*] a voracious, brilliantly colored eel

**mor·bid** (môr′bid) adj. [< L. *morbus*, disease] 1. of or caused by disease; diseased 2. resulting as from a diseased state of mind 3. gruesome [the morbid details] —**mor·bid′i·ty** n. —**mor′bid·ly** adv.

**mor·dant** (môr′d'nt) adj. [< L. *mordere*, to bite] caustic; sarcastic —n. a substance that fixes colors in dyeing —**mor′dan·cy** n. —**mor′dant·ly** adv.

**more** (môr) adj. superl. MOST [OE. *mara*] 1. greater in amount or degree: compar. of MUCH 2. greater in number: compar. of MANY 3. additional [more news later] —n. 1. a greater amount or degree 2. [with pl. v.] a greater number (of) 3. something additional —adv. superl. MOST 1. in or to a greater degree or extent 2. in addition

**more·o·ver** (-ō′vər) adv. in addition to what has been said; besides

**mo·res** (môr′ēz, -āz) n.pl. [L., customs] folkways so basic as to develop the force of law

**morgue** (môrg) n. [Fr.] 1. a place where the bodies of unknown dead or those dead of unknown causes are temporarily kept 2. a newspaper office's file of back copies, etc.

**mor·i·bund** (môr′ə bund′) adj. [< L. *mori*, to die] dying

**Mor·mon** (môr′mən) n. a member of the Church of Jesus Christ of Latter-

---

fat, āpe, cär; ten, ēven; is, bīte; gō, hôrn, t○̄ōl, look; oil, out; up, fur; chin; she; thin, then; zh, leisure; ŋ, ring; ə for a in ago; ′, (ā′b'l); ë, Fr. coeur; ö, Fr. feu; Fr. mon; ü, Fr. duc; kh, G. ich, doch; ‡ foreign; < derived from day Saints, founded (1830) in the U.S.

**morn** (môrn) *n.* [Poet.] morning

**morn·ing** (môr′niŋ) *n.* [OE. *morgen*] the first or early part of the day, from midnight, or esp. dawn, to noon

**morning glory** a twining vine with trumpet-shaped flowers

**Mo·roc·co** (mə rä′kō) kingdom on the NW coast of Africa: 171,300 sq. mi.; pop. 14,140,000 —*n.* [m-] a fine, soft leather made from goatskins —**Mo·roc′can** *adj., n.*

**mo·ron** (môr′än) *n.* [< Gr. *mōros*, foolish] an adult mentally equal to a child between eight and twelve: an obsolescent term —**mo·ron′ic** *adj.*

**mo·rose** (mə rōs′) *adj.* [< L. *mos*, manner] gloomy, sullen, surly, etc. — **mo·rose′ly** *adv.* —**mo·rose′ness** *n.*

**mor·pheme** (môr′fēm) *n.* [< Gr. *morphē*, form] the smallest meaningful language unit, as a base or affix

**mor·phine** (môr′fēn) *n.* [< *Morpheus*, Gr. god of dreams] an alkaloid derived from opium and used in medicine to relieve pain

**mor·phol·o·gy** (môr fäl′ə jē) *n.* [G. < Gr. *morphē*, form + *logie*, -LOGY] form and structure, as in biology

**mor·row** (mär′ō, môr′-) *n.* [< OE. *morgen*, morning] [Archaic or Poet.] 1. morning 2. the following day

**Morse** (môrs) *adj.* [after ff.] [*often* m-] designating or of a code, or alphabet, consisting of a system of dots and dashes, used in telegraphy, etc.

**Morse** (môrs), **Samuel F. B.** 1791-1872; U.S. inventor of the telegraph

**mor·sel** (môr′s'l) *n.* [< L. *morsum*, a bite] 1. a small bite or portion of food 2. a small piece or amount

**mor·tal** (môr′t'l) *adj.* [< L. *mors*, death] 1. that must eventually die 2. of man as a being who must die 3. of death 4. causing or liable to cause death of the body or (*Theol.*) the soul 5. very intense [*mortal* terror] —*n.* a human being —**mor′tal·ly** *adv.*

**mor·tal·i·ty** (môr tal′ə tē) *n.* 1. the mortal nature of man 2. death on a large scale, as from war 3. the ratio of deaths to population; death rate

**mor·tar** (môr′tər) *n.* [< L. *mortarium*] 1. a bowl in which substances are pulverized with a pestle 2. a short-barreled cannon which hurls shells in a high trajectory 3. a mixture of cement or lime with sand and water, used between bricks or stones

**mor·tar·board** (-bôrd′) *n.* 1. a square board for carrying mortar 2. an academic cap with a square, flat top

**mort·gage** (môr′gij) *n.* [< OFr. *mort*, dead + *gage*, pledge] 1. the pledging of property to a creditor as security for the payment of a debt 2. the deed by which this is done —*vt.* -gaged, -gag·ing 1. to pledge (property) by a mortgage 2. to put an advance claim on [to *mortgage* one's future] —**mort′ga·gor, mort′gag·er** *n.*

**mort·ga·gee** (môr′gə jē′) *n.* one to whom property is mortgaged

**mor·ti·cian** (môr tish′ən) *n.* [< L. *mors*, death] a funeral director

**mor·ti·fy** (môr′tə fī′) *vt.* -fied′, -fy′ing [< L. *mors*, death + *facere*, make] 1. to subdue (physical desires) by self-denial, fasting, etc. 2. to humiliate —**mor′ti·fi·ca′tion** *n.*

**mor·tise** (môr′tis) *n.* [< Ar. *murtazza*, joined] a notch or hole cut in a piece of wood to receive a projecting part (*tenon*) shaped to fit

**mor·tu·ar·y** (môr′choo wer′ē) *n., pl.* -ies [< L. *mortuus*, dead] *same as* FUNERAL HOME

**Mo·sa·ic** (mō zā′ik) *adj.* of Moses or the laws, etc. attributed to him

**mo·sa·ic** (mō zā′ik) *n.* [< L. *musivus*, artistic] 1. the making of pictures or designs by inlaying small bits of colored stone, etc. in mortar 2. a picture or design so made

**Mos·cow** (mäs′kou, -kō) capital of the U.S.S.R. in the WC European part: pop. 6,464,000

**Mo·ses** (mō′ziz) *Bible* the leader and lawgiver who brought the Israelites out of slavery in Egypt

**mo·sey** (mō′zē) *vi.* [< VAMOOSE] [Slang] to amble along

**Mos·lem** (mäz′ləm, muz′-) *n.* [ult. < Ar. *aslama*, resign oneself (to God)] an adherent of Islam —*adj.* of Islam or the Moslems

**mosque** (mäsk) *n.* [ult. < Ar. *sajada*, pray] a Moslem place of worship

**mos·qui·to** (mə skēt′ō) *n., pl.* -toes, -tos [Sp. < L. *musca*, a fly] a two-winged insect, the female of which bites animals and sucks blood

**moss** (môs, mäs) *n.* [OE. *mos*, a swamp] a very small green plant that grows in velvety clusters on rocks, moist ground, etc. —**moss′y** *adj.*

**moss·back** (-bak′) *n.* 1. an old turtle or shellfish with a back overgrown with algae 2. [Colloq.] an old-fashioned or very conservative person

**most** (mōst) *adj. compar.* MORE [OE. *mast*] 1. greatest in amount or degree: superl. of MUCH 2. greatest in number: superl. of MANY 3. in the greatest number of instances —*n.* 1. the greatest amount or degree 2. [*with pl. v.*] the greatest number (*of*) —*adv. compar.* MORE in or to the greatest degree or extent

**most′ly** *adv.* 1. for the most part 2. chiefly 3. usually

**mote** (mōt) *n.* [OE. *mot*] a speck, as of dust

**mo·tel** (mō tel′) *n.* [MO(TORIST) + (HO)TEL] a hotel for motorists

**moth** (môth) *n., pl.* moths (môthz, môths) [OE. *moththe*] a four-winged, chiefly night-flying insect related to the butterfly: the larvae of one kind eat holes in woolens, furs, etc.

**moth′ball′** *n.* a small ball of naphthalene or camphor, the fumes of which repel clothes moths —**in mothballs** put into storage or reserve

**moth·er** (mu*th*′ər) *n.* [OE. *modor*] 1. a female parent 2. an origin or source 3. a woman who is the head (**mother superior**) of a religious establishment —*adj.* 1. of or like a mother 2. native *[mother* tongue*] —vt.* to be the mother of or a mother to —**moth'er·hood'** *n.* —**moth'er·less** *adj.*

**Mother Goose** the imaginary creator of a collection of nursery rhymes

**moth'er-in-law'** *n., pl.* **moth'ers-in-law'** the mother of one's husband or wife

**moth'er·land'** *n.* one's native land

**moth'er·ly** *adj.* of or like a mother; maternal —**moth'er·li·ness** *n.*

**moth'er-of-pearl'** *n.* the hard internal layer of the shell of the pearl oyster, etc., used to make buttons, etc.

**mother tongue** one's native language

**mo·tif** (mō tēf') *n.* [Fr.: see MOTIVE] *Art, Literature,* & *Music* a main theme or subject for development

**mo·tile** (mōt'l) *adj.* [< L. *movere,* to move] *Biol.* capable of or exhibiting spontaneous motion —**mo·til'i·ty** *n.*

**mo·tion** (mō'shən) *n.* [< L. *movere,* to move] **1.** a moving from one place to another; movement **2.** a moving of a part of the body; specif., a gesture **3.** a proposal formally made in an assembly —*vi.* to make a meaningful movement of the hand, etc. —*vt.* to direct by a meaningful gesture —**go through the motions** to do something mechanically, without real meaning —**in motion** moving —**mo'tion·less** *adj.*

**motion picture 1.** a series of still pictures on film projected on a screen in such rapid succession as to create the illusion of moving persons and objects **2.** a play, etc. in this form

**mo·ti·vate** (mōt'ə vāt') *vt.* **-vat'ed, -vat'ing** to provide with, or affect as, a motive; incite —**mo'ti·va'tion** *n.*

**mo·tive** (mōt'iv) *n.* [< L. *movere,* to move] **1.** an inner drive, impulse, etc. that causes one to act; incentive **2.** a motif —*adj.* of or causing motion

**-mo·tive** (mōt'iv) *a suffix meaning* moving, of motion *[automotive]*

**mot·ley** (mät'lē) *adj.* [< ?] **1.** of many colors **2.** of many different or clashing elements *[a motley group]*

**mo·to·cross** (mō'tō krôs') *n.* [Fr.] a cross-country race for lightweight motorcycles

**mo·tor** (mōt'ər) *n.* [L. < *movere,* to move] **1.** anything that produces motion **2.** an engine; esp., an internal-combustion engine **3.** a machine for converting electrical energy into mechanical energy —*adj.* **1.** producing motion **2.** of or powered by a motor **3.** of, by, or for motor vehicles **4.** of or involving muscular movements —*vi.* to travel by automobile

**mo'tor·bike'** *n.* [Colloq.] **1.** a motor-driven bicycle **2.** a light motorcycle

**mo'tor·boat'** *n.* a boat propelled by a motor or gasoline engine

**mo'tor·cade'** (-kād') *n.* [MOTOR + (CAVAL)CADE] an automobile procession

**mo'tor·car'** *n.* an automobile

**mo'tor·cy·cle** (-sī'k'l) *n.* a two-wheeled vehicle propelled by an internal-combustion engine

**motor home** an automotive vehicle with a truck chassis, outfitted as a traveling home

**mo'tor·ist** *n.* one who drives an automobile or travels by automobile

**mo'tor·ize'** (-ə rīz') *vt.* **-ized', -iz'-ing** to equip with a motor or with motor-driven vehicles

**mo'tor·man** (-mən) *n., pl.* **-men** one who drives an electric railway car

**motor vehicle** an automotive vehicle, esp. an automobile, truck, or bus

**mot·tle** (mät'l) *vt.* **-tled, -tling** [< MOTLEY] to mark with blotches, etc. of different colors —**mot'tled** *adj.*

**mot·to** (mät'ō) *n., pl.* **-toes, -tos** [It., a word] a word or saying that expresses one's aims, ideals, or guiding rule

**mould, mould'er, mould'ing, mould'y, moult** (mōld, *etc.*) *chiefly Brit. sp.* of MOLD, MOLDER, MOLDING, MOLDY, MOLT

**mound** (mound) *n.* [< ? MDu. *mond,* protection] a heap or bank of earth, sand, etc. —*vt.* to heap up

**mount¹** (mount) *n.* [< L. *mons*] a mountain

**mount²** (mount) *vi.* [< L. *mons,* mountain] **1.** to climb; ascend **2.** to climb up on something, as a horse **3.** to increase in amount —*vt.* **1.** to go up; ascend *[to mount* stairs*]* **2.** to get up on (a horse, platform, etc.) **3.** to provide with horses *[mounted* police*]* **4.** to fix (a jewel, picture, etc.) on or in the proper support, backing, setting, etc. **5.** to arrange (a dead animal, etc.) for exhibition **6.** to place (a gun) into position ready for use —*n.* **1.** the act of mounting **2.** a horse, etc. for riding **3.** the support, setting, etc. on or in which a thing is mounted

**moun·tain** (moun't'n) *n.* [ult. < L. *mons*] **1.** a natural raised part of the earth, larger than a hill **2.** a big pile, amount, etc. —*adj.* of or in mountains

**moun'tain·eer'** (-ir') *n.* **1.** one who lives in a mountainous region **2.** a mountain climber

**mountain goat** a long-haired, goat-like antelope of the Rocky Mountains

**mountain lion** *same as* COUGAR

**moun'tain·ous** *adj.* **1.** full of mountains **2.** like a mountain; huge

**moun·te·bank** (moun'tə baŋk') *n.* [< It. *montare,* to mount + *in,* on + *banco,* bench] a charlatan; quack

**mount'ing** *n.* something serving as a backing, support, setting, etc.

**mourn** (môrn) *vi., vt.* [OE. *murnan*] **1.** to feel or express sorrow for (something regrettable) **2.** to grieve for (someone dead) —**mourn'er** *n.*

**mourn'ful** *adj.* **1.** feeling or expressing grief or sorrow **2.** causing sorrow

**mourn'ing** *n.* **1.** a sorrowing; specif., the expression of grief at someone's death **2.** black clothes, etc., worn as a sign of grief for the dead

**mouse** (mous; *for v.* mouz) *n., pl.* **mice** [OE. *mus*] **1.** any of many small rodents, esp. the **house mouse** that infests human dwellings **2.** a timid person **3.** [Slang] a black eye — *vi.* **moused, mous'ing** to hunt mice

**mousse** (mōōs) *n.* [Fr., foam] a light, chilled dessert made with egg white, gelatin, whipped cream, etc.

**mous·tache** (mə stash', mus'tash) *n. var. of* MUSTACHE

**mous·y, mous·ey** (mou'sē, -zē) *adj.* **-i·er, -i·est** of or like a mouse; specif., quiet, timid, drab, etc. — **mous'i·ness** *n.*

**mouth** (mouth) *n., pl.* **mouths** (mou*th*z) [OE. *muth*] **1.** an opening in the head through which food is taken in and sounds are made **2.** any opening regarded as like this [*the mouth* of a jar, river, etc.] —*vt.* (mouth) **1.** to say, esp. insincerely **2.** to rub with the mouth —**down in** (or at) **the mouth** [Colloq.] unhappy

**mouth'ful'** *n., pl.* **-fuls'** **1.** all the mouth can hold **2.** the usual amount taken into the mouth **3.** a small amount **4.** [Slang] a pertinent remark: chiefly in **say a mouthful**

**mouth organ** *same as* HARMONICA

**mouth'piece'** *n.* **1.** a part, as of a musical instrument, held to or in the mouth **2.** a person, periodical, etc. serving as a spokesman for others

**mouth'wash'** *n.* a flavored, often antiseptic liquid for rinsing the mouth

**mouth'wa'ter·ing** (-wôt'ər iŋ, -wät'-) *adj.* appetizing enough to make the mouth water; tasty

**mouth'y** *adj.* **-i·er, -i·est** talkative esp. in a rude or bombastic way

**mou·ton** (mōō'tän) *n.* [Fr., sheep] lamb fur made to resemble seal, beaver, etc.

**mov·a·ble, move·a·ble** (mōō'və b'l) *adj.* that can be moved from one place to another —*n.* **1.** something movable **2.** *Law* personal property, esp. furniture: *usually used in pl.*

**move** (mōōv) *vt.* **moved, mov'ing** [< L. *movere*] **1.** to change the place or position of **2.** to set or keep in motion **3.** to cause (to do, say, etc.) **4.** to arouse the emotions, etc. of **5.** to propose formally, as in a meeting —*vi.* **1.** to change place or position **2.** to change one's residence **3.** to be active **4.** to make progress **5.** to take action **6.** to be, or be set, in motion **7.** to make a formal application (*for*) **8.** to evacuate: said of the bowels **9.** *Commerce* to be sold: said of goods —*n.* **1.** act of moving **2.** an action toward some goal **3.** *Chess, Checkers,* etc. the act of moving a piece, or one's turn to move —**move up** to promote or be promoted —**on the move** [Colloq.] moving about or active

**move'ment** *n.* **1.** a moving or manner of moving **2.** an evacuation (of the bowels) **3.** a change in the location of troops, etc. **4.** organized action by people working toward a goal **5.** the moving parts of a mechanism, as of a clock **6.** *Music a)* a principal division of a symphony, etc. *b)* rhythm

**mov'er** *n.* one that moves; specif., one whose work is moving furniture, etc. for those changing residence

**mov·ie** (mōō'vē) *n.* [< *moving picture*] a motion picture —**the movies 1.** the motion-picture industry **2.** the showing of a motion picture

**moving picture** *same as* MOTION PICTURE

**mow**[1] (mō) *vt., vi.* **mowed, mowed** or **mown** (mōn), **mow'ing** [OE. *mawan*] to cut down (grass, etc.) from (a lawn, etc.) with a sickle or lawn mower —**mow down** to cause to fall like cut grass —**mow'er** *n.*

**mow**[2] (mou) *n.* [OE. *muga*] **1.** a heap of hay, etc., esp. in a barn **2.** the part of a barn where hay, etc. is stored

**Mo·zam·bique** (mō'zəm bēk') country in SE Africa: c. 302,300 sq. mi.; pop. 8,519,000

**Mo·zart** (mō'tsärt), **Wolf·gang A·ma·de·us** (vôlf'gäŋk' ä'mä dā'oos) 1756–91; Austrian composer

**MP, M.P.** Military Police

**M.P.** Member of Parliament

**mph, m.p.h.** miles per hour

**Mr.** (mis'tər) *pl.* **Messrs.** (mes'ərz) mister: before a man's name or title

**Mrs.** (mis'iz) *pl.* **Mmes.** (mā däm') mistress: before a married woman's name

**MS** Mississippi

**MS., ms., ms** *pl.* **MSS., mss., mss** manuscript

**Ms.** (miz, em'es') a title, free of reference to marital status, used in place of either *Miss* or *Mrs.*

**M.S., M.Sc.** Master of Science

**Msgr.** Monsignor

**MSgt, M/Sgt** Master Sergeant

**MST, M.S.T.** Mountain Standard Time

**MT** Montana

**Mt., mt.** *pl.* **Mts., mts. 1.** mount **2.** mountain

**mu** (myōō) *n.* the twelfth letter of the Greek alphabet (M, μ)

**much** (much) *adj.* **more, most** [< OE. *mycel*] great in quantity, degree, etc. —*adv.* **more, most 1.** to a great degree or extent [*much* happier] **2.** nearly [*much* the same] —*n.* **1.** a great amount **2.** anything great or outstanding [not *much* to look at]

**mu·ci·lage** (myōō's'l ij) *n.* [< L. *mucus,* mucus] **1.** a thick, sticky substance in some plants **2.** any watery solution of gum, glue, etc. used as an adhesive

**muck** (muk) *n.* [< ON. *myki*] **1.** moist manure **2.** black earth with decaying matter, used as manure **3.** mud; dirt; filth —**muck'y** *adj.*

**muck'rake'** *vi.* **-raked', -rak'ing** [see prec. & RAKE[1]] to search for and publicize real or alleged corruption in politics, etc. —**muck'rak'er** *n.*

**mu·cous** (myōō'kəs) *adj.* **1.** of, containing, or secreting mucus **2.** slimy

**mucous membrane** a mucus-secreting lining of body cavities

**mu·cus** (myōō'kəs) *n.* [L.] the slimy secretion of mucous membranes

**mud** (mud) *n.* [prob. < a LowG. source] wet, soft, sticky earth

**mud·dle** (mud′'l) *vt.* **-dled, -dling**
[ < prec.] **1.** to mix up; bungle **2.** to
confuse mentally; befuddle —*vi.* to
act or think confusedly —*n.* **1.** a
mess, jumble, etc. **2.** mental confusion

**mud′dle·head′ed** *adj.* confused;
blundering

**mud·dy** (mud′ē) *adj.* **-di·er, -di·est**
**1.** full of or spattered with mud **2.** not
clear; cloudy [*muddy* coffee] **3.** confused, obscure, etc. [*muddy* thinking]
—*vt., vi.* **-died, -dy·ing** to make or
become muddy —**mud′di·ness** *n.*

**mud′sling′ing** *n.* the practice of
making unscrupulous verbal attacks, as against a political opponent
—**mud′sling′er** *n.*

**mu·ez·zin** (myoo ez′in) *n.* [ < Ar.
*mu'adhdhin*, proclaiming] a Moslem
crier who calls the people to prayer

**muff** (muf) *n.* [< Fr. *moufle*, mitten]
**1.** a cylindrical covering of fur, etc.
to keep the hands warm **2.** *a) Baseball*, etc. a failure to hold the ball
when catching it *b)* any bungle —*vt.,
vi.* **1.** to miss (a catch, etc.) **2.** to
bungle

**muf·fin** (muf′'n) *n.* [ < ?] a quick
bread baked in a cup-shaped mold

**muf·fle** (muf′'l) *vt.* **-fled, -fling**
[prob. < OFr. *moufle*, mitten] **1.** to
wrap or cover closely so as to keep
warm, etc. **2.** to cover so as to deaden
sound **3.** to deaden (a sound)

**muf·fler** (muf′lər) *n.* **1.** a scarf worn
around the throat, as for warmth **2.** a
device for deadening noise

**muf·ti** (muf′tē) *n., pl.* **-tis** [ < Ar.]
ordinary clothes, not a uniform

**mug** (mug) *n.* [prob. < Scand.] **1.** a
cup of earthenware or metal, with a
handle **2.** as much as a mug will hold
**3.** [Slang] the face —*vt.* **mugged,
mug′ging** to assault, usually with
intent to rob —*vi.* [Slang] to grimace,
esp. in overacting —**mug′ger** *n.*

**mug·gy** (mug′ē) *adj.* **-gi·er, -gi·est**
[ < dial. *mug*, mist] hot, damp, and
close —**mug′gi·ness** *n.*

**Mu·ham·mad** (moo ham′əd) *same
as* MOHAMMED

**muk·luk** (muk′luk′) *n.* [Esk. *muklok*,
a seal] **1.** an Eskimo boot of sealskin
or reindeer skin **2.** any similar boot

**mu·lat·to** (mə lat′ō) *n., pl.* **-toes**
[Sp. & Port. *mulato*, of mixed breed]
a person who has one Negro parent
and one white parent

**mul·ber·ry** (mul′ber′ē, -bər ē) *n., pl.*
**-ries** [OE. *morberie*] **1.** a tree with
purplish-red, edible, berrylike fruit
**2.** the fruit **3.** purplish red

**mulch** (mulch) *n.* [ME. *molsh*, soft]
leaves, straw, etc., spread around
plants to prevent freezing of roots, etc.
—*vt.* to apply mulch to

**mulct** (mulkt) *vt.* [ < L. *mul(c)ta*, a
fine] **1.** to fine **2.** to take (money,
etc.) from by fraud —*n.* a fine; penalty

**mule¹** (myool) *n.* [ < L. *mulus*] **1.** the
(usually sterile) offspring of a male
donkey and a female horse **2.** a ma-

chine that spins cotton fibers into yarn
**3.** [Colloq.] a stubborn person

**mule²** (myool) *n.* [ < L. *mulleus*, red
shoe] a lounging slipper that does not
cover the heel

**mu·le·teer** (myoo′lə tir′) *n.* [ <
OFr.] a driver of mules: also [Colloq.]
**mule skin′ner**

**mul′ish** *adj.* like a mule; stubborn;
obstinate —**mul′ish·ly** *adv.*

**mull¹** (mul) *vt., vi.* [ME. *mullen*, to
grind] [Colloq.] to ponder (*over*)

**mull²** (mul) *vt.* [ < ?] to heat, sweeten,
and spice (ale, wine, etc.)

**mul·lein** (mul′in) *n.* [ < OFr.
*moleine*] a tall plant with spikes of
variously colored flowers

**mul·let** (mul′it) *n.* [ < L. *mullus*] any
of a family of edible, spiny-finned
fishes of fresh and salt waters

**mul·li·gan (stew)** (mul′i g'n) [prob.
< name *Mulligan*] [Slang] a kind of
meat stew

**mul·li·ga·taw·ny** (mul′i gə tô′nē)
*n.* [Tamil *milagutannir*, lit., pepper
water] an East Indian soup of meat,
etc., flavored with curry

**mul·lion** (mul′yən) *n.* [ult. < L.
*medianus*, middle] a vertical dividing
bar, as between windowpanes

**multi-** [L. < *multus*, much] *a combining form meaning:* **1.** having many
**2.** more than two **3.** many times

**mul·ti·far·i·ous** (mul′tə far′ē əs)
*adj.* [ < L.] having many kinds of
parts or elements; diverse

**mul′ti·mil′lion·aire′** *n.* a person
whose wealth amounts to many millions of dollars, pounds, etc.

**mul′ti·na′tion·al** *adj.* **1.** of many
nations **2.** designating or of a corporation with branches in many countries
—*n.* a multinational corporation

**mul·ti·ple** (mul′tə p'l) *adj.* [ < L.
*multus*, many + *picare*, fold] having
many parts, elements, etc. —*n.* a number that is a product of some specified
number and another number

**mul′ti·ple-choice′** *adj.* listing several answers from which the correct
one is to be chosen

**multiple sclerosis** a disease of the
central nervous system, with loss of
muscular coordination, etc.

**mul·ti·plex** (mul′tə pleks′) *adj.* [L.,
multiple] designating a system for
sending two or more signals simultaneously over a single circuit, etc.

**mul′ti·pli·cand′** (-pli kand′) *n.* a
number to be multiplied by another

**mul′ti·pli·ca′tion** (-pli kā′shən) *n.*
a multiplying or being multiplied;
specif., the process of finding the
quantity obtained by repeating a
specified quantity a specified number
of times

**mul′ti·plic′i·ty** (-plis′ə tē) *n.* a
great number or variety (*of*)

**mul′ti·pli′er** (-pli′ər) *n.* one that
multiplies; specif., the number by
which another is to be multiplied

**mul·ti·ply** (mul′tə plī′) *vt., vi.*

fat, āpe, cär; ten, ēven; is, bīte; gō, hôrn, tōōl, look; oil, out; up, fur;
chin; she; thin, then; zh, leisure; ŋ, ring; ə for a in ago; ′, (ā′b'l); ë, Fr. coeur;
ö, Fr. feu; Fr. mon; ü, Fr. duc; kh, G. ich; doch. ‡foreign; < derived from

**-plied′, -ply′ing** [see MULTIPLE] **1.** to increase in number, degree, etc. **2.** to find the product (of) by multiplication

**mul·ti·stage′** *adj.* having, or operating in, more than one stage; specif., having several propulsion systems, as a rocket or missile

**mul·ti·tude** (mul′tə tōōd′) *n.* [< L. *multus*, many] a large number; host

**mul·ti·tu′di·nous** (-tōōd′n əs) *adj.* very numerous; many

**mum¹** (mum) *n.* [Colloq.] a chrysanthemum

**mum²** (mum) *adj.* [ME. *momme*] silent; not speaking

**mum·ble** (mum′b'l) *vt., vi.* -bled, -bling [ME. *momelen*] to speak or say indistinctly; mutter —*n.* a mumbled utterance —**mum′bler** *n.*

**mum·bo jum·bo** (mum′bō jum′bō) [of Afr. origin] **1.** an idol or fetish **2.** meaningless ritual, talk, etc.

**mum·mer** (mum′ər) *n.* [< OFr. *momo*, grimace] one who wears a mask or costume, esp. in a pantomime

**mum′mer·y** *n., pl.* -ies **1.** performance by mummers **2.** a hypocritical display or ceremony

**mum·mi·fy** (mum′ə fī′) *vt., vi.* -fied′, -fy′ing to make into or become a mummy

**mum·my** (mum′ē) *n., pl.* -mies [ult. < Per. *mum*, wax] a carefully preserved dead body; esp., an embalmed corpse of ancient Egypt

**mumps** (mumps) *n.pl.* [*with sing. v.*] [< obs. *mump*, a grimace] an acute communicable disease characterized by swelling of the salivary glands

**mun.** municipal

**munch** (munch) *vt., vi.* [ME. *monchen*] to chew steadily, often with a crunching sound

**mun·dane** (mun dān′, mun′dān) *adj.* [< L. *mundus*, world] **1.** of the world; worldly **2.** commonplace; ordinary

**Mu·nich** (myōō′nik) city in SE West Germany: pop. 1,215,000

**mu·nic·i·pal** (myoo nis′ə p'l) *adj.* [< L. *municeps*, inhabitant of a free town] of or concerning a city, town, etc., or its local government

**mu·nic′i·pal′i·ty** (-pal′ə tē) *n., pl.* -ties a city, town, etc. having its own incorporated government

**mu·nif·i·cent** (myoo nif′ə s'nt) *adj.* [< L. *munus*, gift + *facere*, make] very generous in giving; lavish —**mu·nif′i·cence** *n.*

**mu·ni·tions** (myōō nish′ənz) *n.pl.* [< L. *munire*, fortify] war supplies; esp., weapons and ammunition

**mu·ral** (myoor′əl) *adj.* [< L. *murus*, wall] of, on, or for a wall —*n.* a picture, esp. a large one, painted directly on a wall —**mu′ral·ist** *n.*

**mur·der** (mur′dər) *n.* [OE. *morthor*] **1.** the unlawful and malicious or premeditated killing of a person **2.** [Colloq.] something very hard, unsafe, etc. to do or deal with —*vt.* **1.** to kill (a person) unlawfully and with malice **2.** to spoil, as in performance [to *murder* a song] —**mur′der·er** *n.* —**mur′der·ess** *n.fem.*

**mur′der·ous** *adj.* **1.** of or characteristic of murder; brutal **2.** capable or guilty of, or intending, murder —**mur′der·ous·ly** *adv.*

**murk** (murk) *n.* [< ON. *myrkr*, dark] darkness; gloom

**murk·y** (mur′kē) *adj.* -i·er, -i·est dark or gloomy —**murk′i·ness** *n.*

**mur·mur** (mur′mər) *n.* [< L.] **1.** a low, indistinct, continuous sound **2.** a mumbled complaint **3.** *Med.* an abnormal sound in the body, esp. in the region of the heart —*vi.* to make a murmur —*vt.* to say in a murmur

**mur·rain** (mur′in) *n.* [< L. *mori*, die] a plague, specif. of cattle

**mus·cat** (mus′kət) *n.* [Fr. < LL. *muscus*, musk] a sweet European grape

**mus·ca·tel** (mus′kə tel′) *n.* a rich, sweet wine made from the muscat

**mus·cle** (mus′'l) *n.* [< L. < dim. of *mus*, mouse] **1.** any body organ consisting of fibrous tissue that can be contracted and expanded to produce bodily movements **2.** this tissue **3.** muscular strength —*vi.* -cled, -cling [Colloq.] to force one's way (*in*)

**mus′cle-bound′** *adj.* having some of the muscles enlarged and less elastic, as from too much exercise

**mus·cu·lar** (mus′kyə lər) *adj.* **1.** of or done by muscles **2.** having well-developed muscles; strong —**mus′cu·lar′i·ty** (-lar′ə tē) *n.*

**muscular dys·tro·phy** (dis′trə fē) [prec. + *dystrophy*, faulty nutrition] a disease characterized by a progressive wasting of the muscles

**mus·cu·la·ture** (-lə chər) *n.* [Fr.] the arrangement of the muscles of a body, limb, etc.; muscular system

**Muse** (myōōz) *n.* [< Gr. *mousa*] **1.** *Gr. Myth.* any of the nine goddesses who presided over literature and the arts and sciences **2.** [m-] the spirit regarded as inspiring a poet

**muse** (myōōz) *vi.* mused, mus′ing [< OFr. *muser*, ponder] to meditate —*vt.* to think or say meditatively

**mu·sette** (bag) (myoo zet′) [< OFr., bagpipe] a bag with a shoulder strap, worn as by soldiers to carry supplies

**mu·se·um** (myōō zē′əm) *n.* [< Gr. *mousa*, Muse] a building, room, etc. for exhibiting artistic, historical, or scientific objects

**mush¹** (mush) *n.* [prob. var. of MASH] **1.** a thick porridge of boiled meal **2.** any thick, soft mass **3.** [Colloq.] maudlin sentimentality —**mush′y** *adj.* -i·er, -i·est

**mush²** (mush) *interj.* [< ? Fr. *marcher*, go] a shout to urge on sled dogs —*vi.* to travel on foot over snow, usually with a dog sled

**mush′room′** (-rōōm′) *n.* [< LL. *mussirio*] any of various fleshy fungi, typically with a stalk capped by an umbrellalike top; esp., any edible variety —*adj.* of or like a mushroom —*vi.* to grow or spread rapidly

**mu·sic** (myōō′zik) *n.* [< Gr. *mousikē (technē)*, art of the Muses] **1.** the art of combining tones to form expressive compositions 2. such compositions 3. any rhythmic sequence of pleasing sounds —face the music [Colloq.] to accept the consequences.

**mu·si·cal** (myōō'zə kal') *adj.* 1. of or for music 2. melodious or harmonious 3. fond of or skilled in music 4. set to music —*n.* a light play or movie with dialogue, songs, and dances: often, **musical comedy, musical play** —**mu'·si·cal·ly** *adv.*

**mu·si·cale** (myōō'zə kal') *n.* [Fr.] a social affair featuring music

**mu·si·cian** (myōō zish'ən) *n.* one skilled in music; esp., a performer

**mu·si·col·o·gy** (myōō'zi käl'ə jē) *n.* the study of the history, forms, etc. of music —**mu'si·col'o·gist** *n.*

**musk** (musk) *n.* [< Sans. *mus*, mouse] an animal secretion having a strong odor: used in making perfumes —**musk'y** *adj.* —**musk'i·ness** *n.*

**mus·kel·lunge** (mus'kə lunj') *n., pl.* **-lunge** [< AmInd.] a very large, edible pike of N.America: also **mus'·kie** (-kē)

**mus·ket** (mus'kit) *n.* [< L. *musca*, a fly] a former kind of firearm with a long barrel and smooth bore

**mus·ket·eer** (mus'kə tir') *n.* a soldier armed with a musket

**musk'mel'on** *n.* any of various sweet, juicy melons, as the cantaloupe

**musk·rat** (musk'rat') *n.* 1. a N.American water rodent with brown fur and a musky odor 2. its fur

MUSKRAT

**Mus·lim** (muz'ləm) *n.* same as MOSLEM

**mus·lin** (muz'lin) *n.* [< *Mosul*, city in Iraq] a strong cotton cloth; esp., a heavy kind used for sheets, etc.

**muss** (mus) *n.* [prob. var. of MESS] to make messy or disordered; disarrange —*n.* a mess; disorder — **muss'y** *adj.* **-i·er, -i·est**

**mus·sel** (mus'l) *n.* [< OE. *muscle*] any of various saltwater or freshwater bivalve mollusks

**must** (must) *v.aux. pt.* **must** [< OE. *moste*] an auxiliary expressing: 1. necessity *[I must go]* 2. probability *[it must be Joe]* 3. certainty *[all must die]* —*n.* [Colloq.] something that must be done, had, etc.

**mus·tache** (mə stash', mus'tash) *n.* [ult. < Gr. *mastax*, mouth] the hair on the upper lip of men

**mus·tang** (mus'tang) *n.* [< L. *mixtus*, a mingling] a small wild horse of the SW plains

**mus·tard** (mus'tərd) *n.* [< OFr.] 1. a plant with yellow flowers and slender pods 2. the yellow powder made from its ground seeds, often used in paste form as a condiment

**mustard gas** [< its mustardlike odor] an oily liquid used in warfare for its blistering, disabling effects

**mus·ter** (mus'tər) *vt.* [< L. *monere*, warn] 1. to assemble (troops, etc.) 2. to collect; summon *[to muster up strength]* —*vi.* to assemble, as troops —*n.* 1. a gathering or assembling, as of troops for inspection 2. the persons or things assembled —**muster in** (or **out**) to enlist in (or discharge from) military service

**must·n't** (mus'nt) must not

**mus·ty** (mus'tē) *adj.* **-ti·er, -ti·est** [< ? MOIST] 1. having a stale, moldy smell or taste 2. stale or trite; antiquated —**mus'ti·ly** *adv.* —**mus'ti·ness** *n.*

**mu·ta·ble** (myōōt'ə b'l) *adj.* [< L. *mutare*, to change] 1. that can be changed 2. inconstant; fickle —**mu'·ta·bil'i·ty** *n.* —**mu'ta·bly** *adv.*

**mu·tant** (-'nt) *adj.* of mutation —*n.* an animal or plant with inheritable characteristics that differ from those of the parents; sport

**mu·ta·tion** (myōō tā'shən) *n.* 1. a change, as in form, nature, etc. 2. a sudden variation in some inheritable characteristic of a plant or animal — **mu'tate** *vi., vt.* **-tat·ed, -tat·ing**

**mute** (myōōt) *adj.* [< L. *mutus*] 1. not speaking; silent 2. unable to speak —*n.* 1. a deaf-mute 2. a device that softens the sound of a musical instrument —*vt.* **mut'ed, mut'ing** to soften the sound of (an instrument) —**mute'ly** *adv.* —**mute'ness** *n.*

**mu·ti·late** (myōōt'l āt') *vt.* **-lat·ed, -lat·ing** [< L. *mutilus*, maimed] to cut off, damage, or spoil an important part of —**mu'ti·la'tion** *n.* —**mu'ti·la'tor** *n.*

**mu·ti·ny** (myōōt'n ē) *n., pl.* **-nies** [< L. *movere*, to move] revolt against constituted authority; esp., rebellion of soldiers or sailors against their officers —*vi.* **-nied, -ny·ing** to revolt in this way —**mu'ti·neer'** *n.* —**mu'ti·nous** *adj.*

**mutt** (mut) *n.* [Slang] a mongrel dog

**mut·ter** (mut'ər) *vi., vt.* [ME. *moteren*] 1. to speak or say in low, indistinct tones 2. to grumble —*n.* 1. a muttering 2. something muttered

**mut·ton** (mut'n) *n.* [< ML. *multo*, sheep] the flesh of a sheep, esp. a grown sheep, used as food

**mu·tu·al** (myōō'choo wəl) *adj.* [< L. *mutare*, to change] 1. *a)* done, felt, etc. by each of two or more for or toward the other or others *b)* of each other 2. shared in common *[our mutual friend]* —**mu'tu·al·ly** *adv.*

**mutual fund** a corporation that invests its shareholders' funds in diversified securities

**muu·muu** (mōō'mōō) *n.* [Haw.] a long, loose dress of Hawaiian style

**muz·zle** (muz'l) *n.* [< ML. *musum*] 1. the nose and jaws of a dog, horse, etc. 2. a device put over the mouth of an animal to prevent its biting or eating 3. the front end of the barrel of a firearm —*vt.* **-zled, -zling** 1. to

fat, āpe, cär; ten, ēven; is, bīte; gō, hôrn, tōōl, look; oil, out; up, fur; chin; she; thin, then; zh, leisure; ŋ, ring; ə for a in ago; ', (ä'b'l); ë, Fr. coeur; ö, Fr. feu; Fr. mon; ü, Fr. duc; kh, G. ich, doch; ‡ foreign; < derived from put a muzzle on (an animal) **2.** to prevent from talking

**my** (mī) *possessive pronominal adj.* [< OE. *min*] of, belonging to, or done by me

**my·e·li·tis** (mī′ə līt′is) *n.* [< Gr. *myelos*, marrow + -ITIS] inflammation of the spinal cord or the bone marrow

**My·lar** (mī′lär) *a trademark* for a strong, thin polyester used for recording tapes, fabrics, etc. —*n.* [m-] this substance

**my·na, my·nah** (mī′nə) *n.* [Hindi *mainā*] any of certain tropical birds of SE Asia related to starlings, esp. one that can mimic human speech

**my·o·pi·a** (mī ō′pē ə) *n.* [< Gr. *myein*, to close + *ōps*, eye] nearsightedness —**my·op′ic** (-äp′ik) *adj.*

**myr·i·ad** (mir′ē əd) *n.* [< Gr. *myrios*, countless] a great number of persons or things —*adj.* very many

**myr·mi·don** (mur′mə dän′, -dən) *n.* [after name of a Gr. tribe led by Achilles] an unquestioning follower

**myrrh** (mur) *n.* [< Ar. *murr*] a fragrant gum resin of Arabia and E Africa, used in incense, perfume, etc.

**myr·tle** (mur′t'l) *n.* [< Gr. *myrtos*] **1.** an evergreen shrub with white or pink flowers and dark berries **2.** any of various other plants, as the periwinkle

**my·self** (mī self′) *pron.* **1.** *the intensive or reflexive form of* I [I myself went, I hurt *myself*] **2.** my true self [I am not *myself* today]

**mys·te·ri·ous** (mis tir′ē əs) *adj.* of,

containing, implying, or characterized by mystery —**mys·te′ri·ous·ly** *adv.* —**mys·te′ri·ous·ness** *n.*

**mys·ter·y** (mis′tə rē) *n., pl.* -ies [< Gr. *mystērion*, secret rite] **1.** something unexplained, unknown, or kept secret **2.** a story or play about a secret crime, etc. [a murder *mystery*] **3.** obscurity or secrecy

**mys·tic** (mis′tik) *adj.* **1.** of esoteric rites or doctrines **2.** *same as* MYSTICAL **3.** mysterious —*n.* one professing to undergo profound spiritual experiences

**mys·ti·cal** *adj.* **1.** spiritually significant or symbolic **2.** of mystics or mysticism **3.** occult —**mys′ti·cal·ly** *adv.*

**mys·ti·cism** (mis′tə siz′m) *n.* **1.** belief in direct or intuitive attainment of communion with God or of spiritual truths **2.** obscure thinking or belief

**mys·ti·fy** (-fī′) *vt.* -fied′, -fy′ing **1.** to puzzle or perplex **2.** to involve in mystery —**mys′ti·fi·ca′tion** *n.*

**mys·tique** (mis tēk′) *n.* [Fr., mystic] a complex of quasi-mystical attitudes and feelings surrounding some person, institution, etc.

**myth** (mith) *n.* [< Gr. *mythos*] **1.** a traditional story serving to explain some phenomenon, custom, etc. **2.** mythology **3.** any fictitious story, person, or thing —**myth′i·cal** *adj.*

**my·thol·o·gy** (mi thäl′ə jē) *n., pl.* -gies **1.** the study of myths **2.** myths collectively, as of a specific people —**myth·o·log·i·cal** (mith′ə läj′i k'l) *adj.* —**my·thol′o·gist** *n.*

# N

**N, n** (en) *n., pl.* **N's, n's** the 14th letter of the English alphabet

**N** *Chem.* nitrogen

**N, N., n, N. n.** **1.** north **2.** northern

**N.** Norse

**N., n.** **1.** name **2.** navy **3.** neuter **4.** new **5.** nominative **6.** noun

**Na** [L. *natrium*] *Chem.* sodium

**N.A.** North America

**nab** (nab) *vt.* nabbed, nab′bing [prob. < dial. *nap*, snatch] [Colloq.] **1.** to snatch or seize **2.** to arrest or catch (a felon or wrongdoer)

**na·bob** (nā′bäb) *n.* [< Hindi < Ar. *na'ib*, deputy] a very rich or important man

**na·cre** (nā′kər) *n.* [Fr. < Ar.] *same as* MOTHER-OF-PEARL

**na·dir** (nā′dər, -dir) *n.* [< Ar. *nazir*, opposite] **1.** the point opposite the zenith and directly below the observer **2.** the lowest point

**nae** (nā) *adv.* [Scot.] no; not —*adj.* no

**nag¹** (nag) *vt., vi.* nagged, nag′ging [< Scand.] **1.** to annoy by continual scolding, faultfinding, etc. **2.** to keep troubling [nagged by doubts] —*n.* one who nags: also **nag′ger**

**nag²** (nag) *n.* [ME. *nagge*] an inferior horse, esp. an old one

**Na·ga·sa·ki** (nä′gə sä′kē) seaport in

SW Japan: U.S. atomic-bomb target (1945): pop. 405,000

**Na·go·ya** (nä′gō yä′) seaport in S Honshu, Japan: pop. 1,935,000

**nai·ad** (nā′ad, nī′-) *n.* [< Gr. *naein*, flow] [also N-] *Gr. & Rom. Myth.* any nymph living in springs, rivers, etc.

**nail** (nāl) *n.* [< OE. *nægl*] **1.** the thin, horny growth at the ends of fingers and toes **2.** a slender, pointed piece of metal driven with a hammer to hold pieces of wood together —*vt.* **1.** to fasten, secure, etc. with or as with nails **2.** [Colloq.] to catch or hit

**Nai·ro·bi** (nī rō′bē) capital of Kenya: pop., 297,000

**na·ive, na·ïve** (nä ēv′) *adj.* [Fr. < L. *nativus*, natural] unaffectedly simple; artless; unsophisticated —**na·ive′ly, na·ïve′ly** *adv.* —**na·ive·té′, na·ive·té′** (-tā′) *n.*

**na·ked** (nā′kid) *adj.* [OE. *nacod*] **1.** completely unclothed; nude **2.** without covering [a *naked* sword] **3.** without additions, disguises, etc.; plain [the *naked* truth] —**na′ked·ly** *adv.* —**na′ked·ness** *n.*

**nam·by·pam·by** (nam′bē pam′bē) *adj.* [18th-c. play on name *Ambrose*] weak, insipid, indecisive, etc. —*n., pl.* -bies a namby-pamby person

**name** (nām) *n.* [OE. *nama*] **1.** a word or phrase by which a person, thing, or class is known; title **2.** a word or words considered descriptive; epithet, often an abusive one **3.** fame or reputation **4.** appearance only, not reality *[chief in name only]* —*adj.* well-known —*vt.* **named, nam'ing 1.** to give a name to **2.** to mention by name **3.** to identify by the right name *[name the States]* **4.** to appoint to an office, etc. **5.** to specify (a date, price, etc.) —**in the name of 1.** in appeal to **2.** by the authority of

**name'less** *adj.* **1.** not having a name **2.** left unnamed **3.** indescribable

**name'ly** *adv.* that is to say; to wit

**name'sake'** (-sāk') *n.* a person with the same name as another, esp. if named after the other

**Nan·king** (nan'kiŋ') city in E China, on the Yangtze: pop. 2,700,000

**nan·ny goat** (nan'ē) [< fem. name *Nan*] [Colloq.] a female goat

**nap¹** (nap) *vi.* **napped, nap'ping** [OE. *hnappian*] to sleep lightly for a short time —*n.* a brief, light sleep

**nap²** (nap) *n.* [ME. *noppe*] the downy or hairy surface of cloth or suede formed by short hairs or fibers — **nap'less** *adj.* —**napped** *adj.*

**na·palm** (nā'päm) *n.* [< constituents *na(phthene)* & *palm(itate)*] **1.** a substance added to gasoline to form a jelly-like compound used in flame throwers and fire bombs **2.** this compound —*vt.* to attack or burn with napalm

**nape** (nāp) *n.* [ME.] the back of the neck

**naph·tha** (naf'thə, nap'-) *n.* [< Per. *neft,* pitch] a flammable liquid distilled from petroleum, coal tar, etc.: it is used as a fuel, solvent, etc.

**naph'tha·lene'** (-lēn') *n.* [< prec.] a white, crystalline hydrocarbon produced from coal tar: it is used in moth repellents, in certain dyes, etc.

**nap·kin** (nap'kin) *n.* [< L. *mappa*] **1.** a small piece of cloth or paper used while eating to protect the clothes and wipe the lips, etc. **2.** any small cloth or towel

**Na·ples** (nā'p'lz) seaport in S Italy: pop. 1,236,000

**Na·po·le·on I** (nə pō'lē ən) (*Napoléon Bonaparte*) 1769–1821; Fr. general and emperor (1804–15) —**Na·po·le·on'ic** (-än'ik) *adj.*

**narc, nark** (närk) *n.* [Slang] a police agent who enforces laws dealing with narcotics

**nar·cis·sism** (när'sə siz'm) *n.* [< ff.] self-love —**nar'cis·sist** *n.* —**nar'cis·sis'tic** *adj.*

**Nar·cis·sus** (när sis'əs) *Gr. Myth.* a youth who fell in love with his reflection in a pool and was changed into the narcissus —*n.* [n-] *pl.* **-sus, -sus·es, -si** (-ī) a bulb plant with white, yellow, or orange flowers

**nar·co·sis** (när kō'sis) *n.* unconsciousness caused by a narcotic

**nar·cot·ic** (när kät'ik) *n.* [< Gr. *narkē,* numbness] a drug, as morphine, used to relieve pain and induce sleep: narcotics are often addictive —*adj.* of or having to do with narcotics

**nar·co·tize** (när'kə tīz') *vt.* **-tized', -tiz'ing** to subject to a narcotic —**nar'co·ti·za'tion** *n.*

**nar·rate** (nar'āt, na rāt') *vt., vi.* **-rat·ed, -rat·ing** [< L. *narrare,* tell] to tell (a story), relate (events), etc. —**nar'ra·tor** *n.*

**nar·ra·tion** (na rā'shən) *n.* **1.** a narrating **2.** a narrative

**nar·ra·tive** (nar'ə tiv) *adj.* in story form —*n.* **1.** a story; account **2.** the art or practice of narrating

**nar·row** (nar'ō) *adj.* [OE. *nearu*] **1.** small in width; not wide **2.** limited in meaning, size, amount, etc. *[a narrow majority]* **3.** limited in outlook; not liberal **4.** with limited margin *[a narrow escape]* —*vi., vt.* to decrease or limit in width, extent, etc. —*n.* [*usually pl.*] a narrow passage; strait —**nar'row·ly** *adv.* —**nar'row·ness** *n.*

**nar'row-mind'ed** *adj.* limited in outlook; bigoted; prejudiced —**nar'row-mind'ed·ness** *n.*

**nar·whal** (när'wəl) *n.* [< ON. *nahvalr,* lit. corpse whale: from its white coloring] a small arctic whale: the male has a long tusk

**nar·y** (ner'ē) *adj.* [< *ne'er a,* never a] [Dial.] not any; no (with *a* or *an*)

**NASA** (nas'ə) National Aeronautics and Space Administration

**na·sal** (nā'z'l) *adj.* [< L. *nasus,* nose] **1.** of the nose **2.** uttered with the breath passing through the nose

**na'sal·ize'** *vt., vi.* **-ized', -iz'ing** to pronounce or speak with a nasal sound —**na'sal·i·za'tion** *n.*

**na·scent** (nas'nt, nā's'nt) *adj.* [< L. *nasci,* be born] **1.** coming into being **2.** beginning to form or develop

**Nash·ville** (nash'vil) capital of Tenn.: pop. 448,000

**na·stur·tium** (nə stur'shəm) *n.* [< L. *nasus,* nose + *torquere,* to twist] a plant with red, yellow, or orange flowers and a pungent odor

**nas·ty** (nas'tē) *adj.* **-ti·er, -ti·est** [< ?] **1.** filthy **2.** morally offensive; indecent **3.** very unpleasant *[nasty weather]* **4.** mean; malicious —**nas'ti·ly** *adv.* —**nas'ti·ness** *n.*

**na·tal** (nāt'l) *adj.* [< L. *nasci,* be born] of or relating to one's birth

**na·tes** (nā'tēz) *n.pl.* [L.] the buttocks

**na·tion** (nā'shən) *n.* [< L. *natus,* born] **1.** a stable community of people with a territory, history, culture, and language in common **2.** people united under a single government; country

**na·tion·al** (nash'ə n'l) *adj.* of or affecting a nation as a whole —*n.* a citizen or subject —**na'tion·al·ly** *adv.*

**National Guard** in the U.S., the organized militia of the individual States: it can be activated as part of the U.S. Army

fat, āpe, cär; ten, ēven; is, bīte; gō, hôrn, tōōl, look; oil, out; up, fur; chin; she; thin, *then*; zh, leisure; ŋ, ring; ə for *a* in *ago*; ¸ (ā'b'l); ë, Fr. coeur; ö, Fr. feu; Fr. mon; ü, Fr. duc; kh, G. ich, doch; ‡ foreign; < derived from

**na·tion·al·ism** n. 1. devotion to one's nation, its interests, etc.; patriotism or chauvinism 2. the advocacy of national independence —**na'tion·al·ist** n., adj. —**na'tion·al·is'tic** adj.

**na·tion·al·i·ty** (nash'ə nal'ə tē) n., pl. -ties 1. the status of belonging to a nation by birth or naturalization 2. a nation or national group

**na·tion·al·ize'** (-nə liz') vt. -ized', -iz'ing 1. to make national 2. to transfer ownership or control of (land, industries, etc.) to the nation —**na'tion·al·i·za'tion** n.

**na'tion·wide'** adj. by or throughout the whole nation; national

**na·tive** (nāt'iv) adj. [< L. natus, born] 1. inborn 2. belonging to a locality or country by birth, production, or growth 3. being, or associated with, the place of one's birth [one's native land or language] 4. as found in nature; natural 5. of or characteristic of the original inhabitants of a place —n. 1. a person born in the place indicated 2. an original inhabitant 3. an indigenous plant or animal

**na'tive-born'** adj. born in a specified place or country

**na·tiv·i·ty** (nə tiv'ə tē) n., pl. -ties [see NATIVE] birth —**the Nativity** the birth of Jesus

**natl.** national

**NATO** (nā'tō) North Atlantic Treaty Organization

**nat·ty** (nat'ē) adj. -ti·er, -ti·est [< ? NEAT] trim and stylish —**nat'ti·ly** adv.

**nat·u·ral** (nach'ər əl) adj. [< L. naturalis, by birth] 1. of or dealing with nature 2. produced or existing in nature; not artificial 3. innate; not acquired 4. true to nature; lifelike 5. normal [a natural result] 6. free from affectation; at ease 7. Music neither sharped nor flatted —n. [Colloq.] a person or thing sure to be successful —**nat'u·ral·ness** n.

**natural childbirth** childbirth without anesthesia through prior training

**natural history** the study of the animal, vegetable, and mineral world, esp. in a popular way

**nat'u·ral·ism** n. 1. action or thought based on natural desires 2. Literature, Art, etc. the portrayal of people and things as they really are

**nat'u·ral·ist** n. 1. one who studies animals and plants 2. an advocate of naturalism —**nat'u·ral·is'tic** adj.

**nat'u·ral·ize'** (-ə liz') vt. -ized', -iz'ing to confer citizenship upon (an alien) —**nat'u·ral·i·za'tion** n.

**nat'u·ral·ly** adv. 1. in a natural manner 2. by nature; innately 3. as one might expect; of course

**natural resources** those forms of wealth supplied by nature, as coal, oil, water power, etc.

**natural science** the systematized knowledge of nature, including biology, chemistry, physics, etc.

**na·ture** (nā'chər) n. [< L. nasci, be born] 1. the essential quality of a thing; essence 2. inherent tendencies of a person 3. kind; type 4. a) the entire physical universe b) [sometimes N-] the power, force, etc. that seems to regulate this 5. the primitive state of man 6. natural scenery —**by nature** inherently

**Naug·a·hyde** (nôg'ə hīd') [arbitrary coinage] a trademark for an imitation leather, used for upholstery —n. [n-] this material

**naught** (nôt) n. [< OE. na wiht, no person] 1. nothing 2. a zero (0)

**naugh·ty** (nôt'ē) adj. -ti·er, -ti·est [< obs. naught, wicked] 1. mischievous or disobedient 2. indelicate —**naugh'ti·ly** adv. —**naugh'ti·ness** n.

**nau·se·a** (nô'shə, -sē ə) n. [< Gr. nausia, seasickness] 1. a feeling of sickness at the stomach, with an impulse to vomit 2. disgust; loathing

**nau'se·ate'** (-shē āt', -sē-, -zē-) vt. -at'ed, -at'ing to cause to feel nausea

**nau·seous** (nô'shəs, -zē əs) adj. 1. causing nausea 2. [Colloq.] nauseated

**nau·ti·cal** (nôt'i k'l) adj. [< Gr. naus, ship] of sailors, ships, or navigation —**nau'ti·cal·ly** adv.

**nau·ti·lus** (nôt'l əs) n., pl. -lus·es, -li' (-l') [< Gr. naus, ship] a tropical mollusk with a spiral shell

**Nav·a·ho, Nav·a·jo** (nav'ə hō') n., pl. -hos', -ho', -hoes' a member of a tribe of SW U.S. Indians

NAUTILUS

**na·val** (nā'v'l) adj. [< L. navis, ship] of, having, characteristic of, or for a navy, its ships, etc.

**nave** (nāv) n. [< L. navis, ship] the main part of a church, from the chancel to the principal entrance

**na·vel** (nā'v'l) n. [OE. nafela] the small scar in the abdomen, marking the place where the umbilical cord was attached to the fetus

**navel orange** a seedless orange with a navellike hollow at its apex

**nav·i·ga·ble** (nav'i gə b'l) adj. 1. wide or deep enough to be traveled on by ships 2. that can be steered —**nav'i·ga·bil'i·ty** n.

**nav·i·gate** (nav'ə gāt') vt., vi. -gat'ed, -gat'ing [< L. navis, ship + agere, to lead] 1. to steer or direct (a ship or aircraft) 2. to travel through or over (water, air, etc.) in a ship or aircraft 3. [Colloq.] to walk

**nav'i·ga'tion** (-gā'shən) n. a navigating; esp., the science of locating the position and plotting the course of ships and aircraft

**nav'i·ga'tor** n. one skilled in the navigation of a ship or aircraft

**na·vy** (nā'vē) n., pl. -vies [< L. navis, ship] 1. all the warships of a nation 2. [often N-] a nation's entire sea force, including ships, men, stores, etc. 3. very dark blue: also **navy blue**

**navy bean** [from use in U.S. Navy] a small, white variety of bean

**navy blue** very dark, purplish blue

**nay** (nā) adv. [< ON. ne, not + ei, ever] not only that, but beyond that [he's well-off, nay rich] —n. 1. a denial 2. a negative vote or voter

**Na·zi** (nät′sē) *adj.* [G. contr. of the party name] designating or of the German fascist political party which ruled Germany under Hitler (1933–1945) —*n.* a member of this party

**NB** Nebraska

**N.B.** New Brunswick

**N.B., n.b.** [L. *nota bene*] note well

**N.C., NC** North Carolina

**NCO, N.C.O.** noncommissioned officer

**N.Dak., ND** North Dakota

**NE, N.E., n.e.** 1. northeast 2. northeastern

**Ne·an·der·thal** (nē an′dər thôl′) *adj.* [ < a G. valley] designating or of a form of early man of the Stone Age

**neap** (nēp) *adj.* [OE. *nep-* in *nepflod*, neap tide] designating either of the two lowest high tides in the month —*n.* neap tide

**Ne·a·pol·i·tan** (nē′ə päl′ə t′n) *adj.* of Naples —*n.* a native or inhabitant of Naples

**Neapolitan ice cream** brick ice cream in layers of different colors and flavors

**near** (nir) *adv.* [OE. compar. of *neah*, nigh] 1. at a short distance in space or time 2. almost *[near* right*]* 3. closely; intimately —*adj.* 1. close in distance or time 2. close in relationship; akin 3. close in friendship; intimate 4. close in degree *[a near escape]* 5. short or direct *[the near* way*]* —*prep.* close to —*vt., vi.* to draw near (to); approach —**near′ness** *n.*

**near′by′** *adj., adv.* near; close at hand

**Near East** countries near the E end of the Mediterranean, including those of Arabia, &, sometimes, the Balkans

**near′ly** *adv.* almost; not quite

**near miss** a result that is nearly but not quite successful

**near′sight′ed** *adj.* having better vision for near objects than for distant ones; myopic —**near′sight′ed·ness** *n.*

**neat** (nēt) *adj.* [ < L. *nitere*, to shine] 1. unmixed; undiluted *[whiskey neat]* 2. clean and tidy 3. skillful and precise 4. well-proportioned 5. cleverly done or said 6. [Slang] nice, pleasing, etc. —**neat′ly** *adv.* —**neat′ness** *n.*

**'neath, neath** (nēth) *prep. poet. var. of* BENEATH

**Ne·bras·ka** (nə bras′kə) Middle Western State of the U.S.: 77,227 sq. mi.; pop. 1,484,000; cap. Lincoln: abbrev. Nebr. —**Ne·bras′kan** *adj., n.*

**neb·u·la** (neb′yə lə) *n., pl.* **-lae′** (-lē′), **-las** [L., mist] any of the cloud-like patches in the sky consisting of gaseous matter, far distant stars, or external galaxies —**neb′u·lar** *adj.*

**neb′u·lous** (-ləs) *adj.* unclear; vague —**nec·es·sar·i·ly** (nes′ə ser′ə lē) *adv.* 1. because of necessity 2. as a necessary result

**nec·es·sar′y** (-ser′ē) *adj.* [ < L. *ne-*, not + *cedere*, give way] 1. essential; indispensable 2. inevitable 3. required —*n., pl.* **-ies** something necessary

**ne·ces·si·tate** (nə ses′ə tāt′) *vt.* **-tat′ed, -tat′ing** to make necessary or unavoidable

**ne·ces′si·ty** (-tē) *n., pl.* **-ties** [see NECESSARY] 1. natural causation; fate 2. great need 3. something that cannot be done without 4. want; poverty —**of necessity** necessarily

**neck** (nek) *n.* [OE. *hnecca*] 1. that part of man or animal joining the head to the body 2. that part of a garment nearest the neck 3. a necklike part; specif., *a)* a narrow strip of land *b)* the narrowest part of a bottle, etc. *c)* a strait —*vt., vi.* [Slang] to kiss and caress in making love —**neck and neck** very close, as in a contest —**stick one's neck out** to act boldly, risking possible failure

**neck·er·chief** (nek′ər chif, -chēf′) *n.* [see NECK & KERCHIEF] a handkerchief or scarf worn around the neck

**neck′lace** (-lis) *n.* [NECK + LACE, *n.* 1] an ornamental chain of gold, beads, etc., worn around the neck

**neck′tie′** *n.* a band worn around the neck under a collar and tied in front

**neck′wear′** *n.* articles worn about the neck, as neckties, scarfs, etc.

**ne·crol·o·gy** (ne kräl′ə jē) *n., pl.* **-gies** [ < Gr. *nekros*, dead body + -LOGY] a list of people who have died

**nec·ro·man·cy** (nek′rə man′sē) *n.* [ < Gr. *nekros*, corpse + *manteia*, divination] 1. divination by alleged communication with the dead 2. sorcery

**ne·cro·sis** (ne krō′sis) *n.* [ < Gr. *nekros*, dead body] the death or decay of tissue in a part of the body

**nec·tar** (nek′tər) *n.* [ < Gr. *nektar*] 1. *Gr. Myth.* the drink of the gods 2. any very delicious beverage 3. the sweetish liquid in many flowers, used by bees to make honey

**nec·tar·ine** (nek′tə rēn′) *n.* [ < prec.] a kind of smooth-skinned peach

**nee, née** (nā; *now often* nē) *adj.* [Fr.] born *[Mrs. Helen Jones, nee Smith]*

**need** (nēd) *n.* [OE. *nied*] 1. necessity 2. lack of something required or desired *[the need of a rest]* 3. something required or desired that is lacking *[my daily needs]* 4. *a)* a time or condition when help is required *[a friend in need]* *b)* poverty —*vt.* 1. to have need of; require 2. to be obliged *[I need to be careful]* —**have need to** to be required to —**if need be** if it is required

**need′ful** *adj.* necessary; required

**nee·dle** (nēd′'l) *n.* [OE. *nædl*] 1. a slender, pointed piece of steel with a hole for thread, used for sewing 2. a slender rod of steel, bone, etc. used for crocheting or knitting 3. the short, pointed piece that moves in the groove of a phonograph record and transmits vibrations 4. the pointer of a compass, gauge, etc. 5. the thin, short leaf of the pine, spruce, etc. 6. the sharp, slender metal tube at the end of a hypodermic syringe —*vt.* **-dled,**

**-dling** [Colloq.] **1.** to goad; prod **2.** to tease

**nee′dle·point′** *n.* **1.** embroidery of woolen threads upon canvas **2.** lace made on a paper pattern with a needle: in full **needlepoint lace**

**need′less** *adj.* not needed; unnecessary —**need′less·ly** *adv.*

**nee′dle·work′** *n.* work done with a needle; embroidery, needlepoint, etc.

**need′n′t** (nēd′nt) need not

**needs** (nēdz) *adv.* [OE. *nedes*] of necessity [I must *needs* go]

**need′y** *adj.* **-i·er, -i·est** in need; very poor; destitute —**need′i·ness** *n.*

**ne′er** (ner) *adv.* [Poet.] never

**ne′er′-do-well′** *n.* a shiftless, irresponsible person

**ne·far·i·ous** (ni fer′ē əs) *adj.* [ < L. *ne-*, not + *fas*, lawful] very wicked — **ne·far′i·ous·ly** *adv.* —**ne·far′i·ous·ness** *n.*

**ne·gate** (ni gāt′) *vt.* **-gat′ed, -gat′ing** [ < L. *negare*, deny] **1.** to deny **2.** to make ineffective; nullify

**ne·ga·tion** (ni gā′shən) *n.* **1.** act or instance of denying **2.** the lack or opposite of something positive

**neg·a·tive** (neg′ə tiv) *adj.* **1.** expressing denial or refusal; saying "no" **2.** opposite to or lacking in that which is positive [a *negative* force] **3.** Math. designating a quantity less than zero, or one to be subtracted **4.** *Photography* reversing the light and shade of the original subject **5.** *Elec.* a) of electricity predominating in a body of resin that has been rubbed with wool b) charged with negative electricity c) having an excess of electrons —*n.* **1.** a negative word, reply, etc. **2.** the point of view that opposes the positive **3.** the plate in a voltaic battery where the lower potential is **4.** an exposed and developed photographic plate or film on which light and shadow are reversed —*vt.* **-tived, -tiv·ing** to reject or deny —**in the negative** in refusal or denial of a plan, etc. — **neg′a·tive·ly** *adv.*

**neg·lect** (ni glekt′) *vt.* [ < L. *neg-*, not + *legere*, gather] **1.** to ignore or disregard **2.** to fail to attend to properly **3.** to leave undone —*n.* **1.** a neglecting **2.** lack of proper care **3.** a being neglected —**neg·lect′ful** *adj.*

**neg·li·gee** (neg′lə zhā′) *n.* [ < Fr. *négliger*, to neglect] a woman's loosely fitting dressing gown

**neg·li·gent** (neg′li jənt) *adj.* **1.** habitually failing to do the required thing; neglectful **2.** careless, inattentive, etc. —**neg′li·gence** *n.*

**neg′li·gi·ble** (-jə b'l) *adj.* that can be neglected or disregarded; trifling

**ne·go·ti·ate** (ni gō′shē āt′) *vi.* **-at′ed, -at′ing** [ < L. *negotium*, business] to discuss with a view to reaching agreement —*vt.* **1.** to settle (a transaction, treaty, etc.) **2.** to transfer or sell (bonds, stocks, etc.) **3.** to succeed in crossing, passing, etc. —**ne·go′ti·a·ble** (-shē ə b'l, -shə b'l) *adj.* — **ne·go′ti·a′tion** *n.* —**ne·go′ti·a′tor** *n.*

**ne·gri·tude** (neg′rə tōōd′, nē′grə-) *n.* [Fr. *négritude*] an awareness and affirmation by blacks of their distinctive cultural heritage

**Ne·gro** (nē′grō) *n., pl.* **-groes** [Sp. & Port. *negro*, black] **1.** a member of the dominant group of mankind in Africa, characterized generally by a dark skin **2.** a member of the Negroid group **3.** any person with some Negro ancestors —*adj.* of or for Negroes

**Ne′groid** (-groid) *adj.* designating or of one of the major groups of mankind, including most of the peoples of Africa south of the Sahara

**Neh·ru** (nā′rōō), **Ja·wa·har·lal** (jə wä′hər läl′) 1889–1964; prime minister of India (1947–64)

**neigh** (nā) *vi.* [OE. *hnægan*] to utter the characteristic cry of a horse —*n.* this cry; whinny

**neigh·bor** (nā′bər) *n.* [OE. *neah*, nigh + hyp. *gebur*, freeholder] **1.** one who lives or is situated near another **2.** a fellow man —*adj.* nearby —*vt., vi.* to live or be situated nearby Brit. sp. **neighbour** —**neigh′bor·ing** *adj.*

**neigh′bor·hood′** *n.* **1.** a particular community, district, or area **2.** the people living near one another —**in the neighborhood of** [Colloq.] **1.** near **2.** about; approximately

**neigh′bor·ly** *adj.* like or appropriate to neighbors; friendly, helpful, etc. —**neigh′bor·li·ness** *n.*

**nei·ther** (nē′thər, nī′-) *adj., pron.* [OE. *na-hwæther*, lit., not whether] not one or the other (of two); not either [*neither* boy went, *neither* of them was invited] —*conj.* not either [I can *neither* go nor stay]

**nem·e·sis** (nem′ə sis) *n., pl.* **-ses′** (-sēz′) [Gr. < *nemein*, deal out] **1.** a) just punishment b) one who imposes it **2.** anyone or anything that seems inevitably to defeat or frustrate one

**neo-** [ < Gr. *neos*] [often N-] a combining form meaning: **1.** new; recent **2.** in a new or different way

**ne·o·clas·sic** (nē′ō klas′ik) *adj.* designating or of a revival of classic style and form in art, literature, etc.

**ne′o·co·lo′ni·al·ism** *n.* the exploiting of a supposedly independent region, as by imposing a puppet government

**ne·ol·o·gism** (nē äl′ə jiz′m) *n.* [see NEO-, -LOGY, & -ISM] a new word or a new meaning for an established word

**ne·on** (nē′än) *n.* [ < Gr. *neos*, new] a rare, inert gaseous chemical element found in the earth's atmosphere

**neon lamp** a glass tube containing neon, which glows red when an electric current is sent through it

**ne·o·phyte** (nē′ə fīt′) *n.* [ < Gr. *neos*, new + *phyein*, to produce] **1.** a new convert **2.** a beginner; novice

**ne′o·plasm** (-plaz′m) *n.* [ < NEO- + Gr. *plassein*, to mold] an abnormal growth of tissue, as a tumor

**ne′o·prene′** (-prēn′) *n.* a synthetic rubber resistant to oil, heat, etc.

**Ne·pal** (ni pôl′) country in the Himalayas: 54,362 sq. mi.; pop. 10,294,000 —**Nep·a·lese** (nep′ə lēz′) *adj., n., pl.* **-lese′**

**ne·pen·the** (ni pen′thē) *n.* [ < Gr.

ne-, not + *penthos*, sorrow] anything that causes forgetfulness of sorrow

**neph·ew** (nef′yōō) *n.* [< L. *nepos*] the son of one's brother or sister, or of one's brother-in-law or sister-in-law

**ne·phri·tis** (ne frīt′əs) *n.* [< Gr. *nephros*, kidney + -ITIS] disease of the kidneys, accompanied by inflammation

**ne plus ul·tra** (nē plus ul′trə) [L., no more beyond] the utmost limit

**nep·o·tism** (nep′ə tiz′m) *n.* [< L. *nepos*, nephew] favoritism shown to relatives, esp. in securing jobs

**Nep·tune** (nep′tōōn) **1.** the Roman god of the sea **2.** the planet eighth in distance from the sun: see PLANET

**nep·tu·ni·um** (nep tōō′nē əm) *n.* a radioactive chemical element produced from uranium

**nerd** (nurd) *n.* [Slang] a person regarded as contemptibly dull, ineffective, etc.

**Ne·ro** (nir′ō) 37–68 A.D.; emperor of Rome (54–68)

**nerve** (nurv) *n.* [< L. *nervus*] **1.** any of the cordlike fibers carrying impulses between body organs and the central nervous system **2.** coolness in danger; courage **3.** [*pl.*] nervousness **4.** [Colloq.] impudent boldness —*vt.* **nerved, nerv′ing** to give strength or courage to —**get on one's nerves** [Colloq.] to make one irritable — **nerve oneself** to collect one's energies or courage for an effort

**nerve center 1.** any group of nerve cells that work together in controlling a specific sense or bodily activity **2.** a control center; headquarters

**nerve gas** a poisonous gas causing paralysis of the respiratory and central nervous systems

**nerve·less** *adj.* **1.** without strength, vigor, etc.; weak **2.** not nervous; cool; controlled —**nerve′less·ly** *adv.* —**nerve′less·ness** *n.*

**nerve′-rack·ing, nerve′-wrack′-ing** (-rak′iŋ) *adj.* very trying to one's patience or equanimity

**nerv·ous** (nur′vəs) *adj.* **1.** animated **2.** of or made up of nerves **3.** emotionally tense, restless, etc. **4.** fearful — **nerv′ous·ly** *adv.* —**nerv′ous·ness** *n.*

**nervous system** all the nerve cells and nervous tissues in an organism, including, in the vertebrates, the brain, spinal cord, nerves, etc.

**nerv·y** *adj.* **-i·er, -i·est 1.** bold **2.** [Colloq.] brazen; impudent

**-ness** (nis, nəs) [OE. *-nes(s)*] *a suffix meaning* state, quality, or instance of being [*sadness*]

**nest** (nest) *n.* [OE.] **1.** the structure or place where a bird lays its eggs and shelters its young **2.** the place used by insects, fish, etc. for spawning or breeding **3.** a cozy place; retreat **4.** a resort or its frequenters [*a nest of criminals*] **5.** a set of things, each fitting within the one next larger —*vi., vt.* **1.** to build or settle in (a nest) **2.** to fit (an object) closely within another

**nest egg** money, etc. put aside as a reserve or to establish a fund

**nes·tle** (nes′'l) *vi.* **-tled, -tling** [OE. *nestlian*] **1.** to settle down comfortably **2.** to press close for comfort or in affection **3.** to lie sheltered, as a house among trees —*vt.* to rest snugly

**nest·ling** (nest′liŋ, nes′-) *n.* a young bird not yet ready to leave the nest

**net**[1] (net) *n.* [OE. *nett*] **1.** an openwork fabric, as of string, used to snare birds, fish, etc. **2.** a trap; snare **3.** a meshed fabric, esp. one used to hold, protect, etc. [*a hairnet*] —*vt.* **net′ted, net′-ting** to snare or enclose as with a net

**net**[2] (net) *adj.* [Fr., clear] left over after deductions or allowances have been made —*n.* a net amount, profit, weight, price, etc. —*vt.* **net′ted, net′ting** to clear as profit, etc.

**neth·er** (neth′ər) *adj.* [OE. *neothera*] lower or under [*the nether world*]

**Neth·er·lands** (neth′ər ləndz) country in W Europe: 12,978 sq. mi.; pop. 12,597,000

**neth′er·most′** *adj.* lowest

**net′ting** *n.* netted material

**net·tle** (net′'l) *n.* [OE. *netele*] a weed with stinging hairs —*vt.* **-tled, -tling** to irritate; annoy; vex

**net′tle·some** *adj.* annoying; vexing

**net′work′** (-wurk′) *n.* **1.** an arrangement of parallel wires, etc. crossed at intervals by others so as to leave open spaces **2.** anything like this, as a system of interconnected roads, individuals, etc. **3.** *Radio & TV* a chain of transmitting stations —*adj.* broadcast over the stations of a network

**neu·ral** (noor′əl) *adj.* [NEUR(O)- + -AL] of a nerve or the nervous system

**neu·ral·gia** (noo ral′jə) *n.* [see NEURO- & -ALGIA] severe pain along the course of a nerve —**neu·ral′gic** (-jik) *adj.*

**neu·ras·the·ni·a** (noor′əs thē′nē ə) *n.* [< NEUR(O)- + Gr. *asthenia*, weakness] a type of neurosis characterized by fatigue, anxiety, etc. —**neu′ras·then′ic** (-then′ik) *adj., n.*

**neu·ri·tis** (noo rīt′əs) *n.* [NEUR(O)- + -ITIS] inflammation of a nerve or nerves —**neu·rit′ic** (-rit′ik) *adj.*

**neuro-** [< Gr. *neuron*, nerve] *a combining form meaning* of a nerve or the nervous system: also **neur-**

**neu·rol·o·gy** (noo räl′ə jē) *n.* [prec. + -LOGY] the branch of medicine dealing with the nervous system and its diseases —**neu·ro·log·i·cal** (noor′ə läj′i k'l) *adj.* —**neu·rol′o·gist** *n.*

**neu·ron** (noor′än) *n.* the nerve cell body and all its processes

**neu·ro·sis** (noo rō′sis) *n., pl.* **-ses** (-sēz) [NEUR(O)- + -OSIS] a mental disorder characterized by anxieties, compulsions, obsessions, phobias, etc.

**neu·rot·ic** (-rät′ik) *adj.* of, characteristic of, or having a neurosis —*n.* a neurotic person —**neu·rot′i·cal·ly** *adv.*

**neu·ter** (nōōt′ər) *adj.* [< L. *ne-*, not + *uter*, either] **1.** *Biol. a)* having no sexual organ *b)* having undeveloped sexual organs in the adult **2.** *Gram.* designating or of the gender of words neither masculine nor feminine —*vt.* to castrate or spay (an animal)

**neu·tral** (nōō′trəl) *adj.* [see prec.] **1.** supporting neither side in a quarrel or war **2.** of neither extreme in type, kind, etc.; indifferent **3.** having little or no decided color **4.** *Chem.* neither acid nor alkaline —*n.* **1.** a neutral person or nation **2.** a neutral color **3.** *Mechanics* a disengaged position of gears —**neu′tral·ly** *adv.*

**neu·tral·ism** (-iz′m) *n.* a policy of remaining neutral, esp. in international conflicts —**neu′tral·ist** *adj., n.*

**neu·tral·i·ty** (-tral′ə tē) *n.* **1.** a being neutral **2.** the status or policy of a neutral nation

**neu·tral·ize** (nōō′trə līz′) *vt.* **-ized′, -iz′ing** **1.** to declare (a nation, etc.) neutral in war **2.** to destroy or counteract the effectiveness, force, etc. of —**neu′tral·i·za′tion** *n.*

**neutral spirits** ethyl alcohol of 190 proof or over, used in blended whiskeys, liqueurs, etc.

**neu·tri·no** (nōō trē′nō) *n., pl.* **-nos** [It., little neutron] *Physics* an uncharged particle with almost no mass

**neu·tron** (nōō′trän) *n.* [ < NEUTRAL] one of the elementary, uncharged particles of an atom

**neutron bomb** a small thermonuclear bomb, that would release radioactive neutrons that could kill people without destroying buildings, etc.

**Ne·vad·a** (nə vad′ə, -vä′də) Western State of the U.S.: 110,540 sq. mi.; pop. 489,000; cap. Carson City: abbrev. Nev. —**Ne·vad′an** *adj., n.*

**nev·er** (nev′ər) *adv.* [ < OE. *ne,* not + *æfre,* ever] **1.** not ever; at no time **2.** not at all; in no case

**nev′er·more′** *adv.* never again

**never-never land** an unreal or imaginary place or situation

**nev′er·the·less′** (-thə les′) *adv.* in spite of that; however

**ne·vus** (nē′vəs) *n., pl.* **ne′vi** (-vī) [L. *naevus*] a birthmark or mole

**new** (nōō) *adj.* [OE. *niwe*] **1.** appearing, thought of, discovered, made, etc. for the first time **2.** different from (the) one in the past *[a new* hairdo*]* **3.** strange; unfamiliar **4.** recently grown; fresh *[new* potatoes*]* **5.** unused **6.** modern; recent **7.** more; additional **8.** starting as a repetition of a cycle, series, etc. *[the new* moon*]* **9.** having just reached a position, rank, place, etc. *[a new* arrival*]* —*adv.* **1.** again **2.** newly; recently —**new′ness** *n.*

**New·ark** (nōō′ərk) city in NE N.J.: pop. 382,000

**New Bed·ford** (bed′fərd) seaport in SE Mass.: pop. 102,000

**new blood** new people as a possible source of new ideas, vigor, etc.

**new′born′** *adj.* **1.** just born **2.** reborn

**New Bruns·wick** (brunz′wik) province of SE Canada: 28,354 sq. mi.; pop. 617,000

**new′com′er** *n.* a recent arrival

**New Deal** the principles and policies adopted by President F. D. Roosevelt in the 1930's to advance economic recovery and social welfare

**New Delhi** capital of India, adjacent to Delhi: pop. 261,000

**new·el** (nōō′əl) *n.* [ult. < L. *nux,* nut] **1.** the pillar around which the steps of a winding staircase turn **2.** the post that supports the handrail of a flight of stairs: also **newel post**

**New England** the six NE States of the U.S.: Me., Vt., N.H., Mass., R.I., & Conn. —**New Englander**

**new′fan′gled** (-fan′g'ld) *adj.* [ME. < *newe,* new + *-fangel* < OE. *fon,* to take] new; novel: contemptuous term

**new′-fash′ioned** *adj.* **1.** recently come into fashion **2.** new in form

**New·found·land** (nōō′fənd land′, -lənd) province of Canada, including an island off the E coast & Labrador: 156,185 sq. mi.; pop. 494,000

**New Guinea** large island in the East Indies, north of Australia

**New Hamp·shire** (hamp′shir) New England State of the U.S.: 9,304 sq. mi.; pop. 738,000; cap. Concord

**New Ha·ven** (hā′vən) city in S Conn.: pop. 138,000

**New Jersey** Eastern State of the U.S.: 7,836 sq. mi.; pop. 7,168,000; cap. Trenton

**new′ly** *adv.* recently; lately

**new′ly·wed′** *n.* a recently married person

**New Mexico** Southwestern State of the U.S.: 121,666 sq. mi.; pop. 1,016,000; cap. Santa Fe

**new moon** the moon when it is between the earth and the sun, with its dark side toward the earth: in a few days it reappears as a thin crescent

**New Or·le·ans** (ôr′lē əns, ôr lēnz′) city & port in SE La.: pop. 593,000

**New·port News** (nōō′pôrt′) seaport in SE Va.: pop. 138,000

**news** (nōōz) *n.pl.* [with sing. v.] **1.** new information; information previously unknown **2.** *a)* recent happenings *b)* reports of these **3.** a newscast — **make news** to do something reported as news

**news′boy′** *n.* a paperboy

**news′cast′** *n.* a radio or television news broadcast —**news′cast′er** *n.*

**news′deal′er** *n.* a retailer of newspapers, magazines, etc.

**news′let′ter** *n.* a bulletin issued regularly, containing news, often of interest to a special group

**news′man′** (-man′, -mən) *n., pl.* **-men** (-men′, -mən) **1.** *same as* NEWSDEALER **2.** one who gathers and reports news for a newspaper, TV station, etc.

**news′pa′per** *n.* a regular publication, usually daily or weekly, containing news, opinions, advertising, etc.

**news′pa′per·man′** *n., pl.* **-men′ 1.** a man working for a newspaper, esp. a reporter, editor, etc. **2.** a newspaper owner or publisher —**news′pa′per·wom′an** *n.fem., pl.* **-wom′en**

**news′print′** *n.* a cheap paper used chiefly for newspapers

**news′stand′** *n.* a stand at which

newspapers, magazines, etc. are sold

**news·wor·thy** (-wur/*th*ē) *adj.* timely and important or interesting

**news·y** *adj.* **-i·er, -i·est** [Colloq.] containing much news

**newt** (nōōt, nyōōt) *n.* [by merging of ME. *an eute,* a newt] any of various small amphibious salamanders

NEWT

**New Testament** the part of the Bible that contains the life and teachings of Jesus and his followers

**New·ton** (nōōt/'n), Sir Isaac 1642–1727; Eng. mathematician

**New World** the Western Hemisphere —**new/-world/, New/-World/** *adj.*

**New Year's (Day)** January 1

**New Year's Eve** the evening before New Year's Day

**New York** (yôrk) **1.** State of the NE U.S.: 49,576 sq. mi.; pop. 18,191,000; cap. Albany **2.** city & port in SE N.Y.: often **New York City:** pop. 7,868,000 —**New York/er**

**New Zea·land** (zē/lənd) country in the Brit. Commonwealth, including two large islands in the S Pacific: 103,736 sq. mi.; pop. 2,726,000 — **New Zea/land·er**

**next** (nekst) *adj.* [OE. *neahst,* superl. of *neah,* nigh] nearest; immediately preceding or following —*adv.* **1.** in the nearest time, place, rank, etc. **2.** on the first subsequent occasion —*prep.* nearest to *[sit next the tree]*

**next/-door/** *adj.* in or at the next house, building, etc.

**nex·us** (nek/səs) *n., pl.* **-us·es, nex/us** [L.] a link or connection

**Nfld., Nfd.** Newfoundland

**N.G., n.g.** [Slang] no good

**N.H., NH** New Hampshire

**ni·a·cin** (nī/ə sin) *n.* NI(COTINIC) AC(ID) + *-in*] *same as* NICOTINIC ACID

**Ni·ag·a·ra Falls** (nī ag/rə, -ag/ər ə) **1.** large waterfall on a river (**Niagara River**) flowing from Lake Erie into Lake Ontario **2.** city in W N.Y.: pop. 86,000

**nib** (nib) *n.* [< ME. *nebb*] **1.** a bird's beak **2.** a point, esp. a pen point

**nib·ble** (nib/'l) *vt., vi.* **-bled, -bling** [LME. *nebyllen*] **1.** to eat (food) with quick, small bites **2.** to bite (*at*) lightly and intermittently —*n.* a small bite —**nib/bler** *n.*

**nibs** (nibz) *n.* [< ?] [Colloq.] an important, esp. a self-important, person (with *his*)

**Nic·a·ra·gua** (nik/ə rä/gwə) country in Central America: 54,342 sq. mi.; pop. 1,715,000 —**Nic/a·ra/guan** *adj., n.*

**nice** (nīs) *adj.* **nic/er, nic/est** [< L. *nescius,* ignorant] **1.** fastidious; refined **2.** delicate; precise; subtle *[a nice distinction]* **3.** calling for care, tact, etc. **4.** finely discriminating or

minutely accurate **5.** pleasant, attractive, kind, good, etc.: a generalized term of approval —**nice/ly** *adv.*

**ni·ce·ty** (nī/sə tē) *n., pl.* **-ties 1.** precision; accuracy **2.** fastidiousness; refinement **3.** a subtle or minute detail, distinction, etc. **4.** something choice or dainty

**niche** (nich) *n.* [Fr. < L. *nidus,* a nest] **1.** a recess in a wall, for a statue, vase, etc. **2.** an especially suitable place or position

**‡nicht wahr?** (nikht vär/) [G., not true?] isn't that so?

**nick** (nik) *n.* [LME. *nyke*] a small cut, chip, etc. made on a surface —*vt.* **1.** to make a nick or nicks in **2.** to wound superficially —**in the nick of time** exactly when needed

**nick·el** (nik/'l) *n.* [< G. *kupfernickel,* copper demon: the copperlike ore contained no copper] **1.** a hard, silverwhite, metallic chemical element, much used in alloys **2.** a U.S. or Canadian coin of nickel and copper, equal to five cents

**nick·el·o·de·on** (nik/ə lō/dē ən) *n.* [NICKEL + (*mel*)*odeon,* a small keyboard organ] a coin-operated player piano or early type of jukebox

**nick·er** (nik/ər) *vi., n. same as* NEIGH

**nick·name** (nik/nām/) *n.* [by merging of ME. *an ekename,* a surname] **1.** a substitute, often descriptive name given in fun, etc., as "Shorty" **2.** a familiar form of a proper name, as "Jim" for "James" —*vt.* **-named/, -nam/ing** to give a nickname to

**nic·o·tine** (nik/ə tēn/) *n.* [Fr. < J. *Nicot,* 16th-c. Fr. diplomat who took tobacco into France] a poisonous, oily liquid from tobacco leaves

**nic/o·tin/ic acid** (-tin/ik, -tē/nik) a member of the vitamin B complex

**niece** (nēs) *n.* [< L. *neptis*] the daughter of one's brother or sister or of one's brother-in-law or sister-in-law

**Nie·tzsche** (nē/chə), **Frie·drich** (frē/drikh) 1844–1900; Ger. philosopher

**nif·ty** (nif/tē) *adj.* **-ti·er, -ti·est** [prob. < MAGNIFICENT] [Slang] attractive, smart, stylish, etc.

**Ni·ger** (nī/jər) country in WC Africa: 458,500 sq. mi.; pop. 3,546,000

**Ni·ger·i·a** (nī jir/ē ə) country in WC Africa, in the Brit. Commonwealth: 327,186 sq. mi.; pop. 43,265,000 — **Ni·ger/i·an** *adj., n.*

**nig·gard** (nig/ərd) *n.* [prob. < Scand.] a stingy person; miser —*adj.* stingy —**nig/gard·li·ness** *n.* —**nig/gard·ly** *adj., adv.*

**nig·gle** (nig/'l) *vi.* **-gled, -gling** [prob. akin to Norw. *nigla*] to work fussily; be finicky —**nig/gler** *n.* — **nig/gling** *adj.*

**nigh** (nī) *adj., adv., prep.* [OE. *neah*] [Chiefly Archaic or Dial.] near

**night** (nīt) *n.* [OE. *niht*] **1.** the period of darkness from sunset to sunrise **2.** any period or condition of darkness or gloom

---

fat, āpe, cär; ten, ēven; is, bīte; gō, hôrn, tōōl, look; oil, out; up, fur; chin; she; thin, *th*en; zh, leisure; ŋ, ring; ə for *a* in *ago;* ', (ā/b'l); ë, Fr. coeur; ö, Fr. feu; Fr. mon; ü, Fr. duc; kh, G. ich, doch; ‡ foreign; < derived from

**night blindness** poor vision in near darkness or dim light

**night′cap′** n. 1. a cap worn in bed 2. [Colloq.] an alcoholic drink taken just before going to bed

**night clothes** clothes to be worn in bed, as pajamas

**night′club′** n. a place of entertainment for drinking, dancing, etc. at night

**night crawl′er** a large earthworm that comes to the surface at night

**night′dress′** n. same as NIGHTGOWN

**night′fall′** n. the close of the day

**night′gown′** n. a loose gown worn in bed by women or girls

**night′hawk′** n. 1. any of a group of night birds related to the whippoorwill 2. same as NIGHT OWL

**night′ie** (-ē) n. [Colloq.] a nightgown

**night·in·gale** (nīt′′n gāl′) n. [ < OE. niht, night + galan, sing] a small European thrush, the male of which sings melodiously, esp. at night

**Night·in·gale** (nīt′′n gāl′), **Florence** 1820-1910; Eng. pioneer in modern nursing

**night life** pleasure-seeking activity at night, as in nightclubs

**night′ly** adj. 1. of or like the night 2. done or occurring every night —adv. 1. at night 2. every night

**night′mare′** (-mer′) n. [ < ME. < niht, night + mare, demon] 1. a frightening dream 2. any frightening experience

**night owl** a person who works at night or otherwise stays up late

**night′shade′** (-shād′) n. any of various flowering plants related to the potato and tomato; esp., a poisonous variety, as the belladonna

**night′shirt′** n. a kind of nightgown worn, esp. formerly, by men or boys

**night′spot′** n. [Colloq.] a nightclub

**night stand** a small bedside table

**night stick** a long, heavy club carried by a policeman

**night′time′** n. the period of darkness from sunset to sunrise

**night′wear′** n. same as NIGHT CLOTHES

**ni·hil·ism** (nī′ə liz′m) n. [ < L. nihil, nothing] the general rejection of customary beliefs in morality, religion, etc. —ni′hil·ist n. —ni′hil·is′tic adj.

**nil** (nil) n. [L. < nihil] nothing

**Nile** (nīl) river in NE Africa, flowing through Egypt into the Mediterranean

**nim·ble** (nim′b'l) adj. -bler, -blest [ < OE. niman, to take] 1. quick-witted; alert 2. moving or acting quickly and lightly —nim′bly adv.

**nim·bus** (nim′bəs) n., pl. -bi (-bī), -bus·es [L.] 1. any rain-producing cloud 2. a halo around the head of a saint, etc., as on a picture

**Nim·rod** (nim′räd) Bible a mighty hunter

**nin·com·poop** (nin′kəm poōp′) n. [ < ?] a stupid, silly person; fool

**nine** (nīn) adj., n. [OE. nigon] one more than eight; 9; IX —**ninth** (nīnth) adj., n.

**nine′pins′** n.pl. [with sing. v.] a British version of the game of tenpins, played with nine wooden pins

**nine′teen′** (-tēn′) adj., n. nine more than ten; 19; XIX —**nine′teenth′** (-tēnth′) adj., n.

**nine′ty** (-tē) adj., n., pl. -ties nine times ten; 90; XC (or LXXXX) —**the nineties** the numbers or years, as of a century, from 90 through 99 —**nine′ti·eth** (-ith) adj., n.

**nin·ny** (nin′ē) n., pl. -nies [prob. contr. of an innocent] a fool; dolt

**nip¹** (nip) vt. **nipped, nip′ping** [prob. < MLowG. nippen] 1. to pinch or bite 2. to sever (shoots, etc.) as by clipping 3. to check the growth of 4. to have a painful or injurious effect on because of cold —n. 1. a nipping; pinch; bite 2. a stinging, as in cold air 3. stinging cold; frost —**nip and tuck** so close as to leave the outcome in doubt

**nip²** (nip) n. [prob. < Du. nippen, to sip] a small drink of liquor —vt., vi. **nipped, nip′ping** to drink in nips

**nip·per** (nip′ər) n. 1. anything that nips 2. [pl.] pliers, pincers, etc. 3. the claw of a crab or lobster

**nip·ple** (nip′'l) n. [prob. < neb, a beak] 1. the small protuberance on a breast or udder, through which the milk passes; teat 2. a teatlike, rubber part in the cap of a baby's bottle

**Nip·pon** (nip′än, ni pän′) Jap. name for JAPAN —**Nip′pon·ese′** (-ə nēz′) adj., n., pl. -ese′

**nip·py** (nip′ē) adj. -pi·er, -pi·est 1. sharp; biting 2. cold in a stinging way

**nir·va·na** (nir vä′nə, nər-, -van′ə) n. [ < Sans.] [also N-] 1. Buddhism the state of perfect blessedness achieved by the absorption of the soul into the supreme spirit 2. great bliss

**nit** (nit) n. [OE. hnitu] 1. the egg of a louse or similar insect 2. a young louse, etc.

**ni·ter** (nīt′ər) n. [ < Gr. nitron] potassium nitrate or sodium nitrate, used in making explosives, fertilizers, etc.; saltpeter: also, esp. Brit., **ni′tre**

**nit-pick·ing** (nit′pik′iŋ) adj., n. paying too much attention to petty details; niggling —**nit′-pick′er** n.

**ni·trate** (nī′trāt) n. a salt of nitric acid, as sodium nitrate —vt. -trat·ed, -trat·ing to combine with nitric acid or, esp., to make into a nitrate

**ni·tric acid** (nī′trik) a colorless, corrosive acid containing nitrogen

**ni·tro·cel·lu·lose** (nī′trō sel′yoo lōs′) n. a substance obtained by treating cellulose with nitric acid, used in making explosives, lacquers, etc.

**ni·tro·gen** (nī′trə jən) n. [ < Fr.: see NITER & -GEN] a colorless, odorless, gaseous chemical element forming nearly four fifths of the atmosphere —**ni·trog′e·nous** (-träj′ə nəs) adj.

**ni·tro·glyc·er·in, ni·tro·glyc·er·ine** (nī′trə glis′ər in) n. a thick, explosive oil, prepared by treating glycerin with nitric and sulfuric acids; used in dynamite

**ni·trous oxide** (nī′trəs) a colorless gas containing nitrogen, used as an anesthetic and in aerosols

**nit·ty-grit·ty** (nit′ē grit′ē) n. [Slang] the actual basic facts, issues, etc.

**nit'wit'** *n.* [? NIT + WIT[1]] a stupid person

**nix** (niks) *adv.* [G. *nichts*] [Slang] 1. no 2. not at all —*interj.* [Slang] 1. stop! 2. I forbid, disagree, etc. —*vt.* [Slang] to disapprove of or stop

**Nix·on** (nik's'n), **Richard M.** (1913– ); 37th president of the U.S. (1969–74): resigned

**N.J., NJ** New Jersey

**N.Mex.** New Mexico: also **N.M., NM**

**no** (nō) *adv.* [< OE. *ne a*, not ever] 1. not at all [*no worse*] 2. nay; not so: used to deny, refuse, or disagree —*adj.* not a; not one [*no errors*] —*n.*, *pl.* **noes, nos** 1. a refusal or denial 2. a negative vote or voter

**No., no.** number

**No·ah** (nō'ə) *Bible* the patriarch commanded by God to build the ark: see ARK (sense 1)

**No·bel'ist, No·bel'list** *n.* a person who has won a Nobel prize

**No·bel prizes** (nō bel') [after A. B. *Nobel*, 19th-c. Swed. inventor who established them] annual international prizes given for distinction in physics, chemistry, medicine, and literature, and for the promotion of peace

**no·bil·i·ty** (nō bil'ə tē) *n.*, *pl.* **-ties** 1. a being noble 2. high rank in society 3. the class of people of noble rank

**no·ble** (nō'b'l) *adj.* **-bler, -blest** [< L. *nobilis*, well-known] 1. famous or renowned 2. having high moral qualities 3. excellent 4. grand; stately 5. of high hereditary rank —*n.* one having hereditary rank or title —**no'-ble·ness** *n.* —**no'bly** *adv.*

**no'ble·man** (-mən) *n.*, *pl.* **-men** a member of the nobility; peer

**no·blesse o·blige** (nō bles' ō blēzh') [Fr., nobility obliges] the inferred obligation of people of high rank to behave nobly toward others

**no·bod·y** (nō'bud'ē, -bäd'ē; -bə dē) *pron.* not anybody; no one —*n.*, *pl.* **-ies** a person of no importance

**noc·tur·nal** (näk tur'n'l) *adj.* [< L. *nox*, night] 1. of the night 2. functioning, done, or active during the night —**noc·tur'nal·ly** *adv.*

**noc·turne** (näk'tərn) *n.* [Fr.] a romantic or dreamy musical composition thought appropriate to night

**nod** (näd) *vi.* **nod'ded, nod'ding** [ME. *nodden*] 1. to bend the head forward quickly, as in agreement, greeting, etc. 2. to let the head fall forward because of drowsiness —*vt.* 1. to bend (the head) forward quickly 2. to signify (assent, etc.) by doing this —*n.* a nodding

**node** (nōd) *n.* [L. *nodus*] 1. a knot; knob; swelling 2. that part of a stem from which a leaf starts to grow —**nod·al** (nōd''l) *adj.*

**nod·ule** (näj'ōol) *n.* [L. *nodulus*] a small knot or rounded lump

**No·el, No·ël** (nō el') *n.* [Fr. < L. *natalis*, natal] *same as* CHRISTMAS

**no'-fault'** *adj.* 1. being a form of automobile insurance in which the insured collects damages without blame being fixed 2. being a form of divorce granted without blame being charged

**nog·gin** (näg'in) *n.* [prob. < nog, strong ale] 1. a small cup or mug 2. [Colloq.] the head

**no'-good'** *adj.* [Slang] contemptible

**noise** (noiz) *n.* [< OFr.] 1. clamor; din 2. sound; esp., any loud disagreeable sound —*vt.* noised, nois'ing to spread (a rumor, report, etc.)

**noise'less** *adj.* with little or no noise; silent —**noise'less·ly** *adv.*

**noi·some** (noi'səm) *adj.* [see ANNOY & -SOME[1]] 1. injurious to health; harmful 2. foul-smelling; offensive

**nois·y** (noi'zē) *adj.* **-i·er, -i·est** 1. making noise 2. full of noise —**nois'-i·ly** *adv.* —**nois'i·ness** *n.*

**no-knock** (nō'näk') *adj.* [Colloq.] letting police with search warrants enter private dwellings by force without announcing or identifying themselves [*a no-knock law*]

**no·mad** (nō'mad) *n.* [< Gr. *nemein*, to pasture] 1. any of a people having no permanent home, but moving about constantly, as in search of pasture 2. a wanderer —**no·mad'ic** *adj.*

**no man's land** the area on a battlefield separating the combatants

**nom de plume** (näm' də ploom') [Fr.] a pen name

**no·men·cla·ture** (nō'mən klā'chər) *n.* [< L. *nomen*, name + *calare*, call] the system of names used in a science, etc. or for parts of a device, etc.

**nom·i·nal** (näm'i n'l) *adj.* [< L. *nomen*, a name] 1. of or like a name 2. in name only, not in fact [*a nominal* leader] 3. relatively very small [*a nominal* fee] —**nom'i·nal·ly** *adv.*

**nom·i·nate** (näm'ə nāt') *vt.* **-nat'ed, -nat'ing** 1. to appoint to an office or position 2. to name as a candidate for election —**nom'i·na'tion** *n.*

**nom·i·na·tive** (näm'ə nə tiv) *adj.* *Gram.* designating or of the case of the subject of a verb and the words that agree with it —*n.* 1. this case 2. a word in this case

**nom·i·nee** (näm'ə nē') *n.* a person who is nominated

**non-** [< L. *non*] a prefix meaning not: less emphatic than *in-* and *un-*, which often give a word an opposite meaning The terms in the following list will be understood if *not* is used before the meaning of the base word

| | |
|---|---|
| nonabrasive | nonbeliever |
| nonabsorbent | nonbelligerent |
| nonactive | nonbreakable |
| nonadministrative | nonburnable |
| nonaggression | non-Catholic |
| nonalcoholic | nonchargeable |
| nonallergenic | nonclerical |
| nonassignable | nonclinical |
| nonattendance | noncollectable |
| nonbasic | noncombustible |

noncommercial
noncommunicable
non-Communist
noncompeting
noncompetitive
noncompliance
noncomplying
nonconducting
nonconforming
nonconsecutive
nonconstructive
noncontagious
noncontributory
noncontroversial
nonconvertible
noncorroding
noncritical
noncrystalline
noncumulative
nondeductible
nondelivery
nondepartmental
nondepreciating
nondestructive
nondetachable
nondisciplinary
nondiscrimination
nondramatic
nondrinker
nondrying
noneducational
noneffective
nonenforceable
non-English
nonessential
nonexchangeable
nonexclusive
nonexempt
nonexistence
nonexistent
nonexplosive
nonfactual
nonfading
nonfat
nonfatal
nonfiction
nonfictional
nonflammable
nonflowering
nonfluctuating
nonflying
nonfreezing
nonfunctional
nongovernmental
nongranular
nonhazardous
nonhereditary
nonhuman
nonidentical
noninclusive
nonindependent
noninductive
nonindustrial
noninfected
noninflammatory
noninflationary
nonintellectual
noninterchangeable
noninterference
nonintoxicating
nonirritating
nonjudicial
nonlegal
nonliterary
nonmagnetic
nonmalignant

nonmigratory
nonmilitant
nonmilitary
nonnegotiable
nonobjective
nonobligatory
nonobservance
nonoccupational
nonofficial
nonoperational
nonoperative
nonpaying
nonpayment
nonperishable
nonphysical
nonpoisonous
nonpolitical
nonporous
nonprejudicial
nonproductive
nonprofessional
nonprofitable
nonpunishable
nonracial
nonreciprocal
nonreciprocating
nonrecoverable
nonrecurring
nonredeemable
nonrefillable
nonreligious
nonrepresentational
nonresidential
nonresidual
nonresistant
nonreturnable
nonrhythmic
nonrigid
nonsalaried
nonscientific
nonscoring
nonseasonal
nonsecular
nonsensitive
nonsmoker
nonsocial
nonspeaking
nonspecializing
nonspiritual
nonstaining
nonstandard
nonstrategic
nonstriking
nonstructural
nonsuccessive
nonsupporting
nonsustaining
nonsympathizer
nontarnishable
nontaxable
nontechnical
nontheatrical
nonthinking
nontoxic
nontransferable
nontransparent
nontropical
nonuser
nonvenomous
nonvirulent
nonvocal
nonvocational
nonvoter
nonvoting
nonwhite
nonyielding

**non·age** (nän'ij, nō'nij) *n.* [see NON- & AGE] the state of being under full legal age (usually 21)

**non·a·ge·nar·i·an** (nän'ə jə ner'ē ən, nō'nə-) *n.* [ < L. *nonaginta,* ninety] a person between the ages of 90 and 100

**non'a·ligned'** *adj.* not aligned with either side in a conflict of power, esp. power politics —**non'a·lign'ment** *n.*

**nonce** (näns) *n.* [by merging of ME. *(for then) ones,* lit., (for the) once] the present use, occasion, or time: chiefly in **for the nonce**

**non·cha·lant** (nän'shə länt') *adj.* [Fr., ult. < L. *non,* not + *calere,* be warm] 1. without warmth or enthusiasm 2. casually indifferent —**non'cha·lance'** *n.* —**non'cha·lant'ly** *adv.*

**non·com** (nän'käm') *n. colloq. clipped form of* NONCOMMISSIONED OFFICER

**non·com·bat·ant** (nän käm'bə tənt, nän'kəm bat'ənt) *n.* 1. a member of the armed forces not engaged in actual combat 2. any civilian in wartime

**non·com·mis'sioned officer** an enlisted person of any of various grades in the armed forces: in the U.S. Army, from corporal to sergeant major inclusive

**non·com·mit·tal** (nän'kə mit''l) *adj.* not committing one to a definite point of view or course of action

**non com·pos men·tis** (nän' käm'pəs men'tis) [L.] not of sound mind

**non'con·duc'tor** *n.* a substance that does not readily transmit sound, heat, and, esp., electricity

**non'con·form'ist** *n.* one who does not conform to prevailing attitudes, behavior, etc.; esp., [N-] in England, a Protestant who is not an Anglican —**non'con·form'i·ty** *n.*

**non·de·script** (nän'di skript') *adj.* [ < L. *non,* not + *describere,* describe] belonging to no definite class or type; hard to classify or describe

**none** (nun) *pron.* [ < OE. *ne,* not + *an,* one] 1. no one; not anyone 2. [*usually with pl. v.*] not any [*none* are his] —*n.* not any; no part [I want *none* of it] —*adv.* not at all [*none* too soon]

**non·en·ti·ty** (nän en'tə tē) *n., pl.* **-ties** a person or thing of little or no importance

**none·such** (nun'such') *n.* a person or thing unrivaled or unequaled

**none·the·less** (nun'thə les') *adv.* nevertheless: also **none the less**

**non·fer·rous** (nän fer'əs) *adj.* 1. not containing iron 2. designating or of metals other than iron

**non·he'ro** *n. same as* ANTIHERO

**non·in·ter·ven'tion** *n.* refusal to intervene; esp., a refusal by one nation to interfere in another's affairs

**non·met'al** *n.* an element lacking the characteristics of a metal, as oxygen, carbon, nitrogen, fluorine, etc. —**non'me·tal'lic** *adj.*

**non·pa·reil** (nän'pə rel') *adj.* [Fr. < *non,* not + *pareil,* equal] unequaled; unrivaled; peerless

**non·par'ti·san** *adj.* not partisan; esp., not connected with any single political party: also **non·par'ti·zan**

**non·plus** (nän′plus′) *vt.* **-plused′** or **-plussed′**, **-plus′ing** or **-plus′sing** [L. *non*, not + *plus*, more] to cause to be so perplexed that one cannot go, speak, or act further

**non·prof′it** *adj.* not intending or intended to earn a profit

**non·res′i·dent** *adj.* not residing in the locality where one works, attends school, etc. —*n.* a nonresident person

**non′re·stric′tive** (-ri strik′tiv) *adj. Gram.* designating a clause, phrase, or word felt as not essential to the sense, usually set off by commas (Ex.: John, *who is tall*, is Bill's brother)

**non·sched′uled** *adj.* licensed for commercial air flights as demand warrants rather than on a schedule

**non′sec·tar′i·an** (-sek ter′ē ən) *adj.* not confined to any specific religion

**non·sense** (nän′sens, -səns) *n.* words, actions, etc. that are absurd or meaningless —**non·sen′si·cal** *adj.*

**non se·qui·tur** (nän sek′wi tər) [L., it does not follow] **1.** a conclusion that does not follow from the premises **2.** a remark having no bearing on what has just been said

**non′stop′** *adj., adv.* without a stop

**non′sup·port′** *n.* failure to provide for a legal dependent

**non·un′ion** *adj.* **1.** not belonging to a labor union **2.** not made or serviced under labor-union conditions **3.** refusing to recognize a labor union

**non·vi′o·lence** *n.* an abstaining from violence, as in the struggle for civil rights —**non·vi′o·lent** *adj.*

**noo·dle¹** (nōō′d′l) *n.* [< ?] [Slang] the head

**noo·dle²** (nōō′d′l) *n.* [G. *nudel*] a flat, narrow strip of dry dough, usually made with egg and served in soups, etc.

**nook** (nook) *n.* [ME. *nok*] **1.** a corner, esp. of a room **2.** a small, secluded spot

**noon** (nōōn) *n.* [< L. *nona* (*hora*), ninth (hour)] twelve o'clock in the daytime; midday —*adj.* of or at noon Also **noon′day′**, **noon′time′**

**no one** not anybody; nobody

**noose** (nōōs) *n.* [< L. *nodus*, a knot] a loop formed in a rope, etc. by means of a slipknot so that the loop tightens as the rope is pulled

NOOSE

**nor** (nôr) *conj.* [ME., contr. of *nother*, neither] and not; and not either [I can neither go *nor* stay]

**Nor·dic** (nôr′dik) *adj.* [OE. *north*] of a Caucasoid physical type exemplified by the tall, blond Scandinavians

**Nor·folk** (nôr′fək) seaport in SE Va.; pop. 308,000

**norm** (nôrm) *n.* [< L. *norma*, rule] a standard or model; esp., the standard of achievement of a large group

**nor·mal** (nôr′m′l) *adj.* **1.** conforming with an accepted standard or norm; natural; usual **2.** average in intelligence, etc. —*n.* **1.** anything normal **2.**

the usual state, amount, etc. —**nor′mal·cy, nor·mal′i·ty** (-mal′ə tē) *n.* —**nor′mal·ize** *vt., vi.* **-ized′**, **-iz′ing** —**nor′mal·i·za′tion** *n.*

**nor′mal·ly** *adv.* **1.** in a normal manner **2.** under normal circumstances

**Nor·man** (nôr′mən) *n.* [< OFr.] **1.** any of the people of Normandy who conquered England in 1066 **2.** a native of Normandy —*adj.* of Normandy, the Normans, their language, etc.

**Nor·man·dy** (nôr′mən dē) region in NW France, on the English Channel

**norm·a·tive** (nôr′mə tiv) *adj.* of or establishing a norm

**Norse** (nôrs) *adj., n.* [prob. < Du. *noord*, north] **1.** Scandinavian **2.** (of) the languages of W Scandinavia

**Norse′man** (-mən) *n., pl.* **-men** any of the ancient Scandinavian people

**north** (nôrth) *n.* [OE.] **1.** the direction to the right of one facing the sunset (0° or 360° on the compass) **2.** a region in or toward this direction **3.** [*often* N-] the northern part of the earth —*adj.* **1.** in, of, or toward the north **2.** from the north —*adv.* in or toward the north —**the North** that part of the U.S. north of Maryland, the Ohio River, and Missouri

**North America** N continent in the Western Hemisphere: c.9,330,000 sq. mi.; pop. 299,000,000 —**North American**

**North Car·o·li·na** (kar′ə lī′nə) Southern State of the U.S.; 52,712 sq. mi.; pop. 5,082,000; cap. Raleigh —**North Car′o·lin′i·an** (-lin′ē ən)

**North Da·ko·ta** (də kōt′ə) Middle Western State of the U.S.; 70,665 sq. mi.; pop. 618,000; cap. Bismarck —**North Da·ko′tan**

**north′east′** *n.* **1.** the direction halfway between north and east **2.** a region in or toward this direction —*adj.* in, of, or toward the northeast **2.** from the northeast —*adv.* in, toward, or from the northeast —**north′east′er·ly** *adj., adv.* —**north′east′ern** *adj.* —**north′east′ward** (-wərd) *adv., adj.* —**north′east′wards** *adv.*

**north·er** (nôr′thər) *n.* a storm or strong wind from the north

**north·er·ly** (nôr′thər lē) *adj., adv.* **1.** toward the north **2.** from the north

**north·ern** (nôr′thərn) *adj.* **1.** in, of, or toward the north **2.** from the north **3.** [N-] of the North

**north′ern·er** *n.* a native or inhabitant of the north

**Northern Hemisphere** that half of the earth north of the equator

**Northern Ireland** division of the United Kingdom, in NE Ireland: 5,462 sq. mi.; pop. 1,487,000

**northern lights** aurora borealis

**North Pole** the northern end of the earth's axis

**North Sea** arm of the Atlantic, between Great Britain & the European mainland

**North Star** Polaris, the bright star

---

fat, āpe, cär; ten, ēven; is, bīte; gō, hôrn, tōōl, look; oil, out; up, fur; chin; she; thin, *then*; zh, leisure; ŋ, ring; ə for *a* in *ago*; ′, (ā′b'l); ë, Fr. coeur; ö, Fr. feu; Fr. mon; ü, Fr. duc; kh, G. ich, doch; ‡ foreign; < derived from

almost directly above the North Pole
**north'ward** (-wərd) *adv., adj.* toward the north: also **north'wards** *adv.*
**north'west'** *n.* 1. the direction halfway between north and west 2. a
region in or toward this direction —
*adj.* 1. in, of, or toward the northwest
2. from the northwest —*adv.* in,
toward, or from the northwest —**the
Northwest** the 'northwestern U.S.,
esp. Wash., Oreg., and Ida. —**north'-
west'er·ly** *adj., adv.* —**north'west'-
ern** *adj.* —**north'west'ward** (-wərd)
*adv., adj.* —**north'west'wards** *adv.*
**Northwest Territories** division of
N Canada: 1,304,903 sq. mi.
**Norw.** 1. Norway 2. Norwegian
**Nor·way** (nôr'wā') country in N
Europe: 125,064 sq. mi.; pop. 3,769,000
**Nor·we·gian** (nôr wē'jən) *adj.* of
Norway, its people, language, etc. —*n.*
1. a native or inhabitant of Norway
2. the language of Norway
**nose** (nōz) *n.* [OE. *nosu*] 1. the part of
the face above the mouth, having two
openings for breathing and smelling:
in animals, the snout, muzzle, etc. 2.
the sense of smell 3. anything like a
nose in shape or position —*vt.* **nosed,**
**nos'ing** 1. to discover as by smell 2.
to nuzzle 3. to push (a way, etc.) with
the front forward —*vi.* 1. to pry
inquisitively 2. to move forward —
**nose out** to defeat by a very small
margin —**on the nose** [Slang] precisely; exactly —**pay through the
nose** to pay more for something than
it is worth —**turn up one's nose
at** to sneer at; scorn —**under one's
(very) nose** in plain view
**nose'bleed'** *n.* a bleeding from the
nose
**nose cone** the cone-shaped foremost
part of a rocket or missile
**nose dive** 1. a swift downward plunge
of an airplane, nose first 2. any
sudden, sharp drop, as in prices —
**nose'-dive'** *vi.* **-dived', -div'ing**
**nose drops** medication administered
through the nose with a dropper
**nose'gay'** *n.* [NOSE + GAY (obs. "gay
object")] a small bunch of flowers
**nos·tal·gia** (näs tal'jə) *n.* [< Gr.
*nostos*, a return + -ALGIA] a longing
for something far away or long ago
—**nos·tal'gic** (-jik) *adj.*
**nos·tril** (näs'trəl) *n.* [< OE. *nosu*,
the nose + *thyrel*, hole] either of the
external openings of the nose
**nos·trum** (näs'trəm) *n.* [L., ours] 1.
a quack medicine 2. a panacea
**nos·y, nos·ey** (nō'zē) *adj.* **-i·er,
-i·est** [Colloq.] prying; inquisitive
**not** (nät) *adv.* [< ME. *nought*] in no
manner, degree, etc.: a word expressing negation or the idea of *no*
**no·ta·ble** (nōt'ə b'l) *adj.* [< L.
*notare*, to note] worthy of notice;
remarkable; outstanding —*n.* a person
of distinction —**no'ta·bly** *adv.*
**no·ta·rize** (nōt'ə rīz') *vt.* **-rized',
-riz'ing** to certify or attest (a document) as a notary
**no·ta·ry** (nōt'ər ē) *n., pl.* **-ries** [< L.
*notare*, to note] an official authorized
to certify or attest documents, take

affidavits, etc.: in full **notary public**
**no·ta·tion** (nō tā'shən) *n.* 1. the use
of signs or symbols to represent words,
quantities, etc. 2. any such system of
signs or symbols, as in mathematics,
music, etc. 3. a brief note or noting
**notch** (näch) *n.* [by merging of ME.
*an oche*, a notch] 1. a V-shaped cut in
an edge or surface 2. a narrow pass
with steep sides 3. [Colloq.] a step;
degree —*vt.* to cut notches in
**note** (nōt) *n.* [< L. *nota*, a mark] 1. a
distinguishing feature [*a note* of sad-
ness] 2. importance, distinction, etc.
[*a man of note*] 3. a brief writing to
aid the memory; memorandum 4. a
comment or explanation; annotation
5. notice; heed [worthy of *note*] 6. a
short letter 7. a written acknowledgment of a debt 8. a cry or call, as of a
bird 9. *Music a)* a tone of definite
pitch *b)* a symbol for a tone, indicating
its duration and pitch —*vt.* **not'ed,
not'ing** 1. to heed; observe 2. to set
down in writing 3. to mention particularly —**compare notes** to exchange views
**note'book'** *n.* a book in which notes,
or memorandums, are kept
**not·ed** (nōt'id) *adj.* distinguished;
renowned; eminent
**note'wor'thy** *adj.* worthy of note;
outstanding; remarkable
**noth·ing** (nuth'iŋ) *n.* [OE. *na thing*]
1. no thing; not anything 2. nothing-
ness 3. a thing that does not exist 4. a
person or thing considered of little or
no importance 5. a zero —*adv.* not at
all; in no way —**for nothing** 1. free
2. in vain 3. without reason —**think
nothing of** 1. to attach no importance to 2. to regard as easy to do
**noth'ing·ness** *n.* 1. nonexistence 2.
insignificance 3. unconsciousness
**no·tice** (nōt'is) *n.* [see NOTE] 1. an
announcement or warning 2. a short
article about a book, play, etc. 3. a
sign giving some public information,
warning, etc. 4. attention; heed 5. a
formal warning of intention to end an
agreement or contract at a certain
time —*vt.* **-ticed, -tic·ing** 1. to
mention; refer to 2. to observe; pay
attention to —**take notice** to observe
**no'tice·a·ble** *adj.* readily noticed;
conspicuous —**no'tice·a·bly** *adv.*
**no·ti·fy** (nōt'ə fī') *vt.* **-fied', -fy'ing**
[< L. *notus*, known + *facere*, make] to
give notice to; inform —**no'ti·fi·ca'-
tion** (-fi kā'shən) *n.*
**no·tion** (nō'shən) *n.* [see NOTE] 1. a
general idea 2. a belief; opinion 3. an
inclination; whim 4. [*pl.*] small, useful
articles, as needles, thread, etc., sold
in a store —**no'tion·al** *adj.*
**no·to·ri·e·ty** (nōt'ə rī'ə tē) *n.* a
being notorious
**no·to·ri·ous** (nō tôr'ē əs) *adj.* [see
NOTE] widely known, esp. unfavorably
—**no·to'ri·ous·ly** *adv.*
**no'-trump'** *n.* Bridge a bid to play
with no suit being trumps
**not·with·stand·ing** (nät'with
stan'diŋ, -with-) *prep.* in spite of —
*adv.* nevertheless —*conj.* although
**nou·gat** (nōō'gət) *n.* [< Pr. *noga*,

nut] a confection of sugar paste with nuts

**nought** (nôt) *n.* [< OE. *ne,* not + *awiht,* aught] 1. nothing 2. the figure zero

**noun** (noun) *n.* [< L. *nomen,* a name] *Gram.* a word that names or denotes a person, thing, action, etc.

**nour·ish** (nur'ish) *vt.* [< L. *nutrire*] 1. to provide with substances necessary to life and growth 2. to foster; promote —**nour'ish·ing** *adj.*

**nour·ish·ment** (-mənt) *n.* 1. a nourishing or being nourished 2. food

**nou·veau riche** (nōō'vō rēsh') *pl.* **-veaux riches** (-vō rēsh') [Fr.] a newly rich person, esp. one lacking cultural taste or social grace

**Nov.** November

**no·va** (nō'və) *n., pl.* **-vas, -vae** (-vē) [< L., new] a star that brightens intensely and then gradually dims

**No·va Sco·tia** (nō'və skō'shə) province of SE Canada: 21,425 sq. mi.; pop. 756,000; cap. Halifax

**nov·el** (näv'l) *adj.* [< L. dim. of *novus,* new] new and unusual —*n.* a relatively long fictional prose narrative

**nov·el·ette** (-ə let') *n.* a short novel

**nov·el·ist** *n.* one who writes novels

**nov·el·ty** (-tē) *n., pl.* **-ties** 1. the quality of being novel; newness 2. something new, fresh, or unusual 3. a small, often cheap, cleverly made article: *usually used in pl.*

**No·vem·ber** (nō vem'bər) *n.* [< L. *novem,* nine: 9th month in Roman year] the eleventh month of the year, having 30 days

**no·ve·na** (nō vē'nə) *n.* [< L. *novem,* nine] *R.C.Ch.* special prayers for nine days

**nov·ice** (näv'is) *n.* [< L. *novus,* new] 1. a person on probation in a religious order before taking final vows 2. a person new to something; beginner

**no·vi·ti·ate** (nō vish'ē it) *n.* the period or state of being a novice

**No·vo·cain** (nō'və kān') [L. *nov(us),* new + (c)ocain(e)] *a trademark for* PROCAINE: also sp. **Novocaine**

**now** (nou) *adv.* [OE. *nu*] 1. a) at the present time b) at once 2. at that time; then 3. with things as they are [now we'll never know] —*conj.* since; seeing that —*n.* the present time [that's all for now] —*adj.* of the present time —**just now** recently —**now and then** (or **again**) occasionally

**now'a·days'** (-ə dāz') *adv.* in these days; at the present time

**no·where** (nō'hwer', -wer') *adv.* not in, at, or to any place —**nowhere** near not by a wide margin

**no'wise'** (-wīz') *adv.* in no way: also **no'way', no'ways'**

**nox·ious** (näk'shəs) *adj.* [< L. *nocere,* to hurt] harmful to health or morals; injurious or unwholesome

**noz·zle** (näz'l) *n.* [dim. of *nose*] the spout at the end of a hose, pipe, etc.

**N.S.** Nova Scotia

**NT., NT, N.T.** New Testament

**nth** (enth) *adj.* of an indefinitely great number, amount, or degree

**nt. wt.** net weight

**nu** (nōō, nyōō) *n.* the 13th letter of the Greek alphabet (N, ν)

**nu·ance** (nōō'äns) *n.* [Fr. < *nuer,* to shade] a slight variation in tone, color, meaning, etc. —**nu'anced** *adj.*

**nub** (nub) *n.* [var. of *knub,* knob] 1. a lump or small piece 2. [Colloq.] the main point; gist

**nub·bin** (nub'in) *n.* [dim. of prec.] 1. a small ear of corn 2. a small piece

**nub·by** (nub'ē) *adj.* **-bi·er, -bi·est** having a rough, knotted surface [a *nubby* fabric]

**nu·bile** (nōō'b'l, -bīl) *adj.* [< L. *nubere,* marry] ready for marriage: said of a girl

**nu·cle·ar** (nōō'klē ər) *adj.* 1. of, like, or forming a nucleus 2. of, involving, or using atomic nuclei or atomic energy, bombs, power, etc.

**nuclear family** a family unit consisting of parents and their children living in one household

**nuclear fission** the splitting of the nuclei of atoms, accompanied by conversion of part of the mass into energy: the principle of the atomic bomb

**nuclear fusion** the fusion of lightweight atomic nuclei into a nucleus of heavier mass, with a resultant loss in the combined mass converted into energy, as in the hydrogen bomb

**nuclear physics** the branch of physics dealing with the structure of atomic nuclei, nuclear forces, etc.

**nuclear reactor** a device for creating a controlled nuclear chain reaction in a fissionable fuel, as for the production of energy

**nu·cle·ate** (nōō'klē it; *for v.* -āt') *adj.* having a nucleus —*vt., vi.* **-at'ed, -at'ing** to form into a nucleus —**nu'cle·a'tion** *n.*

**nu·cle·us** (nōō'klē əs) *n., pl.* **-cle·i'** (-ī') [L., kernel] 1. a central thing or part around which others are grouped; core 2. any center of growth or development 3. the central part of an atom 4. the central mass of protoplasm in a cell

**nude** (nōōd) *adj.* [L. *nudus*] naked; bare —*n.* 1. a nude human figure, esp. in a work of art 2. the state of being nude [in the *nude*] —**nu'di·ty** *n.*

**nudge** (nuj) *vt.* **nudged, nudg'ing** [< ?] to push gently, esp. with the elbow, in order to get attention, hint slyly, etc. —*n.* a gentle push

**nud'ism** *n.* the practice or cult of going nude —**nud'ist** *n., adj.*

**nu·ga·to·ry** (nōō'gə tôr'ē) *adj.* [< L. *nugari,* to trifle] 1. trifling; worthless 2. not operative; invalid

**nug·get** (nug'it) *n.* [prob. < dial. *nug,* lump] a lump, esp. of native gold

**nui·sance** (nōō's'ns) *n.* [< L. *nocere,* annoy] an act, thing, or person causing trouble, annoyance, etc.

---

fat, āpe, cär; ten, ēven; is, bīte; gō, hôrn, tōōl, look; oil, out; up, fur; chin; she; thin, then; zh, leisure; ŋ, ring; ə for a in ago; ', (ā'b'l); ë, Fr. coeur; ö, Fr. feu; Fr. mon; ü, Fr. duc; kh, G. ich, doch; ‡ foreign; < derived from

**null** (nul) *adj.* [< L. *nullus*, none] **1.** without legal force; invalid: usually in phrase **null and void 2.** amounting to nought **3.** of no value, effect, etc.

**nul·li·fy** (nul′ə fī′) *vt.* **-fied′, -fy′ing** [< L. *nullus*, none + *facere*, make] **1.** to make legally null or valueless **2.** to cancel out **—nul′li·fi·ca′tion** *n.*

**numb** (num) *adj.* [< ME. *nimen*, take] deadened; insensible [*numb* with grief] **—** *vt.* to make numb **—numb′ly** *adv.* **—numb′ness** *n.*

**num·ber** (num′bər) *n.* [< L. *numerus*] **1.** a symbol or word showing how many or which one in a series (Ex.: 2, 27, four, sixth) **2.** [*pl.*] arithmetic **3.** the sum of persons or things; total **4.** *a)* [*often pl.*] many *b)* [*pl.*] numerical superiority **5.** quantity **6.** *a)* a single issue of a periodical *b)* a single song, dance, etc. in a program of entertainment **7.** [Colloq.] a person or thing singled out [a smart *number*] **8.** Gram. the form of a word as indicating either singular or plural **—** *vt.* **1.** to count; enumerate **2.** to give a number to **3.** to include as one of a group **4.** to limit the number of **5.** to have or comprise; total **—** *vi.* **1.** to be included **— a number of** several or many; some **— beyond (or without) number** too numerous to be counted **—the numbers** an illegal lottery based on certain numbers published in newspapers: also **numbers pool (or racket)**

**num′ber·less** *adj. same as* COUNTLESS

**Num·bers** (num′bərz) *n.* the 4th book of the Pentateuch in the Bible: abbrev. **Num.**

**nu·mer·al** (nōō′mər əl) *adj.* [< L. *numerus*, number] of or denoting a number or numbers **—** *n.* a figure, letter, or word expressing a number

**nu′mer·ate** (-mə rāt′) *vt.* **-at′ed, -at′ing** to count one by one; enumerate

**nu′mer·a′tor** (-mə rāt′ər) *n.* the part of a fraction above the line

**nu·mer·i·cal** (noo mer′i k′l) *adj.* **1.** of, or having the nature of, number **2.** in or by numbers **3.** expressed by numbers **—nu·mer′i·cal·ly** *adv.*

**nu·mer·ol·o·gy** (nōō′mə räl′ə jē) *n.* the attributing of occult meaning to numbers, as in birth dates

**nu·mer·ous** (nōō′mər əs) *adj.* **1.** of great number **2.** very many

**nu·mis·mat·ics** (nōō′miz mat′iks, -mis-) *n.pl.* [*with sing. v.*] [< L. *numisma*, a coin] the study or collection of coins, medals, paper money, etc. **—nu·mis′ma·tist** (-mə tist) *n.*

**num·skull, numb·skull** (num′ skul′) *n.* [NUM(B) + SKULL] a dunce

**nun** (nun) *n.* [< LL. *nonna*] a woman devoted to a religious life, esp. one living in a convent under vows

**nun·ci·o** (nun′shē ō′, -sē-) *n., pl.* **-os′** [< It. < L. *nuntius*, messenger] a papal ambassador to a foreign state

**nun·ner·y** (nun′ər ē) *n., pl.* **-ies** a *former name for* CONVENT

**nup·tial** (nup′shəl, -chəl) *adj.* [< L. *nubere*, marry] of marriage or a wedding **—** *n.* [*pl.*] a wedding

**nurse** (nurs) *n.* [< L. *nutrire*, nourish] **1.** a woman hired to care for another's children **2.** a person trained to care for the sick, assist surgeons, etc. **—** *vt.* **nursed, nurs′ing 1.** to suckle (an infant) **2.** to take care of (a child, invalid, etc.) **3.** to nourish, foster, etc. **4.** to try to cure [to *nurse* a cold] **5.** to use or handle so as to protect or conserve **—** *vi.* **1.** to feed at the breast; suckle **2.** to serve as a nurse

**nurse′maid′** *n.* a woman hired to care for a child or children

**nurs·er·y** (nur′sə rē) *n., pl.* **-ies 1.** a room set aside for children **2.** a place where parents may temporarily leave children to be cared for **3.** a place where young trees or plants are raised for transplanting, etc.

**nurs′er·y·man** (-mən) *n., pl.* **-men** one who owns or works in a tree nursery

**nursery rhyme** a poem for children

**nursery school** a prekindergarten school for young children

**nursing home** a residence providing care for the infirm, chronically ill, disabled, etc.

**nur·ture** (nur′chər) *n.* [< L. *nutrire*, nourish] **1.** food **2.** training; rearing **—** *vt.* **-tured, -tur·ing 1.** to feed or nourish **2.** to train, educate, rear, etc. **—nur′tur·er** *n.*

**nut** (nut) *n.* [OE. *hnutu*] **1.** a dry, one-seeded fruit, consisting of a kernel, often edible, in a woody shell, as the walnut **2.** the kernel itself **3.** loosely, any hard-shelled, relatively non-perishable fruit, as the peanut **4.** a small metal block with a threaded hole, for screwing onto a bolt, etc. **5.** [Slang] *a)* a crazy or eccentric person *b)* a devotee; fan

NUT ON A BOLT

**nut′crack′er** *n.* **1.** an instrument for cracking nutshells **2.** a bird of the crow family that feeds on nuts

**nut′hatch′** (-hach′) *n.* a small, nut-eating bird with a sharp beak

**nut′meat′** *n.* the kernel of a nut

**nut′meg′** (-meg′) *n.* [< L. *nux*, nut + LL. *muscus*, musk] the aromatic seed of an East Indian tree, grated and used as a spice

**nut′pick′** *n.* a small, sharp instrument for digging out the kernels of cracked nuts

**nu·tri·a** (nōō′trē ə) *n.* [Sp. < L. *lutra*, otter] the soft, brown fur of a S.American rodent

**nu·tri·ent** (nōō′trē ənt) *adj.* [< L. *nutrire*, nourish] nourishing **—** *n.* anything nutritious

**nu′tri·ment** (-trə mənt) *n.* anything that nourishes; food

**nu·tri·tion** (nōō trish′ən) *n.* [see NUTRIENT] **1.** the process by which an organism takes in and assimilates food **2.** anything that nourishes; food **3.** the study of diet and health **—nu·tri′tion·al** *adj.* **—nu·tri′tion·al·ly** *adv.* **—nu′tri·tive** (-trə tiv) *adj.*

**nu·tri·tious** (-shəs) *adj.* nourishing

**nuts** *adj.* [Slang] crazy; foolish **—** *interj.* [Slang] an exclamation of dis-

gust, scorn, etc.: often in the phrase
**nuts to (someone or something)**
—**be nuts about** [Slang] 1. to be very
enthusiastic about 2. to be greatly in
love with

**nut·shell** n. the shell enclosing the
kernel of a nut —**in a nutshell** in
concise form; in a few words

**nut·ty** adj. -ti·er, -ti·est 1. containing or producing nuts 2. having a
nutlike flavor 3. [Slang] a) very
enthusiastic b) queer, crazy, etc. —
**nut′ti·ness** n.

**nuz·zle** (nuz′'l) vt., vi. -zled, -zling
[< NOSE] 1. to push (against) or rub
with the nose or snout 2. to nestle;
snuggle —**nuz′zler** n.

**NV** Nevada

**NW, N.W., n.w.** 1. northwest 2.
northwestern

**N.Y., NY** New York

**N.Y.C.** New York City

**ny·lon** (nī′län) n. [arbitrary coinage]
1. an elastic, very strong, synthetic
material made into fiber, bristles, etc.
2. [pl.] stockings made of this

**nymph** (nimf) n. [< Gr. nymphē] 1.
Gr. & Rom. Myth. any of a group of
minor nature goddesses, living in
rivers, trees, etc. 2. a lovely young
woman 3. the young of an insect with
incomplete metamorphosis

**nym·pho·ma·ni·a** (nim′fə mā′nē ə)
n. uncontrollable desire by a woman
for sexual intercourse —**nym′pho·
ma′ni·ac′** (-ak′) n., adj.


# O

**O, o** (ō) n., pl. **O's, o's** 1. the fifteenth
letter of the English alphabet 2. the
numeral zero 3. Physics ohm

**O** (ō) interj. 1. an exclamation in
direct address [O Lord!] 2. oh

**O** 1. Old 2. Chem. oxygen

**O.** 1. Ocean 2. October 3. Ohio

**oaf** (ōf) n. [< ON. alfr, elf] a stupid,
clumsy fellow —**oaf′ish** adj.

**O·a·hu** (ō ä′hōō) chief island of
Hawaii

**oak** (ōk) n. [OE. ac] 1. a large hardwood tree with nuts called acorns 2.
its wood —adj. of oak —**oak′en** adj.

**Oak·land** (ōk′lənd) seaport in W
Calif.: pop. 362,000

**Oak Ridge** city in E Tenn.: a center
for atomic research: pop. 28,000

**oa·kum** (ō′kəm) n. [< OE. a-, out
+ camb, a comb] hemp fiber got by
taking apart old ropes, for caulking
boat seams

**oar** (ôr) n. [OE. ar] a long pole with a
broad blade at one end, used in rowing
—**rest on one's oars** to stop to rest
—**oars·man** (ôrz′mən) n., pl. -men

**oar′lock′** n. a device, often U-shaped,
for holding an oar in place in rowing

**OAS, O.A.S.** Organization of American States

**o·a·sis** (ō ā′sis) n., pl. -ses (-sēz) [<
Gr. ŏasis] a fertile place in a desert,
due to the presence of water

**oat** (ōt) n. [OE. ate] [usually pl.] 1. a
hardy cereal grass 2. its edible grain
—**oat′en** adj.

**oat′cake′** n. a thin, flat cake of oatmeal

**oath** (ōth) n., pl. **oaths** (ōthz, ōths)
[OE. ath] 1. a declaration based on an
appeal to God that one will speak the
truth, keep a promise, etc. 2. the
profane use of God's name, as in anger
3. a swearword; curse

**oat′meal′** n. 1. oats crushed into
meal or flakes 2. a porridge of this

**ob-** [< L. ob] a prefix meaning: 1. to,
toward, before [object] 2. against
[obnoxious] 3. upon, over [obfuscate]
4. completely [obsolete]

**OB, O.B.** 1. obstetrician 2. obstetrics

**ob.** [L. obiit] he (or she) died

**ob·bli·ga·to** (äb′lə gät′ō) n., pl. -tos,
-ti (-ē) [see OBLIGE] an elaborate
musical accompaniment, orig. thought
necessary to the performance of a
piece

**ob·du·rate** (äb′door ət) adj. [< L.
ob-, intens. + durus, hard] 1. hardhearted 2. stubborn; obstinate —**ob′-
du·ra·cy** (-ə sē) n. —**ob′du·rate·ly**
adv.

**o·be·di·ent** (ō bē′dē ənt) adj. obeying or willing to obey —**o·be′di·ence**
n. —**o·be′di·ent·ly** adv.

**o·bei·sance** (ō bā′s'ns, -bē′-) n. [<
OFr. obeir, obey] 1. a gesture of
respect, as a bow 2. homage; deference
—**o·bei′sant** adj.

**ob·e·lisk** (äb′ə lisk, ō′bə-) n. [< Gr.
obelos, needle] a tall, four-sided stone
pillar tapering to its pyramidal top

**o·bese** (ō bēs′) adj. [< L. ob- (see
OB-) + edere, eat] very fat; stout
—**o·bes′i·ty** (-ə tē) n.

**o·bey** (ō bā′) vt. [< L. ob- (see OB-)
+ audire, hear] 1. to carry out the
orders of 2. to carry out (an order,
etc.) 3. to be guided by [to obey one's
conscience] —vi. to be obedient

**ob·fus·cate** (äb′fəs kāt′, äb fus′kāt)
vt. -cat′ed, -cat′ing [< L. ob- (see
OB-) + fuscus, dark] to obscure; confuse; bewilder —**ob′fus·ca′tion** n.

**o·bit·u·ar·y** (ō bich′oo wer′ē) n., pl.
-ies [< L. obire, die] a notice of
someone's death, usually with a brief
biography: also **o·bit** (ō′bit)

**obj.** 1. object 2. objective

**ob·ject** (äb′jikt; for v. əb jekt′, äb-)
n. [< ML. objectum, thing thrown in
the way < L. ob- (see OB-) + jacere,

fat, āpe, cär; ten, ēven; is, bīte; gō, hôrn, tōōl, look; oil, out; up, fur;
chin; she; thin, then; zh, leisure; ŋ, ring; ə for a in ago; ', (ā'b'l); ë, Fr. coeur;
ö, Fr. feu; Fr. mon; ü, Fr. duc; kh, G. ich, doch; ‡ foreign; < derived from

to throw] **1.** a thing that can be seen or touched **2.** a person or thing to which action, feeling, etc. is directed **3.** purpose; goal **4.** *Gram.* a noun or substantive that receives the action of a verb or is governed by a preposition —*vt.* to state by way of objection —*vi.* to feel or express disapproval or opposition —**ob·jec′tor** *n.*

**ob·jec·tion** (əb jek′shən) *n.* **1.** a feeling or expression of opposition or disapproval **2.** a reason for objecting

**ob·jec′tion·a·ble** *adj.* **1.** open to objection **2.** disagreeable; offensive

**ob·jec′tive** *adj.* **1.** existing as an object or fact, independent of the mind; real **2.** concerned with the realities of the thing dealt with rather than the thoughts of the artist, writer, etc. **3.** without bias or prejudice **4.** *Gram.* designating or of the case of an object of a preposition or verb —*n.* something aimed at —**ob·jec′tive·ly** *adv.* —**ob·jec·tiv·i·ty** (äb′jek tiv′ə tē), **ob·jec′tive·ness** *n.*

**object lesson** an actual or practical demonstration or exemplification of some principle

**ob·jet d'art** (äb′zhä där′) *pl.* **ob·jets d'art** (äb′zhä) [Fr.] a small object of artistic value

**ob·jur·gate** (äb′jər gāt′) *vt.* **-gat′ed, -gat′ing** [< L. *ob-* (see OB-) + *jurgare,* chide] to upbraid sharply; rebuke

**ob·late** (äb′lāt) *adj.* [< ModL. *oblatus,* thrust forward] *Geom.* flattened at the poles [an *oblate* spheroid]

**ob·la·tion** (ä blā′shən) *n.* [< L. *oblatus,* offered] an offering or sacrifice to God or a god

**ob·li·gate** (äb′lə gāt′) *vt.* **-gat′ed, -gat′ing** [see OBLIGE] to bind by a contract, promise, sense of duty, etc.

**ob′li·ga′tion** *n.* **1.** an obligating or being obligated **2.** a binding contract, promise, responsibility, etc. **3.** the binding power of a contract, etc. **4.** a being indebted for a favor, etc.

**ob·lig·a·to·ry** (ə blig′ə tôr′ē, äb′lig ə-) *adj.* legally or morally binding

**o·blige** (ə blīj′, ō-) *vt.* **o·bliged′, o·blig′ing** [< L. *ob-* (see OB-) + *ligare,* bind] **1.** to compel by moral, legal, or physical force **2.** to make indebted for a favor; do a favor for

**o·blig′ing** *adj.* ready to do favors; helpful —**o·blig′ing·ly** *adv.*

**ob·lique** (ə blēk′, ō-; *also, esp. in mil. use,* -blīk′) *adj.* [< L. *ob-* (see OB-) + *liquus,* awry] **1.** slanting **2.** indirect or evasive —**ob·lique′ly** *adv.* —**ob·liq·ui·ty** (ə blik′wə tē), **ob·lique′ness** *n.*

**ob·lit·er·ate** (ə blit′ə rāt′) *vt.* **-at′ed, -at′ing** [< L. *ob-* (see OB-) + *litera,* a letter] **1.** to blot out; efface **2.** to destroy —**ob·lit′er·a′tion** *n.*

**ob·liv·i·on** (ə bliv′ē ən) *n.* [< L. *oblivisci,* forget] **1.** forgetfulness **2.** the condition of being forgotten

**ob·liv′i·ous** *adj.* forgetful or unmindful (usually with *of* or *to*)

**ob·long** (äb′lôŋ) *adj.* [< L. *ob-* (see OB-) + *longus,* long] longer than broad; specif., rectangular and longer in one direction —*n.* an oblong figure

**ob·lo·quy** (äb′lə kwē) *n., pl.* **-quies** [< L. *ob-* (see OB-) + *loqui,* speak] **1.** widespread censure or abuse **2.** disgrace or infamy resulting from this

**ob·nox·ious** (əb näk′shəs) *adj.* [< L. *ob-* (see OB-) + *noxa,* harm] very unpleasant; offensive —**ob·nox′ious·ly** *adv.* —**ob·nox′ious·ness** *n.*

**o·boe** (ō′bō) *n.* [< Fr. *haut,* high (pitch) + *bois,* wood] a double-reed woodwind instrument having a high, penetrating tone —**o′bo·ist** *n.*

**Obs., obs.** obsolete

**ob·scene** (äb sēn′) *adj.* [< L. *obscenus,* filthy] **1.** offensive to modesty or decency; lewd **2.** repulsive —**ob·scen′i·ty** (-sen′ə tē) *n., pl.* **-ties**

OBOE

**ob·scure** (əb skyoor′) *adj.* [< L. *obscurus,* covered over] **1.** dim; dark **2.** not easily seen; faint **3.** vague; ambiguous [an *obscure* answer] **4.** inconspicuous; hidden **5.** not well-known [an *obscure* actor] —*vt.* **-scured′, -scur′ing** to make obscure —**ob·scure′ly** *adv.* —**ob·scu′ri·ty** *n.*

**ob·se·quies** (äb′sə kwēz) *n.pl.* [< L. *obsequium,* compliance, substituted for L. *exsequiae,* funeral] funeral rites

**ob·se·qui·ous** (əb sē′kwē əs) *adj.* [< L. *obsequi,* comply with] much too willing to serve or obey; fawning

**ob·serv·ance** (əb zur′vəns) *n.* **1.** the observing of a law, duty, custom, etc. **2.** a customary act, rite, etc.

**ob·serv′ant** *adj.* **1.** strict in observing a law, custom, etc. **2.** paying careful attention **3.** perceptive or alert

**ob·ser·va·tion** (äb′zər vā′shən) *n.* **1.** *a)* the act or power of noticing *b)* something noticed **2.** a being seen **3.** a noting and recording of facts, as for research **4.** a comment or remark

**ob·serv·a·to·ry** (əb zur′və tôr′ē) *n., pl.* **-ries** a building equipped for astronomical research, esp. one with a large telescope

**ob·serve** (əb zurv′) *vt.* **-served′, -serv′ing** [< L. *ob-* (see OB-) + *servare,* keep] **1.** to adhere to (a law, custom, etc.) **2.** to celebrate (a holiday, etc.) **3.** *a)* to notice (something) *b)* to pay special attention to **4.** to arrive at as a conclusion **5.** to say casually; remark **6.** to examine scientifically —**ob·serv′a·ble** *adj.* —**ob·serv′er** *n.*

**ob·sess** (əb ses′) *vt.* [< L. *ob-* (see OB-) + *sedere,* sit] to haunt or trouble in mind; preoccupy —**ob·ses′sive** *adj.* —**ob·ses′sive·ly** *adv.*

**ob·ses·sion** *n.* **1.** a being obsessed **2.** an idea, desire, etc. that obsesses one

**ob·sid·i·an** (əb sid′ē ən) *n.* [after one *Obsius,* its alleged discoverer] a hard, dark, volcanic glass

**ob·so·lesce** (äb′sə les′) *vi.* **-lesced′, -lesc′ing** to be obsolescent

**ob·so·les·cent** (äb'sə les''nt) *adj.* becoming obsolete —**ob'so·les'cence** *n.*

**ob·so·lete** (äb'sə lēt') *adj.* [ < L. *ob-* (see OB-) + *solere*, become accustomed] 1. no longer in use 2. out-of-date

**ob·sta·cle** (äb'sti k'l) *n.* [ < L. *ob-* (see OB-) + *stare*, to stand] anything that stands in the way; obstruction

**ob·stet·rics** (əb stet'riks) *n.pl.* [*with sing. v.*] [ < L. *obstetrix*, midwife] the branch of medicine concerned with the care and treatment of women during pregnancy and childbirth —**ob·stet'ric, ob·stet'ri·cal** *adj.* —**ob·ste·tri·cian** (äb'stə trish'ən) *n.*

**ob·sti·nate** (äb'stə nit) *adj.* [ < L. *obstinare*, resolve on] 1. determined to have one's own way; stubborn 2. resisting treatment [an *obstinate* fever] —**ob'sti·na·cy** (-nə sē) *n.* —**ob'sti·nate·ly** *adv.*

**ob·strep·er·ous** (əb strep'ər əs) *adj.* [ < L. *ob-* (see OB-) + *strepere*, to roar] noisy or unruly, esp. in resisting —**ob·strep'er·ous·ly** *adv.* —**ob·strep'er·ous·ness** *n.*

**ob·struct** (əb strukt') *vt.* [ < L. *ob-* (see OB-) + *struere*, pile up] 1. to block or stop up (a passage) 2. to hinder (progress, etc.) 3. to cut off from view —**ob·struc'tive** *adj.* —**ob·struc'tive·ly** *adv.* —**ob·struc'tive·ness** *n.*

**ob·struc·tion** *n.* 1. an obstructing 2. anything that obstructs; hindrance

**ob·struc·tion·ist** *n.* one who obstructs progress —*adj.* that obstructs

**ob·tain** (əb tān') *vt.* [ < L. *ob-* (see OB-) + *tenere*, to hold] to get possession of by trying; procure —*vi.* to prevail [peace will *obtain*] —**ob·tain'a·ble** *adj.* —**ob·tain'ment** *n.*

**ob·trude** (əb trood') *vt.* **-trud'ed, -trud'ing** [ < L. *ob-* (see OB-) + *trudere*, to thrust] 1. to push out; eject 2. to force (oneself, etc.) upon others unasked or unwanted —*vi.* to obtrude oneself —**ob·tru'sion** (-trōō'zhən) *n.* —**ob·tru'sive** *adj.* —**ob·tru'sive·ly** *adv.* —**ob·tru'sive·ness** *n.*

**ob·tuse** (äb tōōs', əb-) *adj.* [ < L. *obtundere*, to strike upon, blunt] 1. not sharp; blunt 2. greater than 90° and less than 180° [an *obtuse* angle] 3. slow to understand or perceive —**ob·tuse'ly** *adv.* —**ob·tuse'ness** *n.*

**ob·verse** (äb vurs'; *for n.* äb'vərs) *adj.* [ < L. *ob-* (see OB-) + *vertere*, to turn] 1. turned toward the observer 2. forming a counterpart —*n.* 1. the side, as of a coin or medal, bearing the main design 2. a counterpart

**ob·vi·ate** (äb'vē āt') *vt.* **-at'ed, -at'ing** [see ff.] to do away with or prevent by effective measures; make unnecessary —**ob'vi·a'tion** *n.*

**ob·vi·ous** (äb'vē əs) *adj.* [L. *obvius*, in the way] easy to see or understand; evident —**ob'vi·ous·ly** *adv.* —**ob'vi·ous·ness** *n.*

**oc-** *same as* OB-: used before *c*

**oc·a·ri·na** (äk'ə rē'nə) *n.* [It. < LL.

*auca*, goose: from its shape] a small wind instrument with finger holes and a mouthpiece

**occas.** occasional(ly)

**oc·ca·sion** (ə kā'zhən) *n.* [ < L. *ob-* (see OB-) + *cadere*, to fall] 1. a favorable time; opportunity 2. an event, etc. that makes something else possible 3. *a)* a happening *b)* a particular time 4. a special time or event 5. need arising from circumstances —*vt.* to cause —**on occasion** sometimes

**oc·ca'sion·al** *adj.* 1. of or for special occasions 2. happening now and then; infrequent —**oc·ca'sion·al·ly** *adv.*

**oc·ci·dent** (äk'sə dənt) *n.* [ < L. *occidere*, to fall: with reference to the setting sun] [Poet.] the west —[O-] Europe and the Americas —**oc'ci·den'tal, Oc'ci·den'tal** *adj., n.*

**Oc'ci·den'tal·ize** (-den't'l īz') *vt., vi.* **-ized', -iz'ing** to turn to the ways of the Occident

**oc·clude** (ə klōōd') *vt.* **-clud'ed, -clud'ing** [ < L. *ob-* (see OB-) + *claudere*, shut] 1. to close or block (a passage) 2. to shut in or out —*vi. Dentistry* to meet with the cusps fitting closely —**oc·clu'sion** (-klōō'zhən) *n.* —**oc·clu'sive** *adj.*

**oc·cult** (ə kult', ä'kult) *adj.* [ < L. *occulere*, conceal] 1. hidden 2. secret 3. mysterious 4. of mystic arts, such as magic, astrology, etc.

**oc·cu·pan·cy** (äk'yə pən sē) *n., pl.* **-cies** an occupying; a taking or keeping in possession

**oc'cu·pant** *n.* one who occupies

**oc·cu·pa·tion** (äk'yə pā'shən) *n.* 1. an occupying or being occupied 2. that which occupies one's time; work; profession —**oc'cu·pa'tion·al** *adj.*

**occupational therapy** therapy by means of work in the arts and crafts, as for hospital patients

**oc·cu·py** (äk'yə pī') *vt.* **-pied', -py'ing** [ < L. *ob-* (see OB-) + *capere*, seize] 1. to take possession of by settlement or seizure 2. to hold possession of; specif., *a)* to dwell in *b)* to hold (a position or office) 3. to take up (space, time, etc.) 4. to employ (oneself, one's mind, etc.)

**oc·cur** (ə kur') *vi.* **-curred', -cur'ring** [ < L. *ob-* (see OB-) + *currere*, to run] 1. to be or be met with; exist 2. to come to mind 3. to take place; happen

**oc·cur'rence** *n.* 1. the act or fact of occurring 2. an event; incident

**o·cean** (ō'shən) *n.* [ < Gr. *Ōkeanos*] 1. the body of salt water that covers about 71% of the earth's surface 2. any of its five principal divisions: the Atlantic, Pacific, Indian, Arctic, or Antarctic Ocean 3. a great quantity —**o·ce·an·ic** (ō'shē an'ik) *adj.*

**o'cean·aut** (-ôt') *n.* [ < OCEAN + Gr. *nautēs*, sailor] *same as* AQUANAUT

**o'cean·go·ing** *adj.* of or for ocean travel

**O·ce·an·i·a** (ō'shē an'ē ə) islands in

the Pacific, including Melanesia, Micronesia, & Polynesia

**o·cean·og·ra·phy** (ō'shə näg'rə fē) *n.* the study of the environment in the ocean, its plants and animals, etc. — **o'cean·o·graph'ic** (-nə graf'ik) *adj.*

**o·cel·lus** (ō sel'əs) *n., pl.* **-li** (-ī) [L. < *oculus,* eye] the simple eye of certain invertebrates

**o·ce·lot** (äs'ə lät', ō'sə-) *n.* [Fr. < Mex. *ocelotl,* jaguar] a medium-sized, spotted wildcat of N. and S.America

**o·cher, o·chre** (ō'kər) *n.* [< Gr. *ōchros,* pale-yellow] **1.** a yellow or reddish-brown clay containing iron, used as a pigment **2.** its color

**o'clock** (ə kläk', ō-) *adv.* of or according to the clock

**octa-** [< Gr. *oktō,* eight] *a combining form meaning* eight: also **octo-, oct-**

**oc·ta·gon** (äk'tə gän') *n.* [< Gr.: see prec. & -GON] a plane figure with eight angles and eight sides —**oc·tag'o·nal** (-tag'ə n'l) *adj.*

**oc·tane number** (or **rating**) (äk'tān) a number representing the antiknock properties of a gasoline, etc.

**oc·tave** (äk'tiv, -tāv) *n.* [< L. *octavus,* eighth] **1.** any group of eight **2.** *Music a)* the eighth full tone above or below a given tone *b)* the interval of eight degrees between a tone and either of its octaves *c)* the series of tones within this interval, or the keys of an instrument producing such a series

**oc·ta·vo** (äk tā'vō, -tä'-) *n., pl.* **-vos** [< L. (*in*) *octavo,* (in) eight] **1.** the page size (about 6 by 9 in.) of a book made up of printer's sheets folded into eight leaves **2.** a book of such pages

**oc·tet, oc·tette** (äk tet') *n.* [OCT(A)- + (DU)ET] *Music* **1.** a composition for eight voices or instruments **2.** the eight performers of this

**Oc·to·ber** (äk tō'bər) *n.* [< L. *octo-,* eight: eighth month in Rom. calendar] the tenth month of the year, having 31 days: abbrev. **Oct., O.**

**oc·to·ge·nar·i·an** (äk'tə ji ner'ē ən) *adj.* [< L. *octoginta,* eighty] between the ages of eighty and ninety —*n.* a person of this age

**oc·to·pus** (äk'tə pəs) *n., pl.* **-pus·es, -pi'** (-pī') [< Gr. *oktō,* eight + *pous,* foot] a mollusk with a soft body and eight arms covered with suckers

**oc·u·lar** (äk'yə lər) *adj.* [< L. *oculus,* eye] **1.** of, for, or like the eye **2.** by eyesight

**oc'u·list** (-list) *n. earlier term for* OPHTHALMOLOGIST

**OD** (ō'dē') *n., pl.* **ODs, OD's** [Slang] an overdose, esp. of a narcotic —*vi.* **OD'd, ODed, OD'ing, ODing** [Slang] to take an overdose, esp. a fatal dose of a narcotic

**OD, O.D.** **1.** Officer of the Day **2.** overdraft **3.** overdrawn

**o·da·lisque, o·da·lisk** (ōd'l isk) *n.* [Fr. < Turk. *ōdalik,* chambermaid] a female slave or concubine in an Oriental harem

**odd** (äd) *adj.* [< ON. *oddi*] **1.** with the other of the pair missing [an *odd* glove] **2.** having a remainder of one

when divided by two **3.** left over after taking a round number **4.** with a few more [sixty *odd* years ago] **5.** occasional [*odd* jobs] **6.** *a)* peculiar *b)* queer; eccentric —**odd'ly** *adv.* —**odd'ness** *n.*

**odd'ball** *adj.* [Slang] strange or eccentric —*n.* [Slang] one who is oddball

**odd'i·ty** (-ə tē) *n.* **1.** strangeness **2.** *pl.* **-ties** an odd person or thing

**odds** (ädz) *n.pl.* **1.** difference in favor of one side over the other; advantage **2.** advantage given by a bettor or competitor in proportion to the assumed chances in his favor —**at odds** quarreling —**by (all) odds** by far

**odds and ends** scraps; remnants

**odds'-on** *adj.* having a very good chance of winning [an *odds-on* favorite]

**ode** (ōd) *n.* [< Gr. *ōidē,* song] a lyric poem characterized by lofty feeling and dignified style

**-ode** (ōd) [< Gr. *hodos*] *a suffix meaning* way, path [anode, cathode]

**O·des·sa** (ō des'ə) seaport in S Ukrainian S.S.R.: pop. 753,000

**O·din** (ō'din) *Norse Myth.* the chief god

**o·di·ous** (ō'dē əs) *adj.* [< L. *odium,* hatred] disgusting; offensive —**o'di·ous·ly** *adv.* —**o'di·ous·ness** *n.*

**o·di·um** (ō'dē əm) *n.* [< L. *odi,* I hate] **1.** hatred **2.** the disgrace brought on by hateful action

**o·dom·e·ter** (ō däm'ə tər) *n.* [< Gr. *hodos,* way + *metron,* a measure] an instrument for measuring the distance traveled by a vehicle

**o·dor** (ō'dər) *n.* [L.] a smell; scent; aroma: Brit. sp. **odour** —**be in bad** (or **ill**) **odor** to be in ill repute —**o'dor·less** *adj.* —**o'dor·ous** *adj.*

**o·dor·if·er·ous** (ō'də rif'ər əs) *adj.* [< L. *odor,* odor + *ferre,* to bear] giving off an odor, esp. a fragrant one

**O·dys·se·us** (ō dis'yōōs, -ē əs) the hero of the *Odyssey,* one of the Greek leaders in the Trojan War

**Od·ys·sey** (äd'ə sē) an ancient Greek epic poem, ascribed to Homer, about the wanderings of Odysseus after the fall of Troy —*n.* [*sometimes* **o-**] *pl.* **-seys** any extended journey

**OE., OE, O.E.** Old English

**Oed·i·pus** (ed'ə pəs, ē'də-) *Gr. Myth.* a king who unwittingly killed his father and married his mother

**o'er** (ōr) *prep., adv.* [Poet.] over

**of** (uv, äv, əv) *prep.* [OE.] **1.** from; specif., *a)* coming from [men *of* Ohio] *b)* resulting from [to die *of* fever] *c)* at a distance from [east *of* the city] *d)* by [the poems *of* Poe] *e)* separated from [robbed *of* his money] *f)* from the whole constituting [one *of* her hats] *g)* made from [a sheet *of* paper] **2.** belonging to **3.** *a)* possessing [a man *of* wealth] *b)* containing [a bag *of* nuts] **4.** specified as [a height *of* six feet] **5.** characterized by [a man *of* honor] **6.** concerning; about **7.** during [*of* recent years]

**of-** *same as* OB-: used before *f*

**off** (ôf) *adv.* [LME. var. of *of*] **1.** so as to be away, at a distance, etc. **2.** so as to be no longer on, attached, etc.

*[take off your hat]* **3.** (a specified distance) away in space or time *[20 yards off]* **4.** so as to be no longer in operation, etc. *[turn the motor off]* **5.** so as to be less, etc. *[5% off for cash]* **6.** away from one's work —*prep.* **1.** (so as to be) no longer (or not) on, attached, etc. *[off the road]* **2.** from the substance of *[live off the land]* **3.** away from *[a mile off shore]* **4.** branching out from *[an alley off Main Street]* **5.** relieved from *[off duty]* **6.** not up to the usual standard, etc. of *[off one's game]* —*adj.* **1.** not on or attached **2.** not in operation **3.** on the way *[off to bed]* **4.** away from work *[we are off today]* **5.** not up to the usual standard, etc. **6.** more remote *[on the off chance]* **7.** in (specified) circumstances *[to be well off]* **8.** wrong *[his figures are off]* —*vt.* [Slang] to kill; murder —*interj.* go away! —**off and on** now and then

**of·fal** (ôf′'l, äf′-) *n.* [ME. *ofal,* lit., off-fall] **1.** *[with sing. or pl. v.]* the entrails, etc. of a butchered animal **2.** refuse; garbage

**off′beat′** *n. Music* a beat having a weak accent —*adj.* [Colloq.] unconventional, unusual, strange, etc.

**off′-col′or** *adj.* **1.** varying from the standard color **2.** improper; risqué

**of·fend** (ə fend′) *vi.* [< L. *ob-* (see OB-) + *-fendere,* to hit] **1.** to commit a sin or crime **2.** to create resentment, anger, etc. —*vt.* **1.** to hurt the feelings of; insult **2.** to be displeasing to (the taste, sense, etc.) —**of·fend′er** *n.*

**of·fense** (ə fens′, ô′fens) *n.* **1.** a sin or crime **2.** a creating of resentment, displeasure, etc. **3.** a feeling hurt, angry, etc. **4.** something that causes anger, etc. **5.** the act of attacking **6.** the side that is attacking or seeking to score in a contest Brit. sp. **offence** —**take offense** to be offended

**of·fen′sive** *adj.* **1.** attacking or for attack **2.** unpleasant; disgusting **3.** insulting —*n.* attitude or position of attack (often with *the*) —**of·fen′sive·ly** *adv.* —**of·fen′sive·ness** *n.*

**of·fer** (ôf′ər, äf′-) *vt.* [< L. *ob-* (see OB-) + *ferre,* bring] **1.** to present in worship *[to offer prayers]* **2.** to present for acceptance *[to offer help]* **3.** to suggest; propose **4.** to show or give signs of *[to offer resistance]* **5.** to bid (a price, etc.) —*vi.* to present itself —*n.* the act of offering or thing offered

**of′fer·ing** *n.* **1.** the act of making an offer **2.** something offered; specif., *a)* a gift *b)* presentation in worship

**of′fer·to′ry** (-tôr′ē) *n., pl.* **-ries** *[often O-]* **1.** the offering of the bread and wine to God in the Eucharist **2.** money collected at a church service, or the prayers or music during the collection

**off′hand′** *adv.* without preparation —*adj.* **1.** said or done offhand **2.** casual, curt, etc. Also **off′hand′ed**

**of·fice** (ôf′is, äf′-) *n.* [< L. *officium*]

**1.** a service done for another **2.** a duty, esp. as a part of one's work **3.** a position of authority or trust, as in government **4.** *a)* the place where the affairs of a business, etc. are carried on *b)* the people working there **5.** a religious ceremony or rite

**of′fice·hold′er** *n.* a government official

**of·fi·cer** (ôf′ə sər, äf′-) *n.* **1.** anyone holding an office, or position of authority, in a government, business, club, etc. **2.** a policeman **3.** one holding a position of authority, esp. by commission, in the armed forces

**officer of the day** *Mil.* the officer in charge of the interior guard and security of his garrison for the day

**of·fi·cial** (ə fish′əl) *adj.* **1.** of or holding an office, or position of authority **2.** authorized or authoritative **3.** formal —*n.* a person holding office —**of·fi′cial·dom** (-dəm), **of·fi′cial·ism** *n.* —**of·fi′cial·ly** *adv.*

**of·fi·ci·ant** (ə fish′ē ənt) *n.* an officiating priest, minister, etc.

**of·fi·ci·ate** (ə fish′ē āt′) *vi.* **-at′ed, -at′ing** **1.** to perform the duties of an office **2.** to perform the functions of a priest, minister, rabbi, etc.

**of·fi·cious** (ə fish′əs) *adj.* [see OFFICE] offering unwanted advice or services; meddlesome, esp. highhandedly so —**of·fi′cious·ly** *adv.* —**of·fi′cious·ness** *n.*

**off·ing** (ôf′iŋ) *n.* [< OFF] the distant part of the sea visible from the shore —**in the offing** **1.** far but in sight **2.** at some vague future time

**off′-key′** (-kē′) *adj.* **1.** *Music* flat or sharp **2.** not harmonious

**off′-lim′its** *adj.* ruled a place not to be gone to by a specified group

**off′-put′ting** *adj.* [Chiefly Brit.] distracting, annoying, etc.

**off′-sea′son** (-sē′z'n) *n.* a time of the year when the usual activity is reduced or not carried on

**off·set** (ôf set′; *for n.* ôf′set′) *vt.* **-set′, -set′ting** to balance, compensate for, etc. —*n.* **1.** a thing that offsets another **2.** offset printing

**offset printing** a printing process in which the inked impression is first made on a rubber-covered roller, then transferred to paper

**off′shoot′** *n.* anything that derives from a main source; specif., a shoot growing from the main stem of a plant

**off′shore′** *adj.* **1.** moving away from the shore **2.** at some distance from the shore —*adv.* away from the shore

**off′side′** *adj. Sports* not in proper position for play

**off′spring′** *n., pl.* **-spring′, -springs′** a child or children; progeny; young

**off′stage′** *n.* the part of the stage not seen by the audience —*adj.* in or from this —*adv.* to the offstage

**off′-track′** *adj.* designating or of legalized betting on horse races, carried on away from the race track

**off′-white′** *adj.* grayish-white or yellowish-white

**off year** 1. a year in which a major election does not take place 2. a year of little production

**oft** (ôft) *adv.* [OE.] [Poet.] often

**of·ten** (ôf′n) *adv.* [ME. var. of prec.] many times; frequently: also **of′ten-times′**

**o·gle** (ō′g'l) *vi., vt.* **o′gled, o′gling** [prob. < LowG. *oog*, an eye] to keep looking (at) flirtatiously —*n.* an ogling look —**o′gler** *n.*

**o·gre** (ō′gər) *n.* [Fr.] 1. in fairy tales and folklore, a man-eating giant 2. a hideous, cruel man

**oh** (ō) *interj., n., pl.* **oh's, ohs** an exclamation of surprise, fear, pain, etc.

**OH** Ohio

**O·hi·o** (ō hī′ō) 1. Middle Western State of the U.S.: 41,222 sq. mi.; pop. 10,652,000; cap. Columbus 2. river flowing from W Pa. into the Mississippi —**O·hi′o·an** *adj., n.*

**ohm** (ōm) *n.* [< G.S. *Ohm*, 19th-c. G. physicist] unit of electrical resistance

**o·ho** (ō hō′) *interj.* an exclamation of surprise, taunting, triumph, etc.

**-oid** (oid) [< Gr. *eidos*, form] *a suffix meaning* like, resembling [*spheroid*]

**oil** (oil) *n.* [< L. *oleum*] 1. any of various greasy, combustible, liquid substances obtained from animal, vegetable, and mineral matter 2. *same as* PETROLEUM 3. *same as: a)* OIL COLOR *b)* OIL PAINTING —*vt.* to lubricate or supply with oil —*adj.* of, from, or like oil

**oil′cloth′** *n.* cloth made waterproof by being treated with oil or paint

**oil color** paint made by grinding a pigment in oil

**oil painting** 1. a picture painted in oil colors 2. painting in oil colors

**oil shale** shale from which oil can be extracted by distillation

**oil′skin′** *n.* 1. cloth made waterproof by treatment with oil 2. [*often pl.*] a garment or outfit made of this

**oil well** a well bored through layers of rock, etc. to a supply of petroleum

**oil′y** *adj.* **-i·er, -i·est** 1. of, like, or containing oil 2. greasy 3. too suave or smooth; unctuous —**oil′i·ness** *n.*

**oink** (oink) *n., interj.* [echoic] the grunt of a pig —*vi.* to make this sound

**oint·ment** (oint′mənt) *n.* [< L. *unguentum*, a salve] a fatty substance used on the skin for healing or cosmetic purposes; salve

**OK, O.K.** (ō′kā′, ō′kā′) *adj., adv., interj.* [< "oll korrect," facetious misspelling of *all correct*] all right; correct —*n., pl.* **OK's, O.K.'s** approval —*vt.* **OK'd, O.K.'d, OK'ing, O.K.'-ing** to put an OK on; approve Also [Colloq.] **o′kay′**

**o·key-doke** (ō′kē dōk′) *adj., interj. slang var.* of OK: also **o′key-do′key** (-ē)

**O·kla·ho·ma** (ō′klə hō′mə) State of the SC U.S.: 69,919 sq. mi.; pop. 2,559,000; cap. Oklahoma City: abbrev. Okla., OK —**O′kla·ho′man** *adj., n.*

**Oklahoma City** capital of Okla.: pop. 366,000

**o·kra** (ō′krə) *n.* [< WAfr. name] 1. a plant with sticky green pods 2. the pods, used in soups, etc.

OKRA

**old** (ōld) *adj.* **old′er or eld′er, old′est or eld′est** [OE. *ald*] 1. having lived or existed for a long time 2. of aged people 3. of a certain age [*two years old*] 4. not new 5. worn out by age or use 6. former 7. experienced [*an old hand*] 8. ancient 9. of long standing 10. designating the earlier or earliest of two or more [*the Old World*] —*n.* 1. time long past [*days of old*] 2. something old (*with the*) —**old′ness** *n.*

**old country** the country, esp. in Europe, from which an immigrant came

**old·en** (ōl′d'n) *adj.* [Poet.] (of) old

**Old English** the Germanic language of the Anglo-Saxons, spoken in England from c.400 to c.1100 A.D.

**old′-fash′ioned** *adj.* suited to or favoring the methods, ideas, etc. of past times —*n.* a cocktail made with whiskey, bitters, soda, and bits of fruit

**old fogy, old fogey** *see* FOGY

**Old French** the French language from c.800 to c.1550 A.D.

**Old Glory** the flag of the U.S.

**old hand** a person with much skill or experience

**old hat** [Slang] old-fashioned or stale

**Old High German** the High German language before the 12th c.

**old·ie, old′y** (-ē) *n., pl.* **-ies** [Colloq.] an old joke, song, movie, etc.

**old lady** [Slang] 1. one's mother 2. one's wife

**old′-line′** *adj.* long-established, traditional, conservative, etc.

**Old Low German** the Low German language before the 12th c.

**old maid** 1. a woman, esp. an older woman, who has never married 2. a prim, prudish, fussy person

**old man** [Slang] 1. one's father 2. one's husband 3. [*usually* O- M-] a man in authority: *with the*

**old master** 1. any of the great European painters before the 18th century 2. a painting by any of these

**Old Norse** the Germanic language of the Scandinavians before the 14th c.

**Old Saxon** the Low German dialect of the Saxons before the 10th c.

**old school** a group of people who cling to traditional or conservative ideas —**old′-school′** *adj.*

**old′ster** (-stər) *n.* [Colloq.] an old or elderly person

**Old Testament** Christian designation for the Holy Scriptures of Judaism, the first of the two general divisions of the Christian Bible

**old′-time′** *adj.* 1. of past times 2. of long standing

**old′-tim′er** *n.* [Colloq.] a long-time resident, employee, member, etc.

**Old World** Europe, Asia, and Africa: often with reference to European culture, customs, etc. —**old'-world'**, **Old'-World'** *adj.*

†**o·lé** (ō lā') *interj., n.* [Sp.] a shout of approval, triumph, etc.

**o·le·ag·i·nous** (ō'lē aj'i nəs) *adj.* [< L. *olea,* olive tree] oily; unctuous

**o·le·an·der** (ō'lē an'dər) *n.* [ML.] a poisonous evergreen shrub with fragrant white or red flowers and narrow, leathery leaves

**o·le·o·mar·ga·rine** (ō'lē ō mär'jə rin) *n.* [< L. *oleum,* oil + MARGARINE] *same as* MARGARINE: also **o'le·o'**

**ol·fac·to·ry** (äl fak'tər ē, ōl-) *adj.* [< L. *olere,* have a smell + *facere,* make] of the sense of smell

**ol·i·gar·chy** (äl'ə gär'kē) *n., pl.* **-ies** [< Gr. *oligos,* few + -ARCHY] 1. (a) government in which a few persons have the ruling power 2. the ruling persons —**ol'i·gar'chic** *adj.*

**ol·ive** (äl'iv) *n.* [< L. *oliva*] 1. *a*) an evergreen tree of S Europe and the Near East *b*) its small oval fruit, eaten as a relish or pressed, when ripe, to extract its light-yellow oil (**olive oil**) 2. the yellowish-green color of the unripe fruit

**olive branch** the branch of the olive tree, a symbol of peace

**O·lym·pi·a** (ō lim'pē ə) capital of Wash.: pop. 23,000

**O·lym·pic games** (ō lim'pik) [< *Olympia,* plain in Greece, site of ancient games] an international athletic competition generally held every four years: also **the O·lym'pics** (-piks)

**O·lym'pus** (-pəs) mountain in N Greece: *Gr. Myth.* the home of the gods —**O·lym'pi·an** (-pē ən) *adj.*

**om** (ōm, ōn) *n.* [Sans.] *Hinduism* a word intoned as during meditation

**O·ma·ha** (ō'mə hô) city in E Nebr.: pop. 347,000

**om·buds·man** (äm'bədz mən) *n., pl.* **-men** [Sw. < *ombud,* deputy] a public official appointed to investigate citizens' complaints against the government

**o·me·ga** (ō mā'gə, -mē'gə) *n.* the 24th & last letter of the Greek alphabet (Ω, ω)

**om·e·let, om·e·lette** (äm'lit, äm'ə let) *n.* [< L. *lamella,* small plate] eggs beaten up, often with water or milk, and cooked as a pancake in a pan

**o·men** (ō'mən) *n.* [L.] a thing or happening supposed to foretell a future event, either good or evil

**om·i·cron** (äm'ə krän', ō'mə-) *n.* the 15th letter of the Greek alphabet (O, o)

**om·i·nous** (äm'ə nəs) *adj.* of or serving as an evil omen; threatening —**om'i·nous·ly** *adv.*

**o·mis·sion** (ō mish'ən) *n.* 1. an omitting 2. anything omitted

**o·mit** (ō mit') *vt.* **o·mit'ted, o·mit'ting** [< L. *ob-* (see OB-) + *mittere,* send] 1. to leave out; fail to include 2. to neglect; fail to do

**omni-** [L. < *omnis,* all] *a combining form meaning* all, everywhere

**om·ni·bus** (äm'nə bəs) *n., pl.* **-bus·es** [< L., for all] *same as* BUS —*adj.* dealing with many things at once

**om·nip·o·tent** (äm nip'ə tənt) *adj.* [< L. *omnis,* all + *potens,* able] having unlimited power or authority; all-powerful —**om·nip'o·tence** *n.*

**om·ni·pres·ent** (äm'ni prez''nt) *adj.* present in all places at the same time —**om'ni·pres'ence** *n.*

**om·nis·cient** (äm nish'ənt) *adj.* [< L. *omnis,* all + *sciens,* knowing] knowing all things —**om·nis'cience** *n.*

**om·niv·o·rous** (äm niv'ər əs) *adj.* [< L. *omnis,* all + *vorare,* devour] 1. eating any sort of food, esp. both animal and vegetable food 2. taking in everything indiscriminately [an *omnivorous* reader] —**om·niv'o·rous·ly** *adv.* —**om·niv'o·rous·ness** *n.*

**on** (än, ôn) *prep.* [OE.] 1. in contact with, supported by, or covering 2. in the surface of [scars *on* it] 3. near to [*on* my left] 4. at the time of [*on* Monday] 5. connected with [*on* the team] 6. engaged in [*on* a trip] 7. in a state of [*on* parole] 8. as a result of [a profit *on* the sale] 9. in the direction of [light shone *on* us] 10. through the use of [live *on* bread] 11. concerning [an essay *on* war] 12. [Colloq.] at the expense of [a drink *on* the house] 13. [Slang] using; addicted to [*on* drugs] —*adv.* 1. in a situation of contacting, being supported by, or covering 2. in a direction toward [he looked *on*] 3. forward [move *on*] 4. without stopping [she sang *on*] 5. into action or operation [turn *on* the light] —*adj.* in action or operation [the play is *on*] —**and so on** and more like the preceding —**on and off** intermittently —**on and on** for a long time; continuously —**on to** [Slang] aware of the real nature or meaning of

**once** (wuns) *adv.* [ME. *ones*] 1. one time only 2. at any time; ever 3. formerly 4. by one degree [cousin *once* removed] —*conj.* as soon as [*once* he hears, he'll tell] —*n.* one time [go this *once*] —**at once** 1. immediately 2. at the same time —**once (and) for all** conclusively —**once in a while** now and then

**once'-o'ver** *n.* [Colloq.] a quick look, examination, etc.

**on·com·ing** (än'kum'iŋ) *adj.* coming nearer in position or time

**one** (wun) *adj.* [OE. *an*] 1. being a single thing 2. united [with *one* accord] 3. a certain but not named; some [take *one* path or the other, *one* day last week] 4. the same 5. being uniquely such [the *one* solution] —*n.* 1. the first and lowest cardinal number; 1; I 2. a single person or thing —*pron.* 1. a certain person or thing 2. any person or thing —**at one** in accord —**one by one** individually in succession

**O'Neill** (ō nēl′), **Eugene** 1888–1953; U.S. playwright

**one′ness** (-nis) *n.* 1. singleness; unity 2. unity of mind, feeling, etc.

**on·er·ous** (än′ər əs) *adj.* [< L. *onus,* a load] burdensome; oppressive

**one·self** (wun′self′) *pron.* a person's own self: also **one's self** —**be oneself** 1. to function normally 2. to be natural —**by oneself** alone

**one′-sid·ed** (-sīd′id) *adj.* 1. on, having, or involving only one side 2. unfair 3. unequal [a *one-sided* race]

**one′-time′** *adj.* former

**one′-track′** *adj.* [Colloq.] limited in scope [a *one-track* mind]

**one′-up′** *adj.* [Colloq.] having superiority or an advantage (over another)

**one′-way′** *adj.* moving, or allowing movement, in one direction only

**on′go·ing** *adj.* going on; progressing

**on·ion** (un′yən) *n.* [< L. *unus,* one] 1. a plant of the lily family with an edible bulb 2. this bulb, having a sharp smell and taste

**on′ion-skin′** *n.* a tough, thin, translucent, glossy paper

**on′look′er** *n.* a spectator

**on·ly** (ōn′lē) *adj.* [< OE. *an,* one + *-lic,* -ly] 1. alone of its or their kind; sole 2. alone in superiority; best —*adv.* 1. and no other; and no more; solely 2. (but) in the end 3. as recently as —*conj.* [Colloq.] except that; but —**only too** very

**on·o·mat·o·poe·ia** (än′ə mat′ə pē′ə, -mät′-) *n.* [< Gr. *onoma,* a name + *poiein,* make] the formation of words by imitating sounds (Ex.: *buzz*)

**on′rush′** *n.* a headlong rush forward

**on′set′** *n.* 1. an attack 2. a start

**on·slaught** (än′slôt′) *n.* [< Du. *slagen,* to strike] a violent attack

**On·tar·i·o** (än ter′ē ō) 1. province of SE Canada: 412,582 sq. mi.; pop. 6,961,000; cap. Toronto: abbrev. **Ont.** 2. **Lake,** smallest of the Great Lakes, between N.Y. and Ontario

**on·to** (än′tōō) *prep.* 1. to a position on 2. [Slang] aware of Also **on to**

**on·tog·e·ny** (än täj′ə nē) *n.* [ult. < Gr. *einei,* be + *-genēs,* born] the life cycle of a single organism

**o·nus** (ō′nəs) *n.* [L.] 1. a burden, unpleasant duty, etc. 2. blame

**on·ward** (än′wərd) *adv.* toward or at a position ahead; forward: also **on·wards** —*adj.* advancing

**on·yx** (än′iks) *n.* [< Gr. *onyx,* fingernail] a type of agate with alternate colored layers

**oo·dles** (ōō′d′lz) *n.pl.* [< ?] [Colloq.] a great amount; very many

**ooze¹** (ōōz) *n.* [OE. *wos,* sap] something that oozes —*vi.* **oozed, ooz′ing** to flow or leak out slowly —*vt.* to exude

**ooze²** (ōōz) *n.* [OE. *wase*] soft mud or slime, as at the bottom of a lake

**op-** *same as* OB-: used before *p*

**o·pal** (ō′p′l) *n.* [< Sans. *upala,* gem] an iridescent silica of various colors: some varieties are semiprecious — **o·pal·es·cent** (ō′pə les′′nt) *adj.*

**o·paque** (ō pāk′) *adj.* [< L. *opacus,* shady] 1. not transparent 2. not reflecting light; dull 3. hard to understand —**o·pac·i·ty** (ō pas′ə tē), **o·paque′ness** *n.* —**o·paque′ly** *adv.*

**op** (art) (äp) a style of abstract painting creating optical illusions

**op. cit.** [L. *opere citato*] in the work cited

**OPEC** Organization of Petroleum Exporting Countries

**Op′-Ed′** *adj.* [*Op*(*posite*) *Ed*(*itorial page*)] designating or on a page in a newspaper, featuring a wide variety of columns, articles, letters, etc.

**o·pen** (ō′p′n) *adj.* [OE.] 1. not closed, covered, clogged, or shut 2. not enclosed [*open* fields] 3. spread out; unfolded [an *open* book] 4. having gaps, holes, etc. 5. free to be entered, used, etc. [an *open* meeting] 6. not decided [an *open* question] 7. not closed to new ideas, etc. [an *open* mind] 8. generous 9. free from legal or discriminatory restrictions [*open* season, *open* housing] 10. not conventional [*open* marriage] 11. not already taken [the job is *open*] 12. not secret; public 13. frank; candid [an *open* manner] —*vt., vi.* 1. to cause to be, or to become, open 2. to spread out; expand; unfold 3. to make or become available for use, etc. without restriction 4. to begin; start 5. to start operating —**open to** 1. willing to receive, discuss, etc. 2. available to —**the open** 1. the outdoors 2. public knowledge —**o′pen·er** *n.* —**o′pen·ly** *adv.* —**o′pen·ness** *n.*

**o′pen-air′** *adj.* outdoor

**o′pen-and-shut′** *adj.* easily decided

**o′pen-end′ed** *adj.* unlimited

**o′pen-eyed′** *adj.* with the eyes wide open, as in surprise or watchfulness

**o′pen-faced′** *adj.* 1. having a frank, honest face 2. designating a sandwich without a top slice of bread: also **o′pen-face′**

**o′pen-hand′ed** *adj.* generous

**o′pen-hearth′** *adj.* designating or using a furnace with a wide hearth and low roof, for making steel

**o′pen-heart′ surgery** surgery on the heart during which the blood is circulated by a mechanical apparatus

**open house** 1. an informal reception at one's home 2. a time when an institution is open to visitors

**o′pen·ing** *n.* 1. an open place; gap; hole 2. a clearing 3. a beginning 4. start of operations 5. a favorable chance 6. an unfilled job

**o′pen-mind′ed** *adj.* having a mind open to new ideas; unprejudiced

**o′pen·work′** *n.* ornamental work, as in cloth, with openings in it

**op·er·a¹** (äp′ər ə) *n.* [< L., a work] a play having its text set to music and sung to orchestral accompaniment — **op′er·at′ic** (-ə rat′ik) *adj.*

**op·er·a²** (äp′ər ə) *n. pl. of* OPUS

**op·er·a·ble** (äp′ər ə b′l) *adj.* [see OPERATE + -ABLE] 1. feasible 2. that can be treated by a surgical operation

**opera glasses** a small binocular telescope used in theaters, etc.

**op·er·ate** (äp′ə rāt′) *vi.* -at′ed, -at′ing [< L. *operari,* to work] 1. to be in action; act; work 2. to bring about a certain effect **3.** to perform a surgical operation —*vt.* **1.** to put or keep in action **2.** to direct; manage

**op'er·a'tion** *n.* **1.** the act or method of operating **2.** a being in action or at work **3.** any of a series of procedures in some work or plan, as in industry, warfare, etc. **4.** any surgical procedure to remedy a physical ailment

**op'er·a'tion·al** (-'l) *adj.* **1.** of, or having to do with, the operation of a device, system, etc. **2.** *a)* that can be used or operated *b)* in use; operating

**op'er·a·tive** (äp'ə rā'tiv, äp'ər ə-) *adj.* **1.** in operation; active **2.** effective **3.** connected with physical work or mechanical action

**op'er·a'tor** (-rāt'ər) *n.* **1.** a person who operates a machine [a telephone *operator*] **2.** a person engaged in business or industrial operations

**op·er·et·ta** (äp'ə ret'ə) *n.* [It. < *opera*] a short, amusing musical play

**oph·thal·mic** (äf thal'mik) *adj.* [< Gr. *ophthalmos*, the eye] of or connected with the eyes

**oph·thal·mol·o·gy** (äf'thal mäl'ə jē, äp'-; -thə-) *n.* the branch of medicine dealing with the eye and its diseases —**oph'thal·mol'o·gist** *n.*

**o·pi·ate** (ō'pē it) *n.* **1.** a narcotic drug containing opium or any of its derivatives **2.** anything quieting

**o·pine** (ō pīn') *vt., vi.* **o·pined', o·pin'ing** [ < L. *opinari*, think] to think; suppose: usually humorous

**o·pin·ion** (ə pin'yən) *n.* [< L. *opinari*, think] **1.** a belief not based on certainty but on what seems true or probable **2.** an evaluation, estimation, etc. **3.** formal expert judgment

**o·pin'ion·at'ed** (-āt'id) *adj.* holding obstinately to one's opinions

**o·pi·um** (ō'pē əm) *n.* [ < Gr. *opos*, vegetable juice] a narcotic drug prepared from the seed of a certain poppy

**o·pos·sum** (ə päs'əm) *n.* [ < AmInd.] a small, tree-dwelling mammal that carries its young in a pouch

**op·po·nent** (ə pō'nənt) *n.* [< L. *ob-* (see OB-) + *ponere*, to place] one who opposes, as in a fight, game, etc.; adversary

**op·por·tune** (äp'ər tōōn') *adj.* [< L. *opportunus*, lit., before the port] **1.** suitable: said of time **2.** well-timed

OPOSSUM

**op'por·tun'ism** *n.* the adapting of one's actions, thoughts, etc. to circumstances, as in politics, without regard for principles —**op'por·tun'ist** *n.*— **op'por·tun·is'tic** *adj.*

**op·por·tu·ni·ty** (äp'ər tōō'nə tē) *n.,* *pl.* **-ties** **1.** a combination of circumstances favorable for the purpose **2.** a good chance

**op·pose** (ə pōz') *vt.* **-posed', -pos'ing** [see OB- & POSITION] **1.** to place

opposite, in balance or contrast **2.** to contend with; resist

**op·po·site** (äp'ə zit) *adj.* [see OB- & POSITION] **1.** set against; in a contrary direction (often with *to*) **2.** entirely different; exactly contrary —*n.* anything opposed —*prep.* across from — **op'po·site·ly** *adv.*

**opposite number** a person whose position, rank, etc. parallels another's in a different place or organization

**op·po·si·tion** (-zish'ən) *n.* **1.** an opposing **2.** resistance, contrast, hostility, etc. **3.** one that opposes; specif., *[often O-]* a political party opposing the party in power

**op·press** (ə pres') *vt.* [ < L. *ob-* (see OB-) + *premere*, to press] **1.** to weigh heavily on the mind of; worry **2.** to keep down by the cruel or unjust use of authority —**op·pres'sor** *n.*

**op·pres·sion** (ə presh'ən) *n.* **1.** an oppressing or being oppressed **2.** a thing that oppresses **3.** physical or mental distress

**op·pres·sive** (ə pres'iv) *adj.* **1.** causing discomfort **2.** tyrannical **3.** distressing —**op·pres'sive·ly** *adv.*

**op·pro·bri·ous** (ə prō'brē əs) *adj.* expressing opprobrium; abusive

**op·pro·bri·um** (-əm) *n.* [ < L. *opprobrare*, to reproach] **1.** the disgrace attached to shameful conduct **2.** anything bringing shame

**opt** (äpt) *vi.* [see OPTION] to make a choice (often with *for*) —**opt out (of)** to choose not to be or continue in (some activity, organization, etc.)

**op·ta·tive** (äp'tə tiv) *adj.* [see OPTION] designating or of that mood of a verb expressing wish or desire

**op·tic** (äp'tik) *adj.* [ < Gr. *optikos*] of the eye or sense of sight

**op'ti·cal** (-'l) *adj.* **1.** of the sense of sight; visual **2.** of optics **3.** for aiding vision —**op'ti·cal·ly** *adv.*

**op·ti·cian** (äp tish'ən) *n.* one who makes or sells eyeglasses, etc.

**op·tics** (äp'tiks) *n.pl.* [*with sing. v.*] the branch of physics dealing with light and vision

**op·ti·mism** (äp'tə miz'm) *n.* [ < L. *optimus*, best] **1.** the belief that good ultimately prevails over evil **2.** the tendency to take the most hopeful view of matters —**op'ti·mist** (-mist) *n.* —**op'ti·mis'tic** (-mis'tik) *adj.*

**op'ti·mum** (-məm) *n.* [see prec.] the best or most favorable degree, condition, etc. —*adj.* most favorable; best: also **op'ti·mal** (-məl)

**op·tion** (äp'shən) *n.* [ < L. *optare*, to wish] **1.** a choosing; choice **2.** the right of choosing **3.** something that is or can be chosen **4.** the right to buy, sell, or lease at a fixed price within a specified time —**op·tion·al** *adj.*

**op·tom·e·try** (äp täm'ə trē) *n.* [ < Gr. *optikos*, optic + *metron*, a measure] the profession of testing the vision and prescribing glasses to correct eye-defects —**op·tom'e·trist** *n.*

**op·u·lent** (äp′yə lənt) *adj.* [ < L. *ops*, riches] 1. having much wealth; rich 2. abundant —**op′u·lence** *n.*

**o·pus** (ō′pəs) *n., pl.* **op·er·a** (äp′ər ə), **o′pus·es** [L., a work] a work; composition; esp., any of the numbered musical works of a composer

**or** (ôr) *conj.* [ < OE. *oththe*] a coordinating conjunction introducing: *a*) an alternative [red or blue] or the last in a series of choices *b*) a synonymous word or phrase [oral, or spoken]

**-or** (ər) [ < L.] *a suffix meaning:* 1. a person or thing that [inventor] 2. quality or condition [error]

**OR** Oregon

**or·a·cle** (ôr′ə k′l, är′-) *n.* [ < L. *orare*, pray] 1. *a*) in ancient Greece and Rome, the place where, or medium by which, deities were consulted *b*) the revelation of a medium or priest 2. *a*) a person of great knowledge *b*) statements of such a person —**o·rac·u·lar** (ô rak′yoo lər) *adj.*

**o·ral** (ôr′əl) *adj.* [ < L. *os*, mouth] 1. uttered; spoken 2. of or near the mouth —**o′ral·ly** *adv.*

**or·ange** (ôr′inj, är′-) *n.* [ult. < Sans. *naranga*] 1. a reddish-yellow, round citrus fruit with a sweet, juicy pulp 2. the evergreen tree it grows on 3. reddish yellow

**or′ange·ade′** (-ād′) *n.* a drink made of orange juice, water, and sugar

**orange stick** a pointed stick of wood of the orange tree, for manicuring

**o·rang·u·tan** (ô raŋ′oo tan′, -taŋ′) *n.* [ < Malay *oraŋ*, man + *utan*, forest] a manlike ape with reddish-brown hair, found only in Borneo and Sumatra

**o·rate** (ô rāt′, ôr′āt) *vi.* **-rat′ed, -rat′ing** to make an oration; speak in a pompous or bombastic way

**o·ra·tion** (ô rā′shən) *n.* [ < L. *orare*, speak] a formal speech, esp. one given at a ceremony

**or·a·tor** (ôr′ət ər, är′-) *n.* an eloquent public speaker; expert in oratory

**or·a·to·ri·o** (ôr′ə tôr′ē ō′, är′-) *n., pl.* **-os′** [It., small chapel] a long, dramatic musical work, usually on a religious theme, but not acted out

**or·a·to·ry** (ôr′ə tôr′ē, är′-) *n., pl.* **-ries** [ < L. *oratoria*] skill in public speaking —**or′a·tor′i·cal** *adj.*

**orb** (ôrb) *n.* [ < L. *orbis*, a circle] 1. a sphere, or globe 2. any heavenly sphere, as the sun or moon

**or·bit** (ôr′bit) *n.* [ < L. *orbis*, a circle] 1. the path of a heavenly body in its revolution around another 2. the path of an artificial satellite or spacecraft around a heavenly body —*vi., vt.* to move in, or put into, an orbit —**or′bit·al** *adj.*

**or·chard** (ôr′chərd) *n.* [OE. *ortgeard*] 1. an area for growing fruit trees 2. the trees

**or·ches·tra** (ôr′kis trə) *n.* [ < Gr. *orcheisthai*, to dance] 1. the space in front of a theater stage, where the musicians sit: in full **orchestra pit** 2. the seats on the main floor of a theater 3. *a*) a group of musicians playing together *b*) their instruments —**or·ches′tral** (-kes′trəl) *adj.*

**or·ches·trate** (-trāt′) *vt., vi.* **-trat′ed, -trat′ing** to arrange (music) for an orchestra —**or′ches·tra′tion** *n.*

**or·chid** (ôr′kid) *n.* [ < Gr. *orchis*, testicle: from the shape of the roots] 1. any of certain plants having flowers with three petals, one of which is lip-shaped 2. this flower 3. pale purple

**or·dain** (ôr dān′) *vt.* [ < L. *ordo*, an order] 1. to decree; establish; enact 2. to invest with the office of minister, priest, or rabbi —*vi.* to command —**or·dain′ment** *n.*

**or·deal** (ôr dēl′) *n.* [OE. *ordal*] any difficult or painful experience

**or·der** (ôr′dər) *n.* [ < L. *ordo*, straight row] 1. social position 2. a state of peace; orderly conduct 3. arrangement of things or events; series 4. a definite plan; system 5. a military, monastic, or social brotherhood 6. a condition in which everything is in its place and functioning properly 7. condition in general [in good order] 8. an authoritative command, instruction, etc. 9. a class; kind 10. an established method, as of conduct in meetings, etc. 11. *a*) a request to supply something [an order for books] *b*) the goods supplied 12. [*pl.*] the position of ordained minister [to take holy orders] —*vt., vi.* 1. to put or keep (things) in order; arrange 2. to command 3. to request (something to be supplied) —**in** (or **out of**) **order** 1. in (or out of) proper position 2. in (or not in) working condition 3. in (or not in) accordance with the rules —**in order that** so that —**in order to** for the purpose of —**in short order** quickly —**on the order of** similar to —**to order** in accordance with the buyer's specifications

**or′der·ly** *adj.* 1. neat or tidy 2. well-behaved; law-abiding —*adv.* methodically —*n., pl.* **-lies** 1. an enlisted man assigned to render personal services to an officer 2. a male hospital attendant —**or′der·li·ness** *n.*

**or·di·nal** (ôr′d′n əl) *adj.* [ < L. *ordo*, order] expressing order in a series —*n.* any number showing order in a series (e.g., first, third): in full **ordinal number**

**or·di·nance** (ôr′d′n əns) *n.* [ < L. *ordo*, an order] a statute or regulation, esp. a municipal one

**or·di·nar·i·ly** (ôr′d′n er′ə lē) *adv.* usually; as a rule

**or·di·nar·y** (ôr′d′n er′ē) *adj.* [ < L. *ordo*, an order] 1. customary; usual 2. familiar; unexceptional; common —**out of the ordinary** unusual

**or·di·na·tion** (ôr′d′n ā′shən) *n.* an ordaining or being ordained to the clergy

**ord·nance** (ôrd′nəns) *n.* [ < ORDINANCE] 1. artillery 2. all military weapons, ammunition, vehicles, etc.

**or·do** (ôr′dō) *n., pl.* **-dos, -di·nes′** (-də nēz′) [L., order] *R.C.Ch.* an annual calendar giving directions for each day's Mass and Office

**or·dure** (ôr′jər) *n.* [ult. < L. *horridus*, horrid] dung; excrement

**ore** (ôr) *n.* [OE. *ar*, brass] a natural combination of minerals, esp. one from which a metal or metals can be profitably extracted

**o·reg·a·no** (ô reg′ə nō) *n.* [< Sp. < Gr. *origanon*] any of certain plants of the mint family, with fragrant leaves used for seasoning

**Or·e·gon** (ôr′i gən, -gän′) Northwestern State of the U.S.: 96,981 sq. mi.; pop. 2,091,000; cap. Salem: abbrev. **Oreg.** —**Or′e·go′ni·an** (-gō′nē ən) *adj., n.*

**or·gan** (ôr′gən) *n.* [< Gr. *organon*, implement] **1.** a keyboard musical instrument with sets of graduated pipes through which compressed air is passed, causing sound by vibration **2.** in animals and plants, a part adapted to perform a specific function **3.** a means for performing some action **4.** a means of communicating ideas or opinions, as a periodical

**or·gan·dy, or·gan·die** (ôr′gən dē) *n., pl.* -**dies** [Fr. *organdi*] a very sheer, crisp cotton fabric

**or·gan·ic** (ôr gan′ik) *adj.* **1.** of or having to do with a bodily organ **2.** inherent; inborn **3.** systematically arranged **4.** designating or of any chemical compound containing carbon **5.** of, like, or derived from living organisms —**or·gan′i·cal·ly** *adv.*

**or·gan·ism** (ôr′gə niz′m) *n.* any living thing —**or·gan·is′mic** *adj.*

**or′gan·ist** *n.* a player of the organ

**or·gan·i·za·tion** (ôr′gə ni zā′shən) *n.* **1.** an organizing or being organized **2.** any organized group, as a club — **or′gan·i·za′tion·al** *adj.*

**or·gan·ize** (ôr′gə nīz′) *vt.* -**ized′**, -**iz′ing 1.** to provide with an organic structure **2.** to arrange for **3.** to establish; institute **4.** to persuade to join a cause, group, etc. —*vi.* to become organized —**or′gan·iz′er** *n.*

**or·gan·za** (ôr gan′zə) *n.* [< ?] a thin, stiff fabric of rayon, silk, etc.

**or·gasm** (ôr′gaz′m) *n.* [< Gr. *organ*, to swell] the climax of a sexual act

**or·gy** (ôr′jē) *n., pl.* -**gies** [< Gr. *orgia*, secret rites] **1.** a wild merrymaking **2.** an overindulgence in any activity

**o·ri·el** (ôr′i əl) *n.* [< ? ML. *oriolum*, gallery] a bay window resting on a bracket or a corbel

**o·ri·ent** (ôr′ē ənt; *also, esp. for v.* -ent′) *n.* [< L. *oriri*, arise: used of the rising sun] [O-] the East, or Asia; esp., the Far East —*vt., vi.* to adjust (oneself) to a particular situation —**o′ri·en·ta′tion** *n.*

**O′ri·en′tal** (-en′t'l) *adj.* of the Orient, its people, etc. —*n.* a member of a people native to the Orient

**or·i·fice** (ôr′ə fis, är′-) *n.* [< L. *os*, mouth + *facere*, make] a mouth of a tube, cavity, etc.; opening

**orig.** **1.** origin **2.** original(ly)

**o·ri·ga·mi** (ôr′ə gä′mē) *n.* [Jap.] a Japanese art of folding paper to form flowers, animal figures, etc.

**or·i·gin** (ôr′ə jin, är′-) *n.* [< L. *oriri*, to rise] **1.** a coming into existence or

use; beginning **2.** parentage; birth **3.** source; root; cause

**o·rig·i·nal** (ə rij′ə n'l) *adj.* **1.** first; earliest **2.** never having been before; new; novel **3.** capable of creating something new; inventive **4.** being that from which copies are made —*n.* **1.** a primary type that has given rise to varieties **2.** an original work, as of art or literature —**o·rig′i·nal′i·ty** (-nal′ə tē) *n.* —**o·rig′i·nal·ly** *adv.*

**o·rig·i·nate** (-nāt′) *vt.* -**nat′ed**, -**nat′ing** to bring into being; esp., to invent —*vi.* to begin; start —**o·rig′i·na′tion** *n.* —**o·rig′i·na′tor** *n.*

**o·ri·ole** (ôr′ē ōl′) *n.* [ult. < L. *aurum*, gold] any of a genus of American birds with bright-orange and black plumage: they build hanging nests

**O·ri·on** (ō rī′ən, ô-) a very bright equatorial constellation

**Or·lon** (ôr′län) *a trademark for a* synthetic fiber similar to nylon

**or·mo·lu** (ôr′mə lōo′) *n.* [Fr. *or moulu*, ground gold] an imitation gold made of a copper and tin alloy, used in ornaments, gilding, etc.

**or·na·ment** (ôr′nə mənt; *for v.* -ment′) *n.* [< L. *ornare*, adorn] **1.** anything that adorns; decoration **2.** one whose character or talent adds luster to his surroundings, etc. —*vt.* to decorate —**or′na·men′tal** *adj.* — **or′na·men·ta′tion** *n.*

**or·nate** (ôr nāt′) *adj.* [< L. *ornare*, adorn] heavily ornamented; showy — **or·nate′ly** *adv.* —**or·nate′ness** *n.*

**or·ner·y** (ôr′nər ē) *adj.* [< ORDINARY] [Chiefly Dial.] **1.** having a mean disposition **2.** obstinate —**or′ner·i·ness** *n.*

**or·ni·thol·o·gy** (ôr′nə thäl′ə jē) *n.* [< Gr. *ornis*, bird + -LOGY] the branch of zoology dealing with birds —**or′ni·thol′o·gist** *n.*

**o·ro·tund** (ôr′ə tund′) *adj.* [< L. *os*, mouth + *rotundus*, round] **1.** resonant: said of the voice **2.** bombastic

**or·phan** (ôr′fən) *n.* [< Gr.] a child whose parents are dead —*adj.* **1.** being an orphan **2.** of or for orphans —*vt.* to cause to become an orphan

**or′phan·age** (-ij) *n.* an institution that is a home for orphans

**Or·phe·us** (ôr′fē əs) *Gr. Myth.* a poet-musician with magic musical powers

**or·ris** (ôr′is, är′-) *n.* [prob. < L. *iris*, iris] any of several European irises, esp. the one yielding a root (**or′ris-root′**) pulverized for perfumery, etc.

**ortho-** [< Gr. *orthos*, straight] *a combining form meaning:* **1.** straight [*orthodontics*] **2.** proper; correct [*orthography*] Also **orth-**

**or·tho·don·tics** (ôr′thə dän′tiks) *n.pl.* [*with sing. v.*] [< ORTH(O)- + Gr. *odōn*, tooth + -ICS] the branch of dentistry concerned with correcting tooth irregularities —**or′tho·don′tist** *n.*

**or·tho·dox** (ôr′thə däks′) *adj.* [< Gr. *orthos*, straight + *doxa*, opinion] conforming to the usual beliefs or established doctrines, as in religion; conventional —**or′tho·dox′y** n.

**Orthodox (Eastern) Church** the Christian church dominant in E Europe, W Asia, and N Africa

**or·thog·ra·phy** (ôr thäg′rə fē) n., pl. **-phies** [ < Gr.: see ORTHO- & -GRAPHY] **1.** correct spelling **2.** spelling as a subject for study —**or·tho·graph·ic** (ôr′thə graf′ik) adj.

**or·tho·pe·dics** (ôr′thə pē′diks) n.pl. [with sing. v.] [ < Gr. orthos, straight + pais, child] the branch of surgery dealing with deformities, diseases, and injuries of the bones and joints —**or′tho·pe′dic** adj. —**or′tho·pe′dist** n.

**-o·ry** (ôr′ē, ər ē) [ < L. -orius] a suffix meaning: **1.** of, having the nature of [commendatory] **2.** a place or thing for [laboratory]

**OS, OS, O.S.** Old Saxon

**O·sa·ka** (ō sä′kə) seaport in S Honshu, Japan: pop. 3,156,000

**os·cil·late** (äs′ə lāt′) vi. **-lat′ed, -lat′ing** [ < L. oscillare, to swing] **1.** to swing to and fro **2.** to vacillate **3.** Physics to vary regularly between high and low values, as an electric current —**os′cil·la′tion** n. —**os′cil·la′tor** n.

**os·cil·lo·scope** (ä sil′ə skōp′) n. [ < L. oscillare, swing + -SCOPE] an instrument that visually displays an electrical wave on a fluorescent screen

**os·cu·late** (äs′kyə lāt′) vt., vi. **-lat′ed, -lat′ing** [ < L. osculum, a kiss] to kiss —**os′cu·la′tion** n.

**-ose¹** (ōs) [Fr. < (gluc)ose] a suffix designating: **1.** a carbohydrate [cellulose] **2.** the product of a protein hydrolysis

**-ose²** (ōs) [L. -osus] a suffix meaning full of, like [bellicose, verbose]

**o·sier** (ō′zhər) n. [ < ML. ausaria, bed of willows] a willow with lithe branches used for baskets and furniture

**-o·sis** (ō′sis) [ < Gr.] a suffix meaning: **1.** condition, action [osmosis] **2.** an abnormal or diseased condition [neurosis]

**Os·lo** (äs′lō, äz′-) capital of Norway: pop. 483,000

**os·mi·um** (äz′mē əm) n. [ < Gr. osmē, odor] a hard, bluish-white metallic chemical element, occurring as an alloy with platinum

**os·mo·sis** (äs mō′sis, äz-) n. [ < Gr. ōsmos, impulse] the tendency of fluids to pass through a membrane and so equalize concentrations on both sides —**os·mot′ic** (-mät′ik) adj.

**os·prey** (äs′prē) n., pl. **-preys** [ < L. os, a bone + frangere, to break] a large hawk that feeds solely on fish

**os·si·fy** (äs′ə fī′) vt., vi. **-fied′, -fy′ing** [ < L. os, a bone + -FY] **1.** to change into bone **2.** to fix rigidly in a custom, etc. —**os′si·fi·ca′tion** n.

**os·ten·si·ble** (äs ten′sə b′l) adj. [ < L. ostendere, to show] apparent; seeming —**os·ten′si·bly** adv.

**os·ten·ta·tion** (äs′tən tā′shən) n. [see prec.] showy display; pretentiousness —**os′ten·ta′tious** adj.

**os·te·op·a·thy** (äs′tē äp′ə thē) n. [ < Gr. osteon, a bone + -PATHY] a school of medicine and surgery that emphasizes the interrelationship of the muscles and bones to all other body systems —**os′te·o·path′** (-ə path′) n.

**os·tra·cize** (äs′trə sīz′) vt. **-cized′, -ciz′ing** [ < Gr. ostrakon, a shell (cast as a ballot)] to banish from a group, society, etc. —**os′tra·cism** n.

**os·trich** (ôs′trich, äs′-) n. [ < L. avis, bird + struthio, ostrich] a large, swift-running, nonflying bird of Africa and the Near East

**OT., OT, O.T.** Old Testament

**O·thel·lo** (ə thel′ō) a tragedy by Shakespeare in which the title character, madly jealous, kills his wife

**oth·er** (uth′ər) adj. [OE.] **1.** being the remaining one or ones [Bill and the other boy(s)] **2.** different or distinct from that or those implied [use your other foot] **3.** additional [he has no other coat] —pron. **1.** the other one **2.** some other one [to do as others do] —adv. otherwise [he can't do other than go] —the other day (or night, etc.) not long ago; recently

**oth′er·wise′** (-wīz′) adv. **1.** in another manner; differently [I believe otherwise] **2.** in all other respects [he is otherwise intelligent] **3.** in other circumstances —adj. different

**oth′er·world′ly** (-wurld′lē) adj. being apart from earthly interests

**o·ti·ose** (ō′shē ōs′) adj. [ < L. otium, leisure] **1.** idle **2.** futile **3.** useless

**Ot·ta·wa** (ät′ə wə, -wä′) capital of Canada, in SE Ontario: pop. 291,000

**ot·ter** (ät′ər) n. [OE. oter] **1.** a furry, swimming mammal related to the weasel and mink **2.** its fur

**ot·to·man** (ät′ə mən) n. [ < Fr.] a low, cushioned seat or footstool

**ouch** (ouch) interj. an exclamation of sudden pain

**ought** (ôt) v.aux. [OE. agan, owe] an auxiliary verb to express: **1.** obligation, duty, or desirability [she ought to stay home] **2.** probability [it ought to be over soon]

**oui** (wē) adv. [Fr.] yes

**Oui·ja** (wē′jə, -jē) [ < prec. + G. ja, yes] a trademark for a supposedly spiritualistic device consisting of a board with the alphabet, and a sliding, three-legged pointer

**ounce** (ouns) n. [ < L. uncia, a twelfth] **1.** a unit of weight, 1/16 pound avoirdupois or 1/12 pound troy **2.** a fluid ounce, 1/16 pint

**our** (our) poss. pronominal adj. [OE. ure] of, belonging to, or done by us

**ours** (ourz) pron. that or those belonging to us [a friend of ours]

**our·selves** (our selvz′) pron. **1.** the intensive form of WE [we went ourselves] **2.** the reflexive form of WE [we hurt ourselves] **3.** our true selves [we are not ourselves when sick]

**-ous** [ < L. -osus] a suffix meaning having, full of, characterized by [hazardous, dangerous]

**oust** (oust) vt. [ < L. ostare, obstruct] to force out; expel; dispossess

**oust′er** n. an ousting or being ousted

**out** (out) *adv.* [< OE. *ūt*] **1.** away or forth from a place, position, etc. **2.** into the open air **3.** into existence or activity [disease broke *out*] **4.** *a*) to a conclusion [argue it *out*] *b*) completely [tired *out*] **5.** into sight or notice [the moon came *out*] **6.** from existence or activity [fade *out*] **7.** aloud [sing *out*] **8.** beyond a regular surface, condition, etc. [stand *out*] **9.** into disuse [long skirts went *out*] **10.** from a group or stock [pick *out*] **11.** [Slang] into unconsciousness **12.** [Slang] in a manner producing an out [to fly *out*] —*adj.* **1.** external: usually in combination [*out*post] **2.** beyond regular limits **3.** away from work, etc. **4.** in error [*out* in my estimates] **5.** not in operation, use, etc. **6.** [Colloq.] having suffered a financial loss [*out* five dollars] **7.** [Colloq.] outmoded **8.** *Baseball* having failed to get on base —*prep.* **1.** out of **2.** along the way of —*n.* **1.** something that is out **2.** [Slang] a way out; excuse **3.** *Baseball* the failure of a player to reach base safely —*vi.* to become known [the truth will *out*] —**all out** wholeheartedly —**on the outs** [Colloq.] on unfriendly terms —**out for** trying to get or do —**out of 1.** from inside of **2.** from (material, etc.) [made *out of* stone] **4.** because of [*out of* spite] **5.** having no [*out of* gas] **6.** so as to deprive —**out to** trying to

**out-** *a combining form meaning:* **1.** at or from a point away; outside [*out*patient] **2.** going away or forth; outward [*out*bound] **3.** better or more than [*out*do, *out*play]

**out′age** (-ij) *n.* an accidental suspension of operation, as of electric power
**out′-and-out′** *adj.* thorough
**out′back′** *n.* any remote, sparsely settled region viewed as uncivilized
**out′bal′ance** *vt.* -anced, -anc·ing to be greater than in weight, value, etc.
**out′bid′** *vt.* -bid′, -bid′ding to bid or offer more than (someone else)
**out′board′** *adj.* outside the hull of a ship, boat, etc. [an *outboard* motor]
**out′bound′** *adj.* outward bound
**out′break′** *n.* a breaking out; sudden occurrence, as of disease, rioting, etc.
**out′build′ing** *n.* a structure, as a barn, separate from the main building
**out′burst′** *n.* a sudden release, as of feeling, energy, etc.
**out′cast′** *adj.* driven out; rejected —*n.* a person rejected, as by society
**out′class′** *vt.* to surpass
**out′come′** *n.* result; consequence
**out′crop′** *n.* **1.** the emergence of a mineral at the earth's surface **2.** the mineral thus exposed
**out′cry′** *n.*, *pl.* -cries′ **1.** a crying out **2.** a strong protest
**out′dat′ed** *adj.* no longer current
**out′dis′tance** *vt.* -tanced, -tanc-ing to get ahead of, as in a race
**out′do′** *vt.* -did′, -done′, -do′ing to exceed or surpass —**outdo oneself** to

do better than one expected to do
**out′door′** (-dôr′) *adj.* **1.** being or occurring outdoors **2.** of or fond of the outdoors
**out′doors′** *adv.* in or into the open; outside —*n.* the outdoor world
**out′er** *adj.* farther out or away
**out′er·most′** *adj.* farthest out
**outer space** space beyond the earth's atmosphere or beyond the solar system
**out′er·wear′** *n.* garments, as overcoats, worn over the usual clothing
**out′field′** *n. Baseball* **1.** the playing area beyond the infield **2.** the players (**outfielders**) positioned there
**out′fit′** *n.* **1.** the equipment used in an activity **2.** clothes worn together; ensemble **3.** a group of people associated in an activity —*vt.* -fit′ted, -fit′ting to furnish with an outfit —**out′fit′ter** *n.*
**out′flank′** *vt.* to go around and beyond the flank of (enemy troops)
**out′fox′** (-fäks′) *vt.* to outwit
**out′go′** *n.*, *pl.* -goes′ that which is paid out; expenditure
**out′go′ing** *adj.* **1.** *a*) leaving *b*) retiring from office **2.** sociable
**out′grow′** *vt.* -grew′, -grown′, -grow′ing **1.** to grow faster or larger than **2.** to lose in becoming mature [he *outgrew* his credulity] **3.** to grow too large for
**out′growth′** *n.* **1.** a growing out or that which grows out **2.** a consequence, result, or development
**out′guess′** *vt.* to outwit
**out′house′** *n.* a boothlike shelter outdoors, used as a toilet
**out′ing** *n.* **1.** a pleasure trip **2.** an outdoor walk, ride, picnic, etc.
**out·land′ish** (-lan′dish) *adj.* very odd or strange; fantastic; bizarre
**out′last′** *vt.* to endure longer than
**out′law′** (-lô′) *n.* **1.** orig., a person deprived of legal rights and protection **2.** a habitual or notorious criminal —*vt.* **1.** orig., to declare to be an outlaw **2.** to declare illegal
**out′lay′** (-lā′) *n.* **1.** a spending (of money, etc.) **2.** money, etc. spent
**out′let′** *n.* **1.** a passage for letting something out **2.** a means of expression [an *outlet* for anger] **3.** a market for goods
**out′line′** *n.* **1.** a line bounding the limits of an object **2.** a sketch showing only contours **3.** a general plan **4.** a systematic summary —*vt.* -lined′, -lin′ing **1.** to draw in outline **2.** to make an outline of
**out′live′** *vt.* -lived′, -liv′ing to live or endure longer than; outlast
**out′look′** *n.* **1.** the view from a place **2.** viewpoint **3.** expectation or prospect
**out′ly′ing** (-lī′iŋ) *adj.* relatively far out from a certain point; remote
**out′ma·neu′ver, out′ma·noeu′-vre′** *vt.* -vered *or* -vred, -ver·ing *or* -vring to outwit by maneuvering
**out′mod′ed** (-mōd′id) *adj.* no longer in fashion or accepted; obsolete

**out/num/ber** *vt.* to exceed in number

**out/-of-date/** *adj.* no longer in style or use; old-fashioned

**out/-of-door/** *adj.* outdoor

**out/-of-doors/** *adv., n.* outdoors

**out/-of-the-way/** *adj.* 1. secluded 2. not common; unusual

**out/-of-town/er** *n.* a visitor from another town or city

**out/pa/tient** *n.* a patient, not an inmate, being treated at a hospital

**out/play/** *vt.* to play better than

**out/post/** *n.* 1. *Mil. a)* a small group stationed at a distance from the main force *b)* the station so occupied *c)* a foreign base 2. a frontier settlement

**out/put/** *n.* 1. the work done or amount produced, esp. over a given period 2. information delivered by a computer 3. *Elec.* the useful voltage, current, or power delivered

**out·rage** (out'rāj') *n.* [ult. < L. *ultra*, beyond] 1. an extremely vicious or violent act 2. a grave insult or offense 3. great anger, etc. aroused by this —*vt.* **-raged/, -rag/ing** 1. to commit an outrage upon or against 2. to cause outrage in

**out·ra/geous** (-rā/jəs) *adj.* 1. involving or doing great injury or wrong 2. very offensive or shocking — **out·ra/geous·ly** *adv.*

**out/rank/** *vt.* to exceed in rank

**‡out·ré** (ōō trā/) *adj.* [Fr.] 1. exaggerated 2. outlandish; bizarre

**out/reach/** *vt., vi.* 1. to reach beyond; surpass 2. to reach out; extend —*n.* a reaching out —*adj.* designating or of a branch away from the main office of a social agency, etc.

**out/rid/er** *n.* 1. a rider on horseback who accompanies a stagecoach, etc. 2. a cowboy riding a range to keep cattle from straying 3. a forerunner

**out/rig/ger** (-rig'ər) *n.* a timber rigged out from the side of a canoe to prevent tipping; also, a canoe of this type

**out/right/** (-rīt') *adj.* 1. utter; downright 2. complete —*adv.* 1. entirely 2. openly 3. at once

OUTRIGGER

**out/run/** *vt.* **-ran/, -run/, -run/ning** 1. to run faster than 2. to exceed

**out/sell/** *vt.* **-sold/, -sell/ing** to sell in greater amounts than

**out/set/** *n.* a setting out; beginning

**out/shine/** *vt.* **-shone/** or **-shined/, -shin/ing** 1. to shine brighter or longer than 2. to surpass; excel

**out/side/** *n.* 1. the outer side or part; exterior 2. outward appearance 3. any area not inside —*adj.* 1. of, on, or from the outside; outer 2. extreme [an *outside* estimate] 3. slight [an *outside* chance] —*adv.* 1. on or to the outside 2. outdoors —*prep.* 1. on or to the outer side of 2. beyond the limits of —**outside of** 1. outside 2. [Colloq.] other than

**out/sid/er** *n.* one who is not included in a given group

**out/size/** *n.* an odd size, esp. an unusually large one

**out/skirts/** (-skurts') *n.pl.* districts remote from the center, as of a city

**out/smart/** *vt.* [Colloq.] to overcome by cunning or cleverness; outwit — **outsmart oneself** to have one's efforts at cunning or cleverness result in one's own disadvantage

**out/spo/ken** *adj.* 1. unrestrained in speech 2. spoken boldly or candidly

**out/spread/** *adj.* spread out; extended

**out/stand/ing** *adj.* 1. projecting 2. prominent; distinguished 3. unpaid; uncollected 4. issued and sold: said of stocks and bonds

**out/sta/tion** *n.* a post or station in a remote or unsettled area

**out/stretch/** *vt.* 1. to stretch out; extend 2. to stretch beyond

**out/strip/** *vt.* **-stripped/, -strip/-ping** 1. to go at a faster pace than 2. to excel; surpass

**out/vote/** *vt.* **-vot/ed, -vot/ing** to defeat or surpass in voting

**out/ward** (-wərd) *adj.* 1. having to do with the outside; outer 2. clearly apparent 3. away from the interior —*adv.* toward the outside: also **out/wards** —**out/ward·ly** *adv.*

**out/wear/** *vt.* **-wore/, -worn/, -wear/-ing** 1. to wear out 2. to outlast

**out/weigh/** *vt.* 1. to weigh more than 2. to be more important than

**out/wit/** *vt.* **-wit/ted, -wit/ting** to get the better of by cleverness

**o·va** (ō/və) *n. pl. of* OVUM

**o·val** (ō/v'l) *adj.* [< L. *ovum*, egg] shaped like an egg in longitudinal cross section —*n.* anything oval

**o·va·ry** (ō/vər ē) *n., pl.* **-ries** [< L. *ovum*, egg] 1. either of two female reproductive glands producing eggs 2. *Botany* the enlarged hollow part of the pistil, containing ovules —**o·var·i·an** (ō ver/ē ən) *adj.*

**o·vate** (ō/vāt) *adj.* egg-shaped; oval

**o·va·tion** (ō vā/shən) *n.* [< L. *ovare*, celebrate a triumph] an enthusiastic burst of applause or public welcome

**ov·en** (uv/ən) *n.* [OE. *ofen*] a receptacle or compartment for baking, drying, or heating

**o·ver** (ō/vər) *prep.* [OE. *ofer*] 1. *a)* in, at, or to a position above *b)* across and down from [to fall *over* a cliff] 2. so as to cover [a board *over* the well] 3. upon, as an effect [to cast a spell *over* someone] 4. above in authority, power, etc. 5. on or to the other side of [fly *over* the lake] 6. throughout [*over* the whole city] 7. during [*over* the year] 8. more than [*over* ten cents] 9. in preference to 10. concerning —*adv.* 1. *a)* above or across *b)* across the brim or edge 2. more [three hours or *over*] 3. from start to finish [talk it *over*] 4. *a)* from an upright position [to fall *over*] *b)* upside down [turn the cup *over*] 5. again [do it *over*] 6. at, on, to, or in a specified place [*over* in Spain] 7. from one belief, etc. to another [win him *over*] —*adj.* 1. upper, outer, superior, excessive, or extra 2. finished; past 3. having reached the other side 4. [Colloq.] as a surplus

**o·ver-** *a combining form meaning:* 1. above in position, rank, etc. [*overlord*]

2. passing across or beyond [*overrun*]
3. excessive(ly) [*overrate*]: the list below includes some common compounds formed with *over-* that can be understood if *too much* or *excessively* is added to the meaning of the base word

| | |
|---|---|
| overabundance | overheat |
| overactive | overindulge |
| overambitious | overload |
| overanxious | overpay |
| overbid | overpopulate |
| overburden | overprice |
| overcautious | overproduce |
| overconfident | overproduction |
| overcook | overrefined |
| overcritical | overripe |
| overcrowd | oversell |
| overdevelop | oversensitive |
| overeager | overspecialize |
| overeat | overspend |
| overemphasize | overstimulate |
| overenthusiastic | overstock |
| overexercise | overstrict |
| overexert | oversupply |
| overexpose | overtire |

**o'ver·act'** *vt.*, *vi.* to act with exaggeration

**o·ver·age¹** (ō'vər āj') *adj.* over the age fixed as a standard

**o·ver·age²** (ō'vər ij) *n.* [OVER- + -AGE] a surplus or excess

**o'ver·all'** *adj.* 1. from end to end 2. including everything; total —*adv.* 1. from end to end 2. in general

**o'ver·alls'** (-ôlz') *n.pl.* loose trousers, often with an attached bib, worn over other clothes as a protection

**o'ver·awe'** *vt.* -awed', -aw'ing to overcome or subdue by inspiring awe

**o'ver·bal'ance** *vt.* -anced, -anc·ing 1. *same as* OUTWEIGH 2. to throw off balance

**o'ver·bear'ing** (-ber'iŋ) *adj.* arrogant; domineering

**o'ver·board'** *adv.* from a ship into the water —**go overboard** [Colloq.] to go to extremes

**o'ver·cast'** (-kast') *adj.* cloudy; dark: said of the sky

**o'ver·charge'** *vt.*, *vi.* -charged', -charg'ing 1. to charge too much 2. to overload —*n.* (ō'vər chärj') 1. an excessive charge 2. too full a load

**o'ver·clothes'** *n.pl. same as* OUTERWEAR

**o'ver·cloud'** *vt.*, *vi.* to make or become cloudy, gloomy, etc.

**o'ver·coat'** *n.* a heavy coat worn over the usual clothing for warmth

**o'ver·come'** *vt.* -came', -come', -com'ing 1. to get the better of in competition, etc. 2. to master, surmount, overwhelm, etc. —*vi.* to win

**o'ver·do'** *vt.* -did', -done', -do'ing 1. to do too much 2. to exaggerate 3. to overcook —*vi.* to exhaust oneself by doing too much

**o'ver·dose'** *n.* too large a dose

**o'ver·draw'** *vt.* -drew', -drawn', -draw'ing to draw on in excess of the amount credited to the drawer — **o'ver·draft'** *n.*

**o'ver·dress'** *vt.*, *vi.* to dress too warmly, too showily, or too formally

**o'ver·due'** *adj.* past the time set for payment, arrival, etc.

**o'ver·es'ti·mate'** (-es'tə māt') *vt.* to set too high an estimate on or for

**o'ver·flight'** *n.* the flight of an aircraft over a foreign territory, as in reconnaissance

**o'ver·flow'** *vt.* 1. to flow across; flood 2. to flow over the brim of —*vi.* 1. to run over 2. to be superabundant —*n.* (ō'vər flō') 1. an overflowing 2. the amount that overflows 3. an outlet for overflowing liquids

**o'ver·grow'** *vt.* -grew', -grown', -grow'ing to overspread, as with foliage, so as to cover —*vi.* to grow too fast or beyond normal —**o'ver·grown'** *adj.* —**o'ver·growth'** *n.*

**o'ver·hand'** *adj., adv.* with the hand raised above the elbow or the arm above the shoulder

**o'ver·hang'** *vt.*, *vi.* -hung', -hang'ing to hang over or project beyond (something) —*n.* (ō'vər haŋ') the projection of one thing over another

**o'ver·haul'** (-hôl') *vt.* 1. *a)* to check thoroughly as for needed repairs *b)* to make such repairs, etc., as on a motor 2. to catch up with —*n.* (ō'vər hôl') an overhauling

**o'ver·head'** *adj.* 1. above the head 2. in the sky 3. on a higher level, with reference to related objects —*n.* the general, continuing costs of a business, as of rent, taxes, etc. —*adv.* (ō'vər hed') above the head; aloft

**o'ver·hear'** *vt.* -heard', -hear'ing to hear (something spoken or a speaker) without the speaker's knowledge

**o'ver·joy'** *vt.* to give great joy to; delight —**o'ver·joyed'** *adj.*

**o'ver·kill'** *n.* the capacity of a nuclear stockpile to kill more than the total population of a given nation

**o'ver·land'** *adv., adj.* by, on, or across land

**o'ver·lap'** *vt.*, *vi.* -lapped', -lap'ping to lap over; extend over (a thing or each other) so as to coincide in part

**o'ver·lay'** *vt.* -laid', -lay'ing 1. to lay or spread over 2. to cover, as with a decorative layer

**o'ver·lie'** *vt.* -lay', -lain', -ly'ing to lie on or over

**o'ver·look'** *vt.* 1. to look at from above 2. to give a view of from above 3. *a)* to fail to notice *b)* to ignore; neglect 4. to excuse 5. to supervise

**o'ver·lord'** *n.* a lord ranking above other lords

**o'ver·ly** (-lē) *adv.* too or too much

**o'ver·mas'ter** *vt.* to overcome

**o'ver·much'** *adj., adv., n.* too much

**o'ver·night'** *adv.* 1. during the night 2. suddenly —*adj.* (ō'vər nīt') 1. done or going on during the night 2. for one night [an *overnight* guest] 3. of or for a brief trip [an *overnight* bag]

**o'ver·pass'** *n.* a bridge, etc. over a road, railway, etc.

**o·ver·play'** vt. 1. to overact, overdo, or overemphasize 2. to overestimate the strength of (one's card hand)

**o·ver·pow'er** vt. to get the better of; subdue or overwhelm

**o·ver·rate'** vt. **-rat'ed, -rat'ing** to rate or estimate too highly

**o·ver·reach'** vt. to reach beyond or above —**overreach oneself** to fail because of trying to do too much

**o·ver·re·act'** vi. to react in an excessively emotional way

**o·ver·ride'** vt. **-rode', -rid'den, -rid'ing** 1. to ride over 2. to prevail over 3. to disregard or nullify

**o·ver·rule'** vt. **-ruled', -rul'ing** 1. to rule out or set aside, as by higher authority 2. to prevail over

**o·ver·run'** vt. **-ran', -run', -run'ning** 1. to spread out over so as to cover 2. to swarm over, as vermin 3. to extend beyond (certain limits)

**o·ver·seas'** adv. over or beyond the sea —adj. 1. foreign 2. over or across the sea Also **o'ver·sea'**

**o·ver·see'** vt. **-saw', -seen', -see'ing** to supervise; superintend —**o'ver·se'er** n.

**o·ver·sexed'** adj. having exceptional sexual drive or interest

**o·ver·shad'ow** vt. 1. a) to cast a shadow over b) to darken 2. to be more important than by comparison

**o·ver·shoe'** n. a boot of rubber or fabric, worn over the regular shoe to protect from cold or dampness

**o·ver·shoot'** vt. **-shot', -shoot'ing** 1. to shoot or pass over or beyond (a target, mark, etc.) 2. to exceed

**o·ver·sight'** (-sīt') n. a careless mistake or omission

**o·ver·sim'pli·fy'** vt., vi. **-fied', -fy'ing** to simplify to the point of distortion —**o'ver·sim'pli·fi·ca'tion** n.

**o·ver·size'** adj. 1. too large 2. larger than the usual Also **o'ver·sized'**

**o·ver·sleep'** vi. **-slept', -sleep'ing** to sleep longer than intended

**o·ver·spread'** vt. **-spread', -spread'ing** to spread or cover over

**o·ver·state'** vt. **-stat'ed, -stat'ing** to exaggerate —**o'ver·state'ment** n.

**o·ver·stay'** vt. to stay beyond the time or limit of

**o·ver·step'** vt. **-stepped', -step'ping** to go beyond the limits of

**o·ver·stuff'** vt. 1. to stuff with too much of something 2. to upholster (furniture) with deep stuffing

**o·vert** (ō vurt', ō'vurt) adj. [< L. aperire, to open] 1. not hidden; manifest 2. Law done openly, with evident intent —**o·vert'ly** adv.

**o·ver·take'** vt. **-took', -tak'en, -tak'ing** 1. to catch up with 2. to come upon suddenly

**o·ver·tax'** vt. 1. to tax too heavily 2. to make excessive demands on

**o·ver·throw'** vt. **-threw', -thrown', -throw'ing** 1. to throw or turn over 2. to conquer 3. to throw beyond —n. (ō'vər thrō') 1. an overthrowing or being overthrown 2. destruction; end

**o·ver·time'** n. 1. time beyond the established limit, as of working hours 2. pay for work done in such time —adj., adv. of, for, or during overtime

**o·ver·tone'** n. 1. a faint, higher tone accompanying a fundamental tone produced by a musical instrument 2. an implication; nuance

**o·ver·ture** (ō'vər chər) n. [< L. apertura, aperture] 1. an introductory proposal or offer 2. a musical introduction to an opera, etc.

**o·ver·turn'** vt. 1. to turn over 2. to conquer —vi. to tip over; capsize

**o·ver·ween'ing** (-wē'niŋ) adj. [< OE. ofer, over + wenan, to hope] 1. arrogant 2. excessive

**o·ver·weight'** adj. above the normal or allowed weight

**o·ver·whelm'** (-hwelm') vt. [see OVER & WHELM] 1. to pour down on and bury beneath 2. to crush; overpower —**o'ver·whelm'ing** adj.

**o·ver·work'** vt. to work or use to excess —vi. to work too hard or too long —n. (ō'vər wurk') severe or burdensome work

**o·ver·wrought'** (-rôt') adj. 1. very nervous or excited 2. too elaborate

**Ov·id** (äv'id) 43 B.C.–17? A.D.; Rom. poet

**ov·i·duct** (ō'vi dukt') n. [< L. ovum, egg + DUCT] a tube through which the ova pass from an ovary to the uterus

**o·vip·a·rous** (ō vip'ər əs) adj. [< L. ovum, egg + parere, to bear] producing eggs which hatch after leaving the body

**o·void** (ō'void) adj. [< L. ovum, egg] egg-shaped —n. anything ovoid

**o·vu·late** (ō'vyə lāt', äv'yə-) vi. **-lat'ed, -lat'ing** [< L. ovum, egg] to produce and discharge ova from the ovary —**o'vu·la'tion** n.

**o·vule** (ō'vyool) n. [< L. ovum, egg] 1. Bot. the part of a plant which develops into a seed 2. Zool. the immature ovum —**o'vu·lar** adj.

**o·vum** (ō'vəm) n., pl. **o·va** (ō'və) [L., egg] a female germ cell

**ow** (ou) interj. a cry of pain

**owe** (ō) vt. **owed, ow'ing** [OE. agan, to own] 1. to be indebted to the amount of 2. to have the need to give, do, etc., as because of gratitude 3. to be indebted (to)

**ow·ing** (ō'iŋ) adj. 1. that owes 2. due; unpaid —**owing to** because of

**owl** (oul) n. [OE. ule] 1. a night bird of prey having a large head, large eyes, and a short, hooked beak 2. a person of nocturnal habits, solemn appearance, etc. —**owl'ish** adj.

**owl'et** (-it) n. a young or small owl

**own** (ōn) adj. [< OE. agan, possess] belonging or relating to oneself or itself [his own car] —n. that which belongs to oneself [that is his own] —vt. 1. to possess; have 2. to admit; acknowledge —vi. to confess (to) —**on one's own** [Colloq.] by one's own efforts —**own'er** n. —**own'er·ship'** n.

**ox** (äks) n., pl. **ox'en** [OE. oxa] 1. any of various cud-chewing mammals of the cattle family, as the buffalo, yak, etc. 2. a castrated bull

**ox'blood'** n. a deep red color

**ox'bow'** (-bō') n. the U-shaped part of an ox yoke which passes under and around the animal's neck

**Ox·ford** (äks′fərd) city in SC England: pop. 110,000

**ox·ford** (äks′fərd) *n.* [after prec.] [*sometimes* O–] 1. a low shoe laced over the instep: also **oxford shoe** 2. a cotton or rayon fabric with a basket-like weave: also **oxford cloth**

**ox·i·dant** (äk′sə dənt) *n.* an oxidizing agent

**ox·i·da·tion** (äk′sə dā′shən) *n.* an oxidizing or being oxidized

**ox·ide** (äk′sīd) *n.* [ < Gr. *oxys*, sour + Fr. (ac)*ide*, acid] a compound of oxygen with another element or a radical

**ox·i·dize** (äk′sə dīz′) *vt.* -dized′, -diz′ing to unite with oxygen, as in burning or rusting —*vi.* to become oxidized —ox′i·diz′er *n.*

**ox·y·acet·y·lene** (äk′sē ə set′′l ēn′) *adj.* of or using a mixture of oxygen and acetylene, as for producing a hot flame used in welding

**ox·y·gen** (äk′si jən) *n.* [ < Fr. < Gr. *oxys*, acid + Fr. -*gène*, -GEN] a color-less, odorless, gaseous chemical element, the most abundant of all elements: it is essential to life processes and to combustion

**ox′y·gen·ate′** (-jə nāt′) *vt.* -at′ed, -at′ing to combine or treat with oxygen —ox′y·gen·a′tion *n.*

**oxygen tent** a transparent enclosure supplied with oxygen, fitted around a bed patient to facilitate breathing

**oys·ter** (oi′stər) *n.* [ < Gr. *ostreon*] an edible marine mollusk with an irregular, hinged shell

**oyster cracker** a very small, round, salted soda cracker

**oz.** *pl.* **oz., ozs.** ounce

**o·zone** (ō′zōn) *n.* [Fr. < Gr. *ozein*, to smell] 1. a form of oxygen with a strong odor, formed by an electrical discharge in air and used as a bleaching agent, water purifier, etc. 2. [Slang] pure, fresh air

# P

**P, p** (pē) *n.*, *pl.* **P's, p's** the 16th letter of the English alphabet —**mind one's p's and q's** to be careful of what one says and does

**P** *Chem.* phosphorus

**p.** 1. *pl.* **pp.** page 2. participle 3. past 4. per 5. pint

**pa** (pä) *n.* [Colloq.] father

**Pa., PA** Pennsylvania

**P.A.** public address (system)

**pace** (pās) *n.* [ < L. *passus*, a step] 1. a step in walking, etc. 2. the length of a step or stride 3. the rate of speed in walking, etc. 4. rate of progress, etc. 5. a gait 6. the gait of a horse in which both legs on the same side are raised together —*vt.* **paced, pac′ing** 1. to walk back and forth across 2. to measure by paces 3. to set the pace for (a runner, etc.) —*vi.* 1. to walk with regular steps 2. to move at a pace: said of a horse —**put through one's paces** to test one's abilities or skills —**pac′er** *n.*

**pace′mak′er** *n.* 1. a person, horse, automobile, etc. that leads the way: also **pace′set′ter** 2. an electronic device placed in the body to regulate the heartbeat

**pach·y·derm** (pak′ə durm′) *n.* [ < Gr. *pachys*, thick + *derma*, skin] a large, thick-skinned, hoofed animal, as the elephant, rhinoceros, etc.

**pach·y·san·dra** (pak′ə san′drə) *n.* [ < ModL. name of genus] a low, hardy evergreen plant often grown as ground cover

**Pa·cif·ic** (pə sif′ik) largest of the earth's oceans, between Asia & the American continents —*adj.* of, in, on, or near this ocean

**pa·cif·ic** (pə sif′ik) *adj.* [see PACIFY] 1. making peace 2. of a peaceful nature; tranquil; calm

**pac·i·fi·er** (pas′ə fī′ər) *n.* 1. a person or thing that pacifies 2. a nipple or teething ring for babies

**pac·i·fism** (-fiz′m) *n.* opposition to the use of force under any circumstances; specif., refusal to participate in war —**pac′i·fist** *n.*, *adj.*

**pac·i·fy** (pas′ə fī′) *vt.* -fied′, -fy′ing [ < L. *pax*, peace + *facere*, make] to make peaceful, calm, nonhostile, etc. —**pac′i·fi·ca′tion** *n.*

**pack¹** (pak) *n.* [ < MDu. *pak*] 1. a bundle of things tied up for carrying 2. a group or mass [a *pack* of lies] 3. a package of a standard number [a *pack* of cigarettes or of playing cards] 4. a number of wild animals living together —*vt.* 1. to make a pack of 2. *a)* to put together in a box, trunk, etc. *b)* to fill (a box, etc.) 3. to crowd; cram [the hall was *packed*] 4. to fill in tight'y, as for prevention of leaks 5. to carry in a pack 6. to send (*off*) [to *pack* him off to school] 7. [Slang] *a)* to carry (a gun, etc.) *b)* to deliver (a punch, etc.) with force —*vi.* 1. to make up packs 2. to put one's clothes, etc. into luggage for a trip 3. to crowd together 4. to settle into a compact mass —*adj.* used for carrying packs, loads, etc. [a *pack* animal] —**send packing** to dismiss abruptly

**pack²** (pak) *vt.* to choose (a jury, etc.) dishonestly so as to get desired results

**pack·age** (pak′ij) *n.* 1. a wrapped or boxed thing or group of things; parcel 2. a number of items, plans, etc. offered as a unit —*vt.* -aged, -ag·ing to make a package of —**pack′ag·er** *n.*

**package store** a store where alcoholic liquor is sold by the bottle

**pack′er** *n.* one who packs; specif., one who operates a packing house

**pack′et** (-it) *n.* **1.** a small package **2.** a boat that travels a regular route carrying passengers, freight, and mail: in full **packet boat**

**pack′ing house** a plant where meats, etc. are processed and packed for sale

**pack rat** a N.American rat that often hides small articles in its nest

**pack′sad′dle** *n.* a saddle with fastenings to secure the load carried by a pack animal

**pact** (pakt) *n.* [< L. *pax*, peace] a compact or agreement

**pad¹** (pad) *n.* [echoic] the dull sound of a footstep —*vi.* **pad′ded, pad′ding** to walk, esp. with a soft step

**pad²** (pad) *n.* [? var. of POD] **1.** anything soft used to protect against friction, blows, etc.; cushion **2.** the cushionlike sole of an animal's paw **3.** the floating leaf of a water lily **4.** a number of sheets of paper glued along one edge; tablet **5.** [Slang] the place where one lives —*vt.* **pad′ded, pad′ding 1.** to stuff or cover with soft material **2.** to expand (a speech, etc.) with superfluous matter or (an expense account, etc.) with fraudulent entries

**pad′ding** *n.* any material used to pad

**pad·dle¹** (pad′'l) *n.* [ME. *padell*, small spade] **1.** a short oar with a wide blade at one or both ends, used without an oarlock **2.** an implement shaped like this, used to beat someone, hit a ball, etc. —*vt., vi.* **-dled, -dling 1.** to propel (a canoe, etc.) by a paddle **2.** to beat as with a paddle; spank

**pad·dle²** (pad′'l) *vi.* **-dled, -dling** [prob. < PAD¹] to move the hands or feet about in the water, as in playing

**paddle wheel** a wheel with boards around it for propelling a steam-boat

PADDLE WHEEL

**pad·dock** (pad′ək) *n.* [< OE. *pearruc*, enclosure] **1.** a small enclosure near a stable, where horses are exercised **2.** an enclosure at a race track, where horses are saddled before a race

**pad·dy** (pad′ē) *n.,* *pl.* **-dies** [Malay *padi*] a rice field

**pad·lock** (pad′läk′) *n.* a removable lock with a hinged link to be passed through a staple, chain, or eye —*vt.* to fasten or close up as with a padlock

**pa·dre** (pä′drā) *n.* [< L. *pater*, father] **1.** father: the title of a priest in Italy, Spain, etc. **2.** [Slang] a priest or chaplain

**pae·an** (pē′ən) *n.* [< Gr. *paian*, hymn] a song of joy, triumph, etc.

**pa·gan** (pā′gən) *n.* [< L. *paganus*, peasant] **1.** *same as* HEATHEN (sense 1) **2.** one who has no religion —*adj.* of pagans —**pa′gan·ism** *n.*

**page¹** (pāj) *n.* [< L. *pangere*, fasten] **1.** *a)* one side of a leaf of a book, etc. *b)* an entire leaf **2.** [*often pl.*] a record of events —*vt.* **paged, pag′ing** to number the pages of

**page²** (pāj) *n.* [< It. *paggio*] a boy attendant, esp. now one who runs errands, etc., as in a hotel —*vt.* **paged, pag′ing** to try to find (a person) by calling his name, as a hotel page does

**pag·eant** (paj′ənt) *n.* [< ME. *pagent*, stage scene] **1.** a spectacular exhibition, parade, etc. **2.** an outdoor drama celebrating historical events

**pag′eant·ry** (-ən trē) *n., pl.* **-ries 1.** grand spectacle; gorgeous display **2.** empty show or display

**pag·i·na·tion** (paj′ə nā′shən) *n.* **1.** the numbering of pages **2.** the arrangement and number of pages

**pa·go·da** (pə gō′də) *n.* [prob. < Per. *but*, idol + *kadah*, house] in India and the Far East, a several-storied temple in the form of a pyramidal tower

**paid** (pād) *pt. & pp.* of PAY

**pail** (pāl) *n.* [< OE. *pægel*, wine vessel] **1.** a cylindrical container, usually with a handle, for holding liquids, etc.; bucket **2.** the amount held by a pail: also **pail′ful′,** *pl.* **-fuls′**

**pain** (pān) *n.* [< Gr. *poinē*, penalty] **1.** physical or mental suffering caused by injury, disease, anxiety, grief, etc. **2.** [*pl.*] great care [take *pains* with the work] —*vt.* to cause pain to; hurt —**on** (or **under**) **pain of** at the risk of a penalty —**pain′ful** *adj.* —**pain′ful·ly** *adv.* —**pain′less** *adj.*

**Paine** (pān), **Thomas** 1737–1809; Am. Revolutionary patriot & writer

**pain′kill′er** (-kil′ər) *n.* [Colloq.] a medicine that relieves pain

**pains·tak·ing** (pānz′tā′kiŋ) *adj.* requiring or showing great care; very careful —**pains′tak′ing·ly** *adv.*

**paint** (pānt) *vt.* [< L. *pingere*] **1.** *a)* to make (a picture) using oil pigments, etc. *b)* to depict with paints **2.** to describe vividly **3.** to cover or decorate with paint —*vi.* to paint pictures —*n.* **1.** a mixture of pigment with oil, water, etc. used as a covering or coloring **2.** a dried coat of paint

**paint′er** *n.* **1.** an artist who paints pictures **2.** one whose work is covering surfaces, as walls, with paint

**paint′ing** *n.* a painted picture

**pair** (per) *n., pl.* **pairs;** occas. after a number **pair** [< L. *par*, equal] **1.** two corresponding things associated or used together [a *pair* of shoes] **2.** a single unit of two corresponding parts [a *pair* of pants] **3.** any two persons or animals regarded as a unit —*vi., vt.* **1.** to form a pair (of) **2.** to mate

**pais·ley** (pāz′lē) *adj.* [< *Paisley,* Scotland] [*also* P-] having an elaborate, colorful pattern of swirls, etc.

**pa·ja·mas** (pə jam′əz, -jä′məz) *n.pl.* [< Per. *pāi,* leg + *jāma,* garment] a loosely fitting sleeping or lounging suit consisting of jacket and trousers

**Pa·ki·stan** (pä′ki stän′, pak′i stan′) country in S Asia, at the head of the Arabian Sea: 310,403 sq. mi.; pop. 66,749,000 —**Pa′ki·stan′i** (-ē) *adj., n.*

**pal** (pal) *n.* [Eng. Gypsy, brother, ult. < Sans.] [Colloq.] a close friend

**pal·ace** (pal'is) *n.* [< L. *Palatium*, one of the seven hills of Rome] 1. the official residence of a king, etc. 2. any large, magnificent building

**pal·at·a·ble** (pal'it ə b'l) *adj.* pleasant or acceptable to the taste or mind

**pal·ate** (pal'it) *n.* [< L. *palatum*] 1. the roof of the mouth 2. taste — **pal'a·tal** (-'l) *adj.*

**pa·la·tial** (pə lā'shəl) *adj.* [see PALACE] 1. of, suitable for, or like a palace 2. magnificent; stately

**pal·a·tine** (pal'ə tīn', -tin) *adj.* [see PALACE] designating or of a count or earl who ruled in his own territory

**pa·lav·er** (pə lav'ər) *n.* [Port. *palavra*, a word] talk, esp. profuse or idle talk —*vi.* to talk idly or profusely

**pale¹** (pāl) *adj.* [< L. *pallere*, be pale] 1. of a whitish or colorless complexion 2. lacking intensity, as color, light, etc. —*vi., vt.* paled, pal'ing to become or make pale —**pale'ness** *n.*

**pale²** (pāl) *n.* [< L. *palus*, a stake] 1. a pointed stake used in fences 2. a boundary: now chiefly figurative

**pa·le·on·tol·o·gy** (pā'lē än täl'ə jē) *n.* [< Gr. *palaios*, ancient + *ōn*, a being + -LOGY] the branch of geology dealing with prehistoric life through the study of fossils —**pa'le·on·tol'o·gist** *n.*

**Pa'le·o·zo'ic** (-ə zō'ik) *adj.* [< Gr. *palaios*, ancient + ZO(O)- + -IC] designating the geologic era (c.600-230 million years ago) characterized by the development of the first fishes, reptiles, and land plants

**Pal·es·tine** (pal'əs tīn') region on the E coast of the Mediterranean, including modern Israel —**Pal'es·tin'i·an** (-tin'ē ən) *adj., n.*

**pal·ette** (pal'it) *n.* [Fr. < L. *pala*, a shovel] a thin board on which an artist mixes his paints

**pal·frey** (pôl'frē) *n., pl.* -freys [ult. < Gr. *para*, beside + L. *veredus*, post horse] [Archaic] a saddle horse, esp. a gentle one for a woman

**pal·imp·sest** (pal'imp sest') *n.* [< Gr. *palimpsēstos*, lit., rubbed again] a parchment that has been written upon previously and that bears traces of the imperfectly erased texts

**pal·in·drome** (pal'in drōm') *n.* [< Gr. *palindromos*, running back] a word, phrase, or sentence that reads the same backward and forward (Ex.: name no one man)

**pal·ing** (pāl'iŋ) *n.* 1. a fence made of pales 2. pales collectively

**pal·i·sade** (pal'ə sād') *n.* [< Fr. < L. *palus*, a stake] 1. any of a row of large pointed stakes forming a fence as for fortification 2. such a fence 3. [*pl.*] a line of steep cliffs

**pall¹** (pôl) *vi.* palled, pall'ing [ME. *pallen*, appall] 1. to become cloying, insipid, etc. 2. to become satiated

**pall²** (pôl) *n.* [< L. *pallium*, a cover]

1. a piece of velvet, etc. used to cover a coffin 2. a dark or gloomy covering

**pall·bear·er** (pôl'ber'ər) *n.* [PALL² + BEARER] one of the persons who attend or carry the coffin at a funeral

**pal·let¹** (pal'it) *n.* [see PALETTE] a low, portable platform used for stacking materials, as in a warehouse

**pal·let²** (pal'it) *n.* [< L. *palea*, chaff] a simple bed, esp. a straw-filled pad or mattress on the floor

**pal·li·ate** (pal'ē āt', ) *vt.* -at'ed, -at'ing [< L. *pallium*, a cloak] 1. to lessen the severity of without curing; alleviate 2. to make (an offense) appear less serious; excuse —**pal'li·a'tion** *n.* —**pal'li·a·tive** *adj., n.*

**pal·lid** (pal'id) *adj.* [L. *pallidus*, pale] faint in color; pale

**pal·lor** (pal'ər) *n.* [L. < *pallere*, be pale] unnatural paleness

**palm¹** (päm; *occas.* pälm) *n.* [< L. *palma*: from its handlike leaf] 1. any of numerous tropical or subtropical trees or shrubs with a branchless trunk and a bunch of huge leaves at the top 2. a leaf of this tree carried as a symbol of victory

**palm²** (päm; *occas.* pälm) *n.* [< L. *palma*] the inner surface of the hand between the fingers and wrist —*vt.* to hide (something) in the palm, as in a sleight-of-hand trick —**palm off** to pass off by fraud

**pal·met·to** (pal met'ō) *n., pl.* -tos, -toes any of certain palms with fan-shaped leaves

**palm·is·try** (päm'is trē, päl'mis-) *n.* [prob. < ME. *paume*, PALM² + *maistrie*, mastery] fortunetelling by means of the lines, etc. on the palm of a person's hand —**palm'ist** *n.*

**Palm Sunday** the Sunday before Easter, commemorating Jesus' entry into Jerusalem, when palm branches were strewn before him

**palm'y** *adj.* -i·er, -i·est 1. of, like, or full of palm trees 2. prosperous

**pal·o·mi·no** (pal'ə mē'nō) *n., pl.* -nos [AmSp. < Sp., dove-colored] a pale-yellow horse with a white mane and tail

**pal·pa·ble** (pal'pə b'l) *adj.* [< L. *palpare*, to touch] 1. that can be touched, felt, etc. 2. easily perceived by the senses; perceptible 3. obvious; plain —**pal'pa·bly** *adv.*

**pal·pi·tate** (pal'pə tāt') *vi.* -tat'ed, -tat'ing [< L. *palpare*, to feel] 1. to beat rapidly, as the heart 2. to throb —**pal'pi·ta'tion** *n.*

**pal·sy** (pôl'zē) *n., pl.* -sies [see PARALYSIS] paralysis of any muscle, sometimes with involuntary tremors —*vt.* -sied, -sy·ing to paralyze

**pal·try** (pôl'trē) *adj.* -tri·er, -tri·est [prob. < LowG. *palte*, rag] almost worthless; trifling —**pal'tri·ness** *n.*

**pam·pas** (pam'pəz) *n.pl.* [< SAm.-Ind. *pampa*, plain, field] the extensive treeless plains of Argentina

**pam·per** (pam'pər) *vt.* [< LowG.] to

be overindulgent with; coddle; humor

**pam·phlet** (pam′flit) *n.* [ < OFr. *Pamphilet*, shortened name of a ML. poem] a thin, unbound booklet, often on some topic of current interest — **pam′phlet·eer′** (-flə tir′) *n.*

**Pan** (pan) *Gr. Myth.* a god of fields, forests, flocks, and shepherds, represented with the legs of a goat

**pan¹** (pan) *n.* [OE. *panne*] **1.** any broad, shallow container used in cooking, etc. **2.** a pan-shaped part or object —*vt., vi.* **panned, pan′ning 1.** [Colloq.] to criticize unfavorably **2.** *Mining* to wash (gravel) in a pan in order to separate (gold, etc.) —**pan out** [Colloq.] to turn out; esp., to turn out well; succeed

**pan²** (pan) *vt., vi.* **panned, pan′ning** [ < PAN(ORAMA)] to move a movie or television camera so as to get a panoramic effect —*n.* the act of panning

**pan-** [ < Gr. *pan*, all] *a combining form meaning:* **1.** all [*pantheism*] **2.** [P-] of, comprising, or uniting every [*Pan-American*]

**pan·a·ce·a** (pan′ə sē′ə) *n.* [ < Gr. *pan*, all + *akeisthai*, to cure] a supposed remedy for all ills

**pa·nache** (pə nash′, -näsh′) *n.* [Fr., ult. < L. *penna*, a feather] **1.** a plume, esp. on a helmet **2.** dashing elegance of manner or style

**Pan·a·ma** (pan′ə mä′, -mô′) Central American country on a strip of land connecting Central & South America: 29,201 sq. mi.; pop. 1,329,000 — **Pan′a·ma′ni·an** (-mä′nē ən) *adj., n.*

**Panama Canal** ship canal across Panama, joining the Atlantic & Pacific

**Panama (hat)** [*also* p-] a handwoven hat made with strawlike strips of the leaves of a tropical plant

**Pan′-A·mer′i·can** *adj.* of the Americas

**pan′cake′** *n.* a flat cake of batter fried on a griddle or in a pan

**pan·chro·mat·ic** (pan′krō mat′ik) *adj.* sensitive to light of all colors [*panchromatic* film]

**pan·cre·as** (paŋ′krē əs, paŋ′-) *n.* [ < Gr. *pan*, all + *kreas*, flesh] a large gland that secretes a digestive juice into the intestine and also produces insulin —**pan′cre·at′ic** (-at′ik) *adj.*

**pan·da** (pan′də) *n.* [ < native name] **1.** a black-and-white, bearlike mammal of China: also **giant panda 2.** a reddish, raccoonlike animal of the Himalayas: also **lesser panda**

**pan·dem·ic** (pan dem′ik) *adj.* [ < Gr. *pan*, all + *dēmos*, people] epidemic over a large region

**pan·de·mo·ni·um** (pan′də mō′nē əm) *n.* [ < name of demons' abode in Milton's *Paradise Lost* < PAN- + Gr. *daimōn*, demon] wild disorder or noise

**pan·der** (pan′dər) *n.* [ < L. *Pandarus*, lovers' go-between in Chaucer, etc.] **1.** a procurer; pimp **2.** one who helps others to satisfy their vices, etc. Also **pan′der·er** —*vi.* to act as a pander (*to*)

**Pan·do·ra** (pan dôr′ə) *n.* [ < Gr. *pan*, all + *dōron*, gift] *Gr. Myth.* the first mortal woman: she opened a box letting all human ills into the world

**pane** (pān) *n.* [ < L. *pannus*, piece of cloth] a sheet of glass in a frame of a window, door, etc.

**pan·e·gyr·ic** (pan′ə jir′ik) *n.* [ < Gr. *panēgyris*, public meeting] **1.** a formal speech or writing praising a person or event **2.** high praise

**pan·el** (pan′'l) *n.* [see PANE] **1.** *a)* a section or division, usually rectangular, forming a part of a wall, door, etc. *b)* a board for instruments or controls **2.** a lengthwise strip in a skirt, etc. **3.** a list of persons summoned for jury duty **4.** a group of people selected for judging, discussing, etc. —*vt.* **-eled** or **-elled, -el·ing** or **-el·ling** to provide with panels

**pan′el·ing, pan′el·ling** *n.* **1.** panels collectively **2.** sheets of plastic, wood, etc. used for panels

**pan′el·ist** *n.* a member of a panel (*n.* 4)

**panel truck** an enclosed pickup truck

**pang** (paŋ) *n.* [ < ?] a sudden, sharp pain or feeling, as of hunger or regret

**pan·han·dle¹** (pan′han′d'l) *n.* [*often* P-] a strip of land projecting like the handle of a pan

**pan·han·dle²** (pan′han′d'l) *vt., vi.* **-dled, -dling** [Colloq.] to beg (from) on the streets —**pan′han′dler** *n.*

**pan·ic** (pan′ik) *n.* [ < Gr. *panikos*, of Pan, as inspirer of sudden fear] a sudden, unreasoning fear, often spreading quickly —*vt.* **-icked, -ick·ing 1.** to affect with panic **2.** [Slang] to convulse (an audience, etc.) with delight —*vi.* to show panic —**pan′ick·y** *adj.*

**pan′ic-strick′en** *adj.* badly frightened: also **pan′ic-struck′**

**pan·nier, pan·ier** (pan′yər, -ē ər) *n.* [ < L. *panis*, bread] a large basket for carrying loads on the back

**pa·no·cha** (pə nō′chə) *n.* [AmSp., ult. < L. *panis*, bread] **1.** a coarse Mexican sugar **2.** *var. of* PENUCHE

**pan·o·ply** (pan′ə plē) *n., pl.* **-plies** [ < Gr. *pan*, all + *hopla*, arms] **1.** a complete suit of armor **2.** any magnificent covering or array

**pan·o·ra·ma** (pan′ə ram′ə) *n.* [ < PAN- + Gr. *horama*, a view] **1.** a wide view in all directions **2.** a constantly changing scene —**pan′o·ram′ic** *adj.*

**pan·sy** (pan′zē) *n., pl.* **-sies** [ < Fr. *penser*, think] a small plant of the violet family, with velvety petals

**pant** (pant) *vi.* [ult. < L. *phantasia*, nightmare] **1.** to breathe rapidly and heavily, as from running fast **2.** to yearn eagerly (with *for* or *after*) —*vt.* to gasp out —*n.* any of a series of rapid, heavy breaths; gasp

**pan·ta·loons** (pan′t'l ōonz′) *n.pl.* [ < It.: ult. after St. *Pantalone*] formerly, a kind of tight trousers

**pan·the·ism** (pan′thē iz′m) *n.* [PAN- + THEISM] the doctrine that all forces, manifestations, etc. of the universe are God —**pan′the·ist** *n.*

**pan·the·on** (pan′thē än′) *n.* [ < Gr. *pan*, all + *theos*, a god] **1.** a temple for all the gods **2.** [*often* P-] a building in which the famous dead of a nation are entombed or commemorated

**pan·ther** (pan′thər) *n.* [ < Gr.

**pan·ther**] 1. a leopard, specif. one that is black 2. a cougar or a jaguar

**pan·ties** (pan'tēz) *n.pl.* women's or children's short underpants: also **pan'tie, pan'ty**

**pan·to·mime** (pan'tə mīm') *n.* [< Gr.: see PAN- & MIME] 1. a drama without words, using only action and gestures 2. action or gestures without words —*vt., vi.* -mimed', -mim'ing to express or act in pantomime — **pan'to·mim'ic** (-mim'ik) *adj.* — **pan'to·mim'ist** (-mī'mist, -mim'-ist) *n.*

**pan·try** (pan'trē) *n., pl.* -tries [< L. *panis*, bread] a small room off the kitchen, where cooking ingredients and utensils, china, etc. are kept

**pants** (pants) *n.pl.* [< PANTALOONS] 1. trousers 2. drawers or panties

**pant'suit'** *n.* matched jacket and pants for women: also **pants suit**

**panty hose** a woman's undergarment combining panties and hose

**pap** (pap) *n.* [ME.] 1. any soft food for babies or invalids 2. any oversimplified or insipid writing, ideas, etc.

**pa·pa** (pä'pə) *n.* father: a child's word

**pa·pa·cy** (pā'pə sē) *n., pl.* -cies [< LL. *papa*, pope] 1. the position or authority of the Pope 2. the period during which a pope rules 3. [also P-] the government of the Roman Catholic Church, headed by the Pope

**pa·pal** (pā'pəl) *adj.* 1. of the Pope or the papacy 2. of the Roman Catholic Church

**pa·paw** (pô'pô) *n.* [prob. < ff.] 1. same as PAPAYA 2. a) a tree of the C and S U.S. with an oblong, yellowish, edible fruit b) its fruit

**pa·pa·ya** (pə pä'yə) *n.* [< SAmInd.] 1. a tropical American tree with a large yellowish-orange fruit 2. its fruit

**pa·per** (pā'pər) *n.* [see PAPYRUS] 1. a thin, flexible material in sheets, made from rags, wood, etc. and used to write or print on, wrap, etc. 2. a single sheet of this 3. an official document 4. an essay, dissertation, etc. 5. a newspaper 6. wallpaper 7. [*pl.*] credentials —*adj.* 1. of, or made of, paper 2. like paper; thin —*vt.* to cover with wallpaper —**pa'per·y** *adj.*

**pa'per·back'** *n.* a book bound in paper

**pa'per·boy'** *n.* a boy who sells or delivers newspapers

**paper clip** a flexible clasp for holding loose sheets of paper together

**pa'per·hang'er** *n.* a person whose work is covering walls with wallpaper

**paper tiger** a person, nation, etc. that seems to pose a threat but is really powerless

**pa'per·weight'** (-wāt') *n.* any small, heavy object set on papers to keep them from being scattered

**paper work** the keeping of records, etc. incidental to some task

**pa·pier-mâ·ché** (pā'pər mə shā') *n.*

[Fr. < *papier*, paper + *mâcher*, to chew] a material made of paper pulp mixed with size, glue, etc. and molded into various objects when moist

**pa·pil·la** (pə pil'ə) *n., pl.* -lae (-ē) [L. < *papula*, pimple] any small, nipplelike projection of tissue, as on the tongue —**pap·il·lar·y** (pap'ə ler'ē) *adj.*

**pa·poose** (pa pōōs') *n.* [< AmInd.] a N.American Indian baby

**pap·ri·ka** (pa prē'kə, pap'ri-) *n.* [ult. < Gr. *peperi*, a pepper] a mild red condiment ground from the fruit of certain peppers

**Pap test** (pap) [< G. *Papanicolaou*, 20th-c. U.S. anatomist who developed it] a test for uterine cancer

**pa·py·rus** (pə pī'rəs) *n., pl.* -ri (-rī), -rus·es [< Gr. *papyros*] 1. a tall water plant of Egypt 2. a writing material made from the pith of this plant by the ancients

**par** (pär) *n.* [L., an equal] 1. the established value of a currency in foreign-exchange rates 2. an equal status, level, etc.: usually in phrase **on a par (with)** 3. the average state, condition, etc. [his work is above *par*] 4. the face value of stocks, etc. 5. *Golf* the number of strokes established as a skillful score for a hole or course —*adj.* 1. of or at par 2. average

**par.** 1. paragraph 2. parish

**par·a-** *a prefix meaning:* 1. beside, beyond [*parapsychology*] 2. helping in a secondary way, accessory [*paramedical*]

**par·a·ble** (par'ə b'l) *n.* [< Gr. *para-*, beside + *ballein*, to throw] a short, simple story teaching a moral lesson

**pa·rab·o·la** (pə rab'ə lə) *n.* [see prec.] *Math.* a curve formed by the intersection of a cone with a plane parallel to its side —**par·a·bol·ic** (par'ə bäl'ik) *adj.*

**par·a·chute** (par'ə shōōt') *n.* [Fr. < *para-*, protecting + *chute*, a fall] a large cloth contrivance, umbrella-shaped when unfolded, used to retard the speed of one dropping from an airplane, etc. —*vt., vi.* -chut'ed, -chut'-ing to drop by parachute —**par'a·chut'ist** *n.*

**pa·rade** (pə rād') *n.* [< L. *parare*, prepare] 1. ostentatious display 2. a review of troops 3. any organized procession or march, as for display —*vt.* -rad'ed, -rad'ing 1. to march or walk through, as for display 2. to show off [to *parade* one's knowledge] —*vi.* 1. to march in a parade 2. to walk about ostentatiously

**par·a·digm** (par'ə dim, -dīm') *n.* [< Gr. *para-*, beside + *deigma*, example] 1. an example or model 2. *Gram.* an example of a declension or conjugation, giving all the inflections of a word

**par·a·dise** (par'ə dīs') *n.* [< Gr. *paradeisos*, garden] 1. [P-] the garden of Eden 2. heaven 3. any place or state of great happiness

**par·a·dox** (par'ə däks') n. [< Gr. *para-*, beyond + *doxa*, opinion] 1. a statement that seems contradictory, etc. but may be true in fact 2. a statement that is self-contradictory and, hence, false —**par'a·dox'i·cal** adj.

**par·af·fin** (par'ə fin) n. [G. < L. *parum*, too little + *affinis*, akin: from its inertness] a white, waxy substance used for making candles, sealing jars, etc.: also **par'af·fine** (-fin, -fēn)

**par·a·gon** (par'ə gän', -gən) n. [< It. *paragone*, touchstone] a model of perfection or excellence

**par·a·graph** (par'ə graf') n. [< Gr. *para-*, beside + *graphein*, write] 1. a distinct section of a writing, begun on a new line and often indented 2. a brief item in a newspaper, etc. —vt. to arrange in paragraphs

**Par·a·guay** (par'ə gwā', -gwī') country in SC S.America: 157,042 sq. mi.; pop. 2,161,000 —**Par'a·guay'an** adj., n.

**par·a·keet** (par'ə kēt') n. [see PARROT] a small, slender parrot with a long, tapering tail

**par·a·le·gal** (par'ə lē'gəl) adj. designating or of persons trained to aid lawyers but not licensed to practice law —n. such a person

**par·al·lax** (par'ə laks') n. [< Gr. *para-*, beyond + *allassein*, to change] the apparent change in the position of an object resulting from a change in the viewer's position

**par·al·lel** (par'ə lel') adj. [< Gr. *para-*, side by side + *allēlos*, one another] 1. extending in the same direction and at a constant distance apart, so as never to meet 2. similar or corresponding —n. 1. a parallel line, surface, etc. 2. any person or thing similar to another; counterpart 3. any comparison showing likeness 4. any of the imaginary lines parallel to the equator and representing degrees of latitude —vt. **-leled'** or **-lelled'**, **-lel'ing** or **-lel'ling** 1. to be parallel with [the road *parallels* the river] 2. to compare 3. to match; equal —**par'al·lel'ism** (-iz'm) n.

**par'al·lel'o·gram'** (-ə gram') n. a four-sided plane figure having the opposite sides parallel and equal

**pa·ral·y·sis** (pə ral'ə sis) n., pl. **-ses'** (-sēz') [< Gr. *para-*, beside + *lyein*, to loose] 1. partial or complete loss of voluntary motion or of sensation in part or all of the body 2. a condition of helpless inactivity —**par·a·lyt·ic** (par'ə lit'ik) adj., n.

PARALLEL-OGRAM

**par·a·lyze** (par'ə līz') vt. **-lyzed'**, **-lyz'ing** 1. to cause paralysis in 2. to make ineffective or powerless

**par·a·me·ci·um** (par'ə mē'shē əm, -sē-) n., pl. **-ci·a** (-ə) [< Gr. *paramēkēs*, oval] an oval freshwater protozoan that moves by means of cilia

**par·a·med·i·cal** (par'ə med'i k'l) adj. [PARA- + MEDICAL] of auxiliary medical personnel, as midwives, aidmen, nurses' aides, etc.

**pa·ram·e·ter** (pə ram'ə tər) n. [< Gr. *para-*, beside + *metron*, a measure] a constant with variable values

**par·a·mil·i·tar·y** (par'ə mil'ə ter'ē) adj. [PARA- + MILITARY] of a private quasimilitary organization

**par·a·mount** (par'ə mount') adj. [< OFr. *par*, by + *amont*, uphill] ranking higher than any other; chief

**par·a·mour** (par'ə moor') n. [< OFr. *par amour*, with love] a lover or mistress in an illicit relation

**par·a·noi·a** (par'ə noi'ə) n. [< Gr. *para-*, beside + *nous*, the mind] a mental disorder characterized by delusions, as of grandeur or, esp., persecution —**par'a·noid'** adj., n.

**par·a·pet** (par'ə pit, -pet') n. [< It. *parare*, to guard + *petto*, breast] 1. a wall or bank for screening troops from enemy fire 2. a low wall or railing

**par·a·pher·na·li·a** (par'ə fər nāl'yə) n.pl. [often with sing. v.] [< Gr. *para-*, beyond + *phernē*, dowry] 1. personal belongings 2. equipment

**par·a·phrase** (par'ə frāz') n. [< Gr. *para-*, beyond + *phrazein*, say] a rewording of the meaning of something spoken or written —vt., vi. **-phrased'**, **-phras'ing** to express in a paraphrase

**par·a·ple·gi·a** (par'ə plē'jē ə) n. [< Gr. *para-*, beside + *plēgē*, a stroke] paralysis of the lower half of the body —**par'a·pleg'ic** (-plē'jik) adj., n.

**par'a·pro·fes'sion·al** n. [see PARA-] a trained assistant to licensed professionals, as in medicine or education

**par'a·psy·chol'o·gy** (-sī kal'ə jē) n. [see PARA-] psychology dealing with psychic phenomena such as telepathy

**par·a·site** (par'ə sīt') n. [< Gr. *para-*, beside + *sitos*, food] 1. one who lives at others' expense without making any useful return 2. a plant or animal that lives on or within another —**par'a·sit'ic** (-sit'ik) adj.

**par·a·sol** (par'ə sôl') n. [< It. *parare*, ward off + *sole*, sun] a lightweight umbrella used as a sunshade

**par·a·thi·on** (par'ə thī'än) n. [< PARA- + *theion*, sulfur] a highly poisonous insecticide

**par'a·thy'roid** (-thī'roid) adj. [see PARA-] designating or of the small glands near the thyroid that regulate calcium and phosphorus metabolism

**par·a·troops** (par'ə troops') n.pl. [< PARA(CHUTE) + TROOP] troops trained and equipped to parachute into a combat area —**par'a·troop'er** n.

**par·boil** (pär'boil') vt. [< L. *per*, through + *bullire*, to boil: infl. by *par*] to boil until partly cooked

**par·cel** (pär's'l) n. [see PARTICLE] 1. a small bundle; package 2. a piece (of land) —vt. **-celed** or **-celled**, **-cel·ing** or **-cel·ling** to divide into parts and distribute (with *out*)

**parcel post** a mail service for parcels of a specified weight and size

**parch** (pärch) vt. [< ?] 1. to expose to great heat so as to dry or roast 2. to make very thirsty —vi. to become very dry and hot

**parch·ment** (pärch'mənt) n. [< L. (*charta*) *Pergamenum*, (paper) of Pergamum, city in Asia Minor] 1. the skin of a sheep, goat, etc. prepared as a surface for writing **2.** paper like parchment **3.** a manuscript on this

**par·don** (pär′d'n) *vt.* [< L. *per-*, through + *donare*, give] **1.** to release from further punishment **2.** to forgive (an offense) **3.** to excuse (a person) for a fault, etc. —*n.* **1.** forgiveness **2.** an official document granting a pardon — **par′don·a·ble** *adj.* —**par′don·er** *n.*

**pare** (per) *vt.* **pared, par′ing** [< L. *parare*, prepare] **1.** to cut or trim away (the rind, skin, etc.) of; peel **2.** to reduce gradually (often with *down*)

**par·e·gor·ic** (par′ə gôr′ik) *n.* [< Gr. *parēgoros*, soothing] a tincture of opium, used to relieve diarrhea

**par·ent** (per′ənt) *n.* [< L. *parere*, beget] **1.** a father or mother **2.** any organism in relation to its offspring **3.** a source; origin —**pa·ren·tal** (pə ren′t'l) *adj.* —**par′ent·hood″** *n.*

**par′ent·age** (-ij) *n.* descent from parents or ancestors; lineage

**pa·ren·the·sis** (pə ren′thə sis) *n.*, *pl.* **-ses′** (-sēz′) [< Gr. *para-*, beside + *entithenai*, insert] **1.** a word, clause, etc. added as an explanation or comment within a sentence **2.** either of the curved lines ( ) used to set this off — **par·en·thet·i·cal** (par′ən thet′i k'l), **par′en·thet′ic** *adj.*

**par′ent·ing** (-iŋ) *n.* the work of a parent in raising a child or children

**pa·re·sis** (pə rē′sis) *n.* [Gr. < *parienai*, relax] **1.** partial paralysis **2.** a brain disease caused by syphilis of the central nervous system

**par·fait** (pär fā′) *n.* [Fr., perfect] a frozen dessert of rich cream and eggs, or ice cream, syrup, fruit, etc.

**pa·ri·ah** (pə rī′ə) *n.* [Tamil *paraiyan*] **1.** a member of one of the lowest social castes in India **2.** any outcast

**par·i·mu·tu·el** (par′ə myoo̅′choo wəl) *n.* [Fr., lit., a mutual bet] a system of betting on races in which the winning bettors share the net of each pool in proportion to their wagers

**par·ing** (per′iŋ) *n.* a piece pared off

**Par·is**[1] (par′is) *Gr. Legend* a prince of Troy: see HELEN OF TROY

**Par·is**[2] (par′is; *Fr.* pä′rē′) capital of France: pop. 2,790,000 —**Pa·ri·sian** (pə rizh′ən, -rē′zhən) *adj., n.*

**par·ish** (par′ish) *n.* [< LGr. *paroikia*, diocese] **1.** a part of a diocese, under the charge of a priest or minister **2.** the congregation of a church **3.** a civil division in Louisiana, like a county

**pa·rish·ion·er** (pə rish′ə nər) *n.* a member of a parish

**par·i·ty** (par′ə tē) *n.* [< L. *par*, equal] **1.** equality in power, value, etc. **2.** equality of value at a given ratio between different kinds of money, etc.

**park** (pärk) *n.* [< ML. *parricus*] **1.** wooded land held as part of an estate or preserve **2.** an area of public land, with playgrounds, etc. for recreation —*vt., vi.* **1.** to leave (a vehicle) in a certain place temporarily **2.** to maneu-

ver (a vehicle) into a parking space

**par·ka** (pär′kə) *n.* [Aleutian < Russ., fur coat] a heavy, hooded jacket

**parking meter** a coin-operated device for indicating the amount of time a parking space may be occupied

**Par·kin·son's disease** (pär′kin sənz) [< J. *Parkinson* (1755-1824), Eng. physician] a degenerative disease of later life, causing rhythmic tremor and muscular rigidity

**Parkinson's Law** [stated by C. *Parkinson* (1909- ), Brit. economist] a parody of economic laws, such as that work expands to fill the allotted time

**park′way′** *n.* a broad roadway landscaped with trees, bushes, etc.

**par·lance** (pär′ləns) *n.* [< OFr. *parler*, speak] language or idiom

**par·lay** (pär′lā, -lē; *for v. also* pär lā′) *vt., vi.* [< It. *paro*, a pair] to bet (an original wager plus its winnings) on another race, etc. —*n.* a parlayed bet

**par·ley** (pär′lē) *vi.* [< Fr. *parler*, speak] to confer, esp. with an enemy —*n.*, *pl.* **-leys** a conference, as to settle a dispute or discuss terms

**par·lia·ment** (pär′lə mənt) *n.* [< OFr. *parler*, speak] **1.** an official government council **2.** [P-] the national legislative body of certain countries, esp. Great Britain

**par′lia·men·tar′i·an** (-men ter′ē ən) *n.* one skilled in parliamentary rules

**par′lia·men′ta·ry** (-men′tər ē) *adj.* **1.** of or by a parliament **2.** conforming to the rules of a parliament

**par·lor** (pär′lər) *n.* [< OFr. *parler*, speak] **1.** a living room **2.** any of certain business establishments [a beauty *parlor*] Brit. sp. **parlour**

**Par·me·san** (**cheese**) (pär′mə zän′) [< *Parma*, an It. city] a very hard, dry Italian cheese, usually grated

**pa·ro·chi·al** (pə rō′kē əl) *adj.* [see PARISH] **1.** of or in a parish or parishes **2.** narrow in scope; provincial

**parochial school** a school supported and controlled by a church

**par·o·dy** (par′ə dē) *n.*, *pl.* **-dies** [< Gr. *para-*, beside + *ōidē*, song] a farcical imitation of a literary or musical work or style —*vt.* **-died, -dy·ing** to make a parody of

**pa·role** (pə rōl′) *n.* [< LL. *parabola*, a speech] the release of a prisoner before his sentence has expired, on condition of future good behavior —*vt.* **-roled′, -rol′ing** to release on parole

**par·ox·ysm** (par′ək siz′m) *n.* [< Gr. *para-*, beyond + *oxynein*, sharpen] **1.** a sudden attack of a disease **2.** a sudden outburst, as of laughter

**par·quet** (pär kā′) *n.* [Fr. < MFr. *parc*, a park] **1.** the main floor of a theater: usually called *orchestra* **2.** a flooring of parquetry —*vt.* **-queted′** (-kād′), **-quet′ing** (-kā′iŋ) to make of parquetry

**parquet circle** the part of a theater below the balcony and behind the parquet

**par·quet·ry** (pär′kə trē) *n.* inlaid flooring in geometric forms

**par·ri·cide** (par′ə sīd′) *n.* [< L. *paricida:* see -CIDE] 1. one who murders his parent, close relative, etc. 2. the act of a parricide

**par·rot** (par′ət) *n.* [Fr. *perrot*] 1. a bird with a hooked bill and brightly colored feathers: some parrots can learn to imitate speech 2. one who parrots what others say —*vt.* to repeat without understanding

**par·ry** (par′ē) *vt.* -ried, -ry·ing [< L. *parare,* prepare] 1. to ward off (a blow, etc.) 2. to evade (a question, etc.) —*n., pl.* -ries a parrying

**parse** (pärs) *vt.* parsed, pars′ing [< L. *pars* (*orationis*), part (of speech)] to break (a sentence) down, giving the form and function of each part

**par·si·mo·ny** (pär′sə mō′nē) *n.* [< L. *parcere,* to spare] stinginess; extreme frugality —**par′si·mo′ni·ous** *adj.*

**pars·ley** (pärs′lē) *n.* [< Gr. *petros,* a rock + *selinon,* celery] a plant with aromatic, often curled leaves used to flavor or garnish some foods

**pars·nip** (pärs′nip) *n.* [< L. *pastinare,* dig up] 1. a plant with a long, white root used as a vegetable 2. its root

**par·son** (pär′s'n) *n.* [see PERSON] a clergyman, esp. one having a parish

**par′son·age** (-ij) *n.* the dwelling provided for a parson by his church

**part** (pärt) *n.* [< L. *pars*] 1. a portion, segment, etc. of a whole [a *part* of a book] 2. an essential, separable element [automobile *parts*] 3. a portion or share; specif., *a*) duty [to do one's *part*] *b*) [*usually pl.*] talent; ability [a man of *parts*] *c*) a role in a play *d*) any of the voices or instruments in a musical ensemble, or the score for this 4. a region; esp., [*usually pl.*] a district 5. one of the sides in a conflict, etc. 6. a dividing line formed in combing the hair —*vt.* 1. to break or divide into parts 2. to comb (the hair) so as to leave a part 3. to break or hold apart —*vi.* 1. to break or divide into parts 2. to separate and go different ways 3. to cease associating 4. to go away; leave (with *from*) —*adj.* partial —**for one's part** so far as one is concerned —**for the most part** mostly —**in part** partly —**part with** to relinquish —**take part** to participate

**par·take** (pär tāk′) *vi.* -took′, -tak′en, -tak′ing [< *part taker*] 1. to participate (*in* an activity) 2. to eat or drink something, esp. with others (usually with *of*)

**part·ed** (pär′tid) *adj.* separated

**par·terre** (pär ter′) *n.* [Fr. < *par,* on + *terre,* earth] 1. a garden with beds and path in a pattern 2. *same as* PARTERRE CIRCLE

**par·the·no·gen·e·sis** (pär′thə nō jen′ə sis) *n.* [see ff. & GENESIS] reproduction from an unfertilized ovum, seed, or spore

**Par′the·non′** (-nän′) [< Gr. *parthenos,* a virgin (i.e., Athena)] the Doric temple of Athena on the Acropolis

**par·tial** (pär′shəl) *adj.* [< L. *pars,* a part] 1. favoring one person, faction,

etc. more than another; biased 2. not complete —**partial to** fond of —**par′ti·al′i·ty** (-shē al′ə tē) *n.* —**par′tial·ly** *adv.*

**par·tic·i·pate** (pär tis′ə pāt′) *vi.* -pat′ed, -pat′ing [< L. *pars,* part + *capere,* take] to have or take a share with others (in some activity) —**par·tic′i·pant** *adj., n.* —**par·tic′i·pa′tion** *n.* —**par·tic′i·pa′tor** *n.* —**par·tic′i·pa·to′ry** (-pə tôr′ē) *adj.*

**par·ti·ci·ple** (pär′tə sip′'l) *n.* [see prec.] a verbal form having the qualities of both verb and adjective —**par′ti·cip′i·al** (-sip′ē əl) *adj.*

**par·ti·cle** (pär′ti k'l) *n.* [< L. *pars,* part] 1. a tiny fragment or trace 2. a short, invariable part of speech, as an article, preposition, etc.

**par·ti·col·ored** (pär′tē kul′ərd) *adj.* [< Fr. *parti,* divided + COLORED] having different colors in different parts

**par·tic·u·lar** (pər tik′yə lər) *adj.* [see PARTICLE] 1. of or belonging to a single group, person, or thing 2. regarded separately; specific 3. unusual 4. exacting; fastidious —*n.* a distinct fact, item, detail, etc. —**in particular** especially —**par·tic′u·lar′i·ty** (-lar′ə tē) *n.*

**par·tic′u·lar·ize′** (-lə rīz′) *vt., vi.* -ized′, -iz′ing to give particulars or details (of); specify

**par·tic′u·lar·ly** *adv.* 1. in detail 2. especially 3. specifically

**par·tic′u·late** (-lit, -lāt′) *adj.* of or formed of tiny, separate particles

**part′ing** *adj.* 1. dividing; separating 2. departing 3. given, spoken, etc. at parting —*n.* 1. a breaking or separating 2. a departure

**par·ti·san** (pärt′ə z'n) *n.* [< L. *pars,* a part] 1. a strong supporter of a faction, party, etc. 2. a guerrilla fighter —*adj.* of or like a partisan Also **partizan** —**part′i·san·ship′** *n.*

**par·ti·tion** (pär tish′ən) *n.* [< L. *partitio*] 1. division into parts 2. something that divides, as a wall separating rooms —*vt.* 1. to divide into parts; apportion 2. to divide by a partition

**part′ly** *adv.* not fully or completely

**part·ner** (pärt′nər) *n.* [< ME.] 1. one who joins in an activity with another or others; specif., one of two or more persons owning jointly a business 2. a spouse 3. either of two persons dancing together 4. a player on the same team —**part′ner·ship′** *n.*

**part of speech** any of the classes to which words can be assigned by form, function, etc., as noun, verb, etc.

**par·tridge** (pär′trij) *n.* [< Gr. *perdix*] any of several game birds, as the grouse, pheasant, etc.

**part song** a song for several voices, usually without accompaniment

**part′-time′** *adj.* of a period of work, study, etc. for less than the usual time

PARTRIDGE

**par·tu·ri·tion** (pär′choo rish′ən) *n.* [ < L. *parere*, to bear] childbirth

**part′way′** *adv.* to a degree but not fully

**par·ty** (pär′tē) *n., pl.* **-ties** [ < L. *pars*, a part] 1. a group of people working to promote a political platform or slate, a cause, etc. 2. a group acting together to accomplish a task 3. a gathering for social entertainment 4. one concerned in an action, plan, lawsuit, etc. [a *party* to the action] 5. [Colloq.] a person —*vi.* **-tied, -ty·ing** to attend social parties —*vt.* to give a party for

**party line** 1. a single circuit connecting two or more telephone users with the exchange 2. the policies of a political party

**par·ve·nu** (pär′və nōō′) *n.* [ < L. *pervenire*, arrive] a newly rich person considered an upstart

**Pas·a·de·na** (pas′ə dē′nə) city in SW Calif.: pop. 113,000

**pas·chal** (pas′k′l) *adj.* [ < LL. < Gr. < Heb. *pesah*, Passover] 1. of Passover 2. of Easter

**pa·sha** (pə shä′, pä′shə) *n.* [Turk.] formerly, in Turkey, a title of rank or honor placed after the name

**pass** (pas) *vi.* [ < L. *passus*, a step] 1. to go or move forward, through, etc. 2. to go or be conveyed from one place, form, condition, etc. to another 3. *a)* to cease *b)* to depart 4. to die (usually with *away, on,* or *out*) 5. to go by 6. to elapse [an hour *passed*] 7. to make a way (*through* or *by*) 8. to be accepted without question 9. to be approved, as by a legislative body 10. to go through a test, course, etc. successfully 11. to give a judgment, sentence, etc. 12. *Card Games* to decline a chance to bid —*vt.* 1. to go by, beyond, over, or through; specif., *a)* to leave behind *b)* to go through (a test, course, etc.) successfully 2. to cause or allow to go, move, or proceed; specif., *a)* to ratify; enact *b)* to spend (time) *c)* to excrete 3. to cause to move from place to place; circulate 4. to give (an opinion or judgment) —*n.* 1. an act of passing; passage 2. a state; situation [a strange *pass*] 3. *a)* a ticket, etc. giving permission to come or go freely or without charge *b) Mil.* a brief leave of absence 4. a motion of the hands 5. a tentative attempt 6. a narrow passage, etc., esp. between mountains 7. [Slang] an over-familiar attempt to embrace or kiss 8. *Sports* a transfer of a ball, etc. to another player during play —**come** (or **bring**) **to pass** to (cause to) happen —**pass for** to be accepted as —**pass off** to cause to be accepted through deceit —**pass out** 1. to distribute 2. to faint —**pass over** to disregard; ignore —**pass up** [Colloq.] to refuse or let go by —**pass′er** *n.*

**pass′a·ble** *adj.* 1. that can be passed, traveled over, etc. 2. adequate; fair —**pass′a·bly** *adv.*

**pas·sage** (pas′ij) *n.* 1. a passing; specif., *a)* migration *b)* transition *c)* the enactment of a law 2. permission or right to pass 3. a voyage 4. a means of passing; road, passageway, etc. 5. an exchange, as of blows 6. a portion of a book, composition, etc.

**pas′sage·way′** *n.* a narrow way for passage, as a hall, alley, etc.

**pass′book′** *n. same as* BANKBOOK

**pas·sé** (pa sā′) *adj.* [Fr., past] 1. out-of-date; old-fashioned 2. rather old

**pas·sel** (pas′′l) *n.* [ < PARCEL] [Colloq.] a group, esp. a fairly large one

**pas·sen·ger** (pas′n jər) *n.* [ < OFr. *passage*, passage] a person traveling in a train, boat, etc.

**pass′er-by′** *n., pl.* **pass′ers-by′** one who passes by

**pass′ing** *adj.* 1. going by, beyond, etc. 2. fleeting 3. casual [a *passing* remark] 4. satisfying given requirements [a *passing* grade] 5. current —*n.* the act of one that passes; specif., death —**in passing** incidentally

**pas·sion** (pash′ən) *n.* [ < L. *pati*, endure] 1. [P-] the sufferings of Jesus on the cross or after the Last Supper 2. any emotion, as hate, love, etc. 3. intense emotional excitement, as rage, enthusiasm, lust, etc. 4. the object of any strong desire

**pas′sion·ate** (-it) *adj.* 1. having or showing strong feelings 2. hot-tempered 3. ardent; intense 4. sensual —**pas′sion·ate·ly** *adv.*

**pas·sive** (pas′iv) *adj.* [see PASSION] 1. inactive, but acted upon 2. offering no resistance; submissive 3. *Gram.* denoting the voice of a verb whose subject receives the action —**pas′-sive·ly** *adv.* —**pas·siv′i·ty** *n.*

**passive resistance** opposition to a law, tax, etc. by refusal to comply or by nonviolent acts, as fasting

**pass′key′** *n.* 1. a key that fits a number of locks 2. one's own key to something

**Pass·o·ver** (pas′ō′vər) *n.* a holiday for Jews, celebrating their deliverance from slavery in ancient Egypt

**pass′port′** *n.* a government document carried by a citizen traveling abroad, certifying identity and citizenship

**pass′word′** *n.* 1. a secret term used for identification, as in passing a guard 2. any means of admission

**past** (past) *rare pp. of* PASS —*adj.* 1. gone by; ended 2. of a former time 3. immediately preceding 4. *Gram.* indicating a time gone by [the *past* tense] —*n.* 1. time gone by 2. the history of a person, group, etc. 3. a personal background that is hidden or questionable —*prep.* beyond in time, space, amount, etc. —*adv.* to and beyond

**pas·ta** (päs′tə) *n.* [It.] 1. the flour paste of which spaghetti, etc. is made 2. any food made of this paste

**paste** (pāst) *n.* [ < Gr. *pastē*, porridge] 1. dough for making rich pastry 2. any soft, moist, smooth preparation [tooth-

*paste*] 3. a mixture of flour, water, etc. used as an adhesive 4. the hard, brilliant glass of artificial gems —*vt.* past'ed, past'ing 1. to make adhere, as with paste 2. [Slang] to hit

**paste'board'** *n.* a stiff material made of layers of paper pasted together

**pas·tel** (pas tel') *n.* [< LL. *pasta,* paste] 1. a crayon of ground coloring matter 2. a picture drawn with such crayons 3. a soft, pale shade of color

**Pas·teur** (pas tur'), **Louis** 1822–95; Fr. bacteriologist & chemist

**pas·teur·ize** (pas'chə rīz', -tə-) *vt.* -ized', -iz'ing [< prec.] to destroy bacteria in (milk, etc.) by heating to a prescribed temperature for a specified time —**pas'teur·i·za'tion** *n.*

**pas·tiche** (pas tēsh') *n.* [Fr.] 1. an artistic composition drawn from various sources 2. a hodgepodge

**pas·time** (pas'tīm') *n.* a way of spending spare time; diversion

**past master** a person of long experience in an occupation, art, etc.; expert

**pas·tor** (pas'tər) *n.* [L., a shepherd] a clergyman in charge of a congregation —**pas'tor·ate** (-it) *n.*

**pas'to·ral** *adj.* 1. of a pastor or his duties 2. of shepherds 3. of rustic life 4. peaceful; simple

**past participle** a participle used: *a)* to signify a past time or state (as *gone* in "he has *gone*") *b)* as an adjective (as *grown* in "a *grown* man")

**pas·tra·mi** (pə strä'mē) *n.* [Vid. < Romanian] highly spiced, smoked beef

**pas·try** (pās'trē) *n., pl.* -tries [see PASTE] 1. pies, tarts, etc. with crusts baked from flour dough made with shortening 2. all fancy baked goods

**pas'tur·age** (-ij) *n. same as* PASTURE

**pas·ture** (pas'chər) *n.* [< L. *pascere,* to feed] 1. grass, etc. used as food by grazing animals 2. ground suitable for grazing —*vt.* -tured, -tur·ing to put (cattle, etc.) out to graze in a pasture

**past·y** (pās'tē) *adj.* -i·er, -i·est of or like paste in color or texture

**pat** (pat) *n.* [prob. echoic] 1. a gentle tap or stroke with a flat surface 2. a sound made by this 3. a small lump, as of butter —*vt.* pat'ted, pat'ting 1. to tap or stroke gently with the hand or a flat surface 2. to shape or apply by patting —*adj.* 1. exactly suitable [a *pat* hand in poker] 2. so glib as to seem contrived —**pat on the back** 1. a compliment 2. to praise —**stand pat** to refuse to change an opinion, etc.

**pat.** 1. patent 2. patented

**patch** (pach) *n.* [ME. *pacche*] 1. a piece of material applied to mend a hole or strengthen a weak spot 2. a bandage 3. an area or spot [*patches* of blue sky] 4. a small plot of land 5. a scrap; bit —*vt.* 1. to put a patch on 2. to produce crudely or hurriedly —**patch up** to settle (a quarrel, etc.)

**patch'work'** *n.* needlework, as a quilt, made of odd patches of cloth

**patch'y** *adj.* -i·er, -i·est 1. made up of patches 2. not consistent or uniform; irregular —**patch'i·ness** *n.*

**pate** (pāt) *n.* [< ?] the top of the head: a humorous term

**pâ·té** (pä tā') *n.* [Fr.] a meat paste

**pa·tel·la** (pə tel'ə) *n., pl.* -las, -lae (-ē) [L., a pan] *same as* KNEECAP

**pat·ent** (pat''nt; *also for adj. 1 & 2,* pāt'-) *adj.* [< L. *patere,* be open] 1. open to all 2. obvious; plain 3. protected by a patent —*n.* 1. a document granting the exclusive right to produce or sell an invention, etc. for a certain time 2. *a)* the right so granted *b)* the thing protected by such a right —*vt.* to secure a patent for

**patent leather** leather with a hard, glossy finish: formerly patented

**patent medicine** a trademarked medical preparation

**pa·ter·nal** (pə tur'n'l) *adj.* [< L. *pater,* father] 1. fatherly 2. inherited from a father 3. on the father's side

**pa·ter'nal·ism** *n.* the governing of subjects, employees, etc. in a manner suggesting a father's relationship with his children —**pa·ter'nal·is'tic** *adj.*

**pa·ter'ni·ty** (-nə tē) *n.* 1. the state of being a father 2. male parentage

**pa·ter·nos·ter** (pāt'ər nŏs'tər, pät'-) *n.* [L., our father] the Lord's Prayer, esp. in Latin: often **Pater Noster**

**Pat·er·son** (pat'ər s'n) city in NE N.J.: pop. 145,000

**path** (path) *n.* [OE. *pæth*] 1. a way worn by footsteps 2. a walk for the use of people on foot 3. a line of movement 4. a course of conduct, thought, etc. —**path'less** *adj.*

**path.** 1. pathological 2. pathology

**pa·thet·ic** (pə thet'ik) *adj.* [see PATHOS] 1. arousing pity, sorrow, etc.; pitiful 2. pitifully unsuccessful, etc. —**pa·thet'i·cal·ly** *adv.*

**path·o·gen·ic** (path'ə jen'ik) *adj.* producing disease

**pa·thol·o·gy** (pə thäl'ə jē) *n.* [< Gr. *pathos,* suffering + -LOGY] 1. the branch of medicine that deals with the nature of disease, esp. with structural and functional effects 2. any abnormal variation from a sound condition —**path·o·log·i·cal** (path'ə läj'i k'l) *adj.* —**pa·thol'o·gist** *n.*

**pa·thos** (pā'thäs) *n.* [Gr., suffering] the quality in something which arouses pity, sorrow, sympathy, etc.

**path'way'** *n. same as* PATH

**-pa·thy** (pə thē) [< Gr. *pathos,* suffering] *a combining form meaning:* 1. feeling [*telepathy*] 2. disease [*osteopathy*] —**-path·ic** (path'ik)

**pa·tience** (pā'shəns) *n.* a being patient; calm endurance

**pa'tient** (-shənt) *adj.* [< L. *pati,* endure] 1. enduring pain, trouble, etc. without complaining 2. calmly tolerating delay, confusion, etc. 3. diligent; persevering —*n.* one receiving medical care —**pa'tient·ly** *adv.*

**pat·i·na** (pat''n ə, pə tē'nə) *n.* [Fr. < It.] a fine greenish crust on bronze or copper, formed by oxidation

**pa·ti·o** (pat'ē ō', pät'-) *n., pl.* -os' [Sp.] 1. a courtyard open to the sky 2. a paved area adjoining a house, for outdoor lounging, dining, etc.

**pat·ois** (pat'wä) *n., pl.* -ois (-wäz) [Fr.] a provincial dialect

**pat. pend.** patent pending

**patri-** [ < Gr. *patēr*] *a combining form meaning* father

**pa·tri·arch** (pā'trē ärk') *n.* [ < Gr. *patēr*, father + *archein*, rule] 1. the father and head of a family or tribe, as Abraham, Isaac, or Jacob in the Bible 2. a man of great age and dignity 3. a high-ranking bishop, as in the Orthodox Eastern Church —**pa'·tri·ar'chal** *adj.*

**pa'tri·ar'chate** (-är'kit, -kāt) *n.* the rank, jurisdiction, etc. of a patriarch

**pa'tri·ar'chy** (-kē) *n., pl.* -**chies** 1. a social organization in which the father is head of the family, descent being traced through the male line 2. rule or domination by men

**pa·tri·cian** (pə trish'ən) *n.* [ < L. *pater*, father] an aristocrat

**pat·ri·mo·ny** (pat'rə mō'nē) *n., pl.* -**nies** [ < L. *pater*, father] property inherited from one's father or ancestors —**pat'ri·mo'ni·al** *adj.*

**pa·tri·ot** (pā'trē ət) *n.* [ < Gr. *patris*, fatherland] one who loves and zealously supports his country —**pa'tri·ot'ic** (-ät'ik) *adj.* —**pa'tri·ot'i·cal·ly** *adv.* —**pa'tri·ot·ism** *n.*

**pa·trol** (pə trōl') *vt., vi.* -**trolled'**, -**trol'ling** [Fr. *patrouiller*] to make a regular, repeated circuit (of) in guarding —*n.* 1. a patrolling 2. a person or group patrolling

**pa·trol'man** (-mən) *n., pl.* -**men** a policeman who patrols a certain area

**patrol wagon** an enclosed truck used by police to carry prisoners

**pa·tron** (pā'trən) *n.* [ < L. *pater*, father] 1. a protector; benefactor 2. one who sponsors and supports some person, activity, etc. 3. a regular customer —**pa'tron·ess** *n.fem.*

**pa·tron·age** (pā'trən ij, pat'rən-) *n.* 1. support, encouragement, etc. given by a patron 2. *a)* clientele *b)* business; trade 3. *a)* the power to grant political favors *b)* such favors

**pa·tron·ize** (pā'trə nīz', pat'rə-) *vt.* -**ized'**, -**iz'ing** 1. to sponsor; support 2. to treat in a condescending manner 3. to be a regular customer of

**patron saint** a saint looked upon as a special guardian

**pat·ro·nym·ic** (pat'rə nim'ik) *n.* [ < Gr. *patēr*, father + *onyma*, name] a name showing descent from a given person (e.g., *Johnson*, son of John)

**pat·sy** (pat'sē) *n., pl.* -**sies** [Slang] a person easily imposed upon

**pat·ter¹** (pat'ər) *vi.* [ < PAT] to make, or move so as to make, a patter —*n.* a series of quick, light taps

**pat·ter²** (pat'ər) *vt., vi.* [ < PATERNOSTER] to speak rapidly or glibly —*n.* glib, rapid speech, as of salesmen

**pat·tern** (pat'ərn) *n.* [ < OFr. *patron*] 1. a person or thing worthy of imitation 2. a model or plan used in making things 3. a design 4. a regular way of acting or doing 5. a predictable route, movement, etc. —*vt.* to make or do in imitation of a pattern

**pat·ty** (pat'ē) *n., pl.* -**ties** [Fr. *pâté*, pie] 1. a small pie 2. a small, flat cake of ground meat, fish, etc., usually fried

**patty shell** a pastry shell for a single portion of creamed food, etc.

**pau·ci·ty** (pô'sə tē) *n.* [ < L. *paucus*, few] 1. fewness 2. scarcity

**Paul** (pôl), Saint ?–67? A.D.; an early Christian apostle: author of several Epistles in the New Testament

**Paul Bun·yan** (bun'yən) *American Folklore* a giant lumberjack who performed superhuman feats

**paunch** (pônch) *n.* [ < L. *pantex*, belly] the abdomen, or belly; esp., a potbelly —**paunch'y** *adj.*

**pau·per** (pô'pər) *n.* [L.] an extremely poor person, esp. one who lives on charity —**pau'per·ism** *n.* —**pau'per·ize'** *vt.* -**ized'**, -**iz'ing**

**pause** (pôz) *n.* [ < Gr. *pauein*, to stop] a temporary stop or rest —*vi.* **paused**, **paus'ing** to make a pause; stop

**pave** (pāv) *vt.* **paved**, **pav'ing** [ < L. *pavire*, beat] to cover the surface of (a road, etc.) as with concrete —**pave the way (for)** to prepare the way (for)

**pave'ment** *n.* a paved surface, as of concrete; specif., a paved road, etc.

**pa·vil·ion** (pə vil'yən) *n.* [ < L. *papilio*, tent] 1. a large tent 2. a building, often partly open, for exhibits, etc., as at a fair or park 3. any of a group of related buildings

**pav·ing** (pā'viŋ) *n.* a pavement

**Pav·lov** (pav'lôv, päv'-), **I·van** (i vän') 1849–1936; Russ. physiologist

**paw** (pô) *n.* [ < OFr. *poue*] 1. the foot of a four-footed animal having claws 2. [Colloq.] a hand —*vt., vi.* 1. to touch, dig, hit, etc. with paws or feet 2. to handle clumsily or roughly

**pawl** (pôl) *n.* [ < ?] a device, as a hinged tongue which engages cogs in a wheel, allowing rotation in only one direction

PAWL

**pawn¹** (pôn) *n.* [ < MFr. *pan*] 1. anything given as security, as for a debt 2. the state of being pledged —*vt.* 1. to give as security 2. to wager or risk

**pawn²** (pôn) *n.* [ML. *pedo*, foot soldier] 1. a chessman of the lowest value 2. a person used to advance another's purposes

**pawn'bro·ker** *n.* a person licensed to lend money at interest on personal property left with him as security

**pawn'shop** *n.* a pawnbroker's shop

**paw·paw** (pô'pô') *n. same as* PAPAW

**pay** (pā) *vt.* **paid**, **pay'ing** [ < L. *pacare*, pacify] 1. to give to (a person) what is due, as for goods or services 2. to give (what is due) in return, as for goods or services 3. to settle (a debt, etc.) 4. *a)* to give (a compliment, attention, etc.) *b)* to make (a visit, etc.) 5. to be profitable to —*vi.* 1. to give due compensation 2. to be profitable —*n.* money paid; esp., wages or salary —*adj.* 1. operated by inserting money [a *pay* phone] 2. designating a service, etc. paid for by fees [*pay* TV] —**in the pay of** employed and paid by —**pay back** 1. to repay 2. to retaliate upon —**pay down** to pay (part of the price) at purchase as an installment —**pay for** to suffer or atone for (a wrong) —**pay off** to pay all that is owed —**pay out** (pt. **payed out**) to let out (a rope, cable, etc.) —**pay up** to pay in full or on time —**pay'er** *n.*

**pay'a·ble** *adj.* 1. that can be paid 2. due to be paid (on a specified date)

**pay'check'** *n.* a check in payment of wages or salary

**pay'day'** *n.* the day on which wages or salary is paid

**pay dirt** soil, ore, etc. rich enough in minerals to make mining profitable

**pay·ee** (pā ē') *n.* one to whom a check, note, money, etc. is payable

**pay'load'** *n.* 1. a cargo 2. the warhead of a ballistic missile, the instruments of an artificial satellite, etc.

**pay'mas'ter** *n.* the official in charge of paying employees

**pay'ment** *n.* 1. a paying or being paid 2. something paid

**pay'off'** *n.* 1. settlement, reckoning, or payment 2. [Colloq.] a bribe 3. [Colloq.] an unexpected climax

**pay phone** (or **station**) a public telephone, usually coin-operated

**pay'roll'** *n.* 1. a list of employees to be paid, with the amount due to each 2. the total amount needed for this

**Pb** [L. *plumbum*] *Chem.* lead

**PBX, P.B.X.** [< *p*(*rivate*) *b*(*ranch*) *ex*(*change*)] a telephone system within an organization, having outside lines

**pct.** percent

**pd.** paid

**pea** (pē) *n., pl.* **peas,** archaic **pease** [< ME. *pese,* a pea, mistaken as pl.; ult. < Gr.] 1. a climbing plant with green pods 2. its small, round seed, used as a vegetable

**peace** (pēs) *n.* [< L. *pax*] 1. freedom from war 2. an agreement to end war 3. law and order 4. harmony; concord 5. serenity, calm, or quiet —**hold** (or **keep**) **one's peace** to be silent —**peace'a·ble** *adj.*

**peace'ful** *adj.* 1. not quarrelsome 2. free from disturbance; calm 3. of or in a time of peace —**peace'ful·ly** *adv.*

**peace'mak'er** *n.* a person who makes peace, as by settling disagreements or quarrels —**peace'mak'ing** *n., adj.*

**peace officer** an officer entrusted with maintaining law and order

**peace pipe** same as CALUMET

**peace'time'** *n.* a time of peace —*adj.* of or characteristic of such a time

**peach** (pēch) *n.* [< L. *Persicum* (*malum*), Persian (apple)] 1. a tree with round, juicy, orange-yellow fruit having a fuzzy skin and a rough pit 2. its fruit 3. the color of this fruit 4. [Slang] a well-liked person or thing

**pea·cock** (pē'käk') *n.* [< L. *pavo,* peacock] the male of a pheasantlike bird (**pea'fowl'**), with a long, showy

tail which can be spread out like a fan —**pea'hen'** *n.fem.*

**pea jacket** [< Du. *pijjekker*] a hiplength, double-breasted coat of heavy woolen cloth, worn by seamen

**peak** (pēk) *n.* [ult. < PIKE²] 1. a pointed end or top, as of a cap, roof, etc. 2. *a*) the summit of a hill or mountain ending in a point *b*) a mountain with such a summit 3. the highest or utmost point of anything —*vi., vt.* to come or bring to a peak

**peak·ed** (pē'kid) *adj.* [< ?] thin and drawn, as from illness

**peal** (pēl) *n.* [ME. *apele,* appeal] 1. the loud ringing of a bell or bells 2. a set of bells 3. a loud, prolonged sound, as of thunder, laughter, etc. —*vi., vt.* to sound in a peal; ring

**pea'nut'** *n.* 1. a vine of the legume family, with underground pods containing edible seeds 2. the pod or any of its seeds 3. [*pl.*] [Slang] a trifling sum

**peanut butter** a food paste or spread made by grinding roasted peanuts

**pear** (per) *n.* [< L. *pirum*] 1. a tree with greenish-yellow or brownish fruit 2. the juicy fruit, round at the base and narrowing toward the stem

**pearl** (purl) *n.* [< L. *perna,* sea mussel] 1. a smooth, hard, usually white or bluish-gray, roundish growth, formed within the shell of some oysters and other mollusks: it is used as a gem 2. same as MOTHER-OF-PEARL 3. anything pearllike in shape, beauty, value, etc. 4. a bluish gray —**pearl'y** *adj.*

**Pearl Harbor** inlet on the S coast of Oahu, Hawaii: site of U.S. naval base bombed by Japan, Dec. 7, 1941

**peas·ant** (pez'nt) *n.* [< LL. *pagus,* district] 1. a small farmer or farm laborer, as in Europe or Asia 2. a person regarded as boorish, ignorant, etc. —**peas'ant·ry** *n.*

**peat** (pēt) *n.* [< ML. *peta,* piece of turf] partly decayed plant matter from ancient swamps, used for fuel

**peat moss** peat composed of residues of mosses, used as a mulch

**peb·ble** (peb''l) *n.* [< OE. *papol(stan),* pebble (stone)] a small stone worn smooth and round, as by running water —**peb'bly** *adj.* **-bli·er, -bli·est**

**pe·can** (pi kan', -kän'; pē'kan) *n.* [< AmInd.] 1. an edible nut with a thin, smooth shell 2. the tree it grows on

**pec·ca·dil·lo** (pek'ə dil'ō) *n., pl.* **-loes, -los** [< Sp. < L. *peccare,* to sin] a small fault or offense

**pec·ca·ry** (pek'ər ē) *n.* [< SAmInd. name] a piglike animal of N. and S.America, with sharp tusks

**peck¹** (pek) *vt.* [ME. *pikken,* to pick] 1. to strike (at), as with a beak 2. to make by doing this [to *peck* a hole] 3. to pick up with the beak —*vi.* to make strokes as with a pointed object —*n.* 1. a stroke so made 2. [Colloq.] a quick, casual kiss —**peck at** 1. to eat very little of 2. to criticize constantly

**peck²** (pek) *n.* [< OFr. *pek*] a unit of dry measure, 1/4 bushel, or 8 quarts

**pec·tin** (pek'tin) *n.* [< Gr. *pēktos,* congealed] a carbohydrate obtained from certain fruits, which yields a gel that is the basis of jellies

**pec·to·ral** (pek′tər əl) *adj.* [< L. *pectus*, breast] of or located in or on the chest or breast

**pec·u·late** (pek′yə lāt′) *vt., vi.* -**lat′ed**, -**lat′ing** [< L. *peculari*] to embezzle —**pec′u·la′tion** *n.*

**pe·cu·liar** (pi kyōōl′yər) *adj.* [< L. *peculium*, private property] **1.** of only one person, thing, etc.; exclusive **2.** particular; special **3.** odd; strange —**pe·cul′iar·ly** *adv.*

**pe·cu·li·ar·i·ty** (pi kyōō′lē ar′ə tē) *n.* **1.** a being peculiar **2.** *pl.* -**ties** something that is peculiar, as a trait

**pe·cu·ni·ar·y** (pi kyōō′nē er′ē) *adj.* [< L. *pecunia*, money] of or involving money

**ped·a·gogue, ped·a·gog** (ped′ə gäg′, -gôg′) *n.* [< Gr. *pais*, child + *agein*, to lead] a teacher, esp. a pedantic one

**ped·a·go·gy** (-gō′jē, -gäj′ē) *n.* the art or science of teaching —**ped′a·gog′ic** (-gäj′ik), **ped′a·gog′i·cal** *adj.*

**ped·al** (ped′′l) *adj.* [< L. *pes*, foot] of the foot or feet —*n.* a lever operated by the foot, as on a bicycle, organ, etc. —*vt., vi.* -**aled** or -**alled**, -**al·ing** or -**al·ling** to operate by pedals

**ped·ant** (ped′nt) *n.* [ult. < Gr. *paidagōgos*, teacher] **1.** one who emphasizes trivial points of learning **2.** a narrow-minded teacher who insists on exact adherence to rules —**pe·dan′tic** (pi dan′tik) *adj.* —**ped′ant·ry** *n.*

**ped·dle** (ped′′l) *vt., vi.* -**dled**, -**dling** [< ? ME. *ped*, basket] to go from place to place selling (small articles) —**ped′dler** *n.*

-**pede** (pēd) [< L. *pes*] *a combining form meaning* foot *or* feet [*centipede*]

**ped·er·as·ty** (ped′ə ras′tē) *n.* [< Gr. *paiderastēs*, lover of boys] sodomy between males, esp. between a man and a boy —**ped′er·ast′** *n.*

**ped·es·tal** (ped′is t′l) *n.* [< It. *piè*, foot + *di*, of + *stal*, a rest] a bottom support or base of a pillar, statue, etc.

**pe·des·tri·an** (pə des′trē ən) *adj.* [< L. *pes*, foot] **1.** going or done on foot **2.** of or for pedestrians **3.** ordinary and dull; prosaic —*n.* a walker

**pe·di·at·rics** (pē′dē at′riks) *n.pl.* [with *sing. v.*] [< Gr. *pais*, child + *iatros*, physician] the branch of medicine dealing with the care and treatment of infants and children →**pe′di·a·tri′cian** (-ə trish′ən) *n.*

**ped·i·cab** (ped′i kab′) *n.* [< L. *pes*, foot + CAB] a 3-wheeled carriage, esp. in SE Asia, pedaled by the driver

**ped·i·cure** (ped′i kyoor′) *n.* [< L. *pes*, foot + *cura*, care] a trimming, cleaning, etc. of the toenails

**ped·i·gree** (ped′ə grē′) *n.* [< MFr. *pié de grue*, lit., crane's foot: from lines in genealogical tree] **1.** a list of ancestors **2.** descent; lineage **3.** a known line of descent, esp. of a purebred animal —**ped′i·greed′** *adj.*

**ped·i·ment** (ped′ə mənt) *n.* [< earlier *periment*, prob. < PYRAMID] an ornamental gable or triangular piece on the front of a building, over a doorway, etc.

PEDIMENT

**pe·dom·e·ter** (pi däm′ə tər) *n.* [< L. *pes*, foot + Gr. *metron*, a measure] an instrument carried to measure the distance walked

**pe·dun·cle** (pi dun′k′l, pē′dun-) *n.* [< L. *pes*, foot] a stalklike organ or process in some plants, animals, etc.

**peek** (pēk) *vi.* [ME. *piken*] to look quickly and furtively —*n.* such a look

**peel** (pēl) *vt.* [< L. *pilare*, make bald] to cut away (the skin, rind, etc.) of —*vi.* **1.** to shed skin, etc. **2.** to come off in layers or flakes —*n.* the rind or skin of fruit

**peel′ing** *n.* a peeled-off strip

**peen** (pēn) *n.* [prob. < Scand.] the end of a hammerhead opposite the flat striking surface, usually ball-shaped (**ball peen**) or wedge-shaped

**peep¹** (pēp) *vi.* [echoic] to make the short, high-pitched cry of a young bird —*n.* a peeping sound

**peep²** (pēp) *vi.* [ME. *pepen*] **1.** to look through a small opening or from a place of hiding **2.** to show gradually or partially —*n.* a brief look; furtive glimpse —**peep′er** *n.*

**peep′hole′** *n.* a hole to peep through

**peeping Tom** [< legendary peeper at Lady Godiva] one who gets sexual pleasure from furtively watching others

**peer¹** (pir) *n.* [< L. *par*, an equal] **1.** a person or thing of the same rank, ability, etc.; an equal **2.** a British noble —**peer′age** (-ij) *n.* —**peer′ess** *n.fem.*

**peer²** (pir) *vi.* [< ? APPEAR] **1.** to look closely, as in trying to see more clearly **2.** to show slightly

**peer′less** *adj.* without equal

**peeve** (pēv) *vt.* peeved, peev′ing to make peevish —*n.* an annoyance

**pee·vish** (pē′vish) *adj.* [ME. *pevische*] irritable; fretful; cross —**pee′vish·ly** *adv.* —**pee′vish·ness** *n.*

**pee·wee** (pē′wē′) *n.* [< ?] [Colloq.] an unusually small person or thing

**peg** (peg) *n.* [ME. *pegge*] **1.** a short pin or bolt used to hold parts together, hang things on, etc. **2.** a step or degree **3.** [Colloq.] a throw —*vt.* **pegged**, **peg′ging 1.** to fasten, fix, secure, mark, etc. as with pegs **2.** [Colloq.] to throw —**peg away (at)** to work steadily (at)

**Peg·a·sus** (peg′ə səs) *Gr. Myth.* a winged horse

**peign·oir** (pān′wär′, pen-) *n.* [Fr.] a woman's loose, full dressing gown

**Pei·ping** (bā′piŋ′) *former name of* PEKING

**pe·jo·ra·tion** (pē′jə rā′shən, pej′ə-) *n.* [< L. *pejor*, worse] a worsening —**pe·jo·ra·tive** (pi jôr′ə tiv) *adj.*

---

fat, āpe, cär; ten, ēven; is, bīte; gō, hôrn, tōōl, look; oil, out; up, fur; chin; she; thin, *then*; zh, leisure; ŋ, ring; ə for a in *ago*; ′, (ä′b′l); ë, Fr. coeur; ö, Fr. feu; Fr. mon; ü, Fr. duc; kh, G. ich, doch; ‡ foreign; < derived from

**Pe·king** (pē'kiŋ'; *Chin.* bā'jiŋ') capital of China: pop. c. 4,000,000

**Pe·king·ese** (pē'kə nēz') *n., pl.* **-ese'** a small dog with long, silky hair, short legs, and a pug nose: also **Pe'kin·ese'**

**pe·koe** (pē'kō) *n.* [< Chin. *pek-ho*, white down (on the leaves used)] a black tea of Ceylon and India

**pel·age** (pel'ij) *n.* [Fr. < L. *pilus*, hair] a mammal's hairy or furry coat

**pelf** (pelf) *n.* [< ? MFr. *pelfre*, booty] money or wealth regarded with contempt

**pel·i·can** (pel'i kən) *n.* [< Gr. *pelekan*] a large, web-footed water bird with an expandable pouch in the lower bill for scooping up fish

**pel·la·gra** (pə lag'rə) *n.* [It. < *pelle*, skin + Gr. *agra*, seizure] a chronic disease caused by lack of nicotinic acid in the diet, characterized by skin eruptions and nervous disorders

**pel·let** (pel'ət) *n.* [< L. *pila*, a ball] 1. a little ball, as of clay or medicine 2. a bullet, small lead shot, etc.

**pell-mell, pell·mell** (pel'mel') *adv., adj.* [ult. < OFr. *mesler*, to mix] 1. in a jumble 2. with reckless speed

**pel·lu·cid** (pə loo'sid) *adj.* [< L. *per*, through + *lucere*, to shine] 1. transparent; clear 2. easy to understand

**pelt¹** (pelt) *vt.* [? < L. *pillare*, to drive] 1. to throw things at 2. to beat repeatedly —*vi.* to strike heavily or steadily, as hard rain

**pelt²** (pelt) *n.* [prob. < OFr. *pel*, a skin] the skin of a fur-bearing animal, esp. when stripped from the carcass

**pel·vis** (pel'vis) *n.* [L., a basin] 1. the basinlike cavity in the posterior part of the trunk in man and many other vertebrates 2. the bones forming this cavity —**pel'vic** *adj.*

**pem·mi·can** (pem'i kən) *n.* [< AmInd.] a concentrated food of dried beef, suet, dried fruit, etc.

**pen¹** (pen) *n.* [OE. *penn*] 1. a small enclosure for domestic animals 2. any small enclosure —*vt.* **penned** or **pent**, **pen'ning** to enclose as in a pen

**pen²** (pen) *n.* [< L. *penna*, feather] 1. a device used in writing, etc. with ink, often with a metal point split into two nibs 2. the metal point —*vt.* **penned**, **pen'ning** to write with a pen

**pen³** (pen) *n.* [Slang] a penitentiary

**Pen., pen.** peninsula

**pe·nal** (pē'n'l) *adj.* [< Gr. *poinē*, penalty] of, for, constituting, or deserving punishment

**pe'nal·ize'** (-īz', pen'l-) *vt.* **-ized'**, **-iz'ing** to impose a penalty on; punish —**pe'nal·i·za'tion** *n.*

**pen·al·ty** (pen'l tē) *n., pl.* **-ties** 1. a punishment 2. the handicap, etc. imposed on an offender, as a fine

**pen·ance** (pen'əns) *n.* [see PENITENT] voluntary self-punishment to show repentance for wrongdoing, sins, etc.

**penates** see LARES AND PENATES

**pence** (pens) *n.* [Brit.] *pl. of* PENNY

**pen·chant** (pen'chənt) *n.* [Fr. < L. *pendere*, hang] a strong liking

**pen·cil** (pen's'l) *n.* [< L. *penis*, tail] a pointed, rod-shaped instrument with a core of graphite or crayon that is sharpened to a point for writing, etc. —*vt.* **-ciled** or **-cilled**, **-cil·ing** or **-cil·ling** to write, etc. with a pencil

**pend** (pend) *vi.* [< L. *pendere*, hang] to await judgment or decision

**pend·ant** (pen'dənt) *n.* [see prec.] an ornamental hanging object, as a locket or earring

**pend·ent** (pen'dənt) *adj.* [see PEND] 1. suspended 2. overhanging 3. undecided; pending

**pend'ing** *adj.* 1. not decided 2. impending —*prep.* 1. during 2. until

**pen·du·lous** (pen'joo ləs) *adj.* [see PEND] hanging freely; drooping

**pen·du·lum** (pen'joo ləm) *n.* [see PEND] a body hung so as to swing freely to and fro: used to regulate clock movements

**pen·e·trate** (pen'ə trāt') *vt., vi.* **-trat'ed**, **-trat'ing** [< L. *penitus*, inward] 1. to enter by piercing 2. to have an effect throughout 3. to affect deeply. 4. to understand —**pen'e·tra·ble** *adj.* —**pen'e·tra'tion** *n.*

**pen'e·trat'ing** *adj.* 1. that penetrates 2. sharp; piercing 3. acute; discerning Also **pen'e·tra'tive**

**pen·guin** (peŋ'gwin, pen'-) *n.* [prob. < W. *pen gwyn*, white head] a flightless bird of the S Hemisphere with webbed feet and flippers for swimming

**pen·i·cil·lin** (pen'ə sil'in) *n.* [< L. *penicillus*, brush] an antibiotic obtained from certain molds or produced synthetically

PENGUIN

**pen·in·su·la** (pə nin'sə lə) *n.* [< L. *paene*, almost + *insula*, isle] a land area almost surrounded by water —**pen·in'su·lar** *adj.*

**pe·nis** (pē'nis) *n., pl.* **-nis·es**, **-nes** (-nēz) [L.] the male organ of sexual intercourse —**pe'nile** (-nīl) *adj.*

**pen·i·tent** (pen'ə tənt) *adj.* [< L. *paenitere*, repent] sorry for having done wrong and willing to atone —*n.* a penitent person —**pen'i·tence** *n.* —**pen'i·ten'tial** (-ten'shəl) *adj.* —**pen'i·tent·ly** *adv.*

**pen·i·ten·tia·ry** (pen'ə ten'shə rē) *adj.* making one liable to imprisonment in a penitentiary —*n., pl.* **-ries** a State or Federal prison for persons convicted of serious crimes

**pen'knife'** *n., pl.* **-knives'** (-nīvz') a small pocketknife

**pen'light', pen'lite'** *n.* a flashlight about the size of a fountain pen

**pen'man** (-mən) *n., pl.* **-men** one skilled in penmanship

**pen'man·ship'** (-ship') *n.* handwriting as an art or skill

**Penn** (pen), **William** 1644-1718; Eng. Quaker: founder of Pennsylvania

**Penn., Penna.** Pennsylvania

**pen name** a pseudonym

**pen·nant** (pen'ənt) *n.* [< PENNON] 1. any long, narrow flag 2. such a flag symbolizing a championship

**pen·ni·less** (pen'i lis) *adj.* without even a penny; extremely poor

**pen·non** (pen′ən) n. [< L. *penna*, a feather] a flag or pennant

**Penn·syl·va·ni·a** (pen′s'l vān′yə, -vā′nē ə) E State of the U.S.: 45,333 sq. mi.; pop. 11,794,000; cap. Harrisburg —**Penn′syl·va′ni·an** *adj.*, *n.*

**pen·ny** (pen′ē) n., *pl.* **-nies**; for 1 (esp. collectively), **pence** [< OE. *pening*] 1. a coin of the United Kingdom equal to a) 1/12 shilling b) one 100th of a pound as of Feb., 1971 2. a U.S. or Canadian cent —**a pretty penny** [Colloq.] a large sum of money

**penny arcade** a public amusement hall with coin-operated games, etc.

**penny pincher** a very frugal or stingy person —**pen′ny-pinch′ing** *n.*, *adj.*

**pen′ny·weight′** *n.* a unit of weight, equal to 1/20 ounce troy weight

**pen′ny-wise′** *adj.* thrifty in small matters —**penny-wise and pound-foolish** thrifty in small matters but wasteful in major ones

**pe·nol·o·gy** (pē näl′ə jē) n. [< Gr. *poinē*, penalty + -LOGY] the study of prison management and prison reform

**pen pal** a person, esp. one abroad, with whom one exchanges letters

**pen·sion** (pen′shən) n. [< L. *pensio*, a paying] a regular payment, not wages, as to one who is retired or disabled —*vt.* to grant a pension to —**pen′sion·er** *n.*

**pen·sive** (pen′siv) *adj.* [< L. *pensare*, consider] thoughtful or reflective, often in a melancholy way —**pen′sive·ly** *adv.* —**pen′sive·ness** *n.*

**pent** (pent) *alt. pt. & pp. of* PEN¹ —*adj.* held or kept in; penned (often with *up*)

**penta-** [< Gr. *pente*, five] a combining form meaning five

**pen·ta·cle** (pen′tə k'l) n. [see PENTA-] a symbol, usually a five-pointed star, formerly used in magic

**pen·ta·gon** (pen′tə gän′) n. [< Gr. *penta-*, five + *gōnia*, an angle] 1. a plane figure with five angles and five sides 2. [P-] the pentagonal office building of the Defense Department, near Washington, D.C. —**pen·tag′o·nal** (-tag′ə n'l) *adj.*

**pen·tam·e·ter** (pen tam′ə tər) n. [see PENTA- & METER¹] a line of verse containing five metrical feet

**Pen·ta·teuch** (pen′tə tōōk′) n. [< Gr. *penta-*, five + *teuchos*, book] the first five books of the Bible

**pen·tath·lon** (pen tath′län) n. [PENTA- + Gr. *athlon*, a contest] a contest in which each contestant takes part in five different events

**Pen·te·cost** (pen′tə kôst′) n. [< Gr. *pentēkostē* (*hēmera*), the fiftieth (day)] a Christian festival on the seventh Sunday after Easter

**pent·house** (pent′hous′) n. [ult. < L. *appendere*, append] a house or apartment on the roof of a building

**Pen·to·thal Sodium** (pen′tə thal) *a trademark for* a yellowish substance injected as a general anesthetic

**pent-up** (pent′up′) *adj.* held in check; curbed [*pent-up* emotion]

**pe·nu·che, pe·nu·chi** (pə nōō′chē) n. [var. of PANOCHA] a fudgelike candy

**pe·nul·ti·mate** (pi nul′tə mit) *adj.* [< L. *paene*, almost + ULTIMATE] next to the last —*n.* the penultimate one

**pe·nu·ri·ous** (pə nyoor′ē əs, -noor′-) *adj.* [see ff.] miserly; stingy —**pe·nu′ri·ous·ly** *adv.* —**pe·nu′ri·ous·ness** *n.*

**pen·u·ry** (pen′yə rē) n. [< L. *penuria*, want] extreme poverty

**pe·on** (pē′än, -ən) n. [< ML. *pedo*, foot soldier] 1. in Latin America, a member of the laboring class 2. in the SW U.S., a person forced into servitude to work off a debt —**pe′on·age** *n.*

**pe·o·ny** (pē′ə nē) n., *pl.* **-nies** [< Gr. *Paiōn*, Apollo as god of medicine: from its former medicinal use] 1. a plant with large pink, white, red, or yellow, showy flowers 2. the flower

**peo·ple** (pē′p'l) n., *pl.* **-ple**; for 1 **-ples** [< L. *populus*, nation] 1. all the persons of a racial or ethnic group; nation, race, etc. 2. the persons of a certain place, group, or class 3. one's family; relatives 4. the populace 5. persons considered indefinitely [what will *people* say?] 6. human beings —*vt.* **-pled, -pling** to populate

**Pe·o·ri·a** (pē ôr′ē ə) city in C Ill.: pop. 127,000

**pep** (pep) n. [< ff.] [Colloq.] energy; vigor —*vt.* **pepped, pep′ping** [Colloq.] to fill with pep; invigorate (with *up*) —**pep′py** *adj.*

**pep·per** (pep′ər) n. [< Gr. *peperi*] 1. a) a pungent condiment ground from the dried fruits of an East Indian plant b) this plant 2. the fruit of the red pepper plant, red, yellow, or green, sweet or hot —*vt.* 1. to season with ground pepper 2. to pelt with small objects

**pep′per·corn′** *n.* the dried berry of the pepper, ground as a condiment

**pepper mill** a hand mill used to grind peppercorns

**pep′per·mint′** *n.* 1. a plant of the mint family that yields a pungent oil used for flavoring 2. the oil 3. a candy flavored with this oil

**pep·per·o·ni** (pep′ə rō′nē) n., *pl.* **-nis, -ni** [< It. *peperoni*] a highly spiced Italian sausage

**pepper shaker** a container for ground pepper, with a perforated top

**pep′per·y** *adj.* 1. of, like, or highly seasoned with pepper 2. sharp or fiery, as words 3. hot-tempered

**pep·sin** (pep′s'n) n. [G. < Gr. *peptein*, to digest] a stomach enzyme, aiding in the digestion of proteins

**pep talk** a talk, as to an athletic team by its coach, to instill enthusiasm and determination

**pep·tic** (-tik) *adj.* [see prec.] 1. of or aiding digestion 2. caused by digestive secretions [a *peptic* ulcer]

**per** (pur, pər) *prep.* [L.] 1. through;

by; by means of **2.** for each *[fifty cents yd.]* **3.** [Colloq.] according to

**per-** [< PER] *a prefix meaning:* **1.** through; throughout **2.** thoroughly

**Per. 1.** Persia **2.** Persian

**per·ad·ven·ture** (pur'əd ven'chər) *adv.* [< OFr. *par*, by + *aventure*, chance] [Archaic] possibly

**per·am·bu·late** (pər am'byoo lāt') *vt., vi.* **-lat'ed, -lat'ing** [< L. *per*, through + *ambulare*, to walk] to walk (through, over, etc.)

**per·am·bu·la·tor** (-lāt'ər) *n.* [Chiefly Brit.] a baby carriage

**per an·num** (pər an'əm) [L.] yearly

**per·cale** (pər kāl', -kal') *n.* [Fr. < Per. *pargāla*] fine, closely woven cotton cloth, used for sheets, etc.

**per cap·i·ta** (pər kap'ə tə) [ML., lit., by heads] for each person

**per·ceive** (pər sēv') *vt., vi.* **-ceived', -ceiv'ing** [< L. *per*, through + *capere*, take] **1.** to understand **2.** to become aware (of) through the senses

**per·cent** (pər sent') *adv., adj.* [< L. *per centum*] in, to, or for every hundred: symbol, %: also **per cent** —*n.* [Colloq.] percentage

**per·cent·age** (-ij) *n.* **1.** a given part in every hundred **2.** part; portion **3.** [Colloq.] advantage; profit

**per·cen·tile** (pər sen'tīl, -sent''l) *n. Statistics* any of 100 divisions of a series, each of equal frequency

**per·cep·ti·ble** (pər sep'tə b'l) *adj.* that can be perceived —**per·cep'ti·bly** *adv.*

**per·cep·tion** (-shən) *n.* [< L. *per·cipere*, perceive] **1.** the mental grasp of objects, etc. through the senses **2.** insight or intuition **3.** the knowledge, etc. got by perceiving —**per·cep'tu·al** (-chōō əl) *adj.*

**per·cep·tive** *adj.* **1.** of perception **2.** able to perceive quickly —**per·cep'tive·ly** *adv.* —**per·cep'tive·ness** *n.*

**per·cep'tu·al** (-chōō əl) *adj.* of or involving perception

**perch**[1] (purch) *n., pl.* **perch, perch'es** [< Gr. *perkē*] **1.** a small, spiny-finned, freshwater food fish **2.** a similar bony, usually saltwater, fish

**perch**[2] (purch) *n.* [< L. *pertica*, pole] **1.** a horizontal pole, etc. serving as a roost for birds **2.** any high resting place **3.** a measure of length equal to 5 1/2 yards —*vi., vt.* to rest or place on or as on a perch

**per·chance** (pər chans') *adv.* [< OFr. *par*, by + *chance*, chance] [Archaic] **1.** by chance **2.** perhaps

**per·co·late** (pur'kə lāt') *vt.* **-lat'ed, -lat'ing** [< L. *per*, through + *colare*, to strain] to pass (a liquid) through a porous substance; filter —*vi.* to ooze through a porous substance

**per'co·la'tor** *n.* a coffeepot in which boiling water bubbles up through a tube and filters back down through the ground coffee

**per·cus·sion** (pər kush'ən) *n.* [< L. *per-*, thoroughly + *quatere*, shake] the hitting of one body against another, as the hammer of a firearm against a powder cap (**percussion cap**)

**percussion instrument** a musical

instrument producing a tone when struck, as a drum, cymbal, etc.

**per·cus·sion·ist** *n.* a musician who plays percussion instruments

**per di·em** (pər dē'əm, dī'-) [L.] daily

**per·di·tion** (pər dish'ən) *n.* [< L. *perdere*, to lose] *Theol.* **1.** the loss of the soul **2.** *same as* HELL

**per·dure** (pər door') *vi.* **-dured', -dur'ing** [< L. *perdurare*, to endure] to remain in existence; last

**per·e·gri·na·tion** (per'ə gri nā'shən) *n.* [see PILGRIM] a traveling about

**per·emp·to·ry** (pə remp'tər ē) *adj.* [< L. *perimere*, destroy] **1.** *Law* barring further action; final **2.** that cannot be denied, delayed, etc., as a command **3.** dogmatic; imperious

**per·en·ni·al** (pə ren'ē əl) *adj.* [< L. *per*, through + *annus*, year] **1.** lasting throughout the whole year **2.** continuing for a long time **3.** living more than two years: said of plants —*n.* a perennial plant —**pe·ren'ni·al·ly** *adv.*

**per·fect** (pur'fikt; *for v. usually* pər fekt') *adj.* [< L. *per-*, through + *facere*, do] **1.** complete in all respects; flawless **2.** excellent, as in skill or quality **3.** completely accurate **4.** sheer; utter *[a perfect fool]* **5.** *Gram.* expressing a state or action completed at the time of speaking —*vt.* **1.** to complete **2.** to make perfect or nearly perfect —*n.* **1.** the perfect tense **2.** a verb form in this tense —**per'fect·ly** *adv.* —**per'fect·ness** *n.*

**per·fec·ta** (pər fek'tə) *n.* [Sp., perfect] a bet in which one wins if one picks correctly the first and second place finishers in a race

**per·fect·i·ble** (pər fek'tə b'l) *adj.* that can become or be made perfect

**per·fec·tion** (pər fek'shən) *n.* **1.** the act of perfecting **2.** being perfect **3.** a person or thing that is the perfect embodiment of some quality

**per·fec'tion·ist** *n.* one who strives for perfection

**per·fi·dy** (pur'fə dē) *n., pl.* **-dies** [< L. *per*, through + *fides*, faith] betrayal of trust; treachery —**per·fid·i·ous** (pər fid'ē əs) *adj.*

**per·fo·rate** (pur'fə rāt') *vt., vi.* **-rat'ed, -rat'ing** [< L. *per*, through + *forare*, to bore] **1.** to make a hole or holes through, as by boring **2.** to pierce with holes in a row, as a pattern, etc. —**per'fo·ra'tion** *n.*

**per·force** (pər fôrs') *adv.* [< OFr.: see PER & FORCE] necessarily

**per·form** (pər fôrm') *vt.* [< OFr. *parfournir*] **1.** to do (a task, etc.) **2.** to fulfill (a promise, etc.) **3.** to render or enact (a piece of music, dramatic role, etc.) —*vi.* to execute an action or process, esp. in a performance (sense 4) —**per·form'er** *n.*

**per·form·ance** *n.* **1.** the act of performing **2.** functional effectiveness **3.** deed or feat **4.** *a)* a formal exhibition or presentation, as a play *b)* one's part in this

**performing arts** arts, such as drama, for performance before an audience

**per·fume** (pər fyoom'; *for n. usually* pur'fyoom) *vt.* **-fumed', -fum'ing**

[ < L. *per-*, intens. + *fumare*, to smoke] 1. to scent 2. to put perfume on —*n*. a pleasing odor, or a substance producing this, as a volatile oil extracted from flowers

**per·fum′er·y** (-ər ē) *n., pl.* -ies perfumes collectively

**per·func·to·ry** (pər fuŋk′tər ē) *adj.* [ < L. *per-*, intens. + *fungi*, perform] 1. done merely as a routine; superficial 2. without concern; indifferent — **per·func′to·ri·ly** *adv.*

**per·go·la** (pur′gə lə) *n.* [L. *pergula*] an arbor with a latticework roof

**per·haps** (pər haps′) *adv.* [PER + pl. of *hap*, chance] possibly; maybe

**peri-** [Gr.] *a prefix meaning:* 1. around; about 2. near

**Per·i·cles** (per′ə klēz′) 495?-429 B.C.; Athenian statesman & general

**per·i·gee** (per′ə jē′) *n.* [ < Gr. *peri-*, near + *gē*, earth] the point nearest a heavenly body, as the earth, in the orbit of a satellite around it

**per·i·he·li·on** (per′ə hē′lē ən) *n., pl.* -li·ons, -li·a (-ə) [ < Gr. *peri-*, around + *hēlios*, sun] the point nearest the sun in the orbit of a planet or comet or of a man-made satellite

**per·il** (per′əl) *n.* [ < L. *periculum*, danger] 1. exposure to harm or injury 2. something that may cause harm —*vt.* -iled or -illed, -il·ing or -il·ling to expose to danger

**per′il·ous** *adj.* involving peril or risk; dangerous —**per′il·ous·ly** *adv.*

**pe·rim·e·ter** (pə rim′ə tər) *n.* [ < Gr. *peri-*, around + *metron*, measure] 1. the outer boundary of a figure or area 2. the total length of this

**per·i·ne·um** (per′ə nē′əm) *n., pl.* -ne′a (-ə) [ < Gr. *perineon*] the small area between the anus and the genitals

**pe·ri·od** (pir′ē əd) *n.* [ < Gr. *periodos*, a cycle] 1. the interval between successive occurrences of an event 2. a portion of time characterized by certain processes, etc. [a *period* of change] 3. any of the portions of time into which a game, school day, etc. is divided 4. the menses 5. an end or conclusion 6. *a)* the pause in speaking or the mark of punctuation (.) used at the end of a sentence *b)* the dot (.) following many abbreviations —*interj.* an exclamation used for emphasis [you can't go, *period!*]

**pe·ri·od·ic** (pir′ē äd′ik) *adj.* 1. appearing or recurring at regular intervals 2. intermittent

**pe′ri·od′i·cal** *adj.* 1. same as PERIODIC 2. published at regular intervals, as weekly, etc. 3. of a periodical —*n.* a periodical publication —**pe′ri·od′i·cal·ly** *adv.*

**per·i·o·don·tal** (per′ē ə dän′t'l) *adj.* [ < PERI- + Gr. *odōn*, tooth] occurring around a tooth or affecting the gums

**per·i·pa·tet·ic** (per′i pə tet′ik) *adj.* [ < Gr. *peri-*, around + *patein*, walk] walking or moving about; itinerant

**pe·riph·er·y** (pə rif′ər ē) *n., pl.* -ies

[ < Gr. *peri-*, around + *pherein*, to bear] 1. an outer boundary, esp. of a rounded object 2. surrounding space or area —**pe·riph′er·al** *adj.*

**per·i·scope** (per′ə skōp′) *n.* [PERI- + -SCOPE] an optical instrument which allows one to see around or over an obstacle: used on submarines, etc.

**per·ish** (per′ish) *vi.* [ < L. *per-*, through + *ire*, go] 1. to be destroyed or ruined 2. to die, esp. violently

**per′ish·a·ble** *adj.* that may perish; esp., liable to spoil, as some foods —*n.* something perishable, esp. food

**per·i·stal·sis** (per′ə stôl′sis, -stal′-) *n., pl.* -ses [ < Gr. *peri-*, around + *stallein*, to place] contractions and dilations of the intestines, moving the contents onward —**per′i·stal′tic** *adj.*

**per·i·to·ne·um** (per′it'n ē′əm) *n.* [ < Gr. *peri-*, around + *teinein*, to stretch] the serous membrane lining the abdominal cavity

**per·i·to·ni·tis** (-īt′əs) *n.* inflammation of the peritoneum

**per·i·wig** (per′ə wig′) *n.* [alt. < Fr. *perruque*] a wig

**per·i·win·kle¹** (per′ə wiŋ′k'l) *n.* [ < L. *pervincire*, entwine] a creeping plant with blue, white, or pink flowers

**per·i·win·kle²** (per′ə wiŋ′k'l) *n.* [OE. *pinewincle*] a small saltwater snail with a thick, cone-shaped shell

PERIWINKLE SHELL

**per·jure** (pur′jər) *vt.* -jured, -jur·ing [ < L. *per*, through + *jurare*, swear] to make (oneself) guilty of perjury —**per′-jur·er** *n.*

**per·ju·ry** (-jər ē) *n., pl.* -ries [ < L. *perjurus*, false] the willful telling of a lie while under oath

**perk¹** (purk) *vt.* [ME. *perken*] 1. to raise (the head, etc.) briskly 2. to give a smart, fresh, or vigorous look to (often with *up*) —*vi.* to become lively (with *up*) —**perk′y** *adj.* -i·er, -i·est

**perk²** (purk) *vt., vi.* colloq. *clip of* PERCOLATE

**per·ma·frost** (pur′mə frôst′, -fräst′) *n.* permanently frozen subsoil

**per·ma·nent** (pur′mə nənt) *adj.* [ < L. *per*, through + *manere*, remain] lasting or intended to last indefinitely or for a long time —**per′ma·nence** *n.* —**per′ma·nent·ly** *adv.*

**permanent wave** a hair wave produced by use of chemicals or heat and lasting through many washings

**per·me·a·ble** (pur′mē ə b'l) *adj.* that can be permeated, as by fluids —**per′me·a·bil′i·ty** *n.*

**per·me·ate** (pur′mē āt′) *vt., vi.* -at′ed, -at′ing [ < L. *per*, through + *meare*, to glide] to spread or diffuse; penetrate (*through* or *among*)

**per·mis·si·ble** (pər mis′ə b'l) *adj.* that can be permitted; allowable

**per·mis·sion** (pər mish′ən) *n.* the act of permitting; esp., formal consent

**per·mis·sive** (-mis'iv) *adj.* 1. that permits 2. allowing freedom; lenient —**per·mis'sive·ly** *adv.* —**per·mis'sive·ness** *n.*

**per·mit** (pər mit'; *for n. usually* pur'mit) *vt.* **-mit'ted, -mit'ting** [< L. *per*, through + *mittere*, send] 1. to allow to be done; consent to 2. to authorize —*vi.* to give opportunity *[if time permits]* —*n.* a license

**per·mu·ta·tion** (pur'myoo tā'shən) *n.* [< L. *per-*, thoroughly + *mutare*, change] 1. any radical alteration 2. any of the total number of groupings possible within a group

**per·ni·cious** (pər nish'əs) *adj.* [< L. *per*, thoroughly + *necare*, kill] causing great injury, destruction, etc.; fatal —**per·ni'cious·ly** *adv.*

**per·o·ra·tion** (per'ə rā'shən) *n.* [< L. *per*, through + *orare*, speak] the concluding part of a speech

**per·ox·ide** (pə räk'sīd) *n.* [< L. *per*, through + OXIDE] any oxide containing the oxygen group linked by a single bond; specif., hydrogen peroxide

**per·pen·dic·u·lar** (pur'pən dik'yə lər) *adj.* [< L. *perpendiculum*, plumb line] 1. at right angles to a given line or plane 2. exactly upright; vertical —*n.* a line or plane at right angles to another line or plane

**per·pe·trate** (pur'pə trāt') *vt.* **-trat'ed, -trat'ing** [< L. *per*, thoroughly + *patrare*, to effect] 1. to do (something evil, criminal, etc.) 2. to commit (a blunder, etc.) —**per'pe·tra'tion** *n.* —**per'pe·tra'tor** *n.*

**per·pet·u·al** (pər pech'oo wəl) *adj.* [< L. *perpetuus*, constant] 1. lasting forever or for a long time 2. continuing without interruption; constant —**per·pet'u·al·ly** *adv.*

**per·pet·u·ate** (-wāt') *vt.* **-at'ed, -at'ing** to make perpetual; cause to continue or be remembered —**per·pet'u·a'tion** *n.*

**per·pe·tu·i·ty** (pur'pə too'ə tē) *n., pl.* **-ties** unlimited time; eternity —**in perpetuity** forever

**per·plex** (pər pleks') *vt.* [< L. *per*, through + *plectere*, to twist] to make (a person) uncertain, hesitant, etc.; confuse —**per·plex'ing** *adj.* —**per·plex'i·ty** *n., pl.* **-ties**

**per·qui·site** (pur'kwə zit) *n.* [< L. *per-*, intens. + *quaerere*, seek] something in addition to regular pay for one's work, as a tip

**per se** (pur'sē', sā') [L.] by (or in) itself; intrinsically

**per·se·cute** (pur'sə kyoot') *vt.* **-cut'ed, -cut'ing** [< L. *per*, through + *sequi*, follow] to afflict constantly so as to injure or distress, as for reasons of religion, race, etc. —**per'se·cu'tion** *n.* —**per'se·cu'tor** *n.*

**per·se·vere** (pur'sə vir') *vi.* **-vered', -ver'ing** [< L. *per-*, intens. + *severus*, severe] to continue a course of action, etc. in spite of difficulty, opposition, etc. —**per'se·ver'ance** *n.*

**Per·sia** (pur'zhə) *former official name of* IRAN —**Per'sian** *adj., n.*

**Persian cat** a variety of domestic cat with long, silky hair

**Persian Gulf** arm of the Indian Ocean, between Iran & Arabia

**Persian lamb** the pelt of karakul lambs

**per·si·flage** (pur'sə fläzh') *n.* [Fr. < L. *per*, through + *sifilare*, to whistle] frivolous talk or writing; banter

**per·sim·mon** (pər sim'ən) *n.* [< AmInd.] 1. a hardwood tree with plumlike fruit 2. the fruit

**per·sist** (pər sist', -zist') *vi.* [< L. *per*, through + *sistere*, cause to stand] 1. to refuse to give up, esp. when faced with opposition 2. to continue insistently 3. to endure; remain

**per·sist'ent** *adj.* 1. continuing, esp. in the face of opposition, etc. 2. continuing to exist or endure 3. constantly repeated —**per·sist'ence** *n.*

**per·snick·e·ty** (pər snik'ə tē) *adj.* [< Scot. dial.] [Colloq.] 1. too particular; fussy 2. showing or requiring careful treatment

**per·son** (pur's'n) *n.* [< L. *persona*] 1. a human being 2. the human body 3. personality; self 4. *Gram.* division into three specified sets of pronouns and corresponding verb forms: see FIRST PERSON, SECOND PERSON, THIRD PERSON —**in person** actually present

**-per·son** (pur's'n) *a combining form meaning* person in a specified activity: used to avoid the masculine implications of *-man [chairperson]*

**per·son·a·ble** (-ə b'l) *adj.* having a pleasing appearance and personality

**per·son·age** (-ij) *n.* a person; esp., an important person; notable

**per·son·al** (-əl) *adj.* 1. private; individual 2. done in person 3. involving human beings 4. of the body or physical appearance 5. *a)* having to do with the character, conduct, etc. of a person *[a personal remark] b)* tending to make personal, esp. derogatory, remarks 6. *Gram.* indicating person (sense 4) 7. *Law* of property (**personal property**) that is movable

**personal effects** personal belongings, esp. those worn or carried

**per·son·al·i·ty** (pur'sə nal'ə tē) *n., pl.* **-ties** 1. the quality or fact of being a person or a particular person 2. distinctive individual qualities of a person, considered collectively 3. a notable person 4. *[pl.]* offensive remarks aimed at a person

**per·son·al·ize** (pur's'n ə līz') *vt.* **-ized', -iz'ing** 1. to make personal 2. to have marked with one's name, etc.

**per·son·al·ly** *adv.* 1. in person 2. as a person *[I dislike him personally]* 3. in one's own opinion 4. as though directed at oneself

**‡per·so·na non gra·ta** (pər sō'nə nän grät'ə) [L.] an unwelcome person

**per·son·i·fy** (pər sän'ə fī') *vt.* **-fied', -fy'ing** 1. to think of or represent (a thing) as a person 2. to typify; embody —**per·son'i·fi·ca'tion** *n.*

**per·son·nel** (pur'sə nel') *n.* [Fr.] 1. persons employed in any work, enterprise, service, etc. 2. a department for hiring employees, etc.

**per·spec·tive** (pər spek'tiv) *n.* [< L. *per*, through + *specere*, look] 1. the art of picturing objects so as to show relative distance or depth 2. the appearance of objects as determined by their relative distance and positions 3. sense of proportion

**per·spi·ca·cious** (pur'spə kā'shəs) *adj.* [see prec.] having keen judgment; discerning —**per'spi·ca'cious·ly** *adv.* —**per'spi·cac'i·ty** (-kas'ə tē) *n.*

**per·spic·u·ous** (pər spik'yoo wəs) *adj.* [see PERSPECTIVE] easily understood; lucid —**per·spi·cu·i·ty** (pur'spə kyōō'ə tē) *n.*

**per·spi·ra·tion** (pur'spə rā'shən) *n.* 1. the act of perspiring 2. sweat

**per·spire** (pər spīr') *vt., vi.* -**spired'**, -**spir'ing** [< L. *per-*, through + *spirare*, breathe] to sweat

**per·suade** (pər swād') *vt.* -**suad'ed**, -**suad'ing** [< L. *per*, intens. + *suadere*, to urge] to cause (someone) to do or believe something, esp. by reasoning, urging, etc.; convince —**per·suad'a·ble** *adj.* —**per·suad'er** *n.*

**per·sua·sion** (pər swā'zhən) *n.* 1. a persuading or being persuaded 2. power of persuading 3. a strong belief 4. a particular religious belief

**per·sua·sive** *adj.* having the power, or tending, to persuade

**pert** (purt) *adj.* [< L. *apertus*, open] bold; impudent; saucy —**pert'ly** *adv.*

**per·tain** (pər tān') *vi.* [< L. *per-*, intens. + *tenere*, hold] 1. to belong; be connected or associated 2. to be appropriate 3. to have reference

**per·ti·na·cious** (pur'tə nā'shəs) *adj.* [< L. *per-*, intens. + *tenax*, holding fast] 1. holding firmly to some purpose, belief, etc. 2. hard to get rid of —**per'ti·nac'i·ty** (-nas'ə tē) *n.*

**per·ti·nent** (pur't'n ənt) *adj.* [see PERTAIN] connected with the matter at hand —**per'ti·nence** *n.*

**per·turb** (pər turb') *vt.* [< L. *per-*, intens. + *turbare*, disturb] to cause to be alarmed, agitated, or upset —**per·tur·ba·tion** (pur'tər bā'shən) *n.*

**per·tus·sis** (pər tus'is) *n.* [< L. *per-*, intens. + *tussis*, a cough] *same as* WHOOPING COUGH

**Pe·ru** (pə rōō') country in W. S. America: 496,222 sq. mi.; pop. 12,385,000 —**Pe·ru'vi·an** *adj., n.*

**pe·ruke** (pə rōōk') *n.* [Fr. *perruque*] a wig

**pe·ruse** (pə rōōz') *vt.* -**rused'**, -**rus'ing** [prob. < L. *per-*, intens. + ME. *usen*, to use] 1. to read carefully; study 2. to read —**pe·rus'al** *n.*

**per·vade** (pər vād') *vt.* -**vad'ed**, -**vad'ing** [< L. *per*, through + *vadere*, go] to spread or be prevalent throughout —**per·va'sive** *adj.*

**per·verse** (pər vurs') *adj.* [see PERVERT] 1. deviating from what is considered right or good 2. stubbornly contrary 3. obstinately disobedient —**per·verse'ly** *adv.* —**per·verse'ness**, **per·ver'si·ty** *n.*

**per·ver·sion** (pər vur'zhən) *n.* 1. a perverting or being perverted 2. something perverted 3. any sexual act or practice considered abnormal

**per·vert** (pər vurt'; *for n.* pur'vurt) *vt.* [< L. *per-*, intens. + *vertere*, turn] 1. to lead astray; corrupt 2. to misuse 3. to distort 4. to debase —*n.* one practicing sexual perversion

**pes·ky** (pes'kē) *adj.* -**ki·er**, -**ki·est** [prob. var. of *pesty*] [Colloq.] annoying; troublesome —**pes'ki·ness** *n.*

**pe·so** (pā'sō) *n., pl.* -**sos** [Sp. < L. *pensum*, something weighed] the monetary unit and a coin of various Spanish-speaking countries

**pes·si·mism** (pes'ə miz'm) *n.* [< L. *pejor*, worse] 1. the belief that the evil in life outweighs the good 2. the tendency to always expect the worst —**pes'si·mist** *n.* —**pes'si·mis'tic** *adj.* —**pes'si·mis'ti·cal·ly** *adv.*

**pest** (pest) *n.* [< L. *pestis*, plague] 1. a person or thing that is troublesome, destructive, etc.; specif., a rat, fly, weed, etc. 2. [Now Rare] a plague

**pes·ter** (pes'tər) *vt.* [< OFr. *empestrer*, entangle] to annoy; vex

**pest'hole'** *n.* a place infested with an epidemic disease

**pes·ti·cide** (pes'tə sīd') *n.* any chemical for killing insects, weeds, etc.

**pes·tif·er·ous** (pes tif'ər əs) *adj.* [< L. *pestis*, plague + *ferre*, to bear] 1. orig., infectious or diseased 2. noxious 3. [Colloq.] annoying

**pes·ti·lence** (pes't'l əns) *n.* 1. a deadly epidemic disease; plague 2. anything regarded as harmful

**pes'ti·lent** *adj.* [< L. *pestis*, plague] 1. likely to cause death 2. dangerous to society; pernicious 3. annoying

**pes·tle** (pes''l) *n.* [< L. *pinsere*, to pound] a tool used to pound or grind substances, esp. in a mortar

**pet**[1] (pet) *n.* [orig. Scot. dial.] 1. an animal that is domesticated and kept as a companion 2. a person treated with particular indulgence —*adj.* 1. kept or treated as a pet 2. especially liked 3. particular [a pet peeve] 4. showing fondness [a pet name] —*vt.* pet'ted, pet'ting to stroke or pat gently; caress —*vi.* [Colloq.] to kiss, embrace, etc. in making love

**pet**[2] (pet) *n.* [< ?] a sulky mood

**pet·al** (pet''l) *n.* [< Gr. *petalos*, outspread] any of the leaflike parts of a blossom

**pe·tard** (pi tärd') *n.* [< Fr.] an explosive device formerly used to break down doors, walls, etc. —**hoist with (or by) one's own petard** destroyed by the very thing with which one meant to destroy others

**pet·cock** (pet'käk') *n.* [< L. *pedere*, break wind + *cock*, valve] a small valve for draining pipes, radiators, etc.

**Pe·ter** (pēt'ər) 1. ?-64? A.D.; one of the twelve Apostles; reputed author of two Epistles: also *Saint Peter* 2. **Peter I** 1672-1725; czar of Russia (1682-1725): called *Peter the Great*

**pe·ter** (pēt'ər) *vi.* [< ?] [Colloq.] to

become gradually smaller, weaker, etc. and then disappear (with *out*)

**pe·tite** (pə tēt′) *adj.* [Fr.] small and trim in figure: said of a woman

**pe·tit four** (pet′ē fôr′), *pl.* **pe′tits fours′** (pet′ē fôrz′), **pe′tit fours′** [Fr., lit., small oven] a tiny frosted cake

**pe·ti·tion** (pə tish′ən) *n.* [ < L. *petere*, ask ] 1. a solemn, earnest request; entreaty 2. a formal document embodying such a request, often signed by many people —*vt.* 1. to address a petition to 2. to ask for —*vi.* to make a petition —**pe·ti′tion·er** *n.*

**petit jury** a group of citizens picked to weigh the evidence in and decide the issues of a trial in court

**pet·rel** (pet′rəl) *n.* [ < ? St. *Peter:* cf. Matt. 14:29] a small, dark sea bird

**pet·ri·fy** (pet′rə fī′) *vt.* -**fied′**, -**fy′ing** [ < L. *petra*, rock + *facere*, make] 1. to turn into stone 2. to harden or deaden 3. to paralyze, as with fear —**pet′ri·fac′tion** (-fak′shən) *n.*

**pet·ro·chem·i·cal** (pet′rō kem′i k'l) *n.* a chemical ultimately derived from petroleum

**pet·ro·dol·lars** *n.pl.* the revenue gotten by some Middle Eastern countries from the sale of petroleum

**pet·rol** (pet′rəl) *n.* [see PETROLEUM] *Brit. term for* gasoline

**pet·ro·la·tum** (pet′rə lāt′əm) *n.* [ < ff.] a greasy, jellylike substance derived from petroleum and used for ointments, etc. Also **petroleum jelly**

**pe·tro·le·um** (pə trō′lē əm) *n.* [ < L. *petra*, rock + *oleum*, oil] an oily, liquid solution of hydrocarbons occurring naturally in certain rock strata: it yields kerosene, gasoline, etc.

**pet·ti·coat** (pet′i kōt′) *n.* [ < PETTY + COAT] a woman's underskirt

**pet·ti·fog·ger** (pet′ē fäg′ər, -fôg′-) *n.* [ < ff. + *fogger* < ?] a lawyer who handles petty cases, esp. unethically —**pet′ti·fog′** *vi.* -**fogged′**, -**fog′ging**

**pet·tish** (pet′ish) *adj.* [ < PET²] peevish; petulant —**pet′tish·ly** *adv.*

**pet·ty** (pet′ē) *adj.* -**ti·er**, -**ti·est** [ < OFr. *petit*] 1. relatively unimportant 2. small-minded; mean 3. relatively low in rank —**pet′ti·ness** *n.*

**petty cash** a cash fund for incidentals

**petty officer** a naval enlisted man whose rank corresponds to that of a noncommissioned army officer

**pet·u·lant** (pech′oo lənt) *adj.* [ < L. *petere*, to attack] impatient or irritable, esp. over a petty annoyance —**pet′u·lance** *n.* —**pet′u·lant·ly** *adv.*

**pe·tu·ni·a** (pə tōōn′yə, -ē ə) *n.* [ < Braz. *petun*, tobacco] a plant with showy, funnel-shaped flowers

**pew** (pyōō) *n.* [ult. < Gr. *pous*, foot] any of the benches with a back that are fixed in rows in a church

**pew·ter** (pyōōt′ər) *n.* [OFr. *peautre*] 1. a dull, silvery-gray alloy of tin with lead, etc. 2. articles made of this

**pe·yo·te** (pā ōt′ē; *Sp.* pe yō′te) *n.* [AmSp. < AmInd. *peyotl*, caterpillar] the cactus plant mescal: see MESCALINE

**pf., pfd.** preferred

**Pfc, Pfc., PFC** Private First Class

**PG** a motion-picture rating for a film

that parents may find unsuitable for children

**pg.** page

**pha·e·ton** (fā′ət 'n) *n.* [ < *Phaëthon*, son of Helios, Gr. sun god] 1. a light, four-wheeled carriage 2. an early type of open automobile

**pha·lanx** (fā′laŋks) *n., pl.* -**lanx·es**, **pha·lan·ges** (fə lan′jēz) [Gr., line of battle] 1. an ancient close-ranked infantry formation 2. any massed group 3. *pl.* -**lan′ges** any of the bones forming the fingers or toes

**phal·lus** (fal′əs) *n., pl.* -**li** (-ī), -**lus·es** [ < Gr. *phallos*] an image of the penis as the reproductive organ —**phal′lic** *adj.*

**phan·tasm** (fan′taz'm) *n.* [ < Gr. *phantazein*, to show] 1. a figment of the mind 2. a deceptive likeness

**phan·tas·ma·go·ri·a** (fan taz′mə gôr′ē ə) *n.* [ < Gr. *phantasma*, phantasm + *ageirein*, assemble] a rapidly changing series of things seen or imagined, as in a dream

**phan·ta·sy** (fan′tə sē) *n., pl.* -**sies** *same as* FANTASY

**phan·tom** (fan′təm) *n.* [see FANTASY] 1. an apparition; specter 2. an illusion —*adj.* of or like a phantom; illusory

**Phar·aoh** (fer′ō) *n.* the title of the rulers of ancient Egypt

**Phar·i·see** (far′ə sē′) *n.* 1. a member of an ancient Jewish group that observed both the written and oral law 2. [p-] [ < characterization in NT.] a self-righteous, hypocritical person —**phar′i·sa′ic** (-sā′ik) *adj.*

**phar·ma·ceu·ti·cal** (fär′mə sōōt′i k'l) *adj.* [ < Gr. *pharmakon*, a drug] of pharmacy or drugs: also **phar′ma·ceu′tic** —*n.* a drug or medicine

**phar′ma·ceu′tics** (-iks) *n.pl.* [*with sing. v.*] *same as* PHARMACY (sense 1)

**phar·ma·cist** (fär′mə sist) *n.* one licensed to practice pharmacy

**phar′ma·col′o·gy** (-käl′ə jē) *n.* [ < Gr. *pharmakon*, a drug] the science dealing with the effect of drugs on living organisms

**phar′ma·co·pe′ia, phar′ma·co·poe′ia** (-kə pē′ə) *n.* [ < Gr. *pharmakon*, a drug + *poiein*, make] an official book listing drugs and medicines

**phar·ma·cy** (fär′mə sē) *n., pl.* -**cies** [ < Gr. *pharmakon*, a drug] 1. the art or profession of preparing and dispensing drugs and medicines 2. a drugstore

**phar·yn·gi·tis** (far′in jīt′əs) *n.* inflammation of the pharynx

**phar·ynx** (far′iŋks) *n., pl.* **phar′ynx·es**, **pha·ryn·ges** (fə rin′jēz) [Gr.] the cavity leading from the mouth and nasal passages to the larynx and esophagus —**pha·ryn·ge·al** (fə rin′jē əl) *adj.*

**phase** (fāz) *n.* [ < Gr. *phasis*] 1. any stage in a series or cycle of changes, as of the moon's illumination 2. an aspect or side, as of a problem —*vt.* phased, phas′ing to introduce or carry out in stages (often with *in*, *into*, etc.) —**in** (or **out of**) **phase** in (or not in) a synchronized state

**phase out** to terminate (an activity) by stages

**phase'-out'** *n.* a phasing out; gradual termination, withdrawal, etc.

**Ph.D.** Doctor of Philosophy

**pheas·ant** (fez'nt) *n.* [< Gr. *phasianos*, (bird) of *Phasis*, river in Asia] a chickenlike game bird with a long tail and brilliant feathers

**phe·no·bar·bi·tal** (fē'nə bär'bə tôl')-*n.* a white crystalline powder used as a sedative

**phe·nol** (fē'nōl, -nôl) *n.* a white crystalline compound, corrosive and poisonous, used to make synthetic resins, etc., and, in dilute solution (*carbolic acid*), as an antiseptic

**phe·nom·e·non** (fi näm'ə nän', -nən) *n., pl.* **-na** (-nə); also, esp. for 2 & usually for 3, **-nons'** [< Gr. *phainesthai*, appear] **1.** any observable fact or event that can be scientifically described **2.** anything very unusual **3.** [Colloq.] an extraordinary person; prodigy **—phe·nom'e·nal** *adj.*

**phi** (fī, fē) *n.* the 21st letter of the Greek alphabet (Φ, φ)

**phi·al** (fī'əl) *n.* [< Gr. *phialē*, shallow bowl] a small glass bottle; vial

**Phil·a·del·phi·a** (fil'ə del'fē ə) city & port in SE Pa.: pop. 1,949,000

**Philadelphia lawyer** [Colloq.] a shrewd or tricky lawyer

**phi·lan·der** (fi lan'dər) *vi.* [< Gr. *philos*, loving + *anēr*, man] to engage lightly in love affairs: said of a man **—phi·lan'der·er** *n.*

**phi·lan·thro·py** (fi lan'thrə pē) *n.* [< Gr. *philein*, to love + *anthrōpos*, man] **1.** a desire to help mankind, esp. as shown by endowments to institutions, etc. **2.** *pl.* **-pies** a philanthropic gift, institution, etc. **—phil·an·throp·ic** (fil'ən thräp'ik) *adj.* **—phi·lan'thro·pist** *n.*

**phi·lat·e·ly** (fi lat'l ē) *n.* [< Fr. < Gr. *philos*, loving + *ateleia*, exemption from (further) tax (i.e., postage prepaid)] the collection and study of postage stamps, postmarks, etc. **—phi·lat'e·list** *n.*

**-phile** (fīl) [< Gr. *philos*, loving] *a combining form meaning* loving, liking

**phil·har·mon·ic** (fil'här män'ik) *adj.* [< Gr. *philos*, loving + *harmonia*, harmony] devoted to music **—n. 1.** a society sponsoring a symphony orchestra **2.** [Colloq.] such an orchestra

**phi·lip·pic** (fi lip'ik) *n.* [< Gr. *Philippos*, Philip, Macedonian king denounced by Demosthenes] a bitter verbal attack

**Phil·ip·pines** (fil'ə pēnz') country consisting of c.7,100 islands (**Philippine Islands**) off the SE coast of Asia: 114,830 sq. mi.; pop. 34,656,000 **—Phil'ip·pine** *adj.*

**Phil·is·tine** (fil'is tēn', fi lis'tin) *n.* **1.** any of a non-Semitic people of SW Palestine in Biblical times **2.** [*often* **p-**] a person smugly conventional, narrow, lacking culture, etc.

**phil·o·den·dron** (fil'ə den'drən) *n.* [< Gr. *philos*, loving + *dendron*, tree] a tropical American vine

**phi·lol·o·gy** (fi läl'ə jē) *n.* [< Gr. *philein*, to love + *logos*, word] *earlier term for* LINGUISTICS **—phil·o·log·i·cal** (fil'ə läj'i k'l) *adj.* **—phi·lol'o·gist** *n.*

**phi·los·o·pher** (fi läs'ə fər) *n.* [< Gr. *philos*, loving + *sophos*, wise] **1.** one who is learned in philosophy **2.** one who lives by or expounds a system of philosophy **3.** one who meets difficulties with calm composure

**phil·o·soph·ic** (fil'ə säf'ik) *adj.* **1.** of philosophy or philosophers **2.** sensibly composed or calm Also **phil'o·soph'i·cal**

**phi·los·o·phize** (fi läs'ə fīz') *vi.* **-phized', -phiz'ing 1.** to think or reason like a philosopher **2.** to moralize, express truisms, etc.

**phi·los'o·phy** (-fē) *n., pl.* **-phies** [see PHILOSOPHER] **1.** study of the principles underlying conduct, thought, and the nature of the universe **2.** general principles of a field of knowledge **3.** a particular system of ethics **4.** composure; calmness

**phil·ter, phil·tre** (fil'tər) *n.* [< Gr. *philein*, to love] a magic potion, esp. one to arouse sexual love

**phle·bi·tis** (fli bīt'is) *n.* [< Gr. *phleps*, vein + -ITIS] inflammation of a vein

**phlegm** (flem) *n.* [< Gr. *phlegma*, inflammation] **1.** thick mucus discharged from the throat, as during a cold **2.** sluggishness; apathy

**phleg·mat·ic** (fleg mat'ik) *adj.* [see prec.] sluggish or unexcited **—phleg·mat'i·cal·ly** *adv.*

**phlo·em** (flō'em) *n.* [G. < Gr. *phloos*, bark] the vascular tissue through which food is distributed in a plant

**phlox** (fläks) *n.* [Gr., lit., a flame] a N.American plant with clusters of white, red, or bluish flowers

**-phobe** (fōb) [< Gr. *phobos*, fear] *a suffix meaning* one who fears or hates

**pho·bi·a** (fō'bē ə) *n.* [see prec.] an irrational, excessive, and persistent fear of some thing or situation

**-pho·bi·a** (fō'bē ə) *a combining form meaning* fear, hatred [*claustrophobia*]

**phoe·be** (fē'bē) *n.* [< Gr. *phoibos*, bright] a small American bird that catches insects in flight

**Phoe·ni·cia** (fə nish'ə, -nē'shə) ancient country at E end of the Mediterranean **—Phoe·ni'cian** *adj., n.*

**Phoe·nix** (fē'niks) capital of Ariz.: pop. 582,000

**phoe·nix** (fē'niks) *n.* [< Gr. *phoinix*] *Egypt. Myth.* a bird which lived for 500 years and then consumed itself in fire, rising renewed from the ashes

**phone** (fōn) *n., vt., vi.* **phoned, phon'ing** [Colloq.] telephone

**-phone** (fōn) [< Gr. *phōnē*, a sound] *a combining form meaning:* **1.** producing or transmitting sound **2.** telephone

**pho·neme** (fō′nēm) *n.* [< Fr. < Gr. *phōnē,* voice] a set of language sounds with slight variations but heard as the same sound by native speakers —**pho·ne·mic** (fə nē′mik) *adj.*

**pho·net·ics** (fə net′iks) *n.pl.* [*with sing. v.*] [< Gr. *phōnē,* a sound] the study of the production and written representation of speech sounds — **pho·net′ic** *adj.* —**pho·ne·ti·cian** (fō′nə tish′ən) *n.*

**phon·ics** (fän′iks) *n.pl.* [*with sing. v.*] [< Gr. *phōnē,* a sound] a phonetic method of teaching reading —**phon′ic** *adj.* —**phon′i·cal·ly** *adv.*

**pho·no·graph** (fō′nə graf′) *n.* [< Gr. *phōnē,* sound + -GRAPH] an instrument for reproducing sound recorded in a spiral groove on a revolving disk —**pho′no·graph′ic** *adj.*

**pho·nol·o·gy** (fō näl′ə jē) *n.* [< Gr. *phōnē,* sound + -LOGY] **1.** the speech sounds of a language **2.** the study of changes in these —**pho′no·log′i·cal** (-nə läj′i k′l) *adj.*—**pho·nol′o·gist** *n.*

**pho·ny** (fō′nē) *adj.* -**ni·er,** -**ni·est** [< Brit. thieves' argot *fawney,* gilt ring] [Colloq.] not genuine; false —*n., pl.* -**nies** [Colloq.] something or someone not genuine; fraud; fake Also sp. **phoney** —**pho′ni·ness** *n.*

**phoo·ey** (fōō′ē) *interj.* [echoic] an exclamation of scorn, disgust, etc.

**phos·phate** (fäs′fāt) *n.* [Fr.] **1.** a salt or ester of phosphoric acid **2.** a fertilizer that contains phosphates **3.** a flavored carbonated beverage

**phos·pho·res·cence** (fäs′fə res′ns) *n.* **1.** the property of giving off light without noticeable heat, as phosphorus does **2.** such light —**phos′pho·res′cent** *adj.*

**phos·phor·ic acid** (fäs fôr′ik) any of three colorless, crystalline acids with a phosphorus and oxygen radical

**phos·pho·rus** (fäs′fər əs) *n.* [< Gr. *phōs,* a light + *pherein,* to bear] a nonmetallic chemical element, a phosphorescent, waxy solid that ignites spontaneously at room temperature

**pho·to** (fōt′ō) *n., pl.* -**tos** *clipped form of* PHOTOGRAPH

**photo-** *a combining form meaning:* **1.** [< Gr. *phōs,* a light] of or produced by light **2.** [< PHOTOGRAPH] of photography

**pho·to·cop·y** (fōt′ə käp′ē) *n., pl.* -**ies** a photographic reproduction, as of a book page, made by a special device (**pho′to·cop′i·er**)

**pho·to·e·lec·tric cell** (fōt′ō i lek′ trik) any device in which light controls an electric circuit which operates a mechanical device, as for opening doors

**pho′to·en·grav′ing** *n.* **1.** a process by which photographs are reproduced on relief printing plates **2.** such a plate, or a print made from it —**pho′· to·en·grave′** *vt.* -**graved′,** -**grav′ing** —**pho′to·en·grav′er** *n.*

**photo finish** a race finish so close that the winner can be determined only from a photograph of the finish

**pho·to·flash** (fōt′ə flash′) *adj.* designating a flashbulb, etc. electrically synchronized with the camera shutter

**pho·to·gen·ic** (fōt′ə jen′ik) *adj.* [PHOTO- + -GEN + -IC] likely to look attractive in photographs

**pho·to·graph** (fōt′ə graf′) *n.* a picture made by photography —*vt.* to take a photograph of —*vi.* to appear (as specified) in photographs — **pho·tog·ra·pher** (fə täg′rə fər) *n.*

**pho·tog·ra·phy** (fə täg′rə fē) *n.* [PHOTO- + -GRAPHY] the art or process of producing pictorial images on a surface sensitive to light or other radiant energy, as on film in a camera —**pho·to·graph·ic** (fōt′ə graf′ik) *adj.*

**pho·ton** (fō′tän) *n.* [PHOT(O)- + (ELECTR)ON] a quantum of electromagnetic energy

**pho·to·off·set** (fōt′ō ôf′set′) *n.* offset printing in which the text or pictures are photographically transferred to a metal plate from which inked impressions are made on the roller

**Pho·to·stat** (fōt′ə stat′) *a trademark for* a device making photographic copies of printed material, drawings, etc. directly as positives on special paper —*n.* [**p-**] a copy so made —*vt.* [**p-**] -**stat′ed** or -**stat′ted,** -**stat′ing** or -**stat′ting** to make a photostat of

**pho·to·syn·the·sis** (fōt′ə sin′thə sis) *n.* production of organic substances, esp. sugars, from carbon dioxide and water by the action of light on the chlorophyll in green plant cells

**pho′to·syn′the·size** (-sīz′) *vt., vi.* -**sized′,** -**siz′ing** to carry on, or produce by, photosynthesis

**phrase** (frāz) *n.* [< Gr. *phrazein,* speak] **1.** a short, colorful expression **2.** a group of words, not a full sentence or clause, conveying a single thought **3.** a short, distinct musical passage —*vt.* **phrased, phras′ing** to express in words or in a phrase —**phras·al** (frā′z′l) *adj.*

**phra·se·ol·o·gy** (frā′zē äl′ə jē) *n., pl.* -**gies** choice and pattern of words

**phre·net·ic** (fri net′ik) *adj.* [< Gr. *phrenētikos,* mad] *same as* FRENETIC

**phre·nol·o·gy** (fri näl′ə jē) *n.* [< Gr. *phrēn,* mind + -LOGY] a system, now rejected, of analyzing character from the shape of the skull

**phy·lac·ter·y** (fi lak′tər ē) *n., pl.* -**ies** [< Gr. *phylax,* watchman] either of two small leather cases holding Scripture texts, worn in prayer on the forehead and arm by orthodox Jewish men

**phy·log·e·ny** (fi läj′ə nē) *n., pl.* -**nies** [< Gr. *phylon,* tribe + -*geneia,* origin] the origin and evolution of a group or race of animals or plants

**phy·lum** (fi′ləm) *n., pl.* -**la** (-lə) [< Gr. *phylon,* tribe] a main division of the animal kingdom or, loosely, of the plant kingdom

**phys·ic** (fiz′ik) *n.* [< Gr. *physis,* nature] a medicine, esp. a cathartic —*vt.* -**icked,** -**ick·ing** to dose with this

**phys·i·cal** (fiz′i k′l) *adj.* **1.** of nature and all matter; material **2.** of or according to the laws of nature **3.** of, or produced by the forces of, physics **4.** of the body —*n.* a general medical examination —**phys′i·cal·ly** *adv.*

**physical education** instruction in the exercise and care of the body; esp., a course in gymnastics, etc.

**physical science** any science dealing with nonliving matter or energy, as physics, chemistry, or astronomy

**physical therapy** the treatment of disease, injury, etc. by physical means, as by exercise, massage, etc.

**phy·si·cian** (fə zish'ən) *n.* [see PHYSIC] a doctor of medicine

**phys·ics** (fiz'iks) *n.pl.* [*with sing. v.*] [see PHYSIC] the science dealing with the properties, changes, interactions, etc. of matter and energy —**phys'i·cist** (-ə sist) *n.*

**phys·i·og·no·my** (fiz'ē äg'nə mē) *n.* [< Gr. *physis*, nature + *gnōmōn*, judge] facial features and expression

**phys·i·og·ra·phy** (-äg'rə fē) *n.* [see prec. & -GRAPHY] the study of the earth's surface and oceans, atmosphere, etc.

**phys·i·ol·o·gy** (-äl'ə jē) *n.* [< Gr. *physis*, nature + -LOGY] the science dealing with the functions and vital processes of living organisms —**phys'i·o·log'i·cal** (-ə läj'i k'l) *adj.* —**phys'i·ol'o·gist** *n.*

**phys·i·o·ther·a·py** (fiz'ē ō ther'ə pē) *n. same as* PHYSICAL THERAPY

**phy·sique** (fi zēk') *n.* [Fr.] the structure or form of the body; build

**pi¹** (pī) *n., pl.* **pies** [see PIE] 1. jumbled printing type 2. any jumble —*vt.* **pied, pie'ing** or **pi'ing** to jumble

**pi²** (pī) *n.* 1. the sixteenth letter of the Greek alphabet (Π, π) 2. the symbol (π) designating the ratio of the circumference of a circle to its diameter, about 3.1416

**pi·a·nis·si·mo** (pē'ə nis'ə mō') *adj., adv.* [It.] *Music* very soft

**pi·a·nist** (pē an'ist, pyan'-, pē'ən-) *n.* one who plays the piano

**pi·an·o¹** (pē an'ō, pyan'ō) *n., pl.* **-os** [< PIANOFORTE] a large, stringed keyboard instrument: each key operates a felt-covered hammer that strikes a corresponding steel wire or wires

**pi·an·o²** (pē ä'nō, pyä'-) *adj., adv.* [It.] *Music* soft

**pi·an·o·for·te** (pē an'ə fôrt', pyan'ə fôr'tē) *n.* [It. < *piano*, soft + *forte*, strong] *same as* PIANO¹

**pi·as·ter, pi·as·tre** (pē as'tər) *n.* [ult. < L. *emplastrum*, plaster] a unit of currency in Egypt, Syria, etc.

**pi·az·za** (pē at'sə, pyät'-; *for 2* pē az'ə) *n.* 1. in Italy, a public square 2. a veranda

**pi·broch** (pē'bräk) *n.* [< Gael. < *piob*, bagpipe] music for the bagpipe, usually of a martial kind

**pi·ca** (pī'kə) *n.* [< ? ML., directory] a size of printing type, 12 point

**pic·a·resque** (pik'ə resk') *adj.* [< Sp. *pícaro*, rascal] dealing with sharpwitted vagabonds and their adventures [*a picaresque* novel]

**Pi·cas·so** (pi kä'sō), **Pa·blo** (pä'blō) 1881–1973; Sp. artist in France

**pic·a·yune** (pik'ē ōōn') *adj.* [< Fr. *picaillon*, small coin] trivial; petty

**pic·ca·lil·li** (pik'ə lil'ē) *n.* [prob. < PICKLE] a relish of chopped vegetables, mustard, and spices

**pic·co·lo** (pik'ə lō') *n., pl.* **-los** [It., small] a small flute, pitched an octave above the ordinary flute

**pick¹** (pik) *n.* [ME. *pic*, PIKE²] 1. any of several pointed tools for picking, esp. a heavy one used in breaking up soil, rock, etc. 2. a plectrum

**pick²** (pik) *vt.* [ME. *picken*] 1. to pierce, dig up, etc. with something pointed 2. to probe, scratch at, etc. so as to remove or clear something from 3. to gather (flowers, berries, etc.) 4. to prepare (a fowl) by removing the feathers 5. to pull (fibers, rags, etc.) apart 6. to choose; select 7. to provoke (a quarrel or fight) 8. to pluck (the strings) of (a guitar, etc.) 9. to open (a lock) with a wire, etc. instead of a key 10. to steal from (another's pocket, etc.) —*vi.* 1. to use a pick 2. to select, esp. in a fussy way —*n.* 1. the act of choosing or the choice made 2. the best —**pick at** to eat sparingly of —**pick off** 1. to remove by picking 2. to hit with a carefully aimed shot —**pick on** [Colloq.] to single out for criticism or abuse; annoy; tease —**pick out** to choose —**pick up** 1. to grasp and lift 2. to get, find, or learn, esp. by chance 3. to stop for and take along 4. to gain (speed) 5. to improve 6. [Colloq.] to become acquainted with casually, esp. for lovemaking —**pick'er** *n.*

**pick·a·back** (pik'ə bak') *adv., adj. same as* PIGGYBACK

**pick·ax, pick·axe** (pik'aks') *n.* [< OFr. *picquois*] a pick with a point at one end of the head and a chisel-like edge at the other

**pick·er·el** (pik'ər əl) *n., pl.* **-el, -els** [< PIKE³] any of various small, N. American freshwater fishes

**pick·et** (pik'it) *n.* [< Fr. *pic*, PIKE¹] 1. a pointed stake

PICKAX

used in a fence, as a hitching post, etc. 2. a soldier or soldiers stationed to guard against surprise attack 3. a person, as a member of a striking labor union, stationed outside a factory, etc. to demonstrate protest —*vt.* 1. to enclose with a picket fence 2. to hitch (an animal) to a picket 3. to post as a military picket 4. to place pickets, or serve as a picket, at (a factory, etc.)

**picket line** a line or cordon of people serving as pickets

**pick'ings** *n.pl.* something picked; specif., *a)* scraps; remains *b)* something got by effort, often dishonestly

**pick·le** (pik′l) *n.* [< MDu. *pekel*]
1. any brine, vinegar, etc. used to
preserve or marinate food 2. a vegetable, esp. a cucumber, preserved in
this 3. [Colloq.] an awkward situation
—*vt.* -led, -ling to put in a pickle
solution

**pick′pock′et** *n.* a thief who steals
from pockets, as in a crowd

**pick′up′** *n.* 1. a picking up 2. the
process or power of increasing speed
3. a small, open delivery truck 4.
[Colloq.] a casual acquaintance 5.
[Colloq.] improvement 6. a device for
producing electric currents from the
vibrations of a phonograph needle

**pick·y** (pik′ē) *adj.* -i·er, -i·est [Col-
loq.] overly fastidious; fussy

**pic·nic** (pik′nik) *n.* [< Fr.] a pleasure
outing at which a meal is eaten outdoors —*vi.* -nicked, -nick·ing to
have a picnic —**pic′nick·er** *n.*

**pi·cot** (pē′kō) *n.* [< Fr. *pic*, a point]
any of the small loops forming a fancy
edge as on lace

**pic·to·graph** (pik′tə graf′) *n.* 1. a
picture or picturelike symbol used in
a system of writing 2. a graph using
pictures to give data

**pic·to·ri·al** (pik tôr′ē əl) *adj.* 1. of,
containing, or expressed in pictures
2. suggesting a mental image; vivid
—**pic·to′ri·al·ly** *adv.*

**pic·ture** (pik′chər) *n.* [< L. *pingere*,
to paint] 1. a likeness of a person,
scene, etc. produced by drawing,
painting, photography, etc. 2. a perfect likeness or image [the *picture* of
health] 3. anything suggestive of a
beautiful painting, drawing, etc. 4. a
vivid description 5. a motion picture
6. the image on a TV screen —*vt.*
-tured, -tur·ing 1. to make a picture
of 2. to show visibly 3. to describe
4. to imagine —**in** (or **out**) **of the
picture** considered (or not considered)
as involved in a situation

**pic′tur·esque′** (-chə resk′) *adj.* like
or suggestive of a picture; beautiful,
vivid, quaint, etc.

**picture window** a large window that
seems to frame the outside view

**pid·dle** (pid′'l) *vi., vt.* -dled, -dling
[< ?] to dawdle; trifle

**pidg·in** (pij′in) *n.* [supposed Chin.
pronun. of *business*] a jargon for trade
purposes, using words and grammar
from different languages: **pidgin English** uses English words and Chinese
or Melanesian syntax

**pie** (pī) *n.* [ME.] a baked dish of fruit,
meat, etc., with an under or upper
crust, or both —(as) **easy as pie**
[Colloq.] extremely easy

**pie·bald** (pī′bôld′) *adj.* [< *pie*, mag-
pie + BALD] covered with patches of
two colors —*n.* a piebald horse, etc.

**piece** (pēs) *n.* [OFr. *pece*] 1. a part
broken or separated from the whole
2. a section of a whole regarded as
complete in itself 3. any single thing,
specimen, example, etc. [a *piece* of
music] 4. a quantity, as of cloth,
manufactured as a unit —*vt.* **pieced,
piec′ing** 1. to add pieces to, as in
repairing 2. to join (*together*) the

pieces of —**go to pieces** 1. to fall
apart 2. to lose self-control

‡**pièce de ré·sis·tance** (pyes′ də
rā zēs täns′) [Fr., piece of resistance]
1. the principal dish of a meal 2. the
main item in a series

**piece goods** *same as* YARD GOODS

**piece′meal′** (-mēl′) *adv.* [< ME.
*pece*, a piece + -*mele*, part] piece by
piece —*adj.* made or done piecemeal

**piece′work′** *n.* work paid for at a
fixed rate per piece of work done

**pied** (pīd) *adj.* [< *pie*, magpie]
spotted with various colors

**pie′-eyed′** *adj.* [Slang] intoxicated

**pier** (pir) *n.* [< ML. *pera*] 1. a structure supporting the spans of a bridge
2. a structure built out over water
and supported by pillars: used as a
landing place, pavilion, etc. 3. *Archit.*
a heavy column used to support weight

**pierce** (pirs) *vt.* **pierced, pierc′ing**
[< OFr. *percer*] 1. to pass into or
through as a pointed instrument does;
stab 2. to make a hole in 3. to force
a way into; break through 4. to sound
sharply through 5. to penetrate with
the sight or mind —*vi.* to penetrate

**Pierce** (pirs), **Franklin** 1804–69; 14th
president of the U.S. (1853–57)

**Pierre** (pir) capital of S.Dak.: pop.
10,000

**pi·e·ty** (pī′ə tē) *n., pl.* -ties [< L.
*pius*, pious] 1. devotion to religious
duties, etc. 2. devotion to parents,
family, etc. 3. a pious act

**pif·fle** (pif′'l) *n.* [Colloq.] anything
considered trivial or nonsensical —
**pif′fling** *adj.*

**pig** (pig) *n.* [OE. *pigge*] 1. a domesticated animal with a broad snout and a
fat body; swine; hog 2. a young hog
3. a greedy or filthy person 4. an
oblong casting of metal poured from
the smelting furnace

**pi·geon** (pij′ən) *n.* [< LL. *pipire*, to
chirp] any of various related birds
with a small head, plump body, and
short legs

**pi′geon·hole′** *n.* a small open compartment, as in a desk, for filing papers,
etc. —*vt.* -holed′, -hol′ing 1. to put
in the pigeonhole of a desk, etc. 2. to
put aside indefinitely 3. to classify

**pi′geon-toed′** (-tōd′) *adj.* having
the toes or feet turned in

**pig·gish** (pig′ish) *adj.* like a pig; gluttonous; filthy —**pig′gish·ness** *n.*

**pig·gy** (pig′ē) *n., pl.* -gies a little pig
—*adj.* -gi·er, -gi·est *same as* PIGGISH

**pig′gy·back′** *adv., adj.* 1. on the
shoulders or back 2. of or by a transportation system in which loaded truck
trailers are carried on railroad cars

**pig′head′ed** *adj.* stubborn

**pig iron** [see PIG, sense 4] crude iron,
as it comes from the blast furnace

**pig·ment** (pig′mənt) *n.* [< L. *pingere*,
to paint] 1. coloring matter used to
make paints 2. any coloring matter
in the tissues of plants or animals

**pig·men·ta·tion** (pig′mən tā′shən)
*n.* coloration in plants or animals due
to pigment in the tissue

**Pig·my** (pig′mē) *adj., n., pl.* -mies
*same as* PYGMY

**pig′pen′** *n.* a pen where pigs are confined: also **pig′sty′** (-stī′) *pl.* **-sties′**

**pig′skin′** *n.* **1.** leather made from the skin of a pig **2.** [Colloq.] a football

**pig′tail′** (-tāl′) *n.* a long braid of hair hanging at the back of the head

**pike**[1] (pīk) *n. clipped form of* TURNPIKE

**pike**[2] (pīk) *n.* [Fr. *pique*] a former weapon consisting of a metal spearhead on a long wooden shaft (**pikestaff**)

**pike**[3] (pīk) *n., pl.* **pike, pikes** [ME. *pik*] a slender, freshwater fish with a pointed head

**pik·er** (pī′kər) *n.* [< ? Pike County, Missouri] [Slang] one who does things in a petty or niggardly way

**pi·laf, pi·laff** (pi läf′, pē′läf) *n.* [Per. & Turk. *pilāw*] rice boiled in a seasoned liquid and usually containing meat or fish: also **pi·lau′** (-lô′)

**pi·las·ter** (pi las′tər) *n.* [< L. *pila*, a pile] a supporting column projecting slightly from a wall

**Pi·late** (pī′lət), **Pon·tius** (pän′shəs, -chəs) Rom. procurator of Judea who condemned Jesus to be crucified

**pil·chard** (pil′chərd) *n.* [< ?] **1.** a small saltwater fish of the herring family, the commercial sardine of W Europe **2.** any of several related fishes; esp., the **Pacific sardine** found off the W coast of the U.S.

**pile**[1] (pīl) *n.* [< L. *pila*, a pillar] **1.** a mass of things heaped together **2.** a heap of wood, etc. on which a corpse or sacrifice is burned **3.** a large building. **4.** [Colloq.] a large amount **5.** *earlier name for* NUCLEAR REACTOR —*vt.* **piled, pil′ing 1.** to heap up **2.** to load **3.** to accumulate Often with *up* —*vi.* **1.** to form a pile **2.** to move confusedly in a mass (with *in, out, on,* etc.)

**pile**[2] (pīl) *n.* [< L. *pilus*, a hair] a soft, velvety, raised surface of yarn loops, often sheared, as on a rug

**pile**[3] (pīl) *n.* [OE. *pil*] a long, heavy beam driven into the ground to support a bridge, dock, etc.

**pile driver** (or **engine**) a machine for driving piles by raising and dropping a heavy weight on them

**piles** (pīlz) *n.pl.* [< L. *pila*, a ball] *same as* HEMORRHOIDS

**pile′up′** *n.* **1.** an accumulation of tasks, etc. **2.** [Colloq.] a collision involving several vehicles

**pil·fer** (pil′fər) *vt., vi.* [< MFr. *pelfre*, booty] to steal (esp. small sums, etc.) —**pil′fer·age** (-ij) *n.* —**pil′fer·er** *n.*

**pil·grim** (pil′grəm) *n.* [< L. *peregrinus*, foreigner] **1.** a wanderer **2.** one who travels to a shrine or holy place as a religious act **3.** [P-] one of the band of English Puritans who founded Plymouth Colony in 1620

**pil′grim·age** (-ij) *n.* **1.** a journey made by a pilgrim to a shrine or holy place **2.** any long journey

**pill** (pil) *n.* [< L. *pila*, ball] a small ball, tablet, etc. of medicine to be swallowed whole —**the pill** (or **Pill**) [Colloq.] any contraceptive drug for women, in pill form

**pil·lage** (pil′ij) *n.* [< MFr. *piller*, rob] **1.** a plundering **2.** loot —*vt., vi.* **-laged, -lag·ing** to plunder

**pil·lar** (pil′ər) *n.* [< L. *pila*, column] **1.** a slender, vertical structure used as a support or monument; column **2.** a main support of something

**pill′box′** *n.* **1.** a small box for holding pills **2.** an enclosed gun emplacement of concrete and steel

**pil·lion** (pil′yən) *n.* [< L. *pellis*, skin] an extra seat behind the saddle on a horse or motorcycle

**pil·lo·ry** (pil′ər ē) *n., pl.* **-ries** [< OFr. *pilori*] a device with holes for the head and hands, in which petty offenders were formerly locked and exposed to public scorn —*vt.* **-ried, -ry·ing 1.** to punish by placing in a pillory **2.** to lay open to public scorn

**pil·low** (pil′ō) *n.* [OE. *pyle*] a cloth case filled with feathers, etc. used esp. to support the head in sleeping —*vt.* to rest as on a pillow

**pil′low·case′** *n.* a removable covering for a pillow: also **pil′low·slip′**

**pi·lot** (pī′lət) *n.* [< Gr. *pēdon*, oar] **1.** a steersman; specif., one licensed to steer ships into or out of a harbor or through difficult waters **2.** a qualified operator of aircraft **3.** a guide; leader —*vt.* **1.** to act as a pilot of, on, etc. **2.** to guide —*adj.* serving as a trial unit in testing

**pilot film** (or **tape**) a film (or video tape) of a single segment of a projected television series

**pi′lot·house′** *n.* an enclosure for the helmsman on the upper deck of a ship

**pilot light** a small gas burner which is kept lighted to rekindle the principal burner when needed

**pi·men·to** (pi men′tō) *n., pl.* **-tos** [< Sp. < L. *pigmentum*, pigment] a variety of sweet red pepper: also **pi·mien′to** (-myen′-, -men′-)

**pimp** (pimp) *n.* [< ?] a prostitute's agent —*vi.* to act as a pimp

**pim·ple** (pim′p'l) *n.* [< ?] a small, often inflamed, swelling of the skin —**pim′ply** *adj.* **-pli·er, -pli·est**

**pin** (pin) *n.* [OE. *pinn*] **1.** a peg, as of wood, or a pointed piece of stiff wire, for fastening things together, etc. **2.** anything like a pin **3.** an ornament or badge with a pin or clasp for fastening to clothing **4.** Bowling one of the clubs at which the ball is rolled —*vt.* **pinned, pin′ning 1.** to fasten as with a pin **2.** to hold firmly in one position —**on pins and needles** anxious —**pin down 1.** to get (someone) to commit himself as to his plans, etc. **2.** to establish (a fact, etc.) —**pin (something) on someone** [Colloq.] to lay the blame for (something) on someone

**pin·a·fore** (pin′ə fôr′) *n.* [prec. + archaic *afore*, before] a sleeveless garment worn over a dress

**pin′ball′ machine** a game machine

with an inclined board having pins, holes, etc. for scoring automatically the contacts of a spring-driven ball

**pince-nez** (pans'nā', pins'-) *n., pl.* **pince-nez** (-nāz') [Fr., nose-pincher] eyeglasses kept in place by a spring gripping the bridge of the nose

**pin·cers** (pin'sərz) *n.pl.* [*occas. with sing. v.*] [ < OFr. *pincier*, to pinch] **1.** a tool formed of two pivoted parts, used in gripping things **2.** a grasping claw, as of a crab

**pinch** (pinch) *vt.* [ME. *pinchen*] **1.** to squeeze between two surfaces, edges, etc. **2.** to press painfully upon (a toe, etc.) **3.** to make thin, cramped, etc., as by hunger **4.** [Slang] *a)* to steal *b)* to arrest —*vi.* **1.** to squeeze painfully **2.** to be stingy or frugal —*n.* **1.** a squeeze or nip **2.** an amount grasped between finger and thumb **3.** distress or difficulty **4.** an emergency

PINCERS

**pinch·ers** *n.pl.* *same as* PINCERS

**pinch-hit** *vi.* -hit', -hit'ting **1.** *Baseball* to bat in place of the player whose turn it is **2.** to substitute in an emergency (*for*) —**pinch hitter**

**pin curl** a strand of hair kept curled with a bobby pin while it sets

**pin'cush'ion** *n.* a small cushion to stick pins in to keep them handy

**pine**[1] (pīn) *n.* [ < L. *pinus*] **1.** an evergreen tree with cones and needle-shaped leaves **2.** its wood

**pine**[2] (pīn) *vi.* **pined, pin'ing** [ < L. *poena, pain*] **1.** to waste (*away*) through grief, etc. **2.** to yearn

**pin·e·al body** (pin'ē əl) [ < L. *pinea*, pine cone] a small, cone-shaped body in the brain: its function is obscure

**pine'ap'ple** (pīn'ap''l) *n.* [ME. *pinappel*, pine cone] **1.** a juicy, edible tropical fruit somewhat resembling a pine cone **2.** the plant it grows on

**pine tar** a thick, dark liquid obtained from pine wood, used in disinfectants, paints, etc.

**pin'feath'er** *n.* an undeveloped feather just emerging through the skin

**ping** (piŋ) *n.* [echoic] the sound as of a bullet striking something sharply —*vi., vt.* to strike with a ping

**Ping-Pong** (piŋ'pôŋ', -päŋ') [echoic] a trademark for table tennis equipment —*n.* [p- p-] *same as* TABLE TENNIS

**pin'head'** **1.** the head of a pin **2.** a stupid or silly person

**pin'hole'** *n.* **1.** a tiny hole as from a pin **2.** a hole to stick a pin into

**pin·ion** (pin'yən) *n.* [ < L. *pinna*, a feather] **1.** a small cogwheel which meshes with a larger one **2.** the end joint of a bird's wing **3.** a wing **4.** any wing feather —*vt.* **1.** to bind the wings or arms of **2.** to shackle

**pink**[1] (piŋk) *n.* [ < ?] **1.** any of certain plants with white, pink, or red flowers **2.** the flower **3.** pale red **4.** the highest degree, finest example, etc. —*adj.* **1.** pale-red **2.** [Colloq.] somewhat radical —**in the pink** [Colloq.] healthy; fit

**pink**[2] (piŋk) *vt.* [ME. *pynken*] **1.** to cut a saw-toothed edge on (cloth, etc.) **2.** to prick or stab

**pink'eye'** *n.* a contagious eye infection in which the eyeball and the lining of the eyelid are red and inflamed

**pink·ie, pink·y** (piŋ'kē) *n., pl.* -ies the smallest finger

**pink'ing shears** shears with notched blades, for pinking edges of cloth

**pin money** a small sum of money, as for incidental minor expenses

**pin·na·cle** (pin'ə k'l) *n.* [ < L. *pinna*, wing] **1.** a small turret or spire **2.** a slender, pointed formation, as a mountain peak **3.** the highest point

**pin·nate** (pin'āt) *adj.* [ < L. *pinna*, a feather] *Bot.* with leaflets on each side of a common stem

**pi·noch·le, pi·noc·le** (pē'nuk''l) *n.* [ < Fr. *binocle*, eyeglasses] a card game played with a deck of 48 cards (two of every card above the eight)

**pin'point'** *vt.* to locate precisely

**pin'prick'** *n.* **1.** a tiny puncture as from a pin **2.** a minor annoyance

**pins and needles** a tingling feeling as in a numb limb —**on pins and needles** in anxious suspense

**pin'set'ter** *n.* a person or automatic device that sets up bowling pins on the alley: also **pin'spot'ter**

**pin stripe** a pattern of very narrow stripes in suit fabrics, etc.

**pint** (pīnt) *n.* [ < ML.] a measure of capacity equal to 1/2 quart

**pin·to** (pin'tō) *adj.* [ < Sp., spotted] having patches of white and some other color —*n., pl.* -tos a pinto horse

**pinto bean** a mottled kidney bean grown in the SW U.S.

**pin'up'** *adj.* **1.** that is or can be fastened to a wall **2.** [Colloq.] designating an attractive girl whose picture is often pinned up on walls

**pin'wheel'** *n.* **1.** a small wheel with vanes of paper, etc., pinned to a stick so as to revolve in the wind **2.** a revolving firework

**pi·o·neer** (pī'ə nir') *n.* [ < OFr. *peonier*, foot soldier] one who goes before, preparing the way for others, as an early settler —*vi.* to be a pioneer —*vt.* to be a pioneer in or of

**pi·os·i·ty** (pī äs'ə tē) *n., pl.* -ties the quality or state of being overly or insincerely pious

**pi·ous** (pī'əs) *adj.* [ < L. *pius*] **1.** having or showing religious devotion **2.** pretending religious devotion **3.** sacred —**pi'ous·ly** *adv.*

**pip**[1] (pip) *n.* [ < PIPPIN] a small seed, as of an apple

**pip**[2] (pip) *n.* [ < ?] any of the figures or spots on playing cards, dice, etc.

**pip**[3] (pip) *n.* [ < L. *pituita*, phlegm] a contagious disease of fowl

**pipe** (pīp) *n.* [ < L. *pipare*, chirp] **1.** a tube of wood, metal, etc. for making musical sounds **2.** [*pl.*] the bagpipe **3.** a long tube for conveying water, gas, etc. **4.** a tube with a small bowl at one end in which tobacco is smoked **5.** any tubular part, organ, etc. —*vi.* **piped, pip'ing 1.** to play on a pipe **2.** to utter shrill sounds —*vt.* **1.** to play (a tune) on a pipe **2.** to utter in a shrill voice **3.** to bring, call, etc. by piping **4.** to convey (water, gas, etc.) by pipes —**pipe down** [Slang] to shout or talk less —**pip'er** n.

**pipe dream** [Colloq.] a fantastic idea, vain hope or plan, etc.

**pipe fitter** a mechanic who installs and maintains plumbing pipes, etc.

**pipe'line'** n. **1.** a line of pipes for conveying water, gas, etc. **2.** any means whereby something is conveyed

**pipe organ** same as ORGAN (sense 1)

**pip·ing** (pīp'iŋ) n. **1.** music made by pipes **2.** a shrill sound **3.** a pipelike fold of material for trimming seams, etc. —**piping hot** so hot as to sizzle

**pip·it** (pip'it) n. [echoic] a small N.American singing bird

**pip·pin** (pip'in) n. [< OFr. pepin, seed] any of several varieties of apple

**pip·squeak** (pip'skwēk') n. [Colloq.] anyone or anything regarded as small or insignificant

**pi·quant** (pē'kənt) adj. [Fr. < piquer, to prick] **1.** agreeably pungent to the taste **2.** exciting interest; stimulating —**pi'quan·cy** n.

**pique** (pēk) n. [see prec.] resentment at being slighted —vt. **piqued, piqu'-ing** **1.** to arouse such resentment in; offend **2.** to excite; arouse

**pi·qué** (pē kā') n. [see PIQUANT] a cotton fabric with ribbed or corded wales: also **pi·que'**

**pi·ra·cy** (pī'rə sē) n., pl. **-cies** **1.** robbery of ships on the high seas **2.** the unauthorized use of copyrighted or patented work

**pi·ra·nha** (pi rän'yə, -ran'-) n. [< SAmInd. piro, a fish + sainha, tooth] any of several small, voracious, fresh-water, S.American fishes that in schools attack any animal

**pi·rate** (pī'rət) n. [< Gr. peirān, to attack] one who practices piracy —vt., vi. **-rat·ed, -rat·ing** **1.** to take (something) by piracy **2.** to publish or reproduce (a book, recording, etc.) in violation of a copyright —**pi·rat'i·cal** (-rat'i k'l) adj.

**pi·ro·gi** (pi rō'gē) n.pl. [Russ.] small pastry turnovers filled with meat, cheese, etc.; also **pi·ro'gen** (-rō'gən)

**pir·ou·ette** (pir'oo wet') n. [Fr., spinning top] a whirling on one foot or the point of the toe —vi. **-et'ted, -et'ting** to do a pirouette

**pis·ca·to·ri·al** (pis'kə tôr'ē əl) adj. [< L. piscator, fisherman] of fishes, fishermen, or fishing

**Pis·ces** (pī'sēz, pis'ēz) [< L. pl. pisces, fish] the twelfth sign of the zodiac

**pis·mire** (pis'mīr', piz'-) n. [< ME. pisse, urine + mire, ant] an ant

**pis·ta·chi·o** (pi stä'shē ō', -stash'ē ō') n., pl. **-os'** [< OPer. pistah] **1.** a small tree of the cashew family **2.** its edible, greenish seed (**pistachio nut**)

**pis·til** (pis't'l) n. [< L. pistillum, pestle] the seed-bearing organ of a flower —**pis'til·late'** adj.

**pis·tol** (pis't'l) n. [< Czech pist'al] a small firearm held and fired with one hand

**pis'tol·whip'** vt. **-whipped', -whip'-ping** to beat with a pistol, esp. about the head

**pis·ton** (pis't'n) n. [ult. < L. pinsere, to pound] a disk or short cylinder fitted in a hollow cylinder and moved back and forth by the pressure of a fluid so as to transmit motion to a rod (**piston rod**) or moved by the rod so as to exert pressure on the fluid

**piston ring** a split metal ring around a piston to make it fit the cylinder closely

**pit¹** (pit) n. [< MDu. pitte] the hard stone, as of the plum, peach, etc., containing the seed —vt. **pit'ted, pit'-ting** to remove the pit from

**pit²** (pit) n. [< L. puteus, a well] **1.** a hole in the ground **2.** an abyss **3.** a pitfall **4.** any concealed danger **5.** an enclosed area in which animals are kept or made to fight **6.** a small hollow in a surface, as a scar left by smallpox **7.** the section for the orchestra in front of the stage —vt. **pit'ted, pit'-ting** **1.** to make pits or scars in **2.** to set in competition (against) —vi. to become marked with pits

**pit·a·pat** (pit'ə pat') adv. with rapid, strong beating —n. a rapid succession of beats

**pitch¹** (pich) n. [< L. pix] a black, sticky substance formed from coal tar, etc., and used for roofing, etc.

**pitch²** (pich) vt. [ME. picchen] **1.** to set up [pitch a tent] **2.** to throw or toss **3.** to fix at a certain point, degree, key, etc. **4.** Baseball a) to throw (the ball) to the batter b) to assign (a pitcher) c) to act as pitcher for (a game) —vi. **1.** to pitch a ball, etc. **2.** to plunge forward or dip downward **3.** to rise and fall, as a ship in rough water —n. **1.** act or manner of pitching **2.** a throw or toss **3.** anything pitched **4.** a point or degree **5.** the degree of slope **6.** [Slang] a line of talk for persuading **7.** Music, etc. the highness or lowness of a sound due to vibrations of sound waves —**pitch in** [Colloq.] **1.** to begin working hard **2.** to make a contribution —**pitch into** [Colloq.] to attack

**pitch'-black'** adj. very black

**pitch'blende'** (-blend') n. [< G. pech, PITCH¹ + blenden, dazzle] a dark, lustrous mineral containing radium, uranium, etc.

**pitch'-dark'** adj. very dark

**pitched battle** **1.** a battle in which troop placement is relatively fixed beforehand **2.** a hard-fought battle

**pitch·er¹** (pich'ər) n. [< OFr. pichier] a container, usually with a handle and lip, for holding and pouring liquids —**pitch'er·ful'** n.

**pitch·er²** (pich'ər) n. one who pitches; specif., Baseball the player who pitches the ball to the batters

**pitcher plant** a plant with pitcher-like leaves that trap and digest insects

**pitch'fork'** *n.* a large, long-handled fork for lifting and tossing hay, etc.

**pitch'man** (-mən) *n., pl.* **-men** 1. a hawker of novelties, as at a carnival 2. [Slang] any high-pressure salesman

**pitch pipe** a small pipe which produces a fixed tone as a standard for tuning instruments, etc.

**pit·e·ous** (pit'ē əs) *adj.* arousing or deserving pity —**pit'e·ous·ly** *adv.*

**pit'fall'** (-fôl') *n.* [ < PIT² + OE. *fealle*, a trap] 1. a covered pit for trapping animals 2. any unsuspected danger

**pith** (pith) *n.* [OE. *pitha*] 1. the soft, spongy tissue in the center of certain plant stems 2. the essential part; gist

**pith'y** (-ē) *adj.* **-i·er, -i·est** 1. of, like, or full of pith 2. terse and full of meaning —**pith'i·ly** *adv.*

**pit·i·ful** (pit'i fəl) *adj.* 1. arousing or deserving pity 2. contemptible Also **pit'i·a·ble** (-ē ə b'l) —**pit'i·ful·ly** *adv.*

**pit'i·less** (-lis) *adj.* without pity

**pi·ton** (pē'tän) *n.* [Fr. < MFr., a spike] a metal spike with an eye for a rope, driven into rock or ice for support in mountain climbing

**pit·tance** (pit'ns) *n.* [ < OFr. *pitance*, food allowed a monk] 1. a meager allowance of money 2. any small amount or share

**pit·ter-pat·ter** (pit'ər pat'ər) *n.* [echoic] a rapid succession of light tapping sounds

**Pitts·burgh** (pits'bərg) city in SW Pa.; pop. 520,000

**pi·tu·i·tar·y** (pi tōō'ə ter'ē) *adj.* [ < L. *pituita*, phlegm] of a small, oval endocrine gland (**pituitary gland**) attached to the brain: it secretes hormones affecting growth, etc.

**pit·y** (pit'ē) *n., pl.* **-ies** [ < L. *pietas*, piety] 1. sorrow for another's suffering or misfortune 2. a cause for sorrow —*vt., vi.* **-ied, -y·ing** to feel pity (for)

**piv·ot** (piv'ət) *n.* [Fr.] 1. a point, shaft, etc. on which something turns 2. a person or thing something depends on 3. a pivoting movement —*vt.* to provide with a pivot —*vi.* to turn as on a pivot —**piv'ot·al** *adj.*

**pix·ie, pix·y** (pik'sē) *n., pl.* **-ies** [ < Brit. dial.] a fairy or sprite

**pi·zazz, piz·zazz** (pə zaz') *n.* [Slang] 1. energy; vigor 2. style, dash, etc.

**piz·za** (pēt'sə) *n.* [It.] an Italian dish made by baking thin dough covered with tomatoes, cheese, etc.

**piz·ze·ri·a** (pēt'sə rē'ə) *n.* [It.] a place where pizzas are made and sold

**piz·zi·ca·to** (pit'sə kät'ō) *adj.* [It.] *Music* plucked: a direction to pluck the strings of a violin, etc.

**pj's** (pē'jāz') *n.pl.* [Colloq.] pajamas

**pk.** *pl.* **pks.** 1. park 2. peck

**pkg.** package(s)

**pkwy.** parkway

**pl.** 1. place 2. plural

**plac·ard** (plak'ärd, -ərd) *n.* [ < MDu. *placke*, a piece] a notice for display in a public place —*vt.* to place placards on or in

**pla·cate** (plā'kāt, plak'āt) *vt.* **-cat·ed, -cat·ing** [ < L. *placare*] to appease; pacify —**plac·a·ble** (plak'ə b'l, plā'kə-) *adj.* —**pla·ca'tion** *n.*

**place** (plās) *n.* [ < Gr. *plateia*, street] 1. a court or short street in a city 2. space; room 3. a region 4. *a*) the part of space occupied by a person or thing *b*) situation 5. a city, town, etc. 6. a residence 7. a building or space devoted to a special purpose [a *place* of amusement] 8. a particular point, part, position, etc. [a sore *place* on the leg, a *place* in history] 9. a step or point in a sequence 10. the customary or proper position, time, etc. 11. a space, seat, etc. reserved or occupied by a person 12. an office; employment 13. the duties of any position 14. *Racing* the second position at the finish —*vt.* **placed, plac'ing** 1. *a*) to put in a particular place, condition, or relation *b*) to recognize or identify 2. to find employment for 3. to repose (trust) *in* a person or thing 4. to finish in (a specified position) in a race —*vi.* to finish second or among the first three in a race —**take place** to occur

**pla·ce·bo** (plə sē'bō) *n., pl.* **-bos, -boes** [ < L., I shall please] a neutral preparation given as a medicine, as to humor a patient

**place mat** a small mat serving as an individual table cover for a person at a meal

**place'ment** *n.* 1. a placing or being placed 2. location or arrangement

**pla·cen·ta** (plə sen'tə) *n., pl.* **-tas, -tae** (-tē) [ult. < Gr. *plax*, flat object] the structure in the uterus through which the fetus is nourished: cf. AFTERBIRTH —**pla·cen'tal** *adj.*

**plac·er** (plas'ər) *n.* [ < Sp. *placel*] a deposit of gravel or sand containing particles of gold, platinum, etc. that can be washed out

**place setting** the china, silverware, etc. for one place at table

**plac·id** (plas'id) *adj.* [L. *placidus*] calm; quiet —**pla·cid·i·ty** (plə sid'ə tē) *n.* —**plac'id·ly** *adv.*

**plack·et** (plak'it) *n.* [ < ?] a slit at the waist of a skirt or dress to make it easy to put on and take off

**pla·gia·rize** (plā'jə rīz') *vt., vi.* **-rized', -riz'ing** [ < L. *plagiarius*, kidnapper] to take (ideas, writings, etc.) from (another) and offer them as one's own —**pla'gia·rism** (-riz'm), **pla'gia·ry** (-rē) *n.* —**pla'gia·rist** *n.*

**plague** (plāg) *n.* [ < Gr. *plēgē*, misfortune] 1. any affliction or calamity 2. any deadly epidemic disease —*vt.* **plagued, plagu'ing** 1. to afflict with a plague 2. to vex; torment

**plaice** (plās) *n., pl.* **plaice, plaic'es** [ < Gr. *platys*, broad] a kind of flatfish

**plaid** (plad) *n.* [Gael. *plaide*, a blanket] 1. cloth with a crossbarred pattern 2. any pattern of this kind

**plain** (plān) *adj.* [ < L. *planus*, flat] 1. open; clear [in *plain* view] 2. clearly understood; obvious 3. outspoken; straightforward 4. not ornate or luxurious 5. not complicated;

simple **6.** homely **7.** pure; unmixed **8.** common; ordinary *[a plain man]* —*n.* an extent of level country —*adv.* clearly —**plain′ly** *adv.* —**plain′ness** *n.*

**plain′clothes′ man** a detective or policeman who wears civilian clothes on duty: also **plain′clothes′man** (-mən) *n., pl.* -**men**

**plains·man** (plānz′mən) *n., pl.* -**men** an American frontiersman on the western plains

**plain′song′** *n.* a very old, plain kind of church music chanted in unison

**plaint** (plānt) *n.* [< L. *plangere*, to lament] a complaint or lament

**plain·tiff** (plān′tif) *n.* [see prec.] one who brings a lawsuit into a court

**plain·tive** (-tiv) *adj.* [see PLAINT] expressing sorrow or melancholy; sad —**plain′tive·ly** *adv.*

**plait** (plāt) *n.* [< L. *plicare*, to fold] **1.** *same as* PLEAT **2.** a braid of hair, etc. —*vt.* **1.** *same as* PLEAT **2.** to braid

**plan** (plan) *n.* [Fr., plan, foundation] **1.** a diagram showing the arrangement of a structure, piece of ground, etc. **2.** a scheme for making, doing, or arranging something **3.** any outline or sketch —*vt.* **planned, plan′ning 1.** to make a plan of (a structure, etc.) **2.** to devise a scheme for doing, etc. **3.** to have in mind as a project or purpose —*vi.* to make plans —**plan′ner** *n.*

**plane¹** (plān) *adj.* [L. *planus*] **1.** flat; level **2.** of or having to do with flat surfaces or points, lines, etc. on them *[plane* geometry*]* —*n.* **1.** a flat, level surface **2.** a level of achievement, etc. **3.** an airplane **4.** a wing of an airplane

**plane²** (plān) *n.* [< L. *planus,* level] a carpenter's tool for leveling or smoothing wood —*vt.* **planed, plan′ing** to smooth or level with a plane

PLANE

**plan·et** (plan′it) *n.* [< Gr. *planan,* wander] any heavenly body that revolves about the sun: the major planets, in their order from the sun, are Mercury, Venus, Earth, Mars, Jupiter, Saturn, Uranus, Neptune, and Pluto —**plan′e·tar′y** (-ə ter′ē) *adj.*

**plan·e·tar·i·um** (plan′ə ter′ē əm) *n., pl.* -**ums, -a** (-ə) a room with a large dome on which the images of the sun, planets, stars, etc. are projected by a complex optical instrument that revolves to show the principal celestial motions

**plane tree** the American sycamore or a related old-world tree like it

**plank** (plaŋk) *n.* [< LL. *planca*] **1.** a long, broad, thick board **2.** an item in the platform of a political party —*vt.* **1.** to cover with planks **2.** to broil and serve on a board **3.** [Colloq.] to set (*down*) with force

**plank′ing** *n.* **1.** planks in quantity **2.** the planks of a structure

**plank·ton** (plaŋk′tən) *n.* [< Gr. *plazesthai,* wander] the microscopic animal and plant life found floating in bodies of water

**plant** (plant) *n.* [< L. *planta,* a sprout] **1.** a living thing that cannot move voluntarily, has no sense organs, and synthesizes food from carbon dioxide **2.** a soft-stemmed organism of this kind, as distinguished from a tree or shrub **3.** the machinery, buildings, etc. of a factory, etc. —*vt.* **1.** to put into the ground to grow **2.** to set firmly in position **3.** to settle; establish **4.** [Slang] to place (a person or thing) in such a way as to trick, trap, etc.

**plan·tain¹** (plan′tin) *n.* [< L. *plantago*] a plant with basal leaves and spikes of tiny, greenish flowers

**plan·tain²** (plan′tin) *n.* [< Sp. *plá(n)tano,* banana tree] a tropical banana plant yielding a coarse fruit

**plan·tar** (plan′tər) *adj.* [< L. *planta,* sole] of or on the sole of the foot

**plan·ta·tion** (plan tā′shən) *n.* [< L. *plantare,* to plant] **1.** an estate in a warm climate, with crops cultivated by workers living on it **2.** a large, cultivated planting of trees

**plant′er** *n.* **1.** the owner of a plantation **2.** a machine that plants **3.** a decorative container for plants

**plant louse** *same as* APHID

**plaque** (plak) *n.* [Fr. < MDu. *placke,* disk] **1.** a thin, flat piece of metal, wood, etc. with decoration or lettering on it, hung on a wall, etc. **2.** a thin film of matter on uncleaned teeth

**plash** (plash) *vt., vi., n.* [echoic] *same as* SPLASH

**plas·ma** (plaz′mə) *n.* [G. < Gr., something molded] **1.** the fluid part of blood, lymph, or milk **2.** a high-temperature, ionized gas that is electrically neutral

**plas·ter** (plas′tər) *n.* [< Gr. *emplassein,* to daub over] **1.** a pasty mixture of lime, sand, and water, hard when dry, for coating walls, etc. **2.** a pasty preparation spread on cloth and applied to the body as a medicine —*vt.* **1.** to cover as with plaster **2.** to apply like a plaster *[to plaster* posters on walls*]* **3.** to make lie smooth and flat —**plas′ter·er** *n.*

**plas′ter·board′** *n.* thin board formed of layers of plaster and paper, used in wide sheets for walls, etc.

**plaster of Paris** [from use of gypsum from Paris, France] a thick paste of gypsum and water that sets quickly: used for casts, statuary, etc.

**plas·tic** (plas′tik) *adj.* [< Gr. *plassein,* to form] **1.** molding or shaping matter; formative **2.** that can be molded or shaped **3.** made of a plastic —*n.* any of various nonmetallic compounds, synthetically produced, which can be molded and hardened for commercial use —**plas·tic′i·ty** (-tis′ə tē) *n.*

**plas'ti·cize'** (-tə sīz'), *vt.*, *vi.* **-cized',** **-ciz'ing** to make or become plastic

**plastic surgery** surgery dealing with the repair of deformed or destroyed parts of the body, as by transferring skin, bone, etc. from other parts

**plat** (plat) *n.* [var. of PLOT] 1. a small piece of ground 2. a map or plan, as of a subdivision —*vt.* **plat'ted, plat'ting** to make a map or plan of

**plate** (plāt) *n.* [< Gr. *platys,* broad] 1. a smooth, flat, thin piece of metal, etc., specif. one on which an engraving is cut 2. an impression taken from an engraved surface 3. dishes, utensils, etc. of, or plated with, silver or gold 4. a shallow dish 5. the food in a dish; a course 6. a denture, specif. that part of it which fits to the mouth 7. *Baseball* short for HOME PLATE 8. *Photography* a sheet of glass, metal, etc. coated with a film sensitive to light 9. *Printing* a cast made from a mold of set type —*vt.* **plat'ed, plat'ing** 1. to coat with gold, tin, etc. 2. to cover with metal plates

**pla·teau** (pla tō') *n.* [Fr.: see prec.] 1. an elevated tract of level land 2. a temporary halt in progress

**plate glass** polished, clear glass in thick-sheets, for windows, doors, etc.

**plat·en** (plat'ʼn) *n.* [< OFr. *plat,* flat] 1. in a printing press, a flat metal plate which presses the paper against the type 2. in a typewriter, the roller against which the keys strike

**plat·form** (plat'fôrm') *n.* [Fr. *plate-forme,* lit., flat form] 1. a raised horizontal surface, as a stage for speakers, etc. 2. a statement of policy, esp. of a political party

**plat·i·num** (plat'ʼn əm) *n.* [< Sp. *plata,* silver] a steel-gray metallic chemical element, resistant to corrosion: used for jewelry, etc.

**plat·i·tude** (plat'ə tōōd') *n.* [Fr. < *plat,* flat, after *latitude,* etc.] a commonplace or trite remark

**Pla·to** (plā'tō) 427?-347? B.C.; Gr. philosopher

**Pla·ton·ic** (plə tän'ik) *adj.* 1. of Plato or his philosophy 2. [*usually* p-] not sexual but purely spiritual

**pla·toon** (plə tōōn') *n.* [Fr. *peloton,* a group] 1. a military unit composed of two or more squads 2. *Sports* any of the specialized squads making up a team —*vt. Sports* to alternate (players) at a position

**plat·ter** (plat'ər) *n.* [< OFr. *plat,* flat] a large, shallow dish, usually oval, for serving food

**plat·y·pus** (plat'ə pəs) *n., pl.* **-pus·es, -pi** (-pī') [< Gr. *platys,* flat + *pous,* foot] a small, egg-laying water mammal of Australia, with webbed feet and a bill like a duck's: in full **duckbill platypus**

PLATYPUS

**plau·dit** (plô'dit) *n.* [< L. *plaudere,* applaud] [*usually pl.*] applause

**plau·si·ble** (plô'zə b'l) *adj.* [< L. *plaudere,* applaud] seemingly true, trustworthy, etc. —**plau'si·bil'i·ty** *n.*

**play** (plā) *vi.* [OE. *plegan*] 1. to move lightly, rapidly, etc. [*sunlight plays* on the water] 2. to engage in recreation 3. to take part in a game or sport 4. to trifle (*with* a thing or person) 5. to perform on a musical instrument 6. to give out sounds 7. to act in a specified way [*play* dumb] 8. to act in a drama 9. to impose unscrupulously (*on* another's feelings) —*vt.* 1. to take part in (a game or sport) 2. to oppose (a person, etc.) in a game 3. to do, as in fun [*play* tricks] 4. to bet on 5. to cause to move, etc.; wield 6. to cause [*to play* havoc] 7. to perform (music, a drama, etc.) 8. to perform on (an instrument) 9. to act the part of [*to play* Hamlet] —*n.* 1. motion or activity, esp. when free or rapid 2. freedom for motion or action 3. recreation; sport 4. fun; joking 5. the playing of a game 6. a move or act in a game 7. a dramatic composition or performance; drama —**play down to** attach little importance to —**played out** exhausted —**play up to** give prominence to —**play up to** [Colloq.] to try to please by flattery

**play'act'** *vi.* 1. to pretend; make believe 2. to behave in an affected or dramatic manner

**play'back'** *n.* the playing of a disc or tape just after recording on it

**play'boy'** *n.* a man of means who is given to pleasure-seeking

**play'er** *n.* 1. one who plays a specified game, instrument, etc. 2. an actor

**play'ful** *adj.* 1. fond of play or fun 2. jocular —**play'ful·ly** *adv.* —**play'ful·ness** *n.*

**play'go'er** *n.* one who goes to the theater frequently or regularly

**play'ground'** *n.* a place, often near a school, for outdoor recreation

**play'house'** *n.* 1. a theater for live dramatic productions 2. a small house for children to play in

**playing cards** cards used in playing various games, arranged in four suits

**play'mate'** *n.* a companion in games and recreation: also **play'fel'low**

**play'-off'** *n.* a contest to break a tie or to decide a championship

**play on words** a pun or punning

**play'pen'** *n.* a portable enclosure for an infant to play or crawl in safely

**play'thing'** *n.* a toy

**play'wright'** *n.* a person who writes plays; dramatist

**pla·za** (plä'zə, plaz'ə) *n.* [Sp. < L. *platea,* street] 1. a public square in a city or town 2. a shopping center 3. a service area along a superhighway

**plea** (plē) *n.* [< L. *placere,* to please] 1. a statement in defense; excuse 2. a request; appeal 3. *Law* a defendant's answer to charges against him

**plea bargaining** pretrial negotiations in which the defendant agrees to plead guilty to lesser charges if more serious charges are dropped

**plead** (plēd) *vi.* **plead'ed** or (colloq.) **pled** or **plead** (pled), **plead'ing** 1.

to present a plea in a law court 2. to make an appeal; beg —*vt.* 1. to argue (a law case) 2. to answer (guilty or not guilty) to a charge 3. to offer as an excuse —**plead′er** *n.*

**pleas·ant** (plez′nt) *adj.* [< MFr. *plaisir*, to please] 1. agreeable to the mind or senses; pleasing 2. having an agreeable manner, look, etc. —**pleas′ant·ly** *adv.* —**pleas′ant·ness** *n.*

**pleas·ant·ry** (-'n trē) *n., pl.* -ries 1. a humorous remark 2. a polite social remark [exchange *pleasantries*]

**please** (plēz) *vt.* **pleased, pleas′ing** [< L. *placere*] 1. to be agreeable to; satisfy 2. to be the wish of [it *pleased* him to go] —*vi.* 1. to be agreeable; satisfy 2. to have the wish; like [I'll do as I *please*] *Please* is also used in polite requests [please sit]

**pleas·ing** *adj.* giving pleasure; agreeable —**pleas′ing·ly** *adv.*

**pleas·ur·a·ble** (plezh′ər ə b'l) *adj.* pleasant; enjoyable

**pleas·ure** (plezh′ər) *n.* 1. a pleased feeling; delight 2. one's wish, will, or choice 3. a thing that gives delight or satisfaction —**pleas′ure·ful** *adj.*

**pleat** (plēt) *n.* [ME. *pleten*] a flat double fold in cloth, etc., pressed or stitched in place —*vt.* to lay and press (cloth) in a pleat or pleats

**ple·be·ian** (pli bē′ən) *n.* [< L. *plebs*, common people] 1. one of the common people 2. a vulgar, coarse person —*adj.* vulgar or common

**pleb·i·scite** (pleb′ə sīt′) *n.* [< L. *plebs*, common people + *scitum*, decree] a direct vote of the people on a political issue such as annexation, independent nationhood, etc.

**plec·trum** (plek′trəm) *n., pl.* -**trums, -tra** (-trə) [L. < Gr. *plēssein*, to strike] a thin piece of metal, etc. for plucking the strings of a guitar, etc.

**pledge** (plej) *n.* [prob. < OS. *plegan*, to guarantee] 1. the condition of being given or held as security for a contract, payment, etc. 2. a person or thing given or held as such security 3. a promise or agreement 4. something promised —*vt.* **pledged, pledg′ing** 1. to give as security 2. to bind by a promise 3. to promise to give

**ple·na·ry** (plē′nə rē, plen′ə-) *adj.* [< L. *plenus*, full] 1. full; complete 2. for attendance by all members [a *plenary* session]

**plen·i·po·ten·ti·ar·y** (plen′i pə ten′shē er′ē, -shə rē) *adj.* [< L. *plenus*, full + *potens*, powerful] having or conferring full authority —*n., pl.* -**ies** a diplomat given full authority

**plen·i·tude** (plen′ə tōōd′) *n.* [< L. *plenus*, full] 1. fullness; completeness 2. abundance; plenty

**plen·te·ous** (plen′tē əs) *adj.* plentiful

**plen·ti·ful** (plen′ti fəl) *adj.* 1. having or yielding plenty 2. abundant —**plen′ti·ful·ly** *adv.*

**plen·ty** (plen′tē) *n.* [< L. *plenus*, full] 1. prosperity; opulence 2. a

sufficient supply 3. a large number —*adv.* [Colloq.] very; quite

**pleth·o·ra** (pleth′ə rə) *n.* [< Gr. *plēthos*, fullness] an overabundance

**pleu·ri·sy** (ploor′ə sē) *n.* [< L. *pleura*, a rib] inflammation of the thin membrane which lines the chest and covers the lungs, characterized by painful breathing

**Plex·i·glas** (plek′sə glas′) *a trademark for* a lightweight, transparent thermoplastic substance —*n.* this material: also **plex′i·glass**

**plex·us** (plek′səs) *n., pl.* -**us·es, -us** [< L. *plectere*, to twine] a network, as of blood vessels, nerves, etc.

**pli·a·ble** (plī′ə b'l) *adj.* [< L. *plicare*, to fold] 1. easily bent; flexible 2. easily influenced or persuaded 3. adaptable —**pli′a·bil′i·ty** *n.*

**pli·ant** (plī′ənt) *adj.* 1. easily bent; pliable 2. compliant —**pli′an·cy** *n.*

**pli·ers** (plī′ərz) *n.pl.* [< PLY¹] small pincers for gripping small objects, bending wire, etc.

**plight¹** (plīt) *n.* [< OFr. *pleit*, a fold] a distressing situation

**plight²** (plīt) *vt.* [OE. *pliht*, danger] to pledge, or bind by a pledge

**plinth** (plinth) *n.* [< Gr. *plinthos*, a brick] the square block at the base of a column, pedestal, etc.

**plod** (pläd) *vi.* **plod′ded, plod′ding** [prob. echoic] 1. to move heavily and laboriously; trudge 2. to work steadily; drudge —**plod′der** *n.*

**plop** (pläp) *vt., vi.* **plopped, plop′ping** [echoic] to drop with a sound like that of something flat falling into water —*n.* such a sound

**plot** (plät) *n.* [OE.] 1. a small area of ground 2. a secret, usually evil, scheme 3. the plan of action of a play, novel, etc. —*vt.* **plot′ted, plot′ting** 1. to mark or trace on a chart or map 2. to make secret plans for —*vi.* to scheme —**plot′ter** *n.*

**plov·er** (pluv′ər, plō′vər) *n.* [< L. *pluvia*, rain] a shore bird with a short tail and long, pointed wings

**plow** (plou) *n.* [OE. *ploh*] 1. a farm implement used to cut and turn up the soil 2. any implement like this, as a snowplow —*vt.* 1. to cut and turn up (soil) with a plow 2. to make (one's way) through as if by plowing —*vi.* 1. to use a plow 2. to move (*through, into,* etc.) with force 3. to plod 4. to begin work vigorously (with *into*) Also, chiefly Brit., **plough** —**plow′-man** (-mən) *n., pl.* -**men**

**plow′share′** (-sher′) *n.* the cutting blade of a plow

**ploy** (ploi) *n.* [< ? (EM)PLOY] an action intended to outwit someone

**pluck** (pluk) *vt.* [OE. *pluccian*] 1. to pull off or out; pick 2. to snatch 3. to pull feathers or hair from 4. to pull at (a taut string, etc.) and release quickly —*vi.* to pull (*at*) —*n.* 1. a pulling 2. courage

**pluck·y** *adj.* -**i·er, -i·est** brave;

spirited; resolute —**pluck'i·ness** n.
**plug** (plug) n. [MDu. *plugge*] 1. an object used to stop up a hole, etc. 2. a cake of tobacco 3. an electrical device, as with prongs, for making contact or closing a circuit 4. a kind of fishing lure 5. [Colloq.] a free boost, advertisement, etc. 6. [Slang] an old, worn-out horse —vt. **plugged, plug'ging** 1. to fill (a hole, etc.) with a plug 2. to insert a plug of 3. [Colloq.] to advertise with a plug 4. [Slang] to shoot a bullet into —vi. [Colloq.] to work doggedly

**plug·o'la** (-ō'lə) n. [< PLUG, n. 5] [Slang] the paying of a bribe, or a bribe paid, for underhanded promotion on radio or TV

**plum** (plum) n. [OE. *plume*] 1. a) a tree bearing a smooth-skinned fruit with a flattened stone b) the fruit 2. a raisin 3. the bluish-red color of some plums 4. something desirable

**plum·age** (plōō'mij) n. [MFr. < *plume*, a feather] a bird's feathers

**plumb** (plum) n. [< L. *plumbum*, LEAD²] a lead weight hung at the end of a line (**plumb line**), used to determine how deep water is or whether a wall, etc. is vertical —adj. perfectly vertical —adv. 1. straight down 2. [Colloq.] entirely —vt. 1. to test or sound with a plumb 2. to probe or fathom —**out of plumb** not vertical

**plumb·er** (plum'ər) n. [see prec.] a worker who installs and repairs pipes, fixtures, etc., as of water systems
**plumber's helper** (or **friend**) [Colloq.] same as PLUNGER (sense 2)

**plumb·ing** (plum'iŋ) n. 1. the work of a plumber 2. the pipes and fixtures with which a plumber works

**plume** (plōōm) n. [< L. *pluma*] 1. a feather, esp. a large, showy one 2. a group of these —vt. **plumed, plum'ing** 1. to adorn with plumes 2. to preen —**plum'y** adj. **-i·er, -i·est**

**plum·met** (plum'it) n. [see PLUMB] 1. a plumb 2. a thing that weighs heavily —vi. to fall straight downward

**plump¹** (plump) adj. [< MDu. *plomp*, bulky] full and rounded in form; chubby —**plump'ness** n.

**plump²** (plump) vi., vt. [echoic] to drop or bump suddenly or heavily —n. 1. a falling, bumping, etc. 2. the sound of this —adv. 1. suddenly; heavily 2. straight down

**plun·der** (plun'dər) vt., vi. [< G. *plunder*, baggage] 1. to rob or pillage 2. to take (property) by force or fraud —n. 1. a plundering 2. things taken by force or fraud

**plunge** (plunj) vt. **plunged, plung'ing** [see PLUMB] to thrust or throw suddenly (*into* a liquid, condition, etc.) —vi. 1. to dive or rush 2. to move violently and rapidly downward or forward 3. [Colloq.] to gamble heavily —n. 1. a dive or fall 2. [Colloq.] a gamble

**plung'er** n. 1. one who plunges 2. a large, rubber suction cup used to free clogged drains 3. any cylindrical device that operates with a plunging motion, as a piston

**plunk** (pluŋk) vt. [echoic] 1. to strum (a banjo, etc.) 2. to throw or put down heavily —vi. 1. to give out a twanging sound 2. to fall heavily —n. the sound made by plunking —**plunk down** [Colloq.] to give in payment

**plu·ral** (ploor'əl) adj. [< L. *plus*, more] more than one —n. *Gram.* the form of a word designating more than one (e.g., *hands, men*)

**plu·ral·i·ty** (ploo ral'ə tē) n., pl. **-ties** 1. a being plural or numerous 2. a) the excess of votes in an election that the leading candidate has over his nearest rival b) a majority

**plu·ral·ize** (ploor'ə līz') vt. **-ized', -iz'ing** to make plural

**plus** (plus) prep. [L., more] 1. added to [2 plus 2] 2. in addition to —adj. 1. indicating addition 2. positive [a *plus* quantity] 3. somewhat higher than [graded B *plus*] 4. involving extra gain [a *plus* factor] 5. [Colloq.] and more [personality *plus*] —n., pl. **plus'es, plus'ses** 1. a sign (**plus sign**, +) indicating addition or positive quantity 2. something added 3. an advantage; benefit

**plush** (plush) n. [< L. *pilus*, hair] a fabric with a soft, thick pile —adj. [Slang] luxurious: also **plush'y**

**Plu·tarch** (plōō'tärk) 46?–120? A.D.; Gr. biographer

**Plu·to** (plōōt'ō) 1. *Gr. & Rom. Myth.* the god of the lower world 2. the outermost planet: cf. PLANET

**plu·toc·ra·cy** (plōō täk'rə sē) n., pl. **-cies** [< Gr. *ploutos*, wealth + *kratein*, to rule] 1. government by the wealthy 2. a group of wealthy people who control a government

**plu·to·crat** (plōōt'ə krat') n. 1. a member of a plutocracy 2. one whose wealth gives him control or influence —**plu'to·crat'ic** adj.

**plu·to·ni·um** (plōō tō'nē əm) n. [< PLUTO (planet)] a radioactive, metallic chemical element

**plu·vi·al** (plōō'vē əl) adj. [< L. *pluvia*, rain] of, or having much, rain

**ply¹** (plī) vt. **plied, ply'ing** [< L. *plicare*, to fold] to twist, fold, etc. —n., pl. **plies** 1. a thickness or layer, as of cloth, plywood, etc. 2. any of the twisted strands in rope, etc.

**ply²** (plī) vt. **plied, ply'ing** [contr. < APPLY] 1. to use (a tool, faculty, etc.), esp. with energy 2. to work at (a trade) 3. to keep supplying, assailing, etc. (*with*) 4. to sail back and forth across —vi. 1. to keep busy 2. to travel regularly (*between* places), as a ship or bus

**Plym·outh** (plim'əth) village on the SE coast of Mass.: settled by the Pilgrims (1620)

**ply'wood'** n. [PLY¹ + WOOD] a construction material made of thin layers of wood glued together

**P.M., p.m., PM** [L. *post meridiem*] after noon: used to designate the time from noon to midnight

**pneu·mat·ic** (nōō mat'ik) adj. [< Gr. *pneuma*, breath] 1. of or containing wind, air, or gases 2. filled with or worked by compressed air

**pneu·mo·ni·a** (noo mōn′yə) *n.* [< Gr. *pneumōn*, a lung < *pnein*, breathe] inflammation of the lungs caused as by bacteria or viruses

**Po** (pō) river in N Italy

**P.O., p.o.** post office

**poach**[1] (pōch) *vt.* [< MFr. *poche*, a pocket: the yolk is "pocketed" in the white] to cook (an egg without its shell, fish, etc.) in or over boiling water

**poach**[2] (pōch) *vt., vi.* [< MHG. *puchen*, to plunder] 1. to trespass on (private property), esp. for hunting or fishing 2. to hunt or catch (game or fish) illegally —**poach′er** *n.*

**pock** (päk) *n.* [OE. *pocc*] 1. a pustule caused by smallpox, etc. 2. *same as* POCKMARK —**pocked** *adj.*

**pock·et** (päk′it) *n.* [< OFr. *poke*, a bag] 1. a little bag or pouch, esp. one sewn into clothing, for carrying small articles 2. a pouchlike cavity or hollow 3. a small area or group *[a pocket of poverty]* 4. *Geology* a cavity filled as with ore —*adj.* 1. that can be carried in a pocket 2. small —*vt.* 1. to put into a pocket 2. to envelop; enclose 3. to take (money, etc.) dishonestly 4. to suppress *[to pocket one's pride]* —**pock′et·ful′** *n., pl.* -**fuls′**

**pock′et·book′** *n.* 1. a woman's purse 2. monetary resources

**pock′et·knife′** *n., pl.* -**knives′** a knife with a blade or blades that fold into the handle

**pock·mark** (päk′märk′) *n.* a scar left by a pustule, as of smallpox

**pod** (päd) *n.* [< ?] a dry fruit or seed vessel, as of peas, beans, etc.

**-pod** (päd) [< Gr. *pous*, foot] *a combining form meaning:* 1. foot 2. (one) having a (specified number or kind of) feet Also —**pode** (pōd)

**po·di·a·try** (pō dī′ə trē) *n.* [< Gr. *pous*, foot + -IATRY] the profession dealing with the care and treatment of the feet —**po·di′a·trist** *n.*

**po·di·um** (pō′dē əm) *n., pl.* -**di·a** (-ə) [L. < Gr. *pous*, foot] a small platform, as for an orchestra conductor

**Poe** (pō), **Edgar Allan** 1809–49; U.S. poet & short-story writer

**po·em** (pō′əm) *n.* [< Gr. *poiein*, to make] an arrangement of words, esp. a rhythmical composition, sometimes rhymed, in a style more imaginative than ordinary speech

**po·e·sy** (pō′ə sē′) *n. old-fashioned var. of POETRY*

**po′et** (-ət) *n.* 1. one who writes poems 2. one who expresses himself with beauty of thought and language —**po′et·ess** *n.fem.* (now rare)

**po·et·as·ter** (pō′ə tas′tər) *n.* [< prec. + Gr. *-aster*, dim. suffix] a writer of mediocre verse

**po·et·ic** (pō et′ik) *adj.* 1. of or for poets or poetry 2. having the beauty, imagination, etc. of poetry Also **po·et′i·cal** —**po·et′i·cal·ly** *adv.*

**poetic license** disregard of strict fact or rules, for artistic effect

**poet laureate** the official poet of a nation, appointed to write poems celebrating national events, etc.

**po·et·ry** (pō′ə trē) *n.* 1. the writing of poems 2. poems 3. poetic qualities

**po·grom** (pō gräm′, pō′grəm) *n.* [< Russ., desolation] an organized massacre, as of Jews in Czarist Russia

**poi** (poi) *n.* [Haw.] a pastelike Hawaiian food made of taro root

**poign·ant** (poin′yənt) *adj.* [< L. *pungere*, to prick] 1. pungent 2. *a)* sharply painful to the feelings *b)* emotionally moving 3. sharp, biting, pointed, etc. —**poign′an·cy** *n.*

**poin·ci·a·na** (poin′sē an′ə) *n.* [< M. de *Poinci*, a governor of the Fr. West Indies] a small tropical tree or shrub with showy red or yellow flowers

**poin·set·ti·a** (poin set′ē ə, -set′ə) *n.* [< J. R. *Poinsett*, 19th-c. U.S. ambassador to Mexico] a tropical shrub with yellow flowers and petallike, red leaves

**point** (point) *n.* [< L. *pungere*, to prick] 1. a dot in writing, etc. *[a decimal point]* 2. a position or location 3. the exact moment 4. a condition reached *[boiling point]* 5. a detail; item *[point by point]* 6. a distinguishing feature 7. a unit, as of value, game scores, etc. 8. a sharp end 9. a projecting piece of land; cape 10. the essential fact or idea *[the point of a joke]* 11. a purpose; object 12. a convincing idea or fact 13. a helpful hint 14. a mark showing direction on a compass 15. *Printing* a measuring unit for type, about 1/72 of an inch —*vt.* 1. to sharpen to a point 2. to give (a story, etc.) emphasis (usually with *up*) 3. to show (usually with *out*) *[point out the way]* 4. to aim —*vi.* 1. to direct one's finger (*at* or *to*) 2. to call attention (*to*) 3. to be directed (*to* or *toward*) —**at the point of** very close to —**beside the point** irrelevant —**to the point** pertinent; apt: also **in point**

**point′-blank′** *adj., adv.* [prec. + *blank* (white center of a target)] 1. (aimed) straight at a mark 2. direct(ly); blunt(ly)

**point′ed** *adj.* 1. having a sharp end 2. sharp; incisive 3. aimed at someone, as a remark 4. very evident —**point′ed·ly** *adv.*

**point′er** *n.* 1. a long, tapered rod for pointing to things 2. an indicator on a meter, etc. 3. a large, lean hunting dog with a smooth coat 4. [Colloq.] a helpful hint or suggestion

**poin·til·lism** (pwan′t'l iz′m, -tē iz′m; point′l-) *n.* [Fr.] a style of painting using dots of color that blend together when seen from a distance —**poin·til·list** *n., adj.*

**point′less** *adj.* 1. without a point 2. without meaning or force; senseless

**point of view** 1. the way in which something is viewed 2. a mental attitude or opinion

**point′y** *adj.* -**i·er**, -**i·est** 1. coming to a sharp point 2. many-pointed

**poise** (poiz) n. [< L. pendere, weigh]
1. balance; stability  2. ease and dignity of manner  3. carriage, as of the body —vt., vi. poised, pois'ing to balance or be balanced

**poi·son** (poi'z'n) n. [< L. potio, potion] a substance which in small quantities can cause illness or death —vt. 1. to harm or kill with poison  2. to put poison into  3. to influence wrongfully —adj. poisonous

**poison ivy** a plant having leaves of three leaflets and ivory-colored berries: it can cause a severe rash

**poi'son·ous** adj. that can injure or kill by or as by poison —poi'son·ous·ly adv.

**poke¹** (pōk) vt. poked, pok'ing [< MDu. poken] 1. a) to prod, as with a stick  b) [Slang] to hit  2. to make (a hole, etc.) by poking —vi. 1. to jab (at)  2. to pry or search (about or around)  3. to move slowly (along) —n. 1. a jab; thrust  2. [Slang] a blow with the fist —poke fun (at) to ridicule

**poke²** (pōk) n. [OFr.] [Dial.] a sack

**pok·er¹** (pō'kər) n. [< ? Fr. poque] a gambling game at cards

**pok·er²** (pō'kər) n. a bar, usually of iron, for stirring a fire

**poker face** [Colloq.] an expressionless face, as of a poker player trying to conceal the nature of his hand

**pok·y** (pō'kē) adj. -i·er, -i·est [< POKE¹ + -Y²] 1. slow; dull  2. small and uncomfortable, as a room  Also pok'ey

**pol** (päl) n. [Slang] a politician

**Pol.** 1. Poland  2. Polish

**Po·land** (pō'lənd) country in C Europe: 120,625 sq. mi.; pop. 31,944,000; cap. Warsaw

**po·lar** (pō'lər) adj. 1. of or near the North or South Pole  2. of a pole

**polar bear** a large, white bear of the arctic regions

**Po·la·ris** (pō lar'is) same as NORTH STAR

**po·lar·i·ty** (pō lar'ə tē) n., pl. -ties 1. the property of having opposite magnetic poles  2. the tendency to turn, grow, think, etc. in contrary directions, as if because of magnetic repulsion

POLAR BEAR

**po·lar·i·za·tion** (pō'lər i zā'shən) n. 1. a polarizing or being polarized  2. Optics a condition, or the production of a condition, of light in which the vibrations of the waves are confined to one plane or one direction

**po·lar·ize** (pō'lə rīz') vt. -ized', -iz'ing to give polarity to —vi. to acquire polarity; specif., to separate into opposed or antagonistic groups, viewpoints, etc.

**Po·lar·oid** (pō'lə roid') a trademark for: 1. a transparent material capable of polarizing light  2. a camera that produces a print within seconds: in full Polaroid (Land) camera

**Pole** (pōl) n. a native or inhabitant of Poland

**pole¹** (pōl) n. [< L. palus, a stake] a long, slender piece of wood, metal, etc.

—vt., vi. poled, pol'ing to propel (a boat or raft) with a pole —pol'er n.

**pole²** (pōl) n. [< Gr. polos] 1. either end of any axis, as of the earth  2. either of two opposed forces, parts, etc., as the ends of a magnet, the terminals of a battery, etc.

**pole·cat** (pōl'kat') n. [prob. < OFr. poule, hen + CAT] 1. a small, weasel-like animal of Europe  2. a skunk

**po·lem·ic** (pə lem'ik) adj. [< Gr. polemos, war] of or involving dispute: also **po·lem'i·cal** —n. (a) controversy

**po·lem'ics** n.pl. [with sing. v.] the art or practice of disputation —**po·lem'i·cist** (-ə sist) n.

**pole'star'** n. 1. Polaris, the North Star  2. a guiding principle

**pole vault** a leap for height by vaulting over a bar with the aid of a long pole —**pole'-vault'** vi. —**pole'-vault'er** n.

**po·lice** (pə lēs') n. [Fr., ult. < Gr. polis, city] 1. the governmental department (of a city, state, etc.) for keeping order, detecting crime, etc.  2. [with pl. v.] the members of such a department —vt. -liced', -lic'ing 1. to control, protect, etc. with police or a similar force  2. to keep (a military camp, etc.) clean and orderly

**po·lice'man** (-mən) n., pl. -men a member of a police force —**po·lice'wom'an** n.fem., pl. -wom'en

**police state** a government that seeks to suppress political opposition by means of police

**pol·i·cy¹** (päl'ə sē) n., pl. -cies [see POLICE] 1. wise management  2. a principle, plan, etc., as of a government

**pol·i·cy²** (päl'ə sē) n., pl. -cies [< Gr. apodeixis, proof] a written insurance contract: in full **insurance policy**

**po·li·o·my·e·li·tis** (pō'lē ō mī'ə lī'təs) n. [< Gr. polios, gray + MYELITIS] an acute infectious disease caused by a virus inflammation of the gray matter of the spinal cord, often resulting in muscular paralysis: also **po'li·o'**

**Pol·ish** (pō'lish) adj. of Poland, its people, their language, etc. —n. the Slavic language of the Poles

**pol·ish** (päl'ish) vt. [< L. polire] 1. to smooth and brighten, as by rubbing  2. to refine (manners, style, etc.) —vi. to take a polish —n. 1. surface gloss  2. elegance, refinement, etc.  3. a substance used to polish —**polish off** [Colloq.] to finish (a meal, job, etc.) completely

**po·lite** (pə līt') adj. [< L. polire, to polish] 1. cultured; refined  2. having good manners; courteous —**po·lite'ly** adv. —**po·lite'ness** n.

**pol·i·tesse** (päl'ə tes') n. [Fr.] politeness; courtesy

**pol·i·tic** (päl'ə tik) adj. [see POLICE] 1. having practical wisdom; prudent  2. expedient, as a plan —vi. -ticked, -tick·ing to campaign in politics

**po·lit·i·cal** (pə lit'i k'l) adj. 1. of, concerned with, or engaged in government, politics, etc.  2. of or characteristic of political parties or politicians —**po·lit'i·cal·ly** adv.

**political science** the science of the

principles, organization, and methods of government —**political scientist**

**pol·i·ti·cian** (päl'ə tish'ən) *n.* one actively engaged in politics: often used with implications of seeking personal or partisan gain, scheming, etc.

**po·lit·i·cize** (pə lit'ə sīz') *vt.* -**cized'**, -**ciz'ing** to make political

**po·lit·i·co** (pə lit'i kō') *n., pl.* -**cos'** [< Sp. or It.] a politician

**pol·i·tics** (päl'ə tiks) *n.pl.* [*with sing. or pl. v.*] 1. the science of government 2. political affairs 3. political methods, tactics, etc. 4. political opinions, etc. 5. factional scheming for power

**pol'i·ty** *n., pl.* -**ties** [see POLICE] 1. governmental organization 2. a society with a government; state

**Polk** (pōk), **James K.** 1795-1849; 11th president of the U.S. (1845-49)

**pol·ka** (pōl'kə) *n.* [Czech, Polish dance] 1. a fast dance for couples 2. music for this dance

**pol·ka dot** (pō'kə) any of a pattern of small, round dots on cloth

**poll** (pōl) *n.* [ME. *pol*] 1. the head 2. a counting, listing, etc. of persons, esp. of voters 3. the number of votes recorded 4. [*pl.*] a place where votes are cast 5. a canvassing of people's opinions on some question —*vt.* 1. to cut off or cut short the wool, hair, horns, etc. of 2. to register the votes of 3. to receive (a specified number of votes) 4. to cast (a vote) 5. to canvass in a poll (sense 5)

**pol·len** (päl'ən) *n.* [L., dust] the yellow, powderlike male sex cells in the anther of the stamen of a flower

**pollen count** the number of grains of pollen, esp. of ragweed, in a given volume of air at a specified time and place

**pol·li·nate** (päl'ə nāt') *vt.* -**nat'ed**, -**nat'ing** to transfer pollen to the pistil of (a flower) —**pol'li·na'tion** *n.*

**pol·li·wog** (päl'ē wäg') *n.* [< ME.: see POLL & WIGGLE] a tadpole

**poll·ster** (pōl'stər) *n.* one whose work is taking public opinion polls

**pol·lute** (pə lōōt') *vt.* -**lut'ed**, -**lut'ing** [< L. *polluere*] to make unclean or impure; defile —**pol·lu'tant** *n.* —**pol·lu'tion** *n.*

**po·lo** (pō'lō) *n.* [prob. < Tibetan *pulu*, ball] a game played on horseback by two teams, using a wooden ball and long-handled mallets

**Po·lo** (pō'lō), **Mar·co** (mär'kō) 1254?-1324?; Venetian traveler in E Asia

**po·lo·naise** (päl'ə nāz') *n.* [Fr. (fem.), Polish] a stately Polish dance

**pol·ter·geist** (pōl'tər gīst') *n.* [G. < *poltern*, to rumble + *geist*, ghost] a ghost supposed to be responsible for mysterious noisy disturbances

**pol·troon** (päl trōōn') *n.* [< It. *poltrone*] a thorough coward

**poly-** [< Gr. *polys*] a combining form meaning much, many

**pol·y·clin·ic** (päl'i klin'ik) *n.* [POLY- + CLINIC] a clinic or hospital for the

treatment of various kinds of diseases

**pol·y·es·ter** (päl'ē es'tər) *n.* [POLY(MER) + ESTER] a polymeric resin used in making plastics, fibers, etc.

**pol·y·eth·yl·ene** (päl'ē eth'ə lēn') *n.* [POLY(MER) + ETHYLENE] a thermoplastic resin used in making plastics, films, etc.

**po·lyg·a·my** (pə lig'ə mē) *n.* [< Gr. *poly-*, many + *gamos*, marriage] the practice of having two or more wives or husbands at the same time —**po·lyg'a·mist** *n.* —**po·lyg'a·mous** *adj.*

**pol·y·glot** (päl'i glät') *adj.* [< Gr. *poly-*, many + *glōtta*, tongue] 1. speaking or writing several languages 2. written in several languages —*n.* 1. a polyglot person 2. a polyglot book

**pol·y·gon** (päl'i gän') *n.* [< Gr.: see POLY- & -GON] a plane figure, esp. one with more than four sides and angles —**po·lyg·o·nal** (pə lig'ə n'l) *adj.*

**pol·y·graph** (-graf') *n.* [see POLY- & -GRAPH] a device measuring changes in respiration, pulse rate, etc., used on persons suspected of lying

**pol·y·math** (-math') *n.* [< Gr. *poly-*, much + *manthanein*, learn] a person of great and varied learning

**pol·y·mer** (-mər) *n.* [G. < Gr. *poly-*, many + *meros*, part] a substance consisting of giant molecules formed from smaller molecules of the same kind —**po·lym·er·ize** (pə lim'ər īz', päl'i mər-) *vt., vi.* -**ized'**, -**iz'ing**

**Pol·y·ne·sia** (päl'ə nē'zhə) group of Pacific islands, east of Micronesia —**Pol'y·ne'sian** *adj., n.*

**pol·yp** (päl'ip) *n.* [< Gr. *poly-*, many + *pous*, foot] 1. a small water animal with tentacles at the top of a tubelike body 2. a growth on mucous membrane, as in the bladder

**po·lyph·o·ny** (pə lif'ə nē) *n.* [< Gr. *poly-*, many + *phōnē*, a sound] *Music* a combining of individual, harmonizing tones, as in a fugue; counterpoint —**pol·y·phon·ic** (päl'i fän'ik) *adj.* —**pol·y·phon'i·cal·ly** *adv.*

**pol·y·syl·lab·ic** (päl'i si lab'ik) *adj.* 1. having four or more syllables 2. characterized by polysyllabic words —**pol'y·syl'la·ble** (-sil'ə b'l) *n.*

**pol·y·tech·nic** (-tek'nik) *adj.* [< Gr. *poly-*, many + *technē*, an art] of or providing instruction in many scientific and technical subjects

**pol'y·the·ism** (-thē iz'm) *n.* [< Gr. *poly-*, many + *theos*, god] belief in more than one god —**pol'y·the·ist** *adj., n.* —**pol'y·the·is'tic** *adj.*

**pol'y·un·sat'u·rat'ed** (-un sach'ə rāt'id) *adj.* designating any of certain plant and animal fats and oils with a low cholesterol content

**pol·y·vi·nyl** (-vī'n'l) *adj.* designating or of any of a group of polymerized vinyl compounds: see VINYL

**po·made** (pä mād', pō-; -mäd') *n.* [< It. *pomo*, apple (orig. an ingredient)] a perfumed ointment, as for the hair

**pome·gran·ate** (päm'gran'it, päm'

ə-; pum**/**-) *n.* [ult. < L. *pomum,* fruit + *granum,* seed] 1. a round, red fruit with a hard rind and many seeds 2. the bush or tree it grows on

**pom·mel** (pum**/**l; *also, for n.,* päm**/**l) *n.* [< L. *pomum,* fruit] the rounded, upward-projecting front part of a saddle —*vt.* -**meled** or -**melled,** -**mel·ing** or -**mel·ling** to pummel

**pomp** (pämp) *n.* [< Gr. *pompē,* solemn procession] 1. stately display 2. ostentatious show or display

**pom·pa·dour** (päm**/**pə dôr**/**) *n.* [< Mme. *Pompadour,* mistress of Louis XV] a hairdo in which the hair is brushed up high from the forehead

**pom·pa·no** (päm**/**pə nō**/**) *n., pl.* -**no/, -nos/** [< Sp.] a spiny-finned food fish of N.America and the West Indies

**pom·pon** (päm**/**pän**/**, -päm**/**) *n.* [Fr.] 1. an ornamental tuft of silk, etc., as worn on hats 2. a chrysanthemum or dahlia with small, round flowers

**pom·pous** (päm**/**pəs) *adj.* 1. full of pomp 2. pretentious; self-important —**pom·pos/i·ty** (-päs**/**ə tē) *n.*

**pon·cho** (pän**/**chō) *n., pl.* -**chos** [Am-Sp. < SAmInd.] a cloak like a blanket with a hole in the middle for the head, esp. one worn as a raincoat

**pond** (pänd) *n.* [< ME. *pounde,* enclosure] a body of standing water smaller than a lake

**pon·der** (pän**/**dər) *vi., vt.* [< L. *ponderare,* weigh] to think deeply (about); consider carefully

**pon·der·o·sa** (**pine**) (pän**/**də rō**/**sə) [< L. *ponderosus,* heavy] a yellow pine of western N. America

**pon/der·ous** *adj.* 1. very heavy 2. unwieldy 3. labored and dull

**pone** (pōn) *n.* [<AmInd.] corn bread in the form of small ovals

**pon·gee** (pän jē**/**) *n.* [< Chin. dial. *pen-chi,* domestic loom] a soft, thin silk cloth, usually in its natural tan

**pon·iard** (pän**/**yərd) *n.* [ult. < L. *pugnus,* fist] a dagger

**pon·tiff** (pän**/**tif) *n.* [< L. *pontifex,* high priest] a bishop; specif., [P-] the Pope —**pon·tif/i·cal** *adj.*

**pon·tif/i·cate** (-i kit; *for v.* -i kāt**/**) *n.* the office or term of a pontiff —*vi.* -**cat/ed,** -**cat/ing** 1. to officiate as a pontiff 2. to be pompous or dogmatic

**pon·toon** (pän tōōn**/**) *n.* [< L. *pons,* a bridge] 1. a flat-bottomed boat 2. any of a row of boats or floating objects used to support a temporary bridge 3. a boatlike float on an aircraft's landing gear

**po·ny** (pō**/**nē) *n., pl.* -**nies** [prob. < L. *pullus,* foal] 1. a horse of any small breed 2. a small liqueur glass 3. [Colloq.] a literal translation of a foreign work, used in doing schoolwork

**po/ny·tail/** *n.* a hair style in which the hair is tied tightly at the back and hangs down like a pony's tail

**pooch** (pōōch) *n.* [< ?] [Slang] a dog

**poo·dle** (pōō**/**d'l) *n.* [G. *pudel*] a dog with a solid-colored, curly coat

**pooh** (pōō) *interj.* an exclamation of disdain, disbelief, or impatience

**pooh-pooh** (pōō**/**pōō**/**) *vt.* to treat disdainfully; make light of

**pool¹** (pōōl) *n.* [OE. *pol*] 1. a small pond 2. a puddle 3. a small collection of liquid 4. a tank for swimming

**pool²** (pōōl) *n.* [< LL. *pulla,* hen] 1. a game of billiards played on a table with six pockets 2. a combination of resources, funds, supplies, etc. for some common purpose 3. the parties forming such a combination —*vt., vi.* to contribute to a common fund

**poop¹** (pōōp) *n.* [< L. *puppis,* stern of a ship] a raised deck at the stern of a ship: also **poop deck**

**poop²** (pōōp) *vt.* [Slang] to tire

**poor** (poor) *adj.* [< L. *pauper,* poor] 1. having little or no means of support; needy 2. lacking in some quality; specif., *a*) inadequate *b*) inferior or worthless *c*) contemptible 3. worthy of pity; unfortunate —**the poor** poor, or needy people —**poor/ly** *adv.*

**poor/house/** *n.* formerly, a publicly supported institution for paupers

**poor/-mouth/** *vi.* [Colloq.] to complain about one's lack of money

**pop¹** (päp) *n.* [echoic] 1. a sudden, light, explosive sound 2. any carbonated, nonalcoholic beverage —*vi.* **popped, pop/ping** 1. to make, or burst with, a pop 2. to move, go, etc. suddenly 3. to bulge: said of the eyes 4. *Baseball* to hit the ball high into the infield —*vt.* 1. to cause to pop, as corn by roasting 2. to put suddenly [he *popped* his head in] —**pop/per** *n.*

**pop²** (päp) *n.* [< PAPA] [Slang] father

**pop³** (päp) *adj. clip of* POPULAR

**pop.** 1. popular 2. population

**pop (art)** a realistic art style using techniques and subjects from commercial art, comic strips, posters, etc.

**pop/corn/** *n.* 1. a variety of corn with hard grains which pop open into a white, puffy mass when heated 2. the popped grains

**pope** (pōp) *n.* [< Gr. *papas,* father] [*usually* P-] R.C.Ch. the bishop of Rome and head of the Church

**Pope** (pōp), **Alexander** 1688-1744; Eng. poet

**pop/gun/** *n.* a toy gun that shoots pellets by air compression, with a pop

**pop·in·jay** (päp/in jā**/**) *n.* [< Ar. *babaghā,* parrot] a conceited person

**pop·lar** (päp**/**lər) *n.* [< L. *populus*] 1. a tall tree of the willow family having soft, fibrous wood 2. its wood

**pop·lin** (päp**/**lən) *n.* [prob. < *Poperinge,* city in Flanders] a sturdy ribbed fabric of cotton, silk, etc.

**pop/o/ver** (-ō**/**vər) *n.* a very light, puffy, hollow muffin

**pop·py** (päp**/**ē) *n., pl.* -**pies** [< L. *papaver*] a plant with a milky juice and variously colored flowers

**pop/py·cock/** (-käk**/**) *n.* [Colloq.] foolish talk; nonsense

**poppy seed** the small, dark seed of the poppy, used in baking, etc.

**pop·u·lace** (päp**/**yə lis) *n.* [< L. *populus*] 1. the common people; the masses 2. population (sense 1*a*)

**pop·u·lar** (päp**/**yə lər) *adj.* [< L. *populus,* the people] 1. of, carried on by, or intended for people generally 2. not expensive [*popular* prices] 3.

commonly accepted; prevalent **4.** liked by many people —**pop'u·lar'i·ty** (-lar'ə tē) *n.* —**pop'u·lar·ly** *adv.*

**pop·u·lar·ize** (päp'yə lə rīz') *vt.* **-ized', -iz'ing** to make popular —**pop'u·lar·i·za'tion** *n.*

**pop·u·late** (päp'yə lāt') *vt.* **-lat'ed, -lat'ing** [< L. *populus*, the people] **1.** to inhabit **2.** to supply with inhabitants

**pop'u·la'tion** *n.* **1.** *a)* all the people in a country, region, etc. *b)* the number of these **2.** a populating or being populated

**population explosion** the great and rapid increase in human population in modern times

**pop·u·lism** (päp'yə liz'm) *n.* any movement to advance the interests of the common people —**pop'u·list** *adj., n.*

**pop·u·lous** (päp'yə ləs) *adj.* full of people; thickly populated

**por·ce·lain** (pôr's'l in) *n.* [< It. *porcellana*] a hard, white, translucent variety of ceramic ware

**porch** (pôrch) *n.* [< L. *porta*, gate] **1.** a covered entrance to a building **2.** an open or enclosed gallery or room on the outside of a building

**por·cine** (pôr'sīn, -sin) *adj.* [< L. *porcus*, a hog] of or like pigs or hogs

**por·cu·pine** (pôr'kyə pīn') *n.* [< L. *porcus*, pig + *spina*, spine] a rodent having coarse hair mixed with long, stiff, sharp spines

**pore¹** (pôr) *vi.* **pored, por'ing** [ME. *poren*] **1.** to study carefully (with *over*) **2.** to ponder (with *over*)

**pore²** (pôr) *n.* [< Gr. *poros*, passage] a tiny opening, as in plant leaves, skin, etc. for absorbing or discharging fluids

**pork** (pôrk) *n.* [< L. *porcus*, pig] the flesh of a pig used as food

**pork barrel** [Colloq.] government appropriations for political patronage

**pork'y** *adj.* **-i·er, -i·est** **1.** of or like pork **2.** [Slang] saucy, cocky, etc.

**por·no** (pôr'nō) *n., adj. clipped form* of PORNOGRAPHY, PORNOGRAPHIC: also **porn** (pôrn)

**por·nog·ra·phy** (pôr näg'rə fē) *n.* [< Gr. *pornē*, a prostitute + *graphein*, write] writings, pictures, etc. intended primarily to arouse sexual desire — **por'no·graph'ic** (-nə graf'ik) *adj.*

**po·rous** (pôr'əs) *adj.* full of pores, through which fluids, air, or light may pass —**po·ros·i·ty** (pô räs'ə tē) *n.*

**por·phy·ry** (pôr'fər ē) *n., pl.* **-ries** [< Gr. *porphyros*, purple] any igneous rock with large, distinct crystals

**por·poise** (pôr'pəs) *n.* [< L. *porcus*, pig + *piscis*, a fish] **1.** a small whale with a blunt snout **2.** a dolphin

**por·ridge** (pôr'ij) *n.* [< POTTAGE by confusion with VL. *porrata*, leek broth] [Chiefly Brit.] a soft food of cereal or meal boiled in water or milk

**por'rin·ger** (-in jər) *n.* [< Fr. *potager*, soup dish: infl. by prec.] a bowl for porridge, cereal, etc.

**port¹** (pôrt) *n.* [< L. *portus*, haven] **1.** a harbor **2.** a city with a harbor where ships load and unload cargo

**port²** (pôrt) *n.* [< *Oporto*, city in Portugal] a sweet, dark-red wine

**port³** (pôrt) *vt.* [< L. *portare*, carry] to hold (a rifle, etc.) diagonally in front of one, as for inspection

**port⁴** (pôrt) *n.* [prob. < PORT¹] the left side of a ship, etc. as one faces the bow —*adj.* of or on the port —*vt., vi.* to turn (the helm) to the port side

**port⁵** (pôrt) *n.* [< L. *porta*, door] **1.** a porthole **2.** an opening, as in a valve face, for the passage of steam, etc.

**Port. 1.** Portugal **2.** Portuguese

**port·a·ble** (pôr'tə b'l) *adj.* [< L. *portare*, carry] **1.** that can be carried **2.** easily carried —*n.* something portable —**port'a·bil'i·ty** *n.*

**por·tage** (pôr'tij) *n.* [< L. *portare*, carry] **1.** a carrying of boats and supplies overland between navigable rivers, lakes, etc. **2.** any route over which this is done —*vt., vi.* **-taged, -tag·ing** to carry (boats, etc.) over a portage

**por·tal** (pôr't'l) *n.* [< L. *porta*, door] a doorway, gate, or entrance

**port·cul·lis** (pôrt kul'is) *n.* [< MFr. *porte*, gate + *coleice*, sliding] a heavy iron grating lowered to bar the gateway of a castle or fortified town

**por·tend** (pôr tend') *vt.* [< L. *por-*, forth + *tendere*, to stretch] **1.** to be an omen of; presage **2.** to signify

**por·tent** (pôr'tent) *n.* **1.** something that portends an event **2.** significance

**por·ten·tous** (pôr ten'təs) *adj.* **1.** portending evil; ominous **2.** amazing **3.** pompous; self-important —**por·ten'tous·ly** *adv.*

**por·ter¹** (pôr'tər) *n.* [< L. *porta*, gate] a doorman or gatekeeper

**por·ter²** (pôr'tər) *n.* [< L. *portare*, carry] **1.** a man who carries luggage, etc. for hire **2.** a man who sweeps, cleans, etc. in a bank, store, etc. **3.** a railroad attendant for passengers as on a sleeper **4.** a dark-brown beer

**por'ter·house'** (**steak**) (-hous') [orig., a tavern: see PORTER², sense 4] a choice cut of beef between the tenderloin and the sirloin

**port·fo·li·o** (pôrt fō'lē ō') *n., pl.* **-os'** [< L. *portare*, carry + *folium*, leaf] **1.** a flat, portable case for loose papers, etc.; briefcase **2.** the office of a minister of state **3.** a list of an investor's securities

**port·hole** (pôrt'hōl') *n.* an opening in a ship's side to admit light and air

**por·ti·co** (pôr'tə kō') *n., pl.* **-coes', -cos'** [< L. *porticus*] a porch or covered walk, consisting of a roof supported by columns

**por·tiere, por·tière** (pôr tyer') *n.* [Fr. < *porte*, door] a curtain hung in a doorway

**por·tion** (pôr'shən) *n.* [< L. *portio*] **1.** a part, esp. that allotted to a person; share **2.** a dowry **3.** one's lot; destiny

---

fat, āpe, cär; ten, ēven; is, bīte; gō, hôrn, tōōl, look; oil, out; up, fur; chin; she; thin, then; zh, leisure; ŋ, ring; ə for *a* in *ago*; ', (ā'b'l); ë, Fr. coeur; ö, Fr. feu; Fr. mon; ü, Fr. duc; kh, G. ich, doch; ‡ foreign; < derived from

—*vt.* 1. to divide into portions 2. to give as a portion to

**Port·land** (pôrt′lənd) 1. city & port in NW Oreg.: pop. 383,000 2. seaport in SE Maine: pop. 65,000

**port·ly** (pôrt′lē) *adj.* -**li·er**, -**li·est** 1. large and stately 2. stout; corpulent —**port′li·ness** *n.*

**port·man·teau** (pôrt man′tō) *n., pl.* -**teaus**, -**teaux** (-tōz) [< Fr. *porter*, carry + *manteau*, a cloak] a stiff suitcase that opens into two compartments

**portmanteau word** a word that is a combination of two other words (Ex.: *smog*, from *smoke* and *fog*)

**Por·to Ri·co** (pôr′tə rē′kō) *former name of* PUERTO RICO —**Por′to Ri′can**

**por·trait** (pôr′trit, -trāt) *n.* [see PORTRAY] 1. a painting, photograph, etc. of a person, esp. of his face 2. a description, portrayal, etc.

**por′trai·ture** (-tri chər) *n.* the practice or art of portraying

**por·tray** (pôr trā′) *vt.* [< L. *pro-*, forth + *trahere*, draw] 1. to make a portrait of 2. to describe graphically 3. to play the part of in a play, movie, etc. —**por·tray′al** *n.*

**Ports·mouth** (pôrts′məth) seaport in SE Va.: pop. 111,000

**Por·tu·gal** (pôr′chə gəl) country in SW Europe, on the Atlantic: 35,509 sq. mi.; pop. 9,228,000

**Por′tu·guese′** (-gēz′) *adj.* of Portugal, its people, their language, etc. —*n.* 1. *pl.* -**guese′** a native or inhabitant of Portugal 2. the Romance language of Portugal and Brazil

**por·tu·lac·a** (pôr′chə lak′ə) *n.* [< L. *portula*, small door: from opening in its seed capsule] a fleshy plant with yellow, pink, or purple flowers

**pose** (pōz) *vt.* posed, pos′ing [< LL. *pausare*, to rest] 1. to propose (a question, etc.) 2. to put (a model, etc.) in a certain attitude —*vi.* 1. to assume a certain attitude, as in modeling for an artist 2. to strike attitudes for effect 3. to set oneself up (*as*) [to pose as an officer] —*n.* 1. a bodily attitude, esp. one held for an artist, etc. 2. behavior assumed for effect

**Po·sei·don** (pō sī′d′n) the Greek god of the sea

**pos·er** (pō′zər) *n.* 1. one who poses; affected person: also **po·seur** (pō zur′) 2. a baffling question

**posh** (päsh) *adj.* [< ?] [Colloq.] luxurious and fashionable —**posh′ly** *adv.* —**posh′ness** *n.*

**pos·it** (päz′it) *vt.* [see ff.] to suppose to be a fact; postulate

**po·si·tion** (pə zish′ən) *n.* [< L. *ponere*, to place] 1. the way in which a person or thing is placed or arranged 2. one's attitude or opinion 3. the place where one is; location 4. the usual or proper place 5. rank, esp. high rank 6. a post of employment; job —*vt.* to put in a certain position

**pos·i·tive** (päz′ə tiv) *adj.* [see prec.] 1. definitely set; explicit [*positive* instructions] 2. *a)* having the mind set; confident *b)* overconfident or dogmatic 3. showing agreement; affirmative 4. constructive [*positive* criticism]

5. regarded as having real existence [a *positive* good] 6. based on facts [*positive* proof] 7. *Elec. a)* of electricity predominating in a glass body after it has been rubbed with silk *b)* charged with positive electricity *c)* having a deficiency of electrons 8. *Gram.* of an adjective or adverb in its uncompared degree 9. *Math.* greater than zero 10. *Photog.* with the lights and shades corresponding to those of the subject —*n.* something positive, as a degree, quality, quantity, photographic print, etc. —**pos′i·tive·ly** *adv.*

**pos·i·tron** (päz′ə trän′) *n.* [POSI(TIVE) + (ELEC)TRON] the positive antiparticle of an electron, having the same mass and magnitude of charge

**poss.** possessive

**pos·se** (päs′ē) *n.* [L., be able] the body of men summoned by a sheriff to assist him in keeping the peace, etc.

**pos·sess** (pə zes′) *vt.* [< L. *possidere*] 1. to have as belonging to one; own 2. to have as an attribute, quality, etc. 3. to gain control over [*possessed* by an idea] —**pos·ses′sor** *n.*

**pos·sessed′** *adj.* 1. owned 2. controlled as if by a demon; crazed

**pos·ses·sion** (-zesh′ən) *n.* 1. a possessing or being possessed 2. anything possessed 3. [*pl.*] property; wealth 4. territory ruled by an outside country

**pos·ses′sive** (-zes′iv) *adj.* 1. of possession 2. showing or desiring possession 3. *Gram.* designating or of a case, form, or construction expressing possession (Ex.: *my*, *Bill's*) —*n. Gram.* the possessive case, form, or construction —**pos·ses′sive·ness** *n.*

**pos·si·ble** (päs′ə b′l) *adj.* [< L. *posse*, be able] 1. that can be or exist 2. that may or may not happen 3. that can be done, selected, etc. 4. permissible —**pos′si·bil′i·ty** (-bil′ə tē) *n., pl.* -**ties**

**pos′si·bly** (-blē) *adv.* 1. by any possible means 2. perhaps; maybe

**pos·sum** (päs′əm) *n.* [Colloq.] *same as* OPOSSUM —**play possum** to pretend to be asleep, dead, ill, etc.

**post¹** (pōst) *n.* [< L. *postis*] 1. a piece of wood, metal, etc., set upright to support a building, sign, etc. 2. the starting point of a horse race —*vt.* 1. to put up (a poster, etc.) on (a wall, etc.) 2. to announce by posting notices 3. to warn against trespassing on by posted notices 4. to put (a name) into a posted or published list

**post²** (pōst) *n.* [< Fr. < It. *posto*] 1. the place where a soldier, guard, etc. is stationed 2. *a)* a place where troops are garrisoned *b)* the troops at such a place 3. the place assigned to one 4. a job or duty —*vt.* 1. to assign to a post 2. to put up (a bond, etc.)

**post³** (pōst) *n.* [< Fr. < It. *posta*] [Chiefly Brit.] (the) mail —*vi.* to travel fast; hasten —*vt.* 1. [Chiefly Brit.] to mail 2. to inform [keep me *posted*]

**post-** [L. < *post*, after] *a prefix meaning*: 1. after in time, later (than) [*postgraduate*] 2. after in space, behind

**post·age** (pōs′tij) *n.* the amount

charged for mailing a letter, etc., esp. as represented by stamps

**post·al** (pōs′t′l) *adj.* [Fr.] of mail or post offices

**postal card** a card with a printed postage stamp, for use in the mails

**post card** a card, often a picture card, that can be sent through the mail when a postage stamp is affixed

**post·date′** *vt.* -dat′ed, -dat′ing 1. to assign a later date to than the actual date 2. to be subsequent to

**post·er** (pōs′tər) *n.* a large advertisement or notice posted publicly

**pos·te·ri·or** (pās tir′ē ər) *adj.* [L. < *post*, after] 1. later; following 2. at the rear; behind —*n.* the buttocks

**pos·ter·i·ty** (pās ter′ə tē) *n.* [see prec.] 1. all of a person's descendants 2. all future generations

**post exchange** a nonprofit general store at an army post or camp

**post′grad′u·ate** *adj.* of or taking a course of study after graduation —*n.* a student taking such courses

**post′haste′** *adv.* with great haste

**post·hu·mous** (pās′choo məs) *adj.* [< L. *postumus*, last] 1. born after the father's death 2. published after the author's death 3. arising or continuing after one's death —**post′hu·mous·ly** *adv.*

**post·hyp·not·ic** (pōst′hip nät′ik) *adj.* in or for the period following a hypnotic trance [*posthypnotic* suggestion]

**pos·til·ion, pos·til·lion** (pōs til′yən, pās-) *n.* [Fr. < It. *posta*, a post] one who rides the leading left-hand horse of a team drawing a carriage

**post·lude** (pōst′lōōd′) *n.* [POST- + (PRE)LUDE] a concluding musical piece

**post′man** (-mən) *n., pl.* -men same as MAILMAN

**post′mark′** *n.* a post-office mark stamped on mail, canceling the postage stamp and recording the date and place —*vt.* to stamp with a postmark

**post′mas′ter** *n.* a manager of a post office —**post′mis′tress** *n.fem.*

**postmaster general** *pl.* postmasters general, postmaster generals the head of a government's postal system

**post me·ri·di·em** (mə rid′ē əm) [L.] after noon: abbrev. **P.M.**

**post-mor·tem** (pōst môr′təm) *adj.* [L.] 1. after death 2. of a postmortem —*n.* 1. an examination of a body after death 2. an evaluation of some event just ended

**post·na·sal drip** (pōst′nā′z′l) a discharge of mucus from behind the nose onto the pharynx, due to a cold, etc.

**post′na′tal** (-nāt′′l) *adj.* after birth

**post office** 1. the governmental department in charge of the mails 2. a place where mail is sorted, postage stamps are sold, etc.

**post′op′er·a·tive** (-āp′ər ə tiv) *adj.* occurring after a surgical operation

**post′paid′** *adj.* with postage prepaid

**post·pone** (pōst pōn′) *vt.* -poned′, -pon′ing [< L. *post-*, after + *ponere*, put] to put off until later; delay —**post·pone′ment** *n.*

**post·script** (pōst′skript′) *n.* [< L. *post-*, after + *scribere*, write] a note added below the signature of a letter

**post time** the scheduled starting time of a horse race

**pos·tu·late** (pās′chə lāt′; *for n.* -lit) *vt.* -lat′ed, -lat′ing [< L. *postulare*, to demand] 1. to assume to be true, real, etc., esp. as a basis for argument 2. to take for granted —*n.* 1. something postulated 2. a prerequisite

**pos·ture** (pās′chər) *n.* [MFr. < L. *ponere*, to place] 1. the position or carriage of the body 2. a position assumed as in posing 3. an official stand or position [*our national posture*] —*vi.* -tured, -tur·ing to pose or assume an attitude: also **pos′tur·ize′** -ized′, -iz′ing

**post′war′** *adj.* after the (or a) war

**po·sy** (pō′zē) *n., pl.* -sies [< POESY] a flower or bouquet: old-fashioned term

**pot** (pät) *n.* [OE. *pott*] 1. a round vessel for holding liquids, cooking, etc. 2. a pot with its contents 3. [Colloq.] all the money bet at a single time 4. [Slang] marijuana —*vt.* pot′ted, pot′ting 1. to put into a pot 2. to cook or preserve in a pot —**go to pot** to go to ruin —**pot′ful′** *n., pl.* -fuls′

**po·ta·ble** (pōt′ə b′l) *adj.* [< L. *potare*, to drink] drinkable —*n.* something drinkable —**po′ta·bil′i·ty** *n.*

**pot·ash** (pät′ash′) *n.* [< Du. *pot*, pot + *asch*, ASH[1]] a potassium compound obtained from wood ashes, etc. and used in fertilizers, soaps, etc.

**po·tas·si·um** (pə tas′ē əm) *n.* [see prec.] a soft, silver-white, metallic chemical element: its salts are used in fertilizers, glass, etc.

**po·ta·to** (pə tāt′ō) *n., pl.* -toes [< WInd.] 1. the starchy tuber of a widely cultivated plant, eaten as a cooked vegetable 2. this plant

**potato chip** a very thin slice of potato fried crisp and then salted

**pot′bel′ly** *n., pl.* -lies a protruding belly —**pot′bel′lied** *adj.*

**pot′boil′er** *n.* a piece of writing, etc. done quickly to earn money

**po·tent** (pōt′′nt) *adj.* [< L. *posse*, be able] 1. having authority or power 2. convincing; cogent 3. effective, as a drug 4. able to have sexual intercourse: said of a male —**po′ten·cy** *n.*

**po·ten·tate** (pōt′′n tāt′) *n.* a person having great power; ruler; monarch

**po·ten·tial** (pə ten′shəl) *adj.* [see POTENT] that can come into being; possible; latent —*n.* 1. something potential 2. the relative voltage at a point in an electric circuit with respect to some reference point in the same circuit —**po·ten′ti·al′i·ty** (-shē al′ə tē) *n., pl.* -ties —**po·ten′tial·ly** *adv.*

**po·ten′ti·ate′** (-shē āt′) *vt.* -at′ed, -at′ing [see POTENT] to increase the

**pother** (päth'ər) *n.* [< ?] a fuss; commotion —*vt., vi.* to fuss or bother

**pot'herb'** *n.* any plant or herb whose leaves are used as a cooked vegetable or as flavoring in cooking

**pot'hold'er** *n.* a small pad, or piece of cloth, for handling hot pots, etc.

**pot'hook'** *n.* 1. an S-shaped hook for hanging a pot over a fire 2. a curved or S-shaped mark in writing

**po·tion** (pō'shən) *n.* [< L. *potare,* to drink] a drink, as of medicine, poison, or a supposedly magic substance

**pot'luck'** *n.* whatever the family meal happens to be [to take *potluck*]

**Po·to·mac** (pə tō'mək) river in the E U.S., flowing into Chesapeake Bay

**pot'pie'** *n.* 1. a meat pie made in a deep dish 2. a stew with dumplings

**pot·pour·ri** (pō'poo rē', pät'poor'ē) *n.* [Fr. < *pot,* a pot + *pourrir,* to rot] a medley or miscellany; mixture

**pot roast** a large cut of beef cooked in one piece by braising

**pot'sherd'** (pät'shʉrd') *n.* [< ME. *pot,* pot + *shard,* broken] a piece of broken pottery

**pot'shot'** (-shät') *n.* 1. an easy shot 2. a random shot 3. a haphazard try

**pot·tage** (pät'ij) *n.* [< Du. *pot,* a pot] a kind of thick soup or stew

**pot'ter** *n.* one who makes earthenware pots, dishes, etc.

**potter's field** a burial ground for paupers or unknown persons

**potter's wheel** a rotating disk upon which clay is molded into bowls, etc.

**pot'ter·y** *n., pl.* **-ies** 1. a potter's workshop 2. the art of a potter 3. pots, dishes, etc. made of clay hardened by heat

POTTER'S
WHEEL

**pouch** (pouch) *n.* [< MFr. *poche*] 1. a small bag or sack [a tobacco *pouch*] 2. a mailbag 3. a saclike structure, as that on the abdomen of the kangaroo, etc. for carrying young —*vt., vi.* to form (into) a pouch

**poul·tice** (pōl'tis) *n.* [< ML. *pultes,* pap] a hot, soft mass applied to a sore part of the body —*vt.* **-ticed, -tic·ing** to apply a poultice

**poul·try** (pōl'trē) *n.* [< L. *pullus,* chicken] domestic fowls; chickens, ducks, etc.

**pounce** (pouns) *n.* [ME. *pownce,* talon] a pouncing —*vi.* **pounced, pounc'ing** to swoop down or leap (on, upon, or at) as if to seize

**pound¹** (pound) *n., pl.* **pounds,** collectively **pound** [< L. *pondus,* a weight] 1. a unit of weight, equal to 16 oz. avoirdupois or 12 oz. troy: abbrev. **lb.** 2. the monetary unit of the United Kingdom and various other countries: symbol, £

**pound²** (pound) *vt.* [OE. *punian*] 1. to beat to a pulp, powder, etc. 2. to hit hard —*vi.* 1. to deliver repeated, heavy blows (*at* or *on*) 2. to move with heavy steps 3. to throb

**pound³** (pound) *n.* [< OE. *pund-*] a municipal enclosure for stray animals

**pound'cake'** *n.* a rich cake made (orig. with a pound each) of flour, butter, sugar, etc.

**pour** (pôr) *vt.* [ME. *pouren*] 1. to cause to flow in a continuous stream 2. to emit, utter, etc. profusely or steadily —*vi.* 1. to flow freely, continuously, etc. 2. to rain heavily

**pout** (pout) *vi.* [ME. *pouten*] 1. to thrust out the lips, as in sullenness 2. to sulk —*n.* a pouting —*pout'er n.*

**pov·er·ty** (päv'ər tē) *n.* [< L. *pauper,* poor] 1. the condition or quality of being poor; need 2. deficiency; inadequacy 3. scarcity

**pov'er·ty-strick'en** *adj.* very poor

**POW, P.O.W.** prisoner of war

**pow·der** (pou'dər) *n.* [< L. *pulvis*] 1. any dry substance in the form of fine, dustlike particles, produced by crushing, grinding, etc. 2. a specific kind of powder [bath *powder*] —*vt.* 1. to sprinkle, etc. with powder 2. to make into a powder —**pow'der·y** *adj.*

**powder keg** 1. a keg for gunpowder 2. an explosive situation

**powder room** a lavatory for women

**pow·er** (pou'ər) *n.* [ult. < L. *posse,* be able] 1. ability to do or act 2. vigor; force; strength 3. *a)* authority; influence *b)* legal authority 4. physical force or energy [*electric* power] 5. a person or thing having great influence, force, or authority 6. a nation with influence over other nations 7. the product of the multiplication of a quantity by itself 8. the degree of magnification of a lens —*vt.* to supply with a source of power —*adj.* 1. operated by electricity, a fuel engine, etc. [*power* tools] 2. served by an auxiliary system that reduces effort [*power* steering] 3. carrying electricity

**power dive** *Aeron.* a dive speeded by engine power —**pow'er-dive'** *vi., vt.* **-dived', -div'ing**

**pow'er·ful** *adj.* strong; mighty; influential —**pow'er·ful·ly** *adv.*

**pow'er·house'** *n.* 1. a building where electric power is generated 2. [Colloq.] a strong or energetic person, team, etc.

**pow'er·less** *adj.* without power; weak; unable —**pow'er·less·ly** *adv.*

**power of attorney** written legal authority to act for another person

**pow·wow** (pou'wou') *n.* [< AmInd.] 1. a conference of or with N. American Indians 2. [Colloq.] any conference

**pox** (päks) *n.* [for *pocks:* see POCK] a disease characterized by skin eruptions, as smallpox; specif., syphilis

**pp.** 1. pages 2. past participle

**P.P., p.p.** 1. parcel post 2. *a)* postpaid *b)* prepaid: also **ppd.**

**ppr., p.pr.** present participle

**P.P.S., p.p.s.** [L. *post postscriptum*] an additional postscript

**Pr.** Provençal

**pr.** pair(s)

**P.R., PR** 1. Puerto Rico 2. public relations

**prac·ti·ca·ble** (prak'ti kə b'l) *adj.* 1. that can be put into practice; feasible 2. that can be used; usable;

useful —**prac′ti·ca·bil′i·ty** *n.* — **prac′ti·ca·bly** *adv.*

**prac·ti·cal** (prak′ti k'l) *adj.* **1.** of or obtained through practice or action **2.** useful **3.** concerned with the application of knowledge to useful ends [*practical* science] **4.** given to actual practice [a *practical* farmer] **5.** that is so in practice, if not in theory, law, etc. **6.** matter-of-fact —**prac′ti·cal′i·ty** (-kal′ə tē) *n.*, *pl.* **-ties**

**practical joke** a trick played on someone in fun —**practical joker**

**prac′ti·cal·ly** *adv.* **1.** in a practical manner **2.** from a practical viewpoint **3.** in effect; virtually

**practical nurse** a nurse with less training than a registered nurse, often one licensed by the State (**licensed practical nurse**) for specified duties

**prac·tice** (prak′tis) *vt.* **-ticed, -tic′ing** [< Gr. *prassein*, do] **1.** to do or engage in frequently; make a habit of **2.** to do repeatedly so as to become proficient **3.** to work at, esp. as a profession —*vi.* **1.** to do something repeatedly so as to become proficient; drill *Chiefly Brit. sp.* **practise** —*n.* **1.** a practicing; habit, custom, etc. **2.** *a)* repeated action to acquire proficiency *b)* proficiency so acquired **3.** the actual doing of something **4.** *a)* the exercise of a profession *b)* a business based on this

**prac′ticed** *adj.* skilled

**prac·ti·tion·er** (prak tish′ə nər) *n.* one who practices a profession

**Prae·to·ri·an** (pri tôr′ē ən) *adj.* [< L. *praetor*, magistrate] of or belonging to the bodyguard (**Praetorian Guard**) of a Roman emperor —*n.* a member of the Praetorian Guard

**prag·mat·ic** (prag mat′ik) *adj.* [< Gr. *pragma*, thing done] **1.** practical **2.** testing the validity of all concepts by their practical results —**prag·mat′i·cal·ly** *adv.* —**prag′ma·tism** (-mə tiz′m) *n.* —**prag′ma·tist** *n.*

**Prague** (präg) capital of Czechoslovakia: pop. 1,025,000

**prai·rie** (prer′ē) *n.* [Fr. < L. *pratum*, meadow] a large area of level or rolling grassy land

**prairie dog** a small, squirrellike, burrowing rodent of N.America

**prairie schooner** a covered wagon

**praise** (prāz) *vt.* **praised, prais′ing** [< L. *pretium*, worth] **1.** to commend the worth of **2.** to glorify (God, a god, etc.) as in song —*n.* a praising or being praised; commendation

**praise′wor′thy** *adj.* worthy of praise —**praise′wor′thi·ly** *adv.* —**praise′wor′thi·ness** *n.*

**pra·line** (prā′lēn, prä′-) *n.* [Fr.] any of various soft or crisp candies made of nuts, sugar, etc.

**prance** (prans) *vi.* **pranced, pranc′ing** [< ?] **1.** to rise up, or move along, on the hind legs, as a horse **2.** to caper or strut —*n.* a prancing —**pranc′er** *n.* —**pranc′ing·ly** *adv.*

**prank** (praŋk) *n.* [< ?] a mischievous trick —**prank′ster** *n.*

**prate** (prāt) *vi.*, *vt.* **prat′ed, prat′ing** [< MDu. *praien*] to talk much and foolishly; chatter

**prat·tle** (prat′'l) *vi.*, *vt.* **-tled, -tling** [MLowG. *pratelen*] to prate or babble —*n.* chatter or babble

**prawn** (prôn) *n.* [< ?] an edible, shrimplike crustacean

**pray** (prā) *vt.* [< L. *prex*, prayer] **1.** to implore [(I) *pray* (you) tell me] **2.** to ask for by prayer —*vi.* to say prayers, as to God —**pray′er** *n.*

**prayer** (prer) *n.* **1.** the act of praying **2.** an entreaty; supplication **3.** *a)* a humble request, as to God *b)* any set formula for this **4.** [often *pl.*] a devotional service chiefly of prayers **5.** something prayed for —**prayer′ful** *adj.* —**prayer′ful·ly** *adv.*

**praying mantis** same as MANTIS

**pre-** [< L. *prae*, before] a prefix meaning before in time, place, rank, etc.

**preach** (prēch) *vi.* [< L. *prae-*, before + *dicare*, proclaim] **1.** to give a religious sermon **2.** to give moral advice, esp. in a tiresome way —*vt.* **1.** to urge as by preaching **2.** to deliver (a sermon) —**preach′ment** *n.*

**preach′er** *n.* one who preaches; esp., a clergyman

**preach′y** *adj.* **-i·er, -i·est** [Colloq.] given to or marked by preaching

**pre·am·ble** (prē′am′b'l) *n.* [< L. *prae-*, before + *ambulare*, go] an introduction, esp. one to a constitution, statute, etc., stating its purpose

**pre′ar·range′** (-ə rānj′) *vt.* **-ranged′, -rang′ing** to arrange beforehand

**pre·can′cer·ous** (prē kan′sər əs) *adj.* likely to become cancerous

**pre·car·i·ous** (pri ker′ē əs) *adj.* [see PRAY] dependent upon circumstances or chance; uncertain; risky —**pre·car′i·ous·ly** *adv.*

**pre·cau·tion** (pri kô′shən) *n.* [< L. *prae-*, before + *cavere*, take care] care taken beforehand, as against danger, failure, etc. —**pre·cau′tion·ar′y** *adj.*

**pre·cede** (pri sēd′) *vt.*, *vi.* **-ced′ed, -ced′ing** [< L. *prae-*, before + *cedere*, to move] to be, come, or go before in time, place, rank, etc.

**prec·e·dence** (pres′ə dəns, pri sēd′'ns) *n.* the act, right, or fact of preceding in time, place, rank, etc.

**pre·ced·ent** (pri sēd′'nt; for *n.* pres′ə dənt) *adj.* preceding —*n.* an act, statement, etc. that may serve as an example or justification for a later one

**pre·ced′ing** *adj.* that precedes

**pre·cept** (prē′sept) *n.* [< L. *prae-*, before + *capere*, take] a rule of moral conduct; maxim

**pre·cep·tor** (pri sep′tər) *n.* a teacher

**pre·cinct** (prē′siŋkt) *n.* [< L. *prae-*, before + *cingere*, surround] **1.** [usually *pl.*] an enclosure between buildings, walls, etc. **2.** [*pl.*] environs **3.** *a)* a police district *b)* a subdivision of a voting ward **4.** a limited area

---

fat, āpe, cär; ten, ēven; is, bīte; gō, hôrn, tōōl, look; oil, out; up, fur; chin; she; thin, *then*; zh, leisure; ŋ, ring; ə for *a* in *ago*; ', (ā′b'l); ë, Fr. coeur; ö, Fr. feu; Fr. mon; ü, Fr. duc; kh, G. ich, doch; ‡ foreign; < derived from

**pre·cious** (presh'əs) *adj.* [< L. *pretium*, a price] 1. of great price or value; costly 2. beloved; dear 3. very fastidious, affected, etc. —**pre'cious·ly** *adv.* —**pre'cious·ness** *n.*

**prec·i·pice** (pres'ə pis) *n.* [< L. *prae-*, before + *caput*, a head] a vertical or overhanging rock·face

**pre·cip·i·tant** (pri sip'ə tənt) *adj.* [see prec.] *same as* PRECIPITATE

**pre·cip·i·tate'** (-tāt'; *also for adj. &* *n.* -tit) *vt.* -tat'ed, -tat'ing [see PRECIPICE] 1. to hurl downward 2. to cause to happen before expected, needed, etc. 3. *Chem.* to separate (a soluble substance) out of a solution —*vi.* 1. *Chem.* to be precipitated 2. *Meteorol.* to condense and fall as rain, snow, etc. —*adj.* 1. acting or done hastily or rashly 2. very sudden or abrupt —*n.* a substance precipitated out from a solution

**pre·cip·i·ta'tion** *n.* 1. a headlong fall or rush 2. rash haste; impetuosity 3. a bringing on suddenly 4. *Chem.* a precipitating or being precipitated from a solution 5. *Meteorol. a)* rain, snow, etc. *b)* the amount of this

**pre·cip·i·tous** (-ə təs) *adj.* 1. steep like a precipice 2. rash; impetuous

**pré·cis** (prā sē', prā'sē) *n., pl.* **-cis** (-sēz', -sēz) [Fr.: see ff.] a concise abridgment; summary

**pre·cise** (pri sīs') *adj.* [< L. *prae-*, before + *caedere*, to cut] 1. accurately stated; definite 2. minutely exact 3. strict; scrupulous; fastidious — **pre·cise'ly** *adv.* —**pre·cise'ness** *n.*

**pre·ci·sion** (pri sizh'ən) *n.* the quality of being precise; exactness —*adj.* requiring exactness [*precision* work]

**pre·clude** (pri klood') *vt.* -clud'ed, -clud'ing [< L. *prae-*, before + *claudere*, to close] to make impossible, esp. in advance; prevent —**pre·clu'sion** (-kloo'zhən) *n.*

**pre·co·cious** (pri kō'shəs) *adj.* [< L. *prae-*, before + *coquere*, to cook] matured earlier than usual [a *precocious* child] —**pre·coc'i·ty** (-käs'ə tē) *n.*

**pre·cog·ni·tion** (prē'käg nish'ən) *n.* [see PRE- & COGNITION] the supposed extrasensory perception of a future event —**pre·cog'ni·tive** *adj.*

**pre'-Co·lum'bi·an** (-kə lum'bē ən) *adj.* of any period in the Americas before Columbus's voyages

**pre·con·ceive** (prē'kən sēv') *vt.* -ceived', -ceiv'ing to form an opinion of beforehand —**pre'con·cep'tion** *n.*

**pre'con·di'tion** (-dish'ən) *vt.* to prepare to behave or react in a certain way under certain conditions

**pre·cur·sor** (pri kur'sər) *n.* [< L. *praecurrere*, run ahead] 1. a forerunner 2. a predecessor —**pre·cur'so·ry** *adj.*

**pred·a·to·ry** (pred'ə tôr'ē) *adj.* [< L. *praeda*, a prey] 1. of or living by plundering or robbing 2. preying on other animals —**pred'a·tor** (-tər) *n.*

**pre·de·cease** (prē'di sēs') *vt.* -ceased', -ceas'ing to die before (someone else)

**pred·e·ces·sor** (pred'ə ses'ər) *n.* [< L. *prae-*, before + *decedere*, go away] a person preceding another, as in office

**pre·des·ti·na·tion** (prē des'tə nā'shən) *n.* 1. *Theol.* the doctrine that *a)* God foreordained everything that would happen to *b)* God predestines souls to salvation or to damnation 2. destiny

**pre·des'tine** (-tin) *vt.* -tined, -tining to destine beforehand; foreordain

**pre'de·ter'mine** *vt.* -mined, -mining to determine beforehand

**pre·dic·a·ment** (pri dik'ə mənt) *n.* [see PREACH] an unpleasant or embarrassing situation

**pred·i·cate** (pred'ə kāt'; *for n. &* *adj.* -kit) *vt.* -cat'ed, -cat'ing [see PREACH] 1. to affirm as a quality or attribute 2. to base (*on* or *upon* facts, conditions, etc.) —*n. Gram.* the word or words that make a statement about the subject —*adj. Gram.* of or involved in a predicate —**pred'i·ca'tion** *n.*

**pre·dict** (pri dikt') *vt., vi.* [< L. *prae-*, before + *dicere*, tell] to state (what one believes will happen); foretell —**pre·dict'a·ble** *adj.* —**pre·dic'tion** *n.* —**pre·dic'tor** *n.*

**pre·di·gest** (prē'di jest', -dī-) *vt.* to treat (food) as with enzymes for easier digestion when eaten

**pre·di·lec·tion** (pred''l ek'shən, prēd'-) *n.* [< L. *prae-*, before + *diligere*, prefer] a partiality or preference

**pre·dis·pose** (prē'dis pōz') *vt.* -posed', -pos'ing to make susceptible (*to*); incline —**pre'dis·po·si'tion** *n.*

**pre·dom·i·nant** (pri däm'ə nənt) *adj.* 1. having authority or influence over others; superior 2. most frequent; prevailing —**pre·dom'i·nance** *n.* —**pre·dom'i·nant·ly** *adv.*

**pre·dom'i·nate'** (-nāt') *vi.* -nat'ed, -nat'ing 1. to have authority or influence (*over* others) 2. to be dominant in amount, number, etc.; prevail

**pre·em·i·nent** (prē em'ə nənt) *adj.* eminent above others; surpassing: also **pre-eminent** —**pre·em'i·nence** *n.* —**pre·em'i·nent·ly** *adv.*

**pre·empt** (prē empt') *vt.* [< L. *prae-*, before + *emere*, buy] 1. to gain the right to buy (public land) by settling on it 2. to seize before anyone else can 3. *Radio, TV* to replace (a scheduled program) Also **pre-empt**

**pre·emp'tion** *n.* 1. a preempting 2. action taken to check other action beforehand —**pre·emp'tive** *adj.*

**preen** (prēn) *vt.* [< ME. *proinen*, PRUNE²] 1. to clean and trim (the feathers) with the beak 2. to dress up or adorn (oneself) 3. to pride (oneself)

**pref.** 1. preface 2. preferred

**pre·fab** (prē'fab') *n.* [Colloq.] a prefabricated building

**pre·fab·ri·cate** (prē fab'rə kāt') *vt.* -cat'ed, -cat'ing to build (a house, etc.) in standardized sections for shipment and quick assembly

**pref·ace** (pref'is) *n.* [< L. *prae-*, before + *fari*, speak] an introduction to a book, speech, etc. —*vt.* -aced, -ac·ing 1. to furnish with a preface 2. to introduce —**pref'a·to·ry** (-ə tôr'ē) *adj.*

**pre·fect** (prē'fekt) *n.* [< L. *praeficere*, to set over] any of various administrators —**pre'fec·ture** (-fek chər) *n.*

**pre·fer** (pri fur′) *vt.* **-ferred′, -fer′-ring** [< L. *prae-*, before + *ferre*, to bear] **1.** to promote; advance **2.** to put before a court, etc. for consideration **3.** to like better

**pref·er·a·ble** (pref′ər ə b'l) *adj.* more desirable —**pref′er·a·bly** *adv.*

**pref·er·ence** (-əns) *n.* **1.** a preferring or being preferred **2.** something preferred **3.** advantage given to one person, country, etc. over others —**pref′er·en′tial** (-ə ren′shəl) *adj.*

**pre·fer·ment** (pri fur′mənt) *n.* an advancement in rank, etc.; promotion

**pre·fig·ure** (prē fig′yər) *vt.* **-ured, -ur·ing** to foreshadow

**pre·fix** (prē′fiks; *also for v.* prē fiks′) *vt.* [< L. *prae-*, before + *figere*, fix] to fix to the beginning; esp., to add as a prefix —*n.* a syllable or group of syllables joined to the beginning of a word to alter its meaning

**preg·nant** (preg′nənt) *adj.* [< L. *pregnans*] **1.** having (an) offspring developing in the uterus; with child **2.** mentally fertile; inventive **3.** full of meaning, etc. **4.** filled (*with*) or rich (*in*) —**preg′nan·cy** *n., pl.* **-cies**

**pre·hen·sile** (pri hen′s'l) *adj.* [< L. *prehendere*, take] adapted for seizing or grasping, esp. by wrapping around something, as a monkey's tail

**pre·his·tor·ic** (prē′his tôr′ik) *adj.* of the period before recorded history

**pre·judge** *vt.* **-judged′, -judg′ing** to judge beforehand, or without all the evidence —**pre·judg′ment** *n.*

**prej·u·dice** (prej′ə dis) *n.* [< L. *prae-*, before + *judicium*, judgment] **1.** a preconceived, usually unfavorable, idea **2.** an opinion held in disregard of facts that contradict it; bias **3.** intolerance or hatred of other races, etc. **4.** injury or harm —*vt.* **-diced, -dic·ing 1.** to injure or harm **2.** to cause to have prejudice; bias —**prej′u·di′cial** (-dish′əl) *adj.*

**prel·ate** (prel′it) *n.* [< L. *praelatus*, placed before] a high-ranking ecclesiastic, as a bishop —**prel′a·cy** (-ə sē) *n.*

**pre·lim·i·nar·y** (pri lim′ə ner′ē) *adj.* [< L. *prae*, before + *limen*, threshold] leading up to the main action, etc.; introductory —*n., pl.* **-ies** [*often pl.*] a preliminary step, test, etc.

**pre·lit·er·ate** (prē lit′ər it) *adj.* of a society lacking a written language

**prel·ude** (prel′yood, prā′lood) *n.* [< L. *prae*, before + *ludere*, to play] **1.** a preliminary part **2.** *Music a*) an introductory section of a suite, fugue, etc. *b*) a short, romantic composition

**pre·mar·i·tal** (prē mar′ə t'l) *adj.* before marriage

**pre·ma·ture** (prē′mə toor′, -choor′, -tyoor′) *adj.* [< L. *prae-*, before + *maturus*, ripe] happening, done, arriving, etc. before the proper or usual time; too early —**pre′ma·ture′ly** *adv.*

**pre·med·i·tate** (-med′ə tāt′) *vt., vi.* **-tat′ed, -tat′ing** to plan or think out beforehand —**pre·med′i·ta′tion** *n.*

**pre·mier** (pri mir′, -myir′) *adj.* [< L. *primus*, first] first in importance; foremost —*n.* a chief official; specif., a prime minister —**pre·mier′ship** *n.*

**pre·mière, pre·miere** (pri myer′, -mir′) *n.* [Fr.: see prec.] a first performance of a play, movie, etc.

**prem·ise** (prem′is) *n.* [< L. *prae-*, before + *mittere*, send] **1.** a previous statement serving as a basis for an argument **2.** [*pl.*] a piece of real estate —*vt.* **-ised, -is·ing** to state as a premise; postulate

**pre·mi·um** (prē′mē əm) *n.* [< L. *prae*, before + *emere*, take] **1.** a reward or prize, esp. as an inducement to buy **2.** an additional amount paid or charged **3.** a payment, as for an insurance policy **4.** very high value [he put a *premium* on wit] —**at a premium** very valuable because of scarcity

**pre·mo·ni·tion** (prē′mə nish′ən, prem′ə-) *n.* [< L. *prae-*, before + *monere*, warn] **1.** a forewarning **2.** a foreboding —**pre·mon·i·to·ry** (pri mān′ə tôr′ē) *adj.*

**pre·na·tal** (prē nāt′l) *adj.* [PRE- + NATAL] before birth

**pre·oc·cu·py** (prē äk′yə pī′) *vt.* **-pied′, -py′ing** [< L. *prae-*, before + *occupare*, seize] **1.** to wholly occupy the thoughts of; engross **2.** to take possession of before someone else or beforehand —**pre·oc′cu·pa′tion** (-pā′shən) *n.* —**pre·oc′cu·pied′** *adj.*

**pre·or·dain** (prē′ôr dān′) *vt.* to ordain or decree beforehand

**prep** (prep) *adj.* [Colloq.] clipped form of PREPARATORY [a *prep* school] —*vt.* **prepped, prep′ping** to prepare (esp. a patient for surgery)

**prep. 1.** preparatory **2.** preposition

**pre·pack·age** (prē pak′ij) *vt.* **-aged, -ag·ing** to package (foods, etc.) in standard units before selling

**pre·paid′** *pt. & pp.* of PREPAY

**prep·a·ra·tion** (prep′ə rā′shən) *n.* **1.** a preparing or being prepared **2.** a preparatory measure **3.** something prepared, as a medicine, cosmetic, etc.

**pre·par·a·to·ry** (pri par′ə tôr′ē) *adj.* serving to prepare; introductory

**preparatory school** a private school that prepares students for college.

**pre·pare** (pri par′, -per′) *vt.* **-pared′, -par′ing** [< L. *prae-*, before + *parare*, get ready] **1.** to make ready **2.** to equip or furnish **3.** to put together [*prepare* dinner] —*vi.* **1.** to make things ready **2.** to make oneself ready

**pre·par′ed·ness** *n.* the state of being prepared, esp. for waging war

**pre·pay′** *vt.* **-paid′, -pay′ing** to pay or pay for in advance

**pre·pon·der·ate** (pri pän′də rāt′) *vi.* **-at′ed, -at′ing** [< L. *prae-*, before + *ponderare*, weigh] to be superior in amount, power, etc. —**pre·pon′der·ance** *n.* —**pre·pon′der·ant** *adj.*

**prep·o·si·tion** (prep′ə zish′ən) *n.* [< L. *prae-*, before + *ponere*, to place] a word, as *in, by, to,* etc., that connects a noun or pronoun to another word —**prep′o·si′tion·al** *adj.*

**pre·pos·sess** (prē′pə zes′) *vt.* 1. to prejudice 2. to impress favorably

**pre′pos·sess′ing** *adj.* that impresses favorably; pleasing

**pre·pos·ter·ous** (pri päs′tər əs) *adj.* [< L. *prae-,* before + *posterus,* coming after] contrary to nature, reason, etc.; absurd; ridiculous

**pre·puce** (prē′pyōōs) *n.* [< L. *prae-putium*] same as FORESKIN

**pre·re·cord** (prē′ri kôrd′) *vt. Radio & TV* to record (a program, etc.) in advance, for later broadcasting

**pre·req·ui·site** (pri rek′wə zit) *adj.* required beforehand as a necessary condition —*n.* something prerequisite

**pre·rog·a·tive** (pri räg′ə tiv) *n.* [< L. *prae-,* before + *rogare,* ask] an exclusive privilege, esp. one peculiar to a rank, class, etc.

**Pres.** President

**pres.** present

**pres·age** (pres′ij; *for v. usually* pri sāj′) *n.* [< L. *prae-,* before + *sagire,* perceive] 1. an omen; portent 2. a foreboding —*vt.* -**aged′,** -**ag′ing** to give warning of; portend

**pres·by·ter** (prez′bi tər) *n.* [see PRIEST] 1. in the Presbyterian Church, an elder 2. in the Episcopal Church, a priest or minister

**Pres·by·te·ri·an** (prez′bə tir′ē ən) *adj.* designating or of a church of a traditionally Calvinistic denomination governed by presbyters —*n.* a member of a Presbyterian church

**pre′school′** *adj.* of or for a child between infancy and school age

**pre·sci·ence** (prē′shē əns) *n.* [< L. *prae-,* before + *scire,* know] foreknowledge; foresight —**pre′sci·ent** *adj.*

**pre·scribe** (pri skrib′) *vt.* -**scribed′,** -**scrib′ing** [< L. *prae-,* before + *scribere,* write] 1. to order; direct 2. to order or advise as a medicine or treatment: said of physicians, etc.

**pre·script** (prē′skript) *n.* a prescribed rule —**pre·scrip′tive** *adj.*

**pre·scrip·tion** (pri skrip′shən) *n.* 1. something prescribed; order 2. *a)* a doctor's written direction for the preparation and use of a medicine *b)* a medicine so prescribed

**pres·ence** (prez′′ns) *n.* 1. the fact or state of being present 2. immediate surroundings [in his *presence*] 3. *a)* a person's bearing or appearance *b)* impressive bearing, personality, etc.

**presence of mind** ability to think and act quickly in an emergency

**pres·ent** (prez′′nt; *for v.* pri zent′) *adj.* [< L. *prae-,* before + *esse,* be] 1. being at the specified place 2. existing or happening now 3. *Gram.* indicating action or state now or action that is always true [*present* tense] —*n.* 1. the present time or occasion 2. the present tense 3. a gift —*vt.* 1. to introduce (a person) 2. to exhibit; show 3. to offer for consideration 4. to give (a gift, etc.) to (a person, etc.) —**present arms** to hold a rifle vertically in front of the body

**pre·sent·a·ble** (pri zen′tə b′l) *adj.* 1. suitable for presentation 2. suitably groomed for meeting people

**pre·sen·ta·tion** (prē′zen tā′shən, prez′′n-) *n.* 1. a presenting or being presented 2. something presented

**pres′ent-day′** *adj.* of the present time

**pre·sen·ti·ment** (pri zen′tə mənt) *n.* [see PRE- & SENTIMENT] a feeling that something, esp. of an unfortunate nature, is about to happen

**pres′ent·ly** *adv.* 1. soon; shortly 2. at present; now

**pre·sent·ment** (pri zent′mənt) *n.* presentation

**present participle** a participle used to express present or continuing action or state of being, as in "the boy is *growing*"

**pre·serv·a·tive** (pri zur′və tiv) *adj.* preserving —*n.* anything that preserves [a *preservative* added to foods]

**pre·serve** (pri zurv′) *vt.* -**served′,** -**serv′ing** [< L. *prae-,* before + *servare,* keep] 1. to protect from harm, damage, etc. 2. to keep from spoiling 3. to prepare (food), as by canning, for future use 4. to carry on; maintain —*n.* 1. [*usually pl.*] fruit preserved by cooking with sugar 2. a place where game, fish, etc. are maintained —**pres·er·va·tion** (prez′ər vā′shən) *n.* —**pre·serv′er** *n.*

**pre·set** (prē set′) *vt.* -**set′,** -**set′ting** to set (automatic controls) beforehand

**pre′-shrunk′** *adj.* shrunk by a special process in manufacture, to minimize further shrinkage in laundering

**pre·side** (pri zid′) *vi.* -**sid′ed,** -**sid′ing** [< L. *prae-,* before + *sedere,* sit] 1. to serve as chairman 2. to have control or authority (*over*)

**pres·i·dent** (prez′i dənt) *n.* [see prec.] 1. the highest officer of a company, club, etc. 2. [*often* P-] the chief executive (as in the U.S.), or the nominal head (as in France), of a republic —**pres′i·den·cy** *n., pl.* -**cies** —**pres′i·den′tial** (-den′shəl) *adj.*

**press** [1] (pres) *vt.* [< L. *premere*] 1. to act on with steady force or weight; push against, squeeze, compress, etc. 2. to squeeze (juice, etc.) from 3. to iron (clothes, etc.) 4. to embrace closely 5. to force; compel 6. to urge persistently; entreat 7. to try to force 8. to emphasize 9. to distress or trouble [*pressed* for time] 10. to urge on —*vi.* 1. to weigh down 2. to go forward with determination 3. to crowd —*n.* 1. pressure, urgency, etc. 2. a crowd 3. a machine for crushing, stamping, etc. 4. smoothness, etc. of clothes after pressing 5. *a) clipped form of* PRINTING PRESS *b)* a printing establishment *c)* newspapers, magazines, etc., or the persons who write for them *d)* publicity, etc. in newspapers, etc. 6. an upright closet for storing clothes, etc. —**press′er** *n.*

**press** [2] (pres) *vt.* [< L. *praes,* surety + *stare,* to stand] to force into service, esp. military or naval service

**press agent** one whose work is to get publicity for his client

**press box** a place for reporters at sports events, etc.

**press conference** a group interview granted to newsmen as by a celebrity

**press'ing** adj. calling for immediate attention; urgent

**pres·sure** (presh'ər) n. 1. a pressing or being pressed 2. a state of distress 3. a compelling influence *[social pressure]* 4. urgent demands; urgency 5. *Physics* force per unit of area exerted upon a surface, etc. —vt. -sured, -sur·ing to exert pressure on

**pressure cooker** a container for quick cooking by steam under pressure

**pres'sur·ize'** (-ìz') vt. -ized', -iz'ing to keep nearly normal atmospheric pressure inside (an airplane, etc.), as at high altitudes —pres'sur·i·za'tion n. —pres'sur·iz'er n.

**pres·ti·dig·i·ta·tion** (pres'tə dij'i tā'shən) n. [Fr. < *preste*, quick + L. *digitus*, finger] sleight of hand

**pres·tige** (pres tēzh') n. [Fr. < L. *praestrigiae*, deceptions] 1. the power to impress or influence 2. reputation based on high achievement, character, etc. —pres·tige'ful adj.

**pres·ti'gious** (-tij'əs, -tēj'-) adj. having or imparting prestige or distinction

**pres·to** (pres'tō) adv., adj. [It., quick] fast or at once

**pre'stressed' concrete** containing tensed steel cables for strength

**pre·sume** (pri zōōm') vt. -sumed', -sum'ing [< L. *prae-*, before + *sumere*, take] 1. to dare (to say or do something); venture 2. to take for granted; suppose —vi. to act presumptuously; take liberties —pre·sum'a·ble adj. —pre·sum'a·bly adv.

**pre·sump·tion** (pri zump'shən) n. 1. a presuming; specif., a) an overstepping of proper bounds b) a taking of something for granted 2. the thing presumed 3. a reason for presuming —pre·sump'tive adj.

**pre·sump'tu·ous** (-choo wəs) adj. too bold or forward

**pre·sup·pose** (prē'sə pōz') vt. -posed', -pos'ing 1. to suppose or assume beforehand 2. to require or imply as a preceding condition —pre'sup·po·si'tion (-sup ə zish'ən) n.

**pre·teen** (prē'tēn') n. a child nearly a teen-ager

**pre·tend** (pri tend') vt. [< L. *prae-*, before + *tendere*, to stretch] 1. to profess *[to pretend infallibility]* 2. to feign; simulate *[to pretend anger]* 3. to make believe *[pretend I'm you]* —vi. to lay claim (to) —pre·tend'er n.

**pre·tense** (pri tens', prē'tens) n. 1. a claim; pretension 2. a false claim 3. a false show of something 4. a pretending, as at play Brit. sp. **pretence**

**pre·ten·sion** (pri ten'shən) n. 1. a pretext 2. a claim 3. assertion of a claim 4. pretentiousness

**pre·ten'tious** (-shəs) adj. 1. making claims to some distinction, importance, etc. 2. affectedly grand; ostentatious —pre·ten'tious·ly adv. —pre·ten'tious·ness n.

**pret·er·it, pret·er·ite** (pret'ər it) adj. [< L. *praeter-*, beyond + *ire*, go] *Gram.* expressing past action or state —n. the past tense

**pre·ter·nat·u·ral** (prēt'ər nach'ər əl) adj. [ML. *praeternaturalis*] 1. differing from or beyond what is natural; abnormal 2. supernatural

**pre·test** (prē'test') vt., vi. to test in advance

**pre·text** (prē'tekst) n. [< L. *prae-*, before + *texere*, weave] a false reason put forth to hide the real one

**Pre·to·ri·a** (pri tôr'ē ə) a capital of South Africa: pop. 423,000

**pret·ti·fy** (prit'ə fī') vt. -fied', -fy'ing to make pretty

**pret·ty** (prit'ē, pur'tē) adj. -ti·er, -ti·est [OE. *prættig*, crafty] attractive in a dainty, graceful way —adv. fairly; somewhat —vt. -tied, -ty·ing to make pretty (usually with *up*) —pret'ti·ly adv. —pret'ti·ness n.

**pret·zel** (pret's'l) n. [< L. *brachium*, an arm] a hard, brittle, salted biscuit, often formed in a loose knot

**pre·vail** (pri vāl') vi. [< L. *prae-*, before + *valere*, be strong] 1. to be victorious (*over* or *against*) 2. to succeed 3. to be or become more widespread 4. to be prevalent —**prevail on** (or **upon**, **with**) to persuade

**pre·vail'ing** adj. 1. superior in strength or influence 2. prevalent

**prev·a·lent** (prev'ə lənt) adj. [see PREVAIL] widely existing; generally accepted, used, etc. —prev'a·lence n.

**pre·var·i·cate** (pri var'ə kāt') vi. -cat'ed, -cat'ing [< L. *prae-*, before + *varicare*, straddle] 1. to evade the truth 2. to lie —pre·var'i·ca'tion n. —pre·var'i·ca'tor n.

**pre·vent** (pri vent') vt. [< L. *prae-*, before + *venire*, come] to stop or keep from doing or happening; hinder —pre·vent'a·ble, pre·vent'i·ble adj. —pre·ven'tion n.

**pre·ven'tive** (-ven'tiv) adj. preventing or serving to prevent —n. anything that prevents Also **pre·vent'a·tive**

**pre·view** (prē'vyōō) n. 1. an advance, restricted showing, as of a movie 2. a showing of scenes from a movie to advertise it Also **pre'vue** (-vyōō)

**pre·vi·ous** (prē'vē əs) adj. [< L. *prae-*, before + *via*, a way] occurring before; prior —**previous to** before —pre'vi·ous·ly adv.

**pre·war** (prē'wôr') adj. before a (or the) war

**prex·y** (prek'sē) n., pl. -ies the president, esp. of a college, etc.

**prey** (prā) n. [< L. *prehendere*, seize] 1. an animal hunted for food by another animal 2. a victim 3. the act or habit of preying on other animals *[a bird of prey]* —vi. 1. to plunder 2. to hunt other animals for food

**3.** to weigh as an obsession  Usually used with *on* or *upon*

**pri·ap·ic** (prī ap′ik) *adj.* [ < *Priapos*, Gr. god of procreation] of or relating to the phallus; phallic

**price** (prīs) *n.* [ < L. *pretium*] **1.** the amount of money, etc. asked or paid for something; cost  **2.** value or worth  **3.** the cost, as in life, labor, etc., of obtaining some benefit —*vt.* **priced, pric′ing  1.** to fix the price of  **2.** [Colloq.] to find out the price of

**price′less** *adj.* of inestimable value; invaluable

**prick** (prik) *n.* [OE. *prica*, a point]  **1.** a tiny puncture made by a sharp point  **2.** a sharp pain caused as by being pricked —*vt.*  **1.** to make (a hole) in (something) with a sharp point  **2.** to pain sharply —**prick up one's** (or **its**) **ears  1.** to raise the ears erect  **2.** to listen closely

**prick·le** (prik′'l) *n.* [OE. *prica*, a point]  **1.** a small, sharply pointed growth, as a thorn: also **prick′er  2.** a tingling sensation —*vt.*, *vi.* **-led, -ling** to tingle —**prick′ly** *adj.*

**prickly heat** a skin eruption caused by inflammation of the sweat glands

**pride** (prīd) *n.* [ < OE. *prut*, proud]  **1.** *a)* an overhigh opinion of oneself  *b)* haughtiness; arrogance  **2.** dignity and self-respect  **3.** satisfaction in something done, owned, etc.  **4.** a person or thing in which pride is taken —**pride oneself on** to be proud of —**pride′ful** *adj.* —**pride′ful·ly** *adv.*

**pri·er** (prī′ər) *n.* one that pries

**priest** (prēst) *n.* [ < Gr. *presbys*, old]  **1.** a person of special rank who performs religious rites in a temple of God or a god  **2.** *R.C.Ch.*, etc. a clergyman ranking next below a bishop —**priest′ess** *n.fem.* —**priest′hood** *n.* —**priest′ly** *adj.*

**prig** (prig) *n.* [ < 16th-c. cant] one who smugly affects great propriety or morality —**prig′gish** *adj.*

**prim** (prim) *adj.* **prim′mer, prim′mest** [ < ?] stiffly formal, precise, or moral —**prim′ly** *adv.* —**prim′ness** *n.*

**pri·ma·cy** (prī′mə sē) *n.*, *pl.* **-cies** [ < L. *primus*, first]  **1.** a being first in time, rank, etc.; supremacy  **2.** the rank or office of a primate

**pri·ma don·na** (prē′mə dän′ə) *pl.* **pri′ma don′nas** [It., first lady] the principal woman singer in an opera

**pri·ma fa·ci·e** (prī′mə fā′shi ē′) [L., at first sight] adequate to establish a fact unless refuted: said of evidence

**pri·mal** (prī′m'l) *adj.* [ < L. *primus*, first]  **1.** first in time; original  **2.** first in importance; chief

**pri·ma·ri·ly** (prī mer′ə lē, prī′mer′-) *adv.* **1.** mainly; principally  **2.** at first; originally

**pri·ma·ry** (prī′mer′ē, -mər ē) *adj.* [ < L. *primus*, first]  **1.** first in time or order; original  **2.** from which others are derived; fundamental [*primary* colors]  **3.** first in importance; chief —*n.*, *pl.* **-ries  1.** something first in order, importance, etc.  **2.** a preliminary election at which candidates are chosen for the final election

**primary accent** the heaviest accent (′) in pronouncing a word

**pri·mate** (prī′māt; *also for 1* -mit) *n.* [ < L. *primus*, first]  **1.** an archbishop, or the highest-ranking bishop in a province, etc.  **2.** any member of the most highly developed order of animals, including man, the apes, etc.

**prime** (prīm) *adj.* [ < L. *primus*, first]  **1.** first in time; original  **2.** first in rank or importance; chief; principal  **3.** first in quality  **4.** fundamental  **5.** *Math.* that can be evenly divided by no other whole number than itself and 1 —*n.* **1.** the first or earliest part  **2.** the best or most vigorous period  **3.** the best part —*vt.* **primed, prim′ing  1.** to make ready; prepare  **2.** to get (a pump) into operation by pouring water into it  **3.** to undercoat, size, etc. before painting  **4.** to provide with facts, answers, etc. beforehand

**prime meridian** the meridian at Greenwich, England, from which longitude is measured east and west

**prime minister** in some countries, the chief executive of the government

**prim·er¹** (prim′ər) *n.* [ < L. *primus*, first]  **1.** a simple book for teaching reading  **2.** any elementary textbook

**prim·er²** (prī′mər) *n.* a thing that primes; specif., *a)* an explosive cap, etc. used to set off a main charge  *b)* a preliminary coat of paint, etc.

**prime time** *Radio & TV* the hours when the largest audience is available

**pri·me·val** (prī mē′v'l) *adj.* [ < L. *primus*, first + *aevum*, an age] of the earliest times or ages; primordial

**prim·i·tive** (prim′ə tiv) *adj.* [ < L. *primus*, first]  **1.** of the earliest times; original  **2.** crude; simple  **3.** primary; basic —*n.* a primitive person or thing

**pri·mo·gen·i·ture** (prī′mə jen′i chər) *n.* [ < L. *primus*, first + *gignere*, beget]  **1.** the condition of being the firstborn of the same parents  **2.** the right of inheritance of the eldest son

**pri·mor·di·al** (prī môr′dē əl) *adj.* [ < L. *primus*, first + *ordiri*, begin] primitive; fundamental; original

**primp** (primp) *vt.*, *vi.* [prob. < PRIM] to groom or dress up in a fussy way

**prim·rose** (prim′rōz′) *n.* [alt. (after *rose*) < ML. *primula*] a plant with tubelike, often yellow flowers

**primrose path  1.** the path of pleasure, self-indulgence, etc.  **2.** a course that seems easy but that could lead to disaster

**prince** (prins) *n.* [ < L. *princeps*, chief]  **1.** a ruler ranking below a king; head of a principality  **2.** a son of a sovereign  **3.** any preeminent person

**prince consort** the husband of a reigning queen

**Prince Edward Island** island province of SE Canada: 2,184 sq. mi.; pop. 109,000

**prince′ly** *adj.* **-li·er, -li·est  1.** of a prince  **2.** magnificent; generous —**prince′li·ness** *n.*

**prin·cess** (prin′sis, -ses) *n.*  **1.** a daughter of a sovereign  **2.** the wife of a prince

**prin·ci·pal** (prin′sə pəl) *adj.* [see

PRINCE] first in rank, importance, etc.
—*n.* 1. a principal person or thing
2. the head of a school 3. the amount
of a debt, etc. minus the interest
—**prin′ci·pal·ly** *adv.*

**prin′ci·pal′i·ty** (-pal′ə tē) *n., pl.*
**-ties** the territory ruled by a prince

**principal parts** the principal inflected forms of a verb: in English, the
present infinitive, past tense, and past
participle (Ex.: *drink, drank, drunk*)

**prin·ci·ple** (prin′sə pəl) *n.* [see
PRINCE] 1. a fundamental truth, law,
etc. on which others are based 2. *a)* a
rule of conduct *b)* adherence to such
rules; integrity 3. a basic part
4. *a)* the scientific law explaining a
natural action *b)* the method of a
thing's operation —**prin′ci·pled** *adj.*

**print** (print) *n.* [< L. *premere*, to
press] 1. a mark made on a surface
by pressing or stamping 2. cloth
printed with a design 3. the impression
of letters, designs, etc. made by inked
type or from a plate, block, etc. 4. a
photograph, esp. one made from a
negative —*vt., vi.* 1. to stamp (a
mark, letter, etc.) on a surface 2. to
produce on (paper, etc.) the impression
of inked type, etc. 3. to produce (a
book, etc.) 4. to write in letters resembling printed ones 5. to make (a photographic print) —**in** (or **out of**) **print**
still (or no longer) being sold by the publisher: said of books, etc. —**print′er** *n.*

**printed circuit** an electrical circuit
formed by applying conductive material, as in fine lines, to an insulating
sheet

**print′ing** *n.* 1. the act of one that
prints 2. something printed 3. all
the copies printed at one time

**printing press** a machine for printing from inked type, plates, etc.

**print′out′** *n.* the printed or typewritten output of a computer

**pri·or¹** (prī′ər) *adj.* [L.] 1. earlier;
previous 2. preceding in order or importance —**prior to** before in time

**pri·or²** (prī′ər) *n.* [L., superior] the
head of a priory —**pri′or·ess** *n.fem.*

**pri·or·i·tize** (prī ôr′ə tīz′) *vt.* **-tized′,
-tiz′ing** to arrange in order of importance

**pri·or·i·ty** (prī ôr′ə tē) *n., pl.* **-ties**
1. a being prior; precedence 2. a prior
right to get, buy, or do something 3.
something given prior attention

**pri′o·ry** *n., pl.* **-ries** a monastery
governed by a prior, or a nunnery
governed by a prioress

**prism** (priz′m) *n.* [< Gr. *prizein*, to
saw] 1. a solid figure
whose ends are equal and
parallel polygons and
whose faces are paral-
lelograms 2. a trans-
parent prism whose ends
are triangles: used to disperse light
into the spectrum —**pris·mat′ic**
(priz mat′ik) *adj.*

PRISM

**pris·on** (priz′'n) *n.* [< L. *prehendere,*

take] a place of confinement for those
convicted by or awaiting trial

**pris′on·er** *n.* one held captive or
confined, esp. in prison

**pris·sy** (pris′ē) *adj.* **-si·er, -si·est**
[prob. PR(IM) + (S)ISSY] [Colloq.]
very prim or prudish —**pris′si·ness** *n.*

**pris·tine** (pris′tēn, pris tēn′) *adj.* [L.
*pristinus*] 1. characteristic of the
earliest period 2. unspoiled

**prithee** (prith′ē) *interj.* [< *pray
thee*] [Archaic] I pray thee; please

**pri·va·cy** (prī′və sē) *n., pl.* **-cies** 1. a
being private; seclusion 2. secrecy
3. one's private life

**pri·vate** (prī′vit) *adj.* [< L. *privus,*
separate] 1. of or concerning a particular person or group 2. not open to
or controlled by the public [a *private*
school] 3. for an individual person [a
*private* room] 4. not holding public
office [a *private* citizen] 5. secret [a
*private* matter] —*n.* 1. [*pl.*] the external sex organs; the genitals: also
**private parts** 2. an enlisted man
of either of the two lowest ranks in the
U.S. Army or of the lowest rank in the
U.S. Marine Corps —**in private** not
publicly —**pri′vate·ly** *adv.*

**pri·va·teer** (prī′və tir′) *n.* 1. a
privately owned ship commissioned in
war to capture enemy ships 2. a commander or crew member of a privateer

**private eye** [Slang] a private detective

**pri·va·tion** (prī vā′shən) *n.* the lack
of ordinary necessities or comforts

**priv·et** (priv′it) *n.* [< ?] an evergreen
shrub used for hedges

**priv·i·lege** (priv′'l ij, priv′lij) *n.* [<
L. *privus,* separate + *lex,* law] a
special right, favor, etc. granted to
some person or group —*vt.* **-leged,
-leg·ing** to give a privilege to

**priv·y** (priv′ē) *adj.* private: now only
in such phrases as **privy council,** a
body of confidential advisers named
by a ruler —*n., pl.* **-ies** an outhouse
—**privy to** formally informed about

**prize¹** (prīz) *vt.* **prized, priz′ing** [see
PRICE] to value highly; esteem —*n.* 1.
something given to one winning a
contest, etc. 2. anything worth striving for —*adj.* 1. that has won or is
worthy of a prize 2. given as a prize

**prize²** (prīz) *n.* [< L. *prehendere,* to
take] something, esp. a warship, taken
by force

**prize′fight′** *n.* a professional boxing
match —**prize′fight′er** *n.*

**pro¹** (prō) *adv.* [L., for] favorably
—*adj.* favorable —*n., pl.* **pros** 1. a
person or vote on the affirmative side
2. an argument for something

**pro²** (prō) *adj., n., pl.* **pros** *clipped form
of* PROFESSIONAL

**pro-¹** [Gr. < *pro,* before] *a prefix
meaning* before in place or time

**pro-²** [L. < *pro,* forward] *a prefix
meaning:* 1. moving forward [*pro-
clivity*] 2. substituting for [*pronoun*]
3. supporting [*prolabor*]

fat, āpe, cär; ten, ēven; is, bīte; gō, hôrn, tōōl, look; oil, out; up, fur;
chin; she; thin, *then*; zh, leisure; ŋ, ring;ə for *a* in ago; ′, (ā′b'l); ë, Fr. coeur;
ö, Fr. feu; Fr. mon; ü, Fr. duc; kh, G. ich; doch. ‡foreign; <derived from

**prob.** 1. probably 2. problem

**prob·a·bil·i·ty** (präb'ə bil'ə tē) *n.*, *pl.* **-ties** 1. a being probable; likelihood 2. something probable

**prob·a·ble** (präb'ə b'l) *adj.* [ < L. *probare*, prove] 1. likely to occur or be 2. reasonably so, but not proved — **prob'a·bly** *adv.*

**pro·bate** (prō'bāt) *n.* [see PROBE] the act or process of probating —*adj.* having to do with probating [*probate court*] —*vt.* **-bat·ed**, **-bat·ing** to establish officially that (a document, esp. a will) is genuine

**pro·ba·tion** (prō bā'shən) *n.* [see PROBE] 1. a testing, as of one's character, ability, etc. 2. the conditional suspension of a convicted person's sentence —**pro·ba'tion·ar'y** *adj.* **pro·ba'tion·er** *n.* a person on probation

**probation officer** an official whose duty is to watch over persons on probation

**probe** (prōb) *n.* [ < L. *probare*, to test] 1. a surgical instrument for exploring a wound, etc. 2. a searching examination 3. a device, as an instrumented spacecraft, used to get information about an environment —*vt.* **probed**, **prob'ing** 1. to explore (a wound, etc.) with a probe 2. to investigate thoroughly —*vi.* to search

**prob·i·ty** (prō'bə tē, präb'ə-) *n.* [ < L. *probus*, good] honesty; integrity

**prob·lem** (präb'ləm) *n.* [ < Gr. *problēma*] 1. a question proposed for solution 2. a perplexing or difficult matter, person, etc.

**prob·lem·at·ic** (präb'lə mat'ik) *adj.* 1. of the nature of a problem 2. uncertain Also **prob'lem·at'i·cal**

**pro·bos·cis** (prō bäs'is) *n.*, *pl.* **-cis·es** [ < Gr. *pro-*, before + *boskein*, to feed] an elephant's trunk, or any similar long, flexible snout

**pro·caine** (prō'kān) *n.* [PRO-² + CO(CAINE)] a synthetic compound used as a local anesthetic

**pro·ce·dure** (prə sē'jər) *n.* the act or method of proceeding in an action — **pro·ce'dur·al** *adj.*

**pro·ceed** (prə sēd') *vi.* [ < L. *pro-*, forward + *cedere*, go] 1. to go on, esp. after stopping 2. to carry on some action 3. to take legal action (*against*) 4. to come forth or issue (*from*)

**pro·ceed'ing** *n.* 1. a going on with what one has been doing 2. a course of action 3. [*pl.*] a record of transactions 4. [*pl.*] legal action

**pro·ceeds** (prō'sēdz) *n.pl.* the sum derived from a sale, venture, etc.

**proc·ess** (präs'es) *n.* [see PROCEED] 1. the course of being done: chiefly in **in process** 2. course (*of* time, etc.) 3. a continuing development involving many changes [*the process* of digestion] 4. a method of doing something, with all the steps involved 5. *Biol.* a projecting part 6. *Law* a court summons —*vt.* to prepare by or subject to a special process

**pro·ces·sion** (prə sesh'ən) *n.* [see PROCEED] a number of persons or things moving forward, as in a parade

**pro·ces'sion·al** *n.* a hymn sung at the beginning of a church service during the entrance of the clergy

**pro·claim** (prō klām') *vt.* [ < L. *pro-*, before + *clamare*, cry out] to announce officially; announce to be

**proc·la·ma·tion** (präk'lə mā'shən) *n.* 1. a proclaiming 2. something that is proclaimed

**pro·cliv·i·ty** (prō kliv'ə tē) *n.*, *pl.* **-ties** [ < L. *pro-*, before + *clivus*, a slope] a tendency or inclination

**pro·cras·ti·nate** (prō kras'tə nāt') *vi.*, *vt.* **-nat'ed**, **-nat'ing** [ < L. *pro-*, forward + *cras*, tomorrow] to put off doing (something) until later; delay —**pro·cras'ti·na'tion** *n.* —**pro·cras'ti·na'tor** *n.*

**pro·cre·ate** (prō'krē āt') *vt.*, *vi.* **-at'ed**, **-at'ing** [ < L. *pro-*, before + *creare*, create] to produce (young); beget (offspring) —**pro'cre·a'tion** *n.*

**proc·tor** (präk'tər) *n.* [see PROCURE] a college official who maintains order, supervises examinations, etc.

**proc·u·ra·tor** (präk'yə rāt'ər) *n.* [see ff.] in the Roman Empire, the governor of a territory

**pro·cure** (prō kyoor') *vt.* **-cured'**, **-cur'ing** [ < L. *pro-*, for + *curare*, attend to] to obtain; get —**pro·cur'a·ble** *adj.* —**pro·cure'ment** *n.*

**pro·cur'er** *n.* a pimp

**prod** (präd) *vt.* [ < ?] **prod'ded**, **prod'ding** 1. to jab as with a pointed stick 2. to goad into action —*n.* 1. a jab or thrust 2. something that prods

**prod·i·gal** (präd'i gəl) *adj.* [ < L. *pro-*, forth + *agere*, to drive] 1. exceedingly or recklessly wasteful 2. extremely abundant —*n.* a spendthrift —**prod'i·gal'i·ty** (-gal'ə tē) *n.*

**pro·di·gious** (prə dij'əs) *adj.* [see PRODIGY] 1. wonderful; amazing 2. enormous —**pro·di'gious·ly** *adv.*

**prod·i·gy** (präd'ə jē) *n.*, *pl.* **-gies** [ < L. *prodigium*, omen] an extraordinary person, thing, or act; specif., a child of genius

**pro·duce** (prə dōōs', prō'dōōs) *vt.* **-duced'**, **-duc'ing** [ < L. *pro-*, forward + *ducere*, to lead] 1. to bring to view; show [*produce* your license] 2. to bring forth; bear 3. to make or manufacture 4. to cause 5. to get (a play, etc.) ready for presentation —*vi.* to yield something —*n.* something produced; esp., fruit and vegetables —**pro·duc'er** *n.*

**prod·uct** (präd'əkt) *n.* 1. something produced by nature, industry, or art 2. result; outgrowth 3. *Math.* the number obtained by multiplying two or more numbers together

**pro·duc·tion** (prə duk'shən) *n.* a producing or something produced

**pro·duc·tive** *adj.* 1. fertile 2. marked by abundant production 3. bringing as a result (with *of*) [*war is productive* of misery] —**pro·duc'tive·ly** *adv.* —**pro·duc·tiv·i·ty** (prō'dək tiv'ə tē), **pro·duc'tive·ness** *n.*

**Prof.** Professor

**pro·fane** (prə fān') *adj.* [ < L. *pro-*, before + *fanum*, temple] 1. not connected with religion; secular 2. showing disrespect or contempt for sacred things —*vt.* -**faned′, -fan′ing** 1. to treat (sacred things) with irreverence or contempt 2. to debase; defile — **prof·a·na·tion** (präf′ə nā′shən) *n.* — **pro·fane′ly** *adv.* —**pro·fane′ness** *n.*

**pro·fan·i·ty** (-fan′ə tē) *n.* 1. a being profane 2. *pl.* -**ties** profane language; swearing

**pro·fess** (prə fes′) *vt.* [< L. *pro-*, before + *fateri*, avow] 1. to declare openly; affirm 2. to lay claim to (some feeling, etc.) insincerely 3. to declare one's belief in —**pro·fessed′** *adj.*

**pro·fes·sion** (prə fesh′ən) *n.* 1. a professing, or declaring; avowal 2. an occupation requiring advanced academic training, as medicine, law, etc. 3. all the persons in such an occupation

**pro·fes·sion·al** *adj.* 1. of or engaged in a profession 2. engaged in some sport or in a specified occupation for pay —*n.* a person who is professional (esp. in sense 2) —**pro·fes′sion·al·ly** *adv.*

**pro·fes·sor** (prə fes′ər) *n.* a teacher; esp., a college teacher of the highest rank —**pro·fes·so·ri·al** (prō′fə sôr′ē əl) *adj.* —**pro·fes′sor·ship** *n.*

**prof·fer** (präf′ər) *vt.* [< OFr.: see PRO-[2] + OFFER] to offer (usually something intangible) *[to* **proffer** *friendship]* —*n.* an offer

**pro·fi·cient** (prə fish′ənt) *adj.* [< L. *pro-*, forward + *facere*, make] highly competent; skilled —**pro·fi′cien·cy** *n.* —**pro·fi′cient·ly** *adv.*

**pro·file** (prō′fīl) *n.* [< It. *profilare*, to outline] 1. a side view of the face 2. a drawing of this 3. an outline 4. a short, vivid biography

**prof·it** (präf′it) *n.* [see PROFICIENT] 1. advantage; gain 2. *[often pl.]* financial gain; esp., the sum remaining after deducting costs —*vt., vi.* 1. to be of advantage (to) 2. to benefit — **prof′it·a·ble** *adj.* —**prof′it·a·bly** *adv.* —**prof′it·less** *adj.*

**prof·i·teer** (präf′ə tir′) *n.* one who makes excessive profits by charging exorbitant prices —*vi.* to be a profiteer

**prof·li·gate** (präf′lə git) *adj.* [< L. *pro-*, forward + *fligere*, to drive] 1. dissolute 2. recklessly wasteful — **prof′li·ga·cy** (-gə sē) *n.*

†**pro for·ma** (prō fôr′mə) [L., for form] as a matter of form

**pro·found** (prə found′) *adj.* [< L. *pro-*, forward + *fundus*, bottom] 1. very deep *[a profound sleep or sigh]* 2. marked by intellectual depth 3. deeply felt *[profound grief]* 4. thoroughgoing *[profound changes]* — **pro·found′ly** *adv.* —**pro·fun′di·ty** (-fun′də tē) *n., pl.* -**ties**

**pro·fuse** (prə fyōōs′) *adj.* [< L. *pro-*, forth + *fundere*, pour] giving or given freely and abundantly —**pro·fuse′ly** *adv.* —**pro·fu′sion** (-fyōō′zhən) *n.*

**pro·gen·i·tor** (prō jen′ə tər) *n.* [< L. *pro-*, forth + *gignere*, beget] 1. an ancestor in direct line 2. a precursor

**prog·e·ny** (präj′ə nē) *n., pl.* -**nies** [see prec.] children; offspring

**prog·na·thous** (präg′nə thəs) *adj.* [PRO-[1] + Gr. *gnathos*, jaw] having the jaws projecting beyond the upper face

**prog·no·sis** (präg nō′sis) *n., pl.* -**no·ses** (-sēz) [< Gr. *pro-*, before + *gignōskein*, know] a prediction, esp. of the course of a disease

**prog·nos′ti·cate′** (-näs′tə kāt′) *vt.* -**cat′ed**, -**cat′ing** [see prec.] to foretell —**prog·nos′ti·ca′tion** *n.* —**prog·nos′ti·ca′tor** *n.*

**pro·gram** (prō′gram, -grəm) *n.* [< Gr. *pro-*, before + *graphein*, write] 1. a list of the acts, speeches, pieces, etc., as of an entertainment 2. a plan or procedure 3. a scheduled radio or TV broadcast 4. *a)* a logical séquence of operations to be performed by an electronic computer *b)* the coded instructions and data for this —*vt.* -**grammed** or -**gramed**, -**gram·ming** or -**gram·ing** 1. to schedule in a program 2. to prepare (a textbook) for use in programmed learning 3. to plan a computer program for 4. to furnish (a computer) with a program Brit. sp. **pro′gramme** —**pro′gram·mer, pro′gram·er** *n.*

**programmed learning** independent learning by a pupil who advances through a series of questions, the answers to which are given elsewhere in his programmed textbook

**prog·ress** (präg′res; *for v.* prə gres′) *n.* [< L. *pro-*, before + *gradi*, to step] 1. a moving forward 2. development 3. improvement —*vi.* 1. to move forward 2. to move forward toward completion 3. to improve

**pro·gres·sion** (prə gresh′ən) *n.* 1. a moving forward 2. a succession, as of events 3. *Math.* a series of numbers increasing or decreasing by a constant difference between terms

**pro·gres·sive** (-gres′iv) *adj.* 1. moving forward 2. continuing by successive steps 3. of or favoring progress, reform, etc. —*n.* one who is progressive —**pro·gres′sive·ly** *adv.*

**pro·hib·it** (prō hib′it) *vt.* [< L. *pro-*, before + *habere*, have] 1. to forbid by law or an order 2. to prevent; hinder —**pro·hib′i·tive, pro·hib′i·to′ry** *adj.*

**pro·hi·bi·tion** (prō′ə hibish′ən) *n.* 1. a prohibiting 2. the forbidding by law of the manufacture or sale of alcoholic liquors —**pro′hi·bi′tion·ist** *n.*

**proj·ect** (präj′ekt; *for v.* prə jekt′) *n.* [< L. *pro-*, before + *jacere*, to throw] 1. a proposal; scheme 2. an organized undertaking —*vt.* 1. to propose (a plan) 2. to throw forward 3. to cause to jut out 4. to cause (a shadow, image, etc.) to fall upon a surface —*vi.* to jut out —**pro·jec′tion** *n.*

**pro·jec·tile** (prə jek′t'l) *n.* 1. an object designed to be shot forward, as a bullet 2. anything thrown or hurled forward

**projection booth** the small chamber in a motion-picture theater from which the pictures are projected

**pro·jec'tion·ist** *n.* the operator of a motion-picture or slide projector

**pro·jec'tor** *n.* a machine for projecting images on a screen

**pro·lapse** (prō laps', for *n.* prō'laps) *vi.* -lapsed', -laps'ing [< L. *prolabi,* to slip out] *Med.* to fall or slip out of place —*n.* a prolapsed condition

**pro·le·tar·i·at** (prō'lə ter'ē ət) *n.* [< L. *proletarius,* a citizen of the lowest class] the working class; esp., the industrial working class —**pro'le·tar'i·an** *adj.*

**pro·lif·er·ate** (prō lif'ə rāt') *vi.* -at'ed, -at'ing [< L. *proles,* offspring + *ferre,* to BEAR[1]] to increase rapidly —**pro·lif'er·a'tion** *n.*

**pro·lif·ic** (prə lif'ik) *adj.* [< L. *proles,* offspring + *facere,* make] 1. producing many young or much fruit 2. creating many products of the mind —**pro·lif'i·cal·ly** *adv.*

**pro·lix** (prō liks') *adj.* [< L. *prolixus,* extended] wordy or long-winded —**pro·lix'i·ty** *n.* —**pro·lix'ly** *adv.*

**pro·logue** (prō'lôg) *n.* [< Gr. *pro-,* before + *logos,* a discourse] 1. an introduction to a poem, play, etc. 2. any preliminary act, event, etc.

**pro·long** (prə lôŋ') *vt.* [< L. *pro-,* forth + *longus,* long] to lengthen in time or space: also **pro·lon'gate** (-gāt) -gat·ed, -gat·ing —**pro'lon·ga'tion** (prō'-) *n.*

**prom** (präm) *n.* [< ff.] [Colloq.] a dance, as of a particular class at a school or college

**prom·e·nade** (präm'ə nād', -näd') *n.* [Fr. < L. *pro-,* forth + *minare,* to herd] 1. a leisurely walk taken for pleasure, display, etc. 2. a public place for walking 3. a ball or dance —*vi., vt.* -nad'ed, -nad'ing to take a promenade (along or through)

**Pro·me·theus** (prə mē'thyōos, -thē əs) *Gr. Myth.* a Titan who stole fire from heaven for the benefit of mankind

**prom·i·nent** (präm'ə nənt) *adj.* [< L. *prominere,* to project] 1. sticking out; projecting 2. noticeable; conspicuous 3. widely and favorably known —**prom'i·nence** *n.* —**prom'i·nent·ly** *adv.*

**pro·mis·cu·ous** (prə mis'kyōo wəs) *adj.* [< L. *pro-,* forth + *miscere,* to mix] 1. consisting of different elements indiscriminately mingled 2. characterized by a lack of discrimination, esp. in sexual liaisons —**prom·is·cu·i·ty** (präm'is kyōō'ə tē) *n., pl.* -ties —**pro·mis'cu·ous·ly** *adv.*

**prom·ise** (präm'is) *n.* [< L. *pro-,* forth + *mittere,* send] 1. an agreement to do or not to do something 2. indication, as of a successful future 3. something promised —*vi., vt.* -ised, -is·ing 1. to make a promise of (something) 2. to give a basis for expecting

**Promised Land** *Bible* Canaan, promised by God to Abraham and his descendants: Gen. 17:8

**prom·is·so·ry** (präm'i sôr'ē) *adj.* containing or being a promise

**prom·on·to·ry** (präm'ən tôr'ē) *n.,*

*pl.* -ries [prob. < L. *prominere,* to project] a peak of high land that juts out into a body of water; headland

**pro·mote** (prə mōt') *vt.* -mot'ed, -mot'ing [< L. *pro-,* forward + *movere,* to move] 1. to raise to a higher rank or position 2. to further the growth, establishment, sales, etc. of —**pro·mo'tion** *n.* —**pro·mo'tion·al** *adj.*

**pro·mot'er** *n.* one who begins, organizes, and furthers an undertaking

**prompt** (prämpt) *adj.* [< L. *pro-,* forth + *emere,* take] 1. ready, punctual, etc. 2. done, spoken, etc. without delay —*vt.* 1. to urge into action 2. to remind (a person) of something he has forgotten; specif., to help (an actor, etc.) with a cue 3. to inspire —**prompt'er** *n.* —**prompt'ly** *adv.* —**prompt'ness, promp'ti·tude'** *n.*

**prom·ul·gate** (präm'əl gāt', prō mul'gāt) *vt.* -gat'ed, -gat'ing [< L. *pro-,* before + *vulgus,* the people] 1. to make known officially 2. to make widespread —**prom'ul·ga'tion** *n.*

**pron.** 1. pronoun 2. pronunciation

**prone** (prōn) *adj.* [< L. *pronus*] 1. lying face downward or prostrate 2. disposed or inclined (*to*) [*prone* to err]

**prong** (prôŋ) *n.* [LME. *pronge*] 1. any of the pointed ends of a fork 2. any projecting part —**pronged** *adj.*

**prong'horn'** *n.* an antelopelike deer of the western U.S., having curved horns

**pro·noun** (prō'noun) *n.* [< L. *pro,* for + *nomen,* noun] a word used in place of a noun (Ex.: *l, he, it,* etc.) —**pro·nom'i·nal** (-näm'ī n'l) *adj.*

**pro·nounce** (prə nouns') *vt.* -nounced', -nounc'ing [< L. *pro-,* before + *nuntiare,* announce] 1. to declare officially, solemnly, etc. [he was *pronounced* dead] 2. to utter or articulate (a sound or word) —**pro·nounce'a·ble** *adj.*

**pro·nounced'** *adj.* clearly marked; decided [a *pronounced* change]

**pro·nounce'ment** *n.* a formal statement, as of an opinion

**pron·to** (prän'tō) *adv.* [Sp.: see PROMPT] [Slang] at once; quickly

**pro·nun·ci·a·tion** (prə nun'sē ā' shən) *n.* 1. the act or way of pronouncing words 2. the way a word is usually pronounced, esp. in phonetic symbols

**proof** (prōōf) *n.* [see PROBE] 1. a proving or testing of something 2. evidence that establishes the truth of something 3. the relative strength of an alcoholic liquor 4. *Photog.* a trial print of a negative 5. a sheet printed from set type, for checking errors, etc. —*adj.* of tested strength in resisting (with *against*)

**-proof** (prōōf) [< prec.] *a suffix meaning:* 1. impervious to [*waterproof*] 2. protected from [*rustproof*]

**proof'read'** *vt., vi.* to read and mark corrections on (printers' proofs, etc.) —**proof'read'er** *n.*

**prop[1]** (präp) *n.* [< MDu. *proppe*] a support, as a pole, placed under or against something: often used figuratively —*vt.* **propped, prop′ping 1.** to support, as with a prop **2.** to lean (something) *against* a support

**prop²** (präp) *n.* property (sense 4)

**prop³** (präp) *n.* clip of propeller

**prop. 1.** proposition **2.** proprietor

**prop·a·gan·da** (präp′ə gan′də) *n.* [ModL.: see ff.] **1.** any widespread promotion of particular ideas, doctrines, etc. **2.** ideas, etc. so spread —**prop′a·gan′dist** *n., adj.* —**prop′a·gan′dize** (-dīz) *vt., vi.*

**prop·a·gate** (präp′ə gāt′) *vt. -gat′ed, -gat′ing* [< L. *propago*, slip (of a plant)] **1.** to cause (a plant or animal) to reproduce itself **2.** to reproduce (itself): said of a plant or animal **3.** to spread (ideas, customs, etc.) —*vt.* to reproduce, as plants or animals —**prop′a·ga′tion** *n.*

**pro·pane** (prō′pān) *n.* a gaseous hydrocarbon from petroleum, used as a fuel

**pro·pel** (prə pel′) *vt.* **-pelled′, -pel′-ling** [< L. *pro-*, forward + *pellere*, drive] to drive onward or forward

**pro·pel′lant, pro·pel′lent** *n.* one that propels; specif., the fuel for a rocket

**pro·pel′ler** *n.* a device having two or more blades in a revolving hub for propelling a ship or aircraft

**pro·pen·si·ty** (prə pen′sə tē) *n., pl.* **-ties** [< L. *propendere*, hang forward] a natural inclination or tendency

**prop·er** (präp′ər) *adj.* [< L. *proprius*, one's own] **1.** specially suitable; appropriate; fitting **2.** naturally belonging (*to*) **3.** conforming to a standard; correct **4.** decent; decorous **5.** in the most restricted sense [Chicago *proper* (i.e., apart from its suburbs)] **6.** designating a noun that names a specific individual, place, etc. [Ex.: *Jim, Paris*] —**prop′er·ly** *adv.*

**prop·er·ty** (präp′ər tē) *n., pl.* **-ties** [see prec.] **1.** ownership **2.** something owned, esp. real estate **3.** a characteristic or attribute **4.** any of the movable articles used in a stage setting —**prop′er·tied** (-tēd) *adj.*

**proph·e·cy** (präf′ə sē) *n., pl.* **-cies** [see PROPHET] **1.** prediction of the future **2.** something predicted

**proph′e·sy′** (-sī′) *vt., vi.* **-sied′, -sy′ing 1.** to predict as by divine guidance **2.** to predict in any way

**proph·et** (präf′it) *n.* [< Gr. *pro-*, before + *phanai*, speak] **1.** a religious leader regarded as, or claiming to be, divinely inspired **2.** one who predicts the future —**proph′et·ess** *n.fem.*

**pro·phet·ic** (prə fet′ik) *adj.* **1.** of or like a prophet **2.** like or containing a prophecy —**pro·phet′i·cal·ly** *adv.*

**pro·phy·lac·tic** (prō′fə lak′tik) *adj.* [< Gr. *pro-*, before + *phylassein*, to guard] preventive or protective; esp., preventing disease —*n.* a prophylactic medicine, device, etc.

**pro′phy·lax′is** (-sis) *n., pl.* **-lax′es** (-sēz) prophylactic treatment; specif.,

*Dentistry* a cleaning of the teeth to remove plaque and tartar

**pro·pin·qui·ty** (prō pin′kwə tē) *n.* [< L. *propinquus*, near] nearness

**pro·pi·ti·ate** (prə pish′ē āt′) *vt.* **-at′ed, -at′ing** [see ff.] to win the good will of; appease —**pro·pi′ti·a′tion** *n.* —**pro·pi′ti·a·to′ry** (-ə tôr′ē) *adj.*

**pro·pi·tious** (prə pish′əs) *adj.* [< L. *pro-*, before + *petere*, seek] **1.** favorably inclined **2.** favorable; auspicious

**prop·jet** (präp′jet) *n.* same as TURBO-PROP

**pro·po·nent** (prə pō′nənt) *n.* [see PROPOSE] one who espouses or supports a cause, etc.

**pro·por·tion** (prə pôr′shən) *n.* [< L. *pro*, for + *portio*, a part] **1.** the comparative relation in size, amount, etc. between things; ratio **2.** a part, share, etc. in its relation to the whole **3.** balance or symmetry **4.** [*pl.*] dimensions —*vt.* **1.** to put in proper relation with something else **2.** to arrange the parts of (a whole) so as to be harmonious —**pro·por′tion·al, pro·por′tion·ate** (-shə nit) *adj.*

**pro·pos·al** (prə pōz′l) *n.* **1.** a proposing **2.** a proposed plan **3.** an offer of marriage

**pro·pose** (prə pōz′) *vt.* **-posed′, -pos′ing** [< L. *pro-*, forth + *ponere*, to place] **1.** to put forth for consideration, approval, etc. **2.** to plan or intend **3.** to present as a toast in drinking —*vi.* to offer marriage

**prop·o·si·tion** (präp′ə zish′ən) *n.* **1.** something proposed; plan **2.** [Colloq.] a proposed deal, as in business **3.** [Colloq.] an undertaking, etc. to be dealt with **4.** a subject to be discussed **5.** *Math.* a problem to be solved —*vt.* [Colloq.] to make a proposition to

**pro·pound** (prə pound′) *vt.* [see PROPOSE] to set forth for consideration

**pro·pri·e·tar·y** (prə prī′ə ter′ē) *adj.* [see PROPERTY] belonging to a proprietor, as under a patent or copyright

**pro·pri′e·tor** *n.* an owner —**pro·pri′e·tor·ship′** *n.* —**pro·pri′e·tress** *n.fem.*

**pro·pri′e·ty** (-ə tē) *n., pl.* **-ties** [see PROPER] **1.** the quality of being proper, fitting, etc. **2.** conformity with accepted standards of behavior

**pro·pul·sion** (prə pul′shən) *n.* [see PROPEL] **1.** a propelling or being propelled **2.** something that propels —**pro·pul′sive** *adj.*

**pro·rate** (prō rāt′) *vt., vi.* **-rat′ed, -rat′ing** [< L. *pro rata*, in proportion] to divide or assess proportionally

**pro·sa·ic** (prō zā′ik) *adj.* [< L. *prosa*, prose] commonplace; dull

**pro·sce·ni·um** (prō sē′nē əm) *n., pl.* **-ni·ums, -ni·a** (-ə) [< Gr. *pro-*, before + *skēnē*, tent] the arch framing a conventional stage

**pro·scribe** (prō skrīb′) *vt.* **-scribed′, -scrib′ing** [< L. *pro-*, before + *scribere*, write] **1.** to outlaw or banish; exile **3.** to denounce or forbid the use, etc. of —**pro·scrip'tion** (-skrip'shən) *n.*

**prose** (prōz) *n.* [ < L. *prosa,* direct] ordinary language, not_poetry

**pros·e·cute** (präs'ə kyōōt') *vt.* -cut'ed, -cut'ing [ < L. *pro-,* before + *sequi,* follow] 1. to carry on; engage in 2. to conduct legal proceedings against —**pros'e·cu'tion** *n.* —**pros'e·cu'tor** *n.*

**pros·e·lyte** (präs'ə līt') *n.* [ < Gr. *prosēlytos,* a stranger] one who has been converted from one religion, sect, etc. to another —*vt., vi.* -lyt'ed, -lyt'ing to try to make a convert (of): also **pros'e·lyt·ize'** (-li tīz') -ized', -iz'ing —**pros'e·lyt·ism** (-li tiz'm) *n.*

**pros·o·dy** (präs'ə dē) *n., pl.* -dies [ < Gr. *prosōidia,* accent] versification; study of meter, rhyme, etc.

**pros·pect** (präs'pekt) *n.* [ < L. *pro-,* forward + *specere,* look] 1. a broad view; scene 2. viewpoint; outlook 3. anticipation 4. *a)* something expected *b)* [*usually pl.*] apparent chance for success 5. a likely customer, candidate, etc. —*vt., vi.* to explore or search (*for*) —**pros'pec·tor** *n.*

**pro·spec·tive** (prə spek'tiv) *adj.* expected; likely

**pro·spec·tus** (prə spek'təs) *n.* [L.: see PROSPECT] a statement of the features of a new work, enterprise, etc.

**pros·per** (präs'pər) *vi.* [ < L. *prospere,* fortunately] to succeed; thrive

**pros·per·i·ty** (prä sper'ə tē) *n., pl.* -ties prosperous condition; wealth

**pros·per·ous** (präs'pər əs) *adj.* 1. prospering; successful 2. wealthy 3. favorable —**pros'per·ous·ly** *adv.*

**pros·tate** (präs'tāt) *adj.* [ < Gr. *prostatēs,* one standing before] designating a gland surrounding the male urethra at the base of the bladder

**pros·the·sis** (präs'thə sis, präs thē'-) *n., pl.* -ses' (-sēz') an artificial substitute for a missing part of the body —**pros·thet'ic** (-thet'ik) *adj.*

**pros·ti·tute** (präs'tə tōōt') *n.* [ < L. *pro-,* before + *statuere,* cause to stand] a woman who engages in promiscuous sexual intercourse for pay —*vt.* -tut'ed, -tut'ing 1. to offer (oneself) as a prostitute 2. to sell (oneself, one's talents, etc.) for base purposes —**pros'ti·tu'tion** *n.*

**pros·trate** (präs'trāt) *adj.* [ < L. *pro-,* before + *sternere,* stretch out] 1. lying face downward 2. lying prone or supine 3. laid low; overcome —*vt.* -trat·ed, -trat·ing 1. to lay flat on the ground 2. to lay low; subjugate —**pros·tra'tion** *n.*

**pros·y** (prō'zē) *adj.* -i·er, -i·est 1. like prose 2. prosaic; dull

**pro·tag·o·nist** (prō tag'ə nist) *n.* [ < Gr. *prōtos,* first + *agōnistēs,* actor] the main character in a drama, novel, etc.

**pro·te·an** (prōt'ē ən) *adj.* [ < *Proteus,* Gr. god who changed his form at will] readily taking on many forms

**pro·tect** (prə tekt') *vt.* [ < L. *pro-,* before + *legere,* to cover] to shield from injury, danger, etc.; defend —**pro·tec'tor** *n.*

**pro·tec'tion** *n.* 1. a protecting or being protected 2. a person or thing that protects

**pro·tec'tive** *adj.* 1. protecting 2. intended to guard domestic industry from foreign competition [*protective tariffs*] —**pro·tec'tive·ly** *adv.* —**pro·tec'tive·ness** *n.*

**pro·tec'tor·ate** (-tər it) *n.* a weak state under the control and protection of a strong state

**pro·té·gé** (prōt'ə zhā') *n.* [Fr.: see PROTECT] a person guided and helped in his career by another person

**pro·tein** (prō'tēn, prōt'ē in) *n.* [ < Gr. *prōtos,* first] any of numerous nitrogenous substances occurring in all living matter and essential to diet

**pro tem·po·re** (prō tem'pə rē') [L.] for the time (being); temporarily: shortened to **pro tem**

**pro·test** (prə test'; *for n.* prō'test) *vt.* [ < L. *pro-,* forth + *testari,* affirm] 1. to state positively 2. to speak strongly against —*vi.* to express disapproval; object —*n.* 1. an objection 2. a formal statement of objection —**prot·es·ta·tion** (prät'is tā'shən) *n.*

**Prot·es·tant** (prät'is tənt) *n.* [see prec.] any Christian not belonging to the Roman Catholic or Orthodox Eastern Church —**Prot'es·tant·ism** *n.*

**proto-** [ < Gr. *prōtos,* first] *a combining form meaning:* 1. first in time, original 2. first in importance, chief

**pro·to·col** (prōt'ə kôl') *n.* [ < LGr. *prōtokollon,* contents page] 1. an original draft of a document, etc. 2. the ceremonial forms accepted as correct in official dealings, as between heads of state or diplomatic officials

**pro·ton** (prō'tän) *n.* [ < Gr. *prōtos,* first] an elementary particle in the nucleus of all atoms, carrying a unit positive charge of electricity

**pro·to·plasm** (prōt'ə plaz'm) *n.* [see PROTO- & PLASMA] a semifluid viscous colloid, the essential living matter of all animal and plant cells —**pro'to·plas'mic** (-plaz'mik) *adj.*

**pro·to·type** (prōt'ə tīp') *n.* the first thing or being of its kind; model

**pro·to·zo·an** (prōt'ə zō'ən) *n.* [ < Gr. *prōtos,* first + *zōion,* animal] any of various, mostly microscopic, single-celled animals: also **pro'to·zo'on** (-än), *pl.* -zo'a (-ə)

**pro·tract** (prō trakt') *vt.* [ < L. *pro-,* forward + *trahere,* draw] to draw out; prolong —**pro·trac'tion** *n.*

**pro·trac'tor** *n.* a graduated semicircular instrument for plotting and measuring angles

**pro·trude** (prō trōōd') *vt., vi.* -trud'ed, -trud'ing [ < L. *pro-,* forth + *trudere,* to thrust] to jut out; project —**pro·tru'sion** (-trōō'zhən) *n.*

**pro·tru·sile** (-trōō's'l) *adj.* that can be protruded, or thrust out: also **pro·trac'tile** (-trak't'l)

**pro·tu·ber·ance** (prō tōō'bər əns) *n.* [ < L. *pro-,* forth + *tuber,* a bump] a part or thing that protrudes; bulge —**pro·tu'ber·ant** *adj.*

**proud** (proud) *adj.* [ < LL. *prode,* beneficial] 1. having a proper pride in oneself **2.** arrogant; haughty **3.** feeling great pride or joy **4.** that is a cause of pride **5.** caused by pride **6.** stately; magnificent —**proud of** highly pleased with —**proud′ly** adv.

**proud flesh** [from notion of swelling up] an excessive growth of flesh around a healing wound

**prove** (prōōv) vt. **proved, proved** or **prov′en, prov′ing** [ < L. probare, to test] **1.** to test by experiment, a standard, etc. **2.** to establish as true —vi. to be found by experience or trial —**prov′a·bil′i·ty** n.—**prov′a·ble** adj.

**prov·e·nance** (präv′ə nəns) n. [ < L. provenire, come forth] origin; source: also **pro·ve·ni·ence** (prō vē′nē əns)

**Pro·ven·çal** (prō′vən säl′, präv′ən-) n. the vernacular of S France, a distinct Romance language of literary importance in the Middle Ages

**prov·en·der** (präv′ən dər) n. [ < L. praebere, give] **1.** dry food for livestock **2.** [Colloq.] food

**prov·erb** (präv′ərb) n. [ < L. pro-, before + verbum, word] a short, popular saying expressing an obvious truth —**pro·ver·bi·al** (prə vur′bē əl) adj.

**Prov′erbs** a book of the Bible containing maxims

**pro·vide** (prə vīd′) vt. **-vid′ed, -vid′ing** [ < L. pro-, before + videre, see] **1.** to make available; supply **2.** to furnish with **3.** to stipulate —vi. **1.** to prepare (for or against) a possible situation, etc. **2.** to furnish support (for) —**pro·vid′er** n.

**pro·vid′ed, pro·vid′ing** conj. on the condition or understanding (that)

**Prov·i·dence** (präv′ə dəns) capital of Rhode Island: pop. 207,000

**prov·i·dence** (präv′ə dəns) n. **1.** provident management **2.** the benevolent guidance of God or nature **3.** [P-] God

**prov′i·dent** adj. [see PROVIDE] **1.** providing for the future **2.** prudent or economical —**prov′i·dent·ly** adv.

**prov′i·den′tial** (-den′shəl) adj. of, by, or as if decreed by divine providence —**prov′i·den′tial·ly** adv.

**prov·ince** (präv′ins) n. [ < L. provincia] **1.** an administrative division of a country, specif. of Canada **2.** a) a district; territory b) [pl.] the parts of a country removed from the major cities **3.** range of duties or work; sphere

**pro·vin·cial** (prə vin′shəl) adj. **1.** of the provinces **2.** having the ways, speech, etc. of a certain province **3.** countrylike; rustic **4.** narrow; limited —**pro·vin′cial·ism** n.

**proving ground** a place for testing new equipment, new theories, etc.

**pro·vi·sion** (prə vizh′ən) n. **1.** a providing or preparing **2.** something provided for the future **3.** [pl.] a stock of food **4.** a stipulation; proviso —vt. to supply with provisions

**pro·vi′sion·al** adj. temporary —**pro·vi′sion·al·ly** adv.

**pro·vi·so** (prə vī′zō) n., pl. **-sos, -soes**

[see PROVIDE] a clause, as in a document or statute, making some condition or stipulation

**prov·o·ca·tion** (präv′ə kā′shən) n. **1.** a provoking **2.** something that provokes; incitement

**pro·voc·a·tive** (prə väk′ə tiv) adj. provoking or tending to provoke to action, thought, anger, desire, etc. —**pro·voc′a·tive·ly** adv.

**pro·voke** (prə vōk′) vt. **-voked′, -vok′ing** [ < L. pro-, forth + vocare, to call] **1.** to excite to some action or feeling **2.** to anger or irritate **3.** to stir up (action or feeling) **4.** to evoke —**pro·vok′er** n. —**pro·vok′ing** adj.

**pro·vost** (prō′vōst) n. [ < L. praepositus, chief] a high executive official, as in some churches or colleges

**pro·vost guard** (prō′vō) a detail of military police under the command of an officer (provost marshal)

**prow** (prou) n. [ < Gr. prōira] the forward part of a ship

**prow·ess** (prou′is) n. [ < OFr. prouesse] **1.** bravery; valor **2.** superior ability, skill, etc.

**prowl** (proul) vi., vt. [ < ?] to roam about furtively, as in search of prey or loot —n. a prowling —**prowl′er** n.

**prowl car** same as SQUAD CAR

**prox·im·i·ty** (präk sim′ə tē) n. [ < L. prope, near] nearness

**prox·y** (präk′sē) n., pl. **-ies** [ < ME. procuracie, office of a procurator] **1.** the authority to act for another, as in voting **2.** a person so authorized

**prude** (prōōd) n. [Fr. < prudefemme, excellent woman] one who is overly modest or proper in behavior, speech, etc. —**prud′er·y** n. —**prud′ish** adj.

**pru·dent** (prōōd′nt) adj. [ < L. providens, provident] **1.** exercising sound judgment in practical matters **2.** cautious in conduct; not rash **3.** managing carefully —**pru′dence** n. —**pru·den′tial** (-den′shəl) adj.

**prune**[1] (prōōn) n. [ < Gr. prounon, plum] a dried plum

**prune**[2] (prōōn) vt., vi. **pruned, prun′ing** [ < MFr. prooignier] **1.** to trim dead or living parts from (a plant) **2.** to cut out (unnecessary parts, etc.)

**pru·ri·ent** (proor′ē ənt) adj. [ < L. prurire, to itch] tending to excite lust; lewd —**pru′ri·ence** n.

**Prus·sia** (prush′ə) former kingdom in N Europe & dominant state of the former German Empire —**Prus′sian** adj., n.

**pry**[1] (prī) n., pl. **pries** [ < PRIZE[2]] a lever or crowbar —vt. **pried, pry′ing** **1.** to raise or move with a pry **2.** to obtain with difficulty

**pry**[2] (prī) vi. **pried, pry′ing** [ < ?] to look closely and inquisitively; snoop

**pry′er** n. same as PRIER

**P.S.** Public School

**P.S., p.s., PS** postscript

**psalm** (säm) n. [ < Gr. psallein, to pluck (a harp)] **1.** a sacred song or poem **2.** [usually P-] any of the songs

**✂** in praise of God constituting the Book of Psalms —*pl. praise* n.

**Psalms** (sämz) a book of the Bible, consisting of 150 psalms

**Psal·ter** (sôl'tər) [< Gr. *psaltērion*, a harp] the Book of Psalms —*n.* [*also* p-] a version of the Psalms for use in religious services

**pseu·do-** (sōō'dō, syōō'-) [< Gr. *pseudein*, deceive] *a prefix meaning* sham, counterfeit

**pseu·do·nym** (sōō'də nim') n. [< Gr. *pseudēs*, false + *onyma*, a name] a fictitious name, esp. one assumed by an author; pen name

**pshaw** (shô) *interj., n.* an exclamation of impatience, disgust, etc.

**psi** (sī) n. the twenty-third letter of the Greek alphabet (Ψ, ψ)

**pso·ri·a·sis** (sə rī'ə sis) n. [ult. < Gr. *psōra*, an itch] a chronic skin disease characterized by scaly, reddish patches

**psst** (pst) *interj.* sound made to get another's attention quietly

**PST, P.S.T.** Pacific Standard Time

**psych** (sīk) *vt.* psyched, psych'ing [< PSYCHOANALYZE] [Slang] to probe the behavior of by psychological means, esp. so as to outwit or control (often with *out*)

**psych.** psychology

**Psy·che** (sī'kē) [< Gr. *psychē*, soul] *Rom. Folklore* the wife of Cupid —*n.* [p-] 1. the soul 2. the mind, esp. as a functional entity governing the total organism and its interactions with the environment

**psy·che·del·ic** (sī'kə del'ik) adj. [< prec. + Gr. *delein*, make manifest] 1. of or causing extreme changes in the conscious mind 2. of or like the auditory or visual effects experienced with psychedelic drugs

**psy·chi·a·try** (sə kī'ə trē, sī-) n. [see PSYCHO- & -IATRY] the branch of medicine dealing with disorders of the mind, including psychoses and neuroses —**psy·chi·at·ric** (sī'kē at'rik) adj. —**psy·chi'a·trist** n.

**psy·chic** (sī'kik) adj. [see PSYCHE] 1. of the psyche, or mind 2. beyond known physical processes 3. apparently sensitive to forces beyond the physical world  Also **psy'chi·cal** —**psy'chi·cal·ly** adv.

**psy·cho** (sī'kō) n. colloq. clipped form of PSYCHOPATH or PSYCHOPATHIC

**psycho-** [see PSYCHE] *a combining form meaning* the mind or mental processes: also **psych·**

**psy·cho·a·nal·y·sis** (sī'kō ə nal'ə sis) n. a method of treating neuroses and some other mental disorders by analyzing emotional conflicts, repressions, etc. through the use of free association, dream analysis, etc. —**psy'cho·an'a·lyst** (-an'ə list) n. —**psy'cho·an'a·lyze'** (-līz') vt. -lyzed', -lyz'ing

**psy·cho·gen·ic** (sī'kə jen'ik) adj. [PSYCHO- + -GEN + -IC] originating in the mind or in mental conflicts

**psy·chol·o·gy** (sī käl'ə jē) n., pl. -gies [see PSYCHO- & -LOGY] 1. the science dealing with the mind and with mental and emotional processes 2. the

science of human and animal behavior —**psy'cho·log'i·cal** (-kə läj'i k'l) adj. —**psy·chol'o·gist** n.

**psy'cho·neu·ro'sis** (-noo rō'sis) n., pl. -ses (-sēz) same as NEUROSIS

**psy'cho·path'** (-path') n. [see PSYCHO- & -PATHY] one suffering from emotional disorders with amoral and asocial behavior —**psy'cho·path'ic** adj.

**psy·cho·sis** (sī kō'sis) n., pl. -ses (-sēz) [see PSYCHO- & -OSIS] any major mental disorder in which the personality is very seriously disorganized and contact with reality is usually impaired —**psy·chot'ic** (-kät'ik) adj.

**psy·cho·so·mat·ic** (sī'kō sō mat'ik) adj. [PSYCHO- + SOMATIC] designating or of a physical disorder originating in or aggravated by emotional processes

**psy'cho·ther'a·py** (-ther'ə pē) n. [PSYCHO- + THERAPY] treatment of mental disorders by counseling, psychoanalysis, etc. —**psy'cho·ther'a·pist** n.

**pt.** pl. **pts.** 1. part 2. pint 3. point

**pt., p.t.** past tense

**P.T.A.** Parent-Teacher Association

**ptar·mi·gan** (tär'mə gən) n. [< Scot. *tarmachan*] a northern grouse

**pter·o·dac·tyl** (ter'ə dak't'l) n. [< Gr. *pteron*, wing + *daktylos*, finger] an extinct flying reptile with wings of skin stretched from the hind limb to a digit of the front limb

**Ptol·e·my** (täl'ə mē) 2d c. A.D.; Greco-Egyptian astronomer

**pto·maine** (tō'mān) n. [< Gr. *ptōma*, corpse] an alkaloid substance, often poisonous, found in decaying matter

**pub** (pub) n. [< *pub*(*lic house*)] [Chiefly Brit. Colloq.] a bar or tavern

**pu·ber·ty** (pyōō'bər tē) n. [< L. *puber*, adult] the state of physical development when sexual reproduction first becomes possible —**pu'ber·tal** adj.

**pu·bic** (pyōō'bik) adj. [see prec.] of or in the region of the genitals

**pub·lic** (pub'lik) adj. [ult. < L. *populus*, the people] 1. of people as a whole 2. for the use or benefit of all [a *public* park] 3. acting officially for the people [a *public* prosecutor] 4. known by most people —*n.* 1. the people as a whole 2. a specific part of the people [the reading *public*] —**in public** openly —**pub'lic·ly** adv.

**pub·li·can** (pub'li kən) n. 1. in ancient Rome, a tax collector 2. [Brit.] a saloonkeeper; innkeeper

**pub·li·ca·tion** (pub'lə kā'shən) n. [see PUBLISH] 1. public notification 2. the printing and distribution of books, magazines, etc. 3. something published, as a periodical, book, etc.

**public domain** the condition of being free from copyright or patent

**pub·li·cist** (pub'lə sist) n. a person whose business is publicity

**pub·lic·i·ty** (pə blis'ə tē) n. 1. a) any information or action that brings a person, cause, etc. to public notice b) work concerned with such promotional matters 2. notice by the public

**pub·li·cize** (pub'lə sīz') vt. -cized', -ciz'ing to give publicity to

**public relations** relations of an organization, etc. with the general public as through publicity

**public school** 1. in the U.S., an elementary or secondary school maintained by public taxes and supervised by local authorities 2. in England, a private boarding school for boys

**public servant** a government official or a civil-service employee

**pub·lic-spir′it·ed** *adj.* having or showing zeal for the public welfare

**public utility** an organization supplying water, electricity, transportation, etc. to the public

**pub·lish** (pub′lish) *vt.* [ < L. *publicare*] 1. to make publicly known; announce 2. to issue (a printed work) for sale —*vi.* to write books, etc. that are published —**pub′lish·er** *n.*

**puck**[1] (puk) *n.* [akin to POKE[1]] the hard rubber disk used in ice hockey

**puck**[2] (puk) *n.* [OE. *puca*] a mischievous sprite or elf —**puck′ish** *adj.*

**puck·er** (puk′ər) *vt., vi.* [ < POKE[1]] to gather into wrinkles —*n.* a wrinkle or small fold made by puckering

**pud·ding** (pood′iŋ) *n.* [ME. *puddyng*] a soft, sweet food variously made with flour, eggs, milk, fruit, etc.

**pud·dle** (pud′'l) *n.* [dim. < OE. *pudd,* a ditch] a small pool of water, esp. stagnant, spilled, or muddy water

**pud′dling** (-liŋ) *n.* the making of wrought iron from pig iron melted and stirred in an oxidizing atmosphere

**pudg·y** (puj′ē) *adj.* -i·er, -i·est [? < Scot. *pud,* belly] short and fat

**pueb·lo** (pweb′lō) *n., pl.* -los [Sp. < L. *populus,* people] a type of communal Indian village in the SW U.S., consisting of terraced structures, as of adobe, housing many families

**pu·er·ile** (pyoo′ər əl) *adj.* [ < L. *puer,* boy] childish; silly —**pu′er·il′i·ty** *n.*

**Puer·to Ri·co** (pwer′tə rē′kō, pôr′-) island commonwealth in the West Indies, associated with the U.S.; 3,421 sq. mi.; pop. 2,350,000; cap. San Juan —**Puer′to Ri′can**

**puff** (puf) *n.* [OE. *pyff*] 1. a short, sudden gust or expulsion of wind, breath, smoke, etc. 2. a draw at a cigarette, etc. 3. a light pastry filled with whipped cream, etc. 4. a soft pad [a powder *puff*] 5. exaggerated praise, as of a book —*vi.* 1. to blow in puffs 2. to breathe rapidly 3. to fill or swell (*out* or *up*) 4. to take puffs at a cigarette, etc. —*vt.* 1. to blow, smoke, etc. in or with puffs 2. to swell; inflate 3. to praise unduly —**puff′i·ness** *n.* —**puff′y** *adj.* -i·er, -i·est

**puff′ball′** *n.* a round, white-fleshed fungus that bursts at the touch

**puf·fin** (puf′in) *n.* [ME. *poffin*] a northern sea bird with a triangular beak

**pug** (pug) *n.* [ < ? PUCK[2]] a small, short-haired dog with a snub nose

**pu·gil·ism** (pyoo′jə liz′m) *n.* [L.

*pugil,* boxer] the sport of boxing —**pu′gil·ist** *n.* —**pu′gil·is′tic** *adj.*

**pug·na·cious** (pug nā′shəs) *adj.* [ < L. *pugnare,* to fight] eager and ready to fight; quarrelsome —**pug·na′cious·ly** *adv.* —**pug·nac′i·ty** (-nas′ə tē) *n.*

**pug nose** a short, thick, turned-up nose —**pug′-nosed′** *adj.*

**puke** (pyook) *n., vi., vt.* puked, puk′ing [ < ?] [Colloq.] vomit

**puk·ka** (puk′ə) *adj.* [Hindi *pakkā,* ripe] 1. first-rate 2. genuine; real

**pul·chri·tude** (pul′krə tood′) *n.* [ < L. *pulcher,* beautiful] beauty

**pule** (pyool) *vi.* puled, pul′ing [echoic] to whimper or whine, as a sick or fretful child

**pull** (pool) *vt.* [OE. *pullian,* to pluck] 1. to exert force on so as to move toward the source of the force 2. to pluck out [to *pull* a tooth] 3. to rip; tear 4. to strain (a muscle) 5. [Colloq.] to carry out; perform [to *pull* a raid] 6. [Colloq.] to restrain [to *pull* a punch] 7. [Colloq.] to draw out (a gun, etc.) —*vi.* 1. to exert force in dragging, tugging, or attracting 2. to be capable of being pulled 3. to move (*away, ahead,* etc.) —*n.* 1. the act or force of pulling; a tugging, attracting, etc. 2. a difficult, continuous effort 3. something to be pulled, as a handle 4. [Colloq.] *a)* influence *b)* drawing power —**pull for** [Colloq.] to cheer on —**pull off** [Colloq.] to accomplish —**pull oneself together** to regain one's poise, etc. —**pull out** to depart or withdraw —**pull through** [Colloq.] to get over (an illness, difficulty, etc.) —**pull up** 1. to bring or come to a stop 2. to move ahead —**pull′er** *n.*

**pull′back′** *n.* a pulling back; esp., a planned military withdrawal

**pul·let** (pool′it) *n.* [ < L. *pullus,* chicken] a young hen

**pul·ley** (pool′ē) *n., pl.* -leys [ < MGr. *polos,* axis] a small wheel with a grooved rim in which a rope, belt, etc. runs, as to raise weights or transmit power

**Pull·man** (pool′mən) *n.* [ < G. *Pullman,* 19th-c. U.S. inventor] a railroad car with private compartments or berths for sleeping: also **Pullman car**

**pull′out′** *n.* 1. a pulling out; esp., a removal, withdrawal, etc. 2. something to be pulled out, as a magazine insert

**pull′o′ver** *adj.* that is put on by being pulled over the head —*n.* a pullover sweater, shirt, etc.

**pull′up′** *n.* the act of chinning oneself

**pul·mo·nar·y** (pul′mə ner′ē) *adj.* [ < L. *pulmo,* lung] of the lungs

**Pul·mo·tor** (pool′mōt′ər, pul′-) [see prec. & MOTOR] *a trademark for* an apparatus for applying artificial respiration —*n.* [p-] such an apparatus

**pulp** (pulp) *n.* [ < L. *pulpa,* flesh] 1. a soft, moist, sticky mass 2. the soft, juicy part of a fruit or soft pith of a plant stem 3. the sensitive substance under the dentine of a tooth 4. ground-up, moistened fibers of wood, rags, etc. used to make paper —**pulp'y** adj.

**pul·pit** (pool'pit) n. [< L. pulpitum, a stage] 1. a raised platform from which a clergyman preaches in a church 2. preachers collectively

**pul·sar** (pul'sär) n. [< PULSE] any of several small, heavenly objects in the Milky Way that emit radio pulses at regular intervals

**pul·sate** (pul'sāt) vi. -sat·ed, -sat·ing [< L. pulsare, to beat] 1. to beat or throb rhythmically 2. to vibrate; quiver —**pul·sa'tion** n.

**pulse** (puls) n. [< L. pulsus, a beating] 1. the regular beating in the arteries, caused by the contractions of the heart 2. any regular beat

**pul·ver·ize** (pul'və rīz') vt., vi. -ized', -iz'ing [< L. pulvis, powder] to grind or be ground into a powder

**pu·ma** (pyōō'mə) n. [AmSp.] a cougar

**pum·ice** (pum'is) n. [< L. pumex] a light, porous volcanic rock, used for removing stains, polishing, etc.

**pum·mel** (pum'l) vt. -meled or -melled, -mel·ing or -mel·ling [< POMMEL] to hit with repeated blows

**pump¹** (pump) n. [< Sp. bomba] a machine that forces a liquid or gas into, or draws it out of, something —vt. 1. to move (fluids) with a pump 2. to remove water, etc. from 3. to drive air into with a pump 4. to draw out, move up and down, pour forth, etc. as a pump does 5. [Colloq.] to question persistently, or elicit by this —**pump'er** n.

**pump²** (pump) n. [< ? Fr. pompe, ornament] a low-cut shoe without straps or ties

**pump·er·nick·el** (pum'pər nik''l) n. [G.] a coarse, dark rye bread

**pump·kin** (pum'kin, pun'-) n. [< Gr. pepōn, ripe] a large, round, orange-yellow, edible gourdlike fruit that grows on a vine

**pun** (pun) n. [< ? It. puntiglio, fine point] the humorous use of a word, or of different words sounded alike, so as to play on the various meanings —vi. **punned, pun'ning** to make puns

**punch¹** (punch) n. [see PUNCHEON] a tool driven against a surface that is to be pierced, shaped, or stamped —vt. 1. to pierce, stamp, etc. with a punch 2. to make (a hole) with a punch

**punch²** (punch) vt. [ME. punchen] 1. to prod with a stick 2. to herd (cattle) as by prodding 3. to strike with the fist —n. 1. a thrusting blow with the fist 2. [Colloq.] effective force

**punch³** (punch) n. [Hind. pāc, five: it orig. had five ingredients] a sweet drink made with fruit juices, sherbet, etc., often mixed with wine or liquor

**punch card** in data processing, a card with holes punched in it to signal specific information

**punch'-drunk'** adj. confused, unsteady, etc., as from many blows to the head in boxing

**punch line** the final line carrying the point of a joke

**punch'y** adj. -i·er, -i·est [Colloq.]

1. forceful; vigorous 2. punch-drunk

**punc·til·i·ous** (puŋk til'ē əs) adj. [see ff.] 1. careful about nice points of behavior 2. very exact; scrupulous

**punc·tu·al** (puŋk'choo wəl) adj. [< L. punctus, a point] on time; prompt —**punc'tu·al'i·ty** (-wal'ə tē) n. —**punc'tu·al·ly** adv.

**punc·tu·ate** (-wāt') vt., vi. -at·ed, -at·ing [see prec.] 1. to use certain standardized marks (**punctuation marks**), as the period, comma, etc. in (written matter) to clarify meaning 2. to interrupt [a speech punctuated with applause] 3. to emphasize —**punc'tu·a'tion** n.

**punc·ture** (puŋk'chər) n. [< L. pungere, pierce] 1. a piercing 2. a hole made by a sharp point —vt., vi. -tured, -tur·ing to pierce or be pierced as with a sharp point

**pun·dit** (pun'dit) n. [< Sans. pandita] a person of great learning

**pun·gent** (pun'jənt) adj. [< L. pungere, pierce] 1. producing a sharp sensation of taste and smell 2. sharp, biting, or stimulating [pungent wit] —**pun'gen·cy** n. —**pun'gent·ly** adv.

**pun·ish** (pun'ish) vt. [< L. punire] 1. to cause to undergo pain, loss, etc., as for a crime 2. to impose a penalty for (an offense) —**pun'ish·a·ble** adj.

**pun'ish·ment** n. 1. a punishing or being punished 2. the penalty imposed 3. harsh treatment

**pu·ni·tive** (pyōō'nə tiv) adj. inflicting, or concerned with, punishment

**punk¹** (puŋk) n. [< SPUNK] 1. decayed wood used as tinder 2. a fungous substance that smolders when ignited, used to light fireworks, etc.

**punk²** (puŋk) n. [< ?] [Slang] 1. a young hoodlum 2. a young person regarded as inexperienced, insignificant, etc. —adj. [Slang] poor; inferior

**punk rock** [see PUNK² (n. 1)] a form of rock music, usually performed in a hostile, coarse, offensive way

**pun·ster** (pun'stər) n. a person who is fond of making puns

**punt¹** (punt) n. [< ? dial. bunt, to kick] Football a kick in which the ball is dropped from the hands and kicked before it strikes the ground —vt., vi. to kick (a football) in a punt

**punt²** (punt) n. [< L. pons, a bridge] a flat-bottomed boat with square ends —vt., vi. to propel (a punt) with a long pole

**pu·ny** (pyōō'nē) adj. -ni·er, -ni·est [< OFr. puis, after + né, born] of inferior size, strength, or importance —**pu'ni·ness** n.

**pup** (pup) n. 1. a young dog; puppy 2. a young fox, seal, etc.

**pu·pa** (pyōō'pə) n., pl. -pae (-pē), -pas [L., doll] an insect in the stage between the last larval and adult forms

PUPA

**pu·pil¹** (pyōō'p'l) n. [< L. pupillus, orphan, ward] a person taught under the supervision of a teacher or tutor

**pu·pil²** (pyōō'p'l) n. [< L. pupilla, figure reflected in the eye] the contractile circular opening, apparently black, in the center of the iris of the eye

**pup·pet** (pup'it) n. [ < L. *pupa*, doll] 1. a small figure, as of a human being, moved by strings or the hands in a performance (**puppet show**) 2. one whose actions, ideas, etc. are controlled by another —**pup'pet·ry** n.

**pup'pet·eer'** (-i tir') n. an operator, designer, etc. of puppets

**pup·py** (pup'ē) n., pl. **-pies** [ < MFr. *popee*, doll] *same as* PUP

**pup tent** a small, portable tent

**pur·blind** (pur'blīnd') adj. [ME. *pur blind*, quite blind] 1. partly blind 2. slow in understanding

**pur·chase** (pur'chas) vt. **-chased, -chas·ing** [ < OFr. *pour*, for + *chacier*, chase] to buy —n. 1. anything bought 2. the act of buying 3. a fast hold applied to move something heavy or to keep from slipping — **pur'chas·a·ble** adj. —**pur'chas·er** n.

**pure** (pyoor) adj. [ < L. *purus*] 1. free from anything that adulterates, taints, etc.; unmixed 2. simple; mere 3. utter; absolute 4. faultless 5. blameless 6. virgin or chaste 7. abstract or theoretical [*pure* physics] —**pure'ly** adv. —**pure'ness** n.

**pu·rée** (pyoo rā') n. [Fr.: see prec.] 1. cooked food pressed through a sieve or whipped in a blender to a soft, smooth consistency 2. a thick soup of this — vt. **-réed', -rée'ing** to make a purée of Also sp. **puree**

**pur·ga·tive** (pur'gə tiv) adj. purging —n. a purging substance; cathartic

**pur·ga·to·ry** (pur'gə tôr'ē) n., pl. **-ries** [see ff.] [*often* P-] Christian Theol. a state or place after death for expiating sins by suffering —**pur'ga·to'ri·al** adj.

**purge** (purj) vt. **purged, purg'ing** [ < L. *purus*, clean + *agere*, do] 1. to cleanse of impurities, etc. 2. to cleanse of sin 3. to rid (a nation, party, etc.) of (individuals held to be disloyal) 4. to empty (the bowels) —n. 1. a purging 2. that which purges; esp., a cathartic —**purg'er** n.

**pu·ri·fy** (pyoor'ə fī') vt. **-fied', -fy'ing** [ < L. *purus*, pure + *facere*, make] 1. to rid of impurities, etc. 2. to free from guilt, sin, etc. —vi. to become purified —**pu'ri·fi·ca'tion** n.

**Pu·rim** (poor'im) n. [Heb.] a Jewish holiday commemorating the deliverance of the Jews by Esther from a massacre

**pur·ism** (pyoor'iz'm) n. strict or excessive observance of precise usage in language, style, etc. —**pur'ist** n.

**Pu·ri·tan** (pyoor'ə t'n) n. [see ff.] 1. a member of a group in 16th–17th-c. England who wanted to purify the Church of England from elaborate forms 2. [p-] a person regarded as very strict in morals and religion —**pu'ri·tan'i·cal** (-tan'i k'l) adj. —**Pur'i·tan·ism, pur'i·tan·ism** n.

**pu·ri·ty** (pyoor'ə tē) n. [ < LL.

*puritas*] a being pure; specif., a) freedom from adulterating matter b) cleanness c) freedom from sin; chastity

**purl**[1] (purl) vi. [ < ? Scand.] to move in ripples or with a murmuring sound —n. the sound of purling water

**purl**[2] (purl) vt., vi. [ < obs. *pirl*, twirl] to invert (stitches) in knitting so as to form ribbing

**pur·lieu** (pur'lōō) n. [ < OFr. *pur-through* + *aler*, go] 1. an outlying part, as of a city 2. [*pl.*] environs

**pur·loin** (pər loin') vt., vi. [ < OFr. *pur-*, for + *loin*, far] to steal

**pur·ple** (pur'p'l) n. [ < Gr. *porphyra*, shellfish yielding a dye] 1. a dark bluish red 2. crimson cloth or clothing, esp. as a former emblem of royalty —adj. 1. bluish-red 2. imperial 3. ornate [*purple* prose] 4. offensively strong [*purple* language]

**pur·port** (pər pôrt'; *for n.* pur'pôrt) vt. [ < OFr. *por-*, forth + *porter*, to bear] 1. to profess or claim as its meaning 2. to give the appearance, often falsely, of being, intending, etc. —n. 1. meaning; sense 2. intention

**pur·pose** (pur'pəs) vt., vi. **-posed, -pos·ing** [ < OFr. *porposer*: see PROPOSE] to intend or plan —n. 1. something one intends to get or do; aim 2. determination 3. the object for which something exists or is done —**on purpose** intentionally —**pur'pose·ful** adj. —**pur'pose·less** adj.

**pur'pose·ly** adv. with a definite purpose; intentionally; deliberately

**purr** (pur) n. [echoic] a low, vibratory sound made by a cat at ease —vi., vt. to make, or express by, such a sound

**purse** (purs) n. [ < Gr. *byrsa*, a hide] 1. a small bag for carrying money 2. finances; money 3. a sum of money for a present or prize 4. a woman's handbag —vt. **pursed, purs'ing** to pucker

**purs·er** (pur'sər) n. [ME., a pursebearer] an officer on a passenger ship, in charge of accounts, tickets, etc.

**pur·su·ance** (pər sōō'əns) n. a pursuing of a project, plan, etc.

**pur·su'ant** adj. [Now Rare] pursuing —**pursuant to** in accordance with

**pur·sue** (pər sōō') vt. **-sued', -su'ing** [ < L. *pro-*, forth + *sequi*, follow] 1. to follow in order to overtake or capture; chase 2. to follow (a specified course, action, etc.) 3. to strive for 4. to continue to annoy —**pur·su'er** n.

**pur·suit'** (-sōōt') n. 1. a pursuing 2. an occupation; interest

**pu·ru·lent** (pyoor'ə lənt, -yoo-) adj. [ < L. < *pus*, PUS] of, like, or discharging pus —**pu'ru·lence** n.

**pur·vey** (pər vā') vt. [see PROVIDE] to supply (esp. food) —**pur·vey'or** n.

**pur·view** (pur'vyōō) n. [ < Anglo-Fr. *purveu est*, it is provided] scope or extent, as of control, activity, etc.

**pus** (pus) n. [L.] the yellowish-white matter produced by an infection

**push** (poosh) vt., vi. [ < L. *pulsare*, to beat] 1. to press against so as to move

---

fat, āpe, cär; ten, ēven; is, bīte; gō, hôrn, tōōl, look; oil, out; up, fur; chin; she; thin, *then*; zh, leisure; ŋ, ring; ə for *a* in *ago*; ', (ā'b'l); ë, Fr. coeur; ö, Fr. feu; Fr. mon; ü, Fr. duc; kh, G. ich, doch; ‡ foreign; < derived from

**2.** to press or urge on **3.** to urge the use, sale, etc. of —*n.* **1.** a pushing **2.** a vigorous effort **3.** an advance against opposition **4.** [Colloq.] aggressiveness; drive —**push′er** n.

**push button** a small knob pushed to operate something electrically

**push′o′ver** n. [Slang] **1.** anything very easy to do **2.** a person, group, etc. easily persuaded, defeated, etc.

**push′-up′, push′up′** n. an exercise in which a prone person, with hands under the shoulders, raises his body by pushing down with his palms

**push′y** adj. **-i·er, -i·est** [Colloq.] annoyingly aggressive and persistent —**push′i·ness** n.

**pu·sil·lan·i·mous** (pyōō′s'l an′ə məs) adj. [< L. *pusillus*, tiny + *animus*, the mind] timid; cowardly —**pu′sil·la·nim′i·ty** (-ə nim′ə tē) n.

**puss** (poos) n. [< ?] a cat: also **puss′y,** pl. **-ies, puss′y·cat′**

**puss′y·foot′** vi. [Colloq.] **1.** to move with stealth or caution, as a cat does **2.** to avoid committing oneself

**pussy willow** a willow bearing velvetlike, silvery catkins

**pus·tule** (pus′chool) n. [L. *pustula*] a pus-filled pimple or blister

**put** (poot) vt. **put, put′ting** [< OE. *potian,* to push] **1.** a) to thrust; drive b) to propel with an overhand thrust [to *put* the shot] **2.** to cause to be in a certain place, condition, relation, etc.; place; set **3.** to impose (a tax, etc.) **4.** to attribute; ascribe **5.** to express [*put* it plainly] **6.** to present for decision [*put* the question] **7.** to bet (money) on —vi. to go (in, out, etc.) —adj. [Colloq.] fixed [stay *put*] —**put across** to cause to be understood, accepted, etc. —**put aside** (or by) to reserve for later use —**put down 1.** to crush; repress **2.** to write down **3.** [Slang] to belittle or humiliate —**put in for** to apply for —**put it** (or **something**) **over on** [Colloq.] to deceive; trick —**put off 1.** to delay; postpone **2.** to evade; divert —**put on 1.** to clothe oneself with **2.** to pretend **3.** to stage (a play) **4.** [Slang] to hoax —**put out 1.** to expel; dismiss **2.** to extinguish (a fire or light) **3.** to inconvenience **4.** *Baseball* to retire (a batter or runner) —**put through 1.** to carry out **2.** to cause to do or undergo —**put up 1.** to offer **2.** to preserve (fruits, etc.) **3.** to build **4.** to provide lodgings for **5.** to provide (money) **6.** to arrange (the hair) with curlers, etc. **7.** [Colloq.] to incite *to* some action —**put up with** to tolerate

**pu·ta·tive** (pyōōt′ə tiv) adj. [< L. *putare,* suppose] generally thought of as such; supposed

**put′-down′** n. [Slang] a belittling remark or crushing retort

**put′-on′** n. [Slang] a hoax

**pu·tre·fy** (pyōō′trə fī′) vt., vi. **-fied′, -fy′ing** [< L. *putris,* putrid + *facere,* make] to make or become putrid; rot —**pu′tre·fac′tion** (-fak′shən) n.

**pu·tres·cent** (pyōō tres′'nt) adj. putrefying; rotting —**pu·tres′cence** n.

**pu·trid** (pyōō′trid) adj. [< L.

*putrere,* to rot] rotten and foul-smelling

**putt** (put) n. [< PUT, v.] *Golf* a light stroke made to roll the ball into the hole —vt., vi. to hit (a ball) with a putt

**putt·er¹** (put′ər) n. *Golf* a straight-faced club used in putting

**put·ter²** (put′ər) vi. [< OE. *potian,* to push] to busy oneself in an ineffective or aimless way (with *along, around,* etc.) —vt. to fritter (away)

**put·ty** (put′ē) n. [< Fr. *potée,* lit., potful] a soft, plastic mixture of powdered chalk and linseed oil, used to fill small cracks, etc. —vt. **-tied, -ty·ing** to cement or fill with putty

**puz·zle** (puz′'l) vt. **-zled, -zling** [< ?] to perplex; bewilder —vi. **1.** to be perplexed **2.** to exercise one's mind, as over a problem —n. **1.** something that puzzles **2.** a toy or problem for testing skill or ingenuity —**puzzle out** to solve by deep study —**puz′zle·ment** n. —**puz′zler** n.

**Pvt.** *Mil.* Private

**PX** post exchange

**Pyg·my** (pig′mē) n., pl. **-mies** [< Gr. *pygmaios,* of the length of the forearm] **1.** a member of any of several very short peoples of Africa and Asia **2.** [p-] a dwarf —adj. **1.** of the Pygmies **2.** [p-] very small

**py·ja·mas** (pə jam′əz, -jä′məz) n.pl. *Brit. sp.* of PAJAMAS

**py·lon** (pī′län) n. [Gr. *pylōn,* gateway] **1.** a gateway, as of an Egyptian temple **2.** a towerlike structure supporting electric lines, marking a flight course, etc.

**py·lo·rus** (pī lôr′əs) n., pl. **-ri** (-ī) [< Gr. *pylōros,* gatekeeper] the opening from the stomach into the duodenum —**py·lor′ic** adj.

**py·or·rhe·a** (pī′ə rē′ə) n. [< Gr. *pyon,* pus + *rhein,* to flow] an infection of the gums and tooth sockets, with formation of pus

**pyr·a·mid** (pir′ə mid) n. [< Gr. *pyramis*] **1.** a huge structure with a square base and four triangular sides meeting at the top, as a royal tomb of ancient Egypt **2.** *Geom.* a solid figure with a polygonal base, the sides of which form the bases of triangular surfaces meeting at a common vertex —vi., vt. to build up as in a pyramid —**py·ram′i·dal** (pi ram′ə d'l) adj.

EGYPTIAN PYRAMID

**pyre** (pīr) n. [< Gr. *pyr,* fire] a pile of wood for burning a dead body

**Pyr·e·nees** (pir′ə nēz′) mountain range between France & Spain

**Py·rex** (pī′reks) [arbitrary coinage < PIE] *a trademark for* a heat-resistant glassware for cooking, etc.

**py·rite** (pī′rīt) n., pl. **py·ri·tes** (pə rīt′ēz, pī′rīts) [< Gr. *pyritēs,* flint] iron sulfide, a lustrous, yellow mineral: also called **iron pyrites**

**pyro-** [< Gr. *pyr,* fire] *a combining form meaning* fire, heat

**py·ro·ma·ni·a** (pī′rə mā′nē ə) n. [prec. + -MANIA] a compulsion to start destructive fires —**py′ro·ma′ni·ac′** *n., adj.*

**py·ro·tech·nics** (pī′rə tek′niks) *n.pl.* [ < Gr. *pyr*, fire + *technē*, art] 1. a display of fireworks 2. a dazzling display, as of wit

**Pyr′rhic victory** (pir′ik) [ < *Pyrrhus*, Gr. king who won such a victory over Romans, 279 B.C.] a too costly victory

**Py·thag·o·ras** (pi thag′ər əs) 6th c. B.C.; Gr. philosopher & mathematician —**Py·thag′o·re′an** (-ə rē′ən) *adj., n.*

**py·thon** (pī′thän, -thən) *n.* [ < Gr. *Pythōn*, a serpent slain by Apollo] a large, nonpoisonous snake of SE Asia & Africa that crushes its prey to death

**pyx** (piks) *n.* [ < Gr. *pyxis*, a box] a container for Eucharistic wafers

# Q

**Q, q** (kyōō) *n., pl.* **Q's, q's** the 17th letter of the English alphabet

**q.** 1. quart 2. queen 3. question

**Q.E.D.** [L. *quod erat demonstrandum*] which was to be proved

**QM, Q.M.** Quartermaster

**qt.** quart(s)

**Q.T., q.t.** [Slang] quiet: usually in **on the Q.T.** (or **q.t.**) in secret

**quack**[1] (kwak) *vi.* [echoic] to utter the sound or cry of a duck —*n.* this sound

**quack**[2] (kwak) *n.* [ < earlier *quacksalver* ( < Du. *quacken*, to brag + *zalf*, salve)] 1. an untrained person who practices medicine fraudulently 2. one who pretends to have knowledge or skill he does not have —*adj.* fraudulent —**quack′er·y** *n.*

**quad** (kwäd) *n. clipped form of:* 1. QUADRANGLE 2. QUADRUPLET

**quad·ran·gle** (kwäd′raŋ′g'l) *n.* [see QUADRI- & ANGLE[1]] 1. *Geom.* a plane figure with four angles and four sides 2. an area surrounded on its four sides by buildings —**quad′ran′gu·lar** *adj.*

**quad·rant** (kwäd′rənt) *n.* [ < L. *quadrans*, fourth part] 1. an arc of 90° 2. a quarter section of a circle 3. an instrument for measuring altitudes in astronomy and navigation

**quad·ra·phon·ic** (kwäd′rə fän′ik) *adj.* [ < L. *quadra*, a square + Gr. *phōnē*, a sound] using four channels to record and reproduce sound

**quad·rat·ic** (kwäd rat′ik) *adj. Algebra* involving a quantity or quantities that are squared but none that are raised to a higher power

**quad·ren·ni·al** (kwäd ren′ē əl) *adj.* [ < L. *quadri-* (see ff.) + *annus*, a year] 1. lasting four years 2. occurring once every four years

**quadri-** [L. < *quattuor*, four] *a combining form meaning* four times

**quad·ri·lat·er·al** (kwäd′rə lat′ər əl) *adj.* [see prec. & LATERAL] four-sided —*n.* a plane figure having four angles and four sides

**qua·drille** (kwə dril′, kwä-) *n.* [Fr.; ult. < L. *quadra*, a square] a square dance performed by four couples

**quad·ru·ped** (kwäd′roo ped′) *n.* [ < L. *quadru-*, four + *pes*, foot] an animal, esp. a mammal, with four feet

**quad·ru·ple** (kwä drōō′p'l, kwäd′roo-) *adj.* [ < L. *quadru-*, four + *-plus*, -fold] 1. consisting of four 2. four times as much or as many —*n.* an amount four times as much or as many —*vt., vi.* -**pled**, -**pling** to make or become four times as much or as many

**quad·ru·plet** (kwä drup′lit, -drōō′plit; kwäd′roo plit) *n.* 1. any of four offspring born at a single birth 2. a group of four, usually of one kind

**quad·ru·pli·cate** (kwä drōō′plə kit; *for v.* -kāt′) *adj.* 1. fourfold 2. being the last of four identical copies —*n.* any one of such copies —*vt.* -**cat′ed**, -**cat′ing** to make four such copies of —**in quadruplicate** in four such copies —**quad·ru′pli·ca′tion** *n.*

**quaff** (kwäf, kwaf) *vt., vi.* [prob. < LowG. *quassen*, overindulge] to drink deeply and heartily —*n.* a quaffing

**quag·mire** (kwag′mīr′) *n.* [ < *quag*, bog + MIRE] wet, boggy ground

**qua·hog** (kwô′hôg, kō′-) *n.* [ < Am-Ind.] a hard-shelled clam of the E coast: also sp. **quahaug**

**quail**[1] (kwāl) *vi.* [prob. ult. < L. *coagulare*, coagulate] to recoil in fear

**quail**[2] (kwāl) *n.* [ < OFr.] a small game bird resembling a partridge

**quaint** (kwānt) *adj.* [ < OFr. *cointe* < L. *cognitus*, known] 1. pleasingly odd and old-fashioned 2. unusual; curious 3. fanciful; whimsical —**quaint′ly** *adv.* —**quaint′ness** *n.*

**quake** (kwāk) *vi.* **quaked, quak′ing** [ < OE. *cwacian*] 1. to tremble or shake 2. to shiver, as from fear or cold —*n.* 1. a shaking or tremor 2. an earthquake —**quak′y** *adj.*

**Quak·er** (kwāk′ər) *n.* [ < founder's admonition to "quake" at the word of the Lord] *a popular name for* a member of the SOCIETY OF FRIENDS

**qual·i·fi·ca·tion** (kwäl′ə fi kā′shən) *n.* 1. a qualifying or being qualified 2. a restriction 3. any skill, etc. that fits one for a job, office, etc.

**qual·i·fied** (kwäl′ə fīd′) *adj.* 1. fit; competent 2. limited; modified

**qual′i·fi′er** (-fī′ər) *n.* 1. one that qualifies 2. an adjective or adverb

**qual′i·fy′** (-fī′) *vt.* -**fied′**, -**fy′ing** [ < L. *qualis*, of what kind + *facere*, make]

1. to make fit for a job, etc. 2. to make legally capable 3. to modify; restrict 4. to moderate; soften —*vi.* to be or become qualified

**qual·i·ta·tive** (-tāt'iv) *adj.* having to do with quality or qualities —**qual'i·ta'tive·ly** *adv.*

**qual·i·ty** (kwäl'ə tē) *n., pl.* **-ties** [< L. *qualis*, of what kind] 1. that which makes something what it is; characteristic element 2. basic nature; kind 3. the degree of excellence of a thing 4. excellence; superiority

**qualm** (kwäm) *n.* [OE. *cwealm*, disaster] 1. a sudden feeling of sickness, faintness, etc. 2. a doubt; misgiving 3. a twinge of conscience

**quan·da·ry** (kwän'drē, -dər ē) *n., pl.* **-ries** [prob. < L.] a state of uncertainty; dilemma

**quan·ti·ta·tive** (kwän'tə tāt'iv) *adj.* having to do with quantity

**quan·ti·ty** (kwän'tə tē) *n., pl.* **-ties** [< L. *quantus*, how great] 1. an amount; portion 2. any indeterminate bulk or number 3. [*also pl.*] a great amount 4. that property by which a thing can be measured 5. a number or symbol expressing this property

**quan·tum** (kwän'təm) *n., pl.* **-ta** (-tə) [L., how much] a fixed, elemental unit of energy: the **quantum theory** states that energy is radiated discontinuously in quanta

**quar·an·tine** (kwôr'ən tēn') *n.* [< L. *quadraginta*, forty] 1. the period, orig. forty days, during which a vessel suspected of carrying a contagious disease is detained in port 2. any isolation imposed to keep contagious disease, etc. from spreading 3. a place for such isolation —*vt.* **-tined'**, **-tin'ing** to place under quarantine

**quark** (kwôrk) *n.* [arbitrary coinage] any of three hypothetical particles assumed as the basic units of matter

**quar·rel** (kwôr'əl) *n.* [< L. *queri*, complain] 1. a cause for dispute 2. a dispute, esp. an angry one —*vi.* **-reled** or **-relled**, **-rel·ing** or **-rel·ling** 1. to find fault 2. to dispute heatedly 3. to have a breach in friendship —**quar'rel·er**, **quar'rel·ier** *n.* —**quar'rel·some** *adj.*

**quar·ry¹** (kwôr'ē) *n., pl.* **-ries** [< OFr. *curer*, eviscerate] an animal, etc. being hunted down

**quar·ry²** (kwôr'ē) *n., pl.* **-ries** [< L. *quadrare*, to square] a place where stone or slate is excavated —*vt.* **-ried**, **-ry·ing** to excavate from a quarry

**quart** (kwôrt) *n.* [< L. *quartus*, fourth] 1. a liquid measure, equal to 1/4 gallon 2. a dry measure, equal to 1/8 peck

**quar·ter** (kwôr'tər) *n.* [< L. *quartus*, fourth] 1. a fourth of something 2. one fourth of a year 3. one fourth of an hour 4. one fourth of a dollar; 25 cents, or a coin of this value 5. any leg of a four-legged animal, with the adjoining parts 6. a certain district or section 7. [*pl.*] lodgings 8. a particular source [news from high *quarters*] 9. mercy —*vt.* 1. to divide into four equal parts 2. to provide lodgings for —*adj.* constituting a quarter —at

**close quarters** at close range —**cry quarter** to beg for mercy

**quar'ter·back'** *n. Football* the back who calls the signals

**quar'ter·deck', quar'ter·deck'** *n.* the after part of the upper deck of a ship, usually for officers

**quar'ter·fi'nal** *adj.* coming just before the semifinals in a tournament —*n.* a quarterfinal match

**quarter horse** any of a breed of thickset, muscular horse capable of a sprinting speed up to ¼ mile

**quar'ter·ly** *adj.* occurring regularly four times a year —*adv.* once every quarter of the year —*n., pl.* **-lies** a publication issued every three months

**quar'ter·mas'ter** *n.* 1. *Mil.* an officer who provides troops with quarters, clothing, equipment, etc. 2. *Naut.* a petty officer or mate who tends to the compass, navigation, etc.

**quarter note** *Music* a note ( ♩ ) having one fourth the duration of a whole note

**quar·tet, quar·tette** (kwôr tet') *n.* [Fr. < L. *quartus*, a fourth] 1. a group of four 2. *Music* a) a composition for four voices or instruments b) the four performers of this

**quar·to** (kwôr'tō) *n., pl.* **-tos** [< L. (*in*) *quarto*, (in) a fourth] 1. the page size (about 9 by 12 in.) of a book made up of sheets each of which is folded twice to form four leaves, or eight pages 2. a book of this size of page

**quartz** (kwôrts) *n.* [G. *quarz*] a crystalline mineral, a form of silica, usually colorless and transparent

**quartz crystal** *Electronics* a piece of quartz accurately cut and ground to vibrate at a particular frequency

**qua·sar** (kwā'sär, -sər) *n.* [*quas(i-)stell)-ar* (radio source)] a distant, starlike, celestial object that emits much light or powerful radio waves

**quash¹** (kwäsh) *vt.* [< L. *cassus*, empty] to set aside (an indictment)

**quash²** (kwäsh) *vt.* [< L. *quassare*, to break] to suppress (an uprising)

**qua·si** (kwā'sī, -zī; kwä'sē) *adv.* [L.] as if; seemingly —*adj.* seeming Often hyphenated as a prefix [*quasi-legal*]

**quat·rain** (kwä'trān) *n.* [Fr. < L. *quatiuor*, four] a stanza of four lines

**qua·ver** (kwā'vər) *vi.* [ME. *cwafien*] 1. to shake or tremble 2. to be tremulous: said of the voice —*n.* a tremulous quality in a voice or tone

**quay** (kē) *n.* [< OFr. *cai*] a wharf, usually of concrete or stone

**quea·sy** (kwē'zē) *adj.* **-si·er**, **-si·est** [< Scand.] 1. affected with nausea 2. squeamish; easily nauseated

**Que·bec** (kwi bek') 1. province of E Canada: 594,860 sq. mi.; pop. 5,781,000: abbrev. **Que.** 2. its capital, on the St. Lawrence: pop. 167,000

**queen** (kwēn) *n.* [OE. *cwen*] 1. the wife of a king 2. a woman monarch in her own right 3. a woman noted for her beauty or accomplishments 4. the fully developed, reproductive female in a colony of bees, ants, etc. 5. a playing card with a picture of a queen on it 6. *Chess* the most powerful piece —**queen'ly** *adj.* **-li·er**, **-li·est**

**Queens** (kwēnz) borough of New York City: pop. 1,974,000

**queer** (kwir) *adj.* [ < ? G. *quer*, crosswise] **1.** different from the usual; strange **2.** [Colloq.] eccentric —*vt.* [Slang] to spoil the success of —*n.* [Slang] **1.** a strange person **2.** a homosexual —**queer'ly** *adv.*

**quell** (kwel) *vt.* [OE. *cwellan*, kill] **1.** to subdue **2.** to quiet; allay

**quench** (kwench) *vt.* [OE. *cwencan*, to put out] **1.** to extinguish [water *quenched* the fire] **2.** to satisfy [to *quench* one's thirst] **3.** to cool (hot steel, etc.) suddenly by plunging into water, etc. —**quench'less** *adj.*

**quer·u·lous** (kwer'ə ləs, -yə-) *adj.* [ < L. *queri*, complain] **1.** inclined to find fault **2.** full of complaint; peevish —**quer'u·lous·ly** *adv.*

**que·ry** (kwir'ē) *n., pl.* **-ries** [ < L. *quaerere*, ask] **1.** a question; inquiry **2.** a question mark —*vt., vi.* **-ried, -ry·ing** to question

**quest** (kwest) *n.* [see prec.] **1.** a seeking **2.** a journey for adventure

**ques·tion** (kwes'chən) *n.* [see QUERY] **1.** an asking; inquiry **2.** something asked **3.** doubt; uncertainty **4.** a matter open to discussion **5.** a difficult matter [not a *question* of money] **6.** a point being debated before an assembly —*vt.* **1.** to ask questions of **2.** to express doubt about **3.** to dispute; challenge —*vi.* to ask questions —**out of the question** impossible —**ques'tion·er** *n.*

**ques'tion·a·ble** *adj.* **1.** that can be questioned **2.** suspected of being immoral, dishonest, etc. **3.** uncertain

**question mark** a mark of punctuation (?) put after a sentence or word to indicate a direct question, or to express doubt, uncertainty, etc.

**ques'tion·naire'** (-chə ner') *n.* a written or printed set of questions used in gathering information from people

**queue** (kyōō) *n.* [ < L. *cauda*, tail] **1.** a pigtail **2.** [Chiefly Brit.] a line, as of persons waiting to be served —*vi.* **queued, queu'ing** [Chiefly Brit.] to line up in a queue (often with *up*)

**quib·ble** (kwib''l) *n.* [ < L. *qui*, who] a petty evasion; cavil —*vi.* **-bled, -bling** to evade the truth of a point under discussion by caviling

‡**quiche Lor·raine** (kēsh lô ren') [Fr., Lorraine (France) pastry] a custard pie baked with cheese, bacon, etc.

**quick** (kwik) *adj.* [ < OE. *cwicu*, living] **1.** *a)* rapid; swift [a quick walk] *b)* prompt [a *quick* reply] **2.** prompt to understand or learn **3.** easily stirred [a *quick* temper] —*adv.* quickly; rapidly —*n.* **1.** the living, esp. in the **quick and the dead 2.** the sensitive flesh under the nails **3.** the deepest feelings [hurt to the *quick*] —**quick'·ly** *adv.* —**quick'ness** *n.*

**quick bread** any bread leavened with baking powder, soda, etc. and baked as soon as the batter is mixed

**quick'en** *vt., vi.* **1.** to animate; revive **2.** to move more rapidly; hasten **3.** to show signs of life, as a fetus

**quick'-freeze'** *vt.* **-froze', -froz'en, -freez'ing** to subject (food) to sudden freezing for long storage at low temperatures

**quick'ie** *n.* [Slang] anything done or made quickly and, often, cheaply

**quick'lime'** *n. same as* LIME

**quick'sand'** *n.* [ < ME.: see QUICK & SAND] a loose, wet, deep sand deposit, engulfing heavy objects easily

**quick'sil'ver** *n. same as* MERCURY

**quick'-tem'pered** *adj.* easily angered

**quick'-wit'ted** *adj.* nimble of mind

**quid** (kwid) *n.* [var. of CUD] a piece, as of tobacco, to be chewed

**quid pro quo** (kwid' prō kwō') [ModL.] one thing in return for another

**qui·es·cent** (kwī es''nt) *adj.* [ < L. *quiescere*, become quiet] quiet; still; inactive —**qui·es'cence** *n.*

**qui·et** (kwī'ət) *adj.* [ < L. *quies*, rest] **1.** still; motionless **2.** *a)* not noisy; hushed *b)* not speaking; silent **3.** not easily excited **4.** not showy [quiet clothes] **5.** not forward; unobtrusive **6.** peaceful and relaxing —*n.* **1.** calmness, stillness, etc. **2.** a quiet or peaceful quality —*vt., vi.* to make or become quiet —**qui'et·ly** *adv.*

**qui·e·tude** (kwī'ə tōōd') *n.* a state of being quiet; calmness

**qui·e·tus** (kwī ēt'əs) *n.* [ < ML. *quietus* (*est*), (he is) quit] **1.** discharge from debt, etc. **2.** death

**quill** (kwil) *n.* [prob. < MLowG. or MDu.] **1.** a large, stiff feather **2.** *a)* the hollow stem of a feather *b)* anything made from this, as a pen **3.** a spine of a porcupine or hedgehog

**quilt** (kwilt) *n.* [ < L. *culcita*, bed] a bedcover filled with down, cotton, etc. and stitched together in lines or patterns —*vt.* to stitch like a quilt —*vi.* to make a quilt —**quilt'er** *n.*

**quince** (kwins) *n.* [ < Gr. *kydōnion*] **1.** a yellowish, apple-shaped fruit, used in preserves **2.** the tree it grows on

**qui·nine** (kwī'nīn) *n.* [ < *quina*, cinchona bark] a bitter, crystalline alkaloid extracted from cinchona bark, used esp. for treating malaria

**quin·sy** (kwin'zē) *n.* [ < Gr. *kyōn*, dog + *anchein*, choke] *an earlier term for* TONSILLITIS

**quin·tes·sence** (kwin tes''ns) *n.* [ < ML. *quinta essentia*, fifth essence] the pure essence or perfect type

**quin·tet, quin·tette** (kwin tet') *n.* [ult. < L. *quintus*, a fifth] **1.** a group of five **2.** *Music a)* a composition for five voices or instruments *b)* the five performers of this

**quin·tu·plet** (kwin tup'lit, -tōō'plit; kwin'too plit) *n.* **1.** any of five offspring born at a single birth **2.** a group of five, usually of one kind

**quip** (kwip) *n.* [ < L. *quippe*, indeed]

a witty or sarcastic remark; jest —*vi.* **quipped, quip′ping** to utter quips —**quip′ster** *n.*

**quire** (kwīr) *n.* [< L. *quaterni,* four each] a set of 24 or 25 sheets of paper of the same size

**quirk** (kwurk) *n.* [< ?] **1.** a sudden turn or twist **2.** a peculiarity — **quirk′i·ness** *n.* —**quirk′y** *adj.*

**quirt** (kwurt) *n.* [AmSp. *cuarta*] a riding whip with a braided leather lash and a short handle

**quis·ling** (kwiz′liŋ) *n.* [< V. *Quisling,* Norw. collaborator with the Nazis] *same as* TRAITOR

**quit** (kwit) *vt.* **quit, quit′ted, quit′-ting** [< ML. *quietus,* free] **1.** to free (oneself) of **2.** to give up **3.** to leave; depart from **4.** to stop or resign from —*vi.* **1.** to stop doing something **2.** to give up one's job —*adj.* clear; free

**quit·claim** (kwit′klām′) *n.* a deed relinquishing a claim, as to property

**quite** (kwīt) *adv.* [see QUIT] **1.** completely **2.** really; positively **3.** very or fairly [*quite* warm] —**quite a few** (or **bit,** etc.) [Colloq.] more than a few (or bit, etc.)

**Qui·to** (kē′tō) capital of Ecuador: pop. 355,000

**quits** (kwits) *adj.* [see QUIETUS] on even terms, as by discharge of a debt, retaliation, etc. —**call it quits** [Colloq.] **1.** to stop working, etc. **2.** to stop being friendly

**quit·tance** (kwit′ns) *n.* [see QUIT] **1.** discharge from a debt **2.** recompense

**quit′ter** *n.* [Colloq.] one who quits or gives up easily, without trying hard

**quiv·er¹** (kwiv′ər) *vi.* [see QUICK] to shake tremulously; tremble —*n.* a quivering; tremor

**quiv·er²** (kwiv′ər) *n.* [< OFr. *coivre*] a case for holding arrows

**quix·ot·ic** (kwik sät′ik) *adj.* [< DON QUIXOTE] extravagantly chivalrous or romantically idealistic

**quiz** (kwiz) *n., pl.* **quiz′zes** [< ? L. *quis,* what, who] a questioning; esp., a

short examination to test one's knowledge —*vt.* **quizzed, quiz′zing** to ask questions of —**quiz′zer** *n.*

**quiz′zi·cal** (-i k'l) *adj.* **1.** odd; comical **2.** perplexed —**quiz′zi·cal·ly** *adv.*

**quoin** (koin, kwoin) *n.* [var. of COIN]
**1.** the external corner of a building; esp., any of the large stones at such a corner **2.** a wedge-shaped block

**quoit** (kwoit) *n.* [prob. < OFr. *coite,* a cushion] **1.** a ring thrown in quoits **2.** [*pl.,* with *sing. v.*] a game somewhat like horseshoes,

QUOINS

in which rings are thrown at a peg

**quon·dam** (kwän′dəm) *adj.* [L.] former [a *quondam* companion]

**Quon·set hut** (kwän′sit) [< *Quonset* Point, R.I., where first made] *a trademark for* a prefabricated, metal shelter like a half cylinder on its flat side

**quo·rum** (kwôr′əm) *n.* [< L. *qui,* who] the minimum number of members required to be present before an assembly can transact its business

**quot.** quotation

**quo·ta** (kwōt′ə) *n.* [< L. *quota pars,* how large a part] a share or proportion assigned to each of a number

**quotation mark** either of a pair of punctuation marks (" . . . ") used to enclose a direct quotation

**quote** (kwōt) *vt.* **quot′ed, quot′ing** [< ML. *quotare,* to number (chapters)] **1.** to repeat a passage from or statement of **2.** to repeat (a passage, statement, etc.) **3.** to state the price of (something) —*n.* [Colloq.] **1.** something quoted **2.** *same as* QUOTATION MARK —**quot′a·ble** *adj.* —**quo·ta-tion** (kwō tā′shən) *n.*

**quoth** (kwōth) *vt.* [< OE. *cwethan,* speak] [Archaic] said

**quo·tient** (kwō′shənt) *n.* [< L. *quot,* how many] the number obtained when one quantity is divided by another

**q.v.** [L. *quod vide*] which see

# R

**R, r** (är) *n., pl.* **R's, r's** the 18th letter of the English alphabet

**R** (är) *n. Elec.* resistance —**the three R's** reading, writing, and arithmetic, regarded as the basic studies

**R** a motion-picture rating for a film restricted to persons seventeen and over and to persons under seventeen if accompanied by a parent

**r** *Math.* radius

**R., r. 1.** radius **2.** railroad **3.** right **4.** river **5.** road **6.** *Baseball* runs

**Ra** *Chem.* radium

**rab·bet** (rab′it) *n.* [< OFr. *rabattre,* beat down] a cut made in the edge of a board so that another piece may be fitted into it —*vt., vi.* to cut, or be joined by, a rabbet

**rab·bi** (rab′ī) *n., pl.* **-bis, -bies** [< Heb. *rabbi,* my master] an ordained teacher of the Jewish law —**rab·bin·i-cal** (rə bin′i k'l) *adj.* —**rab′bin·ate′** *n.*

**rab·bit** (rab′it) *n.* [ME. *rabette*] a burrowing mammal of the hare family, having soft fur and long ears

**rabbit punch** *Boxing* a short, sharp blow to the back of the neck

**rab·ble** (rab′'l) *n.* [< ?] a mob

**rab′ble-rous′er** *n.* a person who tries to arouse people to violent action by appeals to emotions, prejudices, etc.

**Rab·e·lais** (rab′ə lā′), **Fran·çois** (frän swä′) 1490?-1553; Fr. satirist

**Rab′e·lai′si·an** (-zhən, -zē ən) *adj.* of or like Rabelais; broadly and coarsely humorous, satirical, etc.

**rab·id** (rab′id) *adj.* [< L. *rabere*, to rage] 1. violent; raging 2. fanatical 3. of or having rabies

**ra·bies** (rā′bēz) *n.* [L., madness] an infectious disease with convulsions, transmitted to man by the bite of an infected animal

**rac·coon** (ra kōōn′) *n.* [< AmInd. *arakunem*, scratcher] 1. a small, tree-climbing mammal of N.America, having yellowish gray fur and a black-ringed tail 2. its fur

**race**[1] (rās) *n.* [< ON. *rās*, a running] 1. a competition of speed, as in running 2. any contest like a race [the *race* for mayor] 3. a swift current of water, or its channel —*vi.* **raced, rac′ing** 1. to take part in a race 2. to go or move swiftly —*vt.* 1. to compete with in a race 2. to enter (a horse, etc.) in a race 3. to cause to go swiftly —**rac′-er** *n.*

**race**[2] (rās) *n.* [Fr. < It. *razza*] 1. any of the three primary divisions of mankind distinguished esp. by color of skin 2. any geographical, national, or tribal ethnic grouping 3. any distinct group of people [the *race* of artists]

**race′horse′** *n.* a horse bred and trained for racing

**ra·ceme** (rā sēm′, rə-) *n.* [L. *racemus*, cluster of grapes] a flower cluster, having a central stem along which individual flowers grow on small stems

**race track** a course prepared for racing, esp. an oval track for horse races: also **race′course′** *n.*

**race′way′** *n.* 1. a narrow channel 2. a race track for harness races or one for drag races, etc.

**ra·chi·tis** (rə kīt′əs) *n.* [< Gr. *rhachitis*, spine inflammation] *same as* RICKETS —**ra·chit′ic** (-kit′ik) *adj.*

**ra·cial** (rā′shəl) *adj.* of or characteristic of a race, or ethnic group

**rac·i·ness** (rā′sē nis) *n.* racy quality

**rac·ism** (rā′siz′m) *n.* the practice of racial discrimination, persecution, etc. —**rac′ist** *n., adj.*

**rack**[1] (rak) *n.* [prob. < MDu. *recken*, to stretch] 1. a framework, etc. for holding or displaying various things [tie *rack*, pipe *rack*] 2. a toothed bar into which a pinion, etc. meshes 3. an instrument of torture which stretches the victim's limbs 4. any great torment —*vt.* 1. to arrange in or on a rack 2. to torture on a rack 3. to torment —**on the rack** in a difficult situation —**rack one's brains** to try hard to think of something —**rack up** [Slang] to score or achieve

**rack**[2] (rak) *n.* [var. of WRACK] destruction: now only in **go to rack and ruin**, to become ruined

**rack·et**[1] (rak′it) *n.* [prob. echoic] 1. a noisy confusion 2. *a)* an obtaining of money illegally *b)* [Colloq.] any dishonest practice

**rack·et**[2] (rak′it) *n.* [MFr. < Ar. *rāhah*, palm of the hand] a light bat for tennis, etc. with a network, as of cat-

gut, in a frame attached to a handle: also sp. **rac′quet**

**rack·et·eer** (rak′ə tir′) *n.* one who obtains money illegally, as by fraud, extortion, etc. —**rack′et·eer′ing** *n.*

**rac·on·teur** (rak′än tur′) *n.* [Fr. < *raconter*, to recount] a person skilled at telling stories or anecdotes

**rac′quet·ball′** *n.* a game played like handball, but with a racket

**rac·y** (rā′sē) *adj.* **-i·er, -i·est** [< RACE[2]] 1. having the taste or quality of the genuine type [*racy* fruit] 2. lively; spirited 3. pungent 4. risqué

**ra·dar** (rā′där) *n.* [*ra(dio) d(etecting) a(nd) r(anging)*] a system or device that transmits radio waves to a reflecting object, as an aircraft, to determine its location, speed, etc. by the reflected waves

**ra′dar·scope′** (-skōp′) *n.* an oscilloscope that picks up radar waves

**ra·di·al** (rā′dē əl) *adj.* [see RADIUS] 1. of or like a ray or rays; branching out from a center 2. of a radius

**radial (ply) tire** an automobile tire with ply cords nearly at right angles to the center line of the tread

**ra·di·ant** (rā′dē ənt) *adj.* [see RADIUS] 1. shining brightly 2. showing pleasure, etc.; beaming 3. issuing (from a source) in or as in rays —**ra′di·ance** *n.* —**ra′di·ant·ly** *adv.*

**ra·di·ate** (rā′dē āt′) *vi.* **-at′ed, -at′ing** [see RADIUS] 1. to send out rays of heat, light, etc. 2. to branch out in lines from a center —*vt.* 1. to send out (heat, light, etc.) in rays 2. to give forth (happiness, love, etc.)

**ra′di·a′tion** *n.* 1. a radiating 2. the rays sent out 3. nuclear particles

**radiation sickness** sickness produced by overexposure to X-rays, radioactive matter, etc.

**ra′di·a′tor** *n.* an apparatus for radiating heat, as into a room or from an automobile engine

**rad·i·cal** (rad′i k'l) *adj.* [< L. *radix*, root] 1. of or from the root; fundamental 2. favoring basic change, as in the social or economic structure —*n.* 1. a person holding radical views 2. *Chem.* a group of two or more atoms acting as a single atom 3. *Math.* the sign (√) used with a quantity to show that its root is to be extracted —**rad′i·cal·ism** *n.* —**rad′i·cal·ly** *adv.*

**ra·di·i** (rā′dē ī′) *n.* *alt. pl. of* RADIUS

**ra·di·o** (rā′dē ō′) *n., pl.* **-os′** [ult. < L. *radius:* see RADIUS] 1. *a)* the transmission of sounds or signals by electromagnetic waves through space, without wires, to a receiving set *b)* such a set 2. broadcasting by radio as an industry, entertainment, etc. —*adj.* of, using, used in, or sent by radio —*vt., vi.* **-oed′, -o′ing** to transmit, or communicate with, by radio

**radio-** [see RADIUS] *a combining form meaning:* 1. radial 2. by radio 3. using radiant energy [*radiotherapy*]

**ra′di·o·ac′tive** *adj.* giving off radiant

energy in the form of particles or rays by the disintegration of atomic nuclei —**ra/di·o·ac·tiv/i·ty** *n.*

**radio astronomy** astronomy dealing with radio waves in space in order to obtain information about the universe

**ra/di·o·gram/** (-gram/) *n.* a message sent by radio

**ra/di·o·i/so·tope/** *n.* a radioactive isotope of a chemical element

**ra/di·ol/o·gy** (-äl/ə jē) *n.* the use of radiant energy, as X-rays, in medical diagnosis and therapy —**ra/di·ol/o·gist** *n.*

**ra/di·o·paque/** (-ō pāk/) *adj.* not allowing the passage of X-rays, etc.

**ra/di·os/co·py** (-äs/kə pē) *n.* the examination of the inside structure of opaque objects, as by means of X-rays —**ra/di·o·scop/ic** (-ə skäp/ik) *adj.*

**ra/di·o·ther/a·py** *n.* the treatment of disease by the use of X-rays or rays from a radioactive substance

**rad·ish** (rad/ish) *n.* [ < L. *radix*, root] 1. a plant of the mustard family, with an edible root 2. the pungent root, eaten raw

**ra·di·um** (rā/dē əm) *n.* [see ff.] a radioactive metallic chemical element, found in some uranium, which undergoes spontaneous atomic disintegration

**radium therapy** the treatment of cancer, etc. by the use of radium

**ra·di·us** (rā/dē əs) *n., pl.* **-di·i/** (-ī/), **-us·es** [L., spoke (of a wheel), hence ray] 1. any straight line from the center to the periphery of a circle or sphere 2. the circular area limited by the sweep of such a line [within a *radius* of two miles]

**ra·dome** (rā/dōm/) *n.* [RA(DAR) + DOME] a housing to protect a radar antenna

**RAF, R.A.F.** Royal Air Force

**raf·fi·a** (raf/ē ə) *n.* [ < native name] 1. a palm tree of Madagascar with large leaves 2. fiber from its leaves, used for weaving

**raff·ish** (raf/ish) *adj.* [(RIFF)RAFF + -ISH] 1. disreputable 2. tawdry

**raf·fle** (raf/'l) *n.* [ < MFr. *rafle*, dice game] a lottery in which each participant buys a chance to win a prize —*vt.* **-fled, -fling** to offer as a prize in a raffle (often with *off*)

**raft¹** (raft) *n.* [ < ON. *raptr*, a log] 1. a floating structure of logs, boards, etc. fastened together 2. an inflatable boat

**raft²** (raft) *n.* [ < Brit. dial. *raff*, rubbish] [Colloq.] a large quantity

**raft·er** (raf/tər) *n.* [OE. *ræfter*] any of the beams that slope from the ridge of a roof to the eaves

**rag¹** (rag) *n.* [ < ON. *rögg*, tuft of hair] 1. a waste piece of cloth, esp. one old or torn 2. a small piece of cloth for dusting, etc. 3. [*pl.*] old, worn clothes

**rag²** (rag) *n.* a tune in ragtime

**rag³** (rag) *vt.* [ < ?] **ragged, rag'ging** to tease or scold

**ra·ga** (rä/gə) *n.* [Sans. *rāga*, color] any of various melody patterns improvised on by Hindu musicians

**rag·a·muf·fin** (rag/ə muf/in) *n.* [ME. *Ragamoffyn*, name of a demon] a dirty, ragged person, esp. such a child

**rag/bag/** *n.* 1. a bag for rags 2. a collection of odds and ends

**rage** (rāj) *n.* [ < LL. *rabia*, madness] 1. a furious, uncontrolled anger 2. a great violence or intensity —*vi.* 1. to show violent anger, as in speech 2. to be forceful, violent, etc. 3. to spread unchecked, as a disease —(all) **the rage** a fad

**rag·ged** (rag/id) *adj.* 1. shabby or torn from wear 2. wearing shabby or torn clothes 3. uneven; imperfect 4. shaggy [*ragged* hair] —**run ragged** to tire out; exhaust —**rag/ged·ness** *n.*

**rag/ged·y** (-ē) *adj.* somewhat ragged

**rag·lan** (rag/lən) *n.* [ < Lord *Raglan*, 19th-c. Brit. general] a loose coat with sleeves that continue in one piece to the collar —*adj.* designating such a sleeve

**ra·gout** (ra goō/) *n.* [ < Fr. *ragouter*, revive the appetite of] a highly seasoned stew of meat and vegetables

**rag·time** (rag/tīm/) *n.* [prob. < *ragged time*] 1. a type of American music (c. 1890–1915), with strong syncopation in fast, even time 2. its rhythm

RAGLAN SLEEVE

**rag/weed/** *n.* [ < its ragged-looking leaves] a weed whose pollen is a common cause of hay fever

**rah** (rä) *interj.* hurrah

**raid** (rād) *n.* [dial. var. of ROAD] 1. a sudden, hostile attack, as by troops, bandits, etc. 2. a sudden invasion of a place by police, for discovering violations of the law —*vt., vi.* to make a raid (on) —**raid/er** *n.*

**rail¹** (rāl) *n.* [ < L. *regula*, a rule] 1. a bar of wood, metal, etc. placed between posts as a barrier or support 2. any of the parallel metal bars forming a track, as for railroad cars 3. a railroad —*vt.* to supply with rails

**rail²** (rāl) *vi.* [ < LL. *ragere*, to bellow] to speak bitterly; inveigh; complain

**rail³** (rāl) *n.* [ < MFr. *raale*, to screech] a small wading bird

**rail/ing** *n.* 1. material for rails 2. a fence, etc. made of rails and posts

**rail·ler·y** (rāl/ər ē) *n., pl.* **-ies** [see RAIL²] light, good-natured ridicule

**rail/road/** *n.* 1. a road laid with parallel steel rails along which cars are drawn by locomotives 2. a complete system of such roads —*vt.* 1. to transport by railroad 2. [Colloq.] to rush through (a bill) or convict (a person) hastily, without careful consideration —*vi.* to work on a railroad —**rail/road/er** *n.* —**rail/road/ing** *n.*

**rail/way/** *n.* 1. [Brit.] a railroad 2. any track with rails to guide wheels

**rai·ment** (rā/mənt) *n.* [see ARRAY & -MENT] [Archaic] clothing; attire

**rain** (rān) *n.* [OE. *regn*] 1. water falling in drops condensed from the atmosphere 2. the falling of such drops 3. a rapid falling of many small objects —*vi.* 1. to fall: said of rain 2. to fall like rain —*vt.* 1. to pour down (rain, etc.) 2. to give in large quantities —

**rain out** to cause (an event) to be canceled because of rain —**rain′y** adj. **-i·er, -i·est**

**rain′bow′** (-bō′) n. the arc containing the colors of the spectrum formed in the sky by the refraction of the sun's rays in falling rain or in mist

**rain check** the stub of a ticket to a ball game, etc. allowing future admission if the event is rained out

**rain′coat′** n. a water-repellent coat

**rain′drop′** n. a single drop of rain

**rain′fall′** n. 1. a falling of rain 2. the amount of water falling over a given area during a given time

**rain forest** a dense, evergreen forest in a tropical area with much rainfall

**rain′storm′** n. a storm with a heavy rain

**raise** (rāz) vt. **raised, rais′ing** [< ON. reisa] 1. to cause to rise; lift 2. to construct; build 3. to increase in size, amount, degree, intensity, etc. [raise prices, raise one's voice] 4. to provoke; inspire 5. to present for consideration [raise a question] 6. to collect (an army, money, etc.) 7. to end (a siege, etc.) 8. a) to cause to grow b) to rear (children) —n. 1. a raising 2. an increase, as in salary or a bet —**raise Cain** (or **hell, etc.**) [Slang] to create a disturbance

**rai·sin** (rā′z'n) n. [< L. racemus, cluster of grapes] a sweet dried grape

**rai·son d'etre** (rā′zōn det′, det′rə) [Fr.] reason for being

**ra·jah, ra·ja** (rä′jə) n. [< Sans. rāj, to rule] a prince in India

**rake¹** (rāk) n. [OE. raca] a long-handled tool with teeth at one end, for gathering loose hay, leaves, etc. —vt. **raked, rak′ing** 1. to gather or smooth with a rake 2. to search through minutely 3. to direct gunfire along (a line of troops, etc.) —**rake in** to gather a great amount of rapidly —**rake up** to uncover facts or gossip about (the past, a scandal, etc.)

**rake²** (rāk) n. [< earlier rakehell] a dissolute, debauched man

**rake³** (rāk) vi., vt. **raked, rak′ing** [< ?] to slant —n. a slanting

**rake′-off′** n. [Slang] a commission or rebate, esp. when illegitimate

**rak·ish** (rā′kish) adj. [< RAKE³ + -ISH] 1. having a trim appearance, suggesting speed: said of a ship 2. gay and dashing; jaunty —**rak′ish·ly** adv.

**Ra·leigh** (rô′lē, rä′-) capital of N.C.: pop. 122,000

**Ra·leigh** (rô′lē, rä′-), Sir **Walter** 1552?-1618; Eng. explorer & poet

**ral·ly¹** (ral′ē) vt., vi. **-lied, -ly·ing** [< OFr. re-, again + aleier, join] 1. to bring back together in, or come back to, a state of order, as troops 2. to bring or come together for a common purpose 3. to revive; recover —n., pl. **-lies** 1. a rallying or being rallied; esp., a gathering of people for some purpose 2. an organized automobile run designed to test driving skills

**ral·ly²** (ral′ē) vt., vi. **-lied, -ly·ing** [see RAIL²] to tease or banter

**ram** (ram) n. [OE. ramm] 1. a male sheep 2. same as BATTERING RAM —vt. **rammed, ram′ming** 1. to strike against with great force 2. to force into place; press down

**ram·ble** (ram′b'l) vi. **-bled, -bling** [< ME. romen] 1. to roam about; esp., to stroll about idly 2. to talk or write aimlessly 3. to spread in all directions, as a vine —n. a stroll

**ram′bler** n. a person or thing that rambles; esp., a climbing rose

**ram·bunc·tious** (ram buŋk′shəs) adj. [alt., after RAM, < earlier robustious] disorderly, boisterous, unruly, etc. —**ram·bunc′tious·ness** n.

**ram·e·kin** (ram′ə kin) n. [< Fr. < MDu.] a small, individual baking dish

**ram·i·fy** (ram′ə fī′) vt., vi. **-fied′, -fy′ing** [< L. ramus, a branch + facere, make] to divide or spread out into branches or branchlike divisions —**ram′i·fi·ca′tion** n.

**ramp** (ramp) n. [< OFr. ramper, climb] 1. a sloping walk or road joining different levels 2. a wheeled staircase for boarding an airplane 3. a sloping runway for launching boats, as from trailers

**ram·page** (ram pāj′; for n. ram′pāj) vi. **-paged′, -pag′ing** [prob. akin to prec.] to rush violently about; rage —n. an outbreak of wild, raging behavior: chiefly in **on a rampage**

**ramp·ant** (ram′pənt) adj. [see RAMP] growing unchecked; widespread

**ram·part** (ram′pärt, -pərt) n. [< Fr. re-, again + emparer, fortify] an embankment of earth surmounted by a parapet for defending a fort, etc.

**ram′rod′** n. a rod for ramming down the charge in a muzzle-loading gun

**ram·shack·le** (ram′shak″l) adj. [< RANSACK] loose and rickety; likely to fall to pieces

**ran** (ran) pt. of RUN

**ranch** (ranch) n. [< Sp. rancho, small farm] 1. a large farm, esp. in W States, for raising cattle, horses, or sheep 2. a style of house with all the rooms on one floor: in full **ranch house** —vi. to work on or manage a ranch —**ranch′er, ranch′man** n., pl. **-men**

**ran·cid** (ran′sid) adj. [< L. rancere, to be rank] having the bad smell or taste of stale fats or oils; spoiled

**ran·cor** (raŋ′kər) n. [< L. rancere, to be rank] a continuing and bitter hate or ill will: Brit. sp. **ran′cour** —**ran′cor·ous** adj. —**ran′cor·ous·ly** adv.

**R & D, R and D** research and development

**ran·dom** (ran′dəm) adj. [< OFr. randon, violence, speed] purposeless; haphazard —**at random** haphazardly —**ran′dom·ly** adv.

**ran·dom·ize′** (-īz′) vt. **-ized′, -iz′ing** to select or choose (items of a group) in a random order

**ran·dy** (ran′dē) *adj.* **-i·er, -i·est**
[prob. < RANT] amorous; lustful

**rang** (raŋ) *pt. of* RING[1]

**range** (rānj) *vt.* **ranged, rang′ing** [<
OFr. *renc*, a ring] **1.** to arrange in
order; set in a row or rows **2.** to place
(oneself) with others in a cause, etc. **3.**
to roam about — *vi.* **1.** to extend in a
given direction **2.** to roam **3.** to vary
between stated limits — *n.* **1.** a row,
line, or series **2.** a series of connected
mountains **3.** the distance that a
weapon can fire its projectile **4.** *a)* a
place for shooting practice *b)* a place
for testing rockets in flight **5.** extent;
scope **6.** a large, open area for grazing
livestock **7.** the limits of possible
variations of amount, degree, pitch,
etc. [a wide *range* in price] **8.** a
cooking stove

**rang′er** *n.* **1.** *a)* a mounted trooper
who patrols a region *b)* [often R-] a
soldier trained for close-combat raids
**2.** a warden who patrols forests

**Ran·goon** (raŋ go͞on′) capital of
Burma: pop. 1,530,000

**rang·y** (rān′jē) *adj.* **-i·er, -i·est** long-
limbed and slender —**rang′i·ness** *n.*

**rank**[1] (raŋk) *n.* [< OFr. *ranc*] **1.** a
row, line, or series **2.** a social class **3.**
high position in society **4.** an official
grade [the *rank* of major] **5.** a relative
position in a scale [a poet of the first
*rank*] **6.** *a)* a row of soldiers, etc.
placed side by side *b)* [pl.] the army;
esp., enlisted soldiers — *vt.* **1.** to place
in a rank **2.** to assign a position to **3.**
to outrank — *vi.* to hold a certain
position —**rank and file 1.** enlisted
soldiers **2.** ordinary members, as
distinguished from their leaders

**rank**[2] (raŋk) *adj.* [OE. *ranc*, strong] **1.**
growing vigorously and coarsely [*rank*
grass] **2.** strong and offensive in smell
or taste **3.** in bad taste **4.** extreme;
utter [*rank* deceit] —**rank′ness** *n.*

**rank′ing** *adj.* **1.** of the highest rank
**2.** prominent or outstanding

**ran·kle** (raŋ′k'l) *vi., vt.* **-kled, -kling**
[< ML. *dracunculus*, ulcer] **1.** orig.,
to fester **2.** to cause or cause to have
long-lasting anger, rancor, etc.

**ran·sack** (ran′sak) *vt.* [< ON. *rann*,
house + *sækja*, seek] **1.** to search
thoroughly **2.** to plunder; pillage

**ran·som** (ran′səm) *n.* [see REDEEM]
**1.** the redeeming of a captive by paying money or complying with demands
**2.** the price demanded for this — *vt.* to
obtain the release of (a captive, etc.)
by paying the price demanded

**rant** (rant) *vi., vt.* [< obs. Du. *ranten*]
to talk or say in a loud, wild, extravagant way — *n.* loud, wild speech

**rap**[1] (rap) *vt.* **rapped, rap′ping** [prob.
echoic] **1.** to strike quickly and
sharply; tap **2.** [Slang] to criticize
sharply — *vi.* **1.** to knock sharply **2.**
[Slang] to chat — *n.* **1.** a quick, sharp
knock **2.** [Slang] blame or punishment
**3.** [Slang] a talking; chat

**ra·pa·cious** (rə pā′shəs) *adj.* [< L.
*rapere*, seize] **1.** greedy; voracious **2.**
predatory —**ra·pac′i·ty** (-pas′ə tē) *n.*

**rape**[1] (rāp) *n.* [prob. < L. *rapere*,
seize] **1.** the crime of having sexual

intercourse with a woman forcibly and
without her consent **2.** the plundering
(of a city, etc.), as in warfare — *vt.*
**raped, rap′ing 1.** to commit rape on;
ravish **2.** to plunder or destroy — *vi.*
to commit rape —**rap′ist** *n.*

**rape**[2] (rāp) *n.* [< L. *rapa*, turnip] a
plant of the mustard family, whose
leaves are used for fodder

**Raph·a·el** (raf′ē əl, rā′fē-) 1483-
1520; It. painter

**rap·id** (rap′id) *adj.* [< L. *rapere*, to
rush] moving or occurring with speed;
swift; quick — *n.* [usually *pl.*] a part of
a river where the current is swift —
**ra·pid·i·ty** (rə pid′ə tē) *n.* —**rap′-
id·ly** *adv.*

**rapid transit** a system of rapid
public transportation in an urban
area, using electric trains along an
unimpeded right of way

**ra·pi·er** (rā′pē ər) *n.* [Fr. *rapière*] a
light, sharp-pointed sword used only
for thrusting

**rap·ine** (rap′in) *n.* [< L. *rapere*,
seize] plunder; pillage

**rap·port** (ra pôr′, -pôrt′) *n.* [Fr. < L.
*ad-*, to + *portare*, carry] sympathetic
relationship; harmony

**rap·proche·ment** (ra prōsh′mäɴ) *n.*
[Fr.] an establishing of friendly relations

**rap·scal·lion** (rap skal′yən) *n.* [<
RASCAL] a rascal; rogue

**rapt** (rapt) *adj.* [< L. *rapere*, seize] **1.**
carried away with joy, love, etc. **2.**
completely engrossed (in)

**rap·ture** (rap′chər) *n.* the state of
being carried away with joy, love, etc.;
ecstasy —**rap′tur·ous** *adj.*

**ra·ra a·vis** (rer′ə ā′vis) [L., rare bird]
an extraordinary person or thing

**rare**[1] (rer) *adj.* **rar′er, rar′est** [< L.
*rarus*] **1.** not frequently encountered;
scarce; uncommon **2.** unusually good;
excellent **3.** not dense [*rare* atmos-
phere] —**rare′ness** *n.*

**rare**[2] (rer) *adj.* **rar′er, rar′est** [OE.
*hrere*] not completely cooked; partly
raw: esp. of meat —**rare′ness** *n.*

**rare**[3] (rer) *vi.* **rared, rar′ing** [var. of
REAR[2]] [Colloq.] to be eager: used in
prp. [*raring* to go]

**rare·bit** (rer′bit) *n.* same as WELSH
RABBIT

**rar·e·fy** (rer′ə fī′) *vt., vi.* **-fied′, -fy′-
ing** [< L. *rarus*, rare + *facere*, make]
to make or become less dense —**rar′-
e·fac′tion** (-fak′shən) *n.*

**rare·ly** (rer′lē) *adv.* **1.** infrequently;
seldom **2.** uncommonly

**rar·i·ty** (rer′ə tē) *n.* **1.** a being rare;
specif., *a)* scarcity *b)* lack of density;
thinness **2.** *pl.* **-ties** something remarkable or valuable because rare

**ras·cal** (ras′k'l) *n.* [< OFr. *rascaille*,
rabble] **1.** a rogue **2.** a mischievous
child —**ras·cal′i·ty** (-kal′ə tē) *n.* —
**ras′cal·ly** *adj., adv.*

**rash**[1] (rash) *adj.* [ME. *rasch*] too hasty
in acting or speaking; reckless —
**rash′ly** *adv.* —**rash′ness** *n.*

**rash**[2] (rash) *n.* [see RASCAL] **1.** an
eruption of red spots on the skin **2.** a
sudden appearance of a great number

**rash·er** (rash′ər) *n.* [< ? obs. *rash*, to

cut] a thin slice of bacon, etc., or a serving of several such slices

**rasp** (rasp) *vt.* [< OHG. *raspon*, scrape together] 1. to scrape as with a file 2. to grate upon; irritate —*vi.* 1. to grate 2. to make a rough, grating sound —*n.* 1. a type of rough file 2. a rough, grating sound —**rasp′y** *adj.*

**rasp·ber·ry** (raz′ber′ē, -bər-) *n.*, *pl.* **-ries** [< earlier *rasp(is)*] 1. a small, red or purple, juicy fruit of the rose family 2. a plant bearing this fruit 3. [Slang] a sound of derision

**rat** (rat) *n.* [OE. *ræt*] 1. a long-tailed rodent, resembling, but larger than, the mouse 2. [Slang] a sneaky, contemptible person; esp., an informer —*vi.* **rat′ted, rat′ting** [Slang] to inform (*on*) —**smell a rat** to suspect a trick, plot, etc.

**ratch·et** (rach′it) *n.* [< It. *rocca*, distaff] 1. a toothed wheel (in full **ratchet wheel**) or bar whose sloping teeth catch a pawl, preventing backward motion 2. such a pawl

**rate**[1] (rāt) *n.* [< L. *reri*, reckon] 1. the amount, degree, etc. of anything in relation to units of something else [*rate* of pay] 2. price, esp. per unit 3. a class or rank —*vt.* **rat′ed, rat′ing** 1. to appraise 2. to consider; esteem 3. [Colloq.] to deserve —*vi.* to have value, status, etc. —**at any rate** 1. in any event 2. anyway

**rate**[2] (rāt) *vt.*, *vi.* **rat′ed, rat′ing** [ME. *raten*] to scold; chide

**rath·er** (rath′ər) *adv.* [< OE. *hræthe*, quickly] 1. more willingly; preferably 2. with more justice, reason, etc. [I, *rather* than you, should pay] 3. more accurately [my son, or *rather*, stepson] 4. on the contrary 5. somewhat [*rather* hungry]

**raths·kel·ler** (rät′skel′ər, rath′-) *n.* [G. < *rat*, council + *keller*, cellar] a restaurant of the German type, usually below street level

**rat·i·fy** (rat′ə fī′) *vt.* **-fied′, -fy′ing** [< L. *ratus*, reckoned + *facere*, make] to approve; esp., to give official sanction to —**rat′i·fi·ca′tion** *n.*

**rat·ing** (rāt′iŋ) *n.* 1. a rank, or grade, as of military personnel 2. a placement in a certain rank or class 3. an evaluation; appraisal 4. Radio & TV the relative popularity of a program according to sample polls

**ra·tio** (rā′shō, -shē ō′) *n.*, *pl.* **-tios** [L., a reckoning] a fixed relation in degree, number, etc. between two similar things; proportion

**ra·ti·o·ci·nate** (rash′ē ō′sə nāt′, rat′ē-; -äs′ə-) *vi.* **-nat′ed, -nat′ing** [see prec.] to reason, esp. using formal logic —**ra′ti·o′ci·na′tion** *n.*

**ra·tion** (rash′ən, rā′shən) *n.* [see RATIO] 1. a fixed portion; share 2. a fixed allowance of food, as a daily allowance for one soldier 3. [*pl.*] food supply —*vt.* 1. to supply with rations 2. to distribute (food, clothing, etc.) in rations, as in times of scarcity

**ra·tion·al** (rash′ən 'l) *adj.* [see RATIO] 1. of or based on reasoning 2. able to reason; reasoning 3. sensible or sane —**ra′tion·al′i·ty** (-ə nal′ə tē) *n.* —**ra′tion·al·ly** *adv.*

**ra·tion·ale** (rash′ə nal′) *n.* [L., rational] 1. the reasons or rational basis for something 2. an explanation of principles

**ra′tion·al·ism** *n.* the practice of accepting reason as the only authority in determining one's opinions or a course of action —**ra′tion·al·ist** *n.* —**ra′tion·al·is′tic** *adj.*

**ra′tion·al·ize′** (-īz′) *vt.*, *vi.* **-ized′, -iz′ing** 1. to make or be rational or reasonable 2. to devise plausible explanations for (one's acts, beliefs, etc.), usually in self-deception —**ra′tion·al·i·za′tion** *n.*

**rat·line, rat·lin** (rat′lin) *n.* [< ?] any of the small ropes which join the shrouds of a ship and serve as a ladder

RATLINES

**rat race** [Slang] a mad scramble or intense struggle to survive, succeed, etc.

**rat·tan** (ra tan′) *n.* [< Malay *rawt*, to strip] 1. a climbing palm with long, slender, tough stems 2. these stems, used in wickerwork, canes, etc.

**rat·tle** (rat′'l) *vi.* **-tled, -tling** [prob. echoic] 1. to make a series of sharp, short sounds 2. to chatter (often with *on*) —*vt.* 1. to cause to rattle 2. to confuse or upset —*n.* 1. a series of sharp, short sounds 2. a series of horny rings at the end of a rattlesnake's tail 3. a baby's toy, etc. made to rattle when shaken

**rat′tle·brain′** *n.* a frivolous, talkative person —**rat′tle·brained′** *adj.*

**rat′tler** *n.* a rattlesnake

**rat′tle·snake′** *n.* a poisonous American snake with horny rings at the end of the tail that rattle when shaken

**rat′tle·trap′** *n.* a rickety, old car

**rat′tling** *adj.* 1. that rattles 2. [Colloq.] very fast, good, etc. —*adv.* [Colloq.] very [a *rattling* good time]

**rat′trap′** *n.* 1. a trap for rats 2. [Colloq.] a dirty, run-down building

**rat·ty** (rat′ē) *adj.* **-ti·er, -ti·est** [Slang] shabby or mean

**rau·cous** (rô′kəs) *adj.* [L. *raucus*] 1. hoarse 2. loud and rowdy —**rau′cous·ly** *adv.* —**rau′cous·ness** *n.*

**raun·chy** (rôn′chē) *adj.* **-chi·er, -chi·est** [< ?] [Slang] 1. dirty, sloppy, etc. 2. risqué, lustful, etc.

**rav·age** (rav′ij) *n.* [see RAVISH] destruction; ruin —*vt.* **-aged, -ag·ing** to destroy violently; devastate; ruin —*vi.* to commit ravages

**rave** (rāv) *vi.* **raved, rav′ing** [OFr. *raver*] 1. to talk incoherently or wildly 2. to talk with great enthusiasm *(about)* —*n.* [Colloq.] a very enthusiastic commendation

**rav·el** (rav''l) *vt., vi.* **-eled** or **-elled, -el·ing** or **-el·ling** [MDu. *ravelen*] to separate into its parts, esp. threads; untwist; fray —*n.* a raveled part or thread

**rav·en** (rā'vən) *n.* [OE. *hræfn*] a large, black bird of the crow family —*adj.* black and lustrous

**rav·en·ing** (rav'n̄ iŋ) *adj.* [ult. < L. *rapere*, seize] greedily searching for prey *[ravening* wolves]

**rav·e·nous** (rav'ə nəs) *adj.* [see RAVISH] 1. greedily hungry 2. rapacious —**rav'e·nous·ly** *adv.*

**ra·vine** (rə vēn') *n.* [Fr., flood: ult. < L.] a long, deep hollow in the earth, esp. one worn by a stream; gorge

**rav'ing** *adj.* 1. that raves; frenzied 2. [Colloq.] exciting enthusiastic admiration *[a raving* beauty] —*adv.* so as to make rave *[raving* mad]

**ra·vi·o·li** (rav'ē ō'lē) *n.pl. [with sing. v.]* [It.] small casings of dough containing ground meat, cheese, etc.

**rav·ish** (rav'ish) *vt.* [< L. *rapere*, seize] 1. to seize and carry away forcibly 2. to rape 3. to transport with joy or delight —**rav'ish·ment** *n.*

**rav'ish·ing** *adj.* giving much delight

**raw** (rô) *adj.* [OE. *hreaw*] 1. not cooked 2. in its natural condition; not processed *[raw* silk] 3. inexperienced *[a raw* recruit] 4. abraded and sore 5. uncomfortably cold and damp *[a raw* wind] 6. coarse, indecent, bawdy, etc. 7. [Colloq.] harsh or unfair *[a raw* deal] —**in the raw** 1. untamed or unprocessed 2. naked —**raw'ness** *n.*

**raw'boned'** (-bōnd') *adj.* lean; gaunt

**raw'hide'** *n.* 1. an untanned cattle hide 2. a whip made of this

**ray¹** (rā) *n.* [see RADIUS] 1. any of the thin lines, or beams, of light that appear to come from a bright source 2. any of several lines radiating from a center 3. a beam of radiant energy, radioactive particles, etc. 4. a tiny amount *[a ray* of hope]

**ray²** (rā) *n.* [< L. *raia*] a fish with a broad, flat body, widely expanded fins at each side, and a whiplike tail

**ray·on** (rā'än) *n.* [coined < RAY¹] 1. a textile fiber made from a cellulose solution 2. a fabric of such fibers

**raze** (rāz) *vt.* razed, raz'ing [< L. *radere*, to scrape] to tear down completely; demolish

**ra·zor** (rā'zər) *n.* [see prec.] 1. a sharp-edged instrument for shaving 2. *same as* SHAVER

**razz** (raz) *vt., vi.* [< RASPBERRY] [Slang] to tease, ridicule, etc.

**raz·zle-daz·zle** (raz''l daz''l) *n.* [Slang] a flashy, deceptive display

**razz-ma·tazz** (raz'mə taz') *n.* [prob. < prec.] [Slang] 1. liveliness; vigor 2. flashiness; showiness

**rbi, RBI, r.b.i.** *Baseball* run(s) batted in

**R.C.Ch.** Roman Catholic Church

**Rd., rd.** 1. road 2. rod

**R.D.** Rural Delivery

**re¹** (rā) *n.* [It.] *Music* the second tone of the diatonic scale

**re²** (rē, rā) *prep.* [L. < *res*, thing] in the case or matter of; as regards

**re-** [< Fr. or L.] *a prefix meaning:* 1. back 2. again; anew *Re-* is sometimes hyphenated, as before a word beginning with *e* or to distinguish such forms as *re-cover* (to cover again) and RECOVER In the following list, *re-* means *again* or *anew*

| | |
|---|---|
| reacquaint | rehire |
| readjust | reimpose |
| readmit | reinfect |
| reaffirm | reinoculate |
| realign | reinsert |
| reappear | reinspect |
| reappoint | reinvest |
| reappraise | reissue |
| rearm | rekindle |
| reassemble | relearn |
| reassess | relive |
| reassign | reload |
| reawaken | relocate |
| reborn | remake |
| rebroadcast | remarry |
| rebuild | rematch |
| recharge | rename |
| recheck | renegotiate |
| reclassify | renominate |
| recommence | renumber |
| reconquer | reopen |
| reconsign | reorder |
| reconvene | repack |
| reconvert | repackage |
| recopy | repaint |
| re-cover | rephrase |
| redecorate | replant |
| rededicate | replay |
| redetermine | re-press |
| redirect | reprint |
| rediscover | republish |
| redivide | reread |
| redraw | reroute |
| reeducate | resell |
| reelect | reset |
| reembark | resettle |
| reembody | reshuffle |
| reemerge | respell |
| reenact | restate |
| reengage | restring |
| reenlist | restudy |
| reenter | restyle |
| reestablish | retell |
| reexamine | rethink |
| reexplain | retrain |
| refashion | retrial |
| refasten | reunite |
| refinance | reupholster |
| reformulate | reuse |
| refuel | revisit |
| refurnish | revitalize |
| rehear | reweigh |
| reheat | rework |

**reach** (rēch) *vt.* [OE. *ræcan*] 1. to thrust out (the hand, etc.) 2. to extend to by thrusting out, etc. 3. to obtain and hand over *[reach* me the salt] 4. to go as far as; attain 5. to influence; affect 6. to get in touch with, as by telephone —*vi.* 1. to thrust out the hand, etc. 2. to extend in influence, space, etc. 3. to carry, as sight, sound, etc. 4. to try to get something —*n.* 1. a stretching or thrusting out 2. the power of, or the extent covered in, stretching, obtaining, etc. 3. a continuous extent, esp. of water

**re·act** (rē akt′) *vi.* **1.** to act in return or reciprocally **2.** to act in a reverse way; go back to a former condition, stage, etc. **3.** to respond to a stimulus **4.** *Chem.* to act with another substance in producing a chemical change

**re·act·ant** (rē ak′tənt) *n.* any substance involved in a chemical reaction

**re·ac·tion** (rē ak′shən) *n.* **1.** a return or opposing action, etc. **2.** a response, as to a stimulus or influence **3.** a movement back to a former or less advanced condition **4.** a chemical change

**re·ac′tion·ar′y** (-shə ner′ē) *adj.* of, characterized by, or advocating reaction, esp. in politics —*n.*, *pl.* **-ies** an advocate of reaction, esp. in politics

**re·ac·ti·vate** (rē ak′tə vāt′) *vt.*, *vi.* **-vat′ed, -vat′ing** to make or be made active again; specif., to return (a military unit, ship, etc.) to active status —**re·ac′ti·va′tion** *n.*

**re·ac′tive** (-tiv) *adj.* **1.** tending to react **2.** of, from, or showing reaction —**re′ac·tiv′i·ty** *n.*

**re·ac·tor** (rē ak′tər) *n.* *same as* NUCLEAR REACTOR

**read¹** (rēd) *vt.* **read** (red), **read·ing** (rēd′iŋ) [< OE. *rædan*, to counsel] **1.** to get the meaning of (writing) by interpreting the characters **2.** to utter aloud (written matter) **3.** to understand or interpret **4.** to foretell (the future) **5.** to study [to *read* law] **6.** to register, as a gauge **7.** to obtain (information) from (punch cards, tape, etc.): said of a computer **8.** [Slang] to hear and understand (a radio communication, etc.) —*vi.* **1.** to read something written **2.** to learn by reading (with *about* or *of*) **3.** to be phrased in certain words —**read into** (or **in**) to attribute (a particular meaning) to —**read out of** to expel from (an organization) —**read′a·bil′i·ty** *n.* —**read′a·ble** *adj.*

**read²** (red) *pt.* & *pp.* of READ¹ —*adj.* informed by reading [well-*read*]

**read′er** *n.* **1.** one who reads **2.** a book for instruction in reading

**read′er·ship′** *n.* all the readers of a certain publication, author, etc.

**read·ing** (rēd′iŋ) *n.* **1.** the act of one who reads **2.** any material to be read **3.** the amount registered by a barometer, electric meter, etc. **4.** a particular interpretation or performance

**read′out′** *n.* **1.** the retrieving of information from a computer **2.** the information retrieved, as in typewritten form **3.** reading (sense 3)

**read·y** (red′ē) *adj.* **-i·er, -i·est** [OE. *ræde*] **1.** prepared to act or be used immediately **2.** willing **3.** likely or liable; apt [*ready* to cry] **4.** dexterous **5.** prompt [a *ready* reply] **6.** available at once [*ready* cash] —*vt.* **-ied, -y·ing** to make ready; prepare —**read′i·ly** *adv.* —**read′i·ness** *n.*

**read′y-made′** *adj.* made so as to be ready for use or sale at once: also (as applied to clothing) **read′y-to-wear′**

**re·a·gent** (rē ā′jənt) *n. Chem.* a substance used to detect, measure, or react with another substance

**re·al** (rē′əl, rēl) *adj.* [< L. *res*, thing] **1.** existing as or in fact; actual; true **2.** authentic; genuine **3.** *Law* of or relating to immovable things [*real* property] —*adv.* [Colloq.] very —**for real** [Slang] real or really

**real estate** land, including the buildings or improvements on it

**re·al·ism** (rē′ə liz′m) *n.* **1.** a tendency to face facts and be practical **2.** *Art* & *Literature* the portrayal of people and things as they really are —**re′al·ist** *n.* —**re′al·is′tic** *adj.* —**re′al·is′ti·cal·ly** *adv.*

**re·al·i·ty** (rē al′ə tē) *n.*, *pl.* **-ties** **1.** the quality or fact of being real **2.** a person or thing that is real; fact —**in reality** in fact; actually

**re·al·ize** (rē′ə līz′) *vt.* **-ized′, -iz′-ing** **1.** to make real **2.** to understand fully **3.** to convert (assets, rights, etc.) into money **4.** to gain; obtain [*realize* a profit] **5.** to be sold for (a specified sum) —**re′al·i·za′tion** *n.*

**real′-life′** *adj.* actual; not imaginary

**re′al·ly** *adv.* **1.** in reality; actually **2.** truly —*interj.* indeed

**realm** (relm) *n.* [see REGAL] **1.** a kingdom **2.** a region; sphere

**Re·al·tor** (rē′əl tər) *n.* a certified real estate broker, appraiser, etc.

**re·al·ty** (rē′əl tē) *n.* *same as* REAL ESTATE

**ream¹** (rēm) *n.* [< Ar. *rizma*, a bale] **1.** a quantity of paper varying from 480 to 516 sheets **2.** [*pl.*] [Colloq.] a great amount

**ream²** (rēm) *vt.* [< OE. *reman*, widen] to enlarge (a hole) with a reamer

**ream′er** *n.* a sharp-edged tool for enlarging or tapering holes [a juicer]

**re·an·i·mate** (rē an′ə māt′) *vt.* **-mat′ed, -mat′ing** to give new life, power, or vigor to —**re·an′i·ma′tion** *n.*

**reap** (rēp) *vt.*, *vi.* [OE. *ripan*] **1.** to cut (grain) with a scythe, reaper, etc. **2.** to gather (a harvest) **3.** to obtain as the reward of action, etc.

**reap′er** *n.* **1.** one who reaps **2.** a machine for reaping grain

**re·ap·por·tion** (rē′ə pôr′shən) *vt.* to apportion again; specif., to adjust the representation pattern of (a legislature) —**re′ap·por′tion·ment** *n.*

**rear¹** (rir) *n.* [< ARREARS] **1.** the back part **2.** the position behind or at the back **3.** the part of an army, etc. farthest from the battle front —*adj.* of, at, or in the rear —**bring up the rear** to come at the end

**rear²** (rir) *vt.* [OE. *ræran*] **1.** to put upright; elevate **2.** to build; erect **3.** to grow or breed **4.** to educate, nourish, etc. [to *rear* children] —*vi.* **1.** to rise on the hind legs, as a horse **2.** to rise (*up*) in anger, etc. **3.** to rise high

**rear admiral** a naval officer next in rank above a captain

---

fat, āpe, cär; ten, ēven; is, bīte; gō, hôrn, tōōl, look; oil, out; up, fur; chin; she; thin, then; zh, leisure; ŋ, ring; ə for a in ago; ', (ā′b'l); ë, Fr. coeur; ö, Fr. feu; Fr. mon; ü, Fr. duc; kh, G. ich, doch; ‡ foreign; < derived from

**rear'most'** -adj. farthest to the rear

**re'ar·range'** vt. -ranged', -rang'ing to arrange again or in a different way

**rear'ward** (-wərd) adj. at, in, or toward the rear —adv. toward the rear: also **rear'wards**

**rea·son** (rē'z'n) n. [ult. < L. reri, think] 1. an explanation of an act, idea, etc. 2. a cause or motive 3. the ability to think, draw conclusions, etc. 4. good sense 5. sanity —vi., vt. 1. to think logically (about); analyze 2. to argue or infer —**stand to reason** to be logical —**rea'son·ing** n.

**rea'son·a·ble** adj. 1. able to reason 2. just; fair 3. sensible; wise 4. not excessive —**rea'son·a·bly** adv.

**re'as·sure'** vt. -sured', -sur'ing 1. to assure again 2. to restore to confidence —**re'as·sur'ance** n.

**re·bate** (rē'bāt) vt. -bat·ed, -bat·ing [< OFr.: see RE- & ABATE] to give back (part of a payment) —n. a return of part of a payment

**Re·bec·ca, Re·bek·ah** (ri bek'ə) Bible the wife of Isaac

**reb·el** (reb''l; for v. ri bel') n. [< L. re-, again + bellare, wage war] one who openly resists authority —adj. 1. rebellious 2. of rebels —vi. -elled', -el'ling 1. to resist authority 2. to feel or show strong aversion

**re·bel·lion** (ri bel'yən) n. 1. armed resistance to one's government 2. a defiance of any authority

**re·bel'lious** (-yəs) adj. 1. resisting authority 2. opposing any control

**re'birth'** n. 1. a new or second birth 2. a reawakening; revival

**re·bound** (ri bound'; for n. rē'bound') vi. to spring back, as upon impact —n. a rebounding, or ball, etc. that rebounds —**on the rebound** 1. after bouncing back 2. after being jilted

**re·buff** (ri buf') n. [< It. rabuffo] 1. an abrupt refusal of offered advice, help, etc. 2. any repulse —vt. 1. to snub 2. to check or repulse

**re·buke** (ri byōōk') vt. -buked', -buk'ing [< OFr. re-, back + buchier, to beat] to scold in a sharp way; reprimand —n. a reprimand

**re·bus** (rē'bəs) n. [L., lit., by things] a puzzle consisting of pictures, etc. combined to suggest words or phrases

**re·but** (ri but') vt. -but'ted, -but'ting [< OFr. < re-, back + buter, to push] to contradict or oppose, esp. in a formal manner by argument, proof, etc. —**re·but'tal** (-'l) n.

**rec** (rek) n. recreation: used in compounds, as **rec room, rec hall**

**re·cal·ci·trant** (ri kal'si trənt) adj. [< L. re-, back + calcitrare, to kick] 1. refusing to obey authority, etc. 2. hard to handle —**re·cal'ci·trance** n.

**re·call** (ri kôl'; for n. also rē'kôl') vt. 1. to call back 2. to remember 3. to take back; revoke 4. to bring back to memory —n. 1. a recalling 2. memory 3. the removal of, or right to remove, an official from office by popular vote

**re·cant** (ri kant') vt., vi. [< L. re-, back + canere, sing] to renounce formally (one's beliefs, remarks, etc.) —**re·can·ta·tion** (rē'kan tā'shən) n.

**re·cap¹** (rē kap'; for n. rē'kap') vt. -capped', -cap'ping to put a new tread on (a worn tire) —n. such a tire

**re·cap²** (rē'kap') n. a recapitulation, or summary —vt., vi. -capped', -cap'ping to recapitulate

**re·ca·pit·u·late** (rē'kə pich'ə lāt') vi., vt. -lat'ed, -lat'ing [see RE- & CAPITULATE] to summarize; repeat briefly —**re'ca·pit'u·la'tion** n.

**re·cap'ture** vt. -tured, -tur·ing 1. to capture again; retake 2. to remember —n. a recapturing

**recd., rec'd** received

**re·cede** (ri sēd') vi. -ced'ed, -ced'ing [see RE- & CEDE] 1. to go, move, or slope backward 2. to diminish

**re·ceipt** (ri sēt') n. [see RECEIVE] 1. old term for RECIPE 2. a receiving or being received 3. a written acknowledgment that something has been received 4. [pl.] the amount received —vt. 1. to mark (a bill) paid 2. to write a receipt for

**re·ceiv·a·ble** (ri sē'və b'l) adj. 1. that can be received 2. due

**re·ceive** (ri sēv') vt. -ceived', -ceiv'ing [< L. re-, back + capere, take] 1. to take or get (something given, sent, thrown, etc.) 2. to experience or undergo [to receive acclaim] 3. to react to in a specified way 4. to learn (some news, information, etc.) 5. to bear or hold 6. to let enter 7. to greet (visitors, etc.)

**re·ceiv'er** n. 1. one who receives 2. in radio, TV, telephony, etc., a device that converts electrical waves or signals back into sound or images 3. Football the player designated to receive a forward pass 4. Law one appointed to administer or hold in trust property in bankruptcy or in a lawsuit —**re·ceiv'er·ship'** n.

**re·cen·sion** (ri sen'shən) n. [< L. recensere, revise] a revision of a text based on a study of sources

**re·cent** (rē's'nt) adj. [< L. recens] 1. done, made, etc. just before the present; new 2. of a time just before the present —**re'cent·ly** adv.

**re·cep·ta·cle** (ri sep'tə k'l) n. [see RECEIVE] a container

**re·cep·tion** (ri sep'shən) n. 1. a) a receiving or being received b) the manner of this 2. a social function for the receiving of guests 3. Radio & TV the receiving of signals with reference to the quality of reproduction

**re·cep'tion·ist** n. an office employee who receives callers, etc.

**re·cep'tive** adj. able or ready to accept suggestions, new ideas, etc.

**re·cep'tor** n. a nerve ending or group of nerve endings specialized for receiving stimuli; sense organ

**re·cess** (rē'ses; also, and for v. usually, ri ses') n. [< L. recedere, recede] 1. a hollow place, as in a wall 2. a hidden or inner place 3. a temporary halting of work, a session, etc. —vt. 1. to place in a recess 2. to form a recess in —vi. to take a recess

**re·ces·sion** (ri sesh'ən) n. 1. a going back; withdrawal 2. a temporary falling off of business activity

**re·ces·sion·al** (-'l) *n.* a hymn sung at the end of a church service when the clergy and the choir march out

**re·ces·sive** *adj.* tending to recede

**re·cher·ché** (rə sher/shā, -sher/shā/) *adj.* 1. rare; choice 2. refined; esp., too refined

**rec·i·pe** (res/ə pē) *n.* [L. < *recipere*, receive] 1. a list of materials and directions for preparing a dish or drink 2. a way to achieve something

**re·cip·i·ent** (ri sip/ē ənt) *n.* [see RECEIVE] one that receives

**re·cip·ro·cal** (ri sip/rə k'l) *adj.* [< L. *reciprocus*, returning] 1. done, given, etc. in return 2. mutual *[reciprocal love]* 3. corresponding but reversed 4. corresponding or complementary —*n.* 1. a complement, counterpart, etc. 2. *Math.* the quantity resulting from the division of 1 by the given quantity *[the reciprocal of 7 is 1/7]*

**re·cip·ro·cate** (-kāt/) *vt., vi.* -cat´ed, -cat´ing 1. to give and get reciprocally 2. to do, feel, etc. in return 3. to move alternately back and forth —**re·cip/ro·ca/tion** *n.*

**rec·i·proc·i·ty** (res/ə präs/ə tē) *n., pl.* -ties 1. reciprocal state 2. mutual exchange; esp., exchange of special privileges between two countries

**re·cit·al** (ri sīt/'l) *n.* 1. a reciting 2. the account, story, etc. told 3. a musical or dance program

**rec·i·ta·tion** (res/ə tā/shən) *n.* 1. a recital (senses 1 & 2) 2. *a.)* the speaking aloud in public of something memorized *b)* a piece so presented 3. a reciting by pupils of answers to questions on a prepared lesson

**rec/i·ta·tive/** (-tə tēv/) *n.* [< It.: see ff.] a type of declamation, as for operatic dialogue, with the rhythms of speech, but in musical tones

**re·cite** (ri sīt/) *vt., vi.* -cit´ed, -cit´ing [see RE- & CITE] 1. to speak aloud from memory, as a poem, lesson, etc. 2. to tell in detail; relate

**reck/less** *adj.* heedless; rash —**reck/less·ly** *adv.* —**reck/less·ness** *n.*

**reck·on** (rek/ən) *vt.* [OE. *recenian*] 1. to count; compute 2. to regard as being 3. to estimate 4. [Colloq. or Dial.] to suppose —*vi.* 1. to count up 2. [Colloq.] to rely (*on*) —**reckon with** to take into consideration

**reck/on·ing** *n.* 1. count or computation 2. the settlement of an account

**re·claim** (ri klām/) *vt.* [see RE- & CLAIM] 1. to bring back from error, vice, etc. 2. to make (wasteland, etc.) usable 3. to recover (useful materials, etc.) from waste products —**rec·la·ma·tion** (rek/lə mā/shən) *n.*

**re·cline** (ri klīn/) *vt., vi.* -clined/, -clin/ing [< L. *re-*, back + *clinare*, lean] to lie or cause to lie down

**rec·luse** (rek/lōos, ri klōos/) *n.* [< L. *re-*, back + *claudere*, to shut] one who lives a secluded, solitary life

**rec·og·ni·tion** (rek/əg nish/ən) *n.* 1. a recognizing or being recognized 2.

identification of a person or thing as having been known to one

**re·cog·ni·zance** (ri käg/ni zəns, -kän/i-) *n.* [< L. *re-*, again + *cognoscere*, know] *Law* a bond binding one to some act, as to appear in court

**rec·og·nize** (rek/əg nīz/) *vt.* -nized/, -niz/ing [< prec.] 1. to be aware of as known before 2. to know by some detail, as of appearance 3. to perceive 4. to accept as a fact *[to recognize defeat]* 5. to acknowledge as worthy of commendation 6. to acknowledge the status of (a government, etc.) 7. to grant the right to speak in a meeting —**rec/og·niz/a·ble** *adj.*

**re·coil** (ri koil/; *also for n.* rē/koil/) *vi.* [< L. *re-*, back + *culus*, buttocks] 1. to draw back, as in fear, etc. 2. to spring or kick back, as a gun when fired —*n.* a recoiling

**rec·ol·lect** (rek/ə lekt/) *vt., vi.* [see RE- & COLLECT] to remember, esp. with some effort —**rec/ol·lec/tion** *n.*

**rec·om·mend** (rek/ə mend/) *vt.* [see RE- & COMMEND] 1. to entrust 2. to suggest favorably as suited to some position, etc. 3. to make acceptable 4. to advise; counsel —**rec/om·men·da/tion** *n.*

**re/com·mit/** *vt.* -mit/ted, -mit/ting 1. to commit again 2. to refer (a bill, etc.) back to a committee

**rec·om·pense** (rek/əm pens/) *vt.* -pensed/, -pens/ing [see RE- & COMPENSATE] 1. to repay or reward 2. to compensate (a loss, etc.) —*n.* 1. requital; reward 2. compensation

**rec·on·cile** (rek/ən sīl/) *vt.* -ciled/, -cil/ing [see RE- & CONCILIATE] 1. to make friendly again 2. to settle (a quarrel, etc.) 3. to make (ideas, texts, etc.) consistent 4. to make content, or acquiescent (*to*) —**rec/on·cil/a·ble** *adj.* —**rec/on·cil/i·a/tion** (-sil/ē ā/shən) *n.*

**rec·on·dite** (rek/ən dīt/) *adj.* [< L. *re-*, back + *condere*, to hide] beyond ordinary understanding; abstruse

**re/con·di/tion** *vt.* to put back in good condition by repairing, etc.

**re·con·nais·sance** (ri kän/ə səns) *n.* [Fr.: see RECOGNIZANCE] the survey of a region, esp. for obtaining military information about an enemy

**rec·on·noi·ter** (rē/kə noit/ər, rek/ə-) *vt., vi.* to make a reconnaissance (of): Brit. sp. **rec/on·noi/tre**, -tred, -tring

**re·con·sid·er** (rē/kən sid/ər) *vt., vi.* to think over again, esp. with a view to changing a decision

**re·con/sti·tute/** *vt.* -tut/ed, -tut/ing to constitute again; esp., to restore (a dried or condensed substance) to its original form by adding water

**re/con·struct/** *vt.* 1. to construct again; remake 2. to build up, as from remains, an image of the original

**re/con·struc/tion** *n.* 1. a reconstructing 2. [R-] the process or period, after the Civil War, of reestablishing the Southern States in the Union

---

fat, āpe, cär; ten, ēven; is, bīte; gō, hôrn, tōōl, look; oil, out; up, fur; chin; she; thin, *th*en; zh, leisure; ŋ, ring; ə for *a* in *ago*; ', (ā/b'l); ë, Fr. coeur; ö, Fr. feu; Fr. mon; ü, Fr. duc; kh, G. ich, doch; ‡ foreign; < derived from

**re·cord** (ri kôrd'; *for n. & adj.* rek'ərd) *vt.* [ < L. *recordari*, remember] **1.** to write down for future use **2.** to register, as on a graph **3.** to register (sound or visual images) on a disc, tape, etc. for later reproduction —*n.* **1.** a recording or being recorded **2.** any registered evidence of an event, etc. **3.** the known facts about anything or anyone **4.** a grooved disc for playing on a phonograph **5.** the best official performance attained —*adj.* being the best, largest, etc. —**on** (or **off the**) **record** publicly (or confidentially) declared

**re·cord'er** *n.* **1.** an official who keeps records **2.** a machine or device that records; esp., *same as* TAPE RECORDER **3.** an early form of flute

**re·cord'ing** *n.* **1.** what is recorded, as on a disc or tape **2.** the record

**re·count** (ri kount') *vt.* [see RE- & COUNT[1]] to tell in detail; narrate

**re·count** (rē'kount'; *for n.* rē'kount') *vt.* to count again —*n.* a second count, as of votes: also written **recount**

**re·coup** (ri kōōp') *vt.* [ < Fr. *re-*, again + *couper*, to cut] **1.** to make up for [*to recoup* a loss] **2.** to regain

**re·course** (rē'kôrs, ri kôrs') *n.* [see RE- & COURSE] **1.** a turning for aid, safety, etc. **2.** that to which one turns seeking aid, etc.

**re·cov·er** (ri kuv'ər) *vt.* [ < L. *recuperare*] **1.** to get back (something lost, etc.) **2.** to regain (health, etc.) **3.** to make up for [*to recover* losses] **4.** to save (oneself) from a fall, etc. **5.** to reclaim (land from the sea, etc.) **6.** *Sports* to regain control of (a fumbled or wild ball, etc.) —*vi.* **1.** to regain health, balance, control, etc. **2.** *Sports* to recover a ball, etc.

**re·cov·er·y** *n., pl.* **-ies** a recovering; specif., *a*) a return to health *b*) a regaining of something lost, balance, etc. *c*) a retrieval of a capsule, etc. after a space flight

**recovery room** a hospital room where postoperative patients are kept for close observation and care

**rec·re·ant** (rek'rē ənt) *adj.* [ < OFr. *recreire*, surrender allegiance] **1.** cowardly **2.** disloyal —*n.* **1.** a coward **2.** a traitor

**rec·re·a·tion** (rek'rē ā'shən) *n.* [ < L. *recreare*, refresh] any play, amusement, etc. used for refreshment of body or mind —**rec're·ate'** *vt., vi.* **-at'ed, -at'ing** —**rec're·a'tion·al** *adj.*

**re·crim·i·nate** (ri krim'ə nāt') *vi.* **-nat'ed, -nat'ing** [ < L. *re-*, back + *crimen*, offense] to answer an accuser by accusing him in return —**re·crim'i·na'tion** *n.*

**re·cru·des·cence** (rē'krōō des''ns) *n.* [ < L. *re-*, again + *crudus*, raw] a breaking out again, esp. of something bad —**re'cru·des'cent** *adj.*

**re·cruit** (ri krōōt') *vt., vi.* [ < L. *re-*, again + *crescere*, grow] **1.** to enlist (personnel) into an army or navy **2.** to enlist (new members) for an organization —*n.* **1.** a recently enlisted or drafted soldier, etc. **2.** a new member of any group —**re·cruit'er** *n.*

**rec·tal** (rek't'l) *adj.* of, for, or near the rectum

**rec·tan·gle** (rek'taŋ'g'l) *n.* [ < L. *rectus*, straight + *angulus*, a corner] a four-sided plane figure with four right angles —**rec·tan'gu·lar** (-gyə lər) *adj.*

**rec·ti·fy** (rek'tə fī') *vt.* **-fied', -fy'ing** [ < L. *rectus*, straight + *facere*, make] **1.** to put right; correct **2.** *Elec.* to convert (alternating current) into direct current —**rec'ti·fi·ca'tion** *n.*

**rec·ti·lin·e·ar** (rek'tə lin'ē ər) *adj.* bounded or formed by straight lines

**rec·ti·tude** (rek'tə tōōd') *n.* moral uprightness; strict honesty

**rec·tor** (rek'tər) *n.* [ < L. *regere*, to rule] **1.** in some churches, a clergyman in charge of a parish **2.** the head of certain schools, colleges, etc.

**rec·to·ry** (rek'tər ē) *n., pl.* **-ries** the house of a minister or priest

**rec·tum** (rek'təm) *n., pl.* **-tums, -ta** (-tə) [ < L. *rectum* (*intestinum*), straight (intestine)] the lowest segment of the large intestine

**re·cum·bent** (ri kum'bənt) *adj.* [ < L. *re-*, back + *cumbere*, lie down] lying down; reclining

**re·cu·per·ate** (ri kōō'pə rāt') *vt., vi.* **-at'ed, -at'ing** [ < L. *recuperare*, recover] **1.** to get well again **2.** to recover (losses, etc.) —**re·cu'per·a'tion** *n.* —**re·cu'per·a'tive** *adj.*

**re·cur** (ri kur') *vi.* **-curred', -cur'ring** [ < L. *re-*, back + *currere*, run] **1.** to return in thought, talk, etc. **2.** to occur again or at intervals —**re·cur'rence** *n.* —**re·cur'rent** *adj.*

**re·cy·cle** (rē sī'k'l) *vt.* **-cled, -cling** **1.** to pass through a cycle again **2.** to use again and again, as the same water

**red** (red) *n.* [OE. *read*] **1.** the color of blood **2.** any red pigment **3.** [*often* R-] a political radical; esp., a communist —*adj.* **red'der, red'dest** **1.** of the color red **2.** [R-] politically radical; esp., communist —**in the red** losing money —**see red** [Colloq.] to become angry —**red'dish** *adj.* —**red'ness** *n.*

**re·dact** (ri dakt') *vt.* [ < L. *redigere*, get in order] to edit —**re·dac'tion** *n.* —**re·dac'tor** *n.*

**red blood cell** (or **corpuscle**) *same as* ERYTHROCYTE

**red'-blood'ed** *adj.* high-spirited and strong-willed; vigorous

**red'cap'** *n.* a porter in a railway station, air terminal, etc.

**red carpet** a very grand or impressive welcome or entertainment (with *the*) —**red'-car'pet** *adj.*

**red'coat'** *n.* a British soldier in a uniform with a red coat

**Red Cross** an international society for the relief of suffering in time of war or disaster

**red deer** a deer of Europe and Asia

**red·den** (red''n) *vt.* to make red —*vi.* to become red; esp., to blush

**re·deem** (ri dēm') *vt.* [ < L. *re(d)-*, back + *emere*, get] **1.** to get or buy back; recover **2.** to pay off (a mortgage, etc.) **3.** to turn in (coupons) for premiums **4.** to ransom **5.** to deliver from sin **6.** to fulfill (a promise) **7.** *a*) to make amends or atone for  *b*) to restore (oneself) to favor —**re-deem'-a-ble** *adj.* —**re-deem'er** *n.* —**re-demp'-tion** (ri demp'shən) *n.*

**re-de-ploy** (rē'di ploi') *vt., vi.* to move (troops, etc.) from one area to another —**re'de-ploy'ment** *n.*

**re'de-vel'op** (-vel'əp) *vt.* 1. to develop again 2. to rebuild or restore

**red'-hand'ed** *adv., adj.* in the very commission of crime or wrongdoing

**red'head'** *n.* a person with red hair

**red herring** [< herring drawn across the trace in hunting to divert the hounds] something used to divert attention from the basic issue

**red'-hot'** *adj.* 1. hot enough to glow 2. very excited, angry, etc. 3. very new

**re-dis'trict** *vt.* to divide anew into districts

**red'-let'ter** *adj.* designating a memorable or joyous day or event

**red-lin-ing** (red'lī'niŋ) *n.* [from outlining such areas in red on a map] the refusal by some banks and companies to issue loans or insurance on property in certain neighborhoods

**re-do'** *vt.* -**did'**, -**done'**, -**do'ing** 1. to do again 2. to redecorate

**red-o-lent** (red''l ənt) *adj.* [< L. *re*(d)-, intens. + *olere*, to smell] 1. sweet-smelling 2. smelling (*of*), suggestive (*of*) —**red'o-lence** *n.*

**re-dou-ble** (rē dub''l) *vt., vi.* -**bled**, -**bling** 1. to double again 2. to make or become twice as much

**re-doubt** (ri dout') *n.* [see REDUCE] 1. a breastwork 2. any stronghold

**re-doubt'a-ble** (-ə b'l) *adj.* [< L. *re-*, intens. + *dubitare*, to doubt] formidable —**re-doubt'a-bly** *adv.*

**re-dound** (ri dound') *vi.* [< L. *re*(d)-, intens. + *undare*, to surge] 1. to have a result (*to* the credit or discredit of) 2. to come back; react (*upon*)

**red pepper** 1. a plant with a red, many-seeded fruit 2. the ground fruit or seeds, used for seasoning

**re-dress** (ri dres'; *for n. usually* rē'-dres) *vt.* [see RE- & DRESS] to compensate for (a wrong, etc.); remedy —*n.* 1. compensation 2. a redressing

**Red Sea** sea between NE Africa & W Arabia

**red snapper** a reddish, deep-water food fish

**red tape** [< tape for tying official papers] rigid adherence to routine and regulations, causing delay

**red tide** sea water discolored by red protozoans poisonous to marine life

**re-duce** (ri doos') *vt.* -**duced'**, -**duc'-ing** [< L. *re-*, back + *ducere*, to lead] 1. to lessen, as in size, price, etc. 2. to change to a different form 3. to lower, as in rank or condition 4. to subdue or conquer —*vi.* to lose weight, as by dieting —**re-duc'er** *n.*

**re-duc-tion** (ri duk'shən) *n.* 1. a reducing or being reduced 2. anything made by reducing 3. the amount by which something is reduced

**re-dun-dant** (ri dun'dənt) *adj.* [see REDOUND] 1. excess; superfluous 2. wordy 3. unnecessary to the meaning: said of words —**re-dun'dance** *n.*

**red'wood'** *n.* 1. a giant evergreen of the Pacific coast 2. its reddish wood

**re-ech-o, re-ech-o** (rē ek'ō) *vt., vi.* -**oed**, -**o-ing** to echo back or again —*n., pl.* -**oes** the echo of an echo

**reed** (rēd) *n.* [OE. *hreod*] 1. a tall, slender grass 2. a musical instrument made from a hollow stem 3. *Music* a thin strip of wood, plastic, etc. placed against the mouthpiece, as of a clarinet, and vibrated by the breath to produce a tone —**reed'y** *adj.* -**i-er**, -**i-est**

**reef¹** (rēf) *n.* [prob. < ON. *rif*, a rib] a ridge of rock, coral, or sand at or near the surface of the water

**reef²** (rēf) *n.* [ME. *riff*] a part of a sail which can be folded and tied down to reduce the area exposed to the wind —*vt., vi.* to reduce the size of (a sail) by taking in part of it

**reef'er** *n.* 1. one who reefs 2. a short, thick, double-breasted coat 3. [Slang] a marijuana cigarette

**reek** (rēk) *n.* [OE. *rec*] a strong, unpleasant smell —*vi.* to have a strong, offensive smell —**reek'y** *adj.*

**reel¹** (rēl) *n.* [OE. *hreol*] a spool on which wire, film, fishing line, etc. is wound 2. the quantity of wire, film, etc. usually wound on one reel —*vt.* to wind on a reel —*vi.* 1. to sway, stagger, etc., as from drunkenness or dizziness 2. to spin; whirl —**reel in** 1. to wind on a reel 2. to pull in (a fish) by winding a reel —**reel off** to tell, write, etc. fluently —**reel out** to unwind from a reel

**reel²** (rēl) *n.* [prob. < prec.] a lively dance

**re-en-try, re-en-try** (rē en'trē) *n., pl.* -**tries** a coming back, as of a spacecraft, into earth's atmosphere

**ref** (ref) *n., vt., vi.* same as REFEREE

**re-face** (rē fās') *vt.* -**faced'**, -**fac'ing** to put a new front or covering on

**re-fec-tion** (ri fek'shən) *n.* [< L. *re-* again + *facere*, make] a light meal

**re-fec'to-ry** (-tər ē) *n., pl.* -**ries** a dining hall, as in a monastery

**re-fer** (ri fur') *vt.* -**ferred'**, -**fer'ring** [< L. *re-*, back + *ferre*, to bear] 1. to submit (a quarrel, etc.) for settlement 2. to direct (to someone or something) for aid, information, etc. —*vi.* 1. to relate or apply (*to*) 2. to direct attention (*to*) 3. to turn (*to*) for information, aid, etc. —**ref-er-a-ble** (ref'ər ə b'l, ri fur'-) *adj.* —**re-fer'rer** *n.*

**ref-er-ee** (ref'ə rē') *n.* 1. one to whom something is referred for decision 2. an official who enforces the rules in certain sports contests —*vt., vi.* -**eed'**, -**ee'ing** to act as referee (in)

**ref-er-ence** (ref'ər əns) *n.* 1. a referring or being referred 2. relation [in *reference* to his letter] 3. *a*) the directing of attention to a person or thing *b*) a mention 4. *a*) an indication, as in a book, of some other source of information b) such a source 5. a) one who can offer information or recommendation b) a statement of character, ability, etc. by such a person

**ref·er·en·dum** (ref'ə ren'dəm) n., pl. **-dums** or **-da** (-də) [L., see REFER] 1. the submission of a law to the direct vote of the people 2. the right of the people to vote directly on such laws

**ref'er·ent** adj. the thing referred to, esp. by a word or expression

**re·fer'ral** (ri fur'əl) n. 1. a referring or being referred 2. a person who is referred to another person

**re·fill** (rē fil'; for n. rē'fil) vt., vi. to fill again —n. 1. a unit to refill a special container 2. a refilling of a medical prescription —**re·fill'a·ble** adj.

**re·fine** (ri fīn') vt., vi. **-fined', -fin'-ing** [RE- + fine, make fine] 1. to free or become free from impurities, etc. 2. to make or become more polished or elegant —**re·fin'er** n.

**re·fined'** adj. 1. made free from impurities; purified 2. cultivated; elegant 3. subtle, precise, etc.

**re·fine'ment** n. 1. a) a refining or being refined b) the result of this 2. delicacy or elegance of manners, etc. 3. an improvement 4. a subtlety

**re·fin'er·y** n., pl. **-ies** a plant for purifying materials, as oil, sugar, etc.

**re·fin·ish** (rē fin'ish) vt. to put a new surface on (wood, metal, etc.)

**re·fit** (rē fit') vt., vi. **-fit'ted, -fit'ting** to make or become fit for use again by repairing, reequipping, etc.

**re·flect** (ri flekt') vt. [< L. re-, back + flectere, to bend] 1. to throw back (light, heat, or sound) 2. to give back an image of 3. to bring as a result [to reflect honor] —vi. 1. to throw back light, heat, etc. 2. to give back an image 3. to think seriously (on or upon) 4. to cast blame or discredit (on or upon) —**re·flec'tive** adj.

**re·flec'tion** n. 1. a reflecting or being reflected 2. anything reflected 3. contemplation 4. an idea or remark 5. blame; discredit

**re·flec'tor** n. a surface, object, etc. that reflects light, sound, heat, etc.

**re·flex** (rē'fleks) adj. [see REFLECT] designating or of an involuntary action, as a sneeze, due to the direct transmission of a stimulus to a muscle or gland —n. a reflex action

**re·flex·ive** (ri flek'siv) adj. 1. designating a verb whose subject and object refer to the same person or thing (Ex.: I wash myself) 2. designating a pronoun used as the object of such a verb —**re·flex'ive·ly** adv.

**re·for·est** (rē fôr'ist) vt., vi. to plant new trees on (land once forested) —**re'for·est·a'tion** n.

**re·form** (ri fôrm') vt. [see RE- & FORM] 1. to make better as by stopping abuses; improve 2. to cause (a person) to behave better —vi. to become better in behavior —n. a reforming

**re-form** (rē'fôrm') vt., vi. to form again

**ref·or·ma·tion** (ref'ər mā'shən) n. 1. a reforming or being reformed 2.

[R-] the 16th-c. religious movement that resulted in establishing the Protestant churches

**re·form·a·to·ry** (ri fôr'mə tôr'ē) n., pl. **-ries** an institution for reforming young law offenders: also **reform school**

**re·form'er** n. one who seeks to bring about political or social reform

**re·fract** (ri frakt') vt. [< L. re-, back + frangere, to break] to cause (a ray of light, etc.) to undergo refraction

**re·frac'tion** n. the bending of a ray or wave of light, heat, or sound as it passes from one medium into another

**re·frac·to·ry** (ri frak'tər ē) adj. [see REFRACT] hard to manage; obstinate

**re·frain**[1] (ri frān') vi. [< L. re-, back + frenare, to curb] to hold back; keep oneself (from doing something)

**re·frain**[2] (ri frān') n. [see REFRACT] a phrase or verse repeated at intervals in a song or poem

**re·fresh** (ri fresh') vt. 1. to make fresh by cooling, wetting, etc. 2. to make (a person) feel cooler, stronger, etc., as by food, sleep, etc. 3. to replenish 4. to stimulate —vi. to revive

**re·fresh'ing** adj. 1. that refreshes 2. pleasingly new or different

**re·fresh'ment** n. 1. a refreshing or being refreshed 2. that which refreshes 3. [pl.] food or drink or both

**re·frig·er·ate** (ri frij'ə rāt') vt. **-at'-ed, -at'ing** [< L. re-, intens. + frigus, cold] to make or keep cool or cold, as for preserving —**re·frig'er·ant** adj., n. —**re·frig'er·a'tion** n.

**re·frig·er·a'tor** n. a box or room in which food, etc. is kept cool

**reft** (reft) adj. same as BEREFT

**ref·uge** (ref'yōōj) n. [< L. re-, back + fugere, flee] a) shelter or protection from danger, etc.

**ref·u·gee** (ref'yōō jē', ref'yōō jē') n. one who flees from his home or country to seek refuge elsewhere

**re·ful·gent** (ri ful'jənt) adj. [< L. re-, back + fulgere, shine] shining; radiant; glowing —**re·ful'gence** n.

**re·fund** (ri fund'; for n. rē'fund') vt., vi. [< L. re-, back + fundere, pour] to give back (money, etc.); repay —n. a refunding or the amount refunded

**re·fur·bish** (ri fur'bish) vt. [RE- + FURBISH] to freshen or polish up again; renovate —**re·fur'bish·ment** n.

**re·fuse**[1] (ri fyōōz') vt., vi. **-fused', -fus'ing** [< L. re-, back + fundere, pour] 1. to decline to accept; reject 2. to decline (to do, grant, etc.) —**re·fus'al** n.

**ref·use**[2] (ref'yōōs, -yōōz) n. [see prec.] waste; rubbish

**re·fute** (ri fyōōt') vt. **-fut'ed, -fut'ing** [L. refutare, repel] to prove to be false or wrong —**re·fut'a·ble** adj. —**ref·u·ta·tion** (ref'yə tā'shən) n.

**re·gain** (ri gān') vt. 1. to get back; recover 2. to get back to

**re·gal** (rē'gəl) adj. [< L. rex, king] of, like, or fit for a king; royal —**re'gal·ly** adv.

**re·gale** (ri gāl') vt. **-galed', -gal'ing** [< Fr. ré- (see RE-) + OFr. gale, joy] to entertain as with a feast

**re·ga·li·a** (ri gāl′yə, -gā′lē ə) *n.pl.*
[see REGAL] **1.** royal insignia **2.** the
insignia of a society, etc. **3.** finery
**re·gard** (ri gärd′) *n.* [see RE- & GUARD]
**1.** a steady look; gaze **2.** consideration; concern **3.** respect and affection
**4.** reference; relation *[in regard to
peace plans]* **5.** *[pl.]* good wishes —*vt.*
**1.** to look at attentively **2.** to consider
**3.** to hold in affection and respect **4.**
to concern or involve —**as regards**
concerning —**re·gard′ful** *adj.*
**re·gard′ing** *prep.* concerning; about
**re·gard′less** *adv.* [Colloq.] without
regard for objections, etc.; anyway
—**regardless of** in spite of
**re·gat·ta** (ri gät′ə) *n.* [< It.] **1.** a
boat race **2.** a series of boat races
**re·gen·er·ate** (ri jen′ər it; *for v.*
-ə rāt′) *adj.* [see RE- & GENERATE]
renewed or restored —*vt.* -**at′ed**, -**at′**-
**ing 1.** to cause to be spiritually reborn
**2.** to cause to be completely reformed
**3.** to bring into existence again; reproduce —**re·gen′er·a′tion** *n.* —**re·**
**gen′er·a′tive** *adj.*
**re·gent** (rē′jənt) *n.* [< L. *regere,* to
rule] **1.** a person appointed to rule
when a monarch is absent, too young,
etc. **2.** a member of a governing board,
as of a university —**re′gen·cy** *n.*
**reg·gae** (reg′ā) *n.* [< ?] a form of
popular Jamaican music influenced by
rock-and-roll and calypso
**reg·i·cide** (rej′ə sīd′) *n.* **1.** a killer of
a king **2.** the killing of a king
**re·gime, ré·gime** (rə zhēm′, rā-) *n.*
[see ff.] **1.** a political or ruling system
**2.** *same as* REGIMEN
**reg·i·men** (rej′ə mən) *n.* [< L.
*regere,* to rule] a system of diet, exercise, etc. for improving the health
**reg·i·ment** (rej′ə mənt; *for v.* -ment′)
*n.* [< L. *regere,* to rule] a military unit,
smaller than a division —*vt.* **1.** to
organize systematically **2.** to subject
to strict discipline and control —**reg′i·**
**men′tal** *adj.* —**reg′i·men·ta′tion** *n.*
**Re·gi·na** (ri jī′nə) capital of Saskatchewan: pop. 131,000
**re·gion** (rē′jən) *n.* [see REGAL] **1.** a
large, indefinite part of the earth's
surface **2.** any division or part, as of
an organism —**re′gion·al** *adj.*
**re′gion·al·ism** *n.* **1.** regional quality
or character in life or literature **2.** a
word, etc. peculiar to some region
**reg·is·ter** (rej′is tər) *n.* [< L.
*regerere,* to record] **1.** *a)* a list of
names, items, etc. *b)* a book in which
this is kept **2.** a device for recording *[a
cash register]* **3.** an opening into a room
by which the amount of air passing
through can be controlled **4.** *Music* a
part of the range of a voice or instrument —*vt.* **1.** to enter in a list **2.** to
indicate as on a scale **3.** to show, as by
facial expression *[to register joy]* **4.** to
safeguard (mail) by having its committal to the postal system recorded,
for a fee —*vi.* **1.** to enter one's name
in a list, as of voters **2.** to make an

impression —**reg′is·trant** (-trənt) *n.*
**registered nurse** a trained nurse
who has passed a State examination
**reg·is·trar** (rej′i strär′) *n.* one who
keeps records, as in a college
**reg·is·tra·tion** (rej′i strā′shən) *n.*
**1.** a registering or being registered **2.**
an entry in a register **3.** the number
of persons registered
**reg·is·try** (-is trē) *n., pl.* -**tries 1.** a
registering **2.** an office where registers
are kept **3.** *same as* REGISTER (*n.* 1)
**reg·nant** (reg′nənt) *adj.* **1.** ruling **2.**
predominant **3.** prevalent
**re·gress** (ri gres′) *vi.* [< L. re-, back
+ *gradi,* go] to go back —**re·gres′sion**
*n.* —**re·gres′sive** *adj.*
**re·gret** (ri gret′) *vt.* -**gret′ted**, -**gret′**-
**ting** [< OFr. *regreter,* mourn] to feel
sorrow or remorse over (an occurrence,
one's acts, etc.) —*n.* sorrow, esp. over
one's acts or omissions —**(one's)
regrets** a polite expression of regret,
as at declining an invitation —**re·**
**gret′ful** *adj.* —**re·gret′ta·ble** *adj.*
**re·group′** *vt., vi.* to group again; specif., *Mil.* to reorganize (one's
forces), as after a battle
**reg·u·lar** (reg′yə lər) *adj.* [< L.
*regula,* a rule] **1.** conforming to a rule,
type, etc.; orderly; symmetrical **2.**
conforming to a fixed principle or procedure **3.** customary or established **4.**
consistent *[a regular customer]* **5.**
functioning in a normal way *[a
regular pulse]* **6.** properly qualified *[a
regular doctor]* **7.** designating or of the
standing army of a country **8.** [Colloq.]
*a)* thorough; complete *[a regular
nuisance]* *b)* pleasant, friendly, etc.
—*n.* **1.** a regular soldier or player **2.**
[Colloq.] one who is regular in attendance **3.** *Politics* one loyal to his party
—**reg′u·lar′i·ty** (-lar′ə tē) *n.* —**reg′·**
**u·lar·ize′** *vt.* -**ized′**, -**iz′ing** —
**reg′u·lar·ly** *adv.*
**reg·u·late** (reg′yə lāt′) *vt.* -**lat′ed**,
-**lat′ing** [< L. *regula,* a rule] **1.** to
control or direct according to a rule,
principle, etc. **2.** to adjust to a standard, rate, etc. **3.** to adjust so as to
make work accurately —**reg′u·la′**-
**tive, reg′u·la·to′ry** (-lə tôr′ē) *adj.*
—**reg′u·la′tor** *n.*
**reg·u·la·tion** *n.* **1.** a regulating or
being regulated **2.** a rule or law by
which conduct, etc. is regulated —*adj.*
usual; normal; regular
**re·gur·gi·tate** (ri gur′jə tāt′) *vi., vt.*
-**tat′ed**, -**tat′ing** [< ML. re-, back
+ LL. *gurgitare,* to flood] to bring
(partly digested food) from the stomach back to the mouth —**re·gur′gi·**
**ta′tion** *n.*
**re·ha·bil·i·tate** (rē′hə bil′ə tāt′) *vt.*
-**tat′ed**, -**tat′ing** [< L. re-, back +
*habere,* have] **1.** to restore to rank,
reputation, etc. which one has lost **2.**
to put back in good condition **3.** to
bring or restore to a state of health or
constructive activity —**re′ha·bil′i·**
**ta′tion** *n.* —**re′ha·bil′i·ta′tive** *adj.*

fat, āpe, cär; ten, ēven; is, bīte; gō, hôrn, tōōl, look; oil, out; up, fur;
chin; she; thin, *then*; zh, leisure; ŋ, ring; ə for *a* in ago; ', (ā'b'l); ĕ, Fr. coeur;
ö, Fr. feu; Fr. mon; ü, Fr. duc; kh, G. ich, doch; ‡ foreign; < derived from

**re·hash** (rē hash′; *for n.* rē′hash) *vt.* [RE- + HASH] to work up again or go over again —*n.* a rehashing

**re·hear** *vt.* -**heard′**, -**hear′ing** *Law* to hear (a case) a second time

**re·hearse** (ri hurs′) *vt., vi.* -**hearsed′**, -**hears′ing** [< OFr. *re-*, again + *hercer*, to harrow] **1.** to recite in detail **2.** to practice (a play, etc.), for public performance —**re·hears′al** *n.*

**reign** (rān) *n.* [< L. *regere*, to rule] **1.** royal power **2.** dominance or sway **3.** the period of rule, dominance, etc. —*vi.* **1.** to rule as a sovereign **2.** to prevail [*peace reigns*]

**re·im·burse** (rē′im burs′) *vt.* -**bursed′**, -**burs′ing** [RE- + *imburse*, to pay] to pay back —**re′·im·burse′ment** *n.*

**rein** (rān) *n.* [see RETAIN] **1.** [*usually pl.*] a narrow strap of leather attached in pairs to a horse's bit and manipulated to control the animal **2.** [*pl.*] a means of controlling, etc. —*vt.* to guide or control as with reins —**give rein to** to free from restraint

**re·in·car·na·tion** (rē′in kär nā′shən) *n.* [see RE- & INCARNATE] rebirth of the soul in another body —**re′in·car′nate** *vt.* -**nat·ed**, -**nat·ing**

**rein·deer** (rān′dir′) *n., pl.* -**deer′** [< ON. *hreinn*, reindeer + *dyr*, deer] a large deer found in northern regions, and domesticated there as a beast of burden

REINDEER

**re·in·force** (rē′in fôrs′) *vt.* -**forced′**, -**forc′ing** [RE- + var. of ENFORCE] **1.** to strengthen (a military force) with more troops, ships, etc. **2.** to strengthen, as by propping, adding new material, etc. —**re′in·force′ment** *n.*

**re·in·state** (rē′in stāt′) *vt.* -**stat·ed**, -**stat′ing** to restore to a former state, position, etc. —**re·in·state′ment** *n.*

**re·it·er·ate** (rē it′ə rāt′) *vt.* -**at·ed**, -**at′ing** [see RE- & ITERATE] to say or do again or repeatedly —**re·it′er·a′tion** *n.* —**re·it′er·a′tive** *adj.*

**re·ject** (ri jekt′; *for n.* rē′jekt) *vt.* [< L. *re-*, back + *jacere*, to throw] **1.** to refuse to take, agree to, use, believe, etc. **2.** to discard —*n.* a rejected person or thing —**re·jec′tion** *n.*

**re·joice** (ri jois′) *vi., vt.* -**joiced′**, -**joic′ing** [< OFr. *rejoir*] to be or make glad or happy —**re·joic′ing** *n.*

**re·join** (rē join′) *vt., vi.* **1.** to join again; reunite **2.** to answer

**re·join·der** (ri join′dər) *n.* [see RE- & JOIN] an answer, esp. to a reply

**re·ju·ve·nate** (ri joo′və nāt′) *vt.* -**nat′ed**, -**nat′ing** [< RE- + L. *juvenis*, young] to make feel or seem young again —**re·ju′ve·na′tion** *n.*

**re·lapse** (ri laps′; *for n. also* rē′laps) *vi.* -**lapsed′**, -**laps′ing** [see RE- & LAPSE] to slip back into a former state, esp. into illness after apparent recovery —*n.* a relapsing

**re·late** (ri lāt′) *vt.* -**lat′ed**, -**lat′ing** [< L. *relatus*, brought back] **1.** to tell the story of; narrate **2.** to connect, as in thought or meaning —*vi.* to have reference or some relation (*to*)

**re·lat′ed** *adj.* connected, as by origin, kinship, marriage, etc.

**re·la′tion** *n.* **1.** a narrating **2.** a narrative; recital **3.** connection, as in thought, meaning, etc. **4.** connection by blood or marriage **5.** a relative **6.** [*pl.*] the connections between or among persons, nations, etc. —**in** (or **with**) **relation to** concerning; regarding —**re·la′tion·ship′** *n.*

**rel·a·tive** (rel′ə tiv) *adj.* **1.** related each to the other **2.** having to do with; relevant **3.** comparative [*relative comfort*] **4.** meaningful only in relationship ["cold" is a *relative* term] **5.** *Gram.* that refers to an antecedent [a *relative* pronoun] —*n.* a person related by blood or marriage —**rel′a·tive·ly** *adv.* —**rel′a·tive·ness** *n.*

**relative humidity** the ratio of the amount of moisture in the air to the top amount possible at the temperature

**rel·a·tiv·i·ty** (rel′ə tiv′ə tē) *n.* **1.** a being relative **2.** *Physics* the theory of the relative, rather than absolute, character of motion, velocity, mass, etc., and the interdependence of matter, time, and space

**re·lax** (ri laks′) *vt., vi.* [< L. *re-*, back + *laxare*, loosen] **1.** to make or become less firm, tense, severe, etc. **2.** to rest, as from work —**re·lax′er** *n.*

**re·lax′ant** *adj.* causing relaxation, esp. of muscles —*n.* a relaxant drug

**re·lax·a·tion** (rē′lak sā′shən) *n.* **1.** a relaxing or being relaxed **2.** *a)* rest from work or effort *b)* recreation

**re·lay** (rē′lā; *for v. also* ri lā′) *n.* [< MFr. *re-*, back + *laier*, to leave] **1.** a fresh supply of horses, etc., as for a stage of a journey **2.** a relief crew of workers; shift **3.** a race (in full **relay race**) between teams, each member of which goes a part of the distance —*vt.* -**layed′**, -**lay′ing** to convey as by relays [to *relay* news]

**re·lease** (ri lēs′) *vt.* -**leased′**, -**leas′ing** [see RELAX] **1.** to set free, as from confinement, work, pain, etc. **2.** to let go [to *release* an arrow] **3.** to permit to be issued, published, etc. —*n.* **1.** a releasing, as from prison, work, etc. **2.** a device to release a catch, etc., as on a machine **3.** a book, news item, etc. released to the public **4.** *Law* a written surrender of a claim, etc.

**rel·e·gate** (rel′ə gāt′) *vt.* -**gat·ed**, -**gat′ing** [< L. *re-*, away + *legare*, send] **1.** to exile or banish (*to*) **2.** to consign or assign, esp. to an inferior position **3.** to refer or hand over for decision —**rel′e·ga′tion** *n.*

**re·lent** (ri lent′) *vi.* [< L. *re-*, again + *lentus*, pliant] to become less stern, severe, or stubborn; soften

**re·lent′less** *adj.* **1.** harsh; pitiless **2.** not letting up; persistent —**re·lent′less·ly** *adv.* —**re·lent′less·ness** *n.*

**rel·e·vant** (rel′ə vənt) *adj.* [see RELIEVE] relating to the matter under consideration; pertinent —**rel′e·vance, rel′e·van·cy** *n.*

**re·li·a·ble** (ri lī′ə b'l) *adj.* that can be relied on —**re·li′a·bil′i·ty** *n.* —**re·li′a·bly** *adv.*

**re·li·ance** (-əns) *n.* 1. trust, dependence, or confidence 2. a thing relied on —**re·li′ant** *adj.*

**rel·ic** (rel′ik) *n.* [see RELINQUISH] 1. an object, custom, etc. surviving from the past 2. a souvenir 3. [*pl.*] ruins 4. the venerated remains, etc. of a saint

**rel·ict** (rel′ikt) *n.* [L. *relictus*, left behind] 1. [Archaic] a widow 2. a species surviving from an earlier period

**re·lief** (ri lēf′) *n.* 1. a relieving, as of pain, anxiety, a burden, etc. 2. anything that eases tension, or offers a pleasing change 3. aid, esp. by a public agency to the needy 4. release from work or duty, or those bringing it 5. the projection of sculptured forms from a flat surface 6. the differences in height, collectively, of land forms shown as by lines on a map (**relief map**) —*adj. Baseball* designating a pitcher who replaces another during a game —**in relief** carved so as to project from a surface

**re·lieve** (ri lēv′) *vt.* **-lieved′, -liev′ing** [< L. *re-*, again + *levare*, to raise] 1. to ease (pain, anxiety, etc.) 2. to free from pain, distress, a burden, etc. 3. to give or bring aid to 4. to set free from duty or work by replacing 5. to make less tedious, etc. by providing a pleasing change

**re·li·gion** (ri lij′ən) *n.* [< L. *religio*] 1. belief in and worship of God or gods 2. a specific system of belief or worship, etc. built around God, a code of ethics, a philosophy of life, etc.

**re·li′gious** (-əs) *adj.* 1. devout; pious 2. of or concerned with religion 3. conscientiously exact; scrupulous —*n.* a nun or monk —**re·li′gious·ly** *adv.*

**re·lin·quish** (ri lin′kwish) *vt.* [< L. *re-*, from + *linquere*, leave] 1. to give up, as a plan, or let go, as one's grasp 2. to renounce or surrender (property, a right, etc.) —**re·lin′quish·ment** *n.*

**rel·ish** (rel′ish) *n.* [< OFr. *relais*, something remaining] 1. an appetizing flavor 2. enjoyment; zest [to listen with *relish*] 3. pickles, etc. served with a meal or as an appetizer —*vt.* to enjoy; like

**re·live** (rē liv′) *vt.* **-lived′, -liv′ing** to experience (a past event) again, as in imagination

**re·lo·cate** (rē lō′kāt) *vt., vi.* **-cat·ed, -cat·ing** to move to a new location —**re′lo·ca′tion** *n.*

**re·luc·tant** (ri luk′tənt) *adj.* [< L. *re-*, against + *luctari*, to struggle] 1. unwilling; disinclined 2. marked by unwillingness [a *reluctant* answer] —**re·luc′tance** *n.* —**re·luc′tant·ly** *adv.*

**re·ly** (ri lī′) *vi.* **-lied′, -ly′ing** [< L.

*re-*, back + *ligare*, bind] to trust or depend Used with *on* or *upon*

**REM** (rem) *n., pl.* **REMs** [*r*(*apid*) *e*(*ye*) *m*(*ovement*)] the rapid, jerky movements of the eyeballs during stages of sleep associated with dreaming

**rem** (rem) *n.* [*r*(*oentgen*) *e*(*quivalent*), *m*(*an*)] a dosage of ionizing radiation with a biological effect about equal to that of one roentgen of X-rays

**re·main** (ri mān′) *vi.* [< L. *re-*, back + *manere*, to stay] 1. to be left over when the rest has been taken away, etc. 2. to stay 3. to continue [to *remain* a cynic] 4. to be left to be dealt with, done, etc.

**re·main′der** *n.* 1. those remaining 2. what is left when a part is taken away 3. what is left when a smaller number is subtracted from a larger

**re·mains′** *n.pl.* 1. what is left after use, destruction, etc. 2. a dead body

**re·mand** (ri mand′) *vt.* [< L. *re-*, back + *mandare*, to order] to send back, as a prisoner into custody

**re·mark** (ri märk′) *vt., vi.* [< Fr. *re-*, again + *marquer*, to mark] to notice, observe, or comment; make (as) an observation —*n.* a brief comment

**re·mark′a·ble** *adj.* worthy of notice: extraordinary —**re·mark′a·bly** *adv.*

**Rem·brandt** (rem′brant) 1606–69; Du. painter & etcher

**re·me·di·al** (ri mē′dē əl) *adj.* 1. providing a remedy 2. corrective, as some study courses

**rem·e·dy** (rem′ə dē) *n., pl.* **-dies** [< L. *re-*, again + *mederi*, heal] 1. any medicine or treatment for a disease 2. something to correct a wrong —*vt.* **-died, -dy·ing** to cure, correct, etc.

**re·mem·ber** (ri mem′bər) *vt.* [< L. *re-*, again + *memorare*, bring to mind] 1. to think of again 2. to bring back to mind by an effort; recall 3. to be careful not to forget 4. to mention (a person) to another as sending regards —*vi.* to bear in, or call back to, mind

**re·mem′brance** (-brəns) *n.* 1. a remembering or being remembered 2. the power to remember 3. a souvenir

**re·mind** (ri mīnd′) *vt., vi.* to put (a person) in mind (of something); cause to remember —**re·mind′er** *n.*

**rem·i·nisce** (rem′ə nis′) *vi.* **-nisced′, -nis′cing** [< ff.] to think, talk, or write about past events

**rem′i·nis′cence** (-′ns) *n.* [Fr. < L. *re-*, again + *memini*, remember] 1. a remembering 2. a memory 3. [*pl.*] an account of remembered experiences —**rem′i·nis′cent** *adj.*

**re·miss** (ri mis′) *adj.* [see REMIT] careless; negligent —**re·miss′ness** *n.*

**re·mis·sion** (ri mish′ən) *n.* [see REMIT] 1. forgiveness; pardon 2. release from a debt, tax, etc. 3. an abating of (pain, a disease, etc.)

**re·mit** (ri mit′) *vt.* **-mit′ted, -mit′ting** [< L. *re-*, back + *mittere*, send] 1. to forgive or pardon 2. to refrain from exacting (a payment), inflicting (punishment), etc. 3. to slacken; abate 4. to send (money) in payment —re·mit'tance n. —re·mit'tent adj.

rem·nant (rem'nənt) n. [see REMAIN] what is left over, as a piece of cloth at the end of a bolt

re·mod·el (rē mäd''l) vt. -eled or -elled, -el·ing or -el·ling to make over; rebuild

re·mon·strate (ri män'strāt) vt. -strat·ed, -strat·ing [< L. re-, again + monstrare, to show] to say in protest, objection, etc. —vi. to protest; object —re·mon'strance (-strəns) n.

re·morse (ri môrs') n. [< L. re-, again + mordere, to bite] a torturing sense of guilt for one's actions —re·morse'ful adj. —re·morse'less adj.

re·mote (ri mōt') adj. -mot'er, -mot'est [< L. remotus, removed] 1. distant in space or time 2. distant in relation, connection, etc. 3. distantly related [a remote cousin] 4. slight [a remote chance] —re·mote'ly adv.

remote control control of aircraft, missiles, etc. from a distance, as by radio waves

re·move (ri mōōv') vt. -moved', -mov'ing [see RE- & MOVE] 1. to move (something) from where it is; take away or off 2. to dismiss, as from office 3. to get rid of 4. to kill —vi. to move away, as to another residence —n. a step or degree away —re·mov'a·ble adj. —re·mov'al n.

re·mu·ner·ate (ri myōō'nə rāt') vt. -at'ed, -at'ing [< L. re-, again + munus, gift] to pay (a person) for (work, a loss, etc.) —re·mu'ner·a'tion n. —re·mu'ner·a'tive adj.

ren·ais·sance (ren'ə säns') n. [Fr.] 1. a rebirth; revival 2. [R-] the great revival of art and learning in Europe in the 14th, 15th, and 16th centuries

re·nal (rē'n'l) adj. [< L. renes, kidneys] of or near the kidneys

re·nas·cence (ri nas''ns, -nās'-) n. a rebirth; revival —re·nas'cent adj.

rend (rend) vt. rent, rend'ing [OE. rendan] to tear apart or split with violence —vi. to tear; split apart

ren·der (ren'dər) vt. [ult. < L. re(d)-, back + dare, give] 1. to submit, as for approval, payment, etc. 2. to give in return or pay as due [render thanks] 3. to cause to be 4. to give (aid) or do (a service) 5. to depict, as by drawing 6. to play (music), act (a role), etc. 7. to translate 8. to melt down (fat)

ren·dez·vous (rän'dā vōō') n., pl. -vous' (-vōōz') [< Fr. rendez-vous, betake yourself] 1. a meeting place 2. an agreement to meet 3. such a meeting —vi., vt. -voused' (-vōōd'), -vous'ing to assemble as prearranged

ren·di·tion (ren dish'ən) n. a rendering; performance, translation, etc.

ren·e·gade (ren'ə gād') n. [< L. re-, again + negare, deny] one who abandons a party, movement, etc. to join the opposition; turncoat

re·nege (ri nig') vi. -neged', -neg'ing [see prec.] to go back on a promise 2. to play a card not of the suit called for —re·neg'er n.

re·new (ri nōō') vt. 1. to make new or fresh again 2. to reestablish; revive 3. to resume 4. to put in a fresh supply of 5. to give or get an extension of [renew a lease] —re·new'al n.

ren·net (ren'it) n. [ME. rennen, coagulate] an extract from the stomach of calves, etc. used to curdle milk

Re·no (rē'nō) city in W Nev.: pop. 73,000

Re·noir (ren'wär), Pierre Auguste 1841–1919; Fr. painter

re·nounce (ri nouns') vt. -nounced', -nounc'ing [< L. re-, back + nuntiare, tell] 1. to give up formally (a claim, etc.) 2. to give up (a habit, etc.) 3. to disown —re·nounce'ment n.

ren·o·vate (ren'ə vāt') vt. -vat'ed, -vat'ing [< L. re-, again + novus, new] to make as good as new; restore —ren'o·va'tion n. —ren'o·va'tor n.

re·nown (ri noun') n. [< OFr. re-, again + nom(m)er, to name] great fame or reputation —re·nowned' adj.

rent¹ (rent) n. [< L. reddita, paid] a stated payment at fixed intervals for the use of a house, land, etc. —vt. to get or give use of in return for rent —vi. to be let for rent —for rent available to be rented —rent'er n.

rent² (rent) pt. & pp. of REND —n. a hole or gap made by tearing

rent·al (ren't'l) n. 1. an amount paid or received as rent 2. a house, car, etc. for rent 3. a renting —adj. of or for rent

re·nun·ci·a·tion (ri nun'sē ā'shən) n. a renouncing, as of a right

re·or·gan·ize (rē ôr'gə nīz') vt., vi. -ized', -iz'ing to organize anew, as a business —re·or'gan·i·za'tion n.

rep (rep) n. [Fr. reps < Eng. ribs] a ribbed or corded fabric

Rep. 1. Representative 2. Republican

re·paid (rē pād') pt. & pp. of REPAY

re·pair¹ (ri per') vt. [< L. re-, again + parare, prepare] 1. to put back in good condition; fix; renew 2. to make amends for —n. 1. a repairing 2. [usually pl.] work done in repairing 3. the state of being repaired [kept in repair] —re·pair'a·ble adj.

re·pair² (ri per') vi. [< L. re-, back + patria, native land] to go (to a place)

re·pair'man n., pl. -men a man whose work is repairing things

rep·a·ra·tion (rep'ə rā'shən) n. 1. a making of amends 2. [usually pl.] compensation, as for war damage

rep·ar·tee (rep'ər tē', -tā') n. [< Fr. re-, back + partir, to part] quick, witty retort(s); banter

re·past (ri past') n. [< OFr. re-, RE- + past, food] food and drink; a meal

re·pa·tri·ate (rē pā'trē āt') vt., vi. -at'ed, -at'ing [see REPAIR²] to return to the country of birth, citizenship, etc. —re·pa'tri·a'tion n.

re·pay (ri pā') vt. -paid', -pay'ing 1. to pay back 2. to make return to for (a favor, etc.) —re·pay'ment n.

re·peal (ri pēl') vt. [see RE- & APPEAL] to revoke; cancel; annul —n. revocation; abrogation, etc.

re·peat (ri pēt') vt. [< L. re-, again + petere, seek] 1. to say again 2. to recite (a poem, etc.) **3.** to say (something) as said by someone else **4.** to tell to someone else [*repeat* a secret] **5.** to do or make again —*vi.* to say or do again —*n.* **1.** a repeating **2.** anything said or done again, as a rebroadcast of a television program **3.** *Music a)* a passage to be repeated *b)* a symbol for this —**re·peat′er** *n.*

**re·peat′ed** *adj.* said, made, or done again, or often —**re·peat′ed·ly** *adv.*

**re·pel** (ri pel′) *vt.* -**pelled′**, -**pel′ling** [ < L. *re-*, back + *pellere*, to drive] **1.** to drive or force back **2.** to reject **3.** to cause dislike in; disgust **4.** to be resistant to (water, dirt, etc.) —**re·pel′lent** *adj., n.*

**re·pent** (ri pent′) *vi., vt.* [ < L. *re-*, again + *poenitere*, repent] **1.** to feel sorry for (a sin, error, etc.) **2.** to feel such regret over (an action, intention, etc.) as to change one's mind —**re·pent′ance** *n.* —**re·pent′ant** *adj.*

**re·per·cus·sion** (rē′pər kush′ən) *n.* [see RE- & PERCUSSION] **1.** a rebound **2.** reverberation **3.** a far-reaching, often indirect reaction to some event —**re′per·cus′sive** *adj.*

**rep·er·toire** (rep′ər twär′) *n.* [ < Fr. < L. *repertire*, discover] the stock of plays, songs, etc. that a company, singer, etc. is prepared to perform

**rep′er·to·ry** (-tôr′ē) *n., pl.* -**ries 1.** *same as* REPERTOIRE **2.** the system of alternating several plays throughout a season with a permanent acting group

**rep·e·ti·tion** (rep′ə tish′ən) *n.* [ < L. *repetitio*] **1.** a repeating **2.** something repeated —**rep′e·ti′tious** *adj.* —**re·pet·i·tive** (ri pet′ə tiv) *adj.*

**re·pine** (ri pīn′) *vi.* -**pined′**, -**pin′ing** [RE- + PINE²] to feel or express discontent; complain —**re·pin′er** *n.*

**re·place** (ri plās′) *vt.* -**placed′**, -**plac′ing 1.** to put back in a former or the proper place **2.** to take the place of **3.** to provide an equivalent for —**re·place′a·ble** *adj.* —**re·place′ment** *n.*

**re·plen·ish** (ri plen′ish) *vt.* [ < L. *re-*, again + *plenus*, full] **1.** to make full or complete again **2.** to supply again —**re·plen′ish·ment** *n.*

**re·plete** (ri plēt′) *adj.* [ < L. *re-*, again + *plere*, to fill] plentifully supplied; filled or stuffed —**re·ple′tion** *n.*

**rep·li·ca** (rep′li kə) *n.* [see ff.] a copy of a work of art, etc., esp. one done by the maker of the original

**rep·li·cate** (rep′li kāt′) *vt.* -**cat′ed**, -**cat′ing** [see REPLY] to repeat or duplicate

**rep′li·ca′tion** *n.* **1.** a replicating **2.** a reply; answer **3.** a copy; reproduction

**re·ply** (ri plī′) *vi.* -**plied′**, -**ply′ing** [ < L. *re-*, back + *plicare*, to fold] to answer or respond —*n., pl.* -**plies′** an answer or response

**re·port** (ri pôrt′) *vt.* [ < L. *re-*, back + *portare*, carry] **1.** to give an account of, as for publication **2.** to carry and repeat (a message, etc.) **3.** to announce formally **4.** to make a charge about

(something) or against (someone) to one in authority —*vi.* **1.** to make a report **2.** to present oneself, as for work —*n.* **1.** rumor **2.** a statement or account **3.** a formal presentation of facts **4.** the noise of an explosion —**re·port′ed·ly** *adv.*

**re·port′age** (-ij) *n.* **1.** the reporting of the news **2.** reporterlike accounts

**report card** a periodic written report on a pupil's progress

**re·port′er** *n.* one who reports; specif., one who gathers information and writes reports for a newspaper, etc. —**rep·or·to·ri·al** (rep′ər tôr′ē əl) *adj.*

**re·pose¹** (ri pōz′) *vt.* -**posed′**, -**pos′ing** [ < L. *re-*, again + LL. *pausare*, to rest] to lay or place for rest —*vi.* **1.** to lie at rest **2.** to rest **3.** to lie dead —*n.* **1.** *a)* rest *b)* sleep **2.** composure **3.** calm; peace —**re·pose′ful** *adj.*

**re·pose²** (ri pōz′) *vt.* -**posed′**, -**pos′ing** [see ff.] **1.** to place (trust, etc.) *in* someone **2.** to place (power, etc.) *in* the control of some person or group

**re·pos·i·to·ry** (ri päz′ə tôr′ē) *n., pl.* -**ries** [ < L. *re-*, back + *ponere*, place] a box, room, etc. in which things may be put for safekeeping

**re·pos·sess** (rē′pə zes′) *vt.* to get possession of again —**re′pos·ses′sion** *n.*

**rep·re·hend** (rep′ri hend′) *vt.* [ < L. *re-*, back + *prehendere*, take] to rebuke, blame, or censure

**rep′re·hen′si·ble** (-hen′sə b'l) *adj.* deserving to be reprehended —**rep′re·hen′si·bly** *adv.*

**rep·re·sent** (rep′ri zent′) *vt.* [see RE- & PRESENT, *v.*] **1.** to present to the mind **2.** to present a likeness of **3.** to describe **4.** to stand for; symbolize **5.** to be the equivalent of **6.** to act (a role) **7.** to act in place of, esp. by conferred authority **8.** to serve as a specimen, example, etc. of

**rep′re·sen·ta′tion** *n.* **1.** a representing or being represented, as in a legislative assembly **2.** legislative representatives, collectively **3.** a likeness, image, picture, etc. **4.** [*often pl.*] a statement of claims, protest, etc. —**rep′re·sen·ta′tion·al** *adj.*

**rep′re·sent′a·tive** *adj.* **1.** representing **2.** of or based on representation of the people by elected delegates **3.** typical —*n.* **1.** an example or type **2.** one authorized to act for others; delegate, agent, salesman, etc. **3.** [R-] a member of the lower house of Congress or of a State legislature

**re·press** (ri pres′) *vt.* [see RE- & PRESS¹] **1.** to hold back; restrain **2.** to put down; subdue **3.** *Psychiatry* to force (painful ideas, etc.) into the unconscious —**re·pres′sion** *n.* —**re·pres′sive** *adj.*

**re·prieve** (ri prēv′) *vt.* -**prieved′**, -**priev′ing** [ < Fr. *reprendre*, take back] **1.** to postpone the execution of (a condemned person) **2.** to give temporary relief to —*n.* a reprieving or being reprieved

**rep·ri·mand** (rep'rə mand') *n.* [< L. *reprimere*, repress] a severe or formal rebuke —*vt.* to rebuke severely or formally

**re·pris·al** (ri prī'z'l) *n.* [see REPREHEND] injury done for injury received

**re·proach** (ri prōch') *vt.* [< L. *re-*, back + *prope*, near] to accuse of a fault; rebuke —*n.* 1. shame, disgrace, etc. or a cause of this 2. rebuke or censure —**re·proach'ful** *adj.*

**rep·ro·bate** (rep'rə bāt') *adj.* [< LL. *reprobare*, reprove] depraved; unprincipled —*n.* a depraved person

**re·pro·duce** (rē'prə dōōs') *vt.* -duced', -duc'ing to produce again; specif., *a*) to produce by propagation *b*) to make a copy of —*vi.* to produce offspring —**re'pro·duc'i·ble** *adj.*

**re'pro·duc'tion** (-duk'shən) *n.* 1. a copy, imitation, etc. 2. the process by which animals and plants produce new individuals —**re'pro·duc'tive** *adj.*

**re·proof** (ri prōōf') *n.* a reproving; rebuke: also **re·prov'al** (-prōō'v'l)

**re·prove** (ri prōōv') *vt.* -proved', -prov'ing [see RE- & PROVE] 1. to rebuke 2. to express disapproval of

**rep·tile** (rep't'l, -tīl) *n.* [< L. *repere*, to creep] a coldblooded, crawling vertebrate, as a snake, lizard, turtle, etc. —**rep·til·i·an** (rep tīl'ē ən) *adj.*

**re·pub·lic** (ri pub'lik) *n.* [< L. *res publica*, public thing] a state or government, specif. one headed by a president, in which the power is exercised by officials elected by the voters

**re·pub'li·can** (-li kən) *adj.* 1. of or like a republic 2. [R-] of or belonging to the Republican Party —*n.* 1. one who favors a republic 2. [R-] a member of the Republican Party

**Republican Party** one of the two major U.S. political parties

**re·pu·di·ate** (ri pyōō'dē āt') *vt.* -at'ed, -at'ing [< L. *repudium*, separation] 1. to disown 2. to disavow (a treaty, etc.) —**re·pu'di·a'tion** *n.*

**re·pug·nant** (ri pug'nənt) *adj.* [< L. *re-*, back + *pugnare*, fight] 1. contradictory 2. opposed 3. distasteful; offensive —**re·pug'nance** *n.*

**re·pulse** (ri puls') *vt.* -pulsed', -puls'ing [see REPEL] 1. to drive back (an attack, etc.) 2. to refuse or reject with discourtesy, etc.; rebuff —*n.* a repelling or being repelled

**re·pul'sion** *n.* 1. a repelling or being repelled 2. strong dislike 3. *Physics* the mutual action by which bodies tend to repel each other

**re·pul'sive** *adj.* causing strong dislike or aversion; disgusting —**re·pul'sive·ly** *adv.* —**re·pul'sive·ness** *n.*

**rep·u·ta·ble** (rep'yoo tə b'l) *adj.* having a good reputation —**rep'u·ta·bil'i·ty** *n.* —**rep'u·ta·bly** *adv.*

**rep·u·ta·tion** (rep'yoo tā'shən) *n.* [see ff.] 1. estimation in which a person or thing is commonly held 2. favorable estimation 3. fame

**re·pute** (ri pyōōt') *vt.* -put'ed, -put'ing [< L. *re-*, again + *putare*, think] to consider or regard [*reputed* to be rich] —*n.* reputation; esp., fame —**re·put'ed** *adj.* —**re·put'ed·ly** *adv.*

**re·quest** (ri kwest') *n.* [see REQUIRE] 1. an asking for something 2. a thing asked for 3. the state of being asked for; demand —*vt.* 1. to ask for 2. to ask (a person) to do something

**Re·qui·em** (rek'wē əm, rāk'-) *n.* [< L., rest] [*also* r-] *R.C.Ch.* 1. a Mass for the repose of the dead 2. its musical setting

**re·quire** (ri kwīr') *vt.* -quired', -quir'ing [< L. *re-*, again + *quaerere*, ask] 1. to insist upon; demand; order 2. to need —**re·quire'ment** *n.*

**req·ui·site** (rek'wə zit) *adj.* [see prec.] required; necessary; indispensable —*n.* something requisite

**req'ui·si'tion** (-zish'ən) *n.* 1. a requiring; formal demand 2. a formal written order, as for equipment —*vt.* to demand or take, as by authority

**re·quite** (ri kwīt') *vt.* -quit'ed, -quit'ing [RE- + *quite*, obs. var. of QUIT] to repay (someone) for (a benefit, service, etc., or an injury, wrong, etc.) —**re·quit'al** *n.*

**re·run** (rē'run') *n.* a showing of a motion picture or television program after the first showing

**re'sale'** (-sāl') *n.* a selling again, specif., to a third party

**re·scind** (ri sind') *vt.* [< L. *re-*, back + *scindere*, to cut] to revoke or cancel (a law, etc.) —**re·scis'sion** (-sizh'ən) *n.*

**res·cue** (res'kyōō) *vt.* -cued, -cu·ing [ult. < L. *re-*, again + *ex-*, off + *quatere*, to shake] to free or save from danger, confinement, evil, etc. —*n.* a rescuing —**res'cu·er** *n.*

**re·search** (ri surch', rē'surch) *n.* [see RE- & SEARCH] careful, systematic study and investigation in some field of knowledge —*vi., vt.* to do research on or in —**re·search'er** *n.*

**re·sec·tion** (ri sek'shən) *n.* [< L. *re-*, back + *secare*, to cut] the surgical removal of part of an organ, etc.

**re·sem·blance** (ri zem'bləns) *n.* a similarity of appearance; likeness

**re·sem·ble** (ri zem'b'l) *vt.* -bled, -bling [ult. < L. *re-*, again + *simulare*, feign] to be like or similar to

**re·sent** (ri zent') *vt.* [ult. < L. *re-*, again + *sentire*, feel] to feel or show a bitter hurt or indignation at —**re·sent'ful** *adj.* —**re·sent'ful·ly** *adv.* —**re·sent'ment** *n.*

**res·er·pine** (res'ər'pin, -pēn) *n.* [G.] a crystalline alkaloid used in treating hypertension, mental illness, etc.

**res·er·va·tion** (rez'ər vā'shən) *n.* 1. a reserving or that which is reserved; specif., *a*) a withholding *b*) public land set aside for a special use, as for Indians *c*) a holding of a hotel room, etc. until called for 2. a limiting condition

**re·serve** (ri zurv') *vt.* -served', -serv'ing [< L. *re-*, back + *servare*, to keep] 1. to keep back or set apart for later or special use 2. to keep back for oneself —*n.* 1. something kept back or stored up, as for later use 2. a limitation [*without reserve*] 3. the keeping of one's thoughts, feelings, etc. to oneself 4. reticence; silence 5. [*pl.*] troops not on active duty but subject to call **6.** land set apart for some purpose —**in reserve** reserved for later use —**re·serv'ist** *n.*

**re·served'** *adj.* **1.** kept in reserve; set apart **2.** self-restrained; reticent

**res·er·voir** (rez'ər vwär') *n.* [< Fr.: see RESERVE] **1.** a place where water is collected and stored for use **2.** a large supply or store of something

**re·side** (ri zīd') *vi.* **-sid'ed, -sid'ing** [< L. *re-*, back + *sedere*, sit] **1.** to dwell for some time; live (*in* or *at*) **2.** to be present or inherent (*in*): said of qualities, etc.

**res·i·dence** (rez'i dəns) *n.* **1.** a residing **2.** the place where one resides —**res'i·den'tial** (-ə den'shəl) *adj.*

**res'i·den·cy** (-dən sē) *n., pl.* **-cies 1.** *same as* RESIDENCE **2.** a period of advanced, specialized medical or surgical training in a hospital

**res'i·dent** *adj.* residing; esp., living in a place while working, etc. —*n.* **1.** one who lives in a place, not a visitor **2.** a doctor who is serving a residency

**re·sid·u·al** (ri zij'ōo wəl) *adj.* of or being a residue; remaining —*n.* **1.** something left over **2.** [*pl.*] fees paid for reruns on television, etc.

**res·i·due** (rez'ə dōō') *n.* [< L. *residuus*, remaining] that which is left after part is removed; remainder

**re·sid·u·um** (ri zij'ōo wəm) *n., pl.* **-u·a** (-wə) *same as* RESIDUE

**re·sign** (ri zīn') *vt., vi.* [< L. *re-*, back + *signare*, to sign] to give up (a claim, or an office, position, etc.) —**resign oneself** (*to*) to submit (*to*)

**res·ig·na·tion** (rez'ig nā'shən) *n.* **1.** *a)* the act of resigning *b)* formal notice of this **2.** patient submission

**re·signed** (ri zīnd') *adj.* feeling or showing resignation; submissive —**re·sign'ed·ly** (-zīn'id lē) *adv.*

**re·sil·ient** (ri zil'yənt) *adj.* [< L. *re-*, back + *salire*, to jump] **1.** springing back into shape, etc.; elastic **2.** recovering strength, spirits, etc. quickly —**re·sil'ience, re·sil'ien·cy** *n.*

**res·in** (rez''n) *n.* [L. *resina*] **1.** a substance exuded from various plants and trees and used in varnishes, plastics, etc. **2.** *same as* ROSIN —**res'in·ous** *adj.*

**re·sist** (ri zist') *vt.* [< L. *re-*, back + *sistere*, to set] **1.** to withstand; fend off **2.** to oppose actively; fight against —*vi.* to oppose or withstand something —**re·sist'er** *n.* —**re·sist'i·ble** *adj.*

**re·sist'ance** *n.* **1.** a resisting **2.** power to resist, as to ward off disease **3.** opposition of some force, thing, etc. to another, as to the flow of an electric current —**re·sist'ant** *adj.*

**re·sis'tive** *adj.* resisting, tending to resist, or capable of resistance

**re·sist'less** *adj.* **1.** irresistible **2.** unable to resist; unresisting

**re·sis'tor** *n.* a device used in an electrical circuit to provide resistance

**re'sole'** *vt.* **-soled', -sol'ing** to put a new sole on (a shoe, etc.)

**res·o·lute** (rez'ə lōōt') *adj.* [see RE-

& SOLVE] fixed and firm in purpose; determined —**res'o·lute'ly** *adv.*

**res'o·lu'tion** *n.* **1.** the act or result of resolving something **2.** the thing determined upon; decision as to future action **3.** a resolute quality of mind **4.** a formal statement of opinion or determination by an assembly, etc.

**re·solve** (ri zälv') *vt.* **-solved', -solv'-ing** [see RE- & SOLVE] **1.** to break up into separate parts; analyze **2.** to reach a decision; determine **3.** to solve (a problem) **4.** to decide by vote —*vi.* **1.** to be resolved, as by analysis **2.** to come to a decision; determine —*n.* **1.** firm determination **2.** a formal resolution —**re·solv'a·ble** *adj.*

**re·solved'** *adj.* determined; resolute

**res·o·nant** (rez'ə nənt) *adj.* [< L. *resonare*, resound] **1.** resounding **2.** intensifying sound [*resonant walls*] **3.** vibrant; sonorous [*a resonant voice*] —**res'o·nance** *n.* —**res·o·nate'** (-nāt') *vi., vt.* **-nat'ed, -nat'ing**

**res'o·na'tor** *n.* a device that produces, or increases sound by, resonance

**re·sort** (ri zôrt') *vi.* [< OFr. *re-*, again + *sortir*, go out] **1.** to have recourse; turn (*to*) for help, etc. [*to resort to tears*] —*n.* **1.** a place to which people go often, as on vacation **2.** a source of help, support, etc.; recourse —**as a** (or **the**) **last resort** as the last available means

**re·sound** (ri zound') *vi.* [< L. *resonare*] **1.** to reverberate **2.** to make a loud, echoing sound —**re·sound'-ing** *adj.* —**re·sound'ing·ly** *adv.*

**re·source** (rē'sôrs, ri sôrs') *n.* [< OFr. *re-*, again + *sourdre*, spring up] **1.** something that lies ready for use or can be drawn upon for aid **2.** [*pl.*] wealth; assets **3.** resourcefulness

**re·source'ful** *adj.* able to deal effectively with problems, etc. —**re·source'ful·ness** *n.*

**re·spect** (ri spekt') *vt.* [< L. *re-*, back + *specere*, look at] **1.** to feel or show honor or esteem for **2.** to show consideration for —*n.* **1.** honor or esteem **2.** consideration; regard **3.** [*pl.*] expressions of regard **4.** a particular detail **5.** reference; relation [*with respect to his job*] —**re·spect'ful** *adj.* —**re·spect'ful·ly** *adv.*

**re·spect'a·ble** *adj.* **1.** worthy of respect or esteem **2.** proper; correct **3.** of moderate quality or size **4.** presentable —**re·spect'a·bil'i·ty** *n.*

**re·spect'ing** *prep.* concerning; about

**re·spec'tive** *adj.* as relates individually to each one —**re·spec'tive·ly** *adv.*

**res·pi·ra·tion** (res'pə rā'shən) *n.* act or process of breathing —**res·pi·ra·to·ry** (res'pər ə tôr'ē, ri spir'ə-) *adj.*

**res'pi·ra'tor** *n.* **1.** a mask, as of gauze, to prevent the inhaling of harmful substances **2.** an apparatus to maintain breathing by artificial means

**re·spire** (ri spīr') *vt., vi.* **-spired', -spir'ing** [< L. *re-*, back + *spirare*, breathe] to breathe

**res·pite** (res'pit) *n.* [see RESPECT] 1. a delay or postponement 2. temporary relief, as from work or pain

**re·splend·ent** (ri splen'dənt) *adj.* [< L. *re-*, again + *splendere*, to shine] shining brightly; dazzling —**re·splend'ence** *n.* —**re·splend'ent·ly** *adv.*

**re·spond** (ri spänd') *vi.* [< L. *re-*, back + *spondere*, to pledge] 1. to answer; reply 2. to react 3. to have a favorable reaction

**re·spond'ent** *adj.* responding - *n. Law* a defendant

**re·sponse** (ri späns') *n.* 1. something said or done in answer; reply 2. words sung or spoken by the congregation or choir replying to the clergyman 3. any reaction to a stimulus

**re·spon·si·bil·i·ty** (ri spän'sə bil'ə tē) *n., pl.* **-ties** 1. a being responsible; obligation 2. a thing or person for whom one is responsible

**re·spon·si·ble** (-b'l) *adj.* 1. obliged to account (*for*); answerable (*to*) 2. involving obligation or duties 3. accountable for one's behavior or for an act 4. dependable; reliable —**re·spon'si·bly** *adv.*

**re·spon·sive** *adj.* reacting readily, as to appeal —**re·spon'sive·ness** *n.*

**rest¹** (rest) *n.* [OE.] 1. sleep or repose 2. ease or inactivity after exertion 3. relief from anything distressing, tiring, etc. 4. absence of motion 5. a resting place 6. a supporting device 7. *Music* a measured interval of silence between tones, or a symbol for this —*vi.* 1. to get ease and refreshment by sleeping or by ceasing from work 2. to be at ease 3. to be or become still 4. to be supported; lie or lean (*in, on,* etc.) 5. to be found (*the fault rests* with him) 6. to rely; depend —*vt.* 1. to cause to rest 2. to put for ease, etc. [*rest* your head here] —**lay to rest** to bury

**rest²** (rest) *n.* [< L. *restare*, remain] 1. what is left 2. [*with pl. v.*] the others —*vi.* to go on being [*rest* assured]

**res·tau·rant** (res'tə rənt, -ränt') *n.* [Fr.: see RESTORE] a place where meals can be bought and eaten

**res·tau·ra·teur** (res'tər ə tur') *n.* [Fr.] one who operates a restaurant

**rest·ful** (rest'fəl) *adj.* 1. full of or giving rest 2. quiet; peaceful

**res·ti·tu·tion** (res'tə tōō'shən) *n.* [< L. *re-*, again + *statuere*, set up] 1. a giving back of something that has been lost or taken away; restoration 2. reimbursement, as for loss

**res·tive** (res'tiv) *adj.* [< OFr. *rester*, remain] 1. unruly or balky 2. nervous under restraint; restless —**res'tive·ly** *adv.* —**res'tive·ness** *n.*

**rest·less** *adj.* 1. unable to relax; uneasy 2. giving no rest; disturbed [*restless* sleep] 3. rarely quiet or still; active 4. discontented —**rest'less·ly** *adv.* —**rest'less·ness** *n.*

**res·to·ra·tion** (res'tə rā'shən) *n.* 1. a restoring or being restored 2. something restored, as by rebuilding

**re·stor·a·tive** (ri stôr'ə tiv) *adj.* restoring health, consciousness, etc. —*n.* something that is restorative

**re·store** (ri stôr') *vt.* **-stored', -stor'-ing** [< L. *re-*, again + *-staurare*, to erect] 1. to give back (something taken, lost, etc.) 2. to return to a former or normal state, or to a position, rank, use, etc. 3. to bring back to health, strength, etc.

**re·strain** (ri strān') *vt.* [< L. *re-*, back + *stringere*, draw tight] to hold back from action; check; suppress

**re·straint** (ri strānt') *n.* 1. a re-straining or being restrained 2. a means of restraining 3. confinement 4. control of emotions, impulses, etc.; reserve

**re·strict** (ri strikt') *vt.* [see RESTRAIN] to keep within limits; confine —**re·strict'ed** *adj.* —**re·stric'tion** *n.*

**re·stric·tive** *adj.* 1. restricting 2. *Gram.* designating a subordinate clause or phrase felt as limiting the application of the word it modifies, and not set off by commas (Ex.: a man *with money* is needed)

**rest'room'** *n.* a room in a public building, equipped with toilets, wash-bowls, etc.: also **rest room**

**re·struc·ture** (rē struk'chər) *vt.* **-tured, -tur·ing** to plan or provide a new structure or organization for

**re·sult** (ri zult') *vi.* [< L. *resultare*, rebound] 1. to happen as an effect 2. to end as a consequence (*in* something) —*n.* 1. a) anything that issues as an effect b) [*pl.*] a desired effect 2. the number, etc. obtained by mathematical calculation —**re·sult'ant** *adj., n.*

**re·sume** (ri zōōm') *vt.* **-sumed', -sum'ing** [< L. *re-*, again + *sumere*, take] 1. to take or occupy again 2. to continue after interruption —*vi.* to proceed after interruption —**re·sump'tion** (ri zump'shən) *n.*

**ré·su·mé, re·su·me** (rez'oo mā', rä'zoo mā') *n.* [Fr.: see prec.] a sum-mary, esp. of employment experience

**re·sur·face** *vt.* **-faced, -fac·ing** to put a new surface on —*vi.* to come to the surface again

**re·sur·gent** (ri sur'jənt) *adj.* [see ff.] tending to rise again —**re·sur'gence** *n.*

**res·ur·rec·tion** (rez'ə rek'shən) *n.* [< L. *resurgere*, rise again] 1. *Theol.* a rising from the dead; specif., [**the R-**] the rising of Jesus from the dead 2. a coming back into use, etc.; revival —**res'ur·rect'** *vt.*

**re·sus·ci·tate** (ri sus'ə tāt') *vt., vi.* **-tat'ed, -tat'ing** [< L. *re-*, again + *suscitare*, revive] to revive when ap-parently dead or in a faint, etc. —**re·sus'ci·ta'tion** *n.* —**re·sus'ci·ta'tor** *n.*

**re·tail** (rē'tāl) *n.* [< OFr. *re-*, again + *tailler*, to cut] the sale of goods in small quantities directly to the consumer —*adj.* of or engaged in such sale —*adv.* at a retail price —*vt., vi.* to sell or be sold at retail —**re'tail·er** *n.*

**re·tain** (ri tān') *vt.* [< L. *re-*, back + *tenere*, to hold] 1. to keep in posses-sion, use, etc. 2. to hold in 3. to keep in mind 4. to hire by paying a retainer

**re·tain'er** *n.* 1. something that re-tains 2. a servant, attendant, etc. 3. a fee paid to engage a lawyer's services

**retaining wall** a wall built to hold back earth or water

**re·take** (rē tāk′; *for n.* rē′tāk′) *vt.* -took′, -tak′en, -tak′ing 1. to take again; recapture 2. to photograph again —*n.* a scene, etc. rephotographed

**re·tal·i·ate** (ri tal′ē āt′) *vi.* -at′ed, -at′ing [< L. *re-*, back + *talio*, punishment in kind] to return like for like, esp. injury for injury —**re·tal′i·a′tion** *n.* —**re·tal′i·a·to′ry** *adj.*

**re·tard** (ri tärd′) *vt.* [< L. *re-*, back + *tardare*, make slow] to hinder, delay, or slow the progress of —**re·tar·da·tion** (rē′tär dā′shən) *n.*

**re·tard′ant** *n.*, something that retards; esp., a substance that delays a chemical reaction —*adj.* that retards

**re·tard·ate** (ri tär′dāt) *n.* a mentally retarded person

**re·tard′ed** *adj.* slow or delayed in development, esp. mentally

**retch** (rech) *vi.* [OE. *hræcan*, clear the throat] to strain to vomit, esp. without bringing anything up

**re·ten·tion** (ri ten′shən) *n.* 1. a retaining or being retained 2. capacity for retaining —**re·ten′tive** *adj.*

**ret·i·cent** (ret′ə s′nt) *adj.* [< L. *re-*, again + *tacere*, be silent] disinclined to speak; taciturn —**ret′i·cence** *n.*

**ret·i·na** (ret′′n ə) *n., pl.* -nas *or* -nae′ (-ē′) [prob. < L. *rete*, a net] the innermost coat of the back part of the eyeball, on which the image is formed

**ret·i·nue** (ret′′n ōō′, -yōō′) *n.* [see RETAIN] a group of persons attending a person of rank or importance

**re·tire** (ri tīr′) *vi.* -tired′, -tir′ing [< Fr. *re-*, back + *tirer*, draw] 1. to withdraw to a secluded place 2. to go to bed 3. to retreat, as in battle 4. to give up one's work, business, etc., esp. because of age —*vt.* 1. to withdraw (troops, etc.) 2. to pay off (bonds, etc.) 3. to cause to retire from a position, office, etc. 4. to withdraw from use 5. *Baseball*, etc. to put out (a batter, side, etc.) —**re·tir′ee′** *n.* —**re·tire′ment** *n.*

**re·tired′** *adj.* 1. secluded 2. *a)* no longer working, etc., as because of age *b)* of or for such retired persons

**re·tir′ing** *adj.* reserved; modest; shy

**re·tool′** *vt., vi.* to adapt (factory machinery) for a different product

**re·tort** (ri tôrt′) *vt.* [< L. *re-*, back + *torquere*, to twist] 1. to turn (an insult, etc.) back upon its originator 2. to say in reply —*vi.* to make a sharp, witty reply —*n.* a sharp, witty reply

**re·tort²** (ri tôrt′) *n.* [< ML. *retorta:* see prec.] a glass container in which substances are distilled

**re·touch** (rē tuch′) *vt.* to touch up details in (a picture, writing, etc.) so as to improve or change it

RETORT

**re·trace** (ri trās′) *vt.* -traced′, -trac′ing [see RE- & TRACE¹] to go back over again [to *retrace* one's steps]

**re·tract** (ri trakt′) *vt., vi.* [< L. *re-*, back + *trahere*, draw] 1. to draw back or in 2. to withdraw (a statement, charge, etc.) —**re·tract′a·ble**, **re·trac′tile** (-t′l) *adj.* —**re·trac′tion** *n.*

**re·tread** (rē tred′; *for n.* rē′tred′) *vt., n. same as* RECAP

**re·treat** (ri trēt′) *n.* [see RETRACT] 1. a withdrawal, as from danger 2. a safe, quiet place 3. a period of seclusion, esp. for contemplation 4. *a)* the forced withdrawal of troops under attack *b)* a signal for this *c)* a signal, as by bugle, or ceremony at sunset for lowering the national flag —*vi.* to withdraw; go back

**re·trench** (rē trench′) *vt., vi.* [see RE- & TRENCH] to cut down (esp. expenses); economize —**re·trench′ment** *n.*

**ret·ri·bu·tion** (ret′rə byōō′shən) *n.* [< L. *re-*, back + *tribuere*, to pay] deserved reward or, esp., punishment —**re·trib·u·tive** (ri trib′yoo tiv) *adj.*

**re·trieve** (ri trēv′) *vt.* -trieved′, -triev′ing [< OFr. *re-*, again + *trouver*, find] 1. to get back; recover 2. to restore 3. to make good (a loss, error, etc.) 4. to recover (information) from data stored in a computer 5. to find and bring back (killed or wounded game): said of dogs —*vi.* to retrieve game —**re·triev′al** *n.*

**re·triev′er** *n.* a dog trained to retrieve game

**retro-** [< L.] *a combining form meaning* backward, back, behind

**ret·ro·ac·tive** (ret′rō ak′tiv) *adj.* having effect on things that are already past —**ret′ro·ac′tive·ly** *adv.*

**ret·ro·fire** (ret′rə fir′) *vt.* -fired′, -fir′ing to fire (a retrorocket)

**ret·ro·grade** (ret′rə grād′) *adj.* [see RETRO- & GRADE] 1. moving backward 2. going back to a worse condition —*vi.* -grad′ed, -grad′ing 1. to go backward 2. to become worse

**ret·ro·gress** (ret′rə gres′) *vi.* [see prec.] to move backward, esp. into a worse condition —**ret′ro·gres′sion** *n.* —**ret′ro·gres′sive** *adj.*

**ret·ro·rock·et** (ret′rō räk′it) *n.* a small rocket, as on a spacecraft, producing thrust opposite to the direction of flight to reduce landing speed, etc.

**ret·ro·spect** (ret′rə spekt′) *n.* [< L. *retro-* + *specere*, to look] contemplation of the past —**ret′ro·spec′tion** *n.*

**ret·ro·spec′tive** *adj.* looking back on the past —*n.* a representative show of an artist's lifetime work

**ret·si·na**, **ret·zi·na** (ret′si nə) *n.* [Mod. Gr., prob. < L. *resina*, resin] a white or red wine of Greece, flavored with pine resin

**re·turn** (ri turn′) *vi.* [see RE- & TURN] 1. to go or come back 2. to reply —*vt.* 1. to bring, send, or put back 2. to do in reciprocation [to *return* a visit] 3.

to yield (a profit, etc.) **4.** to report officially **5.** to elect or reelect —*n.* **1.** a coming or going back **2.** a bringing, sending, or putting back **3.** something returned **4.** a recurrence **5.** repayment; requital **6.** [*often pl.*] yield or profit, as from investments **7.** a reply **8.** *a)* an official report [*election returns*] *b)* a form for computing (income) tax —*adj.* **1.** of or for a return [*a return ticket*] **2.** given, done, etc. in return —**in return** as a return —**re·turn′a·ble** *adj.*

**re·turn·ee′** *n.* one who returns, as home from military service or to school after dropping out

**re·u·ni·fy** (rē yōō′nə fī′) *vt.*, *vi.* **-fied′, -fy′ing** to unify again after being divided —**re·u′ni·fi·ca′tion** *n.*

**re·un·ion** (rē yōōn′yən) *n.* a coming together again, as after separation

**re-up** (rē′up′) *vi.* **-upped′, -up′ping** [RE- + (SIGN) UP] [Mil. Slang] to reenlist

**rev** (rev) *vt.* revved, rev′ving [Colloq.] to increase the speed of (an engine): usually with *up*

**Rev.** *pl.* **Revs.** Reverend

**re·vamp** (rē vamp′) *vt.* to vamp again; specif., to revise; redo

**re·veal** (ri vēl′) *vt.* [< L. *re-*, back + *velum*, a veil] **1.** to make known (something hidden or secret) **2.** to show; exhibit; display

**re·veil·le** (rev′ə lē) *n.* [< Fr. < L. *re-*, again + *vigilare*, to watch] a signal on a bugle, drum, etc. in the morning to waken soldiers, etc.

**rev·el** (rev′'l) *vi.* **-eled** or **-elled, -el·ing** or **-el·ling** [see REBEL] **1.** to make merry **2.** to take much pleasure (*in*) —*n.* merrymaking —**rev′el·er, rev′el·ler** *n.* —**rev′el·ry** *n.*

**rev·e·la·tion** (rev′ə lā′shən) *n.* **1.** a revealing **2.** something disclosed; esp., a striking disclosure **3.** *Theol.* God's disclosure to man of himself —[R-] the last book of the New Testament

**re·venge** (ri venj′) *vt.* **-venged′, -veng′ing** [< OFr.: see RE- & VENGEANCE] to inflict harm in return for (an injury, etc.) —*n.* **1.** the act or result of revenging **2.** desire to take vengeance —**re·venge′ful** *adj.*

**rev·e·nue** (rev′ə nōō′) *n.* [< MFr., returned] the income from taxes, licenses, etc., as of a city, state, or nation

**re·ver·ber·ate** (ri vur′bə rāt′) *vt.*, *vi.* **-at′ed, -at′ing** [< L. *re-*, again + *verberare*, to beat] to reecho or cause to reecho —**re·ver′ber·a′tion** *n.*

**re·vere** (ri vir′) *vt.* **-vered′, -ver′ing** [< L. *re-*, again + *vereri*, to fear] to regard with deep respect, love, etc.

**Re·vere** (ri vir′), **Paul** 1735–1818; Am. silversmith and patriot

**rev·er·ence** (rev′ər əns) *n.* a feeling of deep respect, love, and awe —*vt.* **-enced, -enc·ing** to revere —**rev′er·ent, rev′er·en′tial** (-ə ren′shəl) *adj.* —**rev′er·ent·ly** *adv.*

**rev·er·end** (rev′ər ənd) *adj.* worthy of reverence: used [*usually* **the R-**] as a title of respect for a clergyman

**rev·er·ie, rev·er·y** (rev′ər ē) *n.*, *pl.*

**-ies** [< Fr.] daydreaming or a daydream

**re·vers** (ri vir′, -ver′) *n.*, *pl.* **-vers′** (-virz′, -verz′) [Fr.: see ff.] a part (of a garment) turned back to show the reverse side, as a lapel: also **re·vere** (-vir′)

**re·verse** (ri vurs′) *adj.* [see ff.] **1.** turned backward; opposite or contrary **2.** causing movement in the opposite direction —*n.* **1.** the opposite or contrary **2.** the back of a coin, medal, etc. **3.** a change from good fortune to bad **4.** a mechanism for reversing, as a gear on a machine —*vt.* **-versed′, -vers′ing 1.** to turn backward, in an opposite position or direction, upside down, or inside out **2.** to change to the opposite **3.** *Law* to revoke or turn in the opposite direction —*vi.* to go or turn in the opposite direction —**re·ver·sal** (-vur′s'l) *n.* —**re·vers′i·ble** *adj.* —**re·vers′i·bly** *adv.*

**re·vert** (ri vurt′) *vi.* [< L. *re-*, back + *vertere*, to turn] **1.** to go back, as to a former practice, state, subject, etc. **2.** *Biol.* to return to a former or primitive type **3.** *Law* to go back to a former owner or his heirs —**re·ver′sion** (-vur′zhən) *n.* —**re·vert′i·ble** *adj.*

**re·vet·ment** (ri vet′mənt) *n.* [< Fr.] **1.** a facing of stone, cement, etc. to protect an embankment **2.** *same as* RETAINING WALL

**re·view** (ri vyōō′) *n.* [< L. *re-*, again + *videre*, see] **1.** a looking at or looking over again **2.** a general survey or report **3.** a looking back on (past events, etc.) **4.** a reexamination, as of the decision of a lower court **5.** a critical evaluation of a book, play, etc. **6.** a formal inspection, as of troops on parade —*vt.* **1.** to look back on **2.** to survey in thought, speech, etc. **3.** to inspect (troops, etc.) formally **4.** to give a critical evaluation of (a book, etc.) **5.** to study again —**re·view′er** *n.*

**re·vile** (ri vīl′) *vt.*, *vi.* **-viled′, -vil′ing** [see RE- & VILE] to use abusive language (to or about) —**re·vile′ment** *n.* —**re·vil′er** *n.*

**re·vise** (ri vīz′) *vt.* **-vised′, -vis′ing** [< L. *re-*, back + *visere*, to survey] **1.** to read over carefully and correct, improve, or update **2.** to change or amend —**re·vi·sion** (ri vizh′ən) *n.*

**Revised Standard Version** a 20th-c. revision of the Bible

**re·viv·al** (ri vī′v'l) *n.* **1.** a reviving or being revived **2.** a bringing or coming back into use, being, etc. **3.** a new presentation of an earlier play, etc. **4.** restoration to vigor or activity **5.** a meeting led by an evangelist to stir up religious feeling —**re·viv′al·ist** *n.*

**re·vive** (ri vīv′) *vi.*, *vt.* **-vived′, -viv′ing** [< L. *re-*, again + *vivere*, to live] **1.** to return to life or consciousness **2.** to return to health and vigor **3.** to bring back or come back into use, attention, popularity, exhibition, etc. —**re·viv′i·fy** (ri viv′ə fī′) *vt.* **-fied′, -fy′ing** to put new life or vigor into —*vi.* to revive —**re·viv′i·fi·ca′tion** *n.*

**re·voke** (ri vōk′) *vt.* **-voked′, -vok′-ing** [< L. *re-*, back + *vocare*, to call] to withdraw; repeal, or cancel (a law, etc.) —**re·vo·ca·ble** (rev′ə kə b'l) adj. —**rev′o·ca′tion** (-kā′shən) n.

**re·volt** (ri vōlt′) n. [see REVOLVE] a rebelling against the government or any authority —vi. 1. to rebel against authority 2. to turn (from or against) in revulsion; be shocked (at) —vt. to disgust —**re·volt′ing** adj.

**rev·o·lu·tion** (rev′ə lōō′shən) n. [see REVOLVE] 1. a movement of a body in an orbit 2. a turning around an axis; rotation 3. a complete cycle of events 4. a complete change 5. overthrow of a government, social system, etc. — **rev′o·lu′tion·ar′y** (-er′ē) adj., n., pl. **-ies** —**rev′o·lu′tion·ist** n.

**Revolutionary War** same as AMERICAN REVOLUTION

**rev′o·lu′tion·ize′** (-īz′) vt. **-ized′**, **-iz′ing** to make a drastic change in

**re·volve** (ri välv′) vt. **-volved′**, **-volv′ing** [< L. re-, back + volvere, to roll] 1. to turn over in the mind 2. to cause to travel in a circle or orbit 3. to cause to rotate —vi. 1. to move in a circle or orbit 2. to rotate 3. to recur at intervals —**re·volv′a·ble** adj.

**re·volv′er** n. a handgun with a revolving cylinder holding cartridges

**re·vue** (ri vyōō′) n. [Fr.: see REVIEW] a musical show with skits, dances, etc., often parodying recent events, etc.

**re·vul·sion** (ri vul′shən) n. [< L. re-, back + vellere, to pull] an abrupt, strong reaction; esp., disgust

**re·ward** (ri wôrd′) n. [see REGARD] 1. something given in return for something done 2. money offered, as for capturing a criminal —vt. to give a reward to (someone) for (service, etc.)

**re·ward′ing** adj. giving a sense of reward or worthwhile return

**re·wind′** vt. **-wound′**, **-wind′ing** to wind again, specif. (film or tape) back on the original reel

**re·word′** vt. to change the wording of

**re·write′** vt., vi. **-wrote′**, **-writ′ten**, **-writ′ing** 1. to write again 2. to revise 3. to write (news turned in) in a form suitable for publication

**Rey·kja·vík** (rā′kyə vēk′) capital of Iceland; a seaport; pop. 78,000

**RFD, R.F.D.** Rural Free Delivery

**rhap·so·dize** (rap′sə dīz′) vi., vt. **-dized′**, **-diz′ing** to speak or write in a rhapsodic manner

**rhap′so·dy** (-dē) n., pl. **-dies** [< Gr. rhaptein, stitch together + ōidē, song] 1. any ecstatic or enthusiastic speech or writing 2. an instrumental composition of free, irregular form, suggesting improvisation —**rhap·sod′ic** (-säd′ik), **rhap·sod′i·cal** adj.

**rhe·a** (rē′ə) n. [< Gr.] a large S.American nonflying bird, like the ostrich but smaller

**rhe·o·stat** (rē′ə stat′) n. [< Gr. rheos, current + -STAT] a device for varying the resistance of an electric circuit, used as for dimming or brightening electric lights

**rhe·sus (monkey)** (rē′səs) [< Gr. proper name] a brownish-yellow monkey of India: used in medical research

**rhet·o·ric** (ret′ər ik) n. [< Gr. rhētōr, orator] 1. the art of using words effectively; esp., the art of prose composition 2. artificial eloquence —**rhe·tor·i·cal** (ri tôr′i k'l) adj. —**rhet′o·ri′cian** (-ə rish′ən) n.

**rhetorical question** a question asked only for rhetorical effect, no answer being expected

**rheum** (rōōm) n. [< Gr. rheuma, a flow] watery discharge from the eyes, nose, etc., as in a cold

**rheumatic fever** an acute or chronic disease, usually of children, with fever, swelling of the joints, inflammation of the heart, etc.

**rheu·ma·tism** (rōō′mə tiz'm) n. [see RHEUM] a popular term for a painful condition of the joints and muscles —**rheu·mat′ic** (-mat′ik) adj., n. — **rheu′ma·toid′** (-mə toid′) adj.

**rheumatoid arthritis** a chronic disease with painful swelling of joints

**Rh factor** (är′āch′) [first discovered in rhesus monkeys] a group of antigens, usually present in human blood: people who have this factor are **Rh positive**; those who do not are **Rh negative**

**Rhine** (rīn) river in W Europe, flowing through Switzerland, Germany, and the Netherlands into the North Sea

**rhine·stone** (rīn′stōn′) n. an artificial gem of hard glass, often cut in imitation of a diamond

**rhi·ni·tis** (rī nīt′əs) n. [< Gr. rhis, nose + -ITIS] inflammation of the nasal mucous membrane

**rhi·no** (rī′nō) n., pl. **-nos**, **-no** clipped form of RHINOCEROS

**rhi·noc·er·os** (rī näs′ər əs) n. [< Gr. rhis, nose + keras, horn] a large, thick-skinned, plant-eating mammal of Africa and Asia, with one or two upright horns on the snout

**rhi·zome** (rī′zōm) n. [< Gr. rhiza, a root] a horizontal stem on or under soil, bearing leaves near its tips and roots from its undersurface

**rho** (rō) n. the 17th letter of the Greek alphabet (P, ρ)

**Rhode Island** (rōd) New England State of the U.S.: 1,214 sq. mi.; pop. 950,000; cap. Providence

**Rho·de·sia** (rō dē′zhə) country in S Africa: 150,333 sq. mi.; pop. 6,100,000 —**Rho·de′sian** adj., n.

**rho·do·den·dron** (rō′də den′drən) n. [< Gr. rhodon, rose + dendron, tree] a tree or shrub, mainly evergreen, with pink, white, or purple flowers

**rhom·boid** (räm′boid) n. [see ff. & -OID] a parallelogram with oblique angles and only the opposite sides equal

**rhom·bus** (räm′bəs) n., pl. **-bus·es**, **-bi** (-bī) RHOMBOID

[L. < Gr. *rhombos*, turnable object] an equilateral parallelogram, esp. one with oblique angles

**Rhone, Rhône** (rōn) river flowing through SW Switzerland & France into the Mediterranean

**rhu·barb** (rōō'bärb) *n.* RHOMBUS [< Gr. *rhēon*, rhubarb + *barbaron*, foreign] 1. a plant with long thick stalks cooked into a sauce, etc. 2. [Slang] a heated argument

**rhyme** (rīm) *n.* [< OFr.] 1. a poem or verse with recurring correspondence of end sounds, esp. at ends of lines 2. such poetry or verse or such correspondence of sounds 3. a word corresponding with another in end sound —*vi.* rhymed, rhym'ing 1. to make (rhyming) verse 2. to form a rhyme ["more" *rhymes* with "door"] —*vt.* 1. to put into rhyme 2. to use as a rhyme

**rhym'er, rhyme'ster** *n.* a maker of rhymes, esp. of trivial rhyming verse

**rhythm** (ri*th*'m) *n.* [< Gr. *rhythmos*, measure] 1. movement characterized by regular recurrence of beat, accent, etc. 2. the pattern of this in music, verse, etc. —**rhyth'mic** (-mik), **rhyth'mi·cal** *adj.* —**rhyth'mi·cal·ly** *adv.*

**rhythm and blues** the form of black American popular music from which rock-and-roll derives

**rhythm method** a method of birth control by abstaining from intercourse during the probable ovulation period

**R.I., RI** Rhode Island

**rib** (rib) *n.* [OE.] 1. any of the arched bones attached to the spine and enclosing the chest cavity 2. anything like a rib in appearance or function —*vt.* ribbed, rib'bing 1. to form with ribs 2. [Slang] to tease or make fun of; kid

**rib·ald** (rib'əld) *adj.* [< OHG. *riban*, to rub] coarse or vulgar in joking, speaking, etc. —**rib'ald·ry** *n.*

**rib·bon** (rib'ən) *n.* [< MFr. *riban*] 1. a narrow strip of silk, rayon, etc. used for decoration, tying, etc. 2. [*pl.*] torn shreds 3. a strip of cloth inked for use, as in a typewriter

**ri·bo·fla·vin** (rī'bə flā'vin) *n.* [< *ribose*, a sugar + L. *flavus*, yellow] a factor of the vitamin B complex found in milk, eggs, fruits, etc.

**rice** (rīs) *n.* [< Gr. *oryza*] 1. an aquatic cereal grass grown widely in warm climates, esp. in the Orient 2. the starchy grains of this grass, used as food —*vt.* riced, ric'ing to reduce (cooked potatoes, etc.) to ricelike granules —**ric'er** *n.*

**rich** (rich) *adj.* [OHG. *richi*] 1. owning much money or property; wealthy 2. well-supplied (*with*); abounding (*in*) 3. valuable or costly 4. full of choice ingredients, as butter, sugar, etc. 5. *a*) full and mellow: said of sounds *b*) deep; vivid: said of colors *c*) very fragrant 6. abundant 7. yielding in abundance, as soil 8. [Colloq.] very amusing —**the rich** wealthy people collectively —**rich'ly** *adv.* —**rich'ness** *n.*

**Rich·ard I** (rich'ərd) 1157–99; king of England (1189–99): called **Richard the Lion-Hearted**

**rich·es** (rich'iz) *n.pl.* [< OFr. *richesse*] wealth

**Rich·mond** (rich'mənd) 1. borough of New York City: pop. 295,000 2. capital of Va.: pop. 250,000

**rick** (rik) *n.* [OE. *hreac*] a stack of hay, straw, etc.

**rick·ets** (rik'its) *n.* [< ? Gr. *rachis*, spine] a disease, chiefly of children, characterized by a softening and, often, bending of the bones

**rick·et·y** (rik'it ē) *adj.* 1. having rickets 2. feeble; weak; shaky

**rick·rack** (rik'rak') *n.* [redupl. of RACK[1]] flat, zigzag braid for trimming dresses, etc.

**rick·shaw, rick·sha** (rik'shô) *n. same as* JINRIKISHA

**ric·o·chet** (rik'ə shā') *n.* [Fr.] the glancing rebound or skipping of an object after striking a surface at an angle —*vt.* -cheted' (-shād'), -chet'ing (-shā'iŋ) to make a ricochet

**rid** (rid) *vt.* rid or rid'ded, rid'ding [< ON. *rythja*, to clear (land)] to free or relieve, as of something undesirable —**get rid of** to dispose of

**rid·dance** (rid'ns) *n.* a ridding or being rid; clearance or removal

**rid·den** (rid'n) *pp.* of RIDE

**rid·dle[1]** (rid'l) *n.* [OE. *rædels*] 1. a puzzling question, etc. requiring some ingenuity to answer 2. any puzzling person or thing

**rid·dle[2]** (rid'l) *vt.* -dled, -dling [OE. *hriddel*, a sieve] to make many holes in; puncture throughout

**ride** (rīd) *vi.* rode, rid'den, rid'ing [OE. *ridan*] 1. to be carried along by a horse, in a vehicle, etc. 2. to be supported in motion (*on* or *upon*) [tanks *ride* on treads] 3. to admit of being ridden [the car *rides* smoothly] 4. to move or float on the water 5. [Colloq.] to continue undisturbed [let the matter *ride*] —*vt.* 1. to sit on or in and control so as to move along 2. to move over, along, or through (a road, area, etc.) by horse, car, etc. 3. to control, dominate, etc. [*ridden* by doubts] 4. [Colloq.] to tease with ridicule, etc. —*n.* 1. a riding 2. a thing to ride at an amusement park

**rid'er** *n.* 1. one who rides 2. an addition or amendment to a document

**rid'er·ship'** *n.* the passengers of a particular transportation system

**ridge** (rij) *n.* [OE. *hrycg*] 1. the long, narrow crest of something 2. a long, narrow elevation of land 3. any narrow raised strip 4. the horizontal line formed by the meeting of two sloping surfaces —*vt., vi.* ridged, ridg'ing to mark with, or form into, ridges

**ridge'pole'** *n.* the horizontal beam at the ridge of a roof, to which the rafters are attached

**rid·i·cule** (rid'i kyōōl') *n.* [< L. *ridere*, to laugh] 1. the act of making one the object of scornful laughter 2. words or actions intended to produce such laughter —*vt.* -culed', -cul'ing to make fun of; deride; mock

**ri·dic·u·lous** (ri dik′yə ləs) *adj.* deserving ridicule; absurd —**ri·dic′u·lous·ly** *adv.* —**ri·dic′u·lous·ness** *n.*

**rife** (rīf) *adj.* [OE. *ryfe*] 1. widespread 2. abounding [*rife* with error]

**riff** (rif) *n.* [prob. alt. < REFRAIN?] *Jazz* a constantly repeated musical phrase —*vi.* to perform a riff

**rif·fle** (rif′′l) *n.* [< ?] 1. a ripple in a stream, produced by a reef, etc. 2. a certain way of shuffling cards —*vt.* -**fled, -fling** to shuffle (cards) by letting a divided deck fall together as the corners are slipped through the thumbs

**riff·raff** (rif′raf′) *n.* [< OFr.: see RIFLE² & RAFFLE] those people regarded as worthless, disreputable, etc.

**ri·fle¹** (rī′f′l) *vt.* -**fled, -fling** [Fr. *rifler*, to scrape] to cut spiral grooves within (a gun barrel, etc.) —*n.* a shoulder gun with a rifled barrel to spin the bullet for greater accuracy

**ri·fle²** (rī′f′l) *vt.* -**fled, -fling** [< Fr. *rifler*] to ransack and rob —**ri′fler** *n.*

**ri·fle·man** (-mən) *n., pl.* -**men** a soldier armed with a rifle

**rift** (rift) *n.* [< Dan., a fissure] an opening caused by splitting; cleft —*vt., vi.* to burst open; split

**rig** (rig) *vt.* **rigged, rig′ging** [< Scand.] 1. to fit (a ship, mast, etc.) with (sails, shrouds, etc.) 2. to assemble 3. to equip 4. to arrange dishonestly 5. [Colloq.] to dress (with *out*) —*n.* 1. the way sails, etc. are rigged 2. equipment; gear 3. a tractor-trailer

**rig·a·ma·role** (rig′ə mə rōl′) *n. alt. sp. of* RIGMAROLE

**rig′ging** *n.* chains, ropes, etc. for a vessel's masts, sails, etc.

**right** (rīt) *adj.* [< OE. *riht*, straight] 1. with a straight or perpendicular line 2. upright; virtuous 3. correct 4. fitting; suitable 5. designating the side meant to be seen 6. mentally or physically sound 7. *a)* designating or of that side toward the east when one faces north *b)* designating or of the corresponding side of something *c)* closer to the **right** side of one facing the thing mentioned —*n.* 1. what is right, just, etc. 2. a power, privilege, etc. belonging to one by law, nature, etc. 3. the right side 4. the right hand 5. [*often* R-] *Politics* a conservative or reactionary position, party, etc. (often with *the*) —*adv.* 1. straight; directly [*go right* home] 2. properly; fittingly 3. completely 4. exactly [*right here*] 5. according to law, justice, etc. 6. correctly 7. on or toward the right side 8. very: in certain titles [the *right* honorable] —*vt.* 1. to put upright 2. to correct 3. to put in order —**right away** (or **off**) at once —**right on!** [Slang] that's right! —**right′ly** *adv.* —**right′ness** *n*

**right′a·bout′-face′** *n. same as* ABOUT-FACE

**right angle** an angle of 90 degrees

**right·eous** (rī′chəs) *adj.* 1. acting in a just, upright manner; virtuous 2. morally right or justifiable —**right′eous·ly** *adv.* —**right′eous·ness** *n.*

**right′ful** *adj.* 1. fair and just; right 2. having a lawful claim —**right′ful·ly** *adv.* —**right′ful·ness** *n.*

**right′-hand′** *adj.* 1. on or toward the right 2. of, for, or with the right hand 3. most helpful or reliable [the president's *right-hand* man]

**right′-hand′ed** *adj.* 1. using the right hand more skillfully than the left 2. done with or made for use with the right hand —*adv.* with the right hand

**right′ist** *n., adj.* conservative or reactionary

**right′-mind′ed** *adj.* having correct views or sound principles

**right of way** 1. the right to move first at intersections 2. land over which a road, power line, etc. passes

**right wing** the more conservative or reactionary section of a political party, group, etc. —**right′-wing′** *adj.* —**right′-wing′er** *n.*

**rig·id** (rij′id) *adj.* [< L. *rigere*, be stiff] 1. not bending or flexible; stiff 2. not moving; set 3. severe; strict 4. having a rigid framework: said of a dirigible —**ri·gid·i·ty** (ri jid′ə tē), **rig′id·ness** *n.* —**rig′id·ly** *adv.*

**rig·ma·role** (rig′mə rōl′) *n.* [< ME. *rageman rolle*, long list] 1. nonsense 2. a foolishly involved procedure

**rig·or** (rig′ər) *n.* [see RIGID] severity; strictness; hardship Brit. sp. **rigour** —**rig′or·ous** *adj.* —**rig′or·ous·ly** *adv.*

**rig·or mor·tis** (rig′ər môr′tis, rī′gôr) [ModL.], stiffness of death] the stiffening of the muscles after death

**rile** (rīl) *vt.* **riled, ril′ing** [< ROIL] [Colloq.] to anger; irritate

**rill** (ril) *n.* [< Du. *ril*] a rivulet

**rim** (rim) *n.* [OE. *rima*] 1. an edge, border, or margin, esp. of something circular 2. the outer part of a wheel —*vt.* **rimmed, rim′ming** to put or form a rim on or around

**rime¹** (rīm) *n., vt., vi.* **rimed, rim′ing** *same as* RHYME

**rime²** (rīm) *n.* [OE. *hrim*] hoarfrost

**rind** (rīnd) *n.* [OE.] a hard outer layer or covering, as of fruit or cheese

**ring¹** (riŋ) *vi.* **rang** or *chiefly dial.* **rung, rung, ring′ing** [OE. *hringan*] 1. to give forth a resonant sound, as a bell 2. to seem [to *ring* true] 3. to sound a bell, esp. as a summons 4. to resound [to *ring* with laughter] 5. to have a ringing sensation, as the ears —*vt.* 1. to cause (a bell, etc.) to ring 2. to signal, announce, etc., as by ringing 3. to call by telephone —*n.* 1. the sound of a bell 2. a characteristic quality [the *ring* of truth] 3. the act of ringing a bell 4. a telephone call —**ring a bell** to stir up a memory

**ring²** (riŋ) *n.* [OE. *hring*] 1. an ornamental circular band worn on a finger 2. any similar band [a key *ring*] 3. a

---

fat, āpe, cär; ten, ēven; is, bīte; gō, hôrn, tōōl, look; oil, out; up, fur; chin; she; thin, *then*; zh, leisure; ŋ, ring; ə for *a* in *ago*; ′, (ā′b′l); ë, Fr. coeur; ö, Fr. feu; Fr. mon; ü, Fr. duc; kh, G. ich, doch; ‡ foreign; < derived from circular line, mark, figure, or course **4.** a group of people or things in a circle **5.** a group working to advance its own interests, esp. in dishonest ways **6.** an enclosed area for contests, exhibitions, etc. *[a circus ring]* **7.** prizefighting (with *the*) —*vt.* **ringed, ring'ing 1.** to encircle **2.** to form into, or furnish with, a ring or rings —**run rings around** [Colloq.] **1.** to outrun easily **2.** to excel greatly

**ring'er**[1] *n.* a horseshoe, etc. thrown so that it encircles the peg

**ring'er**[2] *n.* **1.** one that rings a bell, etc. **2.** [Slang] *a)* a person or thing closely resembling another *b)* a fraudulent substitute in a competition

**ring'lead'er** *n.* one who leads others, esp. in unlawful acts, etc.

**ring'let** (-lit) *n.* **1.** a little ring or circle **2.** a curl of hair

**ring'mas'ter** *n.* a man who directs the performances in a circus ring

**ring'side'** *n.* the place just outside the ring, as at a boxing match

**ring'worm'** *n.* a contagious skin disease caused by a fungus

**rink** (riŋk) *n.* [< OFr. *renc*, a rank] **1.** an expanse of ice for skating **2.** a smooth floor for roller-skating

**rinse** (rins) *vt.* **rinsed, rins'ing** [ult. < L. *recens*, fresh] **1.** to wash or flush lightly **2.** to remove soap, etc. from with clean water —*n.* **1.** a rinsing or the liquid used **2.** a solution used to rinse or tint hair

**Ri·o de Ja·nei·ro** (rē'ō dā' zhə ner'ō) seaport in SE Brazil: pop. 3,307,000

**Rio Grande** (grand, gran'dē) river flowing from S Colo. into the Gulf of Mexico: the S border of Tex.

**ri·ot** (rī'ət) *n.* [< OFr. *riote*, dispute] **1.** wild or violent disorder, confusion, etc.; esp., a violent public disturbance **2.** a brilliant display of color **3.** [Colloq.] something very funny —*vi.* to take part in a riot —**read the riot act** to give very strict orders to so as to make obey —**run riot 1.** to act in a wild way **2.** to grow wild in abundance —**ri'ot·er** *n.* —**ri'ot·ous** *adj.*

**rip** (rip) *vt.* **ripped, rip'ping** [LME. *rippen*] **1.** *a)* to cut or tear apart roughly *b)* to remove in this way (with *off*, *out*, etc.) *c)* to sever the threads of (a seam) **2.** to saw (wood) along the grain —*vi.* **1.** to become ripped **2.** [Colloq.] to rush; speed —*n.* a ripped place —**rip into** [Colloq.] to attack, esp. verbally —**rip off** [Slang] **1.** to steal **2.** to cheat or exploit —**rip'per** *n.*

**rip cord** a cord, etc. pulled to open a parachute during descent

**ripe** (rīp) *adj.* [OE.] **1.** ready to be harvested, as grain or fruit **2.** of sufficient age, etc. to be used *[ripe cheese]* **3.** fully developed; mature **4.** fully prepared; ready *[ripe for action]* —**ripe'ly** *adv.* —**ripe'ness** *n.*

**rip·en** (rī'pən) *vi., vt.* to become or make ripe; mature, age, cure, etc.

**rip'-off'** *n.* [Slang] the act or a means of stealing, cheating, etc.

**ri·poste, ri·post** (ri pōst') *n.* [Fr. <

L. *respondere*, to answer] a sharp, swift response; retort

**rip·ple** (rip''l) *vi., vt.* **-pled, -pling** [prob. < RIP] to have or form little waves on the surface (of) —*n.* **1.** a little wave **2.** a rippling

**rip'-roar'ing** (-rôr'iŋ) *adj.* [Slang] very lively and noisy; boisterous

**rip'saw'** *n.* a saw with coarse teeth, for cutting wood along the grain

**rise** (rīz) *vi.* **rose, ris'en** (riz'n), **ris'ing** [< OE. *risan*] **1.** to stand or sit up after sitting, kneeling, or lying **2.** to rebel; revolt **3.** to go up; ascend **4.** to appear above the horizon, as the sun **5.** to attain a higher level, rank, etc. **6.** to extend, slant, or move upward **7.** to increase in amount, degree, etc. **8.** to expand and swell, as dough with yeast **9.** to originate; begin **10.** *Theol.* to return to life —*n.* **1.** upward movement; ascent **2.** an advance in status, rank, etc. **3.** a slope upward **4.** an increase in degree, amount, etc. **5.** origin; beginning —**give rise to** to bring about

**ris·er** (rīz'ər) *n.* **1.** a person or thing that rises **2.** a vertical piece between the steps in a stairway

**ris·i·ble** (riz'ə b'l) *adj.* [< L. *ridere*, to laugh] causing laughter; funny —**ris'i·bil'i·ty** *n., pl.* **-ties**

**risk** (risk) *n.* [< Fr. < It. *risco*] the chance of injury, damage, or loss —*vt.* **1.** to expose to risk *[to risk one's life]* **2.** to incur the risk of *[to risk a war]* —**risk'y** *adj.* **-i·er, -i·est**

**ris·qué** (ris kā') *adj.* [Fr. < *risquer*, to risk] very close to being improper or indecent; suggestive

**rite** (rīt) *n.* [< L. *ritus*] a ceremonial or solemn act, as in religious use

**rit·u·al** (rich'oo wəl) *adj.* of, like, or done as a rite —*n.* a system or form of rites, religious or otherwise —**rit'u·al·ism** *n.* —**rit'u·al·ly** *adv.*

**ri·val** (rī'v'l) *n.* [< L. *rivalis*] one who tries to get or do the same thing as another i.e. to equal or surpass another; competitor —*adj.* acting as a rival; competing —*vt.* **-valed** or **-valled, -val·ing** or **-val·ling 1.** to try to equal or surpass **2.** to equal in some way —**ri'val·ry** *n., pl.* **-ries**

**rive** (rīv) *vt., vi.* **rived, rived** or **riv·en** (riv''n), **riv'ing** [< ON. *rifa*] **1.** to tear apart; rend **2.** to split

**riv·er** (riv'ər) *n.* [< L. *ripa*, a bank] a natural stream of water flowing into an ocean, lake, etc.

**river basin** the area drained by a river and its tributaries

**Riv'er·side'** city in S Calif.: pop. 140,000

**riv'er·side'** *n.* the bank of a river

**riv·et** (riv'it) *n.* [MFr. < *river*, to clinch] a metal bolt with a head and a plain end that is flattened after the bolt is passed through parts to be held together —*vt.* to fasten with or as with rivets —**riv'et·er** *n.*

**Ri·vie·ra** (riv'ē er'ə) strip of the Mediterranean coast of SE France & NW Italy: a resort area

**riv·u·let** (riv'yoo lit) *n.* [< L. *rivus*, a brook] a little stream

**rm.** *pl.* **rms.** 1. ream 2. room

**R.N., RN** Registered Nurse

**RNA** [< *r(ibo)n(ucleic) a(cid)*] an essential component of all living matter: one form carries genetic information

**roach**[1] (rōch) *n.* *short for* COCKROACH

**roach**[2] (rōch) *n., pl.* **roach, roach′es** [< OFr. *roche*] a freshwater fish of the carp family

**road** (rōd) *n.* [OE. *rad*, a ride] 1. a way made for traveling; highway 2. a way; course [*the road* to fortune] 3. [*often pl.*] a place near shore where ships can ride at anchor —**on the road** traveling, as a salesman

**road′bed′** *n.* the foundation laid for railroad tracks or for a highway, etc.

**road′block′** *n.* 1. a blockade set up in a road to prevent movement of vehicles 2. any hindrance

**road runner** a long-tailed, swift-running desert bird of the SW U.S. and N Mexico

**road′show′** *n.* 1. a touring theatrical show 2. a reserved-seat film showing

**road′side′** *n.* the side of a road —*adj.* on or at the side of a road

**road′way′** *n.* 1. a road 2. the part of a road along which vehicles move

**road′work′** *n.* jogging or running as an exercise, esp. by a prizefighter

**roam** (rōm) *vi., vt.* [ME. *romen*] to wander aimlessly (over or through) —**roam′er** *n.*

**roan** (rōn) *adj.* [< Sp. *roano*] bay, black, etc. thickly sprinkled with white or gray —*n.* a roan horse

**roar** (rôr) *vi.* [OE. *rarian*] 1. to make a loud, deep, rumbling sound 2. to laugh boisterously —*vt.* to express with a roar —*n.* a loud, deep, rumbling sound

**roast** (rōst) *vt.* [< OFr. *rostir*] 1. to cook (meat, etc.) with little or no moisture, as in an oven or over an open fire 2. to process (coffee, etc.) by exposure to heat 3. to expose to great heat 4. [Colloq.] to criticize severely —*vi.* 1. to undergo roasting 2. to be or become very hot —*n.* 1. roasted meat 2. a cut of meat for roasting 3. a picnic at which food is roasted —*adj.* roasted [*roast* pork] —**roast′er** *n.*

**rob** (räb) *vt.* **robbed, rob′bing** [< OFr. *rober*] 1. to take money, etc. from unlawfully by force; steal from 2. to deprive of something unjustly or injuriously —*vi.* to commit robbery —**rob′ber** *n.* —**rob′ber·y** *n., pl.* -**ies**

**robe** (rōb) *n.* [< OFr.] a long, loose outer garment 2. such a garment worn to show rank or office, as by a judge 3. a bathrobe or dressing gown 4. a covering or wrap [a lap *robe*] —*vt., vi.* **robed, rob′ing** to dress in a robe

**rob·in** (räb′in) *n.* [< OFr. dim. of *Robert*] a large N.American thrush with a dull-red breast

**Robin Hood** *Eng. Legend* the leader of a band of outlaws that robbed the rich to help the poor

**Rob·in·son Cru·soe** (räb′in s'n

kroō′sō) the title hero of Defoe's novel (1719) about a shipwrecked sailor

**ro·bot** (rō′bət, -bät) *n.* [< Czech < OBulg. *rabu*, servant] 1. a mechanical device operating in a seemingly human way 2. a person acting like a robot

**ro·bust** (rō bust′, rō′bust) *adj.* [< L. *robur*, oak] strong and healthy —**ro·bust′ly** *adv.* —**ro·bust′ness** *n.*

**Roch·es·ter** (rä′ches′tər) city in W N.Y.: pop. 296,000

**rock**[1] (räk) *n.* [< ML. *rocca*] 1. a large mass of stone 2. broken pieces of stone 3. mineral matter formed in masses in the earth's crust 4. anything like a rock; esp., a firm support 5. [Colloq.] a stone —**on the rocks** [Colloq.] 1. ruined; bankrupt 2. served over ice cubes, as whiskey

**rock**[2] (räk) *vt., vi.* [OE. *roccian*] 1. to move back and forth or from side to side 2. to sway strongly; shake —*n.* 1. a rocking motion 2. rock-and-roll

**rock′-and-roll′** *n.* a form of popular music with a strong, regular beat, which evolved from jazz and the blues

**rock bottom** the lowest level

**rock′-bound′** *adj.* surrounded or covered by rocks

**rock candy** large, hard, clear crystals of sugar formed on a string

**rock′er** *n.* 1. either of the curved pieces on which a cradle, etc. rocks 2. a chair mounted on such pieces: also **rocking chair**

**rocker panel** any panel section below the doors of an automobile

**rock·et** (räk′it) *n.* [It. *rocchetta*, spool] any device driven forward by gases escaping through a rear vent, as a firework, projectile, or the propulsion mechanism of a spacecraft —*vi.* to move in or like a rocket; soar

**rock′et·ry** (-rē) *n.* the science of building and launching rockets

**Rock·ford** (räk′fərd) city in N Ill.: pop. 147,000

**rock garden** a garden of flowers, etc. in ground studded with rocks

**rocking horse** a toy horse on rockers or springs, for a child to ride

**rock lobster** *same as* SPINY LOBSTER

**rock′-ribbed′** *adj.* 1. having rocky ridges 2. firm; unyielding

**rock salt** common salt in masses

**rock wool** a fibrous material made from molten rock, used for insulation

**rock·y**[1] (räk′ē) *adj.* -**i·er, -i·est** 1. full of rocks 2. consisting of rock 3. like a rock; firm, hard, etc. —**rock′i·ness** *n.*

**rock·y**[2] (räk′ē) *adj.* -**i·er, -i·est** inclined to rock; unsteady —**rock′i·ness** *n.*

**Rocky Mountains** mountain system in W N.America, extending from N.Mex. to Alaska: also **Rock′ies**

**Rocky Mountain sheep** *same as* BIGHORN

**ro·co·co** (rə kō′kō) *n.* [Fr. < *rocaille*, shell work] an elaborate style of architecture and decoration, imitating foliage, scrolls, etc. —*adj.* 1. of or in rococo 2. too elaborate

**rod** (räd) *n.* [ < OE. *rodd*] 1. a straight stick or bar 2. a stick for beating as punishment 3. a scepter carried as a symbol of office 4. a measure of length equal to 5 1/2 yards 5. a pole for fishing 6. [Slang] a pistol

**rode** (rōd) *pt. of* RIDE

**ro·dent** (rōd′nt) *n.* [ < L. *rodere*, gnaw] any of an order of gnawing mammals, as rats, mice, beavers, etc.

**ro·de·o** (rō′dē ō′, rō dā′ō) *n., pl.* -os′ [Sp. < L. *rotare*, to turn] a public exhibition of the skills of cowboys, as broncobusting, lassoing, etc.

**Ro·din** (rō dan′), (François) Auguste (René) 1840–1917; Fr. sculptor

**roe**[1] (rō) *n.* [ME. *rowe*] fish eggs

**roe**[2] (rō) *n., pl.* roe, roes [ < OE. *rā*] a small, agile deer of Europe and Asia

**roe·buck** (rō′buk′) *n.* the male of the roe deer

**roent·gen** (rent′gən) *n.* [ < W. K. *Roentgen*, 1845–1923, G. physicist] the unit for measuring the radiation of X-rays (Roentgen rays) or gamma rays

**Rog·er** (räj′ər) *interj.* [ < name of signal flag for R] [*also* r-] 1. received: used to indicate reception of a radio message 2. [Colloq.] right! OK!

**rogue** (rōg) *n.* [ < ?] 1. a scoundrel 2. a mischievous fellow —**ro·guer·y** (rō′gər ē) *n.* —**ro·guish** (rō′gish) *adj.*

**rogues' gallery** a police collection of photographs of criminals

**roil** (roil) *vt.* [ < L. *robigo*, rust] 1. to make (a liquid) cloudy, muddy, etc. by stirring up sediment 2. to vex

**roist·er** (rois′tər) *vi.* [see RUSTIC] to revel noisily —**roist′er·er** *n.*

**role, rôle** (rōl) *n.* [Fr.] 1. the part played by an actor 2. a function assumed by someone [an advisory *role*]

**roll** (rōl) *vi.* [ < L. *rota*, a wheel] 1. to move by turning around or over and over 2. to move on wheels or rollers 3. to pass [the years *roll by*] 4. to extend in gentle swells 5. to make a loud, rising and falling sound [thunder *rolls*] 6. to move or rock from side to side —*vt.* 1. to make move by turning around or over and over 2. to make move on wheels or rollers 3. to utter with full, flowing sound 4. to say with a trill [to *roll* one's r's] 5. to give a swaying motion to 6. to move around or from side to side [to *roll* one's eyes] 7. to wind into a ball or cylinder [*roll* up the rug] 8. to flatten or spread with a roller, etc. —*n.* 1. a rolling 2. a scroll 3. a list of names 4. something rolled into a cylinder 5. a small cake of bread, etc. 6. a swaying motion 7. a loud, reverberating sound, as of thunder 8. a slight swell on a surface

**roll′back′** *n.* a moving back, esp. of prices to a previous level

**roll call** the reading aloud of a roll to find out who is absent

**roll′er** *n.* 1. one that rolls 2. a cylinder of metal, wood, etc. on which something is rolled, or one used to crush, smooth, or spread something 3. a heavy, swelling wave

**roller coaster** an amusement ride in which small cars move on tracks that curve and dip sharply

**roller skate** *see* SKATE[1] (sense 2) —**roll′er-skate′** *vi.*

**rol·lick** (räl′ik) *vi.* [ < ? FROLIC] to play or behave in a gay, carefree way —**rol′lick·ing** *adj.*

**rolling pin** a heavy, smooth cylinder of wood, etc. used to roll out dough

**rolling stock** all the vehicles of a railroad or a trucking company

**roll′-top′** *adj.* having a flexible, sliding top of parallel slats [a *roll-top* desk]

**ro·ly-po·ly** (rō′lē pō′lē) *adj.* [ < ROLL] short and plump; pudgy

**Rom.** Roman

**ro·maine** (rō mān′) *n.* [ult. < L. *Romanus*, Roman] a type of lettuce with long leaves forming a head

**Ro·man** (rō′mən) *adj.* 1. of or characteristic of ancient or modern Rome, its people, etc. 2. of the Roman Catholic Church 3. [*usually* r-] designating or of the usual upright style of printing types —*n.* a native or inhabitant of ancient or modern Rome

**Roman candle** a firework consisting of a tube shooting balls of fire, etc.

**Roman Catholic** 1. of the Christian church (**Roman Catholic Church**) headed by the Pope 2. a member of this church

**ro·mance** (rō mans′; *also for n.* rō′mans) *adj.* [ult. < L. *Romanicus*] [R-] designating or of any of the languages derived mainly from Latin, as Italian, Spanish, French, etc. —*n.* 1. a long poem or tale, orig. written in a Romance dialect, about the adventures of knights 2. a novel of love, adventure, etc. 3. excitement, love, etc. of the kind found in such literature 4. a love affair —*vi., vt.* -**manced′**, -**manc′ing** [Colloq.] to make love (to)

**Roman Empire** empire of the ancient Romans (27 B.C.–395 A.D.), including W & S Europe, N Africa, & SW Asia

**Ro·ma·ni·a** (rō mān′yə, -mā′nē ə) country in SE Europe: 91,700 sq. mi.; pop. 19,287,000; cap. Bucharest —**Ro·ma′nian** *adj., n.*

**Roman numerals** Roman letters used as numerals: I = 1, V = 5, X = 10, L = 50, C = 100, D = 500, and M = 1,000

**ro·man·tic** (rō man′tik) *adj.* 1. of, like, or characterized by romance 2. fanciful or fictitious 3. not practical; visionary 4. full of thoughts, feelings, etc. of romance 5. suited for romance 6. [*often* R-] of a 19th-c. cultural movement characterized by freedom of form and spirit, emphasis on feeling and originality, etc. —*n.* a romantic person —**ro·man′ti·cal·ly** *adv.* —**ro·man′ti·cism** (-tə siz′m) *n.*

**ro·man′ti·cize′** (-tə sīz′) *vt., vi.* -**cized′**, -**ciz′ing** to treat, regard, or act in a romantic way

**Rom·a·ny** (räm′ə nē, rō′mə-) *n.* the language of the Gypsies

**Rome** (rōm) capital of Italy, & formerly, of the Roman Empire: pop. 2,514,000

**Ro·me·o** (rō′mē ō′) the young lover in Shakespeare's *Romeo and Juliet*

**romp** (rämp) *n.* [prob. < OFr. *ramper*, climb] boisterous, lively play —*vi.* to play in a boisterous, lively way

**romp'er** *n.* 1. one who romps 2. [*pl.*] a loose, one-piece outer garment with bloomerlike pants, for a small child

**Rom·u·lus** (räm'yoo ləs) *Rom. Myth.* founder and first king of Rome: he and his twin brother Remus were suckled by a she-wolf

**rood** (rōōd) *n.* [OE. *rod*] 1. a crucifix 2. a measure of area equal to 1/4 acre

**roof** (rōōf, roof) *n., pl.* **roofs** [OE. *hrof*] 1. the outside top covering of a building 2. anything like this [the *roof* of the mouth] —*vt.* to cover as with a roof —**roof'less** *adj.*

**roof'er** *n.* a roof maker or repairer

**roof'ing** *n.* material for roofs

**roof'top'** *n.* the roof of a building

**rook**[1] (rook) *n.* [OE. *hroc*] a European crow —*vt., vi.* to swindle; cheat

**rook**[2] (rook) *n.* [< Per. *rukh*] a chess piece moving horizontally or vertically

**rook'er·y** *n., pl.* **-ies** a breeding place or colony of rooks

**rook·ie** (rook'ē) *n.* [Slang] 1. an inexperienced army recruit 2. any novice

**room** (rōōm, room) *n.* [OE. *rum*] 1. space to contain something 2. suitable scope [room for doubt] 3. an interior space enclosed or set apart by walls 4. [*pl.*] living quarters 5. the people in a room —*vt., vi.* to have or provide with lodgings —**room'ful** *n.* —**room'y** *adj.* **-i·er, -i·est** —**room'i·ness** *n.*

**room and board** lodging and meals

**room'er** *n.* one who rents a room or rooms to live in; lodger

**room·ette** (rōō met') *n.* a small compartment in a railroad sleeping car

**rooming house** a house with furnished rooms for renting

**room'mate'** *n.* a person with whom one shares a room or rooms

**Roo·se·velt** (rō'zə velt', rōz'velt) 1. **Franklin Del·a·no** (del'ə nō'), 1882-1945; 32d president of the U.S. (1933-45) 2. **Theodore**, 1858-1919; 26th president of the U.S. (1901-09)

**roost** (rōōst) *n.* [OE. *hrost*] 1. a perch on which birds, esp. domestic fowls, can rest 2. a place with perches for birds 3. a place for resting, sleeping, etc. —*vi.* 1. to perch on a roost 2. to settle down, as for the night

**roos'ter** (-ər) *n.* a male chicken

**root**[1] (rōōt, root) *n.* [< ON. *rot*] 1. the part of a plant, usually underground, that anchors the plant, draws water from the soil, etc. 2. the embedded part of a tooth, a hair, etc. 3. a source or cause 4. a supporting or essential part 5. a quantity that, multiplied by itself a specified number of times, produces a given quantity 6. *same as* BASE (*n.* 3) —*vi.* to take root —*vt.* 1. to fix the roots of in the ground 2. to establish; settle —**take root** 1. to begin growing by putting out roots 2. to become fixed, settled, etc.

**root**[2] (rōōt, root) *vt.* [< OE. *wrot*,

snout] to dig (*up, out*) as with the snout —*vi.* 1. to search about; rummage 2. [Colloq.] to encourage a team, etc.: usually used *for*

**root beer** a carbonated drink made of root extracts from certain plants

**rope** (rōp) *n.* [OE. *rap*] 1. a thick, strong cord made of intertwisted strands of fiber, etc. 2. a ropelike string, as of beads —*vt.* **roped, rop'ing** 1. to fasten or tie with a rope 2. to mark off or enclose with a rope 3. to catch with a lasso —**know the ropes** [Colloq.] to be acquainted with a procedure —**rope in** [Slang] to entice or trick into doing something

**Roque·fort (cheese)** (rōk'fərt) [< *Roquefort*, France, where orig. made] a strong cheese with a bluish mold

**Ror·schach test** (rôr'shäk) [< H. *Rorschach* (1884-1922), Swiss psychiatrist] *Psychol.* a personality test in which the subject's interpretations of standard inkblot designs are analyzed

**ro·sa·ry** (rō'zər ē) *n., pl.* **-ries** [ML. *rosarium*] *R.C.Ch.* a string of beads used to keep count in saying prayers

**rose**[1] (rōz) *n.* [< L. *rosa*] 1. a shrub with prickly stems and flowers of red, pink, white, yellow, etc. 2. its flower 3. pinkish red or purplish red —*adj.* of this color

**rose**[2] (rōz) *pt. of* RISE

**ro·sé** (rō zā') *n.* [Fr.] a light, pink wine

**ro·se·ate** (rō'zē it) *adj.* rose-colored

**rose'bud'** *n.* the bud of a rose

**rose'bush'** *n.* a shrub bearing roses

**rose'-col'ored** *adj.* 1. *same as* ROSE 2. optimistic —**through rose-colored glasses** with optimism

**rose·mar·y** (rōz'mer'ē) *n.* [< L. *ros marinus*, sea dew] an evergreen plant of the mint family, with fragrant leaves used in cooking, etc.

**ro·sette** (rō zet') *n.* a roselike ornament or arrangement, as of ribbon

**rose water** a preparation of water and attar of roses, used as a perfume

**rose window** a circular window with a pattern of roselike tracery

**rose'wood'** *n.* [< its odor] 1. a hard, reddish wood, used in furniture, etc. 2. a tropical tree yielding this wood

**Rosh Ha·sha·na** (rōsh' hə shō'nə, -shä'-) the Jewish New Year

**ros·in** (räz'n) *n.* [see RESIN] the hard resin left after the distillation of crude turpentine: it is rubbed on violin bows, used in varnish, etc.

**ros·ter** (räs'tər) *n.* [< Du. *rooster*] a list or roll, as of military personnel

**ros·trum** (räs'trəm) *n., pl.* **-trums, -tra** (-trə) [L., beak] a platform for public speaking

**ros·y** (rō'zē) *adj.* **-i·er, -i·est** 1. rose in color 2. bright, promising, etc. — **ros'i·ly** *adv.* —**ros'i·ness** *n.*

**rot** (rät) *vi., vt.* **rot'ted, rot'ting** [OE. *rotian*] to decompose; decay —*n.* 1. a rotting or something rotten 2. a disease characterized by decay 3. [Slang] nonsense

**ro·ta·ry** (rōt′ər ē) *adj.* [< L. *rota*, wheel] 1. turning around a central axis, as a wheel 2. having rotating parts [a *rotary* press] —*n., pl.* **-ries** 1. a rotary machine 2. *same as* TRAFFIC CIRCLE

**ro·tate** (rō′tāt) *vi., vt.* **-tat·ed, -tat·ing** [< L. *rota*, wheel] 1. to turn around an axis 2. to change in regular succession —**ro·ta′tion** *n.* —**ro′ta·to′ry** (-tə tôr′ē) *adj.*

**ROTC, R.O.T.C.** Reserve Officers' Training Corps

**rote** (rōt) *n.* [ME.] a fixed, mechanical way of doing something —**by rote** by memory alone, without thought

**ro·tis·ser·ie** (rō tis′ər ē) *n.* [Fr. < MFr. *rostir*, to roast] a grill with an electrically turned spit

**ro·to·gra·vure** (rō′tə grə vyoor′) *n.* [< L. *rota*, wheel + Fr. *gravure*, engraving] 1. a process of printing pictures, etc. on a rotary press using cylinders etched from photographic plates 2. a newspaper pictorial section printed by this process

**ro·tor** (rōt′ər) *n.* 1. the rotating part of a motor, etc. 2. a system of rotating airfoils, as on a helicopter

**rot·ten** (rät′'n) *adj.* [< ON. *rotinn*] 1. decayed; spoiled 2. foul-smelling 3. morally corrupt 4. unsound, as if decayed within 5. [Slang] very bad, unpleasant, etc. —**rot′ten·ness** *n.*

**Rot·ter·dam** (rät′ər dam′) seaport in SW Netherlands: pop. 728,000

**ro·tund** (rō tund′) *adj.* [L. *rotundus*] round or rounded out; plump —**ro·tun′di·ty, ro·tund′ness** *n.*

**ro·tun·da** (rō tun′də) *n.* [see prec.] a round building, hall, or room, esp. one with a dome

**rou·é** (rōō ā′) *n.* [Fr. < L. *rota*, wheel] a dissipated man; rake

**rouge** (rōōzh) *n.* [Fr., red] 1. a reddish cosmetic powder, paste, etc. for coloring the cheeks and lips 2. a reddish powder for polishing jewelry, etc. —*vt., vi.* **rouged, roug′ing** to use cosmetic rouge (on)

**rough** (ruf) *adj.* [OE. *ruh*] 1. not smooth or level; uneven 2. shaggy [a *rough* coat] 3. stormy [*rough* weather] 4. disorderly [*rough* play] 5. harsh or coarse 6. lacking comforts and conveniences 7. not polished or finished; crude 8. approximate [a *rough* guess] 9. [Colloq.] difficult [a *rough* time] —*n.* 1. rough ground, material, condition, etc. 2. *Golf* any part of the course with grass, etc. left uncut —*adv.* in a rough way —*vt.* 1. to roughen (often with *up*) 2. to treat roughly (usually with *up*) 3. to sketch, shape, etc. roughly (usually with *in* or *out*) —**rough it** to live without customary comforts, etc. —**rough′ly** *adv.* —**rough′ness** *n.*

**rough′age** (-ij) *n.* rough or coarse food or fodder, as bran, straw, etc.

**rough′en** *vt., vi.* to make or become rough

**rough′-hew′** *vt.* **-hewed′, -hewed′** or **-hewn′, -hew′ing** 1. to hew (timber, stone, etc.) roughly, or without smoothing 2. to form roughly Also **roughhew**

**rough′house′** *n.* [Slang] rough, boisterous play, fighting, etc. —*vt., vi.* **-housed′, -hous′ing** [Slang] to treat or act roughly or boisterously

**rough′neck′** *n.* [Slang] a rowdy

**rough′shod′** *adj.* shod with horseshoes having metal points —**ride roughshod over** to treat harshly

**rou·lette** (rōō let′) *n.* [Fr. < L. *rota*, wheel] a gambling game played with a small ball in a whirling shallow bowl (**roulette wheel**) with red and black, numbered compartments

**round** (round) *adj.* [< L. *rotundus*, rotund] 1. shaped like a ball, circle, or cylinder 2. plump 3. full; complete [a *round* dozen] 4. expressed by a whole number or in tens, hundreds, etc. 5. large; considerable [a *round* sum] 6. brisk; vigorous [a *round* pace] —*n.* 1. something round, as the rung of a ladder 2. the part of a beef animal between the rump and the leg 3. movement in a circular course 4. a series or succession [a *round* of parties] 5. [often *pl.*] a regular, customary circuit, as by a watchman 6. a single shot from a gun, or from several guns together; also, the ammunition for this 7. a single outburst, as of applause 8. a single period of action, as in boxing 9. a short song which one group begins singing when another has reached the second phrase, etc. —*vt.* 1. to make round 2. to make plump 3. to express as a round number 4. to complete; finish 5. to go or pass around —*vi.* 1. to make a circuit 2. to turn; reverse direction 3. to become plump —*adv.* 1. in a circle 2. through a recurring period of time [to work the year *round*] 3. from one to another 4. in circumference [ten feet *round*] 5. on all sides 6. about; near 7. in a roundabout way 8. here and there 9. with a rotating movement 10. in the opposite direction —*prep.* 1. so as to encircle 2. on all sides of 3. in the vicinity of 4. in a circuit through In the U.S. *round* (*adv.* & *prep.*) is generally superseded by *around* —**in the round** 1. in an arena theater 2. in full, rounded form: said of sculpture 3. in full detail —**round about** in or to the opposite direction —**round up** to collect in a herd, group, etc. —**round′ness** *n.*

**round′a·bout′** *adj.* 1. indirect; circuitous 2. encircling; enclosing

**round′house′** *n.* a circular building with a turntable, for storing and repairing locomotives

**round′ly** *adv.* 1. in a round form 2. vigorously 3. fully; completely and thoroughly

**round′-shoul′dered** *adj.* having the shoulders bent forward

**Round Table** 1. the circular table around which King Arthur and his knights sat 2. [r- t-] a group gathered for an informal discussion

**round′-the-clock′** *adj., adv.* throughout the day and night; continuous(ly)

**round trip** a trip to a place and back again —**round′-trip′** *adj.*

**round′up′** *n.* 1. a driving together of cattle, etc. on the range, as for branding 2. any similar collecting 3. a summary, as of news

**round′worm′** *n.* a hookworm or similar round, unsegmented worm

**rouse** (rouz) *vt., vi.* roused, rous′ing [LME. *rowsen*] 1. to stir up; excite or become excited 2. to wake

**Rous·seau** (rōō sō′), **Jean Jacques** 1712–78; Fr. writer

**roust·a·bout** (roust′ə bout′) *n.* [< ROUSE + ABOUT] an unskilled, transient laborer, as on wharves

**rout¹** (rout) *n.* [< L. *rupta*, broken] 1. a disorderly flight 2. an overwhelming defeat —*vt.* 1. to put to flight 2. to defeat overwhelmingly

**rout²** (rout) *vt.* [< ROOT²] to force out —**rout out** 1. to gouge out 2. to make (a person) get out

**route** (rōōt, rout) *n.* [< L. *rupta* (*via*), broken (path)] a road or course for traveling; often, a regular course, as in delivering mail, etc. —*vt.* rout′ed, rout′ing 1. to send by a certain route 2. to arrange the route for

**rou·tine** (rōō tēn′) *n.* [see prec.] a regular procedure, customary or prescribed —*adj.* like or using routine —**rou·tine′ly** *adv.*

**rou·tin·ize** (-tē′nīz) *vt.* -ized, -iz-ing to make or bring into a routine

**rove** (rōv) *vi., vt.* roved, rov′ing [ME. *roven*] to roam —**rov′er** *n.*

**row¹** (rō) *n.* [OE. *ræw*] 1. a number of people or things in a line 2. any of the lines of seats in a theater, etc. —**in a row** in succession; consecutively

**row²** (rō) *vt., vi.* [OE. *rowan*] 1. to propel (a boat) with oars 2. to carry in a rowboat —*n.* a trip by rowboat

**row³** (rou) *n., vi.* [< ? ROUSE] quarrel, squabble, or brawl

**row′boat′** (rō′-) *n.* a small boat made for rowing

**row·dy** (rou′dē) *n., pl.* -dies [< ? ROW³] a rough, quarrelsome, and disorderly person —*adj.* -di·er, -di·est rough, quarrelsome, etc. —**row′di-ness** *n.* —**row′dy·ism** *n.*

**row·el** (rou′əl) *n.* [ult. < L. *rota*, wheel] a small wheel with sharp points, forming the end of a spur

**row house** (rō) any of a line of identical houses joined by common walls

**roy·al** (roi′əl) *adj.* [< L. *regalis*] 1. of a king or queen 2. like, or fit for, a king or queen; magnificent, majestic, etc. 3. of a kingdom, its government, etc. —**roy′al·ly** *adv.*

**roy′al·ist** *n.* one who supports a monarch or monarchy

**roy′al·ty** *n., pl.* -ties 1. the rank or power of a king or queen 2. a royal person or persons 3. royal quality 4. a share of the proceeds from a patent, book, etc. paid to the owner, author, etc.

**rpm, r.p.m.** revolutions per minute

**rps, r.p.s.** revolutions per second

**R.R.** RR railroad

**R.S.F.S.R.,** RSFSR Russian Soviet Federated Socialist Republic

**RSV, R.S.V.** Revised Standard Version (of the Bible)

**R.S.V.P., r.s.v.p.** [Fr. *répondez s'il vous plaît*] please reply

**rub** (rub) *vt.* rubbed, rub′bing [ME. *rubben*] 1. to move (one's hand, a cloth, etc.) over (something) with pressure and friction 2. to apply (polish, etc.) in this way 3. to move (things) over each other with pressure and friction 4. to make sore by rubbing 5. to remove by rubbing (*out, off,* etc.) —*vi.* 1. to move with pressure and friction (*on,* etc.) 2. to rub something —*n.* 1. a rubbing 2. an obstacle, difficulty, or source of irritation —**rub down** 1. to massage 2. to smooth, polish, etc. by rubbing —**rub the wrong way** to irritate or annoy

**ru·ba·to** (rōō bät′ō) *adj., adv.* [It., stolen] *Music* intentionally and temporarily not in strict tempo

**rub′ber¹** *n.* 1. one that rubs 2. [< use as eraser] an elastic substance made from the milky sap of various tropical plants, or synthetically 3. something made of this substance; specif., a low-cut overshoe —*adj.* made of rubber —**rub′ber·y** *adj.*

**rub·ber²** (rub′ər) *n.* [< ?] the deciding game in a series: also **rubber game**

**rubber band** a narrow, continuous band of rubber as for holding small objects together

**rubber cement** an adhesive of unvulcanized rubber in a solvent that quickly evaporates when exposed to air

**rub′ber·ize′** (-īz′) *vt.* -ized′, -iz′ing to impregnate with rubber

**rubber plant** 1. any plant yielding latex 2. a house plant with large, glossy, leathery leaves

**rubber stamp** 1. a stamp of rubber, inked for printing signatures, etc. 2. [Colloq.] *a*) a person, bureau, etc. that gives automatic approval *b*) such approval —**rub′ber-stamp′** *vt.*

**rub·bish** (rub′ish) *n.* [ME. *robys*] 1. any material thrown away as worthless; trash 2. nonsense

**rub·ble** (rub′'l) *n.* [ME. *robel*] rough, broken pieces of stone, brick, etc.

**rub′down′** *n.* a massage

**rube** (rōōb) *n.* [< name *Reuben*] [Slang] an unsophisticated rustic

**ru·bel·la** (rōō bel′ə) *n.* [< L. *ruber,* red] an infectious disease causing small red spots on the skin

**Ru·bens** (rōō′bənz), **Peter Paul** 1577–1640; Fl. painter

**ru·bi·cund** (rōō′bi kund′) *adj.* [< L. *ruber,* red] reddish; ruddy

**ru·ble** (rōō′b'l) *n.* [Russ. *rubl'*] the monetary unit of the U.S.S.R.

**ru·bric** (rōō′brik) *n.* [< L. *ruber,* red] 1. a section heading, direction, etc. often in red (as in a prayer book) 2. any rule, explanatory comment, etc.

**ru·by** (rōō′bē) *n., pl.* -bies [ult. < L. *rubeus,* reddish] 1. a clear, deep-red precious stone: a variety of corundum 2. deep red —*adj.* deep-red

fat, āpe, cär; ten, ēven; is, bīte; gō, hôrn, tōōl, look; oil, out; up, fer; chin; she; thin, then; zh, leisure; ŋ, ring; ə for *a* in *ago;* ', (ā'b'l); ë, Fr. coeur; ö, Fr. feu; Fr. mon; ü, Fr. duc; kh, G. ich, doch; ‡ foreign; < derived from

**ruck·sack** (ruk′sak′) *n.* [G., back sack] a kind of knapsack

**ruck·us** (ruk′əs) *n.* [prob. merging of RUMPUS & *ruction*, uproar] [Colloq.] noisy confusion; disturbance

**rud·der** (rud′ər) *n.* [OE. *rother*] a broad, flat, movable piece hinged to the rear of a ship or aircraft, used for steering —**rud′der·less** *adj.*

**rud·dy** (rud′ē) *adj.* -**di·er**, -**di·est** [OE. *rudig*] 1. having a healthy red color 2. reddish —**rud′di·ness** *n.*

**rude** (rōōd) *adj.* **rud′er**, **rud′est** [< L. *rudis*] 1. crude; rough 2. barbarous 3. unrefined; uncouth 4. discourteous 5. primitive; unskillful —**rude′ly** *adv.* —**rude′ness** *n.*

**ru·di·ment** (rōō′də mənt) *n.* [see prec.] 1. a first principle, as of a subject to be learned 2. a first slight beginning of something —**ru′di·men′ta·ry** (-men′tər ē) *adj.*

**rue**[1] (rōō) *vt., vi.* **rued**, **ru′ing** [OE. *hreowan*] 1. to feel remorse for (a sin, fault, etc.) 2. to regret (an act, etc.) —*n.* [Archaic] sorrow —**rue′ful** *adj.* —**rue′ful·ly** *adv.*

**rue**[2] (rōō) *n.* [< Gr. *rhytē*] a strong-scented plant with bitter leaves

**ruff** (ruf) *n.* [< RUFFLE] 1. a high, frilled, starched collar of the 16th–17th c. 2. a band of colored or protruding feathers or fur about an animal's neck

RUFF

**ruf·fi·an** (ruf′ē ən) *n.* [< It. *ruffiano*, a pander] a rowdy or hoodlum

**ruf·fle** (ruf′'l) *vt.* -**fled**, -**fling** [< ON. or MLowG.] 1. to disturb the smoothness of 2. to gather into ruffles 3. to make (feathers, etc.) stand up 4. to disturb or annoy —*vi.* 1. to become uneven 2. to become disturbed, irritated, etc. —*n.* 1. a pleated strip of cloth, lace, etc. 2. a disturbance 3. a ripple

**rug** (rug) *n.* [< Scand.] 1. a piece of thick fabric used as a floor covering 2. [Chiefly Brit.] a lap robe

**rug·by** (rug′bē) *n.* [first played at *Rugby* School in England] a game from which American football developed

**rug·ged** (rug′id) *adj.* [ME.] 1. uneven; rough 2. stormy 3. harsh; severe; hard 4. not polished or refined 5. strong; robust —**rug′ged·ly** *adv.* —**rug′ged·ness** *n.*

**Ruhr** (roor) 1. river in West Germany 2. coal-mining & industrial region along this river: also **Ruhr Basin**

**ru·in** (rōō′in) *n.* [< L. *ruere*, to fall] 1. [*pl.*] the remains of something destroyed, decayed, etc. 2. anything destroyed, decayed, etc. 3. downfall, destruction, etc. 4. anything causing this —*vt.* to bring to ruin; destroy, spoil, bankrupt, etc. —*vi.* to come to ruin —**ru′in·a′tion** *n.* —**ru′in·ous** *adj.*

**rule** (rōōl) *n.* [< L. *regere*, to rule] 1. an established regulation or guide for conduct, procedure, usage, etc. 2.

custom 3. the customary course 4. government; reign 5. a ruler (sense 2) —*vt., vi.* **ruled**, **rul′ing** 1. to have an influence (over); guide 2. to govern 3. to determine officially 4. to mark lines (on) as with a ruler —**as a rule** usually —**rule out** to exclude

**rule of thumb** a practical, though crude or unscientific method

**rul′er** *n.* 1. one who governs 2. a strip of wood, etc. with a straight edge, used in drawing lines, measuring, etc.

**rul′ing** *adj.* that rules —*n.* an official decision, as of a court

**rum** (rum) *n.* [< ?] 1. an alcoholic liquor made from fermented molasses, sugar cane, etc. 2. any alcoholic liquor

**Ru·ma·nia** (rōō mān′yə) *same as* ROMANIA —**Ru·ma′nian** *adj., n.*

**rum·ba** (rum′bə) *n.* [AmSp.] a dance of Cuban Negro origin, or music for it —*vi.* to dance the rumba

**rum·ble** (rum′b'l) *vi., vt.* -**bled**, -**bling** [ME. *romblen*] 1. to make or cause to make a deep, continuous, rolling sound 2. to move with such a sound —*n.* 1. a rumbling sound 2. [Slang] a fight between teen-age gangs

**ru·mi·nant** (rōō′mə nənt) *adj.* [see ff.] 1. chewing the cud 2. meditative —*n.* any of a group of cud-chewing mammals, as cattle, deer, camels, etc.

**ru′mi·nate′** (-nāt′) *vt., vi.* -**nat′ed**, -**nat′ing** [< L. *ruminare*] 1. to chew (the cud) 2. to meditate or reflect (on) —**ru′mi·na′tion** *n.*

**rum·mage** (rum′ij) *n.* [< MFr. *rum*, ship's hold] 1. odds and ends 2. a rummaging —*vt., vi.* to search through (a place) thoroughly

**rummage sale** a sale of contributed miscellaneous articles, as for charity

**rum·my** (rum′ē) *n.* [< ?] any of certain card games whose object is to match sets and sequences

**ru·mor** (rōō′mər) *n.* [L., noise] 1. general talk not based on definite knowledge 2. an unconfirmed report, story, etc. in general circulation —*vt.* to tell or spread by rumor Brit. sp. **rumour**

**rump** (rump) *n.* [< ON. *rumpr*] 1. the hind part of an animal, where the legs and back join 2. the buttocks

**rum·ple** (rum′p'l) *n.* [< MDu. *rompe*] an uneven crease; wrinkle —*vt., vi.* -**pled**, -**pling** to wrinkle; muss

**rum·pus** (rum′pəs) *n.* [< ?] [Colloq.] noisy disturbance; uproar

**run** (run) *vi.* **ran**, **run**, **run′ning** [< ON. & OE.] 1. to go by moving the legs faster than in walking 2. to go, move, etc. easily and freely 3. to flee 4. to make a quick trip (*up to, down to,* etc.) 5. to compete in a race, election, etc. 6. to ply (between two points), as a train 7. to climb or creep, as a vine 8. to ravel, as a stocking 9. to operate, as a machine 10. to flow 11. to spread over cloth, etc. when moistened, as colors 12. to discharge pus, etc. 13. to extend in time or space; continue 14. to pass into a specified condition, as *[he ran into trouble]* 15. to be written, etc. in a specified way 16. to be at a specified size, price, etc. [eggs *run* high] —*vt.* 1. to follow (a specified course) 2. to perform as by running [to *run* a race] 3. to incur (a risk) 4. to get past [to *run* a blockade] 5. to cause to run, move, compete, etc. 6. to drive into a specified condition, place, etc. 7. to drive (an object) into or against (something) 8. to make flow in a specified way, place, etc. 9. to manage (a business, etc.) 10. to trace 11. to undergo (a fever, etc.) 12. to publish (a story, etc.) in a newspaper —*n.* 1. an act or period of running 2. the distance covered in running 3. a trip; journey 4. a route [a milkman's *run*] 5. *a)* a movement onward, progression, or trend [the *run* of events] *b)* a continuous course or period [a *run* of good luck] 6. a continuous course of performances, etc., as of a play 7. a continued series of demands, as on a bank 8. a brook 9. a kind or class; esp., the average kind 10. the output during a period of operation 11. an enclosed area for domestic animals 12. freedom to move about at will [the *run* of the house] 13. a large number of fish migrating together 14. a ravel, as in a stocking 15. *Baseball* a scoring point, made by a successful circuit of the bases —**in the long run** ultimately —**on the run** running or running away —**run across** to encounter by chance: also **run into** —**run down** 1. to stop operating 2. to run against so as to knock down 3. to pursue and capture or kill 4. to speak of disparagingly —**run out** to come to an end; expire —**run out of** to use up —**run over** 1. to ride over 2. to overflow 3. to examine, rehearse, etc. rapidly —**run through** 1. to use up quickly or recklessly 2. to pierce —**run up** 1. to raise, rise, or accumulate rapidly 2. to sew rapidly

**run′a·round′** *n.* [Colloq.] a series of evasions

**run′a·way′** *n.* 1. a fugitive 2. a horse, etc. that runs away —*adj.* 1. escaping, fleeing, etc. 2. easily won, as a race 3. rising rapidly, as prices

**run′-down′** *adj.* 1. not wound and therefore not running, as a watch 2. in poor physical condition, as from overwork 3. fallen into disrepair

**run′down′** *n.* a concise summary

**rune** (rōōn) *n.* [OE. *run*] 1. any of the characters of an ancient Germanic alphabet 2. a mystical or obscure poem or song —**ru′nic** *adj.*

**rung**[1] (rung) *n.* [OE. *hrung*, a staff] a rod forming a step of a ladder, a crosspiece on a chair, etc.

**rung**[2] (rung) *pp. of* RING[1]

**run′-in′** *n.* [*Printing*] matter added without a break or new paragraph: also **run′-on′** 2. [Colloq.] a quarrel, fight, etc.

**run·nel** (run′'l) *n.* [OE. *rynel*] a small stream; brook: also **run′let**

**run′ner** *n.* 1. one that runs, as a racer, messenger, etc. 2. a long, narrow cloth or rug 3. a ravel, as in hose 4. a long, trailing stem, as of a strawberry 5. either of the long, narrow pieces on which a sled, etc. slides

**run′ner-up′** *n.*, *pl.* **-ners′-up′** a person or team that finishes second, etc. in a contest

**run′ning** *n.* the act of one that runs; racing, managing, etc. —*adj.* 1. that runs (in various senses) 2. measured in a straight line [a *running* foot] 3. continuous [a *running* commentary] —*adv.* in succession [for five days *running*] —**in** (or **out of**) **the running** having a (or no) chance to win

**running gear** the wheels, axles, and frame of a motor vehicle

**running lights** the lights that a ship or aircraft must display at night

**running mate** a candidate for the lesser of two closely associated offices in his relationship to the candidate for the greater office

**run′ny** *adj.* **-ni·er, -ni·est** 1. flowing, esp. too freely 2. discharging mucus [a *runny* nose]

**run′off′** *n.* a deciding, final contest

**run′-of-the-mill′** *adj.* not selected or special; ordinary; average

**runt** (runt) *n.* [< ?] a stunted animal, plant, or (contemptuously) person —**runt′y** *adj.* **-i·er, -i·est**

**run′-through′** *n.* a complete rehearsal, from beginning to end

**run′way′** *n.* a channel, track, etc. in, on, or along which something moves; esp., a strip of leveled ground used by airplanes in taking off and landing

**ru·pee** (rōō pē′) *n.* [< Sans. *rūpya*, wrought silver] the monetary unit of India, Pakistan, Ceylon, etc.

**rup·ture** (rup′chər) *n.* [< L. *rumpere*, to break] 1. a breaking apart or being broken apart; breach 2. a hernia —*vt.*, *vi.* **-tured, -tur·ing** to cause or suffer a rupture

**ru·ral** (roor′əl) *adj.* [< L. *rus*, the country] of, like, or living in the country; rustic —**ru′ral·ism** *n.*

**ruse** (rōōz) *n.* [< OFr. *reuser*, deceive] a stratagem, trick, or artifice

**rush**[1] (rush) *vi.*, *vt.* [< MFr. *ruser*, repel] 1. to move, push, drive, etc. swiftly or impetuously 2. to make a sudden attack (on) 3. to pass, go, send, act, do, etc. with unusual haste; hurry —*n.* 1. a rushing 2. an eager movement of many people to get to a place 3. busyness; haste [the *rush* of modern life] 4. a press, as of business, necessitating unusual haste

**rush**[2] (rush) *n.* [OE. *rysce*] a grasslike marsh plant, with round stems used in making mats, etc.

**rush hour** a time of the day when business, traffic, etc. are heavy

**rusk** (rusk) *n.* [Sp. *rosca*, twisted bread roll] 1. a sweet, raised bread or cake toasted until browned and crisp 2. a piece of this

**Russ.** 1. Russia 2. Russian

**rus·set** (rus′it) *n.* [< L. *russus*, reddish] **1.** yellowish (or reddish) brown **2.** a winter apple with a mottled skin

**Rus·sia** (rush′ə) **1.** czarist empire (**Russian Empire**) in E Europe & N Asia (1547–1917) **2.** popularly, U.S.S.R.

**Rus·sian** *adj.* of Russia, its people, language, etc. —*n.* **1.** a native or inhabitant of Russia **2.** the East Slavic language of the Russians

**Russian Soviet Federated Socialist Republic** largest republic of the U.S.S.R., stretching from the Baltic Sea to the Pacific

**rust** (rust) *n.* [OE.] **1.** the reddish-brown coating formed on iron or steel during exposure to air and moisture **2.** any stain resembling this **3.** a reddish brown **4.** a plant disease caused by parasitic fungi, spotting stems and leaves —*vi., vt.* **1.** to form rust (on) **2.** to deteriorate, as through disuse

**rus·tic** (rus′tik) *adj.* [< L. *rus*, the country] **1.** of the country; rural **2.** simple or artless **3.** rough or uncouth —*n.* a country person —**rus′ti·cal·ly** *adv.* —**rus·tic′i·ty** (-tis′ə tē) *n.*

**rus·ti·cate** (rus′ti kāt′) *vi., vt.* -**cat′ed**, -**cat′ing 1.** to go or send to live in the country **2.** to become or make rustic —**rus′ti·ca′tion** *n.*

**rus·tle¹** (rus′l) *vi., vt.* -**tled**, -**tling** [ult. echoic] to make or cause to make soft sounds as of moving leaves, etc. —*n.* a series of such sounds

**rus·tle²** (rus′l) *vi., vt.* -**tled**, -**tling**

[< ?] [Colloq.] to steal (cattle, etc.) —**rustle up** [Colloq.] to collect or get together —**rus′tler** *n.*

**rust·y** (rus′tē) *adj.* -**i·er**, -**i·est 1.** coated with rust, as a metal **2.** *a)* impaired by disuse, neglect, etc. *b)* having lost facility through lack of practice **3.** rust-colored

**rut¹** (rut) *n.* [< ? MFr. *route*, route] **1.** a groove, track, etc., as made by wheels **2.** a fixed, routine procedure, course of action, etc. —*vt.* **rut′ted**, **rut′ting** to make ruts in —**rut′ty** *adj.* -**ti·er**, -**ti·est** —**rut′ti·ness** *n.*

**rut²** (rut) *n.* [< L. *rugire*, to roar] the periodic sexual excitement of certain male mammals —**rut′tish** *adj.*

**ru·ta·ba·ga** (rōōt′ə bā′gə) *n.* [Sw. dial. *rotabagge*] **1.** a turnip with a large, yellow root **2.** this root

**Ruth** (rōōth) *Bible* a woman who left her own people out of devotion to her mother-in-law, Naomi

**ruth·less** (rōōth′lis) *adj.* [OE. *hreowan*, to rue] without pity or compassion —**ruth′less·ly** *adv.* —**ruth′less·ness** *n.*

**Rwan·da** (ʊr wän′də) country in EC Africa: 10,169 sq. mi.; pop. 3,306,000

**Rwy., Ry.** Railway

-**ry** (rē) *shortened form of* -ERY [*dentistry*]

**ry·a rug** (rē′ə) [< Sw.] a decorative, hand-woven, thick area rug of Scandinavian origin

**rye** (rī) *n.* [OE. *ryge*] **1.** a hardy cereal grass **2.** its grain or seeds, used for making flour, etc. **3.** whiskey distilled from this grain

# S

**S, s** (es) *n., pl.* **S's, s's** the 19th letter of the English alphabet

**S** *Chem.* sulfur —*adj.* shaped like *S*

-**s** [alt. of -ES] **1.** the plural ending of most nouns [*lips*] **2.** the ending of the third person singular, present indicative, of verbs [*tells*]

-'**s¹** [OE. *-es*] the ending of the possessive singular of nouns (and some pronouns) and of the possessive plural of nouns not ending in *s* [*boy's, men's*]

-'**s²** the assimilated form of: **1.** is [*he's here*] **2.** has [*she's won*] **3.** does [*what's it matter?*] **4.** us [*let's go*]

**S, S., s, s. 1.** south **2.** southern

**S., s. 1.** *pl.* **SS., ss.** saint **2.** school **s. 1.** second(s) **2.** shilling(s)

**S.A.** South America

**Saar** (sär, zär) rich coal-mining region in a river valley of SW West Germany: also called **Saar Basin**

**Sab·bath** (sab′əth) *n.* [< Heb. *shābath*, to rest] **1.** the seventh day of the week (Saturday), set aside in Jewish Scripture for rest and worship **2.** Sunday as the usual Christian day of rest and worship

**Sab·bat·i·cal** (sə bat′i k'l) *adj.* **1.** of the Sabbath **2.** [s-] bringing a period

of rest [a *sabbatical* leave] —*n.* [s-] a sabbatical year or leave

**sabbatical year** a period of absence with pay, for study, travel, etc., given as to teachers, orig. every 7 years

**sa·ber, sa·bre** (sā′bər) *n.* [< Hung. *szabni*, to cut] a heavy cavalry sword with a slightly curved blade

**Sa·bin vaccine** (sā′bin) [< Dr. A. B. *Sabin* (1906– ), its U.S. developer] a polio vaccine taken orally

**sa·ble** (sā′b'l) *n.* [< Russ. *sobol'*] **1.** *same as* MARTEN **2.** its costly fur pelt

**sab·o·tage** (sab′ə täzh′) *n.* [Fr. < *sabot*, wooden shoe + -AGE: from damage done to machinery by sabots] deliberate destruction of machines, etc. by employees in labor disputes or of railroads, bridges, etc. by enemy agents or by underground resistance —*vt., vi.* -**taged**, -**tag′ing** to commit sabotage (on) —**sab′o·teur′** (-tʊr′) *n.*

**sa·bra** (sä′brə) *n.* [Mod. Heb. *sābrāh*, a native cactus fruit] a native-born Israeli

**sa·bre saw** (sā′bər) a portable electric saw with a narrow, oscillating blade

**sac** (sak) *n.* [see SACK¹] a pouchlike part in a plant or animal

**SAC, S.A.C.** Strategic Air Command

**sac·cha·rin** (sak'ə rin) *n.* [< Gr. *sakcharon*] a white, crystalline coal-tar compound used as a sugar substitute

**sac'cha·rine** (-rin) *adj.* 1. of or like sugar 2. too sweet [a *saccharine* voice]

**sac·er·do·tal** (sas'ər dōt'l, sak'-) *adj.* [< L. *sacerdos*, priest] of priests or the office of priest; priestly

**sa·chem** (sā'chəm) *n.* [AmInd.] among some Indian tribes, the chief

**sa·chet** (sa shā') *n.* [Fr.] a small bag, pad, etc. filled with perfumed powder and stored with clothes

**sack¹** (sak) *n.* [ult. < Heb. *śaq*] 1. a bag, esp. a large one of coarse cloth 2. [Slang] dismissal (with *the*) 3. [Slang] a bed —*vt.* 1. to put into sacks 2. [Slang] to fire (a person)

**sack²** (sak) *n.* [see prec.] the plundering of a captured city, etc. —*vt.* to plunder; pillage

**sack³** (sak) *n.* [< Fr. (*vin*)*sec*, dry (wine) < L.] a dry, white Spanish wine formerly popular in England

**sack'cloth'** *n.* 1. burlap: also **sack'-ing** 2. coarse cloth worn as a symbol of mourning, as in Biblical times

**sack'ful'** *n., pl.* -fuls' the amount that a sack will hold

**sack'ing** *n.* a coarse cloth, as burlap, used for making sacks

**sac·ra·ment** (sak'rə mənt) *n.* [< L. *sacer*, sacred] 1. any of certain Christian rites, as baptism, the Eucharist, etc. 2. something regarded as sacred —**sac'ra·men'tal** *adj.*

**Sac·ra·men·to** (sak'rə men'tō) capital of Calif.: pop. 254,000

**sa·cred** (sā'krid) *adj.* [< L. *sacer*, holy] 1. consecrated to a god or God; holy 2. having to do with religion 3. venerated; hallowed 4. inviolate —**sa'cred·ly** *adv.* —**sa'cred·ness** *n.*

**sac·ri·fice** (sak'rə fīs') *n.* [< L. *sacer*, sacred + *facere*, make] 1. an offering, as of a life or object, to a deity 2. a giving up of one thing for the sake of another 3. a loss incurred in selling —*vt., vi.* -ficed', -fic'ing 1. to offer as a sacrifice to a deity 2. to give up (one thing) for the sake of another 3. to sell at less than the supposed value —**sac'ri·fi'cial** (-fish'əl) *adj.*

**sac·ri·lege** (sak'rə lij) *n.* [< L. *sacer*, sacred + *legere*, take away] desecration of what is sacred —**sac'ri·le'gious** (-lij'əs, -lē'jəs) *adj.*

**sac·ris·tan** (sak'ris tən) *n.* an official in charge of a sacristy

**sac·ris·ty** (sak'ris tē) *n., pl.* -ties [ult. < L. *sacer*, sacred] a room in a church for sacred vessels, etc.

**sa·cro·il·i·ac** (sā'krō il'ē ak', sak'rō-) *n.* the joint between the top part (il'l·um) of the hipbone and the fused bottom vertebrae (**sa'crum**)

**sac·ro·sanct** (sak'rō saŋkt') *adj.* [< L. *sacer*, sacred + *sanctus*, holy] very sacred, holy, or inviolable

**sad** (sad) *adj.* **sad'der, sad'dest** [OE. *sæd*, sated] 1. having or expressing low spirits; unhappy; sorrowful 2. causing dejection, sorrow, etc. — **sad'ly** *adv.* —**sad'ness** *n.*

**sad·den** (*vt., vi.*) to make or become sad

**sad·dle** (sad'l) *n.* [OE. *sadol*] 1. a seat for a rider on a horse, bicycle, etc., usually padded and of leather 2. a cut of lamb, etc. including part of the backbone and the two loins —*vt.* -died, -dling 1. to put a saddle upon 2. to encumber or burden —**in the saddle** in control

**sad'dle·bag'** *n.* 1. a bag hung behind the saddle of a horse, etc. 2. a similar bag carried on a bicycle, etc.

**saddle horse** a horse for riding

**saddle shoes** white oxford shoes with a contrasting band across the instep

**Sad·du·cee** (saj'oo sē') *n.* a member of an ancient Jewish party that accepted only the written law

SADDLE SHOES

**sad·ism** (sad'iz'm, sā'diz'm) *n.* [< marquis de *Sade*, 18th-c. Fr. writer] the getting of pleasure from mistreating others —**sad'ist** *n.* —**sa·dis'tic** *adj.* —**sa·dis'ti·cal·ly** *adv.*

**sad·o·mas·o·chism** (sā'dō mas'ə kiz'm, sad'ō-) *n.* sadism and masochism coexisting in the same person — **sad'o·mas'o·chist** *n.* —**sad'o·mas'·o·chis'tic** *adj.*

**sa·fa·ri** (sə fär'ē) *n., pl.* -ris [< Ar. *safara*, to travel] a journey or hunting expedition, esp. in Africa

**safe** (sāf) *adj.* **saf'er, saf'est** [< L. *salvus*] 1. *a)* free from damage, danger, etc.; secure *b)* having escaped injury; unharmed 2. *a)* giving protection *b)* trustworthy 3. prudent; cautious —*n.* a locking metal container for valuables —**safe'ly** *adv.* —**safe'ness** *n.*

**safe'-con'duct** *n.* permission to travel safely through enemy regions

**safe'-de·pos'it** *adj.* designating or of a box or vault, as in a bank, for storing valuables: also **safe'ty-de·pos'it**

**safe'guard'** *n.* a protection; precaution —*vt.* to protect or guard

**safe'keep'ing** *n.* a keeping or being kept in safety; protection

**safe·ty** (sāf'tē) *n., pl.* -ties 1. a being safe; security 2. any device for preventing an accident 3. *Football a)* the grounding of the ball by the offense behind its own goal line *b)* a defensive back farthest from the line of scrimmage: also **safety man** —*adj.* giving safety

**safety glass** shatterproof glass

**safety match** a match that strikes only on a prepared surface

**safety pin** a pin bent back on itself and having the point held in a guard

**safety razor** a razor with a detachable blade held between guards

**safety valve** an automatic valve which releases steam if the pressure in a boiler, etc. becomes excessive

**saf·flow·er** (saf′lou′ər) *n.* [ult. < Ar.] a flowering thistlelike plant whose seeds yield an edible oil

**saf·fron** (saf′rən) *n.* [ < Ar. *za'farān*] 1. a plant having orange stigmas 2. the dried stigmas, used as a dye and flavoring 3. orange yellow

**sag** (sag) *vi.* **sagged, sag′ging** [prob. < Scand.] 1. to sink, esp. in the middle, from weight or pressure 2. to hang down unevenly 3. to weaken through weariness, age, etc. —*n.* 1. a sagging 2. a sagging place

**sa·ga** (sä′gə) *n.* [ON., a tale] 1. a medieval Scandinavian story of battles, legends, etc. 2. any long story of heroic deeds

**sa·ga·cious** (sə gā′shəs) *adj.* [ < L. *sagax*, wise] keenly perceptive; shrewd —**sa·gac′i·ty** (-gas′ə tē) *n.*

**sage¹** (sāj) *adj.* **sag′er, sag′est** [ult. < L. *sapere*, know] 1. wise, discerning, etc. 2. showing wisdom [a *sage* comment] —*n.* a very wise man

**sage²** (sāj) *n.* [ < L. *salvus*, safe: from its reputed healing powers] 1. a plant of the mint family with leaves used for seasoning meats, etc. 2. sagebrush

**sage′brush′** *n.* a plant with aromatic leaves, common in dry, alkaline areas of the W U.S.

**sag′gy** *adj.* **-gi·er, -gi·est** tending to sag —**sag′gi·ness** *n.*

**Sag·it·ta·ri·us** (saj′i ter′ē əs) [L., archer] the ninth sign of the zodiac

**sa·gua·ro** (sə gwä′rō) *n., pl.* **-ros** [ < native name] a giant cactus of the SW U.S. and N Mexico

**Sa·ha·ra** (sə har′ə) vast desert region extending across N Africa

**said** (sed) *pt. & pp.* of SAY —*adj.* aforesaid

**Sai·gon** (sī gän′) city in S Vietnam: pop. 2,200,000: also called **Ho Chi Minh City** (hō′ chē′ min′)

**sail** (sāl) *n.* [OE. *segl*] 1. a sheet, as of canvas, spread to catch the wind so as to drive a vessel forward 2. sails collectively 3. a trip in a ship or boat 4. anything like a sail —*vi.* 1. to be moved forward by means of sails 2. to travel on water 3. to begin a trip by water 4. to manage a sailboat 5. to glide or move smoothly, like a ship in full sail —*vt.* 1. to move upon (a body of water) in a vessel 2. to manage (a vessel) —**sail into** [Colloq.] to attack vigorously —**set sail** to begin a trip by water —**under sail** sailing

**sail′boat′** *n.* a boat that is propelled by means of a sail or sails

**sail′cloth′** *n.* canvas or other cloth for making sails, tents, etc.

**sail′fish′** *n., pl.:* see FISH a large, tropical, marine fish with a large sail-like dorsal fin

**sail′or** *n.* 1. a person who makes his living by sailing 2. an enlisted man in the navy

**saint** (sānt) *n.* [ < L. *sanctus*, holy] 1. a holy person 2. a person who is exceptionally charitable, patient, etc. 3. in certain Christian churches, a person officially recognized and venerated for having attained heaven after an exceptionally holy life —**saint′li-** ness *n.* —**saint′ly** *adj.* **-li·er, -li·est**

**Saint Ber·nard** (bər närd′) a large dog of a breed once used in the Swiss Alps to rescue lost travelers

**Saint Pat·rick's Day** (pat′riks) March 17, observed by the Irish in honor of the patron saint of Ireland

**Saint Valentine's Day** February 14, observed in honor of a martyr of the 3d c. and as a day for sending valentines to sweethearts, etc.

**saith** (seth) [Archaic] says

**sake¹** (sāk) *n.* [OE. *sacu*, suit at law] 1. motive; cause [for the *sake* of money] 2. behalf [for my *sake*]

**sa·ke²** (sä′kē) *n.* [Jap.] a Japanese alcoholic beverage made from rice: also sp. **saki**

**sa·laam** (sə läm′) *n.* [Ar. *salām*, peace] an Oriental greeting, etc. made by bowing low in respect or obeisance

**sal·a·ble** (sāl′ə b'l) *adj.* that can be sold; marketable: also sp. **saleable**

**sa·la·cious** (sə lā′shəs) *adj.* [ < L. *salire*, to leap] 1. lustful 2. obscene —**sa·la′cious·ly** *adv.* —**sa·la′cious·** ness *n.*

**sal·ad** (sal′əd) *n.* [ < L. *salare*, to salt] a dish, usually cold, of fruits, vegetables (esp. lettuce), meat, eggs, etc. usually mixed with salad dressing

**salad dressing** a preparation of oil, vinegar, spices, etc. put on a salad

**sal·a·man·der** (sal′ə man′dər) *n.* [ < Gr. *salamandra*] 1. a mythological reptile said to live in fire 2. a scaleless, tailed amphibian

**sa·la·mi** (sə lä′mē) *n.* [It. < L. *sal*, salt] a spiced, salted sausage

**sal·a·ry** (sal′ə rē) *n., pl.* **-ries** [ < L. *salarium*, orig. part of a soldier's pay for buying salt < *sal*, salt] a fixed payment at regular intervals for work —**sal′a·ried** (-rēd) *adj.*

**sale** (sāl) *n.* [ < ON. *sala*] 1. a selling 2. opportunity to sell; market 3. an auction 4. a special offering of goods at reduced prices —**for** (or **on**) **sale** to be sold

**sales·clerk** (sālz′klurk′) *n.* a person employed to sell goods in a store

**sales′man** (-mən) *n., pl.* **-men** a man employed to sell goods —**sales′wom′-** an, **sales′la′dy, sales′girl′** *n. fem.* —**sales′man·ship′** *n.*

**sales′per′son** *n.* a person employed to sell goods; esp., a salesclerk

**sales slip** a receipt or bill of sale

**sales talk** 1. talk aimed at selling something 2. any talk to persuade

**sales tax** a tax on sales

**sal·i·cyl·ic acid** (sal′ə sil′ik) [ < *salicin* (substance from certain willows)] a crystalline compound, as in aspirin, for relieving pain, etc.

**sa·lient** (sāl′yənt) *adj.* [ < L. *salire*, to leap] 1. pointing outward; jutting 2. conspicuous; prominent —*n.* a salient angle, part, etc. —**sa′lience** *n.*

**sa·line** (sā′līn) *adj.* [ < L. *sal*, salt] of, like, or containing salt; salty —**sa·** lin·i·ty (sə lin′ə tē) *n.*

**sa·li·va** (sə lī′və) *n.* [L.] the watery fluid secreted by glands in the mouth: it aids in digestion —**sal·i·var·y** (sal′ə ver′ē) *adj.*

**sal·i·vate** (sal′ə vāt′) *vi.* **-vat′ed,** **-vat′ing** [< L. *salivare*] to secrete saliva —**sal′i·va′tion** *n.*

**sal·low** (sal′ō) *adj.* [ME. *salou*] of a sickly, pale-yellowish complexion

**sal·ly** (sal′ē) *n., pl.* **-lies** [< L. *salire,* to leap] **1.** a sudden rushing forth, as to attack **2.** a quick witticism; quip **3.** an excursion —*vi.* **-lied, -ly·ing** to rush or set *(forth* or *out)* on a sally

**salm·on** (sam′ən) *n., pl.* **-on, -ons** [< L. *salmo*] **1.** a game and food fish with yellowish-pink flesh, that lives in salt water and spawns in fresh water **2.** yellowish pink: also **salmon pink**

**sal·mo·nel·la** (sal′mə nel′ə) *n., pl.* **-nel′lae** (-ē), **-nel′la, -nel′las** [< D. E. *Salmon* (d. 1914), U.S. doctor] any of a genus of bacilli that cause typhoid fever, food poisoning, etc.

**sa·lon** (sə län′) *n.* [Fr.: see ff.] **1.** a large reception hall or drawing room **2.** a regular gathering of distinguished guests **3.** a parlor *[beauty salon]*

**sa·loon** (sə lōōn′) *n.* [< Fr. < It. *sala,* hall] **1.** any large room or hall for receptions, etc. **2.** a place where alcoholic drinks are sold; bar

**sal soda** crystallized sodium carbonate

**salt** (sôlt) *n.* [OE. *sealt*] **1.** a white, crystalline substance, sodium chloride, found in natural beds, in sea water, etc., and used for seasoning food, etc. **2.** a chemical compound derived from an acid by replacing hydrogen with a metal **3.** piquancy; esp., pungent wit **4.** *[pl.]* mineral salts used as a cathartic or restorative **5.** [Colloq.] a sailor —*adj.* containing, preserved with, or tasting of salt —*vt.* to sprinkle, season, or preserve with salt —**salt of the earth** any person or persons regarded as the finest, etc. —**with a grain of salt** with allowance for exaggeration, etc. —**salt′ed** *adj.* —**salt′i·ness** *n.* —**salt′y** *adj.* **-i·er, -i·est**

**SALT** (sôlt) Strategic Arms Limitation Talks

**salt′cel′lar** (-sel′ər) *n.* [< prec. + MFr. *salière,* saltcellar] **1.** a small dish for holding salt **2.** a saltshaker

**salt·ine** (sôl tēn′) *n.* [SALT + -INE³] a flat, crisp, salted cracker

**Salt Lake City** capital of Utah: pop. 176,000

**salt lick** a natural deposit or a block of rock salt which animals lick

**salt′pe′ter** (-pēt′ər) *n.* [< L. *sal,* salt + *petra,* a rock] *same as* NITER

**salt pork** pork cured in salt

**salt′shak′er** *n.* a container for salt, with a perforated top

**salt′wa′ter** *adj.* of or living in salt water or the sea

**sa·lu·bri·ous** (sə lōō′brē əs) *adj.* [< L. *salus,* health] healthful; wholesome

**sal·u·tar·y** (sal′yoo ter′ē) *adj.* [see prec.] **1.** healthful **2.** beneficial

**sal·u·ta·tion** (sal′yoo tā′shən) *n.* [see ff.] **1.** the act of greeting, addressing, etc. **2.** a form of greeting, as the "Dear Sir" of a letter

**sa·lute** (sə lōōt′) *vt., vi.* **-lut′ed,** **-lut′ing** [< L. *salus,* health] **1.** to greet with friendly words or ceremonial gesture **2.** to honor by performing a prescribed act, such as raising the hand to the head, in military and naval practice **3.** to commend —*n.* an act or remark made in saluting

**sal·vage** (sal′vij) *n.* [see SAVE¹] **1.** *a)* the rescue of a ship and cargo from shipwreck, etc. *b)* compensation paid for such rescue **2.** *a)* the rescue of any property from destruction or waste *b)* the property saved —*vt.* **-vaged, -vag·ing** to save or rescue from shipwreck, fire, etc.

**sal·va·tion** (sal vā′shən) *n.* [< L. *salvare,* save] **1.** a saving or being saved **2.** a person or thing that saves **3.** *Theol.* spiritual rescue from sin and death; redemption

**salve** (sav) *n.* [OE. *sealf*] **1.** any soothing or healing ointment for wounds, burns, etc. **2.** anything that soothes —*vt.* **salved, salv′ing** to soothe

**sal·ver** (sal′vər) *n.* [ult. < L. *salvare,* save] a tray

**sal·vo** (sal′vō) *n., pl.* **-vos, -voes** [< It. < L. *salve,* hail!] a discharge of a number of guns, in salute or at a target

**SAM** (sam) surface-to-air missile

**sam·ba** (sam′bə) *n.* [Port.] a Brazilian dance of African origin, or music for it —*vi.* to dance the samba

**same** (sām) *adj.* [< ON. *samr*] **1.** being the very one; identical **2.** alike in kind, quality, amount, etc. **3.** unchanged *[to keep the same look]* **4.** before-mentioned —*pron.* the same person or thing —*adv.* in like manner —**same′ness** *n.*

**†sam·iz·dat** (säm′iz dät′) *n.* [Russ., self-published] in the U.S.S.R., a system by which writings officially disapproved of are circulated secretly

**Sa·mo·a** (sə mō′ə) group of islands in the S. Pacific, seven of which constitute a U.S. possession (**American Samoa**) —**Sa·mo′an** *adj., n.*

**sam·o·var** (sam′ə vär′) *n.* [Russ.] a Russian metal urn with an internal tube for heating water in making tea

**sam·pan** (sam′pan) *n.* [< Chin.] a small boat used in China and Japan, rowed with a scull from the stern

**sam·ple** (sam′p'l) *n.* [see EXAMPLE] **1.** a part taken as representative of a whole thing, group, etc.; specimen **2.** an example —*vt.* **-pled, -pling** to take or test a sample of

**sam′pler** *n.* **1.** one who samples **2.** a cloth embroidered with designs, mottoes, etc. in different stitches

**Sam·son** (sam′s'n) *Bible* an Israelite with great strength

**Sam·u·el** (sam′yoo wəl) *Bible* a Hebrew judge and prophet

**sam·u·rai** (sam′ə rī′) *n., pl.* **-rai** [Jap.] a member of a military class in feudal Japan

---

**San An·to·ni·o** (san' ən tō'nē ō') city in SC Tex.: pop. 654,000

**san·a·to·ri·um** (san'ə tôr'ē əm) n. chiefly Brit. var. of SANITARIUM

**San Ber·nar·di·no** (bur'nər dē'nō) city in S Calif.: pop. 104,000

**sanc·ti·fy** (saŋk'tə fī') vt. -fied', -fy'ing [see SAINT & -FY] 1. to set apart as holy; consecrate 2. to make free from sin —**sanc'ti·fi·ca'tion** n.

**sanc·ti·mo·ni·ous** (saŋk'tə mō'nē əs) adj. pretending to be pious —**sanc'ti·mo'ni·ous·ly** adv.

**sanc·ti·mo·ny** n. [< L. sanctus, holy] pretended piety

**sanc·tion** (saŋk'shən) n. [see SAINT] 1. authorization 2. support; approval 3. [usually pl.] a punitive measure, as an official trade boycott, against a nation defying international law —vt. 1. to confirm 2. to authorize; permit

**sanc·ti·ty** (saŋk'tə tē) n., pl. -ties [< L. sanctus, holy] 1. holiness 2. sacredness

**sanc·tu·ar·y** (saŋk'choo wer'ē) n., pl. -ies [< L. sanctus, sacred] 1. a holy place; specif., a church, temple, etc. 2. a place of refuge or protection

**sanc·tum** (saŋk'təm) n. [L.] 1. a sacred place 2. a private room where one is not to be disturbed

**sand** (sand) n. [OE.] 1. loose, gritty grains of disintegrated rock, as on beaches, in deserts, etc. 2. [usually pl.] a tract of sand —vt. 1. to sprinkle or fill with sand 2. to smooth or polish, as with sandpaper —**sand'er** n.

**Sand** (sand), **George** (pseud. of Baronne Dudevant) 1804–76; Fr. woman novelist

**san·dal** (san'd'l) n. [< Gr. sandalon] 1. a shoe made of a sole fastened to the foot by straps 2. any of various low slippers or shoes

**san·dal·wood'** n. [ult. < Sans.] 1. the hard, sweet-smelling heartwood of an Asiatic tree 2. this tree

**sand'bag'** n. a bag filled with sand, used for ballast, protecting levees, etc. —vt. 1. to put sandbags in or around 2. to hit with a sandbag 3. [Colloq.] to force into doing something

**sand bar** a ridge of sand formed in a river or along a shore: also **sandbank**

**sand'blast'** n. a current of air or steam carrying sand at a high velocity, used in cleaning stone, etc. —vt. to clean with a sandblast

**sand'box'** n. a box containing sand, as for children to play in

**sand'hog'** n. a laborer in underground or underwater construction

**San Di·e·go** (san' dē ā'gō) seaport in S Calif.: pop. 697,000

**sand'lot'** adj. of or having to do with games, esp. baseball, played by amateurs, orig. on a sandy lot

**sand'man'** n. a mythical person supposed to make children sleepy by dusting sand in their eyes

**sand'pa'per** n. paper coated on one side with sand, used for smoothing and polishing —vt. to rub with sandpaper

**sand'pip'er** (-pī'pər) n. a small shore bird with a long, soft-tipped bill

**sand'stone'** n. a sedimentary rock composed of sand grains cemented together, as by silica

**sand'storm'** n. a windstorm in which large quantities of sand are blown about in the air

**sand·wich** (sand'wich, san'-) n. [< 4th Earl of Sandwich (1718–92)] slices of bread with meat, cheese, etc. between them —vt. to place between other persons, things, etc.

**sand·y** (san'dē) adj. -i·er, -i·est 1. of or like sand 2. pale reddish-yellow

**sane** (sān) adj. [L. sanus, healthy] 1. mentally healthy; rational 2. sound; sensible —**sane'ly** adv.

**San·for·ize** (san'fə rīz') vt. -ized', -iz'ing [< Sanford L. Cluett (1874–1968), the inventor] to preshrink (cloth) permanently by a patented process before making garments

**San Fran·cis·co** (san' frən sis'kō) seaport in W Calif.: pop. 716,000

**sang** (saŋ) pt. of SING

**sang-froid** (saŋ'frwä') n. [Fr., lit., cold blood] cool self-possession

**san·gui·nar·y** (saŋ'gwi ner'ē) adj. [see ff.] 1. accompanied by much bloodshed or murder 2. bloodthirsty

**san·guine** (saŋ'gwin) adj. [< L. sanguis, blood] 1. of the color of blood; ruddy 2. cheerful; confident

**san·i·tar·i·um** (san'ə ter'ē əm) n., pl. -ums, -a (-ə) [ModL. < L. sanitas, health] 1. a resort where people go to regain health 2. an institution for the care of invalids or convalescents

**san·i·tar·y** (san'ə ter'ē) adj. [< L. sanitas, health] 1. of or bringing about health or healthful conditions 2. in a clean, healthy condition

**sanitary napkin** an absorbent pad worn by women during menstruation

**san·i·ta·tion** (san'ə tā'shən) n. 1. the science and practice of effecting hygienic conditions 2. drainage and disposal of sewage

**san·i·tize** (san'ə tīz') vt. -tized', -tiz'ing to make sanitary

**san·i·ty** (san'ə tē) n. 1. the state of being sane 2. soundness of judgment

**San Jo·se** (san' hō zā') city in W Calif.: pop. 446,000

**San Juan** (san' hwän') capital of Puerto Rico: pop. 432,000

**sank** (saŋk) pt. of SINK

**San Ma·ri·no** (sän' mä rē'nō) country within E Italy: 23 sq. mi.; pop. 18,000

**sans** (sanz; Fr. sän) prep. [Fr. < L. sine] without

**San·skrit** (san'skrit) n. the classical literary language of ancient India: also **Sanscrit**

**San·ta An·a** (san'tə an'ə) city in SW Calif.: pop. 157,000

**San·ta Claus, San·ta Klaus** (san'tə klôz') [< Du. Sant Nikolaas, St. Nicholas] Folklore a fat, white-bearded, jolly old man in a red suit, who distributes gifts at Christmas

**San·ta Fe** (san'tə fā') capital of N.Mex.: pop. 41,000

**San·ti·a·go** (sän'tē ä'gō) capital of Chile: pop. 1,169,000

**São Pau·lo** (soun pou'loo) city in SE Brazil: pop. 3,825,000

**sap¹** (sap) *n.* [OE. *sæp*] **1.** the juice that circulates through a plant, bearing water, food, etc. **2.** vigor; energy **3.** [Slang] a fool —**sap′less** *adj.*

**sap²** (sap) *vt.* sapped, sap′ping [ < It. *zappe*, a hoe] **1.** to dig beneath; undermine **2.** to weaken; exhaust

**sa·pi·ent** (sā′pē ənt) *adj.* [ < L. *sapere*, to taste, know] full of knowledge; wise —**sa′pi·ence** *n.*

**sap·ling** (sap′liŋ) *n.* a young tree

**sap·phire** (saf′īr) *n.* [ < Sans. *śanipriya*] a hard precious stone of a clear, deep-blue corundum

**sap·py** (sap′ē) *adj.* -pi·er, -pi·est **1.** full of sap; juicy **2.** [Slang] foolish; silly —**sap′pi·ness** *n.*

**sap·ro·phyte** (sap′rə fīt′) *n.* [ < Gr. *sapros*, rotten + *phyton*, a plant] any plant that lives on dead or decaying organic matter, as some fungi

**sap′suck′er** *n.* a small American woodpecker that drills holes in trees and drinks the sap

**Sar·a·cen** (sar′ə s'n) *n.* formerly, any Arab or Moslem, esp. during the Crusades

**Sar·ah** (ser′ə) *Bible* the wife of Abraham and mother of Isaac

**sa·ran** (sə ran′) *n.* [a coinage] a thermoplastic substance used in various fabrics, wrapping material, etc.

**sar·casm** (sär′kaz'm) *n.* [ < Gr. *sarkazein*, to tear flesh] **1.** a taunting or caustic remark, generally ironical **2.** the making of such remarks —**sar·cas′tic** (-kas′tik) *adj.* —**sar·cas′ti·cal·ly** *adv.*

**sar·co·ma** (sär kō′mə) *n., pl.* -mas, -ma·ta (-mə tə) [ < Gr. *sarx*, flesh] a malignant tumor in connective tissue

**sar·coph·a·gus** (sär käf′ə gəs) *n., pl.* -gi (-jī′), -gus·es [ < Gr. *sarx*, flesh + *phagein*, to eat] limestone coffins hastened disintegration] a stone coffin, esp. one exposed to view, as in a tomb

**sar·dine** (sär dēn′) *n.* [ < L. *sarda*, a fish] any of various small ocean fishes preserved in cans for eating

**Sar·din·i·a** (sär din′ē ə) It. island in the Mediterranean, south of Corsica

**sar·don·ic** (sär dän′ik) *adj.* [ < Gr. *sardonios*, bitter] scornfully or bitterly sarcastic —**sar·don′i·cal·ly** *adv.*

**sa·ri** (sä′rē) *n.* [ < Sans.] an outer garment of Hindu women, a long cloth wrapped around the body

**sa·rong** (sə rôŋ′) *n.* [Malay *sārung*] a garment of men and women of the East Indies, etc., consisting of a cloth worn like a skirt

**sar·sa·pa·ril·la** (sas′pə ril′ə, särs′-) *n.* [ < Sp. *zarza*, bramble + *parra*, vine] **1.** a tropical American vine with fragrant roots **2.** a carbonated drink flavored with the dried roots

**sar·to·ri·al** (sär tôr′ē əl) *adj.* [ < LL. *sartor*, tailor] **1.** of tailors or their work **2.** of men's dress

**sash¹** (sash) *n.* [Ar. *shāsh*, muslin] an ornamental band, ribbon, etc. worn over the shoulder or around the waist

**sash²** (sash) *n.* [ < Fr. *chāssis*, a frame] a frame for holding the glass pane of a window or door, esp. a sliding frame

**sa·shay** (sa shā′) *vi.* [ < Fr. *chassé*, a dance step] [Colloq.] to walk or go, esp. casually

**Sas·katch·e·wan** (sas kach′ə wän′) province of SW Canada: 251,700 sq. mi.; pop. 955,000; cap. Regina: abbrev. **Sask.**

**sass** (sas) *n.* [var. of SAUCE] [Colloq.] impudent talk —*vt.* [Colloq.] to talk impudently to

**sas·sa·fras** (sas′ə fras′) *n.* [Sp. *sasafras*] **1.** a small tree having small bluish fruits **2.** its dried root bark used for flavoring

**sass·y** (sas′ē) *adj.* -i·er, -i·est [var. of SAUCY] [Colloq.] impudent; saucy

**sat** (sat) *pt. & pp. of* SIT

**Sat.** Saturday

**Sa·tan** (sāt′'n) [ < Heb. *sātān*, enemy] the Devil

**sa·tan·ic** (sā tan′ik, sə-) *adj.* like Satan; wicked —**sa·tan′i·cal·ly** *adv.*

**satch·el** (sach′əl) *n.* [ < L. *saccus*, a bag] a small bag for carrying clothes, books, etc.

**sate** (sāt) *vt.* sat′ed, sat′ing [prob. < L. *satiare*, fill full] **1.** to satisfy (an appetite, etc.) completely **2.** to satiate

**sa·teen** (sa tēn′) *n.* [ < SATIN] a cotton cloth made to imitate satin

**sat·el·lite** (sat′'l īt′) *n.* [ < L. *satelles*, an attendant] **1.** an attendant of some important person **2.** *a)* a small planet revolving around a larger one *b)* a man-made object put into orbit around the earth, moon, etc. **3.** a small state economically dependent on a larger one

**sa·ti·ate** (sā′shē āt′) *vt.* -at′ed, -at′ing [ < L. *satis*, sufficient] to provide with more than enough, so as to weary or disgust; glut

**sa·ti·e·ty** (sə tī′ə tē) *n.* a being satiated

**sat·in** (sat′'n) *n.* [ < Ar. *zaitūnī*, of *Zaitūn*, former name of a Chinese seaport] a fabric of silk, nylon, rayon, etc. with a smooth, glossy finish on one side —**sat′in·y** *adj.*

**sat′in·wood′** *n.* **1.** a smooth wood used in fine furniture **2.** any of a number of trees yielding such wood

**sat·ire** (sat′īr) *n.* [ < L. *satira*] **1.** a literary work in which vices, follies, etc. are held up to ridicule and contempt **2.** the use of ridicule, sarcasm, etc. to attack vices, follies, etc. —**sa·tir·i·cal** (sə tir′i k'l) *adj.* —**sat′i·rist** (-ə rist) *n.*

**sat·i·rize** (sat′ə rīz′) *vt.* -rized′, -riz′ing to attack with satire

**sat·is·fac·tion** (sat′is fak′shən) *n.* **1.** a satisfying or being satisfied **2.** something that satisfies; specif., *a)* anything that brings pleasure or contentment *b)* settlement of debt

SARI

**sat·is·fac·to·ry** (-tə rē) *adj.* good enough to fulfill a need, wish, etc.; satisfying —**sat'is·fac'to·ri·ly** *adv.*

**sat·is·fy** (sat'is fī') *vt.* -**fied'**, -**fy'ing** [< L. *satis*, enough + *facere*, make] **1.** to fulfill the needs or desires of; content **2.** to fulfill the requirements of **3.** to free from doubt; convince **4.** *a)* to give what is due to *b)* to discharge (a debt, etc.)

**sa·to·ri** (sä tôr'ē) *n.* [Jap.] *Buddhism* spiritual enlightenment

**sa·trap** (sā'trap, sat'rap) *n.* [< OPer.] a petty tyrant

**sat·u·rate** (sach'ə rāt') *vt.* -**rat'ed**, -**rat'ing** [< L. *satur*, full] **1.** to make thoroughly soaked **2.** to cause to be filled, charged, etc. with the most it can absorb —**sat'u·ra'tion** *n.*

**Sat·ur·day** (sat'ər dē, -dā') *n.* [< OE. *Sæterdæg*, Saturn's day] the seventh and last day of the week

**Saturday night special** [from their use in weekend crimes] [Slang] any small, cheap handgun

**Sat·urn** (sat'ərn) **1.** the Roman god of agriculture **2.** the second largest planet in the solar system, with three rings revolving about it: see PLANET

**sat·ur·nine** (sat'ər nīn') *adj.* [< supposed influence of planet Saturn] sluggish, gloomy, grave, etc

**sat·yr** (sāt'ər, sat'-) *n.* [< Gr. *satyros*] **1.** *Gr. Myth.* a lecherous woodland deity, represented as a man with a goat's legs, ears, and horns **2.** a lecherous man

**sat·y·ri·a·sis** (sat'ə rī'ə sis) *n.* [< Gr.: see prec.] uncontrollable desire by a man for sexual intercourse

**sauce** (sôs) *n.* [< L. *sal*, salt] **1.** a liquid or soft dressing served as a relish with food **2.** stewed or preserved fruit **3.** [Colloq.] impudence

**sauce·pan'** *n.* a small metal pot with a projecting handle, used for cooking

**sau·cer** (sô'sər) *n.* [see SAUCE] a small, round, shallow dish, esp. one designed to hold a cup

**sau·cy** (sô'sē) *adj.* -**ci·er**, -**ci·est** [SAUCE(E) + -Y²] **1.** rude; impudent **2.** pert; sprightly —**sau'ci·ly** *adv.* —**sau'ci·ness** *n.*

**Sa·u·di Arabia** (sä ōō'dē) kingdom occupying most of Arabia: c.617,000 sq. mi.; pop. 6,036,000

**sau·er·bra·ten** (sour'brät'n, zou'ər-) *n.* [G. *sauer*, sour + *braten*, roast] beef marinated before cooking

**sau·er·kraut** (sour'krout') *n.* [G. *sauer*, sour + *kraut*, cabbage] chopped cabbage fermented in brine

**Saul** (sôl) *Bible* first king of Israel

**sau·na** (sou'nə, sô'-) *n.* [Finn.] a Finnish bath with exposure to hot, dry air

**saun·ter** (sôn'tər) *vi.* [LME. *santren*, to muse] to walk about idly; stroll —*n.* a leisurely walk

**sau·sage** (sô'sij) *n.* [see SAUCE] pork or other meat, chopped fine, seasoned, and often stuffed into a casing

**sau·té** (sō tā', sô-) *vt.* -**téed'**, -**té'ing** [Fr. < *sauter*, to leap] to fry quickly with a little fat

**sau·terne** (sō tern') *n.* [< *Sauternes*, town in France] a white table wine

**sav·age** (sav'ij) *adj.* [< L. *silva*, a wood] **1.** wild; uncultivated [*a savage* jungle] **2.** fierce; untamed [*a savage* tiger] **3.** primitive; barbarous **4.** cruel; pitiless —*n.* **1.** a member of a primitive society **2.** a brutal or crude person —**sav'age·ly** *adv.* —**sav'age·ry** *n.*

**Sa·van·nah** (sə van'ə) seaport in SE Ga.: pop. 118,000

**sa·vant** (sə vänt', sav'ənt) *n.* [Fr. < *savoir*, know] a learned person

**save¹** (sāv) *vt.* **saved**, **sav'ing** [< L. *salvus*, safe] **1.** to rescue or preserve from harm or danger **2.** to preserve for future use **3.** to prevent loss or waste of [to *save* time] **4.** to prevent or lessen [to *save* expense] **5.** *Theol.* to deliver from sin —*vi.* **1.** to avoid expense, waste, etc. **2.** to store up money or goods —*n. Sports* an action that keeps an opponent from scoring or winning —**sav'er** *n.*

**save²** (sāv) *prep., conj.* [< OFr. *sauf*, safe] except; but

**sav·ing** (sā'viŋ) *adj.* that saves; specif., *a)* economizing or economical *b)* redeeming —*n.* **1.** [*often pl.* with *sing. v.*] any reduction in expense, time, etc. **2.** [*pl.*] sums of money saved

**sav·ior, sav·iour** (sāv'yər) *n.* [< LL. *salvare*, to save] one who saves —**the Saviour** (or Savior) Jesus Christ

**sa·voir-faire** (sav'wär fer') *n.* [Fr., to know (how) to do] ready knowledge of what to do or say in any situation

**sa·vor** (sā'vər) *n.* [< L. *sapor*] **1.** a particular taste or smell **2.** distinctive quality —*vi.* to have the distinctive taste, smell, or quality (*of*) —*vt.* to taste with delight Brit. sp. **savour**

**sa'vor·y** *adj.* -**i·er**, -**i·est 1.** pleasing to the taste or smell **2.** pleasant, agreeable, etc. Brit. sp. **savoury**

**sav·vy** (sav'ē) *n.* [alt. < Sp. *sabe* (*usted*), do (you) know?] [Slang] shrewdness or understanding

**saw¹** (sô) *n.* [OE. *sagu*] a cutting tool consisting of a thin metal blade or disk with sharp teeth —*vt.* to cut or shape with a saw —*vi.* **1.** to cut with or as a saw **2.** to be cut with a saw

**saw²** (sô) *n.* [OE. *sagu*] a maxim

**saw³** (sô) *pt.* of SEE¹

**saw'dust'** *n.* fine particles of wood formed in sawing wood

**sawed'-off'** *adj.* short or shortened

**saw'horse'** *n.* a rack on which wood is placed while being sawed

**saw'mill'** *n.* a factory where logs are sawed into boards

**saw'-toothed'** *adj.* having notches along the edge like the teeth of a saw

**saw·yer** (sô'yər) *n.* one whose work is sawing wood

**sax** (saks) *n. short form of* SAXOPHONE

**Sax·on** (sak's'n) *n.* **1.** any of an ancient Germanic people, some of whom settled in England **2.** an Anglo-Saxon **3.** any dialect of the Saxons

**sax·o·phone** (sak'sə fōn') *n.* [< A. J. *Sax*, 19th-c. Belgian inventor + -PHONE] a single-reed, keyed woodwind instrument with a metal body

**say** (sā) *vt.* **said**, **say'ing** [OE. *secgan*] **1.** to utter or speak **2.** to express in words; state **3.** to state positively or as an opinion **4.** to recite [to *say* one's prayers] **5.** to estimate; assume [he is, I'd *say*, forty] —*n.* **1.** a chance to speak [I had my *say*] **2.** authority, as to make a final decision: often with *the* —**that is to say** in other words

**say′·ing** *n.* something said; esp., an adage, proverb, or maxim

**say′·so′** *n.* [Colloq.] **1.** (one's) word, assurance, etc. **2.** right of decision

**Sb** [L. *stibium*] *Chem.* antimony

**S.C., SC** South Carolina

**s.c.** *Printing* small capitals

**scab** (skab) *n.* [< ON. *skabb*] **1.** a crust forming over a sore during healing **2.** a worker who refuses to join a union, or who replaces a striking worker —*vi.* **scabbed, scab′bing 1.** to become covered with a scab **2.** to act as a scab —**scab′by** *adj.* **-bi·er, -bi·est** —**scab′bi·ness** *n.*

**scab·bard** (skab′ərd) *n.* [< ? OHG. *scar*, sword + *bergan*, hide] a sheath for the blade of a sword, dagger, etc.

**sca·bies** (skā′bēz) *n.* [L., the itch] a contagious, itching skin disease caused by a mite that burrows under the skin to lay its eggs

**scab·rous** (skab′rəs, skāb′-) *adj.* [< L. *scabere*, to scratch] **1.** scaly or scabby **2.** indecent, shocking, etc.

**scads** (skadz) *n.pl.* [< ?] [Colloq.] a very large number or amount

**scaf·fold** (skaf′'ld, -ōld) *n.* [< OFr. *escafalt*] **1.** a temporary framework for supporting men working on a building, etc. **2.** a raised platform on which criminals are executed

**scaf′fold·ing** *n.* **1.** the materials forming a scaffold **2.** a scaffold

**scal·a·wag** (skal′ə wag′) *n.* [< ?] a scamp; rascal

**scald** (skôld) *vt.* [< L. *ex-*, intens. + *calidus*, hot] **1.** to burn with hot liquid or steam **2.** to heat almost to the boiling point **3.** to use boiling liquid on —*n.* a burn caused by scalding

**scale¹** (skāl) *n.* [< L. *scala*, ladder] **1.** *a)* a series of marks along a line used in measuring [the *scale* of a thermometer] *b)* any instrument so marked **2.** the proportion that a map, etc. bears to the thing it represents [a *scale* of one inch to a mile] **3.** *a)* a series of degrees classified by size, amount, etc. [a wage *scale*] *b)* any degree in such a series **4.** *Music* a sequence of tones, rising or falling in pitch, according to a system of intervals —*vt.* **scaled, scal′ing 1.** to climb up or over **2.** to make according to a scale —**scale down** (or **up**) to reduce (or increase) according to a fixed ratio

**scale²** (skāl) *n.* [< OFr. *escale*, shell] **1.** any of the thin, flat, horny plates covering many fishes, reptiles, etc. **2.** any thin, platelike layer or piece —*vt.* **scaled, scal′ing** to scrape scales from —*vi.* to flake or peel off in scales —**scal′y** *adj.* **-i·er, -i·est**

**scale³** (skāl) *n.* [< ON. *skal*, bowl] **1.** either pan of a balance **2.** [often *pl.*]

*a)* a balance *b)* any weighing machine —*vt.* **scaled, scal′ing** to weigh —**turn the scales** to decide or settle

**sca·lene** (skā lēn′, skā′lēn) *adj.* [< Gr. *skalēnos*, uneven] having unequal sides [a *scalene* triangle]

**scal·lion** (skal′yən) *n.* [< L. (*caepa*) *Ascalonia*, (onion of) Ascalon (Philistine city)] any of various onions, as the leek or a green onion with an almost bulbless root

**scal·lop** (skäl′əp, skal′-) *n.* [< OFr. *escalope*] **1.** *a)* any of various edible mollusks with two curved, hinged shells *b)* one of the shells **2.** any of a series of curves, etc. forming an ornamental edge —*vt.* **1.** to cut the edge of in scallops **2.** to bake with a milk sauce and bread crumbs

 SCALLOP

**scalp** (skalp) *n.* [< Scand.] the skin on the top and back of the head, usually covered with hair —*vt.* **1.** to cut or tear the scalp from **2.** [Colloq.] to buy (theater tickets, etc.) and resell them at higher prices —**scalp′er** *n.*

**scal·pel** (skal′pəl) *n.* [< L. *scalprum*, a knife] a small, sharp, straight knife used in surgery, etc.

**scamp** (skamp) *n.* [< It. *scampare*, flee] a mischievous fellow; rascal

**scam·per** (skam′pər) *vi.* [see prec.] to run or go quickly —*n.* a scampering

**scam·pi** (skam′pē) *n., pl.* **-pi, -pies** [It.] a large, greenish, edible prawn

**scan** (skan) *vt.* **scanned, scan′ning** [< L. *scandere*, climb] **1.** to analyze (verse) by marking the metrical feet **2.** to look at closely **3.** to glance at quickly —*vi.* to conform to metrical principles: said of verse —*n.* the act or an instance of scanning

**Scan., Scand.** Scandinavia(n)

**scan·dal** (skan′d'l) *n.* [< Gr. *skandalon*, a snare] **1.** anything that offends moral feelings and leads to disgrace **2.** shame, outrage, etc. caused by this **3.** disgrace **4.** malicious gossip

**scan′dal·ize′** *vt.* **-ized′, -iz′ing** to outrage the moral feelings of by improper conduct —**scan′dal·iz′er** *n.*

**scan′dal·mon′ger** (-muŋ′gər,-mäŋ′-) *n.* one who spreads scandal, or gossip

**scan′dal·ous** *adj.* **1.** causing scandal; shameful **2.** spreading slander —**scan′dal·ous·ly** *adv.*

**Scan·di·na·vi·a** (skan′də nā′vē ə) region including Norway, Sweden, Denmark, and, sometimes, Iceland

**Scan′di·na′vi·an** *adj.* of Scandinavia, its people, languages, etc. —*n.* **1.** any of the people of Scandinavia **2.** the subbranch of the Germanic languages spoken by them

**scant** (skant) *adj.* [< ON. *skammr*, short] **1.** inadequate; meager **2.** not quite up to full measure

**scant′y** *adj.* **-i·er, -i·est 1.** barely sufficient **2.** insufficient; not enough —**scant′i·ly** *adv.* —**scant′i·ness** *n.*

**scape·goat** (skāp′gōt′) n. [ < ESCAPE + GOAT: see Lev. 16:7-26] one who bears the blame for mistakes of others

**scape·grace′** n. [ < ESCAPE + GRACE] a graceless rogue; scamp

**scap·u·la** (skap′yoo lə) n., pl. **-lae′** (-lē′), **-las** [L.] the shoulder blade

**scar** (skär) n. [ < Gr. eschara, orig., fireplace] a mark left after a wound, burn, etc. has healed —vt. **scarred**, **scar′ring** to mark as with a scar —vi. to form a scar in healing

**scar·ab** (skar′əb) n. [ < L. scarabaeus] 1. a large, black beetle 2. a carved image of such a beetle

**scarce** (skers) adj. [ult. < L. excerpere, pick out] 1. not common; rarely seen 2. not plentiful; hard to get —make oneself scarce [Colloq.] to go or stay away —scarce′ness n.

**scarce′ly** adv. 1. hardly; only just 2. probably not or certainly not

**scar·ci·ty** (sker′sə tē) n., pl. **-ties** 1. a being scarce; inadequate supply; dearth 2. rarity; uncommonness

**scare** (sker) vt. **scared**, **scar′ing** [ < ON. skjarr, timid] to fill with sudden fear —vi. to become frightened —n. a sudden fear —scare away (or off) to drive away (or off) by frightening —scare up [Colloq.] to produce or gather quickly

**scare′crow′** n. a human figure made with sticks, old clothes, etc., put in a field to scare birds from crops

**scarf** (skärf) n., pl. **scarfs, scarves** (skärvz) [ < OFr. escharpe, purse hung from the neck] 1. a piece of cloth worn about the neck, head, etc. 2. a long, narrow covering for a table, etc.

**scar·i·fy** (skar′ə fī′) vt. **-fied′, -fy′ing** [ < L. scarifare] to make small cuts in (the skin, etc.) —scar′i·fi·ca′tion n.

**scar·let** (skär′lit) n. [ < ML. scarlatum] very bright red —adj. 1. of this color 2. sinful; specif., whorish

**scarlet fever** an acute contagious disease characterized by sore throat, fever, and a scarlet rash

**scar·y** (sker′ē) adj. **-i·er, -i·est** [Colloq.] 1. frightening 2. easily frightened —scar′i·ness n.

**scat¹** (skat) vi. **scat′ted, scat′ting** [? a hiss + CAT] [Colloq.] to go away: usually in the imperative

**scat²** (skat) adj. [ < ?] Jazz using improvised, meaningless syllables in singing —n. such singing —vi. **scat′ted, scat′ting** to sing scat

**scath·ing** (skā′thiŋ) adj. [ < ON. skathi, harm] harsh or caustic [scathing words] —scath′ing·ly adv.

**sca·tol·o·gy** (skə täl′ə jē) n. [ < Gr. skōr, excrement + -LOGY] obsession with excrement or excretion, as in literature —scat′o·log′i·cal adj.

**scat·ter** (skat′ər) vt. [ME. skateren] 1. to throw here and there; sprinkle 2. to separate and drive in many directions; disperse —vi. to separate and go off in several directions

**scat′ter·brain′** n. one who is incapable of concentrated thinking

**scatter rug** a small rug

**scav·eng·er** (skav′in jər) n. [ < ONormFr. escauwer, inspect] 1. one who gathers things discarded by others 2. any animal that eats refuse and decaying matter —scav′enge (-inj) vt., vi. -enged, -eng·ing

**sce·nar·i·o** (si ner′ē ō′) n., pl. **-os′** [see ff.] 1. the working script of a motion picture, television play, etc. 2. an outline for any planned series of events, real or imagined —sce·nar′-ist n.

**scene** (sēn) n. [ < Gr. skēnē, stage] 1. the place where an event occurs 2. the setting of a play, story, etc. 3. a division of a play, usually part of an act 4. a unit of action in a motion picture, story, etc. 5. same as SCENERY (sense 1) 6. a view of people or places 7. a display of strong feeling [to make a scene] 8. [Colloq.] the locale for a specified activity

**scen·er·y** (sē′nər ē) n. 1. painted screens, backdrops, etc. used on the stage to represent places, as in a play 2. the features of a landscape

**sce·nic** (sē′nik) adj. 1. of stage scenery 2. a) of natural scenery b) having beautiful scenery —sce′ni·cal·ly adv.

**scent** (sent) vt. [ < L. sentire, to feel] 1. to smell 2. to get a hint of 3. to fill with an odor; perfume —n. 1. an odor 2. the sense of smell 3. a perfume 4. an odor left by an animal, by which it is tracked —scent′ed adj.

**scep·ter** (sep′tər) n. [ < Gr. skēptron, staff] a staff held by a ruler as a symbol of sovereignty: chiefly Brit. sp. **sceptre**

**scep·tic** (skep′tik) n., adj. chiefly Brit. sp. of SKEPTIC —scep′ti·cal adj. —scep′ti·cism n.

**sched·ule** (skej′ool; Brit. shed′yool) n. [ < L. scheda, strip of papyrus] 1. a list of details 2. a list of times of recurring events, projected operations, etc.; timetable 3. a timed plan for a project —vt. **-uled, -ul·ing** 1. to place in a schedule 2. to plan for a certain time

**Scheduled Castes** the groups of people in India formerly untouchables

**sche·mat·ic** (skē mat′ik) adj. of or like a scheme, diagram, etc.

**scheme** (skēm) n. [ < Gr. schēma, a form] 1. a) a systematic program for attaining some object b) a secret plan; plot 2. an orderly combination of things on a definite plan 3. a diagram —vt., vi. **schemed, schem′ing** to devise or plot —schem′er n.

**scher·zo** (sker′tsō) n., pl. **-zos, -zi** (-tsē) [It., a jest] a lively movement, as of a symphony, in 3/4 time

**schism** (siz′'m) n. [ < Gr. schizein, cleave] a split, as in a church, because of difference of opinion, doctrine, etc. —schis·mat′ic (-mat′ik) adj.

**schist** (shist) n. [ < Gr. schistos, easily cleft] a crystalline rock easily split into layers

**schiz·o·phre·ni·a** (skit′sə frē′nē ə) n. [ < Gr. schizein, cleave + phrēn, mind] a mental disorder characterized by separation between thought and emotions, by delusions, bizarre behavior, etc. —schiz′oid (-soid), schiz′o·phren′ic (-fren′ik) adj., n.

**schle·miel** (shlə mēl′) *n.* [Yid.] [Slang] a bungling person who habitually fails or is easily victimized

**schlep, schlepp** (shlep) *n.* [via Yid. < G. *schleppen,* to drag] [Slang] an ineffectual person

**schlock** (shläk) *n.* [via Yid. < G. *schlacke,* dregs] [Slang] anything cheap or inferior; trash —*adj.* [Slang] cheap; inferior

**schmaltz** (shmälts) *n.* [via Yid. < G. *schmalz,* rendered fat] [Slang] highly sentimental music, literature, etc.

**schmo** (shmō) *n., pl.* **schmoes, schmos** [< Yid.] [Slang] a foolish or stupid person: also sp. **schmoe**

**schnapps** (shnäps) *n., pl.* **schnapps** [G., a nip < Du. *snaps,* a gulp] strong alcoholic liquor: also sp. **schnaps**

**schnau·zer** (shnou′zər) *n.* [G. < *schnauzen,* to snarl] a small terrier with a wiry coat

**schnoz·zle** (shnäz′'l) *n.* [via Yid. < G. *schnauze*] [Slang] the nose: also **schnoz**

**schol·ar** (skäl′ər) *n.* [< L. *schola,* a school] 1. a learned person 2. a student or pupil —**schol′ar·ly** *adj.*

**schol′ar·ship′** *n.* 1. the quality of knowledge a student shows 2. the systematized knowledge of a scholar 3. a gift of money, etc. to help a student

**scho·las·tic** (skə las′tik) *adj.* [see ff.] of schools, colleges, students, etc.; educational; academic

**school¹** (skōōl) *n.* [< Gr. *scholē*] 1. a place or institution, with its buildings, etc., for teaching and learning 2. all of its students and teachers 3. a regular session of teaching 4. formal education; schooling 5. a particular division of a university 6. a group following the same beliefs, methods, etc. —*vt.* 1. to train; teach 2. to discipline or control —*adj.* of a school or schools

**school²** (skōōl) *n.* [Du., a crowd] a group of fish, etc. swimming together

**school board** a group of people in charge of local public schools

**school′book′** *n.* a textbook

**school′boy′** *n.* a boy attending school —**school′girl′** *n.fem.*

**school′house′** *n.* a building used as a school

**school′ing** *n.* training or education; esp., formal instruction at school

**school′marm′** (-märm′, -mäm′) *n.* [Colloq.] a woman schoolteacher, hence any person, who tends to be prudish and pedantic: also **school′ma′am′** (-mäm′, -mam′)

**school′mas′ter** *n.* a man who teaches in a school: an old-fashioned term —**school′mis′tress** *n.fem.*

**school′mate′** *n.* a person going to the same school at the same time as another: also **school′fel′low**

**school′room′** *n.* a room in which pupils are taught, as in a school

**school′teach′er** *n.* one who teaches in a school

**school′yard′** *n.* the ground about a school, used as a playground, etc.

**school year** the part of a year when school is in session

**schoon·er** (skōō′nər) *n.* [< ?] 1. a ship with two or more masts, rigged fore and aft 2. a large beer glass

**Schu·bert** (shōō′bərt), **Franz** (fränts) 1797–1828; Austrian composer

**schuss** (shoos) *n.* [G., lit., shot] *Skiing* a straight, fast run downhill —*vi.* to do a schuss

**schuss′boom′er** (-bōōm′ər) *n.* a skier, esp. one who schusses expertly

**schwa** (shwä) *n.* [G. < Heb. *sh′wā*] 1. the neutral vowel sound of most unstressed syllables in English, as of *a* in *ago* 2. the symbol (ə) for this

**sci·at·ic** (sī at′ik) *adj.* [see ff.] of or in the hip or its nerves

**sci·at·i·ca** (sī at′i kə) *n.* [< Gr. *ischion,* hip] any painful condition in the hip or thighs; esp., neuritis of the long nerve (**sciatic nerve**) down the back of the thigh

**sci·ence** (sī′əns) *n.* [< L. *scire,* know] 1. systematized knowledge derived from observation, study, etc. 2. a branch of knowledge, esp. one that systematizes facts, principles, and methods 3. skill or technique

**science fiction** highly imaginative fiction typically involving some actual or projected scientific phenomenon

**sci·en·tif·ic** (sī′ən tif′ik) *adj.* 1. of or dealing with science 2. based on, or using, the principles and methods of science; systematic and exact —**sci·en·tif′i·cal·ly** *adv.*

**sci′en·tist** *n.* a specialist in science, as in biology, chemistry, etc.

**sci-fi** (sī′fī′) *adj., n. clipped form of* SCIENCE FICTION

**scim·i·tar, scim·i·ter** (sim′ə tər) *n.* [It. *scimitarra*] a short, curved sword used by Turks, Arabs, etc.

**scin·til·la** (sin til′ə) *n.* [L.] 1. a spark 2. a particle; the least trace

**scin·til·late** (sin′t'l āt′) *vi.* -**lat′ed, -lat′ing** [< L. *scintilla,* a spark] 1. to sparkle or twinkle 2. to be brilliant and witty —**scin′til·la′tion** *n.*

**sci·on** (sī′ən) *n.* [< OFr. *cion*] 1. a shoot or bud of a plant, esp. one for grafting 2. a descendant; heir

**scis·sor** (siz′ər) *vt.* [< ff.] to cut, cut off, or cut out with scissors —*n. same as* SCISSORS, esp. in adjectival use

**scis·sors** (siz′ərz) *n.pl.* [< LL. *cisorium,* cutting tool] [*also with sing. v.*] a cutting instrument with two opposing blades pivoted together so that they can work against each other: also **pair of scissors**

**scle·ro·sis** (skli rō′sis) *n., pl.* -**ses** (-sēz) [< Gr. *sklēros,* hard] an abnormal hardening of body tissues —**scle·rot′ic** (-rät′ik) *adj.*

**scoff** (skôf, skäf) *n.* [prob. < Scand.] an expression of scorn or derision —*vt., vi.* to mock or jeer (at) —**scoff′er** *n.*

**scoff'law'** n. [Colloq.] one who flouts traffic laws, liquor laws, etc.

**scold** (skōld) n. [< ON. skald, poet (prob. because of satirical verses)] a woman who habitually uses abusive language —vt. to find fault with angrily; rebuke —vi. 1. to find fault angrily 2. to use abusive language —**scold'ing** adj./n.

**scol·lop** (skäl'əp) n., vt. var. of SCALLOP

**sconce** (skäns) n. [ult. < L. absconsus, hidden] a wall bracket for candles

**scone** (skōn) n. [Scot.] a biscuit, often quadrant-shaped and sweetened

**scoop** (skōop) n. [< MDu. schope, bucket, schoppe, a shovel] 1. any of various small, shovellike utensils, as for taking up flour, ice cream, etc. 2. the deep bucket of a dredge, etc. 3. the act or motion of scooping 4. the amount scooped up at one time 5. [Colloq.] a) advantage gained by being first, as in publishing a news item b) such a news item —vt. 1. to take up or out as with a scoop 2. to hollow (out) 3. [Colloq.] to publish news before (a rival)

**scoot** (skōot) vi., vt. [prob. < ON. skjóta, to shoot] [Colloq.] to hurry (off)

**scoot'er** n. 1. a child's two-wheeled vehicle moved by pushing one foot against the ground 2. a similar vehicle propelled by a motor: in full **motor scooter**

**scope** (skōp) n. [< Gr. skopos, watcher] 1. the extent of the mind's grasp 2. range or extent of action, inquiry, inclusion, etc. 3. room or opportunity for freedom of action or thought

**-scope** (skōp) [< Gr. skopein, to see] a combining form meaning an instrument, etc. for observing [telescope]

**scor·bu·tic** (skôr byōot'ik) adj. [< ModL. < Russ. skórbnut, wither] of, like, or having scurvy

**scorch** (skôrch) vt. [< ? Scand.] 1. to burn slightly or superficially 2. to parch by intense heat —vi. to become scorched —n. a superficial burn

**score** (skōr) n. [< ON. skor] 1. a scratch, mark, notch, incision, etc. 2. an account or debt 3. a grievance one seeks to settle 4. a reason or motive 5. the number of points made, as in a game 6. a grade, as on a test 7. a) twenty people or things b) [pl.] very many 8. a copy of a musical composition, showing all parts for the instruments or voices 9. [Colloq.] the real facts [to know the score] —vt. **scored, scor'ing** 1. to mark with cuts, lines, etc. 2. a) to make (runs, points, etc.) in a game b) to record the score of 3. to achieve [score a success] 4. to evaluate, as in testing 5. Music to arrange in a score —vi. 1. to make points, as in a game 2. to keep the score of a game 3. to gain an advantage, a success, etc. —**scor'er** n.

**score'board'** n. a large board posting scores, etc., as in a stadium

**score'less** adj. having scored no points

**scorn** (skôrn) n. [< OFr. escharnir, to scorn] extreme, often indignant, contempt —vt. 1. to regard with scorn 2.

to refuse or reject with scorn —**scorn'ful** adj. —**scorn'ful·ly** adv.

**Scor·pi·o** (skôr'pē ō') [L., scorpion] the eighth sign of the zodiac

**scor'pi·on** (-ən) n. [< Gr. skorpios] an arachnid with a long tail ending in a poisonous sting

**Scot** (skät) n. a native or inhabitant of Scotland

**Scot.** 1. Scotland 2. Scottish

**Scotch** (skäch) adj. Scottish —n. 1. Scottish 2. same as SCOTCH WHISKY

**scotch** (skäch) vt. [prob. < OFr. coche, a nick] 1. to maim 2. to put an end to; stifle [to scotch a rumor]

**Scotch grain** a coarse, pebble-grained finish given to heavy leather

**Scotch'man** (-mən) n., pl. -men var. of SCOTSMAN

**Scotch tape** [< Scotch, a trademark] a thin, transparent adhesive tape

**Scotch whisky** whisky distilled in Scotland from malted barley

**scot-free** (skät'frē') adj. [< earlier scot, a tax] unharmed or unpunished

**Scot·land** (skät'lənd) division of the United Kingdom, north of England: 30,405 sq. mi.; pop. 5,187,000

**Scotland Yard** the London police headquarters, esp. its detective bureau

**Scots** (skäts) adj., n. Scottish

**Scots'man** (-mən) n., pl. -men a native or inhabitant of Scotland: Scotsman or Scot is preferred to Scotchman in Scotland

**Scot·tie, Scot·ty** (skät'ē) n., pl. -ties [Colloq.] same as SCOTTISH TERRIER

**Scot·tish** (skät'ish) adj. of Scotland, its people, their English dialect, etc.: Scottish is formal usage, but with some words, Scotch is used (e.g., tweed, whisky), with others, Scots (e.g., law) —n. the English spoken in Scotland —**the Scottish** the Scottish people

**Scottish** (or **Scotch**) **terrier** a short-legged terrier with wiry hair

**scoun·drel** (skoun'drəl) n. [prob. ult. < L. ab(s)-, from + condere, to hide] a mean, immoral, or wicked person

**scour¹** (skour) vt., vi. [< ? L. ex-, intens. + cura, care] 1. to clean by rubbing hard, as with abrasives 2. to clean or clear out as by a flow of water

**scour²** (skour) vt. [< L. ex-, out + currere, to run] to pass over quickly, or range over, as in search [to scour a library for a book]

**scourge** (skurj) n. [< L. ex, off + corrigia, a whip] 1. a whip 2. any cause of serious affliction —vt. **scourged, scourg'ing** 1. to whip or flog 2. to punish or afflict severely

**scout** (skout) n. [< L. auscultare, listen] 1. a person, plane, etc. sent to spy out the enemy's strength, actions, etc. 2. a person sent out to survey a competitor, find new talent, etc. 3. a Boy Scout or Girl Scout —vt., vi. 1. to reconnoiter 2. to go in search of (something)

**scout'ing** n. 1. the act of one who scouts 2. the activities of the Boy Scouts or Girl Scouts

**scout'mas'ter** n. the adult leader of a troop of Boy Scouts

**scow** (skou) *n.* [Du. *schouw*] a large, flat-bottomed boat used for carrying loads, often towed by a tug

**scowl** (skoul) *vi.* [prob. < Scand.] to look angry, sullen, etc., as by contracting the eyebrows —*n.* a scowling look —**scowl′er** *n.*

**scrab·ble** (skrab′'l) *vi.* -**bled**, -**bling** [< Du. *schrabben*, to scrape] 1. to scratch, scrape, etc. as though looking for something 2. to struggle

**scrag·gly** (skrag′lē) *adj.* -**gli·er**, -**gli·est** [prob. < ON.] uneven, ragged, etc. in growth or form

**scram** (skram) *vi.* **scrammed**, **scram′ming** [< ff.] [Slang] to get out

**scram·ble** (skram′b'l) *vi.* -**bled**, -**bling** [< ?] 1. to climb, crawl, etc. hurriedly 2. to scuffle or struggle for something —*vt.* 1. to mix haphazardly 2. to stir and cook (slightly beaten eggs) 3. to make (transmitted signals) unintelligible in transit —*n.* 1. a hard climb or advance 2. a disorderly struggle, as for something prized

**Scran·ton** (skrant′'n) city in NE Pa.; pop. 104,000

**scrap**[1] (skrap) *n.* [< ON. *skrap*] 1. a small piece; fragment 2. discarded material 3. [*pl.*] bits of food —*adj.* 1. in the form of pieces, leftovers, etc. 2. used and discarded —*vt.* **scrapped**, **scrap′ping** 1. to make into scraps 2. to discard; junk —**scrap′per** *n.*

**scrap**[2] (skrap) *n.*, *vi.* **scrapped**, **scrap′ping** [< ?] [Colloq.] fight or quarrel —**scrap′per** *n.* —**scrap′py** *adj.* -**i·er**, -**i·est** —**scrap′pi·ness** *n.*

**scrap′book′** *n.* a book in which to mount clippings, pictures, etc.

**scrape** (skrāp) *vt.* **scraped**, **scrap′ing** [< ON. *skrapa*] 1. to make smooth or clean by rubbing with a tool or abrasive 2. to remove in this way (with *off*, *out*, etc.) 3. to scratch or abrade 4. to gather slowly and with difficulty [to *scrape* up some money] —*vi.* 1. to rub against something harshly; grate 2. to manage to get by (with *through*, *along*, *by*) —*n.* 1. a scraping 2. a scraped place 3. a harsh, grating sound 4. a predicament —**scrap′er** *n.*

**scrap′heap′** (-hēp′) *n.* a pile of discarded material or things —**throw** (or **toss**, **cast**, etc.) **on the scrapheap** to get rid of as useless

**scratch** (skrach) *vt.* [LME. *scracchen*] 1. to scrape or cut the surface of slightly 2. to tear or dig with the nails or claws 3. to scrape lightly to relieve itching 4. to scrape with a grating noise 5. to write hurriedly or carelessly 6. to strike out (writing, etc.) 7. *Sports* to withdraw (a contestant, etc.) —*vi.* 1. to use nails or claws in digging, wounding, etc. 2. to scrape —*n.* 1. a scratching 2. a mark, tear, etc. made by scratching 3. a grating or scraping sound —*adj.* used for hasty notes, figuring, etc. [*scratch* paper] —**from scratch** from nothing; without advantage —**up to scratch** [Colloq.]

up to standard —**scratch′y** *adj.* -**i·er**, -**i·est** —**scratch′i·ly** *adv.* —**scratch′i·ness** *n.*

**scrawl** (skrôl) *vt.*, *vi.* [< ?] to write or draw hastily, carelessly, etc. —*n.* sprawling, often illegible handwriting

**scraw·ny** (skrô′nē) *adj.* -**ni·er**, -**ni·est** [prob. < Scand.] very thin —**scrawn′i·ness** *n.*

**scream** (skrēm) *vi.* [ME. *screamen*] 1. to utter a shrill, piercing cry in fright, pain, etc. 2. to shout, laugh, etc. wildly —*vt.* to utter as with a scream —*n.* 1. a sharp, piercing cry or sound 2. [Colloq.] a very funny person or thing

**screech** (skrēch) *vi.*, *vt.* [< ON. *skrækja*] to utter (with) a shrill, high-pitched sound —*n.* such a sound —**screech′y** *adj.* -**i·er**, -**i·est**

**screen** (skrēn) *n.* [< OFr. *escren*] 1. a curtain or partition used to separate, conceal, etc. 2. anything that shields, conceals, etc. [a smoke *screen*] 3. a coarse mesh of wire, etc., used as a sieve 4. a frame covered with a mesh [a window *screen*] 5. a surface on which motion pictures, etc. are projected 6. the motion-picture industry —*vt.* 1. to conceal or protect, as with a screen 2. to sift through a screen 3. to separate according to skills, etc. 4. to show (a motion picture, etc.) on a screen

**screen′play′** *n.* a story written in a form suitable for a motion picture

**screw** (skrŏŏ) *n.* [< MFr. *escroue*, hole in which a screw turns] 1. a cylindrical or conical metal piece threaded in an advancing spiral, for fastening things by being turned 2. any spiral thing like this 3. anything operating or threaded like a screw, as a screw propeller —*vt.* 1. to twist; turn 2. to fasten, tighten, etc. as with a screw 3. to contort —*vi.* 1. to go together or come apart by being turned like a screw [the lid *screws* on] 2. to twist or turn —**put the screws on** (or **to**) to subject to great pressure —**screw up** [Slang] to bungle

**screw′ball′** *n.* [Slang] an erratic, irrational, or unconventional person

**screw′driv′er** *n.* a tool used for turning screws

**screw′y** *adj.* -**i·er**, -**i·est** [Slang] 1. crazy 2. peculiar; eccentric

**scrib·ble** (skrib′'l) *vt.*, *vi.* -**bled**, -**bling** [< L. *scribere*, write] 1. to write carelessly, hastily, etc. 2. to make meaningless or illegible marks (on) —*n.* scribbled writing

**scribe** (skrīb) *n.* [< L. *scribere*, write] 1. one who copied manuscripts before the invention of printing 2. a writer

**scrim** (skrim) *n.* [< ?] 1. a light, sheer, loosely woven cotton or linen cloth 2. such a cloth used as a stage backdrop or semitransparent curtain

**scrim·mage** (skrim′ij) *n.* [< SKIR-MISH] *Football* 1. the play that follows the pass from center 2. a practice game —*vi.* -**maged**, -**mag·ing** to take part in a scrimmage —**line of scrimmage** *Football* an imaginary line along which the teams line up for play

**scrimp** (skrimp) *vt., vi.* [ < ? Scand.] to be sparing or frugal (with)

**scrip** (skrip) *n.* [ < ff.] a certificate of a right to receive something, as stocks, money, etc.

**script** (skript) *n.* [ < L. *scribere,* write] 1. handwriting 2. a copy of the text of a play, film, etc.

**Scrip·ture** (skrip'chər) *n.* [see prec.] 1. [*often pl.*] *a)* the Jewish Bible: see OLD TESTAMENT *b)* the Christian Bible; Old and New Testaments 2. [s-] any sacred writing —**scrip'tur·al** *adj.*

**scrod** (skräd) *n.* [prob. < MDu. *schrode,* strip] a young codfish or haddock, esp. one filleted for cooking

**scrof·u·la** (skräf'yə lə) *n.* [ < L. *scrofa,* a sow] tuberculosis of the lymphatic glands, esp. of the neck —**scrof'u·lous** *adj.*

**scroll** (skrōl) *n.* [ < ME. *scrowe*] 1. a roll of parchment, paper, etc. usually with writing on it 2. an ornamental design in coiled or spiral form

SCROLL

**scro·tum** (skrōt'əm) *n., pl.* -**ta** (-ə), -**tums** [L.] the pouch of skin containing the testicles

**scrounge** (skrounj) *vt.* **scrounged,** **scroung'ing** [ < ?] [Colloq.] 1. to get by begging or sponging 2. to pilfer —*vi.* [Colloq.] to seek (around) for something —**scroung'er** *n.*

**scrub¹** (skrub) *n.* [ME., var. of *shrubbe,* shrub] 1. a thick growth of stunted trees or bushes 2. any person or thing smaller than the usual, or inferior 3. *Sports* a substitute player —*adj.* small, stunted, inferior, etc. —**scrub'by** *adj.* **-bi·er, -bi·est**

**scrub²** (skrub) *vt., vi.* **scrubbed,** **scrub'bing** [prob. < Scand.] 1. to clean or wash by rubbing hard 2. to rub hard —*n.* a scrubbing

**scrub'wom'an** *n., pl.* **-wom'en** a woman who does cleaning, as in offices

**scruff** (skruf) *n.* [ < ON. *skrufr,* a tuft] the nape of the neck

**scruff·y** (skruf'ē) *adj.* **-i·er, -i·est** [ < SCURF + -Y²] shabby; unkempt

**scrump·tious** (skrump'shəs) *adj.* [ < SUMPTUOUS] [Colloq.] very pleasing, esp. to the taste

**scrunch** (skrunch) *vt., vi.* [ < CRUNCH] 1. to crunch, crush, etc. 2. to huddle, squeeze, etc. —*n.* a crunching or crumpling sound

**scru·ple** (skrōō'p'l) *n.* [ < L. *scrupulus,* small stone] 1. a very small quantity 2. a doubt arising from difficulty in deciding what is right, proper, etc. —*vt., vi.* **-pled, -pling** to hesitate (at) from doubt

**scru'pu·lous** (-pyə ləs) *adj.* 1. having or showing scruples; conscientiously honest 2. careful of details; precise —**scru'pu·los'i·ty** (-läs'ə tē) *n.* —**scru'pu·lous·ly** *adv.*

**scru·ti·nize** (skrōōt'n īz') *vt.*

**-nized', -niz'ing** to examine closely

**scru·ti·ny** (-'n ē) *n., pl.* **-nies** [ < L. *scrutari,* examine] 1. a close examination or watch 2. a lengthy, searching look

**scu·ba** (skōō'bə) *n.* [*s(elf)-c(ontained) u(nderwater) b(reathing) a(pparatus)*] a diver's equipment with compressed-air tanks for breathing under water

**scud** (skud) *vi.* **scud'ded,** **scud'ding** [prob. < ON.] 1. to move swiftly 2. to be driven before the wind —*n.* 1. a scudding 2. clouds, etc. driven by wind

**scuff** (skuf) *vt., vi.* [prob. < ON. *skufa,* to shove] 1. to wear or get a rough place on the surface (of) 2. to drag (the feet) —*n.* 1. a worn or rough spot 2. a flat-heeled house slipper with no back upper part

**scuf·fle** (skuf'l) *vi.* **-fled, -fling** [ < prec.] 1. to struggle or fight in rough confusion 2. to drag the feet —*n.* 1. a rough, confused fight 2. a shuffling of feet

**scull** (skul) *n.* [ME. *skulle*] 1. an oar worked from side to side over the stern of a boat 2. a light rowboat for racing —*vt., vi.* to propel with a scull

**scul·ler·y** (skul'ər ē) *n., pl.* **-ies** [ < L. *scutella,* tray] a room where the kitchen utensils, etc. are cleaned

**scul·lion** (skul'yən) *n.* [ult. < L. *scopa,* a broom] [Archaic] a servant doing rough kitchen work

**sculpt** *vt., vi.* same as SCULPTURE

**sculp·tor** (skulp'tər) *n.* an artist who creates works of sculpture

**sculp·ture** (skulp'chər) *n.* [ < L. *sculpere,* carve] 1. the art of forming stone, clay, wood, etc. into statues, figures, etc. 2. a work or works of sculpture —*vt., vi.* **-tured, -tur·ing** 1. to cut, carve, chisel, etc. (statues, figures, etc.) 2. to make or form like sculpture —**sculp'tur·al** *adj.*

**scum** (skum) *n.* [ < MDu. *schum*] 1. a thin layer of impurities on the top of a liquid 2. refuse 3. despicable people —*vi.* **scummed, scum'ming** to become covered with scum —**scum'my** *adj.* **-mi·er, -mi·est**

**scup·per** (skup'ər) *n.* [ < ?] an opening in a ship's side to let water run off the deck

**scurf** (skurf) *n.* [ < ON.] 1. little, dry scales shed by the skin, as dandruff 2. any scaly coating —**scurf'y** *adj.*

**scur·ril·ous** (skur'ə ləs) *adj.* [ < L. *scurra,* buffoon] vulgarly abusive —**scur·ril·i·ty** (skə ril'ə tē) *n., pl.* **-ties** —**scur'ril·ous·ly** *adv.*

**scur·ry** (skur'ē) *vi.* **-ried, -ry·ing** [ < ?] to scamper —*n.* a scampering

**scur·vy** (skur'vē) *adj.* **-vi·er, -vi·est** [ < SCURF] low; mean —*n.* a disease resulting from a vitamin C deficiency, characterized by weakness, anemia, spongy gums, etc. —**scur'vi·ly** *adv.*

**scutch·eon** (skuch'ən) *n.* same as ESCUTCHEON

**scut·tle¹** (skut'l) *n.* [ < L. *scutella,* a salver] a bucket for carrying coal

**scut·tle²** (skut'l) *vi.* **-tled, -tling** [ME. *scutlen*] to scamper —*n.* a scamper

**scut·tle³** (skut'l) *n.* [ < Sp. *escotilla,*

an indentation] an opening fitted with a cover, as in the hull or deck of a ship —*vt.* **-tied, -tling** to cut holes through the lower hull of (a ship) to sink it

**scut·tle·butt'** (-but') *n.* [ < *scuttled butt,* lidded cask] 1. a drinking fountain on shipboard 2. [Colloq.] rumor

**scuz·zy** (skuz'ē) *adj.* **-zi·er, -zi·est** [Slang] dirty, shabby, etc.

**scythe** (sī*th*) *n.* [OE. *sithe*] a tool with a long, single-edged blade on a long, curved handle, for cutting grass, etc.

**S.Dak., SD** South Dakota

**SE, S.E., s.e.** southeast(ern)

**sea** (sē) *n.* [OE. *sæ*] 1. the ocean 2. any of various smaller bodies of salt water [the Red *Sea*] 3. a large body of fresh water [*Sea* of Galilee] 4. the state of the surface of the ocean [a calm *sea*] 5. a heavy wave 6. a very great amount —**at sea** 1. on the open sea 2. uncertain; bewildered

**sea anemone** a sea polyp with a gelatinous body and petallike tentacles

**sea'board'** *n.* land bordering on the sea —*adj.* bordering on the sea

**sea'coast'** *n.* land along the sea

**sea'far'er** (-fer'ər) *n.* a sea traveler; esp., a sailor —**sea'far'ing** *adj., n.*

**sea'food'** *n.* food prepared from or consisting of saltwater fish or shellfish

**sea'go'ing** *adj.* 1. made for use on the open sea 2. *same as* SEAFARING

**sea gull** *same as* GULL¹

**sea horse** a small, semitropical, plated fish with a head somewhat like that of a horse

**seal¹** (sēl) *n.* [ < L. *sigillum*] 1. *a)* a design or initial impressed, often over wax, on a letter or document as a mark of authenticity *b)* a stamp or ring for making such an impression 2. a piece of paper, etc. bearing an impressed design recognized as official 3. something that seals or closes tightly 4. anything that guarantees; pledge 5. an ornamental paper stamp [Easter *seals*] —*vt.* 1. to mark with a seal, as to authenticate or certify 2. to close or shut tight as with a seal 3. to confirm the truth of (a promise, etc.) 4. to decide finally

**seal²** (sēl) *n.* [OE. *seolh*] 1. a sea mammal with a torpedo-shaped body and four flippers 2. the fur of some seals —*vi.* to hunt seals —**seal'er** *n.*

**Sea·lab** (sē'lab') *n.* any of a series of U.S. Navy undersea laboratories for research in oceanography

**seal'ant** (-ənt) *n.* a substance, as a wax, plastic, etc., used for sealing

**sea legs** the ability to walk without loss of balance on board ship

**sea level** the mean level of the sea's surface: used in measuring heights

**sea lion** a seal of the North Pacific

**seal'skin'** *n.* 1. the skin of the seal 2. a garment made of this

SEA HORSE

**seam** (sēm) *n.* [OE.] 1. a line formed by sewing together two pieces of material 2. a line that marks joining edges 3. a mark like this, as a scar or wrinkle 4. a stratum of ore, coal, etc. —*vt.* 1. to join together so as to form a seam 2. to mark with a seamlike line, etc. —**seam'less** *adj.*

**sea·man** (sē'mən) *n., pl.* **-men** 1. a sailor 2. an enlisted man ranking below a petty officer in the navy — **sea'man·ship'** *n.*

**seam·stress** (sēm'stris) *n.* a woman whose occupation is sewing

**seam'y** *adj.* **-i·er, -i·est** unpleasant or sordid [the *seamy* side of life]

**sé·ance** (sā'äns) *n.* [Fr. < L. *sedere,* sit] a meeting at which spiritualists try to communicate with the dead

**sea'plane'** *n.* an airplane designed to land on or take off from water

**sea'port'** *n.* a port or harbor used by ocean ships

**sear** (sir) *vt.* [OE.] 1. to wither 2. to burn the surface of 3. to brand

**search** (surch) *vt.* [ < L. *circare,* go about] 1. to look through in order to find something 2. to examine (a person) for something concealed 3. to examine carefully; probe —*vi.* to make a search —*n.* a searching —**in search of** making a search for —**search'er** *n.*

**search'ing** *adj.* 1. examining thoroughly 2. piercing; penetrating

**search'light'** *n.* 1. an apparatus on a swivel that projects a strong beam of light 2. the beam of light

**search warrant** a legal document authorizing a police search

**sea·scape'** (-skāp') *n.* [SEA + (LAND)-SCAPE] 1. a sea view 2. a drawing, painting, etc. of this

**sea'shell'** *n.* a saltwater mollusk shell

**sea'shore'** *n.* land along the sea

**sea'sick'ness** *n.* nausea, dizziness, etc. caused by the rolling of a ship at sea —**sea'sick'** *adj.*

**sea'side'** *n. same as* SEASHORE

**sea·son** (sē'z'n) *n.* [ < VL. *satio,* sowing time] 1. any of the four divisions of the year; spring, summer, fall, or winter 2. the time when something takes place, is popular, permitted, etc. 3. the fitting time —*vt.* 1. to make (food) more tasty by adding salt, spices, etc. 2. to add zest to 3. to make more usable, as by aging 4. to make used to; accustom —*vi.* to become seasoned

**sea'son·a·ble** *adj.* 1. suitable to the season 2. opportune; timely

**sea'son·al** *adj.* of or depending on the season —**sea'son·al·ly** *adv.*

**sea'son·ing** *n.* anything that adds zest; esp., salt, etc. added to food

**season ticket** a ticket or set of tickets, as for a series of concerts, baseball games, etc.

**seat** (sēt) *n.* [ON. *sæti*] 1. *a)* a place to sit *b)* a thing to sit on; chair, etc. 2. *a)* the buttocks *b)* the part of a chair, garment, etc. that one sits on

**3.** the right to sit as a member [a *seat* on the council] **4.** the chief location, or center [the *seat* of government] — *vt.* **1.** to set in or on a seat **2.** to have seats for [the car *seats* six] —**be seated 1.** to sit down **2.** to be sitting **3.** to be located or settled

**seat belt** anchored straps that buckle across the hips to protect a seated passenger from an abrupt jolt

**Se·at·tle** (sē at'l) seaport in WC Wash.: pop. 531,000

**sea urchin** a small sea animal with a round body in a shell covered with sharp spines

**sea'ward** (-wərd) *adj., adv.* toward the sea: also **sea'wards** *adv.*

**sea'way'** *n.* an inland waterway to the sea for oceangoing ships

**sea'weed'** *n.* a sea plant, esp. an alga

**sea'wor'thy** (-wur'thē) *adj.* fit for travel on the sea: said of a ship

**se·ba·ceous** (si bā'shəs) *adj.* [ < L. *sebum*, tallow] of, like, or secreting fat, etc. [*sebaceous* glands]

**SEC, S.E.C.** Securities and Exchange Commission

**sec. 1.** second(s) **2.** secretary **3.** section(s)

**se·cede** (si sēd') *vi.* -**ced'ed, -ced'ing** [ < L. *se-*, apart + *cedere*, to go] to withdraw formally from a group, federation, organization, etc.

**se·ces·sion** (si sesh'ən) *n.* a seceding, specif. [often S-] by the Southern States from the Federal Union (1860-61) —**se·ces'sion·ist** *n.*

**se·clude** (si klōōd') *vt.* -**clud'ed, -clud'ing** [ < L. *se-*, apart + *claudere*, shut] to shut off from others; isolate

**se·clu·sion** (si klōō'zhən) *n.* a secluding or being secluded; retirement; isolation —**se·clu'sive** *adj.*

**sec·ond**[1] (sek'ənd) *adj.* [ < L. *sequi*, follow] **1.** coming next after the first; 2d or 2nd **2.** another of the same kind; other [a *second* chance] **3.** next below the first in rank, value, etc. —*n.* **1.** one that is second **2.** an article of merchandise not of first quality **3.** an aid or assistant, as to a boxer **4.** the gear next after low gear —*vt.* **1.** to assist **2.** to indicate formal support of (a motion) before discussion or a vote —*adv.* in the second place, group, etc.

**sec·ond**[2] (sek'ənd) *n.* [ < ML. (*pars minuta*) *secunda*, second (small part): from being a further division] **1.** 1/60 of a minute of time or of angular measure **2.** a moment; instant

**sec·ond·ar·y** (sek'ən der'ē) *adj.* **1.** second in order, rank, sequence, importance, etc. **2.** subordinate; minor **3.** derived, not primary; derivative — *n., pl.* -**ies 1.** a secondary person or thing **2.** *Football* the defensive backfield —**sec'ond·ar'i·ly** *adv.*

**secondary accent** a weaker accent (') than the primary accent of a word

**secondary school** a school, as a high school, coming after elementary school

**sec'ond-class'** *adj.* **1.** of the class, rank, etc. next below the highest **2.** of a cheaper mail class, as for periodicals **3.** inferior —*adv.* by second-class mail or travel accommodations

**sec'ond-guess'** *vt., vi.* [Colloq.] to use hindsight in criticizing (someone), remaking (a decision), etc.

**sec'ond-hand'** *adj.* **1.** not from the original source **2.** used before; not new **3.** dealing in used merchandise

**second lieutenant** *Mil.* a commissioned officer of the lowest rank

**sec'ond·ly** *adv.* in the second place

**second nature** an acquired habit, etc. deeply fixed in one's nature

**second person** that form of a pronoun (as *you*) or verb (as *are*) which refers to the person spoken to

**sec'ond-rate'** *adj.* **1.** second in quality, etc. **2.** inferior

**sec'ond-string'** *adj.* [Colloq.] *Sports* that is a substitute player at a specified position —**sec'ond-string'er** *n.*

**second thought** a change in thought after reconsidering —**on second thought** after reconsidering

**second wind 1.** the return of easy breathing after initial exhaustion, as while running **2.** any fresh ability to continue

**se·cre·cy** (sē'krə sē) *n., pl.* -**cies 1.** a being secret **2.** a tendency to keep things secret

**se·cret** (sē'krit) *adj.* [ < L. *se-*, apart + *cernere*, sift] **1.** kept from, or acting without, the knowledge of others **2.** beyond general understanding; mysterious **3.** concealed from sight; hidden —*n.* a secret fact, cause, process, etc. —**se'cret·ly** *adv.*

**sec·re·tar·i·at** (sek'rə ter'ē ət) *n.* a secretarial staff; esp., an administrative staff, as in a government

**sec·re·tar·y** (sek'rə ter'ē) *n., pl.* -**ies** [ < ML. *secretarius*, one entrusted with secrets] **1.** one who keeps records, handles correspondence, etc. for an organization or person **2.** the head of a government department **3.** a writing desk —**sec're·tar'i·al** *adj.*

**se·crete** (si krēt') *vt.* -**cret'ed, -cret'ing** [see SECRET] **1.** to hide; conceal **2.** to form and release (a substance) as a gland, etc. does

**se·cre·tion** (si krē'shən) *n.* **1.** a secretion **2.** a substance secreted by an animal or plant

**se·cre·tive** (sē'krə tiv, si krēt'iv) *adj.* concealing one's thoughts, etc.; not frank or open —**se'cre·tive·ly** *adv.* —**se'cre·tive·ness** *n.*

**se·cre·to·ry** (si krēt'ər ē) *adj.* having the function of secreting, as a gland

**Secret Service** a U.S. agency for uncovering counterfeiters, guarding the President, etc.

**sect** (sekt) *n.* [ < L. *sequi*, follow] **1.** a religious denomination **2.** a group of people having a common philosophy, set of beliefs, etc.

**sec·tar·i·an** (sek ter'ē ən) *adj.* **1.** of or devoted to some sect **2.** narrowminded —*n.* a sectarian person —**sec·tar'i·an·ism** *n.*

**sec·tion** (sek'shən) *n.* [ < L. *secare*, to cut] **1.** a cutting apart **2.** a part cut off; portion **3.** any distinct part, group, etc. **4.** a drawing, etc. of a thing as it would appear if cut straight through —*vt.* to cut into sections

**sec′tion·al** *adj.* 1. of or characteristic of a given section or district 2. made up of sections —**sec′tion·al·ism** *n.*

**sec·tor** (sek′tər) *n.* [< L. *secare,* to cut] 1. part of a circle bounded by any two radii and the included arc 2. any of the districts into which an area is divided for military operations

**sec·u·lar** (sek′yə lər) *adj.* [< LL. *saecularis,* worldly] 1. not religious; not connected with a church 2. not bound by a monastic vow [*secular* clergy] —**sec′u·lar·ism** *n.*

**sec′u·lar·ize** (-īz′) *vt.* -ized′, -iz′-ing to change from religious to civil use or control —**sec′u·lar·i·za′tion** *n.*

**se·cure** (si kyoor′) *adj.* [< L. *se-,* free from + *cura,* care] 1. free from fear, care, etc. 2. free from danger, risk, etc.; safe 3. firm [make the knot *secure*] —*vt.* -cured′, -cur′ing 1. to make secure; protect 2. to make certain, as with a pledge [to *secure* a loan] 3. to make firm, fast, etc. 4. to obtain —**se·cure′ly** *adv.*

**se·cu·ri·ty** (si kyoor′ə tē) *n., pl.* -ties 1. a feeling secure; freedom from fear, doubt, etc. 2. protection; safeguard 3. something given as a pledge of repayment, etc. 4. [*pl.*] bonds, stocks, etc.

**secy., sec′y.** secretary

**se·dan** (si dan′) *n.* [< ? L. *sedere,* sit] an enclosed automobile with front and rear seats and two or four doors

**se·date¹** (si dāt′) *adj.* [< L. *sedare,* settle] calm or composed; esp., serious and unemotional —**se·date′ly** *adv.*

**se·date²** (si dāt′) *vt.* -dat′ed, -dat′-ing to dose with a sedative —**se·da′-tion** *n.*

**sed·a·tive** (sed′ə tiv) *adj.* [see SEDATE¹] tending to soothe or quiet; lessening excitement, irritation, etc. —*n.* a sedative medicine

**sed·en·tar·y** (sed′′n ter′ē) *adj.* [< L. *sedere,* sit] marked by much sitting

**Se·der** (sā′dər) *n.* [< Heb., lit., arrangement] the feast of Passover as observed in the home on the eve of the first (by some also of the second) day of the holiday

**sedge** (sej) *n.* [OE. *secg*] a coarse, grasslike plant growing in wet ground

**sed·i·ment** (sed′ə mənt) *n.* [< L. *sedere,* sit] 1. matter that settles to the bottom of a liquid 2. *Geol.* matter deposited by water or wind

**sed′i·men′ta·ry** (-men′tər ē) *adj.* 1. of or containing sediment 2. formed by the deposit of sediment, as rocks

**se·di·tion** (si dish′ən) *n.* [< L. *sed-,* apart + *itio,* a going] a stirring up of rebellion 'against the government —**se·di′tion·ist** *n.* —**se·di′tious** *adj.*

**se·duce** (si doos′) *vt.* -duced′, -duc′-ing [< L. *se-,* apart + *ducere,* to lead] 1. to tempt to wrongdoing 2. to entice into unlawful sexual intercourse, esp. for the first time —**se·duc′er** *n.* —**se·duc′tion** *n.* —**se·duc′tive** *adj.* —**se·duc′tress** *n.fem.*

**sed·u·lous** (sej′oo ləs) *adj.* [L. *sedulus*] 1. diligent 2. persistent

**see¹** (sē) *vt.* **saw, seen, see′ing** [OE. *seon*] 1. to get knowledge of through the eyes; look at 2. to understand 3. to learn; find out 4. to experience 5. to make sure [see that he goes] 6. to escort [see her home] 7. to encounter 8. to call on; consult 9. to receive [too ill to see anyone] —*vi.* 1. to have the power of sight 2. to understand 3. to think [let me see, who's next?] —**see after** to take care of —**see through** 1. to perceive the true nature of 2. to finish 3. to help through difficulty —**see to** (or **about**) to attend to

**see²** (sē) *n.* [< L. *sedes,* a seat] the official seat or jurisdiction of a bishop

**seed** (sēd) *n., pl.* **seeds, seed** [OE. *sæd*] 1. *a*) the part of a plant, containing the embryo, from which a new plant can grow *b*) such seeds collectively 2. the source of anything 3. descendants; posterity 4. sperm or semen —*vt.* 1. to plant with seed 2. to remove the seeds from 3. to distribute (contestants in a tournament) so that the best players are not matched in early rounds —*vi.* to produce seed —**go** (or **run**) **to seed** 1. to shed seeds after flowering 2. to deteriorate, weaken, etc. —**seed′er** *n.* —**seed′less** *adj.*

**seed′ling** (-liŋ) *n.* 1. a plant grown from a seed 2. a young tree

**seed money** money to begin a long-term project or get more funds for it

**seed vessel** any dry, hollow fruit containing seed: also **seed′case′** *n.*

**seed′y** *adj.* -i·er, -i·est 1. full of seed 2. gone to seed 3. shabby, rundown, etc. —**seed′i·ness** *n.*

**seek** (sēk) *vt.* **sought, seek′ing** [OE. *secan*] 1. to try to find; search for 2. to try to get 3. to aim at 4. to try; attempt [to *seek* to please]

**seem** (sēm) *vi.* [prob. < ON. *sœma,* conform to] 1. to appear to be [seems glad] 2. to appear [seems to know] 3. to have the impression (with an infinitive) [I seem to have lost it]

**seem′ing** *adj.* that seems real, true, etc.; apparent —**seem′ing·ly** *adv.*

**seem′ly** *adj.* -li·er, -li·est suitable, proper, etc. —**seem′li·ness** *n.*

**seen** (sēn) *pp. of* SEE¹

**seep** (sēp) *vi.* [OE. *sipian,* to soak] to leak through small openings; ooze —**seep′age** (-ij) *n.*

**seer** (sir) *n.* one who supposedly foretells the future —**seer′ess** *n.fem.*

**seer·suck·er** (sir′suk′ər) *n.* [< Per. *shir u shakar,* lit., milk and sugar] a crinkled fabric of linen, cotton, etc.

**see·saw** (sē′sô′) *n.* [redupl. of SAW¹] 1. a plank balanced at the middle on which children at play, riding the ends, rise and fall alternately 2. any up-and-down or back-and-forth motion or change —*vt., vi.* to move up and down or back and forth

**seethe** (sēth) *vi.* **seethed, seeth′ing**

[OE. *sēothan*] 1. to boil, surge, or bubble 2. to be violently agitated

**seg·ment** (seg'mənt; *for v.* -ment) *n.* [< L. *secare*, to cut] any of the parts into which something is separated; section —*vt., vi.* to divide into segments —**seg'men·ta'tion** *n.*

**seg·re·gate** (seg'rə gāt') *vt.* -gat'ed, -gat'ing [< L. *se-*, apart + *grex*, a flock] to set apart from others; specif., to impose racial segregation on

**seg·re·ga'tion** *n.* the policy of compelling racial groups to live apart and use separate schools, facilities, etc. —**seg're·ga'tion·ist** *n.*

**se·gue** (seg'wā) *vi.* -gued, -gue·ing [It., (it) follows < L. *sequi*, to follow] to pass without break (*to* or *into* the next part) —*n.* an immediate transition to the next part

**sei·gnior** (sēn'yər) *n.* [OFr. < L. *senior*, older] a feudal lord

**Seine** (sān; *Fr.* sen) river in N France, flowing through Paris

**seine** (sān) *n.* [< Gr. *sagēnē*] a large fishing net weighted along the bottom —*vt., vi.* seined, sein'ing to fish with a seine —**sein'er** *n.*

**seis·mic** (sīz'mik) *adj.* [< Gr. *seismos*, earthquake] of or caused by an earthquake —**seis'mi·cal·ly** *adv.*

**seis'mo·graph'** (-mə graf') *n.* [see prec. & -GRAPH] an instrument that records the direction, intensity, and time of earthquakes —**seis'mo·graph'ic** *adj.*

**seize** (sēz) *vt.* seized, seiz'ing [< ML. *sacire*] 1. *a)* to take legal possession of *b)* to capture; arrest 2. to take forcibly and quickly 3. to grasp suddenly 4. to attack or afflict suddenly [*seized* with pain] —**sei'zure** (sē'zhər) *n.*

**sel·dom** (sel'dəm) *adv.* [OE. *seldan*, strange] rarely; infrequently

**se·lect** (sə lekt') *adj.* [< L. *se-*, apart + *legere*, to choose] 1. chosen in preference to others 2. choice; excellent 3. careful in choosing 4. exclusive —*vt., vi.* to choose or pick out —**select'ness** *n.* —**se·lec'tor** *n.*

**se·lec'tion** (-lek'shən) *n.* 1. a selecting or being selected 2. that or those selected —**se·lec'tive** *adj.* —**se·lec'tiv'i·ty** *n.*

**selective service** compulsory military service set by age, fitness, etc.

**se·lect'man** (-mən) *n., pl.* -men one of a board of governing officers in New England towns

**se·le·ni·um** (sə lē'nē əm) *n.* [ModL. < Gr. *selēnē*, moon] a gray, nonmetallic chemical element: used in photoelectric devices

**sel·e·nog·ra·phy** (sel'ə näg'rə fē) *n.* [< Gr. *selēnē*, moon + -GRAPHY] the study of the physical features of the moon —**sel'e·nog'ra·pher** *n.*

**self** (self) *n., pl.* selves [OE.] 1. the identity, character, etc. of any person or thing 2. one's own person as distinct from all others 3. one's own welfare or interest [Colloq.] myself, himself, etc. [*for self* and *wife*] —*adj.* of the same kind, color, etc. [*self* trim]

**self-** a prefix meaning of, by, in, to, or with oneself or itself   The following

list includes some common compounds formed with *self-* that do not have special meanings:

| | |
|---|---|
| self-appointed | self-improvement |
| self-assertion | self-induced |
| self-command | self-indulgence |
| self-complacent | self-indulgent |
| self-deceit | self-inflicted |
| self-deception | self-love |
| self-defeating | self-pity |
| self-destruction | self-pollination |
| self-discipline | self-preservation |
| self-effacement | self-protection |
| self-employed | self-reproach |
| self-examination | self-sealing |
| self-fertilization | self-support |
| self-help | self-supporting |
| self-imposed | self-sustaining |

**self'-ad·dressed'** *adj.* addressed to oneself [a *self-addressed* envelope]

**self'-as·sur'ance** *n.* confidence in oneself —**self'-as·sured'** *adj.*

**self'-cen'tered** *adj.* concerned only with one's own affairs; selfish

**self'-con·ceit'** *n.* too high an opinion of oneself; vanity

**self'-con·fi·dence** *n.* confidence in one's own abilities, etc. —**self'-con'fi·dent** *adj.*

**self'-con'scious** *adj.* unduly conscious of oneself as an object of notice; ill at ease —**self'-con'scious·ly** *adv.* —**self'-con'scious·ness** *n.*

**self'-con·tained'** *adj.* 1. keeping one's affairs to oneself 2. showing self-control 3. complete within itself

**self'-con·tra·dic'tion** *n.* 1. contradiction of oneself or itself 2. any statement having elements that contradict each other —**self'-con'tra·dic'to·ry** *adj.*

**self'-con·trol'** *n.* control of one's emotions, desires, etc. —**self'-con·trolled'** *adj.*

**self'-de·fense'** *n.* defense of oneself or of one's rights, actions, etc.

**self'-de·ni'al** *n.* denial or sacrifice of one's own desires or pleasures

**self'-de·struct'** *vi. same as* DESTRUCT

**self'-de·ter'mi·na'tion** *n.* 1. determination according to one's own mind; free will 2. the right of a people to choose its own form of government —**self'-de·ter'mined** *adj.*

**self'-dis·cov'er·y** *n.* a becoming aware of one's true potential, character, etc.

**self'-ed'u·cat'ed** *adj.* educated by oneself, with little formal schooling

**self'-es·teem'** *n.* 1. belief in oneself 2. undue pride in oneself

**self'-ev'i·dent** *adj.* evident without explanation or proof

**self'-ex·plan'a·to'ry** *adj.* explaining itself; obvious

**self'-ex·pres'sion** *n.* the expression of one's personality, esp. in the arts

**self'-ful·fill'ing** *adj.* 1. bringing about one's personal goals 2. brought about chiefly as an effect of having been expected or predicted

**self'-gov'ern·ment** *n.* government of a group by the action of its own members —**self'-gov'ern·ing** *adj.*

**self'-im'age** *n.* a person's conception of himself, his abilities, worth, etc.

**self'-im·por'tant** *adj.* having an exaggerated opinion of one's own importance —**self'-im·por'tance** *n.*

**self'-in'ter·est** *n.* 1. one's own interest or advantage 2. an exaggerated regard for this

**self'ish** *adj.* overly concerned with one's own interests, etc. and having little concern for others —**self'ish·ly** *adv.* —**self'ish·ness** *n.*

**self'less** *adj.* devoted to others' welfare; unselfish —**self'less·ly** *adv.* —**self'less·ness** *n.*

**self'-made'** *adj.* 1. made by oneself or itself 2. successful through one's own efforts

**self'-pos·ses'sion** *n.* full control of one's feelings, actions, etc. —**self'-pos·sessed'** *adj.*

**self'-pro·pelled'** *adj.* propelled by its own motor or power

**self'-re·li'ance** *n.* reliance on one's own judgment, abilities, etc. —**self'-re·li'ant** *adj.*

**self'-re·spect'** *n.* proper respect for oneself —**self'-re·spect'ing** *adj.*

**self'-re·straint'** *n.* restraint imposed on oneself by oneself; self-control

**self'-right'eous** *adj.* righteous, moral, etc. in one's own opinion —**self'-right'eous·ly** *adv.* —**self'-right'eous·ness** *n.*

**self'-sac'ri·fice'** *n.* the sacrifice of oneself or one's interests for the benefit of others —**self'-sac'ri·fic'ing** *adj.*

**self'same'** *adj.* identical

**self'-sat'is·fied'** *adj.* feeling or showing satisfaction with oneself —**self'-sat'is·fac'tion** *n.*

**self'-seek'er** *n.* one who seeks mainly to further his own interests —**self'-seek'ing** *n., adj.*

**self'-serv'ice** *n.* the practice of serving oneself in a cafeteria, store, etc.

**self'-serv'ing** *adj.* serving one's own selfish interests

**self'-start'er** *n.* a device for starting an internal-combustion engine automatically

**self'-styled'** *adj.* so named by oneself

**self'-suf·fi'cient** *adj.* able to get along without help; independent —**self'-suf·fi'cien·cy** *n.*

**self'-taught'** *adj.* having taught oneself through one's own efforts

**self'-willed'** *adj.* stubborn; obstinate

**self'-wind'ing** *adj.* wound automatically, as some watches

**sell** (sel) *vt.* **sold, sell'ing** [OE. *sellan,* give] 1. to exchange (goods, services, etc.) for money, etc. 2. to offer for sale 3. to promote the sale of —*vi.* 1. to engage in selling 2. to be sold (*for* or *at*) 3. to attract buyers —**sell out** 1. to get rid of completely by selling 2. [Colloq.] to betray —**sell'er** *n.*

**sell'out'** *n.* [Colloq.] 1. a selling out; betrayal 2. a show, game, etc. for which all the seats have been sold

**Selt·zer** (water) (selt'sər) [< *Niederselters,* Germany] 1. a mineral water 2. [*often* **s-**] carbonated water

**sel·vage, sel·vedge** (sel'vij) *n.* [< SELF + EDGE] a specially woven edge that prevents cloth from raveling

**selves** (selvz) *n., pl.* of SELF

**se·man·tics** (sə man'tiks) *n.pl.* [*with sing. v.*] [< Gr. *sēmainein,* to show] the study of the development and changes of the meanings of words —**se·man'tic** *adj.*

**sem·a·phore** (sem'ə fôr') *n.* [< Gr. *sēma,* a sign + *pherein,* to bear] any apparatus or system for signaling, as by lights, flags, etc.

**sem·blance** (sem'bləns) *n.* [< L. *similis,* like] 1. outward appearance 2. resemblance 3. a likeness or copy

**se·men** (sē'mən) *n., pl.* **sem·i·na** (sem'ə nə) [L., seed] the fluid secreted by the male reproductive organs

**se·mes·ter** (sə mes'tər) *n.* [< L. *sex,* six + *mensis,* month] either of the two terms usually making up a school year

**sem·i** (sem'ī) *n.* [Colloq.] a tractor (sense 2) and an attached semitrailer

**semi-** [L.] *a prefix meaning:* 1. half 2. partly, not fully 3. twice in a (specified period)

**sem·i·an·nu·al** (sem'ē an'yoo wəl) *adj.* 1. happening, coming, etc. every half year 2. lasting half a year

**sem·i·cir·cle** (sem'i sur'k'l) *n.* a half circle —**sem'i·cir'cu·lar** (-kyə lər) *adj.*

**sem'i·co'lon** (-kō'lən) *n.* a mark of punctuation (;) indicating a degree of separation greater than that marked by the comma

**sem'i·con·duc'tor** (-kən duk'tər) *n.* a substance, as germanium, used as in transistors to control current flow

**sem'i·con'scious** *adj.* not fully conscious or awake

**sem'i·fi'nal** *adj.* coming just before the final match, as of a contest —*n.* a semifinal match, etc.

**sem'i·month'ly** *adj.* coming, done, etc. twice a month —*adv.* twice monthly

**sem·i·nal** (sem'ə n'l) *adj.* [see SEMEN] 1. of seed or semen 2. that is a source

**sem·i·nar** (sem'ə när') *n.* 1. a group of supervised students doing research 2. a course for such a group

**sem·i·nar·y** (sem'ə ner'ē) *n., pl.* **-ies** [< L. *seminarium,* nursery] 1. a school, esp. a private school for young women 2. a school where priests, ministers, etc. are trained

**Sem·i·nole** (sem'ə nōl') *n., pl.* **-noles, -nole** a member of an American Indian people of S Florida and Oklahoma

**sem'i·pre'cious** *adj.* designating gems, as the garnet, turquoise, etc., of lower value than precious gems

**sem'i·pri'vate** *adj.* of a hospital room with two, three, or sometimes four beds

**sem'i·pro·fes'sion·al** *n.* one who engages in a sport for pay but not as a regular occupation: also **sem'i·pro'**

**sem'i·skilled'** *adj.* of or doing man-

---

fat, āpe, cär; ten, ēven; is, bīte; gō, hôrn, tōōl, look; oil, out; up, fur; chin; she; thin, *then*; zh, leisure; ŋ, ring; ə for *a* in *ago*; ', (ā'b'l); ĕ, Fr. coeur; ö, Fr. feu; Fr. mon; ü, Fr. duc; kh, G. ich, doch; ‡ foreign; < derived from ual work requiring only limited training

**Sem·ite** (sem′ĭt) *n.* [ < *Shēm*, son of Noah] a member of any of the peoples whose language is Semitic

**Se·mit·ic** (sə mĭt′ik) *adj.* **1.** of or relating to the Semites **2.** designating or of a group of Afro-Asiatic languages, including Hebrew, Arabic, etc.

**sem′i·trail′er** *n.* a detachable trailer attached to a coupling at the rear of a truck cab

**sem′i·trans·par′ent** *adj.* not perfectly or completely transparent

**sem′i·trop′i·cal** *adj.* partly tropical

**sem′i·week′ly** *adj.* coming, done, etc. twice a week —*adv.* twice weekly

**sen. 1.** senate **2.** senator **3.** senior

**sen·ate** (sen′ĭt) *n.* [ < L. *senex*, old] **1.** a lawmaking assembly **2.** [S-] the upper branch of the U.S. Congress or of most of the State legislatures

**sen·a·tor** (sen′ə tər) *n.* a member of a senate —**sen′a·to′ri·al** (-tôr′ē əl) *adj.*

**send** (send) *vt.* **sent, send′ing** [OE. *sendan*] **1.** to cause to go or be transmitted; dispatch **2.** to cause (a person) to go **3.** to impel; drive **4.** to cause to happen, come, etc. **5.** [Slang] to thrill —**send for 1.** to summon **2.** to place an order for —**send′er** *n.*

**send′-off′** *n.* [Colloq.] **1.** a farewell demonstration for someone starting out on a trip, career, etc. **2.** a start given to someone or something

**Sen·e·gal** (sen′i gôl′) country in W Africa: 76,124 sq. mi.; pop. 3,490,000

**se·nile** (sē′nĭl) *adj.* [ < L. *senex*, old] **1.** of or resulting from old age **2.** showing signs of old age; weak in mind and body —**se·nil·i·ty** (si nil′ə tē) *n.*

**sen·ior** (sēn′yər) *adj.* [L. < *senex*, old] **1.** older: written *Sr.* after a father's name if his son's name is the same **2.** of higher rank or longer service **3.** of or for seniors —*n.* **1.** one who is older, of higher rank, etc. **2.** a student in the last year of a high school or college

**senior citizen** an elderly person, esp. one who is retired

**senior high school** high school (usually grades 10, 11, & 12)

**sen·ior·i·ty** (sēn yôr′ə tē) *n., pl.* -ties **1.** a being senior **2.** status, priority, etc. achieved by length of service in a given job

**sen·na** (sen′ə) *n.* [ < Ar. *sanā*, cassia plant] the dried leaflets of a tropical cassia plant, used as a laxative

**‡se·ñor** (se nyôr′) *n., pl.* se·**ñor′-es** (-nyô′res) [Sp.] a man; gentleman: as a title, equivalent to *Mr.* or *Sir*

**‡se·ño·ra** (se nyô′rä) *n.* [Sp.] a married woman: as a title, equivalent to *Mrs.* or *Madam*

**‡se·ño·ri·ta** (se′nyô rē′tä) *n.* [Sp.] an unmarried woman or girl: as a title, equivalent to *Miss*

**sen·sa·tion** (sen sā′shən) *n.* [ < L. *sensus*, sense] **1.** the receiving of sense impressions through hearing, seeing, etc. **2.** a conscious sense impression **3.** a generalized feeling [a *sensation* of joy] **4.** a feeling of excitement or its cause [the play is a *sensation*]

**sen·sa′tion·al** *adj.* **1.** arousing intense interest **2.** intended to shock, thrill, etc. —**sen·sa′tion·al·ism** *n.*

**sense** (sens) *n.* [ < L. *sentire*, to feel] **1.** any faculty of receiving impressions through body organs; sight, hearing, taste, smell, or touch **2.** *a)* feeling, perception, etc. through the senses *b)* a generalized feeling or awareness **3.** an ability to understand some quality, as humor, honor, etc. **4.** normal intelligence and judgment **5.** meaning, as of a word —*vt.* **sensed, sens′ing 1.** to perceive **2.** to detect, as by sensors —**in a sense** in one aspect —**make sense** to be intelligible or logical

**sense′less** *adj.* **1.** unconscious **2.** stupid; foolish **3.** meaningless

**sen·si·bil·i·ty** (sen′sə bil′ə tē) *n., pl.* -ties **1.** the capacity for physical sensation **2.** [*often pl.*] delicate, sensitive awareness or feelings

**sen′si·ble** *adj.* **1.** that can cause physical sensation **2.** easily perceived **3.** aware **4.** having or showing good sense; wise —**sen′si·bly** *adv.*

**sen·si·tive** (sen′sə tiv) *adj.* **1.** sensory **2.** very keenly susceptible to stimuli **3.** tender; raw **4.** having keen sensibilities **5.** easily offended; touchy —**sen′si·tiv′i·ty, sen′si·tive·ness** *n.*

**sen′si·tize′** (-tīz′) *vt.* **-tized′, -tiz′-ing** to make sensitive

**sen·sor** (sen′sər) *n.* a device to detect, measure, or record physical phenomena, as heat, pulse, etc.

**sen·so·ry** (sen′sər ē) *adj.* of the senses or sensation

**sen·su·al** (sen′shoo wəl) *adj.* [ < L. *sensus*, sense] **1.** of the body and the senses as distinguished from the intellect **2.** connected with or preoccupied with sexual pleasures —**sen′su·al′i·ty** (-wal′ə tē) *n.* —**sen′su·al·ly** *adv.*

**sen·su·ous** (sen′shoo wəs) *adj.* **1.** of, derived from, or perceived by the senses **2.** enjoying sensation

**sent** (sent) *pt. & pp.* of SEND

**sen·tence** (sen′t'ns) *n.* [ < L. *sententia*, opinion] **1.** *a)* a decision, as of a court; esp., the determination by a court of a punishment *b)* the punishment **2.** a group of words stating something, usually containing a subject and predicate —*vt.* **-tenced, -tenc-ing** to pronounce punishment upon (a convicted person)

**sen·ten·tious** (sen ten′shəs) *adj.* **1.** full of, or fond of using, maxims, proverbs, etc. **2.** ponderously trite

**sen·tient** (sen′shənt) *adj.* [see SENSE] of or capable of feeling; conscious

**sen·ti·ment** (sen′tə mənt) *n.* [see SENSE] **1.** a complex combination of feelings and opinions **2.** an opinion, etc., often colored by emotion **3.** appeal to the emotions, or sensitivity to this **4.** maudlin emotion

**sen·ti·men·tal** (sen′tə men′t'l) *adj.* **1.** having or showing tender or delicate feelings **2.** maudlin; mawkish **3.** of or resulting from sentiment —**sen′ti·men′tal·ism** *n.* —**sen′ti·men′tal·ist** *n.* —**sen′ti·men·tal′i·ty** (-tal′ə tē) *n.* —**sen′ti·men′tal·ly** *adv.*

**sen·ti·men·tal·ize** *vi.*, *vt.* **-ized′,**
**-iz′ing** to be sentimental or treat in
a sentimental way

**sen·ti·nel** (sen′ti n'l) *n.* [ < L. *sentire*,
to sense] a guard or sentry

**sen·try** (sen′trē) *n.*, *pl.* **-tries** [ < ?
obs. *centery*, sanctuary] a sentinel;
esp., a soldier posted to guard against
danger

**Seoul** (sōl) capital of South Korea:
pop. 3,376,000

**se·pal** (sē′p'l) *n.* [ < Gr. *skepē*, a
covering + L. *petalum*, petal] any of
the leaflike parts of the calyx

**sep·a·ra·ble** (sep′ər ə b'l) *adj.* that
can be separated —**sep′a·ra·bly** *adv.*

**sep·a·rate** (sep′ə rāt′; *for adj.* -ər it)
*vt.* **-rat′ed, -rat′ing** [ < L. *se-*, apart
+ *parare*, arrange] **1.** to set apart into
sections, groups, etc.; divide **2.** to keep
apart by being between —*vi.* **1.** to
withdraw **2.** to part, become disconnected, etc. **3.** to go in different directions —*adj.* **1.** set apart from the rest
or others **2.** not associated with others;
distinct **3.** not shared *[separate beds]*
—**sep′a·rate·ly** *adv.* —**sep′a·ra′tor** *n.*

**sep·a·ra·tion** (sep′ə rā′shən) *n.* **1.** a
separating or being separated **2.** the
place where this occurs; break; division
**3.** something that separates

**sep·a·ra·tism** (-ər ə tiz′m) *n.* the
advocacy of separation, racially, politically, etc. —**sep′a·ra·tist** *n.*

**se·pi·a** (sē′pē ə) *n.*, *adj.* [ < Gr. *sēpia*,
cuttlefish secreting inky fluid] (of)
dark reddish brown

**sep·sis** (sep′sis) *n.* [see SEPTIC] poisoning caused by the absorption into the
blood of pathogenic microorganisms

**Sep·tem·ber** (sep tem′bər) *n.* [ < L.
*septem*, seven: seventh month in Rom.
calendar] the ninth month of the year,
having 30 days: abbrev. **Sept.**

**sep·tic** (sep′tik) *adj.* [ < Gr. *sēpein*,
make putrid] causing, or resulting
from, sepsis or putrefaction

**sep·ti·ce·mi·a** (sep′tə sē′mē ə) *n.*
[see prec.] *same as* BLOOD POISONING

**septic tank** an underground tank in
which waste matter is putrefied and
decomposed through bacterial action

**Sep·tu·a·gint** (sep′too wə jint) *n.*
[ < L. *septuaginta*, seventy: in tradition, done in 70 days] a translation
into Greek of the Old Testament

**sep·tum** (sep′təm) *n.*, *pl.* **-tums, -ta**
(-tə) [L., fence] a dividing wall or
part as in the nose, a fruit, etc.

**sep·ul·cher** (sep′'l kər) *n.* [ < L.
*sepelire*, bury] a vault for burial; tomb

**se·pul·chral** (sə pul′krəl) *adj.* **1.** of
sepulchers, burial, etc. **2.** suggestive
of the grave or burial; gloomy **3.** deep
and melancholy: said of sound

**seq.** [L. *sequentes*] the following

**se·quel** (sē′kwəl) *n.* [ < L. *sequi*,
follow] **1.** something that follows;
continuation **2.** something coming as
a result of something else; aftermath;
effect **3.** any literary work continuing
a story begun in an earlier work

**se·quence** (sē′kwəns) *n.* [ < L. *sequi*,
follow] **1.** *a)* the coming of one thing
after another; succession *b)* the order
in which this occurs **2.** a series **3.** a
resulting event **4.** a single, uninterrupted episode, as in a movie

**se·ques·ter** (si kwes′tər) *vt.* [ < LL.
*sequestrare*, remove] **1.** to set off or
apart **2.** to withdraw; seclude —
**se·ques·tra·tion** (sē′kwes trā′shən) *n.*

**se·quin** (sē′kwin) *n.* [Fr.; ult. < Ar.
*sikkah*, a stamp] a small, shiny spangle,
esp. one of many sewn on fabric for
decoration —**se′quined** *adj.*

**se·quoi·a** (si kwoi′ə) *n.* [ < *Sikwâyi*,
Indian inventor of Cherokee writing]
a giant evergreen tree of the W U.S.

**se·rag·lio** (si ral′yō) *n.*, *pl.* **-lios** [ult.
< L. *sera*, a lock] a harem (sense 1)

**se·ra·pe** (sə rä′pē) *n.* [MexSp.] a
bright-colored woolen blanket used as
a garment by men in Mexico, etc.

**ser·aph** (ser′əf) *n.*, *pl.* **-aphs, -a·phim′**
(-ə fim′) [ < Heb. *serāphīm*, *pl.*] *Theol.*
a heavenly being, or any of the highest
order of angels —**se·raph·ic** (sə raf′ik)
*adj.* —**se·raph′i·cal·ly** *adv.*

**Serb** (surb) *n.* a native or inhabitant
of Serbia; esp., any of a Slavic people
of Serbia —*adj.* Serbian

**Ser·bi·a** (sur′bē ə) republic of Yugoslavia —**Ser′bi·an** *adj.*, *n.*

**sere** (sir) *adj.* [var. of SEAR] [Poet.]
dried up; withered

**ser·e·nade** (ser′ə nād′) *n.* [ult. < L.
*serenus*, clear] music played or sung at
night, esp. by a lover under his sweetheart's window —*vt.*, *vi.* **-nad′ed,**
**-nad′ing** to play or sing a serenade
(to).

**ser·en·dip·i·ty** (ser′ən dip′ə tē) *n.*
[ < a Persian tale *The Three Princes
of Serendip*] an apparent aptitude for
making accidental fortunate discoveries

**se·rene** (sə rēn′) *adj.* [L. *serenus*]
**1.** clear; unclouded **2.** undisturbed;
calm —**se·rene′ly** *adv.* —**se·ren′i·ty**
(-ren′ə tē), **se·rene′ness** *n.*

**serf** (surf) *n.* [ < L. *servus*, a slave]
a person in feudal servitude, bound
to his master's land and transferred
with it to a new owner —**serf′dom** *n.*

**serge** (surj) *n.* [ < L. *sericus*, silken]
a strong twilled fabric

**ser·geant** (sär′jənt) *n.* [ < L. *servire*,
serve] **1.** a noncommissioned officer
ranking above a corporal **2.** a police
officer ranking next below a captain
or a lieutenant

**ser′geant-at-arms′** *n.*, *pl.* **ser′-**
**geants-at-arms′** an officer appointed
to keep order, as in a court

**se·ri·al** (sir′ē əl) *adj.* [ < L. *series*, an
order] appearing in a series of continuous parts at regular intervals —*n.* a
story, etc. presented in serial form
—**se′ri·al·i·za′tion** *n.* —**se′ri·al·ize′**
*vt.*, **-ized′, -iz′ing**

**serial number** one of a series of
numbers given for identification

**se·ries** (sir′ēz) *n.*, *pl.* **-ries** [L. <
*serere*, join together] a number of

fat, āpe, cär; ten, ēven; is, bīte; gō, hôrn, tōol, look; oil, out; up, fur;
chin; she; thin, then; zh, leisure; ŋ, ring; ə for *a* in *ago*; ′, (ā′b'l); ë, Fr. coeur;
ö, Fr. feu; Fr. mon; ü, Fr. duc; kh, G. ich, doch; ‡ foreign; < derived from

similar things or persons arranged in a row or coming one after another

**se·ri·ous** (sir′ē əs) *adj.* [< L. *serius*] 1. earnest, grave, sober, etc. 2. not joking; sincere 3. requiring careful consideration; important 4. dangerous [a *serious* wound] —**se′ri·ous·ly** *adv.* —**se′ri·ous·ness** *n.*

**ser·mon** (sur′mən) *n.* [< L. *sermo*] 1. a speech on religion or morals, esp. by a clergyman 2. any serious talk on behavior, duty, etc., esp. a tedious one —**ser′mon·ize′** *vi.* -**ized′**, -**iz′ing**

**Sermon on the Mount** the sermon delivered by Jesus to his disciples

**se·rous** (sir′əs) *adj.* 1. of or containing serum 2. thin and watery

**ser·pent** (sur′pənt) *n.* [< L. *serpere*, to creep] a snake

**ser′pen·tine′** (-pən tēn′, -tīn′) *adj.* of or like a serpent; esp., *a*) cunning; treacherous *b*) coiled; winding

**ser·rate** (ser′āt) *adj.* [< L. *serra*, a saw] having sawlike notches along the edge, as some leaves: also **ser·rat′ed** —**ser·ra′tion** *n.*

**ser·ried** (ser′ēd) *adj.* [< LL. *serare*, to lock] placed close together

**se·rum** (sir′əm) *n., pl.* -**rums**, -**ra** (-ə) [L., whey] 1. any watery animal fluid, as the yellowish fluid (**blood serum**) separating from a blood clot after coagulation 2. blood serum used as an antitoxin, taken from an animal inoculated for a specific disease

**ser·vant** (sur′vənt) *n.* [ult. < L. *servire*, serve] 1. a person employed by another, esp. to do household duties 2. a person devoted to another or to a cause, creed, etc.

**serve** (surv) *vt.* **served, serv′ing** [< L. *servus*, a slave] 1. to work for as a servant 2. to do services for; aid; help 3. to do military or naval service for 4. to spend (a term of imprisonment, etc.) [to *serve* ten years] 5. to provide (customers) with (goods or services) 6. to set (food, etc.) before (a person) 7. to meet the needs of 8. to be used by [one hospital *serves* the city] 9. to function for [if memory *serves* me well] 10. to deliver (a summons, etc.) to 11. to hit (a tennis ball, etc.) in order to start play —*vi.* 1. to work as a servant 2. to do service [to *serve* in the navy] 3. to carry out the duties of an office 4. to be of service 5. to meet needs 6. to provide guests with food or drink 7. to be favorable: said of weather, etc. —*n.* a serving of the ball in tennis —**serve** (**someone**) **right** to be what (someone) deserves —**serv′er** *n.*

**serv·ice** (sur′vis) *n.* [< L. *servus*, a slave] 1. the occupation of a servant 2. *a*) public employment [diplomatic *service*] *b*) a branch of this; specif., the armed forces 3. work done for others [repair *service*] 4. any religious ceremony 5. *a*) benefit; advantage *b*) [*pl.*] friendly help; also, professional aid 6. the act or manner of serving food 7. a set of articles used in serving [a tea *service*] 8. a system of providing people with some utility, as water or gas 9. the act or manner of serving in

tennis, etc. —*vt.* -**iced**, -**ic·ing** 1. to furnish with a service 2. to make fit for service, as by repairing —**at one's service** 1. ready to serve one 2. ready for one's use —**of service** helpful

**serv′ice·a·ble** *adj.* 1. that can be of service; useful 2. that will give good service; durable

**serv′ice·man′** *n., pl.* -**men′** 1. a member of the armed forces 2. a person whose work is repairing something [a radio *serviceman*]: also **service man**

**service mark** a word, etc. used like a trademark by a supplier of services

**service station** a place selling gasoline, oil, etc. for motor vehicles

**ser·vile** (sur′v'l, -vīl) *adj.* [< L. *servus*, a slave] 1. of slaves 2. like that of slaves 3. humbly submissive —**ser·vil·i·ty** (sər vil′ə tē) *n.*

**ser·vi·tor** (sur′və tər) *n.* a servant

**ser·vi·tude** (sur′və tōōd′) *n.* [see SERVILE] 1. slavery or bondage 2. work imposed as punishment for crime

**ser·vo** (sur′vō) *n., pl.* -**vos** *short for:* 1. SERVOMECHANISM 2. SERVOMOTOR

**ser′vo·mech′a·nism** *n.* an automatic control system of low power, used to exercise remote but accurate mechanical control

**ser′vo·mo′tor** *n.* a device, as an electric motor, for changing a small force into a large force, as in a servomechanism

**ses·a·me** (ses′ə mē′) *n.* [< Sem. origin] 1. an East Indian plant whose edible seeds yield an oil 2. its seeds

**ses·qui·cen·ten·ni·al** (ses′kwi sen ten′ē əl) *adj.* [< L. *sesqui-*, more by a half + CENTENNIAL] of a period of 150 years —*n.* a 150th anniversary

**ses·sion** (sesh′ən) *n.* [< L. *sedere*, sit] 1. *a*) the meeting of a court, legislature, etc. *b*) a series of such meetings *c*) the period of these 2. a period of study, classes, etc. 3. a period of activity of any kind

**set** (set) *vt.* **set, set′ting** [OE. *settan*] 1. to cause to sit; seat 2. to put in a specified place, condition, etc. [*set* books on a shelf, *set* slaves free] 3. to put in proper condition; fix (a trap for animals), adjust (a clock or dial), arrange (a table for a meal), fix (hair) in a desired style, etc., put (a broken bone, etc.) into normal position, etc. 4. to make settled, rigid, or fixed [pectin *sets* jelly] 5. to mount (gems) 6. to direct 7. to appoint; establish; fix (boundaries, the time for an event, a rule, a quota, etc.) 8. to furnish (an example) for others 9. to fit (words *to* music or music *to* words) 10. to arrange (type) for printing —*vi.* 1. to sit on eggs: said of a fowl 2. to become firm, hard, or fixed [the cement *set*] 3. to begin to move (*out, forth, off,* etc.) 4. to sink below the horizon [the sun *sets*] 5. to have a certain direction; tend —*adj.* 1. fixed; established [a *set* time] 2. intentional 3. fixed; rigid; firm 4. obstinate 5. ready [get *set*] —*n.* 1. a setting or being set 2. the way in which a thing is set [the *set* of his jaw] 3. direction; tendency 4. the scenery for a play, etc. 5. a group of persons or things classed or belonging together 6. assembled equipment for radio or television reception, etc. 7. *Tennis* a group of six or more games won by a margin of at least two —**set about** (or **in, to**) to begin —**set down** 1. to put in writing 2. to establish (rules, etc.) —**set forth** 1. to publish 2. to state —**set off** 1. to make prominent or enhance by contrast 2. to make explode —**set on** (or **upon**) to attack —**set up** 1. to erect 2. to establish; found

**set′back′** *n.* a reversal in progress

**set·tee** (se tē′) *n.* 1. a seat or bench with a back 2. a small sofa

**set′ter** *n.* a long-haired dog trained to hunt game

**set′ting** *n.* 1. the act of one that sets 2. the position of a dial, etc. that has been set 3. a mounting, as of a gem 4. the time, place, etc. as of a story 5. actual physical surroundings

**set·tle** (set′′l) *vt.* **-tled, -tling** [OE. *setlan*] 1. to put in order; arrange *[to settle* one's affairs*]* 2. to set in place firmly or comfortably 3. to colonize 4. to cause to sink and become more compact 5. to free (the nerves, etc.) from disturbance 6. to decide (a dispute, etc.) 7. to pay (a debt, etc.) —*vi.* 1. to stop moving and stay in one place 2. to descend, as fog over a landscape, or gloom over a person 3. to become localized, as pain 4. to take up permanent residence 5. to sink *[the house settled]* 6. to become more dense by sinking, as sediment 7. to become more stable 8. to reach an agreement or decision (*with* or *on*) —**set′tler** *n.*

**set·tle·ment** *n.* 1. a settling or being settled 2. a new colony 3. a village 4. an agreement 5. a community center for the underprivileged

**set′-to′** (-tōō′) *n., pl.* **-tos′** [Colloq.] 1. a fight 2. an argument

**set′up′** *n.* 1. *a)* the plan, makeup, etc. of equipment, an organization, etc. *b)* the details of a situation, plan, etc. 2. [Colloq.] a contest, etc. arranged to result in an easy victory

**sev·en** (sev′'n) *adj., n.* [OE. *seofon*] one more than six; 7; VII —**sev′enth** *adj., n.*

**seven seas** the oceans of the world

**sev·en·teen′** (-tēn′) *adj., n.* seven more than ten; 17; XVII —**sev′en·teenth′** (-tēnth′) *adj., n.*

**sev′en·teen′-year′ locust** a cicada which lives underground for 13-17 years before emerging as an adult

**seventh heaven** perfect happiness

**sev·en·ty** (sev′'n tē) *adj., n., pl.* **-ties** seven times ten; 70; LXX —**the seventies** the years from 70 through 79, as of a century —**sev′en·ti·eth** (-ith) *adj., n.*

**sev·er** (sev′ər) *vt., vi.* [ < L. *separare*] to separate, divide, or break off —**sev′er·ance** *n.*

**sev·er·al** (sev′ər əl) *adj.* [ < L. *separ*] 1. separate; distinct 2. different;

respective 3. more than two but not many; few —*n.* [*with pl. v.*] a small number (*of*) —*pron.* [*with pl. v.*] a few —**sev′er·al·ly** *adv.*

**se·vere** (sə vir′) *adj.* [ < L. *severus*] 1. harsh or strict, as in treatment 2. serious; grave, as in expression 3. rigidly accurate or demanding 4. extremely plain: said of style 5. intense *[severe* pain*]* 6. rigorous; trying —**se·vere′ly** *adv.* —**se·vere′ness, sever′i·ty** (-ver′ə tē) *n.*

**Se·ville** (sə vil′) city in SW Spain: pop. 532,000

**Sè·vres** (sev′rə) *n.* [ < *Sèvres*, Paris suburb where made] a type of fine French porcelain

**sew** (sō) *vt., vi.* **sewed, sewn** (sōn) or **sewed, sew′ing** [OE. *siwian*] 1. to fasten with stitches made with needle and thread 2. to make, mend, etc. by sewing —**sew up** [Colloq.] 1. to get full control of 2. to make sure of success in —**sew′er** *n.*

**sew·age** (sōō′ij) *n.* the waste matter carried off by sewers

**sew·er** (sōō′ər) *n.* [ult. < L. *ex*, out + *aqua*, water] a pipe or drain, usually underground, used to carry off water and waste matter

**sew′er·age** (-ij) *n.* 1. a system of sewers 2. *same as* SEWAGE

**sew·ing** (sō′iŋ) *n.* 1. the act of one who sews 2. something to be sewn

**sewing machine** a machine with a mechanically driven needle for sewing

**sex** (seks) *n.* [ < L. *sexus*] 1. either of the two divisions of organisms distinguished as male and female 2. the character of being male or female 3. the attraction between the sexes 4. sexual intercourse

**sex-** [ < L. *sex*, six] *a combining form meaning* six

**sex appeal** the physical charm that attracts members of the opposite sex

**sex chromosome** a sex-determining chromosome in the germ cells: eggs carry an X chromosome and spermatozoa either an X or Y chromosome, with a female resulting from an XX pairing and a male from an XY

**sex′ism** *n.* exploitation and domination of one sex by the other, specif., of women by men —**sex′ist** *adj., n.*

**sex·tant** (seks′tənt) *n.* [ < L. *sextans*, a sixth part (of a circle) ] an instrument for measuring the angular distance of the sun, a star, etc. from the horizon, as to determine position at sea

**sex·tet, sex·tette** (seks tet′) *n.* [ < L. *sex*, six] 1. a group of six 2. *Music* a composition for six voices or instruments, or the six performers of this

**sex·ton** (seks′tən) *n.* [ult. < L. *sacer*, sacred] a church official in charge of the maintenance of church property

**sex·u·al** (sek′shoo wəl) *adj.* of or involving sex, the sexes, the sex organs, etc. —**sex′u·al·ly** *adv.* —**sex′u·al′i·ty** *n.*

**sex′y** *adj.* **-i·er, -i·est** [Colloq.] exciting or intended to excite sexual desire —**sex′i·ly** *adv.* —**sex′i·ness** *n.*

**s.f., sf., SF** science fiction

**Sgt, Sgt.** Sergeant

**sh** (sh) *interj.* hush! be quiet!

**shab·by** (shab′ē) *adj.* **-bi·er, -bi·est** [< OE. *sceabb,* a scab] **1.** run down; dilapidated **2.** *a)* ragged; worn *b)* wearing worn clothing **3.** mean; shameful *[shabby* behavior] —**shab′-bi·ly** *adv.* —**shab′bi·ness** *n.*

**shack** (shak) *n.* [< ?] a small, crudely built house or cabin; shanty

**shack·le** (shak′'l) *n.* [OE. *sceacel*] **1.** a metal fastening, usually in pairs, for the wrists or ankles of a prisoner; fetter **2.** anything that restrains freedom, as of expression **3.** a device for coupling, etc. —*vt.* **-led, -ling 1.** to put shackles on **2.** to restrain in freedom of expression or action

**shad** (shad) *n., pl.* **shad, shads** [OE. *sceadd*] a saltwater fish related to the herring but spawning in rivers

**shade** (shād) *n.* [OE. *sceadu*] **1.** comparative darkness caused by cutting off rays of light **2.** an area with less light than its surroundings **3.** degree of darkness of a color **4.** *a)* a small difference *[shades* of opinion] *b)* a slight amount or degree **5.** [*Poet.*] a ghost **6.** a device used to screen from light *[a* lamp *shade,* window *shade]* **7.** [*pl.*] [Slang] sunglasses —*vt.* **shad′ed, shad′ing 1.** to screen from light **2.** to darken; dim **3.** to represent shade in (a painting, etc.) —*vi.* to change slightly or by degrees

**shad·ing** (shād′iŋ) *n.* **1.** a shielding against light **2.** the representation of shade in a picture **3.** a small variation

**shad·ow** (shad′ō) *n.* [< OE. *sceadu,* shade] **1.** (a) shade cast by a body intercepting light rays **2.** gloom or that which causes gloom **3.** a shaded area in a picture **4.** a ghost **5.** a remnant; trace —*vt.* **1.** to throw a shadow upon **2.** to follow closely, esp. in secret —**shad′ow·y** *adj.*

**shad′ow-box′** *vi. Boxing* to spar with an imaginary opponent for exercise

**shad·y** (shād′ē) *adj.* **-i·er, -i·est 1.** giving shade **2.** shaded; full of shade **3.** [Colloq.] of questionable character —**on the shady side of** beyond (a given age) —**shad′i·ness** *n.*

**shaft** (shaft) *n.* [OE. *sceaft*] **1.** an arrow or spear, or its stem **2.** anything hurled like a missile *[shafts* of wit] **3.** a long, slender part or object, as a pillar, either of the poles between which an animal is harnessed to a vehicle, a bar transmitting motion to a mechanical part, etc. **4.** a long, narrow passage sunk into the earth **5.** a vertical opening passing through a building, as for an elevator

**shag¹** (shag) *n.* [OE. *sceaga*] a heavy, rough nap, as on some cloth

**shag²** (shag) *vt.* **shagged, shag′ging** [< ?] to chase after and retrieve (baseballs hit in batting practice)

**shag′gy** (shag′ē) *adj.* **-gi·er, -gi·est 1.** covered with long, coarse hair or wool **2.** unkempt, straggly, etc. **3.** having a rough nap

**shah** (shä) *n.* [Per. *shāh*] a title of the ruler of Iran

**shake** (shāk) *vt., vi.* **shook, shak′en, shak′ing** [OE. *sceacan*] **1.** to move quickly up and down, back and forth, etc. **2.** to bring, force, mix, etc. by brisk movement **3.** to tremble or cause to tremble **4.** *a)* to become or cause to become unsteady *b)* to unnerve or become unnerved **5.** to clasp (another's hand), as in greeting —*n.* **1.** an act of shaking **2.** a wood shingle **3.** *short for* MILKSHAKE **4.** [*pl.*] [Colloq.] a convulsive trembling (usually with *the*) **5.** [Colloq.] deal *[a* fair *shake]* —**no great shakes** not outstanding —**shake down 1.** to cause to fall by shaking **2.** [Slang] to extort money from —**shake off** to get rid of —**shak′y** *adj.* **-i·er, -i·est**

**shake′down′** *n.* **1.** [Slang] an extortion of money, as by blackmail **2.** a thorough search —*adj.* for testing new equipment, etc. *[a shakedown* cruise]

**shak′er** *n.* **1.** a person or thing that shakes **2.** a device used in shaking **3.** [S-] a member of a religious sect that lived in celibate communities in the U.S.

**Shake·speare** (shāk′spir), **William** 1564–1616; Eng. poet & dramatist —**Shake·spear′e·an** *adj.*, *n.*

**shake′-up′** *n.* a shaking up; specif., an extensive reorganization

**shak·o** (shak′ō) *n., pl.* **-os** [< Hung.] a high, stiff military dress hat, with a flat top and a plume

**shale** (shāl) *n.* [< OE. *scealu,* a shell] a rock formed of hardened clay: it splits easily into thin layers

**shale oil** oil distilled from a hard shale containing veins of a greasy organic solid

**shall** (shal) *v. pt.* **should** [OE. *sceal*] an auxiliary used in formal speech to express futurity in the first person, and determination, obligation, or necessity in the second and third persons *Shall* is now ordinarily replaced by *will* in all persons

**shal·lot** (shə lät′) *n.* [< OFr. *eschaloigne,* scallion] **1.** a small onion whose clustered bulbs are used for flavoring **2.** a green onion

**shal·low** (shal′ō) *adj.* [ME. *shalow*] **1.** not deep **2.** lacking depth of character, intellect, etc. —*n.* a shoal

**shalt** (shalt) *archaic 2d pers. sing., pres. indic.,* of SHALL: used with *thou*

**sham** (sham) *n.* [< ? SHAME] something false or fake; person or thing that is a fraud —*adj.* false or fake —*vt., vi.* **shammed, sham′ming** to pretend; feign —**sham′mer** *n.*

**sham·ble** (sham′b'l) *vi.* **-bled, -bling** [< obs. use in *"shamble* legs," bench legs] to walk clumsily; shuffle —*n.* a shambling walk

**sham′bles** (-b'lz) *n.pl.* [*with sing. v.*] [ME. *schamel,* butcher's bench; ult. < L.] **1.** a slaughterhouse **2.** a scene of great slaughter, destruction, or disorder

**shame** (shām) *n.* [OE. *scamu*] **1.** a painful feeling of guilt for improper behavior, etc. **2.** dishonor or disgrace **3.** something regrettable or outrageous —*vt.* **shamed, sham'ing** 1. to cause to feel shame 2. to dishonor or disgrace 3. to force by a sense of shame —**put to shame** 1. to cause to feel shame 2. to surpass —**shame'ful** *adj.* —**shame'ful·ly** *adv.* — **shame'ful·ness** *n.*

**shame'faced'** *adj.* 1. bashful; shy 2. showing shame; ashamed

**shame'less** *adj.* having or showing no shame, modesty, or decency; brazen

**sham·poo** (sham poo') *vt.* **-pooed', -poo'ing** [Hind. *chāmpnā,* to press] 1. to wash (the hair) 2. to wash (a rug, sofa, etc.) —*n.* 1. a shampooing 2. a liquid soap, etc. used for this

**sham·rock** (sham'räk') *n.* [Ir. *seamar,* clover] a cloverlike plant with leaflets in groups of three: the emblem of Ireland

**Shang·hai** (shaŋ'hī') seaport in E China: pop. c.10,000,000

**shang·hai** (shaŋ'hī') *vt.* **-haied', -hai'ing** [< such kidnapping for crews on the China run] to kidnap, usually by drugging, for service aboard ship

**shank** (shaŋk) *n.* [OE. *scanca*] 1. the part of the leg between the knee and the ankle in man, or a corresponding part in animals 2. the whole leg 3. the part between the handle and the working part (of a tool, etc.) —**shank of the evening** early evening

**shan't** (shant) shall not

**shan·tung** (shan'tuŋ') *n.* [< *Shantung,* province of China] a silk or silky fabric with an uneven surface

**shan·ty** (shan'tē) *n., pl.* **-ties** [< CanadFr. *chantier,* workshop] a small, shabby dwelling; shack; hut

**shape** (shāp) *n.* [< OE. (ge)*sceap,* a form] 1. that quality of a thing which depends on the relative position of all the points on its surface; physical form 2. the contour of the body 3. definite or regular form [to begin to take *shape*] 4. [Colloq.] physical condition —*vt.* **shaped, shap'ing** 1. to give definite shape to 2. to arrange, express, etc. in definite form 3. to adapt [*shaped* to our needs] —**shape up** to develop to a definite or satisfactory form, etc. —**take shape** to show distinct development —**shape'less** *adj.* —**shape'less·ness** *n.*

**shape'ly** *adj.* **-li·er, -li·est** having a pleasing figure: esp. of a woman

**shard** (shärd) *n.* [OE. *sceard*] a broken piece, esp. of pottery

**share¹** (sher) *n.* [< OE. *scearu*] 1. a portion that belongs to an individual 2. any of the equal parts of capital stock of a corporation —*vt.* **shared, shar'ing** 1. to distribute in shares 2. to have or use in common with others —*vi.* to have a share (*in*)

**share²** (sher) *n.* [OE. *scear*] a plowshare

**share'crop'** *vi., vt.* **-cropped', -crop'ping** to work (land) for a share of the crop —**share'crop'per** *n.*

**share'hold'er** *n.* a person who owns shares of stock in a corporation

**shark¹** (shärk) *n.* [prob. < G. *schurke,* scoundrel] 1. a swindler 2. [Slang] an expert in a given activity

**shark²** (shärk) *n.* [< ?] a large, predatory sea fish with a tough, gray skin

**shark'skin'** (-skin') *n.* a smooth, silky cloth of wool, rayon, etc.

**sharp** (shärp) *adj.* [OE. *scearp*] 1. having a fine edge or

SHARK

point for cutting or piercing 2. having a point or edge; not rounded 3. not gradual; abrupt 4. clearly defined; distinct [a *sharp* contrast] 5. quick in perception; clever 6. attentive; vigilant 7. crafty; underhanded 8. harsh; severe, as temper 9. violent, as an attack 10. brisk; active 11. intense, as a pain 12. pungent 13. nippy, as a wind 14. [Slang] smartly dressed 15. *Music* above the true pitch —*n.* 1. [Colloq.] an expert 2. *Music a*) a tone one half step above another *b*) the symbol (♯) for such a note —*vt., vi. Music* to make or become sharp —*adv.* 1. in a sharp manner; specif., *a*) abruptly or briskly *b*) attentively or alertly *c*) *Music* above the true pitch 2. precisely [one o'clock *sharp*] —**sharp'ly** *adv.* —**sharp'ness** *n.*

**sharp'en** *vt., vi.* to make or become sharp —**sharp'en·er** *n.*

**sharp'er** *n.* a swindler or cheat

**sharp'-eyed'** *adj.* having keen sight or perception: also **sharp'-sight'ed**

**sharp'ie** (-ē) *n.* [Colloq.] a shrewd, cunning person, esp. a sharper

**sharp'shoot'er** *n.* a good marksman

**sharp'-tongued'** *adj.* using sharp or harshly critical speech

**sharp'-wit'ted** *adj.* thinking quickly and effectively

**shat·ter** (shat'ər) *vt., vi.* [ME. *schateren,* scatter] 1. to break or burst into pieces suddenly 2. to damage or be damaged severely

**shat'ter·proof'** *adj.* that will resist shattering [*shatterproof* glass]

**shave** (shāv) *vt.* **shaved, shaved** or **shav'en, shav'ing** [OE. *sceafan*] 1. to cut away thin slices or sections from 2. *a*) to cut off (hair) at the surface of the skin *b*) to cut the hair to the surface of (the face, etc.) *c*) to cut the beard of (a person) 3. to barely touch in passing; graze —*vi.* to cut off a beard with a razor, etc. —*n.* the act or an instance of shaving

**shav'er** *n.* 1. one who shaves 2. an instrument used in shaving, esp. one with electrically operated cutters 3. [Colloq.] a boy; lad

**shav'ing** *n.* 1. the act of one who shaves 2. a thin piece of wood, metal, etc. shaved off

**Shaw** (shô), George Bernard 1856–

1950; Brit. dramatist & critic —**Sha·vi·an** (shā′vē ən) *adj., n.*

**shawl** (shôl) *n.* [< Per. *shāl*] an oblong or square cloth worn as a covering for the head or shoulders

**shay** (shā) *n.* [< CHAISE, assumed as pl.] [Dial.] a light carriage; chaise

**she** (shē) *pron. for pl. see* THEY [< OE. *seo*] the woman, girl, or female animal previously mentioned —*n.* a woman, girl, or female animal

**sheaf** (shēf) *n., pl.* **sheaves** (shēvz) [OE. *sceaf*] 1. a bundle of cut stalks of grain, etc. 2. a collection, as of papers, bound in a bundle

**shear** (shir) *vt.* **sheared, sheared** or **shorn, shear′ing** [OE. *scieran*] 1. to cut as with shears 2. to clip (hair) from (the head), (wool) from (sheep), etc. 3. to divest [*shorn* of power] —*n.* 1. a machine for cutting metal 2. a shearing —**shear′er** *n.*

**shears** *n.pl.* 1. large scissors 2. a large tool or machine with two opposed blades, used to cut metal, etc.

**sheath** (shēth) *n., pl.* **sheaths** (shēthz, shēths) [OE. *sceath*] 1. a case for the blade of a knife, sword, etc. 2. a covering resembling this 3. a woman's closefitting dress

**sheathe** (shēth) *vt.* **sheathed, sheath′ing** 1. to put into a sheath 2. to enclose in a case or covering

**sheath·ing** (shē′thin) *n.* something that sheathes, as boards, etc. forming the base for roofing or siding

**she·bang** (shə ban′) *n.* [Colloq.] an affair, business, contrivance, etc.: in phrase **the whole shebang**

**shed**[1] (shed) *n.* [OE. *scead*] a small structure for shelter or storage

**shed**[2] (shed) *vt.* **shed, shed′ding** [OE. *sceadan*, to separate] 1. to pour out 2. to cause to flow [to *shed* tears] 3. to radiate [to *shed* confidence] 4. to cause to flow off [oilskin *sheds* water] 5. to cast off (a natural growth, as hair, etc.) —*vi.* to shed hair, etc. —**shed blood** to kill violently

**she′d** (shēd) 1. she had 2. she would

**sheen** (shēn) *n.* [< OE. *sciene*, beautiful] brightness; luster —**sheen′y** *adj.*

**sheep** (shēp) *n., pl.* **sheep** [OE. *sceap*] 1. a cud-chewing mammal related to the goats, with heavy wool and edible flesh called mutton 2. one who is meek, timid, submissive, etc.

**sheep dog** a dog trained to herd sheep

**sheep′fold**′ *n.* a pen or enclosure for sheep: also **sheep′cote**′ (-kōt′)

**sheep′ish** *adj.* 1. embarrassed or chagrined 2. shy or bashful —**sheep′ish·ly** *adv.* —**sheep′ish·ness** *n.*

**sheep′skin**′ *n.* 1. the skin of a sheep 2. parchment or leather made from it 3. [Colloq.] a diploma

**sheer**[1] (shir) *vi., vt.* [var. of SHEAR] to turn aside or cause to turn aside from a course; swerve

**sheer**[2] (shir) *adj.* [< ON. *skærr*, bright] 1. very thin; transparent: said of textiles 2. absolute; utter [*sheer* folly] 3. extremely steep —*adv.* 1. completely; utterly 2. very steeply

**sheet**[1] (shēt) *n.* [OE. *sceat*] a large piece of cotton, linen, etc., used on a bed 2. *a*) a single piece of paper *b*) [Colloq.] a newspaper 3. a broad, continuous surface or expanse, as of flame, ice, etc. 4. a broad, thin piece of any material, as glass, plywood, metal, etc.

**sheet**[2] (shēt) *n.* [short for OE. *sceat·line*] a rope for controlling the set of a sail

**sheet′ing** *n.* 1. cotton or linen material used for making sheets 2. material used to cover or line a surface [copper *sheeting*]

**sheet metal** metal rolled thin in the form of a sheet

**sheet music** music printed on unbound sheets of paper

**sheik, sheikh** (shēk) *n.* [Ar. *shaikh*, lit., old man] the chief of an Arab family, tribe, or village

**shek·el** (shek′′l) *n.* [< Heb. *shāqal*, weigh] 1. a gold or silver coin of the ancient Hebrews 2. [*pl.*] [Slang] money

**shelf** (shelf) *n., pl.* **shelves** (shelvz) [< MLowG. *schelf*] 1. a thin, flat board fixed horizontally to a wall, used for holding things 2. something like a shelf, as *a*) a ledge *b*) a sand bar —**on the shelf** out of use, activity, etc.

**shell** (shel) *n.* [OE. *sciel*] 1. a hard outer covering, as of a turtle, egg, nut, etc. 2. something like a shell in being hollow, empty, a covering, etc. 3. a light, narrow racing boat rowed by a team 4. an explosive artillery projectile 5. a small-arms cartridge —*vt.* 1. to remove the shell or covering from [to *shell* peas] 2. to bombard —**shell out** [Colloq.] to pay out (money)

**she′ll** (shēl) 1. she shall 2. she will

**shel·lac, shel·lack** (shə lak′) *n.* [< SHELL & LAC] 1. a resin usually produced in thin, flaky layers or shells 2. a thin varnish containing this resin and alcohol —*vt.* -**lacked′**, -**lack′ing** 1. to apply shellac to 2. [Slang] *a*) to beat *b*) to defeat decisively

-**shelled** (sheld) *a combining form meaning* having a (specified kind of) shell

**Shel·ley** (shel′ē), **Per·cy Bysshe** (pur′sē bish) 1792–1822; Eng. poet

**shell′fire**′ *n.* the firing of artillery shells

**shell′fish**′ *n., pl.:* see FISH any aquatic animal with a shell, esp. an edible one, as the clam, lobster, etc.

**shel·ter** (shel′tər) *n.* [< ? OE. *scield*, shield + *truma*, a troop] 1. something that protects, as from the elements, danger, etc. 2. a being covered, protected, etc. —*vt.* to provide shelter for; protect —*vi.* to find shelter

**shelve** (shelv) *vt.* **shelved, shelv′ing** 1. to furnish with shelves 2. to put on a shelf 3. to put aside; defer

**shelves** (shelvz) *n. pl. of* SHELF

**shelv′ing** *n.* 1. material for shelves 2. shelves collectively

**she·nan·i·gan** (shi nan′i g′n) *n.* [< ? Ir. *sionnachuighim*, I play the fox] [*usually pl.*] [Colloq.] trickery; mischief

**Shen·yang** (shun′yän′) city in NE China: pop. 2,423,000

**shep·herd** (shep′ərd) *n.* [see SHEEP & HERD] 1. one who herds sheep 2. a clergyman —vt. to herd, lead, etc. as a shepherd —**shep′herd·ess** n.fem.

**sher·bet** (shur′bət) n. [< Ar. *sharbah*, a drink] a frozen dessert like an ice, but with gelatin added, often, milk added

**sher·iff** (sher′if) n. [< OE. *scir*, shire, + *gerefa*, chief officer] the chief law-enforcement officer of a county

**Sher·pa** (shur′pə, sher′-) n., pl. **-pas**, **-pa** any of a Tibetan people of Nepal, famous as mountain climbers

**sher·ry** (sher′ē) n., pl. **-ries** [< *Jerez*, Spain] 1. a strong, yellow or brown Spanish wine 2. any similar wine

**she's** (shēz) 1. she is 2. she has

**shew** (shō) n., vt., vi. **shewed**, **shewn** or **shewed**, **shew′ing** archaic sp. of SHOW

**shib·bo·leth** (shib′ə ləth) n. [< Heb. *shibbōleth*, a stream] 1. *Bible* the test word used to distinguish the enemy: Judg. 12:4–6 2. any password 3. any phrase, custom, etc. peculiar to a certain class, faction, etc.

**shied** (shīd) pt. & pp. of SHY¹

**shield** (shēld) n. [OE. *scield*] 1. a piece of armor worn on the forearm to ward off blows, etc. 2. one that guards, protects, etc. 3. anything shaped like a shield —vt., vi. to defend; protect

**shift** (shift) vt. [OE. *sciftan*, divide] 1. to move from one person or place to another 2. to replace by another or others 3. to change the arrangement of (gears) —vi. 1. to change position, direction, etc. 2. to get along [to shift for oneself] —n. 1. a shifting; transfer 2. a plan of conduct, esp. for an emergency 3. an evasion; trick 4. a gearshift 5. a) a group of people working in relay with another b) their regular work period —**make shift** to manage (*with* the means at hand)

**shift′less** adj. incapable, inefficient, lazy, etc. —**shift′less·ness** n.

**shift′y** adj. **-i·er**, **-i·est** of a tricky or deceitful nature; evasive —**shift′i·ly** adv. —**shift′i·ness** n.

**Shih Tzu** (shē′ dzōō′) pl. **Shih Tzu**, **Shih Tzus** [< Chin. *shin*, lion + *tzu*, son] a small dog with long, silky hair and short legs

**shill** (shil) n. [Slang] a confederate, as of a carnival operator, who pretends to buy, bet, etc. so as to lure others

**shil·le·lagh** (shi lā′lē, -lə) n. [< *Shillelagh*, Ir. village] a cudgel

**shil·ling** (shil′iŋ) n. [OE. *scylling*] a former British money of account and silver coin, equal to 1/20 of a pound

**shil·ly-shal·ly** (shil′ē shal′ē) vi. **-lied**, **-ly·ing** [< *shall I*?] to be irresolute; vacillate, esp. over trifles

**shim** (shim) n. [< ?] a thin wedge of wood, metal, etc. as for filling space

**shim·mer** (shim′ər) vi. [OE. *scymrian*] to shine with an unsteady light; glimmer —n. a shimmering light

**shim·my** (shim′ē) n. [< a jazz dance < CHEMISE] a marked vibration or wobble, as in a car's front wheels —vi.

**-mied**, **-my·ing** to vibrate or wobble

**shin** (shin) n. [OE. *scinu*] the front part of the leg between the knee and the ankle —vt., vi. **shinned**, **shin′ning** to climb (a pole, etc.) by gripping with hands and legs: also **shin′ny**

**shin′bone′** n. same as TIBIA

**shin·dig** (shin′dig′) n. [< colloq. *shindy*, commotion] [Colloq.] a dance, party, or other informal gathering

**shine** (shīn) vi. **shone**, or, esp. for vt. 2, **shined**, **shin′ing** [OE. *scinan*] 1. to emit or reflect light 2. to stand out; excel 3. to exhibit itself clearly [love *shining* from her face] —vt. 1. to direct the light of 2. to make shiny by polishing —n. 1. brightness; radiance 2. luster; gloss

**shin′er** (-ər) n. 1. a silvery minnow 2. [Slang] same as BLACK EYE

**shin·gle¹** (shiŋ′g'l) n. [prob. < Scand.] 1. coarse, waterworn gravel, as on a beach 2. an area covered with this —**shin′gly** adj. **-gli·er**, **-gli·est**

**shin·gle²** (shiŋ′g'l) n. [< OE. *scindel*] 1. a thin, wedge-shaped piece of wood, slate, etc. laid with others in overlapping rows, as for roofs 2. a short haircut, tapered at the nape 3. [Colloq.] a small signboard, as of a doctor —vt. **-gled**, **-gling** to cover (a roof, etc.) with shingles

**shin·gles** (shiŋ′g'lz) n. [< L. *cingere*, to gird] a virus disease with skin blisters along the course of a nerve

**shin′guard′** n. a padded guard worn to protect the shins in some sports

**shin′splints′** (-splints′) n.pl. [with sing. v.] [< SHIN + ? *splint*, growth on bone of a horse's leg] painful strain of muscles of the lower leg

**Shin·to** (shin′tō) n. [Jap. < Chin. *shin*, god + *tao*, way] a religion of Japan, emphasizing ancestor worship

**shin·y** (shīn′ē) adj. **-i·er**, **-i·est** 1. bright; shining 2. highly polished —**shin′i·ness** n.

**ship** (ship) n. [OE. *scip*] 1. any large vessel navigating deep water 2. a ship's officers and crew 3. an aircraft —vt. **shipped**, **ship′ping** 1. to put or take on board a ship 2. to send or transport by any carrier [to *ship* coal by rail] 3. a) to take in (water) over the side in a heavy sea b) to put in place on a vessel [ship the oars] —vi. to go aboard ship; embark —**ship′per** n.

**-ship** (ship) [OE. *-scipe*] a suffix meaning: 1. the quality or state of [*friendship*] 2. a) the rank or office of [*governorship*] b) one having the rank of [*lordship*] 3. skill as [*leadership*] 4. all persons (of a specified group) collectively [*readership*]

**ship′board′** n. a ship: chiefly in on shipboard aboard a ship

**ship′build′er** n. one whose business is building ships —**ship′build′ing** n.

**ship′mate′** n. a fellow sailor

**ship′ment** n. 1. the shipping of goods 2. goods shipped

**ship′ping** n. 1. the act or business of

transporting goods 2. ships collectively, as of a nation, port, etc.

**shipping clerk** an employee who supervises the shipping of goods and keeps records of shipments

**ship'shape'** *adj.* having everything neatly in place; trim

**ship'wreck'** *n.* 1. the remains of a wrecked ship 2. the loss of a ship through storm, etc. 3. ruin; failure —*vt.* to cause to undergo shipwreck

**ship'yard'** *n.* a place where ships are built and repaired

**shire** (shir) *n.* [OE. *scir*, office] in Great Britain, a county

**shirk** (shurk) *vt., vi.* [< ?] to neglect or evade (a duty, etc.) —**shirk'er** *n.*

**shirr** (shur) *n.* [< ?] *same as* SHIRRING —*vt.* 1. to make shirring in (cloth) 2. to bake (eggs) in buttered dishes

**shirr'ing** *n.* a gathering made in cloth by drawing the material up on parallel rows of short stitches

**shirt** (shurt) *n.* [OE. *scyrte*] 1. a garment worn by men on the upper part of the body 2. an undershirt —**keep one's shirt on** [Slang] to remain patient or calm

**shirt'tail'** (-tāl') *n.* the part of a shirt extending below the waist

**shirt'waist'** (-wāst') *n.* a woman's blouse tailored like a shirt

**shish ke·bab** (shish' kə bäb') [< Ar. *shish*, skewer + *kabāb*, kebab] a dish of kebabs, esp. of lamb

**shiv** (shiv) *n.* [prob. < Romany *chiv*, blade] [Slang] a knife

**shiv·er¹** (shiv'ər) *n.* [ME. *schivere*] a fragment or splinter —*vt., vi.* to break into fragments or splinters

**shiv·er²** (shiv'ər) *vi.* [< ? OE. *ceafl*, jaw] to shake or tremble, as from fear or cold —*n.* a shaking, trembling, etc. —**shiv'er·y** *adj.*

**shlep, shlepp** (shlep) *n.* [Slang] *var. of* SCHLEP

**shmaltz** (shmälts) *n.* [Slang] *var. of* SCHMALTZ

**shoal¹** (shōl) *n.* [OE. *scolu*] 1. a large group; crowd 2. a school of fish

**shoal²** (shōl) *n.* [< OE. *sceald*, shallow] 1. a shallow place in a river, sea, etc. 2. a sand bar forming a shallow place

**shoat** (shōt) *n.* a young hog

**shock¹** (shäk) *n.* [MFr. *choquer*, collide] 1. a sudden, powerful blow, shake, etc. 2. *a*) a sudden emotional disturbance *b*) the cause of this 3. an extreme stimulation of the nerves through the passage of electric current through the body 4. a disorder of the blood circulation, produced by hemorrhage, disturbance of heart function, etc. —*vt.* 1. to astonish, horrify, etc. 2. to produce electrical shock in

**shock²** (shäk) *n.* [ME. *schokke*] bundles of grain stacked together

**shock³** (shäk) *n.* [< ? prec.] a thick, bushy or tangled mass, as of hair

**shock absorber** a device, as on the springs of a car, that absorbs the force of bumps and jarring

**shock'er** *n.* 1. anything that shocks 2. a sensational story, play, etc.

**shock'ing** *adj.* 1. causing great surprise and distress 2. disgusting

**shock'proof'** *adj.* able to absorb shock without being damaged

**shock therapy** the treatment of certain severe mental illnesses by using electricity, drugs, etc., producing convulsions or coma

**shock troops** troops trained to lead an attack

**shod** (shäd) *pt. & pp. of* SHOE

**shod·dy** (shäd'ē) *n., pl.* -dies [< ?] 1. an inferior woolen cloth made from used fabrics 2. anything worth less than it seems to be —*adj.* -di·er, -di·est 1. made of inferior material 2. poorly done or made 3. sham —**shod'di·ly** *adv.* —**shod'di·ness** *n.*

**shoe** (shōō) *n.* [< OE. *sceoh*] 1. an outer covering for the foot 2. a horseshoe 3. the part of a brake that presses against a wheel 4. the casing of a pneumatic tire —*vt.* shod or shoed, **shoe'ing** to furnish with shoes —**fill one's shoes** to take one's place

**shoe'horn'** *n.* an implement used to help slip one's heel into a shoe

**shoe'lace'** *n.* a length of cord, etc. used for lacing and fastening a shoe

**shoe'mak'er** *n.* one whose business is making or repairing shoes

**shoe'shine'** *n.* the cleaning and polishing of a pair of shoes

**shoe'string'** *n.* 1. a shoelace 2. a small amount of capital —*adj.* at or near the ankles [a *shoestring* catch]

**shoe tree** a form inserted in a shoe to stretch it or preserve its shape

**shone** (shōn) *alt. pt. & pp. of* SHINE

**shoo** (shōō) *interj.* go away! get out! —*vt.* shooed, **shoo'ing** to drive away, as by crying "shoo"

**shoo'-in'** *n.* [Colloq.] one expected to win easily in a race, etc.

**shook** (shook) *pt. of* SHAKE —**shook up** [Slang] upset; agitated

**shoot** (shoot) *vt.* shot, **shoot'ing** [OE. *sceotan*] 1. to move swiftly over, by, etc. [to *shoot* the rapids] 2. to variegate (with another color, etc.) 3. to thrust or put forth 4. to discharge or fire (a bullet, arrow, gun, etc.) 5. to send forth swiftly, or with force 6. to hit, wound, etc. with a bullet, arrow, etc. 7. to photograph 8. *Sports a*) to throw or drive (a ball, etc.) toward the objective *b*) to score (a goal, points, etc.) —*vi.* 1. to move swiftly 2. to be felt suddenly, as pain 3. to grow rapidly 4. to jut out 5. to send forth a missile; discharge bullets, etc. 6. to use guns, etc., as in hunting —*n.* 1. a shooting trip, contest, etc. 2. a new growth; sprout —**shoot at** (or **for**) [Colloq.] to strive for

**shoot'-out', shoot'out'** *n.* [Slang] a battle, as between police and criminals, in which small arms are used

**shop** (shäp) *n.* [< OE. *sceoppa*, booth] 1. a place where certain things are offered for sale; esp., a small store 2. a place where a particular kind of work is done —*vi.* shopped, **shop'ping** to visit shops to examine or buy goods —**talk shop** to discuss one's work

**shop'keep'er** *n.* one who owns or operates a shop, or small store

**shop'lift'er** *n.* one who steals articles

from a store during shopping hours —**shop′lift′** *vt., vi.*

**shoppe** (shäp) *n. old sp.* of SHOP (sense 1): now used only in names of such shops

**shop′per** *n.* 1. one who shops 2. one hired by a store to shop for others 3. one hired by a store to compare competitors' prices, etc.

**shopping center** a complex of stores, restaurants, etc. with a common parking area

**shop′talk′** *n.* 1. the specialized words and idioms of those in the same work 2. talk about work, esp. after hours

**shop′worn′** *adj.* soiled, faded, etc. from being displayed in a shop

**shore**[1] (shôr) *n.* [ME. *schore*] land at the edge of a body of water

**shore**[2] (shôr) *n.* [ME. *schore*] a prop, beam, etc. used for support, etc. —*vt.* **shored, shor′ing** to support as with shores; prop (*up*)

**shore patrol** a detail of the U.S. Navy, Coast Guard, or Marine Corps acting as military police on shore

SHORES

**shorn** (shôrn) *alt. pp.* of SHEAR

**short** (shôrt) *adj.* [OE. *scort*] 1. not measuring much from end to end in space or time 2. not great in range or scope 3. not tall 4. brief; concise 5. not retentive [a *short* memory] 6. curt; abrupt 7. less than a sufficient or correct amount 8. crisp or flaky, as pastry rich in shortening 9. designating a sale of securities, etc. which the seller does not yet own but expects to buy later at a lower price —*n.* 1. something short 2. [*pl.*] *a)* short trousers *b)* a man's undergarment like these 3. *same as:* *a)* SHORTSTOP *b)* SHORT CIRCUIT —*adv.* 1. abruptly; suddenly 2. briefly; concisely 3. so as to be short in length —*vt., vi.* 1. to give less than what is needed or usual 2. *same as:* *a)* SHORTCHANGE *b)* SHORT-CIRCUIT —**fall** (or **come**) **short** to fail to reach, suffice, etc. —**in short** briefly —**run short** to have less than enough —**short of** less than or lacking —**short′ness** *n.*

**short′age** *n.* a deficiency in the amount needed or expected; deficit

**short′bread′** *n.* a rich, crumbly cake or cookie made with much shortening

**short′cake′** *n.* a light biscuit or a sweet cake served with fruit, etc. as a dessert

**short′change′** *vt., vi.* **-changed′, -chang′ing** [Colloq.] to give less money than is due in change

**short circuit** 1. a connection between two points in an electric circuit resulting in a side circuit that deflects current or in excessive current flow causing damage 2. popularly, a disrupted electric current caused by this —**short′-cir′cuit** *vt., vi.*

**short′com′ing** *n.* a defect or deficiency

**short′cut′** *n.* 1. a shorter route 2. any way of saving time, effort, etc.

**short′en** *vt., vi.* to make or become short or shorter

**short′en·ing** *n.* edible fat used to make pastry, etc. crisp or flaky

**short′hand′** *n.* any system of speed writing using symbols for letters, words, and phrases

**short′-hand′ed** *adj.* short of workers

**short′horn′** *n.* any of a breed of cattle with short, curved horns

**short′-lived′** (-līvd′, -livd′) *adj.* having a short life span or existence

**short′ly** *adv.* 1. briefly 2. soon 3. abruptly and rudely; curtly

**short order** any food that can be cooked or served quickly when ordered

**short′-range′** *adj.* reaching over a short distance or period of time

**short ribs** rib ends of beef from the forequarter

**short shrift** very little care or attention —**make short shrift of** to make short work of

**short′sight′ed** *adj.* 1. nearsighted 2. lacking in foresight —**short′sight′-ed·ly** *adv.* —**short′sight′ed·ness** *n.*

**short′-spo′ken** *adj.* using few words, esp. to the point of rudeness; curt

**short′stop′** *n. Baseball* the infielder between second and third base

**short story** a piece of prose fiction shorter than a short novel

**short subject** a short film, as an animated cartoon, shown along with a featured motion picture

**short′-tem′pered** *adj.* easily or quickly angered

**short′-term′** *adj.* for or extending over a short time

**short ton** 2,000 pounds: see TON

**short′wave′** *n.* a radio wave 60 meters or less in length

**short′-wind′ed** (-win′did) *adj.* easily put out of breath by exertion

**shot**[1] (shät) *n.* [OE. *sceot*] 1. the act of shooting 2. range; scope 3. an attempt; try 4. a pointed, critical remark 5. the path of an object thrown, etc. 6. *a)* a projectile for a gun *b)* projectiles collectively 7. small pellets of lead for a shotgun 8. the heavy metal ball used in the shot put 9. a marksman 10. a photograph or a continuous film sequence 11. a hypodermic injection, as of vaccine 12. a drink of liquor —**call the shots** to direct or control what is done

**shot**[2] (shät) *adj. & pp.* of SHOOT —*adj.* [Colloq.] ruined or worn out

**shot′gun′** *n.* a gun for firing small shot at close range

**shot put** a contest in which a heavy metal ball is propelled with an overhand thrust from the shoulder —**shot′-put′ter** *n.* —**shot′-put′ting** *n.*

**should** (shood) *v.* [OE. *sceolde*] 1. *pt.* of SHALL 2. an auxiliary used to express: *a)* obligation, duty, etc. *[you should* help*] b)* expectation or probability *[he should* be here soon*] c)* a future condition *[if I should die]*

**shoul·der** (shōl'dər) *n.* [OE. *sculder*] 1. *a)* the joint connecting the arm or forelimb with the body *b)* the part of the body including this joint 2. *[pl.]* the two shoulders and the part of the back between them 3. a shoulderlike projection 4. the land along the edge of a road —*vt.* 1. to push through, as with the shoulder 2. to carry upon the shoulder 3. to assume the burden of —**straight from the shoulder** without reserve; frankly —**turn (or give) a cold shoulder to** to snub or shun

**shoulder blade** either of the two flat bones in the upper back

**shoulder harness** an anchored strap passing across the upper body and used with a seat belt, as in a car

**should·n't** should not

**shout** (shout) *n.* [ME. *schoute*] a loud cry or call —*vt., vi.* to utter or cry out in a shout —**shout'er** *n.*

**shove** (shuv) *vt., vi.* shoved, shov'ing [OE. *scufan*] 1. to push, as along a surface 2. to push roughly —*n.* a push —**shove off** 1. to push (a boat) away from shore 2. [Colloq.] to leave

**shov·el** (shuv'l) *n.* [OE. *sceofl*] a tool with a broad scoop and a long handle, for lifting and moving loose material —*vt.* -eled or -elled, -el·ing or -el·ling 1. to move with a shovel 2. to dig out with a shovel

**shov'el·ful'** *n., pl.* -fuls' as much as a shovel will hold

**show** (shō) *vt.* showed, shown or showed, show'ing [< OE. *sceawian*] 1. to bring or put in sight 2. to guide; conduct 3. to point out 4. to reveal, as by behavior 5. to prove; demonstrate 6. to bestow (favor, mercy, etc.) —*vi.* 1. to be or become seen; appear 2. to be noticeable 3. to finish third in a horse race —*n.* 1. a showing or demonstration 2. pompous display 3. pretense *[his anger was mere show]* 4. a public display or exhibition 5. a presentation of entertainment —**show off** to make a display of, esp. a vain display —**show up** 1. to expose 2. to be seen 3. to arrive

**show'boat'** *n.* a boat with a theater and actors who play river towns

**show'case'** *n.* a glass-enclosed case for displaying things, as in a store

**show'down'** *n.* [Colloq.] an action that brings matters to a climax

**show·er** (shou'ər) *n.* [OE. *scur*] 1. a brief fall of rain, sleet, etc. 2. a sudden, abundant fall, as of sparks 3. a party at which gifts are presented to the guest of honor 4. a bath in which the body is sprayed with fine streams of water: in full **shower bath** —*vt.* 1. to spray with water, etc. 2. to pour forth as in a shower —*vi.* 1. to fall or come as a shower 2. to take a shower bath —**show'er·y** *adj.*

**show'ing** *n.* 1. a bringing to view or notice; exhibition 2. a performance, appearance, etc. *[a good showing in the contest]*

**show·man** (shō'mən) *n., pl.* -men 1. one whose business is producing shows 2. a person skilled at presenting anything in a striking manner —**show'man·ship'** *n.*

**shown** (shōn) *alt. pp.* of SHOW

**show'off'** *n.* one who shows off

**show of hands** a raising of hands, as in voting or volunteering

**show'piece'** *n.* 1. something displayed or exhibited 2. something that is a fine example of its kind

**show'place'** *n.* 1. a place displayed to the public for its beauty, etc. 2. any beautiful place

**show'room'** *n.* a room where goods are displayed for advertising or sale

**show window** a store window in which merchandise is displayed

**show'y** *adj.* -i·er, -i·est 1. of striking appearance 2. attracting attention in a gaudy way —**show'i·ness** *n.*

**snrank** (shrank) *alt. pt.* of SHRINK

**shrap·nel** (shrap'n'l) *n.* [< Gen. *Shrapnel* (1761–1842), its Brit. inventor] 1. an artillery shell filled with an explosive charge and small metal balls 2. these balls or the shell fragments scattered on explosion

**shred** (shred) *n.* [OE. *screade*] 1. a narrow strip cut or torn off 2. a fragment —*vt.* shred'ded or shred, shred'ding to cut or tear into shreds —**shred'da·ble** *adj.* —**shred'der** *n.*

**Shreve·port** (shrēv'pôrt) city in NW La.: pop. 182,000

**shrew** (shrōō) *n.* [< OE. *screawa*] 1. a small, mouselike mammal with a long snout 2. a nagging, evil-tempered woman —**shrew'ish** *n.*

**shrewd** (shrōōd) *adj.* [see prec.] clever or sharp in practical affairs; astute —**shrewd'ly** *adv.* —**shrewd'ness** *n.*

**shriek** (shrēk) *vi., vt.* [ME. *schriken*] to make or utter with a loud, piercing cry; screech —*n.* such a cry

**shrift** (shrift) *n.* [ult. < L. *scribere*, write] [Archaic] confession to and absolution by a priest See also SHORT SHRIFT

**shrike** (shrīk) *n.* [OE. *scric*] a shrill-voiced bird of prey with a hooked beak

**shrill** (shril) *adj.* [echoic] producing a high, thin piercing sound —*vt., vi.* to utter (with) a shrill sound —**shrill'-ness** *n.* —**shril'ly** *adv.*

**shrimp** (shrimp) *n.* [OE. *scrimman*, shrink] 1. a small, long-tailed crustacean, valued as food 2. [Colloq.] a small or insignificant person

**shrine** (shrīn) *n.* [< L. *scrinium*, box] 1. a container holding sacred relics 2. a saint's tomb 3. a place of worship 4. any hallowed place

**shrink** (shrink) *vi.* shrank or shrunk, shrunk or shrunk'en, shrink'ing [OE. *scrincan*] 1. to contract, as from cold, wetting, etc. 2. to lessen, as in amount 3. to draw back; flinch —*vt.* to make shrink —**shrink'a·ble** *adj.*

**shrink'age** *n.* 1. a shrinking 2. the amount of shrinking

**shrinking violet** a very shy person

**shrive** (shrīv) *vt.* shrived or shrove (shrōv), shriv·en (shriv''n) or shrived, shriv'ing [OE. *scrifan*] [Archaic] to hear the confession of and give absolution to

**shriv·el** (shriv′'l) *vt., vi.* -eled or -elled, -el·ing or -el·ling [prob. < Scand.] to shrink and wrinkle or wither

**shroud** (shroud) *n.* [OE. *scrud*] 1. a cloth used to wrap a corpse for burial 2. something that covers, veils, etc. 3. any of the ropes from a ship's side to a masthead —*vt.* to hide; cover

**Shrove Tuesday** [see SHRIVE] the last day before Lent

**shrub** (shrub) *n.* [OE. *scrybb*, brushwood] a low, woody plant with several stems; bush —**shrub′by** *adj.*

**shrub′ber·y** *n.* shrubs collectively

**shrug** (shrug) *vt., vi.* shrugged, shrug′ging [ME. *schruggen*] to draw up (the shoulders), as in indifference, doubt, etc. —*n.* the gesture made

**shrunk** (shruŋk) *alt. pt. & pp. of* SHRINK

**shrunk′en** *alt. pp. of* SHRINK —*adj.* contracted in size

**shtg.** shortage

**shtick** (shtik) *n.* [Yid.] [Slang] a comic bit or special gimmick

**shuck** (shuk) *n.* [ < ?] a shell, pod, or husk —*vt.* to remove the shucks of

**shucks** (shuks) *interj.* [ < prec.] an exclamation of disappointment, disgust, etc.

**shud·der** (shud′ər) *vi.* [ME. *schoderen*] to shake or tremble, as in horror —*n.* a shuddering

**shuf·fle** (shuf′'l) *vt., vi.* -fled, -fling [prob. < LowG. *schuffeln*] 1. to move (the feet) with a dragging gait 2. to mix (playing cards) 3. to mix together in a jumble —*n.* a shuffling

**shuf′fle·board′** *n.* [ < *shovel board*] a game in which disks are pushed with a cue toward numbered squares

**shun** (shun) *vt.* shunned, shun′ning [OE. *scunian*] to keep away from; avoid scrupulously

**shun′pike′** *adj.* avoiding turnpikes and expressways —**shun′pik′er** *n.*

**shunt** (shunt) *vt., vi.* [ME. *schunten*] 1. to move or turn to one side 2. to switch, as a train, from one track to another —*n.* 1. a shunting 2. a railroad switch

**shush** (shush) *interj.* [echoic] hush! be quiet! —*vt.* to say "shush" to

**shut** (shut) *vt.* shut, shut′ting [OE. *scyttan*] 1. to move (a door, lid, etc.) so as to close (an opening, container, etc.) 2. *a)* to prevent entrance to or exit from *b)* to confine (*in* a room, etc.) 3. to bring together the parts of (an umbrella, etc.) —*vi.* to be or become shut —*adj.* closed, fastened, etc. —**shut down** to cease or cause to cease operating —**shut off** to prevent passage of or through —**shut out** 1. to deny entrance to 2. to prevent from scoring —**shut up** 1. to confine 2. [Colloq.] to stop or make stop talking

**shut′down′** *n.* a stoppage of work or activity, as in a factory

**shut′eye′** *n.* [Slang] sleep

**shut′-in′** *adj.* confined indoors by illness —*n.* an invalid who is shut-in

**shut′out′** *n.* a preventing of the opposing side or team from scoring

**shut′ter** *n.* 1. a person or thing that shuts 2. a movable cover for a window 3. a device for opening and closing the aperture of a camera lens —*vt.* to close or furnish with shutters

**shut·tle** (shut′'l) *n.* [OE. *scytel*, missile] 1. a device that carries thread back and forth, as in weaving 2. a bus, etc. making back-and-forth trips over a short route —*vt., vi.* -tled, -tling to move back and forth rapidly

**shut′tle·cock′** *n.* a rounded piece of cork having a flat end stuck with feathers: used in badminton

**shy**[1] (shī) *adj.* shy′er or shi′er, shy′est or shi′est [OE. *sceoh*] 1. easily frightened; timid 2. not at ease with others; bashful 3. distrustful; wary 4. [Slang] lacking —*vi.* shied, shy′ing 1. to move suddenly as when startled 2. to be or become cautious, etc. —shy′ly *adv.* —shy′ness *n.*

**shy**[2] (shī) *vt., vi.* shied, shy′ing [ < ?] to fling, esp. sideways

**shy·ster** (shī′stər) *n.* [ < ?] [Slang] a lawyer who uses unethical or tricky methods

**Si** *Chem.* silicon

**Si·am** (sī am′) *former name of* THAILAND

**Si·a·mese** (sī′ə mēz′) *adj., n., pl.* -mese′ *same as* THAI

**Siamese twins** [after such a pair born in Siam] any pair of twins born with bodies joined together

**Si·ber·i·a** (sī bir′ē ə) N Asiatic section of the U.S.S.R., between the Urals & the Pacific —Si·ber′i·an *adj., n.*

**sib·i·lant** (sib′'l ənt) *adj.* [ < L. *sibilare*, hiss] having or making a hissing sound —*n.* a sibilant consonant, as (s) or (z) —sib′i·late′ (-āt′) *vt., vi.* -lat′ed, -lat′ing

**sib·ling** (sib′liŋ) *n.* [ < OE. *sib*, kinsman + -LING] a brother or sister

**sib·yl** (sib′'l) *n.* [ < Gr. *sibylla*] a prophetess of ancient Greece or Rome —sib′yl·line′ (-l′ln′, -ēn′) *adj.*

**‡sic**[1] (sik) *adj.* [L.] thus; so: used within brackets, [*sic*], to show that a quoted passage, esp. one containing some error, is precisely reproduced

**sic**[2] (sik) *vt.* [ < SEEK] sicked, sick′ing to incite (a dog) to attack

**Sic·i·ly** (sis′'l ē) island of Italy, off its S tip —Si·cil·ian (si sil′yən) *adj., n.*

**sick**[1] (sik) *adj.* [OE. *seoc*] 1. suffering from disease; ill 2. having nausea 3. of or for sick people [*sick* leave] 4. deeply disturbed, as by grief 5. disgusted by an excess [*sick* of excuses] 6. [Colloq.] morbid [a *sick* joke] —the sick sick people —sick′ish *adj.*

**sick**[2] (sik) *vt. same as* SIC[2]

**sick bay** a hospital and dispensary, esp. on board ship

**sick′bed′** *n.* the bed of a sick person

**sick′en** *vt., vi.* to make or become ill, disgusted, etc. —sick′en·ing *adj.*

**sick·le** (sik'l) *n.* [ult. < L. *secare*, to cut] a tool having a crescent-shaped blade on a short handle, for cutting tall grasses and weeds

**sick'le-cell' anemia** an inherited anemia, found chiefly among blacks, in which red blood cells become sickle-shaped due to defective hemoglobin

**sick·ly** (sik'lē) *adj.* **-li·er, -li·est** **1.** in poor health **2.** produced by sickness [a sickly pallor] **3.** faint; pale [a sickly light] **4.** weak; insipid SICKLE

**sick'ness** *n.* **1.** a being sick or diseased **2.** a malady **3.** nausea

**sick'out'** *n.* a staying out of work on the claim of illness, as by a group of employees trying to win demands

**sick'room'** *n.* the room of a sick person

**side** (sīd) *n.* [OE.] **1.** the right or left half, as of the body **2.** a position beside one **3.** *a)* any of the lines or surfaces that bound something *b)* either of the two bounding surfaces of an object that are not the front, back, top, or bottom **4.** either of the two surfaces of paper, cloth, etc. **5.** an aspect [his cruel *side*] **6.** any location, etc. with reference to a central point **7.** the position or attitude of one person or faction opposing another **8.** one of the parties in a contest, conflict, etc. **9.** a line of descent —*adj.* **1.** of, at, or on a side **2.** to or from one side [a *side* glance] **3.** secondary [a *side* issue] —**side by side** together —**side with** to support (a faction, etc.) —**take sides** to support a faction, etc.

**side'arm'** *adj., adv.* with a sweeping forward motion of the arm at or below shoulder level

**side arms** weapons worn at the side or waist, as swords, pistols, etc.

**side'board'** *n.* a piece of furniture for holding linen, china, etc.

**side'burns'** (-burnz') *n.pl.* [< *burnsides*, side whiskers worn by A. E. *Burnside*, Civil War general] the hair growing on the sides of a man's face, just in front of the ears

**side'car'** *n.* a small car attached to the side of a motorcycle

**side dish** any food served along with the main course, as in a separate dish

**side'kick'** *n.* [Slang] **1.** a close friend **2.** a partner; confederate

**side'light'** *n.* a bit of incidental information or knowledge

**side'line'** *n.* **1.** either of two lines marking the side limits of a playing area, as in football **2.** a secondary line of merchandise, work, etc.

**side'long'** *adv.* toward the side —*adj.* directed to the side, as a glance

**side'man'** *n., pl.* **-men'** a band member other than the leader or soloist

**si·de·re·al** (sī dir'ē əl) *adj.* [< L. *sidus*, star] of or expressed in reference to, the stars

**side'sad'dle** *n.* a saddle designed for a rider sitting with both legs on the same side of the animal —*adv.* on or as if on a sidesaddle

**side'show'** *n.* a small show apart from the main show, as of a circus

**side'slip'** *vi.* to slip or skid sideways —*vt.* to make sideslip —*n.* a slip or skid to the side

**side'split'ting** *adj.* **1.** very hearty: said of laughter **2.** very funny

**side'step'** *vt., vi.* **-stepped', -step'ping** to dodge as by stepping aside

**side'swipe'** (-swīp') *vt., vi.* **-swiped', -swip'ing** to hit along the side in passing —*n.* such a glancing blow

**side'track'** *vt., vi.* **1.** to switch (a train) to a siding **2.** to turn away from the main issue

**side'walk'** *n.* a path for pedestrians, usually paved, at the side of a street

**side'wall'** *n.* the side of a tire, between the tread and the wheel rim

**side'ways'** (-wāz') *adj., adv.* **1.** toward or from one side **2.** with one side forward Also **side'wise'** (-wīz')

**sid·ing** (sīd'iŋ) *n.* **1.** a covering, as of overlapping boards, for the outside of a frame building **2.** a short railway track, for unloading, etc., connected with a main track by a switch

**si·dle** (sī'd'l) *vi.* **-dled, -dling** [< *sideling*, sideways] to move sideways, esp. shyly or stealthily

**siege** (sēj) *n.* [< L. *sedere*, sit] **1.** the encirclement of a fortified place by an enemy intending to take it **2.** a persistent attempt to gain control, etc. **3.** a long, distressing period, as of illness —**lay siege to** to subject to a siege

**si·er·ra** (sē er'ə) *n.* [Sp. < L. *serra*, a saw] a range of mountains with a saw-toothed appearance

**Si·er·ra Le·one** (sē er'ə lē ōn') country in W Africa: 27,925 sq. mi.; pop. 2,439,000

**si·es·ta** (sē es'tə) *n.* [Sp. < L. *sexta* (*hora*), sixth (hour), noon] a brief nap or rest after the noon meal

**sieve** (siv) *n.* [OE. *sife*] a utensil with many small holes for straining liquids or fine particles of matter

**sift** (sift) *vt.* [OE. *siftan*] **1.** to pass (flour, etc.) through a sieve **2.** to examine (evidence, etc.) with care **3.** to separate [to *sift* fact from fable] —*vi.* to pass as through a sieve

**sigh** (sī) *vi.* [< OE. *sican*] **1.** to take in and let out a long, deep, audible breath, as in sorrow, relief, etc. **2.** to feel longing or grief (*for*) —*n.* the act or sound of sighing

**sight** (sīt) *n.* [< OE. *seon*, to see] **1.** something seen or worth seeing **2.** the act of seeing **3.** a device to aid the eyes in aiming a gun, etc. **4.** aim or an observation taken, as on a sextant **5.** the power or range of seeing; eyesight **6.** [Colloq.] anything that looks unpleasant, odd, etc. —*vt.* **1.** to observe **2.** to glimpse **3.** to aim at **4.** to adjust the sights of —*vi.* to look carefully [*sight* along the line] —**a sight for sore eyes** [Colloq.] a welcome sight —**at** (or **on**) **sight** as soon as seen —**by sight** by appearance —**not by a long sight** **1.** not nearly **2.** not at all —**out of sight** **1.** not in sight **2.** far off **3.** [Colloq.] beyond reach **4.** [Slang] excellent; wonderful

**sight′ed** *adj.* **1.** having sight; not blind **2.** having a (specified kind of) sight [*farsighted*]

**sight′less** *adj.* blind

**sight′ly** *adj.* **-li·er, -li·est** pleasant to the sight —**sight′li·ness** *n.*

**sight reading** the skill of performing written music on sight, without previous study —**sight′-read′** *vt., vi.*

**sight′see′ing** *n.* a visiting of places of interest —**sight′se′er** (-sē′ər) *n.*

**sig·ma** (sig′mə) *n.* the eighteenth letter of the Greek alphabet (Σ, σ, s)

**sign** (sīn) *n.* [< L. *signum*] **1.** something that indicates a fact, quality, etc.; token **2.** a gesture that conveys information, etc. **3.** a mark or symbol having a specific meaning [a dollar *sign* ($)] **4.** a placard, etc. bearing information, advertising, etc. **5.** any trace or indication —*vt.* **1.** to write (one's name) on [a letter, check, contract, etc.) **2.** to engage by written contract —*vi.* to write one's signature —**sign off** to stop broadcasting

**sig·nal** (sig′n'l) *n.* [< L. *signum*, a sign] **1.** a sign or event that initiates action [a bugle *signal* to attack] **2.** a gesture, device, etc. that conveys command, warning, etc. **3.** in radio, etc., the electrical impulses transmitted or received —*adj.* **1.** remarkable; notable **2.** used as a signal —*vt., vi.* **-naled** or **-nalled**, **-nal·ing** or **-nal·ling 1.** to make a signal or signals (to) **2.** to communicate by signals

**sig·nal·ize′** (-īz′) *vt.* **-ized′, -iz′ing 1.** to make noteworthy **2.** to make known or draw attention to

**sig·nal·ly** *adv.* in a signal way; notably

**sig·na·to·ry** (sig′nə tôr′ē) *adj.* having joined in signing something —*n., pl.* **-ries** a signatory person, nation, etc.

**sig·na·ture** (sig′nə chər) *n.* [< L. *signare*, to sign] **1.** a person's name written by himself **2.** *Music* a staff sign showing key or time

**sign·board** (sīn′bôrd′) *n.* a board bearing a sign or advertisement

**sig·net** (sig′nit) *n.* [< MFr. *signe*, a sign] a seal, as on a ring, used in marking documents as official, etc.

**sig·nif·i·cance** (sig nif′ə kəns) *n.* **1.** that which is signified; meaning **2.** the quality of being significant; expressiveness **3.** importance

**sig·nif′i·cant** (-kənt) *adj.* [< L. *significare*, signify] **1.** having or expressing a meaning, esp. a special or hidden one **2.** full of meaning **3.** important —**sig·nif′i·cant·ly** *adv.*

**sig·ni·fy** (sig′nə fī′) *vt.* **-fied′, -fy′ing** [< L. *signum*, a sign + *facere*, make] **1.** to be an indication of; mean **2.** to make known, as by a sign, words, etc. —*vi.* to be important —**sig′ni·fi·ca′tion** *n.*

**sign of the cross** an outline of a cross (sense 2) made symbolically by moving the hand or fingers

**sign of the zodiac** any of the twelve parts of the zodiac, each represented by a symbol: see ZODIAC

**‡si·gnor** (sē nyôr′) *n., pl.* **-gno′ri** (-nyô′rē) [It.] a man; gentleman: as a title [S-], equivalent to *Mr.* or *Sir*

**‡si·gno·ra** (sē nyô′rä) *n., pl.* **-re** (-re) [It.] a married woman: as a title [S-], equivalent to *Mrs.* or *Madam*

**‡si·gno·ri·na** (sē′nyô rē′nä) *n., pl.* **-ne** (-ne) [It.] an unmarried woman or girl: as a title [S-], equivalent to *Miss*

**sign′post′** *n.* **1.** a post bearing a sign **2.** an obvious clue, symptom, etc.

**si·lage** (sī′lij) *n.* green fodder preserved in a silo

**sild** (sild) *n., pl.* **sild, silds** [Norw., herring] a small or young herring canned as a Norwegian sardine

**si·lence** (sī′ləns) *n.* **1.** a keeping silent **2.** absence of sound **3.** omission of mention —*vt.* **-lenced, -lenc·ing 1.** to make silent **2.** to put down; repress —*interj.* be silent!

**si·lenc·er** *n.* **1.** one that silences **2.** a device to muffle the sound of a gun

**si·lent** (sī′lənt) *adj.* [< L. *silere*, be silent] **1.** making no vocal sound; mute **2.** not talkative **3.** noiseless; still **4.** not expressed; tacit **5.** inactive [a *silent* partner] —**si′lent·ly** *adv.*

**sil·hou·ette** (sil′oo wet′) *n.* [< E. de *Silhouette*, 18th-c. Fr. statesman] **1.** a solid, usually black, outline drawing, esp. a profile **2.** any dark shape seen against a light background —*vt.* **-et′ted, -et′ting** to show in silhouette

**sil·i·ca** (sil′i kə) *n.* [< L. *silex*, flint] a hard, glassy mineral found in various forms, as in quartz, sand, etc. —**si·li·ceous** (sə lish′əs) *adj.*

SILHOUETTE

**sil′i·cate** (-kit, -kāt′) *n.* a salt or ester derived from silica

**sil·i·con** (sil′i kən, -kän′) *n.* [< L. *silex*, flint] a nonmetallic chemical element found always in combination

**sil′i·cone′** (-kōn′) *n.* an organic silicon compound highly resistant to temperature changes, water, etc.

**sil′i·co′sis** (-kō′sis) *n.* [< SILICON + -OSIS] a chronic lung disease caused by inhaling silica dust

**silk** (silk) *n.* [ult. < ? L. *sericus*, (fabric) of the Seres, the Chinese] **1.** *a)* the fine, soft fiber produced by silkworms *b)* thread or fabric made from this **2.** any silklike substance —**silk′en** *adj.* —**silk′y** *adj.* **-i·er, -i·est**

**silk screen** a stencil method of printing a color design through the meshes of a fabric, as silk, in which the parts not to be printed have been blocked up —**silk′-screen′** *vt.*

**silk′worm′** *n.* any of certain moth caterpillars that produce cocoons of silk fiber

**sill** (sil) *n.* [OE. *syll*] **1.** a heavy,

horizontal timber or line of masonry supporting a house wall, etc. **2.** a horizontal piece forming the bottom frame of a door or window opening

**sil·ly** (sil′ē) *adj.* **-li·er, -li·est** [ < OE. *sælig,* happy] having or showing little sense or judgment; foolish, absurd, etc. —**sil′li·ness** *n.*

**si·lo** (sī′lō) *n., pl.* **-los** [ < Gr. *siros*] an airtight pit or tower in which green fodder is preserved

**silt** (silt) *n.* [prob. < Scand.] a fine-grained, sandy sediment carried or deposited by water —*vt., vi.* to fill or choke up with silt

**sil·ver** (sil′vər) *n.* [ < OE. *seolfer*] **1.** a white, precious, metallic chemical element that is very ductile and malleable **2.** *a)* silver coin *b)* money; riches **3.** silverware **4.** a lustrous, grayish white —*adj.* **1.** of, containing, or plated with silver **2.** silvery —*vt.* to cover as with silver

**sil′ver·fish′** *n.* a wingless insect with silvery scales, found in damp places

**silver lining** a basis for hope or comfort in the midst of despair

**silver nitrate** a colorless, crystalline salt, used in photography, as an antiseptic, etc.

**sil′ver·smith′** *n.* a craftsman who makes and repairs silver articles

**sil′ver-tongued′** *adj.* eloquent

**sil′ver·ware′** *n.* **1.** articles, esp. tableware, made of or coated with silver **2.** any metal tableware

**sil′ver·y** *adj.* **1.** of, like, or containing silver **2.** soft and silvery in tone

**sim·i·an** (sim′ē ən) *adj.* [ < L. *simia,* an ape] of or like an ape or monkey —*n.* an ape or monkey

**sim·i·lar** (sim′ə lər) *adj.* [ < L. *similis*] nearly but not exactly the same or alike —**sim′i·lar′i·ty** (-lar′ə tē) *n., pl.* **-ties** —**sim′i·lar·ly** *adv.*

**sim·i·le** (sim′ə lē′) *n.* [ < L., a likeness] a figure of speech likening one thing to another by the use of *like, as,* etc. (Ex.: tears flowed like wine)

**si·mil·i·tude** (sə mil′ə tōōd′) *n.* [ < L. *similitudo*] likeness; resemblance

**sim·mer** (sim′ər) *vi.* [echoic] **1.** to remain at or just below the boiling point **2.** to be about to break out, as in anger —*vt.* to keep at or just below the boiling point —*n.* a simmering

**si·mon-pure** (sī′mən pyoor′) *adj.* [ < *Simon Pure,* a character in an 18th-c. play] genuine; authentic

**si·mo·ny** (sī′mə nē, sim′ə-) *n.* [ < *Simon* Magus: Acts 8:9–24] the buying or selling of sacraments or benefices

**sim·pa·ti·co** (sim pät′i kō) *adj.* [ < It. or Sp.] compatible or congenial

**sim·per** (sim′pər) *vi.* [Early ModE.] to smile in a silly or affected way; smirk —*n.* such a smile

**sim·ple** (sim′p'l) *adj.* **-pler, -plest** [ < L. *simplex*] **1.** having only one or a few parts; uncomplicated **2.** easy to do or understand **3.** without additions [the *simple* facts] **4.** not ornate or luxurious; plain **5.** without guile or deceit **6.** without ostentation; natural **7.** of low rank or position; common **8.** stupid or foolish —**sim′ple·ness** *n.*

**simple interest** interest computed on principal alone and not on principal plus interest

**sim′ple-mind′ed** *adj.* **1.** naive **2.** foolish **3.** mentally retarded

**sim·ple·ton** (sim′p'l tən) *n.* a fool

**sim·plic·i·ty** (sim plis′ə tē) *n., pl.* **-ties 1.** a simple state or quality; freedom from complexity, etc. **2.** absence of elegance, luxury, etc.; plainness **3.** artlessness **4.** foolishness

**sim·pli·fy** (sim′plə fī′) *vt.* **-fied′, -fy′ing** to make simpler, or less complex —**sim′pli·fi·ca′tion** *n.*

**sim·plis·tic** (sim plis′tik) *adj.* making complex problems unrealistically simple —**sim·plis′ti·cal·ly** *adv.*

**sim·ply** (sim′plē) *adv.* **1.** in a simple way **2.** merely [*simply* trying] **3.** completely [*simply* overwhelmed]

**sim·u·late** (sim′yoo lāt′) *vt.* **-lat′ed, -lat′ing** [ < L. *simulare*] **1.** to give a false appearance of; feign **2.** to look or act like —**sim′u·la′tion** *n.*

**si·mul·cast** (sī′m'l kast′) *vt.* **-cast′** or **-cast′ed, -cast′ing** to broadcast (a program) simultaneously by radio and television —*n.* a program so broadcast

**si·mul·ta·ne·ous** (sī′m'l tā′nē əs) *adj.* [ < L. *simul,* together] occurring, done, etc. at the same time —**si′mul·ta′ne·ous·ly** *adv.*

**sin** (sin) *n.* [OE. *synne*] **1.** the willful breaking of religious or moral law **2.** any offense or fault —*vi.* **sinned, sin′ning** to commit a sin —**sin′ful** *adj.* —**sin′ner** *n.*

**Si·nai, Mount** (sī′nī) *Bible* the mountain where Moses received the law from God

**since** (sins) *adv.* [ult. < OE. *sith,* after + *thæt,* that] **1.** from then until now [remained ever *since*] **2.** at some time between then and now [has *since* recovered] **3.** before now; ago [long *since* gone] —*prep.* **1.** continuously from (then) until now [*since* noon] **2.** during the period between (then) and now [twice *since* May] —*conj.* **1.** after the time that [two years *since* they met] **2.** continuously from the time when [lonely ever *since* he left ] **3.** because [*since* I can, I will]

**sin·cere** (sin sir′) *adj.* **-cer′er, -cer′est** [ < L. *sincerus,* pure] **1.** without deceit or pretense **2.** genuine [*sincere* grief] —**sin·cere′ly** *adv.* —**sin·cer′i·ty** (-ser′ə tē) *n.*

**si·ne·cure** (sī′nə kyoor′, sin′ə-) *n.* [ < L. *sine,* without + *cura,* care] any position that brings profit without involving much work

**si·ne di·e** (sī′nē dī′ē) [LL., without a day] for an indefinite period

**si′ne qua non′** (kwä nän′) [L., without which not] an indispensable condition or thing

**sin·ew** (sin′yoo) *n.* [OE. *seonwe*] **1.** a tendon **2.** muscular power; strength —**sin′ew·y** (-yoo wē) *adj.*

**sing** (siŋ) *vi.* **sang** or rarely **sung, sung, sing′ing** [OE. *singan*] **1.** to produce musical sounds with the voice **2.** to use song or verse in praise, etc. [of thee I *sing*] **3.** to make musical sounds, as a songbird 4. to hum, buzz, etc., as a bee 5. [Slang] to confess to a crime, esp. implicating others —*vt.* 1. to render (a song, etc.) by singing 2. to extol, etc. in song 3. to bring or put by singing [to *sing* to sleep] —*n.* [Colloq.] group singing —**sing′er** *n.*

**sing.** singular

**sing′-a-long′** *n.* [Colloq.] an informal gathering of people to sing songs

**Sin-ga-pore** (sin′gə pôr′) island country off the Malay Peninsula: 225 sq. mi.; pop. 1,956,000

**singe** (sinj) *vt.* **singed, singe′ing** [OE. *sengan*] 1. to burn superficially or slightly 2. to expose (a carcass) to flame in removing feathers, etc. —*n.* 1. a singeing 2. a slight burn

**sin-gle** (sin′g'l) *adj.* [ < L. *singulus*] 1. *a)* one only *b)* separate and distinct [every *single* time] 2. solitary 3. of or for one person or family 4. between two persons only [*single* combat] 5. unmarried 6. having only one part; not multiple, etc. 7. whole; unbroken [a *single* front] —*vt.* **-gled, -gling** to select from others (usually with *out*) —*vi. Baseball* to hit a single —*n.* 1. a single person or thing 2. *Baseball* a hit by which the batter reaches first base 3. [*pl.*] *Tennis*, etc. a match with only one player on each side

**sin′gle-breast′ed** *adj.* overlapping the front of the body only enough to fasten [a *single-breasted* coat]

**single file** a single column of persons or things, one behind another

**sin′gle-hand′ed** *adj., adv.* 1. using only one hand 2. without help

**sin′gle-mind′ed** *adj.* with only one aim or purpose

**sin′gle-ton** (-tən) *n.* 1. a playing card that is the only one of its suit held by a player 2. a single thing

**sin′gle-track′** *adj.* [Colloq.] same as ONE-TRACK

**sin′gle-tree′** (-trē′) *n.* [ < ME. *swingle*, rod + *tre*, tree] the crossbar on a wagon, etc. to which the traces of a horse's harness are hooked

**sin-gly** (sin′glē) *adv.* 1. alone 2. one by one 3. unaided

**sing′song′** *n.* a rise and fall of tone in an unvarying cadence

**sin-gu-lar** (sin′gyə lər) *adj.* [ < L. *singulus*, single] 1. unique 2. extraordinary; remarkable 3. peculiar; odd 4. *Gram.* designating only one —*n. Gram.* the singular number or form of a word —**sin′gu-lar′i-ty** (-lar′ə tē) *n.* —**sin′gu-lar-ly** *adv.*

**Sin-ha-lese** (sin′hə lēz′) *adj.* of Ceylon, its people, language, etc. —*n., pl.* **-lese′** 1. any of the Sinhalese people 2. their language

**sin-is-ter** (sin′is tər) *adj.* [ < L. *sinister*, left-hand] 1. orig., on or to the left-hand side 2. threatening harm, evil, etc. 3. wicked; evil

**sink** (sink) *vi.* **sank** or **sunk, sunk, sink′ing** [OE. *sincan*] 1. to go beneath the surface of water, etc. 2.

to go down slowly 3. to appear to descend, as the sun 4. to become lower, as in level, value, or rank 5. to subside, as wind or sound 6. to become hollow, as the cheeks 7. to pass gradually (into sleep, etc.) 8. to approach death —*vt.* 1. to make sink 2. to make (a mine, engraving, etc.) by digging, cutting, etc. 3. to invest 4. to defeat; undo —*n.* 1. a cesspool or sewer 2. a basin, as in a kitchen, with a drainpipe 3. an area of sunken land —**sink in** [Colloq.] to be understood in full —**sink′a-ble** *adj.*

**sink′er** *n.* 1. one that sinks 2. a lead weight used in fishing

**sinking fund** a fund built up to pay off a debt, as of a corporation

**Sino-** [ < Gr. *Sinai*] a combining form meaning Chinese and

**sin-u-ous** (sin′yoo wəs) *adj.* [ < L. *sinus*, a bend] 1. bending or winding in or out; wavy 2. devious; crooked —**sin′u-os′i-ty** (-wäs′ə tē) *n.*

**si-nus** (sī′nəs) *n.* [L., bent surface] a cavity, hollow, etc.; specif., any of the air cavities in the skull which open into the nasal cavities

**si-nus-i-tis** (sī′nəs sīt′əs) *n.* inflammation of the sinuses, esp. of the skull

**-sion** (shən, zhən) [L. *-sio*] a suffix meaning act, state, or result of [fusion]

**Sioux** (soo) *n., pl.* **Sioux** (soo, sooz) a member of a group of Indian tribes of the N U.S. and S Canada —*adj.* of these tribes: also **Siou-an** (soo′ən)

**sip** (sip) *vt., vi.* **sipped, sip′ping** [ME. *sippen*] to drink a little at a time —*n.* 1. the act of sipping 2. a small quantity sipped —**sip′per** *n.*

**si-phon** (sī′fən) *n.* [ < Gr. *siphōn*, tube] 1. a bent tube for carrying liquid out over the edge of a container to a lower level, through the force of air pressure on the liquid 2. a sealed bottle from which carbonated water is released: in full **siphon bottle** —*vt.* to draw off through a siphon

**sir** (sur) *n.* [see ff.] 1. [sometimes S-] a respectful term of address used to a man: not followed by the name 2. [S-] the title used before the name of a knight or baronet

**sire** (sīr) *n.* [ < L. *senior*, compar. of *senex*, old] 1. a title of respect used in addressing a king 2. [Poet.] a father or forefather 3. the male parent of a four-legged mammal —*vt.* **sired, sir′ing** to beget

**si-ren** (sī′rən) *n.* [ < Gr. *Seirēn*] 1. *Gr. & Rom. Myth.* any of several sea nymphs whose singing lured sailors to their death on rocky coasts 2. a seductive woman 3. a warning device, etc. producing a loud, wailing sound

**sir-loin** (sur′loin) *n.* [ < OFr. *sur*, over + *loigne*, loin] a choice cut of beef from the loin end in front of the rump

**si-roc-co** (sə räk′ō) *n., pl.* **-cos** [It. < Ar. *sharq*, the east] a hot, oppressive wind blowing from the deserts of N Africa into S Europe

**sir·ree, sir·ee** (sə rē′) *interj.* [ < SIR] an interjection used for emphasis after *yes* or *no*

**sir·up** (sir′əp, sur′-) *n. same as* SYRUP

**sis** (sis) *n. colloq. form of* SISTER

**si·sal** (sī′s'l) *n.* [after *Sisal*, in SE Mexico] a strong fiber obtained from the leaves of an agave

**sis·sy** (sis′ē) *n., pl.* **-sies** [dim. of SIS] [Colloq.] 1. an effeminate boy or man 2. a timid person —**sis′si·fied′** *adj.*

**sis·ter** (sis′tər) *n.* [ < ON. *systir*] 1. a female related to one by having the same parents 2. a friend who is like a sister 3. a female fellow member of the same race, creed, etc. 4. a nun 5. one of the same kind, model, etc. —**sis′-ter·hood′** *n.* **sis′ter·ly** *adj.*

**sis·ter-in-law** *n., pl.* **sis′ters-in-law** 1. the sister of one's spouse 2. the wife of one's brother 3. the wife of the brother of one's spouse

**Sis·y·phus** (sis′ə fəs) *Gr. Myth.* a king of Corinth doomed in Hades to roll uphill a stone which always rolled down again

**sit** (sit) *vi.* **sat**, **sit′ting** [ < OE. *sittan*] 1. *a)* to rest oneself upon the buttocks, as on a chair *b)* to rest on the haunches with the forelegs braced, as a dog *c)* to perch, as a bird 2. to cover eggs for hatching, as a hen 3. *a)* to occupy a seat as a judge, legislator, etc. *b)* to be in session, as a court 4. to pose, as for a portrait 5. to be located 6. to rest or lie *[cares sit lightly on him]* 7. *same as* BABY-SIT —*vt.* 1. to cause to sit 2. to keep one's seat on (a horse, etc.) —**sit down** to take a seat —**sit in (on)** to attend —**sit up** 1. to sit erect 2. to postpone going to bed 3. [Colloq.] to become suddenly alert —**sit′ter** *n.*

**si·tar** (si tär′) *n.* [Hind. *sitār*] a lute-like instrument of India

**sit′-down′** *n.* 1. a strike in which the strikers refuse to leave the premises 2. civil disobedience in which demonstrators sit down in streets, etc. and refuse to leave voluntarily

**site** (sīt) *n.* [ < L. *situs*, position] location or scene

SITAR

**sit′-in′** *n.* a sit-down inside a public place, as by a civil-rights group

**sit′ting** *n.* 1. the act or position of one that sits 2. a session, as of a court 3. a period of being seated

**sitting duck** [Colloq.] a person or thing easily attacked; easy target

**sit·u·ate** (sich′ōō wāt′) *vt.* **-at′ed, -at′ing** [see SITE] to put in a certain place or position; locate

**sit′u·a′tion** *n.* 1. location; position; place 2. condition with regard to circumstances 3. a state of affairs 4. a position of employment

**situation comedy** a comic television series made up of episodes involving the same group of stock characters

**sit′-up′, sit′up′** *n.* an exercise of sitting up from a lying position without using hands or legs

**sitz bath** (sits, zits) [ < G.] a therapeutic bath in a sitting position, with the hips and buttocks immersed

**Si·va** (sē′və) Hindu god of destruction and reproduction: see BRAHMA

**six** (siks) *adj., n.* [OE. *sex*] one more than five; 6; VI —**sixth** *adj., n.*

**six′-pack′** *n.* a package of six units, as of six cans of beer

**six′-shoot′er** *n.* [Colloq.] a revolver firing six shots without reloading

**six′teen′** (-tēn′) *adj., n.* [OE. *syxtene*] six more than ten; 16; XVI —**six′-teenth′** *adj., n.*

**sixth sense** intuitive power

**six·ty** (siks′tē) *adj., n., pl.* **-ties** [OE. *sixtig*] six times ten; 60; LX —**the sixties** the numbers or years, as of a century, from 60 through 69 —**six′ti-eth** (-ith) *adj., n.*

**siz·a·ble** (sī′zə b'l) *adj.* quite large or bulky: also **size′a·ble**

**size¹** (sīz) *n.* [ult. < L. *sedere*, sit] 1. that quality of a thing which determines how much space it occupies; dimensions or magnitude 2. any of a series of graded classifications of measure into which merchandise is divided —*vt.* **sized, siz′ing** to make or grade according to size —**size up** [Colloq.] 1. to make an estimate or judgment of 2. to meet requirements

**size²** (sīz) *n.* [ME. *syse*] a pasty substance used as a glaze or filler on paper, cloth, etc. —*vt.* **sized, siz′ing** to fill, stiffen, or glaze with size

**-sized** (sīzd) *a combining form meaning* of (a specified) size *[small-sized]*

**siz′ing** *n.* 1. *same as* SIZE² 2. the act or process of applying size

**siz·zle** (siz′'l) *vi.* **-zled, -zling** [echoic] 1. to make a hissing sound when in contact with heat 2. to be extremely hot —*n.* a sizzling sound

**S.J.** Society of Jesus: see JESUIT

**skate¹** (skāt) *n.* [ < OFr. *eschace*, stilt] 1. *a)* a metal runner in a frame, fastened to a shoe for gliding on ice *b)* a shoe with such a runner attached Also **ice skate** 2. a similar frame or shoe with two pairs of small wheels, for gliding on a floor, sidewalk, etc.: also **roller skate** —*vi.* **skat′ed, skat′ing** to glide or roll on skates —**skat′er** *n.*

**skate²** (skāt) *n.* [ < ON. *skata*] a fish of the ray family with a broad, flat body and short, spineless tail

**skate′board′** *n.* a short, oblong board with two wheels at each end, ridden as down an incline —*vi.* to ride on a skateboard

**ske·dad·dle** (ski dad′'l) *vi.* **-died, -dling** [ < ?] [Colloq.] to run away

**skeet** (skēt) *n.* [ < ON. *skeyti*, projectile] trapshooting in which the shooter fires from different angles

**skein** (skān) *n.* [ < MFr. *escaigne*] a quantity of thread or yarn in a coil

**skel·e·ton** (skel′ə t'n) *n.* [ < Gr. *skeletos*, dried up] 1. the hard framework of bones of an animal body 2. *a)* a supporting framework *b)* an outline, as of a book —**skel′e·tal** *adj.*

**skeleton key** a key with a slender bit that can open many simple locks

**skep·tic** (skep′tik) adj. [< Gr. skeptikos, inquiring] var. of SKEPTICAL —n. 1. an adherent of skepticism 2. one who habitually questions matters generally accepted 3. one who doubts religious doctrines

**skep′ti·cal** (-ti k′l) adj. doubting; questioning —**skep′ti·cal·ly** adv.

**skep′ti·cism** (-siz′m) n. 1. the doctrine that the truth of all knowledge must always be in question 2. skeptical attitude 3. doubt about religious doctrines

**sketch** (skech) n. [ult. < Gr. schedios, extempore] 1. a rough drawing or design, done rapidly 2. a brief outline 3. a short, light story, play, etc. —vt., vi. to make a sketch (of) —**sketch′y** adj. -i·er, -i·est

**skew** (skyoo) vi., vt. [< OFr. eschiver, shun < Gmc.] to slant or set at a slant —adj. slanting —n. a slant or twist

**skew·er** (skyoo′ər) n. [< ON. skifa, a slice] a long pin used to hold meat together while cooking —vt. to fasten or pierce with skewers

**ski** (skē) n., pl. **skis**, **ski** [Norw. < ON. skith, snowshoe] one of a pair of long runners of wood, etc., fastened to shoes for gliding over snow —vi. **skied**, **ski′ing** to glide on skis —**ski′er** n.

**skid** (skid) n. [prob. < ON. skith, snowshoe] 1. a plank, log, etc. used as a track upon which to slide a heavy object 2. a low, wooden platform for holding loads 3. a runner on an aircraft landing gear 4. a sliding wedge used to brake a wheel 5. the act of skidding —vt., vi. **skid′ded**, **skid′ding** to slide or slip, as a vehicle on ice —**be on** (or **hit**) **the skids** [Slang] to be on the decline, or to fail

**skid′dy** adj. -di·er, -di·est having a slippery surface on which vehicles are liable to skid

**skid row** [alt. < skid road, trail to skid logs along] a city area where vagrants, derelicts, etc. gather

**skiff** (skif) n. [< It. schifo] a light rowboat, esp. one with a small sail

**ski lift** an endless cable with seats, for carrying skiers up a slope

**skill** (skil) n. [< ON. skil, distinction] 1. great ability or proficiency 2. a) an art, craft, etc., esp. one involving the use of the hands or body b) ability in such an art, etc. —**skilled** adj. —**skill′ful**, **skil′ful** adj.

**skil·let** (skil′it) n. [< ? L. scutra, dish] a pan for frying

**skim** (skim) vt., vi. **skimmed**, **skim′ming** [ME. skimen] 1. to remove (floating matter) from (a liquid) 2. to glance through (a book, etc.) rapidly 3. to glide lightly (over)

**skim milk** milk with the cream removed: also **skimmed milk**

**skimp** (skimp) vi., vt. [Colloq.] same as SCRIMP

**skimp′y** adj. -i·er, -i·est [Colloq.] barely enough; scanty

**skin** (skin) n. [< ON. skinn] 1. the outer covering of the animal body 2. a pelt 3. something like skin, as fruit rind, etc. —vt. **skinned**, **skin′ning** 1. to remove the skin of 2. to injure by scraping (one's knee, etc.) 3. [Colloq.] to swindle —**get under one's skin** [Colloq.] to irritate one —**skin′less** adj.

**skin diving** underwater swimming with air supplied by snorkel, scuba equipment, etc. —**skin′-dive′** vi. **-dived′**, **-div′ing** —**skin diver**

**skin′flick′** n. [Slang] a pornographic motion picture

**skin′flint′** n. [lit., one who would skin a flint for economy] a miser

**skinned** (skind) adj. having skin (of a specified kind) [dark-skinned]

**skin′ny** adj. -ni·er, -ni·est emaciated; thin —**skin′ni·ness** n.

**skin′ny-dip′** (-dip′) vi. **-dipped′**, **-dip′ping** [Colloq.] to swim nude —n. [Colloq.] a swim in the nude

**skip** (skip) vi., vt. **skipped**, **skip′ping** [ME. skippen] 1. to leap lightly (over) 2. to ricochet or bounce 3. to pass from one point to another, omitting or ignoring (what lies between) 4. [Colloq.] to leave (town, etc.) hurriedly —n. a skipping; specif., a gait alternating light hops on each foot

**skip·per** (skip′ər) n. [< MDu. schip, a ship] the captain of a ship

**skir·mish** (skur′mish) n. [< It. schermire < Gmc.] 1. a brief fight between small groups, as in a battle 2. any slight, unimportant conflict —vi. to take part in a skirmish

**skirt** (skurt) n. [< ON. skyrt, shirt] 1. that part of a dress, coat, etc. that hangs below the waist 2. a woman's garment that hangs from the waist 3. something like a skirt —vt., vi. to be on, or move along, the edge (of)

**ski run** a slope or course used for skiing

**skit** (skit) n. [prob. ult. < ON. skjota, to shoot] a short, humorous sketch, as in the theater

**ski touring** the sport of cross-country skiing

**ski tow** an endless cable towing skiers on their skis up a slope

**skit·tish** (skit′ish) adj. [see prec. & -ISH] 1. lively; playful 2. easily frightened; jumpy 3. fickle

**skiv·vy** (skiv′ē) n., pl. **-vies** [< ?] [Slang] a man's, esp. a sailor's, short-sleeved undershirt: usually **skivvy shirt** 2. [pl.] men's underwear

**skoal** (skōl) interj. [< ON. skāl, a bowl] to your health: a toast

**skul·dug·ger·y**, **skull·dug·ger·y** (skul dug′ər ē) n. [< ?] [Colloq.] sneaky behavior; trickery

**skulk** (skulk) vi. [ME. sculken] to move in a stealthy manner; slink

**skull** (skul) n. [< Scand.] 1. the entire bony framework of the head,

---

fat, āpe, cär; ten, ēven; is, bīte; gō, hôrn, tōōl, look; oil, out; up, fur; chin; she; thin, then; zh, leisure; ŋ, ring; ə for a in ago; ′, (ā′b′l); ë, Fr. coeur; ö, Fr. feu; Fr. mon; ü, Fr. duc; kh, G. ich, doch; ‡ foreign; < derived from enclosing the brain 2. the head; mind

**skull'cap'** n. a light, closefitting, brimless cap, usually worn indoors

**skunk** (skuŋk) n. [< AmInd.] 1. a small, bushy tailed mammal having black fur with white stripes down the back: it ejects a foul-smelling liquid when molested 2. its fur 3. [Colloq.] a despicable person

**sky** (skī) n., pl. **skies** [< ON., a cloud] 1. [often pl.] the upper atmosphere [blue skies, a cloudy sky] 2. the firmament 3. heaven

**sky'cap'** n. a porter at an air terminal

**sky diving** parachute jumping involving free-fall maneuvers

**sky'-high'** adj., adv. 1. very high 2. so as to be blasted to pieces

**sky'jack'** vt. [Colloq.] to hijack (an aircraft) —**sky'jack'er** n.

**Sky·lab** (skī'lab') n. U.S. earth-orbiting laboratory launched in 1973, housing alternating crews of astronauts

**sky'lark'** n. a Eurasian lark, famous for the song it utters as it soars —vi. to romp or frolic

**sky'light'** n. a window in a roof or ceiling

**sky'line'** n. 1. the visible horizon 2. the outline, as of a city, seen against the sky

**sky marshal** a Federal officer assigned to guard against skyjacking

**sky'rock'et** n. a firework rocket that explodes aloft —vi., vt. to rise or make rise rapidly

**sky'scrap'er** n. a very tall building

**sky'ward** (-wərd) adv., adj. toward the sky: also **sky'wards** adv.

**sky'ways'** n.pl. routes of air travel

**sky'writ'ing** n. the tracing of words, etc. in the sky by trailing smoke from an airplane —**sky'writ'er** n.

**slab** (slab) n. [ME. sclabbe] a flat, broad, and fairly thick piece

**slack¹** (slak) adj. [< OE. slæc] 1. slow; sluggish 2. not busy; dull [a slack period] 3. loose; not tight 4. careless [a slack workman] —vt., vi. to slacken —n. 1. a part that hangs loose 2. a lack of tension 3. a dull period; lull —**slack off** to slacken —**slack up** to go more slowly —**slack'ness** n.

**slack²** (slak) n. [ME. sleck] a mixture of small pieces of coal, coal dust, etc. left from screening coal

**slack·en** (slak'n) vt., vi. 1. to make or become less active, brisk, etc. 2. to loosen or relax, as rope

**slack'er** n. one who shirks

**slacks** (slaks) n.pl. trousers for men or women

**slag** (slag) n. [< MLowG. slagge] 1. fused refuse separated from metal in smelting 2. lava resembling this

**slain** (slān) pp. of SLAY

**slake** (slāk) vt. slaked, slak'ing [< OE. slæc, SLACK¹] 1. to satisfy (thirst, etc.) 2. to produce a chemical change in (lime) by mixing with water

**sla·lom** (slä'ləm) n. [Norw.] a downhill skiing race over a zigzag course

**slam** (slam) vt., vi. slammed, slam'-ming [prob. < Scand.] 1. to shut, hit, throw, put, etc. with force and

noise 2. [Colloq.] to criticize severely —n. 1. the act or sound of slamming 2. [Colloq.] a severe criticism See also GRAND SLAM

**slam'-bang'** adv. [Colloq.] 1. swiftly or abruptly and recklessly 2. noisily —adj. [Colloq.] lively, noisy, etc.

**slam·mer** (slam'ər) n. [Slang] a prison or jail

**slan·der** (slan'dər) n. [see SCANDAL] 1. the utterance of a falsehood that damages another's reputation 2. such a statement —vt. to utter such a statement about —**slan'der·er** n. —**slan'der·ous** adj.

**slang** (slaŋ) n. [< ?] highly informal language, usually short-lived, that is outside standard usage —**slang'y** adj. -i·er, -i·est

**slant** (slant) vt., vi. [< Scand.] 1. to incline; slope 2. to tell so as to express a particular bias —n. 1. an oblique surface, line, etc. 2. a point of view or attitude —adj. sloping

**slap** (slap) n. [echoic] 1. a blow with something flat, as the palm of the hand 2. an insult; rebuff —vt. slapped, slap'ping 1. to strike with something flat 2. to put, hit, etc. with force

**slap'dash'** adj., adv. hurried(ly), careless(ly), haphazard(ly), etc.

**slap'-hap'py** adj. [Slang] 1. dazed, as by blows 2. silly or giddy

**slap'stick'** n. crude comedy full of horseplay —adj. of or like such comedy

**slash** (slash) vt. [< Fr. esclachier, break] 1. to cut with sweeping strokes, as of a knife 2. to cut slits in 3. to reduce drastically, as prices —vi. to make a sweeping stroke as with a knife —n. 1. a slashing 2. a cut made by slashing —**slash'er** n.

**slash pocket** a pocket (in a garment) with a finished diagonal opening

**slat** (slat) n. [< OFr. esclat, fragment] a narrow strip of wood, etc.

**slate** (slāt) n. [see prec.] 1. a hard rock that cleaves into thin, smooth layers 2. its bluish-gray color 3. a roofing tile, etc. of slate 4. a list of proposed candidates —vt. slat'ed, slat'ing 1. to cover with slate 2. to designate, as for candidacy —**a clean slate** [< blackboard of slate] a record that shows no faults, mistakes, etc.

**slath·er** (slath'ər) vt. [< ?] [Colloq.] to spread on thickly

**slat·tern** (slat'ərn) n. [< dial. slatter, slop] a slovenly or sluttish woman —**slat'tern·ly** adj.

**slaugh·ter** (slôt'ər) n. [< ON. slātr, lit., slain flesh] 1. the killing of animals for food 2. the brutal killing of a person 3. the killing of many people, as in battle —vt. 1. to kill (animals) for food 2. to kill (people) brutally or in large numbers —**slaugh'ter·er** n.

**slaugh'ter·house'** n. a place where animals are butchered for food

**Slav** (släv, slav) n. a member of a group of peoples of E and SE Europe, including Russians, Poles, Czechs, Serbs, etc. —adj. same as SLAVIC

**slave** (slāv) n. [< LGr. Sklabos: first applied to captive Slavs] 1. a human being who is owned by another 2. one dominated by some influence, etc. 3. one who slaves —*vi.* **slaved, slav'ing** to work like a slave; drudge

**slave driver** 1. one who oversees slaves 2. any merciless taskmaster

**slav·er** (slav'ər) *vi.* [ < Scand.] to drool

**slav·er·y** (slā'və rē) *n.* 1. the owning of slaves as a practice 2. the condition of a slave; bondage 3. drudgery; toil

**Slav·ic** (släv'ik, slav'-) *adj.* of the Slavs, their languages, etc. —*n.* a family of languages including Russian, Polish, Czech, Bulgarian, etc.

**slav·ish** (slā'vish) *adj.* 1. of or like slaves; servile 2. blindly dependent or imitative —**slav'ish·ly** *adv.*

**slaw** (slô) *n.* [Du. *sla* < Fr. *salade,* salad] *short for* COLESLAW

**slay** (slā) *vt.* **slew, slain, slay'ing** [OE. *slean*] to kill in a violent way —**slay'er** *n.*

**sleaze** (slēz) *n.* [<SLEAZY] [Slang] 1. sleaziness 2. anything shoddy

**slea·zy** (slē'zē) *adj.* -**zi·er, -zi·est** [< *silesia,* orig.: cloth made in C Europe] 1. flimsy or thin in substance 2. shoddy —**slea'zi·ly** *adv.* —**slea'zi·ness** *n.*

**sled** (sled) *n.* [ME. *sledde*] a vehicle on runners for moving over snow, ice, etc. —*vt., vi.* **sled'ded, sled'ding** to carry or ride on a sled —**sled'der** *n.*

**sledge**[1] (slej) *n.* [OE. *slecge*] a long, heavy hammer, usually held with both hands: also **sledge'ham'mer**

**sledge**[2] (slej) *n.* [MDu. *sleedse*] a sled or sleigh

**sleek** (slēk) *adj.* [var. of SLICK] 1. smooth and shiny; glossy 2. of well-fed or well-groomed appearance 3. suave —*vt.* to make sleek —**sleek'ly** *adv.* —**sleek'ness** *n.*

**sleep** (slēp) *n.* [OE. *slæp*] 1. a natural, regularly recurring rest for the body, during which there is little or no conscious thought 2. any state like this —*vi.* **slept, sleep'ing** to be in the state of, or a state like, sleep —**sleep off** to rid oneself of by sleeping —**sleep'less** *adj.* —**sleep'less·ness** *n.*

**sleep'er** *n.* 1. one who sleeps 2. a railway car with berths for sleeping: also **sleeping car** 3. a beam laid flat to support something 4. something that achieves an unexpected success

**sleeping bag** a warmly lined, zippered bag for sleeping in outdoors

**sleeping sickness** an infectious disease, esp. in Africa, characterized by lethargy, prolonged coma, etc.

**sleep'walk'ing** *n.* the act of walking while asleep —**sleep'walk'er** *n.*

**sleep'wear'** *n. same as* NIGHT CLOTHES

**sleep'y** *adj.* -**i·er, -i·est** 1. ready or inclined to sleep; drowsy 2. dull; idle [a *sleepy* town] —**sleep'i·ly** *adv.* —**sleep'i·ness** *n.*

**sleet** (slēt) *n.* [ME. *slete*] 1. partly frozen rain 2. a mixture of rain with snow —*vi.* to shower in the form of sleet —**sleet'y** *adj.*

**sleeve** (slēv) *n.* [OE. *sliefe*] 1. that part of a garment that covers the arm 2. a tubelike part fitting around another part —**up one's sleeve** hidden but ready at hand —**sleeve'less** *adj.*

**sleigh** (slā) *n.* [Du. *slee*] a light vehicle on runners, for travel on snow

**sleight of hand** (slīt) [ < ON. *slœgr,* crafty] 1. skill with the hands, esp. in deceiving onlookers, as in magic 2. tricks thus performed

**slen·der** (slen'dər) *adj.* [ME. *s(c)len-dre*] 1. long and thin 2. slim of figure 3. small in amount, size, etc. 4. of little force; feeble —**slen'der·ness** *n.*

**slen'der·ize'** *vt., vi.* -**ized', -iz'ing** to make or become slender

**slept** (slept) *pt. & pp.* of SLEEP

**sleuth** (slooth) *n.* [ < ON. *sloth,* a trail] [Colloq.] a detective

**slew**[1] (sloo) *n.* [Ir. *sluagh,* a host] [Colloq.] a large number or amount

**slew**[2] (sloo) *pt.* of SLAY

**slice** (slīs) *n.* [ < OFr. *esclicier*] 1. a relatively thin, broad piece cut from something 2. a part or share —*vt.* **sliced, slic'ing** 1. to cut into slices 2. to cut as in a slice (with *off, from, away,* etc.) 3. to hit (a ball) so that it curves to the right if right-handed or to the left if left-handed —**slic'er** *n.*

**slick** (slik) *vt.* [OE. *slician*] 1. to make smooth 2. [Colloq.] to make smart, neat, etc. (with *up*) —*adj.* 1. sleek; smooth 2. slippery 3. adept; clever 4. [Colloq.] smooth but superficial, tricky, etc. —*n.* a smooth area on the water, as from a film of oil —**slick'ly** *adv.* —**slick'ness** *n.*

**slick'er** *n.* 1. a loose, waterproof coat 2. [Colloq.] a tricky person

**slide** (slīd) *vi.* **slid** (slid), **slid'ing** [OE. *slidan*] 1. to move along in constant contact with a smooth surface, as on ice 2. to glide 3. to slip [it *slid* from his hand] —*vt.* 1. to cause to slide 2. to place quietly or deftly (*in* or *into*) —*n.* 1. a sliding 2. a smooth, often inclined, surface for sliding 3. something that works by sliding 4. a photographic transparency for use with a projector or viewer 5. a small glass plate on which objects are mounted for microscopic study 6. the fall of a mass of rock, snow, etc. down a slope —**let slide** to fail to attend to properly

**slide fastener** a zipper or a zipper-like device with two grooved plastic edges joined or separated by a slide

**slid'er** *n.* 1. one that slides 2. *Baseball* a curve ball that breaks only slightly

**slide rule** an instrument for rapid calculations, consisting of a ruler with a central sliding piece, both marked with logarithmic scales

**sliding scale** a schedule of costs, wages. etc. that varies with given conditions

**slight** (slīt) *adj.* [OE. *sliht*] 1. *a)* light

in build; slender *b)* frail; fragile **2.** lacking strength, importance, etc. **3.** small in amount or extent —*vt.* **1.** to neglect **2.** to treat with disrespect **3.** to treat as unimportant —*n.* a slighting or being slighted —**slight'-ly** *adv.* —**slight'ness** *n.*

**slim** (slim) *adj.* **slim'mer, slim'mest** [< Du., bad] **1.** small in girth; slender **2.** small in amount, degree, etc. —*vt., vi.* **slimmed, slim'ming** to make or become slim —**slim'ness** *n.*

**slime** (slim) *n.* [OE. *slim*] any soft, moist, slippery, often sticky matter —**slim'y** *adj.* **-i·er, -i·est**

**sling** (slip) *n.* [prob. < ON. *slyngva*, to throw] **1.** a primitive instrument whirled by hand for throwing stones **2.** a cast; throw; fling **3.** *a)* a supporting band, etc. as for raising a heavy object *b)* a cloth looped from the neck under an injured arm for support —*vt.* **slung, sling'ing 1.** to throw as with a sling **2.** to hang in a sling

**sling'shot'** *n.* a Y-shaped piece of wood, etc. with an elastic band attached to it for shooting stones, etc.

**slink** (sliŋk) *vi.* **slunk, slink'ing** [OE. *slincan*, to creep] to move in a furtive or sneaking way; sneak

**slink'y** *adj.* **-i·er, -i·est 1.** sneaking **2.** [Slang] sinuous in line or movement

**slip¹** (slip) *vi.* **slipped, slip'ping** [< MLowG. *slippen*] **1.** to go quietly or secretly [to *slip* out of a room] **2.** to pass smoothly or easily **3.** to escape from one's memory, grasp, etc. **4.** to slide, lose footing, etc. **5.** to make a mistake; err **6.** to become worse —*vt.* **1.** to cause to slip **2.** to put, pass, etc. quickly or deftly [to *slip* one's shoes on] **3.** to escape from (the memory) —*n.* **1.** a space between piers for docking ships **2.** a woman's undergarment the length of a skirt **3.** a pillowcase **4.** a slipping or falling down **5.** an error or mistake —**let slip** to say without intending to

**slip²** (slip) *n.* [< MDu. *slippen*, to cut] **1.** a stem, root, etc. of a plant, used for planting or grafting **2.** a young, slim person **3.** a small piece of paper

**slip'case'** *n.* a boxlike container for a book or books, open at one end

**slip'cov·er** *n.* a removable, fitted cloth cover for a sofa, chair, etc.

**slip'knot'** *n.* a knot that will slip along the rope around which it is tied

**slip noose** a noose made with a slipknot

**slip·page** (slip'ij) *n.* a slipping, as of one gear past another

**slipped disk** a ruptured cartilaginous disk between vertebrae

**slip·per** (slip'ər) *n.* a light, low shoe easily slipped on the foot

**slip·per·y** (slip'ə rē) *adj.* **-i·er, -i·est 1.** liable to cause slipping, as a wet surface **2.** tending to slip away, as from a grasp **3.** unreliable; deceitful

**slip·shod** (slip'shäd') *adj.* [after obs. *slip-shoe*, a slipper] careless or slovenly

**slip'-up'** *n.* [Colloq.] an error

**slit** (slit) *vt.* **slit, slit'ting** [ME. *slitten*] **1.** to cut or split open, esp. by a lengthwise incision **2.** to cut into

strips —*n.* a straight, narrow cut, opening, etc.

**slith·er** (sli<i>th</i>'ər) *vi.* [< OE. *slidan*, to slide] to slip, slide, or glide along

**sliv·er** (sliv'ər) *n.* [< OE. *slifan*, to cut] a thin, sharp piece cut or split off; splinter —*vt., vi.* to cut or split into slivers

**slob** (släb) *n.* [< Ir. *slab*, mud] [Colloq.] a sloppy or coarse person

**slob·ber** (släb'ər) *vi.* [prob. < LowG. *slubberen*, to swig] **1.** to drool **2.** to speak in a maudlin way —*n.* slaver

**sloe** (slō) *n.* [OE. *sla*] **1.** the blackthorn **2.** its small, plumlike fruit

**sloe'-eyed'** *adj.* **1.** having large, dark eyes **2.** having almond-shaped eyes

**sloe gin** a red liqueur made of dry gin flavored with sloes

**slog** (släg) *vt., vi.* **slogged, slog'ging** [ME. *sluggen*, go slowly] **1.** to make (one's way) with great effort; plod **2.** to toil (*at*)

**slo·gan** (slō'gən) *n.* [< Gael. *sluagh*, a host + *gairm*, a call: orig., a battle cry] **1.** a catchword or motto associated with a political party, etc. **2.** a catch phrase used in advertising

**sloop** (slōōp) *n.* [< Du. < LowG. *slupen*, to glide] a small sailing vessel with a single mast and a jib

**slop** (släp) *n.* [OE. *sloppe*] **1.** watery snow or mud; slush **2.** a puddle of spilled liquid **3.** unappetizing liquid or semiliquid food **4.** [*often pl.*] liquid waste of any kind —*vt., vi.* **slopped, slop'ping** to spill or splash

SLOOP

**slope** (slōp) *n.* [< OE. *slupan*, to glide] **1.** rising or falling ground **2.** any inclined line, surface, etc.; slant **3.** the amount or degree of this —*vi.* sloped, slop'ing to have an upward or downward inclination; incline; slant —*vt.* to cause to slope

**slop·py** (släp'ē) *adj.* **-pi·er, -pi·est 1.** splashy; slushy **2.** *a)* slovenly *b)* slipshod **3.** [Colloq.] gushingly sentimental

**sloppy Joe** (jō) ground meat cooked with tomato sauce, spices, etc. and served on a bun

**slop sink** a deep sink for filling scrub pails, washing out mops, etc.

**slosh** (släsh) *vi.* [var. of SLUSH] **1.** to splash through water, mud, etc. **2.** to splash about: said of a liquid

**slot** (slät) *n.* [< OFr. *esclot*, hollow between the breasts] **1.** a narrow opening, as for a coin in a vending machine **2.** [Colloq.] a position in a group, etc. —*vt.* **slot'ted, slot'ting 1.** to make a slot in **2.** [Colloq.] to place in a series

**sloth** (slôth, slōth) *n.* [< OE. *slaw*, slow] **1.** disinclination to work or exert oneself; laziness **2.** a slow-moving, tree-dwelling S. American mammal that hangs, back down, from branches —**sloth'ful** *adj.* —**sloth'ful·ness** *n.*

**slot machine** a machine, specif. a gambling device, worked by inserting a coin in a slot

**slouch** (slouch) *n.* [< ON. *slōka*, to droop] **1.** a lazy or incompetent person **2.** a drooping or slovenly posture —*vi.* to sit, stand, walk, etc. in a slouch —**slouch′y** *adj.*

**slough**[1] (sluf) *n.* [ME. *slouh*, skin] a castoff layer or covering, as the skin of a snake —*vt.* to throw off; discard

**slough**[2] (slou) *n.* [OE. *sloh*] **1.** a place full of soft, deep mud **2.** deep, hopeless dejection

**Slo·vak** (slō′väk, -vak) *n.* **1.** any of a Slavic people living chiefly in E Czechoslovakia **2.** their language —*adj.* of the Slovaks, their language, etc.

**slov·en** (sluv′ən) *n.* [prob. < MDu. *slof*, lax] a careless, untidy person —**slov′en·ly** *adj.* -**li·er**, -**li·est**

**Slo·ve·ni·a** (slō vē′nē ə) *n.* a republic of Yugoslavia —**Slo·ve′ni·an**, **Slo′vene** (-vēn) *adj., n.*

**slow** (slō) *adj.* [OE. *slaw*] **1.** not quick in understanding **2.** taking a longer time than is usual **3.** marked by low speed, etc.; not fast **4.** behind the correct time, as a clock **5.** passing tediously; dull —*vt., vi.* to make or become slow or slower (often with *up* or *down*) —*adv.* in a slow manner —**slow′ly** *adv.* —**slow′ness** *n.*

**slow burn** [Slang] a gradual working up of anger: often in **do a slow burn**

**slow′down′** *n.* a slowing down, as of production

**slow′-mo′tion** *adj.* **1.** moving slowly **2.** designating a filmed or taped scene with the original action slowed down

**slow′poke′** (-pōk′) *n.* [Slang] a person who acts or moves slowly

**slow′-wit′ted** *adj.* mentally slow; dull

**sludge** (sluj) *n.* [var. of *slutch*, mud] **1.** mud, mire, or ooze **2.** any heavy, slimy deposit, sediment, etc.

**slue** (slōō) *n., vt., vi.* **slued**, **slu′ing** [< ?] turn, twist, or swerve

**slug**[1] (slug) *n.* [ME. *slugge*, clumsy one] a small mollusk resembling a land snail but having no outer shell

**slug**[2] (slug) *n.* [prob. < prec.] a small piece of metal; specif., a bullet

**slug**[3] (slug) *n.* [< ? Dan. *sluge*, to gulp] [Slang] a drink of liquor

**slug**[4] (slug) *vt.* **slugged**, **slug′ging** [< ON. *slag*] [Colloq.] to hit hard, esp. with the fist or a bat —*n.* [Colloq.] a hard blow or hit —**slug′ger** *n.*

**slug·gard** (slug′ərd) *n.* [< ME. *sluggen*, be lazy] a lazy person

**slug′gish** (-ish) *adj.* [< SLUG[1]] **1.** lacking energy; lazy **2.** slow or slow-moving **3.** not functioning with normal vigor —**slug′gish·ness** *n.*

**sluice** (slōōs) *n.* [< L. *excludere*, to shut out] **1.** an artificial channel for water, with a gate to regulate the flow **2.** such a gate: also **sluice gate 3.** any channel for excess water **4.** a sloping trough, as for washing gold ore —*vt.* **sluiced**, **sluic′ing 1.** to draw off

through a sluice **2.** to wash with water from a sluice

**slum** (slum) *n.* [< ?] a populous area characterized by poverty, poor housing, etc. —*vi.* **slummed**, **slum′ming** to visit slums in a condescending way

**slum·ber** (slum′bər) *vi.* [OE. *sluma*] **1.** to sleep **2.** to be inactive —*n.* **1.** sleep **2.** an inactive state

**slum′lord′** *n.* [Slang] an absentee landlord who exploits slum property

**slump** (slump) *vi.* [prob. < MLowG. *slumpen*, occur by accident] **1.** to fall or sink suddenly **2.** to have a drooping posture —*n.* a sudden decline

**slung** (slung) *pt. & pp.* of SLING

**slunk** (slunk) *pt. & pp.* of SLINK

**slur** (slur) *vt.* **slurred**, **slur′ring** [prob. < MDu. *sleuren*, to drag] **1.** to pass (*over*) quickly and carelessly **2.** to pronounce indistinctly **3.** to disparage **4.** *Music* to produce (successive notes) by gliding without a break —*n.* **1.** a slurring **2.** something slurred, as a pronunciation **3.** an aspersion **4.** *Music* a symbol (⌣) or (⌢) connecting notes to be slurred

**slurp** (slurp) *vt., vi.* [Du. *slurpen*, to sip] [Slang] to drink or eat noisily —*n.* [Slang] a loud sipping or sucking sound

**slush** (slush) *n.* [prob. < Scand.] **1.** partly melted snow **2.** soft mud **3.** sentimentality —**slush′y** *adj.*

**slut** (slut) *n.* [ME. *slutte*] **1.** a dirty, slovenly woman **2.** a sexually immoral woman —**slut′tish** *adj.*

**sly** (slī) *adj.* **sli′er** or **sly′er**, **sli′est** or **sly′est** [< ON. *slœgr*] **1.** skillful at trickery; crafty **2.** cunningly underhanded **3.** playfully mischievous —**on the sly** secretly —**sly′ly**, **sli′ly** *adv.* —**sly′ness** *n.*

**smack**[1] (smak) *n.* [OE. *smæc*] **1.** a slight taste or flavor **2.** a small amount; trace —*vi.* to have a smack (*of*)

**smack**[2] (smak) *n.* [< ?] **1.** a sharp noise made by parting the lips suddenly **2.** a loud kiss **3.** a slapping blow —*vt.* **1.** to part (the lips) so as to make a smack **2.** to kiss or slap loudly —*adv.* **1.** with a smack **2.** directly; precisely

**smack**[3] (smak) *n.* [prob. < Du. *smak*] a fishing vessel fitted with a well for keeping fish alive

**smack′er** *n.* [Slang] a dollar bill

**small** (smôl) *adj.* [OE. *smæl*] **1.** comparatively little in size; not big **2.** little in quantity, extent, duration, etc. **3.** of little importance; trivial **4.** young [*small* children] **5.** mean; petty —*n.* the small part [the *small* of the back] —**feel small** to feel shame —**small′ness** *n.*

**small arms** firearms of small caliber, as pistols, rifles, etc.

**small′-mind′ed** *adj.* selfish, mean, or narrow-minded

**small′pox′** (-päks′) *n.* an acute, contagious virus disease characterized by fever and pustular eruptions

**small talk** light conversation about common, everyday things; chitchat

**smart** (smärt) *vi.* [OE. *smeortan*] **1.** *a*) to cause sharp, stinging pain, as a slap *b*) to feel such pain **2.** to feel distress or irritation —*n.* a smarting sensation **2.** *pl.* [Slang] intelligence —*adj.* **1.** causing sharp pain [a *smart* blow] **2.** sharp, as pain **3.** brisk; lively [a *smart* pace] **4.** intelligent; clever **5.** neat; trim **6.** stylish —**smart'ly** *adv.* —**smart'ness** *n.*

**smart al·eck, smart al·ec** (al'ik) [< masc. name *Alexander*] [Colloq.] an offensively conceited person

**smart bomb** [Mil. Slang] a bomb that is guided precisely to its target from an airplane by electronic means

**smart'en** *vt., vi.* to make or become smart or smarter

**smash** (smash) *vt., vi.* [prob. < MASH] **1.** to break into pieces with noise or violence **2.** to hit, collide, or move with force **3.** to destroy or be destroyed —*n.* **1.** a hard, heavy hit **2.** a violent, noisy breaking **3.** a violent collision **4.** total failure, esp. in business **5.** a popular success

**smash'up'** *n.* **1.** a violent wreck or collision **2.** total failure; ruin

**smat·ter·ing** (smat'ər iŋ) *n.* [ME. *smateren*, chatter] **1.** superficial knowledge **2.** a small number

**smear** (smir) *vt.* [< OE. *smerian*, anoint] **1.** to cover or soil with something greasy, sticky, etc. **2.** to apply (something greasy, etc.) **3.** to slander —*vi.* to be or become smeared —*n.* **1.** a mark made by smearing **2.** slander —**smear'y** *adj.* -i·er, -i·est

**smear'case'** *n.* [G. *schmier-käse*] same as COTTAGE CHEESE

**smell** (smel) *vt.* **smelled** or **smelt**, **smell'ing** [ME. *smellen*] **1.** to be aware of through the nose; detect the odor of **2.** to sense the presence of [to *smell* trouble] —*vi.* **1.** to use the sense of smell; sniff **2.** to have an odor [to *smell* fresh] —*n.* **1.** the sense by which odors are perceived **2.** odor; scent **3.** an act of smelling

**smelling salts** an ammonia compound sniffed to relieve faintness

**smell'y** *adj.* -i·er, -i·est having an unpleasant smell

**smelt¹** (smelt) *n.* [OE.] a small, silvery food fish found esp. in northern seas

**smelt²** (smelt) *vt.* [< MDu. *smelten*] **1.** to melt or fuse (ore, etc.) so as to separate impurities from pure metal **2.** to refine (metal) in this way

**smelt'er** *n.* **1.** one whose work is smelting **2.** a place for smelting

**smidg·en** (smij'ən) *n.* [prob. < dial. *smidge*, particle] [Colloq.] a small amount; bit: also **smidg'in, smidg'eon**

**smile** (smīl) *vi.* **smiled, smil'ing** [ME. *smilen*] to show pleasure, amusement, affection, etc. by an upward curving of the mouth —*vt.* to express with a smile —*n.* the act or expression of smiling —**smil'ing·ly** *adv.*

**smirch** (smurch) *vt.* [prob. < OFr. *esmorcher*, to hurt] **1.** to soil or stain **2.** to dishonor —*n.* **1.** a smudge; smear **2.** a stain on reputation

**smirk** (smurk) *vi.* [< OE. *smearcian*, to smile] to smile in a conceited or complacent way —*n.* such a smile

**smite** (smīt) *vt.* **smote, smit'ten** (smit'n) or **smote, smit'ing** [OE. *smitan*] **1.** to strike with powerful effect **2.** to affect or impress strongly

**smith** (smith) *n.* [OE.] **1.** one who makes or repairs metal objects; metalworker **2.** *short for* BLACKSMITH

**Smith,** Captain John 1580-1631; Eng. colonist in America

**smith·er·eens** (smith'ə rēnz') *n.pl.* [Ir. *smidirin*] [Colloq.] fragments

**smith·y** (smith'ē) *n., pl.* -ies the workshop of a smith, esp. a blacksmith

**smock** (smäk) *n.* [< OE. *smoc* or ON. *smokkr*] a loose, shirtlike outer garment worn to protect the clothes

**smog** (smôg, smäg) *n.* [SM(OKE) + (F)OG] a mixture of fog and smoke

**smoke** (smōk) *n.* [OE. *smoca*] **1.** the vaporous matter arising from something burning **2.** any vapor, etc. like this **3.** an act of smoking tobacco, etc. **4.** a cigarette, cigar, etc. —*vi.* **smoked, smok'ing 1.** to give off smoke **2.** to draw in and exhale the smoke of tobacco; use cigarettes, etc. —*vt.* **1.** to cure (meat, etc.) with smoke **2.** to use (a pipe, cigarette, etc.) in smoking **3.** to drive out or stupefy as with smoke —**smoke out** to force out of hiding, secrecy, etc. —**smoke'less** *adj.* —**smok'er** *n.*

**smoke'house'** *n.* a building where meats, fish, etc. are cured with smoke

**smoke screen** a cloud of smoke for hiding the movements of troops, etc.

**smoke'stack'** (-stak') *n.* a pipe for discharging smoke from a factory, etc.

**smok·y** (smō'kē) *adj.* -i·er, -i·est **1.** giving off smoke **2.** of, like, or of the color of, smoke **3.** filled with smoke —**smok'i·ness** *n.*

**smol·der** (smōl'dər) *vi.* [ME. *smoldren*] **1.** to burn and smoke without flame **2.** to exist in a suppressed state Brit. sp. **smoulder**

**smooch** (smooch) *n., vt., vi.* [Slang] kiss —**smooch'y** *adj.*

**smooth** (smooth) *adj.* [OE. *smoth*] **1.** having an even surface, with no roughness **2.** without lumps **3.** even or gentle in movement [a *smooth* voyage] **4.** free from interruptions, obstacles, etc. **5.** pleasing to the taste; bland **6.** having an easy, flowing rhythm or sound **7.** polished or ingratiating, esp. in an insincere way —*vt.* **1.** to make level or even **2.** to remove lumps or wrinkles from **3.** to free from difficulties, etc. **4.** to make calm; soothe **5.** to polish or refine —*adv.* in a smooth manner —**smooth over** to make light of —**smooth'ly** *adv.* —**smooth'ness** *n.*

**smor·gas·bord, smör·gas·bord** (smôr'gas bôrd', smur'-) *n.* [Sw.] **1.** a wide variety of appetizers, cheeses, meats, etc. served buffet style **2.** a restaurant serving these

**smote** (smōt) *pt. & alt. pp.* of SMITE

**smoth·er** (smuth'ər) *vt.* [< ME. *smorther*, dense smoke] **1.** to keep from getting air; suffocate **2.** to cover over thickly 3. to stifle (a yawn) —*vi.* to be suffocated

**smudge** (smuj) *vt., vi.* **smudged, smudg'ing** [ME. *smogen*] to make or become dirty; smear —*n.* 1. a dirty spot 2. a fire made to produce dense smoke 3. such smoke, used to protect plants from frost, etc. —**smudg'y** *adj.*

**smug** (smug) *adj.* **smug'ger, smug'gest** [prob. < LowG. *smuk*, neat, trim] annoyingly self-satisfied; complacent —**smug'ly** *adv.* —**smug'ness** *n.*

**smug·gle** (smug''l) *vt., vi.* **-gled, -gling** [< LowG. *smuggeln*] 1. to bring into or take out of a country secretly or illegally 2. to bring, take, etc. secretly —**smug'gler** *n.*

**smut** (smut) *n.* [< LowG. *smutt*] 1. sooty matter 2. a soiled spot 3. indecent talk or writing 4. a fungous disease of plants —**smut'ty** *adj.* **-ti·er, -ti·est**

**Sn** [L. *stannum*] *Chem.* tin

**snack** (snak) *n.* [< ME. *snaken*, to bite] a light meal between regular meals —*vi.* to eat a snack

**snack bar** a lunch counter, cafeteria, etc. serving snacks

**snaf·fle** (snaf''l) *n.* [prob. < Du. *snavel*, horse's muzzle] a bit for a horse's mouth, having a joint in the middle and no curb

**snag** (snag) *n.* [< Scand.] 1. a sharp point or projection 2. an underwater tree stump or branch 3. a tear, as in cloth, made by a snag, etc. 4. an unexpected or hidden difficulty —*vt.* **snagged, snag'ging** 1. to damage on a snag 2. to impede with a snag

**snail** (snāl) *n.* [OE. *snægl*] a slow-moving mollusk having a wormlike body and a spiral protective shell

**snake** (snāk) *n.* [OE. *snaca*] 1. a long, scaly, limbless reptile with a tapering tail 2. a treacherous or deceitful person —*vi.* **snaked, snak'ing** to move, curve, twist, etc. like a snake —**snake'like** *adj.*

**snak'y** *adj.* **-i·er, -i·est** 1. of or like a snake or snakes 2. winding; twisting 3. cunningly treacherous

**snap** (snap) *vi., vt.* **snapped, snap'ping** [< MDu. *snappen*] 1. to bite or grasp suddenly (with *at*) 2. to speak or utter sharply (with *at*) 3. to break suddenly 4. to make or cause to make a sudden, cracking sound 5. to close, fasten, etc. with this sound 6. to move or cause to move suddenly and sharply [to *snap* to attention] 7. to take a snapshot (of) —*n.* 1. a sudden bite, grasp, etc. 2. a sharp cracking sound 3. a short, angry utterance 4. a brief period of cold weather 5. a fastening that closes with a click 6. a hard, thin cookie 7. [Colloq.] alertness or vigor 8. [Slang] an easy job, problem, etc. —*adj.* 1. made or done quickly [a *snap* decision] 2. that fastens with a snap 3. [Slang] easy —**snap out of** it to improve or recover quickly —**snap'per** *n.* —**snap'pish** *adj.*

**snap bean** a green bean or wax bean

**snap'drag'on** *n.* [SNAP + DRAGON: from the mouth-shaped flowers] a plant with saclike, two-lipped flowers

**snap'py** *adj.* **-pi·er, -pi·est** 1. cross; irritable 2. that snaps 3. [Colloq.] *a)* brisk or lively *b)* sharply chilly 4. [Colloq.] stylish; smart

**snap'shot'** *n.* an informal photograph taken quickly with a hand camera

**snare** (sner) *n.* [< ON. *snara*] 1. a trap for small animals 2. anything dangerous, etc. that tempts or attracts 3. a length of wire or gut across the bottom of a drum —*vt.* **snared, snar'ing** to catch as in a snare; trap

**snarl¹** (snärl) *vi.* [< earlier *snar*, to growl] 1. to growl, baring the teeth, as a dog 2. to speak sharply, as in anger —*vt.* to utter with a snarl —*n.* 1. a fierce growl 2. an angry utterance —**snarl'ing·ly** *adv.*

**snarl²** (snärl) *n., vt., vi.* [< SNARE] tangle; disorder —**snarl'y** *adj.*

**snatch** (snach) *vt.* [ME. *snacchen*] to take suddenly, without right, etc.; grab —*vi.* 1. to try to seize; grab (*at*) 2. to take advantage of a chance, etc. eagerly (with *at*) —*n.* 1. a snatching 2. a brief period 3. a fragment; bit

**sneak** (snēk) *vi., vt.* [OE. *snican*] to move, act, give, put, take, etc. secretly or stealthily —*n.* 1. one who sneaks 2. an act of sneaking —*adj.* without warning [a *sneak* attack] —**sneak'y** *adj.* **-i·er, -i·est**

**sneak'er** *n.* a shoe with a cloth upper and a soft rubber sole

**sneak preview** an advance showing of a movie, as to get audience reaction

**sneer** (snir) *vi.* [ME. *sneren*] 1. to show scorn as by curling the upper lip 2. to express derision, etc. in speech or writing —*n.* 1. an act of sneering 2. a sneering expression, etc.

**sneeze** (snēz) *vi.* **sneezed, sneez'ing** [ME. *snesen*] to exhale breath from the nose and mouth in an involuntary, explosive action —*n.* a sneezing

**snick·er** (snik'ər) *vi., vt.* [echoic] to laugh or smile with a sly, partly stifled manner —*n.* a snickering

**snide** (snīd) *adj.* [prob. < Du. dial.] slyly malicious or derisive

**sniff** (snif) *vi., vt.* [ME. *sniffen*] 1. to draw in (air) forcibly through the nose 2. to express (disdain, etc.) by sniffing 3. to smell by sniffing —*n.* 1. an act or sound of sniffing 2. something sniffed

**snif·fle** (snif''l) *vi.* **-fled, -fling** to sniff repeatedly, as in checking mucus running from the nose —*n.* an act or sound of sniffling —**the sniffles** [Colloq.] a head cold

**snif·ter** (snif'tər) *n.* [< *snift*, var. of SNIFF] a goblet tapering to a small opening to concentrate the aroma, as of brandy

**snig·ger** (snig'ər) *vi., vt., n.* [echoic] *same as* SNICKER

**snip** (snip) *vt., vi.* **snipped, snip'ping** [Du. *snippen*] to cut or cut off in a short, quick stroke, as with scissors

—*n.* **1.** a small piece cut off **2.** [Colloq.] a small or young person

**snipe** (snīp) *n.* [< ON. *snipa*] a long-billed wading bird —*vi.* **sniped, snip'ing 1.** to hunt snipe **2.** to shoot at individuals from a hidden position —**snip'er** *n.*

**snip·pet** (snip'it) *n.* [dim. of SNIP] a small, snipped piece; scrap, specif. of information, a writing, etc.

**snip·py** (snip'ē) *adj.* **-pi·er, -pi·est** [Colloq.] insolently curt, sharp, etc.

**snitch** (snich) *vt.* [Slang] to steal; pilfer —*vi.* [Slang] to tattle (*on*)

**sniv·el** (sniv''l) *vi.* **-eled** or **-elled, -el·ing** or **-el·ling** [ME. *snivelen*] **1.** to cry and sniffle **2.** to complain and whine **3.** to make a tearful, often false display of grief, etc.

**snob** (snäb) *n.* [< ?] one who thinks that money and rank are very important, and has contempt for those he considers inferior —**snob'bish** *adj.* —**snob'bish·ness, snob'ber·y** *n.*

**snood** (sn̄ood) *n.* [OE. *snod*] a baglike net worn on the back of a woman's head to hold the hair

**snoop** (sn̄oop) *vi.* [Du. *snoepen*, eat snacks on the sly] [Colloq.] to pry about in a sneaking way —*n.* [Colloq.] one who snoops —**snoop'y** *adj.* **-i·er, -i·est**

**snoot** (sn̄oot) *n.* [see SNOUT] [Colloq.] **1.** the nose **2.** the face

**snoot'y** *adj.* **-i·er, -i·est** [Colloq.] haughty; snobbish —**snoot'i·ness** *n.*

**snooze** (sn̄oōz) *n.* [< ? LowG. *snusen*, to snore] [Colloq.] a brief sleep; nap —*vi.* **snoozed, snooz'ing** [Colloq.] to nap; doze

**snore** (snôr) *vi.* **snored, snor'ing** [see SNARL¹] to breathe, while asleep, with harsh sounds —*n.* the act or sound of snoring —**snor'er** *n.*

**snor·kel** (snôr'k'l) *n.* [G. *schnörkel*, spiral] a breathing tube extending above the water, used in swimming just below the surface

**snort** (snôrt) *vi.* [prob. < SNORE] **1.** to force breath audibly through the nostrils **2.** to express contempt, etc. by a snort —*n.* **1.** the act of snorting **2.** [Slang] a quick drink of liquor

SNORKEL

**snot** (snät) *n.* [OE. (*ge*)*snot*, mucus] **1.** nasal mucus: vulgar term **2.** [Slang] an impudent young person —**snot'ty** *adj.* **-ti·er, -ti·est**

**snout** (snout) *n.* [prob. < MDu. *snute*] the projecting nose and jaws of an animal

**snow** (snō) *n.* [OE. *snaw*] **1.** frozen particles of water vapor that fall to earth as white flakes **2.** a falling of snow —*vi.* to fall as or like snow —*vt.* **1.** to cover or obstruct with snow (with *in, under*) **2.** [Slang] to deceive or mislead —**snow under 1.** to overwhelm with work, etc. **2.** to defeat decisively —**snow'y** *adj.* **-i·er, -i·est**

**snow'ball'** *n.* a mass of snow pressed into a ball —*vi.* to increase rapidly like a rolling ball of snow

**snow'bank'** *n.* a large mass of snow

**snow'-bound'** *adj.* shut in or blocked off by snow

**snow'drift'** *n.* a pile of snow heaped up by the wind

**snow'drop'** (-dräp') *n.* a small plant with small, white, bell-shaped flowers

**snow'fall'** *n.* a fall of snow or the amount of this in a given area or time

**snow fence** a light fence of lath and wire to control the drifting of snow

**snow'flake'** *n.* a single snow crystal

**snow'man'** *n., pl.* **-men'** a crude human figure made of snow packed together

**snow'mo·bile'** *n.* a motor vehicle with steerable runners in front and tractor treads at the rear

**snow'plow'** *n.* a plowlike machine used to clear snow off a road, etc.

**snow'shoe'** *n.* a racket-shaped wooden frame crisscrossed with leather strips, etc., worn on the feet to prevent sinking in deep snow

**snow'storm'** *n.* a storm with a heavy snowfall

**snow'suit'** *n.* a child's heavily lined garment, often with a hood, worn in cold weather

**snow tire** a tire with a deep tread for added traction on snow or ice

**snub** (snub) *vt.* **snubbed, snub'bing** [< ON. *snubba*, chide] **1.** to treat with scorn, disdain, etc. **2.** to check suddenly the movement of (a rope, etc.) —*n.* a scornful treatment —*adj.* short and turned up, as a nose

**snub'-nosed'** *adj.* having a snub nose

**snuff¹** (snuf) *vt.* [ME.] **1.** to trim off the charred end of (a wick) **2.** to put out (a candle) —**snuff out 1.** to extinguish **2.** to destroy —**snuff'er** *n.*

**snuff²** (snuf) *vt., vi.* [MDu. *snuffen*] to sniff or smell —*n.* **1.** a sniff **2.** powdered tobacco taken up into the nose or put on the gums —**up to snuff** [Colloq.] up to the usual standard

**snuff'box'** *n.* a small box for snuff

**snuf·fle** (snuf''l) *n., vi.* **-fled, -fling** [< SNUFF²] *same as* SNIFFLE

**snug** (snug) *adj.* **snug'ger, snug'gest** [prob. < Scand.] **1.** warm and cozy **2.** neat; trim [a *snug* cottage] **3.** tight in fit [a *snug* coat] **4.** hidden [to lie *snug*] —**snug'ly** *adv.*

**snug'gle** (-'l) *vt., vi.* **-gled, -gling** [< prec.] to cuddle; nestle

**so** (sō) *adv.* [OE. *swa*] **1.** as shown or described [hold the bat so] **2.** *a)* to such an extent [why are you so late?] *b)* very [they are so happy] *c)* [Colloq.] very much **3.** therefore [they were tired, and so left] **4.** more or less [ten dollars or so] **5.** also; likewise [I am going and so are you] **6.** then [and so to bed] —*conj.* **1.** in order (that) **2.** [Colloq.] with the result that —*pron.* that which has been specified or named [he is a friend and will remain so] —*interj.* an exclamation of surprise, triumph, etc. —*adj.* true [that's so] —**and so on** (or **forth**) and the rest; et cetera —**so as** with the purpose or result —**so what?** [Colloq.] even if so, what then?

**soak** (sōk) *vt.* [OE. *sociąn*] **1.** to make thoroughly wet **2.** to take in; absorb (with *up*) **3.** [Colloq.] to charge excessively —*vi.* **1.** to stay in a liquid for wetting, softening, etc. **2.** to penetrate —*n.* **1.** a soaking or being soaked **2.** [Slang] a drunkard

**so-and-so** (sō'ən sō') *n., pl.* **so'-and-sos'** [Colloq.] an unspecified person or thing: often euphemistic

**soap** (sōp) *n.* [OE. *sāpe*] **1.** a substance used with water to produce suds for washing: made by the action of an alkali on a fat **2.** [Slang] *same as* SOAP OPERA: also **soap'er** —*vt.* to scrub with soap —**no soap** [Slang] (it is) not acceptable —**soap'y** *adj.* **-i-er, -i-est**

**soap'box'** *n.* any improvised platform used in speaking to a street audience

**soap opera** [Colloq.] a daytime radio or television serial drama of a melodramatic, sentimental nature

**soap'stone'** *n.* a soft, impure talc in rock form, used as an abrasive, etc.

**soap'suds'** *n.pl.* foamy, soapy water

**soar** (sôr) *vi.* [ult. < L. *ex-*, out + *aura*, air] **1.** to rise or fly high into the air **2.** to glide along high in the air **3.** to rise above the usual level

**sob** (säb) *vi.* **sobbed, sob'bing** [ME. *sobben*] to weep aloud with short, gasping breaths —*vt.* to utter with sobs —*n.* the act or sound of sobbing

**so-ber** (sō'bər) *adj.* [ < L. *sobrius*] **1.** temperate, esp. in the use of liquor **2.** not drunk **3.** serious, sedate, reasonable, etc. **4.** not flashy; plain, as color, clothes, etc. —*vt., vi.* to make or become sober (often with *up* or *down*) —**so'ber-ly** *adv.* —**so'ber-ness** *n.*

**so-bri-e-ty** (sə brī'ə tē) *n.* a being sober; specif., *a)* temperance, esp. in the use of liquor *b)* seriousness

**so-bri-quet** (sō'brə kā') *n.* [Fr.] **1.** a nickname **2.** an assumed name

**Soc., soc.** **1.** socialist **2.** society

**so'-called'** *adj.* **1.** known by this term **2.** inaccurately or questionably designated as such

**soc-cer** (säk'ər) *n.* [alt. < *(as)soc(iation football)*] a kind of football played by kicking a round ball

**so-cia-ble** (sō'shə b'l) *adj.* [see ff.] **1.** friendly; gregarious **2.** characterized by informal conversation and companionship —*n.* a social —**so'cia-bil'i-ty** *n.* —**so'cia-bly** *adv.*

**so-cial** (sō'shəl) *adj.* [ < L. *socius*, companion] **1.** of or having to do with human beings in their living together **2.** living with others; gregarious *[man as a social being]* **3.** of or having to do with society, esp. fashionable society **4.** sociable **5.** of or for companionship **6.** of or doing welfare work —*n.* an informal gathering —**so'cial-ly** *adv.*

**social disease** any venereal disease

**so'cial-ism** (-iz'm) *n.* **1.** a theory of the ownership and operation of the means of production and distribution by society, with all members sharing in the work and the products **2.** [often S-] a political movement for establishing such a system —**so'cial-ist** *n., adj.* —**so'cial-is'tic** *adj.*

**so-cial-ite** (sō'shə līt') *n.* a person prominent in fashionable society

**so'cial-ize'** (-līz') *vt.* **-ized', -iz'ing** **1.** to make social **2.** to subject to government ownership or control —*vi.* to take part in social activity —**so'cial-i-za'tion** *n.*

**socialized medicine** a system giving complete medical and hospital care to all through public funds

**social science** sociology, history, or any study of social structure

**social security** a Federal system of old-age, unemployment, or disability insurance

**social work** the promotion of the welfare of the community and the individual, as through counseling services, etc. —**social worker**

**so-ci-e-ty** (sə sī'ə tē) *n., pl.* **-ties** [ < L. *socius*, companion] **1.** a group of persons forming a single community **2.** the system of living together in such a group **3.** all people, collectively **4.** companionship **5.** an organized group with some interest in common **6.** the wealthy, dominant class —**so-ci'e-tal** (-t'l) *adj.*

**Society of Friends** a Christian religious sect that believes in plainness of manners and worship, pacifism, etc.: see QUAKER

**so-ci-o-eco-nom-ic** (sō'sē ō ē'kə näm'ik, -ek'ə-) *adj.* involving both social and economic factors

**so-ci-ol-o-gy** (sō'sē äl'ə jē, -shē-) *n.* [see -LOGY] the science of social relations, organization, and change —**so'ci-o-log'i-cal** (-ə läj'i k'l) *adj.* —**so'ci-ol'o-gist** *n.*

**so-ci-o-path** (sō'sē ə path') *n.* an aggressively antisocial psychopath

**sock**[1] (säk) *n., pl.* **socks, sox** [ < L. *soccus*, light shoe] a short stocking

**sock**[2] (säk) *vt.* [Slang] to hit with force —*n.* [Slang] a blow

**sock-et** (säk'it) *n.* [ < OFr. *soc*, plowshare] a hollow part into which something fits *[an eye socket]*

**sock-eye** (säk'ī') *n.* [ < AmInd.] a red salmon of the N Pacific

**Soc-ra-tes** (säk'rə tēz') 470?-399 B.C.: Athenian philosopher & teacher —**So-crat-ic** (sə krat'ik) *adj., n.*

**sod** (säd) *n.* [prob. < MDu. *sode*] **1.** a surface layer of earth containing grass; turf **2.** a piece of this —*vt.* **sod'ded, sod'ding** to cover with sod

**so-da** (sō'də) *n.* [ML.] **1.** *same as: a)* SODIUM BICARBONATE *b)* SODIUM CARBONATE *c)* SODA WATER **2.** a confection of soda water, syrup, and ice cream

**soda biscuit** **1.** a biscuit made with baking soda and sour milk or buttermilk **2.** [Chiefly Brit.] a soda cracker

**soda cracker** a light, crisp cracker, usually salted, made from flour, water, and leavening, orig. baking soda

**soda fountain** a counter for making and serving soft drinks, sodas, etc.

**so-dal-i-ty** (sō dal'ə tē) *n., pl.* **-ties** [ < L. *sodalis*, companion] a society of

# soda pop — 568 — solemn

Roman Catholic Church members for religious or charitable purposes

**soda pop** a flavored, carbonated soft drink

**soda water** water charged under pressure with carbon dioxide gas

**sod·den** (säd'n) *adj.* 1. soaked through 2. soggy from improper cooking 3. dull or stupefied, as from liquor —**sod'den·ly** *adv.* —**sod'den·ness** *n.*

**so·di·um** (sō'dē əm) *n.* [< *soda*] an alkaline metallic chemical element

**sodium bicarbonate** a white crystalline compound, NaHCO₃, used in baking powder, as an antacid, etc.

**sodium carbonate** a hydrated carbonate of sodium, used in washing

**sodium chloride** common salt

**sodium hydroxide** a white, strongly alkaline substance: also called *lye*

**sodium nitrate** a clear, crystalline salt used in explosives, fertilizers, etc.

**sodium pentothal** *see* PENTOTHAL SODIUM

**Sod·om and Go·mor·rah** (säd'əm and gə môr'ə) *Bible* two sinful cities destroyed by fire

**sod·om·y** (säd'əm ē) *n.* [< SODOM] any sexual intercourse considered abnormal, as between two male persons —**sod'om·ite'** (-īt') *n.*

**so·ev·er** (sō ev'ər) *adv.* 1. in any way 2. of any kind; at all

**so·fa** (sō'fə) *n.* [< Ar. *ṣuffah*, bench] an upholstered couch with a fixed back and arms

**sofa bed** a sofa that can be opened into a double bed

**So·fi·a** (sō'fē ə, sō fē'ə) capital of Bulgaria: pop. 801,000

**soft** (sôft) *adj.* [OE. *softe*, gentle] 1. giving way easily under pressure 2. easily cut, shaped, etc. [a *soft* metal] 3. not as hard as is normal, desirable, etc. [*soft* butter] 4. smooth to the touch 5. easy to digest: said of a diet 6. nonalcoholic: said of drinks 7. having few of the mineral salts that keep soap from lathering 8. mild, as a breeze 9. weak; not vigorous 10. easy [a *soft* job] 11. kind or gentle 12. not bright: said of color or light 13. gentle; low: said of sound —*adv.* gently; quietly —**soft'ly** *adv.* —**soft'ness** *n.*

**soft'ball'** *n.* 1. a game like baseball played with a larger and softer ball, for seven innings 2. this ball

**soft'-boiled'** *adj.* boiled a short time to keep the yolk soft: said of eggs

**soft drink** a nonalcoholic, esp. carbonated drink

**sof·ten** (sôf'n) *vt., vi.* to make or become soft or softer —**soft'en·er** *n.*

**soft'heart'ed** *adj.* 1. full of compassion 2. not strict or severe; lenient

**soft landing** a safe landing, as of a spacecraft on the moon, with the craft and its contents unharmed

**soft'-ped'al** *vt.* -aled or -alled, -al·ing or -al·ling [from pedal action in piano, etc.] [Colloq.] to make less emphatic; tone down; play down

**soft sell** selling that relies on subtle inducement or suggestion

**soft soap** [Colloq.] flattery or smooth talk —**soft'-soap'** *vt.*

**soft'ware'** (-wer') *n.* the programs, data, etc. for a digital computer

**soft'wood'** *n.* 1. any light, easily cut wood 2. the wood of any tree with cones, as the pine

**soft'y** *n., pl.* -ies [Colloq.] one who is too sentimental or trusting

**sog·gy** (säg'ē) *adj.* -gi·er, -gi·est [prob. < ON. *sog*, a sucking] soaked; moist and heavy —**sog'gi·ness** *n.*

**soil¹** (soil) *n.* [< L. *solum*] 1. the surface layer of earth, supporting plant life 2. land; country [native *soil*] 3. ground or earth [barren *soil*]

**soil²** (soil) *vt.* [ult. < L. *sus*, pig] 1. to make dirty; stain 2. to disgrace —*vi.* to become soiled or dirty —*n.* a soiled spot

**soi·ree, soi·rée** (swä rā') *n.* [< Fr. *soir*, evening] an evening party

**so·journ** (sō'jurn; *also, for v.* sō jurn') *vi.* [< L. *sub-*, under + *diurnus*, of a day] to live somewhere temporarily —*n.* a brief stay; visit

**sol** (sōl) *n.* [< ML.] *Music* the fifth tone of the diatonic scale

**Sol** (säl) [L.] 1. the Roman sun god 2. the sun personified

**sol·ace** (säl'is) *n.* [< L. *solacium*] 1. an easing of grief, loneliness, etc. 2. a comfort or consolation —*vt.* -aced, -ac·ing to comfort; console

**so·lar** (sō'lər) *adj.* [< L. *sol*, sun] 1. of or having to do with the sun 2. produced by or coming from the sun

**solar battery** an assembly of cells (solar cells) for changing solar energy into electric power

**so·lar·i·um** (sō ler'ē əm) *n., pl.* -i·a (-ə) [L. < *sol*, sun] a glassed-in room, etc. for sunning

**solar plexus** a network of nerves in the abdomen behind the stomach

**solar system** the sun and all the heavenly bodies revolving around it

**sold** (sōld) *pt. & pp. of* SELL

**sol·der** (säd'ər) *n.* [< L. *solidus*, solid] a metal alloy used when melted to join or patch metal parts, etc. —*vt., vi.* to join with solder

**sol·dier** (sōl'jər) *n.* [< LL. *solidus*, a coin] 1. a member of an army 2. an enlisted man, as distinguished from an officer 3. one who works for a specified cause —*vi.* 1. to serve as a soldier 2. to shirk one's duty, as by feigning illness —**sol'dier·ly** *adj.*

**soldier of fortune** a mercenary or any adventurer

**sole¹** (sōl) *n.* [< L. *solum*, a base] 1. the bottom surface of the foot 2. the part of a shoe, etc. corresponding to this —*vt.* soled, sol'ing to furnish (a shoe) with a sole

**sole²** (sōl) *adj.* [< L. *solus*] without another; single; one and only

**sole³** (sōl) *n.* [< L. *solea*, SOLE¹: from its shape] a sea flatfish valued as food

**sol·e·cism** (säl'ə siz'm) *n.* [< Gr. *soloikos*, speaking incorrectly] a violation of the conventional usage, grammar, etc. of a language

**sole·ly** (sōl'lē) *adv.* 1. alone 2. only, exclusively, or merely

**sol·emn** (säl'əm) *adj.* [< L. *sollus*, all + *annus*, year] 1. sacred 2. formal

3. serious; grave; earnest  4. awe-inspiring —**sol'emn·ly** adv.

**so·lem·ni·ty** (sə lem'nə tē) n., pl. -ties 1. solemn ceremony, ritual, etc. 2. seriousness; gravity; impressiveness

**sol·em·nize** (säl'əm nīz') vt. -nized', -niz'ing 1. to celebrate formally or according to ritual 2. to perform the ceremony of (marriage, etc.)

**so·le·noid** (sō'lə noid', säl'ə-) n. [Gr. sōlēn, tube + eidos, a form] a coil of wire that acts like a bar magnet when carrying a current

**so·lic·it** (sə lis'it) vt., vi. [see SOLICI-TOUS] 1. to appeal to (persons) for (aid, donations, etc.) 2. to entice or lure —**so·lic'i·ta'tion** n.

**so·lic'i·tor** n. 1. one who solicits trade, contributions, etc. 2. in England, a lawyer other than a barrister 3. the law officer for a city, etc.

**so·lic·i·tous** (sə lis'ə təs) adj. [ < L. sollus, whole + ciere, set in motion] 1. showing care or concern [solicitous for her welfare] 2. desirous; eager —**so·lic'i·tude'** (-tōōd') n. a being solicitous; care, concern, etc.

**sol·id** (säl'id) adj. [ < L. solidus] 1. relatively firm or compact; neither liquid nor gaseous 2. not hollow 3. having three dimensions 4. firm; strong; substantial 5. having no breaks or divisions 6. of one color, material, etc. throughout 7. showing unity; unanimous 8. reliable or dependable —n. 1. a solid substance, not a liquid or a gas 2. an object having length, breadth, and thickness —**sol'id·ly** adv. —**sol'id·ness** n.

**sol·i·dar·i·ty** (säl'ə dar'ə tē) n. complete unity, as of purpose, feeling, etc.

**so·lid·i·fy** (sə lid'ə fī') vt., vi. -fied', -fy'ing to make or become solid, hard, etc. —**so·lid'i·fi·ca'tion** n.

**so·lid·i·ty** (-tē) n. a being solid

**sol·id-state'** adj. 1. of the branch of physics dealing with the structure, properties, etc. of solids 2. equipped with transistors, etc.

**so·lil·o·quy** (sə lil'ə kwē) n., pl. -quies [ < L. solus, alone + loqui, speak] 1. a talking to oneself 2. lines in a drama spoken by a character as if to himself —**so·lil'o·quize'** (-kwīz') vi., vt. -quized', -quiz'ing

**sol·i·taire** (säl'ə ter') n. [Fr.: see ff.] 1. a diamond or other gem set by itself 2. a card game for one player

**sol·i·tar·y** (säl'ə ter'ē) adj. [ < L. solus, alone] 1. living or being alone 2. single; only [a solitary example] 3. lonely; remote 4. done in solitude

**sol'i·tude'** (-tōōd') n. [see prec.] 1. a being solitary, or alone; seclusion 2. a secluded place

**so·lo** (sō'lō) n., pl. -los [It. < L. solus, alone] 1. a musical piece or passage to be performed by one person 2. any performance by one person alone —adj. for or by a single person —adv. alone —vi. to perform a solo —**so'lo·ist** n.

**Sol·o·mon** (säl'ə mən) Bible king of Israel noted for his wisdom

**So·lon** (sō'lən, -län) c.640–559? B.C.; Athenian lawgiver —n. [sometimes s-] a wise lawmaker

**so long** colloq. term for GOODBYE

**sol·stice** (säl'stis) n. [ < L. sol, sun + sistere, halt] the time of year when the sun reaches the point farthest north (June 21 or 22) or farthest south (Dec. 21 or 22) of the equator: in the Northern Hemisphere, the **summer solstice** and **winter solstice**, respectively

**sol·u·ble** (säl'yoo b'l) adj. [see SOLVE] 1. that can be dissolved 2. that can be solved —**sol'u·bil'i·ty** n.

**sol·ute** (säl'yōōt, sō'lōōt) n. the substance dissolved in a solution —adj. dissolved; in solution

**so·lu·tion** (sə lōō'shən) n. [see ff.] 1. the solving of a problem 2. an answer, explanation, etc. 3. the dispersion of one substance in another, usually a liquid, so as to form a homogeneous mixture 4. the mixture so produced

**solve** (sälv) vt. solved, solv'ing [ < L. se-, apart + luere, let go] to find the answer to (a problem, etc.); explain —**solv'a·ble** adj. —**solv'er** n.

**sol·vent** (säl'vənt) adj. [see prec.] 1. able to pay all one's debts 2. that can dissolve another substance —n. a substance that can dissolve another substance —**sol'ven·cy** n.

**So·ma·li·a** (sō mä'lē ə) country in E Africa: 246,201 sq. mi.; pop. 2,500,000

**so·mat·ic** (sō mat'ik) adj. [ < Gr. sōma, the body] of the body; physical

**somatic cell** any of the cells that form the tissues and organs of the body: opposed to GERM CELL

**som·ber** (säm'bər) adj. [ < L. sub, under + umbra, shade] 1. dark and gloomy or dull 2. dismal; sad Chiefly Brit. sp. **som·bre** —**som'ber·ly** adv.

**som·bre·ro** (säm brer'ō) n., pl. -ros [Sp. < sombra, shade: see prec.] a broad-brimmed, tall-crowned hat worn in Mexico, the Southwest, etc.

**some** (sum) adj. [OE. sum] 1. certain but not specified or known [open some evenings] 2. of a certain unspecified quantity, degree, etc. [have some candy] 3. about [some ten of them] 4. [Colloq.] remarkable, striking, etc. [it was some fight] —pron. a certain unspecified quantity, number, etc. [some of them agree] —adv. 1. approximately [some ten men] 2. [Colloq.] to some extent; somewhat [slept some] 3. [Colloq.] to a great extent or at a great rate [must run some to catch up] —**and then some** [Colloq.] and more than that

**-some¹** (səm) [OE. -sum] a suffix meaning tending to (be) [tiresome]

**-some²** (sōm) [< Gr. sōma, body] a

SOMBRERO

combining form meaning body [chromo-some]

**some·bod·y** (sum'bud'ē, -bäd'ē) pron. a person unknown or not named; some person; someone —n., pl. -ies a person of importance

**some'day'** adv. at some future day or time

**some'how'** (-hou') adv. in a way or by a method not known or stated: often in somehow or other

**some'one'** pron. same as SOMEBODY

**som·er·sault** (sum'ər sôlt') n. [< L. supra, over + saltus, a leap] an acrobatic stunt performed by turning the body one full revolution, heels over head —vi. to perform a somersault

**some'thing** n. 1. a thing not definitely known, understood, etc. [something went wrong] 2. a definite but unspecified thing [have something to eat] 3. a bit; a little 4. [Colloq.] an important or remarkable person or thing —adv. 1. somewhat [looks something like me] 2. [Colloq.] really; quite [sounds something awful] —make something of 1. to get use or profit from 2. to treat as very important 3. [Colloq.] to treat as a point of dispute —something else [Slang] one that is quite remarkable

**some'time'** adv. at some unspecified or future time —adj. former

**some'times'** adv. occasionally

**some'way'** adv. same as SOMEHOW: also some'ways'

**some'what'** n. some degree, amount, part, etc. —adv. to some extent, degree, etc.; a little

**some'where'** adv. 1. in, to, or at some place not known or specified 2. at some time, degree, figure, etc. (with about, around, between, etc.)

**som·nam·bu·lism** (säm nam'byoo liz'm) n. [< L. somnus, sleep + ambulare, to walk] sleepwalking —som·nam'bu·list n.

**som·no·lent** (säm'nə lənt) adj. [< L. somnus, sleep] 1. sleepy 2. inducing drowsiness —som'no·lence n.

**son** (sun) n. [OE. sunu] 1. a boy or man in his relationship to his parents 2. a male descendant —the Son Jesus

**so·nar** (sō'när) n. [so(und) n(avigation) a(nd) r(anging)] an apparatus that transmits sound waves in water, used in locating submarines, finding depths, etc.

**so·na·ta** (sə nät'ə) n. [It. < L. sonare, to sound] a musical composition for one or two instruments, having several movements related by similarity or contrast of tempo, key, style, etc.

**sonde** (sänd) n. [Fr., sounding line] a device for measuring and usually telemetering meteorological conditions at high altitudes

**song** (sôŋ) n. [OE. sang] 1. the act or art of singing 2. a piece of music for singing 3. a) poetry b) a ballad or lyric set to music 4. a singing sound —for a song for a small sum

**song'bird'** n. a bird that makes vocal sounds that are like music

**song'fest'** (-fest') n. [SONG + -FEST] an informal gathering of people to sing songs, esp. folk songs

**song'ster** (-stər) n. a singer —song'stress (-stris) n.fem.

**son·ic** (sän'ik) adj. [< L. sonus, sound] of or having to do with sound or the speed of sound

**sonic barrier** the large increase of air resistance met by some aircraft flying near the speed of sound

**sonic boom** the explosive sound of supersonic jets passing overhead

**son'-in-law'** n., pl. sons'-in-law' the husband of one's daughter

**son·net** (sän'it) n. [< L. sonus, a sound] a poem normally of fourteen lines in any of several rhyme schemes

**son·ny** (sun'ē) n., pl. -nies little son: used in addressing a young boy

**so·no·rous** (sə nôr'əs, sän'ər əs) adj. [< L. sonor, a sound] 1. producing sound; resonant 2. full, deep, or rich in sound —so·nor'i·ty (-ə tē) n.

**soon** (soon) adv. [OE. sona, at once] 1. in a short time [come see us soon] 2. promptly; quickly [as soon as possible] 3. ahead of time; early [he left too soon] 4. readily; willingly [I would as soon go as stay] —sooner or later eventually

**soot** (soot) n. [OE. sot] a black substance consisting chiefly of carbon particles, in the smoke of burning matter —soot'y adj. -i·er, -i·est

**sooth** (sooth) n. [OE. soth] [Archaic] truth

**soothe** (sooth) vt. soothed, sooth'ing [OE. sothian, prove true] 1. to make calm or composed, as by gentleness, flattery, etc. 2. to relieve (pain, etc.) —sooth'er n. —sooth'ing adj.

**sooth·say·er** (sooth'sā'ər) n. [see SOOTH] one who claims to predict the future —sooth'say'ing n.

**sop** (säp) n. [ME. sopp] 1. a piece of food, as bread, soaked in milk, etc. 2. a) something given to appease b) a bribe —vt., vi. sopped, sop'ping 1. to soak; steep, etc. 2. to take (up), as water, by absorption

**SOP, S.O.P.** standing (or standard) operating procedure

**soph·ism** (säf'iz'm) n. [ult. < Gr. sophos, clever] a clever and plausible but fallacious argument

**soph·ist** (-ist) n. one who uses clever, specious reasoning

**so·phis·ti·cate** (sə fis'tə kāt'; for n. -kit) vt. -cat'ed, -cat'ing [see prec.] to change from a natural or simple state; make worldly-wise —n. a sophisticated person

**so·phis'ti·cat'ed** adj. 1. not simple, naive, etc.; worldly-wise or knowledgeable, subtle, etc. 2. for sophisticates 3. highly complex or developed in form, technique, etc., as equipment —so·phis'ti·ca'tion n.

**soph·is·try** (säf'is trē) n., pl. -tries misleading but clever reasoning

**Soph·o·cles** (säf'ə klēz') 496?-406 B.C.; Gr. writer of tragic dramas

**soph·o·more** (säf'ə môr') n. [< obs. sophumer, sophist] a student in the second year of college or in the tenth grade at high school

**soph'o·mor'ic** *adj.* of or like sophomores; opinionated, immature, etc.

**-so·phy** (sə fē) [< Gr. *sophia*, skill] *a suffix meaning* knowledge [*philosophy*]

**sop·o·rif·ic** (säp'ə rif'ik, sō'pə-) *adj.* [< L. *sopor*, sleep + -FIC] causing sleep —*n.* a soporific drug, etc.

**sop'py** *adj.* -pi·er, -pi·est 1. very wet: also **sop'ping** 2. [Colloq.] maudlin

**so·pra·no** (sə pran'ō) *n.*, *pl.* -nos [It. < *sopra*, above] 1. the highest singing voice of women or boys 2. a singer with such a range 3. a part for a soprano —*adj.* of or for a soprano

**sor·cer·y** (sôr'sər ē) *n.*, *pl.* -ies [< L. *sors*, a lot, share] the supposed use of an evil, supernatural power over people; witchcraft —**sor'cer·er** *n.* —**sor'cer·ess** *n.fem.*

**sor·did** (sôr'did) *adj.* [< L. *sordes*, filth] 1. dirty; filthy 2. squalid; wretched 3. base; mean; ignoble —**sor'did·ly** *adv.* —**sor'did·ness** *n.*

**sore** (sôr) *adj.* **sor'er, sor'est** [OE. *sar*] 1. giving or feeling pain; painful 2. *a)* filled with grief *b)* causing sadness, misery, etc. [*a sore* task] 3. causing irritation [*a sore* point] 4. [Colloq.] angry; offended —*n.* a sore, usually infected spot on the body —*adv.* [Archaic] greatly —**sore'ness** *n.*

**sore'head'** *n.* [Colloq.] a person easily angered or made resentful, etc.

**sore'ly** *adv.* 1. grievously; painfully 2. urgently [*sorely* needed]

**sor·ghum** (sôr'gəm) *n.* [< It. *sorgo*] 1. a cereal grass grown for grain, syrup, fodder, etc. 2. syrup made from its juices

**so·ror·i·ty** (sə rôr'ə tē) *n.*, *pl.* -ties [< L. *soror*, sister] a group of women or girls joined together for fellowship, etc., as in some colleges

**sor·rel**[1] (sôr'əl, sär'-) *n.* [< Frank. *sur*, sour] any of various plants with sour-tasting leaves

**sor·rel**[2] (sôr'əl, sär'-) *n.* [< OFr. *sor*, light brown] 1. a light reddish brown 2. a horse, etc. of this color

**sor·row** (sär'ō) *n.* [OE. *sorg*] 1. mental suffering caused by loss, disappointment, etc.; grief 2. that which causes grief —*vi.* to grieve —**sor'row·ful** *adj.* —**sor'row·ful·ly** *adv.*

**sor·ry** (sär'ē) *adj.* -ri·er, -ri·est [< OE. *sar*, sore] 1. full of sorrow, pity, or regret 2. inferior; poor 3. wretched —**sor'ri·ly** *adv.* —**sor'ri·ness** *n.*

**sort** (sôrt) *n.* [< L. *sors*, chance] 1. any group of related things; kind; class 2. quality or type 3. [Archaic] manner; way —*vt.* to arrange according to class or kind —**of sorts** or **of a sort** —**out of sorts** [Colloq.] not in good humor or health —**sort of** [Colloq.] somewhat

**sor·tie** (sôr'tē) *n.* [Fr. < *sortir*, go out] 1. a quick raid by forces of a besieged place 2. one mission by a single military plane

**SOS** (es'ō'es') a signal of distress, as in wireless telegraphy

**so-so** (sō'sō') *adv.*, *adj.* just passably or passable; fair Also **so so**

**sot** (sät) *n.* [< VL. *sottus*, a fool] a habitual drunkard —**sot'tish** *adj.*

**sot·to vo·ce** (sät'ō vō'chē) [It., under the voice] in a low voice, so as not to be overheard

**souf·flé** (sō̄ flā') *n.* [Fr. < L. *sufflare*, puff out] a baked food made light and puffy by adding beaten egg whites before baking

**sough** (sou, suf) *n.* [OE. *swogan*, to sound] a soft sighing or rustling sound —*n.* to make a sough

**sought** (sôt) *pt.* & *pp.* of SEEK

**soul** (sōl) *n.* [OE. *sawol*] 1. an entity without material reality, regarded as the spiritual part of a person 2. the moral or emotional nature of man 3. spiritual or emotional warmth, force, etc. 4. vital or essential part, quality, etc. 5. a person [I didn't see a *soul*] 6. [Colloq.] a feeling by U.S. blacks of racial pride and solidarity —*adj.* [Colloq.] of, for, or by U.S. blacks

**soul food** [Colloq.] certain food, as chitterlings or ham hocks, popular esp. among Southern Negroes

**soul'ful** *adj.* full of deep feeling —**soul'ful·ly** *adv.* —**soul'ful·ness** *n.*

**sound**[1] (sound) *n.* [< L. *sonus*] 1. that which is heard, resulting from stimulation of auditory nerves by vibrations (**sound waves**) in the air 2. the distance within which a sound may be heard 3. mental impression produced by wording [the *sound* of his report] —*vi.* 1. to make a sound 2. to seem upon being heard —*vt.* 1. to cause to sound 2. to signal, express, etc. 3. to utter distinctly [to *sound* one's r's] —**sound'less** *adj.*

**sound**[2] (sound) *adj.* [OE. *ge(sund)*] 1. free from defect, damage, or decay 2. healthy [a *sound* body] 3. safe; stable [a *sound* bank] 4. based on valid reasoning; sensible 5. thorough; forceful [a *sound* defeat] 6. deep and undisturbed: said of sleep 7. honest, loyal, etc. —*adv.* deeply [*sound* asleep] —**sound'ly** *adv.* —**sound'ness** *n.*

**sound**[3] (sound) *n.* [< OE. & ON. *sund*] 1. a wide channel linking two large bodies of water or separating an island from the mainland 2. a long arm of the sea

**sound**[4] (sound) *vt.*, *vi.* [< L. *sub*, under + *unda*, a wave] 1. to measure the depth of (water), esp. with a weighted line 2. to probe (the air or space) for data 3. to try to find out the opinions of (a person), usually subtly (often with *out*) —**sound'ing** *n.*

**sound barrier** *same as* SONIC BARRIER

**sounding board** 1. something to increase resonance or reflect sound: also **sound'board'** *n.* 2. a person used to test ideas on

**sound'proof'** *adj.* that keeps sound

from coming through —*vt.* to make soundproof

**sound track** the sound record along one side of a motion-picture film

**soup** (soōp) *n.* [Fr. *soupe*] a liquid food made by cooking meat, vegetables, etc. in water, milk, etc. —**soup up** [Slang] to increase the capacity for speed of (an engine, etc.)

**soup·çon** (soōp sōn′, soōp′sōn′) *n.* [Fr. < L. *suspicio*, suspicion] 1. a slight trace, as of a flavor 2. a tiny bit

**soup′y** *adj.* **-i·er, -i·est** 1. like soup 2. [Colloq.] foggy

**sour** (sour) *adj.* [OE. *sur*] 1. having the sharp, acid taste of vinegar, etc. 2. spoiled by fermentation 3. cross; bad-tempered 4. distasteful or unpleasant —*vt., vi.* to make or become sour —**sour′ly** *adv.* —**sour′ness** *n.*

**sour′ball′** *n.* a small ball of tart, hard candy

**source** (sôrs) *n.* [ < L. *surgere*, to rise] 1. a spring, etc. from which a stream arises 2. place of origin; prime cause 3. a person, book, etc. that provides information

**sour′dough′** *n.* 1. [Dial.] fermented dough saved for use as leaven 2. a lone prospector, as in the West

**sour grapes** a scorning of something only because it cannot be had or done

**souse** (sous) *n.* [ < OHG. *sulza*, brine] 1. a pickled food, as pig's feet 2. liquid for pickling; brine 3. a plunging into a liquid 4. [Slang] a drunkard —*vt., vi.* soused, sous′ing 1. to pickle 2. to plunge in a liquid 3. to make or become soaking wet

**south** (south) *n.* [OE. *suth*] 1. the direction to the left of one facing the sunset (180° on the compass) 2. a region in or toward this direction —*adj.* 1. in, of, or toward the south 2. from the south —*adv.* in or toward the south —**the South** the part of the U.S. south of Pennsylvania, the Ohio River, and N Missouri

**South Africa** country in S Africa: 472,358 sq. mi.; pop. 18,733,000; caps. Cape Town, Pretoria

**South America** S continent in the Western Hemisphere: c.6,864,000 sq. mi.; pop. 174,000,000 —**South American**

**South Bend** city in N Ind.: pop. 126,000

**South Car·o·li·na** (kar′ə li′nə) Southern State of the U.S.: 31,055 sq. mi.; pop. 2,591,000; cap. Columbia —**South Car′o·lin′i·an** (-lin′ē ən)

**South China Sea** part of the Pacific Ocean, between SE Asia & the Philippines

**South Da·ko·ta** (də kō′tə) Middle Western State of the U.S.: 77,047 sq. mi.; pop. 666,000; cap. Pierre —**South Da·ko′tan**

**south′east′** *n.* 1. the direction halfway between south and east 2. a region in or toward this direction —*adj.* 1. in, of, or toward the southeast 2. from the southeast —*adv.* in, toward, or from the southeast —**south′east′er·ly** *adj., adv.* —**south′-east′ern** *adj.* —**south′east′ward**

(-wərd) *adv., adj.* —**south′east′-wards** *adv.*

**south·er·ly** (su*th*′ər lē) *adj., adv.* 1. toward the south 2. from the south

**south·ern** (su*th*′ərn) *adj.* 1. in, of, or toward the south 2. from the south 3. [S-] of the South

**south′ern·er** *n.* a native or inhabitant of the south

**Southern Hemisphere** the half of the earth south of the equator

**southern lights** aurora australis

**south·paw** (south′pô′) *n.* [Slang] a left-handed person; esp., a left-handed baseball pitcher

**South Pole** the southern end of the earth's axis

**South Sea Islands** the islands in the South Pacific

**south′ward** (-wərd) *adv., adj.* toward the south: also **south′wards** *adv.*

**south′west′** *n.* 1. the direction halfway between south and west 2. a region in or toward this direction —*adj.* 1. in, of, or toward the southwest 2. from the southwest —*adv.* in, toward, or from the southwest —**the Southwest** the southwestern U.S. —**south′west′er·ly** *adj., adv.* —**south′west′ern** *adj.* —**south′west′-ward** (-wərd) *adv., adj.* —**south′-west′wards** *adv.*

**sou·ve·nir** (soō′və nir′) *n.* [Fr. < L. *subvenire*, come to mind] something kept as a reminder; memento

**sov·er·eign** (säv′rən, -ər in) *adj.* [ < L. *super*, above] 1. above all others; chief; supreme 2. supreme in power, rank, etc. 3. independent of all others [a *sovereign* state] —*n.* 1. a monarch or ruler 2. esp. formerly, a British gold coin worth one pound

**sov′er·eign·ty** *n.* 1. the status, rule, etc. of a sovereign 2. supreme and independent political authority

**so·vi·et** (sō′vē it, -et′) *n.* [Russ., lit., council] 1. in the Soviet Union, any of the various elected governing councils from the village and town soviets up to the Supreme Soviet 2. a similar council in a socialist governing system —*adj.* [S-] of or connected with the Soviet Union —**so′vi·et·ism** *n.*

**Soviet Union** same as UNION OF SOVIET SOCIALIST REPUBLICS

**sow¹** (sou) *n.* [OE. *sugu*] an adult female pig

**sow²** (sō) *vt.* **sowed, sown** (sōn) or **sowed, sow′ing** [OE. *sawan*] 1. to scatter (seed) for growing 2. to plant seed in (a field, etc.) 3. to spread or scatter —*vi.* to sow seed —**sow′er** *n.*

**sox** (säks) *n. alt. pl. of* SOCK¹

**soy** (soi) *n.* [Jap. < Chin. *chiang*, salted bean + *yu*, oil] a dark, salty sauce made from fermented soybeans

**soy′bean′** *n.* 1. a plant widely grown for its seeds, which contain much protein and oil 2. its seed

**Sp.** 1. Spain 2. Spaniard 3. Spanish

**spa** (spä) *n.* [ < *Spa*, resort in Belgium] 1. a mineral spring 2. a health resort having a mineral spring

**space** (spās) *n.* [ < L. *spatium*] 1. *a)* the boundless expanse within which all

things are contained b) *same as* OUTER
SPACE 2. a) distance, area, etc.
between or within things b) room for
something [a parking *space*] 3. an
interval of time —vt. **spaced, spac'-**
**ing** to arrange with spaces between
**space'craft'** n., pl. **-craft'** a spaceship or satellite designed for travel,
exploration, etc. in outer space
**spaced'-out'** adj. [Slang] under the
influence of a drug, marijuana, etc.:
also **spaced, space'y**
**space'flight'** n. a flight through
outer space
**space heater** a small heating unit
for a room or small area
**space'man'** n., pl. **-men'** an astronaut or any of the crew of a spaceship
**space'port'** n. a center for testing
and launching spacecraft
**space'ship'** n. a rocket-propelled
vehicle for travel in outer space
**space shuttle** a spacecraft for transporting persons and equipment between earth and a space station
**space station** (or **platform**) an
orbiting structure for use as a launch
pad, observation center, etc.
**space'suit'** n. a garment pressurized
for use by spacemen
**space'walk'** n. an astronaut's moving
about in space outside his spacecraft
—vi. to engage in a spacewalk
**spa·cious** (spā'shəs) adj. having more
than enough space; vast —**spa'-**
**cious·ly** adv. —**spa'cious·ness** n.
**spade**[1] (spād) n. [OE. *spadu*] a flat-
bladed, long-handled digging tool, like
a shovel —vt., vi. **spad'ed, spad'ing**
to dig with a spade —**spade'ful** n.
**spade**[2] (spād) n. [ult. < Gr. *spathē,*
flat blade] 1. the black figure (♠)
marking one of the four suits of playing cards 2. a card of this suit
**spade'work'** n. preparatory work for
some main project, esp. when tiresome
**spa·ghet·ti** (spə get'ē) n. [It. <
*spago,* small cord] pasta in long, thin
strings, cooked by boiling or steaming
**Spain** (spān) country in SW Europe:
194,346 sq. mi.; pop. 32,411,000; cap.
Madrid
**spake** (spāk) archaic pt. of SPEAK
**span** (span) n. [OE. *sponn*] 1. the
distance (about 9 in.) between the tips
of the thumb and little finger when
extended 2. a) the full extent between
any two limits b) the full duration of
[*span* of attention] 3. a part between
two supports 4. a team of two animals
—vt. **spanned, span'ning** 1. to
measure, esp. by the span of the hand
2. to extend over
**Span.** Spanish
**span·dex** (span'deks) n. [< EXPAND]
an elastic synthetic fiber used in
girdles, etc.
**span·gle** (span'g'l) n. [< OE. *spang,*
a clasp] a small piece of bright metal
sewn on fabric for decoration —vt.
**-gled, -gling** to decorate with spangles
or other bright objects

**Span·iard** (span'yərd) n. a native
or inhabitant of Spain
**span·iel** (span'yəl) n. [< MFr.
*espagnol,* lit., Spanish] any of several
breeds of dog with a silky coat, large,
drooping ears, and short legs
**Span·ish** (span'ish) adj. of Spain, its
people, their language, etc. —n. the
language of Spain and Spanish America —**the Spanish** the people of Spain
**Spanish America** those countries
south of the U.S. in which Spanish
is the chief language —**Span'ish-**
**A·mer'i·can** adj., n.
**Spanish moss** a rootless plant that
grows in long, graceful strands from
tree branches in the southern U.S.
**spank** (spaŋk) vt. [echoic] to strike
with the open hand, etc., esp. on the
buttocks, as in punishment —n. a
smack given in spanking
**spank'ing** adj. 1. swiftly moving;
rapid 2. brisk: said of a breeze —adv.
[Colloq.] completely [*spanking* new]
**spar**[1] (spär) n. [< ON. *sparri* or MDu.
*sparre*] any pole, as a mast or yard,
supporting a sail of a ship
**spar**[2] (spär) vi. **sparred, spar'ring**
[prob. < It. *parare,* to parry] 1. to
box with feinting movements, landing
few heavy blows 2. to wrangle
**spare** (sper) vt. **spared, spar'ing**
[OE. *sparian*] 1. to refrain from killing, hurting, etc. 2. to save or free a
person from (something) 3. to avoid
using or use frugally 4. to part with
conveniently —adj. 1. not in regular
use; extra 2. free [*spare* time] 3.
meager; scanty 4. lean; thin —n. 1. a
spare, or extra, thing 2. *Bowling* a
knocking down of all the pins with two
rolls of the ball —**spare'ly** adv.
**spare'ribs'** n.pl. a cut of pork, consisting of the thin end of the ribs
**spar'ing** adj. 1. careful; frugal 2.
scanty or meager —**spar'ing·ly** adv.
**spark** (spärk) n. [OE. *spearca*] 1. a
glowing bit of matter, esp. one thrown
off by a fire 2. any flash or sparkle 3.
a particle or trace 4. a brief flash of
light accompanying an electric discharge as through air —vi. to make
sparks —vt. to stir up; activate
**spar·kle** (spär'k'l) vi. **-kled, -kling**
1. to throw off sparks 2. to glitter 3.
to effervesce —n. 1. a sparkling 2.
brilliance —**spar'kler** (-klər) n.
**spark plug** a piece fitted into a
cylinder of an engine to ignite the fuel
mixture by making sparks
**spar·row** (spar'ō) n. [OE. *spearwa*]
any of numerous finches
**sparse** (spärs) adj. [< L. *spargere,*
scatter] thinly spread; not dense —
**sparse'ly** adv. —**sparse'ness, spar'-**
**si·ty** (-sə tē) n.
**Spar·ta** (spär'tə) city in S Greece: a
military power in ancient times
**Spar'tan** adj. 1. of ancient Sparta, its
people, culture, etc. 2. like the
Spartans; warlike, hardy, disciplined,
etc. —n. a Spartan person

fat, āpe, cär; ten, ēven; is, bīte; gō, hôrn, tōol, look; oil, out; up, fur;
chin; she; thin, then; zh, leisure; ŋ, ring; ə for a in ago; ', (ā'b'l); ë, Fr. coeur;
ö, Fr. feu; Fr. mon; ü, Fr. duc; kh, G. ich, doch; ‡ foreign; < derived from

**spasm** (spaz'm) *n.* [< Gr. *spasmos*] 1. a sudden, involuntary muscular contraction 2. any sudden, violent, temporary activity, feeling, etc.

**spas·mod·ic** (spaz mäd'ik) *adj.* [see prec. & -OID] of or like spasms; fitful —**spas·mod'i·cal·ly** *adv.*

**spas·tic** (spas'tik) *adj.* of or characterized by muscular spasms —*n.* one having a spastic condition

**spat¹** (spat) *n.* [prob. echoic] [Colloq.] a brief, petty quarrel —*vi.* **spat'ted, spat'ting** [Colloq.] to engage in a spat

**spat²** (spat) *n.* [< *spatterdash*, a legging] a gaiterlike covering for the instep and ankle

**spat³** (spat) *alt. pt. & pp. of* SPIT²

**spat⁴** (spat) *n.* [< ?] the spawn of the oyster or other bivalve shellfish

**spate** (spāt) *n.* [< ?] an unusually large outpouring, as of words

**spa·tial** (spā'shəl) *adj.* [< L. *spatium*, space] of, or existing in, space

**spat·ter** (spat'ər) *vt., vi.* [< ?] 1. to scatter or spurt out in drops 2. to splash —*n.* 1. a spattering 2. a mark caused by spattering

**spat·u·la** (spach'ə lə) *n.* [< Gr. *spathē*, flat blade] an implement with a broad, flexible blade for spreading or blending foods, paints, etc.

**spav·in** (spav'in) *n.* [< MFr. *esparvain*] a disease laming horses in the hock joint —**spav'ined** *adj.*

**spawn** (spôn) *vt., vi.* [see EXPAND] 1. to produce or deposit (eggs, sperm, or young) 2. to bring forth or produce prolifically —*n.* 1. the mass of eggs or young produced by fishes, mollusks, etc. 2. something produced, esp. in great quantity, as offspring

**spay** (spā) *vt.* [< Gr. *spathē*, flat blade] to sterilize (a female animal) by removing the ovaries

**speak** (spēk) *vi.* **spoke** or archaic **spake, spo'ken, speak'ing** [OE. *sp(r)ecan*] 1. to utter words; talk 2. to communicate as by talking 3. to make a request (*for*) 4. to make a speech —*vt.* 1. to make known as by speaking 2. to use (a given language) in speaking 3. to utter (words) orally —**speak out** (or **up**) to speak clearly or freely —**speak well for** to say·or indicate something favorable about

**speak'·eas'y** (-ē'zē) *n., pl.* **-ies** [Slang] a place where alcoholic drinks are sold illegally

**speak'er** *n.* one who speaks; esp. *a)* an orator *b)* the presiding officer of various lawmaking bodies, specif. [S-] of the U.S. House of Representatives

**spear** (spir) *n.* [OE. *spere*] 1. a weapon with a long shaft and a sharp point, for thrusting or throwing 2. [var. of SPIRE] a long blade or shoot, as of grass —*vt.* to pierce or stab with or as with a spear

**spear'head'** *n.* 1. the pointed head of a spear 2. the leading person or group, as in an attack —*vt.* to take the lead in (a drive, attack, etc.)

**spear'mint'** *n.* [prob. after the shape of its flowers] a fragrant plant of the mint family, used for flavoring

**spe·cial** (spesh'əl) *adj.* [< L. *species*,

kind] 1. distinctive or unique 2. exceptional; unusual 3. highly valued 4. of or for a particular purpose, etc. 5. not general; specific —*n.* a special person or thing —**spe'cial·ly** *adv.*

**special delivery** mail delivery by a special messenger, for an extra fee

**spe'cial·ist** *n.* one who specializes in a particular study, work, etc.

**spe'cial·ize'** *vi.* **-ized', -iz'ing** to concentrate on a special branch of study, work, etc. —**spe'cial·i·za'·tion** *n.*

**spe'cial·ty** (-tē) *n., pl.* **-ties** 1. a special quality, feature, etc. 2. a special interest, study, etc. 3. an article with special features, etc.

**spe·cie** (spē'shē) *n.* [< L. *species*] coin, rather than paper money

**spe'cies** (-shēz) *n., pl.* **-cies** [L., appearance] 1. a distinct kind; sort 2. the fundamental biological classification, consisting of a number of highly similar plants or animals

**specif.** specifically

**spe·cif·ic** (spi sif'ik) *.adj.* [< L. *species* (see SPECIES) + *-ficus*, -FIC] 1. definite; explicit 2. peculiar to or characteristic of something 3. of a particular kind 4. specially indicated as a cure for some disease —*n.* a specific cure —**spe·cif'i·cal·ly** *adv.*

**spec·i·fi·ca·tion** (spes'ə fi kā'shən) *n.* 1. [*usually pl.*] an enumeration of particulars, as to size, quality, etc. 2. something specified

**specific gravity** the ratio of the weight of a given volume of a substance to that of an equal volume of another substance (as water) used as a standard

**spec·i·fy** (spes'ə fī') *vt.* **-fied', -fy'ing** [< LL. *specificus*, SPECIFIC] 1. to mention or describe in detail 2. to state explicitly

**spec·i·men** (spes'ə mən) *n.* [L. < *specere*, see] a part or individual used as a sample of a whole or group

**spe·cious** (spē'shəs) *adj.* [< L. *species*, appearance] seeming to be good, sound, correct, etc. without really being so —**spe'cious·ly** *adv.*

**speck** (spek) *n.* [OE. *specca*] 1. a small spot, mark, etc. 2. a very small bit —*vt.* to mark with specks

**speck·le** (spek'l) *n.* a small speck —*vt.* **-led, -ling** to mark with speckles

**specs** (speks) *n.pl.* [Colloq.] 1. spectacles; eyeglasses 2. specifications

**spec·ta·cle** (spek'tə k'l) *n.* [< L. *specere*, see] 1. a remarkable sight 2. a large public show 3. [*pl.*] a pair of eyeglasses: old-fashioned term

**spec·tac·u·lar** (spek tak'yə lər) *adj.* unusual to a striking degree —*n.* an elaborate show or display —**spec·tac'·u·lar·ly** *adv.*

**spec·ta·tor** (spek'tāt ər) *n.* [L. < *spectare*, behold] one who watches without taking an active part

**spec·ter** (spek'tər) *n.* [< L. *spectare*, behold] a ghost; apparition: Brit. sp. **spectre** —**spec'tral** (-trəl) *adj.*

**spec·tro·scope** (spek'trə skōp') *n.* [< L. *spectare*, behold + -SCOPE] an optical instrument used for forming spectra for study —**spec′tro·scop′ic** (-skäp′ik) *adj.* —**spec·tros′co·py** (-träs′kə pē) *n.*

**spec·trum** (spek′trəm) *n., pl.* **-tra** (-trə), **-trums** [< L.: see SPECTER] **1.** a series of colored bands diffracted and arranged in order of their respective wavelengths, by the passage of white light through a prism, etc. **2.** a continuous range or entire extent —**spec′tral** (-trəl) *adj.*

**spec·u·late** (spek′yə lāt′) *vi.* **-lat′ed, -lat′ing** [< L. *specere*, see] **1.** to think reflectively; ponder; esp., to conjecture **2.** to engage in a risky venture on the chance of making huge profits —**spec′u·la′tion** *n.* —**spec′u·la′tive** *adj.* —**spec′u·la′tor** *n.*

**speech** (spēch) *n.* [< OE. *sprecan*, speak] **1.** the act or manner of speaking **2.** the power to speak **3.** that which is spoken; utterance, remark, etc. **4.** a talk given to an audience **5.** the language of a certain people

**speech′less** *adj.* **1.** incapable of speech **2.** silent, as from shock

**speed** (spēd) *n.* [OE. *spæd*, success] **1.** quick motion; swiftness **2.** rate of movement; velocity **3.** [Slang] any of various amphetamine compounds —*vi.* **sped** (sped) or **speed′ed, speed′ing** to move rapidly, esp. too rapidly —*vt.* **1.** to cause to speed **2.** to help to succeed; aid —**speed up** to increase in speed —**speed′er** *n.*

**speed′boat′** *n.* a fast motorboat

**speed·om·e·ter** (spi däm′ə tər) *n.* a device attached to a motor vehicle, etc. to indicate speed

**speed′ster** (-stər) *n.* a very fast driver, runner, etc.

**speed′way′** *n.* a track for racing automobiles or motorcycles

**speed′y** *adj.* **-i·er, -i·est 1.** rapid; fast; swift **2.** without delay; prompt *[a speedy reply]* —**speed′i·ly** *adv.*

**spe·le·ol·o·gy** (spē′lē äl′ə jē) *n.* the scientific study and exploration of caves —**spe′le·ol′o·gist** *n.*

**spell¹** (spel) *n.* [OE., a saying] **1.** a word or formula supposed to have some magic power **2.** irresistible influence; charm; fascination

**spell²** (spel) *vt.* **spelled** or **spelt**, **spell′ing** [< OFr. *espeller*, explain] **1.** to name in order the letters of (a word) **2.** to make up (a word, etc.): said of specified letters **3.** to mean *[red spells danger]* —*vi.* to spell words —**spell out** to explain in detail

**spell³** (spel) *vt.* **spelled, spell′ing** [OE. *spelian*] [Colloq.] to work in place of (another) for an interval; relieve —*n.* **1.** a period of work, duty, etc. **2.** a period of anything *[a spell of brooding]* **3.** [Colloq.] a fit of illness

**spell′bind′** (-bīnd′) *vt.* **-bound′, -bind′ing** to cause to be spellbound; fascinate —**spell′bind′er** *n.*

**spell′bound′** (-bound′) *adj.* held by or as by a spell; fascinated

**spell′down′** *n.* a spelling match, esp.

one eliminating a contestant when he misspells one or more words

**spell′er** *n.* **1.** one who spells words **2.** a textbook for teaching spelling

**spell′ing** *n.* **1.** the act of one who spells words **2.** the way a word is spelled

**spe·lunk·er** (spi luŋ′kər) *n.* [< Gr. *spēlynx*, a cave] a cave explorer

**spend** (spend) *vt.* **spent, spend′ing** [see EXPEND] **1.** to use up, exhaust, etc. *[his fury was spent]* **2.** to pay out (money) **3.** to devote (time, labor, etc.) to something **4.** to pass (time) —*vi.* to pay out or use up money, etc. —**spend′er** *n.*

**spend′thrift′** (-thrift′) *n.* one who wastes money —*adj.* wasteful

**spent** (spent) *pt. & pp.* of SPEND —*adj.* **1.** tired out; physically exhausted **2.** used up; worn out

**sperm** (spurm) *n.* [< Gr. *sperma*, seed] **1.** the male generative fluid; semen **2.** *same as* SPERMATOZOON

**sper·mat·o·zo·on** (spər mat′ə zō′än) *n., pl.* **-zo′a** (-ə) [< Gr. *sperma*, seed + *zōion*, animal] the male germ cell, found in semen, which penetrates the female egg to fertilize it

**sperm whale** a large, toothed whale found in warm seas: its head yields a valuable lubricating oil (**sperm oil**)

**spew** (spyōō) *vt., vi.* [OE. *spiwan*] **1.** to throw up as from the stomach; vomit **2.** to flow or gush forth —*n.* something spewed

**sp. gr.** specific gravity

**sphere** (sfir) *n.* [< Gr. *sphaira*] **1.** any round body having the surface equally distant from the center at all points; globe; ball **2.** the place, range, or extent of action, existence, knowledge, experience, etc. —**spher·i·cal** (sfer′i k′l, sfir′-) *adj.*

**sphe·roid** (sfir′oid) *n.* a body that is almost but not quite a sphere —*adj.* of this shape: also **sphe·roid′al**

**sphinc·ter** (sfiŋk′tər) *n.* [< Gr. *sphingein*, to draw close] a ring-shaped muscle at a body orifice

**sphinx** (sfiŋks) *n.* [< Gr., strangler] **1.** [S-] a statue with a lion's body and a man's head, near Cairo, Egypt **2.** *a)* [S-] *Gr. Myth.* a winged monster with a lion's body and a woman's head: it strangled passers-by unable to guess its riddle *b)* one who is difficult to know or understand

**spice** (spīs) *n.* [< L. *species*, kind] **1.** an aromatic vegetable substance, as clove, pepper, etc., used to season food **2.** that which adds zest or interest —*vt.* **spiced, spic′ing 1.** to season with spice **2.** to add zest to —**spic′y** *adj.* **-i·er, -i·est**

**spick-and-span** (spik″n span′) *adj.* [< *spike*, nail + ON. *spānn*, a chip] **1.** new or fresh **2.** neat and clean

**spic·ule** (spik′yōōl) *n.* [L. *spiculum*, a point] a hard, needlelike part

**spi·der** (spī′dər) *n.* [< OE. *spinnan*, spin] **1.** any of various arachnids that spin webs **2.** a cast-iron frying pan

**spi·der·y** (spī′dər ē) *adj.* like a spider

**spiel** (spēl) *n.* {G., play} [Slang] a talk or harangue, as in selling

**spiff·y** (spif′ē) *adj.* -**i·er**, -**i·est** [< dial. *spiff*, well-dressed person] [Slang] spruce, smart, or dapper

**spig·ot** (spig′ət, spik′-) *n.* [ME. *spigote*] 1. a plug to stop the vent in a cask, etc. 2. a faucet

**spike¹** (spīk) *n.* [< ON. *spīkr* or MDu. & MLowG. *spiker*] 1. a long, heavy nail 2. a sharp-pointed projection, as on the sole of a shoe to prevent slipping —*vt.* **spiked, spik′ing** 1. to fasten or fit as with spikes 2. to pierce with, or impale on, a spike 3. to thwart (a scheme, etc.) 4. [Slang] to add alcoholic liquor to (a drink)

**spike²** (spīk) *n.* [L. *spica*] 1. an ear of grain 2. a long flower cluster

**spill** (spil) *vt.* **spilled** or **spilt** (spilt), **spill′ing** [OE. *spillan*, destroy] 1. to allow, esp. unintentionally, to run, scatter, or flow over from a container 2. to shed (blood) 3. [Colloq.] to throw off (a rider, etc.) —*vi.* to be spilled; overflow —*n.* 1. a spilling 2. [Colloq.] a fall or tumble —**spill′age** *n.*

**spill′way′** *n.* a channel to carry off excess water, as around a dam

**spin** (spin) *vt.* **spun, spin′ning** [OE. *spinnan*] 1. *a)* to draw out and twist fibers of (wool, cotton, etc.) into thread *b)* to make (thread, etc.) thus 2. to make (a web, cocoon, etc.), as a spider 3. to draw *out* (a story) to a great length 4. to rotate swiftly —*vi.* 1. to spin thread or yarn 2. to form a web, cocoon, etc. 3. to whirl 4. to seem to be spinning from dizziness 5. to move along swiftly and smoothly —*n.* 1. a spinning or rotating movement 2. a ride in a motor vehicle 3. a descent of an airplane, nose first along a spiral path —**spin′ner** *n.*

**spin·ach** (spin′ich) *n.* [ult. < Per. *aspanākh*] a plant with dark-green, juicy, edible leaves

**spi·nal** (spī′n'l) *adj.* of or having to do with the spine or spinal cord

**spinal column** the series of joined vertebrae forming the axial support for the skeleton; backbone

**spinal cord** the thick cord of nerve tissue in the spinal column

**spin·dle** (spin′d'l) *n.* [< OE. *spinnan*, spin] 1. a slender rod used in spinning for twisting, winding, or holding thread 2. a spindlelike thing 3. any rod or pin that revolves or serves as an axis for a revolving part

**spin·dly** (spin′dlē) *adj.* -**dli·er**, -**dli·est** long or tall and very thin

**spine** (spīn) *n.* [< L. *spina*, thorn] 1. *a)* a sharp, stiff projection, as a thorn of the cactus *b)* anything like this 2. *a)* same as SPINAL COLUMN *b)* anything like this, as the back of a book —**spin′y** *adj.* -**i·er**, -**i·est**

**spine′less** *adj.* 1. having no spine or spines 2. lacking courage or willpower

**spin·et** (spin′it) *n.* [< It. *spinetta*] a small upright piano

**spin·ner·et** (spin′ə ret′) *n.* the organ in spiders, caterpillars, etc. with which they spin silky threads

**spinning wheel** a simple spinning machine with a single spindle driven by a large wheel

**spin-off** (spin′ôf′) *n.* a secondary benefit, product, development, etc.

**spin·ster** (spin′stər) *n.* [ME. < *spinnen*, to spin] an unmarried woman, esp. an elderly one —**spin′ster·hood′** *n.*

**spiny lobster** a sea crustacean similar to the lobster, but lacking large pincers and having a spiny shell

**spi·ra·cle** (spī′rə k'l) *n.* [< L. *spirare*, breathe] an opening for breathing, as on the sides of an insect's body or on top of a whale's head

**spi·ral** (spī′rəl) *adj.* [< Gr. *speira*, a coil] circling around a point in constantly increasing (or decreasing) curves, or in constantly changing planes —*n.* a spiral curve or coil —*vi., vt.* -**raled** or -**ralled, -ral·ing** or -**ral·ling** to move in or form (into) a spiral —**spi′ral·ly** *adv.*

**spire** (spīr) *n.* [OE. *spir*] 1. a sprout or stalk of a plant 2. the top part of a pointed, tapering object 3. anything tapering to a point, as a steeple

**spi·re·a** (spī rē′ə) *n.* [see SPIRAL] a plant of the rose family, with clusters of small flowers: also **spi·rae′a**

**spir·it** (spir′it) *n.* [< L. *spirare*, breathe] 1. *same as* SOUL (sense 1) 2. [*also* S-] life, will, thought, etc., regarded as separate from matter 3. a supernatural being, as a ghost, angel, etc. 4. an individual [a brave *spirit*] 5. [*usually pl.*] disposition; mood [high *spirits*] 6. vivacity, courage, etc. 7. enthusiastic loyalty [school *spirit*] 8. real meaning [the *spirit* of the law] 9. a pervading animating principle; essential quality [the *spirit* of the times] 10. [*usually pl.*] distilled alcoholic liquor —*vt.* to carry (*away, off*, etc.) secretly and swiftly —**spir′it·less** *adj.*

**spir′it·ed** *adj.* lively; vigorous

**spir·it·u·al** (spir′i choo wəl) *adj.* 1. of the spirit or the soul 2. of or consisting of spirit; not corporeal 3. religious; sacred —*n.* a religious folk song of U.S. Negro origin —**spir′it·u·al′i·ty** (-wal′ə tē) *n.* —**spir′it·u·al·ly** *adv.*

**spir·it·u·al·ism** *n.* the belief that the dead survive as spirits which can communicate with the living —**spir′it·u·al·ist** *n.* —**spir′it·u·al·is′tic** *adj.*

**spir·it·u·ous** (spir′i choo wəs) *n.* of or containing distilled alcohol

**spi·ro·chete** (spī′rə kēt′) *n.* [< Gr. *speira*, spiral + *chaitē*, hair] any of various spiral-shaped bacteria

**spit¹** (spit) *n.* [OE. *spitu*] 1. a thin, pointed rod on which meat is roasted over a fire, etc. 2. a narrow point of land extending into the water —*vt.* **spit′ted, spit′ting** to fix as on a spit

**spit²** (spit) *vt.* **spit** or **spat, spit′ting** [OE. *spittan*] 1. to eject from the mouth 2. to eject explosively —*vi.* to eject saliva from the mouth —*n.* 1. a spitting 2. saliva —**spit and image** [Colloq.] perfect likeness

**spit′ball′** *n.* 1. paper chewed up into a wad for throwing 2. *Baseball* an illegal pitch made to curve by wetting one side of the ball, as with spit

**spite** (spīt) *n.* [see DESPITE] 1. ill will; malice 2. a grudge —*vt.* **spit′ed, spit′ing** to vent one's spite upon by hurting, frustrating, etc. —**in spite of** regardless of —**spite′ful** *adj.*

**spit·tle** (spit′'l) *n.* saliva; spit

**spit·toon** (spi tōōn′) *n.* a jarlike container to spit into; cuspidor

**splash** (splash) *vt.* [echoic] 1. to cause (a liquid) to scatter 2. to dash a liquid, mud, etc. on, so as to wet or soil —*vi.* to move, strike, etc. with a splash —*n.* 1. a splashing 2. a spot made by splashing —**make a splash** [Colloq.] to attract great attention

**splash′down′** *n.* the landing of a spacecraft on water

**splash′y** *adj.* **-i·er, -i·est** 1. splashing or apt to splash: wet, muddy, etc. 2. [Colloq.] getting much attention; spectacular —**splash′i·ly** *adv.* —**splash′i·ness** *n.*

**splat¹** (splat) *n.* [< SPLIT] a thin slat of wood, as in a chair back

**splat²** (splat) *n., interj.* a splattering or wet, slapping sound

**splat·ter** (splat′ər) *n., vt., vi.* spatter or splash

**splay** (splā) *vt., vi.* [ME. *splaien*] to spread out —*adj.* spreading outward

**splay′foot′** *n., pl.* **-feet′** a foot that is flat and turned outward —**splay′-foot′ed** *adj.*

**spleen** (splēn) *n.* [< Gr. *splēn*] 1. a large lymphatic organ in the upper left part of the abdomen: it modifies the blood structure 2. malice; spite

**splen·did** (splen′did) *adj.* [< L. *splendere,* to shine] 1. shining; brilliant 2. magnificent; gorgeous 3. grand; illustrious 4. [Colloq.] very good; fine —**splen′did·ly** *adv.*

**splen·dor** (splen′dər) *n.* [see prec.] 1. great luster; brilliance 2. pomp; grandeur Brit. sp. **splendour**

**sple·net·ic** (spli net′ik) *adj.* 1. of the spleen 2. irritable; bad-tempered

**splice** (splīs) *vt.* **spliced, splic′ing** [MDu. *splissen*] 1. to join (ropes) by weaving together the end strands 2. to join the ends of (timbers) by overlapping 3. to fasten the ends of (wire, film, etc.) together, as by soldering, etc. —*n.* a joint made by splicing

**splint** (splint) *n.* [< MDu. or MLowG. *splinte*] 1. a thin strip of wood, etc. woven with others to make baskets, etc. 2. a strip of wood, etc. used to hold a broken bone in place

SPLICE

**splin·ter** (splin′tər) *vt., vi.* [see prec.] to break or split into thin, sharp pieces —*n.* a thin, sharp piece, as of wood, made by splitting, etc.

**split** (split) *vt., vi.* **split, split′ting** [MDu. *splitten*] 1. to separate lengthwise into two or more parts 2. to break or tear apart 3. to divide into shares 4. to disunite 5. *a)* to break (a mole-

cule) into atoms *b)* to produce nuclear fission in (an atom) —*n.* 1. a splitting 2. a break; crack 3. a division in a group, etc. —*adj.* divided; separated

**split′-lev′el** *adj.* having adjacent floor levels staggered about a half-story apart

**split′ting** *adj.* 1. that splits 2. severe, as a headache

**splotch** (spläch) *n.* [prob. < SPOT + BLOTCH] an irregular spot, splash, or stain —*vt., vi.* to mark or be marked with splotches —**splotch′y** *adj.*

**splurge** (splurj) *n.* [echoic] [Colloq.] 1. any very showy display or effort 2. a spell of extravagant spending —*vi.* **splurged, splurg′ing** [Colloq.] 1. to show off 2. to spend money freely

**splut·ter** (splut′ər) *n.* [var. of SPUTTER] 1. to make hissing or spitting sounds 2. to speak hurriedly and confusedly —*n.* a spluttering

**spoil** (spoil) *vt.* **spoiled** or **spoilt, spoil′ing** [< L. *spolium,* plunder] 1. to damage so as to make useless, etc. 2. to impair the enjoyment, etc. of 3. to cause to expect too much by overindulgence 4. [Archaic] to rob; plunder —*vi.* to become spoiled; decay, etc., as food —*n.* [*usually pl.*] plunder; booty —**spoil′age** *n.* —**spoil′er** *n.*

**spoil′sport′** *n.* one whose actions ruin the pleasure of others

**spoils system** the treating of public offices as the booty of a successful political party

**Spo·kane** (spō kan′) city in E Wash.: pop. 171,000

**spoke¹** (spōk) *n.* [OE. *spaca*] any of the braces extending from the hub to the rim of a wheel

**spoke²** (spōk) *pt. of* SPEAK

**spo·ken** (spō′k'n) *pp. of* SPEAK —*adj.* 1. uttered; oral 2. having a (specified) kind of voice [*soft-spoken*]

**spokes·man** (spōks′mən) *n., pl.* **-men** one who speaks for another or for a group

**spo·li·a·tion** (spō′lē ā′shən) *n.* [< L. *spoliatio*] robbery; plundering

**sponge** (spunj) *n.* [< Gr. *spongia*] 1. a plantlike sea animal with a porous structure 2. the highly absorbent skeleton of such animals, used for washing surfaces, etc. 3. any substance like this, as a piece of spongy rubber, etc. —*vt.* **sponged, spong′ing** 1. to wipe, dampen, absorb, etc. as with a sponge 2. [Colloq.] to get as by begging, imposition, etc. —*vi.* [Colloq.] to live as a parasite upon others —**spong′er** *n.* —**spon′gy** *adj.*

**sponge bath** a bath taken by using a wet sponge or cloth without getting into water

**sponge′cake′** *n.* a light, spongy cake without shortening: also **sponge cake**

**spon·sor** (spän′sər) *n.* [L. < *spondere,* promise solemnly] 1. one who assumes responsibility as surety for, or endorser of, some person or thing 2. a godparent 3. a business firm, etc. that pays for a radio or TV program advertising its

product —*vt.* to act as sponsor for
—**spon′sor·ship′** *n.*

**spon·ta·ne·i·ty** (spän′tə nē′ə tē) *n.*
1. a being spontaneous 2. *pl.* -**ties** spontaneous behavior, action, etc.

**spon·ta·ne·ous** (spän tā′nē əs) *adj.* [< L. *sponte*, of free will] 1. acting or resulting from a natural feeling or impulse, without constraint, effort, etc. 2. occurring through internal causes

**spontaneous combustion** the process of catching fire through heat generated by internal chemical action

**spoof** (spo͞of) *n.* [Slang] 1. a hoax or joke 2. a light satire —*vt., vi.* [Slang] 1. to fool; deceive 2. to satirize playfully

**spook** (spo͞ok) *n.* [Du.] [Colloq.] a ghost —*vt., vi.* [Colloq.] to frighten or become frightened —**spook′y** *adj.*

**spool** (spo͞ol) *n.* [< MDu. *spoele*] 1. a cylinder on which thread, wire, etc. is wound 2. the material wound

**spoon** (spo͞on) *n.* [< OE. *spon*, a chip] 1. a utensil consisting of a small, shallow bowl with a handle, used for eating, stirring, etc. 2. something shaped like a spoon, as a shiny, curved fishing lure —*vt.* to take up with a spoon —**spoon′ful′** *n., pl.* -**fuls′**

**spoon′bill′** *n.* a wading bird whose flat bill is spoon-shaped at the tip

**spoon·er·ism** (spo͞on′ər iz′m) *n.* [< Rev. W. A. *Spooner* (1844-1930), of England, who made such slips] the accidental interchange of the initial sounds of words (Ex.: "a well-boiled icicle" for "a well-oiled bicycle")

**spoor** (spoor, spôr) *n.* [Afrikaans] the track or trail of a wild animal

**spo·rad·ic** (spô rad′ik) *adj.* [< Gr. *sporas*, scattered] happening or appearing in isolated instances [*sporadic* storms] —**spo·rad′i·cal·ly** *adv.*

**spore** (spôr) *n.* [< Gr. *spora*, a seed] a small reproductive body produced by mosses, ferns, etc. and capable of giving rise to a new individual —*vi.* spored, spor′ing to bear spores

**sport** (spôrt) *n.* [< DISPORT] 1. any recreational activity; specif., a game, competition, etc. requiring bodily exertion 2. fun or play 3. a thing joked about 4. [Colloq.] a sportsmanlike person 5. [Colloq.] a showy, flashy fellow 6. *Biol.* a plant or animal markedly different from the normal type —*vt.* [Colloq.] to display [to *sport* a new tie] —*vi.* 1. to play 2. to joke —*adj.* 1. of or for sports 2. suitable for casual wear: also **sports** [*sport(s)* clothes] —**in** (or **for**) **sport** in jest —**make sport of** to mock or ridicule

**sport′ing** *adj.* 1. of or interested in sports 2. sportsmanlike; fair 3. of games, races, etc. involving gambling or betting

**sport′ive** *adj.* 1. full of sport or fun 2. done in fun —**spor′tive·ly** *adv.*

**sports car** a low, small automobile with a high-compression engine

**sports′cast′** *n.* a broadcast of sports news on radio or TV —**sports′cast′er** *n.*

**sports′man** *n., pl.* -**men** 1. a man who takes part in sports, esp. hunting, fishing, etc. 2. one who plays fair and can lose without complaint or win

without gloating —**sports′man·like′** *adj.* —**sports′man·ship′** *n.*

**sport′y** *adj.* -**i·er**, -**i·est** 1. sporting or sportsmanlike 2. flashy or showy

**spot** (spät) *n.* [prob. < MDu. *spotte*] 1. *a*) a small area differing in color, etc. from the surrounding area *b*) a stain, speck, etc. 2. a flaw or defect 3. a locality; place —*vt.* **spot′ted, spot′ting** 1. to mark with spots 2. to stain; blemish 3. to place; locate 4. to see; recognize 5. [Colloq.] to allow as a handicap —*vi.* 1. to become marked with spots 2. to make a stain, as ink —*adj.* 1. ready [*spot* cash] 2. made at random [a *spot* survey] —**hit the spot** [Colloq.] to satisfy a craving —**in a** (**bad**) **spot** [Slang] in trouble —**on the spot** [Slang] in a bad or demanding situation —**spot′less** *adj.* —**spot′ted** *adj.*

**spot′-check′** *vt.* to check or examine at random —*n.* such a checking

**spot′light′** *n.* 1. *a*) a strong beam of light focused on a particular person, thing, etc. *b*) a lamp used to project such a light 2. public notice —*vt.* to draw attention to, as by a spotlight

**spot′ter** *n.* one who spots, as an assistant in the stands who reports on plays in a football game

**spot′ty** *adj.* -**ti·er**, -**ti·est** 1. having, occurring in, or marked with spots 2. not uniform or consistent

**spouse** (spous) *n.* [< L. *sponsus*, betrothed] (one's) husband or wife

**spout** (spout) *n.* [ME. *spouten*, to spout] 1. a projecting tube or orifice by which a liquid is poured 2. a stream, etc. as of a liquid from a spout —*vt., vi.* 1. to shoot out (liquid, etc.) as from a spout 2. to speak or utter in a loud, pompous manner

**sprain** (sprān) *vt.* [< ? L. *ex-*, out + *premere*, press] to wrench a ligament or muscle of (a joint) without dislocating the bones —*n.* an injury resulting from this

**sprang** (spraŋ) *alt. pt. of* SPRING

**sprat** (sprat) *n.* [OE. *sprott*] a small European fish of the herring family

**sprawl** (sprôl) *vi.* [OE. *spreawlian*] 1. to sit or lie with the limbs in a relaxed or awkward position 2. to spread out awkwardly or unevenly, as handwriting, etc. —*n.* a sprawling movement or position

**spray**[1] (sprā) *n.* [prob. < MDu. *spraeien*] 1. a mist of fine liquid particles 2. *a*) a jet of such particles, as from a spray gun *b*) a device for spraying 3. something likened to a spray —*vt., vi.* 1. to direct a spray (on) 2. to shoot out in a spray —**spray′er** *n.*

**spray**[2] (sprā) *n.* [ME.] a small branch or sprig of a tree, etc., with leaves, flowers, etc.

**spray can** a can in which gas under pressure sprays out the contents

**spray gun** a device that shoots out a spray of liquid, as paint, etc.

**spread** (spred) *vt., vi.* **spread, spread′ing** [OE. *sprædan*] 1. to open or stretch out; unfold 2. to move (the fingers, wings, etc.) apart 3. to distribute or be distributed over an area 4. to extend in time 5. to make or be made widely known, felt, etc. **6.** to cover or be covered (*with* something), as in a thin layer **7.** to set (a table) for a meal **8.** to push or be pushed apart —*n.* **1.** the act or extent of spreading **2.** an expanse **3.** a cloth cover for a table, bed, etc. **4.** jam, butter, etc. used on bread **5.** [Colloq.] a meal with many different foods

**spree** (sprē) *n.* [< earlier *spray*] **1.** a noisy frolic **2.** a period of drunkenness **3.** a period of uninhibited activity [a shopping *spree*]

**sprig** (sprig) *n.* [ME. *sprigge*] a little twig or spray

**spright·ly** (sprīt′lē) *adj.* **-li·er, -li·est** [see SPRITE] gay; lively —*adv.* gaily; briskly —**spright′li·ness** *n.*

**spring** (sprin) *vi.* **sprang** or **sprung, spring′ing** [OE. *springan*] **1.** to leap; bound **2.** to come, appear, etc. suddenly **3.** to bounce **4.** to arise as from some source; grow or develop **5.** to become warped, split, etc. **6.** to rise up above surrounding objects Often followed by *up* —*vt.* **1.** to cause to leap forth suddenly **2.** to cause (a trap, etc.) to snap shut **3.** to cause to warp, split, etc. **4.** to make known suddenly **5.** [Slang] to get (someone) released from jail —*n.* **1.** a leap, or the distance so covered **2.** a sudden flying back **3.** elasticity; resilience **4.** a device, as a coil of wire, that returns to its original form after being forced out of shape **5.** a flow of water from the ground **6.** a source or origin **7.** *a*) that season of the year following winter, in which plants begin to grow again *b*) any period of beginning —*adj.* **1.** of, for, appearing in, or planted in the spring **2.** having, or supported on, springs **3.** coming from a spring [*spring* water] —**spring a leak** to begin to leak suddenly

**spring′board′** *n.* a springy board used as a takeoff in leaping or diving

**spring fever** a laziness that many people feel in early days of spring

**Spring·field** (sprin′fēld′) **1.** city in SW Mass.: pop. 164,000 **2.** capital of Ill.: pop. 92,000 **3.** city in SW Mo.: pop. 120,000

**spring′time′** *n.* the season of spring

**spring′y** *adj.* **-i·er, -i·est** elastic, resilient, etc. —**spring′i·ness** *n.*

**sprin·kle** (sprin′k'l) *vt., vi.* **-kled, -kling** [ME. *sprinklen*] **1.** to scatter or fall in drops or particles **2.** to scatter drops or particles (upon) **3.** to rain lightly —*n.* **1.** a sprinkling **2.** a light rain —**sprin′kler** *n.*

**sprin′kling** (-kliŋ) *n.* a small, scattered number or amount

**sprint** (sprint) *vi., n.* [ME. *sprenten*] run or race at full speed for a short distance —**sprint′er** *n.*

**sprite** (sprīt) *n.* [< L. *spiritus*, spirit] an elf, pixie, fairy, or goblin

**spritz** (sprits; *G.* shprits) *vt., vi., n.* [< *G. spritze*] squirt or spray

**sprock·et** (spräk′it) *n.* [< ?] **1.** any

of the teeth, as on a wheel rim, arranged to fit the links of a chain **2.** such a wheel: in full **sprocket wheel**

**sprout** (sprout) *vi.* [OE. *sprutan*] to begin to grow; give off shoots or buds —*vt.* to cause to sprout —*n.* **1.** a young growth on a plant; shoot **2.** a new growth from a bud, etc.

**spruce**[1] (sproos) *n.* [ME. *Spruce,* Prussia] **1.** an evergreen tree with slender needles **2.** its wood

**spruce**[2] (sproos) *adj.* **spruc′er, spruc′est** [< *Spruce* leather (see prec.)] neat and trim in a smart way —*vt., vi.* **spruced, spruc′ing** to make or become spruce (with *up*)

**sprung** (sprun) *pp., &* alt. *pt.* of SPRING

**spry** (sprī) *adj.* **spri′er** or **spry′er, spri′est** or **spry′est** [< Scand.] full of life; active, esp. though elderly —**spry′ly** *adv.* —**spry′ness** *n.*

**spud** (spud) *n.* [Colloq.] a potato

**spume** (spyoom) *n.* [< L. *spuma*] foam, froth, or scum —*vi.* **spumed, spum′ing** to foam; froth

**spu·mo·ni** (spə mō′nē) *n.* [It. < L. *spuma,* foam] Italian ice cream in variously flavored layers

**spun** (spun) *pt. &* pp. of SPIN

**spunk** (spunk) *n.* [IrGael. *sponc,* tinder] [Colloq.] courage; spirit —**spunk′y** *adj.* **-i·er, -i·est**

**spur** (spur) *n.* [OE. *spura*] **1.** a pointed device worn on the heel by horsemen, used to urge the horse forward **2.** anything that urges; stimulus **3.** any spurlike projection **4.** a short railroad track connected with the main track —*vt.* **spurred, spur′ring 1.** to prick with spurs **2.** to urge or incite —*vi.* to hurry; hasten —**on the spur of the moment** abruptly and impulsively

**spurge** (spurj) *n.* [< MFr. *espurger,* to purge] any of a group of plants with milky juice and tiny flowers

**spu·ri·ous** (spyoor′ē əs) *adj.* [LL. *spurius*] not genuine; false —**spu′ri·ous·ly** *adv.* —**spu′ri·ous·ness** *n.*

**spurn** (spurn) *vt.* [OE. *spurnan*] to reject with contempt; scorn

**spurt** (spurt) *vt., vi.* [OE. *sprutan*] **1.** to gush forth in a stream or jet **2.** to show a sudden, brief burst of energy —*n.* **1.** a sudden shooting forth; jet **2.** a sudden, brief burst of energy, increased activity, etc.

**sput·nik** (spoot′nik, sput′-) *n.* [Russ., lit., co-traveler] an artificial satellite in space, esp. any of the U.S.S.R.

**sput·ter** (sput′ər) *vi., vt.* [< MDu. *spotten,* to spit] **1.** to spit or throw out (bits or drops) in an explosive manner **2.** to speak or say in a confused, explosive manner **3.** to make sharp, sizzling sounds, as frying fat —*n.* a sputtering

**spu·tum** (spyoot′əm) *n., pl.* **-ta** (-ə) [< L. *spuere,* to spit] saliva, usually mixed with mucus, spat out

**spy** (spī) *vt.* **spied, spy′ing** [< OHG. *spehōn,* examine] **1.** to watch closely and secretly (often with *out*) **2.** to catch sight of; see —*vi.* **1.** to watch

---

fat, āpe, cär; ten, ēven; is, bīte; gō, hôrn, tōōl, look; oil, out; up, fur; chin; she; thin, *then;* zh, leisure; ŋ, ring; ə for *a* in ago; ′, (ā′b'l); ë, Fr. coeur; ö, Fr. feu; Fr. mon; ü, Fr. duc; kh, G. ich, doch; ‡ foreign; < derived from closely and secretly; act as a spy —*n.*, *pl.* **spies** 1. one who keeps close and secret watch on others 2. one employed by a government to get secret information about the affairs, esp. the military affairs, of another government

**spy'glass'** *n.* a small telescope

**sq.** square

**sqq.** [L. *sequentes*] the following ones

**squab** (skwäb) *n.* [prob. < Scand.] a nestling pigeon

**squab·ble** (skwäb''l) *vi.* **-bled, -bling** [< Scand.] to quarrel noisily over a small matter; wrangle —*n.* a noisy, petty quarrel

**squad** (skwäd) *n.* [see SQUARE] 1. a small group of soldiers, often a subdivision of a platoon 2. any small group of people working together

**squad car** a police patrol car

**squad'ron** (-rən) *n.* [< It. *squadra*, a square] a unit of warships, cavalry, military aircraft, etc.

**squal·id** (skwäl'id) *adj.* [< L. *squalere*, be foul] 1. foul or unclean 2. wretched

**squall¹** (skwôl) *n.* [< Scand.] a brief, violent windstorm, usually with rain or snow —**squall'y** *adj.*

**squall²** (skwôl) *vi., vt.* [< ON. *skvala*] to cry or scream loudly and harshly —*n.* a harsh, loud cry or scream

**squal·or** (skwäl'ər) *n.* a being squalid; filth and wretchedness

**squa·mous** (skwā'məs) *adj.* [< L. *squama*, a scale] like, formed of, or covered with scales

**squan·der** (skwän'dər) *vt.* [prob. < dial. *squander*, to scatter] to spend or use wastefully or extravagantly

**square** (skwer) *n.* [< L. *ex-*, out + *quadrare*, to square] 1. *a*) a plane figure having four equal sides and four right angles *b*) anything of or approximating this shape 2. *a*) an area bounded by streets or buildings on four sides *b*) any side of such an area 3. an open area bounded by several streets, used as a park, etc. 4. an instrument for drawing or testing right angles 5. the product of a quantity multiplied by itself 6. [Slang] a person who is square (*adj.* 10) —*vt.* **squared, squar'ing** 1. to make into a square (sense 1) 2. to make straight, even, right-angled, etc. 3. to settle; adjust [to *square* accounts] 4. to make conform [to *square* a statement with the facts] 5. to multiply (a quantity) by itself —*vi.* to fit; agree; accord (*with*) —*adj.* 1. having four equal sides and four right angles 2. forming a right angle 3. straight, level, even, etc. 4. leaving no balance; balanced 5. just; fair 6. direct; straightforward 7. designating or of a unit of surface measure in the form of a square [a *square* foot] 8. solid; sturdy [a *square* joint] 9. [Colloq.] satisfying; substantial [a *square* meal] 10. [Slang] old-fashioned, unsophisticated, etc. —*adv.* in a square manner —**square off** (or **away**) to assume a posture of attack or self-defense —**square oneself** [Colloq.] to make amends —**square'ly** *adv.* —**square'-ness** *n.* —**squar'ish** *adj.*

**square dance** a dance in which the couples are grouped in a given form, as a square —**square'-dance'** *vi.*

**square'-rigged'** *adj.* rigged with square sails as the principal sails

**square root** the quantity which when squared will produce a given quantity [3 is the *square root* of 9]

**squash¹** (skwäsh) *vt.* [< L. *ex-*, intens. + *quatere*, to shake] 1. to crush into a soft, flat mass; press 2. to suppress; quash —*vi.* 1. to be squashed 2. to make a sound of squashing —*n.* 1. something squashed 2. the act or sound of squashing 3. a game played in a walled court with rackets and a rubber ball —**squash'y** *adj.*

**squash²** (skwäsh) *n.* [< AmInd.] the fleshy fruit of various plants of the gourd family, eaten as a vegetable

**squat** (skwät) *vi.* **squat'ted, squat'-ting** [< L. *ex-*, intens. + *cogere*, to force] 1. to sit on the heels with the knees bent 2. to crouch close to the ground 3. to settle on land without right or title 4. to settle on public land in order to get title to it —*adj.* short and heavy or thick: also **squat'ty** —*n.* the act or position of squatting —**squat'ness** *n.* —**squat'ter** *n.*

**squaw** (skwô) *n.* [< AmInd.] a N.American Indian woman, esp. a wife

**squawk** (skwôk) *vi.* [echoic] 1. to utter a loud, harsh cry 2. [Colloq.] to complain loudly —*n.* 1. a loud, harsh cry 2. [Slang] a raucous complaint

**squeak** (skwēk) *vi.* [ME. *squeken*] to make or utter a sharp, high-pitched sound or cry —*vt.* to say in a squeak —*n.* a thin, sharp sound or cry —**narrow** (or **close, near**) **squeak** [Colloq.] a narrow escape —**squeak through** (or **by**) [Colloq.] to succeed, get through, etc. with difficulty —**squeak'y** *adj.* **-i·er, -i·est**

**squeal** (skwēl) *vi.* [ME. *squelen*] 1. to utter or make a high, shrill cry or sound 2. [Slang] to act as an informer —*vt.* to utter in a squeal —*n.* a squealing —**squeal'er** *n.*

**squeam·ish** (skwēm'ish) *adj.* [ME. *squaimous*] 1. easily nauseated 2. easily shocked; prudish 3. fastidious —**squeam'ish·ness** *n.*

**squee·gee** (skwē'jē) *n.* [prob. < ff.] a rubber-edged tool for scraping water from a flat surface

**squeeze** (skwēz) *vt.* **squeezed, squeez'-ing** [OE. *cwysan*] 1. to press hard, esp. from two or more sides 2. to extract (juice, etc.) from (fruit, etc.) 3. to force (*into, out*, etc.) by pressing 4. to embrace closely; hug —*vi.* 1. to yield to pressure 2. to exert pressure 3. to force one's way by pushing —*n.* 1. a squeezing or being squeezed 2. a close embrace; hug 3. the state of being closely pressed or packed; crush 4. a period of scarcity, hardship, etc.

**squeeze bottle** a plastic bottle that is squeezed to eject its contents

**squelch** (skwelch) *n.* [< ?] [Colloq.] a crushing retort, rebuke, etc. —*vt.* [Colloq.] to suppress or silence completely

**squib** (skwib) *n.* [prob. echoic] 1. a firecracker that burns with a hissing noise before exploding 2. a short, witty verbal attack; lampoon

**squid** (skwid) *n.* [prob. < dial. for SQUIRT] a long, slender sea mollusk with ten arms, two longer than the others

**squig·gle** (skwig'l) *n.* [SQU(IRM) + (W)IGGLE] a short, wavy line or illegible scrawl —*vt., vi.* -gled, -gling to write as, or make, a squiggle or squiggles

**squint** (skwint) *vi.* [akin to Du. *schuin*, sideways] 1. to peer with the eyes partly closed 2. to look sideways or askance 3. to be cross-eyed —*n.* 1. a squinting 2. a being cross-eyed 3. [Colloq.] a quick look or sidelong glance

SQUID

**squire** (skwir) *n.* [< ESQUIRE] 1. in England, the owner of a large rural estate 2. a title of respect for a justice of the peace, etc. 3. an attendant; esp., a man escorting a woman —*vt., vi.* squired, squir'ing to act as a squire (to)

**squirm** (skwurm) *vi.* [prob. echoic] 1. to twist and turn the body; wriggle 2. to show or feel distress —*n.* a squirming —squirm'y *adj.* -i·er, -i·est

**squir·rel** (skwur'əl) *n.* [< Gr. *skia*, a shadow + *oura*, tail] 1. a small, tree-dwelling rodent with heavy fur and a long, bushy tail 2. its fur

**squirt** (skwurt) *vt., vi.* [prob. < LowG. *swirtjen*] 1. to shoot out (a liquid) in a jet; spurt 2. to wet with liquid so shot out —*n.* 1. a jet of liquid 2. [Colloq.] an insignificant person

**Sr.** Senior

**Sri Lan·ka** (srē läŋ'kə) *official name of* CEYLON

**S.R.O.** standing room only

**S.S., SS, S/S** steamship

**SST** supersonic transport

**St.** 1. Saint 2. Strait 3. Street

**stab** (stab) *n.* [prob. < ME. *stubbe*, stub] 1. a wound made by stabbing 2. a thrust, as with a knife 3. a sharp pain 4. an attempt —*vt., vi.* stabbed, stab'bing 1. to pierce or wound as with a knife 2. to thrust (a knife, etc.) into a thing 3. to pain sharply

**sta·bil·i·ty** (stə bil'ə tē) *n.* 1. a being stable; steadiness 2. firmness of purpose, etc. 3. permanence

**sta·bi·lize** (stā'bə līz') *vt.* -lized', -liz'ing 1. to make stable 2. to keep from changing 3. to give stability to (a plane or ship) —sta'bi·li·za'tion *n.* —sta'bi·liz'er *n.*

**sta·ble**[1] (stā'b'l) *adj.* -bler, -blest [< L. *stare*, to stand] 1. not likely to give way; firm; fixed 2. firm in character, purpose, etc.; steadfast 3. not likely to change; lasting

**sta·ble**[2] (stā'b'l) *n.* [see prec.] 1. a

building in which horses or cattle are sheltered and fed 2. all the racehorses belonging to one owner —*vt., vi.* -bled, -bling to lodge, keep, or be kept in a stable

**stac·ca·to** (stə kät'ō) *adj.* [It., detached] *Music* with distinct breaks between successive tones

**stack** (stak) *n.* [< ON. *stakkr*] 1. a large, neatly arranged pile of straw, hay, etc. 2. any orderly pile 3. a smokestack 4. [*pl.*] a series of bookshelves —*vt.* 1. to arrange in a stack 2. to arrange (cards, etc.) secretly so as to cheat —stack up to stand in comparison (*with* or *against*)

**stack'up'** *n.* an arrangement of aircraft circling at various altitudes, awaiting their turn to land

**sta·di·um** (stā'dē əm) *n.* [Gr. *stadion*, unit of length, c.607 ft.] a large structure for football, baseball, etc., surrounded by tiers of seats

**staff** (staf) *n., pl.* staffs; also, for senses 1 & 4, staves [OE. *stæf*] 1. a stick or rod used as a support, a symbol of authority, etc. 2. a group of people assisting a leader 3. a specific group of workers [a teaching *staff*] 4. the five horizontal lines and four intermediate spaces on which music is written —*vt.* to provide with a staff, as of workers

**staff'er** *n.* a member of a staff, as of a newspaper

**stag** (stag) *n.* [OE. *stagga*] a full-grown male deer —*adj.* for men only [a *stag* party] —*adv.* unaccompanied by a woman

**stage** (stāj) *n.* [< L. *stare*, to stand] 1. a platform 2. *a)* an area or platform upon which plays, etc. are presented *b)* the theater, or acting as a profession (*with the*) 3. the scene of an event 4. a stopping place, or the distance between stops, on a journey 5. *short for* STAGE-COACH 6. a period or level in a process of development [the larval *stage*] 7. any of the units used in sequence to propel a missile, spacecraft, etc. —*vt.* staged, stag'ing 1. to present as on a stage 2. to plan and carry out [to *stage* an attack]

**stage'coach'** *n.* a horse-drawn public coach that traveled a regular route

**stage'hand'** *n.* one who sets up scenery, furniture, lights, etc. for a stage play

**stage'-struck'** *adj.* intensely eager to become an actor or actress

**stag·ger** (stag'ər) *vi.* [< ON. *stakra*, totter] to totter, reel, etc. as from a blow, fatigue, etc. —*vt.* 1. to cause to stagger, as with a blow 2. to affect strongly with grief, etc. 3. to make zigzag or alternating 4. to arrange so as to come at different times [to *stagger* vacations] —*n.* [*pl.*, *with sing. v.*] a nervous disease of horses, etc., causing staggering

**stag·nant** (stag'nənt) *adj.* [< L. *stagnare*, stagnate] 1. not flowing or moving 2. foul from lack of movement, as water 3. dull; sluggish

**stag·nate** (stag'nāt) vi., vt. **-nat·ed, -nat·ing** to become or make stagnant —**stag·na'tion** n.

**staid** (stād) archaic pt. & pp. of STAY¹ —adj. sober; sedate —**staid'ly** adv.

**stain** (stān) vt. [ult. < L. dis-, from + tingere, to color] 1. to spoil by discoloring or spotting 2. to disgrace; dishonor 3. to color (wood, etc.) with a dye —n. 1. a color or spot resulting from staining 2. a moral blemish 3. a dye for staining wood, etc.

**stain'less steel** steel alloyed with chromium, etc., virtually immune to rust and corrosion

**stair** (ster) n. [OE. stæger] 1. [usually pl.] a staircase 2. one of a series of steps between levels

**stair'case'** (-kās') n. a flight of stairs with a handrail: also **stair'way'**

**stair'well'** n. a vertical shaft (in a building) for a staircase

**stake** (stāk) n. [OE. staca] 1. a pointed length of wood or metal for driving into the ground 2. the post to which a person was tied for execution by burning 3. [often pl.] money, etc. risked as in a wager 4. [often pl.] the winner's prize in a race, etc. —vt. **staked, stak'ing** 1. to mark the boundaries of [to stake out a claim] 2. to fasten to stakes 3. to gamble 4. [Colloq.] to furnish with money or resources —**at stake** being risked — **pull up stakes** [Colloq.] to change one's residence, etc. —**stake out** to put under police surveillance

**sta·lac·tite** (sta lak'tīt) n. [< Gr. stalaktos, trickling] an icicle-shaped lime deposit hanging from a cave roof

**sta·lag·mite** (sta lag'mīt) n. [< Gr. stalagmos, a dropping] a cone-shaped lime deposit on the floor of a cave, often beneath a stalactite

**stale** (stāl) adj. **stal'er, stal'est** [prob. < LowG.] 1. no longer fresh; flat, dry, etc. 2. trite, as a joke 3. out of condition, bored, etc. —vt., vi. **staled, stal'ing** to make or become stale —**stale'ness** n.

**stale·mate** (stāl'māt') n. [ult. < OHG. stal, a place + (CHECK)MATE] 1. Chess a situation in which a player cannot move, resulting in a draw 2. any deadlock —vt. **-mat'ed, -mat'-ing** to bring into a stalemate

**Sta·lin** (stä'lin), Joseph 1879–1953; Soviet premier (1941–53)

**stalk¹** (stôk) vi., vt. [OE. stealcian] 1. to walk (through) in a stiff, haughty manner 2. to advance grimly 3. to pursue (game, etc.) stealthily —n. 1. a stiff, haughty stride 2. a stalking

**stalk²** (stôk) n. [OE. stela] 1. the stem of a plant 2. any part like this

**stall¹** (stôl) n. [OE. steall] 1. a section for one animal in a stable 2. a) a booth, etc. as at a market b) a pew in a church 3. a stop or standstill, esp. due to malfunction —vt., vi. 1. to keep or be kept in a stall 2. to bring or come to a standstill, esp. unintentionally

**stall²** (stôl) vt., vi. [< obs. stale, one

who lures] to act evasively so as to deceive or delay —n. [Colloq.] any action used in stalling

**stal·lion** (stal'yən) n. [< Gmc. stal, a stall] an uncastrated male horse

**stal·wart** (stôl'wərt) adj. [< OE. stathol, foundation + wyrthe, worth] 1. strong; sturdy 2. brave; valiant 3. resolute; firm —n. a stalwart person

**sta·men** (stā'mən) n. [L., thread] the pollen-bearing organ in a flower

**Stam·ford** (stam'fərd) city in SW Conn.; pop. 109,000

**stam·i·na** (stam'ə nə) n. [L., pl. of STAMEN] resistance to fatigue, illness, hardship, etc.; endurance

**stam·mer** (stam'ər) vt., vi. [OE. stamerian] to speak or say with involuntary pauses and rapid repetitions —n. a stammering —**stam'mer·er** n.

**stamp** (stamp) vt. [ME. stampen] 1. to bring (the foot) down forcibly or crush or pound with the foot 2. to imprint or cut out (a design, etc.) 4. to cut (out) by pressing with a die 5. to put a stamp on 6. to characterize —vi. 1. to bring the foot down forcibly 2. to walk with loud, heavy steps —n. 1. a stamping 2. a) a machine, tool, or die for stamping b) a mark or form made by stamping 3. any of various seals, gummed pieces of paper, etc. used to show that a fee, as for postage, has been paid 4. any similar seal [trading stamp] 5. class; kind —**stamp out** 1. to crush by treading on forcibly 2. to suppress, or put down —**stamp'er** n.

**stam·pede** (stam pēd') n. [< Sp. estampar, to stamp] a sudden, headlong rush or flight, as of a herd of cattle —vt., vi. **-ped'ed, -ped'ing** to move, or take part, in a stampede

**stamp'ing ground** [Colloq.] a regular or favorite gathering place

**stance** (stans) n. [< L. stare, to stand] 1. the way one stands, esp. the placement of the feet 2. the attitude taken in a given situation

**stanch** (stônch, stanch) vt., vi., adj. see STAUNCH

**stan·chion** (stan'chən) n. [see STANCE] 1. an upright post or support 2. a device to confine a cow

**stand** (stand) vi. **stood, stand'ing** [OE. standan] 1. to be in, or assume, an upright position on the feet 2. to be supported on a base, pedestal, etc. 3. to take or be in a (specified) position, attitude, etc. 4. to have a (specified) height when standing 5. to be placed or situated 6. to gather and remain, as water 7. to remain unchanged 8. to make resistance 9. a) to halt b) to be stationary —vi. 1. to place upright 2. to endure 3. to withstand 4. to undergo [to stand trial] —n. 1. a standing; esp., a halt or stop 2. a position; station 3. a view, opinion, etc. 4. a structure to stand or sit on 5. a place of business 6. a rack, small table, etc. for holding things 7. a growth of trees, etc. —**stand by** 1. to be near and ready if needed 2. to aid —**stand for** 1. to represent 2. [Colloq.] to tolerate —**stand off** to keep at a distance —**stand out 1.** to project **2.** to be distinct, prominent, etc. —**stand up 1.** to rise to a standing position **2.** to prove valid, durable, etc. **3.** [Slang] to fail to keep a date with —**stand′er** n.

**stand·ard** (stan′dərd) n. [ < OFr. *estendard*] **1.** a flag, banner, etc. as an emblem of a military unit, etc. **2.** something established for use as a rule or basis of comparison in measuring quantity, quality, value, etc. **3.** an upright support —adj. **1.** used as, or conforming to, a standard, rule, model, etc. **2.** generally accepted as reliable or authoritative **3.** typical; ordinary

**stand′ard-bear′er** n. **1.** one who carries the flag **2.** the leader of a movement, political party, etc.

**stand′ard-ize′** vt. -ized′, -iz′ing to make standard or uniform —**stand′-ard·i·za′tion** n.

**standard time** the official civil time for any given region: the earth is divided into 24 time zones, one hour apart (*Eastern, Central, Mountain,* and *Pacific* fall within the conterminous U.S.)

**stand′by′** n., pl. -bys′ a person or thing that is dependable, a possible substitute, etc.

**stand·ee** (stan dē′) n. [Colloq.] one who stands, as in a bus, theater, etc.

**stand′-in′** n. a temporary substitute, as for an actor at rehearsals

**stand′ing** n. **1.** status or reputation [in good *standing*] **2.** duration [a rule of long *standing*] —adj. **1.** that stands; upright **2.** from a standing position [a *standing* jump] **3.** stagnant, as water [a *standing* order] **4.** lasting; permanent [a *standing* order] **5.** not in use

**stand′off′** n. a tie in a contest

**stand′off′ish** adj. aloof; reserved

**stand′point′** n. point of view

**stand′still′** n. a stop or halt

**stand′-up′** adj. **1.** in a standing position **2.** specializing in monologues made up of jokes, as a comedian

**stank** (staŋk) alt. pt. of STINK

**stan·za** (stan′zə) n. [It.: ult. < L. *stare,* to stand] a group of lines of verse forming a division of a poem or song

**staph** (staf) n. *clipped form of* STAPHYLOCOCCUS

**staph·y·lo·coc·cus** (staf′ə lō kāk′əs) n., pl. -coc′ci (-kāk′sī) [ < Gr. *staphylē,* bunch of grapes + *kokkos,* a grain] any of certain spherical bacteria, in clusters or chains

**sta·ple¹** (stā′p'l) n. [ < MDu. *stapel,* mart] **1.** a chief commodity made or grown in a particular place **2.** raw material **3.** a regularly stocked item of trade, as flour, salt, etc. **4.** the fiber of cotton, wool, etc. —adj. **1.** regularly stocked, produced, or used **2.** most important; principal

**sta·ple²** (stā′p'l) n. [OE. *stapol,* a post] a U-shaped piece of metal with sharp ends, driven into wood, etc. as to hold

a hook, wire, etc., or through papers as a binding —vt. **-pled, -pling** to fasten with a staple —**sta′pler** n.

**star** (stär) n. [OE. *steorra*] **1.** a) any heavenly body seen as a small fixed point of light, esp. a far-off sun b) a star or stars regarded as influencing one's fate **2.** a conventionalized figure with five or six points, or anything like this **3.** an asterisk **4.** one who excels, as in a sport **5.** a leading actor or actress —vt. **starred, star′ring 1.** to mark with stars as a decoration, etc. **2.** to present (an actor or actress) in a leading role —vi. **1.** to perform brilliantly **2.** to perform as a star —adj. **1.** having great skill; outstanding **2.** of a star —**star′less** adj.

**star·board** (stär′bərd, -bôrd′) n. [ < OE. *steoran,* to steer (the old rudder was on the right side)] the right side of a ship, etc. as one faces forward —adj. of or on the starboard

**starch** (stärch) n. [OE. *stearc,* stiff] **1.** a white, tasteless, odorless food substance found in potatoes, cereals, etc. **2.** a powdered form of this used in laundering for stiffening cloth, etc. —vt. to stiffen as with starch —**starch′y** adj. **-i·er, -i·est**

**star′dom** (-dəm) n. the status of a star in the theater, etc.

**stare** (ster) vi. **stared, star′ing** [OE. *starian*] to gaze steadily and intently —vt. to look fixedly at —n. a steady, intent look —**star′er** n.

**star′fish′** n., pl.: see FISH a small, star-shaped sea animal

**star′gaze′** vi. **-gazed′, -gaz′ing 1.** to gaze at the stars **2.** to indulge in dreamy thought —**star′gaz′er** n.

**stark** (stärk) adj. [OE. *stearc*] **1.** rigid, as a corpse **2.** sharply outlined **3.** bleak; desolate **4.** sheer; downright —adv. utterly; wholly

**stark′-nak′ed** adj. entirely naked

**star′let** (-lit) n. a young actress being promoted as a future star

**star′light′** n. light given by the stars —**star′lit′** (-lit′) adj.

**star·ling** (stär′liŋ) n. [OE. *stær*] any of a family of old-world birds; esp., the **common starling** with iridescent plumage, introduced into the U.S.

**star′ry** adj. **-ri·er, -ri·est 1.** shining; bright **2.** lighted by or full of stars

**star′ry-eyed′** adj. with sparkling eyes

**Stars and Stripes** the U.S. flag

**star′-span′gled** adj. studded or spangled with stars

**Star-Spangled Banner 1.** the U.S. flag **2.** the U.S. national anthem

**start** (stärt) vi. [OE. *styrtan*] **1.** to make a sudden or involuntary move **2.** to go into action or motion; begin; commence **3.** to spring into being, activity, etc. —vt. **1.** to flush (game) **2.** to displace, loosen, etc. [to *start* a seam] **3.** a) to begin to play, be, do, etc. b) to set into motion, action, etc. **4.** to cause to be an entrant in a race, etc. —n. **1.** a sudden, brief shock or startled movement 2. a starting, or beginning 3. a) a place or time of beginning b) a lead or other advantage 4. an opportunity of beginning a career —**start out** (or **off**) to start a journey, project, etc. —**start′er** n.

**star·tle** (stärt′'l) vt. **-tled, -tling** [< ME. *stertlen*, to start] to surprise, frighten, or alarm suddenly; esp., to cause to start —vi. to be startled

**starve** (stärv) vi. **starved, starv′ing** [< OE. *steorfan*, to die] 1. to die from lack of food 2. to suffer from hunger 3. to suffer great need (with *for*) —vt. 1. to cause to starve 2. to force by starvation —**star·va·tion** (stär vā′shən) n.

**starve′ling** (-liŋ) n. a person or animal that is weak from lack of food

**stash** (stash) vt., vi. [< ?] [Colloq.] 1. to put or hide away (money, etc.) —n. [Slang] 1. a place for hiding things 2. something hidden away

**-stat** (stat) [< Gr. *-statēs*] a combining form meaning stationary [thermostat]

**state** (stāt) n. [< L. *stare*, to stand] 1. a set of circumstances, etc. characterizing a person or thing; condition 2. condition as regards structure, form, etc. 3. rich display; pomp 4. [sometimes S-] a body of people politically organized under one government; nation 5. [usually S-] any of the political units forming a federal government, as in the U.S. 6. civil government [matters of state] —adj. 1. formal; ceremonial 2. [sometimes S-] of the government or a state —vt. **stat′ed, stat′ing** 1. to establish by specifying 2. a) to set forth in words b) to express —**in a state** in an excited condition —**He in state** to be displayed formally before burial —**the States** the United States

**State′house′** n. the building in which the legislature of a State meets

**state′less** adj. having no state or nationality

**state′ly** adj. **-li·er, -li·est** 1. imposing; majestic 2. slow, dignified, etc. —**state′li·ness** n.

**state′ment** n. 1. a) a stating b) an assertion, declaration, etc. 2. a) a financial account b) an invoice; bill

**state′room′** n. 1. a private cabin on a ship 2. a private room on a train

**state′side′** adj. [Colloq.] of or in the U.S. (as viewed from abroad) —adv. [Colloq.] in or to the U.S.

**states′man** n., pl. **-men** one who is wise or experienced in the business of government —**states′man·ship′** n.

**stat·ic** (stat′ik) adj. [< Gr. *statikos*, causing to stand] 1. of masses, forces, etc. at rest or in equilibrium 2. at rest; inactive 3. of or producing stationary electrical charges, as from friction 4. of or having to do with static —n. 1. atmospheric electrical discharges causing noise on radio or TV 2. such noise 3. [Slang] adverse criticism —**stat′i·cal·ly** adv.

**sta·tion** (stā′shən) n. [< L. *stare*, to stand] 1. the place or building where one stands or is located; esp., an assigned post 2. a regular stopping

place, as on a bus line or railroad 3. social standing 4. a place equipped for radio or TV transmission, or its frequency —vt. to assign to a station

**sta·tion·ar·y** (stā′shən er′ē) adj. 1. not moving or not movable; fixed; still 2. unchanging

**station break** a pause in radio or TV programs for station identification

**sta·tion·er** (stā′shə nər) n. [< ML. *stationarius*, shopkeeper] a dealer in stationery, office supplies, etc.

**sta·tion·er·y** (-ner′ē) n. writing materials; esp., paper and envelopes

**station wagon** an automobile with folding or removable rear seats and a back end that opens

**sta·tis·tics** (stə tis′tiks) n.pl. [< L. *status*, standing] 1. numerical data assembled and classified so as to present significant information 2. [with sing. v.] the science of compiling such data —**sta·tis′ti·cal** adj. —**stat·is·ti·cian** (stat′is tish′ən) n.

**stat·u·ar·y** (stach′ōo wer′ē) n. statues collectively

**stat·ue** (stach′ōo) n. [< L. *statuere*, to set] the form of a person or animal carved in stone, etc., modeled in clay, or cast in plaster, metal, etc.

**stat·u·esque** (stach′ōo wesk′) adj. of or like a statue; stately and dignified

**stat′u·ette′** (-wet′) n. a small statue

**stat·ure** (stach′ər) n. [< L. *statura*] 1. the standing height of the body 2. level of attainment [moral stature]

**sta·tus** (stāt′əs, stat′-) n., pl. **-tus·es** [L., standing] 1. legal condition [the status of a minor] 2. position; rank 3. state, as of affairs

**status quo** (kwō′) [L., the state in which] the existing state of affairs

**status symbol** a possession regarded as a sign of (high) social status

**stat·ute** (stach′ōot) n. [see STATUE] 1. an established rule or law 2. a law passed by a legislative body

**statute of limitations** a statute limiting the time within which legal action may be taken

**stat·u·to·ry** (stach′ōo tôr′ē) adj. 1. fixed or authorized by statute 2. punishable by statute, as an offense

**staunch** (stônch, stänch) vt. [< L. *stare*, to stand] to check the flow of (blood, etc.) from (a cut, etc.) —vi. to stop flowing Also **stanch** —adj. 1. seaworthy 2. steadfast; loyal 3. strong; solid —**staunch′ly** adv.

**stave** (stāv) n. [< *staves*, pl. of STAFF] 1. one of the shaped strips of wood that form the walls of a barrel, bucket, etc. 2. a stick or staff 3. a stanza —vt. **staved** or **stove, stav′ing** to puncture, as by breaking in staves —**stave off** to hold or put off

**staves** (stāvz) n. 1. alt. pl. of STAFF 2. pl. of STAVE

**stay**[1] (stā) n. [OE. *stæg*] a heavy rope or cable, used as a brace or support, as for a mast of a ship; guy

**stay**[2] (stā) n. [MFr. *estaie*] 1. a support, or prop 2. a strip of stiffening material used in a corset, shirt collar, etc. —vt. to support, or prop up

**stay**[3] (stā) vi. [< L. *stare*, to stand] 1.

to continue in the place or condition specified; remain 2. to live; dwell 3. to stop; halt 4. to pause; delay 5. [Colloq.] to continue; last —*vt.* 1. to stop or check 2. to hinder or detain 3. to postpone (legal action) 4. to satisfy (thirst, etc.) for a time 5. to remain to the end of —*n.* 1. *a)* a stopping or being stopped *b)* a halt or pause 2. a postponement in legal action 3. the action of remaining, or the time spent, in a place —**stay put** [Colloq.] to remain in place or unchanged

**stay'ing power** power to last; endurance

**Ste.** [Fr. *Sainte*] Saint (female)

**stead** (sted) *n.* [OE. *stede*] the place of a person or thing as filled by a substitute —**stand** (one) **in good stead** to give (one) good service

**stead·fast** (sted'fast') *adj.* [OE. *stedefæste*] 1. firm; fixed 2. constant —**stead'fast'ly** *adv.*

**stead·y** (sted'ē) *adj.* **-i·er, -i·est** [see STEAD + -Y³] 1. firm; stable; not shaky 2. constant, regular, or uniform 3. constant in behavior, loyalty, etc. 4. calm and controlled [*steady* nerves] 5. sober; reliable —*vt., vi.* **-ied, -y·ing** to make or become steady —*n.* [Colloq.] a sweetheart —*adv.* in a steady manner —**go steady** [Colloq.] to be sweethearts —**stead'i·ly** *adv.*

**steady-state theory** a theory that as the universe is expanding new matter is continuously being created

**steak** (stāk) *n.* [< ON. *steikja*, roast on a spit] a slice of meat, esp. beef, or fish, for broiling or frying

**steal** (stēl) *vt.* **stole, stol'en, steal'ing** [OE. *stælan*] 1. to take (another's property, etc.) dishonestly, esp. in a secret manner 2. to take (a look, etc.) slyly 3. to gain insidiously or artfully [he *stole* her heart] 4. to move, put, etc. stealthily (*in, from,* etc.) 5. *Baseball* to gain (a base) as by running to it from another base while a pitch is being delivered —*vi.* 1. to be a thief 2. to move stealthily —*n.* [Colloq.] an extraordinary bargain

**stealth** (stelth) *n.* [< ME. *stelen,* to steal] secret or furtive action —**stealth'i·ly** *adv.* —**stealth'y** *adj.*

**steam** (stēm) *n.* [OE.] 1. water converted into a vapor by being heated to the boiling point 2. the power of steam under pressure 3. condensed water vapor 4. [Colloq.] vigor; energy —*adj.* using or operated by steam —*vi.* 1. to give off steam 2. to become covered with condensed steam 3. to move by steam power —*vt.* to expose to steam, as in cooking —**steam'y** *adj.*

**steam'boat'** *n.* a small steamship

**steam engine** an engine using pressurized steam to supply mechanical energy

**steam'er** *n.* 1. something operated by steam, as a steamship 2. a container for cooking, cleaning, etc. with steam

**steam fitter** a mechanic whose work (**steam fitting**) is installing boilers, pipes, etc. in steam-pressure systems

**steam'roll'er** *n.* a heavy, steam-driven roller used in building roads —*vi., vt.* to move, crush, override, etc. as (with) a steamroller

**steam'ship'** *n.* a ship driven by steam power

**steam shovel** a large, mechanically operated digger, powered by steam

**steed** (stēd) *n.* [OE. *steda*] a horse

**steel** (stēl) *n.* [OE. *stiele*] 1. a hard, tough alloy of iron with carbon 2. a thing of steel 3. great strength or hardness —*adj.* of or like steel —*vt.* to make hard, tough, etc. —**steel'y** *adj.*

**steel band** a percussion band, orig. in Trinidad, beating on steel oil drums

**steel wool** long, thin shavings of steel in a pad, used for scouring, smoothing, and polishing

**steel'yard'** (-yärd') *n.* [STEEL + obs. *yard,* rod] a balance scale consisting of a metal arm suspended from above

**STEELYARD**

**steep¹** (stēp) *adj.* [OE. *steap,* lofty] 1. having a sharp rise or slope; precipitous 2. [Colloq.] excessive; extreme —**steep'ly** *adv.* —**steep'ness** *n.*

**steep²** (stēp) *vt., vi.* [ME. *stepen*] to soak, saturate, imbue, etc.

**stee·ple** (stē'p'l) *n.* [OE. *stepel*] 1. a tower rising above the main structure, as of a church 2. a spire

**stee'ple·chase'** *n.* a horse race over a course obstructed with ditches, hedges, etc.

**stee'ple·jack'** *n.* one who builds or repairs steeples, smokestacks, etc.

**steer¹** (stir) *vt., vi.* [OE. *stieran*] 1. to guide (a ship, etc.) with a rudder 2. to direct the course of (an automobile, etc.) 3. to follow (a course) —**steer clear of** to avoid —**steer'a·ble** *adj.*

**steer²** (stir) *n.* [OE. *steor*] a castrated male of the cattle family 2. loosely, any male of beef cattle

**steer'age** (-ij) *n.* 1. a steering 2. formerly, a section in a ship occupied by passengers paying the lowest fare

**steers·man** (stirz'mən) *n., pl.* **-men** one who steers a ship; helmsman

**steg·o·sau·rus** (steg'ə sôr'əs) *n. pl.* **-ri** (-ī) [< Gr. *stegos,* a roof + *sauros,* lizard] a large dinosaur with pointed bony plates along the backbone

**stein** (stīn) *n.* [G.] a beer mug

**stel·lar** (stel'ər) *adj.* [< L. *stella,* star] 1. of a star 2. excellent 3. leading; chief [a *stellar* role]

**stem¹** (stem) *n.* [OE. *stemn*] 1. *a)* the main stalk of a plant *b)* any stalk supporting leaves, flowers, or fruit 2. a stemlike part, as of a pipe, goblet, etc. 3. the prow of a ship; bow 4. the part of a word to which inflectional endings are added —*vt.* **stemmed,** **stem′ming** to make headway against [to stem the tide] —*vi.* to derive

**stem²** (stem) *vt.* **stemmed, stem′-** **ming** [< ON. *stemma*] to stop or check by or as if by damming up

**stem′ware′** *n.* goblets, wine glasses, etc. having stems

**stench** (stench) *n.* [< OE. *stincan*, to stink] an offensive smell; stink

**sten·cil** (sten′s'l) *vt.* **-ciled** or **-cilled,** **-cil·ing** or **-cil·ling** [ult. < L. *scintilla*, a spark] to make or mark with a stencil —*n.* **1.** a thin sheet, as of paper, cut through so that when ink, etc. is applied, designs, letters, etc. form on the surface beneath **2.** a design, etc. so made

**ste·nog·ra·phy** (stə näg′rə fē) *n.* [< Gr. *stenos*, narrow + -GRAPHY] shorthand writing for later typewritten transcription —**ste·nog′ra·pher** *n.* —**sten·o·graph·ic** (sten′ə graf′ik) *adj.*

**sten·to·ri·an** (sten tôr′ē ən) *adj.* [< *Stentor*, a Greek herald in the *Iliad*] very loud

**step** (step) *n.* [OE. *stepe*] **1.** a single movement of the foot, as in walking **2.** the distance covered by such a movement **3.** a short distance **4.** a manner of stepping **5.** the sound of stepping **6.** a rest for the foot in climbing, as a stair **7.** a degree; level; stage **8.** any of a series of acts, processes, etc. —*vi.* **stepped, step′-** **ping 1.** to move by executing a step **2.** to walk a short distance **3.** to move briskly (*along*) **4.** to enter (*into* a situation, etc.) **5.** to press the foot down (*on*) —*vt.* to measure by taking steps (with *off*) —**in** (or **out of**) **step** (not) conforming to a marching rhythm, a regular procedure, etc. — **step up 1.** to advance **2.** to increase, as in rate —**take steps** to do the things needed —**step′per** *n.*

**step-broth·er** (step′bruth′ər) *n.* one's stepparent's son by a former marriage

**step′child′** *n., pl.* **-chil′dren** [OE. *steop-*, orphaned] one's spouse's child (**stepdaughter** or **stepson**) by a former marriage

**step′-down′** *n.* a decrease, as in amount, intensity, etc.

**step′lad′der** *n.* a four-legged ladder having broad, flat steps

**step′par′ent** *n.* the person (**step-** **father** or **stepmother**) who has married one's parent after the death or divorce of the other parent

**steppe** (step) *n.* [Russ. *step′*] one of the great plains of SE Europe and Asia, having few trees

**step′ping-stone′** *n.* **1.** a stone to step on, as in crossing a stream **2.** a means of bettering oneself

**step-sis·ter** (step′sis′tər) *n.* one's stepparent's daughter by a former marriage

**step′-up′** *n.* an increase, as in amount, intensity, etc.

**-ster** (stər) [OE. *-estre*] a suffix meaning one who is, does, creates, or is associated with (something specified) [*trickster, gangster*]

**ster·e·o** (ster′ē ō′, stir′-) *n., pl.* **-os′ 1.** a stereophonic record player, radio, system, etc. **2.** a stereoscopic system, effect, picture, etc. —*adj. clipped form of* STEREOPHONIC

**stereo-** [< Gr. *stereos*, solid] *a combining form meaning* solid, firm, three-dimensional [*stereoscope*]

**ster·e·o·phon·ic** (ster′ē ə fän′ik, stir′-) *adj.* [< prec. + Gr. *phōnē*, a sound] designating sound reproduction using two or more channels to carry and reproduce the sounds from the directions in which they were recorded

**ster′e·o·scope′** (-ə sköp′) *n.* [STEREO- + -SCOPE] an instrument with two eyepieces that gives a three-dimensional effect to photographs viewed through it

**ster′e·o·type′** (-ə tīp′) *n.* [see STEREO- & -TYPE] **1.** a printing plate cast from a mold, as a page of set type **2.** a fixed or conventional notion or conception —*vt.* **-typed′, -typ′ing** to make a stereotype of —**ster′e·o·typed′** *adj.*

**ster·ile** (ster′l) *adj.* [L. *sterilis*] **1.** incapable of producing offspring, fruit, etc.; barren **2.** free from living microorganisms —**ste·ril·i·ty** (stə ril′ə tē) *n.*

**ster′i·lize′** (-ə līz′) *vt.* **-lized′, -liz′-** **ing** to make sterile; specif., *a)* to make incapable of reproduction *b)* to free from living microorganisms — **ster′i·li·za′tion** *n.* —**ster′i·liz′er** *n.*

**ster·ling** (stur′liŋ) *n.* [ME. *sterlinge*, Norman coin] **1.** sterling silver **2.** British money —*adj.* **1.** of silver that is at least 92.5% pure **2.** of British money **3.** made of sterling silver **4.** excellent [*sterling principles*]

**stern¹** (sturn) *adj.* [OE. *styrne*] **1.** severe; strict [*stern measures*] **2.** grim [*a stern face*] **3.** relentless; firm — **stern′ly** *adv.* —**stern′ness** *n.*

**stern²** *n.* [< ON. *styra*, to steer] the rear end of a ship, etc.

**ster·num** (stur′nəm) *n., pl.* **-nums,** **-na** (-nə) [< Gr. *sternon*] a flat, bony structure to which most of the ribs are attached in the front of the chest; breastbone

**ster·oid** (stir′oid, ster′-) *n.* [< (CHOLE)STER(OL) + -OID] any of a group of compounds that include the sex hormones, cortisone, bile acids, etc.

**ster·to·rous** (stur′tər əs) *adj.* [L. *stertere*, to snore] characterized by raspy, labored breathing

**stet** (stet) [L.] let it stand: printer's term to show that matter orig. marked for deletion is to be kept —*vt.* **stet′ted,** **stet′ting** to mark with "stet"

**steth·o·scope** (steth′ə skōp′) *n.* [< Gr. *stēthos*, the chest + -SCOPE] *Med.* an instrument used to examine the heart, lungs, etc. by listening to the sounds they make

**ste·ve·dore** (stē′və dôr′) *n.* [< Sp. < L. *stipare*, cram] a person employed at loading and unloading ships

**stew** (stoo, styoo) *vt., vi.* [ult. < L. *ex-*, out + Gr. *typhos*, steam] **1.** to cook by simmering or boiling slowly 2. to worry —*n.* 1. a dish, esp. of meat and vegetables, cooked by stewing 2. a state of worry

**stew·ard** (stōō′ərd, styōō′-) *n.* [< OE. *stig*, hall + *weard*, keeper] 1. a person put in charge of a large estate 2. an administrator, as of finances and property 3. one responsible for the food and drink, etc. in a club, restaurant, etc. 4. an attendant, as on a ship or airplane —**stew′ard·ship′** *n.*

**stew′ard·ess** (-ər dis) *n.* a woman steward, esp. on an airplane

**stick** (stik) *n.* [OE. *sticca*] 1. a twig or small branch broken or cut off 2. a long, slender piece of wood, as a club, cane, etc. 3. any sticklike piece [a *stick* of gum] —*vt.* **stuck, stick′ing** 1. to pierce, as with a pointed instrument 2. to pierce with (a knife, pin, etc.) 3. to thrust (*in, into, out*, etc.) 4. to attach as by gluing, pinning, etc. 5. to obstruct, detain, etc. [the wheels were *stuck*] 6. [Colloq.] to put, set, etc. 7. [Colloq.] to puzzle; baffle 8. [Slang] *a*) to impose a burden, etc. upon *b*) to defraud —*vi.* 1. to be fixed by a pointed end, as a nail 2. to adhere; cling; remain 3. to persevere [to *stick* at a job] 4. to remain firm and resolute [he *stuck* with us] 5. to become embedded, jammed, etc. 6. to be puzzled 7. to hesitate; scruple [he'll *stick* at nothing] 8. to protrude or project (*out, up*, etc.) —**stick by** to remain loyal to —**stick up for** [Colloq.] to uphold; defend —**the sticks** [Colloq.] the rural districts

**stick′er** *n.* a person or thing that sticks; specif., a gummed label

**stick′-in-the-mud′** *n.* [Colloq.] a person who resists change

**stick·le·back** (stik′'l bak′) *n.* a small fish having sharp spines on its back and no scales: the male builds a nest for the female's eggs

**stick·ler** (stik′lər) *n.* [< OE. *stihtan*, arrange] 1. one who insists on a certain way of doing things [a *stickler* for discipline] 2. [Colloq.] something difficult to solve

**stick′pin′** *n.* an ornamental pin worn in a necktie, etc.

**stick shift** a gearshift, as on a car, operated manually by a lever

**stick′up′** *n. slang term for* HOLDUP (sense 2)

**stick′y** *adj.* **-i·er, -i·est** 1. that sticks; adhesive 2. [Colloq.] hot and humid 3. [Colloq.] troublesome

**stiff** (stif) *adj.* [OE. *stif*] 1. hard to bend or move; rigid; firm 2. sore or limited in movement: said of joints and muscles 3. not fluid; thick 4. strong; powerful [a *stiff* breeze] 5. harsh [*stiff* punishment] 6. difficult [a *stiff* climb] 7. very formal or awkward 8. [Colloq.] high [a *stiff* price] —**stiff′ly** *adv.* —**stiff′ness** *n.*

**stiff′-arm′** *vt.* to push (someone) away with one's arm out straight

**stiff′en** *vt., vi.* to make or become stiff or stiffer —**stiff′en·er** *n.*

**stiff′-necked′** (-nekt′) *adj.* stubborn

**sti·fle** (stī′f'l) *vt.* **-fled, -fling** [< MFr. *estouffer*] 1. to smother; suffocate 2. to suppress; hold back; stop [to *stifle* a sob] —*vi.* to die or suffer from lack of air —**sti′fling·ly** *adv.*

**stig·ma** (stig′mə) *n., pl.* **-mas, stig·ma′ta** (-mät′ə) [L. < Gr., a mark] 1. a mark of disgrace or reproach 2. a spot on the skin, esp. one that bleeds in certain nervous tensions 3. the upper tip of the pistil of a flower, receiving the pollen —**stig·mat′ic** (-mat′ik) *adj.*

**stig′ma·tize′** (-tīz′) *vt.* **-tized′, -tiz′ing** 1. to mark with a stigma 2. to mark as disgraceful

**stil·bes·trol** (stil bes′trōl) *n.* a synthetic estrogen

**stile** (stīl) *n.* [< OE. *stigan*, to climb] a step or set of steps used in climbing over a fence or wall

**sti·let·to** (sti let′ō) *n., pl.* **-tos, -toes** [It. < L. *stilus*, pointed tool] a small dagger with a slender blade

**still**[1] (stil) *adj.* [OE. *stille*] 1. without sound; silent 2. not moving; stationary 3. tranquil; calm 4. designating or of a single photograph taken from a motion-picture film —*n.* 1. silence; quiet 2. a still photograph —*adv.* 1. at or up to the time indicated 2. even; yet [*still* colder] 3. nevertheless; yet [rich but *still* unhappy] —*conj.* nevertheless; yet —*vt., vi.* to make or become still —**still′ness** *n.*

**still**[2] (stil) *n.* [< obs. *still*, to distill] an apparatus used for distilling liquids, esp. alcoholic liquors

**still′birth′** *n.* the birth of a stillborn fetus

**still′born′** *adj.* dead when born

**still life** a painting of inanimate objects, as fruit, flowers, etc.

**stilt** (stilt) *n.* [ME. *stilte*] 1. either of a pair of poles fitted with a footrest along its length and used for walking, as in play 2. any of a number of long posts used to hold a building, etc. above the ground or out of the water

**stilt·ed** (stil′tid) *adj.* artificially formal or dignified; pompous

**stim·u·lant** (stim′yə lənt) *n.* anything, as a drug, that stimulates

**stim′u·late′** (-lāt′) *vt.* **-lat′ed, -lat′ing** [< L. *stimulus*, a goad] to rouse or excite to activity or increased activity —**stim′u·la′tion** *n.*

**stim′u·lus** (-ləs) *n., pl.* **-li′** (-lī′ (-lī′) [L., a goad] 1. an incentive 2. any action or agent that causes an activity in an organism, organ, etc.

**sting** (stiŋ) *vt.* **stung, sting′ing** [OE. *stingan*] 1. to prick or wound with a sting 2. to cause sudden, pricking pain to 3. to cause to suffer mentally 4. to stimulate suddenly and sharply 5. [Slang] to cheat —*vi.* to cause or feel sharp, smarting pain —*n.* 1. a stinging

**2.** a pain or wound resulting from stinging **3.** a sharp-pointed organ, as in insects and plants, that pricks, wounds, etc. —**sting′er** *n.*

**stin·gy** (stin′jē) *adj.* **-gi·er, -gi·est** [< dial. form of prec.] **1.** giving or spending grudgingly; miserly **2.** less than needed; scanty —**stin′gi·ly** *adv.* —**stin′gi·ness** *n.*

**stink** (stiŋk) *vi.* **stank** or **stunk, stunk, stink′ing** [OE. *stincan*] to give off a strong, unpleasant smell —*n.* a strong, unpleasant smell; stench —**stink′er** *n.*

**stint** (stint) *vt.* [< OE. *styntan,* to blunt] to restrict to a certain quantity, often small —*vi.* to be sparing in giving or using —*n.* **1.** restriction; limit **2.** an assigned task or period of work —**stint′er** *n.* —**stint′ing** *adj.*

**sti·pend** (stī′pend) *n.* [< L. *stips,* small coin + *pendere,* to pay] a regular or fixed payment, as a salary

**stip·ple** (stip′'l) *vt.* **-pled, -pling** [< Du. *stippel,* a speckle] to paint, draw, or engrave in small dots

**stip·u·late** (stip′yə lāt′) *vt.* **-lat′ed, -lat′ing** [< L. *stipulari,* to bargain] **1.** to arrange definitely **2.** to specify as an essential condition of an agreement —**stip′u·la′tion** *n.*

**stir** (stur) *vt., vi.* **stirred, stir′ring** [OE. *styrian*] **1.** to move, esp. slightly **2.** to rouse from lethargy, sleep, etc.; be busy and active **3.** to mix (a liquid, etc.) as by agitating with a spoon **4.** to excite the feelings (of) **5.** to incite (often with *up*) —*n.* **1.** a stirring **2.** movement; activity **3.** excitement; tumult —**stir′rer** *n.*

**stir′-fry′** *vt.* **-fried′, -fry′ing** to fry (diced or sliced vegetables, meat, etc.) very quickly in a wok, with a little oil, stirring constantly

**stir′ring** *adj.* **1.** active; busy **2.** rousing; exciting [*stirring music*]

**stir·rup** (stur′əp) *n.* [OE. *stigrap*] a flat-bottomed ring hung from a saddle and used as a footrest

**stitch** (stich) *n.* [OE. *stice,* a puncture] **1.** a single complete in-and-out movement of a needle in sewing, knitting, etc. **2.** a loop, etc. made by stitching **3.** a particular kind of stitch or stitching **4.** a sudden, sharp pain **5.** a bit —*vi., vt.* to make stitches (in); sew

**stitch′er·y** (-ər ē) *n.* ornamental needlework

**St. Lawrence** river flowing from Lake Ontario into the Atlantic: the main section of an inland waterway (**St. Lawrence Seaway**) connecting the Great Lakes with the Atlantic

**St. Lou·is** (lōō′is, lōō′ē) city in E Mo.: pop. 622,000

**stoat** (stōt) *n.* [ME. *stote*] a large European weasel, in its brown coat

**stock** (stäk) *n.* [OE. *stocc*] **1.** the trunk of a tree **2.** *a)* descent; lineage *b)* a strain, race, etc. of animals or plants **3.** a supporting or main part of an implement, etc., as the part of a rifle containing the barrel **4.** [*pl.*] a wooden frame with holes for confining the ankles or wrists, formerly used for punishment **5.** raw material **6.** water

in which meat, fish, etc. has been boiled, used in soups **7.** livestock **8.** a supply of goods on hand in a store, etc. **9.** shares of corporate capital, or the certificates showing such ownership **10.** *same as* STOCK COMPANY (sense 2) —*vt.* **1.** to furnish (a farm, shop, etc.) with stock **2.** to keep a supply of, as for sale or for future use —*vi.* to put in a stock, or supply (with *up*) —*adj.* **1.** kept in stock [*stock sizes*] **2.** common or trite [a *stock* joke] **3.** that deals with stock **4.** relating to a stock company —**in** (or **out**) **of stock** (not) available for sale or use —**take stock 1.** to inventory the stock on hand **2.** to make an appraisal —**take** (or **put**) **stock in** [Colloq.] to have faith in

**stock·ade** (stä kād′) *n.* [< Pr. *estaca,* a stake] **1.** a defensive barrier of stakes driven into the ground side by side **2.** an enclosure, as a fort, made of such stakes

**stock′bro′ker** *n.* a broker who buys and sells stocks and bonds

**stock car** a standard automobile, modified for racing

**stock company 1.** a company whose capital is in shares **2.** a theatrical company presenting a repertoire

**stock exchange 1.** a place where stocks and bonds are bought and sold **2.** an association of stockbrokers. Also **stock market**

**stock′hold′er** (-hōl′dər) *n.* one owning stock in a given company

**Stock·holm** (stäk′hōm′, -hōlm′) capital of Sweden: pop. 792,000

**stock·ing** (stäk′iŋ) *n.* [< obs. sense of STOCK] a closefitting covering, usually knitted, for the foot and leg

**stocking cap** a long, tapered, knitted cap, often with a tassel at the end

**stock′pile′** (-pīl′) *n.* a reserve supply of goods, raw material, etc. —*vt., vi.* **-piled′, -pil′ing** to accumulate a stock-pile (of)

**stock′-still′** *adj.* motionless

**stock′y** *adj.* **-i·er, -i·est** heavily built; short and thick et —**stock′i·ness** *n.*

**stock′yard′** *n.* an enclosure for keeping cattle, hogs, etc. to be slaughtered

**stodg·y** (stäj′ē) *adj.* **-i·er, -i·est** [< dial. *stodge,* heavy food] dull; uninteresting —**stodg′i·ness** *n.*

**sto·gie, sto·gy** (stō′gē) *n., pl.* **-gies** [< *Conestoga,* town in Pa.] a long, thin, inexpensive cigar

**Sto·ic** (stō′ik) *n.* [< Gr. *stoa,* colonnade: the first Stoics met in a colonnade] **1.** a member of an ancient Greek school of philosophy **2.** [s-] a stoical person —*adj.* [s-] *same as* STOICAL —**sto′i·cism** *n.*

**sto′i·cal** (-i k′l) *adj.* showing indifference to joy, grief, pain, etc.; impassive —**sto′i·cal·ly** *adv.*

**stoke** (stōk) *vt., vi.* **stoked, stok′ing** [< Du. *stoken,* to poke] **1.** to stir up and feed fuel to (a fire) **2.** to tend (a furnace, etc.) —**stok′er** *n.*

**STOL** (stōl) *adj.* [*s(hort) t(ake)o(ff and) l(anding)*] designating, of, or for an aircraft that can take off and land on a short airstrip —*n.* a STOL aircraft, airstrip, etc.

**stole¹** (stōl) *n.* [< Gr. *stolē*, garment] 1. a long strip of cloth worn like a scarf by some clergymen 2. a woman's long scarf of cloth or fur worn around the shoulders

**stole²** (stōl) *pt.* of STEAL

**stol·en** (stō′lən) *pp.* of STEAL

**stol·id** (stäl′id) *adj.* [L. *stolidus*, slow] having or showing little or no emotion; unexcitable —**sto·lid·i·ty** (stə lid′ə tē) *n.* —**stol′id·ly** *adv.*

**stom·ach** (stum′ək) *n.* [ult. < Gr. *stoma*, mouth] 1. the saclike digestive organ into which food passes from the esophagus 2. the abdomen, or belly 3. appetite for food 4. desire or inclination —*vt.* 1. to be able to eat or digest 2. to tolerate; bear

**stom′ach·ache′** *n.* a pain in the stomach or abdomen

**stom′ach·er** *n.* an ornamented piece of cloth formerly worn over the chest and abdomen, esp. by women

**stomp** (stämp) *vt., vi. var.* of STAMP

**stone** (stōn) *n.* [OE. *stan*] 1. the hard, solid, nonmetallic mineral matter of rock 2. a piece of rock 3. the seed of certain fruits 4. a precious gem 5. *pl.* stone in Great Britain, 14 pounds avoirdupois 6. an abnormal stony mass formed in the kidney, gall bladder, etc. —*vt.* **stoned, ston′ing** 1. to throw stones at 2. to remove the stone from (a peach, etc.)

**stone-** [< prec.] *a combining form meaning* completely [*stone*-blind]

**Stone Age** the period in human culture when stone tools were used

**stoned** (stōnd) *adj.* [Slang] under the influence of liquor, a drug, etc.

**stone's throw** a short distance

**stone′wall′** *vi.* [Colloq.] to obstruct by various tactics, as by withholding information, by denials, etc.

**ston·y** (stō′nē) *adj.* **-i·er, -i·est** 1. full of stones 2. of or like stone; specif., unfeeling; pitiless —**ston′i·ness** *n.*

**stood** (stood) *pt. & pp.* of STAND

**stooge** (stooj) *n.* [< ?] [Colloq.] 1. an actor who serves as the victim of a comedian's jokes, pranks, etc. 2. anyone who acts as a foil or underling

**stool** (stool) *n.* [OE. *stol*] 1. a single seat having no back or arms 2. feces

**stool pigeon** [Colloq.] a spy or informer, esp. for the police

**stoop¹** (stoop) *vi.* [OE. *stupian*] 1. to bend the body forward 2. to carry the head and shoulders habitually bent forward 3. to degrade oneself —*n.* the act or position of stooping

**stoop²** (stoop) *n.* [Du. *stoep*] a small porch at the door of a house

**stoop labor** work done by stooping, as in picking crops

**stop** (stäp) *vt.* **stopped, stop′ping** [< VL. *stuppare*, stop up] 1. to close by filling, shutting off, etc. 2. to cause to cease motion, activity, etc. 3. to block; intercept; prevent 4. to cease; desist from [*stop* talking] —*vi.* 1. to cease moving, etc.; halt 2. to leave off

doing something 3. to cease operating 4. to become clogged 5. to tarry or stay —*n.* 1. a stopping or being stopped 2. a finish; end 3. a stay or sojourn 4. a place stopped at, as on a bus route 5. an obstruction, plug, etc. 6. a finger hole in a wind instrument, closed to produce a desired tone 7. a pull, lever, etc. for controlling a set of organ pipes —**stop off** to stop for a while en route to a place —**stop over** to visit for a while: also **stop in** (or **by**)

**stop′cock′** *n.* a cock or valve to stop or regulate the flow of a liquid

**stop′gap′** *n.* a person or thing serving as a temporary substitute

**stop′light′** *n.* 1. a traffic light, esp. when red to signal vehicles to stop 2. a rear light on a vehicle that lights up when the brakes are applied

**stop′o′ver** *n.* a brief stop or stay at a place in the course of a journey

**stop′page** (-ij) *n.* 1. a stopping or being stopped 2. an obstructed condition; block

**stop′per** *n.* something inserted to close an opening; plug

**stop′ple** (-'l) *n.* a stopper or plug —*vt.* **-pled, -pling** to close with a stopple

**stop′watch′** *n.* a watch with a hand that can be started and stopped instantly, for timing races, etc.

**stor·age** (stôr′ij) *n.* 1. a storing or being stored 2. *a)* a place for storing goods *b)* the cost of storing goods

**storage battery** a battery of cells generating electric current and capable of being recharged

**store** (stôr) *vt.* **stored, stor′ing** [< L. *instaurare*, restore] 1. to put aside for use when needed 2. to furnish with a supply 3. to put in a warehouse, etc. for safekeeping —*n.* 1. a supply (*of* something) for use when needed; stock 2. [*pl.*] supplies, esp. of food, clothing, etc. 3. a retail establishment where goods are offered for sale 4. a storehouse —**in store** set aside for the future; in reserve —**set** (or **put** or **lay**) **store by** to value

**store′front′** *n.* a front room on the ground floor of a building, designed for use as a retail store

**store′house′** *n.* a place where things are stored; esp., a warehouse

**store′keep′er** *n.* 1. a person in charge of military or naval stores 2. one who operates a retail store

**store′room′** *n.* a room where things are stored

**sto·rey** (stôr′ē) *n., pl.* **-reys** *Brit. sp.* of STORY²

**sto·ried** (stôr′ēd) *adj.* famous in story or history

**stork** (stôrk) *n.* [OE. *storc*] a large, long-legged wading bird with a long neck and bill

**storm** (stôrm) *n.* [OE.] 1. a strong wind, with rain, snow, thunder, etc. 2. any heavy fall of snow, rain, etc. 3. a strong emotional outburst 4. any strong disturbance 5. a sudden, strong attack on a fortified place —*vi.* **1.** to blow violently, rain, snow, etc. **2.** to rage; rant **3.** to rush violently *[to storm* into a room*]* —*vt.* to attack vigorously

**storm door** (or **window**) a door (or window) placed outside the regular one as added protection

**storm'y** *adj.* **-i·er, -i·est 1.** of or characterized by storms **2.** violent, raging, etc. —**storm'i·ly** *adv.* — **storm'i·ness** *n.*

**sto·ry¹** (stôr'ē) *n., pl.* **-ries** [ < Gr. *historia,* narrative] **1.** the telling of an event or events; account; narration **2.** a joke **3.** a fictitious narrative shorter than a novel **4.** the plot of a novel, play, etc. **5.** [Colloq.] a falsehood **6.** *Journalism* a news report

**sto·ry²** (stôr'ē) *n., pl.* **-ries** [ < prec.] a horizontal division of a building, from a floor to the ceiling above it

**sto'ry·book'** *n.* a book of stories, esp. one for children

**sto'ry·tell'er** *n.* one who narrates stories —**sto'ry·tell'ing** *n.*

**stoup** (stoop) *n.* [ON. *staup,* cup] a church basin for water blessed by a priest

**stout** (stout) *adj.* [ < OFr. *estout,* bold] **1.** courageous **2.** strong; sturdy; firm **3.** powerful; forceful **4.** fat; thickset —*n.* a heavy, dark-brown beer — **stout'ly** *adv.* —**stout'ness** *n.*

**stove¹** (stōv) *n.* [ < MDu., heated room] an apparatus for heating, cooking, etc.

**stove²** (stōv) *alt. pt. & pp. of* STAVE

**stove'pipe'** *n.* a metal pipe used to carry off smoke from a stove

**stow** (stō) *vt.* [ < OE. *stowe,* a place] to pack in an orderly way —**stow away 1.** to put or hide away **2.** to be a stowaway —**stow'age** *n.*

**stow'a·way'** *n.* one who hides aboard a ship, airplane, etc. to get free passage, evade port officials, etc.

**STP** [ < ? STP, motor oil additive] a hallucinogenic drug like mescaline

**St. Paul** capital of Minn.: pop. 310,000

**St. Pe·ters·burg** (pē'tərz burg') city in WC Fla.: pop. 216,000

**strad·dle** (strad''l) *vt., vi.* **-dled, -dling** [ < STRIDE] **1.** to sit or stand astride of, or stand with the legs wide apart **2.** to appear to take both sides of (an issue) —*n.* a straddling — **strad'dler** *n.*

**strafe** (strāf) *vt.* **strafed, straf'ing** [ < G. *Gott strafe England* (God punish England)] to attack with machine-gun fire from low-flying aircraft

**strag·gle** (strag''l) *vi.* **-gled, -gling** [prob. < ME. *straken,* roam] **1.** to wander from the main group **2.** to be scattered over a wide area; ramble **3.** to hang in an unkempt way, as hair — **strag'gler** *n.* —**strag'gly** *adj.*

**straight** (strāt) *adj.* [ < ME. *strecchen,* stretch] **1.** having the same direction throughout its length; not crooked, bent, etc. **2.** direct, undeviating, etc. **3.** in order; properly arranged, etc. **4.** honest; sincere **5.** unmixed; undiluted *[straight* whiskey*]*

**6.** [Slang] normal or conventional — *adv.* **1.** in a straight line **2.** upright; erectly **3.** without detour, delay, etc. —*n. Poker* a hand of five cards in sequence —**straight away** (or **off**) without delay —**straight'ness** *n.*

**straight arrow** [Slang] a person who is proper, righteous, conscientious, etc. and thought of as conservative, stodgy, etc. —**straight'-ar'row** *adj.*

**straight'en** *vt., vi.* to make or become straight —**straighten out 1.** to make or become less confused, easier to deal with, etc. **2.** to reform

**straight face** a facial expression showing no amusement or other emotion —**straight'-faced'** *adj.*

**straight'for'ward** *adj.* **1.** moving or leading straight ahead; direct **2.** honest; frank —*adv.* in a straightforward manner: also **straight'for'- wards**

**straight time 1.** the standard number of working hours, as per week **2.** the rate of pay for these hours

**straight'way'** *adv.* at once

**strain¹** (strān) *vt.* [ < L. *stringere*] **1.** to draw or stretch tight **2.** to exert, use, etc. to the utmost **3.** to injure by overexertion *[to strain* a muscle*]* **4.** to stretch beyond normal limits **5.** to pass through a screen, sieve, etc.; filter —*vi.* **1.** to make violent efforts; strive hard **2.** to filter, ooze, etc. —*n.* **1.** a straining or being strained **2.** great effort, exertion, etc. **3.** a bodily injury from overexertion **4.** stress or force **5.** a great demand on one's emotions, resources, etc.

**strain²** (strān) *n.* [ < OE. *strynan,* to produce] **1.** ancestry; lineage **2.** race; stock; line **3.** a line of individuals differentiated from its main species **4.** an inherited tendency **5.** a trace; streak **6.** a musical tune

**strained** (strānd) *adj.* not natural or relaxed

**strain'er** *n.* a device for straining, sifting, or filtering; sieve, filter, etc.

**strait** (strāt) *adj.* [ < L. *stringere,* draw tight] [Archaic] narrow or strict —*n.* **1.** [*often pl.*] a narrow waterway connecting two large bodies of water **2.** [*often pl.*] difficulty; distress

**strait'en** *vt.* **1.** esp. formerly, to make strait or narrow **2.** to bring into difficulties: esp. in **in straitened circumstances,** lacking enough money

**strait'jack'et** *n.* a coatlike device for restraining violent persons

**strait'-laced'** (-lāst') *adj.* narrowly strict in behavior or moral views

**strand¹** (strand) *n.* [OE.] shore, esp. ocean shore —*vt., vi.* **1.** to run or drive aground, as a ship **2.** to put or be put into a helpless position *[stranded* in a desert*]*

**strand²** (strand) *n.* [ME. *stronde*] **1.** any of the threads, wires, etc. that are twisted together to form a string, cable, etc. **2.** a ropelike length of anything *[a strand* of pearls*]*

**strange** (strānj) *adj.* **strang'er, strang'est** [ < L. *extraneus,* foreign] **1.** not previously known, seen, etc.; unfamiliar **2.** unusual; extraordinary

3. peculiar; odd  4. reserved or distant
5. unaccustomed (to) —**strange′ly**
adv. —**strange′ness** n.

**stran·ger** (strān′jər) n. 1. a newcomer
2. a person not known to one

**stran·gle** (straŋ′g'l) vt., vi. **-gled,**
**-gling** [< Gr. strangos, twisted] 1. to
choke to death  2. to suppress; stifle
—**stran′gler** n.

**stran′gle·hold′** n. 1. an illegal
wrestling hold choking an opponent
2. a force or action suppressing freedom

**stran·gu·late** (straŋ′gyə lāt′) vt.
**-lat′ed, -lat′ing** Med. to block (a
tube) by constricting

**strap** (strap) n. [dial. form of STROP]
a narrow strip of leather, etc., as
for binding or securing things —vt.
**strapped, strap′ping** to fasten with
a strap

**strap′less** adj. having no straps;
specif., having no shoulder straps

**strapped** (strapt) adj. [Colloq.] without money

**strap′ping** adj. [Colloq.] tall and
well-built; robust

**stra·ta** (strāt′ə, strat′ə) n. alt. pl.
of STRATUM

**strat·a·gem** (strat′ə jəm) n. [< Gr.
stratos, army + agein, to lead] 1. a
trick, plan, etc. for deceiving an
enemy in war  2. any tricky ruse

**strat·e·gy** (strat′ə jē) n., pl. **-gies**
1. the science of planning and directing
military operations  2. skill in managing or planning, esp. by using strata-
gems  3. a stratagem, plan, etc. —
**stra·te·gic** (strə tē′jik) adj. —**stra-
te′gi·cal·ly** adv. —**strat′e·gist** n.

**strat·i·fy** (strat′ə fī′) vt., vi. **-fied′,**
**-fy′ing** [< L. stratum, layer + facere,
make] to form in layers or strata
—**strat′i·fi·ca′tion** n.

**strat′o·sphere** (-ə sfir′) n. [< ModL.
stratum, layer + Fr. sphère, SPHERE]
the atmospheric zone extending from 6
to 15 miles above the earth's surface

**stra·tum** (strāt′əm, strat′-) n., pl.
**-ta** (-ə), **-tums** [ModL. < L. stratus,
a spreading] 1. a horizontal layer of
matter; specif., a single layer of sedimentary rock  2. a level of society

**stra′tus** (-əs) n., pl. **-ti** (-ī) [see prec.]
a long, low, gray cloud layer

**Strauss** (strous), **Jo·hann** (yō′hän)
1825-99; Austrian composer

**Stra·vin·sky** (strə vin′skē), **I·gor**
(ē′gôr) 1882-1971; U.S. composer,
born in Russia

**straw** (strô) n. [OE. streaw] 1. hollow
stalks of grain after threshing  2. a
single one of these  3. a tube used for
sucking beverages  4. a trifle —adj.
1. straw-colored; yellowish  2. made
of straw  3. worthless

**straw′ber′ry** (-ber′ē, -bər ē) n., pl.
**-ries** [prob. from the strawlike particles on the fruit] 1. the small, red,
fleshy fruit of a vinelike plant of the
rose family  2. this plant

**straw boss** [Colloq.] a person having
subordinate authority

**straw vote** an unofficial vote taken to
determine general group opinion

**stray** (strā) vi. [prob. < L. extra
vagari, wander outside] 1. to wander
from a given place, course, etc.  2. to
deviate (from what is right) —n. one
that strays; esp., a lost domestic
animal —adj. 1. having strayed; lost
2. isolated [a few stray words]

**streak** (strēk) n. [< OE. strica] 1. a
long, thin mark or stripe  2. a layer, as
of fat in meat  3. a tendency in
behavior, etc. [a nervous streak]  4. a
period, as of luck —vt. to mark with
streaks —vi. 1. to become streaked
2. to go fast  3. to make a short dash
naked in public as a prank —**streak′-
er** n. —**streak′y** adj.

**stream** (strēm) n. [OE.] 1. a current
of water; specif., a small river  2. any
steady flow, as of air, light, etc.
3. a continuous series [a stream of
cars] —vi. 1. to flow as in a stream
2. to flow (with)  3. to move swiftly

**stream′er** n. 1. a long, narrow flag
2. any long, narrow, flowing strip

**stream′line′** vt. **-lined′, -lin′ing**
1. to give a streamlined contour to
2. to organize for simplicity and efficiency —adj. same as STREAMLINED

**stream′lined′** adj. 1. having a contour designed to offer the least resistance in moving through air, water, etc.
2. efficient, simplified, trim, etc.

**street** (strēt) n. [< L. strata (via),
paved (road)] 1. a public road in a
town or city, esp. a paved one  2. such
a road with its sidewalks and buildings
3. the people living, working, etc.
along a given street

**street′car′** n. a car on rails for public
transportation along the streets

**street′walk′er** n. a prostitute

**street′wise′** adj. [Colloq.] experienced in dealing with people in urban
poverty areas where crime is common

**strength** (streŋkth) n. [OE. strengthu]
1. the state or quality of being strong;
force  2. toughness; durability  3. the
power to resist attack  4. potency, as of
drugs  5. intensity, as of sound, etc.
6. force of an army, etc., as measured
in numbers —**on the strength of**
based or relying on

**strength′en** vt., vi. to make or become stronger —**strength′en·er** n.

**stren·u·ous** (stren′yoo wəs) adj. [L.
strenuus] requiring or characterized by
great effort or energy —**stren′u·
ous·ly** adv. —**stren′u·ous·ness** n.

**strep throat** (strep) [Colloq.] a sore
throat caused by a streptococcus,
with inflammation and fever

**strep·to·coc·cus** (strep′tə käk′əs) n.,
pl. **-coc′ci** (-käk′sī) [< Gr. streptos,
twisted + kokkos, kernel] any of various
spherical bacteria occurring in chains:
some cause serious diseases

**strep′to·my′cin** (-mī′sin) n. [< Gr.
streptos, bent + mykēs, fungus] an
antibiotic drug obtained from molds
and used in treating various diseases

---

fat, āpe, cär; ten, ēven; is, bīte; gō, hôrn, tōōl, look; oil, out; up, fur;
chin; she; thin, then; zh, leisure; ŋ, ring; ə for a in ago; ′, (ā′b'l); ĕ, Fr. coeur;
ö, Fr. feu; Fr. mon; ü, Fr. duc; kh, G. ich, doch; ‡ foreign; < derived from

**stress** (stres) *n.* [< L. *strictus*, strict]
1. strain; specif., force that strains or
deforms 2. emphasis; importance
3. *a)* mental or physical tension *b)* urgency, pressure, etc. causing this 4. the
relative force of utterance given a
syllable or word; accent —*vt.* 1. to put
stress or pressure on 2. to accent
3. to emphasize

**stretch** (strech) *vt.* [OE. *streccan*]
1. to reach out; extend 2. to draw out
to full extent or to greater size 3. to
cause to extend too far; strain 4. to
strain in interpretation, scope, etc.
—*vi.* 1. *a)* to spread out to full extent
or beyond normal limits *b)* to extend
over a given distance or time 2. *a)* to
extend the body or limbs to full length
*b)* to lie down (usually with *out*) 3. to
become stretched —*n.* 1. a stretching
or being stretched 2. an unbroken
period [a ten-year *stretch*] 3. an unbroken length, tract, etc. 4. short for
HOMESTRETCH —*adj.* made of elastic
fabric so as to stretch easily —
**stretch′a·ble** *adj.* —**stretch′y** *adj.*

**stretch′er** *n.* 1. one that stretches
2. a light, canvas-covered frame for
carrying the sick, injured, etc.

**strew** (strōō) *vt.* strewed, strewed or
strewn, strew′ing [OE. *streawian*]
1. to spread here and there; scatter
2. to cover as by scattering

**stri·at·ed** (strī′āt id) *adj.* [< L.
*striare*, to groove] marked with parallel
lines, bands, furrows, etc.

**strick·en** (strik′'n) *alt. pp.* of STRIKE
—*adj.* 1. struck or wounded 2. afflicted, as by something painful

**strict** (strikt) *adj.* [< L. *stringere*,
draw tight] 1. exact or precise 2. perfect; absolute 3. *a)* enforcing rules
carefully *b)* closely enforced —**strict′-
ly** *adv.* —**strict′ness** *n.*

**stric·ture** (strik′chər) *n.* [see prec.]
1. adverse criticism 2. an abnormal
narrowing of a passage in the body

**stride** (strīd) *vi., vt.* strode, strid′den
(strid′'n), strid′ing [OE. *stridan*] 1.
to walk with long steps 2. to cross with
a single, long step —*n.* 1. a long step
2. the distance covered by a stride 3.
[*usually pl.*] progress [to make *strides*]

**stri·dent** (strīd′'nt) *adj.* [< L. *stridere*,
to rasp] harsh-sounding; shrill; grating
—**stri′dent·ly** *adv.*

**strife** (strīf) *n.* [< OFr. *estrif*] 1. contention 2. fight or quarrel; struggle

**strike** (strīk) *vt.* struck, struck or,
esp. for vt. 7 & 10, strick′en, strik′ing
[< OE. *strican*, to go] 1. to give a
blow, etc.) to 2. to make by stamping,
etc. [to *strike* coins] 3. to announce
(time), as with a bell: said of clocks,
etc. 4. to ignite (a match) or produce
(a light, etc.) by friction 5. to collide
with or cause to collide [he *struck* his
arm on the door] 6. to attack 7. to
afflict, as with disease, pain, etc. 8. to
come upon; notice, find, etc. 9. to
affect as if by a blow, etc.; occur to
[*struck* by an idea] 10. to remove *from*
a list, record, etc. 11. to make (a
bargain, truce, etc.) 12. to lower (a
sail, flag, etc.) 13. to assume (a pose,
etc.) —*vi.* 1. to hit (*at*) 2. to attack

3. to make sounds as by being struck:
said of a bell, clock, etc. 4. to collide:
hit (*against, on,* or *upon*) 5. to seize
at a bait: said of fish 6. to come
suddenly (*on* or *upon*) 7. to refuse to
continue to work until certain demands
are met 8. to proceed in a new direction —*n.* 1. a striking; specif., a
military attack 2. a refusal by employees to go on working, in an attempt
to gain better working conditions
3. the discovery of a rich deposit of oil,
etc. 4. *Baseball* a pitched ball which
is struck at but missed, fairly delivered
but not struck at, etc. 5. *Bowling* a
knocking down of all the pins on the
first bowl —**strike out** 1. to erase
2. to start out 3. *Baseball* to put out,
or be put out, on three strikes —**strike
up** to begin —**strik′er** *n.*

**strik′ing** *adj.* very impressive; outstanding, remarkable, etc.

**string** (strin) *n.* [OE. *streng*] 1. a
thin line of fiber, leather, etc. used as
for tying or pulling 2. a length of like
things on a string [a *string* of pearls]
3. a row or series or number of like
things [a *string* of houses] 4. *a)* a
slender cord bowed, plucked, etc. to
make a musical sound, as on a violin
*b)* [*pl.*] all the stringed instruments of
an orchestra 5. a fiber of a plant
6. [Colloq.] a condition attached to a
plan, offer, etc. —*vt.* strung, string′-
ing 1. to provide with strings 2. to
thread on a string 3. to tie, hang, etc.
with a string 4. to remove the strings
from (beans, etc.) 5. to arrange in a
row 6. to extend [*string* a cable] —**pull
strings** to use influence, often secretly,
to gain advantage —**string′y** *adj.*
**-i·er, -i·est**

**string bean** a bean whose thick, unripe pods are eaten as a vegetable

**stringed** (strind) *adj.* having strings

**strin·gent** (strin′jənt) *adj.* [see STRICT]
strict; severe —**strin′gen·cy** *n.*

**string′er** *n.* 1. a long horizontal piece
in a structure 2. a part-time local
news correspondent for a newspaper,
etc. elsewhere

**strip¹** (strip) *vt.* stripped, strip′ping
[OE. *strypan*] 1. to remove (the
clothing, etc.) from (a person) 2. to
dispossess of (honors, titles, etc.) 3. to
plunder; rob 4. to take off (a covering)
from (a person or thing) 5. to make
bare by taking away removable parts,
etc. 6. to break the thread of (a bolt,
etc.) or the teeth of (a gear) —*vi.* to
take off all clothing

**strip²** (strip) *n.* [< ff.] 1. a long, narrow piece, as of land, tape, etc. 2. a runway for airplanes: also **landing strip**

**stripe** (strīp) *n.* [< MDu. *strijp*] 1. a
long, narrow band differing from the
surrounding area 2. a strip of cloth on
a uniform to show rank, years served,
etc. 3. kind; sort —*vt.* striped,
strip′ing to mark with stripes

**strip·ling** (strip′lin) *n.* a youth

**strip-tease** (strip′tēz′) *n.* a burlesque
performance with music, in which a
woman takes off her clothes slowly and
with suggestive movements

**strive** (strīv) *vi.* strove, striv·en

(striv′n) or **strived, striv′ing** [< OFr. *estrif*, effort] 1. to make great efforts; try very hard 2. to struggle [*strive* against tyranny]

**strobe (light)** (strōb) [< Gr. *strobus*, a twisting around] an electronic tube emitting rapid, brief, and brilliant flashes of light: also **stro·bo·scope** (strō′bə skōp′) *n.*

**strode** (strōd) *pt.* of STRIDE

**stroke** (strōk) *n.* [ME.] 1. the act of striking; blow, as of an ax 2. a sudden action or event [a *stroke* of luck] 3. a sudden attack, esp. of apoplexy 4. a single, strong effort 5. the sound of striking, as of a clock 6. *a*) a single movement, as with a tool, racket, etc. *b*) any of a series of motions made in swimming, rowing, etc. 7. a mark made by a pen, etc. —*vt.* **stroked, strok′ing** to draw one's hand, etc. gently over the surface of

**stroll** (strōl) *vi.* [prob. < G. *strolchen*] 1. to walk about leisurely; saunter 2. to wander —*vt.* to stroll along or through —*n.* a leisurely walk

**stroll′er** *n.* 1. one who strolls 2. a light, chairlike baby carriage

**strong** (strôŋ) *adj.* [OE. *strang*] 1. *a*) physically powerful *b*) healthy; sound 2. morally or intellectually powerful [a *strong* will] 3. firm; durable [a *strong* fort] 4. powerful in wealth, numbers, etc. 5. of a specified number [troops 50,000 *strong*] 6. having a powerful effect 7. intense in degree or quality [*strong* coffee, a *strong* light, *strong* colors, etc.] 8. forceful, vigorous, etc. —**strong′ly** *adv.*

**strong′-arm′** *adj.* [Colloq.] using physical force —*vt.* [Colloq.] to use force upon

**strong′box′** *n.* a heavily made box or safe for storing valuables

**strong′hold′** *n.* a place having strong defenses; fortress

**strong′-mind′ed** *adj.* determined; unyielding: also **strong′-willed′**

**strong′room′** *n.* a strongly built room used for safeguarding valuables

**stron·ti·um** (strän′shē əm, -tē-) *n.* [< *Strontian*, Scotland, where first found] a metallic chemical element resembling calcium in properties

**strop** (sträp) *n.* [OE.] a leather band for sharpening razors —*vt.* **stropped, strop′ping** to sharpen on a strop

**stro·phe** (strō′fē) *n.* [Gr. *strophē*, a turning] a stanza of a poem

**strove** (strōv) *alt. pt.* of STRIVE

**struck** (struk) *pt. & pp.* of STRIKE —*adj.* closed or otherwise affected by a labor strike

**struc·ture** (struk′chər) *n.* [< L. *struere*, arrange] 1. something built or constructed; building, etc. 2. the arrangement of all the parts of a whole 3. something composed of related parts —*vt.* **-tured, -tur·ing** to put together systematically —**struc′tur·al** *adj.*

**stru·del** (strōō′d'l) *n.* [G.] a pastry made of a thin sheet of dough filled with apples, etc., rolled up, and baked

**strug·gle** (strug′l) *vi.* **-gled, -gling** [ME. *strogelen*] 1. to fight violently with an opponent 2. to make great efforts; strive; labor —*n.* 1. great effort 2. conflict; strife

**strum** (strum) *vt., vi.* **strummed, strum′ming** [echoic] to play (a guitar, etc.) casually or unskillfully

**strum·pet** (strum′pit) *n.* [ME.] a prostitute

**strung** (struŋ) *pt. & pp.* of STRING

**strut** (strut) *vi.* **strut′ted, strut′ting** [OE. *strutian*, stand rigid] to walk swaggeringly —*n.* 1. a strutting walk 2. a brace fitted into a framework to resist lengthwise pressure

**strych·nine** (strik′nin, -nīn, -nēn) *n.* [< Gr. *strychnos*, nightshade] a highly poisonous crystalline alkaloid: used in small doses as a stimulant

**stub** (stub) *n.* [OE. *stybb*] 1. a tree or plant stump 2. a short piece left over 3. any short or blunt projection or thing 4. the part of a ticket, bank check, etc. kept as a record —*vt.* **stubbed, stub′bing** 1. to strike (one's toe, etc.) against something 2. to put out (a cigarette, etc.) by pressing the end against a surface

**stub·ble** (stub′l) *n.* [< L. *stipula*, a stalk] 1. short stumps of grain left after harvesting 2. any short, bristly growth, as of beard

**stub·born** (stub′ərn) *adj.* [ME. *stoburn*] 1. refusing to yield or comply; obstinate 2. done in an obstinate or persistent way 3. hard to handle, etc. —**stub′born·ness** *n.*

**stub·by** (stub′ē) *adj.* **-bi·er, -bi·est** 1. covered with stubs or stubble 2. short and dense 3. short and thickset

**stuc·co** (stuk′ō) *n., pl.* **-coes, -cos** [It.] plaster or cement for surfacing walls, etc. —*vt.* **-coed, -co·ing** to cover with stucco

**stuck** (stuk) *pt. & pp.* of STICK

**stuck′-up′** *adj.* [Colloq.] snobbish

**stud¹** (stud) *n.* [OE. *studu*, post] 1. any of a series of small knobs, etc. used to ornament a surface 2. a small, buttonlike device for fastening collars, etc. 3. an upright piece in a building frame, to which laths, etc. are nailed —*vt.* **stud′ded, stud′ding** 1. to set or decorate with studs, etc. 2. to be set thickly on [rocks *stud* the hill]

**stud²** (stud) *n.* [OE. *stod*] a male animal, esp. a horse (**stud′horse′**), kept for breeding

**stud′book′** *n.* a register of purebred animals, esp. racehorses

**stud′ding** *n.* 1. studs, esp. for walls 2. material for studs

**stu·dent** (stōōd′'nt) *n.* [< L. *studere*, to study] 1. one who studies or investigates 2. one who is enrolled for study at a school, college, etc.

**stud·ied** (stud′ēd) *adj.* 1. prepared by careful study 2. deliberate

**stu·di·o** (stōō′dē ō′) *n., pl.* **-os′** [It., a study] 1. a place where an artist, etc.

works or where dancing lessons, etc. are given  2. a place where movies, radio or TV programs, etc. are produced

**studio couch** a couch that can be opened into a full-size bed

**stu·di·ous** (stōō'dē əs) *adj.* 1. fond of study  2. attentive; zealous

**stud·y** (stud'ē) *n., pl.* **-ies** [< L. *studere*, to study] 1. the acquiring of knowledge, as by reading 2. careful examination of a subject, event, etc. 3. a branch of learning 4. [*pl.*] education; schooling 5. earnest effort or deep thought 6. a room for study, etc. —*vt.* **-ied, -y·ing** 1. to try to learn by reading, etc. 2. to investigate carefully 3. to read (a book, etc.) intently —*vi.* 1. to study something 2. to be a student 3. to meditate

**stuff** (stuf) *n.* [< OFr. *estoffe*] 1. the material out of which anything is made 2. essence; character  3. matter in general 4. cloth, esp. woolen cloth 5. objects; things  6. worthless objects; junk  7. [Colloq.] ability, skill, etc. —*vt.* 1. to fill or pack; specif., *a)* to fill the skin of (a dead animal) in taxidermy *b)* to fill (a fowl, etc.) with seasoning, bread crumbs, etc. before roasting 2. to fill too full; cram 3. to plug; block —*vi.* to eat too much

**stuffed shirt** [Slang] a pompous, pretentious person

**stuff·ing** *n.* something used to stuff, as padding in upholstery, a seasoned mixture for stuffing fowl, etc.

**stuff·y** *adj.* **-i·er, -i·est** 1. poorly ventilated; close 2. having the nasal passages stopped up, as from a cold 3. [Colloq.] dull or stodgy

**stul·ti·fy** (stul'tə fī') *vt.* **-fied', -fy'-ing** [< L. *stultus*, foolish + *facere*, make] 1. to make seem foolish, stupid, etc. 2. to make worthless, etc.

**stum·ble** (stum'b'l) *vi.* **-bled, -bling** [ME. *stumblen*] 1. to trip in walking, running, etc. 2. to walk unsteadily 3. to speak, act, etc. in a blundering way 4. to do wrong 5. to come by chance —*n.* a stumbling —**stum'bler** *n.*

**stumbling block** a difficulty

**stump** (stump) *n.* [ME. *stumpe*] 1. the end of a tree or plant left in the ground after the upper part has been cut off 2. the part of a leg, tooth, etc. left after the rest has been removed 3. the place where a political speech is made —*vt.* 1. to travel over (a district) making political speeches 2. [Colloq.] to puzzle or perplex —*vi.* 1. to walk heavily 2. to travel about making political speeches —**stump'y** *adj.*

**stun** (stun) *vt.* **stunned, stun'ning** [< L. *ex-*, intens. + *tonare*, to crash] 1. to make unconscious, as by a blow 2. to daze; shock

**stung** (stuŋ) *pt. & pp.* of STING

**stunk** (stuŋk) *pp. & alt. pt.* of STINK

**stun·ning** (stun'iŋ) *adj.* [Colloq.] remarkably attractive, excellent, etc.

**stunt¹** (stunt) *vt.* [OE., stupid] 1. to check the growth or development of 2. to hinder (growth, etc.)

**stunt²** (stunt) *n.* [< ?] something done to show one's skill or daring, get attention, etc. —*vi.* to do a stunt

**stu·pe·fy** (stōō'pə fī', styōō'-) *vt.* **-fied', -fy'ing** [< L. *stupere*, be stunned + *facere*, make] 1. to produce stupor in; stun 2. to amaze; bewilder —**stu'pe·fac'tion** (-fak'shən) *n.*

**stu·pen·dous** (stōō pen'dəs, styōō-) *adj.* [< L. *stupere*, be stunned] 1. astonishing 2. astonishingly great

**stu·pid** (stōō'pid, styōō'-) *adj.* [see prec.] 1. lacking normal intelligence 2. foolish; silly [*a stupid idea*] 3. dull and boring —**stu·pid'i·ty** *n., pl.* **-ties**

**stu·por** (stōō'pər, styōō'-) *n.* [L.] a state in which the mind and senses are dulled; loss of sensibility

**stur·dy** (stur'dē) *adj.* **-di·er, -di·est** [< OFr. *estourdi*, stunned] 1. firm; resolute 2. strong; vigorous —**stur'di·ly** *adv.* —**stur'di·ness** *n.*

**stur·geon** (stur'jən) *n.* [< OFr. *esturjon*] a large food fish valuable as a source of caviar

**stut·ter** (stut'ər) *n., vt., vi.* [< ME. *stutten*] stammer

STURGEON

**sty¹** (stī) *n., pl.* **sties** [< OE. *sti, hall*] 1. a pen for pigs 2. any foul place

**sty², stye** (stī) *n., pl.* **sties** [ult. < OE. *stigan*, to rise] a small, inflamed swelling on the rim of an eyelid

**Styg·i·an** (stij'ē ən, stij'ən) *adj.* 1. of the Styx 2. [*also* **s-**] *a)* infernal *b)* dark or gloomy

**style** (stīl) *n.* [< L. *stilus*, pointed writing tool] 1. a stylus 2. *a)* manner of expression in language *b)* characteristic manner of expression, design, etc., in an art, period, etc. *c)* excellence of expression 3. *a)* fashion *b)* something stylish —*vt.* **styled, styl'ing** 1. to name; call 2. to design the style of

**styl·ish** (stīl'ish) *adj.* conforming to current style, as in dress; fashionable

**styl·ist** *n.* a writer, etc. whose work has style and distinction —**sty·lis'tic** *adj.* —**sty·lis'ti·cal·ly** *adv.*

**styl·ize** (stīl'īz) *vt.* **-ized, -iz·ing** to design or depict according to a style rather than nature

**sty·lus** (stī'ləs) *n., pl.* **-lus·es, -li** (-lī) [L., for *stilus*, pointed tool] 1. a sharp, pointed marking device 2. *a)* a pointed device for cutting the grooves of a phonograph record *b)* a phonograph needle

**sty·mie** (stī'mē) *n.* [prob. < Scot., person partially blind] *Golf* a situation in which a ball to be putted has another ball between it and the hole —*vt.* **-mied, -mie·ing** to block; impede Also **stymy** **-mied, -my·ing**

**styp·tic** (stip'tik) *adj.* [< Gr. *styphein*, to contract] tending to halt bleeding; astringent —**styp'sis** *n.*

**styptic pencil** a piece of a styptic substance to stop minor bleeding

**Sty·ro·foam** (stī'rə fōm') *a trademark for* a rigid, foamy-looking, lightweight plastic —*n.* [*also* **s-**] this plastic

**Styx** (stiks) *Gr. Myth.* the river crossed by dead souls entering Hades

**suave** (swäv) *adj.* [ < L. *suavis*, sweet] smoothly gracious or polite; polished —**suave'ly** *adv.* —**suav'i·ty** *n.*

**sub** (sub) *n. clipped form of:* 1. SUB-MARINE 2. SUBSTITUTE —*vi.* **subbed, sub'bing** [Colloq.] to be a substitute (*for* someone)

**sub-** [ < L. *sub*, under] *a prefix meaning:* 1. beneath [*subsoil*] 2. lower than [*subaltern*] 3. to a lesser degree than [*subtropical*]

**sub.** 1. substitute(s) 2. suburb(an)

**sub·a·tom·ic** (sub'ə täm'ik) *adj.* smaller than an atom

**sub'branch'** *n.* a branch division

**sub'com·mit'tee** *n.* a small committee chosen from a main committee

**sub'com'pact** *n.* a model of automobile smaller than a compact

**sub·con'scious** *adj.* occurring with little or no conscious perception on the part of the individual: said of mental processes —**the subconscious** subconscious mental activity —**sub·con'scious·ly** *adv.*

**sub·con'ti·nent** *n.* a large land mass smaller than a continent

**sub·con'tract** *n.* a secondary contract undertaking some or all obligations of another contract —*vt.*, *vi.* to make a subcontract (for) —**sub·con'trac·tor** (-ər) *n.*

**sub'cul'ture** *n.* 1. a distinctive social group within a larger social group 2. its cultural patterns

**sub·cu·ta·ne·ous** (sub'kyoō tā'nē əs) *adj.* beneath the skin

**sub·dea'con** *n.* a cleric ranking just below a deacon

**sub'deb'** (-deb') *n.* a girl not quite of debutante age

**sub'dis'trict** *n.* a subdivision of a district

**sub'di·vide'** *vt.*, *vi.* **-vid'ed, -vid'ing** 1. to divide further 2. to divide (land) into small parcels —**sub'di·vi'sion** *n.*

**sub·due** (səb dōō', -dyōō') *vt.* **-dued', -du'ing** [ < L. *subducere*, take away] 1. to conquer 2. to overcome; control 3. to make less intense; diminish

**sub'head'** *n.* a subordinate heading or title, as for part of an article

**subj.** 1. subject 2. subjunctive

**sub·ject** (sub'jikt; *for v.* səb jekt') *adj.* [ < L. *sub-*, under + *jacere*, throw] 1. under the authority or control of another 2. having a tendency [*subject* to anger] 3. exposed [*subject* to censure] 4. contingent upon [*subject* to approval] —*n.* 1. one under the authority or control of another 2. one made to undergo a treatment, experiment, etc. 3. something dealt with in discussion, study, etc.; theme 4. *Gram.* the word or words in a sentence about which something is said —*vt.* 1. to bring under the authority or control of 2. to cause to undergo something [to *subject* him to questioning] —**sub·jec'tion** *n.*

**sub·jec·tive** (səb jek'tiv) *adj.* of or resulting from the feelings of the person

thinking; not objective; personal —**sub·jec·tiv·i·ty** (sub'jek tiv'ə tē) *n.*

**sub·join** (səb join') *vt.* [see SUB- & JOIN] to append

**sub·ju·gate** (sub'jə gāt') *vt.* **-gat'ed, -gat'ing** [ < L. *sub-*, under + *jugum*, a yoke] to conquer or make subservient —**sub'ju·ga'tion** *n.*

**sub·junc·tive** (səb juŋk'tiv) *adj.* [ < L. *subjungere*, subjoin] designating or of that mood of a verb used to express supposition, desire, possibility, etc., rather than to state an actual fact

**sub·lease** (sub'lēs'; *for v.* sub lēs') *n.* a lease granted by a lessee —*vt.* **-leased', -leas'ing** to grant or hold a sublease of

**sub·let** (sub let') *vt.* **-let', -let'ting** 1. to let to another (property which one is renting) 2. to let out (work) to a subcontractor

**sub·li·mate** (sub'lə māt') *vt.* **-mat'ed, -mat'ing** 1. to sublime (a solid) 2. to express (unacceptable impulses) in acceptable forms, often unconsciously —**sub'li·ma'tion** *n.*

**sub·lime** (sə blīm') *adj.* [ < L. *sub-*, up to + *limen*, lintel] 1. noble; exalted 2. inspiring awe or admiration —*vt.* **-limed', -lim'ing** to purify (a solid) by heating to a gaseous state and condensing the vapor back into solid form —**sub·lim'i·ty** (-blim'ə tē) *n.*

**sub·lim·i·nal** (sub lim'ə n'l) *adj.* [ < SUB- + L. *limen*, threshold + -AL] below the threshold of conscious awareness

**sub·ma·chine gun** (sub'mə shēn') a portable, automatic firearm

**sub·mar·gin·al** (sub mär'ji n'l) *adj.* below minimum standards

**sub·ma·rine** (sub'mə rēn'; *for n.* usually sub'mə rēn') *adj.* being, living, etc. underwater —*n.* a ship, esp. a warship, that can operate underwater

**submarine sandwich** *same as* HERO SANDWICH

**sub·merge** (səb murj') *vt.*, *vi.* **-merged', -merg'ing** [ < L. *sub-*, under + *mergere*, to plunge] to place or sink beneath the surface, as of water —**sub·mer'gence** *n.*

**sub·merse'** (-murs') *vt.* **-mersed', -mers'ing** *same as* SUBMERGE —**sub·mers'i·ble** *adj.* —**sub·mer'sion** *n.*

**sub·mis·sion** (səb mish'ən) *n.* 1. a submitting or surrendering 2. obedience; resignation —**sub·mis'sive** *adj.*

**sub·mit'** (-mit') *vt.* **-mit'ted, -mit'ting** [ < L. *sub-*, under + *mittere*, send] 1. to present to others for consideration, etc. 2. to yield to the power or control of another 3. to offer as an opinion —*vi.* to yield; give in

**sub·nor·mal** (sub nôr'm'l) *adj.* below normal, esp. in intelligence

**sub·or·bit·al** (-ôr'bit 'l) *adj.* designating a space flight in which the spacecraft follows a short-range trajectory instead of going into orbit

**sub·or·di·nate** (sə bôr'də nit; *for v.* -nāt') *adj.* [ < L. *sub-*, under + *ordinare*, to order] 1. below another in rank, importance, etc. **2.** under the authority of another **3.** *Gram.* that cannot function syntactically without other elements [a *subordinate* clause] —*n.* a subordinate person or thing —*vt.* **-nat'ed, -nat'ing** to place in a subordinate position —**sub·or'di·na'tion** *n.*

**sub·orn** (sə bôrn') *vt.* [< L. *sub-*, under + *ornare*, adorn] to induce (another) to commit perjury —**sub·or·na·tion** (sub'ôr nā'shən) *n.*

**sub'plot'** *n.* a secondary plot in a play, novel, etc.

**sub·poe·na** (sə pē'nə) *n.* [< L. *sub poena*, under penalty] a written legal order directing a person to appear in court to testify, etc. —*vt.* **-naed, -na·ing** to summon with such an order *Also sp.* **sub·pe'na**

**sub·pro·fes·sion·al** (sub'prə fesh'-ən 'l) *n. same as* PARAPROFESSIONAL

**sub ro·sa** (sub rō'zə) [L., under the rose] secretly; privately

**sub·scribe** (səb skrīb') *vt., vi.* **-scribed', -scrib'ing** [< L. *sub-*, under + *scribere*, write] **1.** to sign (one's name) on a document, etc. **2.** to give support or consent (to) **3.** to promise to contribute (money) **4.** to agree to receive and pay for a periodical, service, etc. (with *to*) —**sub·scrib'er** *n.*

**sub'script'** (-skript') *n.* [see prec.] a figure, letter, or symbol written below and to the side of another

**sub·scrip·tion** (-skrip'shən) *n.* **1.** a subscribing **2.** money subscribed **3.** a formal agreement to receive and pay for a periodical, etc.

**sub·se·quent** (sub'si kwənt) *adj.* [< L. *sub-*, after + *sequi*, follow] coming after; following —**subsequent to** after —**sub'se·quent·ly** *adv.*

**sub·ser·vi·ent** (səb sur'vē ənt) *adj.* **1.** that is of service, esp. in a subordinate capacity **2.** submissive; servile —**sub·ser'vi·ence** *n.*

**sub·side** (səb sīd') *vi.* **-sid'ed, -sid'-ing** [< L. *sub-*, under + *sidere*, settle] **1.** to sink to a lower level or to the bottom **2.** to become less active, intense, etc. —**sub·sid'ence** *n.*

**sub·sid·i·ar·y** (səb sid'ē er'ē) *adj.* [see SUBSIDY] **1.** giving aid, service, etc.; auxiliary **2.** being in a subordinate relationship —*n., pl.* **-ies** one that is subsidiary; specif., a company controlled by another company

**sub·si·dize** (sub'sə dīz') *vt.* **-dized', -diz'ing** to support with a subsidy —**sub'si·di·za'tion** *n.*

**sub·si·dy** (sub'sə dē) *n., pl.* **-dies** [< L. *subsidium*, auxiliary forces] a grant of money, as from a government to a private enterprise

**sub·sist** (səb sist') *vi.* [< L. *sub-*, under + *sistere*, stand] **1.** to continue to be or exist **2.** to continue to live; remain alive (*on* or *by*)

**sub·sist'ence** *n.* **1.** existence **2.** the act of providing support or livelihood **3.** means of support or livelihood, esp. the barest means

**sub·soil** (sub'soil') *n.* the layer of soil beneath the surface soil

**sub·son·ic** (sub sän'ik) *adj.* designat-

ing, of, or moving at a speed less than that of sound

**sub·stance** (sub'stəns) *n.* [< L. *substare*, exist] **1.** the real or essential part of anything; essence **2.** the physical matter of which a thing consists; material **3.** *a)* solid or substantial quality *b)* consistency; body **4.** the real meaning; gist **5.** wealth

**sub·stand'ard** *adj.* below standard

**sub·stan·tial** (səb stan'shəl) *adj.* **1.** having substance **2.** real; true **3.** strong; solid **4.** ample; large **5.** important **6.** wealthy **7.** with regard to essential elements —**sub·stan'tial·ly** *adv.*

**sub·stan·ti·ate** (-stan'shē āt') *vt.* **-at'ed, -at'ing** [see SUBSTANCE] to show to be true or real by giving evidence —**sub·stan'ti·a'tion** *n.*

**sub·stan·tive** (sub'stən tiv) *adj.* [see SUBSTANCE] of or dealing with essentials —*n. Gram.* a noun or any word or group of words used as a noun

**sub·sta·tion** *n.* a branch station, as of a post office

**sub·sti·tute** (sub'stə tōōt') *n.* [< L. *sub-*, under + *statuere*, put] a person or thing serving or used in place of another —*vt., vi.* **-tut'ed, -tut'ing** to put, use, or serve in place of (another) —**sub'sti·tu'tion** *n.*

**sub·stra·tum** (sub'strāt'əm) *n., pl.* **-ta** (-ə), **-tums** [see SUB- & STRATUM] a part, substance, etc. which lies beneath and supports another

**sub·struc·ture** *n.* a part or structure that is a support, base, etc.

**sub·sume** (səb sōōm') *vt.* **-sumed', -sum'ing** [< L. *sub-*, under + *sumere*, take] to include within a larger class

**sub'teen'** *n.* a child who is nearly a teen-ager

**sub·ten·ant** *n.* a person who rents from a tenant —**sub·ten'an·cy** *n.*

**sub·ter·fuge** (sub'tər fyōōj') *n.* [< L. *subter-*, below + *fugere*, flee] any plan or action used to evade something difficult or unpleasant

**sub·ter·ra·ne·an** (sub'tə rā'nē ən) *adj.* [< L. *sub-*, under + *terra*, earth] **1.** underground **2.** secret; hidden

**sub'ti·tle** *n.* **1.** a secondary or explanatory title **2.** a line or lines as of dialogue shown on a movie screen or TV tube —*vt.* **-tl'tled, -ti'tling** to add a subtitle or subtitles to

**sub·tle** (sut''l) *adj.* **-tler, -tlest** [< L. *subtilis*, fine, thin] **1.** thin; not dense **2.** mentally keen **3.** delicately skillful **4.** crafty **5.** not obvious —**sub'tle·ty** *n., pl.* **-ties** —**sub'tly** *adv.*

**sub'to'tal** *n.* a total that is part of a complete total —*vt., vi.* **-taled** or **-talled, -tal·ing** or **-tal·ling** to add up so as to form a subtotal

**sub·tract** (səb trakt') *vt., vi.* [< L. *sub-*, under + *trahere*, to draw] to take away or deduct, as one quantity from another —**sub·trac'tion** *n.*

**sub·tra·hend** (sub'trə hend') *n.* a quantity to be subtracted from another

**sub·trop'i·cal** *adj.* of, characteristic of, or bordering on the tropics

**sub·urb** (sub'ərb) *n.* [< L. *sub-*, near + *urbs*, town] a district, town, etc. on the outskirts of a city —**sub·ur·ban** (sə bʉr′bən) *adj.*

**sub·ur·ban·ite** (-īt′) *n.* a person living in a suburb

**sub·ur·bi·a** (sə bʉr′bē ə) *n.* the suburbs or suburbanites collectively

**sub·ven·tion** (səb ven′shən) *n.* [< LL. *subventio*, aid] a subsidy

**sub·ver·sive** (səb vʉr′siv) *adj.* tending to subvert —*n.* a subversive person

**sub·vert** (səb vʉrt′) *vt.* [< L. *sub-*, under + *vertere*, to turn] 1. to overthrow or destroy (something established) 2. to corrupt, as in morals —**sub·ver′sion** *n.*

**sub·way** (sub′wā′) *n.* an underground, metropolitan electric railway

**suc-** *same as* SUB-: used before *c*

**suc·ceed** (sək sēd′) *vi.* [< L. *sub-*, under + *cedere*, to go] 1. to follow, as in office 2. to be successful —*vt.* to come after; follow

**suc·cess** (sək ses′) *n.* 1. a favorable result 2. the gaining of wealth, fame, etc. 3. a successful person or thing

**suc·cess·ful** (sək ses′fəl) *adj.* 1. turning out as was hoped for 2. having gained wealth, fame, etc. —**suc·cess′ful·ly** *adv.*

**suc·ces·sion** (sək sesh′ən) *n.* 1. *a)* the act of succeeding another, as to an office *b)* the right to do this 2. a number of persons or things coming one after another

**suc·ces·sive** (-ses′iv) *adj.* coming one after another —**suc·ces′sive·ly** *adv.*

**suc·ces′sor** *n.* one who succeeds another, as to an office

**suc·cinct** (sək siŋkt′) *adj.* [< L. *sub-*, under + *cingere*, to gird] clear and brief; terse —**suc·cinct′ly** *adv.* —**suc·cinct′ness** *n.*

**suc·cor** (suk′ər) *vt.* [< L. *sub-*, under + *currere*, to run] to help in time of need or distress —*n.* aid; relief

**suc·co·tash** (suk′ə tash′) *n.* [< AmInd.] a dish consisting of lima beans and corn kernels cooked together

**suc·cu·lent** (suk′yoo lənt) *adj.* [< L. *sucus*, juice] full of juice; juicy —**suc′cu·lence, suc′cu·len·cy** *n.*

**suc·cumb** (sə kum′) *vi.* [< L. *sub-*, under + *cumbere*, to lie] 1. to give way (*to*); yield 2. to die

**such** (such) *adj.* [OE. *swilc*] 1. *a)* of the kind mentioned *b)* of the same or a similar kind 2. whatever [*at such time as you go]* 3. so extreme, so much, etc. [*such an honor] —adv.* to so great a degree [*such good news] —pron.* 1. such a person or thing 2. that suggested [*such was his nature] —as such* 1. as being what is indicated 2. in itself —**such as** for example

**such and such** (being) something particular but not named or specified [*such and such a place]*

**such/like′** *adj.* of such a kind —*n.* persons or things of such a kind

**suck** (suk) *vt.* [< OE. *sucan*] 1. to draw (liquid) into the mouth 2. to take in as if by sucking 3. to suck liquid from (fruit, etc.) 4. *a)* to

dissolve by holding in the mouth and licking *b)* to hold in the mouth and draw on —*vi.* to suck something —*n.* the act of sucking

**suck′er** *n.* 1. one that sucks 2. a freshwater, bony fish with a mouth adapted for sucking 3. a part used for sucking or for holding fast by suction 4. a lollipop 5. a shoot from the roots or stem of a plant 6. [Slang] one easily cheated

**suck·le** (suk′'l) *vt., vi.* -led, -ling [ME. *sokelen*] 1. to feed at the breast or udder 2. to rear; foster

**suck′ling** *n.* an unweaned child or young animal

**su·crose** (sōō′krōs) *n.* [< Fr. *sucre*, sugar] a sugar extracted from sugar cane or sugar beets

**suc·tion** (suk′shən) *n.* [< L. *sugere*, to suck] 1. a sucking 2. production of a partial vacuum so that external pressure forces fluid in or causes something to adhere to a surface

**Su·dan** (sōō dan′) country in NE Africa: 967,500 sq. mi.; pop. 14,770,000; cap. Khartoum —**Su′da·nese′** (-də nēz′) *adj., n.*

**sud·den** (sud′'n) *adj.* [ult. < L. *sub-*, under + *ire*, go] 1. happening or coming unexpectedly 2. sharp or abrupt 3. quick or hasty —**all of a sudden** unexpectedly —**sud′den·ly** *adv.* —**sud′den·ness** *n.*

**sudden death** *Sports* an extra period added to a tied game, the game ending as soon as one side scores

**suds** (sudz) *n.pl.* [prob. < MDu. *sudse*, marsh water] 1. soapy, frothy water 2. foam —**suds′y** *adj.*

**sue** (sōō) *vt., vi.* sued, su′ing [< L. *sequi*, follow] 1. to appeal (to); petition 2. to prosecute in a court in seeking redress of wrongs, etc.

**suede, suède** (swād) *n.* [< Fr. *gants de Suède*, Swedish gloves] 1. tanned leather with the flesh side buffed into a nap 2. a cloth like this

**su·et** (sōō′it) *n.* [< L. *sebum*, fat] the hard fat of cattle and sheep: used in cooking and as tallow

**Su·ez Canal** (sōō ez′) ship canal joining the Mediterranean & Red seas

**suf-** *same as* SUB-: used before *f*

**suf·fer** (suf′ər) *vt., vi.* [< L. *sub-*, under + *ferre*, to bear] 1. to undergo or endure (pain, injury, loss, etc.) 2. to experience (any process) 3. to permit; tolerate —**suf′fer·er** *n.*

**suf·fer·ance** *n.* 1. the capacity to endure pain, etc. 2. consent, permission, etc. implied by failure to prohibit

**suf·fer·ing** *n.* 1. the bearing of pain, distress, etc. 2. something suffered

**suf·fice** (sə fīs′) *vi.* -ficed′, -fic′ing [< L. *sub-*, under + *facere*, make] to be enough or adequate

**suf·fi·cient** (sə fish′ənt) *adj.* as much as is needed; enough; adequate —**suf·fi′cien·cy** *n.* —**suf·fi′cient·ly** *adv.*

**suf·fix** (suf′iks) *n.* [< L. *sub-*, under

+ *figere*, fix] a syllable or syllables added at the end of a word to alter its meaning, etc. (Ex.: *-ness* in *darkness*)

**suf·fo·cate** (suf′ə kāt′) *vt.* -cat′ed, -cat′ing [< L. *sub-*, under + *fauces*, throat] **1.** to kill by cutting off the supply of air for breathing **2.** to smother, stifle, etc. —*vi.* **1.** to die by being suffocated **2.** to choke; stifle —suf′fo·ca′tion *n.*

**suf·fra·gan** (suf′rə gən) *n.* [< ML. *suffraganus*] a bishop who is an assistant to another bishop

**suf·frage** (suf′rij) *n.* [< L. *suffragium*] **1.** a vote or voting **2.** the right to vote; franchise —suf′fra·gist *n.*

**suf·fra·gette** (suf′rə jet′) *n.* a woman who advocates female suffrage

**suf·fuse** (sə fyōōz′) *vt.* -fused′, -fus′ing [< L. *sub-*, under + *fundere*, pour] to overspread so as to fill with a glow, etc. —suf·fu′sion *n.*

**sug·ar** (shoog′ər) *n.* [< Sans. *śárkarā*] any of a class of sweet, soluble carbohydrates, as sucrose, glucose, etc.; specif., sucrose from sugar cane and sugar beets, used for sweetening —*vt.* to sweeten, cover, etc. with sugar —*vi.* to form sugar crystals —sug′ar·less *adj.* —sug′ar·y *adj.*

**sugar beet** a beet having a white root with a high sugar content

**sugar cane** a very tall tropical grass cultivated as a source of sugar

**sug′ar·coat′** *vt.* **1.** to coat with sugar **2.** to make seem more pleasant

**sug′ar·plum′** (-plum′) *n.* a round piece of sugary candy; bonbon

**sug·gest** (səg jest′, sə-) *vt.* [< L. *sub-*, under + *gerere*, carry] **1.** to bring to the mind for consideration **2.** to call to mind by association of ideas **3.** to propose as a possibility **4.** to show indirectly; imply

**sug·gest′i·ble** *adj.* readily influenced by suggestion —sug·gest′i·bil′i·ty *n.*

**sug·ges′tion** (-jes′chən) *n.* **1.** a suggesting or being suggested **2.** something suggested **3.** a hint or trace

**sug·ges′tive** *adj.* **1.** that tends to suggest ideas **2.** tending to suggest something considered improper or indecent —sug·ges′tive·ly *adv.*

**su·i·cide** (sōō′ə sīd′) *n.* [L. *sui*, of oneself + *-CIDE*] **1.** the act of killing oneself intentionally **2.** one who commits suicide —su′i·cid′al *adj.*

**su·i·ci·dol·o·gy** (-sī däl′ə jē) *n.* the study of suicide, its causes, and its prevention

**su·i ge·ne·ris** (sōō′ē jen′ər is) [L., of his own kind] altogether unique

**suit** (sōōt) *n.* [< L. *sequi*, follow] **1.** a set of clothes; esp., a coat and trousers (or skirt) **2.** any of the four sets of playing cards **3.** action to secure justice in a court of law **4.** an act of suing, pleading, etc. **5.** courtship —*vt.* **1.** to be appropriate to **2.** to make right or appropriate; fit **3.** to please; satisfy [nothing *suits* him] —follow suit to follow the example set —suit oneself to act according to one's own wishes —suit up to put on a spacesuit, an athletic

uniform, etc. in preparing for a particular activity

**suit′a·ble** *adj.* that suits a given purpose, etc.; appropriate —suit′a·bil′i·ty *n.* —suit′a·bly *adv.*

**suit′case′** *n.* a rectangular case for clothes, etc. when traveling

**suite** (swēt; *for 3, occas.* sōōt) *n.* [Fr.: see SUIT] **1.** a group of attendants; staff **2.** a set of connected rooms, as an apartment **3.** a set of matched furniture for a given room

**suit′ing** *n.* cloth for making suits

**suit′or** *n.* a man courting a woman

**su·ki·ya·ki** (sōō′kē yä′kē) *n.* [Jap.] a Japanese dish of thinly sliced meat and vegetables, cooked quickly

**Suk·kot, Suk·koth** (sōō kōt′, sook′-ōs) *n.* [Heb., lit., tabernacles] a Jewish fall festival commemorating the wandering of the Jews after the Exodus

**sul·fa** (sul′fə) *adj.* designating or of drugs of the sulfanilamide type, used against some bacterial infections

**sul·fa·nil·a·mide** (sul′fə nil′ə mīd′) *n.* a white crystalline compound once used in treating certain infections

**sul·fate** (sul′fāt) *n.* a salt or ester of sulfuric acid

**sul′fide** (-fīd) *n.* a compound of sulfur with another element or a radical

**sul·fur** (sul′fər) *n.* [L. *sulphur*] a pale-yellow, nonmetallic chemical element: it burns with a blue flame and a stifling odor: also **sulphur**

**sul·fu·ric** (sul fyoor′ik) *adj.* of or containing sulfur

**sulfuric acid** an oily, colorless, corrosive liquid used in making dyes, explosives, fertilizers, etc.

**sul·fu·rous** (sul′fər əs; *for 1, usually* sul fyoor′əs) *adj.* **1.** of or containing sulfur **2.** like burning sulfur in odor, color, etc.

**sulk** (sulk) *vi.* [< ff.] to be sulky —*n.* [*often pl.*] a sulky mood (with *the*)

**sulk·y** (sul′kē) *adj.* -i·er, -i·est [prob. < OE. *-seolcan*, become slack] sullen; glum —*n.*, *pl.* -ies a light, two-wheeled carriage for one person —sulk′i·ly *adv.* —sulk′i·ness *n.*

**sul·len** (sul′ən) *adj.* [< L. *solus*, alone] **1.** showing resentment and ill humor by morose, unsociable withdrawal; glum **2.** gloomy; dismal —sul′len·ly *adv.* —sul′len·ness *n.*

**sul·ly** (sul′ē) *vt.* -lied, -ly·ing [prob. < OFr. *souiller*] to soil, tarnish, besmirch, etc., esp. by disgracing

**sul·phur** (sul′fər) *n. var. of* SULFUR

**sul·tan** (sul′t′n) *n.* [Fr. < Ar. *sulṭān*] a Moslem ruler

**sul·tan·a** (sul tan′ə) *n.* a sultan's wife, mother, sister, or daughter

**sul·tan·ate** (sul′t′n it, -āt′) *n.* a sultan's authority, office, or domain

**sul·try** (sul′trē) *adj.* -tri·er, -tri·est [< SWELTER] **1.** oppressively hot and moist **2.** inflamed, as with passion

**sum** (sum) *n.* [< L. *summus*, highest] **1.** an amount of money **2.** gist; summary **3.** the result obtained by adding quantities; total **4.** a problem in arithmetic —*vt.* summed, sum′-ming to get the sum of by adding —sum up to summarize

**su·mac, su·mach** (shōō'mak, sōō'-) *n.* [< Ar. *summāq*] 1. any of numerous nonpoisonous plants with cone-shaped clusters of red fruit 2. any of several related poisonous plants

**Su·ma·tra** (soo mä'trə) large island of Indonesia —**Su·ma'tran** *adj., n.*

**sum·ma·rize** (sum'ə rīz') *vt.* -**rized'**, -**riz'ing** to make or be a summary of

**sum·ma·ry** (sum'ə rē) *adj.* [< L. *summa*, a sum] 1. summarizing; concise 2. prompt and unceremonious 3. hasty and arbitrary —*n., pl.* -**ries** a brief report covering the main points; digest —**sum·mar·i·ly** (sə mer'ə lē, sum'ə rə lē) *adv.*

**sum·ma·tion** (sə mā'shən) *n.* a final summary of arguments, as in a trial

**sum·mer** (sum'ər) *n.* [< OE. *sumor*] the warmest season of the year, following spring —*adj.* of or for summer —*vi.* to pass the summer —**sum'mer·y** *adj.*

**sum'mer·house'** *n.* a small, open structure in a garden, park, etc.

**summer sausage** a type of hard, dried and smoked sausage

**sum'mer·time'** *n.* the season of summer

**sum·mit** (sum'it) *n.* [< L. *summus*, highest] 1. the highest point; top 2. the highest degree or state; acme

**sum'mit·ry** (-i trē) *n.* the use of conferences between the heads of state to resolve problems of diplomacy

**sum·mon** (sum'ən) *vt.* [< L. *sub-*, secretly + *monere*, warn] 1. to call together; order to convene 2. to call or send for with authority 3. to call forth; rouse [*summon* (up) your strength] —**sum'mon·er** *n.*

**sum·mons** (-ənz) *n., pl.* -**mons·es** [see prec.] 1. an order or command to come, attend, etc. 2. *Law* an official order to appear in court

**su·mo** (**wrestling**) (sōō'mō) [Jap.] [*sometimes* S-] a Japanese kind of formalized wrestling by heavy men

**sump·tu·ous** (sump'choo wəs) *adj.* [< L. *sumptus*, expense] 1. costly; lavish 2. magnificent or splendid

**sun** (sun) *n.* [OE. *sunne*] 1. the self-luminous, gaseous sphere about which the earth and other planets revolve 2. the heat or light of the sun 3. any star that is the center of a planetary system —*vt.* sunned, **sun'ning** to warm, dry, tan, etc. in the sunlight

**Sun.** Sunday

**sun'bathe'** (-bāth') *vi.* -**bathed'**, -**bath'ing** to expose the body to direct sunlight —**sun bath**

**sun'beam'** *n.* a beam of sunlight

**Sun'belt'** *n.* those States of the South and Southwest with a sunny climate and expanding economy: also **Sun Belt**

**sun'bon'net** *n.* a bonnet for shading the face and neck from the sun

**sun'burn'** (-burn') *n.* inflammation of the skin from exposure to the sun's rays or to a sunlamp —*vi., vt.* -**burned'** or -**burnt'**, -**burn'ing**

to get or cause to get a sunburn

**sun'burst'** *n.* 1. sudden sunlight 2. a decoration representing the sun with spreading rays

**sun·dae** (sun'dē, -dā) *n.* [prob. < ff.] a serving of ice cream covered with a syrup, fruit, nuts, etc.

**Sun·day** (sun'dē, -dā) *n.* [OE. *sunnandæg*, lit., sun day] the first day of the week: set aside as a day of worship by most Christians

**sun·der** (sun'dər) *vt., vi.* [< OE. *sunder*, asunder] to break apart; split

**sun'di'al** *n.* an instrument that shows time by the shadow of a pointer cast by the sun on a dial

**sun'down'** (-doun') *n.* *same as* SUNSET

**sun'dries** (-drēz) *n.pl.* sundry items

**sun'dry** (-drē) *adj.* [< OE. *sunder*, apart] miscellaneous

SUNDIAL

**sun'fish'** *n., pl.:* see FISH 1. any of a family of freshwater fishes of N.America 2. a large, sluggish ocean fish

**sun'flow'er** *n.* a tall plant having yellow, daisylike flowers

**sung** (suŋ) *pp. & rare pt.* of SING

**sun'glass'es** *n.pl.* eyeglasses with tinted lenses to shade the eyes

**sunk** (suŋk) *pp. & alt. pt.* of SINK

**sunk'en** (-ən) *adj.* 1. submerged 2. below the general level [a *sunken* patio] 3. fallen in; hollow [*sunken* cheeks]

**sun'lamp'** *n.* an ultraviolet-ray lamp, used therapeutically

**sun'light'** *n.* the light of the sun

**sun'lit'** *adj.* lighted by the sun

**sun'ny** (-ē) *adj.* -**ni·er**, -**ni·est** 1. full of sunshine 2. bright; cheerful 3. of or like the sun —**sun'ni·ness** *n.*

**sunny side** 1. the sunlit side 2. the brighter aspect —**on the sunny side of** (younger than (a given age) —**sunny side up** fried unturned and with unbroken yolk [eggs *sunny side up*]

**sun'rise'** (-rīz') *n.* 1. the daily appearance of the sun above the eastern horizon 2. the time of this

**sun'set'** (-set') *n.* 1. the daily disappearance of the sun below the western horizon 2. the time of this

**sun'shine'** *n.* 1. the shining of the sun 2. the light and heat from the sun 3. cheerfulness, happiness, etc. —**sun'shin'y** *adj.*

**sun'spot'** *n.* any of the temporarily cooler regions appearing as dark spots on the sun

**sun'stroke'** *n.* a condition caused by excessive exposure to the sun, characterized by fever and collapse

**sun'suit'** (-sōot') *n.* short pants with a bib and shoulder straps, worn by babies and young children

**sun′tan′** (-tan′) *n.* darkened skin resulting from exposure to the sun

**sun′up′** *n. same as* SUNRISE

**Sun Yat-sen** (soon′ yät′sen′) 1866-1925; Chin. revolutionary leader

**sup** (sup) *vi.* **supped, sup′ping** [< OFr. *soupe*, soup] to have supper

**su·per** (soo′pər) *n.* [< ff.] *clipped form of:* **1.** SUPERNUMERARY (esp. sense 2) **2.** SUPERINTENDENT (esp. sense 2) —*adj.* **1.** outstanding; exceptionally fine **2.** great, extreme, or excessive

**super-** [L. < *super*, above] *a prefix meaning:* **1.** over, above [*superstructure*] **2.** superior to [*superintendent*] **3.** *a)* surpassing [*superabundance*] *b)* greater than others of its kind [*supermarket*] **4.** additional [*supertax*]

**su·per·a·bun·dant** (soo′pər ə bun′dənt) *adj.* being more than enough —**su′per·a·bun′dance** *n.*

**su·per·an′nu·at′ed** (-an′yoo wāt′id) *adj.* [< L. *super*, above + *annus*, year] **1.** too old for work **2.** retired on a pension, as because of old age

**su·perb** (soo purb′, soo-) *adj.* [see SUPER-] **1.** noble or majestic **2.** rich or magnificent **3.** extremely fine; excellent —**su·perb′ly** *adv.*

**su·per·car·go** (soo′pər kär′gō) *n.,* *pl.* **-goes, -gos** an officer on a merchant ship in charge of the cargo

**su′per·charge′** (-chärj′) *vt.* **-charged′, -charg′ing** to increase the power of (an engine), as with a device (**supercharger**) that forces air into the cylinders

**su·per·cil·i·ous** (soo′pər sil′ē əs) *adj.* [< L. *super*, above + *cilium*, eyelid, hence (in allusion to raised eyebrows) haughtiness] disdainful or contemptuous; haughty

**su′per·cit′y** (-sit′ē) *n., pl.* **-ies** *same as* MEGALOPOLIS

**su′per·con·duc·tiv·i·ty** (-kän′dək tiv′ə tē) *n.* the lack of resistance to electrical current in certain metals when cooled to near absolute zero

**su·per·e′go** (-ē′gō) *n., pl.* **-gos** *Psychoanalysis* that part of the psyche which enforces moral standards

**su·per·em′i·nent** *adj.* supremely eminent, distinguished, etc.

**su′per·er′o·ga′tion** (-er′ə gā′shən) *n.* [< L. *super*, above + *erogare*, pay] a doing more than is needed —**su′per·e·rog′a·to·ry** (-i räg′ə tôr′ē) *adj.*

**su′per·fi′cial** (-fish′əl) *adj.* [< L. *super-*, above + *facies*, face] **1.** of or being on the surface **2.** concerned with and understanding only the obvious; shallow **3.** quick and cursory **4.** merely apparent —**su′per·fi′ci·al′i·ty** (-ē al′ə tē) *n., pl.* **-ties** —**su′per·fi′cial·ly** *adv.*

**su·per·flu·ous** (soo pur′floo wəs) *adj.* [< L. *super-*, above + *fluere*, to flow] unnecessary or excessive —**su·per·flu·i·ty** (soo′pər floo′ə tē) *n., pl.* **-ties**

**su′per·high′way′** *n.* an expressway

**su·per·hu·man** (soo′pər hyoo′mən) *adj.* **1.** having a nature above that of man; divine **2.** greater than that of a normal human being

**su′per·im·pose′** (-im pōz′) *vt.* **-posed′, -pos′ing** to put or lay on top of something else

**su′per·in·tend′** (-in tend′) *vt.* to act as superintendent of; supervise —**su′per·in·tend′ence** *n.*

**su′per·in·tend′ent** *n.* [see SUPER- & INTEND] **1.** a person in charge of a department, institution, etc.; director **2.** a person responsible for the maintenance of a building

**su·pe·ri·or** (sə pir′ē ər, soo-) *adj.* [see SUPER-] **1.** higher in space, order, rank, etc. **2.** greater in quality or value than (with *to*) **3.** good or excellent in quality **4.** unaffected by (something painful, etc.): with *to* **5.** showing a feeling of being better than others; haughty —*n.* **1.** a superior person or thing **2.** the head of a religious community —**su·pe′ri·or′i·ty** (-ôr′ə tē) *n.*

**Su·pe·ri·or** (sə pir′ē ər, soo-), Lake largest of the Great Lakes, between Mich. & Ontario, Canada

**superl.** superlative

**su·per·la·tive** (sə purl′ə tiv, soo-) *adj.* [< L. *super-*, above + *latus*, pp. of *ferre*, carry] **1.** superior to all others; supreme **2.** *Gram.* designating the extreme degree of comparison of adjectives and adverbs —*n.* **1.** the highest degree; acme **2.** *Gram.* the superlative degree [*coolest* is the superlative of *cool*] —**su·per′la·tive·ly** *adv.*

**su·per·man** (soo′pər man′) *n., pl.* **-men** an apparently superhuman man

**su′per·mar′ket** *n.* a large, self-service retail food store or market

**su·per·nal** (soo pur′n'l) *adj.* [< L. *supernus,* upper] celestial; heavenly

**su·per·nat·u·ral** (soo′pər nach′ər əl) *adj.* not explainable by known natural forces or laws; specif., of or involving God or ghosts, spirits, etc.

**su′per·nu′mer·ar′y** (-noo′mə rer′ē, -nyoo′-) *n., pl.* **-ies** [< L. *super,* above + *numerus,* number] **1.** an extra person or thing **2.** *Theater* a person with a small, nonspeaking part

**su′per·pose′** (-pōz′) *vt.* **-posed′, -pos′ing** [see SUPER- & POSE] to place on or over something else —**su′per·pos′a·ble** *adj.* —**su′per·po·si′tion** *n.*

**su′per·sat′u·rate′** *vt.* **-rat′ed, -rat′ing** to make more highly concentrated than in normal saturation —**su′per·sat′u·ra′tion** *n.*

**su′per·scribe′** (-skrīb′) *vt.* **-scribed′, -scrib′ing** [see SUPER- & SCRIBE] to write (something) at the top or on an outer surface of (something) —**su′per·scrip′tion** (-skrip′shən) *n.*

**su′per·script′** (-skript′) *n.* [see prec.] a figure, letter, or symbol written above and to the side of another

**su′per·sede′** (-sēd′) *vt.* **-sed′ed, -sed′ing** [< L. *supersedere,* sit over] to replace or succeed

**su′per·son′ic** (-sän′ik) *adj.* [SUPER- + SONIC] **1.** of or moving at a speed faster than that of sound **2.** ultrasonic

**su′per·star′** *n.* a star performer of topmost rank in sports or entertainment

**su·per·sti·tion** (sōō′pər stish′ən) n. [ < L. superstitio, lit., a standing (in awe) over] 1. any belief that is inconsistent with known facts or rational thought, esp. such a belief in omens, the supernatural, etc. 2. any action or practice based on such a belief —**su′per·sti′tious** adj.

**su′per·struc′ture** n. 1. a structure built on top of another, as above the main deck of a ship 2. that part of a building above the foundation

**su′per·tank′er** n. an extremely large oil tanker, of 300,000 tons or more

**su·per·vene** (sōō′pər vēn′) vi. -vened′, -ven′ing [ < L. super-, over + venire, come] to come or happen as something additional or unexpected

**su·per·vise** (sōō′pər vīz′) vt., vi. -vised′, -vis′ing [ < L. super-, over + videre, see] to oversee or direct (work, workers, etc.); superintend —**su′per·vi′sion** (-vizh′ən) n. —**su′per·vi′sor** n. —**su′per·vi′so·ry** adj.

**su·pine** (sōō pīn′) adj. [L. supinus] 1. lying on the back, face upward 2. inactive; sluggish; listless

**supp., suppl.** supplement

**sup·per** (sup′ər) n. [see SUP] an evening meal

**supper club** an expensive nightclub

**sup·plant** (sə plant′) vt. [ < L. sub-, under + planta, sole of the foot] 1. to take the place of, esp. by force or plotting 2. to remove in order to replace with something else

**sup·ple** (sup′'l) adj. [ < L. supplex, submissive] 1. easily bent; flexible 2. lithe; limber 3. easily influenced 4. adaptable: said of the mind, etc.

**sup·ple·ment** (sup′lə mənt; for v. -ment′) n. [see SUPPLY] 1. something added, esp. to make up for a lack 2. a section of additional material in a book, newspaper, etc. —vt. to provide a supplement to —**sup′ple·men′ta·ry, sup′ple·men′tal** adj.

**sup·pli·ant** (sup′lē ənt) n. one who supplicates —adj. supplicating Also **sup′pli·cant** (-lə kənt)

**sup·pli·cate** (sup′lə kāt′) vt., vi. -cat′ed, -cat′ing [ < L. sub-, under + plicare, to fold] 1. to ask for (something) humbly 2. to make a humble request (of) —**sup′pli·ca′tion** n.

**sup·ply** (sə plī′) vt. -plied′, -ply′ing [ < L. sub-, under + plere, fill] 1. to furnish or provide (what is needed) to (someone) 2. to compensate for (a deficiency, etc.) —n., pl. -plies′ 1. the amount available for use or sale; stock 2. [pl.] needed materials, provisions, etc. —**sup·pli′er** n.

**sup·port** (sə pôrt′) vt. [ < L. sub-, under + portare, carry] 1. to carry the weight of; hold up 2. to encourage; help 3. to advocate; uphold 4. to maintain (a person, institution, etc.) with money or subsistence 5. to help prove, vindicate, etc. 6. to bear; endure 7. to keep up; maintain 8. to have a role subordinate to (a star) in a play —n. 1. a supporting or being supported 2. a person or thing that supports 3. a means of support —**support′a·ble** adj. —**sup·port′er** n.

**sup·port′ive** adj. giving support or help

**sup·pose** (sə pōz′) vt. -posed′, -pos′ing [ < L. sub-, under + ponere, put] 1. to assume to be true, as for argument's sake 2. to imagine, think, etc. 3. to consider as a possibility [suppose I go] 4. to expect [I'm supposed to sing] —vi. to conjecture —**sup·posed′** adj. —**sup·pos′ed·ly** adv.

**sup·po·si·tion** (sup′ə zish′ən) n. 1. a supposing 2. something supposed

**sup·pos·i·to·ry** (sə päz′ə tôr′ē) n., pl. -ries [see SUPPOSE] a small piece of medicated substance, placed in the rectum, vagina, etc. where it melts

**sup·press** (sə pres′) vt. [ < L. sub-, under + premere, to press] 1. to put down by force; quell 2. to keep from being known, published, etc. 3. to keep back; restrain 4. Psychiatry to consciously dismiss from the mind —**sup·pres′sion** (-presh′ən) n.

**sup·pu·rate** (sup′yoo rāt′) vi. -rat′ed, -rat′ing [ < L. sub-, under + pus, pus] to form or discharge pus

**supra-** [ < L. supra, above] a prefix meaning above, over, beyond

**su·pra·na·tion·al** (sōō′prə nash′ə-n'l) adj. of, for, or above all or a number of nations [supranational authority]

**su·prem·a·cist** (sə prem′ə sist, soo-) n. one who believes in the supremacy of a particular group

**su·prem·a·cy** (-sē) n., pl. -cies supreme condition or power

**su·preme** (sə prēm′, soo-) adj. [ < L. superus, that is above] 1. highest in rank, power, etc. 2. highest in quality, achievement, etc. 3. highest in degree 4. final; ultimate —**su·preme′ly** adv.

**Supreme Being** God

**Supreme Court** 1. the highest Federal court 2. the highest court in most States

**Supreme Soviet** the parliament of the Soviet Union

**Supt., supt.** Superintendent

**sur-¹** [ < L. super, over] a prefix meaning over, upon, above, beyond

**sur-²** same as SUB-: used before r

**sur·cease** (sur′sēs) n. [ < L. supersedere, refrain from] an end, or cessation

**sur·charge** (sur′chärj; also, for v., sur chärj′) vt. -charged′, -charg′ing [see SUR-¹ & CHARGE] 1. to overcharge 2. to mark (a postage stamp) with a surcharge —n. 1. an additional charge 2. a new valuation printed over the original valuation on a postage stamp

**sur·cin·gle** (sur′sin′g'l) n. [ < MFr. sur-, over + L. cingulum, a belt] a strap passed around a horse's body to bind on a saddle, pack, etc.

**sure** (shoor) adj. sur′er, sur′est [ < L. securus] 1. that will not fail [a sure method] 2. that cannot be doubted or questioned **3.** having no doubt; confident *[sure* of the facts*]* **4.** bound to be or happen *[a sure defeat]* **5.** bound (to do, be, etc.) *[sure to lose]* —*adv.* [Colloq.] surely —**for sure** certain(ly) —**sure enough** [Colloq.] without doubt —**sure'ness** *n.*

**sure'-fire'** (-fīr') *adj.* [Colloq.] sure to be successful or as expected

**sure'-foot'ed** *adj.* not likely to stumble, slip, fall, or err

**sure'ly** *adv.* **1.** with confidence **2.** without a doubt; certainly

**sur·e·ty** (shoor'ə tē, shoor'tē) *n., pl.* **-ties 1.** a being sure **2.** something that gives assurance, as against loss, etc. **3.** one who makes himself responsible for another

**surf** (surf) *n.* [prob. < *sough*, rustle] the waves of the sea breaking on the shore or a reef —*vi.* to engage in surfing —**surf'er** *n.*

**sur·face** (sur'fis) *n.* [< Fr. *sur-*, over + *face*, a face] **1.** *a)* the exterior or an object *b)* any of the faces of a solid **2.** superficial features —*adj.* **1.** of, on, or at the surface **2.** external; superficial —*vt.* **-faced, -fac·ing** to give a surface to, as in paving —*vi.* to rise to the surface of the water

**surf'board'** *n.* a long, narrow board used in the sport of surfing

**sur·feit** (sur'fit) *n.* [< OFr. *sur-*, over + *faire*, make] **1.** too great an amount **2.** overindulgence, esp. in food or drink **3.** disgust, nausea, etc. resulting from excess —*vt.* to feed or supply to excess

**surf·ing** (sur'fiŋ) *n.* the sport of riding in toward shore on the crest of a wave, esp. on a surfboard

**surge** (surj) *n.* [< L. *surgere*, to rise] **1.** a large wave of water, or its motion **2.** a sudden, strong increase, as of power —*vi.* **surged, surg'ing** to move in or as in a surge

**sur·geon** (sur'jən) *n.* a doctor who specializes in surgery

**sur·ger·y** (sur'jər ē) *n., pl.* **-ies** [< Gr. *cheir*, the hand + *ergein*, to work] **1.** the treatment of disease, injury, etc. by manual or instrumental operations **2.** the operating room of a surgeon or hospital

**sur'gi·cal** (-ji k'l) *adj.* of surgeons or surgery —**sur'gi·cal·ly** *adv.*

**Su·ri·nam** (soor'i näm') country in NE S. America: 55,144 sq. mi.; pop. 385,000

**sur·ly** (sur'lē) *adj.* **-li·er, -li·est** [earlier *sirly*, imperious < *sir*, sir] bad-tempered; sullenly rude; uncivil

**sur·mise** (sər mīz') *n.* [< OFr. *sur-*, upon + *mettre*, put] a conjecture —*vt., vi.* **-mised', -mis'ing** to guess

**sur·mount** (sər mount') *vt.* [SUR-¹ + MOUNT²] **1.** to overcome (a difficulty) **2.** to be at the top of; rise above **3.** to climb up and across (a height, etc.) —**sur·mount'a·ble** *adj.*

**sur·name** (sur'nām') *n.* [< OFr. *sur-* (see SUR-¹) + *nom*, name] the family name, or last name

**sur·pass** (sər pas') *vt.* [< MFr. *sur-* (see SUR-¹) + *passer*, to pass] **1.** to excel or be superior to **2.** to go beyond the limit, capacity, etc. of

**sur·plice** (sur'plis) *n.* [< L. *super-*, above + *pelliceum*, fur robe] a loose, white outer vestment worn by the clergy and choir in some churches

SURPLICE

**sur·plus** (sur'plus) *n.* [< OFr. < *sur-* (see SUR-¹) + L. *plus*, more] a quantity over and above what is needed or used —*adj.* forming a surplus

**sur·prise** (sər prīz') *vt.* **-prised', -pris'ing** [< OFr. *sur-* (see SUR-¹) + *prendre*, to take] **1.** to come upon suddenly or unexpectedly; take unawares **2.** to attack without warning **3.** to amaze; astonish —*n.* **1.** a being surprised **2.** something that surprises

**sur·re·al** (sə rē'əl, -rēl') *adj.* **1.** surrealistic **2.** bizarre; fantastic

**sur·re·al·ism** (sə rē'ə liz'm) *n.* [see SUR-¹ & REAL] a modern movement in the arts, trying to depict the workings of the unconscious mind —**sur·re'al·ist** *adj., n.* —**sur·re'al·is'tic** *adj.*

**sur·ren·der** (sə ren'dər) *vt.* [< MFr. *sur-*, up + *rendre*, render] **1.** to give up possession of; yield to another on compulsion **2.** to give up or abandon —*vi.* to give oneself up, esp. as a prisoner —*n.* the act of surrendering

**sur·rep·ti·tious** (sur'əp tish'əs) *adj.* [< L. *sub-*, under + *rapere*, seize] done, got, acting, etc. in a stealthy way

**sur·rey** (sur'ē) *n., pl.* **-reys** [< *Surrey*, county in England] a light, four-wheeled carriage with two seats

**sur·ro·gate** (sur'ə gāt', -git) *n.* [< L. *sub-*, in place of + *rogare*, elect] **1.** a deputy or substitute **2.** in some States, a probate court judge

**sur·round** (sə round') *vt.* [< L. *super-*, over + *undare*, to rise] to encircle on all or nearly all sides

**sur·round'ings** *n.pl.* the things, conditions, etc. around a person or thing

**sur·tax** (sur'taks') *n.* an extra tax on top of the regular tax

**sur·veil·lance** (sər vāl'əns) *n.* [Fr. < *sur-* (see SUR-¹) + *veiller*, to watch] watch kept over a person, esp. a suspect

**sur·vey** (sər vā'; *for n.* sur'vā) *vt.* [< OFr. *sur-* (see SUR-¹) + *veoir*, see] **1.** to examine or consider in detail or comprehensively **2.** to determine the location, form, or boundaries of (a tract of land) —*n., pl.* **-veys 1.** a detailed study, as by gathering information and analyzing it **2.** a general view **3.** *a)* the process of surveying an area *b)* a written description of the area —**sur·vey'or** *n.*

**sur·vey'ing** *n.* the science or work of making land surveys

**sur·vive** (sər vīv') *vt.* **-vived', -viv'ing** [< L. *super-*, above + *vivere*, to live] to remain alive or in existence after —*vi.* to continue living or existing —**sur·viv'al** *n.* —**sur·vi'vor** *n.*

**sus·cep·ti·ble** (sə sep'tə b'l) *adj.* [<

L. *sus-*, under + *capere*, take] easily affected emotionally —**susceptible of** admitting; allowing [taking *susceptible of* error] —**susceptible to** easily influenced or affected by —**sus·cep'ti·bil'i·ty** *n.*

**sus·pect** (sə spekt'; *for adj. & n.* sus'pekt) *vt.* [< L. *sus-*, under + *spicere*, to look] 1. to believe to be guilty on little or no evidence 2. to believe to be bad, wrong, etc.; distrust 3. to guess; surmise —*adj.* suspected —*n.* one suspected of a crime, etc.

**sus·pend** (sə spend') *vt.* [< L. *sus-*, under + *pendere*, hang] 1. to exclude for a time from an office, school, etc. as a penalty 2. to make inoperative for a time 3. to hold back (judgment, etc.) 4. to hang by a support from above 5. to hold (dust in the air, etc.) without attachment —*vi.* to stop temporarily

**sus·pend'ers** *n.pl.* 1. a pair of straps passed over the shoulders to hold up the trousers 2. [Brit.] garters

**sus·pense** (sə spens') *n.* [< L. *suspendere*, suspend] 1. a state of uncertainty 2. the growing excitement felt while awaiting a climax of a play, etc. —**sus·pense'ful** *adj.*

**sus·pen·sion** (sə spen'shən) *n.* 1. a suspending or being suspended 2. a supporting device upon or from which something is suspended

**suspension bridge** a bridge suspended from cables anchored at either end and supported by towers at intervals

**sus·pi·cion** (sə spish'ən) *n.* [< L. *suspicere*, to suspect] 1. a suspecting or being suspected 2. the feeling or state of mind of one who suspects 3. a very small amount; trace —*vt.* [Dial.] to suspect

**sus·pi·cious** *adj.* 1. arousing suspicion 2. showing or feeling suspicion —**sus·pi'cious·ly** *adv.*

**sus·tain** (sə stān') *vt.* [< L. *sus-*, under + *tenere*, to hold] 1. to keep in existence; maintain or prolong 2. to provide sustenance for 3. to carry the weight of; support 4. to endure; withstand 5. to suffer (an injury, loss, etc.) 6. to uphold the validity of 7. to confirm; corroborate

**sus·te·nance** (sus'ti nəns) *n.* 1. a sustaining 2. means of livelihood 3. that which sustains life; food

**sut·ler** (sut'lər) *n.* [< Early ModDu.] a person who followed an army to sell things to its soldiers

**su·ture** (sōō'chər) *n.* [< L. *suere*, sew] 1. the line of junction of two parts, esp. of bones of the skull 2. *a*) the stitching together of the two edges of a wound or incision *b*) the thread, etc., or any of the stitches so used

**su·ze·rain** (sōō'zə rin, -rān') *n.* [Fr. < L. *sursum*, above] 1. a feudal lord 2. a state in relation to another over which it has some political control —**su'ze·rain·ty** *n.*

**svelte** (svelt) *adj.* [Fr.] 1. slender; lithe 2. suave

**SW, S.W., s.w.** 1. southwest 2. southwestern

**Sw.** 1. Sweden 2. Swedish

**swab** (swäb) *n.* [< Du. *zwabben*, do dirty work] 1. a mop 2. a small piece of cotton, etc. used to medicate or clean the throat, mouth, etc. —*vt.* swabbed, swab'bing to use a swab on

**swad·dle** (swäd'l) *vt.* -dled, -dling [prob. < OE. *swathian*, swathe] formerly, to wrap (a newborn baby) in long, narrow bands of cloth

**swag** (swag) *vt.* swagged, swag'ging [see ff.] to hang in a swag —*n.* 1. a valance, garland, etc. hanging decoratively in a curve 2. [Slang] loot

**swage** (swāj) *n.* [< OFr.] a tool for shaping or bending metal —*vt.* swaged, -swag'ing to shape, bend, etc. with a swage

**swag·ger** (swag'ər) *vi.* [prob. < Norw. *svagga*, sway] 1. to walk with a bold, arrogant stride 2. to boast or brag loudly —*n.* swaggering walk or manner

**Swa·hi·li** (swä hē'lē) *n.* [< Ar. *sawāhil*, the coasts] a Bantu language of the east coast of Africa

**swain** (swān) *n.* [< ON. *sveinn*, boy] [Poet.] 1. a country youth 2. a lover

**swal·low¹** (swäl'ō) *n.* [OE. *swealwe*] a small, swift-flying bird with long, pointed wings and a forked tail

**swal·low²** (swäl'ō) *vt.* [OE. *swelgan*] 1. to pass (food, etc.) from the mouth into the stomach 2. to absorb (often with *up*) 3. to retract (words said) 4. to put up with [to *swallow* insults] 5. to suppress [to *swallow* one's pride] 6. [Colloq.] to accept as true without question —*vi.* to perform the actions of swallowing something, esp. as in emotion —*n.* 1. a swallowing 2. the amount swallowed at one time

BARN SWALLOW

**swal·low-tailed' coat** *same as* CUTAWAY: also **swal'low-tail'** *n.*

**swam** (swam) *pt.* of SWIM

**swa·mi** (swä'mē) *n., pl.* -mis [< Sans. *svāmin*, a lord] a Hindu religious teacher, pundit, or seer

**swamp** (swämp, swômp) *n.* [prob. < LowG.] a piece of wet, spongy land; bog; marsh —*vt.* 1. to plunge in a swamp, water, etc. 2. to flood as with water 3. to overwhelm [*swamped* by debts] 4. to sink (a boat) by filling with water —**swamp'y** *adj.*

**swamp buggy** a vehicle for traveling over swampy land, often amphibious

**swamp fever** *same as* MALARIA

**swan** (swän, swôn) *n.* [OE.] a large, web-footed water bird, usually white, with a long, graceful neck

**swank** (swank) *n.* [akin to OE. *swancor*, pliant] [Colloq.] ostentatious display

—*adj.* [Colloq.] ostentatiously stylish: also **swank'y, -i·er, -i·est**

**swan's'-down'** *n.* **1.** the soft down of the swan, used for trimming clothes, etc. **2.** a soft, thick flannel Also **swans/down'**

**swan song** [after the song sung, in ancient fable, by a dying swan] the last act, final work, etc. of a person

**swap** (swäp, swôp) *n., vt., vi.* **swapped, swap'ping** [ME. *swappen*, to strike] [Colloq.] trade; barter

**sward** (swôrd) *n.* [< OE. *sweard*, a skin] grass-covered soil; turf

**swarm** (swôrm) *n.* [OE. *swearm*] **1.** a large number of bees, with a queen, leaving a hive to start a new colony **2.** a colony of bees in a hive **3.** a moving mass, crowd, or throng —*vi.* **1.** to fly off in a swarm: said of bees **2.** to move, be present, etc. in large numbers **3.** to be crowded

**swart** (swôrt) *adj. same as* SWARTHY

**swarth·y** (swôr'*th*ē, -*th*ē) *adj.* **-i·er, -i·est** [< OE. *sweart*] dark-skinned

**swash** (swäsh, swôsh) *vi.* [echoic] to dash, strike, etc. with a splash

**swash'buck'ler** (-buk'lər) *n.* [< *swash*, to swagger + *buckler*, a shield] a blustering, swaggering fighting man —**swash'buck'ling** *n., adj.*

**swas·ti·ka** (swäs'ti kə) *n.* [< Sans. *svasti*, well-being] **1.** an ancient design in the form of a cross with arms of equal length bent in a right angle **2.** this design with the arms bent clockwise: used as a Nazi emblem

**swat** (swät) *vt.* **swat'ted, swat'ting** [echoic] [Colloq.] to hit with a quick, sharp blow —*n.* [Colloq.] a quick, sharp blow —**swat'ter** *n.*

**swatch** (swäch) *n.* [orig., a cloth tally] a sample piece of cloth, etc.

**swath** (swäth, swôth) *n.* [OE. *swathu*, a track] **1.** the width covered by one cut of a scythe or other mowing device **2.** a strip, row, etc. mowed

**swathe** (swā*th*) *vt.* **swathed, swath'ing** [OE. *swathian*] **1.** to wrap up in a bandage **2.** to envelop; enclose

**sway** (swā) *vi.* [< ON. *sveigja*] **1.** to swing or move from side to side or to and fro **2.** to lean to one side; veer **3.** to incline in judgment or opinion —*vt.* **1.** to cause to sway **2.** to influence or divert [*swayed* by promises] —*n.* **1.** a swaying or being swayed **2.** influence; control [the *sway* of lust]

**sway'backed'** (-bakt') *adj.* having an abnormal sagging of the spine, as some horses, etc.

**Swa·zi·land** (swä'zē land') country in SE Africa: 6,705 sq. mi.; pop. 375,000

**swear** (swer) *vi.* **swore, sworn, swear'ing** [OE. *swerian*] **1.** to make a solemn declaration with an appeal to God to confirm it **2.** to make a solemn promise; vow **3.** to use profane language; curse —*vt.* **1.** to declare, pledge, or vow on oath **2.** to administer a legal oath to —**swear off** to renounce —**swear out** to obtain (a warrant for arrest) by making a charge under oath —**swear'er** *n.*

**swear'word'** *n.* a profane or obscene word or phrase

**sweat** (swet) *vi., vt.* **sweat or sweat'ed, sweat'ing** [OE. *swat*, sweat] **1.** to give forth or cause to give forth a salty moisture through the pores of the skin; perspire **2.** to give forth or condense (moisture) on its surface **3.** to work hard enough to cause sweating —*n.* **1.** the salty liquid given forth in perspiration **2.** moisture collected in droplets on a surface **3.** a sweating or being sweated **4.** a condition of eagerness, anxiety, etc. —**sweat out** [Slang] to wait anxiously for or through —**sweat'y** *adj.* **-i·er, -i·est**

**sweat'er** *n.* a knitted or crocheted outer garment for the upper body

**sweat shirt** a heavy cotton jersey worn to absorb sweat, as after exercise

**sweat'shop'** *n.* a shop where employees work long hours at low wages under poor working conditions

**Swed.** **1.** Sweden **2.** Swedish

**Swede** (swēd) *n.* a native or inhabitant of Sweden

**Swe·den** (swē'd'n) country in N Europe: 173,620 sq. mi.; pop. 7,869,000; cap. Stockholm

**Swed·ish** (swē'dish) *adj.* of Sweden, its people, language, etc. —*n.* the Germanic language of the Swedes

**sweep** (swēp) *vt.* **swept, sweep'ing** [OE. *swapan*] **1.** to clean (a floor, etc.) as by brushing with a broom **2.** to remove (dirt, etc.) as with a broom **3.** to strip, carry away, or destroy with a forceful movement **4.** to touch in moving across [hands *sweeping* the keyboard] **5.** to pass swiftly over or across **6.** to win overwhelmingly —*vi.* **1.** to clean a floor, etc. as with a broom **2.** to move steadily with speed, force, or gracefulness **3.** to extend in a long curve or line [a road *sweeping* up the hill] —*n.* **1.** the act of sweeping **2.** a steady, sweeping movement **3.** range or scope **4.** extent, as of land; stretch **5.** a line, curve, etc. that seems to flow or move **6.** one whose work is sweeping —**sweep'er** *n.* —**sweep'ing** *adj.* —**sweep'ing·ly** *adv.*

**sweep'ings** *n.pl.* things swept up, as dirt from a floor

**sweep'stakes'** *n., pl.* **-stakes'** a lottery in which each participant puts up money in a common fund which is given as a prize to the winner or winners of a horse race or other contest

**sweet** (swēt) *adj.* [OE. *swete*] **1.** having a taste of, or like that of, sugar **2.** *a)* agreeable in taste, smell, sound, etc. *b)* gratifying *c)* friendly, kind, etc. **3.** *a)* not rancid or sour *b)* not salty or salted —*n.* a sweet food —**sweet'ish** *adj.* —**sweet'ly** *adv.* —**sweet'ness** *n.*

**sweet'bread'** (-bred') *n.* the thymus or sometimes the pancreas of a calf, lamb, etc., when used as food

**sweet'bri'er, sweet'bri'ar** (-brī'ər) *n. same as* EGLANTINE

**sweet corn** a variety of Indian corn eaten unripe as a table vegetable

**sweet'en** *vt.* **1.** to make sweet **2.** to make pleasant or agreeable

**sweet'en·er** *n.* a sweetening agent, esp. a synthetic one, as saccharin

**sweet'heart'** *n.* a loved one; lover

**sweetheart contract** a contract arranged by collusion between union officials and an employer without consulting the union membership

**sweet'meat'** n. a candy

**sweet pea** a climbing plant with variously colored, fragrant flowers

**sweet pepper** 1. a red pepper producing a large, mild fruit 2. the fruit

**sweet potato** 1. a tropical, trailing plant with a large, fleshy, orange root used as a vegetable 2. its root

**sweet'-talk'** vt., vi. [Colloq.] one who to flatter

**sweet tooth** [Colloq.] a fondness or craving for sweets

**swell** (swel) vi., vt. **swelled, swelled** or **swol'len, swell'ing** [OE. swellan] 1. to expand as a result of pressure from within 2. to curve out; bulge 3. to fill (with pride, etc.) 4. to increase in size, force, intensity, etc. —n. 1. a part that swells; specif., a large, rolling wave 2. an increase in size, amount, degree, etc. 3. a crescendo 4. [Colloq.] one who is strikingly stylish —adj. 1. [Colloq.] stylish 2. [Slang] excellent

**swell'head'** n. a conceited person

**swell'ing** n. 1. an increase in size, volume, etc. 2. a swollen part

**swel·ter** (swel'tər) vi. [< OE. sweltan, to die] to be oppressed by great heat

**swel'ter·ing** adj. very hot; sultry

**swept** (swept) pt. & pp. of SWEEP

**swept'back'** adj. having a backward slant, as the wings of an aircraft

**swerve** (swurv) vi., vt. **swerved, swerv'ing** [< OE. sweorfan, to scour] to turn aside from a straight line, course, etc. —n. a swerving

**swift** (swift) adj. [OE.] 1. moving with great speed; fast 2. coming, acting, etc. quickly —n. a swift-flying bird resembling the swallow —**swift'ly** adv. —**swift'ness** n.

**Swift** (swift), **Jonathan** 1667-1745; Eng. satirist, born in Ireland

**swig** (swig) vt., vi. **swigged, swig'ging** [< ?] [Colloq.] to drink in gulps —n. [Colloq.] a deep draft, as of liquor

**swill** (swil) vt., vi. [OE. swilian, wash] 1. to drink greedily 2. to feed swill to (pigs, etc.) —n. 1. liquid garbage fed to pigs 2. garbage

**swim¹** (swim) vi. **swam, swum, swim'ming** [OE. swimman] 1. to move through water by moving arms, legs, fins, etc. 2. to move along smoothly 3. to float on or in a liquid 4. to overflow [eyes swimming with tears] —vt. to swim in or across —n. the act of swimming —**in the swim** active in, or conforming to, current fashions, etc. —**swim'mer** n.

**swim²** (swim) n. [OE. swima] a dizzy spell —vi. **swam, swum, swim'ming** to be dizzy

**swimming hole** a deep place in a river, creek, etc. used for swimming

**swim'suit'** (-sōōt') n. a garment worn for swimming

**swin·dle** (swin'd'l) vt., vi. **-dled, -dling** [< G. schwindeln] to defraud

(another) of money or property; cheat —n. an act of swindling; trick; fraud —**swin'dler** n.

**swine** (swīn) n., pl. **swine** [OE. swin] 1. a pig or hog: usually used collectively 2. a vicious, contemptible person —**swin'ish** adj.

**swing** (swiŋ) vi., vt. **swung, swing'ing** [OE. swingan] 1. to sway or move backward and forward 2. to walk, trot, etc. with relaxed movements 3. to strike (at) 4. to turn, as on a hinge 5. to hang; be suspended 6. to move in a curve [swing the car around] 7. [Colloq.] to cause to come about successfully [to swing an election] 8. [Slang] to be ultra-fashionable, esp. in seeking pleasure —n. 1. a swinging 2. the arc through which something swings 3. the manner of swinging a golf club, etc. 4. a relaxed motion, as in walking 5. a sweeping blow or stroke 6. the course of some activity 7. rhythm, as of music 8. a seat hanging from ropes, etc., on which one can swing 9. a trip or tour 10. jazz music (c. 1935-45) characterized by large bands, strong rhythms, etc.

**swing'er** n. 1. one that swings 2. [Slang] a person who swings (vi. 8)

**swing shift** [Colloq.] a work shift from midafternoon to about midnight

**swipe** (swīp) n. [prob. var. of SWEEP] [Colloq.] a hard, sweeping blow —vt. **swiped, swip'ing** 1. [Colloq.] to hit with a swipe 2. [Slang] to steal

**swirl** (swurl) vi., vt. [ME. swyrl] to move or cause to move with a whirling motion —n. 1. a whirl; eddy 2. a twist; curl —**swirl'y** adj.

**swish** (swish) vi., vt. [echoic] 1. to move with a sharp, hissing sound, as a cane swung through the air 2. to rustle, as skirts —n. a swishing sound or movement

**Swiss** (swis) adj. of Switzerland, its people, etc. —n., pl. **Swiss** a native or inhabitant of Switzerland

**Swiss chard** same as CHARD

**Swiss (cheese)** a pale-yellow, hard cheese with many large holes

**Swiss steak** a thick cut of round steak pounded with flour and braised

**switch** (swich) n. [Early ModE. swits] 1. a thin, flexible stick used for whipping 2. a sharp lash, as with a whip 3. a device used to open, close, or divert an electric circuit 4. a device used in transferring a train from one track to another 5. a shift; change 6. a tress of detached hair, often used as part of a coiffure —vt. 1. to whip as with a switch 2. to jerk sharply 3. to shift; change 4. to turn (an electric light, etc.) on or off 5. to transfer (a train, etc.) to another track 6. [Colloq.] to change or exchange —vi. to shift —**switch'er** n.

**switch'back'** n. a road or railroad following a zigzag course up a steep grade

**switch'-blade' knife** a large jack-

knife that snaps open when a release
button on the handle is pressed

**switch'board'** (-bôrd') *n.* a panel for
controlling a system of electric circuits,
as in a telephone exchange

**switch'-hit'ter** *n.* a baseball player
who bats right-handed or left-handed

**Switz·er·land** (swit'sər lənd) country in WC Europe: 15,941 sq. mi.;
pop. 6,036,000; cap. Bern

**swiv·el** (swiv''l) *n.* [< OE. *swifan*,
to revolve] a coupling device that
allows free turning of the parts attached to it —*vi.*, *vt.* **-eled** or **-elled,
-el·ing** or **-el·ling** to turn or cause
to turn as on a swivel or pivot

**swiz·zle stick** (swiz''l) [< ?] a small
rod for stirring mixed drinks

**swob** (swäb) *n., vt.* **swobbed, swob'-
bing** *var. sp. of* SWAB

**swol·len** (swō'lən) *alt. pp. of* SWELL
—*adj.* blown up; distended; bulging

**swoon** (swo͞on) *vi., n.* [< OE. *geswogen*,
unconscious] *same as* FAINT

**swoop** (swo͞op) *vi.* [< OE. *swapan*,
sweep along] to pounce or sweep
(*down* or *upon*), as a bird in hunting
—*n.* the act of swooping

**swop** (swäp) *n., vt., vi.* **swopped,
swop'ping** *var. sp. of* SWAP

**sword** (sôrd) *n.* [OE. *sweord*] a hand
weapon with a long, sharp-pointed
blade set in a hilt —**at swords' points**
ready to quarrel or fight

**sword'fish'** *n., pl.:* see FISH a large
marine food fish
with the upper
jawbone extend-
ing in a swordlike
point

**sword'play'**
(-plā') *n.* the act
or skill of using
a sword, as in
fencing

**swords'man**
(-mən) *n., pl.*
**-men** 1. one who
uses a sword in
fencing or fight-
ing 2. one skilled
in using a sword

SWORDFISH

**swore** (swôr) *pt. of* SWEAR

**sworn** (swôrn) *pp. of* SWEAR —*adj.*
bound, pledged, etc. by an oath

**swum** (swum) *pp. of* SWIM

**swung** (swung) *pp. & pt. of* SWING

**syb·a·rite** (sib'ə rīt') *n.* [< *Sybaris*,
ancient Gr. city in Italy] anyone very
fond of luxury and pleasure —**syb'a·
rit'ic** (-rit'ik) *adj.*

**syc·a·more** (sik'ə môr') *n.* [< Gr.
*sykomoros*] 1. a maple tree of Europe
and Asia 2. an American tree with
bark that sheds in patches

**syc·o·phant** (sik'ə fənt) *n.* [< Gr.
*sykophantēs*, informer] one who seeks
favor by flattering people of wealth
or influence —**syc'o·phan·cy** *n.*

**Syd·ney** (sid'nē) seaport in SE Australia: pop. 2,431,000

**syl·lab·i·cate** (si lab'ə kāt') *vt.*
**-cat'ed, -cat'ing** *same as* SYLLABIFY
—**syl·lab'i·ca'tion** *n.*

**syl·lab·i·fy** (si lab'ə fī') *vt.* **-fied',
-fy'ing** [< L. *syllaba*, syllable +

*facere*, make] to form or divide into
syllables —**syl·lab'i·fi·ca'tion** *n.*

**syl·la·ble** (sil'ə b'l) *n.* [< Gr. *syn-*,
together + *lambanein*, to hold] 1. a
word or part of a word pronounced
with a single, uninterrupted sounding
of the voice 2. one or more letters
written to represent a spoken syllable
—**syl·lab·ic** (si lab'ik) *adj.*

**syl·la·bus** (sil'ə bəs) *n., pl.* **-bus·es,
-bi'** (-bī') [< Gr. *sillybos*, parchment
label] a summary or outline, esp. of
a course of study

**syl·lo·gism** (sil'ə jiz'm) *n.* [< Gr.
*syn-*, together + *logizesthai*, to reason]
a form of reasoning in which two
premises are made and a logical conclusion drawn from them

**sylph** (silf) *n.* [ModL. *sylphus*, a
spirit] 1. any of a class of imaginary
beings supposed to inhabit the air
2. a slender, graceful woman or girl

**syl·van** (sil'vən) *adj.* [< L. *silva*, a
wood] 1. of, characteristic of, or living
in the woods or forest 2. wooded

**sym·bi·o·sis** (sim'bī ō'sis, -bē-) *n.*
[< Gr. *symbioun*, to live together] the
living together of two kinds of organisms to their mutual advantage —
**sym'bi·ot'ic** (-ät'ik) *adj.*

**sym·bol** (sim'b'l) *n.* [< Gr. *syn-*,
together + *ballein*, to throw] 1. an
object used to represent something
abstract [the dove is a *symbol* of peace]
2. a mark, letter, etc. standing for a
quality, process, etc., as in music
or chemistry —**sym·bol·ic** (-bäl'ik),
**sym·bol'i·cal** *adj.* —**sym·bol'i·cal·
ly** *adv.*

**sym·bol·ism** (sim'b'l iz'm) *n.* 1. representation by symbols 2. a system of
symbols 3. a symbolic meaning

**sym'bol·ize'** *vt.* **-ized', -iz'ing** 1.
to be a symbol of; stand for 2. to
represent by a symbol or symbols

**sym·me·try** (sim'ə trē) *n., pl.* **-tries**
[< Gr. *syn-*, together + *metron*, a
measure] 1. correspondence of opposite parts in size, shape, and position
2. balance or beauty of form resulting
from this —**sym·met·ri·cal** (si met'
ri k'l) *adj.* —**sym·met'ri·cal·ly** *adv.*

**sym·pa·thet·ic** (sim'pə thet'ik) *adj.*
1. of, feeling, or showing sympathy
2. in agreement with one's tastes,
mood, etc. —**sym'pa·thet'i·cal·ly**
*adv.*

**sym'pa·thize'** (-thīz') *vi.* **-thized',
-thiz'ing** 1. to share the feelings or
ideas of another 2. to feel or express
sympathy —**sym'pa·thiz'er** *n.*

**sym·pa·thy** (sim'pə thē) *n., pl.* **-thies**
[< Gr. *syn-*, together + *pathos*, feeling]
1. sameness of feeling 2. agreement in
qualities; accord 3. mutual liking or
understanding 4. ability to share
another's ideas, emotions, etc.; esp.,
pity or compassion

**sym·pho·ny** (sim'fə nē) *n., pl.* **-nies**
[< Gr. *syn-*, together + *phōnē*, sound]
1. harmony, as of sounds, color, etc.
2. an extended musical composition in
several movements, for full orchestra
3. a large orchestra for playing sym-
phonic works: in full **symphony
orchestra** 4. [Colloq.] a symphony

concert —**sym·phon′ic** (-fän′ik) *adj.*

**sym·po·si·um** (sim pō′zē əm) *n., pl.* **-si·ums, -si·a** (-ə) [< Gr. *syn-*, together + *posis*, a drinking] 1. a conference for discussing some subject 2. a collection of opinions on some subject

**symp·tom** (simp′təm) *n.* [< Gr. *syn-*, together + *piptein*, to fall] any circumstance or condition that indicates the existence of something, esp. of a particular disease —**symp′to·mat′ic** (-tə mat′ik) *adj.*

**symp·tom·a·tize′** (-tə mə tīz′) *vt.* **-tized′, -tiz′ing** to be a symptom or sign of: also **symp′tom·ize′**

**syn-** [Gr.] *a prefix meaning* with, together with, at the same time

**syn.** 1. synonym 2. synonymy

**syn·a·gogue** (sin′ə gäg′, -gôg′) *n.* [< Gr. *syn-*, together + *agein*, bring] 1. an assembly of Jews for worship and religious study 2. a building or place for such assembly —**syn′a·gog′al** *adj.*

**syn·apse** (si naps′) *n.* [< Gr. *syn-*, together + *apsis*, a joining] the point of contact where nerve impulses are transmitted from one neuron to another

**sync, synch** (siŋk) *vt., vi.* *clipped form of* SYNCHRONIZE —*n.* *clipped form of* SYNCHRONIZATION

**syn·chro·nize** (siŋ′krə nīz′) *vi.* **-nized′, -niz′ing** [< Gr. *syn-*, together + *chronos*, time] to move or occur at the same time or rate —*vt.* to cause to agree in time or rate of speed

**syn′chro·nous** *adj.* happening at the same time or at the same rate

**syn·co·pate** (siŋ′kə pāt′) *vt.* **-pat′ed, -pat′ing** [< Gr. *syn-*, together + *koptein*, cut] *Music* to begin (a tone) on an unaccented beat and continue it through the next accented beat —**syn′co·pa′tion** *n.*

**syn·di·cate** (sin′də kit; *for v.* -kāt′) *n.* [< Gr. *syn-*, together + *dikē*, justice] 1. an association of individuals or corporations formed for a project requiring much capital 2. any group, as of criminals, organized for some undertaking 3. an organization selling articles or features to many newspapers, etc. —*vt.* **-cat′ed, -cat′ing** 1. to manage as or form into a syndicate 2. to sell (an article, etc.) through a syndicate —*vi.* to form a syndicate —**syn′di·ca′tion** *n.*

**syn·drome** (sin′drōm) *n.* [< Gr. *syn-*, with + *dramein*, run] a set of symptoms characterizing a disease or condition

**syn·er·gism** (sin′ər jiz′m) *n.* [< Gr. *syn-*, together + *ergon*, work] combined action, as of several drugs, greater in total effect than the sum of their effects —**syn′er·gis′tic** *adj.*

**syn·od** (sin′əd) *n.* [< Gr. *syn-*, together + *hodos*, way] 1. a council of churches or church officials 2. any council

**syn·o·nym** (sin′ə nim) *n.* [< Gr. *syn-*, together + *onyma*, name] a word having the same or nearly the same meaning

as another in the same language —**syn·on·y·mous** (si näp′səs) *adj.*

**syn·op·sis** (si näp′sis) *n., pl.* **-ses** (-sēz) [< Gr. *syn-*, together + *opsis*, a seeing] a brief, general review or condensation; summary

**syn·tax** (sin′taks) *n.* [< Gr. *syn-*, together + *tassein*, arrange] the arrangement of words as elements in a sentence to show their relationship —**syn·tac′tic** (-tak′tik), **syn·tac′ti·cal** *adj.*

**syn·the·sis** (sin′thə sis) *n., pl.* **-ses** (-sēz′) [< Gr. *syn-*, together + *tithenai*, to place] the combining of parts or elements so as to form a whole, a compound, etc. —**syn′the·size′** (-sīz′) *vt.* **-sized′, -siz′ing**

**syn′the·siz′er** *n.* an electronic device producing sounds unobtainable from ordinary musical instruments

**syn·thet′ic** (-thet′ik) *adj.* 1. of or involving synthesis 2. produced by chemical synthesis, rather than of natural origin 3. not real; artificial —*n.* something synthetic —**syn·thet′i·cal·ly** *adv.*

**syph·i·lis** (sif′ə lis) *n.* [< *Syphilus*, hero of a L. poem (1530)] an infectious venereal disease —**syph′i·lit′ic** (-lit′ik) *adj., n.*

**Syr·a·cuse** (sir′ə kyōōs′, -kyōōz′) city in C N.Y.: pop. 197,000

**Syr·i·a** (sir′ē ə) country in SW Asia: 71,227 sq. mi.; pop. 7,114,000; cap. Damascus —**Syr′i·an** *adj., n.*

**sy·ringe** (sə rinj′, sir′inj) *n.* [< Gr. *syrinx*, a pipe] a device consisting of a tube with a rubber bulb or piston at one end for drawing in a liquid and then ejecting it in a stream: used to inject fluids into the body, etc. —*vt.* **-ringed′, -ring′ing** to cleanse, inject, etc. by using a syringe

**syr·up** (sir′əp, sur′-) *n.* [< Ar. *sharāb*, a drink] any sweet, thick liquid; specif., a solution made by boiling sugar with water —**syr′up·y** *adj.*

**sys·tem** (sis′təm) *n.* [< Gr. *syn-*, together + *histanai*, to set] 1. a set or arrangement of things so related as to form a whole [a solar *system*, school *system*] 2. a set of facts, rules, etc. arranged to show a plan 3. a method or plan 4. an established, orderly way of doing something 5. the body, or a number of bodily organs, functioning as a unit

**sys′tem·at′ic** (-tə mat′ik) *adj.* 1. constituting or based on a system 2. according to a system; orderly; methodical —**sys′tem·at′i·cal·ly** *adv.*

**sys′tem·a·tize′** (-təm ə tīz′) *vt.* **-tized′, -tiz′ing** to arrange according to a system; make systematic

**sys·tem·ic** (sis tem′ik) *adj.* of or affecting the body as a whole

**sys·to·le** (sis′tə lē′) *n.* [< Gr. *syn-*, together + *stellein*, send] the usual rhythmic contraction of the heart —**sys·tol′ic** (-täl′ik) *adj.*

---

# T

**T, t** (tē) *n., pl.* **T's, t's** the twentieth letter of the English alphabet —**to a T** to perfection

**T.** tablespoon(s)

**t.** 1. teaspoon(s) 2. temperature 3. ton(s) 4. transitive

**tab**[1] (tab) *n.* [< ?] 1. a small, flat loop or strap fastened to something 2. a projecting piece of a card or paper, useful in filing

**tab**[2] (tab) *n.* [prob. < TABULATION] [Colloq.] 1. a bill, as for expenses 2. total cost —**keep tabs (or a tab) on** [Colloq.] to keep a check on

**tab·by** (tab'ē) *n., pl.* **-bies** [ult. < Ar.] a domestic cat, esp. a female

**tab·er·nac·le** (tab'ər nak''l) *n.* [< L. *taberna*, hut] 1. [T-] the portable sanctuary carried by the Jews during the Exodus 2. a large place of worship

**tab·la** (täb'lä) *n.* [< Ar. *ṭabl*, drum] a set of two small drums whose pitch can be varied, used esp. in India and played with the hands

**ta·ble** (tā'b'l) *n.* [< L. *tabula*, a board] 1. orig., a thin slab of metal, stone, etc. 2. *a)* a piece of furniture having a flat top set on legs *b)* such a table set with food *c)* food served *d)* the people seated at a table 3. *a)* a systematic list of details, contents, etc. *b)* an orderly arrangement of facts, figures, etc. 4. any flat, horizontal surface, piece, etc. —*vt.* **-bled, -bling** to postpone consideration of (a legislative bill, etc.) —**at table** at a meal —**turn the tables** to reverse a situation

**tab·leau** (tab'lō) *n., pl.* **-leaux** (-lōz), **-leaus** [Fr. < OFr., dim. of *table*] a representation of a scene, etc. by a group posed in costume

**ta'ble·cloth'** *n.* a cloth for covering a table, esp. at meals

**ta·ble d'hôte** (tä'b'l dōt') [Fr., table of the host] a complete meal served at a restaurant for a set price

**ta'ble-hop'** (-häp') *vi.* **-hopped', -hop'ping** to leave one's table, as at a nightclub, and visit about at other tables —**ta'ble-hop'per** *n.*

**ta·ble·land** (tā'b'l land') *n.* a plateau

**ta'ble·spoon'** *n.* a large spoon for serving, measuring, etc., holding 1/2 fluid ounce —**ta'ble·spoon'ful** *n., pl.* **-fuls**

**tab·let** (tab'lit) *n.* [see TABLE] 1. a flat, thin piece of stone, metal, etc. with an inscription 2. a writing pad of paper sheets glued together at one edge 3. a small, flat piece of compressed material, as of medicine

**table tennis** a game somewhat like tennis, played on a table, with a small celluloid ball

**ta'ble·ware'** (-wer') *n.* dishes, silverware, glassware, etc. for use at a meal

**tab·loid** (tab'loid) *n.* [TABL(ET) + -OID] a newspaper, usually half size, with many pictures and short, often sensational, news stories

**ta·boo** (ta bōō', tə-) *n.* [S Pacific native term *tabu*] 1. among primitive peoples, a sacred prohibition making certain people or things untouchable, etc. 2. any conventional social restriction —*adj.* prohibited by taboo —*vt.* 1. to put under taboo 2. to prohibit or forbid Also **tabu**

**tab·u·lar** (tab'yə lər) *adj.* [see TABLE] 1. flat 2. of, arranged in, or computed from a table or list

**tab'u·late'** (-lāt') *vt.* **-lat'ed, -lat'ing** to put (facts, statistics, etc.) in a table —**tab'u·la'tion** *n.* —**tab'u·la'tor** *n.*

**ta·chom·e·ter** (ta käm'ə tər, tə-) *n.* [< Gr. *tachos*, speed + -METER] a device that measures the revolutions per minute of a revolving shaft

**tac·it** (tas'it) *adj.* [< L. *tacere*, be silent] 1. unspoken; silent 2. not expressed openly, but implied —**tac'it·ly** *adv.* —**tac'it·ness** *n.*

**tac·i·turn** (tas'ə turn') *adj.* [see prec.] almost always silent; not liking to talk —**tac'i·tur'ni·ty** *n.*

**tack** (tak) *n.* [< MDu. *tacke*, twig] 1. a short nail with a sharp point and a large, flat head 2. a temporary stitch 3. a zigzag course 4. a course of action 5. *a)* the direction a ship goes in relation to the position of the sails *b)* a change of a ship's direction —*vt.* 1. to fasten with tacks 2. to attach or add 3. to change the course of (a ship) —*vi.* to change course suddenly

**tack·le** (tak''l) *n.* [< MDu. *takel*] 1. equipment; gear 2. a system of ropes and pulleys for moving weights 3. a tackling, as in football 4. *Football* a player next to the end in the line —*vt.* **-led, -ling** 1. to take hold of; seize 2. to try to do; undertake 3. *Football* to throw (the ball carrier) to the ground —**tack'ler** *n.*

**tack·y** (tak'ē) *adj.* **-i·er, -i·est** 1. sticky, as glue 2. [Colloq.] shabby or dowdy —**tack'i·ness** *n.*

**ta·co** (tä'kō) *n., pl.* **-cos** [Sp., light lunch] a fried tortilla filled with chopped meat, lettuce, etc.

**Ta·co·ma** (tə kō'mə) seaport in W Wash.: pop. 155,000

**tac·o·nite** (tak'ə nīt') *n.* [< *Taconic* Range in Vt. & Mass.] a kind of rock mined as a low-grade iron ore: the iron-bearing particles from the crushed rock are formed into pellets

**tact** (takt) *n.* [< L. *tangere*, touch] delicate perception of the right thing to say or do without offending —**tact'ful** *adj.* —**tact'ful·ly** *adv.* —**tact'less** *adj.* —**tact'less·ly** *adv.*

**tac·tics** (tak'tiks) *n.pl.* [< Gr. *tassein*, arrange] 1. [*with sing. v.*] the science of maneuvering military and naval forces 2. any skillful methods to gain an end —**tac′ti·cal** adj. —**tac·ti′cian** (-tish′ən) n.

**tac·tile** (tak′t'l) adj. [< L. tangere, to touch] of, having, or perceived by the sense of touch

**tad** (tad) n. [prob. < TAD(POLE)] a little child, esp. a boy

**tad·pole** (tad′pōl′) n. [ME. tadde, toad + poll, head] the larva of a frog or toad, having gills and a tail and living in water

**taf·fe·ta** (taf′i tə) n. [< Per. tāftan, to weave] a fine, stiff fabric of silk, nylon, etc., with a sheen

**taff·rail** (taf′rāl′) n. [< Du.] a rail around a ship's stern

**taf·fy** (taf′ē) n. [< ?] a chewy candy made of sugar or molasses

**Taft** (taft), **William Howard** 1857-1930; 27th president of the U.S. (1909-13)

**tag** (tag) n. [prob. < Scand.] 1. a hanging end or part 2. a hard-tipped end on a cord or lace 3. a card, etc. attached as a label 4. an epithet 5. the last line or lines of a story, speech, etc. 6. a children's game in which one player chases the others until he touches one —vt. **tagged, tag′ging** 1. to provide with a tag; label 2. to touch in playing tag 3. to choose; select —vi. [Colloq.] to follow closely (with along, after, etc.) —**tag′ger** n.

**Ta·ga·log** (tä gä′läg, -lôg) n. 1. pl. **-logs, -log** a member of a Malayan people of the Philippine Islands 2. their Indonesian language

**Ta·hi·ti** (tə hēt′ē) Fr. island in the South Pacific —**Ta·hi′tian** (-hēsh′ən) adj., n.

**tai chi** (tī′ jē′) [Chin.] a system of exercise developed in China, consisting of a series of slow, ritual movements: in full, **t'ai chi ch'uan** (chwän)

**tai·ga** (tī′gə) n. [Russ.] the coniferous forests in far northern regions

**tail** (tāl) n. [OE. tægel] 1. the rear end of an animal's body, esp. when a distinct appendage 2. anything like an animal's tail in form or position 3. the hind, bottom, last, or inferior part of anything 4. [often pl.] the reverse side of a coin 5. [pl.] [Colloq.] full-dress attire for men 6. [Colloq.] a person that follows another, esp. in surveillance —adj. 1. at the rear or end 2. from the rear [a tail wind] —vt., vi. [Colloq.] to follow close behind —**tail′less** adj.

**tail′gate′** n. the hinged or removable gate at the back of a wagon, truck, etc. —vi., vt. **-gat′ed, -gat′ing** to drive too closely behind (another vehicle)

**tail′light′** n. a light, usually red, at the rear of a vehicle to warn vehicles coming from behind

TAILGATE

**tai·lor** (tā′lər) n. [< LL. taliare, to cut] one who makes, repairs, or alters clothes —vi. to work as a tailor —vt. 1. to make by tailor's work 2. to form, alter, etc. for a certain purpose [a novel tailored for TV]

**tail′pipe′** n. an exhaust pipe at the rear of an automotive vehicle

**tail′spin′** n. same as SPIN (n. 3)

**taint** (tānt) vt. [< ?] 1. to affect with something injurious, unpleasant, etc.; infect; spoil 2. to make morally corrupt —n. a trace of contamination, corruption, etc.

**Tai·wan** (tī′wän′) island province of SE China: seat of the Nationalist government: 13,885 sq. mi.; pop. 13,466,000

**take** (tāk) vt. **took, tak′en, tak′ing** [< ON. taka] 1. to get possession of; capture, seize, etc. 2. to get hold of 3. to capture the fancy of 4. to obtain, acquire, assume, etc. 5. to use, consume, etc. 6. to buy, rent, subscribe to, etc. 7. to join with (one side in a disagreement, etc.) 8. to choose; select 9. to travel by [to take a bus] 10. to deal with; consider 11. to occupy [take a chair] 12. to require; demand [it takes money] 13. to derive (a name, quality, etc.) from 14. to excerpt 15. to study 16. to write down [take notes] 17. to make by photographing 18. to win (a prize, etc.) 19. to undergo [take punishment] 20. to engage in [take a nap] 21. to accept (an offer, bet, etc.) 22. to react to [to take a joke in earnest] 23. to contract (a disease, etc.) 24. to understand 25. to suppose; presume 26. to feel [take pity] 27. to lead, escort, etc. 28. to carry 29. to remove, as by stealing 30. to subtract 31. [Slang] to cheat; trick 32. Gram. to be used with [the verb "hit" takes an object] —vi. 1. to take root: said of a plant 2. to catch [the fire took] 3. to gain favor, success, etc. 4. to be effective [the vaccination took] 5. to go [to take to the hills] 6. [Colloq.] to become (sick) —n. 1. a taking 2. a) the amount taken b) [Slang] receipts or profit —on the take [Slang] taking bribes, etc. —take after to be, act, or look like —take back to retract (something said, etc.) —take down 1. to put in writing; record —take in 1. to admit; receive 2. to make smaller 3. to understand 4. to cheat; trick —take off 1. to leave the ground, etc. in flight: said of an airplane 2. [Colloq.] to start 3. [Colloq.] to imitate in a burlesque manner —take on 1. to acquire; assume 2. to employ 3. to undertake (a task, etc.) —take over to begin controlling, managing, etc. —take to to become fond of —take up 1. to make tighter or shorter 2. to become interested in (an occupation, study, etc.) —tak′er n.

**take′off′** n. 1. the act of leaving the ground, as in jumping or flight 2. [Colloq.] a caricature; burlesque

**take'o'ver** *n.* the usurpation of power in a nation, organization, etc.

**tak·ing** (tāk'iŋ) *adj.* attractive; winning —*n.* 1. the act of one that takes 2. [*pl.*] earnings; profits

**talc** (talk) *n.* [< Ar. *ṭalq*] 1. a soft mineral used to make talcum powder, etc. 2. talcum powder

**tal'cum (powder)** (-əm) *n.* a powder for the body made of purified talc

**tale** (tāl) *n.* [OE. *talu*] 1. a true or fictitious story; narrative 2. idle or malicious gossip 3. a fiction; lie

**tale'bear'er** (-ber'er) *n.* one who spreads scandal, etc.; gossip

**tal·ent** (tal'ənt) *n.* [< Gr. *talanton*, a weight] 1. an ancient unit of weight or money 2. any natural ability or power 3. a superior ability in an art, etc. 4. people, or a person, with talent —**tal'ent·ed** *adj.*

**tal·is·man** (tal'is mən, -iz-) *n., pl.* -**mans** [< LGr. *telesma*, religious rite] 1. a ring, stone, etc. bearing engraved figures supposed to bring good luck, avert evil, etc. 2. a charm

**talk** (tôk) *vi.* [prob. < OE. *talian*, reckon] 1. to put ideas into words; speak 2. to express ideas by speech substitutes [*talk* by signs] 3. to chatter; gossip 4. to confer; consult 5. to confess or inform on someone —*vt.* 1. to use in speaking [*to talk* French] 2. to discuss 3. to put into a specified condition, etc. by talking —*n.* 1. the act of talking 2. conversation 3. a speech 4. a conference 5. gossip 6. the subject of conversation, gossip, etc. 7. speech; dialect —**talk back** to answer impertinently —**talk down to** to talk patronizingly to, as by simple speech —**talk up** to promote in discussion —**talk'er** *n.*

**talk'a·tive** (-ə tiv) *adj.* talking a great deal; loquacious: also **talk'y**

**talking book** a book, etc. recorded for use on a phonograph by the blind

**talk'ing-to'** *n.* [Colloq.] a scolding

**tall** (tôl) *adj.* [< OE. (*ge*)*tæl*, swift] 1. higher in stature than the average 2. having a specified height 3. [Colloq.] exaggerated [a *tall* tale] 4. [Colloq.] large [a *tall* drink] —**tall'ness** *n.*

**Tal·la·has·see** (tal'ə has'ē) capital of Fla.: pop. 72,000

**tal·low** (tal'ō) *n.* [prob. < MLowG. *talg*] the solid fat taken from the natural fat of cattle, sheep, etc., used to make candles, soaps, etc.

**tal·ly** (tal'ē) *n., pl.* -**lies** [< L. *talea*, a stick (notched to keep accounts)] 1. anything used as a record for an account or score 2. an account, score, etc. 3. a tag or label —*vt.* -**lied**, -**ly·ing** 1. to put on or as on a tally 2. to add (*up*) —*vi.* 1. to score a point 2. to agree; correspond

**tal·ly·ho** (tal'ē hō') *interj.* [< Fr. *taiaut*] the cry of a hunter on sighting the fox

**Tal·mud** (täl'mood, tal'məd) *n.* [< Heb. *lāmadh*, learn] the body of early Jewish civil and religious law

**tal·on** (tal'ən) *n.* [< L. *talus*, an ankle] the claw of a bird of prey

**tam** (tam) *n.* same as TAM-O'-SHANTER

**ta·ma·le** (tə mä'lē) *n.* [< MexSp.] a Mexican food of minced meat and red peppers cooked in corn husks

**tam·a·rack** (tam'ə rak') *n.* [< Am-Ind.] 1. an American larch tree usually found in swamps 2. its wood

**tam·a·rind** (tam'ə rind) *n.* [< Ar. *tamr hindī*, date of India] 1. a tropical tree with yellow flowers and brown, acid pods 2. its edible fruit

**tam·bou·rine** (tam'bə rēn') *n.* [< Ar. *ṭanbūr*, stringed instrument] a shallow, one-headed hand drum with jingling metal disks in the rim: played by shaking, hitting, etc.

**tame** (tām) *adj.* **tam'er**, **tam'est** [OE. *tam*] 1. changed from a wild state and trained for man's use 2. gentle; docile 3. without spirit or force; dull —*vt.* **tamed**, **tam'ing** 1. to make tame, or domestic 2. to make gentle; subdue —**tam'a·ble**, **tame'a·ble** *adj.* —**tame'ly** *adv.* —**tame'ness** *n.* —**tam'er** *n.*

**Tam·il** (tam'l, tum'-) *n.* the non-Indo-European language of the Tamils, a people of S India and N Ceylon

**tam-o'-shan·ter** (tam'ə shan'tər) *n.* [< title character of Burns's poem] a Scottish cap with a round, flat top

**tamp** (tamp) *vt.* [< ? Fr. *tampon*, a plug] to pack or pound (*down*) by a series of blows or taps

**Tam·pa** (tam'pə) seaport in WC Fla.: pop. 278,000

TAM-O'-SHANTER

**tam·per** (tam'pər) *vi.* [< TEMPER] 1. to make secret, illegal arrangements (*with*) 2. to interfere (*with*) or meddle (*with*)

**tam·pon** (tam'pän) *n.* [Fr.] a plug of cotton, etc. put into a body cavity or wound to stop bleeding, etc.

**tan** (tan) *n.* [< ML. *tanum*, TANBARK] 1. a yellowish-brown color 2. the color of suntan —*adj.* **tan'ner**, **tan'nest** yellowish-brown —*vt.* **tanned**, **tan'ning** 1. to change (hide) into leather by soaking in tannic acid 2. to produce a suntan in 3. [Colloq.] to whip severely —*vi.* to become tanned

**tan·a·ger** (tan'ə jər) *n.* [< SAmInd. *tangara*] any of a family of small American songbirds with brightly colored males

**tan'bark'** *n.* any bark containing tannic acid, used to tan hides, etc.

**tan·dem** (tan'dəm) *adv.* [< punning use of L. *tandem*, at length (of time)] one behind another; in single file

**tang** (taŋ) *n.* [< ON. *tangi*, a sting] 1. a prong on a file, etc. that fits into the handle 2. a strong, penetrating taste or odor —**tang'y** *adj.*

**tan·ge·lo** (tan'jə lō') *n., pl.* -**los** [TANG(ERINE) + (*pom*)*elo*, grapefruit] a fruit produced by crossing a tangerine with a grapefruit

**tan·gent** (tan'jənt) *adj.* [< L. *tangere*, to touch] 1. touching 2. *Geom.* touching a curved surface at one point but not intersecting it —*n.* a tangent line, curve, or surface —**go off at** (or **on**) **a tangent** to change suddenly to another line of action, etc. —**tan·gen′tial** (-jen′shəl) *adj.*

**tan·ge·rine** (tan′jə rēn′) *n.* [< *Tangier,* city in N Africa] a small, loose-skinned, reddish-yellow orange with easily separated segments

**tan·gi·ble** (tan′jə b'l) *adj.* [< L. *tangere,* to touch] 1. that can be touched or felt 2. definite; objective —*n.pl.* property that can be appraised for value —**tan′gi·bil′i·ty** *n.*

**tan·gle** (taŋ′g'l) *vt.* **-gled, -gling** [< ? Sw.] 1. to catch as in a snare; trap 2. to make a snarl of; intertwine —*vi.* 1. to become tangled 2. [Colloq.] to argue —*n.* 1. an intertwined, confused mass 2. a confused condition

**tan·go** (taŋ′gō) *n., pl.* **-gos** [AmSp.] 1. a S.American dance with long gliding steps 2. music for this in 2/4 or 4/4 time —*vi.* to dance the tango

**tank** (taŋk) *n.* [< Sans.] 1. any large container for liquid or gas 2. an armored vehicle with guns and full tractor treads —**tank′ful** *n.*

**tank·ard** (taŋ′kərd) *n.* [ME.] a large drinking cup with a handle

**tank·er** (taŋ′kər) *n.* 1. a ship equipped to transport oil or other liquids 2. a plane designed to refuel another plane in flight

**tank farming** *same as* HYDROPONICS

**tank top** [orig. worn in swimming tanks] a casual shirt like an undershirt with wide shoulder straps

**tank truck** a motor truck built to transport gasoline, oil, etc.

**tan·ner** (tan′ər) *n.* one whose work is making leather by tanning hides

**tan′ner·y** *n., pl.* **-ies** a place where leather is made by tanning hides

**tan·nic acid** (tan′ik) a yellowish, astringent substance used in tanning, dyeing, etc.: also **tan′nin** (-in) *n.*

**tan·sy** (tan′zē) *n., pl.* **-sies** [< LL. *tanacetum*] a plant with a strong smell and small, yellow flowers

**tan·ta·lize** (tan′tə līz′) *vt.* **-lized′, -liz′ing** [< *Tantalus,* in Gr. Myth., a king doomed in Hades to stand in water which receded when he wished to drink and under fruit he could not reach] to promise or show something desirable and then withhold it; tease

**tan·ta·lum** (tan′tə ləm) *n.* [< *Tantalus* (see prec.): from difficulty in extracting it] a rare, steel-blue, corrosion-resisting chemical element

**tan·ta·mount** (tan′tə mount′) *adj.* [< OFr. *tant,* so much + *amount,* upward] equal (*to*) in value, effect, etc.

**tan·tra** (tun′trə, tän′-) *n.* [Sans.] [*often* T-] any of a class of Hindu or Buddhist mystical writings

**tan·trum** (tan′trəm) *n.* [< ?] a violent, willful outburst of rage, etc.

**Tan·za·ni·a** (tan′zə nē′ə) country in E Africa: 362,820 sq. mi.; pop. 12,231,000 —**Tan′za·ni′an** *adj., n.*

**Tao·ism** (dou′iz'm, tou′-) *n.* [Chin.

*tao,* the way] a Chinese religion and philosophy advocating simplicity, selflessness, etc. —**Tao′ist** *n., adj.*

**tap¹** (tap) *vt., vi.* **tapped, tap′ping** [echoic] 1. to strike lightly 2. to make or do by tapping [*to tap* a message] 3. to choose, as for membership in a club —*n.* a light, rapid blow

**tap²** (tap) *n.* [OE. *tæppa*] 1. a faucet or spigot 2. a plug, cork, etc. for stopping a hole in a cask, etc. 3. a tool used to cut threads in a female screw 4. *Elec.* a place in a circuit where a connection can be made —*vt.* **tapped, tap′ping** 1. to put a hole in, or pull the plug from, for drawing off liquid 2. to draw off (liquid) 3. to make use of [*to tap* new resources] 4. to make a connection with (a pipe, circuit, etc.); specif., to wiretap

**tap dance** a dance done with sharp taps of the foot, toe, or heel at each step —**tap′-dance′** *vi.* **-danced′, -danc′ing** —**tap′-danc′er** *n.*

**tape** (tāp) *n.* [OE. *tæppe,* a fillet] 1. a strong, narrow strip of cloth, paper, etc. used for binding, tying, etc. 2. *same as* MAGNETIC TAPE 3. *same as* TAPE MEASURE —*vt.* **taped, tap′ing** 1. to bind, tie, etc. with tape 2. to record on magnetic tape

**tape measure** a tape with marks in inches, feet, etc. for measuring

**ta·per** (tā′pər) *n.* [OE. *tapur*] 1. a slender candle 2. a gradual decrease in width or thickness —*vt., vi.* 1. to decrease gradually in width or thickness 2. to lessen; diminish Often *with off*

**tape recorder** a device for recording on magnetic tape and for playing back such recordings

**tap·es·try** (tap′is trē) *n., pl.* **-tries** [< Gr. *tapēs,* a carpet] a heavy woven cloth with decorative designs and pictures, used as a wall hanging, etc.

**tape′worm′** *n.* a tapelike worm that lives as a parasite in the intestines

**tap·i·o·ca** (tap′ē ō′kə) *n.* [< SAmInd.] a starchy substance from cassava roots, used for puddings, etc.

**ta·pir** (tā′pər) *n.* [< SAmInd.] a large, hoglike mammal of tropical America and the Malay Peninsula

**tap′room′** *n.* a barroom

**tap′root′** *n.* [TAP² + ROOT¹] a main root, growing downward, from which small branch roots spread out

**taps** (taps) *n.* [< TAP¹, because orig. a drum signal] a bugle call to put out lights in retiring for the night

**tar¹** (tär) *n.* [OE. *teru*] a thick, sticky, black liquid obtained by the destructive distillation of wood, coal, etc. —*vt.* tarred, tar′ring to cover or smear with tar —**tar′ry** *adj.*

**tar²** (tär) *n.* [< TAR(PAULIN)] [Colloq.] a sailor

**ta·ran·tu·la** (tə ran′choo lə) *n.* [< *Taranto,* Italy] any of several large, hairy, somewhat poisonous spiders of S Europe and tropical America

**tar·dy** (tär′dē) *adj.* **-di·er, -di·est** [<

L. *tardus*, slow] **1.** slow in moving, acting, etc. **2.** late; delayed; dilatory —**tar′di·ly** *adv.* —**tar′di·ness** *n.*

**tare**[1] (ter) *n.* [ME.] **1.** the vetch **2.** *Bible* an undesirable weed

**tare**[2] (ter) *n.* [ < Ar. *taraha*, to reject] the weight of a container deducted from the total weight to determine the weight of the contents

**tar·get** (tär′git) *n.* [ < MFr. *targe*, a shield] **1.** a board, etc. marked as with concentric circles, aimed at in archery, rifle practice, etc. **2.** any object that is shot at **3.** an objective; goal **4.** an object of attack, criticism, etc.

**tar·iff** (tar′if) *n.* [ < Ar. *ta′rif*, information] **1.** a list or system of taxes upon exports or, esp., imports **2.** a tax of this kind, or its rate **3.** any list or scale of prices, charges, etc. **4.** [Colloq.] any bill, charge, etc.

**tar·nish** (tär′nish) *vt.* [ < Fr. *ternir*, make dim] **1.** to dull the luster of **2.** to sully or mar —*vi.* **1.** to lose luster **2.** to become sullied —*n.* dullness; stain —**tar′nish·a·ble** *adj.*

**ta·ro** (tä′rō) *n., pl.* **-ros** [Tahitian] a tropical Asiatic plant with a starchy, edible root

**ta·rot** (tar′ō, -ət) *n.* [Fr. < Ar. *taraha*, remove] [*often* T-] any of a set of fortunetelling cards

**tar·pau·lin** (tär pô′lin, tär′pə-) *n.* [ < TAR[1] + PALL[2]] canvas coated with a waterproofing compound, or a protective cover of this

**tar·pon** (tär′pən) *n.* [ < ?] a large, silvery game fish of the W Atlantic

**tar·ra·gon** (tar′ə gän′) *n.* [ < Sp. < Ar. < Gr. *drakōn*, dragon] an old-world plant with fragrant leaves used for seasoning

**tar·ry** (tar′ē) *vi.* **-ried, -ry·ing** [prob. < OE. *tergan*, to vex & OFr. *targer*, to delay] **1.** to delay; linger **2.** to stay for a time **3.** to wait

**tart**[1] (tärt) *adj.* [OE. *teart*] **1.** sharp in taste; sour; acid **2.** sharp in meaning; cutting [a *tart* reply] —**tart′ly** *adv.* —**tart′ness** *n.*

**tart**[2] (tärt) *n.* [ < MFr. *tarte*] a small pastry shell filled with jam, fruit, etc.

**tart**[3] (tärt) *n.* [ < prec., orig., slang term of endearment] a prostitute

**tar·tan** (tär′t'n) *n.* [cf. MFr. *tiretaine*, mixed fabric] a woolen cloth in any of various woven plaid patterns, worn esp. in the Scottish Highlands

**Tar·tar** (tär′tər) *n.* same as TATAR

**tar·tar** (tär′tər) *n.* [ < MGr. *tartaron*] **1.** a potassium salt forming a crustlike deposit in wine casks: in purified form, called **cream of tartar 2.** a hard deposit on the teeth

**tartar sauce** [ < Fr.] a sauce of mayonnaise with chopped pickles, olives, etc.: also **tartare sauce**

**task** (task) *n.* [ult. < L. *taxare*, to rate] **1.** a piece of work to be done **2.** any difficult undertaking —*vt.* to burden; strain —**take to task** to scold

**task force** a group, esp. a military unit, assigned a specific task

**task′mas′ter** *n.* one who assigns tasks to others, esp. when severe

**Tas·ma·ni·a** (taz mā′nē ə) island

State of Australia, off its SE coast — **Tas·ma′ni·an** *adj., n.*

**tas·sel** (tas′'l) *n.* [OFr., a knob] **1.** an ornamental tuft of threads, etc. hanging loosely from a knob **2.** something like this, as a tuft of corn silk

**taste** (tāst) *vt.* **tast′ed, tast′ing** [ < OFr. *taster*] **1.** to test the flavor of by putting a little in one's mouth **2.** to detect the flavor of by the sense of taste **3.** to eat or drink a small amount of **4.** to experience [to *taste* success] —*vi.* to have a specific flavor —*n.* **1.** the sense by which flavor is perceived through the taste buds on the tongue **2.** the quality so perceived; flavor **3.** a small amount tasted as a sample **4.** a bit; trace **5.** the ability to appreciate what is beautiful, appropriate, etc. **6.** a specific preference **7.** a liking; inclination —**in bad (or good) taste** in a style showing a bad (or good) sense of beauty, fitness, etc. —**taste′less** *adj.* —**tast′er** *n.*

**taste bud** any of the cells in the tongue that are the organs of taste

**taste′ful** *adj.* having or showing good taste (*n.* 5) —**taste′ful·ly** *adv.*

**tast′y** *adj.* **-i·er, -i·est** that tastes good —**tast′i·ness** *n.*

**tat** (tat) *vt.* **tat′ted, tat′ting** to make by tatting —*vi.* to do tatting

**ta·ta·mi** (tə tä′mē) *n., pl.* **-mi, -mis** [Jap.] a floor mat of rice straw, used in Japanese homes for sitting on

**Ta·tar** (tät′ər) *n.* **1.** a member of any of the E Asiatic tribes who invaded W Asia and E Europe in the Middle Ages **2.** a Turkic language

**tat·ter** (tat′ər) *n.* [prob. < ON. *töturr*, rags] **1.** a torn and hanging piece, as of a garment **2.** [*pl.*] torn, ragged clothes —*vt., vi.* to make or become ragged —**tat′tered** *adj.*

**tat′ter·de·mal′ion** (-di mäl′yən) *n.* [< prec. + ?] a person in ragged clothing

**tat·ting** (tat′iŋ) *n.* [prob. < Brit. dial. *tat*, to tangle] **1.** a fine lace made by looping and knotting thread **2.** the process of making this

**tat·tle** (tat′'l) *vi.* **-tled, -tling** [prob. < MDu. *tatelen*] **1.** to talk idly **2.** to reveal others' secrets —*vt.* to reveal (a secret) by gossiping —**tat′tler** *n.*

**tat′tle·tale′** *n.* a talebearer; informer

**tat·too**[1] (ta tōō′) *vt.* **-tooed′, -too′ing** [Tahitian *tatau*] to make (permanent designs) on (the skin) by puncturing it and inserting indelible colors —*n., pl.* **-toos′** a tattooed design

**tat·too**[2] (ta tōō′) *n., pl.* **-toos′** [ < Du. *tap toe*, shut the tap: a signal for closing barrooms] **1.** a signal on a drum, bugle, etc. summoning soldiers, etc. to their quarters at night **2.** a drumming, rapping, etc.

**tau** (tô, tou) *n.* the nineteenth letter of the Greek alphabet (T, τ)

**taught** (tôt) *pt. & pp.* of TEACH

**taunt** (tônt, tänt) *vt.* [ < ? Fr. *tant pour tant*, tit for tat] to reproach scornfully or sarcastically; mock —*n.* a scornful or jeering remark

**taupe** (tōp) *n.* [Fr. < L. *talpa*, a mole] a dark, brownish gray

**Tau·rus** (tôr′əs) [L., a bull] the second sign of the zodiac

**taut** (tôt) *adj.* [ME. *toght*, tight] 1. tightly stretched, as a rope 2. tense [a *taut* smile] 3. trim, tidy, etc. —**taut′ly** *adv.* —**taut′ness** *n.*

**tau·tol·o·gy** (tô täl′ə jē) *n.* [< Gr. < *to auto*, the same + -LOGY] needless repetition of an idea, using a redundant word, phrase, etc. —**tau′to·log′i·cal** *adj.*

**tav·ern** (tav′ərn) *n.* [< L. *taberna*] 1. a saloon; bar 2. an inn

**taw·dry** (tô′drē) *adj.* -**dri·er, -dri·est** [< *St. Audrey laces*, sold at St. Audrey's fair, Norwich, England] cheap and gaudy

**taw·ny** (tô′nē) *adj.* -**ni·er, -ni·est** [< OFr. *tanner*, to tan] brownish-yellow; tan

**tax** (taks) *vt.* [< L. *taxare*, appraise] 1. to require to pay a tax 2. to assess a tax on (income, purchases, etc.) 3. to put a strain on 4. to accuse; charge —*n.* 1. a compulsory payment of a percentage of income, property value, etc. for the support of a government 2. a) heavy demand; burden —**tax′a·ble** *adj.* —**tax·a′tion** *n.*

**tax·i** (tak′sē) *n., pl.* -**is** *clipped form of* TAXICAB —*vi.* -**ied, -i·ing** *or* -**y·ing** 1. to go in a taxi 2. to move along the ground or water under its own power: said of an airplane

**tax′i·cab′** *n.* [< *taxi(meter) cab*] an automobile in which passengers are carried for a fare

**tax·i·der·my** (tak′si dur′mē) *n.* [< Gr. *taxis*, arrangement + *derma*, skin] the art of preparing, stuffing, etc. the skins of animals to make them appear lifelike —**tax′i·der′mist** *n.*

**tax·i·me·ter** (tak′sē mēt′ər) *n.* [< Fr. *taxe*, a tax + *mètre*, meter] a device in taxicabs to register fare due

**tax′i·way′** *n.* any of the paved strips used by airplanes in taxiing to and from the runways

**tax·on·o·my** (tak sän′ə mē) *n.* [< Gr. *taxis*, arrangement + *nomos*, law] classification, esp. of animals and plants —**tax·on′o·mist** *n.*

**tax′pay′er** *n.* one who pays a tax

**Tay·lor** (tā′lər), **Zach·a·ry** (zak′ər ē) 1784–1850; 12th president of the U.S. (1849–50)

**TB, T.B., tb, t.b.** tuberculosis

**T-bone steak** (tē′bōn′) a steak with a T-shaped bone, containing some tenderloin

**tbs., tbsp.** tablespoon(s)

**Tchai·kov·sky** (chī kôf′skē), **Peter** 1840–93; Russ. composer

**tea** (tē) *n.* [< Chin. dial. *t′e*] 1. an evergreen plant grown in Asia 2. its dried leaves, steeped in boiling water to make a beverage 3. this beverage 4. a tealike beverage made as from other plants 5. [Chiefly Brit.] a meal in the late afternoon at which tea is the drink 6. an afternoon party at which tea, etc. is served

**tea·ber·ry** (tē′ber′ē) *n., pl.* -**ries** 1. *same as* WINTERGREEN (sense 1) 2. the fruit of the wintergreen

**teach** (tēch) *vt.* **taught, teach′ing** [OE. *tæcan*] 1. to show how to do something; give lessons to 2. to give lessons in (a subject) 3. to provide with knowledge, insight, etc. —*vi.* to be a teacher —**teach′a·ble** *adj.*

**teach′er** *n.* one who teaches, esp. as a profession

**teaching machine** a mechanical device with a corrective feedback, for presenting programmed educational material to a student

**tea′cup′** *n.* a cup for drinking tea, etc. —**tea′cup·ful′** *n., pl.* -**fuls′**

**teak** (tēk) *n.* [< Malayalam *tēkka*] 1. a large East Indian tree with hard, yellowish-brown wood 2. its wood

**tea′ket′tle** *n.* a kettle with a spout, for boiling water for tea, etc.

**teal** (tēl) *n.* [ME. *tele*] 1. a small, short-necked, freshwater duck 2. a dark grayish or greenish blue

**team** (tēm) *n.* [OE., offspring] 1. two or more horses, oxen, etc. harnessed to the same plow, etc. 2. a group of people working or playing together —*vi.* to join in cooperative activity (with *up*) —*adj.* of a team

**team′mate′** *n.* one on the same team

**team′ster** (-stər) *n.* one whose work is hauling loads with a team or truck

**team′work′** *n.* joint action by a group of people

**tea′pot′** *n.* a pot with a spout and handle, for brewing and pouring tea

**tear¹** (ter) *vt.* **tore, torn, tear′ing** [OE. *teran*, rend] 1. to pull apart into pieces by force; rip 2. to make by tearing [to *tear* a hole] 3. to lacerate 4. to disrupt; split [*torn* by civil war] 5. to divide with doubt, etc. 6. to pull with force (with *out, off, up*, etc.) —*vi.* 1. to be torn 2. to move with force or speed —*n.* 1. a tearing 2. a torn place; rent —**tear down** 1. to wreck 2. to dismantle

**tear²** (tir) *n.* [OE.] a drop of the salty fluid which flows from the eye, as in weeping —**in tears** weeping —**tear′ful** *adj.* —**tear′ful·ly** *adv.* —**tear′y** *adj.*

**tear′drop′** *n.* a tear

**tear gas** (tir) a gas causing irritation to the eyes, a heavy flow of tears, etc. —**tear′-gas′** *vt.* -**gassed′, -gas′sing**

**tea′room′** *n.* a restaurant that serves tea, coffee, light lunches, etc.

**tease** (tēz) *vt.* **teased, teas′ing** [OE. *tæsan*] 1. a) to card or comb (flax, wool, etc.) b) to fluff (the hair) by combing toward the scalp 2. to raise a nap on (cloth) by brushing with teasels 3. to annoy by mocking, poking fun, etc. 4. to beg; importune 5. to tantalize —*vi.* to indulge in teasing —*n.* one who teases

**tea·sel** (tē′z'l) *n.* [see prec.] 1. a bristly plant with prickly flowers 2. the dried flower, or any device, used to raise a nap on cloth

**teas′er** *n.* 1. a person or thing that teases 2. a puzzling problem

**tea′spoon′** *n.* a spoon for use at meals, holding 1 1/3 fluid drams —**teaspoon·ful′** *n., pl.* **-fuls′**

**teat** (tēt, tit) *n.* [< OFr. *tete*] the nipple on a breast or udder

**tech.** 1. technical(ly) 2. technology

**tech·ni·cal** (tek′ni k′l) *adj.* [< Gr. *technē*, an art] 1. dealing with the industrial or mechanical arts or the applied sciences 2. of a specific science, art, craft, etc. 3. of, in, or showing technique 4. concerned with minute details —**tech′ni·cal·ly** *adv.*

**tech′ni·cal′i·ty** (-nə kal′ə tē) *n., pl.* **-ties** 1. the state or quality of being technical 2. a technical point, detail, etc. 3. a minute point, detail, etc. brought to bear on a main issue

**tech·ni·cian** (tek nish′ən) *n.* one skilled in the technique of some art, craft, or science

**Tech·ni·col·or** (tek′ni kul′ər) *a trademark for* a process of making color motion pictures —*n.* [t-] this process

**tech·nique** (tek nēk′) *n.* [Fr.] 1. the method of procedure in artistic work, scientific activity, etc. 2. the degree of expertness in following this

**tech·noc·ra·cy** (tek näk′rə sē) *n.* [< Gr. *technē*, an art + -CRACY] government by scientists and engineers —**tech′no·crat′** (-nə krat′) *n.*

**tech·nol·o·gy** (tek näl′ə jē) *n.* [Gr. *technologia*, systematic treatment] 1. the science of the practical or industrial arts 2. applied science —**tech′no·log′i·cal** (-nə läj′i k′l) *adj.*

**ted·dy bear** (ted′ē) [< *Teddy* (Theodore) Roosevelt] a child's stuffed toy that looks like a bear cub

**te·di·ous** (tē′dē əs) *adj.* full of tedium; long and dull —**te′di·ous·ly** *adv.*

**te′di·um** (-əm) *n.* [< L. *taedet*, it offends] the condition or quality of being tiresome, wearisome, etc.

**tee** (tē) *n.* [prob. < Scot. dial. *teaz*] *Golf* 1. a small peg from which the ball is driven 2. the place from which a player makes the first stroke on each hole —*vt., vi.* **teed′, tee′ing** to place (a ball) on a tee —**tee off** 1. to play a golf ball from a tee 2. [Slang] to make angry or disgusted

**teem** (tēm) *vi.* [< OE. *team*, progeny] to be prolific; abound; swarm

**teen** (tēn) *n.* [OE. *tien*, ten] 1. [*pl.*] the years from 13 through 19, as of a person's age 2. *same as* TEEN-AGER

**teen-age** (tēn′āj′) *adj.* 1. in one's teens 2. of or for persons in their teens Also **teenage** —**teen′-ag′er** *n.*

**tee·ny** (tē′nē) *adj.* **-ni·er, -ni·est** *colloq. var. of* TINY: also **teen′sy, tee′ny-wee′ny, teen′sy-ween′sy**

**teen·y-bop·per** (tē′nē bäp′ər) *n.* [Slang] a faddish young teen-ager, esp. a girl, of the 1960's

**tee·pee** (tē′pē) *n. alt. sp. of* TEPEE

**tee shirt** *same as* T-SHIRT

**tee·ter** (tēt′ər) *vi., vt., n.* [< ON. *titra*, tremble] seesaw or wobble

**tee′ter-tot′ter** (-tät′ər) *n., vi.* seesaw

**teeth** (tēth) *n. pl. of* TOOTH

**teethe** (tēth) *vi.* **teethed, teeth′ing** to grow teeth; cut one's teeth

**tee·to·tal·er** (tē tōt′′l ər) *n.* [< doubling of initial *t* in *total*] one who practices total abstinence from alcoholic liquor: also **tee·to′tal·ler**

**Tef′lon** (tef′län) *a trademark for* a tough polymer, used for nonsticking coatings as on cooking utensils

**Teh·ran, Te·her·an** (te hrän′; E. te ə rän′) capital of Iran: pop. 2,803,000

**tek·tite** (tek′tīt) *n.* [< Gr. *tēktos*, molten] a small, dark, glassy body, thought to be from outer space

**tel.** 1. telegram 2. telephone

**Tel A·viv** (tel′ ä vēv′) seaport in W Israel: pop. 394,000: in full **Tel′ A·viv′-Jaf′fa** (-yäf′ə)

**tele-** *a combining form meaning:* 1. [< Gr. *tēle*, far off] at, over, etc. a distance [*telegraph*] 2. [< TELE(VISION)] of, in, or by television [*telecast*]

**tel·e·cast** (tel′ə kast′) *vt., vi.* **-cast′** or **-cast′ed, -cast′ing** to broadcast by television —*n.* a television broadcast —**tel′e·cast′er** *n.*

**tel·e·gram** (tel′ə gram′) *n.* a message transmitted by telegraph

**tel′e·graph′** (-graf′) *n.* [see TELE- & -GRAPH] an apparatus or system that transmits messages by electric impulses sent by wire or radio —*vt., vi.* to send (a message) to (a person) by telegraph —**tel′e·graph′ic** *adj.*

**te·leg·ra·phy** (tə leg′rə fē) *n.* the operation of telegraph apparatus —**te·leg′ra·pher** *n.*

**tel·e·ki·ne·sis** (tel′ə ki nē′sis) *n.* [see TELE- & KINETIC] the apparent causing of movement in an object by unexplainable means, as by some mental process

**tel·e·me·ter** (tel′ə mēt′ər, tə lem′ə tər) *n.* a device for measuring and transmitting data about radiation, temperature, etc. from a remote point

**te·lep·a·thy** (tə lep′ə thē) *n.* [TELE- + -PATHY] supposed communication between minds by means other than the normal sensory channels —**tel·e·path·ic** (tel′ə path′ik) *adj.*

**tel·e·phone** (tel′ə fōn′) *n.* [TELE- + -PHONE] an instrument or system for conveying speech over distances by converting sound into electric impulses sent through a wire —*vt., vi.* **-phoned′, -phon′ing** to convey (a message) to (a person) by telephone —**tel′e·phon′ic** (-fän′ik) *adj.*

**te·leph·o·ny** (tə lef′ə nē) *n.* the making or operation of telephones

**tel·e·pho·to** (tel′ə fōt′ō) *adj.* designating or of a camera lens that produces a large image of a distant object

**tel′e·pho′to·graph′** *n.* 1. a photograph taken with a telephoto lens 2. a photograph transmitted by telegraph or radio —*vt., vi.* 1. to take (photographs) with a telephoto lens 2. to transmit (telephotographs) —**tel′e·pho·tog′ra·phy** (-fə täg′rə fē) *n.*

**tel′e·scope** (-skōp′) *n.* [see TELE- & -SCOPE] an instrument with lenses for making distant objects appear nearer and larger —*vi., vt.* **-scoped′, -scop′-ing** to slide one into another like the tubes of a collapsible telescope — **tel′e·scop′ic** (-skäp′ik) *adj.*

**tel·e·thon′** (-thän²) *n.* [TELE(VISION) + (MARA)THON] a lengthy telecast

**Tele·type′** (-tīp′) *a trademark for a* form of telegraph in which the receiver prints messages typed on the transmitter —**tel′e·type′writ′er** *n.*

**tel·e·vise** (tel′ə viz′) *vt., vi.* **-vised′, -vis′ing** to transmit by television

**tel·e·vi′sion** (-vizh′ən) *n.* 1. the process of transmitting images by converting light rays into electrical signals: the receiver reconverts the signals so that the images are reproduced on a screen 2. television broadcasting 3. a television receiving set

**tell** (tel) *vt.* **told, tell′ing** [OE. *tellan,* calculate] 1. orig., to count 2. to narrate; relate *[tell a story]* 3. to express in words; say *[tell the facts]* 4. to reveal; disclose 5. to recognize; distinguish *[to tell twins apart]* 6. to inform *[tell me later]* 7. to order *[tell her to go]* —*vi.* 1. to give an account or evidence (*of* something) 2. to be effective *[each blow told]* —**tell off** [Colloq.] to rebuke severely —**tell on** 1. to tire 2. [Colloq.] to inform against

**tell′er** *n.* 1. one who tells (a story, etc.) 2. one who counts, as a bank clerk who pays out or receives money

**tell′ing** *adj.* forceful; striking — **tell′ing·ly** *adv.*

**tell′tale′** *adj.* revealing what is meant to be kept hidden or secret

**tell·y** (tel′ē) *n.* Brit. colloq. term for TELEVISION

**Tel·star** (tel′stär′) a communications satellite, placed in orbit in 1962

**tem·blor** (tem′blôr, -blər) *n.* [Sp. < *temblar,* to tremble] an earthquake

**te·mer·i·ty** (tə mer′ə tē) *n.* [< L. *temere,* rashly] foolish or rash boldness

**temp.** temperature

**tem·per** (tem′pər) *vt.* [< L. *temperare,* regulate] 1. to moderate, as by mingling with something else *[temper blame with praise]* 2. to bring to the proper condition by some treatment *[to temper steel]* 3. to toughen —*n.* 1. the degree of hardness and resiliency of a metal 2. frame of mind; disposition 3. calmness of mind: in **lose** (or **keep**) **one's temper** 4. anger; rage

**tem·per·a** (tem′pər ə) *n.* [It.: see prec.] a process of painting with pigments mixed with size, casein, or egg

**tem·per·a·ment** (tem′prə mənt, -pər ə mənt) *n.* [see TEMPER] 1. one's natural disposition; nature 2. a nature that is excitable, moody, etc. — **tem′per·a·men′tal** *adj.*

**tem·per·ance** (tem′pər əns) *n.* 1. self-restraint in conduct, indulgence of the appetites, etc.; moderation 2. moderation in drinking alcoholic liquors or total abstinence from them

**tem·per·ate** (tem′pər it) *adj.* [see TEMPER] 1. moderate, as in eating or drinking 2. self-restrained in actions, speech, etc. 3. neither very hot nor very cold: said of climate, etc.

**Temperate Zone** either of two zones (**North** or **South Temperate Zone**) between the tropics and the polar circles

**tem·per·a·ture** (tem′prə chər, tem′pər ə-) *n.* [< L. *temperatus,* temperate] 1. the degree of hotness or coldness of anything 2. excess of body heat over the normal; fever

**tem·pered** (tem′pərd) *adj.* 1. having been given the desired temper (*n.* 1) 2. having a (specified) temper (*n.* 2)

**tem·pest** (tem′pist) *n.* [< L. *tempus,* time] a violent storm with high winds, esp. one accompanied by rain

**tem·pes·tu·ous** (tem pes′choo wəs) *adj.* of or like a tempest; violent

**tem·plate** (tem′plit) *n.* [< L. *templum,* a timber] a pattern, as a thin metal plate, for making an exact copy

**tem·ple¹** (tem′p'l) *n.* [< L. *templum*] 1. a building for the worship of God or gods 2. a large building for some special purpose *[a temple of art]*

**tem·ple²** (tem′p'l) *n.* [< L. *tempus*] 1. the flat surface beside the forehead, in front of each ear 2. one sidepiece of a pair of glasses

**tem·po** (tem′pō) *n., pl.* **-pos, -pi** (-pē) [It. < L. *tempus,* time] 1. the rate of speed at which a musical work is played 2. rate of activity

**tem·po·ral¹** (tem′pər əl) *adj.* [< L. *tempus,* time] 1. temporary; transitory 2. of this world; worldly 3. secular 4. of or limited by time

**tem·po·ral²** (tem′pər əl) *adj.* of or near the temples (of the head)

**tem′po·rar′y** (-pə rer′ē) *adj.* [< L. *tempus,* time] lasting only a while; not permanent —**tem′po·rar′i·ly** *adv.*

**tem·po·rize** (tem′pə rīz′) *vt.* **-rized′, -riz′ing** to give temporary compliance, evade decision, etc. so as to gain time or avoid argument

**tempt** (tempt) *vt.* [< L. *temptare,* to test] 1. to entice or induce, as to something immoral 2. to be inviting to; attract 3. to provoke or risk provoking (fate, etc.) 4. to incline strongly *[I am tempted to go]* —**temp·ta·tion** (temp tā′shən) *n.* —**tempt′er** *n.* —**tempt′ress** *n.fem.*

**tem·pu·ra** (tem′poo rä′, tem poor′ə) *n.* [Jap.] a Japanese dish of deep-fried shrimp, fish, vegetables, etc.

**ten** (ten) *adj., n.* [OE.] one more than nine; 10; X

**ten·a·ble** (ten′ə b'l) *adj.* [< L. *tenere,* hold] that can be held, defended, or maintained —**ten′a·bil′i·ty** *n.*

**te·na·cious** (tə nā′shəs) *adj.* [< L. *tenere,* to hold] 1. holding firmly *[a tenacious grip]* 2. retentive *[a tenacious memory]* 3. strongly cohesive or adhesive 4. persistent; stubborn *[tenacious courage]* — **te·na′cious·ly**

*adv.* **—te·nac·i·ty** (tə nas′ə tē) *n.*

**ten·ant** (ten′ənt) *n.* [see prec.] **1.** one who pays rent to occupy land, a building, etc. **2.** an occupant —*vt.* to hold as a tenant **—ten′an·cy** *n.*

**tenant farmer** one who farms land that he pays rent for or sharecrops

**Ten Commandments** the ten laws of moral and religious conduct given to Moses by God: Ex. 20:2–17

**tend**[1] (tend) *vt.* [see ATTEND] **1.** to take care of **2.** to manage or operate

**tend**[2] (tend) *vi.* [ < L. *tendere*, to stretch] **1.** to be inclined, disposed, etc. (*to*) **2.** to be directed (*to* or *toward*)

**tend·en·cy** (ten′dən sē) *n.*, *pl.* **-cies** [see prec.] **1.** an inclination to move or act in a particular direction or way **2.** a course toward some object

**ten·den·tious** (ten den′shəs) *adj.* [ < Gr. < *tendenz*, TENDENCY] advancing a definite point of view **—ten·den′tious·ly** *adv.*

**ten·der**[1] (ten′dər) *adj.* [ < L. *tener*, soft] **1.** soft and easily chewed, broken, cut, etc. **2.** physically weak **3.** immature **4.** that requires careful handling **5.** gentle or light **6.** acutely sensitive, as to pain **7.** sensitive to emotions, others' feelings, etc. **—ten′der·ly** *adv.* **—ten′der·ness** *n.*

**ten·der**[2] (ten′dər) *vt.* [see TEND[2]] to present for acceptance —*n.* **1.** a formal offer **2.** something offered in payment, esp. money

**tend·er**[3] (ten′dər) *n.* **1.** one who tends something **2.** a small ship for supplying a larger one **3.** a railroad car attached behind, and carrying coal and water for, a steam locomotive

**ten′der·foot′** *n.*, *pl.* **-foots′, -feet′** **1.** a newcomer to the ranching country of the West, unused to hardships **2.** any newcomer, novice, etc.

**ten′der·heart′ed** *adj.* quick to feel pity or compassion

**ten·der·ize** (ten′də rīz′) *vt.* **-ized′, -iz′ing** to make (meat) tender

**ten′der·loin′** *n.* the tenderest part of a loin of beef, pork, etc.

**ten·don** (ten′dən) *n.* [ < Gr. *teinein*, to stretch] any of the inelastic cords of tough connective tissue by which muscles are attached to bones, etc.

**ten·dril** (ten′drəl) *n.* [prob. ult. < L. *tener*, delicate] a threadlike, clinging part of a climbing plant

**ten·e·ment** (ten′ə mənt) *n.* [ < L. *tenere*, to hold] **1.** a room or suite tenanted as a separate dwelling **2.** a building divided into tenements; now specif., one that is run-down, overcrowded, etc.: also **tenement house**

**ten·et** (ten′it) *n.* [L., he holds] a principle, doctrine, or belief held as a truth, as by some group

**Ten·nes·see** (ten′ə sē′) EC State of the U.S.: 42,244 sq. mi.; pop. 3,924,000; cap. Nashville: abbrev. **Tenn.** **— Ten′nes·se′an** *adj.*, *n.*

**ten·nis** (ten′is) *n.* [prob. < OFr. *tenez*, hold (imperative)] a game in which players in a marked area (**tennis court**) hit a ball back and forth with rackets over a net

**tennis shoe** a sneaker

**Ten·ny·son** (ten′ə s'n), Alfred 1809–92; Eng. poet

**ten·on** (ten′ən) *n.* [ult. < L. *tenere*, to hold] a projecting part cut on the end of a piece of wood for insertion into a mortise to make a joint

**ten·or** (ten′ər) *n.* [ < L. *tenere*, to hold] **1.** general tendency **2.** general meaning; drift **3.** *a)* the highest regular adult male singing voice *b)* a singer with such a voice *c)* a part for a tenor

**ten′pins′** *n.pl.* **1.** [*with sing. v.*] the game of bowling in which ten pins are used **2.** the pins

**tense**[1] (tens) *adj.* **tens′er, tens′est** [ < L. *tendere*, stretch] **1.** stretched tight; taut **2.** undergoing or showing tension —*vt.*, *vi.* tensed, tens′ing to make or become tense **—tense′ly** *adv.* **—tense′ness, ten·si·ty** (ten′sə tē) *n.*

**tense**[2] (tens) *n.* [ < L. *tempus*, time] any of the forms of a verb that show the time of its action or existence

**ten·sile** (ten′s'l) *adj.* **1.** of, undergoing, or exerting tension **2.** capable of being stretched

**ten·sion** (ten′shən) *n.* **1.** a tensing or being tensed **2.** mental or nervous strain **3.** a state of strained relations due to mutual hostility **4.** voltage **5.** stress on a material produced by the pull of forces causing extension

**tent** (tent) *n.* [ < L. *tendere*, to stretch] a portable shelter made of canvas, etc. stretched over poles —*vi.*, *vt.* to lodge in a tent or tents

**ten·ta·cle** (ten′tə k'l) *n.* [ < L. *tentare*, to touch] a long, slender, flexible growth about the head of some invertebrates, used to grasp, feel, etc.

**ten·ta·tive** (ten′tə tiv) *adj.* [ < L. *tentare*, try] made, done, etc. as a test or experiment **—ten′ta·tive·ly** *adv.*

**ten·ter·hook** (ten′tər hook′) *n.* [ < L: *tendere*, to stretch + HOOK] any of the hooked nails holding cloth stretched on a drying frame (**tenter**) **—on tenterhooks** in anxious suspense

**tenth** (tenth) *adj.* [OE. *teogotha*] preceded by nine others in a series; 10th —*n.* **1.** the one following the ninth **2.** any of the ten equal parts of something; 1/10 **3.** a tenth of a gallon

**ten·u·ous** (ten′yoo wəs) *adj.* [ < L. *tenuis*, thin] **1.** slender or fine, as a fiber **2.** rare, as air at high altitudes **3.** not substantial; flimsy

**ten·ure** (ten′yər, -yoor) *n.* [ < MFr. *tenir*, to hold] **1.** the act or right of holding property, an office, etc. **2.** the length of time, or the conditions under which, something is held

**te·pee** (tē′pē) *n.* [ < Siouan *ti*, dwell + *pi*, used for] a cone-shaped tent used by American Indians

**tep·id** (tep′id) *adj.* [ < L. *tepidus*] **1.** lukewarm **2.** lacking enthusiasm

**te·qui·la** (tə kē′lə) *n.* [ < *Tequila*, Mex. district] an alcoholic liquor distilled from a Mexican agave

TEPEE

**ter·cen·te·nar·y** (tur'sen ten'ər ē, tər sen'tə ner'ē) *adj., n., pl.* **-ies** [L. *ter*, three times + CENTENARY] tricentennial

**term** (turm) *n.* [< L. *terminus*, a limit] **1.** a set date, as for payment, etc. **2.** a set period of time [school *term*, *term* of office] **3.** [*pl.*] conditions of a contract, etc. **4.** [*pl.*] mutual relationship between persons [on speaking *terms*] **5.** a word or phrase, esp. as used in some science, art, etc. **6.** [*pl.*] words; speech [unkind *terms*] **7.** *Math.* *a*) either quantity of a fraction or a ratio *b*) each quantity in a series or algebraic expression —*vt.* to call by a term; name —**bring** (or **come**) **to terms** to force into (or arrive at) an agreement —**in terms of** regarding; concerning

**ter·ma·gant** (tur'mə gənt) *n.* [< OFr. *Tervagant*, imaginary Moslem deity] a quarrelsome, scolding woman —*adj.* quarrelsome; scolding

**ter·mi·na·ble** (tur'mi nə b'l) *adj.* that can be, or is, terminated

**ter·mi·nal** (tur'mə n'l) *adj.* [L. *terminalis*] **1.** of, at, or forming the end or extremity **2.** concluding; final **3.** close to causing death, as cancer **4.** of or at the end of a transportation line —*n.* **1.** an end; extremity **2.** a connective point on an electric circuit **3.** either end of a transportation line, or a main station on it

**ter·mi·nate** (tur'mə nāt') *vt.* **-nat'-ed, -nat'ing** [< L. *terminus*, a limit] **1.** to form the end of **2.** to put an end to; stop —*vi.* **1.** to come to an end **2.** to have its end (*in* something) —**ter'mi·na'tion** *n.*

**ter·mi·nol·o·gy** (tur'mə näl'ə jē) *n., pl.* **-gies** the terms used in a specific science, art, etc.

**term insurance** life insurance that expires after a specified period

**ter·mi·nus** (tur'mə nəs) *n., pl.* **-ni'** (-nī'), **-nus·es** [L., a limit] **1.** a limit **2.** an end; extremity or goal **3.** either end of a transportation line

**ter·mite** (tur'mīt) *n.* [L. *termes*, wood-boring worm] a social insect very destructive to wooden structures

**tern** (turn) *n.* [< ON. *therna*] a sea bird related to the gull, but smaller

**terp·si·cho·re·an** (turp'si kə rē'ən) *adj.* [< *Terpsichore*, Muse of dancing] having to do with dancing

**ter·race** (ter'əs) *n.* [< L. *terra*, earth] **1.** a raised, flat mound of earth with sloping sides, esp. one in a series on a hillside **2.** an unroofed, paved area next to a house and overlooking a garden **3.** a row of houses on ground above street level, or the street below it —*vt.* **-raced, -rac·ing** to form into a terrace or terraces

**ter·ra cot·ta** (ter'ə kät'ə) [It., lit. baked earth] a hard, brown-red earthenware, or its color

**terra fir·ma** (fur'mə) [L.] firm earth; solid ground

**ter·rain** (tə rān', ter'ān) *n.* [< L. *terra*, earth] a tract of ground, esp. with regard to its fitness for some use

**ter·ra·pin** (ter'ə pin) *n.* [< Algonquian] **1.** any of various freshwater or tidewater turtles **2.** its edible flesh

**ter·rar·i·um** (tə rer'ē əm) *n., pl.* **-i·ums, -i·a** (-ə) [< L. *terra*, earth + (AQU)ARIUM] an enclosure, as of glass, in which small plants are grown or small land animals are kept

**ter·raz·zo** (tə raz'ō, -rät'sō) *n.* [It.] flooring of small chips of marble set in cement and polished

**ter·res·tri·al** (tə res'trē əl) *adj.* [< L. *terra*, earth] **1.** worldly; mundane **2.** of the earth **3.** consisting of land, not water **4.** living on land

**ter·ri·ble** (ter'ə b'l) *adj.* [< L. *terrere*, frighten] **1.** causing terror; dreadful **2.** extreme; intense **3.** [Colloq.] very unpleasant, etc. —**ter'ri·bly** *adv.*

**ter·ri·er** (ter'ē ər) *n.* [< MFr. (*chien*) *terrier*, hunting (dog)] any of various breeds of active, typically small dog

**ter·rif·ic** (tə rif'ik) *adj.* [< L. *terrere*, frighten] **1.** causing great fear **2.** [Colloq.] *a*) very great, intense, etc. *b*) unusually fine, admirable, etc.

**ter·ri·fy** (ter'ə fī') *vt.* **-fied', -fy'ing** to fill with terror; frighten greatly

**ter·ri·to·ry** (ter'ə tôr'ē) *n., pl.* **-ries** [< L. *terra*, earth] **1.** an area under the jurisdiction of a nation, ruler, etc. **2.** a part of a country or empire that does not have full status **3.** any large tract of land **4.** an assigned area **5.** a sphere of action, thought, etc. —**ter'ri·to'ri·al** *adj.*

**ter·ror** (ter'ər) *n.* [< L. *terrere*, frighten] **1.** intense fear **2.** *a*) one that causes intense fear *b*) the quality of causing such fear

**ter·ror·ism** *n.* the use of force or threats to intimidate, etc., esp. as a political policy —**ter'ror·ist** *n., adj.*

**ter·ror·ize'** (-īz') *vt.* **-ized', -iz'ing** **1.** to terrify **2.** to coerce, make submit, etc. by filling with terror

**ter·ry** (ter'ē) *n.* [prob. < Fr. *tirer*, to draw] cloth having a pile of uncut loops, esp. cotton cloth used for toweling: also **terry cloth**

**terse** (turs) *adj.* **ters'er, ters'est** [L. *tersus*, wiped off] free of superfluous words; concise; succinct —**terse'ly** *adv.* —**terse'ness** *n.*

**ter·ti·ar·y** (tur'shē er'ē) *adj.* [< L. *tertius*, third] third in order

**tes·sel·late** (tes'ə lāt') *vt.* **-lat'ed, -lat'ing** [< L. *tessella*, little square stone] to lay out in a mosaic pattern of small, square blocks

**test** (test) *n.* [< OFr., assaying cup] **1.** *a*) an examination or trial, as of something's value *b*) the method or a criterion used in this **2.** an event, etc. that tries one's qualities **3.** a set of questions, etc. for determining one's knowledge, etc. **4.** *Chem.* a trial or reaction for identifying a substance

—*vt.* to subject to a test; try —*vi.* to be rated by a test —**test′er** *n.*

**tes·ta·ment** (tes′tə mənt) *n.* [< L. *testis,* a witness] **1.** [T-] either of the two parts of the Bible, the *Old Testament* and the *New Testament* **2.** *a)* a testimonial *b)* an affirmation of beliefs **3.** *Law* a will —**tes′ta·men·ta·ry** (-men′tə rē) *adj.*

**tes′ta·tor** *n.* one who has made a will

**tes·ti·cle** (tes′ti k'l) *n.* [< L. *testis*] either of two male sex glands

**tes·ti·fy** (tes′tə fī′) *vi.* -fied′, -fy′ing [< L. *testis,* a witness + *facere,* make] **1.** to give evidence, esp. under oath in court **2.** to serve as evidence —*vt.* **1.** to affirm; declare, esp. under oath in court **2.** to indicate

**tes·ti·mo·ni·al** (tes′tə mō′nē əl) *n.* **1.** a statement recommending a person or thing **2.** something given or done to show gratitude or appreciation

**tes·ti·mo·ny** (tes′tə mō′nē) *n., pl.* **-nies** [< L. *testis,* a witness] **1.** a statement made under oath to establish a fact **2.** any declaration **3.** any form of evidence; proof

**tes·tis** (tes′tis) *n., pl.* **-tes** (-tēz) *same as* TESTICLE

**tes·tos·ter·one** (tes täs′tə rōn′) *n.* [see TESTICLE] a male sex hormone

**test tube** a tube of thin, transparent glass closed at one end, used in chemical experiments, etc.

**tes·ty** (tes′tē) *adj.* -ti·er, -ti·est [< L. *testa,* the head] irritable; touchy

**tet·a·nus** (tet′'n əs) *n.* [< Gr. *tetanos,* spasm] an acute infectious disease, often fatal, caused by a toxin and characterized by spasmodic contractions and rigidity of muscles

**tête-à-tête** (tāt′ə tāt′) *n.* [Fr., lit., head-to-head] a private conversation between two people

**teth·er** (teth′ər) *n.* [< ON. *tjōthr*] **1.** a rope or chain fastened to an animal to keep it from roaming **2.** the limit of one's abilities, resources, etc. —*vt.* to fasten with a tether

**tet·ra** (tet′rə) *n.* [< ModL.] a brightly colored, tropical American fish

**tetra-** [Gr. < *tettares,* four] *a combining form meaning* four

**tet·ra·eth·yl lead** (tet′rə eth′'l) a poisonous lead compound added to gasoline to prevent engine knock

**tet·ra·he·dron** (tet′rə hē′drən) *n., pl.* **-drons, -dra** (-drə) [see TETRA- & -HEDRON] a solid figure with four triangular faces

**Teut. 1.** Teuton **2.** Teutonic

**Teu·ton·ic** (tōō tän′ik) *adj.* designating of or of a group of north European peoples, esp. the Germans —**Teu·ton** (tōōt′'n) *n.*

TETRA-
HEDRON

**Tex·as** (tek′səs) SW State of the U.S.: 267,339 sq. mi.; pop. 11,197,000; cap. Austin: abbrev. **Tex.** —**Tex′an** *adj., n.*

**text** (tekst) *n.* [< L. *texere,* to weave] **1.** the actual words of an author, as distinguished from notes, etc. **2.** any form in which a written work exists **3.** the principal matter on a printed page,

as distinguished from notes, headings, etc. **4.** *a)* a Biblical passage used as the topic of a sermon, etc. *b)* any topic or subject **5.** a textbook —**tex·tu·al** (teks′choo wəl) *adj.*

**text′book′** *n.* a book giving instructions in a subject of study

**tex·tile** (teks′til, -t'l) *adj.* [see TEXT] **1.** having to do with weaving **2.** that has been or can be woven —*n.* **1.** a woven or knitted fabric; cloth **2.** raw material suitable for this

**tex·ture** (teks′chər) *n.* [< L. *texere,* to weave] **1.** the character of a fabric, determined by the arrangement, size, etc. of its threads **2.** the arrangement of the constituent parts of anything —**tex′tur·al** *adj.*

**-th¹** [OE.] *a suffix meaning:* **1.** the act of *[stealth]* **2.** the state or quality of being or having *[wealth]*

**-th²** [< OE.] a suffix used in forming ordinal numbers *[fourth, ninth]*

**Th.** Thursday

**Thai** (tī) *n.* **1.** a subbranch of the Sino-Tibetan language **2.** the language of Thailand **3.** *pl.* **Thais, Thai** *a)* a member of a group of Thai-speaking peoples of SE Asia *b)* a native or inhabitant of Thailand —*adj.* of Thailand, its people, culture, etc.

**Thai·land** (tī′land) country in SE Asia: 198,456 sq. mi.; pop. 33,693,000

**thal·a·mus** (thal′ə məs) *n., pl.* **-mi′** (-mī′) [< Gr. *thalamos,* inner chamber] a mass of gray matter at the base of the brain, involved in the transmission of certain sensations

**tha·lid·o·mide** (thə lid′ə mīd′) *n.* a drug formerly used as a sedative, but found to cause severe birth deformities when taken in pregnancy

**thal·lo·phyte** (thal′ə fīt′) *n.* [< Gr. *thallos,* green shoot + *phyton,* a plant] any of a large division of plants including the bacteria, algae, fungi, and lichens

**Thames** (temz) river in S England, flowing through London into the North Sea

**than** (*th*an, *th*en) *conj.* [OE. *thenne*] a particle used to introduce the second element in a comparison *[I am taller than Bill]*

**thank** (*th*aŋk) *vt.* [OE. *thancian*] **1.** to give one's thanks to **2.** to hold responsible; blame: an ironic use — **thank you** *short for* I thank you

**thank′ful** *adj.* feeling or expressing thanks —**thank′ful·ly** *adv.*

**thank′less** *adj.* **1.** not feeling or expressing thanks; ungrateful **2.** unappreciated —**thank′less·ly** *adv.*

**thanks** *n.pl.* an expression of gratitude —*interj.* I thank you —**thanks to 1.** thanks be given to **2.** on account of; because of

**thanks·giv′ing** *n.* **1.** a formal public expression of thanks to God **2.** [T-] an annual U.S. holiday observed on the fourth Thursday of November

**that** (*th*at) *pron., adj.* **those** [OE. *thæt*] **1.** the person or thing mentioned *[that is John]* **2.** the farther one or other one *[this is better than that]* **3.** who, whom, or which *[the road that we* took/ **4.** where /the place that I saw him/ **5.** when /the year that he died/ —*adj.*, *pl.* **those 1.** designating the one mentioned /that man is John/ **2.** designating the farther one or other one /this house is larger than that one/ —*conj.*, *used to introduce:* **1.** a noun clause /that he's gone is obvious/ **2.** an adverbial clause expressing purpose /they died that we might live/, result /he ran so fast that I lost him/, or cause /I'm sorry that I won/ **3.** an elliptical sentence expressing surprise, desire, etc. /oh, that he were here!/ —*adv.* to that extent; so /I can't see that far/ —**at that** [Colloq.] **1.** at that point: also **with that 2.** even so —**that is 1.** to be specific **2.** in other words

**thatch** (thach) *n.* [OE. *thæc*] **1.** a roof of straw, rushes, etc. **2.** material for such a roof: also **thatch′ing** —*vt.* to cover as with thatch

**thaw** (thô) *vi.* [OE. *thawian*] **1.** *a)* to melt, as ice, snow, etc. *b)* to become unfrozen: said of frozen foods **2.** to become warmer so that snow, etc. melts **3.** to lose one's coldness of manner —*vt.* to cause to thaw —*n.* **1.** a thawing **2.** a spell of weather warm enough to allow thawing

**THC** [*t*(*etra*)*h*(*ydro*)*c*(*annabinol*)] the principal and most active chemical in marijuana

**Th.D.** Doctor of Theology

**the** (thə; *before vowels* thi, thē) *adj.*, *definite article* [< OE. *se*, with *th*-from other forms] *the* (as opposed to *a*, *an*) refers to: **1.** a particular person or thing /the story ended, the President/ **2.** a person or thing considered generically /the cow is a domestic animal, the poor/ —*adv.* **1.** that much /the better to see you/ **2.** by how much . . . by that much /the sooner the better/

**the·a·ter, the·a·tre** (thē′ə tər) *n.* [< Gr. *theasthai*, to view] **1.** a place or building where plays, motion pictures, etc. are presented **2.** any similar place with banked rows of seats **3.** any scene of events **4.** *a)* the dramatic art *b)* the theatrical world

**the·at·ri·cal** (thē at′ri k'l) *adj.* **1.** having to do with the theater **2.** dramatic; esp. (in disparagement), melodramatic —**the·at′ri·cal·ly** *adv.*

**thee** (thē) *pron.* [OE. *the*] objective case of THOU

**theft** (theft) *n.* [OE. *thiefth*] the act or an instance of stealing; larceny

**their** (ther) *poss. pronominal adj.* [< ON. *theirra*] of, belonging to, made by, or done by them

**theirs** (therz) *pron.* that or those belonging to them /theirs are better/

**the·ism** (thē′iz'm) *n.* [< Gr. *theos*, god] **1.** belief in a god or gods **2.** monotheism —**the′ist** *n.* —**the·is′tic** *adj.*

**them** (them) *pron.* [< ON. *theim*] objective case of THEY

**theme** (thēm) *n.* [< Gr. *thema*, what is laid down] **1.** a topic, as of an essay **2.** a short essay **3.** a short melody used

as the subject of a musical composition **4.** a recurring or identifying song in a film, musical, radio or TV series, etc.: also **theme song** —**the·mat·ic** (thē mat′ik) *adj.*

**them·selves** (them selvz′) *pron.* **1.** intensive form of THEY /they went themselves/ **2.** reflexive form of THEY /they hurt themselves/

**then** (then) *adv.* [see THAN] **1.** at that time /I did it then/ **2.** next in time or order /he ate and then slept/ **3.** in that case; accordingly /if he read it, then he knows/, **4.** besides; moreover /I like to walk, and then it's cheaper/ **5.** at another time /now she's happy, then sad/ —*adj.* being such at that time /the then director/ —*n.* that time /by then, they were gone/

**thence** (thens, thens) *adv.* [OE. *thanan*] **1.** from that place **2.** from that time; thenceforth **3.** therefore

**thence′forth′** (-fôrth′) *adv.* from that time onward; thereafter: also **thence′for′ward, thence′for′wards**

**the·oc·ra·cy** (thē äk′rə sē) *n.*, *pl.* **-cies** [< Gr. *theos*, god + *kratos*, power] (a) government by priests claiming to rule with divine authority

**the·o·lo·gi·an** (thē′ə lō′jən, -jē ən) *n.* a student of or specialist in theology

**the·ol·o·gy** (thē äl′ə jē) *n.*, *pl.* **-gies** [< Gr. *theos*, god + *logos*, discourse] the study of God and of religious doctrines and matters of divinity —**the′o·log′i·cal** (-ə läj′i k'l) *adj.*

**the·o·rem** (thē′ə rəm) *n.* [< Gr. *theōrein*, to view] **1.** a proposition that can be proved from accepted premises; law or principle **2.** a proposition embodying something to be proved

**the·o·ret·i·cal** (thē′ə ret′i k'l) *adj.* **1.** limited to or based on theory; hypothetical **2.** tending to theorize; speculative Also **the′o·ret′ic** —**the′o·ret′i·cal·ly** *adv.*

**the·o·rize** (thē′ə rīz′) *vi.* **-rized′, -riz′ing** to form a theory or theories; speculate —**the′o·re·ti′cian** (-rə tish′ən), **the′o·rist** (-rist) *n.*

**the·o·ry** (thē′ə rē, thir′ē) *n.*, *pl.* **-ries** [< Gr. *theōrein*, to view] **1.** a speculative plan **2.** a formulation of underlying principles of certain observed phenomena which has been verified to some degree **3.** the principles of an art or science rather than its practice **4.** a conjecture; guess

**the·os·o·phy** (thē äs′ə fē) *n.*, *pl.* **-phies** [< Gr. *theos*, god + *sophos*, wise] a religious system proposing to establish direct, mystical contact with the divine spirit —**the′o·soph′ic** (-ə säf′ik) *adj.* —**the′o·soph′i·cal·ly** *adv.* —**the·os′o·phist** *n.*

**ther·a·peu·tic** (ther′ə pyoot′ik) *adj.* [< Gr. *therapeuein*, to nurse] serving to cure or heal or to preserve health

**ther′a·peu′tics** *n.pl.* [with sing. v.] the branch of medicine dealing with the treatment of disease; therapy

**ther'a·py** (-pē) *n.*, *pl.* **-pies** [see THERAPEUTIC] the treatment of any physical or mental disorder by medical or physical means, usually excluding surgery —**ther'a·pist** *n.*

**there** (*th*er) *adv.* [OE. *ther*] 1. at or in that place: often used as an intensive [John *there* is a good player] 2. to or into that place [go *there*] 3. at that point; then 4. in that respect [*there* you are wrong] *There* is also used in clauses in which the real subject follows the verb [*there* is little time] —at that place [we left *there* at six] —*interj.* an exclamation of defiance, satisfaction, sympathy, etc. —(not) all **there** (not) mentally sound

**there'a·bouts'** (-ə bouts') *adv.* 1. near that place 2. near that time, number, degree, etc. Also **there'a·bout'**

**there·af'ter** *adv.* from then on

**there·at'** *adv.* 1. at that place; there 2. at that time 3. for that reason

**there·by'** *adv.* 1. by that means 2. connected with that

**there·for'** *adv.* for this or that; for it

**there'fore'** (-fôr') *adv.* for this or that reason; hence

**there·in'** *adv.* 1. in or into that place 2. in that matter, detail, etc.

**there·of'** *adv.* 1. of that 2. from that as a cause, reason, etc.

**there·on'** *adv.* 1. on that or it 2. immediately following that

**there·to'** *adv.* to that place, thing, etc.: also **there·un'to** (-un'tōō)

**there'to·fore'** *adv.* until that time

**there'up·on'** *adv.* 1. immediately following that 2. as a consequence of that 3. concerning that subject, etc.

**there·with'** *adv.* 1. along with that 2. immediately thereafter

**ther·mal** (thur'm'l) *adj.* [< Gr. *thermē*, heat] 1. having to do with heat 2. designating a loosely knitted material with air spaces for insulation

**thermal pollution** the discharge of heated liquid into lakes, rivers, etc., as by industries, that is harmful to the ecosystems

**thermo-** [< Gr. *thermē*, heat] *a combining form meaning* heat

**ther·mo·dy·nam·ics** (thur'mō dī nam'iks) *n.pl.* [*with sing. v.*] the science dealing with the reversible transformation of heat into mechanical energy —**ther'mo·dy·nam'ic** *adj.*

**ther·mom·e·ter** (thər mäm'ə tər) *n.* [THERMO- + -METER] an instrument for measuring temperatures, as a graduated glass tube in which mercury, etc. rises or falls as it expands or contracts from changes in temperature

**ther·mo·nu·cle·ar** (thur'mō nōō'klē ər) *adj.* *Physics* 1. designating a reaction in which isotopes of a light element fuse, at extreme heat, into heavier nuclei 2. of or using the heat released in nuclear fusion

**ther·mo·plas·tic** (thur'mō plas'tik) *adj.* soft and moldable when subjected to heat: said of certain plastics —*n.* a thermoplastic substance

**ther·mos** (thur'məs) *n.* [orig. a trademark < Gr. *thermos*, hot] a bottle or jug for keeping liquids at almost their original temperature: in full **thermos bottle** (or **jug**)

**ther·mo·stat** (thur'mə stat') *n.* [THERMO- + -STAT] an apparatus for regulating temperature, esp. one that automatically controls a heating unit

**the·sau·rus** (thi sôr'əs) *n.*, *pl.* **-ri** (-ī), **-rus·es** [< Gr. *thēsauros*, a treasure] a book of synonyms and antonyms

**these** (*th*ēz) *pron.*, *adj. pl.* of THIS

**The·seus** (thē'sōōs, -sē əs) *Gr. Legend* a hero who killed the Minotaur

**the·sis** (thē'sis) *n.*, *pl.* **-ses** (-sēz) [< Gr. *tithenai*, to put] 1. a proposition to be defended in argument 2. a research paper, esp. one written by a candidate for a master's degree

**Thes·pi·an** (thes'pē ən) *adj.* [< *Thespis*, ancient Gr. poet] having to do with the drama; dramatic —*n.* [*often* t-] an actor

**the·ta** (thāt'ə, thēt'-) *n.* the eighth letter of the Greek alphabet (Θ, θ)

**thews** (thyōōz) *n.pl.*, *sing.* **thew** [< OE. *thēaw*, habit] muscles or sinews

**they** (*th*ā) *pron.* [for sing. see HE, SHE, IT] [< ON. *their*] 1. the persons, animals, or things previously mentioned 2. people generally or indefinitely [*they* say it's so]

**they'd** (*th*ād) 1. they had 2. they would

**they'll** (*th*āl) 1. they will 2. they shall

**they're** (*th*er) they are

**they've** (*th*āv) they have

**thi·a·mine** (thī'ə mēn', -min) *n.* [ult. < Gr. *theion*, brimstone + (VIT)AMIN] a factor of the vitamin B complex, found in cereal, egg yolk, liver, etc.; vitamin B₁: also **thi'a·min** (-min)

**thick** (thik) *adj.* [OE. *thicce*] 1. of relatively great extent from side to side 2. measured between opposite surfaces [one inch *thick*] 3. close and abundant [*thick* hair] 4. viscous [*thick* soup] 5. dense [*thick* smoke] 6. husky; hoarse; blurred [*thick* speech] 7. [Colloq.] stupid 8. [Colloq.] very friendly —*n.* the thickest part —**thick'ly** *adv.* —**thick'ness** *n.*

**thick'en** *vt.*, *vi.* 1. to make or become thick or thicker 2. to make or become more complex —**thick'en·ing** *n.*

**thick·et** (thik'it) *n.* [see THICK] a thick growth of shrubs or small trees

**thick'set'** *adj.* 1. planted thickly or closely 2. thick in body; stocky

**thick'-skinned'** *adj.* 1. having a thick skin 2. insensitive, as to insult

**thief** (thēf) *n.*, *pl.* **thieves** (thēvz) [OE. *theof*] one who steals

**thieve** (thēv) *vt.*, *vi.* **thieved**, **thiev'ing** to steal —**thiev'ish** *adj.*

**thiev·er·y** (-ər ē) *n.*, *pl.* **-ies** the act or an instance of stealing; theft

**thigh** (thī) *n.* [OE. *theoh*] the part of the leg between the knee and the hip

**thigh'bone'** *n.* the bone extending from the hip to the knee

**thim·ble** (thim'b'l) *n.* [< OE. *thuma*, thumb] a small cap worn to protect the finger that pushes the needle in sewing —**thim'ble·ful'** *n.*, *pl.* **-fuls'**

**thin** (thin) *adj.* **thin'ner**, **thin'nest** [OE. *thynne*] 1. of relatively little extent from side to side 2. lean;

slender 3. not dense or compact [thin hair, thin smoke] 4. very fluid or watery [thin soup] 5. high-pitched and weak [a thin voice] 6. sheer, as fabric 7. flimsy or unconvincing [a thin excuse] 8. lacking substance, depth, etc.; weak —vt., vi. **thinned, thin′ning** to make or become thin or thinner —**thin′ly** adv. —**thin′ness** n.

**thine** (ᵺīn) pron. [OE. thīn] poss. form of THOU: chiefly before a vowel

**thing** (thiŋ) n. [OE., council] 1. any matter, affair, or concern 2. a happening, act, incident, etc. 3. a tangible or an inanimate object 4. an item, detail, etc. 5. a) [pl.] personal belongings b) a garment 6. [Colloq.] a person [poor thing] 7. [Colloq.] a point of contention; issue 8. [Colloq.] an irrational liking, fear, etc. 9. [Colloq.] what one wants to do or is adept at [do one's own thing] —see **things** [Colloq.] to have hallucinations

**think** (thiŋk) vt. **thought, think′ing** [OE. thencan] 1. to form or have in the mind [to think ill of one] 2. to judge; consider [he is thought wise] 3. to believe; expect [I think I can] —vi. 1. to use the mind; reason 2. to have an opinion (often with of or about) 3. to remember or consider (with of or about) 4. to conceive (of) —**think up** to invent, plan, etc. by thinking —**think′er** n.

**think tank** (or **factory**) [Slang] a group or center organized to do intensive research and problem-solving

**thin·ner** (thin′ər) n. a substance added to paint, shellac, etc. to thin it

**thin′-skinned′** adj. 1. having a thin skin 2. sensitive, as to insult

**third** (thurd) adj. [OE. thridda] preceded by two others in a series; 3d or 3rd —n. 1. the one following the second 2. any of the three equal parts of something; 1/3 —adv. in the third place: also **third′ly**

**third′-class′** adj. 1. of the class, rank, etc. next below the second 2. of a low-cost mail class, as for advertisements —adv. by third-class mail or travel accommodations

**third degree** [Colloq.] cruel treatment and questioning to force confession

**third dimension** 1. depth or solidity 2. the quality of seeming real

**third person** that form of a pronoun (as he) or verb (as is) which refers to the person or thing spoken of

**third′-rate′** adj. 1. third in quality or other rating 2. very poor

**third world** [often T- W-] the underdeveloped countries of the world

**thirst** (thurst) n. [OE. thurst] 1. the discomfort caused by a need for drink 2. a strong desire; craving —vi. 1. to feel thirst 2. to have a strong desire or craving —**thirst′i·ly** adv. —**thirst′y** adj. -i·er, -i·est

**thir·teen** (thur′tēn′) adj., n. [OE. threotyne] three more than ten; 13; XIII —**thir′teenth′** adj., n.

**thir·ty** (thurt′ē) adj., n., pl. -ties [OE. thritig] three times ten; 30; XXX —**the thirties** the numbers or years, as of a century, from 30 through 39 —**thir′ti·eth** (-ith) adj., n.

**this** (ᵺis) pron., adj., pl. **these** [OE. thes] 1. (designating) the person or thing mentioned [this (man) is John] 2. (designating) the nearer one or another one [this (desk) is older than that] 3. (designating) something about to be presented [hear this (news)] —adv. to this extent [it was this big]

**this·tle** (this′'l) n. [OE. thistel] a plant with prickly leaves and white, purple, etc. flowers

**this′tle·down′** n. the down growing from the flowers of a thistle

**thith·er** (thith′ər, thith′-) adv. [OE. thider] to or toward that place; there

**tho, tho′** (thō) conj., adv. though

**thole** (thōl) n. [OE. thol] one of a pair of pins set as an oarlock into the gunwale of a boat: also **thole′pin′**

**thong** (thôŋ) n. [OE. thwang] a narrow strip of leather, etc. used as a lace, strap, etc.

**Thor** (thôr) Norse Myth. the god of thunder, war, and strength

**tho·rax** (thôr′aks) n., pl. -rax·es, -ra·ces′ (-ə sēz′) [< Gr.] 1. the part of the body between the neck and the abdomen; chest 2. the middle one of the three main segments of an insect —**tho·rac·ic** (thō ras′ik) adj.

**Thor·eau** (thôr′ō, thə rō′), **Henry David** 1817–62; U.S. writer

**tho·ri·um** (thôr′ē əm) n. [< THOR] a rare, grayish, radioactive chemical element, used as a nuclear fuel

**thorn** (thôrn) n. [OE.] 1. a) a very short, hard, leafless stem with a sharp point b) any small tree or shrub bearing thorns 2. source of constant trouble or irritation —**thorn′y** adj.

**thor·ough** (thur′ō) adj. [var. of THROUGH] 1. done or proceeding through to the end; complete 2. absolute [a thorough rascal] 3. very exact, accurate, or painstaking —**thor′ough·ly** adv. —**thor′ough·ness** n.

**thor·ough·bred** (thur′ō bred′) adj. of pure stock; pedigreed —n. a thoroughbred animal; specif., [T-] any of a breed of racehorses

**thor′ough·fare′** (-fer′) n. a public street open at both ends, esp. a main highway

**thor′ough·go′ing** adj. very thorough

**those** (ᵺōz) adj., pron. pl. of THAT

**thou** (ᵺou) pron. [OE. thū] you (sing.): in poetic or religious use

**though** (ᵺō) conj. [OE. theah] 1. in spite of the fact that [though it rained, he went] 2. and yet; however [they did it, though badly] 3. even if [though he may fail, he will have tried] —adv. however; nevertheless

**thought¹** (thôt) n. [OE. thoht] 1. the act or process of thinking 2. the power of reasoning 3. an idea, concept, etc. 4. attention; consideration 5. a little; trifle [be a *thought* more careful]

**thought²** (thôt) *pt. & pp.* of THINK

**thought'ful** *adj.* 1. full of thought; meditative 2. considerate —**thought'-ful·ly** *adv.* —**thought'ful·ness** *n.*

**thought'less** *adj.* 1. not stopping to think; careless 2. ill-considered; rash 3. inconsiderate —**thought'less·ly** *adv.* —**thought'less·ness** *n.*

**thou·sand** (thou'z'nd) *adj., n.* [OE. *thusend*] ten hundred; 1,000; M —**thou'sandth** (-z'ndth) *adj., n.*

**thrall** (thrôl) *n.* [ < ON. *thræll*] 1. a slave 2. slavery —**thrall'dom, thral'dom** (-dəm) *n.*

**thrash** (thrash) *vt., vi.* [OE. *threscan*] 1. *same as* THRESH 2. to beat; flog 3. to toss about violently 4. to defeat overwhelmingly —**thrash out** to settle by detailed discussion —**thrash'er** *n.*

**thrash'er** *n.* [Eng. dial. *thresher*] a thrushlike American songbird

**thread** (thred) *n.* [OE. *thræd*] 1. a fine, stringlike length of spun cotton, silk, nylon, etc., used in sewing 2. any thin line, vein, etc. 3. something like a thread in its length, sequence, etc. [the *thread* of a story] 4. the spiral ridge of a screw, nut, etc. —*vt.* 1. to put a thread through (a needle, etc.) 2. to make (one's way) by twisting, weaving, etc. 3. to fashion a thread (sense 4) on or in —**thread'y** *adj.*

**thread'bare'** *adj.* 1. worn down so that the threads show 2. wearing worn clothes; shabby 3. stale; trite

**threat** (thret) *n.* [OE. *threat*, pressure] 1. an expression of intention to hurt, destroy, punish, etc. 2. an indication of, or a source of, imminent danger

**threat'en** *vt., vi.* 1. to make threats, as of injury (against) 2. to indicate (danger, etc.) 3. to be a source of danger (to)

**three** (thrē) *adj., n.* [OE. *threo*] one more than two; 3; III

**three'-deck'er** (-dek'ər) *n.* anything having three levels, layers, etc.

**three'-di·men'sion·al** *adj.* having or seeming to have depth or thickness

**three'fold'** *adj.* 1. having three parts 2. having three times as much or as many —*adv.* three times as much or as many

**three·score** (thrē'skôr') *adj.* sixty

**thren·o·dy** (thren'ə dē) *n., pl.* -dies [ < Gr. *thrēnos*, lamentation + *ōidē*, song] a song of lamentation; dirge

**thresh** (thresh) *vt., vi.* [ME. *threschen*] 1. to beat out (grain) from (husks), as with a flail 2. *same as* THRASH —**thresh'er** *n.*

**thresh·old** (thresh'ōld, -hōld) *n.* [OE. *therscwold*] 1. a length of wood, stone, etc. along the bottom of a doorway 2. the beginning point

**threw** (thrōō) *pt.* of THROW

**thrice** (thrīs) *adv.* [OE. *thriwa*] 1. three times 2. threefold

**thrift** (thrift) *n.* [ < ON. *thrifa*, to grasp] economy; frugality —**thrift'i·ly** *adv.* —**thrift'less** *adj.* —**thrift'y** *adj.*, -**i·er**, -**i·est** —**thrift'i·ness** *n.*

**thrift shop** a store where castoff clothes, etc. are sold, as for charity

**thrill** (thril) *vi., vt.* [ < OE. *thurh*, through] 1. to feel or cause to feel emotional excitement 2. to quiver or cause to quiver; tremble —*n.* 1. a thrilling or being thrilled 2. a tremor; quiver —**thrill'er** *n.*

**thrive** (thrīv) *vi.* **thrived** or **throve, thrived** or **thriv·en** (thriv''n), **thriv'ing** [ < ON. *thrifa*, to grasp] 1. to prosper or flourish; be successful 2. to grow robustly

**throat** (thrōt) *n.* [OE. *throte*] 1. the front part of the neck 2. the upper passage from the mouth to the stomach and lungs 3. any narrow passage

**throat'y** *adj.* -**i·er**, -**i·est** produced in the throat, as some sounds; husky

**throb** (thräb) *vi.* **throbbed, throb'bing** [ME. *throbben*] 1. to beat, pulsate, vibrate, etc., esp. strongly or fast 2. to feel excitement —*n.* 1. a throbbing 2. a strong beat or pulsation

**throe** (thrō) *n.* [prob. < OE. *thrawu*, pain] 1. a spasm or pang of pain 2. [*pl.*] agony

**throm·bo·sis** (thräm bō'sis) *n.* [ < Gr. *thrombos*, a clot] coagulation of the blood in the heart or a blood vessel, forming a clot (**thrombus**)

**throne** (thrōn) *n.* [ < Gr. *thronos*, a seat] 1. the chair on which a king, cardinal, etc. sits on formal occasions 2. the power or rank of a king, etc. 3. a sovereign, ruler, etc.

**throng** (thrôŋ) *n.* [OE. *thringan*, to crowd] 1. a crowd 2. any great number of things considered together —*vi.* to gather together in a throng; crowd —*vt.* to crowd into

**throt·tle** (thrät''l) *n.* [ < ? THROAT] the valve that regulates the amount of fuel vapor entering an engine, or its control lever or pedal —*vt.* -**tled, -tling** 1. to choke; strangle 2. to censor or suppress 3. *a)* to reduce the flow of (fuel vapor) by means of a throttle *b)* to slow by this means

**through** (thrōō) *prep.* [OE. *thurh*] 1. in one side and out the other side of 2. in the midst of; among 3. by way of 4. around [touring *through* France] 5. *a)* from beginning to end of *b)* up to and including 6. by means of 7. as a result of —*adv.* 1. in one side and out the other 2. from the beginning to the end 3. completely to the end [see it *through*] 4. completely [soaked *through*] —*adj.* 1. extending from one place to another [a *through* street] 2. traveling to the destination without stops [a *through* train] 3. finished

**through'out'** *prep.* all the way through —*adv.* in every part; everywhere

**through'way'** (-wā') *n.* an expressway: also **thru'way'**

**throve** (thrōv) *alt. pt.* of THRIVE

**throw** (thrō) *vt.* **threw, thrown, throw'ing** [OE. *thrawan*, to twist] 1. to send through the air by a rapid motion of the arm, etc. 2. to cause to fall; upset 3. to send rapidly [to *throw* troops into battle] 4. to put suddenly into a specified state, etc. [*thrown* into confusion] 5. to move (a switch, etc.) so as to connect, disconnect, etc. 6. to direct, cast, etc. [*throw* a glance] 7.

[Colloq.] to lose (a game, etc.) deliberately **8.** [Colloq.] to give (a party, etc.) **9.** [Colloq.] to confuse or disconcert *[the question threw him]* —*vi.* to cast or hurl something —*n.* **1.** the act of one who throws **2.** the distance something is or can be thrown **3.** a spread for a bed, etc. —**throw away 1.** to discard **2.** to waste —**throw in** to add extra or free —**throw off 1.** to rid oneself of **2.** to mislead or confuse **3.** to expel, emit, etc. —**throw oneself at** to try very hard to win the love of — **throw out 1.** to discard **2.** to reject or remove —**throw over 1.** to give up; abandon **2.** to jilt —**throw together** to make or assemble hurriedly — **throw up 1.** to give up; abandon **2.** to vomit —**throw'er** *n.*

**throw'a·way'** *n.* a leaflet, handbill, etc. given out on streets, at houses, etc. —*adj.* designed to be discarded after use *[a throwaway bottle]*

**throw'back'** *n.* (a) reversion to an ancestral type

**throw rug** a small rug; scatter rug

**thru** (thrōō) *prep., adv., adj.* shortened *sp.* of THROUGH

**thrum** (thrum) *vt., vi.* **thrummed,** **thrum'ming** [echoic] *same as* STRUM

**thrush** (thrush) *n.* [OE. *thrysce*] any of a large family of songbirds, including the robin

**thrust** (thrust) *vt., vi.* **thrust,** **thrust'ing** [< ON. *thrysta*] **1.** to push with sudden force **2.** to stab **3.** to force or impose —*n.* **1.** a sudden, forceful push **2.** a stab **3.** continuous pressure, as of a rafter against a wall **4.** *a)* the driving force of a propeller *b)* the forward force produced by a jet or rocket engine **5.** forward movement **6.** the basic meaning; point

**Thu·cyd·i·des** (thōō sid'ə dēz') 460?-400? B.C.; Athenian historian

**thud** (thud) *vi.* **thud'ded, thud'-ding** [prob. < OE. *thyddan,* to strike] to hit with a dull sound —*n.* a dull sound, as of an object dropping on a soft surface

**thug** (thug) *n.* [Hindi *ṭhag,* swindler] a brutal hoodlum, gangster, etc.

**thumb** (thum) *n.* [OE. *thuma*] the short, thick digit of the hand —*vt.* **1.** to handle, soil, etc. as with the thumb **2.** [Colloq.] to solicit or get (a ride) in hitchhiking by signaling with the thumb —**all thumbs** clumsy —**under one's thumb** under one's influence

**thumb'nail'** *n.* the nail of the thumb —*adj.* very small, brief, or concise

**thumb'screw'** *n.* a screw that can be turned by the thumb and forefinger

**thumb'tack'** *n.* a tack with a wide, flat head, that can be pressed into a board, etc. with the thumb

THUMBSCREW

**thump** (thump) *n.* [echoic] **1.** a blow with something heavy and blunt **2.**

the dull sound made by such a blow —*vt.* to strike with a thump —*vi.* **1.** to hit or fall with a thump **2.** to make a dull, heavy sound

**thump'ing** *adj.* **1.** that thumps **2.** [Colloq.] very large; whopping

**thun·der** (thun'dər) *n.* [OE. *thunor*] **1.** the sound following a flash of lightning **2.** any similar sound —*vi.* to produce thunder or a sound like this —*vt.* to utter, etc. with a thundering sound —**thun·der·ous** *adj.*

**thun'der·bolt'** (-bōlt') *n.* **1.** a flash of lightning and the accompanying thunder **2.** something sudden and shocking, as bad news

**thun'der·clap'** *n.* a clap, or loud crash, of thunder

**thun'der·cloud'** *n.* a storm cloud charged with electricity and producing lightning and thunder

**thun'der·head'** (-hed') *n.* a round mass of cumulus clouds appearing before a thunderstorm

**thun'der·show'er** *n.* a shower accompanied by thunder and lightning

**thun'der·storm'** *n.* a storm accompanied by thunder and lightning

**thun'der·struck'** *adj.* struck with amazement, terror, etc.: also **thun'-der·strick'en** (-strik''n)

**Thurs., Thur.** Thursday

**Thurs·day** (thurz'dē, -dā) *n.* [< THOR] the fifth day of the week

**thus** (thus) *adv.* [OE.] **1.** in this or that manner **2.** to this or that degree or extent; so **3.** therefore

**thwack** (thwak) *vt., n.* [prob. echoic] *same as* WHACK

**thwart** (thwôrt) *n.* [< ON. *thvert,* transverse] a seat across a boat —*vt.* to obstruct, frustrate, or defeat (a person, plans, etc.)

**thy** (thī) *poss. pronominal adj.* [< ME. *thin*] of, belonging to, or done by thee: archaic or poet. var. of *your*

**thyme** (tīm) *n.* [< Gr. *thymon*] a plant of the mint family, with leaves used for seasoning

**thy·mus** (thī'məs) *n.* [< Gr. *thymos*] a ductless, glandlike body situated near the throat: also **thymus gland**

**thy·roid** (thī'roid) *adj.* [< Gr. *thyreos,* large shield] designating or of a large ductless gland near the trachea, secreting a hormone which regulates growth —*n.* **1.** the thyroid gland **2.** an animal extract of this gland, used in treating goiter, etc.

**thy·self** (thī self') *pron. reflexive or intensive form of* THOU

**ti** (tē) *n. Music* the seventh tone of the diatonic scale

**Ti·a Jua·na** (tē'ə hwän'ə, -wän'ə) *former name of* TIJUANA

**ti·ar·a** (tē er'ə, -ar'-) *n.* [< Gr. *tiara,* headdress] **1.** the Pope's triple crown **2.** a woman's crownlike headdress of jewels or flowers

**Ti·ber** (tī'bər) river in C Italy, flowing through Rome

**Ti·bet** (ti bet') plateau region of SW

China, north of the Himalayas — **Ti·bet'an** *adj.*, *n.*

**tib·i·a** (tib'ē ə) *n.*, *pl.* **-ae'** (-ē'), **-as** [L.] the inner and thicker of the two bones of the lower leg

**tic** (tik) *n.* [Fr. < ?] any involuntary, regularly repeated, spasmodic contraction of a muscle

**tick¹** (tik) *n.* [prob. echoic] 1. a light clicking sound, as of a clock 2. a mark made to check off items —*vi.* to make a tick or ticks —*vt.* to record, mark, or check by ticks

**tick²** (tik) *n.* [OE. *ticia*] any of various wingless, bloodsucking insects that infest man, cattle, etc.

**tick³** (tik) *n.* [ < ? L. *theca*, a cover] the cloth case of a mattress or pillow

**tick'er** *n.* 1. one that ticks 2. a telegraphic device that records stock market quotations, etc. on paper tape (**ticker tape**) 3. [Slang] the heart

**tick·et** (tik'it) *n.* [ < obs. Fr. *etiquet*, etiquette] 1. a printed card, etc. that gives one a right, as to attend a theater 2. a license or certificate 3. a label on merchandise giving size, price, etc. 4. the list of candidates nominated by a political party 5. [Colloq.] a court summons for a traffic violation —*vt.* 1. to label with a ticket 2. to give a ticket to

**tick'ing** *n.* strong cloth, often striped, used for pillow ticks, etc.

**tick·le** (tik''l) *vt.* **-led, -ling** [ME. *tikelen*] 1. to please, gratify, delight, etc. 2. to stroke lightly so as to cause involuntary twitching, laughter, etc. —*vi.* to have or cause a twitching or tingling sensation —*n.* a sensation of being tickled

**tick'ler** (tik'lər) *n.* a pad, file, etc. for noting items to be remembered

**tick'lish** (-lish) *adj.* 1. sensitive to tickling 2. needing careful handling; precarious; delicate

**tick-tack-toe, tic-tac-toe** (tik'-tak tō') *n.* a game for two, each marking X (or O) in turn in a 9-square block so as to complete any one row before the other can

**tick·tock** (tik'täk') *n.* the sound made by a clock or watch

**tid·al** (tīd''l) *adj.* of, having, or caused by a tide or tides

**tidal wave** 1. an unusually great, destructive wave sent inshore by an earthquake or very strong wind 2. any widespread movement, feeling, etc.

**tid·bit** (tid'bit') *n.* [dial. *tid*, tiny object] a choice bit of food, gossip, etc.

**tid·dly·winks** (tid'lē wiŋks') *n.* [ < ?] a game in which little disks are snapped into a cup by pressing their edges with a larger disk

**tide** (tīd) *n.* [OE. *tid*, time] 1. a period of time [*Eastertide*] 2. the alternate rise and fall, about twice a day, of the surface of oceans, seas, etc., caused by the attraction of the moon and sun 3. something that rises and falls like the tide 4. a stream, trend, etc. —*vt.* **tid'ed, tid'ing** to help along temporarily (with *over*)

**tide'land'** *n.* 1. land covered when the tide is in 2. [*pl.*] land under the sea within territorial waters of a country

**tide'wa'ter** *n.* 1. water that is affected by the tide 2. a seaboard —*adj.* of or along a tidewater

**ti·dings** (tī'diŋz) *n.pl.* [OE. *tidung*] news; information

**ti·dy** (tī'dē) *adj.* **-di·er, -di·est** [ < OE. *tid*, time] 1. neat in appearance, arrangement, etc.; orderly 2. [Colloq.] rather large [a *tidy sum*] —*vt.*, *vi.* **-died, -dy·ing** to make tidy (often with *up*) —**ti'di·ness** *n.*

**tie** (tī) *vt.* **tied, ty'ing** [ < OE. *teag*, rope] 1. to bind, as with string, rope, etc. 2. to knot the laces, etc. of 3. to make (a knot) in 4. to bind in any way 5. to equal the score of, as in a contest —*vi.* to make an equal score, as in a contest —*n.* 1. a string, cord, etc. used to tie things 2. something that connects, binds, etc. 3. a necktie 4. a beam, rod, etc. that holds parts together 5. any of the crossbeams to which the rails of a railroad are fastened 6. *a)* an equality of scores, etc. *b)* a contest in which this occurs —*adj.* that has been made equal [a *tie score*] —**tie down** to confine; restrict —**tie up** 1. to wrap up and tie 2. to moor to a dock 3. to obstruct; hinder 4. to cause to be already in use, committed, etc.

**tie'back'** *n.* a band or ribbon used to tie curtains, etc. to one side

**tie clasp** a decorative clasp for fastening a necktie to a shirt: also **tie clip, tie bar**

**tie'-dye'** (-dī') *n.* a method of dyeing designs on cloth by tying bunches of it so that the dye affects only exposed parts —*vt.* **-dyed', -dye'ing** to dye in this way

**tie'-in'** *n.* a connection or relation

**Tien·tsin** (tin'tsin') seaport in NE China: pop. 3,278,000

**tier** (tir) *n.* [ < OFr. *tire*, order] any of a series of rows, as of seats, arranged one above or behind another

**tie rod** a rod connecting a front wheel of an automotive vehicle to the steering mechanism

**tie tack** a decorative pin fitted into a snap to fasten a necktie to a shirt

**tie-up** (tī'up') *n.* 1. a temporary stoppage of production, traffic, etc. 2. a connection or relation

**tiff** (tif) *n.* [ < ?] 1. a slight fit of anger 2. a slight quarrel

**ti·ger** (tī'gər) *n.* [ < Gr. *tigris*] a large, flesh-eating animal of the cat family, native to Asia, having a tawny coat striped with black

**tight** (tīt) *adj.* [ < OE. *-thight*, strong] 1. so compact in structure that water, air, etc. cannot pass through 2. drawn, packed, etc. closely together 3. fixed securely; firm 4. fully stretched; taut 5. fitting so closely as to be uncomfortable 6. difficult: esp. **in a tight corner, squeeze,** etc., a difficult situation 7. difficult to get; scarce 8. [Colloq.] stingy 9. [Slang] drunk —*adv.* 1. securely 2. soundly [*sleep tight*] —**sit tight** to maintain one's position, etc. —**tight'ly** *adv.* — **tight'ness** *n.*

**tight′en** vt., vi. to make or become tight or tighter —**tight′en·er** n.

**tight′fist′ed** adj. stingy

**tight′fit′ting** adj. fitting very tight

**tight′-lipped′** adj. secretive

**tight′rope′** n. a tightly stretched rope on which acrobats perform

**tights** n.pl. a tightly fitting garment for the lower half of the body, worn by acrobats, dancers, etc.

**tight′wad′** n. [TIGHT + wad, roll of money] [Slang] a stingy person

**ti·glon** (tī′glän′, -glən) n. [TIG(ER) + L(I)ON] the offspring of a male tiger and a female lion

**ti·gress** (tī′gris) n. a female tiger

**Ti·gris** (tī′gris) river flowing from EC Turkey to a juncture with the Euphrates in SE Iraq

**Ti·jua·na** (tē·wä′nə, -hwä′nä) city in NW Mexico, on the U.S. border: pop. 203,000

**til·de** (til′də) n. [Sp. < L. titulus, sign] a diacritical mark (~)

**tile** (tīl) n. [< L. tegula] 1. a thin piece of fired clay, stone, etc., used for roofing, flooring, walls, etc. 2. a similar piece of plastic, etc. 3. a drain of earthenware pipe —vt. **tiled, til′ing** to cover with tiles

**til′ing** n. tiles collectively

**till¹** (til) prep., conj. [OE. til] until

**till²** (til) vt., vi. [< OE. tilian, strive for] to prepare (land) for raising crops, as by plowing, etc. —**till′er** n.

**till³** (til) n. [< ? ME. tillen, to draw] a drawer for keeping money

**till′age** (-ij) n. 1. the tilling of land 2. land that is tilled

**till·er** (til′ər) n. [< ML. telarium, weaver's beam] a bar or handle for turning a boat's rudder

**tilt** (tilt) vt. [ME. tilten, totter] to cause to slope; tip —vi. 1. to slope; incline 2. to charge (at an opponent) 3. to engage in a tilt —n. 1. a medieval contest in which two horsemen fight with lances 2. any spirited contest 3. a slope —(at) **full tilt** at full speed

**tilt′-top′** adj. of a table with a hinged top that can be tipped vertically

**tim·bale** (tim′b'l) n. [Fr.] 1. a custardlike dish of chicken, lobster, etc. baked in a small drum-shaped mold 2. a pastry shell, filled with cooked food: also **timbale case**

**tim·ber** (tim′bər) n. [OE.] 1. wood for building houses, ships, etc. 2. a wooden beam used in building 3. trees collectively —**tim′bered** adj.

**tim′ber·line′** n. the line above or beyond which trees do not grow, as on mountains or in polar regions

**tim·bre** (tam′bər, tim′-) n. [< OFr. timbre, kind of drum] the quality of sound that distinguishes one voice or musical instrument from another

**time** (tīm) n. [OE. tima] 1. every moment there has ever been or ever will be 2. a system of measuring duration [standard time] 3. the period during which something exists, hap-pens, etc. 4. [usually pl.] a period of history; age, era, etc. 5. [usually pl.] prevailing conditions [times are good] 6. a set period or term, as of work, confinement, etc. 7. standard rate of pay 8. rate of speed in marching, driving, etc. 9. a precise or designated instant, moment, day, etc. 10. an occasion or repeated occasion [the fifth time it's been on TV] 11. Music a) rhythm as determined by the grouping of beats into measures b) tempo —vt. **timed, tim′ing** 1. to arrange the time so as to be suitable, opportune, etc. 2. to adjust, set, etc. so as to coincide in time [time our watches] 3. to record the pace, speed, etc. of —adj. 1. having to do with time 2. set to explode, open, etc. at a given time 3. having to do with paying in installments —**ahead of time** early —**at the same time** however —**at times** occasionally —**do time** [Colloq.] to serve a prison term —**for the time being** temporarily —**from time to time** now and then —**in time** 1. eventually 2. before it is too late 3. keeping the set tempo, pace, etc. —**make time** to travel, work, etc. rapidly —**on time** 1. at the appointed time 2. for or by payment by install-ments —**time after time** again and again: also **time and again**

**time clock** a clock with a mechanism for recording the time an employee begins and ends a work period

**time′-hon′ored** adj. honored be-cause of long existence or usage

**time′keep′er** n. one who keeps account of hours worked by employees, or of elapsed time in races, games, etc.

**time′less** (-lis) adj. eternal

**time′ly** adj. -li·er, -li·est well-timed; opportune —**time′li·ness** n.

**time′out′** n. Sports, etc. any tem-porary suspension of play

**time′piece′** n. a clock or watch

**tim′er** n. a device for controlling the timing of some mechanism

**times** (tīmz) prep. multiplied by

**time′serv′er** n. one who abandons his principles only to suit the times or to gain favor —**time′serv′ing** n., adj.

**time sharing** a system for the simul-taneous use of a computer by many users at remote locations

**time sheet** a sheet on which are recorded the hours an employee works

**time′ta′ble** (-tā′b'l) n. a schedule of the times of arrival and departure of airplanes, trains, buses, etc.

**time′worn′** adj. 1. worn out by long use 2. trite; hackneyed

**time zone** see STANDARD TIME

**tim·id** (tim′id) adj. [< L. timere, to fear] lacking poise or self-confidence; shy, fearful, or hesitant —**ti·mid·i·ty** (tə mid′ə tē) n. —**tim′id·ly** adv.

**tim·ing** (tī′miŋ) n. the regulation of the time or speed so as to achieve the most effective performance

**tim·or·ous** (tim′ər əs) adj. [< L.

*timor,* fear] full of fear; timid; afraid

**tim·o·thy** (tim′ə thē) *n.* [< a *Timothy* Hanson, c.1720] a grass with dense spikes, grown for hay

**tim·pa·ni** (tim′pə nē) *n.pl.* [It.: see TYMPANUM] kettledrums, esp. a set of them played by one performer

**tin** (tin) *n.* [OE.] 1. a soft, silver-white, metallic chemical element 2. *same as* TIN PLATE 3. *a)* a pan, box, etc. made of tin plate *b)* [Chiefly Brit.] *same as* CAN² (*n.* 2, 3) Variously used to connote cheapness, etc. of something —*vt.* tinned, tin′ning 1. to plate with tin 2. [Chiefly Brit.] *same as* CAN² (*vt.* 1)

**tin can** *same as* CAN² (*n.* 2)

**tinct.** tincture

**tinc·ture** (tiŋk′chər) *n.* [< L. *tingere,* to dye] 1. a light color; tinge 2. a slight trace 3. a medicinal substance in an alcoholic solution —*vt.* -tured, -tur·ing to tinge

**tin·der** (tin′dər) *n.* [OE. *tynder*] any dry, easily flammable material

**tin′der·box′** *n.* 1. orig., a box to hold tinder 2. a highly flammable building, etc. 3. a potential source of war, rebellion, etc.

**tine** (tīn) *n.* [OE. *tind*] a slender, projecting point; prong [fork *tines*]

**tin′foil′** (-foil′) *n.* a thin sheet of tin or a tin alloy used as wrapping

**tinge** (tinj) *n.* [see TINT] 1. a slight coloring; tint 2. a slight trace, flavor, etc. —*vt.* tinged, tinge′ing or ting′ing to give a tinge of to

**tin·gle** (tiŋ′g'l) *vi.* -gled, -gling [var. of TINKLE] to have a prickling or stinging feeling, as from cold, excitement, etc. —*n.* this feeling

**tin·ker** (tiŋ′kər) *n.* [ME. *tinkere*] 1. one who mends pots, pans, etc. 2. a bungler —*vi.* 1. to attempt clumsily to mend something 2. to putter

**tin·kle** (tiŋ′k'l) *vi.* -kled, -kling [echoic] to make a series of light sounds as of a small bell —*vt.* to cause to tinkle —*n.* a tinkling sound

**tin·ny** (tin′ē) *adj.* -ni·er, -ni·est 1. of tin 2. like tin, as in appearance, sound, value, etc. —tin′ni·ness *n.*

**tin plate** thin sheets of iron or steel plated with tin

**tin·sel** (tin′s'l) *n.* [< L. *scintilla,* a spark] 1. thin strips of tin, metal foil, etc., as for decoration 2. something of little worth that glitters

**tin′smith′** *n.* a person who works in tin or tin plate

**tint** (tint) *n.* [< L. *tingere,* to dye] 1. a delicate color 2. a gradation of a color; shade 3. a hair dye —*vt.* to give a tint to

**tin·tin·nab·u·la·tion** (tin′ti nab′ yoo lā′shən) *n.* [< L. *tintinnabulum,* little bell] the ringing sound of bells

**tin′type′** *n.* an old kind of photograph taken directly as a positive print on a treated plate of tin or iron

**ti·ny** (tī′nē) *adj.* -ni·er, -ni·est [< ME. *tine,* a little] very small

**-tion** (shən) [< Fr. < L.] *a suffix meaning:* 1. the act of [*correction*] 2. the state of being [*elation*] 3. the thing that is [*creation*]

**-tious** (shəs) a suffix forming adjectives corresponding to -TION [*cautious*]

**tip¹** (tip) *n.* [ME. *tippe*] 1. the point or end of something 2. something attached to the end, as a cap, etc. —*vt.* tipped, tip′ping 1. to form a tip on 2. to cover the tip of

**tip²** (tip) *vt.* tipped, tip′ping [< ?] 1. to strike lightly and sharply 2. to give a gratuity to (a waiter, etc.) 3. [Colloq.] to give secret information to (often with *off*) —*vi.* to give a tip or tips —*n.* 1. a light, sharp blow 2. a piece of confidential information 3. a hint, warning, etc. 4. a gratuity —tip one's hand [Slang] to reveal a secret, one's plans, etc., often without meaning to —tip′per *n.*

**tip³** (tip) *vt.,* *vi.* tipped, tip′ping [ME. *tipen*] 1. to overturn or upset (often with *over*) 2. to tilt or slant —*n.* a tilt; slant

**tip′-off′** *n.* a tip; confidential disclosure, hint, or warning

**tip·ple** (tip′'l) *vi.,* *vt.* -pled, -pling [< ?] to drink (alcoholic liquor) habitually —tip′pler *n.*

**tip·ster** (tip′stər) *n.* [Colloq.] one who sells tips, as on horse races

**tip·sy** (tip′sē) *adj.* -si·er, -si·est 1. that tips easily; not steady 2. somewhat drunk —tip′si·ly *adv.*

**tip′toe′** *n.* the tip of a toe —*vi.* -toed′, -toe′ing to walk carefully on one's tiptoes —on tiptoe 1. on one's tiptoes 2. eager(ly) 3. silently

**tip′top′** *n.* [TIP¹ + TOP¹] the highest point —*adj.,* *adv.* 1. at the highest point 2. [Colloq.] at the highest point of excellence, health, etc.

**ti·rade** (tī′rād, tī rād′) *n.* [< It. *tirare,* to fire] a long, vehement speech or denunciation; harangue

**tire¹** (tīr) *vt.,* *vi.* tired, tir′ing [OE. *tiorian*] to make or become weary, exhausted, bored, etc.

**tire²** (tīr) *n.* [ME. *tyre*] a hoop of iron or rubber, or a rubber tube filled with air, fixed around the wheel of a vehicle

**tired** (tīrd) *adj.* 1. weary 2. hackneyed

**tire′less** *adj.* that does not become tired —tire′less·ly *adv.*

**tire′some** *adj.* tiring; boring —tire′some·ly *adv.* —tire′some·ness *n.*

**Tir·ol** (tir′äl, tī′rōl) E Alpine region in W Austria & N Italy —Ti·ro·le·an (ti rō′lē ən) *adj.,* *n.*

**tis·sue** (tish′ōō) *n.* [< L. *texere,* to weave] 1. light, thin cloth 2. an interwoven mass; mesh; web 3. a piece of soft, absorbent paper, used as a disposable handkerchief, etc. 4. *same as* TISSUE PAPER 5. the substance of an organic body, consisting of cells and intercellular material

**tissue paper** very thin, unsized paper, as for wrapping things, etc.

**tit¹** (tit) *n.* a titmouse

**tit²** (tit) *n.* [OE.] 1. *same as* TEAT 2. a breast: now vulgar

**ti·tan** (tīt′'n) *n.* [< Gr. *Titan,* a giant deity] any person or thing of great size or power

**ti·tan·ic** (tī tan′ik) *adj.* of great size, strength, or power

**ti·ta·ni·um** (tī tā′nē əm, ti-) *n.* [see TITAN] a metallic chemical element used as a deoxidizing agent in molten steel, etc.

**tit for tat** [earlier *tip for tap*] blow for blow

**tithe** (tīth) *n.* [OE. *teothe*, a tenth] a tenth of one's income paid to a church —*vt.*, *vi.* tithed, tith′ing to pay a tithe of (one's income, etc.)

**ti·tian** (tish′ən) *n.* [< *Titian* (1490?-1576), Venetian painter] reddish yellow; auburn

**tit·il·late** (tit′'l āt′) *vt.* -lat′ed, -lat′ing [< L. *titillare*, tickle] to excite pleasurably —**tit′il·la′tion** *n.*

**ti·tle** (tīt′'l) *n.* [< L. *titulus*] 1. the name of a poem, book, picture, etc. 2. an epithet 3. an appellation indicating one's rank, profession, etc. 4. a claim 5. *Law a)* a right to ownership, esp. to real estate *b)* a deed 6. *Motion Pictures, TV* a subtitle, credit, etc. 7. *Sports*, etc. a championship —*vt.* -tled, -tling to give a title to

**ti′tled** *adj.* having a title, esp. of nobility

**ti′tle·hold′er** *n.* the holder of a title; specif., (also **titlist**) the champion in some sport

**title role** (or **part** or **character**) the character in a play, movie, etc. whose name is used as or in the title

**tit·mouse** (tit′mous′) *n.*, *pl.* -mice′ [ME. *titemose*] a small bird with ashy-gray feathers

**tit·ter** (tit′ər) *vi.* [echoic] to laugh in a half-suppressed way; giggle —*n.* a tittering; giggle

**tit·tle** (tit′'l) *n.* [ME. *title*] a very small particle; iota; jot

**tit·u·lar** (tich′ə lər) *adj.* [see TITLE] 1. of a title 2. having a title 3. in name only [a *titular* leader]

**tiz·zy** (tiz′ē) *n.*, *pl.* -zies [< ?] [Colloq.] a state of frenzied excitement

**TN** Tennessee

**tn.** ton(s)

**TNT, T.N.T.** [< *trinitrotoluene*] a high explosive used for blasting, etc.

**to** (tōō, too, tə) *prep.* [OE.] 1. toward [turn *to* the left] 2. so as to reach [he went *to* Boston] 3. as far as [wet *to* the skin] 4. into a condition of [a rise *to* fame] 5. on, onto, at, etc. [tied *to* a post] 6. *a)* until [from noon *to* night] *b)* before [the time is 10 *to* 6] 7. for the purpose of [come *to* my aid] 8. in regard to [open *to* attack] 9. so as to produce [torn *to* bits] 10. along with [add this *to* the rest] 11. belonging with [a key *to* the lock] 12. as compared with [a score of 7 *to* 0] 13. in agreement with [not *to* my taste] 14. constituting [ten *to* a peck] 15. with (a specified person or thing) as the recipient of the action [give it *to* me] 16. in honor of [a toast *to* you] *To* is also a sign of the infinitive (Ex.: I want *to* stay) —*adv.* 1. forward [wrong side *to*] 2. shut; closed [pull the door *to*] 3. to the matter at hand [fall

*to!*] —**to and fro** first in one direction and then in the opposite

**toad** (tōd) *n.* [OE. *tade*] a froglike animal that lives on moist land

**toad′stool′** (-stōōl′) *n.* a mushroom, esp. any poisonous mushroom

**toad·y** (tōd′ē) *n.*, *pl.* -ies [short for *toadeater*, quack doctor's assistant] a servile flatterer —*vt.*, *vi.* -ied, -y·ing to be a toady (to)

**toast¹** (tōst) *vt.* [< L. *torrere*, parch] 1. to brown the surface of (bread, etc.) by heating 2. to warm thoroughly —*vi.* to become toasted —*n.* sliced bread made brown by heat —**toast′er** *n.*

**toast²** (tōst) *n.* [< the toasted bread formerly put in wine] 1. a person or thing in honor of which persons raise their glasses and drink 2. a proposal to drink, or a drink, in honor of some person, etc. —*vt.*, *vi.* to propose or drink a toast (to)

**toast′mas′ter** *n.* the person at a banquet who proposes toasts, introduces after-dinner speakers, etc.

**to·bac·co** (tə bak′ō) *n.*, *pl.* -cos [< WInd. *tabaco*, smoking pipe] 1. a plant with large leaves that are prepared for smoking, chewing, or snuffing 2. cigars, cigarettes, snuff, etc.

**to·bac·co·nist** (-ə nist) *n.* [Chiefly Brit.] a dealer in tobacco

**to·bog·gan** (tə bäg′ən) *n.* [< AmInd.] a long, flat sled without runners, for coasting downhill —*vi.* 1. to coast on a toboggan 2. to decline rapidly

TOBOGGAN

**toc·sin** (täk′sin) *n.* [Fr. < Pr. *toc*, a stroke + *senh*, a bell] an alarm bell

**to·day** (tə dā′) *adv.* [OE. *to dæg*] 1. on or during the present day 2. in the present time —*n.* 1. the present day 2. the present time

**tod·dle** (täd′'l) *vi.* -dled, -dling [? < *totter*] to walk with short, uncertain steps, as a child —**tod′dler** *n.*

**tod·dy** (täd′ē) *n.*, *pl.* -dies [< Hindi] a drink of whiskey, etc. mixed with hot water, sugar, etc.: also **hot toddy**

**to-do** (tə dōō′) *n.* [Colloq.] a commotion; stir; fuss

**toe** (tō) *n.* [OE. *ta*] 1. *a)* any of the digits of the foot *b)* the fore part of the foot 2. anything like a toe in location, shape, or use —*vt.* toed, toe′ing to touch, kick, etc. with the toes in a specified position [he *toes* in] —**on one's toes** [Colloq.] alert —**toe the line** (or **mark**) to follow orders or rules strictly

**toed** (tōd) *adj.* having (a specified kind or number of) toes [two-*toed*]

**toe dance** a dance performed on the tips of the toes, as in ballet —**toe′-dance′** *vi.* —**toe′-danc′er** *n.*

**toe′hold′** *n.* 1. just enough space to support the toe in climbing, etc. 2. a slight footing or advantage

---

fat, āpe, cär; ten, ēven; is, bīte; gō, hôrn, tōōl, look; oil, out; up, fur; chin; she; thin, *then*; zh, leisure; ŋ, ring; ə for *a* in *ago;* ', (ā′b'l); ë, Fr. coeur; ö, Fr. feu; Fr. mon; ü, Fr. duc; kh, G. ich, doch; ‡ foreign; < derived from

**toe·nail** (tō'nāl') *n.* the nail of a toe

**tof·fee, tof·fy** (tôf'ē, täf'ē) *n.* [< TAFFY] a kind of taffy

**to·ga** (tō'gə) *n., pl.* **-gas, -gae** (-jē) [L. < *tegere,* to cover] in ancient Rome, a loose outer garment worn in public by citizens

**to·geth·er** (tə geth'ər) *adv.* [< OE. *to,* to + *gædre,* together] **1.** in or into one group, place, etc. *[we ate together]* **2.** in or into contact, union, etc. *[they bumped together]* **3.** considered collectively *[he lost more than all of us together]* **4.** at the same time *[shots fired together]* **5.** in succession *[sulking for three whole days together]* **6.** in or into agreement, cooperation, etc. *[to get together on a deal]* —*adj.* [Slang] having a fully integrated personality

**to·geth·er·ness** *n.* the spending of much time together, as by family members, in seeking a more unified, stable relationship

**tog·gle switch** (täg''l) [prob. < TUG] a switch consisting of a lever moved back and forth to open or close an electric circuit

**To·go** (tō'gō) country in W Africa: 21,853 sq. mi.; pop. 1,772,000

**toga** (tägz, tôgz) *n.pl.* [prob. < L. *toga,* toga] [Colloq.] clothes

**toil** (toil) *vi.* [< L. *tudiculare,* stir about] **1.** to work hard and continuously **2.** to proceed laboriously —*n.* hard, tiring work —**toil'er** *n.*

**toi·let** (toi'lit) *n.* [< MFr. *toile,* cloth < L. *tela,* a web] **1.** the act of dressing or grooming oneself **2.** dress; attire **3.** *a)* a room with a bowl-shaped fixture for defecation or urination *b)* such a fixture

**toilet paper** (or **tissue**) soft paper for cleaning oneself after evacuation

**toi'let·ry** (-lə trē) *n., pl.* **-ries** soap, lotion, etc. used in grooming oneself

**toi·lette** (twä let', toi-) *n.* [Fr.] **1.** the process of grooming oneself: said of a woman **2.** dress; attire

**toilet water** a perfumed, slightly alcoholic liquid, applied to the skin

**toils** (toilz) *n.pl.* [< L. *tela,* a web] any snare suggestive of a net

**toil·some** (toil'səm) *adj.* laborious

**toke** (tōk) *n.* [? < ff.] [Slang] a puff on a cigarette, esp. of marijuana or hashish —*vt.* **toked, tok'ing** [Slang] to take a puff on (such a cigarette)

**to·ken** (tō'k'n) *n.* [OE. *tacn*] **1.** a sign, indication, symbol, etc. *[a token of affection]* **2.** a keepsake **3.** a metal disk to be used in place of currency, for transportation fares, etc. —*adj.* merely simulated *[token resistance]* —**by the same** (or **this**) **token** following from this

**to'ken·ism** (-iz'm) *n.* the making of small, merely formal concessions to a demand, etc.; specif., token integration of Negroes, as in jobs

**To·ky·o** (tō'kē ō') capital of Japan, on Honshu: pop. 8,991,000

**tol·bu·ta·mide** (täl byōōt'ə mīd') *n.* an oral drug for treating diabetes

**told** (tōld) *pt. & pp.* of TELL —**all told** all (being) counted

**tole** (tōl) *n.* [Fr. *tôle,* sheet iron] a type of lacquered or enameled metalware, usually dark-green, ivory, or black, used for lamps, trays, etc.

**To·le·do** (tə lē'dō) city and port in NW Ohio: pop. 384,000

**tol·er·a·ble** (täl'ər ə b'l) *adj.* **1.** endurable **2.** fairly good; passable —**tol'er·a·bly** *adv.*

**tol'er·ance** (-əns) *n.* **1.** a being tolerant of others' beliefs, practices, etc. **2.** the amount of variation allowed from a standard, accuracy, etc. **3.** *Med.* the ability to endure the effects of a drug, poison, etc.

**tol'er·ant** *adj.* having or showing tolerance of others' beliefs, etc.

**tol·er·ate** (täl'ə rāt') *vt.* **-at'ed, -at'ing** [< L. *tolerare,* to bear] **1.** to allow **2.** to respect (others' beliefs, practices, etc.) without sharing them **3.** to put up with **4.** *Med.* to have a tolerance for —**tol'er·a'tion** *n.*

**toll¹** (tōl) *n.* [ult. < Gr. *telos,* tax] **1.** a tax or charge for a privilege, as for the use of a bridge **2.** a charge for a service, as for a long-distance telephone call **3.** the number lost, etc. *[the tornado took a heavy toll of lives]*

**toll²** (tōl) *vt.* [ME. *tollen,* to pull] **1.** to ring (a bell, etc.) with slow, regular strokes **2.** to announce, summon, etc. by this —*vi.* to ring slowly: said of a bell —*n.* the sound of tolling a bell

**toll'gate'** *n.* a gate for stopping travel at a point where toll is taken

**toll road** a road on which tolls must be paid: also **toll'way'** (-wā') *n.*

**Tol·stoy** (tōl'stoi, tôl'-), Count **Leo** 1828–1910; Russ. novelist

**tom** (täm) *adj.* [< the name *Tom*] male *[tomcat, tom turkey]*

**tom·a·hawk** (täm'ə hôk') *n.* [< AmInd.] a light ax used by N.American Indians as a tool and a weapon

**to·ma·to** (tə māt'ō, -mät'ō) *n., pl.* **-toes** [< MexInd.] **1.** a red or yellowish fruit with a juicy pulp, used as a vegetable **2.** the plant it grows on

**tomb** (tōōm) *n.* [< Gr. *tymbos*] **1.** a vault or grave for the dead **2.** a tombstone —**the tomb** death

**tom·boy** (täm'boi') *n.* a girl who behaves like a boisterous boy

**tomb·stone** (tōōm'stōn') *n.* a stone or monument marking a tomb or grave

**tom·cat** (täm'kat') *n.* a male cat

**tome** (tōm) *n.* [< Gr. *tomos,* piece cut off] a book, esp. a large one

**tom·fool·er·y** (täm'fōōl'ər ē) *n., pl.* **-ies** foolish behavior; silliness

**to·mor·row** (tə mär'ō, -môr'-) *adv.* [OE. *to morgen*] on the day after today —*n.* the day after today

**tom·tit** (täm'tit') *n.* [Chiefly Brit.] a titmouse or other small bird

**tom-tom** (täm'täm') *n.* [Hind. *tam-tam*] a primitive drum, usually beaten with the hands

**-to·my** [< Gr. *tomē,* a cutting] *a combining form meaning* surgical operation

**ton** (tun) *n.* [var. of TUN] **1.** a unit of weight equal to 2,000 pounds: in full **short ton 2.** in Great Britain, a unit of weight equal to 2,240 pounds: in full **long ton**

**ton·al** (tō'n'l) *adj.* of a tone

**to·nal·i·ty** (tō nal'ə tē) *n., pl.* **-ties**
*Music* **1.** *same as* KEY¹ (*n.* 6) **2.** tonal
character, as determined by the relationship of the tones to the keynote

**tone** (tōn) *n.* [ < Gr. *teinein*, to
stretch] **1.** a vocal or musical sound,
or its quality as to pitch, intensity, etc.
**2.** a manner of expression showing a
certain attitude [a friendly *tone*] **3.**
style, character, spirit, etc. **4.** elegant
style **5.** a quality of color; shade **6.**
normal, healthy condition of a muscle,
organ, etc. **7.** *Music* *a*) a sound of
distinct pitch *b*) any of the full intervals of a diatonic scale —*vt.* **toned,**
**ton'ing** to give a tone to —**tone**
**down** (or **up**) to give a less (or more)
intense tone to —**tone'less** *adj.*

**tone arm** the pivoted arm containing
the pickup on a phonograph

**tone'-deaf'** *adj.* unable to distinguish
differences in musical pitch

**tone row** (or **series**) *see* TWELVE-
TONE

**tong** (tôŋ, täŋ) *n.* [Chin. *t'ang*, meeting place] in the U.S., a secret, fraternal society of Chinese

**Ton·ga** (täŋ'gə) country on a group
of islands (**Tonga Islands**) in the
South Pacific, east of Fiji: 270 sq. mi.;
pop. 86,000 —**Ton'gan** *n.*

**tongs** (tôŋz, täŋz) *n.pl.* [*sometimes
with sing. v.*] [OE. *tange*] a device for
seizing or lifting, having two long arms
pivoted or hinged together

**tongue** (tuŋ) *n.* [OE. *tunge*] **1.** the
movable, muscular structure in the
mouth, used in eating, tasting, and (in
man) speaking **2.** talk; speech **3.** the
act, power, or manner of speaking **4.** a
language or dialect **5.** something like
a tongue in shape, position, use, etc.,
as the flap under the laces of a shoe
—**hold one's tongue** to keep from
speaking —**speak in tongues** to utter
unintelligible sounds, as while in a
religious trance —**tongue'less** *adj.*

**tongue-and-groove joint** a kind
of joint in which a projection on one
board fits into a groove in another

**tongue'-lash'ing** *n.* [Colloq.] a
harsh scolding or reproving; reprimand

**tongue'-tied'** *adj.* speechless from
amazement, embarrassment, etc.

**tongue twister** a phrase or sentence
hard to say fast (Ex.: six sick shieks)

**ton·ic** (tän'ik) *adj.* [see TONE] **1.** of or
producing good muscular tone **2.**
*Music* designating or based on a keynote —*n.* **1.** anything that invigorates,
as a drug or medicine **2.** a quinine-
flavored beverage served with gin,
vodka, etc. **3.** *Music* a keynote

**to·night** (tə nīt') *adv.* [OE. *to niht*]
on or during the present or coming
night —*n.* the present or the coming
night

**ton·nage** (tun'ij) *n.* **1.** the total
amount of shipping of a country or
port, calculated in tons **2.** the carrying
capacity of a ship

**ton·sil** (tän's'l) *n.* [L. *tonsillae, pl.*]
either of a pair of oval masses of tissue
at the back of the mouth

**ton·sil·lec·to·my** (tän'sə lek'tə mē)
*n., pl.* **-mies** [ < prec. & -ECTOMY] the
surgical removal of the tonsils

**ton'sil·li'tis** (-līt'əs) *n.* [see -ITIS]
inflammation of the tonsils

**ton·so·ri·al** (tän sôr'ē əl) *adj.* [see
ff.] of a barber or barbering: often
humorous [a *tonsorial* artist]

**ton·sure** (tän'shər) *n.* [ < L. *tondere*,
to clip] **1.** the act of shaving the head
or crown of one becoming a cleric or
entering a monastic order **2.** the part
of the head so shaven —*vt.* **-sured,**
**-sur'ing** to shave the head of in a
tonsure

**ton·y** (tō'nē) *adj.* **-i·er, -i·est** [ <
TONE + -Y²] [Slang] very elegant

**too** (tōō) *adv.* [stressed form of TO] **1.**
in addition; also **2.** more than enough
[the hat is *too* big] **3.** extremely; very
[you're *too* kind]

**took** (took) *pt. of* TAKE

**tool** (tōōl) *n.* [OE. *tol*] **1.** any hand
implement, instrument, etc. used for
some work **2.** any similar instrument
that is the working part of a machine,
as a drill **3.** anything that serves as a
means **4.** a stooge —*vt.* **1.** to form or
shape with a tool **2.** to impress designs
on (leather, etc.) with a tool —*vi.* to
install tools, equipment, etc. needed
(often with *up*)

**toot** (tōōt) *vi., vt.* [echoic] to sound (a
horn, whistle, etc.) in short blasts —*n.*
a short blast of a horn, etc.

**tooth** (tōōth) *n., pl.* **teeth** [OE. *toth*]
**1.** any of the hard, bonelike structures
in the jaws, used for biting, chewing,
etc. **2.** a toothlike part, as on a saw,
comb, gearwheel, etc. **3.** [*pl.*] effective
means of enforcing [a law with *teeth*]
—**in the teeth of 1.** directly against
**2.** defying —**tooth and nail** with all
one's strength —**toothed** *adj.* —
**tooth'less** *adj.*

**tooth'ache'** *n.* a pain in a tooth

**tooth'brush'** *n.* a small brush for
cleaning the teeth

**tooth'paste'** (or **tooth powder**) *n.*
a paste (or powder) for brushing the
teeth

**tooth'pick'** *n.* a slender, pointed
instrument for dislodging food particles from between the teeth

**tooth'some** (-səm) *adj.* tasty; savory

**tooth'y** *adj.* **-i·er, -i·est** having or
exposing teeth that show prominently
[a *toothy* smile] —**tooth'i·ly** *adv.*

**top¹** (täp) *n.* [OE.] **1.** the head or
crown **2.** the highest point or surface
of anything **3.** the part of a plant
above ground **4.** the uppermost part
or covering, as a lid, cap, etc. **5.** the
highest degree [at the *top* of his voice]
**6.** the highest rank [the *top* of the
class] —*adj.* of, at, or being the top;
highest or foremost —*vt.* **topped,**
**top'ping 1.** to take off the top of (a
plant, etc.) **2.** to provide with a top
**3.** to be a top for **4.** to reach the top of

fat, āpe, cär; ten, ēven; is, bīte; gō, hôrn, tōōl, look; oil, out; up, fur;
chin; she; thin, then; zh, leisure; ŋ, ring; ə for a in ago; ', (ā'b'l); ë, Fr. coeur;
ö, Fr. feu; Fr. mon; ü, Fr. duc; kh, G. ich, doch; ‡ foreign; < derived from

**5.** to exceed in amount, etc. **6.** to surpass; outdo —**blow one's top** [Slang] to lose one's temper —**on top of 1.** resting upon **2.** besides **3.** controlling successfully —**top off** to complete by adding a finishing touch —**top′per** *n.*

**top**[2] (täp) *n.* [OE.] a cone-shaped toy with a point upon which it is spun

**to·paz** (tō′paz) *n.* [ < Gr. *topazos*] any of various yellow gems, esp. a variety of aluminum silicate

**top brass** important officials

**top′coat′** *n.* a lightweight overcoat

**top′-draw′er** *adj.* of first importance

**To·pe·ka** (tə pē′kə) capital of Kans.: pop. 125,000

**top·er** (tō′pər) *n.* [ < archaic *tope*, to drink (much liquor)] a drunkard

**top′-flight′** *adj.* [Colloq.] first-rate

**top hat** a man's tall, black, cylindrical silk hat, worn in formal dress

**top′-heav′y** *adj.* too heavy at the top, so as to be unstable

**top·ic** (täp′ik) *n.* [ult. < Gr. *topos*, place] the subject of an essay, speech, discussion, etc.

**top′i·cal** *adj.* dealing with topics of the day; of current or local interest

**top′knot′** (-nät′) *n.* a tuft of hair or feathers on the top of the head

**top′less** (-lis) *adj.* without a top, as a costume exposing the breasts

**top′-lev′el** *adj.* of or by persons of the highest office or rank

**top′mast′** *n.* the second mast above the deck of a sailing ship

**top′most** *adj.* at the very top

**top′-notch′** *adj.* [Colloq.] first-rate; excellent

**to·pog·ra·phy** (tə päg′rə fē) *n.*, *pl.* **-phies** [ < Gr. *topos*, a place + *graphein*, write] **1.** the science of representing surface features of a region on maps and charts **2.** these surface features —**top·o·graph·i·cal** (täp′ə graf′i k'l), **top′o·graph′ic** *adj.*

**top·ping** (täp′in) *n.* something put on top of something else

**top·ple** (täp′'l) *vi.* **-pled, -pling** [ < TOP[1]] to fall top forward; fall (*over*) because top-heavy, etc. —*vt.* to cause to topple; overturn

**top·sail** (täp′s'l, -sāl′) *n.* in a square-rigged vessel, the square sail next above the lowest sail on a mast

**top′-se′cret** *adj.* designating or of the most secret information

**top′side′** *adv.* on or to an upper deck or the main deck of a ship

**top′soil′** *n.* the upper layer of soil, usually richer than the subsoil

**top·sy-tur·vy** (täp′sē tur′vē) *adv.*, *adj.* [prob. < *top*, highest part + ME. *terven*, to roll] **1.** upside down; in a reversed condition **2.** in disorder

**toque** (tōk) *n.* [Fr.] a woman's small, round hat, with or without a brim

**to·rah** (tō′rə) *n.* [ < Heb., law] **1.** [*also* T-] the body of Jewish scriptures **2.** [*usually* T-] *a*) the Pentateuch *b*) *pl.* **-roth, -rot** (-rəs, tō rōt′) a scroll containing it

**torch** (tôrch) *n.* [see TORQUE] **1.** a portable flaming light **2.** a source of enlightenment, etc. **3.** a device for producing a very hot flame, as in welding **4.** [Brit.] a flashlight —*vt.* [Slang] to set fire to, as in arson

**torch′bear′er** *n.* **1.** one who carries a torch **2.** *a*) one who brings enlightenment, truth, etc. *b*) an inspirational leader, as of a movement

**torch′light′** *n.* the light of a torch or torches —*adj.* done by torchlight

**tore** (tôr) *alt. pt. of* TEAR[1]

**tor·e·a·dor** (tôr′ē ə dôr′) *n.* [Sp. < L. *taurus*, a bull] a bullfighter

**tor·ment** (tôr′ment; *for v.* tôr ment′) *n.* [see TORQUE] **1.** great pain or anguish **2.** a source of pain, anxiety, etc. —*vt.* **1.** to cause great physical or mental anguish in **2.** to annoy; harass —**tor·men′tor, tor·ment′er** *n.*

**torn** (tôrn) *alt. pp. of* TEAR[1]

**tor·na·do** (tôr nā′dō) *n.*, *pl.* **-does, -dos** [ < Sp. < L. *tonare*, to thunder] a violently whirling column of air seen as a funnel-shaped cloud that usually destroys everything in its narrow path

**To·ron·to** (tə rän′tō) capital of Ontario, Canada: pop. 665,000

**tor·pe·do** (tôr pē′dō) *n.*, *pl.* **-does** [see ff.] **1.** a large, cigar-shaped, self-propelled, underwater projectile containing explosives **2.** any of various explosive devices —*vt.* to attack, destroy, etc. as with a torpedo

**tor·pid** (tôr′pid) *adj.* [ < L. *torpere*, be numb] **1.** without sensation or motion; dormant **2.** dull; sluggish

**tor·por** (tôr′pər) *n.* [L.] **1.** a torpid state; stupor **2.** dullness; apathy

**torque** (tôrk) *n.* [ < L. *torquere*, to twist] *Physics* a force that produces a twisting or wrenching effect

**Tor·rance** (tôr′əns) city in SW Calif.: pop. 135,000

**tor·rent** (tôr′ənt, tär′-) *n.* [ < L. *torrens*, rushing] **1.** a swift, violent stream, esp. of water **2.** a rapid or violent flow, as of words —**tor·ren′tial** (tō ren′shəl) *adj.*

**tor·rid** (tôr′id, tär′-) *adj.* [ < L. *torrere*, to dry] **1.** subjected to intense heat, esp. of the sun; parched **2.** very hot; scorching **3.** passionate; ardent

**Torrid Zone** the area of the earth's surface between the Tropic of Cancer and the Tropic of Capricorn

**tor·sion** (tôr′shən) *n.* [see TORQUE] **1.** a twisting or being twisted **2.** the stress produced in a rod, wire, etc. by twisting along a longitudinal axis

**torsion bar** a metal bar exhibiting resilience under torsion

**tor·so** (tôr′sō) *n.*, *pl.* **-sos, -si** (-sē) [ < Gr. *thyrsos*, a stem] the trunk of the human body

**tort** (tôrt) *n.* [ < L. *torquere*, to twist] *Law* a wrongful act or damage (not involving a breach of contract), for which a civil action can be brought

**torte** (tôrt; *G.* tôr′tə) *n.*, *pl.* **tortes,** *G.* **tor·ten** (tôr′tən) [G. < It. < LL. *torta,* a twisted bread] a rich cake, as one made of eggs, finely chopped nuts, crumbs, etc.

**tor·til·la** (tôr tē′ə) *n.* [Sp., dim. of *torta,* a cake] a flat cake of unleavened cornmeal, or of flour: a Mexican food

**tor·toise** (tôr′təs) *n.* [ < ? LGr.

*tartarouchos*, demon] a turtle, esp. one that lives on land

**tortoise shell** the hard, mottled, yellow-and-brown shell of some turtles —**tor′toise-shell′** adj.

**tor·to·ni** (tôr tō′nē) n. [prob. alt. < It. *tortone*, big pastry tart] an ice cream made with heavy cream, maraschino cherries, almonds, etc.

**tor·tu·ous** (tôr′choo wəs) adj. [see TORQUE] 1. full of twists, turns, etc.; crooked 2. deceitful or tricky

**tor·ture** (tôr′chər) n. [see TORQUE] 1. the inflicting of severe pain, as to force information or confession 2. any severe physical or mental pain; agony —vt. **-tured, -tur·ing** 1. to subject to torture 2. to twist or distort (meaning, etc.) —**tor′tur·er** n.

**To·ry** (tôr′ē) n., pl. **-ries** [Ir. *tōruidhe*, robber] 1. formerly, a member of the major conservative party of England 2. in the American Revolution, one loyal to Great Britain

**toss** (tôs) vt. [prob. < Scand.] 1. to throw about [waves *tossed* the boat] 2. to throw lightly from the hand 3. to jerk upward [to *toss* one's head] —vi. 1. to be thrown about 2. to fling oneself about in sleep, etc. —n. a tossing or being tossed —**toss up** to toss a coin for deciding something according to which side lands uppermost

**toss′up′** n. 1. the act of tossing up 2. an even chance

**tot¹** (tät) n. [prob. < ON.] 1. a young child 2. [Chiefly Brit.] a small amount

**tot²** (tät) vt. **tot′ted, tot′ting** [Chiefly Brit. Colloq.] to total (with *up*)

**to·tal** (tōt′'l) adj. [< L. *totus*, all] 1. constituting a whole 2. complete; utter [a *total* loss] —n. the whole amount; sum —vt. **-taled** or **-talled, -tal·ing** or **-tal·ling** 1. to find the total of 2. to add up to —vi. to amount (*to*) as a whole —**to′tal·ly** adv.

**to·tal·i·tar·i·an** (tō tal′ə ter′ē ən) adj. [prec. + (AUTHOR)ITARIAN] designating or of a government in which one political group maintains complete control, esp. under a dictator —n. one who favors such a government —**to·tal′i·tar′i·an·ism** n.

**to·tal·i·ty** (tō tal′ə tē) n., pl. **-ties** the total amount or sum

**to·tal·i·za·tor** (tōt′'l i zāt′ər) n. a machine for registering bets and computing the odds and payoffs, as at a horse race: also **to′tal·iz′er** (-ī′zər)

**tote** (tōt) vt. **tot′ed, tot′ing** [< ?] [Colloq.] to carry or haul

**to·tem** (tōt′əm) n. [< Algonquian] 1. among primitive peoples, an animal or natural object taken as the symbol of a family or clan 2. an image of this

**totem pole** a pole carved and painted with totems by Indian tribes of NW N.America

**tot·ter** (tät′ər) vi. [prob. < Scand.] 1. to rock as if about to fall 2. to be unsteady on one's feet; stagger

**tou·can** (tōō′kan) n. [ < SAmInd.] a brightly colored bird of tropical America, with a very large beak

TOUCAN

**touch** (tuch) vt. [< OFr. *tochier*] 1. to put the hand, etc. on, so as to feel 2. to bring (something), or come, into contact with (something else) 3. to border on 4. to strike lightly 5. to give a light tint, aspect, etc. to [*touched* with pink] 6. to stop at (a port) 7. to handle; use 8. to come up to; reach 9. to compare with; equal 10. to affect; concern 11. to arouse sympathy, gratitude, etc. in 12. [Slang] to seek a loan or gift of money from —vi. 1. to touch a person or thing 2. to be or come into contact 3. to verge (*on* or *upon*) 4. to pertain; bear (*on* or *upon*) 5. to treat in passing (with *on* or *upon*) —n. 1. a touching or being touched; specif., a light tap 2. the sense by which physical objects are felt 3. a special quality or skill 4. a subtle change or addition in a painting, story, etc. 5. a trace, tinge, etc. 6. a slight attack [a *touch* of the flu] 7. contact or communication [keep in *touch*] 8. [Slang] the act of seeking or getting a gift or loan of money 9. *Music* the manner of striking the keys of a piano, etc. —**touch down** to land: said of an aircraft or spacecraft —**touch up** to improve or finish (a painting, story, etc.) by minor changes

**touch and go** a risky or precarious situation —**touch′-and-go′** adj.

**touch′down′** n. 1. the moment at which an aircraft or spacecraft lands 2. *Football* a play, scoring six points, in which a player grounds the ball on or past the opponent's goal line

**tou·ché** (tōō shā′) interj. [Fr.] touched: said when one's opponent in fencing scores a point, or to acknowledge a point in debate or a witty retort

**touched** (tucht) adj. 1. emotionally affected; moved 2. slightly demented

**touch′ing** adj. arousing tender emotions; moving

**touch′stone′** n. 1. a stone formerly used to test the purity of gold or silver 2. any test of genuineness

**touch′-type′** vi. **-typed′, -typ′ing** to typewrite without looking at the keyboard by regularly touching a given key with a specific finger

**touch′y** adj. **-i·er, -i·est** 1. easily offended; oversensitive; irritable 2. very risky or precarious

**tough** (tuf) adj. [OE. *toh*] 1. that will bend, etc. without tearing or breaking 2. not easily cut or chewed [*tough* steak] 3. strong; hardy 4. stubborn 5. brutal or rough 6. very difficult; laborious —n. a tough person; thug

**tough′en** vt., vi. to make or become tough or tougher —**tough′en·er** n.

**tou·pee** (tōō pā′) n. [ < Fr. < OFr.

*toup*, tuft of hair] a man's small wig

**tour** (toor) *n.* [ < OFr. *torner*, to turn]
1. a turn, period, etc., as of military duty 2. a long trip, as for sightseeing 3. any trip, as for inspection, giving performances, etc. —*vt.*, *vi.* to go on a tour (through)

**tour de force** (toor' də fôrs') *pl.* **tours de force** (toor') [Fr.] an unusually skillful or ingenious creation or performance, sometimes a merely clever one

**tour/ism** *n.* tourist travel

**tour/ist** *n.* one who tours, esp. for pleasure —*adj.* of or for tourists

**tour·ma·line** (toor'mə lin, -lēn') *n.* [ < Sinhalese] a semiprecious mineral

**tour·na·ment** (toor'nə mənt, tur'-) *n.* [ < OFr. *tourner*, to turn] 1. a contest between knights on horseback who tried to unseat each other with lances 2. a series of contests in competition for a championship Also **tour/ney** (-nē), *pl.* **-neys**

**tour·ni·quet** (toor'nə kit, tur'-) *n.* [Fr. < L. *tunica*, tunic] a device for compressing a blood vessel to stop bleeding, as a bandage twisted about a limb and released at intervals

**tou·sle** (tou'z'l) *vt.* **-sled**, **-sling** [ < ME. *tusen*, to pull] to disorder, dishevel, muss, etc.

**tout** (tout) *vi.*, *vt.* [OE. *totian*, to peep] [Colloq.] 1. to praise highly 2. to sell betting tips on (race horses) —*n.* [Colloq.] one who touts

**tow** (tō) *vt.* [OE. *togian*] to pull as by a rope or chain —*n.* 1. a towing or being towed 2. something towed 3. *same as* TOWLINE —**in tow** 1. being towed 2. in one's company or charge

**to·ward** (tôrd, tə wôrd') *prep.* [see TO & -WARD] 1. in the direction of 2. facing 3. along a likely course to [steps *toward* peace] 4. concerning 5. just before [*toward* noon] 6. for [save *toward* a car] Also **towards**

**tow·el** (tou''l) *n.* [ < OFr. *toaille*] a piece of cloth or paper for wiping or drying things —*vt.* **-eled** or **-elled**, **-el·ing** or **-el·ling** to wipe or dry with a towel —**throw** (or **toss**) **in the towel** [Colloq.] to admit defeat

**tow·el·ing**, **tow·el·ling** *n.* material for making towels

**tow·er** (tou'ər) *n.* [ < L. *turris*] 1. a high structure, often part of another building 2. such a structure used as a fortress, etc. —*vi.* to rise high like a tower —**tow'er·ing** *adj.*

**tow·head** (tō'hed') *n.* [ < *tow*, fibers of flax, etc.] 1. a head of pale-yellow hair 2. a person with such hair —**tow'head'ed** *adj.*

**tow·hee** (tou'hē, tō'-) *n.* [echoic] a small N.American sparrow

**tow/line'** *n.* a rope, etc. for towing

**town** (toun) *n.* [OE. *tun*] 1. a concentration of houses, etc. somewhat larger than a village 2. a city 3. a township 4. the business center of a city 5. the people of a town —**go to town** [Slang] to act fast and efficiently —**on the town** [Colloq.] out for a good time

**town crier** one who formerly cried

public announcements through the streets of a village or town

**town hall** a building in a town, housing the offices of officials, etc.

**town house** a two-story dwelling, a unit in a complex of such dwellings

**town meeting** a meeting of the voters of a town, as in New England

**town/ship** *n.* 1. a division of a county, constituting a unit of local government 2. in the U.S. land survey, a unit generally 6 miles square

**towns·man** (tounz'mən) *n.*, *pl.* **-men** 1. one who lives, or was reared, in a town 2. a fellow resident of one's town

**towns/peo'ple** *n.pl.* the people of a town: also **towns/folk'** (-fōk')

**tow/path'** *n.* a path along a canal, used by men or animals towing freight-carrying boats

**tow/rope'** *n.* a rope used in towing

**tox·e·mi·a** (täk sē'mē ə) *n.* [see ff. & -EMIA] a condition in which the blood contains poison substances, esp. toxins produced by pathogenic bacteria

**tox·ic** (täk'sik) *adj.* [ < Gr. *toxikon*, a poison] 1. of, affected by, or caused by a toxin 2. poisonous

**tox·i·col·o·gy** (täk'si käl'ə jē) *n.* [see prec. & -LOGY] the science of poisons, their effects, antidotes, etc. —**tox'i·col'o·gist** *n.*

**tox·in** (täk'sin) *n.* [ < TOXIC] 1. a poison produced by microorganisms and causing certain diseases 2. any poison secreted by plants or animals

**toy** (toi) *n.* [ < ? MDu. *toi*, finery] 1. a trifle 2. a bauble; trinket 3. a plaything for children —*adj.* 1. like a toy in size, use, etc. 2. made as a toy —*vi.* to trifle (*with* a thing, an idea, etc.)

**tr.** 1. transpose 2. treasurer

**trace**[1] (trās) *n.* [ < L. *trahere*, to draw] 1. a mark, track, sign, etc. left by a person, animal, or thing 2. a barely perceptible amount —*vt.* **traced**, **trac'ing** 1. to follow the trail of; track 2. *a*) to follow the development or history of *b*) to determine (a source, etc.) thus 3. to draw, outline, etc. 4. to copy (a drawing, etc.) by following its lines on a superimposed transparent sheet —**trace'a·ble** *adj.* —**trac'er** *n.*

**trace**[2] (trās) *n.* [see TRAIT] either of two straps, etc. connecting a draft animal's harness to the vehicle

**trace element** a chemical element, as copper, zinc, etc., essential in nutrition but only in minute amounts

**trac·er·y** (trās'ər ē) *n.*, *pl.* **-ies** [ < TRACE[1] + -ERY] ornamental work of interlacing or branching lines

**tra·che·a** (trā'kē ə) *n.*, *pl.* **-ae'** (-ē'), **-as** [ < Gr. *tracheia* (*arteria*), rough (windpipe)] the passage that conveys air from the larynx to the bronchi; windpipe —**tra'che·al** *adj.*

**tra·che·ot·o·my** (trā'kē ät'ə mē) *n.* [see prec. & -TOMY] an incision of the trachea to aid breathing in an emergency

**tra·cho·ma** (trə kō'mə) *n.* [Gr. *trachōma*, roughness] a contagious viral infection of the conjunctiva and cornea, causing granulation and scarring

**trac·ing** (trā′siŋ) *n.* something traced; specif., a copy of a drawing, etc.

**track** (trak) *n.* [ < MFr. *trac*] **1.** a mark left in passing, as a footprint, wheel rut, etc. **2.** a path or trail **3.** a sequence of ideas, events, etc. **4.** a path or circuit laid out for racing, etc. **5.** a pair of parallel metal rails on which trains, etc. run **6.** *a)* sports performed on a track, as running, hurdling, etc. *b)* these sports along with other contests in jumping, throwing, etc. **7.** a separate, parallel recording surface along a magnetic tape —*vt.* **1.** to follow the track of **2.** to trace by means of evidence, etc. **3.** to observe or plot the path of, as with radar **4.** to leave tracks of (mud, etc.) on (often with *up*) —**in one's tracks** where one is at the moment —**keep (or lose) track of** to stay (or fail to stay) informed about —**track′less** *adj.*

**tract¹** (trakt) *n.* [ < L. *trahere*, to draw] **1.** a continuous expanse of land **2.** a system of organs having some special function *[the digestive tract]*

**tract²** (trakt) *n.* [ < LL. *tractatus*, treatise] a propagandizing pamphlet, esp. one on a religious subject

**trac·ta·ble** (trak′tə b'l) *adj.* [ < L. *trahere*, to draw] **1.** easily managed; docile **2.** easily worked; malleable

**trac·tion** (trak′shən) *n.* [ < L. *trahere*, to draw] **1.** *a)* a pulling or drawing *b)* a being pulled or drawn **2.** the kind of power used by a locomotive, etc. **3.** adhesive friction

**trac·tor** (trak′tər) *n.* [see prec.] **1.** a powerful, motor-driven vehicle for pulling farm machinery, etc. **2.** a truck with a driver's cab and no body, for hauling large trailers

**trade** (trād) *n.* [ < MLowG., a track] **1.** an occupation; esp., skilled work **2.** all the persons in a particular business **3.** buying and selling; commerce **4.** customers **5.** a purchase or sale **6.** an exchange; swap —*vi.* trad′ed, trad′ing **1.** to carry on a business **2.** to have business dealings (*with*) **3.** to make an exchange (*with*) **4.** [Colloq.] to be a customer (*at* a certain store) —*vt.* to exchange; barter —**trade on (or upon)** to take advantage of

**trade′-in′** *n.* a thing given or taken as part payment for something else

**trade journal** a magazine devoted to a specific trade or industry

**trade′mark′** *n.* a symbol, word, etc. used by a manufacturer or dealer to distinguish his product: usually protected by law

**trade name** **1.** a name used as a trademark **2.** the name used for a certain article by those who deal in it **3.** the business name of a company

**trade′-off′** *n.* an exchange in which one benefit is given up for another considered more desirable: also **trade′off′**

**trad′er** *n.* **1.** one who trades; merchant **2.** a ship used in trade

**trades·man** (trādz′mən) *n., pl.* **-men** [Chiefly Brit.] a storekeeper

**trade union** same as LABOR UNION

**trade wind** a wind that blows toward the equator from either side of it

**trading post** a store in an outpost, settlement, etc., where trading is done

**trading stamp** a stamp redeemable for merchandise, given as a premium by some merchants

**tra·di·tion** (trə dish′ən) *n.* [ < L. *tradere*, deliver] **1.** the handing down orally of customs, beliefs, etc. from generation to generation **2.** a story, belief, etc. handed down in this way

**tra·di′tion·al** *adj.* of, handed down by, or conforming to tradition

**tra·duce** (trə dōōs′, -dyōōs′) *vt.* **-duced′, -duc′ing** [ < L. *trans*, across + *ducere*, to lead] to slander

**traf·fic** (traf′ik) *n.* [ < It. < L. *trans*, across + It. *ficcare*, bring] **1.** buying and selling; trade **2.** dealings (*with* someone) **3.** the movement or number of automobiles, pedestrians, etc. along a street, etc. **4.** the business done by a transportation company —*adj.* of or having to do with the regulation of traffic —*vi.* **-ficked, -fick·ing** **1.** to carry on traffic (*in* a commodity) **2.** to have dealings (*with* someone)

**traffic circle** a circular road at the intersection of several streets: vehicles move on it in one direction only

**traffic light** (or **signal**) a set of signal lights at a street intersection to regulate traffic

**tra·ge·di·an** (trə je′dē ən) *n.* an actor or writer of tragedy

**trag·e·dy** (traj′ə dē) *n., pl.* **-dies** [ < Gr. *tragos*, goat + *ōidē*, song] **1.** a serious play with an unhappy ending **2.** a very sad or tragic event

**trag·ic** (traj′ik) *adj.* **1.** of, or having the nature of, tragedy **2.** disastrous, fatal, etc. —**trag′i·cal·ly** *adv.*

**trail** (trāl) *vt.* [ < L. *trahere*, to draw] **1.** to drag or let drag behind one **2.** to follow the tracks of **3.** to hunt by tracking **4.** to follow behind —*vi.* **1.** to drag along on the ground, etc. **2.** to grow along the ground, etc., as some plants **3.** to flow behind, as smoke **4.** to follow or lag behind; straggle **5.** to grow weaker, dimmer, etc. (with *off* or *away*) —*n.* **1.** something that trails behind **2.** a mark, scent, etc. left by a person, animal, or thing that has passed **3.** a beaten path

**trail′blaz′er** *n.* **1.** one who blazes a trail **2.** a pioneer in any field

**trail′er** *n.* **1.** one that trails **2.** *a)* a wagon, van, etc. designed to be pulled by an automobile, truck, etc. *b)* such a vehicle designed to be lived in

**trailer park** an area, usually with piped water, electricity, etc., for trailers, esp. mobile homes: also **trailer camp, trailer court**

**train** (trān) *n.* [ < L. *trahere*, to pull] **1.** something that drags along behind, as a trailing skirt **2.** a group of followers; retinue **3.** a procession; caravan **4.** any connected order; sequence [a *train* of thought] **5.** a line of connected railroad cars pulled by a locomotive —*vt.* **1.** to guide the growth of (a plant) **2.** to guide the mental, moral, etc. development of; rear **3.** to instruct so as to make proficient **4.** to make fit for an athletic contest, etc. **5.** to aim (a gun, etc.) —*vi.* to undergo training —**train·ee** (trā nē') *n.* —**train'er** *n.* —**train'ing** *n.*

**train'man** (-mən) *n., pl.* -**men** one who works on a railroad train

**traipse** (trāps) *vi., vt.* **traipsed, traips'ing** [< ?] [Dial. or Colloq.] to walk, wander, or tramp

**trait** (trāt) *n.* [< L. *trahere*, to draw] a distinguishing characteristic

**trai·tor** (trāt'ər) *n.* [< L. *tradere*, betray] one who betrays his country, friends, etc. —**trai'tor·ous** *adj.*

**tra·jec·to·ry** (trə jek'tə rē) *n., pl.* -**ries** [< L. *trans*, across + *jacere*, to throw] the curved path of something hurtling through space

**tram** (tram) *n.* [prob. < LowG. *traam*, a beam] **1.** an open railway car used in mines **2.** [Brit.] a streetcar

**tram·mel** (tram'l) *n.* [< L. *tres*, three + *macula*, a mesh] [*usually pl.*] something that confines or restrains —*vt.* -**meled** or -**melled**, -**mel·ing** or -**mel·ling** to confine, restrain, etc.

**tramp** (tramp) *vi.* [ME. *trampen*] **1.** to walk or step heavily **2.** to travel about on foot —*vt.* **1.** to step on heavily **2.** to walk through —*n.* **1.** a hobo; vagrant **2.** the sound of heavy steps **3.** a journey on foot; hike **4.** a freight ship that picks up cargo wherever it may be **5.** [Slang] a loose woman

**tram·ple** (tram'p'l) *vi.* -**pled, -pling** [see prec.] to tread heavily —*vt.* to crush as by treading heavily

**tram·po·line** (tram'pə lēn', -lin) *n.* [< It.] a sheet of strong canvas stretched tightly on a frame, used in acrobatic tumbling

**trance** (trans) *n.* [< L. *transire*, to die] **1.** a state of altered consciousness, resembling sleep, as in hypnosis **2.** a daze; stupor **3.** a state of great mental abstraction

**tran·quil** (traŋ'kwəl) *adj.* [L. *tranquillus*] calm, serene, placid, etc. — **tran·quil'li·ty, tran·quil'i·ty** (-kwil'ə tē) *n.* —**tran'quil·ly** *adv.*

**tran'quil·ize', tran'quil·lize'** (-īz') *vt., vi.* -**ized'** or -**lized', -iz'-ing** or -**liz'ing** to make or become tranquil

**tran'quil·iz'er, tran'quil·liz'er** *n.* a drug used to tranquilize the emotionally disturbed, etc.

**trans-** [L. < *trans*, across] *a prefix meaning* over, across, beyond

**trans. 1.** translated **2.** translation

**trans·act** (tran sakt', -zakt') *vt.* [< L. *trans*-, over + *agere*, to drive] to carry on or complete (business, etc.)

**trans·ac'tion** *n.* **1.** a transacting **2.** something transacted; specif., *a)* a business deal *b)* [*pl.*] a record of the proceedings of a society, etc.

**trans·ac'tion·al analysis** a form of popular psychotherapy dealing with hypothetical states of the ego

**trans·at·lan·tic** (trans'ət lan'tik) *adj.* **1.** crossing the Atlantic **2.** on the other side of the Atlantic

**trans·ceiv·er** (tran sē'vər) *n.* a radio transmitter and receiver in a single housing

**tran·scend** (tran send') *vt.* [< L. *trans*-, over + *scandere*, climb] **1.** to go beyond the limits of; exceed **2.** to surpass; excel —**tran·scend'ent** *adj.*

**tran·scen·den·tal** (tran'sen den't'l) *adj.* **1.** supernatural **2.** abstract

**tran'scen·den'tal·ism** *n.* a philosophy based on a search for reality through spiritual intuition

**trans·con·ti·nen·tal** (trans'-) *adj.* **1.** that crosses a continent **2.** on the other side of a continent

**tran·scribe** (tran skrīb') *vt.* -**scribed', -scrib'ing** [< L. *trans*-, over + *scribere*, write] **1.** to make a written or typewritten copy of (shorthand notes, etc.) **2.** *Music, Radio & TV* to make a transcription of

**tran·script** (tran'skript') *n.* **1.** a written or typewritten copy **2.** a copy, esp. an official copy

**tran·scrip'tion** (-skrip'shən) *n.* **1.** a transcribing **2.** a transcript **3.** an arrangement of a piece of music for some other instrument or voice **4.** a recording made for radio or television broadcasting

**tran·sept** (tran'sept) *n.* [< L. *trans*-, across + *septum*, enclosure] the part of a cross-shaped church at right angles to the nave

**trans·fer** (trans fur'; *esp. for n.* trans'fər) *vt.* -**ferred', -fer'ring** [< L. *trans*-, across + *ferre*, to bear] **1.** to carry, send, etc. to another person or place **2.** to make over (property, etc.) to another **3.** to convey (a picture, etc.) from one surface to another —*vi.* **1.** to transfer oneself or be transferred **2.** to change to another school, etc. or to another bus, etc. —*n.* **1.** a transferring or being transferred **2.** one that is transferred **3.** a ticket entitling the bearer to change to another bus, etc. —**trans·fer'a·ble** *adj.*

**trans·fer'ence** (-əns) *n.* a transferring or being transferred

**trans·fig·ure** (trans fig'yər) *vt.* -**ured, -ur·ing** [< L. *trans*-, across + *figura*, figure] **1.** to change the form or appearance of **2.** to transform so as to glorify —**trans·fig'u·ra'tion** *n.*

**trans·fix** (trans fiks') *vt.* [< L. *trans*-, through + *figere*, to fix] **1.** to pierce through; impale **2.** to make motionless, as if impaled

**trans·form** (trans fôrm') *vt.* [ult. < L. *trans*-, over + *forma*, a form] **1.** to change the form or appearance of **2.** to change the condition, character, or function of —**trans'for·ma'tion** *n.*

**trans·form'er** *n.* **1.** one that transforms **2.** a device for changing electrical energy to a different voltage

**trans·fuse** (trans fyōoz') *vt.* -**fused', -fus'ing** [< L. *trans*-, across + *fundere*, pour] **1.** to instill; imbue **2.**

to transfer (blood, etc.) into a blood vessel —**trans·fu′sion** n.

**trans·gress** (trans gres′) vt., vi. [< L. trans-, over + gradi, to step] 1. to break (a law, command, etc.); sin (against) 2. to go beyond (a limit, etc.) —**trans·gres′sion** (-gresh′ən) n. —**trans·gres′sor** n.

**tran·sient** (tran′shənt) adj. [< L. trans-, over + ire, to go] 1. passing away with time; temporary 2. passing quickly; fleeting —n. a transient person; esp., a temporary lodger, etc. —**tran′sience, tran′sien·cy** n.

**tran·sis·tor** (tran zis′tər, -sis′-) n. [TRAN(SFER) + (RE)SISTOR] a compact electronic device, composed of semiconductor material, that controls current flow —**tran·sis′tor·ize′** vt. -ized′, -iz′ing

**trans·it** (tran′sit) n. [< L. trans-, over + ire, go] 1. passage through or across 2. a carrying through or across; conveyance 3. a surveying instrument for measuring horizontal angles

**tran·si·tion** (tran zish′ən) n. a passing from one condition, place, etc. to another —**tran·si′tion·al** adj.

**tran·si·tive** (tran′sə tiv) adj. designating a verb taking a direct object

**tran·si·to·ry** (tran′sə tôr′ē) adj. not enduring; temporary; fleeting

**transl.** 1. translated 2. translation

**trans·late** (trans lāt′) vt. -lat′ed, -lat′ing [< L. translatus, transferred] 1. to change from one place, condition, etc. to another 2. to put into words of a different language 3. to put into different words —**trans·la′tor** n.

**trans·la·tion** n. 1. a translating 2. writing or speech translated into another language

**trans·lit·er·ate** (trans lit′ə rāt′) vt. -at′ed, -at′ing [< TRANS- + L. litera, letter] to write (words, etc.) in the characters of another alphabet

**trans·lu·cent** (trans lōō′s'nt) adj. [< L. trans-, through + lucere, to shine] letting light pass through but not transparent

**trans·mi·grate** (trans mī′grāt) vi. -grat·ed, -grat·ing [see TRANS- & MIGRATE] in some religions, to pass into another body at death: said of the soul —**trans′mi·gra′tion** n.

**trans·mis·si·ble** (trans mis′ə b'l) adj. capable of being transmitted

**trans·mis·sion** (trans mish′ən) n. 1. a transmitting 2. something transmitted 3. the part of an automobile, etc. that transmits motive force to the wheels, as by gears

**trans·mit** (-mit′) vt. -mit′ted, -mit′ting [< L. trans-, over + mittere, send] 1. to cause to go to another person or place; transfer 2. to hand down by heredity, inheritance, etc. 3. a) to pass (light, heat, etc.) through some medium b) to conduct 4. to convey (force, movement, etc.) to 5. to send out (radio or television signals) —**trans·mit′tal, trans·mit′-**

**tance** n. —**trans·mit′ti·ble, trans·mit′ta·ble** adj.

**trans·mit·ter** n. one that transmits; specif., the apparatus that transmits signals in telephony, radio, etc.

**trans·mute** (trans myōōt′) vt., vi. -mut′ed, -mut′ing [< L. trans-, over + mutare, change] to change from one form, nature, substance, etc. into another —**trans′mu·ta′tion** n.

**trans·na·tion·al** adj. transcending the interests, etc. of a single nation

**trans·o·ce·an·ic** (trans′ō shē an′ik) adj. across the ocean

**tran·som** (tran′səm) n. [prob. < L. transtrum, crossbeam] 1. a horizontal crossbar, as across the top of a door or window 2. a small window just above a door or window

**tran·son·ic** (tran sän′ik) adj. of or moving at a speed within the range of change from subsonic to supersonic speed: also sp. **transsonic**

**trans·pa·cif·ic** (trans′pə sif′ik) adj. 1. crossing the Pacific 2. on the other side of the Pacific

**trans·par·ent** (trans per′ənt) adj. [< L. trans-, through + parere, appear] 1. transmitting light rays so that objects on the other side may be seen 2. so fine in texture as to be seen through 3. easily understood or detected; obvious —**trans·par′en·cy** n., pl. -**cies** —**trans·par′ent·ly** adv.

**tran·spire** (tran spīr′) vi. -spired′, -spir′ing [< L. trans-, through + spirare, breathe] 1. to give off vapor, moisture, etc., as through pores 2. to become known 3. to happen: regarded by some as a loose usage —**tran′spi·ra′tion** (-spə rā′shən) n.

**trans·plant** (trans plant′) vt. 1. to remove from one place and plant, resettle, etc. in another 2. Surgery to graft (tissue, an organ, etc.)

**tran·spon·der** (tran spän′dər) n. [< TRANSMITTER & RESPOND] a transceiver that transmits signals automatically

**trans·port** (trans pôrt′; for n. trans′pôrt) vt. [< L. trans-, over + portare, carry] 1. to carry from one place to another 2. to carry away with emotion 3. to banish to a penal colony, etc. —n. 1. a transporting; transportation 2. rapture 3. a ship, airplane, etc. used for transporting

**trans·por·ta·tion** (trans′pər tā′shən) n. 1. a transporting or being transported 2. a means of conveyance 3. fare or a ticket for being transported

**trans·pose** (trans pōz′) vt., vi. -posed′, -pos′ing [see TRANS- & POSE] 1. to change the usual order or position of; interchange 2. to rewrite or play (a musical composition) in another key —**trans′po·si′tion** (-pə zish′ən) n.

**trans·sex·u·al** (tran sek′shoo wəl) n. a person who is predisposed to identify with the opposite sex, sometimes to the point of undergoing sex-change surgery

**trans·ship** (tran ship′) *vt.* **-shipped′, -ship′ping** to transfer from one ship, train, truck, etc. to another for further shipment —**trans·ship′ment** *n.*

**trans·verse** (trans vʉrs′; *esp. for n.* trans′vʉrs) *adj.* [< L. *trans-*, across + *vertere*, to turn] situated across; crosswise —*n.* a transverse part, etc.

**trans·ves·tite** (trans ves′tīt) *n.* [< TRANS- + L. *vestire*, to dress] a person who gets sexual pleasure from dressing in clothes of the opposite sex

**trap¹** (trap) *n.* [< OE. *træppe*] **1.** a device for trapping animals **2.** any stratagem designed to catch or trick **3.** a device, as in a drainpipe, for preventing the escape of gas, etc. **4.** a light, two-wheeled carriage **5.** [*pl.*] percussion devices, as in a band —*vt.* **trapped, trap′ping** to catch as in a trap —*vi.* to trap animals, esp. for their furs —**trap′per** *n.*

**trap²** (trap) *n.* [Sw. *trapp*] darkcolored, igneous rock, used in road making: also **trap′rock′**

**trap³** (trap) *vt.* **trapped, trap′ping** [< OFr. *drap*, cloth] to cover, equip, or adorn with trappings

**trap′door′** *n.* a hinged or sliding door in a roof, ceiling, or floor

**tra·peze** (tra pēz′, trə-) *n.* [see ff.] a short horizontal bar, hung high by two ropes, on which gymnasts, etc. swing

**trap·e·zoid** (trap′ə zoid′) *n.* [< Gr. *trapeza*, table] a plane figure with four sides, two of which are parallel — **trap′e·zoi′dal** *adj.*

TRAPEZOID

**trap·pings** (trap′iŋz) *n.pl.* [< OFr. *drap*, cloth] **1.** an ornamental covering for a horse **2.** adornments

**trap′shoot′ing** *n.* the sport of shooting at clay disks sprung into the air from throwing devices (**traps**)

**trash** (trash) *n.* [prob. < Scand.] **1.** worthless or waste things; rubbish **2.** a disreputable person or people — **trash′y** *adj.* **-i·er, -i·est**

**trau·ma** (trou′mə, trô′-) *n., pl.* **-mas, -ma·ta** (-mə tə) [Gr.] **1.** a bodily injury or shock **2.** an emotional shock, often having a lasting psychic effect —**trau·mat′ic** (-mat′ik) *adj.*

**trau′ma·tize′** (-tīz′) *vt.* **-tized′, -tiz′ing** to subject to a physical or mental trauma

**trav·ail** (trav′āl, trə vāl′) *n.* [< VL. *tri-*, three + *palus*, stake: referring to a torture device] **1.** very hard work **2.** intense pain; agony

**trav·el** (trav′l) *vi.* **-eled** or **-elled, -el·ing** or **-el·ling** [var. of TRAVAIL] **1.** to go from one place to another **2.** to move, pass, or be transmitted —*vt.* to make a journey over or through —*n.* **a.** traveling; trip —**trav′el·er, trav′el·ier** *n.*

**trav·e·logue, trav·e·log** (trav′ə lôg′) *n.* an illustrated lecture or motion picture of travels

**trav·erse** (tra vʉrs′; *for n. & adj.* trav′ərs) *vt.* **-ersed′, -ers′ing** [see TRANSVERSE] to pass over, across, or through —*n.* something that traverses

or crosses, as a crossbar —*adj.* **1.** extending across **2.** designating or of drapes drawn by pulling a cord at the side

**trav·es·ty** (trav′is tē) *n., pl.* **-ties** [< L. *trans-*, over + *vestire*, to dress] **1.** a farcical imitation in ridicule **2.** a ridiculous representation —*vt.* **-tied, -ty·ing** to make a travesty of

**trawl** (trôl) *n.* [< ? MDu. *traghel, dragnet*] **1.** a large net dragged along the bottom of a fishing bank **2.** a long line supported by buoys, from which fishing lines are hung —*vt., vi.* to fish or catch with a trawl

**trawl′er** *n.* a boat used in trawling

**tray** (trā) *n.* [< OE. *treg*, wooden board] a flat receptacle with raised edges, for holding or carrying things

**treach·er·ous** (trech′ər əs) *adj.* **1.** characterized by treachery **2.** untrustworthy —**treach′er·ous·ly** *adv.*

**treach·er·y** *n., pl.* **-er·ies** [< OFr. *trichier*, to cheat] **1.** betrayal of trust; disloyalty **2.** treason

**trea·cle** (trē′k'l) *n.* [< Gr. *thēriakē*, antidote for venom] [Brit.] molasses

**tread** (tred) *vt.* **trod, trod′den** or **trod, tread′ing** [OE. *tredan*] **1.** to walk on, in, along, etc. **2.** to do or follow by walking, dancing, etc. **3.** to press or beat with the feet —*vi.* **1.** to walk **2.** to set one's foot (*on, across,* etc.) **3.** to trample (*on* or *upon*) —*n.* **1.** the manner or sound of treading **2.** something on which a person or thing treads or moves, as a shoe sole, wheel rim, surface of a stair, etc. —**tread water** *pt. usually* **tread′ed** to stay upright in swimming by moving the legs up and down

**trea·dle** (tred′'l) *n.* [< OE. *tredan*, to tread] a lever moved by the foot as to turn a wheel

**tread′mill′** *n.* a mill wheel turned by an animal treading an endless belt

**treas.** **1.** treasurer **2.** treasury

**trea·son** (trē′z'n) *n.* [< L. *trans-*, over + *dare*, give] betrayal of one's country to an enemy —**trea′son·a·ble, trea′son·ous** *adj.*

**treas·ure** (trezh′ər, trā′zhər) *n.* [< Gr. *thēsauros*] **1.** accumulated wealth, as money, jewels, etc. **2.** any person or thing considered valuable —*vt.* **-ured, -ur·ing** **1.** to save up for future use **2.** to value greatly

**treas′ur·er** *n.* one in charge of a treasury, as of a government, corporation, club, etc.

**treas′ure-trove′** (-trōv′) *n.* [*trove* < OFr. *trover*, find] treasure found hidden, the owner of which is unknown

**treas′ur·y** (-ē) *n., pl.* **-ies** **1.** a place where treasure or funds are kept **2.** the funds or revenues of a state, corporation, etc. **3.** [T-] the governmental department in charge of revenue, taxation, etc.

**treat** (trēt) *vt.* [ult. < L. *trahere*, to draw] **1.** to discuss terms (*with*) **2.** to speak or write (*of*) —*vt.* **1.** to deal with (a subject) in writing, music, etc. in a specified manner **2.** to act toward (someone or something) in a specified manner **3.** to pay for the food, etc. of (another) **4.** to subject to some process, chemical, etc. **5.** to give medical care to —*n.* **1.** a meal, drink, etc. paid for by another **2.** anything that gives great pleasure

**trea·tise** (trēt′is) *n.* [see prec.] a formal writing on some subject

**treat·ment** (trēt′mənt) *n.* **1.** act, manner, method, etc. of treating **2.** medical or surgical care

**trea·ty** (trēt′ē) *n., pl.* **-ties** [< L. *trahere*, to draw] a formal agreement between two or more nations

**tre·ble** (treb′'l) *adj.* [< L. *triplus*, triple] **1.** threefold; triple **2.** of, for, or performing the treble —*n.* **1.** the highest part in musical harmony; soprano **2.** a high-pitched voice or sound —*vt., vi.* **-bled, -bling** to make or become threefold

**tree** (trē) *n.* [OE. *treow*] **1.** a large, woody perennial plant with one main trunk and many branches **2.** anything resembling a tree; specif., a diagram of family descent (**family tree**) —*vt.* **treed, tree′ing** to chase up a tree —**tree′less** *adj.*

**tre·foil** (trē′foil) *n.* [< L. *tri-*, three + *folium*, leaf] **1.** a plant with leaves divided into three leaflets, as the clover **2.** a design, etc. shaped like such a leaf

**trek** (trek) *vi.* **trekked, trek′king** [Afrik. < Du. *trekken*, to draw] **1.** to travel slowly or laboriously **2.** [Colloq.] to go on foot —*n.* **1.** a journey **2.** a migration

**trel·lis** (trel′is) *n.* [< L. *trilix*, triple-twilled] a lattice on which vines are trained

**trem·ble** (trem′b'l) *vi.* **-bled, -bling** [< L. *tremere*] **1.** to shake or shiver, as from cold, fear, etc. **2.** to feel great fear or anxiety **3.** to quiver, vibrate, etc. —*n.* **1.** a trembling **2.** [*sometimes pl.*] a fit or state of trembling

**tre·men·dous** (tri men′dəs) *adj.* [< L. *tremere*, tremble] **1.** terrifying; dreadful **2.** *a)* very large; great *b)* [Colloq.] wonderful, amazing, etc. — **tre·men′dous·ly** *adv.*

**trem·o·lo** (trem′ə lō′) *n., pl.* **-los′** [It.] a tremulous effect produced by rapid reiteration of the same tone

**trem·or** (trem′ər) *n.* [< L. *tremere*, tremble] **1.** a trembling, shaking, etc. **2.** a nervous thrill

**trem·u·lous** (trem′yoo ləs) *adj.* [< L. *tremere*, to tremble] **1.** trembling; quivering **2.** fearful; timid—**trem′u·lous·ly** *adv.*

**trench** (trench) *vt.* [< OFr. *trenchier*, to cut] to dig a ditch or ditches in —*n.* **1.** a deep furrow **2.** a long, narrow ditch with earth banked in front, used in battle for cover, etc.

**trench·ant** (tren′chənt) *adj.* [see prec.] **1.** sharp; keen; incisive [*trenchant* words] **2.** forceful; vigorous [*a trenchant* argument]

**trench coat** a belted raincoat in a military style

**trench·er** (tren′chər) *n.* [see TRENCH] [Archaic] a wooden platter for meat

**trench′er·man** (-mən) *n., pl.* **-men** an eater; esp., a heavy eater

**trench foot** a circulatory disorder of the feet from long exposure to wet and cold with inactivity

**trench mouth** an infectious disease of the mucous membranes of the mouth and throat

**trend** (trend) *vi.* [OE. *trendan*] to have a general direction or tendency —*n.* **1.** the general tendency or course; drift **2.** a current style

**trend′y** (-ē) *adj.* **-i·er, -i·est** [Colloq.] of or in the latest style, or trend

**Tren·ton** (tren′tən) capital of N.J.: pop. 105,000

**tre·pan** (tri pan′) *n.* [< Gr. *trypan*, to bore] an early form of the trephine —*vt.* **-panned′, -pan′ning** *same as* TREPHINE

**tre·phine** (tri fīn′, -fēn′) *n.* [< L. *tres*, three + *fines*, ends] a surgical saw for removing disks of bone from the skull —*vt.* **-phined′, -phin′ing** to operate on with a trephine

**trep·i·da·tion** (trep′ə dā′shən) *n.* [< L. *trepidus*, disturbed] **1.** trembling movement **2.** fearful uncertainty

**tres·pass** (tres′pəs, -pas′) *vi.* [< L. *trans-*, across + *passus*, a step] **1.** to go beyond the limits of what is considered right; do wrong; transgress **2.** to enter another's property without permission or right —*n.* a trespassing; specif., a moral offense —**tres′pass·er** *n.*

**tress** (tres) *n.* [< OFr. *tresce*, braid of hair] **1.** a lock of hair **2.** [*pl.*] a woman's or girl's hair, esp. when long

**tres·tle** (tres′'l) *n.* [< L. *transtrum*, a beam] **1.** a horizontal beam fastened to two pairs of spreading legs, used as a support **2.** a framework of uprights and crosspieces, supporting a bridge, etc.

TRESTLE

**trey** (trā) *n.* [< L. *tres*, three] a playing card, etc. with three spots

**tri-** [< Fr., L., or Gr.] *a combining form meaning:* **1.** having or involving three **2.** three times, into three **3.** every third

**tri·ad** (trī′ad) *n.* [< Gr. *treis*, three] a group of three

**tri·al** (trī′əl) *n.* [see TRY] **1.** the act or process of trying, testing, etc.; test; probation **2.** a hardship, suffering, etc. **3.** a source of annoyance **4.** a formal examination to decide a case by a court of law **5.** an attempt; effort —*adj.* **1.** of a trial **2.** for the purpose of trying, testing, etc.

**trial and error** the process of making repeated trials, tests, etc. to find a desired result or solution

**trial balloon** something said or done to test public opinion on an issue

**tri·an·gle** (trī'aŋ'g'l) *n.* [see TRI- & ANGLE[1]] 1. a plane figure having three angles and three sides 2. any three-sided or three-cornered object 3. a situation involving three persons [a love *triangle*] —**tri·an'gu·lar** (-gyə lər) *adj.*

**tri·an'gu·late'** (-gyə lāt') *vt.* -**lat'ed, -lat'ing** to divide into triangles to compute distance or relative positions —**tri·an'gu·la'tion** *n.*

**tribe** (trīb) *n.* [ < L. *tribus*] 1. a group of persons or clans descended from a common ancestor and living under a leader or chief 2. a natural group of plants or animals —**trib'al** *adj.* —**tribes'man** *n.*

**trib·u·la·tion** (trib'yə lā'shən) *n.* [ < L. *tribulare*, to press] great misery or distress, or the cause of it

**tri·bu·nal** (trī byōō'n'l, tri-) *n.* [see ff.] 1. a seat for a judge in a court 2. a court of justice

**trib·une** (trib'yōon, tri byōon') *n.* [ < L. *tribus*, tribe] 1. in ancient Rome, a magistrate appointed to protect the rights of plebeians 2. a champion of the people: often a newspaper name

**trib·u·tar·y** (trib'yoo ter'ē) *adj.* 1. paying tribute 2. subject [a *tributary* nation] 3. *a)* making additions *b)* flowing into a larger one [a *tributary* stream] —*n.*, *pl.* -**ies** 1. a tributary nation 2. a tributary river

**trib·ute** (trib'yoot) *n.* [ < L. *tribuere*, allot] 1. money paid regularly by one nation to another as acknowledgment of subjugation, for protection, etc. 2. any forced payment 3. something given, done, or said to show gratitude, respect, honor, or praise

**trice** (trīs) *n.* [ < MDu. *trisen*, to pull] an instant: now only in **in a trice**

**tri·cen·ten·ni·al** (trī'sen ten'ē əl) *adj.* happening once every 300 years —*n.* a 300th anniversary

**tri·ceps** (trī'seps) *n.*, *pl.* -**cep·ses, -ceps** [L. < *tri*, three + *caput*, head] a muscle with three points of origin; esp., the large muscle at the back of the upper arm

**tri·cer·a·tops** (trī ser'ə täps') *n.* [ < TRI- + Gr. *keras*, horn + *ōps*, eye] a plant-eating dinosaur with a long horn above each eye and a short horn on the nose

**trich·i·no·sis** (trik'ə nō'sis) *n.* [ < Gr. *trichinos*, hairy] a disease caused by small worms in the intestines and muscle tissues, usually acquired by eating pork from an infested hog

**trick** (trik) *n.* [ < OFr. *trichier*, v.] 1. something designed to deceive, cheat, etc. 2. a practical joke; prank 3. a clever act intended to amuse 4. any feat requiring skill 5. a personal mannerism 6. a round of duty; shift 7. *Card Games* the cards won in a single round —*vt.* to deceive or cheat —*adj.* apt to malfunction [a *trick* knee] —**do (or turn) the trick** to produce the desired result —**trick'er·y** *n.*, *pl.* -**ies** —**trick'ster** *n.*

**trick·le** (trik''l) *vi.* -**led, -ling** [prob. < ME. *striken*, to strike] 1. to flow slowly in a thin stream or fall in drops 2. to move slowly [the crowd *trickled* away] —*n.* a slow, small flow

**trick'y** *adj.* -**i·er, -i·est** 1. given to or characterized by trickery 2. like a trick; intricate; difficult

**tri·col·or** (trī'kul'ər) *n.* a flag having three colors in large areas; esp., the flag of France

**tri·cy·cle** (trī'si k'l) *n.* [Fr.: see TRI- & CYCLE] a child's three-wheeled vehicle operated by pedals

**tri·dent** (trīd''nt) *n.* [ < L. *tri-*, TRI- + *dens*, tooth] a three-pronged spear —*adj.* three-pronged

**tried** (trīd) *pt. & pp.* of TRY —*adj.* 1. tested; proved 2. trustworthy

**tri·en·ni·al** (trī en'ē əl) *adj.* [ < L. *tri-*, TRI- + *annus*, a year] 1. happening every three years 2. lasting three years —**tri·en'ni·al·ly** *adv.*

**Tri·este** (trē est') seaport in NE Italy: pop. 281,000

**tri·fle** (trī'f'l) *n.* [ < OFr. *truffe*, deception] 1. something of little value or importance 2. a small amount or sum —*vi.* -**fled, -fling** 1. to talk or act jokingly 2. to play or toy (*with*) —*vt.* to spend idly; waste (time, etc.) —**tri'fler** *n.*

**tri'fling** *adj.* 1. frivolous; shallow 2. of little importance; trivial

**tri·fo·cals** (trī fō'k'lz) *n.pl.* a pair of glasses like bifocals, but with a third area in the lens ground for intermediate distance

**trig**[1] (trig) *adj.* [< ON. *tryggr*, trusty] [Chiefly Brit.] 1. trim; neat; spruce 2. in good condition; sound

**trig**[2] (trig) *n. clipped form of* TRIG-ONOMETRY

**trig·ger** (trig'ər) *n.* [ < Du. *trekken*, to pull] a lever pulled to release a catch, etc., esp. one pressed to activate the firing mechanism on a firearm —*vt.* to initiate (an action)

**trig·o·nom·e·try** (trig'ə näm'ə trē) *n.* [ < Gr. *trigōnon*, triangle + *-metria*, measurement] the branch of mathematics analyzing, and making calculations from, the relations between the sides and angles of triangles —**trig'o·no·met'ric** (-nə met'rik) *adj.*

**trill** (tril) *n.* [ult. echoic] 1. a rapid alternation of a musical tone with the tone immediately above it 2. a warble 3. a rapid vibration of the tongue or uvula —*vt.*, *vi.* to sound, speak, sing, or play with a trill

**tril·lion** (tril'yən) *n.* 1. in the U.S. and France, 1 followed by 12 zeros 2. in Great Britain and Germany, 1 followed by 18 zeros —**tril'lionth** *adj.*, *n.*

**tril·o·gy** (tril'ə jē) *n.*, *pl.* -**gies** [see TRI- & -LOGY] a set of three related plays, novels, etc.

**trim** (trim) *vt.* **trimmed, trim'ming** [ < OE. *trymman*, make firm] 1. to put in proper order; make neat or tidy [to *trim* hair] 2. to clip, lop, cut, etc. 3. to decorate as by adding ornaments, etc. 4. *a)* to balance (a ship) by ballasting, etc. *b)* to put (sails) in order for sailing 5. to balance (an aircraft) in flight 6. [Colloq.] to beat, punish, defeat, cheat, etc. —*vi.* to adjust according to expediency —*n.* 1. order; arrangement 2. good condition 3. a trimming 4. decorative parts or borders —*adj.* trim′mer, trim′mest 1. orderly; neat 2. well-proportioned 3. in good condition —trim′ly *adv.* —trim′mer *n.*

**tri·ma·ran** (trī′mə ran′) *n.* a boat like a catamaran, but with three hulls

**tri·mes·ter** (trī mes′tər, trī′mes-) *n.* [< L. *tri-*, three + *mensis*, month] in some colleges, any of the three periods of the academic year

**trim′ming** *n.* 1. decoration; ornament 2. [*pl.*] *a)* the side dishes of a meal *b)* parts trimmed off 3. [Colloq.] a beating, defeat, cheating, etc.

**Trin·i·dad and To·ba·go** (trin′ə dad′, tō bā′gō) island country in the West Indies: 1,980 sq. mi.; pop. 1,010,000

**trin·i·ty** (trin′ə tē) *n., pl.* -ties [< L. *trinitas*] 1. a set of three 2. [T-] *Christian Theol.* the union of Father, Son, and Holy Ghost in one Godhead

**trin·ket** (trin′kit) *n.* [ME. *trenket*] 1. a small ornament, piece of jewelry, etc. 2. a trifle or toy

**tri·o** (trē′ō) *n., pl.* -os [< L. *tres*, three] 1. a group of three 2. *Music a)* a composition for three voices or three instruments *b)* the three performers of such a composition

**trip** (trip) *vi., vt.* tripped, trip′ping [< OFr. *treper*] 1. to move or perform with light, rapid steps 2. to stumble or cause to stumble 3. to make or cause to make a mistake 4. to release or run past (a spring, wheel, etc.) —*n.* 1. a light, quick tread 2. a journey, voyage, etc. 3. a stumble or a causing to stumble 4. [Slang] the experience of being under the influence of a psychedelic drug, esp. LSD 5. [Slang] an experience that is pleasing, exciting, etc. —trip up to catch in a lie, error, etc. —trip′per *n.*

**tri·par·tite** (trī pär′tīt) *adj.* [< L. *tri-*, three + *partire*, to part] 1. having three parts 2. made between three parties, as an agreement

**tripe** (trīp) *n.* [prob. ult. < Ar. *tharb*, entrails] 1. part of the stomach of an ox, etc. used as food 2. [Slang] anything worthless, etc.; nonsense

**trip′ham′mer** *n.* a heavy, power-driven hammer, alternately raised and allowed to fall by a tripping device

**tri·ple** (trip′'l) *adj.* [< L. *triplus*] 1. consisting of three; threefold 2. three times as much or as many —*n.* 1. an amount three times as much or as many 2. *Baseball* a hit on which the batter reaches third base —*vt., vi.* -pled, -pling 1. to make or become three times as much or as many 2. to hit a triple —trip′ply *adv.*

**trip·let** (trip′lit) *n.* any of three offspring born at a single birth

**trip·li·cate** (trip′lə kit; *for v.* -kāt′) *adj.* [< L. *triplex*] 1. threefold 2. being the last of three identical copies

—*n.* any one of such copies —*vt.* -cat′ed, -cat′ing to make three copies of —in triplicate in three copies

**tri·pod** (trī′päd) *n.* [< Gr. *tri-*, three + *pous*, a foot] a three-legged caldron, stool, support, etc.

**trip·tych** (trip′tik) *n.* [< Gr. *tri-*, three + *ptychē*, a fold] a set of three panels with pictures, etc. often hinged: used as an altarpiece

**tri·sect** (trī sekt′, trī′sekt) *vt.* [< TRI- + L. *secare*, to cut] to cut or divide into three equal parts

**trite** (trīt) *adj.* trit′er, trit′est [< L. *terere*, wear out] worn out by constant use; stale —trite′ness *n.*

**trit·i·um** (trit′ē əm, trish′-) *n.* a radioactive isotope of hydrogen having an atomic weight of three

**tri·umph** (trī′əmf) *n.* [< L. *triumphus*] 1. a victory; success 2. exaltation or joy over a victory, etc. —*vi.* 1. to gain victory or success 2. to rejoice over victory, etc. —tri·um′phal (-um′f'l) *adj.*

**tri·um·phant** (-um′fənt) *adj.* 1. successful; victorious 2. rejoicing for victory —tri·um′phant·ly *adv.*

**tri·um·vir** (trī um′vər) *n., pl.* -virs, -vir·i′ (-vi rī′) [L. < *trium virum*, of three men] in ancient Rome, any of three administrators sharing authority

**tri·um′vi·rate** (-it) *n.* government by a group of three men

**triv·et** (triv′it) *n.* [< L. *tripes*, tripod] 1. a three-legged stand for holding pots, etc. near a fire 2. a short-legged stand for hot dishes to rest on

**triv·i·a** (triv′ē ə) *n.pl.* [*often with sing. v.*] unimportant matters

**triv·i·al** (triv′ē əl) *adj.* [< L. *trivialis*, commonplace] unimportant; insignificant —triv′i·al′i·ty (-al′ə tē) *n.*

**-trix** (triks) *pl.* -trix′es, -tri·ces′ (tri sēz′, trī′sēz) [L.] an ending of some feminine nouns of agent [*aviatrix*]

**tro·che** (trō′kē) *n.* [< Gr. *trochos*, a wheel] a small, medicinal lozenge

**tro·chee** (trō′kē) *n.* [< Gr. *trechein*, to run] a metrical foot of an accented syllable followed by an unaccented one —tro·cha′ic (-kā′ik) *adj.*

**trod** (träd) *pt. & alt. pp.* of TREAD

**trod′den** (-'n) *alt. pp.* of TREAD

**trog·lo·dyte** (träg′lə dīt′) *n.* [< Gr. *trōglē*, hold + *dyein*, enter] 1. any of the prehistoric people who lived in caves 2. a recluse

**troi·ka** (troi′kə) *n.* [Russ.] 1. a vehicle drawn by three horses abreast 2. an association of three in authority

**Tro·jan** (trō′jən) *adj.* of Troy, its people, etc. —*n.* 1. a native or inhabitant of ancient Troy 2. a strong, hard-working, determined person

**Tro·jan horse** *Gr. Legend* a huge, hollow wooden horse filled with Greek soldiers: it was taken into Troy as an ostensible gift, thus leading to the destruction of the city

**troll**[1] (trōl) *vt., vi.* [ME. *trollen*, to roll] 1. to sing the parts of (a round, etc.) in succession 2. to sing in a full voice 3. to fish (for) with a moving line — *n.* a lure and line used in trolling

**troll**[2] (trōl) *n.* [ON.] in Scand. folklore, a supernatural being, as a giant or dwarf, living in a cave

**trol·ley** (träl'ē) *n., pl.* **-leys** [< TROLL[1]] 1. a wheeled basket, etc. that runs suspended from an overhead track 2. a grooved wheel at the end of a pole, that transmits electric current from an overhead wire to a streetcar, etc. 3. *same as* TROLLEY CAR

**trolley car** (or **bus**) an electric streetcar (or bus) powered from an overhead wire by means of a trolley

**trol·lop** (träl'əp) *n.* [prob. < G. *trolle*, wench] a prostitute

**trom·bone** (träm bōn', träm'bōn) *n.* [It. < *tromba*, a trumpet] a large, brass-wind instrument, usually with a slide, or movable section: also **slide trombone**

TROMBONE

**troop** (trōōp) *n.* [< ML. *troppus*, a flock] 1. a group of persons or animals 2. [*pl.*] soldiers 3. a subdivision of a cavalry regiment 4. a unit of Boy Scouts or Girl Scouts — *vi.* to gather or go as in a group

**troop'er** *n.* [prec. + -ER] 1. a cavalryman 2. a mounted policeman 3. [Colloq.] a State policeman

**trope** (trōp) *n.* [< Gr. *tropos*, a turning] figurative language or a word used in a figurative sense

**tro·phy** (trō'fē) *n., pl.* **-phies** [< Gr. *tropaion*] a memorial of victory in war, sports competition, etc.; prize

**trop·ic** (träp'ik) *n.* [< Gr. *tropikos*, of a turn (of the sun at the solstices)] 1. either of two parallels of latitude, one, the **Tropic of Cancer**, 23 1/2° north of the equator, and the other, the **Tropic of Capricorn**, 23 1/2° south 2. [*also* T-] [*pl.*] the region between these latitudes — *adj.* of the tropics; tropical

**trop'i·cal** (-i k'l) *adj.* 1. of, in, characteristic of, or suitable for the tropics 2. very hot; sultry; torrid

**tro·pism** (trō'piz'm) *n.* [< Gr. *tropē*, a turn] the tendency of a plant or animal to grow or turn in response to an external stimulus, as light

**trop·o·sphere** (träp'ə sfir', trō'pə-) *n.* [see TROPE & SPHERE] the atmosphere from the earth's surface to about 6 to 12 miles above

**trot** (trät) *vt., vi.* **trot'ted, trot'ting** [< OHG. *trottōn*, to tread] 1. to move, ride, go, etc. at a trot 2. to hurry; run — *n.* 1. a gait of a horse, etc. in which the legs are lifted in alternating diagonal pairs 2. a jogging gait of a person — **trot'ter** *n.*

**troth** (trôth, trōth) *n.* [ME. *trouthe*] [Archaic] 1. faithfulness; loyalty 2. truth 3. a promise, esp. to marry

**trou·ba·dour** (trōō'bə dôr') *n.* [Fr. < Pr. *trobar*, compose in verse] any of a class of poet-musicians of S France & N Italy in the 11th–13th cent.

**trou·ble** (trub''l) *vt.* **-bled, -bling** [< L. *turba*, crowd] 1. to disturb or agitate 2. to worry; harass 3. to cause inconvenience to [don't trouble yourself] — *vi.* to take pains; bother — *n.* 1. a state of mental distress; worry 2. a misfortune; calamity 3. a person, event, etc. causing annoyance, distress, etc. 4. public disturbance 5. effort; bother [take the trouble to listen]

**trou'ble·mak'er** *n.* one who incites others to quarrel, rebel, etc.

**trou'ble·shoot'er** *n.* one whose work is to locate and eliminate the source of trouble in any flow of work

**trou'ble·some** (-səm) *adj.* characterized by or causing trouble

**trough** (trôf) *n.* [OE. *trog*] 1. a long, narrow, open container, esp. one for holding water or food for animals 2. a channel or gutter for carrying off rain water 3. a long, narrow hollow, as between waves 4. a long, narrow area of low barometric pressure

**trounce** (trouns) *vt.* **trounced, trounc'ing** [< ?] 1. to beat; flog 2. [Colloq.] to defeat — **trounc'er** *n.*

**troupe** (trōōp) *n.* [Fr.] a troop, esp. of actors, singers, etc. — *vi.* **trouped, troup'ing** to travel as a member of such a company — **troup'er** *n.*

**trou·sers** (trou'zərz) *n.pl.* [< Scot-Gael. *triubhas*] a two-legged outer garment, esp. for men and boys, extending from the waist to the ankles

**trous·seau** (trōō'sō) *n., pl.* **-seaux** (-sōz), **-seaus** [Fr. < OFr. *trousse*, a bundle] a bride's clothes, linen, etc.

**trout** (trout) *n., pl.* **trout, trouts** [< Gr. *trōgein*, gnaw] any of various food and game fishes of the salmon family, found chiefly in fresh water

**trow** (trō, trou) *vi., vt.* [< OE. *treowe*, faith] [Archaic] to believe

**trow·el** (trou'əl) *n.* [< L. *trua*, ladle] 1. a flat hand tool for smoothing plaster or applying mortar 2. a scooplike tool for loosening soil, etc. — *vt.* **-eled** or **-elled, -el·ing** or **-el·ling** to spread, smooth, dig, etc. with a trowel

**Troy** (troi) ancient city in NW Asia Minor

**troy** (troi) *adj.* [< *Troyes*, Fr. city where first used] of or by a system of weights (**troy weight**) for gold, silver, gems, etc., based on a pound of 12 oz.

**tru·ant** (trōō'ənt) *n.* [< OFr., beggar] 1. a pupil who stays away from school without permission 2. one who shirks his duties — *adj.* 1. that is a truant 2. errant; straying — **tru'an·cy** *n., pl.* **-cies**

**truce** (trōōs) *n.* [< OE. *treowa*, faith] 1. a temporary cessation of warfare by agreement between the belligerents 2. respite from conflict, trouble, etc.

**truck**[1] (truk) *n.* [prob. < Gr. *trochos*, wheel] 1. a kind of two-wheeled barrow or a low, wheeled frame, for carrying heavy articles 2. an automotive vehicle for hauling loads 3. a swiveling, wheeled frame under each end of a railroad car, etc. —*vt.* to carry on a truck —*vi.* to drive a truck — **truck'er** *n.*

**truck**[2] (truk) *vt., vi.* [< MFr. *troquer*] to exchange; barter —*n.* **1.** small articles of little value **2.** vegetables raised for market **3.** [Colloq.] dealings **4.** [Colloq.] rubbish

**truck farm** a farm where vegetables are grown to be marketed

**truck·le** (truk'l) *n.* [< Gr. *trochos*, a wheel] *same as* TRUNDLE BED: in full **truckle bed** —*vi.* **-led, -ling** to be servile; submit (*to*)

**truc·u·lent** (truk'yoo lənt) *adj.* [< L. *trux*] fierce; cruel; savage —**truc'u·lence** *n.* —**truc'u·lent·ly** *adv.*

**trudge** (truj) *vi.* **trudged, trudg'ing** [< ?] to walk, esp. wearily or laboriously —*n.* a wearying walk

**true** (trōō) *adj.* **tru'er, tru'est** [OE. *treowe*] **1.** faithful; loyal **2.** in accordance with fact; not false **3.** conforming to standard, etc.; correct **4.** rightful; lawful **5.** accurately fitted, shaped, etc. **6.** real; genuine —*adv.* **1.** truly **2.** *Biol.* without variation from type —*vt.* **trued, tru'ing** or **true'ing** to make true; esp., to fit, shape, etc. accurately —*n.* that which is true (with *the*)

**true bill** a bill of indictment endorsed by a grand jury

**true'-blue'** *adj.* very loyal; staunch

**truf·fle** (truf'l) *n.* [< L. *tuber*, knob] a fleshy, edible underground fungus

**tru·ism** (trōō'iz'm) *n.* a statement the truth of which is obvious

**tru'ly** *adv.* **1.** in a true manner; accurately, genuinely, etc. **2.** really **3.** sincerely [yours *truly*]

**Tru·man** (trōō'mən), **Harry S.** 1884–1972; 33d president of the U.S. (1945–53)

**trump** (trump) *n.* [< TRIUMPH] **1.** any playing card of a suit ranked higher than any other suit for a given hand **2.** such a suit —*vt., vi.* to play a trump on (a trick, etc.) —**trump up** to devise fraudulently

**trump·er·y** (trum'pər ē) *n., pl.* **-ies** [< Fr. *tromper*, deceive] **1.** something showy but worthless **2.** nonsense

**trum·pet** (trum'pit) *n.* [< OFr. *trompe*] **1.** a brass-wind instrument consisting of a looped tube ending in a flared bell **2.** a trumpetlike device for channeling sound, as an early kind of hearing aid **3.** a sound like that of a trumpet —*vi.* to make the sound of a trumpet —*vt.* to proclaim loudly — **trum'pet·er** *n.*

**trun·cate** (trun'kāt) *vt.* **-cat·ed -cat·ing** [< L. *truncus*, stem] to cut off a part of; lop —**trun·ca'tion** *n.*

**trun·cheon** (trun'chən) *n.* [< L. *truncus*, stem] a short, thick club

**trun·dle** (trun'd'l) *vt., vi.* **-dled, -dling** [< OE. *trendan*, to roll] to roll along —**trun'dler** *n.*

**trundle bed** a low bed on small wheels, that can be rolled under another bed when not in use

**trunk** (trunk) *n.* [< L. *truncus*] **1.** the main stem of a tree **2.** a human or animal body, not including the head and limbs **3.** a long snout, as of an elephant **4.** a large, reinforced box to hold clothes, etc. in travel **5.** [*pl.*] shorts worn by men for athletics **6.** a compartment in a car, usually in the rear, for a spare tire, luggage, etc.

**trunk line** a main line of a railroad, telephone system, etc.

**truss** (trus) *vt.* [< OFr. *trousser*] **1.** orig., to bundle **2.** to tie; bind (*up*) **3.** to support with a truss —*n.* **1.** a bundle or pack **2.** a framework for supporting a roof, bridge, etc. **3.** a padded device for giving support in cases of rupture or hernia

**trust** (trust) *n.* [< ON. *traust*] **1.** *a*) firm belief in the honesty, reliability, etc. of another; faith *b*) the one trusted **2.** confident expectation, hope, etc. **3.** responsibility resulting from confidence placed in one **4.** care; custody **5.** something entrusted to one **6.** faith in one's ability to pay; credit **7.** a combination of corporations to establish a monopoly **8.** *Law a*) the fact of having nominal ownership of property to keep, use, or administer for another *b*) such property —*vi.* to be confident in **2.** to have confidence in **2.** to commit (something) (*to* another's care) **3.** to allow to do something without misgivings **4.** to believe **5.** to hope; expect **6.** to grant business credit to —*adj.* **1.** relating to a trust **2.** acting as trustee —**in trust** entrusted to another's care

**trus·tee** (trus tē') *n.* **1.** one to whom another's property or its management is entrusted **2.** a member of a board managing the affairs of a college, hospital, etc. —**trus·tee'ship** *n.*

**trust'ful** *adj.* full of trust; ready to confide —**trust'ful·ly** *adv.*

**trust fund** money, stock, etc. held in trust

**trust'ing** *adj.* that trusts; trustful

**trust territory** a territory placed under the administrative authority of a country by the United Nations

**trust'wor'thy** *adj.* worthy of trust; reliable —**trust'wor'thi·ness** *n.*

**trust·y** (trus'tē) *adj.* **-i·er, -i·est** dependable; trustworthy —*n., pl.* **-ies** a convict granted special privileges as a trustworthy person

**truth** (trōōth) *n.* [OE. *treowth*] **1.** a being true; specif., *a*) sincerity; honesty *b*) conformity with fact *c*) reality; actual existence *d*) correctness; accuracy **2.** that which is true **3.** an established fact —**in truth** truly

**truth'ful** *adj.* **1.** telling the truth; honest **2.** corresponding with fact or reality —**truth'ful·ly** *adv.* —**truth'ful·ness** *n.*

**try** (trī) *vt.* **tried, try'ing** [< OFr. *trier*] **1.** to melt out or render (fat, etc.) **2.** to conduct the trial of in a law court **3.** to put to the proof; test **4.** to subject to trials, etc.; **afflict** **5.** to experiment with [to *try* a recipe] **6.** to attempt; endeavor —*vi.* to make an effort, attempt, etc. —*n., pl.* **tries** an attempt; effort; trial —**try on** to test the fit of (something to wear) by putting it on —**try out** **1.** to test by putting into use **2.** to test one's fitness, as for a place on a team or a part in a play

**try′ing** *adj.* that tries one's patience; annoying; irksome

**try′out′** *n.* [Colloq.] a test to determine fitness, qualifications, etc.

**tryst** (trist) *n.* [< OFr. *triste*, hunting station] **1.** an appointment to meet, esp. one made by lovers **2.** an appointed meeting or meeting place

**tsar** (tsär, zär) *n. var. of* CZAR

**tset·se fly** (tset′sē, tsēt′-) [< native name] a small fly of C and S Africa: one kind carries sleeping sickness

**T′-shirt′** *n.* a collarless, pullover knit shirt with short sleeves

**tsp.** **1.** teaspoon(s) **2.** teaspoonful(s)

**T square** a T-shaped ruler for drawing parallel lines

**tsu·na·mi** (tsŏŏ nä′mē) *n.* [Jap. < *tsu*, a harbor + *nami*, a wave] a huge sea wave caused by an undersea earthquake, volcanic eruption, etc.

**tub** (tub) *n.* [< MDu. *tubbe*] **1.** a round wooden container, usually with staves and hoops **2.** any large, open container, as of metal **3.** a bathtub

**tu·ba** (tŏŏ′bə) *n.* [L., a trumpet] a large, deep-toned brass-wind instrument

**tub·by** (tub′ē) *adj.* **-bi·er, -bi·est** **1.** shaped like a tub **2.** fat and short

**tube** (tŏŏb) *n.* [< L. *tubus*, pipe] **1.** a slender pipe of metal, glass, etc., for conveying fluids **2.** a tubelike part, organ, etc. **3.** a pliable cylinder with a screw cap, for holding paste, etc. **4.** *short for:* a) ELECTRON TUBE b) VACUUM TUBE **5.** [Brit. Colloq.] a subway —**the tube** [Colloq.] television —**tube′less** *adj.*

**tu·ber** (tŏŏ′bər) *n.* [L., lit., a swelling] a short, thickened, fleshy part of an underground stem, as a potato — **tu′ber·ous** *adj.*

**tu′ber·cle** (-k′l) *n.* [see prec.] **1.** a small, rounded projection, as on a bone or a plant root **2.** any abnormal hard nodule or swelling; specif., the typical lesion of tuberculosis

**tu·ber·cu·lin** (too bur′kyə lin) *n.* a solution injected into the skin as a test for tuberculosis

**tu·ber·cu·lo·sis** (-lō′sis) *n.* [< ModL.: see TUBERCLE & -OSIS] an infectious disease characterized by the formation of tubercles in body tissue; specif., tuberculosis of the lungs —**tu·ber′cu·lar, tu·ber′cu·lous** *adj.*

**tub·ing** (tŏŏb′iŋ) *n.* **1.** a series or system of tubes **2.** material in the form of a tube **3.** a piece of tube

**tu·bu·lar** (tŏŏ′byə lər) *adj.* [< L. *tubus*, pipe] **1.** of or like a tube **2.** made with a tube or tubes

**tu′bule** (-byool) *n.* a small tube

**tuck** (tuk) *vt.* [< MDu. *tucken*] **1.** to pull or gather (*up*) in a fold or folds

2. to sew a fold or folds in (a garment) **3.** to fold the edges of (a sheet, etc.) under or in, to make secure **4.** to press snugly into a small space —*n.* a sewed fold in a garment

**tuck′er** *vt.* [prob. < obs. *tuck*, punish] [Colloq.] to tire (*out*); weary

**Tuc·son** (tŏŏ′sän, tŏŏ sän′) city in S Ariz.: pop. 263,000

**-tude** (tŏŏd, tyŏŏd) [< L. *-tudo*] a suffix corresponding to -NESS [*certitude*]

**Tues·day** (tŏŏz′dē, -dā) *n.* [OE. *Tiwes dæg*, day of the god of war *Tiu*] the third day of the week

**tuft** (tuft) *n.* [< OFr. *tufe*] **1.** a bunch of hairs, grass, etc. growing closely together **2.** any cluster, as the fluffy ball forming the end of a cluster of threads drawn through a mattress, etc. —*vt.* **1.** to provide with tufts **2.** to secure the padding of (a mattress, etc.) with tufts —**tuft′ed** *adj.*

**tug** (tug) *vi., vt.* **tugged, tug′ging** [prob. < ON. *toga*, pull] **1.** to pull hard; drag; haul **2.** to tow with a tugboat —*n.* **1.** a hard pull **2.** a tugboat

**tug′boat′** *n.* a small, sturdy boat for towing or pushing ships, etc.

**tug of war** **1.** a contest in which two teams pull at opposite ends of a rope **2.** any struggle for supremacy

**tu·i·tion** (too wish′ən) *n.* [< L. *tueri*, protect] the charge for instruction, as at a college

**tu·la·re·mi·a** (tŏŏ′lə rē′mē ə) *n.* [ModL. < *Tulare* County, Calif.] an infectious disease of rabbits, etc., sometimes transmitted to man

**tu·lip** (tŏŏ′lip) *n.* [< Turk. *tülbend*, turban: from its shape] **1.** a bulb plant with a large, cup-shaped flower **2.** the flower

**tulle** (tŏŏl) *n.* [< *Tulle*, city in France] a fine netting of silk, rayon, nylon, etc., used for veils, scarfs, etc.

**Tul·sa** (tul′sə) city in NE Okla.: pop. 332,000

**tum·ble** (tum′b'l) *vi.* **-bled, -bling** [< OE. *tumbian*, to jump] **1.** to do somersaults or similar acrobatic feats **2.** to fall suddenly or helplessly **3.** to toss or roll about **4.** to move in a hasty, disorderly manner —*vt.* **1.** to cause to tumble **2.** to put into disorder; disarrange —*n.* **1.** a fall **2.** disorder

**tum′ble·down′** *adj.* dilapidated

**tum′bler** (-blər) *n.* **1.** an acrobat who does somersaults, etc. **2.** a drinking glass **3.** a part of a lock whose position must be changed by a key in order to release the bolt

**tum′ble·weed′** *n.* a plant that breaks off near the ground in autumn and is blown about by the wind

**tum·brel, tum·bril** (tum′brəl) *n.* [< MFr. *tomber*, to fall] a cart, esp. one that can be tilted for emptying

**tu·mid** (tŏŏ′mid) *adj.* [< L. *tumere*, to swell] **1.** swollen; bulging **2.** inflated or pompous; bombastic

**tum·my** (tum′ē) *n., pl.* **-mies** stomach: a child's word

**tu·mor** (tŏŏ′mər) *n.* [L., a swelling] an abnormal growth of new tissue, independent of its surrounding structures: Brit. sp. **tumour**

**tu·mult** (tōō′mult) *n.* [< L. *tumere,* to swell] 1. noisy commotion; uproar 2. confusion; disturbance

**tu·mul·tu·ous** (too mul′choo wəs) *adj.* full of tumult, uproar, etc.

**tun** (tun) *n.* [OE. *tunne*] a large cask

**tu·na** (tōō′nə) *n., pl.* **-na, -nas** [AmSp.] 1. a large ocean fish of the mackerel group 2. any related fish, as the albacore 3. the flesh of the tuna, canned for food: also **tuna fish**

**tun·dra** (tun′drə) *n.* [Russ.] any of the vast, treeless arctic plains

**tune** (tōōn) *n.* [see TONE] 1. a rhythmic succession of musical tones; melody 2. correct musical pitch 3. agreement; concord [out of *tune* with the times] —*vt.* **tuned, tun′ing** 1. to adjust (a musical instrument) to some standard of pitch 2. to adapt to some condition, mood, etc. 3. to adjust (a motor, circuit, etc.) for proper performance —**tune in** to adjust a radio or TV receiver so as to receive (a station, etc.) —**tun′er** *n.*

**tune′ful** *adj.* full of music; melodious

**tune′up′, tune′-up′** *n.* an adjusting, as of an engine, to the proper condition

**tung·sten** (tun′stən) *n.* [Sw. < *tung,* heavy + *sten,* stone] a hard, heavy, metallic chemical element, used in steel, etc.

**tu·nic** (tōō′nik, tyōō′-) *n.* [L. *tunica*] 1. a loose, gownlike garment worn by men and women in ancient Greece and Rome 2. a blouselike garment extending to the hips, often belted

**tuning fork** a two-pronged steel instrument which when struck sounds a fixed tone in perfect pitch

**Tu·nis** (tōō′nis) seaport and capital of Tunisia: pop. 662,000

**Tu·ni·sia** (too nē′zhə) country in N Africa: 48,332 sq. mi.; pop. 4,533,000 —**Tu·ni′sian** *adj., n.*

**tun·nel** (tun′l) *n.* [< MFr. *tonnelle,* a vault] 1. an underground passageway, as for autos, etc. 2. any tunnellike passage, as in a mine —*vt., vi.* **-neled** or **-nelled, -nel·ing** or **-nel·ling** to make a tunnel (through or under) —**tun′nel·er, tun′nel·ler** *n.*

**tunnel vision** a narrow outlook, as on a particular problem

**tun·ny** (tun′ē) *n., pl.* **-nies, -ny** same as TUNA

**tur·ban** (tur′bən) *n.* [< Per. *dulbänd*] 1. a Moslem headdress, consisting of cloth wound in folds about the head 2. any similar headdress

**tur·bid** (tur′bid) *adj.* [< L. *turba,* a crowd] 1. muddy or cloudy from having the sediment stirred up 2. thick, dense, or dark, as clouds 3. confused

TURBAN

**tur·bine** (tur′bin, -bīn) *n.* [< L. *turbo,* whirl] an engine driven by the pressure of steam, water, air, etc. against the curved vanes of a wheel

**tur·bo·jet** (tur′bō jet′) *n.* a jet engine in which the energy of the jet operates a turbine which drives the air compressor: in full **turbojet engine**

**tur·bo·prop** (-präp′) *n.* a turbojet engine whose turbine shaft drives a propeller: in full **turboprop engine**

**tur·bot** (tur′bət) *n., pl.* **-bot, -bots** [< OFr. *tourbout*] a large, edible European flatfish

**tur·bu·lent** (tur′byə lənt) *adj.* [see TURBID] 1. wild or disorderly 2. full of violent motion —**tur′bu·lence** *n.* —**tur′bu·lent·ly** *adv.*

**tu·reen** (too rēn′) *n.* [< MFr. *terrine,* earthen vessel] a large, deep dish with a lid, for serving soup, etc.

**turf** (turf) *n.* [OE.] 1. *a)* a top layer of earth containing grass with its roots; sod *b)* a piece of this 2. peat 3. a track for horse racing; also *horse racing:* usually with *the* —*vt.* to cover with turf —**turf′y** *adj.*

**tur·gid** (tur′jid) *adj.* [< L. *turgere,* to swell] 1. swollen; distended 2. bombastic; pompous —**tur·gid′i·ty** *n.*

**Tu·rin** (toor′in, too rin′) city in NW Italy: pop. 1,107,000

**Turk** (turk) *n.* a native or inhabitant of Turkey

**Turk.** 1. Turkey 2. Turkish

**Tur·key** (tur′kē) country occupying Asia Minor & part of the Balkan Peninsula: 301,381 sq. mi.; pop. 33,823,000

**tur′key** *n.* [< similarity to a fowl formerly imported through Turkey] 1. a large N.American bird with a small head and spreading tail 2. its flesh, used as food

**turkey buzzard** a dark-colored vulture of temperate and tropical America

**Tur·kic** (tur′kik) *adj.* designating or of a subfamily of languages, including Turkish, Tatar, etc.

**Turk·ish** (tur′kish) *adj.* of Turkey, the Turks, etc. —*n.* language of Turkey

**Turkish bath** a bath with steam rooms, showers, massage, etc.

**Turkish towel** [also t-] a thick cotton towel of terry cloth

**tur·mer·ic** (tur′mər ik) *n.* [< ML. *terra merita,* deserving earth] an East Indian plant whose powdered root is used as a yellow dye, seasoning, etc.

**tur·moil** (tur′moil) *n.* [< ?] tumult; commotion; confusion

**turn** (turn) *vt.* [ult. < Gr. *tornos,* lathe] 1. to rotate (a wheel, etc.) 2. to move around or partly around [turn the key] 3. to give form to as in a lathe 4. to change the position or direction of 5. to reverse [to *turn* pages] 6. to wrench (one's ankle) 7. to upset (the stomach) 8. to divert; deflect 9. to cause to change one's actions, beliefs, aims, etc. 10. to go around (a corner, etc.) 11. to pass (a certain age, amount, etc.) **12.** to repel (an attack, etc.) **13.** to drive, set, let go, etc. [to turn loose] **14.** to direct, point, aim, etc. **15.** to change [to turn cream into butter] **16.** to make sour **17.** to affect in some way —vi. **1.** to rotate or revolve; pivot **2.** to move around or partly around **3.** to reel; whirl **4.** to become curved or bent **5.** to become upset: said of the stomach **6.** to change or reverse course, direction, etc., or one's feelings, allegiance, etc. **7.** to refer (to) **8.** to apply (to) for help **9.** to shift one's attention [he turned to music] **10.** to make a sudden attack (on) **11.** to be contingent (on or upon) **12.** to become [to turn cold] **13.** to change to another form [the rain turned to snow] **14.** to become rancid, sour, etc. —n. **1.** a turning around; rotation; revolution **2.** a single twist, winding, etc. **3.** a change or reversal of course or direction **4.** a short walk, ride, etc. **5.** a bend; curve [a turn in a road] **6.** a change in trend, events, etc. **7.** a sudden shock or fright **8.** an action or deed [a good turn] **9.** the right, duty, or chance to do something in regular order [my turn to go] **10.** a distinctive form, detail, etc. [an odd turn of speech] **11.** natural inclination —in (or out of) turn (not) in proper sequence —**turn down 1.** to reject (a request, etc.) —**turn in 1.** to deliver; hand in **2.** [Colloq.] to go to bed —**turn off 1.** to shut off **2.** to make (an electrical device) stop functioning **3.** [Slang] to cause to be bored, depressed, etc. —**turn on 1.** to start the flow of **2.** to make (an electrical device) start functioning **3.** [Slang] to make or become elated, euphoric, etc. —**turn out 1.** to put out (a light, etc.) **2.** to put outside **3.** to dismiss **4.** to come or go out **5.** to produce **6.** to result **7.** to prove to be **8.** to become —**turn over 1.** to ponder **2.** to hand over; transfer —**turn up** to happen, appear, arrive, etc. —**turn′er** n.

**turn′a·bout′** n. a shift or reversal of position, allegiance, opinion, etc.

**turn′a·round′** n. **1.** same as TURNABOUT **2.** a wide area, as in a driveway, to allow turning a vehicle around

**turn′buck·le** (-buk″'l) n. an adjustable coupling for two rods, etc., consisting of a metal sleeve with opposite internal threads at each end

**turn′coat′** n. a renegade; traitor

**turn′ing** n. **1.** the action of one that turns **2.** a place where a road, etc. turns

**turning point** a point in time at which a decisive change occurs

**tur·nip** (tur′nip) n. [prob. < Fr. tour, round + ME. nepe, turnip] **1.** a plant of the mustard family with a roundish, light-colored, edible root **2.** the root

TURN-
BUCKLE

**turn′key′** n., pl. **-keys** a jailer

**turn′off′** n. **1.** a turning off **2.** a place to turn off, as a road ramp

**turn′out′** n. **1.** a gathering of people, as for a meeting **2.** a wider part of a narrow road, for vehicles to pass

**turn′o′ver** n. **1.** a turning over; upset **2.** a small pie with half the crust folded back over the other **3.** a) the selling out and replenishing of a stock of goods b) the amount of business done during a given period **4.** the rate of replacement of workers

**turn′pike′** (-pīk′) n. [ME. turnpyke, a spiked road barrier] a toll road, esp. one that is an expressway

**turn′stile′** (-stīl′) n. a device, as a post with revolving horizontal bars, placed in an entrance to allow the passage of persons one at a time

**turn′ta′ble** n. a circular rotating platform, as for playing a phonograph record

**tur·pen·tine** (tur′pən tīn′) n. [< Gr. terebinthos, tree yielding this substance] a colorless, volatile oil distilled from a substance extracted from various coniferous trees: used in paints, etc.

**tur·pi·tude** (tur′pə tōōd′) n. [< L. turpis, vile] baseness; vileness

**tur·quoise** (tur′koiz, -kwoiz) n. [< OFr. turqueis, Turkish] a greenish-blue semiprecious stone, or its color

**tur·ret** (tur′it) n. [see TOWER] **1.** a small tower projecting from a building, usually at a corner **2.** a dome or revolving structure for guns, as on a warship, tank, or airplane **3.** a rotating attachment for a lathe, etc. holding cutting tools for successive use

**tur·tle** (tur′t'l) n. [< Fr. tortue, tortoise] any of various land and water reptiles having a soft body encased in a hard shell —**turn turtle** to turn upside down

**tur′tle·dove′** n. [< L. echoic turtur] a wild dove with a plaintive call

**tur′tle·neck′** n. **1.** a high, snug, turned-down collar, as on a sweater **2.** a sweater, etc. with such a neck

**tusk** (tusk) n. [OE. tucs] a long, large, pointed tooth projecting outside the mouth, as of the elephant

**tus·sle** (tus″'l) n., vi. -sled, -sling [< LME. tusen, to pull] struggle; scuffle

**tus·sock** (tus′ək) n. [prob. < ME. (to)tusen, to rumple] a thick tuft or clump of grass, sedge, etc.

**tu·te·lage** (tōōt″'l ij, tyōōt′-) n. [< L. tutela, protection] **1.** guardianship; care, protection, etc. **2.** instruction —**tu′te·lar·y** (-er′ē) adj.

**tu·tor** (tōōt′ər, tyōōt′-) n. [< L. tueri, to guard] a private teacher —vt., vi. to act as a tutor (to); teach —**tu·to·ri·al** (tōō tôr′ē əl, tyōō-) adj.

**tut·ti-frut·ti** (tōōt′ē frōōt′ē) n. [It., all fruits] an ice cream, candy, etc. made or flavored with mixed fruits

**tu·tu** (tōō′tōō) n. [Fr.] a short, projecting skirt worn by ballerinas

**tux** (tuks) n. clipped form of TUXEDO

**tux·e·do** (tək sē′dō) n., pl. -dos [< a country club near Tuxedo Lake, N.Y.] a man's semiformal suit with a tailless jacket

**TV** (tē′vē′) n., pl. TVs, TV's television or a television receiving set

**TVA** Tennessee Valley Authority

**TV dinner** a frozen, precooked dinner packaged in the tray in which it is heated and served

**twad·dle** (twäd'l) *n.* [akin to *tattle*] foolish, empty talk or writing; nonsense

**twain** (twān) *n., adj.* [OE. *twegen,* two] *archaic var. of* TWO

**Twain, Mark** *see* CLEMENS

**twang** (twaŋ) *n.* [echoic] **1.** a sharp, vibrating sound, as of a plucked string **2.** a sharply nasal way of speaking —*vi., vt.* **1.** to make or cause to make a twang **2.** to utter with a twang —**twang′y** *adj.* **-i·er, -i·est**

**tweak** (twēk) *vt.* [OE. *twiccan,* to twitch] to give a twisting pinch to (the nose, ear, etc.) —*n.* such a pinch

**tweed** (twēd) *n.* [< misreading of *tweel,* Scot. form of TWILL] **1.** a rough wool fabric in a weave of two or more colors **2.** [*pl.*] clothes of tweed

**tweed′y** *adj.* **1.** of, like, or wearing tweeds **2.** of an informal, outdoor type

**tweet** (twēt) *n., interj.* [echoic] the chirping sound of a small bird —*vi.* to make this sound

**tweet′er** *n.* a small loudspeaker for reproducing high-frequency sounds: cf. WOOFER

**tweez·ers** (twē′zərz) *n.pl.* [*with sing. or pl. v.*] [< obs. *tweeze,* surgical set] small pincers for plucking out hairs, etc.

**twelfth** (twelfth) *adj.* [OE. *twelfta*] preceded by eleven others; 12th —*n.* **1.** the one following the eleventh **2.** any of the twelve equal parts of something; 1/12

**Twelfth Day** Epiphany, the twelfth day after Christmas: **Twelfth Night** is the evening before, or of, Epiphany

**twelve** (twelv) *adj., n.* [OE. *twelf*] two more than ten; 12; XII

**twelve′-tone** *adj. Music* of composition in which twelve tones of the chromatic scale are fixed in some arbitrary succession (*tone row*)

**twen·ty** (twen′tē) *adj., n., pl.* **-ties** [OE. *twegentig*] two times ten; 20; XX —**the twenties** the numbers or years, as of a century, from 20 through 29 —**twen′ti·eth** (-ith) *adj., n.*

**twen′ty-one′** *n.* a card game in which the object is to total 21 points

**twerp** (twerp) *n.* [ult. < ? Dan. *tver,* perverse] [Slang] a person regarded as insignificant, contemptible, etc.

**twice** (twīs) *adv.* [OE. *twiga*] **1.** two times **2.** two times as much or as many

**twid·dle** (twid′l) *vt., vi.* **-dled, -dling** [prob. < TW(IST) + (D)IDDLE] to twirl or play with lightly —**twiddle one's thumbs** to be idle

**twig** (twig) *n.* [OE. *twigge*] a small branch of a tree or shrub

**twi·light** (twī′līt′) *n.* [ME.] **1.** the subdued light just after sunset or, sometimes, just before sunrise **2.** the period from sunset to dark **3.** a gradual decline —*adj.* of twilight

**twill** (twil) *n.* [OE. *twilic,* woven of double thread] a cloth woven with parallel diagonal lines —**twilled** *adj.*

**twin** (twin) *adj.* [OE. *twinn,* double] **1.** consisting of, or being one of a pair of, two similar things **2.** being a twin or twins —*n.* **1.** either of two born at the same birth **2.** either of two persons or things much alike

**twine** (twīn) *n.* [OE. *twin*] strong thread, string, etc. of strands twisted together —*vt., vi.* **twined, twin′ing 1.** to twist together **2.** to wind around

**twinge** (twinj) *vt., vi.* **twinged, twing′ing** [OE. *twengan,* to squeeze] to have or give a sudden, sharp pain, qualm, etc. —*n.* such a pain, etc.

**twi-night, twi-night** (twī′nīt′) *adj.* [TWI(LIGHT) + NIGHT] *Baseball* designating a double-header starting in late afternoon and going into evening

**twin·kle** (twiŋ′k'l) *vi.* **-kled, -kling** [OE. *twinclian*] **1.** to shine with quick, intermittent gleams **2.** to light up with amusement: said of the eyes **3.** to move to and fro quickly, as dancers' feet —*n.* **1.** a glint in the eye **2.** a gleam; sparkle **3.** an instant

**twin′kling** *n.* an instant

**twirl** (twurl) *vt., vi.* [prob. < Scand.] **1.** to rotate rapidly; spin **2.** to whirl in a circle —*n.* **1.** a twirling **2.** a twist, coil, etc. —**twirl′er** *n.*

**twist** (twist) *vt.* [OE. *-twist,* a rope] **1.** to wind (strands, etc.) around one another **2.** to wind (rope, etc.) around something **3.** to give spiral shape to **4.** *a)* to subject to torsion *b)* to wrench; sprain **5.** to contort or distort **6.** to confuse **7.** to pervert the meaning of **8.** to revolve or rotate **9.** to break (*off*) by turning the end —*vi.* **1.** to undergo twisting **2.** to spiral, twine, etc. (*around* or *about*) **3.** to revolve or rotate **4.** to turn to one side **5.** to wind, as a path **6.** to squirm; writhe —*n.* **1.** something twisted, as cord or thread, a roll of tobacco, etc. **2.** a twisting or being twisted **3.** torsional stress **4.** a contortion **5.** a wrench or sprain **6.** a turn; bend **7.** distortion, as of meaning **8.** an unexpected or different direction, method, slant, etc.

**twist′er** *n.* **1.** a person or thing that twists **2.** a tornado or cyclone

**twit** (twit) *vt.* **twit′ted, twit′ting** [< OE. *æt,* at + *witan,* accuse] to reproach, taunt, etc. —*n.* a taunt

**twitch** (twich) *vt., vi.* [< OE. *twiccian,* to pluck] to pull (at) or move with a quick, slight jerk —*n.* **1.** a twitching **2.** a sudden quick motion, esp. a spasmodic one

**twit·ter** (twit′ər) *vi.* [ME. *twiteren*] **1.** to chirp rapidly **2.** *a)* to chatter *b)* to giggle **3.** to tremble with excitement —*n.* **1.** a twittering **2.** a condition of tremulous excitement

**two** (tōō) *adj., n.* [OE. *twa*] one more than one; 2; II —**in two** in two parts

**two′-bit′** (-bit′) *adj.* [Slang] cheap

**two bits** [Colloq.] twenty-five cents

**two′-by-four′** *n.* a piece of lumber two inches thick and four inches wide untrimmed (1 5/8″ by 3 5/8″ trimmed)

**two′-edged′** *adj.* 1. having two cutting edges 2. that can be taken two ways, as a remark

**two′-faced′** *adj.* 1. having two faces 2. deceitful; hypocritical

**two·fer** (tōō′fər) *n.* [alt. < *two for*] [*usually* pl.] [Colloq.] two (esp. theater tickets) for the price of one

**two′-fist′ed** *adj.* [Colloq.] 1. able to use both fists 2. vigorous; virile

**two·fold′** *adj.* 1. having two parts 2. having twice as much or as many —*adv.* twice as much or as many

**two·pence** (tup′ns) *n.* two pence

**two′-ply′** *adj.* having two layers, strands, etc.

**two·some** (-səm) *n.* 1. two people; a couple 2. a golf match for two

**two′-time′** *vt.* -timed′, -tim′ing [Slang] to be unfaithful to

**two′-way′** *adj.* 1. allowing passage in either direction 2. involving two or used in two ways

**twp.** township

**TX** Texas

**-ty** (tē, ti) [< L. *-tas*] a suffix meaning quality, of condition of

**ty·coon** (tī kōōn′) *n.* [< Jap. < Chin. *ta*, great + *kiun*, prince] a powerful industrialist, etc.

**ty·ing** (tī′iŋ) *prp. of* TIE

**tyke** (tīk) *n.* [< ON. *tik*, a bitch] [Colloq.] a small child

**Ty·ler** (tī′lər), **John** 1790–1862; 10th president of the U.S. (1841–45)

**tym·pa·ni** (tim′pə nē) *n.pl. var. of* TIMPANI— **tym′pa·nist** *n.*

**tym·pan·ic membrane** (tim pan′ik) a thin membrane inside the ear, that vibrates when struck by sound waves

**tym·pa·num** (tim′pə nəm) *n.*, *pl.* -nums, -na (-nə) [L., a drum] *same as:* 1. MIDDLE EAR 2. TYMPANIC MEMBRANE

**type** (tīp) *n.* [< Gr. *typos*, a mark] 1. the characteristic form, plan, style, etc. of a class or group 2. a class, group, etc. with characteristics in common 3. a person, animal, or thing representative of a class 4. a perfect example; model 5. *a)* a piece of metal or wood with a raised letter, etc. in reverse on its top, used in printing *b)* such pieces collectively *c)* a printed or photographically reproduced character or characters —*vt.* typed, typ′ing 1. to classify 2. to typewrite —*vi.* to typewrite

**-type** (tīp) *a combining form meaning:* 1. type, example [*prototype*] 2. stamp, print [*daguerreotype*]

**type′cast′** *vt.* -cast′, -cast′ing to cast (an actor) repeatedly in the same type of part

**type′script′** *n.* typewritten matter

**type′set′** *vt.* -set′, -set′ting to set in type; compose

**type′set′ter** *n.* 1. a person who sets type 2. a machine for setting type

**type′write′** *vt.*, *vi.* -wrote′, -writ′-ten, -writ′ing to write with a typewriter: now usually *type*

**type′writ′er** *n.* a writing machine with a keyboard for reproducing letters resembling printed ones

**ty·phoid** (tī′foid) *n.* [TYPH(US) + -OID] an acute infectious disease acquired by ingesting contaminated food or water: characterized by fever, intestinal disorders, etc.: in full **typhoid fever**

**ty·phoon** (tī fōōn′) *n.* [< Chin. *tai-fung*, great wind] a violent tropical cyclone originating in the W Pacific

**ty·phus** (tī′fəs) *n.* [< Gr. *typhos*, fever] an acute infectious disease transmitted by fleas, lice, etc. and characterized by fever, skin rash, etc.: in full **typhus fever**

**typ·i·cal** (tip′i k'l) *adj.* 1. serving as a type 2. having the distinguishing characteristics of a class, group, etc.; representative 3. belonging to a type; characteristic —**typ′i·cal·ly** *adv.*

**typ·i·fy** (tip′ə fī′) *vt.* -fied′, -fy′ing 1. to be a type of; symbolize 2. to have the characteristics of; be typical of; exemplify

**typ·ist** (tīp′ist) *n.* a person who operates a typewriter

**ty·po** (tī′pō) *n.* [Colloq.] an error made in setting type or in typing

**ty·pog·ra·phy** (tī päg′rə fē) *n.* [see TYPE & -GRAPHY] 1. the setting of, and printing with, type 2. the arrangement, style, etc. of matter printed from type —**ty·pog′ra·pher** *n.* —**ty′po·graph′i·cal** (-pə graf′i k'l) *adj.*

**ty·ran·ni·cal** (ti ran′i k'l) *adj.* 1. of or suited to a tyrant 2. harsh, cruel, unjust, etc. Also **ty·ran′nic** —**ty·ran′ni·cal·ly** *adv.*

**tyr·an·nize** (tir′ə nīz′) *vi.* -nized′, -niz′ing 1. to govern as a tyrant 2. to govern or use authority harshly or cruelly —*vt.* to treat tyrannically

**ty·ran·no·saur** (ti ran′ə sôr′, tī-) *n.* [< Gr. *tyrannos*, tyrant + *sauros*, lizard] a huge, two footed, flesh-eating dinosaur: also **ty·ran′no·saur′us** (-əs)

**tyr·an·ny** (-nē) *n.*, *pl.* -nies 1. the authority, government, etc. of a tyrant 2. cruel and unjust use of power 3. a tyrannical act

**ty·rant** (tī′rənt) *n.* [< Gr. *tyrannos*] 1. an absolute ruler 2. a cruel, oppressive ruler, etc.

**ty·ro** (tī′rō) *n.*, *pl.* -ros [< L. *tiro*, young soldier] a beginner in learning something; novice

**Tyr·ol** (tir′äl, tī′rōl) *same as* TIROL

**tzar** (tsär, zär) *n. var. of* CZAR —**tza·ri·na** (tsä rē′nə) *n.fem.*

# U

**U, u** (yoō) *n., pl.* **U's, u's** the 21st letter of the English alphabet

**U** *Chem.* uranium

**U. U** 1. Union 2. University

**U., U, u.,** u unit; units

**u·biq·ui·tous** (yoo bik′wə təs) *adj.* [< L. *ubique*, everywhere] (seemingly) present everywhere at the same time —**u·biq′ui·ty** *n.*

**U-boat** (yoō′bōt′) *n.* [< G. *Untersee-boot*, undersea boat] a German submarine

**ud·der** (ud′ər) *n.* [OE. *udr*] a large, pendulous, milk-secreting gland with two or more teats, as in cows

**UFO** (yoō′fō, yoō′ef ō′) *n., pl.* **UFOs, UFO's** an unidentified flying object

**u·fol·o·gist** (yoō fäl′ə jist) *n.* [< UFO + -LOGY + -IST] a person interested in UFOs, esp. as supposed craft from outer space —**u·fol′o·gy** *n.*

**U·gan·da** (yoō gan′də, oō gän′dä) country in EC Africa: 93,981 sq. mi.; pop. 7,934,000 —**U·gan′dan** *adj., n.*

**ugh** (ookh, oo, ug, etc.) *interj.* an exclamation of disgust, horror, etc.

**ug·li** (ug′lē) *n.* [< ff.] an odd-shaped fruit that is a cross between a grape-fruit, orange, and tangerine

**ug·ly** (ug′lē) *adj.* **-li·er, -li·est** [< ON. *uggr*, fear] 1. unpleasing to look at 2. bad, vile, repulsive, etc. 3. ominous; dangerous 4. [Colloq.] cross; quarrelsome —**ug′li·ness** *n.*

**uh** (u, un) *interj.* 1. *same as* HUH 2. a sound indicating hesitation

**UHF, uhf** ultrahigh frequency

**U.K.** United Kingdom

**u·kase** (yoō′kās, yoō kāz′) *n.* [Russ. *ukaz*, edict] an official decree

**U·krain·i·an** **So·vi·et** **So·cial·ist Republic** (yoō krā′nē ən) republic of the U.S.S.R., in the SW part: 231,990 sq. mi.; pop. 46,600,000: also the **U·kraine′** (-krān′)

**u·ku·le·le** (yoō′kə lā′lē) *n.* [Haw., flea] a small, four-stringed, guitarlike musical instrument

**ul·cer** (ul′sər) *n.* [L. *ulcus*] 1. an open sore on the skin or some mucous membrane, discharging pus 2. any corrupt condition —**ul′cer·ous** *adj.*

**ul·cer·ate** (ul′sə rāt′) *vt., vi.* **-at·ed, -at′ing** to make or become ulcerous —**ul′cer·a′tion** *n.*

**ul·na** (ul′nə) *n., pl.* **-nae** (-nē) **-nas** [L., the elbow] the larger of the two bones of the forearm —**ul′nar** *adj.*

**ul·ster** (ul′stər) *n.* [< *Ulster*, in N Ireland] a long, loose, heavy overcoat

**ul·te·ri·or** (ul tir′ē ər) *adj.* [L. < *ulter*, beyond] 1. lying beyond or on the farther side 2. beyond what is expressed or implied; undisclosed

**ult.** ultimate(ly)

**ul·ti·mate** (ul′tə mit) *adj.* [< L. *ultimus*, last] 1. beyond which it is impossible to go 2. final; conclusive 3. beyond further analysis; fundamental 4. greatest possible —*n.* a final point or result —**ul′ti·mate·ly** *adv.*

**ul·ti·ma·tum** (ul′tə māt′əm) *n., pl.* **-tums, -ta** (-ə) [see prec.] a final offer or demand, as in negotiations

**ul·tra** (ul′trə) *adj.* [< ff.] going beyond the usual limit; extreme

**ultra-** [L. < *ultra*, beyond] *a prefix meaning:* 1. beyond [*ultraviolet*] 2. excessively [*ultramodern*]

**ul·tra·con·serv·a·tive** (ul′trə kən-sur′və tiv) *adj.* extremely conservative

**ul·tra·high frequency** (ul′trə hī′) any radio frequency between 300 and 3,000 megahertz

**ul′tra·ma·rine′** (-mə rēn′) *adj.* deep-blue —*n.* deep blue

**ul′tra·son′ic** (-sän′ik) *adj.* above the range of sound audible to the human ear

**ul′tra·sound′** *n.* ultrasonic waves, used in medical diagnosis and therapy, in surgery, etc.

**ul′tra·vi′o·let** *adj.* lying just beyond the violet end of the visible spectrum: said of certain light rays

**ul·u·late** (yoō′yoo lāt′, ul′-) *vi.* **-lat′ed, -lat′ing** [< L. *ululare*, howl] to howl, hoot, or wail loudly —**ul′u·la′tion** *n.*

**U·lys·ses** (yoo lis′ēz) [ML.] *same as* ODYSSEUS

**um·bel** (um′b'l) *n.* [see UMBRELLA] a cluster of flowers with stalks of equal length which spring from the main stem

**um·ber** (um′bər) *n.* [< It. (*terra d′*) *ombra*, (earth of) shade] 1. a kind of earth used as a reddish-brown pigment 2. a reddish-brown color

**um·bil·i·cal** (um bil′i k'l) *adj.* [< L. *umbilicus*, navel] of a cordlike structure (**umbilical cord**) connecting a fetus with the placenta and serving to convey food to the fetus

**um·bra** (um′brə) *n., pl.* **-brae** (-brē) **-bras** [L., a shade] 1. shade or a shadow 2. the dark cone of shadow from a planet or satellite on the side opposite the sun

**um·brage** (um′brij) *n.* [< L. *umbra*, a shade] 1. [Obs.] shade 2. foliage 3. offense or resentment

**um·brel·la** (um brel′ə) *n.* [< L. *umbra*, shade] 1. a screen, usually of cloth on a folding frame, carried for protection against the rain or sun 2. any comprehensive, protective alliance, device, etc.

---

fat, āpe, cär; ten, ēven; is, bīte; gō, hôrn, toōl, look; oil, out; up, fur; chin; she; thin, *then*; zh, leisure; ŋ, ring; ə for *a* in ago; ′, (ā′b'l); ë, Fr. coeur; ö, Fr. feu; Fr. mon; ü, Fr. duc; kh, G. ich, doch; ‡ foreign; < derived from

**u·mi·ak** (ōō′mē ak′) *n.* [Esk.] a large, open boat made of skins on a wooden frame, used by Eskimos

UMIAK

**um·laut** (oom′lout) *n.* [G. < *um*, about + *laut*, a sound] *Linguistics* **1.** a vowel changed in sound by its assimilation to another vowel **2.** the mark (¨) placed over such a vowel

**ump** (ump) *n., vt., vi. clip of* UMPIRE

**um·pire** (um′pīr) *n.* [< MFr. *nomper*, uneven, hence a third person] a person chosen to judge a dispute; esp., an official who administers the rules in certain sports —*vt., vi.* **-pired, -pir·ing** to act as umpire (in or of)

**ump·teen** (ump′tēn′) *adj.* [Slang] very many —**ump′teenth′** *adj.*

**un-** *either of two prefixes, meaning:* **1.** [OE.] not, lack of, the opposite of *[untruth, unhappily]* **2.** [OE. *un-, on-]* back: indicating a reversal of action *[unfasten]* The following list includes some common compounds formed with *un-* (either prefix) that do not have special meanings:

| | |
|---|---|
| unabashed | undeclared |
| unable | undefeated |
| unabridged | undefended |
| unaccented | undefined |
| unaccompanied | undemocratic |
| unacquainted | undeserved |
| unadorned | undesirable |
| unaffected | undeveloped |
| unafraid | undiscipined |
| unaided | undiscovered |
| unannounced | undisguised |
| unanswerable | undisputed |
| unashamed | undisturbed |
| unasked | undivided |
| unassailable | unearned |
| unassisted | uneducated |
| unattainable | unemotional |
| unattractive | unending |
| unauthorized | unenlightened |
| unavailable | uneventful |
| unavoidable | unexceptional |
| unbearable | unexpired |
| unbeaten | unexplained |
| unbiased | unexplored |
| unbind | unexpressed |
| unbleached | unexpurgated |
| unbreakable | unfair |
| unbroken | unfasten |
| unbutton | unfavorable |
| uncap | unfit |
| unceasing | unflattering |
| uncensored | unforeseen |
| unchallenged | unforgivable |
| unchanged | unfulfilled |
| unchecked | unfurnished |
| uncivil | ungrateful |
| uncivilized | unhampered |
| unclassified | unhandy |
| unclean | unharmed |
| unconnected | unhealthful |
| uncontrollable | unheeded |
| unconventional | unhitch |
| uncooked | unhook |
| uncultivated | unhurried |
| uncultured | unhurt |
| undamaged | unidentified |

| | |
|---|---|
| unimaginative | unrealistic |
| unimpaired | unrecorded |
| unimportant | unrelated |
| unimproved | unreliable |
| unincorporated | unrelieved |
| uninformed | unrequited |
| uninhabited | unrighteous |
| uninhibited | unripe |
| uninjured | unsafe |
| uninspired | unsanitary |
| uninsured | unsatisfactory |
| unintelligent | unsatisfied |
| unintelligible | unsaturated |
| unintentional | unscientific |
| uninteresting | unseasoned |
| uninterrupted | unseeing |
| uninvited | unseen |
| unknowing | unselfish |
| unlace | unshackle |
| unlatch | unshakable |
| unleavened | unshaven |
| unlisted | unshod |
| unmanageable | unshorn |
| unmannerly | unsightly |
| unmarked | unsociable |
| unmarried | unsold |
| unmatched | unsolicited |
| unmindful | unsought |
| unmolested | unspoiled |
| unmoved | unsuccessful |
| unnamed | unsuitable |
| unnoticed | unsupported |
| unobserved | unsurpassed |
| unobstructed | unsuspected |
| unobtrusive | unsweetened |
| unoccupied | unswerving |
| unofficial | unsympathetic |
| unopened | untainted |
| unorthodox | untamed |
| unpaid | untarnished |
| unpardonable | untasted |
| unpaved | untenable |
| unperturbed | unthankful |
| unpin | untiring |
| unplanned | untouched |
| unplowed | untrained |
| unpolished | untried |
| unpredictable | untroubled |
| unprejudiced | untrue |
| unpremeditated | unverified |
| unprepared | unvisited |
| unpretentious | unwanted |
| unprofitable | unwarranted |
| unpromising | unwashed |
| unprotected | unwavering |
| unprovoked | unwed |
| unpublished | unworkable |
| unpunished | unworldly |
| unquestioned | unyielding |
| unquiet | unzip |

**un·ac·count·a·ble** (un′ə koun′tə b'l) *adj.* **1.** that cannot be explained; strange **2.** not responsible

**un′ac·cus′tomed** *adj.* **1.** not accustomed (*to*) **2.** not usual; strange

**un′ad·vised′** *adj.* **1.** without counsel or advice **2.** indiscreet; rash

**un′-A·mer′i·can** *adj.* regarded as not properly American, i.e., as opposed to the U.S., its institutions, etc.

**u·nan·i·mous** (yoo nan′ə məs) *adj.* [< L. *unus*, one + *animus*, the mind] in complete agreement; without dissent —**u·na·nim·i·ty** (yoo′nə nim′ə tē) *n.* —**u·nan′i·mous·ly** *adv.*

**un′ap·proach′a·ble** *adj.* **1.** not to

be approached; inaccessible; aloof **2.** having no equal; unmatched

**un·armed′** *adj.* having no weapons

**un′as·sum′ing** *adj.* not assuming, pretentious, or forward; modest

**un′at·tached′** *adj.* **1.** not attached **2.** not engaged or married

**un′at·tend′ed** *adj.* **1.** not waited on **2.** unaccompanied (*by*) **3.** neglected

**un′a·vail′ing** (-ə vā′liŋ) *adj.* futile; useless

**un′a·ware′** *adj.* not aware or conscious —*adv.* same as UNAWARES

**un′a·wares′** (-werz′) *adv.* **1.** unintentionally **2.** unexpectedly

**un·backed′** *adj.* **1.** not backed, supported, etc. **2.** without a back or backing

**un·bal′anced** *adj.* **1.** not in balance **2.** *a)* mentally deranged *b)* erratic

**un·bar′** *vt.* **-barred′, -bar′ring** to unbolt; unlock; open

**un′be·com′ing** *adj.* not appropriate or suited to one's appearance, character, etc.; unattractive, indecorous, etc.

**un′be·known′** *adj.* without one's knowledge; unknown (usually with *to*): also **un′be·knownst′** (-nōnst′)

**un·be·lief′** *n.* lack of belief, esp. in religion —**un′be·liev′er** *n.*

**un′be·liev′a·ble** *adj.* beyond belief; astounding; incredible

**un·bend′** *vt., vi.* **-bent′** or **-bend′ed, -bend′ing 1.** to release or be released from tension **2.** to relax, as from formality **3.** to straighten

**un·bend′ing** *adj.* **1.** rigid; stiff **2.** firm; resolute **3.** aloof; austere

**un·bid′den** *adj.* **1.** not commanded **2.** not invited

**un·blush′ing** *adj.* **1.** not blushing **2.** without any feeling of shame —**un·blush′ing·ly** *adv.*

**un·bolt′** *vt., vi.* to withdraw the bolt or bolts of (a door, etc.); open

**un·born′** *adj.* **1.** not born **2.** still in the mother's womb **3.** yet to be

**un·bos′om** (-booz′əm, -boo′zəm) *vt., vi.* to tell or reveal (feelings, secrets, etc.) —**unbosom oneself** to reveal one's feelings, secrets, etc.

**un·bound′ed** *adj.* **1.** without bounds or limits **2.** not restrained

**un·bri′dled** *adj.* **1.** having no bridle on, as a horse **2.** not controlled

**un·bur′den** *vt.* **1.** to free from a burden **2.** to relieve (one's soul, mind, etc.) by disclosing (guilt, etc.)

**un·called′-for′** *adj.* **1.** not called for **2.** unnecessary and out of place

**un·can·ny** (un kan′ē) *adj.* **1.** mysterious and eerie; weird **2.** so good, acute, etc. as to seem preternatural

**un·cared′-for′** *adj.* not cared for or looked after; neglected

**un′cer·e·mo′ni·ous** *adj.* **1.** not ceremonious; informal **2.** curt; abrupt

**un·cer′tain** *adj.* **1.** *a)* not surely or certainly known *b)* not sure or certain in knowledge; doubtful **2.** vague **3.** not dependable or reliable **4.** varying —**un·cer′tain·ty** *n., pl.* **-ties**

**un·char′i·ta·ble** *adj.* harsh or severe, as in opinion —**un·char′i·ta·bly** *adv.*

**un·chart′ed** *adj.* not marked on a chart or map; unexplored or unknown

**un·chris′tian** *adj.* **1.** not Christian **2.** [Colloq.] outrageous; dreadful

**un·ci·al** (un′shē əl, -shəl) *adj.* [L. *uncialis*, inch-high] of or in the large, rounded letters of Greek and Latin manuscripts between 300 and 900 A.D. —*n.* uncial script or letter

**un·cir′cum·cised′** *adj.* **1.** not circumcised; gentile **2.** [Archaic] heathen

**un·cle** (uŋ′k'l) *n.* [< L. *avunculus*] **1.** the brother of one's father or mother **2.** the husband of one's aunt

**Uncle Sam** [< abbrev. *U.S.*] [Colloq.] the U.S. (government or people) personified as a tall man with whiskers

**Uncle Tom** [< main character in novel *Uncle Tom's Cabin* (1852)] [Colloq.] a Negro regarded as servile toward whites: a term of contempt

**un·cloak′** *vt., vi.* **1.** to remove a cloak (from) **2.** to reveal; expose

**un·clothe′** *vt.* **-clothed′** or **-clad′, -cloth′ing** to undress, uncover, etc.

**un·coil′** *vt., vi.* to unwind

**un·com′fort·a·ble** *adj.* **1.** feeling discomfort **2.** causing discomfort **3.** ill at ease —**un·com′fort·a·bly** *adv.*

**un·com·mit′ted** *adj.* **1.** not committed or pledged **2.** not taking a stand

**un·com′mon** *adj.* **1.** rare; not common or usual **2.** strange; remarkable

**un′com·mu′ni·ca′tive** *adj.* not communicative; reserved; taciturn

**un′com·pro·mis′ing** *adj.* not yielding; firm; inflexible

**un′con·cern′** *n.* **1.** indifference; apathy **2.** lack of concern, or worry

**un′con·cerned′** *adj.* **1.** indifferent **2.** not solicitous or anxious

**un′con·di′tion·al** *adj.* without conditions or reservations; absolute

**un′con·scion·a·ble** (un kän′shən ə b'l) *adj.* **1.** not guided or restrained by conscience **2.** unreasonable or excessive —**un′con·scion·a·bly** *adv.*

**un·con′scious** *adj.* **1.** deprived of consciousness **2.** not aware (*of*) **3.** not realized or intended [an *unconscious* habit] —**the unconscious** *Psychoanalysis* the sum of all thoughts, impulses, etc. of which the individual is not conscious but which influence his behavior

**un′con·sti·tu′tion·al** *adj.* not in accordance with a constitution

**un·cork′** *vt.* to pull the cork out of

**un·count′ed** *adj.* **1.** not counted **2.** inconceivably numerous

**un·cou′ple** *vt.* **-pled, -pling** to unfasten (things coupled together)

**un·couth** (un kooth′) *adj.* [OE. < *un-*, not + *cunnan*, know] **1.** awkward; ungainly **2.** uncultured; crude

**un·cov′er** *vt.* **1.** to disclose **2.** to remove the cover from **3.** to remove the hat, etc. from (the head) —*vi.* to bare the head, as in respect

---

fat, āpe, cär; ten, ēven; is, bīte; gō, hôrn, tōōl, look; oil, out; up, fur; chin; she; thin, then; zh, leisure; ŋ, ring; ə for a in *ago*; ', (ā′b'l); ë, Fr. coeur; ö, Fr. feu; Fr. mon; ü, Fr. duc; kh, G. ich, doch; ‡ foreign; < derived from

**unc·tion** (uŋk′shən) *n.* [< L. *ungere*, anoint] 1. *a)* the act of anointing, as for medical or religious purposes *b)* the oil, ointment, etc. used for this 2. anything that soothes or comforts

**unc·tu·ous** (uŋk′choo wəs) *adj.* [see prec.] 1. oily or greasy 2. characterized by a smooth pretense of fervor or earnestness; too suave or oily —**unc′tu·ous·ness** *n.*

**un·cut′** *adj.* not cut; specif., *a)* not ground to shape: said of a gem *b)* not shortened or abridged

**un·daunt′ed** *adj.* not daunted; fearless, not disheartened

**un·de·ceive′** *vt.* -ceived′, -ceiv′ing to cause to be no longer deceived or misled

**un·de·cid′ed** *adj.* 1. not decided 2. not having come to a decision

**un·de·mon′stra·tive** *adj.* not demonstrative; not showing feelings openly; reserved —**un′de·mon′stra·tive·ly** *adv.*

**un·de·ni′a·ble** *adj.* 1. that cannot be denied; indisputable 2. unquestionably good —**un′de·ni′a·bly** *adv.*

**un·der** (un′dər) *prep.* [OE.] 1. in, at, or to a position down from; below 2. beneath the surface of 3. below and to the other side of [drive *under* the bridge] 4. covered by [a vest *under* his coat] 5. *a)* lower in rank, position, amount, etc. than *b)* lower than the required degree of [*under* age] 6. subject to the control, limitations, etc. of [*under* oath] 7. undergoing [*under* repair] 8. with the disguise of [*under* an alias] 9. in (the designated category) 10. in the time of [*under* Lincoln] 11. being the subject of [a topic *under* debate] 12. because of [*under* the circumstances] 13. authorized by —*adv.* 1. in or to a lower position or state 2. so as to be covered, concealed, etc. —*adj.* lower in position, authority, amount, etc.

**under-** *a prefix meaning:* 1. in, on, to, or from a lower place, beneath [*undershirt*] 2. in a subordinate position [*undergraduate*] 3. too little, insufficiently [*underpay*]

**un′der·a·chieve′** *vi.* -chieved′, -chiev′ing to fail to do as well in school as might be expected from intelligence tests

**un′der·act′** *vt., vi.* to act (a theatrical role) with not enough emphasis or with too much restraint

**un′der·age′** *adj.* 1. not of mature age 2. below the age required by law

**un′der·arm′** *adj.* 1. of, for, in, or used on the area under the arm, or the armpit 2. *same as* UNDERHAND (sense 1) —*adv.* *same as* UNDERHAND (sense 1)

**un′der·bel′ly** *n.* 1. the lower, posterior part of an animal's belly 2. any vulnerable area, point, etc.

**un′der·bid′** *vt., vi.* -bid′, -bid′ding 1. to bid lower than (another person) 2. to bid less than the worth of (as one's hand in bridge)

**un′der·brush′** *n.* small trees, shrubs, etc. growing in woods or forests

**un′der·car′riage** *n.* a supporting frame, as of an automobile

**un′der·charge′** *vt., vi.* -charged′, -charg′ing 1. to charge too low a price (to) 2. to load insufficiently —*n.* (un′dər chärj′) an insufficient charge

**un′der·class′** *n.* the class with incomes below subsistence level, including esp. the underprivileged

**un′der·class′man** (-mən) *n., pl.* -men a freshman or sophomore in high school or college

**un′der·clothes′** *n.pl.* *same as* UNDERWEAR: also **un′der·cloth′ing**

**un′der·coat′** *n.* 1. a tarlike coating applied to the underside of an automobile to retard rust, etc. 2. a coat of paint, etc. applied before the final coat Also **un′der·coat′ing** —*vt.* to apply an undercoat to

**un′der·cov′er** *adj.* acting or carried out in secret

**un′der·cur′rent** *n.* 1. a current flowing beneath the surface 2. an underlying tendency, opinion, etc.

**un′der·cut′** *vt.* -cut′, -cut′ting 1. to make a cut below or under 2. to undersell or work for lower wages than

**un′der·de·vel′oped** *adj.* inadequately developed, esp. economically and industrially

**un′der·dog′** *n.* one that is underprivileged, unfavored, losing, etc.

**un′der·done′** *adj.* not cooked enough

**un′der·es′ti·mate′** *vt., vi.* -mat′ed, -mat′ing to set too low an estimate on or for

**un′der·foot′** *adv., adj.* 1. under the foot or feet 2. in the way

**un′der·gar′ment** (-gär′mənt) *n.* a piece of underwear

**un′der·go′** *vt.* -went′, -gone′, -go′ing to experience; go through

**un′der·grad′u·ate** *n.* a college student who does not yet have a degree

**un′der·ground′** *adj.* 1. under the earth's surface 2. secret; hidden 3. of noncommercial newspapers, movies, etc. that are unconventional, radical, etc. —*adv.* 1. under the earth's surface 2. in or into secrecy —*n.* 1. the region under the earth's surface 2. a secret movement in a country to oppose the government or occupying enemy forces 3. [Brit.] a subway

**un′der·growth′** *n.* underbrush

**un′der·hand′** *adj.* 1. done with the hand below the level of the elbow or shoulder 2. underhanded —*adv.* 1. with an underhand motion 2. underhandedly

**un′der·hand′ed** *adj.* sly, deceitful, etc. —**un′der·hand′ed·ly** *adv.*

**un′der·lie′** *vt.* -lay′, -lain′, -ly′ing 1. to lie beneath 2. to be the basis for; form the foundation of

**un′der·line′** *vt.* -lined′, -lin′ing 1. to draw a line beneath 2. to stress

**un·der·ling** (un′dər liŋ) *n.* [OE.: see UNDER- & -LING] a person in a subordinate position; inferior

**un′der·ly′ing** *adj.* 1. lying under 2. fundamental; basic

**un′der·mine′** *vt.* -mined′, -min′ing 1. to dig beneath, so as to form a tunnel or mine 2. to wear away at the foundation 3. to injure or weaken, esp. by subtle or insidious means

**un·der·most** *adj., adv.* lowest in place, position, rank, etc.

**un·der·neath** (un'dər nēth') *adv., prep.* under; below; beneath

**un'der·nour'ished** *adj.* not getting the food needed for health and growth

**un'der·pants'** *n.pl.* an undergarment of long or short pants

**un'der·pass'** *n.* a passage under something, as a road under a railway

**un'der·pin'ning** (-pin'iŋ) *n.* 1. a support or prop 2. [*pl.*] [Colloq.] the legs

**un'der·play'** *vt., vi.* 1. *same as* UNDERACT 2. to make seem not too important

**un'der·priv'i·leged** *adj.* deprived of basic social rights and security through poverty, discrimination, etc.

**un'der·pro·duce'** *vt., vi.* -duced', -duc'ing to produce less than is needed or wanted

**un'der·rate'** *vt.* -rat'ed, -rat'ing to rate or estimate too low

**un'der·score'** *vt.* -scored', -scor'ing to underline

**un'der·sea'** *adj., adv.* beneath the surface of the sea: also **un'der·seas'** *adv.*

**un'der·sec're·tar'y** *n., pl.* -ies an assistant secretary

**un'der·sell'** *vt.* -sold', -sell'ing to sell at a lower price than

**un'der·shirt'** *n.* a collarless undergarment worn under an outer shirt

**un'der·shorts'** *n.pl.* short underpants worn by men and boys

**un'der·shot'** *adj.* 1. with the lower part extending past the upper [an *undershot* jaw] 2. driven by water flowing along the lower part

**un'der·side'** *n.* the side or surface that is underneath

**un'der·signed'** *adj.* 1. signed at the end 2. whose name is signed at the end —**the undersigned** the person or persons having signed at the end

**un'der·staffed'** *adj.* having fewer workers on the staff than are needed

**un'der·stand'** *vt.* -stood' (-stood'), -stand'ing [OE. *understandan*, stand under] 1. to perceive the meaning of 2. to assume from what is heard, etc.; infer 3. to take as meant; interpret 4. to take as a fact 5. to learn 6. to know the nature, character, etc. of 7. to be sympathetic with —*vi.* 1. to have understanding, comprehension, etc. 2. to be informed; believe —**un'der·stand'a·ble** *adj.* —**un'der·stand'a·bly** *adv.*

**un'der·stand'ing** *n.* 1. comprehension 2. the power to think and learn; intelligence 3. a specific interpretation 4. mutual agreement, esp. one that settles differences —*adj.* that understands; sympathetic

**un'der·state'** *vt.* -stat'ed, -stat'ing 1. to state too weakly 2. to state in a restrained style —**un'der·state'·ment** *n.*

**un'der·stud'y** *n., pl.* -ies an actor prepared to substitute for another —*vt., vi.* -ied, -y·ing to learn (a part) as an understudy (to)

**un'der·take'** *vt.* -took', -tak'en, -tak'ing 1. to take upon oneself (a task, etc.) 2. to promise; guarantee

**un'der·tak'er** *n. earlier term for* FUNERAL DIRECTOR

**un'der·tak'ing** (*also* un'dər tā'kiŋ) *n.* 1. something undertaken; task; enterprise 2. a promise; guarantee

**un'der-the-count'er** *adj.* [Colloq.] done secretly in an unlawful way: also **un'der-the-ta'ble**

**un'der·things'** *n.pl.* women's or girls' underwear

**un'der·tone'** *n.* 1. a low tone of voice 2. a subdued color 3. an underlying quality, factor, etc.

**un'der·tow'** (-tō') *n.* a current of water moving beneath the surface water and in a different direction

**un'der·waist'** *n.* an undergarment worn under a blouse, or waist

**un'der·wa'ter** *adj.* being, done, etc. beneath the surface of the water

**un'der·wear'** *n.* clothing worn under one's outer clothes, usually next to the skin, as undershirts

**un'der·weight'** *adj.* below the normal or allowed weight

**un'der·world'** *n.* 1. Hades; hell 2. criminals as an organized group

**un'der·write'** *vt.* -wrote', -writ'ten, -writ'ing 1. to agree to market (an issue of securities, and to buy any part remaining unsubscribed) 2. to agree to finance (an undertaking, etc.) 3. to sign one's name to (an insurance policy), thus assuming liability —**un'der·writ'er** *n.*

**un·dies** (un'dēz) *n.pl.* [Colloq.] women's or girls' underwear

**un·do'** *vt.* -did', -done', -do'ing 1. to untie, open, etc. 2. to do away with; annul 3. to bring to ruin

**un·do'ing** *n.* 1. an annulling 2. a bringing to ruin 3. the cause of ruin

**un·done'** *adj.* 1. not done; not performed, accomplished, etc. 2. ruined

**un·doubt'ed** *adj.* that cannot be doubted; certain —**un·doubt'ed·ly** *adv.*

**un·dreamed'** *adj.* not even dreamed (*of*) or thought (*of*) as possible: also **un·dreamt'** (-dremt')

**un·dress'** *vt.* to take off the clothing of —*vi.* to take off one's clothing

**un·due'** *adj.* 1. not appropriate; improper 2. excessive; unreasonable

**un·du·lant** (un'joo lənt, -dyoo-) *adj.* undulating

**un·du·late'** (-lāt') *vi., vt.* -lat'ed, -lat'ing [< L. *unda*, a wave] 1. to move or cause to move in waves 2. to have or cause to have a wavy form or surface —**un·du·la'tion** *n.*

**un·du·ly** (un doo'lē) *adv.* 1. improperly; unjustly 2. excessively

**un·dy'ing** *adj.* immortal or eternal

**un·earth'** *vt.* 1. to dig up from the earth 2. to bring to light; disclose

**un·earth·ly** *adj.* 1. supernatural 2. weird; mysterious 3. [Colloq.] fantastic, outlandish, etc.

**un·eas·y** *adj.* -i·er, -i·est 1. having, showing, or allowing no ease of body or mind; uncomfortable, disturbed, perturbed, etc. 2. awkward; constrained —**un·eas′i·ly** *adv.* —**un·eas′i·ness** *n.*

**un·em·ployed′** *adj.* 1. not employed; without a job 2. not being used; idle —**un′em·ploy′ment** *n.*

**un·e′qual** *adj.* 1. not equal, as in size, strength, ability, value, etc. 2. not balanced, even, regular, etc. 3. not adequate (*to*) 4. [Rare] unjust

**un·e′qualed, un·e′qualled** *adj.* not equaled; unmatched; unrivaled

**un·e·quiv′o·cal** *adj.* not equivocal; plain; clear

**un·err′ing** *adj.* 1. free from error 2. not missing or failing; sure; exact

**UNESCO** (yoo nes′kō) United Nations Educational, Scientific, and Cultural Organization

**un·e′ven** *adj.* 1. not even, level, smooth, regular, etc. 2. unequal 3. *Math.* odd —**un·e′ven·ly** *adv.*

**un·ex·am′pled** *adj.* having no parallel or precedent; unprecedented

**un·ex·cep′tion·a·ble** *adj.* not exceptionable; without fault; beyond criticism —**un′ex·cep′tion·a·bly** *adv.*

**un·ex·pect′ed** *adj.* not expected; unforeseen —**un·ex·pect′ed·ly** *adv.*

**un·fail′ing** *adj.* 1. not failing 2. never ceasing or falling short; inexhaustible 3. always reliable

**un·faith′ful** *adj.* 1. lacking or breaking faith or loyalty 2. not true, accurate, etc. 3. adulterous

**un·fa·mil′iar** *adj.* 1. not well-known; strange 2. not acquainted (*with*)

**un·feel′ing** *adj.* 1. incapable of feeling; insensible 2. hardhearted; cruel —**un·feel′ing·ly** *adv.*

**un·feigned′** (-fānd′) *adj.* genuine

**un·fin′ished** *adj.* 1. not finished; incomplete 2. having no finish, or final coat, as of paint

**un·flap′pa·ble** (-flap′ə b'l) *adj.* [UN- + FLAP (*n.* 4) + -ABLE] [Colloq.] not easily excited; imperturbable

**un·flinch′ing** *adj.* steadfast; firm

**un·fold′** *vt.* 1. to open and spread out (something folded) 2. to lay open to view; reveal, explain, etc. —*vi.* 1. to become unfolded 2. to develop fully

**un·for·get′ta·ble** *adj.* so important, forceful, etc. as never to be forgotten

**un·for·tu·nate** *adj.* 1. having or bringing bad luck; unlucky 2. not suitable —*n.* an unfortunate person

**un·found′ed** *adj.* 1. not founded on fact or truth 2. not established

**un·friend′ly** *adj.* 1. not friendly or kind 2. not favorable

**un·frock′** (-fräk′) *vt.* to deprive of the rank of priest or minister

**un·furl′** *vt., vi.* to open or spread out from a furled state; unfold

**un·gain·ly** (un gān′lē) *adj.* [< ME. *un-*, not + ON. *gegn*, ready] awkward; clumsy

**un·god′ly** *adj.* 1. not godly or religious 2. [Colloq.] outrageous

**un·gov′ern·a·ble** *adj.* that cannot be governed or controlled; unruly

**un·gra′cious** *adj.* 1. not gracious; rude 2. unpleasant; unattractive

**un·guard′ed** *adj.* 1. unprotected 2. guileless 3. careless; imprudent

**un·guent** (uŋ′gwənt) *n.* [< L. *un-guere*, anoint] a salve or ointment

**un·gu·late** (uŋ′gyoo lit, -lāt′) *adj.* [< L. *unguis*, a nail] having hoofs —*n.* a mammal having hoofs

**un·hand′** *vt.* to loose or release from the hand or hands; let go of

**un·hap′py** *adj.* -pi·er, -pi·est 1. unfortunate 2. sad; wretched 3. not suitable —**un·hap′pi·ly** *adv.*

**un·health′y** *adj.* -i·er, -i·est 1. sickly; not well 2. harmful to health 3. harmful to morals 4. dangerous

**un·heard′** *adj.* 1. not perceived by the ear 2. not given a hearing

**un·heard′-of′** *adj.* 1. not heard of before; unprecedented or unknown 2. unacceptable or outrageous

**un·hinge′** *vt.* -hinged′, -hing′ing 1. to remove from the hinges 2. to dislodge 3. to unbalance (the mind)

**un·ho′ly** *adj.* -li·er, -li·est 1. not sacred, hallowed, etc. 2. wicked; profane 3. [Colloq.] outrageous; dreadful

**un·horse′** *vt.* -horsed′, -hors′ing to throw (a rider) from a horse

**uni-** [L. < *unus*, one] *a combining form meaning* united, having one only

**u·ni·cam·er·al** (yoo′nə kam′ər əl) *adj.* [< *uni-* + L. *camera*, chamber] of or having a single legislative chamber

**UNICEF** (yoo′nə sef′) United Nations International Children's Emergency Fund

**u·ni·corn** (yoo′nə kôrn′) *n.* [< L. *unus*, one + *cornu*, horn] a mythical horselike animal with a single horn in its forehead

UNICORN

**u·ni·form** (yoo′nə fôrm′) *adj.* [< L. *unus*, one + *-formis*, -FORM] 1. not varying in form, rate, degree, etc. 2. like others of the same class —*n.* the distinctive clothes of a particular group, as soldiers —*vt.* to supply with a uniform —**u′ni·form′i·ty** (-fôr′mə tē) *n.* —**u′ni·form′ly** *adv.*

**u·ni·fy** (yoo′nə fī′) *vt., vi.* -fied′, -fy′ing [see UNI- & -FY] to become or make united —**u′ni·fi·ca′tion** *n.*

**u·ni·lat·er·al** (yoo′nə lat′ər əl) *adj.* 1. of, occurring on, or affecting one side only 2. involving one only of several parties; not reciprocal

**un·im·peach·a·ble** (un′im pēch′ə b'l) *adj.* that cannot be doubted or discredited; irreproachable

**un·in·ter·est·ed** *adj.* not interested; indifferent

**un·ion** (yoon′yən) *n.* [< L. *unus*, one] 1. a uniting or being united; combination 2. a grouping together of nations, etc. for some specific purpose 3. marriage 4. something united 5. *short for* LABOR UNION 6. a device symbolizing political union, used as in a flag **7.** a device for uniting parts — **the Union** the United States

**un·ion·ize** (-īz′) *vt., vi.* **-ized′, -iz′ing** to organize into a labor union

**union jack 1.** a flag, esp. a national flag, consisting only of a union **2.** [U-J-] the flag of the United Kingdom

**Union of Soviet Socialist Republics** country in E Europe & N Asia, consisting of 15 federated republics: 8,603,000 sq. mi.; pop. 237,300,000

**u·nique** (yōō nēk′) *adj.* [< L. *unus*, one] **1.** one and only; sole **2.** without like or equal **3.** very unusual

**u·ni·sex** (yōō′nə seks′) *adj.* [Colloq.] not differentiated for the sexes, as a style of clothing

**u·ni·son** (yōō′nə sən, -zən) *n.* [< L. *unus*, one + *sonus*, a sound] **1.** identity of musical pitch, as of two or more tones **2.** agreement; harmony — **in unison with** all the voices or instruments performing the same part

**u·nit** (yōō′nit) *n.* [< UNITY] **1.** the smallest whole number; one **2.** a standard basic quantity, measure, etc. **3.** a single person or group, esp. as a part of a whole **4.** a distinct part or object with a specific purpose

**U·ni·tar·i·an** (yōō′nə ter′ē ən) *n.* a member of a Christian sect holding that God is a single being

**u·nite** (yōō nīt′) *vt., vi.* **-nit′ed, -nit′ing** [< L. *unus*, one] **1.** to put or join together so as to make one; combine **2.** to bring or come together in common cause, action, etc.

**United Arab Republic** *former name* of EGYPT (1961–71)

**United Kingdom** country in W Europe, consisting of Great Britain & Northern Ireland: 94,217 sq. mi.; pop. 55,229,000

**United Nations** an international organization of nations for world peace and security: formed (1945) and having, in 1976, a membership of 146

**United States (of America)** country including 49 States in N.America, & Hawaii: 3,615,211 sq. mi.; pop. 203,185,000; cap. Washington

**u·nit·ize** (yōō′nə tīz′) *vt.* **-ized′, -iz′ing** to make into a single unit

**unit pricing** a system of showing prices in terms of standard units such as the ounce and pint

**u·ni·ty** (yōō′nə tē) *n., pl.* **-ties** [< L. *unus*, one] **1.** a being united; oneness **2.** a single, separate thing **3.** harmony; agreement **4.** a complex that is a union of related parts **5.** a harmonious, unified arrangement of parts in an artistic work **6.** continuity of purpose, action, etc. **7.** *Math.* any quantity, etc. identified as a unit, or 1

**u·ni·valve** (yōō′nə valv′) *n.* a mollusk with a one-piece shell, as a snail

**u·ni·ver·sal** (yōō′nə vur′s'l) *adj.* **1.** of the universe; present everywhere **2.** of, for, or including all or the whole **3.** used, or intended to be used, for all kinds, sizes, etc. or by all people —**u′ni·ver·sal′i·ty** (-vər sal′ə tē) *n.*

**u′ni·ver·sal·ize′** *vt.* **-ized′, -iz′ing** to make universal

**universal joint (or coupling)** a joint or coupling that permits a swing of limited angle in any direction

**u′ni·ver′sal·ly** *adv.* **1.** in every instance **2.** in every part or place

**u·ni·verse** (yōō′nə vurs′) *n.* [< L. *unus*, one + *versus*, to turn] **1.** the totality of all things that exist **2.** the world

**u·ni·ver·si·ty** (yōō′nə vur′sə tē) *n., pl.* **-ties** [see prec.] an educational institution of the highest level, variously composed of undergraduate and graduate colleges

**un·just** (un just′) *adj.* not just or right; unfair —**un·just′ly** *adv.*

**un·kempt′** (-kempt′) *adj.* [UN- + *kempt* < dial. *kemben*, to comb] **1.** not combed **2.** not tidy; slovenly

**un·kind′** *adj.* not kind; specif., *a)* not considerate of others *b)* harsh, severe, cruel, etc. —**un·kind′ness** *n.*

**un·kind′ly** *adj. same as* UNKIND — *adv.* in an unkind way

**un·known′** *adj.* not known; specif., *a)* unfamiliar *b)* not discovered, identified, etc. —*n.* an unknown person or thing

**un·law′ful** *adj.* **1.** against the law; illegal **2.** immoral —**un·law′ful·ly** *adv.* —**un·law′ful·ness** *n.*

**un·lead′ed** *adj.* not mixed with tetraethyl lead: said of gasoline

**un·learn′** *vt., vi.* to seek to forget (something learned)

**un·learn′ed** (-lur′nid; *for 2* -lurnd′) *adj.* **1.** not learned or educated **2.** not learned or mastered

**un·leash′** *vt.* to release from or as from a leash

**un·less** (ən les′) *conj.* [< earlier *on lesse that*, at less than] in any case other than that; except that

**un·let′tered** *adj.* **1.** not lettered; ignorant; uneducated **2.** illiterate

**un·like′** *adj.* not alike; different — *prep.* not like; different from

**un·like′ly** *adj.* **1.** not likely; improbable **2.** not likely to succeed — **un·like′li·hood′** *n.*

**un·lim′ber** (-lim′bər) *vt., vi.* to get ready for use or action

**un·lim′it·ed** *adj.* **1.** without limits or restrictions **2.** vast; illimitable

**un·load′** *vt., vi.* **1.** *a)* to remove (a load) *b)* to take a load from **2.** *a)* to tell (one's troubles, etc.) without restraint *b)* to relieve of something that troubles, etc. **3.** to remove the charge from (a gun) **4.** to get rid of

**un·lock′** *vt.* **1.** *a)* to open (a lock) *b)* to open the lock of (a door, etc.) **2.** to let loose; release **3.** to reveal

**un·looked′-for′** *adj.* not expected

**un·loose′** *vt.* **-loosed′, -loos′ing** to set loose; loosen, release, etc.

**un·luck′y** *adj.* **-i·er, -i·est** having or bringing bad luck; unfortunate

**un·make′** vt. -made′, -mak′ing 1. to cause to be as before; undo 2. to ruin; destroy 3. to depose from a position, rank, or authority

**un·man′** vt. -manned′, -man′ning to deprive of manly courage, nerve, etc. —un·man′ly adj.

**un·manned′** adj. without men aboard and operating by remote control

**un·mask′** vi., vt. 1. to remove a mask or disguise (from) 2. to disclose the true nature or character (of)

**un·mean′ing** adj. lacking in meaning or sense

**un·men′tion·a·ble** adj. not fit to be mentioned in polite conversation

**un·mer′ci·ful** adj. having or showing no mercy; cruel; pitiless

**un·mis·tak′a·ble** adj. that cannot be mistaken or misinterpreted; clear —un′mis·tak′a·bly adv.

**un·mit′i·gat′ed** adj. 1. not lessened or eased 2. out-and-out; absolute

**un·mor′al** adj. var. of AMORAL

**un·nat′u·ral** adj. 1. contrary to nature; abnormal 2. artificial 3. very cruel —un·nat′u·ral·ly adv.

**un·nec′es·sar′y** adj. not necessary; needless —un·nec′es·sar′i·ly adv.

**un·nerve′** vt. -nerved′, -nerv′ing to cause to lose one's nerve, courage, etc.

**un·num′bered** adj. 1. not counted 2. innumerable 3. not numbered

**un·or′gan·ized′** adj. not organized; specif., not belonging to a labor union

**un·pack′** vt., vi. 1. to remove (the contents of a trunk, package, etc.) 2. to take things out of (a trunk, etc.)

**un·par′al·leled** adj. that has no parallel, equal, or counterpart

**un·pleas′ant** adj. not pleasant; offensive; disagreeable —un·pleas′ant·ly adv. —un·pleas′ant·ness n.

**un·plumbed′** adj. 1. not measured with a plumb 2. not fully understood

**un·pop′u·lar** adj. not liked by the public or by the majority —un′pop·u·lar′i·ty (-lar′ə tē) n.

**un·prac′ticed** (-prak′tist) adj. 1. not habitually or repeatedly done 2. not skilled or experienced; inexpert

**un·prec′e·dent′ed** adj. having no precedent or parallel; unheard-of

**un·prin′ci·pled** (-p′ld) adj. lacking moral principles; unscrupulous

**un·print′a·ble** adj. not fit to be printed, as because of obscenity

**un′pro·fes′sion·al** adj. not professional; esp., violating the ethical code of a given profession

**un·qual′i·fied′** adj. 1. lacking the necessary qualifications 2. not limited or modified; absolute

**un·ques′tion·a·ble** adj. not to be questioned, doubted, or disputed; certain —un·ques′tion·a·bly adv.

**un′quote′** interj. I end the quotation

**un·rav′el** vt. -eled or -elled, -el·ing or -el·ling 1. to separate the threads of (something woven, tangled, etc.) 2. to make clear; solve —vi. to become unraveled

**un·read′** (-red′) adj. 1. not having been read, as a book 2. having read little or nothing

**un·re′al** adj. not real or actual; imaginary, fanciful, false, etc.

**un·rea′son·a·ble** adj. 1. not reasonable or rational 2. excessive; immoderate —un·rea′son·a·bly adv.

**un·rea′son·ing** adj. not reasoning or reasoned; irrational

**un′re·con·struct′ed** adj. 1. not reconstructed 2. holding to an earlier, outmoded practice or attitude and not reconciled to change

**un′re·gen′er·ate** adj. 1. not spiritually reborn 2. stubbornly defiant

**un′re·lent′ing** adj. 1. inflexible; relentless 2. without mercy; cruel 3. not relaxing in effort, speed, etc.

**un′re·mit′ting** adj. not stopping, relaxing, etc.; incessant; persistent

**un′re·served′** adj. not reserved; specif., a) frank or open in speech b) not restricted or qualified —un′re·serv′ed·ly (-zur′vid lē) adv.

**un·rest′** n. 1. restlessness; disquiet 2. angry discontent verging on revolt

**un·ri′valed, un·ri′valled** adj. having no rival, equal, or competitor

**un·roll′** vt. 1. to open (something rolled up) 2. to display —vi. to become unrolled

**un·ruf′fled** adj. not ruffled or disturbed; calm; smooth; serene

**un·ru′ly** (un rōō′lē) adj. -i·er, -i·est hard to control, restrain, or keep in order; disobedient —un·rul′i·ness n.

**un·sad′dle** vt. -dled, -dling to take the saddle off (a horse, etc.)

**un·said′** adj. not expressed; unspoken

**un·sa′vor·y** adj. 1. unpleasant to taste or smell 2. morally offensive

**un·scathed′** (-skāth̄d′) adj. [ < un- + ON. skathi, harm] uninjured

**un·schooled′** adj. not educated or trained, esp. by formal schooling

**un·scram′ble** vt. -bled, -bling to cause to be no longer scrambled, mixed up, or unintelligible

**un·screw′** vt. to detach or loosen by removing screws, or by turning

**un·scru′pu·lous** adj. not restrained by moral scruples; unprincipled

**un·seal′** vt. to break the seal of; open

**un·sea′son·a·ble** adj. 1. not usual for the season 2. at the wrong time

**un·seat′** vt. 1. to dislodge from a seat 2. to remove from office

**un·seem′ly** adj. not seemly; not decent or proper; unbecoming

**un·set′tle** vt., vi. -tled, -tling to make or become unstable; disturb, displace, or disorder

**un·set′tled** adj. 1. not settled; not fixed, orderly, stable, calm, decided, etc. 2. not paid 3. having no settlers

**un·sheathe′** (-shēth̄′) vt. -sheathed′, -sheath′ing to remove (a sword, etc.) from a sheath

**un·sight′ly** adj. not sightly, or pleasant to look at; ugly

**un·skilled′** adj. having or requiring no special skill or training

**un·skill′ful** adj. having little or no skill; awkward; clumsy

**un·snap′** vt. -snapped′, -snap′ping to undo the snaps of, so as to detach

**un·snarl′** (-snärl′) vt. to untangle

**un′so·phis′ti·cat′ed** adj. not sophisticated; simple, ingenuous, etc.

**un·sound/** *adj.* not sound; specif., *a)* not healthy, safe, firm, etc. *b)* not reliable, sensible, etc.

**un·spar/ing** *adj.* 1. not sparing; lavish 2. not merciful; severe

**un·speak/a·ble** *adj.* 1. that cannot be spoken 2. so bad, evil, etc. as to defy description —**un·speak/a·bly** *adv.*

**un·sta/ble** *adj.* 1. not stable; easily upset 2. changeable 3. unreliable 4. emotionally unsettled    5. *Chem.* tending to decompose

**un·stead/y** *adj.* 1. not steady or firm; shaky 2. changeable; inconstant 3. erratic in habits, purpose, etc.

**un·stop/** *vt.* -**stopped/,** -**stop/ping** 1. to remove the stopper from 2. to clear (a pipe, etc.) of an obstruction

**un·struc/tured** *adj.* not formally organized; loose, free, open, etc.

**un·strung/** *adj.* 1. nervous or upset 2. with the strings loosened or detached, as a bow, racket, etc.

**un·stuck/** *adj.* loosened or freed from being stuck

**un·stud/ied** *adj.* not got by study or conscious effort; spontaneous; natural

**un/sub·stan/tial** *adj.* 1. having no material substance 2. not solid; flimsy 3. unreal; visionary

**un·sung/** (-sun/) *adj.* not honored or celebrated; as in song or poetry

**un·tan/gle** *vt.* -**gled,** -**gling** 1. to free from a snarl or tangle 2. to free from confusion; put in order

**un·taught/** *adj.* 1. not taught; uneducated 2. got without teaching

**un·think/a·ble** *adj.* not to be considered or thought of; impossible

**un·think/ing** *adj.* 1. thoughtless; heedless 2. unable to think

**un·ti/dy** *adj.* -**di·er,** -**di·est** not tidy; slovenly; messy

**un·tie/** *vt.* -**tied/,** -**ty/ing** or -**tie/-ing** 1. to unfasten (a thing tied or knotted) 2. to free, as from restraint

**un·til** (un til/, ən-) *prep.* [ME. *untill*] 1. up to the time of [*until* death] 2. before [not *until* tomorrow] —*conj.* 1. up to the time when or that [*until* you leave] 2. to the point, degree, etc. that [cook *until* it is done] 3. before [not *until* I die]

**un·time/ly** *adj.* 1. before the proper time; premature 2. at the wrong time; inopportune —*adv.* 1. inopportunely 2. prematurely —**un·time/li·ness** *n.*

**un·to** (un/tōō, -too) *prep.* [ME.] *archaic var. of:* 1. to 2. until

**un·told/** *adj.* 1. not told or revealed 2. too many to be counted; vast

**un·touch/a·ble** *adj.* that cannot or should not be touched —*n.* in India, formerly, a member of the lowest caste

**un·to·ward** (un tō/ərd, -tôrd/) *adj.* 1. improper, unseemly, etc. 2. not favorable; adverse

**un·trav/eled, un·trav/elled** *adj.* 1. not used or frequented by travelers 2. not having done much traveling

**un·truth/** *n.* 1. falsity 2. a falsehood; lie —**un·truth/ful** *adj.*

**un·tu/tored** *adj.* uneducated

**un·twist/** *vt., vi.* to separate, as something twisted together; unwind; also **un·twine/,** -**twined/,** -**twin/ing**

**un·used/** *adj.* 1. not in use 2. never used before 3. unaccustomed (*to*)

**un·u/su·al** *adj.* not usual or common; rare —**un·u/su·al·ly** *adv.*

**un·ut/ter·a·ble** *adj.* inexpressible

**un·var/nished** *adj.* 1. not varnished 2. plain; simple; unadorned

**un·veil/** *vt.* to reveal as by removing a veil from —*vi.* to take off one's veil

**un·voiced/** *adj.* not expressed; not spoken

**un·war/y** *adj.* not wary or cautious

**un·well/** *adj.* not well; sick

**un·whole/some** *adj.* 1. harmful to body or mind 2. of unsound health or unhealthy appearance 3. morally harmful —**un·whole/some·ness** *n.*

**un·wield/y** *adj.* hard to wield, manage, etc., as because of large size

**un·will/ing** *adj.* 1. not willing; reluctant 2. done, said, etc. reluctantly —**un·will/ing·ly** *adv.*

**un·wind/** *vt.* -**wound/,** -**wind/ing** 1. to wind off or undo (something wound) 2. to untangle (something involved) —*vi.* 1. to become unwound 2. to become relaxed

**un·wise/** *adj.* having or showing a lack of wisdom or sound judgment

**un·wit·ting** (un wit/in) *adj.* 1. not knowing or aware 2. unintentional

**un·wont·ed** (un won/tid, -wōn/-) *adj.* not common or usual; rare

**un·wor/thy** *adj.* -**thi·er,** -**thi·est** 1. lacking merit or value; worthless 2. not deserving (*of*) 3. not fit or becoming (with *of*) —**un·wor/thi·ness** *n.*

**un·wrap/** *vt.* -**wrapped/,** -**wrap/-ping** to take off the wrapping of

**un·writ/ten** *adj.* 1. not in writing 2. operating only through custom or tradition [an *unwritten* law]

**up¹** (up) *adv.* [OE.] 1. to, in, or on a higher place or level 2. to a later period 3. in or to a higher condition, amount, etc. 4. in or into a standing position 5. in or into action, view, consideration, etc. 6. aside; away [lay *up* wealth] 7. so as to be even with in time, degree, etc. 8. so as to be tightly closed, bound, etc. [tie *up* the package] 9. completely; thoroughly 10. *Baseball* to one's turn at batting   The adverb *up* is also used *a)* to alter the meaning of a verb (Ex.: look *up* this word) *b)* as an intensive with verbs (Ex.: dress *up*) —*prep.* up to, toward, along, through, into, or upon —*adj.* 1. directed toward a higher position 2. in a higher place or position 3. advanced in amount, degree, etc. [rents are *up*] 4. in a standing position 5. in an active or excited state 6. at an end; over [time's *up*] 7. [Colloq.] going on [what's *up*?] 8. *Baseball* at bat —*n.* 1. an upward slope 2. an

---

upward movement, etc. —*vi.* **upped**, **up′ping** [Colloq.] to get up; rise —*vt.* [Colloq.] **1.** to put up, lift up, etc. **2.** to cause to rise [to *up* prices] —**on the up and up** [Slang] honest —**up against** [Colloq.] confronted with —**up on** (or **in**) [Colloq.] well-informed concerning —**ups and downs** good periods and bad periods —**up to** [Colloq.] **1.** doing or scheming **2.** capable of (doing, etc.) **3.** as many as **4.** as far as **5.** dependent upon —**up with!** put in or restore to power, authority, etc.!

**up²** (up) *adv.* [phonetic respelling of *apiece*] apiece [a score of two *up*]

**up-** *a combining form meaning* up

**up-and-com·ing** (up′'n kum′iŋ) *adj.* **1.** enterprising, promising, etc. **2.** gaining in prominence

**up′beat′** *n. Music* an unaccented beat, esp. when on the last note of a bar —*adj.* cheerful; optimistic

**up·braid** (up brād′) *vt.* [ < OE. *up-*, up + *bregdan*, to pull] to rebuke severely; censure; scold

**up′bring′ing** *n.* the training and education received while growing up

**up′chuck′** (-chuk′) *vi., vt., n.* [Slang] *same as* VOMIT

**up′com·ing** *adj.* coming soon

**up′coun·try** *adj., adv.* in or toward the interior of a country —*n.* the interior of a country

**up·date′** *vt.* -dat′ed, -dat′ing to make up-to-date; make conform to the most recent facts, methods, ideas, etc.

**up·end′** *vt., vi.* to set, turn, or stand on end

**up′-front′** *adj.* [Colloq.] **1.** forthright **2.** in advance [up-front money]

**up′grade′** *n.* an upward slope —*adj., adv.* uphill; upward —*vt.* -grad′ed, -grad′ing to raise in value, grade, rank, quality, etc.

**up·heav·al** (up hē′v'l) *n.* **1.** a heaving up **2.** a sudden, violent change

**up′hill′** *adj.* **1.** going or sloping up **2.** laborious; tiring —*adv.* **1.** upward as on a hillside **2.** with difficulty

**up·hold′** *vt.* -held′, -hold′ing **1.** to hold up **2.** to keep from falling; support **3.** to confirm; sustain

**up·hol·ster** (up hōl′stər, ə pōl′-) *vt.* [ult. < ME. *upholder*, tradesman] to fit out (furniture, etc.) with coverings, padding, springs, etc. —**up·hol′ster·er** *n.*

**up·hol·ster·y** *n., pl.* -ies **1.** the material used in upholstering **2.** the work of an upholsterer

**up′keep′** *n.* **1.** maintenance **2.** state of repair **3.** the cost of maintenance

**up′land** (-lənd, -land′) *n.* land elevated above other land —*adj.* of or situated in upland

**up·lift′** *vt.* **1.** to lift up **2.** to raise to a higher moral, social, or cultural level —*n.* (up′lift′) **1.** a lifting up **2.** a movement for moral, social, or cultural betterment —**up·lift′ment** *n.*

**up′man·ship′** *n. short for* ONE-UPMANSHIP

**up·on** (ə pän′) *prep.* on, or up and on: used interchangeably with *on* —*adv.* on

**up·per** (up′ər) *adj.* **1.** higher in place **2.** higher in rank; superior —*n.* **1.** the part of a shoe above the sole **2.** [Slang] any drug that is a stimulant; esp., an amphetamine

**upper case** capital-letter type used in printing, as distinguished from small letters —**up′per-case′** *adj.*

**upper class** the rich or aristocratic class —**up′per-class′** *adj.*

**up′per·class′man** (-mən) *n., pl.* -men a junior or senior in high school or college

**up′per-cut′** *n. Boxing* a short, swinging blow directed upward

**upper hand** the position of advantage or control

**up′per·most′** *adj.* highest in place, power, authority, etc. —*adv.* in the highest place, rank, etc.; first

**Upper Vol·ta** (väl′tə) country in W Africa: 108,880 sq. mi.; pop. 5,155,000

**up·pish** (up′ish) *adj.* [Colloq.] haughty, snobbish, arrogant, etc.: also **up′pi·ty**

**up·raise′** *vt.* -raised′, -rais′ing to raise up; lift; elevate

**up·rear′** *vt.* **1.** to raise or lift up **2.** to exalt **3.** to bring up; rear

**up′right′** *adj.* **1.** standing, pointing, etc. straight up; erect **2.** honest and just —*adv.* (*also* up rīt′) in an upright position or direction —*n.* something having an upright position

**upright piano** a piano with a vertical, rectangular body

**up′ris·ing** (-rīz′iŋ) *n.* a revolt

**up·roar** (up′rôr′) *n.* [Du. *oproer*, a stirring up] **1.** violent disturbance; tumult **2.** loud, confused noise

**up·roar′i·ous** *adj.* **1.** making, or full of, an uproar **2.** loud and boisterous, as laughter

**up·root′** *vt.* **1.** to tear up by the roots **2.** to destroy or remove utterly

**up·set** (up set′; *for n.* up′set′) *vt.* -set′, -set′ting **1.** *a)* to tip over; overturn *b)* to defeat unexpectedly **2.** *a)* to disturb the functioning of [to *upset* a schedule] *b)* to disturb emotionally —*vi.* to become overturned or upset —*n.* **1.** an upsetting **2.** an unexpected defeat **3.** a disturbance —*adj.* **1.** tipped over **2.** overthrown or defeated **3.** disturbed or disordered

**up′shot′** *n.* [orig., final shot in an archery match] the conclusion; result

**up′side′** *n.* the upper side or part

**upside down 1.** with the top side or part underneath **2.** in disorder —**up′side′-down′** *adj.*

**up·si·lon** (yōōp′sə län′) *n.* the twentieth letter of the Greek alphabet (Υ, υ)

**up′stage′** *adv., adj.* toward or at the rear of a stage —*vt.* -staged′, -stag′ing to draw attention away from (another), as by moving upstage

**up′stairs′** *adv.* **1.** up the stairs **2.** on or to an upper floor —*adj.* on an upper floor —*n.* an upper floor

**up·stand′ing** *adj.* **1.** erect **2.** upright in character; honorable

**up′start′** *n.* one who has recently come into wealth, power, etc., esp. one who is presumptuous, aggressive, etc. —*adj.* of or like an upstart

**up'state'** *adj., adv.* in, to, or from the northerly part of a State

**up'stream'** *adv., adj.* in the direction against the current of a stream

**up'surge'** (-surj') *n.* a sudden rise

**up'swing'** *n.* a swing, trend, or movement upward

**up'take'** *n.* a taking up —**quick (or slow) on the uptake** [Colloq.] quick (or slow) to comprehend

**up'-tight', up'tight'** *adj.* [Slang] very tense, nervous, etc.

**up'-to-date'** *adj.* 1. extending to the present time 2. keeping up with what is most recent

**up'town'** *adj., adv.* of, in, or toward the upper part of a city or town

**up-turn** (up turn'; *for n.* up'turn') *vt., vi.* to turn up or over —*n.* an upward turn or trend —**up'turned'** *adj.*

**up'ward** (-wərd) *adv., adj.* toward a higher place, position, etc.: also **up'wards** *adv.* —**upwards (or upward) of** more than —**up'ward-ly** *adv.*

**upward mobility** movement to a higher social and economic status

**U.rals** (yoor'əlz) mountain range in W U.S.S.R., regarded as the boundary between Europe & Asia: also **Ural Mountains**

**u.ra.ni.um** (yoo rā'nē əm) *n.* [< ff.] a very hard, heavy, radioactive metallic chemical element: used in work on atomic energy

**U.ra.nus** (yoor'ə nəs, yoo rā'-) [< Gr. *Ouranos*, heaven] a planet of the solar system: see PLANET

**urb** (urb) *n.* an urban area, esp. as contrasted with its suburbs

**ur-ban** (ur'bən) *adj.* [< L. *urbs*, city] 1. of, in, or constituting a city 2. characteristic of cities

**ur-bane** (ur bān') *adj.* [see prec.] polite in a smooth, polished way; refined —**ur-ban'i-ty** (-ban'ə tē) *n.*

**ur-ban-ize** (ur'bə nīz') *vt.* **-ized', -iz'ing** to change from rural to urban —**ur'ban-i-za'tion** *n.*

**ur'ban-ol'o-gist** (-näl'ə jist) *n.* a specialist in urban problems —**ur'ban-ol'o-gy** *n.*

**urban renewal** rehabilitation of deteriorated urban areas, as by slum clearance and housing construction

**urban sprawl** the spread of urban congestion into surrounding areas

**ur-chin** (ur'chin) *n.* [< L. *ericius*, hedgehog] a small child; esp., a mischievous boy

**-ure** (ər) [Fr. < L. *-ura*] a suffix meaning: 1. act or result of being [*exposure*] 2. agent of [*legislature*] 3. state of being [*composure*]

**u.re.a** (yoo rē'ə) *n.* [< Gr. *ouron*, urine] a soluble, crystalline solid found in urine or made synthetically

**u.re.mi.a** (yoo rē'mē ə) *n.* [< Gr. *ouron*, urine + *haima*, blood] a toxic condition caused by the presence in the blood of waste products normally eliminated in the urine —**u.re'mic** *adj.*

**u.re.ter** (yoo rēt'ər) *n.* [< Gr. *ourein*,

urinate] a tube carrying urine from a kidney to the bladder

**u.re.thra** (yoo rē'thrə) *n., pl.* **-thrae** (-thrē), **-thras** [< Gr. *ouron*, urine] the canal through which urine is discharged from the bladder: in males, also the duct for semen

**urge** (urj) *vt.* **urged, urg'ing** [L. *urgere*, press hard] 1. *a)* to press upon the attention; advocate *b)* to plead with; ask earnestly 2. to incite; provoke 3. to drive or force onward —*n.* 1. an urging 2. an impulse

**ur-gent** (ur'jənt) *adj.* [see prec.] 1. calling for haste, immediate action, etc. 2. insistent —**ur'gen-cy** *n., pl.* **-cies** —**ur'gent-ly** *adv.*

**-ur-gy** (ur'jē) [< Gr. *ergon*, work] a combining form meaning a working with or by means of [*zymurgy*]

**u.ric** (yoor'ik) *adj.* of, contained in, or derived from urine

**u.ri.nal** (yoor'ə n'l) *n.* 1. a receptacle for urine 2. a place for urinating

**u.ri.nal.y.sis** (yoor'ə nal'ə sis) *n.* chemical or microscopic analysis of the urine

**u.ri.nar.y** (yoor'ə ner'ē) *adj.* 1. of urine 2. of the organs that secrete and discharge urine

**u.ri.nate** (yoor'ə nāt') *vi.* **-nat'ed, -nat'ing** to discharge urine from the body —**u'ri.na'tion** *n.*

**u.rine** (yoor'in) *n.* [< L. *urina*] the yellowish liquid containing waste products secreted by the kidneys and discharged through the urethra

**urn** (urn) *n.* [< L. *urna*] 1. *a)* a vase with a pedestal *b)* such a vase used to hold ashes after cremation 2. a metal container with a faucet, for making or serving hot coffee, tea, etc.

**u.rol.o.gy** (yoo räl'ə jē) *n.* [< Gr. *ouron*, urine + -LOGY] the branch of medicine dealing with the urinary and genital organs and their diseases —**u.rol'o.gist** *n.*

**ur.sine** (ur'sīn, -sin) *adj.* [< L. *ursus*, a bear] of or like a bear

**ur.ti.car.i.a** (ur'tə ker'ē ə) *n.* [< L. *urtica*, a nettle] a skin condition characterized by itching, burning, and the formation of smooth patches

**U.ru.guay** (yoor'ə gwā', -gwī') country in SE S.America: 72,171 sq. mi.; pop. 2,818,000

**us** (us) *pron.* [OE.] objective case of WE

**U.S., US** United States

**USA, U.S.A.** 1. United States of America 2. United States Army

**us.a.ble, use.a.ble** (yoo'zə b'l) *adj.* that can be used; fit for use —**us'a-bil'i-ty, use'a-bil'i-ty** (-bil'ə tē) *n.*

**USAF, U.S.A.F.** United States Air Force

**us.age** (yoo'sij, -zij) *n.* 1. the act, way, or extent of using; treatment 2. established practice; custom; habit 3. the way in which a word, phrase, etc. is used to express a particular idea

**use** (yooz; *for n.* yoos) *vt.* **used, us'ing** [< L. *uti*] 1. to put into action or service **2.** to exercise [*use* your judgment] **3.** to deal with; treat **4.** to consume; expend (often with *up*) —*n.* **1.** a using or being used **2.** the ability to use **3.** the right to use **4.** the need or opportunity to use **5.** way of using **6.** usefulness; utility **7.** the purpose for which something is used **8.** function or service —**used** to (yoos'tə, -too) **1.** did at one time [I *used* to live here] **2.** accustomed to [he's *used* to the cold] —**us'er** *n.*

**used** (yoozd) *adj.* not new; second-hand

**use·ful** (yoos'fəl) *adj.* that can be used; serviceable; helpful —**use'ful·ly** *adv.* —**use'ful·ness** *n.*

**use'less** (-lis) *adj.* **1.** having no use **2.** to no purpose —**use'less·ly** *adv.* —**use'less·ness** *n.*

**ush·er** (ush'ər) *n.* [< L. *ostiarius*, doorkeeper] **1.** one who shows people to their seats in a theater, church, etc. **2.** a bridegroom's attendant —*vt.* **1.** to escort (others) to seats, etc. **2.** to be a forerunner of (often with *in*)

**USMC, U.S.M.C.** United States Marine Corps

**USN, U.S.N.** United States Navy

**USO, U.S.O.** United Service Organizations

**U.S.P.** United States Pharmacopoeia

**U.S.S.** United States Ship

**U.S.S.R., USSR** Union of Soviet Socialist Republics

**u·su·al** (yoo'zhoo wəl) *adj.* [see USE] such as is most often seen, used, etc.; common; customary —**u'su·al·ly** *adv.*

**u·surp** (yoo surp', -zurp') *vt., vi.* [< L. *usus*, a use + *rapere*, seize] to take and hold (power, a position, etc.) by force or without right —**u·sur·pa·tion** (yoo'sər pā'shən, -zər-) *n.* —**u·surp'er** *n.*

**u·su·ry** (yoo'zhoo rē) *n.* [see USE] **1.** the lending of money at an excessive rate of interest **2.** an excessive interest rate —**u'su·rer** *n.* —**u·su·ri·ous** (yoo zhoor'ē əs) *adj.*

**U·tah** (yoo'tô, -tä) Western State of the U.S.: 84,916 sq. mi.; pop. 1,059,000; cap. Salt Lake City: abbrev. Ut., UT

**u·ten·sil** (yoo ten's'l) *n.* [< L. *uti*, to use] an implement or container, esp. one for use in a kitchen

**u·ter·us** (yoo'tər əs) *n., pl.* **-ter·i** (-ī') [L.] a hollow organ of female mammals in which the embryo and fetus are developed; womb —**u'ter·ine** (-in, yoo'tə rīn') *adj.*

**U·ti·ca** (yoo'ti kə) city in C N.Y.: pop. 92,000

**u·til·i·tar·i·an** (yoo til'ə ter'ē ən) *adj.* **1.** of or having to do with utility **2.** stressing usefulness over beauty or other considerations

**u·til·i·ty** (yoo til'ə tē) *n., pl.* **-ties** [< L. *uti*, to use] **1.** usefulness **2.** something useful, as the service to the public of gas, water, etc. **3.** a company providing such a service

**utility room** a room containing laundry appliances, heating equipment, etc.

**u·ti·lize** (yoot''l īz') *vt.* **-lized', -liz'-ing** to put to profitable use; make use of —**u'ti·li·za'tion** *n.*

**ut·most** (ut'mōst') *adj.* [< OE. superl. of *ut*, out] **1.** most extreme; farthest **2.** of the greatest degree, amount, etc. —*n.* the most possible

**U·to·pi·a** (yoo tō'pē ə) [< Gr. *ou*, not + *topos*, a place] an imaginary island in T. More's *Utopia* (1516), with a perfect political and social system —*n.* [*often* **u-**] **1.** any idealized place of perfection **2.** any visionary scheme for a perfect society —**U·to'pi·an, u·to'-pi·an** *adj., n.*

**ut·ter**[1] (ut'ər) *adj.* [< OE. compar. of *ut*, out] **1.** complete; total **2.** unqualified; absolute; unconditional —**ut'ter·ly** *adv.*

**ut·ter**[2] (ut'ər) *vt.* [< ME. *utter*, outward] **1.** to speak or express audibly (words, sounds, etc.) **2.** to express in any way

**ut'ter·ance** *n.* **1.** an uttering **2.** the power or style of speaking **3.** that which is uttered

**ut'ter·most'** (-mōst') *adj., n.* same *as* UTMOST

**u·vu·la** (yoo'vyə lə) *n., pl.* **-las, -lae'** (-lē') [< L. *uva*, grape] the small, fleshy process hanging down from the soft palate above the back of the tongue —**u'vu·lar** *adj.*

**ux·o·ri·ous** (uk sôr'ē əs, ug zôr'-) *adj.* [< L. < *uxor*, wife] dotingly fond of or submissive to one's wife

# V

**V, v** (vē) *n., pl.* **V's, v's** the 22d letter of the English alphabet

**V** (vē) *n.* a Roman numeral for 5

**V, v 1.** velocity **2.** volt(s)

**v. 1.** verb **2.** versus **3.** volume

**VA, V.A.** Veterans Administration

**Va., VA** Virginia

**va·can·cy** (vā'kən sē) *n., pl.* **-cies 1.** a being vacant **2.** empty or vacant space **3.** an unoccupied position, office, quarters, etc.

**va·cant** (vā'kənt) *adj.* [< L. *vacare*, be empty] **1.** having nothing in it **2.** not held, filled, etc., as a seat, house,

etc. **3.** free from work; leisure **4.** foolish or stupid —**va'cant·ly** *adv.*

**va'cate** (-kāt) *vt.* **-cat·ed, -cat·ing 1.** to cause (an office, house, etc.) to be vacant **2.** to make void; annul

**va·ca·tion** (və kā'shən, vā-) *n.* [< L. *vacatio*] a period of rest from work, study, etc. —*vi.* to take one's vacation —**va·ca'tion·er, va·ca'tion·ist** *n.*

**vac·ci·nate** (vak'sə nāt') *vt., vi.* **-nat'ed, -nat'ing** to inoculate with a vaccine to prevent a disease, specif. smallpox —**vac'ci·na'tion** *n.*

**vac·cine** (vak sēn', vak'sēn) *n.* [< L.

*vacca*, cow] **1.** a substance containing the cowpox virus, used in vaccination against smallpox **2.** any preparation so used to produce immunity to a specific disease

**vac·il·late** (vas′ə lāt′) *vi.* **-lat′ed, -lat′ing** [< L. *vacillare*] **1.** to sway to and fro; waver **2.** to fluctuate **3.** to show indecision —**vac′il·la′tion** *n.*

**va·cu·i·ty** (va kyōō′ə tē) *n., pl.* **-ties** [< L. *vacuus*, empty] **1.** emptiness **2.** an empty space **3.** emptiness of mind **4.** an inane or senseless remark, thing, etc.

**vac·u·ous** (vak′yōō wəs) *adj.* [see prec.] **1.** empty **2.** stupid; senseless —**vac′u·ous·ly** *adv.*

**vac·u·um** (vak′yōō wəm, vak′yōōm) *n., pl.* **-ums, -a** (-ə) [L.] **1.** space with nothing at all in it **2.** a space from which most of the air or gas has been taken **3.** any void —*adj.* **1.** of, or used to make, a vacuum **2.** having or working by a vacuum —*vt., vi.* to clean with a vacuum cleaner

**vacuum cleaner** a machine for cleaning carpets, floors, etc. by suction

**vacuum-packed** *adj.* packed in an airtight container to maintain freshness

**vacuum tube** an electron tube from which most of the air has been evacuated, containing one or more grids and used as an amplifier, etc.

**vag·a·bond** (vag′ə bänd′) *adj.* [< L. *vagari*, wander] **1.** wandering **2.** living a drifting or irresponsible life **3.** shiftless; worthless —*n.* **1.** one who wanders from place to place **2.** a wandering beggar **3.** an idle or shiftless person —**vag′a·bond′age** *n.*

**va·gar·y** (və ger′ē, vā′gər ē) *n., pl.* **-ies** [see prec.] **1.** an odd or eccentric action **2.** a whimsical or freakish notion; caprice —**va·gar′i·ous** *adj.*

**va·gi·na** (və jī′nə) *n., pl.* **-nas, -nae** (-nē) [L., sheath] in female mammals, the canal from the vulva to the uterus —**vag·i·nal** (vaj′ə n′l) *adj.*

**va·grant** (vā′grənt) *n.* [prob. < OFr. *walcrer*, wander] one who wanders from place to place, esp. one without a regular job, supporting himself by begging, etc. —*adj.* **1.** wandering; nomadic **2.** of or like a vagrant **3.** wayward, erratic, etc. —**va′gran·cy** *n., pl.* **-cies**

**vague** (vāg) *adj.* [< L. *vagus*, wandering] **1.** indefinite in shape or form **2.** not sharp, certain, or precise in thought or expression —**vague′ly** *adv.* —**vague′ness** *n.*

**vain** (vān) *adj.* [< L. *vanus*, empty] **1.** having no real value; worthless [*vain* pomp] **2.** without effect; futile [a *vain* endeavor] **3.** having an excessively high regard for one's self, looks, etc.; conceited —**in vain 1.** fruitlessly **2.** profanely —**vain′ly** *adv.*

**vain′glo′ry** (-glôr′ē) *n.* [< L. *vana gloria*, empty boasting] excessive vanity —**vain′glo′ri·ous** *adj.*

**val. 1.** valuation **2.** value

**val·ance** (val′əns, vāl′-) *n.* [ME. < ?]

a short curtain forming a border, esp. across the top of a window

**vale** (vāl) *n. poet. var. of* VALLEY

**val·e·dic·to·ri·an** (val′ə dik tôr′ē ən) *n.* the student who delivers the valedictory at graduation

**val′e·dic′to·ry** (-tər ē) *n., pl.* **-ries** [< L. *vale*, farewell + *dicere*, to say] a farewell speech, esp. at a graduation

**va·lence** (vā′ləns) *n.* [< L. *valere*, be strong] *Chem.* the combining capacity of an element or radical as measured by the number of hydrogen or chlorine atoms which one radical or atom of the element will combine with or replace: also **va′len·cy**

**Va·len·ci·a** (və len′shē ə, -shə) seaport in E Spain: pop. 583,000

**val·en·tine** (val′ən tīn′) *n.* **1.** a sweetheart chosen or complimented on Saint Valentine's Day **2.** a greeting card or gift sent on this day

**val·et** (val′it, -ā) *n.* [Fr., a groom] **1.** a personal manservant who takes care of a man's clothes, helps him dress, etc. **2.** an employee, as of a hotel, who cleans or presses clothes, etc.

**Val·hal·la** (val hal′ə) *Norse Myth.* the great hall where Odin feasts the souls of heroes slain in battle

**val·iant** (val′yənt) *adj.* [< L. *valere*, be strong] brave; courageous —**val′iance** *n.* —**val′iant·ly** *adv.*

**val·id** (val′id) *adj.* [< L. *valere*, be strong] **1.** having legal force **2.** based on evidence or sound reasoning —**val′id·ly** *adv.* —**val′id·ness** *n.*

**val·i·date** (val′ə dāt′) *vt.* **-dat′ed, -dat′ing 1.** to make legally valid **2.** to prove to be valid

**va·lid·i·ty** (və lid′ə tē) *n.* the quality or fact of being valid in law or in argument, proof, etc.

**va·lise** (və lēs′) *n.* [Fr. < It. *valigia*] a piece of hand luggage

**Val·i·um** (val′ē əm) *a trademark for* a tranquilizing drug

**Val·kyr·ie** (val kir′ē, val′ki rē) *n. Norse Myth.* any of the maidens of Odin who conduct the souls of heroes slain in battle to Valhalla

**val·ley** (val′ē) *n., pl.* **-leys** [< L. *vallis*] **1.** low land lying between hills or mountains **2.** the land drained by a river system **3.** any valleylike dip

**Valley Forge** village in SE Pa.: scene of Washington's winter encampment (1777–78)

**val·or** (val′ər) *n.* [< L. *valere*, be strong] marked courage or bravery: Brit. sp. **valour** —**val′or·ous** *adj.*

**Val·pa·rai·so** (val′pə rā′zō, -rī′sō) seaport in C Chile: pop. 262,000

**val·u·a·ble** (val′yōō b′l, -yōō wə b′l) *adj.* **1.** *o)* having material value *b)* of great monetary value **2.** highly important, esteemed, etc. —*n.* an article of value: *usually used in pl.*

**val·u·a·tion** (val′yōō wā′shən) *n.* **1.** the determining of the value of anything **2.** determined or estimated value

**val·ue** (val'yōō) *n.* [< L. *valere*, be worth] **1.** the worth of a thing in money or goods **2.** estimated worth **3.** purchasing power **4.** that quality of a thing which makes it more or less desirable, useful, etc. **5.** a thing or quality having intrinsic worth **6.** [*pl.*] beliefs or standards **7.** relative duration, intensity, etc. —*vt.* **-ued, -u·ing 1.** to estimate the value of; appraise **2.** to place an estimate of worth on [to *value* health above wealth] **3.** to think highly of —**val'ue·less** *adj.*

**val'ue-add'ed tax** a tax based and paid on the value added at each stage of production and distribution, and included in the cost to the consumer

**val'ued** *adj.* highly thought of

**valve** (valv) *n.* [< L. *valva*, leaf of a folding door] **1.** *Anat.* a membranous structure which permits body fluids to flow in one direction only, or opens and closes a tube, etc. **2.** any device in a pipe, etc. that regulates the flow by means of a flap, lid, etc. **3.** *Music* a device, as in the trumpet, that changes the tube length so as to change the pitch **4.** *Zoology* one of the parts making up the shell of a mollusk, clam, etc. **5.** *Brit.* term for ELECTRON TUBE

VALVE

**va·moose** (va mōōs') *vi.* **-moosed', -moos'ing** [Sp. *vamos*, let us go] [Old Slang] to leave quickly

**vamp** (vamp) *n.* [< OFr. *avant*, before + *pié*, a foot] **1.** the part of a boot or shoe covering the instep **2.** *Music* a simple, short improvisation, as by a dance band —*vt.* **1.** to put a vamp on **2.** *Music* to improvise —*vi.* *Music* to play a vamp

**vam·pire** (vam'pīr) *n.* [< Slav.] **1.** in folklore, a reanimated corpse that sucks the blood of sleeping persons **2.** one who preys ruthlessly on others **3.** *clipped form of* VAMPIRE BAT

**vampire bat** a tropical American bat that lives on the blood of animals

**van¹** (van) *n.* *same as* VANGUARD

**van²** (van) *n.* [< CARAVAN] a large, closed truck or wagon

**va·na·di·um** (və nā'dē əm) *n.* [< ON. *Vanadis*, goddess of love] a ductile metallic element used in steel alloys, etc.

**Van Al·len (radiation) belt** (van al'ən) [< J. *Van Allen* (1914–  ), U.S. physicist] a broad belt of radiation encircling the earth at varying levels

**Van Bu·ren** (van byoor'ən), **Martin** 1782–1862; 8th president of the U.S. (1837–41)

**Van·cou·ver** (van kōō'vər) city in SW British Columbia, Canada: pop. 410,000

**Van·dal** (van'd'l) *n.* **1.** a member of a Germanic tribe that sacked Rome (455 A.D.) **2.** [v-] one who maliciously destroys works of art, public property, etc.

**van'dal·ize'** *vt.* **-ized', -iz'ing** to destroy or damage (property) maliciously —**van'dal·ism** *n.*

**Van·dyke (beard)** (van dīk') a closely trimmed, pointed beard

**vane** (vān) *n.* [< OE. *fana*, a flag] **1.** a free-swinging piece of metal, etc. that shows which way the wind is blowing; weather vane **2.** any of the flat pieces set around an axle and rotated about it by moving air, water, etc. or rotated to move the air or water

**van Gogh** (van gō'), **Vincent** 1853–90; Du. painter

**van·guard** (van'gärd') *n.* [< OFr. *avant*, before + *garde*, guard] **1.** the front part of an army in an advance **2.** the leading position or persons in a movement

**va·nil·la** (və nil'ə) *n.* [< Sp. *vaina*, pod] **1.** a climbing orchid with podlike capsules (**vanilla beans**) **2.** a flavoring made from these capsules

**van·ish** (van'ish) *vi.* [see EVANESCENT] **1.** to pass suddenly from sight; disappear **2.** to cease to exist

**van·i·ty** (van'ə tē) *n., pl.* **-ties** [< L. *vanus*, vain] **1.** anything vain or futile **2.** worthlessness; futility **3.** a being vain, or too proud of oneself **4.** a small table with a mirror, for use while putting on cosmetics, etc.

**vanity case** a woman's small traveling case for carrying cosmetics, toilet articles, etc.

**van·quish** (van'kwish, van'-) *vt.* [< L. *vincere*] to conquer or defeat

**van·tage** (van'tij) *n.* [see ADVANTAGE] **1.** a favorable position **2.** a position allowing a clear view or understanding: also **vantage point**

**vap·id** (vap'id) *adj.* [L. *vapidus*] tasteless; flavorless; dull —**va·pid·i·ty** (va pid'ə tē), **vap'id·ness** *n.*

**va·por** (vā'pər) *n.* [L.] **1.** *a)* visible particles of moisture floating in the air, as fog or steam *b)* smoke, fumes, etc. **2.** the gaseous form of any substance normally a liquid or solid Brit. sp. **vapour**

**va'por·ize'** (-pə rīz') *vt., vi.* **-ized', -iz'ing** to change into vapor —**va'por·i·za'tion** *n.* —**va'por·iz'er** *n.*

**va'por·ous** *adj.* **1.** forming or full of vapor **2.** like vapor

**vapor trail** *same as* CONTRAIL

**va·que·ro** (vä ker'ō) *n., pl.* **-ros** [Sp. < *vaca*, a cow] in the Southwest, a man who herds cattle; cowboy

**var. 1.** variant(s) **2.** various

**var·i·a·ble** (ver'ē ə b'l) *adj.* **1.** apt to change or vary; changeable, inconstant, etc. **2.** that can be changed or varied —*n.* anything changeable; thing that varies —**var'i·a·bil'i·ty** *n.*

**var'i·ance** (-əns) *n.* **1.** a varying or being variant **2.** degree of change or difference; discrepancy —**at variance** not in agreement or accord

**var'i·ant** (-ənt) *adj.* varying; different in some way from others of the same kind —*n.* anything variant, as a different spelling of the same word

**var'i·a'tion** (-ā'shən) *n.* **1.** a varying; change in form, extent, etc. **2.** the degree of such change **3.** a thing somewhat different from another of the same kind **4.** *Music* the repetition of a theme with changes in rhythm, key, etc.

**var·i·col·ored** (ver′i kul′ərd) *adj.* of several or many colors

**var·i·cose** (var′ə kōs′) *adj.* [< L. *varix*, enlarged vein] abnormally and irregularly swollen [*varicose* veins]

**var·ied** (ver′ēd) *adj.* **1.** of different kinds; various **2.** changed; altered

**var′i·e·gat′ed** (-ē ə gāt′id) *adj.* [< L. *varius*, various] **1.** marked with different colors in spots, streaks, etc. **2.** having variety; varied

**va·ri·e·ty** (və rī′ə tē) *n., pl.* **-ties 1.** a being various or varied **2.** a different form of some thing, condition, etc.; kind [*varieties* of cloth] **3.** a collection of different things

**variety store** a retail store selling many small, inexpensive items

**var·i·ous** (ver′ē əs) *adj.* [L. *varius*, diverse] **1.** differing one from another; of several kinds **2.** several or many **3.** individual —**var′i·ous·ly** *adv.*

**var·let** (vär′lit) *n.* [OFr., a page] [Archaic] a scoundrel; knave

**var·mint, var·ment** (vär′mənt) *n.* [var. of VERMIN] [Dial.] a person or animal regarded as objectionable

**var·nish** (vär′nish) *n.* [< ML. *veronix*, resin] **1.** a preparation of resinous substances dissolved in oil, alcohol, etc., used to give a glossy surface to wood, metal, etc. **2.** this smooth, glossy surface **3.** a surface smoothness, as of manner —*vt.* **1.** to cover with varnish **2.** to make superficially attractive

**var·si·ty** (vär′sə tē) *n., pl.* **-ties** [< UNIVERSITY] the main team representing a university, school, etc., as in a sport

**var·y** (ver′ē) *vt.* **-ied, -y·ing** [< L. *varius*, various] **1.** to change; alter **2.** to make different from one another **3.** to give variety to [*vary* your reading] —*vi.* **1.** to undergo change **2.** to be different **3.** to deviate, diverge, or depart (*from*)

**vas·cu·lar** (vas′kyə lər) *adj.* [< L. *vas*, vessel] of or having vessels or ducts for conveying blood, sap, etc.

**vase** (vās, vāz) *n.* [< L. *vas*, vessel] an open container used for decoration, displaying flowers, etc.

**vas·ec·to·my** (vas ek′tə mē) *n., pl.* **-mies** [< L. *vas*, vessel + -ECTOMY] surgical removal of all, or esp. part, of the ducts carrying sperm from the testicles

**Vas·e·line** (vas′ə lēn′) [< G. *wasser*, water + Gr. *elaion*, oil] a trademark for petrolatum —*n.* [v-] petrolatum

**vas·o·mo·tor** (vas′ō mōt′ər) *adj.* [< L. *vas*, vessel + MOTOR] regulating the size in diameter of blood vessels: said of a nerve, drug, etc.

**vas·sal** (vas′'l) *n.* [< ML. *vassus*, servant] **1.** in the Middle Ages, one who held land under the feudal system, pledging fealty to an overlord **2.** a subordinate, servant, slave, etc. — **vas′sal·age** (-ij) *n.*

**vast** (vast) *adj.* [L. *vastus*] very great

in size, extent, number, degree, etc. —**vast′ly** *adv.* —**vast′ness** *n.*

**vat** (vat) *n.* [< OE. *fæt*, cask] a large tank, tub, or cask for liquids

**vat·ic** (vat′ik) *adj.* [< L. *vates*, prophet] prophetic

**Vat·i·can City** (vat′i k'n) papal state, an enclave in Rome, including the papal palace (**the Vatican**): 108 acres

**vaude·ville** (vôd′vil, vôd′-; -ə vil) *n.* [Fr. < *Vau-de-Vire*, a valley in Normandy, famous for convivial songs] a stage show consisting of various acts of songs, dances, skits, etc.

**vault**[1] (vôlt) *n.* [< L. *volvere*, to roll] **1.** an arched roof or ceiling **2.** an arched chamber or space **3.** a cellar room used for storage **4.** a burial chamber **5.** a room for the safekeeping of valuables, as in a bank —*vt.* to cover with, or build as, a vault —*vi.* to curve like a vault

VAULT

**vault**[2] (vôlt) *vi., vt.* [< OIt. *voltare*] to jump, leap, etc.; esp., to leap over (a barrier) with the hands supported on the barrier, or holding a long pole —*n.* a vaulting —**vault′er** *n.*

**vault′ing** *adj.* **1.** leaping **2.** unduly confident [*vaulting* ambition]

**vaunt** (vônt) *vt., n.* [< L. *vanus*, vain] boast —**vaunt′ed** *adj.*

**VD, V.D.** venereal disease

**veal** (vēl) *n.* [< L. *vitulus*, a calf] the flesh of a young calf used as food

**vec·tor** (vek′tər) *n.* [< L. *vehere*, to carry] any animal that transmits a disease-producing organism

**Ve·da** (vā′də, vē′-) *n.* [Sans. *veda*, knowledge] any of the four ancient sacred books of Hinduism —**Ve′dic** *adj.*

**Veep** (vēp) *n.* [also v-] vice-president

**veer** (vir) *vi., vt.* [< Fr. *virer*, turn around] to change in direction; shift; turn —*n.* a change of direction

**veg·e·ta·ble** (vej′tə b'l, vej′ə tə-) *adj.* [see VEGETATE] **1.** of plants in general **2.** of, from, or like edible vegetables —*n.* **1.** any plant, as distinguished from animal or inorganic matter **2.** a plant eaten whole or in part as with an entree or in a salad, as the tomato, potato, lettuce, etc.

**veg′e·tar′i·an** (-ə ter′ē ən) *n.* one who eats no meat —*adj.* **1.** of vegetarians **2.** consisting only of vegetables

**veg·e·tate** (vej′ə tāt′) *vi.* **-tat′ed, -tat′ing** [< L. *vegere*, quicken] **1.** to grow as plants **2.** to lead a dull, inactive life —**veg′e·ta′tive** *adj.*

**veg′e·ta′tion** *n.* **1.** a vegetating **2.** plant life in general

**ve·he·ment** (vē′ə mənt) *adj.* [< L. *vehere*, carry] **1.** violent; impetuous **2.** full of intense feeling or strong passion —**ve′he·mence, ve′he·men·cy** *n.* —**ve′he·ment·ly** *adv.*

**ve·hi·cle** (vē′ə k'l) *n.* [< L. *vehere*, carry] **1.** any device for carrying or conveying persons or objects **2.** a

means of communicating thoughts, etc.
—ve·hic′u·lar (-hik′yoo lər) *adj.*

veil (vāl) *n.* [ < L. *velum,* cloth] 1. a piece of light fabric, as of net, worn, esp. by women, over the face or head 2. anything used to conceal, cover, separate, etc. [a *veil* of silence] 3. a part of a nun's headdress —*vt.* 1. to cover with a veil 2. to hide or disguise —**take the veil** to become a nun

veiled (vāld) *adj.* 1. wearing, or covered with, a veil 2. concealed, hidden, etc. 3. not openly expressed

vein (vān) *n.* [ < L. *vena*] 1. any blood vessel carrying blood to the heart 2. any of the ribs of an insect's wing or of a leaf blade 3. a body of minerals occupying a fissure in rock 4. a lode 5. a streak of a different color, etc., as in marble 6. a distinctive quality in one's character, speech, etc. 7. a mood —*vt.* to mark as with veins

Vel·cro (vel′krō) *a trademark for* a nylon material for fastenings, made up of matching strips with tiny hooks and adhesive pile, that are easily pressed together or pulled apart

veld, veldt (velt) *n.* [Afrik. < MDu. *veld,* field] in S. Africa, open grassy country with few bushes or trees

vel·lum (vel′əm) *n.* [ < L. *vitulus,* calf] 1. a fine parchment prepared from calfskin, lambskin, etc. used for writing on or for binding books 2. a strong paper made to resemble this

ve·loc·i·ty (və läs′ə tē) *n., pl.* -ties [ < L. *velox,* swift] 1. quickness of motion; swiftness 2. rate of motion

ve·lour, ve·lours (və loor′) *n., pl.* -lours′ [Fr.: see VELURE] a fabric with a soft nap like velvet

ve·lum (vē′ləm) *n., pl.* -la (-lə) [L., a veil] the soft, fleshy, rear part of the palate —ve′lar (-lər) *adj.*

ve·lure (və loor′) *n.* [LL. *villosus,* shaggy] velvet or a fabric like velvet

vel·vet (vel′vit) *n.* [see prec.] 1. a rich fabric of silk, rayon, etc. with a soft, thick pile 2. anything like velvet in texture —*adj.* 1. made of velvet 2. like velvet —vel′vet·y *adj.*

vel′vet·een′ (-və tēn′) *n.* a cotton cloth with a short, thick pile like velvet

ve·nal (vē′n'l) *adj.* [ < L. *venus,* sale] open to, or characterized by, corruption or bribery —ve·nal′i·ty(-nal′ə tē) *n.* —ve′nal·ly *adv.*

vend (vend) *vt., vi.* [ < L. *venum dare,* offer for sale] to sell (goods) —ven′dor, vend′er *n.*

ven·det·ta (ven det′ə) *n.* [It. < L. *vindicta,* vengeance] a family feud

vending machine a coin-operated machine for selling certain small articles

ve·neer (və nir′) *vt.* [ < Fr. *fournir,* furnish] to cover with a thin layer of more costly material; esp., to cover (wood) with wood of a finer quality —*n.* 1. a thin surface layer, as of fine wood, laid over a base of common material 2. superficial appearance [a *veneer* of culture]

ven·er·a·ble (ven′ər ə b'l) *adj.* worthy of respect or reverence because of age, dignity, etc. —ven′er·a·bil′i·ty *n.*

ven·er·ate (ven′ə rāt′) *vt.* -at′ed,

-at′ing [ < L. *venerari,* to worship] to look upon with feelings of deep respect; revere —ven′er·a′tion *n.*

ve·ne·re·al (və nir′ē əl) *adj.* [ < L. *venus,* love] 1. of sexual intercourse 2. transmitted by sexual intercourse [a *venereal* disease]

Ve·ne·tian (və nē′shən) *adj.* of Venice, its people, etc. —*n.* a native or inhabitant of Venice

Venetian blind [*also* v- b-] a window blind made of a number of thin slats that can be set at any angle

Ven·e·zue·la (ven′i zwā′lə) country in N S.America: 352,143 sq. mi.; pop. 9,686,000 —Ven′e·zue′lan *adj., n.*

venge·ance (ven′jəns) *n.* [ < L. *vindicare,* avenge] the return of an injury for an injury, as in retribution; revenge —**with a vengeance** 1. with great force or fury 2. excessively

venge·ful (venj′fəl) *adj.* seeking vengeance; vindictive —venge′ful·ly *adv.*

ve·ni·al (vē′nē əl, vēn′yəl) *adj.* [ < L. *venia,* grace] that may be forgiven; pardonable [a *venial* sin]

Ven·ice (ven′is) seaport in N Italy: pop. 364,000

ve·ni·re·man (və nī′rē mən) *n., pl.* -men [ < ML. *venire facias,* cause to come] one of a group of people from among whom a jury will be selected

ven·i·son (ven′i s'n, -z'n) *n.* [ < L. *venari,* to hunt] the flesh of a deer, used as food

ven·om (ven′əm) *n.* [ < L. *venenum,* a poison] 1. the poison secreted by some snakes, spiders, etc. 2. malice

ven′om·ous *adj.* 1. full of venom; poisonous 2. spiteful; malicious

ve·nous (vē′nəs) *adj.* [L. *venosus*] 1. of veins 2. designating blood carried in veins

vent¹ (vent) *n.* [ < L. *ventus,* wind] 1. a means of escaping; outlet 2. expression; release [giving *vent* to emotion] 3. a small opening to permit passage, as of a gas —*vt.* 1. to make a vent in or for 2. to give release to; let out

vent² (vent) *n.* [ < L. *findere,* to split] a vertical slit in a garment

ven·ti·late (ven′t'l āt′) *vt.* -lat′ed, -lat′ing [ < L. *ventus,* wind] 1. to circulate fresh air in (a room, etc.) 2. to provide with an opening for the escape of air, gas, etc. —ven′ti·la′tion *n.*

ven′ti·la′tor *n.* an opening or a device for replacing foul air

ven·tral (ven′trəl) *adj.* [ < L. *venter,* belly] of, near, or on the belly

ven·tri·cle (ven′tri k'l) *n.* [see prec.] either of the two lower chambers of the heart

ven·tril·o·quism (ven tril′ə kwiz′m) *n.* [ < L. *venter,* belly + *loqui,* speak] the art of speaking so that the voice seems to come from a source other than the speaker —ven·tril′o·quist *n.*

ven·ture (ven′chər) *n.* [see ADVENTURE] 1. a risky undertaking, as in business 2. something on which a risk is taken —*vt.* -tured, -tur·ing 1. to expose to danger or chance of loss 2. to express at the risk of criticism *[to venture* an opinion*]* —*vi.* to do or go at some risk

**ven′ture·some** (-səm) *adj.* 1. inclined to venture; daring 2. risky; hazardous Also **ven′tur·ous** (-chər əs)

**ven·ue** (ven′yōō, -ōō) *n.* [< OFr. *venir*, come] *Law* 1. the locality in which a cause of action or a crime occurs 2. the locality in which a jury is drawn and a case tried

**Ve·nus** (vē′nəs) *n.* 1. the Roman goddess of love and beauty 2. the most brilliant planet in the solar system: see PLANET

**Venus′ fly′trap′** a swamp plant of N.Carolina and S.Carolina with leaves snapping shut to trap insects

**Ve·nu·sian** (vi nōō′shən) *adj.* of the planet Venus —*n.* an imaginary inhabitant of Venus

**ve·ra·cious** (və rā′shəs) *adj.* [< L. *verus*, true] 1. habitually truthful; honest 2. true; accurate

**ve·rac·i·ty** (və ras′ə tē) *n.* 1. honesty 2. accuracy 3. truth

**ve·ran·da, ve·ran·dah** (və ran′də) *n.* [< Port. *varanda*, balcony] a long, open porch, usually roofed

**verb** (vurb) *n.* [< L. *verbum*, a word] a word expressing action, existence, or occurrence

**ver·bal** (vur′b'l) *adj.* 1. of, in, or by means of words 2. in speech; oral 3. of, having the nature of, or derived from a verb —**ver′bal·ly** *adv.*

**ver′bal·ize′** (-bə līz′) *vi.* -ized′, -iz′-ing to use words for communication —*vt.* to express in words

**verbal noun** *Gram.* a noun derived from a verb (Ex.: *swimming* is fun, to *err* is human)

**ver·ba·tim** (vər bāt′əm) *adv., adj.* [< L. *verbum*, a word] word for word

**ver·be·na** (vər bē′nə) *n.* [L., foliage] an ornamental plant with spikes or clusters of showy red, white, or purplish flowers

**ver·bi·age** (vur′bē ij) *n.* [Fr. < L. *verbum*, a word] an excess of words; wordiness

**ver·bose** (vər bōs′) *adj.* [< L. *verbum*, a word] using too many words; wordy —**ver·bos′i·ty** (-bäs′ə tē) *n.*

**ver·dant** (vur′d'nt) *adj.* [prob. VERD(URE) + -ANT] 1. green 2. covered with green vegetation

**Ver·di** (ver′dē), **Giu·sep·pe** (jōō zep′pe) 1813–1901; It. operatic composer

**ver·dict** (vur′dikt) *n.* [< L. *vere*, truly + *dicere*, say] 1. the formal finding of a jury 2. any decision or judgment

**ver·di·gris** (vur′di grēs′, -gris) *n.* [< MFr. *verd de Grece*, green of Greece] a greenish coating that forms on brass, bronze, or copper

**ver·dure** (vur′jər) *n.* [OFr. < *verd*, green] 1. the fresh green color of growing things 2. green vegetation

**verge¹** (vurj) *n.* [< L. *virga*, rod] the edge, brink, or margin (*of* something) —*vi.* verged, verg′ing to be on the verge; border (with *on* or *upon*)

**verge²** (vurj) *vi.* verged, verg′ing [L. *vergere*, to bend, turn] 1. to tend or incline (*to* or *toward*) 2. to change or pass gradually (*into*) [dawn *verging* into daylight]

**ver·i·fy** (ver′ə fī′) *vt.* -fied′, -fy′ing [< L. *verus*, true + *facere*, make] 1. to prove to be true by evidence, etc.; confirm 2. to test the accuracy of —**ver′i·fi′a·ble** *adj.* —**ver′i·fi·ca′tion** *n.*

**ver·i·ly** (ver′ə lē) *adv.* [Archaic] in very truth; truly

**ver·i·si·mil·i·tude** (ver′ə si mil′ə tōōd′, -tyōōd′) *n.* [< L. *verus*, true + *similis*, like] the appearance of being true or real

**ver·i·ta·ble** (ver′i tə b'l) *adj.* [< L. *veritas*, truth] true; actual

**ver·i·ty** (ver′ə tē) *n., pl.* -ties [< L. *verus*, true] 1. truth; reality 2. a principle, belief, etc. taken to be fundamentally true; a truth

**ver·mi·cel·li** (vur′mə sel′ē, -chel′ē) *n.* [It. < L. *vermis*, a worm] pasta like spaghetti, but in thinner strings

**ver·mi·form** (vur′mə fôrm′) *adj.* [< L. *vermis*, a worm + -FORM] shaped like a worm

**vermiform appendix** same as APPENDIX (sense 2)

**ver·mil·ion** (vər mil′yən) *n.* [< L. *vermis*, a worm] 1. a bright-red pigment 2. a bright red or scarlet —*adj.* of this color

**ver·min** (vur′min) *n., pl.* -min [< L. *vermis*, a worm] 1. any of various destructive insects or small animals, as lice, rats, etc. 2. a vile person

**Ver·mont** (vər mänt′) New England State of the U.S.: 9,609 sq. mi.; pop. 444,000; cap. Montpelier —**Ver·mont′er** *n.*

**ver·mouth** (vər mōōth′) *n.* [< G. *wermut*, wormwood] a fortified white wine flavored with herbs, used in cocktails and as an aperitif

**ver·nac·u·lar** (vər nak′yə lər) *adj.* [< L. *vernaculus*, native] 1. of, in, or using the native language of a place 2. native to a country —*n.* 1. the native language or dialect of a country or place 2. the common, everyday language of a people 3. the jargon of a profession or trade

**ver·nal** (vur′n'l) *adj.* [< L. *ver*, spring] 1. of or in the spring 2. springlike 3. youthful

**ver·ni·er** (vur′nē ər) *n.* [after P. *Vernier*, 17th-c. Fr. mathematician] a short scale sliding along a longer graduated instrument to indicate parts of divisions: also **vernier scale**

**Ver·sailles** (vər sī′) city in NC France, near Paris: pop. 95,000

**ver·sa·tile** (vur′sə t'l) *adj.* [< L. *vertere*, to turn] competent in many things —**ver′sa·til′i·ty** (-til′ə tē) *n.*

**verse** (vurs) *n.* [< L. *vertere*, to turn] 1. a single line of poetry 2. poetry 3. a particular form of poetry 4. a poem 5. a stanza 6. *Bible* any of the short divisions of a chapter

**versed** (vʉrst) *adj.* [ < L. *versari*, be busy] skilled or learned (*in* a subject)

**ver·si·fy** (vʉr′sə fī′) *vi.* **-fied′, -fy′ing** [ < L. *versus*, a verse + *facere*, make] to compose verses —*vt.* 1. to tell in verse 2. to put into verse form —**ver′si·fi·ca′tion** (-fi kā′shən) *n.* —**ver′si·fi′er** *n.*

**ver·sion** (vʉr′zhən) *n.* [see VERSE] 1. a translation, esp. of the Bible 2. an account showing one point of view 3. a particular form of something

**ver·sus** (vʉr′səs) *prep.* [ML. < L., toward] 1. against 2. in contrast with

**ver·te·bra** (vʉr′tə brə) *n., pl.* **-brae′** (-brē′), **-bras** [L. < *vertere*, to turn] any of the single bones of the spinal column —**ver′te·bral** *adj.*

**ver·te·brate** (-brit, -brāt′) *adj.* 1. having a backbone, or spinal column 2. of the vertebrates —*n.* any of a large division of animals having a spinal column, as mammals, birds, etc.

**ver·tex** (vʉr′teks) *n., pl.* **-tex·es, -ti·ces′** (-tə sēz′) [L.] 1. the highest point; top 2. *Geom.* the point of intersection of the two sides of an angle

**ver·ti·cal** (vʉr′ti k'l) *adj.* 1. of or at the vertex 2. upright; straight up and down —*n.* a vertical line, plane, etc. —**ver′ti·cal·ly** *adv.*

**ver·tig·i·nous** (vər tij′ə nəs) *adj.* of, having, or causing vertigo

**ver·ti·go** (vʉr′ti gō′) *n.* [L. < *vertere*, to turn] a sensation of dizziness

**verve** (vʉrv) *n.* [Fr. < OFr., manner of speech] vigor; energy; enthusiasm

**ver·y** (ver′ē) *adj.* [ < L. *verus*, true] 1. complete; absolute *[the very opposite]* 2. same *[the very hat I lost]* 3. being just what is needed 4. even *[the very rafters shook]* 5. actual *[caught in the very act]* —*adv.* 1. extremely 2. truly; really *[the very same man]*

**very high frequency** any radio frequency between 30 and 300 megahertz

**very low frequency** any radio frequency between 10 and 30 kilohertz

**ves·i·cle** (ves′i k'l) *n.* [ < L. *vesica*, bladder] a small membranous cavity, sac, or cyst —**ve·sic·u·lar** (və sik′yə lər), **ve·sic′u·late** (-lit) *adj.*

**ves·per** (ves′pər) *n.* [L., evening] [*usually pl.*] an evening prayer or service: also **Vespers**

**Ves·puc·ci** (ves pōōt′chē), **A·mer·i·go** (ä′me rē′gō) (L. name *Americus Vespucius*) 1451?-1512; It. navigator

**ves·sel** (ves′'l) *n.* [ < L. *vas*] 1. a utensil for holding something, as a bowl, kettle, etc. 2. a ship or boat 3. a tube or duct of the body, as a vein, containing or circulating a fluid

**vest** (vest) *n.* [ < L. *vestis*, garment] a short, sleeveless garment, esp. one worn under a suit coat by men —*vt.* 1. to dress, as in clerical robes 2. to place (authority, etc.) *in* someone 3. to put (a person) in control of, as power, etc. —*vi.* to become vested (*in* a person), as property

**ves·tal** (ves′t'l) *adj.* [ < L. *Vesta*, goddess of the hearth] chaste; pure —*n.* a virgin priestess of the Roman goddess Vesta: in full **vestal virgin**

**vest·ed** (ves′tid) *adj.* 1. clothed, esp. in vestments 2. *Law* fixed; settled; absolute *[vested right]*

**ves·ti·bule** (ves′tə byōōl′) *n.* [L. *vestibulum*] a small entrance hall, as to a building

**ves·tige** (ves′tij) *n.* [ < L. *vestigium*, footprint] 1. a trace, mark, or sign, esp. of something that has passed away 2. *Biol.* a degenerate part, more fully developed in an earlier stage —**ves·tig′i·al** (-tij′ē əl) *adj.*

**vest·ing** (ves′tiŋ) *n.* the retention by an employee of all or part of his pension rights, regardless of changes in employment, early retirement, etc.

**vest·ment** (vest′mənt) *n.* [ < L. *vestire*, clothe] a garment or robe, esp. one worn by a clergyman

**vest′pock′et** *adj.* very small, or unusually small for its kind

**ves·try** (ves′trē) *n., pl.* **-tries** [ < L. *vestis*, garment] 1. a room in a church, where vestments, etc. are kept 2. a room in a church, used as a chapel 3. a group of church members who manage temporal affairs —**ves′try·man** (-mən) *n., pl.* **-men**

**Ve·su·vi·us** (və sōō′vē əs) active volcano in S Italy, near Naples

**vet[1]** (vet) *n. clip for* VETERINARIAN

**vet[2]** (vet) *n. clip for* VETERAN

**vetch** (vech) *n.* [ < L. *vicia*] a plant of the legume family, grown for fodder

**vet·er·an** (vet′ər ən) *adj.* [ < L. *vetus*, old] 1. old and experienced 2. of veterans —*n.* 1. a person of ·long service in some position 2. one who has served in the armed forces

**Veterans Day** a legal holiday in the U.S. honoring all veterans of the armed forces: observed on Nov. 11 (Armistice Day), the anniversary of the armistice of World War I

**vet·er·i·nar·i·an** (vet′ər ə ner′ē ən) *n.* one who practices veterinary medicine or surgery

**vet′er·i·nar′y** (-ē) *adj.* [ < L. *veterina*, beasts of burden] designating or of the medical or surgical treatment of animals —*n., pl.* **-ies** a veterinarian

**ve·to** (vē′tō) *n., pl.* **-toes** [L., I forbid] 1. *a*) an order prohibiting some act *b*) the power to prohibit action 2. *a*) the right of one branch of a government to reject bills passed by another *b*) the exercise of this right —*vt.* **-toed, -to·ing** 1. to prevent (a bill) from becoming law by a veto 2. to forbid

**vex** (veks) *vt.* [ < L. *vexare*, agitate] 1. to disturb; annoy, esp. in a petty way 2. to distress; afflict

**vex·a·tion** (vek sā′shən) *n.* 1. a vexing or being vexed 2. something that vexes —**vex·a′tious** (-shəs) *adj.*

**VHF, vhf** very high frequency

**vi., v.i.** intransitive verb

**V.I., VI** Virgin Islands

**vi·a** (vī′ə, vē′ə) *prep.* [L., way] by way of

**vi·a·ble** (vī′ə b'l) *adj.* [ < L. *vita*, life] 1. sufficiently developed to be able to live outside the uterus 2. workable *[viable ideas]* —**vi′a·bil′i·ty** *n.*

**vi·a·duct** (vī′ə dukt′) *n.* [ < VIA + (AQUE)DUCT] a bridge consisting of a series of short spans, supported on piers or towers

**vi·al** (vī′əl) *n.* [ < Gr. *phialē*, PHIAL] a small vessel or bottle for containing medicines or other liquids

**vi·and** (vī′ənd) *n.* [ < L. *vivere*, live] an article of food

**vibes** (vībz) *n.pl.* **1.** [Colloq.] *same as* VIBRAPHONE **2.** [Slang] attractive or unattractive qualities in a person or thing, thought of as setting up vibrations that can be sensed

**vi·bra·harp** (vī′brə härp′) *n. same as* VIBRAPHONE

**vi·brant** (vī′brənt) *adj.* **1.** quivering or vibrating **2.** produced by vibration; resonant: said of sound **3.** vigorous, energetic —**vi′bran·cy** *n.* —**vi′brant·ly** *adv.*

**vi·bra·phone** (vī′brə fōn′) *n.* a musical instrument like the marimba, but with electrically operated valves in the resonant tubes

**vi·brate** (vī′brāt) *vt.* -brat·ed, -brat·ing [ < L. *vibrare*] to set in to-and-fro motion —*vi.* **1.** to swing back and forth; oscillate **2.** to move rapidly back and forth; quiver **3.** to resound **4.** to be emotionally stirred —**vi·bra′tion** *n.* —**vi′bra·tor** *n.*

**vi·bra·to** (vi brät′ō) *n., pl.* -tos [It.] a pulsating effect produced by rapid alternation of a given tone

**vic·ar** (vik′ər) *n.* [ < L. *vicis*, a change] **1.** *Anglican Ch.* a parish priest who receives a stipend instead of the tithes **2.** *R.C.Ch.* a priest or other deputy of a bishop —**vic′ar·age** *n.*

**vi·car·i·ous** (vī ker′ē əs) *adj.* [ < L. *vicis*, a change] **1.** taking the place of another **2.** endured or performed by one person in place of another **3.** shared in by imagined participation in another's experience [a *vicarious* thrill] —**vi·car′i·ous·ly** *adv.*

**vice¹** (vīs) *n.* [ < L. *vitium*] **1.** *a)* an evil action or habit *b)* evil conduct; depravity *c)* prostitution **2.** a trivial fault or failing

**vi·ce²** (vī′sē) *prep.* [L. < *vicis*, a change] in the place of

**vice-** [see prec.] a *prefix meaning* subordinate, deputy [*vice*-president]

**vice·ge·rent** (vīs′jir′ənt) *n.* [ < prec. + L. *gerere*, to direct] a deputy

**vice′-pres′i·dent** *n.* an executive assistant to a president, acting in his place during his absence: for the U.S. official, usually Vice President —**vice′-pres′i·den·cy** *n.*

**vice·roy** (vīs′roi) *n.* [MFr. < *vice-* (see VICE-) + *roy*, king] a person ruling a country, province, etc. as the deputy of a sovereign

**vi·ce ver·sa** (vī′sē vur′sə, vīs′ vur′sə) [L.] the relation being reversed

**vi·chy·ssoise** (vē′shē swäz′, vish′ē-) *n.* [Fr.] a cream soup of potatoes, onions, etc., usually served cold

**vic·i·nage** (vis′ə nij) *n.* neighborhood

**vi·cin·i·ty** (və sin′ə tē) *n., pl.* -ties [ < L. *vicus*, village] **1.** nearness;

proximity **2.** a nearby region; neighborhood

**vi·cious** (vish′əs) *adj.* [ < L. *vitium*, vice] **1.** characterized by vice; evil or depraved **2.** faulty; flawed **3.** unruly [a *vicious* horse] **4.** malicious; spiteful [a *vicious* rumor] **5.** very intense, forceful, etc. [a *vicious* blow] —**vi′cious·ly** *adv.* —**vi′cious·ness** *n.*

**vicious circle** a situation in which the solution to each problem gives rise to another, eventually bringing back the first problem

**vi·cis·si·tudes** (vi sis′ə tōōdz′) *n.pl.* [ < L. *vicis*, a turn] unpredictable changes in life, fortune, etc.; ups and downs

**vic·tim** (vik′təm) *n.* [L. *victima*] **1.** someone or something killed, destroyed, sacrificed, etc. **2.** one who suffers some loss, esp. by being swindled

**vic′tim·ize′** (-tə mīz′) *vt.* -ized′, -iz′ing to make a victim of

**vic·tor** (vik′tər) *n.* [L. < *vincere*, conquer] a winner or conqueror

**Vic·to·ri·a** (vik tôr′ē ə) 1819–1901; queen of England (1837–1901)

**Vic·to′ri·an** *adj.* **1.** of or characteristic of the time of Queen Victoria **2.** showing the respectability, prudery, etc. attributed to the Victorians —*n.* a person of that time

**vic·to·ri·ous** (vik tôr′ē əs) *adj.* **1.** having won a victory; triumphant **2.** of or bringing about victory

**vic·to·ry** (vik′tər ē, -trē) *n., pl.* -ries [ < L. *vincere*, conquer] **1.** final supremacy in battle or war **2.** success in any struggle

**vict·uals** (vit′lz) *n.pl.* [ < L. *victus*, food] [Dial. or Colloq.] articles of food

**vi·cu·ña** (vī kōōn′yə, -ə) *n.* [Sp.] **1.** a S.American animal related to the llama **2.** its soft, shaggy wool

**‡vi·de** (vī′dē) [L.] see; refer to [a certain page, etc.]: abbrev. v., **vid.**

**vid·e·o** (vid′ē ō) *adj.* [L., I see] of television, esp. of the picture portion of a telecast —*n.* television

VICUNA

**vid′e·o·disc′** (-disk′) *n.* a disc on which images and sounds, as of a movie, can be recorded for reproduction on a home TV set: also **video disc**

**video game** an electronic device for producing images on a TV screen, controlled by players of various games

**vid′e·o·phone′** *n.* a telephone combined with television so that users can see, as well as speak with, one another

**video tape** a magnetic tape on which the electronic impulses of a TV program can be recorded

**vie** (vī) *vi.* vied, vy′ing [ < L. *invitare*, invite] to struggle for superiority (*with* someone); compete

**Vi·en·na** (vē en'ə) capital of Austria: pop. 1,628,000 —**Vi·en·nese** (vē'ə nēz') adj., n., pl. **-nese'**

**Vi·et·nam** (vē'ət näm') country on the E coast of Indochina: 129,607 sq. mi.; pop. 43,752,000 —**Vi·et·nam·ese'** (-nə mēz'), adj., n., pl. **-ese'**

**view** (vyōō) n. [< L. videre, to see] 1. a seeing or looking, as in inspection 2. range of vision 3. mental survey [a correct view of a situation] 4. a) a scene or prospect [a room with a view] b) a picture of such a scene 5. manner of regarding something; opinion —vt. 1. to inspect; scrutinize 2. to see; behold 3. to survey mentally; consider —**in view** 1. in sight 2. under consideration 3. as a goal or hope —**in view of** because of —**on view** displayed publicly —**with a view to** with the purpose or hope of

**view'er** n. 1. a person who views something 2. an optical device for individual viewing of slides

**view'find'er** n. same as FINDER (sense 2)

**view'point'** n. the mental position from which things are viewed and judged; point of view

**vig·il** (vij'əl) n. [< L., awake] 1. a) a watchful staying awake b) a watch kept 2. the eve of a church festival

**vig·i·lant** (vij'ə lənt) adj. [< L. vigil, awake] staying watchful or alert to danger or trouble —**vig'i·lance** n.

**vig·i·lan·te** (vij'ə lan'tē) n. [Sp., watchman] one of an unauthorized group organized professedly to keep order and punish crime —**vig'i·lan·tism** n. —**vig'i·lan'tist** adj.

**vi·gnette** (vin yet') n. [Fr. < vigne, vine] 1. an ornamental design used as a border, inset, etc. on a page 2. a picture shading off gradually at the edges 3. a short, delicate literary sketch —**vi·gnet'tist** n.

**vig·or** (vig'ər) n. [L. < vigere, be strong] active force or strength; vitality; energy: Brit. **vigour** —**vig'or·ous** adj. —**vig'or·ous·ly** adv.

**vik·ing** (vī'kiŋ) n. [ON. vikingr] [also V-] any of the Scandinavian pirates of the 8th to 10th centuries

**vile** (vīl) adj. [< L. vilis, cheap, base] 1. morally evil; wicked 2. repulsive; disgusting 3. degrading; mean 4. highly disagreeable; very bad [vile weather] —**vile'ness** n.

**vil·i·fy** (vil'ə fī') vt. **-fied', -fy'ing** [see prec. & -FY] to use abusive language about or of; defame —**vil'i·fi·ca'tion** n.

**vil·la** (vil'ə) n. [It. < L., a farm] a country house or estate, esp. a large one used as a retreat

**vil·lage** (vil'ij) n. [see prec.] 1. a community smaller than a town 2. the people of a village, collectively —**vil'lag·er** n.

**vil·lain** (vil'ən) n. [< VL. villanus, a farm servant] a wicked or evil person, or such a character in a play, etc. —**vil'lain·ous** adj.

**vil'lain·y** n., pl. **-ies** 1. wickedness; evil 2. a villainous act

**vil·lein** (vil'ən) n. [see VILLAIN] an English serf in the late Middle Ages who was a freeman in some ways

**vim** (vim) n. [prob. echoic] vigor

**vin** (van; Anglicized vin) n. [Fr.] wine

**Vin·ci** (vin'chē), **Le·o·nar·do da** (lē'ə när'dō də) 1452–1519; It. painter, sculptor, & scientist

**vin·di·cate** (vin'də kāt') vt. **-cat'ed, -cat'ing** [< L. vis, force + dicere, say] 1. to clear from criticism, blame, etc. 2. to defend against opposition 3. to justify —**vin'di·ca'tion** n. —**vin'di·ca'tor** n.

**vin·dic·tive** (vin dik'tiv) adj. [see prec.] 1. revengeful in spirit 2. said or done in revenge —**vin·dic'tive·ly** adv. —**vin·dic'tive·ness** n.

**vine** (vīn) n. [< L. vinum, wine] 1. a plant with a long, thin stem that grows along the ground or climbs a support 2. the stem of such a plant 3. a grapevine

**vin·e·gar** (vin'i gər) n. [< MFr. < vin, wine + aigre, sour] a sour liquid made by fermenting cider, wine, etc. and used as a condiment and preservative —**vin'e·gar·y** adj.

**vine·yard** (vin'yərd) n. land devoted to cultivating grapevines

**vi·no** (vē'nō) n. [It. & Sp.] wine

**vin rosé** [Fr.] same as ROSÉ

**vin·tage** (vin'tij) n. [< L. vinum, wine + demere, remove] 1. the crop of grapes of a single season 2. the wine of a particular region and year 3. an earlier model [a car of prewar vintage] —adj. 1. of choice vintage [vintage wine] 2. representative of the best [vintage short stories] 3. of a past period [vintage clothes]

**vint·ner** (vint'nər) n. [< ME. < L. vinum, wine] a wine merchant

**vi·nyl** (vī'n'l) n. [< L. vinum, wine] any of various compounds polymerized to form resins and plastics (**vinyl plastics**)

**vi·ol** (vī'əl) n. [< OPr. viula < ?] any of an early family of stringed instruments, usually having six strings, frets, and a flat back

**vi·o·la** (vē ō'lə, vī-) n. [It.] a stringed instrument of the violin family, slightly larger than a violin

**vi·o·la·ble** (vī'ə lə b'l) adj. that can be, or is likely to be, violated

**vi·o·late** (vī'ə lāt') vt. **-lat'ed, -lat'ing** [< L. violare, use violence] 1. to break (a law, promise, etc.) 2. to rape 3. to desecrate (something sacred) 4. to break in upon; disturb —**vi'o·la'tor** n.

**vi'o·la'tion** (-lā'shən) n. a violating or being violated; specif., a) infringement, as of a law b) rape c) desecration of something sacred d) disturbance

**vi·o·lence** (-ləns) n. [< L. violentus, violent] 1. physical force used so as to injure 2. powerful force, as of a hurricane 3. a violent act or deed 4. harm done by violating rights, etc.

**vi·o·lent** adj. 1. acting with or having great physical force 2. caused by violence 3. furious [violent language] 4. intense; extreme; very strong [a violent storm] —**vi'o·lent·ly** adv.

**vi·o·let** (vī′ə lit) *n.* [< L. *viola*] **1.** a plant with white, blue, purple, or yellow flowers **2.** a bluish-purple color —*adj.* bluish-purple

**vi·o·lin** (vī′ə lin′) *n.* [< It. *viola*, viol] any instrument of the modern family of four-stringed instruments played with a bow; specif., the smallest and highest pitched instrument of this family —**vi′o·lin′ist** *n.*

**vi·ol·ist** (vī′əl ist; *for 2* vē ō′list) *n.* **1.** a viol player **2.** a viola player

**vi·o·lon·cel·lo** (vē′ə län chel′ō, vī′ə lən-) *n., pl.* **-los** same as CELLO

**VIP, V.I.P.** [Colloq.] very important person

**vi·per** (vī′pər) *n.* [OFr. < L.] **1.** a venomous snake **2.** a malicious or treacherous person —**vi′per·ous** *adj.*

**vi·ra·go** (vi rä′gō, vī rā′-) *n., pl.* **-goes, -gos** [< L. *vir*, a man] a quarrelsome, shrewish woman; scold

**vi·ral** (vī′rəl) *adj.* of, involving, or caused by a virus

**vir·e·o** (vir′ē ō′) *n., pl.* **-os′** [L.] a small American songbird, with olive-green or gray plumage

**Vir·gil** (vur′jəl) 70–19 B.C.: Rom. poet; wrote the *Aeneid*: also **Vergil**

**vir·gin** (vur′jin) *n.* [< L. *virgo*, a maiden] a person, esp. a young woman, who has never had sexual intercourse —*adj.* **1.** being a virgin **2.** chaste; modest **3.** untouched, unused, pure, etc. —**the Virgin** Mary, the mother of Jesus

**vir′gi·nal** *adj.* same as VIRGIN

**Vir·gin·ia** (vər jin′yə) Southern State of the U.S.: 40,815 sq. mi.; pop. 4,648,000; cap. Richmond —**Vir·gin′ian** *adj., n.*

**Virginia creeper** same as WOODBINE (sense 2)

**Virginia reel** an American reel danced by couples facing in two lines

**Virgin Islands** group of islands in the West Indies, divided between those forming a Brit. colony & those constituting a U.S. territory

**vir·gin·i·ty** (vər jin′ə tē) *n.* a virgin state; maidenhood, chastity, etc.

**Virgin Mary** the mother of Jesus

**Vir·go** (vur′gō) [L., virgin] the sixth sign of the zodiac

**vir·gule** (vur′gyōōl) *n.* [< L. *virgula*, small rod] a diagonal line (/) used in dates or fractions (3/8) and also standing for "or" (and/or), "per" (feet/second), etc.

**vir·ile** (vir′əl) *adj.* [< L. *vir*, a man] **1.** of or characteristic of a man; masculine **2.** having manly strength or vigor **3.** capable of copulation —**vi·ril·i·ty** (vi ril′ə tē) *n.*

**vi·rol·o·gy** (vī räl′ə jē) *n.* [< VIR(US) + -LOGY] the study of viruses and virus diseases —**vi·rol′o·gist** *n.*

**vir·tu·al** (vur′choo wəl) *adj.* being so in effect, although not in actual fact or name —**vir′tu·al·ly** *adv.*

**vir·tue** (vur′choo) *n.* [< L. *virtus*, manliness, worth] **1.** general moral excellence **2.** a specific moral quality regarded as good **3.** chastity **4.** *a)* excellence in general *b)* a good quality **5.** efficacy, as of a medicine —**by (or in)** virtue of because of

**vir·tu·o·so** (vur′choo wō′sō) *n., pl.* **-sos, -si** (-sē) [It., skilled] a person with great technical skill in some fine art, esp. in playing music —**vir′tu·os′i·ty** (-wäs′ə tē) *n.*

**vir·tu·ous** (vur′choo wəs) *adj.* **1.** having, or characterized by, moral virtue **2.** chaste: said of a woman —**vir′tu·ous·ly** *adv.* —**vir′tu·ous·ness** *n.*

**vir·u·lent** (vir′yoo lənt, -oo-) *adj.* [see ff.] **1.** *a)* extremely poisonous; deadly *b)* bitterly antagonistic; full of hate **2.** *Med.* *a)* violent and rapid in its course: said of a disease *b)* highly infectious —**vir′u·lence** *n.*

**vi·rus** (vī′rəs) *n.* [L., a poison] **1.** any of a group of very small infective agents that cause various diseases, as measles **2.** a harmful influence

**vi·sa** (vē′zə) *n.* [< L. *videre*, see] an endorsement on a passport, granting entry into a country

**vis·age** (viz′ij) *n.* [see prec.] **1.** the face; countenance **2.** aspect; look

**vis-à-vis** (vē′zə vē′) *adj., adv.* [Fr.] face to face; opposite —*prep.* **1.** opposite to **2.** in relation to

**vis·cer·a** (vis′ər ə) *n.pl., sing.* **vis′cus** (-kəs) [L.] the internal organs of the body, as the heart, lungs, intestines, etc.

**vis′cer·al** *adj.* **1.** of the viscera **2.** intuitive, emotional, etc. rather than intellectual

**vis·cid** (vis′id) *adj.* [< L. *viscum*, birdlime] thick, syrupy, and sticky

**vis·cose** (vis′kōs) *n.* [see VISCOUS] a syruplike solution of cellulose, used in making rayon, cellophane, etc.

**vis·cos·i·ty** (vis käs′ə tē) *n., pl.* **-ties** **1.** a viscous quality **2.** *Physics* the resistance of a fluid to flowing freely, caused by friction of its molecules

**vis·count** (vī′kount) *n.* [see VICE- & COUNT²] a nobleman next below an earl or count and above a baron —**vis′count·ess** *n.fem.*

**vis·cous** (vis′kəs) *adj.* [see VISCID] **1.** thick, syrupy, and sticky. **2.** *Physics* having viscosity

**vise** (vīs) *n.* [< L. *vitis*, vine, lit., that which winds] a device having two jaws opened and closed as by a screw, used for holding firmly an object being worked on

**VISE**

**Vish·nu** (vish′nōō) the second member of the Hindu trinity (Brahma, Vishnu, and Siva), called "the Preserver"

**vis·i·bil·i·ty** (viz′ə bil′ə tē) n., pl. **-ties** 1. a being visible 2. a) the relative possibility of being seen under the prevailing conditions of distance, light, etc. b) range of vision

**vis·i·ble** (viz′ə b'l) adj. [< L. videre, to see] 1. that can be seen 2. evident —**vis′i·bly** adv.

**vi·sion** (vizh′ən) n. [< L. videre, to see] 1. the power of seeing 2. something supposedly seen in a dream, trance, etc. 3. a mental image 4. the ability to foresee something as through mental acuteness 5. something or someone of great beauty

**vi′sion·ar·y** (-er′ē) adj. 1. seen in a vision 2. not realistic; impractical [visionary schemes] —n., pl. **-ies** 1. one who sees visions 2. one whose ideas, etc. are impractical

**vis·it** (viz′it) vt. [< L. videre, to see] 1. to go or come to see 2. to stay with as a guest 3. to afflict or trouble —vi. 1. to make a visit, esp. a social call 2. [Colloq.] to chat —n. a visiting; specif., a) a social call b) a stay as a guest

**vis′it·ant** (-ənt) n. a visitor

**vis·it·a′tion** (-ə tā′shən) n. 1. an official visit as to inspect 2. a reward or punishment, as sent by God

**vis′i·tor** n. a person making a visit

**vi·sor** (vī′zər) n. [< OFr. vis, a face] 1. the movable part of a helmet, covering the face 2. a projecting brim, as on a cap, for shading the eyes

**vis·ta** (vis′tə) n. [< L. videre, to see] 1. a view, esp. as seen through a long passage 2. a mental view of events

**vis·u·al** (vizh′oo wəl) adj. [< L. videre, to see] 1. of or used in seeing 2. based on the use of sight 3. that can be seen; visible

**vis′u·al·ize′** vt., vi. **-ized′, -iz′ing** to form a mental image of (something not present to the sight) —**vis′u·al·i·za′tion** n.

**vi·tal** (vīt′'l) adj. [< L. vita, life] 1. of or concerned with life 2. essential to life 3. fatal 4. a) essential; indispensable b) very important 5. full of life; energetic —n. [pl.] 1. the vital organs, as heart, brain, etc. 2. any essential parts —**vi′tal·ly** adv.

**vital capacity** the volume of air one can forcibly expel from the lungs after taking a full breath

**vi·tal·i·ty** (vī tal′ə tē) n., pl. **-ties** 1. power to live 2. power to endure 3. mental or physical vigor

**vi·tal·ize** (vīt′'l īz′) vt. **-ized′, -iz′ing** to make vital; give life or vigor to

**vital signs** the pulse, respiration, and body temperature

**vital statistics** data on births, deaths, marriages, etc.

**vi·ta·min** (vīt′ə min) n. [< L. vita, life] any of certain complex substances found variously in foods and essential to good health: some of the important vitamins are: —**vitamin A**, a fat-soluble alcohol found in fish-liver oil, egg yolk, carrots, etc.: a deficiency of this results in imperfect vision in the dark —**vitamin B (complex)** a group of unrelated water-soluble substances including a) **vitamin B₁** (see THIA-

MINE) b) **vitamin B₂** (see RIBOFLAVIN) c) NICOTINIC ACID d) **vitamin B₁₂** a vitamin containing cobalt, used in treating anemia —**vitamin C** a compound occurring in citrus fruits, tomatoes, etc.: a deficiency of this produces scurvy —**vitamin D** any of several fat-soluble vitamins found esp. in fish-liver oils, milk, etc.: a deficiency of this produces rickets —**vitamin E** a substance occurring in wheat germ, etc., vital to the reproductive processes in some animals —**vitamin K** a substance occurring in green vegetables, fish meal, etc., that clots blood

**vi·ti·ate** (vish′ē āt′) vt. **-at′ed, -at′ing** [< L. vitium, a vice] 1. to spoil; corrupt; pervert 2. to invalidate (a contract, etc.) —**vi′ti·a′tion** n.

**vit·i·cul·ture** (vit′ə kul′chər) n. [< L. vitis, vine] cultivation of grapes

**vit·re·ous** (vit′rē əs) adj. [< L. vitrum, glass] 1. of or like glass 2. derived from or made of glass

**vitreous humor** the transparent, jellylike substance filling the eyeball between the retina and the lens

**vit·ri·fy** (vit′rə fī′) vt., vi. **-fied′, -fy′ing** [< L. vitrum, glass + Fr. -fier, -FY] to change into glass or a glasslike substance by heat

**vit·rine** (vi trēn′) n. [see VITREOUS] a glass or glass-paneled display case

**vit·ri·ol** (vit′rē əl) n. [< L. vitreus, glassy] 1. any of several sulfates of metals, as of copper (blue vitriol), or iron (green vitriol) 2. same as SULFURIC ACID 3. sharp or bitter speech, etc. —**vit′ri·ol′ic** (-äl′ik) adj.

**vi·tu·per·ate** (vī too′pə rāt′, vi-) vt. **-at′ed, -at′ing** [< L. vitium, fault + parare, prepare] to speak abusively to or about —**vi·tu′per·a′tion** n. —**vi·tu′per·a′tive** adj.

**†vi·va** (vē′vä) interj. [It., Sp.] (long) live (someone specified)!

**vi·va·ce** (vi vä′chä) adj., adv. [It.] Music in a lively, spirited manner

**vi·va·cious** (vi vā′shəs, vī-) adj. [< L. vivere, to live] full of animation; lively —**vi·va′cious·ly** adv. —**vi·vac′i·ty** (-vas′ə tē), **vi·va′cious·ness** n.

**†vive** (vēv) interj. [Fr.] (long) live (someone specified)!

**viv·id** (viv′id) adj. [< L. vivere, to live] 1. full of life; vigorous 2. bright; intense, as colors 3. strong and clear; active [a vivid imagination] —**viv′id·ly** adv. —**viv′id·ness** n.

**viv·i·fy** (viv′ə fī′) vt. **-fied′, -fy′ing** [< L. vivus, alive + facere, make] to give life to; animate

**vi·vip·a·rous** (vī vip′ər əs) adj. [< L. vivus, alive + parere, produce] bearing living young instead of laying eggs

**viv·i·sec·tion** (viv′ə sek′shən) n. [< L. vivus, alive + SECTION] surgery performed on a living animal in medical research —**viv′i·sect′** vt., vi. —**viv′i·sec′tion·ist** n.

**vix·en** (vik′s'n) n. [OE. fyxe] 1. a female fox 2. an ill-tempered, shrewish, or malicious woman —**vix′en·ish** adj. —**vix′en·ish·ly** adv.

**viz., viz** (viz) [< L. videlicet] that is; namely

**vi·zier, vi·zir** (vi zir′) *n.* [< Ar. *wazara*, bear a burden] in Moslem countries, a high government official

**viz·or** (vī′zər) *n. alt. sp. of* VISOR

**VLF, vlf** very low frequency

**vo·cab·u·lar·y** (vō kab′yə ler′ē) *n., pl.* **-ies** [ult. < L. *vocare*, to call] 1. a list of words, etc., as in a dictionary or glossary 2. all the words used in a language or by a person, class, etc.

**vo·cal** (vō′k'l) *adj.* [< L. *vox*, a voice] 1. of or produced by the voice 2. sung 3. capable of making oral sounds 4. speaking freely —**vo′cal·ly** *adv.*

**vocal cords** membranous folds in the larynx that vibrate to produce voice

**vo·cal·ic** (vō kal′ik) *adj.* of, like, or involving a vowel or vowels

**vo′cal·ist** *n.* a singer

**vo′cal·ize′** (-īz′) *vt., vi.* **-ized′, -iz′ing** to utter, speak, or sing

**vo·ca·tion** (vō kā′shən) *n.* [< L. *vocare*, to call] 1. the career to which one feels he is called 2. any occupation —**vo·ca′tion·al** *adj.*

**voc·a·tive** (väk′ə tiv) *adj.* [see prec.] *Gram.* designating the case indicating the one addressed

**vo·cif·er·ate** (vō sif′ə rāt′) *vt., vi.* **-at′ed, -at′ing** [< L. *vox*, voice + *ferre*, to bear] to shout loudly; clamor —**vo·cif′er·a′tion** *n.*

**vo·cif·er·ous** (vō sif′ər əs) *adj.* noisy; clamorous —**vo·cif′er·ous·ly** *adv.*

**vod·ka** (väd′kə) *n.* [Russ. < *voda*, water] a colorless alcoholic liquor distilled from wheat, rye, etc.

**vogue** (vōg) *n.* [Fr.] 1. the fashion at any particular time 2. popularity

**voice** (vois) *n.* [< L. *vox*] 1. sound made through the mouth, esp. by human beings 2. the ability to make such sounds 3. anything regarded as like vocal utterance 4. an expressed wish, opinion, etc. 5. the right to express one's wish, etc.; vote 6. utterance or expression 7. *Gram.* a form of a verb showing it as active or passive 8. *Music a)* singing ability *b)* any of the parts in a composition —*vt.* **voiced, voic′ing** to give utterance or expression to —**with one voice** unanimously —**voice′less** *adj.*

**voice′-o′ver** *n.* the voice of an unseen announcer or narrator as on TV

**void** (void) *adj.* [< L. *vacare*, be empty] 1. containing nothing 2. devoid of [*void* of sense] 3. ineffective; useless 4. of no legal force —*n.* 1. an empty space 2. a feeling of emptiness —*vt.* 1. to empty out 2. to make void; annul —**void′a·ble** *adj.*

‡**voi·là** (vwa lä′) [Fr.] behold; there it is: often used as an interjection

**voile** (voil) *n.* [Fr., a veil] a thin, sheer fabric, as of cotton

**vol.** *pl.* **vols.** volume

**vol·a·tile** (väl′ə t'l) *adj.* [< L. *volare*, to fly] 1. evaporating quickly 2. unstable or fickle —**vol′a·til′i·ty** (-til′i·tē) *n.* —**vol′a·til·ize′** (-īz′) *vt., vi.* **-ized′, -iz′ing**

**vol·can·ic** (väl kan′ik) *adj.* 1. of or caused by a volcano 2. like a volcano; violently explosive

**vol·ca·no** (väl kā′nō) *n., pl.* **-noes, -nos** [< L. *Volcanus*, Vulcan] 1. a vent in the earth's crust through which molten rock, ashes, etc. are ejected 2. a cone-shaped mountain of this material built up around the vent

**Vol·ga** (väl′gə, vōl′-) river in W R.S.F.S.R.

**vo·li·tion** (vō lish′ən) *n.* [ult. < L. *velle*, be willing] the act or power of using the will —**vo·li′tion·al** *adj.*

**vol·ley** (väl′ē) *n., pl.* **-leys** [< L. *volare*, to fly] 1. the simultaneous discharge of a number of weapons 2. the missiles so discharged 3. a rapid burst of words, etc. 4. *Tennis*, etc. a return of a ball, etc. before it touches the ground —*vt., vi.* **-leyed, -ley·ing** 1. to discharge or be discharged as in a volley 2. *Sports* to return (the ball, etc.) as a volley

**vol′ley·ball′** *n.* 1. a team game played by hitting a large, light, inflated ball back and forth over a net with the hands 2. the ball

**vol·plane** (väl′plān′) *vi.* **-planed′, -plan′ing** [< Fr. *voler*, to fly + *planer*, to glide] to glide down, as an airplane with the engine cut off

**volt** (vōlt) *n.* [< A. *Volta* (1745-1827), It. physicist] the unit of electromotive force

**volt·age** (vōl′tij) *n.* electromotive force expressed in volts

**vol·ta·ic** (väl tā′ik, vōl-) *adj.* of or producing electricity by chemical action [a *voltaic* battery]

**Vol·taire** (vōl ter′, väl-) 1694-1778; Fr. writer and philosopher

**volt·me·ter** (vōlt′mēt′ər) *n.* an instrument for measuring voltage

**vol·u·ble** (väl′yoo b'l) *adj.* [< L. *volvere*, to roll] characterized by a great flow of words; talkative —**vol′u·bil′i·ty** *n.* —**vol′u·bly** *adv.*

**vol·ume** (väl′yoom) *n.* [< L. *volumen*, scroll] 1. *a)* a book *b)* one of a set of books 2. the amount of space occupied in three dimensions 3. *a)* a quantity, bulk, or amount *b)* a large quantity 4. the loudness of sound

**vo·lu·mi·nous** (və loo′mə nəs) *adj.* 1. producing or consisting of enough to fill volumes 2. large; bulky; full —**vo·lu′mi·nous·ly** *adv.*

**vol·un·ta·rism** (väl′ən tər iz′m) *n.* voluntary participation in a certain action, or a system based on this

**vol′un·tar′y** (-ter′ē) *adj.* [< L. *voluntas*, free will] 1. brought about by one's own free choice 2. acting of one's own accord 3. intentional; not accidental 4. controlled by one's mind or will —**vol′un·tar′i·ly** *adv.*

**vol′un·tar′y·ism** *n.* the theory or system of support of churches, schools, etc. by voluntary contributions only

**vol·un·teer** (väl′ən tir′) *n.* one who offers to enter into service, as military service, of his own free will —*adj.* **1.** of volunteers **2.** voluntary —*vt.* to offer or give of one's own free will —*vi.* to offer to enter into any service of one's own free will

**vo·lup·tu·ar·y** (və lup′choo wer′ē) *n.*, *pl.* **-ies** [< L. *voluptas*, pleasure] one devoted to sensual pleasures

**vo·lup′tu·ous** (-choo wəs) *adj.* full of, producing, or fond of sensual pleasures —**vo·lup′tu·ous·ness** *n.*

**vo·lute** (və lōōt′) *n.* [< L. *volvere*, to roll] a spiral or whorl

**vom·it** (väm′it) *n.* [< L. *vomere*, to vomit] matter ejected from the stomach through the mouth —*vt.*, *vi.* **1.** to eject (the contents of the stomach) through the mouth; throw up **2.** to discharge or be discharged with force

**voo·doo** (vōō′dōō) *n.*, *pl.* **-doos** [of WAfr. origin] **1.** a primitive religion in the West Indies, based on a belief in sorcery, etc. **2.** a charm, fetish, etc. used in voodoo —*vt.* to affect by voodoo magic —**voo′doo·ism** *n.*

**vo·ra·cious** (vô rā′shəs) *adj.* [< L. *vorare*, devour] **1.** greedy in eating; ravenous **2.** very eager [a *voracious* reader] —**vo·rac′i·ty** (-ras′ə tē) *n.*

**vor·tex** (vôr′teks) *n.*, *pl.* **-tex·es**, **-ti·ces′** (-tə sēz′) [L.: see VERTEX] **1.** a whirlpool **2.** a whirlwind **3.** anything like a whirl in its rush, catastrophic power, etc.

**vo·ta·ry** (vōt′ə rē) *n.*, *pl.* **-ries** [< L. *vovere*, to vow] **1.** one bound by a vow, esp. by religious vows **2.** one devoted to a cause, study, etc.

**vote** (vōt) *n.* [< L. *votum*, a vow] **1.** a decision on a proposal, etc., or a choice between candidates for office **2.** *a)* the expression of such a decision or choice *b)* a ballot, etc. by which it is expressed **3.** the right to vote **4.** votes collectively —*vi.* vot′ed, vot′ing to give or cast a vote —*vt.* to decide or enact by vote —**vot′er** *n.*

**vo·tive** (vōt′iv) *adj.* [see prec.] given, done, etc. in fulfillment of a vow

**vouch** (vouch) *vi.* [< L. *vocare*, to call] to give, or serve as, assurance, a guarantee, etc. (*for*) [to *vouch* for one's honesty]

**vouch′er** *n.* **1.** one who vouches **2.** a paper serving as evidence or proof, as a receipt

**vouch·safe** *vt.* **-safed′**, **-saf′ing** [< ME. *vouchen safe*, vouch as safe] to condescend to give or grant

**vow** (vou) *n.* [< L. *votum*] **1.** a solemn promise, esp. one made to God **2.** a promise of love and fidelity [marriage *vows*] —*vt.* to promise or declare solemnly —*vi.* to make a vow —**take vows** to enter a religious order

**vow·el** (vou′əl) *n.* [< L. *vocalis*, vocal] **1.** a speech sound in which the air passes in a continuous stream through the open mouth **2.** a letter representing such a sound, as *a, e, i, o, u*

**voy·age** (voi′ij) *n.* [< L. *via*, way] **1.** a relatively long journey, esp. by water **2.** a journey by aircraft or spacecraft —*vi.*, *vt.* **-aged, -ag·ing** to make a voyage (over or on) —**voy′ag·er** *n.*

**†vo·ya·geur** (vwä yá zhèr′) *n.*, *pl.* **-geurs′** (-zh‑r′) [Fr., a traveler] a woodsman or boatman of Canada

**vo·yeur** (vwä yur′) *n.* [Fr. < L. *videre*, see] one who has an excessive interest in sexual objects or activities —**vo·yeur′ism** *n.* —**vo′yeur·is′tic** *adj.*

**V.P., VP** Vice-President

**vs.** versus

**V/STOL** [*v(ertical)* or *s(hort)* *t(ake)-o(ff* and) *l(anding)*] an aircraft that can take off and land either vertically or on a short airstrip

**Vt., VT** Vermont

**vt., v.t.** transitive verb

**VTOL** [*v(ertical)* *t(ake)o(ff* and) *l(and-ing)*] an aircraft that can take off and land vertically

**Vul·can** (vul′k'n) the Roman god of fire and of metalworking

**vul·can·ite** (vul′kə nīt′) *n.* [prec. + -ITE] a hard rubber

**vul′can·ize′** *vt.*, *vi.* **-ized′**, **-iz′ing** to treat (crude rubber) with sulfur under heat to increase its strength and elasticity —**vul′can·i·za′tion** *n.*

**Vulg.** Vulgate

**vul·gar** (vul′gər) *adj.* [< L. *vulgus*, common people] **1.** of people in general; popular **2.** vernacular **3.** lacking culture, taste, etc.; crude; boorish **4.** obscene —**vul′gar·ly** *adv.*

**vul·gar′i·an** (-ger′ē ən) *n.* a rich person with coarse, vulgar tastes

**vul′gar·ism** *n.* **1.** a word, phrase, etc. used widely but regarded as nonstandard, coarse, or obscene **2.** vulgarity

**vul·gar′i·ty** (-gar′ə tē) *n.* **1.** a being vulgar **2.** *pl.* **-ties** a vulgar act, habit, usage in speech, etc.

**vul′gar·ize′** (vul′gə rīz′) *vt.* **-ized′, -iz′ing 1.** to make popular **2.** to make vulgar, coarse, obscene, etc. —**vul′gar·iz′er** *n.*

**Vulgar Latin** the everyday Latin spoken by ancient Romans as distinguished from standard written Latin

**Vul·gate** (vul′gāt) *n.* [ML. *vulgata (editio)*, popular (edition)] **1.** a Latin version of the Bible, used in the Roman Catholic Church **2.** [v-] the vernacular

**vul·ner·a·ble** (vul′nər ə b'l) *adj.* [< L. *vulnus*, a wound] **1.** that can be wounded or injured **2.** open to, or easily hurt by, criticism or attack **3.** *Bridge* subject to increased penalties and bonuses —**vul′ner·a·bil′i·ty** *n.* —**vul′ner·a·bly** *adv.*

**vul·pine** (vul′pīn) *adj.* [< L. *vulpes*, a fox] of or like a fox; cunning

**vul·ture** (vul′chər) *n.* [< L. *vultur*] **1.** a large bird that lives chiefly on carrion **2.** a greedy, ruthless person —**vul′tur·ous** *adj.*

**vul·va** (vul′və) *n.* [L., womb] the external genital organs of the female

**vy·ing** (vī′iŋ) *adj.* that vies

VULTURE

# W

**W, w** (dub′'l yōō) n., pl. **W's, w's** the 23d letter of the English alphabet

**W** Chem. tungsten

**W., w** watt(s)

**W., W., w., W. 1.** west **2.** western

**W. 1.** Wednesday **2.** Welsh

**W., w. 1.** watt(s) **2.** weight **3.** width

**w. 1.** week(s) **2.** wide **3.** wife **4.** with

**WA** Washington (State)

**wab·ble** (wäb′'l) n., vi., vt. -bled, -bling var. of WOBBLE

**Wac** (wak) n. a member of the Women's Army Corps (**WAC**)

**wack·y** (wak′ē) adj. -i·er, -i·est [ < ?] [Slang] erratic; eccentric; irrational

**wad** (wäd, wôd) n. [ML. wadda, wadding] **1.** a small, soft mass, as of cotton or paper **2.** a lump or small, compact roll —vt. **wad′ded, wad′ding 1.** to compress, or roll up, into a wad **2.** to plug or stuff with a wad or wadding

**wad′ding** n. any soft material for use in padding, packing, etc.

**wad·dle** (wäd′'l, wôd′-) vi. -dled, -dling [ < ff.] to walk with short steps, swaying from side to side, as a duck —n. a waddling gait

**wade** (wäd) vi. **wad′ed, wad′ing** [ < OE. waden, go] **1.** to walk through any resisting substance, as water, mud, etc. **2.** to proceed with difficulty [to wade through a dull book] **3.** [Colloq.] to attack with vigor (with in or into) —vt. to cross by wading

**wad·er** (wād′ər) n. **1.** one who wades **2.** same as WADING BIRD **3.** [pl.] high waterproof boots, often with trousers

**wa·di** (wä′dē) n., pl. -dis, -dies [Ar. wādī] in N Africa, a river valley that is usually dry

**wading bird** a long-legged shore bird that wades the shallows and marshes for food

**wa·fer** (wā′fər) n. [ < MDu. wafel] **1.** a thin, flat, crisp cracker or cookie **2.** any disklike thing resembling this

**waf·fle** (wäf′'l) n. [see prec.] a crisp batter cake baked in a waffle iron

**waffle iron** a utensil with two flat, studded plates pressed together so that the waffle bakes between them

**waft** (waft) vt., vi. [ < Du. wachter, watcher] to move or carry (sounds, odors, etc.) lightly through the air or over water —n. **1.** an odor, sound, etc. carried through the air **2.** a gust of wind **3.** a wafting movement

**wag¹** (wag) vi., vt. **wagged, wag′ging** [prob. < ON. vaga] to move rapidly back and forth, up and down, etc. —n. a wagging

**wag²** (wag) n. [prob. < obs. waghalter, joker] a comical person; wit —**wag′ger·y** n., pl. -ies —**wag′gish** adj.

**wage** (wāj) vt. **waged, wag′ing** [ < OFr. gage, a pledge] to engage in or carry on (a war, etc.) —n. **1.** [often pl.] money paid for work done **2.** [usually pl.] what is given in return

**wag·er** (wā′jər) n. [see prec.] a bet —vt., vi. to bet

**wag·gle** (wag′'l) vt., vi. -gled, -gling to wag, esp. with short, quick movements —n. a waggling

**Wag·ner** (väg′nər), **Rich·ard** (rikh′ärt) 1813–83; Ger. composer

**wag·on** (wag′ən) n. [Du. wagen] **1.** a four-wheeled vehicle, esp. one for hauling heavy loads **2.** short for STATION WAGON —**on** (or **off**) **the wagon** [Slang] no longer (or once again) drinking alcoholic liquor

**waif** (wāf) n. [ < ONormFr.] **1.** anything found that is without an owner **2.** a homeless person, esp. a child

**wail** (wāl) vi. [ < ON. væ, woe] to make a long, loud, sad cry, as in grief or pain —n. such a cry

**wain·scot** (wān′skət, -skät′) n. [ < MDu. wagenschot] a paneling of wood, etc. on the walls of a room, sometimes on the lower part only —vt. -scot·ed or -scot·ted, -scot·ing or -scot·ting to panel with wood, etc.

**wain·wright** (wān′rīt′) n. [wain (wagon) + WRIGHT] one who builds wagons

**waist** (wāst) n. [ < OE. weaxan, grow] **1.** the part of the body between the ribs and the hips **2.** the part of a garment that covers the body from the shoulders to the waistline **3.** a blouse **4.** the narrow part of any object that is wider at the ends

**waist′band′** n. a band fitting around the waist, as on slacks or a skirt

**waist·coat** (wes′kət, wāst′kōt′) n. [Brit.] a man's vest

**waist·line** (wāst′līn′) n. the line at the narrowest part of the waist

**wait** (wāt) vi. [ < ONormFr. waitier] **1.** to remain (until something expected happens) **2.** to be ready **3.** to remain undone [it can wait] **4.** to serve food at a meal (with at or on) —vt. **1.** to await **2.** [Colloq.] to delay serving (a meal) —n. act or period of waiting —**lie in wait (for)** to wait so as to catch after planning a trap (for) —**wait on** (or **upon**) **1.** to act as a servant to **2.** to serve (a customer) —**wait table** to serve food to people at a table —**wait up** to delay going to bed until someone arrives, etc.

**wait′er** n. one who waits; esp., a man who waits table in a restaurant

**wait′ing** adj. **1.** that waits **2.** of or for a wait —n. **1.** the act of one that

**waits 2.** a period of waiting —**in waiting** in attendance, as on a king

**waiting game** a strategy by which one wins out over another by delaying action until one has an advantage

**waiting list** a list of applicants, in order of their application

**waiting room** a room where people wait, as in a bus station or dentist's office

**wait'ress** (-ris) n. a woman waiter

**waive** (wāv) vt. **waived, waiv'ing** [< ON. veifa, fluctuate] **1.** to give up or forgo (a right, etc.) **2.** to postpone; defer

**waiv·er** (wā'vər) n. Law a waiving of a right, claim, etc.

**wake**[1] (wāk) vi. **woke** or **waked, waked** or **wo'ken, wak'ing** [< OE. wacian, be awake & wacan, arise] **1.** to come out of sleep; awake (often with up) **2.** to stay awake **3.** to become active **4.** to become alert (to a realization, etc.) —vt. **1.** to cause to wake: often with up **2.** to arouse (passions, etc.) —n. an all-night vigil over a corpse before burial

**wake**[2] (wāk) n. [< ON. vök, hole] the track left in water by a moving ship —**in the wake of** following closely

**wake'ful** adj. **1.** alert; watchful **2.** unable to sleep —**wake'ful·ness** n.

**wak·en** (wāk'′n) vi., vt. to wake

**wale** (wāl) n. [OE. walu, weal] **1.** a welt raised by a whip, etc. **2.** a ridge on the surface of cloth —vt. **waled, wal'ing** to mark with wales

**Wales** (wālz) division of the United Kingdom, west of England: 8,016 sq. mi.; pop. 2,662,000

**walk** (wôk) vi. [OE. wealcan, to roll] **1.** to go on foot at a moderate pace **2.** to follow a certain course [to walk in peace] **3.** Baseball to go to first base on four balls —vt. **1.** to go along, over, etc. on foot **2.** to cause (a horse, etc.) to walk **3.** to accompany on a walk or stroll [I'll walk you home] **4.** Baseball to advance (a batter) to first base by pitching four balls —n. **1.** the act or manner of walking **2.** a stroll or hike **3.** a distance walked [an hour's walk] **4.** a sphere of activity, occupation, etc. [people from all walks of life] **5.** a path for walking **6.** Baseball a walking —**walk away** (or **off**) **with 1.** to steal **2.** to win easily —**walk out 1.** to go on strike —**walk out on** [Colloq.] to leave; desert —**walk'er** n.

**walk·ie-talk·ie** (wôk'ē tôk'ē) n. a compact radio transmitter and receiver that can be carried by one person

**walking stick** a stick carried when walking; cane

**walk'-on'** n. a bit role in which an actor has few if any words to speak

**walk'out'** n. a labor strike

**walk'up'** n. an apartment house without an elevator

**wall** (wôl) n. [< L. vallum] **1.** an upright structure of wood, stone, etc., serving to enclose, divide, or protect **2.** something like a wall in function —vt. **1.** to enclose, divide, etc. with or as with a wall **2.** to close up (an opening) with a wall (usually with up)

—**drive** (or **push**) **to the wall** to place in a desperate position —**off the wall** [Slang] **1.** insane; crazy **2.** very odd or unconventional

**wal·la·by** (wäl'ə bē) n., pl. **-bies, -by** [< Australian name] a small kangaroo

**wal·let** (wôl'it) n. [< ?] a flat pocketbook for paper money, cards, etc.

**wall-eye** (wôl'ī') n. [< ON. vagl, a beam + eygr, eye] **1.** an eye that turns outward, showing much white **2.** a fish with large, staring eyes, esp. a N. American freshwater fish of the perch family: in full **wall'eyed' pike**

**wall'flow'er** n. [Colloq.] a shy person who merely looks on at a dance

**Wal·loon** (wä loōn') n. **1.** any of a people of Celtic descent in S Belgium **2.** their French dialect

**wal·lop** (wäl'əp, wôl'-) vt. [< OFr. galoper, to gallop] [Colloq.] **1.** to beat or defeat soundly **2.** to strike hard —n. [Colloq.] **1.** a hard blow **2.** a thrill

**wal·low** (wäl'ō, wôl'ō) vi. [OE. wealwian, roll around] **1.** to roll about, as in mud, etc. **2.** to indulge oneself fully (in a specified thing) —n. **1.** a wallowing **2.** a muddy or dusty place

**wall'pa'per** n. paper for covering walls —vt. to put wallpaper on or in

**Wall Street** a street in New York City: financial center of the U.S.

**wall'-to-wall'** adj. **1.** covering a floor completely **2.** [Colloq.] a) pervasive b) comprehensive; all-inclusive

**wal·nut** (wôl'nut') n. [< OE. wealh, foreign + hnutu, nut] **1.** a tree valued for its nuts and its wood **2.** its edible nut with a two-lobed seed **3.** its brown wood, used in furniture

**wal·rus** (wôl'rəs, wäl'-) n. [prob. < ON. hrosshvair, horse whale] a massive sea mammal related to the seals and having two projecting tusks

**WALRUS**

**waltz** (wôlts, wôls) n. [< G. walzen, dance about] **1.** a ballroom dance for couples in 3/4 time **2.** music for this —vi. **1.** to dance a waltz **2.** to move lightly

**wam·pum** (wäm'pəm) n. [< Algonquian] shell beads used by N.American Indians as money

**wan** (wän, wôn) adj. **wan'ner, wan'nest** [OE. wann, dark] **1.** sickly pale **2.** feeble or weak [a wan smile]

**wand** (wänd, wônd) n. [ON. vondr] **1.** a staff symbolizing authority **2.** a rod of supposed magical power

**wan·der** (wän'dər, wôn'-) vi. [OE. wandrian] **1.** to roam idly about; ramble **2.** to stray (from a path, etc.) **3.** to go astray; speak, etc. **4.** to meander, as a river —vt. to roam in or over —**wan'der·er** n.

**wan'der·lust'** (-lust') n. [G.] an urge to wander or travel

**wane** (wān) vi. **waned, wan'ing** [OE. wanian, to decrease] **1.** to grow gradually less in extent, as the moon after it is full **2.** to grow dim, as a light

3. to decline in power, etc. 4. to approach the end —*n.* a waning

**wan·gle** (waŋ'g'l) *vt.* -gled, -gling [< ?] [Colloq.] to get or cause by persuasion, tricks, etc.

**Wan·kel engine** (vän'k'l, waŋ'-) [after F. *Wankel* (1902– ), G. engineer] a rotary combustion engine with a spinning piston, needing fewer parts and less fuel than used in a turbine engine

**want** (wänt, wônt) *vt.* [ < ON. *vanta*] 1. to lack 2. to crave [he wants love] 3. to desire [he wants to travel] 4. to wish to see or apprehend [wanted by the police] 5. [Chiefly Brit.] to require —*vi.* 1. to have a need or lack (with *for*) 2. to be destitute —*n.* 1. a lack; shortage 2. poverty 3. a craving 4. something needed

**want ad** [Colloq.] an advertisement for something wanted, as a job, etc.

**want'ing** *adj.* 1. lacking 2. not up to standard —*prep.* less; minus — **wanting in** deficient in (a quality)

**wan·ton** (wän't'n, wôn'-) *adj.* [ < OE. *wan*, lacking + *teon*, bring up] 1. sexually loose 2. [Poet.] playful 3. unprovoked or malicious 4. recklessly ignoring justice, etc. —*n.* a wanton person; esp., a sexually loose woman —*vi.* to be wanton —**wan'ton·ness** *n.*

**wap·i·ti** (wäp'ə tē) *n.* [ < Algonquian] an elk, the largest N.American deer, with widely branching antlers

**war** (wôr) *n.* [ < ONormFr. *werre*] 1. open armed conflict as between nations 2. any active hostility or struggle 3. military operations as a science —*adj.* of, in, or from war —*vi.* warred, war'ring 1. to carry on war 2. to contend; strive —**at war** in a state of active armed conflict

**war·ble** (wôr'b'l) *vt., vi.* -bled, -bling [ < ONormFr. *werbler*] to sing (a song, etc.) with trills, quavers, etc., as a bird —*n.* a warbling; trill

**war'bler** *n.* 1. one that warbles 2. any of various songbirds

**ward** (wôrd) *vt.* [OE. *weardian*, to guard] to turn aside; fend (*off*) —*n.* 1. a being under guard 2. one under the care of a guardian or court 3. a division of a jail, hospital, etc. 4. a division of a city or town, for purposes of voting, etc.

**-ward** (wərd) [OE. *-weard*] *a suffix* meaning in a (specified) direction [backward]: also **-wards** (-wərdz)

**war·den** (wôr'd'n) *n.* [ < OFr. *gardein*] 1. one who guards, or has charge of, something [game warden] 2. the chief official of a prison

**ward·er** (wôr'dər) *n.* a watchman

**ward heeler** a hanger-on of a politician, who solicits votes, etc.

**ward·robe** (wôrd'rōb') *n.* 1. a closet, cabinet, etc. for holding clothes 2. one's supply of clothes

**ward'room'** *n.* a room on a warship used by commissioned officers, except the captain, for eating and lounging

**ware** (wer) *n.* [OE. *waru*] 1. anything for sale: *usually in pl.* 2. pottery

**ware'house'** *n.* a building where goods are stored —*vt.* -housed', -hous'ing to store in a warehouse

**war·fare** (wôr'fer') *n.* 1. the action of waging war 2. conflict of any kind

**war'head'** (-hed') *n.* the front part of a torpedo, etc. containing the charge

**war'horse'** *n.* [Colloq.] one who has been through many struggles; veteran

**war·i·ly** (wer'ə lē) *adv.* in a wary manner —**war'i·ness** *n.*

**war'like'** *adj.* 1. fond of or ready for war 2. of war 3. threatening war

**war·lock** (wôr'läk') *n.* [OE. *wærloga*, liar] the male equivalent of a witch

**war'lord'** *n.* 1. a warlike high military officer 2. an aggressive local ruler or bandit leader, as formerly in China

**warm** (wôrm) *adj.* [OE. *wearm*] 1. *a)* having or giving off a moderate degree of heat *b)* hot [a warm night] 2. that keeps body heat in [warm clothing] 3. ardent; enthusiastic 4. lively, vigorous, etc. 5. quick to anger 6. *a)* genial; cordial [a warm welcome] *b)* sympathetic or loving 7. newly made; fresh, as a trail 8. [Colloq.] close to discovering something —*vt., vi.* to make or become warm — **warm up** to practice or exercise, as before playing in a game —**warm'ish** *adj.* —**warm'ly** *adv.*

**warm'blood'ed** *adj.* having a body temperature that is relatively constant and usually warmer than the surroundings, as mammals and birds

**warmed-o·ver** (wôrmd'ō'vər) *adj.* 1. reheated 2. presented again, without significant change, as ideas

**warm'heart'ed** *adj.* kind, sympathetic, friendly, loving, etc.

**war'mon'ger** (-muŋ'gər, -mäŋ'-) *n.* one who advocates, or tries to cause, war —**war'mon'ger·ing** *adj., n.*

**warmth** (wôrmth) *n.* 1. *a)* a being warm *b)* mild heat 2. *a)* enthusiasm, ardor, etc. *b)* affectionate feelings

**warm'-up'** *n.* the act of warming up

**warn** (wôrn) *vt., vi.* [OE. *wearnian*] 1. to tell of a danger, coming evil, etc. 2. to advise to be wary or cautious 3. to notify in advance; inform

**warn'ing** *n.* 1. the act of one that warns 2. that which warns —*adj.* that warns

**warp** (wôrp) *n.* [< OE. *weorpan*, to throw] 1. *a)* a distortion, as a twist or bend, in wood *b)* any similar distortion 2. a mental quirk, bias, etc. 3. *Weaving* the threads running lengthwise in the loom —*vt.* 1. to bend or twist out of shape 2. to distort, pervert, etc. [a warped mind] —*vi.* to become bent or twisted

**war'path'** *n.* the path taken by N.American Indians on a warlike expedition —**on the warpath** 1. ready for war 2. actively angry; ready to fight

**war·rant** (wôr'ənt, wär'-) *n.* [ < OFr. *garant*] 1. authorization, as by law *b*) justification for some act, belief, etc. **2.** something serving as a guarantee of some event or result **3.** *Law* a writ authorizing an arrest, search, etc. —*vt.* **1.** to authorize **2.** to serve as justification for (an act, belief, etc.) **3.** to guarantee

**warrant officer** a military officer ranking above an enlisted man but below a commissioned officer

**war'ran·ty** *n., pl.* **-ties** a guarantee (*n. 2a*)

**War·ren** (wôr'ən, wär'-) city in SE Mich.: pop. 179,000

**war·ren** (wôr'ən, wär'-) *n.* [< ONorm-Fr. *warir*, to preserve] **1.** an area in which rabbits breed or are numerous **2.** any crowded building or buildings

**war·ri·or** (wôr'ē ər, wär'-) *n.* [see WAR] a fighting man; soldier

**War·saw** (wôr'sô) capital of Poland: pop. 1,249,000

**war·ship** (wôr'ship') *n.* any ship for combat use, as a battleship

**wart** (wôrt) *n.* [OE. *wearte*] **1.** a small, usually hard, tumorous growth on the skin **2.** a small protuberance, as on a plant —**wart'y** *adj.*

**wart hog** a wild African hog with large tusks, and warts below the eyes

**war·y** (wer'ē) *adj.* **-i·er, -i·est** [OE. *wær*, aware] full of or characterized by caution —**wary of** careful of

**was** (wuz, wäz) [OE. *wæs*] *1st & 3d pers. sing., pt.,* of BE

**wash** (wôsh, wäsh) *vt.* [OE. *wæscan*] **1.** to clean with water or other liquid **2.** to purify **3.** to wet or moisten **4.** to flow over, past, or against: said of a sea, waves, etc. **5.** to soak (*out*), flush (*off*), or carry (*away*) with water **6.** to erode (*with out* or *away*) [the flood *washed* out the road] **7.** to cover with a thin coating of paint or metal —*vi.* **1.** to wash oneself **2.** to wash clothes **3.** to undergo washing **4.** to be removed by washing (*with out* or *away*) **5.** to be worn or carried (*out* or *away*) by the action of water [the bridge had *washed* out] —*n.* **1.** a washing of a quantity of clothes washed, or to be washed **3.** the rush or surge of water **4.** the eddy of water or air caused by a propeller, etc. **5.** silt, mud, etc. carried and dropped by running water **6.** a thin coating of paint or metal **7.** a liquid for cosmetic or toilet use [*mouthwash*] —*adj.* that can be washed without damage [a *wash* dress] —**wash down** to follow (food) with a drink —**wash'a·ble** *adj., n.*

**wash'-and-wear'** *adj.* needing little or no ironing after washing

**wash'board'** *n.* a ridged board for scrubbing dirt out of clothes

**wash'bowl'** *n.* a bowl, esp. a bathroom fixture, for use in washing one's hands, etc.: also **wash'ba'sin**

**wash'cloth'** *n.* a small cloth used in washing the body: also **wash'rag'**

**washed'-out'** *adj.* **1.** faded **2.** [Colloq.] tired; spiritless; pale and wan

**washed'-up'** *adj.* **1.** [Colloq.] tired; exhausted **2.** [Slang] finished; done for; having failed

**wash'er** *n.* **1.** one who washes **2.** a

flat ring of metal, rubber, etc. used to make a seat as for a nut or faucet valve, etc. **3.** a machine for washing

**wash'er·wom'an** *n., pl.* **-wom'en** a woman whose work is washing clothes

**wash'ing** *n.* **1.** the act of one that washes **2.** clothes, etc. to be washed

**washing machine** a machine for washing clothes, etc.

**Wash·ing·ton** (wôsh'iŋ tən, wäsh'-) **1.** NW State of the U.S.: 68,192 sq. mi.; pop. 3,409,000; cap. Olympia: abbrev. **Wash., WA 2.** capital of the U.S., coextensive with the District of Columbia: pop. 757,000 —**Wash'ing·to'ni·an** (-tō'nē ən) *adj., n.*

**Washington, George** 1732–99; 1st president of the U.S. (1789–97)

**wash'out'** *n.* **1.** a washing away of soil, etc. by water **2.** [Slang] a failure

**wash'room'** *n.* **1.** a room for washing **2.** same as RESTROOM

**wash'stand'** *n.* a table or plumbing fixture with a washbowl, etc.

**wash'tub'** *n.* a tub, often with faucets and drain, to wash clothes, etc.

**wash'y** *adj.* **-i·er, -i·est 1.** watery; diluted **2.** insipid; feeble

**was·n't** (wuz'ənt, wäz'-) was not

**WASP, Wasp** (wäsp, wôsp) *n.* a white Anglo-Saxon Protestant

**wasp** (wäsp, wôsp) *n.* [OE. *wæsp*] a winged insect with a slender body and, in the females and workers, a vicious sting

**wasp'ish** *adj.* **1.** of or like a wasp **2.** bad-tempered; snappish

**was·sail** (wäs''l, -āl) *n.* [< ON. *ves heill*, be hearty] **1.** a former toast in drinking healths **2.** the spiced ale, etc. with which such healths were drunk **3.** a drinking party —*vi., vt.* to drink a wassail (to)

**wast·age** (wās'tij) *n.* **1.** loss by use, decay, etc. **2.** anything wasted

**waste** (wāst) *vt.* **wast'ed, wast'ing** [< L. *vastare*] **1.** to devastate; ruin **2.** to wear away **3.** to make weak or emaciated [wasted by age] **4.** to use up needlessly; squander **5.** to fail to take advantage of —*vi.* **1.** to lose strength, etc., as by disease **2.** to be used up or worn down gradually —*adj.* **1.** uncultivated or uninhabited; desolate **2.** left over or superfluous **3.** excreted from the body **4.** used for waste —*n.* **1.** uncultivated or uninhabited land **2.** a devastated area **3.** a wasting or being wasted **4.** discarded material, as ashes, etc. **5.** excretions from the body, as urine —**go to waste** to be wasted —**lay waste (to)** to destroy —**wast'er** *n.*

**waste'bas'ket** *n.* a container for wastepaper, etc.

**waste'ful** *adj.* characterized by waste; squandering —**waste'ful·ly** *adv.* —**waste'ful·ness** *n.*

**waste'land'** *n.* **1.** barren land **2.** unproductive activity

**waste'pa'per** *n.* paper thrown away after use: also **waste paper**

**was'trel** (wās'trəl) *n.* one who wastes; esp., a spendthrift

**watch** (wäch, wôch) *n.* [OE. *wæcce*] **1.** a keeping awake, esp. in order to guard **2.** close observation for a time **3.** a guard, or the period of duty of a guard **4.** a small timepiece carried in the pocket or worn on the wrist **5.** *a)* any of the periods of duty (usually four hours) on shipboard *b)* the crew on duty during such a period —*vi.* **1.** to stay awake; keep vigil **2.** to be on the alert **3.** to look or observe **4.** to be looking or waiting attentively (*for*) —*vt.* **1.** to guard or tend **2.** to observe carefully **3.** to wait and look for — **watch oneself** to be careful —**watch out** to be alert or careful —**watch'·er** *n.*

**watch'band'** *n.* a band of leather, metal, etc. to hold a watch on the wrist

**watch'dog'** *n.* **1.** a dog kept to guard property **2.** one that keeps watch in order to prevent or expose waste, etc.

**watch'ful** *adj.* watching closely; vigilant; alert —**watch'ful·ly** *adv.*

**watch'man** (-mən) *n., pl.* -men a person hired to guard property

**watch'tow'er** *n.* a high tower from which watch is kept, as for forest fires

**watch'word'** *n.* **1.** a password **2.** a slogan or cry of a group, etc.

**wa·ter** (wôt'ər, wät'-) *n.* [OE. *wæter*] **1.** the colorless liquid of rivers, lakes, etc., which falls as rain **2.** water with reference to its depth, surface, or level *[above water]* **3.** a body secretion, as urine **4.** a wavy, lustrous finish given to linen, silk, metal, etc. —*vt.* **1.** to give (animals) water to drink **2.** to supply (crops, etc.) with water **3.** to moisten, soak, or dilute with water **4.** to give a wavy luster to (silk, etc.)—*vi.* **1.** to fill with tears, as the eyes **2.** to secrete saliva *[his mouth watered]* **3.** to take on a supply of water **4.** to drink water —*adj.* of, for, in, on, near, from, or by water —**hold water** to prove sound, logical, etc.

**water bed** a heavy vinyl bag filled with water and used as a bed or as a mattress in a special bed frame: also **wa'ter·bed'** *n.*

**water buffalo** a slow, powerful, oxlike draft animal of S Asia

**Wa·ter·bur·y** (wôt'ər ber'ē, wät'-) city in WC Conn.: pop. 108,000

**water chestnut 1.** a Chinese sedge with a nutlike tuber **2.** this tuber

**water closet** a TOILET (sense 3)

**wa'ter·col'or** *n.* **1.** a pigment mixed with water to make a paint **2.** a painting done with such paints

**wa'ter·cooled'** *adj.* cooled by water circulated around or through it

**wa'ter·course'** *n.* **1.** a stream, river, etc. **2.** a channel for water, as a canal

**wa'ter·craft'** *n., pl.* -craft' a boat, ship, or other water vehicle

**wa'ter·cress'** (-kres') *n.* a plant of the mustard family, growing in water: its leaves are used in salads, etc.

**wa'ter·cy'cle** (-sī'k'l) *n.* a small watercraft moved by pedals or treadles

**wa'ter·fall'** *n.* a steep fall of water, as of a stream, from a height

**wa'ter·fowl'** *n.* a water bird, esp. one that swims

**wa'ter·front'** *n.* land or docks at the edge of a stream, harbor, etc.

**Wa·ter·gate** (wôt'ər gāt', wät'-) *n.* [< *Watergate*, where Dem. Party hdqrs. in Washington were burglarized (June, 1972)] a scandal involving criminal abuses of power by officials —*vt.* -gat'ed, -gat'ing to deal with in a criminal manner

**water glass 1.** a drinking glass **2.** a silicate of sodium or potassium, dissolved in water to form a syrupy liquid used as a preservative for eggs, etc.

**water hole** a pond or pool

**wa'ter·lil'y** *n., pl.* -ies **1.** a water plant with large, flat, floating leaves and showy flowers **2.** the flower

**wa'ter·line'** *n.* the line to which the surface of the water comes on the side of a ship or boat

WATERLILY

**wa'ter·logged'** (-lôgd', -lägd') *adj.* soaked or filled with water so as to be heavy and sluggish, as a boat

**Wa·ter·loo** (wôt'ər loo', wät'-) town in C Belgium: scene of Napoleon's final defeat (1815) —*n.* any disastrous or decisive defeat

**water main** a main pipe in a system of pipes for carrying water

**wa'ter·mark'** *n.* **1.** a mark showing the limit to which water has risen **2.** a mark in paper, produced by the impression of a design, as in the mold —*vt.* to mark (paper) with a watermark

**wa'ter·mel'on** *n.* a large, seedy, green melon with a juicy, red pulp

**water moccasin** a large, poisonous water snake of the SE U.S.

**water pipe 1.** a pipe for water **2.** a hookah

**water polo** a water game played with a ball by two teams of swimmers

**water power** the power of running or falling water, used to drive machinery

**wa'ter·proof'** *adj.* that keeps out water, as by being treated with rubber, etc. —*vt.* to make waterproof

**wa'ter·re·pel'lent** *adj.* that repels water but is not fully waterproof

**wa'ter·shed'** (-shed') *n.* **1.** a ridge dividing the areas drained by different river systems **2.** the area drained by a river system

**wa'ter·side'** *n.* land at the edge of a body of water; shore

**wa'ter·ski'** *vi.* -skied', -ski'ing to be towed on skilike boards (**water skis**) by a line attached to a speedboat

**wa'ter·spout'** *n.* a tornado occurring over water, and appearing as a rotating, tubelike column of air full of mist and spray

**water table** the level below which the ground is saturated with water

**wa·ter·tight′** *adj.* **1.** so tight that no water can get through **2.** that cannot be misconstrued, nullified, etc.; flawless *[a watertight plan]*

**water tower** an elevated tank for water storage, etc.

**wa′ter·way′** *n.* **1.** a channel through which water runs **2.** any body of water on which boats, ships, etc. can travel

**water wheel** a wheel turned by running water, as for power

**water wings** an inflated device to keep one afloat in the water

**wa′ter·works′** *n.pl. [often with sing. v.]* a system of reservoirs, pumps, etc. supplying water to a city

**wa′ter·y** *adj.* **1.** of or like water **2.** full of water **3.** thin; diluted **4.** tearful **5.** weak —**wa′ter·i·ness** *n.*

**WATS** (wäts) *n. [w(ide) a(rea) t(ele-communications) s(ervice)]* a telephone service that ties a customer into the long-distance network through special lines, at special rates

**watt** (wät, wôt) *n.* [< James *Watt* (1736–1819), Scot. inventor of steam engine] a unit of electrical power, equal to the power developed in a circuit by a current of one ampere flowing through a potential difference of one volt

**watt′age** (-ij) *n.* amount of electrical power, expressed in watts

**wat·tle** (wät′'l, wôt′-) *n.* [OE. *watul*] **1.** a woven work of sticks intertwined with twigs or branches **2.** a fleshy flap of skin hanging from the throat of a cock, etc. —*vt.* **-tled, -tling 1.** to intertwine (sticks, twigs, etc.) **2.** to construct of wattle

**Wave** (wāv) *n.* [orig. < *W(omen) A(ppointed for) V(oluntary) E(mergency) S(ervice)]* a member of the women's branch of the U.S. Navy (WAVES)

**wave** (wāv) *vi.* **waved, wav′ing** [OE. *wafian*] **1.** to move or sway to and fro **2.** to signal by moving a hand, arm, etc. to and fro **3.** to have the form of a series of curves —*vt.* **1.** to cause to wave **2.** to brandish (a weapon) **3.** *a)* to move or swing (something) as a signal *b)* to signal (something) to (someone) by doing this **4.** to give an undulating form to (hair, etc.) —*n.* **1.** a ridge or swell moving along the surface of the ocean, etc. **2.** an undulation or curve, as in the hair **3.** a motion to and fro, as with the hand in signaling **4.** a thing like a wave in effect; specif., an upsurge *[a crime wave]* **5.** *Physics* a periodic disturbance, as in the propagation of light, sound, etc., that is transmitted progressively through a medium

**wave′length** *n. Physics* the distance, measured in the direction of progression of a wave, from any given point to the next point in the same phase

**wave′let** (-lit) *n.* a little wave

**wa·ver** (wā′vər) *vi.* [< ME. *waven,* to wave] **1.** to sway to and fro **2.** to show indecision; vacillate **3.** to falter, flicker, or tremble —*n.* a wavering

**wav·y** (wā′vē) *adj.* **-i·er, -i·est 1.** having or like waves **2.** moving in a wavelike motion —**wav′i·ness** *n.*

**wax¹** (waks) *n.* [OE. *weax*] **1.** a plastic, dull-yellow substance secreted by bees; beeswax **2.** any plastic substance like this, as paraffin —*vt.* to rub, polish, cover, or treat with wax

**wax²** (waks) *vi.* [OE. *weaxan,* grow] **1.** to increase in strength, size, etc. **2.** to become gradually full: said of the moon **3.** to become *[to wax angry]*

**wax bean** a variety of bean with long, edible, yellow pods

**wax·en** (wak′s'n) *adj.* **1.** made of wax **2.** like wax; pale, plastic, etc.

**wax myrtle** an evergreen shrub with grayish-white, wax-coated berries

**wax paper** a paper made moisture-proof by a wax coating

**wax′wing′** *n.* a bird with silky-brown plumage and scarlet spines at the ends of the wings

**wax′works′** *n.pl. [with sing. v.]* an exhibition of wax figures

**wax′y** *adj.* **-i·er, -i·est** of, full of, or like wax —**wax′i·ness** *n.*

**way** (wā) *n.* [OE. *weg*] **1.** a road, street, path, etc. **2.** room for passing **3.** a route or course **4.** movement forward *[lead the way]* **5.** habits of life *[give up evil ways]* **6.** a method of doing something **7.** a manner of living, acting, etc. *[his ways are odd]* **8.** distance *[a long way off]* **9.** direction of movement **10.** respect; particular *[right in some ways]* **11.** wish; will *[I had my way]* **12.** *[pl.]* a timber framework on which a ship is built **13.** [Colloq.] *a)* a condition *[he's in a bad way] b)* a locality *[out our way]* —*adv.* [Colloq.] away; far *[way behind]* —*by the way* incidentally —*by way of* **1.** passing through **2.** as a method, etc. of —*give way* **1.** to yield **2.** to break down —*make way* **1.** to clear a passage **2.** to make progress —*under way* moving; advancing

**way′far·er** (-fer′ər) *n.* a traveler, esp. on foot —**way′far·ing** *adj., n.*

**way′lay′** *vt.* **-laid′, -lay′ing 1.** to lie in wait for and attack; ambush **2.** to wait for and accost by surprise

**way′-out′** *adj.* [Colloq.] very unusual or unconventional

**-ways** (wāz) [< WAY] *a suffix meaning in a (specified) direction, position, or manner [endways]*

**ways and means** methods of raising money, specif. such methods, including legislation, in government

**way′side′** *n.* the edge of a road

**way′ward** (-wərd) *adj.* [see AWAY & -WARD] **1.** headstrong, willful, disobedient, etc. **2.** unpredictable; erratic —**way′ward·ness** *n.*

**W.C.T.U.** Women's Christian Temperance Union

**we** (wē) *pron.* [for sing. see I] [OE.] the persons speaking or writing: sometimes used by a person in referring to a group of which he is one, or, in place of *I,* by a monarch, editor, etc.

**weak** (wēk) *adj.* [< ON. *veikr*] **1.** lacking physical strength; frail; feeble **2.** lacking moral strength or will power **3.** lacking mental power **4.** lacking force, power, etc. *[weak discipline]* **5.**

easily torn, broken, etc. [a *weak* railing] 6. lacking intensity, etc. [a *weak* voice] 7. diluted [*weak* tea] 8. unconvincing [a *weak* argument]

**weak'en** *vt.*, *vi.* to make or become weak or weaker —**weak'en·er** *n.*

**weak'-kneed'** *adj.* lacking in courage, determination, resistance, etc.

**weak'ling** *n.* one lacking physical or moral strength

**weak'ly** *adj.* -li·er, -li·est sickly; feeble —*adv.* in a weak manner

**weak'ness** *n.* 1. a being weak 2. a weak point; fault 3. an unreasonable fondness (*for* something)

**weal**¹ (wēl) *n.* [< WALE] a mark raised on the skin, as by a blow; welt

**weal**² (wēl) *n.* [OE. *wela*] well-being; welfare [the public *weal*]

**wealth** (welth) *n.* [< prec.] 1. much money or property; riches 2. a large amount [a *wealth* of ideas] 3. valuable products, contents, etc. 4. everything having value in money

**wealth'y** *adj.* -i·er, -i·est having wealth; rich —**wealth'i·ness** *n.*

**wean** (wēn) *vt.* [OE. *wenian*] 1. to accustom (a child or young animal) to take food other than by suckling 2. to withdraw (a person) as from a habit

**weap·on** (wep'ən) *n.* [OE. *wæpen*] 1. any instrument used for fighting 2. any means of attack or defense

**weap'on·ry** (-rē) *n.* 1. the design and production of weapons 2. weapons collectively

**wear** (wer) *vt.* wore, worn, wear'ing [OE. *werian*] 1. to bear (clothing, etc.) on the body 2. to show in one's appearance [she *wore* a smile] 3. to impair or diminish by use, friction, etc. 4. to make by rubbing, flowing, etc. [to *wear* a hole in the rug] 5. to tire or exhaust —*vi.* 1. to become impaired or diminished, as by use 2. to hold up in use [that suit *wears* well] 3. to have an irritating effect (*on*) —*n.* 1. a wearing or being worn 2. things worn; clothes [men's *wear*] 3. impairment or loss, as from use, friction, etc. —**wear off** to diminish by degrees —**wear'a·ble** *adj.* —**wear'er** *n.*

**wear and tear** loss and damage resulting from use

**wea·ri·some** (wir'ē səm) *adj.* causing weariness; tiresome or tedious

**wea·ry** (wir'ē) *adj.* -ri·er, -ri·est [OE. *werig*] 1. tired; worn-out 2. without further patience, zeal, etc. 3. tiring [*weary* work] —*vt.*, *vi.* -ried, -ry·ing to make or become weary —**wea'ri·ly** *adv.* —**wea'ri·ness** *n.*

**wea·sel** (wē'z'l) *n.* [OE. *wesle*] an agile, flesh-eating mammal, with a long, slender body and short legs —*vi.* to be evasive or deliberately misleading —**wea'sel·ly** *adj.*

**weath·er** (we*th*'ər) *n.* [OE. *weder*] 1. the condition of the atmosphere with regard to temperature, moisture, etc. 2. storm, rain, etc. —*vt.* 1. to expose to the action of weather 2. to pass

through safely [to *weather* a storm] 3. *Naut.* to pass to the windward of —*vi.* to become discolored, worn, etc. by exposure to the weather —**under the weather** [Colloq.] ill

**weath'er-beat'en** *adj.* showing the effect of exposure to sun, rain, etc.

**weath'er·cock'** *n.* a weather vane in the form of a cock

**weath'er·man'** *n.*, *pl.* -men' one whose work is forecasting the weather

**weath'er·proof'** *adj.* that can withstand exposure to the weather without damage —*vt.* to make weatherproof

**weath'er·strip'** *n.* a strip of metal, felt, etc. covering the joint between a door or window and the casing to keep out drafts, etc.: also **weath'er·strip'ping** —*vt.* -stripped', -strip'ping to provide with weatherstrips

**weather vane** a vane for showing which way the wind is blowing

**weave** (wēv) *vt.* wove or, chiefly for *vt.* 5 & *vi.* 3, weaved, wov'en or wove or, chiefly for *vt.* 5 & *vi.* 3, weaved, weav'ing [OE. *wefan*] 1. to make (a fabric, basket, etc.) by interlacing (threads, reeds, etc.), as on a loom 2. to construct in the mind [to *weave* a tale] 3. to twist (something) into or through 4. to spin (a web), as spiders do 5. to make (one's way) by moving from side to side or in and out —*vi.* 1. to do weaving 2. to become interlaced 3. to move from side to side or in and out —*n.* a method or pattern of weaving —**weav'er** *n.*

**web** (web) *n.* [OE. *webb*] 1. any woven fabric 2. the network spun by a spider, etc. 3. a carefully woven trap 4. a network 5. a membrane joining the digits of various water birds, animals, etc. —*vt.* webbed, web'bing to join by, or cover as with, a web

**web'bing** *n.* a strong fabric woven in strips and used for belts, etc.

**web'foot'** *n.*, *pl.* -feet' a foot with webbed toes —**web'-foot'ed** *adj.*

**Web·ster** (web'stər), **Noah** 1758-1843; U.S. lexicographer

**wed** (wed) *vt.*, *vi.* wed'ded, wed'ded or wed, wed'ding [OE. *weddian*] 1. to marry 2. to unite or join

**we'd** (wēd) 1. we had 2. we should 3. we would

**Wed.** Wednesday

**wed·ding** *n.* 1. the marriage ceremony 2. a marriage anniversary

**wedge** (wej) *n.* [OE. *wecg*] 1. a piece of wood, metal, etc. tapering to a thin edge: used to split wood, lift weights, etc. 2. anything shaped like a wedge 3. any act serving to open the way for change, etc. —*vt.* **wedged, wedg'ing** 1. to force apart, or fix in place, with a wedge 2. to crowd together or pack (*in*) —*vi.* to be forced as a wedge

WEDGE

**wed·lock** (wed′läk) n. [OE. wedlac] the state of being married

**Wednes·day** (wenz′dē, -dā) n. [< Woden, Germanic god] the fourth day of the week

**wee** (wē) adj. we′er, we′est [OE. wege] 1. very small; tiny 2. very early [wee hours of the morning]

**weed** (wēd) n. [OE. weod] any undesired, uncultivated plant, esp. one that crowds out desired plants —vt., vi. 1. to remove weeds from (a garden, etc.) 2. to remove as useless, harmful, etc.: often with out —weed′er n.

**weeds** (wēdz) n.pl. [< OE. wæde, garment] black mourning clothes

**weed′y** adj. -i·er, -i·est 1. full of weeds 2. of or like a weed

**week** (wēk) n. [OE. wicu] 1. a period of seven days, esp. the period from Sunday through Saturday 2. the hours or days of work in this period

**week′day′** n. any day of the week except Sunday and, often, Saturday

**week′end′, week′-end** n. the period from Friday night or Saturday to Monday morning: also week end —vi. to spend the weekend (at or in)

**week′ly** adj. 1. of, for, or lasting a week 2. done, happening, etc. once every week —adv. once a week; every week —n., pl. -lies a periodical published once a week

**ween** (wēn) vi., vt. [OE. wenan] [Archaic] to think; suppose; imagine

**weep** (wēp) vi., vt. wept, weep′ing [OE. wepan] 1. to shed (tears) in grief, etc. 2. to mourn (for) 3. to drip or exude (water, etc.) —weep′er n.

**weep′ing** n. the act of one who weeps —adj. 1. that weeps 2. having graceful, drooping branches

**weep′y** adj. -i·er, -i·est weeping or inclined to weep

**wee·vil** (wē′v'l) n. [OE. wifel] a beetle whose larvae feed on grain, etc.

**weft** (weft) n. [< OE. wefan, to weave] Weaving the woof

**weigh** (wā) vt. [OE. wegan, carry] 1. to determine the heaviness of 2. to have (a specified weight) 3. to consider and choose carefully [weigh one's words] 4. to hoist (an anchor) —vi. 1. to have significance, importance, etc. 2. to be a burden —weigh down to burden or bear down on

**weight** (wāt) n. [OE. wiht] 1. a quantity weighing a definite amount 2. heaviness; specif., Physics the force exerted on a mass by gravity 3. amount of heaviness 4. a) any unit of heaviness b) any system of such units c) a piece of standard heaviness used in weighing 5. any body used for its heaviness [a paperweight] 6. a burden, as of sorrow 7. importance; consequence 8. influence; power —vt. 1. to add weight to 2. to burden

**weight′less** adj. having little or no apparent weight; specif., lacking acceleration of gravity

**weight lifting** the athletic exercise or sport of lifting barbells

**weight′y** adj. -i·er, -i·est 1. very heavy 2. burdensome 3. significant; important —weight′i·ness n.

**weir** (wir) n. [OE. wer] 1. a low dam built to back up water, as for a mill 2. a fence, as of brushwood, in a stream, etc., for catching fish

**weird** (wird) adj. [< OE. wyrd, fate] 1. suggestive of ghosts, etc.; mysterious 2. queer; bizarre —weird′ly adv. —weird′ness n.

**weird·o** (wir′dō) n., pl. -os [Slang] a queer or bizarre person or thing: also weird′ie

**wel·come** (wel′kəm) adj. [< OE. wilcuma, welcome guest] 1. gladly received [a welcome guest, welcome news] 2. freely permitted [welcome to use my car] 3. under no obligation [you're welcome] —n. a welcoming —vt. -comed, -com·ing to greet or receive with pleasure, etc.

**weld** (weld) vt. [< obs. well] 1. to unite (pieces of metal) by heating until fused or soft enough to hammer together 2. to unite closely —vi. to be welded —n. 1. a welding 2. the joint formed by welding —weld′er n.

**wel·fare** (wel′fer′) n. [< ME. wel, well + OE. faran, to go] 1. state of health, prosperity, etc.; well-being 2. those government agencies which grant aid to the poor, the unemployed, etc. —on welfare receiving government aid because of poverty, etc.

**wel·kin** (wel′kin) n. [< OE. wolcen, cloud] [Archaic] the vault of the sky

**well¹** (wel) n. [OE. wella] 1. a natural spring and pool 2. a hole sunk into the earth to get water, oil, etc. 3. a source of abundant supply 4. a shaft, etc. resembling a well 5. a container for a liquid, as an inkwell —vi., vt. to gush or flow as from a well

**well²** (wel) adv. bet′ter, best [OE. wel] 1. in a satisfactory, proper, or excellent manner [treat him well, to sing well] 2. prosperously [to live well] 3. with good reason [one may well ask] 4. to a considerable degree [well advanced] 5. thoroughly [stir it well] 6. with certainty; definitely 7. familiarly [I know him well] —adj. 1. suitable, proper, etc. 2. in good health 3. favorable; comfortable —interj. an exclamation of surprise, agreement, etc. —as well (as) 1. in addition (to) 2. equally (with)

**we'll** (wēl) 1. we shall 2. we will

**well-ap·point·ed** (wel′ə poin′tid) adj. excellently furnished

**well′-bal·anced** adj. 1. nicely adjusted 2. sane, sensible, etc.

**well′-be·haved′** adj. behaving well; displaying good manners

**well′-be·ing** n. the state of being well, happy, or prosperous; welfare

**well′-bred′** adj. showing good breeding; courteous and considerate

**well′-dis·posed′** adj. friendly (toward a person) or receptive (to an idea, etc.)

**well′-done′** adj. 1. performed with skill 2. thoroughly cooked, as meat

**well′-fed′** adj. plump, or fat

**well′-fixed′** adj. [Colloq.] rich

**well′-found′ed** adj. based on facts, good evidence, or sound judgment

**well′-groomed′** adj. clean and neat

**well′-ground′ed** adj. having a thorough basic knowledge of a subject
**well′-heeled′** adj. [Slang] rich
**well′-in·formed′** adj. having considerable knowledge of a subject or of many subjects
**well′-in·ten′tioned** adj. having or showing good or kindly intentions
**well′-knit′** adj. 1. well constructed 2. sturdy in body build
**well′-known′** adj. 1. widely known; famous 2. thoroughly known
**well′-made′** adj. skillfully and soundly put together
**well′-man′nered** adj. having good manners; polite; courteous
**well′-mean′ing** adj. 1. having good intentions 2. said or done with good intentions: also **well′-meant′**
**well′-nigh′** adv. very nearly; almost
**well′-off′** adj. 1. in a fortunate condition 2. prosperous
**well′-pre·served′** adj. in good condition or looking good, in spite of age
**well′-read′** adj. having read much
**well′-round′ed** adj. 1. well planned for proper balance 2. showing diverse talents 3. shapely
**well′-spo′ken** adj. 1. speaking easily, graciously, etc. 2. spoken well
**well′spring′** n. 1. a spring 2. a source of abundant supply
**well′-thought′-of** adj. having a good reputation
**well′-timed′** adj. timely; opportune
**well′-to-do′** adj. prosperous; wealthy
**well′-turned′** adj. 1. gracefully shaped [a well-turned ankle] 2. expressed well [a well-turned phrase]
**well′-wish′er** n. one who wishes well to another, or to a cause, etc.
**well′-worn′** adj. much worn or used
**Welsh** (welsh) adj. of Wales, its people, etc. —n. the Celtic language of Wales —**the Welsh** the Welsh people —**Welsh′man** (-mən) n., pl. **-men**
**welsh** (welsh) vi. [Slang] to fail to pay a debt, fulfill an obligation, etc. (often with on) —**welsh′er** n.
**Welsh rabbit** a dish of melted cheese served on crackers or toast: also **Welsh rarebit**
**welt** (welt) n. [ME. welte] 1. a strip of leather in the seam between the sole and upper of a shoe 2. a ridge raised on the skin by a slash or blow
**welt·er** (wel′tər) vi. [< MDu. welteren] to roll about or wallow —n. a confusion; turmoil
**welt·er·weight** (wel′tər wāt′) n. [prob. < welt (to thrash)] a boxer or wrestler weighing 136 to 147 lb.
**wen** (wen) n. [OE. wenn] a benign skin tumor, esp. of the scalp
**wench** (wench) n. [< OE. wencel, child] 1. a young woman: derogatory term 2. [Archaic] a female servant
**wend** (wend) vt. [OE. wendan, to turn] to go on (one's way)
**went** (went) pt. of GO
**wept** (wept) pt. & pp. of WEEP
**were** (wur) [OE. wæron] pl. & 2d pers.

sing., past indic., and the past subj., of BE
**we're** (wir) we are
**weren't** (wurnt) were not
**were·wolf** (wir′woolf′, wur′-) n., pl. **-wolves′** [< OE. wer, man + wulf, wolf] Folklore a person changed into a wolf: also **werwolf**
**Wes·ley** (wes′lē, wez′-), **John** 1703-91; Eng. clergyman: founder of Methodism —**Wes′ley·an** adj., n.
**west** (west) n. [OE.] 1. the direction in which sunset occurs (270° on the compass, opposite east) 2. a region in or toward this direction 3. [W-] Europe and the Western Hemisphere —adj. 1. in, of, or toward the west 2. from the west —adv. in or toward the west
**West Berlin** W section of Berlin, associated with West Germany: pop. 2,200,000
**west′er·ly** adj., adv. 1. toward the west 2. from the west
**west′ern** adj. 1. in, of, or toward the west 2. from the west 3. [W-] of the West —n. a story or motion picture about cowboys, etc. in the western U.S.
**west′ern·er** n. a native or inhabitant of the west
**Western Hemisphere** that half of the earth including N. and S.America
**west′ern·ize′** (-īz′) vt. **-ized′, -iz′-ing** to make western in ways or ideas
**Western Samoa** island country in S. Pacific: 1,130 sq. mi.; pop. 134,000
**West Germany** W section of Germany; country in NC Europe: 95,735 sq. mi.; pop. 59,674,000
**West Indies** large group of islands extending from Florida to Venezuela —**West Indian**
**West Point** military reservation in SE N.Y.: site of U.S. Military Academy
**West Virginia** E State of the U.S.: 24,181 sq. mi.; pop. 1,744,000; cap. Charleston —**West Virginian**
**west′ward** (-wərd) adv., adj. toward the west Also **west′wards** adv.
**wet** (wet) adj. **wet′ter, wet′test** [OE. wæt] 1. covered or saturated with water or other liquid 2. rainy; misty 3. not yet dry [wet paint] 4. permitting the sale of alcoholic liquor —n. 1. water or other liquid 2. rain or rainy weather 3. one who favors the sale of alcoholic liquor —vt., vi. **wet** or **wet′ted, wet′ting** to make or become wet —**all wet** [Slang] wrong —**wet′ly** adv. —**wet′ness** n. —**wet′ter** n.
**wet′back′** n. [Colloq.] a Mexican who illegally enters the U.S. to work
**wet blanket** one who lessens the enthusiasm or gaiety of others
**wet nurse** a woman hired to suckle another's child —**wet′-nurse′** vt. **-nursed′, -nurs′ing**
**wet suit** a closefitting suit of rubber worn by skindivers for warmth
**we've** (wēv) we have

**whack** (hwak) *vt., vi.* [echoic] [Colloq.] to strike or slap with a sharp, resounding blow —*n.* [Colloq.] 1. *a)* a sharp, resounding blow *b)* the sound of this 2. a share 3. an attempt —**out of whack** [Colloq.] not in proper condition —**whack′er** *n.*

**whack′ing** *adj.* [Colloq.] very large

**whack′y** *adj.* **-i·er, -i·est** *same as* WACKY

**whale**[1] (hwāl) *n.* [OE. *hwæl*] a large, warmblooded sea mammal that breathes air —*vi.* **whaled, whal′ing** to hunt whales —**a whale of a** [Colloq.] an exceptionally large, impressive, etc. example of

**whale**[2] (hwāl) *vt.* **whaled, whal′ing** [prob. < WALE] [Colloq.] to thrash

**whale′bone′** *n.* the horny, elastic material hanging from the upper jaw of some whales (**whalebone whales**): used, esp. formerly, for corset stays, etc.

**whal′er** *n.* 1. a whaling ship 2. a man whose work is whaling

**wham** (hwam) *interj.* a sound imitating a heavy blow or explosion —*n.* a heavy blow or impact —*vt., vi.* **whammed, wham′ming** to strike, explode, etc. with a loud, sharp sound

**wham·my** (hwam′ē) *n., pl.* **-mies** [Slang] a jinx; the evil eye

**wharf** (hwôrf) *n., pl.* **wharves** (hwôrvz), **wharfs** [< OE. *hwerf*, a dam] a structure on a shore, at which ships are loaded or unloaded

**what** (hwut, hwät) *pron.* [< OE. *hwa, who*] 1. which thing, event, etc.? *[what* is that object?*]* 2. that or those which *[do what* you will*]* —*adj.* 1. which or which kind of: used interrogatively or relatively 2. as much, or as many, as *[take what* men you need*]* 3. how great, surprising, etc. *[what* nonsense!*]* —*adv.* 1. in what way? how? *[what* does it matter?*]* 2. partly *[what* with singing and joking, the time passed*]* 3. how greatly, etc. *[what* tragic news!*]* —*interj.* an exclamation of surprise, anger, etc. —**what about** what do you think, feel, etc. concerning? —**what for** why?

**what·ev·er** (hwət ev′ər) *pron.* 1. what: an emphatic variant 2. anything that *[say whatever* you like*]* 3. no matter what *[whatever* you do, don't hurry*]* —*adj.* 1. of any kind *[no plans whatever]* 2. being who it may be *[whatever* man said that, it's false*]*

**what′not′** *n.* a set of open shelves, as for bric-a-brac

**what′so·ev′er** (-sō ev′ər) *pron., adj.* whatever: an emphatic form

**wheal**[1] (hwēl) *n.* [ME. *whele*] a small, raised patch of skin, as from an insect bite

**wheal**[2] (hwēl) *n. same as* WEAL[1]

**wheat** (hwēt) *n.* [OE. *hwæte*] a cereal grass having spikes containing grains used in making flour, cereals, etc.

**wheat germ** the embryo of the wheat kernel, rich in vitamins

**whee·dle** (hwē′d'l) *vt., vi.* **-dled, -dling** [< ?] to influence or persuade (a person) or get (something) by flattery, coaxing, etc.

**wheel** (hwēl) *n.* [OE. *hweol*] 1. a circular disk or frame turning on a central axis 2. anything like a wheel in shape, movement, etc. 3. the steering wheel of a motor vehicle 4. *[pl.]* [Slang] an automobile 5. *[usually pl.]* the moving forces *[the wheels* of progress*]* 6. a turning movement 7. [Slang] an important person —*vt., vi.* 1. to move on or in a wheeled vehicle 2. to turn, revolve, etc. 3. to turn so as to change direction —**at the wheel** steering a motor vehicle, etc.

**wheel′bar′row** (-bar′ō, -ber′ō) *n.* a shallow, open box for moving small loads, having a wheel in front, and two shafts in back for moving the vehicle

**wheel′base′** *n.* in a motor vehicle, the distance in inches from the front axle to the rear axle

**wheel′chair′** *n.* a chair mounted on wheels, for persons unable to walk

**wheeled** (hwēld) *adj.* having wheels

**wheel·er-deal·er** (hwēl′ər dēl′ər) *n.* [Slang] one who is showily aggressive, as in arranging business deals

**wheel′wright′** (-rīt′) *n.* one who makes and repairs wheels and wheeled vehicles

**wheeze** (hwēz) *vi.* **wheezed, wheez′ing** [< ON. *hvæsa,* to hiss] to make a whistling, breathy sound, as in asthma —*n.* a wheezing —**wheez′y** *adj.* **-i·er, -i·est**

**whelk** (hwelk) *n.* [OE. *wioluc*] a large marine snail with a spiral shell, esp. a variety used in Europe for food

**whelm** (hwelm) *vt.* [ME. *welmen*] 1. to submerge 2. to overpower or crush

**whelp** (hwelp) *n.* [OE. *hwelp*] the young of a dog, etc. —*vt., vi.* to bring forth (young): said of animals

**when** (hwen) *adv.* [OE. *hwænne*] 1. at what time? *[when* did he leave?*]* 2. on what occasion? —*conj.* 1. at what time *[tell me when* to go*]* 2. at which time *[he* came at six, *when* the sun rose*]* 3. at the time that *[when* we were young*]* 4. as soon as *[we will eat when* he comes*]* 5. although —*pron.* what or which time *[until when* will you stay?*]* —*n.* the time *(of* an event*)*

**whence** (hwens) *adv.* [ME. *whennes*] from what place, source, cause, etc.; from where *[whence* do you come?*]*

**when·ev′er** *adv.* [Colloq.] when: an emphatic form —*conj.* at whatever time *[leave whenever* you like*]*

**where** (hwer) *adv.* [OE. *hwær*] 1. in or at what place? *[where* is it?*]* 2. to or toward what place? *[where* did he go?*]* 3. in what respect? *[where* is he at fault?*]* 4. from what place or source? *[where* did he learn it?*]* —*conj.* 1. at what place *[I see where* it is*]* 2. at which place *[I* came home, *where* I ate*]* 3. wherever 4. to the place to which *[we* go *where* you go*]* —*pron.* 1. the place at which *[a* mile to *where* I live*]* 2. what place *[where* are you from?*]* —*n.* the place *(of* an event*)*

**where′a·bouts′** (-ə bouts′) *adv.* near

what place? where? —*n.* the place where a person or thing is

**where·as'** (-az') *conj.* **1.** in view of the fact that **2.** while on the contrary [she is slim, *whereas* he is fat]

**where·at'** *conj.* [Archaic] at which point

**where·by'** *conj.* by which [a device *whereby* to make money]

**where'fore'** (-fôr') *adv.* [Archaic] for what reason? why? —*conj.* **1.** for which **2.** because of which —*n.* the reason

**where·in'** *conj.* in which

**where·of'** *adv.*, *conj.* of what, which, or whom

**where·on'** *conj.* on which

**where'up·on'** *conj.* **1.** upon which **2.** at which

**wher·ev·er** (hwer ev'ər) *adv.* [Colloq.] where: an emphatic form —*conj.* in, at, or to whatever place [go *wherever* you like]

**where·with'** *conj.* with which

**where'with·al'** (-with ôl') *n.* the necessary means, esp. money

**wher·ry** (hwer'ē) *n.*, *pl.* **-ries** [ME. *whery*] a light rowboat

**whet** (hwet) *vt.* **whet'ted, whet'ting** [< OE. *hwæt*, keen] **1.** to sharpen by rubbing or grinding, as a knife **2.** to stimulate, as the appetite

**wheth·er** (hweth'ər) *conj.* [OE. *hwæther*] **1.** if it be the case that [ask *whether* she sings] **2.** in case; in either case that: introducing alternatives [*whether* it rains or snows]

**whet·stone** (hwet'stōn') *n.* an abrasive stone for sharpening knives, etc.

**whew** (hyōō) *interj.* [echoic] an exclamation of relief, surprise, etc.

**whey** (hwā) *n.* [OE. *hwæg*] the thin, watery part of milk that separates from the curds

**which** (hwich) *pron.* [OE. *hwylc*] **1.** what one (or ones) of several? [which do you want?] **2.** the one (or ones) that [I know *which* I want] **3.** that [the boat *which* sank] **4.** any that [take *which* you like] —*adj.* what one or ones [*which* man (or men) came?]

**which·ev'er** *pron.*, *adj.* **1.** any one [take *whichever* (desk) you like] **2.** no matter which [*whichever* (horse) wins, he loses]

**whiff** (hwif) *n.* [echoic] **1.** a light puff or gust of air, etc. **2.** a slight odor

**whif·fle·tree** (hwif''l trē') *n.* same as SINGLETREE

**Whig** (hwig) *n.* [< *whiggamore* (contemptuous term for Scot. Presbyterians)] **1.** a member of a former English political party which championed reform and parliamentary rights **2.** a supporter of the American Revolution **3.** a member of a U.S. political party (c.1836–1856)

**while** (hwīl) *n.* [OE. *hwīl*] a period of time —*conj.* **1.** during the time that [I read *while* I eat] **2.** although; whereas [*while* not poor, he's not rich]

—*vt.* **whiled, whil'ing** to spend (time) pleasantly (often with *away*)

**whi·lom** (hwī'ləm) *adj.* [< OE.] former

**whilst** (hwīlst) *conj.* [Chiefly Brit. or U.S. Dial.] same as WHILE

**whim** (hwim) *n.* [< ?] a sudden fancy; idle and passing notion

**whim·per** (hwim'pər) *vi.*, *vt.* [? akin to WHINE] to cry or utter with low, whining, broken sounds —*n.* a whimpering sound or cry

**whim·si·cal** (hwim'zi k'l) *adj.* **1.** full of whims or whimsy **2.** oddly out of the ordinary —**whim'si·cal·i·ty** (-kal'ə tē) *n.* —**whim'si·cal·ly** *adv.*

**whim·sy** (hwim'zē) *n.*, *pl.* **-sies** [< ?] **1.** an odd fancy; idle notion; whim **2.** quaint or fanciful humor Also **whimsey,** *pl.* **-seys**

**whine** (hwīn) *vi.* **whined, whin'ing** [OE. *hwīnan*] **1.** *a)* to utter a high-pitched, nasal sound, as in complaint *b)* to make a prolonged sound like this **2.** to complain in a childish way —*n.* **1.** a whining **2.** a complaint uttered in a whining tone —**whin'y** *adj.*

**whin·ny** (hwin'ē) *vi.* **-nied, -ny·ing** [prob. < prec.] to neigh in a low, gentle way: said of a horse —*n.*, *pl.* **-nies** a whinnying

**whip** (hwip) *vt.* **whipped, whip'-ping** [< MDu. *wippen*, to swing] **1.** to move, pull, throw, etc. suddenly [to *whip* out a knife] **2.** to strike, as with a strap; lash **3.** to wind (cord, etc.) around a rope to prevent fraying **4.** to beat into a froth [to *whip* cream] **5.** [Colloq.] to defeat —*vi.* **1.** to move quickly and suddenly **2.** [to flap about —*n.* **1.** a flexible instrument for striking or flogging **2.** a blow, etc. as with a whip **3.** an officer of a political party in a legislature who maintains discipline, etc. **4.** a whipping motion —**whip up 1.** to rouse (interest, etc.) **2.** [Colloq.] to prepare quickly

**whip'cord'** *n.* **1.** a hard, twisted or braided cord **2.** a strong worsted cloth with a diagonally ribbed surface

**whip hand** control or advantage

**whip'lash'** *n.* **1.** the lash of a whip **2.** a sudden, severe jolting of the neck back and forth, as caused by the impact of an automobile collision

**whip'per·snap'per** *n.* an insignificant but presumptuous person

**whip·pet** (hwip'it) *n.* [< WHIP] a swift dog resembling a small greyhound, used in racing

**whip·ple·tree** (hwip''l trē') *n.* [< WHIP + TREE] same as SINGLETREE

**whip·poor·will** (hwip'ər wil') *n.* [echoic] a grayish bird of E N. America, active at night

**whir, whirr** (hwur) *vi.*, *vt.* **whirred, whir'ring** [ME. *quirren*] to fly, revolve, vibrate, etc. with a buzzing sound —*n.* such a sound

**whirl** (hwurl) *vi.* [< ON. *hvirfla*] **1.** to move rapidly in a circle or orbit **2.** to rotate or spin fast **3.** to seem to spin *[my head is whirling]* —*vt.* to cause to move, rotate, revolve, etc. rapidly —*n.* 1. a whirling or whirling motion 2. a tumult; uproar 3. a confused or giddy condition —**give it a whirl** [Colloq.] to make an attempt

**whirl·i·gig** (hwur'li gig') *n.* a child's toy that whirls or spins

**whirl'pool'** *n.* water in violent, whirling motion tending to draw floating objects into its center

**whirlpool bath** a bath in which an agitator drives a current of warm or hot water in a swirling motion

**whirl'wind'** *n.* 1. a current of air whirling violently around and around and moving forward 2. anything like a whirlwind —*adj.* impetuous; speedy

**whirl'y·bird'** *n.* [Colloq.] a helicopter

**whisk** (hwisk) *n.* [< ON. *visk*, a brush] 1. a brushing with a quick, light, sweeping motion 2. such a motion —*vt.*, *vi.* to move, carry, brush (*away, off,* etc.) with a quick, sweeping motion

**whisk broom** a small, short-handled broom for brushing clothes, etc.

**whisk'er** *n.* 1. [*pl.*] the hair growing on a man's face, esp. on the cheeks 2. any of the long, bristly hairs on the upper lip of a cat, rat, etc.

**whis·key** (hwis'kē) *n., pl.* **-keys, -kies** [< IrGael. *uisce*, water + *beathadh*, life] a strong alcoholic liquor distilled from the fermented mash of grain: also, esp. for Brit. and Canad. usage, **whisky**, *pl.* **-kies**

**whis·per** (hwis'pər) *vi., vt.* [OE. *hwisprian*] 1. to speak or say very softly, esp. without vibrating the vocal cords 2. to talk or tell furtively, as in gossip 3. to make a rustling sound —*n.* 1. a whispering 2. something whispered 3. a rustling sound

**whist** (hwist) *n.* [< Whist.] a card game: forerunner of bridge

**whis·tle** (hwis''l) *vi.* **-tled, -tling** [ME. *hwistlian*] 1. to make a clear, shrill sound as by forcing breath through the contracted lips 2. to move with a shrill sound, as the wind 3. *a)* to blow a whistle *b)* to have its whistle blown, as a train —*vt.* 1. to produce (a tune, etc.) by whistling 2. to signal, etc. by whistling —*n.* 1. an instrument for making whistling sounds 2. a whistling —**whis'tler** *n.*

**whistle stop** 1. a small town 2. a brief stop in a small town on a tour

**whit** (hwit) *n.* [< OE. *wiht*, a wight] the least bit; jot; iota

**white** (hwit) *adj.* **whit'er, whit'est** [OE. *hwit*] 1. having the color of pure snow or milk; opposite to black 2. of a light or pale color 3. pale; wan 4. lacking color 5. pure; innocent 6. having a light-colored skin —*n.* 1. *a)* white color *b)* a white pigment 2. a white or light-colored part, as the albumen of an egg or the white part of the eyeball 3. a person with a light-colored skin —**white'ness** *n.*

**white blood cell** (or **corpuscle**) same as LEUKOCYTE

**white'cap'** *n.* a wave with its crest broken into white foam

**white'-col'lar** *adj.* designating or of office and professional workers

**white-collar crime** fraud, embezzlement, etc. committed in business, government, or a profession

**white elephant** 1. an albino elephant, held as sacred in SE Asia 2. a thing of little use, but expensive to maintain 3. any object not wanted by its owner, but of possible value to others

**white feather** symbol of cowardice

**white'fish'** *n., pl.:* see FISH a white or silvery lake fish of the salmon family, found in N U.S. and Canada

**white flag** a white banner hoisted as a signal of truce or surrender

**white gold** a gold alloy that looks like platinum

**white goods** 1. household linens, as sheets, towels, etc. 2. large household appliances, as refrigerators

**white heat** 1. the degree of intense heat at which metal, etc. glows white 2. a state of intense emotion, etc. —**white'-hot'** *adj.*

**White House, the** 1. official residence of the President of the U.S., in Washington, D.C. 2. the executive branch of the U.S. government

**white lead** a poisonous, white powder, lead carbonate, used in paint

**white lie** a lie about a trivial matter, often told to spare someone's feelings

**whit·en** (hwīt''n) *vt., vi.* to make or become white or whiter —**whit'en·er** *n.* —**whit'en·ing** *n.*

**white race** loosely, the Caucasoid group of mankind

**white sale** a sale of household linens

**white slave** a woman forced into prostitution for others' profit — **white'-slave'** *adj.* —**white slavery**

**white'wall'** *adj.* designating or of a tire with a white band on the outer sidewall —*n.* a whitewall tire

**white'wash'** *n.* 1. a mixture of lime, chalk, water, etc. as for whitening walls, etc. 2. a concealing of faults in order to exonerate —*vt.* 1. to cover with whitewash 2. to conceal the faults of 3. [Colloq.] to defeat (an opponent) without letting him score

**whith·er** (hwi*th*'ər) *adv.* [OE. *hwider*] to what place, condition, result, etc.? where? —*conj.* 1. to which place, condition, result, etc. 2. wherever

**whit·ing**[1] (hwīt'iŋ) *n.* [< MDu. *wit*, white] 1. any of many unrelated food fishes of N.America, Europe, and Australia 2. a variety of European cod

**whit·ing**[2] (hwīt'iŋ) *n.* [ME. *whytyng*] powdered chalk used in paints, etc.

**whit'ish** *adj.* somewhat white

**Whit·man** (hwit'mən), **Walt(er)** 1819–92; U.S. poet

**Whit·ney** (hwit'nē), **Mount** mountain in EC Calif.

**Whit·sun·day** (hwit'sun'dē) *n.* [OE. *Hwita Sunnandæg*, lit., white Sunday] same as PENTECOST

---

**Where the sound (hw) occurs for wh, the sound (w) is also heard.**

**whit·tle** (hwit'l) *vt.* **-tled, -tling** [< OE. *thwitan*, to cut] 1. *a)* to cut thin shavings from (wood) with a knife *b)* to carve (an object) thus 2. to reduce gradually —*vi.* to whittle wood

**whiz, whizz** (hwiz) *vi.* **whizzed, whiz'zing** [echoic] 1. to make the hissing sound of something rushing through the air 2. to speed by with this sound —*n.* 1. this sound 2. [Slang] an expert [a *whiz* at football]

**who** (hōō) *pron.,* obj. **whom,** poss. **whose** [OE. *hwa*] 1. what or which person or persons [*who* is he? I know *who* came] 2. (the, or a, person or persons) that [a man *who* knows]

**WHO** World Health Organization

**whoa** (hwō) *interj.* stop!: used esp. in directing a horse to stand still

**who·dun·it** (hōō dun'it) *n.* [Colloq.] *same as* MYSTERY (sense 2)

**who·ev·er** (hōō ev'ər) *pron.* 1. any person that 2. no matter who [*whoever* said it, it's not so] 3. who?: an emphatic usage

**whole** (hōl) *adj.* [OE. *hal*] 1. healthy; not diseased or injured 2. not broken, damaged, etc.; intact 3. containing all the parts; complete 4. not divided up; in a single unit 5. *Arith.* not a fraction —*n.* 1. the entire amount 2. a thing complete in itself —**on the whole** all things considered; in general —**whole'ness** *n.*

**whole'heart'ed** *adj.* with all one's energy, enthusiasm, etc.; sincere

**whole milk** milk from which no butterfat, etc. has been removed

**whole note** *Music* a note (◯) having four times the duration of a quarter note

**whole'sale'** *n.* the selling of goods in large quantities and at lower prices, esp. to retailers —*adj.* 1. of or having to do with such selling 2. extensive or indiscriminate [*wholesale* criticism] —*adv.* 1. at wholesale prices 2. extensively or indiscriminately —*vt., vi.* **-saled', -sal'ing** to sell wholesale —**whole'sal'er** *n.*

**whole'some** (-səm) *adj.* [ME. *holsom*] 1. promoting good health or well-being; healthful 2. improving the mind or character 3. having health and vigor —**whole'some·ness** *n.*

**who'll** (hōōl) 1. who shall 2. who will

**whol·ly** (hō'lē) *adv.* to the whole amount or extent; entirely

**whom** (hōōm) *pron.* obj. *case of* WHO

**whoop** (hōōp, hwōōp) *n.* [< OFr. *houper,* cry out] 1. a loud shout, cry, etc., as of joy 2. the convulsive intake of air following a fit of coughing in whooping cough —*vt., vi.* to utter (with) a whoop or whoops

**whooping cough** an acute infectious disease, esp. of children, with coughing fits that end in a whoop

**whop·per** (hwäp'ər) *n.* [< colloq. *whop,* to beat] [Colloq.] 1. anything extraordinarily large 2. a great lie

**whop'ping** (-iŋ) *adj.* [Colloq.] extraordinarily large or great

**whore** (hôr) *n.* [OE. *hore*] a prostitute —**whor'ish** *adj.*

**whorl** (hwôrl, hwurl) *n.* [ME. *whorwyl*] anything with a coiled or spiral appearance, as any of the circular ridges forming the design of a fingerprint —**whorled** *adj.*

**who's** (hōōz) 1. who is 2. who has

**whose** (hōōz) *pron.* [OE. *hwæs*] that or those belonging to whom —*poss. pronominal adj.* of, belonging to, or done by whom or which

**who·so·ev·er** (hōō'sō ev'ər) *pron.* whoever: an emphatic form

**why** (hwi) *adv.* [< OE. *hwæt,* what] for what reason, cause, or purpose [*why* eat?] —*conj.* 1. because of which [no reason *why* I must] 2. the reason for which [that is *why* he went] —*n., pl.* **whys** the reason, cause, etc. [this is the *why* of it] —*interj.* an exclamation of surprise, impatience, etc.

**WI** Wisconsin

**Wich·i·ta** (wich'ə tô') city in S Kans.: pop. 277,000

**Wichita Falls** city in NC Tex.: pop. 98,000

**wick** (wik) *n.* [OE. *weoca*] a piece of cord, tape, etc., as in a candle or oil lamp, that absorbs the fuel and, when lighted, burns

**wick·ed** (wik'id) *adj.* [ME. < *wikke,* evil] 1. morally bad; evil 2. generally bad, unpleasant, etc. [a *wicked* storm] 3. mischievous 4. [Slang] showing great skill —**wick'ed·ly** *adv.* —**wick'ed·ness** *n.*

**wick·er** (wik'ər) *n.* [< Scand.] 1. a thin, flexible twig 2. *a)* such twigs or long, woody strips woven together, as in making baskets or furniture *b)* *same as* WICKERWORK (sense 1) —*adj.* made of wicker

**wick'er·work'** *n.* 1. things made of wicker 2. *same as* WICKER (sense 2*a*)

**wick·et** (wik'it) *n.* [ME. *wiket*] 1. a small door or gate, esp. one in or near a larger one 2. a small window, as in a box office 3. *Croquet* any of the small wire arches through which the balls must be hit

**wide** (wid) *adj.* [OE. *wid*] 1. extending over a large area, esp. from side to side 2. of a specified extent from side to side 3. of great extent [a *wide* variety] 4. open fully [eyes *wide* with fear] 5. far from the point, etc. aimed at [*wide* of the mark] —*adv.* 1. over a relatively large area 2. to a large or full extent [*wide* open] 3. so as to miss the point, etc. aimed at; astray —**wide'ly** *adv.* —**wide'ness** *n.*

**-wide** (wid) *a combining form meaning* extending throughout [statewide]

**wide'-an'gle** *adj. Photog.* having a wider angle of view than usual

**wide'-a·wake'** *adj.* 1. completely awake 2. alert

**wide'-eyed'** *adj.* with the eyes opened widely, as in surprise

**wid·en** (wīd''n) *vt.*, *vi.* to make or become wide or wider

**wide'spread'** *adj.* occurring over a wide area or extent

**widg·eon**, **wi·geon** (wij'ən) *n.* [prob. < MFr. *vigeon*] a wild, fresh-water duck

**wid·ow** (wid'ō) *n.* [OE. *widewe*] a woman whose husband has died and who has not remarried —*vt.* to cause to become a widow —**wid'ow·hood'** *n.*

**wid·ow·er** *n.* a man whose wife has died and who has not remarried

**width** (width) *n.* 1. distance from side to side 2. a piece of a certain width

**wield** (wēld) *vt.* [OE. *wealdan*] 1. to handle (a tool, etc.), esp. with skill 2. to exercise (power, control, etc.)

**wie·ner** (wē'nər) *n.* [< G. *Wiener wurst*, Vienna sausage] a smoked link sausage; frankfurter

**wie'nie** (-nē) *n.* [Colloq.] a wiener

**wife** (wīf) *n.*, *pl.* **wives** [OE. *wif*, woman] a married woman —**wife'less** *adj.* —**wife'ly** *adj.*

**wig** (wig) *n.* [< PERIWIG] a false covering of real or synthetic hair for the head —*vt.* **wigged**, **wig'ging** 1. to furnish with a wig 2. [Slang] *a)* to annoy, upset, etc. *b)* to excite, craze, etc. —*vi.* [Slang] to be or become upset, excited, etc.

**wig·gle** (wig''l) *vt.*, *vi.* **-gled**, **-gling** [ME. *wigelen*] to move with short, jerky motions from side to side —*n.* a wiggling —**wig'gler** *n.* —**wig'gly** *adj.* **-gli·er**, **-gli·est**

**wight** (wīt) *n.* [OE. *wiht*] [Archaic] a human being; person

**wig·let** (wig'lit) *n.* a small wig

**wig·wag** (wig'wag') *vt.*, *vi.* **-wagged'**, **-wag'ging** [< obs. *wig*, to move + WAG¹] 1. to move back and forth; wag 2. to send (a message) by waving flags, lights, etc. according to a code —*n.* the sending of messages in this way

**wig·wam** (wig'wäm) *n.* [< Algonquian] a N.American Indian shelter consisting of a framework of arched poles covered with bark, leaves, branches, etc.

**wild** (wīld) *adj.* [OE. *wilde*] 1. living or growing in its original, natural state 2. not lived in or cultivated; waste 3. not civilized; savage 4. not easily controlled [a *wild* boy] 5. lacking social or moral restraint; dissolute [a *wild* time] 6. turbulent; stormy 7. enthusiastic [*wild* about golf] 8. fantastically impractical; reckless 9. missing the target [a *wild* shot] 10. Card Games having any desired value: said of a card —*adv.* in a wild manner —*n.* [*usually pl.*] wilderness or wasteland —**wild'ly** *adv.* —**wild'ness** *n.*

**wild'cat'** *n.* 1. any fierce, medium-sized, undomesticated animal of the cat family 2. a fierce, aggressive person 3. a productive oil well in an area not previously known to have oil —*adj.* 1. unsound or risky 2. illegal or unauthorized —*vi.* **-cat'ted**, **-cat'-ting** to drill for oil in an area previously considered unproductive

**wil·de·beest** (wil'də bēst', vil'-) *n.*, *pl.* **-beests'**, **-beest'** [Afrik.] same as GNU

**wil·der·ness** (wil'dər nis) *n.* [< OE. *wilde*, wild + *deor*, animal] an uncultivated, uninhabited region; waste

**wild'-eyed'** *adj.* 1. staring in a wild way 2. very impractical or foolish

**wild'fire'** *n.* a fire that spreads fast and is hard to put out

**wild'fowl'** *n.* a wild bird, esp. a game bird: also **wild fowl**

**wild'-goose' chase** a futile search, pursuit, or endeavor

**wild'life'** *n.* wild animals and birds

**wild oats** (or **oat**) a wild grass common in the W U.S. —**sow one's wild oats** to be promiscuous or dissolute in youth

**wild rice** 1. an aquatic grass of the U.S. and Canada 2. its edible grain

**Wild West** the Western U.S. in its early, lawless frontier period

**wile** (wīl) *n.* [< OE. *wigle*, magic] 1. a sly trick; stratagem 2. a beguiling trick: *usually used in pl.* —*vt.* **wiled**, **wil'ing** to beguile; lure —**wile away** to while away (time, etc.)

**will¹** (wil) *n.* [OE. *willa*] 1. the power of making a reasoned choice or of controlling one's own actions 2. determination 3. attitude toward others [good *will*] 4. *a)* a particular desire, choice, etc. of someone *b)* mandate [the *will* of the people] 5. a legal document directing the disposal of one's property after death —*vt.* 1. to desire; want [to *will* to live] 2. to control by the power of the will 3. to bequeath by a will —*vi.* to wish, desire, or choose —**at will** when one wishes

**will²** (wil) *v.*, *pt.* **would** [OE. *willan*, to desire] an auxiliary used: 1. to express simple futurity 2. in formal speech, to express determination, obligation, etc. in the first person and futurity in the second and third persons See note at SHALL 3. to express: *a)* willingness [*will* you go?] *b)* ability or capacity [it *will* hold a pint] —*vt.*, *vi.* to wish; desire [do as you *will*]

**will·ful** (wil'fəl) *adj.* 1. said or done deliberately 2. obstinate; stubborn Also **wilful** —**will'ful·ly** *adv.* —**will'ful·ness** *n.*

**Wil·liam I** (wil'yəm) 1027?-87; king of England (1066-87): called *William the Conqueror*

**wil·lies** (wil'ēz) *n.pl.* [< ?] [Slang] a nervous feeling: with *the*

**will·ing** (wil'iŋ) *adj.* 1. favorably disposed; consenting [*willing* to play] 2. acting, giving, etc., or done, given, etc., readily and cheerfully —**will'ing·ly** *adv.* —**will'ing·ness** *n.*

**will·li·waw** (wil'i wô') *n.* 1. a violent, cold wind blowing from mountain to coast in far north or south latitudes 2. confusion; turmoil

**will-o'-the-wisp** (wil'ə thə wisp') *n.* 1. a light seen over marshes at night, believed to be marsh gas burning 2. a delusive hope or goal

**wil·low** (wil'ō) *n.* [OE. *welig*] 1. a tree with narrow leaves, and flexible twigs used in weaving baskets, etc. 2. its wood

**wil·low·y** (wil′ə wē) *adj.* like a willow; slender, lithe, etc.

**will′pow′er** *n.* strength of will, mind, or determination; self-control

**wil·ly-nil·ly** (wil′ē nil′ē) *adv., adj.* [contr. < *will I, nill I: nill* < OE. *nyllan,* be unwilling] (happening) whether one wishes it or not

**Wil·son** (wil′s′n), **(Thomas) Woodrow** 1856–1924; 28th president of the U.S. (1913–21)

**wilt** (wilt) *vi.* [< obs. *welk,* wither] **1.** to become limp, as from heat or lack of water; droop, as a plant **2.** to become weak or faint; lose strength or courage —*vt.* to cause to wilt

**Wil·ton** (**carpet** or **rug**) (wil′t′n) [< *Wilton,* England] a kind of carpet with a velvety pile of cut loops

**wi·ly** (wī′lē) *adj.* -li·er, -li·est full of wiles; crafty; sly —**wi′li·ness** *n.*

**wim·ple** (wim′p′l) *n.* [OE. *wimpel*] a nun's head covering so arranged as to leave only the face exposed

**win** (win) *vi.* **won, win′ning** [< OE. *winnan,* to fight] **1.** *a)* to gain a victory *b)* to finish first in a race, etc. **2.** to become by effort; get [*he won* loose from the crowd] —*vt.* **1.** to get by labor, struggle, etc. **2.** to be victorious in (a contest, etc.) **3.** to get to with effort [they *won* the camp by noon] **4.** to influence; persuade: often with *over* **5.** to gain (the sympathy, favor, etc.) of (someone) **6.** to persuade to marry one —*n.* [Colloq.] a victory, as in a contest

**wince** (wins) *vi.* **winced, winc′ing** [< OFr. *guenchir*] to shrink or draw back slightly, usually with a grimace, as in pain —*n.* a wincing

**winch** (winch) *n.* [OE. *wince*] **1.** a crank with a handle for transmitting motion **2.** an apparatus for hoisting or hauling, having a cylinder upon which is wound the rope, etc. attached to the object to be lifted or moved

**wind¹** (wīnd) *vt.* **wound, wind′ing** [OE. *windan*] **1.** to turn [*wind* the crank] **2.** to coil into a ball or around something else; twine **3.** to cover by entwining **4.** *a)* to make (one's way) in a twisting course *b)* to cause to move in a twisting course **5.** to tighten the spring of (a clock, etc.) as by turning a stem —*vi.* **1.** to move or go in a curving or sinuous manner **2.** to take a devious course **3.** to coil (*about* or *around* something) —*n.* a turn; twist —**wind up 1.** to wind into a ball, etc. **2.** to bring to an end; settle **3.** to make very tense, excited, etc. **4.** *Baseball* to swing the arm preparatory to pitching —**wind′er** *n.*

**wind²** (wind) *n.* [OE.] **1.** air in motion **2.** a strong current of air; gale **3.** air bearing a scent, as in hunting **4.** air regarded as bearing information, etc. [a rumor in the *wind*] **5.** breath or the power of breathing **6.** empty talk **7.** gas in the intestines **8.** [*pl.*] the wind instruments of an orchestra —*vt.* **1.** to

get the scent of **2.** to put out of breath —**get wind of** to hear of —**in the wind** happening or about to happen

**wind′break′** *n.* a hedge, fence, or trees serving as a protection from wind

**wind·ed** (win′did) *adj.* out of breath

**wind′fall** *n.* **1.** something blown down by the wind, as fruit from a tree **2.** an unexpected stroke of good luck

**wind′ing sheet** (wīn′diŋ) a shroud

**wind instrument** (wind) a musical instrument played by blowing air, esp. breath, through it, as a flute

**wind·jam·mer** (wind′jam′ər) *n.* a large sailing ship or one of its crew

**wind·lass** (wind′ləs) *n.* [< ON. *vinda,* to WIND¹ + *ass,* a beam] a winch, esp. one worked by a crank

WINDLASS

**wind′mill′** *n.* a mill operated by wind's rotation of large vanes radiating from a shaft

**win·dow** (win′dō) *n.* [< ON. *vindr,* WIND² + *auga,* an eye] **1.** an opening in a building, vehicle, etc. for letting in light or air or for looking through, usually having a pane of glass in a movable frame **2.** a windowpane **3.** an opening resembling a window

**window dressing 1.** the display of goods in a store window **2.** that which is meant to make something seem better than it really is —**win′dow-dress′** *vt.* —**window dresser**

**win′dow-pane′** *n.* a pane of glass in a window

**win′dow-shop′** *vi.* -shopped′, -shop′ping to look at goods in store windows without entering to buy

**win′dow-sill′** *n.* the sill of a window

**wind′pipe′** *n.* the trachea

**wind·row** (wind′rō′) *n.* a row of hay, etc. raked together to dry

**wind′shield** (wind′shēld′) *n.* in automobiles, etc., a glass screen in front, to protect from wind, etc.

**wind′sock′** (-säk′) *n.* a long cloth cone flown at an airfield to show wind direction: also **wind sleeve**

**Wind·sor** (win′zər) port in SE Ontario, Canada: pop. 193,000

**Wind·sor knot** (win′zər) a double slipknot in a four-in-hand necktie

**wind′storm′** *n.* a storm with a strong wind but little or no rain, etc.

**wind·up** (wīnd′up′) *n.* **1.** a conclusion; end **2.** *Baseball* the swinging of the arm preparatory to pitching

**wind·ward** (wind′wərd) *n.* the direction from which the wind blows —*adv.* toward the wind —*adj.* **1.** moving windward **2.** on the side from which the wind blows

**Windward Islands** group of islands in the West Indies, south of the Leeward Islands

**wind·y** (win′dē) *adj.* -i·er, -i·est **1.** with much wind [a *windy* city] **2.**

stormy, blustery, etc. 3. *a)* flimsy, intangible, weak, etc. *b)* long-winded, boastful, etc. —**wind′i·ness** *n.*

**wine** (wīn) *n.* [< L. *vinum*] 1. the fermented juice of grapes, used as an alcoholic beverage 2. the fermented juice of other fruits or plants —*vt.*, *vi.* **wined, win′ing** to provide with or drink wine: usually in **wine and dine** to entertain lavishly

**wine′-col′ored** *adj.* having the color of red wine; dark purplish-red

**win·er·y** (-ər ē) *n., pl.* **-ies** an establishment where wine is made

**wing** (wiŋ) *n.* [< ON. *vaengr*] 1. either of the paired organs of flight of a bird, bat, insect, etc. 2. something like a wing in use, position, etc.; esp., *a)* a (or the) main lateral supporting surface of an airplane *b)* a subordinate, projecting part of a building *c)* either side of the stage out of sight of the audience 3. the section of an army, fleet, etc. to the right (or left) of the center 4. a section, as of a political party, with reference to its radicalism or conservatism 5. a unit in an air force 6. a flying, or manner of flying —*vt.* 1. to provide with wings 2. *a)* to send swiftly as on wings *b)* to make (one's way) by flying *c)* to pass through or over as by flying 3. to wound in the wing, arm, etc. —*vi.* to fly —**on the wing** (while) flying —**take wing** to fly away —**under one's wing** under one's protection, etc. —**wing it** [Colloq.] to improvise in acting, speaking, etc. —**winged** (wiŋd; *poet.* wiŋ′id) *adj.* —**wing′less** *adj.*

**wing′span′** (-span′) *n.* the distance between the tips of an airplane's wings

**wing′spread′** *n.* 1. the distance between the tips of a pair of fully spread wings 2. *same as* WINGSPAN

**wink** (wiŋk) *vi.* [OE. *wincian*] 1. to close the eyelids and open them again quickly 2. to close and open one eyelid quickly, as a signal, etc. 3. to twinkle —*vt.* to make (an eye) wink —*n.* 1. a winking 2. an instant 3. a signal given by winking 4. a twinkle —**wink at** to pretend not to see

**win·ner** (win′ər) *n.* one that wins

**win·ning** (win′iŋ) *adj.* 1. victorious 2. attractive; charming —*n.* 1. a victory 2. [*pl.*] money that is won

**Win·ni·peg** (win′ə peg′) capital of Manitoba, Canada: pop. 257,000

**win·now** (win′ō) *vt., vi.* [< OE. *wind*, WIND²] 1. to blow (the chaff) from (grain) 2. to scatter 3. to sift out

**win·o** (wī′nō) *n., pl.* **-os** [Slang] an alcoholic who drinks cheap wine

**win·some** (win′səm) *adj.* [OE. *wynsum*, pleasant] sweetly attractive; charming —**win′some·ly** *adv.*

**Win·ston-Sa·lem** (win′stən sā′ləm) city in NC N.C.: pop. 133,000

**win·ter** (win′tər) *n.* [OE.] 1. the coldest season of the year, following autumn 2. a period of decline, distress, etc. —*adj.* of, during, or for winter —*vi.* to pass the winter —*vt.* to keep or maintain during the winter

**win′ter·green′** *n.* 1. an evergreen plant with white flowers and red berries

2. an aromatic oil (**oil of wintergreen**) made from its leaves and used as a flavoring 3. the flavor

**win′ter·ize′** (-īz′) *vt.* **-ized′, -iz′ing** to put into condition for winter

**win′ter·time′** *n.* the winter season

**win·try** (win′trē) *adj.* **-tri·er, -tri·est** of or like winter; cold, bleak, etc.

**win·y** (wī′nē) *adj.* **-i·er, -i·est** like wine in taste, smell, color, etc.

**wipe** (wīp) *vt.* **wiped, wip′ing** [OE. *wīpian*] 1. to clean or dry by rubbing with a cloth, etc. 2. to rub (a cloth, etc.) over something 3. to apply or remove by wiping —*n.* a wiping —**wipe out** 1. to remove; erase 2. to kill off 3. to destroy —**wip′er** *n.*

**wire** (wīr) *n.* [OE. *wīr*] 1. metal drawn into a long thread 2. a length of this 3. *a)* telegraph *b)* a telegram 4. the finish line of a race —*adj.* made of wire —*vt.* **wired, wir′ing** 1. to furnish, connect, bind, etc. with wire 2. to telegraph —*vi.* to telegraph

**wire′hair′** *n.* a fox terrier with a wiry coat: also **wire-haired terrier**

**wire′less** *adj.* without wire; specif., operating by electromagnetic waves, not with conducting wire —*n.* 1. wireless telegraphy or telephony 2. [Chiefly Brit.] radio

**Wire′pho′to** *a trademark for* a system of reproducing photographs, or a photograph reproduced, by electric impulses transmitted by wire

**wire service** an agency that sends news stories, etc. by telegraph to subscribers, as newspapers

**wire′tap′** *vi., vt.* **-tapped′, -tap′ping** to tap (a telephone wire, etc.) to get information secretly —*n.* 1. a wiretapping 2. a device for wiretapping

**wir′ing** *n.* a system of wires, as for carrying electricity

**wir·y** *adj.* **-i·er, -i·est** 1. of wire 2. like wire; stiff 3. lean and strong —**wir′i·ness** *n.*

**Wis·con·sin** (wis kän′s'n) Middle Western State of the U.S.: 56,154 sq. mi.; pop. 4,418,000; cap. Madison: abbrev. **Wis.**

**wis·dom** (wiz′dəm) *n.* [OE.: see WISE¹ & -DOM] 1. the quality of being wise; good judgment 2. learning; knowledge

**wisdom tooth** the back tooth on each side of each jaw

**wise¹** (wīz) *adj.* **wis′er, wis′est** [OE. *wīs*] 1. having or showing good judgment 2. informed 3. learned 4. shrewd; cunning 5. [Slang] conceited, impudent, fresh, etc. —**wise′ly** *adv.*

**wise²** (wīz) *n.* [OE.] way; manner —**wise** (wīz) [< prec.] *a suffix meaning:* 1. in a specified direction, position, or manner [*sidewise*] 2. in a manner characteristic of [*clockwise*] 3. with regard to [*weatherwise*]

**wise·a·cre** (wīz′ā′kər) *n.* [ult. < OHG. *wizzago*, prophet] one who pretends to be wiser than he really is

**wise′crack′** *n.* [Slang] a flippant or facetious remark —*vi.* [Slang] to make wisecracks

**wish** (wish) *vt.* [OE. *wyscan*] 1. to have a longing for; want 2. to express a desire concerning [I *wish* you well]

3. to request *[I wish you to go]* —*vi.*
1. to long; yearn 2. to make a wish
—*n.* 1. a wishing 2. something wished
for 3. a polite request, almost an order
4. *[pl.]* expressed desire for a person's
health, etc. *[best wishes]* —**wish'er** *n.*

**wish'bone'** *n.* the forked bone in
front of a bird's breastbone

**wish'ful** *adj.* having or showing a
wish; desirous —**wish'ful·ly** *adv.*

**wish·y-wash·y** (wish'ē wŏsh'ē) *adj.*
[Colloq.] 1. watery; thin 2. *a)* weak;
feeble *b)* vacillating; indecisive

**wisp** (wisp) *n.* [prob. < Scand.] 1. a
small bundle, as of straw 2. a thin or
filmy piece, strand, etc. *[a wisp of
smoke]* 3. something delicate, frail,
etc. —**wisp'y** *adj.* **-i·er, -i·est**

**wis·te·ri·a** (wis tîr'ē ə) *n.* [< C.
*Wistar*, 19th-c. U.S. anatomist] a
twining vine with showy clusters of
flowers: also **wis·tar'i·a** (-ter'-)

**wist·ful** (wist'fəl) *adj.* [< earlier
*wistly*, intently] showing or expressing
vague yearnings —**wist'ful·ly** *adv.*
—**wist'ful·ness** *n.*

**wit**[1] (wit) *n.* [OE.] 1. *[pl.]* powers of
thinking; mental faculties 2. good
sense 3. *a)* the ability to make clever
remarks in a sharp, amusing way
*b)* one characterized by wit

**wit**[2] (wit) *vt., vi.* **wist** (wist), **wit'ting**
[OE. *witan]* [Archaic] to know or learn
—**to wit** that is to say

**witch** (wich) *n.* [OE. *wicce*] 1. a
woman supposedly having supernatural
power by a compact with evil spirits
2. an ugly old shrew 3. [Colloq.] a
fascinating woman

**witch'craft'** *n.* the power or practices
of witches

**witch doctor** a person who practices
primitive medicine involving the use
of magic, as among tribes in Africa

**witch'er·y** (-ər ē) *n.* 1. witchcraft;
sorcery 2. bewitching charm

**witch hazel** [< OE. *wice*] 1. a shrub
with yellow flowers 2. a lotion made
from its leaves and bark

**with** (wi*th*, with) *prep.* [OE.] 1. in
opposition to *[he argued with me]*
2. *a)* alongside of; near to *b)* in the
company of *c)* into; among *[mix blue
with red]* 3. as a member of *[he plays
with a trio]* 4. concerning *[happy with
his lot]* 5. compared to 6. as well as
*[he rides with the best]* 7. in the
opinion of *[it's OK with me]* 8. as a
result of *[faint with hunger]* 9. by
means of 10. having received *[with
your consent, I'll go]* 11. having as a
possession, attribute, etc. 12. in the
keeping, care, etc. of *[leave it with me]*
13. in spite of 14. at the same time as
15. in proportion to *[wages that vary
with skill]* 16. to; onto *[join this end
with that one]* 17. from *[to part with
one's gains]* —**with that** after, or as a
consequence of, that

**with-** *a combining form meaning:* 1.
away, back *[withdraw]* 2. against,
from *[withhold]*

**with·al** (wi*th* ôl', with-) *adv.* 1. besides 2. despite that

**with·draw'** (-drô') *vt.* **-drew',
-drawn', -draw'ing** 1. to take back;
remove 2. to retract or recall (a
statement, etc.) —*vi.* 1. to move
back; go away; retreat 2. to remove
oneself *(from* an organization, activity,
etc.) —**with·draw'al** *n.*

**with·drawn'** *adj.* shy, reserved, etc.

**withe** (with, wī*th*) *n.* [< OE.] a
tough, flexible twig, as of willow, used
for binding things —*vt.* **withed,
with'ing** to bind with withes

**with·er** (wi*th*'ər) *vi.* [< ME. *wederen,*
to weather] 1. to dry up; wilt, as
plants 2. to become wasted or decayed
3. to weaken; languish —*vt.* 1. to cause
to wither 2. to cause to feel abashed

**with·ers** (wi*th*'ərz) *n.pl.* [< OE.
*wither,* against] the part of a horse's
back between the shoulder blades

**with·hold'** (with hōld', wi*th*-) *vt.*
**-held', -hold'ing** 1. *a)* to hold back;
restrain *b)* to deduct (taxes, etc.) from
wages 2. to refrain from granting

**withholding tax** the amount of income tax withheld from wages, etc.

**with·in** (wi*th* in', with-) *adv.* [OE.
*withinnan]* 1. on or into the inside
2. indoors 3. inside the body, mind,
etc. —*prep.* 1. in the inner part of
2. not beyond 3. inside the limits of
—*n.* the inside *[from within]*

**with·out'** *adv.* [OE. *withutan]* 1. on
the outside 2. out-of-doors —*prep.*
1. at, on, or to the outside of 2. lacking
3. free from 4. with avoidance of *[to
pass by without speaking]*

**with·stand'** (with stand', wi*th*-) *vt.,
vi.* **-stood', -stand'ing** to oppose,
resist, or endure, esp. successfully

**wit·less** (wit'lis) *adj.* lacking wit;
foolish —**wit'less·ly** *adv.*

**wit·ness** (wit'nis) *n.* [< OE. *witan,*
know] 1. evidence; testimony 2. one
who saw, or can give a firsthand account
of, something 3. one who testifies in
court 4. one who observes, and attests
to, a signing, etc. —*vt.* 1. to testify to
2. to serve as evidence of 3. to act as
witness of 4. to be present at —**bear
witness** to testify

**wit·ti·cism** (wit'ə siz'm) *n.* [< WITTY]
a witty remark

**wit·ting** (wit'ĭŋ) *adj.* [ME. *wytting]*
intentional —**wit'ting·ly** *adv.*

**wit'ty** *adj.* **-ti·er, -ti·est** [OE. *wittig]*
having or showing wit; cleverly amus-
ing —**wit'ti·ly** *adv.* —**wit'ti·ness** *n.*

**wive** (wīv) *vi., vt.* **wived, wiv'ing** [<
*wīfian]* [Archaic] to marry (a woman)

**wives** (wīvz) *n. pl. of* WIFE

**wiz·ard** (wiz'ərd) *n.* [ME. *wisard]* 1.
a magician; sorcerer 2. [Colloq.] one
very skilled at a certain activity

**wiz'ard·ry** *n.* magic; sorcery

**wiz·ened** (wiz'nd) *adj.* [< OE.
*wīsnian,* wither] dried up; withered

**wk.** *pl.* **wks.** 1. week 2. work

**wkly.** weekly

**WO, W.O.** Warrant Officer

---

fat, āpe, cär; ten, ēven; is, bīte; gō, hôrn, tōōl, look; oil, out; up, fur;
chin; she; thin, *then;* zh, leisure; ŋ, ring; ə for *a* in *ago;* ', (ā'b'l); ë, Fr. coeur;
ö, Fr. feu; Fr. mon; ü, Fr. duc; kh, G. ich, doch; ‡ foreign; < derived from

**wob·ble** (wäb′'l) *vi.* **-bled, -bling** [prob. < LowG. *wabbeln*] **1.** to move unsteadily from side to side; shake **2.** to vacillate —*vt.* to cause to wobble —*n.* wobbling motion —**wob′bly** *adj.* **-bli·er, -bli·est** —**wob′bli·ness** *n.*

**woe** (wō) *n.* [OE. *wa*] **1.** great sorrow; grief **2.** trouble —*interj.* alas!

**woe·be·gone′** (-bi gôn′) *adj.* of woeful appearance; looking sad or wretched

**woe′ful** (-fəl) *adj.* **1.** full of woe; sad **2.** of, causing, or involving woe **3.** pitiful; wretched —**woe′ful·ly** *adv.*

**wok** (wäk) *n.* [Chin.] a bowl-shaped cooking pan used, as in a ringlike stand, for frying, braising, etc.

**woke** (wōk) *alt. pt.* of WAKE[1]

**wolf** (woolf) *n., pl.* **wolves** [OE. *wulf*] **1.** a wild, flesh-eating, doglike mammal of the Northern Hemisphere **2.** *a)* a cruel or greedy person *b)* [Slang] a man who flirts with many women —*vt.* to eat greedily —**cry wolf** to give a false alarm —**wolf′ish** *adj.*

**wolf′hound′** (-hound′) *n.* a breed of large dog, once used for hunting wolves

**wolf·ram** (wool′frəm) *n.* [G.] *same as* TUNGSTEN

**wol·ver·ine** (wool′və rēn′) *n.* [< WOLF] a stocky, flesh-eating mammal of N.America and Eurasia

**wolves** (woolvz) *n., pl.* of WOLF

**wom·an** (woom′ən) *n., pl.* **wom′en** [< OE. *wif*, a female + *mann*, human being] **1.** an adult, female human being, or women collectively **2.** a female servant **3.** womanly qualities

**wom′an·hood′** *n.* **1.** the state of being a woman **2.** womanly qualities **3.** womankind

**wom′an·ish** *adj.* like a woman

**wom′an·ize′** *vt.* **-ized′, -iz′ing** to make effeminate —*vi.* [Colloq.] to be sexually promiscuous with women —**wom′an·iz′er** *n.*

**wom′an·kind′** *n.* women in general

**wom′an·like′** *adj.* womanly

**wom′an·ly** *adj.* **1.** womanish **2.** characteristic of or fit for a woman

**womb** (woom) *n.* [OE. *wamb*] uterus

**wom·bat** (wäm′bat) *n.* [< native name] a burrowing Australian marsupial resembling a small bear

**wom·en** (wim′in) *n., pl.* of WOMAN

**wom′en·folk′** *n.pl.* [Dial. or Colloq.] womankind: also **wom′en·folks′**

**won** (wun) *pt. & pp.* of WIN

**won·der** (wun′dər) *n.* [OE. *wundor*] **1.** a person, thing, or event causing astonishment and admiration; marvel **2.** the feeling aroused by something strange, unexpected, etc. —*vi.* **1.** to be filled with wonder; marvel **2.** to have curiosity, sometimes mingled with doubt —*vt.* to have curiosity or doubt about [I *wonder* why he came]

**won′der·ful** *adj.* **1.** that causes wonder; marvelous **2.** [Colloq.] fine, excellent, etc. —**won′der·ful·ly** *adv.*

**won′der·land′** *n.* an imaginary land full of wonders, or a real place like this

**won′der·ment** *n.* amazement

**won·drous** (wun′drəs) *adj.* wonderful —*adv.* surprisingly Now only literary —**won′drous·ly** *adv.*

**wont** (wônt, wônt) *adj.* [< OE. *wunian*, to dwell] accustomed [he was *wont* to eat late] —*n.* usual practice; habit

**won′t** (wōnt) will not

**wont·ed** (wōn′tid, wôn′-) *adj.* customary; accustomed

**won ton** (wän′ tän′) a Chinese dish of noodle casings filled with meat, often served in a broth (**won-ton soup**)

**woo** (woo) *vt.* [OE. *wogian*] **1.** to seek the love of, usually in order to propose marriage **2.** to seek [to woo fame] —*vi.* to woo a person —**woo′er** *n.*

**wood** (wood) *n.* [OE. *wudu*] **1.** [*usually pl.*] a thick growth of trees; forest **2.** the hard, fibrous substance beneath the bark of trees and shrubs **3.** lumber or timber **4.** any of certain golf clubs with wooden heads —*adj.* **1.** made of wood; wooden **2.** growing or living in woods —**out of the woods** [Colloq.] out of difficulty, danger, etc. —**wood′ed** *adj.*

**wood alcohol** a colorless, poisonous liquid obtained by the distillation of wood and used as a fuel, etc.

**wood′bine′** (-bīn′) *n.* [< OE. *wudu*, wood + *binde*, to bind] **1.** a climbing honeysuckle **2.** a climbing vine with dark-blue berries

**wood′carv′ing** (-kär′viŋ) *n.* **1.** the art of carving wood by hand **2.** an art object so made —**wood′carv′er** *n.*

**wood′chuck′** (-chuk′) *n.* [< AmInd. name] a N.American burrowing and hibernating marmot

**wood′cock′** (-käk′) *n.* a small game bird with short legs and a long bill

**wood′craft′** *n.* **1.** matters relating to the woods, as camping, hunting, etc. **2.** *same as* WOODWORKING

**wood′cut′** (-kut′) *n.* **1.** a wooden block engraved with a design, etc. **2.** a print made from this

**wood′cut′ter** *n.* one who fells trees, cuts wood, etc. —**wood′cut′ting** *n.*

**wood′en** (-'n) *adj.* **1.** made of wood **2.** stiff, lifeless, etc. **3.** dull; insensitive —**wood′en·ly** *adv.*

**wood′land′** (-land′, -lənd) *n.* land covered with woods —*adj.* of the woods

**wood′man** (-mən) *n., pl.* **-men** *same as* WOODSMAN

**wood′peck′er** (-pek′ər) *n.* a climbing bird with a strong, pointed bill used to peck holes in bark to get insects

**wood′pile′** *n.* a pile of wood, esp. of firewood

**wood screw** a sharp-pointed metal screw for use in wood

**wood′shed′** *n.* a shed for firewood

**woods·man** (woodz′mən) *n., pl.* **-men** **1.** one who lives or works in the woods **2.** one skilled in woodcraft

**wood′sy** (-zē) *adj.* **-si·er, -si·est** of or like the woods —**wood′si·ness** *n.*

**wood′wind′** *n.* any of the wind instruments of an orchestra made, esp. orig., of wood: flute, clarinet, oboe, English horn, and bassoon

**wood′work′** *n.* **1.** work done in wood **2.** things made of wood, esp. the moldings, doors, etc. of a house

**wood′work′ing** *n.* the art or work of making things of wood

**wood′y** *adj.* **-i·er, -i·est** **1.** covered with trees **2.** consisting of or forming wood **3.** like wood —**wood′i·ness** *n.*

**woof** (woof, woof) *n.* [ult. < OE. *wefan*, to weave] the horizontal threads crossing the warp in a woven fabric

**woof′er** *n.* in an assembly of two or more loudspeakers, a large speaker for reproducing low-frequency sounds

**wool** (wool) *n.* [OE. *wull*] **1.** the soft, curly hair of sheep or of some other animals, as the goat **2.** woolen yarn, cloth, clothing, etc. **3.** anything that looks or feels like wool

**wool′en, wool′len** (-ən) *adj.* **1.** made of wool **2.** relating to wool or woolen cloth —*n.* [*pl.*] woolen goods

**wool′gath′er·ing** (-gath′ər iŋ) *n.* absent-mindedness or daydreaming

**wool·ly** (wool′ē) *adj.* **-li·er, -li·est 1.** of or like wool **2.** bearing or covered with wool **3.** rough and uncivilized: chiefly in **wild and woolly 4.** confused [*woolly* ideas] Also **wool′y**

**wooz·y** (woo′zē) *adj.* **-i·er, -i·est** [Colloq.] dizzy or befuddled, as from drink —**wooz′i·ness** *n.*

**Worces·ter** (woos′tər) city in C Mass.: pop. 177,000

**word** (wurd) *n.* [OE.] **1.** *a)* a speech sound, or series of them, having meaning as a unit of language *b)* the written or printed representation of this **2.** a brief remark [a *word* of advice] **3.** a promise [he gave his *word*] **4.** news; information **5.** *a)* a password or signal *b)* a command, order, etc. **6.** [*pl.*] *a)* talk; speech *b)* lyrics; text *c)* a quarrel; dispute —*vt.* to express in words; phrase —**in a word** briefly —**the Word** the Bible —**word for word** in precisely the same words

**word′age** (-ij) *n.* quantity of words

**word′ing** *n.* choice of words; diction

**word of honor** solemn promise

**Words·worth** (wurdz′wurth), **Wil·liam** 1770–1850; Eng. poet

**word·y** (wur′dē) *adj.* **-i·er, -i·est** containing or using many or too many words; verbose —**word′i·ness** *n.*

**wore** (wôr) *pt.* of WEAR

**work** (wurk) *n.* [OE. *weorc*] **1.** effort exerted to do or make something; labor; toil **2.** employment; occupation **3.** something one is making or doing; task **4.** something made or done; specif., *a)* an act; deed: *usually used in pl.* [good *works*] *b)* [*pl.*] collected writings *c)* [*pl.*] engineering structures **5.** [*pl.*] a place where work is done, as a factory **6.** workmanship —*adj.* of, for, or used in work —*vi.* **worked** or **wrought, work′ing 1.** to do work; labor; toil **2.** to be employed **3.** to function or operate, esp. effectively **4.** to ferment **5.** to move, proceed, etc. slowly and with difficulty **6.** to come or become, as by repeated movement [the door *worked* loose] —*vt.* **1.** to cause; bring about [his idea *worked* wonders] **2.** to mold; shape **3.** to sew, embroider, etc. **4.** to solve (a mathematical problem, etc.) **5.** to manipulate; knead **6.** to bring into a specified condition [they *worked* it loose] **7.** to cultivate (soil) **8.** to operate; use **9.** to cause to work [to *work* a crew hard] **10.** to make (one's way, etc.) by effort **11.** to provoke; rouse [he *worked* her into a rage] —**at work** working —**out of work** unemployed —**the works 1.** the working parts (*of* a watch, etc.) **2.** [Colloq.] everything: also **the whole works** —**work off** to get rid of —**work on** (or **upon**) **1.** to influence **2.** to try to persuade —**work out 1.** to accomplish **2.** to solve **3.** to result **4.** to develop **5.** to have a workout —**work up 1.** to advance **2.** to develop **3.** to excite

**work′a·ble** (-ə b'l) *adj.* **1.** that can be worked **2.** practicable or feasible

**work·a·day** (wur′kə dā′) *adj.* **1.** of workdays; everyday **2.** ordinary

**work·a·hol·ic** (wur′kə hôl′ik) *n.* [<WORK & ALCOHOLIC] a person having a compulsive need to work

**work′bench′** (-bench′) *n.* a table at which work is done, as by a carpenter

**work′book′** *n.* a book of questions, exercises, etc. for use by students

**work′day′** *n.* **1.** a day on which work is done **2.** the part of the day during which work is done

**work·er** (wur′kər) *n.* **1.** one who works for a living **2.** one who works for a cause **3.** a sterile ant, bee, etc. that does work for the colony

**work′horse′** *n.* **1.** a horse used for working **2.** a steady, responsible worker

**work′house′** *n.* a prison where petty offenders are confined and made to work

**work′ing** *adj.* **1.** that works **2.** of, for, or used in work **3.** sufficient to get work done [a *working* majority] —*n.* the act of one that works

**work′ing·man′** *n.,* *pl.* **-men′** a worker, esp. an industrial worker

**work′man** (-mən) *n.,* *pl.* **-men 1.** *same as* WORKINGMAN **2.** a craftsman

**work′man·like′** *adj.* skillful

**work′man·ship′** *n.* skill of a workman, or the quality of his work

**work′out′** *n.* **1.** a training session of physical exercises **2.** any strenuous exercise, work, etc.

**work sheet 1.** a paper sheet on which work records, working notes, etc. are kept **2.** a paper sheet with problems to be worked on by students

**work′shop′** *n.* **1.** a room or building where work is done **2.** a seminar for specified intensive study, work, etc.

**work′up′** *n.* a complete medical study of a patient, including tests

**work′week′** *n.* the total number of hours or days worked in a week

**world** (wurld) *n.* [OE. *werold*] **1.** *a)* the earth *b)* the universe **2.** *a)* mankind *b)* people generally; the public **3.** *a)* [*also* **W-**] some part of the earth [the Old *World*] *b)* any sphere or domain [the dog *world*] **4.** individual experience, outlook, etc. [his *world* is narrow] **5.** secular life and interests, or people concerned with these **6.** [*often pl.*] a large amount [a *world* of good] —**for all the world** exactly

**world·ly** adj. **-li·er, -li·est 1.** of this world; secular **2.** devoted to the affairs, pleasures, etc. of this world **3.** worldly-wise —**world'li·ness** n.

**world·ly-wise'** adj. wise in the ways or affairs of the world; sophisticated

**World War I** the war (1914–18) involving Great Britain, France, Russia, the U.S., etc. on one side and Germany, Austria-Hungary, etc. on the other

**World War II** the war (1939–45) involving Great Britain, France, the Soviet Union, the U.S., etc. on one side and Germany, Italy, Japan, etc. on the other

**world'wide'** adj. extending throughout the world

**worm** (wurm) n. [< OE. *wyrm,* serpent] **1.** a long, slender, soft-bodied, creeping animal **2.** an abject or contemptible person **3.** something wormlike or spiral in shape, etc., as the thread of a screw **4.** [pl.] any disease caused by parasitic worms in the intestines, etc. —vi. to proceed like a worm, in a winding or devious manner —vt. **1.** to bring about, make, etc. in a winding or devious manner **2.** to purge of intestinal worms —**worm'y** adj.

**worm gear** a gear consisting of a rotating screw meshed with a toothed wheel

**worm'wood'** (-wood') n. [< OE. *wermōd*] **1.** a strong-smelling plant that yields a bitter-tasting oil used in making absinthe **2.** a bitter experience

WORM GEAR

**worn** (wôrn) pp. of WEAR —adj. **1.** damaged by use or wear **2.** exhausted

**worn'-out'** adj. **1.** used until no longer effective, usable, etc. **2.** exhausted; tired out

**wor·ri·ment** (wur'ē mənt) n. **1.** a worrying or being worried; anxiety **2.** a cause of worry

**wor·ri·some** (wur'ē səm) adj. **1.** causing worry or anxiety **2.** tending to worry —**wor'ri·some·ly** adv.

**wor·ry** (wur'ē) vt. **-ried, -ry·ing** [< OE. *wyrgan,* to struggle] **1.** to bite and shake with the teeth [the dog *worried* a shoe] **2.** to annoy, bother, etc. **3.** to make troubled or uneasy —vi. **1.** to bite or tear (at an object) **2.** to be anxious, troubled, etc. —n., pl. **-ries 1.** a troubled state of mind; anxiety **2.** a cause of this —**wor'ri·er** n.

**wor'ry·wart'** (-wôrt') n. [prec. + WART] one who tends to worry much

**worse** (wurs) adj. compar. of BAD[1] & ILL [OE. *wiersa*]. **1.** a) bad, evil, harmful, etc. in a greater degree b) of inferior quality **2.** in poorer health; more ill **3.** in a less satisfactory condition —adv. compar. of BADLY & ILL in a worse manner; to a worse extent —n. that which is worse —**worse off** in worse circumstances

**wors·en** (wur's'n) vt., vi. to make or become worse

**wor·ship** (wur'ship) n. [OE. *weorth-scipe*] **1.** a service or rite showing reverence for a deity **2.** intense love or admiration **3.** [Brit.] a title of honor, in addressing magistrates, etc. —vt. **-shiped** or **-shipped, -ship·ing** or **-ship·ping 1.** to show religious reverence for **2.** to have intense love or admiration for —vi. to engage in worship —**wor'ship·er, wor'ship·per** n.

**wor·ship·ful** adj. **1.** [Brit.] honorable; respected **2.** worshiping

**worst** (wurst) adj. superl. of BAD[1] & ILL [OE. *wyrsta*] **1.** bad, evil, harmful, etc. in the highest degree **2.** of the lowest quality —adv. superl. of BADLY & ILL in the worst manner; to the worst extent —n. that which is worst —vt. to defeat —**at worst** under the most unfavorable conditions —**if (the) worst comes to (the) worst** if the worst possible thing happens —**(in) the worst way** [Slang] very much; greatly —**make the worst of** to be pessimistic about

**wor·sted** (woos'tid, wur'stid) n. [< *Worstead,* England] **1.** a smooth, hard-twisted wool thread or yarn **2.** fabric made from this

**wort** (wurt) n. [OE. *wyrt-*] a liquid prepared with malt which, after fermenting, becomes beer, ale, etc.

**worth** (wurth) n. [OE. *weorth*] **1.** material value, esp. as expressed in money **2.** importance, value, merit, etc. **3.** the quantity to be had for a given sum [a dime's *worth*] —adj. **1.** deserving or worthy of **2.** equal in value to **3.** having wealth totaling

**worth'less** adj. without worth or merit; useless —**worth'less·ness** n.

**worth'while'** adj. worth the time or effort spent; of true value

**wor·thy** (wur'thē) adj. **-thi·er, -thi·est 1.** having worth, value, or merit **2.** meriting —n., pl. **-thies** a person of outstanding worth, etc. —**wor'thi·ly** adv. —**wor'thi·ness** n.

**would** (wood) v. [OE. *wolde*] **1.** pt. of WILL[2] **2.** an auxiliary used to express: a) condition [if you *would*] b) futurity [he said he *would* come] c) habitual action [Sundays he would rest] d) a request [*would* you help me?] **3.** I wish [*would* that I could]

**would'-be'** adj. **1.** wishing or pretending to be **2.** intended to be

**would·n't** (wood'nt) would not

**wound**[1] (woond) n. [OE. *wund*] **1.** an injury in which tissue is cut, torn, etc. **2.** any hurt to the feelings, honor, etc. —vt., vi. to inflict a wound (on or upon); injure

**wound**[2] (wound) pt. & pp. of WIND[1]

**wove** (wōv) pt. & alt. pp. of WEAVE

**wo·ven** (wōv'n) alt. pp. of WEAVE

**wow** (wou) interj. an exclamation of surprise, pleasure, etc. —vt. [Slang] to arouse enthusiasm in

**wpm** words per minute

**wrack** (rak) n. [< MDu. *wrak,* wreck] ruin; destruction [*wrack* and ruin]

**wraith** (rāth) n. [Scot.] a ghost

**wran·gle** (raŋ'g'l) vi. **-gled, -gling** [< OE. *wringan,* to press] to argue; quarrel; esp. angrily and noisily —n. an angry, noisy dispute —**wran'gler** n.

**wran·gler** (-glər) n. [< AmSp. *cabal-*

*lerango*, a groom] a cowboy who herds livestock, esp. saddle horses —**wran′-gle** *vt.* **-gled, -gling**

**wrap** (rap) *vt.* **wrapped** or **wrapt,** **wrap′ping** [ME. *wrappen*] 1. to wind or fold a (covering) around (something) 2. to enclose and fasten in paper, etc. —*vi.* to twine, coil, etc. (*over, around,* etc.) —*n.* 1. an outer covering or garment 2. [*pl.*] secrecy; censorship —**wrapped up** in absorbed in —**wrap up** [Colloq.] to conclude; settle

**wrap′per** *n.* 1. one that wraps 2. that in which something is wrapped 3. a woman's dressing gown

**wrap′ping** *n.* [often *pl.*] the material in which something is wrapped

**wrap′-up′** *n.* [Colloq.] a concluding, summarizing statement, report, etc.

**wrath** (rath) *n.* [OE., angry] 1. intense anger; rage; fury 2. any action of vengeance —**wrath′ful** *adj.*

**wreak** (rēk) *vt.* [OE. *wrecan,* to revenge] 1. to give vent to (anger, etc.) 2. to inflict (vengeance, etc.)

**wreath** (rēth) *n.,* *pl.* **wreaths** (rēthz) [OE. *writha*] 1. a twisted ring of leaves, flowers, etc. 2. something like this in shape [*wreaths* of smoke]

**wreathe** (rēth) *vt.* **wreathed, wreath′-ing** 1. to form into a wreath 2. to coil or twist around; encircle 3. to decorate with wreaths

**wreck** (rek) *n.* [< ON. *vrek,* driftwood] 1. a shipwreck 2. the remains of something destroyed 3. a run-down person 4. a wrecking or being wrecked —*vt.* 1. to destroy or damage badly; ruin 2. to tear down (a building, etc.) 3. to overthrow; thwart

**wreck′age** (-ij) *n.* 1. a wrecking or being wrecked 2. the remains of something wrecked

**wreck′er** *n.* 1. one who wrecks 2. one that salvages or removes wrecks

**wren** (ren) *n.* [OE. *wrenna*] a small songbird with a stubby, erect tail

**wrench** (rench) *n.* [OE. *wrenc,* a trick] 1. a sudden, sharp twist or pull 2. an injury caused by a twist, as to the back 3. a sudden feeling of grief, etc. 4. a tool for turning nuts, bolts, pipes, etc. —*vt.* 1. to twist or jerk violently 2. to injure with a twist 3. to distort (a meaning, etc.)

STILLSON WRENCH

MONKEY WRENCH

SINGLE-HEADED END WRENCH

**wrest** (rest) *vt.* [OE. *wræstan*] 1. to pull or force away violently with a twisting motion 2. to take by force; usurp —*n.* a wresting; twist

**wres·tle** (res′'l) *vi., vt.* **-tled, -tling** [see prec.] 1. to struggle hand to hand with (an opponent) in an attempt to throw him 2. to contend (with) —*n.* a wrestling —**wres′tler** *n.*

**wretch** (rech) *n.* [OE. *wrecca,* outcast] 1. a miserable or unhappy person 2. a person despised or scorned

**wretch′ed** (-id) *adj.* 1. very unhappy; miserable 2. distressing; dismal 3. poor in quality 4. contemptible; despicable —**wretch′ed·ly** *adv.* —**wretch′ed·ness** *n.*

**wrig·gle** (rig′'l) *vi.* **-gled, -gling** [MLowG. *wriggeln*] 1. to twist and turn; squirm 2. to move along with a twisting motion 3. to make one's way by shifty means —*n.* a wriggling —**wrig′gler** *n.* —**wrig′gly** *adj.*

**wright** (rīt) *n.* [< OE. *wyrcan,* to work] one who makes or constructs

**wring** (rin) *vt.* **wrung, wring′ing** [OE. *wringan*] 1. a) to squeeze, press, or twist b) to force (out water, etc.) by this means 2. to extract by force, threats, etc. 3. to twist (the hands) in distress 4. to clasp (another's hand) in greeting —*n.* a wringing

**wring′er** *n.* a machine with rollers to squeeze water from wet clothes

**wrin·kle¹** (rin′k'l) *n.* [ME. *wrinkel*] 1. a small furrow in a normally smooth surface 2. a crease in the skin —*vt., vi.* **-kled, -kling** to form wrinkles (in); pucker; crease —**wrin′kly** *adj.* **-kli-er, -kli-est**

**wrin·kle²** (rin′k'l) *n.* [< OE. *wrenc,* a trick] [Colloq.] a clever trick, idea, etc.

**wrist** (rist) *n.* [OE.] the joint between the hand and forearm —**a slap on the wrist** a token punishment

**wrist′band′** *n.* a band that goes around the wrist, as on a cuff

**wrist′watch′** *n.* a watch worn on a strap or band around the wrist

**writ** (rit) *n.* [OE. < *writan,* write] a formal legal document ordering or prohibiting some action

**write** (rīt) *vt.* **wrote, writ′ten, writ′-ing** [OE. *writan*] 1. to form (words, letters, etc.) on a surface, as with a pen 2. to compose (literary or musical material) 3. to communicate (with) in writing [he *wrote* (me) that he was ill] 4. to record (information) in a computer —*vi.* to write words, books, a letter, etc. —**write off** 1. to remove from accounts (bad debts, etc.) 2. to drop from consideration 3. to amortize —**write out** 1. to put into writing 2. to write in full —**write up** to write an account of

**write′-in′** *n.* a candidate whose name is not on the ballot, but is written in by a voter

**write′-off′** *n.* something written off, amortized, etc.

**writ′er** *n.* one who writes, esp. as an occupation; author

**write′-up′** *n.* [Colloq.] a written report, specif. a favorable one

**writhe** (rīth) *vt.* **writhed, writh′ing** [OE. *writhan,* to twist] to cause to twist or turn; contort —*vi.* **1.** to twist or turn; squirm **2.** to suffer great emotional distress —*n.* a writhing

**writ·ing** (rīt′iŋ) *n.* **1.** the act of one who writes **2.** something written **3.** written form **4.** handwriting

**writing paper** paper for writing on, esp. stationery

**writ′ten** (rit′'n) *pp.* of WRITE

**wrong** (rôŋ) *adj.* [< ON. *rangr*, twisted] **1.** not in accordance with justice, law, morality, an established standard, etc. **2.** not suitable or appropriate **3.** *a)* contrary to fact, etc.; incorrect *b)* mistaken **4.** not functioning properly **5.** not meant to be seen [the *wrong* side of a fabric] —*adv.* in a wrong manner, direction, etc. —*n.* something wrong; esp., an unjust, immoral, or illegal act —*vt.* to treat badly or unjustly —**in the wrong** wrong, immoral, etc. —**wrong′ly** *adv.* —**wrong′ness** *n.*

**wrong′do·ing** *n.* any wrong act or behavior —**wrong′do′er** *n.*

**wrong′ful** *adj.* **1.** unjust, unfair, or injurious **2.** unlawful —**wrong′ful·ly** *adv.* —**wrong′ful·ness** *n.*

**wrong′head′ed** *adj.* stubborn or per-

verse —**wrong′head′ed·ly** *adv.* —**wrong′head′ed·ness** *n.*

**wrote** (rōt) *pt.* of WRITE

**wroth** (rôth) *adj.* [OE. *wrath*] angry; wrathful; incensed

**wrought** (rôt) *alt. pt. & pp.* of WORK —*adj.* **1.** formed; made **2.** shaped by hammering, etc.: said of metals

**wrought iron** tough, ductile iron containing very little carbon — **wrought′-i′ron** *adj.*

**wrought′-up′** *adj.* very disturbed or excited

**wrung** (ruŋ) *pt. & pp.* of WRING

**wry** (rī) *adj.* wri′er, wri′est [< OE. *wrigian*, to turn] **1.** twisted; distorted **2.** distorted in a grimace [a *wry* face] **3.** ironic, sardonic, etc. [*wry* humor] —**wry′ly** *adv.* —**wry′ness** *n.*

**wt.** weight

**Wu·han** (wōō′hän′) city in EC China: pop. 2,500,000

**W.Va., WV** West Virginia

**WWI** World War I

**WWII** World War II

**Wy·o·ming** (wī ō′miŋ) Western State of the U.S.: 97,914 sq. mi.; pop. 332,000; cap. Cheyenne: abbrev. **Wyo., WY**

# X, Y, Z

**X, x** (eks) *n., pl.* **X's, x's** the 24th letter of the English alphabet

**X** (eks) *n.* the Roman numeral 10

**X** a motion-picture rating for a film to which no one under seventeen is to be admitted

**x** *Math.* **1.** an unknown quantity **2.** times (in multiplication)

**X chromosome** *see* SEX CHROMOSOME

**xe·non** (zē′nän) *n.* a colorless, gaseous chemical element: symbol, Xe

**xen·o·pho·bi·a** (zen′ə fō′bē ə) *n.* [< Gr. *xenos*, strange + -PHOBIA] fear or hatred of strangers or foreigners — **xen′o·phobe′** (-fōb′) *n.* —**xen′o·pho′bic** (-fō′bik, -fäb′ik) *adj.*

**xe·rog·ra·phy** (zi räg′rə fē) *n.* [< ff. + -GRAPHY] a process for copying printed material, etc. by the action of light on an electrically charged surface —**xe·ro·graph·ic** (zir′ə graf′ik) *adj.*

**Xe·rox** (zir′äks) *a trademark for a* process of xerography —*vt., vi.* to reproduce by this process

**Xer·xes I** (zurk′sēz) 519?-465? B.C.; king of Persia (486?-465?)

**xi** (zī, sī) *n.* the 14th letter of the Greek alphabet (Ξ, ξ)

**XL** extra large

**Xmas** (kris′məs) *n.* Christmas

**X-ray** (eks′rā′) *n.* **1.** a ray or radiation of very short wavelength, that can penetrate solid substances: used to study internal body structures and treat various disorders **2.** a photograph made with X-rays —*adj.* of or by X-rays —*vt.* to examine, treat, or photograph with X-rays Also **X ray, x-ray, x ray**

**xy·lem** (zī′ləm) *n.* [< Gr. *xylon*, wood] the woody tissue of a plant

**xy·lo·phone** (zī′lə fōn′) *n.* [< Gr. *xylon*, wood + -PHONE] a musical percussion instrument having a series of graduated wooden bars struck with small, wooden hammers —**xy′lo·phon′ist** (-fō′nist, zī läf′ə nist). *n.*

**Y, y** (wī) *n., pl.* **Y's, y's** the 25th letter of the English alphabet

**-y¹** (ē, i) [ME.] *a suffix meaning* little, dear [*kitty, daddy*]

**-y²** (ē, i) [OE. *-ig*] *a suffix meaning:* **1.** full of, like, etc. [*dirty*] **2.** rather [*dusky*] **3.** tending to [*sticky*]

**-y³** (ē, i) [< L. *-ia*] *a suffix meaning:* **1.** quality or condition [*jealousy*] **2.** a specified shop, group, etc. [*bakery*]

**-y⁴** (ē, i) [< L. *-ium*] *a suffix meaning* action of [*inquiry, entreaty*]

**yacht** (yät) *n.* [Du. *jacht*] a small ship for cruises, racing, etc.

**yacht′ing** *n.* the sport of sailing a yacht —**yachts′man** (-mən) *n.*

**Ya·hoo** (yä′hōō, yä′-) *n.* in Swift's *Gulliver's Travels*, any of a race of brutish, degraded creatures

**Yah·weh, Yah·we** (yä′we) [Heb.: see JEHOVAH] God

**yak¹** (yak) *n.* [Tibetan *gyak*] a long-haired wild ox of Tibet and C Asia

**yak²** (yak) *vi.* **yakked, yak′king** [echoic] [Slang] to talk much or idly —*n.* [Slang] **1.** a yakking **2.** a laugh

**yam** (yam) *n.* [< WAfr.] **1.** the edible, starchy, tuberous root of a tropical climbing plant **2.** [South] a large variety of sweet potato

**yam·mer** (yam'ər) *vi.* [ < OE. *geomor*, sad] 1. to whine, whimper, or complain 2. to shout, yell, etc. —*vt.* to say complainingly —**yam'mer·er** *n.*

**yang** (yäŋ, yaŋ) *n.* [Chin.] in Chinese philosophy, the masculine force or principle in the universe: cf. YIN

**Yang·tze** (yaŋ'sē) river in C China, flowing into the East China Sea

**Yank** (yaŋk) *n.* [Slang] a Yankee; esp., a U.S. soldier in World Wars I and II —*adj.* of or like Yanks

**yank** (yaŋk) *n., vt., vi.* [ < ?] [Colloq.] jerk

**Yan·kee** (yaŋ'kē) *n.* [ < ? Du. *Jan Kees*, a disparaging nickname] 1. a New Englander 2. a native of a Northern State 3. a citizen of the U.S. —*adj.* of or like Yankees

**yap** (yap) *vi.* yapped, yap'ping [echoic] 1. to make a sharp, shrill bark 2. [Slang] to talk noisily and stupidly —*n.* 1. a sharp, shrill bark 2. [Slang] *a*) jabber *b*) the mouth

**yard**[1] (yärd) *n.* [OE. *gierd*, rod] 1. a measure of length, 3 feet or 36 inches 2. *Naut.* a slender rod or spar fastened across a mast to support a sail

**yard**[2] (yärd) *n.* [OE. *geard*, enclosure] 1. the ground around or next to a house or other building 2. an enclosed place for a particular purpose [*shipyard*] 3. a rail center where trains are switched, etc.

**yard·age** (yär'dij) *n.* 1. measurement in yards 2. the extent so measured

**yard'arm**' *n. Naut.* either end of a yard supporting a square sail, etc.

**yard goods** textiles made in standard widths, usually sold by the yard

**yard'man** (-mən) *n., pl.* -men a man who works in a yard, esp. a railroad yard

**yard'stick**' *n.* 1. a graduated measuring stick one yard in length 2. any standard used in judging, etc.

**yar·mul·ke, yar·mal·ke** (yär'məlkə) *n.* [Yid. < Pol.] a skullcap often worn by Jewish men, as at prayer

**yarn** (yärn) *n.* [OE. *gearn*] 1. fibers of wool, cotton, etc., spun into strands for weaving, knitting, etc. 2. [Colloq.] a tale or story

**yaw** (yô) *vi.* [ON. *jaga*, sway] to turn from the planned heading, as a ship, spacecraft, etc. —*n.* a yawing

**yawl** (yôl) *n.* [ < Du. *jol*] a small, two-masted sailboat rigged fore-and-aft

**yawn** (yôn) *vi.* [ME. *yanen*] 1. to open the mouth wide involuntarily, as a result of fatigue, drowsiness, etc. 2. to open wide; gape —*n.* a yawning

**yaws** (yôz) *n.pl.* [*with sing. v.*] [of WInd. origin] a tropical, infectious skin disease

**Y chromosome** *see* SEX CHROMOSOME

**y·clept, y·clept** (i klept') *pp.* [ < OE. *clipian*, to call] [Archaic] called; named: also **ycleped, y·cleped**

**yd.** *pl.* **yds., yds.** yard

**ye**[1] (thə, thi, thē; *now often erroneously* yē) *adj. archaic form of* THE

**ye**[2] (yē) *pron.* [OE. *ge*] *archaic form of* YOU

**yea** (yā) *adv.* [OE. *gea*] 1. yes 2. indeed; truly —*n.* 1. an affirmative vote 2. a person voting affirmatively

**yeah** (ya, ye) *adv.* [Colloq.] yes

**year** (yir) *n.* [OE. *gear*] 1. a period of 365 days (366 in leap year) beginning Jan. 1 2. the period (365 days, 5 hours, 48 minutes, 46 seconds) of one revolution of the earth around the sun: also **solar year** 3. a period of 12 calendar months reckoned from any date 4. an annual period of less than 365 days [a school *year*] 5. [*pl.*] *a*) age [old for his *years*] *b*) a long time —**year after year** every year

**year'book**' *n.* an annual book, as one giving data of the preceding year

**year·ling** (yir'liŋ, yur'-) *n.* an animal one year old or in its second year

**year·ly** (yir'lē) *adj.* 1. lasting a year 2. once a year or every year 3. of a year, or each year —*adv.* every year

**yearn** (yurn) *vi.* [ < OE. *georn*, eager] 1. to be filled with longing or desire 2. to be deeply moved, esp. with tenderness —**yearn'ing** *n.*

**year'-round**' *adj.* open, in use, operating, etc. throughout the year

**yeast** (yēst) *n.* [OE. *gist*] 1. a yellowish, moist mass of minute fungi that cause fermentation: used in making beer, etc., and as leavening 2. yeast dried in flakes or granules or compressed into cakes 3. foam; froth 4. ferment; agitation

**yeast'y** *adj.* -i·er, -i·est 1. of, like, or containing yeast 2. frothy; light

**yegg** (yeg) *n.* [ < ?] [Slang] a criminal, esp. a burglar, etc.

**yell** (yel) *vi., vt.* [OE. *giellan*] to cry out loudly; scream —*n.* 1. a loud outcry 2. a rhythmic cheer in unison

**yel·low** (yel'ō) *adj.* [OE. *geolu*] 1. of the color of ripe lemons 2. having a somewhat yellow skin 3. [Colloq.] cowardly 4. sensational, as a newspaper —*n.* 1. a yellow color 2. an egg yolk —*vt., vi.* to make or become yellow —**yel'low·ish** *adj.*

**yellow fever** an infectious tropical disease caused by a virus transmitted by the bite of a certain mosquito

**yellow jacket** a wasp or hornet having bright-yellow markings

**Yellow River** *same as* HWANG HO

**Yellow Sea** arm of the East China Sea, between China and Korea

**yelp** (yelp) *vi., vt.* [OE. *gielpan*, to boast] to utter or express in a short, sharp cry or bark, as a dog —*n.* a short, sharp cry or bark

**Yem·en** (yem'ən) 1. country in S Arabia, on the Red Sea: 75,000 sq. mi.; pop. 5,000,000: in full **Yemen Arab Republic** 2. country just east of this: 110,000 sq. mi.; pop. 1,475,000: in full **People's Democratic Republic of Yemen**

**yen**[1] (yen) *n., pl.* **yen** [Jap.] the monetary unit of Japan

---

fat, āpe, cär; ten, ēven; ĭs, bīte; gō, hôrn, tōōl, look; oil, out; up, fur; chin; she; thin, then; zh, leisure; ŋ, ring; ə for a in ago; ', (ā'b'l); ë, Fr. coeur; ö, Fr. feu; ü, Fr. mon; kh, G. ich, doch; ‡ foreign; < derived from

**yen²** (yen) *n.* [Chin. *yan*, opium] [Colloq.] a strong longing or desire

**yeo·man** (yō′mən) *n., pl.* **-men** [ME. *yeman*] 1. orig., a freeholder of a class below the gentry 2. *U.S. Navy* a petty officer assigned to clerical duty

**yeo′man·ry** *n.* yeomen collectively

**yes** (yes) *adv.* [OE. *gese*] 1. aye; it is so: expressing agreement, consent, etc. 2. not only that, but more [ready, yes, glad to go] —*n., pl.* **yes′es** an affirmative reply, vote, etc. —*vt., vi.* yessed, yes′sing to say *yes* (to)

**yes man** [Slang] a person always approving what his superior says

**yes·ter** (yes′tər) *adj.* of yesterday or previous to this [yestereve]

**yes·ter·day** (yes′tər dē, -dā′) *n.* [< OE. *geostran*, yesterday + *dæg*, day] 1. the day before today 2. a recent day or time —*adv.* 1. on the day before today 2. recently

**yet** (yet) *adv.* [OE. *giet*] 1. up to now; thus far [he hasn't gone *yet*] 2. at the present time; now [we can't go just *yet*] 3. still [there is *yet* a chance] 4. in addition; even [he was *yet* more kind] 5. nevertheless [she's kind, *yet* dull] —*conj.* nevertheless; however [she seems well, *yet* she is ill] —as *yet* up to now

**yew** (yōo) *n.* [OE. *iw*] 1. an evergreen tree with needle leaves 2. its wood

**Yid·dish** (yid′ish) *n.* [< G. *jüdisch*, Jewish < L. *Judaeus*, Jew] a language derived from medieval High German, written in the Hebrew alphabet, and spoken esp. by East European Jews

**yield** (yēld) *vt.* [OE. *gieldan*, to pay] 1. to produce as a crop, result, profit, etc. 2. to surrender 3. to concede —*vi.* 1. to produce 2. to surrender 3. to give way to physical force 4. to lose precedence, etc. (often with *to*) —*n.* the amount yielded

**yield′ing** *adj.* flexible; submissive

**yin** (yin) *n.* [Chin.] in Chinese philosophy, the feminine force or principle in the universe: cf. YANG

**yip** (yip) *n.* [echoic] [Colloq.] a yelp or bark —*vi.* yipped, yip′ping [Colloq.] to yelp or bark

**yip·pie** (yip′ē) *n.* [Slang] a person in the U.S. belonging to a loosely organized group of young radicals

**Y.M.C.A., YMCA** Young Men's Christian Association

**Y.M.H.A., YMHA** Young Men's Hebrew Association

**yo·del** (yō′d'l) *vt., vi.* **-deled** or **-delled, -del·ing** or **-del·ling** [G. *jodeln*] to sing with abrupt alternating changes to the falsetto —*n.* a yodeling

**yo·ga** (yō′gə) *n.* [Sans., union] a Hindu discipline for achieving union with the supreme spirit through intense concentration, prescribed postures, controlled breathing, etc.

**yo·gi** (yō′gē) *n., pl.* **-gis** one who practices yoga: also **yo′gin** (-gin)

**yo·gurt** (yō′gərt) *n.* [Turk. *yōghurt*] a thick, semisolid food made from fermented milk: also **yo′ghurt**

**yoke** (yōk) *n.* [OE. *geoc*] 1. a wooden frame for harnessing together a pair of oxen, etc. 2. such a pair harnessed 3.

bondage; servitude 4. anything like a yoke, as something that binds, unites, etc., or a part of a garment fitted to the shoulders or hips as a support for the gathered parts below —*vt.* yoked, yok′ing 1. to put a yoke on 2. to harness (an animal) to (a plow, etc.) 3. to join together

**yo·kel** (yō′k'l) *n.* a person from the country; bumpkin: contemptuous term

**Yo·ko·ha·ma** (yō′kə hä′mə) seaport in S Honshu, Japan: pop. 1,789,000

**yolk** (yōk) *n.* [OE. *geolca*] the yellow, principal substance of an egg

**Yom Kip·pur** (yäm kip′ər; *Heb.* yōm′ kē pōōr′) the Day of Atonement, a Jewish holiday and day of fasting

**yon** (yän) *adj., adv.* [OE. *geon*] [Archaic or Dial.] yonder

**yon·der** (yän′dər) *adj., adv.* [ME.] (being) at or in that (specified or relatively distant) place; over there

**Yon·kers** (yäŋ′kərz) city in SE N.Y.: pop. 204,000

**yore** (yôr) *adv.* [OE. *geara*] [Obs.] long ago —of *yore* formerly

**you** (yōō) *pron.* [< OE. *eow* < *ge*, YE²] 1. the person or persons spoken to 2. a person or people generally [you can never tell]

**you'd** (yōōd) 1. you had 2. you would

**you'll** (yōōl) 1. you will 2. you shall

**young** (yuŋ) *adj.* [OE. *geong*] 1. being in an early period of life or growth 2. youthful; fresh; vigorous 3. in an early stage 4. inexperienced; immature —*n.* 1. young people 2. offspring, esp. young offspring —with *young* pregnant —**young′ish** *adj.*

**young blood** 1. young people; youth 2. youthful strength, vigor, etc.

**young′ster** (-stər) *n.* a child or youth

**Youngs·town** (yuŋz′toun) city in NE Ohio: pop. 140,000

**your** (yoor, yôr) *poss. pronominal adj.* [OE. *eower*] of, belonging to, or done by you: also used before some titles [your Honor]

**you're** (yoor, yōōr) you are

**yours** (yoorz, yôrz) *pron.* that or those belonging to you [that tie is *yours*]

**your·self** (yər self′, yoor-) *pron., pl.* **-selves′** 1. *the intensive form of* YOU [you *yourself* said so] 2. *the reflexive form of* YOU [you hurt *yourself*] 3. your true self [you're not *yourself* now]

**yours truly** 1. a phrase used in ending a letter 2. [Colloq.] I or me

**youth** (yōōth) *n., pl.* **youths** (yōōths, yōō thz) [OE. *geoguthe*] 1. the state or quality of being young 2. the period of adolescence 3. an early stage of development 4. young people 5. a young person; esp., a young man

**youth′ful** *adj.* 1. young 2. of, like, or fit for youth 3. fresh; vigorous 4. new; early —**youth′ful·ly** *adv.* —**youth′ful·ness** *n.*

**you've** (yōōv) you have

**yowl** (youl) *vi., n.* [< ON. *gaula*] howl; wail

**yo-yo** (yō′yō′) *n.* [< Philippine name] a spoollike toy reeled up and let down by a string

**yr.** 1. year(s) 2. your

**yrs.** 1. years 2. yours

**yuc·ca** (yuk′ə) *n.* [< Sp. *yuca*] 1. a desert plant with stiff leaves and white flowers 2. its flower

**Yu·go·sla·vi·a** (yōō′gō slä′vē ə) country in the NW Balkan Peninsula: 98,766 sq. mi.; pop. 20,186,000 —**Yu′go·slav′, Yu′go·sla′vi·an** *adj., n.*

**Yu·kon** (yōō′kän) territory in NW Canada: in full **Yukon Territory**

**yule** (yōōl) *n.* [OE. *geol*] Christmas or the Christmas season

YUCCA

**yule′tide′** (-tīd′) *n.* Christmas time

**yum·my** (yum′ē) *adj.* **-mi·er, -mi·est** [Colloq.] very tasty; delectable; delicious

**Y.W.C.A., YWCA** Young Women's Christian Association

**Y.W.H.A., YWHA** Young Women's Hebrew Association

**Z, z** (zē; *Brit.* zed) *n., pl.* **Z's, z's** the 26th and last letter of the English alphabet

**Za·ire, Za·ïre** (zä ir′) country in C Africa, on the Congo River: 905,563 sq. mi.; pop. 22,860,000

**Zam·bi·a** (zam′bē ə) country in S Africa: 290,323 sq. mi.; pop. 3,945,000

**za·ny** (zā′nē) *n., pl.* **-nies** [< It. *zanni* < *Giovanni*, John] 1. a clown or buffoon 2. a silly person —*adj.* **-ni·er, -ni·est** of or like a zany; funny, silly, crazy, etc. —**za′ni·ness** *n.*

**Zan·zi·bar** (zan′zə bär′) island territory off the E coast of Africa: part of Tanzania

**zap** (zap) *vt., vi.* **zapped, zap′ping** [echoic] to move, strike, smash, kill, etc. with sudden speed —*n.* [Slang] pep —*interj.* an exclamation expressing sudden swift action or change

**zeal** (zēl) *n.* [< Gr. *zēlos*] intense enthusiasm; ardor; fervor

**zeal·ot** (zel′ət) *n.* one who is zealous, esp. to a fanatic degree

**zeal·ous** (zel′əs) *adj.* full of, characterized by, or showing zeal; fervent; enthusiastic —**zeal′ous·ly** *adv.*

**ze·bra** (zē′brə) *n.* [Port.] an African mammal related to the horse and having dark stripes on a light body

**ze·bu** (zē′byōō) *n.* [Fr. *zébu*] an oxlike domestic animal of Asia and Africa: it has a large hump

**zed** (zed) *n.* [< Gr. *zēta*] *Brit. name for* the letter *Z, z*

**Zeit·geist** (tsīt′gīst′) *n.* [G., time spirit] the trend of thought and feeling in a period of history

**Zen** (zen) *n.* [Jap. ult. < Sans. *dhyāna*, thinking] a Buddhist sect in which enlightenment is sought through introspection and intuition

**ze·nith** (zē′nith) *n.* [ult. < L. *semita*, path] 1. the point in the sky directly overhead 2. the highest point

**zeph·yr** (zef′ər) *n.* [< Gr. *zephyros*] 1. the west wind 2. a gentle breeze

**zep·pe·lin** (zep′ə lin) *n.* [after Count F. von *Zeppelin* (1838–1917), its G. designer] [often Z-] a type of rigid airship designed around 1900

**ze·ro** (zir′ō) *n., pl.* **-ros, -roes** [< Ar. *sifr*, cipher] 1. the symbol 0; cipher; naught 2. the point, marked 0, from which quantities are reckoned on a graduated scale 3. nothing 4. the lowest point —*adj.* of or at zero —**zero in on** to concentrate attention on; focus on

**zero hour** 1. the time set for beginning an attack, etc. 2. crucial point

**zero population growth** a condition in a given population in which the birth rate equals the death rate

**ze′ro-sum′** (-sum′) *adj.* of or being a situation in which a gain for one must result in a loss for another

**zest** (zest) *n.* [Fr. *zeste*, orange peel] 1. something that gives flavor or relish 2. stimulating or exciting quality; piquancy 3. keen enjoyment [*zest* for life] —**zest′ful** *adj.*

**ze·ta** (zāt′ə) *n.* the sixth letter of the Greek alphabet (Z, ζ)

**Zeus** (zōōs) the supreme deity of the ancient Greeks

**zig·zag** (zig′zag′) *n.* [Fr.] 1. a series of short, sharp angles in alternate directions 2. a design, path, etc. in this form —*adj.* having the form of a zigzag —*adv.* so as to form a zigzag —*vt., vi.* **-zagged′, -zag′ging** to move or form in a zigzag

**zilch** (zilch) *n.* [nonsense syllable] [Slang] nothing; zero

**zil·lion** (zil′yən) *n.* [< MILLION] [Colloq.] a very large, indefinite number

**zinc** (ziŋk) *n.* [G. *zink*] a bluish-white, metallic chemical element, used in various alloys, as a protective coating for iron, etc. —*vt.* **zincked** or **zinc·ked, zinck′ing** or **zinc′ing** to coat with zinc

**zinc ointment** a zinc-oxide salve

**zinc oxide** a white powder used in making glass, paints, ointments, cosmetics, etc.

**zing** (ziŋ) *n.* [echoic] [Slang] 1. a shrill whizzing sound 2. zest, vigor, etc.

**zin·ni·a** (zin′ē ə, zin′yə) *n.* [< J. *Zinn* (d. 1759), G. botanist] a plant having colorful, composite flowers

**Zi·on** (zī′ən) 1. a hill in Jerusalem, site of Solomon's Temple 2. Jerusalem 3. Israel 4. heaven

**Zi′on·ism** *n.* a movement that reestablished, and now supports, the state of Israel —**Zi′on·ist** *n., adj.*

**zip** (zip) *n.* [echoic] 1. a short, sharp hissing sound, as of a passing bullet 2. [Colloq.] energy; vigor —*vi.* **zipped, zip′ping** 1. to make, or move with, a zip 2. [Colloq.] to move with speed —*vt.* to fasten with a zipper

**ZIP code** (zip) [z(oning) i(mprovement) p(lan)] a system to speed mail

fat, āpe, cär; ten, ēven; is, bīte; gō, hôrn, tōōl, look; oil, out; up, fur; chin; she; thin, then; zh, leisure; ŋ, ring; ə for a in ago; ʼ, (ä′b′l); ë, Fr. coeur; ö, Fr. feu; Fr. mon; ü, Fr. duc; kh, G. ich, doch; ‡ foreign; < derived from deliveries, using code numbers for zones, or regions

**zip·per** (zip′ər) *n.* a device used to fasten and unfasten two edges of material: it consists of interlocking tabs worked by a sliding part

**zip′py** *adj.* **-pi·er, -pi·est** [Colloq.] full of zip, or energy; brisk

**zir·con** (zur′kän) *n.* [ult. < Per. *zar*, gold] a crystalline silicate mineral, often used as a gem

**zir·co·ni·um** (zər kō′nē əm) *n.* a ductile, metallic chemical element used in alloys, nuclear reactors, etc.: symbol, Zr

**zit** (zit) *n.* [Slang] a pimple, esp. on the face

**zith·er** (zith′ər, zith′-) *n.* [ < Gr. *kithara*, lute] a musical instrument with 30 to 40 strings, played with a plectrum

**Zn** *Chem.* zinc

**zo·di·ac** (zō′dē ak′) *n.* [ < Gr. *zōdiakos (kyklos)*, (circle) of animals] 1. an imaginary belt in the heavens extending on either side of the apparent path of the sun and divided into twelve equal parts, or signs, named for, constellations 2. a diagram representing this —**zo·di·a·cal** (-dī′ə k'l) *adj.*

ZODIAC

**zom·bie, zom·bi** (zam′bē) *n.* [of Afr. orig.] 1. in West Indian superstition, a supernatural power by which a corpse may be reanimated 2. such a corpse

**zone** (zōn) *n.* [Fr. < Gr. *zōnē*] 1. an encircling band, stripe, etc. 2. any of the five great latitudinal divisions of the earth's surface (the **torrid zone**, two **temperate zones**, and two **frigid zones**) 3. any area with reference to a specified use or restriction [a canal zone, postal *zone*] —*vt.* **zoned, zon′ing** 1. to mark off into zones 2. to encircle; surround —**zon′al** *adj.* —**zoned** *adj.*

**zonked** (zäŋkt) *adj.* [Slang] drunk or stupefied, as from alcohol or a drug

**zoo** (zōō) *n.* [ < *zoo(logical garden)*] a place where a collection of wild animals is kept for public showing

**zoo-** [ < Gr. *zōion*, animal] *a combining form meaning* animal(s) [*zoology*] Also **zoö-**

**zo·ol·o·gy** (zō äl′ə jē) *n.* [**zoo-** + **-logy**] the science that deals with animals and animal life —**zo′o·log′i·cal** (-ə läj′i k'l) *adj.* —**zo·ol′o·gist** *n.*

**zoom** (zōōm) *vi.* [echoic] 1. to make a loud, buzzing sound 2. to climb in an airplane sharply 3. to rise rapidly [prices *zoomed*] 4. to focus with a zoom lens: see ff. —*vt.* to cause to zoom —*n.* a zooming

**zoom lens** a system of lenses, as in a motion-picture camera, that can be rapidly adjusted for close or distant shots while keeping the image in focus

**zo·o·phyte** (zō′ə fīt′) *n.* [**zoo-** + Gr. *phyton*, plant] any animal, as a sponge, that looks and grows somewhat like a plant

**Zo·ro·as·ter** (zō′rō as′tər) ?6th or 7th c. B.C.; Per. founder of Zoroastrianism

**Zo′ro·as′tri·an·ism** (-trē ən iz′m) *n.* the religion of the ancient Persians

**Zou·ave** (zōō äv′) *n.* [ < Ar. *Zwāwa*, Algerian tribe] a member of a former French military unit with colorful uniforms or of any similar military group

**zounds** (zoundz) *interj.* [alt. < oath *(by) God's wounds*] [Archaic] a mild oath

**zuc·chi·ni** (zōō kē′nē) *n.* [It.] a cucumberlike summer squash

**Zu·lu** (zōō′lōō) *n.* 1. *pl.* **-lus, -lu** a member of a people of South Africa 2. their language —*adj.* of the Zulus, their language, etc.

**Zu·ñi** (zōō′nyē) *n.* 1. *pl.* **-ñis, -ñi** a member of a pueblo-dwelling Indian tribe of New Mexico 2. their language: pop. 440,000

**Zur·ich** (zoor′ik) city in N Switzerland: pop. 440,000

**zwie·back** (swē′bak, swī′-) *n.* [G. < *zwie-*, twice + *backen*, bake] a kind of biscuit that is sliced and toasted after baking

**zy·gote** (zī′gōt) *n.* [Gr. *zygon*, a yoke] a cell formed by the union of male and female gametes

**zym-, zymo-** [ < Gr. *zymē*, leaven] *a combining form meaning* fermentation

**zy·mur·gy** (zī′mər jē) *n.* [prec. + **-urgy**] the chemistry of fermentation, as applied in brewing, etc.